Implementing Microsoft SharePoint 2019

An expert guide to SharePoint Server for architects, administrators, and project managers

Lewin Wanzer

Angel Wood

BIRMINGHAM—MUMBAI

Implementing Microsoft SharePoint 2019

Group Product Manager: Ashwin Nair
Publishing Product Manager: Rohit Rajkumar
Commissioning Editor: Kunal Chaudhari
Acquisition Editor: Rohit Rajkumar
Senior Editor: Sofi Rogers
Content Development Editor: Divya Vijayan
Technical Editor: Shubham Sharma
Copy Editor: Safis Editing
Project Coordinator: Kinjal Bari
Proofreader: Safis Editing
Indexer: Manju Arasan
Production Designer: Jyoti Chauhan

First published: December 2020

Production reference: 2080421

Published by Packt Publishing Ltd.
Livery Place
35 Livery Street
Birmingham
B3 2PB, UK.

ISBN 978-1-78961-537-1

www.packt.com

To God, for giving me the opportunity to help others, to my mother, Janie Wanzer, and to the memory of my father, Clayton, for their sacrifices and for instilling the values of courage and perseverance. To my wife, Elsi, for being my loving partner, along with all my kids, old and young, who supported me through this effort.

– Lewin Wanzer

I would like to thank God for the goodness he has shown to me and my family. I am grateful to have this opportunity to share this knowledge with the technical community and beyond. I dedicate this book to the memory of my mother, Jaqueline Price, and my grandmother, Mary Price, for instilling in me the belief that strong, smart women can accomplish anything. Lastly, thanks to my son, Jaire, for his support and for sharing me with this book as I spent many hours locked away writing.

– Angel Wood

Packt.com

Subscribe to our online digital library for full access to over 7,000 books and videos, as well as industry leading tools to help you plan your personal development and advance your career. For more information, please visit our website.

Why subscribe?

- Spend less time learning and more time coding with practical eBooks and Videos from over 4,000 industry professionals

- Improve your learning with Skill Plans built especially for you

- Get a free eBook or video every month

- Fully searchable for easy access to vital information

- Copy and paste, print, and bookmark content

Did you know that Packt offers eBook versions of every book published, with PDF and ePub files available? You can upgrade to the eBook version at packt.com and as a print book customer, you are entitled to a discount on the eBook copy. Get in touch with us at customercare@packtpub.com for more details.

At www.packt.com, you can also read a collection of free technical articles, sign up for a range of free newsletters, and receive exclusive discounts and offers on Packt books and eBooks.

Contributors

About the authors

Lewin Wanzer is a seasoned SharePoint architect with over 30 years of IT experience, of which he has spent 16 managing SQL Server and SharePoint environments. As an architect, he specializes in governance, planning, taxonomy, design, infrastructure, implementation, migration, maintenance, and support for SharePoint Enterprise and Microsoft Cloud environments. He also has expertise in IT management, business analysis, and process development, designing solutions and managing large projects, bringing together many years of hands-on experience and knowledge.

It has been a long ride with SharePoint, but I would like to personally thank some key people and entities that have helped my career when I needed it most: Microsoft, for the opportunity to work as a PFE supporting SharePoint from 2011 to 2013, and the PFE who told me I would never make it at Microsoft; Marion and Dallas Bishoff, for giving me an opportunity to push myself to be a consultant; the teachers I have had throughout the years of schooling, who have been positive and negative with me; finally, thanks to those who shared tech concepts without thought or apprehension. These many thanks go to ALL of you!

Angel Wood is a SharePoint architect and communications specialist with over 20 years' experience, specializing in migration planning and implementation, governance, knowledge management, and solution design. Angel has provided project-level implementation and management for large government organizations and private companies alike and has developed SharePoint training programs and worked aggressively to drive user adoption and satisfaction on the SharePoint platform. SharePoint security and its relation to proper governance design and adoption is her passion and drives her work day-to-day consulting with major government agencies. Angel has also edited several books, training materials, and other publications, including NASA KM case studies.

About the reviewer

Sudeep Ghatak has over 17 years of experience working with Microsoft technologies. He started as a .NET programmer, later moving to SharePoint back in 2007. Sudeep currently works as a senior solution architect in New Zealand and designs solutions based on Office 365 and the Azure platform. He is a certified Solutions Developer (MCSD) and holds a postgraduate degree in instrumentation engineering. He is an active member of the Microsoft community in New Zealand and runs an Azure meetup group. He is also an active speaker and advocate of Office 365 and Azure. He is often seen speaking at user groups and conferences in and around Christchurch, New Zealand. Outside of work, Sudeep loves to spend time with his family and has a strong interest in music and astrophysics. He loves playing guitar and is currently taking violin lessons with his 7-year-old daughter.

Packt is searching for authors like you

If you're interested in becoming an author for Packt, please visit authors. packtpub.com and apply today. We have worked with thousands of developers and tech professionals, just like you, to help them share their insight with the global tech community. You can make a general application, apply for a specific hot topic that we are recruiting an author for, or submit your own idea.

Table of Contents

2
Planning and Architecture

3
Creating and Managing Virtual Machines

4
Installation Concepts

5

Farm and Services Configuration

6

Finalizing the Farm – Going Live

7

Finalizing the Farm to Go Live – Part II

8

Post-Implementation Operations and Maintenance

9

Managing Performance and Troubleshooting

10

SharePoint Advanced Reporting and Features

11
Enterprise Social Networking and Collaboration

12
SharePoint Framework

Other Books You May Enjoy

Index

Preface

Implementing Microsoft SharePoint 2019 is a technology book that covers the ins and outs of SharePoint implementations with a view from the field. We give solutions to an array of problems as well as step-by-step guidance to provide an easy-to-read book that helps you plan and manage SharePoint Server 2019 implementations. In this book, we provide insight on questions you may have around planning, assessment, governance, installation, configuration, integration, and a host of developer topics. The book provides the information required to bridge the gap between on-premises and cloud hybrid solutions to support an all-encompassing SharePoint 2019 project.

Who this book is for

This book is for SharePoint administrators, project managers, and architects who have some experience in designing, planning, implementing, and managing SharePoint Farms.

What this book covers

Chapter 1, Understanding Your Current State, helps you figure out the state of your current environment to find out what will change and what you need to have a successful SharePoint 2019 implementation. This includes new environments as well as the governance that these environments need, as we'll discuss in this chapter.

Chapter 2, Planning and Architecture, talks you through reviewing and assessing your current environments, which will help you understand what you need to change and update in your new environment. The planning and design of infrastructure (be it on the cloud or on-premises), server resources, redundancy, and team resources are also explained in this chapter with many other related scenarios.

Chapter 3, Creating and Managing Virtual Machines, sees you creating server resources to support SharePoint Server 2019 using Hyper-V and Windows Server installations. You will also learn to understand how these resources can be configured for the best performance to support SharePoint Server 2019.

Chapter 4, Installation Concepts, teaches you how to best install SQL Server to support SharePoint Server 2019 step by step and also provides a step-by-step guide to SharePoint Server 2019 installation to complete the installation of the server process.

Chapter 5, Farm and Service Configuration, covers SharePoint Server 2019 logging and services, along with instructions on how to configure the services within the farm to achieve the best configuration. We also review MinRoles and how they can be used strategically, along with a good review of the Distributed Cache service.

Chapter 6, Finalizing the Farm – Going Live, sees you do some final configuration of services, specifically the Search and User Profiles services. You will create web applications and learn how to extend web applications using zoning and alternate access mappings.

Chapter 7, Finalizing the Farm to Go Live: Part II, walks you step by step through the installation and teaches you more about integrated applications such as Workflow Manager. We talk more in this chapter about authentication, software and hardware load balancing, and migration concepts, and complete some final checks before we release our environment to our user community.

Chapter 8, Post-Implementation Operations and Maintenance, is dedicated to day-one scenarios and discusses how to prepare and what work needs to happen on the cutover weekend. We pose many common questions at the beginning of this chapter that are answered with our experience from the lessons we've learned to help prepare you. Applying SharePoint updates and other maintenance is also covered in this chapter.

Chapter 9, Managing Performance and Troubleshooting, reviews the client's and developers' roles in maintaining the performance, tools, and stability of your SharePoint 2019 farm. We also discuss administrative responsibilities around the performance of your farm and look at which areas to support for the best possible performance. Troubleshooting is also discussed in the areas with tools and we provide some scenarios and fixes from our own experience.

Chapter 10, SharePoint Advanced Reporting and Features, looks at deprecated reporting features, such as Excel Services and BI, and what new features are offered as replacements in the configuration of SharePoint Server 2019. We also dive into connecting to the cloud and the options available once hybrid connectivity is in place. Since Power Tools are important, we go through each tool that includes Azure integration and how they can be used with your on-premises environment.

Chapter 11, Enterprise Social Networking and Collaboration, is dedicated to showing you Microsoft Teams and how it has changed how we communicate in the new cloud and SharePoint Server 2019 environment. We also show you some other cloud social tools that are easily integrated into SharePoint Server 2019. If you are looking to use Live Meeting, we have included some high-level details on setting up Teams for small auditoriums.

Chapter 12, SharePoint Framework, is dedicated to developers and what they will see has changed in SharePoint Server 2019 farms. We give recommendations on the tools and languages that developers need to get familiar with and some best practices to follow. We also walk through SPFx and the setup of Node.js step by step.

To get the most out of this book

To be prepared for this book and to emulate the concepts discussed, you will need to have access to server resources. Please have an environment you can use to follow the step-by-step instructions as part of the book.

Software/hardware covered in the book	OS requirements
Hyper-V	Windows only
SharePoint Server 2019	Windows only
PowerShell	Windows only
SQL 2017 or Server 2019	Windows and Linux
Visual Studio Code	Windows and Mac
Node.js	Windows, Mac, and Linux
Microsoft 365 subscription	Cloud tenant

You will have to download some of the integrated tools, such as SharePoint Designer 2013, InfoPath 2013, and others mentioned throughout the book, to use them and install them on a desktop. We do not cover these tools within the book, but research and practice with them to learn how to develop workflows and forms.

If you are using the digital version of this book, we advise you to type the code yourself or access the code via the GitHub repository (link available in the next section). Doing so will help you avoid any potential errors related to the copying and pasting of code.

If you are looking to follow along with the book and build while you read, then be prepared to get your own server or a hosted server in Azure or AWS to set up your environment. This will require the purchase of either a used server from eBay or a subscription to one of the cloud services mentioned here.

Download the example code files

You can download the example code files for this book from GitHub at `https://github.com/PacktPublishing/Implementing-Microsoft-SharePoint-2019`. In case there's an update to the code, it will be updated on the existing GitHub repository.

We also have other code bundles from our rich catalog of books and videos available at `https://github.com/PacktPublishing/`. Check them out!

Download the color images

We also provide a PDF file that has color images of the screenshots/diagrams used in this book. You can download it here: `https://static.packt-cdn.com/downloads/9781789615371_ColorImages.pdf`.

Conventions used

There are a number of text conventions used throughout this book.

`Code in text`: Indicates code words in text, database table names, folder names, filenames, file extensions, pathnames, dummy URLs, user input, and Twitter handles. Here is an example: "Mount the downloaded `WebStorm-10*.dmg` disk image file as another disk in your system."

A block of code is set as follows:

```
# Get the Web Application
$WebApp = Get-SPWebApplication "https://my.company.com"
#Loop through all site collections and Set read only status
foreach ($SPsite in $webApp.Sites)
{
$SPsite.ReadOnly = $truePost-implementation 11
#Or : Set-SPSiteAdministration -LockState "Unlock"
-Identity $SPsite.url
}
```

When we wish to draw your attention to a particular part of a code block, the relevant lines or items are set in bold:

```
[default]
exten => s,1,Dial(Zap/1|30)
exten => s,2,Voicemail(u100)
exten => s,102,Voicemail(b100)
exten => i,1,Voicemail(s0)
```

Any command-line input or output is written as follows:

```
Set-SPLogLevel -TraceServerity verboseex
```

Bold: Indicates a new term, an important word, or words that you see onscreen. For example, words in menus or dialog boxes appear in the text like this. Here is an example: "Select **System info** from the **Administration** panel."

> **Tips or important notes**
> Appear like this.

Get in touch

Feedback from our readers is always welcome.

General feedback: If you have questions about any aspect of this book, mention the book title in the subject of your message and email us at customercare@packtpub.com.

Errata: Although we have taken every care to ensure the accuracy of our content, mistakes do happen. If you have found a mistake in this book, we would be grateful if you would report this to us. Please visit www.packtpub.com/support/errata, selecting your book, clicking on the Errata Submission Form link, and entering the details.

Piracy: If you come across any illegal copies of our works in any form on the Internet, we would be grateful if you would provide us with the location address or website name. Please contact us at copyright@packt.com with a link to the material.

If you are interested in becoming an author: If there is a topic that you have expertise in and you are interested in either writing or contributing to a book, please visit authors.packtpub.com.

Reviews

Please leave a review. Once you have read and used this book, why not leave a review on the site that you purchased it from? Potential readers can then see and use your unbiased opinion to make purchase decisions, we at Packt can understand what you think about our products, and our authors can see your feedback on their book. Thank you!

For more information about Packt, please visit packt.com.

1

Understanding Your Current State

The current state of your environment is critical in how you proceed to start a new enterprise SharePoint implementation, migration to a new version of SharePoint, hybrid integration, or migration to the cloud. There are many checks and balances you need to understand before moving forward with your SharePoint project. The reason most projects fail with SharePoint is the lack of understanding and gathering of facts on the environment from the enterprise, governance, content, customizations, errors, and server configuration levels before you begin. Assessing the good and the bad in these areas gives clarity on what needs to be planned, designed, and implemented to be successful. This chapter will help you understand those areas that need to be identified to be changed, updated, documented, and corrected before proceeding to new versions of SharePoint, including the Microsoft 365 cloud.

The following topics will be covered in this chapter:

- Deprecated features
- New features
- Accessing the environment
- Best practices
- Governance

Technical requirements

The following will help you gain a better understanding of this chapter:

- Current experience with SharePoint farm administration to support 2007, 2010, 2013, and 2016

- Current enterprise planning and or project planning to support a collaborative user community with SharePoint

- 2–3 years of collaboration and or system implementation experience

Warning – deprecated features

In my years as a SharePoint architect, I have come across different definitions for various terms, and the meaning of the term "deprecated" always comes up in conversation. When defining the word "deprecated" and Microsoft's use of the word, I want to make sure we are on the same page to ensure we understand Microsoft's intentions before going forward. The features listed in this section will be referred to as either deprecated or removed features.

Microsoft defines deprecated in a couple of different ways, as seen in their documentation online. One definition for the word deprecated as used by Microsoft is *no longer making updates to features listed within SharePoint*. In this definition, we need to understand, as SharePoint professionals, that this means Microsoft is suggesting that customers do not rely on these features if they have not used them before. The features listed are supported in SharePoint Server 2019 as Microsoft still supports these features for those companies still making use of them.

The reason for discouraging customers from investing in these features is that the features listed have the potential of being removed from the product soon or are possibly on the list for removal. If you are new to SharePoint and one of the features that comes up in this section is something you were hoping to use for your environment, please explore other options from a third-party vendor or start using an integrated product that can reclaim the features for use in your environment.

If a feature is referred to in this section as "removed," then we will consider this feature *not available and no longer supported by Microsoft in this version of SharePoint.* This often brings tears to my eyes, as some features can be widely used within your environment by the user community. When relaying this information to a customer, this can be tough, but it is important because you want to present a clear path to success. This also gives us, as consultants and engineers, the opportunity to define how to recover from those features that are lost. It is essential that we give our user community confidence that we will find a way to make up for the lost functionality during our planning process. Third-party solutions can sometimes be the answer to this issue but be careful with what third-party companies you agree to purchase from. We will talk about third-party components later in the book.

As you can see from these first four paragraphs, understanding your new application software product version is one of the keys to success for planning and designing your implementation. When installing fresh with no need for migration of a prior product's content, this section may not be too useful to you; however, for those of you who are upgrading and migrating content to this newer platform, this section is very important to give clarity on the server platform, integrations, user features, administration changes, developer platform changes, and other areas of the product that could have changed between SharePoint 2016 to SharePoint 2019.

If you're migrating from other versions, such as 2007, 2010, or 2013, you will need to go back and make a list of changes from all versions to see what features and changes have happened between those versions as well. The reason we need to do that is that if you're using SharePoint 2007, there will be a lot of change associated with your move to SharePoint 2019. This change will bring a host of user questions, from the UI to site collection features. Admins will see a big change in administration areas and how and what other Microsoft products integrate within the product currently.

As part of understanding this platform, we also want to start making a list of areas lacking in the supportability of the product. We will need to support all aspects to fully integrate this platform into the enterprise.

Training and other aspects of learning are essential for users as well as admins to make sure they do not get lost when implementing the product in the enterprise. Users' understanding of the site features, how to navigate the sites, UI changes, and overall SharePoint product progression through versions are essential use cases for requesting training as part of this implementation. Training is something you do not want to leave out as part of this project, even from a new installation perspective. I have seen one implementation where no training was given to users and the product was not used effectively for 10+ years due to the users not understanding how to effectively use the product.

Customizations you activated as third-party solutions and developed as custom solutions that were used in prior versions of SharePoint may not work in this new version of SharePoint. If you are using customizations in SharePoint versions 2007 up to 2013, you will have to test to make sure those customizations are available through the vendors you purchased them from to support SharePoint 2019. A lot of companies that were thriving with the 2007 SharePoint custom solution market may no longer be around, so this will need some research on the company and/or finding a replacement for the solution.

FAB 40 templates come into play as well in older versions of the product. These templates were retired during the release of SharePoint 2010 and are no longer valid for newer versions of SharePoint. Customized solutions by developers will need to be vetted and redeveloped for SharePoint Server 2019. We talk more about migration in the future chapters of this book, and there I will give you more in-depth information on what you should be migrating and things to watch out for during the process.

Deprecated features

The following listed features are deprecated in SharePoint Server 2019.

Access Services 2010

Access Services 2010 was the first step in taking desktop one-user databases and making them available for sharing through SharePoint. The service gave us the ability to publish an Access file and secure it for viewing and editing for those peers who had access. Access Services 2010 will remain supported but will be deprecated within this new version of the product.

There are alternatives to replacing Access Services 2010 as Microsoft has made available Power Apps and Power Automate. If you're new to SharePoint, this would be a good time to look at the alternative solutions first to provide those same features to replace this service and database type. If you are using these services, I would start migrating data from these databases and creating new solutions using Power Apps or a relevant third-party solution. Another alternative is to use SharePoint lists in place of Access databases, which can help in some small applications developed on that platform that bring better sharing experiences to the application.

Access Services 2013

Access Services 2013 provided data used within these services to be used within SQL tables, while Access Services 2010 data was captured in a SharePoint list. This service is deprecated in the SharePoint Server 2019 release. I recommend that you migrate all Access applications to Power Apps. If these applications require support for business processes, enhance them using Flow. These applications are considered as potential alternatives to support the functionality within SharePoint 2019.

If you are new to SharePoint, I recommend you start with the alternative products, and if you are using these services currently, start migrating from this service to a new solution that can be provided by these new applications and or third-party solutions.

Aggregated newsfeed

The newsfeed was used to post status updates with everyone on a landing page or within specific sites where you had permissions to do so. As users saw your post, they were able to reply and continue responding to the conversation, as seen in similar functionality on other social platforms. Users could also like your posts as well using the newsfeed. The newsfeed functionality, which was made available by way of `newsfeed.aspx` and mainly accessed via the **Newsfeed** tile in the app launcher, will be set to read-only. The tile located in the app launcher will be removed, as well as the option to create newsfeed capability.

If you are currently using the newsfeed capabilities, I recommend other alternatives, such as Microsoft Teams or Yammer, but I would be wary of adopting Yammer as a full solution at this time as I see this being a potential removed or deprecated feature soon.

Help content

In the past, content to support help within sites had been ineffective in supporting users. We as administrators depend on this to give relevant information to users for issues they may run into during their experience or even some instructions for how to manipulate content within SharePoint. This has not been the case from my perspective in older versions of SharePoint and it really needed some fine-tuning to get the type of information to support the product efficiently.

Within this version, enhancements have been completed to make sure users access quality help content. Help content will also be consistent and centralized as it will be accessed by syncing with the Microsoft 365 help engine. Support for the legacy on-premises integrated help engine will be a thing of the past. In this release, the legacy SharePoint help engine will remain supported. The help content in the legacy help engine will be deprecated.

Groove sync client

In past versions of SharePoint, the Groove sync client was used to sync documents between your personal devices and SharePoint Server 2010, 2013, and 2016 team sites. This client was a very unstable syncing mechanism that confused users and had some ups and downs throughout its life cycle. The reliability of this client has been talked about many times in blogs, at customer sites, and at conferences I have attended. This client is something desired for syncing offline synchronization documents when not connected to the network where SharePoint lives. It gives the user the ability to read documents and update documents offline, and when online, these changes are synced with the documents that have been updated.

SharePoint Server 2019 introduces support for a new OneDrive sync client. This client has been known as the new generation client and will provide a more reliable syncing experience. When using the Groove client in this version of the product, it will automatically update any SharePoint 2019 site sync relationships to the new OneDrive sync client. Administrators can also control this migration experience. The sync client will be supported but deprecated in SharePoint Server 2019.

InfoPath client and services

Almost every client I have visited recently and in the past uses InfoPath to build forms to collect information related to business processes. The potential problem is when the company has been relying on InfoPath for many years, taking advantage of developing these custom forms. Companies relying on these forms and heavily using them in their environment see that these forms would take a lot of time to move away from. Companies at this point would have to redesign the forms, build the forms in a new application, and rebuild the business processes around these forms so that they do not miss a step in their business. If I worked for a company that heavily relied on InfoPath, I would be looking at this time to start migrating these forms to alternative applications. These potential migrations can be completed with Power Apps and Power Automate.

There are also other alternatives from other third-party vendors, such as KwizCom, which feature a form replacement solution. Microsoft advises that customers should explore alternatives for InfoPath at this time. InfoPath services have been deprecated in SharePoint 2019 but will be supported. The use of InfoPath 2013 for designing forms is still supported within SharePoint 2019. The InfoPath client will be supported until 2026, but the InfoPath 2013 client will not be supported beyond this date.

Lists Web service

Since Microsoft Sync Framework, which supported the Groove sync client as well as the Lists Web service, depended on this framework, the following SOAP endpoints are deprecated as part of the SharePoint 2019 release:

- `Lists.GetListItemChangesWithKnowledge`
- `Lists.UpdateListItemsWithKnowledge`

Machine Translation service

If you didn't know about and/or are new to how this service works, the Machine Translation service provides language translation text from within the context of SharePoint. The application service will translate text from one language, such as Spanish, for example, to another language, such as English. This service will substitute one word in one language to its corresponding word in another language naturally. The Machine Translation service will remain supported but will be deprecated in this version of SharePoint.

PerformancePoint Services

If you are wondering how to support **Key Performance Indicators** (**KPIs**) and dashboarding in SharePoint, PerformancePoint is an integrated service to support these types of solutions. This service has been around since the 2010 version of the product. It's a cool integration, and as you can see, it will be replaced soon with newer alternatives mentioned in other areas of this section. At this point, it would be great to start migrating your solutions and moving away from this service so that you can be ahead of the game before it's too late. The reason for the deprecation of PerformancePoint Services is that it has dependencies on Microsoft Silverlight. This technology will no longer be supported as of October 12, 2021. PerformancePoint Services will remain supported in this version of the product. I strongly advise you to explore Power BI as an alternative to PerformancePoint Services. There are many new business intelligence enhancements being made due to big investments in Power BI.

SharePoint Designer

If we take a look at the progression of SharePoint over the years, you can see that SharePoint Designer was an essential part of the product versions released for 2007 and 2010. As Microsoft made major changes in 2013, you can see that SharePoint Designer would not be around much longer due to the integration of outside product integrations to manipulate SharePoint sites. We can also see that as the Microsoft 365 platform grows with product announcements, support for the replacement of SharePoint Designer is on the way. Microsoft has announced that there will not be a new SharePoint Designer client shipped with this release. Microsoft has also said that the SharePoint Designer 2013 product will work with SharePoint Server 2019 for the remainder of the client support life cycle, which is until 2026. SharePoint Designer 2013 will not be supported beyond that support life cycle. You can see that things are coming to an end for this product, but the question is when.

Site mailbox

Site mailboxes provide a way to centralize and share email using collaboration with teams and groups. With mailboxes growing due to the amount of email produced, this offers some options for teams, especially related to forwarding mail due to sharing project-related messages. Since this feature's introduction, there has not been much adoption and the feature has seen a decline since it was offered in Microsoft 365. Microsoft has made this feature deprecated in Microsoft 365 and now announced that they will also do the same for SharePoint 2019. The reason behind this is the decline in the use of the feature. Personally, I believe this is a great feature and I am not sure why more companies didn't move toward using it. Just the use of forwarding email within the enterprise probably takes up the majority of mailbox space to manage project and team-shared emails. I can only see good in this feature, but Microsoft has spoken. Shared mailboxes would be the alternative for the replacement of this functionality, and in hybrid scenarios using Microsoft 365 groups as an alternative.

Site manager

The main functionality of the site manager is now available in the modern document library copy/move announced on the Microsoft community website. The site manager feature will be supported, but it is deprecated in SharePoint Server 2019. Only site collection administrators will have permission to access the site manager page and the UI entry points to this page will be removed. You will have to know the page URL to get access to the feature. You can also copy/move content to OneDrive as well, as OneDrive is able to be browsed using this feature.

List of removed features

The following listed features are removed in SharePoint Server 2019.

Code-based sandbox solutions

During my travels as an engineer, I didn't see much use of this feature by corporate clients. I believe there was fear in using this feature as well as supporting the feature fully. There have been some instances I am aware of where this feature has created problems due to administrators being unaware of how it should be implemented and used by the user community. Microsoft announced, in the Microsoft Office Dev Center and in some other articles, that code-based sandbox solutions were deprecated in SharePoint Server 2013. They have also now been removed in SharePoint Online. Microsoft considered keeping this feature in SharePoint Server 2019, but they have decided to also remove support for code-based sandbox solutions in SharePoint Server 2019. Customers are recommended to explore SharePoint add-ons as an alternative, which are fully supported for both SharePoint on-premises and SharePoint Online. You can also take a look at SharePoint Framework Extensions, which have three extension types and can be used to extend the user experience using common scripting frameworks, such as Angular, React, or JavaScript.

Digest authentication

Microsoft will be deprecating the digest authentication feature in **Internet Information Services (IIS)**. This announcement came from the Windows team. When using the SharePoint prerequisite installer to prep the server for SharePoint, the installer will no longer attempt to install this Windows feature. When I have been on the road visiting many companies, I have never seen this authentication used for SharePoint. It seems Microsoft is aware that this isn't a very popular authentication mechanism. There are other alternative mechanism choices that could help those that use this specific mechanism. As alternatives, Kerberos, NTLM, and SAML are available to explore.

Incoming mail automatic mode

While this is a useful feature of SharePoint, I haven't seen this being used in many companies due to the dependency on a separate MX record being configured in the domain. This service also depended on IIS 6 Management Compatibility, which is a feature within IIS. The SMTP service within IIS used IIS APIs for the management of the service when using automatic mode for SharePoint incoming mail. There is no other way to manage the IIS SMTP service. This service is being removed to support automatic mode incoming mail. Customers who currently use incoming mail are advised to use advanced mode instead. The advanced mode gives you options to manually manage the IIS SMTP service and the drop folder.

Multi-tenancy

You may be surprised to hear that this was one removal I was hoping for. I have never been a fan of multi-tenancy. I think it brings too many challenges to the planning and design of the platform. It also brings challenges to the performance, configuration, and support of growing sites. There was the need to provide more support for this platform that just wasn't there, which made me stay away from recommending it to customers. Microsoft continues to innovate this feature in SharePoint Online but there is much more complexity in the configuration and bigger cost in providing this in the on-premises environment. Microsoft has announced that this feature will no longer be supported in the SharePoint Server 2019 release. Customers who are currently using this feature can still be supported up to the SharePoint Server 2016 version. Of course, you can always move to Microsoft 365, where it's fully supported.

PowerPivot Gallery and refresh

The removal of PowerPivot Gallery and refresh is not surprising to me. Since Power BI is now available and built to be standalone-capable, Power BI is now more ready to support SharePoint in a more robust way. Power BI will be a force as now the capabilities can be pushed to the limit, integrating the product as its own server instead of running it as a service, which sets this product up for a great future. Power BI Desktop works with a different file extension, PBIX, which you can then use to migrate Excel workbooks to Power BI Desktop.

Visio Services – Silverlight-based rendering

Silverlight will no longer be supported as of October 12, 2021. Since there are only two options for rendering Visio diagrams – Microsoft Silverlight-based and PNG-based to support SharePoint 2019 – Silverlight is no longer available within SharePoint Server 2019 and you will have to render Visio diagrams using PNG-based technology.

SharePoint business intelligence scenarios

Looking over the SQL Server Reporting Services Team blog post referenced on Microsoft's SharePoint 2019 new and improved features page, I have recently seen the changes related to SharePoint services from the SQL installations. If you refer to SQL 2016 and SQL 2017, you will see the differences in support for SQL Reporting Services, as SQL 2016 only provides integration for SharePoint Reporting Services features. I know from experience after writing many SQL Reporting Services reports that this feature has some issues that need to be improved upon. Microsoft has made some changes as native mode will be a standalone Power BI solution that you can deploy whether you have SharePoint or not. This mode of support for reporting services provided in SQL Server is different, as you can see from the differences between SQL 2016 and SQL 2017. With this new way of integration, you will see a modern web portal, paginated reports, mobile reports, KPIs, and much more. Available as well is an on-premises data gateway for hybrid environments, which gives the capability for users in the cloud to be able to use Flow and Power Apps. You will also be able to interact with Power BI reports in your web browser for the web-based viewing of Excel workbooks. (Watch out for PowerPivot users.) The scenarios that have been supported in this service are the following: embedding reports in SharePoint pages, reporting on data in SharePoint lists, and delivering reports to SharePoint libraries.

There is also a migration script available to migrate your reports from SharePoint integrated mode to native mode. Power View reports can be converted into Power BI reports, and with that evolution, you can also import your Excel workbooks in to Power View and then to Power BI to start converting your content. This sounds like a much better way to tackle reporting in SharePoint and I'm happy to see that they have done something different with SQL Server Reporting Services to alleviate some of the issues we have seen using Reporting Services.

Now that we have seen what features are to be deprecated or removed, let's see what new features SharePoint Server 2019 have to offer.

New features

With the ever-changing SharePoint platform, I want to make sure you understand all of the changes to this new platform before proceeding to the installation of the product. It is easy to get lost in the mix of all the changes and information you may see online. This is not to say do not check behind me. As I write this book, things could be changing at the same time. So, make sure to do that but also make sure to document and plan this implementation well. Leaving out any crucial details during this assessment could bring about a migraine headache, so please be thorough and make sure to work as a team with other IT areas for support of this SharePoint 2019 on-premises implementation.

As part of our assessment to understand your current state, we also need to investigate new features. This is useful for both those new to SharePoint Server and those that have implemented SharePoint with prior versions of the product. New features cover many different areas within the platform, as we saw in the *Depreciated features* section of this chapter. As part of this section, we will list the same areas of changed components so that all bases are covered to start planning and designing your implementation. As we saw in SharePoint 2016, there were many changes to the platform. Integrations that once were common were not common anymore. The installation has become more complex but for good reasons, as server components have been individualized for performance. So, in this version, we need to expect the same types of updates and even more integration with Microsoft 365 using the hybrid features.

Here is the list of new features for SharePoint Server 2019.

Service application enhancements

A change has been added to the Access Services 2013 service application. The service now supports the Send Email action for sending email messages from within the application. This is a nice new feature to have, and I know a lot of users will look forward to using it with this version of SharePoint. I know that when working with customers, this was a feature that was often needed.

Additional documentation links for central administration

As administrators, we always look for the latest and greatest information on the products we support. I can vouch that sometimes finding information that supports SharePoint on the Microsoft website is tough to do. I don't believe it's meant to be tough to find, but sometimes just finding the right information to support something we are trying to accomplish or need for support of new endeavors takes some time. Since so many people blog and try to post what they find out first through Microsoft channels, these sites can weigh in to find reliable information directly. Microsoft, in support of SharePoint using links within central administration, makes it easier for farm administrators to find information and reach the latest SharePoint administration documentation. They can also find the latest public updates by adding links to the SharePoint central administration home page:

SharePoint Server

This guide helps IT Pros plan, deploy, and manage SharePoint Server 2016 and 2013 in their enterprise environments.

Get started

Migration

Hybrid

Community

Product feedback

End user content

Figure 1.1 – SharePoint support home page

The site is well organized and categorized for a quick turnaround on what you're searching for. I really think this will go a long way for admins and developers across the world who support the product and keep things centralized to find reliable information.

Communication sites

Communication sites hit the scene in SharePoint Server 2013. These sites were created to help better share news, showcase stories, or broadcast messages to other users within the site. With communication sites, there is now a new Hero web part that can display up to five items with rich images, wording, and associated links to draw attention to the content you deem as highly visible on your communication site.

Fast Site Creation

Fast Site Creation was introduced in SharePoint Server 2016. Although I have seen performance data captured on this negating the feature of creating sites more quickly, in this version of SharePoint 2019, significant performance areas have been enhanced and you can see a major difference in the creation of sites. Only certain templates can be created using this method and are listed as follows.

Fast Site Creation can use these templates:

- OneDrive personal site [SPSPERS#10]

- Team site (modern only) [STS#3]

- Communication site [SITEPAGEPUBLISHING#0]

Fast Site Creation is used when creating sites in the following entry points:

- OneDrive personal site auto-provisioning
- The **Create Site** button on SharePoint home
- The `New-SPSite` PowerShell cmdlet with the `-CreateFromSiteMaster` switch parameter

Increased storage file size in SharePoint document libraries

Microsoft has increased the file size limitation for files to 15 GB. This gives us a new maximum file size we can support and import into our document libraries. With this, we must be careful and conscious of what we plan for disk sizes during our implementation. We want to make sure that if we are using this maximum size, we account for that with our disk space. Remember, shredded storage is still in play, so when we turn on versioning, we only retain the changes made to the file and not another copy of the file with those changes. There are some best practices you can follow to help relieve your environment from performance issues with these large files.

Modern lists and libraries

Within older versions of SharePoint, we saw lists and libraries as classic experiences. SharePoint 2019 brings a whole new experience to our lists and libraries, which can be seen in the list and library pages. The lists and libraries in this modern experience make it easier to make updates and change what was normally in the list or library settings.

Modern sharing experiences

In older versions of SharePoint, sharing content was a task that took a little time to achieve. Since SharePoint 2019 uses the modern experience you see in SharePoint Online, you will notice that sharing is now at your fingertips with the interface you need to keep security a focus. Another new enhancement is that you will be warned if you are sharing to a large group or sharing a large number of items, which comes in handy when using **Active Directory** (**AD**) groups.

The modern experience is here in SharePoint 2019. You will now see the modern experience in sites and other pages as seen in SharePoint Online. Not all features that SharePoint Online exhibits are available in SharePoint 2019 on-premises. Adding new site pages creates a new modern experience, which gives you enhanced improvements. These pages are easy to create by just clicking in **Site Actions** and clicking **New | Site page**.

Modern search experiences

SharePoint Server 2019 offers an enhanced search experience in addition to the classic experience seen in older versions of SharePoint. In this version of SharePoint, the results are populated as soon as you start to type in the search box. There are some differences we will explore later in this book from a search administrator's point of view but the user experience has been updated for faster search results.

Modern team sites

SharePoint 2019 brings forth the experience of modern team sites, which also brings a new and fresh user experience to SharePoint sites. The home page has been redesigned and improves the display of content so that the most important information is presented. This new page also improves on discovering the most common tasks as well. Again, as stated in the communication site, as a new feature, users can create modern team sites from the SharePoint home site without needing IT to help them. SharePoint Server 2019 continues to support creating classic team sites as well for those who may want to continue using them.

Sharing using modern internet information APIs

With sharing, using modern internet information APIs, I have waited for this API change for many years as we were always stuck using the IIS6 APIs even up to SharePoint 2016. Microsoft has modernized its integration with IIS, which in the past was used in conjunction with legacy IIS6 APIs. In SharePoint 2019, Microsoft has removed all dependencies on II6 API components and now uses the IIS7+ APIs to manage IIS. IIS7+ APIs are the latest and greatest supported APIs from Microsoft. With the integration of these latest and greatest APIs, we can now more easily adopt new IIS features and with this integration, IIS will provide seamless integrations with Windows Server releases. Since this change has altered how we install SharePoint from a backward-compatibility standpoint, the following Windows Server features will no longer be installed by the SharePoint prerequisite installer: IIS 6 Management Compatibility (`Web-Mgmt-Compat`), IIS 6 Metabase Compatibility (`Web-Metabase`), and IIS 6 Scripting Tools (`Web-Lgcy-Scripting`).

SharePoint home page

The SharePoint home page has changed in SharePoint 2019. The home page now uses a modern UI experience that gives users more integrated access to all their sites online and on-premises. This new modern experience saves users' time by bringing everything together in one unified view. It allows users to browse their intranet and see activities across the site, as well as shows a personal view of all team news. The SharePoint home page has now been changed to give users direct access to create new, modern sites using self-service site creation, which was never available in other SharePoint versions. The home page can be reached by clicking the SharePoint icon in the SharePoint app launcher.

Creating sites from the home page

As I have stated in this chapter, the self-service site creation experience now supported in the new SharePoint home page now supports creating new sites in a different web application. The new self-service site creation feature will allow you to decide whether the web application is hosted locally or in a remote environment. When creating site collections, you will see options for creating sites in the same web application or options for other web applications in the same farm. You can also create sites in remote site collections using the remote web application drop-down field.

Site creation support for AAM zones

When creating sites using the self-service creation on the SharePoint home page, it fully supports **Alternate Access Mapping (AAM)** zones. Sites can be created using different web applications from local and remote farms. External resources have to be created on both farms for this type of site creation to be available. This process would apply for the same web application, sites created in a different web application on the local farm, and sites created on a remote farm.

This brings a different experience for site collection admins as they will be able to create a site on any web application they manage. This will help bring faster results when sites are requested, and the site collection admin will be able to reach across platforms and web applications to create these sites.

SMTP authentication when sending emails

Microsoft has made some big changes in how you can use SMTP within a SharePoint farm. SharePoint 2019 now supports authenticating to external SMTP servers when sending email messages for notifications. Authentication for the connection can be configured through the central administration website or through PowerShell. SharePoint Server 2019 also supports connecting to external SMTP servers that accept anonymous connections. This new SMTP feature makes it easier for administrators to adhere to requirements for integration of SharePoint into highly secure environments where authentication is a requirement. Admins will no longer need to configure smart host relays for SharePoint farm environments.

Use of # and % in file and folder names

Microsoft has made changes for document and folder names. SharePoint 2019 now supports the # and % characters being part of naming in lists and libraries. Including these characters makes it easier to sync content from personal storage devices to SharePoint.

Syncing files with the OneDrive sync client (NGSC)

As mentioned in the *Deprecated features* section, the Groove client has been changed. The Next Generation client will now be available and will be used for OneDrive synchronization as well. The client will sync files within your SharePoint Server 2019 team sites and personal sites with all your devices. The client will be a lot easier to use and supports some advanced features, such as push notifications, IRM protection, and Files On-Demand. IRM is a key feature, as this will keep the rights management policies associated with any documents synced to your devices.

PowerShell enhancements

This section lists the new PowerShell cmdlets for SharePoint Server 2019.

New user profile synchronization PowerShell cmdlets

As you can see from this chapter, Microsoft has been in the process of converting the old STSADM commands from SharePoint 2010 and 2007 to PowerShell. In this version, the `stsadm.exe -o sync` command has been converted but has been separated into a few different PowerShell cmdlets, as shown:

- `Get-SPContentDatabase` cmdlet with the optional `-DaysSinceLastProfileSync` parameters: This command is used to return content databases that haven't been synchronized with User Profile Service.

- `Clear-SPContentDatabaseSyncData` cmdlet with optional `-DaysSinceLastProfileSync`: This command is used to clear user profile synchronization information from the content databases in the farms that haven't been synchronized.

- `Update-SPProfileSync` cmdlet: This command is used to update the user profile synchronization settings to update the main synchronization schedule, identify new users in the sweep schedule, and exclude web applications from synchronization.

The `stsadm.exe -o sync` command will also be supported for those who still rely on STSADM.

New Get-SPContentDatabaseOrphanedData PowerShell cmdlet

In older versions of SharePoint, we used the STSADM `stsadm.exe -o enumallwebs` command to enumerate all webs using the command line. This command has now been converted into a PowerShell cmdlet. You can now use the new `Get-SPContentDatabaseOrphanedData` cmdlet and run it against content databases to find any orphaned data within it. The `stsadm.exe -o enumallwebs` command supports backward compatibility.

New Set-SPApplicationCredentialKey PowerShell cmdlet

Due to the changes in SharePoint 2019, Microsoft is converting all `stsadm.exe` commands into PowerShell. The `stsadm.exe -o setapppassword` command has been updated in SharePoint 2019 to be used as a PowerShell cmdlet. You can now use the new `Set-SPApplicationCredentialKey` cmdlet to set the application credential key on the local server. Services affected by this command are the SharePoint People Picker control and SMTP authentication. The `stsadm.exe -o setapppassword` command is still supported as an option for backward compatibility.

New Remove-SPApplicationCredentialKey PowerShell cmdlet

The new `Remove-SPApplicationCredentialKey` cmdlet and administrator user rights give access to remove the application credential key from the local server. The impact level of this cmdlet is set to high due to the fact that removing the application credential key from the local server will either cause a block of functionality or degrade the ability for the service affected to function properly. Examples of services that could be affected are the SharePoint People Picker control and SMTP authentication.

New health analyzer rules

The health analyzer serves as a way to warn us when configurations and other areas of SharePoint are out of line with best practices. These new health rules will help us to support our SharePoint Server 2019 farm in many new ways:

- **People Picker health rule**: The People Picker health analyzer rule has been added to detect whether servers in the farm are missing the encryption key. The encrypted key is needed to retrieve People Picker credentials in SharePoint. The new health analyzer rule detects when the People Picker is configured to find users in another forest or domain with a one-way trust to the SharePoint farm's domain. When the rule is run, it returns information if the rule finds any missing encryption keys. The process will then notify the SharePoint farm administrator.

- **SMTP authentication health rule**: There is a new SMTP authentication health rule that has been added for SMTP authentication. This health analyzer rule notifies the SharePoint farm administrator if any servers in the SharePoint farm are missing the encryption key needed to retrieve the credentials for authentication.

Improved features

The following listed features are improved in SharePoint Server 2019.

Distributed Cache now uses background garbage collection by default: Distributed Cache, during my travels helping customers, has always been a configuration left out and forgotten. This configuration is very important to the stability of your SharePoint farm and should not be left out. Make sure to configure this as one of the first steps once your farm has been created and services are stable. Make sure to follow the Microsoft configuration best practices for this service to work effectively in your environment. In SharePoint Server 2019, Distributed Cache has changed to include AppFabric velocity cache. AppFabric velocity cache will be used for background garbage collection. This new component helps to provide a more sound experience for features that depend on the Distributed Cache service.

File path limit of 400 characters: In SharePoint Server 2019, the file path length limit was increased from 260 characters to 400 characters. The file path is all the characters used when typing in the URL after the domain or server name and port number. This will be helpful as it can help with content that may be nested within sites that require longer URLs.

Hybrid experience improvements: In SharePoint Server 2019, there is a new hybrid status bar located at the top of the central administration page. The minimum requirements for hybrid connectivity are:

- A reverse proxy
- STS certificate
- Inbound connectivity
- Operational Active Directory (AD DS), SharePoint Server Farm, and Microsoft 365 Organization (E1 – minimized functionality with hybrid federated search results only, E3 and E4)

Once the farm has reached the minimum requirements needed to support the hybrid connectivity to Microsoft 365, the page will give you direct access to launch the Hybrid Configuration wizard. The links have also been added throughout the central administration site, so you always have access to get to the Hybrid Configuration wizard.

Recycle bin improvements: In SharePoint Server 2019, users can restore items they have deleted personally, along with other items that other users have deleted. Users would need to have edit permissions on the deleted items for them to be available in the recycle bin.

Sharing email template: Sharing email notifications have been updated to use the modern template design. We can now set the `SPWebApplication.SharingEmailUseSharePoint2016Templates` property to `true` so that if we want to continue using the previous email sharing template, we can do so.

Suite navigation and app launcher improvements: Microsoft has changed the suite navigation and app launcher experience in SharePoint Server 2019. The experience using these interfaces is very similar to the Microsoft 365 experience. Users using the hybrid experience will now have a seamless experience using both SharePoint Server 2019 and SharePoint Online.

The SPFX Framework: This is the latest from Microsoft to support the development of custom web parts for both SharePoint and Teams clients. The SPFX Framework is used to customize modern sites, but modern sites cannot be fully customized. Developers can use Angular, React, or JavaScript with SPFX for customizing SharePoint. We can also integrate many applications with the modern UI easily but the developer has fewer options compared to developing on classic sites. Classic sites are fully customizable using JSOM and CSOM along with the REST API for customizing classic sites. There is now increased support for JSOM and CSOM.

Telemetry privacy experience: SharePoint Server 2019 now has an updated telemetry management experience. As you set up your farm, you can provide an email address that will be used for the telemetry contact as part of your organization. This is in anticipation of future telemetry reporting capabilities that will allow customers to associate SharePoint Server and OneDrive sync client telemetry with their hybrid tenancy. The email address provided cannot be used outside of the SharePoint farm. This address will not be sent to Microsoft for any reason. The farm data will be used to generate a unique hash value that represents your farm. This will make your data unique when uploading telemetry data to Microsoft. As customers start to associate telemetry with hybrid tenancy, the email address will be used as part of the process to show ownership of the data. If you do not want to provide this data to Microsoft, you have a choice to opt in or out at any time.

Visio Services accessibility: Visio Services has introduced a few accessibility improvements. The improvements are for high-contrast displays, keyboard navigation, and Narrator. Within Visio Services, users will be able to use the different panes from the keyboard shortcuts listed:

- Move focus to the **Comments** pane = *Alt + R*
- Move focus to the **Shape Data** pane = *Alt + S*
- Move focus to the canvas = *Alt + C*

Server support updates

Server support updates include updates that have changed in the server creation or what the server supports as part of the installation for SharePoint 2019. There were also a few changes in SharePoint 2016 that are well documented, which if you are upgrading you may want to review as well. This does not include server specifications or configuration information, only newly supported and non-supported updates:

- **Drive filesystem support**: SharePoint Server 2019 provides support for drives that are formatted with the **Resilient File System** (**ReFS**).

- **Single-label domain names**: SharePoint Server 2019 will not support single-label domain names.

- **SQL updates**: In prior versions of SharePoint, SQL Server Express was supported to provide a single server installation for the quick setup of SharePoint Server. In SharePoint Server 2019, SQL Server Express is not supported as you will have to install a separate SQL Server instance to support even a small test or development environment. In Azure, the use of SQL Azure (the SaaS service) is not available for support for any SharePoint databases. Please take note that these changes will change the way you provide lower-level environments.

- **Office client installations**: SharePoint Server 2019 does not support Office applications installed on the same computer. The minimum supported version for SharePoint 2019 is the Office 2010 client.

- **.NET Framework 3.5**: As admins, we are aware of how to install .NET Framework 3.5 on our servers when preparing our operating systems for SharePoint. Prep for .NET Framework 3.5 will continue to be supported using a manual installation as there have been no updates to improve this feature installation for automatic install using the prerequisite process.

Now that we have identified all the areas where there are new features within SharePoint 2019 and have learned about the old features that have been deprecated, we can now focus on how we move forward with our new farm configuration. Moving forward takes documentation and thinking about what our goals are for this project in terms of the administrators and users who use the services.

We will start that process in the next section of this chapter with accessing the environment, which will give us the opportunity to see where we are in the current environment and where we need to be in the new environment. This also gives us the opportunity to understand where features will be enhanced and where features will stay the same or be non-existent in our new environment. Having this laid out now will help you design the right solutions to support the users that currently use the environment so that no interruption to services happens during the migration; or even if you are starting from scratch, this helps to match requirements to the services you are providing in the farm.

Assessing the environment

As stated in this section's title, our first order of business is to find out what we have in our current environment, what's changing in the new environment, and what's new in the new environment with regards to SharePoint Server 2019. We began this chapter by looking at deprecated features, removed features, and new features for SharePoint 2019. Now, we need to look at our current environment to see where we are now and how we can improve it. This is very important to figure out how SharePoint is running if you have a current farm configured in your enterprise before going forward with a new implementation. This should also include multi-cloud deployments that end up eating your costs and you paying more than you were in on-premises financial support.

Assessments can be done in several ways. You can do the assessment yourself using a team within your IT department to find out all the details and assess where your current environment stands, or you can hire an independent contractor to come in and figure out your current state for you. Microsoft also offers these services as well, where they run tools to export your information about your farm and ask questions about your organization's processes and how you manage the environment.

I can vouch for this risk assessment done by Microsoft because I have done these while working at Microsoft as a **Premier Field Engineer (PFE)**. This process is very thorough and you will receive a report after the engagement to let you know of things you have missed and things that you are doing well. This will give you a baseline and you will need this going forward as you start your new project for your move to SharePoint 2019.

Even when you are starting a new SharePoint installation from scratch, it really helps to spend a day with seasoned professionals combing through your environment and figure out all the things that are working and not working to support your new farm. This would include overall configuration, network stability, server performance, network, farm design, best practices, and other IT-related and non-IT organizational information.

The intent of an assessment is to provide findings to help align your farm to best practices in the industry and design your farm accordingly. Even if your current environment is not stable, you can still fix issues that may hinder you from moving forward before starting the project, which will give you a better baseline on how your new environment should be configured.

To understand your SharePoint environment's state, this would mean looking at the details of the farm from these areas and documenting each one of them:

- Authentication methods
- Web applications
- Customizations

- Workflow
- Application services
- Search
- Farm configuration
- DEV, TEST, and production environments
- Content database health (unused, version, and size)
- Orphaned sites and site collections
- Custom and third-party solutions, active and inactive
- Server health (Windows logs)
- Server performance and configuration (SQL and SP)
- Farm Health Analyzer issues
- Microsoft update status
- Governance health
- Organizational health for support of the environment
- Network performance and issues
- Current known issues
- Multi-cloud complexity

Grades should be given to each area assessed so that you can determine the next steps for that particular finding:

Green	Shows that the item was as expected and configured based on best practices	
Yellow	Shows that the item was close to being configured based on best practice state	
Red	Shows that the area needs reconfiguration to bring it to a best practice state	
Purple	Shows that the item was reconfigured during the maintenance and is now in a best practice state	
Orange	Shows that the item was not tested during the assessment	

Figure 1.2 - Grades

An example of an assessed item in our document is as follows:

SharePoint Health Analyzer	
Finding	More cache hosts are running in this deployment than are registered with SharePoint.
Summary Recommendation	Distributed Cache - we need to consolidate all the servers running the service to one Ditrubuted Cache Cluster. One of the servers that is part of the cluster is down and some servers that were configured previously are still registered in the cluster.
Risk Status	

Figure 1.3 – An assessed item

The outcome of this assessment would be to develop a remediation plan based on the findings. This remediation plan could be used to clean up the current environment to support the migration or you could start clean and avoid the potholes you created in the old environment using a migration tool to migrate the content.

One thing I also want to point out is to make sure that your current environment is working and satisfying our user community. We may want to send out a survey or two to see what responses we get from our user community as well. One of the biggest errors we can make is only focusing on the technical aspects of this assessment and not the satisfaction of the users who use it every day.

There are also developers that work on this platform that we need to talk to as well. We want to make sure we are providing all they need in our current or new SharePoint environment to satisfy their workspace. Sometimes, developers are left out of talks as well but they are another big part of the whole equation. There are also servers and processes that they are part of that may need some tweaking in our new environment. These may require servers and software to bring the environment up to speed for them to use effectively.

This assessment process must be thorough and really doesn't have to take a long period of time. You can gather details in a month or so depending on the size of your environment and user community. Email is an effective way to gather interview results with short conversations on the phone. You can also create a SharePoint list to gather those requirements and list details about the solutions these users are looking for to help them with their workload. In the new environment, take some of those requirements for solutions and develop those solutions quickly to show how SharePoint can help, and show those solutions as a demo when you start talking to other departments about new requirements for new solutions.

> **Note**
>
> Remember that some solutions you develop will cross department lines, so we want to be able to know what solutions we have available in case another department asks for a similar solution. Keep a list of those solutions and details in a SharePoint list and on hand for demonstrations.

Other collaborative tools

In our assessment, we also want to look outside of SharePoint and see what applications our users are using in the enterprise for collaborating. Having conversations with your user community is key to moving forward with your new environment. It helps you determine how users want to use the collaborative systems that are currently in place and helps us to design the next environment to support some of their wish lists. This also gives the users a chance to tell you about any pain points or areas of concern they may have currently.

When assessing the user community, we need to talk to our stakeholders and see where we have failed in delivering collaborative support, which should be our first priority. During our governance stakeholder meetings, we should find out what the stakeholders are looking for to help them with their workload as well. There is also the need to see where they are in terms of being able to use the tools approved for use within the environment. This would show whether they have the ability to use the tools effectively on their own, which would have required some training in the past.

In environments I have assessed, there is always the question of "other" collaborative tools but these are never brought up by management or the IT staff that are out of scope with "approved applications." A lot of these departments are out of touch with the user community and have not reached out often enough to keep an eye on what's happening in their part of the enterprise. This is key to why governance is important and why this assessment will kick-start a new beginning for your enterprise application roll-out, now and in the future.

Keeping an eye on what's happening has been a complicated task because as we have moved forward in technology with other mobile apps and cloud applications that have been developed for collaboration, desktops have changed and platforms have been enhanced, such as mobile phones, which give users a computer in the palm of their hands. Users, in most cases, have not been restricted to use these tools either on their phone or through the browser. This brings up the question of what content is being used, how that content is being used, and why it's being used outside of our enterprise.

In this part of the assessment exercise, we need to focus on these outside applications and determine where these applications can either be used or replaced as part of our integrated SharePoint environment. Take, for instance, the case of using Slack; this is a common occurrence because some users use this application at home or for other personal use. So, obviously, they would be used to this application and view it as an alternative for work. If they can bring others on board in their group or department, then you have a rogue app being used for company intellectual property.

My point is not to demonize all apps or say that they're bad because they are not Microsoft-built, but I want to make it clear that we have to set boundaries on what applications are being used in our environment. We want to keep our data within the control of our users but also in control under our enterprise umbrella. The communication of these approved applications should be clear and written on your company's intranet.

Determining how to proceed or go forward is up to you. As in my example, Slack could be one of the mobile apps you see users applying to their business processes. When evaluating your state of collaboration, you may want to keep this in place or determine an alternative for them to use in place of that third-party application. Microsoft has introduced many new applications as part of the Microsoft 365 cloud that can be integrated with SharePoint on-premises and the cloud. Microsoft Teams would be a great alternative instead of using Slack because of its integration with SharePoint.

Make sure to assess all areas of collaboration, which includes wikis, shared drives, mobile apps, cloud applications such as Google Apps, and other areas of collaboration users could be using within your desktop and mobile platforms. Take these to the governance board and determine how to communicate these efforts to create a safe and secure environment for your company enterprise data so that nothing is shared outside of your control. Create requirements and use cases from these assessed areas as well to determine your path forward.

Our assessment is the key to the success of this project and I cannot stress enough the importance of knowing and understanding where you are currently. Again, even if you are starting fresh with SharePoint, this is an important step to go through and you should do what is told in this chapter. This really gives you the opportunity to start fresh and to make improvements to the service.

The biggest failures come from not knowing where you are currently and not being honest about where you are with errors/blotched configurations and where you want to go with the service for the future. Requirements and requests for services are missed. This could mean someone implements a separate system that does one of SharePoint's many processes and you could have included this in the overall SharePoint service agreement to support that new process.

With the assessment, you are looking at all of those areas to make sure you share the capabilities with others so that these duplicate applications do not get implemented. You can also avoid having duplicate solutions within SharePoint, but at the same time duplicate those solutions for others using the platform. Again, this goes for multi-cloud implementations as well as these seem to have spawned at a lot of companies. You need to do a deep evaluation and inventory at this time. This saves money and time!

As we go through our assessment, we will look at best practices that are given by Microsoft along with software limitations. This gives us a guide on what resources are required and their limits that we can use based on services within SharePoint. Best practices help us manage our server resources and understand what we need to run our environment with no processing bottlenecks.

Best practices

SharePoint is being improved by Microsoft within new versions of the software, which brings new features that require us as IT professionals to look at each version with a fresh set of eyes. Microsoft releases best practices for these newer versions of SharePoint to help us plan our environments based on the testing Microsoft does as part of its new product delivery. These tests push the limits and boundaries of the product, and based on those tests, Microsoft gives us a list of areas we need to adhere to so that we get the most out of the product.

Microsoft's boundaries and limits page is dedicated to defining limitations within the versions of SharePoint released. These are best practices shared by Microsoft to give tested areas a maximum threshold for configuration. These tests are done when Microsoft has finished developing the product to gather these points for sharing with the community. These limitations are also valuable to your organization as part of the design and configuration of your SharePoint farm. Communication of these values should be shared with other administrators and users as the items are defined across the board.

Capacity (threshold) limitations are included as part of the boundaries and limits dedicated to SharePoint. Depending on your version, you will see different capacity limitations and available configuration areas. The capacity limitations do give some hard-limit areas and some areas are defined, but you have the ability to go beyond them based on other resources you have defined in your environment, such as servers and other hardware supporting the environment.

Best practices are important to the design of any system as again, they help us provide a stable environment for our users. I can say from experience that not all the best practices and boundaries will be hard limits we cannot go beyond, but they give us a baseline to work from and test in our own environments. In this section, you will see a subset of the list of server best practices I follow when preparing to install the product as part of my assessment.

The reason for defining the best practices listed is that we need to make sure we know the pitfalls as part of the guidance in our assessment. You can describe these best practices as areas you want to avoid, almost like a removed feature in a way. Whether we are looking at our old environment or prepping for a new environment, these best practices will go a long way in avoiding bad situations, configurations, and performance issues.

Best practices can come from Microsoft or other IT technology; as well as these are things we have learned through using SharePoint over the years that have not changed but have stayed true throughout each version of the software, and some new things. Some of these best practices actually void your support for Microsoft as well. You really want to pay good attention to these items and mark them as part of your assessment.

Again, there are a lot more items we can share here, and if you want to review Microsoft's list of best practices, refer to the following link: `https://social.technet.microsoft.com/wiki/contents/articles/12438.sharepoint-community-best-practices.aspx#Performance_related_best_practice`.

The following is a short list of things I always think about when assessing environments and getting geared up for planning and designing my new environment.

Windows Server and VMs

Virtual Machines (VMs) are widely used as servers for environments such as SharePoint. The hosts, and VMs running on the hosts, are very important to the stability of the farm. These are a couple of things to be aware of when setting up your VMs:

- VMs should never be configured with dynamically configured resources (RAM, CPU, and so on). If this is the case, Microsoft can void your support for the farm.

- Do not clone VMs with SharePoint – they are already installed for a quicker VM installation process.

- Create multiple environments for DEV, TEST, and PROD.

- Make sure to plan for efficient disk space, RAM, and CPU to support the environment.

SQL Server

SQL Server is the core data store for a SharePoint farm. This server should be planned very carefully for performance and redundancy. Please review my short list of best practices:

- SQL Server dedicated to SharePoint only per farm.

- Redundant configuration using Always On.

- MAX DOP setting 1 for all SQL servers supporting SharePoint.

- SQL Server 2016 and 2017 support SharePoint 2019.

- SQL Server 2016 comes with support for SharePoint integrated mode Reporting Services.

- SQL Server 2017 uses native mode Reporting Services only but supports the SQL Server Reporting Services reporting web part and Power BI is supported via an on-premises gateway.

- **Logical Unit Number (LUN)**, which is a drive space that should be created separately for Configuration DB, Service, Search, Content, Secure Store, TEMP and other SQL databases that support SharePoint.

- No third parties or databases supporting other applications should be running on a SQL server supporting SharePoint.

- Configure a maintenance plan in SQL Server to support restoring databases in the case of loss of the server.

- Use a naming convention for your databases (for example, `App_ NAMEnTypeofDB_Environment`, that is, `SP_FarmConfig_DEV`).

SharePoint Server

SharePoint is a complex server installation and requires planning and precise configuration. Please review my short list of initial best practices before you start the journey into planning and design:

- 2–3 hard drives for storage SharePoint Server configurations (C drive for the operating system, D drive for applications and install files (optional), and an E drive for SharePoint LOGS and Search Indexes).

- Always provide minimum server resource requirements for all environments.

- Ports for SharePoint need to be defined for communication between the servers within the environment.

- Antivirus exclusions need to be configured so that areas of the hard drive are free from virus protection.

- All service accounts must have names under 20 characters long.

- Make sure to use a separate admin account to install the product (not your personal account) and use several service accounts to define your service application pools.

- Create a farm admins group in AD and assign local admin rights to this group on each server.

- Remember that the farm account only needs admin rights on the server deemed the User Profile Service server and that right can be taken away after the service is started.

- Always use PowerShell to create your farm so that you can name your databases and other resources.

- Use AD groups and assign permissions within the sites for the best performance.

- If doing custom builds of the operating system, make sure you test those builds, doing a full installation before implementing your production farm.

- Always define quotas for your site collections.

I have only mentioned a few things to be aware of in this chapter and have defined many other areas of best practices throughout the book. Some are from Microsoft and others are lessons learned that I follow and have jotted down through my years working with SharePoint.

As we go into our next section, on governance, be aware that all these chapters were put together for a reason. All of these areas outline the pre-installation work you need to do before you design your SharePoint farm. If you move forward without planning and assessments, you will find out later that you totally missed the boat. The problem is, this takes time, and if you want to give your community a great SharePoint service, make sure to follow the guidelines given in this book. I cannot define everything due to the limitations I have on pages in the book, but this will point you in the right direction to have a vision of how you should be implementing SharePoint for a new or migration project in the real world.

Governance

A challenge for companies today is deciding who owns the collaborative and social environments in our company – is it IT or the business? In the case of collaboration tools and social tools, it's the business, as IT is only a part of the governance stakeholder community. SharePoint is included due to how widespread the data that could be included in the content on-premises and on the cloud. This reaches across mobile, desktop, and web platforms presented to our employees every day.

The other challenge is managing those available apps and enterprise solutions and bringing the best solutions to our customers and departments within our entity. We should never go into any project without first seeing how it reflects on our enterprise and the data that is presented in that solution. As stated, if you miss the mark on governance, you will fail the implementation.

As part of our environment assessment in this chapter, we need to take a look at governance policies and standards to support our current and or newly implemented systems. When creating and implementing any new application systems within your enterprise, you need to provide policy guidance around the system to support it using policies. This would include actions such as content updates, role assignment, branding, and even training, as a few of many examples. The support of any system can be easy to complex, and for that reason can stretch over many areas of management.

The areas of support included to be defined are as follows:

- Define technical management.
- Define policies and standards.
- Define guiding principles.
- Define features and web parts.
- Define site deployment and management.
- Define customizations and enhancements.
- Define site and system security.

To provide the best policies and standards to support our new or changing system, we need to include all of the areas mentioned. To support these policies, we would look to governance as the mechanism to provide a composed list of system rules and policies to be established within an organization. These policies would bind to a system or application, and/or standardize these areas from a global perspective. Each can bring an individual scope as well, in which a unique policy standard may be required depending on that application's requirements.

This system of rules known as governance should meet the requirements of the users while keeping administrative and managerial control of that data for compliance, policies, processes, and all associated content. Included in this process is the process to check that the appropriate systems run appropriate applications on their platforms and also give the users on the board the ability to choose the right policies for the applications being developed.

Governance of systems in your enterprise is needed to support applications and processes that bring insight into ultimately all company data. With governance, you can define where content lives, define shared policies across applications, and create policies to protect those data areas. Since this is a centralized process and governing body, you will also catch projects of the same outcome where you can recommend centralizing some applications for different departments in your organization. This will help not to replicate systems of the same kind but to use already developed platforms that can be repeated within the organization to save money.

Stakeholders

The governance rules are created by a team of stakeholders within the company in which everyone provides input to build individual policies that can be related to a certain application or broad policies that affect all applications for individual or multiple platforms. Rules are also created by a host of different stakeholders. They could range from top management personnel to users who actually use the applications within the environment. These rules should be implemented by this team or teams every time a new application or system is requested.

The reason we want stakeholders to come from different areas of the company is to provide different perspectives from all levels of management, the user community, and senior management. This helps to provide total coverage of ideas and a variety of issues that can be recommended to help prevent areas of the applications that may not affect those unaware due to the level of involvement.

As these policies and standards are being created, they also need to be communicated to the user community. With regard to that, I have seen a formal list of applications on intranet sites that were relayed by management but when assessing the environment, there were many other applications being used in the enterprise that were not approved for use. The confusion started when SharePoint was initially released, as no training for the users was given. All users interviewed had many things they could use SharePoint for, but did not know how to create those applications.

This left a big collaborative asset within the enterprise that got no use and was deemed an unusable product. Users were convinced that SharePoint was very hard to use and there was no hope for the platform. This started a revolution of all of the enterprise users and their management to find easier ways to do their work using mobile applications that most users needed for the same issues. You can see, even in this situation, how important training is to users when releasing a system, as well as how governance could have weighed in to solve common application requirements and prevent these rogue applications from being used.

Why governance is important

As a traveling engineer who has visited and spoken to well over 100 customers for SharePoint-related projects, I have noticed that most companies do not implement governance. This is something I find concerning, which is why I have included this as a section in this book. I cannot stress enough how important this process is to a system as sophisticated as SharePoint and other collaborative systems and apps. If you have not implemented a solid governance plan with the new addition of mobile apps and desktop changes due to cloud applications, these need to be looked at now.

The new age of apps and other mobile applications brought to the playing field has really made governance a challenge in enterprises. Compromise of this mobile data could happen because mobile platforms stretch to a wide audience and these apps can also be used from private computers that are secured by home users of these applications. This information is also not governed, which gives the opportunity to share content with a wide audience. If the user is not governing the associated apps, along with the device, and providing security standards, we do not know how data is being secured through these devices. In the event of a device being stolen, we have no idea what data could have lived on the device.

Mobile apps leave a big hole in our control over information and how it's being used within the organization, and now with the cloud, even outside the organization. Using mobile apps leaves data out of the control of the company and intellectual property unmanaged. Internal secrets can be compromised and shared with competitors if these companies that provide support for the apps are compromised. When data isn't centralized and controlled using a centralized security method, data is unable to be secured properly and unable to be shared within the enterprise. Having data centralized or spread over different platforms with policies and standards gives us more reporting capabilities and the ability to set policies to hinder the users of data inside and outside the organization.

In the cloud, we also have hybrid connected SharePoint on-premised environments and OneDrive, which also bring a new element of governed content that crosses networks. Each system has administrative controls, but some of the controls in the cloud are not in our hands. Policies for these types of connected data repositories also need to be considered in our governance document, as well as data compliance and security across networks.

Determining an approach

With systems such as SharePoint, you could have enterprise implementations of SharePoint that have been used for many years and those that are just getting started with the implementation of the product for the first time. If you are in the situation of having a system in place with no governance, it's time to get started. If you are starting fresh, it is also time to get started.

Do not release without governance or a plan in place for a SharePoint environment. SharePoint as a product has many areas to be concerned about for governance stability and the stability of the product. It was created to give users more control of their daily requirements, such as security and other ways of sharing, but can easily get out of hand if you do not provide policies and standards for this environment.

In the next section, we will go through some of the areas of concern and get you started with creating a governance plan. This process takes time and should be factored into your project. Although it is one of many areas of concern in your planning, some of these items can be determined while designing the system. The documentation that needs to be produced during a SharePoint implementation can be time-consuming but it is needed to really build this platform on a solid foundation.

Creating a governance plan

When creating a governance plan, there are a few things that should be included. In these times of additional mobile apps and other integrations between collaborative applications, we should not just be looking at SharePoint. SharePoint could be a big piece of our enterprise pie for collaborative applications, but there are other applications that bring value to our enterprise as well. Including overarching guidance for all governed collaborative areas actually makes sense because they all work together in some way, shape, or form.

When looking at our collaborative environments, we take the biggest piece and build around it. Collaboration can be made up of a centralized solution and many other small solutions that make up a total solution. All solutions will have different governance plans but can be built to integrate those areas related to others, which is what collaboration is. Creating this document is very important and I cannot stress enough how far this dictates the success or failure of a collaborative project.

The following are some guidelines on how to create your document and some high-level details about each area.

Vision statement

Using a vision statement in your governance document describes overall what you want to achieve with SharePoint or any application you are preparing this document for. This document should bring high-level details about the guidance provided within this living policies guide. You should make sure to make your vision statement clear and provide choices and critical guidelines that will be documented here. Again, this document is living and will always change. Keeping ongoing versions of this document is critical to the life cycle of governance in the environment you are writing it for.

This vision statement and details should be shared on the intranet for all users to see. This gives a way to communicate to the whole enterprise and not just SharePoint users.

Roles and responsibilities

Teams, as stated in this section, should be created to manage this document and the governance of any given application. The team can be the same team for all projects, or you can create different teams as needed to support your environment. Having many teams creates diversity and brings more ideas to projects that are in play.

Training also comes into play as these roles are defined, especially when implementing a new or updated software application such as SharePoint. You want to make sure your farm administrators, site administrators, and users get trained on the latest and greatest version of the product so that they understand how to use it before you implement it.

Microsoft has lots of help when it comes to training and getting the help you need for the communication of changes coming to the environment. Please review your Microsoft licensing and have a meeting with your technical account manager to figure out some of Microsoft's freebies and some other cost-effective ways to help you prepare your admins and users.

When looking at the roles, we can see that depending on the size of the project and integration points, there could be more roles needed. Examples of roles are shown in the following table:

Role	Key Responsibilities
Executive Sponsor	Manager is responsible for the solution and is the go-to person when it comes to pushing the agenda of the solution to others in management across departments in the enterprise.
Governance Board	This steering committee would be the governance team responsible for meeting the objectives of the solution. This board comprises of representatives of each of the major businesses represented in the solution, including human resources, communication areas of the company, and IT.
Business Owner	The business owner is the functional designer of the solution and works to make sure that the functionality needed is communicated to the groups. The business owner also does not have to have an IT background as the communication is from a user perspective.
Solution Technology Administrator	This administrator works hand in hand with the business owner to support the functionality and design of the solution from a technical standpoint.

Figure 1.4 – Roles and responsibility

Site collection roles are advised to be implemented as part of governing the sites from the top level. Site collection admin groups are used to create a top-level administrative group for each department or however your sites are distributed:

Role	Key Responsibilities
Site Sponsor	The Site Sponsor role is in place to manage the design and content of the site collection. This role is also responsible for making sure links, web parts, and other designed functionality are in place and working as they should.
Site Admin	Manages site security and day-to-day activities. These include security, retention, policies, data compliance, IRM policies, and content tags used within the site that create search results and or data hierarchies.
Site Designer	The Site Designer role is to make sure security policies are working and make sure that features that are being used work as expected. The role is in place to keep the functional areas intact.
Users	A user has access to the solution to access and share information. Users may have different access permissions in different areas of the solution. They can sometimes act as a contributor and other times acting as a visitor.

Figure 1.5 – Site collection roles

Utilizing a team is important to bring clarity as different ideas are shared to support a project and create policies around content. In governance, roles are always needed to make sure that a hierarchy is in place for those roles and the access they are provided. This also is true with securing information in sites that users access once the platform is available.

Guiding principles

Most companies in their vision of web content have preferences that outline best practices for all users and site designers that they will have to adhere to and understand.

Guiding principles define a company's preferences and support the vision and goals of the company. The critical statements that come out of this exercise best reflect the company's outlook and include best practices that all users and site designers must abide by to ensure the success of the company's implemented solution. It is common for your organization to share many of the same principles that I have seen in successful SharePoint deployments, which would include best practices from Microsoft. In some cases, you may deviate from those best practices, but for the most part, you will include a good majority of those common goals with the implementation.

Policies and standards

Policies define rules around content and use, which can be described as standards within SharePoint. Users are expected to adhere to policies without diverting from these policies. Governance policies are defined and usually driven from statutory, regulatory, or organizational requirements. These standards are set in place to encourage consistent practices. Users can adopt some standards to help define their content depending on the implementation and requirements.

When looking at standards, let's take an example: in a case management requirement, one of the key fields may be a case number. This number may consist of parts of a name and sequential numbers keeping cases in order, or there could be a different approach to this field requirement. All the policies and standards we are after define what this case number will be every time it is assigned and should not have many deviations from the standard once it is set.

Another example could be a branded page with web parts in a certain layout. This could be a standard for the company, but different departments may have wiggle room to change the layout but maybe not the colors, or maybe they are allowed to use a different logo on the site depending on the department. These types of standards need to be discussed as part of our governance process based on the project we are working on.

Content policies and standards

Create a list of policies and standards you will require when users and administrators create content within the SharePoint sites. These policies and standards control how content will be created, who has ownership of the content, and how the information should be managed. Publishing features are also addressed in this section if you plan to use publishing as a way of controlling information posted within the sites.

Creating subsites

When end users have control to create their own content within a SharePoint site, we have given them control to build their own content hierarchies. We need to guide users on best practices when giving them free reign to organize their content. So, in this area of your governance plan, you want to set standards on the areas that are affected by users when they do create new subsites.

They should make sure to set the following:

- **Content ownership**: Provide a content owner who has responsibility for the content and make them aware of any other governance practices related to their job.

- **Security**: Provide security for the new content and create new security groups when needed for highly sensitive information.

- **Content administration**: Someone should be managing the information and making sure that current and new sites are backed up and have the ability to be restored.

- **Navigation**: As information gets added to the site, make sure to not build deep hierarchical content within the site and keep the information easy for access by other users.

Posting content

When posting content, we want to make sure that documents and content posted to the site are not duplicated. There are features within SharePoint that can help with this, but ultimately, this is the job of all users. Duplicated information adds to your content size, especially when documents are concerned, and can also confuse users who may not get the latest version of a document with relevant information.

The site sponsor is ultimately responsible, but users are responsible as well. As a team, everyone should be working to ensure that posted content is accurate and complies with policies that are put in place for record retention.

Things you can do to define these types of policies are as follows:

- **Content cycle for posting**: Updating and validating content should be an ongoing cycle performed by all users. Deleting content that is stale or moving content that may have reached a cycle of completion could be a sign to move it using retention policies.

- **Content formats and naming conventions**: Some content, such as documents, may require templates to make the record a valid record. Naming conventions also weigh in as naming documents in certain formats may be a requirement by the sponsor.

- **Content that contains links**: Define responsibility for who should update links within documents to make sure that the links are still valid.

Content types and metadata

Content types are collections of settings or form details that define information within SharePoint lists. These collections can be used for gathering a collection of data from users or in a project plan. Content types can be defined for the entire enterprise or a site collection. Typically, these collections are used in local pages or sites. Site columns are referred to as property and can be a part of any content within a site as these are defined at the top-level site collection. Both are used as metadata to describe the content within a particular list, library, or even other content.

Managed Metadata is a similar collection of settings as well. This is centrally located on the farm, so all users can access it, and since it is centralized, the management of these terms is easier to keep organized. The metadata can also be segregated as well but this gives SharePoint owners a way to define how data is searched and presented.

In these cases, we need to include policies and standards related to these areas. These would need to be communicated so that users can request to create new content types and site columns, and manage metadata to support their project.

Social tags and ratings

Social tagging in SharePoint became popular in version 2013 and was new in 2010. These capabilities allow users to participate and interact with your SharePoint solution and improve content searchability. This feature allows users to tag information, which then classifies that information within the site that the user finds meaningful to them.

With all social capabilities, you should make sure your users understand the social tagging functionality and how it's used in the search index to provide security trimming. Security trimming provides access to information that a user has access to. If you do not have access to content, you will not see it in search results.

Content auditing

Within SharePoint, there is the ability to audit content changes. You should consider a policy to define a review process of sites and even types of content. Content that is available to all users in your company should be governed using a content management process. This process is used to ensure true, trusted, and vetted content is being displayed to users. The review process should be as frequent as you need but shouldn't be longer than a 1-year period.

Records retention

Records management is becoming a big deal in the SharePoint world. I see a lot of information on these types of solutions popping up everywhere. In the governance of these types of solutions, we need to create clear, defined policies on how records will be used within your solutions. Codes for records should be used to identify content as a record. You need to choose the appropriate method to apply records management policies, which is especially useful because this dictates how users find information as well.

Data compliance

In the latest versions of SharePoint, data compliance has come to the forefront. There are built-in compliance features for administrators for server roles and services. There are also compliance site collection features we need to create policies and standards around as well. These site collections have areas of automation that can be configured to help manage compliance and send notifications on faults with content within our sites. Policies and standards should be created to manage what constitutes a violation of data and what type of data should be protected.

Business process workflow

This is one feature in SharePoint that is getting used more and more within companies. This feature really needs oversight as well as guidance on how workflows should be created. The other side of this is reusability. If a standard workflow has been created for the approval process, then this workflow should not have to be recreated. We need to put in checks and balances as well to make sure we are not recreating the process and wasting developer time. Make sure to set policies and standards on the creation of these processes and provide guidance on what is considered a business process. You don't want to create something that really isn't needed.

Page layouts

Page layouts are very important to present data to your users. Users can easily get confused from the visual layout of a page, especially when data could be in no organized manner. All users with permissions to change and add web parts should be familiar with design and usability best practices.

Branding

Most organizations brand sites to give a look and feel based on the colors and logo of the company. There are sometimes different departments that would like to project a slightly different appeal to their entity within the company. In this case, there should be policies in place to consider slight deviations of branding for these reasons. We also want to keep in mind that users also want to know where they are within the site as well. For these reasons, we need to be careful about how we brand our sites and what we approve as part of our look and feel. Define standards and policies to help guide the branding within your company.

Blogs and wikis

Using blogs and wikis can result in posting wrong information or information that needs approval. End users should be aware of your organization's policies around posting content in these areas. We need to ensure we are not being too restrictive but have checks and balances around this information to ensure the responsibility of the content owner's published works. Consider creating policies and standards around any information published for use within SharePoint.

Announcements

Using the announcement web part to relay information to your users is very useful as a SharePoint feature. With that, we need to make sure the information is projected well and is precise and descriptive. The title and announcement text should encapsulate all that needs to be said within a descriptive title and no more than a few sentences. We should avoid large fonts and not create emphasis on words using italics or underlining.

Picture and video libraries

Picture and video content is very popular now. We see more and more of these files as these types of content become more needed. The size of these files can be very large as well, which brings a new element to how to structure our databases and where we keep this content. There should be policies around types of files, size of files, and types of content, which should always be business-related content. We should also have policies around the ownership of images as well and how we copyright those images created by our users.

Links

The site designer will need to review and edit documents and other content to make sure that links have the option of opening either in the same window or in a new window. Also, there should be policies for links within documents, pages within the sites, and links that go outside to your intranet.

Content-specific guidelines

To really impact your community with accessible content for the end users, we must make content easy to find but also structured. 508 compliance also comes into play because not everyone will have the ability to access content using formal methods. These policies for easily accessible data will include those areas that will be addressed by tagging content. Accessibility is important and is not always a thing we talk about or put a lot of effort into. This is due to the vast majority of our users not usually requiring accessibility features. There are many things we can do to help those who cannot easily access data in an out-of-the-box format. Third parties and other manual ways of including all users can be achieved using these methods.

Security

Security is one of the most important design elements in a SharePoint site. When you think about security during the design process, make sure you understand how content will need to be secured in the site as this will affect how the site is accessed. Site structure and page layout could be affected due to this important element.

It is important to ensure that everyone who has permissions to assign security roles understands how SharePoint security works and has had some type of training to ensure that company policies are followed, especially with the introduction of the cloud and hybrid connectivity.

There are options to create security groups using AD and SharePoint. Users would need to understand when to use these different groups and why they are being used. Please make sure to define policies around your content clearly so that everyone understands how SharePoint security works and understands your policies and procedures.

Training

When it comes to governance, there could be a big learning curve as some users may have never been a part of a process like this before. This brings another area of concern, but you do not want to turn away those that are deemed as part of the team due to this issue. I know of training centers that key on governance as a topic of choice but you can also talk with Microsoft to help you work on your governance plan as well as training those who will be part of the team.

Training for governance is too important to miss! To get the most out of the personnel you select as part of this process, please train your staff to understand what the governance plan is all about.

Summary

Understanding your environment is very important before starting a new installation or upgrading a project to a new version of SharePoint. Again, make sure you know all the deprecated features, new features, boundaries and limits, best practices, and governance. All these areas need to be investigated as part of an assessment to figure out what areas need help in your current environment and what areas are changing.

Remember to document all areas of your environment if you haven't already. It is very important to understand your position. Along with documentation, governance is a very important part of the implementation process and if you do not have this in place currently, make sure you do it now. Please take my advice and implement governance in your SharePoint enterprise. Do not let this slip through the cracks and do not release your environment without it. I have seen too many environments fail or have daily fires because of governance not being implemented.

In the next chapter, we will start to plan our project by reviewing our current architecture and server roles within the environment. Along with that, we will start to look at some scenarios and focus on where we are and where we need to be by the end of our project.

Questions

You can find the answers on GitHub under Assessments at `https://github.com/PacktPublishing/Implementing-Microsoft-SharePoint-2019/blob/master/Assessments.docx`

1. A removed feature is unavailable in SharePoint Server 2019 but is available in older versions of SharePoint. True or False?

2. When migrating from SharePoint 2007 using a deprecated migration tool, new and removed features don't matter to your project from these older versions: 2010, 2013, or 2016. True or False?

3. In SharePoint, governance provides security and farm topology aspects for the project. True or False?

4. Microsoft best practices can change based on the version of SharePoint you are using. True or False?

5. Boundaries and limits are a list of limitations on features that are distributed by Microsoft but have not been tested for accuracy. True or False?

6. VMs can run on hosts in your SharePoint environment using dynamic memory allocation as a Microsoft best practice. True or False?

7. SharePoint training for users is needed to support upgrading to SharePoint Server 2019. True or False?

2
Planning and Architecture

When planning SharePoint architecture and solutions for an enterprise, it takes time and patience to achieve successful requirements that give defined goals and time-frames. During the planning phase, there will be many documents that will need to be produced. These documents will come from the following areas:

- Assessments
- Design
- Research
- Needs
- Use cases
- Project resource scheduling

The planning of tasks also gives metrics on the time to complete them, which involves project milestones and start and end dates for targeted deliveries. This planning will encompass all time-related information needed to move the project forward at a steady pace.

Designing architecture for a SharePoint enterprise requires different resources and is based on a technical set of requirements. These can be found in the new and deprecated features, removed features, and any gathered data provided during the assessment of your current environment that we completed in the previous chapter. The design encompasses detailed information about the network, server platform, SQL and SharePoint configurations, and any area of IT that is configured during the installation and configuration process that will support the product life cycle. This design document should be a living document as it also provides details on those areas for future reference and can be changed as needed when changes are made to the environment to include future changes made to the architecture.

In this chapter, we will cover the following topics:

- Planning – overview
- Planning – how to find the best architecture based on requirements
- Planning – cost of your environment
- Planning – resources
- Planning – SharePoint farm design

You will learn in this chapter how to plan and prepare for a SharePoint implementation. This task is very detailed and there are varying reasons why this is the case. There are many areas to cover to make sure you get a clear understanding and successfully implement a project of small to large size. You will also learn how to manage costs and resources and how to design your farm based on company security and requirements.

Technical requirements

For you to understand this chapter and the knowledge shared, the following requirements must be met:

- Current admin experience on SharePoint farms 2007, 2010, 2013, or 2016
- Current enterprise experience supporting a collaborative user community with SharePoint
- Project planning experience related to SharePoint
- You must be a SharePoint power user

Planning – overview

Planning a new SharePoint environment or a migration from an older SharePoint environment requires us to define future goals for collaboration solutions within our enterprise, as well as research to provide clear requirements and project schedules. Whether it's SharePoint or other collaborative applications, planning to add additional systems to your environment requires great insight. This requires attention to detail and building teams that can do the work to support the scheduling and delivery of the application.

For the record, I am not a project manager in any light but I understand what things should be identified as specific to a SharePoint implementation project. It doesn't take a PMP certification to understand the tasks and timelines needed for a successful implementation. These certified project managers look at these tasks differently from architects and measure against them using other mechanisms. In this planning chapter, I am just going to touch on the areas needed to help you as an engineer or architect understand your responsibilities and what areas need to be concentrated on as part of this process from an IT standpoint.

SharePoint is often a huge piece of the pie or central focus for many enterprise collaboration environments. There could be other cloud apps or large applications that play a part as well, but in this planning exercise, we will concentrate on SharePoint with some caveats where the integration or confirmation of other applications needs to be present in our plan. With SharePoint, there could be integration with the cloud or other Microsoft communication platforms, such as Teams, Skype, or OneDrive, which could play a part in how fast we can provide our environment to our user community. This may also require a different team or consultant who may be providing those services.

As you saw in the first chapter of this book, we assessed our environment, new features, and deprecated features, and did an overall assessment of our current state, be it new or already in place. In our planning process, we will use those documented areas to determine what needs to be completed to finish our project and what resources we may need to do so. We will also determine the time it will take based on these assessed areas by using the data to figure out what tasks are needed to complete the project.

These tasks could range from reporting or the clean up of our old environment to working to create our new environment. Some of our tasks could even relate to our last SharePoint project and the requirements will remain the same or look very similar. If you have an old SharePoint project plan, you can use some of those areas in that plan for a new project for SharePoint Server 2019. SharePoint at its core does not change, as you will see when we install a VM and host servers. Most of everything you have done in the past you will also do now. You will install SQL Server and SharePoint, which works very similarly to in previous installations. This can be said about every SharePoint installation we have installed since SharePoint 2007, with the exception of those environments where SQL Express was used for a single server installation, as this is not supported in SharePoint Server 2016 or 2019.

Goals and objectives

As part of our goals and objectives for our SharePoint project, we should proceed to start our planning by finding out the goals of the enterprise solution from a company standpoint. We want to make sure to understand how, as a company, they would like to use this collaborative environment to support the goals of the company. We also want to find out general information supporting the project, which would include information such as funding, completion expectations, and any other details related to the project.

This project will take a team effort as all requirements and tasks may not be specific to a central group. Coordination of these efforts is very important and should be completed before you start on any project, especially SharePoint projects. During this project, you will have internal meetings with many different teams supporting the project individually and collectively. This would include all external team representatives from the different specialist areas, such as **Active Directory** (**AD**), networking, database, server, governance, management, and user community, and whoever is a stakeholder in this implementation. These teams will need to be assembled, which would be a requirement before starting any technical configurations.

There could also be other projects in progress or in the planning stages that relate to your SharePoint project. This could mean integration points and/or other types of intercommunication that would need to happen to make sure your project is successful. An example of that could be an AD restructuring project. AD would be required to be completed before SharePoint could be installed and configured due to the fact that AD is the method of authentication needed for users and service accounts to be functional. AD restructuring, be it on-premises or on the Azure cloud, as a project could put our overall project on hold because identities needed for administrators and service accounts would not be able to be created. The reason AD restructuring is important is there could be a change in the domain structure or we could be upgrading to a newer level of server, cloud, or integrated authentication method, such as SAML. This could delay your project if you are bound to using this new AD structure.

One of the goals we need to understand before going forward is to determine the architecture and the reason SharePoint is being implemented. The architecture is important because it drives our cost, which also drives what resources we need to support the environment. As part of our assessment, we found out things that we need to change within our current environment and things we need to bring to the table to support our SharePoint 2019 environment. Let's take some fake data and make some determinations from that data to create some architectures to work with.

Planning – how to find the best architecture based on requirements

Planning an enterprise SharePoint farm takes a lot of work. Do not skip the planning phase of your new farm as it will have consequences later during your move to that environment if you are not careful about doing some upfront work. The following exercise examples are based on existing company infrastructure and an acquired company that is merging their SharePoint into your new environment. In the exercises, we will go through some basic examples of how to identify the required architecture and configuration based on different versions of SharePoint and different farm configurations. These exercises will help you to figure out the necessary changes to your new environment and give you recommendations in those areas.

Exercise 1

The current SharePoint 2013 farm architecture used by your company that was assessed is structured as follows.

The architecture is as follows:

- Two web frontends
- One app server
- Redundant database servers (two)

The license details are as follows:

- Windows 2012 R2 Standard: Two CPUs, 8 GB RAM, C drive = 60 GB, E drive = 60 GB
- SharePoint 2013 Standard: Four CPUs, 8 GB RAM, C drive = 60 GB, E drive = 60 GB
- SQL 2012 R2 Standard: Four CPUs, 16 GB RAM, C drive = 60 GB, E drive = 60 GB, H drive = 2 TB, L drive = 500 GB
- NLB load balancing
- Two virtual server hosts: Eight CPUs, 96 GB RAM, C drive = 120 GB, E drive = 2 TB

The content details are as follows:

- 1 TB of data
- No custom applications
- No third-party applications
- File size max: 2 GB
- Claims authentication
- Supports 3,500 users

In our current company's configuration, you will see in the following diagram that we are lacking coverage for all the tiers within our design:

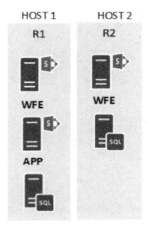

Figure 2.1 – The company's farm design

The acquired business's current 2010 farm architecture used in these exercises is as follows.

The architecture is as follows:

- Two web frontends
- Three app servers (one server dedicated to search)
- Redundant database servers

The license details are as follows:

- Windows 2008 R2 Enterprise: Four CPUs, 8 GB RAM, C drive = 60 GB, E drive = 60 GB
- SharePoint 2010 Enterprise: Four CPUs, 8 GB RAM, C drive = 60 GB, E drive = 60 GB

- SQL 2008 R2 Enterprise: Four CPUs, 8 GB RAM, C drive = 60 GB, E drive = 60 GB, F drive = 3 TB, L drive = 1 TB

- Hardware load balancer

- Four virtual server hosts

The content details are as follows:

- 2 TB of data

- Four custom applications

- One third-party solution

- File size max: 2 GB

- Scan to SharePoint capability

- Classic authentication

- One web application with forms-based authentication

- Supports 6,600 users

In the following diagram, we can see that there are four hosts and VMs are dispersed across the hosts for the best recovery and stability of the SharePoint farm:

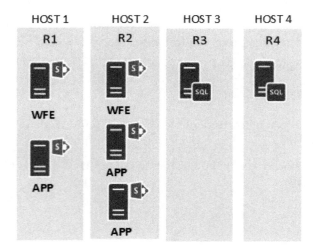

Figure 2.2 – The acquired farm design

Let's look at some scenarios to gain a better understanding of how we can plan our architecture.

Scenario one

In our assessment, we found that we currently support 3,500 users running SharePoint Server 2013 Standard and the company is planning to grow to 5,500 users by the end of the year due to an acquisition of another company. SharePoint adoption is low at this point at your company but the company you acquired uses SharePoint 2010 Enterprise heavily, using **Key Performance Indicators (KPIs)**, SQL Reporting Services, and Power BI. Your management plans to adopt some of their business applications for use within your business processes. Your management would also like you to take into consideration that as the company grows with this acquisition, the understanding is that this will bring more customers, which then brings more revenue for the company. This will, in turn, create more jobs and more users to support the enterprise.

Recommendations

In this situation, we have many things to look at from a planning perspective. We need to take into consideration our environment, the acquired environment, and our move to SharePoint Server 2019. Some of the big things that jump out to me in looking at the requirements are that we have a 2010 Enterprise environment and a 2013 Standard environment. This means we need to make sure that our SharePoint 2019 environment supports the applications developed in the acquired SharePoint farm. This would mean upgrading the SharePoint environment from Standard to Enterprise as well as upgrading SQL Server to Enterprise level. In this case, we would also need to upgrade our Windows operating system to Windows Server 2019.

Authentication stands out as well as we have both farms using different authentication methods. This would need to be resolved as part of the integration of both farms into a single farm. The acquired farm could be using classic authentication, which is obsolete and not supported in SharePoint 2019. The course for upgrading from classic to claims would be to migrate the users over in that environment using the original AD domain. Once the authentication process is completed using PowerShell, we would then migrate the content once it had been updated to claims authentication. Testing this process in your dev and test environments first would reveal any troubleshooting efforts you may need to make before trying this in your production environment.

The next recommendation in planning for the new farm is we would need to resolve areas of the farm architecture that will not support the users from a service standpoint for redundancy. The architecture is also not built for growth as the company could bring on more users in the next year due to the acquisition. In this plan, we need to make sure we can accommodate the new users that come on board, which means we may want to add one or two more web frontends. Adding one would be ideal, but when you have three, it gives you flexibility when doing updates to your servers as there are always two more available to handle the load. We also need to think about MySites and how we approach that configuration. We should look at using OneDrive as our target if no applications are being run against files in SharePoint currently.

When thinking along the lines of redundancy as part of the solutions, we also need to find a new way to support our load balancing for our web frontends, which is more reliable and doesn't take away from our web frontend service performance. We would need to look at a hardware load balancer at this point and maybe even hire a person to handle this from a technology perspective if you do not have someone in-house already. This is very important as you add more users to the platform and spread those users across two or more servers to handle the load. Power BI and other data-related services will need to be considered as well as these could give a much more intense user experience and workload on the web frontends.

There is also the need to redefine the number of hosts that support the VMs in your environment. Currently, we have two hosts with four servers, which provide no redundancy for each area of our platform. In our platform for SharePoint, you will see that we can mock this up with MinRole, as seen in this diagram:

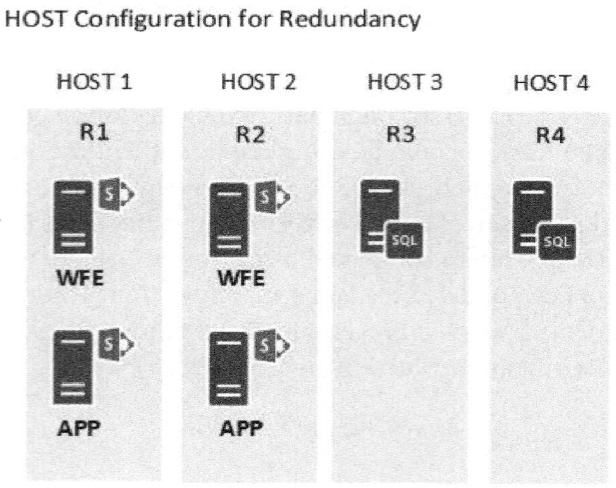

HOST Configuration for Redundancy

Figure 2.3 – A mock-up in MinRole

When following some host best practices, you can see that we need to create redundancy from a host perspective so that if one host server is lost, we could still be somewhat effective at keeping the service up and alive until that host server is brought back online. There are other tools available as well for the cloning and duplication of VMs, which can be considered as a partial solution.

When cloning and duplication tools are used, these tools can help with duplicating servers. One thing to mention is SharePoint doesn't like servers to be duplicated or cloned because of the complexity of the farm/server configuration, so there would be no way to capture the total configuration of a server without some deep recreation and manual steps. It's best to keep servers on standby that are already in a warm standby state. These servers should be part of the farm or at a state where the operating system is installed and configured and SharePoint is ready for connectivity to the farm. In these situations, third-party tools can come in handy, as you can use them to recreate your server farm from scratch – I specifically refer you to AvePoint's tools. At this point, we would install the server as usual with a new server name and configure the server quickly using PowerShell or AutoSPInstaller.

To provide support for SQL Reporting Services and Power BI, which is non-existent in our company farm but does exist in our acquired farm, we would need more server power to support these services, as well as a plan for the installation of these integrations for the farm. When looking at our new features, we can see that SQL configurations have changed in support of SharePoint Server 2019. This would mean that you will have to understand which version of SQL to use (2016 or 2017), which was mentioned in *Chapter 1*, *Understanding Your Current State*. Plan your SQL supported services using the information in the new features area to make sure to architect your solutions based on a new configuration.

Scenario two

In our assessment, we found out that we currently have authentication concerns. Each environment acquired and our company farm support different authorization methods. We also noticed that both environments are currently using separate domains and neither one has trust between them. Both domains are using AD for user login but the acquired farm is also integrated with SAML for authentication within the enterprise.

The acquisition farm uses custom code within the farm to support user profiles. The custom code brings in user identities from the source of employee profiles instead of AD, which this code is established on one server in the farm. We need to find out how we support AD, SAML, claims authentication, and services for user profiles going forward in SharePoint 2019.

Since we are on SharePoint 2010, shredded storage has not been introduced. So, the size of your overall content is one to one. So, if there is a 2 GB file in a library, all versioned documents are 2 GB as well. Once you migrate to the newer version of SharePoint, these documents will change in size if you use a migration tool. If you are using content database migration, these documents will stay the same size in the database and will not change until you start adding versions in the new 2019 library. Once you start using shredded storage, you will see a dramatic decrease in document sizes and storage being used in site collections.

The need to check the sizes of your content databases and site collections is so important as you should have been managing them as you managed your current farm. Some of these databases could be over the best practice limits and may need to be broken up, or site collections may need to be moved to a new content database. Shredded storage will play a part in this as well once you get over to your new environment if you are on an older version of SharePoint. You will see some dramatic downsizing in your file sizes for versioning.

> **Note**
> Make sure to examine some of your data within your libraries. I had one customer who had one Excel spreadsheet that was set to have unlimited versions in SharePoint 2007. When calculating the size of that one file, it came up as a 20 GB footprint in the content database. At this point, with all the versions of this document over the years, they limited the versions and saved over 18 GB of storage on *one file*.

Recommendations

There have been a lot of updates to the SharePoint architecture in the last two versions of the product. As for authentication, SharePoint only supports AD out of the box as of SharePoint 2016 and 2019. This change really limited what authentication methods could be used to connect to SharePoint. Since we already have differences with user accounts using classic and claims identities, we would need to fix that issue first as stated, and then figure out support for SAML. Forms-based authentication is still supported in SharePoint 2019 and is still configured pretty much the same as it always has been.

Microsoft provides a product that gives a solution for these types of issues and integrates with SharePoint seamlessly. Microsoft Identity Manager supports authentication stores that are outside of AD. This server would need to be built and configured to support a final configuration for SharePoint 2019. Migrating to SAML and using PIV cards is a project you would want to plan out thoroughly with a lot of testing.

With this type of security, an **Active Directory Federation Services (ADFS)** or trusted identity provider will come into play, and the ADFS server will be needed for the users to authenticate properly. ADFS is a server that gives access to sites within SharePoint for external access. There are other providers, such as Okta, who also provide these services in the cloud in which the integration is a solution and PowerShell would be used to create realms and connectivity to Okta for authentication.

You can configure this integration after you go through the process of implementing the new farm. This would need to be tested in a lower environment, or even a separate environment, before implementation within the production environment to make sure the authentication works as it should do based on your requirements.

There are many scenarios we can go through with this assessment data but I wanted to point out some obvious details to get you thinking about where you are in your planning and how you can start rebuilding your company's SharePoint environment with Server 2019. Please make sure that you have checked under the covers of every configuration, content database, service database, service, **Global Assembly Cache (GAC)**, and site collection with the utmost granularity. The last thing you want is to be blindsided after your move to the new farm.

Looking at these scenarios gives a sense of what things we need to be aware of to support our environment. Essentially, the standard for a web frontend configured with Microsoft-recommended resources can support up to 15,000 users concurrently. This means that you need to understand your community and how many users you will be supporting with your SharePoint services. If you have more than that number of users, you will need to add web frontends and use a load balancer to distribute traffic between them.

In doing this analysis for web and app tiers, you will notice a cost associated with the hosts that will support your server VMs and costs for software and other incidentals, such as third-party solutions. You would also need to include outside network hardware and software needed for load balancers and other interfaces that may be required in your environment. As you can see, costs will add up.

In the next section, we will talk about costs and how these costs can be lowered by solutions and other known recommendations we can show to help you create a shopping list to get started with. Once you have really gone through your planning process, your shopping cart will be completed and you can order equipment and other software to help get ready for your installation. Right now, we need to make sure we are thinking correctly about what we are building and what we need in place to support our services.

Planning – cost of your environment

We have seen how we use our assessment data to figure out the options to move forward with for our implementation. With those collected details, we need to examine them thoroughly so that we can architect our new farm. Since we have some details that will continue to be defined as we go through the project on how we move forward, we now need to take cost into consideration. The cost will not be your area of expertise because we, as technologists, want the biggest and the best technology to work with, but with feedback from management, we can look for solutions to support our dream environment while still saving money and getting the same stability with other products and services.

Management, however, will be looking at these numbers to make sure they fit within the company's budget. You can get some numbers from them to make sure you are totaling close to where they want to be with hardware and software costs. There needs to be an understanding and an explanation of the new platform so that management understands where the costs are coming from.

As an example, you may add a third-party tool as part of your needs assessment to help you with **Remote Blob Storage** (**RBS**). This solution can be beneficial in a lot of ways that management may not understand, and they may question why you are purchasing this solution. So, we must help management see the big picture of the architecture, which can help you with your case to receive more money if needed so that approvals can be given for your architecture.

While we can be looking for ways to find savings in our project, we know first off that we have little or no choice in using Microsoft platforms in almost all cases, especially SQL Server. There really is no way to leave Microsoft per se, because we know everything is built on Microsoft's platform that supports SharePoint. If we look at this with our eyes wide open and examine the new features mentioned in this book, there have been some big changes with SQL Server 2016, 2017, and 2019. We may be able to take advantage of the fact that SQL Server now runs on Linux, which may save us money on our operating system licenses. Although this is new, we can test the server to make sure we are comfortable with using this platform within our architecture to support the database layer of our farm. We know that we will have to use Enterprise to support the efforts of bringing the acquired farm applications in-house for use.

There are other areas as part of cost savings in hardware and software that we will be looking at next.

Virtualization

Which virtual platform will you use? You have many choices when finding a platform to support your VM servers. Some of the solutions cost a considerable amount, but then there is Hyper-V, which is part of your Windows license. There is also other virtual server technology, such as VMware, which is a valid platform as well. Find your platform for your virtualization and find out which platform is cost-efficient while giving you the support and stability needed for your environment. Host cost can also save you money as the cost for the server resources needed to support a development environment will not be the same as a production or **User Acceptance Testing** (**UAT**) environment. Plan your resources and do not just buy the same amount of resources for all the environments you plan to support.

Disk space and speed

Not all disks used for our host and VM servers or data storage need to be super speedy. There are some areas where we can let go of speed and exchange it for capacity and/or vice versa. Some areas that can use slower disk speed are backup storage locations and record center content for database storage. These areas are usually low usage and do not require speed to get the job done.

Cloud and Services

The Azure cloud is another option for your SharePoint implementation. You can build your infrastructure there and connect it using hybrid configurations if needed for Microsoft 365 and Azure AD. The cost for this platform can be expensive depending on the size of your farm, the number of users, and the horsepower needed for your server builds. You could also hire or train someone to manage the infrastructure, which may be expensive but could provide the goals the company is looking for. Savings for computer rooms, electrical, and other environment support would go down as well for cost savings.

Azure will bring some complexity to your architecture, as stated, due to the expertise needed to set this environment up correctly, along with those skills in the management of this architecture. Azure provides many services and software features that make it seem overwhelming, but with some training and coaching, this environment can be a rewarding experience due to servers being outside our organization and managed in the cloud. With that, it helps to cut costs using this platform, which cuts down on electricity bills, leasing for computer rooms, fire prevention systems, and server hardware costs.

If you are considering Azure, make sure you understand the benefits you can achieve using Azure:

- Deploy a SharePoint farm and scale it up and down as needed.
- Host in a cost-effective environment.
- Advantages of location with minimal investment.
- Disaster recovery.
- Move VMs from on-premises to Azure.
- Run Microsoft applications where they are safe.
- Run Microsoft applications where they have been tested to run effectively.

When configuring your Azure environment, you will want to build in high availability. The following diagram explains how your Azure environment should look for SharePoint Server 2019:

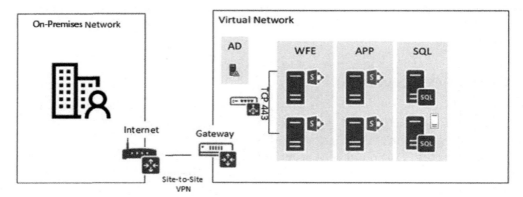

Figure 2.4 – Azure On-Premises Gateway

AD could be located on-premises or in Azure, depending on your configuration. For more information, you can refer to https://docs.microsoft.com/en-us/SharePoint/administration/designing-a-sharepoint-server-2016-farm-in-azure.

AWS

AWS is another cloud offering that can provide a cloud space to implement your infrastructure for your SharePoint environment. AWS provides similar supported cloud infrastructure that can be compared to Azure. While being not as complex as Azure, it takes a large learning curve to get started on both platforms, but as we are technologists, we know how to dig deep to learn new technologies.

Microsoft 365

Migrating to Microsoft 365 is another option to get SharePoint without the server hardware. There are other issues that go along with this type of implementation because you have to think about other Microsoft applications that would need to be moved as a part of this migration. Some of the solutions you use today may need to be rebuilt using other technologies provided with Microsoft 365.

We will see Exchange as part of the offerings for Microsoft 365. This is a migration that will take time and planning, which could lead to putting your SharePoint migration off until this is completed. The Office server would not be needed as part of your planning because it's built into Microsoft 365. This would be one server application we would not need to worry about as the functionality is already available.

As licenses are complex with the offerings in the cloud for the suite, there are different levels of licensing that are available. The higher the cost, the more features and space you receive. The platform also offers government tenants that are specifically created for government entities and do not support some of the flash and glamour that normal tenants support. You would need to look at these options very closely and find something you can move into.

Storage is key in this environment. There may be some splitting up of sites needed before your move. Splitting sites involves taking content from a site collection and moving into another site collection so that the site can grow and stay under a quota. As you sort the sites that are being moved from on-premises to the cloud to make them work as part of Microsoft 365, please be sure to take a look at the size of subsites and areas within the site collection to make the best decisions going forward.

Make sure to make the right decision going forward. Stop here and evaluate where you are and what your future is for SharePoint and other Microsoft ecosystem applications within your environment. Stepping to the cloud makes sense in some cases where you want to save money, but there is more to it than money when you look at the whole picture.

SharePoint licensing

Finding the best licensing for your on-premises implementation can be as easy as asking yourself whether you will be using business intelligence as part of your configuration. If you don't need it, then you should get the licensing for the standard version of SharePoint. Enterprise licenses are expensive, but with the need for data and functionalities that this version provides for reporting, KPIs, and other data reporting, this is your go-to solution.

With development environments, you will want to support the same version of SharePoint so that developers are developing on that same platform. There are versions of SharePoint that are free with Microsoft Partner subscriptions that can be used for this purpose, as well as free versions that can be downloaded as 90-day trials that also work. Ultimately, you want to gravitate to a license that can be sustained with no issues or complex situations coming up in the future. It's better to get a license that works forever than to plan your development on a 90-day license for your operating system, SQL, or SharePoint.

Battling contingency

Backup and **Disaster Recovery (DR)** are some of the most important solutions you will implement within a SharePoint farm. Without it, you will fail and fail miserably. The way you implement backup and DR will impact everything you build in SharePoint and how you could restore it from scratch if the need arose. This can be a rewarding experience in which you get a solution that makes this process easy, or you can stick with SQL backups and make your administrators work harder to restore and provide consistent support for your SharePoint implementation.

To start, as mentioned, SQL server backups are the basic backup plan for a SharePoint farm. Backing up databases, logs, and other areas of the server is very important to recreate the server when a disaster happens. In most cases, you will have an Always On configuration for the data tier of your architecture. Rebuilding this configuration and the associated data can be very complex without a tool to help you manage the databases involved.

If you add RBS to the mix of your supported configurations, you then add a different level of backup support that would need to be in place to support this integration. This solution is very complex and if your backup is not done correctly, you may not be able to restore your farm correctly, which could lead to disaster. The content used in a farm that is supported by RBS is programmatically associated as content within the sites using links to the content to associate the content on the disk within SharePoint.

> **Note**
>
> RBS is a way to keep large files outside of the database on a disk so that the files can be retrieved without disrupting the database and other users working with content in that database. The larger the file, the more work for the database to bring it to a user. If this is kept outside of the database, you get better performance when using large files.

Business intelligence as a service adds complexity to the farm and to the backup and DR solution that supports the farm. Business intelligence integrations need to be planned and even put on their own web application so that they can be used separately from the rest of the users in the farm. Separation using its own application pool separates the web application from the rest of the sites to provide better performance for those using this service. This service pulls on the server resources and will cause a delay in your data rendering if you're not careful to follow some best practices.

Solutions for backup and restore are available but there is only one I recommend and trust as I have seen this solution work and have supported it in many environments. AvePoint has a backup solution that helps in almost all scenarios for contingency planning. Their solution is superior because they have been in this space from the beginning. Over the years, I have seen many solutions they have offered and they really get administrators' pain points.

As I have stated, AvePoint offers a full backup and restore solution. The solution runs from its own server in your environment and uses agents to communicate with your farm and not embedded farm solutions. This is a very good way of integrating a solution from a third party into a farm. The solution is easy to clean up, not like embedded farm solutions I have seen that require troubleshooting to uninstall. Their suite of products gives you many solution options, including backup and restore, blob storage solutions, and so many other ways to support your farm.

AvePoint also has a solution for replicating content to another farm over a data connection. This will sync the content so that all content that is updated in the production farm gets updated in the DR farm. There are many configurations that can be determined for your environment but the bottom line is, you want to make sure you cover all areas with your backup solution that supports the SharePoint farm so that you can recover either from backup or a standby DR site.

Monitoring

Often, we think that as we add products or third-party solutions to our architecture, we are absorbing costs that we could be saving, but we have to look at this under different circumstances to support the farm proactively. The areas where we save money are not always cost savings but also downtime, which may cost you more in the long run. When looking at SCOM, which is a monitoring application used to monitor services and performance in SharePoint, this product can save a lot of cost in downtime, which in some cases can add up to dollar amounts for employees not being able to perform their jobs. If you look at it from a hosting model where we want the best up-time possible for our customers, this is a component we would not want to leave out of our architecture.

The savings monitoring can bring to the table are invaluable to our architecture, as we can find out areas of concern before something happens that can bring down the service. When a service is down, you lose confidence and you also lose money. Most customers will request information on why the service was down and may ask for money back for that downtime, in the end, depending on the severity.

Customers do understand, but when you have a business that depends on a service to work, they expect the service to work as it should. We often take monitoring for granted and use other tools and checks to figure out our pain points, such as Windows logs, ULS logs, and Task Manager, where we can monitor the resources on our servers. This is not the best effort for SharePoint as there are many services that could be in limbo if not monitored consistently.

There are many tools out there that work to provide monitoring, but SCOM is one of the more integrated tools that can work within your farm and other Microsoft products in your enterprise. This product gives you a one-stop solution for your Microsoft products and interface into those enterprise areas that need constant monitoring. There is another tool I really like called SolarWinds that also gives you real-time monitoring of services and server resources.

There are other areas where the benefit of having other applications integrated into our architecture outweighs the costs that come up in the SharePoint cost for hardware and support. Make sure you protect your investment while saving in other areas of the platform.

Now that we have understood how we can manage the cost of our environment, let's look at the aspect of resources.

Planning – resources

Adding resources also adds to the cost of our project, but in most cases, the resources requested will be needed to implement and support the project. Resources are generally handled by your project manager but with full transparency supporting the IT team and management. Everyone involved needs to make sure that there is a good project plan as part of structuring this project and make sure there is the availability of resources, as well as enough team members to support it. The team also needs to make sure that they have the cycles to start and finish the jobs they are assigned to complete.

There could also be concerns with resources that have been assigned to the team where there could be other projects these resources have that could take priority or eat into the time they can spend on the project. One of the biggest errors I have seen in the field is under-resourced SharePoint projects. This is one area where you do want to pay attention and make sure you either hire personnel or contract the positions to get the work completed.

The change management board and operations teams also come into play in planning as since we are adding or changing resources within the environment, these changes need to be confirmed by the owners of the environment. This can also add more pain to the implementation and take up time you were not planning for. Make sure to add in planning for this change review to make sure there are no hidden scenarios where you will get behind on the project. One thing you can do also is talk to this group before you get started. This will help them understand what's coming and they may be able to give you details they may need to move forward successfully. I notice this especially in secured areas where the SharePoint service would be used.

Another issue that is always seen from my experience is that I will run into a SharePoint admin that has not had much experience with the product and/or there is one SharePoint admin supporting a large farm alone. I have also seen cases where SharePoint is running without any real supervision but relied on heavily within the company. In these cases, these scenarios almost always bring to light the issue that the support personnel are overwhelmed and do not know where to start to fix issues and expand when added requirements arise. The team, in some cases, can also be running the help desk, managing customers, applying updates to the servers, and supporting all other areas that come with the SharePoint territory. Make sure you budget for the right size team for the environment you want to support.

Here is an example of a resource matrix to support SharePoint:

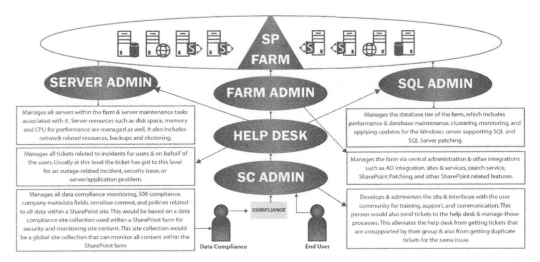

Figure 2.5 – Resource matrix

To avoid scenarios where you have overwhelmed support personnel, management needs to understand that this product is not easy to implement, manage, administer, support, and maintain. The platform requires many skill sets, along with experience, to really support the environment in the right way. There are many best practices that can really drive you crazy if you do not have experience with the product that will creep up on you at a later time. There is a reason why these best practices are used and specified in the Microsoft documentation to support the environment, so do not bypass them.

Being new to the product or not as well seasoned can really cause projects like this to fail. Your resources should be somewhat seasoned in the SharePoint space and you should have a good understanding of the product. Remember that your project is only as good as the people implementing it.

The outcomes of this resource exercise should help create thought processes around gathering resources to support the platform for the help desk, site collection admins, and farm admins. The support for the platform is essential and we should not hesitate to get these resources in place before starting the implementation. Training and knowledge sharing also make a big difference in these roles; do not forget it!

I can't tell you how important it is to have resources available that understand the product and can help make supporting the product easier using separated roles that bring together a team of knowledgeable professionals. You will see a big difference in how users perceive your service and how less complex the support process can be.

Assessment review

An assessment review is a meeting of the minds of IT and management supporting the efforts of the implementation. This could mean your CIO, director, and, in some cases, the CEO would be part of this meeting. The goal of this meeting is to review your assessment and its results. As assessments can be done over intervals of time, these meetings may happen when assessments are needed for the farm environment. The attendees would have a chance to review the document before the meeting so that they can come to the meeting with an understanding and questions about the document as well. This gives those teams a heads up on what the project consists of, gives them an idea of the resources that may be needed during this project, and helps them to plan for what resources can be provided for you to work with during the project.

This is a somewhat difficult task because you do not want to overstate the project goals and you do not want to show huge costs for the project, nor do you want to overstate the requirements with solutions not needed. When management is reviewing whether to approve the work, you want to be cautious and explain things in good detail (where they need to be explained) and leave some areas out that are common and not elaborate on them in great detail if no questions are asked. This is because the scope of the meeting could be directed in the wrong direction due to comments on details that are already clear and understood.

However, we should be prepared for anything during the meeting and questions could come out of the left field. Make sure you know your presentation well and practice it with the other team members so that everyone understands the direction the meeting should go. If things are rehearsed or talked about in depth, there will be no error in the delivery of the message sent during the meeting. Keep the meeting simple and to the point, validating the assessment and areas of concern, how you plan to remediate those concerns, and the direction or path for the future.

Management will be all ears and listening to certain details. In the meetings I have been a part of, most managers and even executives do not want to hear too many technical details. They want to hear concerns, fixes, and costs, as well as how you are addressing those concerns. Those areas of technical concerns help with new solutions you plan to implement, but overall, management has no ears for IP addresses, protocols, and so on in most cases.

Now, I am telling you this from my experience, but there could be some CEOs and upper management who may want to hear more technical details to figure out why you are heading in a certain direction for the platform. Some CEOs and other management are technical, and in some cases, you will need to explain your position more thoroughly. You need to gauge your situation and plan for it accordingly.

Prioritizing requirements

As things change within an organization, the goals set out within an organization may change as well. When an organization makes those changes to its future goals, this can bring changes in personnel, security, structure, and business processes. As part of those effective changes, IT can be affected, which can bring change to the way the IT department delivers solutions and secures data and content, platform support, governance, and other IT policies, which, in turn, will affect the way the technical teams support the enterprise.

As a part of the goals of this planning prioritization exercise, we need to define the purpose and motivation for our new or migrated SharePoint farm to this newer version of SharePoint Server 2019. When defining priorities, please consider the following items:

- Top tasks
- Milestones
- Deliverables
- Schedules
- Organizational charts
- Resources

All these areas can affect our implementation project in ways where we will need to rework our project schedule. We don't want this to happen, so planning around current and long-term projects is a must to avoid any situations where you have to, for example, change your schedule or resources in the midst of implementation. If you want management to get involved and give you some grief, just let that happen and you will see things fall apart.

Another example would be a change in deliverables. If we had a certain set of deliverables and all of a sudden you forgot about RBS, and have to make a change where you have to go back and ask for money, this brings the pain. You want to make sure you prepare all areas, especially technical solutions that form the environment, to support the farm and its functional components.

Prioritizing what's important as part of the implementation is needed because there are logistics involved as well. You need hardware before software, you need a network before you can configure servers, and you need SQL installed and configured before SharePoint can be installed. These examples help you understand how important order is in your project plan.

With that, there will be some tasks that take priority in these examples. In the case of ordering software, finding out when the software would be delivered is an example. The delivery of equipment and software can ruin a project plan as well. It's best to get a list of the items you need to start the process before you get started writing your project plan, so you don't have any items that fall by the wayside. Licensing and even funding sometimes take time to procure, especially in government projects. Make sure to put in requests once you finalize your architecture so that these areas can be in the works while you are finalizing your plan.

This is a good place to start evaluating the timing and prepping resources. Look over your work and make sure you have taken everything into consideration. Changing things now can make a big difference in your timing, so you do not want to change too much at this point. Also, evaluate the platform you are proposing. Make sure you're making the right decisions and press forward.

Planning – SharePoint farm design

Generating a mapping of how site collections per department will be represented in a hierarchical architecture is a task you should carry out with the management and stakeholders. The hierarchical order can make a difference in how users navigate the structure of the sites but can also be confusing to them if not thought about thoroughly.

Creating an intranet of the content doesn't have to be a hard task. Use resources around you to help with the organization of the sites. Where I believe this process goes wrong is when teams who are responsible for this architecture do not take into consideration the landing page. The landing page in all site collections can be used to help users navigate the site collection and even sites within the web application. Users should be able to browse just like when they access content on an internet site, which gives them links to areas within the site collection that are available to everyone. This method gives you the ability to bring content that could be buried in the site to the forefront, but other users outside your site may need access too. Breaking inheritance in a site, list, or library is always looked down upon, but in these cases, this should be considered to secure information that not everyone should have access to. We would also use a separate site to support content that is "for everyone" as well. Presenting hyperlinks that expose the content should be part of this exercise, which is to organize the sites and content for ease of use.

Some sites I have seen have terrible designs and content structure. Content exposure is so important on landing pages; for example, the name of the site is important with a real description of the department's responsibilities in the company. This verbiage makes it clear to the user looking for information that they are in the right place to get the information they are looking for. Listing the name of the site collection administrator and their contact information is another piece of good information that should be a part of the site collection landing page. There should also be some information on some team members and links to the department forms where information is collected, for instance, an employee vacation request form. This could be useful for the users surfing your site where they shouldn't have to have lower-level access to fill out a form that could be used by everyone.

As always, security is another area of concern of most site owners, but it doesn't have to be. Using the landing page as a read-only page is commonplace and in SharePoint 2019, you can use a team or communication site as your landing page as well. If the user is not a team member, then give them access to what they need from the landing page and secure the content they need to have access to with permissions. Make sure to create groups for your department users so that those users do not get mixed in with users with read-only access. All employee groups would get read-only access and internal groups that work behind the scenes within the site could give these users deeper access as needed.

If we look at the external sharing of information in our farm, we could see how some of the components within SharePoint 2019 and the cloud affected as part of your implementation. There are some things we want to be aware of in opening our content for sharing outside the company. Overriding that governance rule will make your admins work a little harder. You also need to trust that your users are sharing information that is OK to share. The security of your content is most important when it comes to sharing. I have seen some bad practices that could cost a company their secrets because external sharing was enabled and other mobile solution apps were being used within the company without IT knowing. Be on top of external sharing and make sure to secure your content.

Site collections are a great way to capture a bulk of content at a time as these can be a one-to-one relationship with content databases. In this configuration, you now have a database that encapsulates all the content for one particular department. Management of a content database is what you would like to work with as a farm admin and not a content database with mixed site collections from different departments. This site hierarchy gives you complete isolation of the content from a security and recovery perspective. All backups are of that database and content can be restored individually without having to interfere with other departments' content if something were to happen to the database. Migration efforts are clean as well, with no mixed site migrations or work beforehand to separate sites into separate content databases.

Database naming conventions should be used, as well as site collection URL names. We should, as administrators, be using good naming conventions to make sure our content is organized and named so that we understand what that content is. This goes along with naming our site collections and providing content in the site collection that describes it. There is nothing like going to a client's office, reviewing their farm with them, and seeing errors where content databases cannot be contacted. In review, I sometimes find out they do not know what the database is supporting, what the content is being used for, or even what department it supports. This all happens because it is named improperly. Please don't be that client.

Site collection templates should also be used to add functionality to your farm's logical structure when needed. One of the big perks of using some of the site templates are data compliance, record center, and document center templates. These templates can enhance how your logical structure works together. These templates can be used to create automated processes that protect content and store content. These processes use key data fields to set policies that automate the protection of data. Make sure to use these features in templates so that you have a well-rounded process in place when needed.

Physical server assessment

As we start our physical planning for servers and roles within the farm, we need to understand what architecture will best support the user community and be the least complex to support. Some solutions may be needed to support our farm, but it's a best practice to really understand your requirements and not just add solutions because they will be used minimally. One example of that would be a distributed cache and web frontend MinRole. If I was providing services for 100,000 users, then I would most likely separate the cache cluster process over several servers, but if I was only supporting 5,000 users, I would most likely keep them together on one server for a small deployment and over two servers if I needed redundancy.

> **Note**
> RAM comes into play as in the initial farm, we will only see 5% of our RAM on each server supporting the MinRole dedicated to this service. The more we play with the configuration of distributed cache, the more RAM you may have to reserve for this service. We talk about this more in *Chapter 9, Managing Performance and Troubleshooting*.

Physical design is not hard like it used to be. Before, we had to worry about services and what services were started on what server. Now, with MinRoles, that issue goes away if you use them. We can now be alerted for compliance based on the role of the server in the farm. If a service is not supposed to be started, we will see that the server will be out of compliance. MinRoles help with these types of scenarios by keeping the services needed to support the role of the server minimal. In the past, we were responsible for managing this ourselves, and I am sure Microsoft saw the writing on the wall from its long list of support tickets, which gave them the idea to put this MinRole in place. The MinRole was created to help administrators and was started in the MOSS version of the product, but was discontinued in SharePoint 2010. The MinRole helps administrators follow best practices and wisely use server resources to support how farm server resources are configured and to support the performance of those resources. Here are some examples of MinRoles:

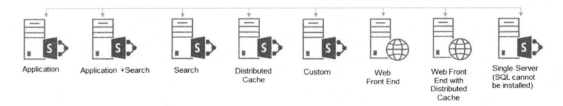

Figure 2.6 – Examples of MinRoles

In creating a physical architecture, we have to know what we are building. If the farm is going to support 5,000 users, then we figure out how important the farm is to our company's application support. Is it a tier 1 application, or is it tier 3, where we don't need redundancy and quick response times? In most of the companies I have worked at, SharePoint was a tier 1 application because everyone used it. I have also seen where it wasn't tier 1, but if one of the applications within SharePoint went down, it was a fire drill. We have to understand how SharePoint needs to be supported and have the company recognize its importance in the enterprise.

Now that we know our architecture will be tier 1, we need to take into consideration redundancy and up-time for the farm. Server resources and topology will mean that we have two servers for each tier and any other services that need to be robust in performance. Looking at our scenarios in this chapter, we know that we are part of an acquisition. The acquisition is bringing Power BI and large files to the table, which means we need a separate BI server redundancy and RBS as part of our architecture. 10,000 users may be a number that may be reached sooner or later, so three web frontends will be great as part of our architecture. A search may be a service we want to duplicate as we do not want this to fail as well.

Looking at these areas of concern, we can create an architecture for the hosts and the farm shown in the following figure for SharePoint Server 2019:

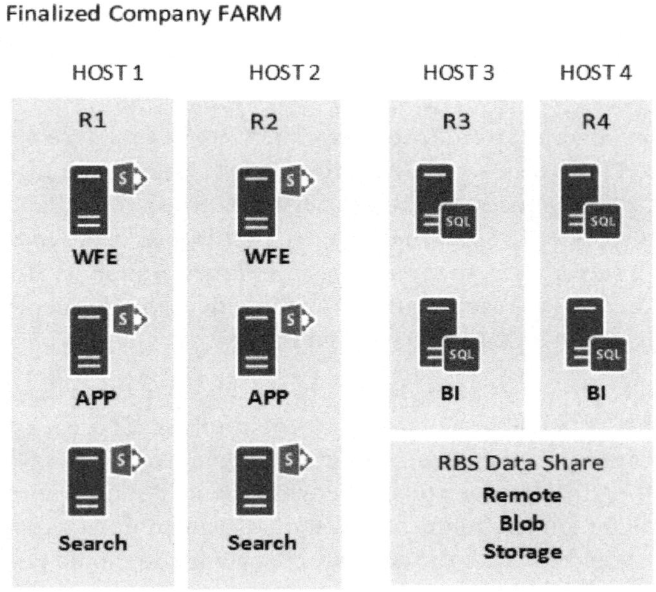

Figure 2.7 – An architecture for the hosts and farm

As you can see, we have redundancy on the hosts and redundancy within the farm. We also have the server resources to run the farm at a minimal requirement for SharePoint servers at 16 GB for each server, and all SQL servers at 64 GB, which is more than enough for this configuration. The SQL server needs this extra boost as we are using Power BI and SQL reporting services within the farm configuration, which can lead to big queries that pull on SQL resources pretty hard. If you remember, there are a couple of new applications we are introducing as part of the acquired farm configuration and these will be used by our users in a few different departments.

Aligning a farm to the requirements of the assessment is key in building a topology for the physical architecture. Make sure to take into consideration all areas of configuration, user traffic, and other areas that can pull on resources. Do not undersize your farm and always test your farm using a load tester as in Visual Studio. This will give you a sense of how the resources are going to perform using the number of users expected to be part of the environment that will use SharePoint.

Dev and test environments will also need to be stood up as part of the architecture. Dev environments vary in size. Usually, we have one SharePoint server and one SQL server as part of this environment just to do some little development on. This would support out-of-the-box development for different departments using separate site collections. Scheduling of reboots and testing should be coordinated with the users that require this development farm.

When talking about larger environments where there are several developers, each developer should get their own server. The problem with SharePoint 2019 is that it is not like older versions where you can install SQL Server on the same box and/or use SQL Express, as it is not supported. So, each developer, in this case, needs to have a separate SQL server for each server farm, or use a large SQL server to support all developers, using separate namespaces. This can work, but having those developers independent makes more sense as each should have their own environment.

Team Foundation Server comes in to play as well, so any code that's developed can be pushed for deployment and tested in the test environment before it's pushed to production. Pre-test environments can also be stood up in some cases where you want to validate before putting the code on your test environment. Test environments should be a duplicate of the production environment and should have minimal use and test content. This environment should be clean and the only changes made should be good changes that were tested previously.

Time and money are always part of the equation, so with that, we need to do our due diligence when planning our IT architecture. We need to review our requirements and make the right decisions to bring the best solution to management for the best cost. Looking at our current state and our acquired farm, we have to combine each of the farms and solutions into one. This can be a complex process depending on your situation.

In this situation, we have some clear guidance, and we understand this from the information that was given in this chapter. We have pointed out the server resources currently in place, and some details on the farm configuration. Assessment data has been gathered and again, all bases have been covered when finding out the information on SharePoint Server 2019.

What role does the cloud play in your environment? Can we build this into our architecture to save on costs? Well, in this scenario, we don't have any requirement to add the cloud to our migration process or even a hybrid solution, but you may find yourself in this situation. If you do, study the cloud thoroughly; there are many subscription models, and within those models, there are solutions that you may need that may not be offered in others.

Call Microsoft for support if you get stumped and do not guess on this type of configuration. Licensing can be very complex and it may not make sense to you. Make sure to ask the experts when coming up with strategies to move to the cloud.

As you can see, building server architecture is not hard but you have to take into consideration all the requirements and research: how you can create a low-cost, extremely robust, and best-performing server farm for your company.

Design – documenting the design

From my experience over the last 15 years, I have seen two design documents while I have been supporting SharePoint. Most environments I have worked and consulted in run in a reactive support method, which is an uncomfortable seat for those that manage the farm. This is a sign that companies are not making the effort and exerting due diligence to document the installation, configuration, and use cases of the SharePoint farms architected to support their company's collaboration efforts. It was often said in the past that installing SharePoint was easy, just throw the disk in and walk away. This was said early on when 2003 and 2007 SharePoint were just getting started, which was not true and showed in so many failed deployments of the product.

Little did these people know that their support for the product would take a considerable amount of time on the phone as they wondered why certain errors and functionality for users of the product were not working as they should in these environments. Early on in the evolution of SharePoint, there weren't a lot of documents or sites you could use to support yourself through a project like this. There was a very minimal amount of information available, even from Microsoft. This happened due to the product really not making much headway during the 2001, 2003, and WSS versions of the product.

When 2007 MOSS hit the market, it seemed like there was a wave of interest in the product, and Microsoft really got caught off guard at how this took off. Once they saw the need to address these issues, we started seeing more support for SharePoint and more websites and blogs. Some of the third-party blogs and sites could not be trusted in those days due to the newness of the product. Someone could have found a solution to an issue with BCS but then you find out it wasn't a best practice on the Microsoft website. There was a lot of pain and learning during those times, and you had to almost do some of the configurations blind and test them yourself to see whether the solution worked.

Now, with the vast information from Microsoft and blogs online, there is no excuse to not have documents in place to support your efforts for the SharePoint enterprise. Yes, it takes more time, but be thorough so that you can be successful and have references on why, what, and how you created this platform. I cannot express the importance of this and other documents that I am walking you through in this book enough. These are needed to support the product and user communities using the SharePoint farms for services and solutions. This also helps you to understand as an admin or architect what you have designed. As you configure and support the farm in the enterprise, this document, which is the foundation of the build, will be able to be referenced and updated in case you need to review a configuration or make changes as you grow.

So, in my efforts to help organizations do the job of supporting their environment with documentation, I have composed an outline of what I use to document the design of my SharePoint environments. This documentation is for the design of the SharePoint environment and is not intended to collect any SharePoint installation step-by-step instructions, but rather to cover the build of the environment that frames the moving parts and how they are working together to support the farm. The document should include an executive summary, solution design, and security.

Executive summary

This section of the document should be used to give an overview of what the document represents in support of the SharePoint project. Here, we would write a summary of the document within this area for executives who may not have the time to read through the entire document. This portion of the document includes the underlying topics listed:

- **Purpose**: This section of the document should be used to give a brief description of the document's purpose. In our case, this document represents the design and configuration for the SharePoint enterprise environment we are deploying.

- **Scope**: This section of the document lists the scope of the environment. This could include the Office server, SQL Server Reporting Services, PerformancePoint, PowerPivot, storage configurations, third-party integration, or anything that is not a native SharePoint installation.

- **Out of scope**: This section of the document lists the services or solutions within the environment that will be out of scope, such as business intelligence, RBS, hybrid connectivity, or third-party tools you may have discussed previously that didn't make it within the budget.

- **Assumptions**: This section of the document describes your design assumptions, which would be based on the requirements you gathered. This would include things such as PPI data restrictions within the environment or that access to the SharePoint environment will be authorized by AD.

- **Terms and abbreviations**: This section of the document should be a table of abbreviations used throughout the document that support protocols or even solutions or frameworks. This gives the reader a list of those abbreviations in case they do not understand them. This should also include the meaning of the abbreviations so that all abbreviations are understood in layman's terms. You could also add a hyperlink to those referenced abbreviations as well to give more detail to the reader.

- **Reference documents**: This section of the document provides a list of documents, which should also be in a table within the document. These documents are supporting documents from other supported IT or project-related areas that will be supporting this SharePoint design. This would include documents such as governance, installation guides, project plans, and any documents you would like to add that will support this work. Links to documents within SharePoint should be used so that documents can be in a centralized location. Referencing documents in shared drives would only confuse people as naming and versioning changes in this solution.

Solution design

This section of the document provides details of each portion of the solution. So, in our case, since we are designing a SharePoint enterprise solution, we will need to mention all the design requirements we reviewed to create this environment. You would want to mention what services will be used to support the environment from a SharePoint perspective.

We would also need to mention how the environment will be supported from a security, capacity, scalability, and availability perspective. You would also include contingency plans as bullets on how you would support the environment in a disaster crisis. Mention any security design considerations you took during your research as well. A summary of these items and then each of the following listed areas would be presented in a more complete explanation:

- **Network**: In this section, you would want to mention best practices; for example, SharePoint Server roles as in a **Web Front End (WFE)** server would not run any SharePoint services or the WFE should have index partitions for search residing on the server as part of the search configuration. You may want to mention any other network-related areas, such as VLAN configuration and domain information that might weigh in on the design. Include any diagrams as well.

- **Hardware**: In this section, you would want to mention best practices related to hardware. This could be related to SQL Server as you may not virtualize this hardware or mention which type of virtualization you will be using, such as Hyper-V or VMware. Make sure to mention anything you are changing in the hardware design from the norm.

- **Software**: In this section, you would want to list any software that would be used for the installation of this enterprise solution. This would also include listing the prerequisites as well as any extra tools, such as ULS Viewer or Fiddler, which are utilities that you might use for administration.

- **Environments**: In this section, we want to list the environments and their purposes supporting the enterprise solution, which could be dev, test, UAT, and production. We would want to mention any best practices, such as any separate service accounts and/or domains that will be used for each environment for security separation. You would also want to mention a release management plan or guidance on how this process will be managed within the environments. Include any diagrams or supporting documentation names and links as well.

- **Virtualization**: In this section, we want to list all servers that will be created in the environment, using a table with names, descriptions, quantity, CPU, memory, operating system type, and other information that can be captured for each server you are creating to support the environment. We also need to mention any best practices that we will use in the configuration of our hosts and VMs to support the environment. As an example, mentioning a best practice such as no VM server will use dynamic memory allocation would be the best practice of what to list here.

- **Availability**: In this section, we want to list all specific service-level agreements that will be defined as part of the customer agreements. Only list sections that are covered through the SharePoint service and components only. This section should not include disaster recovery or data protection. You would mention percentage up-time, redundancy specifically supporting the enterprise solution, and specific services within SharePoint that will be redundant, such as search or application services that support redundancy. Then, include those that do not support redundancy, such as SMTP, from a SharePoint perspective.

- **Load balancing**: In this section, we will list how we plan to support load balancing as part of our enterprise solution. This would include what type of load balancing, hardware, or software (NLB) to use, and how these components will be set up or configured to support the SharePoint environment. This could include mentioning SSL certificates, VIP pools, and distributed cache, to name a few.

- **.NET Framework**: In this section, we will list the .NET Framework that will be used to support the SharePoint Server 2019 installation. We would need to be sure to mention .NET 3.5 if it is still relevant in your installation as well.

- **IIS Settings**: In this section, list all configurations that will be used within IIS and mention the version of IIS being used. We would also want to mention log locations and how often these logs will be captured. Also, list all web service extensions and which are allowed and which are prohibited for use on the SQL and SharePoint servers.

- **Farm services**: In this section, we would need to include a table that lists all SharePoint services, which could include hybrid connectivity. This table also provides columns for server host and state, meaning stopped or started. This gives a precise configuration of the services that will be available within the farm and what servers they will be running under. The use of MinRoles and service compliance, introduced in SharePoint Server 2016, will help to keep your servers compliant at all times.

- **Active Directory**: In this section, mention all AD interaction that will take place and any required objects that will be needed to support the SharePoint farm. This could be mentioning the domain name, **Organizational Unit (OU)** structure, service accounts, and or security groups. Also, Azure AD could come into play, as mentioned here, in this document.

- **Capacity and storage**: In this section, we talk about the databases and storage needed for the overall enterprise solution. User capacity would need to be tested and can be tested using a Visual Studio load testing application. This would be good to use so that you can verify the number of users the hardware you configured will support and give the solution great performance based on best practices. Defining the types of drives could mean OneDrive or search considerations in the cloud that will be used as part of the environment, and their speeds are crucial as well as this can keep the cost down by using slower disks in areas where they can be utilized.

  We should also document the sizes of *all* databases and configuration details and define all database size limitations within this section of the document using a table. If you're pre-creating databases, this is a good place to list those databases, and if you are not, this is a good reference for naming conventions as you install the product. As a documented process, we would also want to document our database maintenance plan here as well.

  Don't forget to define drive sizes for our servers for the expected disk space needed to support search indexing. When defining the search indexing location, we must remember that indexes can be replicated to other servers depending on their role in the farm. This location is defined during the SharePoint Server installation process as a *data* location or will reside on the cloud if you use search in a hybrid configuration.

  We also need to remember logging for each component we are using to support the environment. This includes SQL with Always On, SharePoint, and IIS. We also want to remember that logs grow substantially when migrating content from one farm to another. Make sure to account for these sizes when building your servers.

- **Web applications**: In this section, we define the dedicated web applications that will be used as part of our solution for the administration of SharePoint and for supporting our user community. Web application settings should be captured as part of each of these web applications, which define areas such as authentication type, time zone, file upload size, and others, and should be documented as part of this section of the document.

  You should also define standards that should be followed in naming web applications, the application pools associated, and databases associated. We should also define our sites and what configuration details should be listed here in this document. This should also include all site collection best practices and areas of web applications that should be followed within some guidelines for site collection admins.

> **Note**
> Remember, host-named site collections are discontinued in SharePoint Server 2019.

- **Central administration**: In this section, list all details pertaining to the central administration site, which could be a vanity URL or the port that the site will run on. We would also want to mention access to the site as this could be a limited community of users. With that, an AD group should be created, which should also be listed here.

- **Site collections**: In this section, let's cover how we will create site collections and how they will be used within our organization. You could mention that a site collection will be created for each department or that a site collection will be created for each site as determined by our stakeholders. We also want to mention quotas and other details related to metadata, content types, and site columns.

- **Email**: In this section, we need to define how email will be used within the SharePoint enterprise solution. Define use with workflows and notifications as well as the configuration of TLS using the new configuration settings within SharePoint Server 2019.

- **Search**: In this section, we need to define all that is search. Define the configuration, any content sources that will be configured, redundancy configurations, index and capacity, crawl logs, and any special configurations. Crawling of content should also be captured here as schedules and other targeted content sources as per their requirements. Service accounts and the configuration for using those accounts should be defined as part of this section. Remember, hybrid could come into play in this configuration as well.

- **Profile imports**: In this section, we define profile imports and scheduling for imports within our SharePoint configuration. Any service accounts that are needed that will be used as part of the import would need to be defined in this section as well. Remember, Azure AD could come into play here as well.

- **Monitoring**: In this section, we define how we monitor the enterprise solution and mention what tools we will use to do so. As we define these areas, we want to make sure that we have made mention of any third-party solutions at the beginning of the document that are in scope. This would include monitoring of the network components, services, servers, VMs, and so on. We should also set any thresholds per component that need to be captured in this document so that others that are administrators of this environment understand those thresholds and make sure to adhere to those maximums. These thresholds would be defined by testing using the Visual Studio tools for simulation or other tools as you see fit.

- **Backup and recovery**: In this section, we list all areas of the farm that should be backed up that are essential in recovering the farm in case of disaster (DR). These documented areas should be listed and configured in your backup software. The frequency of these areas should also be documented as some may not need to be backed up as often, such as a records management platform where documents are finalized and in a view-only access area. We would also need to consider SQL database backups, which should be part of a maintenance plan but could also be picked up as part of a daily backup for offsite storage. Timing and frequency should be considered as part of this documentation.

- **Software updates**: In this section, we need to define how software updates will take place, either manually or automatically. In most environments I have been in, most do their patching manually. This would be my recommendation as well. We should be testing our environments through development, test, UAT, and production to make sure these new updates are working as they should. This alleviates the destruction of our production environment as we test through those lower environments for verification of the patches.

  Most companies also have separate teams that support individual IT areas, so in that case, you will have an overlap of support for updating servers, SharePoint, and SQL Server. In this case, scheduling becomes a factor or you have your SharePoint admin update all areas of the server. In a lot of cases, SharePoint admins can have many servers, depending on how their environment is configured, and could have to do updates in a certain order based on the application.

  Some third-party tools require servers as support for their platform. My recommendation is to give the SharePoint admin access to update all servers supporting the environment. If the environment is built for redundancy, then we should be equipped to provide users around-the-clock access to the environment. In this case, we can use what are called zero-downtime methods so that we can update the server without disruption. This would mean all levels of the stack would have redundancy: WFE, the application, and the database.

- **Ports**: There is a pretty detailed list of ports needed for SharePoint to communicate between servers within the enterprise. These ports should be documented here either through diagrams or a table listing those ports and descriptions. With SharePoint, there are intra-server communications, which refer to how SharePoint services communicate, and extra-server communications, which refer to how SharePoint communicates with other servers and applications supporting the platform. We will detail that list and the script to configure them later in this book.

- **Development farm**: In this section, we define how the development environment will be used to support the enterprise solution. In most cases, the development environment, as mentioned, is the first environment to get patches and updates related to the servers and applications supporting the enterprise solution. Using a development environment supports the total solutions from a development standpoint. This is the messiest environment in most cases and there could be multiple servers, depending on the number of developers supporting it.

  Consolidating developed code would be another defining area we would want to add here in this section. If you are using Visual Studio and Azure DevOps Server, then centralizing code is fairly easy to do even if there are multiple developers and servers. From there, we define how code is entered into the testing environment, where there should be only one or at most, a few testers reviewing the functionality of the coded solutions. Once it is tested, there will be a verdict that it either failed to meet the requirements or successfully met the requirements. At that point, we would then move the code to UAT.

- **UAT farm**: In this section, we define how the UAT environment will be used to support the enterprise solution. This environment is used as the name states. Once code or even UI functionality tested in the lower environments is moved to this location, users can log in and test the solutions before they are moved to the production environment.

  We will speak more about this in *Chapter 12, SharePoint Framework*, to provide some lessons learned and best practices. After working as a developer, I saw many things that could lead to disaster, along with choices that need to be made as an admin function or a developer function. This decision could cost you if you are relying on code to build environments for new developers and rebuilding a production environment that was lost due to disaster.

- **Migration**: In this section, define migration and how it will support the enterprise solution. In reality, migration can either come as a tool that requires its own server or workstation and can be a process we follow using our SharePoint server and SQL servers. Document how the tool will be used, especially when it comes to environment migrations, release management processes, and who has access to the servers and tools. Document the selected tools and processes chosen as well to do migrations and the content that will be migrated. Schedules and other areas concerning migration will be documents in project-related documentation.

> **Note**
> Documenting any of these sections with supporting diagrams is also a great way to present solutions as part of this documentation.

Security

This section of the document should be used to give an overview of what the document represents in support of the SharePoint project. Here, we would write a summary of the document within this area for executives who may not have the time to read through the entire document. This portion of the document includes the underlying topics listed here:

- **General**: In this section, we need to define general security practices that will be followed within our SharePoint environment. Some of the areas that could be mentioned in this area would be the central administration location, direct user access to databases, separate accounts being used to separate services used within the environment, and any other SQL or environment general security best practices you will follow that are part of this enterprise solution.

- **Physical security**: In this section, we need to define any physical layers of security, as in server rooms and PIV card security, which would count as physical security accessing servers and desktops. Physical security could also be part of a certification you hold as more companies are using these certifications for government contracting. Any physical security enhancements and authorizations would be good to mention in this section.

- **Authentication and authorization**: In this section, we need to define which types of security you will use for authentication and authorization. If you're using AD, you are most likely going to use claims authentication and Kerberos for integration with AD. There could be a mention of other authentication areas, such as SAML, which provides the integration of PIV cards for more physical security options. Authorization can be mentioned, as in how you use groups within the solutions, either SharePoint groups or AD groups.

> **Note**
> Always use AD groups for your SharePoint security when you can. If there are areas where they just don't work, then use SharePoint groups.

- **Antivirus**: In this section, we need to define the type of antivirus we will use to support the upload and download of documents within our SharePoint farm. This is one area I saw during my travels that was abandoned because everyone thought since they had antivirus on desktops, there would be no need for it to be installed on the farm. My opinion is you always need to be careful and don't take chances with your data.

  With antivirus, there are areas on the server that need to be documented as well, which should be excluded from the antivirus scanning those areas on the hard drive. Those areas are documented on Microsoft's website. These exclusions help to protect files from being compromised by the antivirus program and interrupting the SharePoint service.

- **Auditing and policies**: In this section, we need to define how we will audit users and what policies we will put in place to ensure data compliance. **Information Rights Management (IRM)** and a new feature called Data Compliance that was introduced in SharePoint Server 2016 can be used to flag documents and make sure data is protected from use by users who do not need access.

- **Security principles**: In this section, we need to define how admin and service accounts will be used in the solution for the separation of duties. Document their purpose, local policy settings, and database access in this section. Use a table to pull together the best results. Local service and network service accounts should be documented here as well. Also, document group permissions as well, as out-of-the-box SharePoint creates groups that are used within the configuration. These are often forgotten about. Document these groups and make sure they are a part of your documentation for reference.

- **Group policy**: In this section, we need to define GPO settings. This is one area where a lot of admins get stuck and wonder why security isn't working in the environment. We need to make sure that all of these policies are documented, as well as GPO settings.

- **Blocked file types**: In this section, we need to define a list of file types that will be blocked from use within the SharePoint libraries. These file extensions should be documented so that they are captured for reference.

- **Appendix**: If needed, add an appendix to the document.

You are not finished with creating your design document as this document is a living document created to capture changes in your design. Keep this document safe in a place where only you and your team can get to it. Have someone review it as well to make sure you hit all areas of your design to support the services you are planning to configure in your farm. The key to a successful implementation is getting things right the first time and always checking and rechecking against the Microsoft best practices and your assessment.

Disaster recovery

In this section, we need to look at recovery from the unknown glitches that can happen that bring down the server environment, where the service is unavailable or partially available. This could be the loss of the application services or even just the loss of data. In the case of SharePoint, there are network components that can also cause issues as well, such as load balancers, routers, and DNS, which can alter the availability of the service.

With that, we need to take into consideration the company's policies on the **Recovery Time Objective (RTO)** and **Recovery Point Objective (RPO)**. There are disaster recovery concepts that can be followed that support SharePoint 2019. These concepts have not changed since SharePoint 2013 was in play, which includes standby recovery options, service application redundancy, and third-party solutions specifically for SharePoint:

- The RTO defines the time metric to calculate how quickly we can recover from a disaster. This would be the expectation the company would like to support as part of an **Statement of Work (SOW)**, which supports the service and is given to users or departments using the service. This is so that customers understand all the services provided and situations that may come into play within the environment.

- The RPO defines the point in which you would like to be able to recover. This means that the point of recovery could be a full SQL database backup time and maybe you also have a differential backup that was done later, combining these two backups, so overlaying the differential backup would then bring our point of recovery to a more recent time. This would be defined in the backup strategies, which we will talk about later in the book.

- **Standby recovery options** are provided using separate data center locations to house a system or service so that in the case of a service or group of systems that go down, those systems can be recovered and provide the service from a different set of servers or services. There are three different models for these options:

The first is cold standby, which is a data center that could be back online within hours.

The second is warm standby, which is a data center that could be back online within minutes or hours.

The third is hot standby, which would make the systems redundant, and if something were to happen, the users would not see much of a change in service. This would facilitate an almost-instant recovery, with some caveats of URL changes, DNS updates, and other networking configurations that could be automated or done manually.

- **Service application redundancy** can be configured when you configure services within SharePoint to be redundant as part of an outage, which would then require services to be running on hot standby servers. This is not a bad solution but we have to remember that SharePoint also brings with it a database side. In that case, we also must remember that we can also ship logs to another database server in another data center as well. This would push all database changes from the production farm to the DR farm in another location. These databases that support SharePoint can also be in read-only mode in the event that you do not want any changes to be made once failed over. This could come in handy in some scenarios.

- **Third-party solutions** come into play, and I refer you to AvePoint again as they provide some solutions that provide synchronization of content between locations and disaster recovery solutions just for SharePoint. If you have the funding, these are good to take a look at, but also remember that this comes at the cost of new servers to support the functionality and more time spent by your administrators managing these services as well.

Summary

In conclusion, the design of your SharePoint farm means everything to the support of the service. This means you cannot miss much when implementing a SharePoint farm. Making sure to document your infrastructure is key due to three things you will need now and in the future:

- Having a place to create, share, and save your design for review and changes

- Making sure you do not miss anything during the design process

- Giving someone else a chance to help, troubleshoot, and take over if you leave the company

Again, I cannot stress enough to document! I will say this many times in this book but documentation helps you figure things out because you write it out and don't just keep it in your thoughts. We admins tend to want to be smart off the top of our head but some things need to be written down. Don't keep things hidden in your mind; make sure to put them on paper. I have heard others who I have worked with always ask themselves why their team member doesn't know something, because it's obvious. Well, writing things down will make it even more obvious and get people working independently so that you don't have to hold their hand.

As part of that, always make sure to go through the scenarios when examining your current state. The assessment, best practices, and other planning information help to bring your design into a perfect scenario for your company. Remember that detail needs to be captured. Any little nuances, such as a custom port for incoming mail or as little as a service account used for a custom service – all these items need to be captured so that the design is understood. No one should be hunting you down for information or to see how things were designed.

We learned a lot in this chapter from the many angles that SharePoint has to offer. Some parts I didn't even touch upon. This chapter taught you a few things that will help you plan for success in many different scenarios. Although I didn't go too deeply into some of the areas I wanted to, this gives you a road map on where you need to go and what you need to focus on when designing and planning your architecture. Planning is everything and it creates the design for the farm as it answers many questions for you and your management. Always make sure to focus on planning as this is the *only* way to a successful SharePoint environment. There is no other way.

In the next chapter, we'll look at how we can go about creating and managing VMs.

Questions

You can find the answers on GitHub under Assessments at `https://github.com/PacktPublishing/Implementing-Microsoft-SharePoint-2019/blob/master/Assessments.docx`

1. What standby recovery options would require some configuration to bring online?

2. What Microsoft Server product is used to support the development cycle and uses the three environments to help push and version developed code through those environments?

3. I can configure my SharePoint 2019 farm to use hostname site collections. True or false?

4. As part of our assessment review, what areas of our old farm should we be reviewing?

5. In our logical design, we should use one content database with a site collection and many subsites to support all departments in our company. True or false?

6. In our physical design, MinRoles play a big part in how we build service compliance in our server resources. Which MinRole is used for capturing a mix of services and has no compliance?

7. Should the help desk as a support resource field all SharePoint issues within the environment?

8. When designing our farm, what tier supports user connectivity?

3

Creating and Managing Virtual Machines

Creating a physical architecture to support your SharePoint 2019 farm starts with virtualization and setting up the servers needed to install all the software applications. In this chapter, we will see how to set up our Hyper-V environment using best practices and how to create redundancy using separate hosts. We will define server resources based on our requirements, finalize our configurations, and give guidance on how to maintain our hosts.

We will also discuss, as part of this chapter, understanding the importance of using Microsoft documentation as part of your installation and setup. Following best practices and Microsoft guidance is always the first thing you should do. Although it may not cover all the requirements, you will be able to find out what has fallen through the cracks. This will give you a baseline configuration to help you avoid any mistakes for the future of your environment, such as features, maintenance, and updates needed to support the environment.

We will also take a look at general changes in the Windows server over these past couple of operating system versions to make sure you are caught up and understand where Server 2019 is currently. Changes within the operating system can help you to use new features to support the environment to help bring you better use of your server features.

The following topics will be covered in this chapter:

- Creating hosts and VMs
- Defining needed server roles
- Installing Windows Server 2019 – host configuration
- Configuring Hyper-V Manager on Windows Server 2019
- Creating VMs

Technical requirements

For you to understand this chapter and the knowledge shared, the following requirements must be met:

- General understanding of Windows Server and **Active Directory** (**AD**)
- Experience with Hyper-V installation and configuration
- Experience with host installation and configuration
- Experience with **Virtual Machine** (**VM**) creation and configuration

You can find the code files present in this chapter on GitHub at `https://github.com/PacktPublishing/Implementing-Microsoft-SharePoint-2019`.

Creating hosts and VMs

When we start out trying to find the right hardware to support our SharePoint environment, we must have a SharePoint architecture as described in the first chapters of this book. If you have fully read *Chapter 2, Planning and Architecture*, you will recall that we looked at many scenarios to form an architecture for our SharePoint environment. We looked at our old environments, new features, changing features, and other aspects where there is a need for a change in strategies, such as Remote Blob Storage, so that we plan our new environment according to the needs of our users, administrators, management, and stakeholders, which is based on the current state and new requirements.

Host and VM configurations are the backbone of your server architecture and are the first step in starting to build a platform to support our farm. SharePoint runs well on hardware built to support it, as in any application, but the difference with SharePoint is that it covers many tiers and we need to think about those tiers as we look at starting our project implementation.

Some of your research should have already been completed as you should have already created a design document, but this doesn't mean we can't change a few things along the way as long as you **document**. We need to make sure to play our part in making changes and discussing these changes with other people on our team. Some of the areas that we may need to stop and think about in this portion of our implementation are the following:

- Server feature comparisons (which server is better for my needs: 2016 or 2019?)
- SQL Server version (which server is better for my needs: 2016, 2017, or 2019?)
- SharePoint Server version (which server is better for my needs: 2016, 2019, and/or Microsoft 365?)
- Third-party products, network products, and other data and backup integrations

Do not move forward until you have really finalized your choice of these supporting servers and you understand the differences. You don't want to go down the road of selecting a platform that doesn't support your future plans. You may see that a feature you need is not available in your version of operating system, AD, Exchange, SharePoint, or SQL. You may need a feature to support either an old application or new technology you were hoping to break ground with. Some of the differences in technology also come with added server resources, so make sure you are aware of those areas. Document all shortcomings, especially if you want to move forward with a product but you already know there is a hiccup in the support for the farm; just document this in the design document or in a separate document so that these items are noted.

The reason why I make this point is that there have been so many changes from SharePoint 2007 to SharePoint 2019 and the server platforms that support it, so it is possible that you may overlook some areas. Make sure you go back and look at the changes that have been made and ensure you are making the right decisions. Even some third-party products have areas that you wouldn't think of asking about, such as the product I have used for migration, AvePoint's FLY tool, which does not support SharePoint 2007. You want to make sure not to assume anything.

So, say you were building all this architecture to migrate from 2007 to 2019 and you thought you had the product to do it. Then, you get to the point where you need to use it and find out that it doesn't support your old environment. This would be a big loss of time because now you're back to square one trying to find a solution. One solution that still costs a lot of time would be migrating to 2010 first and then migrating to 2019 from that environment using the tool. This would take time because in SharePoint 2007, the main support was for classic authentication. When moving to 2019, you have to move to claims, so you would need to migrate to 2010 and update all the users from classic to claims and test. This could cause a major setback in the time spent.

So, my take on this is before you start, have a final discussion on these topics with your team and finalize anything you may need to move forward. Look at all aspects of the operating system, software, and third-party integrations before you move forward. This could be getting approvals on builds, approvals on funding, and other areas. You don't want to hold the project up because you didn't do enough research, so I am adding this point to give you a heads up to always do a second round of quick checking and research. This may take a week or two but it will be worth the effort in the long run to minimize time loss.

Server feature comparisons

There have been many changes to the Windows Server (Hyper-V) and SharePoint feature sets in the last two versions of these products. Since most of you reading this book will more than likely be migrating from SharePoint Server 2013, I think as part of this book we need to review the changes in Windows Server 2016 Server and those changes made within Windows Server 2019 to get a clear scope of the overall changes we need to be aware of.

It's important to understand what has been deprecated, what is no longer available, and those new features that have been added that may have even changed from the 2016 operating system version to 2019. Without this comparison, you may lose the functionality that you need to maintain your servers effectively as you would want. This gives you the opportunity to shop and look at other technologies as well. I am using Hyper-V as the example for this book because that is what 90% of my customers use for virtualization, and I use Hyper-V in my environment when setting up virtual servers as well.

Let's start our comparison by looking at Windows Server 2016 and looking at things that were changed from Windows Server 2012. This will give you a good baseline to work with to figure out which platform you want to use for your farm.

Windows Server 2016

If you have not had your ears open to all the changes that have been happening for the different Windows Server releases, here are some updates that you need to be aware of.

There are two support tracks for Windows Server: the **Semi-Annual Channel** (**SAC**) and the **Long-Term Servicing Channel** (**LTSC**). The difference between the two channels is the following:

- **SAC**: Microsoft will release two releases a year for Server Core.
- **LTSC**: Microsoft will release feature updates every 2 to 3 years.

Here is a list of new Hyper-V features on Windows Server 2016:

- Compatible with Connected Standby
- Discrete device assignment
- Operating systems disk encryption support
- Host resource protection
- Network adapters and memory
- Hyper-V Manager improvements
- Integration Services
- Linux secure boot
- Support for resources
- Nested virtualization
- Networking features
- Production checkpoints
- Rolling Hyper-V cluster
- Shared virtual hard disks
- VM backup
- Shielded VMs
- Start order
- Storage **Quality of Service** (**QoS**)
- Configuration file format

- Configuration version
- Virtualization security
- Windows containers
- Windows PowerShell Direct

Windows Server 2019

Here is a list of new Hyper-V features on Windows Server 2019:

- Desktop Experience
- System Insights
- Server Core
- Windows Defender Advanced
- SDN
- Shielded VMs
- HTTP/2
- Storage Migration Service
- Storage Spaces Direct
- Storage Replica
- Failover clustering
- Linux containers
- Kubernetes
- Container improvements
- Network performance
- Windows Time service
- High-performance SDN gateway
- Delay Background Transport
- Memory support

As you can see, there are no real differences here but more additions in Windows Server 2019. I am only adding this information to let you know what changes were implemented in Server 2016 because you need to know these features as they are part of 2019 as well. In most cases, as I have stated in this book, you are moving from an older version of SharePoint, so you really need to understand what has transpired from version to version in your operating system as well as SQL and SharePoint. This will give you an overall understanding of what your systems have the ability to support.

When looking at features and areas to support our environment, we also need to define the roles needed within the farm to support the services. In the next section, we will talk about server roles and the importance of these roles in the environment.

Defining needed server roles

Creating hosts should be the first step in starting the process to build our VMs for the platform. This means we have already completed our assessment and have met with all teams working on our new architecture as well as finalized that architecture so that we can implement it at this point. Making sure you have your architecture is one thing, but we also need to look at environments.

Did we build environments to support DEV, QA, TEST, and production? If not, we need to do so now and we need to make sure we have addressed our support farms. These environments can weigh heavily on how our development and test process is defined for our environment. These other farms can also change the way our environments are secured and managed. These should all be separate environments with their own hardware, admin accounts, service accounts, and in some cases, AD, depending on your defined requirements.

Separation in these areas should be consistent with maintaining the validity of your migrations of code and content through testing those components before bringing them to the production environment. DEV environments are typically small, one-server environments that are managed one to one or developer to developer. You will need more VMs depending on how big the development team you're supporting is. If your team is medium to large for developers, you will want to spread out the resources using Team Foundation Server as the bridge to support the code developed in these cases.

Within our architecture, we must include a design to support redundancy, backup, and restore, build enough resources for performance concerns, as well as build a stable server architecture. The last thing we want in our host configurations is the possibility of error and downtime associated with misconfiguration or calculations of resources. The best thing to do is to take your time and figure out what resources will be needed to support your environment, especially looking at hardware types (Dell, HP, NetApp, EMC), rack space planning, networking equipment, and cabling. We also want to give some measurements to our installation by looking at server resources such as CPU, memory, disk space, types of disks, and disk speed.

When choosing server resources, make sure to look at and evaluate the speed of the hardware resources you choose. These choices make a big difference in how the server responds to processing and deals with memory, as well as the requirements for disk speed. The disk choice could be dependent on what those disks are supporting within your server resource. We could use an SAS drive for our operating system and partitions where you need the fastest response. There are also RAID configurations we could use for redundancy, such as mirroring and/or RAID 10, to make sure our data is always protected. Disk arrays have changed over the years and could be another investment you could bring to the table. These new technologies bring better ways to manage disk space along with the ability for enormous growth using connected hardware.

Logging may not be something we will need the fastest disk for, so we could take a hit on those resources and choose lower-speed disks. We could also use lower-speed disks to support backup file locations and record center locations where there is not much activity or user interaction. This takes planning, coordination, and documentation of those areas to support the configurations you are setting in this case. I can't stress enough in this book about documentation. If you're not already doing it, please start doing it on this project. It will save you a lot of headache and pain down the road.

In another vein, you may not need as much memory for a VM server in certain environments or use cases. I can tell you that I've been in a bad situation before when I used less than the recommended processor and memory for an Exchange and Skype implementation that I carried out in a test environment. It caused a lot of errors within my Outlook and Skype clients due to the server not having enough memory to process presence within the application. So, this can be very important depending on the application. If you have the resources to do so, do as Microsoft recommends because it can save you a headache.

So, let's take my environment as an example and look at all the servers I will be building:

- AD server
- Web frontend servers
- App servers
- Two SQL servers
- Exchange server

You could call this an evaluation, proof of concept, or DEV environment, so not many people will be using this environment. The support for users is very minimal, which means I do not need a lot of resources to really support a lot of overhead. My server footprints will be small and resources will also be minimal. So, when looking at our example, we will create servers that do not need many resources, but we want enough resources to support our environment from a best practice perspective. Please take into consideration that we are not building production in our examples.

When making decisions on hardware, always consult the manufacturer to make sure you are making the right decision. You will need to explain what your project is about and what you want to get out of the hardware you purchase. Tell them about any software you are going to use, in this case, SharePoint and SQL Server, and how many users you will be supporting.

If you believe your CPU will be your biggest worry, then do some research before your conversation; ask the manufacturer about any details you found, test the scenarios, and look at reports from old environments as well to make the best decisions going forward. Make sure you buy/create a server that can provide a better response to your environment needs and not take on the same issues you had in the past from a hardware standpoint.

In my environment, I am using a Dell R710 server and installing Windows Server 2019 to build my host servers. I am doing this to show the new advanced features that Windows Server 2019 offers. In that configuration, my hosts have five **Network Interface Cards (NIC)**, two eight core CPUs, 144 GB of disk space for my C drive, 2 TB of space for my VM locations, and 80 GB of RAM.

My environment has four host servers available and we will use two of the servers as SQL servers to support the database tier. SQL Server is the backbone of our SharePoint environment and we should not skimp on making this tier as strong as possible. For my other two hosts, I will use them as my SharePoint and/or web application tier. On this tier, any third-party applications can always be added as supported applications if needed.

We also need to make sure that as we build our servers, we also relate them to what application services we will be running on our SharePoint servers, especially using MinRoles. We will look into this more in *Chapter 4, Installation Concepts*, which will point out services we need to be careful with. Distributed Cache is one service where we need to be very careful with how it's configured, either as a MinRole as an individual server or accompanied by other services, and assign what resources it needs to run efficiently. MinRoles play a big part in what application services strictly run on a SharePoint server, so defining server resources goes hand in hand with our MinRole choices for our SharePoint servers.

In this environment, I will be using Hyper-V (because I am a Microsoft guy) to support the virtualization within the server builds. The host server will need to have dedicated server resources as well to make sure that the server can not only support the platform but also support itself as it needs resources to keep the server running and process any details used by the Hyper-V host. So, in our configuration, we need to make sure that out of the 80 GB of RAM and eight cores available, we set aside some good resources for our hosts. The host will not be working very hard in my environment because of the light user community.

So, let's get started with configuring our first host that will support AD!

Installing Windows Server 2019 – host configuration

To start our installation, please create a bootable DVD or USB to install Windows Server 2019. After doing so, reboot your system and choose the method with which you would like to start your installation. There are two ways to install Windows Server 2019: one is using Desktop Experience or a GUI interface, and the other is Core, which is all command-line driven. We will use the GUI interface because this is the default interface supported by SharePoint 2019.

The checklist of items we need to create our hosts is the following, and these items should be documented as a best practice for the support of the environment:

- IP addresses for the servers
- Server naming conventions
- Admin and service accounts
- A network supporting the servers
- ISO for installation of Windows Server 2019

- Licenses for *all* product installations
- Any company policy-related configuration details
- Any security policy-related configuration details
- Access to any custom server builds related to your company's policy

Again, to start the Windows installation, use a shared mounted DVD or mounted shared USB or folder. Once you have inserted the media, you will see the Windows setup screen, and then you can take the following steps to start the installation of Windows 2019 Server:

1. Click **Next** to continue the installation:

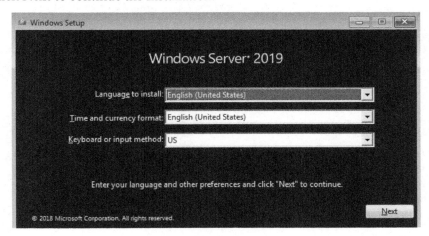

Figure 3.1 – Windows setup screen

2. Click **Install now** to continue the installation:

Figure 3.2 – Installation splash screen

3. Click **Next** to continue the installation, choosing the desired operating system you would like to install:

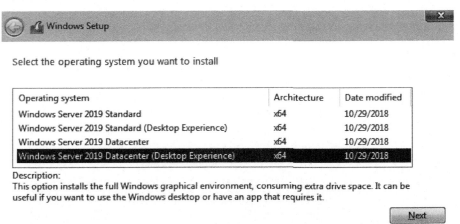

Figure 3.3 – Operating system choices

> **Note**
>
> **Standard (Desktop Experience)** supports small, virtualized environments and **Datacenter (Desktop Experience)** supports highly virtualized and cloud-based environments. The choices without **Desktop Experience** are core, which is supported using the command line only.

4. Click the checkbox and then click **Next** to continue:

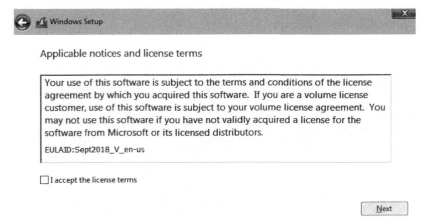

Figure 3.4 – Accepting the license terms

5.   Click **Next** to continue the installation (you may have many drives here and some may need formatting – use the tools as needed):

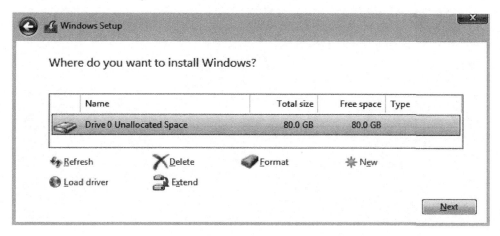

Figure 3.5 – Selecting a drive for installation

6.   Wait for the installation process to complete:

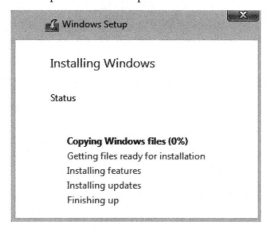

Figure 3.6 – Progress of installation during setup

7. After your server reboots, you will be prompted to supply a password for the administrator credentials:

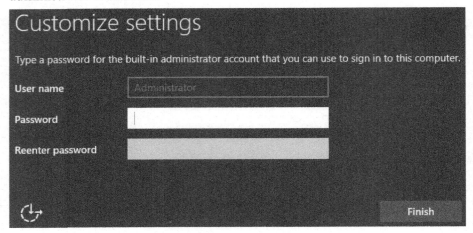

Figure 3.7 – Supply your credentials here

8. Wait for the installation process to complete and you will see your desktop.

We have completed our installation of Windows Server. We will now configure our network and server names for the servers that will support our farm.

Configuring the network and server names

Make sure to update the IP address, server name, and domain before you start the installation! Let's look at the steps to start configuration:

1. On the desktop, press *Ctrl + Alt + Delete* to log in to the server with your admin account.

2. Click the start button to pull up a list of available options. Choose the file manager.

3. Right-click on **This PC** on the Windows menu and choose **Properties**:

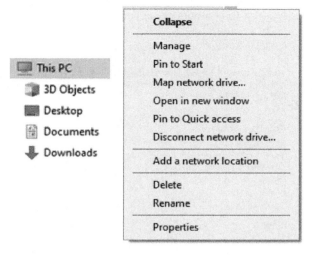

Figure 3.8 – Right-clicking on This PC

Change the server name to the desired name and change the settings.

This window will pop up to show the system properties:

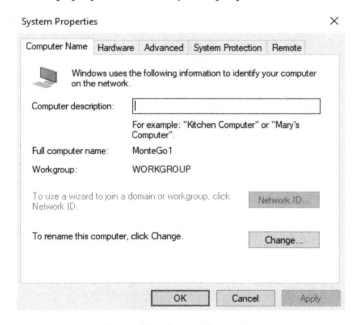

Figure 3.9 – System Properties

4.   Click the **Change…** box to change the server name:

Figure 3.10 – Changing your server name

5.   Click **OK**. Then, reboot the server and your server name will be updated.

Configuring network and internet access

We will start the configuration of network resources on our server at this point in our installation. This will include network configuration, which you will need to finish this configuration. Please have the IP addresses of your gateway, servers, and subnet mask and follow these steps:

1.   Once the server is installed, go to **Control Panel** and choose the **Network and Internet** feature. Next, select **Network and Sharing Center**:

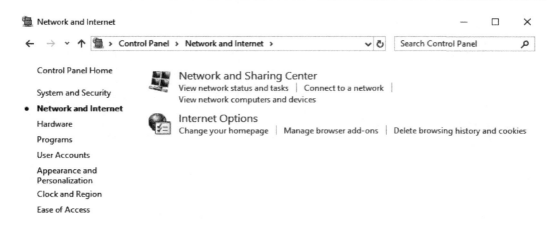

Figure 3.11 – Network and Internet in Control Panel

2. Click on **Change adapter settings**:

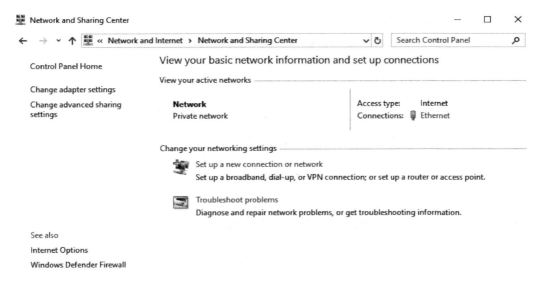

Figure 3.12 – Network connection view

3. Right-click the Ethernet connection you would like to configure and choose **Properties**:

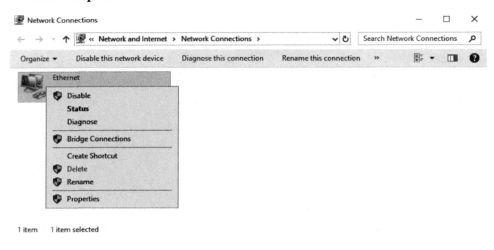

Figure 3.13 – Navigating to the properties of your Ethernet connection

4. Choose **Internet Protocol Version 4** and click **Properties**:

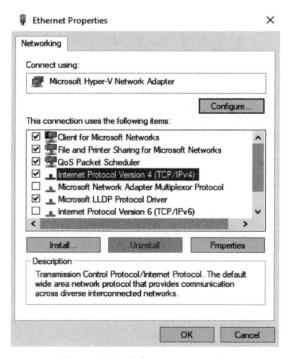

Figure 3.14 – Selecting properties

5. Select **Use the following IP address**. Insert your static IP address for this
    server, the subnet mask, and the default gateway. Also, enter your preferred DNS
    server and alternate DNS server addresses. Then, click **OK**:

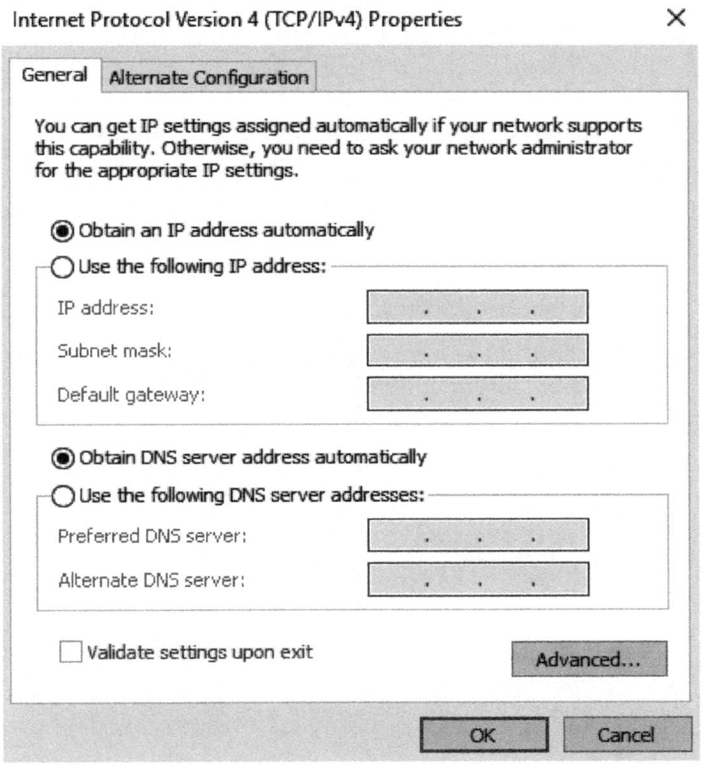

Figure 3.15 – Inserting the required details on this screen

Networking is set up for the server now and you will now be able to see the server on the
network and browse the internet if the server is connected to the internet. Again, you can
also add configurations for NIC teaming, which is more advanced and can easily be found
on Microsoft's website.

Adding the server to the domain

Once you have set up networking on the server and you are able to access other resources
from the server, we need to add the server to the domain. The domain is essential in
centralizing the server farm to use the same authentication method for the farm. This is
also given as SharePoint using AD for authentication.

Remember that in SharePoint 2016, AD is the only method of authentication supported. As in older versions, **Forms Based Authentication (FBA)** and other methods are supported out of the box. You will need to use Microsoft Identity Manager to configure those methods for use within SharePoint Server 2016.

To start adding the server to the domain, follow these steps:

1. Go to **Control Panel** by typing `control panel` in the run or search area of the desktop. You can also find **Control Panel** by clicking **start** as well.

2. Add the domain name you will use in your environment (this should be the name of the AD domain created for your farm) and the correct server name in the **Computer name** area of the form:

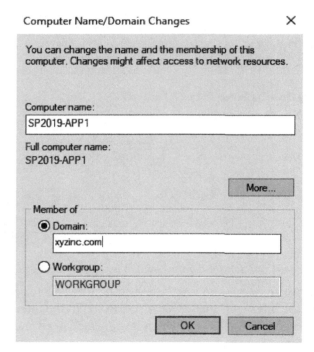

Figure 3.16 – Updating the domain

3. Type in the domain admin account and password and click **OK** (if you do not get this screen and get an error, please check your DNS, and even rebooting may help at this point):

Figure 3.17 – Entering the username and password

4. Click **OK** on the welcome message screen:

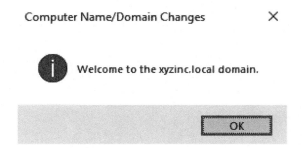

Figure 3.18 – Welcome screen

5. Reboot your server!

We have now added our new server(s) to the domain. Repeat these steps as needed within the configuration of your servers. Now that we have our host established, installing Hyper-V is next on our list to be completed.

Configuring Hyper-V Manager on Windows Server 2019

There are two ways to install Hyper-V on Windows 2019 Server. One is through PowerShell and the other is through the GUI using a visual approach. In my view, it doesn't matter what you use. Although PowerShell is a very powerful set of tools to know and understand, you can get the same results through the GUI in most cases. I know that some admins choose to run everything in PowerShell and don't want to use the GUI, though.

To me, either of the two can get the job done in certain aspects of administration. PowerShell is more powerful and scripts make life easier, so you have to weigh up the benefits of the two. The GUI should be used by beginners so that they understand the platform before venturing down the PowerShell road. I use a mix of both the GUI and PowerShell in this book so that I can cater to both beginner and intermediate admins and others who just want to understand the platform.

To get a basic understanding of Hyper-V networking, there are some areas you may want to research to get more insight into the application. I have provided a list of research terms for you to look up to dig deeper. As we can't cover all of these topics in this book, knowing these terms can at least point you in the right direction:

- Hyper-V virtual switch
- Hyper-V working with DNS
- The OSI model for Hyper-V virtualization
- VLANs and Hyper-V configuration
- Hyper-V teaming
- Hyper-V and load balancing
- Hyper-V storage

If you would like to use PowerShell to install Hyper-V, make sure before running PowerShell that you start the process to get Hyper-V installed and that you are running it with elevated privileges in the GUI-mode installation. You must run as an administrator to run these commands successfully:

- The PowerShell command is as follows:

```
Install-WindowsFeature -Name Hyper-V
-IncludeManagementTools -Restart
```

- Install Hyper-V with **DISM (Deployment Image Servicing and Management)** as follows:

```
dism /Online /Enable-Feature /FeatureName:Microsoft-
Hyper-V /All
```

If you want to see the installation visually, then take the following steps:

1. Open Server Manager from the desktop of your server by searching for `server manager` or click the icon for Server Manager in your start window. Select the following option and click **Next**:

Figure 3.19 – Selecting Installation Type

2. Choose the server and click **Next**:

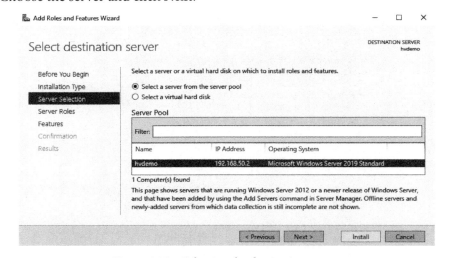

Figure 3.20 – Selecting the destination server

3.   Select **Hyper-V** and click **Next**:

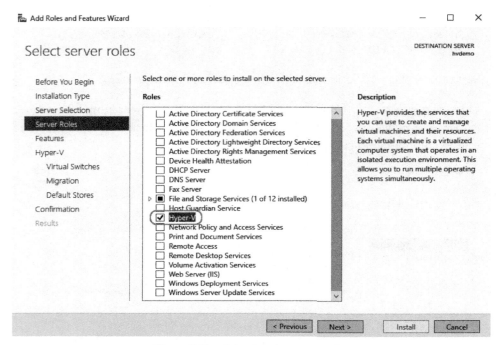

Figure 3.21 – Selecting the server roles

4.   Click the **Add Features** button, like so:

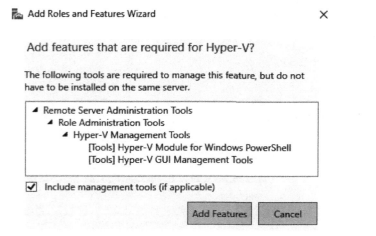

Figure 3.22 – Adding features

5. Make sure to check all the Hyper-V roles, as shown in the following screenshot:

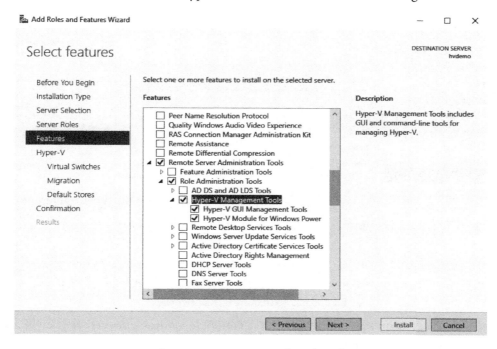

Figure 3.23 – Hyper-V roles selected

6. Click **Next** once you have read the page that explains Hyper-V workloads on VMs:

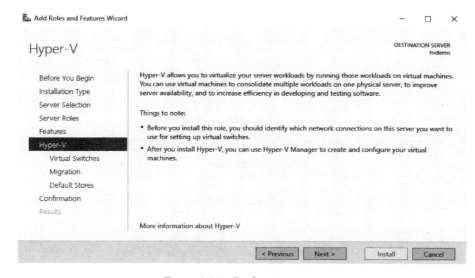

Figure 3.24 – Explanation page

7. Select the **Ethernet** network adapter and click **Next**:

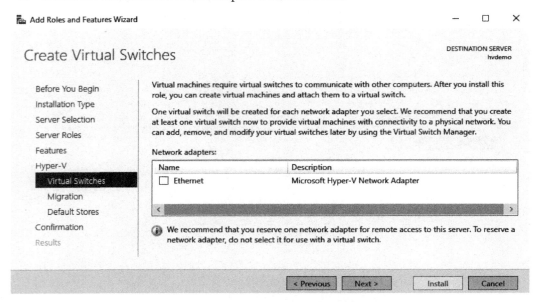

Figure 3.25 – Creating virtual switches

8. In the **Migration** selection, make the selection depending on whether you will be using the live migrations features available within Hyper-V:

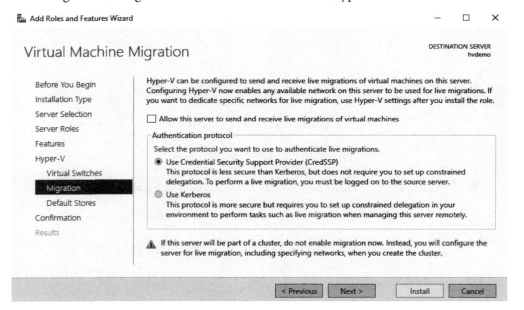

Figure 3.26 – Selecting security

9. Select the default locations for hard disks and configuration files. Choose a location that can grow, not your operating system disk. Once you have added a location for each option, click **Next**:

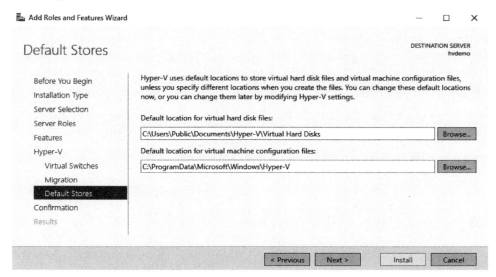

Figure 3.27 – Selecting the default locations

10. Click **Install**:

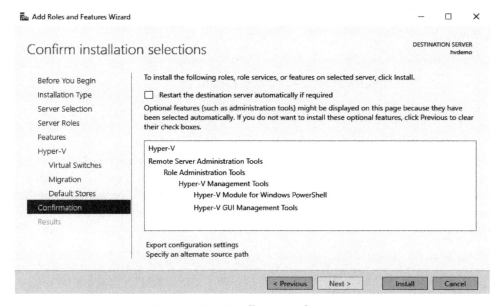

Figure 3.28 – Installation confirmation

When the process completes, **reboot** your server!

Hyper-V advanced post-installation options

Hyper-V used within Windows Server 2019 is a great product and Microsoft continues to build on the server technology by requiring very little post-installation configuration, which was needed in prior versions of the server technology. I will list some of the things you want to check before getting started with using Hyper-V, but from my standpoint, this installation was pretty rock solid.

As for networking, these areas should be addressed as a post-check of the Hyper-V installation depending on the configuration needed within your environment.

The host networking configuration requires the following:

- Create adapter teams.
- Create a virtual switch or create a switch-embedded team.

> **Note**
> These concepts only work in Windows Server 2016 and 2019 and are not supported in earlier versions of the Windows operating system.

As for the overall host configuration, please review this list of checks to make sure you have the locations and settings in place. If you are using live migration, please refer to those items that should be evaluated before starting to use Hyper-V:

- Configure the default virtual configuration storage location.
- Configure the default virtual disk storage location.
- Configure the live migration security settings.
- Configure the live migration performance settings.

There are also commands and other areas of Hyper-V that can be set through the command line and cannot be seen in the GUI. Please look through the list of cmdlets available to you and do some research. You may find that you need to use some of the available cmdlets to configure the Hyper-V configuration further. To list the commands available for Hyper-V, use the following command:

```
Get-Command -Module Hyper-V
```

PowerShell is powerful! Make sure you learn to use it as you go through this book to open your mind to more ways to administer the SharePoint farm and servers in the farm. Most administrators use PowerShell to manage everything.

Now that we have our server host configured, we can create VMs to support the resources needed within the environment.

Creating VMs

Since we now have hosts to create VMs, we can start the process of creating VMs to support our farm.

The checklist of items we need to create our VMs is the following:

- IP addresses for the servers
- Server naming convention
- A network supporting the servers
- Hosts configured for resources
- ISO for installation
- A list of the admin and service accounts with passwords created in AD

The VMs that we will be creating are listed here:

- AD (if you do not already have it)
- SharePoint servers based on MinRoles
- SQL Server
- Office Online Server
- Workflow Manager
- All the installation prerequisites
- Any PowerShell scripts

Creating our first VM

When creating our first VM, we want to locate the Hyper-V VM manager on our server. Let's take a look at how we can do that:

1.   Once opened, right-click the server name and select **New | Virtual Machine…**:

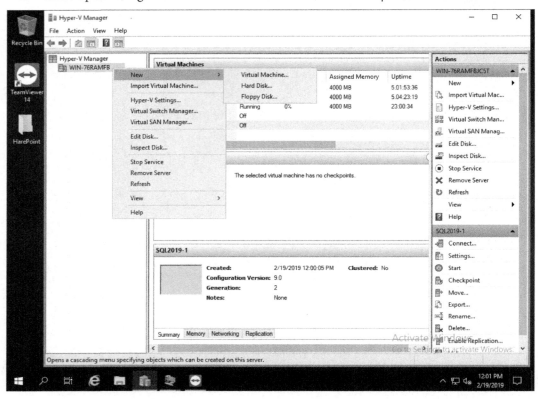

Figure 3.29 – Hyper-V Manager

2. In **Specify Name and Location**, type in the name of your server and browse to select where your VMs will be located on your server. Click **Next** after reading the information about the creation wizard:

> **Note**
> This should be storage you have set aside on separate drive space; please avoid using the C drive!

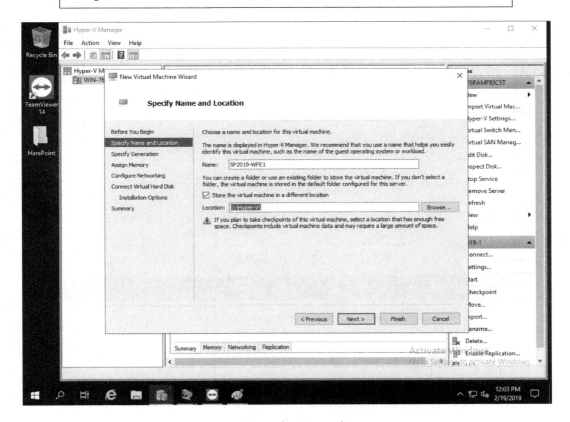

Figure 3.30 – Specify Name and Location

3. Select the generation of server you would like to use as part of your farm. For the latest and greatest features, please select **Generation 2**:

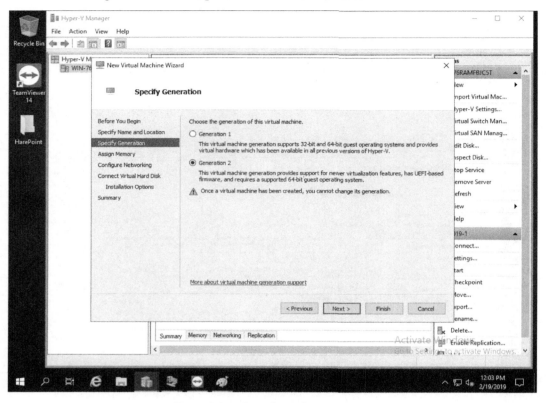

Figure 3.31 – Specifying the generation

4. Select the amount of memory you would like this server to use for support of the farm:

> **Note**
>
> Please do not use Dynamic Memory! This is not a supported feature for the support of SharePoint environments. You will not be supported by Microsoft if you were to call in for support.

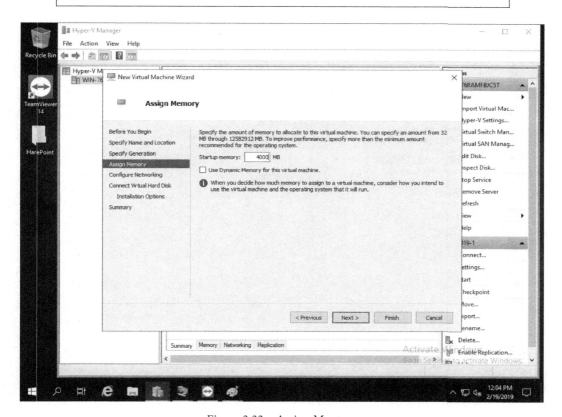

Figure 3.32 – Assign Memory

5.   Select the network adapter you would like to use for networking configuration:

> **Tip**
> You can always change this later by using NIC Teaming or both a switch with NIC teaming. This is just a demonstration of the basic functionality to get you started.

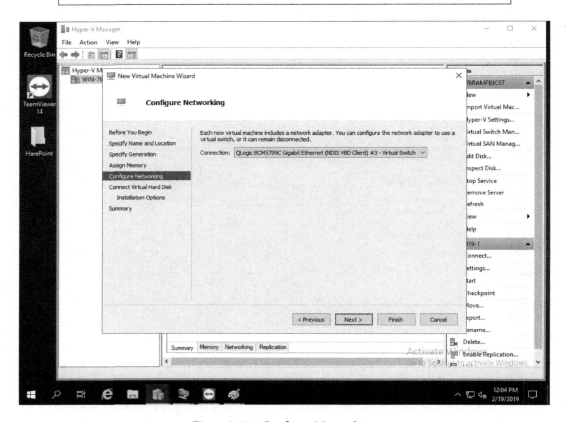

Figure 3.33 – Configure Networking

6. The name of the server file for the VM is shown, as well as the location of the VM and the amount of disk space you would like this server to have for its first drive:

> **Tip**
> Refer back to your drive configurations in your design document to make sure you build your server correctly.

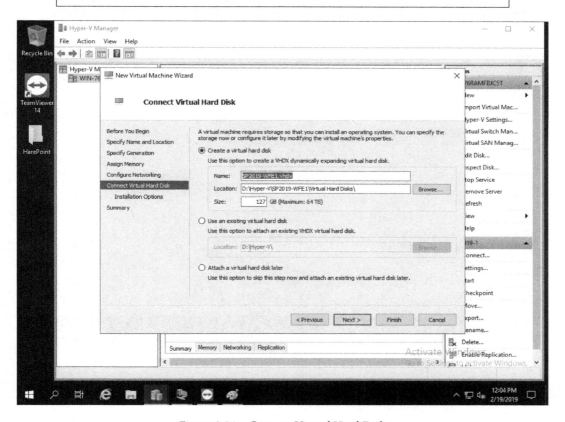

Figure 3.34 – Connect Virtual Hard Disk

7. If you have an ISO image or a DVD of the installation for Windows, please connect it here using the **Browse…** button. If you are just creating the servers, then you can install the operating system later as well:

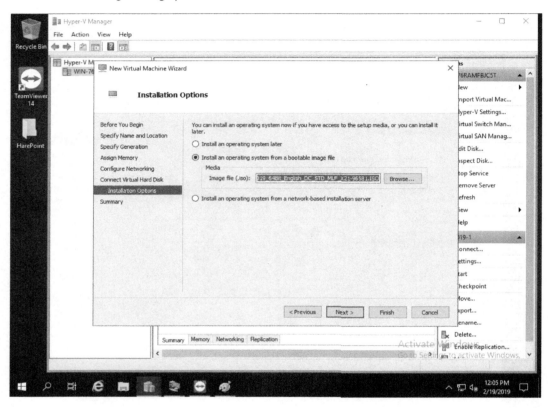

Figure 3.35 – Installation options

8. Complete your server configuration by clicking **Finish**:

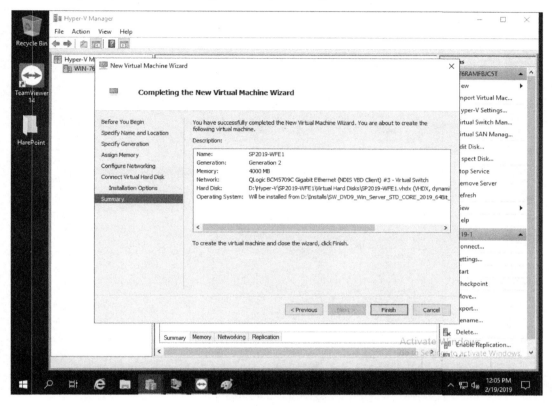

Figure 3.36 – Completing the New Virtual Machine Wizard

Note

This allows the VM to connect to resources on the host computer very easily and even allows drag-and-drop files. This is with Generation 2 VM servers and Windows Server 2016 or 2019 only!

9. Once completed, go back and click on **Integration Services** and select **Guest services**:

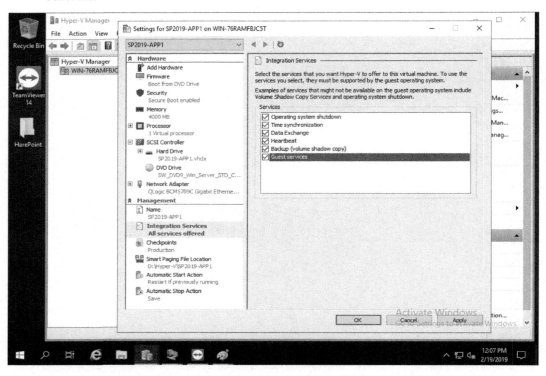

Figure 3.37 – Selecting Guest services

10. Start the installation by choosing your language and keyboard method. Click **Next**:

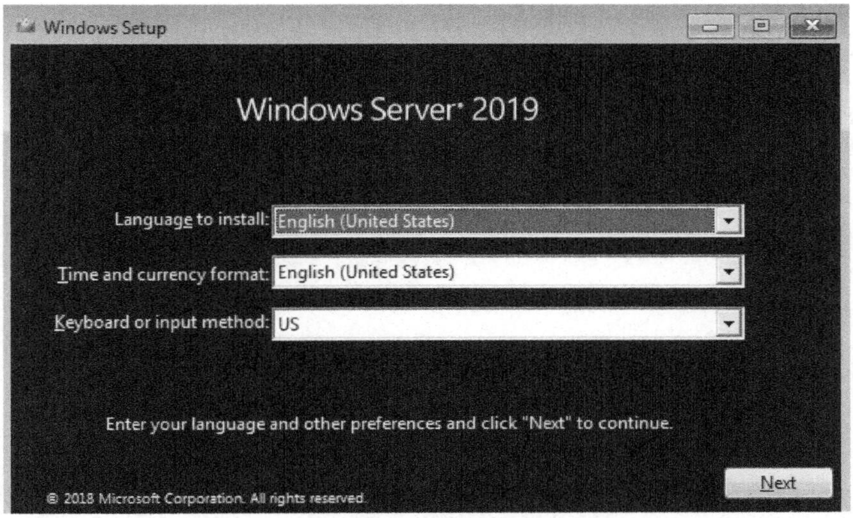

Figure 3.38 – Choosing a language

11. Click **Install now**:

Figure 3.39 – Installation screen

12. Choose the Windows operating system version and experience you would like to use for the server:

> **Tip**
> Remember that for all SharePoint servers, you will need to use the Desktop Experience installation. SharePoint does not support the core installation.

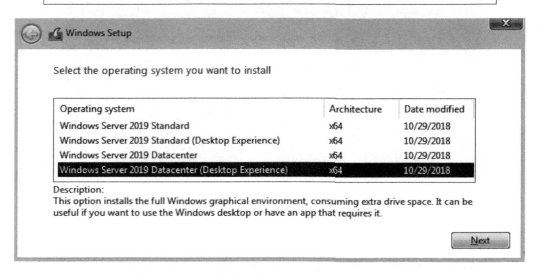

Figure 3.40 – Selecting the operating system to install

13. Click the checkbox to accept the license terms and click **Next**:

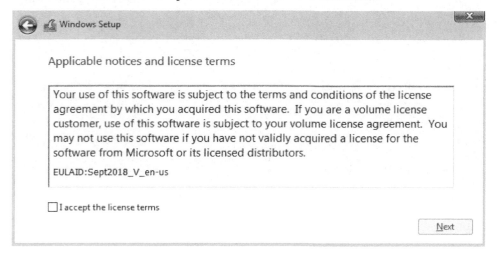

Figure 3.41 – Accepting the terms

14. Choose the drive you would like to install Windows Server on and click **Next**:

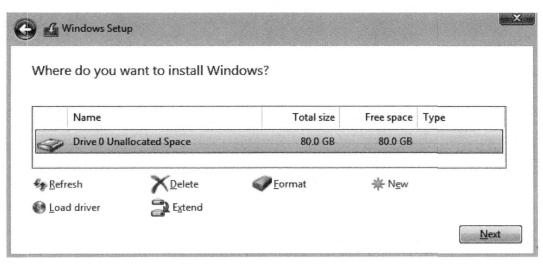

Figure 3.42 – Selecting the install location

You will see the Windows Server in-progress screen:

Figure 3.43 – Installation in progress

Windows is processing the installation:

Figure 3.44 – Progress screen

Finished! You have set up the first VM server on your Hyper-V platform.

Repeat these tasks to set up all your server VMs for the farm, including adding the server to the domain and any other areas covered in this chapter. The servers you plan to install in support of the environment should all use the same configurations on the VMs. Make sure you add one set of servers to one host and the other set to another host for support of redundancy.

Summary

In this chapter, we covered a lot to create the basics of the SharePoint platform. We learned about creating VMs and configuring the host to support the SharePoint resources supporting the platform. We also covered the differences between operating systems and how they have changed over the years in terms of features and support of the environment. Make sure that you understand these details because they will tailor the way that your environment is configured and managed going forward.

Do not under resource your host or VM servers. Make sure you have plenty of disk space and memory to support the environment. Also, remember that dynamic memory is not supported on SharePoint servers. This has changed since the Distributed Cache service was introduced. If you call for Microsoft support, they will not support you with VMs configured in this manner. Don't make mistakes from the beginning. With the low cost of server components, this should not be a limitation any more.

If you really apply yourself in these details, there is much more to research, as you can see from the notes I have provided in this chapter. Please make sure to research the topics I have covered and get a clear understanding of Hyper-V and the technology using the GUI for configuration – and, of course, PowerShell. Do not skip this as a step in your learning as PowerShell is a key way to manage servers and I suspect that it will be the only way to manage servers and cloud resources in the future.

It takes time to learn but, at the same time, it is not rocket science. Do not be intimidated because the more time you spend on it, the better you will be at managing servers with no GUI or visual aspects. Always remember to test your scripts before you run them in a production environment. This is why I have stressed in this chapter and the book to create DEV and TEST environments so that users are not impacted by mistakes. This also applies to SharePoint as there are PowerShell cmdlets for that platform as well. Move toward it openly and embrace its power.

In the next chapter, we will start our installations and do some pre-installation tasks to finalize our server configurations.

Questions

You can find the answers on GitHub under Assessments at `https://github.com/PacktPublishing/Implementing-Microsoft-SharePoint-2019/blob/master/Assessments.docx`

1. What is the difference between the choice of a Standard Desktop Experience and the DataCenter Desktop Experience?

2. The data location for your VMs should be managed on the same drive as your operating system. True or False?

3. When creating the host and VM servers, should you use DHCP or a static address to configure IP addresses for your servers?

4. What are the main three environments we need to have to support our SharePoint development processes ultimately? Why?

5. How do MinRoles relate to server resources?

6. Can the Distributed Cache service be affected by the configuration of your VM?

4

Installation Concepts

In this chapter, we will discuss SQL and SharePoint installation concepts and how to craft installations to fit the requirements your team is trying to build to support the infrastructure. In my travels, I have seen instances where many companies did not pay much attention to these initial steps on how the farm was installed, which later made it difficult to make changes in the infrastructure. We must take into consideration the different versions of software we should be using to make our infrastructure and project successful by implementing features that support our final build goals. Your server resource platform, as well as the version of the software, plays a big part in the infrastructure requirement efforts you are trying to support.

During our build, we must also pay attention to the configuration settings that also come into play to support the users in your community as these settings can make a difference in how the farm supports user requirement efforts. Some settings also play into how we recover from the disasters and hiccups we may face in our farm when the farm is in production use and available to our users.

In this chapter, we will go through the installation and configuration of SharePoint and SQL Server. The issues we have seen in most installations take the form of botched configurations. Looking closely at assessment reports from many different SharePoint farms and SQL Server instances will help bring up some obvious points in this book to help you avoid some pitfalls in the future.

We will also expand on some points that admins and others may gloss over as a non-issue at the beginning because they do this as part of their installation process. From what we have seen, we believe that most of the topics covered in this chapter need to be reviewed as there could be something you might have missed.

The following topics will be covered in this chapter:

- Installation updates
- Configuring SQL Server 2017
- Configuring SharePoint 2019 prerequisites
- SharePoint 2019 installation

Technical requirements

For you to understand this chapter and the knowledge shared, the following requirements must be met. Please review these points to ensure your understanding:

- Installation and configuration experience in SharePoint 2007/2010/2013/2016
- SQL Server experience with installation and configuration

You can find the code files present in this chapter on GitHub at `https://github.com/PacktPublishing/Implementing-Microsoft-SharePoint-2019`.

Let's get started!

Installation updates

We can see a different installation and evaluation process for the new versions of the Windows operating system, SQL, and SharePoint. In this section, we will go through initial installations of SQL Server 2017 Enterprise and SharePoint 2019 Enterprise to show you the step-by-step process of these new installations and point out the new and notable areas to key in on.

When we were writing this book, we really wanted to make sure to get the point across about changes. The reason why we mention this several times in this book is that a lot of you will be coming from a different version of SharePoint to upgrade to SharePoint 2019. So, we want to make sure to cover these areas well as some of you may be skipping versions of SharePoint, SQL, and operating systems to move to new Microsoft applications. Skipping over versions like this requires some research and there will be things you need to understand.

Some of the things in this installation that we need to talk about again are as follows:

- SQL Server and SharePoint do not coexist on the same server in this version.
- SharePoint 2019 only supports these versions of SQL Server: 2016, 2017, and 2019.
- SQL Server Express, SQL Azure, and SQL 2017 on Linux are not supported.
- Windows Server must be installed using Server with Desktop Experience.

As part of our configuration, we are required to use one of these server operating systems:

- Windows Server 2016 Standard or Datacenter (Desktop Experience)
- Windows Server 2019 Standard or Datacenter (Desktop Experience)

For the current installation scenarios, you can refer to the following site: `https://docs.microsoft.com/en-us/sharepoint/install/hardware-and-software-requirements-2019`.

Use one of the following operating systems:

- Microsoft SQL Server 2016 RTM Standard or Enterprise edition
- Microsoft SQL Server 2017 RTM Standard or Enterprise edition for Windows

A list of admin and user accounts needed for the installations of SQL and SharePoint is as follows (could be more depending on your needs):

- **SPAdmin**: Admin account to manage the farm, mainly used for Windows and SharePoint updates
- **SPFarm**: Farm account for the farm
- **SPSearch**: Runs the search application service
- **SPWebApp**: Runs the web applications in the farm; sometimes good to use separate service accounts in some situations
- **SPCTWTS**: Claims to Windows Token Service account needed for this service
- **SPService**: Service account for all services
- **SPProfile**: Runs the User Profile service in the farm
- **SPUPSREP**: For User Profile service connectivity to **Active Directory** (**AD**)
- **SPCacheWrite**: Cache account for the web application that has full control access
- **SPCacheRead**: Cache account for the web application that has read-only access

Now that we have looked at the installation details, let's move on to the configuration details.

List of configuration details

Now that we have created servers for our farm using the methods from *Chapter 3*, *Creating and Managing Virtual Machines*, we need to make sure we have done a check of our list of items that we will need during this process:

- AD domain installation complete.
- NIC card has been set on all **Virtual Machines** (**VMs**) with static IPs.
- All drives have been added to the servers created (second drives for SharePoint servers).
- Admin and service accounts are created.
- All servers have been connected to the AD domain.
- All admin accounts are added to the servers as local admins.
- List of service accounts and passwords.
- License keys for products being installed.

As you can see, this list is short and I am sure there are more items you could need during your installation. There are other items that I could have missed due to my environment being a demo of a basic configuration and not a more secure and sophisticated farm.

In the next section, we will go through the installation of SQL Server 2017 and break down the installation concepts based on requirements.

Configuring SQL Server 2017

The foundation of SharePoint is SQL Server. The database server holds all the data related to your SharePoint installation. SQL Server 2019 is also available for us to test during this proof of concept installation. There are big differences in the two versions of SQL due to updates in the 2019 version that support big data.

Let's talk about the differences for a minute to get you up to speed on SQL Server 2016, 2017, and 2019. SQL Server is supported if installed on the same server as SharePoint 2019. SQL Express is not supported as an automatic installation to support your single server installation. In production environments, we like to see SQL on a separate server for performance reasons.

Installation of SQL Server 2017 can be done on a new platform, which is exciting to see. Linux is now a platform that will support SQL Server 2016, 2017, and 2019, which you can now run on the Linux operating system. What does this mean to me? This could mean a lower cost for operating system licenses and also, Linux is known to be more stable than Windows (depending on who you talk to), so this could give you some benefits of moving your databases to a Linux server.

The installation prerequisites are as follows:

- The SQL admin account has been added to the local administrator group.
- All service accounts have been identified for supporting the installation.
- Local policies have been configured for the SQL admin account.
- Turn off your firewall or configure the port configuration.

Local policies for SQL Server service accounts are as follows:

Name	Description	Local User Rights	Domain Rights	SQL Permission
SQLInstall	Account to install SQL.	Local Administrator... on the SQL server	Doman user	Permission will be assigned when SQL server is being installed on the SQL Server.
SQLUser	This account is for running the following SQLServer services: MSSQLSERVER, SQLSERVERAGENT.	Bypass traverse checking, log on as a service	Domain user	Permission will be assigned when SQL server is being installed on the SQL Server.

Figure 4.1 – SQL Server service accounts

SQL Server Windows Firewall ports can be set for explicit ports, so the firewall does not have to be turned off.

> **Important Note**
>
> REMEMBER: If you are migrating to a cloud service, make sure you check how ports are configured as even if you have the firewall off on the server, the cloud service still requires you to configure the firewall outside the server. This would then allow you to open the ports necessary for the farm to communicate locally and over the internet. Do this configuration at the beginning so that you have no issues with setting up services at the end!

SQL outbound port configuration

Setting the firewall ports is a step you want to make sure to check before installation. Without it, you will not be able to communicate with the SharePoint servers. SharePoint servers will not be able to connect, create, or manage databases. We want to make sure to check the configuration of the server and check to see whether the Windows Firewall is even needed. In some cases, you may not need to have the firewall running. You also want to be sure that the AWS firewall ports are set within the service before you even start your installation.

The outbound ports are listed as follows. Make sure to name your ports specifically so that you know what they are being used for. You can also change the names as needed. The following code can be run in a command window as an administrator:

```
netsh advfirewall firewall add rule name="SQL RPC Transact SQL
TCP Port 135" dir=out action=allow protocol=TCP localport=135

netsh advfirewall firewall add rule name="SQL Default TCP Port
1433" dir=out action=allow protocol=TCP localport=1433

netsh advfirewall firewall add rule name="SQL Named Instance
TCP Port 1434" dir=out action=allow protocol=TCP localport=1434

netsh advfirewall firewall add rule name="SQL Named Instance
UDP Port 1434" dir=out action=allow protocol=UDP localport=1434

netsh advfirewall firewall add rule name="SQL Broker UDP Port
4022" dir=out action=allow protocol=TCP localport=4022

netsh advfirewall firewall add rule name="SQL Analysis Services
TCP Port 2383" dir=out action=allow protocol=TCP localport=2383

netsh advfirewall firewall add rule name="SQL Browser TCP Port
2382" dir=out action=allow protocol=TCP localport=2382

netsh advfirewall firewall add rule name="SQL IPSec UDP Port
500" dir=out action=allow protocol=UDP localport=500

netsh advfirewall firewall add rule name="SQL IPSec DB
Mirroring TCP Port 4500" dir=out action=allow protocol=TCP
localport=4500
```

The SQL outbound ports are now set, so let's set our inbound ports.

SQL inbound port configuration

Inbound ports are just as important as outbound ports, so make sure you update these ports before you start your installation. Name your ports specifically so that you know what they are being used for and change the names as needed.

Inbound ports are listed as follows. The following code can be run in a command window as an administrator:

```
netsh advfirewall firewall add rule name="SQL Default TCP Port
1433" dir=in action=allow protocol=TCP localport=1433

netsh advfirewall firewall add rule name="SQL Named Instance
TCP Port 1434" dir=in action=allow protocol=TCP localport=1434

netsh advfirewall firewall add rule name="SQL Named Instance
UDP Port 1434" dir=in action=allow protocol=UDP localport=1434

netsh advfirewall firewall add rule name="SQL Broker UDP Port
4022" dir=in action=allow protocol=TCP localport=4022

netsh advfirewall firewall add rule name="SQL DB Mirroring TCP
Port 5022" dir=in action=allow protocol=TCP localport=5022

netsh advfirewall firewall add rule name="SQL DB Mirroring TCP
Port 7022" dir=in action=allow protocol=TCP localport=7022

netsh advfirewall firewall add rule name="SQL Analysis Services
TCP Port 2383" dir=in action=allow protocol=TCP localport=2383

netsh advfirewall firewall add rule name="SQL Browser TCP Port
2382" dir=in action=allow protocol=TCP localport=2382

netsh advfirewall firewall add rule name="SQL IPSec UDP Port
500" dir=in action=allow protocol=UDP localport=500

netsh advfirewall firewall add rule name="SQL IPSec DB
Mirroring TCP Port 4500" dir=in action=allow protocol=TCP
localport=4500
```

Now that you have created your VM for SQL Server, we need to set our feature installation, which consists of features being configured on the Windows server to support SQL Server 2017. Open a PowerShell window and run the following command as an administrator:

```
Install-WindowsFeature NET-HTTP-Activation,NET-Non-HTTP-
Activ,NET-WCF-Pipe-Activation45,NET-WCF-HTTP-Activation45,Web-
Server,Web-WebServer,Web-Common-Http,Web-Static-Content,Web-
Default-Doc,Web-Dir-Browsing,Web-Http-Errors,Web-App-
Dev,Web-Asp-Net,Web-Asp-Net45,Web-Net-Ext,Web-Net-Ext45,Web-
ISAPI-Ext,Web-ISAPI-Filter,Web-Health,Web-Http-Logging,Web-
Log-Libraries,Web-Request-Monitor,Web-Http-Tracing,Web-
Security,Web-Basic-Auth,Web-Windows-Auth,Web-Filtering,Web-
Performance,Web-Stat-Compression,Web-Dyn-Compression,Web-
Mgmt-Tools,Web-Mgmt-Console,WAS,WAS-Process-Model,WAS-NET-
Environment,WAS-Config-APIs,Windows-Identity-Foundation,Xps-
Viewer -IncludeManagementTools -Verbose -Source (windows server
installation location\sxs)
```

This command installs the features needed to support SQL Server:

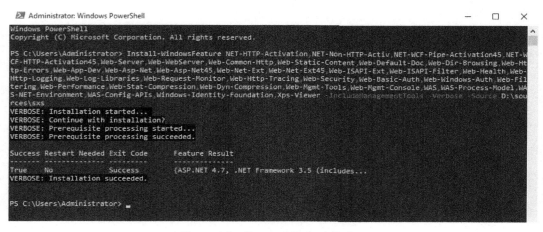

Figure 4.2 – Prerequisite installation

In the past, we had to manually install features using a server manager, which could take up a lot of time depending on how many servers you had to prepare for installation.

To get started with the SQL installation, follow the steps given here:

1. Log in with your SQL admin account only; do not use your personal account to install SQL Server. Also, have the media available on a DVD or USB to get started. After you have started the installation, you will see a window open called **SQL Server Installation Center**, as shown in the following screenshot:

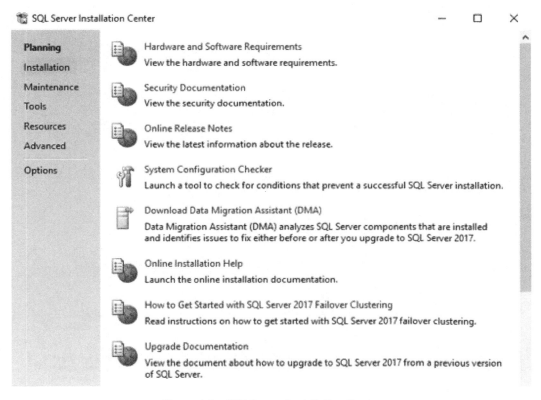

Figure 4.3 – SQL Server Installation Center

2. Click **Installation** on the left main navigation list and click the **New SQL Server stand-alone installation or add features to an existing installation** link in the main area of the screen at the top:

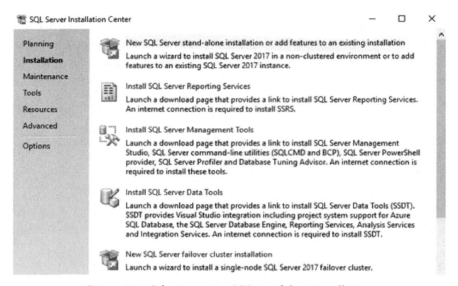

Figure 4.4 – Selecting a new SQL standalone installation

3. Add your product key to continue the installation:

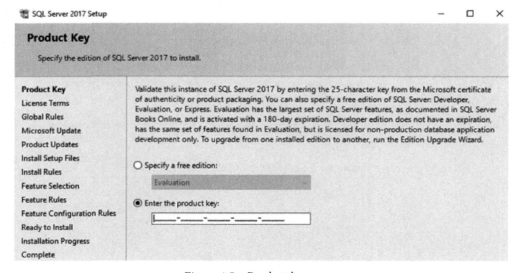

Figure 4.5 – Product key entry

4. Click the checkbox to accept the license terms:

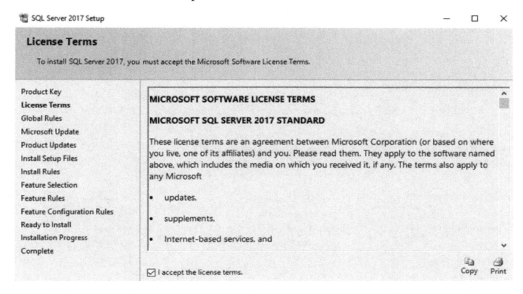

Figure 4.6 – License terms

5. If you would like automatic updates to be provided via Windows Update, select the recommended process, and then select the checkbox. If you plan to use another method such as manual updates, then do not check this box, and just make sure you always download the updates and apply them as needed. Click **Next** to continue with the installation:

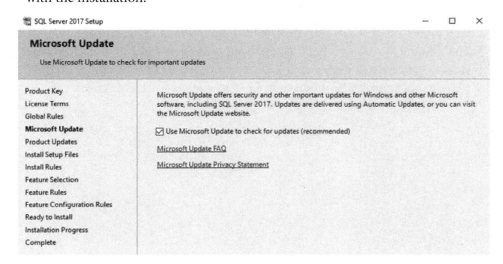

Figure 4.7 – Microsoft Update

6. The SQL Server installation finds any updates and installs them. Your server must be connected to the internet to use Windows Update. Click **Next** to continue the installation:

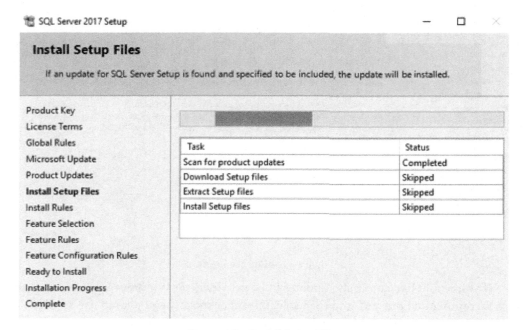

Figure 4.8 – Install Setup Files

7. **Feature Selection** provides the features you would like to install and use within the SQL configuration. Choose your features and select the location for the instance directory, feature directory, and x86 feature directory. More than likely, you will keep the same location on the C drive to support these features, but I have seen instances where there are three drives set up on servers that give an operating system, application, and data drive to support applications and growth:

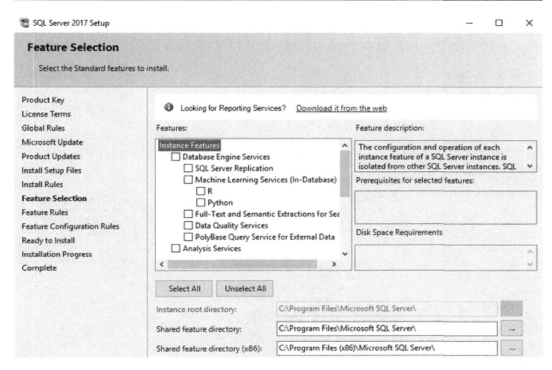

Figure 4.9 – Feature Selection

8. As you can see in the feature choices, we have to select the features we would like to use in our SQL Server 2017 configuration. I chose the following:

- **Database Engine Services**
- **SQL Server Replication**
- **Full-Text and Semantic Extractions for Search**
- **Analysis Services**

9. Some features do not need to be chosen as they do not pertain to SharePoint-supported features. Click **Next** to continue the installation:

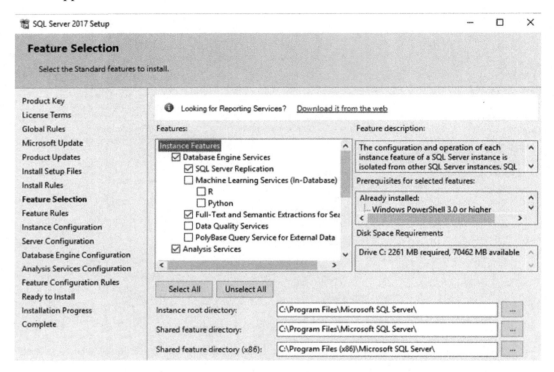

Figure 4.10 – Note the features selected

10. The next step is **Instance Configuration**. Click **Next** to install the default instance of SQL Server:

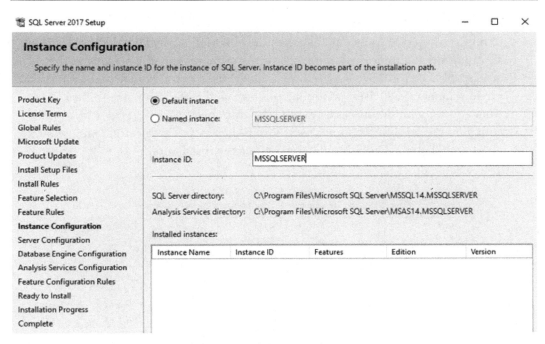

Figure 4.11 – Instance Configuration

11. Since this is our first instance on the server, we will install the default instance. If you want, you can rename it using the instance ID. You can use **Named instance** for the next instances of SQL Server on the same server as a separate service. I have done that in the past when I have had third-party applications that needed a place to live. Since they are associated with SharePoint, I configured a named instance to house those third-party databases. This works great only if you have the resources to support all the components. I would not suggest doing this on a VM but only on a server that is not running virtualization.

12. Service account configuration has not changed. Please add your service accounts to select the service you would like them to run. In my case, I have my SQL admin account, which I am logged into while running the setup and installation. The accounts I need for this configuration are to be used as service accounts. I have an account named **SQL User** mentioned in this chapter. You can name this account what you want but in my case, I named the account SQL Service. I will use it to configure the services. In some cases, admins have separate services using separate accounts. Click the **Collation** tab to continue the installation:

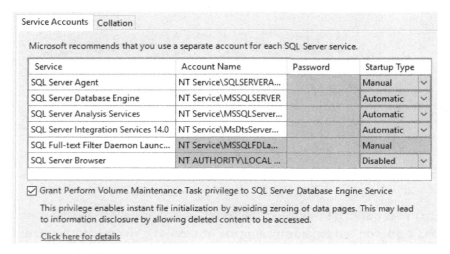

Figure 4.12 – The Service Accounts and Collation tabs

> **Important Note**
> As you select the account, make sure to click and choose them from the people picker; if not, you will receive an error that the account cannot be found.

13. The collation at this point on the server must be configured to be case-insensitive. There have been many blogs talking about this and from a Microsoft standpoint, this does not need to be set to any specific collation as long as it's case-insensitive. The collations of the created databases must be set correctly with the SharePoint default collation, which is Latin1_General_CI_AS_KS_WS. Click **Next** to continue the installation.

14. Setting authentication for administrators should be completed using the current account you are logged in with as a given and adding any other accounts that will be deemed administrators of the SQL instance. We do not want to select **Mixed Mode** for our SQL server. As a best practice, we should only be using **Windows Authentication Mode** to support SharePoint environments. If you plan to use **Mixed Mode**, in most cases, it means you plan to house other databases on the server as well. This goes against Microsoft's best practices as all SQL servers deemed that the data tier for SharePoint should only support that SharePoint farm. Click **Next** to continue the installation.

15. This screen has not changed much with the SQL Server installation process and it still wants you to share the location in which it should hold the files for the configuration. Update the locations as needed in this window.

    In theory, we should have several locations for this and should not have all files created on the same drive. As part of my installation process, I used separate disks to hold the locations of my database files, which are separated by configuration type. So, in theory, this configuration out of the box does not work for me, which is why I pre-create my databases.

    The reason for pre-creating my databases is because I use separate drive spaces to house my config databases, content databases, service databases, search databases, TempDB databases, and any other databases that are part of my installation outside of SharePoint, like how Workflow Manager would be a house on its own drive space. The reason I do this type of setup is I want to get the best performance out of my databases and have them use their own space. So, on this screen, I would set up my targeted locations for these areas but the split will also happen later when more databases are created.

16. Click **TempDB** to see the setting available for configuration and continue the installation:

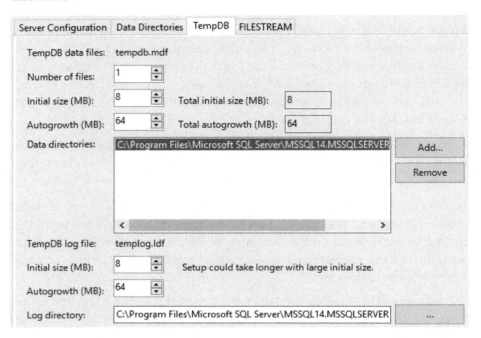

Figure 4.13 – TempDB options

17. Configuring **TempDB**, we will see a different screen than other SQL Server installations in the past. Although this is the same as for SQL Server 2016, I want to make sure that since these two products have been so closely released, you understand this new database engine configuration page. You may be migrating from SQL 2008 or 2012 at this point, so I do not want to miss out anything in the book. Click the **FILESTREAM** tab to continue the installation:

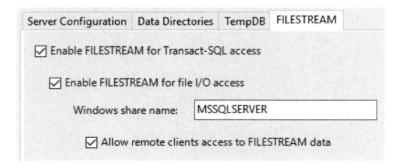

Figure 4.14 – FILESTREAM options

18. FILESTREAM is used for **Remote Blob Storage**, also known as **RBS**. If you are planning to configure that service, you need to click the checkboxes associated with this feature so that it can be installed. Click **Next** to continue the installation:

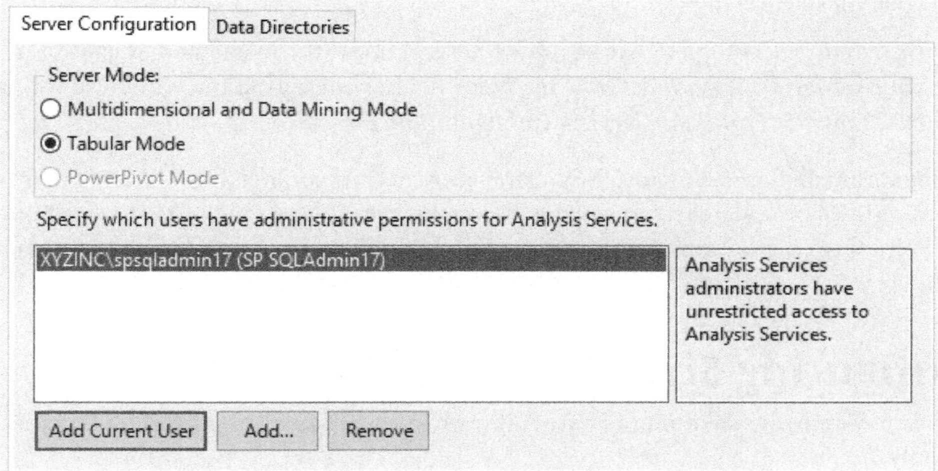

Figure 4.15 – Server configuration

19. Setting administrator rights within Analysis Services should be completed. Please add the admin account you are logged in with as you are performing the installation and any other accounts you will need to have admin access to this feature for administration. Click **Next** to continue the installation:

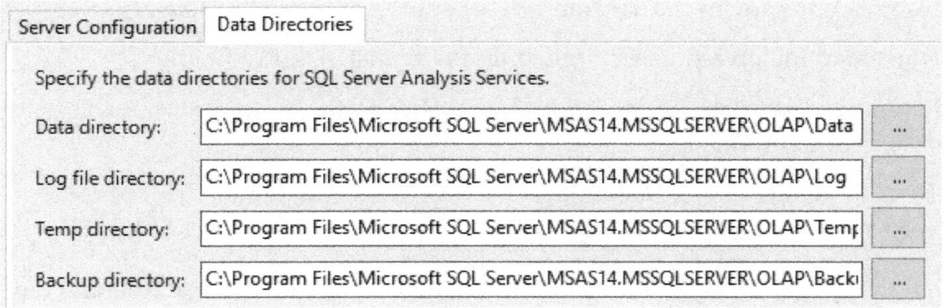

Figure 4.16 – Data Directories

20. Configuring data directories goes back to what I was saying about pre-creating databases as well, which is the way I install and configure my databases. This area is also configured as drive space within my configuration to hold these databases. Choose your locations and click **Next** to continue the installation.

21. Now that all the configurations have been set, we will click on **Install** and start the installation process for the SQL server.

22. The installation is progressing and this does progress slowly, so just be patient and you will start seeing results.

23. Installation is complete. Please click **Close** to finish the install and afterward, reboot your server. Your server is now ready for further configuration, which we will tackle in *Chapter 5*, *Farm and Services Configuration*.

We are not finished installing our SQL database server. If you need to add any other custom utilities or updates to your database server, please do so now. Once we get our SharePoint farm configured, we will set up our maintenance plans to back up our content and services.

Configuring SharePoint 2019 prerequisites

When we start the installation of SharePoint, we need to make sure the following things are available:

- Installation software (DVD, ISO, USB).
- Keys for licensing.
- Accounts created for the service and admin identities.
- AD: SharePoint Server 2019 is only supported with a minimum of AD 2003.
- Admin rights are given to the admin account running the installation.
- Download the prerequisites needed to do the installation.
- Identical hard drive configurations on all SharePoint servers (always at least two drives configured).
- Turn off Windows Firewall unless you have to download my script to configure the ports manually.

Note that the Office 2019 client cannot be installed on the same server as SharePoint Server 2019.

Preparing the server is the same as we did for SQL Server 2017 in the *Configuring SQL Server 2017* section of this chapter. Repeat these steps on all SQL and SharePoint servers:

```
Install-WindowsFeature NET-HTTP-Activation,NET-Non-HTTP-
Activ,NET-WCF-Pipe-Activation45,NET-WCF-HTTP-Activation45,Web-
Server,Web-WebServer,Web-Common-Http,Web-Static-Content,Web-
Default-Doc,Web-Dir-Browsing,Web-Http-Errors,Web-App-
Dev,Web-Asp-Net,Web-Asp-Net45,Web-Net-Ext,Web-Net-Ext45,Web-
ISAPI-Ext,Web-ISAPI-Filter,Web-Health,Web-Http-Logging,Web-
Log-Libraries,Web-Request-Monitor,Web-Http-Tracing,Web-
Security,Web-Basic-Auth,Web-Windows-Auth,Web-Filtering,Web-
Performance,Web-Stat-Compression,Web-Dyn-Compression,Web-
Mgmt-Tools,Web-Mgmt-Console,WAS,WAS-Process-Model,WAS-NET-
Environment,WAS-Config-APIs,Windows-Identity-Foundation,Xps-
Viewer -IncludeManagementTools -Verbose -Source (windows server
installation location\sxs)
```

> **Important Note**
>
> Make sure to include the Windows Server media SXS location in the
> -Source parameter of the script.

Once you have run the feature installation script on the SharePoint server, you will see the confirmation that the installation succeeded, like so:

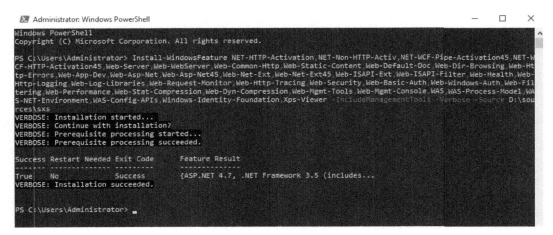

Figure 4.17 – Installation success confirmation

The local policy settings for SharePoint service accounts are as follows:

Name	Description	Local User Rights	Domain Rights	SQL Permission
SPAdmin	Used for installation and to perform product configuration	Local administrator on SharePoint Server, adjust memory quotas for a process, impersonate a client after authentication, log on as a batch job, log on as a service, restore files and directories, and take ownership of files or other objects	Domain user	The public, dbcreator, and security admin SQL roles
SPFarm	It is used for the following tasks: to configure and manage the server farm and to run Microsoft SP Foundation Workflow Timer Service, Central Administration, and the User Profile service	Local administrator on SharePoint Server during UPS provisioning, local administrator (remove after complete configuration), back up files and directories, bypass traverse checking, impersonate a client after authentication, log on as a batch job, log on as a service, replace a process level, and generate security audits	Domain user	The public, dbcreator, and security admin SQL roles
SPWebApps	Used to run web application pools	Adjust memory quotas for a process, impersonate a client after authentication, log on as a batch job, Log on as a service	Domain user	None
SPService Apps	Used to run service application pools	Adjust memory quotas for a process, impersonate a client after authentication, log on as a batch job, and log on as a service	Domain user	None

Name	Description	Local User Rights	Domain Rights	SQL Permission
SPSearch	Used as the default account by the Search Service application to crawl content.	Impersonate a client after authentication, log on as a batch job, and log on as a service	Domain user	None
SPProfile	User for user profile synchronization account.	None	Domain user and Replicated Directory Changes permission on the domain	None

Figure 4.18 – Local policy table

Make sure to create the service accounts you need for your installation. The web application and service application pools can be used many times depending on what you need in your environment. For example, for an additional web application pool, I would add one for mysites to cover that web application separately from my main application pool. All installations of SharePoint, depending on the admin account, require different numbers of service accounts based on what you want to configure in your farm. There are a couple of accounts missing that we will talk about later in the book as those services are created:

- Cache accounts

- Workflow Manager accounts

- Office Online Server accounts

- SharePoint crawl account (only needed if you want to separate at that level for security)

- Business Connectivity service (accounts may be needed to connect to outside data sources)

The local policy is very important as the rights given to each service account are reflected in the local policy settings. If the service account is not given the proper rights, you will see errors in your event logs pertaining to that particular service, which can be misleading. This is due to the errors given not telling you specifically what the issue is in some cases.

Domain policies come into play as well as they can overwrite these local policies set by SharePoint automatically. This usually happens only when the server is rebooted, so you could think you have a great configuration until you reboot one day and then the service is down. Be very careful how you use local and domain policies within a SharePoint and SQL Server configuration. Talk to your AD group to make sure these areas within the domain and local server policies have been covered.

SharePoint outbound port configuration

Port settings for the SharePoint servers are required for communication between the farm servers and the SQL server. It is important that you do not skip this step as this can cause the farm to be non-operational.

As part of our configuration, the firewall is very important to configure as the ports for the server need to be open to support the SharePoint Server configuration. This script configures the firewall port outbound settings for SharePoint servers individually. The following code can be run in a command-line window as an administrator:

```
netsh advfirewall firewall add rule name="SharePoint Open Port
80" dir=out action=allow protocol=TCP localport=80
```
```
netsh advfirewall firewall add rule name="SharePoint Open Port
443" dir=out action=allow protocol=TCP localport=443
```
```
netsh advfirewall firewall add rule name="SharePoint SQL Open
Ports" dir=out action=allow protocol=TCP localport=1433-1434
```
```
netsh advfirewall firewall add rule name="SharePoint SQL Open
Port 445" dir=out action=allow protocol=TCP localport=445
```
```
netsh advfirewall firewall add rule name="SharePoint Open Port
25" dir=out action=allow protocol=TCP localport=25
```
```
netsh advfirewall firewall add rule name="SharePoint
Open Port 16500-16519" dir=out action=allow protocol=TCP
localport=16500-16519
```
```
netsh advfirewall firewall add rule name="SharePoint Open Port
22233" dir=out action=allow protocol=TCP localport=22233-22236
```
```
netsh advfirewall firewall add rule name="SharePoint Open Port
443" dir=out action=allow protocol=TCP localport=443
```
```
netsh advfirewall firewall add rule name="SharePoint Open Port
808" dir=out action=allow protocol=TCP localport=808
```
```
netsh advfirewall firewall add rule name="SharePoint Open Port
32843" dir=out action=allow protocol=TCP localport=32843-32846
```
```
netsh advfirewall firewall add rule name="SharePoint
Workflow Manager Open Port 12290-12291" dir=out action=allow
```

```
protocol=TCP localport=12290-12291

netsh advfirewall firewall add rule name="SharePoint Open Port
5725" dir=out action=allow protocol=TCP localport=5725

netsh advfirewall firewall add rule name="SharePoint Open Port
389" dir=out action=allow protocol=TCP localport=389

netsh advfirewall firewall add rule name="SharePoint Open Port
389" dir=out action=allow protocol=UDP localport=389

netsh advfirewall firewall add rule name="SharePoint Open Port
88" dir=out action=allow protocol=TCP localport=88

netsh advfirewall firewall add rule name="SharePoint Open Port
88" dir=out action=allow protocol=UDP localport=88

netsh advfirewall firewall add rule name="SharePoint Open Port
53" dir=out action=allow protocol=TCP localport=53

netsh advfirewall firewall add rule name="SharePoint Open Port
53" dir=out action=allow protocol=UDP localport=53

netsh advfirewall firewall add rule name="SharePoint Open Port
464" dir=out action=allow protocol=UDP localport=464

netsh advfirewall firewall add rule name="SharePoint Open Port
809" dir=out action=allow protocol=TCP localport=809
```

Once we have completed the outbound ports, let's configure the inbound ports on your SharePoint server next.

SharePoint Server inbound port configuration

Inbound ports are just as important as outbound ports. Communication between the farm server resources is needed to support the infrastructure. This script configures firewall port inbound settings for SharePoint Server. The following code can be run in a command window as an administrator:

```
netsh advfirewall firewall add rule name="SharePoint Open Port
80" dir=in action=allow protocol=TCP localport=80

netsh advfirewall firewall add rule name="SharePoint Open Port
443" dir=in action=allow protocol=TCP localport=443

netsh advfirewall firewall add rule name="SharePoint Open Port
445" dir=in action=allow protocol=TCP localport=445

netsh advfirewall firewall add rule name="SharePoint Open Port
25" dir=in action=allow protocol=TCP localport=25

netsh advfirewall firewall add rule name="SharePoint Open
Port 16500 - 16519" dir=in action=allow protocol=TCP
localport=16500-16519
```

```
netsh advfirewall firewall add rule name="SharePoint Open Port
22233" dir=in action=allow protocol=TCP localport=22233-22236
```

```
netsh advfirewall firewall add rule name="SharePoint Open Port
808" dir=in action=allow protocol=TCP localport=808
```

```
netsh advfirewall firewall add rule name="SharePoint Open Port
32843" dir=in action=allow protocol=TCP localport=32843-32846
```

```
netsh advfirewall firewall add rule name="SharePoint Workflow
Manager Open Port 12290-12291" dir=in action=allow protocol=TCP
localport=12290-12291
```

```
netsh advfirewall firewall add rule name="SharePoint Open Port
5725" dir=in action=allow protocol=TCP localport=5725
```

```
netsh advfirewall firewall add rule name="SharePoint Open Port
389" dir=in action=allow protocol=TCP localport=389
```

```
netsh advfirewall firewall add rule name="SharePoint Open Port
389" dir=in action=allow protocol=UDP localport=389
```

```
netsh advfirewall firewall add rule name="SharePoint Open Port
88" dir=in action=allow protocol=TCP localport=88
```

```
netsh advfirewall firewall add rule name="SharePoint Open Port
88" dir=in action=allow protocol=UDP localport=88
```

```
netsh advfirewall firewall add rule name="SharePoint Open Port
53" dir=in action=allow protocol=TCP localport=53
```

```
netsh advfirewall firewall add rule name="SharePoint Open Port
53" dir=in action=allow protocol=UDP localport=53
```

```
netsh advfirewall firewall add rule name="SharePoint Open Port
464" dir=in action=allow protocol=UDP localport=464
```

```
netsh advfirewall firewall add rule name="SharePoint Open Port
809" dir=in action=allow protocol=TCP localport=809
```

Now that we have completed our outbound and inbound port configuration, let's learn about the preparation toolkit.

Disabling loopback check

By installing SharePoint, you will see that there are many little hidden issues we need to overcome before installing the application, such as ports, for example. When you install SharePoint, you will find that if you leave out this configuration for disabling loopback check, you will not be able to access your SharePoint sites from your servers. You can do this manually by going to the registry and editing the HKLM:\System\CurrentControlSet\Control\Lsa location and adding a new DWORD value of DisableLookbackCheck with a value of 1.

You can also simply use PowerShell:

```
New-ItemProperty HKLM:\System\CurrentControlSet\Control\Lsa
-Name "DisableLoopbackCheck" -Value "1" -PropertyType DWORD
```

Microsoft SharePoint preparation toolkit

The Microsoft SharePoint Products Preparation Tool installs the following prerequisites on SharePoint servers in a farm after server features are installed:

- Web server (IIS) role

- The Windows Process Activation Service feature

- Microsoft .NET Framework version 3.5

- Microsoft .NET Framework version 4.7.2

- Microsoft SQL Server 2012 Service Pack 4 Native Client

- Microsoft WCF Data Services 5.6

- Microsoft Identity Extensions

- **Microsoft Information Protection and Control Client (MSIPC)** 2.1

- Microsoft Sync Framework Runtime v1.0 SP1 (x64)

- Windows Server AppFabric 1.1

- Cumulative Update package 7 for Microsoft AppFabric 1.1 for Windows Server (KB 3092423)

- Visual C++ Redistributable package for Visual Studio 2012

- Visual C++ Redistributable package for Visual Studio 2017

The following are optional software installations that support SharePoint 2019. These are in support of business intelligence service capabilities and may be required to support these services:

- .NET Framework Data Provider for SQL Server (part of Microsoft .NET Framework).

- .NET Framework Data Provider for OLE DB (part of Microsoft .NET Framework).

- SharePoint Workflow Manager: You can install SharePoint Workflow Manager on a dedicated computer.

- Microsoft SQL Server 2008 R2 Reporting Services Add-in for Microsoft SharePoint Technologies: This add-on is used by Access Services for SharePoint Server 2019.

- Microsoft SQL Server 2012 **Data-Tier Application (DAC)** Framework 64-bit edition

- Microsoft SQL Server 2012 Transact-SQL ScriptDom 64-bit edition

- Microsoft System CLR Types for Microsoft SQL Server 2012 64-bit edition

- Microsoft SQL Server 2012 with SP1 LocalDB 64-bit edition

- Microsoft Data Services for.NET Framework 4 and Silverlight 4 (formerly ADO.NET Data Services)

- Exchange Web Services Managed API, version 1.2

There are two ways to install prerequisites:

- Online if your server is connected to the internet

- Offline, where you would need to go and download all the prerequisites beforehand and use PowerShell to install the needed components.

In our case, I will explain both and provide details on how to install them. There is one new way to install via PowerShell as well, which I will also point out as an option.

When installing from our SharePoint DVD, ISO, or USB installation, we will see that Microsoft has included a new choice to install SharePoint Server 2019. Now, instead of needing to access the prerequisite installation from the file manager, we can do this from the splash menu. Add the prerequisites to the folder within the installation, which means you need to copy the installation to the server you are installing from so that these files can be associated with the install.

> **Important Note**
> Before we start the installation preparation using the tools provided by SharePoint Server 2019, we need to make sure we copy our installation to a hard drive location on the server. We need to do this to provide any updates, as in cumulative updates you may want to include during the installation and all the prerequisite files needed to finish the preparation for the server installation.

Once you have added all the updates and prerequisite files to a local installation folder, follow the steps given here:

1. Click on the **Install software prerequisites** link on the splash page to get started:

Figure 4.19 – SharePoint 2019 splash screen

2. Click **Next** to continue the installation of the Products Preparation Tool:

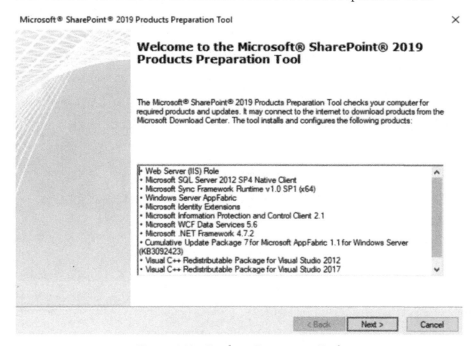

Figure 4.20 – Products Preparation Tool

3. Check the box to accept the license agreement and click **Next**:

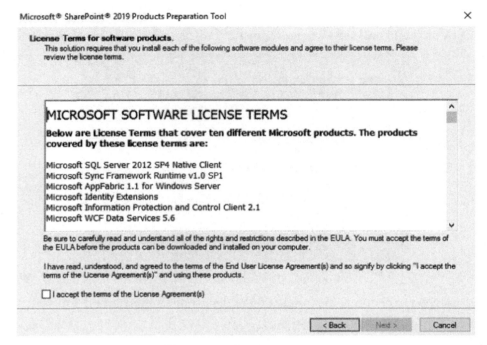

Figure 4.21 – License agreement

4. Monitor the process of the preparation tool until complete:

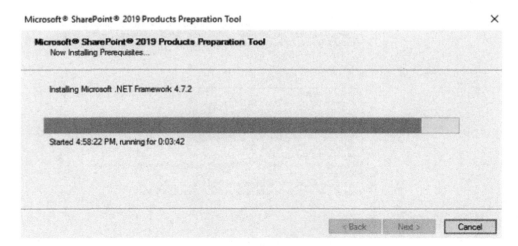

Figure 4.22 – Installing prerequisites

5. The server will reboot automatically during the installation and will continue after the server comes back up. You will be prompted with the following screen of the completed installation; just click **Finish**:

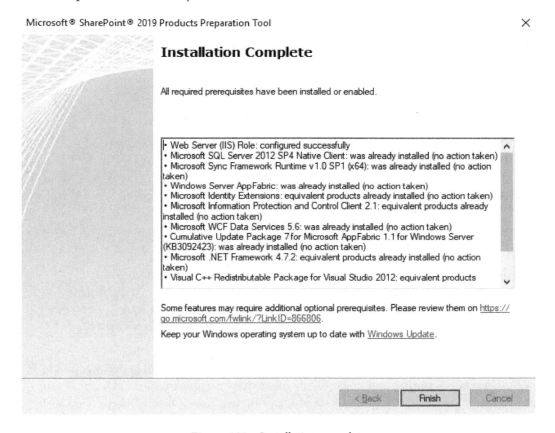

Figure 4.23 – Installation complete

This completes the GUI installation of the prerequisite files using the prerequisite installer from our installation files.

Scripted preparation tool installation

Installing using PowerShell is a different way of doing our installation. This method is used when we want to install the prerequisites offline.

Please run the following script to install the prerequisites using Command Prompt:

```
.\prerequisiteinstaller.exe
  /SQLNCli:c:\(Folder)\sqlncli.msi
 /Sync:c:\(Folder)\Synchronization.msi
 /AppFabric:c:\(Folder)\WindowsServerAppFabricSetup_x64.exe
 /IDFX11:c:\(Folder)\MicrosoftIdentityExtensions-64.msi
 /MSIPCClient:c:\(Folder)\setup_msipc_x64.exe
 /WCFDataServices56:c:\(Folder)\WcfDataServices56.exe
 /MSVCRT11:c:\(Folder)\vcredist_x64.exe
 /MSVCRT141:c:\(Folder)\vc_redist.x64.exe
 /KB3092423:c:\(Folder)\AppFabric-KB3092423-x64-ENU.exe
 /DotNet472:c:\(Folder)\NDP472-KB4054530-x86-x64-AllOS-ENU.exe
 /MSVCRT11:<file> Install Visual C++ Redistributable Package
for    Visual Studio 2012 from <file>.
 /MSVCRT141:<file> Install Visual C++ Redistributable Package
for Visual Studio 2017 from <file>.
```

There is also a new **desired state configuration**, which can be scripted to dynamically specify parameters for the prerequisites instead of the install doing it on its own from the internet. You can read more about that here: https://docs. microsoft.com/en-us/powershell/scripting/dsc/overview/ overview?view=powershell-7.1.

Whether you use scripting or the GUI to install your prerequisites, it is up to you. It is good to practice scripting and PowerShell and as these scripts are elementary, they can help you start your journey to understand scripting and how it works. There is no real benefit in using either one, but best believe PowerShell is something you will need to understand. So, if you are new to it, start working with PowerShell now.

SharePoint 2019 installation

Now that we have finished our preparation for SharePoint Server 2019 installation, we can start our SharePoint Server 2019 install process. There are other tools that you can use to install SharePoint using an automated process. In this book, we will install using the manual method to get an understanding of what is actually going on in that process. Please follow along with the installation process:

1. Once you encounter the splash screen for SharePoint 2019, choose **Install SharePoint Server** under the **Install** menu:

Figure 4.24 – The splash screen Install SharePoint Server option

2. Check the box to accept the terms of the license agreement and click **Continue**:

Figure 4.25 – License agreement

3. Enter the license key for the product:

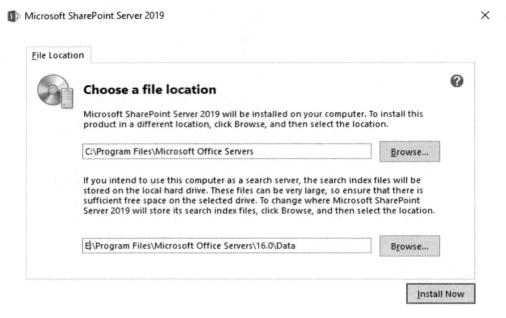

Figure 4.26 – Product key entry

4. Choose the file locations for the installation. This screen is very important for setting up the application file locations and then your data location. Click **Install Now** to continue the installation:

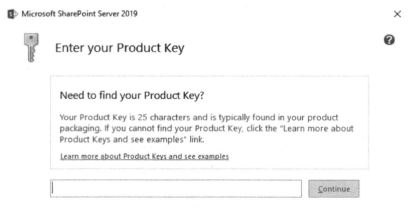

Figure 4.27 – Install Now

> **Tip**
>
> Make sure to change the data location as I have stated earlier to have at least two drives available, one for the operating system and then another for data, which will house your logs and search index. Also, make sure to create the logging and data drive large enough to grow your intended logs and search data, which you will need for now and a 2 to 3 year period.

5. Monitor the progress of the installation for SharePoint Server 2019:

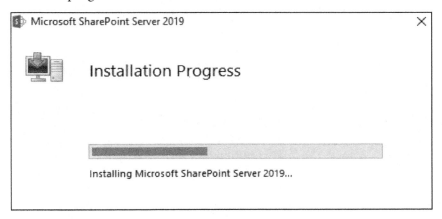

Figure 4.28 – Installation in progress

6. Once the product has been installed, you will come to the **Run Configuration Wizard** screen. Please uncheck the box and click **Close**:

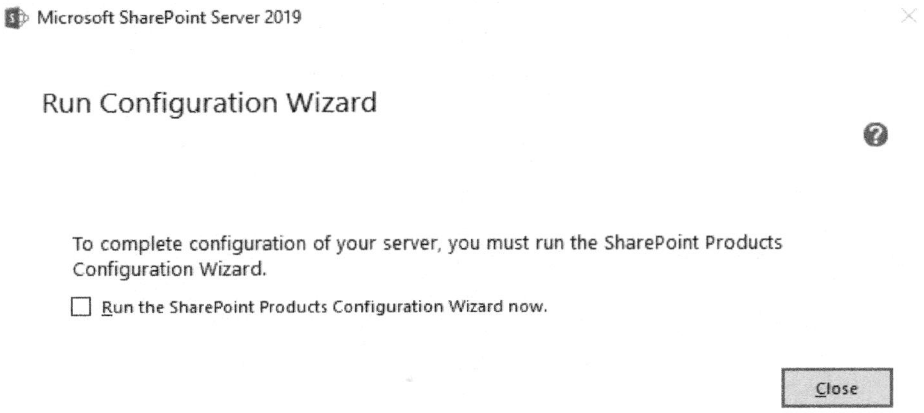

Microsoft SharePoint Server 2019   ✕

Run Configuration Wizard

To complete configuration of your server, you must run the SharePoint Products Configuration Wizard.

☐ Run the SharePoint Products Configuration Wizard now.

Close

Figure 4.29 – Run Configuration Wizard

At this point, we will use a PowerShell script to configure our farm.

Configuration of SQL and SharePoint

So, now that we have all our servers installed, there are a few details we need to configure to make all these components work together for SharePoint and SQL Server. We will start with the following configurations:

- SQL alias creation
- Alias setup on SQL Server

We will use SQL aliases for the connectivity from SharePoint to the SQL server, so if we lose our SQL server, we can recreate the SQL server and use the same alias to connect to the farm from our SharePoint servers, and then our database server name never changes. You cannot do this using a named instance of a SQL server that is being used as the connecting SQL server name in your SharePoint farm.

Other areas of the configuration, such as logging, monitoring, and services, will be explained in *Chapter 5, Farm and Services Configuration*. These will be the SharePoint configurations needed to get ready to install service applications, use databases, and set server locations further. The following steps show the configuration for database connectivity settings so that we can complete the installation of SharePoint Server 2019:

1. Find **cliconfg** in your server to configure your SQL alias connection:

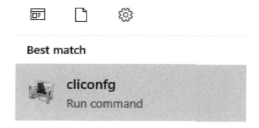

Figure 4.30 – Finding cliconfg

2. Run the application as an administrator:

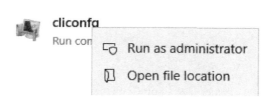

Figure 4.31 – Running as an administrator

3. Enable **TCP/IP**:

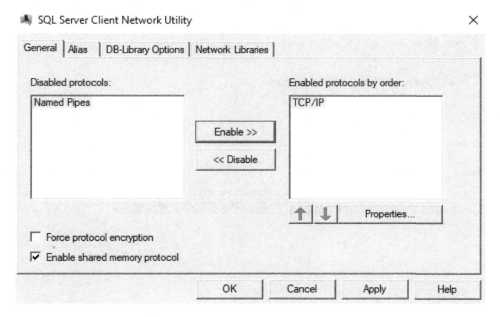

Figure 4.32 – SQL Server Client Network Utility

4. Configure the **TCP/IP** setting, as shown, giving it an alias name and the server name of the SQL server:

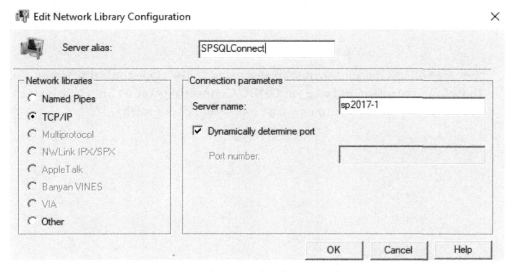

Figure 4.33 – Edit Network Library Configuration

> **Important Note**
>
> You can dynamically determine the port by keeping the checkbox checked, which sets the port on its own, or you can set the port manually to a different port other than 1433, which is the default for SQL connectivity.

5. Click **Apply**, and then **OK** to finish:

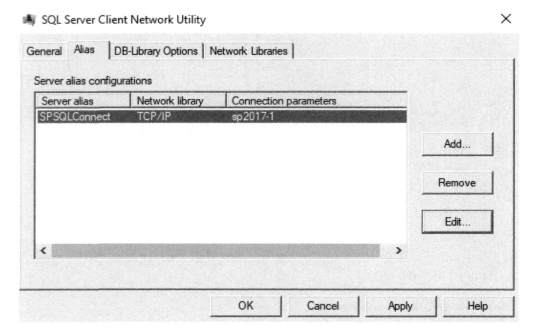

Figure 4.34 – SPSQLConnect server alias

6. Now, we will test the alias we just created using ODBC. Open **Administrator Tools** from the server and click on **ODBC Connectivity for 64 bit**. Once open, select **SQL Server** to create a new data source and click **Finish**:

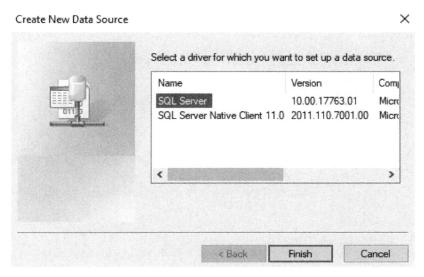

Figure 4.35 – Create New Data Source

7. After clicking **Finish**, you will be prompted with a new window to create a new data source. Input a name and a description of the data source and the SQL server you are connecting to. The connected SQL server you are testing is the alias name you created in *Step 5*. Then, click **Next**:

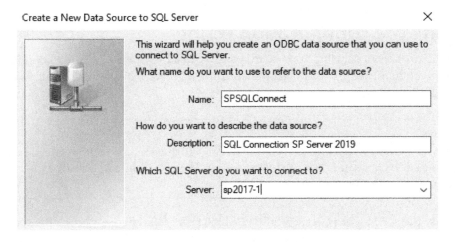

Figure 4.36 – Inputting a name/description/server

8. Click **Next** to continue, which will test connectivity to your SQL server using the alias name:

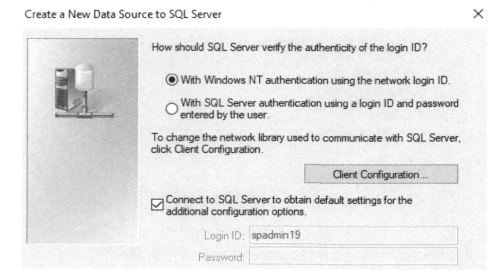

Figure 4.37 – Testing connectivity

We have now successfully connected to SQL Server 2017 to support our SharePoint farm.

Running the configuration script

To start the process of creating your farm, you will need to open PowerShell and follow the steps given here. We will create our farm using a PowerShell script so that we can name all of our databases:

> **Note**
>
> With the new SharePoint 2016 and SharePoint 2019 servers, we now need to use a new parameter: $ServerRole. This determines the MinRole that will be used on this server resource.

1. Copy the script from GitHub called FarmCreation.ps1 and run this script to create your farm. Remember to change the fields where needed:

```
Add-PSSnapin "Microsoft.SharePoint.PowerShell

#Configuration Settings

$DatabaseServer = "SPSQLCONNECT"

$ConfigDatabase = "2019_Farm_Config"
```

```
$AdminContentDB = "2019_Farm_Content_Admin"

$Passphrase = "ENTER A PHRASE"

$FarmAccountName = "Domain\SP_Farm"

$ServerRole="APPLICATION"

#Get the Farm Account Credentials

$FarmAccount = Get-Credential $FarmAccountName

$Passphrase = (ConvertTo-SecureString $Passphrase
-AsPlainText -force)

#Create SharePoint Farm

Write-Host "Creating Configuration Database and Central
Admin Content Database..."

New-SPConfigurationDatabase -DatabaseServer
$DatabaseServer -DatabaseName $ConfigDatabase
-AdministrationContentDatabaseName $AdminContentDB
-Passphrase $Passphrase -FarmCredentials
$FarmAccount -LocalServerRole $ServerRole
-SkipRegisterAsDistributedCacheHost

$Farm = Get-SPFarm -ErrorAction SilentlyContinue
-ErrorVariable err

if ($Farm -ne $null)

{

Write-Host "Installing SharePoint Resources..."

Initialize-SPResourceSecurity

Write-Host "Installing Farm Services ..."

Install-SPService

Write-Host "Installing SharePoint Features..."

Install-SPFeature -AllExistingFeatures

Write-Host "Creating Central Administration..."

New-SPCentralAdministration -Port 2019
-WindowsAuthProvider NTLM

Write-Host "Installing Application Content..."

Install-SPApplicationContent

Write-Host "SharePoint 2019 Farm Created Successfully!"

}
```

> **Important Note**
>
> `Install-SpHelpCollection` is no longer needed in our script as part of the SharePoint 2019 configuration. Also, if `-LocalServerRole $ServerRole` is not specified, the server will be created as a custom role. We also do not want to create a Distributed Cache service on this initial app server. So, we will include `-SkipRegisterAsDistributedCacheHost`.

2. Monitoring progress: As you wait for the script to run, check the SQL server by refreshing the databases to see whether databases have started to be created:

Databases
System Databases
Database Snapshots
2019_Farm_Config
2019_Farm_Content_Admin

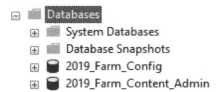

Figure 4.38 – Checking the database creation status

3. Once the script is finished, you will see that that farm was created successfully:

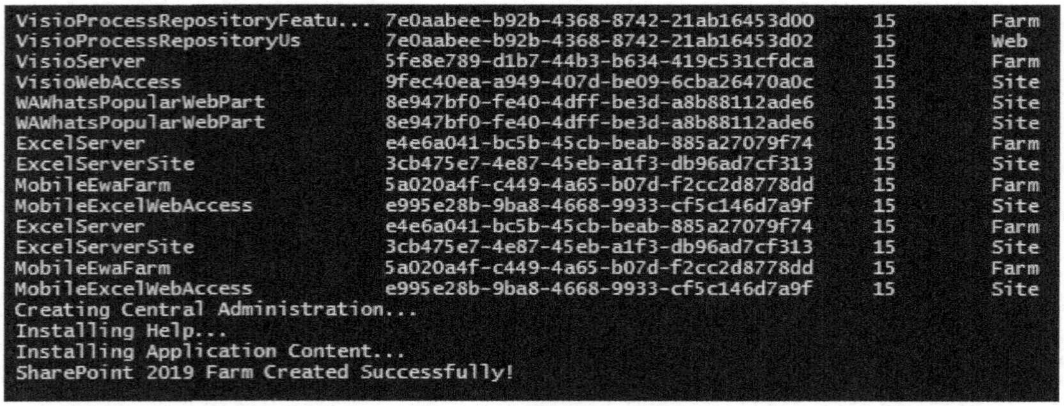

VisioProcessRepositoryFeatu... 7e0aabee-b92b-4368-8742-21ab16453d00 15 Farm
VisioProcessRepositoryUs 7e0aabee-b92b-4368-8742-21ab16453d02 15 Web
VisioServer 5fe8e789-d1b7-44b3-b634-419c531cfdca 15 Farm
VisioWebAccess 9fec40ea-a949-407d-be09-6cba26470a0c 15 Site
WAWhatsPopularWebPart 8e947bf0-fe40-4dff-be3d-a8b88112ade6 15 Site
WAWhatsPopularWebPart 8e947bf0-fe40-4dff-be3d-a8b88112ade6 15 Site
ExcelServer e4e6a041-bc5b-45cb-beab-885a27079f74 15 Farm
ExcelServerSite 3cb475e7-4e87-45eb-a1f3-db96ad7cf313 15 Site
MobileEwaFarm 5a020a4f-c449-4a65-b07d-f2cc2d8778dd 15 Farm
MobileExcelWebAccess e995e28b-9ba8-4668-9933-cf5c146d7a9f 15 Site
ExcelServer e4e6a041-bc5b-45cb-beab-885a27079f74 15 Farm
ExcelServerSite 3cb475e7-4e87-45eb-a1f3-db96ad7cf313 15 Site
MobileEwaFarm 5a020a4f-c449-4a65-b07d-f2cc2d8778dd 15 Farm
MobileExcelWebAccess e995e28b-9ba8-4668-9933-cf5c146d7a9f 15 Site
Creating Central Administration...
Installing Help...
Installing Application Content...
SharePoint 2019 Farm Created Successfully!

Figure 4.39 – Farm created successfully

4. Navigate to **Central Administration,** and now the Central Administration site is ready for configuration:

Figure 4.40 – Central Administration

We will start that configuration in the next chapter.

Remote installations

You can install using remote installations, where you can use `AutoSPInstaller` to install SharePoint on multiple servers using one script from one server. The script first installs SharePoint locally to establish a baseline installation on the local server where the script is being executed. The script then installs SharePoint remotely using PowerShell Remoting and **Windows Remote Management (WinRM)** on the other servers you have configured in the script. These installations can be done all at once in a parallel or serial process based on the configuration file. WinRM must be enabled on the servers where you want SharePoint to be installed remotely. To learn more about remote installation, find `AutoSPInstaller` at the following link or review GitHub for more information: `https://autospinstaller.com/`.

Summary

If you are familiar with SharePoint, you can see that not a lot has changed in the installation process. There have been some cool additions to help with the process, but overall, we can see that if you know SharePoint installation, you can get through this pretty easily. The key things to remember are using the MinRoles, setting logging locations correctly, reviewing scripts, and installing all the prerequisites for the server, SQL and SharePoint, before installing.

In the next chapter, we will go through more configurations and understand how to put this farm altogether. There are many steps and variations to this configuration that we cannot cover in this book. We condensed as much as possible into the scope of the book. Although we are very clear about setting some areas of the configuration, you will see that some areas can be customized, which we will state in the following chapters.

Questions

You can find the answers on GitHub under Assessments at `https://github.com/PacktPublishing/Implementing-Microsoft-SharePoint-2019/blob/master/Assessments.docx`

1. Why should we use a script to create our farm and not the configuration wizard?

2. If we lost our SQL server due to a disaster, we could recover our databases on a named SQL Server instance and reconnect the farm with no issues. True or False?

3. When installing our SharePoint servers, which firewall port supports Office Online Server?

4. Local policy is needed when installing SharePoint. Why?

5. Domain policies can interfere with the configuration of SharePoint and SQL Server. True or False?

6. If I wanted to install my farm and other server resources all in one executed script, can I use PowerShell to do so?

7. What parameter in our farm creation script is needed only for SharePoint Server 2016 and 2019?

5
Farm and Services Configuration

SharePoint's key to success is the services it provides. In this chapter, we'll learn how to make all the necessary performance tweaks, as well as how to configure the services related to logging, monitoring, and integrating services that support content, plus other application integrations. SharePoint, as a product, changes with every version, so expect to see some changes in terms of how these services are configured and supported.

Security will also be reviewed in this chapter: besides the services SharePoint provides, we need to look at the service accounts that support them. Application pool best practices and other areas that can be configured will also be covered; there has always been some speculation on the best practices surrounding these areas of security and application pools.

Knowing which services support which resources of the platform will also be mentioned in this chapter. We need to understand how to use our MinRoles as we add more servers to the farm, as well as what services those applications support. We also need to know how to make the best choices when adding these server roles and resources to the environment. To do this, we need to follow the design for the farm we finished and follow best practices.

The following topics will be covered in this chapter:

- Configuring SQL Server services
- Configuring SharePoint services
- Antivirus and security configurations
- Creating service applications
- SharePoint MinRole resources
- Understanding the Distributed Cache service

Let's get started!

Technical requirements

For you to understand this chapter and the knowledge provided, you will need the following:

- 2-3 years of experience using PowerShell and SharePoint
- 2-3 years of experience using SQL Server
- A good understanding of the SharePoint architecture
- The link to this book's GitHub repository: `https://github.com/PacktPublishing/Implementing-Microsoft-SharePoint-2019`

Configuring SQL Server services

In *Chapter 4, Installation Concepts*, we learned how to install HOSTs and VMs in order to support our environment before installing the main applications for our farm configuration on SQL Server 2017 and SharePoint Server 2019. Although we have done this, there is so much more to do, as we will see in this chapter and others to come. We still have some server configurations to finish and services to configure in the farm before we can create some web applications and test them.

SQL Server is the main component and the foundation of the SharePoint Server Farm. Without it, we cannot support SharePoint in any way. So, since this server supports all the data that will be used for configuration, services, content, and security, we really need to make sure that this part of our farm is performing up to par and has been configured to support the farm through growth, redundancy, and performance.

We have compiled a list of areas we want to change and/or update as part of our SQL Server configuration that help us create databases and improve their perform on existing databases. These changes must be made so that there's better support for SharePoint Farm. This is because SharePoint uses SQL Server as its central repository for configuration, services, and content. Please make the changes mentioned in the following subsections while ensuring they support the servers you have built as part of your farm.

SQL properties

Now that we have successfully installed SQL Server, we need to check its configuration. Start by right-clicking the server's name:

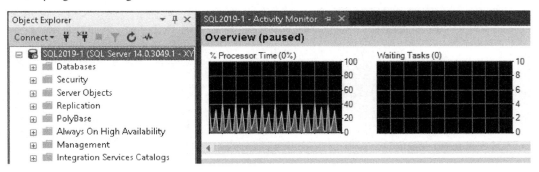

Figure 5.1 – SQL Activity Monitor

Selecting **Properties** in SQL Server Management Studio will present the property settings for the server:

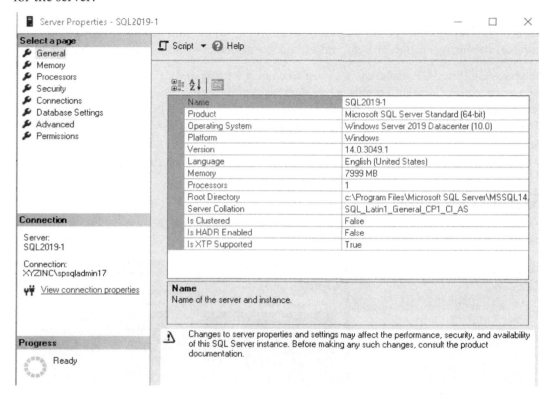

Figure 5.2 – SQL Server properties

These settings show how SQL Server has been configured. Note that some of these properties need to be changed for SQL Server to support SharePoint. We will look at these properties next.

SQL Server MAXDOP settings

As part of SQL Server's configuration, SharePoint is only supported when SQL Server is being used as the backend. It is also a best practice to set the **MAX Degree of Parallelism (MAXDOP)** on any SQL Server to 1. This setting is recommended by Microsoft for SQL servers that support SharePoint Server. As stated in prior chapters, Microsoft tests their products and tunes them to ensure they provide the best performance. Setting MAXDOP to 1 ensures that queries and calls from SharePoint are processed efficiently. This setting is required, and SharePoint will update the SQL configuration when you install the product. We must do this before we start our installation.

Use the following commands to change the value of SQL Server once it has been installed. In newer versions of SharePoint, this setting is set automatically, but if you see that it is not set to 1, please do so using the following SQL query:

```
sp_configure 'show advanced options', 1;
GO
RECONFIGURE WITH OVERRIDE;
GO
sp_configure 'max degree of parallelism', 1;
GO
RECONFIGURE WITH OVERRIDE;
GO
```

Within the configuration, please make sure that the following areas have been updated and set to support SharePoint Server 2016 and the performance of SQL Server:

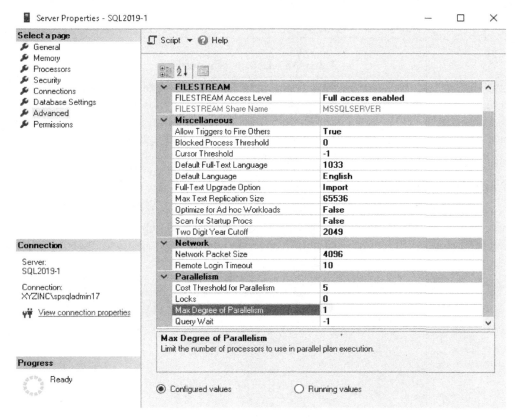

Figure 5.3 – MAXDOP setting in Server Properties

Setting SQL file default locations

To ensure we remain consistent with the configuration that was explained in *Chapter 2, Planning and Architecture*, we need to make sure we define the general areas of our SQL configuration, as shown in the following screenshot. Typically, you will not use this standard configuration, especially if you're following my guidance of using LUNNS for each type of database SharePoint creates. This is typically done using a manual database creation process so that you can set the locations of the databases and logs. This configuration will give you better performance, and using separate drives gives you separation of those processes as well. As we mentioned previously, the following screenshot shows the general areas of your SQL configuration:

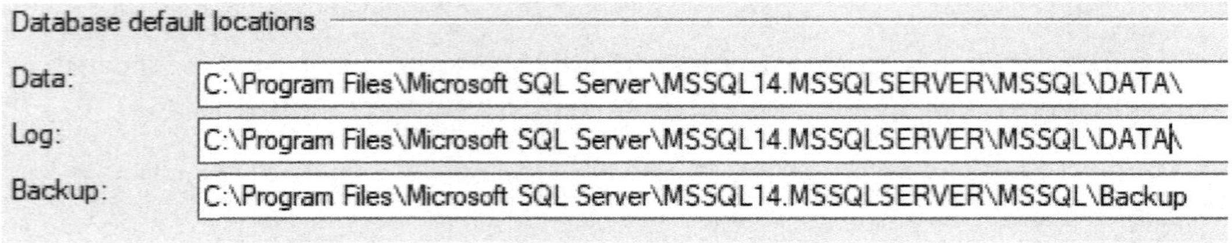

Database default locations	
Data:	C:\Program Files\Microsoft SQL Server\MSSQL14.MSSQLSERVER\MSSQL\DATA\
Log:	C:\Program Files\Microsoft SQL Server\MSSQL14.MSSQLSERVER\MSSQL\DATA\
Backup:	C:\Program Files\Microsoft SQL Server\MSSQL14.MSSQLSERVER\MSSQL\Backup

Figure 5.4 – Default locations

Set the default locations for the **Data** files (.mdf files) and **Log** files (.ldf files). These files need to be separated. Here, the best option is to split the files up by database type, as discussed in the SQL Server Preparation. The backup location should be set using the default setting for any Maintenance Plans you plan to use within SQL Server. If you are using a third-party application to manage your databases, this setting will not matter.

Instant file initialization

We need to make changes to the model database so that it has enough space to create templates for our newly created databases. These changes will help us create databases faster and bring a different level of performance to adding new clients that would like to have separation within content databases:

```
Alter Database [model] MODIFY FILE (NAME = modeldev, SIZE = 
150mb, MAXSIZE = Unlimited
```

Once you have run this SQL command, you will see the following message, stating that you have successfully applied the setting:

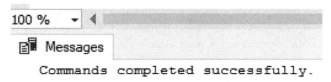

Figure 5.5 – Commands completely successfully message

Now that we have updated the property for the model database, we will review our authentication method.

Reviewing our authentication method

When checking our properties, we will notice that we can set the authentication of SQL Server in two ways; that is, **Windows Authentication mode** or **SQL Server and Windows Authentication mode**:

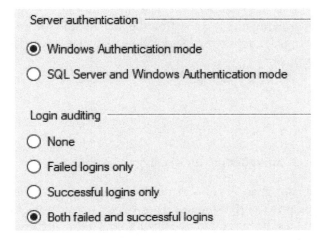

Figure 5.6 – Selecting an authentication method in SQL Server

Windows Authentication mode should be the option that's highlighted. SQL Server mode should not be included in our configuration for SharePoint server since the product is fully integrated with Active Directory. Allowing connections with SQL Server will only bring about vulnerabilities in terms of security.

Our SQL configuration is now complete. If there are other integrations and settings you need to work on so that SQL Server supports SharePoint, please complete them now.

Configuring SharePoint Services

Configuring SharePoint Services is the first thing we must do before creating web applications that hold content for our users. In this section, we will start adding services to our farm and configuring areas for monitoring and logging. The following exercises will help us complete all the preparation we need to do to support the creation of web applications that serve our user's communities. This will allow them to start using the farm to share content and use the services provided.

There are different methods you can use to configure your SharePoint farm; that is, PowerShell, GUI, or AutoSPInstaller. Figure out what works best for you. In this book, we will be using a combination of PowerShell and GUI to show you how things are done from an illustrative perspective, though scripts that show you how to do this manually will also be provided. The reason we will be using both is so that those who may be new to SharePoint can follow along, especially if they are not very familiar with PowerShell.

So, let's get right to it!

Setting server logging locations

To help manage the disk space resources we have created for our servers, we must make sure that we point all growing files to a location that can handle the number of files that are generated by logging. The following areas will be moved to a new location within the server for growth purposes:

- IIS
- Diagnostic Logging
- Usage Logging
- Index (see Search configuration for details)

IIS is the service that runs SharePoint websites on the server and creates logs as part of the service. When you log into the IIS Manager, you will see the sites and application pools that are available and have been created, as shown in the following screenshot:

Application Pools

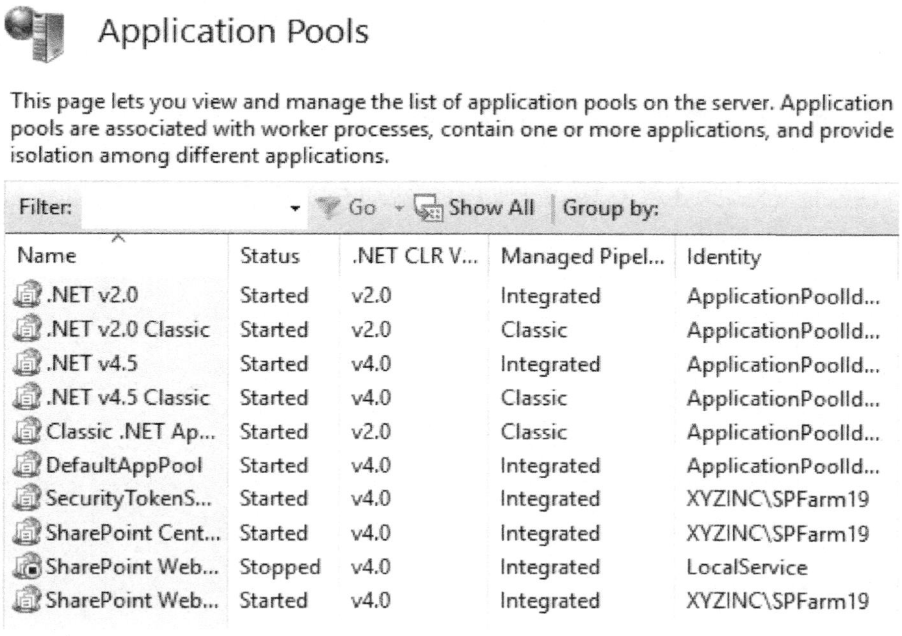

This page lets you view and manage the list of application pools on the server. Application pools are associated with worker processes, contain one or more applications, and provide isolation among different applications.

Name	Status	.NET CLR V...	Managed Pipel...	Identity
.NET v2.0	Started	v2.0	Integrated	ApplicationPoolId...
.NET v2.0 Classic	Started	v2.0	Classic	ApplicationPoolId...
.NET v4.5	Started	v4.0	Integrated	ApplicationPoolId...
.NET v4.5 Classic	Started	v4.0	Classic	ApplicationPoolId...
Classic .NET Ap...	Started	v2.0	Classic	ApplicationPoolId...
DefaultAppPool	Started	v4.0	Integrated	ApplicationPoolId...
SecurityTokenS...	Started	v4.0	Integrated	XYZINC\SPFarm19
SharePoint Cent...	Started	v4.0	Integrated	XYZINC\SPFarm19
SharePoint Web...	Stopped	v4.0	Integrated	LocalService
SharePoint Web...	Started	v4.0	Integrated	XYZINC\SPFarm19

Figure 5.7 – IIS Application Pools window

The preceding screenshot shows what the application pools look like after a fresh install of SharePoint 2019. The SharePoint Web Services application pool should not be started, which is by design. When you select **Sites**, you will also see a list of sites that were created when you created your farm:

∨ ▣ Sites
  ⟩ ⊕ Default Web Site
  ⟩ ⊕ SharePoint Central Administration v4
  ⟩ ⊕ SharePoint Web Services

Figure 5.8 – IIS Default Web Site view

The preceding screenshot shows what you will see once you have performed a fresh installation of SharePoint on your first server. The first server will always include **Central Administration** as it is the key to setting up and configuring the rest of your SharePoint environment.

To get to the logging area of the IIS service, please click on the server's name and then select **Logging** from the list of available configuration areas in the middle of the screen:

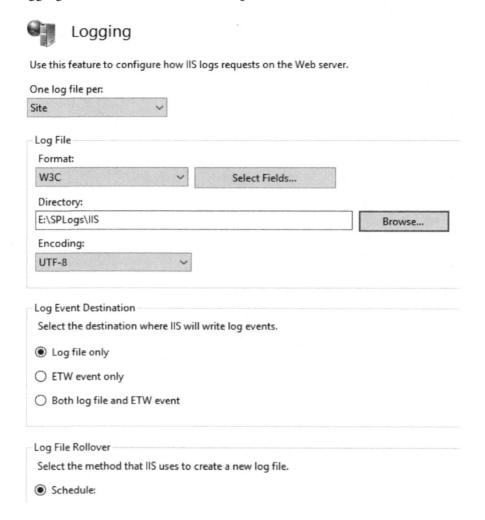

Figure 5.9 – IIS Logging settings

Since we are SharePoint administrators, there is also a tool called ULS Viewer we can use that can help with reading logs and troubleshooting issues that may arise. Please use this tool to view logs as it brings added clarity, along with the functionality to manage logs, considering how large SharePoint logs tend to be.

While we're configuring logging, we want to make sure that all the logs are collected by **Site**, which is the default option. The **Directory** location needs to be changed here. As shown in the preceding screenshot, I have changed mine to reflect the second drive on my server. This should be done on every server in the farm, including SQL, to make sure you set the location to a drive that has the capacity to hold the log. After setting the location of the file, you can set your preferences in terms of **Log Event Destination** and **Schedule**. You can also customize the fields you would like to see in your logs since you may want to add more detail to your log captures.

Select the information you would like to collect, as well as the schedule, from the following configuration parameters:

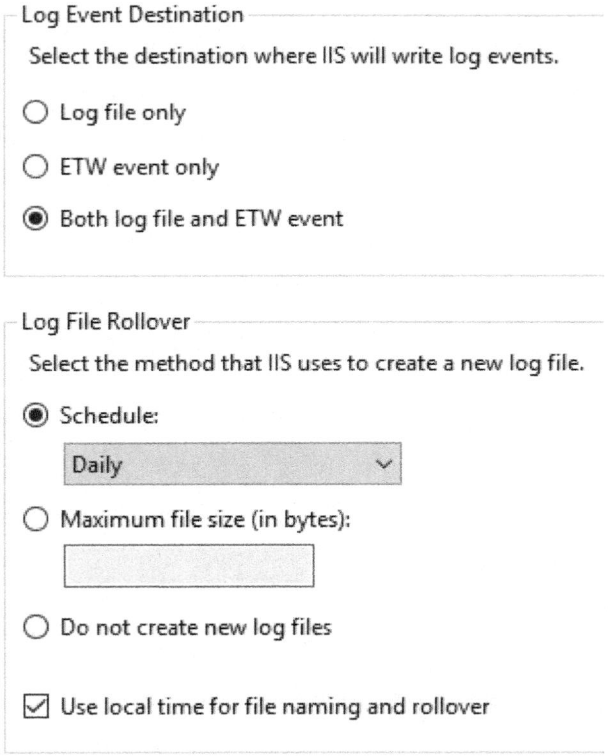

Log Event Destination

Select the destination where IIS will write log events.

○ Log file only

○ ETW event only

◉ Both log file and ETW event

Log File Rollover

Select the method that IIS uses to create a new log file.

◉ Schedule:

Daily ▾

○ Maximum file size (in bytes):

○ Do not create new log files

☑ Use local time for file naming and rollover

Figure 5.10 – Log Event Destination and Log File Rollover settings

I have set **Schedule** to **Daily** so that I get a daily log of the site for troubleshooting if needed. The daily log file's size depends on the user traffic. So, the more users you have, the bigger these files become. Also, remember that these logs are kept by site. You can always change this if you like to place them in one server log file. However, this is not something I recommend.

If you click on the **Select Fields** button on the main screen, you will be brought to the following selection screen:

Figure 5.11 – Selecting IIS Logging Fields

In the **Standard Fields** section of the window, you can set which fields you would or wouldn't like to be displayed in your logs. If you would like to log more information, you can also use the **Add Field** option to include fields that may be missing based on your preference. Again, these fields help you troubleshoot issues that may arise during the farm's existence.

Next, we will learn how to create the state service and logging service. The state service serves as a shared service and is used by some components to store temporary data in SQL databases related to HTTP requests. InfoPath Forms Services requires the state service to be available for it to function correctly. The logging service is used to collect logs about the SharePoint environment for troubleshooting and finding issues within the farm.

Creating the state service

The state service is used as a connectivity service within SharePoint that supports publishing, searching crawl and query components, the Visio service, and various other services within SharePoint. This service is one of the first services I install because it is a foundation service you do not want to forget.

To create this service, you will need to use PowerShell:

```
$db = New-SPStateServiceDatabase -Name "XYZ State Service
Application"
 $sa = New-SPStateServiceApplication - Name "XYZ_State_Service"
-Database $db
 New-SPStateServiceApplicationProxy -Name "XYZ State Service
Application Proxy" -ServiceApplication $sa
 -Default Proxy Group
```

Always run PowerShell using the run as administrator option so that you are using your administrative privileges while running commands and scripts. If you do not, your process will fail.

Creating SharePoint logging services

Central Administration, as its name suggests, is an administrative website that controls all the servers that have been configured as part of the SharePoint farm. When you set logging locations within the Central Administration site, those locations need to be the same on all servers since the location is looked for on all servers associated with the farm. If you change any locations during the farm's existence, please remember to also make those changes and folder updates on all servers.

Let's install the logging services within SharePoint by performing the following steps:

1. Navigate to the **Central Administration** link on your server, right-click it, and run as administrator. Then, click the **Start** button and right-click the SharePoint Central Administration icon and run as administrator. Never open this area without running as administrator. You can also set this up on your taskbar and run as administrator as well. You will see the following screen, which is your **Central Administration** site:

Figure 5.12 – Central Administration site

There are lots of areas within the site. However, we will only be working on a few of these in this book.

2. We will start with the **Monitoring** area of this menu. Click on the **Monitoring** link in the **Central Administration** site:

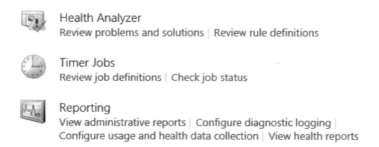

Figure 5.13 – Monitoring configuration

A menu will appear for working with the monitoring aspects of the farm's configuration.

3.   Click on **Configure diagnostic logging**. In this area, we want to select **All Categories** and click the box next to the selection we want to hone in on during our log capture. Find out more about these categories and figure out the areas you are looking to target as part of your troubleshooting efforts:

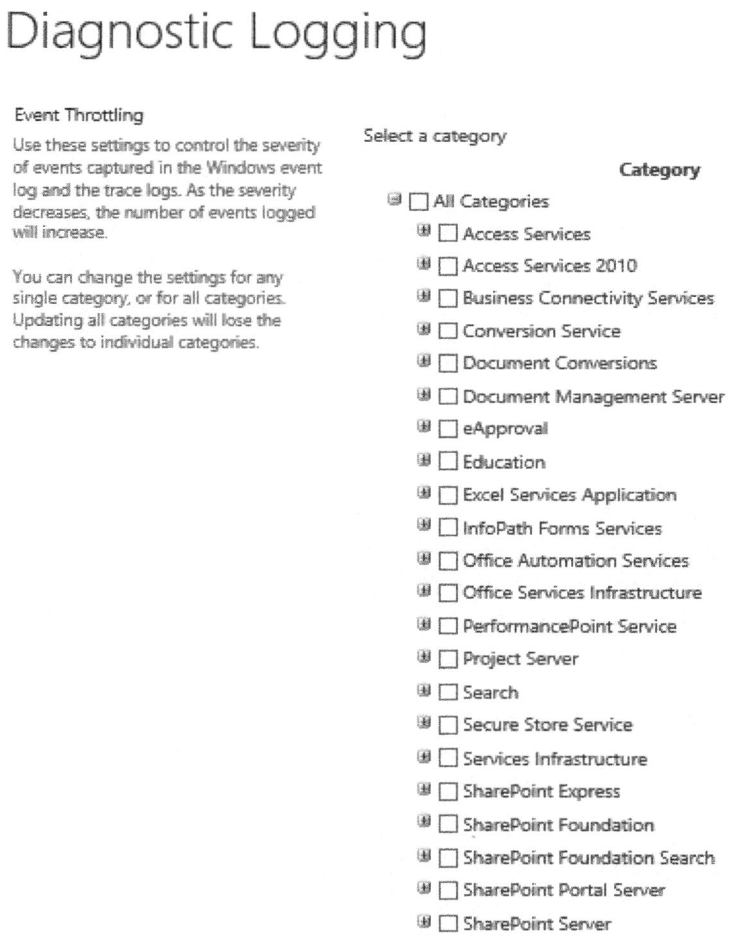

Diagnostic Logging

Event Throttling

Use these settings to control the severity of events captured in the Windows event log and the trace logs. As the severity decreases, the number of events logged will increase.

You can change the settings for any single category, or for all categories. Updating all categories will lose the changes to individual categories.

Select a category

Category

- ☐ All Categories
  - ☐ Access Services
  - ☐ Access Services 2010
  - ☐ Business Connectivity Services
  - ☐ Conversion Service
  - ☐ Document Conversions
  - ☐ Document Management Server
  - ☐ eApproval
  - ☐ Education
  - ☐ Excel Services Application
  - ☐ InfoPath Forms Services
  - ☐ Office Automation Services
  - ☐ Office Services Infrastructure
  - ☐ PerformancePoint Service
  - ☐ Project Server
  - ☐ Search
  - ☐ Secure Store Service
  - ☐ Services Infrastructure
  - ☐ SharePoint Express
  - ☐ SharePoint Foundation
  - ☐ SharePoint Foundation Search
  - ☐ SharePoint Portal Server
  - ☐ SharePoint Server

Figure 5.14 – Diagnostic logging configuration – I

Clicking on **All Categories** will select all the areas within the server.

4. If you have specific areas you would like to monitor, you can select them individually as well:

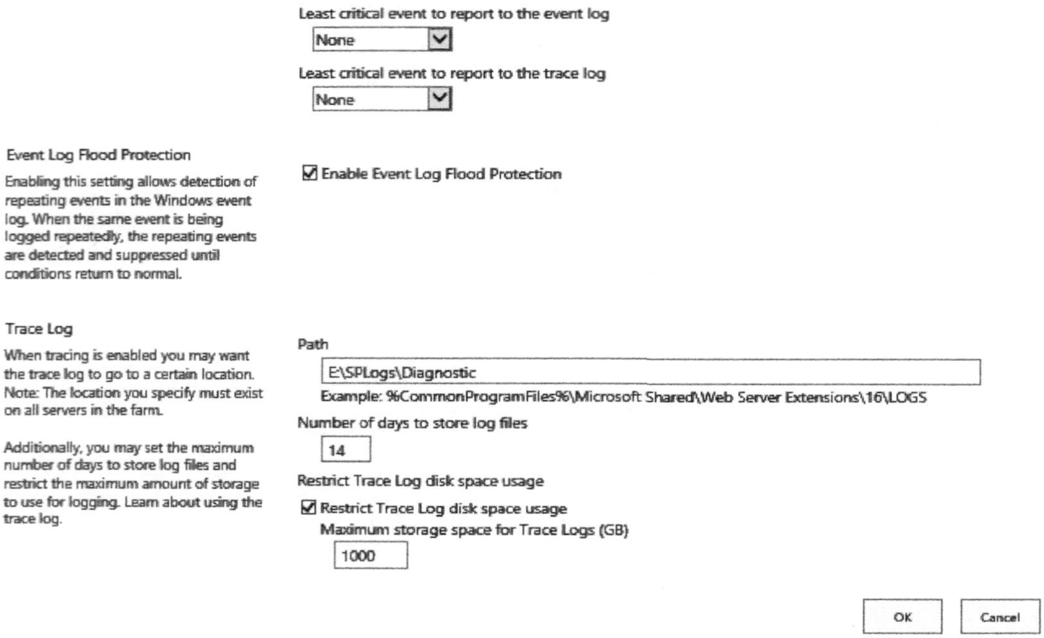

Least critical event to report to the event log

[None ▼]

Least critical event to report to the trace log

[None ▼]

Event Log Flood Protection

Enabling this setting allows detection of repeating events in the Windows event log. When the same event is being logged repeatedly, the repeating events are detected and suppressed until conditions return to normal.

☑ Enable Event Log Flood Protection

Trace Log

When tracing is enabled you may want the trace log to go to a certain location. Note: The location you specify must exist on all servers in the farm.

Additionally, you may set the maximum number of days to store log files and restrict the maximum amount of storage to use for logging. Learn about using the trace log.

Path

[E:\SPLogs\Diagnostic   ]

Example: %CommonProgramFiles%\Microsoft Shared\Web Server Extensions\16\LOGS

Number of days to store log files

[14]

Restrict Trace Log disk space usage

☑ Restrict Trace Log disk space usage

Maximum storage space for Trace Logs (GB)

[1000]

[OK]   [Cancel]

Figure 5.15 – Diagnostic logging configuration – II

5. On the same screen, after selecting your categories, we need to set the event log. Since we have just installed SharePoint, there is no need for detailed logging because we are not troubleshooting. So, for **Least critical event to report to the event log** and **Least critical event to report to the trace log**, select **None**.

As far as **Event Log Flood Protection** goes, you can choose to use this to suppress repeating events. This is your call. It does help with limiting the number of events you pick up in the Windows event log, but some people like it so that they know that the event is present.

6. Now, we need to set the path of our **Trace Log**. We need to set the location of the second drive so that these logs can grow and not jeopardize our operating system.

How many days do you want to keep your logs for? Again, this is your call. Set this setting based on the amount of days you may need to have these logs available. If you have lots of disk space, set the logs for longer periods.

Restrict the space on the trace logs using the next configuration tab. I have it set this to 1 GB. This is great for getting a good chunk of data but not having the system strain to open it on the server or transfer it to others.

7. We will now configure usage logging. Click on **Configure usage and health data collection** under the **Reporting** section:

Monitoring

Health Analyzer
Review problems and solutions | Review rule definitions

Timer Jobs
Review job definitions | Check job status

Reporting
View administrative reports | Configure diagnostic logging |
Configure usage and health data collection | View health reports

Figure 5.16 – Monitoring configuration page

8. At the top of the configuration screen, please check the **Enable usage data collection** box:

Configure usage and health data collection ⓘ

Warning: This page is not encrypted for secure communication. User names, passwords, and any other information will be sent in clear text. For more information, contact your administrator.

Usage Data Collection

Usage data collection will log events whenever various events occur in your SharePoint deployment. Usage Logging enables analysis and reporting, but also uses system resources and can impact performance and disk usage.

☐ Enable usage data collection

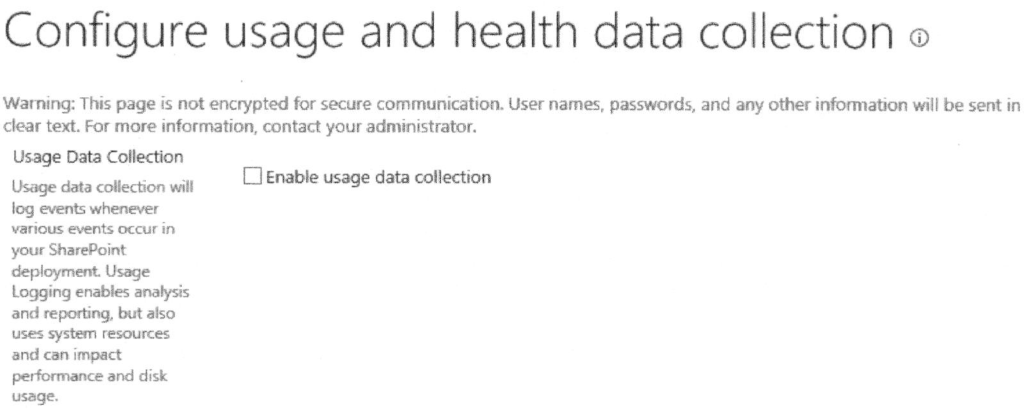

Figure 5.17 – Enable usage data collection box

9.   Choose all the events you would like to log:

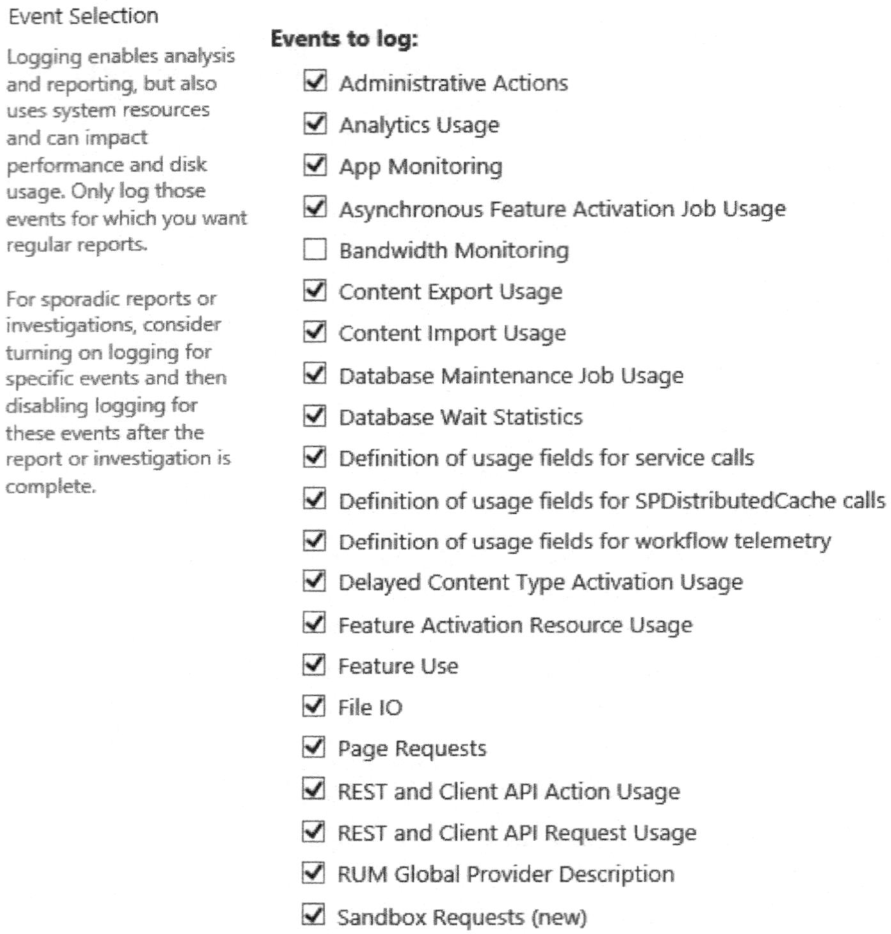

Event Selection

Logging enables analysis and reporting, but also uses system resources and can impact performance and disk usage. Only log those events for which you want regular reports.

For sporadic reports or investigations, consider turning on logging for specific events and then disabling logging for these events after the report or investigation is complete.

Events to log:

☑ Administrative Actions

☑ Analytics Usage

☑ App Monitoring

☑ Asynchronous Feature Activation Job Usage

☐ Bandwidth Monitoring

☑ Content Export Usage

☑ Content Import Usage

☑ Database Maintenance Job Usage

☑ Database Wait Statistics

☑ Definition of usage fields for service calls

☑ Definition of usage fields for SPDistributedCache calls

☑ Definition of usage fields for workflow telemetry

☑ Delayed Content Type Activation Usage

☑ Feature Activation Resource Usage

☑ Feature Use

☑ File IO

☑ Page Requests

☑ REST and Client API Action Usage

☑ REST and Client API Request Usage

☑ RUM Global Provider Description

☑ Sandbox Requests (new)

Figure 5.18 – Event Selection

Most of these events should make sense to you, though some may not. Which ones you choose to log is up to you.

10. Select a location where the log file will exist. We will house these files in the folder on the second drive for our servers:

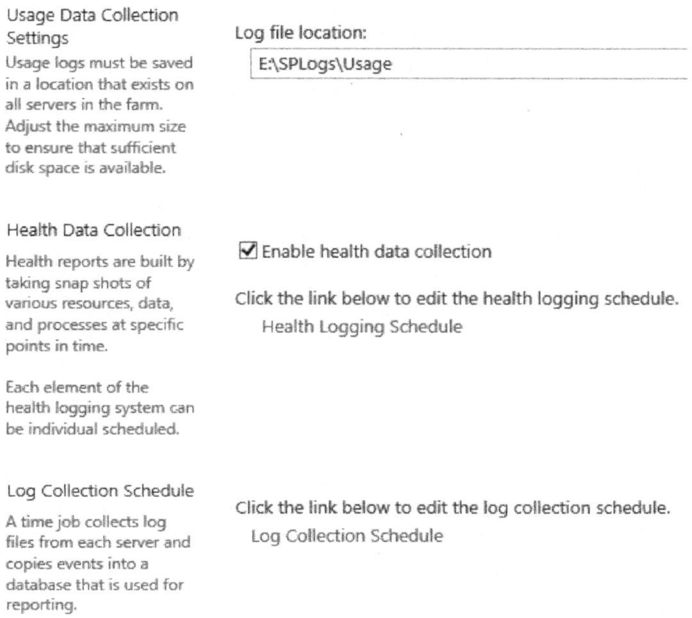

Usage Data Collection
Settings

Usage logs must be saved
in a location that exists on
all servers in the farm.
Adjust the maximum size
to ensure that sufficient
disk space is available.

Log file location:

E:\SPLogs\Usage

Health Data Collection

Health reports are built by
taking snap shots of
various resources, data,
and processes at specific
points in time.

Each element of the
health logging system can
be individual scheduled.

☑ Enable health data collection

Click the link below to edit the health logging schedule.
    Health Logging Schedule

Log Collection Schedule

A time job collects log
files from each server and
copies events into a
database that is used for
reporting.

Click the link below to edit the log collection schedule.
    Log Collection Schedule

Figure 5.19 – Selecting a log location

11. Please connect to the SQL alias database and then add the name of the database
you would like to use. Remember to use the correct naming convention for your
databases so that they are uniform:

Logging Database Server

Use of the default
database server and
database name is
recommended for most
cases. Refer to the
administrator's guide for
advanced scenarios where
specifying database
information is required.

Use of Windows
authentication is strongly
recommended. To use
SQL authentication,
specify the credentials
which will be used to
connect to the database.

Database Server

    SPSQLConnect

Database Name

    2017_UsageLog_Service   ✕

Database authentication

◉ Windows authentication (recommended)
○ SQL authentication
    Account

    [   ]

    Password

    [   ]

Figure 5.20 – Adding a database name

12. Click **OK** to finish.

With that, we have finished setting up our server login locations. Next, we will move on and understand the antivirus and security configurations within SharePoint Server 2019. These will help protect our farm from viruses and vulnerabilities.

Antivirus and security configurations

Antivirus and security help protect content, as well as block content that could potentially be damaging or lead to issues due to files containing viruses. These files can also create vulnerabilities in a SharePoint farm. Some of the areas that we need to look at are related to antivirus and security that protect us from threats from uploaded files, as well as files that can be uploaded onto our sites. The main areas for concern here are as follows:

- Antivirus settings
- Web Part Security
- Blocked File Types

Let's look at these areas in detail.

Antivirus settings

The antivirus settings are configured in the farm, while Web Part Security and Blocked File Types are set at the web application level. These settings should be taken very seriously. Since antivirus is usually related only to the server and its protection, antivirus is typically overlooked and is missed out during the installation process. Another reason for this being missed out on is because almost every admin I have met thinks that having antivirus on all their PCs and servers secures their content from viruses. From my experience, there have been instances where I have seen infected files get into a SharePoint site.

We should always make sure we configure the farm so that it's not vulnerable to the many different types of attacks that can be performed, and also secure it from all types of vulnerabilities. All incidents are created by overlooking steps in the configuration process, and deeming them as minimal can cause incidents. These types of vulnerabilities can be brought on easily, especially when you're hosting a SharePoint environment where the user does not understand security and you do not have control of the users' desktop.

As shown in the following screenshot, antivirus can be set in a few different ways, but again, you must have a product that integrates fully with SharePoint for these settings to work:

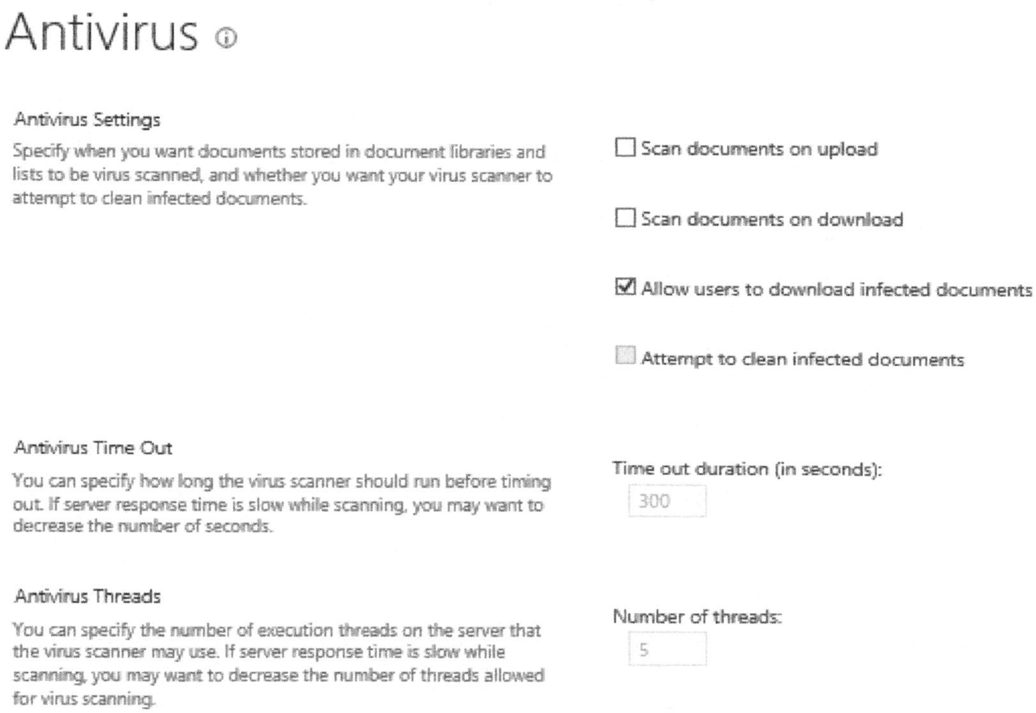

Antivirus ⓘ

Antivirus Settings

Specify when you want documents stored in document libraries and lists to be virus scanned, and whether you want your virus scanner to attempt to clean infected documents.

☐ Scan documents on upload

☐ Scan documents on download

☑ Allow users to download infected documents

☐ Attempt to clean infected documents

Antivirus Time Out

You can specify how long the virus scanner should run before timing out. If server response time is slow while scanning, you may want to decrease the number of seconds.

Time out duration (in seconds):

300

Antivirus Threads

You can specify the number of execution threads on the server that the virus scanner may use. If server response time is slow while scanning, you may want to decrease the number of threads allowed for virus scanning.

Number of threads:

5

Figure 5.21 – Antivirus settings

This is not only the virus scanning tool on the server, but it is an integrated component that works within sites so that files can be scanned.

The ideal configuration would be to install an antivirus scanner that works when integrated with SharePoint. This will allow your farm configuration to scan files when they're either uploaded or downloaded. Fortunately, there are a few top antivirus companies that offer this integration; previously, there was only Microsoft Forefront Server integration, which scanned files within SharePoint lists and libraries. To benefit from these features, you had to install and integrate this product.

SharePoint antivirus protection also occurs at the file level. Here, we need to make sure we not disrupt SharePoint and its file management process. For the following list of folders, we will need to make some exclusions. Configure all the SharePoint Server antivirus software so that the following folders and subfolders are excluded from antivirus scanning:

- `Drive:\Program Files\Common Files\Microsoft Shared\Web Server Extensions`

If you do not want to exclude the whole Web Server Extensions folder from antivirus scanning, you can just exclude the following folders:

- `Drive:\Program Files\Common Files\Microsoft Shared\Web Server Extensions\16`

- `Drive:\Program Files\Common Files\Microsoft Shared\Web Server Extensions\16\Logs`

- `Drive:\Program Files\Microsoft Office Servers\16.0\Data\ Office Server\Applications`

- `Drive:\Windows\Microsoft.NET\Framework64\v4.0.30319\ Temporary ASP.NET Files`

- `Drive:\Windows\Microsoft.NET\Framework64\v4.0.30319\Config`

- `Drive: \Users\ServiceAccount\AppData\Local\Temp\WebTempDir`

   Note: The `WebTempDir` folder is a replacement for the `FrontPageTempDir` folder.

- `Drive:\ProgramData\Microsoft\SharePoint`

- `Drive:\Users\account that the search service is running as\AppData\Local\Temp`

   Note: The search account creates a folder in the `Gthrsvc_spsearch4` Temp folder, which must be periodically written to.

- `Drive:\WINDOWS\System32\LogFiles`

- `Drive:\Windows\Syswow64\LogFiles`

   Note that if you use a specific account for SharePoint services or application pools identities, you may also have to exclude the following folders:

- `Drive:\Users\ServiceAccount\AppData\Local\Temp`

- `Drive:\Users\Default\AppData\Local\Temp`

- Any location where you decided to store the disk-based **binary large object (BLOB)** cache (for example, `C:\Blobcache`).

- `Drive:\inetpub\wwwroot\wss\VirtualDirectories` and all the folders inside it

- `Drive:\inetpub\temp\IIS Temporary Compressed Files`

SQL Server's antivirus settings will need to be configured in the same way on each SQL Server that is being used within the environment. So, if you have three nodes, all three servers would need this configuration on all servers. The exclusions needed for these servers are listed here.

As a best practice and to avoid downtime, please configure your SQL Server antivirus software settings so that the following file locations are not scanned. Doing this will help improve the performance of the server. This will also alleviate any files being locked while the SQL Server service is working. If some of these file types become infected, the antivirus software will not be able to detect this:

- SQL Server data files (`.mdf`, `.ndf`, `.ldf` files)

- SQL Server backup files (`.bak` and `.trn` files)

- Full-text catalog files

- Trace files (`.trc` files)

- SQL audit files for SQL Server 2008 or later versions (`.sqlaudit` files)

- SQL query files (`.sql` files)

- The directory that holds Analysis Services data

- The directory that holds Analysis Services temporary files, which are used during Analysis Services processing

- Analysis Services backup files

- The directory that holds Analysis Services log files

- Directories for any Analysis Services partitions that are not stored in the default data directory

- Filestream data files (SQL 2008 and later versions)

- Remote Blob Storage files (SQL 2008 and later versions)
- The directory that holds Reporting Services temporary files and logs (`RSTempFiles` and `LogFiles`)

The following are the processes you must exclude from virus scanning:

- `%ProgramFiles%\Microsoft SQL Server\<Version.><Instance Name>\MSSQL\Binn\SQLServr.exe`

- `%ProgramFiles%\Microsoft SQL Server\<Version>.<Instance Name>\Reporting Services\ReportServer\Bin\ ReportingServicesService.exe`

- `%ProgramFiles%\Microsoft SQL Server\MSAS13.<Instance Name>\OLAP\Bin\MSMDSrv.exe`

Setting the antivirus on our server is very important and you will face issues if you do not set these areas correctly. There are many areas that need to be excluded, but it is worth configuring these areas so that they support your farm and its services. They will help the server run as it should without hindering performance and availability.

There are also other ways to protect data, including using security methods such as Data Compliance Protection in the cloud and Data Compliance Site Templates, both of which are available within SharePoint. You can find out more by researching these topics online. We will go over some of the aspects of these features later in this book.

Web Part Security

Web Part Security is the next area of concern we must tackle. We won't be configuring this at the moment since we do not have a web application for users yet. However, I am mentioning this here because this is part of how we set security within our sites. The following screenshot shows the available settings for Web Part Security:

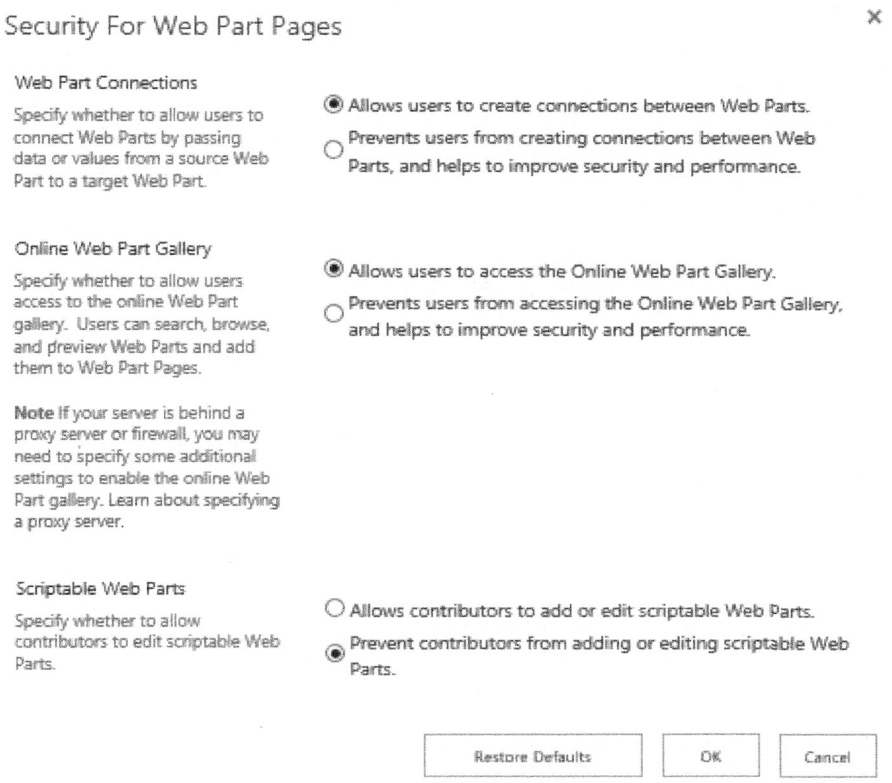

Security For Web Part Pages   ✕

Web Part Connections

Specify whether to allow users to connect Web Parts by passing data or values from a source Web Part to a target Web Part.

◉ Allows users to create connections between Web Parts.

○ Prevents users from creating connections between Web Parts, and helps to improve security and performance.

Online Web Part Gallery

Specify whether to allow users access to the online Web Part gallery. Users can search, browse, and preview Web Parts and add them to Web Part Pages.

◉ Allows users to access the Online Web Part Gallery.

○ Prevents users from accessing the Online Web Part Gallery, and helps to improve security and performance.

Note If your server is behind a proxy server or firewall, you may need to specify some additional settings to enable the online Web Part gallery. Learn about specifying a proxy server.

Scriptable Web Parts

Specify whether to allow contributors to edit scriptable Web Parts.

○ Allows contributors to add or edit scriptable Web Parts.

◉ Prevent contributors from adding or editing scriptable Web Parts.

| Restore Defaults | OK | Cancel |

Figure 5.22 – Security For Web Part Pages

Web Part Security can be set either in the menu under **Security** in the Central Administration site or via web application using the application management area within the Central Administration site. Both options work and are associated with a web application when you choose to configure this setting. The big settings to look at here are the ones that prevent users from creating web part connections within the web application, allowing user access to the Online Web Part Gallery, and allowing contributors to add or edit scriptable Web Parts.

These are choices you should make based on the content within your web application. Within production environments, I would not want any of these settings to be allowed. The last thing you want is a user to make changes to a site that can affect the way it performs, or what the site is actually doing from an application standpoint. For example, you could have connected web parts in an application so that they display filtered content in another web part, but now you have an issue because one of the users made a change to the web part connection. Avoid these scenarios by limiting these areas, especially in production environments.

Block File Types

Configuration settings help prevent certain document extensions from being uploaded to SharePoint sites. This is great because some viruses run within certain types of files, and we can prevent those files from being uploaded programmatically using these settings. As shown in the following screenshot, in the **Blocked File Types** area, we would type the names of each extension; for example, .docx:

Figure 5.23 – Blocked File Types

We are only using .docx files as an example here; we never want to block Word files. The following is a list of best practices when it comes to extensions:

File Type	Description
.ASHX	ASP.NET Web handler file. Web handlers are software modules that handle raw HTTP requests received by ASP.NET.
.ASMX	ASP.NET Web Services source file.
.JSON	JavaScript Object Notation file.
.SOAP	Simple Object Access Protocol file.
.SVC	Windows Communication Foundation (WCF) service file.
.XAMLX	Visual Studio Workflow service file.

Figure 5.24 – Best practices for extensions

Blocked File Types are powerful, especially when you may not want certain types of content in your farm. This helps ensure that files with certain extensions stay out of our libraries and do not get uploaded to the farm. Keeping these settings in check can help us know what kind of data is in our farm, as well as what kind of data should not be in our farm.

Creating service applications

Starting services within our farm is the first big task we need to complete before we can create sites for the user community. We must understand what services are needed for the farm, but also whether more than one web application will be created for the farm. The reason we need this information and why it's important is because if we do want to support more than one web application, we need to know what services are required for each web application.

In this section, you will learn how to configure services and find out what services you really need. In our planning session in *Chapter 2, Planning and Architecture*, I mentioned that this was something we should have looked at while planning. The reason why we must review those areas at the planning stage is because during our assessment, we looked at our old farm. When looking at our old farm, we found out what services were already running and what services will support the farm going forward. So, we have already started our list.

Now, we need to understand what those new services are and how they will be configured to support the farm. If you have not thought about this already, please make sure you do so before starting this section. In *Chapter 2, Planning and Architecture*, we went through this in detail, so you should be ready to start. If not, you will need to understand the following:

- Do I have enough server resources to support the farm?
- Do I need to segregate some of the services within the farm?
- What department needs what services?
- Do I create services that support all or some of the associated web applications?

In this section, we will create a matrix of services that can be individually dispersed across these web applications or shared between them. Whatever the case, we want to make sure we are managing our services so that we support the server resources that have been allocated for the farm, as well as the users who need these services within their sites. If security is a concern, then this will also play into how many services we create and what web applications they will support.

The following screenshot is our first glance at our **Services on Server** since we just created our new farm:

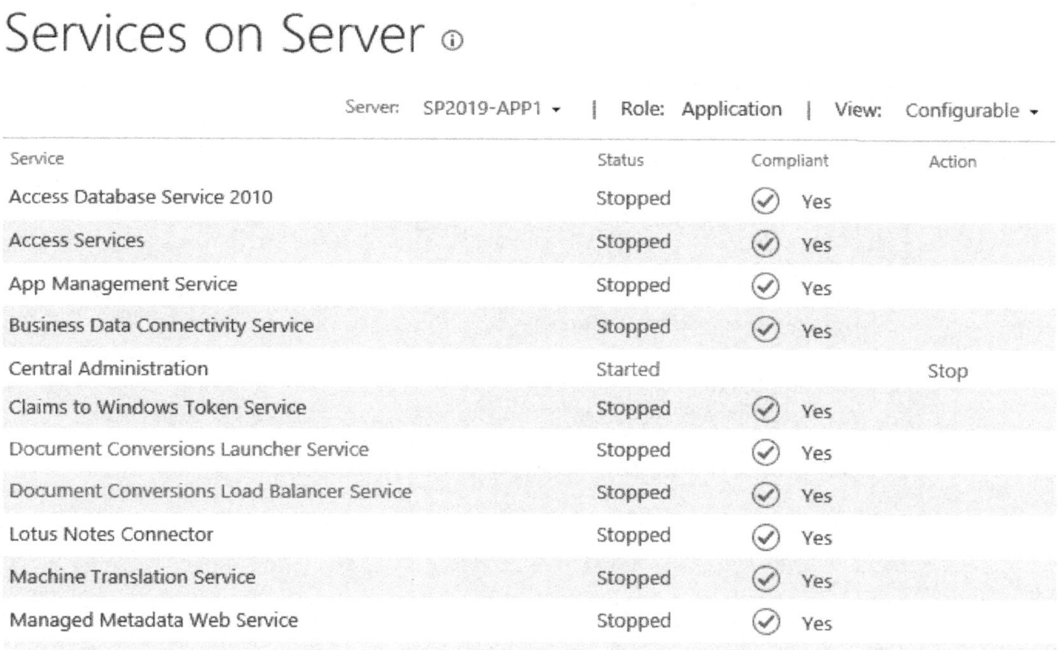

Services on Server ⓘ

| | Server: SP2019-APP1 ▾ | Role: Application | View: Configurable ▾ |

Service	Status	Compliant	Action
Access Database Service 2010	Stopped	✓ Yes	
Access Services	Stopped	✓ Yes	
App Management Service	Stopped	✓ Yes	
Business Data Connectivity Service	Stopped	✓ Yes	
Central Administration	Started		Stop
Claims to Windows Token Service	Stopped	✓ Yes	
Document Conversions Launcher Service	Stopped	✓ Yes	
Document Conversions Load Balancer Service	Stopped	✓ Yes	
Lotus Notes Connector	Stopped	✓ Yes	
Machine Translation Service	Stopped	✓ Yes	
Managed Metadata Web Service	Stopped	✓ Yes	

Figure 5.25 – Services on Server

This shows that we are currently only running the **Central Administration** site. This is because we have only created the farm and the Central Administration site. Because this is the only service that is running on this server, we can start configuring our farm and adding more services to our first server.

Registering service accounts

Before we can create service applications or web applications, we need to register service accounts for our farm so that these accounts can configure these services. This is really important because if these accounts are not available, you will not be able to configure separation of duties between service accounts. The only account that will be available will be the farm account since it was registered during the farm creation process.

To do this via SharePoint's Central Administration site, perform the following steps:

1. Start by opening the **Security** page:

Security

Users
Manage the farm administrators group | Approve or reject distribution groups |
Specify web application user policy

General Security
Configure managed accounts | Configure service accounts | Configure password
Specify authentication providers | Manage trust | Manage antivirus settings | Def
Manage web part security | Configure self-service site creation

Information policy
Configure information rights management | Configure Information Management

Figure 5.26 – Central Administration – account management

2. Click **Configure managed accounts** underneath **General Security**. Once you have filled in the form that appears, click **OK**:

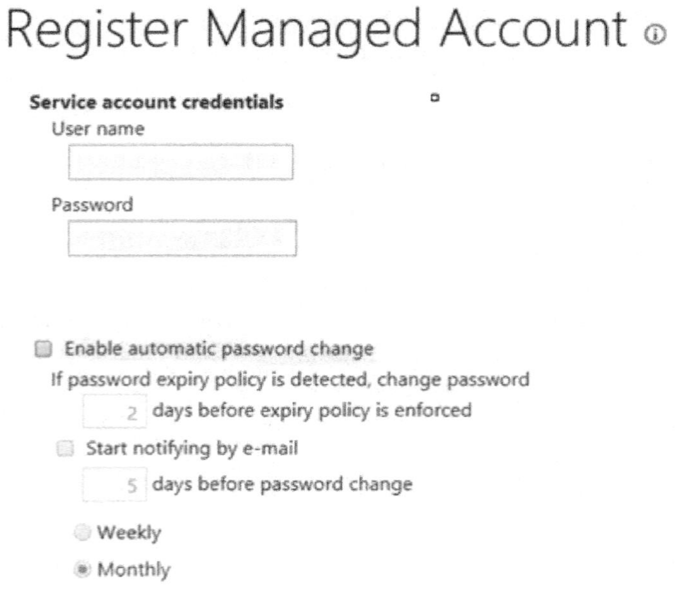

Register Managed Account ⓘ

Service account credentials
User name

Password

☐ Enable automatic password change
If password expiry policy is detected, change password
2 days before expiry policy is enforced
☐ Start notifying by e-mail
5 days before password change

○ Weekly
◉ Monthly

Figure 5.27 – Register Managed Account page

Add the account to the **User name** area of the form. The account must be in the following format: domain\username. You can enable automatic password changes via SharePoint. I have used this in the past to update passwords for my service accounts and it worked like a charm. The only issue that occurs is when you may need to sign in using that account as part of troubleshooting. So, if you want to know your password for the account, just do this as part of your monthly maintenance process and document this password change if you don't want to use the randomly automated password updates.

3. To do this using PowerShell, use the following commands:

```
$Password = "Ki90@T887"
$Account= "XYZ\WebAppPool"
$pass = convertto-securestring $Password -asplaintext
-force
$cred = new-object management.automation.pscredential
$Account ,$pass
$res = New-SPManagedAccount -Credential $cred
```

Make sure that you include a password that is up to your security standards. Remember that user accounts cannot be more than 20 characters in length; if they are, you will never see them added to the list of registered accounts. Now that we have added our accounts, we can use them in our service application and web application configurations.

Under the **Configurable** drop-down, you can view all the accounts that have been created and registered for use with the service applications you will be creating in this section:

Figure 5.28 – Adding registered accounts

Creating our services

The following is the list of services we will be creating in this section:

- Word Automation Services

- Visio Services

- Machine Translation Services

- Managed Metadata Services

- Claims to Windows Token Service

- Business Data Connectivity Service

- Secure Store Service

To ensure we do not include any redundant steps, let's explain the process of adding a service application.

You will find yourself going back to the main menu within the Central Administration Service Application menu to create a new service application once you've created one. Perform the following steps to create a service application. We will be using these steps for all our services since most require the same inputs for creation:

1. From the **Central Administration** site, to get to the service application creation area, click on **Application Management**:

Figure 5.29 – Central Administration

2. Under **Application Management**, click on **Manage Service Applications**:

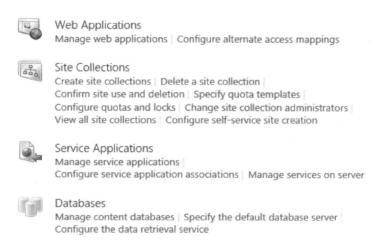

Figure 5.30 – Application Management

3. Upon clicking **Service Applications**, you will see a list of running service applications, as well as various ways to create and manage them within the farm:

Figure 5.31 – Service Applications

This is the main area you will be working from to create your service applications. This is a redundant step, so please remember how to get to these areas if you are not familiar with the process. You can always come back to this section to refresh your memory.

4. Upon clicking on the **New** button in the top-left corner, you will see a list of service applications that can be created:

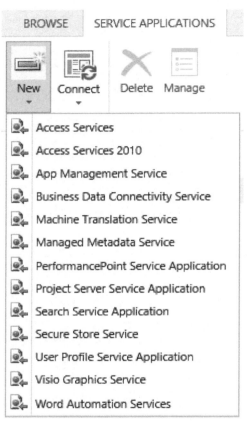

Figure 5.32 – Service Applications – creation selection menu

Next, we will look at Word Automation Services.

Word Automation Services

We will start with our first service: **Word Automation Services**. Word Automation Services is a technology that allows you to provide unattended, server-side conversion for documents that are supported by Microsoft Word. To start creating this service using the GUI, please click on that area within the menu.

Follow these steps to set this up:

1. Create a name for your service. Remember your naming conventions for service applications. Choose a service account that will manage this service and click the checkbox shown in the following screenshot to add this service application to your list of proxies:

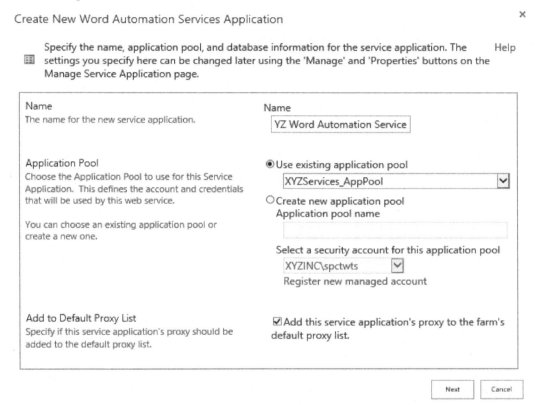

Figure 5.33 – Create New Word Automation Services Application page

2. Provide the SQL Server name for the database server, which is our alias name, and the database name for the database that will be hosting the data for this service:

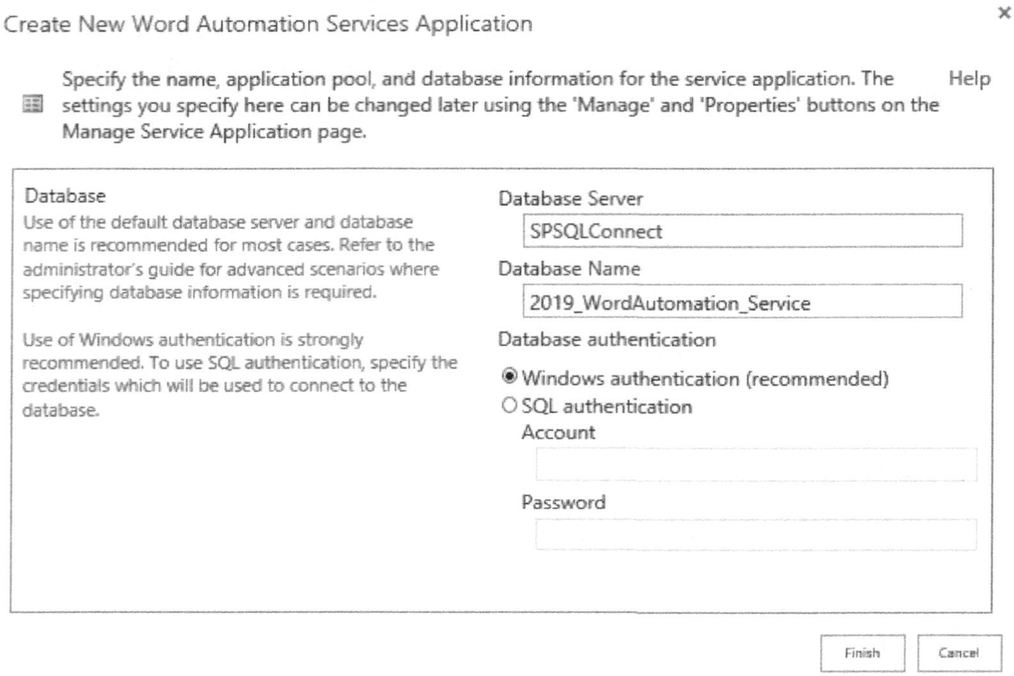

Create New Word Automation Services Application   ✕

Specify the name, application pool, and database information for the service application. The   Help
settings you specify here can be changed later using the 'Manage' and 'Properties' buttons on the
Manage Service Application page.

Database   Database Server
Use of the default database server and database
name is recommended for most cases. Refer to the   SPSQLConnect
administrator's guide for advanced scenarios where   Database Name
specifying database information is required.
                                                       2019_WordAutomation_Service
Use of Windows authentication is strongly
recommended. To use SQL authentication, specify the   Database authentication
credentials which will be used to connect to the
database.   ⦿ Windows authentication (recommended)
                                                       ○ SQL authentication
                                                          Account

                                                          Password

                                                              Finish   Cancel

Figure 5.34 – Providing a name for our SQL Server

Please provide the **Database Server** name, which is your alias name, and a **Database Name**. You should use a naming convention that supports the service being documented.

Important Note

Naming conventions are very important. Remember that service applications can be related to the overall company, a department, or custom segments of your company. Name it so that you understand who this service belongs to. This also stands when you're naming databases. If the service and/or database is just going to be used overall for the farm, then name it similar to how I named it so that it supports a global aspect. Any specifics in your naming are welcome, but try not to make the database names too long.

We can also use PowerShell to create the service. To open the SharePoint Management Shell, type in SharePoint on your desktop; you will see it listed as an application. When using the SharePoint Management Shell, always click **Run As Administrator**. Right-click the application link and choose **Run As Administrator**:

```
Add-pssnapin Microsoft.SharePoint.PowerShell
```
```
New- New-SPServiceApplicationPool -Name "Word Conversion
Services Application Pool" -Account <<service application
account>>
```
```
Get- New-SPServiceApplicationPool -Identity <<application pool
name>> | New-SPWordConversionServiceApplication -Name "Word
Conversion Services"
```

Now, we can create our next application service: **Visio Graphics Service**.

Visio Graphics Services

This service enables you to load, display, and interact programmatically with Microsoft Visio documents on you SharePoint Server. Provide a name for your service and use the service's application pool or create your own, depending on your requirements. Check the checkbox shown in the following screenshot and click **OK**:

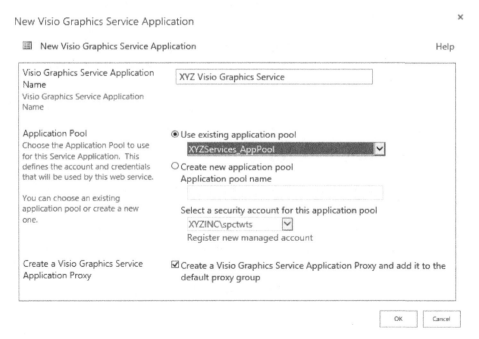

Figure 5.35 – Visio Graphics Service Application

You can also create this service using PowerShell:

```
New-SPVisioServiceApplication -Identity 'Visio Graphics Service
Application' -ApplicationPool 'SharePoint Web Services Default'
-CreateDefaultProxy
```

> **Note**
>
> The SharePoint Web Services Default Application Pool is an application pool that's created by SharePoint when the application is installed. This can be used to support new services you create, though you can create another service application pool to support these services. Please be aware that the Farm Account will run this application pool by default.
>
> There are best practices you need to follow since we do not want to have an overwhelming amount of application pools. In some cases, you can use separate application pools to give individuality to the service you are creating. This would use a different service account other than the farm account to limit access to the service account being compromised. If you can, limit the pools to 10 as that is a best practice.
>
> I have seen some bad configurations in my career. I had one local government client call me to come onsite to take a look at their configuration. The servers they had for the web tier were running out of memory. The client had 34 path-based web applications running with different applications pools and service accounts. This was the shortest call I had while working at Microsoft; I resolved the issue by adding memory and CPU to the servers. This is not a great configuration, but it worked. They could have used Host Named Site Collections but chose not to do so. The moral of the story is that best practices are there for a reason. Choose your path and understand the consequences that may result from your actions.

Business Connectivity Services

Now, will create our next service: **Business Connectivity Services**. Business Connectivity Services is used to help us connect to data that may be outside of SharePoint. This allows us to connect to SQL databases that are hosted on other servers, as well as on the cloud. To create a Business Connectivity Service, add a name for your service application. Enter your database's alias name as the **Database Server** name and provide a name for your service database, under **Database Name**. Then, click **OK**:

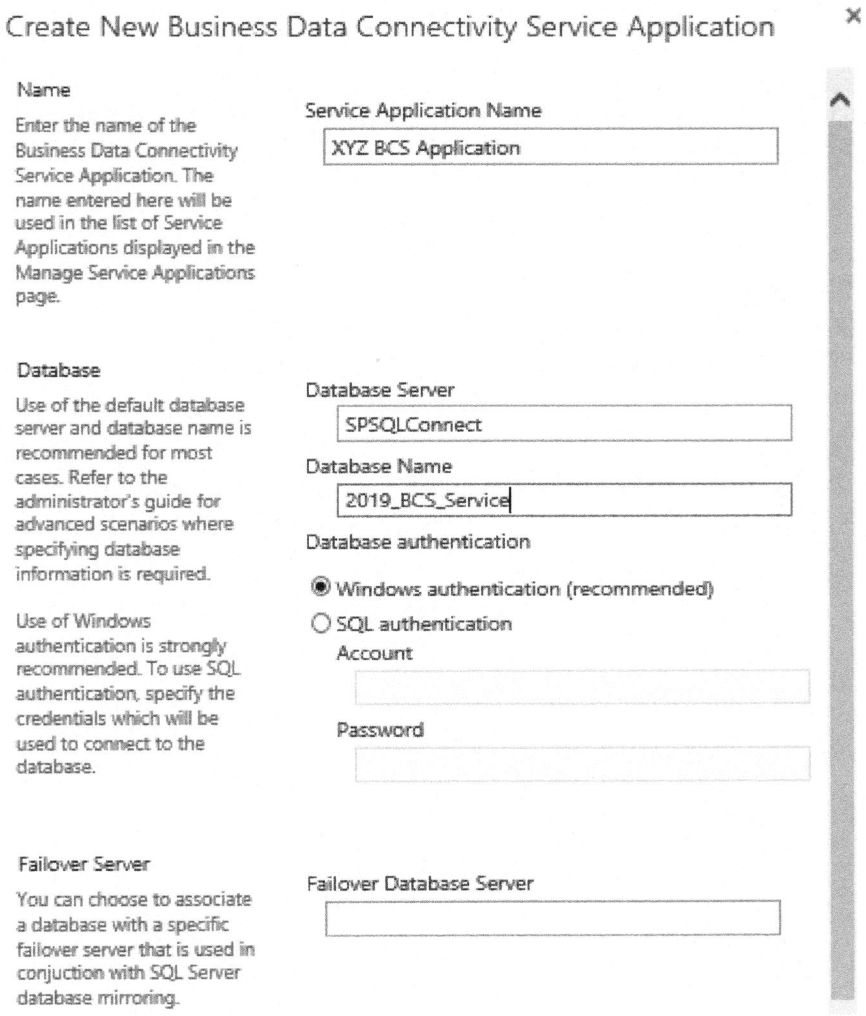

Figure 5.36 – Create New Business Data Connectivity Service Application

Important Note

In my examples, I placed the name of my main service at the end of all the names of my service databases. I did this to categorize them in the list of databases in SQL Server. This way, all my services databases will be in one area and all my content databases will be in another.

To create the service using PowerShell, use the following commands:

```
New-SPBusinessDataCatalogServiceApplication -ApplicationPool
"SharePoint Web Services Default" -DatabaseName "NewBdcDB"
-DatabaseServer "YourDomain\SharePoint" -Name "YourServiceApp"
```

Now, we will create our next service: **Machine Translation Services**.

Machine Translation Services

The Machine Translation Service is used to provide automatic machine translation of files and sites. This service is provided on a cloud hosted machine by Microsoft and powers Office, Lync, Yammer, and Bing's translation features.

If you need this service application and are willing to make sure your users understand how this service works, please add a name for the service application. At this point, you can either create a new services application pool or use the same existing services application pool. Click **OK** once you have completed the form:

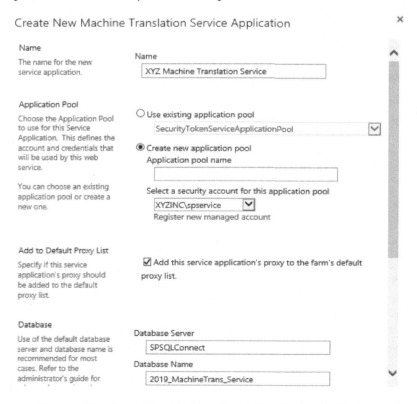

Figure 5.37 – Create New Machine Translation Service Application

You also have the option to create this service application using PowerShell:

```
New-SPTranslationServiceApplication -Name
TranslationService -ApplicationPool 'SharePoint Web
Services Default' -DatabaseServer Server1 -DatabaseName
TranslationServiceDatabase
```

Now, we will create the Managed Metadata Service.

Managed Metadata Services

This service is used to define metadata that can be used to tag information within your content for search and navigation purposes. Follow these steps to create the service:

1. Add a name for the Managed Metadata Service application, along with the SQL alias and **Database Name** you need for the service application:

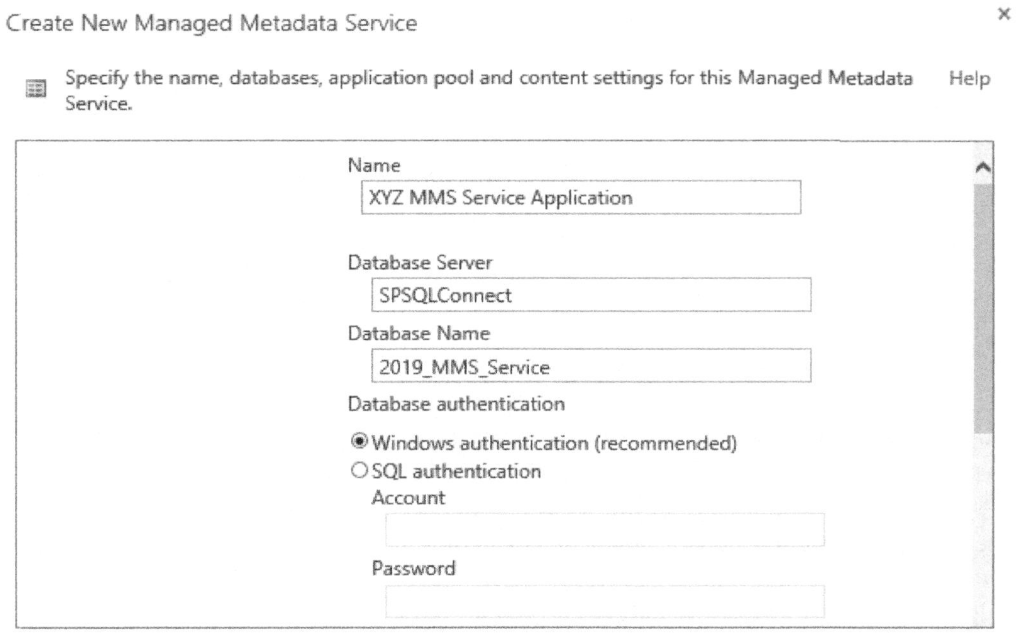

Create New Managed Metadata Service   ×

Specify the name, databases, application pool and content settings for this Managed Metadata   Help
Service.

Name

XYZ MMS Service Application

Database Server

SPSQLConnect

Database Name

2019_MMS_Service

Database authentication

◉ Windows authentication (recommended)
○ SQL authentication
Account

Password

Figure 5.38 – Create New Managed Metadata Service

2. You can also use the same services application pool or create a new one for this service application. Click **OK** to create the service application:

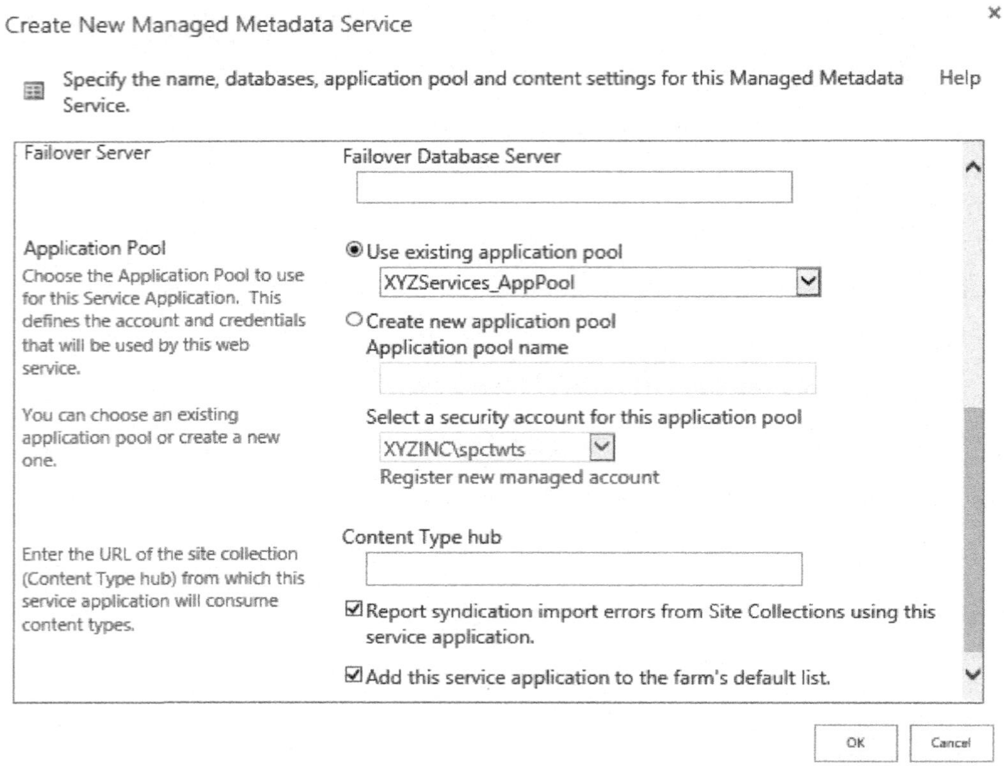

Create New Managed Metadata Service   ✕

Specify the name, databases, application pool and content settings for this Managed Metadata   Help
Service.

Failover Server   Failover Database Server   ⌃

Application Pool   ⦿ Use existing application pool
Choose the Application Pool to use   XYZServices_AppPool   ⌄
for this Service Application. This
defines the account and credentials   ○ Create new application pool
that will be used by this web   Application pool name
service.

You can choose an existing   Select a security account for this application pool
application pool or create a new   XYZINC\spctwts   ⌄
one.   Register new managed account

Enter the URL of the site collection   Content Type hub
(Content Type hub) from which this
service application will consume
content types.   ☑ Report syndication import errors from Site Collections using this
                                          service application.

                                       ☑ Add this service application to the farm's default list.   ⌄

                                                                    OK   Cancel

Figure 5.39 – Application pool options

If you plan on having a dedicated site collection for the Content Type Hub, which distributes content types to web applications, you can set that URL here. However, since we do not have a web application yet, we will come back to this later and set it using PowerShell. You can also add this service application to the farm's default list if this is a default service for the farm.

To create this service using PowerShell, use the following code:

```
New-SPMetadataServiceApplication -Name "MetadataServiceAppName"
 -ApplicationPool "AppPoolName" -DatabaseName "MetadataDBName"
```

To create the Managed Metadata Service with a Content Type Hub, use the following code:

```
New-SPMetadataServiceApplication -Name "MetadataServiceAppName"
-ApplicationPool "AppPoolName" -DatabaseName "MetadataDBName"
-HubUri "https://sitename" -SyndicationErrorReportEnabled
```

Claims to Windows Token Service

SharePoint Server 2019 – in fact, all versions of the product – require Active Directory authentication. This authentication is required for users to access SharePoint resources and apps, and is also used so allow servers to access on-premises SharePoint resources in a farm. If a server has a trust relationship with other servers in the SharePoint farm, they will be able to access secured resources on another SharePoint server in the farm. This is called server-to-server authentication and is done using the STS and OAuth server-to-server protocol.

When outside data sources or application connectivity is needed outside the SharePoint farm, such as with SQL Reporting Services, we need the **Claims to Windows Token Service (C2WTS)** running as it is a required service in SharePoint for connectivity to occur between two applications. This service should run under its own domain identity and should have the following rights assigned:

- Act as part of the operating system
- Impersonate a client after authentication
- Log on as a service

There are other authentication methods available, such as Kerberos and SAML, that we will explain later in this book.

Starting this service can be done using a simple PowerShell command that can be used to start any service in SharePoint. We can use this command for all the services we have created once the service application has been created. Search and User Profiles have different processes that need to be followed.

This service, C2WTS, does not require us to create a service application. We only need to start the service. Open SharePoint Management Shell to run PowerShell commands:

```
Start-SPServiceInstance -Identity <ServiceGUID>
```

To stop a service, use the following command:

```
Stop-SPServiceInstance -Identity <ServiceGUID>
```

When you wish to find the `ServiceGUID` for the service you want to start, run the following command:

```
Get-SPServiceInstance
```

Now, we will create another service: Secure Store Service.

Secure Store Service

The Secure Store Service application provides a claims-aware authorization service. It also provides an encrypted database for storing credentials that is usually kept on another SQL Server for security. This service provides authorization to applications that are running within the SharePoint Server.

To create this service using PowerShell, use the following commands:

```
New-SPSecureStoreServiceApplication -ApplicationPool
'SharePoint Web Services Default' -AuditingEnabled:$false
-DatabaseName 'Secure Store' -Name 'Secure Store Service
Application'
```

Make sure that you only create the services you need. You do not have to follow my creation plan in this book. Creating services you don't need is not a good practice. Finalize the services you think you will need and create them.

Once these service applications have been added, it does not hurt to run `PSconfig` to solidify the farm and make sure all configurations are working as they should. You can do this using the Configuration Wizard, which can be found by typing in SharePoint on your desktop or by using PowerShell and running the following script:

```
PSConfig.exe -cmd upgrade -inplace b2b
```

Once you've done this, shut down/restart or reboot your servers, starting with SharePoint first and then SQL. Make sure SQL is running first before the SharePoint server so that you don't get any connectivity errors. Once completed, we can start adding servers to the farm. Always check your event logs once you've rebooted to see if there are any new errors.

> **Important Note**
>
> Running `PSConfig.exe` with no parameters does not upgrade or do any good to the farm's content. Without any parameters running, this command is useless. Make sure that you add parameters to apply upgrades when running a full upgrade command, not just the initial executable. When you add content to the farm, you will add more parameters to upgrade content and features.

SharePoint MinRole resources

We talked about MinRoles and their importance in *Chapter 2, Planning and Architecture*. Assigning MinRoles at this point in our configuration is essential as we have two big service applications we left out previously: User Profile Services and Search Services. I have different reasons for leaving these for last, all of which will be explained in *Chapter 6, Finalizing the Farm – Going Live*, but to summarize, User Profiles require a server resource in order to run efficiently, as do Search Services. In our configuration, Search requires two servers for redundancy. We can only provide these resources by adding the servers to the farm, which we will do now. Distributed caches will come into play now as well.

Once you have installed SharePoint on all the servers you've created, as we stated in *Chapter 4, Installation Concepts*, we need to start adding them to the farm. Various prerequisites must be met on all the servers, including performing updates that relate to the version the farm is running at currently. All server resources should have similar/the same configurations as other SharePoint servers, including CPU, RAM, and drive configurations (drive letters must be the same; configuring server resources by tier or MinRole is a best practice).

There are two different ways to add a new server to our farm:

- The first is to use the **Configuration Wizard** window, as shown in the following screenshot:

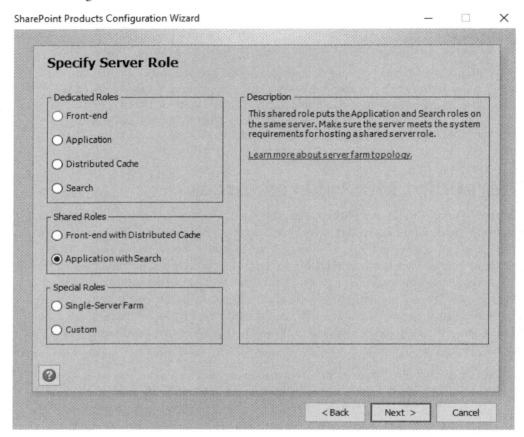

Figure 5.40 – Specify Server Role

- The other is to use PowerShell and add the servers using a stripped-down version of our farm configuration script, as shown in the following example:

```
Add-PSSnapin "Microsoft.SharePoint.PowerShell
#Configuration Settings
$DatabaseServer = "SQL Alias Name"
$ConfigDatabase = "Farm_Config"
$Passphrase = "57J7902KK9Srww$!#LiPQ"
$FarmAccountName = "Montego\SP_Farm"
$ServerRole="Application"
```

```
#"Custom","WebFrontEnd","Application","DistributedCache",
"SingleServerFarm","Search","ApplicationWithSearch",
"WebFrontEndWithDistributedCache"

Connect-SPConfigurationDatabase -DatabaseServer
$DBServer -DatabaseName $DBName -PassPhrase $Passphrase
-LocalServerRole $ServerRole

Write-Host "Installing SharePoint Resources..."
Initialize-SPResourceSecurity

Write-Host "Installing Farm Services ..."
Install-SPService

Write-Host "Installing SharePoint Features..."
Install-SPFeature -AllExistingFeatures

Write-Host "Installing Help..."
Install-SPHelpCollection -All

Write-Host "Installing Application Content..."
Install-SPApplicationContent

Write-Host "Joined the Server to Farm Successfully!"
```

Always remember to update the parameters of this script, as well as the Minrole or Server Role in your script, to make sure you choose the right server roles for your farm. In my farm, I will be adding the following roles:

- Two Application/Search Servers

- Two Web FrontEnd Servers with the Distributed Cache service

Once you've run the script and/or added the servers to the farm using either method, you will see the servers in the **System Settings** area of the **Central Administration** site, under **Servers in the Farm**.

Understanding the Distributed Cache service

The Distributed Cache service is used to improve performance by managing objects and data across MinRole configured servers, as well as servers included in your farm. From past engagements where I've reviewed a farm, I've seen that this service was either not set correctly or was non-existent because it had crashed. In one case, a site was down for many months due to this service and Microsoft Updates failing. It is a very important service, so you cannot leave this out when monitoring or planning a maintenance window that supports updates and/or changing the configuration of the service.

The Distributed Cache service is used to maintain a large amount of information on the server you have chosen to provide these services to in your farm. From a configuration standpoint, these servers can be standalone or used on a WFE tier server, where users interface with the farm at the site level. This service ensures that the information that is gathered for the services is readily available and is provided for the following services running in your farm:

- Authentication

- Newsfeeds, micro blogging, and conversations

- OneNote client access

- Security trimming (Search)

- Page load performance

This service provides caching functionalities that allow users to quickly retrieve data without any dependency on the database. All this information is stored in memory on the servers or MinRoles you have deemed Distributed Cache servers. Distributed Cache spans across these servers as a cache cluster so that each host can save data without duplicating or copying data from other servers running the service.

This service is very important, and in some cases, I have seen where this service was not recoverable. You want to be very careful when working with this service and monitor it as much as possible. Do not administer your AppFabric Caching Service from the services console. It is recommended that you leave this service as-is from your initial configuration. I have seen farms having to be rebuilt due to this service and its parameters being changed.

To check your Distributed Cache, run the following command using PowerShell:

```
Get-CacheHost
```

At the time of installation, 5% of the total physical memory will be assigned to the Distributed Cache service. This is known as the cache's size and can be altered if needed. Since we are setting up a farm, we must have at least one cache host running in the farm. If you have two or more servers that you want to run this service, just know that the size of each cache host is 5% of your physical memory. The maximum size you can make your cache is 16 GB per cache host, so you want to make sure you set aside memory for this service. You should have thought about this when you were planning. We also want to make sure we are aware that we can only have 16 servers running the Distributed Cache service in a farm.

We will learn more about this service and how to make our servers perform well in *Chapter 9, Managing Performance and Troubleshooting.*

Summary

This chapter was the meat of the installation process for SharePoint. Although there is more to come, this chapter laid the foundation for the farm. If we didn't cover these areas, we would not have a base installation to move forward with and, as pertaining to the server resources, have a complete server infrastructure that supports a SharePoint and SQL Server environment.

Be mindful of your settings when you're configuring the performance of SQL Server, especially the MAXDOP settings. If they are changed, the SharePoint environment will not run correctly and you will see performance hits on your SQL servers. This is because SharePoint is built for MAXDOP to be set to 1. Also, building redundancy into your SQL Server platform is also key to supporting the environment. As we mentioned previously, SQL is the key to the data that feeds SharePoint from a configuration, service, and content point of view. Without a fully performant SQL Server, great performance will not exist in your environment.

Make sure that you add servers as needed that support the SharePoint infrastructure that's required for your environment. Separating services as needed and adding user web frontends to support your user community is key to building a farm that can support many users and services. Scaling out your farm is easy to do, and there are many ways to isolate and combine traffic for all your services and user traffic.

We also learned that MinRoles are the key to this separation and service compliance. Never add a server where you do not know what the resource is being used for. If you use a custom MinRole, always make sure to configure it so that it only does what you need it to do and uses the resources it has to only run the services it needs to run. The reason we use MinRoles is so that we can control where services are processed and keep our resources free from running unnecessary processes.

As you can see, paying attention to small details and documenting your configuration is key to updating your farm. It also allows you to ensure you have covered all your requirements, which is the key to success. Configuration management plays a part in all this because you want to make sure the servers match how you want the service to perform. Again, SQL is a big part of SharePoint, and we cannot run SharePoint without it. However, if it's configured incorrectly, we will see performance issues. Follow the guidelines and best practices at hand to make sure you are building the best farm possible. Although this is a lot of work to document, it will pay off in the end.

Questions

You can find the answers on GitHub under Assessments at `https://github.com/PacktPublishing/Implementing-Microsoft-SharePoint-2019/blob/master/Assessments.docx`

1. Why should we separate application pools for different services within our configuration?

2. Antivirus exclusions don't need to be completed before installation. True or False?

3. Which service application is optional to use a separate database server as a best practice?

4. What setting is required on SQL Server to install SharePoint? What is the setting for that configuration?

5. When setting up Blocked File Types, I can set these file types per site collection. True or False?

6. If running `psconfig`, do I need to run the command using extended parameters? If so, when? Why?

6
Finalizing the Farm – Going Live

Finalizing the farm to "go live" is the last step of the process of supporting the release of your new farm. Within this book, you will find two chapters about the "go live" aspects of your implementation. This is due to the amount of instruction needed to prepare you for your "go live" date. There are a few steps that we still need to complete related to installation, the configuration of services, and overall configuration, which we will cover in this chapter; but what you will also see in this chapter is that there are many areas that we still need to configure to complete the core system.

You will see, while dealing with those lingering configurations, that migration is not the last thing we need to do. There are other areas of preparedness that need to be addressed, as is the case with the setup of development and testing environments. We need to handle any custom configurations that may have been missed, out-of-the-box workflows and custom workflows, backup and restore solution integration, and any operating areas that we need to check, update, and pass on to others who will support the new farm and overall environment.

We will also talk a little about stress testing the environment and the overall testing of the new sites, as well as covering other integrations that need to be checked and installed to support sites as they were supported in the older environment (or schedule them for deployment in our new environment).

The checklist is vast, and we need to make sure that we are bringing a solid environment to the company before release. This chapter will follow that checklist and get you prepared for the release of your new SharePoint farm!

The following topics will be covered in this chapter:

- Finalizing services configuration
- Web application configuration
- Web application settings
- Site collection creation
- Site collection configuration and settings
- Cache service accounts

Technical requirements

To follow along with this chapter, the following requirements must be met:

- 3-5 years of SharePoint experience
- 3-5 years of project management experience

You can find the code files for this chapter on GitHub at `https://github.com/PacktPublishing/Implementing-Microsoft-SharePoint-2019`.

Finalizing loose ends

Did we forget something? I am sure we did. That's why I created this chapter to make sure we go back and retrace our steps and find things that may not have been communicated or documented. We want to make sure at this point that we have accounted for everything in our old environment, which includes services and content. This includes everything we noted in our planning and assessments. The last thing you want is a failed SharePoint farm implementation.

These next two chapters were created to finalize the configuration and make sure that we check all the loose ends to finalize our farm. There are a couple of areas that were left out of our service configuration chapter that we need to expand on, as well as web applications, site collections, and general settings for those areas, which we will get into in this chapter.

Here, as a precaution, it's a good idea to go back and assess your users and departments to make sure you have accounted for all developed solutions, out-of-the-box solutions, workflows, identified retired web parts, and anything that could be an area of concern for functionality and could be missed during this change. I can't stress this enough. The more you miss, the more you will pay for it after users start to work on the new farm.

You need to make sure you know what these users are doing in their site collections and sites. Don't sleep until you get all the answers. At the end of the day, this is what makes you, your department, and SharePoint look bad when you don't migrate everything or miss a functionality that users have been using for years and all of a sudden it's gone. If that functionality has changed, make sure you let the department know and give them a new way to make it work in SharePoint Server 2019.

Believe me, I have been caught with my pants down on a couple of migration projects. One time, there was a tool that I used, and I will not mention the name of this tool, but it malfunctioned as it was not adhering to the migration parameters I had chosen. If I chose to move only the top-level site and not subsites, it would just move all sites anyway. This actually made my contract go over hours because I had to go back and delete all the subsites that were not on the list to move. We will talk more about tools later in this chapter, and I will give my opinions and recommendations on tools and how they can play into your migration and help in other ways to support your infrastructure.

Another situation I was in a few years ago was not having got enough information from users and admins. After doing the migration and moving over to the new farm, there were two critical components missing from the new farm. One was a script used for identity management that worked with the User Profile service to clean up those users no longer working in the company, and another was a custom solution that was developed for a site but was not identified during the migration to the new farm. This caused a lot of problems during the post-implementation as some functionality was missing, and it was very stressful.

So, please be careful: your career and reputation can be shattered when you are not attentive to areas that make a difference in a successful migration. Everyone remembers the bad things, and even if it is one little thing, it will outweigh the good things.

Let's look at some things to remember during the final actions before releasing the farm to the community:

- Workflows keep items locked in lists and libraries if it's in progress on the source site.
- Migration tools will not move locked items or custom solutions.

- Release items by having the department finalize the workflow process or stop the workflow on the item.

- Make a list of those items in progress so the department can restart the workflow in the new environment.

- Workflows and solutions may have to be recreated, especially those coming from 2007 and 2010.

- Workflows and solutions created in Visual Studio from earlier versions will have to be updated to support SharePoint 2019's code structure.

- The workflow history does not migrate with the content database or migration tool – If needed, go to the workflow history list (For example, `http://sharepoint/mysite/lists/Workflow%20History/AllItems.aspx`) and make copies of the lists for your records and for the department. You can slice and dice with columns to get information sorted for printing or saving.

- Remember that the workflow history can be captured as part of the default list or a new history list and can be associated with the workflow.

- Make sure to check the settings of lists moved with tools, as all the required settings for advanced and versioning are not set. This can cause some issues with approval processes in the task list and in the list itself.

- Check your old servers for any PowerShell or custom code used to do any server-side functionality, such as backups, or as in my situation, user profile cleanup.

- Check the **Global Assembly Cache (GAC)** on the old server to make sure there are no custom solutions hiding there that do not show up in the farm solutions list.

There are other areas you can check that might not be included in my list of last-minute checks, but the best thing to do is communicate. Double-check with your admins and site collection admins before making any final migrations. We will talk about testing in this chapter, as well as the pre-migration tasks, test migrations, and final migrations that we need to implement. I will show you what these tasks are all about and how they are used to finalize the movement of content.

Search and the User Profile service

As you know, we have not installed Search or the User Profile service, and the reason is that we need to make sure we have servers added to the farm to support these two services. So, in *Chapter 5, Farm and Services Configuration*, we added servers to the farm, and these servers were created as MinRole services in the farm for the services we are about to deploy. We will add and distribute services for these two missing services across the server resources we added. These are the last two service creations and I saved them for last for a reason. These two services, although they have not changed much in any version of SharePoint, are the most involved in terms of configuration and should be the services that you configure last.

Search service creation

When implementing Search, we need to think about the availability of the service as well as the resources we must provide for services within the farm. As stated in our planning, we plan in this environment to have a redundant Search service running on two servers within the farm using a Search MinRole. This gives the service a redundant footprint in the farm and keeps the service up and running in case of the failure of one of the servers.

There could be situations where security comes into play, where you may need two Search service applications. This would separate the indexes and instead of relying on security trimming, you'd rely on a totally different index, service account, and application pool to separate the content from one web application to another. In our configuration, I really want to go through how to create a redundant Search application because this seems to be more of an issue in the field.

To get started with this implementation, we will need to use PowerShell, and as always, we right-click on the PowerShell icon to open and make sure to run as administrator. We also want to make sure our servers are in place to support the configuration for these services to run redundantly. As you can see in the following screenshot, both servers are available and ready to go:

Figure 6.1 – Search app servers

Implementing the Search service with redundancy again cannot be done within the GUI in **Central Administration**. There are also other restrictions in the GUI that will come up in the configuration, such as database names being grayed out for where you cannot update the names. If you are shooting for full naming and custom database names for all service databases, you will have to create this service application using PowerShell. So, let's open up the SharePoint 2019 shell command line and run the following script from a file location on our primary Search server. The script is shown here and is available on the GitHub site for this book:

> **Note**
>
> Download the script and instructions on the GitHub link at the top of the chapter. Please make sure to set the parameters in the script to fit your server names, index locations, and any other areas you need to customize for your environment.

Search successfully installed:

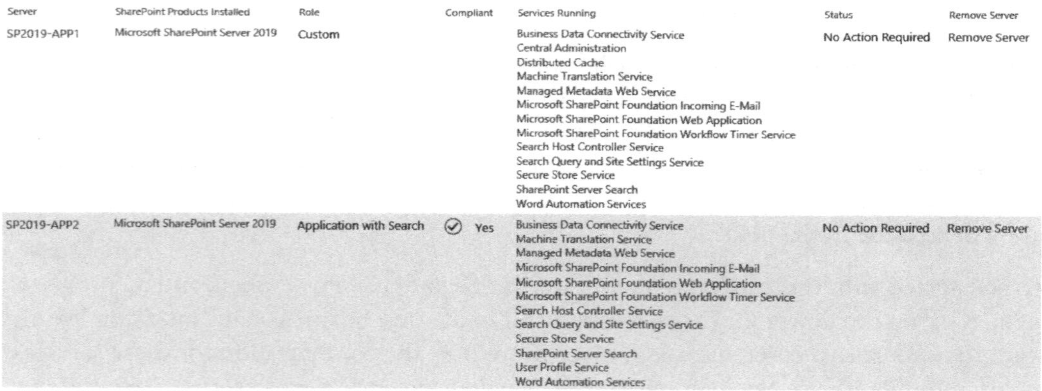

Server	SharePoint Products Installed	Role	Compliant	Services Running	Status	Remove Server
SP2019-APP1	Microsoft SharePoint Server 2019	Custom		Business Data Connectivity Service Central Administration Distributed Cache Machine Translation Service Managed Metadata Web Service Microsoft SharePoint Foundation Incoming E-Mail Microsoft SharePoint Foundation Web Application Microsoft SharePoint Foundation Workflow Timer Service Search Host Controller Service Search Query and Site Settings Service Secure Store Service SharePoint Server Search Word Automation Services	No Action Required	Remove Server
SP2019-APP2	Microsoft SharePoint Server 2019	Application with Search	✓ Yes	Business Data Connectivity Service Machine Translation Service Managed Metadata Web Service Microsoft SharePoint Foundation Incoming E-Mail Microsoft SharePoint Foundation Web Application Microsoft SharePoint Foundation Workflow Timer Service Search Host Controller Service Search Query and Site Settings Service Secure Store Service SharePoint Server Search User Profile Service Word Automation Services	No Action Required	Remove Server

Figure 6.2 – Confirmation of Search being successfully installed

We have successfully installed the Search service! Once you have migrated your content or have your farm stabilized, start your Search crawl to start gathering content to present in the results. You can use continuous crawling, which will keep crawling content. You can also set a schedule for full or incremental crawls, which is ideal for some scenarios.

Search is configured – what now?

There are many things to know about the Search service, and we will get into some detail on Search later in the book from a user perspective, but at the server level, there are some best practices and things to understand about Search.

One of the key things to remember is that users use Search to find information. So, content must be crawled by connecting to content sources to crawl for the information to come up in the search results. The index you create is what the users will search against, so timing is everything, which is why there are a couple of ways to create crawling schedules. You can use continuous crawling or provide a schedule for full or incremental crawls.

Most companies I have worked for have used continuous crawling as their way to get information in the index, but this doesn't mean that the other crawling types are not useful. A full crawl is still useful because it processes and indexes all the items in a content source. It doesn't matter whether the previous crawl did that or not. This keeps your index clean and up to date.

> **Tip**
>
> Remember, it's always good to run a full crawl after you migrate content from another farm or source so that the information is indexed.

The incremental crawl only crawls items that have been newly created or modified since the last crawl. These crawls don't take a lot of time and usually are pretty quick, depending on how much new content has been added. These modifications would include the following updates:

- Content
- Metadata (remember the Managed Metadata service)
- Permissions
- Deletions from the content

The continuous crawl is sort of similar to the incremental crawl. The difference, though, is that the continuous crawl checks the SharePoint change logs about every 15 minutes. If there is an item in the change log, the crawler finds the content and processes the updates to the index. It's good to have a mixture of continuous crawl and incremental crawls, and this is because the continuous crawl does not fix any errors. Please create a schedule to run these as needed, but if you run an incremental every 4 hours, this would help to clean up any errors; use a full crawl as needed.

Users also have tools to make their search results as good as they can be by tagging content. It's best for users to tag their information so that content can be found easily. This leads to relevant search results, and there are tools for users to tune how content is found as well. They can also create silos of results based on content using the Search web part. This can help them to hone in on any content, such as content in a specific site or library, to provide the search results from that specific content only.

SharePoint 2019 Server provides the same modern search experience as Microsoft 365. You will see a big difference, as the search box is placed at the top of the SharePoint site in the header bar. The search experience in SharePoint 2019 is personal. The results for one user will most likely be different than another user's results in this new version of SharePoint. We talk more about it in *Chapter 12, SharePoint Framework*.

One Search consideration to be aware of is that if you actually get close to having 10 million items indexed, you may want to configure your server as I did in this book using cloning. This will help to spread the service over two servers, which will process items faster and bring better performance for your Search service. The Search service may benefit from being assigned as a MinRole service in some environments where you want to isolate the service to server resources for support as well.

Always keep your configuration of Search clean and separate for processing within the farm, along with where the use of those Search components will be located in a cloned configuration. In the Search configuration for my farm, you can see that I have redundancy on my app servers and redundancy on my web frontend servers. My web frontend servers in this configuration provide query processing and index partitions. My index partitions are updated from the application servers that run the crawl, which propagates over the network after every crawl to my web frontend servers. The results from the user queries are compiled on the web frontend from the index, so that the results from the search come back quickly because the user is on that server resource at the time of the search. This is to not have them go over the network to bring back the results. Make sure to make the crawler servers IIS configurations and HOST file understand that the website is local and there is no need to hit a WFE to crawl the website:

Search Application Topology

Server Name	Admin	Crawler	Content Processing	Analytics Processing	Query Processing	Index Partition 0
					✓	✓
	✓	✓	✓	✓		
	✓	✓	✓	✓		
					✓	✓

Figure 6.3 – The Search configuration page

> **Tip**
>
> Always configure your crawling server to crawl sites on the local server using the HOST file and not across the network to hit a web frontend to connect to the sites for crawling. The performance for this process will be very slow for crawling. Your users will be affected as well because of the crawl on the sites they use, and the propagation of the index will also be slowed down if the network is not able to push data from server to server quickly. Remember to check your network connections and configure them to be full duplex and not auto-negotiate.

Now that we have covered the Search service, we can work on setting up the User Profile service. User Profile requires that the Search configuration be completed because there are settings within User Profile that refer to a configured Search service.

Configuring the User Profile service

Before we get started with this configuration, we must make sure to determine which server this service will run on. We can use the first server we created in the farm or another if you have another one that is not running the Search service. These two services are some of the heavy-hitters in terms of resource consumption, so we want to make sure that they are separate in our farm configuration. The first thing we want to do is add our farm account to the local server that we plan to run the User Profile service from. Add the account to the local administrator's group on that server.

> **Important note**
>
> Make sure that you added the farm account to the local administrator's group of the server you choose to run this service! This is part of the configuration process, as you will see in the following steps. Make sure of this!

Once this is completed, you can start the following process:

1.   Under **Service Applications**, select **Manage service applications**:

Figure 6.4 – Application Management

2.   Click on **New** in **SERVICE APPLICATIONS**:

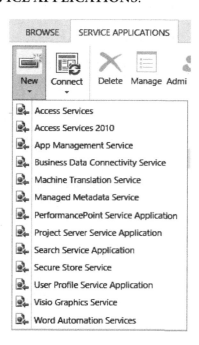

Figure 6.5 – The New button on the SERVICE APPLICATIONS page

Now you could do this the old way in **Central Administration**, but I ran into an error with **User Profile Service Application** using the UI. The error I encountered was a grayed-out screen for the social database. I could not name it or change the SQL Server name in the form. We will create the service using PowerShell; you should get used to using PowerShell. The reason why I added the GUI in this book is to give those who are beginners a way to understand what we are doing. Code sometimes looks foreign and I would rather that all were able to get something out of this book than to just add a bunch of scripts and have people be confused.

3. So, in this case, we will use the following script to create our User Profile service. Please remember to right-click the PowerShell icon and choose to run as administrator.

4. We must create the service application pool first to associate with the User Profile service. Make sure you have added the application pool service account as a managed account before moving forward:

```
$AppPoolAccount = "XYZINC\spuserprofapp"
 $AppPoolName = "UPS_App_Pool"


$AppPool = New-SPServiceApplicationPool -Name
$AppPoolName -Account $AppPoolAccount
```

5. Create the service application:

```
Add-PSSnapin Microsoft.SharePoint.PowerShell
 $UPSName = "XYZ UPS Service Application"
 $ApplicationPool = "UPS_App_Pool"
 $ProfileDBName = "XYZ_UPS_Profile_Service"
 $SocialDBName = "XYZ_UPS_Social_Service"
 $SyncDBName = "XYZ_UPS_Sync_Service"


 New-SPProfileServiceApplication -Name $UPSName
-ApplicationPool $ApplicationPool -ProfileDBName
$ProfileDBName -SocialDBName $SocialDBName
-ProfileSyncDBName $SyncDBName
```

6. As you can see in the following screenshot, when we run the PowerShell script, we get a new service application for the User Profile service:

```
PS C:\Windows\system32> C:\Users\spadmin19\Documents\userprofileservice.ps1

Name                    Type                Id
----                    ----                --
XYZ UPS Application     User Profile Serv... 9b9c4c22-fb99-4f32-88ff-9f66d9f47eb2
```

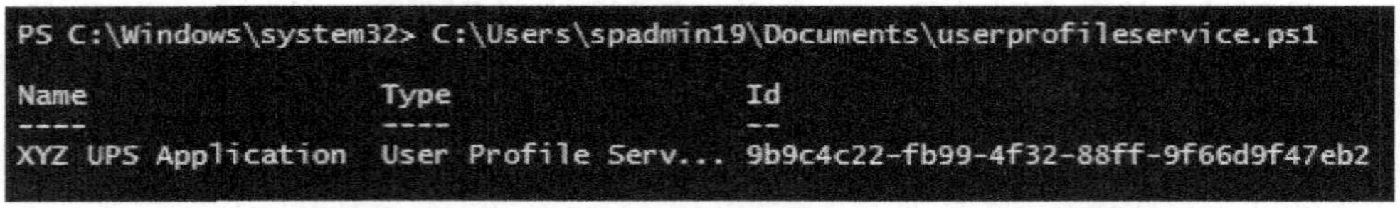

Figure 6.6 – New service application confirmation in PowerShell

7. Then we bind the service application with the proxy for the service:

```
New-SPProfileServiceApplicationProxy -Name 'XYZ UPS
Application Proxy' -ServiceApplication "9b9c4c22-fb99-
4f32-88ff-9f66d9f47eb2"-DefaultProxyGroup
```

8. As you can see in the following screenshot, we now have a proxy for our User Profile service application:

```
PS C:\Windows\system32> New-SPProfileServiceApplicationProxy -Name 'XYZ UPS Application Proxy' -ServiceApplication "9b9c4c22-fb99-4f32-88ff-9f66d9f47eb2" -DefaultProxyGroup
Name            Type                Id
----            ----                --
XYZ UPS Applicati... User Profile Serv... 8fbc0bf3-054e-43dc-ad82-236901dd7352
```

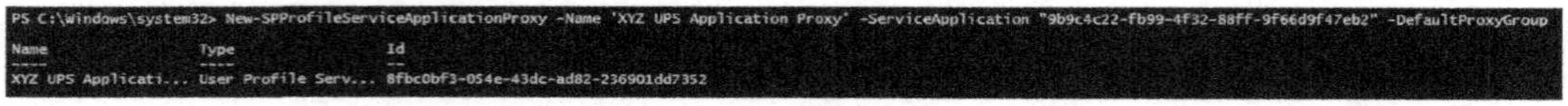

Figure 6.7 – Proxy for the User Profile service application

Go to the `Manage Services on Server` link and start the service on the server you installed the service on during the PowerShell configuration process.

Now that we have created our User Profile service, we need to bring in individual identities or groups of users from Active Directory. Let's look at how we can do that in the next section.

Configuring your connection to Active Directory

Do you understand your **Active Directory** (**AD**) structure? Do you know where the users and groups are located that need access to your SharePoint environment? These are questions you need to ask yourself before you go any further. The last thing you want to do is pull identities into the farm that you do not need. Have a conversation with your AD admin and find out the locations of the users and groups needed so that you can choose those areas within the AD structure and bring in only the users and groups that are necessary. They could be in the cloud!

Now that you have that information, let's get started on connecting to AD!

> **Important Note**
> Please make sure you have accounted for a replication account to connect to AD, as this service account needs to be used as part of the connection settings in this configuration.

Let's look at the steps:

1. Select **Configure Synchronization Connections** under the **Synchronization** section:

Figure 6.8 – Configure Synchronization Connections

2. Click on **Create New Connection**:

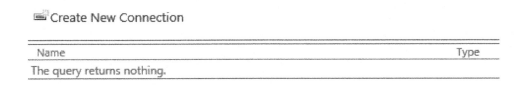

Figure 6.9 – Synchronization Connections

3. Fill out the form to update **Connection Settings**:

Add new synchronization connection

Use this page to configure a connection to a directory service server to synchronize users.

* Indicates a required field

Connection Name

Type

Active Directory Import ▾

Connection Settings

Fully Qualified Domain Name (e.g. contoso.com):

For Active Directory connections to work, this account must have directory sync rights.

Fully Qualified Domain Name (e.g. contoso.com):

Authentication Provider Type:

Windows Authentication ▾

Authentication Provider Instance:

▾

Account name: *

Example: DOMAIN\user_name

Password: *

Confirm password: *

Port:

389

☐ Use SSL-secured connection

☐ Filter out disabled users

Filter in LDAP syntax for Active Directory Import.

Containers

Choose which containers you want to be synchronized.

Populate Containers

Figure 6.10 – Adding a new synchronization connection

4. Start the synchronization using **Start Profile Synchronization** as shown in the following figure:

Manage Profile Service: XYZ UPS Application

People
Manage User Properties | Manage User Profiles | Manage User Sub-types | Manage Audiences | Schedule Audience Compilation | Manage User Permissions | Compile Audiences | Manage Policies

Synchronization
Configure Synchronization Connections | Configure Synchronization Timer Job | Configure Synchronization Settings | Start Profile Synchronization

Organizations
Manage Organization Properties | Manage Organization Profiles | Manage Organization Sub-types

My Site Settings
Setup My Sites | Configure Trusted Host Locations | Manage Promoted Sites | Publish Links to Office Client Applications | Manage Social Tags and Notes | Manage Following

Figure 6.11 – Start Profile Synchronization

5.   Choose **Start Full Synchronization**:

Start Profile Synchronization

Use this page to start a full or incremental Synchronization.

Start Profile Synchronization

Select Incremental Synchronization to start an incremental synchronization now. Only data that has changed in connected sources and User Profile will be synchronized.

Not recommended: In most case, Incremental sync should be sufficient. Selecting Full Synchronization is time and compute intensive and is not recommended unless absolutely required to reset data store in User Profile.

○ Start Incremental Synchronization
◉ Start Full Synchronization

[OK]   [Cancel]

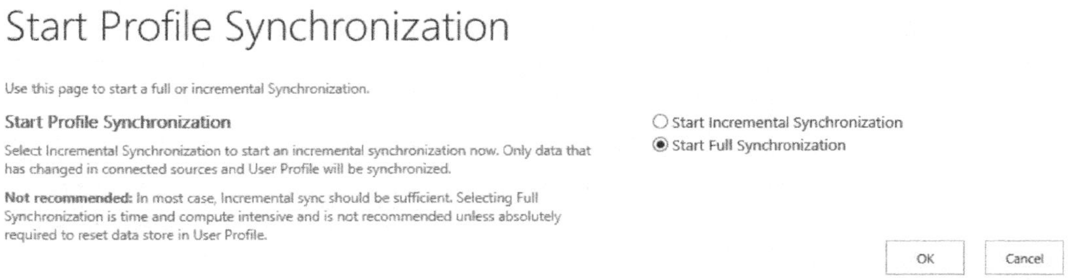

Figure 6.12 – Start Full Synchronization

We will run a full crawl using the search area of the central admin later when we have created our user web application and/or have migrated some content to a site.

Creating web applications and associations

In this section, we will go over the creation of web applications and how we associate services to those web applications. The need for two web applications is immediate. The two we need to create in this section are for the users and the MySite content, which we will talk about as well. MySite is not a mandatory site but it needs to be in place as part of the farm as it is necessary to user profiles, gathering user hierarchical information for use within workflows (such as an identity for a user's manager), and settings for configuration within the farm for search. If you would like an enterprise search web application, you can also do that as well, but it is not mandatory. The site template for that site collection is **Enterprise Search Center** under **Enterprise**:

Figure 6.13 – Enterprise Search Center

There have always been special needs for each customer I have worked with, so there could be a need for more web applications. Follow and repeat the following steps to add more web applications as needed. During this process, we will need IP addresses and SSL certificates, which you have to use during the configuration of the site. Please have those ready as these are prerequisites for this section.

The association of services to web applications is something we need to discuss as well as what constitutes a web application that needs a separate service association. We will also look at server and service compliance for how we can keep our servers running efficiently using the MinRole topology we chose to configure our farms with. We will see how server/service compliance works and how it really helps us to manage resources more efficiently.

Web applications

Web applications define how content is accessed from the network in SharePoint through the web browser. If there is no web application, there is no content. So, in this section, we want to focus on how to create web applications and what needs to be brainstormed before you start creating. In a previous section, we did discuss web applications and the reasons for them (in our planning section), but again we need to make sure at this time that we really have thought everything through and also make any changes that necessary due to new developments as well.

When starting to think about web applications, make sure you have done the following:

- Captured all areas of content you would like to categorize on this URL level
- Handled the zoning of the web application and how it will be accessed
- Associated service applications
- Managed the service accounts and app pools that will run this web application
- Handled the isolation and security of the web application on a server resource

When looking at our company and the departments and functional areas we need to support, one of the reasons why we would split content into separate web applications within SharePoint is to secure it. Securing content within a web application, which is the top-level access point, can be an area of concern. Making this our focus for security gives us a clear security break from other app pool service accounts, users, and groups accessing the web application and service associations at this level. The key to this split at this level is to make sure that access is not given to someone by accident.

Keeping content separate also can be done for performance reasons and/or reasons to do with customization. Customized sites with coding bring a different level of processing and support to a web application. This also can be the case with web applications that host a lot of data, such as PowerPivot or Excel data and other reporting data. Such a web application would be more resource-intensive than other web applications with no coding that are used for normal, out-of-the-box functionality.

Another reason for separation would be to separate groups of content and use separate URLs within the company for departments within the organization. For example, we can have a subdomain such as hr.xyzinc.com to represent the human resources division and another subdomain of it.xyzinc.com to represent the information technology division. This will give a clear separation of sites and content for the company department structure. This type of configuration will make it hard to share information, but I have seen these configurations help in organizing and protecting sensitive information.

To create a web application, follow the steps given here:

1. Go to the **Central Administration** site and click on **Application Management**:

Figure 6.14 – Central Administration

2. Under **Web Applications**, click on **Manage web applications**:

Figure 6.15 – Application Management

3. Click **New** in the top-left corner:

Figure 6.16 – The New button

4. Complete the form presented to configure your web application. Name your web application, `Port` and use a host header if needed:

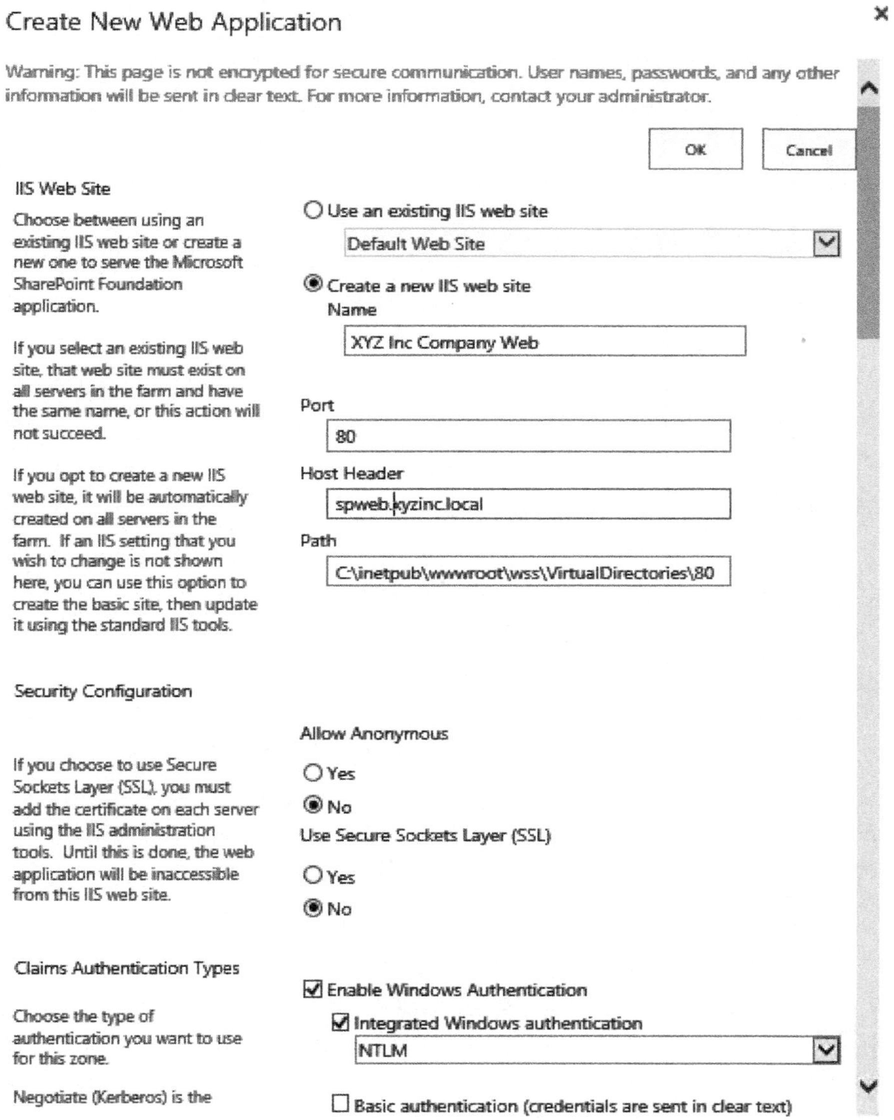

Create New Web Application   ✕

Warning: This page is not encrypted for secure communication. User names, passwords, and any other information will be sent in clear text. For more information, contact your administrator.

[OK]   [Cancel]

IIS Web Site

Choose between using an existing IIS web site or create a new one to serve the Microsoft SharePoint Foundation application.

If you select an existing IIS web site, that web site must exist on all servers in the farm and have the same name, or this action will not succeed.

If you opt to create a new IIS web site, it will be automatically created on all servers in the farm. If an IIS setting that you wish to change is not shown here, you can use this option to create the basic site, then update it using the standard IIS tools.

○ Use an existing IIS web site
   [Default Web Site   ▾]

◉ Create a new IIS web site
   Name
   [XYZ Inc Company Web]

Port
[80]

Host Header
[spweb.kyzinc.local]

Path
[C:\inetpub\wwwroot\wss\VirtualDirectories\80]

Security Configuration

If you choose to use Secure Sockets Layer (SSL), you must add the certificate on each server using the IIS administration tools. Until this is done, the web application will be inaccessible from this IIS web site.

Allow Anonymous
○ Yes
◉ No
Use Secure Sockets Layer (SSL)
○ Yes
◉ No

Claims Authentication Types

Choose the type of authentication you want to use for this zone.

Negotiate (Kerberos) is the

☑ Enable Windows Authentication
   ☑ Integrated Windows authentication
   [NTLM   ▾]

☐ Basic authentication (credentials are sent in clear text)

Figure 6.17 – Creating a new web application

5. Input the URL and choose a new application pool name. Update the service account you will use for the application pool. Input a **Database Server** name and a database name for the content database supporting the initial creation of the web application:

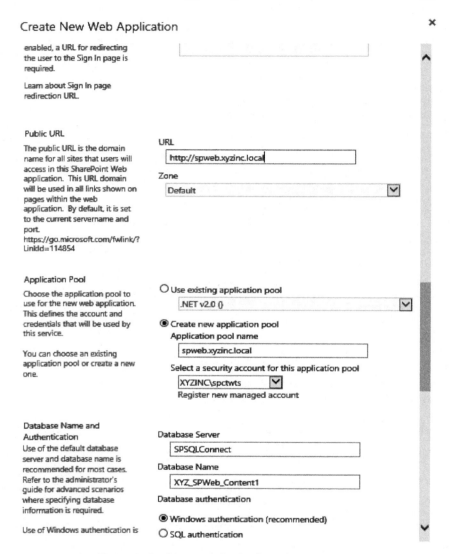

Figure 6.18 – Inputting the database server name

6. Complete this section using the values given in the following screenshot:

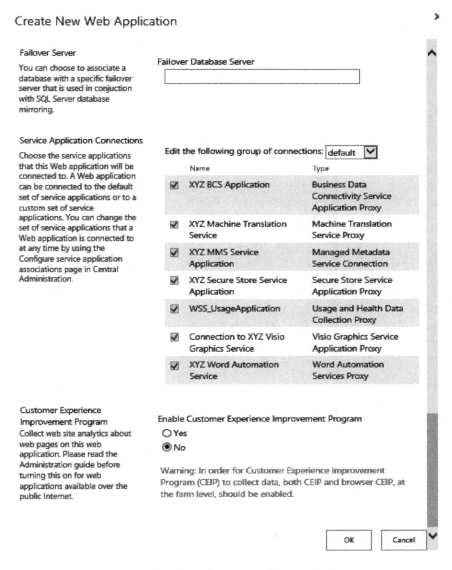

Figure 6.19 – Web application configuration values

Assigning service applications is a part of the web application. If you have separate service applications, you can create new services and assign them to the appropriate web application using Central Administration.

To create a web application using PowerShell, use the following command:

```
New-SPWebApplication -Name "XYZ Company Web Application"
-Port 80 -HostHeader spweb.xyzinc.local -URL "https://
spweb.xyzinc.local" -ApplicationPool "spweb_App_Pool"
-ApplicationPoolAccount (Get-SPManagedAccount "xyzinc\
websrvact")
```

Configuring host named site collections using PowerShell is very similar as there are few differences in the approach for this type of site hierarchy. The top-level site is a path-based site and the site collections below it are host named sites. You create those using the following PowerShell command:

```
New-SPSite 'http://portal.contoso.com'
-HostHeaderWebApplication (Get-SPWebApplication 'Contoso
Sites') -Name 'Portal' -Description 'Customer root' -OwnerAlias
'contoso\administrator' -language 1033 -Template 'STS#0'
```

There are some other configurations needed within the web application you have created. There are selections of features within the web application and within site collections that need to be set. We look at those web application features in the next section.

When you have finished creating web applications in your environment be sure to look at a load balancing strategy to support redundancy within the Web Tier. We talk about load balancers and those technologies in *Chapter 7, Finalizing the Farm to Go Live - Part II*. Also, make sure to define Site Quotas as part of your web application configurations and the site collection level to keep the size of your site collections in a best practice capacity.

Managing features

There are features that we can activate from Central Administration to turn on features related to the web application. As stated, we can separate services and features based on the need within the web application. For example, let's say video processing is not needed in the MySite web application based on company policy. Using these feature activation settings, I can make sure that that feature is deactivated at the web application level:

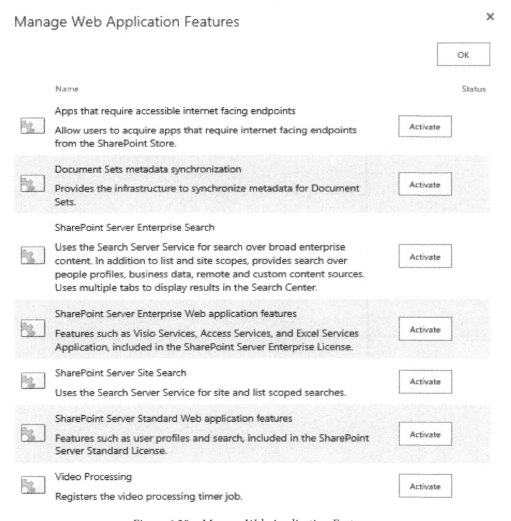

Figure 6.20 – Manage Web Application Features

This helps bring another level of feature separation to content and users for the sake of resources and company policies.

Here is how to turn on features using PowerShell:

```
Enable-SPFeature -identity "Video Processing" -URL http://
spweb.xyzinc.local
```

Knowing the features you want to be enabled on the web application level is key. As you can see, there are some choices. Make sure to choose what level of features you want based on the URL or web application. Now that we have our main web application completed, let's move on to create a MySite web application that will create a host for personal sites used by users in the farm.

Creating a MySite web application

Let's create a MySite web application. In the field, I have noticed that a lot of admins and companies do not like MySites, which is understandable. They are nothing to be afraid of however, with SharePoint 2019 Server you can also integrate OneDrive using a hybrid connected farm. This will give us a place where users can share and store documents easily from a folder based interface similar to Shared Drives with better tools as they have the rights to manage their own files even externally.

The MySite is used to give the user a way of having what I call a SharePoint desktop. They can run applications within SharePoint against their content if they like but this has to be set up as features within the farm in central administration. Yes, they need to be planned for and storage is needed for each site collection, but if planned for properly, these sites help users keep their information centralized and not on a desktop where something might not get backed up or categorized properly. At least with MySites all the data is backed up as part of the overall SharePoint backup and a user can count on having their data restored if needed. You can also control the size of these site with Site Quotas. Please make a choice to use either OneDrive or MySites as you plan out personal files storage for your user community.

Let's look at the steps to create a MySite web application:

1. Create a new web application and name it. Add a host header if needed:

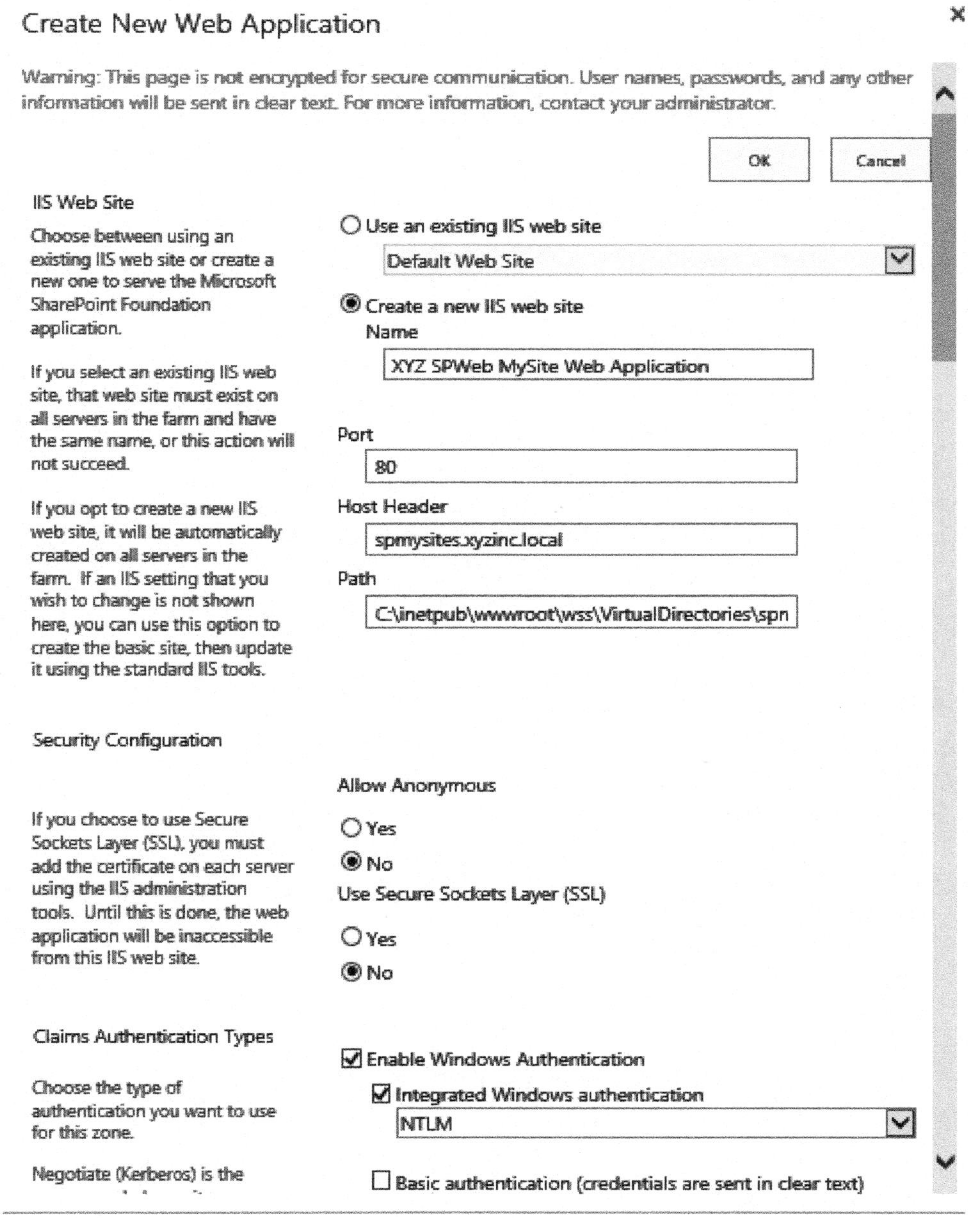

Create New Web Application

Warning: This page is not encrypted for secure communication. User names, passwords, and any other information will be sent in clear text. For more information, contact your administrator.

OK   Cancel

IIS Web Site

Choose between using an existing IIS web site or create a new one to serve the Microsoft SharePoint Foundation application.

If you select an existing IIS web site, that web site must exist on all servers in the farm and have the same name, or this action will not succeed.

If you opt to create a new IIS web site, it will be automatically created on all servers in the farm. If an IIS setting that you wish to change is not shown here, you can use this option to create the basic site, then update it using the standard IIS tools.

○ Use an existing IIS web site
    Default Web Site

◉ Create a new IIS web site
    Name
    XYZ SPWeb MySite Web Application

Port
    80

Host Header
    spmysites.xyzinc.local

Path
    C:\inetpub\wwwroot\wss\VirtualDirectories\spn

Security Configuration

If you choose to use Secure Sockets Layer (SSL), you must add the certificate on each server using the IIS administration tools. Until this is done, the web application will be inaccessible from this IIS web site.

Allow Anonymous
○ Yes
◉ No

Use Secure Sockets Layer (SSL)
○ Yes
◉ No

Claims Authentication Types

Choose the type of authentication you want to use for this zone.

Negotiate (Kerberos) is the

☑ Enable Windows Authentication
    ☑ Integrated Windows authentication
        NTLM

    ☐ Basic authentication (credentials are sent in clear text)

Figure 6.21 – Create New Web Application

2. Update the application pool and assign a service account for the web application:

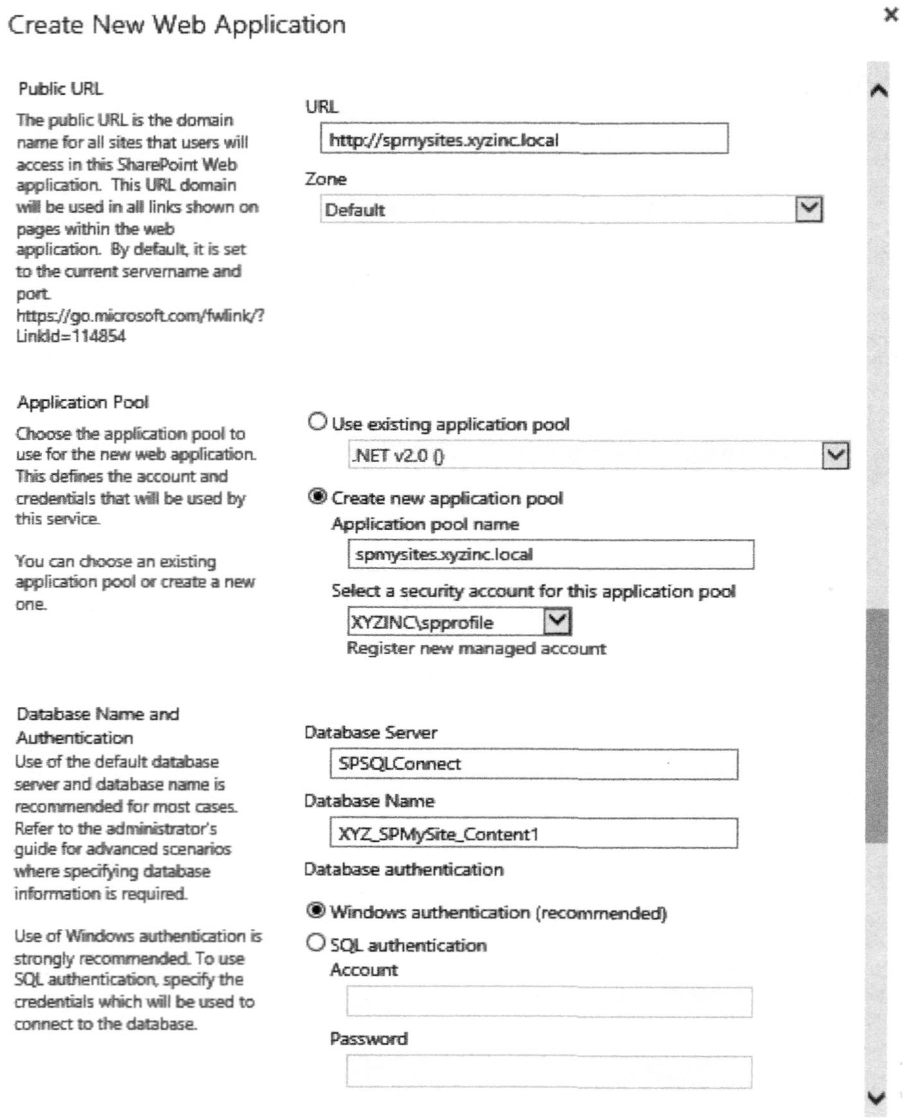

Figure 6.22 – Assign service accounts and a database name

3. Update the **Database Name** field with the name of the database that will hold the site collection. Scrolling down, you will see the next section of the form:

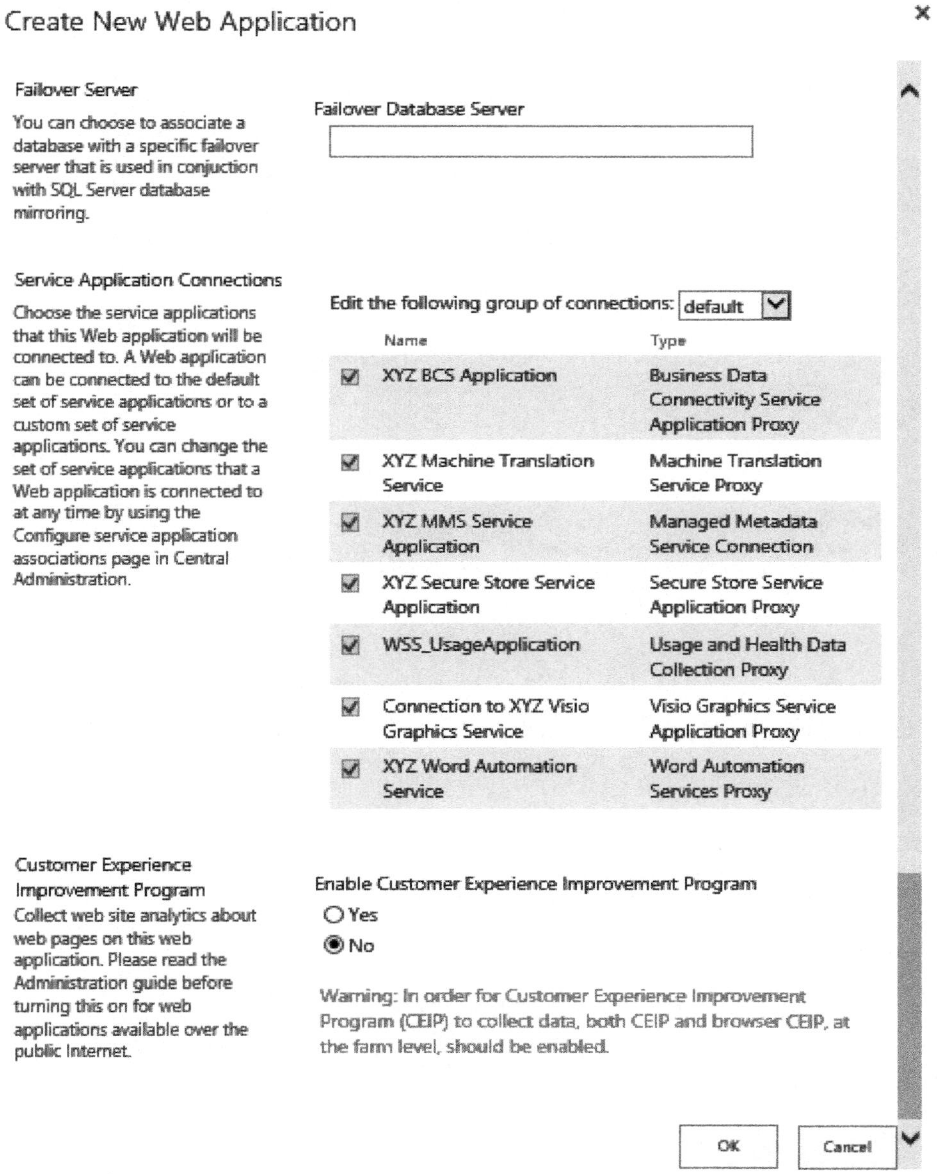

Create New Web Application   ✕

Failover Server

You can choose to associate a database with a specific failover server that is used in conjuction with SQL Server database mirroring.

Failover Database Server

Service Application Connections

Choose the service applications that this Web application will be connected to. A Web application can be connected to the default set of service applications or to a custom set of service applications. You can change the set of service applications that a Web application is connected to at any time by using the Configure service application associations page in Central Administration.

Edit the following group of connections: default ▾

Name	Type
☑ XYZ BCS Application	Business Data Connectivity Service Application Proxy
☑ XYZ Machine Translation Service	Machine Translation Service Proxy
☑ XYZ MMS Service Application	Managed Metadata Service Connection
☑ XYZ Secure Store Service Application	Secure Store Service Application Proxy
☑ WSS_UsageApplication	Usage and Health Data Collection Proxy
☑ Connection to XYZ Visio Graphics Service	Visio Graphics Service Application Proxy
☑ XYZ Word Automation Service	Word Automation Services Proxy

Customer Experience Improvement Program
Collect web site analytics about web pages on this web application. Please read the Administration guide before turning this on for web applications available over the public Internet.

Enable Customer Experience Improvement Program

◯ Yes
◉ No

Warning: In order for Customer Experience Improvement Program (CEIP) to collect data, both CEIP and browser CEIP, at the farm level, should be enabled.

OK   Cancel

Figure 6.23 – Service application connections

4. Assign service applications as part of the web application. If you have separate service applications, we will go over how to create those later in the chapter.

5. Add a default site collection under the MySite web application:

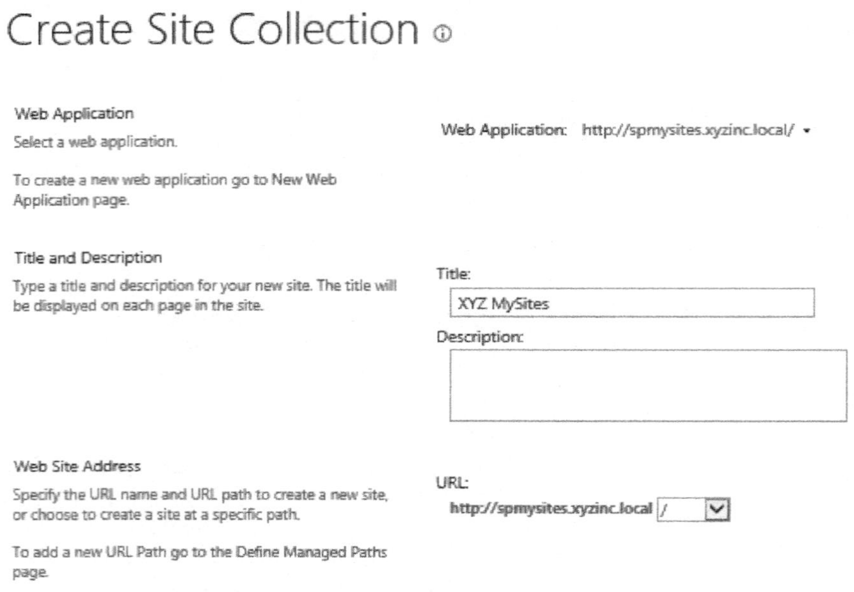

Create Site Collection ⓘ

Web Application

Select a web application.

To create a new web application go to New Web Application page.

Web Application: http://spmysites.xyzinc.local/ ▾

Title and Description

Type a title and description for your new site. The title will be displayed on each page in the site.

Title:

XYZ MySites

Description:

Web Site Address

Specify the URL name and URL path to create a new site, or choose to create a site at a specific path.

To add a new URL Path go to the Define Managed Paths page.

URL:

http://spmysites.xyzinc.local /   ▾

Figure 6.24 – Create Site Collection

6. Choose **My Site Host** as a template:

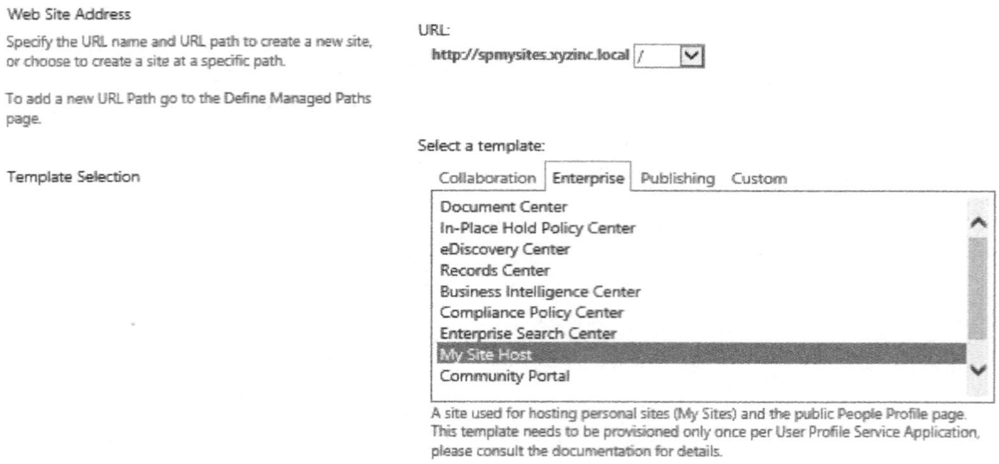

Web Site Address

Specify the URL name and URL path to create a new site, or choose to create a site at a specific path.

To add a new URL Path go to the Define Managed Paths page.

URL:

http://spmysites.xyzinc.local /   ▾

Select a template:

Template Selection

Collaboration | Enterprise | Publishing   Custom

Document Center
In-Place Hold Policy Center
eDiscovery Center
Records Center
Business Intelligence Center
Compliance Policy Center
Enterprise Search Center
My Site Host
Community Portal

A site used for hosting personal sites (My Sites) and the public People Profile page. This template needs to be provisioned only once per User Profile Service Application, please consult the documentation for details.

Figure 6.25 – The My Site Host template

7. Add primary and secondary site collection administrators:

Primary Site Collection Administrator

Specify the administrator for this site collection. Only one user login can be provided; security groups are not supported.

User name:

Secondary Site Collection Administrator

Optionally specify a secondary site collection administrator. Only one user login can be provided; security groups are not supported.

User name:

Quota Template

Select a predefined quota template to limit resources used for this site collection.

To add a new quota template, go to the Manage Quota Templates page.

Select a quota template:

No Quota

Storage limit:

Number of invited users:

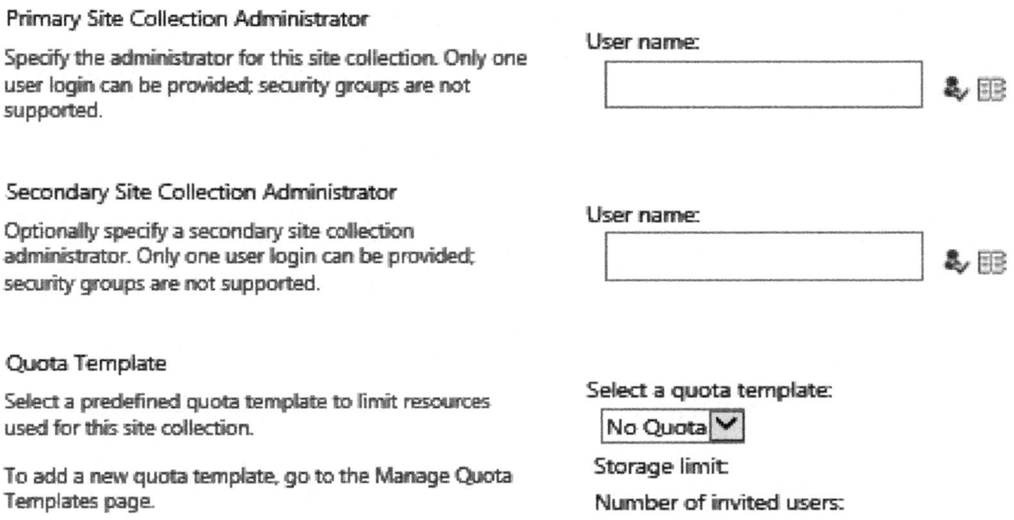

Figure 6.26 – Adding site collection administrators

8. Select a quota template for this site collection.

> **Important Note**
>
> You can create quota templates at the beginning or end of your creation of a site collection. They can be applied to web applications using the tools within Central Administration under **Application Management | Site Collection Quotas and Locks**. Again, these can be created prior to the creation of site collections so they can be applied individually as well.

9. Setting up quotas for your site collections is key to setting limits on your site collection growth. If you followed my recommendation of having individual site collections nested in content databases, then quotas will work well for you from a management perspective. Make sure to set the quotas as per Microsoft's best practices of 2-4 GB limits. If it is a record center site collection you are creating, then you can set this to be unlimited, due to the best practice being a limited number of resources accessing the data:

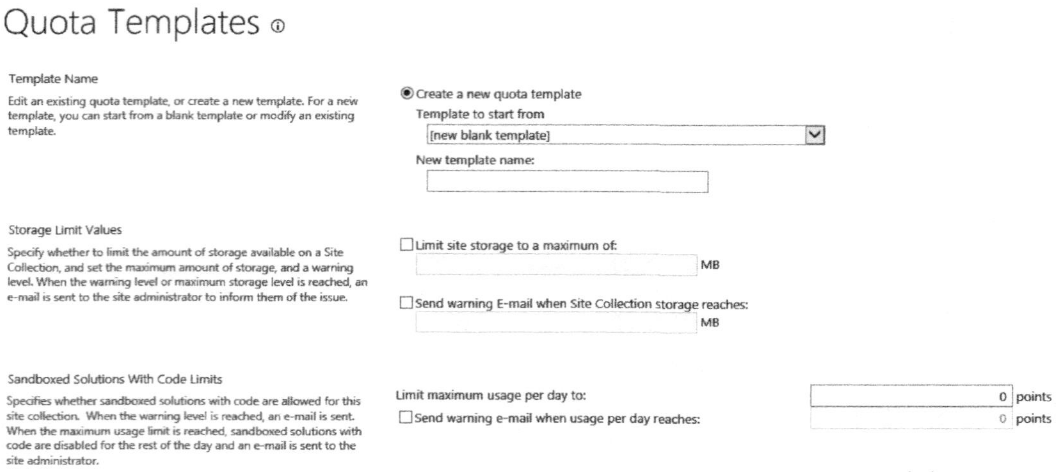

Quota Templates ⓘ

Template Name

Edit an existing quota template, or create a new template. For a new template, you can start from a blank template or modify an existing template.

◉ Create a new quota template
  Template to start from
  [new blank template]   ▾

  New template name:
  [   ]

Storage Limit Values

Specify whether to limit the amount of storage available on a Site Collection, and set the maximum amount of storage, and a warning level. When the warning level or maximum storage level is reached, an e-mail is sent to the site administrator to inform them of the issue.

☐ Limit site storage to a maximum of:
  [   ] MB

☐ Send warning E-mail when Site Collection storage reaches:
  [   ] MB

Sandboxed Solutions With Code Limits

Specifies whether sandboxed solutions with code are allowed for this site collection. When the warning level is reached, an e-mail is sent. When the maximum usage limit is reached, sandboxed solutions with code are disabled for the rest of the day and an e-mail is sent to the site administrator.

Limit maximum usage per day to:
  [0] points

☐ Send warning e-mail when usage per day reaches:
  [0] points

Figure 6.27 – Quota Templates

10. If the quota is being set for MySites, you need to understand how much storage you have available to give all your users. The same storage limits will be used for every individual MySite based on individual site collections. We need to make sure to look at the number of users and the size of the site collections you are allowing them to create.

11. MySites are handled differently once they are created. For example, if you created four content databases and created site collections using the MySite site collection template within those content databases, the sites would load balance themselves over the four databases you created. This makes separates the content well, meaning good performance for those databases.

If you need to do some creation based on departments or other criteria, you need to create these site collections by using PowerShell or by taking the database offline in the SharePoint Content Database utility. This will allow you to place the site collections in the databases you want.

> **Important Note**
>
> MySites should have a set quota due to situations where users may use a MySite to keep all their files. By setting a limit, users will understand how much storage space they have and will only keep relevant files in SharePoint and not keep every file on their desktop in the MySite. Quotas can be set for different types of site collections using the **Application Management** menu in Central Administration.

Quotas are very helpful for identifying the growth of content and creating plans around data size. This also helps when you have those plans identified and made into quota templates so that you can apply them quickly and easily.

Now let's look at self-service policies and how they work in the farm:

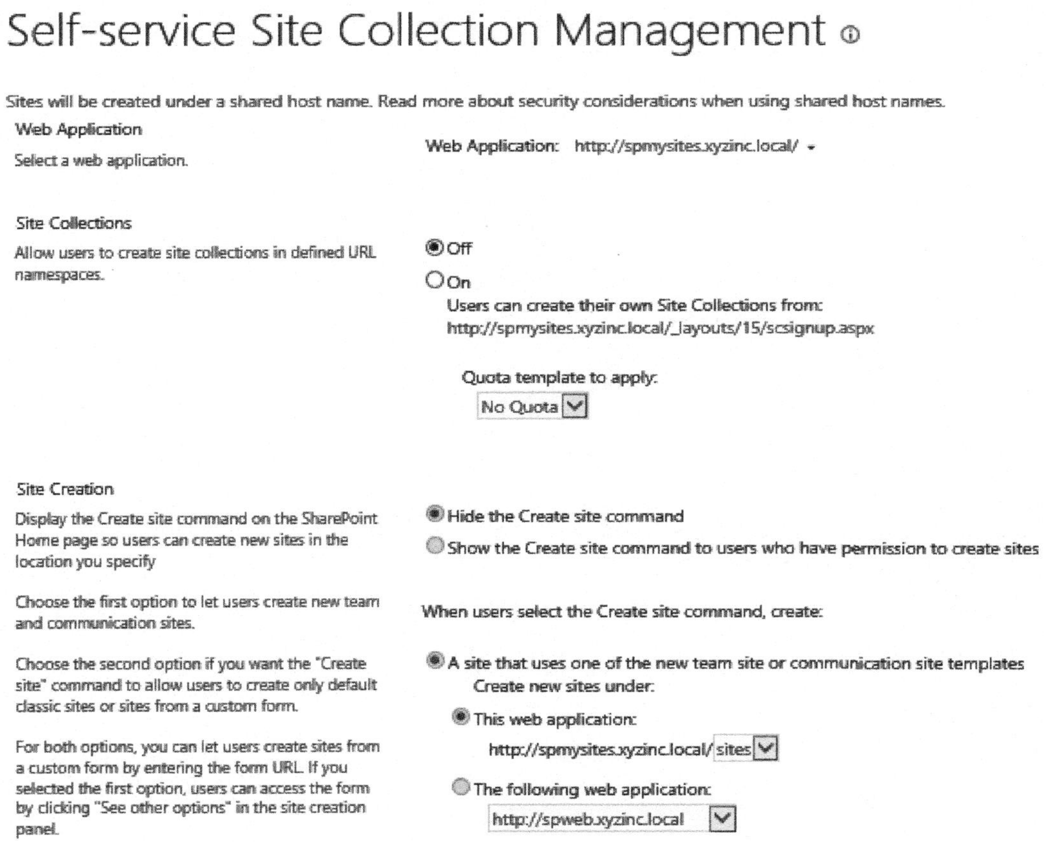

Self-service Site Collection Management ⓘ

Sites will be created under a shared host name. Read more about security considerations when using shared host names.

Web Application
Select a web application.

Web Application: http://spmysites.xyzinc.local/ ▾

Site Collections
Allow users to create site collections in defined URL namespaces.

◉ Off
○ On
Users can create their own Site Collections from:
http://spmysites.xyzinc.local/_layouts/15/scsignup.aspx

Quota template to apply:
No Quota ▾

Site Creation
Display the Create site command on the SharePoint Home page so users can create new sites in the location you specify

Choose the first option to let users create new team and communication sites.

Choose the second option if you want the "Create site" command to allow users to create only default classic sites or sites from a custom form.

For both options, you can let users create sites from a custom form by entering the form URL. If you selected the first option, users can access the form by clicking "See other options" in the site creation panel.

◉ Hide the Create site command
○ Show the Create site command to users who have permission to create sites

When users select the Create site command, create:

◉ A site that uses one of the new team site or communication site templates
Create new sites under:

◉ This web application:
http://spmysites.xyzinc.local/ sites ▾

○ The following web application:
http://spweb.xyzinc.local ▾

Figure 6.28 –Self-service Site Collection Management

Here is how you enable self-site creation using PowerShell:

```
$w = Get-SPWebApplication http://spweb.xyzinc.local
$w.SelfServiceSiteCreationEnabled =$True $w.Update()
```

Setting the self-service site to **On** for MySites means that users will be able to create their own MySite from the SharePoint site. This only happens once, but this setting gives them that ability. We can also set it to **Off** and not have them create a site. This is where I see admins getting scared, but you do not have to use MySites in SharePoint; things only need to be configured so that the searching of profiles works in the environment.

Now that we have finished with the MySites web application settings, let's go back and finish up our User Profile service and MySites configuration using the following form:

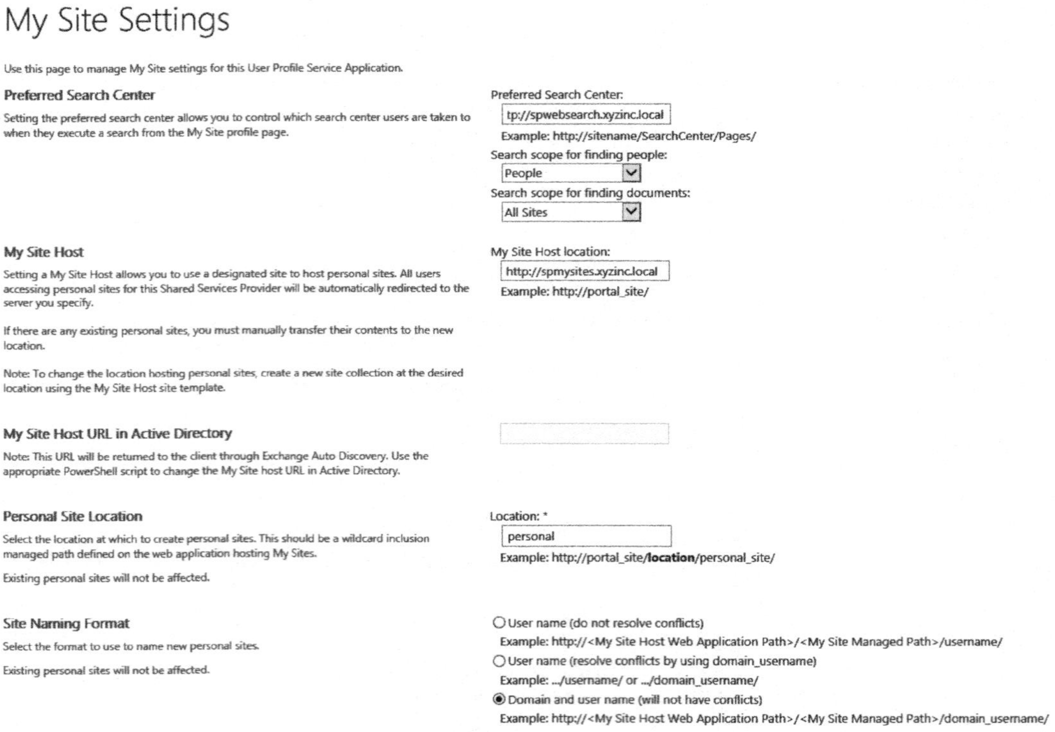

My Site Settings

Use this page to manage My Site settings for this User Profile Service Application.

Preferred Search Center

Setting the preferred search center allows you to control which search center users are taken to when they execute a search from the My Site profile page.

Preferred Search Center:

tp://spwebsearch.xyzinc.local

Example: http://sitename/SearchCenter/Pages/

Search scope for finding people:

People

Search scope for finding documents:

All Sites

My Site Host

Setting a My Site Host allows you to use a designated site to host personal sites. All users accessing personal sites for this Shared Services Provider will be automatically redirected to the server you specify.

If there are any existing personal sites, you must manually transfer their contents to the new location.

Note: To change the location hosting personal sites, create a new site collection at the desired location using the My Site Host site template.

My Site Host location:

http://spmysites.xyzinc.local

Example: http://portal_site/

My Site Host URL in Active Directory

Note: This URL will be returned to the client through Exchange Auto Discovery. Use the appropriate PowerShell script to change the My Site host URL in Active Directory.

Personal Site Location

Select the location at which to create personal sites. This should be a wildcard inclusion managed path defined on the web application hosting My Sites.

Existing personal sites will not be affected.

Location: *

personal

Example: http://portal_site/**location**/personal_site/

Site Naming Format

Select the format to use to name new personal sites.

Existing personal sites will not be affected.

○ User name (do not resolve conflicts)
  Example: http://<My Site Host Web Application Path>/<My Site Managed Path>/username/
○ User name (resolve conflicts by using domain_username)
  Example: .../username/ or .../domain_username/
◉ Domain and user name (will not have conflicts)
  Example: http://<My Site Host Web Application Path>/<My Site Managed Path>/domain_username/

Figure 6.29 – My Site Settings

The form continues:

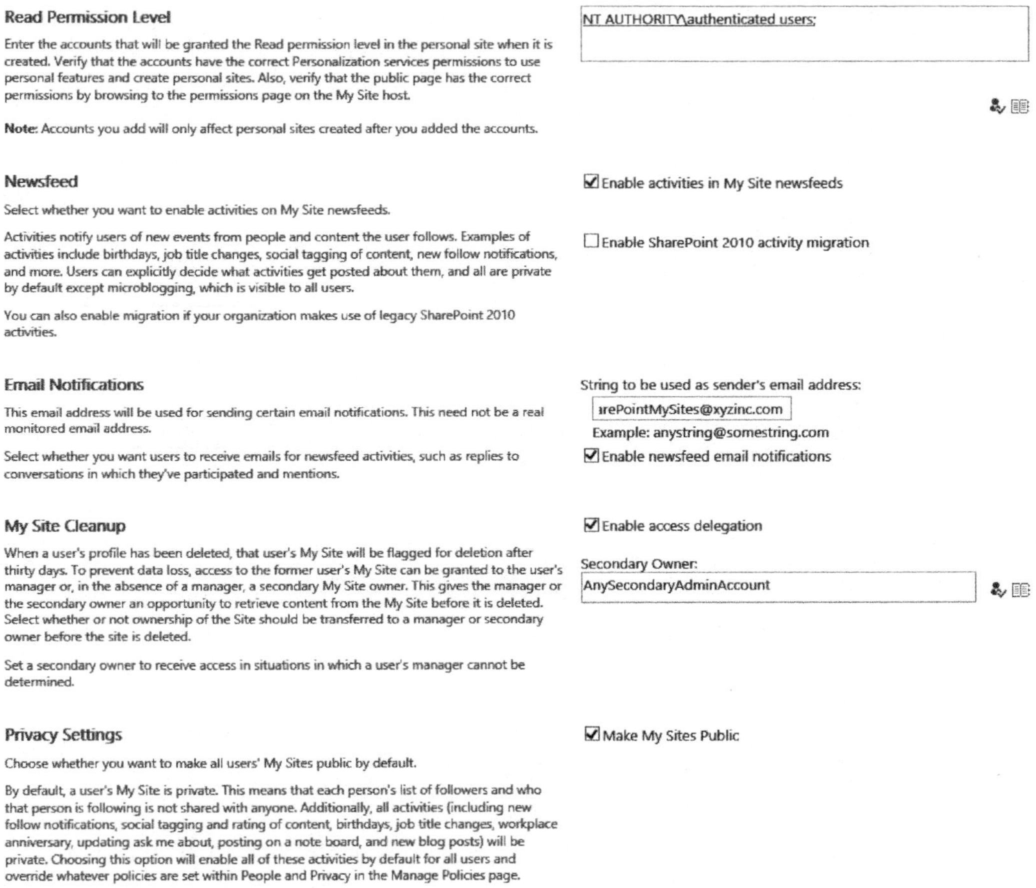

Read Permission Level

Enter the accounts that will be granted the Read permission level in the personal site when it is created. Verify that the accounts have the correct Personalization services permissions to use personal features and create personal sites. Also, verify that the public page has the correct permissions by browsing to the permissions page on the My Site host.

Note: Accounts you add will only affect personal sites created after you added the accounts.

> NT AUTHORITY\authenticated users;

Newsfeed

Select whether you want to enable activities on My Site newsfeeds.

Activities notify users of new events from people and content the user follows. Examples of activities include birthdays, job title changes, social tagging of content, new follow notifications, and more. Users can explicitly decide what activities get posted about them, and all are private by default except microblogging, which is visible to all users.

You can also enable migration if your organization makes use of legacy SharePoint 2010 activities.

> ☑ Enable activities in My Site newsfeeds
>
> ☐ Enable SharePoint 2010 activity migration

Email Notifications

This email address will be used for sending certain email notifications. This need not be a real monitored email address.

Select whether you want users to receive emails for newsfeed activities, such as replies to conversations in which they've participated and mentions.

> String to be used as sender's email address:
>
> | arePointMySites@xyzinc.com |
>
> Example: anystring@somestring.com
>
> ☑ Enable newsfeed email notifications

My Site Cleanup

When a user's profile has been deleted, that user's My Site will be flagged for deletion after thirty days. To prevent data loss, access to the former user's My Site can be granted to the user's manager or, in the absence of a manager, a secondary My Site owner. This gives the manager or the secondary owner an opportunity to retrieve content from the My Site before it is deleted. Select whether or not ownership of the Site should be transferred to a manager or secondary owner before the site is deleted.

Set a secondary owner to receive access in situations in which a user's manager cannot be determined.

> ☑ Enable access delegation
>
> Secondary Owner:
>
> | AnySecondaryAdminAccount |

Privacy Settings

Choose whether you want to make all users' My Sites public by default.

By default, a user's My Site is private. This means that each person's list of followers and who that person is following is not shared with anyone. Additionally, all activities (including new follow notifications, social tagging and rating of content, birthdays, job title changes, workplace anniversary, updating ask me about, posting on a note board, and new blog posts) will be private. Choosing this option will enable all of these activities by default for all users and override whatever policies are set within People and Privacy in the Manage Policies page.

> ☑ Make My Sites Public

Figure 6.30 – My Site Settings (continued)

Input the information according to your requirements to finalize the MySite configuration, then click **OK**.

Now let's configure our managed paths, if there are any you need to configure as part of your web application. You can look at your old farm to make sure you understand how these paths need to be in place during migration processes so that the paths present in your prior environment match up with the content you are migrating:

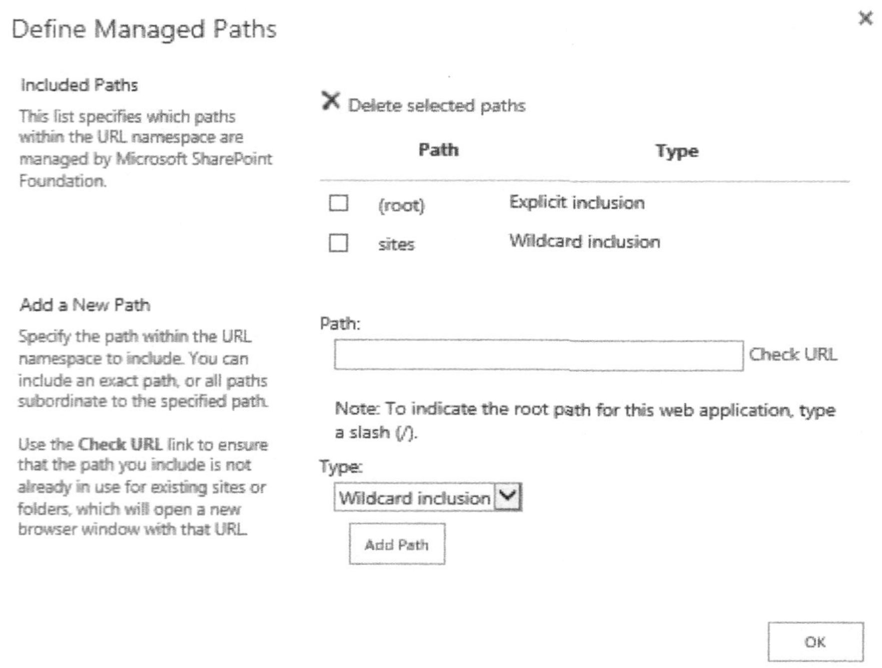

Define Managed Paths   ✕

Included Paths

This list specifies which paths within the URL namespace are managed by Microsoft SharePoint Foundation.

✗ Delete selected paths

	Path	Type
☐	(root)	Explicit inclusion
☐	sites	Wildcard inclusion

Add a New Path

Specify the path within the URL namespace to include. You can include an exact path, or all paths subordinate to the specified path.

Use the **Check URL** link to ensure that the path you include is not already in use for existing sites or folders, which will open a new browser window with that URL.

Path:

[   ] Check URL

Note: To indicate the root path for this web application, type a slash (/).

Type:

[Wildcard inclusion ▼]

[Add Path]

[OK]

Figure 6.31 – Define Managed Paths

Managed paths are paths set when you have areas of a web application that you want to set as a standard path within the URL. So, with MySite, you will want to set the path as **/personal**, or whatever it is that is also in the configuration for MySite. This path is assigned to all MySites within the farm, so the users understand where they are within the web application. It's hardcoded upon creation and will not change, and this means that no mistakes happen when we know where a site collection can be created for MySites outside of this hard-coded path.

This is how you create a managed path using PowerShell:

```
New-SPManagedPath -RelativeUrl "HR" -WebApplication http://
spweb.xyzinc.local
```

```
$wa = Get-SPWebApplication http://spweb.xyzinc.local
$wa.SelfServiceSiteCreationEnabled = $true
$wa.Update()
```

Your web applications should be all set now:

Name	URL	Port
SharePoint Central Administration v4	http://sp2019-app1:29292/	29292
XYZ SPWeb MySite Web Application	http://spmysites.xyzinc.local/	80
XYZ SPWeb Search Web Application	http://spsearch.xyzinc.local/	80
XYZ Company Web Application	http://spweb.xyzinc.local/	80

Figure 6.32 – Web applications

Finally, we need to move our `BlobCache` location within our web application's `default.aspx` pages. This is to make sure that `BlobCache` does not get collected on the C drive where your OS lives. You can do this for all web applications configured to use **Remote Blob Storage** (**RBS**). To do that, follow these instructions (before this, make a copy of the file for safekeeping):

1. Find your `BlobCache` location. In my case, this is `E:\SPLogs\BlobCache`:

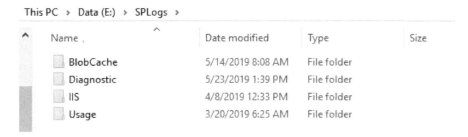

Figure 6.33 – BlobCache

2. Find `inetpub`, which is where your websites for SharePoint are running, and find the site you are looking for. Open the `wwwroot` folder:

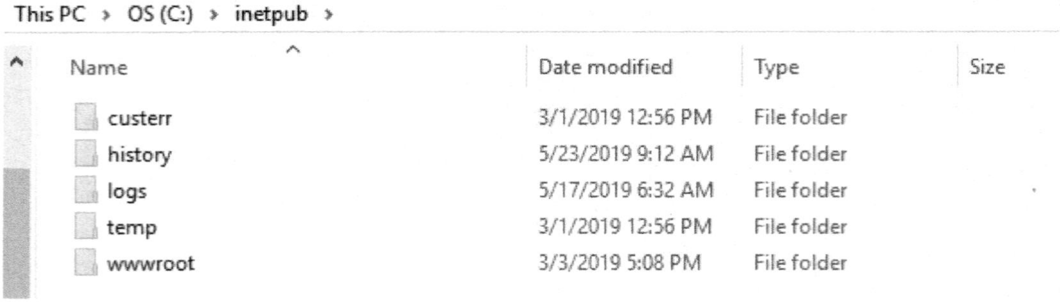

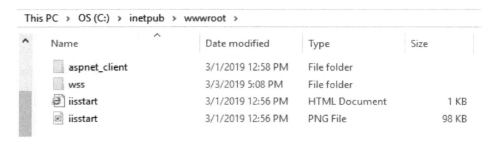

Figure 6.34 – The wwwroot folder

3. Open the `wss` folder:

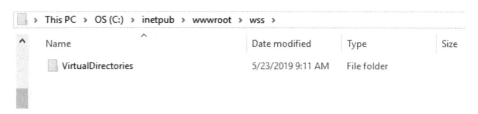

Figure 6.35 – The wss folder

4. Open the `VirtualDirectories` folder:

This PC › OS (C:) › inetpub › wwwroot › wss ›

Name	Date modified	Type	Size
VirtualDirectories	5/23/2019 9:11 AM	File folder	

Figure 6.36 – The virtual directories folder

5. Open the folder where your website is located, which in my case is `spweb.xyzinc.local80`:

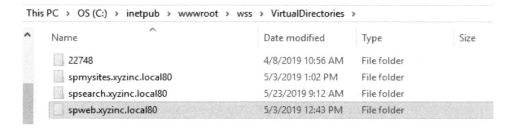

Figure 6.37 – The website location folder

6.   Choose `web.config` and right-click to open and select **Open with**:

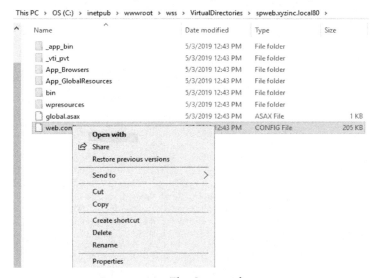

Figure 6.38 – The Open with option

7.   Choose **Notepad**:

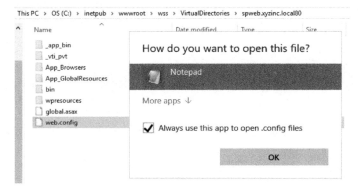

Figure 6.39 – Opening with Notepad

8. Click **Find** and `BlobCache`:

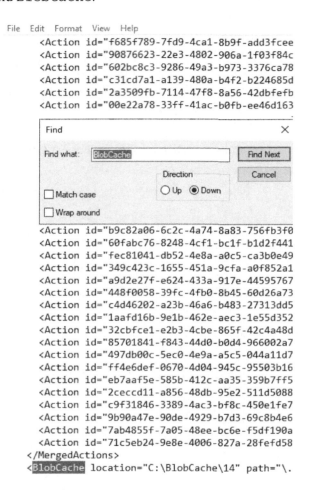

Figure 6.40 – Finding BlobCache

9. Edit the location and click **Save** :

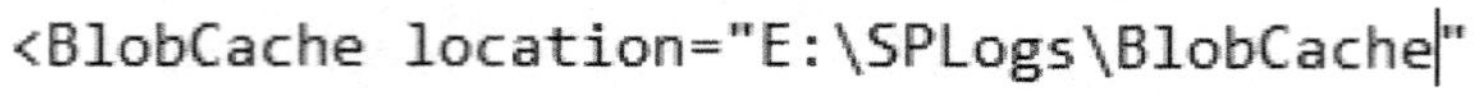

```
<BlobCache location="E:\SPLogs\BlobCache"
```

Figure 6.41 – BlobCache location

All done! This must be completed for every server and every web application
`web.config`!

Web Application General Settings

Each web application has a configuration for features and other areas to set the expectations of the content captured in the web application. Each web application has an area called **Web Application General Settings**. Let's look at the settings for the site collection configuration:

1. Set the time zone for the web application and other parameters:

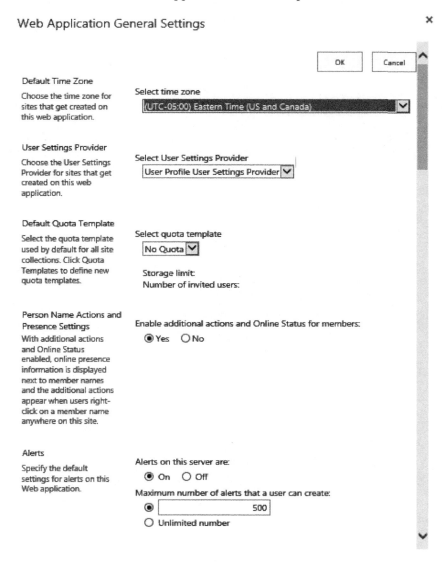

Figure 6.42 – Web Application General Settings

The user settings provider is the setting for the configured User Profile service provider, where you can have one or more User Profile service applications in your environment. This gives you an option to choose.

2. Please set **Browser File Handling** to what you believe it needs to be in your environment. I have mostly used **Permissive** settings as this opens files within document libraries and does not download files to the desktop:

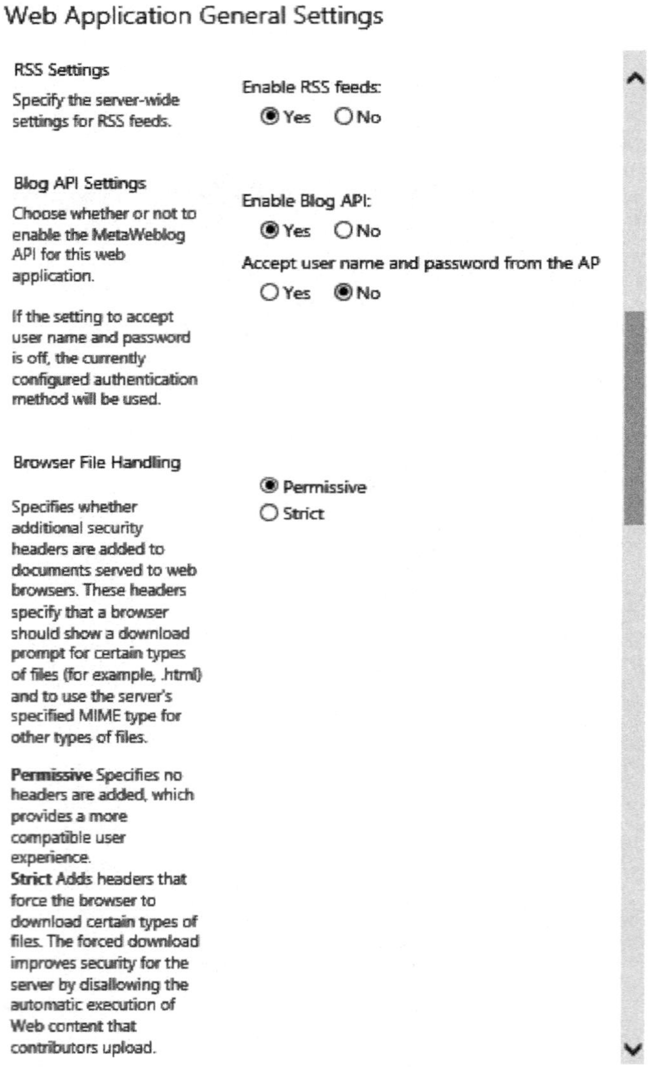

Web Application General Settings

RSS Settings

Specify the server-wide settings for RSS feeds.

Enable RSS feeds:
◉ Yes   ○ No

Blog API Settings

Choose whether or not to enable the MetaWeblog API for this web application.

If the setting to accept user name and password is off, the currently configured authentication method will be used.

Enable Blog API:
◉ Yes   ○ No

Accept user name and password from the AP
○ Yes   ◉ No

Browser File Handling

Specifies whether additional security headers are added to documents served to web browsers. These headers specify that a browser should show a download prompt for certain types of files (for example, .html) and to use the server's specified MIME type for other types of files.

Permissive Specifies no headers are added, which provides a more compatible user experience.
Strict Adds headers that force the browser to download certain types of files. The forced download improves security for the server by disallowing the automatic execution of Web content that contributors upload.

◉ Permissive
○ Strict

Figure 6.43 –Browser File Handling

3. Choose the options carefully:

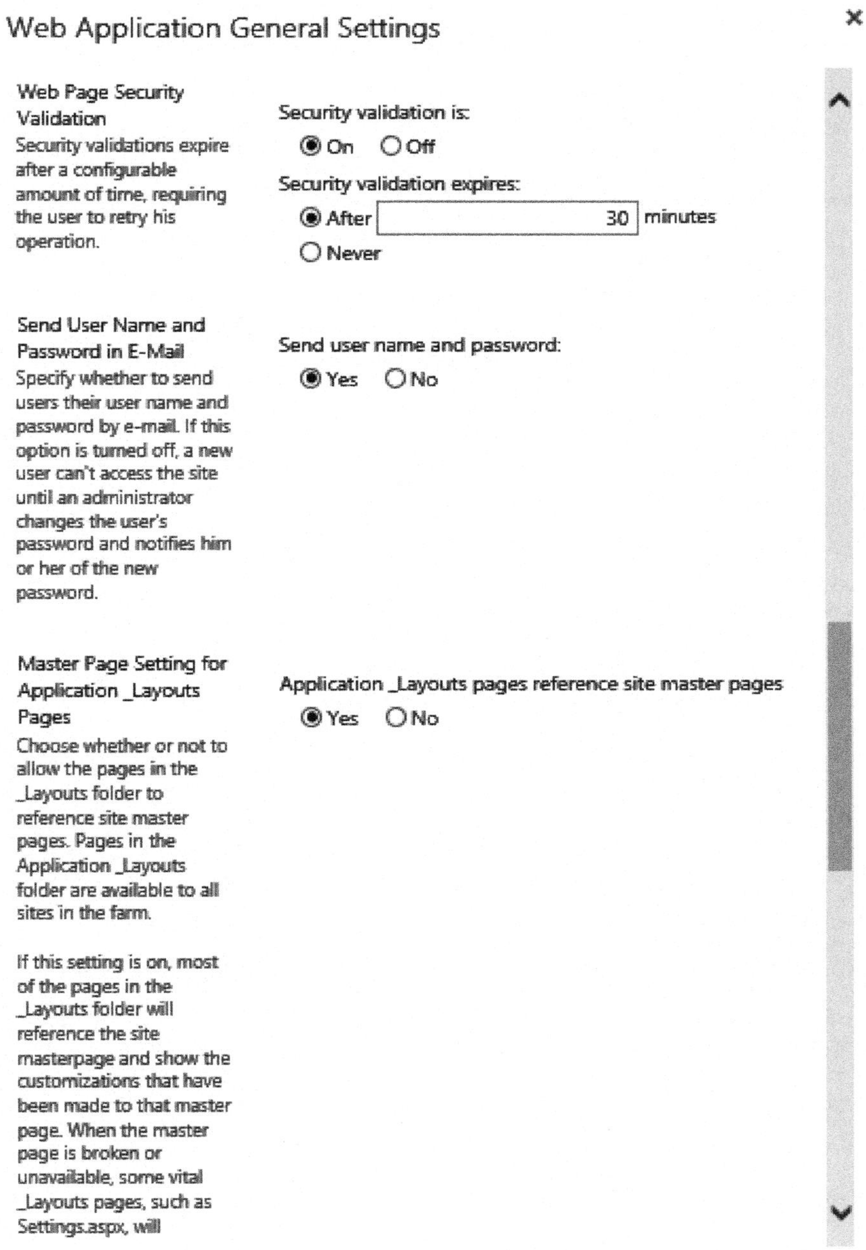

Web Application General Settings   ✕

Web Page Security Validation
Security validations expire after a configurable amount of time, requiring the user to retry his operation.

Security validation is:
◉ On   ○ Off
Security validation expires:
◉ After [30] minutes
○ Never

Send User Name and Password in E-Mail
Specify whether to send users their user name and password by e-mail. If this option is turned off, a new user can't access the site until an administrator changes the user's password and notifies him or her of the new password.

Send user name and password:
◉ Yes   ○ No

Master Page Setting for Application _Layouts Pages
Choose whether or not to allow the pages in the _Layouts folder to reference site master pages. Pages in the Application _Layouts folder are available to all sites in the farm.

Application _Layouts pages reference site master pages
◉ Yes   ○ No

If this setting is on, most of the pages in the _Layouts folder will reference the site masterpage and show the customizations that have been made to that master page. When the master page is broken or unavailable, some vital _Layouts pages, such as Settings.aspx, will

Figure 6.44 – Web Application General Settings

4. Notice the default maximum upload size has changed. Make a change if necessary:

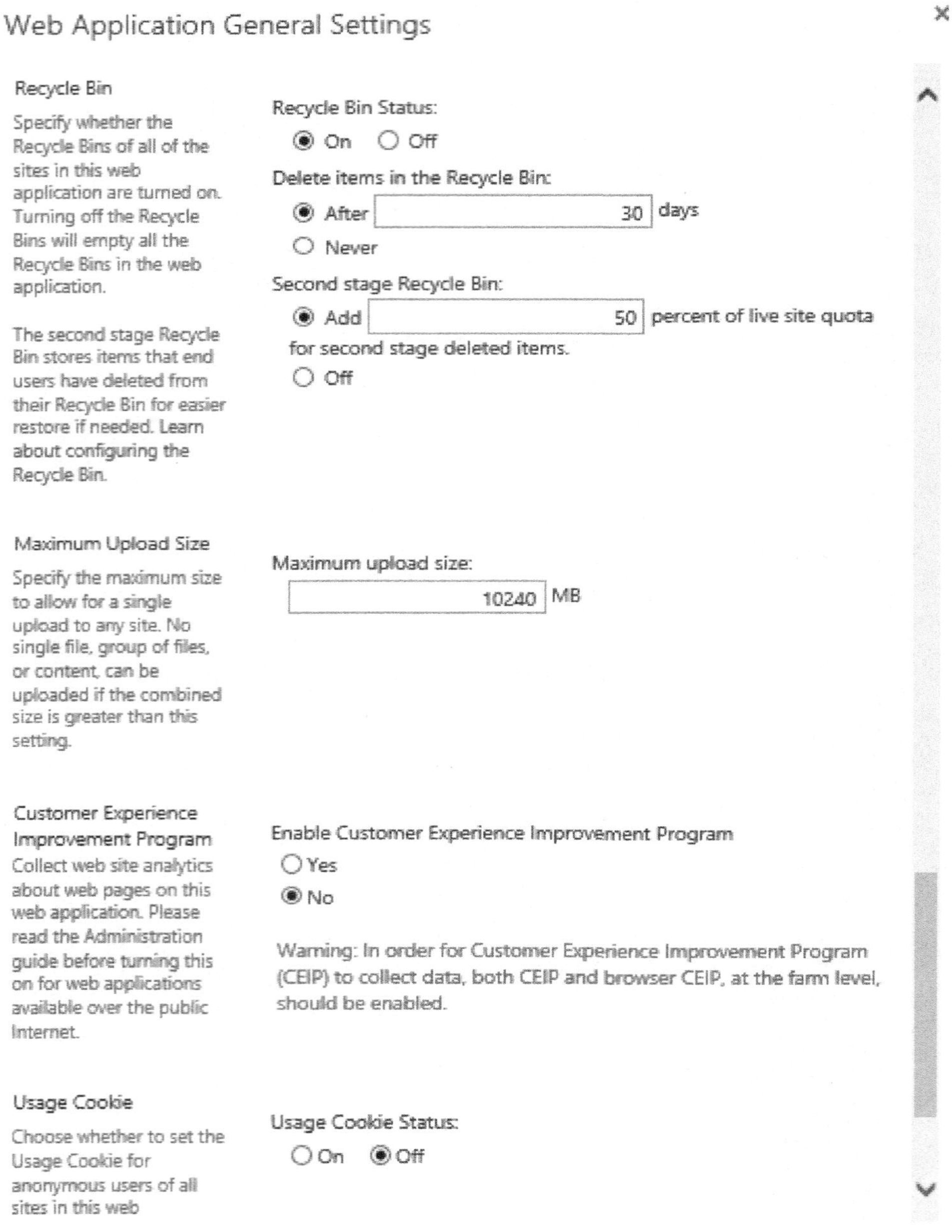

Web Application General Settings   ✕

Recycle Bin

Specify whether the
Recycle Bins of all of the
sites in this web
application are turned on.
Turning off the Recycle
Bins will empty all the
Recycle Bins in the web
application.

The second stage Recycle
Bin stores items that end
users have deleted from
their Recycle Bin for easier
restore if needed. Learn
about configuring the
Recycle Bin.

Recycle Bin Status:

◉ On   ○ Off

Delete items in the Recycle Bin:

◉ After [30] days
○ Never

Second stage Recycle Bin:

◉ Add [50] percent of live site quota
for second stage deleted items.
○ Off

Maximum Upload Size

Specify the maximum size
to allow for a single
upload to any site. No
single file, group of files,
or content, can be
uploaded if the combined
size is greater than this
setting.

Maximum upload size:

[10240] MB

**Customer Experience
Improvement Program**
Collect web site analytics
about web pages on this
web application. Please
read the Administration
guide before turning this
on for web applications
available over the public
Internet.

Enable Customer Experience Improvement Program

○ Yes
◉ No

Warning: In order for Customer Experience Improvement Program
(CEIP) to collect data, both CEIP and browser CEIP, at the farm level,
should be enabled.

Usage Cookie

Choose whether to set the
Usage Cookie for
anonymous users of all
sites in this web

Usage Cookie Status:

○ On   ◉ Off

Figure 6.45 – Recycle bin, maximum upload size, and cookie settings

> **Important Note**
>
> Remember that you only have a certain amount of storage designated for this environment. Set the document upload size to a setting you know you can handle as the documents really add up at these larger sizes. Also, remember that Shredded Storage is used as well to make sure that documents are not duplicated and the subset that was changed is captured in versioning.

5. The following is the PowerShell example for setting parameters within the general settings of a web application:

```
$siteURL = "http://spweb.xyzinc.local" | $webApp =
Get-SPWebApplication $siteURL
```

```
$webApp.BrowserFileHandling = [Microsoft.SharePoint.
SPBrowserFileHandling]::Permissive
```

There are many other parameters for this command using $webapp and the related area of focus to set parameters. The parameters for this command can be found on GitHub.

Zones

When setting up web applications in SharePoint, we have a couple of things to think about. One of them is zoning. Zoning helps us to define web application access from different URLs. Adding a URL to a zone gives the users in that zone a way to access the same content as the default zone but from another URL; for example, hr.xyzinc. local could be accessed through our internet zone using hr.xyzinc.com. Separate access pipelines could be used from a router or an ISA server perspective to have users access a site through a certain URL. This method also creates a separate IIS site as well, so you can configure the site as you would any individual site in IIS.

The different zones available to create these access points are as follows:

- Default
- Intranet
- Internet
- Extranet
- Custom

Use the zones within the configuration to determine what the URL for the alternate access mapping is being used for. This helps users to understand why URLs were created and also to put URLs in some type of category.

Alternate access mappings

Alternate access mappings also relate to zones and can be set up within SharePoint as a separate link to the content using a separate URL. This gives you many access URL points to the same content that can be supported by different zones in SharePoint.

The following figure shows the alternate access mapping that was created for the Central Administration site. The alternate access mapping URL is `http:ca.xyzinc.local:`

Alternate Access Mappings

Internal URL	Zone	Public URL for Zone
http://sp2019-app1:29292	Default	http://sp2019-app1:29292
http://ca.xyzinc.local	Intranet	http://ca.xyzinc.local

Figure 6.46 – Alternate Access Mappings

To set the alternate access mapping using PowerShell, use the following command:

```
Set-SPAlternateURL -Identity http://spweb.xyzinc.local -Zone
"Internet"
```

There is another method you can use to create separate URLs, which is using extended web applications. Let's look at that method in the next section.

Extending a web application

When using the extended web application feature, we are basically creating a new IIS website that directs users to the same content that we are extending in a default zone web application. So, in short, we are duplicating the site with a new zone and URL. This extended site can be configured with a separate IP address in IIS as well because a new site is created within IIS that is separate from the default site. This is powerful because we are given the ability to have separate bindings related to this extended site in IIS. This also helps as an example for you to separate external traffic to a given site and even where this site resides on server resources. Pointing external traffic to that site, for example, it would be easy to direct traffic from external sources to this URL at that point.

The following figure shows how this would look. Two IIS websites are using the same content database:

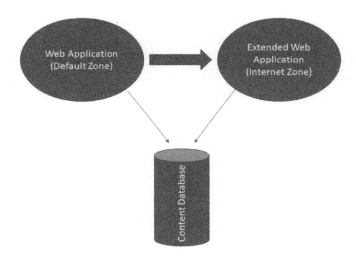

Figure 6.47 – A diagram of two web applications using the same content database

Let's look at the steps:

1. Create your extended web application and name it:

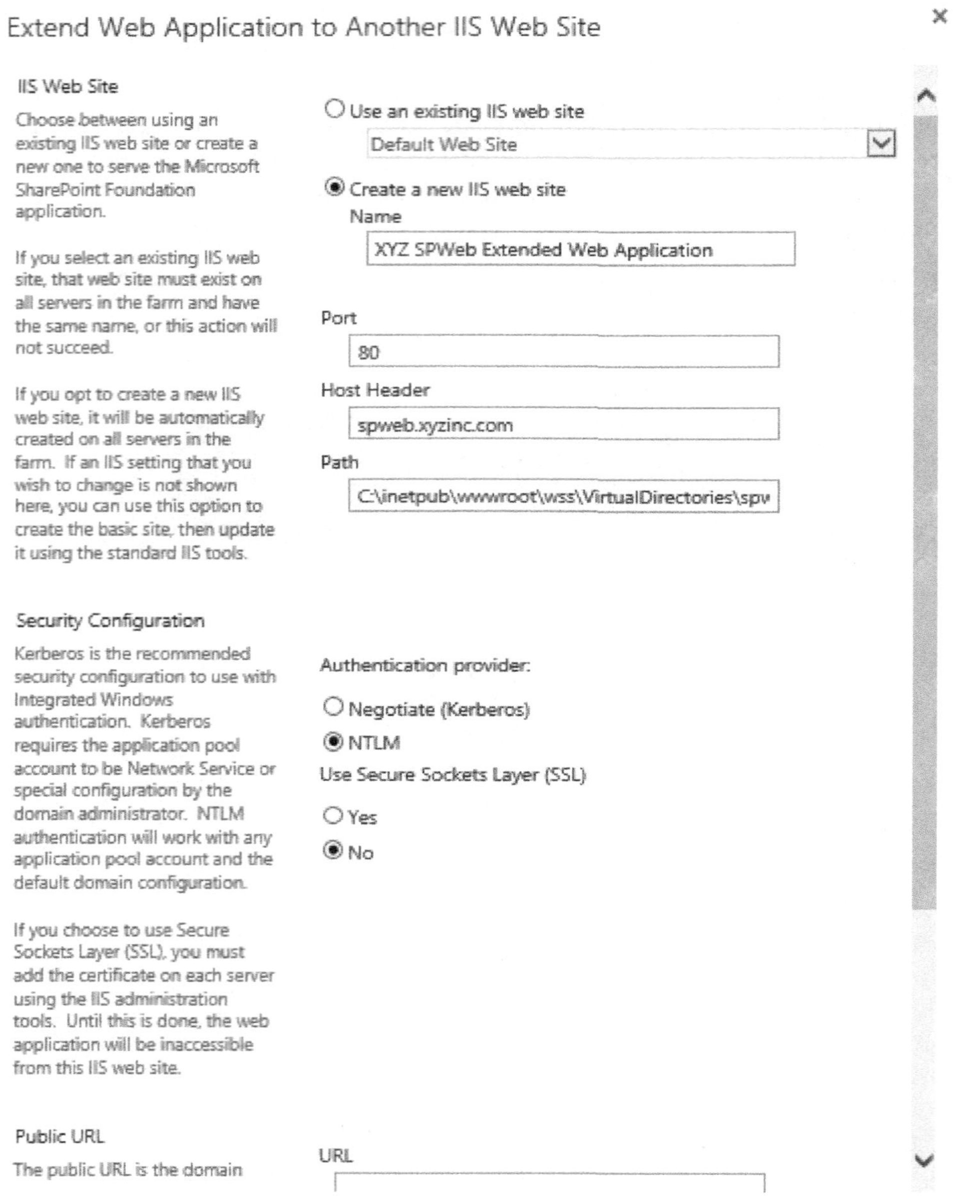

Extend Web Application to Another IIS Web Site   ×

IIS Web Site

Choose between using an existing IIS web site or create a new one to serve the Microsoft SharePoint Foundation application.

If you select an existing IIS web site, that web site must exist on all servers in the farm and have the same name, or this action will not succeed.

If you opt to create a new IIS web site, it will be automatically created on all servers in the farm. If an IIS setting that you wish to change is not shown here, you can use this option to create the basic site, then update it using the standard IIS tools.

○ Use an existing IIS web site

Default Web Site   ⌄

● Create a new IIS web site
Name

XYZ SPWeb Extended Web Application

Port

80

Host Header

spweb.xyzinc.com

Path

C:\inetpub\wwwroot\wss\VirtualDirectories\spv

Security Configuration

Kerberos is the recommended security configuration to use with Integrated Windows authentication. Kerberos requires the application pool account to be Network Service or special configuration by the domain administrator. NTLM authentication will work with any application pool account and the default domain configuration.

If you choose to use Secure Sockets Layer (SSL), you must add the certificate on each server using the IIS administration tools. Until this is done, the web application will be inaccessible from this IIS web site.

Authentication provider:

○ Negotiate (Kerberos)
● NTLM

Use Secure Sockets Layer (SSL)

○ Yes
● No

Public URL

The public URL is the domain

URL

Figure 6.48 – Extend Web Application to Another IIS Web Site

2. Choose your authentication method and the zone that this extended web application should belong to:

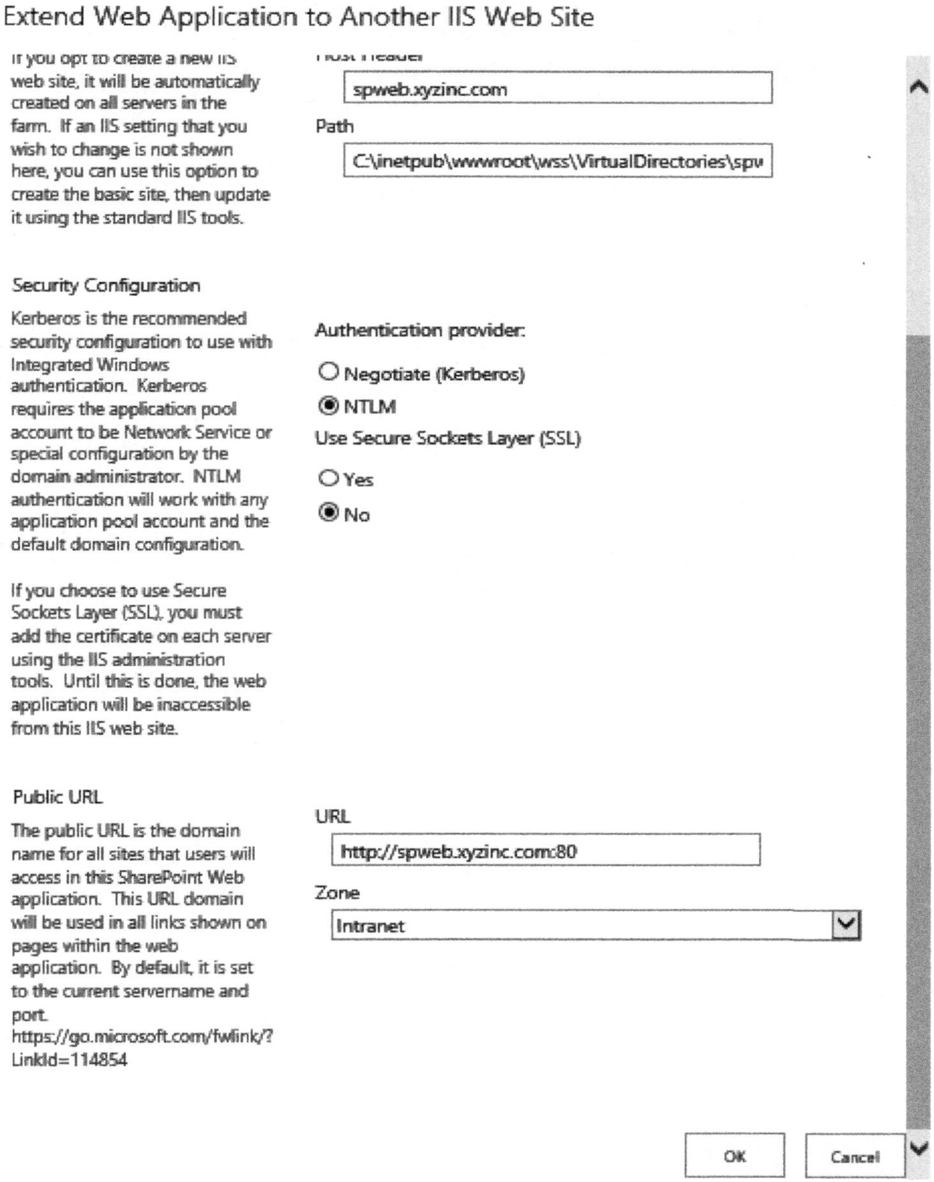

Extend Web Application to Another IIS Web Site

If you opt to create a new IIS web site, it will be automatically created on all servers in the farm. If an IIS setting that you wish to change is not shown here, you can use this option to create the basic site, then update it using the standard IIS tools.

Host Header

spweb.xyzinc.com

Path

C:\inetpub\wwwroot\wss\VirtualDirectories\spv

Security Configuration

Kerberos is the recommended security configuration to use with Integrated Windows authentication. Kerberos requires the application pool account to be Network Service or special configuration by the domain administrator. NTLM authentication will work with any application pool account and the default domain configuration.

If you choose to use Secure Sockets Layer (SSL), you must add the certificate on each server using the IIS administration tools. Until this is done, the web application will be inaccessible from this IIS web site.

Authentication provider:

○ Negotiate (Kerberos)
◉ NTLM

Use Secure Sockets Layer (SSL)

○ Yes
◉ No

Public URL

The public URL is the domain name for all sites that users will access in this SharePoint Web application. This URL domain will be used in all links shown on pages within the web application. By default, it is set to the current servername and port.
https://go.microsoft.com/fwlink/?LinkId=114854

URL

http://spweb.xyzinc.com:80

Zone

Intranet

OK   Cancel

Figure 6.49 – Choose an authentication method

3. To create an extended web application using PowerShell, use the following command:

```
Get-SPWebApplication -Identity https://spweb.xyzinc.com
 | New-SPWebApplicationExtension -Name XYZ SPWeb External
Web Application -HostHeader spwebexternal.xyzinc.com
-Zone Internet -URL https://spwebexternal.xyzinc.com
-Port 443 -AuthenticationProvider NTLM
```

Now that we have finished configuring the web application, let's learn about service associations, which we discussed earlier in this chapter.

Associating services

Service association is very important, and this is a configuration that I do not see a lot of companies using even when they have a bunch of web applications running in a farm. Creating default services is great if you have one web application, but if you have many, we should use this configuration method to help isolate services. Some web application content may not use all the services configured in a farm. So, why should we associate services that they will not use?

Let's associate services in the following steps so that you can see how this can help you in managing your server resources and make better choices in configuring your environment. As you can see, there are two web applications in the following figure:

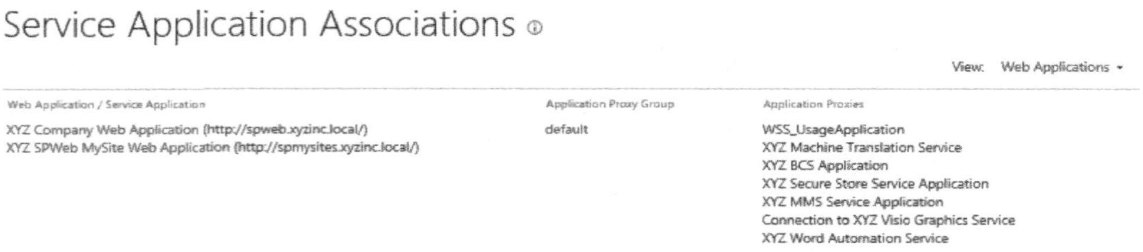

Service Application Associations ⓘ

	View: Web Applications ▾

Web Application / Service Application	Application Proxy Group	Application Proxies
XYZ Company Web Application (http://spweb.xyzinc.local/) XYZ SPWeb MySite Web Application (http://spmysites.xyzinc.local/)	default	WSS_UsageApplication XYZ Machine Translation Service XYZ BCS Application XYZ Secure Store Service Application XYZ MMS Service Application Connection to XYZ Visio Graphics Service XYZ Word Automation Service

Figure 6.50 – Service Application Associations

Right now, there is only one configured proxy group, which needs to be changed based on our requirements. Let's look at the steps:

1. Create your new service application to support your new web application:

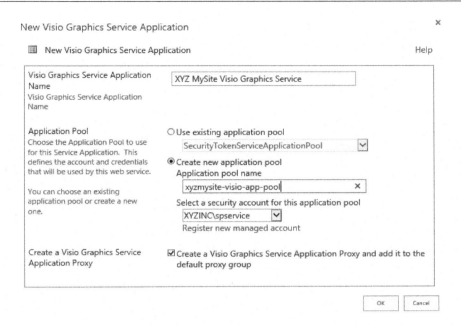

Figure 6.51 – New Visio Graphics Service Application

2.   Choose the [**custom**] configuration in the dropdown for service application associations so that we can separate the services that support each web application:

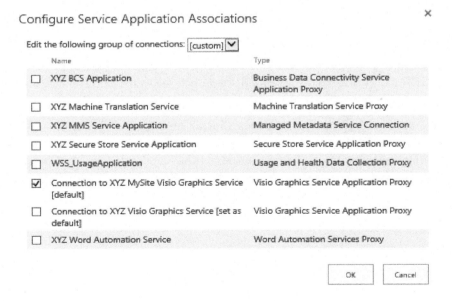

Figure 6.52 – The [custom] option

3. Choosing [**custom**] now allows us to see that we have two separate service association configurations:

Service Application Associations ⓘ

View: Web Applications ▾

Web Application / Service Application	Application Proxy Group	Application Proxies
XYZ Company Web Application (http://spweb.xyzinc.local/)	custom	WSS_UsageApplication Connection to XYZ MySite Visio Graphics Service XYZ Word Automation Service
XYZ SPWeb MySite Web Application (http://spmysites.xyzinc.local/)	custom	Connection to XYZ MySite Visio Graphics Service

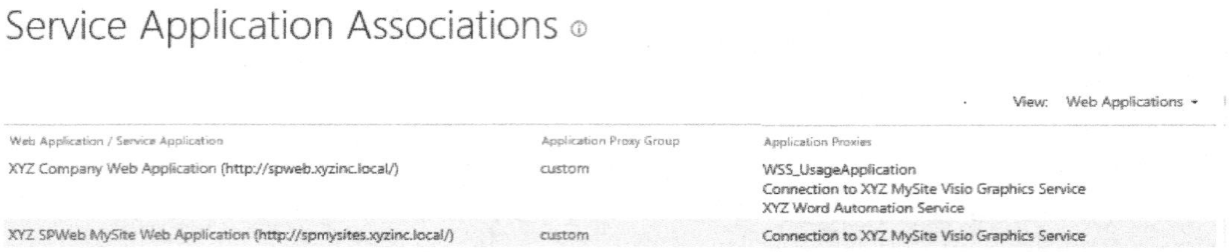

Figure 6.53 – Separate service association configurations

4. Use the following command to do this using PowerShell:

```
Add-SPServiceApplicationProxyGroupMember -Identity < the
service application proxy group > -Member <members to add
to the service application proxy group>
```

Remember to always run PowerShell as administrator. This concludes the configuration for service application associations. Now let's move on to setting cache accounts for our farm.

Setting cache accounts

Cache accounts are very important accounts that serve the web application for duties such as storing properties about items within content in a SharePoint site. This reduces the load on the SQL server supporting the SharePoint farm, which also improves request latency. Items stored in the cache provide the items used by the publishing feature when it renders web pages. If you do not have these accounts, you will see weird things happening on the site, such as you not being able to log in anymore.

Please make sure to add these two accounts, one for super user and one for super reader, before migrating any content and letting users do any testing. These accounts do not need to be managed accounts – as you can see in the PowerShell script, passwords are nonexistent – so to avoid any issues, I personally keep these out of the managed accounts list. To add these accounts, you will need to use PowerShell.

Use this PowerShell command to set cache accounts for your web applications:

```
$wa = Get-SPWebApplication http://spweb.xyzinc.local
$wa.Properties["portalsuperuseraccount"] = "i:o#.w|xyzinc\
swritecache"
$wa.Properties[:portalsuperreaderaccount"] = "i.o#.w|xyzinc\
sreadcache"
$wa.Update()
```

```
$wa = Get-SPWebApplication http://spweb.xyzinc.local
$zp = $wa.ZonePolicies("Default")
$policy = $zp.Add("i.o#.w|xyzinc\swritecache", "Portal Super
User")
$policyRole = $wa.PolicyRoles.GetSpecialRole(:FullControl")
$policy.PolicyRoleBindings.Add($policyRole)
$policy = $zp.Add("i:o#.w|xyzinc\sreadcache", "Portal Super
Reader")
$policyRole = $wa.PolicyRoles.GetSpecialRole("FullRead")
$policy.PolicyRoleBindings.Add($policyRole)
$wa.Update()
```

These settings are key to the performance of the farm. Without them, you could see a slowdown or no response at all. Make sure to complete this step before going live for the new sites in your new farm.

Summary

This chapter showed how SharePoint configuration is not as easy as people would believe. It does take some documentation, design, and thought to make it happen. We didn't even cover all that we need to do. Again, there are varying configurations and other integrations that could have happened here. Our aim in this book is to cover the basics and add some details to get you thinking about how you can make things work in your environment.

We covered a lot in this chapter, but the main point of this chapter was to make sure you have covered all your areas of focus. In the end, you do not want to release a product that is not complete. Make sure you have documented your backup and restore process and that you follow best practices for all your configurations. Double-check things and work with the departments to resolve any issues upfront and make sure to tell them about any foreseen issues beforehand. The more communication before going live, the better.

In the next chapter, we will talk about more final configurations and other integrations needed within the farm. Workflow Manager is a big part of the integrations needed to make this farm work successfully, give the farm some useful tools for the users to collaborate, and automate business processes.

Other topics covered will include authentication and more on migration. We have mentioned migration many times in this book, but in the next chapter, we will cover more on this topic to help you choose the best tool for you or use a content database and other methods that are available.

Questions

You can find the answers on GitHub under Assessments at `https://github.com/PacktPublishing/Implementing-Microsoft-SharePoint-2019/blob/master/Assessments.docx`

1. When creating web applications for users, which web application zone must be created first before we can start extending web applications and adding alternate access mappings?

2. Which method for migration could be used best if there were no custom solutions involved within the content?

3. When crawling content, how does the crawler connect to the content?

4. How many items must be available in the farm's search item count before we need to upgrade the Search service to a cloned service?

5. When configuring the User Profile service, what account must be added to the administrators group of the server running the service?

6. True or false: A MySite is a mandatory web application that needs to be created as part of the SharePoint farm.

7
Finalizing the Farm to Go Live – Part II

As you will see, in this chapter, we still have a lot of areas to account for. These areas are very important to talk about as they relate to finalizing the farm and the content to be presented within our sites. Load balancing is also another area we will talk about. This process is usually planned in advance but is typically saved for last. We will also cover migration as you will need to have your environment set up to migrate your content from the prior farm.

We will also install Workflow Manager in this chapter and show you how to set up the application step by step. We will provide tips on what's important to understand as part of this solution integration. Workflow Manager is pretty easy to install but has some requirements you may need to be aware of before you start the configuration process. We'll address these in this chapter.

Finally, we want to make sure we have covered all our bases. I can't stress this enough, which is why you will hear me say this many times during these last few chapters: we must look at our old environment and make sure we have accounted for everything so that we can move forward gracefully.

In this chapter, the following topics will be covered:

- Understanding workflows and Workflow Manager
- Authentication
- Understanding load balancing
- Exploring SharePoint migration
- Exploring farm solutions
- Carrying out testing
- Performing the final checks
- Backup and restore

Let's get started!

Technical requirements

To understand this chapter and the knowledge provided within, you must meet the following requirements:

- 3-5 years of experience configuring SharePoint
- 3-5 years of experience using SharePoint Server

You can find the code files present in this chapter in this book's GitHub repository at `https://github.com/PacktPublishing/Implementing-Microsoft-SharePoint-2019`.

Understanding workflows and Workflow Manager

Within SharePoint, workflows are a form of automation and provide business processes with documents and content within lists. How do we migrate them from older versions of SharePoint? In some cases, you will have to recreate workflows, especially those created in Visual Studio as custom developed solutions. If you have some out of the box workflows, you can investigate whether the tool you're using will migrate them for you without any other manual involvement. Make sure to use mappings for any accounts missing from **Active Directory (AD)**, mappings that have been retired due to employees leaving the company, and mappings for content types and other columns that may not be present in the newer version of SharePoint.

You will also notice that, in Microsoft 365 SharePoint Designer 2010, workflows have been discontinued. In SharePoint 2019, however, these workflows are still supported. SharePoint 2019 Server gives you the option to move sites back to on-premises if need be. This gives you time to figure out a more suitable way to overcome the discontinuance of 2010 workflows in the cloud. You can also use Power Tools to redevelop them, which is a learning process. I am mentioning this here because you should not confuse Microsoft 365 and SharePoint On-Premises. These platforms are different and abide by different rules and guidance. You control your On-Premises environment and as long as the workflow platform can be configured, you can use it with SharePoint 2019 Server, which I believe will never go away.

One of the main issues I see most customers having during migrations is that they don't know how many workflows they have in their environment. If you want to find out where your workflows are located from a web application perspective, there are PowerShell scripts you can use to find workflows in a web application and even a site collection, but your best bet is to spot check for these manually. I have seen some errors where PowerShell could not find all workflows, so manual checks as well as PowerShell would work in this case. You can also make this a task for your site collection admins as they know their processes and can give you a good count. This is why spreading out responsibility is very important; a farm admin will not know everything. The one thing that can come out of this is identifying unused workflows, which could be flagged for deletion. This helps clean up stale content before migration.

Installing Workflow Manager

You need to install and configure Workflow Manager 1.0 in your SharePoint 2019 environment to support workflows within SharePoint 2019. The choice of what server you want this service to run on is yours. The best choice, however, is to install it on its own server so that the service can be isolated from using resources related to user and other service traffic. On the same note, I recommend setting this up on its own server because of the integration and failures that can happen with the application being installed on a SharePoint server.

Workflow Manager, although related to the SharePoint 2013 and 2016 products, works with SharePoint Server 2019. Do not worry about the outdated release of this product based on its name (year); this product works and is just as stable in the newer version of SharePoint. You can take a backup of your current Workflow Manager databases if you're migrating and restoring them in a SharePoint 2019 environment as part of the SQL Management process. You can then move forward with your configuration as you would with any other service application installation, using those databases to configure the new environment.

To create a farm of Workflow Manager servers, you need to log in as the Setup/Admin account for SharePoint on all servers. As part of this farm, the configuration does not use built-in accounts for the services. Only three servers are needed to support high availability. Please use a separate server for this installation and do not install this application as an addition to any SharePoint Server, although it can be configured that way. **This is highly recommended!**

Remember to create a separate service account and log in with that account to run the workflow manager. You can also run this using the **Web Platform Installer** for the workflow manager 2013 executable and follow the steps given here for its installation:

1. The Web Platform Installer can be found here: `https://docs.microsoft.com/en-us/iis/install/web-platform-installer/web-platform-installer-direct-downloads`. Right-click and install it, making sure to select **Run as administrator**:

Figure 7.1 – Accepting the License Agreement for Web Platform Installer

2. Click **Yes** to allow this app to make changes to your device:

Do you want to allow this app to make changes to your device?
Web Platform Installer
Verified publisher: Microsoft Corporation
File origin: Hard drive on this computer
Show more details
Yes
No

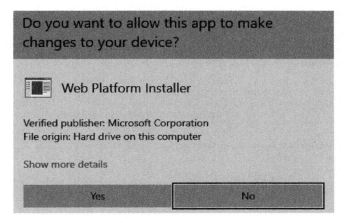

Figure 7.2 – Verifying the installation

3. A splash screen will appear while the installation file is loading:

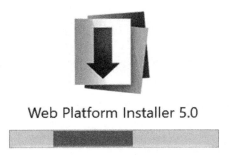

Web Platform Installer 5.0

Figure 7.3 – Installation splash screen

4. Click **Install** to start the installation process:

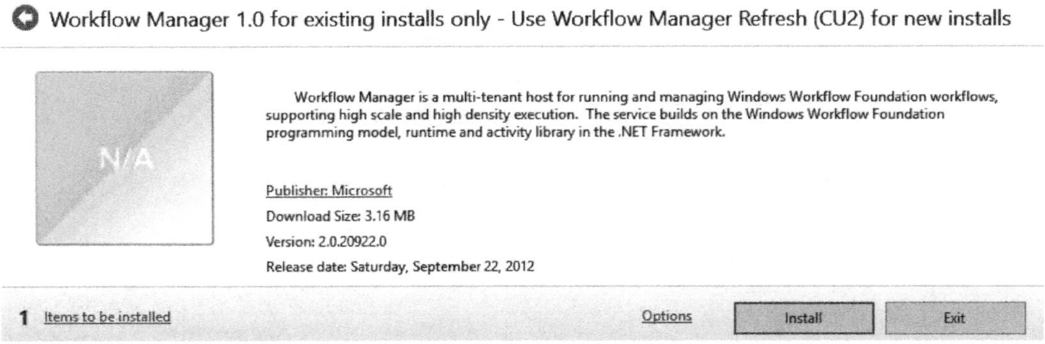
Workflow Manager 1.0 for existing installs only - Use Workflow Manager Refresh (CU2) for new installs
N/A
Workflow Manager is a multi-tenant host for running and managing Windows Workflow Foundation workflows, supporting high scale and high density execution. The service builds on the Windows Workflow Foundation programming model, runtime and activity library in the .NET Framework.
Publisher: Microsoft
Download Size: 3.16 MB
Version: 2.0.20922.0
Release date: Saturday, September 22, 2012
1 Items to be installed
Options
Install
Exit

Figure 7.4 – Choosing to Install Workflow Manager

5. Click **I Accept** to accept the license agreement:

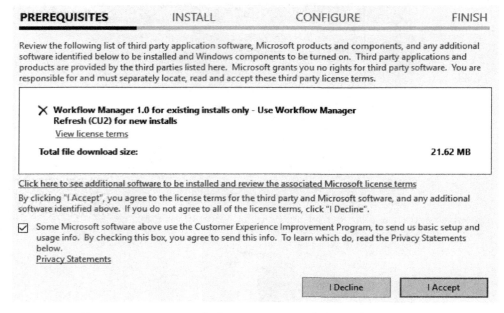

Figure 7.5 – Accepting the license agreement for Workflow Manager

6. A splash page will appear, showing the progress of the installation:

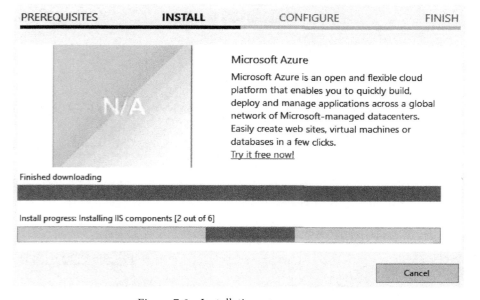

Figure 7.6 – Installation progress screen

7. Click **Continue** to configure Workflow Manager:

PREREQUISITES	INSTALL	**CONFIGURE**	FINISH

The following product(s) have additional work to complete. Clicking the Continue button will continue the installation.

Product	Additional Actions
Workflow Manager 1.0 for existing installs only - Use Workflow Manager Refresh (CU2) for new installs	Launching the Configuration Wizard which helps you configure and get started with Workflow Manager.

Continue

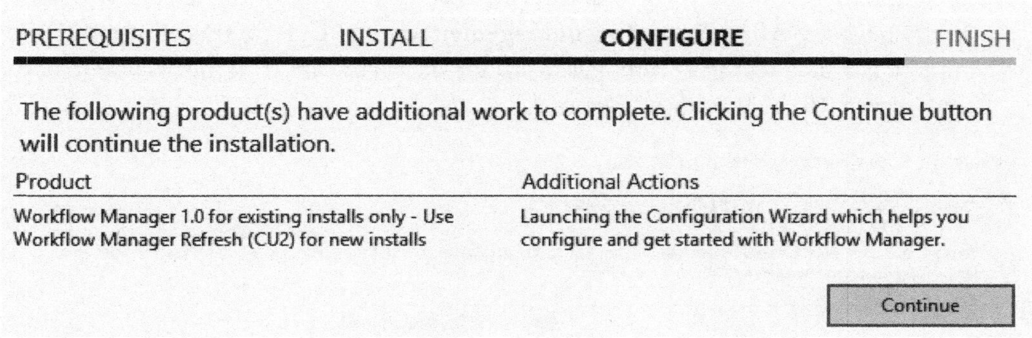

Figure 7.7 – Continuing to configure the service

8. I used the **(Recommended)** default configuration for my installation:

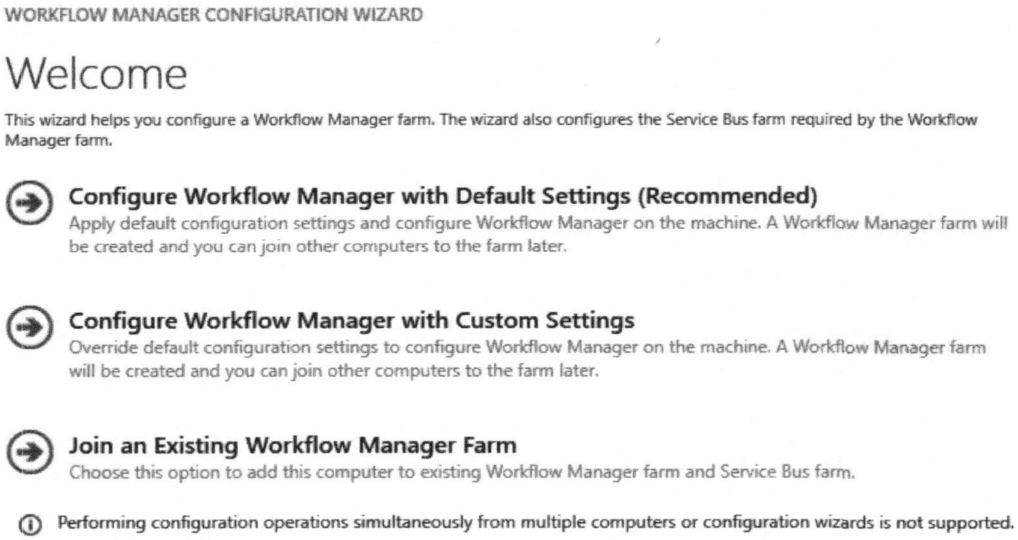

WORKFLOW MANAGER CONFIGURATION WIZARD

Welcome

This wizard helps you configure a Workflow Manager farm. The wizard also configures the Service Bus farm required by the Workflow Manager farm.

 Configure Workflow Manager with Default Settings (Recommended)
Apply default configuration settings and configure Workflow Manager on the machine. A Workflow Manager farm will be created and you can join other computers to the farm later.

 Configure Workflow Manager with Custom Settings
Override default configuration settings to configure Workflow Manager on the machine. A Workflow Manager farm will be created and you can join other computers to the farm later.

 Join an Existing Workflow Manager Farm
Choose this option to add this computer to existing Workflow Manager farm and Service Bus farm.

ⓘ Performing configuration operations simultaneously from multiple computers or configuration wizards is not supported.

Figure 7.8 – Choosing the type of installation

You may want to do make custom configurations, which requires you to use the **Configure Workflow Manager with Custom Settings** option. I recommend using this option if you have any requirements outside of the basic configuration as you can add those to the configuration. You can refer to Microsoft's documentation for further information on the custom installation of Workflow Manager 2013.

9. Update SQL Server, which in my case is a SQL alias name. Also, input the farm's account and password. If you want to run Workflow Manager using HTTP, you must check the **Allow Workflow management over HTTP on this computer** box. Input a key that acts as a secret password for the certificate. This allows you to add new servers to the Workflow Farm:

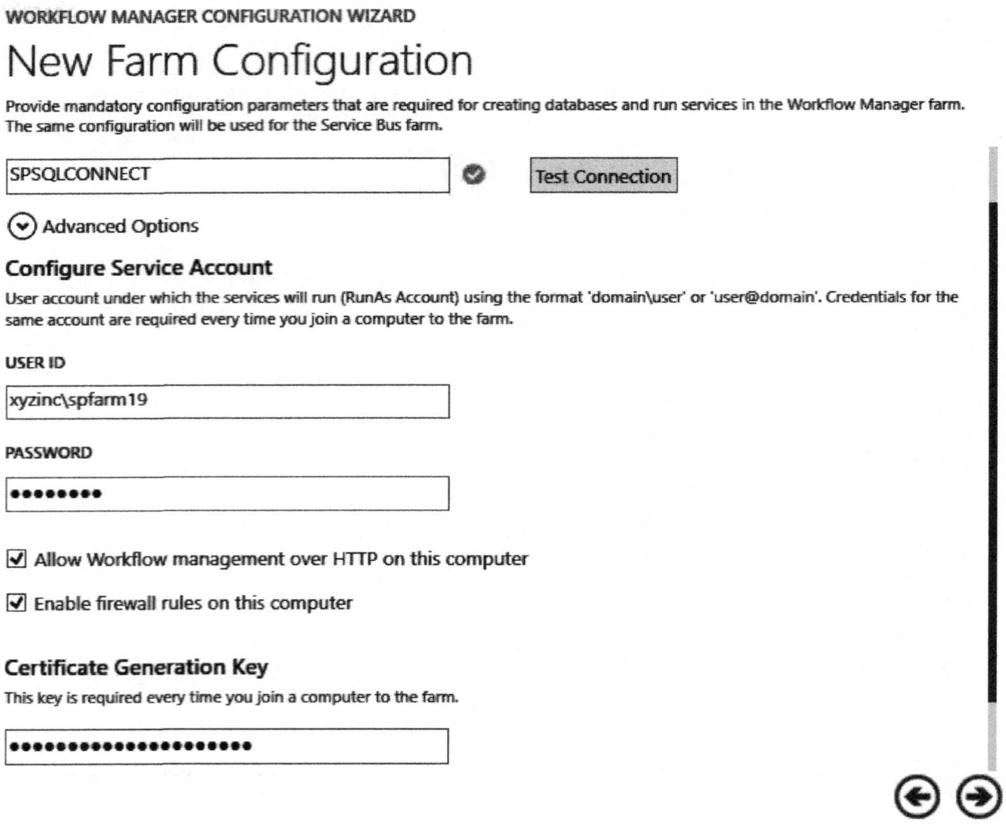

WORKFLOW MANAGER CONFIGURATION WIZARD

New Farm Configuration

Provide mandatory configuration parameters that are required for creating databases and run services in the Workflow Manager farm. The same configuration will be used for the Service Bus farm.

SPSQLCONNECT   ✅   Test Connection

⌄ Advanced Options

Configure Service Account

User account under which the services will run (RunAs Account) using the format 'domain\user' or 'user@domain'. Credentials for the same account are required every time you join a computer to the farm.

USER ID

xyzinc\spfarm19

PASSWORD

••••••••

☑ Allow Workflow management over HTTP on this computer

☑ Enable firewall rules on this computer

Certificate Generation Key

This key is required every time you join a computer to the farm.

••••••••••••••••••••••

Figure 7.9 – Updating the service account and generation key

I used my certificate for Secure Store but changed some of the characters.

10. Once you've input all the configuration details, you have the opportunity to go back and make changes using the back arrow at the bottom-right corner. If you are satisfied with the configuration, just click the tick button to start the configuration process:

WORKFLOW MANAGER CONFIGURATION WIZARD

Summary

This page lists changes that the configuration wizard will apply.

⌃ Configuration for Workflow Manager

Management Database SQL Instance	**SPSQLCONNECT**
Enable SSL connection with SQL Server instance	**False**
Authentication	**Windows Authentication**
Management Database Name	**WFManagementDB**
Instance Management Database SQL Instance	**SPSQLCONNECT**
Enable SSL connection with SQL Server instance	**False**
Authentication	**Windows Authentication**
Instance Management Database Name	**WFInstanceManagementDB**
Resource Management Database SQL Instance	**SPSQLCONNECT**
Enable SSL connection with SQL Server instance	**False**
Authentication	**Windows Authentication**
Resource Management Database Name	**WFResourceManagementDB**
RunAs Account	**xyzinc\spfarm19**
RunAs Password	***********
Certificate Generation Key	***********
Workflow Manager Outbound Signing Certificate	**Auto-generated**
Service SSL Certificate	**Auto-generated**
Encryption Certificate	**Auto-generated**
Workflow Manager Management Port	**12290**
HTTP Port	**12291**

Copy   Get PowerShell Commands

Figure 7.10 – Summary of your configuration settings

11. As the configuration process starts to work, you will notice that it goes through a series of processes that need to be completed:

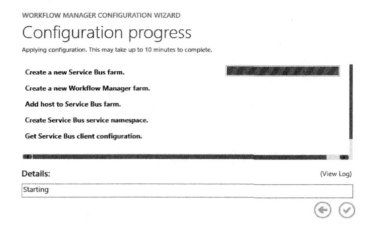

Figure 7.11 – Configuration progress screen

12. Please make sure to install the Workflow Client on all the servers in the farm:

Figure 7.12 – Workflow Manager installation completed successfully

For the client to work, you will need to create a self-signed certificate from the Workflow Server and install it on the SharePoint servers, in the Trusted Provider folder in Certificate Manager.

This is a requirement and will complete the installation process. Please click the checkbox to close the installation screen.

If you didn't use the right service account for Workflow Manager, you can update it using the following PowerShell command:

```
Stop-SBFarm
Set-SBFarm -RunAsAccount Domain\Username
$RunAsPassword = ConvertTo-SecureString -AsPlainText -Force
'<password>'
[RunOnAllNodes] Update-SBHost -RunAsPassword $RunAsPassword
Start-SBFarm
```

If you do not verify that Workflow Manager PowerShell is activated, you will get the following error:

```
Error: The term 'Set-SBFarm' is not recognized as the name of a
cmdlet, function, script file or operable program.
```

So, before you try to update the account, make sure you have PowerShell for Workflow Manager active. To do this, go to **Start** | **All Programs** | **Workflow Manager** | **Workflow Manager PowerShell**.

Then, use the following command to set the Workflow Manager Service Account:

```
Stop-SBFarm Set-SBFarm -RunAsAccount Domain\Username
$RunAsPassword = ConvertTo-SecureString -AsPlainText -Force
'<password>' [RunOnAllNodes] Update-SBHost -RunAsPassword
$RunAsPassword Start-SBFarm
```

To check your installation using the Workflow Manager Shell, use the following command:

```
Get-WFFarm
```

You can also use the following command, which checks the status of your farm:

```
Get-WFFarmStatus
```

To register Workflow Manager to a web application for use with out of the box SharePoint workflows and SharePoint Designer workflows, please use the following command:

```
Register-SPWorkflowService -SPSite "https://site.yourcompany.
com" -WorkflowHostUri "https://your.workflowurl.com:12290"
-force
```

To find your `WorkflowHostUri`, use the following command:

```
Add-PSSnapin Microsoft.SharePoint.Powershell
$wfProxy = Get-SPWorkflowServiceApplicationProxy
$wfProxy.GetWorkflowServiceAddress((Get-SPSite -Limit 1
-WarningAction SilentlyContinue))
```

This will complete the installation of Workflow Manager for integration with SharePoint 2019. Please remember to install this integration on a separate server. It is better to keep all integrations, even Office Web Apps and other server integrations, separate when possible so that if the product fails or has complications, it does not affect your farm as well. How much harm is one more server with a few resources going to do in comparison to having a product you cannot uninstall or may cause damage to your farm? Separate everything you can, and it will save you from issues in the long run.

Authentication

Authentication is used in SharePoint 2019 to validate a user for the purpose of using SharePoint sites, lists, libraries, and documents within the farm. SharePoint then authorizes use after verifying the user has rights to a particular site within the farm. You will see this process when you use Fiddler to troubleshoot issues from a desktop where a user is signing in. You will notice a 401 error right from the start, before the user actually enters their username and password. This is to make sure the authorization has completed. It does this by authenticating to a security source first before access to the site can be given.

The default authentication for SharePoint is Windows authentication. Microsoft has always made Active Directory available for use as an authentication method for user accounts since SharePoint 2007, along with other methods we will talk about in this section. Active Directory is well-known as an authentication provider and used solely in some cases by companies who use SharePoint. It is still used as a valid authentication method in SharePoint 2019. It is also used for the service and administrative accounts that are used to configure and support the farm. In some cases, you will see that service and administrative accounts will be used within Active Directory and that all user accounts may use another claims provider to authenticate to the sites. We will talk about this later in this section.

Forms-based authentication is supported in SharePoint 2019, as well as in SharePoint 2016. Things have changed, and basic authentication and other forms of authentication that were once offered as default methods are no longer offered anymore. **Security Assertion Markup Language (SAML)** is one of the methods that is new to the group of supported authentication methods but not new to SharePoint Admins. **Forms-based authentication (FBA)** is still available if needed for the support of SQL Membership Providers, which is a somewhat common way to configure authentication in SharePoint in some use cases. This method is not very secure but carries some value for external farms and sites due to exposing only trivial accounts, not Active Directory accounts, to the internet.

To integrate with SharePoint 2016 and 2019 using alternative methods that support other authentication providers such as Basic Authentication, you will need to use Microsoft Identity Manager to implement a solution that supports them. There are also cloud providers such as Okta that provide claims-based authentication, which helps in defining processes for authentication using solutions within SharePoint from the cloud. Depending on what you're planning to provide, there are many options out there. Using a cloud-based solution poises you to be ready for any migrations to the cloud in the future.

Claims authentication

There are many ways to integrate claims authentication methods. Out of the box, SharePoint does this automatically using **Active Directory (AD)** and Claims Tokens, changing the user account in Active Directory to claims identities. As we saw in *Chapter 6, Finalizing the Farm – Going Live*, there is a service, called the User Profile Service, that requires you to use a service account for SharePoint to connect to it. This account is given replication rights access to AD to basically store a copy of the user list you choose within SharePoint. In SharePoint, you would then also set up the User Profile Service to pull in user identity profiles from AD into SharePoint. Based on those identities, the accounts can add to sites and content within SharePoint. If they are not listed, they will not be able to authenticate, which is why you should run this process on a schedule.

Within Okta, a cloud-based claims provider, there is a two-fold process for adding users to what is called, in Okta, an Application. You can add a user to a SharePoint site, but they will not get access to the content until that user has been mapped to the Application in Okta. This helps with managing users because if they do not have an account in Okta and are mapped to the application, which is the URL of a Host Named Site Collection or Path-Based Web Application, they still won't get access to the site.

Again, there are some third-party companies that do offer cloud authentication integration with SharePoint. Most companies I have seen, such as Okta for on-premises integration, use farm solutions that have been deployed on the farm to support claims authentication. This is a great way to integrate a solution for authentication, but what happens when a solution breaks or gets retracted by accident? That's when you have an issue. This is my only reservation when using Farm Solutions, because too many things can happen that can cause big problems in the on-premise environment. Some things you can do to control changes are as follows:

- Control the Central Administration site by only adding admins to the Farm Admin Group.

- Implement a change management process to manage changes in the environment.

- Clean up all old identities within your AD, Farm Admin group, and Cloud Provider Admin group.

- **Always** use Service Accounts to run your services on cloud solutions.

- Never use a personal account for your farm installation or any service accounts used in configuration.

Please follow these recommendations to deflect any mishaps within your environment.

Windows authentication

Windows authentication is available in SharePoint 2019 and if you are coming from an older version of SharePoint like SharePoint 2007 which uses Classic Authentication, you will need to update your web applications so that they can use Windows authentication, which is really just Claims Authentication. This has been in place since SharePoint 2010 and the conversion needs to happen now. There is no way around this, and there is a process you need to follow to migrate your accounts. Classic authentication is no longer supported and was deprecated in SharePoint 2013. If you are migrating from one of the older versions of SharePoint, then you want to convert your identities into claims identities using PowerShell.

> **Note**
>
> Refer to the following link for more information on this process:
> ```
> https://docs.microsoft.com/en-us/sharepoint/
> upgrade-and-update/migrate-from-classic-mode-to-
> claims-based-authentication-in-sharepoint-2013
> ```

There are other protocols that integrate with Windows authentication as well. Both NTLM and Kerberos are methods that help users authenticate without prompts for credentials, which in some cases can happen many times until they are fully authenticated. This happens when there are hops within the authentication where it needs to be verified by different content within your site. This could be an image or even a broken inheritance library, but SharePoint will not let you fully be free until you have been verified by all the content within the site.

NTLM

In this protocol, in most cases, no setup or configuration will be needed for this authentication method. The reason for that is it is most likely integrated already if you're using a Windows Server or client. When you set up your web applications, you will see the option for this protocol, which you can select from the list provided.

Kerberos

This is another selection you will see when creating web applications in SharePoint. This is known as a ticketing authentication process and requires some configuration in Active Directory. The client and server computers used within a configuration must have a trusted connection to the domain's **Key Distribution Center** (**KDC**). When configuring Kerberos, you need to set up **Service Principal Names** (**SPNs**) in AD DS. This must be completed before you install SharePoint because these configurations must be available to SharePoint before it is up and running.

The use cases for Kerberos have been listed here so that you can see how it can be used to help secure your environment. This is better than using out of the box authentication methods:

- Kerberos requires the use of the Strongest Integrated Windows authentication protocol, which supports advanced features and allows the mutual authentication of clients and servers.

- Allows the delegation of client credentials.

- Kerberos requires the least amount of network traffic to AD DS domain controllers, and it can increase the number of pages a web frontend server can serve in some scenarios.

- Kerberos is an open protocol supported by many platforms and vendors.

Figure out if Kerberos is the method you want to use for your implementation. This should have been discussed back in the planning stage as well. There is a lot to learn when building SharePoint farms, so make sure you investigate and make the right choice for your environment.

SAML authentication

SAML token-based providers are more than popular these days because most companies have moved to using Federated Authentication methods. You can use single sign-on and smart cards to complete this authentication process for convenience within the environment. This brings a seamless process so that users can authenticate once to many resources and sites within an environment without the need to log in.

Many domains can also be authenticated using this method. It can even be used in collaboration with other companies that may be partners since the authentication to other federated domains can be included in this implementation. This gives users many options when it comes to collaboration, as well as other areas of the business where you may want to share resources.

As you can see, SAML authentication is a good choice as it is an easy and secure way to manage authentication across multiple enterprise domains and other resource domains. One point to mention is that you will lose control of the people picker when using this method in SharePoint. The people picker will search for and find users, but you cannot base this search on a valid user, group, or claim.

Zones are very important in a SharePoint web application configuration as they provide logical areas within a web application that separate authentication based on a web application. Within the web application, you can establish separate URLs across the zones to access the content within one web application.

You can also implement multiple authentication methods in a single zone, which gives you some different ways to create and establish authentication, depending on the method or who you want to access the zone. I have seen cases where there has been code within the site to determine what you see based on your authentication method. If you want to control an anonymous site, then you can control what content users see within the site settings of the site using this method as well.

Some other things to note are that Windows authentication and forms-based authentication are the only methods that you can only have one instance per zone. (Remember that you must have Windows authentication established on the default web application for search crawling to take place! You can also have more than one form of authentication in each zone.)

To architect a SAML token-based solution, you must create some components so that the architecture supports it, such as the following:

- SharePoint Security Token Service
- Token-signing certificate
- Identity claim
- Claims that describe users
- Realms or web application URLs
- `SPTrustedidentityTokenIssuer`

You can use multiple user repositories in order to work within a SAML claims architecture. These all use the Security Token Service to communicate. As you will see when configuring web applications, you will be required to add an entry to establish trust with the Trusted Identity Provider area within the form. Once that has been established, the certificate will need to be copied and/or pulled into SharePoint via Central Administration so that these security validations have a verifiable handshake.

There are other configurations that may also need to take place, such as PowerShell scripting and, in some cases, hardware that supports the configuration. The following links provides help in terms of using SAML and ADFS. You can read more about the process of implementing Federated Authentication at `https://docs.microsoft.com/en-us/sharepoint/security-for-sharepoint-server/implement-saml-based-authentication-in-sharepoint-server`.

As you can see, authentication has changed a bit, but there is a way to get what you want using a third-party tool or even new Microsoft technologies. The methods provided at this link are only supported by SharePoint 2013 farms or newer. The important thing to remember is that you always want to set up for the future. I recommend a cloud-based authentication method so that even if you are thinking about moving to the cloud, it doesn't become a hassle because your cloud provider can be authenticated on-premises or in a cloud environment. It is the best way to be ready for any transitions in the future.

Understanding load balancing

Load balancing is a way of leveraging hardware or software in order to manage connections to web frontend servers in your farm, which are seen as user traffic resources. These servers, when used in two or more configurations, help provide balanced resources for user loads to support connections using the sites within a specific URL. As a MinRole Server, WFE server has redundancy based on the number of WFE MinRoles that have been deployed. Deploying these server resources in two or more server configurations brings redundancy and can support user connections effectively so that they are not overrun by user connections to the sites that are available.

With that, there are, in theory, limitations in terms of how many web applications are supported by best practices – 20 using the Traditional Web Application creation option in SharePoint. There are also bounced around limitations in terms of how many service accounts/app pools are supported, which should really be no more than 10. Each web application you add to a farm with its own application pool will add about 380 MB to the RAM that's consumed on the server it is running on. Adding a web application with a shared application pool will add about 62 MB of RAM that's consumed on the server. In the past, I tested Host Named Site Collections and each was about 2 GB and the RAM was consumed per web application, which is a lot of RAM. So, if you have enough RAM to throw at the server, you will see no performance hit on them.

When working in the field, I have seen a customer who had 34 web applications running SharePoint 2010 and had the minimum CPU and RAM on the server to support the server resources, but the sites were really slow (for obvious reasons). Once they bumped up the RAM to around 64 GB on each WFE and added some more CPU, the server resources worked fine. The sites were speedy, and things worked as they should. So, don't think that you have to have only 10 application pools. Just know that with some creative configurations, you can make this work using MinRoles, server resources, and RAM.

I am not saying that you should do this and bypass best practices because best practices are documented for a reason on Microsoft's website. You can test the waters if you want to, which I have seen others do. I am making this a recommendation but sometimes, these things do not matter, depending on the community's size and other resource factors, as stated previously. There are also configurations you can use to scale out web frontend servers so that they support web applications on individual servers. This stops unnecessary IIS sites from running on certain servers using IIS bindings and IP address assignments, which you can use to isolate traffic to the server based on the URL. This can help with minimizing the number of app pools as well because some sites will not be running. Find your sweet spot and ramp up in areas as needed.

As we mentioned previously, we have two ways of performing load balancing: using hardware load balancers or software load balancers. Next, we will see which one is best for your environment while looking at costs.

Load balancing with hardware

As you may be aware, hardware load balancers used to cost a pretty penny, but this is because they can host many different web applications. F5 is the most popular load balancer for SharePoint because its configuration works well with SharePoint configurations within the farm. Hardware load balancers run on their own and have their own processors and memory. So, there is no need to use them as part of the servers supporting our sites. They can also be configured for redundancy so that the hardware fails over.

With that comes other features that a hardware load balancer can provide, especially over the choice of using NLB as a Windows service load balancer. For one, as mentioned previously, performance would be my first concern as NLB resides on web frontends. Features such as affinity and persistence will be available in the hardware load balancer. A hardware load balancer can also provide certificate management, which can be useful in some use cases. You will also find that hardware load balancers will spread workloads across the web frontends with consistent response times. Due to these and other factors, hardware load balancers are the first choice in my book.

Load balancing with software

Software load balancers are more challenging to set up because they usually run on the servers we are using as web frontends on our farm. When performing the configuration for NLB load balancing, you will see that option works well, but the resources it consumes may not be optimal for the performance of the web frontend. There are also other things to be aware of when using NLB as this service cannot detect failures due to a service outage. It can only detect an outage by IP address. There are also other features that are not available, such as SSL offloading, compression, and caching, which are features I would say are mandatory these days. Performance is the main concern with using NLB, so please figure out the best plan for your environment.

There are other software load balancers that can be run from other servers, but I really see this as a separate managed server that brings more complexity than simply adding a hardware device. A hardware device is specific in its duty, but a server managing this type of feature is a trouble spot in my book. Anything can happen to Windows Updates, server misconfigurations, and more. The choice is yours at the end of the day.

In Azure, there are cloud software load balancers that work but since they are cloud-based, they always perform as they should separate from the web server resources. Realistically, in an on-premises environment, it's best to use a hardware load balancer. This could also be true for the cloud in a hybrid scenario.

Load balancers can play a big role in your network in terms of how the network is configured, what protocols are used to authenticate it, and other configurations we have not mentioned in this book, such as session stickiness. The thing we wanted to point out is that you should make sure you bring this to the table early and map out your process of load balancing your SharePoint sites beforehand. Test and make sure things work before going live.

Exploring SharePoint migration

Migrating content is a tough role in any organization. Overseeing getting all the data from source to destination is a challenging task, especially with SharePoint, mapped drives, and other storage resources. Users will complain about data being missing, even if it is irrelevant. They will be, in some cases, irritated or even combative because they are afraid of change.

You must plan and make sure you understand the data they use, some of their processes, and the content they are using intimately. You will also need to find out what data is relevant and what data may not be relevant before moving to the new environment. You will find this to be a daunting task when dealing with mapped drives because people do not know what the latest versions of files are in most cases; for example, some may be named FinalFinal. To make sure you're using the correct files, you must work with the customer to clean up any irrelevant files before going forward. You have lots of choices when it comes to storage locations due to SharePoint and OneDrive being available. Don't go back to mapped drives if you can avoid it, but if you do, clean up those files before moving them.

When looking at content, you must be prepared to classify and reclassify files as needed and tag them within the new environment correctly. Use of managed metadata and/or columns to describe the content is key for search results. Securing the data based on those classifications comes into play so that once they've been migrated to a document library, they can be secured. Files within the libraries can also be secured individually if needed. Breaking inheritance is also a concern at this point when you're talking to your customer because you do not want to do this a lot when you're setting up content. So, be mindful of how you set up new libraries in the new environment.

Here is a list of areas to pay attention to before migration:

- File Size
- Individual Permission
- URLs (file paths) and file names
- File sizes
- Character limitations
- Custom solutions
- Branding
- InfoPath
- Workflow state and history
- Permissions (do you have access to all the files?)
- Folders with more than 5000 items
- Unsupported site templates
- Orphaned users
- Checked out files
- Unsupported list templates
- File extensions

We must also remember that even with mapped drives, we can also migrate to OneDrive. Security and various options for folder organization will help the customer manage those files. It's not like SharePoint, but if a customer wants to implement this type of storage location, be ready to answer questions. This is contingent with if you are in a hybrid environment where you already have Microsoft 365 set up.

If you're working with SharePoint, you will also need to look at versioning settings, column types, and any updated aspects that are moving from one version of SharePoint to another. Help them understand that moving to this new location will give them more control over the data from a security aspect; waiting for an admin to update security for new and existing users within mapped drives is also possible.

This sometimes gets them excited about moving and helps them relax, which will make your users feel as though everything is going to be OK. Show them that you have investigated everything and build confidence in the migration by having meetings about this migration. You can even suggest the use of retention libraries for holding documents online either with OneDrive or SharePoint so that the customer understands there are choices when it comes to how old documents can be handled. Processes can be put in place for handling new files that need to be moved to a separate location for safe keeping as well.

As we mentioned previously, this is not an easy task. You are in the hot seat to figure out how to get 100% of your content identified from one version to the other. We will talk about some of the areas to focus on and which migration method will work for your migration scenario. I have also identified some migration tools within the method to give you a breakdown of my experiences with those tools.

We will also talk about creating schedules for your departments and testing with users as we also want to break down the use of preliminary migrations and final migration testing. If you have not, and I will say this again, create new dev and test environments to make sure you can provide areas within the environment where users can test their content and have new ways of accessing it.

As part of our environment, we should have dev, test, and production environments, which gives us a completely functional SharePoint environment. This means we have a place we can test out migrations and have the user test them too. If you do not have this development environment set up, then you should not be reading this chapter of this book. The last thing you want to do is test in your test and production environments; always do this during the development phase. If you have these environments set up, then we can move on and find out what we need to do in order to start moving content from our old farm to the new one. Make sure all your farms have been configured correctly and are the same so that the results of the tests will be the same across the board. Configuration management is important!

During migrations, you also want to make sure you put source content in read-only mode when doing final migrations so that nothing is changed during this process. There are many things you need to make sure are in place before we start this migration. Take full backups of content before the migration, as well as once you have got the content over to the new farm. This backup should be taken once you have settled all issues and confirmed that all the errors have been fixed with the customer. This helps create a baseline that acts as a safeguard from the migration of both the source and target farms.

Know your customers

Identify all the departments that are being migrated and create a list of departments and users (if possible). If you have departments that are ready to move and eager to take advantage of new technology, then work with those customers first. These departments are the ones that will be successful and will give you a chance to build a good story going forward. Make sure to interview all departments before picking and choosing a schedule as well.

The following are some example questions you should ask when performing department interviews:

- What are you currently using SharePoint for?
- How big are some of the larger files that you will be migrating?
- Is there anything you want to change in your current site?
- Do you have any automated processes?
- Do you have any custom applications?
- Are there any file shares that will be migrated?
- What do you do day-to-day with SharePoint?
- Do you have any staff that can be contacted and can help drive the migration process?
- When would you like to move?
- Do you have any immediate or future goals for the product?

The biggest thing you will encounter with this part of your project is a failure. The reason why it is more crucial at this point to succeed is that when you fail in front of IT staff, it is OK; you can recover since it's a small subset of the project. However, when you get to the migration stage, this affects the company because everyone is watching. This also brings a spotlight on why some users do not like SharePoint. Do not give them any ammunition to criticize SharePoint because it can cause issues and it's something you will have to live with for a while. Believe me, success is the goal here.

Some of the things you can do to be more in tune with your customers or department include understanding what they do. Knowing what they do and how they use SharePoint can go a long way into supporting the department during the migration process. If possible and if you have time, find out who used to work in those departments that might have data that is still valid in the source content. Knowing some of those user accounts that may not be in Active Directory now will help to troubleshoot errors going forward. Some tools that are used when migrating lists and libraries do not work well when versioning items that could have a user account specified in a people and group column because, when the item is migrated, it will fail. Make sure to account for what you can do beforehand and use the tool mapping component to map users and groups if needed. By doing this, accounts that are not there can be masked with the admin account or another account so that the item does not fail during the migration.

Find out what your customer or department needs from you. Whether it is handholding or more information for them to feel comfortable, make sure you provide it. There might be multiple questions you wish to ask, some of which are as follows:

- Are you migrating a file share or SharePoint site?
- Do you have access to the file share or SharePoint site?
- How large are the files that are being migrated?

This may add more to your workload, which is why you want to make sure you account for any scheduling hold-ups now by interviewing all departments before you finalize your schedule, as stated previously. If there is a person on the staff that would like to help or be that go-to person, find that out now so that they can be your liaison between you and the rest of the team.

Find out the immediate or future goals of the department. This is crucial so that you can get an understanding of where they would like to go with SharePoint. This also gives you the opportunity to discuss how SharePoint can help them manage data more efficiently. Having a demo ready for some of the new features within SharePoint, as discussed earlier in this book, can show you are prepared and that these features are working as they should in the new version. This gives the business analyst some information on what could be done to help them in the future. This is the time to start being proactive and not reactive with your customers. Start fresh and make this transition useful for everyone.

Migration – choosing your weapon of choice

When choosing how we migrate, we must look at the content and versions of SharePoint we are working with. Some questions that you should be asking yourself are as follows:

- What method should I use to get this task completed?
- Should I purchase a tool to perform migration?
- What are some other methods we can use to migrate content from the source to the destination?

There are a few ways to migrate content in SharePoint:

- Content database migration
- Using a migration tool
- PowerShell migration
- Manually using Windows Explorer

Let's take a look at these in more detail.

Content database migration

This is the out of the box task of moving content from one farm to another. This supports migration from version to version and cross-web applications for on-premises environments. There are technical points that need to be addressed as part of both migration paths when using this method. This provides a better capture of the site from a bigger standpoint, but it does not give you some of the more finite capabilities you may need in order to clean up content beforehand. This is best used when custom solutions are not involved, and the content is mostly out of the box.

Using a migration tool

This depends on whether you're using an external application to move content from one SharePoint site to another site. These tools can be used for either on-premises or cloud migrations. This also means we can migrate from one version of a SharePoint farm to another SharePoint farm. Using a migration tool provides us with flexibility for scheduling, picking specific content, using mapping capabilities to map columns in lists, and updating permissions on items that may be held by users who no longer work at the company, to name a few. Governance tools also come into play with tools you select as many companies provide those to help you understand your environment before migration.

One thing I do to speed up the migration process is create as many server named sites as possible to extend my web applications. This will give you many URL points of entry for content migrations so that you can use separate servers to push the content through, instead of using a DNS name where all traffic will hit one or two servers. The server resources are then separate from one another and you can have different admins pointing different tool installations to different servers. You will see no bottlenecks pushing content through as long as your SQL server can keep up with the influx of data.

Tools also allows you to make choices for other Microsoft cloud services and third-party solutions such as Google, Dropbox, and OneDrive. If you have a tool that can connect to those types of services and you want to migrate content from those repositories, this is the way to do it. A migration tool provides such integrations and can be helpful in moving these documents over to a new platform. It will also leave behind database errors found in the content, such as errors with solutions that were left behind from other versions, plus other content that may have faced errors due to database issues.

You can also use the tool in combination with content database migration and migrate your databases first, before using the tool on the weekend to push incremental changes to the content. This cuts down how long it will take you to move content save you money since with most tools, you must pay per GB. Unfortunately, you cannot use this method when moving to the cloud.

> **Important Note**
> Remember: your logging files will grow while you're completing this process, and large amounts of logging data will be created on your SQL and SharePoint servers. Make sure that all your logging services for IIS and SharePoint are pointed to the Data or Log drive on your machine and that it has a lot of space during this process!

PowerShell migration

PowerShell migration is another way we can migrate content. It is more tedious and requires you to be skilled in PowerShell. I do not recommend this method for newbies or admins who do not have this skill set already. The chances of errors occurring is high, and you do not want that when you are on a schedule. It is not time to practice PowerShell at this point.

> **Tip**
> Some examples of PowerShell being used as a migration tool can be found on Microsoft's website at `https://docs.microsoft.com/en-us/sharepointmigration/overview-spmt-ps-cmdlets`.

Manual migrations

As an example, let's say I have a folder on a server that is being used as a shared folder. This folder has documents in it that need to be migrated to a SharePoint library. I can take these files from the shared folder and copy them directly into the library using the Windows Explorer functionality within the SharePoint library. This is an easy way to migrate documents from desktops, but the limitation is that you can only copy up to 100 documents at a time. You also do not have the opportunity to add column information or metadata to these documents as they are being uploaded.

> **Important Note**
>
> Beware! Do not make the mistake of having a live site on a destination farm where you have not finished configuring your services. Make sure you have completed all configurations before you put any new "live" sites in your new production environment. If you need to work with some of the departments and have sites that are live while migrating, ensure your dev and test environments are set up so that you can test any migrated content before it's put into production as a live site. You can then make configuration changes there and not in production to test the farm.

There are other ways we can use manual processes to move data as well. Microsoft Office tools such as Microsoft Access and Microsoft Excel allow us to move content from one list to another or one farm to another. All lists are basically Excel and Access databases. So, capturing columns and pulling data back into another list is fairly straightforward using PowerShell and even just Access itself. Look around and see what you can find. In some instances, this may work when you are just moving small items or concentrating on one document library and don't want to purchase something, or you don't want users bothering the admin when it comes to moving the list through Central Administration.

The Central Administration tool, which can be used to export lists and libraries, can be seen in the following screenshot:

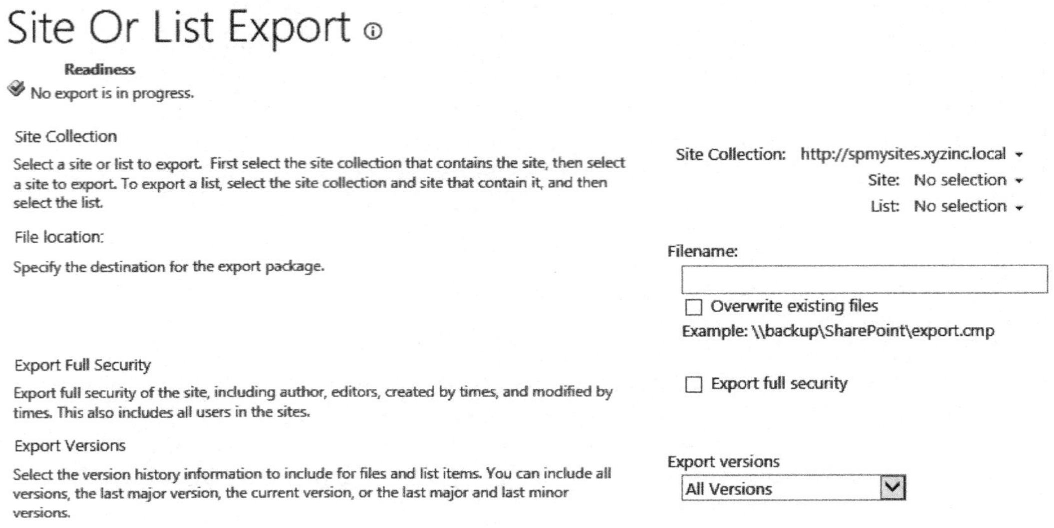

Site Or List Export ⓘ

Readiness
✅ No export is in progress.

Site Collection

Select a site or list to export. First select the site collection that contains the site, then select a site to export. To export a list, select the site collection and site that contain it, and then select the list.

Site Collection: http://spmysites.xyzinc.local ▾
Site: No selection ▾
List: No selection ▾

File location:

Specify the destination for the export package.

Filename:

[   ]

☐ Overwrite existing files

Example: \\backup\SharePoint\export.cmp

Export Full Security

Export full security of the site, including author, editors, created by times, and modified by times. This also includes all users in the sites.

☐ Export full security

Export Versions

Select the version history information to include for files and list items. You can include all versions, the last major version, the current version, or the last major and last minor versions.

Export versions

[All Versions   ▾]

Figure 7.13 – Exporting a site or list

As you can see, there are many ways to migrate content from SharePoint. Using the tools that work for your situation is the name of the game. Do not just take someone else's word for it. Some tools work better for some people than others. It's all about what you want, not how expensive or popular a solution is. Even within SharePoint, I can pull content from top-level areas and import them. In some cases, this would not work, while in others, it could be the best solution to use. Just make sure it works for you and your requirements.

Now that we have talked about the different ways we can perform migrations, next, we will learn about the types of migrations that can be achieved.

Types of migration

In this section, we will cover different types of migration. This will provide you with a use case to follow once you start the migration process. The types of migration that can be achieved are as follows:

- Version to version
- Server to server
- Service to service

- Cross-web applications

- Cloud migrations from on-premises

- Third-party to on-premises and cloud

- Files shares

Version to version: A version-to-version migration is when you migrate from a SharePoint 2013 farm to a SharePoint 2019 farm. However, as part of that migration, you need to validate your content through the in-between version of SharePoint – in this case, SharePoint 2016. This also needs to be a content database migration method.

Server to server: Server-to-server migrations can be easy or become very complex, depending on the way the content was structured in SharePoint. Server-to-server migrations could be when you migrate from one cloud to another cloud where you have the same version of SharePoint, or it could be when you need to upgrade the server platform from Windows Server 2012 R2 to Windows 2016 Server for licensing reasons, supportability, or just to keep your servers up to date with the latest and greatest server technology. If you are migrating from SharePoint 2007 to SharePoint 2019 using the content database migration method, this could be considered a server-to-server migration as well because when lifting content from 2007, you have to take it through the different versions of SharePoint to get the content to 2019.

When moving through 2010, 2013, and 2016, each server would have to be set up and configured to support the migration. There is also a step in the 2010 migration that will upgrade your workflows and InfoPath forms during the process, and there's a tool to migrate you to 2019 from that point. You would have to manually migrate the business data catalog (BCS in 2019) from 2007 to 2010, for which you can refer to `https://docs.microsoft.com/en-us/previous-versions/office/developer/sharepoint-2010/ff817559(v=office.14)`. After that, the services database could be moved through this process as well to keep those services intact as you move through the migration. You will also need to migrate classic users to claims, which occurs during the migration from 2007 to 2010. For more information on migrating from classic-mode to claims-based authentication in SharePoint 2013, refer to `https://docs.microsoft.com/en-us/sharepoint/upgrade-and-update/migrate-from-classic-mode-to-claims-based-authentication-in-sharepoint-2013`.

Service to service: These migrations can be complex. I was recently on a migration from Rackspace to AWS and it was challenging due to the size of the content databases that we had to work with. Getting such databases transferred to a new service is tough, especially when you have small maintenance windows. The one thing to watch out for is the size, but also what type of web application configuration you choose.

Say, for instance, you chose Path-Based Web Applications as your standard application. Now, in terms of migration, all content needs to be migrated all at once, regardless of how many databases you have in that web application. If you do not move all the content databases at once, your users will have no way of getting to the content because there is no way to split the URL so that it talks to two separate farms.

However, you can migrate Host Named Site Collections one at a time or all at once. This is because the Host Name is the key to getting to the content, and it is associated with the site collection and not the web application. This is great when it comes to these types of situations where content can be very hard to move to another service or farm. Plan accordingly so that you do not get caught in a situation like this, especially when you're managing the sizes of your content databases.

Cross-web applications (internal farm): These migrations also happen during the production use of a SharePoint farm. You need to understand how or why you need to use any other migration methods mentioned at the beginning of this section. The approach you should use for list and library migrations would be to use a tool or use the area within Central Administration to extract the site, list, or library and then move the content from one site to another. Some tweaks may be involved here, but this is something you should explore, depending on your requirements.

Migration to the cloud: This can only be achieved using a tool or a very time-consuming manual method. Of course, a tool is preferred in this scenario due to the amount of time you would have to spend going through files and uploading them to SharePoint Online. The manual process would be to download all files to a local system and then upload them back into the new farm libraries. This would mean reapplying all permissions, as well as losing version history. We can see why a tool is very important when migrating to the cloud. Most tools charge you per GB, so please budget for this!

I remember migrating from DocuShare a few years ago and the only tool available was the command line. During that process, you could export all the files, but a lot of information was lost. At the time of writing, there are lots of command-line tools, such as JSOM, that can help define these files and permissions. They are exported in a flat file structure to help pull that information into SharePoint and apply some metadata from the old system, which in some cases is not SharePoint.

You can also migrate many different types of information using tools to SharePoint or OneDrive. Some tools give you different capabilities with different applications. Some connect to Google Docs, Dropbox, and even some other applications. I have seen with some tools, such as Saketa, offer Microsoft Teams migrations as part of their tool set.

Microsoft also has a free tool that can be used to perform migrations from an on-premises environment to the cloud. I have only used this tool once and it works as it should. However, at the time, it didn't have a lot of bells and whistles compared to what other tools offer. I believe they have made updates to this tool, so if you are looking for one, try it and see if it will work for your project.

> **Important Note**
>
> Microsoft has its own migration tool that only migrates to the cloud. You can find more information at `https://docs.microsoft.com/en-us/sharepointmigration/introducing-the-sharepoint-migration-tool`.

File shares: File shares are always forgotten, but the return on investment in migrating these files to SharePoint is huge. When we leave these files shared on servers, you are requiring these files to be hosted by one or many servers with extended storage space. These servers cost you money to run and always require disk space upgrades. Instead, pull these files into SharePoint and use the databases for sharing and managing these files.

OneDrive can also be used to hold personal files and get rid of MySites and the storage comes for free with your plan. The SharePoint 2019 Server must be set up to use a hybrid connection to the cloud, which we talk about in *Chapter 10, SharePoint Advanced Reporting and Features.*

The users win as well because they gain functionality when using SharePoint, and your help desk will love you for it. With this, you have the benefit of versioning and much more control over your files. You can also place the files into segregated site collections/document libraries so that there will be no slips in security, unlike file shares. They will also not be calling the help desk to add users to certain folders, which will cut down administration use as well. Users can also use files for workflow processes, versioning, and other collaborative means. They can include these files in links throughout sites in order to share information using the latest version of the file via Manage Copies.

Migration tools

Most tools run on any OS platform and provide a lot of options when it comes to migrating using mappings, PowerShell, and scheduling. My experience with ShareGate has been great, but it does not offer an array of solutions as it seems to concentrate on the migration and governance space. As far as the tool goes, it is great and provides everything you need to prepare for a smooth migration process. I have not had many issues using the product, and I would say that it is first class!

ShareGate has been the tool of choice for my migrations. I really like both ShareGate and Saketa. Unlike other tools in this space, ShareGate gives you a great desktop and many functionalities you will not see in other tools. The tool is inexpensive and runs on any Windows platform. Again, pricing is tiered, so you can find a comfortable spot that fits your budget based on your data requirements.

> **Important Note**
> If you are performing an on-premises migration, make sure to try out content database migrations first. This will save you money in the long run. You can then use ShareGate to push the deltas needed to finalize the updates to the user's content when performing on-premises migrations.

Some of the features of ShareGate are as follows:

- Auto-generates PowerShell scripts for all types of migrations with copy options.
- You can pre-test your migration to figure out errors before performing a real-time migration.
- Governance reporting features for pinpointing issues with governance.
- Gives you the option to import user and group mappings from Excel files.
- ShareGate Shell can be used to migrate on schedules and allows you to use PowerShell within the tool.
- Advanced options for managing more complex migration strategies.
- Provides a connection manager for performing SharePoint and OneDrive migrations.
- Performance improves when using Insane Mode for migrations.
- General bug fixes and updates are provided regularly.
- Easy to use.

The following is a list of some of the tools that can be used for SharePoint migration:

Tool	Comments	Review
AvePoint	Has an arsenal of solutions for SharePoint On-Premises and Office 365 for migration, governance, backup, RBS, and many others.	Very good support and works as described in most cases. Setup for products can be confusing but once you get it, you'll be fine. Uses agents instead of solutions on the farm which keeps your environment free of application solutions. Lots of bells and whistles and highly recommended on-premise and in the cloud. The only downfall for me is it requires servers to be added to an on-premise farm to function, which can lead to a bigger server footprint on your network which, is more cost. Also, it can be a little pricy but is your farm worth it? Yes!
ShareGate	This solution provides reporting, migration, and governance.	For the money, this is one of the best tools on the market for the areas of focus the tool works for. The only downfall I have seen is it can be confusing for some users who do not have a lot of experience with SharePoint. Other than that, if you want governance, reporting and migration tools this is the tool I would use for that purpose.
Metalogix	The company is out of business but was purchased by Dell. A long-time player in the migration and solution business for SharePoint.	Metalogix, although out of business, has been purchased and we should see some new things happening with the product under a rebranded title. In my experience it has not been the best experience with this product. best experience with this product. I will say early on I had the opportunity to use it when it was first created for Blob management. It worked great and I was impressed but as they moved on with new solutions things became a little more concerning. I would thoroughly test first before moving forward and make sure you have a great sales rep who can get you great support when you need it.
Saketa	A new player in the SharePoint Migration space.	The interface of this product is like no other. I love the speed of the product during migration as in testing this product pushed content faster than others tested. Great pricing for different tiers of migration unlike other tools on the market. Other integrations are included as well for Microsoft Teams migration.

Figure 7.14 – Tools that can be used for SharePoint migration

AvePoint also has a new migration tool called Fly that does not require any server resources. This really changed the game for the company's migration offering from my perspective. It can be installed free of charge from the AvePoints enterprise application interface and is similar to portable applications such as ShareGate. The product is great! I have tested it, but not with a lot of data. Please check this tool out for your next migration and tell them I sent you! Metalogix has been a key player in SharePoint since I can remember. I wrote up some of this information a while back with the first release of the product, and want to make sure you understand that you definitely need to try this product. Although I had a bad experience with it, I have heard good things about the tool now and the features are very impressive. The downside to it is that is not very user friendly, like ShareGate or other tools, so there is a learning curve. This tool, despite its improvement, does not support PowerShell integration. I just wanted to update you on this tool to make it clear that you should try it.

Microsoft also has a free migration tool that allows you to migrate to Microsoft 365 from SharePoint On-Premises platforms, including 2016, 2013 including Foundation, and 2010 including Foundation. It also includes hooks for connecting to network and local file shares. To find out more about this tool, please go to `https://docs.microsoft.com/en-us/sharepointmigration/introducing-the-sharepoint-migration-tool`.

If you are looking for a planning and assessment tool, Microsoft provides the **SharePoint Migration Assessment Tool** (**SMAT**), a command-line tool that scans SharePoint farms to identify issues before you migrate. This will give you a report so that you can go back and fix any issues before migration. This tool can also be found in the preceding link.

Managed metadata: This is a more complex migration. Some of the migration tools that are available allow you to migrate metadata using the methods provided by the tool. The issue with managed metadata is that there is a GUID for each term set, and the term within the service will not change if you migrate the data. So, if you are doing a service and content database migration, this method of migrating the databases works because there is no GUID change. If you cannot get these methods working and you must do a new installation, you will have to recreate the service and the terms within it.

When performing a content database migration, these details for the managed metadata can be brought over by backing up and restoring the managed metadata service database. When you're creating your managed metadata service, you will use that restored backup to create the new service on the new farm. If you are using a content type hub, update that link using the following PowerShell script:

```
Set-SPMetadataServiceApplication -Identity "Managed metadata
Service Application" -HubURI "http://sitename/contenttypehub"
```

If this is not the method you would like to use to restore the service database, you can use the export-import method. When you migrate the service in this way, you will have to create the service first and then import the information using Excel. You can do that using the following PowerShell script:

```
Add-PSSnapin Microsoft.SharePoint.Powershell $metadataApp= Get-
SpServiceApplication | ? {$_.TypeName -eq "Managed metadata
Service"} $mmsAppId = $metadataApp.Id $mmsproxy = Get-
SPServiceApplicationProxy | ?{$_.TypeName -eq "Managed metadata
Service Connection"} Export-SPMetadataWebServicePartitionData
-Identity $mmsAppId -ServiceProxy $mmsproxy -Path "C:\MMD.cab"
```

> **Important Note**
>
> Make sure you do not have any duplicates in your file before moving forward. If you have duplicates, the process will error on import.

The script for importing is as follows:

```
Add-PSSnapin Microsoft.SharePoint.Powershell $metadataApp=
Get-SpServiceApplication | ? {$_.TypeName -eq "Managed
metadata Service"} $mmsAppId = $metadataApp.Id $mmsproxy =
Get-SPServiceApplicationProxy | ?{$_.TypeName -eq "Managed
metadata Service Connection"} Import-SPMetadataWebServiceParti
tionData -Identity $mmsAppId -ServiceProxy $mmsproxy -Path "//
SharedPath/MMD.cab"
```

Remember that if you were using managed metadata previously in your farm, then you need to migrate this service database and create a service application first before migrating any content. The content, when migrated, will find out whether this data is available so that it can populate the data in the fields that use metadata columns. In some cases, it may give you the functionality to migrate this metadata, depending on the tool you are using. When performing content database migrations, you will have to move the metadata first.

You also need to check that there is a content type hub in your past farm. If so, you will want to make sure you configure that in the new SharePoint 2019 farm. You can do this by setting up a new site collection solely for this purpose and adding the URL to the Content Type Hub form field when editing your Managed metadata Service application. You can also update the Content Type Hub using PowerShell, as shown in the preceding script, to create the service application. If you have already created it without it, use this script:

```
Set-SPMetadataServiceApplication -Identity <MMSAppName> -HubURI
<ContentTypeHub>
```

As you can see, there is a sequence you must follow when performing migrations, and scheduling is a big part of this process. Next, we will learn how and when to schedule migrations.

Scheduling migrations

At this point, everyone knows they are moving to the new SharePoint environment. Everyone is on edge to do this because, at the end of the day, most are afraid of change. So, how do we schedule migrations? My take on this is that you start with the departments that are most eager to jump in. The reason you want to do this is that you will get the most help with the process from resources within the department. This creates a team effort that you might not get from another department, which could defeat the migration before it starts.

If you don't have any eager departments, which I doubt you will, take one department that you have some camaraderie with or one of the hardest you will have to move due to complexity and test their migration first. You can at least test migration with this first department and have the users test the migrated content and compare it between the source and the destination. You should be able to give them an error report from any migration type and work with them on how you will mitigate the errors when performing the final migration of the content.

In the *Types of migration* section, we discussed that migration tools have some scheduling automation capabilities that you can use to configure a migration and create a scheduled task when a particular content migration should run. You can also migrate using PowerShell by scheduling a command to execute on the server at a certain time, but most tools have this integrated with the product.

When running scheduled migrations, you do not have to be present. You could migrate several departments at a time if the content size is reasonable. This also depends on what your time frame is because you want to make sure your users have access to the content you're migrating, maybe the next morning or after the weekend on Monday morning.

You will need to support the migration from time to time to monitor the progress of the migrations you are scheduling. Believe me, there are always errors. To help with such errors, you may need to assign tasks to people in your department to help monitor their progress. If you have tested your migrations and are pretty sure you have done the testing well or if you know there is not much complexity in the site you're migrating, then you may be able to let the scheduled migration run on its own.

If you were testing and used the most difficult customer based on the complexity of the content, then this would have given you a realistic look at the tool and any errors that come up, based on this content. Always take this on with all resources on the ground. If it is just you, get support from Microsoft, a third-party company, or from the company that owns the tools you purchased. This can be done successfully if you plan out the migration properly and identify any errors and mitigate them prior in a test migration.

Again, this may take a couple of test migrations, but the mitigation of errors that surface is the key to success and how quickly you can turn them around. Make sure you always account for the time you may have to spend on the backend recreating content in a site. Again, if the solution is not available in the next version of the farm, you have to make sure you recreate it using a new tool and communicate the difficulty and/or discontinuation of the product to the customer.

> **Important Note**
>
> If you have a couple or even a few web applications, NEVER EVER migrate one web application if the services on the new farm are not stable. If you are still in configuration mode and making updates to services, DO NOT migrate anyone to that unstable farm. Once you have a stable service platform and you have tested those services, you can migrate your first set of user content.

Success is the best way to build confidence in the company as you make these migrations. Choose the right department to work with and test your migration. Review your errors and figure out how to fix them before the final migrations. This may take another test migration, but do not let the first migration fail. Do your best to be successful and have the department that is using the new environment brag about how easy it was to migrate so that others will be at ease and want to move immediately.

In the next section, we will look at farm solutions. They play a big part in recreating content in sites. You may have some issues with this, depending on whether you chose a customized or third-party solution.

Exploring farm solutions

Have you identified all the third-party solutions in your current environment that will be migrated to the new environment? Have you checked the GAC? Have you identified new third-party solutions you would like to use or have replace old solutions? Be sure you check this location within your servers to make sure you have not missed anything. This happened mainly in the 2007 and 2010 days when some solutions were not deployed through SharePoint so that they could be seen and documented. So, if you are coming from one of the older versions of SharePoint, please make sure to check the GAC, which can be found in the `Assemblies` folder in `C:\Windows`, for any solutions that have been deployed using this method.

If you have a good list of solutions from third-party vendors, then you are in business. You can take that list of solutions and find out if the company has upgrades for SharePoint Server 2019. If they do have the solutions, which may have changed to the new SharePoint Add-In model, then download and activate them in the new environment. Test them with your content or have your users test them to make sure they work as expected. Ask your third-party vendor questions and gather information about how they test the migration process from older versions of SharePoint. They should supply documentation about how their solutions can be migrated to the new farm. Again, your testing is important as well, so do not discount testing this for yourself once you have the necessary information.

If the company is no longer in business or has discontinued the solution, have we found a new one to replace it? What can we do to find a solution to replace it with? Well, the first thing we can do is find out what the solution does. There could be another company that has a similar solution you can replace it with. The issues you will encounter will be from a content perspective and will depend on how that content was captured within this solution. You may have to rebuild the content within the solution in the new environment. This will have to be accounted for on the backend of the migration as time spent to do this process. Going into this in detail is beyond the scope of this book, but identify the content and how it is presented and try to do the same in the new environment using the new solution.

Test your third-party solution as well, especially any new solutions you may purchase. You want to make sure it works as it should. Document how the users can use it by coming up with use cases and showcasing them in a demo or in a PowerPoint. As always, keeping communication with your users active is the most important thing you can do during this time. The more you can communicate good and bad things, the better off you will be.

We should also be moving away from the Farm Solution model for custom solutions. There is a new model available in SharePoint 2019. This new model is called the SharePoint Add-In Model and it allows us to get away from Farm Solutions. It helps with migrating solutions to the cloud later. This requires transforming your farm solutions into SharePoint Add-in Model solutions. This would involve doing the following:

- Analyzing your existing extensions
- Designing and developing your new SharePoint add-in
- Testing and deploying your add-in
- Deploying your add-in to the production environment

> **Note**
>
> To deploy newly created custom web parts, you must create an App Catalog. Please review *Chapter 12, SharePoint Framework*, and follow the instructions provided to set up an environment for developers.

The biggest thing to be aware of while doing a process like this is downtime and how this will impact your business. If the solutions you are transforming are key to the business, then you will need to be very careful of how you implement this change. You want to make sure your users are aware of this and also understand you are making this change. You can also run Farm Solutions and Add-Ins in parallel. The time needed to complete or even plan would be great to show the user community so that they have documentation of what is going to happen.

There are two ways we can deploy the new add-in to the farm. One is to do this in-place, which is where you deploy the add-in and then, after making sure the site is using the SharePoint Add-In, you can retract the feature.

The other way you can deploy during a cutover would be to swing content, which extracts the content from the existing site collection where the farm solutions are currently deployed. Migrate the content to a new site collection that uses the new SharePoint Add-In that has been configured.

There are advantages and disadvantages to using either of these migrations strategies, but the big thing is to find out what you believe will work for you, test it, and then implement that process during your migration. Farm Solutions can also be tricky, so I believe the cleanest model is Swing Content. This is because I have seen cases where farm solutions get errors once they've been retracted and it takes time to figure out how to get the solution removed from the farm. This would be a terrible thing to happen, but it has happened to me many times. So, we can't get too comfortable. It's always best to build on clean environments.

There is also a process we need to follow to look into the site in general. This is because some of the elements of farm solutions interface with the users in a page. We should do the following to ensure we have done everything to replace our solutions properly:

- Check custom page layouts and master pages
- Replace web parts and controls in the UI
- Implement page manipulation
- Check for created site columns, list definitions, and content types
- Check for customized modules and feature frameworks
- Determine any custom timer jobs

There are steps you can follow to work through this list of UI-related items related to Farm Solutions. Please research those areas to figure out what you need to do to complete this process of moving toward a cloud ready, on-premises platform. Remember to use a naming convention for the new solutions and features you may migrate to the new farm.

Developed custom solutions

Not all companies use developers to build custom solutions. If you have and those developers have left the building, then you will need to either hire a developer to help you recode the custom solutions you have in your current farm for migration, use third-party solution, or find a different way to build the solution out of the box. We will talk about development frameworks in *Chapter 12, SharePoint Framework,* so that developers understand what tools are available in SharePoint Server 2019. There could also be a third-party solution that could be close to functioning as the current custom solution, which you may want to investigate.

Custom solutions really bring a different level of support to your organization's SharePoint farm. If you do not have a development team on-site, I would suggest that you do not build any custom solutions into your environment unless you have full confidence you can support them. This is where many environments fail due to the company not having the money to support efforts for developers to be on-site, or have a development team that has a high turnover where the developer with the appropriate knowledge has left the company.

In both situations, you need to be forward-thinking. As a company, set aside money to support the developed product. Have someone you can call on speed dial that understands the code and can come in and look at it if something goes wrong. Do not wait until the last minute to try and find someone. It is going to take time for them to review the documentation (if you have it), code, and any errors that may be on the server. SharePoint logs will need to be reviewed as well so that the developer has an understanding of what is happening, which could keep your environment down for days. Having a developer looking at these things prior before anything happens is a best practice so that they can review the code and get familiar with what the solution does before anything goes wrong. At this point, they may see where it may fail and may have some suggestions on updating it right away to make your solutions better.

If you have a development team that has a high turnover rate, make sure that all developers are reviewing each other's code. As part of Sprints or developer processes, they should be doing this anyway as there should be code distributed to a Code Source Safe. It could be the Team Foundation Server or other products, but someone must oversee pushing the code to other environments and testing. Having one person do that and rotating a schedule around this process helps developers understand code that has been created by other developers. Upon doing this, we can go back and see very what happened if we come across any errors. Having a high turnover rate does not help the team, so try to figure out what is happening with the team as well. Whatever it is, try and stabilize the team and keep your developers in the long term, especially if you're using a lot of custom solutions that need support.

Carrying out testing

Have you created your dev, test, and production environments? If you have not, this is where you should stop and do this. Do not move on without having these environments in place. These environments help you mitigate errors, especially when you're performing custom development. They also help with maintenance and testing product updates, as well as other updates you may have based on third-party solutions.

Stress and performance testing the environment

Performance and stress testing is a great way to figure out if your farm is suitable for the user community you're building it for. Visual Studio Enterprise Edition is the ultimate product for load testing SharePoint sites. Unfortunately, this feature will be deprecated but there is a new online version of the product that we will talk about in *Chapter 9, Managing Performance and Troubleshooting*. Within this product, there are two features called Web Performance and Load Testing Tools that can be installed using the Visual Studio Installer. You can choose from cloud-based testing to on-premises load testing. I have used this tool in the past for a couple of my clients that wanted to perform reporting before going live and the results were great. This process also performance tests your servers and you will get performance reports from the servers as part of the testing process. If you need a good tool to test your resources and ramp up user stress against the environment, this is the tool to use. Unfortunately, we will not go into this testing in-depth as this would take a whole chapter, but if you are interested in performing load tests on your environment, please take a look at the following link, which tells you how to set up and use the product: `https://docs.microsoft.com/en-us/visualstudio/test/quickstart-create-a-load-test-project?view=vs-2017`.

User testing

One of the best tools for testing workstations or desktops for troubleshooting errors in your environment is Fiddler. Fiddler will interface with the network card to show you how the device is connecting to SharePoint. It will also give you error messages if something is not working correctly from a protocol/port perspective. This is one of the best tools I have seen on the market because of how thorough the tool is with reporting, but also how easy it is to install and run.

Workstation configurations with DHCP are something to also remember. The user's workstations must be configured with the proper network configuration to reach the SharePoint site. If you are using DHCP, take a look at what has been configured for the user's workstations and make sure it is correct. The last thing you want is a user that is unable to work due to a misconfigured workstation.

Mobile devices work well with SharePoint as well. As you already know, SharePoint can be rendered from a mobile device. You want to make sure you have configured the sites so that the mobile view is activated when it is being used for that feature. This will be activated by default, but you want to check these views if you have more than one administrator to make sure it is still active.

User testing should be documented and there should be some type of testing script for the users to follow. This is generally a walkthrough SharePoint functionality that ensures the site is working as it should. It can also look at the department's workload.

As an example, you may wish to upload documents, but there are other tasks that make sense to test as well. Uploading different types of documents would be a great test. This would mean uploading the most popular document types, such as `.docx`, `.pdf`, `.xlsx`, and others. This ensures everything on the farm, as far as uploads are concerned, is working properly.

So, as part of your testing, you could go a step further and try uploading documents you do not want to capture as part of SharePoint libraries. This means that if you have a stipulation where access documents should not be uploaded to SharePoint and you have set the blocked file type, then you want to test this as part of your testing process.

Make sure you step through all the SharePoint default testing steps, as well as the user's department steps, to create your test plan. This also gets users more acquainted with the new SharePoint look and feel and the changes that have been made to the new UI. In *Chapter 5, Farm and Services*, I listed all the areas that should be focused on when it comes to user testing.

Performing the final checks

As we mentioned previously, this is our final chance to look over our sites, content, migrations, server configurations, and any forgotten steps or services. Please make sure you look over your server resources. There are many things to account for from a server perspective, as well as a SQL and SharePoint perspective, that need to line up to give us a well-balanced baseline that supports our environment.

Server resources and configuration

Server performance is one of the biggest hidden issues I have seen in the field. It is not obvious all the time because not many admins really dig deep to see how a server is performing, nor are they even aware that the system is having issues based on a SQL Server and SharePoint-related service. As admins, we need to be aware of those areas where the server can be in bad shape and do something about it.

> **Important Note**
>
> Run `Get-SPProduct -local` on each of your machines on the farm. This command ensures the updated version on your server is currently in the database.

So, to sanity check and solidify our environment as part of testing, we are going to do some server configuration reviews. We have already done a stress test and user testing. You should take this seriously and review what you have learned from the stress tests to see where your servers are falling short. I have a list of performance monitoring parameters we can monitor that can be downloaded from this book's GitHub repository.

Take those performance areas and run performance monitoring on them while testing the system until you have fine-tuned all your server resources. Yes, there are Microsoft best practices for minimum server configurations for resources, but as you know, things can be incorrect in our configuration as well. In this chapter, we're looking at those areas and fine-tuning our environment to make our server resources as responsive as possible. We will look at performance monitoring in more detail in the chapters to follow.

Application creep

Sometimes, in the world of IT, we make a mistake by adding too many applications to a server or database server and do not even realize it. One of the biggest no-nos you can do in SharePoint is add another database from another application to a SQL Server that supports SharePoint. This is a well-known best practice and should not be taken lightly.

In my experience, I have had two different scenarios occur with applications:

- Non SharePoint Database additions being made to a SQL Server instance that supports SharePoint

- Custom applications being developed that overran server resources at given times of the day

This is not to say there are not more scenarios out there that fall into this category. What I learned from these scenarios is the following:

- Database additions from other applications can kill SQL Server performance. You could run every day with no issue but once there is a problem with that application, you have problems with SharePoint. When a database being used by another application is running on a SQL Server supporting SharePoint, depending on how much that application is used in the environment, that application can slow down the performance of your SharePoint Server.

- We must look at one of the best practices for SharePoint, which is MAXDOP. MAXDOP set to 1 is not a usual setting to use for other applications. So, when adding a database that will not run well on a database server with that setting, you are just compounding problems. Make sure you have no other outside application databases running on the SQL Server you're using that supports SharePoint.

In our configuration, we also need to make sure we have selected the proper servers that support our integrations, such as SQL Reporting Services and other BI applications. In most cases, you want to justify having servers that support just these services. Even PWA and Search need to be evaluated for this isolation. This all depends on the size of your user community and how many users are using the service.

Another item to be aware of is stress testing custom developed solutions. When I worked at Microsoft as a PFE, I had a customer at a bank where they were having issues with a process every afternoon. Everyone using SharePoint would complain about slow performance and the system would just slow down dramatically. I witnessed this firsthand the first day I accessed the customer's site. That evening, I set up performance monitoring on all the servers and the next day, we captured data from the incident.

After reviewing the results, it came down to a custom application that had been developed in house to reconcile some list data that had been captured during the day. The process was very resource-intensive and just slowed everything down. The reason why this happened every day is because they performed this reconciliation every day at the same time when the company closed at 3 p.m. So, from 3 p.m. to 5 p.m. SharePoint was dead due to this custom application.

So, make sure you check all your servers at this time and make sure there are no excess applications, databases, or processes that are running that are unnecessary or located on the SharePoint Servers that do not need to be. This also goes for system supported applications such as antivirus and other server applications required by your IT management team. You must make the judgment call on these applications, but know that some can destroy the performance of your server.

NIC settings

Network Interface Cards (**NICs**) can also be a bottleneck. NICs have many parameters and we need to make sure we set our network interfaces properly:

- Updating your NIC firmware and drivers is critical if you wish to support the server. Please make sure you are on the latest version of the firmware and drivers on all your NICs.

- NIC teaming can affect the performance of the server on the network if it's not been configured properly. Make sure you confirm your configurations during your server testing.

- Next, we will look at MinRoles and service compliance.

MinRoles and service compliance

Assigning MinRoles to servers is the best thing that has happened with the introduction of this component in SharePoint Server 2016. MinRoles have done so much to help admins manage services and make sure they are not running services on servers that are not in line with the server's role and the design of the farm. The following screenshot shows a list of services running on the APP1 server. You can also see that this server is running a custom role. So, when testing compliance, try updating the role and adding a non-compliant service to it so that you can see how these compliance tools work.

Services on Server lists all the services based on the MinRole type:

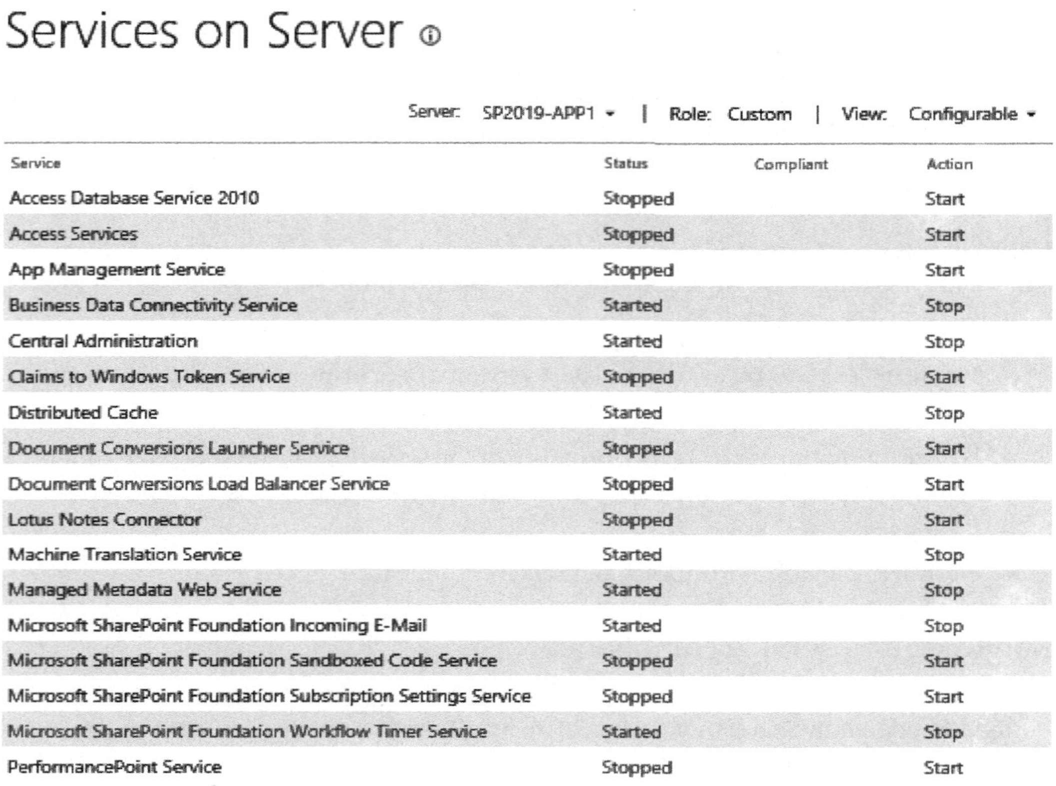

Services on Server ⓘ

| | Server: SP2019-APP1 ▾ | Role: Custom | View: Configurable ▾ |

Service	Status	Compliant	Action
Access Database Service 2010	Stopped		Start
Access Services	Stopped		Start
App Management Service	Stopped		Start
Business Data Connectivity Service	Started		Stop
Central Administration	Started		Stop
Claims to Windows Token Service	Stopped		Start
Distributed Cache	Started		Stop
Document Conversions Launcher Service	Stopped		Start
Document Conversions Load Balancer Service	Stopped		Start
Lotus Notes Connector	Stopped		Start
Machine Translation Service	Started		Stop
Managed Metadata Web Service	Started		Stop
Microsoft SharePoint Foundation Incoming E-Mail	Started		Stop
Microsoft SharePoint Foundation Sandboxed Code Service	Stopped		Start
Microsoft SharePoint Foundation Subscription Settings Service	Stopped		Start
Microsoft SharePoint Foundation Workflow Timer Service	Started		Stop
PerformancePoint Service	Stopped		Start

Figure 7.15 – Services on Server – Central Administration

You can click the **Server** drop-down and change the server you want to view within **Central Administration**.

Services in Farm shows the services and if they are disabled or enabled:

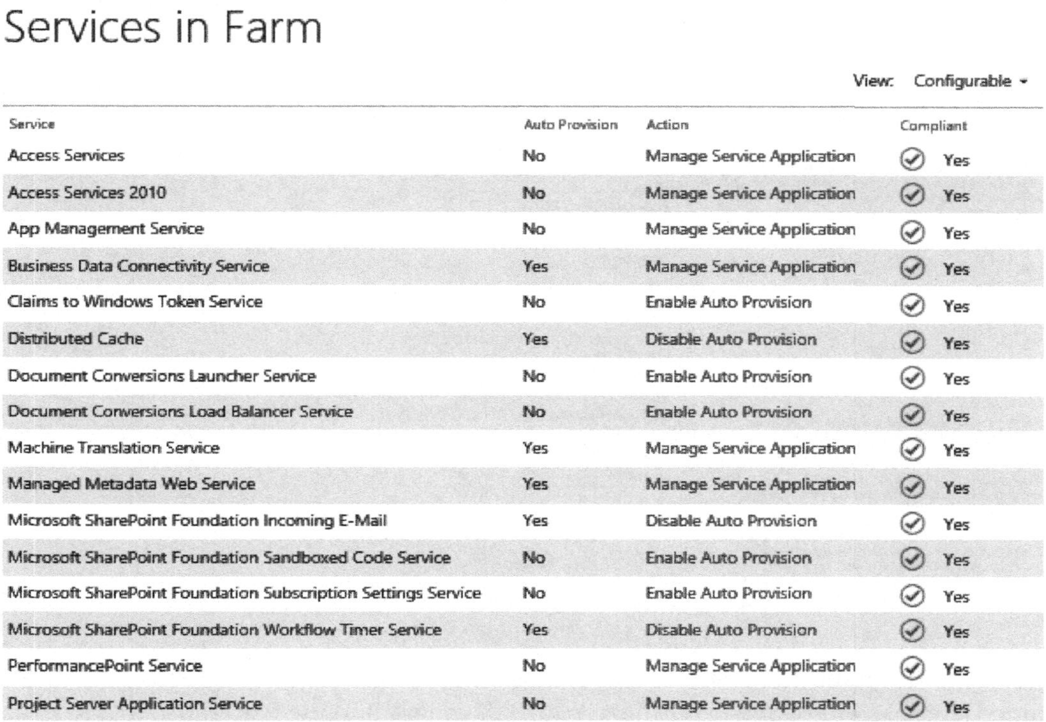

Services in Farm

View: Configurable ▾

Service	Auto Provision	Action	Compliant	
Access Services	No	Manage Service Application	✓	Yes
Access Services 2010	No	Manage Service Application	✓	Yes
App Management Service	No	Manage Service Application	✓	Yes
Business Data Connectivity Service	Yes	Manage Service Application	✓	Yes
Claims to Windows Token Service	No	Enable Auto Provision	✓	Yes
Distributed Cache	Yes	Disable Auto Provision	✓	Yes
Document Conversions Launcher Service	No	Enable Auto Provision	✓	Yes
Document Conversions Load Balancer Service	No	Enable Auto Provision	✓	Yes
Machine Translation Service	Yes	Manage Service Application	✓	Yes
Managed Metadata Web Service	Yes	Manage Service Application	✓	Yes
Microsoft SharePoint Foundation Incoming E-Mail	Yes	Disable Auto Provision	✓	Yes
Microsoft SharePoint Foundation Sandboxed Code Service	No	Enable Auto Provision	✓	Yes
Microsoft SharePoint Foundation Subscription Settings Service	No	Enable Auto Provision	✓	Yes
Microsoft SharePoint Foundation Workflow Timer Service	Yes	Disable Auto Provision	✓	Yes
PerformancePoint Service	No	Manage Service Application	✓	Yes
Project Server Application Service	No	Manage Service Application	✓	Yes

Figure 7.16 – Services in Farm

If the service has not been provisioned, it will show you a link to click to create the service application.

Outgoing mail configuration

The **E-Mail** setting is usually one of the first things I configure. However, I have saved it for last as this service has changed from older versions of SharePoint. You can now do so much more within the configuration since the component can run as a TLS service using connection encryption. You can even change the port you want this service to run on. You can also assign a username and password to the connection, which you could not do in prior versions of SharePoint (excluding 2016). This brings a different level of security to the email traffic that comes from a SharePoint server, from administration messages to workflow messaging.

If you have been using SharePoint Server for a while through different versions over the years, you will have seen that the **Outgoing E-Mail Settings** page has changed significantly:

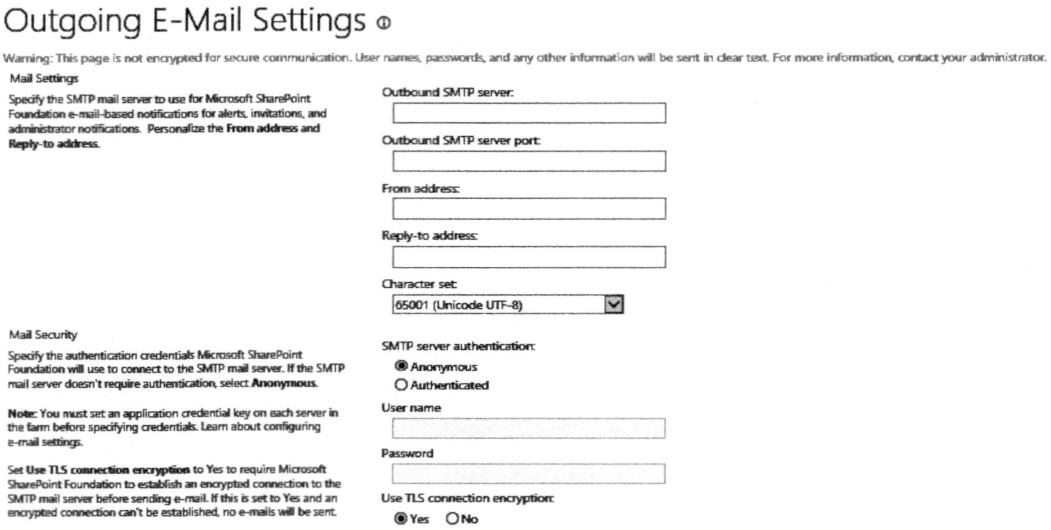

Outgoing E-Mail Settings ⓘ

Warning: This page is not encrypted for secure communication. User names, passwords, and any other information will be sent in clear text. For more information, contact your administrator.

Mail Settings

Specify the SMTP mail server to use for Microsoft SharePoint Foundation e-mail-based notifications for alerts, invitations, and administrator notifications. Personalize the **From address** and **Reply-to address**.

Outbound SMTP server:

Outbound SMTP server port:

From address:

Reply-to address:

Character set:
65001 (Unicode UTF-8)

Mail Security

Specify the authentication credentials Microsoft SharePoint Foundation will use to connect to the SMTP mail server. If the SMTP mail server doesn't require authentication, select **Anonymous**.

Note: You must set an application credential key on each server in the farm before specifying credentials. Learn about configuring e-mail settings.

Set **Use TLS connection encryption** to Yes to require Microsoft SharePoint Foundation to establish an encrypted connection to the SMTP mail server before sending e-mail. If this is set to Yes and an encrypted connection can't be established, no e-mails will be sent.

SMTP server authentication:
◉ Anonymous
○ Authenticated

User name

Password

Use TLS connection encryption:
◉ Yes ○ No

Figure 7.17 – Outgoing E-Mail Settings

Figure out the best configuration for your environment. If security is a concern, there are options for that within SharePoint Server 2019. If you want to use PowerShell to create the configuration for outgoing mail, use the following commands:

```
#Set Outgoing Mail:
$ca = Get-SPWebApplication -IncludeCentralAdministration |
?{$_.ISAdministrationWebApplication -eq $true}
 $sendAd = "SPSMessage@xyzinc.com"
 $replyAd = "SPSMessage@xyzinc.com"
 SsmtpSvr = "mail.xyzinc.com"
 Sca.UpdateMailsettings($smtpServer, $senderAddr, $replyAddr,
65001, $true, 587)


#To Test Outgoing Mail:

Add-PSSnapin Microsoft.SharePoint.PowerShell -ErrorAction
SilentlyContinue

 #Parameters
 $EmailTo = "yourname@company.com"
 $EmailSubject = "Test Email from your company SharePoint Farm"
```

```
$EmailBody = "Test Email Body"

#Get the outgoing Email Server settings:
$SPGlobalAdmin = New-Object Microsoft.SharePoint.
Administration.SPGlobalAdmin
$SMTPServer = $SPGlobalAdmin.OutboundSmtpServer
$EmailFrom = $SPGlobalAdmin.MailFromAddress

#Send-Mail Message:
Send-MailMessage -To $EmailTo -From $EmailFrom -Subject
$EmailSubject -Body $EmailBody -BodyAsHtml -SmtpServer
$SmtpServer
```

Be careful when you're configuring your environment. Just because you set these values using the GUI or PowerShell does not mean they work. There may be some middle configurations with Exchange or other SMTP servers that will need to be completed before this works correctly. Test all incoming and outgoing mail configurations and the functionality within lists and libraries. Notifications for alerts should also be included in your testing to ensure this functionality works as it should.

Backup and restore

We have mentioned backup and restore alongside disaster recovery several times in this book because it's very important. In *Chapter 2, Planning and Architecture*, we showed you how to put together a plan for Disaster Recovery. In *Chapter 6, Finalizing the Farm - Going Live*, we talked about scenarios that will come up as part of setting up a plan of action that are concerned with content size and other things that need to be considered when implementing this retention plan. Let's talk about this again so that we can feel comfortable that we have everything in place to support the content in the farm.

There are a few options in SharePoint that can help with good content management and security to manage access in a better way than just securing the site collections and using broken inheritance as granular security methods. We don't want to get into using these methods because they slow down migrations, even when using SharePoint as a user. The permissions have to be checked more frequently the more individual permissions you give. There are other ways around this, but the root of this is using groups to establish your overarching security within your sites.

I want to make sure to mention the data compliance features that are available within SharePoint Server 2019, Microsoft 365, and Azure. We do not want to omit that in the cloud, there are other features to support our data and how it is accessed and managed as well. We have not covered these areas thoroughly within the book, but we want to make sure to mention them as part of the backup and data protection strategy, because these features can be easily implemented in your SharePoint environment with some planning:

- Data Retention: This controls the life cycle of content within a SharePoint site. It can be a scheduled or in-place action from a user. Files, documents, folders, and content types can be moved, deleted, and managed.

- Records Management: This helps with declaring records within libraries in SharePoint sites. These documents cannot be deleted once declared a record.

- Data Loss Prevention: This helps to protect documents from malicious or accidental sharing. Details within the document can be scanned and identified, such as a social security number to prevent a user from sharing the information, or to limit sharing to only a subset of users.

- eDiscovery: This provides a way to legally hold content within SharePoint sites. You can provide this feature to regulate email and documents to help with legal disputes and other issues that might arise within your company, such as sharing intellectual property.

- Rights Management: This allows admins to set up policies on information within SharePoint and Exchange to protect against sharing outside the organization. It also provides deeper security on documents, and the policies can be valid externally. Azure also has Information Management, which can be used from the cloud and within SharePoint farms as well. The configuration for this integration is not complex but only allows you to create new policies within document libraries on-premises. There is no way to centralize policies when integrating with the cloud.

Please take a look at these areas as part of your backup and restore plan because they can help as you look at creating a plan for supporting the farm. There are strategies with all of these features that will help you understand how they fit into your backup and restore (Disaster Recovery) planning.

How do you plan to back up and restore your environment? The first area I would target would be SQL Server. When looking at SharePoint, you will see that SQL Server captures all your data in a database based on configuration, content, and services. So, in this case, we know what we need to concentrate on to successfully restore our environment if needed.

Storage is the first thing that comes to mind when we start looking at backups. Do you have sufficient storage when starting the planning process to hold the content from the SQL database server? Did you make some adjustments along the way that could have changed how much data is planned for the environment due to migration data? These are questions you need to answer now before going live.

As a process, things change, especially when you're doing migrations. You never know when something may come up during the process; for example, a department may want to bring over a file share or have documents on another system and they would like to move to a SharePoint library. Things change and you must roll with the punches in this type of scenario. There is no way to really plan for some of the challenges that you may face when it comes to personalities, department managers, relationships, and the overall data that can be left out of the mix when dealing with migrations.

Since we have planned for migration of content, we need to circle back and figure out if we have captured everything. Again, our first stop in solving the restoration issue we have with the environment is to back up our SQL Server databases. Next, to really find a sweet spot for total server restoration, we need to back up our servers. While doing this, we need to make sure we do a full server backup, including server state. Next, any components that are third-party need to be fully backed up.

SQL backups are easy to set up as a maintenance plan. They can be scheduled and perform maintenance on the databases as they are going through this scheduled plan. There are a few ways to do this, depending on the size of your environment. For small environments, this is a no-brainer: create a maintenance plan and follow some best practices. If you do not have a lot of processes running on the server or in the environment, nothing should really step on the toes of this process. Schedule it daily with various times for log backups during the day and you are done. You can also use PowerShell backups, which I will mention later in this section, to manage this process.

Larger environments require some thought and details due to other application processes, storage space, responsibility, and overall management of the backup from creation to off-site storage. So, if you are in a larger environment than a two to three server farm, we need to define some of these areas of support for our farm. With larger environments, you need to have some type of application to support the backup of the farm. There are many companies that offer tools that back up servers and have integration with SharePoint as well. Find a tool that works for you or, if you have one, see if they support integration with SharePoint.

As we mentioned previously, SharePoint should be the sole occupant on any SQL Server you deemed to be a SharePoint default SQL Server that holds the databases that support the configuration of the environment. So, in turn, we should not have any issues with outside application processes residing on the database server other than SharePoint. If you do, you need to figure out how to move those processes that support the other servers or be ready for some heavy troubleshooting and complexity when something happens to the performance of the farm.

Make sure to test your management tools for successful backups and restores. I have had an issue a few times where third-party tools lock the databases and SharePoint cannot function at the same time. There have also been issues where the database was in a different format than what SharePoint likes after restoring. Do not take the company's word for it and make sure these processes work before going live.

Since we know that SQL is our main focus point, let's focus on storage space. We defined this earlier, but we need to make sure we have enough space after all the migrations have taken place and new sites with new content come on board later. Let's go back and define how much space each will need and assess the situation so that we can increase the space if needed. Please make sure to define your file sizes when you perform migrations as these will play a big part in how much space is needed. Sometimes, we make mistakes by not setting limits on file sizes, which can eat up our space quickly. This should be discussed as part of your department interview process.

Who is responsible for the backups? Is it the SQL admin, SharePoint admin, or the server admin? Or is there a backup administrator? At this point, you need to figure out who is responsible for what. In the best scenario, one group should be responsible for the backups of the farm. So, if you have a backup team, let them be responsible. However, note that they must take on any best practices the SharePoint or SQL Server teams have to support the process. The more you can divide the responsibility, the better off your teams will function. This takes teamwork and cross training from requirements standpoint so that everyone understands the need of the environment.

Backup scheduling can cause some conflicts as well. Yes, we have scheduled backups, but which backups go offsite, and which backups come back in a certain amount of time? We need to make sure the management of our backups is documented and always monitored so that if we are sending media offsite, we can ensure they are labeled correctly and we know what's on the media leaving the building. Build your process on a spreadsheet or in a database if you like. Just make sure it is always downloaded so that, in the case of a disaster, you always have access to the latest copy. Make sure you have some type of chain of custody sign off within the process as well so that everyone understands what they did with this media as they did it. This is a very important part of our backup and restores the process.

Backup management also plays into how we restore data. Do we have the right media? Was the media labeled correctly? Restoring data from a SQL perspective is a process that has been documented many times on Microsoft's website and other blogs. We will not go into that here, but just know that SQL Server is your friend. It is what helps you restore any SharePoint component. Services, content, and configuration all have databases associated with the farm. Use those backups to restore as needed.

You can also use the Central Administration Backup and Restore area for restoring content from an unattached content database. The word "unattached" in this case means that the content database is part of your SQL Server list of live databases, but it is not part of the farm list of active databases. In this case, you have not attached the database yet. This is a powerful tool for recovering content, but it takes a little longer than a recycle bin or a migration tool due to the steps involved. However, this can be done while users are working on the system. **Unattached Content Database Data Recovery** is located in the **Backup and Restore** section of **Central Administration**:

Unattached Content Database Data Recovery ⓘ

Warning: This page is not encrypted for secure communication. User names, passwords, and any other information will be sent in clear text. For more information, contact your administrator.

Database Name and Authentication

Specify the content database server and content database name to connect to.

Use of Windows authentication is strongly recommended. To use SQL authentication, specify the credentials which will be used to connect to the database.

Database Server

    SPSQLConnect

Database Name

Database authentication

◉ Windows authentication (recommended)

○ SQL authentication

    Account

    Password

Operation to Perform

Select an operation to perform on the content database you selected. You can browse the content of the content database, perform a site collection backup, or export a site or list.

Choose operation:

◉ Browse content

○ Backup site collection

○ Export site or list

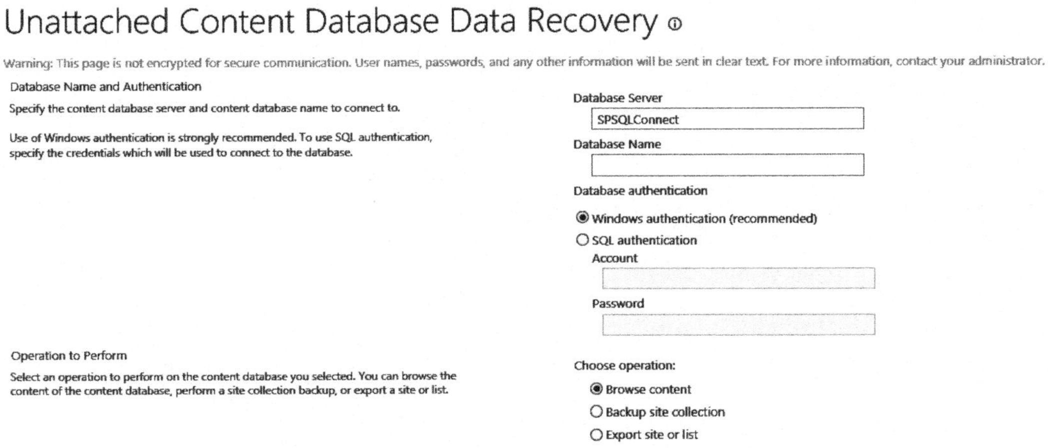

Figure 7.18 – Unattached Content Database Data Recovery

There is also the recycle bin that works for files and other components that have been created in SharePoint. Here, you can find deleted components and documents and restore them back to their original locations. The content is available for as many days as you wish. By default, as shown in the **General Settings** section of any web application, this is 90 days. Once the 90-day period is up, the content is transferred to an admin recycle bin for the number of days you set. So, anyone who deletes any content can go back to those first 90 days and restore the content, after which the admin will have to restore it for them.

As we mentioned previously, there are different ways we can use the PowerShell backup tool to capture content and services. However, this is based on scripting, which can be a little clunky to use and requires your admin to be on their toes. These types of backups need to be monitored and checked daily because they are not 100% functioning applications. They rely on server scheduling and other processes to run. So, do not let this go past you; check the scripts and errors on your server.

Disaster Recovery is not as complex as you may think. If you have a site already, the easiest thing to do is set up a new farm in that location. Figure out how this farm should be configured as a standby. There are a couple of ways to do this using the Hot, Warm, and Cold scenarios for the off-site location. As far as content goes, using SQL Server to push logs to replicate the content to the new SQL Server locations would be the best way to configure the updates of content, either daily or hourly. The timing is up to you.

Having the bandwidth to move the content in big chunks is also another link that is very important. If you don't have the bandwidth, you can expect many delays in terms of how fast the data is moved from one site to another. Make sure to replicate the farm's resources as much as possible. If you have three WFE servers and two app servers, make sure you have that same configuration on the offsite farm. If you have changed and added a service application to the production farm, make sure to add that to the off-site farm. Managing these processes is the key to a successful Disaster Recovery plan for SharePoint.

As a recommendation, AvePoint cannot be beaten for the solutions they bring to the table in terms of overall farm management. If you are looking for a product that can help you manage servers, disaster recovery, content, and retention, look no further. Call them today because this is where you want to invest your time and money to support the environment – especially large environments that have more than three servers. You want to make sure you are covered so that you can sleep sound at night.

Do not forget to investigate solutions, regardless of whether it is the one I am recommending or something different. I have seen too many one-man teams managing a farm and other resources in the network and pulling their hair out. Do not pass this opportunity up at this point, even if you must push your delivery date back for your users. This is everything to your organization at this point, especially if they plan on building tools and other applications within the product.

You are now ready to prepare to go LIVE!

Summary

This chapter has shown you how SharePoint configuration is not as easy as people would believe. It takes some documentation, design, and thought process to make this happen. We covered a lot in this chapter, but the main point was to make sure you have covered all your areas of focus.

In the end, you do not want to release a product that is not complete. Make sure you have your backup and restore process documented and that you follow best practices for all your configuration. Double-check and work with your departments to resolve any issues upfront and make sure to tell them about any foreseen issues beforehand. The better your communication before going live, the better everything will be.

In the next chapter, *Chapter 8, Post-Implementation Operations and Maintenance*, we will discover what to expect on the scheduled cutover day. You will be provided with some tips on how to handle this, as well as some same day things to think about. We will also go over security, responsibilities, and the tools we can use for troubleshooting and maintenance, which will come in handy when we wish to support the environment.

Questions

You can find the answers on GitHub under Assessments at `https://github.com/PacktPublishing/Implementing-Microsoft-SharePoint-2019/blob/master/Assessments.docx`

1. Which ports are used for the Workflow Manager configuration in a SharePoint farm?

2. Which MinRole should your Workflow Manager be installed on as a best practice?

3. When implementing load balancing, which is more cost-effective, a software or a hardware load balancer?

4. NLB does not require any resources from your SharePoint servers. True or False?

5. When meeting with departments about their migration, what should be the main goal of meeting with them?

6. When should I choose content database migration over a SharePoint migration tool?

7. What is one of the new features that can be used with outgoing mail?

8

Post-Implementation Operations and Maintenance

The purpose of this chapter is to let you know what to expect on the release day and things to keep in mind after the release of your environment. We will also focus on processes that should be in place that need to now be executed. These are the tasks that will come into play in supporting the farm immediately and in the future. Within those areas, we will also talk about how to handle the workloads that come from this release, which could mean a very busy day or days to come depending on the fallout from the farm you created and the content you migrated from your old farm. Teams will need to be in place to help support the immediate migration to the new farm. How do we assemble that team? Who needs to be available? These are some of the questions we tackle in this chapter.

As part of the migration, we also go into finalizing those documented errors and updates that need to be documented after the users start using the farm. We need to provide guidance on how they will be handled and how those incidents are pushed through our help desk process as part of the support for the farm. Where do we document those errors? How do we assign those tasks?

As far as the farm, we will look at the system errors and updates that may be needed to the farm configuration. We will look at some ways to troubleshoot and how to document those changes made to correct those errors for future reference. There also could be situations that are unforeseen, for which I will share some of my experiences with you to prepare you for what could happen.

Some of the questions you will ask yourself as part of this process are the following:

- What can I expect on day one?
- What should I have in place to help with that day and days to come?
- How will the help desk be affected?
- How should the team be organized to help with the minimal or large influx of calls?
- What happens if I missed something crucial to the user community?
- How should I handle management questions and outbursts in some cases?
- What if I only did a partial migration of data and there is data missing?
- Do I keep my same URLs from my past farm?
- How do I plan my DNS change?

We will tackle these questions and more in this chapter and make sure to give you guidance and recommendations on how to handle all situations that can come up in this new farm release. The main goal of this release is to be successful so your conduct and technical expertise will come into play in this area to support your deployment.

Remember that maintenance has also started on your farm as well, as this is your first day of release. We will investigate how to keep up your maintenance of the farm and what things are crucial on day one to make sure maintenance is working and any scheduled jobs or manual processes are documented and in place. Maintenance also includes the other environments, DEV and TEST, if you have set them up. We should be monitoring these areas as well to make sure teams using these environments are happy and there are no issues.

This is also a big day and exciting day as well, because of all your hard work. Be prepared and do not be on edge. Stay calm and collected as you will have issues, no matter how big or small the migration was nor how big or small the farm you deployed was. If you have followed this book from a high level and have collected documentation and done due diligence, you are more than 90% there, with some caveats depending on your environment. Now let's go through a day in the life of management, SharePoint admins, and supporting teams on the first day of release.

Technical requirements

For the reader to understand this chapter and the knowledge shared, the following requirements must be met:

- 1 year of SharePoint experience, managing SharePoint or general project management

- 3-5 years of technical experience administering a SharePoint farm

The code files for this chapter are placed at `https://github.com/PacktPublishing/Implementing-Microsoft-SharePoint-2019`.

Post-implementation

In the world of SharePoint, you hear so many horror stories about migrations and implementations that go wrong. These stories are very true. On my way to a customer site, I met a CTO who was doing a SharePoint implementation for 2010. He told me about the issues he faced while using SharePoint and I explained to him that SharePoint is all about planning and understanding what you want from it. He also mentioned he was unaware of some of the best practices I had mentioned, as were his team, and he said they did not use many service accounts in the configuration. They also had slow-running sites and the users were confused about how to use the platform.

So on the first day, please do not be surprised with comments, issues you may run into, or those for which you think you have covered everything thoroughly, because something always happens that cannot be explained in SharePoint in my experience. But you should be able to alleviate most issues that plague implementations if you follow this book, implement my recommendations, and dig deep in the areas mentioned. It is a lot of work in the beginning, but it pays off in the end.

In looking at the chapters that I have written, again I gave you as much information as I have noted and gathered over the years to help you prepare for this kick-off. Again it's up to you on what you use, and what you consider important or trivial, but from my experience, you have to take everything into consideration when standing up a new SharePoint environment or migration. The more thorough you are, the better your deployment. It takes a lot of handholding in some cases and a lot of patience to move forward with these types of releases.

Please make sure you have documented all your configurations and designs for your farm prior to releasing the farm. The more you document, the more information you have to find resolutions to those issues that may come up. Documentation is the key to a successful deployment as I have stated. You need a design document and an installation guide to really make the best of securing the details of your environment. This is necessary and not trivial. I have been to many companies that have documented nothing about their SharePoint environments. Make sure your documentation is up to date with any new changes and make sure to understand what you have built in your farm.

Now that we have that out of the way and have verified that we have documentation, have done testing of the new farm, and trained our users on the new features in the new version of SharePoint, we are now ready to release the farm. We should have updated all required information in all documents and stored these documents in a safe place with roles assigned on who can access, edit, and delete these documents, which is the number-one priority the day before day one. Some of these documents may change during these next few days so we need to make sure we are prepared to update any information necessary. Do not change anything without documenting what you are changing, no matter how rushed you are or how small you may think the change will be.

Our teams should also be prepared and ready to manage whatever situations may arise from this release of SharePoint. This should be their top priority for at least the first two weeks to a month. The teams should be briefed and this should include the following groups:

- Help desk staff
- Site collection admins
- Developers
- SQL administrators
- SharePoint administrators
- Active Directory administrators

- Server administrators

- Management

If you are a one-man shop, then you and your manager should be prepared to handle any calls that come directly to you. The calls related to the new environment are filtered as priority calls. If your team is large you should have already had meetings on how to handle calls and a process flow covering how help desk calls should be routed. We also need to make sure you have guidelines on how these calls should be documented. We will get into these areas later in this chapter.

As an example, you can see in the following figure a guide for how to provide separation of SharePoint duties:

Farm Admin
- Central Administration
- Database Support

Site Collection Admin
- Site Security
- Feature Management
- Page Layouts and Interface

Figure 8.1 – Farm and site collection admin

When following this model, you have feet on the ground with the user's department having a site collection admin take on any calls directly from the department. The site collection admin should have the knowledge to support all applications and structures within the department sites because they work closely with the department or team. This example provides separation between the farm admin and the site collection admin where issues may never make it to the farm admin tier or help desk. So why bug the farm admin when it is not necessary?

A lot of times, site issues are with code, developed functionality, workflows, forms, or just general questions from users who do not understand something. These areas supported are all under the direction of the site collection admin anyway. The site collection admin should organize things in the site collections under that person's direction, so they have a support team as well, and make sure the structure is being followed so that job is easier as well. They can manage one or many site collections, subsites, and projects, which can mean lots of the burden is on this position. This is a recommendation I always relay when talking to companies who use SharePoint and how they should structure their support.

As you can see, communications with users at this time are very crucial for the success of your implementation. Going back to the preceding figure, we have segregated control of the environment based on roles and there are other roles involved as well, who are outside of this example. The example also shows the duties of the farm admin role, who will make sure to check the servers, Central Administration, and any other server areas related to those resources that present the platform and services.

Then, as stated in *Chapter 2, Planning and Architecture*, we should have designated users specific to the departments or site collections that could be technically able to handle the management of the site collection. Again, as stated, this helps you to minimize calls to the help desk and they can keep track of help desk tickets that are local to a site collection admin who understands the department's layout, needs, and security.

One of the other project tasks we talked about was to hire a third-party vendor to help with the deployment and help with tasks in the post-implementation. This would be good for any company to provide an objective, second set of eyes on the process to make sure all things have been captured and make sure you are on the right track. This is especially needed for one-man shops that may not have all the skill sets needed to capture all details as they may not be as experienced in some technical and project functions.

As part of this process, we should build a quick SharePoint site, all of which should be able to be accessed to see posts on common issues. This will give the help desk and site collection admins a way to funnel calls that may need a fix that was already implemented and that the user can do themselves and keep track of the issues that have been called in. The blog post template would be the best way to show this information as it could be a set of step-by-step instructions posted in SharePoint. You can then have the user follow up after they went through that process or go through it with them while on the phone if necessary. The good thing about them having the link to this site is that they will know where to go before calling you for help, alleviating unnecessary phone calls and duplicate tickets. They can also pass this information along to other employees they know have the same issue.

Another way to be successful during post-implementation is to divide and conquer your tasks with the teams you have available. We should also have a page or two dedicated to the same site as the common issues we talked about in the preceding paragraph, which would provide an area where the other teams can manage help desk calls in an isolated area. This could be ServiceNow, another service platform, or SharePoint, and this can be done whichever way you want to handle it. Sometimes making this implementation more isolated from the normal help desk makes sense as it brings a more cohesive and collaborative way to make sure things are being corrected, documented, and seen by everyone on the teams working through the fallout from the implementation.

The hierarchy of support traditionally required to support a company's IT infrastructure is shown in the following figure:

Figure 8.2 – Traditional support model

Having this process isolated does not mean it cannot be kept as documentation and stored for later use. Doing this just means that the process is only available to certain support users and could also have its own phone number for taking calls, which isolates these issues for better tracking and documentation. This would deviate from the traditional support model I have seen in companies. This content could be later backed up and stored or kept open so that it is available, because sometimes we will need to get to this data to see related issues that may come up in the future.

This process is up to you, but I wanted to give some ideas about how I have seen this work in some organizations. All the ideas have a reason behind them and can be helpful depending on your requirements and or the situations your company may be in. You need to find the best solution that can help you work through issues with your users as you implement this new farm. Not following some or all these recommendations can only mean disaster, especially when you are being held accountable for this new environment. It's best to be thorough, and again, **document** everything you can to make sure you have covered all bases.

During the weekend of the cutover, you should also have an individual or team (depending on the size of your farm) testing that all sites are fully migrated if your project included migrations. These migrations would consist of migration tool connectivity, speed, and functionality, while still executing other tasks.

The following is my list of out-of-the-box and superuser functionality that will need to be tested:

- Create a list
- Create a library
- Upload a document
- Create a column
- Create a content type
- Create a workflow 2010 and 2013
- Test existing workflows
- InfoPath Forms
- Create views
- InfoPath publishing
- Create a subsite
- Create a site with a template
- Test site settings (Search settings and Term Store)
- Test Search
- Incoming and outgoing mail
- Notifications in sites and SharePoint Designer workflows
- Find a file (List Search)
- Test People Picker
- Test advanced permissions
- Managed Metadata
- Navigation from Quick Launch and Top Navigation
- Test farm solutions deployed to the site collection
- Verify web parts and other areas in the site are functioning
- Test content and structure
- Syncing tasks
- Open in Windows Explorer
- Recycle Bin

As part of this exercise, you will want to document the functionality for each site tested using a spreadsheet or SharePoint list. This could be a spot check or even a full site list check throughout the farm. It all depends on whether you have enough time and resources to do this. Again, this is very important and will reflect on the support needed on Monday when your users come back to work. This gives you a heads-up on errors, which then gives you a heads-up on fixing issues and documenting how you fixed those issues. I have had some sites not work after migration using out-of-the-box functionality, so please be sure to test these functionalities before releasing.

This exercise with testing also gives you a heads-up on those sites that are working as they should and those that are not. You also can communicate with the department (the site collection admin) that owns the site to have them look through the site as well just to check whether there are some things they do that are more customized so they can verify those specifically and report on them.

Also, capturing images, technical errors, functional errors, and time and date information related to those errors and details on the site where the error happened is also helpful for the tech support team when troubleshooting. There is nothing like having all the information you need so you can really dig deep to find a solution immediately. This should be communicated to the site collection admins, so they know what information they need to supply if this is farm-related.

DNS cutover and on-premise migrations

It is the weekend of your cutover and you may ask, *what should I be doing?* There are steps we need to follow to make sure URLs for our SharePoint sites have been moved and or updated, and are working and functional for the company within the network. This takes involvement from your network team to make sure to set up DNS entries and HOST files for your path-based or host-named site collections. This could be a cloud or on-premise environment we are talking about when it comes to resources needed to provide support for these implementations.

There are a couple of questions that come up when migration comes into play. What if you want new URLs for your web applications? What if you want to preserve your URLs and move them over to the new location? Both have different processes and steps that need to be followed. If you want to know which is the easiest way to move to a new environment, my take on this is that it takes more effort to use the same URL in a different environment.

There is not much that is easy when keeping the same URLs. However, the big benefit is that it does relieve the chore of all your users saving new bookmarks for the new locations of their content. You would think that was easy, but I have run into some issues with this that show a broken rendering of the site. Those issues come from the user's desktop caching, which is seen in *Figure 8.4* in this chapter.

Mind you, you could also have some changes in the content structure as well, which you would need to communicate. When migrating and making changes to any environment, it is the time to make those content changes as well. It could be a new site or even some newly developed functionality, but this is not the time to tell your users about these types of changes. Site mappings and structural changes should have been discussed by the user's site collection admin who should relay these types of events.

These changes should have been done way earlier, during your design phase, and any changes documented at that time. A lot of times admins may change the way sites are mapped during migration because it is a convenient time to make the change, and will move content based on the company's structure. If we have done these types of changes we should have communicated those changes to our users long ago.

Take for instance an acquisition – you may have many sites or changes that need to be merged into your site map. Content and structure could be a big issue as part of your design. This is a good example of when these types of changes would come into play.

When keeping old URLs, we need to also make sure that our old farm is online as well and in read-only mode as we migrate content. We also need to make sure this has been done and is functioning because we do not want any data changing, which would bring the need to do incremental migrations using ShareGate or other migration tools. The worst thing that could happen is a user getting to the old site and making changes to the old site not knowing they are not in the right location.

These types of issues can also be handled with changes to site colors and messages on the front page of the site to make sure people know this is the old site. The reason for the security is that these sites and data cannot change as we try to get the latest and greatest content from the old farm migrated to the new farm.

We also need to change the URL for the old farm and update the DNS entries for these URLs as well after the cutover. If we need to keep the old farm online and in read-only mode for a period, we need to make sure that this task is completed during this weekend of change. This farm could be up and running for another month or more depending on your requirements. Once that point is reached, these servers can be backed up and removed or repurposed as resources for other applications.

Use the following script to update all site collections in a web application to read-only:

```
# Get the Web Application
$WebApp = Get-SPWebApplication "https://my.company.com"
#Loop through all site collections and Set read only status
    foreach ($SPsite in $webApp.Sites)
    {
```

```
    $SPsite.ReadOnly = $true
    #Or : Set-SPSiteAdministration -LockState "Unlock"
-Identity $SPsite.url
  }
```

These changes could take time, as they need to propagate over the network, so all users get the new changes when they log in through the network. These changes consist of IP addresses, network segmentation, routing changes, firewall changes, load balancers, and other areas that may need updating to successfully connect the environment to this new URL.

We must also consider the old location where, in this configuration, we may be updating the name of the URL and associating it with a new IP address. These changes can also take time to be propagated successfully over your network. The bigger your network is, the longer it may take for these changes to take effect.

When using path-based site collections, you will see that there is a one-to-one integration with the site and DNS entry. Path-based sites prepend the site collection to the end of the URL. Preparing your web application is easy in this case, and starts from when you created the web application. Making sure you have the right URL and then the correct choices for the host header, authentication type, and ports, all of which are in that form we used to create the web application. These are very important to get correct because if not, you will have to recreate these web apps, in some cases with information that may not match what you had previously. Naming your web application is also important also so you know what web application it is you are working with specifically.

DNS cutover could mean something totally different to those using host-named site collections. This type of implementation takes a whole other process to complete. To start, each site collection will have its own URL, which is a management nightmare if you look at this at a high level. There are other configurations that are involved with host-named site collections as well, as you have to use realms, many DNS entries for each site collection, and HOST file entries on all servers in the farm, and if you are integrating a cloud-based authentication solution, this could mean extra steps in creating and securing you web application as well, as these will also require setup and installation.

In *Figure 8.3*, you will notice that when keeping the same URL, there are not many changes needed. You could add a server or two to the new environment but under the surface there are many things that need to be configured:

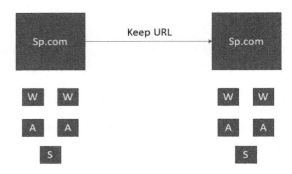

Figure 8.3 – Keeping the same URL (migration)

Remember when you keep the URL from another network segment or network, be it servers in your own environment or a separate cloud service provider, your users may run into issues with rendering sites correctly. The following screenshot shows what your users could see as part of their experience on the first day of using the newly implemented web applications:

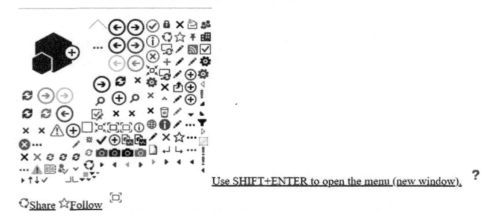

Figure 8.4 – An error rendering the site (first day, same URL)

As you can see in this example of a user going to a migrated site for the first time, when migrated from cloud service to cloud service, the sites could come out garbled or dismantled, and some of the sites may not load fully and look to be in a loop depending on the type of authentication used. Authentication can be messy as well because if you have a cloud provider, this authentication must be in sync with your old farm and your new farm as well. So, there are potential risks with this implementation that will be unforeseen but most can be corrected using the cloud provider's application interface, as we can within Okta. This situation happened to me on a huge migration project, and after six migrations, this situation suddenly reared its ugly head.

I have seen this happen only with cloud-based authentication solutions. You will see a Signing in to Sharepoint loop, as the user is trying to authenticate but cannot due to the authentication process looping.

To resolve this issue, you want the user to clear their cache, the SSL cache, FlushDNS, and even the Windows cache to start fresh when accessing the new URL location. The SSL cache may also need to be cleared as well, as this also keeps a cache for the system. I have had this happen and it is not fun when you have over 90k users having this issue and needing to know this information. It is best to include this in your planning, so everyone is aware prior to the migration by testing sites within the production environment prior to users gaining access. In my case, we were not afforded the time to test before migration.

You might say, *well, why wouldn't you test this in DEV or TEST?* Well, you cannot test in these environments unless you set up the exact same URL in another environment that has its own Active Directory and network structure. The URL can be recreated in an environment where you have a DNS entry for this web application without causing conflicts. Most likely, looking at my experience, not too many people have the luxury of having a whole separate network environment for DEV and TEST. They are usually servers on the same network using the same Active Directory structure.

URL changes using alternate access mappings are an alternative to using the default web applications but again as I stated, you would only be using one IIS site for both the default site and the alternate access mapping if there were two URLs you wanted to use for access to a site. You can have up to five URLs pointing to one IIS site. There are five zones you can use when adding alternate access mappings.

Make sure to catch any of these mappings on the farm you are migrating from, so you can include them in the configurations on the new farm. They are useful when you want to just have an alternate URL to bind against a main web application with a different URL name, maybe using it for a specific department or group of users.

To add a new alternate access mappings, use the following script but also remember you may have several web applications you need to update. The following code will work with traditional web applications or, as stated, path-based web applications:

```
New-SPAlternateURL -WebApplication "http://server.yourcompany.
com" -URL "http://sp.yourcompany.com" -Zone Internet
```

In the case of *Figure 8.3*, we are looking at an internal on-premise SharePoint farm and a migration from one set of servers to another. When using the server-named web applications, this also gives us a way to test our content by connecting to it, testing authentication, and looking through content to make sure all content is migrated and services are working correctly before we even start this DNS change process. When in testing, the URL does not matter too much at that point. This helps us with time management so that we can start this days or weeks before we do our final migration. The URL can be changed later when we need it.

This method of server-named web applications is an easy way to set up a web application quickly without the need for networking teams to get involved. The server already has a DNS name and IP, and is configured on the network, so utilizing this makes sense just to do some testing. It also gives us an opportunity to have users go in and test and review content, workflows, and other areas of their sites we may not know about. They also have the opportunity to do a spot check before the sites have fully been migrated.

In my experience, this is not done often enough and the communication from the SharePoint teams is usually nonexistent for this type of sanity check. In most cases, it happens because of time constraints and a lack of understanding of how necessary these tests really are before going live. Therefore, it is very important to plan and not rush during an implementation like this where it affects almost everyone in your company and even external users in some cases.

We also need to remember that if we are using DEV and TEST environments, this can also be done using those environments to migrate too before bringing content into production. As part of our migration process, this should be number one on our list of tasks as this is so important. Please make sure to set up these environments even if they are just one or two servers.

In my experience, this is not the case as most SharePoint Admins do not have these environments set up for us to use to brainstorm, test configurations, and develop processes. Even if you just have a small DEV environment, it helps you to be able to test something before bringing it to the production farm. There are so many problems you can face later if you do not follow this process. If you don't follow this process, you may end up releasing a farm riddled with errors.

> **Note**
>
> One of my pet peeves is migrating directly to production and potentially having errors in production on services that have not been released yet. Be wise and create DEV and TEST environments to make sure your content and services are working as they should before migrating to production, documenting the configuration for each environment. When you get to PROD it should be pretty much perfect. This also gives you a way to test with users' content prior to releasing to production, which then you can use different URLs to do so. Production should be perfect, or close to it!

So, in our current on-premise enterprise, we would make sure to make changes to the DNS the day you tell the users the systems will be down. So, if you schedule the system to be down on Friday at 6 p.m. and you are expecting the system back up 5 a.m. on Monday morning, then that window of time is to be used to migrate your DNS. This gives a chance for URLs especially to be propagated and updated to where the new IP location of that URL is moving. The best time to migrate is a holiday weekend or over Christmas through New Year's, where there are not many people online due to the holidays.

This also gives you time to make any updates to your firewalls and other areas in your network that could be a concern, especially when it comes to external access. This also gives you time to configure (if you haven't already) and test your load balancer using the URL. Propagation also has time to finish and update all network changes, so users do not get errors when trying to connect to content.

As we are talking about internal enterprise changes, we also need to remember that we also need to test our connectivity to our new URLs and even the old URLs if they are staying in place. This should also be done during this downtime. We want to make sure we do not have any missed DNS entries or weird errors, especially when using ADFS or other intermediate applications for authentication. If you are leaving your old farm in place, we need to make sure to test whether the old farm is working with the current or new URL assigned to it. This is only preserved as a read-only site for verification.

When looking at this scenario from path-based web applications and host-named site collections, we will see that there is a big difference in how we would utilize our time during the cutover. If you have a path-based web application and you are migrating that application, it all needs to come over that weekend. Everything in the content databases associated with the web application must be migrated all at once.

With host-named site collections, you can look at this very differently. The path-based web application at the top of the URL does not have to be migrated; only the site collections with URLs below the web application do, and they do not all have to go at one time. I have seen some instances where there was a mixture of both in a host-named site collection's web application. At that point, you would move all your site collections as you feel but at the end, all path-based web applications could move when the top-level web application is moved, as I have seen before where some of those top-level web applications have had path-based site collections added by accident. Please check before moving this content.

There are more content strategies for on-premise migrations in *Chapter 9, Managing Performance and Troubleshooting*. There are some strategies outlined within the cloud migration details in the following section that can also be used for on-premise migrations when it comes to content structuring.

Cloud migrations and cut over

In the case where you are moving cloud providers, it can be very tricky migrating from one service provider to another. There are so many factors that come into play as part of a migration from one cloud service to another, or even from on-premise to the cloud. Let's talk through some scenarios and figure out what we should be looking for in a cloud provider.

Migrating to a new cloud service sounds easy enough. If you look at this from a high level you would think all you have to do is set up new servers on the new provider, install SharePoint, and migrate your content over to the new SQL server. Sounds like a great plan in theory, but that is easier said than done.

There are so many gray areas that can come into play, where things may be different in the new cloud provider's interface such that you miss something very important that can set you back weeks. When looking at network interfaces – the way servers communicate using the new provider – and maintaining the services and setup, you will be in for a rude awakening even after you have made your migration.

When choosing a cloud provider, you really want to explore what the company offers as services and make sure they fit what you are looking for. Here is a list of a couple of things you can pay attention to when hunting for a new cloud provider, to help you find the right provider for your new SharePoint environment:

- Their **Service-Level Agreement (SLA)**
- Robust security and data protection features
- The range of services they provide
- Migration assistance
- The best in connectivity

From an overall contract position, most cloud providers will send you a long and complicated SLA. This should be read in its entirety by your management and even a company lawyer. This agreement will solidify your relationship with your new service provider, so this SLA is very important. You may have some unique requirements this provider may not understand or even offer support for. Having a clear understanding at the start should be your focus at this point before signing any contracts. If you are looking for compliance at a high level due to your industry, make sure to choose a provider that meets those requirements.

When cloud first came on the scene, security was a big concern. This was due to horror stories that people heard from other companies and the services had not matured to meet the needs of high-profile government agencies. Those worries are gone now, except for maybe a few small gray areas, but overall, you can pretty much now trust your providers with the security of your presence in the cloud.

There are a few things to look for but one of the most important is how data is transmitted from your business and the cloud. Is it secure? Does your provider use some of the best technology to secure your data? This should be the questions you need to investigate by asking your provider about these areas of concern and researching blogs and other companies that may be using this provider's services. Blogs sometimes give you hints on what shortcomings your provider may have.

Other areas that affect data are transfer speeds and how we get our data from one platform to another. Ask yourself, *will this take me weeks or months to complete? How much storage do I need on my new cloud platform?* Questions like these are key to discovering key areas of connectivity. This even weighs on how your users will connect to the new services. Does the platform meet your needs? Most likely, yes, but you must really test drive this platform to see what you uncover, and in most cases, it's going to take you trusting your provider and testing your systems and processes on the platform after migration. At that point, you will be able to tweak as needed to get the most out of the platform. I will explain more later in this section about my experience of moving from RackSpace to AWS.

You also want to see how your new provider handles physical security. Where are they located? Do they have multiple locations? Are these locations dispersed around the world? These are just a few things to think about with physical location. Even with those physical locations, how does the provider handle weather disasters, security breaches, and damage that could happen due to accidents or robbery? This should be the least of your concerns. The provider should make you feel at ease when it comes to the protection of your data and should have disaster recovery in mind and be able to explain how their failover secures your data from disaster. Services could be affected by these incidents as well.

Providers offer such a vast range of services and in some cases, you may have one that provides 80% of what you are looking for and another that provides only 50% of what you are looking for. The 80% provider may have 20% of the services you need out of the box. So do your investigation and wisely choose the best fit for your organization. This may be two providers but that comes as a cost.

The thing to keep in mind is that when moving to the cloud, the first thing you want is a place to expand and exploit new capabilities. The goal in all this is to provide services that expand your business and even bring more continuity to the business using applications and enhancing business processes. Looking at a provider's future goals would be another area of concern. What are they planning to bring to the table in the future? These are all things to think about during this time.

As stated, when looking at cloud providers, you will come across a new platform where your current IT professionals may not have the expertise. This is where you look to your provider to see what professional services may be included in your subscription for their cloud and how you can get your current employees trained on the platform through other training providers. This brings up the questions of, *where do we start? Does the provider have these training services available? How long will it take to get the employees trained?* Talk to them to get more details on a plan moving forward. In most cases, they have done this all before and can provide recommendations.

When looking at training and services, we arrive at another issue that brings all of this together at the bottom line: cost. *What is it going to cost me to move from my current platform to this new platform? How is this going to affect my business and customers?* These are some of the things you need to think about as you walk through the process of choosing a provider and what can transpire as part of this migration that may affect your business.

Choosing a cloud provider and a subscription that fits will give you a total sum for the bottom line and you then can adjust as you see fit. The big thing to consider is yes, you are moving to the cloud, but moving to the cloud is going to enhance your systems, streamline your processes and give you more to offer to your customers. So, the ROI could make the difference in how you see the cloud playing in your migration as well. Think about these things.

Again, in most cases, you will do an incremental migration, migrating areas within your environment separately when possible and moving the services to the new platform. The thing is, I am only talking about SharePoint in this book, but we need to consider other services that are provided in your current environment. Create a plan of action once you have chosen a provider. Move your systems as you see fit and create a plan that works for you and the resources you need to get the job done. If you need help, call a third-party company or some consultants to help you manage the migration.

Reflecting on this section, we covered the following topics:

- Environmental differences
- Training
- Cost

Please make sure to review and ask questions before you make a move to the cloud. This is a pivotal move that can make or break your company. One mistake could leave you with a long-lasting migration where a platform like SharePoint is way behind schedule and you are paying for an engineer to migrate the platform. You have paid for their service and nothing has been migrated. Now you are paying for servers in your current platform and servers on the new platform. This is not cost-effective at all and can lead to you spending a lot more than planned.

This exact situation occurred on a project I was on recently. After I analyzed what happened, I could have saved the company over a million dollars in costs if I had started the project. There was more to this story, but at a high level, I was brought in later in the project to help the current consultant.

I made recommendations the first week I was there, and they were ignored. Fast-forward 4 months later and I am on the project with a third-party vendor now and just starting to migrate content. The other consultant was let go two months prior.

This brings up some great points, but we will not dive into this. I have touched upon a lot of them in the book already but the points I am trying to make here are the following:

- Planning is everything.
- Choosing the right people is everything.
- Experience matters in most cases.
- Always evaluate your position constantly.
- Never overlook a recommendation.

In looking at these points, one stands out to me: planning for cloud migrations with SharePoint. I have focused a lot on planning in this book because it's everything that matters. For instance, you have a large amount of data, so you already know that the connection speed could slow you down for database transfers if doing a content database migration, and even when using a tool such as ShareGate.

Depending on the speed of the connection to your current provider's network, you could see slow transfers of content databases and slow migration of content using a tool. It is best to let your provider know what you are doing and see if they have other pipelines you can use to transfer data. As part of that setup, you would want to include secure tunneling to move the data from point A to point B as well.

In this scenario with SharePoint, you would want to look at your databases as well. You could also come across large databases that need to be minimized as per best practice sizing of 100 GB to 200 GB, which is a reasonable size to get the fastest transfers from one provider to another. On premises, this will not have much bearing on your migration, but over the internet to separate cloud providers, this could be an immediate cause of concern, especially when you are talking about costs and the ability to move the data as you planned to. As stated, the goal is to not have to pay more for your old system than you have to. You want to move and be done with the former services, so you do not have to pay both companies for very long at the same time.

There are services that some cloud providers have available that help with the migration of large data. Amazon offers a few ways of moving these large databases, called Snowball and Snow Mobile, which give you a way to get those extra-large data files moved faster but require some physical logistics to make this happen.

These services are hardware-related and you basically get a piece of hardware and copy the data from your server to this hardware. Once the data is copied, you send it over to your new service provider and they use it to copy the data to your new cloud instance.

Amazon S3 is a transfer acceleration service and has some requirements you must meet as well. I used this to do a 15 TB content database migration and it worked like a charm. Please look for these services online and find out which you can take advantage of in cases where you just cannot or do not have time to downsize content in your databases. If your databases are more than 600 GB, you will have an issue getting those databases copied over in a decent amount of time. There is an upload process and then a download process on the other end.

To elevate some of the stress on content size, there are a few things to remember. Again, the best practice size for content databases, as mentioned previously, is 100 GB to 200 GB, but investigating the content to see what you can do to mitigate issues with content size can help to soften the blow of the time required. This exercise really helps you to load balance the content over the databases to make them less in size. Even creating new databases that will help you manage what sites you want to move and many sites may not want to move at a specific time. There could be plans you need to follow for moving sites by department or even by priority.

Let's look at a couple of things you can do to make size less of an issue when copying a database from one service to another:

- Site collection cleanup
- Moving site collections
- Promotion of sites to site collections (use a tool)

With the cloud, we also have hybrid configurations that come into play when you want to keep your server on premises or in a cloud environment, and connect to a cloud service such as Microsoft 365. This service, along with Azure, really have some cool tools you can take advantage of. We will talk about hybrid configurations and how these come into play in *Chapter 10, SharePoint Advanced Reporting and Features*.

Site collection cleanup: This is the easiest way to delete old content and you should have done this in the planning stages of your implementation. Verifying that a site is still being used and or is valid is something you should do right away. If you have not done this, then you want to try and get this done one evening before your migration weekend as you migrate incrementally. The process consists of validating the site for deletion with the site collection admin and then backing it up for retrieval if something goes wrong is the first step of the process. Then, at that point, you can delete the site collection. This is done in cases where there may be a need for this site later.

Site collection moves: This is the next option we have and is not that hard to do but it takes time and patience to make sure you are validating which sites need to be moved and what database they are moving to. This does require some updating to your current documentation so that we know where the site now resides in case there is a need to move the sites in the future. To do this, you need to use PowerShell. Before we do this though, we need to see what site collections are available within the content databases. We can do that by either looking through Central Administration using **View all site collections** and clicking on the site collection to see what content database it is associated with and making a list or using the following PowerShell script:

```
Get-SPContentDatabase | %{Write-Output "- $($_.Name)";
foreach($site in $_.sites){write-Output $site.url}} > Drive\
Folder\sitecollections.txt
```

Or, alternatively, you could use the following:

```
Get-SPSite -Limit All -ContentDatabase contentdbname | select
url, @{label="Size";Expression={$_.usage.storage}}
```

The difference between each is that from the first PowerShell script, it is understood that it is going through and getting the content database and listing all site collections under it. The second command lists all the site collections and storage used within the database. Choose how you want to do this, but both can be of help in any situation:

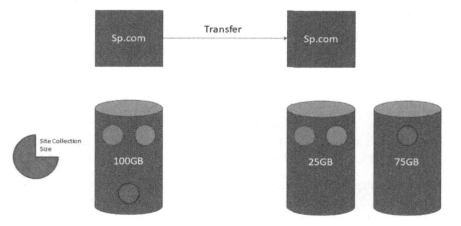

Figure 8.5 – Site collection move

You would then create a new content database as shown in the following snippet:

```
New-SPContentDatabase -identity NEWCONTENTDATABASENAME
```

Once you create that content database using your naming convention, then use this PowerShell command to move the site collection from the current location to the new location (the content database). See the following code for this:

```
Move-SPSite <Site-Collection-URL> –DestinationDatabase
"<Database-Name>"
```

To show you how this would work, take for example a content database named "A", which has site collections running, and a new content database named "B", which was just created and is empty. The total size of content database "A" is 100 GB and it has 3 site collections. The total size of the one red site collection is very large, at 75 GB, as shown in *Figure 8.5*. We would then move that site collection from the current content database to the new one, so we alleviate the size of the current database. Now that we have created a new database "B", where this site collection is able to grow, content database "A" is now able to grow as well with more space.

This is a good practice to follow, especially when you are moving content from one site to another. This also helps with incremental pushes of content if you are using a tool once you get your content database moved to the new location, as the size of those transfers is not large in size, so the amount of time to move is not as long.

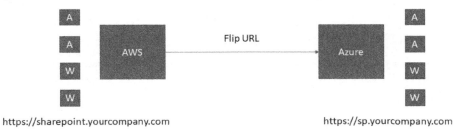

Figure 8.6 – Changing the URL

Again, knowing environmental differences is very important, as the settings within the cloud provider's networks and a basic understanding of that network could be a learning curve. Moving data is a big portion of a migration. This is something you would have to have had discussed previously in your planning stages or you would not be where you are in this book. Knowing how to use AWS, Azure, Rackspace or any cloud environment is a plus and if your admins needed training, they should have already been through this training already. There are so many things that are different in each of these providers' services because they each have their own ecosystems.

One of the things I noticed on AWS, for example, is that just because you set firewall settings on a server doesn't mean that port will work or be open for your servers to communicate through. There are also other layers that control this portion of the AWS network. You do not want to learn this at this stage of the game. This should have been something you learned during installation and configuration.

Before I install SharePoint, I make sure all firewall ports are open and local policies are set correctly for all service accounts that are needed for a successful deployment so I do not have issues later with failed services and trying to figure out and troubleshoot problems after the release of the environment. Make sure you know your platforms before you start, or get help from the service provider immediately for any issues or problems.

Not understanding the environment also affects your plans in other ways. This could happen with unexpected pitfalls and the need for more training. This can also lead to unexpected service costs or migration tools at a cost per GB – it could even be several things that pop up at this time that you did not expect. The biggest is the fact that you must keep the old servers online for a longer period than you expected.

Migrating from cloud to cloud comes with costs, even though you may not be using the service actively. Your provider will understand you're moving, but they will continue to bill you until you have finished moving or deleting your objects or have asked them to shut down your subscription areas. So, while preparing your new environment for use, you need to be preparing your old environment for deletion as well.

This means you need to figure out everything that needs to move, whether it's the databases, folders with files in them, mapped drives with the content on servers you may not know about, or whatever you may have that you may need going forward to protect you from loss of data.

As far as migration tool costs go, you must look at this from a migration perspective. These tools cost us per gigabyte, so we must be careful. We can sit here all day and say all is going to go well, but there is the chance that you start the tool and it doesn't do what you expect, and you have to restart the process of incrementally migrating that content to the new sites. This can add a lot of extra costs depending on how much content you just made a mistake migrating. Test within your internal environment using some trial software for which your provider will give you a certain amount of gigabytes to test. Whether it's on-premise or on the cloud, make sure you understand the settings within the migration tool so you do not have to redo any work. The trial time with the tool will also help you figure out the use of the tool and how it works.

In some cases, old content is usually sitting around on SQL servers, and in some cases, is still running on the database server but not attached to the SharePoint farm. There also may be some content in mapped drives that have been planned as part of the migration. These files need to be vetted and cleaned up as part of this process.

As part of planning, these areas should have been reviewed, deleted, and taken into consideration already in your planning phase but if you have not done this, you will need to finalize the data you want to move. You never know when someone is going to ask for information from a few years back that may not be online or in backups. This way, you have those databases or data that may be unused for a long time but if it is asked for in the future, you will have it.

With this old content, we need to be able to document the content as well. The following questions might pop up in your mind:

- What was that database being used for?

- Was it attached to a web app?

- Was it a part of a department's site?

- What was this folder on the server used for that seems to have scripts or content in it?

- Do we have some PowerShell scripts running as scheduled tasks that need to be moved?

- Did we check the GAC for any custom solutions?

The answers to those questions need to be investigated and you need to make sure they are documented. This goes for services databases as well. If you have an old service database, you should keep it and just label it correctly on a backup drive or some media for review.

Did you take a backup?

As part of the migration from cloud service to cloud service, and even in the case of server-to-server migration within an on-premises implementation, the gathering of old data and content should be the focus when it comes to preserving information. You want to make sure before moving environments, especially in a cloud environment, that you have accounted for everything. If you are not organized and have folders on servers where you keep things and mapped drive locations which has files on other servers, then this is the time for you to search and find data. You could also take a snapshot of old backups from SQL servers as well to make sure you have retention in place where you needed to recover some data. Figure out a good point in time to go back to and take those backups with you.

If you are in this mode of finding data, you want to make sure you do not have to go through this again, so applying a fresh start and clean slate to this new farm environment is the key to a healthy start. Do not go back to bad habits and do things as you used to. If you need help with that and have some resources that can be used to check behind you, make sure to do so at this time. It is time for a change and the beginnings of managing this environment properly.

So, after you have found the files you are looking for and copied them to a central location, what do you do now? You can have your old cloud provider give you backup space, or provide them with a USB drive to get the data copied to a backup location. There are not many choices and it all depends on how you want to move the data. If you do not want to use the service any longer, then the easiest way would be to have the USB or storage added to a server or storage hardware and copy the files there. You can have them send the hardware back to you through the mail and or use OneDrive or another cloud storage service to move files as well, but they all come with a cost depending on the storage needed.

If you use a cloud location, you then have to take the time to copy up and then copy down from the location, which could mean several days or weeks of time spent monitoring, being at risk of losing your connection, and as I stated, cost. Timeouts can happen if the connection is broken, which add to costs because you must start over, which also lengthens the time required to move those files. Choosing a method will be best for you to decide. I can make recommendations, but you know your situation and time frames at this point in your migration. Please just be aware of stumbling blocks and make sure to understand your cloud environment policies.

In *Chapter 2, Planning and Architecture*, we talked about disaster recovery and how to implement a plan for backing up your SharePoint farm. There are many ways to build redundancy in your new farm. If you plan to use our outline to develop a Disaster Recovery Plan then make sure you put in place some of these options to help you build a good backup and recovery plan. As part of the plan, we also want to take into consideration all the locations and files you have gathered that SharePoint used or was involved with in the old farm. These files are important and we should be backing up those locations as well.

As far as databases are concerned, we can use SQL mirroring or SQL Always On to build a redundant system for failover. This will help to prevent any data loss. Of course, this all depends on where your other SQL server is located. If you do not have a great data pipeline built between those two locations, either locally or externally, the connectivity will fail. There are requirements for these systems to be external and the communication speed needed to sustain connectivity between SQL servers. Please investigate these configurations before starting to build a second or third server for geographical purposes.

Database mirroring and replication also work the same way. I believe I mentioned a product from AvePoint, called Replicator, that helps with these scenarios. Please investigate third-party solutions as well, which may give you more in-depth control over the information being pushed to another location or server on your network. Out-of-the-box mirroring works, and so do transfers such as log shipping, but it all depends on your requirements as to how you build the systems to support backup and recovery. Check out all available options before proceeding and also look at the configuration best practices for these areas first before starting any work, as they may not work out depending on your needs.

As far as restoration, you will need to follow some basic rules around your database sizes, which should be around the 200 GB size limit. The smaller your databases, the faster the recovery. Please try to stick to that as much as possible. Always look at a site collection that is getting close to that limit as they need to add a new site collection and not more disk space. You can add links to the new site collection within the original, and use the Portal Connection in site settings to make them site-related.

Labeling your databases properly also helps if there is prioritization during the recovery, where you have an ordered list of what sites are to be online first to last, as this could come into play in some company structures. This has been mentioned throughout the book. Naming is everything, and stops you from deleting something that you need. When restoring, do not leave a restored database name, such as **Restored_11_10_2019**. This is a no-no!

Drive selection for your backup will also come into play. Please use a local drive to provide storage for your SQL backups. Once those backups have been completed, then copy them to cloud storage or another server. Of course, this process needs to be orchestrated and tested, because backups should be captured and then removed so that the next batch of backups have the space to be captured the next day. If you want to capture more than one day's worth of backups, make sure to have the storage available to hold that amount of days multiplied by the database sizes being stored.

Using less costly disk space for backups is fine if there is not a lot of activity and the size of your databases is not too large, but you would need the right amount of space for storage of these files. Using RAID 10 will help to increase the speed of your backup as it does not manage parity. This type of configuration on your disks will read and write faster. This will come at a cost, as this would be looked at as a higher functioning disk configuration.

Avoid running backups when other processes are running or when there is a lot of user traffic on the systems. This could include a process built by a developer that runs at night, or a process where some other maintenance is being captured on SharePoint or SQL Server using PowerShell scheduled jobs, SharePoint custom timer jobs, and other customizations that may take time to process.

Again, as mentioned in *Chapter 2, Planning and Architecture*, please also remember to schedule full, incremental, and differential backups as needed. This will make sure to capture RTO, as a full backup may not pull the most recent data for you once restored. The incremental and differential backups will help to make sure you bring your database up to date with the most recent content that was available before you had a hiccup on the system. Make sure, if you schedule a backup of the database, to include the logs on every backup type as well.

If you are crunched for time, as this process again is orchestrated and needs to have an order to it, please use compression if your backups are taking too long. This can affect the CPU as it does need more processing power to complete the backup process, but time is money, and in this case, sanity. You want to make sure you get backups done every night. Losing data doesn't work when it's needed for restoring operations. Even when using SharePoint Shell cmdlets such as `Export-SPWeb`, the command automatically compresses the exported information. If we use the `-NoFileCompression` parameter as part of this command line, then we see that we have a larger output, which takes up more storage.

Some final thoughts are to always make sure to back up your ULS logs and any other locations needed to support your SharePoint farm. If you lose a server, you want to make sure you have that information available for restoring as well. Blob storage is another location you need to make sure you have tackled as part of the restore process. Depending on the method you used to configure this custom location, make sure to find the right solution for the restoration of these files and structures.

First-day blues

Although I tried to get as much in this book as possible on the configuration, migration, and management of your SharePoint project based on my experiences and lessons learned, there could still be issues that I have not come across. There could also be some things you did not ask about during this process or that others did not mention while in meetings with departments or stakeholders, as I have been in that situation before as well. This book really provides a list of everything you need, which I could think of and noted down to eliminate having anything missed during this process.

If you have done those things and understand where you are and what to look forward to then good for you. Either way, the first day is very stressful because you do not know what to expect. If you have worked with SharePoint long enough, you will understand what I am saying. You could have triple-checked everything, and still, something will happen to blindside you. So, on the first day, be ready for the unexpected and make sure you are notified of things that go wrong immediately.

You should also have a **Release Management Process** in place to make sure that you understand the first versions of customizations that have been changed during this process or updated due to changes in the newer version of SharePoint. The developers should have already tackled this but this process should help us understand what versions of customizations should be deployed in the farm. If you are using Team Foundation Server, the versions of these solutions should be captured there. If not, make sure the developers have a process in place that supports this process. We talk about this more in *Chapter 12, SharePoint Framework*.

Think over your steps thoroughly as you go through this process and if you worked over the weekend as you most likely have, then make sure you prepare for release day. Make sure to get some rest on that Sunday or the day before to prepare for your morning. If your management gets in at 6 a.m., you need to be in at 4-5 a.m. This is to make sure things are *still* working correctly, as you will need to do some spot testing and make sure that any early users do not have issues connecting to the site. Using a warm-up script would help in keeping the site fresh so that those first users connecting are always connected without waiting until the app pool spins up. There are warm-up scripts on the Microsoft Office site that are good and easy to use. We talk about these more in *Chapter 9, Managing Performance and Troubleshooting*.

By getting in early, you could also most likely mitigate any other issues in those first few days of the release before the first users of the system get in the office. It is always good to be in early before the users get in the office to make sure things are working, especially for the first couple of weeks. SharePoint has a way of making the top list of applications, but is never deemed a Tier 1 application, I've noticed. So be ready to be treated like a Tier 1 and expect to have a busy week or month.

As part of those first users connecting to the system, you will also want to look over *Chapter 9, Managing Performance and Troubleshooting*; as stated, warm-up scripts play a big part in ensuring that the site does not take long to load for the first user of the system. There are other things you can do to make content render quickly using database maintenance and other areas we will cover in that chapter as well.

We also want to check the servers as well and make sure all servers are in place, functioning, haven't blue screened, and are performing well with no error messages detected in our Windows logs or ULS logs that might have come up during the evening. A lot of times after the SharePoint jobs run through their schedules (which could be hourly, daily, weekly, and monthly), there could be something that comes up in our SharePoint Health Analyzer.

We should also check the backups and any SharePoint server-side jobs you may have running. You should have a backup of the systems and sites to start so that the content can be baselined before being made available for the user community. If there are any issues or you notice that there are errors in your backups that were not there before, make sure to document those errors and start with the errors that need to be resolved immediately.

Logging errors will be part of your day today. You want to make sure you have a site or list dedicated to this release. You want to tag all errors you encounter as high, medium, or low. These errors also need to be categorized and if they are duplicated, they need to be combined so you don't have a long list of errors you have to report to management that include duplicate errors from different users. Make sure to show related errors as one error, even if it is not the same error. Set priorities on these errors as well to make sure attention is focused on the errors and issues you record as appropriate.

As stated in this section, we want to have a site and pages dedicated to our issues. We should categorize all our issues that are reported and use a system like that in the following figure:

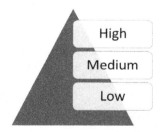

Figure 8.7 – Categorization of issues

Having levels of urgency, whether it's three or five levels, would help in managing those critical issues that may affect more users than a lower-level issue where it may only affect a user's desktop and the version of IE they are using. It is important to manage this, as due to their expectations, your management will really look hard at this, more so than the number of tickets you may have unresolved.

Understanding team dynamics

Supporting this effort will be a challenge depending on how many users you have, the size of the farm, the number of internal sites, the number of external sites, and so on. So, the best efforts to support this environment need to be enthusiastically shared across the team, as well as wanting the best for the users and customers that access this environment. If you are hosting SharePoint services, then you have a bigger task of supplying the best efforts for your platform and support for your customers.

There are many team players as I have pointed out in this chapter and you will need the time of all of them at some point. Make sure you have met with the teams and have gone over your expectations for each of them. They need to understand what you want from them during this time as they will have other areas they will be supporting within the company as well. So, you do not want to overburden them where they are not able to help you or are slow to respond because they didn't know the plans for this new environment or migration project.

In creating the best support efforts for your environment, communication and collaboration are key to a successful implementation. The more you can get the team working together and understanding their jobs in this process, the better off you will be. For example, handing off errors to the technical team is part of the process, but if you are handing over user training issues, trivial issues, or duplicated errors to the technical team, this will not be a good use of their time. Sorting and managing this list of issues is the key to success and you get a quicker turnaround on getting these errors resolved.

As part of this process, centralizing the process and incidents is another area of concern, as I have seen many ways other companies have handled implementation and migration cutover days differently. When reviewing these companies, I found that some of their plans did not work due to the lack of communication between groups and the tools they were using to manage the list of incidents.

When separating the processes visually using different solutions to host the incidents, communication gets lost or misunderstood. It is best to centralize and use a system where others from different teams can view and sort the incidents. The reason is that another team may have the answer, as SharePoint Server resources span many areas of Microsoft technology. We must be aware of that and make sure we do not leave any eyes or ears out of the loop.

In my travels, SharePoint is the best tool to use because of its collaborative nature and the way it helps to centralize the information. It also does not take much time to set up a good prototype to support this process. Most people who support SharePoint already know how it works and they can manage the views and manipulate the data. Processes can be automated if you have time, so that if you assign an issue to someone, they get notified and can document the trail of notes and resolutions.

You can also prioritize items and make sure some have bigger priority over others in the queue. As shown in the following diagram, your team intersects with many other teams:

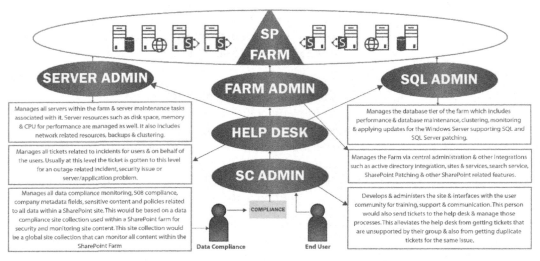

Figure 8.8 – Support structure for a SharePoint farm

I shared this diagram in *Chapter 2, Planning and Architecture,* to help with planning resources. If you have not done this exercise the time is now to get organized before you move forward. Do not go into this unorganized and with no plan. You cannot wing this unless SharePoint is just a sub-system where it's not high in priority in your organization. I have never seen this be true because it's such a sharing tool that even if it's grown out of the wild wild west it will be considered very important. Again, it maybe not considered tier one, but it is to a lot of people.

One product that I have seen that can help take some weight off the teams are Governance Solutions. Governance Solutions can be put in place to give the user the freedom to create sites or site collections as an example to get those types of requests moved from your queue. This puts the power in the hands of the users but also can be streamlined for certain users who have the access to do it.

The big thing with this Governance Solution is that it can also be used to keep things in order, such as naming conventions and use of templates for site collections. This gives the users strict options to move forward with creating something in the farm but you are putting rules around that content to make it useful, size the content and name it based on a naming convention as an example.

Once everything has been completed and you have successfully moved into your new environment there is another resource that will come into play to help guide the development process called the Business Analyst. This role in my travels has been mostly nonexistent. I have only seen this role implemented on two customer sites out of the over 100 I have been to over the years.

The role is a key role in development and interfacing with the user community. When you look at this compared to a site collection admin or someone keeping the interface between the farm admin and the user community this is the role needed to help guide those communications. The site collection admin still has that key role of communication, but the Business Analyst helps to provide information back to developers and the farm admin, so coordination of newly developed solutions is guided and documented correctly.

Their key responsibilities are the following:

- Understand how the business operates
- Understand SharePoint from a technical and user standpoint
- Developer background preferred (not a must)
- Identify gaps and opportunities to improve the service
- Identify where automation can be used to help business processes
- Technically document requirements and user feedback on testing
- Document and help in any areas of this process

The reason I did not have this role documented in the image is because they are not really part of the technical staff that supports the implementation. This role is more to guide new and in process developed solutions. They should have skills to help with the implementation, but their focus is not an administrative task at the farm level. This role helps users and site collection admins come up with solutions to problems to help build the right solution to support the community. This is a key role and there need to be more companies utilizing this skill set in their collaboration space.

Incident management concepts

The farm is down on the first day, what do I do? Good question! Pray it's nothing you missed. Most likely in these cases, it could be anything—storage, network outage, server down—but whatever it is you need to respond quickly. During these first days and really the first month things will be on edge because things are settling in with the team and the user community. As time goes on you will see things start to be more and more stable and users become more and more happy unless they just do not like SharePoint. (We do have some people like that...LOL.)

The technical team again consists of SharePoint Admins, SQL Admins, Network Resources, Storage Resources, and others who may have a part in this wide-ranged system. As stated, the collaboration between these teams needs to be fluent and responses need to be almost immediate, especially for incidents like the preceding one.

For technical issues like the one described previously, with a total outage of services, we must be careful. We must respond quickly and make sure to try and fix the problem as quickly as possible. So, this would include logging the incident within the centralized system and relaying this to the team and management right away. Major outages I would always include management, so they are not blindsided. In the end, you will save your manager some grief.

Next, I would work the incident to see if this is an easy fix or a major outage where it will take time so I can communicate that back to the team and management. Once you figure the issue out and you see that it is a fix that you can resolve, follow your process to fix that issue. This could mean doing it right away for a major outage like the one described, or if it's something that only affects a certain department then we see how it affects the farm, and if it's something where you have to take down resources then maybe it could wait until after hours to be completed. This is all part of your process within your company that could include a change management process as well.

At this point, all teams should be on standby and processes should be streamlined. I know in some companies I have been with it takes time to get approval for calling outside vendors, vendor-customer numbers and or login information is not readily available, and other procurement factors can come into play. At this stage in the game, you do not want to have these types of hiccups. Make sure your teams are ready and have the information needed to make calls on the spot for support.

This help could include some help from outside vendors like Microsoft as well where you may have something a little more involved where you need an expert to look at the issue over your shoulder. This requires time especially dealing with Microsoft because it will take some time to log the call and, depending on your service agreement, you could be waiting 4 hours for a response by contract. So, the quicker you find the issue and what you need to fix the problem the better off you are to get management a solid update.

Make sure again to report success and failures immediately. Even if you are working with an outside vendor, always communicate to keep some updates going. For me, it is bad to have your manager calling you for an update instead of you providing one. It keeps them off your back and fully aware of the status, even if it is using Teams or email.

When to meet and when to include management? All throughout the process. Meeting with management should only take place if there is a failure where your vendor could not fix the issue. This is when you need management to make a decision as this could mean some rework in the configuration and you will have to think of ways to work around the farm so at least some people can continue working if possible, or some type of way to be partially up and running on this new platform.

Exploring troubleshooting tools

I wanted to list some troubleshooting tools to get you thinking about what you need during this event of handing over this new SharePoint environment. We will talk in more detail in *Chapter 9, Managing Performance and Troubleshooting*. For now, we will document some tools you may want to consider for troubleshooting any issues you may encounter during this process of supporting the farm. To download any of these tools, please see my GitHub and find the download link or do a search yourself, but make sure you are going to a reliable source:

- **Netmon**: This is a tool used to monitor communication between App and Web servers, Active Directory, DNS, SQL, and the client, in this case, would be your end users.

- **Event Viewer**: These logs are the go-to for SharePoint admins. These logs, which are located on the server, will point out issues quickly within the OS that is supporting the application, which in this case is SharePoint. I have used these logs to troubleshoot issues, but they do not always give you the answer to an underlying problem.

- **Perfmon**: These are the tools that are built into the Windows Server and Desktop operating systems and can be used to find out core issues with performance on server and desktop resources. Monitoring all aspects of a SharePoint server farm is important when you are troubleshooting so do not forget SQL. Counters for the specific server types and services are viewable via Microsoft's website.

- **PAL**: This is an extension of Perfmon as it helps you to identify issues quickly using the performance monitor capture. This tool was created by a PFE at Microsoft and is used widely for assessments and other reports for SharePoint. It makes your life easier by converting the performance files into something you can read easily. This is a CodePlex download and is available on that site.

- **ULS Viewer**: This is a great tool provided by Microsoft. I would not recommend any of the other tools who provide similar functionality. You can copy logs and send them to others to review (if small enough in size) and the product does not have to be loaded on the server. It's a great tool to find issues with problems in SharePoint.

- **Fiddler**: This is a network monitoring application I have used a lot in the past as well as Netmon. I prefer Fiddler because I am more familiar with it but have heard great things about Netmon.

- **PowerShell**: It has many commands that people may be unaware of, like `Merge-SPLogFile`. This combines all trace log entries from all the servers in the farm into one single file on the local computer. `Merge-SPUsageLog` is also available to merge usage logs.

- **SharePoint Designer**: This tool is very helpful when looking at site related issues and changes you may need to make to sites and related files. I have used SharePoint Designer in some cases to change the look and feel of the site, change filenames, permissions, and many other areas. This tool is used to make life easier managing sites within SharePoint.

These tools will get you started on troubleshooting issues and find solutions to problems within your environments. Most issues come from not following best practices. I have mentioned that several times in this book as well. Microsoft tests the SharePoint environments using these best practices and this list of practices and software limits can really save you when implementing SharePoint. We talk more about how to use a few of these tools in *Chapter 9, Managing Performance and Troubleshooting*.

Maintaining the environments

The first day of your new environment means if you have followed this high-level plan in this book you are doing things differently in most cases. The last thing you want to do is follow old habits and bring them into your new environment. So, when you encounter an issue with content, check it first in production find out what the issue is. Unless this is something simple where you can fix it easily without configuration changes I would not troubleshoot in production. I see a lot of admins guessing on solutions to issues and when they do not work they cause more issues or leave residue from the attempted fix that is not cleaned up.

The way to keep production clean is to create a backup of the site or site collection and migrate it to the DEV environment. Then test the content in DEV and see if you get the same behavior. This alleviates any issues you may cause with PowerShell scripts and other troubleshooting methods that may disturb the production farm. Once you have found a solution, test the solution in the TEST environment and figure out if that fix worked as well.

If you have all three environments, GREAT! If not, it is time to do things differently. Do not make the same mistakes you made in your last farm environment. Work towards keeping Production clean and healthy by illuminating excess from failed development projects and other changes made to the server resources without testing first. This goes for Microsoft Updates as well as we apply those updates to the product and the OS and SQL servers. You want to test these updates before proceeding to apply these updates to your production farm. This is a best practice! Your SharePoint environments should at the least mimic the following image conceptually:

Figure 8.9 – Needed SharePoint environments

Your test (TEST) and production (PROD) environments should have the same server footprint or be similar in server footprint. There are also other environments that can be added, such as DEVINT, which will give you a single source-testing environment where an individual tester can go in and test any updates or changes that were fixed in the code from development first, which then protects your TEST environment. The developers would not deploy the code or even have access to this environment. The code would be deployed and tested independently to avoid any tampering. The code changes made in this environment should work as described, or be backed out of and retested, so we know the code works.

Security is the most important consideration, as I have seen everything you can imagine. I have had customers who have had development environments and used the same service accounts in production environments. They had also deleted accounts as well, and I have even seen customers who have disabled accounts used in all environments, worsening the effects of the mistake of using the same account across all environments. Guess what? SharePoint went down.

To avoid the headache of managing all your service accounts you should separate them. You want to make sure to use separate accounts for each environment. This could even be from separate AD domains as well, which is the ideal situation you would want for this type of configuration. The reason for this is to make sure that accounts being used in DEV work with the resources in DEV and then resources in TEST work with TEST. PROD should be separated as well so the accounts are associated with the proper environment.

If you want to use the same AD domain, make sure to use separate **Organizational Units (OUs)** and separate servers, with groups based on admin, test user accounts, and service accounts to make sure the accounts are separated and have something in the naming convention that indicates the environment that the account is being used for, such as `Domain\DevSPAdmin`. This is a good way to tell where that service account should reside and if it is not in the right place, you can see so immediately and do something about that right away.

To add to that, make sure not to install SharePoint using an account you do not want to own your environment. There is no way to change this, so using personal accounts and for instance, a DEV farm account from the PROD environment, would not be an ideal situation to be in. All accounts should be defined for specific uses and environments. If a personal account was used as the farm admin account to install the service, once that person leaves the organization you are stuck having that account active for the life of the farm.

Again, this is only to help you make sense of what these environments are used for. This is something you must do to maintain your sanity when you are managing three SharePoint farms and any little slip-up could cause you an outage.

Change management processes are an ongoing effort and help to alleviate issues caused by changes to your environment(s). The change process can be involved in controlling when changes are allowed, setting an approval for the change, and scheduling the resources to implement the change request. Implementing a change management process also allows you to document how the change went in terms of its success, and add those documents that show how the change will be implemented. Keeping track of changes within each environment helps to backtrack as well, so you can see what has happened and be able to go back through the history to understand where there could have been a mistake made. Having that history is priceless if you have documentation that shows what was done during that change request, especially concerning the code and developers.

SharePoint can help you with documenting change requests, and I have put together simple change request processes that can be used to manage updates to systems, applications, and services. There are other tools out there as well that do the same thing. I prefer SharePoint because it centralizes your information and makes it available to those that you want to see it. So, requests can be made, and the process can be started and finished using a simple workflow created by your team. Having this process in place is priceless but you must use it.

Zero downtime and patching is a way of keeping your environment up and running without the need for interruptions to your user base due to Windows Update or maintenance processes. One of the big areas you will see change over the course of your farm is the need for monthly maintenance to your farm, which is done to implement changes and updates to features and services within your farm. These updates are published on what is called Patch Tuesday, which is the second Tuesday in the month.

> **Note**
>
> For more detail on zero downtime patching, consult the Microsoft documentation at `https://docs.microsoft.com/en-us/ sharepoint/upgrade-and-update/sharepoint-server- 2016-zero-downtime-patching-steps`.

As stated in prior chapters, you should have already come up with a baseline and schedule for patches and have implemented the following areas for inclusion:

- Identifying patches needed (do not forget Project Server, AppFabric, and third-party integrations)
- Leaving time for testing in DEV environment
- Leaving time for testing in the TEST environment
- Implementing the patches in the production environment
- In the process of this implementation, making sure all servers have each update

When doing a fresh install, as we talked about in prior chapters, you must be aware of changes in the environment. You will see errors in the Health Analyzer that may point to databases being out of sync and servers that may be missing patches. This is the time to upgrade all servers and all databases to make sure the farm is cohesive. This should have been done when doing your installation by applying the latest patches at this time. If a newer patch has come up, then you can apply that if you want as well, but the farm needs to have a baseline at some point.

> **Important note**
>
> This is so important, and I cannot stress enough the importance of making sure your farm is in good standing. Checking the statuses of the database, product, patch, and your Health Analyzer after changes have been applied is critical. Remember to wait a day before checking, or run all the timer jobs that update the status of these components so you can see the effects.

Having a baseline helps in the amount of work you must put in as an admin. This means you do not have to go back and check the farm again because it is understood you will be releasing the farm at a baseline you determine. A mistake made by most admins is they go back and apply updates to a farm and do not remember which servers they applied them to. Documenting and paying attention to detail can be a pain, I know, but you can avoid mistakes by updating all documentation and knowing where you left off if you had to break off before finishing the update task. This could have also slipped through the hands of the Windows admins who control **Windows Server Update Services (WSUS)**. Make sure to only download those patches and not automatically install SharePoint patches.

When you look at your farm from Central Administration, in the **Upgrade and Migration** area you will see a **Check product and path installation status** option:

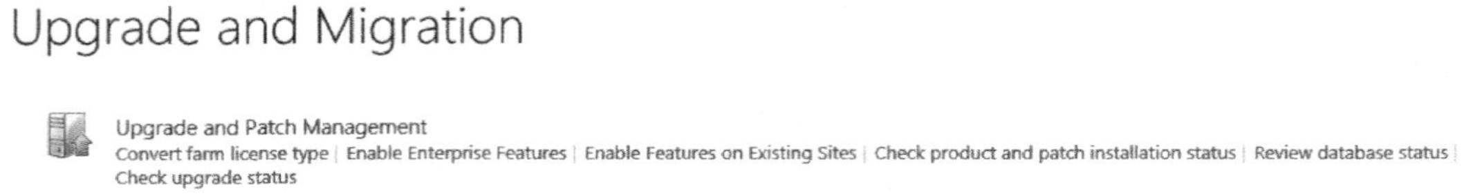

Upgrade and Migration

Upgrade and Patch Management
Convert farm license type | Enable Enterprise Features | Enable Features on Existing Sites | Check product and patch installation status | Review database status |
Check upgrade status

Figure 8.10 – Check the product and path installation status

If your servers are out of compliance as far as the server role is concerned, those issues will come up. When servers are not on the same patch level, you may see some performance issues, as well as feature functionalities being intermittent. Remember, PSConfig is your friend, and make sure to always update your farm using this command by running it on each server so that patches are rolled up and configured. You can also use the SharePoint Configuration Wizard on each server to update them as well.

The following PowerShell command will come in hand:

```
Get-SPProduct -Local
```

The preceding command shows the version of SharePoint you are currently running. This can be run after patching and this will update your system (config db) to the latest version of SharePoint it is running. It also updates operations in the SharePoint database and ensures the information is accurate by updating the SharePoint configuration database information. This is also the equivalent of running the Product Version timer job, as I have had issues with servers updating but still facing an error because of not having the right version when trying to connect to the farm.

> **Note**
>
> Again, for all content databases that need an update, you should refer to `Update-SPContentDatabase "database name"`. Updating services' databases requires different commands based on different services depending on the error given. Please do some research on Microsoft's website.

Configuration management is a term you do not hear much anymore. I used to hear this a lot back in the mainframe days in the 1980s and 90s. Today I believe it is still important, but things have changed so much with technology that I do not see a lot of people doing this and managing it correctly. It is important to remember we need to make sure to keep our farms configured the same in each environment. If we are making changes to those environments, the changes to Central Administration would need to be implemented on the other environments as well. If I make a feature change, I should change it on my other environments as well – and document it!

Updates to all areas of our network, servers, and other areas where we depend on testing these updates in an environment that can be changed – all of these need to be documented. Pushing things through environments can be a challenge if you are not configuring areas where you will need high-level services configured before you can implement a process.

Say you have not implemented Project Server in your lower environment, and you install it and never document the steps for production. The next person who implements it in a higher environment implements it differently than you did. Now we have issues in the higher environment due to not following the process of documenting, testing, and passing the working implementation documentation on to the next environment.

Change management and configuration management are very important, and are here for you to work with to make your life easier. Yes, it takes some extra time but in the long run, this will help you sleep at night and not be awakened by calls from developers complaining that the systems are not working correctly. Make sure to take this recommendation seriously for SharePoint implementations. SharePoint can be a massive pain if you do not manage it correctly.

Tools are also available to push content from one environment to another. The use of replication can keep data fresh and keep all of the environment's content the same as production. This can be a lifesaver in some instances where having content from production will help you in determining the best development process. With this, configuration management is the key to success for this to happen because if you have services running in production that key in on certain content and those same services are not running in a lower environment, you will see errors and content will not be in a good state, which could cause issues that are not recoverable from.

Some of the tools that you can use range from SQL log shipping to AvePoint Replication services. I am sure there are some services and third-party tools that can come into play here as well. My experience has been with AvePoint and although it works in general, you may have to see if it will work for your specific situation and requirements. AvePoint makes great tools that tend to be missing out-of-the-box features such as replication, so please check with them for a demo. I know a couple of my customers in the past used this product and things went well. Cost might also be a factor at this point, if you have not thought about it already. Talk with your management and see if this is something they can provide to help you with migrating content.

Why is a development environment important?

Again, I have mentioned this throughout this book, and this is the final hour. I want to mention this again because I need you to understand how important your DEV environment is to the success of your production environment. In some cases, you may not have developers but you may have people who want to play out-of-the-box development, which also can lead to corruption and sites not working as they should if not managed correctly.

The best bet is to implement a development environment and use it to support any users who want to make changes to the production environment. This way you can have them practice here and implement in the production environment by documenting the steps needed for the implementation. You could even have them document the change they want to implement so you can check it before it is done in production, as in a change management review process.

In some environments, there could be many developers, so you would have to create separate farms for using server resources. This is the best way (and I have seen many ways of doing this) to have some separation and individual ways of supporting the developers. Do not go down the road to having many developers on one farm. There are many issues just with rebooting, and resetting IIS could be a big issue when another project needs to be completed.

Using GitHub as a cloud-based code repository works well for Microsoft 365 and Azure for developers to add code and version-control it. Azure DevOps Server also works and can be used by many developers at a time. If you are using Sprints to move your code through the process, the developers can create folders based on the Sprint and add the code in the folder for that Sprint. Once completed, they can check it in for tests and testers can download the code from this central location to use for testing and implementing in higher environments.

Why do you need a test environment?

Since we discussed the DEV environment, we need to mention why the TEST environment is important as well. The TEST environment should mimic your production environment as far as the server footprint. We may not give this environment the same storage or server resources, but this environment should have the same configuration as your production farm. The reason for this is so you can test how integrations and other configurations and development will be implemented. This also gives the opportunity to users to see how things will work before they are passed on to the production environment.

Testing helps achieve successful deployments either on a schedule or in general use of the practice. Without testing, there would be no way to see if you are affecting areas in SharePoint that maybe you shouldn't, and if the code works you implemented an out-of-the-box development that may not be able to be achieved due to differences in the platforms. Testing is everything to the sanity of your production environment. Let users test before they drive. Make it a point to have this environment available with production data so that the users get a feel for it before you implement it.

Production – why you should be cautious

I have seen production resources used in many ways, and some were not the best. Production to me means the latest source of content that has been updated by the user community. How can we develop our production environment with confidence? Can we expect these developed features and sites to be 100% error-free? If we allow development in production, you will be bound to have an error or two, which could be a small thing or a very intrusive thing.

Production during the later process of migrating from one source to a new destination should always be the final stage. When I say final stage, I mean the following situation:

- All testing is done in other environments.
- All services have been configured and reconfigured in other environments.
- Documented processes for setting up services that work.
- Documented service accounts used for these configurations.
- Documented errors in lower environments have been fixed.

The bottom line is to apply only proven concepts to this environment. Even this method is not foolproof all the time. You may have developers who have developed and pushed code through testing in other environments, but it still fails in the production environment. In these cases, you need to figure out what happened, and if it does not work, then back out of your code in most cases when you can't find a way to correct it. This situation can really complicate things.

The difficulty in this approach is that developers are not perfect, and a lot of times they expect to be able to rebuild an environment based on code that was pushed through testing but there are some gaps. Say you added a new AD group to a site. You gave that group permissions to content within the site during that Sprint. Now you have updated the way this content is viewed; maybe, say we created a list in the beginning but now they are moving to their own subsite as this group needs more functionality. Suddenly you need to make that change – how does the code capture this when going through Sprints? It will apply everything as it was during that Sprint, so now there could be some confusion as to whether to delete the document library they used. So, any number of things can happen to rebuild from code.

Taking that example we know there is no way to recreate an environment from code. So, the best thing is not to rely on code and never implement code that is not tested. The last thing you need is a major slip-up in a Sprint that changes the way the site was designed. My point here is you need the lower environments to make sure you have done your due diligence to provide the best code and updates to your production farm. Once there's a backup, you are golden, with some caveats for updates from code you have deployed, but do not get hooked on your code being your backup.

Summary

Going live with your new farm takes a lot of planning and attention to detail. As you have seen in this chapter, there were lots of references to prior chapters to make you aware of some of the things you may have missed. A lot of the information in this chapter was mentioned way back at the beginning, but if you still didn't take those areas of concern into consideration, you can see how they can come back to haunt you right before deployment. This happens a lot, and if you did run into this issue, you are one of many.

As stated, planning and implementing a SharePoint environment takes patience, organization, teamwork, and cross-team support. Even the best technically sound SharePoint admin will miss things, and this could be due to not being organized or just not having the patience to document the environment. These, as well as other errors, come into play when depending on one person to do all the work. In this type of implementation, do not let one person do this job alone. This is not a job for one person. Make sure to have a team around this person to help, even if it is just to document the process and technical aspects.

The moral of this chapter is that if you missed something, make sure to clean it up before releasing. The effects when you do not pay attention to detail in some cases are devastating. It is better to make sure the environment is sound now than have to answer to your boss later.

In the next chapter, we look at performance and troubleshooting. This chapter will help explain some of the concepts we have covered in this chapter and give you more in-depth information on the topics. The next chapter also takes a thorough look at troubleshooting tools and performance tools.

Questions

You can find the answers on GitHub under Assessments at `https://github.com/PacktPublishing/Implementing-Microsoft-SharePoint-2019/blob/master/Assessments.docx`

1. When making the decision to release your farm to the users in production, what are some of the things you want to check before the cutover?

2. Issues may arise after the cutover. The help desk should have had training to handle these new help desk calls. True or false?

3. What are some of the basic site functionalities that should be tested before the cutover?

4. Why do you need a test environment for your SharePoint farm?

5. When using the zero downtime process to update your environment, what is the key to a successful update process?

6. A user calls and says the SharePoint site looks like it's been dismantled. What do you suggest they do, as the site was migrated using the same URLs from another farm?

9

Managing Performance and Troubleshooting

Managing performance for SharePoint Server has not changed much from prior versions. The same tools and processes you used in the past can be used in this version, though there are some caveats. Some of the things we did with other SharePoint versions have become integrated into the configuration of the platform, which gives us a baseline to make even more performance improvements. SQL and SharePoint settings are automatically configured in some cases, whereas in the past, we had to do it ourselves.

In this chapter, we will talk about ways to get a baseline configuration documented on your environment and what tools there are to help you get there. This includes tools that will help you configure your baseline, as well as things admins forget as part of their environment. There are many ways to slice and dice this and I will not be able to cover all possible areas. However, I will point you in the right direction so that you can move forward with getting your server resources figured out and set up for success.

The following topics will be covered in this chapter:

- Performance overview
- Troubleshooting tips
- SQL Server performance

Let's get started!

Technical requirements

The technical requirements for this chapter are as follows:

- Experience using SharePoint Administration versions 2007, 2010, 2013, and 2016
- Lite coding using Visual Studio

You can find the code present in this chapter in this book's GitHub repository at `https://github.com/PacktPublishing/Implementing-Microsoft-SharePoint-2019`.

Performance overview

All users want is speed and reliability when it comes to satisfying the services provided by SharePoint and your team. I cannot tell you how many times I have been confronted by users and management on why something is performing slowly. Tuning performance ensures that the platform is solid and working as it should, while also giving users the ability to quickly do their work.

When SharePoint runs slowly or is not reliable, you run the risk of users not being able to complete work – there could be major work being done in SharePoint you may know nothing about. I have been on site at a bank where a process ran every day at the same time. No one knew what was going on. We did some performance checks and figured out it was coming from a specific department. It ended up being a reconciliation process that was custom developed for one of the departments.

This type of scenario is common because, as farm administrators, we do not commonly get in the weeds talking to developers all the time or talking with user groups, but we should be. In the previous chapter, I mentioned a hierarchical support model for the SharePoint service. Within that diagram, there were relationships that were built between the support staff and brown bags, as well as information sharing going on between farm admins and users.

This tells us what people are doing, but it also helps us figure out what teams are going to do in the future. This makes everyone aware of those future processes because they could come with modifications that are needed for the systems to perform those duties successfully. This also gives you time to change things as needed to support any content structures, such as web applications, site collections, and other areas, where you can split off a new process to isolation, which also helps with performance.

A lot of times, as admins, we pay too much attention to the high-level requirements, such as Microsoft recommendations on minimum RAM, CPU, and disk space, but there is a lot more to performance that we seem to forget. Sometimes, even with those minimum recommendations, admins still undercut the server resources, thinking it is not a good minimum. They then run servers on less than the minimum specifications, which is a bad choice.

I am here to tell you to make sure you use those minimum specifications. Microsoft tests SharePoint Server builds before releasing the product to give us best practices. Those minimum recommendations are captured for a reason. This is done to set the expectation level of SharePoint running in an environment where you can be comfortable that the product will work as it should.

The performance of your farm all depends on how you created it. Here, again, you use best practices and software boundaries to figure out what is supported. If you are not separating processes, understanding where and how processes run, and figuring out the overhead of related processes that may run in the environment, then you are going to lose the battle. There are also other areas where you can isolate some processes at the web application level, thus giving a site its own IIS space, or even a site collection level, where the site collection is in its own content database.

When systems are slowed by poorly performing configurations, depending on the user or group who encountered the issues while the system was running slowly, you could either have an angry mob or a single user who just puts in a help desk ticket. A single user is not that noticeable in the overall company because it is a single incident that is isolated. There is the factor of who that user is, of course, which depends on their rank and position in the company.

In the case of an angry mob having an issue that is consistent across departments, this will get you and your boss's attention. These incidents are the ones you want to avoid if possible. That is why, in this book, I have been basically preaching about best practices and making sure you have covered every area of configuration. This will save you in the long run.

Client configurations come into play as well, as the user's desktop can be a bottleneck in the environment. The big thing now is that everyone is working from home, so there is a dependency on connectivity from the home to the office. Then, you have a VPN where the users connect to the office from home, which could also slow them down. Understanding these areas as an admin will help you detect what the problem is in most cases.

When site collection admins or developers develop solutions for SharePoint, they can also be bottlenecks for performance. There are best practices they should follow as well. We will touch on them in this chapter, but *Chapter 12, SharePoint Framework*, will explain more about how we support our developers and what we need to ask about in meetings with them.

There are a lot of areas that we will talk about in this section of this book that were not mentioned in other chapters. This is because they are for special configurations or we need to dwell on these topics a little deeper. You will see why I chose to keep these topics separate; I wanted to have room to expand on them.

There is lots to cover in this chapter as we dive into configurations for caching, which will give you some insight into how it can help your users get faster performance from SharePoint. Distributed Cache also helps as the configuration for this service is usually untouched. With this service, there are other caching methods that can really speed up your farm's performance, especially when you're using large files.

So, let's dive into performance for SharePoint!

The client's role in terms of performance

Since the servers provide the services on your farm, we must be conscious of our users and how their desktop is configured and performing with SharePoint. In this section, we will discuss user resources and how they come into play for performance, as well as what settings can really bring down user responsiveness from the desktop.

Most users that work remotely believe they do not have the right tools to get the job done from their home. Positioning employees so that they perform well is very important. In some cases, it's crucial, depending on the company and the position the employee holds. If they have performance issues, we have lost the battle again. The key thing we want for our home users and on-premises users is a great overall employee experience when working.

The desktop is the first key to successful performance on your enterprise network and cloud solutions because it supports your users at a personal level. This is their source of power and where they work every day. One thing I believe is that a SharePoint admin should understand all the clients that attach to the sites and services SharePoint offers.

Client machines can be laptops, desktops, tablets, or mobile phones. The operating systems that are used on them can be either Linux, Apple, or Windows, with all different versions and flavors available. I believe that, as a company, we should be giving out those systems and not having a user go buy a system to use on our networks. The reason why we want to have more control over these clients is due to governance, speed, and performance. Compromising those areas will cost you in the long run.

We also need to know about these so that we can support the environment, which makes us a special breed of admin. The reason why I say that is that SharePoint admins deal with identity, networks, servers, the web, and databases, and that is on top of managing services and content within the platform. We need to have a vast amount of knowledge to support our farms.

When supporting connections across the internet, there are many of client hardware configurations that can make a desktop respond quickly or slowly. When your desktop team is configuring for Microsoft 365, for example, and connecting to the cloud, we would want a fast network speed. We can key in on a few things regarding this topic, but I am just going to key in on the following areas in this section:

- Enterprise network speed
- VPN choice
- Geolocation of the data center
- User's internet speed (home network)
- Desktop configuration

A user's desktop in a large enterprise – and even a small enterprise – should have the resources available to support the workload and connectivity speeds needed for the user to complete their daily job. The network team should have enough equipment and local locations to support the number of users that will be connecting to the network. This would mean that technical resources need to come up with configurations for networking components, servers, and PCs and/or laptops that fit the person's need based on their job description.

If you want to have users test their connectivity to the Microsoft 365 cloud, there is also a Microsoft 365 connectivity test. The reason I am mentioning this is that you could be standing up your SharePoint 2019 server in a hybrid configuration. These tests need to be carried out to ensure connectivity to the cloud works as well. As far as SharePoint 2019 On-Premises goes, this all depends on the data pipes open to the user. To learn more about this tool and this connectivity strategy, please go to `https://docs.microsoft.com/en-us/microsoft-365/enterprise/assessing-network-connectivity?view=o365-worldwide`.

Note

To test client speed, have the users type in the words Speed Test in Bing; they will be prompted to start a test from their location.

When evaluating network connectivity, the equipment being used matters. Creating different configurations of machines can mean different behaviors occurring when they're being used. So, if someone is a developer and needs to run VMs on their machine, you may want to give them a machine that has more RAM and CPU than a normal user would need. This could mean having a four-CPU machine with 32 GB of RAM, as an example.

This configuration could also include other areas of concern, such as disk space. We should choose the right disk space for the user, be it for a laptop, desktop, or Windows Surface machine, which are very good as well. With that, we should also have the maximum speed possible from the NIC card on the devices and/or a speedy wireless network connection on the hardware. When the client machine connects to the network, we want the fastest responses to the network and, in turn, we want to have a network that supports fast speeds for the best response back to the client machine.

When you are hosting SharePoint or using Microsoft 365, you should post hardware requirements to the users of your service. The issues that come into play include that you may not be able to force someone to use a certain type of laptop or desktop, or even a mobile device in some cases. With that, the internet service speed that comes with the customer's mobile carrier also makes a difference, as well as where the mobile device is located.

So, in this case, not much can be done because you can't force your customers to buy a certain machine or a certain internet service. At this point, we just have to support the users in terms of what they bring to the table and if they do not use the minimum required hardware, we need to explain that to them when they call in for support. There must be expectations for connectivity, especially antivirus support for those client machines.

There are some things we need to be aware of when configuring a desktop, especially for SharePoint. SharePoint is a site, but there are things we need to remember. The following is a list of applications you could set up for the employees of your company:

- Syncing from SharePoint to the client device for offline access
- Syncing with Libraries and OneDrive
- Outlook calendar sync
- SharePoint Designer
- InfoPath Designer and its services

- Microsoft Project
- IE and browsers

Special configurations such as syncing content from SharePoint to desktop can be cumbersome. In SharePoint 2019, there have been big changes to make this process faster and more reliable. By using OneDrive Sync instead of Groove, like in older versions of SharePoint, we can see major differences in the process for offline files.

Most organizations I have been with have a terrible time managing their VPNs. I have had so many performance problems using Remote Desktop Manager and connecting and managing multiple servers. I can only imagine the problems that users have gaining access to the enterprise network and utilizing applications from within.

Although we believe the VPN is the only issue when using a VPN, there are other factors that add to our bandwidth at this point. This includes the VPN's software performance, the servers we connect to to establish a connection, and our authentication provider for the network.

In most cases, your VPN is establishing an authentication session with your authentication providers. The last client I worked with used Okta. So, as you are authenticating, you are establishing authentication with Okta and, in most cases, using two-factor authentication to finalize that connectivity. This all takes time and synchronization. The speed of the transactions is based on the applications and servers supporting the process.

With those processes comes the factor of the location of your data center, which can influence very heavily how the user connects to the VPN. At this point, the VPN is most likely not load balanced, meaning that any user can make a choice to use any VPN. So, by chance, location A could have 50 people connected and location B could have 250 people connected.

Having multiple sites does help support downed sites where the network is not functioning. This gives the user the choice to change locations based on their experience. If I were a user, I would test all possible locations to see which one works the best. Just because some VPNs are closer to your current location may not mean they run the fastest for you.

You also can consider switching virtual desktops running in the cloud as a solution to bypass some of the issues you may have due to different user incidents. Even your SharePoint servers can run in Azure or another cloud platform that is local to the support of those virtual desktops, which changes the game in a lot of ways in terms of performance. At this point, the performance, stability, and consistency of configurations would be the same using this method. Maintenance and other administrative processes can be run across those resources consistently to bring a similar experience for the users.

Client resources support the user but also run applications that developers create. So, let's talk about developers and their responsibility in the SharePoint environment.

The developer's role in terms of performance

As a rule, all developers should follow best practices when developing code in SharePoint. There are so many ways that code can affect performance and cause other issues with the security and stability of the farm and sites within SharePoint. Developers must be careful to use best practices and make sure to dispose of objects when using assets within the structure to run processes.

The Dispose Checker tool is used to make sure all locked objects that are used while processing a developed solution are released and not locked or in a process where they can cause looping. Solutions should be checked by admins using this tool to make sure these solutions are indeed releasing objects. Solutions that do not release objects cause memory leaks, which can cause your servers to slow down and their performance to degrade. Sometimes, these types of errors are hard to find and take a lot of troubleshooting and skill.

As I have already stated in this book, it is important to have a separate development farm, which is the best solution if you have developers that use the system daily or even in situations where we have one solution being developed for a company. You do not want any developers working on production systems, even if it's just performing a workflow process in SharePoint Designer. It is best to have them outside of the production farm where they can test and run the customization. I've stressed these best practices many times over the course of this book. This is because I have seen that most companies do not support dev and test environments as they seem to think it's a waste of resources.

We will dive into the SharePoint framework in the final chapter of this book, where we will provide more details about developer responsibilities and what you need to be aware of as a developer in a SharePoint environment.

Farm administrator tips

The responsibilities of a farm administrator are many, as stated previously in this book. We support a varying amount of technology as a SharePoint admin, depending on the size of our farm, what applications are integrated within the environment, what type of authentication we use, and our disaster recovery capabilities. These are only a few things we support on a day-to-day basis.

Supporting SharePoint farms in an environment really is downplayed by companies, management, and others I have encountered as part of my 15 years in my SharePoint career. It really baffles me how SharePoint will be used as a centralized repository for documents but is still not given the priority of a tier 1 application in the enterprise.

I have also seen where a farm administrator is supporting a huge farm with three app servers, four web frontends, and redundant SQL servers, and also provides support for many users, including authentication integration, all by themselves. Yes, if you implement SharePoint correctly and it cruises along for 6 months, that is great. The problem comes when there is an issue or there is a big need for support. How do you support that environment and troubleshoot at the same time?

When supporting SharePoint Server in the cloud or on-premises, we need to make sure we have the staff in place, full time or part-time, or a contractor to help handle anything that comes at us. We need to be able to support our environment with the best support possible while utilizing multiple people. Even in this case, one other admin is always great to have on board. The cost of SharePoint going down definitely outweighs paying one extra person to watch over the farm.

This is also true for performance as areas of administration should be separated, depending on the size of your farm. I know that in my last big SharePoint migration, I was a team of one managing a 15 TB migration, user issues, and the administration of two environments while moving from one cloud to another cloud provider. I did it and was successful, but it cost me a lot of sleep and time away from my family.

The performance of your environment is very important and in my situation, I did not have time to worry about performance or even about whether the farm was having issues. Sometimes, I didn't even have time to help users fix issues they were having within site collections. This made me prioritize each issue and fix them as they came to the surface.

If it was something quick, I did it quickly, but other than that, performance was only something I looked at now and then. If a person could connect, that was enough for me, depending on the situation. If the situation was that one user was having performance issues, then I would put that on the back burner, but if there were several users having issues, then it was bumped up in terms of priority. I had to really work hard and fast, document those issues, and prioritize to make this work.

So, in the vein of giving you thoughts and ideas on how to manage the performance of a SharePoint farm from a farm administrator's perspective, I have put together a list of proactive steps you can take to care for your environment before you release it to the users.

Some of these have been mentioned over the course of this book, but I will explain them in a little more detail in this section. There are many ways to configure this environment and you really do not want to miss anything. So, please take the time to review the expected results so that you can find the solutions and configurations that work for you in your environment.

Load testing

If you have tested and constructed a load test with Visual Studio before, you will have noticed that you get some much needed verification in terms of how the farm will support your user base. It also gives you the opportunity to see how your server resources respond as if users in your company were using the farm on a regular basis. These load tests are essential in finding out performance issues before they happen. These tests help you tune your farm and server resources so that the farm responds to the needs of your users. Always remember to run these tools after hours and/or in a segregated environment.

There are two types of Visual Studio load testing toolkits. One is Visual Studio Online, while the other is using Visual Studio 2013 behind your firewall, which is a tool you can use for on-premises environments. You can use the Online tool with your on-premises environment, but the farm must be accessible from the internet:

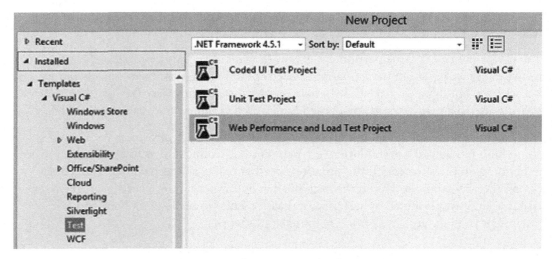

Figure 9.1 – Creating a new load project

Using the load test as an example, you can easily get your farm set up and configured. You can migrate or create new content within sites so that you can use the load testing tool to imitate a user by recording actions as a video screen capture. The capture then reproduces these actions, such as Power Automate actions, in the cloud to create sessions within the environment that simulate as many users as you like. In the following figure, we can add a user count to simulate as many sessions as we need for testing. We can then bring them online in certain scenarios we may find helpful for testing:

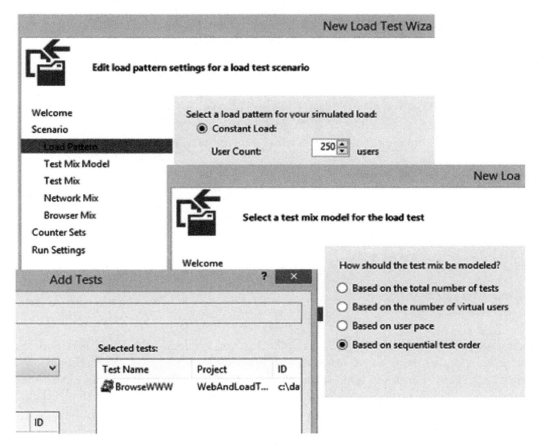

Figure 9.2 – Load testing options

When recording your steps, you can go to different sites, download documents, upload documents, and even test solutions and workflows if you like. Once you've recorded your steps, you can load as many users as you want so that you can perform those same steps as many times as you have users. This gives you a real-time test of your environment based on server resources using solutions that your company may use every day. Configure the options shown in the following screenshot to capture any URL criteria and validate error patterns:

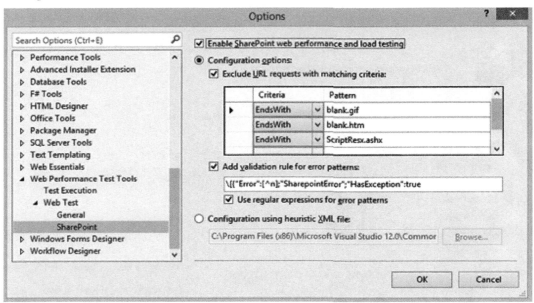

Figure 9.3 – Configuring the options

So, if you realistically have 500 or even 1,000 users, you can load tests using these fictitious user simulations by using a load test script against your farm and sites. When recording these users, who are running your script using the Visual Studio tool, you can record the performance of your servers in real time. This will give you a record of what the server response is as the process runs. You can also customize what processes you grab while the load test script is running to grab what you need or think is necessary. The performance data will be captured during the testing, which you can then export and analyze.

There is also an onboarding process as you can add to your steps at the beginning, which onboards the users based on a certain increment of time. So, if you want to have the first user onboard and start the load testing script, you can stagger the other users by a set time interval. At this point, you could choose times such as 1 minute or even a few seconds. This is when new users jump on board the process and run your load test script. This also tests how many concurrent users the farm will support, as well as how many users can be running scripts at the same time.

I wanted to make sure I shared this tool because lots of people know nothing about it. This process helps you baseline your servers and gives you reports on the different processes running in the environment, as well as information about how the server resources are responding. At this point, once this load test has been successfully run, you can analyze the data you've collected and tweak those areas of concern before running the test again.

This will save you so much time trying to tweak performance and getting ready for Go Live day. There is no need to guess how the servers will perform because you are proving how they will perform with these tests. However, you really want to use content from your environment, and even some developed solutions in your environment, to get a real feel of how these servers will perform. Doing this early in your build process once you've gathered content to test will give you a head start on your server resource configuration. If you want to run against your dev, test, and production environments, then do that. At this point, production is what you really want to understand because that is where the bulk of your users will be using SharePoint the most.

Load testing link: `https://marketplace.visualstudio.com/items?itemName=SharePointTemplates.SharePointLoadGenerationTool`

Warm-up scripts

There is something about being the first person to come into the office in the morning – especially when you're hitting a SharePoint site. Users want instant results and with SharePoint, if you are the first user, then sorry, but you must wait. Application pools take time to spin up. It's like you using the sleep mode on your computer. Even when you hit the power button or the keyboard, the computer still takes time to come back to a point where you can use it.

This is where warm-up scripts come into play. These scripts work on a scheduled basis, depending on the person who wrote the script. It could also be based on a certain time in the morning you have it run or based on server resources or IIS components. They are used to keep sites in SharePoint warm by keeping the application pool fresh and ready for a user to render the site.

Usually, the first person to hit a site in the morning has to take on the responsibility of the application pool being slow to spin up, which creates wait time for the site to come up for the user. Instead of having them wait, we can add a warm-up script to keep the application pool fresh and readily available so that no one ever has to wait for the site to come to life. This requires either scripting and/or Windows Server scheduling to keep this script active.

To learn more about warm-up scripts, please go to `https://gallery.technet.microsoft.com/office/SPBestWarmUp-Warmup-e7c77527`.

Storage

Better known as disk space, this is the next in line as disks can cause slow responses when you're reading or writing data to SharePoint. When we say reading and writing to SharePoint, we really mean SQL Server because that is where all our content, configuration, and services live. We would be more concerned about this on a SQL Server database resource than any other server role. The faster your disk can read and write, the faster information can be relayed back to the user.

We need to choose the proper storage for the proper server resources and, in the case of SQL, the proper components to house our databases. When looking at Web and App servers, you should use a disk with good performance since our operating system, logging, and search indexes will play a big part in how this server responds in the farm. Also, you should take blobs and other files that will be added to the server into consideration, as well as the amount of disk space needed to support the servers.

As far as SQL is concerned, we really need to be mindful of what types of databases SQL Server will support, their size, and how they communicate with each other. If we break this down at a high level, we have configuration, search, services, and content. You can spread just these four areas across separate LUNNs or dig deeper to narrow these databases down into more LUNNs. Believe it or not, this will bring about greater performance for the databases and the resources the server consumes to support the farm.

Disk storage comes in many forms. There are companies that specifically make disk arrays with proprietary software to help us manage disks and configurations that support our server and application needs. NetApp is one that I have used in the past that has helped me design storage and supports the SharePoint server farm. Please check out storage companies that may have something to offer you that can bring about better solutions for support.

Disk types are a great way to gain performance boosts as well, with options for SATA, SAS, SCSI, and SSD available. There are many choices, all of which bring different methods of high performance and specific ways to bring stability to your server. We also have options for RAID, which brings data protection options into play. There are a few different options here, including ones for RAID 0, 1, 5, 6, 10, 50, and 60. For more information, please go to `https://www.dell.com/support/article/en-us/sln129581/ understanding-hard-drive-types-raid-and-raid-controllers-on- dell-poweredge-and-blade-chassis-servers?lang=en`.

More information on Azure disks types for cloud configurations can be found here. However, they come at a cost: `https://docs.microsoft.com/en-us/azure/ virtual-machines/disks-types`.

As you configure your servers, you also need to make sure **ALL** the logs within SharePoint and SQL Server are moved to a separate drive other than your C drive. This can cause servers to stop working altogether. Move IIS logs, especially when you have a large user base. SQL Reporting Services and other integrated applications also have logs. Move them to a separate drive and make sure the drive is big enough to hold your logs and the search index for the farm. Size is important!

The following link talks about Microsoft's recommendations for storage: `https://docs.microsoft.com/en-us/sharepoint/administration/ storage-and-sql-server-capacity-planning-and-configuration`.

Quotas

As we set goals to keep our content at a certain limit, we need to make sure we implement quotas. Site Collection Quotas play a part in the storage's configuration as well. Quotas help you set limits on how much content a user can have in a site collection. There are thresholds you can set here that will help warn users using that site collection that they may be running out of space.

Microsoft has limits on what you can set, which could be a 200 GB minimum to a 400 GB maximum. The reason for these limits is to help the environment recover quickly if you have to restore or perform a migration backup and copy these databases to another server or cloud service. The smaller you can keep these site collections, the better off you will be in the long run when it comes to avoiding issues with backups, restores, and performance due to the size of content databases.

Deleting site collections and subsites

Deleting a site collection from a content database can also cause performance issues you may not be aware of. When the site collection is deleted, it may take a while, depending on the size of the sites supported within that site collection. Other users who have site collections in that content database will be affected once you start this process as well.

There are a couple of ways to do this using `Remove-SPSite` and the `GradualDelete` parameter. When you delete site collections all at once, SQL Server may take some time to process the request, depending on its size and how many databases you are running on the server, as well as the RAM and CPU on the server resources. Using the gradual delete option will put this process at a lower priority so that it does not affect the performance of the server.

Some recommendations when doing this are as follows:

- Run the deletion over a weekend, which would alleviate the issue of other users being affected.

- When setting up the farm, make a rule that all site collections must have a one-to-one relationship with a content database (this helps with restoring processes).

- Move the other site collections in the content database to a new content database if there's more than one site collection per database.

- To recapture the disk space after deletion, run a shrink on the database and log files.

Deleting subsites is done within your site collection. Sometimes, these sites get very big and take up a lot of space within a site collection. At this point, you can see if the site is really needed, move content from this site to another site, or upgrade the subsite to its own site collection. This helps reduce the storage in a site collection as well.

As a site collection admin, you now have the option to create site collections. This is a new feature that was made available in SharePoint 2016 called Self-Service Site Creation. This is different from what you are thinking, because now, we can make web applications use this feature. However, the feature has gone further and lets site collection admins create their own site collections. This does take coordination, documentation, and database management, so make sure to communicate when and if you have these features activated.

RAM

As you set up your server resources, RAM is another area of concern as you will want to make sure you have enough RAM to support the server resources for the farm. Do not use minimums as your point of reference. It is better to test the load on the servers to see how they respond. There are many dynamics that come into play here, such as the following:

- How many web applications are you running?
- Are you running Host Named Site Collections?
- How many content databases are you running?
- How many users are connecting to the farm?
- What processes are running?
- How heavily used are those processes?

There are probably more things you can consider, but these have been mentioned to get you thinking about how to scale your environment with memory so that you do not revisit this right away.

Virtual environments

When setting up my environment, I used VMs within my environment to run all the server resources. One thing you want to make sure of is that you do not want to run RAM dynamically. This causes lots of issues with the servers and is not supported by Microsoft. They will basically stop working with you if you are running your farm with this configuration.

Another thing to be mindful of is the introduction of Distributed Cache. If you have a dedicated MinRole running dynamic RAM, this would negate the use of this service as this has to be configured as static. This is because the RAM cannot fluxgate. Remember to set your Distributed Cache size to an optimal setting. You can set Distributed Cache to a maximum of 16 GB.

More information on this can be found at `https://docs.microsoft.com/en-us/sharepoint/install/deploy-sharepoint-virtual-machines`.

PowerShell Jobs

New to the scene, or somewhat new, are PowerShell Jobs. If you come from a Unix or Linux background, then you will be familiar with these types of processes. With PowerShell, there are two types of code that can be executed:

- Synchronous
- Asynchronous

When using synchronous execution, PowerShell will execute code in the script one line at a time. It will complete each line of code before it starts another line of code. This is usually how I see admins run code so that there is order in the code so that it can complete successfully. It's usually an easy way to write something quickly and think out the strategy in some type of order, while not really taking advantage of the performance of server resources.

When creating scripts, you may want to consider using asynchronous execution and a concept called Jobs. I used a product back in the day called WinCron, when I used to do a lot of SQL and Windows Server automated processes. This type of processing using PowerShell seems to be similar. Jobs are great for performance only when a script does not depend on the results of a prior execution in the code. They run in the background and don't interact with the current session.

The following are some parameters you can use when creating jobs:

- **Start-Job**: Starts a background job on a local computer.
- **Receive-Job**: Gets the results of background jobs.
- **Stop-Job**: Stops a background job.
- **Get-Job**: Gets the background jobs that were started in the current session.
- **Wait-Job**: Suppresses the Command Prompt until one or all jobs are completed.
- **Remove-Job**: Deletes a background job.
- **Invoke-Command**: The `AsJob` parameter runs any command as a background job on a remote computer. This command also runs any job command remotely. The `Start-Job` command can also be started remotely using `Invoke-Command`.

To learn more about PowerShell Jobs, take a look at the following links:

- `https://docs.microsoft.com/en-us/powershell/module/microsoft.powershell.core/about/about_jobs?view=powershell-7`

- `https://docs.microsoft.com/en-us/powershell/module/microsoft.powershell.core/about/about_remote_jobs?view=powershell-7`

Distributed Cache service

When configuring SharePoint server, you will notice that Distributed Cache service is installed on every server you installed SharePoint on. During the installation, if you do not want a server to be updated with the service, use the `skipRegisterAsDistributedCachehost` parameter when creating a new configuration database. Distributed Cache supports the following caching functionalities:

- Claims-based authentication
- Newsfeeds, micro blogging, and conversations
- OneNote client access
- Security trimming
- Page load performance

This service can be run on any server and can be run in dedicated server mode or in collocated server mode. In dedicated mode, all services other than Distributed Cache are stopped on the servers that run Distributed Cache. In collocated mode, the service can run together with other SharePoint services, and it's up to you to manage which servers the service was started on. Microsoft recommends using dedicated mode when you deploy the service.

If this server is not configured properly, you could experience a serious performance hit. We need to figure out the capacity for this server so that it can support the service and how we want to install the service so that it runs within the environment. Here, you can look at the number of users that will be supported and see that, based on the number of users we have, we can determine how Microsoft considers your deployment size. The basic minimum memory for a SharePoint server in a farm is 16 GB. We want to make sure that the size of the server is correct so that we do not have any misconfiguration issues with this service.

If you have less than 10,000 users, then your farm is considered small by Microsoft's standards. If you are running up to 100,000 users, then you are looking at a medium-sized farm. Large farms contain up to 500,000 users. You should look at how much RAM should be configured for your service based on size. 1 GB would be plenty for a small farm, 2.5 GB would be great for a medium-sized farm, and 12 GB would be fine for a large farm.

In a small farm, you have the option to use a dedicated server or collocated server configuration. Medium-sized farms would be best run using a dedicated, but for large farms, you would need to have two cache hosts per farm. When running Distributed Cache service in a collocated configuration, you cannot run Search Services, Excel Services (2013), or Project Server Services on the same server.

Configuring Distributed Cache service is easy, but you really need to understand how to configure the service. To configure the service with any type of command in order to, for example, change the memory allocation, you would need to stop the service first to complete the changes and then start the service again.

From my experience, the best configuration for performance is to use dedicated server mode to run the Distributed Cache service. This takes on the burden of processing the web frontends and is recommended. You can run in collocated mode if you want to, but again, there are some services that cannot be run from that server when you're using that method.

To find out more, please go to `https://docs.microsoft.com/en-us/sharepoint/administration/manage-the-distributed-cache-service`.

Request Management Service

I have not seen this service used in any farms that I have supported, except when the engineer was trying to use this to route incoming requests. It was failing and was not a good choice for this small farm. This service would be better used in larger farms where there is a need to route traffic. This is because there could be latency if SharePoint were used natively to route traffic.

This service is used to do the following:

- Route good requests to available servers within the farm.

- Deny requests entering a SharePoint farm that may be harmful.

- Optimize performance by configuring rules manually.

As an example, if there was a request coming in for an available web application and your web frontend servers were busy, the service would choose the best performing server at that time to route the traffic to that better performing server. The request manager provides three functional components:

- Request routing
- Request throttling and prioritizing
- Request load balancing

The service also provides manageability, accountability, and capacity planning in order to support specific types of services, such as Search, User Profile, and Office Online Server, which means that SharePoint doesn't determine where the request needs to be routed. This makes routing less complex and the service can locate problems within those servers that may be failing or running slow.

The Request Management Service can also be scaled out as needed so that as an admin creates and implements those routing associations in the servers in the farm, the load balancer can quickly determine and load balance at the network level.

The service can be started within Central Administration or by using PowerShell. You can use the following parameters in PowerShell to change the parameters within the service to change the properties of the request management service:

- `RoutingEnabled`
- `ThrottlingEnabled`
- `Set-SPRequestManagementSettings`

The service can be run in two different modes. The first is in dedicated mode, where the web frontends are dedicated exclusively for managing requests. These servers would be created in their own farm, which would be located between the SharePoint farm and the hardware load balancers.

The service can also run in integrated mode, where all the web frontends run the request manager. All web frontends means all servers, as in APP and WFE. All the web frontends receive requests from the hardware load balancers and then determine where the request needs to be routed.

Using this service takes a lot of planning and configuration. You do not want to use this service on smaller farms but on large farms where you need this type of dedicated service routing. Once the service has been started, it adds information to your content databases. Without the service, this content database will be out of support in a new farm.

I have seen some weird behavior when moving a content database from one farm with request management to another farm without the service. You must be careful where you start because it may impact you once you migrate. We noticed that requests that were made to sites that had site collections from a farm with the service running were trying to route to different web applications, even when we entered the right URL in a new farm without the service.

When I worked on a project where the engineer was using this service, we ran into some issues. I was told by a well-known SharePoint architect to not use this service at all. He said he had not seen it used before and that there was no legitimate rationale for using it right from the get-go. He also said that there had been a lot of bad implementations when using this service, though it is an option you can use for performance if you dare.

To find out more, please go to `https://docs.microsoft.com/en-us/SharePoint/security-for-sharepoint-server/configure-request-manager-in-sharepoint-server`.

Document size

When determining document sizes that could potentially be used within your environment, note that they affect many areas. One of these areas is performance, which we will talk about in more detail in the next subsection. These documents can also be affected by search settings. I believe lots of people overlook this setting and then notice they are limited by the results they get from the search.

The max document size in SharePoint 2019 Server is 15GB. The setting for Document Size within the Search component, especially when large files are used, such as Word and Excel files, is set out of the box at 64 MB. This setting can be set to a maximum size of 1 GB if needed on both Excel and Word documents. You will capture more metadata on these large files and the search results will produce more relationships for user search results.

This setting can only be completed using PowerShell:

- `MaxDownLoadSize`
- `MaxDownloadSizeExcel`

Use these commands to maximize the document's crawl size. This is explained in more detail on the Software Boundaries Microsoft page: `https://docs.microsoft.com/en-us/sharepoint/install/software-boundaries-and-limits-0`.

Blob Cache

One of the things you should do when planning your farm is look at the file sizes of the documents that you will be supporting within the farm. Meetings with users should have given you some clue of what is being used now and what is being planned. If your users plan to upload large files, first, you need to make sure your network can support it. You do not want to have your users uploading 1 GB files over a 100 MB network.

Blob Cache helps with finding the easiest ways to bring performance to your farm, especially for those farms using large files within your sites. The new maximum for the file upload size for document libraries is 10 GB, while list item attachments can be 50 MB in size maximum in SharePoint On-Premises. Microsoft 365 is 15 GB for files in document libraries and 250 MB for list attachments. By reviewing those size limits, you can see that 10 GB is a pretty large file. Processing those files for a user to view in the browser would be pretty process-intensive and heavily dependent on the user's connectivity to the farm.

Using Blob Cache can help you by providing a separate flat drive space (not a database) to hold all those large files so that when users request them, they are pulled from the drive space and not placed within the content database. The blob storage space is located on SharePoint servers and you need to make sure you have storage to support those files.

When using this method to support those files, we can use a configuration where the content database would hold the site collection, which would then associate all the document's meeting certain criteria for the blob and its size to a link to the image or document that is larger than the limitation we set. Users would request that content using the same user interface, but the content would be rerouted so that it can be rendered from disk from the Blob Cache location.

There are many third-party companies that offer Blob Cache solutions, such as AvePoint. Storsimple is a product from Microsoft that also works with on-premises SharePoint environments. You can find out more about this solution at `https://docs.microsoft.com/en-us/azure/storsimple/storsimple-adapter-for-sharepoint`.

Microsoft introduced this feature in SharePoint Server 2019 and can be found within the Manage Web Application area of Central Administration: `https://thesharepointfarm.com/2019/05/sharepoint-2019-blobcache/`.

Other resources:

- Caching and performance planning: `https://docs.microsoft.com/en-us/sharepoint/administration/caching-and-performance-planning`

- Cache settings configuration for a web application: `https://docs.microsoft.com/en-us/sharepoint/administration/cache-settings-configuration-for-a-web-application`

Object Cache

As you saw in the installation setup for SharePoint, we have dedicated cache accounts called SuperUser and SuperReader. These accounts support the Object Cache, which stores properties about items in SharePoint Server. You cannot use out of the box accounts because of check in/check out and claims authentication issues that will arise. The service is used as part of the publishing feature and helps reduce the load on SQL servers to improve performance. These accounts must be set up; otherwise, your SharePoint farm can and will come to a complete stop one day with no warning.

Search Services

As part of SharePoint Server, there are services that provide search results based on the content that's been crawled. This product is called Search Services and we talked about it briefly in *Chapter 6, Finalizing the Farm – Going Live*. Some of this information may be redundant but it's good to recap at this time. To make content available based on certain criteria, a user associates metadata or column information within content that is stored in SharePoint sites. The crawler function within Search Services runs the crawler process and finds all the metadata needed to index that information for users to search and find the results of a search. Be sure to stagger your search crawls across sites so that they finish processing before you move on to the next scheduled site for crawling.

Choosing physical or virtual servers for this service is key as this server can be either. If you have a large amount of data and are planning to expand even more, then you may want to consider using a physical server for this service. Cloning, as we talked about previously, will help in defining the components of Search Services for specific server resources, which creates better support for this service.

Isolating Search Services would be yet another way of helping the performance of a SharePoint farm. This is because this service is very intensive on RAM and CPU. Search Services can take over your server because it requires the resources to crawl through all your content. Remembering to divide the search components into separate servers is key as well since they can be spread out among server resources.

You should isolate these processes either on several servers or a couple of servers. However, most importantly, you should configure these services so that they only run on application servers and not the web frontends where users request access to web applications. The services can be split up, especially when you need redundancy.

If you have more than 10 million items, you must clone your search services, which would make them redundant and boost performance for the service as well. This is the most intense service you have, and it can make or break your farm. The faster you can crawl and gather information, the better the results for your users. I haven't covered a lot on search in this book, but please research further if you wish to make this service stable.

To find out more, please go to `https://docs.microsoft.com/en-us/sharepoint/install/software-boundaries-and-limits-0`.

Excel Online

As you may have noticed, Excel Services is not listed in our services for the farm anymore. This service has been moved to Office Online Server and is now called Excel Online. This is a nice move on Microsoft's part. This service, especially when used heavily, needs some isolation as it can weigh heavily on the server's resources.

Another thing I used to see all the time is that no one took advantage of the segregation of Excel Services throughout the farm. In some cases where this service is used heavily, you want to use Excel Services in designated locations of a web application or even segregate it to a separate web application, purely for the purpose of big data and reporting. This takes the service out of the most used areas of the farm and isolates it in one web application, which then has its own IIS site and databases associated with content and resources.

The reason I would do the separation at the web application level is due to heavily using the service and/or related services. These could be SSRS or other third-party integrations that may need to have separate processing and relationships to services in SQL and SharePoint. These can be separated by server as well since you can integrate SharePoint with several SQL servers if you like. On the flip side, you only need to run certain web applications on designated web frontends to give some good separation of processes.

Some things to think about when configuring Excel Services are as follows:

- Use trusted file locations to segregate the use of this service within web applications. You must specify HTTP or HTTPS in your URL and the location limits where Excel can be used within your farm.

- The service also controls the location type, which could be a SharePoint Foundation location or other location types such as UNC and HTTP.

- Configuring options so that child libraries and directories are trusted within the trusted file location.

- Session management, for timeout settings and request duration.

- Calculating Excel data mode, which can be done against a file. This can be a manual calculation or automatic, except when this is done on data tables.

- External data connectivity can be allowed or not allowed and can be for libraries only or embedded connections.

- A refresh rate for the data can be set. You have many options here.

If you are looking to use Excel Online heavily, look at some of my recommendations to spread out your processes so that they do not collide a create a performance bottleneck. We will talk more about Excel Online's features and its installation in *Chapter 10, SharePoint Advanced Reporting and Features*.

InfoPath

If you are still using InfoPath in your farm for users, this brings up another farm service that gets overlooked as a performance bottleneck. There are areas in Central Administration that control these services and are sort of hidden. I believe most admins just keep the default settings and never look at these controls.

The issue I have seen with this service is the settings that are used to support it. I have seen some InfoPath users or developers, especially those new to InfoPath, create forms that are just one-page forms with many form inputs that collect a lot of data. In the real world, you really want to split your form up and make views so that the data settings in the InfoPath service do not have to be made larger for session data.

In some cases, I can see when you may have to do this, but if you are keying in on performance, you really want to limit that data per session from each user. You also want to watch what connections to services you are using as these can slow down forms, especially when you're querying data when the form is open. As an example, interfacing with User Profile Services can help you auto-fill forms, though this can produce issues, depending on how much data you are autoloading. SQL Server databases can also be used to connect to, but then again, you have to look at how much data you are pulling into the form.

Doing this can delay the form from opening due to the service trying to connect to get the data or user you requested, or even connecting to other resources within the domain. These services can be slow sometimes and depending on how many users are using that form at once, this could be a big burden on the farm and server resources.

Depending on how you create your form, getting data through InfoPath processes presents data when the form is opened, such as a user's manager or phone number. This could also be anything that is related to the user profile or even a separate list or database. This process must go out to that data source, gather the required information, and then load it inside the form.

This process can be quick but also a little cumbersome. So, it is better to load as little data as possible so that you do not have to change your settings and put a burden on the server resources. These are just a couple of tips about InfoPath you should think about as we investigate the settings within Central Administration for InfoPath:

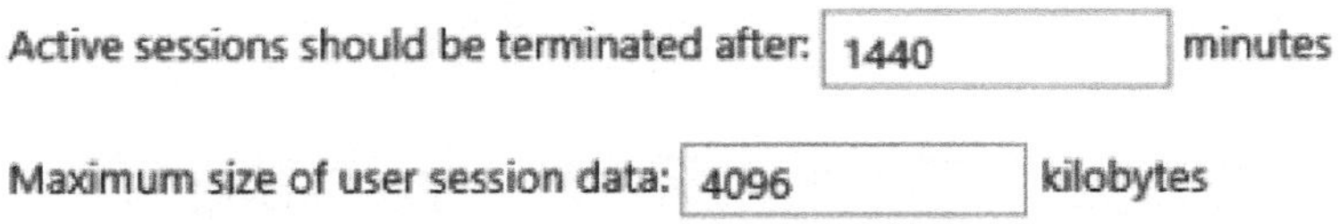

Active sessions should be terminated after: 1440 minutes

Maximum size of user session data: 4096 kilobytes

Figure 9.4 – InfoPath session settings

As you can see, there are many things to consider in terms of the performance of SharePoint. SharePoint has not changed a lot, but you do find some diamond new developments within the structure of the 2019 version that really help change how we configure our servers and manage resources within the environment. Building your farm cleverly and using recommendations from Microsoft, along with following the best practices, helps you get to a point where you can have a solid baseline to support your company's goals.

Farm administrative monitoring

When building and administering a SharePoint environment, you will find you are setting up logging and other aspects that help you report issues and problems. Logging, as you saw when we configured SharePoint, was set up to use a separate disk space so that we had room for these logs to grow and ensured they did not affect our operating system's functionality.

I cannot stress enough that you need to move all logs, even if it is a third-party tool you are deploying, to make sure those logs are moved to a separate drive space. Even IIS falls into this category as those logs can grow quickly, depending on the number of users you have. If you are performing a migration, you will see your logs growing dramatically for IIS and ULS.

Now that our logs have been set up, we need to proactively monitor our SharePoint farm. There are different ways to monitor SharePoint. As a starting point, you can use the Central Administration website, which provides health and reporting features for SharePoint. There is also the System Center Management Packs for SharePoint, which provide out-of-the-box monitoring insights for monitoring SharePoint natively.

Then, there is PowerShell, which may take you some time to get set up. However, it is a very powerful way of making sure your farm services and farm is running well. There are also SQL monitoring tools that you can purchase to monitor the tasks that are being processed on this server, but SQL includes an activity monitor that will feed processes in real time:

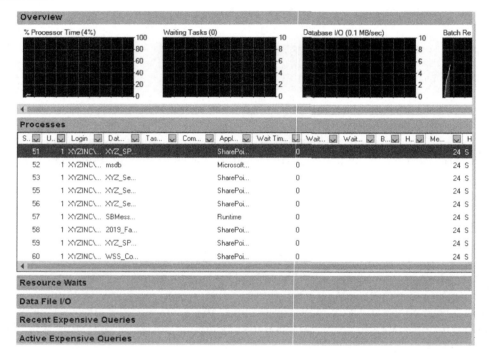

Figure 9.5 – SQL activity monitor

When monitoring SharePoint, there's a host of areas we need to take into consideration:

- **The Health Analyzer**: How to mitigate issues that have been captured

- **Reporting**: Using the reports within Central Administration to find solutions to issues

- Performing regular checks to inspect the current state of the environment

- Defining what is important to your business and what to monitor more frequently

The configurations for logging we set up in the installation are native to SharePoint only. SQL Server is also monitored from a configuration standpoint to help you promote a configuration that supports performance and best practices. SharePoint uses databases that capture logging, as well as diagnostics and usage. There are still server components outside of SharePoint that we use to support troubleshooting and to monitor our services. All of the services we use for SharePoint run on the servers we provision, and how we provision them makes a difference in terms of how the farm performs.

In SharePoint 2016 and 2019, MinRoles come into play. They help us manage roles within our environment so that we can support our server resources. This is because MinRoles limit what services can be run on our servers. These preconfigured and dedicated MinRoles can be added to our environment:

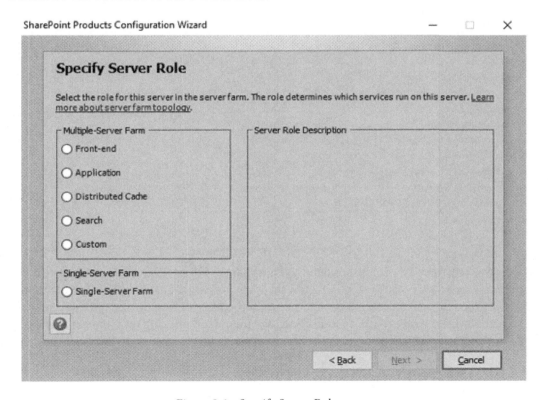

Figure 9.6 – Specify Server Role screen

These were covered in *Chapter 2, Planning and Architecture*. We need to make sure we choose the right MinRole for the server resource. We also have Server Compliance. This is shown in the following figure, which shows the role of the server in the farm. This Central Administration function monitors which services are running on the specific MinRole or server resource. If a server is running a service that is not accounted for by the restrictions within the MinRole, the server will be deemed non-compliant:

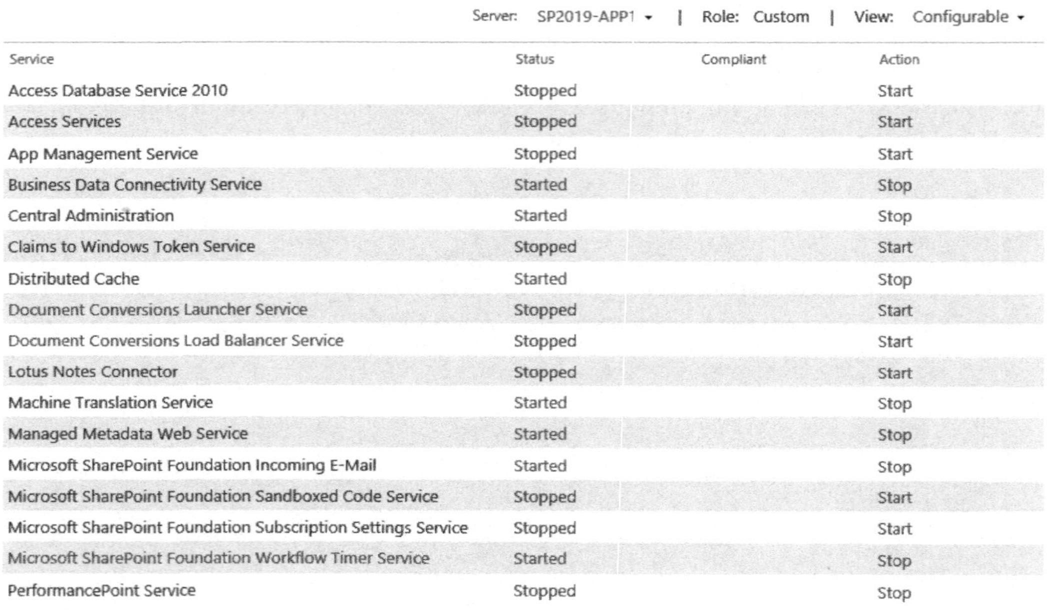

Server: SP2019-APP1 ▾ | Role: Custom | View: Configurable ▾

Service	Status	Compliant	Action
Access Database Service 2010	Stopped		Start
Access Services	Stopped		Start
App Management Service	Stopped		Start
Business Data Connectivity Service	Started		Stop
Central Administration	Started		Stop
Claims to Windows Token Service	Stopped		Start
Distributed Cache	Started		Stop
Document Conversions Launcher Service	Stopped		Start
Document Conversions Load Balancer Service	Stopped		Start
Lotus Notes Connector	Stopped		Start
Machine Translation Service	Started		Stop
Managed Metadata Web Service	Started		Stop
Microsoft SharePoint Foundation Incoming E-Mail	Started		Stop
Microsoft SharePoint Foundation Sandboxed Code Service	Stopped		Start
Microsoft SharePoint Foundation Subscription Settings Service	Stopped		Start
Microsoft SharePoint Foundation Workflow Timer Service	Started		Stop
PerformancePoint Service	Stopped		Stop

Figure 9.7 – Server compliance

As you can see, there is a column related to compliance. If there was a service that was not compliant on this MinRole, you would see it flagged in this list of services. Note that this MinRole is a custom role, so no service would be flagged for non-compliance. I can change the role by going to the **Systems Settings** menu and clicking on **Convert Server Role** in this Farm:

Role Conversion

Server	Current Role	New Role
SP2019-APP1	Custom	Custom ▾

Figure 9.8 – Role Conversion screen

Diagnostic Logging is a log that collects data that is used to troubleshoot SharePoint farm environments. When you set up logging, you will see there are various ways to capture data. These will be provided in a drop-down list. You can select from a list for the least critical events to monitor in the event log and do the same for the trace log. There are also categories you can select from where there's a list of areas you can choose to report on. Since we configured our logging in *Chapter 4, Installation Concepts*, we will give some background on logging here, as well as what to look for in SharePoint that can help with performance and troubleshooting:

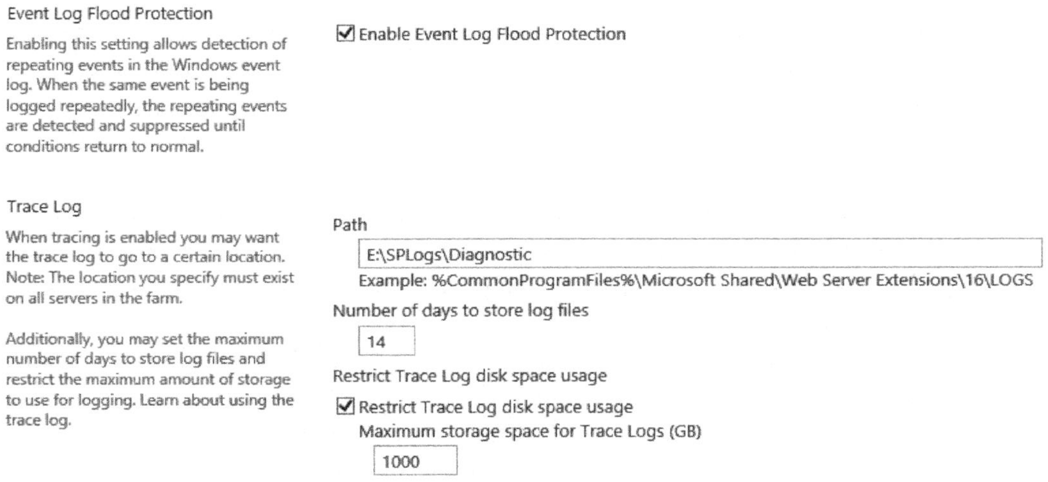

Event Log Flood Protection

Enabling this setting allows detection of repeating events in the Windows event log. When the same event is being logged repeatedly, the repeating events are detected and suppressed until conditions return to normal.

☑ Enable Event Log Flood Protection

Trace Log

When tracing is enabled you may want the trace log to go to a certain location. Note: The location you specify must exist on all servers in the farm.

Additionally, you may set the maximum number of days to store log files and restrict the maximum amount of storage to use for logging. Learn about using the trace log.

Path

E:\SPLogs\Diagnostic

Example: %CommonProgramFiles%\Microsoft Shared\Web Server Extensions\16\LOGS

Number of days to store log files

14

Restrict Trace Log disk space usage

☑ Restrict Trace Log disk space usage

Maximum storage space for Trace Logs (GB)

1000

Figure 9.9 – Log location definitions for ULS logs

When using diagnostics for monitoring, you can select the level of logging you want to perform. If you are performing well and not making any significant changes to the environment, you will want to keep it at a default level, where we are capturing minimal information about the farm and its state. If you are making changes or seeing issues, then you will want to find out detailed information. Here, you would change that setting to **Verbose**, which will create more information in your log. The size of your log will be larger due to those intimate details being captured based on that change.

Some of the best practices for diagnostic logging have been mentioned in this book, but here is a short list to help you remember:

- Update the drive location where the logs are being captured.
- Restrict the trace log disk space's usage (set a quota).
- Back up the logs regularly as part of your server backup.

- Enable event log flooding protection (limits repeating events in the event log).
- Only use the Verbose setting when troubleshooting (more logs will be created and there will be storage issues).

The levels you can set within the diagnostic logging feature limits the types and amounts of information that will be gathered within each log. The level settings for each log are available here:

Event Log Levels:

- **None**: No trace logs are gathered based on this selection.
- **Critical**: This type of information gathering is related to serious errors caused by a major failure.
- **Error**: These messages are gathered based on an urgent condition.
- **Warning**: These messages are gathered based on a potential problem that requires immediate attention.
- **Information**: These messages do not require attention as they are only informational messages.
- **Verbose**: These messages only capture lengthy messages.

Trace Log Levels:

- **None**: No trace logs are gathered based on this selection.
- **Unexpected**: These messages gather only unexpected, assert, and critical message levels.
- **Monitorable**: These messages gather information that limits functionality but does not stop the application.
- **High**: These messages combine all the methods that are gathered at the Unexpected and Monitorable levels.
- **Medium**: These messages combine all the messages that are gathered, except for at the Verbose and VerboseEx levels.
- **Verbose**: These messages combine Medium messages and include most actions. Verbose tracing can contain a vast amount of log messages.
- **VerboseEx**: You can only set this level using the PowerShell `Set-SPLoglevel` command. Microsoft recommends that this level is only used in a development environment. The messages that are gathered here include all trace log levels.

Usage and Health Data Collection is a logging method based on how SharePoint is used from an overall perspective. The information that's gathered here is assembled into a database and placed in the logging folder on the server. This data is used to create the health and administrative reports that are shown on the Central Administration Monitoring page. This includes search usage and performance counter data:

Figure 9.10 – Central Administration Monitoring page

Usage and Health Data Collection features include health and other services, such as SQL Server, all of which rely on timer jobs. These timer jobs are run on schedules that are controlled within Central Administration. These timer jobs monitor tasks and collect data specific to the timer job's relationship to services. These time jobs schedule how frequently these jobs should be run and how frequently services should be started based on their needs. The SharePoint Timer Service is a service that runs on the operating system and is part of every server in the farm.

You can change the settings for these jobs so that they run more frequently or less frequently. Disabling jobs is only recommended if you really understand what that time job is being used for. In some cases, time jobs are not needed, and we do disable them. As an example, Dead Site Deletion may be disabled because you may not want SharePoint to automatically delete sites. If a site is not being used, this timer job would automatically try to delete the site. It will send you a notification to ask you if the site is still being used. You may not want this type of automatic service on your farm, so you would disable this timer job.

It is also important to run Health Analysis jobs after maintenance so that you can see the effects is has on your health report. The Health Analysis rules verify and update health collections so that if anything is not a best practice, it will post that to the health report page, which is called Review Problems and Solutions. By doing this, you can get the status of the environment and clean up any loose ends.

As part of timer Job management, you can do the following from Central Administration:

- View and modify timer job schedules

- Immediately run a timer job

- Disable and enable timer jobs

- View the status of a timer job

- Find what time job has an association with what web application

- View a timer job's history

Always remember to run PSConfig after maintenance to make sure your farm is configured cohesively and successfully. Do not just run the minimum PSConfig command; instead, run the full command so that the configuration is fully updated; for example:

```
PSConfig.exe -cmd upgrade -inplace b2b -wait -cmd
applicationcontent -install -cmd installfeatures -cmd
secureresources -cmd services -install
```

PSConfig finalizes the configurations for the servers and databases, which then get updated. You may see changes in the GUI of Central Administration in some cases or even sites. Next, we will look at monitoring in Central Administration and how that helps us manage the farm proactively.

Monitoring in Central Administration

Health Analyzer within Central Administration is used to view and resolve issues within the farm. Again, Health Analyzer is updated after health timer jobs have been run to trigger the statuses of services within the farm's environment. The rules associated with the timer jobs are located within **Central Administration | Monitoring** and can be edited. These health rules create alerts and give you information about the rule that was run so that you can fix the issue:

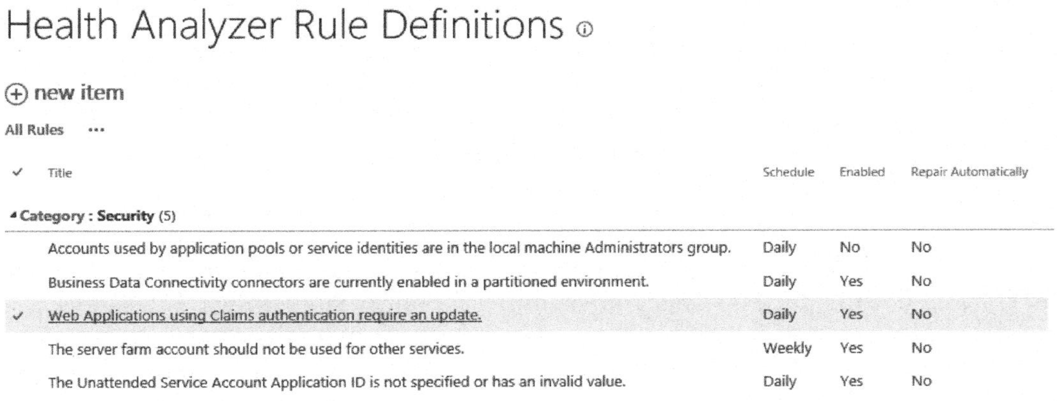

Health Analyzer Rule Definitions ⓘ

⊕ **new item**

All Rules ⋯

✓	Title	Schedule	Enabled	Repair Automatically
▲ **Category : Security** (5)				
	Accounts used by application pools or service identities are in the local machine Administrators group.	Daily	No	No
	Business Data Connectivity connectors are currently enabled in a partitioned environment.	Daily	Yes	No
✓	Web Applications using Claims authentication require an update.	Daily	Yes	No
	The server farm account should not be used for other services.	Weekly	Yes	No
	The Unattended Service Account Application ID is not specified or has an invalid value.	Daily	Yes	No

Figure 9.11 – Health Analyzer

There are specific categories a health rule can fall into, and these categories cannot be changed. You can, however, edit some areas of the rules:

- Title of the rule
- Schedule the rule runs on: Hourly, Daily, Weekly, Monthly, or OnDemandOnly
- Enable or disable the rule
- Enable Repair Automatically
- Change the version of the rule
- Receive alerts about the rule once it has been run

You can also change the way the rules are viewed and add more information using a custom view. You can also export this list to Excel or use the RSS Feed for the list. There is also an **Analyze Now** button in those rules that can be corrected through the Health Analyzer. Not all are successful all the time and they may require some manual intervention. The big thing is that Health Analyzer can help identify potential issues.

Monitoring as a Site Collection Admin

Site Collection Administrators are really the key to creating a cohesive environment and supporting the users in that community or department. As a Farm Admin, we are outside of the user community and cannot possibly know everything users are working on in real time or even any time. I often wonder how large organizations go without these roles and expect Farm Admins to know all and be all to everyone. This is especially true for small SharePoint support shops where you have one person supporting 10,000 – 100,000 users, normal administration duties, updates, and mandates from management.

As a site collection admin, this takes all the guesswork from the farm administrator and makes the load lighter. Again, as stated in *Chapter 2, Planning and Architecture*, you need to make sure you provide site collection administrators to your user community. This can be a side job for one person and strictly the only job for that person. In a perfect world, these teams would meet and find out how to best solve problems for the users in that community or collectively with other farm admins and site collection admins.

As part of a site collection administrator's duties, they should be monitoring how the tools are used within the **Site Collection** admin page, under **Site settings**. These tools give them reporting capabilities for storage and other insights needed to manage the site collection. Storage reports in a site collection will give the administrator the total storage being used in the site collection and break out each subsite, thus giving totals for these areas as well. This way, you will know where most of your content is being kept within the site collection.

As a site collection administrator, there are best practices that you need to follow. These play into how the site collection is managed:

- Keep your content under 200 GB unless you're told otherwise by your Farm Administrator.
- Split subsites across site collections when needed to load balance your storage.
- Organize your subsites across site collections using department or project names.
- Do not turn on features you do not need in your site collection.
- Always uninstall third-party features you do not use or have been abandoned.
- Tag content and come up with metadata that makes sense to describe the content.
- Use Active Directory groups within the security model for your site collection.

These are just a few things site collection administrators can do to support their sites based on best practices. This team really helps Farm Admins do their jobs more efficiently and helps mitigate issues within the environment that are site-related. If a farm admin is administering a farm with over 2,500 sites, you do not want them managing the user community as well. Site Collection admins are a plus in this scenario and a recommendation.

SQL Server performance

Tuning SQL Server has a big bearing on how SharePoint will run as an application. This is the backbone of SharePoint and stores all data for the farm. There are outside configurations that help here, such as blob storage, which we talked about earlier in this section. The easiest way to gain performance on your databases is to follow these recommendations:

- Database maintenance
- Dual NICs to minimize traffic
- Isolate Search Indexing

When creating a maintenance plan, one of the key responsibilities is to make sure you have enough disk space to hold backups of the content you are managing in the SharePoint farm. If you do not have enough space, you will not be able to hold backups for all your databases. You also want to use cheap storage for this location, depending on the size of your content and services. If you have a large amount of data, then you may want to use faster writing disks.

When looking at the size of our databases, what could cause the database to grow? What processes would start making our databases get larger? Well, the answer to that question can have many credible sources. Let's look at some:

- SharePoint migrations can cause databases to grow quickly.
- Users adding content can cause fast growth, depending on the users.
- Moving site collections can cause growth in content size.
- User activity can cause growth in the log file.

I have managed small and large farms where I had up to 3,000 site collections. When you look at space, you may need the same amount of content you have at the moment, or double or triple, depending on how much data you want to retain for direct access if something was to go wrong.

When creating a maintenance plan, the options we must run against our database to keep them healthy are to shrink the databases to clean up any unallocated space. This helps keep the databases at their current size when site collections or many documents are deleted. Indexes can then get fragmented, which then can cause performance issues. We can handle those fragmented indexes by scheduling index defragmentation as part of our maintenance plan.

You can create the steps in a maintenance plan and then clean up to delete old backups. This ensures that your drive space is free from old data that may have already been moved to offsite storage. Make sure to keep backups off your C drive where the OS is located. I have often seen times when SQL was implemented with one huge drive. Lots of things can happen in that configuration.

Another way to help with performance is to create separate service user and database traffic. Web frontends and SQL could be routed through one NIC card, while the other NIC card can be used for user traffic. This separates the traffic so that those networks are dedicated to supporting the processes in separate environments. This could be a VLAN or even a physical network.

Choosing a physical or virtual server for the SQL database server would be another way of boosting performance. Physical servers run with better performance and do not have any contention on other VMs or HOST server processes that may be running on the same server.

Troubleshooting

Troubleshooting SharePoint is a task you will fail at many times, but the good news is that there are others who have experienced the same frustration. It is such a big platform and it touches on so many other applications and systems within the enterprise that it takes dedication to support this platform. You must really understand SharePoint under the hood to take the right steps in fixing issues. As you may have noticed, we keep harping on about best practices. If you can keep those in mind as you go through the implementation, you will be able to configure a stable farm.

This section will be light due to the vast arena of issues we could come across and because this could be a whole other book in itself. If you wish to understand troubleshooting in SharePoint, we recommend the book *Troubleshooting SharePoint* by Stacy Simpkins. It goes through many scenarios to show you how to deeply analyze SharePoint issues. It also provides tips on how to figure out common issues within SharePoint.

So, let's start this section by providing a list of areas you should check when you're monitoring your server daily. Performing daily checks and even consistent checks throughout the day, if you're not using a monitoring tool, is recommended. SharePoint can change at any moment, even when you think things are OK. Just make sure you look at these areas on each server and SQL Server at least once a day to verify you have a good standing of the farm, especially after changes and updates have been made:

- Health Analyzer
- Windows Event Logs
- Windows Application Logs
- Task Manager
- Task Manager – Performance
- Scan a recent diagnostic log
- View Administrative Reports

Finding the issue is the tough part of working with and administrating SharePoint. In some cases, these issues are easy, but in others, you will find yourself surfing the net finding information about what others have done to fix the issue. In SharePoint 2003 and 2007, this type of information was not available because the SharePoint products did not take off immediately until MOSS and once that happened, Microsoft had to catch up and post information. In those days, there were not a lot of blogs and support there to help you. You had to work through the issues and fix them yourself.

Now, there is a lot of readily available information and you have many resources to choose from. However, be aware that some of the issues that were fixed may not have been fixed properly in Blog Posts. The first thing you must do is test the scripts you see in posts and alter them as needed. Test the script in a lower-level environment first to see the effects of the script. Do not trust every blog you see that contains scripts and other fixes that, in your gut, do not seem to be correct. Beware of posts that go against best practices and others that may ask you to run a script to update or change a database.

We mentioned some great tools in the previous chapter but did not really dive into how they are used. We will show you the real-world scenarios of how we found the answers to solving issues within the farm. The following tools can help you troubleshoot issues in SharePoint:

- **Fiddler**: Client-side logging software used to capture events with clients connecting to SharePoint
- **Process Monitor**: Logs all processes running on the server and what the process is processing
- **Network Monitor**: Logs all the network activity of the resource
- **ULS Viewer**: Gathers information from the ULS logs and color codes information that may be critical
- **PowerShell**: Can be used to help manage the ULS files by merging logs, starting a new log, setting the log level, clearing log levels that have been changed for VerboseEx, and so on

When troubleshooting the first area, I always check the Windows event logs, either on the client or the server. Most of the time, you will find the issue or a related issue in these logs right away. Sometimes, it can be hidden among many entries, so you must be thorough in your search. If it's a sporadic issue, you will see that it could be one line in hundreds of entries, so sometimes, it's best to recreate the issue and log the first time to see if anything comes up in the Windows logs while using the other tools mentioned as well.

When capturing logs, you want to set your ULS log level to VerboseEx. The first thing you must do before starting VerboseEx is check your drive space. Depending on the size of your farm, you can generate some big logs if you are not careful. Therefore, we have other commands to help us manage these logs instantly.

So, let's say we have an issue we are about to recreate. The first thing we must do is set the log level to VerboseEx, as shown here:

```
Set-SPLogLevel -TraceServerity verboseex
```

This will help us capture everything SharePoint spits out so that we can gather details about anything happening within the environment. Once we start the log at that level, we must immediately recreate our issue. The reason we must recreate the issue is that we want our log to be as small as possible when capturing information about the error. So, let's perform a quick recreation and then start a new log:

```
New-SPLogFile
```

Now, you will need to clear the log level, which means setting the log level back to the default and not capturing verbose logging anymore:

```
Clear-SPLogLevel
```

If you are unsure of what server the error is happening on due to it being a service or something you just don't understand, then you can also merge the logs to find errors for the same period of time:

```
Merge-SPLogFile -Path "D:\Output\SSRSService.log" -Overwrite
 -StartTime "06/09/2008 16:00" -EndTime "06/09/2008 16:15"
```

Always remember to put all the output from PowerShell and other growing files (logs) on your D drive or a drive that is always separate from the C or OS location. We do not want to fill up our C drive with this type of information – especially growing files that can fill up drive space quickly and stop the server from running. I have seen many horror stories just on this simple use of drive space.

We could really go into a lot of areas here while going through all the methods and applications we could use to troubleshoot issues, but I believe the best use of your time would be to look at some of the scenarios I have come across in my career and give you those fixes. So, in the next section, we will go through some of the issues I have encountered in the past and tell you how to get past them.

Scenarios and fixes

As part of this book, I wanted to go through some scenarios I have encountered to help you discover how to use the tools mentioned previously. In these scenarios, there will be many different types of issues. This will help you understand what tools can be used to figure out fixes quickly.

Let's go over some scenarios.

User desktop issues during migration

Scenario:

You migrate users so that they can use content from one SharePoint farm (or service) in a new SharePoint farm (or Service) using the same URL and SSL certificates. This could be from servers in one cloud service to servers in another cloud service as well.

Behavior:

Users will see issues when connecting to the site where the site will be blank, never connect, won't come up, and/or spin like it is trying to connect but can't. You may even encounter broken user interface issues, such as the page not loading fully.

Fix:

Clearing the cache on the client machine is the answer to this issue. Clear everything in the browser cache in IE since this seems to be the most vulnerable cache in this scenario. Google Chrome and Firefox seem to work well in most cases, but you may have one or two users who need to do the same in those browsers as well.

You also want to clear your machine cache and profile cache. Some information may be stored that could be corrupted as well. Then, if all else fails, clear your SSL cache in the browser. This seems to resolve the issue for those with stubborn desktop configurations.

Please follow these instructions:

> **Note**
> If you are not an admin on your computer, please contact an admin so that they can do this for you.

1. Clear all browser caches completely (if you're using Chrome, make sure you choose all the caches and not just the last 24 hours).
2. In Windows 10, open **Internet Explorer**.
3. Click on the gear icon (tools) and click on **Internet Options**.
4. Click on the **General** tab.
5. In **Browsing History**, do the following:

- **Delete Browsing History** (select the check boxes in the popup for deleting all types of information).
- Click on the **Browsing history** settings and open **View Files** (there were still a bunch there when I did this).
- Delete all those files.

Then, follow these steps to clear the computer's cache:

1. Open **My Computer.**
2. Click the address bar and paste in `%USERPROFILE%\AppData\Local\`
    `Microsoft\WebsiteCache`.
3. Delete everything within this location.
4. Click the address bar and paste in `%APPDATA%\Microsoft\Web Server`
    `Extensions\Cache`.
5. Delete everything in this location.
6. Then, from the command line, run `ipconfig /flushdns`.
7. Reboot your computer.

Site collection issues after migration

Scenario:

You are in the process of performing a database attach migration from an old farm
to a new farm, but users seem to be having issues connecting to the site or rendering the
site clearly.

Behavior:

The user sees garbage where the site is not easy to navigate and broken images and links
are all over the page. They also may have issues connecting to the site.

Fix:

Remove the content database in Central Administration and reset the IIS or reboot the
servers in the farm. Reattach the content database to the web application using the GUI
or PowerShell. You can also run `Repair-SPContentDatbase` as this resolves some
issues once you've migrated over content from another site. These steps have helped me
clear issues where the content database seems to not be fully engaged or seems to cause
trouble in terms of stability.

Content database migration errors

Scenario:

When creating your farm and adding content databases to a web application, you get an
error message stating that the ID of the database is already in use.

Behavior:

When using PowerShell to mount the content database or the GUI within Central Administration, you get an error when you try to add content databases to web applications.

Fix:

Use PowerShell to add the content database to the web application and use a new database ID:

```
Mount-SPContentDatabase "WSS_Content" -DatabaseServer
"DBSERVERNAME or ALIAS" -WebApplication "https://
WebApplication/" -AssignNewDatabaseId
```

SharePoint designer connectivity issues

Scenario:

As a site collection admin, you may see errors like this when you have transitioned to a new SharePoint farm using SharePoint Designer to create workflows and other content:

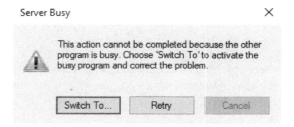

Figure 9.12 – SharePoint Designer connection error

The following is another error example:

Figure 9.13 – SharePoint Designer – possible connection error

Behavior:

You cannot connect to any sites. Individual sites could be a problem here as well. You may be able to open the site, but no content is displayed in Designer. There could be content but workflows, and lists may be missing. There are many issues that can be caused by a corrupted SharePoint Designer installation.

Fix:

Uninstalling and reinstalling the application is the first test you should do to see if there is just something wrong with the application. If this doesn't work, then you should delete all SharePoint Designer caches. You can do this by following these steps:

1. Open **My Computer.**
2. Click the address bar and paste in `%USERPROFILE%\AppData\Local\Microsoft\WebsiteCache`.
3. Delete everything within this location.
4. Click the address bar and paste in `%APPDATA%\Microsoft\Web Server Extensions\Cache`.
5. Delete everything in this location.
6. Then, from the command line, run `ipconfig /flushdns`.
7. Reboot your computer.

Moving site collections

Scenario:

During your migration planning, you've noticed that you have some site collections that are very small and some that are very large in the same content database. You want to consolidate those sites that are smaller into a different content database so that they can grow, and also relieve the space that's been taken up so that the larger site collection has room to grow in the current database.

Behavior:

When you're performing a migration, the worst thing you can come across is several small site collections and some medium-sized site collections in one huge content database where there is one site that is over 100 GB.

Fix:

Migrate the small- and medium-sized databases to other content databases to change the current content database from being very large to being large. This means that small-to medium-sized site collections could total 100 GB themselves; having another very large site collection at 100 GB or more in size makes no sense to move altogether. Breaking these site collections up gives you a faster migration time when moving a database from one server to another or even one service to another. This also helps with scheduling.

To move your site collections, create a new content database using Central Administration (make sure you document your moves during this process). Move the select site collections to one or many new content databases to ensure they can be moved quickly and easily:

```
Move-SPSite http://webapp/sites -DestinationDatabase
NewContentDb
```

Temp path update for Search

Scenario:

You are getting errors in your Windows logs and you have also noticed your C drive is full on the index server.

Behavior:

After creating and running a search crawl, you notice that the server runs out of disk space. After doing some research, you notice that the location of the growing information is from the Search Temp area, which is located on the C drive. This happened to me after one of my colleagues installed it using `AutoSPInstaller`.

Fix:

Change the location of the Temp space after installing it by changing the registry settings for these locations. In the beginning, when you created the farm, the installation process provided a screen that many do not pay attention to:

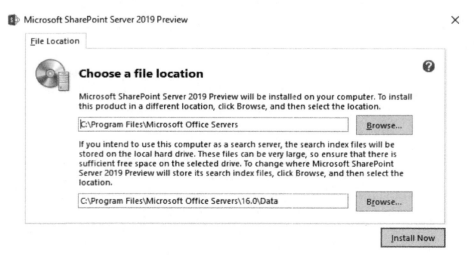

Figure 9.14 – Installation configuration screen for SharePoint

Notice that the second entry is for search index files. This is how we set our location for the search index and Temp space for the crawler. If you choose the default option, it will locate everything on the C drive. However, when you set up your search service, you can change the index location but not the Temp space for the crawler. To update the Temp space, we need to do the following using the registry:

```
HKLM:\Software\Microsoft\Office Server\16.0\Search\Global\
Gathering Manager
```

Update the registry with the new location for the Gathering Manager and reboot your machine. You will see that information will gather in the new path and that the OS drive will be free from clutter and growing index files.

CName versus A records

Scenario:

During the migration process, you've noticed that, when migrating an on-premises farm from one cloud service to another, some DNS records in the source farm for web applications and Host Named Site Collections are using CName records.

Behavior:

When you try to move a Host Named Site Collection, you notice that it's dependent on another site and is not an A record in DNS. This could be happening because the Host Named Site Collection (`https://xyz.example.com`) CName record is configured to relate to `https://xyzroot.example.com` in the source domain.

Fix:

All Host Named Site Collections in the new cloud service should be created with A records that have no association to the root-level web application. This breaks the dependency on the site having to have that site available to support the site being available on the new network. If that root site is not available, the site will not work using CName records in DNS.

Changing the names of databases

Scenario:

You didn't use a naming convention in your source farm and when migrating, you want to change the names of the content databases before adding them to the farm.

Behavior:

Naming conventions are good when you're using databases that support SharePoint. You see where someone could make a mistake by deleting a database by the way it was named. I have seen names such as `Temporary Database, Restore_12-11-2015`, which was a live database, `WSS_Content_Test`, which was a live database in production, and a host of other names that were deceiving when I read them.

Fix:

Before restoring any database, come up with a naming convention. When you have your naming convention, restore the database from a backup and in the properties, put in the correct name you would like for the database. Once you've restored the database, all MDF and LDF files will be named with the name you specified.

For MDF and LDF updates, if you are moving files from one server to another (which I do not like to do because if the file gets corrupted, you have nothing to fall back on), you would just rename both files with the name you want and attach them to the new server.

If the content database is already attached to the farm and you need to update the name, just disconnect it from the SharePoint farm (make sure you find out the location of the MDF and LDF before detaching them), detach the database from SQL Server, rename the MDF and LDF files, and then reattach the database to SQL Server. Once you've done that, you can right-click and rename the database to what you named the MDF and LDF files, unless you want someone to be confused.

HTTP authentication error when using a 2013 SPD workflow

Scenario:

A user's site has been migrated to the new farm and all checks have been made to ensure the site is working correctly. The site collection admin has republished all workflows as needed and has run checks to verify the workflows are working. A user goes to invoke a 2013 workflow on a document in a library and the workflow suspends.

Behavior:

When certain users try to use a 2013 workflow in a site, they get an error stating that there's been an HTTP authentication error.

Fix:

This error occurs due to the user who created the workflow not having a SharePoint user profile or the user who is invoking the workflow does not have a user profile. Please check that the user has a valid profile and, most importantly, that they have a work email address in the profile.

I've had several users who had profiles from the **Active Directory (AD)** domain and from a third-party cloud authentication solution in their user profiles. The problem was that none of the AD domain accounts had email addresses associated with the profiles, only the third-party solution. So, the user was creating workflows and using workflows that were created by the AD domain profile that had no email addresses. None of the workflows would work consistently. In the end, all the caches, including the SSL and SharePoint Designer caches, had to be deleted for this user to authenticate correctly.

This also presents an issue when users log in to their device using an AD account and when using a federated account to log in to SharePoint. Sometimes, the system gets confused. I have seen situations where a user has created workflows using their Active Directory account and have workflows with the federated account listed in the workflow view of SharePoint Designer.

Updating database permissions

Scenario:

After performing a content database migration, some SharePoint services fail on some sites.

Behavior:

Logins fail on certain content databases due to the service accounts' inability to access the content database.

Fix:

Make sure you go back and add the service accounts to the content databases that you added to a new farm due for migration purposes. You will see that when you update them to a web application, only the app pool account will be associated with the database.

To add the service application accounts, farm account, and any other account that would need access to the content database, there is some work that's required. Document the database's security before migration and duplicate it with the new service account names.

Also, remember to delete any other accounts that may have been used in the old farm that are not being used any more. We keep them in place while migrating but once the new security has been applied, we can remove those user accounts as part of the cleanup process.

SMTP mail issues

Scenario:

Users are complaining that mail from all alerts is working and that when they're sending emails within workflows, the emails never get delivered to the users.

Behavior:

The user sets an alert on a library or list and the alert is captured; then, a confirmation email is sent successfully. However, when they add anything to the library, no email is sent to let them know that content was added as part of the alert. This is the same behavior but with a workflow. When a workflow is processed on a document, no email is sent, as defined in the workflow, to the User.

Fix:

Verify that your port is open on the server, as well as your outgoing mail configuration in SharePoint. Then, verify that your outgoing mail works correctly using PowerShell:

```
$site = New-Object Microsoft.SharePoint.SpSite("https://
sitename")

$web = $site.OpenWeb()

$mail = [Microsoft.Sharepoint.Utilities.
SpUtility]::SendEmail($web,0,0,"lewin@xyz.com","Testing from
PowerShell", "This is a test from PowerShell and server APP1")
```

In my case, the SMTP mail was working. All ports were working correctly, even with a custom port, 587. All was working well but no emails were getting to the users from any workflow, even though Alerts were working. I was scratching my head because I did not understand what was happening.

So, I started investigating further and noticed that there were some changes to the server. Upon accessing **Control Panel** and **Uninstall Software**, I noticed that three applications had been installed over the weekend. My users noticed the change in the delivery of mail over the weekend and Monday morning more so.

So, I screenshotted the applications that were installed and used Process Monitor to log processes on the Central Administration server, where outgoing mail is processed. In doing so, I noticed that one of the new applications was blocking all SMTP traffic. I uninstalled the application and voila – the SMTP mail started being delivered again. I also notified the security team to make them aware that this was the cause of my issue. Coordination between teams is very important so that everyone is aware of changes.

Site collection location

Scenario:

You are in the process of migrating content from one site to another farm. You need to understand what site collections are available in each content database so that you can come up with a plan to migrate those sites and let the users of the site know prior to the migration date.

Behavior:

Not all site collections are easy to find through the GUI of Central Administration. Yes, we can go there and find the site, which would give us the information we need, but in this case, we want to find out where the sites are so that we can plan, move sites around if needed, and know the sizes and other information about the site.

Fix:

Use PowerShell to find out information about on-site collections before migration. Have a list of sites, sizes, and content database locations so that you know how large the database is beforehand. This will help you plan and understand the time frames needed to move content from one farm to another farm or one server to another server.

Again, to move a site collection in order to groom the content database of unwanted or smaller site collections, use the `move-spsite` command:

```
Move-SPSite http://webapp/sites -DestinationDatabase
NewContentDb
```

When you want to create a migration plan, we need to know more information. PowerShell comes in handy when you want to know how big the site collection is, as well as the content database's total size.

User migrations to a new domain

Scenario:

You are in the process of migrating and you notice some of the user accounts are failing to log in.

Behavior:

Users will fail to log in to the new site locations within the new farm because they do not have access to the sites.

Fix:

Use the PowerShell `Move-SP-User` command to move the account from one domain to the new domain. This will give the user rights to access the server. Most of the time, I have found that this is due to the account not migrating properly to the new domain.

```
$user = Get-SPUser -Identity "DOMAIN\JaneDoe" -Web https://
webUrl
```

```
Move-SPUser -Identity $user -NewAlias "Domain\JaneSmith"
-IgnoreSid
```

That's it in terms of scenarios and fixes. Now, we will conclude this chapter.

Summary

Performance is one of the most important things you can implement as part of your SharePoint farm and environment. Without it, you will hear from your user community. I have done my best to provide as much information as possible within the confines of this book. Make sure to follow the guidelines we set here and always look at how you can tune your environment based on the ups and downs of concurrent users and services, which could peak at a certain time of the day.

Monitor your environment daily and understand how it is performing. You should also pay attention when tickets for issues come in. This can tell you a lot about your farm and when it has the worst performance. Home in on those time frames and see what is going on; for example, you could have peaked on CPU or memory. Investigating issues like these is crucial to getting in front of problems instead of waiting for them to happen.

Troubleshoot issues with the tools listed in this chapter and make sure to look at obvious locations first before gathering logs and searching through them. Following best practices during configuration saves you from having issues in the first place, so the more you do in the beginning, the less you have to fix in the backend.

If you have delivered the environment and are still having issues, this is the worst situation you can be in. Make sure to test and know your services work before you deliver them. Another thing to watch for is coming behind someone else's work. If someone else set up the farm, make sure to follow along or review all their configurations before delivering the farm. You can get yourself in trouble if you do not because if just one service doesn't work, everyone will be looking at you, not the technician that left after they did the installation.

In the next chapter, we will review reporting and the other features and integrations that are available to support it. We'll also talk about what cloud services are available for reporting via hybrid connectivity.

Questions

You can find the answers on GitHub under Assessments at `https://github.com/PacktPublishing/Implementing-Microsoft-SharePoint-2019/blob/master/Assessments.docx`

1. When you're planning for performance, what are some areas you can key in on that support physical or virtual servers?

2. What can be a key issue when a user connects to the company VPN?

3. Developers can contribute to performance issues. What tool can they use to help mitigate issues with memory leaks?

4. What is the name of the tool that's used to onboard users using a recorded script and receive performance reports before we can go live?

5. Which SharePoint service supports OneNote client access?

6. When large files are kept outside of the content database, what caching solution should you use?

7. If my application pool is slow to respond every morning, how can I keep the application pool live?

8. What are some specific disk types we can use to support the physical performance of our physical server configuration?

10
SharePoint Advanced Reporting and Features

SharePoint 2019 has several advanced reporting features. These advanced reporting features include Excel Online, Power Apps, Power Automate, Power BI, SQL reporting services, and Visio and Visio services. In this chapter, we will explore some of these advanced reporting features in SharePoint 2019. Some of these features also exist in earlier versions of SharePoint, but you will see differences in how they are configured and integrated into SharePoint 2019.

SharePoint Server 2019 brings the cloud closer to customers and vice versa. The cloud features Power Apps, Power BI, and Power Automate, all of which are now available locally and bring the power of the cloud to on-premises farms. SharePoint Server 2019 includes process automation and forms technologies such as Power Apps and Power Automate to connect with your on-premises data. These features need to be configured via an On-Premises Gateway, which we will talk about in this chapter.

We will also briefly touch on various Azure tools and Excel Online, both of which have been built to integrate SharePoint. We will then reference a few third-party reporting applications that you may want to leverage in your SharePoint environment. This chapter is going to provide a brief overview of these reporting features, so do not expect a deep dive or an exhaustive exploration. If you want to do a deep dive into any of these topics, I have added some links to the *Further reading* section that you can explore further on your own.

The following topics will be covered in this chapter:

- Deprecated reporting features
- SQL reporting services
- On-Premises Gateway
- Power Tools
- Office Online Server
- Excel Online

Let's get started!

Technical requirements

To be able to understand this chapter and the knowledge provided, you will need to meet the following requirements:

- 3-5 years of experience using SharePoint
- 2 years of experience using Microsoft 365
- 2 years of experience using Azure

You can find the code files present in this chapter in this book's GitHub repository at https://github.com/PacktPublishing/Implementing-Microsoft-SharePoint-2019.

Advanced reporting and features

With more and more companies looking to move to the cloud in recent years, it seems that consolidation is a new priority. This is usually the largest area of need and has always been the architecture for supporting reporting and applications. The database resources that support those areas of our businesses are large and, if compromised, can put a company at risk. The security of our data is everything and we must keep that in mind as we clean up and figure out where our data should be located.

It is not uncommon for medium- to large-sized enterprises to have their data spread across multiple enterprise systems. These enterprises may have data residing in multiple locations, both on-premises and in the cloud. Data residing in disparate systems across enterprises that have not yet been consolidated can cause data compliance, performance, and redundancy issues. Not to mention, that keeping old database systems in play that are no longer supported by companies due to the company being no longer existent is a very high security risk.

As companies seek to trim their technical overhead by reducing the number of systems that maintain their data, this would be a prime target on the list for consolidation. Database architectures cost the most in any organization, be it cloud or on-premises. The licensing and overall cost for virtual or hardware can be staggering, depending on how much data and redundancy you build in the architectures.

The need for consolidation and integration becomes even more complex as companies merge and incorporate other entities under one umbrella. We are now seeing a trend where companies want to reduce the number of systems that they have and use one or two systems to view and manipulate data enterprise wide.

We are also seeing that user subscriptions are being more scrutinized now than ever because of companies spreading their applications, business processes, and storage over many cloud providers. I have had one customer paying $100 a month per user and they had over 10,000 users. Upon breaking down the subscriptions, they were paying $35 for Microsoft 365 and $65 for a subscription to an enterprise cloud application that was used by everyone. The application could have been built in 365 using the tools available, which could have saved them lots of money.

So, in most cases, these subscriptions and applications being used in the cloud need to be looked at thoroughly. It is not cost-effective and you can run the risk of putting too much at stake by connecting many cloud architectures together. With the cloud being so new, things are changing daily. Your IT staff must understand the risks of securing those risky areas. Since this can be a huge task, especially managing all these clouds and on-premise areas, advanced reporting will be the biggest area of concern due to the size and sensitive nature of the data being exposed.

However, as we mentioned previously, there is the need to have our teams work smarter and put the power in the hands of the users to a certain point. We must empower them to create their own applications and their own reports, which trims the need for development staff and the server footprint to support the database architecture. Doing this helps put data into perspective. If you have a small database, change where you hold the information. Put it into SharePoint, where it can be utilized by everyone. Access databases are a perfect target for migrating to SharePoint, and you can also redo the process using Power Tools.

Advanced reporting has always been a key integrated feature in SharePoint and is now even more powerful. People really use SharePoint effectively when collaborating. Collaboration means we are working together as a team to manage projects, tasks, data, and documents. If we are working as a team, reporting should be easy, right? This is because if we are using a collaborative platform with abilities to connect to other data platforms, then all data can be reached. This is exactly why SharePoint was created.

There are other features, such as Power Automate and Power BI, that also give you easy ways to pull data and report on it – either from databases, Excel spreadsheets, or SharePoint lists – using these new cloud features. Workflow processes can also be built with these tools, which automates processes and captures information based on the process at hand.

Since SharePoint 2019 is built on the same version of SharePoint as SharePoint Online, you will see that using modern sites is available in this 2019 version of SharePoint, which makes it somewhat comparable to Microsoft 365. Microsoft 365 has more features on the backend and is a lot more advanced, but you can accomplish some of the same things in the on-premises version of SharePoint 2019.

The power of this platform is that you can put certain tools in the hands of users who need reports and processes that they can create on their own. Using the tool sets described in this chapter will help users make applications that can be shared across the enterprise. Users can also take advantage of using out of the box views in SharePoint lists. This has been a traditional way of reporting information in lists and libraries. We should not forget that we have the out of the box capabilities and customized capabilities of JSON, which we can use to format views from lists. Remember that although there are many new solutions that can help show and process this data in many different ways, we still can use some of our old customizations to do our work as well.

In this chapter, we will show you how to gather data and how the tools that make applications, business processes, and reports based on specific areas of content are not as hard to use as you may think. Using tools such as SSRS, Power BI, Power Apps, Power Automate, and Excel Services, you can create forms, workflows, and pull reports together quickly.

Deprecated features

With SharePoint changing over the years, we have seen many features come and go that were used in prior versions of the software. We saw a big change from 2010 to 2013, with one of them being the focus on claims authentication. Classic Windows authentication was still available, but this created some extra steps when migrating from that version of SharePoint. It was a real eye opener and let us know to expect change.

The most memorable for me was the FAB 40 templates and the Productivity Hub, which for some people still using SharePoint 2007 and 2010 need to be aware of. These templates will not work in 2013 or later versions of SharePoint. This was a big surprise for a lot of people because Microsoft created them. Everyone was expecting them to be available in the next versions to come but to our surprise, they did not make it.

With SharePoint 2016, we also saw a big shift, with Excel Services being moved from a service in SharePoint to a service within Office Online Server now known as Excel Online. This change makes sense to me because these services do need their own server resources to keep SharePoint running at peak performance. There are already enough services and web applications that SharePoint server farm resources provide, so taking some services and spreading them out over resources is great news, but it will cost you to add another server. However, if this new server is a VM, this will not be that costly.

The following is a list of deprecated and removed reporting features for SharePoint 2019:

Feature	Status
SQL Server Reporting Services Integrated Mode	Removed
Power View	Removed
BISM file connections	Removed
InfoPath Services	Deprecated
PerformancePoint	Deprecated
Power Pivot for SharePoint	Removed
Scheduled workbook data refresh	Removed
Workbook as a data source	Removed
PowerPivot management dashboard	Removed
PowerPivot Gallery	Removed

Figure 10.1 – Deprecated and removed reporting features

So, it never phases me to see that we have many business intelligence features that have been removed and deprecated from within SharePoint natively with replacement applications. These features, which have been renamed and refined, are now integrated with SharePoint but are not native to it. I am sure we will see more of this to come in newer versions of SharePoint and within Microsoft 365.

Some of the removed and deprecated features include PerformancePoint, which is now deprecated in SharePoint 2019. Performance Point services, which included the ability to create scorecards and analytics reports, has also been removed from SharePoint 2019. Most of the functionality of PerformancePoint is available in Power BI and Power BI Report Server, which we will discuss later in this chapter.

PowerPivot for SharePoint has also been removed, which included the Power Pivot management dashboard known as PowerPivot Gallery. This was a huge integrated service that I only saw installed correctly without broken configurations in only a couple farms.

It was a very useful integration and provided users with another way to provide reporting on data. Most users loved this feature because it was built into the desktop version of Excel already. Now, users will need to take advantage of Power BI and Power BI Report Server to get some of the same functionality.

PowerView and BISM file connections have been removed completely from SharePoint. This type of connection is typically used by Excel and SSRS to connect PowerView reports to SQL server analysis services data sources. However, this is no longer included due to PowerView being removed.

We will not go over InfoPath in this book, but we will mention what has taken place as part of the big move to the cloud. InfoPath has been deprecated as well but still works as it did in other versions of SharePoint. It currently works in SharePoint Online. It is still available by default in the installation for SharePoint 2019 and is managed the same as it was in prior versions. You will still need to use InfoPath Designer 2013 to create and publish those forms to SharePoint 2019.

If I were you, I would start moving away from this product as soon as possible. This is because many companies have used this product over the years and have many forms published using InfoPath, along with workflows for creating business processes. I have seen this with my own eyes and one of my latest customers had so many InfoPath forms it would take them years to recreate them.

The problem comes with Microsoft pulling the plug on old applications, as they did with SharePoint Designer 2010 workflows. This means they may pull the plug on InfoPath in the next couple years. Is that enough time for you to recreate all the forms you have in your current farm? Probably not. As I explained previously, there is a learning curve with Power Apps and Power Automate, so you really need to start migrating and planning now.

You may be wondering why this is the case. Well, things change all the time. Your company may change direction and not want to use SharePoint 2019 and go straight to SharePoint Online. In 2021, you will be better off using cloud applications to create your forms and workflows. This will be very helpful when you migrate to the cloud as the core components will be in place, and training for those new tools can be achieved earlier. It is always good to think ahead.

SQL Reporting Services Integrated Mode has also been removed from SharePoint 2019 released version. SSRS Integrated Mode was deprecated in 2016, but it could still be used with SharePoint 2016. With SQL Server 2017, it was completely removed and is not supported in SharePoint 2019.

Next, we will discuss what BI tools work in SharePoint 2019. This will give you the guidance to move forward with integrating BI into your new SharePoint 2019 environment.

Azure Active Directory

Azure Active Directory is Microsoft's identity and access management solution and is required for cloud security and managing user accounts. Your company's Active Directory and human resources rolls can be added to a secure version of Azure Active Directory. This Active Directory access management tool will manage your access to the Microsoft 365 app suite. This is great for hybrid configurations because although your SharePoint 2019 environment is on-premises, you can still leverage the newly updated reporting services and applications that are available in the cloud.

> **Important Note**
> The following link provides an overview of Azure Active Directory:
> `https://docs.microsoft.com/en-us/azure/`
> `architecture/reference-architectures/identity/`
> `azure-ad`.

Most organizations maintain a mixture of on-premises and cloud applications. Azure Active Directory offers a solution for managing access and identity for both. This is more important now than ever because the on-premises deployment of SharePoint 2019, as discussed previously, is unable to use many of the previous on-premises reporting solutions. This fact drives the need for hybrid solutions so that admins and the user base can utilize the features of Microsoft's cloud applications, such as Power Automate and Power BI.

Azure Active Directory uses a **tenant architecture**. Within the Azure Active Directory ecosystem, you must create a tenant. Each tenant is its own instance partitioned within Azure AD. Each tenant represents an organization of users that will access applications. When the Azure AD Tenant is set up, the administrator can choose the source of user accounts. In most instances, the on-premises source within the organization would be Windows Server AD. Azure has a tool called **Azure AD connect** that you can use to synchronize your Azure Tenant with your on-premises Active Directory.

Formally, Azure AD was solely a managed service but due to high demand, Azure recently added Azure ADDS trust. This is important for many organizations and enterprises that want to keep all their identity management on-premises, but also wish to allow Azure AD to utilize those identities to connect to the cloud-based apps that Microsoft 365 provides. I will not go too deep into the one-way outbound forest trust as it is beyond the scope of this book. However, do explore this option, especially if your organization is hesitant to adopt Azure AD. Azure ADDS's one-way trust relationship will allow users and applications to authenticate against the on-premises Active Directory domain environment from the Azure ADDS managed services domain. This may be key to incentivizing hesitant management to begin adopting cloud technologies for use within their on-premises environments.

SQL Reporting Services

SQL Reporting Services is a powerful tool for gathering reports within SharePoint. The service can gather and display reports in many ways and from many data resources. However, when used in SharePoint, you can only pull from SharePoint lists. You cannot combine reporting from SharePoint lists and a database resource at the same time unless you customize the data within the SharePoint list so that it includes an offsite database that uses BCS.

In previous versions of SharePoint, an admin could install **SSRS (SSRS)** in SharePoint integration mode versus Native Mode. SSRS Native mode is when the reporting services are installed to run on a separate application server and the reporting services are supplied to SharePoint through the Report Viewer web part.

In this configuration, all the processes run on the application server. With Integrated Mode configured, these services can be installed on a SharePoint server running internally on the SharePoint farm. Integrated mode installations caused a few issues because if a customer only wanted the BI solution, they would be forced to install SharePoint to get access to reporting features such as PowerView.

The integrated mode for SSRS and SharePoint also left some of the Native Mode features out, such as Linked Reports, My Reports, and subscription and batching. The move away from SSRS integrated mode is in line with Microsoft moving away from heavy on-premises installations to a preference for cloud integration and putting more feature capabilities, such as reporting services, in the hands of the end user.

With SharePoint integrated mode, SSRS was installed on a SharePoint Server. It still requires a SQL Server license. You could use SQL Server 2012 Standard Edition to access many of the reporting features unless you had a need for PowerView, in which case you would have needed to install SQL Server Enterprise Edition. However, now, SQL Server Standard Edition is not available for SharePoint 2019 and it must be installed to leverage SSRS. This is more costly than the standard edition, so keep that in mind when you are planning your deployment architecture and costs.

Also, since SSRS cannot be deployed on a SharePoint Server in SharePoint 2019, this must be another server that must be monitored and maintained. This can add to the admin troubleshooting burden as you will now have to troubleshoot reporting issues from SQL server instead of directly from your SharePoint Server.

The reporting capability now resides outside of SharePoint and is solely native to SSRS so that it can be leveraged by SharePoint. Since **Native** mode is the only way to leverage SSRS in SharePoint 2019, SharePoint connects to this external application server through the SQL Reporting Services Report Viewer Web Part.

The Report Viewer web part enables you to put embedded paginated reports that are stored in SSRS (Native mode) into a page on your SharePoint site or Power BI Report Server into SharePoint Server web part pages. However, you cannot use this web part for Power BI reports. The web part can only be used with classic pages in SharePoint. Modern pages are not supported.

To utilize the Report Viewer web part in your SharePoint farm, you need to download the report for your web part. Then, you need to deploy the web part to your SharePoint farm in order to run the SharePoint management shell from your SharePoint farm. Remember to run the SharePoint management shell as administrator. For this, you can run `Add-SPSolution` to install the `ReportViewerWebpart.wsp` package.

You can download this package from `https://www.microsoft.com/en-us/download/details.aspx?id=55949&751be11f-ede8-5a0c-058c-2ee190a24fa6=True`.

To deploy the package, follow these steps:

1. Open SharePoint Management Shell on SharePoint 2019 Server and choose **Run as Administrator**.

2. Run the `Add-SPSolution` command. This adds the farm solution to the farm. The following is an example of this:

```
Add-SPSolution -LiteralPath "Drive:\*solutionfolder*\
ReportViewerWebPart.wsp"
```

3. Run the `Install-SPSolution` command to deploy the farm solution to the farm. The following is an example of this:

```
Install-SPSolution -Identity ReportViewerWebPart.wsp
 -GACDeployment -AllWebApplications
```

> **Note**
> You can deploy solutions to a specific web application if required by using the `-WebApplication` parameter.

You need to activate this feature from the site collection where you want to view Power BI paginated reports. To do so, follow these steps:

1. Navigate to the site collection.
2. Click the gear icon and select **Site Settings**.
3. Under **Site Collection administration**, click **Site Collection Features**.
4. Scroll down the page until you get to **Report Viewer WebPart**. Click **Activate**.
5. This feature will now be available on your site collection.

Migrating integrated reports from previous versions is supported through the use of a script that Microsoft provides for moving these documents. Microsoft has stated that it will continue to support SharePoint integrated mode in earlier versions of SharePoint. However, if you have SSRS reports from previous versions of SharePoint and you want to migrate them to SharePoint 2019, you will need to leverage the migration script that will change the reports from integrated mode to **Native** mode.

To use the script, follow these steps:

1. Download the `ssrs_migration.rss` script.
2. Download the Reporting Services `RS.exe` migration script from this book's GitHub repository to a local folder.

Note that you will lose your passwords once you migrate your reports. These passwords must be reentered. Make sure you document those passwords if you have not already. Data sources can be located on various SQL servers in our enterprise. Just make sure you have covered all your bases as they contain stored credentials.

> **Note**
>
> For more information, see the section How to use the script section of this article: `https://github.com/Microsoft/sql-server-samples/tree/master/samples/features/reporting-services/ssrs-migration-rss`.

Now that we have installed the solution into the farm, let's configure the sites where we want to use the web part by adding it to the pages within the site.

Site feature configuration

Adding the web part to a page is straightforward and remains the same as it was in older versions of SharePoint. To start this process, follow these steps:

1. In your SharePoint site, select the gear icon in the top-left corner and select **Add a page**:

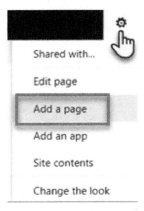

Figure 10.2 – Add a page

2. Give your page a name and select **Create**.

3. Within the page designer, select the **Insert** tab from the ribbon. Then, select **Web Part** within the **Parts** section:

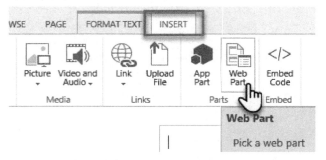

Figure 10.3 – Choosing Web Part from the ribbon

4. Under **Categories**, select **SSRS (Native mode)**. Then, under **Parts**, select **Report Viewer** and select **Add**:

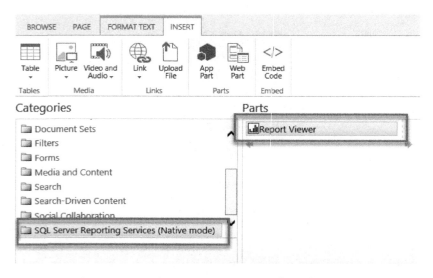

Figure 10.4 – Choosing Report Viewer from the menu

You may see an error initially. This is because the default report server URL is set to `https://localhost` and may not be available at that location.

Configuring the Report Viewer web part

To configure the web part so that it points to your specific report, follow these steps:

1. When editing the SharePoint page, select the down arrow in the top-right of the web part and select **Edit Web Part**:

Figure 10.5 – Edit Web Part

2. Enter your **Report Server URL** for the report server hosting your report. The URL should look similar to `https://myrsserver/reportserver`.

3. Enter the path and name of the report you want to display within the web part. It will look similar to `/AdventureWorks Sample Reports/Company Sales`. In this example, the `Company Sales` report is in a folder called `AdventureWorks Sample Reports`.

4. If your report requires parameters, once you have supplied the report server URL and the name of the report, select **Load Parameters** within the **Parameters** section.

5. Select **OK** to save your changes for our **Web Part**.

6. Select **Save** from within the Office ribbon to save these changes to the SharePoint page.

As you can see, Microsoft thought about those customers who use a lot of reporting features. At one point, I did not think they were going to give us any tools for SSRS so that we could migrate to the cloud. I thought there would have been a conversion or something using a new tool they created. This really confirmed that Microsoft takes everything into consideration and gives us options to move forward.

Using Report Builder

What is Report Builder? **Report Builder** is a tool that allows users to create SSRS reports. This tool is native to SSRS and was integrated with SharePoint 2013 and SharePoint 2016. However, with integrated mode being removed in SharePoint 2019, Report Builder can only be used once your SharePoint site has been configured to work with SSRS and Report Builder has been configured.

Using Report Builder, you can determine what data sources you will pull into your report, the datasets you want to utilize, and how you want that data displayed. Report Builder allows you to create reports using existing datasets and **report parts**, which are parts of already created reports that you have access to pull into your new report. It has a great drag and drop feature that allows you to customize your report fields and layouts.

> **Note**
>
> You can download Report Builder by going to `https://www.microsoft.com/en-us/download/details.aspx?id=53613`.
>
> You can install Report Builder by going to `https://docs.microsoft.com/en-us/sql/reporting-services/install-windows/install-report-builder?view=sql-server-ver15`.

To create a simple report in SharePoint using Report Builder, you must have your SSRS configured and have Report Builder installed. You are on your way to building a report using this tool. It is a good idea you try and utilize the tools that you will be rolling out to your users and document any issues. Ensure you cover them while training. We will discuss this later. The following steps show you how to build a very simple report:

1. Open Report Builder and choose a dataset screen. The default choice will be to create a dataset.

2. Click **Next**.

3. On the **Data source property** screen, click the **Build** button.

4. Next, you will need to enter the **SQL Server** name that you want to connect to.

5. Enter the database name under **Select** and select the name of your database.

6. Click **OK**.

7. In the **Data source property** window, click **Credentials** and enter your **Username** and **Password**.

8. You will see **Use as Windows credentials**. Check this box and click **OK**.

9. Select the following from the list and click **Next**:

   a) **NameCustomer**

   b) **Namelocation**

   c) **Factloanamount**

10. From the fields listed, click **Factloanamount** under **Values**.

11. From the available fields, drag the United States location under the road and click **Next**.

12. Choose the layout you want and click **Next**. Alternatively, you can choose the style you want and click **Next**.

There are some cosmetic changes that you can make to update reports so that they are more attractive and easy to read. Using Report Builder, you can add titles to your report and resize your columns and rows. However, this is beyond the scope of this simple tutorial. More advanced tutorials are available on Microsoft's website: `https://docs.microsoft.com/en-us/sql/reporting-services/report-builder-tutorials?view=sql-server-ver15`. There are even third-party classes available that provide support.

As we can see, we have not really lost a lot of functionality with SSRS, but things have changed. We can migrate reports and even show those reports in our sites using web parts. The interfaces have stayed somewhat the same, but the locations of tools and administration has changed, which has added a new twist to maintaining the farm and what you need to be aware of in SQL Server.

Hybrid configurations

Since SharePoint 2013, we have seen how we can interface our on-premises SharePoint farms with the Microsoft 365 platform. There is no reason not to have a mixture of both cloud and on-premises functionality nowadays. To be quite honest, my recommendation is to stay in this configuration. This gives you control over your data and any content that you may not want to have hosted on systems in the cloud. These configurations also give you bridges to move to the cloud as fast as you like instead of all at once. Also, allowing you to use tools and services in the cloud can be very useful in helping you further collaborate and bring about a broader range of reports, data gathering, and automation.

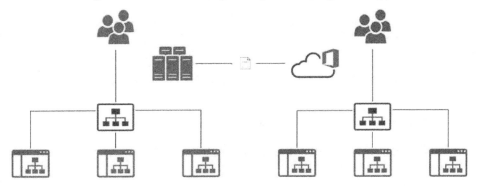

Figure 10.6: Hybrid Configuration

We are going to touch on those areas in this chapter so that you know what is offered mainly on-premises, but we must remember that these services play both ways. So, what I can connect to in the cloud I can also connect back to my on-premises environment. There are endless possibilities that can help you manage the cost of your services and analyze the needs of moving to the cloud instead of moving blindly.

SharePoint hybrid gateways

When deploying SharePoint on-premises, there is a functionality that is needed to create this hybrid connection to the cloud. You can create that connectivity using the Hybrid Picker which is a SharePoint Hybrid Configuration Wizard that you can download from your Microsoft 365 tenant. The trusted communication that must be created can be created from your on-premises enterprise internal SharePoint Server, either in a private cloud that hosts servers or in a public cloud that hosts servers for SharePoint 2019. This goes without the need to use the cloud, so this could be Azure, AWS, or RackSpace. Wherever you are and depending on your network configurations, which may take some toying with, this connection can be made so that you can reap the benefits of this hybrid gateway.

Link to Hybrid Picker Overview: `https://docs.microsoft.com/en-us/ sharepoint/hybrid/hybrid-picker-in-the-sharepoint-online- admin-center`

I highly recommend using the hybrid connectivity provided by the cloud. I really believe that companies should take full advantage of this functionality to move forward in using the cloud for other solutions. This allows you to have the cloud meet your internal server resources and manage those functional areas, which can bring a host of new possibilities.

You have complete control of your on-premises environment, which also means that you have complete authority over it. There is no need to be limited to this environment – just the software boundaries that come with the product. Other than that, follow best practices and provide any customizations you want to deploy in this environment. You get some of the features of the cloud but since they are two different environments, there will be some limitations.

The following are the areas where you will see available features when creating this connection:

- **Hybrid Sites**: Allows users to follow sites on-premises and in the cloud.
- **Hybrid One Drive for Business**: Creates a user's OneDrive for Business profile in the cloud instead of on-premises.
- **Hybrid Self-Site Creation**: Redirects sites to be created in SharePoint Online only.

- **Hybrid Auditing**: All audit logging is pushed from on-premises to the cloud.

- **Hybrid Taxonomy and Content Types**: Allows shared taxonomy and content types between the cloud and on-premises environments.

- **Hybrid Business Connectivity Services**: Allows data to be securely displayed from external systems within the cloud or on-premises.

- **Hybrid Search**: Allows you to search both on-premises and the cloud for function separating indexes that are supported on those systems individually.

When taking advantage of this configuration, we must plan what we expect to gain from this hybrid connectivity. Some questions you need to ask before you go down the road of configuring this connectivity are as follows:

- What are the business's goals for the future?

- What benefits can we, as a company, get from these features?

- Do we even plan to go to the cloud?

- Are our users trained enough to realize the benefits of these features?

- How will we manage this from a topology standpoint?

- Will we be able to support these areas within SharePoint 2019 effectively?

- Will security be an issue if we implement this feature?

- How does governance play a role in this new connectivity at this point?

- Do we need to update our Governance Plan?

These are just some of the questions that need to be answered at this point. You want to make sure you have a plan in place and that that plan is followed so it is documented. Your risks at this point could be the answers to one of these questions. Please understand what you are creating, providing, and managing at this point – a connection to the cloud that you want to be able to leverage. Before including this as a solution for your company, make sure you understand what it brings to the table.

Although there is not a lot of space in this book to write about this subject, I do want to touch on some of the topologies that can be configured when using this Hybrid Gateway for SharePoint 2019:

- **One-Way Outbound Topology**: On-premises to the cloud

- **One-Way Inbound Topology**: The cloud to on-premises

- **Two-Way (Bidirectional) Topology**: Communicate back and forth between the cloud and on-premises environments

To create the connection, we need to know the requirements for these features to exist:

- An on-premises Active Directory Services domain.
- An operational SharePoint Server Farm.
- Have a configured Microsoft 365 organization with E1, E3, or E4 licenses.
- STS certificate in the SharePoint farm that is used by the hybrid picker to establish token signing trust when configuring hybrid workloads.

To set up the Hybrid Picker on your SharePoint Server, you need to meet some other requirements, as follows:

1. Sign up and register your domain with Microsoft 365.
2. Synchronize your user account with Microsoft 365.
3. Assign the respective licenses to users.
4. Create services for User Profile, Managed Metadata, and Application Management Service.
5. Create a web application for My Sites with the My Site Host site collection template.

To find out more about this process, please go to `https://docs.microsoft.com/en-us/sharepoint/hybrid/set-up-sharepoint-services-for-hybrid-environments`.

All inbound connectivity for search, business connectivity services, and Duet Enterprise Online may require further configuration using reverse proxy devices, and internet domain with permissions to create and edit DNS records, and using a wildcard certificate for encryption between Microsoft 365 and the proxy device. On-premises SharePoint SSL certificates also need to be configured on the on-premises SharePoint web application.

The reverse proxy devices that are supported for this are as follows:

- Windows Server 2012 R2 with **Web Application Proxy (WAP)**
- Forefront **Threat Management Gateway (TMG)** 2010
- F5 Big-IP

> **Note**
>
> More information about the configuration you need to do can be found here: `https://docs.microsoft.com/en-us/sharepoint/hybrid/configure-server-to-server-authentication`.

As you can see, there are many configuration steps and areas you need to tend to when creating this connection between your on-premises and Microsoft 365 environment. To install the Hybrid Picker, execute the following steps:

1. Log into the console of a SharePoint Server farm server as a farm admin.
2. From the farm server, connect to Microsoft 365 as a global admin.
3. Navigate to `https://go.microsoft.com/fwlink/?linkid=867176`.
4. To configure your hybrid features, follow the prompts provided by the Hybrid Picker.

There is a lot more to this configuration. You can find out more by taking a look at the links provided in the *Further reading* section. In this chapter, I did not want to focus much on the configuration but expand on the capabilities and applications in the cloud that can bring benefits to your on-premises environment. Unfortunately, I do not have the room in this book to publish the whole configuration.

The configurations for hybrid can be removed if needed but from my experience, this is not easy to do. You may find some residue from these configurations, which is why you should think through this process before moving forward. This can be a great experience, but you really have to plan and make sure your architecture is correct before following through with it.

On-premises data gateways

Opening an on-premises gateway provides secure data transfer between on-premises content and server Microsoft cloud services. This gateway is a bridge that provides cloud services to internal enterprise servers. The applications that can be used with this gateway are as follows:

- Power BI
- Power Apps
- Power Automate
- Azure Analysis Services
- Azure Logic Apps

When utilizing this method of connecting on-premises enterprise systems and cloud services, organizations can keep their databases and other data sources on their enterprise networks. This process was built to be secure so that customers can take advantage of the features that are only available in the cloud.

There are two types of gateways available:

- **On-premises data gateway for multiple users**: This allows multiple people to connect to on-premises data sources. It opens a single gateway for this purpose and can support complex scenarios with multiple people accessing multiple data sources.

- **On-premises data gateway for a single user**: This is a personal mode that allows one user to connect to sources that cannot be shared with anyone else. The Power BI cloud service can only be used with this offering. If your company only has one person creating reports, this would be the gateway you'd use with your company's needs.

There are four main steps to installing the gateway:

1. Download and install the gateway on a local server.
2. Configure the gateway using firewall and other network requirements.
3. Add users as gateway admins to administer the gateway.
4. Troubleshoot any issues you may have when setting up the gateway.

Installing the gateway is fairly easy unless you run into issues. There is a troubleshooting page that can help you if you have problems getting this setup on your server: `https://docs.microsoft.com/en-us/data-integration/gateway/service-gateway-tshoot`.

The requirements for installation are as follows:

- **Minimum requirements**:

  .NET Framework 4.6 (Gateway release August 2019 and earlier)

  .NET Framework 4.7.2 (Gateway release September 2019 and later)

  A 64-bit version of Windows 8 or a 64-bit version of Windows Server 2012 R2

- **Recommended hardware**:

  An 8-core CPU server or workstation

  8 GB of memory minimum

  A 64-bit version of Windows Server 2012 R2 or later

  Solid-state drive storage for spooling

Next, we will look at the best practices for configuring an on-premises gateway.

On-premises gateway configuration best practices

When setting up any IT configurations, you always want to check the best practices for the system you are building. Please review the following best practices when using an on-premises gateway:

- Gateways, as you may have guessed, are not supported on Server Core installations.
- The user installing the gateway must be the admin of the gateway, so using a personal account may not be the best idea. You don't want to tie up the services with an account that could be disabled one day.
- As you know, we do not want to install anything on a domain controller that has connectivity to something outside the organization.
- Remember that if you are planning to use Windows authentication, you must install the gateway on a server that is connected to the domain.
- Do not install the gateway on a computer that may get turned off, such as a personal computer.
- You may want to shy away from installing other applications on this server as those services could stop the gateway or create a slow response.
- Installing one personal mode and one multi-user mode gateway is supported on the same server.

To install the gateway, download the installation files from Microsoft by going to `https://go.microsoft.com/fwlink/?LinkId=2116849&clcid=0x409`.

You can configure an on-premises gateway by following these steps:

1. Provide a location for the installation files and accept the terms of use:

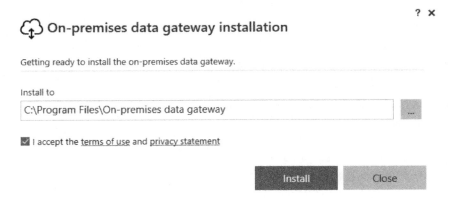

Figure 10.7 – Configuration screen

2. Once the installation is successful, enter an email address to use this gateway. The email address needs to a work or school account that's used to sign into Microsoft 365. This should be your organization's account.

3. You will now be fully signed into your gateway on this computer.

4. Now, you have the option to migrate or register the gateway. As part of the migration process, you can migrate the gateway for one of the following reasons:

   • Move to a new computer

   • Recover a damaged gateway

   • Take ownership of a gateway

5. Insert a name for the gateway and create a recovery key for it. Once completed, click **Configure**.

6. Now that the gateway has been created, click **Close** to exit the setup.

Once you have finished with the setup, you have the option to restart the gateway, give the gateway a service account, perform diagnostics and network setting configurations, and more. You can play around with these once you have this set up in your environment. At the moment, we can use the gateway to create connections to data in our on-premises environment.

Now, let's talk about the tools we will be using to connect to our data sources within the enterprise, starting with Power BI.

Power BI

Power BI is a cloud platform that gives everyday users a way to connect to and visualize many data sources in your enterprise. The interface will be familiar to those users who have worked with Excel and it has deep integration with other Microsoft products. This gives our users the ability to build robust reports using a self-service application that gives them the tools to analyze and aggregate data. The platform is easy to use and can help a company gain better knowledge of the data they are managing using this self-service tool.

Power BI can help a company make decisions based on data since the product allows you to connect to multiple data sources and aggregate data. So, depending on the data and reports generated, this can prevent the company from making bad decisions. With Power BI, you will see that the data is made available through charts, graphs, and other visual ways by modeling data how you want to see it. You can build KPIs and other advanced reports using this tool. The data can also be exported as other formats, such as PDF, Excel, and PowerPoint.

The advantages of Power BI are that you can connect to many data sources individually or multiple data sources to create more advanced reports. There are over 120+ free data connectors that support many other database platforms. With these connectors, you can take advantage of the big data investments your company has put a lot of time and money into to provide insights across your organization. By using Power BI, you can start working smarter. The tool allows you to analyze data and share it while maintaining the consistency and security of your data. Your data is protected even if you share information outside your organization.

Power BI was built to put the manipulation of data in the end users' hands. In the past, users had to rely on the IT department to build reports from the data that resided in database systems. As we have seen, in recent years, Microsoft has decided to put more functionality into the end user's hands so that they do not have to rely on a database programmer, or other development teams, to give them reports. This can be seen in several aspects of Microsoft's strategy, including self-service site creation.

SharePoint is one of the systems that leverages Power BI to accommodate data flowing from various sources. When you are implementing SharePoint within an organization, it is important that you understand not only your current challenges but also your future goals, as well as the vision and direction of the company when it comes to data management.

Next, we will briefly look at Power BI and the tools available for managing and manipulating data.

Power BI admin

This tool allows you to manage organization-wide tools that control how Power BI works. The portal provides settings that allow you to manage and monitor the usage as well as manage tenant settings. Users that have been assigned admin rights can configure, monitor, and provision organizational resources. Power BI admins should be familiar with other related tools and admin centers within Azure and Microsoft 365.

There are a few admin roles to consider when using Power BI. These roles are used to spread security roles across the admin center:

Type of administrator	Administrative scope	Power BI tasks
Global admin	Microsoft 365	Has unlimited access to all management features for the organization
		Assigns roles to other users
Billing admin	Microsoft 365	Manage subscriptions
		Purchase licenses
License admin	Microsoft 365	Assign or remove licenses for users
User admin	Microsoft 365	Create and manage users and groups
		Reset user passwords
Power BI admin	Power BI service	Full access to Power BI management tasks
		Enable and disable Power BI features
		Report on usage and performance
		Review and manage auditing
Power BI Premium Capacity admin	A single Premium capacity	Assign workspaces to the capacity
		Manage user permission to the capacity
		Manage workloads to configure memory usage
		Restart the capacity
Power BI Embedded Capacity admin	A single Embedded capacity	Assign workspaces to the capacity
		Manage user permission to the capacity
		Manage workloads to configure memory usage
		Restart the capacity

Figure 10.8 – Security roles in Microsoft 365

To get to the admin portal, you must have provisioned the Power BI service administrator role or a Global Admin role. These roles can be provided via the web interface or PowerShell. The limitations of this role are as follows:

- The ability to modify users and licenses within the Microsoft 365 Admin Center
- Access to all the audit logs

Using the Power BI Admin Role, you can only see a limited amount of information in the user audit logs. The log only keep activity data that has been collected over a 30-day window. Currently, there is no user interface for searching the activity log currently. Admins can download activity logs using the Power BI REST API and management cmdlets.

Power BI Desktop

There is also a free application called Power BI Desktop. This application runs on Windows 10 and on mobile. It is available for Windows, Android, and iOS devices. There is also a Power BI Report Server that can be used on-premises to support companies that want to maintain their data and reports. This version of the software is called Power BI Desktop for Power BI Report Server.

There are several components that help users get the most out of the platform:

- **Power Query**: A data mashup and transformation tool
- **Power Pivot**: A memory tabular data modeling tool
- **Power View**: A data visualization tool
- **Power Map**: A 3D geospatial data visualization tool
- **Power Q&A**: A natural language question and answering engine

As stated previously, there are over 120+ connectors available, which gives you the ability to connect to most types of databases and data sources. You can also connect to a SharePoint list, a SharePoint Excel file, and a SharePoint folder. From there, you can view the data contained within that list or folder.

To create a Power BI report, you must download the Power BI Desktop application. Once you open the application, you have the option to select **Get Data** and choose your resource. You then need to query the data to create reports based on the needs within the data provided.

Once you have created your report, you can share this report in a secured manner to users both internally and externally. Mobile and cloud users can also see the reports you've created, and the users can interact with the report using these platforms. Security can be set as well since you can give users the ability to read or edit reports based on groups or individual use.

There are three levels of usage that Power BI provides (note that these pricing tiers may change):

- **Power BI Desktop**: Free
- **Power BI Professional**: $9.99 a month
- **Power BI Premium**: Cost determined based on the size of the deployment and the amount of users

There is also a web part that is available within the SharePoint Online Microsoft 365 offering. Unfortunately, the dynamic Power BI web part is only available for SharePoint online and cannot be used with SharePoint 2019 On-Premises. With the Report Viewer web part, you can view paginated reports that are available on the Power BI report server directly in SharePoint.

Since this book is primarily about on-premises resources, I wanted to touch a little more on Power BI Desktop for Power BI Report Server.

Best practices for Power BI

When creating charts and reports using Power BI for your SharePoint sites, there are a few best practices that you must keep in mind. You must be aware of the number of charts and visuals that you embed into your SharePoint site as they can greatly impact performance if you have too many. This is especially important if you are pulling data from a large list in multiple locations or connecting to data sources that reside outside of SharePoint.

Visuals and graphics

Microsoft also recommends that interactions between visuals are limited. Visuals within Power BI can interact with one another by default, though it is best to limit this or eliminate this visual interaction altogether to optimize performance.

Within Power BI, you can create customized visuals, but it is a best practice to use the Microsoft app source certified custom visuals since they have passed rigorous testing and are less likely to negatively impact your SharePoint environment.

Access management

Remember that embedding a Power BI report into SharePoint does not automatically give the user access to your data. Power BI reports are still subject to the security trimming within SharePoint. So, if you are using this function to allow users to view data that is being pulled from a source, you must make sure that they have the access to do so. This access management consideration is important for all aspects of your migration, upgrade, or new solution configuration. However, this is something that the average user may not think about before a feature goes live. You must think about this.

Many companies nowadays are moving toward a centralized Access Management Control Model where access may be configured through the Identity Access Management team and provisioned through Active Directory groups. This may add more of a lead time requirement to your report rollout, so please plan for this ahead of time.

If you have not moved to the cloud yet, the first step you will take is to look at your Active Directory structure and the email you wish to migrate. Once that has been established, you can build from there. If you do have these resources in the cloud, you can still use Active Directory from the cloud to manage resources in your on-premises environment. SharePoint can use these security resources to secure content.

Performance impacts and testing

Calling and retrieving very large datasets can have a real performance impact on your SharePoint environment. Do not underestimate this impact. It may seem slight to you as you set up and configure these services in the environment, but a delay of a few seconds is extremely noticeable for users that are in and out of sites and report many times throughout their workday. Even small lags in performance can impact productivity over time. This impact is exacerbated when you are dealing with businesses that have very tight SLAs, such as banking.

Testing before rollout is the best way to mitigate this issue. In most instances, you will not have access to actual production data in your test environments. If you have the ability to use production data and this does not break any of the policies of the specific enterprise, then this would be the best option to test what effect the load reporting service configurations may have on your live production environment. If testing reports with actual data is not possible, try and replicate the capacity and utilization of the production environment as closely as possible.

Please engage your most intensive reporting users in your testing to gauge real-life scenarios based on how these users perform their day-to-day work. Also, if your enterprise has a Capacity Planning team and Quality Assurance team, it is recommended to involve them when planning and testing reporting solutions.

Performance Analyzer

The **Performance Analyzer** is a tool that can be used to examine report element performance within your environment. The analyzer records logs and measures different reports you have created, looking specifically at the report elements, and capture how they perform when users interact with the reports. The analyzer can also see what areas of the report resource are intensive. This will give you an insight into how these reports impact your environment.

The Performance Analyzer works similarly to the Load Testing product in Visual Studio. You can record your session so that you can interact with the report. When changing the way the report criteria interacts with data, you will see the analyzer recording those performance changes. The analyzer will then collect and display the results of your interactions when you run queries that pertain to the report.

As we've already mentioned in this book, performance is everything, especially when it comes to the support of your users. Always do testing and analyze things before they go into production. The better you can plan for these added reports, especially reports that deal with data, the better off you will be when these reports make it to production resources.

Power BI brings reporting to the forefront in the cloud. It really changes the game for on-premises environments. With the changes to server platforms and their removal, this brings hope for us to continue robustly reporting using cloud tools. There are other changes that have been made to the cloud platform that can help us start thinking about the cloud's direction. With SharePoint Designer 2010 going out of commission on the cloud, we must think about SharePoint Designer 2013, whose changes will be becoming more prominent soon. We will talk about replacements for these tools in the next section, which is all about Power Apps.

Power Apps

To provide rapid development for apps, Microsoft came up with a cloud application known as **Power Apps**. This application empowers users to create apps almost immediately. If you come from an InfoPath background, then this is your new buddy. Power Apps is not the same, nor does it have the same menu, so be prepared for a learning curve. Training is available to kick-start your knowledge at very low reasonable prices since COVID-19 and the push for virtual meetings.

Power Apps can be given to everyone or a subset of users in your company to help them develop applications that work for your organization. You can extend these apps with capabilities using Azure Functions and the use of custom connectors for on-premises systems. This gives the company a business transformation that enables it to see ROI quickly. It also improves employee productivity.

Again, Power Apps can be used with our on-premises environments through the On-Premises Gateway. This brings the power back to our server farms, which can be local to our server rooms or in the cloud. Remember that you must use modern sites and modern lists or libraries to use the tools within SharePoint 2019. We will talk about this in more detail in *Chapter 12, SharePoint Framework*.

When you log into Power Apps for the first time, you will see that there are a few ways to get started. You will have to choose an environment for the app to run in for security purposes. This could be internal for internal users or external if you plan to share information outside the organization. Choosing this option does not limit you because you can move apps between environments as well.

The options for creating new apps are as follows:

- Modern Apps
- Canvas Apps
- Portal Apps

Each option creates a different type of app. The most common is Modern Apps. You can also start from data, which gives you the option to select the data source first and then come back and create your app on top of the data source you've selected.

When you first open Power Apps, you will be prompted to create an app via Data Connection or via the Canvas, Model-driven, or Portal application models. The following screenshot shows these choices:

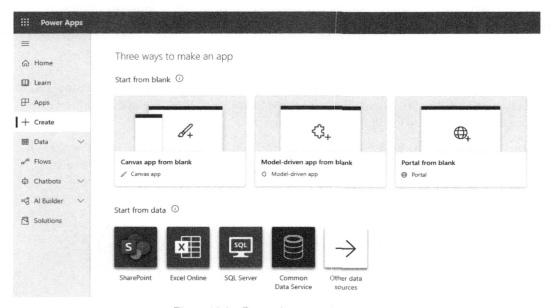

Figure 10.9 – Power Apps creation menu

Your data can come from the following connections:

- **SharePoint**
- **SQL Server**
- **Excel Online**
- **Common Data Service**
- **Other Data Sources** (this is where you will find the On-Premises Gateway)

When using an On-Premises Gateway, you must have set up the gateway first and have the necessary credentials to connect to the resources you plan to use to connect to the data you need. Once you have set up your On-Premises Gateway, you will be prompted to choose your SQL server, if that was the data source you were planning to use, by inputting its name, username, and password and then choosing the gateway you plan to use to connect to the data you are in need of:

SQL Server
Microsoft

Username *

Password *

Choose a gateway

If you don't see a gateway, or want a new one, you can install one now. To see recently installed gateways, refresh this list.

Install a gateway

Cancel   Create

Figure 10.10 – SQL Server connection form

As you can see, the availability of using SQL Server or any other data resources on-premises is easy to configure. Once the gateway is in place, there is no limit to what you can provide as far as reporting using data internally or in the cloud is concerned. Even mixing the data to create robust reports is available in some cases.

Now that we have talked about Power Apps, we will look at other tools that can help automate those apps and make the information that has been collected in those apps come to life. Power Automate provides the tools for creating Flows, which bring data to life.

Power Automate

Power Automate is used as a workflow automation tool and is very useful for creating workflow triggers in SharePoint 2019 and SharePoint Online. Power Automate was known as **Flow** previously, and although the name has changed, its awesome functionality persists. Due to the deprecation of previous workflow solutions, such as SharePoint Designer and InfoPath, users and developers have started to rely more heavily on the new workflow tools available to them.

Although there are a few third-party products that have gained popularity, such as Nintex, if you want to stay within the Microsoft Suite for your workflow solutions, Power Automate is a great option. Keep in mind that if you wish to utilize Power Automate's tools, you will need a subscription. This is not a solution that is deployed directly into your SharePoint Farm and is part of the Microsoft 365 suite of products, which means there are fees associated with this product.

The following are some things you need to know when using Power Automate:

- Use a trigger to start a flow and an action to change data.
- You cannot pause a Flow, but you can KILL a Flow.
- Flows run for 30 days until timeout.
- Use Service Accounts to run your Flows.
- Use Shared Mailboxes when necessary.
- Retry policies on Flows is 90 times.
- Set timeouts on loops.
- You cannot remove an owner of a Flow, but you can change it using PowerShell.
- History is only kept for 28 days.
- Concurrent loops – 50.
- 500 action limits.
- You can call Power Automate Flow from another Flow (determine your strategy).
- REST only returns 100 items – you can use the Get-Item action and return more items using paging.

With the recent announcement of SharePoint 2010 workflows not being able to be created after September 2020 and not able to run at all after October 31, 2020, companies have been scrambling to find solutions that can help recreate those workflows and even InfoPath forms as well. Since it was such a surprise, many companies are utilizing Power Automate to make sure their current workflows and business processes do not fail.

Since this announcement, you may be wondering when InfoPath and SharePoint 2013 are going to be permanently retired from Microsoft 365. I believe it's coming as soon as 2023. I would start preparing those business processes so that they can also be converted. The issues that come into play when you have so many workflows is overwhelming. This also creates a big issue for those who have not migrated yet and have SharePoint 2010 workflows in their on-premises environments.

This brings about one of the big issues I saw, which was training the developers who have been using SharePoint Designer and how they are going to transition to these new tools. They are not the same by any means and you cannot expect developers to jump into this from one day to the next, especially during a migration. It's best to plan this upfront so that users can start playing with the tools early in the planning phases of the implementation. Do not wait until the last minute and expect developers to run with these tools like they have used them before.

I was recently working with a company that was just planning to move SharePoint farm content from 2013 on-premises to Microsoft 365. In the on-premises farm, they had well over 500 workflows within the web application. They had six web applications with many developers. This creates a big stink when you want to migrate and must remember that 2010 workflows do not work almost as soon as you migrate them to Microsoft 365. Support for them is still available in SharePoint 2019, but if your goal is to migrate one day and SharePoint 2019 is your bridge to that goal, make sure to plan early and understand that none of those workflows will move and work in the cloud after the dates I noted previously.

So, to solve this problem, the only thing you can do is recreate your workflows. The Power Automate workflow tool can be utilized by SharePoint On-Premises and SharePoint Online using connectors. In this context, connectors is a prepacked API that is used to communicate with and perform actions in the destination location. The following are some simple step-by-step instructions that show you how to connect Power Automate to a SharePoint list online and on-premises using the On-Premises Gateway.

When you log into Power Automate, you will see the following screen, which gives you options to start creating flows right away. This page also gives you access to templates that were pre-created by Microsoft to help you get started as well:

Figure 10.11 – Power Automate creation screen

The power of Power Automate is its flexibility and how it gives you many options to use the platform to create workflows. I was amazed because it incorporated one of my PowerShell features where you "try-catch". If used correctly in PowerShell, you could end up with errorless scripts. In Power Automate, you can also use the Run After feature to set up relationships and run a sequence of rules between actions. So, if an action has been completed successfully, failed, skipped, or has even timed out, you can set triggers to determine how you handle those types of errors.

There are many ways you can start creating flows within your company. As shown in the preceding screenshot, you can create the following:

- **Automated flow**
- **Instant flow**
- **Scheduled flow**
- **UI flow**
- **Business Process flow**
- **Start from a template**

This should give you a basic overview of how to started with Power Automate. Depending on the solution you are trying to create, you could use any of these to start creating flows to automate business processes. The goal of this book is to let you know about SharePoint 2019 and how we can leverage the cloud so that we can use our on-premises resources with cloud applications. Due to this, I will not be going into these topics in more detail. However, we will learn how to connect Power Automate to our on-premises data sources and SharePoint resources. We will cover this in the next section.

Connecting Power Automate to SharePoint Online

To show you how easy it is to create a workflow using Power Automate, follow these simple steps to create a Power Automate flow that connects to a SharePoint Online site:

1. The **Power Automate** tool must be launched from the **Power Automate** website at `https://flow.microsoft.com/en-us/`. Log into the Power Automate website.

2. In the top-right corner of the **Power Automate** website, you will see a gear icon just like the one you are familiar with from SharePoint. Select it.

3. Once you've selected the gear icon, you will see a dropdown that provides a few options. Select the **Connections** option.

4. Select **Create connection**.

5. You will see a list of available connections. In this instance, we want to select SharePoint.

6. Select the **Create Connection** button. Then, click **Set up your connection to SharePoint**. Once you have selected a connection, choose a site within the SharePoint Online environment.

Connecting to a SharePoint On-Premises environment

To get you more familiar with how easy it is to connect to on-premises environments, follow these simple steps to create a Power Automate flow that connects to a SharePoint On-Premises site:

1. To connect to the SharePoint On-Premises environment, you need to log into the **Power Automate** website at `https://flow.microsoft.com/en-us/`.

2. Select the gear icon and select the **Connections** option.

3. Click **Create connection**.

4. Power Automate will now be connected to your on-premises environment through an on-premises data gateway. Power Automate supports SQL Server and SharePoint Server On-Premises data gateways.

5. From the available connections, list select **SQL** and select the option to connect through the on-premises data gateway or SharePoint On-Premises. This option will be featured as a checkbox.

6. You must provide your connection credentials and then choose the gateway that you want to connect to.

7. To check that the connection is successful, check **My connections**. You should see it listed.

Once connected, you will be able to utilize the tool by connecting to SharePoint On-Premises environments to create workflows that work specifically for your on-premises content. This gives you the opportunity to update those old workflows and build out with the newest tools from Microsoft.

Power Automate Desktop

There is also a new Power Automate Desktop application where Robotics Process Automation is at your fingertips. This new desktop tool was announced in preview September 22, 2020 and is exciting news. The possibilities are endless with this tool in hand, especially for those who aspire to learn about robotics. This platform supports coders and non-coders. To learn more, go to `https://docs.microsoft.com/en-us/power-automate/ui-flows/desktop/introduction`.

Office Online Server

Office Online Server is the next version of Office Web Apps. Office Web Apps was used in older versions of SharePoint so that users could view Microsoft Office application content, including Word documents, PowerPoint presentations, and Excel documents within their browser. Office Online Server is an on-premises product and is compatible with SharePoint 2019.

There have been some updates to the product and one important one to me is the ability to protect the installation of Office Online Server. There is a feature where you can restrict which servers can join the Office Online Server farm, such as SharePoint and other Microsoft products. You can base this on OU membership and prevent unauthorized servers from joining.

There have been some updates to how Office components work as well, and these are distributed across the enterprise. This product allows Exchange Server and Outlook Web App to preview Office file attachments. Excel Online is the replacement tool for Excel Services in SharePoint and has now been moved to Office Online Server as of SharePoint 2016.

The product still allows external data connectivity and data refresh features, as provided in the past versions of SharePoint for services such as Excel Online. Office Online Server only works with SharePoint web applications that use claims authentication. All other authentication methods are not supported.

Office Online Server not only allows you to view content – it also allows you to edit content. It provides support for PCs, tablets, smart phones, and many different mobile device platforms. There may be differences due to the browsers supported by those device platforms, and testing would need to be done to figure out what is supported by Microsoft. Language packs are used to enable users to view files in multiple languages.

Office Online Server has a small footprint on a server and should be set up on its own resource. I do not advise trying to add this component to a SharePoint server or install any other applications with this application when running it on its own server. All integrated products, including Workflow Manager, should all be separated onto their own server resources.

You can install the services on multiple instances of this server to support redundancy. Providing that type of support for the product would depend on how big your organization is. If you need to grow this server platform out, you have the options to do so later as our organization grows as well.

If you are planning to provide redundancy, you will probably want to add a load balancer. **Windows Server (IIS)** solution using Application Request Routing are supported for this. You can run this IIS role on one of the servers Office Online Server is running. DNS will come into play, as well as certificates, to help resolve to the IP address of the load balancer.

As part of the planning process for this product, you should use the same minimum requirements for a server as you would for SharePoint Server 2019. The product is only supported on Windows Server 2016 and Windows Server 2012 R2. So, when installing this server, you cannot use Windows Server 2019 OS to do so. To support the server correctly, you need to install the server OS as Server with Desktop Experience, which is an option for Windows Server 2016 if you're using that OS.

As with any application server, there is maintenance that comes into play when you're supporting this server installation.

> **Note**
> The following is a link to the Office Online Server release schedule: `https://docs.microsoft.com/en-us/officeonlineserver/office-online-server-release-schedule`.

Some of the best practices to follow when running this server are as follows:

- Do not install any applications that need support for ports 80, 443, or 809 on these servers.

- Do not install any versions of Office products on this server. If installed, uninstall Office before you install Office Online Server.

- Do not install Office Online Server on a domain controller as the product will not run on a server hosting Active Directory Services.

- Configure the product for HTTP or HTTPS requests.

To install the application, Office Online Server must be deployed on your network. Then, you can configure the server so that it works with SharePoint 2019. If you are planning to deploy Office Online Server, make sure that you have enough memory on the servers you are deploying.

If you do not have enough memory on your farm's server resources, certain functions, such as previewing documents, will fail to work. I had a failure when deploying a Skype test server and I recommended minimum memory requirements and was given 4 GB of RAM. When I tested Skype, I had issues with the scheduling process within Outlook and kept seeing the presence of users online. After a long 4-week process with Microsoft, it was found that due to not using the minimum amount of memory required as a best practice, these processes were failing.

This all goes back to the earlier warnings and advice that you received in this book – you must make sure you are aware of the best practices and what you are actually building as it could impact the amount of server resources needed; that is, your CPU, RAM, and storage. Make sure to play close attention to these details and test all areas before launching.

Also, it is highly advisable that your farm is configured over a secure port using HTTPS and the latest TLS configuration, This is because Office Online Server uses OAuth tokens to communicate with the SharePoint 2019 server. This can cause an entry point of attack into your environment if your environment is not configured on a secured port. To configure Office Online Server, follow these instructions:

Prerequisites:

- Windows Server 2012 R2 or Windows Server 2016

- 16 GB of RAM, 4 CPUs, and 100 GB or more hard drive space

- Use your SharePoint Admin account to perform the installation (you must have admin rights on the server)

Install:

1. To install **Office Online Server**, you need to get the required license and download it from your **Volume Licensing Service Center**. **Office Online Server** is a component of Office, so it will be included under **Product pages** for Office in your Service Center.

2. Once you have downloaded the product, run the `Setup.exe` file.

3. Accept the terms and licensing terms and click **Continue**.

4. Choose a file location for the installation (it is recommended that you install it on your system drive).

5. Click **Close** to complete the installation.

6. Using Kerberos Constrained Delegation with Excel Online, you must set the Windows Service (Claims to Windows Token Service) so that it starts automatically.

If you are not familiar with Office Online Server and it is not available from your company download location at Microsoft, please remember to get specifics on how to access the download so that you can install and deploy the application.

Deploying Office Online Server:

Before you can use PowerShell to manipulate Office Online Server, you must import the `OfficeWebApps` module into your server using the following command:

```
Import-Module -Name OfficeWebApps
```

Creating the Office Online Server farm:

To create a single farm with a single server, use the following command:

```
HTTP: New-OfficeWebAppsFarm -InternalURL "http://servername"
-AllowHttp -EditingEnabled
```

```
HTTPS: New-OfficeWebAppsFarm -InternalUrl "https://server.
contoso.com" -ExternalUrl "https://wacweb01.contoso.com"
-CertificateName "OfficeWebApps Certificate" -EditingEnabled
```

Verify that the Office Online Server farm was successfully created:

Go to the following URL from a browser on your server: `http://servername/hosting/discovery`.

You should see the following page in your browser:

```xml
<?xml version="1.0" encoding="utf-8" ?>
- <wopi-discovery>
- <net-zone name="internal-http">
- <app name="Excel" favIconUrl="http://servername/x/_layouts/
images/FavIcon_Excel.ico" checkLicense="true">
<action name="view" ext="ods" default="true" urlsrc="http://
servername/x/_layouts/xlviewerinternal.aspx?<ui=UI_
LLCC&amp;><rs=DC_LLCC&amp;>" />
<action name="view" ext="xls" default="true" urlsrc="http://
servername/x/_layouts/xlviewerinternal.aspx?<ui=UI_
LLCC&amp;><rs=DC_LLCC&amp;>" />
<action name="view" ext="xlsb" default="true" urlsrc="http://
servername/x/_layouts/xlviewerinternal.aspx?<ui=UI_
LLCC&amp;><rs=DC_LLCC&amp;>" />
<action name="view" ext="xlsm" default="true" urlsrc="http://
servername/x/_layouts/xlviewerinternal.aspx?<ui=UI_
LLCC&amp;><rs=DC_LLCC&amp;>" />
```

Secure Store Integration (Optional):

If you need to configure Secure Store access for Excel Online, then you need to run the following command for all connections to the Secure Store Service:

```
Set-OfficeWebAppsFarm -AllowHttpSecureStoreConnections:$true
```

Adding servers to the Office Online Server farm:

To add servers to the farm, you can follow the same steps for installing and then use the HTTP or HTTPS method of creating the Office Online Server farm on the new server:

```
HTTP: New-OfficeWebAppsFarm -InternalURL "http://servername"
-AllowHttp -EditingEnabled
HTTPS: New-OfficeWebAppsFarm -InternalUrl "https://server.
contoso.com" -ExternalUrl "https://wacweb01.contoso.com"
-CertificateName "OfficeWebApps Certificate" -EditingEnabled
```

Adding a server to the farm:

Use the following command to add a server to the farm:

```
New-OfficeWebAppsMachine -MachineToJoin "server1.contoso.com"
```

To verify that the server is running, follow the same steps we followed for the first server we created.

Configuring Office Online Server in SharePoint 2019

First, you will need to create a binding between your installation of Office Online Server and SharePoint Server 2019. To do this, follow these steps:

1. Open SharePoint Management Shell and choose **Run as Administrator**:

   ```
   New-SPWOPIBinding -ServerName <WacServerName> -AllowHTTP
   ```

   This command will allow SharePoint Server 2019 to receive information from Office Online Server.

2. Check if WOPI is using the default internal HTTPS zone:

   ```
   Get-SPWOPIZone
   ```

   The result that we are looking for here is internal-http. If the shell results show internal-https and not internal-http, then we must perform an additional step. If your results are showing internal-http, you can skip the next step.

3. Switch WOPI to internal-http:

   ```
   Set-SPWOPIZone -zone "internal-http"
   (Get-SPSecurityTokenServiceConfig).AllowOAuthOverHttp
   ```

Once your deployment is completed, make sure that you have tested Office Online Server in your SharePoint environment. Test the URL for Office Online Server to make sure you can get to the URL successfully. Also, ensure you can connect to this URL from your SharePoint servers: http://servername/hosting/discovery.

Make sure that your users are testing this thoroughly. You should set up your test scripts and make sure that all the functionality of Office Online Server is working properly before it is fully released to the user community.

One you have installed Office Online Server, you can configure the different components within the server. In the next section, we will cover Excel Online to give you a short overview of what this server can provide.

Excel Online

Excel Services has changed immensely and if you offer these services as part of your SharePoint 2019 deployments, there are many changes you need to know about and understand. It was moved outside of SharePoint in the SharePoint 2016 version of the product. Excel Online includes many of the same features Excel Services included in SharePoint Server 2013, such as external data connectivity and data refresh features.

Data refresh in Excel Online is supported only on SQL Server and SQL Analysis Server. There are steps you can follow to setup data refresh, from creating a workbook to setting the workbook's refresh based on the data source. Refreshes can only be triggered in one of two ways:

- The end user opens the workbook
- The end user clicks on the refresh button on an open workbook

Office Online Server can communicate with SharePoint servers, Exchange servers, and Skype for Business servers by using HTTPS protocol. This should be the way environments are set up in a production environment as it helps secure communication between the servers. Certificates will need to be installed either on the server (IIS) or on a load balancer if you're using multiple servers.

With this new version of Excel Online, you can adjust the resource usage of your Office Online Server farm. These PowerShell commands give you the opportunity to enforce governance over the services provided by this server or server farm. This really helps make this farm better suited to support your users and the performance and stability of the services provided.

Excel Online supports the following connections when it comes to connecting to data sources:

- SQL Server Analysis Services
- SQL Server Databases
- OLE DB data sources
- ODBC data sources

Windows authentication and SQL authentication can be used to connect to external data sources through Excel Online. Kerberos delegation can be used as well as but requires that the **Claims to Windows Token Service** is running. Office Online Servers must be allowed to delegate to each backend data source, and the `c2wtshost.exe.config` file must be updated.

When using Excel Online workbooks, you can use two types of connections:

- **Embedded Connections**: Stored as part of the workbook

- **Linked Connections**: Uses an ODC file for enterprise-scale data sources

> **Note**
>
> Link to Plan installation: `https://docs.microsoft.com/en-us/officeonlineserver/plan-office-online-server`.

Applying updates to Office Online Server requires a maintenance window that should be in sync with your SharePoint maintenance. Automatic updates cannot be used for this product because the updates must be applied manually. If the updates are applied automatically, this could result in you having to rebuild your Office Online Server farm. Users may not be able to see documents at this point either. So, you want to make sure you are updating appropriately because in some instances, such as other servers, these servers require a certain process to be followed. PowerShell is used to apply updates to this server. Anything could come into play here, so research and be careful.

Azure reporting capabilities

Another powerful offering in the Microsoft cloud ecosystem is Azure. Azure was designed to help companies build and manage applications. It gives you a choice of tools to use, as well as frameworks. You also have the option to build applications that run across multiple clouds and on-premises enterprise systems while taking full advantage of Microsoft 365.

This platform just brings a solid anchor to the Microsoft cloud offering and allows so much creativity and many forward-thinking solutions to be brought to the table. Using these applications within Azure may rearchitect how you have your current enterprise configured.

With these offerings, we also have the option to report using services such as Analysis Service and Logic App Service. These services allow you to analyze data and build apps across platforms and clouds while you're integrating with your on-premises environment. There are other services that cross the bounds of cloud and on-premises as well, such as Azure Information Protection, which is an RMS. This is another service that's available for security and data compliance. We will keep our focus on reporting in this section.

Azure Analysis Services

The On-Premises Gateway also provides you with access to data so that you can use it with Azure Analysis Services. You can transform complex data by combining data from a singular or even multiple sources into a trusted and secure BI model. Microsoft invested around 1 billion dollars a year into cyber security and has over 3,500 security experts working on this version of Azure alone, all to keep data secure and ease the minds of the users managing their private and sensitive data in this service model. Azure, as a platform, has many compliance certifications that help provide support for companies who require these certifications.

Microsoft guarantees speed and performance with this platform and is promising the fastest responses from the data you have combined to create complex datasets. You can get up and running quickly as you can create a server within minutes using Azure Resource Manager or PowerShell. You have full control of this service and you can scale up or down, pause, and resume the service whenever you need to. You only pay for what you use in cycles.

Azure Analysis Services also integrates with other services, which helps you be creative when planning analytics solutions for your company. There are also integrations with Azure Data Factory. This service is used to orchestrate and operationalize processes to refine enormous stores of raw data. Azure Automation and Azure Functions can be used with custom code for lightweight orchestration models.

Security for authorized users is managed within the Azure service and is role-based for separation of duties. Azure Active Directory is used to support role-based security, which helps keep user management an easy task. Using the cloud as an administrator should help you understand how to use Azure Active Directory and plan security accordingly.

There are three tiers available for use:

- **Developer**: Evaluation, development, and test scenarios.
- **Basic**: Used for production solutions on smaller tabular models and limited user concurrency.
- **Standard**: Mission-critical production applications with growing data models.

The product is supported in regions and there are plans that support query replicas, depending on the region you choose.

> **Tip**
>
> Please check the regions for availability at `https://docs.microsoft.com/en-us/azure/analysis-services/analysis-services-overview`.

Microsoft guarantees 99.9% availability and users can access this data from anywhere in the world. This self-service platform for data discovery can help you define the data in your company and find those areas where data still may need some cleanup. When I say easy to use, I am talking about the interface of Microsoft Visual Studio, which is the interface that's used to work with this product. This way, your developers do not have to learn about any new interfaces in order to work with the data within your environment; they should be familiar with this interface already.

The application is robust and can be scaled to match your business needs. It also provides life cycle management capabilities for the following areas:

- Governance
- Deployment
- Testing
- Delivery

The easy-to-use platform is for those who have used Visual Studio in the past. The application service is free with no obligations but once you start to use it, you will be charged for what you use. You will have to use SQL Server 2016 Enterprise Server to use the product as this is the version of SQL that's supported. If your SQL Server is on your on-premises network, this is when the On-Premises Gateway helps you connect to those databases that hold data, so you may want to fully expose it in the cloud. SQL Analysis Server supports tabular models at the 1,200 and higher levels. Both direct query and in-memory are supported.

Azure is not well-known by some customers because they never planned to use its services. The problem with being closed-minded and only looking at Microsoft 365 as a target solution is that you miss out on some of the benefits Azure provides natively to the cloud platform. It really can open a new world of supported applications and security to your company that you may never actually investigate. Let's look at another option that works with the On-Premises Gateway.

Azure Logic Apps

If you want to use scheduling, automate tasks, and easily create business processes and workflows, get acquainted with using Azure Logic Apps. You can integrate other apps, data, systems, and services across your enterprise or organizations, including on-premises enterprises. This is where the On-Premises Gateway becomes effective.

I really believe that business automation tools are very helpful and can help you build business processes that support your workforce and customers. You can use the tools provided by Azure Logic Apps to do the following in your business:

- Process and route orders
- Send email notifications
- Integrate with Microsoft 365 services and data
- Manage files
- Provide secure access
- Process data
- Monitor other applications
- Use the many connectors to connect to other services, apps, and data

Some of the many connectors available are as follows:

- Azure Service Bus
- Azure Functions
- Azure Storage
- SQL Server
- Microsoft 365
- Dynamics
- Salesforce
- BizTalk
- SAP
- Oracle DB
- File shares and more!

The interface for Azure Logic Apps reminds me of Power Automate. It has a similar interface with deeper functionality than Power Automate, which helps you create robust customized solutions. The process uses triggers that respond to events that happen in the created business process, which could be a choice in the logic of the app by the user. By using the templates and recurrence triggers for more advanced scheduling, no code needed in most instances.

There are a few ways to interface with this product to create automation:

- Logic Apps Portal (Logic Apps Designer)
- Visual Studio
- Visual Studio Code
- ARM Template
- Azure CLI

You will have to create a Logic Apps Custom Connector to use Logic Apps over an On-Premises Gateway. Once the On-Premises Gateway has been created, it will be available in Azure apps and Microsoft 365 apps such as Power Apps, Power Automate, and Power BI. Once you have that resource available, just select it from the menu as your resource group:

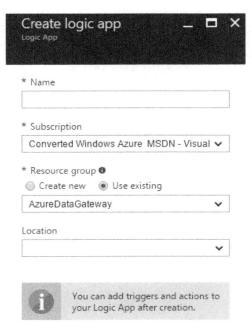

Figure 10.12 – Creation page for Logic Apps

Once you have selected the resources group, create your connection to the SQL server hosting your data or whatever connection your area is looking for within your on-premises environment:

Figure 10.13 – Connection information form

You can then connect to the following supported systems using the On-Premises Gateway:

- BizTalk Server 2016
- File System
- IBM DB2
- IBM Informix
- IBM MQ
- MySQL
- Oracle Database
- PostgreSQL

- SAP Application Server
- SAP Message Server
- SharePoint Server
- SQL Server
- Teradata

This sums up the available options for creating reports and connecting to data from on-premises resources. Again, you can do this using your companies' location, where you have a data center, or through Azure, AWS, or another cloud service provider. There is no end to the possibilities. It is all about what you want as an architecture to support your users and the company's assets.

Summary

In this chapter, we have looked at the many changes that have been made to the BI and application reporting structures in SharePoint 2019. Microsoft has moved in a new direction and removed much of the BI functionality from its former integration into SharePoint. Now, the services must be connected to from the cloud or even separate servers to our SharePoint 2019 farm. This change also complicates your overall migration strategy as these changes must be planned for. This adds a measure of complexity to your migration.

For instance, if you want to migrate SSR reports from previous versions of SharePoint, you would need to do this by utilizing the migration script referenced in this book. This script is provided by Microsoft and is also linked and available on the Microsoft website. It is best to inform your user community of the BI reporting changes that Microsoft has made before migration, and then get your user community accustomed to the deprecated and removed features and the changed functionality of some of the BI processes that they have gotten used to. I am a firm believer that if this is planned for and laid out in the beginning and surprises are minimized, you will greatly increase the satisfaction of your user group.

Microsoft's overall strategy of removing a lot of the BI integration from within SharePoint is a good one from an enterprise standpoint. This perspective can be used as a great selling point when dealing with prospective clients. Most enterprises utilize various applications and if they are explained and demonstrated properly, the enterprise will welcome the opportunity to have these various systems connected to a centralized business intelligence reporting source. Highlight the positive aspect that these centralized business intelligence data and reporting services will help consolidate data reporting within their organization and could also help minimize the redundancy of these types of tools going forward.

In the next chapter, we will talk about the User Interface and Developer frameworks that can be used within SharePoint 2019. Things have changed drastically, and we need to make sure we explain how the modern and classic sites work, as well as how developers can make changes to the sites. This is an important chapter since admins and users need to understand the possibilities this brings to farms and where their skill sets must be updated to support the new platform. The tools listed in the next chapter bring on a whole new level of training and understanding as they are different from the legacy tools that supported SharePoint in the past.

Questions

You can find the answers on GitHub under Assessments at `https://github.com/PacktPublishing/Implementing-Microsoft-SharePoint-2019/blob/master/Assessments.docx`

1. In SharePoint 2019, SSRS can be installed in Integrated Mode on a SharePoint server.

    a) True

    b) False

2. Office Online Server is the new version of which Microsoft product/component? Choose the best answer.

    a) Excel Services

    b) Office Web App

    c) Power Pivot

3. What are "connectors" in the context of Microsoft's Power Automate interaction with SharePoint?

    a) Connectors are the method that SharePoint uses to integrate with Power Automate.

    b) Connectors are prepacked APIs that Power Automate uses to communicate and update SharePoint.

    c) Connectors are used to update Power Automate to the latest version.

4. Using as many graphics/visuals in your Business Intelligence solution will have zero impact on performance.

    a) True

    b) False

5. Report Builder remains integrated with the latest version of SharePoint 2019 On-Premises SharePoint 2019.

    a) True

    b) False

Further reading

Please visit the following links to learn more about Azure AD.

Hybrid identities and authentication:

- `https://docs.microsoft.com/en-us/azure/active-directory/hybrid/whatis-hybrid-identity`
- `https://docs.microsoft.com/en-us/azure/active-directory-domain-services/tutorial-create-forest-trust`
- `https://docs.microsoft.com/en-us/azure/active-directory/fundamentals/active-directory-access-create-new-tenant`

More information about how to install the Hybrid Picker can be found at `https://docs.microsoft.com/en-us/sharepoint/hybrid/configure-inbound-connectivity`.

You can learn more about the Power Automate desktop offering here: `https://flow.microsoft.com/en-us/blog/jumpstart-your-business-with-power-automates-new-desktop-rpa-solution/`.

To create your first Azure Logic App, check out these links:

- **Using the Portal**: `https://docs.microsoft.com/en-us/azure/logic-apps/quickstart-create-first-logic-app-workflow`
- **Visual Studio**: `https://docs.microsoft.com/en-us/azure/logic-apps/quickstart-create-logic-apps-with-visual-studio`
- **Visual Studio Code**: `https://docs.microsoft.com/en-us/azure/logic-apps/quickstart-create-logic-apps-visual-studio-code`
- **ARM Template**: `https://docs.microsoft.com/en-us/azure/logic-apps/quickstart-create-deploy-azure-resource-manager-template?tabs=azure-portal`
- **Azure CLI**: `https://docs.microsoft.com/en-us/azure/logic-apps/quickstart-logic-apps-azure-cli`

11
Enterprise Social Networking and Collaboration

Microsoft Teams has become an instant hit for social collaboration, using SharePoint Online as the backend for the application. The replacement for Skype has brought on new features that make collaborating in the cloud even more collaborative. Microsoft Teams has really taken over the social collaboration space and has overtaken the top sellers in this market, including Slack.

The reason for its success is its features and ease of use. There are so many great things to talk about with this product and we plan to do a thorough job of running through its features. From instant messaging and telephony to integrated apps, the product has really included a list of great features. We will also talk about the downfalls as well where the product could be improved and support an even more collaborative vision.

We will also look at how the product can be used to facilitate meetings and even large live events. The product gives a deeper functionality for providing support for businesses that need to manage events. There is a lot to get into but I will run through the setup of Microsoft Teams, including creating a visual and audio configuration, so that you can see the possibilities and the direction it can take you in supporting those services.

There are some features included that SharePoint offers natively that we will also talk about as some of these features have been deprecated. Yammer has some integrations as well with SharePoint 2019 and there are also Microsoft mobile capabilities that we can walk through that are native to SharePoint on-premises and social collaboration.

In this chapter, we will also look at the features of SharePoint 2019 and show how these products can be bridged together. Although Teams is a key component in the cloud, there are other features available that we can take advantage of to push the platform.

The following topics will be covered in this chapter:

- Social features in SharePoint 2019
- Microsoft Teams

Technical requirements

For you to understand this chapter and the knowledge shared, the following requirements must be met:

- 3–5 years of SharePoint experience
- 1–2 years of Microsoft Teams experience

You can find the code files present in this chapter on GitHub at `https://github.com/PacktPublishing/Implementing-Microsoft-SharePoint-2019`.

Social features in SharePoint 2019

SharePoint 2019 was built to bring a bigger experience to the platform by integrating features that would expand on the collaboration features of the past. SharePoint is configured differently now than it used to be. Earlier, there were restrictions or, technically put, limitations on how you could integrate products and features.

As we look at where SharePoint was and where it is now, we can notice that all integrations are outside of the product and not included in the product's installation, or can't even be installed on the same server. Again, this helps with performance and keeps applications separated that could get messy when troubleshooting if installed together on servers. The cloud now provides some integrations, as seen in *Chapter 10, SharePoint Advanced Reporting and Features*, where we can use applications from the outside to manipulate data in our on-premises environment.

All the social features you have seen in other versions of SharePoint, such as 2016 and SharePoint Online, are available in SharePoint 2019. As we mentioned, where SharePoint 2019 enhances these features is with integration with other applications such as Yammer that push content to SharePoint through web parts and other integrations. We will talk more about this in this chapter but here is a short list of social features that are available in SharePoint 2019:

- Community features
- Company feed
- Follow features
- Microblogging
- One-click sharing
- Personal sites

Developers can extend these features by developing enhancements to make these features do more to support their users. With the use of APIs, the developer can start developing these enhancements. Using Visual Studio 2012 or newer, the platform is available for these enhancements; we will talk more about this in *Chapter 12, SharePoint Framework*. They can also use Power Apps, Power Automate, and other tools within Microsoft 365 to enhance the functionality of social features within SharePoint 2019 using hybrid connectivity.

Microsoft's direction in enterprise social networking

Microsoft's direction in enterprise social networking has become very clear over the last few years. Microsoft has taken a strong move away from collaboration silos. The traditional collaboration methods offered by Microsoft and utilized within many organizations required several different applications to cover the communication and collaboration needs of a company.

Most companies would have their Outlook application, Lync/Skype client, Yammer, and browser Office clients, which of course included SharePoint, primarily for document collaboration. Although there have always been plugin methods to integrate SharePoint and Outlook, most enterprise users have been forced to hop around to different locations to fulfill all their social networking and collaboration needs.

Now we see how, with new social applications, users can stay in one application such as Microsoft Teams and do not have to hop around to find information. A bridge has been created where we can pull in information from other apps and bring them into Microsoft Teams, including SharePoint, which makes the user experience so much easier and saves time when users are looking for information.

The user experience is enhanced by Microsoft offering mobile apps for SharePoint and Microsoft Teams. This gives users access to these applications from their mobile devices and they are able to access meetings and information from anywhere. Yammer also has a mobile app and you could create your own app using Power Apps or, using other development languages, you can create single sign-on access to protect access from the internet into the company tenant, using Intune and Azure to host the mobile connectivity.

We believe we will see more of this as some of the social networking tools get more enhanced and bring more collaborative functionality to the table. It seems the goal of all this is to be able to share anything with people internally or externally securely, which is a great step in the right direction. Everyone seems to love these new features and cannot wait to see what is yet to come.

Microsoft Teams overview

Lync and Skype have been long regarded as the kings of instant messaging and meeting feature applications for Microsoft, until now. Microsoft Teams has come on the scene strong and is bringing a bigger experience and giving tighter integration with SharePoint. When mentioning those applications, we must also mention Yammer. This social app has also been used for social interactions but in a different way. We see the need to explain how Yammer works so that you can see the differences and why they are both used together.

Yammer is used primarily for organizational communication and engagement. You would find Yammer content open to everyone in your organization. As stated, when you work with larger groups of people and content is everywhere, you may see a posting of Yammer content as you surf your SharePoint site. These posts would contain organization-wide information, which can include conversational or professional information and is not suitable for confidential content.

This comes into play where maybe you have IT teams that are separated across the company. In that scenario, you may have SharePoint admins in different departments that run their own farms. Using Yammer, you can create an organizational space where they can share ideas and information through the social networking tool.

We apologize but we do not have enough page space in this book to dig deeper into this to show more ways of how Yammer can be useful in on-premises environments and how it can be easily integrated with SharePoint 2019. Research to find out how Yammer can help your organization along with Microsoft Teams.

There is also another social tool that needs to be mentioned, and that is a mobile app built and supported by Microsoft named Kaizala. Kaizala is a group communication and work management tool used for secure mobile messaging. It provides a chat interface to securely connect to colleagues, vendors, distributors, and other resources a person may need in and out of your enterprise.

Kaizala gives you options to send invoices, and other Kaizala actions can be used within the app. You can schedule work, provide training materials, or even send attachments for review by other colleagues. Polls and surveys are also available and these types of communications can be sent to thousands of people. This app is an alternative to other social media-type applications we can use within the Microsoft 365 cloud. In the case of SharePoint 2019, you must be on a hybrid configuration to take advantage of Yammer, Kaizala, and other apps like SharePoint as well. These all are supported through hybrid connectivity.

If you look at the other tools, Yammer and Kaizala, you will see that they both work for large-scale communication, more like enterprise communication tools. Microsoft Teams works better for projects and smaller teams of people within your organization, as you will see in this section. Those teams that are created are used mostly to support projects or departments within the organization. This is a smaller group of people, so responses would be quick, and you will only find yourself using Teams when you are working on projects or working with these small groups of people.

When Microsoft Teams is rolled out in an organization, so is SharePoint Online, technically, because behind every Microsoft Teams workspace is what we traditionally know as a SharePoint team site. This is important to remember and drive home with your users and management teams as they need to understand that with each team comes a SharePoint site. You could end up with many sites that you know nothing about as an administrator.

The other thing that admins need to be aware of is that Microsoft Teams only authenticates using Microsoft Azure **Active Directory** (**AD**) authentication. So, when using the product for an on-premises SharePoint farm, that farm also needs to use AD in the cloud. So, the dependency on using Teams within your on-premises environment is using Azure AD.

The reason why you want this integration is to get the presence feature working in your on-premises environment seamlessly. This would require user profiles to import users from AD in the cloud, and if you want to make an even tighter integration, use the hybrid features within SharePoint 2019 to bring it all together, integrating OneDrive and other great features.

While Microsoft Teams is an amazing interface that offers a lot of different collaboration tools under a single moniker, it is not a replacement for SharePoint. I have seen some confusion around this as management in certain organizations are solely focused on reducing redundant applications and some may wrongly believe that if Microsoft Teams is adopted, then Microsoft SharePoint disappears, yet that is simply not the case.

Use both collaboration tools for different types of collaborative options. SharePoint is used for a more advanced set of features, such as document sharing, departmental sites, libraries and lists, and automated business processes on a large scale that work to create collaborative interactions with departmental technology.

Use Microsoft Teams for meetings, project calendars, messaging, and keeping related files associated with the project or team in the SharePoint site associated with the team. With this use of collaboration tools, it seems to me to be more project focused but has some organizational areas it supports, such as meeting technology.

Bridging these two applications together creates a full, powerful collaborative experience. This is why you see more and more people flocking to the Microsoft cloud because the tools are powerful and can create a sense of your company being large but you are actually small due to the technology behind your company.

Microsoft Teams in the age of the pandemic

As everyone is aware, we were all recently blindsided by the COVID-19 pandemic. This pandemic illustrated the uncertainty not only in our personal lives but in our working lives as well. Many people were impacted by the onset of COVID-19 and there was a great loss of jobs in many areas. However, this impact was lessened a bit by using virtual technologies and social networking capabilities to keep businesses functioning and to keep people at work and school safe by social distancing using working from home. Microsoft Teams was the shining star in the midst of this need for rapid adaptation. Companies, schools, and government agencies alike leveraged the power of Microsoft Teams to keep functioning.

Users can communicate through Microsoft Teams using the chat functions that Lync and Skype historically provided. Businesses can also host meetings, both video calls and audio, through the Microsoft Teams platform. This function was typically handled by Cisco Webex functionality, GoToMeeting, and other virtual meeting platforms. Microsoft Teams also allows users and groups of users to access, view, and edit SharePoint documents right from the Teams interface. The Microsoft Teams platform can also be integrated with Outlook so that your email messages can be viewed from this single interface. Many other apps can be integrated as well, such as Salesforce, Power Apps, and so much more, which brings a new meaning to collaboration.

SharePoint and Microsoft Teams

With the introduction of Microsoft Teams, organizations are now able to meet all their social networking communication and collaboration needs in one place. This will allow users to focus on the tasks at hand with all the information organized within a single location where all the messages, documents, notes, and chat conversations are accessible in real time to members of the team. For SharePoint, this means that each created team is associated with a SharePoint Online team site and each channel within that team is associated with the SharePoint site's document library. We will explore the concept of a "team" and a "channel" later in this chapter. For now, review the following chart to see a representation of the architecture of teams and channels in relation to SharePoint Online:

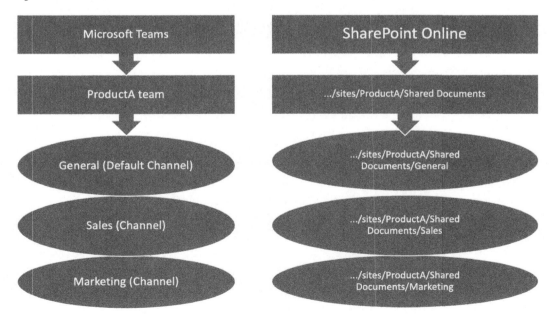

Figure 11.1 – Microsoft Teams versus SharePoint Online

As you can see, Microsoft Teams has very tight integration with SharePoint Online. When dealing with files in Microsoft Teams, any changes made to that file are made directly within SharePoint within the document library. This is not in sync with SharePoint as it is just that the file actually exists in SharePoint. The user also has the option to open the document in SharePoint and using this option will take them directly to their SharePoint Online team site, which corresponds with the team that was created in Microsoft Teams. There is also the option to add a SharePoint page tab in your Teams channel. If a page already exists within the SharePoint site, you can plug it in by adding it as a tab and view the information without having to visit the SharePoint site.

We are all familiar with the SharePoint failed newsfeed in conversations launched in SharePoint 2013. It failed when it was first launched due to the novelty of users playing around with the feature and those of us who presented the features of SharePoint highlighted this innovative feature to our customers. However, there was very low adoption in our opinion, and apparently in Microsoft's opinion as well, and this was due to the placement of the conversation and newsfeed option. It was placed outside of the actual working content and you could see the conversations on a site; however, this placement made the conversations within the newsfeed very general. Now, conversations can be placed alongside a specific document. I think that this is an amazing feature because it allows collaborators on a document to have real-time conversations about that document, thereby eliminating the need for emailing back and forth or Lync/Skype chat sessions that may be interpreted out of context without having the document readily available. The following is just a snapshot of some of the awesome features of Microsoft Teams as it relates to SharePoint:

- Open a document in SharePoint.
- Add a SharePoint page as a tab.
- Add a SharePoint document for view within a tab. This feature is useful for PowerPoint presentations or Excel spreadsheets that may be relevant to the team.
- Conversations alongside documents in real time.
- Coming soon! SharePoint web parts as tabs within Teams. This is great news and will open Microsoft Teams up to SharePoint development.

Understanding the differences between Microsoft Teams and SharePoint is critical because we want to make sure that we use the correct technology for the right purpose. Please make sure to review, document, and train users on how Microsoft Teams and SharePoint are different. It seems to be confusing for users what they can and cannot do in both applications. This is key to rolling out the application across your enterprise and if not explained, you can wind up with many Microsoft Teams SharePoint sites. So, now you are asked to spin up Teams in your company's environment; what do you do? Let's talk about the preparation and areas we need to be concerned about.

Tasked to suddenly roll out teams – now what?

As more people work remotely, many businesses have decided the best way to deal with this change and keep up employee connectivity within their enterprise is to roll out Microsoft Teams or greatly expand its usage if it already existed within their application suite. This change has left many IT administrators, particularly SharePoint administrators, scrambling to learn how to deploy and configure this platform rapidly.

While scrambling to acquire the knowledge to stand up a Microsoft Teams environment for your organization, you must not forget that governance is key to the long-term success of the rollout. All the administrative settings are in the cloud. So, there is no need, as in the case of an on-premises SharePoint 2019 environment, to set up a server or even integrate Teams one to one with SharePoint.

The activation of presence in an on-premises environment is done based on identity, as we talked about in the overview for this chapter. There are also key features in hybrid configurations that can be taken into consideration for further integration with the cloud, which is discussed in *Chapter 10, SharePoint Advanced Reporting and Features*. The key is to figure out how Teams works and what it provides as a service. Let's look at some of the areas we need to know about to move forward.

Governance

In this section, we will explore some of the governance features built into Microsoft Teams. Due to the rapid pace of the Microsoft Teams rollouts in many organizations, the governance of this platform became an afterthought. We highly recommend that if you are in the position to roll out your team's platform from the beginning and have time to do this properly, you consider the governance strategy for this platform beforehand. If you already have a governance strategy for your Microsoft 365 or SharePoint environment, this plan can be augmented to fit your Teams environment.

Since Microsoft Teams is most likely new to a lot of admins, decisions must be made about what type of identity model is supported in your organization, who will have what type of administrative access, whether conditional access provisioning is needed, retention and life cycle management, and a rollout communication strategy.

There are many areas to check but one of my pet peeves is not checking guest and external user access. You want to know who has access to your company's user community within the Microsoft Teams environment. The last thing you want is unwanted users contacting your users or even users sharing files outside the organization that are deemed intellectual property. There are other areas you need to make sure to check as well that concern how the application is set up. These are listed as follows:

- Team naming policies
- Team classification
- Team guest access
- Team creation
- Sensitivity labels
- Team expiration
- Retention
- Archiving

Make sure you do your due diligence on checking these governance areas. There are more as well within the Teams user settings that may need to be looked into to make sure you have complete control of what you want your users to have access to change.

Microsoft 365 licensing

Licensing comes with many options, but it all depends on what you need from the Microsoft 365 cloud, as applications are in some ways split by the following:

- The size of content needed to store
- By application

In a case where we would be looking at storage, this could be for email, OneDrive, or SharePoint, where we know that storage is key for documents and email. These applications that need storage may come at a higher price based on how much content you plan to store per user. In some cases, you may give some users a higher subscription and some a lower subscription depending on these two factors mentioned.

If you feel that by application is the more appropriate way to provide governance over subscriptions, then you would look at what applications are provided by which subscription model. This would be the case when you look at, for example, Microsoft 365 Business Basic, which includes Teams, Exchange, OneDrive, and SharePoint, but your users may need Microsoft Office as part of their subscription. In this case, they would need to buy Microsoft 365 Business Standard, which includes the four applications mentioned plus Microsoft Office apps at a higher price.

Please be aware of these pricing models as the subscriptions and pricing change; although they have not changed at this level lately, you will find that other apps outside of the subscription model, such as Stream, will cost you and those pricing models do change sometimes. You must be aware of these changes so that you understand your monthly bill.

Third-party applications

Microsoft Teams also provides ways to integrate outside applications and pull in data from those applications to present to a team within the Teams desktop. With those applications, you want to make sure that data from those applications is governed, as well as knowing what third-party apps are being used. Microsoft Teams gives you the option to control what apps are integrated with your Teams rollout and what users can or cannot use within the application.

Life cycle management

It is important to plan for life cycle management within Microsoft Teams. It may sound weird but there is a method to using this product where it can save you a lot of headache in the end. This is especially the case when there are a lot of teams and no one knows the status of the project or team's content.

All projects have a beginning, middle, and end because that is the way projects are rolled out in a company. The end date is an important date because that is when you expect the project to be completed and finished so that resources around it, be it IT or personnel, can be relieved from those projects and repurposed for other work.

Looking at Microsoft Teams, there are a few things we need to understand, which are teams and channels. Teams are the groups of users who are collaborating on the project. These users can be from any department within your company. Then there are channels, which split those users into their organizational groups or custom groups for targeted workloads.

Along with these areas, we must look at Teams access from a location standpoint, be it internal (private) or external (public) users. Then, we must also look at the types of roles we plan to include as part of the rollout of Microsoft Teams. Admins need these areas of coverage to support the service:

- Teams service administrator
- Teams communication administrator
- Teams communication specialist
- Teams communication support engineer

There are also other types of roles that need to be assigned to support members of teams, which we will talk about later in this chapter:

- Team creator
- Team owner
- Team member
- Guest

The life cycle follows a pattern as stated where you have a beginning, middle, and end of the project life pattern. Let's look at these three important parts in detail:

- **Beginning**: The beginning of a team would be to create the team. This would include several steps because you can also add an existing Microsoft group to a team or many of them. You can also create a team from scratch or add an existing team along with using APIs for Microsoft Graph teams to create teams programmatically. These teams would be created based on global address book attributes. Within the setup, we should also create channels and assign team members to those channels.

- **Middle**: The middle is used to describe the use of the Microsoft Teams product after it is set up. This would be the management of the application based on the team. Areas that need administration would be to update team members, update channels as needed, manage guests using the Microsoft Teams mobile app, and a few other areas of change and/or adoption with the product. This would also include users being more active using the product, which we want so that they enhance their knowledge of the product and build confidence with using the product successfully.

- **End**: After the use of a team has been completed, we must make decisions on how we handle the team's content. You need to make sure to get confirmation from the project leader or users before removing anything from the team. Closing these ended projects or teams makes sure that users do not get access to old content that is irrelevant to anything they are currently working on.

You can delete teams that you do not need. All teams are deleted as a soft delete, which you then have the option as an admin to reverse within 21 days. If the team is for a Microsoft 365 group, the reverse option is available for 30 days.

Retention policies can also be used to prohibit the deletion of teams. Policies can be added to teams or associated with SharePoint so that information can be retained for further time periods. Teams consist of files and content that need to be examined by the teams. Some teams may see value in different content and only want that content retained. This could be in SharePoint as well where you do not want things changed and kept in state going forward so that the information can be recalled if needed.

Some types of content that are captured by Microsoft Teams are as follows:

- SharePoint document library
- Conversations
- Planner boards
- Wikis
- Forms and the results
- Recorded meetings
- OneNote notebooks

In all the integrated apps, their content is retained in the app and not in Microsoft Teams. If you need that information, you should be able to either migrate it into SharePoint or keep it in the current app and pull it from that application when needed.

There are a host of new features in Microsoft Teams that you may want to look at for this purpose, which are listed as follows:

- Turn off message previews.
- Appear offline in Microsoft Teams.
- Change the notification settings.
- Team templates to change the way you work.
- Switch between devices while in a team meeting.
- The speaker name has been added to live captions.
- New keyboard shortcuts.

Now that we have our governance vision, let's look at access roles and the types of access we need to create.

Access

As we know, Microsoft Teams is a service that is only available in the cloud. However, this does not mean that you must have a cloud-only identity to access Teams. All the identity and access models allowed in Microsoft 365 are compatible with Teams. Even third-party authentication providers such as Okta are available to integrate with Microsoft 365 and your on-premises SharePoint 2019 environment for single sign-on.

However, if your access resides on-premises, for example, Windows AD, it must be configured within Azure AD. Azure AD was discussed in *Chapter 10, SharePoint Advanced Reporting and Features*, and briefly this chapter also offers knowledge on AD services, identity security, and application access management.

The following are the types of identity models supported by Teams:

- **Cloud identity**: Cloud identity is when the user is created and managed within Microsoft 365. Azure AD then stores this identity and manages password verification and security, giving access to various applications – in this instance, Microsoft Teams.

- **Synchronized identity**: The synchronized identity model is when the identity is managed and stored on-premises and accounts and passwords are synchronized to the cloud. This synchronization is done through Azure AD. This is the preferred method of most organizations for security reasons.

- **Federated identity**: With federated identity, the identities are still synchronized; however, the password is verified within the on-premises user store and/or through an online provider such as **Active Directory Federation Services (ADFS)**.

Most organizations go with the synchronized identity model for security reasons as stated. Organizations are becoming more open to cloud offerings; however, many prefer, and some are required by policy, to have their access identities remain on-premises and be managed by an identity access management team within the organization that is separate from the IT organization or the business users. Many organizations are even audited by outside governmental agencies to ensure that access to systems and applications is managed through identities on-premises and that segregation of duties is enforced.

By using Azure AD, these organizations can leverage powerful collaborative tools such as Microsoft Teams. Once Azure AD is configured to sync with on-premises, the identity for Microsoft Teams is then able to use these identities to dole out licenses to those identities, granting them access to the Teams features, such as Exchange mailboxes and phone system licensing.

Teams uses identities used in Azure AD. Groups can be created utilizing these Azure identities and from a governance perspective, different groups can be given access to different features of Microsoft Teams that fit in line with the function of the users within the group.

Structuring these groups properly can create a group-to-Teams relationship, but in a lot of cases, this will not happen. But we want to get to a point where we don't have to do a lot of clean-up work within our Azure AD, so the closer you can relate groups to Teams, the better. As you will see, we can set retention on groups and archive information within Microsoft Teams, so we could have many groups created that are not being used if we are not careful to unprovision these teams and groups consistently.

Admin roles in Microsoft Teams

There are several administration roles in Microsoft Teams. Depending on the administration role that you have, you can perform different tasks:

- **Teams service administrator**: This role has access to manage everything within the Microsoft Teams admin center. Along with managing the Teams service, it also can manage and create Microsoft 365 groups.

- **Teams communication administrator**: This role has access to manage all the calling features of Microsoft Teams, as well as the meetings feature within the service.

- **Teams communication support engineer**: This role is tasked with troubleshooting communications issues within Teams using the advanced troubleshooting tools available. This troubleshooting is done through the Microsoft Teams admin center.

- **Teams communication support specialist**: This role has access to troubleshoot communication issues using more basic tools. The scope of the troubleshooting tools and information available for the Teams communication support specialists is the individual affected user, unlike the Teams communication support engineer who has access to view data from all of the Teams communication users.

- **Teams device administrator**: This role manager is actually a device that utilizes the Teams service.

The following is the Microsoft 365 role that is relevant to Teams:

- **Global administrator**: Has broad access to administer the entire Microsoft 365 suite, including Microsoft Teams

Setting up these high-level administrator identities for support of the product is key to supporting Microsoft Teams. Make sure to remember to look at those areas specifically as you get started working with Microsoft Teams to make the right decisions on who has what admin access.

To learn more about Microsoft Teams administration, please follow this link to try your hand at administration:

```
https://docs.microsoft.com/en-us/microsoftteams/manage-teams-
in-modern-portal
```

User roles within Microsoft Teams

There are two roles that a user can have within Microsoft Teams. A user can be a team owner or a team member. By default, the user who creates the team is given the role of team owner, and a user who joins the team is given the role of team user. All users are given the permissions to create teams by default; this is the recommended setting for Microsoft Teams – however, if this does not fit your in-organization strategy, then the default permissions can be modified to limit who is able to create teams.

As a global administrator, groups can be created in the Microsoft 365 admin console. Groups can also be created within specific applications such as Microsoft Teams. It is important to keep in mind that groups created in the Microsoft 365 admin console are available for use across the Microsoft suite of applications; however, if a group is created natively in the Microsoft Teams application, it is only available for use within Microsoft Teams.

Within the user roles, there are three sets of permissions that can be granted: owner, member, and guest. The owner is the person that creates the team, a member is someone that has joined the team within the organization, and the guest role is typically reserved for those who are outside of the organization, such as vendors or consultants, that the owner invites to join the team:

- **Team owner**: The team owner is the person that created the team.
- **Team member**: A team member is anyone inside of an organization that is invited by the team owner to join.
- **Guest**: Anyone outside of the organization that the team owner invites to join the team. This option may or may not be allowed within an organization and can be suppressed.

The following chart represents the tasks that Teams users can perform based on their role in a particular team. Organizations may limit the out-of-the-box capabilities of each role depending on governance specifications. Please consider whether any limitations are required before deployment:

Tasks allowed to perform	Owner	Member	Guest
Create a team	Yes	No	No
Delete a team	Yes	No	No
Converse in a private chat	Yes	Yes	Yes
Join in conversation	Yes	Yes	Yes
Receive an invitation on any Office 365 Account	No	No	Yes
Create a channel	Yes	Yes	Yes
Delete a channel	Yes	No	No
Create a private channel	Yes	No	No
Add team guests	Yes	No	No
Add a member	Yes	No	No
Change graphics on a team	Yes	No	No
Allow or suppress channel @ mentions	Yes	No	No
Edit private channel name	No	No	No
Configure team permissions on channels, tabs, and connectors	Yes	No	No
Edit team name and description	Yes	No	No
Remove user access from the team	Yes	No	No
Archive a team	Yes	No	No
Restore a team	Yes	No	No
Share a file from the channel	Yes	Yes	Yes
Add an App	Yes	Yes	Yes

Figure 11.2 – Teams tasks by role

> **Note**
>
> Team admins can control what guests within the team can do. Team owners can control some of what members and guests can do if certain functionality is not limited by team admins.

For more information on Microsoft Teams guest access, check out the following link:

`https://docs.microsoft.com/en-us/MicrosoftTeams/guest-access`

Teams and channels within Microsoft Teams

Teams and channels are created within Microsoft Teams. A team is defined as a group of people/content organized around a particular project within an organization. A team can be public, private, or organization-wide. I will discuss a bit more about these options in the *Creating a team* section. The purpose of a team is to bring people together to work closely on a common goal, task, or project; product launches; or ongoing organizational activities. They can be set up to reflect the structure of your company; for instance, each division or department can have its own main team's space.

Channels are segmentations within the team that are dedicated to a specific project, topic, or action. Multiple channels can exist within one team space. Chat conversations, documents, and other files within a team's channels are only accessible to members of the team. Channels can be extended with apps, bots, and connectors, including BI connectors, in Teams.

As mentioned earlier in this chapter, each team within Microsoft Teams corresponds to a SharePoint Online site and each channel within a team corresponds to a folder within that site.

Deployment

Microsoft recommends deploying Teams in stages and not rolling out all the Teams features at once. We wholeheartedly agree and can speak from experience here as we participated in a very rapid rollout of Teams due to the pandemic. The vast number of features and lack of organizational communication (we will go into the need for a firm communication plan in the next section) left users befuddled and overwhelmed and hindered adoption due to confusion about what in fact Microsoft Teams is and what it does. As in all other rollouts, migrations, and upgrades, clear communication and training is key to satisfaction and adoption.

If you can deploy Teams in stages, pick the set of features you want to roll out first. If you already have other technologies that are performing these functions, you can drive adoption by letting the user community know that the older technologies will be phased out and suggest that they begin their transition as soon as possible to Teams for the features that will be replaced. For instance, if you are set to begin your Teams rollout with the chat and meeting features, which is recommended if you plan on making Teams the organization standard for these features, let the user community know when their previous chat and meeting technology, such as Skype or Webex, will no longer be accessible to them.

Training is also an immensely important step in your rollout. Training is made much easier when you focus it on a small set of features that are newly available versus expecting the user community to take Teams training on all the features that are rolled out at once.

Network considerations

Microsoft Teams has many features, including document collaboration, Skype phone services, chat messaging, virtual meetings, and more; each of these components requires network and bandwidth considerations. We will not do a deep dive on network preparation for Microsoft Teams in this book; however, there are some requirements that you must consider:

- Make sure that your organization's network is already optimized for Microsoft 365. If it is not, you must follow the prerequisite steps from Microsoft's site to make sure to prepare the network for this optimization.

- At a minimum, all locations where we use Microsoft Teams must have internet access, of course. For all locations that will access Teams, the following ports must be opened, and the IP must be set:

  Ports: UDP ports `3478` through `3481`

  IP addresses: `13.107.64.0/18`, `52.112.0.0/14`, and `52.120.0.0/14`

- SharePoint Online and Exchange Online must be deployed within your organization.

- Once Microsoft Teams is deployed, please test the following for network optimization as further optimization may be required:

1. Check whether Teams is running slowly.
2. Check whether meetings are connecting slowly.

3. Check whether documents are opening at a sufficient rate.

4. Check whether call audio is clear or whether calls are dropped.

- Utilize the call quality dashboard to understand the quality of calls and meetings within Teams. This will help to identify issues and plan remediation.

To access Microsoft Network Planner, please visit this link: `https://docs.microsoft.com/en-us/microsoftteams/prepare-network`.

Communication

Having a firm communication plan is extremely important to the success of your Microsoft Teams deployment. If you have chosen to roll out only certain features, make sure that this is highlighted in the communication plan and the communications being sent to users. The user community will undoubtedly begin doing research on their own on the features of Microsoft Teams and may be confused as to why certain features are lacking in the initial rollout.

Along with the communication, if there is a long-term strategy within the organization to use Teams as their preferred method of collaboration and communication, make sure this is emphasized in the plan. This emphasis can help drive adoption as users are often hesitant to move to newer technologies when their older counterparts are still in use within the organization. Let the user community know that the older technologies will be phased out.

Also, within your communication, reference or link any training sessions that are available to the user base. I believe it is important to have live overviews and step-by-step training sessions from the beginning. These live sessions are important especially if you are doing a phased rollout or rolling out to a smaller user base at the beginning because it will allow you to gather many of the questions that users may have and ascertain any confusion that the subset of users may have concerning Microsoft Teams. Gathering this information at the beginning will allow you to tailor your environment, communication, and training going forward.

Prerequisite steps

Before you embark on a Microsoft Teams rollout, there are a few steps you need to take to make sure you look at all your environmental dependencies. As we talked about governance over SharePoint, we also need to do the same for Microsoft Teams and this should be taken even more seriously as it really opens huge areas of concern and exposure to unwanted incidents.

When looking at these prerequisite steps, we are really going back to our section on governance. Here, though, we will explain more about the high-level governance needed to be in place to make sure the service is covered and vetted by all stakeholders.

The areas that we want to concentrate on are the following:

- Project stakeholders
- Project scope
- Coexistence and interoperability
- Journey to be successful

There are many things that need to be done as well to get started, such as workloads, configured domain, Azure AD, Exchange configuration, Microsoft 365 groups interaction, and other areas, which include a public switched telephone network if this is the configuration you are implementing. Please make sure to look at this link before you start your journey:

```
https://docs.microsoft.com/en-us/microsoftteams/upgrade-plan-
journey-prerequisites
```

Using Microsoft Teams

Once Microsoft Teams is deployed within your organization, you will need to log in to the Microsoft Teams environment to use the application. Within most organizations, this access will be the same as what is used to log in to your computer and other applications both on-premises and in the cloud, which is a single sign-on. If Microsoft Teams is not yet configured within your organization and you would like to get a preview, Microsoft is currently (at the time of writing this book) offering a 30-day free trial. You will need to sign up for the Microsoft 365 Business version to have access to SharePoint.

In this section, we will go over some of the basic instructions for using Microsoft Teams. You will learn how to create your own team and create a channel within your team. You will also see how to start a conversation within a document to showcase this cool social feature. We will also briefly discuss a bit about tabs, which can be added to channels within the team workspace. This book is by no means an exhaustive resource for Microsoft Teams; however, we will highlight some of the features that you can explore in more depth on your own.

When opening Microsoft Teams, you will see the following sign-on page come up on your computer. The same page renders on your mobile app if using the app on a mobile device:

Figure 11.3 – Microsoft Teams login

Once you are successfully logged in to Microsoft Teams, you will see your Teams workspace as shown in *Figure 11.4*. From this location, you can view, create, upload, and edit documents, make phone calls via Skype, start a Teams meeting, or engage in or start a new conversation. You can also create a new team, a channel within a team, and much more:

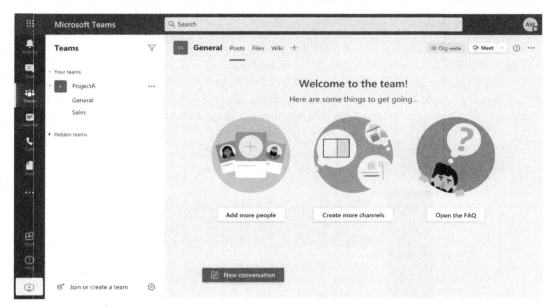

Figure 11.4 – Microsoft Teams home page

- **Teams**: The Teams workspace is the location where you will be able to create more teams, which Microsoft defines as the groups of people that you will collaborate with on projects and assignments.

- **Channels**: Channels help organize your Teams content into specific topics, departments, or projects.

- **Conversations**: Conversations are the chat feature within Teams, which can also take place within a channel. All conversation content, including meetings, is open to the whole team that has access.

- **Meetings**: From the meetings icon, you can start a meeting immediately with your team members or schedule one for another time.

- **Files**: The files feature of Microsoft Teams allows you to manage documents and collaborate on documents within the Teams interface. As you will see, the features within the files location are similar to what you would see on a SharePoint site.

Creating a team

When Microsoft Teams is rolled out within an organization, users will have access to any organizational teams spaces that they are automatically added to by being part of the enterprise organization AD group that is synced to Azure AD. However, there is also an option to create your own group within Microsoft Teams to collaborate with a specific community of users within the organization. Follow these steps to create a new team:

1. Log in to Teams.

2. In the bottom-left corner, click **Join or create a team**:

Figure 11.5 – Invite people and send invitations

3. Click **Create team**:

Figure 11.6 – Link to create a team

For this example, I will create a team from a template. Select **Manage a Project**:

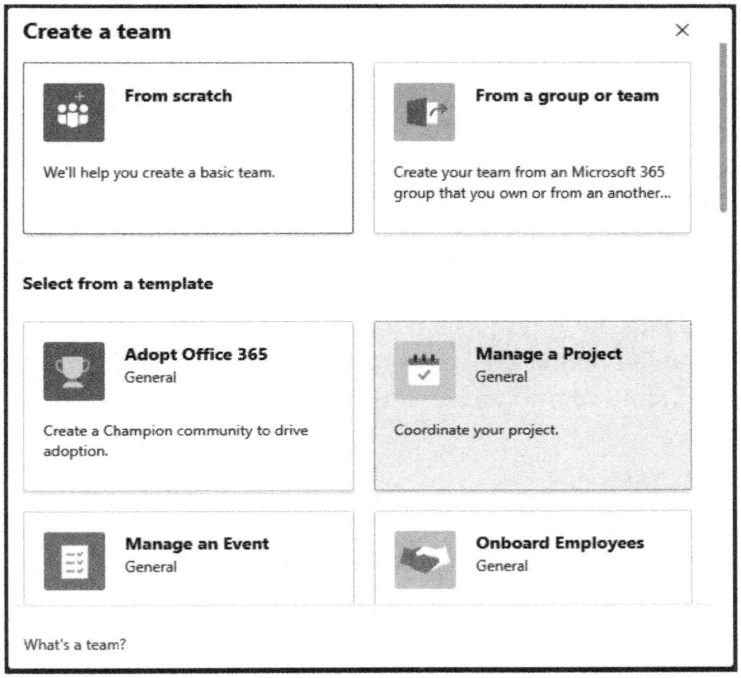

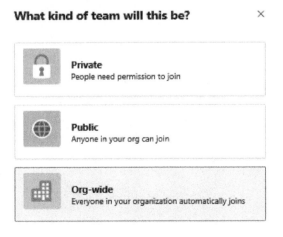

Figure 11.7 – Templates for team creation

4. Here, we see three different settings to determine what type of team you want to create:

Figure 11.8 – Select the type of team to create

- **Private**: You will want to choose the **Private** option if you want to keep this group to a limited audience. With this option, only those with permission to join will be able to access this team and the content native to it.

- **Public**: The **Public** group option allows anyone in the organization to join this group.

- **Org-wide**: The **Org-wide** option automatically gives everyone within the organization access to this group.

  A note on creating an org-wide group. Org-wide teams can only be created by the global administrator. This type of team is synchronized with the organization's AD and is kept up to date as people join and leave the organization. Microsoft imposes limitations on this option; only organizations with less than 5,000 users can create an org-wide team and the number of this specific type of team is limited to five per tenant.

5. Name your new team:

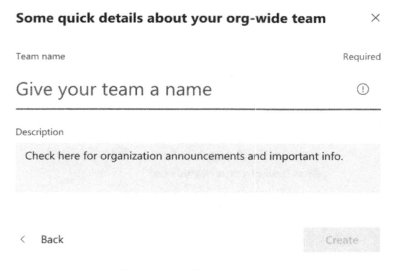

Figure 11.9 – Name your team

6. Your team is now created:

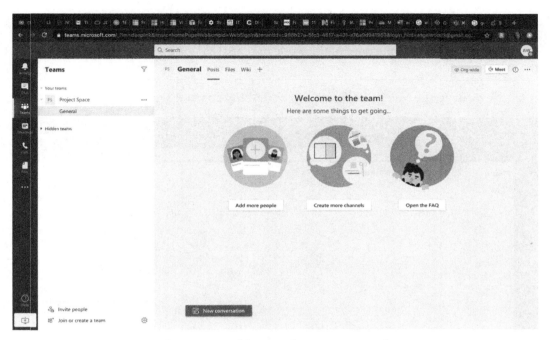

Figure 11.10 – New team home page created

Now that you have added your team, let's create a channel to continue to show you the structure of how Microsoft Teams works.

Creating a channel in Microsoft Teams

The following instructions show you how to create a regular channel and a private channel within your team. Remember, it is best to think of the logical architecture of your team and channels so that the purpose of the workspace makes sense to your users. Let's look at the steps:

1. Navigate to the Microsoft Teams site or desktop app and sign in:

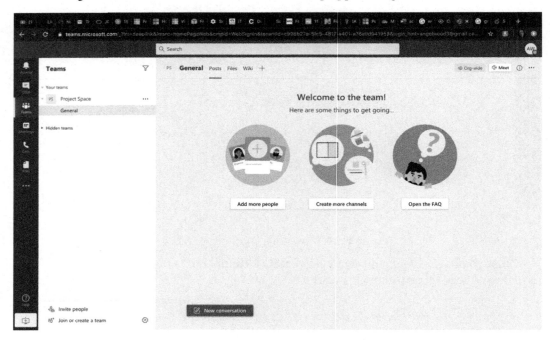

Figure 11.11 – Microsoft Teams home page

2. Select the ellipses (…) to see the list of more options, then select **Add channel**:

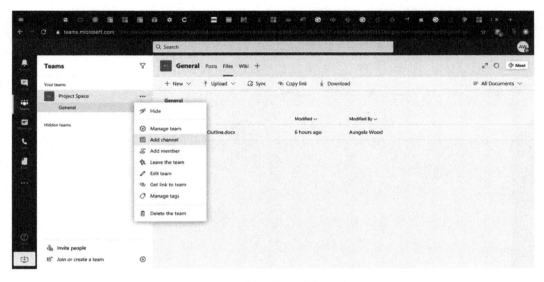

Figure 11.12 – Add a channel from the menu

3. Select a name for your channel, then click the **Add** button:

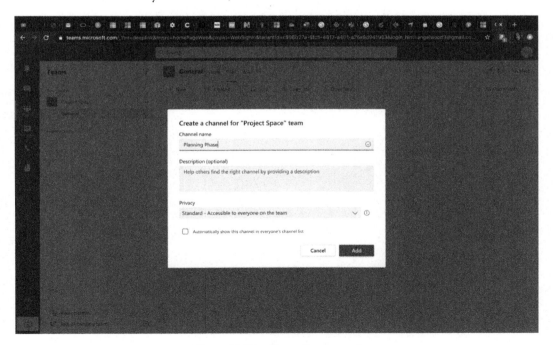

Figure 11.13 – Name the channel

4. Check on the left side of your workspace and you will see the newly created channel:

Figure 11.14 – Channel home page

5. The channels within Teams are very extendable using apps, bots, and custom connections. If you click the **Add tab** button, you will get a list of the many tab options that you can add, by default:

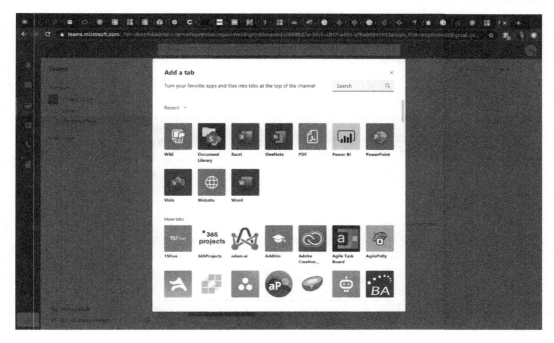

Figure 11.15 – App integration tab

Many of the tabs, including Power BI, must be configured in your Microsoft 365 environment to be utilized as a tab here. You can also limit what apps are seen here by securing this area using the Microsoft Teams administration settings.

These apps come in handy when you want to create a connection to information in another app or even use Power Apps to create a survey for the team to collect information. You can use many forms of storage for the information gathered, such as Excel spreadsheets, SQL databases, and more. It is a very cool tool to help share information within Microsoft Teams!

Opening a document in SharePoint

Let's look at the steps for how we can open a document in SharePoint:

1. Navigate to the document that you want to open in SharePoint.

2. Click the ellipses (...) and select **Open in SharePoint**:

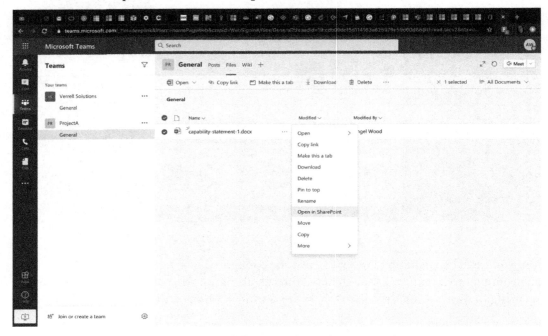

Figure 11.16 – View of SharePoint list within Microsoft Teams

3. You will now see the SharePoint Online library behind Microsoft Teams:

Figure 11.17 – SharePoint list view in Microsoft Teams

Utilizing the **Open in SharePoint** option, you can view the SharePoint document directly from the SharePoint site; however, opening this document in Microsoft Teams offers an extra feature not available in SharePoint Online alone. This is the conversation feature that we mentioned earlier. This is one of the most useful features of Microsoft Teams when it comes to document collaboration in real time. Next, we will go through the steps of starting a conversation within a document in Microsoft Teams.

Starting a conversation within a document

Follow the steps given for creating a new conversation:

1. Navigate to the document that you want to open in Teams:

Figure 11.18 – View of a file in Microsoft Teams

2. Click the **Conversation** button at the top of the page:

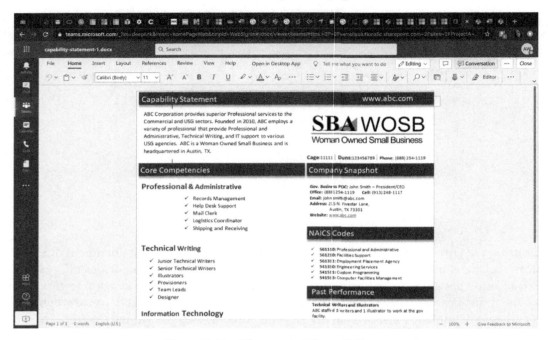

Figure 11.19 – File open in Microsoft Teams

3. The conversation pane will be displayed on the right side of the screen. Type your message in the chat window at the bottom of the pane and click **Send**:

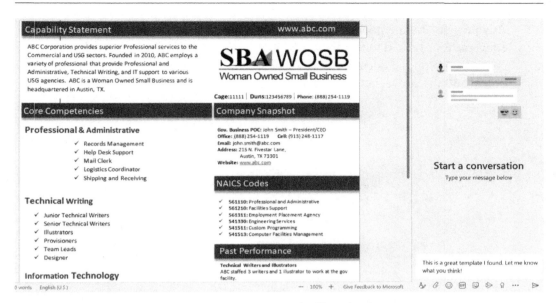

Figure 11.20 – Start a conversation on the file with others in your team

4. See your message displayed in the pane:

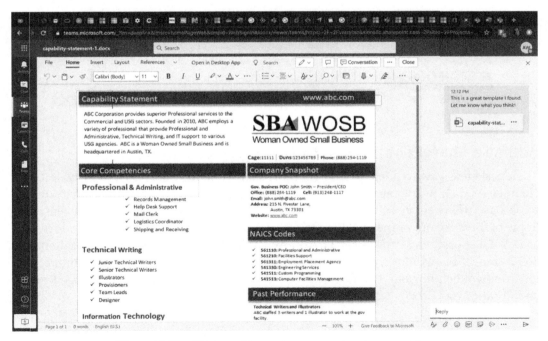

Figure 11.21 – Click send to send a message to a team member

5. Anyone who is a member of your team has access to view the document and the conversations related to the document. If a team member misses the real-time conversation on the document, they will receive a notification with the document linked and the conversation displayed:

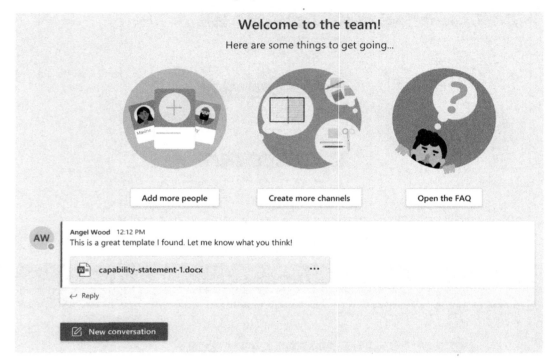

Figure 11.22 – Welcome page for a newbie team member

Adding a SharePoint-related tab to a Teams channel

There are a few ways to integrate content from SharePoint into a tab in your Teams channel. As mentioned, tabs are a way to extend the functionality of a Microsoft Teams workspace. There are various apps that can be added to a tab within your Teams channel. Some of these are out of the box; however, Teams allows customized apps to be added as well. Of course, these apps must be deployed and allowed within your organization's 365 instance. Teams allows you to add a SharePoint page from the SharePoint Online environment behind your Teams workspace. You can also link to SharePoint, page lists, and libraries via URL.

To add a tab in a Teams channel, use the following instructions:

1. Navigate to the channel where you want to add a tab:

Figure 11.23 – Teams menu

2. View the list of available options:

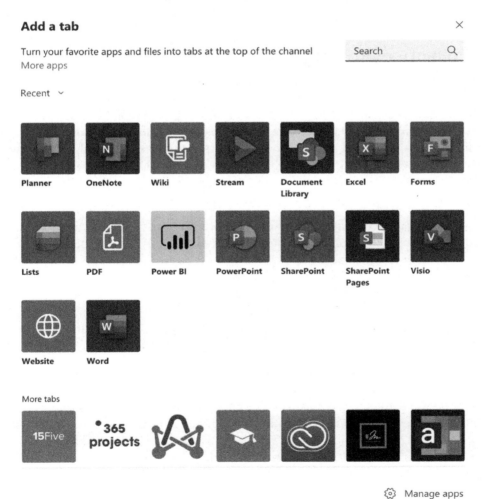

Figure 11.24 – Use apps within Microsoft Teams using tabs

You can see on the **Add a tab** page that there are several default apps that can be added to your Teams channel. Some of these are the standard Microsoft applications, such as **Word, PowerPoint, OneNote**, and **Excel**. However, do take special note of the **Power BI** app, which can be added as a tab, as well as the SharePoint **Document Library** app. There is a **SharePoint Pages** app that will allow you to add a SharePoint page from your SharePoint Online environment that is associated with this team's site. You can also select the **SharePoint** app, which gives you a bit more flexibility in connecting to content outside of the site that simply exists within your Teams channel. In addition to the out-of-the-box apps that are displayed, there is also the option for a developer to create custom applications within your organization, and based on access, those applications will be displayed here as well and can be chosen as a tab.

Best practices for organizing Teams

There are some best practices to consider when organizing a team within Microsoft Teams. Please keep in mind, regarding documents, that these are stored in SharePoint, and that behind every team created in Microsoft Teams is a SharePoint site, and every channel is a document library. There are limitations and restrictions imposed by Microsoft that must be considered. These limitations can be seen in the following chart – you will see that they are very high and, in most organizations, users will be just fine with not breaching these limitations. However, without firm governance and data cleanup, over time these limitations could be breached and cause issues.

If users are arbitrarily creating teams in channels within teams and these are not being used, this could cause the organization to approach these limits rather quickly. If there is a large organization with a lot of users with the ability to create teams, you can imagine how issues can arise over time. Think about how this has been an issue historically in SharePoint and it's still an issue that users have been known to create sites when a library or list would do or creating sites that are abandoned. Users must be aware of this possibility and the best practice of limiting the number of teams and channels created to only those that are purposeful within the organization should be driven home.

The option to allow team owners to create teams and channels can be restricted, although this is not recommended because this can affect the business purpose for which the organization wants to utilize Teams. This is where great communication and training will come into play; team owners must understand their responsibility in maintaining the logistical and purposeful use of Microsoft Teams. This can be likened to, within SharePoint, making sure that your site admins are knowledgeable and maintain their sites and prevent unnecessary sprawl.

Out of the box, team owners can create private channels at will. What administrators must understand is that private channels are their own SharePoint site collections and should be limited in number. You do not want team owners creating a lot of private channels that correlate to SharePoint site collections. The team administrator can limit the ability of team owners to create private channels; this option should be considered. Each team can have up to 100 team owners; if they are all creating private channels, this will become a problem.

Each team and each channel within a team should be created for a purpose, a goal, or a project, and only those that are necessary to contribute to that purpose should be added to that team. Channels and apps and connections within channels should be added solely for the purpose of reaching the goal of that team.

Limits and restriction considerations

There are some limits and restrictions that Microsoft has placed on teams and channels and we have included this information in the following chart. Please check Microsoft's site for updates as these limits can change:

Features	Limits
Number of teams per user	250
Number of team memberships per user	1,000
Maximum members per team	10,000
Owners per team	100
Org-wide teams per Tenant	5
Members in an Org-wide team	5000
Teams created per Global Admin	500,000
Maximum number of teams per organization	500,000
Number of channels per team	200 (includes deleted channels until 30+days)
Maximum members in Private channel	250
Members in Office 365 group that can be converted to a team	10,000
Channel conversation post size limit	28KB in total

Figure 11.25 – Best practices and limitations of Microsoft Teams

Now that we have looked at some of the functional areas of Microsoft Teams, let's take a look at one of the meeting features within Teams called live meetings.

Configuring an auditorium solution with Microsoft Teams

When taking advantage of Microsoft Teams as your go-to meeting application, you can do so much more with this application as it also makes sense to have live events using the application as well. As we noticed while working with the platform, it is open to governance and configuration settings to manage a host of functionalities. The focus of this section will be live events using Microsoft Teams to manage, host, and collaborate during the event.

The configuration I put together that I have implemented is for a company that recently really loved Microsoft Teams. They wanted to use Teams in an auditorium setting and wanted to host their meetings at their location, but they did not leave out those who wanted to either stream the event or call into the event. Some requirements that were stated were there was a band playing during the event and some guest speakers as well. The company also wanted video to be displayed on each side of the stage along with three cameras, one wired and two wireless. These would be used to catch separate angles from the event so that the video producer could pan back and forth between the video cameras.

Unfortunately, I am not going to be able to go through all the technical information in this section, but this will get you started at a high level on the journey to hosting live Teams events. My background in music played a big part in setting this up for the companies I configured this for and we will keep this simple so that you get an idea of what to buy, some small details, and how to set up a live event.

Our event will look like this once we set up all the hardware components:

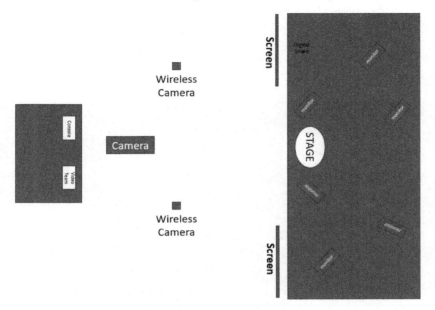

Figure 11.26 – Auditorium setup

The components used in this diagram to make up the solution are the following:

- Behringer X32 mixing console
- Two laptops for the video team
- One HDMI video camera
- Two wireless video cameras
- Two 70-inch monitors
- Six stage monitors
- Two main speakers
- Other microphones and Cat 6, HDMI, and USB cables not shown

Since this is basically a small concert setting, we are going to start with the Behringer X32 console as the first area of focus. The Barringer X32 is an intermediate digital sound console as far as cost and notoriety around the music world go. It's not bad for the price and will give you a great sound with some amazing features to go along with it since the board is digital. The mixer supports many new functions you will not see in analog mixers:

Figure 11.27 – Behringer X32 mixer

Some of the first things you will notice are that the console is large and needs some room to manage the cabling and for someone to manage the mixing. The main things you want to find in a mixer are how many channels it provides because this will play into how many instruments or vocal mics can be provided to the band or hosts while they are doing the event. If you plan on having music, there are AUX inputs that can be used for those connections but make sure to get the right type of cabling to support your source. The mixer comes with a small window console to manage settings and is fairly easy to use, and you will get a manual that is in PDF form and comes in paperback.

This mixer also comes with a network connection for Cat 5 that enables it to be managed on the network from a remote console such as an iPad. Mixing the sound on an iPad can be very useful when there is no one to manage the sound, or the sound person can also be home mixing as well. This is almost the best way to do the mix and that is due to you wanting to check the way the sound is coming out through the speakers at home because this is what your audience will hear when the event is streaming. They will not hear what you hear in the auditorium, so we must do some things outside the auditorium to make sure things are mixed well.

There is also a USB connection that takes the sound input and pushes that sound out digitally to a laptop. In most cases, all mixers will need to have a driver installed on the laptop to make sure it can connect the hardware to the computer. Once you have that driver, you will see the choice for sound sources that comes up in the Microsoft Teams device settings menu for the X32 sound source, which then will project that sound through your Teams event.

The sound needs to be mixed well and you want to make sure you verify that the mix you have created, called a scene, works for the outputs in the auditorium and for those streaming online. Using two separate scenes in the console will provide that capability and give you a way to change settings on the different mixes separately as needed.

This also brings up some other X32 capabilities, for example, you can set mixes for different outputs in the mixer. So, if you have a house mix, which could be the main mix on outputs 1 and 2, this can be set in the mixer and saved as a scene as well. So, when you select that scene or channel configuration, the mix comes back to the board, where you can change it and then save it again if needed. If you have a mix for the USB out and the sound is just not working or you added an instrument, you can also go back and edit the channels you have saved to be received by that output. Overall, the board gives you so much control over everything, but if you come from an analog background like me, then these new mixers will take some getting used to.

If you are having trouble with your X32 console, look at updating the firmware. Old firmware could cause freezes on the board and other weird power issues where the board resets power with no warning. Upgrading the firmware will provide the latest and greatest menus and functionality for the board as well. It will also fix a lot of hardware issues you may have. We suggest doing this as soon as you get your board, so you program your settings on a good foundation and download the compatible Windows drivers for that firmware as well. One thing to remember is that the board settings will be erased on this board once the firmware is upgraded. Save the scenes before you upgrade if you started adding scenes before you upgraded the firmware. You should upgrade the firmware no matter what soundboard you buy!

Headphone amps are also useful for stage sound instead of monitors and help the musicians and others who are part of the event to hear the music clearly and/or even a microphone you may deem as an instruction feed for stage coordinators could help in the production of the event as well. As a musician, I have used these many times and it helps to hear the music more clearly and even instructions from a bandleader. This requires a separate feed from the mixer, which would be from the analog or digital snake where instead of using an input, we would use an output to get the feedback to the headphone amp. Separate mixes can be sent, or you can use one mixer to feed all headphones.

The digital snake is such a lifesaver as far as cabling and getting a true digital sound from the players, singers, or MCs that will be performing at the event goes. The snake sends a signal from the digital input and output mixer on the stage with ¼ and XLR inputs and outputs back to the board so that the sounds from the instruments and vocals can be captured and mixed on the console. The snake costs a lot more than a traditional snake but provides a better quality of sound. This is really all it provides but avoiding having this huge cable from your console to your stage is also a saving as digital snakes can use Cat 5 or 6, depending on your mixing console, or a special cable. This also helps to feed the monitors on stage if needed so that everyone can hear themselves if a headphone amp is not the solution.

Wireless mics are what you see most of the time at events but there are still people that love cabled mics as well. The only thing to look at with wireless microphones is to make sure you either buy different brands of wireless mics or make sure to upgrade the firmware on the wireless microphones' bases. In most cases, the newest brands provide channel separation if there are the same brand wireless microphones on stage. If you do not have the latest and greatest, then updating the firmware may be your answer. It is important to make sure the microphones do not stay on the same channel because when they clash, you lose your sound from the microphone, which means the audience will not hear you and could miss something important you said.

Your video team should investigate what software will work with Microsoft Teams. In some cases, Teams is all you need. When doing a live event, the console changes from the normal Microsoft Teams screen where you see other people to the live interface, where you see a staging area and a live area for presenting the staged content. This is good in some cases but there is other software out there, such as Wirecast, UBS, and others, that give you better functionality to handle many types of feeds. Although Teams does handle some feeds well, some feeds are currently not handled very well. I tested many different types of HDMI adapters to see which one could help with the multiple cameras and figured out that Teams is still in need of some upgrades.

NDI was not available when I did this installation, but I believe it is soon to be available to use with Teams, which will make Teams more compatible with other video management software out there. NDI is a video network protocol that streams video from different network resources but can be captured by a software application so that it can be managed by the producer. It makes cameras that are wireless easy to connect to and brings those feeds back to the video console. You can also connect wireless cameras using IP as well by connecting them to the laptop and then pulling them into your software.

It also creates an environment where if we had a second laptop and had something we wanted to stream from that laptop, then we could use NDI to bring that video back to the main producer console. This is all wireless or you can use Cat 5/Cat 6 to connect all the hardware. With that being said, I still like the Cat 5 or 6 option because when a network protocol fails, it really makes troubleshooting tough, especially when you are live streaming. Knowing a cable could be the problem is a quick switch, so I have been up in the air so far on hardware connection. Network cables also provide reliable streaming, so you do not lose video stream during a production.

Cameras come in so many shapes, sizes, and tech varieties. The main camera used for this setup was an old Sony HVR-HD10000U camera that had HDMI and then I purchased two Mevo wireless cameras. The Sony camera was used as the main camera and was connected using HDMI. This camera did most of the main video captures for the event. It was manned by a cameraman and used to pan and follow the main person on stage. The wireless cameras were focused on other parts of the stage but with the Mevo, you can also do some remote control to zoom in and out. This became very effective for the shots during the event.

The Mevo is very unique as it will connect to your wireless network and make itself available for streaming. It can also be connected directly to some applications, such as Facebook, which it was built to be used with. The camera is small but gets some great video and you can buy a stand for it or mounting hardware to put this camera pretty much anywhere. It is not a high-end camera with a lot of tech bells and whistles but for the price, it is great, small, and compact:

Figure 11.28 – Mevo camera

All video monitors were installed using TV risers and were 70 inches to present a good view from the back of the auditorium. We connected them all through HDMI to a switch and then back to an HDMI switcher in the booth. To get the monitors connected, we used HDMI boosters that used Cat 6 to connect a TX and RX box on each end. Those then convert to HDMI on the other end of the hardware, which is then connected to the TVs. We ran our cables over 100 feet and the feed was solid with no delay or lack of clarity on the screen.

So, let's now look at how to create a live event.

Creating a live event

Follow these steps to create a live event:

1. To create a live meeting, use your calendar in Microsoft Teams to create a new event from the **New meeting** menu:

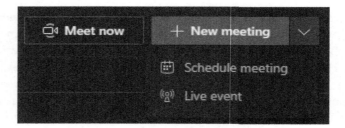

Figure 11.29 – Microsoft meeting creation menu

2. Select **Live event** from the menu. The menu for the live event will come up on your screen:

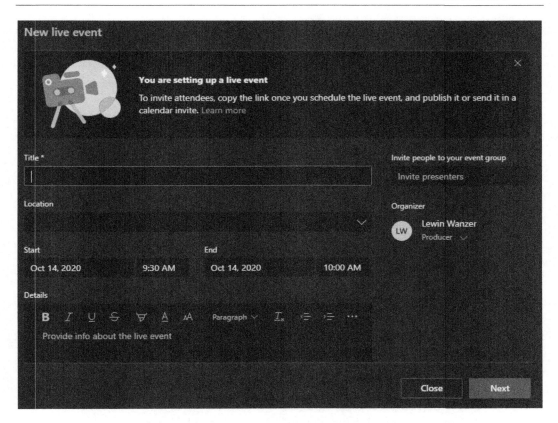

Figure 11.30 – Create a live event screen

3. Fill in the areas of information to give the event a name and provide start and end dates and times. If you have people you would like to invite now, say that are part of the production team or presenting, you can add them in the invite people area of the form.

4. After clicking **Next**, we will get a menu to choose permissions for the event:

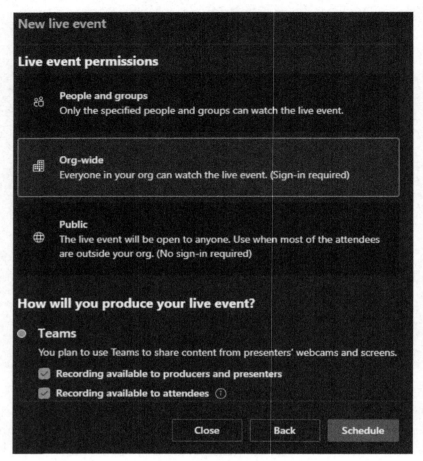

Figure 11.31 – Event permissions and settings

5. When choosing people and groups, you are selecting specific people you want to join that are part of your organization. **Org-wide** is everyone in your organization and **Public** is a mixture of organization and external attendees.

For the event I was working with, we chose **Public** because this was being broadcast to anyone who wanted to attend. We had a sign-up sheet on our website and added those emails to a list so that we could email the link to them. I am sure there are other ways to collect this information, but we did not have time to get into those areas.

6. Once you click **Schedule**, you will see the event details screen. This screen shows you the link for the attendees and gives you options to copy it so that you can share it. You can also join the event or create a chat. You can cancel the meeting if you are having trouble or need to reschedule:

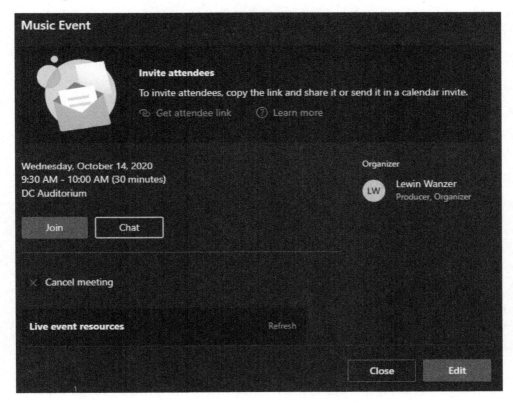

Figure 11.32 – Live event creation screen

7. The event is also placed on your calendar in Teams and Outlook:

Figure 11.33 – Teams calendar view

The link for the event will automatically be sent to those you added as producers and presenters for the event. Their calendars will automatically be updated.

8. Once the event has started, as the producer, you will see the production screen:

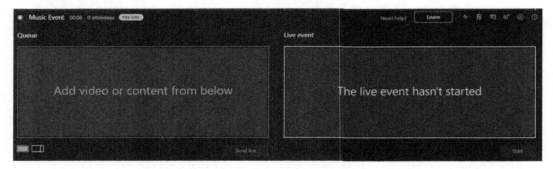

Figure 11.34 – Producer screen

9. You can see the **Queue** area, which is where we need to add a feed from our video camera or other apps to be shared live. This is how we prepare content to send live. This can be an app such as PowerPoint or any open app, video monitor, or HDMI feed. Once you have your content ready for presenting, you would click **Send live** and start the event.

10. If you need to display two content sources such as video and content from another app, Microsoft Teams give you an interface to do that within the live event UI:

Figure 11.35 – Queuing content screen

11. We can see that there are a couple of queue interfaces we can use. One interface is to display just one content source, and the preceding screenshot shows how we can add video and other content in the same feed, which is very good to show variations of content on one screen. We are sure Microsoft will provide more variations with this UI in the future but there is also other software such as UBS that give you better options and more flexibility that can be used with Microsoft Teams.

12. There are also options to share a desktop or an app from the lower menu. You can also mute all users as well, but this is something you can do automatically using the administrator options in Teams to have this set beforehand:

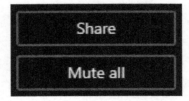

Figure 11.36 – Sharing content

13. Click the gear button in the top-right menu to see the device settings:

Figure 11.37 – Microsoft Teams device settings

14. This is where you set your speaker settings if you use those for playback. This is good for mixing and hearing what the auditorium will sound like. Settings will come up when using a direct mic within your computer or, like we talked about, the X32 mixer. The mixer is our sound source. Video cameras should be set on the primary camera you have set up.

15. To set the auditorium, we can use this in-room audience feature to get reactions, but the more interesting feature that is configured on your X32 soundboard is a mix-minus. What this does is you create a process in the board where people that call in can ask a question, which is then projected on the house speakers so that everyone can hear it. Then, the moderator or MC can answer questions from those who called in or joined in via the Teams app. This is needed when you want to have interactions with your audience.

16. By clicking the first choice on the settings menu, you will find the health and performance menu:

Figure 11.38 – Health and performance menu

17. This information is good to know especially when using video because the network means so much to the performance of the video feeds:

Figure 11.39 – Performance

18. The following menu is for taking notes about the event. This is for the producers and presenters:

Figure 11.40 – Notes

19. IM is used to communicate with those in the meeting:

Figure 11.41 – Chat

20. If you need to add some attendees, you can do so by selecting the following icon on the menu:

Figure 11.42 – Add attendees

There are also other things you can set in the Teams administration that will help events such as this go smoothly. Here is a list of things you can do to better support public events:

- Mute everyone automatically.
- Hide phone numbers from users who call in.
- Auto-accept attendees or make attendees wait in the lobby.
- Set up a call center to support the event using Microsoft Teams.
- Add images in the content, such as logos and other information.
- Create break out sessions and more!

As you can see, Microsoft Teams has a great platform to host live events and meetings and supports up to 10,000 attendees depending on your subscription. I really believe it is only going to get better and I am digging deeper into this because of my music background. I wanted to share at a high level what I did to make this work for my customer as it can shed light on the possibilities for your company looking to provide auditorium-sized events with outside callers. Teams is a great tool and there is so much more you can do with it.

Summary

Microsoft Teams seemingly came out of nowhere as the hero of enterprise social networking and collaboration. During the trying times that people and organizations were dealing with due to the COVID-19 pandemic, many turned to Microsoft Teams as a solution to their social connectivity issues as the workforce and education were driven home into remote working situations that many were facing for the first time. This left many admins scrambling to get up to speed with the Microsoft Teams application and the opportunities for extendibility within this platform.

Microsoft Teams offers phone communication, virtual meeting capabilities, Outlook integration, document management, and chat-in-conversation features all in one place. As amazing as Teams is from a business perspective, from an administrative perspective, it is important to understand that Microsoft Teams is a layer on top of SharePoint and not a replacement for SharePoint. It is very important that as an administrator you drive this point home to management and the decision-makers for your SharePoint project. It is also very important to remember that a solid governance plan should be created prior to rolling out Teams in your organization because although the mini features in one location are great, Microsoft Teams can grow unwieldy without proper governance and use of best practices.

In our next chapter, on SharePoint Framework, we will cover how this all works from a developer standpoint. Developers have such a vast array of tools to use to create customizations that APIs are available to alter any Microsoft application offering. Developers also have access to all SharePoint 2019 sites and content to Microsoft 365 sites, and content using data gateways, which brings this platform to another level. This is so powerful and really takes collaboration to the next level with these integrations, especially with Microsoft Teams as pulling in an app in Teams is very easy. The ideas for collaboration at this point in time are unlimited. "Why leave on-premises?" You may ask yourself whether a hybrid configuration is your best bet after reading this book.

Questions

You can find the answers on GitHub under Assessments at `https://github.com/PacktPublishing/Implementing-Microsoft-SharePoint-2019/blob/master/Assessments.docx`

The answers to these questions can be found in the *Assessments*:

1. When preparing to deploy Microsoft Teams, which of the following is true?

   a) The rollout does not take much thought or planning to be successful.

   b) Governance and best practice considerations are important to the long-term success of the deployment.

   c) There are no network or bandwidth considerations when deploying Microsoft Teams.

2. Your organization must have an a Microsoft 365 license to roll out Microsoft Teams. True or false?

   a) True

   b) False

3. Which of the following is true of the Microsoft Teams site? Choose the best option.

   a) Behind every Microsoft Teams site is a SharePoint Online site.

   b) When a Microsoft Teams site is created, it automatically has a SharePoint 2019 site URL.

   c) Microsoft Teams is completely independent of SharePoint.

   d) None of the above.

4. Having a firm communication plan when rolling out Microsoft Teams is not likely to enhance the success of the rollout. True or false?

   a) True

   b) False

5. Which of the Microsoft Teams roles has access to manage everything within the Microsoft Teams admin center?

   a) Teams communication support engineer

   b) Teams device administrator

   c) Teams communication administrator

   d) Teams service administrator

6. Which of the following can be extended using apps, bots, and custom connectors?

    a) User permissions

    b) Channels

    c) Azure AD

    d) None of the above

7. In Microsoft Teams, live events can be created from which menu? Choose the best answer.

    a) New meeting menu

    b) Privacy settings menu

    c) Add an app menu

    d) None of the above

Further reading

Please check out the following helpful links to further explore Microsoft Teams on your own:

- `https://docs.microsoft.com/en-us/microsoftteams/how-to-roll-out-teams`

- `https://techcommunity.microsoft.com/t5/microsoft-sharepoint-blog/sharepoint-and-teams-better-together/ba-p/189593`

- `https://support.microsoft.com/en-us/office/create-a-channel-in-teams-fda0b75e-5b90-4fb8-8857-7e102b014525`

12
SharePoint Framework

The method of SharePoint development has gone through many iterations since SharePoint 2007. In SharePoint 2007, farm solutions were all the rage. Developers had free rein to create what they wanted – the custom solutions they needed with full integration with services running on the farm. However, this did not come without risk because farm solutions could in fact bring the entire farm to a halt. Next, in SharePoint 2010, we saw the rise of the sandbox solution, which still allowed developers to create customized solutions but limited the scope of the development and the impact on the site collection. Now, of course, we have SharePoint's client-side development, which includes add-in model script infusion and is now the newest of all the SharePoint frameworks.

Although we have seen some very much necessary changes throughout the versions of SharePoint over the years, there are some updates within SharePoint 2019 that put this platform on another level. As developers, there are tools and things we need to know to understand the framework in a platform so that we can go on to develop. In *Chapter 10, SharePoint Advanced Reporting and Features*, we saw the no-code developer tools available within the platform locally and most of them were accessed on-premises environments through gateways using hybrid configurations.

In this chapter, we will look at hardcore development and how it's changed for coders. We will take a quick look at the things that you need to know before you get started on working with SharePoint 2019 development. The topics covered in this chapter could be a book in itself but we just wanted to make sure to cover them as administrators need to know these areas, and if you are an aspiring developer, this may give you some information on how to get started on your quest to become a developer. It is a great time to start because things have changed.

The following topics will be covered in this chapter:

- Developer essentials
- Developer tools and languages
- Developer best practices
- SPFx

Technical requirements

To understand this chapter clearly, you must meet the following requirements:

- Be a beginner with some experience or an intermediate developer

You can find the code files present in this chapter on GitHub at `https://github.com/PacktPublishing/Implementing-Microsoft-SharePoint-2019`.

Developer essentials

Since SharePoint 2019 is a big change from all other versions of SharePoint, there are things you need to know to move forward as a developer. As stated, we have seen so many changes over the years, especially between 2007, 2010, and 2013. These versions brought big functionality changes, which then brought development changes and changes to out-of-the-box functionality.

The same goes for this version; as you will see in this chapter, SharePoint 2019 is bringing the cloud SharePoint Online service to an on-premises environment. Although it's not patched and updated to the standard of the server used in the cloud, we do see most features available for developers. Admins do not have the same configuration features in the on-premises servers that support SharePoint Online. These features will probably never surface in an on-premises build. If they do, these features would be a great addition to environments that need administrative support.

The good thing though is that developers get almost everything SharePoint Online has to offer in SharePoint 2019. Again, things have changed, so the things you need to know and the skills you need to have add to the learning curve. If you have not been keeping up, this can be detrimental to your job search as most SharePoint on-premises work is slowly fading. Do not make the mistake of keeping a job in SharePoint on-premises development and not aspiring to learn more about the new tools.

As developers, we need to have a certain skill set, especially when developing on the SharePoint platform as this is a niche environment. There are certain things you need to know, such as how to use and understand out-of-the-box features, lists, libraries, scripting, design, and other tools that all together will make you a great developer. Business knowledge is a big plus as your background can help you understand requirements when developing solutions.

One thing I have noticed over the years is that many developers do not understand out-of-the-box functionality. I have seen developers develop functionality that is already out of the box in a document library. This is not a great way to develop. It is best to use those out-of-the-box features and code around them using the API. Even some of the best developers you meet may not fit the skill set when working with SharePoint due to this need to know the area of SharePoint.

If you are new to SharePoint, focus on the functionality within the product first. Make sure to look at all the settings within sites, lists, and libraries. Look into features such as document sets, manage copy, versioning, and all the features available that support SharePoint to make sure you do not recreate something that is already available.

The important thing to know is the functional differences between on-premises and SharePoint Online, which are listed as follows:

	SharePoint On-Premises	**SharePoint Online**
New features	New tools are made available using updates.	All new features are provided on the online version first. Does not mean you will see everything on-premises.
Collaboration	Admin is responsible for implementing.	Microsoft works these tools to make them better and available.
Updates	Updates and patching managed by admin.	Managed and installed by Microsoft.
Availability	Configured by the admin but can be an SLA of 99.9%.	SLA with 99.9% availability.
Backup	Backups are managed by the admin.	Microsoft ensures backup and redundancy.
External users	Access can be provided with network availability and risks associated.	Can be configured to support external users and external sites using Power Apps.
Scaling	Admin is responsible for all configuration changes.	Microsoft provides scaling.
Management	Central Administration and PowerShell.	The SharePoint admin center and PowerShell.

Figure 12.1 – On-premises versus SharePoint Online

The list of areas you will need to really understand is as follows. Make sure you study them all in order to be a good developer. There is a lot to learn and we are going to try and cover as much as we can to help those who are new and those who are looking to update their skills. Companies are looking for developers that understand these areas of SharePoint. Here are the out-of-the-box features:

- Creating web pages
- Forms
- Workflows
- SQL databases
- Master pages
- SharePoint apps
- Page layouts
- User store

- Web parts or solutions

- SharePoint ribbon

- Workflow Manager

- InfoPath

- SharePoint Designer

- Power tools in Microsoft 365

- Visio

- Visual Studio

- PowerShell

As you can see, there is a lot here. SharePoint is vast and has a lot of twists and turns. You must really dive in to be a developer on this platform. It takes skill and years of learning on projects to really be a developer on this platform. With this knowledge of just the out-of-the-box features, you will also need to know how to code.

Let's look at the coding languages that support SharePoint:

- **.NET**: Our first coding language that is a basis of the product is .NET and is used with on-premises environments when you want to develop custom web parts. This coding language is very powerful, and it supports a wide variety of features and functionality, so it must be understood to program in SharePoint. .NET is a technology that supports Windows apps and web services. It provides a way to build and run those apps and services while providing a consistent object-oriented programming environment. The code is stored locally on the server and executed locally or can be executed remotely. The latest version of the framework is available, which is 5.0 or greater for new development, and is serviced with monthly security and reliability bug fixes. There are no plans to remove .NET Framework from the Microsoft platform.

- **C#**: Our next coding language is C#, which is also one that gives you the basis to build SharePoint solutions. This is a modern, object-oriented, and type-safe programming language. You may find similarities with other languages, such as C, C++, Java, and JavaScript, as the roots of these languages are very similar. Using both C# and .NET brings the vastest server-side library to build the most robust solutions. For more information, refer to the following links:

Introduction to C#: `https://docs.microsoft.com/en-us/dotnet/csharp/getting-started/`

Get started: `https://docs.microsoft.com/en-us/dotnet/framework/get-started/`

- **JavaScript, the REST API, and jQuery**: Our next coding language is JavaScript, the REST API, and jQuery. These tools can be used to develop custom web parts to alter and control design components on a page. The **SharePoint Framework (SPFx)** is the latest, which enables you to develop web parts for SharePoint and Teams clients. jQuery can also be used in conjunction with JavaScript with C# for web part development depending on the requirements.

- **HTML5**: Coding using this language is standard for all web pages now. This coding changes the way the page is designed, so you can create a unique design for a SharePoint site. Changing the master page using HTML5 will bring a different experience to SharePoint, allowing you to design in a way where you can brand it for your company uniquely instead of using the boxy, out-of-the-box layouts in SharePoint.

- **CSS**: The CSS coding framework is available on all websites and is easy to figure out. You can almost learn this online if you have a little time to spend. CSS provides the capabilities of giving your SharePoint site a facelift and make the site look more pleasing to the eye, which works with HTML to place images and other content on the page. To avoid the boxy style, look, and feel out of the box, learn both HTML5 and CSS and this will help you create a design that works for your customers.

Now, let's turn our attention to some of the helpful tools used in SharePoint development.

Helpful tools

Working with SharePoint, especially when in a development environment, you will need to know some administration basics. Understanding the tools and the different environments where the tools are supported is a big plus. Please make sure to learn more about Azure and Microsoft 365 as you could be working in a hybrid environment where the following tools will be useful:

- **SharePoint PowerShell**: The PowerShell module is provided directly by Microsoft and allows you to manage your Microsoft 365 and Azure environments. As part of SharePoint Server 2019, it is installed on the operating system and provides a great library for administrative tasks for on-premises environments.

  Link to resources: `https://docs.microsoft.com/en-us/powershell/module/sharepoint-online/?view=sharepoint-ps`

- **PnP**: The PnP module, provided by the **Pattern & Practices (PnP)** community, is managed by Microsoft affiliates to help developers and administrators. It is available for many frameworks and is the latest library. There are libraries for SPFx, CSOM, C#-CSOM for SharePoint Online, and PnP for PowerShell. PnP also gives you a way to provision template features on any site with a predefined look and feel.

  Link to resources: `https://docs.microsoft.com/en-us/powershell/module/sharepoint-pnp/?view=sharepoint-ps`

- **Office 365 CLI**: Using the CLI for Microsoft 365 can help manage your Microsoft 365 tenant and SPFx projects from any platform. The platforms supported are Windows, macOS, and Linux. Using the Bash, Cmder, or PowerShell CLIs and the CLI for Microsoft 365, you can manage various configuration settings of Microsoft 365. This tool also helps you manage SPFx and build automation scripts. The tool is provided partially by the PnP community in Microsoft.

  Link to resources: `https://pnp.github.io/office365-cli/`

  CLI blog: `https://developer.microsoft.com/en-us/office/blogs/new-version-of-office-365-cli-040/`

- **Azure CLI**: The Azure CLI can be used across many Azure services and is provided directly by Microsoft, which allows you to manage your Azure resources with an emphasis on automation. The Bash scripting and CLI help you get working fast with Azure. The Azure CLI offers the capability to load extensions provided by Microsoft. Extensions provide access to experimental commands and give you the ability to write your own CLI interfaces as well. It is available to install on Windows, macOS, and Linux environments.

  Link to resources: `https://docs.microsoft.com/en-us/cli/azure/?view=azure-cli-latest`

  Get started: `https://docs.microsoft.com/en-us/cli/azure/get-started-with-azure-cli`

  List of managed services: `https://docs.microsoft.com/en-us/cli/azure/azure-services-the-azure-cli-can-manage`

- **Azure Functions**: This is a powerful way to develop ad hoc functions with serverless computer technology that accelerates and simplifies application development. Azure Functions can be invoked from Power Automate as well to perform operations and it also supports flexible scaling based on your workload volume. The tool can incorporate C# and PowerShell when needed. Use Visual Studio and Visual Studio Code on your local machine, which are integrated fully into the entire Azure platform.

Get started: `https://azure.microsoft.com/en-us/services/functions/#get-started`

Code and tools summary

As you can see, there is a vast amount of information here where all topics could be their own book. This can be frustrating for a newbie or an intermediate developer. The only advice we can give is to jump in with all your determination and win the battle. Try to find a quick way in; for example, start with JavaScript and then build from there. You can add on languages; as you can see, some complement each other and are similar in code structure.

We have not been able to really jump into these topics because of the limitations of the book, but in this section, we wanted to make sure to let you know of the possibilities of the tools available that you can use on-premises and in Microsoft 365. They are all somewhat needed in a hybrid model and some are dedicated to on-premises only, but the goal of this is to make you aware of those tools so that you can investigate and create rich experiences with SharePoint.

If you have some experience, there is still a lot to learn here and you can spend countless hours trying to figure out the best coding solution to start with. Our recommendation again is to start with JavaScript but if you're more experienced, you may already know this coding language. If that is the case, assess what is needed within your job and go for that language or look at some of the tools to see what really aligns with your company's needs. The more you can make yourself available, the more valuable you will be to your company.

If you are not actively developing in SharePoint already, make sure you leave behind all the things you learned previously on other platforms as this is a total start-from-scratch technology. Make sure to learn the basics first (out of the box) and then move on to coding so that you understand the platform. Navigate through a SharePoint site and look at the site settings to make sure you understand the functionality that is already there. We suggest learning JavaScript and PowerShell first because they will give you quick coding solutions that work well with SharePoint 2019 and SharePoint Online. This will bridge the gap from SharePoint on-premises to SharePoint Online to make you more marketable.

To learn more about other on-premises administrative tools that are not mentioned here specifically for SharePoint Server 2019, check out *Chapter 9, Managing Performance and Troubleshooting*. Please refer to that chapter to help you with identifying other administrative tools for on-premises environments.

Developer experience and teamwork

Earlier in this section, we mentioned your job experience as it really plays a big part in how you build a solution or make changes to support the end user experience. You must have a good work ethic to identify end users' problems and then find the right solution. This may take time and some testing, which may include a few different methods and skills, as we will mention in this chapter, but your job and personal experiences come into play because the more you can identify with the users' work, the better you will understand what they are aiming for.

Creating solutions for users, especially those that want a professional look and feel along with functionality, you really need to understand the end user experience. This helps guide the user within the solutions to use the functionality you develop. You need to make sure you think out your processes and make easy-to-use solutions. Again, the more you understand SharePoint and the out-of-the-box features, the better you will be at creating solutions.

When becoming a developer, always gravitate toward your strengths by looking for jobs that include the personal or job experiences you have. For example, if you were a security guard, learn how SharePoint and Microsoft 365 could help a company like that and see what type of solutions you would build for them to make the company more automated and work smarter. This is your strength, not your weakness.

The types of jobs available for developers that you will see all the time in job posts are the following:

- **Full stack engineer**: An engineer who can handle both frontend and backend work where they can create a fully functional web application.

- **Frontend engineer**: User interface developer, which includes visual elements such as layouts and aesthetics.

- **Backend engineer**: Uses APIs to integrate data systems, caches, and email systems and takes on underlying performance and logic in applications.

- **Software engineer (TEST)**: Validates the quality of the application using automated tests, tools, and other methods to validate the product.

- **DevOps engineer**: Builds, deploys, integrates, and administers application infrastructure, database systems, and servers.

- **Security engineer**: Specializes in creating systems, methods, and procedures that test the security of a software system. Exploits and fixes flaws as they penetrate to discover vulnerabilities.

Finding an eagerness to learn really starts with your interests. Find a job you believe you will enjoy. If you love to design things and have an artsy-type background, you may want to stick with trying to aspire to be a frontend engineer. If you love data and working with reports, you may want to look at being a backend engineer. It's all in what you want but it's best to get into something that piques your interest; otherwise, you will end up dropping out of classes and be bored with the work to achieve these goals.

Once you achieve these goals, there are players in the development teams you need to know about. We will explain some other members that become important to your everyday work.

Team members

As we saw earlier when we talked about skill sets and teams, there is a position that helps in these types of situations where you need guidance on the direction of a solution. This is where the business analyst comes in and can help you determine requirements, and since they should have a SharePoint and coding background, they can help you identify those features you may need to research and/or customize to make the solution work. In Agile project management, as explained in the next section, this is a Product Owner. This is a necessary team member in heavily developed SharePoint environments. They interface with the users and meet with them to gather requirements. If you use Jira, you will see the stories these team members create, which are worked on as a team, but the initial stories will be entered by a business analyst.

You could also encounter a Scrum Master as Agile project management is really surging as the go-to project management tool. This project management style is, I have to say, very useful, especially with development. I was on a team that used this methodology and it really helps to keep track of what is going on within the teams associated with the product they support. Daily standup meetings come into play that are centered around stories, which are requirements broken down into stages considering the customers' needs and how we build out those solutions within the SharePoint platform. Please read more on Agile at the following link. I encountered the company Scaled Agile recently and like their approach to learning the craft:

```
https://www.scaledagile.com/
```

Training users

This activity goes right along with requirements as the requirements need to be met so that the user can put two and two together when looking at what they told you and what you bring to them to demo. Your demo will determine whether you have hit the mark when it comes to the development of the solution and if not, they can let you know of any areas that may seem rough that they want to be done a little differently.

Once those areas are updated and tested and you have determined that the user has no other concerns or bugs, then you can have the users test the solution themselves in a test environment, which you would need to vet the changes for first through a tester prior to delivery to the test users. This way, the users have access to the product that was vetted by a separate member of your team or another team. Also, if you want to hold their hand before releasing the solution, you can do a training session with them to make sure they understand the solution.

Your business analyst, or Product Owner, in Agile project management controls the interactions between you and the customer along with the Scrum Master. They also need to be well versed in the product you are supporting as they could have been a developer in the past or worked with a particular software intensely for years. This team member is key because they make recommendations to the customer on the requirements and also create stories about those requirements for you, the developer. Again, this is a very key interaction between customer and developer.

As mentioned, Agile will play heavily in a development team if this project management style is being used within your company. The stories you receive have time limitations and you can help grade the length of developing those areas with the team using story points and using a process called Planning Poker. This helps the team look at what are called backlog stories to help determine what stories should be next in line, as well as determining how much time each will take to complete and who should be responsible for the work. Read more on Agile project management so that you will not be surprised in this environment.

For me, using Agile was a great learning experience and I will tell you that those standup meetings can be brutal if you do not have the work completed in a timely fashion. This method promotes healthy dialog, learning from peers, and an organized development process, and also uncovers those that are not performing. Team dynamics are very important and in the experiences I have had, you really needed to be sharp because, on this side of IT, you can get eaten up quickly. If you want to be a developer, you have to know the craft *well*, especially in this environment.

Documentation

Make sure to document bug fixes; we will get into more detail about developers' best practices later in this chapter. We want to make sure you understand the processes involved and what you are expected to do as a developer. Document any thing and everything is needed so that you can capture where code fails; plus, it helps you to grow as a developer.

Not every shop is the same and some shops use Agile to manage projects, where code will be pushed quickly by separating requirements into chunks. This helps the business analyst to support the users and the developer to understand the requirements for working together as a team. This will also require you to be in daily meetings where you update your team on your assigned tasks. These chunks of coding projects are called Sprints.

We will not get into this much in this book, but we wanted to point Agile out especially for developers because you will be held under a microscope. I was on a contract with this style of project management and it really helped me grow. Being put on display every day to show what you have accomplished face to face with your manager and teammates will keep you on task, but if you are not doing the work or do not understand it, everyone will see your limited skill set openly.

Jobs and certifications

Find jobs at the beginning stages, if you are a newbie, that you can handle easily before you move on to bigger and better ones. This even goes for seasoned professionals because you may not have used the platform or will be new to some of the new coding languages. Gain some experience and then start taking on jobs you cannot yet handle but can get through the interview process for.

Doing this will build your character and your knowledge, especially when working with other developers that can be mentors to you. We should say that this may be hard in some cases as when you work with great developers, they can be the most critical of you. So, you must be tough and withstand the pain and even insults to your skills so that you can grow and exceed their abilities in the future. You must have a thick skin, unfortunately.

If you do not have the ability or time to provide due diligence to learn the platform, you will fail. We can tell you that right away. It takes some time, determination, and bumps and bruises to learn this platform as a newbie for an admin or developer. Even with the changes we are seeing in SharePoint 2019 and SharePoint Online, you will find yourself learning new tools and languages even if you are a seasoned professional.

There are several certifications for SharePoint that you can find on Microsoft's site. These certifications also help you to be more marketable and display your eagerness to learn and provide credible skills needed by a company. You can learn more about certifications at the following link, but we did not want to list them because they change often, so please look at what is available at the time you're reading:

https://docs.microsoft.com/en-us/learn/certifications/browse/

Also, if you want to start to learn from authorized training, please check out the following link:

```
https://www.linkedin.com/learning/subscription/topics/
sharepoint?trk=sem_src.pa-bi_c.bng-lil-sem-b2c-nb-dr-
namer-us-lang-en-biz-beta-desktop-core-tier2-sharepoint_
pkw.%2Bmicrosoft+%2Bsharepoint+%2Btraining_pmt.
bb_pcrid.77240797721612_pdv.c_trg.kwd-77240851810630%3Aloc-190_
net.o_learning&hero=10&veh=sem_src.pa-bi_c.bng-lil-sem-
b2c-nb-dr-namer-us-lang-en-biz-beta-desktop-core-tier2-
sharepoint_pkw.%2Bmicrosoft+%2Bsharepoint+%2Btraining_pmt.
bb_pcrid.77240797721612_pdv.c_trg.kwd-77240851810630%3Aloc-190_
net.o_learning&src=pa-bi&gclid=%5B*GCLID*%5D
```

Where do you start? To get started with working on your skills, you need training and an environment to play in. Let's look at how to set up a development environment and what things we can use to help us get things in place to start our journey.

Setting up a development environment

Before you can start using the tools, look at some training, but you must also have an environment to use to set up SharePoint 2019 and install the tools on the server. When setting up your environment, refer to this book; you can use this book to set up your environment from an installation perspective. If you are using a laptop or desktop, there are several virtual software options available for you to use on those platforms. You can also purchase a used server on eBay, lease a server from a hosting company, or set up a server in the cloud using AWS or Azure (if you have the funds). Some cloud platforms offer free subscriptions for a period.

The SharePoint 2019 download is located on the Microsoft website and offers a free 90-day trial:

```
https://www.microsoft.com/en-us/download/details.aspx?id=57462
```

Again, if you are setting this environment up for a company you are supporting, ask them to give you an individual server. Make sure you are not setting up a server that supports many developers. The reason why is you can step on each other's toes, especially for reboots, and coding can overlap if you are not careful.

The environment should consist of the following server resources:

- 16 GB of RAM or more
- 500 GB of disk space or more
- Four cores of virtual processors or more
- A laptop or desktop compatible with the virtualization
- Licenses for SharePoint 2019 and any other integrated applications

The choices for virtual server host and other options are as follows:

- **VirtualBox**: This is a software platform used for personal usage environments, such as laptops, desktops, or even servers, but we do not recommend this platform for production environments: `https://www.virtualbox.org/`.

- **VMware**: The free version of VMware Player can be sufficient for testing, but for development, this solution can quickly become insufficient: `https://www.vmware.com/products/workstation-player/workstation-player-evaluation.html`.

- **Hyper-V**: This is the option used in this book to set up servers for installation. Microsoft provides this ability within the Microsoft operating system by configuring the server options: `https://docs.microsoft.com/en-us/virtualization/hyper-v-on-windows/quick-start/enable-hyper-v`.

- **Parallels**: This gives you the option to run Windows on macOS but is not free if you want to virtualize Windows environments. The pricing for the product is not bad and you pay by year. We have never used it, so we cannot give any reviews, but it's worth a try if you strictly use macOS: `https://www.parallels.com/`.

- **Azure**: This is a cloud infrastructure environment provided by Microsoft and provides 12 free months of service: `https://azure.microsoft.com/en-us/free/search/?OCID=AID2100131_SEM_1aa5a26fbf5a139881e0fdf61ec56fb0:G:s&ef_id=1aa5a26fbf5a139881e0fdf61ec56fb0:G:s&msclkid=1aa5a26fbf5a139881e0fdf61ec56fb0`.

- **Microsoft Partner Program**: Microsoft offers an Action Pack subscription for those who are looking to work with Microsoft products. This could be a small company or a newbie looking to start developing, but you gain access to licenses for their software products: `https://partner.microsoft.com/en-US/`.

- **AWS**: This is a cloud infrastructure environment provided by Amazon. The service has a free tier that can be used for development and testing: `https://aws.amazon.com/`.

- **Rackspace**: This is another cloud infrastructure environment that has awesome engineers who can support you with using SharePoint. You will not find this in a lot of other offerings: `https://www.rackspace.com`.

- **Team Foundation Server**: This is used to version code and publish code within an environment. It is also used to package code for testing and integrates with Visual Studio: `https://www.microsoft.com/en-us/download/details.aspx?id=48260`.

Let's take a look at the modern and classic SharePoint sites. This book does not thoroughly explore the SharePoint user interface; however, these two types of SharePoint sites are important to discuss because the differences could inform your development choices.

Modern or classic?

This will be our only topic that has to do with the user interface for SharePoint in the book really. The reason for this is very important because you must know what the differences between a classic and a modern site are. There are two experiences you can choose from within SharePoint 2019: one is modern and the other is classic. These experiences bring different functionality and aspects to the SharePoint Server 2019 site experience, which is different from all the other versions of SharePoint. SharePoint Server 2016 has some updates to the classic experience but was never designed like SharePoint 2019.

The reason why these are important is that there are two distinct ways you can create content in SharePoint 2019 sites. When we refer to classic, it is just like referring to what Windows Authentication was called in SharePoint 2007 and 2010. It is the native way of doing things from when a product was created, sort of like a legacy version of a component.

When we refer to modern, we are referring to the most up-to-date way to display content or interact with features within sites. This way of displaying content also brings a new way of using sites, lists, and libraries. Remember, this will take some thought and training before it is exposed to your user community.

Your users need to know about changes implemented like this because everything changes at this point. The classic lists and libraries look and feel goes away and links to areas we used in site actions along with how to navigate to certain actions will change. This could be a learning curve for your users, so you need to really make them aware of what you are doing before you do it.

If you like your classic experience, then stick with the classic, but if you want some cool updates to your sites, lists, libraries, and other areas where the cloud can be supported by SharePoint 2019 using modern features, then you should upgrade. This upgrade brings a new set of Microsoft 365 cloud power tools, which are only made available in this experience. So, if you are using an on-premises gateway, then this is the only way you will be able to take advantage of the tools in the cloud and use them on-premises.

As a developer, this is important because if you do not have access to power tools in the cloud and are asked to develop something on a classic site using those tools, you need to make the users who want this change aware of the changes you have to implement before you can even get started.

Let's see what the differences between the classic and modern experiences are and what they look like in SharePoint 2019.

The modern experience

The modern experience in SharePoint Online and SharePoint 2019 is designed to be mobile, flexible, and easier to use than the prior classic experience. Although SharePoint Server 2019 supports the modern experience, you will notice that it is supported in several areas but not all features within SharePoint 2019. We will not cover all of these new experiences but will cover some you will want to be aware of.

The following experiences are modern by default:

- The SharePoint start page
- Lists and libraries
- New team site and communication site home pages
- New pages
- Site contents
- Site usage
- Recycle bin

In the following screenshot, you can see how the classic feel gives a legacy display of a library:

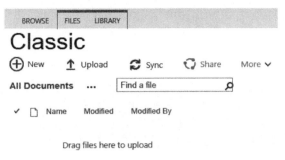

Figure 12.2 – Classic library

The following screenshot shows what the modern library looks like:

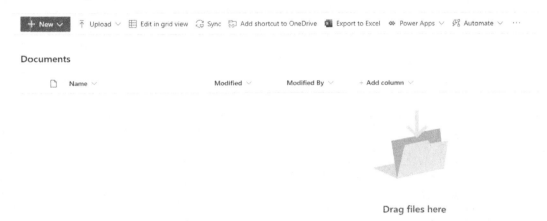

Figure 12.3 – Modern library

You can see from this screenshot of a modern library how the list has changed from the classic list screenshot. Users will be confused right away with how to use this library due to the differences from the classic view.

The SharePoint start page

This page has changed drastically, and you can see from the following screenshots that we have a new way of displaying information on our main page. This is what the classic page looks like:

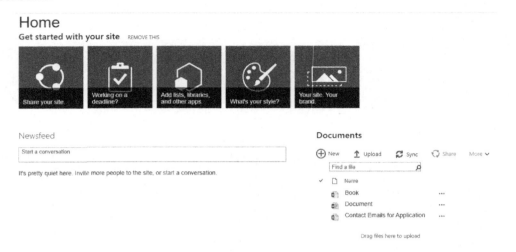

Figure 12.4 – Classic view

Here is what the modern page looks like:

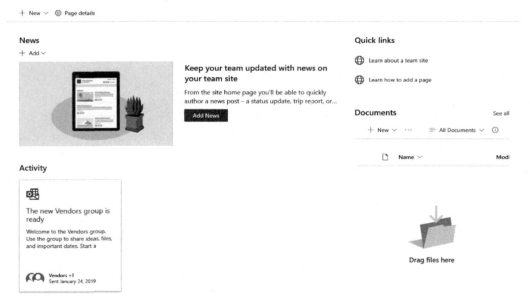

Figure 12.5 – Modern view

There are many areas Microsoft has tackled in using modern templates, but there is still more to be done. As you can see, not everything is customizable using this type of site. We suspect with the change from SharePoint Designer and InfoPath coming soon, there will be no more classic sites and everything will be modern in the next couple of years.

Site usage analytics

This component has a new look. It's very easy to look at analytics and see popular content on the site using this tool:

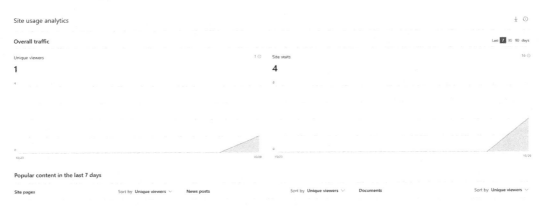

Figure 12.6 – Site analytics

Team sites and communication sites

There is also a new modern team site and an additional new communication site. Team sites got a facelift, as you can see from the SharePoint start page example. Communication sites are new, and they give you the ability to share news, reports, statuses, and other great information you can see in a visual format. Communication sites are like classic publishing sites but are simpler to create and do not need that legacy publishing site infrastructure (but boy do we remember that headache).

Search

Unfortunately, we haven't gone too much into search in this book but we wanted to mention this when it comes to modern sites. SharePoint Server 2019 comes with a modern search experience and you will be able to see results before typing in the search box. The results come in real time, so as you continue to type, the results update and change right on the page.

The modern search boxes can be found on the home page, communication sites, and modern team sites. There will be options to change where the results come from, such as a site you may have searched on but did not mean to search. Then, you have other options to refine your results. There is also a **Show more results** option that expands from the bottom of the search box and you can open the search results page and look at more details:

Figure 12.7 – Modern search experience

Other things for you to research are listed as follows, related to the modern experience:

- List column calculations and column formatting
- SPFx client-side web parts and extensions
- Webhooks
- Asset packaging – hosting your solution assets automatically from app catalog site collection
- Tenant scoped deployment – deploy your web parts across the farm just by installing them to the app catalog
- ALM APIs for add-on and SPFx solution management

What is not supported in modern sites are as follows:

- Site designs and site scripts
- Hub sites
- Custom modern themes – out-of-the-box modern themes are available for team sites and communication sites
- Site collection app catalog (potentially supported by RTM)

Supported browsers

SharePoint supports several web browsers that are most used, such as Internet Explorer, Mozilla Firefox, and Safari. However, some browsers may cause some functionality to be limited or available only through some alternative steps. At times, some of the functionalities may not be available for noncritical administrative tasks.

The following chart quickly summarizes some key points in user interface design:

User Interface Design Framework Key Points	
Classic Sites	Classic sites are fully customized. You can create a master page and page layouts and set up everything inside the master page and page layouts. You can use the REST API, JSON, and CSOM to customize classic sites.
Modern Sites	Modern sites are not fully customized. We can use SPFx to customize modern sites, but we have less options as compared to classic site customization. We can integrate many applications with the modern user interface easily.
SPFx	This is a framework for customizing the modern user interface. We can use the Angular, React, or JavaScript frameworks with SPFx for customizing SharePoint.

Figure 12.8 – Design framework key points

There is so much to learn within this platform, and we have only touched the surface. This section aimed to help explain starting points and what you should be concentrating on as a developer. There are many applications to get used to and even if you are used to them, there are still changes in SharePoint 2019 that you need to address. In this next section, we will talk about SPFx and what it is, some history, what has changed, and how to get started.

SPFx overview

A brief history of SharePoint development follows. In the past, SharePoint development has consisted of the following methods: farm solutions, sandbox solutions, script injection using content editors and script editor web parts, and the SharePoint add-in/app model. The modern way to develop in SharePoint is through SPFx. Before we get into our examination of SPFx, let's go over the previous forms of SharePoint development:

- **Farm solutions**: Farm solutions were the original development method for SharePoint. They involved creating full-trust code and employing **WSP**. WSP is the file extension for the Windows SharePoint solution. This form of development allowed great creativity within SharePoint because developers could do pretty much whatever they wanted to do. Microsoft introduced full-trust farm solutions with SharePoint 2007. Developers were able to write fully customized server-side solutions using ASP.NET. Using SharePoint's API, developers could create solutions that integrated timer jobs and web parts. However, having the ability to write full-trust farm solutions using ASP.NET came with some obvious risks. Farm solutions are hosted in the IIS worker process (`W3WP.exe`), so the scope of possible impact is wide. Fully customized code can, and sometimes does, contain errors. A poorly created web part could bring down an entire SharePoint farm. For this reason, farm solutions are no longer allowed in SharePoint 2019 and SharePoint Online.

- **Sandbox solutions**: Sandbox solutions use `SPUCWorkerProcess.exe`. Code is contained in the SharePoint user code solution worker process. Sandbox solution code cannot affect the entire farm and its impact is contained to the site collection that the solution targets. Since the sandbox solution does not involve the IIS worker process and IIS application pool or IIS server, it does not have to be restarted. With the rollout of sandbox solutions in SharePoint 2010, site collection administrators were able to deploy solutions specific to their site collection without having high-level farm admin rights.

- **Script injection**: With the rollout of SharePoint 2013, Microsoft made the pivot to its preference for using the client-side framework for the development of custom master pages and branding. With this change, we began to see the move toward JavaScript injection. This method allows developers to write custom applications and push those scripts onto the page. Utilizing client-side development, users were able to add, modify, or remove elements from the SharePoint page.

- **App model (add-ins)**: Starting with SharePoint 2013, Microsoft began to recommend that development within SharePoint use the app model. Within the app model, solutions are packaged in a `.APP` file. This file contains many files, including the SharePoint solution packages, any custom actions or customized app parts, web deployment packages, and more. As we stated in *Chapter 7, Finalizing the Farm to Go Live – Part II*, start to migrate your farm solutions to the add-in model to position yourself for migration to the cloud.

Please refer to the links in the *Further reading* section for more information on SPFx.

What is SPFx?

Now that we've explored the previously popular methods of SharePoint development, let's look at Microsoft's current development method, SPFx. SPFx is a Node.js and TypeScript development platform. One of the great benefits of SPFx is that it provides a faster browser experience. Another benefit is that SPFx is automatically responsive, so no matter the device, solutions will render in the appropriate aspect.

SPFx is used in the development of pages and web parts for SharePoint 2019 and SharePoint Online. In this chapter, we will give an overview of the latest SharePoint framework, as it relates to SharePoint 2019 in SharePoint online. We will briefly discuss how this framework is used in Microsoft Teams development as well. The Microsoft SharePoint framework is a client-side tool that gives developers what they need to extend SharePoint and create client-side solutions to best serve their customers' needs. See the following comparison chart, which gives a quick snapshot of the key differences between traditional SharePoint development and SPFx:

Comparison	Dev Server	Package	Templates	Build Tasks	Language	Editor
Traditional SharePoint Development	IIS Express	NuGet	Visual Studios Project Templates	MSBuild	C # and Javascript	Visual Studio
SPFX	Node.js	NPM	Yeoman	Gulp	TypeScript	Visual Studio Code

Figure 12.9 – Traditional SharePoint development versus SPFx

In this chapter, we will not do a deep dive into development methods and coding; however, Packt Publishing has a book that does a deep dive into SPFx. We will give details on how to set up your development environment and discuss some of the best practices to remember when developing solutions. The following are some of the key features of SPFx:

- SPFx client-side solutions can be used on all SharePoint sites, unless limited by the administrator.

- SPFx solutions can be created to extend the functionality of Microsoft Teams.

- Client-side web parts can be built using HTML or JavaScript.

- SPFx applies to both SharePoint Online and on-premises.

- SPFx is framework-agnostic, therefore you can use any JavaScript framework.

- The SharePoint client-side framework is supported both on-premises and online. Therefore, solutions created for the on-premises environment will migrate to SharePoint Online. This is important when road-mapping for the future state of your environment.

- Due to the use of common open source client-side development tools, developers that were not SharePoint developers before can now develop SharePoint solutions using SPFx.

- SPFx web parts can be added to classic and modern pages.

- SPFx can be used to create both client-based web parts and extensions that customize applications, commands set, and fields in lists or libraries.

Now that we have something of an understanding of what a developer can do, let's look at how we can create a server environment to support our new learning. We need to use the environment we created to try and develop on the platform. This will help us to understand how the developer tools are set up but, most importantly, give us a place to play with those tools once they are installed. If you are planning to take classes, this is the best way to get started as while learning, you can also do each lesson on your development servers. This will capture what you learned as well as giving you a way to enhance what you learned by making changes to those lessons within the class later after the class is over. So, let's dive into setting up our development environment!

Setting up a development environment to create SharePoint framework solutions

When setting up your development environment, you could use Visual Studio or a custom development environment to build your SharePoint framework solutions, and you can build these in Windows, macOS, or on the Linux platform. Please take the following listed steps to set up your development environment. Microsoft has recently moved from SPFx version 1.10 to version 1.11. As always, when following the instructions, check the documentation and make sure that you are installing the correct versions of development software. The following steps apply to SPFx 1.11.

The first thing that you need to do to set up a development environment is install Node.js. See the following chart for the Node.js version needed:

SharePoint Version	Node.js Version
SharePoint 2019	v10.x.x
SharePoint Online	v10.x.x
SharePoint 2016	v8.x.x

Figure 12.10 – Determine the version you need

> **Note**
> Node.js v9.x, v11.x, and v12.x are not supported in SPFx development.

You can check to see whether you already have Node.js by using the following steps:

1. Open Command Prompt in PowerShell.

2. Type `Node-v` in the command line.

3. Press *Enter*.

If you have no version of Node.js installed or a version other than the currently supported v10.x.x for SharePoint 2019 and SharePoint Online, you must use the following steps to download the correct Node.js version.

Install Node.js

Let's look at the steps to install Node.js:

1. Navigate to the following link: `https://nodejs.org/en/download/releases/`.

2. Choose **Node.js 10.x**:

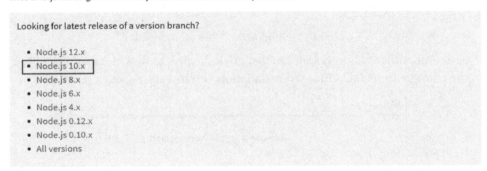

Figure 12.11 – Choosing the version you want to install

3. You will see a list of Node.js versions. At the time of this book's creation, the supported version of Node.js is 10.22.1. If you are using Windows, choose either the 64-bit or 86-bit MSI version depending on your machine:

Figure 12.12 – Finding MSI files for installation

4. My compatible version is x64. Double-click the link to download and double-click the package to install. Once the installation window opens, click **Next**:

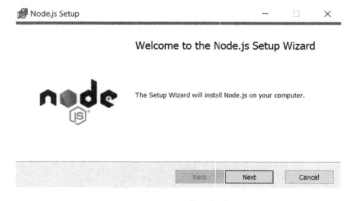

Figure 12.13 – Install splash screen

5.   Read then accept the licensing agreement, and then click **Next**:

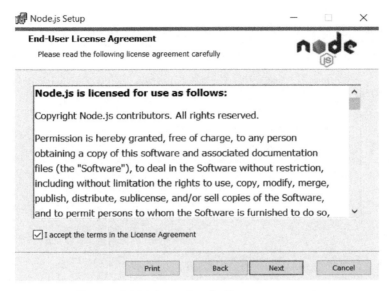

Figure 12.14 – Accepting the license agreement

6.   Choose the location for installation or go with the default:

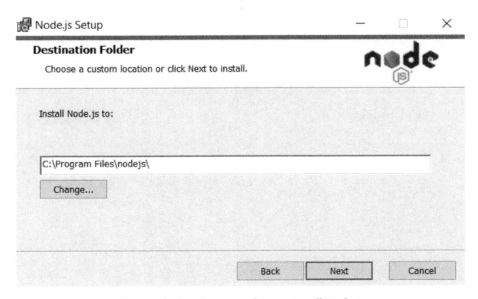

Figure 12.15 – Choosing where to install Node.js

7. Select **Next**:

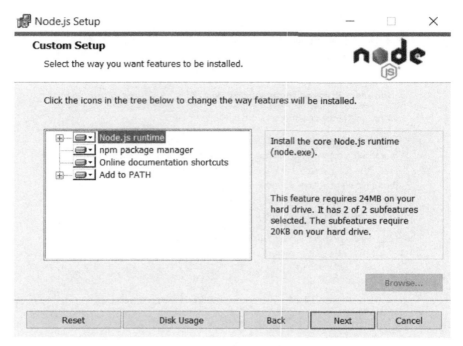

Figure 12.16 – Choosing features

8. Click the **Install** button to begin installation:

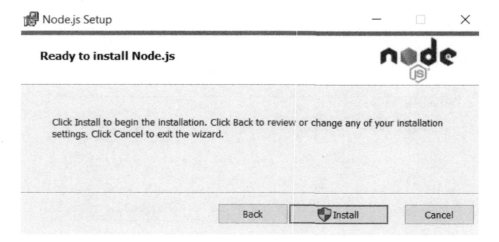

Figure 12.17 – Installation screen

9.   Allow the package to copy files to your machine:

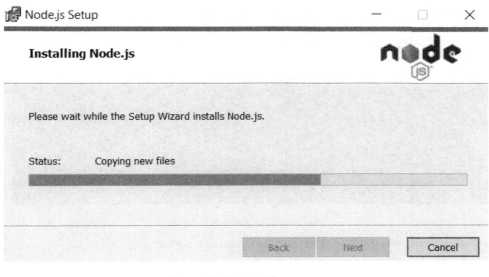

Figure 12.18 – Install progress

10. Click **Finish**:

Figure 12.19 – Finishing setup

11. Verify that Node.js is installed on your computer by using the following command:

```
Node -v
```

And you will see the following as result:

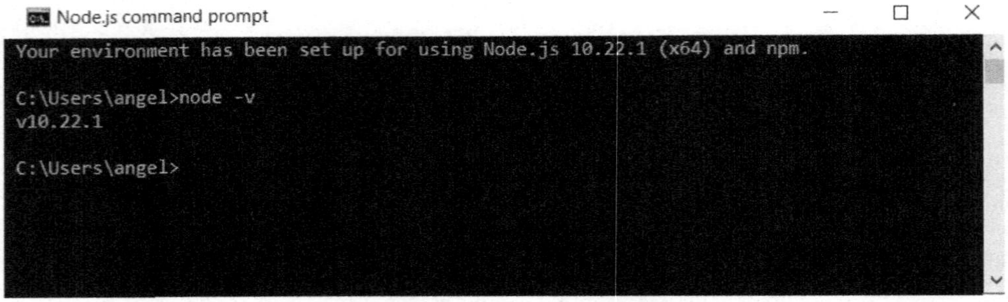

Figure 12.20 – Node.js is ready

Now that we have installed Node.js, let's install a code editor.

Visual Studio setup

Whether you are using Visual Studio or a different product as your code editor, it is important that you have your structure and naming conventions determined. Please take the time up front to design a proper project structure and naming convention within your editor and stick with this throughout not only your current project but also future projects. Having a standardized naming convention will help you organize your projects and provide knowledge transfer when the time comes. There is nothing worse in the world of tech than having an application break and going to view the source code and not being able to make head nor tail of what you find in the code repository.

Installing Visual Studio Code

If you do not have a code editor installed already, you need to install one. In this book, we will use Visual Studio Code as our editor. There are other choices you can look into, such as Atom or WebStorm, so see which one of these works for you. To install Visual Studio Code, follow these steps:

1. Navigate to the Visual Studio Code site located at `https://code/visualstudio.com` and click the **Download for Windows** button:

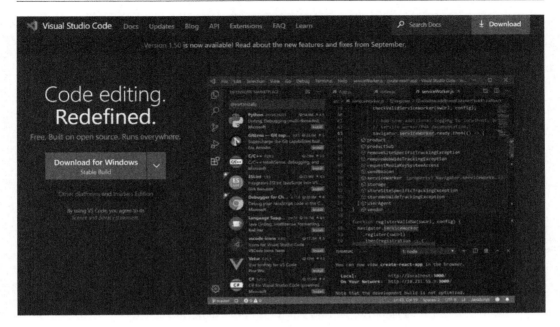

Figure 12.21 – Visual Studio download page

2. Double-click the downloaded package to begin the installation. Accept the license agreement, then click **Next**:

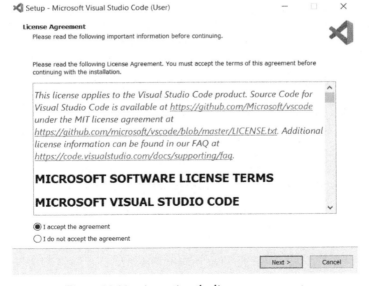

Figure 12.22 – Accepting the license agreement

3. Choose the location of the installation or keep the default:

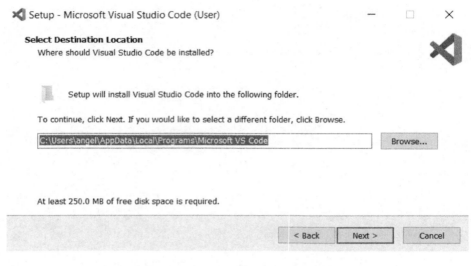

Figure 12.23 – Choosing the location of the install

4. Choose the location of the shortcut or keep the default:

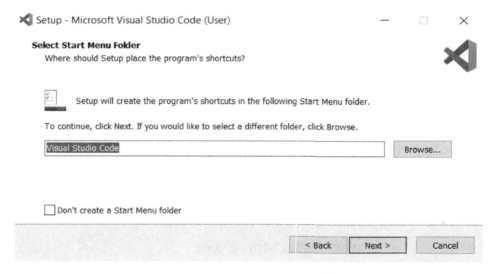

Figure 12.24 – Changing the start menu

5.   Select **Install**:

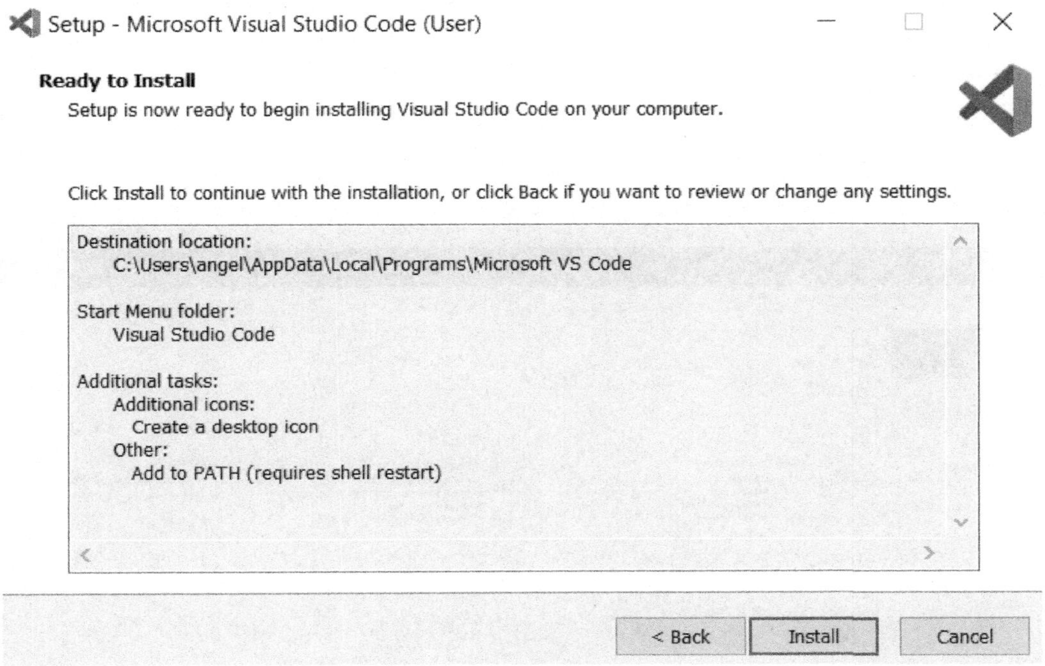

Figure 12.25 – Clicking to install

Visit the following link to learn more about packaging and deploying solutions in Visual Studio:

```
https://docs.microsoft.com/en-us/visualstudio/sharepoint/
packaging-and-deploying-sharepoint-solutions?view=vs-2019
```

Now that we have set up Visual Studio Code, let's look at creating an app catalog within SharePoint to support deploying web parts.

Creating an app catalog

To deploy web parts in SharePoint, you must first create an app catalog site. This is the location where the developed web parts will live. From the app catalog, you can deploy solutions throughout your SharePoint environment. Follow these steps to create an app catalog:

1. Navigate to SharePoint Central Administration.

    From the landing page, click on the **Apps** heading and select **Manage App Catalog**:

Figure 12.26 – Manage App Catalog

2. Select the web application where you want the app catalog.

3. Select **Create a new app catalog site** and click **OK**:

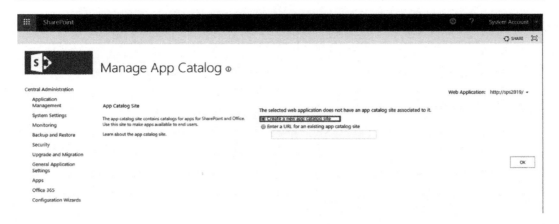

Figure 12.27 – Create a new app catalog

4. Add the details for the app catalog, including **Title**, **URL**, and the site collection admin details, and then click **OK**:

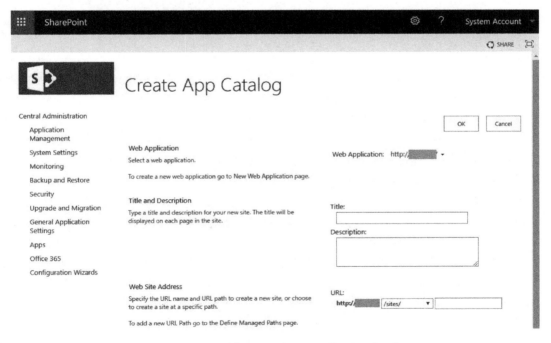

Figure 12.28 – Filling out the site collection details

> **Note.**
>
> The site collection creation may take a few moments. Once it is created, you will be able to install SharePoint framework solutions on the app catalog site.

More prerequisites for SPFx

Yeoman and Gulp are both prerequisites that must be installed for SPFx. Yeoman provides the project templates for your development work and Gulp is the task runner for SPFx.

To install Yeoman and Gulp globally, run the following command:

```
Npm install -g yo gulp
```

In addition to installing Yeoman and Gulp globally, you need to install the Yeoman SharePoint generator. The Yeoman SharePoint generator allows you to create client-side solutions using the correct toolchain and project structure. The generator gives you the common build tools that you will need, as well as the basic code, and supplies the "playground" websites for testing.

To install the Yeoman SharePoint generator, use the following command:

```
Npm i -g @microsoft/generator-sharepoint
```

To call the Yeoman SharePoint generator, use the following command:

```
Yo
```

Additionally, the command line can be used to scaffold projects instead of going through the interface prompts. You can use the following command to return a list of command-line options:

```
yo @microsoft/sharepoint --help
```

To learn more about scaffolding SharePoint development projects using the Yeoman generator, please visit the following link:

```
https://docs.microsoft.com/en-us/sharepoint/dev/spfx/
toolchain/scaffolding-projects-using-yeoman-sharepoint-
generator
```

In the next section, let's go over the steps to upgrade an SPFx project to the latest version.

Upgrading existing SharePoint development projects from SPFx version 1.10 to version 1.11

Microsoft recently upgraded SPFx from version 1.10 to version 1.11. If you already have existing development packages created in version 1.10, you can take the following steps to upgrade your package to version 1.11:

1. Navigate to the `package.json` file to locate all of the packages using SPFx version 1.10. You will need to use the package name in the console.

2. To uninstall version 1.10, use the following:

```
npm uninstall @microsoft/{spfx-package-name}@1.10
```

3. To install version 1.11, use the following:

```
npm install @microsoft/{spfx-package-name}@1.11 --save
--save-exact
```

Make sure that you update the package solution with the developer information. This is a new addition with SPFx and if you do not update this, you will get an error during the Gulp package solution process.

Visit this link to learn more about the process to update the developer info:

```
https://docs.microsoft.com/en-us/sharepoint/dev/spfx/
toolchain/sharepoint-framework-toolchain
```

New features of SPFx version 1.11 are as follows:

- Now supports SharePoint framework solutions via AppSource and Marketplace
- The ability to have your web parts exposed in Teams messages
- Additional developer information metadata fields
- The ability to preview images for a web part

Deprecated features in SPFx version 1.11 are as follows:

- No more support for `system.js` in the local workbench.
- Node.js v8 is no longer supported as discussed earlier; the accepted version is Node. js v10.xx.
- In this new version, Microsoft has removed the Knockout web framework option when creating web parts. Knockout can still be used but the default scaffolding is no longer available.

In the next section, we will discuss the SharePoint Framework toolchain. The vast array of open source development packages available will provide you with a head-start in developing client-side solutions. Be sure to visit the links included in the section to learn more.

The SharePoint Framework toolchain

The SharePoint Framework toolchain is a set of development tools and framework packages that allow the developer to build end-to-end client-side solutions and deploy these projects. Some SharePoint developers may have issues with this new approach to SharePoint development. However, developing via the modern web development toolchain is already very popular throughout the development industry and it is now the way of the future for SharePoint development:

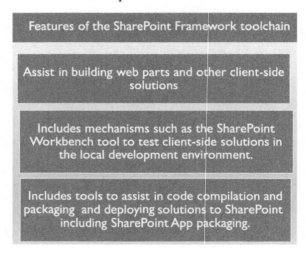

Figure 12.29 – SharePoint Framework features

Node.js changes coming soon

Microsoft now owns NPM, which was the largest software registry in the world. NPM is a package manager for JavaScript. NPM is popular primarily because of the open source Node.js. Microsoft has been betting on open source for the past few years and they have strengthened their position in the open source world by also purchasing GitHub, which is also widely used today. Since the purchase, they plan to integrate NPM with GitHub. Open an account today and get access to learn, see what's trending, access open source guides, and so much more:

```
https://github.com/
```

In addition to being an open source online repository, NPM is also a command-line utility. You have seen many of the commands run in this chapter start with NPM; this is because NPM commands are used to install packages and manage versions and dependencies. If you run the `npm install` command from the root of your package, it will automatically install the dependencies associated with the package. This saves precious time in the development process and helps to minimize dependency errors in your project.

NPM has a large website that contains open source packages from all over the world and, as mentioned, is also now a part of GitHub. Packages from NPM can be adapted to fit your SPFx projects. The CLI is run from your terminal to interact with NPM. NPM also consists of a large registry of JavaScript and the metadata around it.

Visit the following link for NPM open source packages: `https://www.npmjs.com/`.

Next, we will walk through the steps to build your first client-side SPFX web part.

Develop a Client side WebPart

The following steps can be used to create a very simple web part. Of course, the options and complexity of building web parts are endless as your skill set grows. Although, in depth development is beyond the scope of this book, we wanted to show you a quick example to get you started. Follow these steps to begin:

1. From the PowerShell Admin console create a project directory using the following command:

```
Md myfirstspfx-webpart
```

Which results in:

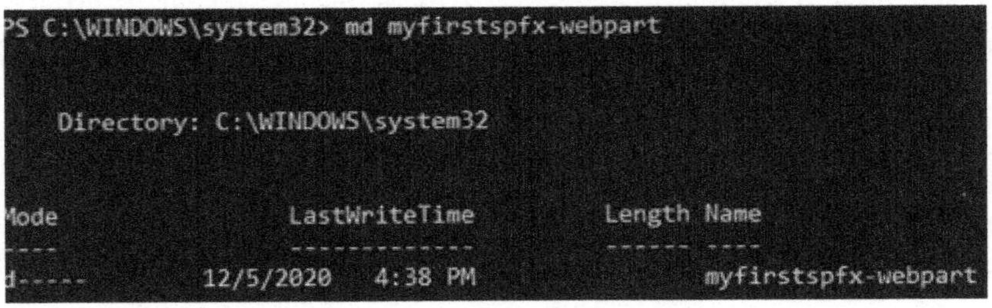

Figure 12.30: Create the project Directory

2. Navigate to the newly created project directory via Powershell:

```
cd myfirstspfx-webpart
```

Which results in:

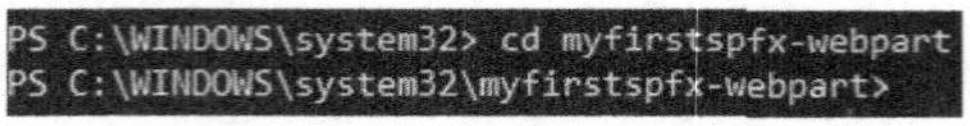

```
PS C:\WINDOWS\system32> cd myfirstspfx-webpart
PS C:\WINDOWS\system32\myfirstspfx-webpart>
```

Figure 12.31: Navigating to the New Directory

3. Run Yeoman SharePoint Generator

```
Yo @microsoft/sharepoint
```

Which gives us the following result:

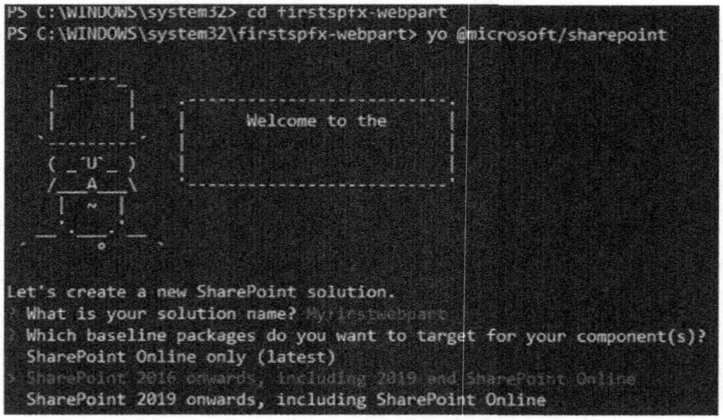

```
PS C:\WINDOWS\system32> cd firstspfx-webpart
PS C:\WINDOWS\system32\firstspfx-webpart> yo @microsoft/sharepoint


    _-----_
   |       |    .--------------------------.
   |       |    |   Welcome to the         |
   ( _'U'_ )    |                          |
   /___A___\    '--------------------------'
    |  ~  |
  __'.___.'__
·´   `  |° ´ Y `

Let's create a new SharePoint solution.
? What is your solution name? Myfirstwebpart
? Which baseline packages do you want to target for your component(s)?
  SharePoint Online only (latest)
  SharePoint 2016 onwards, including 2019 and SharePoint Online
  SharePoint 2019 onwards, including SharePoint Online
```

Figure 12.32: Run Yeoman Generator

Answer the questions about the new webpart, including the solution name, target environment, and whether to allow deployment of this web part to all sites.

4. Once you answer the final question, you will see the creation of the Webpart Scaffolding as shown in the following screen:

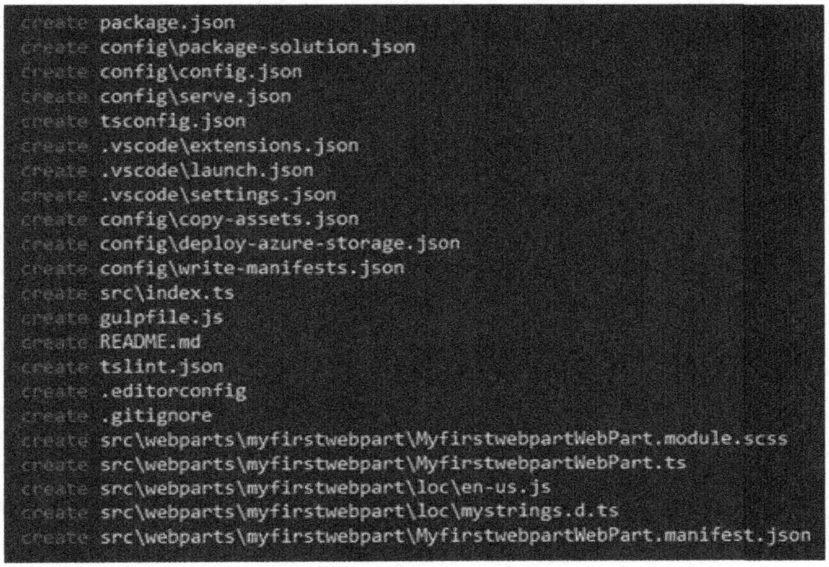

```
create  package.json
create  config\package-solution.json
create  config\config.json
create  config\serve.json
create  tsconfig.json
create  .vscode\extensions.json
create  .vscode\launch.json
create  .vscode\settings.json
create  config\copy-assets.json
create  config\deploy-azure-storage.json
create  config\write-manifests.json
create  src\index.ts
create  gulpfile.js
create  README.md
create  tslint.json
create  .editorconfig
create  .gitignore
create  src\webparts\myfirstwebpart\MyfirstwebpartWebPart.module.scss
create  src\webparts\myfirstwebpart\MyfirstwebpartWebPart.ts
create  src\webparts\myfirstwebpart\loc\en-us.js
create  src\webparts\myfirstwebpart\loc\mystrings.d.ts
create  src\webparts\myfirstwebpart\MyfirstwebpartWebPart.manifest.json
```

Figure 12.33: Scaffolding

5. Once the scaffolding completes, you will see the below message of a successful Web Part creation:

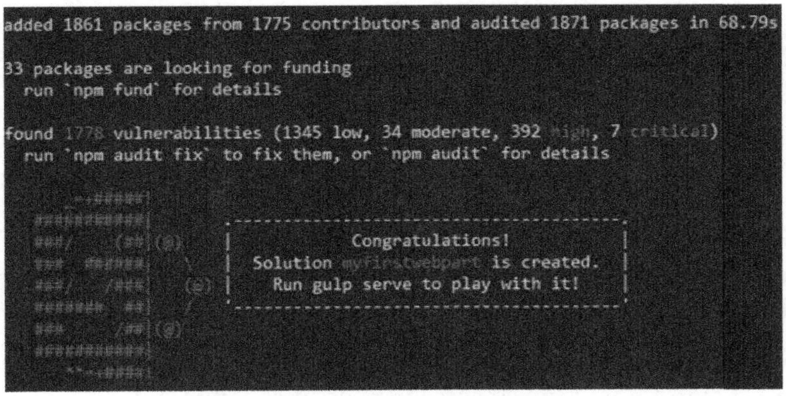

```
added 1861 packages from 1775 contributors and audited 1871 packages in 68.79s

33 packages are looking for funding
  run `npm fund` for details

found 1778 vulnerabilities (1345 low, 34 moderate, 392 high, 7 critical)
  run `npm audit fix` to fix them, or `npm audit` for details


   -+#####|
 #########|
 ###/    (##|(@)              -------------------------------------
 ### ######|    \             |          Congratulations!          |
 ###/  /###|     (@)          |    Solution myfirstwebpart is created. |
 ####### ##|    /             |     Run gulp serve to play with it!  |
 ###     /##|(@)              -------------------------------------
 #########|
   **-+####|
```

Figure 12.34: Solution Creation Successful

6. Since the client-side toolchain uses the HTTPS endpoint, you must install the developer Trust Certificate by using the following command:

```
gulp trust-dev-cert
```

7. Run the following command to preview and build onto the new webpart:

```
gulp serve
```

8. Your Web part preview will open in SharePoint Workbench.

Now that you have the information you need to set up your development environment and create your first SPFx web part, let us turn our attention to developer best practices so that you can create successful solutions and steer clear of any trouble.

Developer best practices

In this section, we will discuss developer best practices. Regardless of your deployment method or the system you are deploying to, it is important to keep in mind deployment best practices. Following best practices will get you much closer to realizing a successful deployment. Ignoring best practices will most definitely get you in a world of hurt eventually. First of all, every development rollout should have a plan; whether you are following the waterfall method where you follow your plan out from beginning to end or you are utilizing an Agile approach where you roll out shorter iterations and improve as you go, you must document your plan from the beginning all the way through to completion.

Requirement gathering

Requirement gathering can seem like the easy part of the development process – after all, you're only speaking with your customers and figuring out what they want and what they need in the development solution. However, this is the portion of development that can lead to a poor product or an upset customer who thought they were requesting one thing and you deliver another. The best way to avoid this is to make sure that you have the proper stakeholders in the room when you are gathering requirements. Make sure that the decision-makers are in the room and that those decision-makers, once you have gathered the full list of requirements, are willing to sign off on the finalized document.

In the statement of work or whatever agreement document it is that will cover this rollout, make sure that clauses are included to ensure that if requirements are changed by the customer, then the timeline and cost will have to be adjusted to accommodate these changes. The stakeholders need to know this from the beginning before you document the set of requirements. Let them know that changes can occur; however, changes will come at a cost, and that cost may be scrapping the entire development project and starting from the beginning.

Take a look at the following chart for a quick-glance view of some important requirement gathering techniques.

The following list is not an exhaustive list of requirement gathering techniques. However, these are the points that you must remember to cover when gathering requirements from clients. As you begin to gather more requirements for solutions, you can add additional techniques to the following list that have worked well for you:

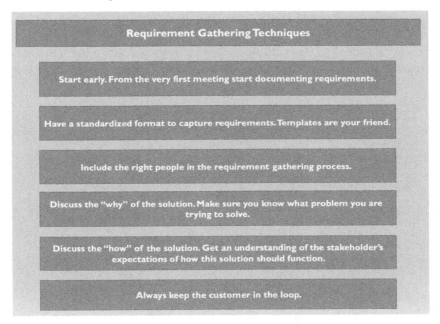

Figure 12.35 – Requirement gathering techniques

Many stakeholders and project teams will want to have the technical specifications for the development process in place before the actual development begins. This is one of the advantages of the waterfall method because you can build in your planning phase; you can build the creation of all of the technical specifications into the project plan before you ever develop your first piece of code for the project.

However, in the world of SharePoint, many of the stakeholders will not know exactly what they want until they see an actual representation of it. So, of course, if you follow this process and build out the development before your stakeholders get to try it, you risk finding out that what you developed was not what they needed. Communication gaps in development between project teams and stakeholders can often lead us down this road. Once you are so far down this road that the stakeholder can actually test the product that you have developed for them, you may find out that it is not indeed what they wanted and it may be too late – and oftentimes it is.

That is why we highly recommend the Agile approach to development. Agile does not mean development done on the fly; you still need a solid plan that outlines all of the stages. However, the iterative nature of Agile development will allow you to roll out the first stage, have your stakeholders test it and see whether you're going down the right path, and make corrections if necessary before you move on to the next stage. This method of development can lead to a successful deployment without the need for scrapping an entire project that did not meet the customers' needs.

Take a look at the following chart to see the stages of a development cycle.

Whether you are following a waterfall development approach or an Agile approach, the standard stages of development still apply. With an Agile approach, you will cycle through the development stages multiple times:

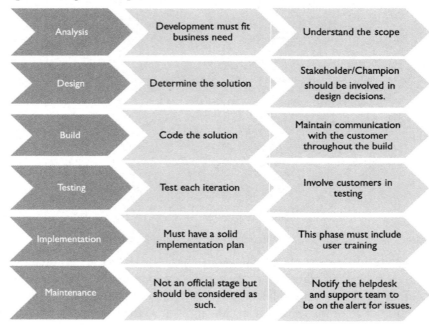

Figure 12.36 – Software development stages

The development cycle is very important to learn. In some organizations, you may see different variations of this or no development process at all. You also want to make sure you follow what works for you within this process to suit the specific processes that you encounter. Make sure you figure out where you can insert your own personal process cycle in there as well. *Figure 12.31* gives you the basics, but remember to always modify it where you have to so that the development cycle works to support successful deployments.

Preproduction environments

The standard preproduction environments that you will be required to stand up and maintain for SharePoint development is the development environment and the **User Acceptance Testing (UAT)** environment. However, the development environment and UAT are the bare minima and these two environments often fail to offer enough testing of the new solution before deployment. It is recommended that in addition to the aforementioned environments, you stand up a **System Integration Testing (SIT)** or performance testing environment and a quality assurance environment:

- **Development environment**: The development environment is usually not an exact replica of the production environment. However, this environment should have all of the necessary elements for the developer to deploy and test the functionality of the newly created solution before deployment to the SIT environment.

- **SIT**: This is an extremely important step to ensure that the newly developed solution will seamlessly integrate into your existing platform. SIT is performed to test that all of the components of the SharePoint system perform to expectations after the deployment of a developed solution to catch any system issues that could occur before the solution is deployed in production. In some organizations, SIT is performed by the administrator of the SharePoint environment; in others, SIT is performed by the quality assurance team.

- **UAT**: UAT may be the most important stage to a successful deployment. Make sure that your UAT environment is in great condition as all of your environments should be. Have patches applied regularly and set up this environment to simulate the production environment as closely as possible. Test scripts should be created for all UATs.

If your organization is small, you may not have a quality assurance team; however, you can include other members of the technical team, including the capacity monitoring team. In most small shops, you would most likely do this testing yourself. This SIT should not be performed by the same person who developed the solution as this can lead to missed issues or reworking of code directly in SIT, which should never happen. The SIT environment should match your production environment. This is very important because if these environments do not match, production issues may not be caught before they reach production.

Most enterprise organizations have a quality assurance team; this team sits apart from your internal IT team and is tasked with rigorously testing solutions before they are deployed into production. Having a quality assurance environment is a bonus as this quality assurance team will maintain access to the environment and can easily test the developed solutions before deployment into production. However, some small companies will not have a separate quality assurance environment but that's OK; the quality assurance team can utilize the UAT environment for their testing.

The success or failure of your deployment depends on having good-quality test scripts that cover all of the functionality expected from the solution. Make sure that you understand how the business will utilize this solution, how they will access this solution, and how they perform their work day to day; these aspects should be covered in the test scripts. When creating test scripts, place yourself in the shoes of the business user and remember to write test scripts to cover the different roles of the users. Testing is an easy place to slack off. Do not get lazy here as it will cost you. Make sure all the functionality has been tested.

Testers

Choosing testers for the developed solution is extremely important. We've already discussed quality assurance performing testing on the solutions that you build; however, quality assurance will be testing the functionality of the solutions and possibly the logistics and ease of use from their perspective. However, members of the quality assurance team are typically very technologically savvy, and this may lead to an ease of use of the product that may not be experienced by the user.

You must have the user community involved in your testing. We caution you not to just hand over the test scripts, go away, and then come back for sign off. Testing your solution is not your users' primary job; they may be busy with other activities and not prioritize fully testing the solution. Users have been known to sign off on solutions that they have not thoroughly tested. This is why it is important to have the stakeholders engaged, as they are actually accountable for the success of this rollout. If the stakeholders are accountable, they are more likely to have a vested interest in the success of the solution. Choose your testers wisely and always get sign off from multiple stakeholders and their management.

Capacity planning

When you are developing and deploying solutions into an on-premises environment, you must consider the performance configuration of the platform before you start development.

Consider jobs running on the servers, search configurations that could drain capacity, and available storage on the platform for logs and data. Many times, developers create solutions in a silo, which can lead to overzealous development that does not take into account the actual limitations of the environment.

For instance, if a large number of users are going to be accessing a developed solution at the same time or the solution will lead to a heavy influx of documents to be stored in SharePoint, as in this example, this must be planned for with the capacity teams. If you are a one-person IT shop, then you must make sure that your environment is configured and revved up to handle the upswing in usage and storage.

List limits

When creating solutions, always keep in mind the SharePoint list limits and be sure that you are not designing a solution that will quickly breach those limitations. Use the following link to learn more about SharePoint limits: `https://docs.microsoft.com/en-us/sharepoint/install/software-boundaries-and-limits-0`.

Timeout issue

If the development solution is meant to ingest large files, you must configure the file upload size limits. Be aware that users can face timeout issues with large file uploads.

SharePoint on-premises is not the best place for extremely large files that eat up tons of storage space. This is where good governance will come into play.

If everyone developing, managing, and using solutions understands the limits, then it will be easier to prevent these types of issues. SharePoint storage is expensive; the use of connectors in your development can help to overcome timeout issues and storage limits. If the organization has access to other storage systems, then connectors can be developed to store the document external to SharePoint while allowing users to view the documents within SharePoint. This is a great method to consider if you run into this sort of issue because it alleviates the large storage expense while still taking advantage of the user interface and features of SharePoint that the users love.

Enterprise security

Begin with enterprise security in mind. You must follow the security standards of your organization. Do not wait until you are halfway through development, or even worse, finished with development and in production, to realize that your application goes against a policy. Make sure that you are familiar with the enterprise security policies before you begin development. It is often a good idea to have a meeting with the enterprise security group in the design phase to get initial approval and check that nothing you are developing is breaking any policies.

Summary

Microsoft has made it clear that the SharePoint development framework is the way of the future. Microsoft over the years has made the steady move from farm solutions to sandbox solutions to app solutions, and this in turn has made developing on the platform less risky and more uniform. Additionally, since SPFx uses common open source client development tools, traditional SharePoint developers who embraced this new way would now not be limited to only developing for SharePoint but could begin developing cross-platform. In the same vein, the agnostic framework has opened up the world of SharePoint development to developers that did not traditionally work in SharePoint. SPFx can be used to develop solutions both on-premises and on SharePoint Online. This standardized development method is great because as many organizations are looking to move their technological footprint from on-premises to the cloud, we must begin to create solutions even while on-premises that will migrate easily when the day comes.

Best practices should always be considered and adhered to when creating solutions. Taking the time to gather clear requirements is extremely important. You must make sure that you are building the solution that the client is expecting. Understanding the client's expectations occurs by listening to your client's needs and understanding the business problem that they need to solve. You need to work with the client throughout the entire development process to be sure that you are on track to providing that solution.

In this book, we tried to cover as much as we could to give you insights on what is new, what has changed, and what tools and knowledge you need to move forward in this new cloud-integrated SharePoint Server 2019 application. There are many people that work in this type of deployment and we hope we have touched on enough topics to give you insight into those teams and responsibilities, and enough technical information to get you moving on your project with confidence. Some of the topics on SharePoint 2019 require deeper knowledge and research, which we pointed out during the course of the book.

There was no way we could add any more to those areas in the book. When talking about technology, there are areas that require another book to learn what those technologies consist of. We recommend researching those areas and learning more about how you can implement SharePoint 2019 effectively from all standpoints. We hope this book has given you a good insight into implementing SharePoint 2019.

Questions

You can find the answers on GitHub under Assessments at `https://github.com/PacktPublishing/Implementing-Microsoft-SharePoint-2019/blob/master/Assessments.docx`

1. In SPFx, Node.js v8.xx is currently supported. True or false?

    a) True

    b) False

2. If you are an engineer who can create both frontend and backend fully functional web applications, which of the following do you qualify as?

    a) DevOps engineer

    b) Full stack engineer

    c) Frontend engineer

3. When dealing with client requirements, what is it best practice to do?

    a) Speak with the client once, midway through development.

    b) Gather requirements early on and continue to communicate with the client as requirements are refined and throughout the development process.

    c) Gather all requirements from a junior member of the client staff and never speak to the decision-makers.

4. What is NPM?

    a) NPM is an open source Node.js software repository.

    b) NPM is a product owned by IBM and is used to configure Azure.

    c) NPM is a project management certification.

5. SharePoint PowerShell allows you to manage Office 365 and Azure. True or false?

    a) True

    b) False

6. What is the proper order of the development cycle?

    a) Implementation, analysis, build, testing, design, maintenance

    b) Analysis, design, testing, build, implementation, testing

    c) Analysis, design, build, testing, implementation, maintenance

7. SPFx web parts can be used on both classic and modern pages. True or false?

    a) True

    b) False

Further reading

For more information on SPFx, check out the following links:

- `https://docs.microsoft.com/en-us/sharepoint/dev/spfx/sharepoint-2019-support`

- `https://docs.microsoft.com/en-us/sharepoint/dev/spfx/sharepoint-framework-overview`

- `https://docs.microsoft.com/en-us/sharepoint/dev/spfx/release-1.11.0`

For more information on the SharePoint client library, check out `https://docs.microsoft.com/en-us/sharepoint/dev/sp-add-ins/complete-basic-operations-using-sharepoint-client-library-code`.

SharePoint code samples: `https://docs.microsoft.com/en-us/sharepoint/dev/general-development/code-samples-for-sharepoint`

SharePoint development center: `https://developer.microsoft.com/en-us/sharepoint`

SharePoint development documentation: `https://docs.microsoft.com/en-us/sharepoint/dev/`

Other Books You May Enjoy

If you enjoyed this book, you may be interested in these other books by Packt:

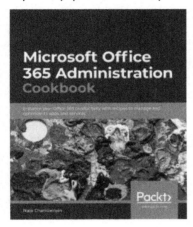

Microsoft Office 365 Administration Cookbook

Nate Chamberlain

ISBN: 978-1-83855-123-0

- Get to grips with basic Office 365 setup and routine administration tasks
- Manage Office 365 identities and groups efficiently and securely
- Harness the capabilities of PowerShell to automate common administrative tasks
- Configure and manage core Office 365 services such as Exchange Online, SharePoint, and OneDrive
- Configure and administer fast-evolving services such as Microsoft Search, Power Platform, Microsoft Teams, and Azure AD

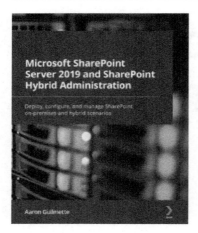

Microsoft SharePoint Server 2019 and SharePoint Hybrid Administration

Aaron Guilmette

ISBN: 978-1-80056-373-5

- Understand how SharePoint Server technologies enable you to collaborate
- Deploy and configure SharePoint Server 2019
- Configure and manage SharePoint site collections
- Manage data migration with SharePoint's migration tools
- Explore Business Connectivity Services (BCS) for working with external data sources
- Get to grips with the different types of authentication available in the SharePoint ecosystem

Leave a review - let other readers know what you think

Please share your thoughts on this book with others by leaving a review on the site that you bought it from. If you purchased the book from Amazon, please leave us an honest review on this book's Amazon page. This is vital so that other potential readers can see and use your unbiased opinion to make purchasing decisions, we can understand what our customers think about our products, and our authors can see your feedback on the title that they have worked with Packt to create. It will only take a few minutes of your time, but is valuable to other potential customers, our authors, and Packt. Thank you!

Index

T

Hittites

MEDITERRANEAN SEA

PHOENICIA

Arameans

Sidon •
• Damascus

Tyre •
△ Mt Hermon

Plain of
Esdraelon

• Megiddo

ISRAEL

Shechem •

Jordan River

GILEAD

AMMON

PHILISTIA

Beth-
shemesh •
Jericho •
• Jerusalem

• Bethlehem

Gaza •
• Hebron •

Dead Sea

JUDAH

• Beersheba

MOAB

Amalekites

• Kadesh-barnea

• Petra

EDOM

• Ezion-geber

Sinai

Gulf of Aqaba

Palestine in the Time of David

Encyclopedia
of **the Bible**

Encyclopedia of the Bible

of the Bible

VOLUME 2 **J–Z**

Walter A. Elwell

General Editor

Associate Editors
Peter C. Craigie
J. D. Douglas
Robert Guelich
R. K. Harrison
Thomas E. McComiskey

Assistant Editors

Barry J. Beitzel
H. Douglas Buckwalter
Walter R. Hearn
Virginia K. Hearn
James S. McClanahan
Robert L. Morrison
Stephen Taylor
R. Milton Winter
Ronald F. Youngblood

MARSHALL PICKERING

Marshall Morgan and Scott
Marshall Pickering
34–42 Cleveland Street, London, W1P 5FB. U.K.

Copyright © 1988

ISBN: 0-551-01970-0 Volume 1
       0-551-02052-0 Volume 2

First published in the UK 1990
by Marshall Morgan and Scott Publications Ltd
Pickering and Inglis Ltd
Part of Marshall Pickering Holdings Group

Portions of the text of this volume were originally prepared by
Tyndale House Publishers, Inc., and have been used with
permission.

Printed in the United States of America

Contributors

Alden, Robert L. Ph.D., Hebrew Union College. Professor of Old Testament, Denver Seminary, Denver, Colorado.

Alexander, Ralph H. Th.D., Dallas Theological Seminary. Professor of Hebrew Scripture, Western Conservative Baptist Seminary, Portland, Oregon.

Allen, Leslie C. Ph.D., University of London. Professor of Old Testament, Fuller Theological Seminary, Pasadena, California.

Allen, Ronald B. Th.D., Dallas Theological Seminary. Chairman, Division of Biblical Studies; Professor of Hebrew Scripture, Western Baptist Seminary, Portland, Oregon.

Archer, Gleason L. Ph.D., Harvard University. Professor Emeritus Old Testament and Semitic Languages, Trinity Evangelical Divinity School, Deerfield, Illinois.

Aune, David E. Ph.D., University of Chicago. Professor of Religious Studies, Saint Xavier College, Chicago, Illinois.

Babcock, James F. M.Div., Trinity Evangelical Divinity School. Senior Technical Training Instructor, Gould Inc., Information Systems Computer Systems Division, Greenbelt, Maryland.

Barber, Cyril J. D.Min., Talbot Theological Seminary. Counselor, Insight for Living, California.

Barker, Kenneth L. Ph.D., Dropsie College for Hebrew and Cognate Learning. Academic Dean and Professor of Old Testament Literature and Exegesis, Capitol Bible Seminary, Lanham, Maryland.

Bass, Clarence B. Ph.D., University of Edinburgh. Professor of Theology and Ethics, Bethel Theological Seminary, St. Paul, Minnesota.

Baylis, Albert H. Th.D., Dallas Theological Seminary. Chairman, Department of Theology, Multnomah School of the Bible, Portland, Oregon.

Beckman, L. David. Th.D., Dallas Theological Seminary. Chancellor, Professor of Biblical Studies, Colorado Christian College; Pastor, Windsor Gardens Community Church, Denver, Colorado.

Beitzel, Barry J. Ph.D., Dropsie University. Associate Dean of Education and Professor of Old Testament and Semitic Languages, Trinity Evangelical Divinity School, Deerfield, Illinois.

Benton, W. Wilson, Jr. Ph.D., University of Edinburgh. Senior Minister, The Kirk of the Hills Presbyterian Church, St. Louis, Missouri.

Bilezikian, Gilbert. Th.D., Boston University. Professor of Biblical Studies, Wheaton College, Wheaton, Illinois.

Blaiklock, E. M. Ph.D., University of Aukland. Sometime Professor Emeritus of Classics, University of Auckland, New Zealand.

Blankenbaker, George. Ph.D., Claremont Graduate School. Vice President and Academic Dean, Associate Professor of Religious Studies, Westmont College, Claremont, California.

Bodey, Richard Allen. D.Min., Trinity Evangelical Divinity School. Associate Professor of Practical Theology, Trinity Evangelical Divinity School, Deerfield, Illinois.

Borchert, Gerald L. Ph.D., Princeton Theological Seminary; LL.B., University of Alberta Law School. Professor of New Testament Interpretation, Southern Baptist Theological Seminary, Louisville, Kentucky.

Contributors

Brauch, Manfred T. Ph.D., McMaster University, Ontario. Maxwell Professor of Biblical Theology, Eastern Baptist Theological Seminary, Philadelphia, Pennsylvania.

Brown, Colin. Ph.D., University of Bristol. Professor of Systematic Theology, Fuller Theological Seminary, Pasadena, California.

Bruce, F. F. M.A., Universities of Aberdeen, Cambridge, Manchester. Emeritus Professor, University of Manchester, England.

Buckwalter, H. Douglas. M.A., Wheaton College. Doctoral student, University of Aberdeen, Scotland.

Buehler, William W. D.Theol., University of Basel. Professor of Biblical and Theological Studies, Gordon College, Wenham, Massachusetts.

Burge, Gary M. Ph.D., King's College, Aberdeen University. Department of Philosophy and Religion, North Park Theological Seminary, Chicago, Illinois.

Bush, Frederic W. Ph.D., Brandeis University. Associate Professor of Old Testament, Fuller Theological Seminary, Pasadena, California.

Campbell, Donald K. Th.D., Dallas Theological Seminary. President and Professor of Bible Exposition, Dallas Theological Seminary, Dallas, Texas.

Cannon, George E. Ph.D., Fuller Theological Seminary. Professor of New Testament, Bethel Theological Seminary, St. Paul, Minnesota.

Carlson, David C. Ph.D., University of Aberdeen. Associate Professor of Philosophy and Religion, Franklin College, Franklin, Indiana.

Carr, G. Lloyd. Ph.D., Boston University. Professor of Biblical and Theological Studies; Chairman, Division of Humanities, Gordon College, Wenham, Massachusetts.

Chamblin, J. Knox. Th.D., Union Theological Seminary in Virginia. Professor of New Testament, Reformed Theological Seminary, Jackson, Mississippi.

Congdon, Roger Douglass. Th.D., Dallas Theological Seminary. Professor of Bible, Multnomah School of the Bible, Portland, Oregon.

Coppenger, Mark T. Ph.D., Vanderbilt University. Pastor, First Baptist Church, El Dorado, Arkansas.

Craigie, Peter C. Ph.D., McMaster University. Formerly Dean, Faculty of Humanities, Calgary, Alberta, Canada.

Culver, Robert D. Th.D., Grace Theological Seminary. Freelance Author and Visiting Professor of Theology, Winnipeg Theological Seminary, Manitoba, Canada.

Davids, Peter H. Ph.D., University of Manchester. Adjunct Professor of New Testament, Regent College, Vancouver, British Columbia, Canada.

de Vries, Paul H. Ph.D., University of Virginia. Associate Professor of Philosophy and Coordinator of General Education, Wheaton College, Wheaton, Illinois.

DeVries, Carl E. Ph.D., University of Chicago. Retired, The Oriental Institute, University of Chicago. Research Associate, The Oriental Institute, University of Chicago. Retired.

DeYoung, James C. Th.D., Free University of Amsterdam. Professor of New Testament, Reformed Theological Seminary, Jackson, Mississippi.

Demarest, Bruce A. Ph.D., University of Manchester. Professor of Systematic Theology, Denver Seminary, Denver, Colorado.

Dillard, Raymond B. Ph.D., Dropsie University. Professor of Old Testament Language and Literature, Westminster Theological Seminary, Philadelphia, Pennsylvania.

Douglas, J. D. Ph.D., Hartford Seminary Foundation. Editor and writer.

Dunn, James D. G. Ph.D., Cambridge University. Professor of Divinity, University of Durham, England.

Earle, Ralph. Th.D., Gordon Divinity School. Emeritus Professor of New Testament, Nazarene Theological Seminary, Kansas City, Missouri.

Ecklebarger, Kermit A. M.A., Wheaton College. Associate Professor of New Testament, Denver Seminary, Denver, Colorado.

Erickson, Millard J. Ph.D., Northwestern University. Dean, Professor of Theology, Bethel Theological Seminary, St. Paul, Minnesota.

Ericson, Norman R. Ph.D., University of Chicago. Professor of New Testament; Chairman, Biblical, Theological, and Archaeological Studies, Wheaton College, Wheaton, Illinois.

Fackler, Mark. Ph.D., University of Illinois. Assistant Professor of Communication, Wheaton College, Wheaton, Illinois.

Farrell, Hobert K. Ph.D., Boston University. Professor of Biblical Studies, LeTourneau College, Longview, Texas.

Feinberg, Charles L. Th.D., Dallas Theological Seminary; Ph.D., Johns Hopkins University. Dean Emeritus and Professor Emeritus of Old Testament, Talbot Theological Seminary, La Mirada, California.

Field, David H. B.A., University of Cambridge. Vice-Principal, Oak Hill College, London, England.

Finley, Harvey E. Ph.D., Johns Hopkins University. Professor of Old Testament, Nazarene Theological Seminary, Kansas City, Missouri.

Fisher, Milton C. Ph.D., Brandeis University. Professor of Old Testament and Academic Dean, Reformed Episcopal Seminary, Philadelphia, Pennsylvania.

Foulkes, Francis. B.D., Oxford. Warden, St. John's College, Auckland, New Zealand.

Fowler, Paul B. Ph.D., University of Edinburgh. Professor of New Testament, Columbia Graduate School of Bible and Missions, Columbia, South Carolina.

Gaffin, Richard B., Jr. Th.D., Westminster Theological Seminary. Professor of Systematic Theology, Westminster Theological Seminary, Philadelphia, Pennsylvania.

Gerig, Wesley L. Ph.D., University of Iowa. Chairperson of the Division of Biblical Studies and Professor of Bible and Theology, Fort Wayne Bible College, Fort Wayne, Indiana.

Goldberg, Louis. Th.D., Grace Theological Seminary. Professor of Theology and Jewish Studies, Moody Bible Institute, Chicago, Illinois.

Guelich, Robert. D. Theol., University of Hamburg. Professor of New Testament, Fuller Theological Seminary, Pasadena, California.

Guthrie, Donald. Ph.D., University of London. Visiting Lecturer, London Bible College, London, England.

Haik, Paul S. Th.D., Dallas Theological Seminary. Profesor of Bible and Chairman, Department of Bible, Moody Bible Institute, Chicago, Illinois.

Harris, J. Gordon. Ph.D., Southern Baptist Seminary. Vice President for Academic Affairs, North American Baptist Seminary, Sioux Falls, South Dakota.

Harrison, R. K. Ph.D., University of London; D.D. (Hon.), Huron College, University of Western Ontario. Emeritus Professor of Old Testament Studies, Wycliffe College, University of Toronto, Ontario, Canada.

Hearn, Walter R. Ph.D., University of Illinois. Editor, American Scientific Affiliation Newsletter and Adjunct Professor of Science, New College for Advanced Christian Studies, Berkeley, California.

Hearn, Virginia K. B.A., Otterbein College. Editor; adjunct professor of communications, New College for Advanced Studies, Berkeley, California.

Helm, Paul. B.A., Oxford University. Senior Lecturer in Philosophy, University of Liverpool, England.

Henry, Carl F. H. Ph.D., Boston University. Lecturer-At-Large, World Division, Monrovia, California.

Hensley, C. L. V. Ph.D., University of Liverpool.

Hensley, Carl Wayne. Ph.D., University of Minnesota. Professor of Speech Communication, Bethel College, St. Paul, Minnesota.

Hill, Andrew E. Ph.D., University of Michigan. Assistant Professor of Old Testament, Wheaton College, Wheaton, Illinois.

Hoehner, Harold W. Ph.D., Cambridge University. Chairman and Professor of New Testament Literature and Exegesis; Director of Th.D. Studies, Dallas Theological Seminary, Dallas, Texas.

Hoffmeier, James K. Ph.D., University of Toronto. Associate Professor of Archaeology and Old Testament, Wheaton College, Wheaton, Illinois.

Holloman, Henry W. Th.D., Dallas Theological Seminary. Professor of Systematic Theology, Talbot School of Theology, La Mirada, California.

Holmes, Arthur F. Ph.D., Northwestern University. Professor of Philosophy, Wheaton College, Wheaton, Illinois.

Hopper, Mary. D.M.A., University of Iowa. Assistant Professor of Music, Wheaton College, Wheaton, Illinois.

Contributors

House, H. Wayne. Th.D., Concordia Theological Seminary; J.D., O.W. Coburn School of Law. Assistant Professor of Systematic Theology, Dallas Theological Seminary, Dallas, Texas.

Houston, James H. D.Phil., Oxford University. Professor of Spiritual Theology, Regent College, Vancouver, British Columbia, Canada.

Howe, E. Margaret. Ph.D., University of Manchester. Professor of Religious Studies, Western Kentucky University, Bowling Green, Kentucky.

Huey, F. B., Jr. Ph.D., Southwestern Baptist Theological Seminary. Professor of Old Testament, Southwestern Baptist Theological Seminary, Fort Worth, Texas.

Hughes, Philip Edgcumbe. Th.D., Australian College of Theology; D.Litt., University of Cape Town. Visiting Professor, Westminster Theological Seminary, Philadelphia; Associate Rector, St. John's Episcopal Church, Huntingdon Valley, Pennsylvania.

Huttar, David K. Ph.D., Brandeis University. Professor of Bible and Greek, Nyack College, Nyack, New York.

Inch, Morris A. Ph.D., Boston University. Executive Director, Institute of Holy Land Studies, Jerusalem, Israel.

James, Edgar C. Th.D., Dallas Theological Seminary. Professor of Bible and Theology, Moody Bible Institute, Chicago, Illinois.

Jewett, Paul K. Ph.D., Harvard University. Professor of Systematic Theology, Fuller Theological Seminary, Pasadena, California.

Johnson, Alan F. Th.D., Dallas Theological Seminary. Professor of New Testament and Christian Ethics, Wheaton College, Wheaton, Illinois.

Jordan, Gregory D. Ph.D., Hebrew Union College—Jewish Institute of Religion. Assistant Professor, Department of Bible and Religion (Old Testament), King College, Bristol, Tennessee.

Kaufman, Paul L. M.A., Wheaton College. Sometime Professor of New Testament Language and Literature, Western Conservative Baptist Seminary, Portland, Oregon.

Kistemaker, Simon J. Th.D., Free University of Amsterdam. Professor of New Testament, Reformed Theological Seminary, Jackson, Mississippi.

Klotz, John W. Ph.D., University of Pittsburgh. Director of Graduate Studies, Concordia Seminary, St. Louis, Missouri.

Klug, Eugene F. A. D.Theol., Free University of Amsterdam. Professor of Systematic Theology, Concordia Theological Seminary, Fort Wayne, Indiana.

Knight, George W., III. Th.D., Free University of Amsterdam. Chairman of New Testament Department, Covenant Theological Seminary, St. Louis, Missouri.

Ladd, George E. Ph.D., Harvard University. Sometime Professor Emeritus of New Testament Theology and Exegesis, Fuller Theological Seminary, Pasadena, California.

Lake, Donald M. Ph.D., University of Iowa. Associate Professor of Bible, Wheaton College, Wheaton, Illinois.

Lane, William L. Th.D., Harvard University. Professor of Religious Studies, Western Kentucky University, Bowling Green, Kentucky.

LaSor, William Sanford. Ph.D., Dropsie College; Th.D., University of Southern California. Professor Emeritus of Old Testament, Fuller Theological Seminary, Pasadena, California.

Liefeld, Walter L. Ph.D., Columbia University. Distinguished Professor of New Testament, Trinity Evangelical Divinity School, Deerfield, Illinois.

Lindsey, F. Duane. Th.D., Dallas Theological Seminary. Assistant Professor of Systematic Theology.

Long, John E. Ph.D., Brandeis University. Associate Professor of Religion, Western Kentucky University, Bowling Green, Kentucky.

Lyon, Robert W. Ph.D., St. Andrews University. Professor of New Testament Interpretation, Asbury Theological Seminary, Wilmore, Kentucky.

MacDonald, William Graham. Th.D., Southern Baptist Theological Seminary. Freelance author, Front Royal, Virginia.

Mare, W. Harold. Ph.D., University of Pennsylvania. Professor of New Testament, Covenant Theological Seminary, St. Louis, Missouri.

Marshall, I. Howard. Ph.D., University of Aberdeen. Professor of New Testament Exegesis, University of Aberdeen, Scotland.

Mason, James L. Ph.D., University of Southern California. Retired Full Professor of Speech Communication, and Adjunct Professor in Greek and Homiletic Courses at Bethel College and Seminary, St. Paul, Minnesota. Semi-retired and Preaching Minister, Oakmont Community Church, Santa Rosa, California.

Mattingly, Gerald L. Ph.D., Southern Baptist Theological Seminary. Professor of Old Testament and Archaeology, Cincinnati Christian Seminary, Cincinnati, Ohio.

McAlister, Paul K. D.Min., Bethel Theological Seminary. Professor of Theology and Social Ethics, Minnesota Bible College, Rochester, Minnesota.

McClanahan, James S. Th.D., Union Theological Seminary in Virginia.

McComiskey, Thomas E. Ph.D., Brandeis University. Professor of Old Testament and Semitic Languages, Trinity Evangelical Divinity School, Deerfield, Illinois.

McConville, J. Gordon. Ph.D., Queen's University, Belfast. Lecturer in Old Testament and Course Leader, Trinity College, Bristol, England.

McDonald, H. D. Ph.D., D.D., University of London. Formerly Vice-Principal, London Bible College, London, England.

McNeely, Richard I. Th.D., Dallas Theological Seminary; Ph.D., University of Southern California. Writer, Educational Consultant, Missoula, Montana.

McRay, John R. Ph.D., University of Chicago. Professor of New Testament and Archaeology, Wheaton College, Wheaton, Illinois.

Merrill, Eugene H. Ph.D., Columbia University. Professor of Semitics and Old Testament Studies, Dallas Theological Seminary, Dallas, Texas.

Mickelsen, A. Berkeley. Ph.D., University of Chicago. Professor Emeritus of Biblical Interpretation, Bethel Theological Seminary, St. Paul, Minnesota.

Miller, Douglas J. Ph.D., Claremont Graduate School and University Center. Professor of Christian Social Ethics, Eastern Baptist Theological Seminary, Philadelphia, Pennsylvania.

Morris, Leon L. Ph.D., University of Cambridge. Formerly Principal, Ridley College, Melbourne, Australia.

Morrison, Robert L. M.A., Wheaton College. Ph.D. candadate, Boston University.

Motyer, Alec. B.D., University of Dublin. Minister of Christ Church, Westbourne, Bournemouth, England.

Motyer, Stephen. M.Litt., University of Bristol. Formerly New Testament Tutor, Oak Hill College, London, England.

Mounce, Robert H. Ph.D., University of Aberdeen. President, Whitworth College, Spokane, Washington.

Norman, James Garth Gifford. B.D., M.Th. Studied at Spurgeon's College, London. Minister of the following Baptist churches: Stourport-on-Severn, Worcestershire, England; George Road, Erdington, Birmingham, England; Shettleston, Glasgow, Scotland; Rosyth, Fife, Scotland.

Osborne, Grant R. Ph.D., University of Aberdeen. Professor of New Testament, Trinity Evangelical Divinity School, Deerfield, Illinois.

Patterson, Richard. Ph.D., University of California—Los Angeles. Chairman, Department of Biblical Studies, Liberty University, Lynchburg, Virginia.

Perkin, Hazel W. M.A., McGill. Principal, St. Clement's School, Toronto, Canada.

Piper, John. D.Theol., University of Munich. Senior Pastor, Bethlehem Baptist Church, Minneapolis, Minnesota.

Potts, Austin H. Ph.D., Dropsie College. Professor of Bible, Philadelphia College of Bible, Langhorne, Pennsylvania.

Powell, Ralph E. Th.D., Northern Baptist Theological Seminary. Distinguished Professor of Theology Emeritus, North American Baptist Seminary, Sioux Falls, South Dakota.

Price, James D. Ph.D., Dropsie College for Hebrew and Cognate Learning. Professor of Old Testament, Temple Baptist Seminary, Chattanooga, Tennessee.

Rainey, Anson F. Ph.D., Brandeis University. Professor of Ancient Near Eastern Cultures and Semitic Linguistics, Tel Aviv University, Ramat Aviv, Israel.

Ramm, Bernard L. Ph.D., University of Southern California. Professor of Christian Theology, American Baptist Seminary of the West, Berkeley, California.

Reymond, Robert L. Ph.D., Bob Jones University. Professor of Systematic Theology and Apologetics, Covenant Theological Seminary, St. Louis, Missouri.

Contributors

Rupprecht, Arthur. Ph.D., University of Pennsylvania. Professor of Classical Languages, Wheaton College, Wheaton, Illinois.

Sacks, Stuart D. Th.D., Southwest Theological Seminary. Senior Pastor, Berith Presbyterian Church, Bryn Mawr, Pennsylvania.

Sailer, William S. S.T.D., Temple University. Professor of Theology, Evangelical School of Theology, Myerstown, Pennsylvania.

Scaer, David P. Th.D., Concordia Seminary, St. Louis. Academic Dean and Professor of Systematic Theology and New Testament, Concordia Theological Seminary, Fort Wayne, Indiana.

Scott, J. Julius, Jr. Ph.D., University of Manchester. Professor of Biblical and Historical Studies, Wheaton College Graduate School, Wheaton, Illinois.

Scott, Jack B. Ph.D., Dropsie University. Professor of Biblical Studies and Chairman of the Division of Biblical Religion and Philosophy, Belhaven College, Jackson, Mississippi.

Shepherd, Norman. Th.M., Westminster Theological Seminary. Senior Pastor, First Christian Reformed Church, Minneapolis, Minnesota.

Shipps, Kenneth W. Ph.D., Yale University. Vice President for Academic Affairs, Phillips University, Enid, Oklahoma.

Sider, John W. Ph.D., University of Notre Dame. Professor of English, Westmont College, Santa Barbara, California.

Silva, Moisés. Ph.D., University of Manchester. Professor of New Testament, Westminster Theological Seminary, Philadelphia, Pennsylvania.

Smick, Elmer B. Ph.D., Dropsie College for Hebrew and Cognate Learning. Professor of Old Testament, Gordon-Conwell Theological Seminary, South Hamilton, Massachusetts.

Smith, Albert J. Ph.D., University of Chicago. Professor of Biology, Wheaton College, Wheaton, Illinois.

Smith, Ralph L. Th.D., Southwestern Baptist Theological Seminary. Professor of Old Testament, Southwestern Baptist Theological Seminary, Fort Worth, Texas.

Snodgrass, Klyne R. Ph.D., University of St. Andrews, Scotland. Professor of Biblical Literature, North Park Theological Seminary, Chicago, Illinois.

Spender, Robert D. Ph.D., Dropsie University. Associate Professor of Biblical Studies, The King's College, Briarcliff Manor, New York.

Stein, Robert H. Ph.D., Princeton Theological Seminary. Professor of New Testament, Bethel Theological Seminary, St. Paul, Minnesota.

Taylor, Stephen. M.A., Wheaton College. Ph.D. candidate, University of Pennsylvania.

Thompson, John A. Ph.D., University of Cambridge. Former Reader and Chairman of the Department of Middle Eastern Studies, University of Melbourne.

Thomson, J. G. S. S. Ph.D., University of Edinburgh. Minister Emeritus, Church of Scotland.

Tolar, William B. Th.D., Southwestern Baptist Theological Seminary. Dean and Professor of Biblical Backgrounds.

Toon, Peter. D.Phil., Oxford University. Rector of Boxford Parish; Director of Post-Ordination Training, Diocese of St. Edmundsbury and Ipswich.

Travis, William. Ph.D., New York University. Professor of Church History, Bethel Theological Seminary, St. Paul, Minnesota.

Turner, George A. Ph.D., Harvard University. Professor of Biblical Literature (Emeritus), Asbury Theological Seminary, Wilmore, Kentucky.

Van Groningen, Gerard. Ph.D., University of Melbourne, Victoria. President Emeritus, Trinity Christian College, Palos Heights, Illinois.

Van Reken, David E. M.D., University of Illinois College of Medicine. Lecturer in Pediatrics, Indiana University School of Medicine, Indianapolis, Indiana.

VanGemeren, Willem A. Ph.D., University of Wisconsin. Professor of Old Testament, Reformed Theological Seminary, Jackson, Mississippi.

Vannoy, J. Robert. Th.D., Free University of Amsterdam. Professor of Old Testament, Biblical Theological Seminary, Hatfield, Pennsylvania.

Vos, Arvin G. Ph.D., University of Toronto. Professor of Philosophy, Department of Philosophy of Religion, Western Kentucky University, Bowling Green, Kentucky.

Vos, Howard F. Th.D., Dallas Theological Seminary; Ph.D., Northwestern University. Professor of History and Archaeology, The King's College, Briarcliff Manor, New York.

Walker, Larry Lee. Ph.D., Dropsie College for Hebrew and Cognate Learning. Professor of Old Testament and Semitic Languages, Mid-America Baptist Theological Seminary, Memphis, Tennessee.

Waltke, Bruce K. Ph.D., Harvard University; Th.D., Dallas Theological Seminary. Professor of Old Testament, Westminster Theological Seminary, Philadelphia, Pennsylvania.

Walton, John H. Ph.D., Hebrew Union College. Assistant Professor of Bible, Moody Bible Institute, Chicago, Illinois.

Wead, David W. D.Theol., Basel University. Senior Minister, First Christian College, Nashville, Tennessee.

Webber, Robert Eugene. Th.D., Concordia. Professor of Theology, Wheaton College, Wheaton, Illinois.

Weigelt, Morris A. Ph.D., Princeton Theological Seminary. Professor of New Testament, Nazarene Theological Seminary, Kansas City, Missouri.

Wenham, Gordon J. Ph.D., King's College, University of London. Senior Lecturer in Religious Studies, The College of St. Paul and St. Mary, Cheltenham, England.

Wheaton, David H. M.A., St. John's College, Oxford. Vicar and Honorary Canon of the Cathedral and Abbey Church of St. Albans, Christ Church, Ware, Herts, United Kingdom.

White, R. E. O. M.A., University of Liverpool; B.D., University of London. Formerly Principal, Baptist Theological College of Scotland, Glasgow.

White, William, Jr. Ph.D., Dropsie College for Hebrew and Cognate Learning. President, Nitech Research Corporation, Warrington, Pennsylvania.

Whitlock, Luder G., Jr. D.Min., Vanderbilt University. President, Reformed Theological Seminary, Jackson, Mississippi.

Wilcock, Michael J. B.A., University of Durham. Vicar, St. Nicholas' Church, Durham, England.

Winter, R. Milton. Th.M., Princeton Theological Seminary. Pastor, First Presbyterian Church, Holly Springs, Mississippi.

Wolf, Herbert M. Ph.D., Brandeis University. Associate Professor of Theological Studies, Wheaton College, Wheaton, Illinois.

Woudstra, Marten H. Th.D., Westminster Theological Seminary. Professor of Old Testament Emeritus, Calvin Theological Seminary, Grand Rapids, Michigan.

Yamauchi, Edwin M. Ph.D., Brandeis University. Professor of History, Miami University, Oxford, Ohio.

Yarbrough, Robert W. Ph.D., University of Aberdeen. Associate Professor of Biblical and Theological Studies, Liberty University, Lynchburg, Virginia.

Young, Warren C. Ph.D., Boston University. Distinguished Professor of Theology and Christian Philosophy Emeritus, Northern Baptist Theological Seminary, Lombard, Illinois.

Youngblood, Ronald F. Ph.D., Dropsie College for Hebrew and Cognate Learning. Professor of Old Testament and Hebrew, Bethel Theological Seminary West, San Diego, California.

Abbreviations

General Abbreviations

c.	about, approximately
cf.	compare
ch	chapter (*pl.* chs)
ed	edition, editor (*pl.* eds)
e.g.	for example
et al.	and others
etc.	and so forth
f.	and following (*pl.* ff.)
Gr.	Greek
Heb.	Hebrew
i.e.	that is
km.	kilometers
lit.	literal(ly)
LXX	Septuagint
m.	meters
mg.	margin
MS	manuscript (*pl.* MSS)
MT	Masoretic Text
N,NE	north, northeast
N,NW	north, northwest
NT	New Testament
OT	Old Testament
p	page (*pl.* pp)
S,SE	south, southeast
S,SW	south, southwest
TR	Textus Receptus
v	verse (*pl.* vv)
vol	volume (*pl.* vols)

Books of the Bible

Old Testament

Gn	Genesis
Ex	Exodus
Lv	Leviticus
Nm	Numbers
Dt	Deuteronomy
Jos	Joshua
Jgs	Judges
Ru	Ruth
1 Sm	1 Samuel
2 Sm	2 Samuel
1 Kgs	1 Kings
2 Kgs	2 Kings
1 Chr	1 Chronicles
2 Chr	2 Chronicles
Ezr	Ezra
Neh	Nehemiah
Est	Esther
Jb	Job
Ps(s)	Psalms
Prv	Proverbs
Eccl	Ecclesiastes
Sg	Song of Solomon
Is	Isaiah
Jer	Jeremiah
Lam	Lamentations
Ez	Ezekiel
Dn	Daniel
Hos	Hosea
Jl	Joel
Am	Amos
Ob	Obadiah
Jon	Jonah
Mi	Micah
Na	Nahum
Hb	Habakkuk
Zep	Zephaniah
Hg	Haggai
Zec	Zechariah
Mal	Malachi

New Testament

Mt	Matthew
Mk	Mark
Lk	Luke
Jn	John
Acts	Acts
Rom	Romans
1 Cor	1 Corinthians
2 Cor	2 Corinthians
Gal	Galatians
Eph	Ephesians

Abbreviations

Phil	Philippians
Col	Colossians
1 Thes	1 Thessalonians
2 Thes	2 Thessalonians
1 Tm	1 Timothy
2 Tm	2 Timothy
Ti	Titus
Phlm	Philemon
Heb	Hebrews
Jas	James
1 Pt	1 Peter
2 Pt	2 Peter
1 Jn	1 John
2 Jn	2 John
3 Jn	3 John
Jude	Jude
Rv	Revelation

Extracanonical Literature

Apocryphal Books

Ecclus	Ecclesiasticus
1 Esd	1 Esdras
Jth	Judith
1 Macc	1 Maccabees
2 Macc	2 Maccabees
Wisd of Sol	Wisdom of Solomon

Pseudepigraphal Books

2 Bar	Syriac Apocalypse of Baruch
1 Enoch	Ethiopic Book of Enoch
4 Ezr	4 Ezra
Life AE	Life of Adam and Eve
Pss of Sol	Psalms of Solomon

Dead Sea Scrolls

CD	Cairo (Genizah text of the) Damascus (Document)
1 QM	War Scroll
1 QS	Manual of Discipline
1 QSa	Rule of the Congregation

Early Christian Writings

1 Clem	1 Clement
2 Clem	2 Clement

Bible Versions and Other Sources

Antiq.	Josephus, Antiquities of the Jews
Dio Cassius	Dio Cassius, Roman History
Ep Fest	Athanasius, Festal Letters
HE	Eusebius, Historia Ecclesiastica
KJV	The King James Version
NASB	The New American Standard Bible
NEB	The New English Bible
NIV	The New International Version
Prol Gal	Jerome, Prologue to Galatians
RSV	The Revised Standard Version
Strabo	Strabo, Geography
Tacitus, Hist.	Tacitus, Histories
War	Josephus, The Jewish War

Jj

Jaakan. Esau's descendant and the son of Ezer the Horite (1 Chr 1:42, KJV Jakan); alternately called Akan in Genesis 36:27.

See BE-EROTH BENE-JAAKAN.

Jaakobah. Leader in Simeon's tribe (1 Chr 4:36).

Jaala, Jaalah. Head of a family that returned to Jerusalem with Zerubbabel after the Babylonian exile (Ezr 2:56, Jaalah; Neh 7:58).

Jaalam. KJV form of Jalam, Esau's son, in Genesis 36:5,14,18 and 1 Chronicles 1:35.

See JALAM.

Jaanai. KJV form of Janai, a Gadite, in 1 Chronicles 5:12.

See JANAI.

Jaar. Most common word in Hebrew for "forest." It refers to forests generally (Is 10:19) and to specific forests, such as the "forest of Ephraim" (2 Sm 18:6), and the "forest of Hereth" (1 Sm 22:5), both associated with King David. It also occurs as the name of one of Solomon's buildings, "the house of the forest of Lebanon" (1 Kgs 7:2), apparently because of its extensive use of cedar. Only one occurrence of "Jaar" seems to be a proper name. Psalm 132:6 alludes to the transfer of the ark from Kiriath-jearim to Jerusalem. Here it is called the field of Jaar (or forest), perhaps a poetic abbreviation.

Jaare-oregim. Textual corruption of Jair in 2 Samuel 21:19.

See JAIR #3.

Jaareshiah. Jeroham's son, a Benjamite leader who lived in Jerusalem (1 Chr 8:27, KJV Jaresiah).

Jaasau. KJV spelling of Jaasu, Bani's son, in Ezra 10:37.

See JAASU.

Jaasiel. 1. Warrior among David's mighty men. He is called "the Mezobaite" (1 Chr 11:47, KJV Jasiel).
2. Abner's son and the leader of Benjamin's tribe during David's reign (1 Chr 27:21).

Jaasu. Bani's son, who obeyed Ezra's exhortation to divorce his pagan wife after the exile (Ezr 10:37, KJV Jaasau).

Jaazaniah. 1. Son of Hoshaiah, who was a Maachathite and a leader in the armies of Judah at the beginning of the exile. These troops received assurance of safety in return for loyalty to the Babylonians (2 Kgs 25:23). Jaazaniah is alternately called Jezaniah in Jeremiah 40:8 and Azariah in Jeremiah 42:1 (KJV Jezaniah) and 43:2.
2. Son of Jeremiah (not the prophet), who was taken by Jeremiah the prophet into the Lord's house where he refused to drink wine because of the command of his ancestor, Jonadab the Rechabite (Jer 35:3–11).
3. Shaphan's son, who led a group of elders in worshiping idols in the temple (Ez 8:11).
4. Azzur's son and one of a group of 25 men who gave bad counsel and plotted evil in Jerusalem near the time of the exile (Ez 11:1).

Jaazer. KJV alternate form of Jazer, an Amorite city in Gilead, in Numbers 21:32 and 32:35.

See JAZER.

Jaaziah. Son of Merari in a list of Levites assigned to temple duty in David's reign (1 Chr 24:26,27).

Jaaziel. One of the eight men appointed to play the harp when the ark was brought up to Jerusalem by David (1 Chr 15:18). He is called Aziel in verse 20.

Jabal. Descendant of Cain and the first son of Lamech and Adah. He was the father of a nomadic people who dwelt in tents (Gn 4:20).

Jabbok. Eastern tributary of the Jordan, the modern Nahr ez-Zerqa or Blue River. Its source is a spring near Amman, capital of modern Jordan (the Decapolis town of Philadelphia in Hellenistic times). From its source the Jabbok loops N,NE before swinging west and cutting a valley which, characteristic of the east Jordan tributary streams, deepens into a canyon. It emerges from this ravine near Tell Deir 'Alla, which may be the ancient Succoth, quiets its flow, and debouches into the Jordan at ed-Damiyeh, the ancient Adam, some 15 miles north of the Dead Sea. The Jabbok ranks next to the Yarmuk, its more northerly companion stream, in the extent of its watershed, a region of well-watered territory blessed with an average rainfall of some 30 inches. The Jabbok has a fast, strong, perennial flow; over a large portion of its 60-mile course the stream averages an 80-foot drop over each mile.

The Jabbok was a natural boundary as implied in the story of Jacob's struggle with the angel of the Lord, and Esau's meeting with his brother (Gn 32:22,23). The loop of the river north of Ammon was an Ammonite frontier (Nm 21:24). Gad occupied the enclave as far as es-Salt. The river divided Sihon and Og (Jgs 11:22), and lower down its course, the two political divisions of Gilead (Dt 3:12,16; Jos 12:2–6).

E.M. BLAIKLOCK

See JORDAN RIVER.

Jabesh (Person). Shallum's father. Shallum assassinated Zechariah, king of Israel (2 Kgs 15:10–14).

Jabesh, Jabesh-gilead (Place). Town appearing in some stormy passages of OT history. The closing chapters of the Book of Judges (19–21), a sorry record of the division and degradation of the land, tell of a base atrocity committed by the men of Gibeah against a Levite's concubine, a sanguinary war against Benjamin in consequence, and savage reprisals against Jabesh-gilead whose community had sent no contingent to the battle. Such is the first mention of the town. The town was repopulated by neighboring Gileadites, and next appears in 1 Samuel 11. East of the Jordan River, Jabesh was exposed to Ammonite attack, and Nahash of Ammon forced Jabesh-gilead to seek terms of surrender. The condition imposed by the barbarous Nahash was the loss of the right eye for all the inhabitants, a mutilation intended to humiliate Israel and destroy the military potential of a border fortress. The sequel was Saul's forced march, a fine piece of military prowess, and a tremendous boost for the new king's prestige. Saul gained in one swift blow the support of the Transjordanian tribes and the reduction of the frontier threat which a militarily powerful Ammon would undoubtedly offer. The men of Jabesh-gilead repaid their deep debt to Saul when the king, now unbalanced and rejected, died on Gilboa with his son Jonathan in a last attempt to blunt the Philistine drive to the northwest. The bodies of Saul and Jonathan, hung headless over the walls of Beth-shan, were cut down and rescued by a commando force from Jabesh-gilead, who made a forced march of nine miles each way to honor their onetime benefactor (1 Sm 31:8–13; 1 Chr 10:8–12). When David became king he repaid the men of Jabesh-gilead with gratitude. Jabesh-gilead, of course, like Beth-shan, lay astride the eastward trade routes between the plateaus on both sides of the river.

The name Jabesh is preserved in that of the Wadi el-Yabis which runs into the Jordan directly south of tbe southern end of the Lake of

The Jabbok River.

Galilee. The town itself, according to Eusebius' generally reliable topography, was about six miles south of Pella on the road to Gerasa. The twin tells of Tell el-Meqhereh and Tell Abu Kharaz on the Wadi el-Yabis correspond with Eusebius' location much better than the other site suggested—Tell el-Maqlub. Tell el-Meqereh and Tell Abu Kharaz are on the eastern rim of the Jordan Valley, and fit the details of the historical record—Saul's forced march from Bezek, and the route of the Jabesh-gilead raiding party to Beth-shan.

E.M. BLAIKLOCK

Jabez (Person). Member of Judah's tribe who was noted for his godliness. He prayed for God's protection and his prayer was answered (1 Chr 4:9,10).

Jabez (Place). City that was probably located in Judah and was inhabited by scribes (1 Chr 2:55).

Jabin. 1. King of Hazor, who led a coalition against Joshua at Merom. Jabin and his allies were destroyed in the battle, and Hazor was burned to the ground (Jos 11:1–14).

2. King of Hazor during the period of the judges (Jgs 4). God allowed him to oppress Israel for 20 years because of their wickedness. His army included 900 chariots of iron. Eventually, God delivered Israel through the prophetess Deborah and Barak, who defeated Sisera, the captain of Jabin's army. While resting after his flight from battle, Sisera himself was killed by a woman. Jabin was no longer a threat after Sisera's death and was soon killed (v 24; Ps 83:9).

Jabneel. 1. Alternate name for the town Jabneh in Judah's tribe (Jos 15:11).

See JABNEH.

2. Town in Galilee near Tiberias which described part of Naphtali's southern border (Jos 19:33). It was located south of modern Jabneel.

Jabneh. Biblical city on the coastal plain between Jaffa and Ashdod, first mentioned as Jabneel, on the northern border of the tribe of Judah (Jos 15:11). It is mentioned together with the Philistine cities Gath and Ashdod, whose walls were breached by Uzziah, king of Judah (2 Chr 26:6). In the Middle Bronze Age a harbor was established at Jabneh-yam, which is probably mentioned by Thutmose III in his list of conquered cities and in the Tell el-Amarna letters (Jabni-ilu). The remains of the harbor show evidence of all periods—from Early Bronze Age down to the Byzantine period. In Hellenistic times Jabneh was called

Jamnia, and was used as a base by foreign armies for subsequent attacks against the Judean territory of the Maccabeans. After the destruction of Jerusalem in AD 70, a small community of learned refugees was located in Jabneh. Their leader was Johanan ben Zakkai, a former member of the Sanhedrin, the supreme court of the Jews in Jerusalem. He founded a school there. His successor was Gamaliel II. Here the canon of the OT was defined. During the second Jewish war (Bar Kochba Revolt, AD 132–135) Jabneh was deserted. The spiritual center of the Jewish life was removed to Galilee. The refugees settled down first in Zippori and later in Tiberias, where the Jerusalem Talmud was codified and the Masoretic Text of the OT was produced.

Jacan, Jachan. Member of Gad's tribe who lived in Bashan during the reign of Jotham, king of Judah (1 Chr 5:13, KJV Jachan).

Jachin. 1. Son of Simeon and leader of the Jachinites, who immigrated to Egypt with his grandfather Jacob (Gn 46:10; Ex 6:15; Nm 26:12). He is called Jarib in 1 Chronicles 4:24.

2. Priest who lived in Jerusalem after the exile (1 Chr 9:10; Neh 11:10). The name "Jachin" may possibly designate a group of priests of which Jachin was the head.

3. Priest assigned to temple duty in David's reign (1 Chr 24:17).

Jachin and Boaz. Names of two pillars Solomon set up before the temple vestibule. He named the south pillar Jachin and the north pillar Boaz (1 Kgs 7:21; 2 Chr 3:17). These hollow pillars were cast of bronze and measured about 27 feet in height and about 18 feet in circumference (or nearly 6 feet in diameter). They were crowned with a capital (ornate cap or top) about 6 feet high that consisted of cast lily-work, chains, and 100 pomegranates each (1 Kgs 7:15–20; 2 Chr 3:15,16).

See TABERNACLE, TEMPLE.

Jachinite. Descendant of Jachin, Simeon's son (Nm 26:12).

See JACHIN #1.

Jacinth. Precious stone mentioned in Revelation 21:20 as a foundation stone in the New Jerusalem.

See MINERALS, METALS, AND PRECIOUS STONES.

Jackal. Wolflike mammal known for its distinctive wail (Mi 1:8).

See ANIMALS.

Jackal's Well. Unknown location along the Jerusalem wall between the Valley Gate and the Dung Gate visited by Nehemiah during his night inspection of the wall (Neh 2:13); perhaps better rendered "Dragon Well" (KJV, NASB). It has been frequently identified with En-rogel (Job's Well; 2 Sm 17:17), where the Valley of Hinnom and the Kidron Valley meet.

Jacob. 1. Younger of twin sons born to Isaac and Rebekah (Gn 25:24–26). Isaac had prayed for his barren wife, Rebekah, and she conceived the twins, who jostled each other in the womb. She inquired about this of the Lord, who told her that she was carrying two nations and that the older son would serve the younger (v 23). Esau was hairy and red (later he was called Edom, "red," v 30; 36:1), but Jacob was born holding the heel of his brother, so that he was named Jacob, "he takes by the heel" (cf. Hos 12:3), with the derived meaning "to supplant, deceive, attack from the rear."

Personal History. Esau and Jacob were very different from each other. Esau was an outdoorsman, the favorite of his father, while Jacob stayed around the tents and was loved by his mother.

One day when Jacob was preparing red pottage, Esau came in famished. Jacob offered to sell Esau some stew in exchange for his birthright as firstborn, and Esau agreed, thus repudiating his birthright (cf. Heb 12:16). The significance of this episode of the red pottage is demonstrated by its association with Esau's second name, Edom ("red") (Gn 26:30).

Isaac became old and blind. One day he asked Esau to take his weapons and get some wild game, of which Isaac was very fond (Gn 27:7; cf. 25:28), so that he could eat and then confer his blessing upon Esau. Rebekah had been eavesdropping, so she called Jacob and told him to go to the flock and select two good kids. She would prepare a dish that would pass for the game while Esau was out hunting. Jacob feared that Isaac would detect the deception, for Esau was very hairy, but Rebekah had everything planned. She placed the skins of the kids on Jacob's hands and neck to give the impression of hairiness (27:16) and clothed him in Esau's best garments, which had the smell of the outdoors on them. Although Isaac recognized the voice of Jacob, his other senses failed him, and he was deceived by the feel of the skins and the smell of the garments. He proceeded to give the blessing to Jacob (vv 27–29).

No sooner had Jacob left than Esau arrived with the game he had cooked. Jacob's ruse was discovered, but the deed could not be undone (Gn 27:33) for, as the Nuzi tablets show,

an oral blessing had legal validity and could not be revoked. Esau was heartbroken (cf. Heb 12:27). Isaac gave him a blessing inferior to the one given to Jacob (Gn 27:39,40).

The animosity between the brothers deepened, and Esau plotted to kill Jacob after the death of their father. Rebekah learned of this, so she instructed Jacob to flee to her brother Laban in Haran (Gn 27:42–45). Esau's Hittite wives meanwhile had been making life miserable for Rebekah; she complained to Isaac, who called Jacob and sent him to Laban to marry one of his uncle's daughters. (v 46–28:4).

Jacob set out for Haran. Using a stone for a pillow, he dreamed one night of a ladder reaching up to heaven, with the angels of God ascending and descending on it. God spoke to Jacob and gave to him the promise he had given to Abraham and Isaac concerning the land and descendants. The next morning Jacob took his stone pillow and set it up as a pillar, anointing it with oil. He named the place Bethel ("house of God") and made a vow that if the Lord would be with him and provide for him he would give a tithe to the Lord (Gn 28:10–22).

When Jacob reached the area of Haran he met shepherds who knew Laban. Rachel, Laban's younger daughter, arrived with her father's flock, and Jacob rolled the large stone from the mouth of the well and watered the sheep for her (Gn 29:1–10). When Rachel learned that Jacob was from their own family, she ran to tell her father, who greeted Jacob warmly. After staying with them for a month, Jacob was hired to tend Laban's flocks. When wages were discussed, Jacob proposed to work seven years to earn Rachel as his wife (vv 15–20).

At the end of seven years Jacob was set to claim his wages, but on the night of the wedding feast Laban gave his older daughter Leah to Jacob; Jacob did not discover the substitution until morning. He felt cheated and protested to Laban, but Laban insisted that according to custom the older daughter must marry first and proposed that Jacob work another seven years for Rachel. Jacob agreed to this and put in his time (Gn 29:21–30).

Genesis 29 and 30 relate the birth of most of Jacob's children. Leah bore Jacob four sons: Reuben, Simeon, Levi, and Judah (Gn 29:31–35). She named her first son Reuben ("see, a son") since she felt that her husband would love her because she bore a son. Simeon is derived from the root "hear," since Leah thought that God had given her this son because he had heard that she was hated. Levi is related to the verb "join," for Leah thought that her husband would be joined to her because of this third son. Judah means "praise," for she praised the Lord at the birth of her fourth son.

Rachel could not conceive any children, so she gave her maid Bilhah to Jacob. She bore him Dan and Naphtali (Gn 30:1–9). Rachel named the first son Dan ("he judged"), because God had judged, that is, vindicated her. Naphtali means "my struggle, my wrestling," for Rachel said she had wrestled with and overcome her sister.

Thereupon Leah gave her maid Zilpah to Jacob as wife; she brought forth Gad and Asher (Gn 30:11). Gad means "fortune"; Leah said "Good fortune" when he was born. Asher ("happy") was so named for Leah said, "Now the women will call me happy."

Reuben found some mandrakes in the field, and Leah traded them to Rachel for Jacob's services. Leah then bore sons five and six, Issachar and Zebulun, followed by a daughter, whom she named Dinah (Gn 30:14–21). Issachar perhaps means "reward," for Leah said that God had rewarded her for giving her maidservant to her husband. Zebulun probably means "honor"; Leah thought that now her husband would honor her.

At last Rachel herself conceived and bore her first child, a son whom she named Joseph. "Joseph" means "he will add" or "may he add," for Rachel wanted God to add another son to her.

Jacob wanted to leave and go back to Canaan, but Laban wanted him to stay, for through divination he had learned that the Lord had blessed him because of Jacob (Gn 30:27). They discussed the matter of wages, and Jacob proposed that every speckled and spotted sheep and goat and every black lamb become his (vv 32,33). Laban considered this a good idea, so he quickly took all the animals marked in that fashion and put them under the care of his sons, some three days' distance from the rest of the flocks (vv 35,36).

Jacob also was contriving to gain an advantage; he tried to influence the genetics of the animals by putting speckled and streaked wooden rods by the water-troughs when the best animals were breeding. The Lord blessed Jacob and he became rich in flocks and herds (Gn 30:37–43).

The sons of Laban became very bitter toward Jacob and Laban's attitude toward him changed also. Jacob noticed this, and now the Lord spoke to Jacob and told him to return to Canaan (Gn 31:8–16). Jacob held a family council with his two wives and told them how God had blessed him, even though their father had cheated him and had changed his wages 10 times (v 7; cf. v 41). Jacob organized his caravan while Laban was away shearing sheep. Rachel stole her father's household gods (v 19),

for their possession would make the holder heir to Laban's estate (cf. Nuzi tablets). The party took off, crossed the Euphrates, and headed for Gilead. Laban and his relatives pursued them, but God spoke to Laban in a dream, warning him not to say anything to Jacob (v 24).

When Laban caught up with Jacob, he upbraided him for sneaking away and inquired about his household gods. Jacob did not know what Rachel had done, so he said that the one found with the gods should be put to death (Gn 31:32). Rachel had hidden them in a camel saddle and was sitting on the saddle when her father searched the tent. Laban did not find the idols. After this, Jacob became angry and complained that he had served Laban for 20 years and Laban had changed his wages 10 times.

Laban suggested a covenant of peace, so the two men gathered stones to make a pillar and called it "heap of witness." Early the next morning Laban said his farewells and returned home.

As Jacob journeyed on, he was met by the angels of God, so he named that place Mahanaim, "the two camps." Jacob sent messengers ahead to inform Esau of his return. They came back with the news that Esau was approaching with 400 men. Jacob was afraid and sought the Lord for protection. To win Esau's favor, Jacob sent ahead gifts of animals, and that night he sent his family and possessions across the ford of the Jabbok River. Jacob was left alone, and "a man" wrestled with him throughout the night. Toward dawn the man touched Jacob's thigh, and his hip was dislocated, but Jacob would not give up until the angel blessed him. Here the Lord changed Jacob's name to Israel ("he strives with God"), and Jacob named the place Peniel ("face of God") because he had seen God face to face and lived (Gn 32:30).

Esau was getting near, so Jacob divided his party into two groups, thinking that if an attack came, possibly one of the groups could escape. But Esau was gracious and forgiving and the meeting was a happy one (Gn 33:4). Esau was surprised at Jacob's large family and property and made every gesture of friendship. Esau returned to Seir and Jacob moved on to Shechem where he bought a piece of land from Hamor, the father of Shechem. Jacob built an altar there and named it El-Elohe-Israel, "God, the god of Israel" (v 20).

Acting on the Lord's instructions, Jacob moved to Bethel and expelled the foreign gods from his household. At Luz (Bethel) the Lord again met him and reaffirmed his new name, renewing his promise of land and descendants (Gn 35:9–15).

As they journeyed south, Rachel died while giving birth to her second son (Gn 35:16–20). She named him Benoni ("son of my sorrow"), but Jacob changed his name to Benjamin ("son of the right hand"). Rachel was buried between Jerusalem and Bethlehem, at a site called Ramat Rahel today. Jacob went on to Hebron and found Isaac was still living. Isaac died at age 180 and was buried by Esau and Jacob (vv 27–29).

Although the story of Jacob continues in the Book of Genesis, the central figure in chapters 37–50 is Joseph, Jacob's favorite son, the firstborn of Rachel. Jacob showed this favoritism so openly that the other sons became jealous of Joseph. They plotted to kill Joseph, but instead sold him to a caravan of traders on their way to Egypt (37:9–28). They took Joseph's coat, dipped it into the blood of a goat, and took it to their father, telling him that they had found the robe. Jacob recognized the coat he had given his son and concluded that he was dead. Jacob was heartbroken and would not be comforted.

When a famine hit Canaan, Jacob sent his sons to Egypt to buy grain (Gn 42:1–5), keeping Benjamin at home. When the brothers returned to Palestine they reported to Jacob that the Egyptian administrator, (who was really Joseph), had kept Simeon as a hostage and demanded that they bring Benjamin with them when they came again for grain (vv 29–34).

The famine became severe, and Jacob sent his sons again to Egypt for grain. Very reluctantly he permitted Benjamin to go with them, sending a gift for the prime minister (Joseph) (Gn 43:11–14).

The next news Jacob received was that Joseph was alive in Egypt and wanted his father and all his family to join him (Gn 45:21–28). Jacob went first to Beersheba and made offerings to the Lord (46:1). The Lord spoke to Jacob, telling him to go down to Egypt and confirming once more the promises he had previously made. The descendants of Jacob that came to Egypt numbered 70, including the two sons of Joseph (vv 8–27).

When Jacob reached Goshen, Joseph came to meet him and there was a joyous reunion (Gn 46:28–30). Joseph reported the arrival of his father and brothers to the pharaoh (47:1), and took five of the brothers and his father to meet the ruler. Israel settled in the area of Goshen and prospered there. Jacob spent 17 years in Egypt and reached the age of 147 (vv 27,28). When Jacob sensed his death was near, he called Joseph and made him swear that he would bury him with his forebears in Canaan (vv 28–31). Joseph took his two sons, Manasseh and Ephraim, to his father for the patriar-

chal blessing. He presented the boys so that Manasseh, the firstborn, would be on Jacob's right and Ephraim on his left. Jacob, however, crossed his hands and gave the younger son the greater blessing (48:13–20). Jacob prophesied that his people would return to Canaan, and he gave Joseph a double portion of the land (v 22). Then Jacob called for all of his sons (49:1) and gave to each of them a blessing (vv 4–7, 13–21). Judah received the place of preeminence, and it is he who appears in the genealogies of Jesus (vv 8–12), and the blessing of Joseph shows the mark of special favor (vv 22–26). Jacob also charged his sons to bury him in the cave of Machpelah in Hebron; then he drew his feet up on the bed and died.

Joseph summoned the physicians to embalm his father according to Egyptian practice; there were 40 days for embalming and 70 days for the period of mourning (Gn 50:1–3). Joseph made arrangements to go to Canaan to bury Jacob as he had promised, and a large funeral procession, including many Egyptian officials and the family of Jacob, went up from Egypt. The company mourned for 7 days at the threshing floor of Atad (vv 10,11); then the sons of Jacob buried him in the cave of Machpelah as he had requested (vv 12,13). The entire group returned to Egypt, and Joseph assured his brothers that he had no intention of avenging the wrong they had done him. God had meant the whole episode for good (vv 50:15–21).

Jacob as the Nation Israel. God made the same promises concerning the land and the nation to Abraham, Isaac, and Jacob, but it is by Jacob's God-given name, Israel, that the nation is known.

The name "Jacob" is used for the nation about 100 times (e.g., Nm 24:5,19; Dt 32:9; Ps 59:13; Is 10:21). It is found as a parallel to Israel (e.g., Nm 23:7; Dt 33:10; Is 14:1; 43:1). "Jacob" is also used specifically of the northern kingdom of Israel (Am 7:2,5). In Isaiah 41:21 "the King of Jacob" refers to God himself.

See PATRIARCHS, PERIOD OF THE; ISRAEL, HISTORY OF; GENESIS, BOOK OF.

2. Father of Joseph, the husband of Mary and stepfather of Jesus (Mt 1:16). This genealogy traces the line of descent from Abraham to Joseph and demonstrates that Jesus had legal right to possess the Promised Land and to sit upon the throne of David.

See GENEALOGY OF JESUS CHRIST.

CARL E. DEVRIES

Jacob's Well. Place mentioned only in John's Gospel (4:5–29). It was here that Jesus sat and talked with the unnamed woman of Samaria, who accepted Jesus' words so readily that she became one of the most effective

Jacob's Well, near Shechem, looking north from Mt Gerizim.

lay-evangelists mentioned in the NT. This well is located in a plot of ground acquired by the patriarch Jacob and about 300 yards southeast from the traditional tomb of Joseph (Gn 33:19; 48:22; Jos 24:32; Jn 4:5,6). The site is about 2 miles southeast of modern Nablus, 600 yards southeast of the site of ancient Shechem (modern Balata), and 1000 yards south of Sychar (modern Askar). It lies at an important crossroad: the road west leads to Nablus, Tulkarm, and the coast; the road east to the Jordan Valley; the road south to Jerusalem; the road north to Beth-shan and Tiberias. Towering over the site on the northwest is Mt Ebal (at the foot of which lies Askar) and on the southwest Mt Gerizim, mountains of cursing and blessing, respectively (Dt 27:12,13; Jos 8:30–33). Near here Abraham built his first altar, and Jacob his second (Gn 12:6,7; 33:18–20). Thus the site is one of the most ancient and sacred in the Holy Land.

The well is about 100 feet in depth and one yard in diameter, cut through limestone. Fed by subterranean streams from the adjacent mountain slopes, the water is pure and plentiful, "the chief pride and joy" of the villagers. A church has existed on the site from at least AD 380. The Greek Orthodox Church acquired the site in 1885 and began a structure; the walls stand without a roof since building stopped during World War I. Access to the well is by steps leading from either side of the church altar to the well curb below.

Jada. Onam's son from Judah's tribe (1 Chr 2:28, 32).

Jaddai, Jadau. Nebo's descendant, who was encouraged by Ezra to divorce his foreign wife during the postexilic era (Ezr 10:43, KJV Jadau).

Jaddua. 1. Leader who set his seal on Ezra's covenant during the postexilic era (Neh 10:21).

2. Eliashib's descendant and a contemporary of Nehemiah (Neh 12:11,22). Jonathan, Jaddua's father, is mentioned in the Elephantine papyri about 410 BC.

Jadon. Workman on the Jerusalem wall after the return from exile. Jadon worked on the section near the Old Gate of the city with men from Gibeon and Mizpah. He was a Meronothite (Neh 3:7).

Jael. Wife of Heber the Kenite. Though the wife of a man belonging to the Kenite tribe which was at peace with Jabin, the Canaanite king, Jael demonstrated her loyalty to Israel, Jabin's enemy. Displaying oriental hospitality, she invited Sisera, Jabin's general, into her tent, gave him milk instead of water, provided a place to sleep, and then drove a tent peg into his temple (Jgs 4:17,18,21,22). Deborah, the inspired poetess, reflecting on the God-given victory over the Canaanites, praises Jael for this deed (5:6,24–31).

Jagur. Place in the extreme southern part of Israel, near Edom, inherited by Judah's tribe soon after the conquest (Jos 15:21). Its location is unknown.

Jah. Abbreviation of the covenant name of God, Yahweh or YHWH (Jehovah, KJV; LORD, most modern translations). The fragment is often used in words and names (e.g., Hallelujah, Jahaziel).

See GOD, NAMES OF.

Jahath. 1. Reaiah's son and the father of Ahumai and Lahad from Judah's tribe (1 Chr 4:2).

2. Gershonite Levite (1 Chr 6:20), appointed by King David to serve as a musician in the temple (v 43).

3. Shimei's son and a descendant of Gershon from Levi's tribe (1 Chr 23:10,11).

4. Shelomoth's son from Levi's tribe (1 Chr 24:22).

5. Merarite Levite, who was one of the supervisors of the temple repairs under Josiah (2 Chr 34:12).

Jahaz, Jahaza, Jahazah. Town east of the Dead Sea (in modern Jordan) where the Israelites defeated Sihon, king of the Amorites, when he refused to permit them to pass through his land (Nm 21:23; Dt 2:32; Jgs 11:20). According to Joshua 13:18 (KJV Jahaza), Moses gave the town to Reuben's tribe as part of its allotment. The town with its surrounding pasture lands was given to the Merarite Levites (Jos 21:36, KJV Jahazah; 1 Chr 6:78, Jahzah).

In later times, it is referred to as a city in the land of Moab in prophetic oracles by both Isaiah (15:4) and Jeremiah (48:21, Jahzah; KJV Jahazah). This may indicate that it was taken from Israel by Moab (to whom it apparently belonged before Sihon conquered it). The town is mentioned on the Moabite Stone (known also as the Dibon Stele and dating c. 845 BC) as the place where Mesha, king of Israel, had lived while at war with Moab. According to Mesha, he took Jahaz from Israel and added it to his own territory. Its exact location is uncertain.

Jahaziah. KJV rendering of Jahzeiah, Tikvah's son, in Ezra 10:15.

See JAHZEIAH.

Jahaziel. 1. Warrior from Benjamin's tribe who joined David at Ziklag in his struggle against King Saul. Jahaziel was one of David's ambidextrous archers and slingers (1 Chr 12:4).

2. One of the two priests David appointed to blow trumpets before the ark as it was brought into the tent in Jerusalem, where it remained until the completion of the temple by Solomon (1 Chr 16:6).

3. Levite belonging to the Kohathite division appointed by David to temple duties (1 Chr 23:19; 24:23).

4. Levite of the sons of Asaph who encouraged Jehoshaphat and the army of Judah not to be dismayed by the size of Moabite and Ammonite armies coming against them, but to stand still and see the victory of the Lord (2 Chr 20:14). Jehoshaphat's response exemplified a godly king encouraging his people to have faith in the Lord their God (vv 18–21).

5. Shecaniah's father. Shecaniah returned to Jerusalem with Ezra after the exile (Ezr 8:5).

Jahdai. Caleb's descendant from Judah's tribe (1 Chr 2:47).

Jahdiel. One of the family heads of Manasseh's half tribe dwelling east of the Jordan following the allotment of the land (1 Chr 5:24). He was noted as one of the mighty warriors in his tribe.

Jahdo. Gadite, son of Buz and a forefather of a number of valiant men who were registered during the reigns of King Jeroboam of Israel (793–753 BC) and King Jotham of Judah (750–732 BC; 1 Chr 5:14).

Jahleel, Jahleelite. Zebulun's son (Gn 46:14) and the founder of the Jahleelite family (Nm 26:26).

Jahmai. Tola's son from Issachar's tribe (1 Chr 7:2).

Jahzah. Alternate form of Jahaz, a town east of the Dead Sea, in 1 Chronicles 6:78 and Jeremiah 48:21.

See JAHAZ, JAHAZA, JAHAZAH.

Jahzeel, Jahzeelite. Naphtali's son (Gn 46:24; 1 Chr 7:13, Jahziel) and founder of the Jahzeelite family (Nm 26:48).

Jahzeiah. Tikvah's son and one of the persons named in connection with the divorce proceedings between the Israelites and their foreign wives (Ezr 10:15, KJV Jahaziah). Opinions differ as to whether he was for or against the proceedings. While the Hebrew text can be justifiably read either way, the grammar favors the former reading.

Jahzerah. Ancestor of a priest who returned to Judah after the Babylonian exile (1 Chr 9:12). He is called Ahzai (KJV Ahasai) in Nehemiah 11:13. Little else is known about him except that he was a great-grandson of a priest named Immer who lived in Jerusalem before the exile.

See AHZAI.

Jahziel. Alternate spelling of Jahzeel, Naphtali's son, in 1 Chronicles 7:13.

See JAHZEEL, JAHZEELITE.

Jair. 1. Descendant of Manasseh (Nm 32:41), who at the time of the conquest took several villages in Bashan and Gilead and called them after his own name, Havvoth-jair ("towns of Jair") (Dt 3:14; cf. Jos 13:30; 1 Kgs 4:13; 1 Chr 2:23). A descendant of his, Ira, is called "the Jairite" (2 Sm 20:26).

See HAVVOTH-JAIR, HAVOTH-JAIR.

2. One of the judges of Israel. He judged Israel 22 years. His being a Gileadite makes it probable that he was a descendant of #1 above (Jgs 10:3–5).

3. Father of Elhanan who killed Lahmi, Goliath's brother (1 Chr 20:5). In 2 Samuel 21:19 he is called Jaare-oregim.

4. Father of Mordecai (Est 2:5). Because of the time lapse from the capture of Jeconiah, king of Judah, to the beginning of the reign of Xerxes, king of Persia (597–486 BC), Jair was either the one taken captive with Jeconiah, or his father Shimei was and Jair was then born in captivity.

Jairite. Descendant of Jair from Manasseh's tribe (2 Sm 20:26).

See JAIR #1.

Jairus. Ruler of the synagogue, perhaps at Capernaum. Jairus sought Jesus among the crowds and petitioned him to come and heal his critically ill daughter. However, delayed by another healing, Jesus learned that Jairus' daughter had died. Jesus, encouraging him not to fear but to believe, went to the ruler's house, dismissed the mourners, and healed the child (Mk 5:22; Lk 8:41).

Jakan. KJV spelling of Jaakan, Esau's descendant, in 1 Chronicles 1:42

See JAAKAN.

Jakeh. Agur's father. Agur authored a series of proverbs addressed to Ithiel and Ucal (Prv 30:1).

Jakim. 1. Elpaal's descendant from Benjamin's tribe (1 Chr 8:19).
2. Levite assigned to temple duty in David's time (1 Chr 24:12).

Jalam. Esau's son and chief of an Edomite clan (Gn 36:5,14,18; 1 Chr 1:35, KJV Jaalam).

Jalon. Ezrah's son from Judah's tribe (1 Chr 4:17).

Jambres. Enemy of Moses, who, along with Jannes, is used by Paul as an example of the type of person to avoid (2 Tm 3:8).

James (Person). Personal name which occurs 38 times in the NT, mostly in the synoptic Gospels. Apart from #1 below, the identities of the other persons bearing the name have been much debated. There may have been as many as four, though some scholars argue for two or three. Jerome (345?–414?), with a somewhat tortuous and question-begging argument, reaches the conclusion that the four are really only one.

1. James the Son of Zebedee. He was a Galilean fisherman (Mk 1:19,20) who was called to be one of the 12 disciples at the same time as his brother John (Mt 4:21; Mk 1:19, 20). It is reasonable to assume that he was older than John—he is nearly always mentioned first, and John is sometimes identified as "the brother of James" (Mt 10:2; 17:1; Mk 3:17; 5:37).

James, John, and Simon (Peter) comprise a trio that attained a place of primacy among the disciples. They are found at the center of things, for example, when Jairus' daughter was raised (Mk 5:37; Lk 8:51), at the transfiguration (Mt 17:1; Mk 9:2; Lk 9:28), on the Mt of Olives (Mk 13:3), and in the Garden of Gethsemane (Mt 26:37; Mk 14:33). It was James and

John, moreover, who had earlier accompanied Jesus to the home of Simon and Andrew (Mk 1:29).

James and John were nicknamed "Boanerges" or "sons of thunder" (Mk 3:17), when they were rebuked by the Lord for impetuous speech and for having totally misconceived the purpose of his coming. This may have been the consequence of their suggestion that they should pray for the destruction of the Samaritan village which had rejected the Lord's messengers (Lk 9:54).

The presumptuous and ill-considered thinking of the two brothers was also obvious when they asked for a place of honor in the kingdom. James was co-recipient of the prophecy that the two would drink the cup their Master was to drink (Mk 10:35–40; cf. Mt 20:20–23). These sons of Zebedee are also assumed to have been present with the other disciples when the risen Christ appeared by the Sea of Tiberias (Jn 21:1,2), though curiously James' name is nowhere mentioned in the fourth Gospel.

We know nothing about James' career subsequently until about AD 44, when Jesus' prophecy was fulfilled: James was "slain with the sword" by Herod Agrippa I, and thus became the first of the 12 whose martyrdom was referred to in the NT.

The wife of Zebedee was Salome (Mt 27:56), who may have been a sister of the Lord's mother (see Jn 19:25). If this is indeed so it would mean that James and John were first

The tomb of the apostle James in the Kidron Valley outside Jerusalem.

cousins of Jesus, and that they may have considered themselves to have been in a privileged position.

An account attributed to Clement of Alexandria (c. 155–c.220) says that when James went on trial for his life, his steadfast testimony led to the conversion of his accuser who, the story goes on, was carried off with him to execution. A much less reliable tradition declares that James preached the gospel in Spain, of which country he is the patron saint.

See APOSTLE, APOSTLESHIP.

2. James, the Son of Alphaeus. Another of the apostles (Mt 10:3; Mk 3:18; Lk 6:15; Acts 1:13), but nothing certain is known about him. As Levi or Matthew is also described as "the son of Alphaeus" (Mk 2:14), he and James may have been brothers.

See APOSTLE, APOSTLESHIP.

3. James "The Less." He was the son of a Mary (Mt 27:56; Mk 15:40; Lk 24:10) who might have been the wife (or the daughter) of Clopas. Assuming that she was the wife, some go on to conclude from a superficial word resemblance that Clopas and Alphaeus are two forms of the same name. This in turn has led on to a suggested identification of this James with #2 above.

The description "the less" seems to have been given to distinguish this James from the son of Zebedee, and may signify that he was either smaller or younger than his namesake (the Greek word can encompass both meanings).

4. James, the Brother of Jesus. The only two references to him in the Gospels mention him with his brothers Joses, Simon, and Judas (Mt 13:55; Mk 6:3). This James may have been, after Jesus, the oldest of the brothers. As with the other brothers, James apparently did not accept Jesus' authority during his earthly life (Jn 7:5).

There is no specific mention of James' conversion; it may have dated from Jesus' appearance to him and the others after the resurrection (1 Cor 15:7). He became head of the Christian church at Jerusalem (Acts 12:17; 21:18; Gal 2:9). Although Jesus had always taught the relative subordination of family ties (Mt 12:48–50; Mk 3:33–35; Lk 8:21), it is hard to believe that James' authority was not somehow enhanced because of his relationship to the Master.

James was regarded as an apostle (Gal 1:19), although he was not one of the 12. Some suggest he was a replacement for the martyred son of Zebedee; others infer his apostleship by widening the scope of that term to embrace both the 12 and "all the apostles" (see the two separate categories cited in 1 Cor 15:5,7).

Tradition states that James was appointed as the first bishop of Jerusalem by the Lord himself and the apostles. It is certain that he presided over the first Council of Jerusalem, called to consider the terms of admission of Gentiles into the Christian church, and he may have formulated the decree which met with the approval of all his colleagues, and was promulgated to the churches of Antioch, Syria, and Cilicia (Acts 15:13–21).

James evidently regarded his own special ministry as being to the Jews, and his was a mediating role in the controversy that arose in the young church around the place of the Law for those who had become Christians, from both gentile and Jewish origins.

That he continued to have strong Jewish Christian sympathies is apparent from the request made to Paul when the latter visited Jerusalem for the last time (Acts 21:18–25). This is also the last mention of James in Acts.

His name occurs again in the NT as the traditional author of the Letter of James, where he describes himself as "a servant of God and of the Lord Jesus Christ" (Jas 1:1).

According to Hegesippus (c. AD 180), James' faithful adherence to the Jewish Law and his austere life-style led to the designation "the Just." It seems clear that he suffered martyrdom; Josephus places it in the year AD 61 when there was a Jewish uprising after the death of Festus the procurator and before his successor had been appointed.

Jerome (c. 345–c.419) speaks of an apocryphal Gospel of the Hebrews (fragments of which appear in various patristic writings), which contained a passage recounting the appearance of the risen Christ to James. In contrast to 1 Corinthians 15:7, this gospel claims that this was the first appearance of the Lord after the resurrection. The same writing is alleged to have noted James' vow to eat no bread from the time of the Last Supper until he had seen the risen Lord. This raises questions about the assumption that James was in fact present at the Last Supper.

See JAMES, BOOK OF; BROTHERS OF JESUS.

5. James, the father of the Apostle Judas. (Judas was "not Iscariot," Jn 14:22; the Thaddaeus of Mt and Mk), according to a more natural rendering of Luke 6:16 and Acts 1:13. The KJV represents him as the *brother* of the apostle, but the RSV rendering given above is preferable. Nothing further is known about him.　　　　　　　　　　J. D. DOUGLAS

James, Letter of.

Author. According to the salutation this letter was written by "James, a servant of God and of the Lord Jesus Christ" (1:1). But who was this James? Of the several James mentioned in the NT, only two have ever been proposed as the author of this letter—James, the son of Zebedee, and James, the Lord's brother. It is not likely that the son of Zebedee wrote it because he was martyred very early (AD 44), and there is no indication that he had attained a leadership role in the early church that would warrant his writing a general letter. The traditional view identifies the author with James, the brother of our Lord, and the head of the Jerusalem church (Acts 12:17; 15:13; 21:18; 1 Cor 15:7; Gal 2:9–12). This identification is supported by: (1) the similarity of the language of the letter with that of James' speech and the circular letter of Acts 15; (2) the consistency of the historical reports of the life and character of the Lord's brother with what is found in the letter; (3) the distinct Judaistic flavor of the letter; and (4) the fact that no other James fits the situation as well as the Lord's brother.

Date, Origin, and Destination. A wide range of opinion exists on the date of James. Those who accept the traditional authorship date it either in the middle 40s or early 60s (shortly before the death of its author). It has been dated as late as AD 150 by those who hold that it was written by an unknown James or that the author was writing in the name of James, the Lord's brother.

Although it is impossible to be certain about the time of writing, there are several factors which point to an earlier date. The social conditions revealed in the letter, especially the sharp cleavage between rich and poor (1:9–11; 2:1–7; 5:1–6), a situation which was markedly changed after AD 70, point to an early date. The strong expectation of the return of Jesus Christ also suggests an early date (5:7,8). There is nothing in the Christian literature of the 2nd century that can match the simple and powerful teaching about the end times found in this letter. Other evidence includes the rather primitive church organization revealed in the book (2:1–6), the absence of the debate concerning the inclusion of the Gentiles, and the fact that it is addressed to the whole church (1:1) and yet primarily to Jews (a situation that existed in the church only before Paul's first missionary journey). But the most crucial passage for dating the letter is the one on faith and works (2:14–26). Whoever wrote these verses must have been acquainted with Paul's teaching. Yet it is impossible to believe that he is trying to refute Paul. This would involve an almost inconceivable misunderstanding of Paul's doctrine of justification by faith. The passage is best explained as having come about as the result of a misunderstanding of Paul, not by James, but by his readers. Such a misunderstanding

would have been more likely at the beginning of Paul's public ministry. The Book of Acts records his first extended public preaching as taking place at Antioch (Acts 11:26). This year-long ministry preceded the famine visit to Jerusalem of about AD 46 (cf. Acts 11:27–29) and the persecution by Herod Agrippa of AD 44. How long it was before the misunderstanding of Paul's doctrine of justification by faith came to the attention of James, we do not know. However, since Jews (both Christian and non-Christian) from all over the Mediterranean world were continually moving in and out of Jerusalem, it probably was not long. A date of about AD 45, immediately following the Herodian persecution, would best fit all the conditions.

Although a number of suggestions have been made from time to time about the origin of the book, there can be little doubt that the letter was written in Palestine. The author makes allusions that are Near Eastern generally and Palestinian particularly (cf. "the early and late rain" 5:7; the spring of brackish water, 3:11; the fig, olive, and vine, 3:12; and the "scorching heat" 1:11).

The only direct section of the letter which might help in discovering who the readers are is found in 1:1: "to the twelve tribes in the Dispersion." This is usually taken to mean Christian Jews living outside of Palestine. The basic difficulty with this position is that "the twelve tribes" is a term which traditionally meant the entirety of the Jewish nation (cf. Ecclus 44:23; Assyrian Moses 2:4–5; Bar 1:2; 62:5, etc.; Acts 26:7), which, no matter how widely it had been scattered, could never have its entire existence outside of Palestine. Furthermore, had James been writing to that part of the Jewish nation which was living in the diaspora (dispersion), he could easily have made that clear. Thus it seems best to take "the twelve tribes" in a symbolical sense and understand it as a reference to the Christian church, conceived of as the new Israel.

An examination of the rest of the contents of the letter indicates clearly that James is writing to Jews who are primarily Christians (cf. 2:1). However, there is one section (5:1–6) that seems to be addressed to non-Christians, and may represent a prophetic attempt to reach non-Christians who were attending Christian assemblies (cf. 1 Cor 14:23,24).

In the shorter disconnected passages of the letter, it is impossible to discover anything about the readers' circumstances. Most of these exhortations are general and relate to social and spiritual conditions one might find among any group of Christians in any age. The more extended passages that deal with social conditions (2:1–12; 5:1–11) do provide information about the readers' situation. James is addressing poor Christians who are employed as farm laborers by wealthy landowners. A few rich may be included among his Jewish Christian readers (cf. 4:13–17), but James is primarily concerned with the poor. His statements denouncing the rich are reminiscent of the OT prophets, especially Amos.

Purpose and Theological Teaching. The letter of James was written: (1) to strengthen Jewish Christians undergoing trial (1:2–4,13–15; 5:7–11); (2) to correct a misunderstanding of the Pauline doctrine of justification by faith (2:14–26); and (3) to pass down to first-generation Christians a wealth of practical wisdom.

James' theology is not dogmatic; it omits the great theological themes that dominate Paul's writings and play such an important role in the rest of the books of the NT. James makes no mention of the incarnation, and the name of Christ appears only twice (1:1; 2:1). No mention is made of Christ's sufferings, death, or resurrection.

James' theology is practical, and has a decided Jewish flavor. The distinctive Christian features, of course, are there. James has simply baptized rabbinical ideas into Christ.

The outstanding theological themes of the letter are:

Temptation (Trials). The typically Jewish teachings—joy in trials and the use of trial for the building and perfecting of character—are both found in the letter (1:2–4). James also discusses the origin of temptation (vv 13–15). Here the author comes into conflict with contemporary Jewish theology. The rabbinical solution to the problem of the origin of sin was that there was an evil tendency in man which enticed man to sin. The rabbis reasoned that since God is the Creator of all things, including the evil impulse in man, man is not responsible for his sin. No, says James, "Let no one say when he is tempted, 'I am tempted by God'; for God cannot be tempted with evil and he himself tempts no one; but each person is tempted when he is lured and enticed by his own desire" (vv 13,14).

Law. The entire letter is concerned with ethical teaching with no mention of the central gospel truths of Christ's death and resurrection. James presupposes the gospel and presents the ethical side of Christianity as a perfect law. He seems to be reassuring his Jewish Christian readers that for them there is still law (the priceless possession of every Jew).

The law (ethical teaching of Christianity) is a perfect law (1:25), because it was perfected by Jesus Christ. It is also a law of freedom (1:25), that is, a law (ethical responsibility) which applies to those who have freedom, not from law, but from sin and self through the "word of truth." Thus "law" is a Palestinian Christian Jew's way of describing the ethical teaching of the Christian faith, the standard of conduct for the believer in Jesus Christ.

This tendency to describe Christian ethical teaching as law is found in 2:8–13, a passage which arises out of a rebuke against the favoritism that James' readers were showing toward the rich. This favoritism was being condoned by an appeal to the law of love to one's neighbor. So James writes: "If you really fulfil the royal law, . . . you do well" (v 8). The "royal law" is to be understood with the statement in verse 5, where James reminds his readers that God has "chosen those who are poor in the world to be rich in faith and heirs of the kingdom which he has promised to those who love him." The "royal law," then, is for those who are of God's kingdom; it is the rule of faith for those who have willingly subjected themselves to God's rule. The identification of law with the ethical side of Christianity runs through the entire letter.

Faith and Faith vs. Works. Faith plays an important role in the theology of James. It is the basic element of piety (1:3; cf. 2:5), belief in God—not merely in his existence, but in his character as being good and benevolent in his dealings with mankind (1:6; cf. v 13). Faith includes belief in the power of God, in his ability to perform miraculous acts, and is closely associated with prayer (5:15,16; cf. 1:6). James has a dynamic concept of faith and clearly goes beyond Judaism when he speaks of faith directed toward the Lord Jesus Christ (2:1).

Similarities exist between the concept of faith in James and in the teachings of Jesus. For our Lord also, faith meant access to the divine power and is often associated with healing (cf. Mt 21:22; Mk 5:34; 11:24).

The best known passage in which faith is mentioned is 2:14–26, where it is contrasted with works. From a study of this passage it is hard to conclude that the author is attempting to refute Paul. The two stand basically in agreement. For both James and Paul faith is directed toward the Lord Jesus Christ; such faith will always produce good works. The faith of which James speaks is not faith simply in the Hebraic sense of trust in God which results in moral action. This is not recognized as *true* faith by James (cf. "if a man says he has faith," 2:14), and Paul would agree with him.

James' use of the word "works" differs significantly from Paul's. For James, "works" are works of faith, the ethical outworking of true spirituality and include especially the "work of love" (2:8). (Paul would probably call such works the fruit of the Spirit.) When Paul uses the word "works" he usually has in mind the works of the law, that is, works righteousness—the attempt by man to establish his own righteousness before God. It is against such theological heresy that Paul's strongest polemics are addressed in the letters to the Galatians and Romans.

It is best then to understand 2:14–26 as a refutation, not of Paul, but of a misunderstanding of his doctrine of justification by faith.

Wisdom. James' concept of wisdom also reveals the Jewish background of the letter. Wisdom is primarily practical, not philosophical. It is not to be identified with reasoning power or the ability to apprehend intellectual problems; it has nothing to do with the questions *how* or *why.* It is to be sought by earnest prayer and is a gift from God (1:5). Both of these ideas find their roots in the wisdom literature of the Jews (cf. Wis of Sol 7:7; Prv 2:6; Ecclus 1:1). The wise man demonstrates his wisdom by his good life (3:13), whereas the wisdom that produces jealousy and selfishness is not God's kind of wisdom (3:15,16).

Doctrine of the Endtime. Three important endtime themes are touched upon in the letter.

THE KINGDOM OF GOD. Mention of the kingdom of God grows out of a discussion of favoritism in the first half of chapter 2. No favoritism is to be shown to the rich, for God has chosen "those who are poor in the world to be rich in faith and heirs of the kingdom which he has promised to those who love him" (2:5). This echoes our Lord's teaching in Luke 6:20: "Blessed are you poor, for yours is the kingdom of God." The kingdom is the reign of God partially realized in this life, but fully realized in the life to come (cf. "promised," 2:5). It is almost synonymous with salvation or eternal life.

JUDGMENT. This is the dominant endtime theme of the letter. In 2:12, the readers are admonished to speak and act, remembering that they will be judged under the law of liberty, and they are reminded that judgment is without mercy to one who has shown no mercy. Judgment, in other words, will be administered according to works. In 3:1, James addresses teachers and reminds them that privilege is another basis on which God judges.

The theme of judgment again appears in 5:1–6, and here the author reaches prophetic heights. God's judgment will fall on the wealthy land owners who have lived self-indulgent, irresponsible lives. Not only have they cheated their poor tenant farmers, they have even "condemned and murdered innocent men, who were not opposing you" (v 6

NIV). All this has made them ripe for judgment ("you have fattened your hearts in a day of slaughter," v 5).

The final passage on judgment (5:9) is addressed to those being exploited by the unscrupulous rich. James' word of exhortation is that they are not to grumble against each other. Judging is God's business and the Judge is close at hand.

THE SECOND COMING. The hope of Christ's coming is presented as the great stimulus for Christian living. Every kind of suffering and trial must be endured because the coming of Christ is at hand (5:8). This expectancy is powerful and immediate and like that found in the Thessalonian letters.

Content. In the true spirit of Wisdom literature, James touches upon many subjects. His short, abrupt paragraphs have been likened to a string of pearls—each is an entity in itself. Some transitions exist, but they are often difficult to find as James moves quickly from one subject to another.

The author begins by identifying himself as the "servant of God and of the Lord Jesus Christ," and his readers as the "twelve tribes in the diaspora," that is, the whole Christian church, which, when James wrote, was overwhelmingly Jewish (1:1).

His first word is one of encouragement. Trials are to be counted as joy because they are God's way of testing the believer, and they produce spiritual maturity. If the reason for trial is not clear, God can and will give the answer. He is a lavish giver of wisdom to those who really want it (1:5–8).

A poor Christian should be proud of his exalted position in Jesus Christ, and a rich Christian should be glad that he has discovered there are more important things than wealth. Riches are transitory—like quickly wilting flowers under the hot Palestine sun (1:9–11).

God promises the man who endures trial life which is life indeed. One must not blame God for temptation, for it is contrary to his very nature to either be tempted or to tempt man. Temptation has its origin in man's selfish desire—a desire which, when brought to full fruition, produces death (vv 12–15).

God is not the origin of temptation but the source of all good in the life of man. He has given to man his best gift, the gift of new life, and this has come through the gospel (1:16–18).

The proper attitude toward the word of truth is receptivity, not anger, and an effective listening to that word involves spiritual preparation of heart and mind. Such a reception of the word brings salvation (1:19–21).

The word is to be acted upon, not merely listened to. To be a passive hearer is to be like a man who sees himself in a mirror and because he takes such a fleeting glance, forgets what he sees. An active hearer, one who takes a long look in the mirror of God's Word, will become a doer, and God will bring great blessing into his life (1:22–25).

True religion is an intensely practical thing. It involves such things as controlling one's tongue, looking after the needs of orphans and widows, and adopting a nonworldly life-style (1:26,27).

Favoritism and faith in Jesus Christ do not go together. It is wrong to show deference to a rich man when he comes into the assembly and ignore the poor man. God has chosen poor people to be heirs of his kingdom. Furthermore, to show favoritism to the rich does not make sense, since they are the very ones who drag Christians into court and blaspheme the name of Christ (2:1–7).

If by showing deference to the rich, the royal law, "to love one's neighbor as oneself," is fulfilled, well and good. But to show favoritism is sin and such sin will be judged by God. In order to be a law-breaker one has only to break one law (2:8–13).

Can a faith that does not produce works save a man? What good is a faith that does not respond to human need? Such a faith is dead. Someone will object by saying that there are "faith Christians" and "works Christians." But this is not so. True faith is always demonstrated by works. It is not enough to have orthodox beliefs. Even the demons are theologically orthodox! Abraham, by offering up Isaac, is an example of how true faith and worship go together. Even Rahab, the prostitute, dem-onstrated her faith by protecting the spies at Jericho. So faith and works are inseparable (2:14–26).

Not many people should become spiritual teachers because of the awesome responsibility involved. All of us are subject to mistakes, and especially mistakes of the tongue, because the tongue is almost impossible to control. It is like a destructive blaze set by hell itself. The tongue is also inconsistent; it is used both to praise God and to curse men. Such inconsistency ought not to be (3:1–12).

True wisdom will always evidence itself in ethical living, whereas false wisdom produces jealousy and selfish ambition (3:13–18).

Strife and conflict arise out of illegitimate desires. Failure to have what one wants arises either from not asking God for it or from asking for the wrong thing. To be a friend of the world is to be an enemy of God, for God is a jealous God and will brook no rivals. He also opposes the proud but offers abundant grace to the humble (4:1–9).

To speak against a brother or to judge him is to speak against God's Law and to judge it. The Christian's proper role is to be a doer of the Law, not a judge. The role of judge belongs to God alone (4:11,12).

Life is at best uncertain. Therefore plans for traveling or doing business should be made with the realization that all are subject to the will of God. To do otherwise is to be boastful and arrogant. When what is right is clearly known and one fails to do it, that is sin (4:13–17).

Judgment is coming to the rich because they are hoarding their wealth instead of us-

Excavations of the ruins at Jericho, the city where Rahab, exercising her faith, "received the messengers and sent them out another way" (Jas 2:25).

ing it for good purposes. God is not unmindful of the cries of the poor farm laborers whom the rich have cheated and unjustly condemned. He is preparing the selfish, unscrupulous rich for a day of awful judgment (5:1–6).

In the midst of suffering and injustice the poor are to be patient for Christ's coming, as a farmer must be patient as he waits for God to send the rains to cause his crop to grow and ripen. The return of Christ is at hand and therefore complaining and judging one another must cease. Job is a good example of patience and endurance in suffering. One need not use oaths to guarantee the truthfulness of his statements. A single yes or no is sufficient (5:7–12).

Suffering should elicit prayer, cheerfulness, and praise. When a believer is sick, he should call the elders of the church to pray for him and anoint him with oil. God has promised to answer such prayers. If the sickness is due to personal sin, and that sin is confessed, God will forgive. Elijah is a classic example of how the prayer of a righteous man has powerful results (5:13–18).

If a fellow Christian sees that his brother has strayed from the truth and is able to bring him back into fellowship with Christ and his church, the consequences will be: (1) he shall save the sinner from death, and (2) God will forgive the erring brother (5:19,20).

WALTER W. WESSEL

See JAMES (PERSON); BROTHERS OF JESUS.

Bibliography. E.D. Hiebert, *The Epistle of James;* R. Johnstone, *Lectures Exegetical and Practical on the Epistle of James;* R. J. Knowling, *The Epistle of St. James;* S. Laws, *A Commentary on the Epistle of James;* J. B. Mayor, *The Epistle of St. James;* A. Plummer, *The General Epistles of St. James and St. Jude.*

Jamin. 1. Simeon's son (Gn 46:10; Ex 6:15; 1 Chr 4:24) and founder of the Jaminite family (Nm 26:12).

2. Ram's son from Judah's tribe (1 Chr 2:27).

3. One of the men (perhaps a Levite) who taught and explained the Law to the people following Ezra's public reading (Neh 8:7).

Jaminite. Descendant of Jamin from Simeon's tribe (Nm 26:12).

See JAMIN #1.

Jamlech. Leader in Simeon's tribe (1 Chr 4:34).

Janai. Gadite chief who settled, along with his kinsmen, in the land of Bashan (1 Chr 5:12, KJV Jaanai).

Janim. City in the hill country of the territory assigned to Judah's tribe for an inheritance (Jos 15:53, KJV Janum). Its location is presumably W,SW of Hebron.

Jannai, Janna. Ancestor of Jesus recorded in Luke's genealogy (3:24, KJV Janna).

See GENEALOGY OF JESUS CHRIST.

Jannes. Enemy of Moses who, along with Jambres, is used by Paul as an example of what type of person to avoid (2 Tm 3:8).

Janoah. 1. City defining the eastern border of Ephraim's territory, located southeast of Shechem and northeast of Shiloh (Jos 16:6,7, KJV Janohah). It has been identified with modern Khirbet Yanun.

2. Town (modern Yanuh) of Naphtali's tribe captured by Tiglath-pileser, king of Assyria, during the reign of King Pekah of Israel in 732 BC (2 Kgs 15:29).

Janohah. KJV spelling of Janoah, a town in Ephraim's territory, in Joshua 16:6,7.

See JANOAH #1.

Janum. KJV spelling of Janim, a town in Judah's territory, in Joshua 15:53.

See JANIM.

Japheth. One of Noah's three sons (Gn 5:32; 7:13; 9:18,23,27; 10:1–5; 1 Chr 1:4–6) who, along with his wife, was among the eight human survivors of the great flood. Because Japheth and his brother Shem acted with respect and modesty in covering their father's nakedness while he was in a drunken condition (Gn 9:20–23), they were both blessed in Noah's prophetic pronouncement of Genesis 9:26,27. Of Japheth, Noah said, "God enlarge Japheth, and let him dwell in the tents of Shem; and let Canaan be his slave." There are two common interpretations of the meaning of this prophecy. Some understand the "enlargement of Japheth" to be a reference to a great increase in numbers of descendants. "To dwell in the tents of Shem" is understood as Japheth's sharing in the blessing of Shem. According to this view there is to be a time when God will work primarily with Shem (the people of Israel); but then at a later time Japheth will be brought into connection with the faith of Israel and share in its promises. In this view fulfillment is found in the opening of the gospel to the Gentiles at the inception of the NT church. Others understand the "enlargement of Japheth" to refer to territorial enlargement and the "dwelling in the tents of Shem" as the conquest of Shemite territory by Japhethites. In this view fulfillment is found in the Greek and Roman conquests of Palestine.

In the table of nations in Genesis 10, Japheth is listed as the father of Gomer, Magog, Madai, Javan, Tubal, Meshech, and Tiras (vv 1–5). These are the ancestors of peoples who lived to the north and west of Israel, and who spoke what today are classified as Indo-European languages.

See NATIONS; NOAH #1.

Japhia (Person). 1. King of Lachish who joined an alliance of four other Amorite kings to punish Gibeon for its treaty with the Jews. Joshua dealt a total defeat to the Amorites at the battle of Beth-horon (aided by hailstones and the sun standing still). Japhia and the four kings hid in a cave at Makkedah, but were discovered and hung by Joshua (Jos 10:3–27).

2. Son born to David while he was king in Jerusalem (2 Sm 5:15; 1 Chr 3:7; 14:6).

Japhia (Place). Town described as the southern border of Zebulun's territory (Jos 19:12). It has been identified with modern Yafa, about two miles southwest of Nazareth.

Japhlet. Heber's son and a chief in Asher's tribe (1 Chr 7:32,33).

Japhletite, Japhleti. Unidentified territory marking part of the southern border of Ephraim's territory in the vicinity of Beth-horon (Jos 16:3, KJV Japhleti).

Japho. KJV form of Joppa in Joshua 19:46.

See JOPPA.

Jar. See POTTERY.

Jarah. Descendant of King Saul (1 Chr 9:42); also called Jehoaddah in 1 Chronicles 8:36 (KJV Jehoadah).

Jareb. Name used by Hosea to designate an Assyrian king (Hos 5:13). Because no such name is to be found in the Assyrian king lists, some have conjectured that it designated Sargon, but this is mere speculation. In all probability Hosea chose this name (which in Hebrew means "contentious") to describe the opposition that Ephraim and Judah would encounter from a contentious king in Assyria because of Israel's sin (Hos 10:6).

Jared. Mahalalel's son and a descendant of Seth. He was the father of Enoch (Gn 5:15–20; 1 Chr 1:2, KJV Jered; Lk 3:37).

See GENEALOGY OF JESUS CHRIST.

Jaresiah. KJV rendering of Jaareshiah, Jeroham's son, in 1 Chronicles 8:27.

See JAARESHIAH.

Jarha. Egyptian slave of Sheshan, Jerahmeel's descendant, who was given his master's daughter in marriage. Sheshan did this because he had no sons (1 Chr 2:34,35).

Jarib. 1. Alternate name for Jachin, Simeon's son, in 1 Chronicles 4:24.

See JACHIN #1.

2. Man who assisted Ezra in securing temple servants before the return to Palestine from exile (Ezr 8:16).

3. Jeshua's son, who obeyed Ezra's exhortation to divorce his pagan wife after the exile (Ezr 10:18).

Jarmuth. 1. Fortified city in the northern part of the Shephelah given to Judah's tribe for an inheritance (Jos 15:35). It was one of five Amorite cities that banded together to attack Gibeon after they had made peace with Joshua and Israel (Jos 10:3,5,23; 12:11). Jarmuth was reinhabited after the exile by Judahites (Neh 11:29), and possibly maintained a population throughout the exile period. It is identified with Khirbet Yarmuk, 18 miles southwest of Jerusalem. Archaeological evidence suggests that the area of the Bronze Age city was 6 to 8 acres and had a population of about 1500 to 2000 people. It is mentioned in the Amarna letters as receiving aid from Lachish.

2. One of four cities of Issachar given to the Levites for their inheritance (Jos 21:28,29). It is apparently identifiable with Ramoth in 1 Chronicles 6:73 and Remeth in Joshua 19:21. A stela of Pharaoh Seti I was found at Beth-shan, referring to the whole area as Mt Jarmuth.

See LEVITICAL CITIES.

Jaroah. Gilead's son from Gad's tribe (1 Chr 5:14).

Jashen. One of David's 30 mighty men (2 Sm 23:32). The Hebrew text reads "the sons of Jashen," and 1 Chronicles 11:34 reads "the sons of Hashem the Gizonite." Scholars are generally agreed that the phrase "the sons of" is dittographic and repeats the last three letters of the preceding word. The reading in the original text probably was either "Jashen the Gizonite" or "Hashem the Gizonite," making him, and not his son, the mighty man of David's army.

Jashobeam. 1. Zabdiel's son who was put in charge of David's mighty men (1 Chr 11:11). He was also appointed chief of a division

(24,000 soldiers) in the first month (1 Chr 27:2). He is the same person as the Tahchemonite "who sat in the seat" (2 Sm 23:8), which is often rendered as a name, Josheb-basshebeth. Jashobeam gained renown by killing 300 men, according to 1 Chronicles 11:11, or 800, according to 2 Samuel 23:8.

2. One of the warriors who joined David at Ziklag (1 Chr 12:6).

Jashub. 1. Issachar's third son (1 Chr 7:1, alternately called Iob in Gn 46:13, KJV Job), and founder of the Jashubite family (Nm 26:34).

2. Bani's son, who obeyed Ezra's exhortation to divorce his pagan wife after the exile (Ezr 10:29).

Jashubi-lehem. KJV translation of a Hebrew phrase (in 1 Chr 4:22) probably meaning "returned to Lehem," as in RSV.

See LEHEM.

Jashubite. Descendant of Jashub, Issachar's third son (Nm 26:24).

See JASHUB #1.

Jasiel. KJV form of Jaasiel the Mezobite in 1 Chronicles 11:47.

See JAASIEL #1.

Jason. 1. Jewish Christian at Thessalonica who hosted the apostle Paul (Acts 17:1,5–9). He and others were called before the city officials on charges of harboring seditionists. He was released when he put up bail.

2. Christian at Corinth who, along with Paul, sent greetings to the church at Rome (Rom 16:21).

Jasper. Variety of green quartz.

See MINERALS, METALS, AND PRECIOUS STONES.

Jathniel. Fourth son of Meshelemiah the Korahite and doorkeeper of the temple in David's time (1 Chr 26:2).

Jattir. Town in the hill country of Judah given to the Levites (Jos 15:48; 21:14; 1 Chr 6:57). David sent spoils from his victory over the Amalekites to Jattir (1 Sm 30:27). It is identified with modern Khirbet 'Attir, 13 miles southeast of Hebron.

See LEVITICAL CITIES.

Javan (Person). Japheth's son whose descendants migrated to the north and west of Canaan (Gn 10:2–4; 1 Chr 1:5,7).

Javan (Place). Location commonly identified with Greece. The name is linguistically associated with Ionia, a region in westernmost Asia Minor that was colonized by Greeks. By extension Javan came to be applied to Greece itself. In most occurrences in the Greek translation of the Bible, Javan appears as Hellas, "Greece."

Some hints as to its location are given as early as the table of nations, where Javan appears as the fourth son of Japheth (Gn 10:2; cf. 1 Chr 1:5); this tends to place it in Europe. Japheth is also said to be the father of Elishah (Cyprus?), Tarshish (Spain?), Kittim (Cyprus?), and Dodanim or Rodanim (Gn 10:4; 1 Chr 1:7). The connections of these areas or peoples is well known.

Most of the references to Ionia (Greece) are in the prophetic books. In Isaiah 66:19 Javan is named along with Tarshish, Put, Lud, and Tubal as places to which the glory of the Lord will be declared. These are taken as representative of the distant nations ("the coastlands afar off").

In a lengthy prophecy against Tyre, Ezekiel refers to Javan, Tubal and Meshech as those who traded slaves and bronze vessels for the merchandise of Tyre (27:13), while in Joel 3:6 Tyre is condemned for having sold the people of Judah and Jerusalem to the Greeks.

In Ezekiel 27:19 the Hebrew text reads "Vedan and Javan." This is followed by the NIV, which says that "Danites and Greeks" from Uzal purchased merchandise from Tyre. The NASB states, "Vedan and Javan paid for your wares from Uzal"; the KJV reads "Dan also and Javan." The RSV follows the Greek translation: "and wine from Uzal." The mention of Uzal has led some interpreters to place this Javan in southwest Arabia.

The Lord also said that he would brandish the sons of Zion over the sons of Greece when God executes judgment and brings in peace (Zec 9:13).

The references in Daniel clearly mean Greece. The he-goat who represents the king of Greece (Dn 8:21) is Alexander the Great, whose empire was divided among his four generals upon his death. "The prince of Greece" (Dn 10:20) is parallel to "the prince of Persia" (Dn 10:13,20). It has been suggested that "prince" means guardian angel, but the prince of Persia's opposition to the archangel Michael makes it evident that "prince" is a demonic spirit of high rank (a "world ruler," Eph 6:12).

Conflict between Persia and Greece is predicted in Daniel 11:2, while the following verse tells of the success of Alexander the Great and the breakup of his empire.

See also GREECE, GREEKS.

Javelin. Light, short, spearlike weapon.

See ARMS AND WARFARE.

Jazer. Town east of the Jordan River in southern Gilead, taken with its surrounding villages by the Israelites under Moses (Nm 21:32, KJV Jaazer). The tribes of Gad and Reuben asked for the lands of "Jazer" and Gilead. They had many cattle and saw that the east side of the Jordan was fertile and best suited for livestock grazing (Nm 32:1–5). They promised to build protection for their women and children, then go with the other tribes to fight in Canaan (Nm 32:7–27). Jazer became a border point marking the inheritance of Gad (Jos 13:25) and was given to the Levites (Jos 21:39; 1 Chr 6:81). When Joab was sent to number the people, he reached the city of Jazer in Gad (2 Sm 24:5). Jazer also became known for its mighty men of valor under King David (1 Chr 26:31). Over 200 years later, however, it was occupied by Moab (Is 16:6–9; Jer 48:32).

See LEVITICAL CITIES.

Jaziz. One of David's royal stewards in charge of the flocks (1 Chr 27:30,31).

Jearim, Mount. Mountain on the northwest border of Judah's territory between Beth-shemesh and Kiriath-jearim. Chesalon was located on its northern slope (Jos 15:10). It is associated with Mt Seir and Mt Ephron.

See CHESALON.

Je-atherai, Jeaterai. Zerah's son, a Gershonite Levite (1 Chr 6:21, KJV Jeaterai), called Ethni in 1 Chronicles 6:41.

Jeberechiah. Father of Zechariah the scribe. Zechariah, with Uriah the priest, witnessed Isaiah's prophecy of the Assyrian conquest of Israel (Is 8:2).

Jebus, Jebusi, Jebusite. Walled city, lying on the boundary between Judah and Benjamin, conquered by David; thereafter it was known as the "city of David," or ancient Jerusalem. Its occupants were Jebusites (KJV Jebusi, Jos 18:16). They were one of the several clans or tribes collectively known as Canaanites (Gn 10:15). Their land, along with that of their neighbors, was repeatedly promised to the Israelites (Ex 3:8; 13:5; 23:23; 33:2; 34:11; Nm 13:29; Dt 7:1; 20:17). This promise was partially fulfilled early in the campaign under Joshua (Jos 3:10; 12:8; 18:28, KJV Jebusi; cf. 24:11). It is said that "the men of Judah fought against Jerusalem, and took it" (Jgs 1:8), but also that "the Benjaminites, however, failed to dislodge the Jebusites, who were living in Jeru-

Middle Bronze wall from pre-Davidic Jerusalem.

salem; to this day the Jebusites live there with the Benjamites" (Jgs 2:21 NIV). Apparently the city was captured by the men of Judah, but its inhabitants were not destroyed and they later reoccupied the site.

Jebus (or Jerusalem) lay on the borderline between two tribes, and this may account for its survival until the time of David. The borders of Judah and Benjamin are thus defined: "The boundary goes up by the valley of the son of Hinnom at the southern shoulder of the Jebusite (that is, Jerusalem); . . . up to the top of the mountain that lies over against the valley of Hinnom" (Jos 15:8); "it then goes down the valley of Hinnom, south of the shoulder of the Jebusites, and downward to En-rogel" (Jos 17:16). The two accounts agree: the survey of Judah follows a westerly direction; the survey of Benjamin moves eastward; both indicate that Jebus lay on the southern slope of the "mountain" north of the valley of Hinnom, the site of East Jerusalem today.

The city's survival was assured by a constant supply of water, the spring of Gihon, and strong natural defenses. It was easily defended by steep valleys on three sides: the Kidron on the east, the Hinnom on the south and west. The Jebusites therefore considered their city impregnable. This gave them a certain arrogance and complacency. After the death of Saul, when David was seeking to consolidate the kingdom, the Jebusites scornfully challenged David to capture their stronghold, saying, "You will not come in here, but the blind and the lame will ward you off" (2 Sm 5:6; cf.

2 Chr 11:5). As the last remaining Canaanite stronghold in the area it presented a unique challenge. Joab apparently led the attack "up the water shaft" and succeeded where previous attempts had failed (2 Sm 5:8).

For political as well as strategic reasons David decided to move his capital from Hebron to Jebus. Politically it lay in neutral territory between Judah and Benjamin and thus aroused no jealousy. Strategically it was easily defended and more centrally located. The choice proved a wise one. In spite of the fact that Jebus-Jerusalem lies on no waterway or major highway, it has become through the centuries the "spiritual capital of the world." Under David and Solomon it became Israel's religious center, and today is of prime importance to the three major monotheistic religions of mankind. In 1947 the United Nations voted to internationalize Jerusalem and thus make available to all peoples the former Jebusite stronghold which became "the mountain of the house of the Lord" (Is 2:2; cf. Rv 21:2).

See JERUSALEM.

Jecamiah. KJV spelling of Jekamiah, King Jehoiachin's son, in 1 Chronicles 3:18.

See JEKAMIAH #2.

Jecholiah. KJV spelling of Jecoliah, King Azariah's mother, in 2 Kings 15:2.

See JECOLIAH.

Jechoniah. Alternate form of Jehoiachin, a Judean king, in Matthew 1:11,12.

See JEHOIACHIN.

Jechonias. KJV form of Jechoniah, an alternate name for Jehoiachin, king of Judah, in Matthew 1:11,12.

See JEHOIACHIN.

Jecoliah. Mother of King Azariah (Uzziah) (2 Kgs 15:2, KJV Jecholiah; 2 Chr 26:3).

Jeconiah. Alternate name for King Jehoiachin of Judah, who was carried into Babylonian exile (1 Chr 3:16,17; Jer 24:1).

See JEHOIACHIN.

Jedaiah. 1. Shimri's son and the father of Allon. He is listed in the genealogical tables of the Simeonites who settled in the valley of Gedor in Hezekiah's time (1 Chr 4:37).

2. Harumaph's son, who helped repair the Jerusalem wall after the exile (Neh 3:10).

3. Aaron's descendant and the head of the second of the 24 priestly divisions in David's time (1 Chr 24:7). His descendants are listed among the returned exiles (1 Chr 9:10; Ezr 2:36; Neh 7:39). The individuals and families listed below are probably a part of this priestly line, but their exact relationships are difficult to determine.

4. Resident priest in postexilic Jerusalem (Neh 11:10).

5. Another priest after the exile. He appears in the same list as #4 above, but as a distinct person (Neh 12:6,7,21). In the next generation this was the name of a family (v 19).

6. One of the exiles taken by Zechariah as witness to the symbolic crowning of Joshua. He may be the same as #4 or #5 above. He came back from captivity bringing gifts for the temple in the days of the high priest Joshua (Zec 6:10–14).

Jediael. 1. Benjamin's son (1 Chr 7:6,10,11), whose descendants were "men of valor" (or warriors) numbering 17,200 by David's time. Some suggest that he is identifiable with Ashbel, also Benjamin's son (Gn 46:21).

See ASHBEL, ASHBELITE.

2. Shimri's son, listed among David's mighty men (1 Chr 11:45).

3. One who deserted Saul to join David at Ziklag (1 Chr 12:20). He may be the same as #2 above.

4. Member of the Levitical family of Korah, appointed a "gatekeeper" (or doorkeeper) of the temple during David's reign (1 Chr 26:2).

Jedidah. Adaiah's daughter, the wife of King Amon of Judah and the mother of King Josiah (2 Kgs 22:1).

Jedidiah. Name meaning "friend of Jehovah" or "beloved of Jehovah"; God told Nathan the prophet to give Solomon, David's second son by Bathsheba, this name soon after his birth (2 Sm 12:24,25).

Jeduthun. Member of the Levitical family of Merar who, along with Asaph and Heman, presided over the music in the sanctuary in David's reign (1 Chr 25:1, 2 Chr 5:12). In other references Asaph and Heman are listed in conjunction with Ethan (1 Chr 15:17), suggesting that perhaps Ethan and Jeduthan are the same person. It may be that Ethan was his original name.

Some of his sons were set apart to prophesy with lyres, harps, and cymbals (1 Chr 25:1,3), apparently following the example of their father, who was called "the King's Seer" (2 Chr 35:15). In 1 Chronicles 16:38,42, he is listed as Obed-edom's father.

Jeduthun is mentioned in the titles of Psalms 39, 62, and 77.

Jeezer, Jeezerite. KJV forms of Iezer and Iezerite, contractions of Abiezer and Abiezerite, the names of Gilead's son and his descendants (Nm 26:30).

See ABIEZER #1.

Jegar-sahadutha. Aramaic name given by Laban to the heap of stones that he and Jacob piled up as a memorial to their covenant (Gn 31:47). The name means "heap of witness" and was called Galeed by Jacob.

See GALEED.

Jehaleleel. KJV spelling of Jehallelel, a Judahite, in 1 Chronicles 4:16.

See JEHALLELEL #1.

Jehalelel. KJV spelling of Jehallelel, a Levite, in 2 Chronicles 29:12.

See JEHALLELEL #2.

Jehallelel. 1. Descendant of Judah who had three sons (1 Chr 4:16, KJV Jehaleleel).

2. Levite of the family of Merari whose son Azariah participated in the cleansing of the temple in Hezekiah's time (2 Chr 29:12, KJV Jehalelel).

Jehdeiah. 1. Shubael's son, a Levite in David's time (1 Chr 24:20).

2. Meronothite and royal steward who was in charge of David's female donkeys (1 Chr 27:30).

Jehezkel, Jehezekel. Levite assigned to temple duty in David's time (1 Chr 24:16, KJV Jehezekel).

Jehiah. Levite who, along with Obed-edom, was appointed as doorkeeper for the ark when David brought it to Jerusalem (1 Chr 15:24).

Jehiel. 1. KJV spelling of Jeiel, King Saul's ancestor, in 1 Chronicles 9:35.

See JEIEL #2.

2. KJV spelling of Jeiel, Hotham's son, in 1 Chronicles 11:44.

See JEIEL #3.

3. A Levite musician who, along with other Levites appointed by David, played a psaltery at the removal of the ark to Jerusalem (1 Chr 15:18,20). Afterwards he was appointed to a permanent ministry of music in the sanctuary (1 Chr 16:5).

4. Levite of the family of Gershon; a chief of the house of Laadan (1 Chr 23:8). He was in charge of the temple treasury in David's reign, an office that seems to have continued in the family (1 Chr 29:8), and he was founder of a

priestly family called Jehieli (or Jehielites) (1 Chr 26:21,22).

5. Hachmoni's son who, with David's uncle Jonathan, "a counselor . . . and a scribe," was appointed to "attend" the king's sons, probably as a tutor or advisor (1 Chr 27:32).

6. Son of King Jehoshaphat of Judah, placed by his father over one of the fortified cities of Judah (2 Chr 21:2). He and five brothers were slain by Jehoram when Jehoram became king.

7. One of the Levites of the family of Kohath who assisted in King Hezekiah's reforms (2 Chr 29:14, Jehuel). He may be the same Levite who was assigned to oversee the reception and distribution of the sacred offerings (2 Chr 31:13).

See JEHUEL.

8. One of the chief officers of the temple at the time of Josiah's religious reformation (2 Chr 35:8); he contributed many sacrifices for the great Passover service.

9. Father of Obadiah from Joab's house. Obadiah returned with Ezra from Babylon (Ezr 8:9).

10. One of the sons of Elam and father of Shecaniah. He was associated with Ezra's marriage reforms (Ezr 10:2) and was perhaps the same Jehiel who was among those who divorced their foreign wives (Ezr 10:26).

11. Priest who was among those Ezra persuaded to divorce their foreign wives (Ezr 10:26).

Jehieli, Jehielite. Alternate spelling of Jehiel, a Levite and founder of the Jehielite family, in 1 Chronicles 26:21,22.

See JEHIEL #4.

Jehizkiah. Shallum's son and chief of Ephraim during the reign of Ahaz. He opposed the enslavement of the men of Judah by victorious Israel (2 Chr 28:12).

Jehoaddah, Jehoadah. Ahaz's son and a descendant of King Saul through Jonathan's line (1 Chr 8:36, KJV Jehoadah); alternately called Jarah in 1 Chronicles 9:42.

Jehoaddin, Jehoaddan. Mother of Amaziah, king of Judah (2 Kgs 14:2; 2 Chr 25:1, Jehoaddan).

Jehoahaz. 1. Twelfth king of Israel, succeeding his father, Jehu, and ruling from 814 BC to 798 BC. Because he was an evil king, God punished Israel by subjecting them to the Aramaean kings Hazael and his son Ben-hadad. The military force in Israel was reduced to 50 cavalrymen, 10 chariots, and 10,000 infantrymen. The oppression became so severe that Jehoahaz prayed to God, who listened to him and delivered Israel from the Aramaeans, but not until the reign of Joash (Jehoash) (2 Kgs 13:2–7,25). During his reign relations between Judah and Israel seem to have been fairly good, since Jehoahaz named his son Joash after his contemporary, Joash king of Judah (2 Kgs 13:1,9; 14:1, Joahaz).

2. Seventeenth king of Judah, ruling 3 months in 609 BC. He succeeded his father, Josiah, who was killed in the battle of Megiddo. His mother's name was Hamutal. Jehoahaz was 23 years old at his coronation. He is also called Shallum (1 Chr 3:15; Jer 22:11,12), and Jehoahaz may well be a throne name. He is characterized as an evil king before God. His rule ended when Pharoah Neco imprisoned him at Riblah in Hamath. Later he was taken to Egypt, where he died (2 Kgs 23:30–34). Jeremiah prophesied that Jehoahaz would never return to Israel but would die in the land of his captivity (Jer 22:11,12).

First Chronicles states that Jehoahaz was the fourth son of Josiah. That the people chose him king rather than Josiah's firstborn son may indicate an attempt to placate the Egyptians following Josiah's unsuccessful battle against them, for it was customary for the firstborn son to succeed his father on the throne.

3. Another form of the name of Ahaziah, the sixth king of Judah, who ruled in 841 BC (2 Chr 21:17; 22:1). Both forms of the name have the same meaning. The difference is the placement of the divine name. In Jehoahaz it comes first, "Jeho-" and in Ahaziah it comes last, "-iah" (-yah).

See AHAZIAH #2.

4. Full name of Ahaz, the twelfth king of Judah, according to an inscription of Tiglathpileser III.

See ISRAEL, HISTORY OF.

Jehoash. Name of two OT kings, occurring only in the Book of 2 Kings. The name means "The Lord is strong" or "The Lord hath bestowed." Joash, the shorter form of the name, frequently appears in the Kings and Chronicles narratives.

1. Son of Ahaziah and ninth king of Judah (835–796 BC). Jehoash ascended the throne after the wicked Athaliah had been slain at the command of Jehoiada the priest. As an infant he was sequestered by his aunt Jehosheba in the temple, and thus survived the earlier slaughter of the king's household by Athaliah (2 Kgs 11:1). After remaining 6 years within the temple precinct, Jehoash was declared king at the age of 7 and ruled for 40 years (2 Kgs 11:21; 12:1).

His major activity during his reign was the renovation of the temple (2 Kgs 12:4,5; 2 Chr 24:4,5). When, by his 23rd year, little progress had been made (2 Kgs 12:6), he revised the taxation schedule, commanded the people of Judah to bring their contributions directly to the Jerusalem temple, and soon restored the Lord's house to its "proper condition." (2 Chr 24:13).

After the death of the priest, Jehoiada, Jehoash and Judah forsook the Lord and served the Asherim and the idols (2 Chr 24:15–18). Not heeding the prophets' warnings of divine judgment (2 Chr 24:20), Jehoash and his people were conquered by the Syrians. Though Jehoash had once been able to avert a Syrian siege of Judah by paying tribute to Hazael (2 Kgs 12:17,18), the same strategy did not work a second time. The Syrians plundered Judah and Jerusalem, sending the spoil to Hazael in Damascus (2 Chr 24:23,24). Jehoash was assassinated by his servants Jozacar and Jehozabad while recuperating from wounds incurred in battle with the Syrians (2 Kgs 12:20,21; 2 Chr 24;25,26).

2. Son of Jehoahaz and 14th king of Israel (798–782 BC). Jehoash enjoyed a measure of military success that had eluded his father. No longer subject to the punitive military exploits of Hazael of Syria, he was able to establish political stability in the northern kingdom. In fact, he subjugated the southern kingdom of Judah, while Amaziah was king in Jerusalem (796–767 BC). The conflict between Amaziah and Jehoash was precipitated mainly by Amaziah. Overconfident with his victories in Edom, Amaziah initiated a military conflict with Israel (2 Kgs 25:17–19). The battle was fought near Beth-shemesh in the Judean Shephelah, and eventually spread into the hill country of Judah until Jehoash finally reached the Judean capital city. When Jehoash entered Jerusalem, he plundered the treasuries of the palace and the temple, and destroyed the outer wall of the city from the Ephraim Gate to the Corner Gate (2 Chr 25:20–24). He was apparently used as an instrument of the Lord to subdue Judah (2 Chr 25:20).

A contemporary of Jehoash was Elisha the prophet. In spite of the pervasive wickedness in Israel and the apostasy of the king himself (2 Kgs 13:10,11), Jehoash still sought the counsel of this prophet of the Lord. While Elisha was on his deathbed, Jehoash sought the prophet's blessing (2 Kgs 13:14). Elisha assured the king that the Syrians would be defeated by Israel at Aphek and that Israel would enjoy three decisive victories over this same enemy (2 Kgs 13:15–19). Jehoash achieved political stability in the northern kingdom for 16 years (798–782 BC). Though considered an evil king, he was used as an instrument of judgment against Amaziah of Judah and enjoyed the blessing of Yahweh against the Syrians.

See ISRAEL, HISTORY OF.

Jehohanan. 1. Levite of the family of Korah who was a gatekeeper of the sanctuary during David's reign (1 Chr 26:3).

2. Commander of thousands in King Jehoshaphat's army (2 Chr 17:15).

3. Father of Ishmael, commander of a unit of soldiers who helped the priest Jehoiada overthrow the wicked queen Athaliah of Judah (2 Chr 23:1).

4. Eliashib's descendant who owned a chamber into which Ezra retired to pray, fast, and mourn for his people (Ezr 10:6, KJV Johanan). He is probably the same as Johanan of Nehemiah 12:22, who apparently was a grandson of Eliashib the high priest, and Jonathan (perhaps a corruption of the text), Joiada's son, in Nehemiah 12:11.

5. One of Bebai's four sons, who was exhorted by Ezra to divorce his foreign wife (Ezr 10:28).

6. Ammonite; Tobiah's son and a contemporary of Nehemiah. He married a Jewish woman whose father, Mashullam, had helped repair the Jerusalem wall (Neh 6:18, KJV Johanan).

7. One of the priests in postexilic Jerusalem during the days of Joiakim the high priest (Neh 12:13).

8. One of the priests who participated in the dedication of the rebuilt Jerusalem wall (Neh 12:42).

Jehoiachin. King of Judah for a very brief time (598–597). He was the son of Jehoiakim and Nehushta, the daughter of Elnathan of Jerusalem (possibly the Elnathan mentioned by Jeremiah, cf. 26:22; 36:12,25). The name Jehoiachin means "Yahweh will uphold," and variations include Coniah (Jer 22:24,28; 37:1), Jeconiah (1 Chr 3:16,17; Est 2:6; Jer 24:1; 27:20; 28:4; 29:2), and Jechoniah (Mt 1:11,12, KJV Jechonias). Jehoiachin was 18 years old when he was installed as king upon his father's death, and he ruled for only 3 months and 10 days in Jerusalem (2 Kgs 24:8; cf. 2 Chr 36:9, where his accession age of 8 must be a scribal error given the evidence of Babylonian documents and the mention of his wives in 2 Kgs 24:15). He inherited a vassal kingdom in revolt. Besieged by the armies of the Babylonian overlord Nebuchadnezzar, Jehoiachin had little choice but to capitulate in the face of insurmountable odds. According to the Babylonian Chronicle, records based on the official annals of the Babylonian kings, Nebu-

chadnezzar entered Syro-Palestine in December of 598 BC and captured Jerusalem on March 16, 597. The Babylonians plundered the palace and temple treasuries, and Jehoiachin, his family, and prominent military leaders, royal officials, and artisans were taken prisoner and led away into exile in Babylon (2 Kgs 24:12–16; 2 Chr 36:10). Before returning to Babylon the victorious king placed Jehoiachin's uncle, Mattaniah, now named Zedekiah, on the throne in Jerusalem.

According to Jeremiah the trauma caused by the Babylonian invasion of Judah, and the consequent political upheaval prompted by a succession of three kings in four months, had little impact on the people spiritually (chs 37,38). This same prophet of God forecast Jehoiachin's exile and predicted he would have no descendants succeeding him on the throne (Jer 22:24–30). In contrast, the false prophet Hananiah prophesied Jehoiachin would be restored to the throne of Judah within two years (Jer 28:3,4,11; cf. vv 12–17).

Jehoiachin's continuing royal status as the legitimate claimant to the Judahite kingship was reflected in the fact that Ezekiel's oracles are dated to the year of Jehoiachin's exile, not Zedekiah's reign (Ez 1:2; 8:1; 20:1; etc.). Babylonian records confirm this recognition of Jehoiachin's former position; he retained his title of king and received favorable treatment from the Babylonians. He is certainly the "Yaukin, king of the land of Yahuda" listed in one of the cuneiform tablets; this tablet contains inventories of rations of oil and barley for the king and his five sons and implies they were not imprisoned but living a fairly normal life in Babylonia. Later, during the reign of Evil-merodach, Jehoiachin was released from prison and granted dining privileges with the Babylonian king (c. 562 BC; cf. 2 Kgs 25:27–30; Jer 52:31–34). Whether he was imprisoned for attempting to escape or because of Judah's rebellion against Babylon under Zedekiah is unclear.

Jehoiachin's name appears in Matthew's genealogy of Jesus Christ (1:11,12), and some contend this contradicts Jeremiah's oracle of judgment against the king's descendants (Jer 22:30). Yet it is possible to understand Haggai's blessing of Zerubbabel (2:20–24) as the rescission of Jeremiah's curse and the reinstatement of Jehoiachin's line on the Davidic (and ultimately Messianic) throne (cf. Is 56:3–5).

ANDREW E. HILL

See ISRAEL, HISTORY OF; EXILE; CHRONOLOGY, OLD TESTAMENT.

Jehoiada. 1. Benaiah's father. Benaiah held a high military office in the latter part of David's reign and commanded David's mercenaries (2 Sm 8:18; 20:23; 23:20,22; 1 Kgs 1:8–2:46). He also served under Solomon (1 Chr 11:22,24; 18:17; 27:5; in the last passage he is called "priest," but not as in KJV "chief priest"). It is this Jehoiada who succeeded Joab after serving under him (1 Kgs 4:4), and it is probably this same Jehoiada who joined forces with David at Hebron and was identified with the house of Aaron (1 Chr 12:27).

2. High priest in Jerusalem who organized and led the coup that overthrew Queen Athaliah of Judah, together with the Baal cult that she supported, and established his nephew Joash (Jehoash) on the throne (2 Kgs 11:4–21). As long as he lived, Jehoiada kept the king true to Jehovah (2 Kgs 11:1–12:16; 2 Chr 22:10–24:14). He died at the age of 130 and was buried in the city of David among the kings.

3. Benaiah's son, who succeeded Ahithophel as King David's counselor (1 Chr 27:33,34); he was thus a grandson of #1 above, although some believe these to be the same.

4. KJV spelling of Joiada, Paseah's son, in Nehemiah 3:6.
See JOIADA #1.

5. Alternate name for Joiada, son of Eliashib the high priest, in Nehemiah 13:28.
See JOIADA #2.

6. Priest during the time of Jeremiah who was succeeded by Zephaniah as overseer of the temple (Jer 29:26).

Jehoiakim. Second son of Josiah by Zebidah (2 Kgs 23:36; 1 Chr 3:15; 2 Chr 36:5) who

This seal impression of the steward of Jehoiakim (c. 597 BC) is a typical seal on a jar handle.

became King of Judah in 609 BC. His given name, Eliakim, means "God will establish" (2 Kgs 23:34; 2 Chr 36:4). He replaced his older brother as king when Jehoahaz was deposed and exiled by Pharaoh Neco after a 3-month reign (2 Kgs 23:31–35). Eliakim was installed as king at age 25, and he ruled for 11 years in Jerusalem. Upon enthroning him, Neco changed his name to Jehoiakim ("Yahweh will establish," 2 Kgs 23:34; cf. Jer 26:20–23).

Neco laid a heavy tribute on Judah, which Jehoiakim raised by levying a tax on the whole land (2 Kgs 23:35; cf. Jer 22:13–17, where the woe oracle against Jehoiakim implies he appropriated some of these funds for personal use). Jehoiakim remained subservient to the Egyptians until the battle of Carchemish in 605 BC, when Nebuchadnezzar and the Neo-Babylonians routed Neco. Judah then became a vassal state of Babylon for three years (2 Kgs 24:1–7). After Nebuchadnezzar's failure to completely subdue Neco in a second fierce battle in 601 BC, Jehoiakim seized the opportunity to throw off the Babylonian yoke when the Babylonian king returned home to reorganize his army. This ill-advised decision proved costly, as Nebuchadnezzar invaded Judah in 598 to punish the rebellious vassal king (2 Kgs 24:8–17; cf. Jer 52:28). The Babylonians destroyed the important Judahite cities of Debir and Lachish, seized control of the Negeb, and deported several thousand of Judah's ablest citizens. This no doubt crippled the economy and left Judah virtually leaderless. The expected help from Egypt never came, and Jehoiakim died during the Babylonian siege of Jerusalem (probably late in 598). His son Jehoiachin was placed on the throne.

Although the details of Jehoiakim's death are not reported, the biblical historian does pass judgment on his reign as one which perpetuated the evils of his fathers (2 Kgs 23:37; 2 Chr 36:5,8; cf. Jer 22:18,19 and 36:27–32, which predicted Jehoiakim's dead body would be cast on the ground outside of Jerusalem without proper burial and he would have no descendants upon the throne). Presumably the reference here is to his predecessors Manasseh, Amon and Jehoahaz. Jeremiah describes the evils that characterized Jehoiakim's rule, including idolatry, social injustice, robbing the wage-earner, greed, murder, oppression, extortion, and forsaking the covenant of the Lord (22:1–17). Despite Jeremiah's extensive activity during his reign (chs 25,26,36) Jehoiakim remained disobedient, unrepentant, smug, and self-sufficient in his ill-gotten prosperity (22:18–23).

See ISRAEL, HISTORY OF; EXILE; CHRONOLOGY, OLD TESTAMENT.

Jehoiarib. 1. Alternate form of Joiarib, a priestly family in Jerusalem, in 1 Chronicles 9:10.

> See JOIARIB #1.

2. Priest in the time of King David, assigned to head the first of 24 divisions of priests for temple duty (1 Chr 24:7).

Jehonadab. Alternate name for Jonadab, Rechab's son, in 2 Kings 10:15,23.

> See JONADAB #2.

Jehonathan. 1. KJV spelling of Jonathan, Uzziah's son, in 1 Chronicles 27:25.

> See JONATHAN #7.

2. One of the Levites appointed by Jehoshaphat to travel about Judah teaching the Law to the people as part of his national religious reform (2 Chr 17:8).

3. Head of Shemaiah's priestly house in postexilic Jerusalem during the days of Joiakim the high priest (Neh 12:18).

Jehoram. 1. Jehoshaphat's son and Judah's 5th king (853–841 BC; also called Joram). Prior to the rule of the Omride dynasty in the northern kingdom of Israel (885–841 BC), the relationship between Judah and Israel had been strained. The political influence and economic stability of the united monarchy had long since vanished. Israel's power and wealth had been diminished by Egyptian overlordship under Shishak (2 Chr 12) and by civil war: the unsuccessful Shechem conference (2 Chr 10); Rehoboam of Judah versus Jeroboam of Israel (2 Chr 12:15); Abijah of Judah versus Jeroboam of Israel (2 Chr 13:2–22); and Asa of Judah versus Baasha of Israel (2 Chr 16:1–4). The Omride dynasty in the mid-9th century BC, however, cast aside familial rivalry and sought to forge a new alliance between the two nations.

The two kingdoms of Judah and Israel were increasingly threatened by the surrounding peoples—the Ammonites, Moabites, Edomites, Syrians, Philistines, Arabs, and Assyrians. In response to this threat Ahab, the second king of the Omride dynasty, secured diplomatic relations with Phoenicia (1 Kgs 16:31) and Judah (1 Kgs 22:4). During this time joint military expeditions by Israel and Judah were not infrequent (1 Kgs 22; 2 Kgs 3; 8:28), though these political alliances were not without their liabilities. The intrusion of the worship of Baal and Asherah led to religious apostasy in Judah and Israel (1 Kgs 16:31–33; 2 Kgs 3:2; 2 Chr 21:11). It was within this political-religious context that Jehoram reigned over Judah.

Though he may have served as co-regent as early as 853 BC, Jehoram was the sole ruler for 8 years (848–841 BC). His reign was marked by unnecessary internecine fighting and religious apostasy. His father had generously provided for his 6 brothers, a decision that Jehoram quickly reversed once he had secured the throne (2 Chr 21:2,3). He executed not only his brothers but also several Israelite princes, thereby removing any political threat to himself (2 Chr 21:2–4). In addition, he reverted to the idolatrous practices that his father had tried to eliminate by restoring forbidden worship sites, "the high places" (2 Chr 21:11). Jehoram had apparently fallen under the influence of his wife, Athaliah, the daughter of Jezebel (2 Kgs 8:18). As her mother had done in Israel, Athaliah imported Baal worship into Judah. As a result, Elijah the prophet pronounced judgment on Jehoram and the people of Judah—a curse which brought a great plague upon his people, children, wives, and possessions, and a gross intestinal disorder upon the king himself. In spite of this pervasive wickedness in Judah, the Lord did not destroy the southern kingdom because of his promise to David (2 Kgs 8:19; cf. 2 Sm 7:12–16).

Politically, Judah was vulnerable, having lost its control of Edom (2 Chr 21:9) and having sustained attacks by the Philistines and the Arabs. Jehoram was left bereft of possessions, wives, and sons except for Jehoahaz (Ahaziah), his youngest (2 Chr 21:16,17).

At his death Jehoram was not accorded honor and was deprived of burial in the tomb of the kings within the city of David (2 Chr 21:19,20).

> See ISRAEL, HISTORY OF; CHRONOLOGY, OLD TESTAMENT.

2. Ahab and Jezebel's son, and Israel's tenth king (852–841 BC; also called Joram). He succeeded his brother Ahaziah, whose premature death led to Jehoram's ascension to the throne in Samaria (2 Kgs 1:2,17); he was a contemporary of the Judean kings Jehoshaphat, Jehoram, and Ahaziah.

Jehoram was preoccupied with the political resurgence of the two neighboring kingdoms of Moab and Syria. When Moab withheld its annual tribute to Israel, he sought assistance from both Jehoshaphat and Judah's vassal kingdom, Edom. Jehoram and Jehoshaphat joined forces with the king of Edom, but were halted in their attack on Moab when they encountered a serious lack of water. Hesitant to advance with their troops, they summoned Elisha the prophet and asked him to inquire of the Lord's will regarding the expedition. Because of the high regard that Elisha held for Jehoshaphat, the prophet sought the Lord on their behalf, gaining both the Lord's blessing and an abundance of water. The account of the battle records the slaughter of the Moabites as well as the horrible incident of a human sacrifice by the Moabite king. Having won the battle, Israel withdrew (2 Kgs 3:4–27).

Jehoram's conflict with Syria was less successful because the Israelite king sustained a wound. Retreating from Ramoth-gilead in Transjordan to his palace in Jezreel (2 Kgs 8:29), he found his problems compounded when one of his generals, Jehu, led an insurrection against him. Commissioned by the Lord and declared to be king of Israel, Jehu confronted Jehoram and his nephew, Ahaziah, king of Judah. The incident culminated in the death of the two reigning monarchs of Israel and Judah (2 Kgs 9:14–24). While Ahaziah was buried in the tomb of the kings in Jerusalem, Jehoram's corpse was cast into Naboth's field outside the city of Jezreel. His end was the appropriate judgment against the last king of the Omride dynasty and their wicked contrivances (2 Kgs 9:25,26).

3. Levite member of a traveling group of scholars who taught the people the Law of God during the reign of Jehoshaphat (2 Chr 17:7–9).   GREGORY D. JORDAN

See ISRAEL, HISTORY OF; CHRONOLOGY, OLD TESTAMENT.

Jehoshabeath. Alternate name for Jehosheba, daughter of Judah's King Jehoram, in 2 Chronicles 22:11.

See JEHOSHEBA.

Jehoshaphat. 1. The fourth king of Judah (872–848 BC), son and successor of Asa (910–869 BC).

Jehoshaphat was 35 years of age when he began his reign; he ruled 25 years, during which time he maintained the stability of the Davidic dynasty (1 Kgs 22:41,42). He was contemporary with King Ahab of Israel (874–853 BC), since his 1st year on the throne corresponds with the 4th year of the reign of Ahab (1 Kgs 22:41). He was also contemporary with Ahaziah (853–852 BC), son of Ahab, and his brother Jehoram (852–841), who succeeded Ahaziah when he died childless (2 Kgs 1:17).

Jehoshaphat is held in high esteem by the Chronicler, along with Hezekiah and Josiah. His successful rule was due to his religious policy. He continued the religious reformation initiated by his father; therefore the Lord firmly established the kingdom under his control, "and all Judah brought tribute to Jehoshaphat; and he had great riches and honor" (2 Chr 17:1–5). The Chronicler praises Jehoshaphat's courageous heart, evidenced in his removing the high places and the Asherim from Judah (2 Chr 17:6). Jehoshaphat is also reported to have closed all the houses of the male prostitutes (1 Kgs 22:46).

The biblical record informs us that Jehoshaphat reversed his father's foreign policy. During his reign Asa warred against Baasha of Israel (908–886), who exterminated the house of Jeroboam I (930–909 BC) and usurped the throne for himself, continuing to keep it for nearly a quarter of a century. The two kingdoms engaged in warfare over the boundaries between the kingdoms. Jehoshaphat, however, discontinued this war and made peace with the king of Israel (1 Kgs 22:2). To confirm this state of peace he made an alliance with Ahab, and married his son and successor Jehoram to Ahab's daughter Athaliah (2 Kgs 8:18; 2 Chr 18:1,2). In accordance with this alliance Jehoshaphat fought on the side of Ahab in his battle against Aram, which took place at Ramoth-gilead (1 Kgs 22; 2 Chr 18). He also was an ally of Jehoram, the younger son of Ahab, against Mesha the king of Moab (2 Kgs 3:4–27).

In his domestic reforms Jehoshaphat sent Obadiah, Zechariah, Nathanel, and Micaiah to teach in the cities of Judah (2 Chr 17:7–9). He is also reported to have organized the use of tribute paid to Judah. The surrounding nations, observing the strength of Jehoshaphat and recognizing the presence of the Lord with him, not only refrained from attacking Judah but even brought tribute to him. He used this tribute to fortify the cities of Judah (2 Chr 17:10–13). Jehoshaphat also reorganized the army and made arrangements for the defense of the kingdom. He had a standing army in the capital as well as garrisons in the fortified cities. It is evident that the organization centered about the tribal association of Judah and Benjamin (2 Chr 17:14–19).

A prophet by the name of Jehu rebuked Jehoshaphat for his alliances with Ahab (2 Chr 19:1–3). Evidently Jehoshaphat took this rebuke to heart and ruled Judah wisely. He swept the Asherim from the land and determined in his mind to seek God. He is reported to have gone regularly among the people from Beersheba to Mt Ephraim to convert them to the Lord. He appointed judges in each of the fortified cities of Judah and admonished them to judge not for man, but for the Lord. He also appointed Levites, priests, and family heads to handle cases pertaining to the worship of the Lord and to make decisions in disputes arising among citizens (2 Chr 19:4–11).

In addition to the fortified cities in Judah, Jehoshaphat placed military forces in the cities of Ephraim which his father Asa had taken (2 Chr 17:1,2). Though his alliances with Phoenicia and Israel were not approved by the prophets and proved dangerous in the long run, they still brought relative peace and temporary prosperity to his realm. He was held in high esteem by the neighboring Philistines and the Arabs (2 Chr 17:10–13), and it is also evident that Edom submitted to him. He won victory over the Moabites, Ammonites, and Meunites at En-gedi (2 Chr 20:1–30). Wishing to emulate Solomon, he constructed ships at Ezion-geber to go to Tarshish, but this did not prove a successful venture (2 Chr 20:35–37).

Jehoshaphat died when he was about 60 years of age and was buried with his fathers in the city of David. His son Jehoram became king in his place (2 Chr 21:1). His name is listed in Matthew's genealogy of Jesus Christ (1:8, KJV Josaphat).

See ISRAEL, HISTORY OF.

2. Son of Ahilud who held the position of recorder (the Hebrew word may imply an official historian or a spokesman for the king) in the days of David and Solomon (2 Sm 8:16; 20:24; 1 Kgs 4:3; 1 Chr 18:15).

3. Son of Paruah and one of Solomon's 12 administrative officials who requisitioned food from the people for the king's household. Each of them arranged provisions for one month of the year. Jehoshaphat was the officer assigned for the tribe of Issachar (1 Kgs 4:7,17).

4. Son of Nimshi and the father of Jehu, who exterminated the dynasty of Omri and became king of Samaria, around 842–815 BC (2 Kgs 9:2,14).

5. KJV spelling of Joshaphat, a priest during David's reign, in 1 Chronicles 15:24.

See JOSHAPHAT #2.

Jehoshaphat, Valley of.

Valley mentioned in prophecy as the place of future judgment (Jl 3:2,12), sometimes called the valley of Decision (Jl 3:14). Its exact location is disputed. Some identify it with the Kidron Valley, east of Jerusalem, pointing to early Christian tradition, notably, Jerome; others prefer the valley of Hinnom, south of Jerusalem. This tradition may be traced back through Eusebius to the

The Kidron Valley, southeast of Jerusalem, perhaps to be identified with the Valley of Jehoshaphat.

book of 1 Enoch (53:1). Still others say the name is symbolic and refers only to coming judgment, not to a specific place.

Jehosheba. Daughter of King Jehoram of Judah (853–841 BC) and Queen Athaliah, sister of King Ahaziah (841 BC), and wife of Jehoiada, the high priest. Upon Ahaziah's death, Athaliah attempted to kill all the remaining royal heirs to the throne; Jehosheba, however, hid young Joash, Ahaziah's son, in a temple bedchamber for the duration of Athaliah's reign (841–835 BC; 2 Kgs 11:2). Jehosheba is alternately spelled Jehoshebeath in 2 Chronicles 22:11.

Jehoshua, Jehoshuah. Alternate KJV names for Joshua, son of Nun, in Numbers 13:16 and 1 Chronicles 7:27, respectively.

See JOSHUA (PERSON) #1.

Jehovah. Name for God formed by adding the vowels of the Hebrew word *Adonai* to the consonants of the Hebrew divine name, YHWH. Out of their respect for God and their fear of defiling his name, the postexilic Jews refused to pronounce the divine name when reading Scripture. Instead they substituted *Adonai*, a word meaning "my Lord." Prior to the 6th century AD, the Hebrew text had no vowels. These were supplied during the reading of the Scripture by one who was familiar with the language. When vowel points were added to the text (AD 600–700), the vowels of *Adonai* were placed below the consonants of YHWH to indicate that *Adonai* should be read.

It is thought that in about AD 1520 Petrus Galatinus conceived the idea of combining the two names, thus creating the new form *YeHoWaH* from which the English term *Jehovah* comes. Although this form was foreign to the Hebrew language, it gained wide acceptance and was included as the translation for God's name in the KJV and ASV. Biblical scholars now agree that the original pronunciation of the divine name was *Yahweh* or *Jahveh*.

See GOD, NAMES OF.

Jehozabad. 1. Shomer's son, who was a servant of King Josiah and later, with another assailant, murdered the king at Millo (2 Kgs 12:21). In a parallel passage, Jehozabad is called the son of Shimrith the Moabitess (2 Chr 24:26). King Amaziah eventually executed Jehozabad for his murder of Josiah (2 Chr 25:3).

2. Obed-edom's second son and a member of a Levitical Korahite family appointed by King David to be gatekeepers in the temple (1 Chr 26:4).

3. Benjamite military commander who served under King Jehoshaphat of Judah and commanded 180,000 men in his army (2 Chr 17:18).

Jehozadak. Alternate name for Jozadak, Seraiah's son (1 Chr 6:14,15; Hg 1:1–14; 2:2,4; Zec 6:11).

See JOZADAK.

Jehu. 1. Prophet in Israel, son of the "seer" Hanani (2 Chr 16:7), who denounced Baasha for following in the ways of Jeroboam (1 Kgs 16:1–7). In addition to continuing the heretical worship of the golden calves at Bethel and Dan, Baasha also assassinated Nadab, the son of Jeroboam (1 Kgs 15:25–32).

Jehu later rebuked Jehoshaphat, king of Judah, for helping Ahab the king of Israel in his wars against the Aramaeans (2 Chr 19:2,3). The writings of this prophet, however, were so profound that his "words" were included in the official records of the reign of Jehoshaphat in the "Book of the Kings of Israel" (2 Chr 20:34).

2. Important army officer during the reigns of Ahab and Jehoram (2 Kgs 9:25), who in reaction to the economic and religious abuses of the house of Omri, was anointed as king of the northern kingdom of Israel (1 Kgs 19:16,17). In the following revolution he exterminated the royal house of Israel, the king of Judah, and a royal party from the south (2 Kgs 9:1–10:36). He executed the worshipers of Baal in order to revive true worship in Israel. As king he ruled in Samaria 28 years (841–814 BC) and began a dynasty that lasted some 100 years.

In the time of Jehu the prophets were engaged in a religious equivalent of war with the adherents of Tyrian Baal-melcarth. Elijah met and defeated the Canaanite priests on Mt Carmel (1 Kgs 18:17–40). Later he and then Elisha were commissioned to anoint Jehu as king. The prophets waited until the time was right (2 Kgs 9:1–10), at which time Elisha sent a "son of the prophets" to Ramoth-gilead to designate Jehu as the monarch.

Jehu left his siege of Ramoth-gilead in northern Transjordan to meet the king of Israel in Jezreel. There he killed King Jehoram and Ahaziah, the king of Judah (2 Kgs 9:17–28). His bloody ways continued as he extinguished the royal house of Ahab (2 Kgs 10:1–17) and 42 ambassadors of goodwill from Judah (apparently without provocation, 10:12–14). Israel's bloodbath finally ended in Samaria. There Jehu cunningly vowed to serve Baal with a zeal greater than that of Ahab. Unsuspecting devotees of Baal-melcarth gathered in great numbers to join in a festival sacrifice. Instead, the devotees themselves became the sacrifice,

and the house of Baal in Samaria was destroyed and desecrated by turning its ruins into a latrine (10:18–27).

Although religious grievances dominate the account of Jehu's revolution, certain political and economic problems contributed to the unrest. Under the reign of Ahab and Jezebel justice was corrupted. The poor lost their land in the drought and their property rights were ignored (1 Kgs 18:5,6). Jehu cast the body of Jehoram into the field of Naboth the Jezreelite as justice for the crime of Ahab and Jezebel (1 Kgs 21:19).

Dissatisfaction in the army probably contributed to the support from the military for the revolt. The soldiers were not particularly interested in the goals of the prophets. To pragmatic officers, these spokesmen of God were "mad men" (2 Kgs 9:11). On the other hand, Jehoram had not been successful against the Aramaeans. He remained in Jezreel while the army fought in Ramoth-gilead on the pretext of being injured.

Nevertheless, religious passions dominated the cause. Jehu called his slaughter of the house of Omri his "zeal for the Lord." Jehonadab, a Rechabite, joined Jehu as he traveled toward Samaria (2 Kgs 10:15–17). Rechabites opposed social and economic developments that took place in the northern kingdom under Ahab. They followed a strict moral code and lived a simple life (Jer 35:2–19). Since Rechabites represented the most conservative elements of Yahwism, they became natural allies for the reform of Jehu.

Jehu's revolution seriously weakened the worship of Baal-melcarth. Although not all of the adherents were eliminated, Baalism no longer remained the official religion of the state (2 Kgs 10:28). Rather, Baalism united with Yahwism to form the sinister syncretistic religion that was denounced by Hosea.

Politically the revolt of Jehu was disastrous. The triple alliance between Tyre, Israel, and Judah was shattered by the atrocities. Israel, now isolated, became easy prey for Assyria and Syria. Jehu attempted to buy some help from Assyria by paying tribute to Shalmaneser III. That event is pictured on the Black Obelisk in a relief from the campaign of 841 BC. An inscription names "Jehu, son of Omri," as the one kneeling before Shalmaneser.

After the Assyrian threat dissipated in 838 BC, Hazael, king of Aram-Damascus, conquered all of Israelite Transjordan as far as the Arnon (2 Kgs 10:32,33). In a second campaign in 815 BC, Hazael moved across the Jordan River, through the Jezreel plain, and down the coast, conquering the land as far as Gath in the northern Shephelah. There the

The portion of the Black Obelisk of Shalmaneser III that shows Jehu (king of Israel) bowing in tribute.

son of Jehu, Jehoahaz, paid tribute to Hazael (2 Kgs 12:18). The revolution weakened Israel both politically and economically.

Later generations spoke of the massacre of the house of Omri with horror (Hos 1:4). Jehu did not destroy the golden calves of Jeroboam, and so continued the syncretistic worship at Bethel and Dan. In the final analysis the revolution, which was meant to purge Israel of oppression and false religion succeeded in doing neither.

3. Member of Judah's tribe, the son of Obed and Azariah's father (1 Chr 2:38).

4. Prince of Simeon's tribe, and the son of Joshibiah, who, along with others, migrated from the approaches to the valley of Gedor eastward in search of good pasture (1 Chr 4:35).

5. One of the skilled warriors who joined David at Ziklag. Interestingly he was of Saul's tribe, Benjamin, and from Anathoth to which Abiathar of the priests of Eli was later banished (1 Chr 12:3).　　　J. GORDON HARRIS

See ISRAEL, HISTORY OF; CHRONOLOGY, OLD TESTAMENT.

Jehubbah.　Shemer's son from Asher's tribe (1 Chr 7:34).

Jehucal.　Son of Shelemiah who was sent by King Zedekiah to request Jeremiah's prayers for Judah (Jer 37:3; Jer 38:1, Jucal). Later, he tried to kill Jeremiah, who continued to prophesy the invasion of Jerusalem by the Babylonians, thereby undermining the confidence of the people and the army (Jer 38:1–6).

Jehud.　One of the border towns given to Dan's tribe after the conquest (Jos 19:45). It has been variously identified with the village of el-Yehudiyeh, about seven miles southeast of Joppa, and with Yazur, about five miles southeast of Joppa.

Jehudi.　Son of Nethaniah and a messenger of King Jehoiakim of Judah. He was sent by a number of princes to summon Baruch to read Jeremiah's scroll privately to them. Later Jehoiakim ordered Jehudi to read the same scroll publicly before him and all the court, after which the writing was burned (Jer 36:14–23).

Jehudijah.　Not a proper name; KJV mistranslation for "Jewish," a descriptive term distinguishing Mered's Jewish wife from his other wife, who was an Egyptian princess (1 Chr 4:18).

Jehuel.　Heman's son, the brother of Shimei and one of the Levites selected to cleanse the sanctuary during Hezekiah's reign (2 Chr 29:14). He is alternately called Jehiel in 2 Chronicles 31:13.

Jehush.　KJV spelling of Jeush, Eshek's son, in 1 Chronicles 8:39.

See JEUSH #3.

Jeiel.　1. Chief in Reuben's tribe (1 Chr 5:7).

2. Benjamite who lived at Gibeon, and an ancestor of Israel's first king, Saul (1 Chr 9:35, KJV Jehiel).

3. One of David's mighty men (1 Chr 11:44, KJV Jehiel). He is perhaps identical with #1 above.

4. Levite gatekeeper in the sanctuary. He may also have served as a musician (1 Chr 15:18,21; 16:5).

5. Levite descended from Asaph and an ancestor of a prophet named Jahaziel (2 Chr 20:14).

6. Royal secretary to King Uzziah who kept or made military "rolls" or "musters" of the king's troops (2 Chr 26:11).

7. KJV spelling of Jeuel, Elizaphan's descendant, in 2 Chronicles 29:13.

See JEUEL #2.

8. Levite who contributed Passover offerings during King Josiah's reign (2 Chr 35:9).

9. KJV spelling of Jeuel, Adonikam's descendant, in Ezra 8:13.

See JEUEL #3.

10. Nebo's descendant who was encouraged to divorce his foreign wife during the postexilic era (Ezr 10:43).

Jekabzeel. Alternate name for Kabzeel, a city in southern Judah, in Nehemiah 11:25.

See KABZEEL.

Jekameam. Hebron's son from Levi's tribe (1 Chr 23:19; 24:23).

Jekamiah. 1. Shallum's son from Judah's tribe (1 Chr 2:41).

2. One of King Jehoiachin's sons (1 Chr 3:18, KJV Jecamiah).

Jekuthiel. Zanoah's father from Judah's tribe (1 Chr 4:18).

Jemimah, Jemima. First of the three daughters born to Job when he was restored after his affliction (Jb 42:14, KJV Jemima).

Jemuel. Simeon's first son (Gn 46:10; Ex 6:15). He is called Nemuel in 1 Chronicles 4:24 and is the founder of the Nemuelite family (Nm 26:12).

Jephthah, Jephthae. Illegitimate son of Gilead (Jgs 11:1) and a leader in the period of the judges. The son of a harlot, Jephthah was dispossessed by his father's other sons and refused a share in their father's home. He moved to the land of Tob, a small Aramaean state east of the Jordan River (11:3,5), and became leader of a band of malcontents and adventurers who went raiding with him.

When war broke out between the Israelites and the Ammonites, the leaders of Gilead begged Jephthah to return and lead their army. At first he refused because of their previous mistreatment of him. When they promised to make him Gilead's king, he accepted and became commander in chief and king (11:4–10). The agreement was ratified before the Lord at a general assembly of the people at Mizpah (11:11) in Gilead, probably south of the Jabbok River.

After diplomatic negotiations with the king of Ammon failed, Jephthah waged war against the Ammonites. Before the fighting started, he vowed to the Lord that if he was victorious, on his return home he would sacrifice to God whoever met him at the door of his house. Then he successfully led his army against the Ammonites, destroying them with a terrible slaughter (11:29–33).

When Jephthah returned home, he was shocked to find that the first person to meet him was his only child, his daughter, playing a tambourine and dancing for joy. When he saw her, he tore his clothes and said, "Alas, my daughter! you have brought me very low, and you have become the cause of great trouble to me; for I have opened my mouth to the Lord, and I cannot take back my vow" (v 35). She submitted to her destiny, but begged that it might be postponed for two months so that she and her companions could retreat to the mountains and lament that she must die a virgin (Jgs 11:34–38). A woman in ancient Israel could suffer no greater disgrace than to die unmarried and childless. When she returned, her father fulfilled his vow, offering her as a burnt sacrifice (Jgs 11:38,39). Human sacrifice was practiced at that time, though it was abhorred by the Hebrews and prohibited in the Mosaic law (Lv 18:21; cf. Ex 13:13). Jephthah lived by the traditions of his time. His dealings with his daughter must be understood in light of patriarchal rule, where the head of a family had absolute power over all within his household.

Jephthah also led the Gileadites against the Ephraimites, who were resentful that they had not been included in the fight against the Ammonites. They had been given a previous chance to ally with Gilead, but had refused. Jephthah captured the fords of the Jordan behind the Ephraimites, and prevented their escape by an ingenious strategy. Gileadite guards put fugitives to a test demanding that they say "shibboleth." If they could not pronounce the *sh*, they were revealed as Ephraimites and killed. The account says that 42,000 Ephraimites died at that time.

Jephthah was judge over Gilead for six years (Jgs 12:1–7), and when he died he was buried in one of the cities of Gilead. In the letter to the Hebrews, Jephthah is named with Gideon, Barak, and others as a hero of faith (Heb 11:32, KJV Jephthae).

See JUDGES, BOOK OF.

Jephunneh. 1. Father of Caleb, one of the 12 spies sent by Moses to search out the land of Canaan (Nm 13:6; 14:6; 26:65; 1 Chr 4:15; 6:56). He is identified variously as a Judahite and a Kenizite.

2. Jether's son from Asher's tribe (1 Chr 7:38).

Jerah. Son of Joktan and nephew of Peleg, during whose lifetime the earth was divided, probably a reference to the dispersion following Babel. Jerah is likely also the name of an Arabian tribe or district (Gn 10:25,26; 1 Chr 1:20).

Jerahmeel. 1. Firstborn of Hezron's three sons, the father of six sons and a descendant of Judah through Perez's line (1 Chr 2:9–42). He was the founder of the family of Jerahmeelites, who in David's time lived in the Negeb region and occupied a number of cities (1 Sm 27:10; 30:29).

2. Kish's son and a Levite who served in the sanctuary during David's reign (1 Chr 24:29).

3. Son of King Jehoiakim of Judah and one who, with Abdeel and Seraiah, was ordered by the king to seize Baruch and Jeremiah (Jer 36:26).

Jerahmeelite. Jerahmeel's descendant from Judah's tribe (1 Sm 27:10; 30:29).

See JERAHMEEL #1.

Jered. 1. KJV spelling of Jared in 1 Chronicles 1:2.

See JARED.

2. Ezrah's son from Judah's tribe (1 Chr 4:18).

Jeremai. Hashum's son who obeyed Ezra's exhortation to divorce his foreign wife after the exile (Ezr 10:33).

Jeremiah (Person). 1. Prophet to Judah before its fall in 586 BC; his name is sometimes spelled Jeremias (Mt 16:14) and Jeremy (Mt 2:17; 27:9) in the KJV.

Jeremiah was born in the village of Anathoth, about three miles northeast of Jerusalem. His father's name was Hilkiah, and he belonged to the tribe of Benjamin. His call came in the 13th year of King Josiah (640–609 BC). He refers to himself as "a child" when called, but this word is not the same as used in Jeremiah 30:6 and 31:8, and cannot be limited to preadolescence. He was probably referring to his inexperience rather than his age. Jeremiah was born about 657 BC during the reign of wicked King Manasseh, while the great Ashurbanipal, who had shaken the world by sacking the ancient Egyptian city of Thebes in 663 BC, ruled a world empire from Assyria.

God informed Jeremiah that he had consecrated and appointed him before birth (1:4,5).

Jeremiah first shrank with a sense of inadequacy and fear: "Ah, Lord God! Behold, I do not know how to speak, for I am only a youth." God would not allow Jeremiah to excuse himself. He was assured that words would be given him to speak, and guidance given for the way (1:7). He was promised protection (1:18) and deliverance (1:8) despite opposition (1:19). God touched his mouth, signifying divine inspiration of his words, and gave the sign of an almond rod, explaining that the Lord is the wakeful One. The third sign was the bubbling pot (1:13) facing from the north, picturing the source and fury of impending disaster.

Thus the tone of Jeremiah's life ministry is set: judgment, disaster, danger, defeat, and impending death for the nation.

Early Ministry. The messages given by Jeremiah during his first five years of ministry may have been instrumental in the great revival of 622 BC. Those cooperating with King Josiah in the reformation and friendly with Jeremiah included Ahikam and his father Shaphan (Jer 26:24); Gedaliah, Ahikam's son (Jer 39:14), who later became governor; Achbor, son of Michaiah, also called Abdon, whose son Elnathan joined the opposition (Jer 26:22) but later repented (36:25); and Asaiah (2 Chr 34:20). The prophets Nahum and Zephaniah also influenced the reform movement, which must have climaxed under the preaching of Habakkuk and Jeremiah, the priestly ministry of Hilkiah, and the prophecies of Huldah the prophetess. During the reign of King Josiah, Jeremiah spoke without the fear of persecution that plagued his later ministry. Though the content of the Book of Jeremiah sometimes appears to be fragmentary, most of chapters 1–19 date to the time of Josiah.

The finding of the lost Law of Moses in the temple debris may be the reason for the words in Jeremiah 15:16: "Thy words were found, and I ate them." The words "So be it, Lord" (11:5) in a context recalling the words of Moses in the Torah may be Jeremiah's response after hearing King Josiah read the newly found book.

Small towns and rural areas now heard Jeremiah's denunciation of high places and idolatry, including his hometown. They sought to kill the young prophet, or at least to intimidate him (11:21). Instead of being silent, Jeremiah asserted that his motivation was for their good and condemned their resistance to the truth as their greatest danger.

Shortly after Jeremiah began his ministry, a number of world-changing events took place. Ashurbanipal died, and the Assyrian Empire rapidly declined. Nabopolassar began a 21-year reign in Babylon, leading an expansion that culminated in his son Nebuchadnez-zar's subjugation of the known world. As the world news filtered in, Jeremiah turned more toward Jerusalem. His temple speeches (7–10) may have been uttered at this time.

Nabopolassar felt his strength sufficient to launch an attack against Assyrian territory in 616 BC, but advanced cautiously because Psamtik I of Egypt appeared ready to aid Assyria. Cyaxares of Media pounced on Assyria when Babylon hesitated and took its most sacred city, Ashur, in 614. Babylon joined Media, along with Scythia, and waged an assault against Nineveh, which fell in late summer of 612. The Assyrian Empire had shriveled to two small holdings, Haran and Carchemish.

Nabopolassar took Haran in 610, but Assur-ballit II, having escaped, appealed to Egypt for help to retake it. Neco II, who had become pharaoh within the year, responded immediately. He marched through Palestine without giving Josiah prior notice of his nonbelligerence and asking that the Jews not bother him in view of his haste northward (2 Chr 35:21). Josiah pursued them to their encampment in the plain beyond Megiddo and was wounded in battle; he died in Jerusalem.

Ministry During the Reign of Jehoiakim. In place of Jehoahaz, Josiah's third son, who reigned only three months, Pharaoh Neco enthroned Jehoiakim (Eliakim). Neco demanded heavy indemnity payments from Israel, and took Jehoahaz prisoner as collateral to assure payment (2 Kgs 23:31–33).

Early in the reign of Jehoiakim, Jeremiah, moved by God's Spirit, delivered his third temple speech (ch 26) on the occasion of one of the annual Jewish feasts. He called for the people to repent, to act on the basis of the revelation they had heard repeatedly from the Law. The barb of the sermon came in the warning: "If you will not listen to me, . . . I [the Lord] will make this house like Shiloh, and I will make this city a curse." Shiloh had been the heart of Jewish worship from Joshua to Samuel, but after being destroyed by the Philistines it never revived. It served as an example of complete desolation following God's judgment in the days of Eli.

The crowd gathered rapidly and reacted angrily against Jeremiah. Priests and princes hurried to the New Gate, where a court was established to bring order and to control violence. Jehoiakim would be no help to Jeremiah, for he had refused to listen to God's messages (Jer 22:21). The priests and false prophets cited the example of Uriah, who had prophesied the same message, then fled to Egypt. Jehoiakim had him extradited and promptly slew him on his return. Rather than risk the same fate, Ahikam hurried Jeremiah off to a place of hiding.

Egypt controlled Palestine and Syria as far as Carchemish after the decay of the Assyrian Empire. In the third year of Jehoiakim a band of Babylonian soldiers appeared at Jerusalem to demand submission and to take hostages (Dn 1:1). In that same year (606 BC) Egypt succeeded in annihilating a garrison city of Babylonian soldiers south of Carchemish and then reoccupied Carchemish to await the return blow from Babylon. This Egyptian victory meant persecution for Jeremiah, who was often accused of false prophecy (cf. Jer 20).

Jeremiah never had confidence in Egypt. Each time a Jewish leader would call for a new alliance with Egypt, Jeremiah repeated God's message against it. Whenever a Jewish group fled to Egypt for security, Jeremiah warned of worse things in that land of false refuge (e.g., 44:26,27). Jeremiah's ode and prophecy in chapter 46 poetically describe Egypt's defeat at Carchemish, when Nabopolassar sent his son Nebuchadnezzar to destroy them (605 BC). After smashing the Egyptian army at Carchemish, Nebuchadnezzar pursued the enemy all the way to the Egyptian borders. "Not a single man escaped to his own country" reads the exaggerated Babylonian record. The following year Nebuchadnezzar, now king of Babylonia, returned to accept the homage of rulers of Israel, Syria, and Phoenicia. On this occasion God gave Jeremiah his great 70-year prophecy (Jer 25:11,12), which became the basis of Daniel 9:2,24–27.

A year after the decisive battle at Carchemish, Baruch, Jeremiah's scribe, finished recording all the dictated poems and oracles of Jeremiah. A report reached the king, who sent Jehudi, a servant, to fetch the scroll and read it to him. When this was done, Jehoiakim burned the book in spite of two counselors who pleaded that the king desist (Jer 36:23–25). God's message, soon rewritten, added a promise of fearful judgment on Jehoiakim (36:24–31).

Ambitious young Nebuchadnezzar determined to add Egypt to his dominion. In 601 he led his forces through Israel again, but Neco II had intelligence information warning him to prepare for the onslaught. In the desert of Shur, Nebuchadnezzar suffered defeat. Encouraged by this display of Egyptian defensive strength, the pro-Egyptian parties in Israel asserted themselves, persuading Jehoiakim to lead them to freedom from Babylon by making an alliance with Egypt (2 Kgs 24:1).

In 599 BC, Nebuchadnezzar armed those surrounding the rebel Jewish kingdom to harass the Jews, which they willingly did (2 Kgs 24:2). Evidently Jehoiakim lost his life on one of these raids. Since the people despised him, his body was thrown out without honorable burial (Jer 22:19) as Jeremiah had predicted.

Ministry During the Reign of Zedekiah. Nebuchadnezzar's siege of Jerusalem lasted only a short time (598 BC) because the new king, Jehoiachin, crowned at age 18, knew resistance was useless. He gave himself up with all his family and court in March of 597 BC after serving as king about three months. The Babylonian Chronicle reads: "He [Nebuchadnezzar] seized the city and captured the king."

Jehoiachin was carried to Babylon along with 18,000 officers, artisans, and executives (Ezekiel among them) and much booty. In his place Nebuchadnezzar appointed Zedekiah, Jehoiachin's uncle, to rule. Zedekiah proceeded to organize his government with the less capable and inexperienced help left after the deportation.

Jeremiah took up his thankless ministry, calling on the Jews to believe God, obey the laws of Babylon, and reject false hopes in Egypt. Zedekiah turned a deaf ear to these appeals, listening rather to the unwise advice of his counselors (Jer 37:1,2). During the first year of Zedekiah's rule, Jeremiah received the vision of the two baskets of figs. The Jews carried to Babylon were like good figs, while Zedekiah and those who trusted in Egypt were like rotten figs (24:1–8). The reason for this reproachful description was that the Jews began plotting rebellion against Babylon along with Edom, Moab, Ammon, Tyre, and Sidon from "the beginning of the reign of Zedekiah" (Jer 27:1–3), thus breaking their oath of loyalty to Nebuchadnezzar and repudiating God's message through Jeremiah.

In Egypt the pharaoh began to renew plans to organize dissidents within the Babylonian Empire to revolt. He hired Jewish soldiers to aid him in protecting his southern border. The Jewish soldiers settled on a Nile island called Yeb (593–410 BC). Jeremiah addressed an oracle to these Jews (ch 44). The treaty for Jews to help in Egypt evidently also assumed that Egyptians would aid Israel. When the Babylonians besieged Jerusalem in 588, Pharaoh Hophra came to the aid of Zedekiah. Nebuchadnezzar, ruling from Riblah, commanded that the siege against Jerusalem be lifted in order to make a surprise attack on Hophra (Jer 37:5). The release gave Jeremiah an opportunity to journey to Anathoth to secure a real estate inheritance (37:12). Irijah, captain of the guard, arrested Jeremiah in the Gate of Benjamin for defecting to the enemy, and he was beaten and flung into a dungeon. King Zedekiah brought him out after many days to obtain a prognostication. With characteristic boldness, Jeremiah told the king he would shortly become a captive. At the same time, Jeremiah requested relief from injustice for himself. He gained part of his request but continued as prisoner in the guard house.

The Babylonian army chased Pharaoh Hophra back to Egypt and returned to crush Jerusalem without further mercy. The siege, which began in January of 588, was restored with rigor in Zedekiah's 9th year (Jer 39:1). During this time the Lord gave Jeremiah foreknowledge of a visit from a cousin who wished to sell a field near Anathoth. Jeremiah bought the field as an object lesson to verify the message of restoration after a captivity of 70 years (29:10).

The armies of Babylon cut off all supplies from Jerusalem, and destroyed the last two outlying Jewish fortresses of Lachish and Azekah (34:7). Food became scarce. Disease spread. Undisposed sewage and impure cistern water caused pestilence. With increased distress came Jeremiah's increased appeal for the city to surrender.

Jeremiah remained in the prison court until the Babylonians breached the city wall in July 586. The king escaped by night and succeeded in reaching the woods of Jericho, but was captured there and taken to Riblah. Zedekiah's family and counselors were slain; he himself was blinded and taken in fetters to Babylon, where he died soon after (Jer 39:6,7).

Back in Jerusalem, Nebuzaradan, the Babylonian general, sent most of the Jews into captivity. Jeremiah, however, was granted special consideration; after being released from prison, he was placed under the care of Gedaliah, son of Ahikam.

After the Fall of Jerusalem. A month after the fall of Jerusalem, the city was burned and the walls broken down. Gedaliah was appointed governor of the remaining agricultural community, with headquarters at Mizpah. Jeremiah returned to Jerusalem, where, according to tradition, he took up his abode in a grotto near what is now known as Gordon's Calvary. There he wrote the Book of Lamentations.

The Ammonite king Baalis, plotting rebellion against Babylon, instigated the murder of Gedaliah. In the reaction that followed, the remaining people followed the leader Johanan ben Kereatz to a camp near Bethlehem. They asked Jeremiah, who joined them at Jerusalem, to give guidance from the Lord, promising obedience. Jeremiah's message required that they remain in Israel, and not go to Egypt. Disobedience was complete and immediate. Fearing Babylon, they departed from Palestine, taking Jeremiah with them, and entered Egypt.

Jeremiah did not stop his ministry in Egypt. His message at Tahpanhes assured a victorious conquest of the land by Nebuchadnezzar, which took place in 568–567 (Jer 43:8–13).

Jews from all parts of Egypt gathered to discuss their future as exiles. Jeremiah took the opportunity to denounce their idolatry. Jewish women as well as men argued that they enjoyed prosperity while serving idols, but suffered since desisting. Jeremiah condemned their obdurate blindness to reality and gave God's indictment. For a verifying sign, Jeremiah predicted that Pharaoh Hophra of Egypt would shortly be assassinated. No later record of Jeremiah's acts exists in the Bible. Tradition says Jeremiah was stoned to death by the people of the Jewish exile settlement in Tahpanhes.

Though Jeremiah suffered continued rejection during his life, he has been honored by numerous apocryphal and traditional embellishments to his history. Jesus could well have had Jeremiah in mind when he said: "You build tombs for the prophets and decorate the graves of the righteous, . . . you are the descendants of those who murdered the prophets" (Mt 23:29–31).

ROGER DOUGLASS CONGDON

See JEREMIAH, BOOK OF; PROPHET, PROPHETESS; ISRAEL, HISTORY OF.

2. Family head in the Transjordan portion of Manasseh whom Tiglath-pileser took captive (2 Kgs 15:29; 1 Chr 5:24).

3. Father of Hamutal, a wife of King Josiah (2 Kgs 23:31; 24:18).

4. Benjamite bowman and slinger who joined David at Ziklag (1 Chr 12:4).

5,6. Two Gadite soldiers who joined David's army (1 Chr 12:10,13).

7. Postexilic prince who helped Nehemiah in rebuilding the Jerusalem wall (Neh 10:2; 12:34).

8. Postexilic priest (Neh 12:1).

9. Father of Jaazaniah, a Rechabite who refused to drink wine (Jer 35:3).

Bibliography. R.P. Carroll, *From Chaos to Covenant*; W.L. Holladay, *Jeremiah: Spokesman Out of Time*; J.P. Hyatt, *Jeremiah: Prophet of Courage and Hope*; W.F. Lofthouse, *Jeremiah and the New Covenant*; H.W. Robinson, *The Cross of Jeremiah*; G.A. Smith, *Jeremiah*.

Jeremiah, Book of.

OT prophetic book, second in the canonical order of the Prophets.

Author. Few doubt that the prophet from Anathoth wrote the Book of Jeremiah, yet questions persist concerning some parts, particularly chapter 52. The use of the third person cannot be used to discredit Jeremiah's authorship, for Jeremiah used the first and third person, and even the second person, in the same context. For example, 32:6,7: "Jeremiah said [third person], 'The word of the Lord came to me [first] . . . your uncle will come to you [second].'

The problem of the passage of time provides the strongest argument against the Jeremian authorship of chapter 52. Jeremiah was born about 657 BC. Evil-merodoch released Jehoiachin (Jer 52:31) about 95 years later. Jeremiah 52:33 summarizes the continuation of events beyond this time. The problem of location also argues against Jeremian authorship, for Jeremiah took up residence in Egypt (43:6,7) while Jehoiachin dwelt in Babylon. Note also that Jeremiah concludes his writing with chapter 51, making chapter 52 a true editorial appendix. Since chapter 52 parallels 2 Kings 24:18–25:30, it may be that other portions of Jeremiah which parallel sections of 2 Kings may have been written by someone other than Jeremiah.

The following table shows such portions, and includes harmonic passages in 2 Chronicles. The first column shows historical (chronological) sequence. The last column provides a brief condensation of content.

Jeremiah's Parallels with 2 Kings and 2 Chronicles*

Order	Jeremiah	2 Kings	2 Chronicles	Content
1	37:1–2	24:17–19	36:10–12	Zedekiah made king
2	39:1–8	25:1–10	36:17,19	Zedekiah rebels; Siege begins
7	39:10 and 40:5b	25:12 and 25:22b		Gedaliah made governor
8	40:7–9	25:23,24		Gedaliah urges fidelity to Babylon
9	41:1–3	25:25		Gedaliah assassinated
10	43:5–7	25:26		Jews flee to Egypt
1	52:1,2 cf. 37:1,2	24:17–19	36:10–12	Zedekiah made king
2	52:3–5	24:20 and	36:13–16	Zedekiah rebels;
	cf. 39:1–3	25:1,2		Siege begins
3	52:6–14	25:3–10	36:17,19	Zedekiah captured; Jerusalem destroyed
6	52:15	25:11	36:20	People deported
5	52:17–23	25:13–17	36:18	Booty taken
4	52:24–27	25:18–21		Nobles slain
11	52:31–34	25:27–30		Later events

*This chart follows the order of passages as they occur in Jeremiah.

Baruch served as the secretary for Jeremiah. The relationship between the two men apparently lasted many years; the prophet gave a word of encouragement as he blessed his helper (45:5). According to the custom of the people, it would have been legitimate for the scribe to write some of the prophet's messages in his own words. This would not deny inspiration.

Authenticity. That Jeremiah lived and actually wrote the major part of the book bearing his name is authenticated by numerous references in both biblical and nonbiblical sources (e.g., Dn 9; Ecclus 49; Josephus *Antiq.* Book 10; Talmud: *Baba Bathra*). The veracity of the historical sections of Jeremiah have abundant confirmation in contemporary biblical books and in the secular histories preserved in Babylon, Egypt, and Persia.

Higher critics sought to discredit portions of Jeremiah omitted by the Septuagint, or to credit passages to a later writer because of style differences (e.g., 30–33), or spelling differences (as found, e.g., in 27–29), or linguistic problems (e.g., 10:11, written in Aramaic, may be a gloss). Another reason given for dating prophecies later than indicated in the context results from requiring that predictive writing follow later than fulfillment. None of these reasons is sufficient cause for doubting authenticity. The Hebrew text deserves priority over the Septuagint. Aramaic contact with the Jews became commonplace during this period (cf. Dn 2–7; Ezr 4–7). Different styles may be expected from the same writer due to differing circumstances and differing purposes. Baruch may have been inspired to write parts of this book. Prediction preceding fulfillment presents no problem for believers.

Jeremiah and the Septuagint. The special problems of the Septuagint translation of Jeremiah demand attention. The Septuagint translators evidently made an inaccurate translation. About 2300 Hebrew words are omitted from the Septuagint. After chapter 23, the mistranslation, omissions, and mixed order indicate confusion. However, the Dead Sea Scrolls contain references to both the Hebrew and the Septuagint order, indicating the antiquity of both editions. Both have suffered corruption at the hands of scribes and the ravages of the ages. The Septuagint evidently veers much further from the original, yet it has invaluable clues to help suggest answers to some textual problems.

The following table shows the relationship between the Hebrew (which is followed also by the Latin Vulgate, the Douay, the KJV, and all commonly used versions in modern languages), and the Greek Septuagint translation (which dates to the 2nd or 3rd century BC).

The Text of Jeremiah

Hebrew	Greek	Hebrew	Greek
1:1–25:13a	1:1–25:13	39:15–18	46:15–18
23:7–8	23:7–8 added after	40–43	47–50
	23:40*	44:1–30	51:1–30
25:13b–14	missing	45	51:1–5 added after
25:15–38	32:15–38		51:30*
26:1–24	33:1–24	46	26
27:2–20	34:2–20	47:1	missing
27:1,7,13,	mostly	47:2–7	29:2–7
15,19–22	missing	48:1–44	31:1–44
28–32	35–39	48:45–47	missing
30:10–11,22	missing	49:1–5	30:1–5
33:1–13	40:1–13	49:6	missing
33:14–26	missing	49:7–22	29:7–22
34–38	41–45	49:23–27	30:12–16
39:1–3	46:1–3	49:28–33	30:6–11
39:4–13	missing	49:34–39	25:34–39
39:14	46:4	50–51	27–28
		52	52

*The Septuagint version of Jeremiah does not have a consistent numbering system for all the chapters and verses.

The most evident major shift in the Septuagint consists of the removal of chapters 46–51 of the Hebrew order, and the placing of them in the spot from which 25:13b–14 was removed. These chapters are renumbered 26–31, but are mixed and changed considerably from the order of the Hebrew Masoretic Text.

Historical and Archaeological Background. The fact that Anathoth existed as a Canaanite village before Joshua's conquest points to the possibility that the village's name may derive from the popular sex and war goddess Anath. Many statues of this goddess prove the depths of depravity practiced by her devotees. Others associate the name Anathoth with a simple Semitic word meaning "answer to prayer."

A dramatic correspondence illustrating Jeremiah 34:7 came to light with the discovery of 21 inscribed sherds at Lachish by the Wellcome Expedition between 1932 and 1938. Some of these letters refer to "the prophet" (Letter 16 includes the last letters of the name, *iah*). The letters were written by Hoshaiah (Jer 42:1; 43:2). The latest letters indicate that fire signals had ceased from Azekah (note the reference to such signals in Jer 6:1). The expected support from Egypt was not able to save either Lachish or Jerusalem.

At Tell Beit Mirsim two jar handles from Jeremiah's time were inscribed "Eliakim, steward of Jehoiachin." A similar jar handle was discovered at Beth-shemesh. Evidently Jehoiachin was considered as the true king even after he was carried to Babylon, and maintained his royal holdings by the steward in charge of his estate.

The seal of Gedaliah found at Lachish by 1935 evidently gives a direct contact with the governor of Judah appointed by Nebuchadnezzar after the fall of Jerusalem (Jer 40:5–12). The seal of Jaazaniah discovered at Tell en-Nasbeh dates to the time of Jeremiah, and probably belonged to the person named in 2 Kings 25:23, though a man of the same name and time is mentioned in Jeremiah 35:3. The Shallum seal found at Lachish may refer to the youngest son of Josiah, or to the Shallum mentioned in the Lachish letters, or to a person mentioned in Jeremiah 32:7 or 35:4. The phrase "son of Mas" on the seal probably does not denote family relationship. The Hilkiah seal also reads "son of Mas." Since the date of origin fits Jeremiah's time, the owner of the seal may have been the father of Jeremiah, or the high priest, or some other person.

One of the most positive identifications comes from the excavation near the Ishtar Gate of Nebuchadnezzar's Babylon, where a cuneiform tablet dating about 585 BC lists "Yaukin (Jehoiachin), king of the land of Yahud (Judah)" as one of the resident captives. The Babylonian record even mentions the five sons (cf. 1 Chr 3:17,18) who were under the care of a certain Kenaiah.

The abundance of archaeological evidence relating to Jeremiah and his times confirms and illustrates the message of the book.

Reconstruction of the Ishtar Gate in Babylon.

Date. The chronological sequence of the messages of Jeremiah constitutes a major problem that cannot be wholly solved. Dated portions give helpful clues, but the content of the remainder does not assure us as to order. The following table presents a suggested order.

A Suggested Chronology of Jeremiah's Messages

Date B.C.	Passage	Chronological Notation
627	Ch 1	13th year of Josiah
626–609	2–12	Dating uncertain
610	47	Before Egypt smote Gaza (609 BC?)
609	26, 27:1	1st year of Jehoiakim (27:1 may be a scribal error)
608	13	Jewish captivity still future
607	14–20	Defeat of Jews appears more imminent
606	(Dan 1:1)	(3rd year of Jehoiakim)
605	25,45,46 36:1–8	4th year of Jehoiakim
604	36:9–32	5th year of Jehoiakim
603	21:11–14; 22; 23; 35	During reign of Jehoiakim, time uncertain.
598–97	22:24–28; 24:1; 27:20; 28:4; 29:2 37:1; 52:31	During the reign of Jehoiakim; time uncertain. Jehoiachin reigned 3 months, end of 598 and early 597 See also Ez 1:2
597	49:34	1st year of Zedekiah
597	24	Jehoiachin has been deported
596	29	Probably a year after Jehoiachin's deportation
593	27–28 50–51 (v. 59)	4th year of Zedekiah (contrary notations in 27:1 and 28:1 probably scribal errors)
588	21:1–10; 34:1–7	Siege of Jerusalem by Babylonian army begins
588	34:8–22; 37	Siege temporarily lifted
587	30–31	Undated message of hope
587	32	10th year of Zedekiah
587	33, 34, 38	During the siege
586	39–42	After the fall of Jerusalem
585	43–44	Jeremiah goes to Egypt
582	48	Moab is desolated by Babylon (582?)
561	52	Historical addenda dated after the accession of Evil-merodoch

Origin and Destination. After beginning his ministry in Anathoth, Jeremiah moved to Jerusalem, where he remained until he joined the disobedient refugees who wandered into Egypt about 584 BC. Until the deportation of

Jehoiachin (597 BC), Jeremiah addressed his messages to the king and the people residing in Judah. Later messages addressed the same group, plus the captives in Babylon (e.g., ch 29). After the departure to Egypt, he addressed Jews in that land.

Purpose. Part of God's commission to Jeremiah stated the purpose: "To root out, and to pull down, and to destroy, and to throw out, to build, and to plant." The first four parts of the commission required that Jeremiah, appointed as a "chief governor" over nations, should wreck the existing religious and social structures by his preaching against moral and spiritual sin. Doubtless God saw the physical destruction caused by Egyptians, Assyrians, and Babylonians to be the natural accoutrement for the truth uttered by the prophet. Jeremiah is consistent in his blasts at moral and religious wickedness, his call to submit to the punishment that God gives through Babylon, and his assurance that such submission will lead to blessing. When Zedekiah asks advice (38:14), we know what Jeremiah will say. When the captains of the refugees ask if they should go to Egypt, we already know the answer (42:3). We may also anticipate the obdurate rejection of God's message on the part of the inquiring people, who apparently want to know God's will but have no desire to obey it.

Nevertheless, part of Jeremiah's purpose focuses on the most distant future when the new covenant will supplant the old (31:31–37), and a transformed people bent on obedience rather than sin will receive God's promised millennium.

Outline and Content. Though many see no logical order, a careful reading of Jeremiah will reveal a grouping on the basis of content, as suggested by the following outline:

I. Introduction
   1
II. Oracles Against Jews
   2–25
III. History—signs and sufferings of Jeremiah before the siege
   26–29
IV. The Book of Hope
   30–33
V. History—signs and sufferings of Jeremiah after the siege
   34–45
VI. Oracles Against Nations
   46–51
VII. Conclusion
   52

The prophet opens his ministry with a series of poetic utterances against the sins of Jerusalem (2:1–3:5), followed by similar messages (partly prose, through ch 4), concluding with judgment poems (5,6). The message in the temple gate (7–10) leads into the proclamation against covenant breakers (11–13). The lamentation over the drought (ch 14) and subsequent miseries (15) compares with many similar expressions of grief. Jeremiah did not differ from other prophets in his use of object lessons. The rotted linen waistband (13), the broken jug (19,20,28), figs (24), and ox yoke (27,28) may be supplemented by human object lessons (35), and even the prophet himself, whose celibacy (16:2,3), resistance to sympathetic consolation (16:5–7), and withdrawal from feasts (16:8,9) all served to illustrate and confirm his message.

Places where Jeremiah proclaimed his messages helped bear home his point. He stood in the public gate where kings came and went to proclaim that judgment (fire) would come through the gate (17:19,27; 39:3). Then he went to the potter's house (18), and then to Hinnom, the Vale of Slaughter or Tophet (19).

The persecution suffered by Jeremiah first hinted at (1:8), then predicted (1:19), expresses its venom privately from his home village (11:19–23). The prophet's kindred join the opposition (12:6). Public opposition brings beatings and the stocks (20:2,3). Jeremiah prefers to keep silent rather than to speak and suffer (20:9), but he cannot withhold the Word which is as fire in his bones. The result: all his familiars reproached, derided, terrorized, denounced him, and sought his death (20:7–18). Jeremiah escaped death at the hands of priests, prophets, and people only because he had a few faithful friends (26:8–24). When his prophecies began to materialize, hatred mounted. He was beaten and put into a cistern-pit dungeon for many days (37:14–17) on a false charge. Temporary relief at the guard house (37:21) lasted only a few days. Officials clamored again for his death (38:4); and put him into a cistern in which he sank in the mire (38:6). His rescue preserved his life but his imprisonment in the guard house continued (38:28). His writings were cut up and burned (36:23); his words were denied and rejected (43:1–7; 44:16).

The Book of Hope does contain some words of judgment (32:28–35), and other sections of the prophecy have a few bright spots (3:11–18; 16:14–16; 23:1–8; 29:10–14); but in a volume otherwise dark, these four chapters (30–33) bring pleasant relief. The climax of hope, as indicated also in the longest NT quotation from Jeremiah, predicts a new covenant (31:31–40). Other prophecies also describe the end of Mosaic law and sacrament (e.g., 3:16), and the new covenant (32:40; 33:19–26).

Little is known of Jeremiah's activity or messages from *c.* 594–589 BC. Zedekiah's counselors made clandestine plans for throwing off Babylon's yoke by alliances with neighbor nations. A traitor may have reported the conspiracy to Babylon (perhaps Edom). After Babylon attacked, Zedekiah sought a hopeful report from Jeremiah but did not get it.

The Rechabite faithfulness to the Nazirite vow (ch 35) dates to the days of Jehoiakim, but as an object lesson fits the siege context. Rechabites received a human command which they obeyed; Jews received a divine command which they rejected. Rechabites will be blessed (35:18,19), Israel judged (35:15,17). The reading of the scroll to Jehoiakim and his scornful rejection of it (ch 36) illustrates the prophetic assertion (35:15) that destruction follows the rejection of God's message given through the prophets.

The siege comes into focus in chapter Jeremiah 37 with another inquiry from Zedekiah (the nonchronological chs 35,36 serve as an illustrative parenthesis). Jeremiah 37:11 moves forward to the time of lifting of the siege when Nebuchadnezzar drove Pharaoh Hophra's army back to Egypt. During the reprieve Jeremiah sought to attend a meeting of relatives to settle an inheritance at or near Anathoth. Perhaps it involved the concluding of the purchase mentioned in 32:6–15. However, as he was leaving the city, he was arrested for desertion to the Babylonians, and jailed in a dungeon pit until Zedekiah granted him privileged prisoner status.

The king's officers had ample cause for the accusation of sedition: Jeremiah had encouraged desertion (21:9; 38:2). Traitors deserved death, and this was their verdict against Jeremiah (38:4,5). The violence of the time encouraged the officers to select a cruel method of execution: let Jeremiah starve and bury himself in the sewage at the bottom of an abandoned pit. A sympathetic Ethiopian, Ebedmelech, made the rescue. Immediately the unadulterated prophecies of judgment came forth again from Jeremiah's lips, including a message to the king which reflected Jeremiah's own recent experience: "Now that your feet are sunk in the mire . . ." (38:22).

Jeremiah 39:1–43:7 records history from the fall of Jerusalem to the flight into Egypt, including the liberation of Jeremiah (39), appointment and assassination of Gedaliah (40, 41), warning from God against going to Egypt (42), and the obdurate disobedience of the people (43:1–7).

The latest writings of Jeremiah are found in chapter 44. The audience consisted of idolatrous Jews (44:4–6) gathered from various parts of Egypt as far as Aswan (Pathros). Jeremiah repeated the appeal of former prophets to reject false gods in favor of Jehovah, but to no avail (44:15,16).

The message to Baruch (45), written about 605 BC, is placed here to round out the main part of the book, which begins with the commission to "break down" and "pluck up" (1:10) and concludes with the same Hebrew words (45:4). If Baruch had ambition to obtain status in the Judean court like his brother Seraiah (51:59), he was advised it would be useless because disaster would come, as the preceding chapters indicate.

The oracles against nations (46–51), introduced by a title superscription (46:1), constitute a distinct stylistic division similar to Isaiah 13–23, Ezekiel 25–32, and Amos 1:3–2:16. The following table shows the relationship of major prophecies against foreign nations.

Prophecies Against Foreign Nations

Foreign nation	Isaiah	Jeremiah	Ezekiel	Amos	Other
Babylon	13:1–14:23 21:1–10	50,51			Habakkuk
Philistia	14:28–32	47	25:15–17	1:6–8	
Moab	15,16	48	25:8–11	2:1–3	
Damascus	17:1–11	49:23–27		1:3–5	
Egypt	19,20	46	29–32		Joel 3:19 Zech 14:18,19
Edom	21:11,12	49:7–22	25:12–14	1:11,12	Obadiah Joel 3:19
Arabia	21:13–17				
Tyre	23	(47:4)	26:1–28:19	1:9,10	Joel 3:4
Sidon	(23:4,12)	(47:4)	28:20–24		Joel 3:4
Ammon		49:1–6	25:1–7	1:13–15	
Kedar and Hazor		49:28–33			
Elam		49:34–39			
Assyria	14:24–27				Jonah, Nahum

Some of the prophecies against foreign nations in Jeremiah carry dates which show that they were written at different points during his ministry, but were collected together for the book.

The prophecy against Egypt opens with a colorful poetic description of Egypt's expulsion from Carchemish (605 BC) after a short occupancy (46:1–12). The second poem (46:13–26) may picture the attack on Egypt in 601 when Neco stopped Nebuchadnezzar at the border, or 588 when Hophra lost in his attempt to aid Zedekiah; or (most probable) it predicts the invasion of Egypt by Nebuchadnezzar in 568, when Babylon took advantage of the weakness of Egypt to occupy it. At that time Nebuchadnezzar set up his judgment throne as predicted (43:10) and meted out death sentences to all rebels, including those Jews who might have been implicated in anti-

Babylonian conspiracies. The conclusion of the Egypt oracle repeats part of the Book of Hope (46:27,28, cf. 30:10,11).

Messages against Edom, Arabia, Phoenician cities, and Ammon generally condemn pride, cruelty, and idolatry. The ode against Elam (dated 597 BC) is unique. No other prophet speaks judgment against this people, whose dwelling east of Babylon meant rare contact with Israel. Jeremiah predicted that Elam would be doomed, then restored. Ezekiel counts Elamites among the inhabitants of Sheol (32:24).

The final judgment indicates the unbiased attitude of the prophet. His messages placed him in an advantageous position with the Babylonians, who treated him with respect and kindness, in contrast to their cruelty to other Jews. But when God spoke against Babylon, Jeremiah uttered God's words without respect to his own comfort, just as he had spoken against Egypt when silence would have been logical for self-preservation.

Chapter 51 concludes "the words of Jeremiah."

Chapter 52 repeats historical facts previously stated prophetically by Jeremiah, and partially recorded also as history in chapter 39 (cf. 2 Kgs 25 and 2 Chr 36). The editor of Jeremiah evidently desired to climax the book with a historical confirmation of Jeremiah's prophecy, but he includes facts beyond those contained elsewhere.

Teaching. National sin brings national punishment. No truth blazes so clearly as this. Gentiles as well as Israel stand under the same judgment, for God is not God of the Jews only.

Individuals are not overlooked in divine judgments on nations. God sets before each the way of life and the way of death (21:8), and appeals to each to choose life ("Why will you die?" 27:13).

Jeremiah illustrates human depravity using the Ethiopian's skin and leopard's spots (13:23). The depths of depravity reach beyond man's ability to measure (17:9,10). People even love falsehood (5:30,31). Yet God promises to transform willing subjects who call on him (33:3) by giving them a "new heart" (24:7; 32:38–41) as the climactic provision of the new covenant (31:33–35). The Messiah who accomplishes this saving work is called the Lord our Righteousness, the King, the Righteous Branch, the Branch of David (23:5,6; 33:15,16).

A future nation will be made up of individuals who accept this salvation. Passing through the night of tribulation as of travail (30:6,7), the Jews will understand the true identity of their Messiah, will believe and receive him with repentant sorrow, and will be cleansed

(33:8) and regathered from all countries (32:37) by the omnipotent God (32:27).

ROGER DOUGLASS CONGDON

See JEREMIAH (PERSON) #1; ISRAEL, HISTORY OF; PROPHECY; PROPHET, PROPHETESS.

Bibliography. C.L. Feinberg, *Jeremiah*; R.K. Harrison, *Jeremiah*; E.A. Leslie, *Jeremiah*; J.A. Thompson, *The Book of Jeremiah*; C. von Orelli, *The Prophecies of Jeremiah*; J. Woods, *Jeremiah*.

Jeremias. KJV spelling of Jeremiah in Matthew 16:14.

See JEREMIAH (PERSON) #1.

Jeremoth. 1. One of Becher's nine sons and a leader in Benjamin's tribe (1 Chr 7:8). His name is rendered Jerimoth in some versions.

2. Benjamite, the son of Beriah and head of his family living in Jerusalem (1 Chr 8:14).

3. Levite of the family at Merari and one of Mushi's three sons registered during David's reign (1 Chr 23:23). His name is alternately spelled Jerimoth in 1 Chronicles 24:30.

4. Heman's son and the leader of the 15th of 24 divisions of musicians trained for service in the house of the Lord (1 Chr 25:22). In 1 Chronicles 25:4 his name is spelled Jerimoth.

5. Azriel's son and the chief official of Naphtali's tribe during David's reign (1 Chr 27:19). His name is spelled Jerimoth in some texts.

6. One of Elam's sons who was encouraged by Ezra to divorce his foreign wife during the postexilic period (Ezr 10:26).

7. One of Zattu's sons who was encouraged by Ezra to divorce his foreign wife (Ezr 10:27).

8. One of Bani's sons who was encouraged by Ezra to divorce his foreign wife (Ezr 10:29). He is named Ramoth (KJV; RSV mg) in some Hebrew manuscripts.

Jeremy. KJV spelling of Jeremiah in Matthew 2:17 and 27:9.

See JEREMIAH (PERSON) #1.

Jeriah. Levite of the family of Kohath and head of Hebron's house (1 Chr 23:19; 24:23). David made Jeriah and other Levites officers and judges to manage the religious and civil affairs of the kingdom (1 Chr 26:31, Jerijah).

Jeribai. Elnaam's son and one of David's mighty men (1 Chr 11:46).

Jericho. The name "Jericho" may be connected to the ancient name of the Canaanite moon god. The Hebrew words for moon, month, or new moon, and Jericho are very similar. Others associate it with the word for spirit or smell, assuming that the pleasant fragrances of the fruits and spices which grew in this oasis occasioned the name of the place.

Excavation showing an old tower at OT Jericho; the Mt of Temptation is in the background.

The OT occasionally calls it "the city of palm trees" (e.g., Dt 34:3; 2 Chr 28:15).

Jericho is on the west side of the Jordan River about 5 miles from the southernmost fords and about 10 miles northwest of the Dead Sea. Being in the broad part of the plain of the Jordan, it lies nearly 1000 feet below sea level and about 3500 feet below Jerusalem, which is a mere 14 miles away. This simple topographical fact explains the incidental words in Jesus' parable of the good Samaritan, "down from Jerusalem to Jericho."

History. *Prebiblical Record.* Jericho was a large and thriving city centuries, even millennia, before the Bible first mentions it in connection with the exodus from Egypt. In fact, Jericho is one of the oldest cities in the world, with remains dating to and before the Neolithic Age 10,000 years ago.

For three reasons primitive people would have chosen this site, first as a settlement and eventually as a key city. (1) It has a copious spring, called the fountain of Elisha (2 Kgs 2:18–22). (2) It has a warm climate in the winter, although "hot" describes it in the summer. (3) It is strategically located at a Jordan ford and at the base of several routes leading westward to the foothills.

The comings and goings of various populations can be reconstructed only sketchily from noninscriptional archaeological data. The civilizations grew more complex over the years, going from a simple food-gathering economy at first to the relatively complex urban society complete with king, soldiers, and guest houses which Joshua encountered. The first certain identification of its inhabitants occurs in Numbers 13:29. "The Hittites, the Jebusites, and the Amorites dwell in the hill country; and the Canaanites dwell by the sea, and along the Jordan."

Old Testament. The Jericho of the OT is best known as the first city taken by the invading Israelites through the miracle of the falling walls. Having spent some time on the east bank of the Jordan in the plains of Moab (Nm 22:1; 26:3,63, etc.), the Israelites targeted it as the first military objective in the conquest. Joshua sent spies to reconnoiter the land and the city. Rahab the harlot took them in and later engineered their escape. For her cooperation she and her family were spared when Israel destroyed the city and put its inhabitants under the ban (Jos 2,6). The fall of the city itself occurred after the Israelites had marched around it in silence once a day for six days and then seven times on the seventh day. Then when the priests blew the trumpets and the people shouted, the walls collapsed.

Joshua laid a curse on anyone who might rebuild Jericho (6:26), which was fulfilled in 1 Kings 16:34 when Hiel rebuilt it at the cost of two of his sons about 500 years later.

Jericho was in the territory of Benjamin but right on the border with the territory of Ephraim to the north (Jos 18:12,21).

Jericho appears in scattered incidents throughout the rest of the OT. In 2 Samuel 10:5 (see also 1 Chr 19:5) David had his humiliated soldiers wait there until their beards grew back. It served as a kind of headquarters for Elisha and apparently was where the "company of the prophets" lived (2 Kgs 2:5). During the time of Ahaz a return of prisoners took place there (2 Chr 28:15). When Jerusalem fell in 586 BC the reigning king, Zedekiah, fled to near Jericho but was caught by the Babylonians, who later put out his eyes at Riblah in Syria (2 Kgs 25:5; Jer 39:5; 52:8). The last OT references to Jericho are in the census lists of Ezra (2:34) and Nehemiah (7:36). Men from Jericho also helped rebuild the Jerusalem wall (Neh 3:2).

New Testament. First, it must be understood that the Jericho of NT times was built by Herod more than a mile to the south of the OT site, at the mouth of the Wadi Qilt. It is possible to sort out the healing of the blind men episodes in the synoptic Gospels by understanding that Jesus was passing from the site of ancient Jericho (Mt 20:29; Mk 10:46) and approaching Herodian Jericho (Lk 18:35). The modern city of Jericho includes both these sites.

Jericho also figures in the parable of the good Samaritan (Lk 10:30–37). And in at least one other instance Jesus passed through Jericho (Lk 19:1). On this occasion he met and ate with Zacchaeus, the wealthy chief tax collector of the new Roman Jericho.

Postbiblical Record. While ancient Jericho was of small consequence after its destruction under Joshua, the Jericho of Herod was a city of beauty and importance. But even this city fell into decay along with the decline of Roman influence in the Middle East. Most of what we know of the city until modern times comes from the writings of pilgrims to the Holy Land. They usually report seeing certain things of biblical significance, such as the tree that Zacchaeus climbed, but they also report that Jericho was a squalid, wretched Muslim village. And such it has been until relatively recent times, when it grew in size and importance as a major west bank city.

Archaeology. Jericho was excavated first by Charles Warren in 1868, then by Ernst Sellin and Carl Watzinger in 1907–11, and then by John Garstang in 1930–36. Garstang thought he had found the wall that fell before the Israelites, but the more thorough, scientific, and widely accepted results of the investigations by Kathleen Kenyon in 1952–56 showed that the topmost level of ruins was already too early to tell anything of the city of Joshua's day. To her goes the credit for uncovering and interpreting the many layers of civilizations which date back to 8000 BC at Jericho.

ROBERT L. ALDEN

See CONQUEST AND ALLOTMENT OF THE LAND.

Jeriel. Tola's son from Benjamin's tribe (1 Chr 7:2).

Jerijah. Alternate spelling of Jeriah, a Kohathite Levite, in 1 Chronicles 26:31.

See JERIAH.

Jerimoth. 1. One of Bela's five sons and a leader in the tribe of Benjamin (1 Chr 7:7).

2. KJV alternate spelling of Jeremoth, Beher's son, in 1 Chronicles 7:8.

See JEREMOTH #1.

3. Benjamite and one of the men of military prowess who came to David's support at Ziklag (1 Chr 12:5).

4. Alternate spelling of Jeremoth, Mushi's son, in 1 Chronicles 24:30.

See JEREMOTH #3.

5. Alternate spelling of Jeremoth, Heman's son, in 1 Chronicles 25:4.

See JEREMOTH #4.

6. KJV alternate spelling of Jeremoth, Azriel's son, in 1 Chronicles 27:19.

See JEREMOTH #5.

7. Son of David and Mahalath's father. Mahalath was married to King Rehoboam of Judah (2 Chr 11:18).

8. One of the Levites who assisted with the administration of the temple contributions during King Hezekiah's reign (2 Chr 31:13).

Jerioth. Obscure Hebrew term in 1 Chronicles 2:18, evoking much controversy because of the difficulty of its grammatical construction. Azubah is obviously the wife of Caleb. The translation "and by Jerioth" (KJV "and of Jerioth") would designate Jerioth as Caleb's wife as well, although the singular pronoun "her" is found in the list of sons. Contextually, Jerioth would better be understood as an object of an implied verb which corresponds to "had" (KJV "begat"), thus making Jerioth a daughter of Caleb and Azubah. The translation would then read: "And Caleb the son of Hezron caused Azubah his wife to conceive and she conceived Jerioth. These are her sons. . . ."

Jeroboam. Name of two kings who reigned in the northern kingdom of Israel: Jeroboam I (930–909 BC), the originator and first monarch of Israel, and Jeroboam II (793–753 BC), the 14th king of the northern kingdom.

1. Jeroboam I was the son of Nebar from Ephraim's tribe. He was also a servant of King Solomon (1 Kgs 11:26). His loyalty to Solomon had been rewarded by his placement as the supervisor of an Ephraimite work force. Jeroboam, therefore, helped rebuild an important section of the defenses of Jerusalem (1 Kgs 11:27,28).

This efficient and energetic young man was not to remain in the employ of Solomon for long, however. Jeroboam's background, his tribe's pride, and the oppression of Solomon produced a young rebel. An assassination plot was brewing and a military coup was on the horizon. Jeroboam participated in the plot (1 Kgs 11:26). The prophet Ahijah met Jeroboam outside Jerusalem one day and did a startling thing—Ahijah grabbed Jeroboam's new outer garment, tore it into 12 pieces, and gave 10 of them to Jeroboam (1 Kgs 11:29,30). Ahijah had symbolically shown Jeroboam that God would give him 10 tribes and would leave the Davidic line intact (1 Kgs 11:31–39). Solomon's idolatry had brought this judgment upon the Davidic line (1 Kgs 11:33). Jeroboam was not satisfied with only 10 tribes, however. He wanted the entire kingdom. God saw to it that Jeroboam's plot failed, and he fled to Egypt in order to save his life (1 Kgs 11:40).

After Solomon's death Jeroboam returned

to Palestine and approached Rehoboam, Solomon's son, with a request that his program of oppression cease (1 Kgs 12:1–4). Rehoboam asked for three days to consult with his advisers before answering (1 Kgs 12:5–11). The counsel of the older advisers was toward clemency, but younger hotheads prevailed with their counsel of increased taxation and forced labor (1 Kgs 12:12–14).

The Israelites responded by rejecting Rehoboam. Jeroboam was quickly elected king of the northern tribes (1 Kgs 12:20), and an uneasy cease-fire temporarily stabilized relationships between the two kingdoms at their division (931 BC).

Being ambitious and skillful, Jeroboam built two capital cities, one at Shechem (cf. Jos 8:30–35) in the territory west of the Jordan and one at Penuel (cf. Jgs 8:17) east of the Jordan (1 Kgs 12:25). He reinstituted the cult of the golden calves, substituting an ancient religion for the worship of Jehovah. He changed the centers of worship, the object of worship, the priesthood, and the time of worship. The new centers became Bethel and Dan (1 Kgs 12:29); Bethel was a place of patriarchal worship (Gn 28:10–22; 31:13; 35:1–7), and Dan was the site of a renegade Levitical worship established for the tribe of Dan in the days of the judges (Jgs 18).

The object of worship became the idol calf (1 Kgs 12:28). The worship was based upon Aaron's participation in the first instance of this idolatry in Israel. Aaron had presented the golden calf at Sinai as a visible representation of the invisible Jehovah who had brought Israel out of Egypt (Ex 32:4,5). This compromise religion would yet have an appeal to the Jehovah worshipers. Aaron's prior establishment of this worship added to the appeal for those who were reluctant to separate from Levitical methodology. The Levites in Dan would also add to the authentication of the calf worship.

Doubtless the Egyptian sojourn of Jeroboam contributed to this turn of events. The Egyptians' worship of Amon-Re, the sun god, included his representation as a bull. The bull in Egyptian worship was intended to visibly represent an invisible deity. This concept could have easily been transferred by the Israelites to their worship of the invisible Jehovah. It seems obvious that the calf worship of Jeroboam was based upon the calf worship of Aaron. Even God's dealings with the false worship are similar. The following similarities may be pointed out: (1) Aaron responded to the people (Ex 32:1–6); Jeroboam responded to counsel (1 Kgs 12:28). (2) The announcement of the calves as the deliverers from Egyptian bondage was made by Aaron (Ex 32:4) and by Jeroboam (1 Kgs 12:28). (3) Altars and feasts were associated with both (Ex 32:5; 1 Kgs 12:32,33; 2 Kgs 23:15). (4) Sacrifices were associated with both (Ex 32:2–6; 1 Kgs 12:32–13:1). (5) A non-Levitical priesthood was established (Ex 32:26–29; 1 Kgs 12:31; 13:33). (6) The resulting sin was disastrous to the entire nation (Ex 32:21,30–34; Dt 9:18–21; 1 Kgs 12:30; 13:34; 14:16; 15:26,30,34; 2 Kgs 3:3; 10:29–31). (7) Divine displeasure and the threat of annihilation came to both Aaron and Jeroboam, though both came to a natural end (Nm 20:28; 33:38, 39; Dt 9:20; 1 Kgs 13:34; 14:20; cf. 2 Chr 13:20). (8) Intercession was made for the sinners in both incidents (Ex 32:11–14; Dt 9:20; 1 Kgs 13:6). (9) The altars were ultimately desecrated (Ex 32:8,20,26–29; Dt 9:21; 1 Kgs 13:2; cf. 2 Kgs 23:16; 2 Chr 34:5). (10) The calves were destroyed in a similar fashion in both incidents (Ex 32:20; Dt 9:21; 2 Kgs 23:15). (11) The punishments upon the people were also similar (Ex 32:35; 2 Chr 13:20). (12) The eldest sons of both men bore essentially identical names—Aaron: Nadab and Abihu (Ex 6:23; Nm 3:2; 26:60); Jeroboam: Nadab and Abijah (1 Kgs 14:1,20; 15:25); and both sets of sons died in the prime of life (Lv 10:2; Nm 3:4; 26:61; 1 Kgs 14:17; 15:25–28; 1 Chr 24:2). (13) The sons of Aaron and Jeroboam contributed to God's being glorified (Lv 10:3,6; 1 Kgs 14:13).

Jeroboam's idolatry would result in the ultimate destruction of his line (1 Kgs 13:33,34). An immediate result was the death of his son Abijah (1 Kgs 14:1–18). Jeroboam's plan to deceive the prophet Ahijah failed and became the means of pronouncing judgment upon the house of Jeroboam and the northern kingdom (1 Kgs 14:7–16). One manifestation of the gradual decline of Israel was the defeat Jeroboam suffered at the hand of Abijah of Judah (2 Chr 13:1–20).

Jeroboam I died after reigning 21 years over Israel (1 Kgs 14:19,20; 2 Chr 13:20). His remaining son, Nadab, ruled for only 2 years before he was assassinated by Baasha of the tribe of Issachar (1 Kgs 14:20; 15:25–31). The whole household of Jeroboam was then slain by Baasha, fulfilling the prophecy of Ahijah concerning the end of the dynasty of Jeroboam. Yet even Baasha walked in the footsteps of Jeroboam's apostasy (1 Kgs 15:34).

2. Jeroboam II, the son of Joash (or Jehoash, 798–782 BC), reigned over Israel longer than any other northern king. His reign of 41 years included an 11-year co-regency with his father. Evidently Joash had taken steps to ensure the stability of his kingdom before meeting Amaziah of Judah in battle (2 Kgs 14:8–14; 2 Chr 25:5–24).

Jeroboam II followed the evil example of his ancestral namesake, Jeroboam I (2 Kgs 14:24). The prophet Ahijah had prophesied the acquisition of power by Jeroboam II (2 Kgs 14:25–27). The time of Jeroboam's reign was late in the history of the northern kingdom, but God was yet desirous of exhibiting his long-suffering and faithful covenant-keeping love, ever offering Israel repentance (2 Kgs 14:27,28).

The northern kingdom reached its greatest extension since the time of Solomon as the result of God's care for Israel during Jeroboam's reign. The boundaries stretched from Hamath on the Orontes River in the north to the Gulf of Aqaba with its cities of Elath and Ezion-geber in the south. Prosperity did not suffice to deliver Israel from internal and external problems, however. The extensive corruption in government and the degenerate spiritual state of the people propelled Israel into the tumultuous days that would end in the utter destruction of the northern kingdom. Jeroboam's own life must have been in danger from conspirators. Amaziah, a priest at Bethel, even accused the prophet Amos of conspiring to assassinate Jeroboam (Am 7:8–17). Amos had actually prophesied the captivity of Israel and the fall of Jeroboam's dynasty. The Word of God had become a threat to Jeroboam because of the hardness of the hearts of all in Israel, including the king.

Jeroboam II ruled in the city of Samaria (2 Kgs 14:23). The archaeological evidence at Samaria indicates a reconstruction program in the royal palace during the prosperous reigns of Joash and Jeroboam II. In 1910 excavators found over 60 inscribed potsherds which were invoices or labels for oil and wine sent to the royal stores for use in the king's service. The limited number of place-names (27) on the potsherds indicates that the shipments of these commodities were not a nationwide levy of taxes, but were probably all

from properties belonging to the royal house. These illustrate the extensive holdings and opulence of the royal house in Israel during the reign of Jeroboam II.

Large numbers of carved decorative plaques and panels of ivory were also found in the ruins of Samaria, a reminder of the wealth of the northern kingdom in its latter days. The influence of the pagan societies of Syria, Assyria, and Egypt can be seen by the various figures of deities on the ivories.

Economic depression, moral deterioration, political weakness, and governmental corruption served to hasten the fall of Israel. The rich landowners, including Jeroboam II, had oppressed the less wealthy citizens and had forced small landowners to migrate from their farms to the cities.

Within six months of the death of Jeroboam II, the prophecy concerning the end of the dynasty of Jehu (Jeroboam was the fourth king of that line) was fulfilled (2 Kgs 15:8–12; cf. 2 Kgs 10:12–31). As the son of Jeroboam I, Nadab, was assassinated, so the son of Jeroboam II, Zechariah, was assassinated. Thirty-one years after the death of Jeroboam II, the prophecies concerning the captivity of Israel were fulfilled (722 BC; 2 Kgs 17:3–41).

See ISRAEL, HISTORY OF; CHRONOLOGY, OLD TESTAMENT.

Jeroham. 1. Levite of the family of Kohath, father of Elkanah and a forefather of the prophet Samuel and Heman the singer. He was a musician in the sanctuary during David's reign (1 Sm 1:1; 1 Chr 6:27,34).

2. Benjamite whose sons lived in Jerusalem and were leaders among their people (1 Chr 8:27). He is perhaps identical with #3 below.

3. Benjamite and Ibneiah's father. Ibneiah, head of his family, resided in Jerusalem during the postexilic period (1 Chr 9:8).

4. Descendant of Pashbur and the father of Adaiah the priest. Adaiah returned to Jerusalem after the exile (1 Chr 9:12; Neh 11:12).

5. Benjamite from Gedor whose two sons, Joelah and Zebadiah, came to David's support at Ziklag (1 Chr 12:7).

6. Father of Azarel, the chief official of the Danites during David's reign (1 Chr 27:22).

7. Father of Azariah, one of the commanders who was instrumental in removing Queen Athaliah from Judah's throne to make way for Joash, the rightful claimant (2 Chr 23:1).

Jerubbaal. Name given to Gideon after he destroyed an altar to Baal (Jgs 6:32). The name means "let Baal contend against him."

See GIDEON; JERUBBESHETH.

A well at Samaria, the city from which Jeroboam II ruled.

Jerubbesheth. Variation of the name Jerubbaal, meaning "let Baal contend" (Jgs 6:32), ascribed to Gideon for his daring feat of destroying his father's altar to Baal. Because of Israel's abhorrence of Baal, the author of 2 Samuel subsequently altered Gideon's cognomen Jerubbaal to Jerubbesheth, meaning "let shame contend," in 1 Samuel 12:11.

See GIDEON.

Jeruel. Wilderness region lying southeast of Tekoa near En-gedi, just above and west of the cliff of Ziz (2 Chr 20:16). Its exact location is unknown, but some identify it with el-Hasasah.

Jerusalem. Historic city sacred to Christians, Jews, and Muslims; the chief city of ancient Palestine and of the modern state of Israel.

Name. *Egyptian Meaning.* The earliest mention of the name occurs in the Egyptian Execration Texts of the 19th and 18th centuries BC in the form probably transliterated *Urusalimum.*

Semitic Meaning. In the 14th century the name appears in the Abdi-Hepa correspondence from Tell el-Amarna, written *Urusalim.* Later it is found in the inscription of the Assyrian monarch Sennacherib, written *Ursalimmu.* The two transparently Semitic elements, *uru* (city) and *salim* (a divine name), have produced the hyphenated composite meaning "the city of (the god) Salim." Hyphenating geographic names to incorporate divine elements was a common practice in the ancient Near Eastern world, and the deity Salim, or Shalem (Akkadian, Shulmanu; cf. Solomon), was a member of the Amorite pantheon (cf. Ez 16:3). Since the oldest textual evidence—Egyptian, West Semitic, and Akkadian—supports only *uru* + *salim*, and the OT itself attests that Jerusalem was not originally a Hebrew city, it is probable that the Semitic etymological origin of this name produced the meaning "the city of (the god) Salim."

Hebrew/Aramaic Meaning. In the Hebrew OT, Jerusalem is written *yerûshālayim*, and in the Aramaic portions the name is rendered *yerûshālēm*. Containing the elements *yarah* (to found, cf. Jb 38:6) and *shalem* (a divine name), it yields the meaning "the foundation of (the god) Shalem," the *sh* of the Hebrew/Aramaic to be taken as the phonemic equivalent of the Akkadian *s*. The eloquence of this alteration is reflected in the word "foundation," indicating the permanent home (in contrast to an impermanent tent, cf. Heb 11:10) of Shalem. From this, one may deduce that Shalem was the patron deity of the city and that he had given his name to it, an onomastic transference frequently seen in the ancient world.

Greek Meaning. In the NT, Jerusalem translates the two Greek words *Ierousalem* and *Hierosoluma.* The former is simply the Greek transliteration of the OT Aramaic form; the latter reflects the word *hieros* (holy), representing a Hellenized paronomasia, corresponding neither with the Semitic root of the name nor with the city's historical reality.

Others. That the Salem of Genesis 14:18 is actually an abbreviated citation of Jerusalem is corroborated by the parallelism of Psalm 76:2, the *Genesis Apocryphon*, and Josephus (*Antiq.* 1.180; cf. Beth-shalem of the Amarna tablets). The name "Jebus" denotes the Jebusite people living in Jerusalem during the conquest and settlement of Canaan by the Israelites, and the city was so designated until the time of David. According to the Bible (Gn 10:15, 16) and Josephus (*Antiq.* 7.3.1), the Jebusites are to be classified as Canaanites (i.e., West Semites).

The name "Zion," whose meaning is unknown, is said to have applied to part of the Jebusite city. The land ridge running south of the temple is usually thought to correspond to Zion. Other ancient names for Jerusalem include Moriah, city of David, Ariel, the City, and the Holy City.

Situation. Jerusalem is situated 31° 46' 45" north latitude and 35° 13' 25" east longitude. The city rises to just over 2500 feet above sea level and rests some 14 miles west of the northern end of the Dead Sea and approximately 33 miles east of the Mediterranean coast. With a 10° southeast aspect, Jerusalem is thoroughly exposed to the rays of the summer sun; one would expect its natural condition to be quite barren.

A Mediterranean climate pervades Jerusalem. From October to May the city experiences its rainy season, with an annual accumulation of about 25 inches. Throughout January and February the rains are often driven by winds, and the mercury drops to near freezing (cf. Ezr 10:9, cold weather coinciding with the days of heaviest rainfall). Snow falls two years out of three. There is no rain between May and September, and a high percentage of solar radiation produces oppressive heat. Frequently in September or October the thermometer soars over 100° F, though prevailing humid breezes provide a welcome, if limited, relief in the evenings. Also in the late fall Jerusalem is sometimes beset by a sirocco, a sweltering wind from the southeastern deserts creating torrid heat and parched dryness.

Like Rome, Jerusalem is a city set on hills. A cluster of five hills comprise the denuded quadrilateral land mass roughly one mile long

Aerial view of Jerusalem.

and one-half mile wide, bordered on all sides, except the north, by deep ravines. Skirting the city on the west and south is the Valley of Hinnom (Greek Gehenna); hedging Jerusalem on the east is the Kidron Valley (cf. the Valley of Jehoshaphat, Jl 3:2,12). Stretching from the Damascus Gate in the north to the pool of Siloam, where it converged with the Kidron, was an interior ravine known as the Tyropean Valley, or "Cheesemakers" Valley. These three principal ravines are connected by a number of lateral valleys, naturally segmenting the configuration of the original terrain.

East of the Tyropean lie 3 hills. The southernmost, historically known as the southeastern hill, was the site of earliest occupation, undoubtedly because of its convenient water supply. It was the hill conquered by David. In the Bible it is variously called Zion, the city of David, and Ophel. This narrow ridge of land is no more than 60 yards across at the top and encompasses no more than 8 acres. Josephus called this land spur "the lower city," signifying its comparative elevation. Today this area is completely outside the walls of the city.

Immediately north of Zion lies the temple hill, dominated today by the sacred rock on which rests the Muslim Dome of the Rock mosque. Some believe this to be the location of Araunah's threshing floor (2 Sm 24:18–25); others aver it to be the site of Moriah (Gn 22:2; 2 Chr 3:1). Jerusalem certainly is a three-day journey from Beersheba, and Genesis 22:4 need not be construed spatially "at a great distance."

A lateral ravine separates the temple hill from the third hill to the east of the Tyropean. Historically known as the northeastern hill, it bears the name Bezetha ("the new city"). It received this name because later, in the Roman period, practical necessity dictated that a third northern wall be constructed to accommodate a growing population. Hence, the Bezetha was added to the city, though, ironically, it always has been a somewhat sparsely populated area.

To the west of the Tyropean stand the two remaining hills. What is historically known as the southwestern hill, sometimes mistakenly referred to as Zion, is called the upper city, a reference to its higher elevation. Today it roughly approximates the Armenian quarter and contains the Tower of David, built on the foundations of Herod's towers, the traditional site of the tomb of David, and the Church of St. James.

The northwest hill largely corresponds to the Christian quarter, with the Church of the Holy Sepulchre at its center.

Stationed astride the crest of Palestine's central plateau and located at the crossroad of the watershed route connecting Hebron, Bethlehem, Shechem (Nablus), and points north with the longitudinal route from the Jordan Valley and the several arteries to the Mediterranean, Jerusalem is commercially central to the country. The lateral highway through the Judean mountains and eastward could not pass south of Jerusalem, being blocked by the Dead Sea and its sheer cliffs. Karmon (*Israel: A Regional Geography*, p. 249) submits that the only possibility for this route existed along the crest of the watershed, passing some three or four miles northwest of Jerusalem. Accordingly, the city lies just off the natural crossroads of Judea. (David's transference of his capital to Jerusalem was as commercially discerning as it was politically and religiously astute.) Because it lacked significant water supply, the city's strategic commercial location was probably the deciding criterion for its original occupation.

Though in the Bible one is said to travel "up to Jerusalem," it is far from the highest point in the immediate vicinity. Nestled among the "hills of Jerusalem" (Ps 125:2), the city is hidden from the eyes of an approaching traveler until he mounts one of the higher ridges.

Eastward from Jerusalem one crosses the Olivet summit to begin the sharp descent toward the Jordan rift and the scorched cliffs of the Dead Sea, where many adherents of a resurgent Judaism sought refuge after AD 70. Westward lie the cultivable lands in the plain of the Rephaim, where David decisively defeated the Philistines (2 Sm 5:18–25). Northward the summit of Mt Scopus dominates the horizon.

Water, a lifeline of civilization, has always been in meager supply at Jerusalem. The only natural source of permanent water was the spring at Gihon, today sometimes called the Virgin's Spring, located in the Kidron immediately east of the ancient fortress conquered by David. Tunnels were burrowed to provide access to the Gihon when Jerusalem was besieged. Later, the Siloam Tunnel was cut through nearly 1800 feet of Cenomanian-Turonian limestone, allowing the waters of the Gihon to pass through the hill of Zion to the pool of Siloam.

Farther south, where the Kidron and Hinnom valleys converge, there was another spring, called in the Bible En-rogel (modern Bir Eyyub). Owing to the lowering of the water table, this source of water ceased to percolate and was subsequently converted into a well. (The jackal's well of Neh 2:13 should be kept separate from these sources and its location is altogether unknown.)

These two sources were clearly insufficient to sustain a sizable population, and both were too deep in the Kidron to be employed for irrigation. Hence, a vast network of cisterns, reservoirs, and water conduits for supplemental supply has been devised since ancient times.

Explorations and Excavations. Modern exploration of Jerusalem dates from the surveying of van Kootwijck in 1598–99. Later, Pocke recognized the Tomb of the Kings of Judah on the Zion summit. The first survey of the temple area was made in 1833 by Bonomi, Catherwood, and Arundale.

But with Edward Robinson the first important exploratory work was inaugurated. This American scholar made a series of topographical surveys of profound significance even today, and his activities mark the beginning of a flood of literature. Robinson's chief contribution lay in his method. He dared to challenge the axiom that ecclesiastical traditions provide the primary source for reconstructing a city's history. Instead, he sought to reconstruct Jerusalem's history on the basis of the "unsuspected evidence of the stones," thereby signaling for the holy city the advent of the archaeological method.

A second creative venture commenced in 1864 when, through the philanthropic contribution of Lady Burdett-Coutts of London, who wished to improve the sanitary conditions and water supply of the city, the Palestine Exploration Fund launched its first archaeological enterprise, under the direction of Charles Wilson. This nascent venture was enlarged between 1867–70 as Charles Warren carried out extensive excavations around the temple area, on the southeastern hill, and in the Tyropean Valley, employing a system of underground shafts and tunnels. Of especial interest is his unearthing of a section of the ancient city wall located near the southeastern sector of the temple. This find led him to postulate that the southeastern hill was the site of original occupation.

While conducting more extensive research within the Siloam Tunnel, Warren discovered an alternate, archaic shaft connecting the Gihon with a plateau of the southeastern hill. Though not specifically discussed by him, the magnitude of this discovery is considerable for Bible history, as it provides an entirely reasonable explanation for David's military strategy (2 Sm 5:8). The cartographic materials amassed by Wilson and Warren still form the basis of much topographic research.

In the wake of the much-publicized discoveries of Wilson and Warren came the quests of Conder, Maudsley, and Clermont-Ganneau. In 1881 Guthe conducted additional excavations on the southeastern hill and at the pool of Siloam, while Schick reported the discovery of the now famous Siloam Inscription. Schick also excavated a number of tombs just off the Nablus Road. At the same time Bliss and Dickie undertook elaborate excavations of the southern wall, isolating for the first time a wall across the mouth of the Tyropean connecting the southwestern and southeastern hills. The southeastern hill was again the subject of excavation when, from 1909 to 1911, Parker engineered a number of underground shaft tunnels. His work brought to light a highly complicated network of canals along the east slope of Zion in the Gihon region.

With the work of Raymond Weill one enters a third creative period. While the territory on the southeastern hill actually excavated by Weill was proportionally small, it was he

The gates of that part of modern Jerusalem that is known as the Old City (clockwise, beginning with the gate that is farthest west): (1) New Gate, (2), Damascus Gate, (3) Herod's Gate, (4) St. Stephen's Gate (Lions' Gate, St. Mary's Gate, Sheep Gate), (5) Golden Gate, (6) Dung Gate, (7) Zion Gate, and (8) Jaffa Gate.

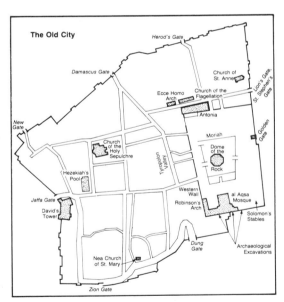

The Old City

Herod's Gate

Damascus Gate

Church of
St. Anne

Ecce Homo
Arch

Church of the
Flagellation

Lion's Gate,
St. Stephen's
Gate

Antonia

New
Gate

Moriah

Golden
Gate

Church
of the Holy
Sepulchre

Dome
of the
Rock

Tyropoeon Valley

Hezekiah's
Pool

Western
Wall

al Aqsa
Mosque

Jaffa Gate

Robinson's
Arch

Solomon's
Stables

David's
Tower

Dung
Gate

Archaeological
Excavations

Nea Church
of St. Mary

Zion Gate

who first employed the stratigraphic excavation method at Jerusalem. Weill's work was interrupted in 1914 by the outbreak of World War I, but his method had already provided penetrating new insights into Jerusalem's history before the time of David. His labors forever dispelled all doubt that the southeastern hill was the most important area in the earliest times.

Following the war, the southeastern hill was the object of a second campaign by Weill, of a team under the direction of Macalister and Duncan, and of an expedition led by Crowfoot and Fitzgerald. From 1925 to 1927 Sukenik, Mayer, and Fisher explored north of the city, discovering sections of the third (northern) wall (i.e., Herod Agrippa's wall). Later, Iliffe unearthed a cemetery and Johns excavated the citadel at the Jaffa Gate. Johns's unstinting efforts were rewarded with the discovery of walls and towers from the pre-Christian era. Just prior to World War II, Hamilton carried out excavations outside the northeastern wall near St. Stephen's Gate. From 1949 to 1953 Testa conducted excavations at Bethphage, where the colt for Jesus' triumphal entry into Jerusalem was obtained (Mt 21:1–11).

An important new period in archaeological research began with the protracted expedition under the leadership of Kathleen Kenyon. From 1961 to 1967, the British School of Archaeology project explored several regions of Jerusalem, focusing principally upon the southeastern hill near the Gihon, the region of the mouth of the Tyropean, the territory immediately south of the temple area, and the Armenian Gardens inside the west wall of the Old City and south of the Citadel atop the southwestern hill.

Excavations begun subsequent to the commencement of Kenyon's labor include Bennett and Hennessy, who toiled in the vicinity of the Damascus Gate, and Mazar, whose surveys were conducted primarily along the southern slope of the temple hill. Since 1968 the Hebrew University Museum, under the direction of Amiran and Eitan, has intermittently conducted archaeological research in and near the city. The Israel Department of Antiquities and Museums has engaged in isolated excavations of what was known prior to the 1967 war as the Jewish Quarter.

History.

The Pre-Israelite Period. Paleolithic and Mesolithic flint implements of an Acheulian type found in the plain of the Rephaim constitute the earliest evidence of the existence of human beings in the area of Jerusalem. Near the beginning of the 4th millennium BC, the southeastern hill was first occupied by a sedentary group, a fact evinced from the artifactual remains recovered from three graves and the pottery type discovered on bedrock. By 1800 BC the crest of the southeastern hill was walled in rudimentary form. Balance of probability favors identifying the ethnic character of these earliest occupants as Semitic, given the cultural similarities attested at Jericho, Ai, and Gezer.

Jerusalem is listed in the Execration Texts of the 12th dynasty of Egypt as a Canaanite city-state.

From the Bible one learns that Abraham paid tithes to Melchizedek, king of Salem (Gn 14:17–20). That the Valley of Shaveh (v 17) was near Jerusalem is supported by the fact that Melchizedek *brought out* the bread and wine and that the king of Sodom likewise participated in the event. Many commentators surmise that Shaveh lay near the convergence of the Kidron and Hinnom valleys. Again the great patriarch visited an area later incorporated into Jerusalem, the site where Isaac was nearly sacrificed (Gn 22). Second Chronicles 3:1 identifies Mt Moriah as the temple hill.

In the 15th century or thereabouts the Hurrians (possibly the biblical Horites) penetrated into Palestine. At about the same time at Jerusalem, extensive building activities were initiated and improved fortification methods were introduced. Accordingly, most writers attribute these projects at Jerusalem to the Hurrian infiltration. Beginning some 160 feet down the eastern slope, the new occupants undertook to construct platform terraces, engineered to be filled up to the level of the top of the hill. These were reinforced by a series of ribs designed to retain the immense fill that was required. A strong masonry rampart was erected near the bottom of the slope, below the spot where a shaft was burrowed to provide access to the waters of the Gihon. This enterprise procured an enlarged land area on the summit, a much stronger and more permanent city wall, and water access during times of siege. Traces of the northern side of this wall were located in 1961 by Kenyon. Apparently the northern perimeter of this fortress extended to just south of the modern south wall. A gate unearthed in 1929 by Crowfoot is attributed to the western sector of this wall, indicating that the western wall ran parallel, and very near, to the western edge of the Zion crest.

To date there is not one shred of conclusive evidence that the Hurrians ever occupied Jerusalem. (The Horites are conspicuously absent from every OT list of peoples who were dispossessed from Palestine.) The extant testimony favors understanding a Semitic occupation throughout the whole of the pre-Israelite period (cf. Gn 10:15,16).

Conquest and Settlement Period. Upon learning of Gibeon's placation of Joshua's army (Jos 9), Adoni-zedek, king of Jerusalem, formed a coalition with the kings of Hebron, Jarmuth, Lachish, and Eglon. In response to their attack on Gibeon, Joshua marshaled his forces and defeated the coalition, killing all five monarchs at Makkedah (Jos 10:17–27). It appears that the tribe of Judah temporarily took control of Jerusalem and burned it in the wake of this victory (Jgs 1:8). However, the Jebusites reoccupied the site (Jos 15:63; 1 Chr 11:5). Later, Judges 19 records the grim details of the plight of the Levite who, though arriving at Jebus (i.e., Jerusalem) at nightfall, disparagingly refused to spend the night in a city of foreigners. Apparently the Jebusites more or less maintained control of Jerusalem until the time of David.

The city appears again as a boundary separating the tribal inheritances of Judah and Benjamin, becoming the southern border of the latter's domain. The identification of "the shoulder of the Jebusite" (Jos 15:8; 18:16) with Jerusalem is usually explained as a reference to the southwestern hill, possibly held also by the Jebusites at this time. A less viable explanation seeks to apply the name "Valley of Hinnom" to the Tyropean Valley.

The Davidic Period. Following the Philistine victory atop Mt Gilboa, where Saul and Jonathan were slain (1 Sm 31), David reigned over the tribe of Judah from Hebron, while a surviving son of Saul, Ish-bosheth, ruled over the northern tribes from Mahanaim. During the two-year struggle that ensued, the house of David grew stronger while the forces of Ish-bosheth shrunk considerably (2 Sm 3:1). This struggle culminated in the death and decapitation of Ish-bosheth and the dispersion of his forces. David became the undisputed monarch of all the tribes of Israel.

But the new monarch recognized that a consolidated national capital acceptable to both the north and the south would have to be created. Jerusalem had remained neutral in the conflict, being the site of a Jebusite enclave. It also represented a location that was militarily desirable, and by being commercially central to the fledgling nation, it was ideally suited.

The capture itself was effected with remarkable ease, though opinions differ concerning the stratagem employed. On the one hand, it is argued that the verb in 2 Samuel 5:8 ("get up") carries the meaning "to touch, to reach" (cf. Ps 42:7), connoting that David's men were being challenged to fight their way up the slope to the water shaft, so as to cut off the Jebusites' water source. On the other hand, a

number of newer excavations made along the east slope of the southeastern hill tend to strengthen the hypothesis that Joab and his men climbed through a water shaft from the Gihon and took the Jebusites by surprise.

In the course of David's 33-year reign at Jerusalem he made the city into the center of an empire that stretched from Egypt to the Euphrates River. He engaged in considerable building and expansion of the city. He fortified the Canaanite walls and prepared an extension of the city by the Millo ("filling"), possibly along the east slope of Zion (cf. the platform terraces of the 15th century occupation). He built a house for his mighty men and prepared a dynastic sepulcher within the city walls, a privileged burial plot accorded only to royalty. According to Nehemiah 3:16, the sepulcher of David was located near the south end of the southeastern hill along the east slope. Remains from tombs excavated in this region by Weill may indicate the place, but the traditional site of David's tomb on the southwestern hill can lay no claim to authenticity. No concrete evidence exists for the occupation of the southwestern hill prior to the 7th century BC.

David also constructed a royal residence, receiving the technology and many materials from Hiram, king of Tyre (2 Sm 5:11). Nehemiah 12:37 suggests that this palace also may have lain near the east side of the southeastern hill. It was from a window of this house that Michal saw David performing in what was, to her, an undignified manner (2 Sm 6:16–23). From the roof of this palace David gazed upon Bathsheba as she bathed (2 Sm 11:2–5), and from this residence he plotted the murder of her husband Uriah (2 Sm 11:14–25).

By bringing the ark of the covenant to Jerusalem (2 Sm 6:1–15), implying that Jehovah would reside here, David displayed his most profound leadership. For in this perceptive act he merged for the first time in Israel's history its political and religious capitals. Jerusalem took on the unique character of a holy city and a royal city. Now the city would be known as the "city of David" (2 Sm 5:7) as well as the "city of God" (Ps 46:4). Now adult male Jews would make their pilgrimages *to Jerusalem* to take part in the feasts and offerings. It only remained for David to make this arrangement permanent, to enshrine Jehovah at Jerusalem forever by building him a temple. David aspired to do so (2 Sm 7), but God responded that such an undertaking was reserved for a son of the king.

The First Temple Period. (1) Under Solomon. A growing national realization of the extent and impact of the Davidic empire was employed by Solomon to full advantage. Himself an innovative and dynamic administrator, this son of David made Jerusalem into a cosmopolitan center. The revenues of caravans from Egypt to Babylonia as well as the Phoenician trade with Elath, the Red Sea, and Ophir passed through his royal capital. Solomon's own naval fleet traveled as far as Tarshish, most likely located on an island along the western coast of Spain. These expeditions returned every three years with such exotic commodities as apes, peacocks, silver, iron, tin, ivory, and gold. The capital swelled with residents and visitors, and the monarch's fame became proverbial (1 Kgs 10).

Solomon was the great OT builder of Jerusalem. His most significant building enterprise was undoubtedly the first temple. Erected on the summit of the temple hill, this edifice required seven years to construct, from April/May, 966 (1 Kgs 6:1), to October/November, 959 (1 Kgs 6:38). Hiram again provided both the technology and the cedar beams. These beams were floated southward on the Mediterranean to Joppa, where they were transported overland to Jerusalem (2 Chr 2:16). With a suggested tripartite floor plan, the temple faced east, the direction of the rising of the sun. Its interior measured approximately 90 feet in length, some 30 feet in width, and about 45 feet in height. Along the entire front (east side) was a portico measuring some 15 feet in depth, with two bronze pillars erected at the center (1 Kgs 7:15). Surrounding the temple on the other three sides were chambers. Following the completion of the temple, Solomon had the furniture of the tabernacle, including the ark, moved from Zion (2 Chr 5) for the feast of tabernacles. This crowning event was climaxed with the coming of the presence of God (1 Kgs 8:10).

Today the temple site is occupied by the Muslim sacred enclosure called Haram-esh-Sherif ("the noble sanctuary"). There inside the Dome of the Rock Mosque, also known as the Mosque of Omar, is embedded a large rock long venerated as the spot over which stood the Holy of Holies of the Solomonic temple. Though the tradition may be based on fact, nothing definitively dating from the Solomonic era has been excavated at the sacred precinct.

Solomon also extended the Late Bronze Age Canaanite walls to enclose the enlarged area of his city (1 Kgs 3:1; 9:15). Though it is unlikely that Solomon expanded the city to the east or south, to encompass the temple hill required constructing an extension wall in the north. Kenyon corroborates that the area north of the southeastern hill was occupied in the Solomonic era. She also asserts that Solomon most likely built the eastern wall extension along the ridge of the southeastern and temple hills, not down the slope where the Canaanite wall was located, thus reducing the width of the city at that point to about 50 yards. His western extension merely continued the Canaanite wall along the western crest of the two hills.

Josephus' description of the ancient walls (*Wars* 5.4.1–2) is not completely understandable today, but it is possible that parts of what he described as the north and west walls were built by Solomon. Kenyon discovered remains of an early occupation on the northern sector

The Dome of the Rock (or Mosque of Omar) stands over the traditional site of Solomon's temple, the site that some believe to be that of Araunah's threshing floor and Mt Moriah.

of the southwestern hill which some writers have attributed to the time of Solomon. If true, this would strongly suggest that a wing extending west of the temple hill was also enclosed by a city wall which, along its northern perimeter, might have run near the modern David Street and, on its southern perimeter, might have crossed the Tyropean Valley near the modern south wall. It is at least reasonable to assume that the promontory (knob) that projected into the Tyropean at the northeastern corner of the southwestern hill was enclosed by the Solomonic wall.

While the king did not extend his city walls to the east, a massive buttressing platform terrace built on bedrock at the foot of the Canaanite terrace complex was discovered in 1962 by Kenyon. Stones weighing up to a ton each and acting as the bedrock support for the older terraces were unearthed. Pottery from this level was dated by Kenyon to a time near to when Solomon reigned.

The building of Millo by Solomon is mentioned three times in the Bible (1 Kgs 9:15,24; 11:27). Whether these references are to the further bolstering of the Canaanite platform terraces or to filling in another section of the city cannot be ascertained.

The Bible records that Solomon erected a royal palace adequate for himself, his 700 wives, and 300 concubines (1 Kgs 7:1–8). He constructed cedared quarters for his guards and chariots, a Hall of the Throne, and a Hall of Pillars. And to cement his single most important political marriage, the king built a house for his wife, the daughter of the Egyptian pharaoh, outside the city, her presence being incompatible with the presence of the ark (2 Chr 8:11). However, he displayed no reticence in building idolatrous shrines to the deities worshiped by his foreign wives (1 Kgs 11:7,8).

One may find in 1 Kings 10:27 a succinct encapsulation of the economic wealth lavished upon Jerusalem by Solomon: silver became as abundant as stone and cedar was as common as sycamore. It is estimated that the annual revenues that coursed to Jerusalem were as high as $17 million. Ironically, it was the fiscal factor which became the burden of Solomon's monarchy. Overextending himself financially, his economic and political programs soon required the levying of heavy taxes (1 Kgs 4:7–19) and the drafting of Israelites into forced labor (1 Kgs 5:13–18; cf. 9:22–23). These were the primary factors which prompted the schism in Israel's political structure after the death of Solomon and resulted in a divided monarchy.

(2) Under the Kings of Judah. The rupture of the monarchy left Judah and Jerusalem extremely weak economically, politically, and militarily. In fact, between the disintegration of the monarchy and the fall of Jerusalem to Nebuchadnezzar's forces, the city's humiliating history was largely a series of foreign assaults and plunderings.

Less than a decade after the schism, Jerusalem's decline was seized upon by Pharaoh Shishak (1 Kgs 14:25,26). Heavy tribute paid to placate the pharaoh further impoverished the city, though it was spared. Although a kind of peace was forged between Jerusalem and the Omri dynasty, the Davidic capital remained so weak that it was plundered by the Philistines and Arabs (2 Chr 21:16,17). In the wake of its renewed alliance with Israel, Jerusalem was permeated with foreign influences; and, in the reign of Athaliah, the daughter of Ahab and Jezebel and granddaughter of Omri, the city became the center of a revived baalism (2 Kgs 11; 2 Chr 22:10–23:15).

During the rule of Joash, Hazael of Syria carried off still more of the temple treasures (2 Chr 24:23,24). Under Amaziah, Jerusalem was temporarily captured by Jehoash, king of Israel, who broke down parts of the north wall (2 Kgs 14:8–14).

A brief respite was granted to the holy city during the reign of Uzziah (2 Chr 26). This king was able to repair the breach in the city wall, to inflict a defeat upon the Philistine-Arab alliance, and to exact tribute from the Ammonites. It was in the time of Uzziah that the voice of Isaiah was heard in Jerusalem, condemning it as the center of moral and social degeneration.

With the accension of Ahaz, Jerusalem was plunged again into humiliation. Rezin, king of Syria, and his ally Pekah, king of Israel, led their forces to besiege the city. Though taking numerous captives, they could not prevail ultimately against Ahaz, who received encouragement from Isaiah (Is 7:4–9). An attempt to confederate with the growing Assyrian empire backfired, and Ahaz was made to pay heavy tribute in gold and silver to Tiglath-pileser in order to avoid complete destruction.

Hezekiah fell heir to a grave situation politically and religiously. In anticipation of an Assyrian assault predicted by Isaiah (Is 10:28–32), he rebuilt parts of the city walls and armed Jerusalem's inhabitants. He engineered the Siloam Tunnel to bring the waters of the Gihon to the western slope of the southeastern hill, inside the city walls, (2 Kgs 20:20; 2 Chr 32:30).

Sennacherib, the Assyrian monarch, did lay siege to Jerusalem around 701 BC, in fulfillment of Isaiah's claim. If, as is reasonable to assume, 2 Kings 20 and Isaiah 38,39 may be construed as a chronological unit, with their events dating to some 15 years prior to Hezekiah's death (c. 703/2), the coincidental outbreak of troubles in Babylon in 703 was not unrelated to Sennacherib's assault of Jerusalem. What is clear from the Bible is that Hezekiah was successful in attempting to curry the favor of his Babylonian contemporary, Merodach-baladan (2 Kgs 20:12–15; Is 39:1–4). But the concerted effort of Babylon and Jerusalem to throw off the Assyrian yoke was unsuccessful, the miracle of 2 Kings 19:35 notwithstanding, and Hezekiah was forced to pay heavy tribute to Sennacherib (2 Kgs 18:14–16).

Hezekiah's son, Manasseh, was also a tributary to the Assyrian Empire. Perhaps it was his fear of complete annihilation at the hands of the Assyrians that led him to fill Jerusalem with pagan shrines. At any rate, this wicked and bloodthirsty monarch ravaged the worship of Jehovah. Eventually he was captured and deported to Babylon in chains by the Assyrian king, probably Ashurbanipal.

Under King Josiah, Jerusalem was returned to its historical religious function. The temple was reopened and renovated, and a copy of the Law of Moses was discovered inside. The Kidron smoked with the burnings of Baal and Asherah, and the sanctuaries of Canaanite deities facing Jerusalem were desecrated, as Josiah carried forth his reform. An instant of religious revival was realized. In the broader historical context, this reformation could occur unimpeded because the Assyrians were preoccupied with the growing menace of the rising Neo-Babylonian empire.

Regrettably, Josiah injected himself into the shifting balance of political power. Having no affinity for the Assyrian aggression, in 609 BC Josiah sought to intercept the northward march of Pharaoh Neco. Neco was proceeding to Carchemish to assist the Assyrian army against the Babylonian hosts under the command of Nebuchadnezzar. Josiah's effort proved fatal. Being greatly outnumbered in manpower and technology, he died at Megiddo in the battle. His death at the hands of the Egyptians had profound influence upon the remainder of the Davidic line. Henceforth, Jerusalem's kings would vacillate between Egyptian and Babylonian loyalties.

Four years after Josiah's death, in 605 BC, Nebuchadnezzar successfully defeated the Assyrian-Egyptian coalition, forever breaking the back of the Assyrian Empire. Shortly thereafter he marched south to Jerusalem (2 Kgs 24:1–4), taking captive King Jehoiakim (2 Chr 36:6), who maintained an Egyptian loyalty (2 Kgs 23:34,35).

Nebuchadnezzar returned to Jerusalem in 597. This time he took Jehoiachin captive and crowned Zedekiah, a son of Josiah. Some 10 years later, in 587, Zedekiah rebelled, and the Babylonian army again laid siege to the city, capturing it after several months. This time the city was completely decimated. The temple and the Solomonic palace were destroyed with fire; the city walls were demolished. The temple treasures were completely plundered, and the citizens were deported in large numbers.

The Second Temple Period. Jerusalem's doom and 70-year captivity had been spelled out by Jeremiah (Jer 25:11; 29:10; cf. 2 Chr 36:21; Dn 9:2). (One might compute this interval of time as lasting from 586 to 516 BC, i.e., from the destruction of the first temple by Nebuchadnezzar's forces to the official opening of the second temple in the 6th year of Darius, cf. Ezr 6:15–18.) On the other hand, from an exilic perspective, Jeremiah's pronouncement came to be understood by the more pious as a signal for return. That is, Jerusalem's doom had been spelled for *only* 70 years (cf. Ps 137).

In 536, after the fall of Babylon, Cyrus, king of Persia, issued his famous proclamation (2 Chr 36:22,23; Ezr 1:1–4; cf. Is 44:28; 45:1). Thereupon, a humble group of Jews returned to Jerusalem under the direction of Sheshbazzar, a prince of Judah (Ezr 1:8–11). Other groups followed, and the resettlement of the city and the rebuilding of the temple were effected gradually. Zerubbabel, the governor, and Joshua, the high priest, initiated a rebuilding expedition (Ezr 3:8–13); but only in the second year of Darius, at the urging of Haggai and Zechariah, was a full-scale work undertaken. Four years later, in 516 BC, the doors of the second temple were opened officially, and the Passover feast was again observed from Jerusalem (Ezr 6:15–18).

Ezra came to Jerusalem in the seventh year of Artaxerxes (Ezr 7:7). Assuming this is a reference to Artaxerxes I, the date of Ezra's return would have been 458. Again, it was only a meager remnant who felt the compelling urge to make that difficult journey (cf. Josephus *Antiq.* 11.1.3). They were permitted to bring gold, silver, and vessels with which to adorn and enrich the temple. But the city remained almost empty; its walls were broken and its gates were burned down.

Moved by reports of these miserable conditions (Neh 1:3,4), Nehemiah, in the 20th year of Artaxerxes (444 BC), decided to leave his post as cupbearer to the king and to go to Jerusalem. If the concern of the earlier returnees focused upon the temple, Nehemiah's was upon the city walls. After being in Jerusalem for three days, he undertook an evening reconnaissance to ascertain the extent of work still required on the walls. His is the most comprehensive description of Jerusalem's postexilic city walls and topography (Neh 2:11–16). Spurred on by his energetic enthusiasm, the people completed the task of rebuilding the walls in 52 days (Neh 6:15). Like Zerubbabel and Joshua before him, the labor of Nehemiah excited the antagonism of the non-Jewish local citizenry who had profited from the Jewish absence from Jerusalem (Neh 6).

In 332 BC Jerusalem, along with the remainder of Judah, peacefully submitted to the army of Alexander the Great. In the wake of Alexander's death, Jerusalem suffered through a series of battles waged between the Ptolemies and the Seleucids for control of Palestine. In 320 Jerusalem was incorporated into the Ptolemaic kingdom, and its economy was stabilized. During the period of comparative prosperity which ensued, the city continued as Judah's administrative center. However, the scene soon changed after 198 BC, when Antiochus III crushed the Ptolemaic hold on Palestine and incorporated Jerusalem into the Seleucid kingdom. For with this, the process of Hellenization of the upper strata of Jewish society was intensified. The more progressive embraced the Hellenistic ideology, while the more traditional saw it as a threat to their ancestral religion. When Antiochus IV Epiphanes ascended to the Seleucid throne in 175, the concerted effort toward Hellenization reached its zenith. At Jerusalem he constructed a gymnasium and converted the Jewish city into a Hellenistic polis, to be known as Antioch. This required a new census. In 168 he erected a fortress in Jerusalem called the Akra, and deployed a Syrian legion. The following year he issued further decrees against Judaism which were carried out with severity in Jerusalem. The temple was desecrated and its treasures were confiscated. The worship of Jehovah was abolished, and a statue of the Olympian Zeus was installed in the temple.

Outraged at this flagrant perversion, Mattathias, a priest from Modin, refused to offer the prescribed heathen sacrifice. Instead, he slew Antiochus' emissary and fled for his life. When word of this action spread throughout Judea, thousands of insurgents, later to be known as the Hasidim ("the pious ones"), under the leadership of Judas Maccabeus openly revolted. Laying siege to Jerusalem, they beat back four successive attempts to relieve the Seleucid legion in the Akra, whereupon a truce was declared. The Hasidim were permitted to occupy the temple hill, to cleanse the temple of pagan objects, and to reinstitute sacrifices to Jehovah. Some three years after its profanation by Antiochus, the temple lamps were again lit in the name of Jehovah. Since that time Jews have solemnly observed the feast of Hanukkah ("lights") in memory of this occasion.

With religious purity now well within view, Judas set out to achieve political freedom as well. This was a far-reaching decision which established an unfortunate precedent. Judas set in motion a regrettable chain of events which culminated some 100 years later in the coming of Rome to Jerusalem. At Judas' death his brother Jonathan was appointed governor and high priest. Not only was a kind of Maccabean political-religious syncretism forged, but henceforth the armies of Jerusalem would be commanded by the high priest. From now on the citizens of Jerusalem could observe their high priest dripping the blood of bulls and goats. But they could also view the high priest dripping human blood as he attempted to conquer and reconquer vast territories in the name of Jehovah.

Simon, the brother of Jonathan and Judas, was the third in this line. He drove the remaining Seleucid soldiers from Akra, making Jerusalem wholly Jewish until AD 70. His successor, John Hyrcanus, assaulted the Idumeans to the south and the Samaritans to the north. Not to be outdone by his father, the next high priest and governor, Aristobulus, added Galilee to the emerging Jewish state, forcibly converting its inhabitants to Judaism. His successor, Alexander Jannaeus, was forced to engage in repeated incursions against the rebellious Samaritans and Idumeans. By this time the question of the advisability of the high priest leading the Jewish armies became so hotly contested that bitter civil strife between several Jewish sects broke out. The Sadducees entertained Hellenistic sympathies; the Pharisees were anti-Hellenistic; the Zealots were prepared to create a Jewish state at all costs. Alexander's wife, Salome Alexandra, succeeded in restoring a temporary peace. But the conditions for renewed civil war were always on the horizon. At Salome's death the Pharisees backed her son Hyrcanus II as the high priest, while the Sadducees backed another son, Aristobulus II, and civil war broke out. In the end this fraticidal war profited only the Romans. In 64 BC, the Roman general Pompey decided in favor of Hyrcanus II. The partisans of Aristobulus isolated themselves in the temple and defied his order, and Pompey was forced to lay siege to Jerusalem. The following year the temple wall was breached and the Romans broke into the temple. Pompey simply dissolved the Maccabean government and added Jerusalem and Judea to the Roman province of Syria, with this act ensuring that law and order would prevail.

The Roman Period. (1) In the Time of Herod. Between the fall of Jerusalem to Pompey and the rise of the Roman Empire in Judea in 37 BC, the two most significant events which molded this era of Jerusalem's history were the death of Pompey in 48 BC and the assassination of Julius Caesar in 44 BC.

Though Pompey had left Hyrcanus in charge of Jerusalem, three times in the next decade Aristobulus or his compatriots attempted to gain control. Throughout these assaults Hyrcanus was supported by Pompey and a wily Idumean (Edomite) named Antipater. At the death of Pompey, Hyrcanus and Antipater aligned themselves with Rome and Julius Caesar, while a son of Aristobulus, Mattathias Antigonus, was welcomed by the Parthians. When Caesar was slain, Mark Antony established Antipater's two sons, Phasael and Herod, as tetrarchs of Judah. However, Roman preoccupation with political affairs outside Palestine provided Antigonus with his opportunity.

In 40 BC, with the aid of the Parthians, Antigonus attacked and seized Jerusalem, forcing Hyrcanus, Herod, and Antipater to seek refuge in the Maccabean palace. Their doom imminent, they made a futile effort to negotiate a truce. Instead Hyrcanus was taken prisoner, and Phasael committed suicide. Herod was able to escape by night. He journeyed to Rome, where the Senate appointed him as "king of the Jews" (cf. Mt 2:1). Armed with this new authority, Herod marshaled two Roman legions, and in 37 BC, he succeeded in forever expelling the Parthians. So began the long and infamous rule of Herod, who reigned at Jerusalem for 33 years (37–4 BC).

Knowing full well how much he was hated by his Jewish constituency, Herod sought to ameliorate his position by providing work, by assessing equitable taxes, and by marrying the Jewess Mariamne. It cannot be denied that Jerusalem enjoyed prosperous and peaceful years during his reign. Herod transformed the external aspect of Jerusalem. He transferred the seat of government to the southwestern hill. Here he erected a lavish palace, an arena for athletic contests, a theater, and a vast aqueduct network. By this time the entire southwestern hill was enclosed with a wall which ran along the rim of the Hinnom Valley, though it is not certain whether it was constructed by Herod or by one of his Maccabean (Hasmonean) predecessors.

Other building projects concerned the temple hill. Herod transformed the old Maccabean fortress into a much larger structure and named it Antonia, in honor of Mark Antony. In the temple area proper he enlarged the esplanade on both the North and south sides, giving it a rectangular shape. Herod's reconstruction of the temple was undertaken in 20 BC,

and it was not completed until around AD 64, just six years prior to its destruction by Titus (cf. Jn 2:20). The dimensions of the enlarged building were approximately 2500 feet by 1000 feet, with two concentric courts giving added dimension to the structure. The outer court, called the Gentile court, was the only area where non-Jews might enter. Archaeology has yielded two Greek inscriptions warning Gentiles not to enter the inner court. The inner court had three subdivisions: one for men, one for women, and the third for priests and Levites.

Surrounding the temple hill, a massive wall of huge stones was constructed. A portion of the western perimeter, known today as the Wailing Wall, still remains intact. Connecting the temple hill with the southwestern hill, Herod erected a huge viaduct across the Tyropean Valley, following a course marked today by the Street of the Chain.

(2) In the Time of Jesus. After Herod's death and the banishment of his son, Judea was made a province of the Roman Empire, ruled over by Roman procurators, the fifth of whom was Pontius Pilate. Though residing in Caesarea, the procurators would occasionally journey to Jerusalem, especially during those times when the streets would be crowded with religious pilgrims; their primary purpose in

The Wailing Wall, with its Herodian stones.

coming was to maintain the peace. Apart from the visit of Jesus to Jerusalem with his parents (Lk 2:41–52), all associations of Jesus with Jerusalem were contemporary with Pilate.

The place of Jesus' crucifixion has been identified, since the 4th century, with the Church of the Holy Sepulchre. A generation of Christian believers contemporary with the emergence of the Christian church continued to live in Jerusalem until AD 66 when, due to the Jewish revolt, they removed to Pella.

Full-scale war erupted that same year as the approaching Roman forces were repelled by the Jewish insurgents. In AD 70, Titus assaulted the north wall of the city, but again the Jewish defenders resisted. Titus thereupon ordered the construction of a siege wall to tightly blockade the city, weakening the inhabitants through hunger. Then, directing a vicious attack upon the Antonia fortress, Titus witnessed the successful scaling of the wall by his armies. They burned the temple in a great conflagration; most of Jerusalem's citizens who had not already died of starvation were killed, though a few were taken as slaves. The city was leveled, except for the three Towers of Herod, which were spared to provide defenses for the 10th Roman legion.

BARRY J. BEITZEL

See JERUSALEM, NEW; ISRAEL, HISTORY OF; JUDAISM; ZION; ZION, DAUGHTER OF.

Bibliography. Y. Aharoni, *The Land of the Bible: A Historical Geography*; M. Avi-Yonah, *Jerusalem*; K.M. Kenyon, *Digging Up Jerusalem* and *Jerusalem: Excavating 3000 Years of History*; R.M. Mackowski, *Jerusalem: City of Jesus*; B. Mazar, *The Mountain of the Lord*; G.A. Smith, *Jerusalem: From the Earliest Times to AD 70*, 2 vols; J. Wilkinson, *Jerusalem as Jesus Knew It.*

Jerusalem, New. Phrase appearing only twice in the Bible, once near the beginning and once near the end of the Book of Revelation (3:12; 21:2). In the first of the great visions of that book, the risen Christ speaks to his people in the midst of their conflict in this world. Among his promises to those who conquer is that they will one day be citizens of the New Jerusalem. The last of the book's visions shows the fulfillment of this promise. There we see not only the victorious people of God, but the city which is to be their home in a new world.

This does not of course answer the question, "What is the New Jerusalem?" A description of what it is like would be relatively simple. An explanation of what it *is* would be more complicated.

Description of the City. An angel takes John to a mountaintop to show him the New Jerusalem. In the account which follows (Rv 21:10–22:5), the first thing John notes is the great jewel-like lamp which lights the city (for that is the true meaning of 21:11). Then he describes its walls and gates (21:12–14). The 12 gates bear the names of the tribes of Israel, and the wall between each gate and the next forms a single "foundation" or block, bearing the name of one of the 12 apostles of Christ. Next, the measurements of the city are given (21:15–17). It is 1500 miles each way—not only in breadth and in length, but also in height—and its wall is 216 feet thick (or high?). By working out these equivalents in miles and feet, however, we miss what John would probably have thought much more important. According to the biblical units of measurement, the city is 12,000 stadia broad and its wall is 144 cubits thick; these numbers may be more significant than the actual dimensions, relating as they do to numbers that appear elsewhere in Revelation (e.g., 7:4–8).

After this, John describes the materials of which the New Jerusalem is built (21:18–21). The wall is of jasper; its foundation layers are encrusted with other precious stones; its gates are pearls; and the streets and buildings within are made of "transparent gold."

As for the city itself, John notes a series of things which it does *not* have (21:22–27)—no temple, no sun or moon, no night, no closing of its gates, and no evil. Finally, there are the three wonderful things that it *does* have (22:1–5)—the river of the water of life, the tree of life, and the throne and presence of God himself.

Such is the New Jerusalem as John describes it. But he wants us not so much to picture what the city looks like as to understand what it means.

Background of the City. OT history presents the city of David, Old Jerusalem, as the place where God's rule over his people and his presence among them was centered. In that Jerusalem stood both the temple, where the priests served, and the throne of the kings who governed as God's deputies. It was the metropolis, or "mother city," of Israel, the people of God. But the whole Bible is about God's redeeming a people for himself, out of all nations, in all ages—a greater Israel of which OT Israel is only the vanguard. So it is natural that the last revelation the Bible gives should be a vision of that greater people—home at last in the true mother city, a new and greater Jerusalem.

The OT prophets witnessed the decline of Old Jerusalem. They watched with grief and anger as it disappointed the hope that it would live up to its high destiny. As it became infected with sin and folly, and its kings and priests increasingly betrayed their calling, two of these prophets in particular began to look forward to a Jerusalem that one day would really be what it was meant to be. Ezekiel (chs 40–48) foresaw the city and its temple reconstructed in detail; Isaiah (chs 52, 60–66) described this latter-day Jerusalem in even more glowing terms. First one prophet's vision and then the other's tie in closely with the vision John records in Revelation 21,22.

In the period between the OT and NT, Jewish writers became yet more disillusioned with the way things were going, and they encouraged their readers not so much with hopes of the renewal of the earthly Jerusalem as with imaginative descriptions of the heavenly one. This, they reckoned, existed already; at the end of the age it would come down from God out of heaven, the metropolis of his people, populous and beautiful, the place of his temple and throne. In fact, what was imagined by these apocalyptic writers is in many respects very like what would in due course actually be seen by John.

Jesus develops all these lines of thought in a quite remarkable way. It is not simply that he foretells the final destruction of Jerusalem and its temple (Mk 13; Lk 19:41–44). If that were all, it would leave a great question unanswered. For Old Jerusalem existed for a purpose, as we have seen; and if it is to be destroyed, how can that purpose then be fulfilled? Where will God's people then find his throne and his temple?

Jesus' answer is that since his incarnation God's rule and God's presence are to be found *in him* (Mt 28:18; Jn 14:9). He himself is the "New Jerusalem"—an entirely new kind of Jerusalem.

This is borne out by the word for "new" which John uses in Revelation. There are two distinct Greek words translated in English Bibles as "new." Some time after the destruction of Jerusalem in AD 70, the emperor Hadrian built a "new" Jerusalem; that was the kind of "new" which simply meant the latest in a series of cities on the same site. But John's vision is of a Jerusalem which is "new" in the sense of being fresh, clean, and different. The NT speaks in the same way of the new covenant and the new commandment (Jn 13:34; Heb 8:8), the new creation and the new man (2 Cor 5:17; Eph 2:15). John's vision brings out the same truth by telling of seven things that will exist "no more" in the new heaven and earth: no more sea, no more death, sorrow, crying, or pain, no more curse, no more night (Rv 21:1,4; 22:3,5). In these respects all will be new and different.

There are five passages elsewhere in the NT which help to fill in the background to Revelation 21. In Galatians 4:26 Paul speaks of "Jerusalem above," the mother city of all who receive salvation by faith, as opposed to the old

Jerusalem, where those belong who seek "to please God by trying to obey the Commandments" (as the LB glosses Gal 4:25). In Ephesians 5:25–32 he speaks of the bride of Christ, by which he means the church; in John's vision the "bride" is the "city" (Rv 21:9,10). In Philippians 3:20 (NASB) we are told that the heavenly city is not simply the future home of believers, but also the place of their present "citizenship." Hebrews 12:22 makes the same point: those who believe have arrived already at the "heavenly Jerusalem." (A separate train of thought is suggested by chs 17 and 18 of Revelation itself, where we see Jerusalem's great rival Babylon, the heathen city which is a picture of godless human society.)

In other words, *this* Jerusalem is the home of all God's believing people, Jew and Gentile, from OT and NT times, and it seems not only to be future, but also to exist already, in some sense, in the present. What then are we to make of John's vision?

Meaning of the City. Some of those who expect a future millennium (1000-year earthly reign of Christ, between his second coming and the final defeat of Satan) hold that the New Jerusalem belongs to the millennium, because of certain indications which they believe suit that period better than the eternal state that will follow it (Rv 21:24,26; 22:2). They visualize it as a literal, material city. It will presumably then be in the shape of a cube, or perhaps a pyramid, and some even picture it hovering like an immense spaceship above the surface of the earth.

Most millennarians, however, and also many who do not believe in a millennium in the sense just mentioned, hold that John is describing the city as it will be in eternity. They too may take it literally. They may on the other hand believe that the literal details given in these chapters—the city's measurements, materials, and so on—are the only way in which John could describe something

A panorama of Jerusalem, with the Dome of the Rock near the center.

which is in fact indescribable (though nonetheless real).

In line with the message of the entire Book of Revelation, many take the New Jerusalem to be the ideal city of God, which belongs not only to the future but also to the present. It exists here and now because it is a spiritual truth, not a material one. It is always "coming down . . . out of heaven" precisely because it comes to men "from God" (21:2). The fact remains, of course, that everything John records in the last two chapters of Revelation belongs to a world which will only appear after the first heaven and the first earth have passed away—a world which is (to us, at any rate) still future.

Taking into account all these Scriptures, we may come closest to understanding the New Jerusalem if we see it as the community of Christ and his people, which will appear in its perfection only when this age has come to an end. Yet in another sense, Christians belong to it already, and it gives them both an ideal to strive for in this world and a hope to anticipate in the next.　MICHAEL J. WILCOCK

See BRIDE OF CHRIST; CHURCH; JERUSALEM; ZION; ZION, DAUGHTER OF.

Jerusalem Council. Meeting described in Acts 15:6–29, held about AD 48–50. Acts records that the conference was held to deal with the question of the requirement for gentile salvation raised by Jews first in Antioch (14:26–15:1) and later in Jerusalem (15:3–5). The matter was subjected to lengthy consideration by "the apostles and the elders" (15:6), with Peter (vv 7–11), Paul and Barnabas (vv 12,22,25,26), and James the brother of Jesus (vv 13–21), who seems to have been the moderator.

Acts gives only a summary of the conclusion (v 6, "after there had been much debate"). The major points clarified and emphasized include: (1) God makes "no distinction" between Jewish and gentile believers (v 9); (2) salvation is by grace through faith (vv 9,11); (3) God has confirmed his acceptance of Gentiles through signs and wonders (vv 8,12); (4) inclusion of the Gentiles among his people was a part of the divine intention revealed in the OT (vv 15–18; quoting Am 9:11,12). The assembly also issued a list (called "the degree") instructing gentile Christians to abstain from (1) "the pollution of idols," (2) "fornication," (3) "things strangled," and (4) "blood" (vs 20). The decision was circulated by letter to churches in "Antioch, Syria and Cilicia" (v 22; cf. 16:4).

The account, when viewed within its place in the Book of Acts as a whole, forms the culmination of the struggle by the early church to understand itself. The Judaism from which Christianity arose was a legalistic religion that sought to earn God's favor by observing ceremonies and keeping laws. It also held to an exclusive nationalistic outlook which regarded Israel alone as "the people of God," and which required non-Jews desiring to be identified with God to submit to circumcision and the Mosaic law, and offer prescribed sacrifices. The earliest Christians in Jerusalem seem to have held at least some of these views even after recognizing Jesus as the Messiah.

Acts portrays a series of events through which the fallacy of the the Jewish legalistic and exclusivistic attitudes were exposed. Stephen questioned the narrow religious view which restricted God's presence, activity, and concern to Jerusalem (Acts 7). Philip led Samaritans and an Ethiopian official, representatives of groups with only loose traditional connections to Judaism, to faith in Jesus (Acts 8). At the direct command of God, Peter proclaimed Jesus as Messiah and Lord to Cornelius, a good, God-fearing, but uncircumcised Gentile (Acts 10). Through this incident Peter came to recognize that God does not discriminate between peoples (Acts 10:34,35). The undeniable coming of the Holy Spirit upon Cornelius and his household (10:44) provided surprising proof of God's acceptance of the Gentiles, which could not be doubted even by members of the scrupulously Jewish, procircumcisionist group who witnessed the event (10:45–48) or to whom it was later reported (11:1–18). The conversion of Cornelius became a precedent later cited by Peter at the council (15:7–11).

God's acceptance of Cornelius might have been regarded as an exceptional case by strict Jewish Christians. This was made impossible by the conversion of Greeks at Antioch (11:20), the establishment of a racially and culturally mixed church in that city (as implied by the diverse backgrounds of the leaders mentioned in Acts 13:1), and the large number of Gentiles converted during Paul's missionary journey into south central Asia Minor (Acts 13,14).

Acts records that at this juncture Jewish Christians from Jerusalem came to Antioch and precipitated the crisis that made necessary the convening of the council. Their insistence that gentile believers be circumcised and submit to the Mosaic law was tantamount to requiring them to become Jews nationally, socially, and religiously in order to become Christians. The early church was thus faced with the necessity of clarifying its relation to Judaism (was it a part of or separate from it?) and the nature of the salvation it proclaimed (nationalistic and legalistic or by grace through faith?).

Modern scholarship has raised a number of questions relating to the account of the Jerusalem Council in Acts. A number of these involve uncertainty about the date of Galatians and the relation of Paul's visits to Jerusalem recorded in Galatians 2:1–10 to those mentioned in Acts 11:30; 15. Many students believe Galatians 2:1–10 to be an alternate (possibly contradictory) account of the meeting also described in Acts 15. A few students suggest that the Galatians passage describes a Jerusalem visit of Paul not mentioned in Acts.

It is probable that Galatians 2:1–10 recounts events which took place (but were not recorded in Acts) on the occasion of the Acts 11:30 visit, when Paul took famine relief to the church in Jerusalem. Within this reconstruction, Galatians is dated just after Paul's first missionary journey (Acts 13,14) and just before the Acts 15 council. Thus, the disruptions in Antioch described in Galatians 2:11–14 are regarded as the same as those of Acts 15:1, and are the immediate reason for calling the council.

Other questions regarding the council are associated with doubts about the historical accuracy of Acts. Some scholars are bothered about apparent inconsistencies within the text of Acts or between Acts and Galatians. Some puzzle over Paul's silence about the council and especially about the decree, even in circumstances in which mention of it might be to his advantage (e.g., 1 Cor). A current branch of scholarly opinion originating in Germany questions the historicity of Acts 15 by suggesting it is an invention of the author to portray his own view of the early church as an essentially harmonious body. Such opinions appear more grounded in philosophical and theological presupposition than in historical research or careful scrutiny of the texts.

One serious question asks why a discussion of the place of circumcision and Law, grace and faith, concludes with such moral and ceremonial issues as those contained in the decree. Further difficulties arise from the differing versions of the decree which appear in some ancient manuscripts (e.g., Codex Bezae omits "things strangled" and adds a negative form of the Golden Rule). Consequently the decree has been interpreted as a new legal requirement for salvation, as either general ceremonial or moral proscriptions for Christians, or as prohibitions against specific pagan religious practices that might appeal to gentile Christians. Some regard the decree as universally and eternally binding, while others believe it was intended to deal with conditions limited to a particular time and place.

The decree has close affinities with OT regulations for Gentiles who wished to live among Israelites in Canaan (e.g., Lv 17,18; cf. Acts 15:21) and with Talmudic legislation regulating contact between Jews and Gentiles (e.g., the Noachin Laws, *TB Sahn* 59b). Thus it seems the decree was intended to regulate contact between Christian Jews and Gentiles in the racially mixed Christian communities to which it was sent. It also provided minimal religious and moral guidelines for newly converted Gentiles of whose background Jewish Christians had good reason to be suspicious. Paul may well have refrained from mentioning the decree because he knew it was not intended to be applied legalistically and universally.

The Jerusalem Council established Christianity as a religion which offers divine favor as a free gift to be received by faith; it rejected human effort as a means of or contributor to salvation. By implication it also dissociated Christianity from any attempt to restrict it to a particular racial, national, cultural, or social group. The council affirmed Christians to be free from the obligation to earn salvation through ceremonies or law-keeping. At the same time it recognized the practical necessity of responsible and appropriate conduct, which takes into account the moral nature of God and the sensitivities and concerns of other Christians. J. JULIUS SCOTT, JR.

See PAUL, THE APOSTLE; JUDAIZERS; GALATIANS, LETTER TO THE; ACTS OF THE APOSTLES, BOOK OF THE.

Jerusha, Jerushah. Zadok's daughter, wife of King Uzziah of Judah and mother of King Jotham (2 Kgs 15:33; 2 Chr 27:1, alternately spelled Jerushah).

Jesaiah. 1. KJV spelling of Jeshaiah, Hananiah's son, in 1 Chronicles 3:21.

See JESHAIAH #1.

2. KJV spelling of Jeshaiah, Ithiel's father, in Nehemiah 11:7.

See JESHAIAH #6.

Jeshaiah. 1. Hananiah's son; the father of Rephaiah and a descendant of David through Zerubbabel's line, who lived in postexilic Palestine (1 Chr 3:21, KJV Jesaiah).

2. Jeduthun's son and the leader of the 8th of 24 divisions of musicians trained for service in the sanctuary during David's reign (1 Chr 25:3,15).

3. Rehabiah's son and one of the Levites in charge of the temple treasury during David's reign (1 Chr 26:25).

4. Son of Athaliah from the house of Elam, who returned with Ezra to Judah following the Babylonian captivity (Ezr 8:7).

5. Levite of the family of Merari, who returned with Ezra to Jerusalem after the exile (Ezr 8:19).

6. Benjamite, Ithiel's father and an ancestor of Sallu. Sallu lived in Jerusalem during the postexilic era (Neh 11:7, KJV Jesaiah).

Jeshanah. Border city in the hill country of Ephraim which King Abijah of Judah (913–910 BC) seized from King Jeroboam 1 (930–909 BC) and the northern kingdom during a civil war (2 Chr 13:19). The Greek and Syriac reading of "Jeshanah" as one of the towns between which Samuel erected the Ebenezer stone is preferred to the more suspect Hebrew "Shen" in 1 Samuel 7:12. Its location is perhaps near Burj el-Isaneh, four miles north of Bethel.

Jesharelah. Probably a scribal mistake for Asharelah, the name of a Levite musician, in 1 Chronicles 25:14.

See ASHARELAH.

Jeshebeab. Levite assigned to temple duty during David's reign (1 Chr 24:13).

Jesher. Caleb's son from Judah's tribe (1 Chr 2:18).

Jeshimon. 1. Desolate wilderness at the end of the Dead Sea, not far from Pisgah and Peor (Nm 21:20; 23:28). In both passages the RSV renders it "desert" in the text, but has "Jeshimon" in the margin, allowing it to be translated as a specific area.

2. Wilderness to the north of the hill of Hachilah and of Maon (1 Sm 23:19,24; 26:1,3); this location was probably just a few miles south of Hebron.

Jeshishai. Descendant of Gad in the days of Jotham, king of Judah (1 Chr 5:14).

Jeshohaiah. One of the 13 Simeonite princes in the days of Hezekiah who participated in the invasion of the valley of Gedor; they killed the inhabitants of the territory and took the land for the pasture of their sheep (1 Chr 4:36).

Jeshua (Person). 1. Levite and head of the 9th of 24 divisions of priests formed during David's reign (1 Chr 24:11, KJV Jeshuah). He was perhaps the forefather of 973 descendants who returned with Zerubbabel to Judah following the exile (Ezr 2:36; Neh 7:39).

2. One of the Levites assisting Kore in the distribution of the offerings among his fellow priests living in the priestly cities of Judah during the days of King Hezekiah (2 Chr 31:15).

3. Son of Jozadak the high priest. Jozadak was deported by Nebuchadnezzar to Babylonia (1 Chr 6:14,15). Jeshua, Jozadak's successor as high priest, returned with Zerubbabel to Jerusalem after the exile (Ezr 2:2; Neh 7:7; 12:1). Upon arrival, he led his brethren in making the altar of God (Ezr 3:2; 5:2) and eventually headed up a reconstruction program to rebuild the temple (Ezr 3:8). Confirmed as God's leader by Haggai and Zechariah (Hg 1:1–14; 2:2,4; Zec 3:1–9; 6:11), Jeshua resolutely resisted attempts by adversaries to infiltrate his people and hinder the work on the temple (Ezr 4:3). During the days of Nehemiah, his sons were encouraged by Ezra to divorce the foreign women they had married since returning to Palestine (Ezr 10:18). Joiakim was Jeshua's son and high-priestly successor, serving in the days of Nehemiah and Ezra (Neh 12:7,26). Jeshua is alternately called Joshua in the Haggai and Zechariah passages.

4. Descendant of Pahath-moab and the forefather of a family of Jews who returned with Zerubbabel to Judah following the Babylonian captivity (Ezr 2:6; Neh 7:11).

5. Father of a family of Levites who returned to Jerusalem with Zerubbabel (Ezr 2:40; Neh 7:43; 12:8). Perhaps he and his sons were responsible for overseeing the workmen building the temple (Ezr 3:9; this Jeshua may be identical with #3 above).

6. Levite and Jozabad's father. Jozabad assisted Meremoth, Eleazar, and Hoadiah with taking inventory of the temple's precious metals and vessels during the days of Ezra (Ezr 8:33).

7. Ezer's father. Ezer was ruler of Mizpah, who repaired the section of the Jerusalem wall "from the point facing the ascent to the armory as far as the angle" (Neh 3:19) during the days of Nehemiah.

8. Azaniah's son and a leader of the Levites in the days of Ezra and Nehemiah. Jeshua assisted Ezra with teaching the people the Law (Neh 8:7) and later set his seal on Ezra's covenant (Neh 10:9). Nehemiah 12:24 reads "Jeshua the son of Kadmiel," which probably reflects a corruption in the Hebrew text where a scribe mistook the proper name Bani or Bunni for *ben*, the Hebrew word for "son" (cf. Neh 9:4,5).

9. Alternate spelling of Joshua, the son of Nun, in Nehemiah 8:17.

See JOSHUA (PERSON) #1.

Jeshua (Place). Town in the Negeb listed before Moladah among the towns where Judeans still lived (Neh 11:26). It may be identical with the Shema mentioned next to Moladah in Joshua 15:26. The name is perhaps preserved in Tell es-Sa'weh, northeast of Beersheba.

Jeshuah. KJV spelling of Jeshua, a priest during David's time, in 1 Chronicles 24:11.

See JESHUA (PERSON) #1

Jeshurun. Poetical name for Israel, possibly derived from the Hebrew root meaning "upright," but according to many scholars a diminutive of Israel. The name Jeshurun is mentioned in Deuteronomy 32:15 and 33:5,26. In the Septuagint, the word is not translated as a proper name but as an adjective, "beloved." In Isaiah 44:2 Jacob (KJV Jesurun) is described as "my servant whom I have chosen," thus linking the name with the idea of election. In Deuteronomy 33:5 Israel is reminded that "the Lord became king in Jeshurun," and in verse 26 it is told that there is none like God. If we follow the Septuagint, there is a link with the term "beloved" used of Christ (Mt 3:17; Mk 1:11; Eph 1:6) and of the church (Col 3:12; 1 Thes 1:4; 2 Thes 2:13; Jude 1).

Jesiah. 1. KJV rendering of Isshiah, one of David's ambidextrous archers, in 1 Chronicles 12:6.
See ISSHIAH #2.
2. KJV rendering of Isshiah, Uzziel's son, in 1 Chronicles 23:20.
See ISSHIAH #3.

Jesimiel. One of the 13 Simeonite princes who participated in the invasion of the Valley of Gedor in King Hezekiah's day, killing the inhabitants and taking the land for the pasture of their sheep (1 Chr 4:36).

Jesse. Son of Obed and grandson of Ruth and Boaz (Ru 4:17,22). Jesse was a shepherd from Bethlehem. He had eight sons, of whom David was the youngest. He had at least two daughters, Zeruiah and Abigail, who became mothers of famous warriors.

When Samuel went to Jesse's home to search for and anoint a king, Jesse did not at first feel it worthwhile to call David for examination (1 Sm 16:11). Later he sent David to play the lyre for Saul (1 Sm 16:19–21). After David became a fugitive from Saul, Jesse and others of the family came to David in the cave of Adullam. David then brought his father and mother to Mizpah in Moab (1 Sm 22:3). Nothing further is heard of Jesse.

After Saul broke with David, he commonly spoke of him derisively as a "son of Jesse" to underscore his humble origins (1 Sm 20:31; 22:7). This same emphasis on Jesse's modest station in life is found in such messianic references as Isaiah 11:1,10, which speak of the "shoot from the stump of Jesse" and "the root of Jesse" (RSV).

See JESSE, ROOT OF; DAVID.

Jesse, Root of. Figure of speech used by Isaiah (11:10) to express the hope of a messianic king from the line of David. The "root" of a family is its progenitor. Jesse, David's father, is listed as an ancestor of the Messiah (Is 11:1,10; Mt 1:5,6; Lk 3:32; Acts 13:22,23). Isaiah pictures God's judgment upon Assyria as the cutting down of a forest (Is 10:33,34); Judah likewise will be felled and the proud tree of David's sovereignty hewn down, but a remnant will remain, described by Isaiah as a shoot from a stump (Is 6:13). The messianic shoot will come forth from the stump of Jesse as a branch from his roots. The Spirit of the Lord will rest upon this one who stands as an ensign to the peoples, so that the nations will seek him in the glory of his dwelling place (Is 11:1–10; see Is 53:2; Jer 23:5; 33:15; Ez 17:22,23; Zec 3:8; 6:12).

The apostle Paul, quoting Isaiah's prophecy, identified Jesus as "the root of Jesse" in

Bethlehem—the hometown of Jesse—looking south, with the Herodium visible on the horizon.

whom the Gentiles hope (Rom 15:12). Christ is not only "a shoot from the stump of Jesse" (Is 11:1), but is himself the "root of Jesse" (Is 11:10; Rom 15:12; see Rv 5:6; 22:16 "root of David") because the family of Jesse would have perished had it not borne within itself the vitality of the Messiah who was to come from it.

The expression "the root of Jesse" suggests Christ's humanity, because of his earthly ancestry; his humiliation, because of the degree to which the royal house of David was humbled; and the hope offered to Israel and the gentile nations, because of his coming to establish righteousness and peace and to fill the earth with the knowledge of the Lord as the waters cover the sea (Is 11:1–10).

See DAVID; JESSE; CHRISTOLOGY; JESUS CHRIST, LIFE AND TEACHING OF; GENEALOGY OF JESUS CHRIST; MESSIAH.

Jesui, Jesuite. KJV forms of Ishvi and Ishvite, one of Asher's descendants and his family, in Numbers 26:44.

See ISHVI #1.

Jesurun. KJV spelling of Jeshurun, a poetical name for Israel, in Isaiah 44:2.

See JESHURUN.

Jesus. 1. Name meaning "savior" or "Jehovah is salvation" given to the Messiah.

See JESUS CHRIST, LIFE AND TEACHING OF.

2. KJV translation of Joshua, son of Nun, in Acts 7:45 and Hebrews 4:8.

See JOSHUA (PERSON) #1.

3. Jewish Christian, surnamed Justus, who sent his greetings to the believers at Colossae in the salutation of Paul's letter to the Colossians (4:11).

Jesus Christ, Life and Teaching of. Center of the Christian faith. Although Christian doctrines are mainly based on the NT letters, their authority is found in their connection with the life of Christ. The main source for his life and teaching is the material recorded in the four Gospels.

There are a few references to Jesus in secular sources, but none of them gives any indication of how he lived or what he taught. The Jewish historian Josephus merely notes his existence in passing, totally unaware of the significance of the one who had lived and died in Palestine. Yet Christians at once recognized his supreme importance and rapidly came to acknowledge his claim to their homage and devotion. So great was the impact of Jesus upon his disciples after his resurrection that they went everywhere proclaiming the good news about him. He was declared to be Savior and Lord. He was called Jesus Christ because believers were convinced that he was the long-looked-for Messiah (Christ) predicted in the OT and other writings. His followers were prepared to suffer hardship and even death in his service. They soon came to be known as Christians, because they were witnesses to him.

The importance of the life and teaching of Jesus cannot be overemphasized. What he was and what he said had a dynamic force which impelled men to write about him. The fact that there are four Gospels in the NT, which overlap in much of the material and yet present unique portraits, is an indication that the early Christians recognized the value of several parallel accounts. The life and teaching of Jesus was too important to be confined to one witness.

History of Life of Jesus Research. Because of the nature of the four Gospels, no real biography of Jesus can be written. There is insufficient material available to enable us to trace the development of his mind, although some scholars have attempted to do this. Once a biographical approach is regarded as impossible, the question arises over how the Gospels should be treated.

The 19th Century. (1) The Historical Approach. Although there is not enough material to construct a proper biography of Jesus, it is widely accepted that the four Gospels provide sufficient information to give an accurate idea of what Jesus did and taught. A large proportion of the Gospels is devoted to the last week of Jesus' life; this apparently lopsided arrangement makes good sense when it is remembered that the announcement of the death and resurrection of Jesus formed an essential feature of all the early Christian sermons recorded in Acts. Moreover, the importance of these events is confirmed by the frequent mention of them in the letters. It was maintained that there was no reason to suppose that the records which focused on these historic events were not reliable.

Those who have treated the Gospels as reliable historical records have not been unmindful of certain difficulties which arise. There are differences in parallel passages which occur in Matthew, Mark, and Luke, or in two of them and not in the third. Moreover, John's Gospel is quite different from the other three. Many of the older traditional interpreters of the life and teaching of Jesus dealt with the differences by bringing about a forced harmony. These harmonizing efforts were often so strained that they provided fuel for rationalistic attacks on the Gospels.

More recent scholars who want to preserve the historical character of the records exercise more reserve over the difficulties and do not attempt to press all the accounts into the same mold. There are some cases where it is better to accept that the information available is not sufficient for a complete reconstruction of events. Even so, the number of such cases is minimal.

The historical approach, when taken seriously, necessarily involves acceptance of miracles as part of the life of Jesus. To those who have come to the conclusion that Jesus was more than man, the performance of supernatural acts does not appear incongruous. But this admittedly involves a prior decision before approaching the life and teaching of Jesus. It is because this prior decision about Jesus Christ has come under attack in various schools of criticism that attempts have been made to develop a non-supernatural approach to his life and teaching.

(2) The Rationalistic Approach. It was not surprising that, with the rise of the Age of Reason, the life and teachings of Jesus were subjected to rationalistic criticism. To the rationalist the intrusion of the supernatural into human life was intolerable, and the Gospels were accordingly stripped of all miracles. This led to a cavalier attitude to the Gospels, as a result of which they ceased to be reliable guides to the historical life and teaching of Jesus. It was inevitable that a rejection of miracles would soon impinge on the nature of Jesus. If miracles were impossible, there was no logical reason for retaining belief in the resurrection of Jesus. The 19th-century German writer H. Reimaris advanced the view that the resurrection of Jesus was an invention of the apostles. This skepticism over the resurrection found its most thoroughgoing 19th-century advocate in H. E. G. Paulus, whose rationalism has left its mark on many later German theories.

· During this period there was a growing tendency to treat John's Gospel as less historical than Matthew, Mark, and Luke, mainly because it was thought to be impossible to harmonize them. It was some time before the fourth Gospel regained any historical credibility in German academic circles. Indeed, German criticism of the Gospels is still affected in some ways by a low view of the historicity of this Gospel.

One of the most radical approaches during the 19th century was that of David Strauss, who treated much of the Gospel materials as myth. Even his own age regarded his opinions as too radical, but the introduction of the idea of myth as a means of explaining anything that could not be explained in historical terms has left its mark on subsequent approaches to the Gospel material.

(3) The Liberal Approach. At the end of the 19th century there was a spate of "lives of Jesus" which were an expression of what has become known as the liberal school. Its main aim was to produce a presentation of Jesus which could serve as a pattern. Indeed, Christianity was seen largely in terms of imitation of Jesus. But this inevitably meant that Jesus had to be reduced to purely human terms. The need for this played havoc with the Gospels, for again any material that was not agreeable to the general aim had to be excised from the records. This liberal movement has more recently been seen as inadequate because it presented Jesus in terms of a 19th-century man, and any consideration of a true historical viewpoint went by the board. The adjective "liberal" is often extended to include later approaches that are in some ways indebted to this older phase of liberalism, in which the Jesus of history was emphasized at the expense of the Christ of faith. During the 20th century the tension between these has played an important part in many different approaches to the life and teaching of Jesus. More often than not the historical Jesus has either been played down or else modified to such an extent that the result bears little resemblance to the Jesus of the Gospels.

The 20th Century. The last 80 years have produced a greater volume of research on the Gospels than on any other aspect of the NT. Much of this may be regarded as a reaction against the liberal view of Jesus in the last century. This liberal view was continued well into this century in the works of those committed to a social gospel. A nonsupernatural Jesus was ideally suited to the view that the life and teaching of Jesus was designed mainly to spur people into action to improve the environment. But this was a one-sided interpretation that left out much of what the Gospels say about Jesus—his supernatural power, his saving mission, and his powerful resurrection. The reaction against this view may be summarized under several different trends which have all in their turn exerted influence on NT scholarship.

(1) The Eschatological View. It was Albert Schweitzer who fired a broadside against the liberal Jesus by claiming that Jesus ended up totally disillusioned. He had been convinced that the kingdom of God would come in his lifetime; when it did not do so, his hopes were shattered. But there is no more basis for this in the Gospels than there was for the liberal Jesus. All that Schweitzer achieved was to make it necessary to provide a satisfactory alternative to the liberal approach. He did at least show that there was need to put Jesus back into the 1st century, even if his own solution was unacceptable.

(2) The Existential Approach. A totally different reaction to the liberal Jesus was one which almost completely swung away from the Jesus of history. This movement was developed by Rudolf Bultmann, who dominated German scholarship for more than half a century. He brought to bear on the life and teaching of Jesus his existential philosophy, which stressed the importance of decision in the present rather than events in the past. The result was that the Gospels came to have far less meaning for him than the letters. In fact, he came to the conclusion that it was impossible to know anything at all about the life of Jesus and very little about his teaching.

Bultmann believed that all the narratives and most of the teachings had been created by Christians. He was convinced that those who had come to believe in Jesus would not be able to report in an unbiased way on what he did and said. But this assumption is based on the view that no Christian who had come to faith in the risen Lord could ever look at the historic Jesus without his judgment being influenced by his faith. This is a fallacy, for it supposes that the earliest Christians could convince themselves that what they had imagined was actually true. But there is no reason to suppose that all the eyewitnesses were equally deluded, nor is it possible to maintain that no eyewitnesses existed to control the traditions. When the reports of Jesus' acts and teachings began to circulate among the earliest churches, it is inconceivable that no eyewitnesses would be present to prevent wrong ideas from gaining ground.

Bultmann's position is an interesting instance of the convergence of several influences on the life and teaching of Jesus. In addition to his existential approach he was also a member of that movement which believed that Christian origins should be studied against the background of other religions. This meant that the Gospels ceased to be regarded as unique records of a unique person. Pagan material was used in interpreting the Christian Gospels. It was not surprising that this movement did nothing to enhance the historical reliability of the records. Because most of the evidence quoted was drawn from later sources, the movement has been largely discredited.

Another of the movements which formed the background to Bultmann's theories was form criticism. This approach is an attempt to explain how the stories about Jesus and the reports of his teaching first circulated among the earliest Christians. It is supposed that traditions were passed on in the form of units, which means that there was no narrative to hold them together or to show any connection between them. This at once resulted in doubt

over whether a reconstruction of the life of Christ was possible. Form critics have expressed various opinions concerning this; the more extreme position (which Bultmann held) posits that any sequence that has been preserved has been due to the invention of the Christian communities.

Even some of Bultmann's closest disciples have recognized that he drove his skepticism too far, and various attempts have been made to restore some modicum of history to the understanding of Jesus. This movement has been dubbed the "new quest"; its aim is to restore to respectability the idea that we can know at least *something* about the Jesus of history. Nevertheless, because this movement begins from the standpoint of skepticism, it insists on accepting only what can be historically proved, which means that its approach to a more historical assessment is painfully slow and inevitably results in a wide variety of interpretations.

Arising out of the unsatisfactory focus on units of tradition, a more recent movement known as redaction criticism (composition criticism) has developed, which has switched attention to the editorial work of the evangelists. Where this movement has built on the radical opinions of the skeptical school, it has merely transferred the creativity from the communities to the evangelists without any appreciable increase in historical reliability. But many more modern scholars have been examining the evangelists' contribution to the history of Jesus without concluding that the records are unreliable. It is reasonable to treat the Gospels as intending to portray actual events unless it can be proved otherwise.

The Problems and Sources. The life of Jesus is known only from the four Gospels, but they raise certain problems. When they are compared with one another, several differences at once become apparent.

The first is that John's Gosepl is arranged on an entirely different plan from the other three, with little common material. Clearly, this demands some explanation. It is generally agreed that John wrote his Gospel after the others wrote theirs and was to some extent supplementing their records. This would be a sufficient explanation for its omission of so much material. John specializes in the teaching of Jesus, and the narratives he includes mainly serve as a framework for this teaching. Nevertheless his passion narrative shows extensive similarities with the other three. This feature is a fitting reminder that the Gospels all work up to a crisis in the death and resurrection of Jesus. Since this was the theme of early Christian preaching, it explains why the records of the life of Jesus are called "Gospels" (i.e., announcements of good news). It would not be too farfetched to regard these books as passion narratives with extended introductions. Any attempt to reconstruct a life of Christ can only be done on this basis.

Another problem arises from the similarities and differences between the Gospels of Matthew, Mark, and Luke (commonly known as the Synoptic Problem). The word "synoptic" gives the key to the similarity in the arrangement of these Gospels. They are all built on the general scheme that the first part of the ministry of Jesus reached its climax with Peter's confession at Caesarea Philippi, and that after this time Jesus devoted himself more particularly to the training of the disciples. There are, however, within this general framework some variations in the order in which common material occurs, although there is a basic similarity. The most extensive variation occurs in Luke's Gospel, where the final section between Peter's confession and the passion narrative is much more extensive and comprises a high proportion of material peculiar to Luke. There are certain variations in order which are due to the individual arrangements of the Evangelists, as for instance Matthew's arrangement of his teaching material in blocks, or the placing of events or sayings in different contexts. We may conclude that there is a substantial measure of agreement between these three Gospels in their structures. Similarities also extend to the language, for where the three Gospels record the same incident, in many cases there is remarkable verbal similarity, although this applies only to a proportion of the total material.

It is the differences, however, which raise the problems. In some instances, parallel accounts differ significantly in wording, and some decision has to be made to explain which wording is preferable. In addition to this, Matthew, Mark, and Luke have all included unique material.

To complicate the matter further, Matthew and Luke share a considerable block of material (mainly consisting of the teaching of Jesus) that is entirely absent from Mark. This has led to the theory that both evangelists used a common source, which has been designated as Q. Such a source has never been found, and the whole idea of Matthew and Luke using it must remain purely speculative. Many scholars use Q as a convenient symbol for this block of material without being convinced that it ever existed as a written source.

There have been various theories attempting to explain the similarities and differences among the synoptic Gospels. Although it was originally supposed that all three Evangelists drew from a common pool of oral tradition, it is now most widely held that Matthew and Luke used Mark. It is clear that our "sources" are the Gospels themselves as they have been preserved, and theories over their origins do not affect this conclusion.

A further problem arises from the fact that John's record seems to require a public ministry of three years, whereas the other three Gospels do not on the surface give the impression that it was more than a year. Whereas no definite solution can be reached, it is most likely that the longer period is correct and that the other Evangelists have telescoped events, with the resulting effect of suggesting a one-year period. It is generally admitted by scholars that none of the evangelists was particularly interested in chronology. It is impossible, in short, to attach precise dates to the life and ministry of Jesus.

In approaching any kind of construction of the life of Christ, there are certain features that must be borne in mind. Each of the Gospels has its unique purpose; this must not be lost sight of when material from that Gospel is used. Matthew, for instance, presents Jesus as the messianic King, whereas the emphasis in Mark is more on Jesus as the servant of all. Luke tends to present Jesus in a softer light, showing particularly his amazing compassion to the less fortunate, whereas John plunges the reader into a deeper and more spiritual understanding of Jesus. These different aims resulted in different selections and arrangements of material, but the fourfold portrait is essentially of the same man. It was undoubtedly for this reason that the Christian church preserved four Gospels instead of one. At an early stage in church history a single harmony of the Gospels was produced, largely by a scissors-and-paste method, but this was not accepted in orthodox Christian circles.

Because of the lack of sufficient information, it is impossible to present a biography of Christ. However, it is possible to delineate the chief stages of his life. These stages show a definite progression from the incarnation to the cross, but the amount of space devoted to each stage in each Gospel is dictated by theological rather than biographical concerns. The whole presentation centers on the cross and the resurrection. It is more an account of God's message to man than a plain historic account of the life of Jesus.

Incarnation and Birth. Only Matthew and Luke give accounts of Jesus' birth, but John goes back beyond it and reflects on his preexistence.

Before Jesus' Birth. It seems strange that John should begin as he does with a reference to the Word. There has been much debate over his reason. Some think he wanted to bring in an idea that was widely current in the Greek world in order to show that Jesus both fulfilled and went beyond it. The main idea in the use of Word (or Logos) was of some kind of divine agent in human affairs. The Alexandrian Jewish philosopher Philo wrote much about "The Word," but he never conceived the idea of the Word becoming flesh, as John does (1:14). It is likely that John was also following up the Hebrew idea of Wisdom as a kind of personalized agent of God. What is most important is that he begins his Gospel with an exalted view of Jesus. He saw him as existing even before the creation of the world. In fact, he saw him as having a part in that creation. Therefore, when Jesus became man, it was an act of humiliation but also of illumination. The light shone, but the world preferred to remain in darkness.

Anyone examining John's records of the life of Jesus would know at once, even before being introduced to the man named Jesus, that here was the record of no ordinary man. The account of his life and teaching which followed could not be properly understood except against the background of his preexistence.

The Birth Stories. Whereas John simply says that the Word became flesh and dwelt among us, Matthew and Luke fill in some of the details of how this happened. There is little in common between the two accounts, for each approaches the subject from a different point of view, but the supernatural character is clear in both. The coming of Jesus is announced beforehand, through dreams to Joseph in Matthew's account and through an angel to Mary in Luke's account. Matthew clearly tells his readers that the one to be born had a mission to accomplish: to save people from their sins (Mt 1:21). Luke sets his story of Jesus' coming in an atmosphere of great rejoicing; he includes some exquisite songs which have formed part of the church's worship ever since. The homage of the wise men in Matthew is significant because it sets the scene for a universalistic emphasis that links the beginning of the Gospel to its ending (cf. Mt 28:19,20). A similar emphasis is introduced in the angels' announcement to the shepherds in Luke 2:14 and in Simeon's song (Lk 2:32), where he predicts that Jesus would be a light for Gentiles as well as glory for Israel. The flight into Egypt for safety shows the contribution of a gentile nation in providing protection for a Jewish child.

One feature of the birth stories in both Matthew and Luke is that they are linked to genealogies. Difficulties arise in attempting to harmonize these, since they appear to be drawn from different sources; but the purpose in both cases is to show that Jesus was descended from both Abraham and David, the latter fact giving rise to the title "Son of David" which was on occasion used of him.

It should be noted that Luke is the only writer who attempts to link the coming of Jesus with events in secular history. He mentions several people; and although problems arise over the census of Quirinius because of its dating, the firm setting of a contemporary background is highly signficant. The Christian faith is a historic faith centered in a historic person.

Childhood in Nazareth. It is remarkable that the years of Jesus' human development are passed over in a few lines, with details of only one incident from his childhood. The discussion of the 12-year-old Jesus with the Jewish teachers in the temple (Lk 2:41–50) points ahead to one of the most characteristic features of his later ministry—his display of irrefutable wisdom in dialogue with his contemporaries. It also reveals that at an early age Jesus was acutely aware, as his parents were not, of a divine mission. Nevertheless, Luke notes that in his formative years Jesus was obedient to his parents (Lk 2:51). The obscurity of the 30 years at Nazareth, during which Jesus learned the carpenter's trade from Joseph, later led to many fantastic imaginings about his childhood recorded in the apocryphal gospels; but Luke's account could not be more unembellished. Its remarkable reserve is a strong indication of its historical reliability.

Preparation for Public Ministry. All the Gospels refer to a brief preparatory period immediately preceding the commencement of Jesus' public ministry. This period focused on three important events.

The Preaching of John the Baptist. The appearance of John the Baptist in the wilderness of Judea, dressed after the manner of Elijah, caused an immediate stir, particularly because of his call to repentance and baptism. He was like one of the prophets, but disclaimed any importance except as a herald of a greater person to come. His stern appearance and uncompromising moral challenge effectively prepared the way for the public appearance of Jesus. It is noteworthy that John the Baptist's announcement of the imminent coming of the kingdom was the same theme with which Jesus began his own ministry. This shows that the Baptist's work was an integral part of the preparation for the public ministry of Jesus. The same may be said of the rite of baptism, although John recognized that Jesus would add a new dimension in that he would baptize with the Holy Spirit and with fire (Mt 3:11). The herald has no doubt that the one to follow would not only be greater than he, but would come with exacting standards of judgment. The stage was therefore set in stern terms for the initial public act of Jesus— his willingness to be baptized.

The Baptism by John. Since John's baptism was a baptism of repentance and Jesus submitted to this, are we to suppose that Jesus himself needed to repent? If we suppose this, it would involve the further assumption that he had sinned, but this is contrary to all other evidence in the NT. Yet if Jesus did not need to repent, what was the point of his requesting baptism at the hands of John? Some kind of identification with the people must be in mind. Jesus had come on a mission to others, and it is not inconceivable that he deliberately submitted to John's baptism in order to show that he was prepared to take the place of others. At least this explanation would be in line with Paul's later understanding of the work of Jesus Christ (cf. 2 Cor 5:21). Matthew is the one evangelist who records John's hesitation (Mt 3:14,15).

The most important part of the baptism of Jesus was the heavenly voice which declared pleasure in the beloved Son. This announcement by God is the real starting point of the public ministry of Jesus. It reveals that Jesus' ministry is no accident or the result of sudden inspiration on his part. He begins his work with the full approval of the Father. A further important feature is the part played by the Holy Spirit in this scene. The dove is full of symbolic meaning. This was not just an inner experience that Jesus had.

The Temptation. If the baptism showed the nature of Jesus' vocation, the temptation showed the nature of the environment in which he was to minister. There is an immediate confrontation with adverse spiritual forces which was to characterize his whole ministry. Matthew and Luke alone record details of the kind of temptation to which Jesus was subjected by the devil. The whole incident is designed to illustrate the spiritual warfare in which he was engaged in the fulfillment of his mission as the Messiah. All the temptations present short-cuts which, if pursued, would have deflected Jesus from his vocation. Jesus gained the victory over temptation by appealing to Scripture. There may again be a representative aspect in these accounts, since it was important that Jesus should be seen to be a real man who, like all other men, was subject to temptation. The writer of the Letter to the Hebrews notes the importance of this when he shows how this qualified Jesus to act as high priest and to intercede on behalf of his people (Heb 2:18; 4:15).

Early Ministry in Judea and Samaria. Only John's Gospel discusses Jesus' work in Judea following his baptism. It also describes

The "pinnacle of the temple," one of the places where Satan tempted Jesus (Mt 4:5; Lk 4:9).

the calling of the first disciples by Jesus. This is set against a background of John the Baptist's announcement to two of his disciples that Jesus was the Lamb of God who was to take away the sin of the world (Jn 1:29). These first two disciples were soon joined by three others, and at once we are confronted with the nucleus of the band of followers whom Jesus gathered around him, which came to be known as the twelve. The initial calling of the five was later followed by a more definite call to leave their present occupations and go on preaching tours with Jesus. One feature of John's account is the disciples' early recognition of Jesus as Messiah (Jn 1:41) and as Son of God (Jn 1:49). There is no knowing what the disciples understood by these titles, but after the resurrection they undoubtedly acquired new meaning.

It is unexpected that so soon after beginning his ministry in Jerusalem an incident is related that is located at Cana of Galilee (Jn 2:1–11). John undoubtedly included this early event, in which water was turned into wine, because of its importance as the first of the signs he records. He saw miracles in terms of their significance for a right appreciation of Jesus rather than as mere wonders. Everything that Jesus did was seen as a manifestation of the glory of God.

In this early period John records two incidents in Jerusalem. The cleansing of the temple, which Matthew, Mark, and Luke all place just before the trial of Jesus, is placed by John at an early stage. The moral intent of Jesus' work is particularly seen in his act of driving out the money changers who were extorting from temple worshipers more than was appropriate. What was apparently acceptable to Judaism was unacceptable to Jesus. In one sense the cleansing of the temple was a kind of parable of what Jesus had come to do. The other Evangelists imply that Jesus' authoritative act was the event which sparked the final hostility of his opponents. John's moving it to an earlier stage in the ministry could only be for a theological reason.

The other incident in Jerusalem is the meeting between Jesus and the Jewish official Nicodemus (Jn 3), a man who was searching for truth although he was closely associated with Judaism. He was unable to understand the spiritual truth of being born again through the Spirit.

John's story then moves from Judea to Samaria. He records the story of the Samaritan woman who recognized that Jesus had something to offer which she had not previously known. Jesus used the reality of physical thirst to point to a deeper spiritual thirst. As a result of the woman's experience and testimony many of the Samaritans came to recognize Jesus as the Savior of the world (Jn 4:42). Again it is clear that John wants his readers to recognize Jesus in the same way that others were coming to see him. Indeed, the readers would have a better opportunity to appreciate the fuller significance of the words, since they would view them in the light of the resurrection.

The Galilean Ministry. Almost all the information on Jesus' ministry in Galilee is found in the synoptic Gospels. It should be noted that although the synoptic Gospels concentrate on Galilee, there were evidently some visits to Jerusalem during this main period, according to John's account.

The First Stage. John records another incident which happened at Cana, the healing of the son of a Capernaum official. This is noted as the second sign which Jesus performed (Jn 4:54). It is important because of the extraordinary faith of the father, who was prepared to take Jesus at his word.

(1) The Call of Disciples. In the synoptic Gospels, there is an account of the initial call to four of the disciples to leave their fishing boats and accompany Jesus (Mt 4:18–22; Mk 1:16–20; Lk 5:1–11). They had already met Jesus and must have had some idea what was involved in following him. Jesus did not at this point appoint them to be disciples. The setting apart of a particular number of disciples formed an important part of the ministry of Jesus. The miraculous catch of fish which preceded the call of the disciples in Luke's account served to highlight the superiority of the spiritual task of catching men rather than fish.

Another significant call came to Levi, otherwise known as Matthew. As a tax collector he was no doubt different than most of the others. He would certainly have been despised by his Jewish contemporaries because of his profession. But his inclusion in the special circle of Jesus' disciples shows the broad basis on which these men were chosen. One of the others, Simon the Zealot, had apparently belonged to the group of revolutionaries. It seems strange that such a man should be chosen. It was even stranger that a man like Judas Iscariot should be numbered among the twelve. In many ways the people whom Jesus chose to be around him were types unlikely to be of much help in the fulfillment of his mission. In training the twelve, Jesus accepted them as they were and molded them into men who later came to learn how to be totally dependent on God and the power of his Spirit.

(2) The Sermon on the Mount. Matthew is particularly impressed with Jesus as a teacher and presents samples of the kind of teaching he gave. Because some of the same material occurs in Luke in a different context, some scholars regard the arrangement of the Sermon on the Mount as Matthew's work. It is possible that Jesus often repeated his teachings on different occasions and in different combinations. Certainly Matthew's version of the Sermon on the Mount presents an impressive body of teaching, mainly of an ethical character, in which Jesus is seen to uphold the Mosaic law and yet at the same time to go beyond it. Some have sought to isolate this teaching of Jesus and make it central to the gospel. It is clear, however, that much of the teaching would have been impossible except for those who were committed to following Jesus. The beatitudes, which stand at the beginning of this sermon, commend moral and spiritual values. The teaching was radical, but not in a political sense. We may take the sermon, therefore, as a fair sample of the kind of discourses which must have abounded in the ministry of Jesus.

(3) Healing. Throughout the Gospels there are a number of cases of healing miracles. Mat-

Karn Hattin, near Capernaum, is the traditional site of the Mt of Beatitudes.

thew has a special section devoted to a sequence of healings (Mt 8:1–9:34). Those healed include a leper, a centurion's servant, Peter's mother-in-law, several sick people, a demoniac, a paralytic, a woman with hemorrhage, blind men, and a dumb man. In addition, Jairus' daughter was raised from the dead. This group of healings demonstrating Jesus' power over physical problems is included to focus on Jesus as a miracle-worker. But throughout the Gospels there is no suggestion that Jesus healed by magical means. In many cases his motive was pure compassion, and the power of healing was to some extent dependent on the faith of the person healed. In at least one incident the healing was accompanied by an announcement of the forgiveness of the sins of the one healed (Mt 9:2; Mk 2:5), which shows that Jesus considered the spiritual problem to be of greater consequence than the physical need.

In view of the widespread belief in the powerful influence of evil spirits over human lives, it is of great significance that Jesus is seen exercising his power over demons. Because his ministry was set in an atmosphere of spiritual conflict, already presented in the temptations, these confrontations between the forces of darkness and Jesus, who was the light of the world, were to be expected. Those who explain away these cases of demon possession in psychiatric terms miss this key feature of Jesus' ministry. Each time he exorcised a demon, he was demonstrating a victory which reached its most dramatic expression in the cross.

In addition to healing miracles in this early ministry, one nature miracle is recorded, that of the stilling of the storm (Mt 8:23–27; Mk 4:35–41; Lk 8:22–25). This miracle focused both on the lack of faith in the disciples and the mysterious power of the presence of Jesus.

(4) The Reaction of the People. In the early stages of his ministry, Jesus became very popular with the ordinary people (e.g., Mt 4:23–25).

Admittedly this popularity was superficial and showed no appreciation for the spiritual purpose of Jesus' mission. Nevertheless it stands in stark contrast to the opposition of the religious leaders. Mark records that such normally uncooperative groups as the Pharisees and Herodians plotted to kill Jesus (Mk 3:6). The Evangelists, especially Mark, realized that in view of the kind of person Jesus was and particularly because of his teaching, opposition was inevitable. The first issue over which Jesus and the religious leaders clashed was the sabbath. Jesus adopted a more liberal view than the rigid and often illogical interpretation of some of his religious contemporaries, as for instance when he compared an act of alleviation of human suffering on the sabbath, which they criticized, with the rescuing of trapped animals, which they allowed (Lk 13:15; Mt 12:11). To the Pharisaic mind Jesus must be regarded as a lawbreaker. If his teaching were permitted to influence popular opinion, the Pharisees feared that it would undermine their authority.

(5) Preparing the Twelve. The synoptic Gospels each supply a full list of the names of the 12 apostles (Mt 10:2–4; Mk 3:16–19; Lk 6:14–16), but John assumes that his readers will know who they are. Both Matthew and Mark name them in the context of their authority over evil spirits. In other words, these men were being called to enter the same spiritual conflict as Jesus.

All the synoptic Gospels detail the special instructions Jesus gave his disciples before sending them out on a preaching tour (Mt 10:5–42; Mk 6:7–13 Lk 9:1–6). Matthew has again included material in his discourse which appears in a different context in Mark and Luke, but the discourse shows the concern of Jesus to prepare his disciples for their future work. They were to proclaim the kingdom as he had done, but they were not to suppose that all would respond to it; they were warned about hostility and even persecution. It is particularly noteworthy that Jesus warned his disciples about encumbering themselves with material possessions while on mission work. Although the instructions given related immediately to a preaching tour, they were laying the foundation for the future work of the church. They are proof that Jesus did not neglect to prepare for the continuation of his work after his death. He may have said little about the church, but it was certainly not absent from his mind.

(6) Relation to John the Baptist. For a while there seems to have been parallel preaching and baptisms by John the Baptist and his followers and Jesus and his disciples. When John was imprisoned by Herod because of his un-

compromising condemnation of Herod's marriage to Herodias, his brother's wife, it is not surprising that he began to have doubts about Jesus (Mt 11:1–19; Lk 7:18–35). He might have expected Jesus, if he really was the Messiah, to have come to his rescue. When he sent some of his disciples to Jesus to express his doubts, he received in reply an account of what Jesus was doing. Jesus took the opportunity to tell the crowds who were present of the greatness of John the Baptist. He even said there was no one born of women who was greater than he. Nevertheless, John belonged to the old order and Jesus had to make clear that his kingdom was so superior it demanded new methods. At the same time he recognized that neither he nor his disciples could expect any different treatment from their contemporaries than John had received.

The Middle Period. This period in the life of Jesus is marked by various controversies, healings, teachings, and miracles, which shed additional light on what Jesus came to accomplish.

(1) Various Controversies. Jesus did not hesitate to confront his contemporaries on issues that involved moral or religious questions. John's Gospel records a controversy that arose over the sabbath when a lame man was healed at the pool of Bethesda (5:1–18). It was typical of the Jewish approach that once again ritual observance of the sabbath was regarded as of greater importance than compassionate concern for the physical welfare of a lame man. This led at once to condemnation of Jesus, particularly because he claimed to be doing the work of God.

A similar clash arose after Jesus' disciples had plucked grain in the cornfields on the sabbath (Mt 12:1–8). The sole grounds for the Pharisees' objection was the assumption that plucking corn constituted work. They saw it as sufficient reason to destroy Jesus, after he again healed a paralytic on the sabbath (Mt 12:9–14). They clearly regarded him as a direct threat to their very existence.

Rising opposition did not deter Jesus from further healings, as is clear from Matthew 12:15–32. Matthew sees these healings as a fulfillment of Scripture. But another controversy arose because of the healing of a blind and dumb demoniac. The Pharisees charged Jesus with casting out demons by the power of Beelzebub, prince of the demons, which led him to remind them that to blaspheme the Holy Spirit was an unforgivable sin. The incident not only brings out the perversity of the religious leaders, but shows that the ministry of Jesus was under the direct control of the Spirit. Other notable miracles were the healing of the centurion's servant (Lk 7:1–10) and the raising from the dead of the widow's son at Nain (Lk 7:11–17). The former is notable because of the remarkable faith of a Gentile in the power of Jesus.

Yet another example of Pharisaic criticism was the occasion when Jesus shared a meal with Simon (Lk 7:36–50). His host had not provided for the usual courtesies toward guests and yet was critical of Jesus for allowing an immoral woman to wash his feet with tears, dry them with her hair, and anoint them with ointment. There is no doubt that most of Simon's Pharisaic colleagues would have shared

The pool of Bethesda in Jerusalem, with the entrance door in the lower center of the picture.

his reaction. Jesus did not prevent the woman because he knew that the motive which impelled her to do it was love.

(2) Teaching in Parables. Matthew's Gospel has already given a sample of a continuous discourse of Jesus. But Jesus more often spoke in parables, and Matthew has collected some of these into a group which treats the theme of the kingdom (Mt 13). Matthew has other kingdom parables besides these, while Luke tends to preserve parables that are not specifically linked to the kingdom. Mark contains the fewest parables, but this is not surprising in view of the fact that his Gospel shows the least interest in the teaching material. There is no doubt that the parable was a form of teaching which was particularly characteristic of Jesus. It is noticeable that John does not relate any parables, although he does preserve two allegories (the sheepfold and the vine) that may be regarded as extended parables. In addition, Jesus interspersed even his discourses with metaphors that are akin to the parabolic form.

The parable was valuable because it could stimulate thought and, because the parable form was easy to retain in the mind, could later challenge the reader. Nevertheless it was true in Jesus' experience that some of the seed of the Word which he preached fell in soil that was not receptive to it. The parable of the sower and the soils was in fact an illustration of the reception which his teaching had experienced.

(3) Some Significant Events. The most striking instance of unwillingness to respond to the ministry of Jesus occurred at Nazareth, where his own people proved so hostile that he could perform only a very few miracles there (Mt 13:53–58; Mk 6:1–6). A measure of faith was needed in the recipients of his healing miracles.

Another notable event was the death of John the Baptist. There is a touching comment in Matthew 14:13 that news of John's death caused Jesus to withdraw to a lonely place, although his desire was thwarted by the crowds following him.

The one miracle performed by Jesus which all four Evangelists describe is the feeding of the five thousand, which must therefore be considered to be of particular importance (Mt 14:13–21; Mk 6:30–44; Lk 9:10–17; Jn 6:1–14). It shows the great popularity of Jesus at this stage of his ministry. It also shows that he was not unmindful of the physical needs of people, although one comment in John's account reveals his awareness of the danger (Jn 6:15). After the miracle some wanted to make Jesus king, which casts considerable light on their real motives. They were more concerned with material and political expediency than with

The general location of Bethesda Julius, perhaps where more than 5000 were miraculously fed by Jesus.

spiritual truth. This explains why Jesus at once withdrew from them and proceeded to instruct his disciples about the spiritual bread which comes from heaven. It is worth noting at this point that in John's Gospel Jesus is often seen in dialogue with his opponents, a style of teaching rather different from the synoptic parables but nevertheless familiar in Jewish debate. At the same time many of the people found the spiritual themes of his teaching (e.g., the giving of his flesh for the life of the world, Jn 6:51) too difficult to accept and consequently ceased to be his disciples. The feeding of the five thousand demonstrates again the uniqueness of the challenge of Jesus.

Another miracle closely linked with the miraculous feeding is the occasion when Jesus walked on the water, again demonstrating his power in the natural world. Many have sought to rationalize the event by supposing that Jesus was really walking on the shore and that the disciples did not realize this in the haze. But this miracle is no more extraordinary than the massive multiplication of loaves and fishes, and neither are inconceivable if the miracle worker was all that he claimed to be.

(4) The Transfiguration. After a brief time spent in the region of Tyre and Sidon, during which further healings were performed and he made clear that his main mission was to the house of Israel, Jesus moved on toward Caesarea Philippi, which was the real turning point of his ministry (Mt 16:13–20; Mk 8:27–38; Lk 9:18–28). It was there that Jesus put a pointed question to his disciples which drew out Peter's well-known confession—"You are the Christ, the Son of the Living God." This led Jesus to say that he would build his church on "this rock" (only in Matthew's account). Much debate has raged about the meaning of this saying. It is uncertain whether Jesus intended to build his church on Peter, or on the confession, or on Peter's making the confession. It is historically true that Peter was God's instrument for the entrance into the

church of both Jews and Gentiles (Acts 2, 10). There is no doubt about Jesus' intention to found a church (the word occurs again in Mt 18:17; see below for further discussion of Jesus' teaching on the church). The confession itself gives an insight into Jesus' true nature, but it was at once followed by a prediction that he was to be killed at Jerusalem.

This revelation of Jesus as the Christ was reinforced by the transfiguration, when he was transformed in the presence of three of his disciples (Mt 17:1–8). It was natural for them to want to keep this glorious vision of Jesus for themselves, but the vision vanished as rapidly as it came. Its purpose was evidently to show the three leading disciples something of the divine nature of Jesus, which was partially obscured by his human form. A further feature of the vision was the appearance of Moses and Elijah, representatives of the Law and the Prophets.

After the transfiguration, two more predictions were made by Jesus concerning his approaching death. These announcements were totally perplexing to the disciples. After the first one, Peter attempted to rebuke Jesus and was himself rebuked. After the second, Matthew notes that the disciples were greatly distressed (Mt 17:23), while Mark and Luke mention the disciples' lack of understanding (Mk 9:32; Lk 9:45). Jesus was approaching the cross with no support from those closest to him. It is not surprising that when the hour arrived they all forsook him.

One incident that illustrates the attitude of Jesus toward the authorities was when he was asked to pay tax (Mt 17:24–27). He paid it, although he did not acknowledge any obligation to do so. The method of payment was extraordinary, for it involved the miracle of the coin in the fish, but the greater importance of the incident is the light it throws on the independence of Jesus.

The Final Period. (1) The Way up to Jerusalem. Luke devotes more than half his Gospel to the events which begin with Jesus leaving Galilee and setting his face toward Jerusalem and end with the cross and resurrection in Jerusalem. In this section of his Gospel Luke introduces a great deal of unique material. In addition to the mission of the twelve, Luke records a mission of the seventy (Lk 10:17–20) which shows an extension of the idea of commissioning. Many of the special parables of Jesus recorded by Luke are inserted into this section—the Good Samaritan, the lost sheep, the lost coin, the prodigal son. Unlike Matthew's collection of parables, Luke's deal with ethical matters rather than specifically with the kingdom.

A notable feature of this period of his ministry is Jesus' concern to develop the religious life of his disciples. There is special teaching on prayer (Lk 11:1–13), teaching about the Father's care for them (Lk 12:13–34), and about being prepared for the coming of the Son of man (Lk 12:35–56). Jesus is clearly mindful of the fact that he will not be with them much longer and wishes to prepare them for the future. There is a mention of Jerusalem in Luke 13:34, which suggests that Jesus must have visited the city at least once before his triumphal entry.

John's record centers around the attendance of Jesus at the feast of tabernacles and the feast of dedication. The presence of Jesus at such feasts throws some light on his religious life. He follows the practices of all devout Jews. John is more interested in what Jesus taught rather than what he did, but the fact that Jesus taught in the temple area and entered into dialogue with the religious leaders shows that he adapted his methods to his environment. The chief priests and Pharisees became alarmed and sent officers to arrest him (Jn 7:32), but they were unable to complete their task and were themselves captivated by the teaching of Jesus. More discussions with the Jews followed, with Jesus being charged with demon possession (Jn 8:48). Both in this case and in the healing of the blind man (Jn 9) the hostility of the Jews to Jesus surfaces. After Jesus had been speaking of himself as the Shepherd, his teaching again raised the anger of his Jewish hearers, who took up stones to kill him (Jn 10:31).

In Luke's account we find a series of incidents in which Jesus alternately speaks specifically to small groups (Pharisees) and then more generally addresses the crowds. Several of his parables contained criticisms of the religious scruples and attitudes of the Pharisees

The two arches in the Wailing Wall are from the temple in Christ's time.

(e.g., the prodigal son). But other parables were intended for his disciples (Lk 16:1–13).

On the way to Jerusalem, Jesus challenged a rich young man to sell his possessions and follow him, but the man could not face the challenge (Mt 19:16–30; Mk 10:17–31; Lk 18:18–30). It offered Jesus an opportunity to tell his followers about his approach to wealth. He gave special promises to those who had made great sacrifices for his sake.

Also on the approach to Jerusalem, Jesus visited both Jericho and Bethany. In Jericho he healed Bartimaeus and had a fruitful encounter with Zacchaeus, who reformed his ways as a tax collector as a result. Bethany is mainly notable for Jesus' friendship with two sisters, Mary and Martha, and their brother Lazarus. There was particular pathos when Lazarus died, and John records the way in which Jesus reacted to that situation and brought him back to life (Jn 11). John even mentions that Jesus wept. As a result of the raising of Lazarus the religious leaders once again determined to put Jesus to death (Jn 11:53).

(2) Jerusalem. All the Gospels relate the triumphal entry into Jerusalem, which shows the importance they attached to it. The multitudes acclaimed Jesus, and the whole scene appears to be widely removed from the one a few days later when crowds cried out for his crucifixion. In spite of appearances, Jesus had not come to reign, as the crowd imagined. He had in fact come to die.

The synoptic Gospels all place the cleansing of the temple as the first main event in which Jesus was involved following his entry into the city. His audacity in clearing out the money changers from the temple area was too much for the authorities. The die was cast, and the crucifixion loomed closer.

It was during this period that further controversies developed with the Pharisees and Sadducees (Mt 21:23–22:46). In several cases trick questions were posed in order to trip Jesus up, but with consummate skill he turned their questions against them. They reached a point when they dared not put any more questions to him (Mt 22:46).

While he had his disciples gathered around him, Jesus took the opportunity to instruct them about certain future events, especially about the end of the world. He again reiterated the certainty of his return, but he mentioned various signs which would have to precede that coming (Mt 24,25; Mk 13; Lk 21). The purpose of the teaching was to provide a challenge to the disciples to be watchful (Mt 25:13) and diligent (Mt 25:14–30). The parable of the sheep and goats comes within the context of this teaching and is intended to focus on social

responsibility. These teachings prepare the way for the events of the arrest, the trial, the scourging, and crucifixion, which follow soon after.

(3) The Last Supper. When Jesus sat at table with his disciples on the night before he died, he gave them a simple means by which the significance of his death could be grasped. The use of the bread and wine for this purpose was a happy choice, since these were elements basic to everyday life. Through this symbolic significance Jesus gave an interpretation of his approaching death—his body broken and his blood poured out for others. It was necessary for Jesus to provide this reminder that his sacrificial death would seal a completely new covenant. It was to be an authentic memorial to prevent the church from losing sight of the centrality of the cross.

John's Gospel, which does not relate the institution of the last supper, nevertheless records a significant act in which Jesus washed the feet of the disciples as an example of humility (Jn 13:1–20). He impressed on the disciples the principle that the master was not above the servant. John follows this display of humility with a series of teachings which Jesus gave on the eve of the passion. The most important feature of this teaching was the promise of the coming of the Holy Spirit upon the disciples after Jesus had gone. With his mind occupied with thoughts of approaching death, Jesus showed himself more concerned about his disciples than about himself. This is evident in his prayer in John 17. All the Evangelists refer in advance to the betrayal by Judas, which prepares readers for the final stages of Jesus' journey to the cross.

(4) Betrayal and Arrest. There is a sense in which the whole Gospel story has been working up to a climax of rejection. The various outbursts of popular support are soon over, and the determined opposition emerges as seemingly in control, until it is recalled that Jesus himself predicted his crucifixion. In John's Gospel, the approaching climax is expressed in terms of "his hour." When this at length comes, the betrayal and arrest are seen as part of a larger plan. From the upper room where the last supper was eaten, Jesus went straight to the garden of Gethsemane, where he prayed to his Father with deep intensity. Luke notes that his perspiration was like drops of blood, so agonizing was the experience. In this we see part of what it cost Jesus to identify himself with human need. He prayed for a change, but at the same time submitted to the Father's will. The three disciples he took with him all fell asleep, while another of his disciples, having betrayed his master, appeared at the head of the group who had

Ruins of the house of Caiaphas, who presided over the Sanhedrin's trial of Jesus.

come to arrest him. At the moment of confrontation with Judas, Jesus exhibits an amazing dignity when he addressed the betrayer as "friend" (Mt 26:50). He offered no resistance when he was arrested and chided the crowd of people for their swords and clubs (Mt 26:55).

Crucifixion and Resurrection. *The Trial.* Jesus was first taken to the house of Annas, one of the high priests, for a preliminary examination. During his trial scorn was poured upon him by his enemies, and one of his disciples, Peter, denied him three times, as Jesus predicted he would. Before the Sanhedrin the official trial was presided over by Caiaphas, who was nonplussed when Jesus at first refused to speak. At length Jesus predicted that the Son of man would come on the clouds of heaven, and this was enough to make the high priest charge him with blasphemy (Mk 14:62–64). Although he was spat upon and his face was struck, Jesus remained calm and his dignity never deserted him. He showed how much greater he was than those who were treating him with contempt.

The further examinations before Pilate and Herod were no better examples of impartial justice. Again Jesus did not answer when asked about the charges, either before Pilate (Mt 27:14) or Herod (Lk 23:9). He remained majestically silent, except to make a comment to Pilate about the true nature of his kingship (Jn 18:33–38). The pathetic governor declared Jesus innocent, offered the crowds the release of either Jesus or Barabbas, publicly disclaimed responsibility by washing his hands, and then cruelly scourged him and handed him over to be crucified.

The Crucifixion. Bearing in mind that so many indications have been given throughout the Gospels that Jesus was more than man, the details of the crucifixion are challenging. The soldiers' ribald mockery, mixing a royal robe with a frightful crown of thorns, the compelling of a passerby to carry the cross, the cruel procedure of nailing Jesus to the cross, the callous casting of lots for his garment, and the scornful challenge to use his power to escape, demonstrate man's inhumanity in vivid light. But over against this is Jesus' concern about the repentant criminal who was crucified with him and for his mother, his prayer for forgiveness for those responsible for the crucifixion, and his final triumphant cry, all of which show a nobility of mind which contrasts strongly with the meanness of those about him. A few observers showed a better appreciation, including the centurion who was convinced of Jesus' innocence and the women who followed him and stood at a distance. There was one dark moment as far as Jesus was concerned—his cry of dereliction. There was an accompanying darkness and an earthquake, as if nature itself were acknowledging the significance of the event. Even the temple veil was torn in two, as if it no longer had any right to bar the way into the Holy of Holies.

The Resurrection. Joseph of Arimathea asked Pilate for Jesus' body. He and Nicodemus prepared Jesus' body and laid it in a new tomb. The evangelists concentrate on the appearances of Jesus not only on Easter day but subsequently. This is not the place to discuss the difficulties of dovetailing the resurrection appearances. There can be no doubt about the historic happening. The disciples were convinced that Jesus was alive. Some, like Thomas, had doubts to overcome. Others, like John, were more ready to believe in face of the empty tomb. It is not without significance that the first to see the risen Lord was a woman, Mary Magdalene, whose presence at the cross put to shame those disciples who had run away.

In his risen state Jesus was in a human form, although he was not at once recognized. There was a definite continuity with

Near Gordon's Calvary is the Garden Tomb, on the north side of Jerusalem, considered by some to be the place of Jesus' burial.

the Jesus the disciples had known. The appearances were occasions of both joy and instruction (cf. Lk 24:44; Acts 1:3). The resurrection transformed the cross from a tragedy into a triumph.

The Teachings of Jesus. Because of the wide variety of forms in which the teaching of Jesus has been preserved, it is difficult to bring out the essence of that teaching in a systematic way. Jesus did not present us with a theological system. His words were essentially practical in intent. Yet from all the variety of sayings it is possible to extract a clear idea of what Jesus thought about a number of important issues. What was his teaching about God? What did he think about himself? What did he mean when he spoke about the kingdom? What light does his teaching throw on the meaning of his death? What did he say about the Holy Spirit? How did he describe human beings and their needs? Did he anticipate the Christian church? Did he teach anything about the end of the world? What were the main features of his moral teaching? The following sections will seek to answer these important questions.

Teaching About God. Anyone who comes to the teaching of Jesus after reading the OT will at once recognize that much of his teaching about God is the same. Since Jesus, as all orthodox Jews of his day, accepted the testimony of the OT as inspired, it is not surprising that his approach to God was similar. This is especially true of his assumption that God was Creator. He taught a special providential care over the created order and affirmed that God watched over such small creatures as the sparrow (Mt 10:31). There is no support in the teaching of Jesus for the view that God is disinterested in the world he made.

One of the most characteristic titles Jesus used for God was Father. This was not new, for the idea occurs in the OT, where God is seen as Father of his people Israel. This kind of fatherhood was national rather than personal. In the intertestamental period the Jews came to regard God as so holy that he was removed from direct contact with human affairs. There had to be mediators between God and man. This exalted notion of God was not conducive to the idea of God as Father, and it is against this background that the uniqueness of the personal fatherhood of God in the teaching of Jesus must be seen. There is some evidence in Judaism that prayer to God as "Our Father" was known, but what distinguishes Jesus' teaching from that of his contemporaries is that the fatherhood of God was central in his teaching.

The father-son relationship is particularly vivid in John's Gospel, where Jesus as Son is seen to be in close communion with God as Father. This comes out strongly in Jesus' prayer in John 17, and in the frequent assertions that the Father had sent the Son and that the Son was doing the will of the Father. It is this strong relation between God and Jesus in terms of fatherhood and sonship that led Jesus to teach men to approach God in the same way. The Lord's Prayer at once recognizes this in its opening words. It is particularly important to note that "Our Father" precedes "hallowed be thy name," for the more intimate idea prepares the way for the more remote. Jesus never taught men to approach God with terror.

Although there is a connection between the way in which Jesus addressed God as Father and the way in which he taught his disciples to approach God, there is also a distinction. Jesus spoke of "my Father and your Father" when he appeared to Mary Magdalene after his resurrection (Jn 20:17), but he did not say "our Father." His sonship was unique, for he claimed that he and the Father were one (Jn 10:30).

In the Sermon on the Mount, Jesus assured his followers that their heavenly Father knows about their needs (Mt 6:32; Lk 12:30), on the strength of which they are exhorted not to be anxious. This gives some insight into the way in which Jesus' teaching about God has a bearing on practical issues.

Teaching About Himself. What Jesus said about himself is of great importance, for this undoubtedly formed the basis of what the early church came to teach about him.

Jesus used certain titles of himself or accepted them as descriptions of himself when they were used by others. The most widely used is "Son of man." This title was used by Jesus to refer to himself, but was not used by anyone else. It was used, moreover, in several different kinds of sayings. Sometimes the sayings related directly to the public ministry of Jesus, like the saying that the Son of man was Lord of the sabbath (Mk 2:28), or that the Son of man had authority to forgive sins (Mk 2:10). Sometimes the sayings had a direct bearing on the passion, as when Jesus said that the Son of man must suffer many things (Mk 8:31; note that Mt 16:21 has "he" instead of "Son of man"). At other times the reference is to a future appearance, as when Jesus declared to the high priest that he would see the Son of man sitting at the right hand of power and coming on the clouds of heaven (Mk 14:62). What did Jesus mean by the title and why did he use it?

The title "Son of man" had been used before. The phrase occurs in Psalm 8:4, where it refers to man. Again, the expression is used many times in Ezekiel as a mode of address to the prophet, but here also it means man. A rather different use occurs in Daniel 7:13, where one like a son of man comes with the clouds before the Ancient of Days. There is a strong similarity between this passage and the words of Jesus in Mark 14:62. But an important difference is that whereas Son of man becomes a title in Mark, it is not so in Daniel. There is some evidence for the title in Jewish apocalyptic literature (e.g., in the Similitudes of Enoch), where it represents a preexistent being who will come to judge and overthrow the enemies of God. It seems evident from this that Jesus' use of Son of man as a title is unique.

The Son of man sayings are distributed throughout the four Gospels, and there are no appreciable differences in their uses. What is at first astonishing is that though the title is so widespread in the Gospels on the lips of Jesus, it never became a name by which Jesus was known by the early Christians. In fact only in Acts 7:56 does the title appear, in this case used by Stephen. It is clear therefore that it had a special meaning for Jesus that it did not have for others. There is no doubt that he was referring to himself and not to someone else, as a careful study of all the Son of man sayings shows. Those who think that Jesus was referring to someone else arrive at this conclusion only after first dispensing with some of the sayings. The most probable reason why he used the title Son of man was because he wanted to avoid a term like Messiah, which carried with it too many political overtones. But what did "Son of man" mean to Jesus? It is rich with the idea of humanness, possible allusions to Daniel's Son of man, and perhaps a touch of the suffering Servant idea from Isaiah 53. It is most likely that Jesus saw it in terms of his mission in a way that his hearers could not fully appreciate. It is also probable that the early church preferred Messiah because this title carried the meaning of a royal deliverer; also, after the death of Jesus there would be no further fear of political misunderstanding.

The term Messiah, or Christ, does not belong strictly to the teaching of Jesus since he himself never used it. The most striking instance where he accepted the ascription of Messiah was in Peter's confession at Caesarea Philippi. All the synoptic Gospels record the confession "Thou art the Christ," while Matthew adds the significant comment by Jesus that flesh and blood had not revealed it but "my Father who is in heaven" (Mt 16:17). He certainly accepted the confession and regarded it as revelation. One other case in the Synoptics where he does not specifically refute mes-

siahship is his answer to the high priest's question, "Are you the Messiah?" (Mk 14:61). In John's Gospel, Andrew tells Peter that he had found the Messiah (Jn 1:41); the woman at Samaria talks to Jesus, and he admits that he is the coming Messiah (Jn 4:25,26). There was a widespread expectation among the Jews that a deliverer would come to overthrow their political enemies, the Romans. There were various ideas about his origin (a military leader or a heavenly warrior) and his methods (the Zealots believed that deliverance could come only through armed revolution). The reticence of Jesus concerning messiahship is therefore readily understandable.

Another title of utmost importance is "Son of God," although it occurs mainly in John's Gospel. That both Mark and John regarded Jesus in this light is clear from explicit statements in their Gospels (cf. Mk 1:1; Jn 20:30, 31). There are certainly passages where Messiah is linked with Son of God and where Jesus rejects neither title (cf. Mt 16:16). But in the teaching of Jesus one passage makes abundantly clear the special relationship that Jesus had with God as Son (Mt 11:27; Lk 10:22). Although the title "Son of God" is not used, the status is there. It is not possible to decide in what sense divine sonship is intended. Many similar passages in John's Gospel are, however, more explicit. The Son is unquestionably preexistent, because he knows he came from the Father and returns to the Father. It is not possible from the many references to sonship in John's Gospel to come to any other conclusion than that Jesus regarded himself as divine. It is particularly important to note that it is also in this Gospel that Jesus is portrayed most clearly in his human nature with its attendant weaknesses. Nowhere in the teaching of Jesus did he explain how God could become man, but he assumed this as a fact. He taught with the authority of God.

Teaching About the Kingdom of God. No one can read the synoptic Gospels without being impressed with the frequency with which the expression "kingdom of God" (or of heaven) occurs. It was clearly an important theme in the whole teaching of Jesus. It is less evident in John's Gospel, but is nevertheless still present. Many of the parables of Jesus are specifically called parables of the kingdom. Jesus' concept of the kingdom provided a foundational idea to the Christian gospel.

The main idea is the rule of God over men rather than a realm that belongs to God. In other words, the emphasis is on the active reigning of the King. This is important because it means that the kingdom is inextricably affected by relationships between the members and the King. It also means the kingdom will not be expressed in institutional terms.

There is one problem with the kingdom teaching that must be faced: its timing. Some sayings imply that it is already present, while others suggest that it will not come until the future. Some scholars disavow the idea that present and future can be held together; therefore they reject one and concentrate on the other. Those who maintained a present understanding of the kingdom developed the idea of a social gospel, since Christianity was defined as the establishment of the kingdom of God on earth. According to this view there is no place for a future arrival of the kingdom. On the other hand, some have denied altogether the present aspect and concentrate on the future. In this case it is difficult to see in what sense the kingdom teaching is relevant.

Yet others have insisted that since both present and future aspects are found in the Gospel records, no explanation is satisfying which denies one at the expense of the other. One possible solution is to regard the present aspects as applying to this age, but as not reaching their fulfillment until the future establishment of the kingdom. A similar solution, expressed differently, is to maintain that the reality is the future kingdom, but that it has spilled over into the present. Jesus intentionally included both present and future aspects.

That the kingdom was a theme of common interest is clear from Luke 17:20,21, where the Pharisees asked Jesus when it was coming. His answer, that it was among them, shows unmistakably a present idea. This is equally true of the statement that in the exorcism of evil spirits the kingdom had arrived (Mt 12:28; Lk 11:20). Moreover Jesus mentioned that men of violence were taking the kingdom by force (Mt 11:12; Lk 7:28), by which he did not mean by revolutionary methods, although he clearly implied that something dynamic was already happening. This idea of dynamic power is one of the most characteristic features of the kingdom. Jesus spoke of binding the strong, armed man (Lk 11:21,22), which shows that in his ministry he expected to give a powerful demonstration against the forces of darkness.

It is evident that the kingdom which Jesus proclaimed was a kingdom in which God was supreme. It was inseparably linked with his redemptive mission, in which God was bringing spiritual deliverance to his people. Moreover, the kingdom teaching of Jesus cannot be regarded in isolation. It is part of the total message; no part of that message can be divorced from any other part without distorting the whole.

The clearest teaching on the future aspect of the kingdom is to be found in some of the parables (Mt 13) and in the discourse on the Mt of Olives (Mt 24,25; Mk 13; Lk 21). In the latter, Jesus spoke of the future using imagery drawn from Jewish literature, like the reference to clouds, to glory, and to angels in relation to the coming of the Son of man (Mk 13:26). In Matthew's account there is reference to a trumpet call, another familiar feature (Mt 24:31).

Various features from the kingdom parables give the clearest idea of the nature of the kingdom. Membership of the kingdom is not considered to be universal, for in the parable of the sower not all the soils are productive. The same cleavage is seen in the parable of the tares and the parable of the dragnet. The tares are destroyed and only the wheat is harvested, while the bad fish are discarded. The members of the kingdom are those who hear and understand the word of the kingdom (Mt 13:23). It is clear, therefore, that a response is necessary if the benefits of the kingdom are to be enjoyed.

There is an emphasis on growth in the parable of the mustard seed, where rapid developments occur from small beginnings. The parables of the treasure and the pearl are intended to underline the value of the kingdom. The universal character of the kingdom comes out sharply in the parable of the vineyard, where the kingdom is said to be taken away from the Jews and given to another "nation," presumably an allusion to the Gentiles (Mt 21:43). This is in line with the great commission Jesus gave to his disciples to preach to all nations (Mt 28:19). A universal kingdom would certainly be entirely different from the messianic kingdom idea in Judaism, in which Israel was to be the central unit. It is not easy to appreciate how revolutionary the idea was of a worldwide kingdom with Gentiles and Jews on the same footing.

Teaching About His Own Death. The announcement of the kingdom must be linked with Jesus' approach to his own death. Did Jesus see his death as an integral part of his mission? Some have maintained that he ended his life in disillusionment, but a brief survey of his teaching about his own destiny is sufficient to dispel such a theory. To the further question, What meaning did Jesus attach to his forthcoming death? He gave a series of passing indications which, when taken together, supply us with a basis on which to reconstruct some idea of the place of his death within the entire range of his mission.

It is important to note that many times Jesus showed his awareness that details of his life were a fulfillment of Scripture (cf. Mt 26:24,56; Mk 9:12; Lk 18:31; 24:25–27,44,45). In

In the present Garden of Gethsemane is the Church of All Nations, completed in 1924 on the site of two earlier churches (the earliest built by Theodosius I in 385).

all the instances cited, the suffering of Jesus is referred to as the subject of OT prophecy. This must mean that he had reflected on OT predictions and recognized that they could be fulfilled only through his own sufferings. In this case the passion must be regarded as an indispensable part of Jesus' consciousness of his own mission.

This emphasis on fulfillment of Scripture is also seen in John's Gospel. His statement that the Son of man must be lifted up even as Moses lifted up the serpent (Jn 3:14) illustrates this point. Most of the passages where fulfillment of Scripture is mentioned are the comments of the Evangelist. But there can be no doubt that the fulfillment motive played a vital part both in Jesus' own understanding of his mission and in the early Christians' understanding of his death. In this connection, some hold that John puts more stress on the incarnation as a means of salvation in that he sees it as an illumination of the mind. But this is only part of the truth, for there is more on the meaning of the death of Jesus in John's Gospel than in the others.

The Gospels emphasize the divine necessity of the death of Jesus. In addition to the fulfillment motive the idea of necessity is strong in the first prediction by Jesus of his approaching death. In John's Gospel Jesus speaks of his "hour" several times in the earlier stages of his ministry as "not yet," but in the later stages as having arrived. There is a sense of definite movement toward a climax, the hour undoubtedly being the hour of the passion (cf. Jn 17:1). There is no room for any disillusionment here. Jesus knew that only through the hour of death could the Father be glorified. The climax was according to an orderly plan.

Jesus evidently regarded his death as in some ways a sacrifice. The clearest indication of this is in the words of institution at the last supper. The cup is connected with the blood of the new covenant, which is said to be for the "remission of sins" (Mt 26:26–28). No explanation is given of the way in which the coming death, signified by the broken bread and poured-out wine, would bring about forgiveness of sins. But the immediate realization by the early church that Christ died for our sins (cf. 1 Cor 15:3) shows that the importance of what Jesus said had been clearly grasped. The new covenant idea is parallel to the old covenant, which according to Exodus 24 was sealed with sacrificial blood; there can be little doubt that Jesus had this in mind when he spoke the words about the new covenant. It was also linked with the ideas expressed in Jeremiah 31, referring to a covenant written on the heart rather than graven in stone.

Another aspect of the death of Christ seen especially in John's Gospel is the sense of completion that went with it. In Jesus' prayer in John 17, as he faces the cross, he declares that he has finished the work which the Father had given him to do (v 4). This is reinforced by the cry from the cross, "It is finished," which only John records (19:30). This sense of accomplishment gives an air of triumph to what might otherwise have been considered a disaster. One passage in Luke (12:32) gives something of the same idea of completion.

An important idea especially developed in the writings of Paul and elsewhere in the NT is that in some senses Jesus was a substitute for man in his fallen state. Can this idea be traced to the teaching of Jesus? In submitting to John's baptism of repentance, Jesus must have been identifying himself with those who needed repentance, since he himself did not. On one occasion he quoted words from Isaiah 53:12—"he was reckoned with transgressors"—and applied them to himself. Since there is a strong emphasis on substitution in the Isaiah Servant passages, it is not unreasonable to suppose that Jesus thought of himself in such terms. Another saying that brings out a strong substitutionary view of the mission, and especially of the death of Jesus, is the ransom passage of Mark 10:45 (Mt 20:28). A ransom was generally thought of in terms of the payment required for freeing a slave. Jesus sees the giving up of his life as a ransom for many. The preposition "for" as used here has the meaning "instead of," which again reinforces the substitutionary idea. Some have tried to reduce the force of this by speaking of Jesus as a representative rather than as a substitute, but the ransom passage does not support this interpretation. A similar passage where substitution appears to be in mind is John 10:15, in which Jesus points out that the good shepherd lays down his life for his sheep.

That the motive for the work of Christ was love is seen especially in such a saying as John 15:13, that no one can show greater love than to give his life for his friends. Jesus is clearly referring to himself in this passage. This is in line with the statement on the love of God in John 3:16. At the same time, Jesus viewed his death as a victory over the devil. Immediately after pointing out that a corn of wheat must die in order to produce fruit, he announced that the prince of this world would be cast out (Jn 12:23,31).

It would not be adequate to outline Jesus' teaching about his death without pointing out that its effectiveness with regard to the individual follower depends on the further demand for repentance and faith which characterized the ministry of Jesus.

Teaching About the Holy Spirit. At several of the major events in the life of Jesus, the Evangelists note the activity of the Spirit (e.g., the virgin birth, the baptism, the temptation). It is to be expected therefore that Jesus would have instructed his disciples about the Spirit. However, there is surprisingly little in the synoptic Gospels on this theme, although there are several sayings in John's Gospel.

When Jesus began his preaching ministry in Nazareth, according to Luke, he read the statement in Isaiah 61:1,2 about the Spirit of God and applied it to himself. He saw his ministry in terms of the Spirit. This becomes clear in the way in which he responded to the charge that he cast out demons by means of Be-elzebub, prince of the demons. He identified the reality of the coming of the kingdom by the fact that he was casting out evil spirits by the Spirit of God (Mt 12:28). He was, more-over, sensitive to the seriousness of blaspheming the Spirit, which he implies his accusers were in danger of doing. Whatever he did in his ministry he saw as an activity of the Spirit, and this was especially so in his contest with evil spirits.

When warning his disciples that they would meet with opposition, Jesus assured them of the Spirit's support when they were forced to appear before kings or governors (Mt 10:19,20; Mk 13:11). Indeed, he told them that the Spirit would speak through them, thus emphasizing that he expected a continuation of the Spirit's activity in the future. Luke records one saying of Jesus in which he comments on what fathers will do for their children and asks whether God will not give the Holy Spirit to those who ask (Lk 11:13). The assumption is that God regards the Holy Spirit as the best gift to give his children (Mt has "good things"). On yet another occasion Jesus recognized that David was inspired by the Holy Spirit when he wrote Psalm 110 (Mk 12:36), which reflects his belief in the Spirit's agency in the production of Scripture.

In the Gospel of John we find both incidental and specific evidence. Indeed, the latter includes five notable sayings about the Spirit in which he is called the Counselor or Spirit of truth. The incidental references are in the earlier section of the Gospel. In the encounter Jesus had with Nicodemus, he required rebirth through the Spirit in a manner that completely baffled Nicodemus (Jn 3:5). Yet it was an important part of Jesus' teaching that man cannot save himself. To be born anew could be accomplished only through God's intervention through the Spirit. At the end of the discourse in John 3, a comment is made that God does not give the Spirit in a stinting manner (3:34).

Two other passages throw light on the Spirit. Because God's nature is spirit, Jesus told the Samaritan woman that his worshipers must worship in spirit and in truth (Jn 4:24), which looks like an allusion to the Spirit. In his teaching at the feast of tabernacles, Jesus promises the Spirit under the analogy of flowing water (Jn 7:37–39).

The passages which record the teaching about the Holy Spirit to the disciples in the upper room are John 14:16,17; 14:25,26; 15:26, 27; 16:7–11; and 16:13–15. These passages contain many important truths about the Holy Spirit which are particularly valuable for a right approach to the teaching of the NT letters. First of all, the Spirit is called "the Spirit of truth" in three of the five passages, and this draws special attention to the function of the Spirit to witness to what is true. That same Spirit of truth is promised to the disciples as a guide into truth (Jn 16:13). The Spirit has a specific witnessing function (Jn 15:26), but the object of the witnessing is to glorify Christ. He does not draw attention to himself.

The Spirit is also called the Counselor or Paraclete, a word derived from the root idea of one who is called alongside to help. In other words, where help is needed the Spirit's presence is promised. More than once the origin of the Counselor is mentioned—he is sent by the Father (Jn 14:26); he proceeds from the Father (Jn 15:26); he is a gift of the Father (Jn 14:16). There is a close association in these passages between Father, Son, and Spirit. The Son prays to the Father and the Father gives the Spirit. The Father sends the Spirit in the Son's name. The Son sends the Spirit from the Father. The Spirit's task is to declare to us what the Father has entrusted to the Son.

One of the important functions of the Spirit is to aid the memory of the disciples (Jn 14:26). This means that Jesus did not intend that the preservation of his teachings should be left to chance. All too often theories attempting to explain the way in which the traditions about Jesus and his teachings were transmitted in the period before there were any written Gospels are suggested without any reference to the Holy Spirit. It is not acceptable to concentrate on so-called laws of oral tradition and pay no attention to the unique factor in this case—the Holy Spirit. It is part of his mission to preserve and transmit the teaching of Jesus. What Jesus says in this passage about the Spirit has far-reaching significance for the formation of the Gospels.

Another important function is the activity of the Spirit in the world. Jesus made it clear that the Spirit would convict of sin, of righteousness, and of judgment (Jn 16:8). Without the activity of the Spirit there would be no possibility of the disciples making any impact on the world. Nevertheless, Jesus warned that the world could not receive the Spirit because it did not know him (Jn 14:17). The mystery of the Spirit is that he dwells in every believer. This indwelling aspect is of great importance, and was particularly developed in the writings of Paul.

One other passage bearing on the Spirit is John 20:22, where Jesus breathed on his disciples and said, "Receive the Holy Spirit." It was at Pentecost that the Spirit was to be given in full measure, and this statement in John seems to be a foretaste. It involves a special power to forgive and to retain sins (Jn 20:23). What this must mean is that God, who alone can forgive sins, works through his Spirit in the disciples. It shows the indispensable character of the Spirit's work in the ongoing work of the church.

Teaching About Man. Jesus taught about God's providential care over all human beings. Man's hairs are all numbered (Mt 10:30), a vivid way of saying that God is concerned about the details of life, as well as indicating God's view of the value of man. This statement does not exclude the view that God has a special concern for those who through faith have become his children (cf. Mt 6:25–33).

Over against any emphasis on physical life or possessions, Jesus made it clear that it would be unprofitable for anyone to gain the world and to lose his soul (Mt 16:26; Mk 8:37; Lk 9:25). The focus falls on what a man is and not what he has. Jesus even said that a maimed body was preferable to a forfeited life (Mk 9:43–47). One's total fulfillment depends on more than environment or physical well-being. He was not, of course, unconcerned about man's physical state, as his many healings show; but his major concern was with man's relation with God. In this context it is worth noting that Jesus did not practice asceticism (cf. Mt 11:19). He taught that it was what came out of a person, not what went in, that defiled him (Mk 7:14–23), contrary to Jewish ritual practices with regard to food.

Jesus never viewed man purely as an individual. Within God's community people were expected to have responsibility toward one another. The Sermon on the Mount illustrated this social emphasis in the teaching of Jesus. Those who are merciful to others will obtain mercy (Mt 5:7). There is special commendation for peacemakers (Mt 5:9). The disciples of Jesus are expected to bring light to others (Mt 5:16). They are expected to share their cloaks with the needy (Mt 5:40). Jesus is clearly saying that people have responsibility beyond themselves.

The relation of man to God is one of dependence. Jesus taught men to pray to God for daily bread (Mt 6:11) as a reminder that they cannot be wholly self-sufficient. He allowed no place in his teaching for man to boast in his own achievements. Man is constantly reminded of his creatureliness.

Jesus had some specific things to say about home life. He accepted the sanctity of the marriage contract (Mt 5:31,32; cf. 19:3–9), and therefore showed a high regard for the honor and rights of the wife. It was more in his actions and attitudes rather than his specific teachings that Jesus showed his regard for the status of women. When he spoke of men he often used the term in the sense of people, including both men and women. There is no suggestion that in matters of faith women were in the least inferior to men. Moreover, Luke points out how many women supported Jesus and his disciples in their travels.

Jesus had a high view of man's potential, but also acknowledged man's present condition. The stress on repentance (Mt 4:17) shows a state of sinfulness of which man needed to repent. This sense of need is implicit in the instances where Jesus pronounces forgiveness (e.g., to the paralytic, Mt 9:1–8; and to the woman who anointed him, Lk 7:47,48). In the Lord's Prayer, Jesus instructs his disciples to pray for forgiveness (Mt 6:12; Lk 11:4). He takes for granted that they need it and desire to obtain it.

Jesus gives no support to any self-righteousness in man. This is the burden of his criticism of the religious leaders in various sayings, but particularly in Matthew 23. He was critical of Jewish teachers because they placed so much importance on works of merit as contributing to salvation. His whole approach depended on man casting himself on the mercy of God. This is vividly illustrated in the parable about the Pharisee and the tax-collector at prayer. It was the latter who threw himself on the mercy of God and who was commended by Jesus.

Undoubtedly Jesus regarded sin as universal. He never suggested that there was anyone who was exempt from it. The major concept of sin in his teaching was alienation from God. This comes out clearly in John's Gospel, with its strong antithesis between light and darkness, life and death (cf. Jn 5:24). Indeed the "world" in John's Gospel represents the system that takes no account of God.

But sin is also seen as enslavement to Satan. The life and teaching of Jesus is seen against the background of spiritual conflict. Jesus can even say to his opponents, "You are of your father the devil" (Jn 8:44). He assumes throughout that there are hostile forces bringing man into subjection.

In the parable of the prodigal son, sin against God is linked with sin before the father. In other words, it is regarded in terms of rebellion and revolt (Lk 15:21). This is a different assessment of the son's offense than the one arrived at by the elder brother, who could see it only in terms of property. The view that man is essentially in a state of rebellion against God is a basic tenet of Paul's theological position, and it is important to note that it finds its roots in the teaching of Jesus.

There is no question that Jesus had much to say about condemnation. Those who did not believe and were therefore outside the provision of salvation which Jesus had made are declared to be already condemned (Jn 3:18). At various times Jesus mentioned judgment to come, which shows that man's destiny is related to his present state. Against this background of man's spiritual need the whole mission of Jesus must be seen. Man if left to himself would be totally unable to achieve salvation, but Jesus came to offer eternal life to those who believe in him (Jn 3:16).

Teaching About the Church. Some have supposed that Jesus did not predict that there would be a church. But on two occasions he used the word "church," which means a people called out by God. On one of the occasions—at Caesarea Philippi—Jesus told Peter that he would build his church upon the rock (Mt 16:16–19). It seems most probable that "rock" was intended to link the foundation of the church to Peter's particular confession about Jesus. It is certain that the later church was a community which affirmed that Jesus was the Christ, the Son of the living God. It is important to note that it is Christ himself who is the builder of the church. He assured his disciples that it would be impregnable (the gates of Hades would not overcome it). Moreover, one of the functions of the church was to proclaim forgiveness of sins, and this is implied in what Jesus said to Peter. That the words were not intended to refer exclusively to him is clear from Matthew 18:18, where similar words were addressed to all the disciples. The church, according to Matthew 18:17, was to be a community that could settle disputes between brethren.

In addition to these specific references to the church, Jesus assumed that his followers would meet together in his name (Mt 18:19,20). In his final words in Matthew's account, he commissioned them to teach what he had taught them and to baptize new disciples (Mt 28:19,20). He promised his presence would be with them. The command to baptize was reinforced by Jesus' own example in submitting to John's baptism. One other special rite that Jesus expected his disciples to observe was the Lord's Supper. His instructions about this presuppose a later community which could observe it. Since the form of words used in the institution point to the meaning of the death of Christ, it is clear that Jesus intended the future community to be frequently reminded of the center of the faith. The Christian church was to be a group of people who knew that through Christ they had entered into a new relationship with God.

Although there are no references to the church in John's Gospel, there are certainly hints which support the community idea. Jesus introduced himself as the Shepherd and conceived of his followers as forming a flock (Jn 10:16). The sheep imagery occurs again in this Gospel when Peter is instructed three times by the risen Lord to feed the sheep (Jn 21:15–17). Another figure of speech which Jesus used to bring out the group idea is that of

Looking eastward toward the city wall, the Jaffa Gate, and the Mt of Olives (in the background), from which Jesus delivered the Olivet Discourse (Mt 24–25), the most concentrated record of what Jesus taught about the future.

the many branches which draw their life from the vine, and therefore belong to each other because of their common life in the vine.

Jesus recognized that the future community would need the aid of the Spirit. His teaching on this subject laid the foundation for the evident dependence of the early church on the leading of the Spirit, as seen in the Book of Acts.

It should be noted that there is a close connection between the church and the kingdom, although they are not identical. The kingdom is more comprehensive than the church, which is included within it.

Teaching About the Future. Jesus thought of the kingdom in terms of both present realization and future hope. The future aspect is related to the end of the age. Although he did not spell it out in specific terms, Jesus did not leave his disciples without any knowledge of how the present age would end. He gave firm assurance that he would return at some time in the future.

He told the disciples that the Son of man would come with his angels in his Father's glory (Mt 16:27). In the discourse in which he answers the disciples' question about the end of the world, he speaks again of the Son of man coming in clouds with power and glory (Mk 13:26), probably drawn from the familiar language of Daniel 7. Jesus described various signs which would precede his own coming. He spoke of wars, conflicts, earthquakes, famines, and disturbances in the heavens. The gospel was to be preached to all nations. At the same time many false Christs would arise.

Jesus gave such details about his return to encourage his disciples in face of persecution. The future hope had a definitely practical purpose. The disciples were urged to watch. The coming would happen as unexpectedly as a thief in the night. Jesus said that even he himself did not know when the coming would take place (Mk 13:32).

Another important theme affecting the future is Jesus' teaching about resurrection. The Sadducees did not believe in the resurrection of the body. They attempted to trap Jesus with a question about a woman who had been married seven times. They wanted to know whose husband she would be at the resurrection (Mk 12:18–27). Jesus pointed out that there would be no marriage when the dead rise. The Sadducees' idea about resurrection was clearly wrong. Jesus' teaching was that the resurrected would be like the angels. There is no doubt about the resurrection of the dead, although no information is given about the resurrection body. Jesus told a story about a rich man and a poor man who both died (Lk 16:19–31). In the afterlife the rich man cries out in torment while the poor man enjoys a state of blessedness. What is most clear from this is the certainty of the afterlife and the fact of a distinction between the two men, although we are not told on what grounds the distinction is made. Elsewhere in his teaching Jesus suggested that the most vital requirement is faith in himself. The conversation between Jesus and the dying thief on the cross suggests that paradise for the latter consisted in an awareness of the presence of Jesus (Lk 23:42,43).

The theme of rewards and punishment occurs in many passages. In Matthew 16:27 Jesus says that the Son of man will reward everyone according to what he has done. Those who are worthless are promised punishment in darkness (Mt 25:30). Moreover, Jesus spoke of a day of judgment on which men must give an account, even of all their careless words (Mt 12:36,37). In the parable of the sheep and the goats, he spoke of a separation which the Son of man will make when he comes. Those commended are those who have shown concern for the "brethren" (Mt 25:31–46).

Among Jesus' most solemn statements are those which speak of hell. There is no way of getting around his teaching about eternal punishment for the unrighteous (as in Mt 25:41,46), which is opposite to the eternal life promised to the righteous. He taught that his disciples would have a place prepared for them in heaven (Jn 14:2), and spoke of a book of life in which the names of his disciples were written (Lk 10:20).

Teaching About Moral Issues. So much of the teaching of Jesus contained in isolated sayings or parables or sometimes in longer discourses (like the Sermon on the Mount) is concerned with moral issues that some have concluded that this was the main burden of his teaching. But the moral teaching cannot be considered apart from the many facets of his teaching outlined above. It has been said that there are close parallels between the teaching of Jesus and the moral teaching of Judaism. What is distinctive about Jesus' teaching is the motive power behind it. It is not conceived in terms of laws that must be obeyed. Right conduct is seen to be the result of a right relationship with God.

Jesus was himself the pattern for moral behavior. He made clear that his aim was to fulfill the will of God. There is no sense of legalism in his approach to ethical decisions. When in the Sermon on the Mount he compared his own teaching with that of Moses, he showed the importance of penetrating to the inner meaning (cf. Mt 5:21,22,27,28,31,32). On the face of it Jesus made more rigorous demands than the Mosaic law, because he was concerned to probe the motives as well as the actions. Many have dismissed the teaching of the Sermon on the Mount as entirely impractical, but Jesus never intended that his teaching would be easy; he set as a target nothing less than the perfection of God himself (Mt 5:48). Nevertheless he called his yoke easy and his burden light (Mt 11:29,30), which suggests that he was not setting out an impossible ethical pattern. It must be remembered that he was not producing a manifesto for society. His concern was that each individual should have powerful motives for right decisions on matters of conduct. His reaction against a rigid application of sabbath observance at the expense of the welfare of a needy person illustrates this point. Concern for others was rated higher than ritual correctness.

Conclusion. No account of the life and teaching of Jesus would be complete without some indication of the place that Jesus Christ gained in the developing church. Such a quest naturally takes us outside the scope of the Gospels into the testimony of the Book of Acts and Paul's letters. There we can see whether the predictions of Jesus were fulfilled and whether in fact the early Christians took his teaching seriously. Although there can be no question that Jesus Christ became central to the faith of the early Christians, he was regarded from many points of view. He was seen as Messiah in the sense of a spiritual deliverer, as Lord in the sense of being sovereign over his people, as Servant in the sense of his obedience to suffering, as Son in his relation to his Father. In many ways the full understanding of what and who he was could not have occurred until after the resurrection; therefore we find that many facets of his teaching about himself were more fully developed in the reflections of his people. This is true in a special sense of the writings of the apostle Paul.

Many have found a problem in linking the Gospels with their detailed presentation of the acts and teachings of Jesus with the Christ who is so central in Paul's beliefs. The problem arises because the apostle does not refer to any specific incident in the life of Jesus and does not reflect in his epistles any acquaintance with the large amount of teaching material in the Gospels. Does this suggest that Paul had no interest in the historical Jesus? Or could it be maintained that he knew nothing about him? Those who have driven a wedge between Paul and Jesus have not given sufficient weight to those incidental indications that Paul knew a great deal more about the historical Jesus than he states in his letters. He writes, for instance, about the meekness and gentleness of Christ (2 Cor 10:1), suggesting that he knew that Jesus had said of himself that he was meek and lowly of heart (Mt 11:29). Moreover, Paul speaks of the poverty of Christ (2 Cor 8:9) and must have known that the Son of man had nowhere to lay his head. He certainly knows the details of how Jesus instituted the Lord's Supper, and he knows of his death by crucifixion. It seems reasonable to conclude that Paul assumes that his readers will be acquainted with the Gospel material.

It is perhaps useful in this connection to enquire whether the life and teaching of Jesus played a significant part in the early Christian proclamation. One passage that is valuable in this respect is Acts 10:36–38. In Peter's address to Cornelius, he spoke of God having anointed Jesus of Nazareth, and that he went about doing good and healing all who were under the power of the devil. It is clear that some account of the acts of Jesus was included in the early preaching, and there is no reason to suppose that this was not a regular procedure.

There is no doubt that the example of Jesus was a powerful motive for promoting right behavior. Peter appeals to it in encouraging Christians who were suffering for their faith (1 Pt 2:21). Paul also knows the value of imitation (1 Cor 11:1; 1 Thes 1:6). Since Jesus was recognized as being a man who did not sin (cf. 2 Cor 5:21), his behavior patterns would have proved invaluable for those who needed a new standard for moral action. While this idea of example is unquestionably present in the epistles, it would be quite wrong to suppose that it formed a major part of Christian doctrine.

There are few references to the teaching of Jesus in the NT. In the letter of James, which is almost wholly practical, there are more allusions to the teaching of Jesus than anywhere else in the NT. This is especially true of echoes of the Sermon on the Mount, and it shows the strong contribution that the moral teaching of Jesus had on the ethical values of the early Christians. Most of the expositions of doctrine in the epistles find their basis in some aspect of the teaching of Jesus. That teaching has an

The Sea of Galilee, looking south from Capernaum. From the Gospel accounts, it seems that it was in Galilee that Jesus spent the most time ministering and teaching.

ongoing significance for the development of the church.

To what extent is knowledge of the life and teaching of Jesus relevant to the 20th century? Existential theologians have driven such a wedge between the Christ of faith and the Jesus of history that the latter has ceased to have any importance for them. Christians today, no less than their first-century predecessors, need to know that the object of their faith is the same one who lived and taught in Galilee and Judea. The Gospels make this clear in their resurrection narratives. Although we might at first consider the way of the existentialists attractive, on reflection we realize that it reduces the Gospels to little more than treasuries of a few genuine sayings of Jesus and a vast amount of church invention.

DONALD GUTHRIE

See PARABLE; KINGDOM OF GOD (HEAVEN); CHRISTOLOGY; VIRGIN BIRTH OF JESUS; INCARNATION; ASCENSION OF CHRIST; MESSIAH; SAVIOR; GENEALOGY OF JESUS CHRIST; REDEEMER, REDEMPTION; CHRIST; SON OF GOD; SON OF MAN; TRANSFIGURATION; BROTHERS OF JESUS.

Bibliography. P. Benoit, *Jesus and the Gospel*, 2 vols; H. Daniel-Rops, *Jesus and His Times*, 2 vols; J. Denney, *Jesus and the Gospel*; G.S. Duncan, *Jesus, Son of Man*; A. Edersheim, *The Life and Times of Jesus the Messiah*; D. Guthrie, *A Shorter Life of Christ*; W. Kasper, *Jesus the Christ*; T.W. Manson, *The Teaching of Jesus*; J.D. Pentecost, *The Words and Works of Jesus Christ*; J.W. Shepard, *The Christ of the Gospels*; D. Smith, *The Days of His Flesh*; R.H. Stein, *The Method and Message of Jesus' Teachings*; G. Vos, *The Self-Disclosure of Jesus*; T. Walker, *The Teaching of Jesus.*

Jesus Justus. Jewish Christian.

See JESUS #4.

Jether. 1. Firstborn son of Gideon who, because of his youth, was afraid to execute the Midianite kings Zebah and Zalmunna at his father's request (Jgs 8:30).

2. Ishmaelite and the father of Amasa (1 Kgs 2:5,32; 1 Chr 2:17). He is alternately called Ithra in 2 Samuel 17:25.

See ITHRA.

3. Firstborn son of Jada, the brother of Jonathan, and a descendant of Judah through Hezron's line. He fathered no children (1 Chr 2:32).

4. Judahite and the firstborn of Ezrah's four sons (1 Chr 4:17)

5. Asherite, the father of three sons (1 Chr 7:38) and probably identical with Ithran, Zophah's son, in 1 Chronicles 7:37.

Jetheth. Chief of Edom (Gn 36:40; 1 Chr 1:51).

Jethlah. KJV form of the Danite city Ithlah in Joshua 19:42.

See ITHLAH.

Jethro. Father-in-law of Moses. Zipporah, Jethro's daughter, became Moses' wife while he was a fugitive in the wilderness (Ex 2:21). When Moses departed for Egypt, he took Zipporah and his sons with him (4:20), but he must have sent them back. Jethro brought them to Moses after the Israelites arrived in Sinai (Ex 18:1–7). Through this familial relationship with Moses, Jethro became involved with Israel.

Jethro's relationship with Israel has been variously interpreted. Scholars who have suggested that Jethro's tribal god, Jahweh, was introduced to Israel by Moses have not been able to establish their case. The biblical record could be understood to teach that Jethro knew of Israel's God because he was a descendant of Abraham (Gn 25:2). Having heard of Jahweh's deliverance of his people from Egypt, Jethro acknowledged him as God, greatest of all gods. He also brought a burnt offering and sacrifices, thereby worshiping Jahweh and identifying with Israel (Ex 18:11). This action has been interpreted as Jethro's acceptance of a covenant with Israel, but this interpretation rests upon a faulty reading of what Jethro actually did and the meaning of sacrifice and a fellowship meal. Upon receiving Jethro's good counsel concerning procedures for judging disputes among the people, Moses appointed able men as heads and judges over the people (Ex 18:13–27). Jethro departed to his own land and seems to have had no further interaction with Israel, but his son (Nm 10:29–33) and other descendants later became a part of Israel (Jgs 1:16; 4:11).

Jethro was a priest of Midian (Ex 2:16; 3:1). It is not definitely known what the religion of the Midianites was, but some scholars have suggested that the Kenites, which were a tribe included in the nation of Midianites (Judg 1:16), had a tribal god named Yahweh whom Jethro served as priest. Biblical evidence does not support this interpretation. That Jethro was a god-fearing and god-serving man is quite clear.

Jethro is referred to by other names, both in the Scriptures and later. The Talmud records that his name was Jether originally, but after his conversion it became Jethro; there is no definite evidence to support this. He is called Reuel, the father of seven daughters whom Moses met at a well (Ex 2:16,18; Nm 10:29, KJV Raguel). He is also referred to by the name Hobab (Jgs 4:11); and he is also said to be the son of Reuel (Nm 29:10). The Scriptures do not explain the use of the different names. Suggestions such as (1) each Midianite tribe he served as priest knew him by a different name; (2) Reuel was a tribal name, not personal; (3) Hobab, the son's name, was used to refer to the father; (4) a gloss appears in the text at Exodus 2:18 and Judges 4:11; and (5) different literary sources account for the differences do not present adequate solutions. It can be quite clearly established, however, that Jethro had a son named Hobab.

See MOSES; MIDIAN, MIDIANITE.

Jetur. Tribe descended from Ishmael (Gn 25:15; 1 Chr 1:31); the Israelite tribes who settled east of the Jordan had to fight them (1 Chr 5:19). Called Itureans, they survived into NT times, giving their name to Ituraea, an area northeast of Galilee (Lk 3:1).

See ITURAEA.

Jeuel. 1. Descendant of Judah residing in postexilic Jersualem (1 Chr 9:6).

2. Levite who took part in Hezekiah's reforms (2 Chr 29:13, KJV Jeiel).

3. Head of a family that returned to Jerusalem with Zerubbabel after the exile (Ezr 8:13, KJV Jeiel).

Jeush. 1. Eldest of three sons borne to Esau by Oholibamah, daughter of the Canaanite Anah, and a chief among Esau's descendants in Edom (Gn 36:5–18; 1 Chr 1:35).

2. Bilhan's son from Jediael's house and a leader in Benjamin's tribe (1 Chr 7:10).

3. Benjamite, Eshek's son and a descendant of Saul (1 Chr 8:39, KJV Jehush).

4. Levite from the family of Gershon and the third of Shimei's four sons. Since he and

his youngest brother, Beriah, had few sons, they were together considered one house during David's reign (1 Chr 23:10,11).

5. Eldest of three sons borne to King Rehoboam by Abihail, Eliab's daughter (2 Chr 11:19).

Jeuz. Shaharaim's son from Benjamin's tribe (1 Chr 8:10).

Jew. Judean, belonging to Judah. The short form of the English word has developed from the French. The underlying Hebrew word is used first in 2 Kings 16:6 as a national term, meaning citizens of Judah. It came into general use in the period of Jeremiah just before the exile (late 6th century BC; see, e.g., Jer 32:12). It reflects a growing sense of national identity over against foreign nations in an international world. In Jeremiah 34:9, a statement of the national principle that an individual citizen had the right to freedom from slavery uses the term "Jew." It is poignantly used in giving the number of deported citizens in Jeremiah 52:28.

Once the people were in exile, the term's national meaning was expanded with a religious one. The Jews were different from surrounding peoples in that they preserved a living religious tradition of the one true God. A Jewish-Gentile polarization developed. Thus in Daniel 3:8,12, certain Jews are accused of deviating from otherwise acceptable Babylonian religious practices. The Book of Esther is concerned with the problem of Jewish identity and survival in a hostile alien environment. Esther 8:17 speaks of Gentiles declaring themselves Jews (RSV) in the religious sense of becoming proselytes.

After the exile the strongly religious meaning of "Jew" is expressed in the prophecy of Zechariah 8:23 that the Jew would be courted by Gentiles because God was with him. In Ezra 4:12 the term "Jews" is the national designation of the returned exiles, as it is in the Book of Nehemiah (e.g., 1:2; 4:2). In Nehemiah 13:24 there is a consciousness of the social exclusiveness of the Jews: on religious grounds (27 RSV) marriage to foreigners is deplored.

In the NT "Jew" continues to have the same national and/or religious meaning. Culturally Jews have their own religious and other customs which NT documents addressed to Gentiles find it necessary to explain (Mk 7:3; Jn 5:1; 19:40). Jews are contrasted with Gentiles (Acts 11:19), Samaritans (Jn 4:9,22) and proselytes (Acts 2:10). Jewish Christians can be called "Jews" (Gal 2:13). But there is an increasing stress on the religious distinctions between Jew and Christian. In Romans 2:17–

29 Paul gives an interesting theological analysis of the term "Jew." He is at pains to emphasize that the true meaning of the word lies not in outward religious profession but in an inward attitude to God. Paul was doubtless thinking of the inadequacy of his own life as a Jew before he was converted to the Christian faith (cf. Phil 3:3–6). His mention of "praise" in verse 29 is the climax of the passage. It is a forceful play on words: in Hebrew, Judah means praise (Gn 29:35; cf. 49:8).

The apostle Paul is here moving in the direction of regarding Christianity as the true heir of the faith of the OT. Revelation 2:9 and 3:9 express similar sentiments: to be truly a Jew is much more than a matter of birth and synagogue observance. Underlying these passages in both Revelation and Romans is obviously the issue of the messianic claims of Jesus (cf. Rom 9:3–5; 10:1–4). The NT bears sad testimony to the opposition of Jews to the Christian message. The gospel proved a cause of offense to the Jews (1 Cor 1:23). Paul himself, despite his claim of impeccable Jewish credentials (Acts 26:4–7), found himself the object of bitter Jewish attacks (Acts 21:11; 23:12,27). Revelation 2:9 and 3:9 describe the Jews' opposition as satanic: they were carrying out the work of God's adversary, Satan.

These negative overtones are especially attached to the use of the word "Jew" in John's Gospel. It is found, some 70 times over against about five or six instances in each of the synoptic Gospels. Some passages, such as those already cited, have no associations of hostility. But in most cases the fourth Gospel uses "Jews" in the sense of the religious authorities, especially those in Jerusalem, who were hostile to Jesus (see, e.g., 5:18; 9:18; 11:8; 18:36.) It is noteworthy that in 9:22 the parents of the blind man, clearly Jews themselves, are said, literally, to fear the investigating Jews. In 18:12 the Jews stand for the chief priests and Pharisees of 18:3. It must be emphasized that the author, who was obviously a Jew himself, was not expressing an anti-Semitic viewpoint as such. He condemned not race or people but opposition to Jesus. He gladly acknowledged that some Jews put their faith in Jesus (8:31; 11:45; 12:11). Nathanael is featured as a type of the Christian Jew, a true Israelite "in whom is no guile" (1:47; cf. 1:31).

See ISRAEL, HISTORY OF; JUDAISM; POSTEXILIC PERIOD, THE; EXILE; ISRAEL, RELIGION OF; PHARISEES; JUDAIZERS; DIASPORA OF THE JEWS.

Jewels, Jewelry.

See FASHION AND DRESS; MINERALS, METALS, AND PRECIOUS STONES.

Jezaniah. Alternate form of Jaazaniah, one of the Judean captains in Jerusalem during the exile (Jer 40:8; 42:1 KJV).

See JAAZANIAH #1.

Jezebel. Daughter of Ethbaal, king of Sidon (1 Kgs 16:31). She became the wife of Ahab, king of the northern kingdom of Israel; the marriage was probably a continuation of the friendly relations between Israel and Phoenicia begun by Omri and confirmed a political alliance between the two nations. Jezebel exerted a strong influence over the life of Israel, as she insisted on establishing the worship of Baal and demanded the absolute rights of the monarchy. So strong was her pagan influence that Scripture attributes the apostasy of Ahab directly to Jezebel (1 Kgs 16:30–34).

Jezebel's efforts to establish Baal worship in Israel began with Ahab's acceptance of Baal following the marriage (1 Kgs 16:31). Ahab followed Jezebel's practices by building a house of worship and altar for Baal in Samaria (32), and by setting aside a grove, probably for worship of the Asherah (33). A campaign was then conducted to exterminate the prophets of God (1 Kgs 18:4), while Jezebel organized and supported large groups of Baal prophets, housing and feeding large numbers of them in the royal palace (1 Kgs 18:19). To meet this challenge God sent Elijah, first to prophesy a drought which lasted three years (1 Kgs 17:1; 18:1).

Elijah's confrontation with Jezebel and Ahab culminated on Mt Carmel, where Elijah demanded that the prophets of Baal meet him (1 Kgs 18:19–40). As they and the people of Israel gathered, Elijah issued the challenge to Israel to follow the true God. To demonstrate who was the true God, Baal's prophets and Elijah each took a bullock for sacrifice. The prophets of Baal then prepared the sacrifice and called on their god to send fire to consume it, but no answer came. Elijah prepared his sacrifice and had it drenched in water. After his prayer, God sent fire which consumed the sacrifice, the wood, the stones of the altar, the dust, and the water that had overflowed. Following this the Israelites fell down in tribute to God. Then Elijah directed the people to take the prophets of Baal to the brook Kishon, and he slaughtered all of them. When Jezebel heard of this, she flew into a rage and threatened Elijah with the same fate. In fear Elijah fled for his life to the wilderness.

Jezebel's unscrupulous nature is revealed in the account of Ahab's desire for Naboth's vineyard (1 Kgs 21:1–16). Although Ahab desired the vineyard, he recognized Naboth's right to retain the family property. Jezebel recognized no such right in view of a monarch's wishes. She arranged to have Naboth falsely accused of blaspheming God and consequently executed, leaving the vineyard for Ahab to seize. For this heinous crime Elijah pronounced a violent death for Ahab and Jezebel (1 Kgs 21:20–24), which was ultimately fulfilled (1 Kgs 22:29–40; 2 Kgs 9:1–37).

The corrupt influence of Jezebel spread to the southern kingdom of Judah through her daughter Athaliah, who married Jehoram, king of Judah. Thus the idolatry of Phoenicia infected both kingdoms of the Hebrews through this evil Sidonian princess.

In Revelation 2:20 the name of Jezebel is used (perhaps symbolically) to refer to a prophetess who seduced the Christians of Thyatira to fornication and to eating things sacrificed to idols.

See AHAB #1; ELIJAH; SIDON, SIDONIAN (PLACE).

Jezer. Naphtali's third son and the founder of the family of Jezerites (Gn 46:24; Nm 26:49; 1 Chr 7:13).

Jeziah. KJV form of Izziah, Parosh's son, in Ezra 10:25.

See IZZIAH.

Jeziel. Warrior from Benjamin's tribe who joined David at Ziklag in his struggle against King Saul. Jeziel was one of David's ambidextrous archers and slingers (1 Chr 12:3).

Jezliah. KJV form of Izliah, Elpaal's son, in 1 Chronicles 8:18.

See IZLIAH.

Jezoar. KJV rendering of Izhar, Helah's son, in 1 Chronicles 4:7.

See IZHAR #2.

Jezrahiah. Leader of the temple singers who participated in the dedication of the rebuilt Jerusalem wall (Neh 12:42).

Jezreel (Person). 1. Eldest of Etam's three sons and a descendant of Judah (1 Chr 4:3). Another possible reading suggests that Jezreel was one of the founding fathers of the town of Etam. Due to numerous scribal alterations within the Hebrew text, it is difficult to discern the original intent of the author.

2. Firstborn son of the prophet Hosea and his wife Gomer. Jezreel's name, meaning "God sows," prefigured the outpouring of God's wrath on the disobedient kingdom of Israel (Hos 1:4,5).

Jezreel (Place). 1. Town originally founded by the tribe of Issachar to the south of Shunem, a site that was abandoned in the el-Amarna period by earlier settlers (Jos 19:18). The city became associated with a number of important events in the history of Israel.

It probably gained some of its importance from the decline of the ancient town of Beth-shan during the Iron Age. Jezreel became the center of an important district in Saul's kingdom (2 Sm 2:9), and a nearby spring served as the rallying point for Saul's army before they met the Philistines in the battle of Mt Gilboa (1 Sm 29:1). After Saul's death the town was for a short time part of Ish-bosheth's kingdom (2 Sm 2:8–11). In Solomon's day it was assigned to the 10th district of Issachar and was excluded from the main Jezreel Valley. It was administered by Jehoshaphat, son of Paruah (1 Kgs 4:12,17).

In the days of Omri (885–874 BC) it was chosen as the site of the king's winter capital, and the four kings of his dynasty down to Joram (852–841 BC) all resided there. It was to this place that Joram retired to recover from wounds received in battle (2 Kgs 8:29). The royal palace at Jezreel had a tower from which the countryside could be surveyed (2 Kgs 9:17), and it was adjacent to the vineyard of Naboth, the Jezreelite, which was seized by King Ahab through an unjust and fraudulent act (1 Kgs 21). For this dastardly deed the dynasty of Ahab received severe retribution. Jezebel, Ahab's Phoenician wife, was thrown to the dogs through an upper window at the time of Jehu's usurpation of the throne. King Joram, wounded in battle, was slain by Jehu along with his courtiers and his body cast into the field of Naboth (2 Kgs 9:24–26). The remnant of Ahab's household were exterminated at the same time (2 Kgs 10:1–11).

Jezreel was a walled city with a gate and a tower, and was administered by a council of elders and nobles (2 Kgs 10:1). After the downfall of Omri's dynasty the town declined in importance, although it is mentioned as a village in a number of writers in the Christian era. Eusebius (AD 260–340) refers to it as a village between Scythopolis and Legio (*Onomasticon* 108:13ff). The Crusaders called it "le Petit Gerim" to distinguish it from "le Grand Gerim" (Jenin).

Today Jezreel is identified with Zer'in, the site of an Israeli kibbutz about 55 miles north of Jerusalem. Archaeological remains found in the area point to an occupation in the Iron Age and the Roman period.

2. Town in the mountains of Judah (Jos 15:56). It was the hometown of Ahinoam, one of David's wives (1 Sm 25:43), but nothing is known about the site today.

The Valley of Jezreel.

Jezreel, Valley of.
Largest and richest valley in the land of Israel. It was named after Jezreel, apparently the only town on the plain where the Israelites had gained a foothold in the early stages of their conquest (cf. Jgs 1:27,28,30). The form of the name in later Greek sources is Esdraelon (Jth 1:8); some scholars have wrongly applied the latter term to the great western plain and the former to the narrow valley leading eastward to Bethshan. Comparison of Joshua 17:16 with Judges 1:27,28 and Joshua 17:11 shows that the Bethshan area was considered as a separate entity from the Valley of Jezreel, which included the cities of Taanach and Megiddo among others (cf. also Hos 1:5).

The Midianites encamped there (Jgs 6:33), between the Hill of Moreh and Tabor (Ps 83:9,10), and later the Philistines gathered there to oppose Saul (1 Sm 29:1,11; 2 Sm 4:4). Under the monarchy the valley was an administrative district (2 Sm 2:9; 1 Kgs 4:12). Another name, perhaps applicable only to the southern half of the valley, is the plain of Megiddo (2 Chr 35:22; Zec 12:11.).

The valley figures in the wars of Thutmose III and Amenhotep II, and the towns there, especially Megiddo, were under Egyptian control in the Late Bronze Age. The southwestern side was famous as a military assembly ground, probably called Harosheth-ha-geiim (Jgs 4:2,13,16).

See PALESTINE.

Jezreelite, Jezreelitess.
Inhabitant of one of two cities named Jezreel. Two such persons are specifically named:

1. Naboth, who lived in the Jezreel in Issachar's territory (1 Kgs 21:1–16; 2 Kgs 9:21,25).
See JEZREEL (PLACE) #2.

2. David's wife Ahinoam, who was a native of the Jezreel in Judah's territory (1 Chr 3:1).
See JEZREEL (PLACE) #1.

Jibsam.
KJV form of Ibsam, Tola's son, in 1 Chronicles 7:2.

See IBSAM.

Jidlaph.
Seventh son of Nahor and Milcah (Gn 22:22).

Jimna, Jimnah, Jimnite.
KJV forms of Imnah and Imnite, Asher's son and his family, in Genesis 46:17 and Numbers 26:44.

See IMNAH #1.

Jiphtah.
KJV rendering of Iphtah, a village in Judah, in Joshua 15:43.

See IPHTAH.

Jiphthah-el.
KJV rendering of Iphtahel, a valley on Zebulun's border, in Joshua 19:14,27.

See IPHTAHEL.

Joab.
1. Son of Zeruiah, the half-sister of David (1 Chr 2:16), who, along with his brothers Abishai and Asahel, was well known for his military valor in Judah (2 Sm 2:18; cf. 1 Sm 26:6). Of the three sons Joab rose to prominence and distinguished himself at the battle of Gibeon when Saul's troops under Abner were vanquished (2 Sm 2:8–32). Because Abner had slain Joab's brother Asahel (2:23), Joab later killed Abner in revenge (2 Sm 3:26–30), despite Abner's new loyalty to David (3:12–19). Possibly Joab sensed that Abner would be his rival. Nevertheless David praised the slain commander as "a prince and a great man" (3:31–39) and set a curse on the house of Joab for his insubordination (3:26–29,39). This incident illumines Joab's sometimes unscrupulous and ruthless behavior.

Joab spearheaded David's siege of the Jebusite city of Jerusalem; and when David consolidated his reign there, Joab became the commander of the king's army (2 Sm 8:16; 11:1; cf. 1 Chr 11:6,8; 18:15). He suppressed a rebellion among the Syrians and Ammonites (2 Sm 10:7–14; 1 Chr 19:8–15). At Rabbah he not only

The stage and part of the 6000 seats in the Roman theater in Amman, Jordan (OT Rabbah), the city that Joab conquered while making sure that Uriah the Hittite died in battle (2 Sm 11–12).

conquered the city (2 Sm 11,12) but arranged for the death of Uriah the Hittite so that David could take Uriah's wife, Bathsheba.

Joab's loyalties to David and shrewd control of the army are seen during Absalom's rebellion (2 Sm 15). Joab suppressed the conspiracy (2 Sm 18), but ignoring a direct order from David not to kill his son (18:5) brutally slew him anyway (18:10–17). When David mourned, Joab rebuked the king, urging that a crisis with the army was imminent (19:5–7). This insubordination led David to replace Joab with Amasa as commander (19:13) but later, at Gibeon, Joab also killed him dishonorably (20:18–10). Joab's influence in the army must have been great, since he regained his former role as military commander (20:23, 24:2, 1 Kgs 1:19).

At the end of David's reign, Joab supported the conspiracy of Adonijah and Abiathar against the throne (1 Kgs 1:7). David's distrust of him led the king to warn Solomon specifically about Joab's repeated treacheries (1 Kgs 2:5–9). Solomon had to resolve the problem of an untrustworthy army. Therefore, upon his father's death, Solomon pursued the conspirators Adonijah (2:23), Abiathar (2:26), and Joab (2:28). Solomon's officer Beniah found Joab at the altar seeking refuge and killed him there (2:28–35), thus cleansing Solomon's reign from the wrongdoing of Joab.

See ISRAEL, HISTORY OF.

2. KJV translation ("Ataroth, the house of Joab") of Atroth-beth-joab in 1 Chronicles 2:54.

See ATROTH-BETH-JOAB.

3. Judahite, Seraiah's son from the house of Kenaz and forefather of the residents of the valley of craftsmen (1 Chr 4:14).

4. Forefather of a clan of Jews who returned to Palestine with Zerubbabel following the exile (Ezr 2:6; Neh 7:11).

5. Forefather of a family of which 219 members returned with Ezra to Palestine following the exile (Ezr 8:9). He is perhaps identifiable with #4 above.

Joah. 1. Asaph's son and a court official under King Hezekiah (2 Kgs 18:18,26; Is 36:3,11, 22). He was one of the officers sent by Hezekiah to deal with the Assyrians during the siege of Jerusalem.

2. Zimmah's son from Levi's tribe (1 Chr 6:21).

3. Levite, Obed-edom's son and a gatekeeper of the sanctuary in David's time (1 Chr 26:4).

4. Joahaz's son and a recorder under King Josiah; he was one of the deputies overseeing the temple repairs (2 Chr 34:8).

Joahaz. 1. Variant spelling of Jehoahaz, Jehu's son, in 2 Kings 14:1.

See JEHOAHAZ #1.

2. Joah's father. Joah was King Josiah's recorder (2 Chr 34:8).

Joanan. Ancestor of Jesus mentioned in Luke's genealogy (3:27, KJV Joanna).

See GENEALOGY OF JESUS CHRIST.

Joanna. 1. KJV form of Joanan in Luke 3:27.

See JOANAN.

2. Wife of Chuza, a steward of Herod the tetrarch. She was among those healed of evil spirits and sicknesses by Jesus, and contributed to his support (Lk 8:2,3). She probably witnessed the crucifixion and prepared spices for the body, later to find Jesus' tomb empty (Lk 23:55–24:10).

Joash. 1. Abiezrite who lived at Ophrah and the father of Gideon. Joash built an altar to Baal and an image of Asherah, which Gideon later destroyed (Jgs 6:11–31; 7:14; 8:13,29,32).

2. Son of King Ahab of Israel (1 Kgs 22:26; 2 Chr 18:25).

3. Alternate name for Jehoash, Ahaziah's son and king of Judah (835–796 BC), in 2 Kings 11:2,3 and 1 Chronicles 3:11.

See JEHOASH #1.

4. Alternate name for Jehoash, Jehoahaz's son and king of Israel (798–782 BC), in 2 Kings 13:10–13.

See JEHOASH #2.

5. Judahite from the house of Shelah (1 Chr 4:22).

6. Second of Becher's nine sons and a leader in Benjamin's tribe (1 Chr 7:8).

7. Benjamite chief who supported David at Ziklag (1 Chr 12:3).

8. Official of David (1 Chr 27:28).

Joatham. KJV spelling of Jotham, king of Judah (750–732 BC), in Matthew 1:9.

See JOTHAM #2.

Job (Person). 1. KJV rendering of Iob, an alternate form of Jashub, Issachar's third son, in Genesis 46:13.

See JASHUB #1.

2. Central character of the Book of Job. The intense suffering endured by Job provides the framework for the main theme of the book, which deals with the role of suffering in the life of the child of God.

The etymology of the name is difficult. Some have seen it as a derivative of a Hebrew word meaning "to be hostile" and have suggested that it reflects Job's adamancy in refusing to bow to God's will. The name occurs in several West Semitic texts as a proper name, however, and it seems best to understand it simply as a common name. The meaning of the name in West Semitic is either "no father" or "where is my father?"

The lack of certainty surrounding the authorship and geographical provenance of the book makes it difficult to place Job in history. The occurrence of Job's name in Ezekiel 14:14,20 seems to support the possibility that he was a personage of great antiquity.

See JOB, BOOK OF.

Job, Book of. OT book belonging to the scriptural category of Writings.

Author. The question of the authorship of the Book of Job is a difficult one. The difficulty is compounded not only by the lack of ascription of authorship to any individual but also by the structure of the book which, according to some scholars, is a composite consisting of several literary works.

Some scholars who hold that the book is a composite work base their views on alleged incongruities existing among the various sections. The prologue (chs 1,2) and the epilogue (42:7–17), for example, are seen as separate from the body of the book because they seem to present Job as a man of perfect moral character. The dialogues, however, picture a somewhat more human Job whose utterances about God are at times brash and shocking.

It is true that Job is depicted as a man of perfect moral character in the prologue. But it should be noted that while he refuses his wife's suggestion to curse God, an account recorded in the prologue (2:9,10), he does not curse God in the dialogues either. The very point of the book seems to be that even one of the highest moral character can struggle with the ways of God in this world. Only after the series of misfortunes recorded in chapters 1 and 2, and the period of inner struggle that no doubt transpired during the seven days and seven nights before he began to speak (2:11–13), did Job find those deep inner questions that the book deals with. Job's high moral character is quite evident in the dialogues, for throughout, even though he cannot comprehend God, he speaks the truth before him.

Other portions alleged to be additions to the book are the speeches of Elihu (32–37), the discourse of God (38–41), and the Wisdom poem in chapter 28. It is held by some that the author of the final version borrowed these existing works to provide a literary structure for his own work.

The main structure of the book, consisting of prologue, dialogues, and epilogue, need not necessarily be regarded as the result of a com-

plex process of editing. The Code of Hammurabi, for example, has a similar structure, as does an ancient Egyptian work called "A Dispute Over Suicide."

With regard to the problem of authorship, it seems best to acknowledge that the author is anonymous. His theology is certainly Yahwistic; thus, he was probably a Hebrew. His literary skills were remarkable, for he has produced one of the finest works known through the ages.

Date. Since the authorship of the book is in question, the date of the book is as well. Most modern scholars place the book in the postexilic period, around the 5th century BC. However, some place it toward the end of the exile. Others put it in the Solomonic era, while still others place it in the period of the patriarchs.

The internal evidence points to a very early setting for the book. There are no levitical institutions cited. Job sacrifices for his family as in the period before the priesthood (1:5). The wealth of Job, given in terms of cattle, seems to reflect the patriarchal milieu (1:3).

The language of the book may also point to an early date. Certain linguistic elements indicate more archaic forms of Hebrew, as preserved in the epic material from Ugarit.

It may be that Job himself lived in the 2nd millennium BC. If the book, or part of it, was written then, it may represent the first written material to find its way into the biblical canon. The book may have come into its final form in the Solomonic era, when so much of the Hebrew Wisdom Literature was produced.

Background. The Book of Job belongs to the body of OT materials known as the Wisdom Literature. This literature deals with the basic issues of human life. The Israelites were not the only ancient people to produce Wisdom Literature. This type of material came out of pagan cultures as well, and often represents efforts to explain the course of human events within the structure of pagan religion.

Several ancient works similar to the OT Book of Job are known from ancient cultures. A Sumerian "Job" exists which does not compare with the biblical book, either in literary scope or depth of feeling. It depicts the plight of a young man whose sorrow was turned to joy as a result of extended pleading to his personal deity. According to Sumerian thought, the gods were responsible for evil as well as good. Only placation of some kind could prevent the evil they might do. There is no attempt to philosophize or expound the problem of the presence of evil in the world.

A Babylonian "Job" also exists. This work, commonly titled "I Will Praise the Lord of Wisdom," is philosophically similar to the Sumerian "Job." In this work the writer describes his suffering in vivid terminology. No one can help him. He wonders whether the ritual obligations of his pagan religion really are pleasing to a god. An emissary of the god Marduk appears to him in a dream and relieves his suffering. The work ends with a section of praise to Marduk in which occurs the affirmation that the offerings he gave the gods served to gladden the hearts of the gods.

Another work, "A Dialogue About Human Misery," is also similar to the biblical Book of Job. It struggles with the fact that worship of the deities seems to make no difference in the quality of one's life. A figure in this book reminds the sufferer that the ways of the gods are difficult to understand, and man is naturally perverse. The sufferer appeals to the gods, but the work ends at that point with no resolution to the problem.

These literary works are not comparable to the OT Book of Job theologically or philosophically. They offer only a fatalistic outlook on life and understand life to be governed by the capricious will of the gods.

However, these documents, which date variously between the 2nd and 1st millennia BC, may provide us with the literary ground from which the Book of Job sprang. That is, the Book of Job may present the inspired answer to the deep questions that were being considered at this time in history. Thus, this type of literature may argue for an early date for the Book of Job.

Content. *The Prologue (1:1–2:13).* This section of the book describes the events which led to the suffering of Job. He is pictured at the outset as a man of wealth with a family for whom he cared deeply.

In a dramatic scene set in heaven Satan appears, and is asked by the Lord, "Have you considered my servant Job, . . . a blameless and upright man?" (1.8). Satan's reply is, "Put forth thy hand now, and touch all that he has, and he will curse thee to thy face" (1:11). There follows the first of Job's great calamities, the loss of his family and his possessions.

Another encounter between the Lord and Satan leads to the physical suffering of Job. It is this loathsome disease that provides the context for the dialogues which follow. In all of this the writer is careful to tell us that Job did not sin. He has resisted his wife's plea to curse God. He has resisted the temptation to forsake God because of the loss of his children. But suddenly the placid picture ends with dialogues as we listen to Job's complaints. We wonder, has Job given up his faith in God?

Three of Job's friends have come to comfort him. They sit silent in his presence for seven days, reluctant to speak. After the period of silence they begin their dialogues with Job.

The Dialogues (3:1–31:40). (1) The First Cycle (3:1–14:22).

Job's complaint, recorded in chapter 1, questions the wisdom of God in allowing him to be born. He wonders why life was given to one whose lot in life is to suffer.

Eliphaz is the first of Job's friends to speak. A polite man on the surface, he is heartless underneath. His answer is that Job must have sinned; why else would he be suffering so (4:7–11)?

Eliphaz clearly believes that Job's questioning represents a negative attitude toward God. He appeals to Job to return to the Lord (4:8) and give up his vexation toward God, since his anger will lead only to ruin (5:2). He sees a positive element in suffering, for he affirms that it is chastening from the Almighty (5:17).

Job responds by pointing out that his vexation is warranted in view of the terrible suffering he is enduring (6:1–7). He also complains that Eliphaz is in the wrong in not showing him kindness, likening him to a wadi in the desert which offers no water in the hot, dry season (6:14–23).

The next comforter, Bildad, is even more heartless than Eliphaz. He too repeats the accusation that Job has sinned. His pitiless attitude is evident in his reference to Job's children, blaming their deaths on probable sin in their lives (8:3).

Bildad, like Eliphaz, appeals to Job to turn to God (8:5), assuring him that God will surely respond (8:6). He pictures Job's misfortunes as the result of turning from God (8:11–19) but assures him that God will not reject a blameless man (8:20).

Job's response to Bildad begins with a poignant question: "Truly I know that it is so: But how can a man be just before God?" (9:2). This question is followed by an eloquent statement in which Job pictures the magnitude of God's power as seen in the universe (9:3–12). Job stands before the might of God completely helpless to withstand that power. He protests that he cannot contend with such a God, or protest his innocence before him, for he is too powerful to oppose.

Job also complains that he cannot gain a fair hearing from God because God believes him guilty. The fact that God has punished him with his affliction proves that he does not regard him as innocent (9:14–24). Job continues his response through chapter 10 and questions God's wisdom in bringing him into existence (10:18–22).

The next to speak is Zophar. He too accuses Job of sin (11:4–6). In an insulting statement he says that God "knows worthless men; when he sees iniquity, will he not consider it? But a stupid man will get understanding, when a wild ass's colt is born a man" (11:11,12).

Job's anger is kindled by Zophar's insulting accusations (12:2,3), and he calls on God to withdraw his hand and answer his demand that God speak (13:20–28).

(2) The Second Cycle (15:1–21:34). The second cycle of discourses continues in the same pattern as the first. Eliphaz, Bildad, and Zophar continue their accusations, attributing Job's misfortune to sin in his life. But as the narrative continues, the speakers begin to become more involved in their own assertions, and they no longer answer each other's arguments as directly as they did in the first series of dialogues.

(3) The Third Cycle (22:1–31:40). In the third series of dialogues only Eliphaz and Bildad speak. The accusations of sin in Job become even more pointed and cruel. Eliphaz says, "Is not your wickedness great? There is no end to your iniquities" (22:5). And Bildad proclaims, "The stars are not clean in his sight; how much less man, who is a maggot" (25:5,6).

This third dialogue is unusual in that Job speaks more than he does in the others. While Bildad's argument extends for only six verses, Job's reply goes on for six chapters (26–31).

Chapter 31 is an important one. In it Job protests his innocence. It is a chapter in which Job's sincerity cannot be doubted. He affirms that he has been morally pure (1–4), he has not been deceitful (5–8), he has not been guilty of adultery (9–12), he has concern for others (13–23), he has not trusted in wealth (24–28). He concludes with a general affirmation of his innocence (29–40).

A pattern begins to develop. Job gradually moves away from his friends in the discussion. They become more insistent on sin as the cause of his misfortunes, and Job more firmly asserts his innocence. The writer of the book deftly weaves the account so that the reader can find little that is unorthodox in the statements of the friends. Yet while we may agree with their words, we cannot approve their attitudes. It is true that sin brings punishment, but the friends emphasize only that. The next friend, Elihu, will point out another function of suffering.

We hear the ring of truth in Job's protestations of innocence. But if we believe Job and also believe the comforters, we have the same dilemma as Job. We do not know where the truth lies. We do not know why Job is suffering.

The Speech of Elihu (32–37). Elihu is a young man who listens to his fellow comforters with growing impatience (32:3). He is overly sensitive about his youth (32:6–22), but when he speaks he reveals an understanding of suffering that is more mature than that of his companions.

Elihu emphasizes the fact that suffering is chastening (33:19) which reveals the goodness of God (33:29–33). While this thought was found in Eliphaz' first speech (5:17), it is given greater prominence by Elihu, who emphasizes a dimension of suffering that reveals the love of God. But still one feels that the whole answer has not been given. Another dimension follows in the words of God.

The Voice from the Whirlwind (38–41). God speaks in this section. He poses one question after another to Job, all having to do with some aspect of the creation. God asks, "Where were you when I laid the foundation of the earth? . . . Who determined its measurements?" Then, in a note of sarcasm, he adds, "Surely you know!" (38:4,5).

God refers to the seas and asks Job who made the ocean basins (38:8–11). He pictures the rising dawn and asks Job if he has "commanded the morning" (38:12). Further questions relate to light (38:19–21), snow (38:22–24), rain (38:25–30), the constellations (38:31–33), storms (38:34–38), and animals (38:39–39:30). Job is made to realize the vastness of God's power as revealed in the creation. Job must have felt rather small and insignificant as he contemplated God's might.

But the questions are meant to accomplish more than to make Job feel small. They are meant to make him feel ashamed of his presumption as well. The sarcasm in this section is particularly biting, and one can imagine Job sinking deeper into the ash heap with each question. In the section dealing with light (38:19–21), the question "Where is the way to the dwelling of light?" is followed by "You know, for you were born then, and the number of your days is great!" And in the section dealing with the constellations God asks Job, "Can you bind the chains of the Pleiades, or loose the cords of Orion?" (38:31).

Job has been somewhat brash in his statements to God in the dialogues. He has demanded that God speak to him (13:22), and has accused God of injustice (19:6,7; 24:1; 27:2). Now, as he is reminded of the power of the Almighty, Job begins to recognize his proper place in the universe.

The crucial questions in this long series are those in 40:15–41:34. Here, in an unusual sequence, God draws Job's attention to Behemoth (40:15) and Leviathan (41:1). While some scholars see these as mythical figures, it is most probable that these, like the others cited throughout this section, are literary depictions of ordinary animals known for their great size and strength. It is suggested by many scholars that Behemoth is the hippopotamus and Leviathan the crocodile. The contexts in which these animals are described seem to support this.

God commands Job, "Behold, Behemoth," (40:15) and at the end of the section asks, "Can one take him with hooks, or pierce his nose with a snare?" After reading the description of Behemoth's power in this section, one has to answer the question negatively.

Leviathan, or the crocodile, is cited next. Again the strength of this animal is set forth. God asks, "Can you fill his skin with harpoons?" (41:7). He describes Leviathan as thrashing in the water (41:25), defying all efforts to capture him (41:26).

These references to two powerful beasts end the section in which the voice of God speaks from the whirlwind. It is a section filled with suspense. At the end of it, the reader finds that Job has learned his lesson (42:1,2).

There is an important reason for these questions that came to Job with such insistent force. Job has been led to see that he does not control the universe—God does. Job is forced to face the power of God and learn that he is only part of this vast structure that reflects God's almighty power. By demanding that God speak to him, Job was attempting to control God. By implying that God was unjust he was making a judgment on God, thus making himself equal, if not superior to God. God demands that Job face the power displayed in the universe and repeat his petulant words. Job wanted a God he could control; God demands submission. Job wanted a world run his way; God created a world to be run his way. Job had manufactured an illusory god, one who should obey his own whims. By recognizing God's sovereign control in this world, he is led to see that suffering has a purpose. Job may not recognize that purpose, but it is part of the creation of the Almighty. It is no wonder that Job begins to enter into a settled peace and acknowledge God's sovereignty (42:1–6).

This section of questions is followed by a poignant response from Job. He confesses God's might (42:2). He admits that he did not fully understand things too wonderful for him (42:3), and he repents in dust and ashes (42:6).

The Epilogue (42:7–17). The final part of the book begins with a denunciation of Job's comforters. They are condemned because they did not speak that which was right (42:7). This seems most unusual, since their words have seemed quite orthodox. Yet, in the final analysis, they did not say what was right because their answer to the problem of suffering was only a partial answer; and because it was partial, it was dangerous. It caricatured God as an austere being who used suffering only to punish sin. It did not allow room for the loving hand of God in suffering, as did Elihu's answer to the problem.

While Job said some things about God that were harsh, he was not berated. In fact, the text says that Job spoke of God that which was right (42:8). This evidently refers to Job's concluding words in 42:1–6 where, purified by suffering, he humbly yielded himself to God's sovereign will.

Purpose and Theological Teaching. The question of the central purpose of the Book of Job has been a serious one in biblical scholarship for ages. It is difficult to assert that the purpose of the book is to present the solution to the problem of evil, for at the very point where an answer is expected, God asks questions instead of giving a reasoned answer.

Some have suggested that the central purpose is to answer the question, "Why do the righteous suffer?" It is true that the book has much to do with this question, but it too presents various problems. When one comes to the end of the book, he has only the words of the comforters and the statements of Elihu relating to that question—not a great deal at all. Then one may wonder why we were given the long dialogues with their record of Job's internal struggles. When God speaks from the whirlwind, we find no concern to explain why the righteous suffer. Job is simply led to accept his place in the universe.

It seems best to adopt another approach to the book. In attempting to find the central theme of any literary work, one should look to the prologue and the epilogue. In the prologue he will see what the author intends to do, and in the epilogue he will find the author's understanding of what he actually has done.

In the prologue of Job, the author deftly establishes an atmosphere of suspense. We are told of Job's perfect moral character. Then Satan taunts, "Put forth thy hand now, and touch all that he has, and he will curse thee to thy face." We wonder whether Job will curse God and thus deny his faith, but then we hear his great affirmation of trust: "The Lord gave, and the Lord has taken away; blessed be the name of the Lord."

The writer then sets up another suspenseful situation when Satan proposes to afflict Job. To this trial is added the discouraging words of Job's wife: "Curse God and die." Again we wonder whether this trial will destroy Job's faith. The suspense is broken when we read that "in all this Job did not sin with his lips."

The writer then introduces Job's friends into the narrative. We are told that they remained silent for seven days. We wonder what is going on in Job's mind. Is he still the man of staunch faith, or is his trust being eroded as the disease eats at his flesh? When Job speaks and curses the day of his birth, the suspense becomes intense. The writer has raised a question in our minds: Will Job's faith remain secure?

At times we think it will. Job makes several great affirmations of faith. He states that God will vindicate him. One of the greatest affirmations of the book occurs in 19:25: "For I know that my Redeemer lives, and at last he will stand upon the earth; and after my skin has been thus destroyed, then from my flesh I shall see God, whom I shall see on my side, and my eyes shall behold, and not another."

At other times Job expresses deep doubts about God's orderly control of the universe. The suspense continues.

Throughout the dialogues we trace the pattern of Job's struggle. It is a deep emotional struggle in which Job speaks from the depth of despair and the heights of triumphant faith.

In the epilogue the suspense is resolved. Job's trials have not destroyed or even eroded his faith. He emerges triumphant, with a humble faith. He can say, "I know that thou canst do all things, and that no purpose of thine can be thwarted."

The purpose of the writer is clear. At the outset he has raised the question, "Will Job's faith endure in spite of trial?" The dialogues have heightened the suspense, and the epilogue resolves it. Job has remained faithful to God in the midst of his suffering. We learn that Job's faith is genuine.

The Book of Job, then, is a treatise on faith and the role that suffering plays in faith. As such, it fits into a distinctive body of biblical material that relates these two concepts. This important teaching may be found, for example, in the prophecy of Habakkuk. The prophet complains about the injustice he sees all around him (1:1–4). He balks at God's response that he will use the Assyrians to punish the evil that the prophet decries (1:12–17). Then in this context of suffering and injustice God speaks: "For still the vision awaits its time. . . . If it seem slow, wait for it. . . . Behold, he whose soul is not upright in him shall fail, but the righteous shall live by his faith" (2:3,4).

The word translated "faith" here connotes in the Hebrew the enduring nature of faith and is best translated "faithfulness." The passage teaches that the truly righteous person will remain faithful to God in spite of the seeming delay of God's justice. He may not be able to comprehend all that God does in history, but his faith in God's good plan and wise providence will remain secure. This aspect of faith is one facet of the total spectrum of faith in the Bible. It does not allow for works but is totally dependent on God.

The same relationship between faith and suffering may be found in the NT as well. In James 1:12 trials and faithfulness are woven together in the words, "Blessed is the man who endures trial, for when he has stood the test he will receive the crown of life which God has promised to those who love him" (see also 1 Pt 1:3–7).

According to these passages trials provide the test of faith, and thus reveal whether one's faith is true or false. Faith that is not true will not stand the test of suffering (Mt 13:20,21). The Book of Job then, is a tapestry of faith. It connects faith and trials, and portrays the nature of a genuine faith, a faith unbroken by suffering.

There are other principles in this rich book. It teaches that sin brings punishment. There is truth in the words of the comforters that is corroborated by Scripture. But this is but a small part of the role of suffering in life. The book also teaches that suffering has a didactic function, for it is chastening from the Almighty. In the section in which God speaks from the whirlwind, we learn that suffering is part of the structure of things and that we must submit to the wisdom of the Creator. In this section God reveals himself personally. Job could say, "Now my eye sees thee" (42:5). In trial we need a God who is near much more than a philosophical treatise on the problem of evil. Another emphasis is the role of suffering in producing true righteousness. While Job was depicted as a righteous man at the beginning of the book, his righteousness lacked what suffering could give it. At the end of the book, Job is a humbler man, who sees his role in the universe and who has submitted to the wisdom of God.   THOMAS E. McCOMISKEY

See JOB (PERSON) #2; WISDOM, WISDOM LITERATURE.

Bibliography. S. Cox, *A Commentary on the Book of Job*; E. Dhorme, *Job*; H.L. Ellison, *From Tragedy to Triumph*; H.H. Rowley, *Job*; A. Van Selms, *Job*; N.H. Snaith, *The Book of Job*; R.A. Watson, *The Book of Job*.

Jobab. 1. Joktam's son in Eber's line (Gn 10:29; 1 Chr 1:23).

2. Early Edomite king. He was the son of Zerah of Bozrah (Gn 36:33,34; 1 Chr 1:44,45).

3. King of Madon who, along with other Canaanite kings, joined Jabin of Hazor in a northern confederacy to stop the Israelites from taking over the northern section of Canaan. He was killed in battle at the waters of Merom (Jos 11:1; 12:19).

4. Shaharaim's son by his wife Hodesh, a member of Benjamin's tribe (1 Chr 8:9).

5. Elpaal's son from Benjamin's tribe (1 Chr 8:18).

Jochebed. Amram's wife and the mother of Moses, Aaron, and Miriam (Ex 6:20; Nm 26:59). On one occasion she is identified merely as "a daughter of Levi" (Ex 2:1).

Joda. Joanan's son, the father of Josech, and a forefather of Jesus Christ living in Palestine during the postexilic era (Lk 3:26, KJV Juda, Judah).

See GENEALOGY OF JESUS CHRIST.

Joed. Descendant of Benjamin living in Jerusalem during the days of Nehemiah (Neh 11:7). His name, meaning "Jehovah is witness," does not appear in a parallel list in 1 Chronicles 9:7.

Joel (Person). 1. Levite from the family of Kohath. He was Azariah's son and an ancestor of Elkanan, the father of Samuel the prophet (1 Sm 1:1; 1 Chr 6:36).
2. Oldest son of Samuel the prophet. He and his brother Abijah so corrupted the office of judge that the elders increased their demands for a king (1 Sm 8:2–5). He was the father of Heman the singer (1 Chr 6:33; 15:17).

Monument at Ramah, 5 miles north of Jerusalem, marking the tomb of Samuel, a descendant of one Joel and the father of another Joel.

His name has been mistakenly translated "Vashni" in the KJV in 1 Chronicles 6:28.
3. Prince from one of the Simeonite families that emigrated to the valley of Gedor (1 Chr 4:35).
4. Member of Reuben's tribe (1 Chr 5:4,8,).
5. Chief of Gad's tribe residing in Bashan (1 Chr 5:12).
6. Third of Izrahiah's four named sons and a chief of Issachar's tribe in David's time (1 Chr 7:3).
7. Nathan's brother and one of David's mighty men (1 Chr 11:38). He is alternately called Igal the son of Nathan in 2 Samuel 23:36.
See IGAL #2.
8. Levite from the family of Gershon who participated in the royal procession that brought the ark of God to Jerusalem during David's reign (1 Chr 15:7,11). He may have administered the treasuries of the temple in Jerusalem (1 Chr 26:22).
9. Pedaiah's son, who acted as tribal chieftain over Manasseh's half tribe during David's reign (1 Chr 27:20).
10. Levite from the family of Kohath who assisted in King Hezekiah's reform of the temple in Jerusalem (2 Chr 29:12).
11. Nebo's son, who was encouraged by Ezra to divorce his foreign wife during the postexilic period (Ezr 10:43).
12. Zichri's son and the supervisor of postexilic Jerusalem (Neh 11:9).
13. Prophet who wrote the second book of the Minor Prophets. Little is known about him except that he was Pethuel's son (Jl 1:1; Acts 2:16).
See JOEL, BOOK OF.

Joel, Book of. OT book; second of the Minor Prophets.
Author. In the first verse the contents of the Book of Joel are described as the "message" of the Lord that "came to Joel, the son of Pethuel." We are told nothing more in Scripture about Joel or Pethuel. The name Joel was common; there are 13 different Joels in the OT. From what is said in the book it would seem that Joel was not a priest but closely associated with the priests of the temple, and in all probability a man of Jerusalem. More than that we cannot say.
Contents. *1:1–12.* A plague of locusts more devastating than any that past generations had experienced had come on the land (vv 2–4). Drinkers were summoned to see the grape vines devastated and the fig trees stripped (vv 5–7). People were called to mourn at the sight of fields laid waste—especially the priests, as they would no longer be able to bring cereal and drink offerings to the Lord

(vv 8–10). Farmers must grieve over the ruin of their harvest, in anguish at the loss of the fruits of the land (vv 11,12).

1:13–20. Because of what had happened the people were called to prayer and fasting; the priests were to come before the Lord in sackcloth, grieving that no offerings could be brought (v 13). Elders and people alike must come to the temple to pray (v 14). Such a time of crisis, with the crops lost and the sheep and cattle having no pasture, was to be seen as foreshadowing the great coming day of the Lord, for which all should prepare (vv 15–18). The prophet himself could only cry out to God at the devastation of the land (vv 19,20).

Much in this chapter and the next seems descriptive of the kind of locust plagues that are still common in lands of the Middle East and North and Central Africa. Millions of locusts may cover hundreds of square miles of land. In flight they are like a cloud above the ground, and the sound they make has been described as "less like the whirring of wings than the rattle of hail or the crackling of bush on fire." Nothing can resist their progress as they devastate field after field, stripping everything that is green, even branches of trees. It is thought that some passages in Joel 1 may speak of drought as well as the plague of locusts, but the devastation described may be simply due to the locusts.

2:1–11. Now the prophet goes on to speak of a time when God's judgment threatens the whole land. It is a time for the alarm to be sounded, when a great and powerful "people" come up on the land, a more threatening foe than any known before. Further, it is a warning of the coming "day of the Lord," "a day of darkness and gloom" (vv 1,2). The land is devastated as by fire; what was like the garden of Eden becomes a wilderness (v 3). This invasion is like that of cavalry and the sound of the insurgents like "the rumbling of chariots." Everyone is in anguish at their advance. They march like warriors, burst through the weapons, scale the walls of the city, and come into the houses like thieves (vv 4–9).

Some have taken this description to be a picture of armies of nations who are the foes of Israel, used by the Lord in judgment on his own people. But in that they are described as "like war horses" and their noise like "the rumbling of chariots," their advance "like a powerful army drawn up for battle," it seems that the locust plague is still in mind. Yet the dark cloud of the locusts in the sky and their terrible effect on the land foreshadows the great day when the Lord will speak and act in judgment on all peoples. Then heaven and earth will tremble; sun, moon, and stars will be darkened (vv 10,11).

2:12–17. The prophet repeatedly calls the people to the Lord in humility and penitence so that his mercy and grace may be found. Then it will be possible to have "grain and wine" to offer to the Lord as before (vv 12–14). A fast is to be appointed, a solemn assembly of young and old called. Even the newlyweds are to come. The priests must lead the people in prayer to God to spare his people (vv 14–17).

2:18–27. It seems that the people did turn to God as the prophet required; in response he had compassion on them and assured them of his renewal of their grain, wine, and oil, and the removal of their reproach (vv 18,19). The "armies from the north" would retreat, and God would restore the pastures of the land, its fruit trees and its vines (vv 20–22). The people would rejoice, and with the blessing of the early and later rains the land would again be abundantly productive. The losses from the locust plague would be made good (vv 23–25). People would eat food in plenty and praise God. They would know that the one great living God was among them, and they would not be put to shame any more (vv 26,27).

2:28–32. The prophet also saw that the blessing experienced in this renewal after the plague of locusts foreshadowed greater blessings to come, just as the judgment experienced brought the warning of the great and terrible day of the Lord to come. God would do greater things for his people in the future; in particular he would pour out his Spirit on men and women, young and old, slave and free (vv 28,29). There would be awe-inspiring signs in heaven and on earth (vv 30,31), but all who called on the name of the Lord would know his salvation (v 32).

3:1–15. The meaning of the day of the Lord for Israel as a nation and its significance for all nations must be realized. God's people in turning to him would find restoration; those who had scattered them, taken their land, and sold them as slaves would come under his judgment (vv 1–3). Tyre and Sidon and the Philistines especially would have to give account for what they had done, taking the Lord's silver and gold, removing his people from their land, and selling them as slaves to the Greeks. The sons and daughters of these slave traders would in turn be sold as slaves (vv 4–8). So the nations must be prepared for war—to melt their plowshares into swords and to beat pruning hooks into spears—but not for a battle between human armies. Those who have fought against the living God must reckon with him as mighty warrior (vv 9–11). He is also judge, and so the figure changes from the battleground to the court of justice. Great crowds will stand before the Lord "in the valley of decision" on the day of the Lord, which is a day of dread darkness for those who have made themselves enemies of the Almighty (vv 12–15).

3:16–21. After men have spoken and done their worst, God will speak and act. He will show himself to be his people's "refuge and strength" (v 16). Their city will then be kept from invasion by strangers (v 17). Their land will be wonderfully productive (v 18). Because of what Egypt and Edom have done in violence to Judah, they will be desolate (v 19). Israel will be avenged and restored, and to all it will be clear that the Lord's home is in Jerusalem with his people (vv 20,21).

This account of the contents of the book is based on the view that Joel experienced a plague of locusts in his day and that he saw this as a warning of a greater judgment of God to come. At the same time, he also spoke of a greater restoration and blessing when the people turned back to God with prayer and fasting. Others see the enemies throughout the book as human foes, at least in chapter 2. Some think of the whole book as prophetic of battles to come, and in particular of a final battle of the Lord against those who have made themselves his enemies. Some think of two prophets, or two parts of the book written at different times. But the view of the book taken above seems exposed to the fewest difficulties and makes good sense and meaning of the whole.

Date. Many different views of the date of Joel have been taken by those who have studied this book carefully; thus it is difficult to be dogmatic. Most likely, however, the book is to be dated to a time after the return to Jerusalem of the Jewish exiles who had been in Babylon; more precisely, after Nehemiah's work of rebuilding the walls of Jerusalem (*c.* 400 BC.) Reasons may be given in support of this as follows:

(1) 3:2 says that the people of Judah and Jerusalem had been scattered among the nations and their land divided up; but they have been brought back, and their city once again has its walls (2:9).

(2) When a call is issued to prayer and fasting, the priests and elders are to give the lead (1:13; 2:16,17). There is no mention of a king at any point in the book. There were kings until the time of the exile, but not for 400 years after it.

(3) The preexilic prophets—Amos, Hosea, Isaiah, Micah, and Jeremiah—were often critical of the people for offering sacrifices while in their daily lives they departed from the ways of the Lord. Postexilic prophets like Haggai and Malachi offer encouragement and deep concern for the offering of sacrifices. In the preexilic prophets there was constant rebuke

of the people for their worship of idols; this was not so much a besetting sin of the people after the exile. In both these concerns Joel seems to fit better the postexilic than the preexilic scene.

(4) There is no reference to the northern kingdom of Israel in this book. Much is said of Judah and Jerusalem; when "Israel" is spoken of, the reference seems to be to the same people (2:27; 3:16). We would expect to find a different way of speaking before the fall of the northern kingdom to the Assyrians in 722 BC.

(5) The other kingdoms referred to are Edom, Tyre and Sidon, the Philistines, and the Greeks. There is no mention of Syria, Assyria, and Babylonia, the inveterate enemies from whom the people suffered so much in preexilic days. Those mentioned were certainly significant to the people in postexilic times, and only then are the Greeks of importance on the Palestinian scene.

(6) There are many close similarities between Joel and other OT books (see below). If Joel was earlier than these other prophets, we must say that Joel's words were taken up by his successors more than were the words of any other prophet. More likely it seems that Joel was a man whose mind was saturated with the utterances of prophets who went before him.

Some feel that there is no great strength in these arguments and that everything in the book can be made to fit a much earlier date. It has sometimes been argued that the book is placed deliberately in the Hebrew Scriptures alongside the two 8th-century prophets Hosea and Amos. But the order of the books in the prophetic canon does not determine their date. The postexilic Obadiah stands between the 8th-century prophets Amos and Micah, and in fact in the Greek OT Joel was placed in a different position from its place in the Hebrew Bible. Most likely Joel and Amos stand together, as Amos 1:2 has the same words found at the close of the Book of Joel (3:16). Some of those who favor a preexilic date for the book place it in the 9th century, in the early period of the reign of Joash when the king was too young to actually function as ruler of the land. Others place it sometime shortly before the death of Josiah in 609 because of the reference to the enemy coming from the north (as in Jeremiah) and because of the appeal to the people (like Jeremiah's appeal) to return to the Lord with all their hearts (2:12).

Joel and the Prophets Before Him. It is probable that Joel knew the prophecies that had been uttered before him, and in the light of these he read the signs of his times and spoke of the future. It is worth following carefully the parallels between Joel and other OT books, whatever significance we may be led to attach to them.

Amos 1:2 and Joel 3:16 are identical: "The Lord roars from Zion, and utters his voice from Jerusalem." Both Amos 9:13 and Joel 3:18 say how "the mountains shall drip sweet wine."

Obadiah has striking similarities with Joel. Joel 1:15 and 2:1 say, as Obadiah 15, "The day of the Lord is near." Obadiah 17 says that "in Mount Zion there shall be those that escape; Joel 2:32 reads "in Mount Zion and in Jerusalem there shall be those who escape" and adds, perhaps consciously referring to an earlier prophecy, "as the Lord has said." Obadiah 15 says, "Your deeds shall return on your own head," while in Joel 3:4,7 we have the word of the Lord, "I will requite your deed upon your own head." Obadiah 10 speaks of the consequences of "violence done to your brother Jacob," and Joel 3:19 rather similarly of "violence done to the people of Judah." Obadiah 11 speaks of the way that "foreigners entered his gates and cast lots for Jerusalem," and Joel 3:3 of those whom the Lord says "cast lots for my people." These parallels with the Book of Obadiah hardly seem accidental.

With the Book of Malachi there are two quite close parallels. Both Joel 2:31 and Malachi 4:5 speak of what must take place "before the great and terrible day of the Lord comes." Joel 2:11 says, "The day of the Lord is great and very terrible; who can endure it?" while Malachi 3:2 asks, "Who can endure the day of his coming?"

Then there are sections of the Book of Isaiah with close parallels in Joel. Most significant is Isaiah 13, speaking as it does of the downfall of Babylon in the mighty judgment of God. "Wail, for the day of the Lord is near; as destruction from the Almighty it will come!" is almost identical to Joel 1:15. In Isaiah 13:10,13 the signs of the great judgment of God are: "The stars of the heavens and their constellations will not give their light; the sun will be dark at its rising and the moon will not shed its light," and, "I will make the heavens tremble, and the earth will be shaken out of its place." Joel 2:10 puts it, "The earth quakes before them, the heavens tremble. The sun and the moon are darkened, and the stars withdraw their shining," and 3:15 speaks similarly of sun, moon, and stars not giving their light.

Joel 3:10 speaks of beating plowshares into swords and pruning hooks into spears, the opposite of that blessing of peace of which Isaiah 2:4 (and its equivalent in Mi 4:3) speaks. There is a similar pair of opposites in Isaiah 51:3, which speaks of the Lord comforting Zion and making "her wilderness like Eden, her desert like the garden of the Lord," and Joel 2:3, where it is said that "the land is like the garden of the Lord before" the plague of locusts, "but after them a desolate wilderness." Joel 2:27 gives the declaration of the Lord, "You shall know that I am in the midst of Israel, and that I, the Lord, am your God and there is none else," a declaration paralleled in such passages as Isaiah 45:5,6,22 and 46:9. There is a parallel in Isaiah 66:18 to Joel's speaking of the Lord's gathering of all the nations (3:2).

The gathering of the nations is not peculiar to Isaiah 66 and the Book of Joel. Zephaniah 3:8 speaks of a similar gathering, and that prophet (1:14), like Joel, speaks of "the great day of the Lord" as "near." Zephaniah parallels Joel more precisely, however, when he goes on to say that it will be "a day of darkness and gloom, a day of clouds and thick darkness" (v 15). Amos (5:18) gave warning in general terms that the day of the Lord would prove to be a day of darkness and not of light, but between the words of Joel (2:2) and Zephaniah (1:15) there is an identity of words in the original language.

The theme of the Lord's gathering of the nations is similarly developed in Zechariah 14; and a further parallel is to be noted between Zechariah 14:8, which speaks of "living waters" flowing out from Jerusalem, and Joel 3:18, speaking of "a fountain" coming forth "from the house of the Lord" to "water the valley of Shittim" (cf. also Ez 47:1).

Other prophetic books have parallels which, though not extensive, are significant. Both Nahum 2:10 and Joel 2:6 speak of the way that "all faces grow pale" and people are in "anguish" at what God is doing. Joel 2:19, like Hosea 2:22, speaks of the "grain, wine, and oil" (both in that order) which the Lord is again giving to his people.

Jeremiah 50:4,20 has an expression strikingly identical with Joel 3:1, "in those days and at that time." Like Joel (3:9), Jeremiah (6:4) speaks of preparing war, literally "sanctifying" war, making holy preparation for it. Joel (2:20) speaks of the hostile threat to Judah, which later in God's mercy was removed, as "the northerner," perhaps because Jeremiah (e.g., in 1:13–15; 4:6; and 6:1,22) spoke so much of the foe coming from the north against the Lord's people.

Ezekiel (e.g., 38:6,15; 39:2) also spoke of the foe advancing on Judah from the north, and there are other striking similarities between his prophecies and those of Joel. Ezekiel (30:2,3) is told to proclaim, "Wail, 'Alas for the day!' For the day is near, the day of the Lord is near; it will be a day of clouds, a time of doom for the nations" (cf. Jl 2:1,2). Joel (3:2) and Ezekiel (17:20) both speak of God "entering into judgment" with his people, but also of the Lord pouring out his Spirit upon men (Jl 2:28; Ez 39:29).

Finally, it is to be noted that there are parallels between Joel and other parts of the OT besides the prophets. The reproach of Israel among the nations in the time of the judgment of God's people was "Where is their God?" (Jl 2:17); this has a parallel in Micah 7:10 but more conspicuously in a number of the psalms (e.g., 42:10; 79:10; 115:2). Similarly the words of Joel 2:13 that speak of the Lord as "gracious and merciful, slow to anger, and abounding in steadfast love" and as repenting of evil are paralleled in Jonah 4:2 and in Exodus 34:6 (see also Pss 103:8; 145:88).

These parallels do not argue decisively for a verbal dependence of one prophet on another; still less do they permit us to argue dogmatically the direction of the dependence. Sometimes the language may be that used frequently not only by prophets but by other people as well. But taken all together these parallels at least point to a consensus in the preaching of the OT messengers of the Lord. There was a proclamation common to a number of the prophets of what would happen in the great coming day of the Lord and how people should prepare for it. Many of the prophets shared in challenging the people to return to the Lord their God and find his grace and mercy, restoring them and taking away their reproach among the nations.

Yet at some points the wording is so close that it is hard to escape the conclusion that either later prophets have a knowledge of Joel (thus to be dated very early among the prophets), or Joel alludes to and quotes the prophets who were before him. The greater probability of the latter, along with the reasons given above for placing Joel as a prophet of postexilic times, suggest that we should see Joel as one of the great messengers of the Lord, whose word, received from God, was often mediated by and under the influence of the prophetic utterances to Israel in former times. This would say something of significance also about the preservation and use of the messages of earlier prophets in the generations before they came to be gathered together and canonized in what we call the OT.

Message. What can be said finally of the abiding significance of the message of Joel? His, like that of most of the OT prophets, was a message of mercy and judgment. Such a catastrophe as a plague of locusts was a warning of God's judgment of all men and nations, within history and ultimately at the great day of the Lord at the consummation of history, when all will be gathered before him. The message of Joel, with its challenge to repentance

arising from the events of his time, can be set alongside the words of Jesus himself when he was asked about those who had suffered in the catastrophic events of his time. When asked whether they were worse sinners than others, he answered in the negative, but with the warning, "Unless you repent, you will all of you come to the same end" (Lk 13:1–5 NEB). The word of God through Joel called people to turn back to him to find his mercy; then to the assurance of mercy was added the hope of the greater things that God in his goodness would do. He would pour out his Spirit freely on all. These words of promise (2:28), made more significant than any others in the Book of Joel by their quotation in the NT in Peter's sermon on the day of Pentecost (Acts 2:16–21), stand true for the Christian church ever since that beginning of their fulfilment; and with them stands Joel's great assurance that God makes his home in the midst of his people and that those who turn to him will never be ashamed.

FRANCIS FOULKES

See ISRAEL, HISTORY OF; PROPHECY; PROPHET, PROPHETESS.

Bibliography. L.C. Allen, *The Books of Joel, Obadiah, Jonah, and Micah*; S.R. Driver, *Joel and Amos*; C.F. Keil, *Biblical Commentary on the OT: The Twelve Minor Prophets*, vol 1; G.A. Smith, *The Book of the Twelve Prophets*, vol 2; C. von Orelli, *The Twelve Minor Prophets*.

Joelah. Warrior who joined David at Ziklag in his struggle against King Saul. Joelah was one of David's ambidextrous archers and slingers (1 Chr 12:7).

Joezer. Warrior who joined David at Ziklag in his struggle against King Saul. He was one of David's ambidextrous archers and slingers (1 Chr 12:6). Korahite probably refers to a place of origin.

Jogbehah. City in Gilead (Transjordan) built and fortified by Gad's tribe (Nm 32:35). During the period of the judges, Gideon, in his pursuit of the Midianites, circled to the east of Jogbehah in order to attack the unsuspecting camp of Midian at Karkor (Jgs 8:11). This ancient city is now identified with Khirbet el-Ajbeihat, seven miles northwest of Amman.

Jogli. Father of Bukki, a Danite leader who helped oversee the distribution of the Promised Land west of the Jordan River (Nm 34:22).

Joha. 1. Benjamite and one of Beriah's six sons (1 Chr 8:16).

2. Tizite, the brother of Jediael and one of David's mighty men (1 Chr 11:45).

Johanan. Name meaning "Yahweh has been gracious." It occurs in the alternate form of

Jehohanan. The name John is derived from these names. Several men of this name appear in the OT.

1. Son of Kareah (2 Kgs 25:23). Johanan was a Jewish leader, a contemporary of Jeremiah, and supportive of Gedaliah, the governor of Judah after the fall of Jerusalem (Jer 40:8,13). He forewarned Gedaliah of Ishmael's plan to assassinate him (Jer 40:13–16). When the warning was ignored and Johanan was refused permission to execute the would-be assassin, Gedaliah was murdered. Johanan took vengeance against Ishmael and rescued those who had been captured (41:14–18), but was unable to pursue Ishmael. In fear of a Babylonian reprisal he made plans to seek asylum in Egypt. Jeremiah, whom he consulted, gave God's word against this move (42:1–22), but Johanan was unwilling to take counsel (43:2,3). He led the Judeans, including Jeremiah and Baruch, to Egypt (43:5–7).

2. Eldest son of Josiah, king of Judah (1 Chr 3:15). He did not succeed his father on his throne, even though he was the firstborn.

3. Son of Elioenai (1 Chr 3:24), a descendant of Jehoiakim, one of the last kings of Judah.

4. Grandson of Ahima-az. He was the son of Azariah, who served as priest in the temple of Solomon (1 Chr 6:9,10).

5. Warrior from Benjamin's tribe. He joined David's 30 special forces at Ziklag (1 Chr 12:4). The special forces could shoot arrows and sling stones with either hand (v 2).

6. Gadite who joined David in the wilderness (1 Chr 12:12). He was also specially trained for war, in that he could handle both shield and spear, could take hardships, and was quick on his feet (v 8).

7. Ephraimite. His son was a leader of the Ephraimites during the regime of Pekah and protested against the enslavement of 200,000 Judeans (2 Chr 28:12), who were subsequently freed.

8. Son of Hakkatan ("the younger" or "the smaller"). The designation may be read as "Johanan the younger." He was a head of a family that claimed their descent from Azgad (Ezr 8:12). He joined Ezra with 110 men from Babylonia to Judah.

9. Priest under Joiakim. He was one of the priests during whose ministry the Levites and priests formally registered (Neh 12:22). He is alternately called Jehohanan in Ezra 10:6 (KJV Johanan).

See JEHOHANAN #4.

10. KJV spelling of Jehohanan, Tobiah's son, in Nehemiah 6:18.

See JEHOHANAN #6.

Johanan Ben Zakkai.
Leading Jewish sage at the end of the second temple period. His place of birth is not known; he went to Jerusalem to study, and after 18 years there spent some time in Galilee. Later he returned to Jerusalem and taught "in the shadow of the temple." He encouraged the Pharisees among the priesthood rather than the Sadducees. During the siege of Jerusalem he managed to leave, in a coffin according to one version. He was a prisoner of Vespasian, probably in AD 68, who gave him leave to settle in Jamnia. There he began quietly to lay the groundwork for the survival of Judaism without its temple.

See JUDAISM; PHARISEES.

John (Person).
1. Father of Simon Peter and Andrew (Jn 1:40,42; 21:15–17). According to Matthew 16:17, Peter's father was named Jona (Jonas, Jonah). Either Jona was an alternate form of the name John or, more probably, two independent traditions existed regarding his name.

2. Member of the high priestly family who, along with Annas, Caiaphas, and Alexander, questioned Peter and John after the two apostles had healed a lame man (Acts 4:6).

3. According to the early church bishop Papias, a member of the larger group of Jesus' disciples outside the 12 (cf. Lk 10:1). Known as "John the elder" (the presbyter), he is often credited with the authorship of 2 and 3 John (2 Jn 1; 3 Jn 1), although the term "elder" there may refer to John the apostle.

See JOHN THE APOSTLE, LIFE AND WRITINGS OF; JOHN THE BAPTIST; MARK, JOHN.

John, Gospel of.

Author. At the end of this Gospel we are told that it was written by "the disciple whom Jesus loved" (Jn 21:20,24), but unfortunately the book nowhere tells us who this disciple was. Evidence shows that the most probable identification is with the beloved disciple, the apostle John. He fills the place we would have expected John to fill from what we know from the other Gospels.

The Gospel appears to have been written by one who knew the Jews and the Palestine of Jesus' day well. He is familiar with Jewish messianic expectations (e.g., Jn 1:20,21; 4:25; 7:40–42; 12:34). He knows of the hostility between Jews and Samaritans (4:9) and the contempt the Pharisees had for "the people of the land" (7:49). He knows of the importance attached to the religious schools (7:15). He knows the way the sabbath is observed and is aware of the provision that the obligation to circumcise on the eighth day overrides the sabbath regulations (7:22,23). Throughout the Gospel he moves with certainty in the vast range of Jewish ideas and customs.

It is the same with topography. The writer mentions many places, and his place-names

Storage jar from Cana, where—as John records—Jesus' first miracle occurred.

all seem to be used correctly. He refers to Cana, a village not mentioned in any earlier literature known to us, which means that the reference almost certainly came from someone who actually knew the place. He locates Bethany with some precision as about 15 stadia from Jerusalem (i.e., about 2 miles, 11:18). He has several references to places in or near Jerusalem, such as Bethesda (5:2), Siloam (9:7), and the Kidron (18:1). Of course, this does not rule out some contemporary of John's, but it makes it difficult to think of the author as a much later individual writing at a distance from Palestine. As B.F. Westcott argued in the late 19th century, the evidence as we have it indicates that the writer was a Jew of the Palestine of Jesus' day.

To many students it seems that the Gospel bears the stamp of an eyewitness. For example, Jesus was teaching "in the treasury" (8:20). Nothing is made of the point; the incident could easily have been told without it. It looks like a reminiscence of someone who sees the scene in his mind's eye as he writes. The fact that the house was filled with fragrance when the woman broke the perfume jar (12:3) does not materially affect the account but is the kind of detail that one who was there would remember. The author notes that the loaves used in the feeding of the multitude were of barley (6:9), that Jesus' tunic was without seam, woven in one piece from the top to bottom (19:23). He tells us that the branches with which Jesus was greeted were palm branches (12:13), and that it was night when Judas went out (13:30). Such touches are found throughout the Gospel, and it seems unjustified to treat them as no more than an attempt to create verisimilitude. They seem much more like indications that the author was writing about events in which he had himself taken part.

The early church seems to have accepted Johannine authorship without question. Irenaeus, Clement of Alexandria, and Tertullian all see the apostle as the author. The first to quote this Gospel by name was Theophilus of Antioch, about AD 180.

Those who object to Johannine authorship emphasize the differences between this Gospel and the Synoptics. The argument is that if Jesus was anything like the Christ portrayed by Matthew, Mark, and Luke, he could not be like the Christ of the fourth Gospel. This is a completely subjective argument, ignoring the fact that any great man will appear differently to different people. The judgment of the church throughout the centuries has been that Jesus was large enough to inspire both portraits. To put the same point another way, we have no reason for holding that the first three Evangelists tell us all there is to know about Jesus. There is no contradiction. John simply brings out other aspects of Jesus' life and teaching.

While we cannot prove beyond all doubt that John the apostle was the author, we can say that there is more reason for holding to this view than to any other.

Date, Origin, and Destination. It has been usual for conservatives and liberals alike to date this writing in the last decade of the 1st century or early in the 2nd. Some liberal scholars have put it well into the 2nd century, but this is not common, and it is remarkable that there has been such a considerable measure of agreement.

It is said that this Gospel is dependent on the Synoptics, which means that it must be dated some time after them. Again it is often urged that there is a very developed theology in John and that therefore we must allow time for the development. But the first of these arguments has been widely abandoned in recent times. There is so much in John that is without parallel in the other three Gospels, and conversely so much in the other three that John might have used had he known it, that it is very difficult indeed to hold that this writer had any of the other Gospels before him when he wrote, or even that he had read them. Such resemblances as there are seem better explained by common use of oral tradition.

Nor is the argument from theological development any stronger. Granted that the theology of this Gospel is profound, this does not require that we must wait for it until the end of the 1st century. The theology of the Letter to the Romans is also profound, and there is no reason for dating that writing later than the 50s. On the ground of development there is no reason for putting John later than Romans. Development is a slippery argument at best, for it usually takes place at uneven rates; and even if it be conceded that there is developed theology in this writing, we have no means of knowing how fast development took place in the area from which it came.

Other arguments for a late date are no more conclusive. For example, it is urged that the ecclesiastical system presupposed by the Gospel is too late for the time of the apostle John, and that the sacramental system of John 3 and 6 must have taken time to develop. But John does not mention any sacrament. It is true that many scholars think these chapters refer to baptism and the Lord's Supper, but the fact is that John mentions neither.

It is not surprising in view of the way the traditional arguments have crumbled away that many in recent times are arguing that John must have been written before the fall of Jerusalem in AD 70. If it were later, why does not John have some reference to it? Some of his language appears to be earlier. Thus in 5:2 he says there "is" (not "was") a pool called Bethesda. Again, he often refers to the 12 as Jesus' disciples, or "his" disciples, or the like. In later times Christians usually said "the" disciples, for they saw no need to say whose the disciples were. But in the early days, when Christians were in contact with rabbis (each of whom had his disciples), it was important to show which disciples were in mind. It is important also that John makes no reference to any of the synoptic Gospels. The simplest explanation is that he had not seen them. They were not yet widely circulated.

None of this enables us to date this Gospel with precision. But the weight of evidence points to an early date (before 70 AD).

The author was John the apostle. However, the writing gives evidence of contact with Greek thought, for example, in the reference to Christ as "the Word" in chapter 1 and the translation of words like "rabbi" (1:38). It is almost universally held that such considerations compel us to see the work as originating in a center of Greek culture, and Ephesus has been traditionally favored. Before the end of the second century we have Irenaeus writing that John published the Gospel during his residence at Ephesus.

Some scholars point to similarities between John and the Odes of Solomon, which they think came from Syria. As there are also some resemblances in the language of Ignatius, bishop of Antioch in the early 2nd century, this is held to show that John was written in Syria, probably at Antioch. Others again think that Egypt was the place, and they support this by

pointing out that the oldest fragment of a manuscript of this Gospel was found there. There is no real evidence, and we are left with probabilities. There is most to be said for accepting the evidence of Irenaeus and seeing Ephesus as the place of origin, but we can scarcely say more.

There is no real indication of the intended destination. From 20:31 we learn that the book was written that the readers might believe that Jesus is the Messiah, God's Son, and that believing they might have life. The Gospel, then, has an evangelistic aim. But it is also possible that "believe" means "keep on believing," "go on in faith," rather than "begin to believe." That is to say, the book may have been meant from the beginning to build people up in the faith. Probably we should not distinguish these aims too sharply. Both may well be in mind.

Background. Several possible backgrounds to the Gospel have been suggested. The Greek interest is obvious, and this writing has sometimes been called the Gospel of the Hellenists. The suggestion is that we should look to Greek writings, perhaps the works of the philosophers or Philo of Alexandria, to find the right background against which to understand what John has written. This approach may be seen in the work of Rudolf Bultmann, who thought specifically of Gnosticism. Indeed for Bultmann one of the sources of this Gospel was a discourse source that he thought was taken from non-Christian Gnosticism. Not many have been prepared to follow Bultmann, but a number of recent commentators have discerned some form of Gnosticism as the backdrop to John.

While such views are put forward seriously, there are some substantial objections. One is that, despite the confident assertions of some scholars, Gnosticism has never been shown to be earlier than Christianity. In the form in which it comes before us in history it is a Christian heresy, and, of course, the Christian faith must appear before a Christian heresy is possible. Another objection is that there is a basic difference between the two systems. Gnosticism is concerned with knowledge (the very word is derived from the Greek word *gnosis*, "knowledge"). Its "redeemer" is one who comes from heaven with knowledge. But John does not subscribe to the view that man is saved by knowledge. The Redeemer comes to take away the sin of the world (1:29). Gnosticism tells man the way he is to struggle upward; Christianity tells of a Savior who came down to raise him. It is not easy to see any form of Gnosticism as the essential background to Christianity.

Much more significant is John's Semitic

background. Especially important here is the OT, accepted as sacred Scripture by Jew and Christian alike. It lies constantly behind John's statements, and it must be studied carefully if John is to be understood. It is plain that John knew and loved the Septuagint, the translation into Greek of the Hebrew OT. Again and again the Septuagint can be shown to lie behind what John says.

In modern times important discoveries have been made at Qumran, in the vicinity of the Dead Sea. Among the scrolls unearthed in the caves of this area are several that have affinities with John. Indeed, one of the interesting facts about the scrolls is that they have more parallels with John than with any other part of the NT, a fact difficult to explain if John was written late and at a distance from Palestine. The resemblances to the Qumran writings must be viewed with care, for there is often a linguistic resemblance where the thinking is quite different. For example, both use the unusual expression "the Spirit of truth." But where John means one of the persons of the Trinity, the scrolls speak of "a spirit of truth" and "a spirit of error" striving in the souls of men. The connection is real, but John is clearly not dependent on the scrolls for his thinking. The contribution of the Dead Sea Scrolls is that they afford additional evidence that this Gospel is basically Palestinian and must be understood against a background of first-century Palestine.

Other backgrounds have been suggested, such as the Hermetic literature. This is a group of writings attributed to Hermes Trismegistus ("Hermes Thrice-greatest"), a designation of the Egyptian god Thoth. There are indeed some points of contact with John, but they are few in comparison with those of writing rooted in Palestine. It is difficult to take such suggestions seriously. John is essentially Palestinian.

Purpose and Theological Teaching. The writer tells us that Jesus did many "signs" (or miracles) that he has not recorded, but "these are written that you may believe that Jesus is the Christ, the Son of God, and that believing you may have life in his name" (Jn 20:31). John writes to show that Jesus is the Messiah. But he does not do this simply with a view to conveying interesting information. He wants his readers to see this knowledge as a challenge to faith; when they believe, they will have life. John seeks to bring men and women to Christ; he has an evangelistic aim. That does not exhaust what he is trying to do, for his words have meaning for believers. It is important that believers have a right knowledge of Jesus and that they continue to believe. Building up the faithful will not be out of

John's mind. But his primary purpose, according to his own words, is evangelistic.

The main theological teaching of this Gospel, then, is that God has sent his Messiah, Jesus. He is the very Son of God, and he comes to bring life (3:16). Though Jesus told the woman at the well that he was the Messiah, this is not often said in exact terms. The avoidance of the term might well be because of the political overtones it had acquired among the Jews at large. They looked for a Messiah who would fight the Romans. He would defeat them and set up a mighty world empire with its capital in Jerusalem. Jesus was not aiming at anything like that, and it was important that he avoid the kind of language that would give that impression. But though the conventional messianic terminology is avoided, John leaves no doubt that Jesus was God's chosen one. Again and again he depicts Jesus as fulfilling messianic functions. For example, in the long discourse in chapter 6 we see Jesus as the bread from heaven, fulfilling the expectation that when Messiah came, he would renew the manna; and in the giving of sight to the blind man (ch 9) we have another messianic function (Is 35:5).

With this greatness of Jesus, John also combines teaching about his lowliness. A continuing, though unobtrusive, strand of Johannine teaching is that Jesus depends on the Father for everything. Apart from the Father, Jesus said, he could do nothing (5:30). His very food is to do the Father's will (4:34). He lives through the Father (6:57). It is the Father who gives him his disciples (6:37,44; 17:6). It is the Father who bears witness to him (5:32,37). John insists that Jesus is in no sense independent of the Father. In the mission of Jesus, John sees the working out of the purpose of the Father.

Content. *Prologue.* John begins with a prologue (1:1–18) that is unlike anything in any of the other Gospels. In it he refers to Jesus as "the Word," a term that has points of contact with both Greek and Hebrew thinking. As John uses it, it conveys the thought that Jesus is the expression of the mind of the Father. John speaks of the Word as God (1:1), sees him as active in creation (1:3–5), goes on to the witness borne to him by John the Baptist (1:6–8), speaks of the coming of the Word into the world (1:9–14), and finishes with a section on the greatness of the Word (1:15–18). In this prologue he briefly introduces some of the great themes that will be developed throughout the Gospel. It is a majestic introduction to the whole.

Next we have the beginnings of Jesus' public ministry (1:19–51). Jesus' work was preceded by that of John the Baptist, and the

Evangelist tells us first about the kind of witness that the Baptist bore to Jesus. Witness is one of his important concepts, and witness is all that John the Baptist does in this Gospel. From this witness we move to the way the first disciples came to Jesus. We learn something of how Andrew and Peter came to know the Lord. We read also of Philip and Nathanael, of whom we learn little or nothing in the other Gospels.

The Signs and Discourses. The public ministry of Jesus is described in a very distinctive way in this Gospel. John has a long section (2:1–12:50) in which he tells of a number of miracles Jesus did, interweaving into his account a series of discourses. Sometimes these are addresses given to groups of people, and sometimes they are talks with individuals. Some scholars call this section of the Gospel the Book of Signs, thus emphasizing the prominent place given to seven miracles. For John they are not simply wonders. They are meaningful; in the literal sense of the term they are *sign*ificant.

The first of them is the turning of the water into wine at a marriage in Cana of Galilee (2:1–11). The water in question is connected with Jewish rites of purification (2:6), and the story is surely to teach us that Jesus transforms life. He changes the water of the law into the wine of the gospel. As a result of this "sign" his disciples "believed on him" (2:11). John goes on to tell how Jesus went up to Jerusalem and drove the traders out of the temple. They were selling animals for sacrifice and changing money. But their business was being done in the court of the Gentiles, the only place in the temple where a Gentile could come to meditate and pray.

The first discourse is on the new birth (3:1–21). Jesus talked with Nicodemus, a leading Pharisee, about the necessity for radical renewal if one is to enter the kingdom. Jesus is speaking of God's regenerating activity, not some human reformation. This leads to a dispute some of John's disciples had with a Jew on the subject of purification and opens the way to further teaching about Jesus.

The second discourse is really a long conversation Jesus had with a woman of Samaria, whom he met by a well (4:1–42). It turns on "the water of life," a term which is not fully explained in this chapter, but which we later find points to the work of the Holy Spirit (7:39). This leads to the story of the second sign, the healing of the nobleman's son (4:46–54), notable for the fact that Jesus healed at a distance.

The third sign is the healing of the lame man by the pool of Bethesda (5:1–18). This man had spent years waiting for healing at the moving of the water. Jesus told him to get up and walk, and he did. Because it was done on a sabbath, the Pharisees objected, and this leads to Jesus' third discourse, that on the divine Son (5:19–47). Here the closeness of the relationship of Jesus to the Father is stressed, and his place in the judgment is brought out. There is emphasis also on the variety of witness borne to Jesus, which shows how reasonable it is to accept him as God's own Son.

John's fourth sign is the one miracle (apart from the resurrection) found in all four Gospels, the feeding of the five thousand (6:1–15). It is followed by Jesus' walking on water (6:16–21), which seems to be meant as the fifth sign (though some scholars think not; if they are right, there are only six signs). Then comes the fourth discourse, the great sermon on the bread of life (6:22–59). Jesus is this bread, and he gives it to men and women. There are references to eating his flesh and drinking his blood (6:50–58), which point to his death. Some have seen in them a reference to communion, but it is hard to see why Jesus should refer in this way to an as-yet nonexistent sacrament. Moreover, much the same effect is attributed in the same discourse to believing (e.g., vv 35,47). It seems best to understand Jesus as meaning that people must believe in him as the one who would die for them.

There is a section detailing Peter's affirmation of loyalty in the face of some who drifted away from the Master (6:67–71). Then we come to the fifth discourse, on the life-giving Spirit (7:1–52). John has an important explanatory point of his own when he tells us that at that time the Spirit had not been given because Jesus had not yet been glorified (7:39). The fullness of the Spirit depends on the completion of the work of Christ in his death and resurrection.

The sixth discourse tells of the light of the world (8:12–59). This aspect of Jesus' person and ministry is dramatically brought out in the sixth sign, the healing of the man born blind (9:1–41). It is a lively narrative, as the healed man conducts a spirited defense against the Pharisees who wished to belittle Jesus.

One of the most beautiful of all the illustrations of Jesus' relations to his people is that on which he dwells in the seventh discourse, where he speaks of himself as the good shepherd (10:1–41). There is the obvious truth that sheep depend entirely on their shepherd, but Jesus says something else. Whereas earthly shepherds live to meet the needs of their sheep, Jesus lays down his life for his own.

The final sign is the raising of Lazarus (11:1–44), a man who had been dead for four days. The story graphically brings out Jesus'

Speaking of himself as the good shepherd of the sheep, Jesus said that he goes "before them, and the sheep follow him, for they know his voice" (Jn 10:4).

power over death and his readiness to confer the gift of life. Jesus speaks of himself as "the resurrection and the life" (11:25); death cannot defeat him. He brings life to the dead, to the spiritually dead as well as to physically dead Lazarus. John goes on to note the reaction to this miracle: some believed, but some opposed Jesus (11:45–57). He includes a notable saying of Caiaphas, the high priest, that one man should die for the people (11:50–52). Caiaphas was speaking as a cynical politician (better one dead, however innocent, than trouble for the nation). But John sees in the words the deeper meaning that Jesus' death would bring salvation to many.

John rounds off his account of the ministry with the story of the anointing of Jesus by a woman in Bethany, the triumphal entry into Jerusalem, the coming of some Greeks to Jesus, and his final summary (ch 12). He cites prophecy to show why some had not believed in Jesus. Clearly he discerns the working out of God's purpose in all Jesus does.

The Last Supper. The account of what went on in the upper room on the night before the crucifixion is the fullest of all the four Gospels. Curiously, John says nothing about the institution of communion, a fact that has never been satisfactorily explained. But he tells us how Jesus washed the feet of the disciples (13:1–17), an action splendidly exemplifying the spirit of lowly service so soon to be shown on the cross. Then comes the prophecy of the betrayal and the giving of the sop to Judas, an action which set in motion the events that would lead to the cross (13:18–30).

In the long discourse that follows, Jesus dealt with some questions posed by his followers and went on to teach them some important truths—for example, that he is the way, the truth, and the life (14:6). He develops the thought that he is the true vine, the disciples being related to him as branches to the vine. It is important for the branches to remain in the vine if they are to have life (15:1–16). Then come some words about suffering that would be of help to them in times of persecution (15:17–25). Jesus goes on to speak about the Holy Spirit (15:26–16:15). This is a very important passage, for it contains much more about the Spirit than we find elsewhere in Jesus' words. Jesus calls the Spirit the "Paraclete," a title not easy to understand. It is in origin a legal term, and at least we can say that it indicates that the Spirit brings friendship and help. Jesus goes on to speak of his approaching departure from the disciples and to prepare them for the trying time ahead (16:16–33). This part of the Gospel concludes with Jesus' great high priestly prayer. He prays for the disciples to be one, as he commends them to the care of the heavenly Father (ch 17).

The Cross and Resurrection. When the soldiers came to arrest Jesus, he went forward to meet them and they fell to the ground (18:1–11). At the outset of his passion narrative, John is making the point that Jesus is sovereign. He is not being defeated by the march of events but is sovereignly doing the will of the Father. John is the only one to tell us that Jesus was taken before Annas, father-in-law to Caiaphas, the reigning high priest (18:12–14,19–24). He tells also of Peter's three denials of Jesus (18:15–27). He does not spend much time on the Jewish trial, but he is much more explicit than the other Evangelists in his account of the Roman trial. Clearly he had some special knowledge of what went on before Pilate. He has a magnificent picture of Jesus talking with Pilate about kingship (18:33–40), the Son of God discussing with the representative of Caesar the meaning of sovereignty.

In his account of the crucifixion John has a number of touches of his own, notably the way Jesus commended Mary to the care of the beloved disciple (19:26,27), the fact that the cry Jesus uttered as he died was "It is finished" (19:30), and the piercing of his side by a soldier's spear (19:31–37).

John proceeds to the narrative of the burial (19:38–42) and of the empty tomb (20:1–10). He

The Sea of Galilee, the site of Jesus' last recorded miracle (Jn 21:1–4).

speaks of appearances of the risen Lord to Mary Magdalene (20:11–18), and to the disciples both without (20:19–23) and with Thomas (20:24–29). The final chapter tells of a miraculous catch of fish (21:1–14) and goes on to the moving account of Peter's threefold declaration of love to Jesus and his restoration.

LEON L. MORRIS

See JOHN THE APOSTLE, LIFE AND WRITINGS OF.

Bibliography. R.E. Brown, *The Gospel According to John*, 2 vols.; C.A. Dodd, *The Fourth Gospel*; F. Godet, *Commentary on John's Gospel*; E.W. Hengstenberg, *Commentary on the Gospel of St. John*, 2 vols.; E. Hoskyns and F.N. Davey, *The Fourth Gospel*; B. Lindars, *The Gospel of John*; G.A.C. MacGregor, *The Gospel of John*; L. Morris, *Commentary on the Gospel of John*; D. Thomas, *The Gospel of John*; C.J. Wright, *Jesus, The Revelation of God.*

John, Letters of. Three brief epistles ascribed to John. Their brevity is deceiving, for they deal with profound and critical questions about the basic nature of Christian religious experience.

The First Letter of John. Occasion and Purpose. First John is a simple yet profound response to a heresy threatening the church. The methodology used is a careful and clear delineation of the truth as it is found in Christ. The two different positions—the correct and the incorrect—are clearly contrasted. The lines of demarcation are definitely drawn.

The letter, however, also has a positive purpose. The author wants his "children" to know the truth and respond in relationship to God who was revealed in Christ: "And we are writing this that our joy may be complete. This is the message we have heard from him and proclaim to you, that God is light and in him is no darkness at all" (1:4,5). The positive purpose is further designated in 5:20: "And we know that the Son of God has come and has given us understanding, to know him who is true; and we are in him who is true, in his Son Jesus Christ." The clear understanding of the nature of Christ is of highest importance to the author. The response of the believer for which the author calls is to be "born of God" and to "abide in him."

The Nature of the Opposition. Assuming that the letter is written to contest the claims of the heretics provides interesting insights into their identity. According to 2:19, the opponents had been members of the Christian community, but had now withdrawn to propagate their own beliefs.

The series of "if" clauses in the last half of chapter 1 imply that the group was teaching the impossibility of walking in fellowship with God who is light; that there is no freedom from the practice of sin; and that there is no forgiveness and cleansing from sins.

The major christological error of the heretics was a denial of the humanity of Jesus, with the implication that he was not the Messiah. The false spirits in the world can be identified by their confession of Jesus: "By this you know the Spirit of God: every spirit which confesses that Jesus Christ has come in the flesh is of God" (4:2). The opening verse of the letter sharply contests the denial of Jesus' humanity. The liar is identified in 2:22 as the one "who denies that Jesus is the Christ. This is the antichrist, he who denies the Father and the Son."

The practical outcome of these positions was a moral irresponsibility that advocated a life of sin and disregard for others. John, therefore, needs to call these apostates back to a life of ethics and brotherly love in Christ.

The opposition has been identified in various ways. The emphasis on secret and esoteric knowledge points toward a gnostic-type heresy. The denial of the humanity of Jesus points toward the docetic heresy. The name of one Cerinthus of Asia Minor (mentioned by Irenaeus) has often been associated with the opposition in 1 John.

The Author. Careful comparison of 1 John with the fourth Gospel reveals a marked resemblance in vocabulary, style, and thought. Characteristic words used by both works include: love, life, truth, light, Son, Spirit, advocate, manifest, sin, world, flesh, abide, know, walk, and commandments. Combinations of words such as "Spirit of truth," "born of God," "children of God," and "overcome the world" also point to a single author. There are also similarities in grammatical usage and patterns of expression. There are marked similarities in theological outlook as well.

It is difficult to deny the close relationship of the two writings. Those who have attempted to distinguish between the two have had to admit that the variations in style and theological method must have come from one who was closely related and deeply influenced by the writer of the other.

The traditional position on authorship has been that the apostle John was the author of both the Gospel and the letter. The opening words of 1 John point clearly in that direction: "That which was from the beginning, which we have heard, which we have seen with our eyes, which we have looked upon and touched with our hands, concerning the word of life." This is clearly intended to let the readers know that the author was an eyewitness of the events. The eyewitness claim is at the same time a claim for the validity of the viewpoint and understanding of the nature of Christ.

The traditional position has been questioned on the basis of a quotation from Papias, who was bishop of Hierapolis in Asia Minor (AD 100–140). His comment, transmitted through Eusebius via Irenaeus, is: "If anywhere one came my way who had been a follower of the elders, I would inquire about the words of the elders—what Andrew and Peter had said, or what Thomas or James or John or Matthew or any other of the Lord's disciples; and I would inquire about the things which Aristion and the elder John, the Lord's disciples, say." A number of significant commentators have argued for the existence of an elder or presbyter John in Asia Minor in distinction from the apostle John. Irenaeus, in *Against Heresies*, and the Muratorian Fragment (both from the end of the second century), however, assign 1 John to the apostle John.

The claim to be an eyewitness and the air of authority of the first letter definitely point toward the apostle John. Tradition speaks of the advanced age of the apostle as he taught at Ephesus, and of his emphasis upon the love of the brethren to the very end of his life. First John reflects just such a situation.

Date. The date for the composition of 1 John is usually placed near the end of the 1st century. This date is confirmed by the nature of the heresy condemned and by the references to it in Polycarp and Irenaeus. Greater precision in fixing the date is not possible with the evidence available.

Text. The text of 1 John has been preserved rather well. The simplicity of the terminology and the clarity of its thought has contributed to this preservation. Three passages deserve mention in the discussion of text.

The words "all things" (2:20) are found in the nominative case in some manuscripts and in the accusative or objective case in others. The KJV translates the verse: "Ye know all things." The best manuscripts use the nominative case, which then modifies "you"—"You all know." The emphasis is on the breadth of the distribution of knowledge and not on the completeness of it.

In 4:19 there is no object for the verb "love" in the earliest manuscripts. Some later manuscripts have inserted either "him" or "God" in this sentence, and the KJV is dependent upon these manuscripts.

The most famous variant in 1 John is found in 5:7,8. "These three agree" is clearly an interpolation added to the text at a fairly late date. The earliest reference comes from the Spanish heretic Priscillian, who died in AD 385. At a later date it was accepted into the Vulgate. Erasmus, who edited the first Greek Testament ever published, eliminated the words on the basis of their absence in Greek manuscripts. The only two Greek manuscripts which contain the words were produced since that date. Thus modern translations have eliminated this verse.

The Second Letter of John. Second John was written in a setting similar to that of 1 John. The author identifies himself as "the elder" and designates his audience as "the elect lady and her children." The "elect lady" is probably a church and the "children" are the members of it. This church is harassed by the heresies that were attacked in 1 John. The heresies are denounced, and the church is warned not to entertain the messengers of the heresy.

The grammar, style, and vocabulary of 2 John compare very closely to 1 John. Eight of the 13 verses of the second letter are almost identical with verses in 1 John.

Information concerning date of writing is inadequate to make any decision. The similarity to 1 John suggests a similar era.

The Third Letter of John. Third John is also written in a similar setting. The occasion, however, is not the threat of heresy. The problem now is a certain Diotrephes, who is repudiating the authority of "the elder" and trying to frustrate his leadership. The letter is addressed to Gaius, who is still loyal to the elder. The elder asks Gaius to provide for the genuine missionaries who are passing through.

Again we have insufficient information to establish date or additional setting. The familiar terminology and writing style tie it closely to the other two letters.

The Message of the Letters. *1 John.* Commentators are unable to agree on the specific plan and structure of the first letter. The simple terminology, the narrow range of vocabulary, the repetition of ideas, and the almost monotonous grammatical construction defy logical analysis in terms of outline and structure. Commentators have characterized the argument of the epistles as "spiral." The picture is that of a venerable and respected elder in the community sharing his wisdom without attempting to provide a closely reasoned argument.

Although chapter designations were not introduced into the text of the NT until AD 1228 and are often misleading divisions of thought, they do provide a convenient method of surveying the content of the letter. It should be noted that the letter also departs from the common letter style of the 1st century so vividly represented in the Pauline letters.

(1) The first chapter is composed of an introduction and a discussion of walking in the light. The nature of God and of man in relationship comes into sharp focus.

The introduction stands in the noble tradition of the prologue to the fourth Gospel and the Letter to the Hebrews. With majestic profundity the basic dependability of the gospel message is declared. The author claims the status of eyewitness at the significant events through which the Father manifested himself. He claims that he is simply proclaiming the events in which he himself participated. The emphasis on hearing, seeing, and touching (the frequent use of the perfect tense emphasizes the continuing results) takes the manifestation out of the ethereal and speculative realm and places it directly in the world of experience.

The purpose of the proclamation is fellowship (the Greek word is *koinonia*). This fellowship operates both on the horizontal plane between believers and on the vertical plane between believers and both Father and Son (v 3). The second element of purpose is "to make our joy complete" (v 4 NIV).

In the opening paragraph of the body of the letter (1:5–10), the author moves immediately to the definitive nature of God as light. God's nature as light has a number of significant implications. First, darkness has no place in God

at all (v 5). Second, those who walk (live, conduct themselves) in darkness cannot be in fellowship with God (v 6). Third, relationship with God (walking in the light) results in fellowship with other believers and cleansing from all sin by Jesus his Son (v 7). Fourth, all have sinned, and denial of that fact does not change the truth (v 8). Fifth, acknowledgement of sin brings forgiveness and cleansing from the faithful and righteous God (v 9). Finally, denial of ever having sinned is a reflection upon God and proves that his word is not present (v 10).

Joy and fellowship are available only to those who walk in the light of God's presence. God who is light through his Son Jesus Christ (we are reminded of the prologue of the fourth Gospel, that the Word manifested light to all men) solves the problem of sin and unrighteousness through forgiveness and cleansing.

(2) The second chapter continues the thought of the final paragraph of chapter 1—the solution to the problem of sin—and then turns to a discussion of the new commandment and, in the final paragraph, the threat of the antichrist.

In the first paragraph (vv 1–6) the solution to the problem of sin in the presence of a pure God is expanded. Jesus Christ not only forgives sin and cleanses unrighteousness, but he is our advocate (the same word used in Jn 14–16 and transliterated "Paraclete") before God. The work of Christ is now designated as "propitiation for our sins." Jesus had satisfied the requirements for complete reconciliation between God and humanity.

The response of the believer is to keep his commandments. The third verse is the first of a number of verses which respond to the question: How can I, the believer, know that all of this is true? The first test is that of obedience. The implications of the test of obedience is stated positively in verses 3 and 5 and negatively in verse 4. Verse 6 clearly points out that the model for the life-style of the believer is to be found in Jesus.

The second paragraph (vv 7–17) outlines the second test of believing ("abiding in him"). The second authentication is love for the brethren. The author clearly states that it is impossible to walk in the light of God and hate your brother at the same time. Here is an expansion on the idea of fellowship found in the opening verses.

After encouraging three different age groups (vv 12–14—the reference may well be to stages in the Christian life rather than to chronological age groups) he warns them of the folly of loving the world (vv 15–17). The world consists of transient lusts and pride and is not a part of the Father who is Light. The only one who survives is the one who is obedient to the total will of God.

Now the author turns to the problem of the end time with its manifestation of the antichrist (vv 18–27). The antichrists (note the use of the plural) once were members of the fellowship (v 19). Anyone who denies that Jesus is the Messiah falls into that category. The author further declares that it is impossible to deny Christ and embrace God (v 23). Those who are born of God have an anointing from him which enables them to recognize the lies of the antichrist (v 27).

The whole epistle to this point has revolved around the implications of walking in God who is Light. God's self-revelation in Jesus provides clear direction and understanding to recognize the true and identify the false.

(3) The last two verses of chapter 2 introduce the new topic for chapter 3, being "born of God" (2:29). The children of God do not fear the final revelation of God at the second coming. Instead they anticipate it, for the full quality of their new birth will be made visible (3:2). The author pauses to revel in the function of God's love in our lives as his children (3:1).

The author quickly comes back from the joy of contemplating our status as children of God to the stark realities of the world in which we must live. The world about us is characterized by sin, which is now defined as lawlessness (v 4). Sin finds its origin in the devil, who "sinned from the beginning" (v 8). The children of the devil reveal their essential nature by living lawless lives—Cain is used as a model (vv 10–12).

Jesus, whose second appearance is noted in the opening verses, came the first time to "take away sins" (v 5) and "destroy the works of the devil" (v 8). Those "who abide in him" and are "born of God" live according to the pattern of their Father, who is righteous (v 7). The righteous life-style is characterized by purity (v 3) and cessation of sin (vv 7,9). The contrast between the two life-styles is obvious (v 10).

The last half of chapter 3 turns to one of the expressions of righteousness—love for one's fellows. The negative was already introduced in verse 12 (Cain). Hatred of the brother is equivalent to murder (v 15). Indifference to the need of the brother is also condemned (vv 17,18). The model for the love of the brother is Jesus, who laid down his life for us (v 16). The positive note is that love for one's brothers is evidence of being born of God—of passing from death into life (v 14). Again the contrast between the children of God and the children of the devil is obvious.

The last half of chapter 3 highlights one of John's favorite emphases. "We know" is repeated in verses 14, 16, 19, and 24. In a world of uncertainties John recognizes the great need for assurance. He thus outlines a variety of tests to establish and maintain assurance in this world filled with hatred and marked by an incomplete revelation of our full nature as children of God (v 1).

(4) The transition to chapter 4 occurs at the end of chapter 3: "And by this we know that he abides in us, by the Spirit which he has given us." The search for assurance must contend with the spirit of error and learn to distinguish between truth and error. The doctrinal test is outlined in this paragraph. The Spirit of God confesses Jesus as the gift of God and acknowledges the full reality of the incarnation (vv 2,3). False prophets who deny these basic truths are reflections of the antichrist (v 3). Obedience to God enables the children of God to recognize and respond to the language of God (vv 4–6).

In verses 7–12 John speaks of the origin of love in God who is Love (v 8). That love was demonstrated unmistakably in Jesus (vv 9,10) in order to solve the problem of sin. The natural response of the children of God, then, is to love one another (v 11), to the end that God's love may be perfected (reach its designated goal) in us (v 12). In this paragraph being born of God, loving God, and knowing God are inextricably intertwined.

Verse 13 picks up the assurance note of verse 1 and goes on to sharpen the relationship (the synthesis) of love for one's fellows and correct Christian doctrine or belief. Recognition of Jesus as the Son of God and the Savior of the world leads us to know the love of God. The love of God flows through us to others and is an evidence of our relationship to God (vv 14–21). The present assurance is so clear that even the fear of final judgment is obviated (vv 17,18).

(5) In the final chapter, John turns to the interrelationship between love and righteousness. Those who are born of God do not find the commandments of God to be burdensome (v 3). The faith of the children of God enables them to find victory over the world which would hinder the fulfillment of his commands (v 4). That faith rests in Jesus as the Son of God (v 5). Again, correct belief enters the picture: Jesus was fully human (v 6), and the Spirit bears witness to the reality of Jesus (vv 7,8). The result is a great inner certitude "that God gave us eternal life, and this life is in his Son" (v 11). Again the line of demarcation between the one who has life and the one who does not is crystal clear (v 12).

Verses 13–16 move from the possession of eternal life to certainty in prayer. A solid confidence in God brings answers to prayer (vv 14, 15). Confidence also extends to prayer on behalf of others who are committing sin (now John defines sin as unrighteousness in light of the early verses of the chapter); God will honor that prayer by giving life to the sinner (v 16).

The final paragraph is a reiteration of major themes of the whole letter. The victory of the one who is born of God through the true God who has come to us in Jesus clearly differentiates the child of God from the life of the world under the power of the evil one. The shining note of assurance continues to the very end of the letter.

2 John. The second letter contains all the elements of first-century letter style. The author is identified as the elder, and the "elect lady and her children" are probably a church and its members. The closing greeting from "your elect sister" confirms this analysis.

The burden of the letter is twofold. In the first place, the "lady" is urged that "we love one another" (v 5). The nature of love is then defined as following "his commandments" (v 6).

The second, and more compelling, element is the warning against the deceivers who refuse to acknowledge Christ and persuade others to do the same. Love indeed has its limits when it comes to even housing those who refuse to acknowledge Christ (vv 8–11). The deceivers are probably the same heretics identified in the first letter.

The letter closes with a promise of further communication in person. The purpose of the visit will be "that your joy may be complete" (cf. 1 Jn 1:4).

3 John. The third letter is directed to one individual, Gaius. Again the first-century letter style is followed carefully. In the thanksgiving section Gaius is commended for his faithfulness to the truth—especially as a "child" of the elder.

The burden of the letter is also twofold. The first paragraph (vv 5–8) commends Gaius for his hospitality to the itinerant missionaries who are traveling "for the sake of the Name." The missionaries have spoken well of Gaius' love for the church.

The second paragraph of the main body of the letter warns against the insubordination of a certain Diotrephes. His love of power and authority has led him not only to defy the authority of the elder, but also to convince others to follow his defiance or be excommunicated. He has refused to entertain the genuine itinerant preachers. Gaius is warned not to be influenced by Diotrephes' example.

The conclusion reflects the anticipation of an immediate personal visit. Normal greetings conclude the little letter.

Conclusion. The brief Johannine letters provide an interesting insight into the state of the church at the end of the 1st century. Heresy is rearing its ugly head. Autonomy and church organization are reflected. The genuine nature of a committed and obedient relationship to God through Christ is powerfully and warmly portrayed and commanded.

MORRIS A. WEIGELT

See JOHN THE APOSTLE, LIFE AND WRITINGS OF.

Bibliography. R.E. Brown, *The Epistles of John;* F.F Bruce, *The Epistles of John;* R.S. Candlish, *The First Epistle of John;* J.L. Houlden, *The Johannine Epistles;* J.J. Lies, *The First Epistle of John;* A. Plummer, *The Epistles of Saint John;* B.F. Westcott, *The Epistles of St. John.*

John, The Revelation of. See REVELATION, BOOK OF.

John Mark. See MARK, JOHN.

John of Gischala.
Leader in the first Jewish revolt, from Gischala (Gush-halab) in Galilee. He was a rival of Josephus Flavius, who had been appointed commander of Galilee. When Vespasian sent his son Titus against Gischala in AD 67, John fled to Jerusalem and took part in the defense of the city. Josephus accuses him of betraying him by inviting the extremist Idumeans into Jerusalem; later, when they had abandoned him, he entered into strife with Simon, a rival Zealot leader. He surrendered to the Romans and was imprisoned in Italy.

See FIRST JEWISH REVOLT.

John the Apostle, Life and Writings of.
Little is known about the early life of John, except that his father was named Zebedee and he had a brother called James (Mt 4:21). Matthew names Mary Magdalene, Mary the mother of James and Joseph, and "the mother of the sons of Zebedee" as the women at the cross (Mt 27:56). Mark names the two Marys and adds Salome (Mk 15:40), from which it appears that this may be the name of John's mother. If Matthew and Mark are naming the same women that John does, then Salome was Jesus' "mother's sister" (Jn 19:25). This would make John a cousin of Jesus. We cannot be certain of this, for there is no way of being sure that Matthew, Mark, and John all name the same three.

John was one of the first disciples, being among those whom Jesus called by the Sea of Galilee (Mt 4:21,22; Mk 1:19,20). It is also possible that he was the unnamed companion of Andrew when he first followed Jesus (Jn 1:35–37). That he was important in the little group around Jesus appears from the fact that he was one of the three who were especially close to the Master, who were selected to be with

Gethsemane, where Jesus singled out John (along with Peter and James) to pray with him (Mt 26:37; Mk 14:33).

him on some great occasions. John, along with his brother James and Peter, was present at the transfiguration (Mt 17:1,2; Mk 9:2; Lk 9:28,29). Jesus took only these three into the house of Jairus when he brought the man's daughter back to life (Mk 5:37; Lk 8:51). And before Jesus' arrest it was this trio of his followers that Jesus took to pray with him in the garden of Gethsemane (Mt 26:37; Mk 14:33). In the time of great difficulty, when Jesus faced the prospect of death on a cross, it was to this group of three that he looked for support.

There are other occasions when John is mentioned in the Gospels. Luke tells us of his surprise when the miraculous catch of fish took place (Lk 5:9,10), this being especially noteworthy as the surprise of a man whose expertise was fishing. Toward the close of Jesus' ministry we find John coming to Jesus with Peter, James, and Andrew, to ask when the end would come and what the sign would be (Mk 13:3,4). And Jesus sent Peter and John to prepare the Passover meal for the little band before his arrest (Lk 22:8).

Passages like these show that John was highly esteemed among the apostles and that he was close to Jesus. Yet there are indications that at first he was far from appreciative of what Jesus stood for. When Mark gives his list of the 12, he tells us that Jesus gave James and John the name "Boanerges," which means "sons of thunder" (Mk 3:17). Some in the early church took this as complimentary, understanding it to mean that their witness to Jesus would be as strong as thunder. Most see it, however, as pointing to the tempestuousness of character we see, for example, when John instructed a man casting out demons in Jesus' name to stop, "for he was not following us" (Mk 9:38; Lk 9:49). This is the only utterance attributed to John in the Gospels; elsewhere he is associated with someone else who is the spokesman.

On another occasion the sons of Zebedee asked Jesus for the two chief places when he came in glory, one to be on his right and the other on his left (Mk 10:35–40). Matthew adds the point that the words were spoken by the men's mother, but there is no doubt that James and John were in on it (Mt 20:20,21). Jesus proceeded to ask them whether they could drink the cup he would drink and be baptized with the baptism he would receive. Clearly these are metaphors for the suffering he would in due course undergo. James and John affirmed that they could, and Jesus assured them that they would indeed do this. But he gave them no assurance about such places of honor; that James and John would suffer for Christ is plain. So is their failure at that time to understand the loving spirit that moved their Master and that was required of them.

Another incident that shows much the same spirit is that in which certain Samaritan villagers refused to receive the little band as they traveled. When they heard of it, James and John asked Jesus whether he wanted them to call down fire from heaven and burn the villagers up (Lk 9:54). In this they were clearly at variance with Jesus, and he rebuked them. But we should not miss the zeal they displayed for their Lord, nor their conviction that if they did call down fire it would come. They were sure that God would not fail to answer the prayer of those who called on him for vengeance.

The Synoptics then show us John as a zealous and loyal follower of Jesus. He is not depicted as gentle and considerate. At this time he knew little of the love that should characterize the follower of Jesus. But he had faith and a passionate conviction that God would prosper Jesus and those who served him.

In the Book of Acts, John's name occurs in a list of the 12 (Acts 1:13). When we are told of James' death, we are told also that he was John's brother (Acts 12:2). In all the other references to him, John is in the company of Peter. These two were the instruments God used in bringing healing to a lame man (Acts 3). That they were going to the temple at the hour of prayer says something about their habits of devotion. Prayer at the ninth hour apparently denotes the service of prayer that was held at the same time as the evening offering (i.e., at about three o'clock in the afternoon). Evidently Peter and John were continuing the devotional habits of pious Jews. On another occasion these two were arrested and jailed on account of their preaching about Jesus' resurrection (Acts 4:1–3). They were brought before the council, where Peter spoke for them. The council saw these two men as "uneducated, common men," (Acts 4:13) which means that they did not have the normal rabbinic education. The council forbade them to speak about Jesus, but the apostles replied, "Whether it is right in the sight of God to listen to you rather than to God, you must judge; for we cannot but speak of what we have seen and heard" (Acts 4:19,20).

John was again associated with Peter when the gospel was first preached in Samaria. Philip was the evangelist, but the apostles in Jerusalem decided to send Peter and John to Samaria when they heard how the people had accepted the gospel message. "When they arrived, they prayed for them that they might receive the Holy Spirit" (Acts 8:15 NIV), a revealing illustration of apostolic priorities. In due course they laid their hands on the new believers and they received the Holy Spirit (v 17). John is not specifically mentioned but he no doubt was included in "the apostles" who were arrested and jailed because of the jealousy of prominent Jews (Acts 5:17,18). That imprisonment did not last long, for an angel released them at night, and they resumed their preaching in the early morning (v 21).

John is mentioned by name in Galatians 2:9, where he is joined with Peter and James and the three are called "the pillars of the church."

John is not mentioned by name in the fourth Gospel, but there are passages that refer to "the disciple Jesus loved" (Jn 13:23; 19:26; 20:2; 21:7,20). We are not told who this was, but the evidence seems to indicate that the apostle John is meant. There is an account of a fishing trip in chapter 21, and the people who went are listed in 21:2. The group includes Peter, who must be ruled out because he is often mentioned along with the beloved disciple. It also includes Thomas and Nathanael, but there seems no reason for seeing either as a likely candidate. Two unnamed men and the sons of Zebedee make up the party. Of these two mentioned last James is excluded by his early death (Acts 12:2). This leaves John or one of the unnamed men. John is favored by the fact that the beloved disciple is linked with Peter on a number of occasions (13:24; 20:2; 21:7), and we know from the other Gos-

pels that Peter and John (together with James) were especially close (cf. Acts 3; 8:14; Gal 2:9). Of course, one of the unnamed disciples may have been the beloved disciple, but such a supposition faces the problem of the omission of the name of John the apostle throughout the entire fourth Gospel. If John wrote this book, we can understand his not mentioning himself (and this would explain why he calls the Baptist simply "John"). But why should anyone else omit all mention of a man as prominent in the apostolic band as the other Gospels show John to have been?

It is argued that "the disciple Jesus loved" is not the kind of title a man would naturally use of himself, but it is not the kind of title a man would naturally use of someone else, either. And it may be that John uses it in a modest fashion, partly because he did not want to draw attention to himself by using his name and partly because he wanted to emphasize the truth that it was the fact that Jesus loved him that made him what he was.

If John may be identified with the beloved disciple, we learn more about the apostle. We should not, of course, press the words as though they meant that Jesus did not love his other disciples. He loved them all. Yet John was indeed beloved, and also recognized that he owed all he had and all he was to that love. That he was specially close to Jesus is indicated by the fact that he leaned on Jesus' breast at the last supper (Jn 13:23). It tells us something of his relationship to the Master that he was there when the crucifixion took place, and that it was to him that Jesus gave the charge to look after his mother (Jn 19:26, 27). One would have expected that Jesus would have selected one of the family for this responsibility. The charge certainly shows that a close relationship existed between Jesus and the disciple he loved.

On the first Easter morning this disciple raced Peter to the tomb when Mary Magdalene told them it was empty. He won the race but stood outside the tomb until Peter came. John followed Peter in, and he "saw, and believed" (Jn 20:8). In the next chapter we read of the beloved disciple on a fishing trip. It was he who recognized that it was Jesus who stood on the shore and told them where to cast the net (21:7).

Such appears to be the NT portrait of John. Clearly he was an important figure in the little band of the early Christians. On almost every occasion on which he comes before us he is in the company of someone else, and usually the speaking is done by his companion, not John. But we may justly conclude that he stood very close to Jesus. Perhaps he had entered into the mind of Jesus more than any of the others had. The best evidence of this is the fourth Gospel. Clearly the man who wrote this had great spiritual insight. John may have been more the thinker than the man of action and the leader of men.

A study of nonscriptural sources for the life of John should probably begin with the suggestion that John was martyred early. If this was the case, he can scarcely have been the author of the the NT books ascribed to him: the Gospel of John, the letters of 1, 2, and 3 John, and Revelation. A number of considerations are brought forward. A summary of history by Philip of Side (*c.* AD 450) contains the statement that Papias, an early Christian, says that John and James were killed by the Jews. One manuscript of the 9th-century George the Sinner also says that John was killed by the Jews. This can scarcely be called impressive evidence. Philip is an unreliable historian, and there is doubt whether he (or his summarizer) has reported Papias correctly. Even if he did, the statement does not say that John was killed at the same time as James. George the Sinner adds nothing of weight, and he may even be copying Philip. There are some ecclesiastical calendars that indicate James and John were commemorated on the same day, from which some have argued that they were martyred together. But the conclusion does not follow. Commemoration on the same day implies nothing about having suffered the same fate; and even if this did happen, there is nothing to say that it was at the same time. The argument is worthless. Other arguments are no stronger, and the whole idea should be dismissed.

There is a tradition that John lived at Ephesus and died a very old man. There is no way of proving or disproving this. We simply do not know. The author of Revelation was on the island of Patmos (Rv 1:9), which is usually un-derstood to mean that he had been exiled for his work as a preacher of the gospel. If this is so, he may well have died there. But there is little that such speculations can tell us. For the rest, we are dependent on what the writings associated with the apostle's name reveal about their author. We have seen reason for thinking that the fourth Gospel was written by the apostle. The letters of John probably came from him also (though as they stand they are anonymous). Revelation claims to have been written by an author named John (Rv 1:1,2,9), though it does not say whether this is the apostle or another John. Many hold that the style is so different from that of the other writings that we cannot claim the same author. The style is certainly different, but we cannot know how much influence an amanuensis had on one or more of these writings. And there are certainly some striking resemblances. Nothing will be lost and much gained if we look at each of these writings to find what its teaching tells us about the author.

Theology of the Fourth Gospel. This Gospel opens with some statements about the Logos (Word) and goes on to say that the Logos became flesh and lived among us. It is not too much to say that the life and work of the incarnate Logos is what the fourth Gospel is all about. From start to finish John is concerned with the great divine act of salvation, which Jesus Christ accomplished.

Christology. John speaks of Jesus as "the Savior of the world" (Jn 4:42), and his Gospel brings this out clearly. Indeed, he tells us that his purpose was to show that Jesus was the Christ, the Son of God, so that men might believe in him and have eternal life (Jn 20:31). "Christ" is the transliteration of a Greek word meaning "anointed," just as "Messiah" transliterates the corresponding Hebrew word. Thus "Christ," "Messiah," and "anointed" all mean the same thing. Certain important OT people were anointed, notably kings (1 Sm 10:1; 15:17; 2 Sm 2:4; 1 Kgs 1:39), priests (Ex 30:30), and sometimes prophets (1 Kgs 19:16). But the men of the OT looked for a day when God would send not simply "an" anointed one but *the* anointed one (Ps 45:6,7; Is 61:1,2), someone who would do the will of God in a special way (Acts 10:38). By NT times this longing for the Messiah had increased, and John is able to tell his readers that Jesus is this long-expected one. Not only does he do this in set terms (Jn 1:41; 4:25,26), but he brings out the truth by drawing attention to aspects of Jesus' ministry that show him to be the Messiah. He reports that John the Baptist claimed not to be the Messiah but to have been sent before him (Jn 3:28). He tells of Jesus' cleansing the temple (Jn 2:13–22), a messianic act (Ps 69:9; see also

The fountain of Memnius in Ephesus, the city where, according to tradition, John lived in his later years and died.

Zec 14:21; Mal 3:1–5). The healing of the lame man (Jn 5:1–9) is probably meant to be seen as messianic, for the leaping of the lame was associated with the time of the Messiah (Is 35:6). Similarly we should see the feeding of the five thousand (Jn 6:1–14) as a messianic work in supplying men's needs (the messianic banquet was a frequent topic in Jewish discussions). Because the rulers knew where Jesus came from, they rejected him as the Messiah. This is a splendid example of John's irony, for if they had really known Jesus' origin, they would have known he was the Messiah (Jn 7:26–29). There are other passages, but these are sufficient to show that it is one of John's prominent emphases that Jesus fulfilled all that is involved in the work of the Messiah. This does not mean a public claim, for that would have been misunderstood. People expected a political deliverer, but Jesus was no politician; he was more, for John tells us that Jesus would be active in final judgment and that he would raise the dead (Jn 5:25–29). Neither function was previously ascribed to the Messiah.

John depicts Jesus as "Son of God" as well as Messiah. The expression might mean much or little (men might be "children of God" or "born . . . of God," Jn 1:12,13). As applied to Jesus it is clear that it has its maximum content. In the discourse recorded in John 5 it is plain that Jesus is the divine Son in a very special way. Deity is ascribed to him at the beginning of the Gospel, when we are told that "the Word was God" (1:1), and at the end, when Thomas greets the risen Lord as "My Lord and my God" (20:28). That John regards Jesus as fully divine is so plain that some recent scholars have claimed that he is depicting a docetic Christ (one who was wholly divine and only appeared to be human). This view is unjustified, but the fact that it can be held shows the strength of the evidence that John saw Jesus as indeed God.

As do the other Evangelists, John tells us that Jesus' favorite title for himself was "the Son of man." This sounds like a statement of his humanity, but the expression is probably taken from Daniel 7:13, where one "like a son of man" was brought before the Ancient of Days and given ruling power. This is a superhuman figure, not to be thought of as simply a man. When Jesus uses the expression, he is not claiming to be just another man. But the title was not a recognized one for the Messiah, so it is likely that he could use it without making people think that he was claiming to be Messiah in the way they understood the term—as a political deliverer. It was well to avoid that kind of conclusion, and "the Son of man" may well have been used at least partly for this purpose. In this Gospel the title seems to be connected either with the heavenly glory of Christ or with the salvation he accomplished. In its first occurrence (Jn 1:51) Jesus speaks the heaven opening and the angels arising and descending on the Son of man. This is surely a poetic way of saying that Jesus is the means of communication between heaven and earth. He brings the salvation that will lift men to God, and he reveals God to men. Sometimes there are references to the Son of man being "lifted up" (3:14; 8:28), which means "lifted up on a cross." They point to the saving death he would die. Thus he is the object of faith (9:35). He gives the food that endures for life eternal (6:27); eating his flesh and drinking his blood are the means of receiving eternal life (6:53,54).

John tells us that on the eve of the crucifixion Jesus said, "The hour has come for the Son of man to be glorified" (Jn 12:23; cf. 13:31). For John, glory, paradoxically, means not something like majesty and splendor, but lowly service. He uses the word in a commonly accepted sense, as when he speaks of the miracles as demonstrating Jesus' glory (2:11; 11:4), but more often he sees the willing performance of service as the true glory. Christ performed that act of lowly service that brought salvation to men most supremely on the cross. When John uses the verb "glorified," we should usually understand it in the sense "crucified." This hammers home the truth that Jesus' concern is not with the kind of things that the world so greatly esteems. True glory is to be understood quite differently. John does not, of course, confine this to the cross, though that is his great example. He tells us in his prologue that "we have beheld his glory" (1:14). The earthly life of the Son of man was lived not in the splendor of some palace, but in obscurity and rejection. But he went where he was needed, and there he did the will of God. In that life of lowliness and service John sees something more glorious by far than any earthly pomp and glitter.

Sometimes the glory is linked with the miracles. John has his own way of dealing with Christ's miracles. To begin with, he does not call them "miracles" at all. He avoids the term "miracle," meaning "mighty works," which is the usual term in the synoptic Gospels. Often he calls them "signs." John uses this term occasionally of other happenings, as in his statement that John the Baptist "did no sign" (Jn 10:41), but mostly of Jesus' miracles. This way of regarding the miracles concentrates not on the aspect of wonder but on the meaning, the *significance*. John does not deny that these great deeds are miraculous in our sense of the term, but he sees it as more important that in them God is teaching us something. For example, the first of his signs, the changing of the water into wine (2:1–11), points to the transformation of all that Judaism means (the water was "for the Jewish rites of purification," 2:6) into all that Christianity means. Jesus is not simply repeating the old but making it completely new. The feeding of the multitude leads to the thought that Jesus is the living bread (5:35). The healing of the man born blind points to Jesus as the Light of the world (8:12). The raising of Lazarus from the dead points to Jesus as the resurrection and the life (11:25).

But this is not the only way John refers to Jesus' miracles. Quite often he calls them "works." He can use this word to refer to human deeds, either good deeds (Jn 3:21; 6:28) or evil deeds (3:19,20; 7:7). But characteristically he uses the term for the works Jesus did. John uses the noun "work" 27 times, and 18 of these refer to Jesus' works. He uses it in the singular, of a particular deed (7:21) or of Jesus' total life work (17:4), and in the plural of a number of deeds. There is a sense in which it is the Father who does the works (5:19,20; 14:10). The unity between the Father and the Son is one of the great ideas of John's Gospel. The works accomplish God's purpose, but they can also be seen as revelatory. They teach important truths. Thus they "testify" of Jesus (5:36). They challenge people to believe in Jesus, for he can tell them to believe the works (10:38)—even if they are not ready to believe him—or to believe him on account of the works (14:11).

It is clear that "work" is an important theological term. It is a reminder that God does not see the miracles as we do. To us they are extraordinary happenings, mystifying. We cannot explain them. To God they are no more than works. The term appears to be used of the nonmiraculous as well as the miraculous, and this indicates that there is a continuity between the two. We cannot divide Jesus up so that he does some things as God and others as man. His works are sometimes the kind of things humans do and sometimes the kind of things they cannot do. Since the term is often used in the OT of the mighty works of God (Gn 2:2,3; Ps 8:3; 73:28; Dn 9:14), John's use of it may indicate that Jesus is carrying on the works God did in ancient times. The work of God goes on.

The closeness of the relationship between the Father and the Son is brought out in another way, in the concept that the Father sent the Son. John's Gospel uses two Greek words meaning "to send," and both occur more often in this Gospel than in any other NT book. In the large majority of cases it involves the fact that the Father sent the Son. "The Father who sent me" is a frequently occurring expression (e.g., Jn 5:23,30; 6:37,39,44; 8:16,18,29), often

without any indication as to the purpose of the sending. But there is the clear declaration that "God sent the Son into the world, not to condemn the world, but that the world might be saved through him" (3:17).

The passages that speak of Jesus as not being alone but having with him the Father who sent him (e.g., 8:16) also draw attention to the close communion with God that marked Jesus' earthly life. It is difficult to separate the Father and the Son, for he that believes the one believes the other (12:44,45; cf. 13:20).

There are important passages that link the mission of the Son with the mission of his followers. Jesus prayed, "As thou didst send me into the world, so I have sent them into the world" (17:18), and he said to them, "As the Father has sent me, even so I send you" (20:21). Earlier he had linked them with himself by using "we" of those who must work the works of the Father who had sent him (9:4).

All the passages so far noted in one way or another draw attention to the oneness of Jesus with the Father, to his deity. But it is clear that Jesus was a man with needs like other men. Thus he could be tired (4:6) and thirsty (19:28). He loved his friends Martha, Mary, and Lazarus (11:5). He was troubled in spirit and he cried (11:33,35). Jesus had a normal life as a member of a family (2:12), and his brothers lectured him in the way brothers do (7:3–

Tradition states that this is the tomb where Jesus raised Lazarus (Jn 11).

5). He was troubled in spirit as he spoke of his betrayal by Judas (13:21; the same verb is used of Jesus again in 11:33; 12:27).

Jesus' whole manner of life as John depicts it is a human life. This is seen especially in the way John refers to him, using the human name Jesus far more often than does any other NT writer—237 times (cf. Mt 150 times, Mk 81 times, Lk 89 times). John accounts for more than a quarter of the uses of this name in the whole NT (905). This is inexplicable apart from a conviction of the reality of Jesus' humanity.

But perhaps the most significant thing in this connection is the way John brings out Jesus' constant dependence on the Father. He quotes Jesus as saying, "The Son can do nothing of his own accord" (5:19), and again, "I can do nothing on my own authority" (5:30). The Father is with him continually (8:29). The life he lives he owes to the Father (5:26; 6:57). His very food is to do the will of God (4:34). He recognizes that the Father gave him the disciples: "all that the Father gives me will come to me" (6:37); "no one can come to me unless the Father who sent me draws him" (6:44). Jesus speaks of the disciples as "the men whom thou gavest me out of the world" (17:6). He refers to "the cup which the Father has given me" (18:11), to the "authority" the Father gave him (17:2), and to the "glory" that came from the same source (17:24). The Father gave him a commandment which Jesus describes in terms of the authority to lay down his life and to take it again (10:18). John depicts Jesus as praying (notably in ch 17), a human trait.

In summary, John writes about a Jesus who was fully human as well as divine. When he tells us that the Word was made flesh (1:14), he means this to be taken with the utmost seriousness. The Son of God came right where men are. He became one with us.

The Father. Throughout this discussion of Christology there has necessarily been much about the Father. John puts strong emphasis on the place of the Son, but that also says something about the Father. The term "Son" is meaningless without a reference to the Father.

In common with all Jewish monotheists John insists that there is one God. There is no dispute with the Jews on this point. But he has his own distinctives. One of them is his emphasis on the fatherhood of God. The Jews accepted this truth, but they did not emphasize it or personalize it as Jesus did. For him it was common to refer to God as "my Father." John reports that on one occasion the Jews sought to kill Jesus because he "called God his own Father, making himself equal with God" (5:18). This the Jews could not stand. When

Jesus drove the traders out of the temple, it was "my Father's house" to which he referred (2:16). The Jews would have said, "our Father's house." We see the same kind of thing in Jesus' words, "I am ascending to my Father and your Father, to my God and your God" (20:17). He does not associate others with himself when he speaks of relationship to the Father. His relationship was not that of anyone else. John does not deny that God is Father to others; for example, he tells us that Jesus called God "Father" when he spoke to the Samaritan woman (4:23). But he places emphasis on Jesus' special sonship.

John's use of the term "Father" is remarkable. He uses the word 137 times, which is more than twice as often as anyone else (next highest is Matthew with 64; there are 63 occurrences in the Pauline letters). Sometimes John refers to human fatherhood, but 122 times the word refers to God. This emphasis may be because it was needed at the time. In OT days people might have been tempted to presume on God's concern for them; the emphasis was then on his holiness and majesty. But the lesson was well and truly learned, and by NT times people were in danger of thinking of God as lofty, removed from his people, remote. There was need for the kind of teaching John supplies. Above all, God is Father to his people. But John does not overlook the holiness aspect. He records Jesus as praying, "Holy Father" and again, "O righteous Father" (17:11,25). However, his stress is on God as Father; this is a new note, and one that has permanently influenced the Christian understanding of God.

John records Jesus' statement, "God is spirit" (4:24). This does not mark a great advance on Judaism, for the Jews were insistent that God is not to be thought of as in any way material. But John makes it clear that Christians too hold this important truth. John also makes much of the love of God. It is true that we must go on to his first epistle before we find the words "God is love" (1 Jn 4:8). But already in the Gospel we find what this means when we read, "God so loved the world that he gave his only Son" (Jn 3:16). It is the cross that shows us the greatness of the Father's love. Love is one of the key thoughts of this Gospel, and it is dwelt on, especially in the latter part.

The Father's ceaseless activity is the justification for Jesus' continuing deeds of mercy even on the sabbath (5:17,18). There is a sense in which God's work was finished at creation, but there is also God's continual sustaining work; the universe could not continue a moment without it. If people really understood what God does constantly and what he taught about the sabbath in the OT, they would see that deeds of mercy on that day were not only permitted but required. The sabbath was a day for doing good.

This Gospel depicts a mighty God whose will is done. There is a predestinarian strain that we see, for example, in the words of Jesus, "No one can come to me unless the Father who sent me draws him" (6:44; cf. v 65). Similarly it is the man who is "of God" who hears Jesus (8:47), or him who is "of the truth" (18:37). "You did not choose me, but I chose you and appointed you that you should go and bear fruit" said Jesus (15:16). These passages affirm that God is a mighty God, working out his purposes.

Holy Spirit. The Gospel of John has more to say about the Holy Spirit than has any of the other Gospels. To begin with, it speaks of John the Baptist seeing the Holy Spirit descend from heaven in the form of a dove and rest on Jesus (Jn 1:32). The Baptist also speaks of Jesus as the one who baptizes with the Holy Spirit (1:33). This is not explained, but it evidently indicates that Jesus would in due course communicate the Spirit to his followers. There is an important statement about this in the passage dealing with Jesus' visit to the temple during the feast of tabernacles. There Jesus spoke of rivers of living water, and John explains: "Now this he said about the Spirit, which those who believed in him were to receive, for as yet the Spirit had not been given, because Jesus was not yet glorified" (7:39). The Spirit then could be given in his fullness only when Jesus' work had come to its consummation. The reason for this is not completely clear, but the facts are there. It would not be true to say that the Holy Spirit did nothing in OT days, or in the lifetime of Jesus. But from the day of Pentecost in Acts 2 the work of the Spirit was on a scale vastly greater than anything that preceded it. The great work of the Spirit followed on the work of the Christ.

The Gospel of John makes it clear that the Spirit is active throughout the Christian life. He is there at its beginning, for "unless one is born of water and the Spirit, he cannot enter the kingdom of God" (3:5). The phrase "born of water" has caused problems, but there are good reasons for holding that "water" must be taken very closely with "Spirit" in this passage. In this case it means very much the same as being "born of the Spirit" in verse 8. John is conveying Jesus' teaching that no one enters the kingdom by his own effort. He must be reborn, and that rebirth is the result of the activity of the Spirit (so also in 6:63).

But Jesus' most significant teaching about the Spirit comes in the farewell discourses.

There the Spirit is given an unusual title that we transliterate as "Paraclete." Originally the term appears to have meant a legal helper, hence translations like "advocate" or "counselor." But the Greek paraclete did more than modern legal helpers, and the term could be used of anyone who came to the help of a man in legal need. The traditional translation is "comforter," correct on at least etymological grounds (the Latin *con fortis* gives the idea of a strengthening together, which is what the word conveys). Many ways of understanding the term have been suggested in modern times, but we can scarcely do better than see it as meaning a friend or helper at court.

The Paraclete is identified with "the Spirit of truth" (Jn 14:16,17; 15:26; 16:13) and with "the Holy Spirit" (14:26). Jesus told the disciples that the Holy Spirit would be with them forever (14:16), bearing witness to Jesus (15:26) and teaching them and reminding them of all that Jesus had told them (14:26). His work among unbelievers would be that of convicting them of sin, righteousness, and judgment (16:8).

A further important passage is Jesus' commission of his followers. "He breathed on them, and said to them, 'Receive the Holy Spirit. If you forgive the sins of any, they are forgiven; if you retain the sins of any, they are retained'" (20:22,23). This gift of the Spirit seems to be made to the group rather than to individuals.

Dualism. John's Gospel includes a number of opposites: light and darkness, flesh and spirit, this world and that to come, God and Satan, life and death. Opposites are found in a number of writings in antiquity—for example, in the Dead Sea Scrolls. Some have reasoned that John is indebted to one or other of the dualistic systems of the day. But this goes beyond the evidence. There is nothing in John's dualism that is not authentically Christian.

Probably the most important aspect of the dualism in John's Gospel is that he presents us with a picture of this world over against that which is above—this world, where Satan is active, and heaven, where God rules. For example, Jesus said to the Jews, "You are from below, I am from above; you are of this world, I am not of this world" (8:23). This sets a sharp distinction between the two worlds and firmly locates Jesus' origin in the other one. This world can be characterized as doing evil deeds (7:7). It does not know God (17:25), nor does it know the Christ (1:10). This does not mean that everyone in this present world is hostile to God, but Jesus and his followers are expressly differentiated from it (17:14). God gave Jesus the disciples out of the world (17:6).

The world is under the influence of an evil

being, described variously as "the devil" (8:44), "Satan" (13:27), and "the ruler of this world" (12:31). John sees this evil one as constantly in opposition to God and to the people of God. He enters into people, as he did into Judas Iscariot (13:27). He opposes Jesus but he "has no power" over him (14:30). The conflict comes to its climax at the cross. The ruler of this world is judged (16:11).

Other aspects of dualism, such as the conflict between light and darkness (1:5), are all to be seen as aspects of the great conflict between God and Satan. Light is a natural symbol for what is good, and darkness for what is evil. Where these two are pictured as in conflict, it is much the same as saying that God and Satan are opposed. So with flesh and spirit. "Flesh" is not something essentially evil, but it does belong to the lower world. What is born of the flesh is flesh (3:6). Flesh cannot rise to the life of the upper world, of heaven. For that it is necessary to be reborn from above, a birth which can be said to be of the Spirit (3:5,8). It is the Spirit who enables humans to enter the life of heaven; flesh can never do this (6:63).

The Christian Life. According to the Gospel of John, life begins with a divine act. Humans do not fit themselves for the kingdom of God. They cannot. They are sinful. The word "sin" occurs 17 times in John's Gospel, a total exceeded in the NT only in Romans and Hebrews. Sin is very real, and to "die in your sins" is the ultimate horror (8:21). But there is no necessity for this, for the Lamb of God came to take away the sins of the world (1:29). Deliverance from sin and entrance into life are divine acts. For this it is necessary to be born of the Spirit (3:5,8). There is dispute about whether we should understand John 3:3 in terms of being "born again" or "born from above." For the present purpose the resolution of the difficulty is not important. Both are involved. To enter the kingdom is, not to continue as one was, but to be born all over again. And this rebirth is not a matter of human striving, but a work of the Spirit. The emphasis is on what God does in bringing about life in men and women.

This life is often called "eternal life," though "life" seems to mean much the same. The adjective "eternal" means literally "pertaining to an age." The Jews divided time into the age before creation, the present age, and the age to come. Theoretically, then, "eternal" could apply to any of these ages, but in practice it was used of the age to come. Sometimes this means "everlasting," for the coming age was thought to have no end. But sometimes the emphasis is on quality—it is the life proper to the coming age, an age that differs in many respects from the present age. John uses the adjective about three times as often as any other NT writer. Scripture nevers says that God has eternal life, only God has life "in himself" (5:26). But God gives eternal life to believers (e.g., Jn 3:15). He gives it at a cost, the cost of the Son (3:16).

Often Jesus speaks simply of "life," and this means much the same in most places. The Father has given to him the property of having life in himself (5:26), but this property is not shared by anything or anyone else. All other life is derivative. It does not even exist by itself, so to speak, after Christ made it. It exists only "in" him. Only those who come to Christ have life (5:40); the same truth may be put in terms of eating his flesh and drinking his blood (6:53,54). He gave his flesh for the life of the world (6:51); thus the reference to eating and drinking is a symbolic way of referring to receiving him in his character as the Savior who died for men. When he gives life, the recipients never perish (10:28). Jesus can speak of coming to give men life, and give it more abundantly (10:10). So closely is life associated with him that twice he is said to be life (11:25; 14:6).

Life is God's gift, and those who enter it do so because of an activity of the Spirit within them. But the other side of this coin is that only those who believe are reborn. John recognizes the importance of believing. His Gospel uses the verb "believe" no less than 98 times (next most frequent in the NT are Acts with 37, then Romans with 21).

"Believe" occurs in a variety of constructions. Sometimes it is followed by "that," referring to truths humans believe; sometimes the idea is simply of believing people or believing facts. A very interesting construction— "believing into" Jesus—is used 36 times. This brings out the element of personal trust.

We should not make firm distinctions between the various usages of "believe." In the last resort they come to mean much the same thing. Really to believe "that" (i.e., the facts about Christ) means trusting him, just as "believing in" him or simply believing him means trusting him. However it is worded, this verb shows the central importance of coming to a place of faith in Christ. There is no substitute for that.

John has a great deal to say about love and emphasizes its importance. Fundamentally this is God's love. The Father loves the Son, a truth that is insisted on a number of times (3:35; 10:17; 15:9; 17:24 etc.). But he loves humans too, and we have the great declaration that he loved the world (3:16). This surpasses anything so far known in Judaism and represents a specifically Christian understanding of

God. God's great and sacrificial love cannot but have its consequences. It awakes an answering love in men, and there are several references to men loving Christ (14:15,21,23).

Christians also have love for one another, and this is the characteristic mark of discipleship. "By this all men will know that you are my disciples, if you have love for one another" (13:35). Jesus repeatedly commanded his followers to love one another (13:34; 15:12,17). There are two Greek verbs for "to love" in the NT and John's Gospel has each of them more than twice as often as any other book of the NT except 1 John. The Christian owes all he has and is to the love of God in Christ; it is the most natural thing that he should respond with an answering love, and such an answering love overflows in love to men.

Like life, light is specially linked with Christ, who is indeed called "the light of the world" (8:12; 9:5). The prologue states, "In him was life, and the life was the light of men" (1:4). The linking of life and light is like that in Psalm 36:9, and it brings out the truth that wherever there is life and light, Christ has been at work. The prologue goes on immediately to say that "the light shines in the darkness, and the darkness has not overcome it" (1:5). This is the conflict between light and darkness discussed above. Light drives darkness away. They cannot coexist. If there is even a little light, there is no longer darkness. The metaphor is a vivid one for the opposition of good and evil.

John carried this through in his exposition of the Christian life. Christ has indeed come "as light into the world" (12:46) and those who follow him will not walk in darkness but "will have the light of life" (8:12). To love darkness rather than light is itself condemnation (3:19), depriving oneself of all the blessing that comes from loving light.

The concept of truth is closely linked with Jesus. Truth is not simply information about Jesus; he *is* the truth (14:6). Or he is said to be "full of grace and truth" (1:14). John the Baptist came to bear witness to Jesus (1:6,7), and he bore witness to the truth (5:33). It is not surprising that truth is connected with salvation, as it is elsewhere in the NT (e.g., Eph 1:13; Gal 2:5). As John reaches the climax of his Gospel, he records that Pilate asked, "What is truth?" (18:38). There is no formal answer, but John's passion narrative clearly shows what truth really is. The cross is in mind also when Jesus says, "For their sake I consecrate myself, that they also may be consecrated in truth" (17:19).

Truth links up with salvation in other ways. Thus Jesus says that if people abide in his word, they are truly his disciples, "and you will know the truth, and the truth will make you free" (8:31,32). Jesus is not speaking of truth as a philosophical concept, the knowledge of which brings genuine intellectual freedom. He is speaking about the life which a person can live free from bondage to evil. That is an immensely liberating experience, and it comes from a right relationship to Jesus. It is in line with this that believers can be said to be "of the truth" (18:37) or to sanctify themselves "in the truth" (17:17). On the other hand, the devil is one who does not stand in the truth, and there is no truth in him (8:44).

Truth is so distinctive of Jesus that he can be said to have come into the world in order to bear witness to the truth (18:37; cf. 8:40). Truth is linked similarly with the Spirit. He is "the Spirit of truth" (14:17), and part of his work is to guide men "into all the truth" (16:13). Moreover, those who approach God must worship "in Spirit and in truth" (4:23, 24).

More could be said. In many circles today there is extensive discussion of the Johannine community. It is true that John's Gospel records Jesus speaking of a fold and also of a vine whereof believers are branches, as well as other indications that believers belong together; but it never uses the word "church." Many scholars think of baptism in connection with John 3 and see communion in John 6, but neither term is used. What is clear is the emphasis on Christ and on the new life provided for believers by his death and resurrection and the gift of the Spirit.

Theology of the Johannine Letters. The letters of John set forth much the same theology as that in the Gospel. Sometimes it is somewhat more explicit, as in the reference to Christ's atoning work: "The blood of Jesus his Son cleanses us from all sin" (1 Jn 1:7); Jesus Christ "is the expiation for our sins, and not for ours only but also for the sins of the whole world (1 Jn 2:2; cf. 4:10). Such statements reaffirm what the Gospel has already said.

The first letter is largely concerned with false teachers who are leading people astray with their wrong ideas about the Christ. John writes: "Many false prophets have gone out into the world. By this you know the Spirit of God: every spirit which confesses that Jesus Christ has come in the flesh is of God, and every spirit which does not confess Jesus is not of God. This is the spirit of antichrist, of which you heard that it was coming, and now it is in the world already" (1 Jn 4:1–3). These false teachers evidently stressed knowledge, and John agrees that knowledge is important. But he is concerned that it be real knowledge and not some sham. He points out that all believers have knowledge as a result of the Holy

Spirit within them (1 Jn 2:20); thus knowledge is not the exclusive possession of the false teachers. Indeed they lack real knowledge. John speaks especially of the knowledge of truth (1 Jn 2:21; 2 Jn 1; 3 Jn 12) and of the knowledge that "we are of the truth" (1 Jn 3:19). Much of the Christian's knowledge has to do with knowing Christ (1 Jn 2:3,13,14; 3:5). First John is written to give the knowledge of life: "I write this to you who believe in the name of the Son of God, that you may know that you have eternal life" (1 Jn 5:13).

John is clear that it is important to have right knowledge, particularly of the incarnation. He speaks of "antichrist" (1 Jn 2:18; 22; 4:3; 2 Jn 7), a term found only in these letters (the idea is found elsewhere but with other terminology). John sees antichrist as one who opposes Christ and tries to replace him. Whereas in other places there is emphasis on the opponent as a single figure (e.g., 2 Thes 2), John recognizes a spirit that might govern many people; and indeed there are many deceivers of this kind (2 Jn 7).

John has some important statements to make about God, notably that "God is light" (1 Jn 1:5) and that "God is love" (1 Jn 4:8,16). The former directs attention to the goodness of God and to his opposition to everything that is evil. The dualism between light and darkness that we found in the Gospel is an important concept in the first letter also. There is no darkness in God (1 Jn 1:5), but it is sadly possible for humans to live in darkness. If they do so, and yet claim to have fellowship with God, they are liars (1 Jn 1:6). There is no fellowship between light and darkness. Darkness is connected with lack of love—in fact, hatred—and with spiritual blindness (1 Jn 2:9,11).

All this shows that for John love is important. In a notable treatment of the theme he twice assures us that God is love. This means more than that God loves. It means that love is part of his very nature. He loves, not because he has found some very attractive people who draw love from him, so to speak. He loves because it is his nature to love, because he is a loving God. We see what love is, in the sense in which John understands it (which is not the sense the world knows), when we see the cross, not when we see human love, such as love for God (1 Jn 4:10).

A major thrust of the first letter is put simply: "Beloved, if God so loved us, we also ought to love one another" (1 Jn 4:11). When we see what God has done for us, we cannot but respond with an answering love. John insists that if there is a real love for God, it will be shown in a love for one's fellows. He uses strong language about this: "If any one says, 'I love God,' and hates his brother, he is a liar" (1 Jn 4:20). Love is practical.

John is insistent that those who belong to God must turn from every evil thing. They must not walk in darkness. He uses some strong terms and goes so far as to say that the one who has been begotten of God "cannot" sin (1 Jn 3:9; cf. vv 3,6). This does not mean that one lacks the physical capacity. It is to be understood of the habitual practice—he does not make a practice of sinning, or he can't keep on sinning. Certainly it is a strong repudiation of sin. Those who are Christ's must walk in the paths of righteousness and of love.

Theology of Revelation. Revelation is a book which tells of the realities of power. It is a theology of power. It is a book that takes us behind the curtain, so to speak, and shows us that when we come to grips with ultimate reality, the might of any earthly empire, be it Rome or any other, is but a petty and insignificant thing. Real power is with God. He works his purposes out in his own way, and that way may perhaps not be the way that men might have expected. The power of Rome may last

The Temple of Vesta in Rome, capital of the empire and center for much persecution of Christians.

for longer than persecuted Christians would have wished. But Rome is doomed, and so is every other earthly power.

The book is full of strange symbolism. Indeed, some of it may be impossible to interpret accurately with the information at our disposal. But the main lines are clear enough. From first to last Revelation tells of a God who is working out his purposes and who will continue to work them out. He is often referred to as "him who is seated upon the throne" (Rv 4:9,10; 5:1,7,13,16; 7:10,15; 19:4; 20:11; 21:5), and this reference to his royalty is important. John is writing about a God who rules heaven and earth. There is much about angels in Revelation, more indeed than in any other biblical book, and this brings out the truth that God has powerful beings who do his bidding.

The book begins with a vision of the glorious Lord (Rv 1:9–20), which sets the tone for what follows. Just as God is referred to in connection with the throne, so Christ is often "the Lamb in the midst of the throne" (5:6; 7:17; see 22:3). He is one with the Father and works out the same purpose. Chapter 4 has a vision of heaven, bringing out the majesty and holiness of God (notice the reserve with which the one on the throne is described, vv 2,3). Then we move into the triumph of the Christ, now called "the Lion of the tribe of Judah" (Rv 5:5). He is pictured as worthy to open the scroll of human destiny, and this leads to an outburst of triumphant praise from all the hosts of heaven and indeed from all creation. The book goes on to unfold something of what this means. The series of judgments linked with the seals, the trumpets, and the bowls present problems, but there can be no doubt about the way they drive home the truth that God is over all. He brings about his judgments as and when he pleases.

The book has a good deal to say about the wrath of God. This is a topic that the modern world finds uncongenial, and there are many who deny that it should be accepted as the teaching of the Bible. It is hard to see how such a verdict could apply to Revelation. John uses the words of wrath a number of times, and he makes it clear from first to last that God is vigorously opposed to every evil thing. And that, of course, is what the wrath of God is all about. It is not an irrational passion but the settled opposition of God's holy nature to everything that is evil. Revelation makes this very clear. The God who is depicted in this book will not tolerate evil. He will oppose it until in the end he destroys it completely.

Thus the book ends with a description of the new heaven and the new earth, rich with the blessing of God and from which every evil thing is excluded. The vision of the great throng of the redeemed (ch 7) and the new heaven and earth (chs 21,22) bring out vividly the complete triumph of God. The writer sees evil as powerful. That is never denied. There are some vivid pictures of a fearsome beast in league with Satan and opposed to God (13:1–10). He is supported by a second beast, not as fearful as he, but frightful enough (13:11–18). John shows us that evil is immensely powerful. But it cannot triumph in the end. John's point is that God is stronger than any evil thing or any evil being. Satan will be completely overthrown (20:10).

Christ is characteristically referred to as "the Lamb," a description that probably carries a sacrificial connotation. This seems even clearer when the Lamb is "as though slain" (e.g., 5:6). The death of Jesus is not out of mind throughout this book; but it is seen as the way of triumph, not as a defeat. Christ overcomes by way of the cross.   LEON L. MORRIS

See JOHN, GOSPEL OF; JOHN, LETTERS OF; REVELATION, BOOK OF; APOSTLE, APOSTLESHIP.

Bibliography. T.E. Crane, *The Message of St John*; J.E. Davey, *The Jesus of St John*; W.F. Howard, *Christianity According to St John*; R. Kysar, *The Fourth Evangelist and His Gospel*; E.K. Lee, *The Religious Thought of St John*; L. Morris, *Studies in the Fourth Gospel*; C.F. Nolloth, *The Fourth Evangelist*; N.J. Painter, *John: Witness and Theologian*; G.B. Stevens, *The Johannine Theology*.

John the Baptist.

Forerunner of the Messiah who prepared the people for Jesus' coming, proclaimed the need for forgiveness of sins, and offered a baptism symbolizing repentance. His ministry included the baptism of Jesus in the Jordan River, where he testified to Jesus being the Expected One from God. John was arrested and beheaded by Herod Antipas in approximately AD 29, while Jesus was still ministering.

Infancy and Boyhood. Luke is our only source of information concerning the birth and boyhood of John. The Gospel writer states that John was born in the hill country of Judah (1:39) of priestly descent, being the son of Zechariah, a priest of the order of Abijah (1:5), and Elizabeth, a daughter of Aaron (1:5b). Both parents were righteous before God, following all the commandments closely (1:6). Like the birth of Jesus, only to a much lesser degree, the birth of John the Baptist is described in Luke as extraordinary. The angel Gabriel announced the coming birth to Zechariah in the temple; to the older, barren Elizabeth it came as an answer to prayer (1:8–13). John's name is announced to Zechariah by the angel, even as his purpose as forerunner is revealed before birth (1:13–17). Such a consecration from birth is reminiscent of the call of the OT prophet Jeremiah (Jer 1:5).

There existed some familial relationship between the families of John and Jesus. Elizabeth is described as a "kinswoman" of Mary (1:36), which may connote cousin or aunt, but may only mean being from the same tribe.

John's childhood, as that of Jesus, is left quite vague in the Gospel account. All that is said is that the "child grew and became strong in spirit, and he was in the wilderness till the day of his manifestation to Israel" (Lk 1:80). Some scholars have suggested that John might have been adopted as a boy by the Essenes (as was their practice) at Qumran and reared in their wilderness community, adjacent to the Dead Sea and near the Jordan River. There are some similarities between the Qumran sect, known through the Dead Sea Scrolls, and the later ministry of John the Baptist. Both practiced a type of asceticism and removed themselves from the life of Jerusalem. Both practiced baptism and associated this rite with initiation and repentance. Finally, John and the Qumran group were both eschatologically minded, awaiting God's final end-time activity in history. Nevertheless, many significant differences exist between John and the Qumran sect.

Appearance and Identity. Mark's Gospel begins with an account of John the Baptist's appearance "in the wilderness, preaching a baptism of repentance for the forgiveness of sins" (Mk 1:4). A rich OT background lies behind John's association with the wilderness, in this case the wilderness of Judea. It was in the wilderness that God revealed himself to Moses (Ex 3), gave the Law, and entered into the covenant with Israel (Ex 19). It was also the site of refuge for David (1 Sm 23–26; Ps 63) and Elijah (1 Kgs 19), and in this light became the anticipated site of God's future deliverance (Hos 2:14,15; Ez 47:1–12; esp. Is 40:3–5).

The strange dress of John the Baptist, "clothing made of camel's hair with a leather belt around his waist" (Mk 1:6 NIV) may have suggested to his audience an association with Elijah in particular (2 Kgs 1:8) or with the prophets in general (Zec 13:4). His diet, "locusts and wild honey" (Mk 1:6), was levitically clean, reflecting one who lived off the desert (such food was also eaten at Qumran) or forming part of the broader asceticism practiced by John and his disciples (Mk 9:14; 11:18). Who did John understand himself to be? In answer to questions by the multitude whether he was the Messiah, Elijah, or the expected prophet (Jn 1:20–23), John only identified himself as "A voice cries: 'In the wilderness prepare the way of the Lord'" (Is 40:3). The background for the question lies at the end of the OT period; prophecy on the one hand was considered to have ceased (Zec 13:2–6), yet on the

other hand was expected to appear again before the coming of the messianic kingdom (see Jl 2:28,29; Mal 3:1–4). Some anticipated this final prophet to be one "like unto Moses" (Dt 18:15), others a returning Elijah as foretold in Malachi 4:5,6. While John personally refrained from identifying himself with these specific expectations (Jn 1:20–23), it is clear that his dress, life-style, and message caused the people to identify him with this end-time prophet (Mt 14:5; Mk 11:32). Jesus also saw John as this final "Elijah-like" prophet (Mt 11:7–15), who from Malachi's prophecy was to be a forerunner to the coming of the Lord (Mal 3:1–4; 4:5,6).

Proclamation. John's proclamation involved three elements: a warning of imminent judgment at the hands of the Coming One, a call for repentance in light of the coming kingdom of heaven, and a demand to express this repentance in concrete ethical terms. Many Jews looked forward confidently to the messianic judgment as a time of blessing for themselves and destruction for the gentile oppressors. John, however, warned that Jewish ancestry was only false security in the coming judgment (Lk 3:8); true repentance was the only means of escaping destruction (Mt 3:2). John anticipated this judgment at the hands of the Coming One, who would baptize the nation with "the Holy Spirit and with fire" (Lk 3:16). Fire represented the OT means of destruction in the end time (Mal 4:1) as well as purification (Mal 3:1–4), while the outpouring of the Holy Spirit in the end time connoted blessing (Is 32:15; Ez 39:29; Jl 2:28) and purification (Is 4:2–4). The judgment anticipated by John was therefore twofold: destruction for the unrepentant and blessing for the penitent and righteous (Mt 3:12).

In light of this imminent event John called for repentance on the part of his listeners (Mt 3:2), a true "turning back" or turning "toward" God in obedience that would bring forgiveness of sin. Such a turnabout in an individual's relation with God should be lived out in one's everyday dealings: fairness on the part of the tax collector (Lk 3:12,113) and soldiers (3:14), and the general requirement of compassion for the poor (3:10,11).

Baptism. The Gospels record that John baptized those repentant of their sins at several locations: the Jordan River (Mk 1:5), Bethany beyond the Jordan (Jn 1:28), and Aenon near Salim (Jn 3:23). This practice was an integral part of John's call for repentance, given in light of the approaching judgment and the appearance of the Coming One. The baptism of the penitent symbolized desire for forgiveness of sin, a renunciation of past life, and a desire to be included in the coming messianic kingdom.

What was the background for John's practice of baptism? From the OT we know of ceremonial lustrations or washings which guaranteed ritual purity (Lv 14, 15; Nm 19). Unlike John's baptism, these washings were repetitive in nature and referred predominantly to ritual rather than moral cleansing. The prophets, however, urged a moral purification associated with the washing of water (Is 1:16–18; Jer 4:14). More significantly, the prophets anticipated a cleansing by God in the end times preceding the day of judgment (Ez 36:25; Zec 13:1; cf. Is 44:3), an eschatological element which John may have assumed was being fulfilled in his water baptism.

Another precedent for John's practice may have been proselyte baptism, a rite along with circumcision and the offering of sacrifices which constituted the conversion of a Gentile to Judaism. Common to both proselyte baptism and John's baptism were the emphasis on an ethical break with the past, a once-for-all character, and the similarity of immersion. Notable differences were that John's baptism was for Jews, not gentile converts, and had a marked eschatological character as a preparation for the new age. Unless John, in light of the imminence of the messianic age, consciously treated all Jews as "pagans" in need of a baptism of repentance (cf. Mt 3:7–10), it is doubtful that proselyte baptism formed the primary background for John's baptismal ministry.

In the Qumran community we know from the Dead Sea Scrolls that baptism, along with penitence, formed part of the initiation of members into this eschatologically oriented community. Assuming John was familiar with this community, it is possible that his similar practice of baptism derived to a degree from that community's practice. Nevertheless, John transformed the meaning of baptism in his administration of it, which was open to the entire nation, once-for-all in character, and had a stronger eschatological flavor.

If John's baptism had this clear association with the forgiveness of sin, the question naturally arises as to why Jesus, the Son of God, sought baptism from John. John himself asks this very question of Jesus (Mt 3:14), to which our Lord responds, "Let it be so now; for thus it is fitting for us to fulfil all righteousness" (15). First, it is clear that Jesus' baptism represented an act of obedience on his part to God's will as he saw it. Second, by submitting to the baptism of John, Jesus was clearly validating the ministry and message of John. The imminent coming of the kingdom and its Messiah, and the need for repentance in anticipation of

this event which John proclaimed, were affirmed by Jesus through baptism. Third, by being baptized, Jesus condemned the self-righteous for their lack of repentance and took a stand with the penitent publicans and sinners awaiting the kingdom of God (Lk 7:29,30). Fourth, Jesus stepped forward for baptism not as an individual in need of forgiveness but as the Messiah, as a representative of the people before God. His baptism therefore demonstrated solidarity with the people in their need of deliverance, even as he is judged in their place on the cross. Finally, the voice from heaven (Mk 1:11) and the descent of the Spirit (Lk 3:21,22) signify the inauguration of Jesus' own ministry through his baptism by John.

John's View of Jesus. Throughout his ministry John pointed beyond himself to one "mightier than I, the thong of whose sandals I am not worthy to stoop down and untie" (Mk 1:7). His self-understanding apparently sprang from the application of Isaiah 40:3 to himself, that he was the preparer or forerunner for God's coming activity through the Messiah (Lk 3:4–6). When asked by curious spectators, John firmly denied that he was the Messiah, and according to the Gospel accounts subordinated himself to the Coming One (Mk 1:7,8; Jn 1:26–28; 3:28–31). The coming of Jesus to baptism seems to represent the first time John identified these expectations with Jesus himself (Jn 1:38). His recognition of Jesus as the Messiah prior to baptism (Mt 3:14) was confirmed by the descent of the Holy Spirit as a dove and the voice from heaven quoting a phrase from an OT messianic psalm (Mk 1:11a from Ps 2:7) together with a phrase from a Suffering Servant song of Isaiah (Mk 1:11b from Is 42:1). In the fourth Gospel, John the Baptist goes even further in acknowledging Jesus to be the "Lamb of God" (1:29,36), an anticipation of Jesus' sacrificial role on the cross, and the "Son of God" (1:34, a probable equating of Jesus with the Messiah; Ps 2:7, see Mk 1:11).

In light of John's strong affirmation, it is at first difficult to understand his questioning of Jesus while imprisoned ("Are you he who is to come, or should we look for another?" Mt 11:2–8). Some have suggested that John was merely asking for the sake of his disciples, or that the question reflected John's own despondency with being imprisoned. It is more likely, however, that the question represents John's own confusion with the activity expected of the Messiah. John had proclaimed a Coming One who would bring a baptism of fire and judgment upon the wicked (Lk 3:16). It may have been difficult for him to understand Jesus' different emphases on forgiveness and acceptance of sinners (Mt 9:9–13) and his healing of the sick (Mt 8,9). When John's disciples bring their master's question to Jesus, asking whether or not he is the Messiah, Jesus responds by quoting Isaiah 35:5,6 (see also Is 61:1). This text proclaims the activities of healing and proclaiming salvation to the poor to indeed be fulfillments of the Messiah's role, even though they may not have been what John or countless other Jews expected.

Jesus' View of John. That Jesus highly regarded John the Baptist is implied by his baptism by John. It is also explicitly stated on several occasions. John "came to you in the way of righteousness" (Mt 21:32), had "borne witness to the truth, . . . a burning and shining lamp" (Jn 5:33–35), and practiced a baptism divinely ordained (Lk 20:1–8).

John's uniqueness, however, lies in the fact that he stood at the turning of the ages. He was the last of the old era, the period of the law and the prophets (Lk 16:16), which was to precede the coming of the messianic age (the kingdom of God). John was the last of the prophets, the greatest of them, the Elijah figure who would prepare the way for the judgment of God (Mt 11:13–15; Lk 1:17). Because John belonged to the era of the law and the prophets, however, he was not as great as the "least" already in the kingdom of God (Mt 11:11)—that is, those who belonged to the era of the kingdom's appearance in Jesus.

Arrest, Imprisonment, and Martyrdom. To understand why John was arrested and beheaded by Herod Antipas, one has to grasp the messianic excitement caused by John's appearance and message (Lk 3:15–18). Herod and other secular rulers were obviously suspicious of anyone who might stir up the crowds with predictions of a coming messianic ruler. Other messianic movements had arisen before John which resulted in outbreaks of violence against the Roman-Herodian rulership. Moreover, Her-

od Antipas was under heavy criticism for his marriage with Herodias, the ex-wife of his brother Philip. His first marriage, with the daughter of Aretus II, constituted a political alliance between the Herodian family and the Nabataean kingdom of Perea. His new relationship with Herodias was perceived as a breach of the political alliance and led to friction between the two families. John's denunciation of Herod's new marriage (Mt 14:3–12) could thus have been interpreted by Herod as a subversive rousing of sentiment against his authority. The Jewish historian Josephus states that Herod did in fact arrest John because he feared John's influence over the crowds. According to Josephus, John was imprisoned at the fortress Machaerus on the eastern side of the Dead Sea. That he was not killed immediately was due to Herod's personal fear of the righteous John (Mk 6:2) and of the people's reaction (Mt 14:5). On a point about which Josephus is silent, the Gospels record that it was Herodias' feelings against John (Mk 6:17) and her plot, through the dancing of her daughter, which brought about the beheading of John (Mk 6:21–29). John was beheaded at Herodias' request in approximately AD 29 or 30.

The Disciples of John. While it is clear that a band of disciples formed around John in his lifetime (Jn 1:35), to suggest that he intended to begin a continuing movement is contradicted by his message on the imminent day of judgment. Apparently his disciples consisted of a small group of those who had been baptized by John and were awaiting the coming Messiah. Some transferred their loyalty after John had identified Jesus as the Coming One (Jn 1:37). Others, however, apparently stayed on with their teacher, communicating with the imprisoned John concerning the activities of Jesus (Lk 7:18–23) and after his death taking the body for burial (Mk 6:29).

The Dead Sea, near where Josephus says John the Baptist was imprisoned.

We know little about the activities and practices of the band of disciples clustered around John. We do know, however, that fasting was one practice specifically associated with the group, and one that marked them as similar to the Pharisees (Mt 9:14). In this practice they no doubt followed the example of John himself (Lk 7:33). Prayer and fasting were often linked in late Judaism. The disciples of John were also known for the prayers taught by their master (Lk 11:1). Seeing this practice, the disciples of Jesus asked the Lord to teach them to pray, to which Jesus responded with the Lord's Prayer (11:2–4).

After his death it is likely that other disciples of John came over to the followers of Jesus (see Lk 7:29,30). Not all did so, however, as is attested by the presence of disciples of John encountered by Paul approximately 25 years later in Ephesus (Acts 18:24–19:7). Upon hearing Paul's witness to Jesus, these Ephesian followers of John responded by being baptized in the name of Jesus and received the Holy Spirit (19:4–7). It is apparent from later documents that various groups continued to honor John, even considering him the Messiah, centuries after the NT period.   DAVID C. CARLSON

Bibliography. F.F. Bruce, *NT History;* C.H. Kraeling, *John the Baptist;* C.H.H. Scobie, *John the Baptist;* J. Steinmann, *St John the Baptist and the Desert Tradition;* W. Wink, *John the Baptist in the Gospel Tradition.*

Joiada.   1. Paseah's son who, with Meshullam, repaired the Old Gate in the Jerusalem wall during the days of Nehemiah (Neh 3:6, KJV Jehoiada).

2. Levite and high priest in Jerusalem during the postexilic era, the great-grandson of Jeshua, son of Eliashib, and father of Jonathan (or Jehohanan, Neh 12:10,11,22). He is alternately called Jehoiada in Nehemiah 13:28, where one of his sons was expelled from the priesthood for marrying a daughter of Sanballat, governor of Samaria.

Joiakim.   Levite; Jeshua's son and the father of Eliashib the high priest, a contemporary of Nehemiah (Neh 12:10,12,26).

Joiarib.   1. One of the Jewish leaders whom Ezra sent to Iddo at Casiphia to gather Levites and temple servants for the caravan of Jews returning to Palestine from Babylon (Ezr 8:16). He is alternately called Jehoiarib in 1 Chronicles 9:10.

2. Zechariah's son, the father of Adaiah, and an ancestor of a Judahite family living in Jerusalem during the postexilic era under Nehemiah (Neh 11:5).

3. Father of Jedaiah, a priest who served in the temple during the days of Nehemiah (Neh

11:10). Perhaps Joiarib's forefather was Jehoiarib, who was the head of the first course of priests ministering in the sanctuary during David's reign (1 Chr 24:7).

4. One of the leaders of the priests who returned with Zerubbabel and Jeshua to Judah after the exile (Neh 12:6). His family in the next generation was headed by Nattenai (v 19).

Jokdeam.   One of the cities located in the hill country allotted to Judah's tribe for an inheritance, mentioned between Jezreel and Zanoah (Jos 15:56). Its site is uncertain.

Jokim.   Descendant of Judah through Shelah's line (1 Chr 4:22).

Jokmeam.   1. City of Zebulun (1 Kgs 4:12); perhaps the same as Jokneam.
  See JOKNEAM.

2. City given to the Kohathite Levites out of Ephraim's inheritance (1 Chr 6:68). A parallel passage in Joshua 21:22 lists the city as Kibzaim. Its site is unknown.
  See KIBZAIM.

Jokneam.   Royal Canaanite city "belonging to Carmel" (Jos 12:22), mentioned also by Thutmose III as "the Well of Q." The border of Zebulun touched on the "stream that is before Jokneam" (Jos 19:11); the town became a levitical city in Zebulun (Jos 21:34). Some think that Jokmean of 1 Kings 4:12 should be amended to Jokneam, but this is not certain. Eusebius placed it six miles from Legio (beside Megiddo) on the way to Ptolemais. This is Tell Qaimun, at the mouth of Wadi Milh on the edge of the Jezreel Valley. It is under excavation by the Hebrew University.

  See LEVITICAL CITIES.

Jokshan.   Son of Abraham and Keturah, and the father of Sheba and Dedan (Gn 25:2,3; 1 Chr 1:32).

Joktan.   Eber's son and younger brother of Peleg. A number of Arabian groups descended from him (Gn 10:25–29; 1 Chr 1:19–23).

Joktheel.   1. Town in the Shephelah of Judah near Lachish (Jos 15:38). Its exact location is unknown.

2. Ancient Edomite stronghold originally named Sela. Amaziah changed its name to Joktheel after defeating the Edomites (2 Kgs 14:7).

Jona.   KJV form of John, father of Simon Peter and Andrew, in John 1:42.

  See JOHN (PERSON) #1.

Jonadab. 1. King David's nephew, the son of David's brother Shimeah. As the friend to David's son Amnon, he devised a scheme by which Amnon seduced his half sister Tamar (2 Sm 13:3,5). Absalom, Tamar's brother, sought revenge by killing Amnon.

2. Rechab's son; descendant of the Kenites and Calebites (1 Chr 2:55; 4:11,12). He founded the religious order of Rechabites, who maintained a strong anti-agriculturalist tradition (Jehonadab, Jer 35:6–19). He encouraged Jehu in his bloody reform of the house of Ahab (2 Kgs 10:15,23, Jehonadab).

Jonah (Person). Prophet of Israel; Amittai's son (Jon 1:1) of the Zebulunite city of Gath-hepher (2 Kgs 14:25). The historian who wrote 2 Kings recorded that Jonah had a major prophetic role in the reign of King Jeroboam II (793–753 BC). Jonah had conveyed a message encouraging expansion to the king of Israel, whose reign was marked by prosperity, expansion, and, unfortunately, moral decline.

In the midst of all the political corruption of Israel, Jonah remained a zealous patriot. His reluctance to go to Nineveh doubtless stemmed partially from his knowledge that the Assyrians would be used as God's instrument for punishing Israel. The prophet, who had been sent to Jeroboam to assure him that his kingdom would prosper, was the same prophet God chose to send to Nineveh to forestall that city's (and thus that nation's) destruction until Assyria could be used to punish Israel in 722 BC. It is no wonder that the prophet reacted emotionally to his commission.

No other prophet was so strongly Jewish (cf. his classic confession, Jon 1:9), yet no other prophet's ministry was so strongly directed to a non-Jewish nation. Jonah's writing is also unusual among the prophets. The book is primarily historical narrative. His actual preaching is recorded in only five words in the Hebrew; eight words in most English translations (Jon 3:4b). In the NT, Jonah is called Jonas (KJV).

See JONAH, BOOK OF; JEROBOAM #2; ISRAEL, HISTORY OF; PROPHET, PROPHETESS.

Jonah, Book of. Fifth book of the 12 Minor Prophets in the traditional arrangement of the books of the OT. It is a literary narrative rather than a series of prophetic oracles, and gives the account of Jonah's experiences after he disobeyed a command of the Lord directing him to preach to the people of Nineveh. Several extraordinary events recorded in the book have made it the center of much controversy as to its interpretation.

Author. The Book of Jonah has been traditionally ascribed to Jonah the son of Amittai, a prophet of great influence who ministered during the reign of Jeroboam II of Israel (2 Kgs 14:25).

The content of the book describes Jonah as an intensely patriotic person, but his misguided patriotism caused him to rebel at the possibility of Israel's former enemies receiving forgiveness from God. One of the most important lessons of the book emerges when God rebukes Jonah's exclusivistic attitude (4:6–11).

Jesus used two of the experiences of Jonah as signs to his generation. The three days and nights spent by Jonah in the great fish served as an analogy of Jesus' death and resurrection (Mt 12:38–41). Also, the positive response of the Ninevites to Jonah's preaching was used by Jesus as a condemnation of the failure of many in his generation to believe in him (Lk 11:32).

Authenticity. The unusual elements in the Book of Jonah have led to widely varying views of its nature. Not only has the account of Jonah being swallowed by the fish led some to think the book to be of a fabulous nature, but the account of the repentance of the people of Nineveh (3:5) has been regarded as highly unlikely as well.

The historicity of the book has been championed by outstanding biblical scholars. The basic approach of these scholars has been to counter the arguments of those who deny its historicity and to point to what is regarded as positive evidence for the historicity of the book in Jesus' allusions to the prophecy and in early Jewish tradition.

Opponents of the authenticity of Jonah point to the following difficulties: (1) The use of the expression "king of Nineveh" (3:6) appears to be an inaccuracy because Nineveh was the capital of Assyria. A contemporary would have referred to the king as the king of Assyria. (2) The use of the past tense to describe the city of Nineveh (3:3) seems to point to a much later date than the traditional view of the authorship of the book would permit. (3) The size of the city of Nineveh is described in greatly exaggerated terms (3:3). (4) The mass repentance of the Ninevites lacks historical support. (5) It is unlikely that a human being could exist within a fish for an extended period of time.

With regard to the use of "king of Nineveh," it should be noted that similar expressions may be found in the OT. Ahab, the king of Israel, is called "king of Samaria" (1 Kgs 21:1), and Ben-hadad, the king of Syria, is designated "king of Damascus" (2 Chr 24:23). The designation "king of Nineveh" is therefore not anomalous.

The use of the past tense to describe the city of Nineveh may be regarded as nothing more than a simple narrative past tense describing the size of the city at the time that Jonah prophesied there.

The description of the size of the city ("three days' journey") may be an indication of the length of time that it would take one to go through the suburbs included in the administrative district of Nineveh.

The repentance of the Ninevites is not to be understood as a mass conversion to Yahweh, the God of Israel. The Book of Jonah describes their response as repentance in view of the impending destruction threatened by Jonah (3:4). While secular history does not record such an event, there is evidence that such a response was possible. In less than a decade (765–759 BC) the city of Nineveh had experienced a total eclipse of the sun and two serious plagues. One can understand how the citizens of Nineveh may have been prepared for the preaching of this prophet who came to them in such an unusual way.

It should also be noted that one of the kings of Assyria, Adad-Nirari III, limited his worship only to the god Nebo. If the prophetic ministry of Jonah was carried on around the time of his reign (810–783 BC), it is possible that the Jewish monotheism represented by Jonah may have found a more favorable climate than one would normally expect in a pagan society.

The participation of the animals in the national penitence that followed Jonah's preaching (3:7,8) is not unknown from history. The historian Herodotus records a similar event in the Persian Empire.

The event that creates the greatest difficulty, however, is the experience of Jonah in the fish. It has often been pointed out that the gullets of most whales are not large enough to admit an object the size of a man. But the book does not say that it was a whale that swallowed Jonah, but simply a great fish (1:17). It is possible, however, for a sperm whale to swallow an object as large as a man.

Numerous examples of individuals being swallowed by whales have been cited in the past. While many of these accounts may be disregarded as fancy, it would be wrong to uncritically reject all of them. (An interesting account of one of these experiences may be found in the *Princeton Theological Review* 25, 1927, p. 636.) The experience of Jonah in the great fish need not be regarded as an absolute impossibility. The activities of God in history have often been accompanied by unusual or miraculous events.

The difficulties of the Book of Jonah have led many to regard the book as a prophetic parable rather than a record of historical fact. The most common interpretation is that the book is an expression of the universal concerns of God. As such it inveighs against the exclusive nationalism of the Jews. This narrow-minded attitude, some suggest, fits best into the postexilic period when the hatred of Israel for its former captors was still very bitter.

There are several difficulties with this view. While there are a number of parables in the OT, none is as extensive as the Book of Jonah. Also, since the major elements of a parable symbolize persons, objects, or concepts that contribute to the main teaching of the parable, the proponents of this view are hard pressed to show how the account of Jonah's experience in the fish contributes to the central lesson of the parable.

Another approach to the book is to regard it as an extended allegory. An allegory is a literary form, the basic elements of which are intended to symbolize or explain aspects of real life to which they are analogous. The intended meaning is usually evident or explained by the author. In the OT, allegories are short literary forms used to lend force to a pronouncement. The Book of Jonah does not seem to fit this category. It is a narrative account with no evident meaning given to the various persons, objects, and events cited.

There seems to be no convincing reason for rejecting the historicity of the Book of Jonah on the basis of the arguments generally given. Jesus referred to the account of Jonah in a way that seems to imply his acceptance of its validity.

Date. If Jonah was the son of Amittai cited in 2 Kings 14:25, the prophecy would have to be dated in the reign of Jeroboam II of Israel (793–753). Jonah would then be one of the great 8th-century prophets who ministered during the Silver Age of Israel.

Those who understand the book to have been written by an author other than Jonah place the writing at various times, from the period following the fall of Nineveh to well into the postexilic period.

Background. Archaeological excavations at the site of ancient Nineveh have yielded many artifacts and literary works indicating that it was a cultural center for a great part of its history. In the Middle Assyrian period, the city of Nineveh was greatly enlarged and became an administrative center. Some of the most powerful Assyrian kings ruled from Nineveh.

The city of Calah, to the south of Nineveh, had an area much smaller than Nineveh but housed almost 70,000 persons. The description of the vast population of Nineveh in the prophecy of Jonah seems to fit with this.

Purpose. The purpose of the Book of Jonah is to teach that God's grace was not limited to the Hebrew people. This lesson is taught in the dramatic climax of the book. Jonah, filled with self-pity, laments that the plant that gave him shade had been withered by the sun. God places Jonah's pity for the plant in stark contrast to God's concern for the thousands of people of Nineveh.

The book clearly sets forth the fact that God's mercy was not the sole possession of the Hebrew people of Jonah's time but was available to all through repentance. Even Israel's enemies could experience God's mercy.

Content. The Book of Jonah begins with a command from the Lord to the prophet directing him to preach to the people of Nineveh. Jonah was reluctant to go to Nineveh because he knew that the Ninevites would repent. He would thus find himself in the dubious position of proclaiming God's mercy to the hated Assyrians. Therefore, he fled from Joppa by ship in a mindless attempt to flee from the presence of God. He boarded a ship bound for Tarshish, a Phoenician colony in southern Spain. It was as far west as Jonah could flee within the scope of the ancient Mediterranean world (1:1–3).

God would not allow his servant to disobey without chastisement, however (1:4–16). God's love demanded Jonah's discipline. The program of discipline commenced with a divinely originated storm (1:4). In the midst of the terrifying rage of this storm the sailors busied themselves with supplications to their individual pagan deities and with casting excess cargo overboard (1:5). Through all the commotion Jonah was asleep in the hold of the ship (1:5).

The sailors were as yet unaware that Jonah was the real problem. The captain of the ship aroused Jonah and told him to pray to his god for deliverance from the tempest (1:6).

Receiving no response to their supplications, the sailors proceeded to cast lots in an attempt to determine who on board was the cause of the wrath of the god who had brought the storm upon them (Jon 1:7); the lot indicated that Jonah was to blame (1:7). The sailors then wanted to know what god was responsible for the storm and why. Jonah's testimony was simple and to the point: he was a Hebrew who worshiped Jehovah, who created both land and sea (1:9).

The sailors asked Jonah what they should do to him since the storm was increasing in its fury (1:11). The captain had previously told Jonah to pray or perish. Now Jonah revealed that praying would not accomplish what his perishing could (1:12). He asked them to throw him into the sea.

Before yielding to Jonah's request, the sailors struggled to save the ship (1:13). Failing in their attempt, they cast him into the sea (1:15). Imagine the impression made on these sailors when the storm ceased as soon as Jonah's body was in the sea. Their experience caused the ship's crew to fear Jehovah, and they offered a sacrifice and made vows to him (1:16).

God was not through with Jonah, for he prepared a great fish to swallow him (1:17). Jonah was in the belly of the fish for three days and nights (1:17; cf. Mt 12:38–41). From within the fish Jonah prayed to God (2:1), and God heard the prayer of the prophet (2:7,8). Jonah's deliverance brought him to the point of renewed devotion to God (2:9). It is significant that his prayer reflected a deep personal acquaintance with the Psalms (cf. Pss 3:8; 5:7; 18:4–19; 30:2,3; 31:6,22; 39:9; 42:6,7; 59:17; 69:1,2; 120:1; 142:3; 144:2).

The ultimate answer to Jonah's prayers came when God provided him with the opportunity of obeying his commission and keeping his vows. The sea creature spit Jonah out upon the shore (Jon 2:10).

The second major section of the book commences with 3:1. The writer now turns his attention to God's dealing with the city of Nineveh (3:1–4:11). Jonah repented of his disobedience and manifested that repentance by obeying the commission to declare God's message to Nineveh (3:1–4). Upon his arrival in Nineveh, he proceeded to proclaim God's message for one full day. The inhabitants of the city were told they had 40 days (3:4), but they evidently responded immediately since the other two days needed for Jonah to cover the city are not recorded.

The people and their king repented in sackcloth and with fasting (3:5,6). Having repented privately, the king made a public proclamation to reinforce the response to God's message (3:7–9). Jonah' previous reluctance and continuing grudging attitude were rebuked (3:10–4:11).

God's acceptance of Nineveh's repentance caused Jonah to complain (4:1–3). His recently uttered psalm of prayerful praise to God (2:1–9) now turned to bitter grumbling. Jonah prayed again to God (4:2), revealing his reason for refusing to obey the first commission. He had personal knowledge of God's loving and forgiving nature, and resented that love and forgiveness being extended to the enemies of his country. In foolish abandon Jonah asked to die rather than to see God's work among the Ninevites (4:3).

God's compassion had been manifested to Nineveh, but he was also to show compassion again to Jonah by illustration and instruction (4:4–11). God's quiet question, "Do you do well to be angry?" must have probed Jonah's innermost being (4:4). But the prophet preferred to pout in a temporary shelter on the east side of Nineveh (4:5).

God added a gourd (some kind of large plant with large leaves, probably the palm-crist plant) to the number of nature's objects which he used in his dealings with Jonah (4:6). This provision for Jonah's comfort brought him joy. But the gourd was destroyed by a worm sent by God (4:7). Then God sent the hot sirocco wind to dry out the air, increase the heat, and add to Jonah's misery (4:8). Again, Jonah begged to die.

For the second time God asked Jonah, "Do you do well to be angry for the plant?" (4:9). The point of the illustration was being driven home to the insensitive prophet. Jonah, however, responded with more bitterness (4:9). Jonah was greatly agitated because the loss of the gourd affected him personally, even though he had nothing to do with its creation (4:10). Jehovah had created man. Jehovah was concerned for the welfare of the Ninevites. Did not the great Creator have the right to be agitated over the destruction of Nineveh with its 120,000 children and all its cattle (4:11)? As Jonah had desired the preservation of the gourd, so God had desired even more exceedingly the preservation of Nineveh.

THOMAS E. McCOMISKEY

See JONAH (PERSON); PROPHECY; PROPHET, PROPHETESS; ISRAEL, HISTORY OF.

Bibliography. G. Ch. Aalders, *The Problem of the Book of Jonah;* L.C. Allen, *The Books of Joel, Obadiah, Jonah, and Micah;* S.C. Burn, *The Prophet Jonah;* G.A. Smith, *The Book of the Twelve Prophets,* vol. 2; C. von Orelli, *The Twelve Minor Prophets.*

Jonam, Jonan. Ancestor of Jesus mentioned in Luke's genealogy (3:30, KJV Jonan).

See GENEALOGY OF JESUS CHRIST.

Jonas. 1. KJV form of Jonah in Matthew 12:39–41 and Luke 11:29–32.

See JONAH (PERSON).

2. KJV form of John, Simon Peter's father, in John 21:15,17.

See JOHN (PERSON) #1.

Jonathan. 1. Levite from Bethlehem in Judah, a descendant of Gershon, son of Moses (cf. 1 Chr 23:14–16); he was a priest first to Micah in Ephraim and later to Dan's tribe during the period of the judges (Jgs 18:30).

2. Benjamite, the firstborn son of Saul and the father of Merib-baal (1 Sm 14:49; 1 Chr 8:33,34). Jonathan was a valiant warrior (1 Sm 13:2–4; 14:1–15; 2 Sm 1:22) and a devoted friend to David (1 Sm 18:1–5; 19:1–7). He was eventually killed, along with his brothers, by the Philistines at Mt Gilboa (1 Sm 31:2; 1 Chr 10:2).

3. Son of the high priest Abiathar and one

Mt Gilboa—where Saul and Jonathan died in battle.

of David's loyal servants (2 Sm 15:27,36; 17:17, 20; 1 Kgs 1:42,43).

4. Shimei's son and the nephew of David (2 Sm 21:21; 1 Chr 20:7).

5. Son of Shagee the Hararite and one of David's mighty warriors (2 Sm 23:32; 1 Chr 11:34).

6. Judahite; Jada's son, the brother of Jether, and the father of Peleth and Zaza (1 Chr 2:32,33).

7. Son of Uzziah and one of David's treasurers (1 Chr 27:25, KJV Jehonathan).

8. David's relative who served as counselor and scribe in the royal household (1 Chr 27:32).

9. Ebed's father. Ebed returned with Ezra to Judah following the Babylonian captivity (Ezr 8:6).

10. Asahel's son, who, with Jahzeiah, opposed Ezra's suggestion that the sons of Israel should divorce the foreign women they had married since returning to Palestine from exile (Ezr 10:15).

11. Levite; the son of Joiada, the father of Jaddua, and a descendant of Jeshua, the high priest (Neh 12:11). He is perhaps the same man as Jehohanan, Eliashib's grandson, in Ezra 10:6.

See JEHOHANAN #4.

12. Priest and the head of Malluchi's house during the days of Joiakim the high priest (Neh 12:14).

13. Priest; father of Zechariah and a descendant of Asaph (Neh 12:35).

14. Secretary in whose house Jeremiah was at one point imprisoned during the reign of King Zedekiah of Judah (Jer 37:15,20; 38:26).

15. Kareah's son, who, with his brother Johanan, sought protection under Gedaliah (Jer 40:8; RSV omits Jonathan).

Jonath-elem-rechokim. Hebrew phrase in the title of Psalm 56 (KJV), translated "according to The Dove on the Far-off Terebinths"

(RSV); perhaps a familiar ancient melody to which the psalm was performed.

See MUSIC AND MUSICAL INSTRUMENTS.

Joppa. City about 35 miles northwest of Jerusalem that served as Jerusalem's seaport. Joppa was built on a rocky hill about 116 feet high, with a cape projecting beyond the coastline into the sea, and was the only natural harbor on the Mediterranean coast between Egypt and the OT town of Acco. Some 300 to 400 feet offshore a series of reefs formed a breakwater so that entrance into the harbor was gained from the north. It is possible that the harbor was larger and better protected in biblical times than is true today. The biblical city was well supplied with water, and the land surrounding it was quite fertile.

Joppa first appears in ancient records in the Egyptian list of Palestinian cities captured by Thutmose III (1490–1432 BC). During the Amarna period it was ruled by a local prince in alliance with Jerusalem. One source from this period describes its beautiful gardens and the craftsmanship of its workers in metal, leather, and wood. When Palestine was divided among the 12 tribes, Joppa was assigned to Dan (Jos 19:46, KJV Japho). It was soon taken by the Philistines, who made it one of their seaports. David's conquest of the Philistines restored Joppa to Israel, and during Solomon's reign it became a major port serving Jerusalem; cedar logs were floated from Lebanon to Joppa and then transported to Jerusalem for use in building the temple (2 Chr 2:16).

Joppa was the seaport to which Jonah fled in an attempt to avoid preaching to Nineveh (Jon 1:3); there, hoping to escape his responsibility, he boarded a ship bound for Tarshish. When Tiglath-pileser III invaded Philistia in 743 BC, Joppa probably was one of the Philistine cities which fell to him. Sennacherib in his campaign of 701 BC lists Joppa as one of the cities he occupied. Subsequent to that little is known of it until the time of Ezra, when

The harbor at Joppa (Jaffa), the seaport to which Jonah fled (Jon 1:3).

once again cedar logs from Lebanon were floated to Joppa and taken to Jerusalem for the rebuilding of the temple (Ezr 3:7). During the 4th century BC, Eshmunazar of Sidon controlled the city. When Sidon revolted against Persia and was destroyed by Artaxerxes III, Joppa apparently became a free city. Alexander the Great changed its name from Yapho (its OT name) to Joppa and established a mint there, making it a city of some importance in the Greek Empire. Following Alexander's death his successors fought over the city several times. It was ruled by Egypt from 301 BC until 197 BC, when Antiochus III made it a part of the Seleucid kingdom.

During the Maccabean period Joppa had varied experiences. When Antiochus Epiphanes moved toward Jerusalem in 168 BC to enforce his program of Hellenization, he landed his troops at Joppa. In 164, because of the success of Judas Maccabeus against the Seleucids, non-Jewish citizens drowned about 200 Jews. Judas retaliated by burning the harbor installations and the boats anchored there, but was unable to conquer the city itself (2 Mc 12:3–9). In 147 Jonathan and Simon defeated Appollonius Taos, the Syrian general, and occupied Joppa as a reward from Alexander Balas, a contender for the Syrian throne. Through a series of political moves in the next few years Simon was able by 142 to fortify the city, expel the Greek inhabitants, and firmly establish Joppa as a Jewish city. During Pompey's Roman occupation, Joppa was declared a free city; it was returned to the Jews by Julius Caesar (47 BC); and it was captured by Herod the Great in 37 BC. Due to the hatred of the residents of Joppa, Herod built a new port at Caesarea, about 40 miles north of Joppa. By the time of Jesus' birth Joppa was under the rule of Caesarea in the province of Syria (Josephus *Antiq.* 17. 13. 2–4).

A Christian congregation appeared quite early in Joppa. Among the disciples living there were Dorcas, whom Peter raised from death (Acts 9:36–41), and Simon the tanner (v 43). From Joppa, Peter was called to Caesarea to present the gospel to the Roman centurion Cornelius (Acts 10:1–48).

Joppa was a primary center of revolt against the Romans. It was destroyed by Vespasian in AD 68 and replaced with a Roman army camp. It was later rebuilt, and is known today as Jaffa, a suburb of Tel Aviv.

WAYNE C. HENSLEY

Jorah. Alternate name for Hariph in Ezra 2:18.

See HARIPH.

Jorai. Member of Gad's tribe (1 Chr 5:13).

Joram.   1. Toi's son and king of Hamath. He was sent by Toi to offer congratulations to David when David won a victory over Hadadezer of Zobah (2 Sm 8:9–12). He is called Hadoram in 1 Chronicles 18:10.

2. Alternate name for Jehoram, king of Judah (853–841 BC).

See JEHORAM #1.

3. Alternate name for Jehoram, king of Israel (852–841 BC).

See JEHORAM #2.

4. Jeshaiah's son from Levi's tribe (1 Chr 26:25).

Jordan River.   River lying in the bottom of a great canyon called the Jordan Rift, an elongated depression stretching from lower southwest Asia Minor (Syria) to the Gulf of Aqaba. The rift was once filled by the Lisan Lake, but significant geologic activity caused it to recede, and the result was the formation of three separate aqueous bodies: the Huleh Lake, the Sea of Galilee, and the Dead Sea. To this day each of these are fed by the Jordan River, the stream whose name in Hebrew means "the descender."

Sources.   Originating at the northern end of the Huleh Basin, the river comprises four separate streams: Nahr Bereighith, Nahr Hasbani, Nahr el-Liddani, and Nahr Baniyas. In the northwest corner of the Huleh Valley the Bereighith emerges within the area of Merj Ayoun, flowing from a spring located on a modest knoll west of Mt Hermon. Slightly to the east is the Hasbani, a stream that descends from a spring 1700 feet above sea level and follows a course of about 24 miles. These two smaller streams merge together less than a mile above their confluence with the el-Liddani and the Baniyas. The el-Liddani, lying between the Nahr Hasbani and the Nahr Baniyas, is located near Tel el-Qadi (the biblical city of Dan). It is the most powerful stream of the four and is fed by 'Ain Leddan, a spring that is nestled among thick underbrush and is fed by the melting snows off Mt Hermon. Flowing quickly and briefly, the el-Liddani rushes to meet the Nahr Baniyas, the last of the four streams. In the northeast corner of the Huleh Valley at the NT site of Caesarea Philippi, the Baniyas originates from a cave approximately 1100 feet above sea level and follows a steep descent to its confluence with the others. These four streams making up the Jordan River then flow together along a southerly course of 10 miles before entering Huleh Lake.

Course and Character of the River.   The course of the Jordan follows a north-south route through the Great Rift, descending gradually from the Huleh Lake (7 feet above sea level) to the Dead Sea (1274 feet below sea

Aerial view of Jordan River that shows its zigzag course.

level). From the Huleh Lake the river follows a 20-mile course, passing though the basaltic lip that forms the southern dam of the Huleh basin (Rosh Pinnah Sill), and descends quickly to the Sea of Galilee (685 feet below sea level). To the south lies the Dead Sea at a distance of approximately 65 miles. The river that connects these 2 seas, however, travels a circuitous route of 200 miles, following a snakelike river bed cut through the Ghor, the canyon floor.

The Jordan has many tributaries, not all of which are perennial. If there is no consistent water source such as a spring at the head of the river bed, then these v-shaped water courses remain dry until a seasonal deluge. When the rain comes, these dry, narrow courses are filled with fast-paced streams that flow off the sides of the canyon into the Jordan River. North of the Sea of Galilee four major systems feed the fluvial system in the Huleh Basin: Nahr Dishon and Nahr Hazor on the west, and Nahr Shuah and Nahr Gilbon on the east. Between the Sea of Galilee and the Dea Sea are the following major tributary systems: on the east—Yarmuq, 'Arab, Tayibeh, Ziqlab, Jurm, Yabis, Kufrinjia, Rajib, Zarqa, Nimrin, Abu Gharuba; on the west—Fejjas, Bireh, Jalud, Malih, Far'ah, Aujah, el-Qelt.

The character of the Ghor varies from north to south as the canyon floor drops farther below sea level. Just south of the Sea of

Galilee arable fields may be cultivated without irrigation, which permits occupation and settlement. South of this and further below sea level, beyond the narrowest constriction of the canyon at Ghor el-Wahadina, the terrain and climate change. Since the floor now consistently approaches 1000 feet below sea level, the climatic conditions approximate that of the desert. In this dry and desolate region the river and its immediate environs now assume a more prominent role, becoming a lifeline to the flora and the fauna that hug its banks. Its course and character are more easily discerned as it has become a veritable stream in the desert. The dense foliage on the banks of the Jordan is still today a wildlife haunt as it was in antiquity, the low-lying shrub and the tamerisk alike providing thick ground cover. This lower section of the canyon, called the Zor, is 150 feet below the Ghor and separated by the *qattara* (a sedimentary deposit of grayish-white marls and clays that form precipitous and barren slopes) from the canyon floor above. Generally inaccessible and extremely dangerous, the Zor and *qattara* form a natural barrier between Cis-Jordan (west) and Transjordan (east). Thus, trade, settlement, and travel were necessarily affected by the various topographical features that characterize this area. And in spite of its difficult terrain south of Ghor el-Wahadina, it was an area in which numerous biblical events occurred.

Biblical Events. The OT Israelites passed across the Jordan upon entry into the Promised Land (Jos 3:14–17); the fords of the Jordan were the sites of conflict in the war of Jephthah and the Gileadites against the Ephraimites (Jgs 12:1–6); the prophet Elijah sought refuge from Ahab king of Israel by the brook of Cherith east of the Jordan (1 Kgs 17:1–5). Elijah was translated up to heaven in a whirlwind after having crossed the Jordan with Elisha on dry ground (2 Kgs 2:6–12); Naaman, the Syrian general, bathed in the Jordan at the command of Elisha and his leprosy was healed (2 Kgs 5:8–14); Elisha made the ax head float here (2 Kgs 6:1–7). In the NT, Jesus was baptized by John the Baptist in the Jordan (Mt 3:13–17); Peter confessed that Jesus was the "Christ, the Son of the living God" at Caesarea Philippi—located on one of the sources of the Jordan, Nahr Baniyas (Mt 16:13–20); Jesus healed two blind men at Jericho, which is near the Jordan (Mt 20:29–34) and visited with Zacchaeus in that same city (Lk 19:1–10).   GREGORY D. JORDAN

See PALESTINE.

Bibliography. N. Glueck, *The Other Side of Jordan* and *The River Jordan.*

The Baniyas, a source of the Jordan River, near which Peter made his memorable confession (Mt 16:16).

Jorim. Ancestor of Jesus listed in Luke's genealogy (3:29).

See GENEALOGY OF JESUS CHRIST.

Jorkeam, Jorkoam. Raham's son and a descendant of Judah through Caleb's line (1 Chr 2:44, KJV Jorkoam). The name should perhaps be understood as a place-name and be identified with Jokdeam (Jos 15:56).

Josabad. KJV spelling of Jozabad, a Benjamite warrior, in 1 Chronicles 12:4.

See JOZABAD #1.

Josaphat. KJV spelling of Jehoshaphat, Asa's son, in Matthew 1:8.

See JEHOSHAPHAT #1.

Jose. KJV spelling of Joshua, Eliezer's son, in Luke 3:29.

See JOSHUA (PERSON) #5.

Josech. Ancestor of Jesus mentioned only in Luke's genealogy (3:26, KJV Joseph).

See GENEALOGY OF JESUS CHRIST.

Josedech. KJV spelling of Jozadak, Joshua's father, in Haggai 1:1,12,14; 2:2,4; and Zechariah 6:11.

See JOZADAK.

Joseph. 1. Jacob's 11th son and the firstborn son of Rachel. Rachel named the boy Joseph, meaning "May he add," expressing her desire that God would give her another son (Gn 30:24).

Nothing more is said about Joseph until, at the age of 17, he is seen tending his father's flocks with his brothers (Gn 37:2). Joseph was the favorite of his father, since he was the son of his old age (Gn 37:3) and the firstborn son of his favorite wife. Because of this his brothers hated Joseph. This envy was magnified when Jacob gave Joseph a ground-length, long-sleeved, and perhaps multicolored robe (Gn 37:3,4). (This type of garment is illustrated by the paintings in the Asiatic tombs of Khnumhotep II at Beni Hasan and of the nobles at Gurneh, near Luxor.) The animosity of his brothers increased still more when Joseph revealed to them his dreams of dominion over them (Gn 37:5–11). Subsequently, when Joseph was sent to check on his brothers and the flocks at Shechem, his brothers sold him to a caravan of traders going down to Egypt (Gn 37:25–28). His brothers then took his robe, dipped it in goat's blood, and brought it to Jacob, who concluded that Joseph had been killed by wild animals (Gn 37:31–33); Jacob was overwhelmed with grief (Gn 37:34,35).

In Egypt, Joseph was sold to Potiphar, an Egyptian officer of the guard (Gn 37:36; 39:1), who eventually put Joseph in charge of his entire household. However, trouble arose from Potiphar's wife, who was attracted to the young Hebrew and tried to seduce him (Gn 39:6–10). He steadfastly resisted her advances, protesting that to comply with her wishes would be a disservice to his master and a sin against God (Gn 39:9). One day she seized his garment, but he left the garment behind and fled. Potiphar's wife accused Joseph of attempted rape; her report was believed, and Joseph was incarcerated in the king's prison (Gn 39:20) where Pharaoh's butler and baker were also confined. While in prison Joseph, with the Lord's help, interpreted these men's troublesome dreams. As Joseph had foretold, the baker was executed and the butler was restored to royal favor (Gn 40:5–23).

Two years later Pharaoh had two dreams which his magicians and wise men could not interpret. The butler, remembering Joseph, had him summoned from prison. God revealed to Joseph that the dreams presaged seven years of abundance, followed by seven years of famine (Gn 41:25–36). Pharaoh, impressed with Joseph's interpretation, made him ruler of Egypt, second only to himself (Gn 41:39–44). Joseph was given the name Zaphenath-paneah (meaning "uncertain," Gn 41:45) and Asenath, the daughter of Potiphera, in marriage.

Joseph was 30 years old when he became ruler of Egypt. During the seven years of prosperity he gathered food supplies for the seven years of famine to come (Gn 41:53–56). When the famine eventually became severe in Palestine, Jacob sent all his sons, except Benjamin, his youngest son, to Egypt to purchase grain. Appearing before Joseph in Egypt, they did not recognize him. But he remembered them and his dream of dominion over his family (Gn 42:8,9). After listening to the report of their family, he accused them of being spies (Gn 42:9–14) and insisted that they leave one of their brothers as hostage and return with Benjamin to verify the truthfulness of their report (Gn 42:19,20). Thus Simeon was bound and left in Egypt (Gn 42:24).

After the famine worsened in Palestine, Jacob asked his sons to go back to Egypt to buy more grain (Gn 43:1,2); reluctantly agreeing to the conditions which the Egyptian administrator had placed on them, Jacob allowed Benjamin to go with them (Gn 43:11). When they arrived in Egypt, they were taken to Joseph's house, where Simeon was restored to them (Gn 43:23) and a meal was prepared for them (Gn 43:33). Joseph at last disclosed his identity and declared that God had sent him before them to preserve their lives (Gn 45:4–8). Arrangements were then made to send for Jacob; wagons were provided, along with provisions for the journey (Gn 45:21). When Jacob came to Goshen in the Nile delta, Joseph went out to meet him, and another great reunion took place (Gn 46:28,29). He also presented his father and brothers to Pharaoh, who let live in the land of Goshen (Gn 47:6).

Upon learning that his father was ill, Joseph took his two sons, Manasseh and Ephraim, to him for his blessing. He presented the sons so that the older would be at Jacob's right hand and the younger at his left in order that Manasseh would receive the blessing of the firstborn, Jacob, however, crossed his hands and gave the greater blessing to Ephraim (Gn 48:14–20). He also gave to Joseph the land which he had taken from the Amorites (Gn 48:22). At Jacob's death, Joseph made the funeral arrangements; and after the customary funerary practices were carried out, a great funeral procession went to Canaan, where Jacob was buried by his sons in the cave of Machpelah at Hebron (Gn 50:1–12).

When Joseph was 110 years old, he called his brothers and told them that he was about

Pylon gateway to the temple of Amun at Karnak, built by Thutmose III (1504–1450 BC) in the years just before Moses took Joseph's bones out of Egypt.

to die. He made them take an oath that when they returned to Canaan they would take his bones with them. So he died, was embalmed, and was placed in a coffin in Egypt (Gn 50:26). Many years later, during the exodus, Moses took the bones of Joseph with him from Egypt (Ex 13:19). Joseph's remains were eventually interred at Shechem in the parcel of land that Jacob had bought from Hamor, the father of Shechem (Jos 24:32).

See PATRIARCHS, PERIOD OF THE; ISRAEL, HISTORY OF.

2. Igal's father from Issachar's tribe. Igal was one of the 12 spies sent by Moses to search out the land of Canaan (Nm 13:7).

3. Asaph's second son and the leader of the first course of priests serving in the sanctuary during David's reign (1 Chr 25:2,9).

4. One of Binnui's sons who was encouraged by Ezra to divorce his foreign wife during the postexilic era (Ezr 10:42).

5. Shebaniah's son and the head of his father's household during the days of Joiakim, the high priest (Neh 12:14).

6. Descendant of David (Mt 1:16; Lk 3:23) and the husband of Mary, the mother of Jesus. Joseph was betrothed to Mary, a young woman of the city of Nazareth. Mary had learned from the angel Gabriel that she was to bear the Son of God, whom she was to name Jesus (Lk 1:31) and that this conception was to be a work of the Holy Spirit (Lk 1:35). Joseph was not aware of this, so when he learned that Mary was pregnant, he decided to divorce her quietly, for he was a just man and did not want to humiliate her publicly (Mt 1:19). An angel subsequently appeared to him in a dream to tell him what was happening (Mt 1:21; cf. Is 7:14). The text of Matthew makes it clear that there was no sexual union between Joseph and Mary until after Jesus was born (1:18,25; see also Lk 1:14).

When Caesar Augustus issued a decree that everyone had to register in his native city for purposes of taxation, Joseph and Mary returned to Bethlehem, where Jesus was subsequently born (Lk 2:1–6). Later, Joseph and Mary took the infant Jesus to the temple to present him to the Lord (Lk 2:33). After the visit of the wise men an angel appeared to Joseph in a dream and instructed him to take Jesus and Mary to Egypt to protect the child from King Herod (Mt 2:13). Upon the death of Herod, an angel similarly advised him to return to Israel, so the family went to live in Nazareth. The last recorded event that involves Joseph is the incident of Jesus in the temple at age 12 (Lk 2:41–51). Joseph is not mentioned by name, but Mary told Jesus that she and his father had been looking for him anxiously.

Jesus was identified by people around Nazareth as "Joseph's son" (Lk 4:22; Jn 1:45; 6:42). It is only through references identifying Jesus that we learn of Joseph's trade. Twice Jesus is referred to as "the carpenter's son" (Mt 13:55; Mk 6:3). Joseph was not a carpenter in our sense of the word, for houses were built mostly of stone and earth. He was a woodworker, or artificer in wood, and probably most of his work was with furniture and agricultural implements.

During the ministry of Jesus it was his mother and his brothers who came to look for him (Mt 12:50; Mk 3:35), so it is assumed that by this time Joseph was dead. Joseph was most likely the father of James, Joseph, Simon, Judas, and unnamed sisters (Mt 13:55; Mk 6:3).　　　　　　　　CARL E. DEVRIES

See GENEALOGY OF JESUS CHRIST; BROTHERS OF JESUS.

7. Joseph and Mary's son and the brother of Jesus (Mt 13:55); alternately called Joses in Mark 6:3.

See BROTHERS OF JESUS.

8. Native of Arimathea and the follower of Jesus who provided for his burial. He was a rich man from the town of Arimathea and a respected member of the Sanhedrin, or council (Mk 15:43). He was a good and righteous man, and did not go along with the decision to crucify Jesus (Lk 23:50,51). Joseph had been a secret follower of Jesus because he was afraid of the Jews (Jn 19:38), but after the crucifixion he took courage and went to Pilate to ask for Jesus' body. He and Nicodemus took the body, treated it with spices, and wrapped it in linen cloths, according to the Jewish burial customs. In a nearby garden was Joseph's own new rock-cut tomb in which no one had ever been buried. Here they placed Jesus and sealed the tomb with a large stone.

9. Mattathias' son and an ancestor of Jesus (Lk 3:24).

See GENEALOGY OF JESUS CHRIST.

10. KJV rendering of Josech, an ancestor of Jesus, in Luke 3:26.

See JOSECH.

11. Jonam's son and an ancestor of Jesus (Lk 3:30).

See GENEALOGY OF JESUS CHRIST.

12. Disciple of Jesus who was "called Barsabbas" and "surnamed Justus" (Acts 1:23). Joseph was one of the candidates put forward by the 11 apostles to replace Judas Iscariot. It was Matthias, however, who was chosen.

13. Cypriot Levite who sold a field and gave the proceeds to the apostles. He was surnamed "Barnabas," meaning "son of encouragement," by the apostles (Acts 4:36).

See BARNABAS.

Joseph Barsabbas. *See* JOSEPH #12.

Joseph of Arimathea. *See* JOSEPH #8.

Joses. 1. Alternate spelling for Joseph, Mary's son, in Mark 6:3.

See JOSEPH #7.

2. KJV spelling for Joseph, surnamed Barnabas, in Acts 4:36.

See BARNABAS.

Joshah. Prince in Simeon's tribe (1 Chr 4:34).

Joshaphat. 1. Mithnite and one of David's mighty men, listed between Hanan and Uzzia (1 Chr 11:43).

2. One of the seven priests assigned to blow a trumpet before the ark of God in the proces-

sion led by David when the ark was brought to Jerusalem (1 Chr 15:24, KJV Jehoshaphat).

Joshaviah. Elnaam's son, the brother of Jeribai and one of David's 30 valiant warriors, listed between Jeribai and Ithmah (1 Chr 11:46).

Joshbekashah. Heman's son and head of the 17th of 24 divisions of priestly musicians for ministry in the sanctuary during David's reign (1 Chr 25:4,24).

Josheb-basshebeth. Alternate spelling of Jashobeam, one of David's mighty men, in 2 Samuel 23:8.

See JASHOBEAM #1.

Joshibiah. Simeonite; Seraiah's son and the father of Jehu (1 Chr 4:35, KJV Josibiah).

Joshua (Person). 1. Son of Nun, Moses' assistant and successor, and the military leader whom God chose to lead the Israelites in the conquest of Canaan (1 Chr 7:27, KJV Jehoshua, Jehoshuah; also spelled Jeshua in Neh 8:17).

Early in the exodus Joshua was sent by Moses to fight against the Amalekites (Ex 17:8–15). Joshua defeated Amalek, and Moses wrote of the event and built an altar which he called "The Lord is my banner."

When Moses sent 12 men from Kadesh-barnea to spy out the land of Canaan, Joshua represented the tribe of Ephraim (Nm 13:8). At that time Joshua was called Hoshea (KJV Oshea), but Moses changed his name to Joshua (Nm 13:8,16, KJV Jehoshua). Joshua and Caleb were the only two spies to bring back an affirmative report concerning an Israelite invasion of the land (Nm 14:6–9). Consequently, of all the adult Israelite males to leave Egypt in the exodus, only these two crossed the Jordan River and entered the Promised Land (Nm 14:30).

When the Lord announced to Moses his impending death, Moses asked about his successor, and the Lord appointed Joshua to that position (Nm 27:12–23). After the death of Moses on Mt Nebo, Joshua's leadership was confirmed (Nm 34:17), and the Lord told Joshua to go over the Jordan and take the land (Jos 1:1,2).

From the Transjordan, Joshua sent two men across the river to reconnoiter Jericho (Jos 2:1–24). In Jericho they were concealed by Rahab and later safely made their way back to Joshua to report that the people of the land were fainthearted because of the Israelites (Jos 2:23,24).

When Israel had crossed the river, the Lord

instructed Joshua to set up a circle of 12 stones at Gilgal to commemorate this passage (Jos 4:1–7). The Lord then commanded that all of the males who had been born during the exodus be circumcised (Jos 5:2–9).

While camped at Gilgal, near Jericho, Joshua was confronted by a man with a drawn sword. When Joshua challenged the man, he learned that it was the Lord, who told him to remove his shoes, for the ground was holy (Jos 5:13–15). The Lord gave Joshua directions for the destruction of Jericho; these were followed explicitly and the city fell (Jos 6). The attack on Ai ended in temporary defeat, until the matter of Achan's sin was discovered and judged (Jos 7:10–26). Then Ai was taken and destroyed.

Joshua built an altar on Mt Ebal (Jos 8:30–32), and the blessing and curse were read, as commanded by God through Moses (Jos 8:33–35; cf. Dt 27).

Because the Israelites failed to ask direction from the Lord (Jos 9:14), Joshua was tricked into making a covenant of peace with the Hivites of Gibeon. Joshua then reduced them to doing menial tasks in Israel (Jos 9:21–27).

The kings of the various Canaanite cities allied themselves against the Israelite threat (Jos 9:1,2) and a league of five Amorite cities (Jerusalem, Hebron, Jarmuth, Lachish, and Eglon) attacked Gibeon (Jos 10:1–5). The Gibeonites appealed to Joshua for help; he responded quickly against this Amorite confederation and routed the Amorite forces. It was on this occasion that Joshua commanded the sun and the moon to stand still so that Israel could have more time to defeat these adversaries (Jos 10:12–14). This victory was followed by a series of successful attacks on enemy towns (Jos 10:28–43).

A northern alliance headed by Jabin, king of Hazor, was the next opposition (Jos 11:1–5).

The Lord assured Joshua of success, and the city of Hazor was taken and destroyed by fire (Jos 11:6–15). Joshua 11:23 summarizes the conquest of the land, and chapter 12 enumerates the kings who were conquered.

Joshua was now old, and the Lord told him that much land remained to be possessed. These territories are listed, but the Lord directed Joshua to proceed with the division of the land among the nine and one-half tribes (Jos 13:7; cf. Jos 13:8–18:28). Joshua himself was given the city he asked for, Timnath-serah, in the hill country of Ephraim, which he rebuilt and settled (Jos 19:49,50).

The Lord told Joshua to appoint cities of refuge to which a person guilty of manslaughter could flee to escape the avenger of blood (Jos 20). The Levites came to Eleazar the priest and Joshua to request that they be given the cities which the Lord had commanded through Moses (Jos 21:1–42).

In his advanced years Joshua summoned all Israel and solemnly charged them to continue in faithfulness to the Lord (Jos 23). Finally, he called all Israel to Shechem, where he gave them his farewell message. He summed up the Lord's dealings with them from the time of Abraham, and again challenged them to serve the Lord, putting before them the well-known choice and decision: "Choose this day whom you will serve, . . . but as for me and my house, we will serve the Lord" (Jos 24:15).

Joshua died at the age of 110 years and was buried in his inheritance at Timnath-serah (Jos 24:29,30; the parallel account in Jgs 2:8,9 reads Timnath-heres).

Israel served the Lord all the days of Joshua and during the time of the elders of Israel who outlived Joshua (Jos 24:31; Jgs 2:7).

CARL E. DeVries

See JOSHUA, BOOK OF; CONQUEST AND ALLOTMENT OF THE LAND; ISRAEL, HISTORY OF.

The Valley of Aijalon, where God gave Joshua a great military victory.

2. Inhabitant of Beth-shemesh. It was his grain field to which the cart carrying the ark sent by the Philistines came. Subsequently a large stone was set up in Joshua's field to commemorate this event (1 Sm 6:14,18).

3. Governor of Jerusalem during King Josiah's reign (2 Kgs 23:8).

4. Jozadak's son and high priest during the days of Zerubbabel in postexilic Jerusalem (Hg 1:1–14; 2:2,4; Zec 3:1–9; 6:11). Joshua is alternately called Jeshua in Ezra and Nehemiah.

See JESHUA (PERSON) #3.

5. Eliezer's son and an ancestor of Jesus Christ (Lk 3:29, KJV Jesus, Jose).

See GENEALOGY OF JESUS CHRIST.

Joshua, Book of.

First of the historical books in the English Bible and the first of the Former Prophets (including Jgs, 1,2 Sm, and 1,2 Kgs) in the Hebrew Bible. It begins with the Lord's commission of Joshua (1:1–9) and concludes with the burial of Joshua, Eleazar, and the bones of Joseph (24:29–33). The purpose of the book is to show how Joshua continued in the footsteps of Moses, how the Lord gave the land to Israel, and how Israel might prosper in the land.

Author and Date. According to the Talmud, Joshua wrote the book. This ancient tradition is probably based on the brief statement that Joshua wrote "these words in the book of the law of God" (24:26). However, this applies only to the renewal of the covenant (ch 24). The issue of authorship is tied up with the dating of the book. Since the book has no unambiguous markers on date and authorship, neither critics nor conservative scholars have been able to come to any agreement on these issues. According to a conservative analysis of Joshua, the book was written between 1375 BC and 1045 BC (premonarchic). The argument is based on the references to the migration of Dan (19:47; cf. Jgs 18:27–31), to Jerusalem as a Jebusite city (15:8,63; 18:16,28), to Sidon rather than Tyre as the prominent Phoenician city (11:8; 13:4–6; 19:28), and also on the eyewitness style (5:1,6 in the Masoretic Text). Critical scholars have raised difficult issues which they considered could best be resolved by positing a 7th-century or even an exilic date. M. Noth viewed Joshua 2–11 essentially as a prologue to the Deuteronomic history of Israel (Jgs–2 Kgs). Critics explain the variations and repetitions in Joshua as evidence of different stages of literary development and transmission, resulting in a composite work filled with internal contradictions. J.A. Soggin concludes that it is an exilic recension of Israel's early history in order to give hope to an exiled people. The emphasis on the land and on Joshua was to inspire the community to covenant renewal and was an anticipation that the Lord would raise up another Joshua in the form of a king or a leader who would give them rest.

Y. Kaufmann rejected the critical approach in favor of the assumption that the historical reflections of the book favor a date close to the events of the conquest. His arguments are persuasive. M. Woudstra has made an attempt to approach the internal difficulties of Joshua from a literary analysis of the narratives, without depending on the contradictory results of archaeology.

Problems. *Holy War.* The morality of the conquest may be explained by the concept of "holy war." The "holy war" motif would explain why Israel was to destroy the indigenous population (Dt 7:16; 20:16–18; Jos 6:21; 8:24–26; 10:10,28,30,35,37,39–42; 11:11). The justification may lie in the "intrusion ethics," according to which Israel was God's instrument of judgment on the Canaanite nations. This argument is related to the mention of the wickedness of the Canaanites (Gn 15:16; Lv 15:24–28; Dt 7:2–5,25,26; 12:30,31; Jos 23:7; Jgs 2:11). However, the canonical narrative of the progression of the conquest puts the responsibility on the Canaanites. They marched and fought against Israel (Nm 21:21–35; Jos 7:4,5; 8:5,16,17; 9:1,2; 10:1–6; 11:1–5; 24:11). Therefore, it could be argued that in the process of war a sincere invitation to make peace was given to the kings (cf. Nm 21:21; Dt 20:10,11), but was refused. Instead, the kings took the initiative in battle. The responsibility for the destruction of the native population thus lay with the leadership. Yet, all this was evidence of God's working in human affairs, which the Bible simply states, "For it was the Lord himself who hardened their hearts to wage war against Israel, so that he might destroy them totally, exterminating them without mercy, as the Lord had commanded Moses" (Jos 11:20 NIV). Even as Pharaoh, whose heart the Lord hardened, was responsible for the plagues in Egypt, so the Canaanite rulers were responsible for the extermination of their populations. The biblical account of the conquest affirms the mystery of human responsibility and divine sovereignty without explaining it.

Nature of the Conquest. Various explanations of the nature of the conquest have been given. The traditional view of a blitzkrieg type of a conquest, which resulted in a complete occupation of the whole land (cf. 10:40; 11:1, 16,19), does not fit within the whole picture of the book. The book presents a realistic description of the areas which still had to be conquered (13:1–7) and of the military strength of the indigenous population (cf. 13:13; 15:63; 16:10; 17:12,13,16,18; 19:47). Moreover, Joshua promised that the Lord would continue to help Israel to occupy the land, as its population and needs developed (23:5). The occupation of Canaan was in two stages: conquest and gradual occupation (cf. Ex 23:29,30; Dt 7:22). Critics have offered alternate models. According to one hypothesis, some Israelite tribes entered Canaan without resistance and settled around Shechem, whereas others fought their way into the land. Another hypothesis posits waves of migrants who ended up in Canaan, made a treaty (amphictyony), and developed traditions which obscured the distinct origins of each tribe.

The Jordan River, which the Israelites, led by Joshua, miraculously crossed (c. 1400 BC).

Purpose. B. S. Childs has made an attempt to look anew at the historical-critical approach to Joshua. He posits the canonical shape of Joshua as the object of study. The role of the final (canonical) form of the book is to present Joshua's obedience to the Law of Moses. Victory and defeat are illustrations of obedience and disobedience, and make a sustained argument leading up to Joshua's final appeals for covenant loyalty. Childs recognizes the tension in the descriptions of the conquest as complete and as incomplete. He does not attempt to harmonize the points in tension, but seeks to uncover how the book is to be understood. He concludes that the tension is a dynamic device to show that the conquest and enjoyment of the land depend wholly on obedience. The period of Joshua is viewed "as a paradigm of obedient Israel." Thus, a holistic reading of the book presents an appeal to covenant loyalty directed to future generations.

Content. *Conquest of the Land, 1:1–12:24.* (1) The Lord's Commission of Joshua, 1:1–9. With the death of Moses (v 1), the Lord himself confirms Moses' ordination of Joshua (Dt 34:9). He charges him with leadership in the conquest of Canaan (vv 2,3), defines the geographical boundaries of the land (v 4), encourages him with his continued presence (vv 5,9), and expects him to devoutly follow in "the law of Moses" (i.e., the law given in Dt; cf. Dt 31:9,24–26; Jos 23:6), so that he may succeed in his mission (vv 7,8). The original mission as well as the ministry of Moses find their continuity in Joshua.

(2) Crossing the Jordan, 1:10–5:12. The first stage calls for the preparation of Israel. As their leader Joshua must demonstrate to the people that he follows in the footsteps of Moses. He does this by reminding the Transjordan tribes to demonstrate loyalty to the command of Moses by joining with the other tribes in the conquest of Canaan (1:13–15; cf. Nm 32:20–27). They submitted to Joshua's authority as to Moses' (1:16–18). He demonstrates his military leadership in sending the two spies to Jericho (2:1–24). His authority is accepted by priests (3:6; 4:10) and people (3:5,9) as they cross the Jordan. The crossing of the Jordan marks the public recognition of Joshua as a leader like Moses (4:14).

The account of the crossing marks an important transition from the era of the exodus/wilderness to the era of the conquest. On the one hand, the story of Rahab illustrates how the Canaanites had heard about the Lord's mighty acts (2:10,11) and reacted with great fear (2:11; cf. Ex 15:15; 23:27,28; Dt 2:25; 7:23; 11:25; 32:30). Rahab's expression of faith in Israel's God (2:11) anticipates the inclusion of the Gentiles in the covenant community as promised to the patriarchs ("all the peoples on earth will be blessed through you," Gn 12:3). By faith Rahab was included in the covenant and was richly rewarded by the inclusion of her name in the lineage of our Lord (Mt 1:5).

The Israelites crossed the Jordan with the knowledge that the fear of God had come on the Canaanites (2:24). However, they were also instructed to show their reverence for the Lord by keeping a safe distance between themselves and the ark of the covenant (3:4) and by consecrating themselves (3:5). The "living God" was among them and required holiness and reverence from his people (3:10). He, in turn, would demonstrate his loyalty in the marvelous passage through the Jordan River (3:13) and in the conquest of the land (3:10). After the tribes had crossed (4:1), each leader of the 12 tribes took up a stone out of the dried-up river bed and set up a memorial at Gilgal (4:1–9,20). Thus, Israel was to remember that the stones, taken from the place where the priests who carried the ark had stood, were reminders of the majestic presence of God. Future generations who were to hear this report (4:21–24) were hereby encouraged because of the fear of God which would fall on all the peoples of the earth (4:24).

The consecration before the conquest of Jericho is also symbolized by the act of circumcision (5:1–9) and by the celebration of the

Passover (5:10–12). The events are not necessarily chronologically related, but were selected as examples of Israel's responsiveness to Joshua's ministry. Moses' appeal to the new generation had its effect (cf. Dt 4:4–14; 6:1–5). The new generation served the Lord as long as Joshua and the elders were alive (24:31). Physical circumcision, neglected during the wilderness journey (5:5) due to unbelief, is a sign of spiritual responsiveness. The responsive nation receives the external sign of the covenant with the anticipation that the Lord of the covenant will bless his people in giving them victory and the fruit of the land. Their reproach was rolled away (5:9). The covenant continuity is also brought out in the brief mention of the Passover celebration. The newness is their eating the fruit of the land. With the taste of the food of Canaan, the manna stopped. The desert experience was over. A new era was ushered in with their presence in the Promised Land (5:11,12).

(3) Conquest of Jericho, 5:13–6:27. The victory is the Lord's. This is the message with which the battle of Jericho begins. The holy God who appeared to Moses in the burning bush (Ex 3:2–4:17) appeared to Joshua as "the commander of the Lord's army" (5:14,15) with a message from the Lord (6:2). The city of Jericho will fall without a siege and ensuing battle. Israel's response to Jericho's preparedness for war (cf. 24:11) was strange, but the presence of the ark and the blowing of the trumpets symbolized that the Lord would fight for Israel, even as he had promised. However, Israel may not take any of the spoils. Because

Yahweh fought for Israel, everything was to be devoted to him (6:17). The Lord honored the vow to Rahab, made by the spies, so that she and her family were kept alive (6:17,25), but were placed temporarily outside the camp (6:23). The valuable metals were placed into the treasury (6:19,24), whereas everything else was burned by fire (6:24). Nothing was to be taken for personal gain; otherwise God's judgment would rest on Israel (6:18). In order to emphasize God's absolute ownership of Jericho, Joshua put a curse on anyone who would attempt to rebuild the city (6:26; cf. 1 Kgs 16:34). The rumors of Jericho's destruction spread, and the peoples of Canaan knew that the Lord was with Joshua (6:27; cf. 1:5,9).

(4) Tragedy and Triumph at Ai, 7:1–8:29. Victory was short-lived, because Achan defied God's "ban," took some of the objects, hid them in the ground under his tent (7:21), and brought God's wrath on all of Israel (7:1). Israel was stunned by their defeat at Ai (7:2–5). Joshua and the elders responded to the disaster by fasting and lamenting (7:6–9). What a contrast between the reports of victory spread through the land and the anguished cry of God's servant, fearful that the Canaanites would amass strength and wipe out Israel (7:9). Only after the people had consecrated themselves (7:13) and Achan was exposed and his memory removed (7:25b,26) could they renew the attack on Ai with the encouraging promise of God's presence and victory (8:1,2). Ai, too, was taken (8:3–19) and the population execrated (8:20–26), but Israel enjoyed the spoils by direct permission from the Lord

The ruins of Jericho, including an ancient wall.

(8:27). The ruins of Ai, the pile of stones covering the body of Ai's king (8:28,29), and the heap of rocks over Achan's body were sobering reminders to Israel that God's faithfulness requires absolute loyalty from his people. To emphasize this, the canonical account interrupts the narrative of the campaign and puts before us the renewal of the covenant at Mt Ebal (8:30–35).

(5) Renewal of the Covenant, 8:30–35. Joshua led Israel in a ceremonial covenant renewal at Shechem, as Moses had instructed (v 31; cf. Dt 11:29; 27:1–26). Joshua took care in the proper preparation of the altar (cf. Ex 20:25) on which dedicatory and communal offerings were presented. He copied the law as a symbol of his royal leadership and his devotion to the Lord (v 32; cf. Dt 17:18). All Israel (officers and people, aliens and native-born Israelites) together presented themselves for the reading of the blessings and the curses (vv 33–35). The whole Book of Deuteronomy (i.e., "the Book of the Law," cf. Dt 31:26) was read in their presence. Half of the tribes stood on Mt Gerizim and said "Amen" to the blessings, and the other six stood on Mt Ebal, saying "Amen" to the curses (cf. Dt 27:9–26).

(6) Covenant with the Gibeonites, 9:1–27. The rumors of God's mighty acts had brought fear on the Canaanite kings (cf. 2:8–11,24; 5:1; 6:27). The first defeat at Ai had given them a ray of hope that Israel could be put down. Rather than submit themselves to Israel and suffer from humiliation as servants of Israel, they joined forces against Joshua and Israel (vv 1,2).

The Hivites from Gibeon, Kephirah, Beeroth, and Kiriath-jearim (vv 7,17) did not join with their fellow Canaanites. Instead, they developed an intricate plan to deceive Israel and to sue for full treaty status. The purpose of the treaty was that of friendship (namely, "peace,"), promising each other to be of mutual assistance in case of attack. The concern was with the preservation of life (v 15). Their deception included a ruse about the great distance they had traveled (vv 11–14) and a feigned report of Israel's victories in Transjordan with no mention of their crossing the Jordan (vv 9,10; cf. 5:1). The law permitted the submissive city to subject its population to a type of suzerainty treaty, in which Israel defined the terms and expected the subjugated populace to serve as its forced laborers (Dt 20:11; cf. Jgs 1:28,30,33,35; 1 Kgs 9:15,20,21). However, the treaty permitted the Hivites to maintain their way of life with the advantage of Israel's military protection (v 15).

The Israelites had acted in good faith and had applied the Law (Dt 20:11). They had no need of inquiring of the Lord and were not rebuked for not doing so. It was now a matter of wisdom—that is, the application of God's Law to life. Soon it was discovered that they were wrong (vv 16–18). The Israelites complained, but the leaders did not revoke the oath made to the Gibeonites (vv 18–20). Instead, the friendship treaty was reduced to that of a suzerainty treaty and the Hivites were forced to be Israel's manual laborers (v 21). The Hivites confessed their subterfuge and willingly submitted themselves to Israel (vv 24,25). They were to support the tabernacle personnel by providing water and wood for the altar. An altar may have been constructed at Gibeon before the dedication of Jerusalem's temple by Solomon. Solomon worshiped the Lord at the Gibeonite altar (1 Kgs 3:4; cf. 1 Chr 16:39; 21:29).

(7) The Southern Campaign, 10:1–43. The king of Jerusalem, Adoni-zedek ("my lord is righteous"), led the cities of Hebron, Jarmuth, Lachish, and Eglon in an alliance against Gibeon as a military ploy to take a stand against Israel (vv 1–5). The Gibeonites appealed to Israel for help based on their covenantal relationship (v 6). Joshua led Israel on a 25-mile hike through the wilderness from Gilgal up to Gibeon during one night (vv 7–9). The Israelite attack surprised the Canaanites, who were already frightened of the Israelites. The camp of the Canaanites was thrown into confusion, and the soldiers fled the hill country via the road of Beth-horon to Azekah and Makkedah (v 10). But while running, they were tormented with large hailstones (v 11). The victory was the Lord's. Miraculously, Israel could push the Canaanites farther from the hill country because of the long day (vv 12–14). The marvel of this day was long remembered in the Book of Jashar (cf. 2 Sm 1:18), because on it "the Lord listened to a man," namely Joshua (v 14).

The five kings hidden in a cave at Makkedah were discovered, killed, hanged on trees, and buried in the cave (vv 16–27). Their foolish attempt to make war on Israel came to a quick end. Since the coalition of large cities had been put down, Joshua led Israel in a rapid campaign of the southern cities (vv 29–43). The region was taken in one campaign with the Lord's help (v 42).

(8) The Northern Campaign, 11:1–15. The Israelites were again forced into battle, this time under the leadership of Jabin, king of Hazor. Jabin rallied the kings of the northern cities to assemble their troops and horses by the waters of Merom against Israel (vv 1–5). The similarity to the southern campaign is a literary way to demonstrate that the kings of the south and north initiated the war and were consequently defeated. So it was with the

The site of Hazor, one of the three cities the Bible specifies were burned by Joshua.

northern kings, who were routed as far as the region of Sidon in Phoenicia (v 8). The horses were hamstrung and their chariots burned (v 9), as the Lord had instructed (v 6). Israel was to depend on the Lord (cf. Ps 20:7). Hazor, the great and ancient city, the center of Canaanite power in the north, was completely destroyed (vv 10,11,13). The burning of Jericho, Ai, and Hazor were exceptions, because Israel had been promised Canaanite houses, wells, and cities (Dt 6:10,11; cf. Jos 24:13). The campaign narrative stresses again the absolute loyalty of Joshua to the Lord and to Moses, the servant of the Lord (vv 9,12,15).

(9) Summary of the Campaigns, 11:16–12:24. Joshua led Israel in victory (v 16) and rest (v 23b) because of his careful adherence to the Lord's directions to Moses (v 23a). Moses had described the land to be conquered in detail (Dt 1:7), and Joshua took the regions of which Moses had spoken (vv 16,17). Though the cities would have sued for a peaceable arrangement under which they would have been forced laborers (Dt 20:11), none of the cities recognized Israel. In fear they plotted and schemed how to destroy Israel. They were the aggressors (chs 10; 11; 24:11). God had hardened their hearts (v 20). The theological reason is a mystery, as it was in the case of Pharaoh. But the net result was that Canaan was conquered and the population exterminated, except for the Hivites at Gibeon and the sur-

rounding cities (vv 19,20). Even the Anakites, who had brought fear on Israel some 40 years before (Nm 13:33; cf. Dt 2:10,21), were execrated (v 21). Yet it is already apparent that not every square mile of land was taken (v 22), even though in a sense "the entire land" was Israel's, because major centers of Canaanite resistance had been broken. The tension between fulfillment and complete fulfillment is apparent in these verses.

The list of the defeated kings (12:1–24) includes the victories over Sihon and Og (vv 2–5) under Moses' leadership (v 6). Their juxtaposition with the list of the conquered kings under Joshua (vv 7–24) demonstrates the continuity of leadership and purpose—two leaders, many campaigns, but one battle. The land of promise is now a fulfillment. Through the campaigns the borders of the land of inheritance were now more transparent. In Transjordan the limits are from the Arnon to Mt Hermon (vv 2–5). In Canaan the boundary extends from the region south of Sidon to the Negeb (vv 7,8).

The Division of the Land, 13:1–22:34. (1) The Command to Divide the Land, 13:1–7. Because of Joshua's advanced age, the "whole" land was not taken. Moses had forewarned Israel that the inheritance would result from conquest and from gradual extension of Israel's narrow boundaries. Slowly Israel was to inherit the whole land, lest it be overwhelmed by the size and be unable properly to use it (Ex 23:29,30; Dt 7:22). The region to the north of Galilee and Mt Hermon to the east of the Sea of Galilee, the area later occupied by the Philistines, and regional Canaanite enclaves were still to be occupied (vv 2–7; cf. Jgs 1). Israel was not to be concerned with the future rights of occupation, because the Lord promised to help them (v 6).

(2) Division of Transjordan, 13:8–33. Joshua did not alter the Mosiac arrangement, according to which part of the tribes of Manasseh, Reuben, and Gad had already received their allotments in Transjordan (vv 8,32,33; cf. Nm 32; Dt 3:12–17). The territory also excluded certain regions still occupied by Canaanites (v 13). The clans of Reuben had received the territory from the Arnon to Heshbon (vv 15–23). The clans of Gad had received the territory of the Gilead, south of the Arnon River (vv 24–28). Several clans of Manasseh received the region south of the Wadi Yarmouk to the Arnon (vv 29–31). The levitical towns are not listed here, but a reference is made to them as not receiving a patrimony, because they are to live off the offerings and sacrifices made to the Lord (v 14; cf. Nm 18:20–24; 35:1–8).

(3) The Tribal Divisions in Canaan, 14:1–19:51. Eleazar, the high priest, and Joshua to-

The Negeb, south of Arad, part of the territory allotted to Judah.

gether cast lots to determine the boundaries, size, and allocation of the remaining nine and a half tribes. Again the inclusion of the tribe of Levi is mentioned (14:4), because their cities will be dealt with in chapters 20,21. Another literary device is special mention of the inheritance of Caleb in the beginning (14:6–15) and of Joshua at the conclusion (19:49,50). These two were the only ones who had left Egypt as adults, had been faithful spies, and had entered into the Promised Land (Nm 14:24,30; Dt 1:36,38).

(a) Judah, 15:1–63 (cf. Jgs 1:10–15,20). The boundaries of Judah extend from the Dead Sea westward to the Mediterranean (vv 2–12). The cities of Judah are listed in its four regions: 29 in the Negeb (vv 21–32), 42 cities in the Shephelah (or western foothills) and coastal plains (vv 33–47), 38 cities in the hill country (vv 48–60), and six cities in the desert (vv 61,62). Judah was unable to take Jerusalem (v 63) until David made it his capital (cf. Jgs 1:21; 2 Sm 5:6–16).

(b) Ephraim and Manasseh, 16:1–17:18. These two tribes, descended from Joseph, were richly blessed (cf. Gn 48; 49:22–26; Dt 33:13–17) and had obtained prominence among the tribes. Part of Manasseh had already received a patrimony in Transjordan (13:29–31). They received *one* allotment as "the allotment for Joseph" (16:1). The limits were from Bethel to Mt Tabor in the north and from the Jordan to the Mediterranean (vv 16:1–3). Ephraim received the smaller portion in the south (16:5–9), but was unable to subdue the Canaanites of Gezer (v 10). The clans of Manasseh are given, including Zelophehad (17:3–6; cf. Nm 27:1–11; 36:1–12), in order to clearly distinguish them from the clans of Manasseh in Transjordan. The region of Manasseh extended from Shechem to Mt Tabor (17:7–11). But Manasseh too was incapable of driving out the Canaanites completely (vv 12,13).

Though they had received the largest portion of the land (more than a third), the tribes of Joseph complained. They knew that the Lord had blessed them (17:14) and expected to get more cultivatable land. But Joshua urged them to use the available land by cutting down the forests (vv 15,17,18). When they came back with a realistic observation of Canaanite military power (v 16), Joshua called on them to do their share in occupying the land (v 18).

(c) Seven Tribes, 18:1–19:51. The Israelites assembled at Shiloh to set up the tabernacle (cf. 1 Sm 1). At that point seven tribes had not yet received their patrimony. Joshua called for each tribe to commission three men to survey the land. When they returned, Joshua cast lots at the tabernacle in Shiloh and divided the land (18:3–10). The territory of Benjamin was between Judah and Ephraim (18:11–28). Simeon's allotment was in southern Judah (19:1–9), resulting in its absorption into Judah (cf. Gn 49:7). Zebulun (19:10–16), Issachar (vv 17–23), Asher (vv 24–31), and Naphtali (vv 32–39) received a portion north of Manasseh in the region of Galilee. Dan received the seventh lot and suffered subsequently, when it could not maintain the allotted territory because of the pressure of Judah on the east and the Philistines to the west (vv 40–48). They migrated northward and found the sources of the Jordan to be a fruitful region (v 47; cf. Jgs 18).

(d) Conclusion, 19:49–51. The conclusion is symmetric with the beginning (14:1–14) in that Joshua, too, received a gift. Again mention is made that all divisions were in the presence of the Lord, witnessed to and executed by the high priest Eleazar and Joshua (v 51; cf. 14:1).

(4) Cities of Refuge and the Levitical Cities, 20:1–21:45. According to the instructions of Moses, six levitical cities were set apart, three on each side of the Jordan, as "cities of refuge" (Nm 35:9–34; Dt 4:41–43; 19:1–10). The purpose was to provide "refuge" (asylum) for those who were guilty of manslaughter but had not intentionally killed someone. This practice was not a way out for someone who was guilty, but it provided for the legal process to be completed (20:1–9).

The Levites received by clan a total of 48 cities, 6 of which also served as cities of refuge (21:1–42). The Levites could not cultivate the soil, because they were dependent on the tithes of the people (Nm 18:21–24). They were permitted to have land for grazing. The dimensions of the land are given in Numbers 35:4,5. A special allocation is made to the descendants of Aaron (vv 9–19), because they served as priests and their 13 cities were in the Judah-Simeon region, in proximity to the Jerusalem temple of the Solomonic era.

With the allocation of the levitical cities, the division of the land is concluded. The promise of the land is fulfilled (vv 43–45). God is faithful! This section emphasizes the fulfillment, the power, and the grace of God, by which Israel entered into its rest. However, the Book of Joshua also knows of the struggle which is still ahead of the Israelites and of the test which ultimately they will fail (cf. Ps 95:11; Heb 3:7–11).

(5) Return of the Transjordan Tribes, 22:1–34. Joshua dismissed the two and a half tribes with a commendation for their loyalty to the other tribes and to the Lord (vv 1–4), with a warning not to succumb to idolatry but to love the Lord in accordance with the Deuteronomic Law (v 5), and with a blessing (vv 6–8). However, on their return they set up a large altar by the Jordan on the eastern side. The other tribes heard about it and met at Shiloh (v 12). They wisely commissioned Phinehas, the son of the high priest, with 10 representatives of the tribes, to investigate the matter. The commission charged the Transjordan tribes with treachery (vv 15–20; cf. Nm 25; Jos 7).

The response of the Transjordan tribes demonstrated their concern for the unity of the tribes and for the worship of God. These tribes feared being excluded from the fellowship of God's people, and had purposefully constructed an altar, identical to that prescribed in the Law, in order to demonstrate their common heritage (vv 21–30). The altar was not for sacrifice or worship, but functioned as a symbol of the covenantal unity of the people of God. Their protestations were strengthened by calling upon God as "the Mighty One," "God, the Lord" (twice, v 22).

Phinehas and the tribal representatives were pleased with the response and left with the assurance of God's presence (vv 30,31). Their report to the tribes led to reconciliation of all the tribes on this matter. The narrative concludes with a mention of the name given to the altar: "A witness between us that the Lord is God."

Epilogue: The Land Is a Sacred Trust, Chs 23,24. The last two chapters contain Joshua's farewell speeches to all the leaders and to all Israel.

(1) Address to the Leaders, ch. 23. Joshua reviews what the Lord has done for Israel in giving the land to the tribes (vv 3,4,9,10,14). He has demonstrated his loyalty. And he will continue to be with his people so that no enemy can stand against them (vv 5,10). He will fulfill every outstanding promise, even as he had already fulfilled the promises (vv 14,15). However, they must persevere in their loyalty to the Lord (vv 7,8,11). Loyalty to the Lord is not apart from loyalty to the Law of Moses (v 6). Apostasy will be severely punished first by

leaving the nations to ensnare Israel (vv 12,13), and then by consuming them in his wrath (v 16).

(2) Address to Israel, 24:1–28. The address ends up in a covenant renewal at Shechem (cf. 8:30–35). Some scholars have proposed a treaty structure here, but this is still a debated issue. The canonical structure of the text requires a narrative analysis.

Joshua reviews Israel's history from the patriarchs to their generation: patriarchs (vv 2–4), exodus (vv 5–7), and conquest (vv 8–13).

The goodness, presence, and loyalty of Yahweh was evident to them. Yahweh also expected "faithfulness" from his people in the form of whole allegiance, without any form of idolatry or syncretism (vv 14,15). Joshua vows as the head of his family to be loyal (v 15). The people respond by covering the reasons for loyalty to the Lord (vv 16–18). But Joshua pushes them to a deeper commitment by challenging their profession (vv 19,20) and by setting up a stone of witness against Israel (vv 26b,27), by recording their vow (vv 25,26a).

(3) End of an Era, 24:29–33. The book began with a reference to the death of Moses (1:1,2) and concludes with the death and burial of Joshua (v 29) and of Eleazar the high priest (v 33). This marks the end of an era. The burial of Joseph's bones (v 32; cf. Gn 50:25; Ex 13:19) in a plot purchased by Jacob (Gn 33:19) brings together the hope characteristic of the epoch of Moses and Joshua. R. K. HARRISON

See CONQUEST AND ALLOTMENT OF THE LAND; ISRAEL, HISTORY OF; JOSHUA (PERSON) #1; CITIES OF REFUGE; LEVITICAL CITIES.

Bibliography. T.C. Butler, *Joshua*; B.S. Childs, *Introduction to the OT as Scripture*; Y. Kaufman, *The Book of Joshua*; J.A. Soggin, *Joshua*; M. Woudstra, *The Book of Joshua*.

Josiah. 1. Sixteenth king of the southern kingdom of Judah (640–609 BC). A godly man, he stood in marked contrast to his grandfather, Manasseh, and his father, Amon. In fact, Scripture declares there was no king either before or after him that was as obedient to the Law of Moses (2 Kgs 23:25). The Greek form of his name, Josias, appears in Matthew 1:10,11 (KJV).

Times of Josiah. When Josiah became king in 640, the international scene was about to change drastically. After the great Assyrian king Ashurbanipal died in 633 mediocre rulers followed him on the throne, and there was considerable unrest in the empire. Nabopolassar, father of Nebuchadnezzar, seized the kingship in Babylon and established the Neo-Babylonian Empire late in 626. Soon Babylonians and Medes combined forces to topple the Assyrian Empire, and in 612 completely destroyed the city of Nineveh. As Babylonian power rose in the east, Assyrian control over the province that had once been the kingdom of Israel relaxed and Assyrian pressure on Judah virtually ceased. After the fall of Nineveh the Assyrians established their capital at Haran. There they were defeated by Babylonians and Scythians in 610. At that point Pharaoh Neco II of Egypt decided to support Assyria. In the late spring of 609 he advanced through Judah, defeated and killed Josiah, and spent the summer campaigning in Syria.

Judah had capitulated to gross idolatry during the reign of Manasseh (696–642 BC). Baalism, Moloch worship, and other pagan religions had invaded the land, as had occultism and astrology. A false altar even stood in the temple in Jerusalem, and human sacrifice to pagan deities was practiced near Jerusalem. The land was thoroughly corrupted. Although some reform occurred in Manasseh's latter days, conditions reverted to their former baseness during the reign of his son Amon (642–640 BC). In 640 officials of Amon's household assassinated him, and the "people of the land" put Josiah on the throne (2 Kgs 21:26; 22:1; 2 Chr 34:1).

Josiah's Reform Activities. Josiah was only 8 years old when he became king. Evidently he had spiritually motivated advisers or regents; by the time he was 16 he began of his own accord "to seek the God of David" (2 Chr 34:3). When he was 20, he became greatly exercised over the idolatry of the land and launched a major effort to eradicate the pagan high places, groves, and images from Judah and Jerusalem. So intense was Josiah's hatred of idolatry that he even opened the tombs of pagan priests and burned their bones on pagan altars before these were destroyed.

Josiah carried his reform movement beyond the borders of Judah, venting his fury especially on the cult center at Bethel, where Jeroboam had set up his false worship. In fulfillment of prophecy (1 Kgs 13:1–3), he destroyed the altar and high place and burned the bones of officiating priests to desecrate the site (2 Kgs 23:15–18). What he did at Bethel, he did everywhere else in the kingdom of Samaria (2 Kgs 23:19,20).

When Josiah was 26, he launched a project to cleanse and repair the temple in Jerusalem (2 Kgs 22:3). Shaphan, the king's administrative assistant, commissioned the work; Hilkiah the priest exercised direct supervision of renovation and construction. In the process of restoring the temple, Hilkiah found the book of the law, the nature and contents of which are otherwise unknown. Possibly in the dark days of Manasseh a deliberate attempt had been made to destroy the Word of God. At any rate, evidently there was little knowledge of Scripture in Judah.

When Shaphan read the book of the law to Josiah, the king was devastated by the pronouncements of judgment against apostasy contained in it; he sent a delegation to Huldah the prophetess to find out what judgments awaited the land. The prophetess replied that the condemnation of God would indeed fall on Judah for its sin, but sent word to Josiah that because his heart was right toward God, the punishment would not come during his lifetime.

The king called together a large representative group for a public reading of the law—evidently sections especially concerned with obligations to God. The king and the people covenanted before God to keep his commandments.

Faced with the importance of maintaining a pure monotheistic faith, the king was spurred on to even more rigorous efforts to cleanse the temple and Jerusalem. He destroyed the vessels used in Baal worship, the monument of horses and chariot of the sun given by the kings of Judah for sun worship, the homosexual community near the temple, and shrines built by Solomon and in use since his day. Moreover, he made stringent efforts to eliminate the pagan shrines and high places in all the towns of Judah (2 Kgs 23:4–14).

Death of Josiah. Precisely why Josiah opposed Pharaoh Neco's advance through Judean territory is unknown. He may have wanted to prevent aid from reaching the hated Assyrians or to maintain his own independence. Josiah was mortally wounded in the conflict and was greatly lamented by Jeremiah and all the people (2 Chr 35:25). Well they might weep, for their godly king was gone, and within a few years the judgment withheld during his lifetime would descend on the nation.   HOWARD F. VOS

See ISRAEL, HISTORY OF; CHRONOLOGY, OLD TESTAMENT.

2. Son of Zephaniah, who returned to Jerusalem with other Jews after the captivity. In his house Zechariah was to crown the high priest Joshua (Zec 6:10,14, KJV Hen in v 14).

Josias. KJV spelling of Josiah, Jechoniah's father, in Matthew 1:10,11.

See JOSIAH #1.

Josibiah. KJV spelling of Joshibiah, Jehu's father, in 1 Chronicles 4:35.

See JOSHIBIAH.

Josiphiah. Father of Shelomith and founder of a house of which 160 members accompanied Ezra back to Palestine (Ezr 8:10).

Jotbah. Hometown of Haruz, the father of Meshullemeth. Meshullemeth was the mother of King Amon of Judah (2 Kgs 21:19). Its location is uncertain; however, some identify it with the town later named Jotapata by the Romans, situated six miles north of Sepphoris (modern Khirbet Jefat).

Jotbathah, Jotbath. Temporary camping place of the Israelites during their wilderness wanderings, located between Hor-haggidgad and Abronah (Nm 33:33,34). Later, following the death of Aaron, Israel journeyed from Gudgodah to this place, noted for its streams of water (Dt 10:7, KJV Jotbath). Its site is unknown.

See WILDERNESS WANDERINGS.

Jotham. 1. Youngest of Gideon's 70 sons and the only survivor of Abimelech's slaughter of Jotham's brothers at Ophrah (Jgs 9:5). Upon learning of Abimelech's intrigue with the Shechemites, which led to the death of his brothers, Jotham traveled to Shechem and addressed its men from atop nearby Mt Gerizim. Using a parable, he portrayed Abimelech's rise as king and concluded his denunciation by issuing a curse on both his half brother (see 8:31) and the men of Shechem for their treachery (9:7). Jotham then fled to Beer for fear of a reprisal from Abimelech (9:21). Later, God fulfilled Jotham's curse; the men of Shechem were killed in revolt and Abimelech was struck down at the hands of a woman (9:57).

2. Eleventh king of Judah (750–732 BC). He was the son of King Azariah of Judah and Jerusa, daughter of Zadok (2 Kgs 15:7; 2 Chr 26:21,23; 27:1), and the father of Ahaz. Jotham, at 25 years of age, ascended Judah's throne in the 2nd year of King Pekah of Israel (752–732 BC) and ruled for 16 years in Jerusalem. Initially he reigned as co-regent with Azariah, who was stricken with leprosy for tolerating pagan worship, until his father's death (2 Kgs 15:5).

Jotham was considered a righteous king in the eyes of the Lord. However, he too failed to cleanse the temple of its pagan influences, and subsequently the people of Judah continued in their evil ways (2 Chr 27:2,6). His building projects included the upper gate of the temple, work on the wall of Ophel, and the fortification of numerous towns in Judah's hill country (2 Chr 27:3,4). Jotham also defeated the troublesome Ammonites in battle (2 Chr 27:5) and registered by genealogy the families of Gad living east of the Jordan (1 Chr 5:17). He was buried in Jerusalem after his death (2 Chr 27:9). The prophets Isaiah and Micah ministered to Judah, and Hosea to Israel, during his

The wall that Jotham strengthened along the eastern edge of the Hill of Ophel in Jerusalem (south of the temple mount).

tenure as king. Jotham is listed as an ancestor of Jesus Christ in Matthew's genealogy (1:9, KJV Joatham).

See ISRAEL, HISTORY OF; GENEALOGY OF JESUS CHRIST; CHRONOLOGY, OLD TESTAMENT.

3. Second of Jaddai's five sons (1 Chr 2:47).

Jot or Tittle. Expression Jesus used in the Sermon on the Mount. In Matthew 5:18 *jot* (KJV) is a transliteration of the Greek letter *iota* (RSV). In this context it originally referred to the Hebrew letter *yod*, the smallest letter in the Hebrew alphabet. *Tittle* is a Middle English word referring to the diacritical dot placed over abbreviated words. The KJV translators used it to render a Greek word meaning "little horn." The Jews used that word to refer to the small marking that distinguished certain Hebrew letters from one another. Jesus used these two terms to emphasize the importance of the Law when he said not one jot or tittle would pass from the Law until all was fulfilled.

See BIBLICAL LANGUAGES.

Joy. Positive human condition that can be either feeling or action. The Bible uses joy in both senses.

Joy as Feeling. Joy is a feeling called forth by well-being, success, or good fortune. A person automatically experiences it because of certain favorable circumstances. It cannot be commanded.

The shepherd experienced joy when he found his lost sheep (Mt 18:13). The multitude felt it when Jesus healed a Jewish woman whom Satan had bound for 18 years (Lk 13:17). The disciples returned to Jerusalem rejoicing after Jesus' ascension (Lk 24:52). Joy was also the feeling of the church at Antioch when its members heard the Jerusalem Council's decision that they did not have to be circumcised and keep the Law (Acts 15:31). Paul mentioned his joy in hearing about the obedience of the Roman Christians (Rom 16:19). He wrote to the Corinthians that love does not rejoice in wrong but rejoices in the right (1 Cor 13:6; see also 1 Sm 2:1; 11:9; 18:6; 2 Sm 6:12; 1 Kgs 1:40; Est 9:17,18,22).

Psalm 137:3 shows that the emotion cannot be commanded. The Jews' captors wanted them to sing in the land of their exile, something they were unable to do. Faraway Jerusalem was their chief joy (Ps 137:6).

Joy as Action. There is a joy that Scripture commands. That joy is action that can be engaged in regardless of how the person feels. Proverbs 5:18 tells the reader to rejoice in the wife of his youth, without reference to what she may be like. Christ instructed his disciples to rejoice when they were persecuted, reviled, and slandered (Mt 5:11,12). The apostle Paul commanded continuous rejoicing (Phil 4:4; 1 Thes 5:16). James said Christians are to reckon it all joy when they fall into various testings because such testings produce endurance (Jas 1:2). First Peter 4:13 seems to include both action and emotion when it says, "But rejoice [the action] in so far as you share Christ's sufferings, that you may also rejoice and be glad [the emotion] when his glory is revealed." Joy in adverse circumstances is possible only as a fruit of the Holy Spirit, who is present in every Christian (Gal 5:22).

Other Meanings. The NT uses joy for that state which Christ saw would be his at the right hand of God and which made him willing to endure the cross (Heb 12:2). It is also the state into which the faithful servants in the parable of the talents were permitted to enter (Mt 25:21,23). In those cases it seems the joy refers to heaven and all the blessings of eternal life.

The Bible uses joy to describe a person or object that brings someone happiness. The good news was said by the angel who brought it to be "of a great joy" (Lk 2:10). Paul called the beloved brethren of Philippi, whom he longed to see, "my joy and crown" "(Phil 4:1). Writing to the Thessalonians he asked, "For what is our hope or joy or crown of boasting before our Lord Jesus at his coming? Is it not you? For you are our glory and joy" (1 Thes 2:19,20).

See FRUIT OF THE SPIRIT.

Jozabad. 1. Benjamite from Gederah and one of the military men who came to David's support at Ziklag (1 Chr 12:4, KJV Josabad).

2. Leader and mighty warrior from Manasseh's tribe who joined David at Ziklag to fight against Saul (1 Chr 12:20).

3. Another leader and man of valor from Manasseh's tribe who joined David at Ziklag (1 Chr 12:20).

4. One of the Levites who assisted with the administration of the temple contributions in Jerusalem during King Hezekiah's reign (2 Chr 31:13).

5. One of the levitical chiefs who generously gave animals to the Levites for celebration of the Passover feast during King Josiah's reign (2 Chr 35:9).

6. Levite, the son of Jeshua, and one who helped Meremoth, Eleazar, and Noadiah take inventory of the temple's precious metals and vessels during the days of Ezra (Ezr 8:33).

7. Priest and one of the six sons of Pashhur who was encouraged by Ezra to divorce his foreign wife during the postexilic era (Ezr 10:22).

8. One of the Levites who was encouraged by Ezra to divorce his foreign wife (Ezr 10:23).

9. One of the Levites who assisted Ezra with teaching the people the Law during the postexilic period (Neh 8:7).

10. One of the leaders of the Levites who were put in charge of the work of the temple during the days of Nehemiah (Neh 11:16).

Jozacar, Jozachar. Son of Shimeath the Ammonitess and one of the royal servants who conspired against and murdered King Joash of Judah (2 Kgs 12:21, KJV Jozachar). He is alternately called Zabad in 2 Chronicles 24:26.

Jozadak. Seraiah's son and one of the exiles transported by Nebuchadnezzar to Babylonia (1 Chr 6:14,15). He was the father of Jeshua (also called Joshua), the high priest in postexilic Jerusalem during the days of Zerubbabel (Ezr 3:2,8; 5:2; 10:18; Neh 12:26; Hg 1:1–14; 2:2,4; Zec 6:11). Jozadak is alternately called Jehozadak in the 1 Chronicles, Haggai, and Zechariah passages (KJV Josedech in Haggai and Zechariah).

"J" Source. Hypothetical document said to be characterized by the use of the name Jehovah or Yahweh. It supposedly was written about 850 BC by an unknown writer in the kingdom of Judah and was one of the source documents for the Pentateuch.

See DOCUMENTARY HYPOTHESIS.

Jubilee Year. Year of emancipation and restoration to be kept every fifty years. For Israel, the seventh year expressed at length the values of the seventh day (Lv 25:1–7). When a series of seventh years reached the perfection of seven sevens, the fiftieth year was heralded by the trumpet of jubilee and a whole additional year was set aside as belonging to the Lord.

The word "jubilee" simply means a ram's horn; it came to mean a trumpet made from or in the shape of a ram's horn. Such horns were exclusively for religious use, as is seen in Joshua 6, where different words express the "ordinary" trumpet used by the people and the ram's horn carried and blown by the priests. The sacred trumpet gave its name to the year of the ram's horn, the jubilee year—a year to which the people of God were summoned in a striking and holy way. It was not simply a release from labor, not just a rest, but a year belonging to the Lord. In Leviticus 25 this exact expression occurs in connection with the seventh year rather than expressly with the jubilee year. Functionally such a year was a sabbath rest "for the land" (v 4), and in its spiritual motivation it was "to the Lord" or "belonging to the Lord" (v 4). But nothing could more directly express the implications and orientations of the 50th year.

Lordship. The first principle of the jubilee is God's lordship over the whole earth, acknowledged by his people in their obedience to his command to set the year aside in this way. Just as the sabbath expressed his right to order life, giving it the shape of six days' work and one day's rest, and just as the seventh year, linked in Deuteronomy 31:9–13 with the reading of his law, expressed his right to command the obedience of his people, so the 50th year expressed his sovereign possession of all: land, people, means of production, and life itself. Take the typical case of debtor and creditor. When God brought his people into possession of the land, he gave to each his inheritance. In a given circumstance a man might be compelled to sell his land in whole or part, but it must come back to him: "The land shall not be sold in perpetuity, for the land is mine; for you are strangers and sojourners with me" (Lv 25:23). In this verse "strangers" carries the meaning "stateless persons," "refugees," "those who have sought political asylum"—in a word, those who have no rights except what mercy concedes. Such are the people of God and such they must

acknowledge themselves to be when the jubilee year comes round. When a piece of real estate changed hands, the seller might congratulate himself on the astuteness with which he had solved his problem and the buyer might rejoice in his skillful acquisitiveness; but in the year of jubilee seller and buyer alike are compelled to confess a different truth: neither is master, either of his own welfare or of the person and goods of another; each has a Master in heaven.

Redemption. According to the ordinance, the trumpet which heralded the year was sounded on the Day of Atonement (Lv 25:9). That was the day on which the Lord proclaimed his people clean before him from all their sins (Lv 16:30). The forgiveness of sins ushered in the jubilee year. The verb "to redeem" and the noun "redemption" had a strong commercial use in the recovery of property pledged against loans of money, and in the 50th year these words would have sounded and resounded as debtors confessed that they could not "redeem" and creditors forewent their "redemption" rights, each using the very vocabulary of the Lord's action at the exodus (Ex 6:6). This is what the Lord had done for his people, and the divine action must be the norm of the human. Brotherly generosity is urged (Lv 25:35–38), liberty is granted (vv 39–43), slavery in perpetuity is forbidden (vv 47–55) simply because the divine redemptive act makes the redeemed into brothers, brings them into the Lord's servitude, and cancels the bondage that would otherwise be theirs forever. In this way too the year is the Lord's: that they should imitate the excellencies of him who brought them out of darkness into his marvellous light (1 Pt 2:9).

Rest. The correlative of redemption is rest. This rest is vividly illustrated and enforced as Moses legislates for rest from all the toil connected with promoting next year's crop (Lv 25:4); rest from the toil of harvesting, for the people of God were to live hand to mouth, gathering only what and when need dictated (vv 5–7); rest from the anxious burden of debts incurred, and rest from slavery (v 10). Like the sabbath this rest would have meant exactly what it said: freedom from toil; relaxation, refreshment, recreation. Very likely tiredness was as endemic among the people of God then as now, and grace drew near to give them a holiday. But equally with the sabbath, release from the preoccupations of staying alive created time to be preoccupied with the Lord, his worship, his Word, and the life which pleases him. We can understand Isaiah 58 as binding the ideals of sabbath and jubilee together. The Lord frees his people not for unbroken idleness, but for the redirection of life toward himself. The jubilee year was thus a deliberate opting out of the rat race; it called a halt to acquisitiveness; it abandoned concern over the pressure to stay alive. It reordered priorities, giving a chance to appraise the use of time and the selection of objectives. For a whole year the people of God stood back, rested, ceased from the good in order to attain the best.

Faith. But this standing back from life was not in the style of a drop-out. It was the action of responsible faith. No one on earth can escape questions such as "What shall we eat?" The Lord foresees and provides (Lv 25:20); grace provides so that God's people can enjoy the ordinances of grace (cf. Ex 16:29). When he commands a year off, he enables them to take it. The fiftieth year was a living testimony to his faithfulness. The last season of sowing and reaping would have been the forty-ninth year; in the final seventh year in the series the people would live off the casual growth; and in the fiftieth year nothing but the sheer attentive faithfulness of their God could provide for them (Lv 25:21). Here indeed their faith would be put to the test, for God spoke a word of majestic promise and called on them to believe. At the heart of their jubilee they took God at his word and found him faithful.

Obedience. Biblically, it is a central characteristic of the people of God that they do what he commands for no other reason than that he commands it. In the ordinance of the 50th year the people of God must show themselves as his obedient ones, and in fact their obedience is the guarantee of continuance in the land he has granted to them. Thus, for example, Leviticus 26:34,35 teaches that loss of tenure and loss of liberty is directly related to contravention of the principle of the sabbath, found on the seventh day, seventh year, and jubilee year. Refusal of the way of obedience goes hand in hand with loss of possession, leaving behind an empty land which then enjoys the sabbath rest it never received from its disobedient inhabitants.

Hope. In the 50th year the people lived in the light of the forgiveness of sins, walked by obedience in harmony with the God who redeemed them, and, in freedom from toil, received from the ground its life-sustaining benefits without any sweat on their brows (Gn 2:16; 3:19). It was a sort of Eden restored, the curse momentarily held in abeyance—but also a prolonged foretaste of the coming day when the promises would all be fulfilled, the blood of the covenant efficacious without hindrance, the prisoners of hope (i.e., who had waited in hope for their release) freed, and the trumpet of liberation heard throughout the world (Zec 9:11–14; Is 27:13). The jubilee year in a limited but real way foreshadowed what would yet be the eternal inheritance and bliss of the people of God.

See FEASTS AND FESTIVALS OF ISRAEL; BIBLICAL THEOLOGY.

Jucal. Alternate name for Jehucal, Shelemiah's son, in Jeremiah 38:1.

See JEHUCAL.

Juda (Person). 1. Alternate KJV spelling of Judas, Jesus' brother, in Mark 6:3. Judas is also called Jude in Jude 1.

See JUDE, THE LORD'S BROTHER.

2. Alternate KJV spelling of Joda, Joanan's son, in Luke 3:26.

See JODA.

3. Alternate KJV spelling of Judah, Joseph's son, in Luke 3:30.

See JUDAH (PERSON) #8.

4. Alternate KJV spelling of Judah, Jacob's son, in Luke 3:33.

See JUDAH (PERSON) #1.

5. Alternate KJV spelling for Judah's tribe (Lk 1:39; Heb 7:14; Rv 5:5; 7:5).

See JUDAH, TRIBE OF.

Juda (Place). See JUDAH, TRIBE OF.

Judah (Person). 1. Fourth of Jacob's 12 sons (Gn 35:23; 1 Chr 2:1) and the 4th son born to Jacob by Leah, who, overjoyed with the thought of bearing Jacob another son, named him Judah, meaning "praise" (Gn 29:35, "This time I will *praise* the Lord"). Judah fathered five sons: Er, Onan, and Shelah by Bathshua the Canaanitess (Gn 38:3–5; 1 Chr 2:3) and the twins, Perez and Zerah, by Tamar, his daughter-in-law (Gn 38:29,30; 1 Chr 2:4). He eventually settled his family in Egypt with his father and brothers (Ex 1:2), although his first two sons, Er and Onan, were divinely killed in Canaan for their disobedience (Gn 46:12). Judah became the founder of one of Israel's 12 tribes (Nm 1:26,27).

Though reckless in his behavior with Tamar (Gn 38:6–30), Judah showed firm resolve in taking personal responsibility for Benjamin's safety in Egypt and acting as intercessor for his brothers before Joseph (Gn 44:14–18). At the time of Jacob's blessing Judah was granted the birthright privileges of the firstborn; the leadership of Jacob's family would come through Judah's seed, as would the promised Messiah of Abraham's covenant (Gn 49:8–12). Later, Judah's house was praised at the time of Ruth's engagement to Boaz (Ru 4:12), and both the Davidic line of kings (1 Chr 2:1–16; 3) and Jesus Christ's ancestors (Mt

1:2,3; KJV Judas; Lk 3:33; KJV Juda) traced their descent from Judah.

See JUDAH, TRIBE OF; GENEALOGY OF JESUS CHRIST.

2. Forefather of a family of Levites who assisted Jeshua, the high priest, with rebuilding the temple during the postexilic era (Ezr 3:9). He is alternately called Hodaviah in Ezra 2:40 and Hodevah in Nehemiah 7:43.

See HODAVIAH #4.

3. One of the Levites who was encouraged by Ezra to divorce his foreign wife (Ezr 10:23).

4. Benjamite, son of Hassenuah, who was second in command over the city of Jerusalem during the days of Nehemiah (Neh 11:9).

5. One of the leaders of the Levites who returned with Zerubbabel and Jeshua to Judah after the exile (Neh 12:8).

6. One of the princes of Judah who participated in the dedication of the Jerusalem wall during the postexilic period (Neh 12:34).

7. One of the priests who played a musical instrument at the dedication of the Jerusalem wall during the days of Nehemiah (Neh 12:36). He is perhaps identical with #5 above.

8. Joseph's son, father of Simeon and an ancestor of Jesus Christ (Lk 3:30; KJV Juda).

See GENEALOGY OF JESUS CHRIST.

Judah, Tribe of.

Geographical Territory. The frontiers of Judah are well defined in Joshua 15, which describes the inheritance of the tribe after the conquest. Second Kings 23:8 describes Judah as extending from Geba to Beersheba: Geba is about 8 miles north of Jerusalem, and Beersheba about 40 miles south. Judah thus held a strip of mountain land on the central spine of southern Palestine, about 50 miles from north to south and 20 miles from east to west. Of this 1000 square miles, half was desert (on the south and east); the rest was stony and not well watered. The central ridge, upon which are situated Jerusalem, Hebron, and Beersheba, rises to over 3000 feet in places before tapering off into the desert in the south. Along this ridge, connecting these towns, runs the

The Levonah Valley, which separates Judea and Samaria.

chief road. To the east, the ridge drops steeply to the Dead Sea, nearly 5000 feet below. To the west it drops less sharply to the "lowlands," actually a plateau some 1000 feet high, before descending to the Philistine plain, which stretches to the sea. To people of today it is staggering that God should have chosen such a small and apparently unpromising area in which to work out his plans.

Judah proper (for Jerusalem was a later addition) was remote and secure in its hills. Its true center and capital was Hebron, 3500 feet up. Only on the north was it vulnerable to attackers marching south along the ridge road. However, three great valleys led up from the western lowlands into the hills: the Valley of Ajalon, the Valley of Sorek, and the Valley of Elah. Battles would rage up and down these valleys from the days of Joshua to the time of David and long afterward. The few roads to the east (the one from Jerusalem to Jericho is the best known) were not so important, although it was by this "back door," that Joshua had invaded the hill country (Jos 10:9). Judah was thus geographically well out of the mainstream of Israelite life, since only the territory of Simeon lay to the south.

The area occupied by Judah falls easily into three natural regions; the central mountain ridge, fairly densely settled, especially on its western side, where rainfall and dew were greatest; the eastern slopes, almost uninhabited and mostly desert; and the southern pastoral region round Beersheba, where the mountains fall away into dry prairie, with sparse settlement throughout.

Economic Life. To Israel, Palestine was a land flowing with milk and honey (Nm 13:27). Half of Judah might be desert, but the rest was reasonably good soil, and on the western slopes the rain was usually adequate. Wheat and barley, olive and fig, and especially vineyards, grew freely. The land might be stony, but stones could be collected and used for walls and buildings. Not as rich as the great northern valleys like Jezreel, Judah was still good mixed farming country, although it required hard work. Sheep and goats were plentiful, and that meant wool and milk. Cattle were probably rarer; Judah was not cattle country like Bashan (Nm 32:1). Wool meant cloth and hides meant leather. In those days the hills were forested, which meant fuel and building materials. Clay for pottery was readily available for domestic utensils. Copper came from Edom in the south, and iron from Philistia in the west; these could be obtained by barter of agricultural produce. Whether they realized it or not, God had dealt graciously with the people of Judah, in giving them an adequate if simple life. The climate was bracing: a cold, wet winter, with snow and hail at times, and a long, rainless summer, with low humidity and cool nights. This brought heavy dews on the eastern slopes (Jgs 6:38), and precious rainwater was conserved in rock-hewn cisterns (Jer 2:13). Permanent streams of any size did not exist in Judah, but springs or "wells" were abundant, from Jerusalem to Beersheba. It was not until Judah got caught up into the economic life of Solomon's trading empire that its simple pattern of life changed; even then, the change in the hills of Judah was far less than elsewhere. Judah had no seaport of its own and controlled no rich caravan routes; it had no coveted raw materials, like the copper of Edom or the cedars of Lebanon; no luxury goods for trade, like the purple dye of Phoenicia or the gold of Ophir; no lush land to tempt the greed of others. In God's mercy Judah's temptations were few. Its faith was also less liable to be corrupted: comparatively few Canaanites had ever settled in this area, while the conquest had been more thorough in the south than in the north.

History and Significance. The earliest blessings on Judah are recorded in Genesis 49:8–12 and Deuteronomy 33:7. After the exodus the tribe of Judah took first place in the desert camping arrangement (Nm 2:3). Caleb, one of the two faithful spies, was a tribal chieftain of Judah (Nm 13:6). In Joshua's invasion of Palestine, the highlands allotted to Judah were the first to be cleared of Canaanites, after the initial fighting around Jericho and Ai (Jos 6,8). The Book of Joshua is a summary account of the whole campaign. Simeon and Judah marched together against the hill country of the south, led by Caleb and Othniel.

Although God's gift to Judah had been the whole land westward as far as the sea, Judah failed to take anything but the hills. The plain was controlled by iron-protected chariots and fortress cities. The king of Jerusalem was killed and Jerusalem was burned (Jgs 1:8), but the Jebusites continued to occupy the area until David's day (Jgs 1:21). The men of Judah, like other Israelites, might burn Canaanite towns, but they did not usually occupy the old sites themselves. Under the judges, the tribe of Judah was still isolated, though Othniel was of Judah (Jgs 3). In the great battle against Sisera, Judah is not even mentioned (Jgs 5). This tribal isolation was soon lost, first through Philistine invasions from the west, and then through David's capture of Jerusalem and the placing of the national and religious capital there. Although in Judges 15:11 the men of Judah are prepared even to hand over Samson to the Philistines, with Samuel as judge all changes. The ark returns (1 Sm 7:1); lost territory is regained (1 Sm 7:14). Indeed, Samuel's sons act as judges in Beersheba (1 Sm 8:2), although they are corrupt.

David finally breaks the power of the Philistines in a series of victories and rules as king first in Hebron, Judah's chief town (2 Sm 2:1–4). When he is crowned king of all Israel, however, he moves the capital to the newly conquered Jerusalem, on the northern frontier of the tribe of Judah (2 Sm 5:6–10). Here the ark was to be brought (2 Sm 6), and here Solomon was to build the temple (2 Sm 7:13). All God's promises will henceforth cluster around Jerusalem, the temple, and David's line, and from Judah was to come the Messiah (Gn 49:10). It is possible that Judah, the royal tribe, had favored treatment; it may not have been included in the list of 12 districts for "taxation" in 1 Kings 4. In any case the chief officials of David's kingdom were all drawn from the tribe of Judah, and this led to jealousy.

The division between the northern and southern tribes had begun in David's lifetime, after Absalom's revolt (2 Sm 20:1); after Solomon's death the rift became complete (1 Kgs 12:16). Henceforth for 200 years, until the fall of the northern kingdom in 722 BC, there were two little kingdoms side by side: a larger one in the north and east, called Israel (the "ten tribes" of 1 Kgs 11:35), and a smaller one in the south, called Judah. With this, the history of Judah as a tribe virtually comes to an end, for although still called by the old tribal name, this little kingdom was really a "Greater Judah." It now contained not only the old tribe of Judah but also the newly conquered Jebusite territory of Jerusalem, some of the old Philistine country, and the tribes of Benjamin and Simeon, as well as many Levites (2 Chr 11:14) and other "loyalists" from the north. Indeed, from now on, "tribe" had far less meaning than before; it was more important where a person lived than of what tribe the person was, although, within the family, tribal origins continued to be remembered. For 250 more years the little kingdom of Judah persisted alone. Even after the exile it was the tiny province of Judah that emerged under Nehemiah (Neh 1:2,3), and Judea still remained as a district in NT days (Lk 3:1). In fact, the vast majority of later Jews were of the tribe of Judah, as the very name "Jew" shows. But the chief glory of the tribe of Judah, now as ever, was that the House of David sprang from it; when Jesus Christ was born, he was to be of David's line and Judah's tribe. So it is that in Revelation 7:5, when 12,000 are sealed from each tribe, Judah, whose very name meant "praise" (Gn 29:35), has pride of place in the list, as it had in Numbers (2:3) so long before.

R. ALAN COLE

See ISRAEL, HISTORY OF; JUDAH (PERSON) #1.

Judaism. Religion and culture of the Jewish people from the beginning of the postexilic period (538 BC) to modern times. The term "Judaism" is derived from "Judah," the name of the southern kingdom of ancient Israel, while "Jew" is a shortened form of "Judeans."

The Period of the Second Temple (516 BC–AD 70). *Historical Survey.*

The united kingdom of Israel under Saul, David, and Solomon, came to an end shortly after the death of Solomon. Rehoboam, his son, provoked a revolt about 933 BC on the part of the 10 northern tribes by levying unreasonably high taxes (1 Kgs 12). From that time on, the kingdoms of Israel, or Samaria (the northern kingdom), and Judah (the southern kingdom) maintained a separate existence. The northern kingdom fell to the Assyrians in 722 BC, and thousands of captives, primarily members of the upper class, were exiled forcibly and taken to Assyria where they presumably intermarried with the native population and disappeared from history. The kingdom of Judah survived as an independent state until 597 BC, when it came under the control of the Babylonians under Nebuchadnezzar. The temple was finally destroyed in 586 BC and many captives were carried off to Babylonia, beginning a period of exile that was to last two generations. The Babylonians were defeated by Cyrus the Persian in 539 BC, and the following year the king issued a decree permitting all captive peoples to return to the lands of their origin (1 Chr 36:22,23; Ezr 1). At least four waves of Jewish expatriates returned from Mesopotamia to Judea during the century following the decree of Cyrus under such leaders as Sheshbazzar, Zerubbabel, Ezra, and Nehemiah. Many Jews chose to remain in their adopted Mesopotamian homeland. The dedication of the second temple in the spring of 516 provided a formal end to the exilic period of 70 years (Jer 29:10), and was a direct result of the prophetic exhortations of Haggai and Zechariah.

In Judea the Jewish people were ruled by governors who held office at the pleasure of the Persian king. One of the earlier governors was Zerubbabel (Hg 1:1; 2:1), a descendant of David (1 Chr 3:10–19). In some way he shared rule with the high priest Jeshua ben Jehozadak. Palestine was part of one of the 20 satrapies of the Persian Empire, which lasted from 539 to 331 BC, when it fell to the Greeks under Alexander the Great. Little is known about the historical developments in Palestine during most of the Persian period. When Alexander died in 323 BC, his empire was divided up among his generals; Egypt and Palestine fell to Ptolemy I. The Ptolemies were benevolent despots who allowed the Jews of Palestine a measure of freedom and autonomy. After the battle of Paneion in 198 BC, Palestine came under the rule of the Seleucid Empire, founded by Seleucus I, another of Alexander's generals.

The Seleucid Empire embraced a very large area with a diverse population, extending from Asia Minor and Palestine in the west to the borders of India on the east. Antiochus IV (Epiphanes) ascended the Seleucid throne in 175 BC and attempted to unify his vast empire by Hellenizing it (i.e., by forcing the adoption of Greek language and culture). Local cultures and religions were forcibly suppressed as a result of this policy, and the Jewish state in Palestine was perhaps the hardest hit of all. In 167 BC Antiochus IV dedicated the temple in Jerusalem to Olympian Zeus, sacrificed a sow on the altar, destroyed scrolls containing the Jewish Scriptures, and forbade the rite of circumcision. This repression triggered a revolt led by an aged priest named Mattathias and his sons. The Seleucids were repulsed, and finally in 164 BC the temple was retaken by Mattathias' son Judas the Maccabee (an epithet meaning "the hammer"). This Jewish victory has been commemorated annually by the festival of Hanukkah ("dedication"). Judas and his brothers, called Maccabees or Hasmoneans (Mattathias was of the house of Hasmon), and their descendants ruled Judea from 164 to 63, when Palestine fell to the Roman general Pompey. Thereafter, Palestine remained a vassal of Rome.

Hyrcanus, a Hasmonean, was high priest after the conquest of Judea by the Romans, though Antipater, an Idumean, was the real power behind Hyrcanus. The sons of Antipater, Phasael and Herod, were governors of Jerusalem and Galilee, respectively. Upon the assassination of Antipater in 43 BC, and through his connections in Rome, Herod (later called Herod the Great) was named king of Judea by the Roman senate; he reigned from 37 to 4 BC. When he died, Palestine was divided up by the emperor Augustus (27 BC–AD 14) and placed under the governorship of three of Herod's sons: Herod Archelaus (ethnarch of Judea, Idumaea, and Samaria from 4 BC to AD 6), Herod Antipas (tetrarch of Galilee and Perea from 4 BC to AD 39), and Herod Philip (tetrarch of Batanea, Trachonitis, and other small states from 4 BC to AD 34). These territories were generally placed under Roman procurators after the sons of Herod had died or been deposed. For a brief period (AD 41–44), Herod Agrippa I, the grandson of Herod the Great, ruled virtually the same territory as his grandfather. Upon his death (narrated in Acts 12:20–23), his territories were placed under Roman procurators. The greed and ineptness of these procurators provoked the Jewish populace to rebel. The ill-fated Jewish revolt of AD 66–73 resulted in the

The Maccabean Genealogy

destruction of the second temple by the Tenth Roman legion under Titus in 70. The revolt was completely quelled in 73, when more than 900 Jews under siege in the desert fortress of Masada near the Dead Sea committed mass suicide rather than fall into Roman hands. These tragic events ended permanently the temple cult and the priestly system in Judaism.

Social and Religious Developments. The Babylonian conquest of Judea and the destruction of the Solomonic temple in 586 BC produced dramatic social and religious changes in Jewish life. The cessation of the temple cult struck a serious blow at the heart of the Israelite religion, since the Jerusalem temple alone was the legitimate and divinely appointed place for discharging much of the ritual requirement of the Mosaic law, chiefly the sacrificial cult. Even the three annual pilgrimage festivals, Succoth ("Tabernacles"), Pesach ("Passover"), and Shavuoth ("Weeks") could no longer be observed by pious Jews who had remained in Judea after 586 BC. When after 538 BC many exiles chose to return to Judea, many others elected to remain in their new homeland. For the latter, the temple cult, even when reinstituted in 516 BC, could no longer play a significant role in their religious lives.

During the exilic and early postexilic period the peculiar Jewish institution of the synagogue (a Greek word meaning "gathering place") began to evolve. The synagogue became such a popular and useful institution for Jewish communities outside Palestine that in the centuries after the dedication of the second temple they sprang up throughout Palestine, many in Jerusalem itself. By the end of the second temple period, the synagogue had come to play three important functions in Jewish life. It served as a house of prayer, a house of study, and a place of assembly. First-

century AD synagogue worship is illustrated in Luke 4:16–30 and Acts 13:13–42. The focus of the service was a reading of a selection from the Torah (Law of Moses), then one from the Haphtorah (Prophets). These readings were followed by a homily based on Scripture. Other elements in first-century AD synagogue worship included the recitation of the Shema ("Hear O Israel"), a combination of biblical passages including Deuteronomy 6:4–9; 11:13–21 and Numbers 15:37–41, and the Shemoneh Esreh ("Eighteen Benedictions") called the Amidah ("standing") because it was recited while standing upright. Jews also wore fringes on their garments in obedience to Numbers 15:38,39 (Mt 23:5), and phylacteries on their foreheads and left arms. Phylacteries are little boxes containing the portions of Scripture recited in the Shema; they were used in literal fulfillment of the command in Deuteronomy 6:8. Archaeologists have discovered actual first-century phylacteries in the ruins of Masada.

Outside of Palestine, Mesopotamia became the second most important center of Judaism. The Babylonian Jewish community was known as the Golah ("captivity"), and its titular head was called the Resh Galuta or Exilarch (both terms mean "leader of the captivity"). By the end of the exilic period, the descendants of the original captives had forgotten Hebrew and adopted Aramaic, the international language of the ancient Near East and a sister language to Hebrew, as their first language. Even in Palestine, Aramaic was the primary language spoken. Thus, when portions of Scripture were read in synagogue services in Hebrew, most of those present were unable to understand what was read. This problem was solved by providing a methurgeman ("translator") who would translate orally short sections of Scripture. Eventually these Targums ("translations") were reduced to writing, beginning in the 2nd century AD.

By the 1st century AD it has been estimated that there were from 4 to 7 million Jews in the Greco-Roman world, perhaps 3 to 4 times the population of Palestine. Jews in lands outside of Palestine came to be known collectively as the Diaspora ("scattering"). After the Greeks dominated the Mediterranean world through Alexander and his successors, Greek became the common language throughout this region. Just as Mesopotamian Jews spoke Aramaic in place of Hebrew, so Jews in the Greco-Roman world came to speak Greek. By the middle of the 3rd century BC Hellenistic Jews began to translate the Hebrew Scriptures into Greek. This translation, called the Septuagint (a term meaning "seventy," based on a legend that it was translated simultaneously by 70 Jewish scholars), contained a more extensive canon of Scripture than that recognized by Palestinian Judaism. This reflects the more liberal attitudes of Hellenistic Jews in contrast with the more conservative cast of Palestinian Judaism.

During the 2nd century BC, most of the major sects within Palestinian Judaism came into being. The Hasidim ("pious") were members of a religious association which aided the Hasmoneans in their revolt against the Seleucids (1 Mc 2:42; 7:13), but later opposed them when they claimed rights to the priesthood. Both the Pharisees and Essenes may have their origin in this religious sect. The Sadducees (a name perhaps connected with Zadok, a high priest appointed by David; Zadok's descendants were regarded as the only legitimate priestly line in Ez 40–48) were a wealthy, aristocratic class which monopolized the high priesthood. They did not believe in angels, spirits, life after death, or the resurrection (Acts 23:8), nor did they accept the validity of the oral law as developed by the Pharisees. They left no writings and disappeared with the destruction of the temple in AD 70.

The Pharisees ("separated ones") first appear in our sources toward the end of the 2nd century BC and are involved primarily in political affairs. They represented the common people against the tyrannical Hasmonean ruler Alexander Janneus (103–76 BC), who had hundreds of Pharisees executed in reprisal. By the 1st century AD the Pharisees seem wholly concerned with religious matters, and were noted for the scrupulous observance of the Mosaic law as traditionally interpreted. On grounds of ritual purity, they separated themselves from other Jews who were not as scrupulous, and might contaminate them. Pharisees went about in groups called Haberim ("associates") in which they were insulated from those who were lax religiously. In their zeal to remain faithful to the Mosaic law, the Pharisees developed an oral law (later erroneously attributed to Moses) which served as a fence around the Torah. This oral law was an interpretation and expansion of the 613 commands in the Mosaic law; it was finally compiled and reduced to written form as the Mishna ("Teaching") in the late 2nd century AD. Paul (Acts 22:3; 23:6; 26:5; Phil 3:5) and many other early Christians were converts from Pharisaism (Acts 15:5). Pharisaic Judaism survived the destruction of Jerusalem in AD 70 to form the rabbinic Judaism that dominated Jewish religious life from the 2nd century AD to modern times.

The Essenes were another religious sect within Judaism which had its origins in the 2nd century BC. Like the Pharisees the Essenes were concerned principally with maintaining ritual purity in obedience to the Law of Moses. The Essenes lived and worked in Jewish society, seeking to influence people by the simple, altruistic life which they followed. Some Essenes also lived in their own communities, to which they returned each night after work. There were numerous religious factions within contemporary Judaism, and one such group, which may only have had vague connections with the Essenes, established a community on the western shore of the Dead Sea. This group regarded itself as the true Israel, and in the wilderness prepared for the final visitation of God by keeping themselves pure from all defilement. Many documents written by members of this sect were discovered in caves near the Dead Sea where they had been hidden just before the Romans destroyed the settlement. These documents, the Dead Sea Scrolls, have provided detailed information about this religious sect and its beliefs.

The Zealots were another Jewish sect, who may be related to the Sicarii ("dagger men"). This group of political activists flourished from AD 6 to 66. Regarding God alone as their sovereign, they attempted to overthrow the Romans and those who collaborated with them by violent means, including assassination. They helped to foment the Jewish revolt of 66–73 and perished with Jerusalem in 70.

Social class and status in first-century Palestine was determined in accordance with the rules of ritual purity. The upper class comprised members of the religious establishment, such as the Sadducees, scribes, Pharisees, and Jerusalem priests. The Sanhedrin was a deliberative body whose membership was drawn from these groups. For all practical purposes there was no middle class. The lower class consisted primarily of the Am Ha Arez ("People of the Land"), Jews who were

A Comparison of Five Jewish Sects

	Essenes	Herodians [Kannai]	Pharisees	Sadducees	Zealots [Boethusians]
Origin	Possibly the Hasidim (1 Mc 2:42; 7:13)	Sadducean aristocracy (Boethus)	Possibly the Hasidim (1 Mc 2:42; 7:13)	Zadok Joshua (priest at time of return from Babylon) Anonymous Leader	Unknown
Dates	2nd cent. BC–AD 70	37 BC–AD 70	2nd cent. BC–present	200 BC(?)–AD 70	37 BC–AD 70
Prominence in Scripture	no mention	3 passages	99 passages	13 passages	1 passage
Characteristics	Legalism Rigorous probation period Exclusivism/ isolationism Communal asceticism Altruism (only toward members of own sect) Daily worship, prayer, and study of Scripture Periods of silence No worship in temple Subjection to superiors Oaths of initiation/ piety/ obedience/ secrecy Marriage eschewed	Partisans of the Herodian dynasty Not a religious or political sect	Legalism (strict observance of Mosaic law) Exclusivism (separation from common people) Flexible liberalism) Ethical emphasis	Disputations, confrontations Exclusivism (aristocratic, political) Rigid, reactionary conservatism (seeing themselves as protectors of the pure Mosaic tradition) Theological (temple cultus) emphasis Political priesthood	Patriotic fanaticism with religious underpinning Violence (including assassination) Zeal—like Mattathias and sons (1 Mc 2:24–27) and Phinehas (Nm 25:11)— for God's law vs. all enemies of Israel
Beliefs	Separate national existence of Israel They are the people of the new covenant Emphasis on purity of life Strict predestination Immortality of soul Preexistence of soul Strict Sabbath observance Purification rites (daily ritual bathing) No war or commerce	Sadducean theology	Scripture and Oral Law are inspired and authoritative Canon = whole OT Nonliteral biblical interpretation Free will + providence Resurrection and afterlife Earthly paradise Angels and demons Messianic expectations (overthrow of Gentiles; restoration of Israel)	Torah alone is inspired and authoritative Canon = Torah Literal biblical interpretation Individual free will No resurrection or afterlife (but Sheol) No angels or demons	God as Israel's true King Total obedience + action = messianic age

ignorant of the Law through lack of education and who did not scrupulously observe those commandments with which they were familiar. The generally hostile attitude of the Pharisees toward the Am Ha Arez is expressed in John 7:49: "But this crowd, who do not know the law, are accursed." There was yet another social class in first-century Palestine, which can be designated as "untouchables." This group was composed of Samaritans, tax collectors, prostitutes, shepherds, those who bought and sold seventh-year produce, lepers, Gentiles, and, perhaps worst of all, Jews who became as Gentiles (e.g., the prodigal son of Lk 15:11–32). The rules of ritual purity as generally observed prevented any form of social contact between the upper class and the untouchables, and made contacts with the Am Ha Arez highly undesirable. Against this background, the horror of the Pharisees over Jesus' association with tax collectors and sinners is thoroughly understandable (Mk 2:15–17).

A further consequence of this religious criterion for determining social class and status was an uneasy tension between Jerusalem and the rural areas of Palestine, particularly Galilee, during the last two centuries of the second temple period. Those in Jerusalem regarded Galilee as a place where ignorance of the Torah was the rule (Jn 1:46). Jerusalem was primarily a religious center, whose major industry was the temple cult. The total population of Jerusalem in the 1st century AD has been estimated at from 25,000 to 40,000. Most of these were either artisans and craftsmen devoted to building and adorning the temple (still incomplete before it was destroyed; Jn 2:20), or priests and Levites involved in the many ritual activities of the temple. Though Jews were expected to travel to Jerusalem for each of the three annual pilgrimage festivals, this requirement proved difficult for rural Palestinian farmers.

Further, the tithe demanded by Mosaic command was only on the produce of the land, not upon wages or bartered goods. The rural farmers, therefore, bore the brunt of this taxation and quite naturally resented the privileged position of urban artisans, merchants, and priests who were not obliged to tithe. The temptation not to tithe the produce of the land was very great, and many farmers succumbed to it. Their untithed produce was not kosher, and thus to be avoided by those, like the Pharisees, who were religiously scrupulous. In addition to the first and second tithes demanded of farmers (the second tithe had to be spent in the vicinity of Jerusalem), it has been estimated that Roman tax levies amounted to 10 to 15 percent of an individual's income. Religious taxes together with Roman taxes added up to a crushing tax burden of from 25 to 30 percent. The fact that the Jews finally revolted against their Roman oppressors in AD 66 is not difficult to comprehend. Throughout the 1st century AD, in fact, minor revolts in Palestine occurred with predictable frequency. Many of these occurred during the 3 annual pilgrimage festivals in Jerusalem, when the normal population of 25,000 to 40,000 swelled to 500,000 or more. These festivals provided ideal opportunities for uprisings, and the Romans were particularly alert for such eventualities. Jesus was executed during one such Passover festival because he was suspected of being a political revolutionary (Mk 15:26).

The second temple period provided the setting for the rise and fall of apocalypticism within Judaism. Apocalypticism (from a Greek word meaning "revelation") was a kind of eschatology ("account of final events") which assumed that ideal conditions could not be restored on earth unless God first intervened climactically to destroy evil (particularly foreign oppressors) and vindicate the righteous (Israel). Apocalyptic visionaries composed many documents, called apocalypses, in which they attempted to read the signs of the times and predict the coming of the visitation of God. Since there was a widespread consciousness that the era of prophecy was over, these apocalyptists wrote not under their own names but under the names of ancient Israelite worthies such as Moses, Abraham, Enoch, and Ezra. Among the more significant expectations of Jewish apocalypticism were: (1) the coming of a Messiah; (2) the coming of a great period of tribulation, sometimes called the messianic woes; (3) the resurrection of the just; (4) the judgment of the wicked and the reward of the righteous. Apocalyptic beliefs probably provided the motivation for most if not all of the Jewish revolts against the Romans.

Some portions of the Hebrew Scriptures were still in the process of composition at the beginning of the second temple period. The last three prophetic books—Haggai, Zechariah, and Malachi—were written from the end of the 6th century to the mid-5th century BC. Later rabbis expressed the opinion that the Spirit of God had been taken from Israel when these prophets ceased their labors. The Chronicler ends his work by referring to the decree of Cyrus (538 BC), and both Ezra-Nehemiah and Esther appear to have been written in the 5th century.

The second temple period witnessed not only the completion of those writings which were later regarded as inspired and authoritative in Judaism, but also the full recognition of all 24 sacred books. Prior to the destruction of Jerusalem in 586 BC, the Mosaic law had not been observed with any consistency (according to 2 Kgs 22 it had been mislaid for an unknown period of time), nor had the classical prophets always received appropriate recognition. But after 586 the Torah occupied a a position of unquestioned sanctity in the lives and thoughts of the Jewish people, replacing in many respects the temple cult even before its final dissolution in AD 70.

The Jewish Scriptures are divided into three sections, designated by Jews with the acrostic "Tenak": (1) Torah ("Law," or "Revelation"), (2) Nebiim ("Prophets"), and (3) Kethubim ("Writings"). It is generally claimed that while the Law and Prophets enjoyed canonical status prior to the 2nd century BC, the Writings were finally declared canonical at the rabbinic council of Jamnia (c. AD 90), the historicity of which is disputed, however. The rabbis are thought to have discussed whether certain biblical books should continue to be part of Scripture. In reality, the Jewish canon of Scripture was fully defined from traditional usage by the 1st century BC. The Law consisted of five books: Genesis, Exodus, Leviticus, Numbers, and Deuteronomy. The Prophets consisted of two sections, the Former Prophets (Joshua, Judges, Samuel and Kings), and the Latter Prophets (Isaiah, Jeremiah, Ezekiel, and the Twelve). The Writings included Chronicles, Ezra-Nehemiah, Esther, Job, Psalms, Proverbs, Ecclesiastes, Song of Songs, Lamentations, Ruth, and Daniel. The total number of books in this canon is 24, identical with the Protestant canon of 39 books, since Samuel, Kings, Chronicles, Ezra-Nehemiah, and the Twelve are each counted as only one book. The Alexandrian canon of Hellenistic Judaism was more extensive, and the extra books (called Apocrypha by Protestants) are all found in the Roman Catholic OT canon of 46 books.

The Talmudic Period (AD 73–425). *Historical Survey.* According to Jewish legend, when the Romans were about to conquer Jerusalem in the revolt of AD 66–73, a prominent Pharisee, Rabbi Johanan ben Zakkai, feigned death and his disciples were permitted to carry him out of the besieged city in a coffin. He received permission from the Romans to move his school from Jerusalem to Jamnia, on the coast of Palestine. The temple cult and the priestly system had disappeared, and rabbinic academies such as that of Rabbi Johanan set themselves to the enormous task of reconstructing Judaism. The older Sanhedrin was reinstituted as the Beth Din ("Court of Law"), and Gamaliel II, a grandson of Hillel, who had presided over the old Sanhedrin, became its leader with the title Nasi ("Prince"), or Patriarch. The patriarchate continued until AD 425, when Emperor Theodosius II abolished the office upon the death of the last patriarch, Gamaliel VI. In Mesopotamia, Babylonian Judaism experienced a renaissance that lasted until the end of the 5th century AD. This period was called the Age of the Gaonim ("Excellencies") after the heads of the two great rabbinic academies at Sura and Pumpeditha. It was there that the great Babylonian Talmud was compiled by the 5th century AD.

In AD 115, various Jewish communities throughout the eastern Mediterranean, including Egypt, Cyprus, and Cyrene, revolted vainly against the Roman emperor Trajan. Without exception these revolts were all put down by Roman legions. Finally, when the emperor Hadrian was on the brink of founding the new city of Aelia Capitolina on the site of old Jerusalem, the Jews again revolted in AD 132, led by a self-proclaimed messiah, Simon bar Kosiba, who was called Bar Kochba ("Son of a Star") by his followers as an allusion to the messianic passage in Numbers 24:17. Bar Kosiba was aided by the famous rabbinic scholar Akiba. This revolt, though initially successful, was put down by the Romans under Julius Severus in 135. Shortly thereafter Hadrian issued a decree banning all Jews from the new Aelia Capitolina.

Social and Religious Developments. During this period the result of generations of rabbinical scholarship bore fruit with the compilation of the Babylonian and Jerusalem Talmuds. The rabbinic sages consciously saw themselves as the heirs of the ancient Israelite prophets, who in turn were the heirs of the Mosaic law. They distinguished consciously between their own legal interpretations of the Mosaic law (which they called Halakah, or "walking," i.e., a guide for life), and the commands in Torah itself (called Mitvah, or "commandment"). The oral law, developed through generations of rabbinic discussion, was finally compiled and written down through the efforts of the patriarch Judah ha-Nasi (*c*. AD 135–220) during the last quarter of the 2nd century AD, and became known as the Mishna ("Teaching"). This is a topical arrangement of rabbinic discussions of such subjects as the sabbath, firstfruits, sacrifices, and women. The Mishna became the basis for further rabbinic discussion in both Palestine and Babylonia. The decisions of sages who flourished after the writing of the Mishna were compiled about AD 450 in Palestine and about 500 in Babylonia. This second stage beyond the Mishna was called the Gemara (meaning either "completion" or "repetition"). The Mishna and the Babylonian Gemara make up the Babylonian Talmud, while the same Mishna with the Jerusalem or Palestinian Gemara comprises the Jerusalem Talmud. Yet another type of rabbinic literature is the Midrashim ("interpretations"), which either follow the order of a particular biblical book or consist of homilies on particular biblical texts. The Targums ("translations"), or paraphrastic translations of Scripture into the Aramaic language, finally came to be written down beginning in the late 2nd century AD.

With the temple cult part of the irretrievable past, rabbinic Judaism concentrated on the religious significance of the Torah, and elevated scholarship to the central role which it still plays in Judaism. Rabbinic Judaism gradually exerted its influence upon diaspora Judaism under the initial leadership of Rabbi Johanan until a kind of rabbinic orthodoxy emerged during the 2nd century. Christianity was one of the major ideological foes of rabbinic Judaism. In order to purge Jewish Christians from their midst, the rabbis introduced an additional benediction to the Eighteen Benedictions customarily recited at synagogue services. This 19th benediction was a curse upon the *minim* (Christians and other heretics) which Jewish Christians who attended synagogue services found impossible to repeat. The line was firmly drawn between Judaism and Christianity by this device, which was employed late in the 1st century.

DAVID E. AUNE

See DEAD SEA SCROLLS; ESSENES; PHARISEES; TRADITION, ORAL; TRADITION; TORAH; PHILO JUDAEUS; SANHEDRIN; ISRAEL, RELIGION OF; POSTEXILIC PERIOD, THE; HELLENISTIC JUDAISM; JEW; ISRAEL, HISTORY OF; JUDAH, TRIBE OF; EXILE; FIRST JEWISH REVOLT; TALMUD.

Bibliography. J. Bonsirven, *Palestinian Judaism in the Time of Jesus Christ;* W. Förster, *Palestinian Judaism in NT Times;* M. Hengel, *Judaism and Hellenism,* 2 vols; G.F. Moore, *Judaism in the First Centuries of the Christian Era,* 3 vols; J. Neusner, *First Century Judaism in Crisis and Judaism;* J. Parkes, *The Foundations of Judaism and Christianity;* S. Schechter, *Studies in Judaism,* 3 vols; E. Schürer, *History of the Jewish People in the Time of Jesus Christ,* 5 vols; D.J. Silva, *A History of Judaism,* vol 1.

Judaizers.

Christian Jews who, during the apostolic and early postapostolic periods, attempted to impose the Jewish way of life on gentile Christians. The Greek verb, which literally means "to Judaize," is found only one time in the NT (Gal 2:14), where it actually means "to live according to Jewish customs and traditions." In that passage Paul quotes part of a brief conversation he had with Peter several years earlier: "If you, though a Jew, live like a Gentile and not like a Jew, how can you compel the Gentiles to live like Jews [to Judaize]?" The issue that concerns Paul is not simply whether or not a person follows the Jewish way of life, but whether one erroneously thinks that salvation is attained thereby.

In the early days of Christianity most if not all Christians were Jews prior to their conversion to Christianity. The few who were originally Gentiles, such as Nicolaus of Antioch (Acts 6:5), had converted to Judaism before turning to Christianity. At that time conversion to Judaism was accomplished through three separate steps: (1) circumcision (for males); (2) a ritual bath in water; and (3) agreement to take upon oneself the "yoke of the law," that is, to obey the 613 commands of the Mosaic law as interpreted and expanded in Jewish halakah (rabbinic legal decisions). Following Jewish customs and traditions and observing Jewish religious laws was a normal way of life for Jewish Christians, whether they were Jews by birth or through conversion. For them, belief in Jesus as the Messiah of Jewish expectation enhanced, but did not replace, their Judaism. Christianity was not regarded as a religion distinct from Judaism, but rather as the truest form of Judaism. These Jewish Christians had all been circumcised as infants, or upon conversion to Judaism, and they also practiced the kosher dietary laws and rules of ritual purity prescribed in Mosaic legislation and rabbinic tradition. Further, they worshiped at the temple in Jerusalem (Acts 3:1; 21:26) until its destruction by the Romans in AD 70 and in Jewish synagogues scattered throughout the Roman world (Acts 13:5,14,42, 43; 14:1; 17:1–5).

While earliest Christianity began as a predominantly Jewish movement, it soon expanded into the Greco-Roman world. Jewish Christians were forced to leave Jerusalem as a result of persecutions (Acts 8:1; 11:19–24), and they proclaimed the gospel wherever they went. Philip was responsible for bringing the gospel to Samaria, where many Samaritans became Christians (Acts 8:4–25). On the day of Pentecost many Jews from places all over the Roman world became converts to the Christian faith (Acts 2:5–11). Presumably, when these newly converted Jewish Christians returned to their homes, they carried the gospel with them. Although the origin of the Christian community in Rome is shrouded in obscurity, this is probably how the gospel first came to Rome. One of the central concerns of Luke, the author of Acts, is to show how Christianity, which began as a small, persecuted sect of Judaism in Jerusalem, spread throughout the Roman world; in so doing, it was rejected by Jews and embraced by Gentiles. The major turning point in Acts is in chapter 10, where Peter is the means whereby the Roman centurion Cornelius, together with his entire household, accepted the gospel and began to manifest the gifts of the Holy Spirit. According to Acts 10:45, "the believers from among the circumcised who came with Peter were amazed, because the gift of the Holy Spirit had been poured out even on the Gentiles."

The growing number of gentile converts to Christianity forced Jewish Christians to face a very difficult problem: Must a Gentile first become a Jew in order to be a Christian? Some Jewish Christians gave a positive answer to this question, and these became known as the circumcision party (Acts 11:2; Gal 2:12). Others, such as Peter and Barnabas, and especially Paul, vigorously disagreed. While these two radically different points of view could have split the early church into two major factions, that possibility did not occur. Luke tells the story of how, after a successful first missionary journey (Acts 13:1–14:28). Paul and Barnabas reported to the church at Antioch how God had opened a door of faith to the Gentiles (Acts 14:27). Opposition from the

Judaizers in the circumcision party was soon felt, however, since some of them had come to Antioch from Judea for the express purpose of advocating the idea that circumcision was absolutely necessary for salvation (Acts 15:1). Many Jewish Christians had, like Paul, once been Pharisees. These former Pharisees were particularly insistent that new converts who were Gentiles be circumcised and charged to keep the Law of Moses (Acts 15:5). They were really demanding that Gentiles become converted to Judaism in order to be Christians.

Paul and Barnabas debated with members of the circumcision party before an assembly of apostles and elders in Jerusalem (Acts 15:4–12). The assembly, led by James the Just (the brother of Jesus), listened to both sides and decided to effect a compromise. A letter to the gentile churches was drafted in which it was recommended that gentile converts to Christianity adhere to only a few absolutely essential obligations: (1) abstention from meat sacrificed to idols, (2) abstention from eating blood or blood-saturated meat, and (3) abstention from unchastity (Acts 15:23–29). These three obligations were probably singled out because they were thought to have been important features of those laws regarded as part of the covenant between God and Noah according to Jewish tradition. Since Noah was the ancestor of all mankind, Gentiles as well as Jews, such laws had universal validity. The Mosaic covenant, on the other hand, was incumbent only upon Jews, not upon Gentiles. For this reason the Jerusalem Council determined that abstension from meat sacrificed to idols, blood-saturated meat, and unchastity applied to all Christians, whereas the obligation of circumcision did not.

Judging from the remainder of the Book of Acts, it might be supposed that the decision of the Jerusalem Council was satisfactory to the Judaizers of the circumcision party. However, from the details provided by Paul in many of his letters, we find that this was not the case. After Paul briefly summarizes the results of the Jerusalem Council for the Galatian Christians (Gal 2:1–10), he relates how, even after the Jerusalem Council, the Judaizers of the circumcision party were sufficiently powerful to cause even Peter and Barnabas to temporarily isolate themselves from gentile Christians. (According to rabbinic purity laws, one would become religiously impure if one ate with Gentiles.) The major reason Paul wrote the Letter to the Galatians was to combat Judaizers who had apparently invaded the Christian communities in Galatia after his departure. These Judaizers appear to have successfully persuaded some of the Galatian Christians that salvation was available only for those who

were circumcised and who kept the Mosaic law (Gal 5:12; 6:13). At least some of the problems experienced by the Corinthian church appear to have been caused by Judaizers (2 Cor 11:12–15,22), and they had infected the Christian community at Philippi (Phil 3:2,3). Judaizers also appear to have made some progress in the church at Colossae. Therefore, according to Colossians 2:16,17, "let no one pass judgment on you in questions of food and drink or with regard to a festival or a new moon or a sabbath. These are only a shadow of what is to come; but the substance belongs to Christ."

Of all the early apostles and elders Paul was the one who most consistently opposed the Judaizers' view that Gentiles must first become Jews in order to be Christians. His dramatic conversion to Christianity, narrated three times in Acts (9:1–9; 22:6–16; 26:12–23) and occasionally referred to by Paul himself (Gal 1:11–17; 1 Cor 9:1; 15:8), convinced him that salvation could only be achieved through faith in Christ. Since Jesus was the *only* way, all other means by which persons sought to obtain salvation were necessarily invalid and illegitimate. Paul was fully aware that it was not because of the fact that he was an observant Jew that he had become justified before God (Phil 3:2–11), but through faith in Christ. Primarily because of the persistent activity of the Judaizers, Paul had to insist frequently on the invalidity of the Law and the validity of faith as the means of being justified before God. This theme dominates his letters to the Romans and the Galatians.

Toward the end of Paul's life the success of the Christian mission to the Gentiles resulted in the fact that the number of gentile Christians began to exceed the number of Jewish Christians. Paul lamented the fact that the Jews had not responded to the gospel as he would have hoped (Rom 9:1–33). In Acts one can see how Paul began his ministry in a new area by preaching at the local Jewish synagogue (Acts 13:5,14,42–43; 14:1; 17:1–5). At that time Judaism had become a very popular religion, since it could offer ethical monotheism to its adherents. Ethical monotheism consisted of a belief in one God (in contrast to pagan polytheism), in association with a highly moral life-style (Greco-Roman religions were largely amoral). While few pagans went so far as to become actual converts to Judaism, many attended synagogue services and kept as many Jewish laws and customs as they felt able. These people were called "God-fearers." Although Paul began by preaching to the Jews in local synagogues, it was usually the gentile God-fearers who responded, while the Jews themselves rejected both Paul and his message. This recurring pattern can be glimpsed in Acts 17:4,5, a scene which took place just after Paul had spent three weeks in the Jewish synagogue at Thessalonica presenting the gospel: "And some of them were persuaded, and joined Paul and Silas; as did a great many of the devout Greeks and not a few of the leading women [the last two groups are God-fearers]. But the Jews were jealous, and taking some wicked fellows of the rabble, they gathered a crowd [and] set the city in uproar."

Jewish Christianity gradually withered and disappeared, and with it went the insistence of the Judaizers that Gentiles live according to Jewish customs and traditions in order to receive salvation. The center of Jewish Christianity had traditionally been Jerusalem. Just before the destruction of Jerusalem and the temple at the end of the Jewish revolt of AD 66–70, many Jewish Christians fled to Pella in obedience to a divine revelation. The ill-fated revolt of Bar Kochba (AD 132–35) further weakened the movement, when Jewish Christians experienced persecution at the hands of the Jewish insurgents. Thereafter Jewish Christianity grew weaker and eventually disappeared. With its disappearance the persistent notion that Gentiles must first become Jews in order to be Christians also died.

DAVID E. AUNE

See JEW; ACTS OF THE APOSTLES, BOOK OF THE; GALATIANS, LETTER TO THE; JERUSALEM COUNCIL; JUDAISM; FIRST JEWISH REVOLT; HELLENISTIC JUDAISM; PAUL, THE APOSTLE.

Judas. 1. Simon's son, surnamed Iscariot; one of the 12 disciples of Jesus. The derivation of Iscariot is uncertain. In all probability it designated the place of his birth—the town of Kerioth. His childhood home was perhaps Kerioth of Moab, east of the Jordan (Jer 48:24; Am 2:2), or Kerioth-hezron of southern Judah, also known as Hazor (Jos 15:25). A less feasible suggestion identifies Iscariot with an Aramaic word meaning "assassin," a word eventually attached to Judas' name because of his betrayal of Jesus.

Judas Iscariot's name appears last in the lists of disciples (Mt 10:4; Mk 3:19; Lk 6:16), perhaps indicating his ignomy in the minds of later believers rather than his original importance among the 12. During Jesus' public ministry he managed the treasury of the company (Jn 13:29), from which he was known to pilfer money (Jn 12:4). As betrayer, Judas contracted to turn Jesus over to the chief priests for 30 pieces of silver. He accomplished this act of treachery by singling out Jesus with a kiss in

The Church of All Nations in the Garden of Gethsemane, a location remembered for Judas' kiss of betrayal.

the Garden of Gethsemane (Mt 26:14–47; Mk 14:10–46; Lk 22:3–48; Jn 18:2–5).

Various suggestions have been offered to explain Judas' traitorous deed. (1) In keeping with his patriotic zeal, Judas turned Jesus over to the authorities after realizing that his Master did not intend to overthrow the Roman order and establish a Jewish state. (2) Judas believed Jesus to be the Messiah and planned his arrest in hopes of urging Jesus to usher in his kingdom. (3) He was a scoundrel who plotted wickedness since the start of Jesus' public ministry. (4) Prompted by a satanic impulse, Judas betrayed Jesus; however, after recognizing that he was deceived, out of remorse he took his own life. (5) With a damaged pride and a humiliated ego from Jesus' caustic rebukes, Judas, originally a loyal disciple, turned against him. (6) Judas, moved by his own greed, yielded to his selfish instincts, not realizing that Jesus would consequently be tried and killed; upon learning the outcome of his betrayal, he repented in dispair and committed suicide.

Judas, despondent over his act of betrayal, went out and hung himself in a field bought with his 30 pieces of silver (Mt 27:3–10). Acts 1:18 gruesomely adds that his body "swelled up" (RSV margin) and burst, spilling forth his intestines; for this reason the field was called the "Field of Blood" (Acts 1:19). Matthias later took Judas Iscariot's place among the 12 (Acts 1:26).

2. Son of Joseph and Mary, and the brother of Jesus, James, Joseph, and Simon (Mt 13:55; Mk 6:3). He is identifiable with Jude.

See JUDE, THE LORD'S BROTHER.

3. Son of James and one of the 12 disciples (Lk 6:16; Jn 14:22; Acts 1:13). He is identifiable with Thaddeus in Matthew 10:3 and Mark 3:18.

See THADDAEUS, THE APOSTLE.

4. Galilean who led a Jewish revolt against the Romans because of the census taken by Quirinius in AD 6. In Acts 5:37 the Pharisee Gamaliel mentioned Judas as an example of one who unsuccessfully tried to gain the support of the Jewish people. Josephus credited him with founding the Jewish Zealot party, an extreme revolutionary movement that attempted to throw off Roman suzerainty and to reestablish Jewish autonomy (*Wars* 2.8.1).

5. Owner of a house along the street called Straight in Damascus. Here, following his conversion, Saul (Paul) found lodging and had his vision restored by Ananias (Acts 9:11).

6. Prophet and leader in the early Jerusalem church. Judas, surnamed Barsabbas, was selected with Silas to accompany Paul and Barnabas to Antioch, where they confirmed the Jerusalem Council's decision regarding the gentile church and subsequently encouraged its believers (Acts 15:22–32).

See JOSEPH #12.

7. KJV spelling of Judah, Jacob's son (Mt. 1:2,3.)

See JUDAH (PERSON) #1.

Judas Barsabbas. *See* JUDAS #6.

Judas Iscariot. *See* JUDAS #1.

Judas of Galilee. *See* JUDAS #4.

Jude, Letter of. Short, hard-hitting letter to a church being infiltrated by teachers who practiced all types of moral evil. Jude reveals the inner situation of a Jewish-Christian community and also presents some great difficulties for the Christian interpreter.

Author. The Letter of Jude states that it was written by "Jude ... [the] brother of James" (Jude 1), meaning Jude, the Lord's brother, whose brother James became the leader of the Jerusalem church. Since Jude, unlike James, probably traveled with his wife and family when evangelizing (1 Cor 9:5), he would have had good reason to write to Christians he knew when in his old age he heard of false teachers in the churches he had founded or visited.

Despite this testimony, however, there has been a large debate as to whether Jude, the Lord's brother, actually wrote this letter. It is thought that perhaps another Jude wrote it, or some later author wrote it in the spirit of the leader whom he revered. The hypothesis that another Jude wrote it seems unlikely, for the apostle Jude (Lk 6:16; Acts 1:13) is the son of a certain James, not a brother of James; besides, Jude 17 appears to distinguish Jude from the apostles. And since there was only one James who was prominent in the early church, James the Lord's brother, it would be hard to believe that some other Jude would have a brother named James and would use such an identification in the title; it would be too confusing. The title "brother of James" must mean that Jude was James of Jerusalem's brother and therefore Jesus' brother; he did not use the title "brother of our Lord," perhaps, as Clement of Alexandria said, out of modesty.

The idea that a later author wrote using Jude's name presents a major problem: Why would he pick such an obscure name, instead of Paul or Peter or James, and why would he not use a more exalted and authoritative title? We must conclude that despite the difficulties of date and background, Jude the Lord's brother wrote this letter.

Date, Origin, Destination. About date, origin, and destination, the letter says nothing directly. Since the content of the faith is clearly fixed (Jude 3) and the recipients have personally heard the apostles (who have apparently died already, Jude 17), the date must be later than AD 60 and earlier than 100.

Jude may have written from Galilee in his old age, or perhaps he had returned to Jerusalem. The best guess we can make about the recipients would be that they were members of Jewish-Christian churches in Syria, which would have been a likely place for the type of heresy that the letter combats. Still, these locations remain little more than guesses.

Background. Three facts about the Letter of Jude make its background difficult for the average reader. First, it is hard to be sure what type of heresy it is combatting. Some scholars believe that this is early Gnosticism, and others that it is simply teaching infiltrated with ethical error. If the heretics were Gnostics, they believed in a hierarchy of angels or demigods. In this case they probably saw Jesus as a lower rung on the way to salvation. Perhaps they also considered God as the lower creator God (the Demiurge) and spoke of wanting to serve the true God (Jude 4). This might explain the interest in angels and demons (Jude 8) and the stress on the unity of God (Jude 25). But probably these were simply people who had found a way to rationalize immoral behavior and were unwisely mocking the evil powers; there is no clear evidence that they were gnostic, while there is plenty of evidence that people turned the freedom of the gospel into an excuse for sin (e.g., Rom 6; 1 Cor 5,6). These teachers probably denied Christ by failing to follow his ethical teaching, and their blasphemy of angels (while they themselves were deep in sin) was another ethical sin. Such depravity is enough to explain the letter; however, knowing that doctrinal and ethical error often go hand in hand, we must not discount the possibility that some doctrinal error was also involved.

Second, Jude surprises us by quoting from two apocryphal books, the Assumption of Moses (Jude 4) and 1 Enoch (Jude 14, 15, which quotes 1 Enoch 1:9). This fact and other allusions in the book reveal that Jude and probably his readers were well read in Jewish apocalyptic literature. Moreover, it also shows that Jude regarded books outside the canon of the OT as transmitting true traditions and authoritative prophecy. That Jude accepted these books is not surprising, since many apocryphal books were used by Jews of that period alongside the OT as a type of devotional literature. Early Christians often included apocryphal literature along with canonical books as part of their Bibles (sometimes they would also omit NT books they either did not yet know or considered inauthentic). The canon of NT Scripture was not firmly established until the 3rd century, long after Jude.

It is important to realize that while Jude probably believed in the historicity of these citations, the teaching of the letter does not depend on that historicity. Jude wrote about neither the history of Moses nor Enoch, but about how one should behave toward authorities (Jude 8) and what God will do to ungodly people (Jude 13). The citations illustrate Jude's teaching, and probably carried weight with his first readers, but the fact that they are apocryphal should bother us no more than Paul's quotations from pagan writers or the writer of Hebrew's allusions to 2 Maccabees (Acts 17; Ti 1:12; Heb 11:35). The authority of Scripture rests in the point the author is making.

Third, Jude shows such a close relationship to 2 Peter 2 that either Jude is an expansion of 2 Peter 2 or 2 Peter 2 is an abbreviation of Jude. Words, phrases, and illustrations are identical in the two works. While it is hard to determine who borrowed from whom, probably the author of 2 Peter has adapted the strong denunciations of Jude to the more instructive tone of his work. It would be hard to imagine anyone writing Jude if 2 Peter already existed. Christians should have no problems with this borrowing, for no writer of Scripture believed himself so original that he could not borrow from other Scriptures, from hymns, or from noncanonical literature. It is no more a problem for God to inspire a quotation or adaptation from another writing than for him to inspire a new composition. Indeed, some passages in Scripture are total repetitions of others (e.g., Ps 18 and 2 Sm 22).

Purpose and Theological Teaching. Jude describes his work in terms of exhortation or encouragement (Jude 3). Obviously he wanted to strengthen the churches against false teachers who were perverting the gospel. Thus he repeatedly urges the believers to hold fast or guard their purity and the gospel (Jude 3,20, 21,24). Yet he does not want the teachers simply kicked out, for he has hopes that the believers will be able to rescue some from this danger, although the rescue itself is dangerous work (Jude 23).

In framing his exhortation the author does not produce any new doctrines, but he does underline some old ones. (1) He stresses the ethical nature of the gospel and the need to maintain purity in life and speech. (2) He shows a high regard for salvation through Christ and a strong belief in one God. (3) He demands respect for authority, both temporal and spiritual (Jude 8–11). (4) He has a clear apocalyptic belief, stressing the coming last judgment (Jude 14,15) and the fact that the last days are not future but have already come (Jude 18). (5) He warns of the necessity to persevere in the faith both doctrinally and ethically (Jude 19–21). (6) He assumes evangelistic zeal to reclaim those who have erred, for they are outside the grace of God (Jude 23).

Content. *Salutation (1,2).* The author identifies himself humbly as a servant of Jesus Christ and addresses his letter to the faithful in the church, those that are loved, guarded, and called by God and Christ.

Call to Hold the Faith (3,4). Jude had been planning to write these Christians about the faith ("our common salvation"). We will never know what instruction he had planned to give, for in the middle of his preparations he heard news that forced him to change his plans. Some people had joined the church, perhaps with ulterior motives ("admission has been secretly gained"), who are a danger to the church. The Christians must fight hard to keep pure the body of doctrine (meaning ethics as well as theology) which they have received from Jude and the apostles. Jude makes two charges against these false believers: (1) they have perverted God's grace into licentiousness, perhaps openly flaunting sexual sins as a sign of the freedom they have in Christ (cf. Rom 6, 1 Cor 5, 6); and (2) they have denied the Lord Jesus (by failing to follow his teachings).

Reminder of God's Judgment (5–7). Since the recipients were probably Jewish Christians, they had learned the OT and Jewish tradition well. The author chooses three illustrations of the results of apostasy: (1) Judgment can come to those once considered as God's people (as it did to those "saved" from Egypt, Ex 32:28; Nm 11:33,34; 14:29,30,35). (2) The consequence of apostasy is eternal damnation (as in the case of the fallen angels of 1 Enoch 6–16, although these ideas appear in other Jewish traditions). (3) Ethical corruption is in fact a type of apostasy and thus merits damnation (as in the case of Sodom, Gn 19; 2 Pt 2:4,6—the author stresses the homosexuality of Sodom rather than its injustice, which Ez 16:49 condemns, so perhaps sexual misbehavior was a problem with the false teachers). These three illustrations drive home the seriousness of the problems that the church is facing.

Denunciation of the False Teachers (8–16; cf. 2 Pt 2:10–17). The false teachers claim revelations in dreams as the basis of their evil behavior. Their sins are: (1) sexual impurity (including, but not limited to, homosexuality); (2) rejection of Christ's authority (as embodied in his ethical teaching); and (3) evil speech about angels (whether good ones, which is

probably the case, or evil). This latter practice is shown to be sin by an example from the Assumption of Moses: even an archangel rebuking the devil himself would not use the language these teachers use about angels. But since these people are unspiritual, they are totally ignorant of what they insult (cf. 1 Cor 2:7–16); yet they are experts in bodily sin, like mere animals, and this sin is destroying them.

Therefore the teachers are just like Cain (the embodiment of violence, lust, greed, and rebellion against God in Jewish tradition), Balaam (who tried to make money by leading people into sin, Nm 31:16; Dt 23:4), and Korah (who rebelled against God's authority in Moses, Nm 16). They are also dangerous to the believers, for they are turning the meal which was part of the Eucharist into an orgy (cf. 1 Cor 11:20–22), and could corrupt the practice of the rest of the church. They care only for themselves and are devoid of real spiritual gifts from God (like waterless clouds or the dead trees of winter, Lk 13:6–9), being ready for the second death (their fate is so sure that it is seen as having already happened). They produce only evil deeds and in this are like the fallen angels (stars are considered angels in Jewish tradition, 1 Enoch 18:13–16; 21:1–10).

The prophecy of Enoch in 1 Enoch 1:9 shows the certainty of their doom. Originally the prophecy spoke of God coming in judgment, but Jude makes it refer to Christ, who for Christians is the coming judge (Mt 25:31). Christ will come with the angelic hosts and wreak justice on sinners for their sins (both evil deeds and evil words). That prophecy includes people who grumble or accuse God as Israel did (Ex 16:7–12; 17:3), do whatever they desire, are loud-mouthed, yet flatter when it is to their advantage.

Instructions for the Faithful (17–23). Faithful Christians must remember that the apostles (here meaning the 12, not the wider circle of apostles which included Paul, Barnabas, and others) had predicted just such a situation when they were alive: in the last days there would be scoffers, who would do any ungodly act they desired (2 Pt 3:3). These false teachers are such people. They divide the church; and, although they claim to be spiritual and receive dreams, they are really totally on the worldly level, for they do not possess the Holy Spirit. The faithful must watch out that they remain in the love of God and do not drift into rebellion as these heretics have. This is done by (1) building themselves up (as opposed to causing divisions) on the basis of the faith, the apostolic teaching, and example; (2) praying in the Holy Spirit (Eph 6:18, which sets them off from those not having the Spirit); and (3) waiting expectantly for the mercy Jesus would show them in the soon-coming last judgment (1 Enoch 27:3,4).

Yet the Christians must still deal with those influenced by the false teaching. While the Greek text here is very uncertain (it is not clear whether Jude had two or three groups in mind), Jude probably intended that the church should act mercifully toward those who were wavering over whether to follow the false teaching, restore those it could from the followers of the false teaching as if snatching them from hell, and, while keeping a merciful attitude (a readiness to accept them back quickly if they repented), strictly avoid any social contact with the unrepentant out of fear of God's judgment.

Benediction (24,25). Jude closes with a doxology which probably reminded the readers of the liturgy of their church (Rom 16:25–27). In the midst of many who have fallen from the faith, God is praised as the one who can not only keep the readers from falling, but bring them safely rejoicing into his very presence. It is to this one who is alone God our Savior through Jesus Christ (meaning God saves us by means of Jesus) that the four attributes (typical in doxologies) glory, majesty, dominion, and authority belong, now and forever.

PETER H. DAVIDS

See APOSTASY; BROTHERS OF JESUS.

Bibliography. J.N.D. Kelly, *A Commentary on the Epistles of Peter and Jude;* T. Manton, *An Exposition on the Epistle of Jude;* J.B. Mayor, *The Epistle of Jude and the Second Epistle of Peter;* E.M. Sidebottom, *James, Jude, and 2 Peter.*

Jude, The Lord's Brother.

Joseph and Mary's son, and the brother of Jesus, James, Joseph, and Simon according to Matthew 13:55 and Mark 6:3 (KJV Juda), where he is called Judas. He should not be confused with Judas the apostle (cf. Lk 6:16; Jn 14:22; Acts 1:13), for Jude and his brothers evidently rejected Jesus as Messiah (Jn 7:5) until after his resurrection (Acts 1:14). Later, Jude authored a general epistle in which he warned believers to beware of false teaching.

See JUDE, LETTER OF; BROTHERS OF JESUS.

Judea.

"Land of the Jews," particularly after the captivity. Since most of the Israelites who returned from the exile were from the tribe of Judah, they were called Jews and their land, Judea. This part of the Holy Land has always been of great interest to the Bible student because of the location of such places as Jerusalem and Bethlehem within the area and because of the events of Christ's life and ministry that occurred here.

Definition. First used in Ezra 5:8, the term there designates a province of the Persian Empire. It is also spoken of in the litera-

Mar Saba, a Greek Orthodox monastery from Byzantine times, is located in the lower Kidron.

ture of the Maccabean period after Greece had taken control of the area from the Persians (1 Mc 5:45; 7:10). In Roman times Judea was annexed to the Roman province of Syria until the time of Herod the Great, who was declared king of Judea in about 37 BC. On occasion the term "Judea" seems to mean all the territory occupied by the Jewish nation, that is, all of western Palestine (Lk 23:5; Acts 10:37; 26:20). Secular writers of NT times, including Strabo, Tacitus, and Philo, used the term in the wider sense, but in its ordinary and strict sense it denoted the southern district of Palestine. The other two districts or divisions were Galilee in the north and Samaria in the center.

Geography. While the geographic boundaries of Judea were not always the same in different historical periods, the province did include the territories once belonging to the tribes of Judah, Dan, Benjamin, and Simeon. The northern boundary, separating Judea and Samaria, is less definite than the others since there is no natural geographic barrier—no valley, no body of water, no break in the terrain to indicate a division. It is thought, however, that the northern boundary line ran from Joppa on the Mediterranean to a point on the Jordan River about 10 or 12 miles north of the Dead Sea.

The southern boundary extended from a point about 7 miles southwest of Gaza near the coast through Beersheba to the Dead Sea. According to Judges 20:1, Beersheba was the southern boundary of the nation, and it is therefore properly considered the southern limit of Judea. The eastern boundary was the Dead Sea, and the western boundary the Mediterranean Sea. Judea therefore was in shape a square of territory approximately 45 miles wide on each side.

History. The history of Judea begins in the Persian period (539–331 BC), when Cyrus allowed the Jews to return to rebuild their temple and their holy city of Jerusalem. In the Greek period (334–167 BC) the area came under the control of the Seleucids, descendants of one of Alexander's generals who ruled in Syria. Their attempts to destroy the Jewish religion led to a Jewish revolt under the leadership of the Hasmonean family, and the Jews enjoyed nearly a hundred years of independence (167–63 BC). In 63 BC Pompey conquered Palestine for Rome, and eventually Herod the Great was made king (37–4 BC), being succeeded by his son Herod Archelaus (4 BC–AD 6). The Romans then appointed a series of imperial governors called procurators, and these ruled Judea, Samaria, and Idumaea (south of Judea) until the Jewish revolt of 66–73, with the exception of the years 41 to 44, when the grandson of Herod the Great, Herod Agrippa I, ruled all of Palestine.

The fate of Judea has been the fate of all Palestine, and it has continued to know many cruel conquerors since the close of NT times. The country continued under the heel of Rome until 330, when it came under Constantinople, or Byzantium, and saw the building of many Christian churches (330–634). The Persians again invaded (607–629), destroying Christian churches and killing many people. The Arab period (634–1099) saw the coming of Moslem control of Judea, which was interrupted by the Crusaders (1099–1263), who were determined to rescue the Holy Land from the Moslems. After the the final defeat of the Crusaders, the Moslems regained control until the modern period (1917–present). After World War I, Judea was a part of the British mandate over Palestine. In 1948 it was partitioned between Israel and Jordan, and as a result of Israel's victories in the Six Day War of June 1967, Judea was reunited and came once again under the control of the Jews.

DONALD K. CAMPBELL

See JUDAISM; EXILE; POSTEXILIC PERIOD, THE; PALESTINE.

Judge. *See* TRADES AND OCCUPATIONS

Judges, Book of. OT book named after the prominent leaders raised up by the Lord to deliver his people. The word "judge" in Hebrew also denotes the activity of governance, including warfare. Some scholars have argued that there were two kinds of judges: charismatic deliverers (or major judges) and local judicial sages (or minor judges). It is uncertain why some judges receive cursory attention, whereas the exploits of other judges are given in great detail.

Author. The book reflects a final editing of the material in the period of the early monarchy. It may well be a polemic for the righteous rule of David over against the kingship of Saul, which was molded by a secular, Canaanite conception of kingship rather than by the Law of God. The author, certainly not Samuel, relied on ancient written materials.

Date. Though the judges succeeded in giving the tribes some rest from the incursions of surrounding enemies, the Israelites were continually harassed over long periods of time. Scholarly opinion differs on the duration of the period of the judges. The dating of the exodus affects the dating of the beginning of the judges. Those who take an early date for the exodus put the beginning around 1370–60 BC, whereas others propose a date close to the end of the 13th century BC. A related issue pertains to the chronology of the judges. Does Judges give a chronological, sequential account of the period, or is the book a representative account of judges from various parts of Canaan and Transjordan who "judged" a region, a tribe, or several tribes simultaneously?

Literary Framework. There is no doubt that the stories in the book bear the marks of literary creativity. The stories are classics in their own right. The poetry of Deborah's song is very moving, and the fable of Jotham is a fine example of figurative speech. The care given to the stories is also reflected in the construction of the book. There are two introductions: a political one (1:1–2:5) and a socioreligious one (2:6–3:6). The political introduction connects Judges with the story of the conquest, when the tribes attempted to occupy the land. It prepares the reader for the political and military problems of the era of the judges. The socioreligious background explains why Israel had so many adversities, why the institution of the judges arose, and why the Lord never gave Israel the promised lasting rest from its enemies. The main body of the book is the story of the judges (3:7–16:31). References to the minor judges (six in all) are set within the stories of the major judges in increasing frequency: As is evident from the schema, the number of minor judges increased in frequency in proportion to the decrease in number of major judges: 2 major—1 minor; 2 major—2 minor; 1 major—3 minor; 1 major. There is a total of 12 judges, representative of the 12 tribes of Israel.

The purpose of the listing of 12 judges, representative of the various parts of Canaan and Transjordan, is to demonstrate that all tribes throughout the conquered territories experienced grave difficulties from a variety of enemies: Aramaeans, Moabites, Ammonites, Amalekites, Canaanites, and Philistines. Israel was hard pressed on nearly all its frontiers. The appendixes (chs 17–21) together with the two introductions form the framework of the book.

The political and socioreligious problems (1:1–3:6) are presented by way of several stories in the last chapters. According to Childs, the final editor who gave the book its canonical shape purposefully framed the stories of the judges so as to show lack of movement. The successes of the previous stages in redemptive history came to a standstill in the ebb and flow of the judges. Though the Lord delivered his people in many ways, they returned to the problems described in 1:1–3:6. The appendixes describe Israel's problems representative of the period of the judges, when "there was no king in Israel" (17:6; 18:1; 19:1; 21:25).

Purpose and Theological Teaching. The cycle of apostasy, judgment, cry for deliverance, and God's raising up of a judge reflects a Deuteronomic perspective with its warnings concerning disobedience and judgment. The repetitiveness of the cycle supports the contention of the anonymous narrator that Israel remained unchanged by the grace of God. The moral, religious, and political anarchy was not significant, as it lacked movement. The last chapter shows that in spite of the civil wars, the tribes are still concerned with each other's welfare. Though the unity of God's people has been gravely challenged, the situation is not hopeless. The book ends on a note of hope, hope for a king who may deliver Israel, bring cohesiveness to the tribes, and lead Israel morally and religiously as well as politically and socially.

Thus, the purposes of the book are: (1) to demonstrate the meaninglessness of this stage in Israel's development; (2) to explain why the tribes did not occupy all the land promised to the patriarchs; (3) to justify the way of God, who was gracious and patient with Israel's repeated acts of disobedience; (4) to set forth the legitimacy of a "shepherd" king in contrast to a despotic form of kingship; and (5) to explain the urgent need for a new momentum, lest Israel succumb to the Philistines and intertribal warfare.

Content. *The Political Introduction (1:1–2:5).* In Joshua 1–12 the warfare under Joshua is portrayed as a mobilization of Canaanite forces against Israel. By the intervention of the Lord the Canaanite resistance was put down and the land was occupied by the tribes (chs 13–21). Joshua 13–21, however, clearly shows that each tribe had problems ridding its territory of pockets of Canaanite resistance, which were usually centered around heavily guarded and well-fortified cities (cf. 13:2–6,13; 15:63; 16:10; 17:12,16,18).

The Book of Joshua emphasizes the successes and minimizes the problems, whereas the prologue to Judges sets the stage for the whole book by openly addressing Israel's problems and failures. As the book unfolds, it is precisely these problems and failures which in due time bring Israel to the brink of disaster.

The period of the judges began with the death of Joshua (Jgs 1:1; 2:8,9). The Israelites had inherited a legacy from Joshua: the Law of the Lord (Jos 23:6; 24:26), the land, a challenge to obey the Lord (24:14–27), and a promise of God's presence and help in subduing the Canaanites (23:5,10).

(1) Judah and Simeon (Jgs 1:2–20). The prominence of Judah and Caleb parallels the position of Judah in Joshua (14:6–15:63; cf. also the house of Joseph, Jgs 1:22–29; cf. Jos 16,17). Judah was victorious over the cruel Adoni-bezek, who ruled over Bezek, a town of uncertain location. Judah successfully occupied the hill country, the Negeb, and the western foothills (v 9). They even took Jerusalem, or an outlying suburb identified with Jerusalem (1:8), but could not retain control there (1:21) until David's conquest of the city (2 Sm 5:6–9). Judah was victorious over the Canaanites in the region of Hebron, already conquered under Joshua (Jos 10:36). Hebron, also known as Kiriath-arba ("city of four" or "tetrapolis"), was a powerful ally of Jerusalem (Jos 10:3) and had been able to rally military support for a new assault on Israel, even after its first defeat. Caleb received Hebron, as Moses had promised (1:20; cf. Jos 15:13). After the victory over Hebron, Judah extended its control over the southern hill country by an attack on Debir (1:11–15; cf. Jos 15:14–19).

The Kenites (1:16), descendants of Jethro and related to Moses by marriage, settled in the Negeb around Arad and the City of Palms, which here probably refers to Tamar rather than Jericho.

Judah secured the southern border by a victory over the Canaanites at Hormah (1:17; cf. Nm 14:45; 21:3; Dt 1:44) and the coastal plain by victories at Gaza, Ashkelon, and Ekron. However, its successes in the coastal plain were resisted by a well-armed Canaanite force (1:18,19). It occupied the Judean hill country and the Negeb, but could not retain control over the plains. The Philistines were soon to take control over Gaza, Ashkelon, and Ekron, and incorporate them into their Pentapolis.

(2) Benjamin (1:21). Jerusalem was situated on the border between Judah and Benjamin. Judah took the city or a suburb (1:8), but was too far removed to retain control over it. Benjamin was too weak to subdue the Jebusites. Only David succeeded in this (2 Sm 5:6–9); he incorporated it into Judah (cf. Jos 15:63), even though it originally was allotted to Benjamin (Jos 18:27).

(3) Joseph: Ephraim and Manasseh (1:22–29). Ephraim took Bethel (vv 22–26), known

from the patriarchal stories as a significant cultic site (Gn 12:8; 13:3,4; 28:19; 31:13; 35:1–15). However, Manasseh was unsuccessful in taking the fortified cities in the Valley of Jezreel (Esdraelon): Beth-shan, Taanach, Dor, Ibleam, and Megiddo (v 27). The cities controlled traffic along the east-west, north-south roads, as well as the important passes through the Carmel range and the ford of the Jordan. Ephraim could not take full possession of the coastal plain, controlled by Gezer (v 29). The success of both Ephraim and Manasseh was limited.

(4) The other four tribes (1:30–36). The other four tribes in Canaan receive brief mention. They too were only partially successful. Zebulun, Asher, Naphtali, and especially Dan did not fully succeed in driving out the Canaanites. At best they later subjected most of them to forced labor (vv 30,33,35).

(5) The failure of Israel (2:1–5). The failure to subdue the land and to wipe out the Canaanites and their culture led to intermarriage and idolatry (cf. Ex 23:33; 34:12–16; Nm 33:55; Dt 7:2,5,16; Jos 23:7,12).

The identity of "the angel of the Lord" is far from certain. It may be a reference to the Lord himself, or to an angelic messenger, or to a prophet (cf. 6:8). He rebuked the people in the prophetic spirit and pronounced God's judgment as taking the form of continual confrontation between Israel and the Canaanites (v 3; cf. Jos 23:13). Their weeping and sacrificing were to no avail (vv 4,5; cf. Mal 2:13). Israel stood condemned within a generation after Joshua's death.

The Theological Introduction (2:6–3:6). The theological introduction begins where Joshua left off (24:28–31). The generation of Joshua was characterized by loyalty, but the loyalty to Yahweh did not last long after the excitement of the conquest and the demonstration of God's presence (2:10). Israel served Canaanite gods (Baal and Astarte) instead. Baal was the storm god, symbolic of rain and fertility, and Astarte was his cohort. The plural (Baals and Ashtaroth, vv 11,13) signifies the many local ways in which the Canaanite gods were worshiped. The religious unity was broken up into a great diversity. Thus Israel angered the Lord (vv 12,14), who sent them enemies and plunderers. Israel was unsuccessful in dealing with them, as Moses and Joshua had forewarned (Dt 28:25,33; Jos 23:13,16). The cycle of apostasy, judgment, cry for mercy, and deliverance is found throughout Judges. The people were rooted in the apostasy of their forefathers, even though the previous generation had been sensitive to God (vv 7,17). Israel did not submit to the leadership of the judges (vv 16–19), except to free itself from the oppressors. In fulfillment of the curses of the covenant God swears not to give his people rest, but to test them (vv 20–23) and to train them for warfare (3:1–4), so that they might learn to respond to the challenges of a real world.

The Judges of Israel (3:7–16:31). (1) Othniel (3:7–11). Othniel is a transitional figure, linking the conquest and the judgment. He had involved himself in the conquest of Kiriath-sepher and was related to Caleb as his cousin and son-in-law (1:13). He repelled the Aramaeans led by Cushan-rishathaim, so that the land enjoyed peace for some 40 years.

(2) Ehud (3:12–30). The Moabites, allied with the Ammonites and Amalekites, came against Israel from the east and oppressed them for 18 years (under the leadership of Eglon, vv 12–14). Ehud led the mission to bring tribute to Eglon at his palace, located probably by Jericho (the City of Palms, v 13). Ehud was uniquely qualified for this mission; being

The Judges of Israel

Judge	Old Testament Passages	New Testament Mention	Years of Rest and Judgeship	Major Enemy
Othniel	Jdg 1:13; 3:7–11	—	40 (Jdg 3:11)	Mesopotamia
Ehud	Jdg 3:12–30	—	80 (Jdg 3:30)	Moabites
Shamgar	Jdg 3:31; 5:6	—	—	Philistines
Deborah/Barak	Jdg 4–5	Heb 11:32 (Barak)	40 (Jdg 5:31)	Canaanites
Gideon	Jdg 6–8	Heb 11:32	40 (Jdg 8:28)	Midianites
Tola	Jdg 10:1–2	—	23 (Jdg 10:2)	—
Jair	Jdg 10:3–5	—	22 (Jdg 10:3)	—
Jephthah	Jdg 10:6–12:7	Heb 11:32	6 (Jdg 12:7)	Ammonites
Ibzan	Jdg 12:8–10	—	7 (Jdg 12:9)	—
Elon	Jdg 12:11–12	—	10 (Jdg 12:11)	—
Abdon	Jdg 12:13–15	—	8 (Jdg 12:14)	—
Samson	Jdg 13–16	Heb 11:32	20 (Jdg 16:31)	Philistines
Eli	1 Sm 1–4; 14:3; 1 Kgs 2:27	—	40 (1 Sm 4:18)	Philistines
Samuel	1 Sm 1:20; 2:18–26; 3–4; 7–13; 15–16; 19; 25:1; 28	Acts 3:24; 13:20; Heb 11:32	20 (1 Sm 7:2)	Philistines

left-handed, he was able to take his double-edged sword in an unsuspecting manner to stab the king (vv 15,21). Ehud's success was the result of careful plotting and the element of surprise. He paid the tribute and left, only to return with a supposed oracle from the gods. The king fell for the deception and was murdered. The details of the murder (vv 21,22) were to create a sense of ridicule. The delay at the Moabite court (vv 24,25) gave the Israelites an opportunity to bring their forces together at the fords of the Jordan. Ehud's success was complete; no Moabite escaped (v 29), and Israel enjoyed peace for 80 years (v 30).

(3) Shamgar (3:31). Shamgar's exploits were against the Philistines in the coastal plains. He had a non-Israelite name, but was probably an Israelite by birth. Like Samson he fought the Philistines with an unconventional weapon (an oxgoad). His name is also mentioned in the song of Deborah (5:6).

(4) Deborah and Barak (4:1–5:31). The narrative now turns to the Canaanite aggressors in the north under the leadership of Jabin, king of Hazor, and Sisera, of Harosheth-ha-goiim (4:1–3). The ruins of Hazor (Jos 11:13) had been rebuilt, and another Jabin (cf. Jos 11:1) ruled over the region. He had regained his military power, as he had as many as 900 chariots of iron. He oppressed Israel for 20 years (4:3).

God had a prophetess in Israel who led his people during this dark time (4:4). She rendered judgments under a palm tree in southern Ephraim near Benjamin (4:5). She called on Barak to muster the armies of Naphtali and Zebulun, the tribes affected by the Canaanite raids, and to engage Sisera in a surprise attack by the Kishon River (4:6,7). Barak's hesitancy led him to request Deborah's presence, which resulted in his forfeiture of the honor of killing Sisera, the commander of the Canaanite forces (4:8–10). The Lord gave success to the surprise attack from Mt Tabor, so that the Canaanites were routed, unable to use their heavy chariots which were mired down in the swamps of the Jezreel Valley (5:20–22). The Canaanites were routed, and Sisera was killed by Jael, the wife of Heber, a Kenite who had separated from the Kenites around Arad (4:17,18; cf. 1:16). She offered him hospitality, as her family had friendly relations with the Canaanites (v 17), but heroically put him to death with a tent peg (4:18–21; 5:26,27). In successive campaigns the Israelites gained freedom from Jabin, until they destroyed his power (4:24).

The song of Deborah (ch 5) celebrates in a poetic way the victory over Jabin. It is one of the oldest poems in the Bible. It praises the God of Israel (vv 2,3) as the King who comes to protect his covenant people, and before whom the mountains move. He is the God of Mt Sinai (vv 4,5; cf. Dt 33:2; Ps 68:7,8; Hb 3:3,4). Though the oppressors had despoiled Israel and had made the roads unsafe for travel, and Israel was unable to defend itself (vv 6–8), the Lord raised up Deborah and Barak to lead the nobles to war (vv 9–13). They came from Ephraim, Benjamin, Zebulun, Issachar, and Naphtali (vv 14,15a,18), but the Transjordan tribes and Asher did not want to get involved (vv 15b–17). The song then moves to the battle scene, where torrential rains bogged the chariots down (vv 19–23). Jael is celebrated as "most blessed of women" who used her simple way of life to bring an end to Sisera (vv 24–27). She stands in contrast to Sisera's mother, who is portrayed with all her culture waiting in vain for Sisera's return with all of his spoils (vv 28–30). The Lord has used the simple to confound the powerful. The conclusion is a prayer for God's judgment on all of Israel's enemies (v 31a; cf. Ps 68:1–3).

(5) Gideon (6:1–8:35). Israel's rest for 40 years (5:31b) was disturbed by the invasion of Midianites and Amalekites from the East (6:1–3). They destroyed the economy by invading the country at harvest time (vv 4–6). In response to Israel's cry, God sent a prophet with a message similar to that of the angel of the Lord (2:1–5). Then an angel appeared to Gideon and called him to lead the people in battle (6:11–14). The Lord assured him of his presence (6:16) by a sign (vv 17–22). Gideon knew that he had been visited by the Lord and built an altar called "The Lord is Peace" in Ophrah (6:24). He responded by destroying the cultic site dedicated to Baal and Asherah at Ophrah (6:25–28) and by initiating worship at the new altar (v 28). Baal did not protect his own altar (6:29–32), even when challenged by Gideon's father (v 31). Consequently, Gideon was known as Jerubbaal ("Let Baal contend with him," v 32).

Next, Gideon mustered an army of 32,000 men from Asher, Zebulun, and Naphtali (v 35; cf. 7:3b). In order to assure himself of the Lord's presence, he asked for another sign: the sign of the fleece (6:36–40). It must be kept in mind that Gideon lived in an era in which the wonders of God had been scarce (v 13) and that he, like Moses, needed reassurance that God was with him. God responded to his growing faith. Gideon went forth with a greatly reduced army of 300 against the enemy. Of his original army 22,000 had left because they were afraid (7:2,3; cf. Dt 20:8). Another 9700 were sent home, though they were valiant men (7:4–8). God used the 300 in a marvelous way to confound the Midianites, after assuring Gideon by a dream of an enemy soldier (7:9–

15). God gave Israel victory over the Midianite leaders Oreb, Zeeb, Zebah, and Zalmunna (7:16–8:21). Gideon wisely avoided a possible military confrontation with Ephraim (8:1–3), pursued the enemy deep into the Transjordan, and punished the leaders of Succoth and Penuel who did not assist him (8:4–9,13–16).

This glorious victory created a new wave of interest in the idea of kingship. The men of Israel wished to establish the family of Gideon as their royal dynasty (8:22). Gideon refused, and instead wrongly set up a ephod, cast from the gold taken in battle (8:23–27). The ephod was probably used for cultic practices, possibly divination (cf. 17:5).

Gideon's era also came to an end. He was God's instrument, giving Israel rest for 40 years (v 28). He fathered 70 sons and died in old age (vv 30–32). God had richly blessed him, even though he had led Israel astray with his ephod. Thereafter Israel returned to Baal worship (vv 33–35).

In the wake of Gideon's era his son Abimelech attempted to establish dynastic continuity by having himself installed as king at Shechem (9:1–6). With the support of his relatives at Shechem, Abimelech had all his brothers killed except Jotham (9:4,5). After Abimelech's coronation (v 6), Jotham set forth his opposition to his brother in a proverbial manner (vv 7–20), and went into hiding (v 21). Three years later Abimelech's evil schemes entrapped him when the citizens of Shechem rebelled. He furiously attacked the city and destroyed it (vv 22–49). A short time later, however, he was wounded at Thebez by a millstone dropped by a woman from the tower in which she had sought refuge from him (vv 50–53). His servant put him out of his misery as per his request (vv 54,55). This episode demonstrates how bad a despotic king may be. Again, God's justice prevailed (vv 56,57).

(6) Tola (10:1–2). Tola was a minor judge from Issachar who judged Israel for 23 years.

(7) Jair (10:3–5). Jair was a minor judge from Gilead who judged Israel for 22 years.

(8) Jephthah (10:6–12:7). A recapitulation (10:6–16) of the cycle (idolatry, enemies, cry for help, momentary repentance) sets the introduction to the Jephthah narrative. Under attack from the Ammonites, the elders of Gilead requested help from Jephthah (10:17–11:8), who promised to help them on the condition that he remain their leader even after the war (11:9,10). At a solemn ceremony he becomes their "head" at Mizpah (v 11). Jephthah opened up correspondence with the Ammonite king, in which he argued for Israel's rights on the basis of the Israelites' historic claim to the land as granted to them by the Lord (vv 12–27). Instead of going out immediately to war, he hoped that "the Lord, the Judge" would settle the dispute (v 27); but the Ammonite king was unimpressed (v 28). When the Spirit of God came over him, Jephthah led Israel into battle, but only after making a rash vow (vv 29–31). He was victorious (vv 32,33), but found out that his vow to sacrifice whatever came first out of his house required him to sacrifice his daughter as a burnt offering (vv 29–35). After she wept with her female companions for two months, Jephthah offered her up (vv 36–40). Regrettably, he had not considered that he could have substituted a payment

Shechem, where Abimelech (Gideon's son) had himself crowned king.

of 10 to 30 shekels of silver, depending on the age of the daughter (cf. Lv 27:4,5).

The Ephraimites seemed to have had an insatiable desire for war. Earlier they had complained to Gideon, who successfully defused their threats (8:1–3). Jephthah fought them, however, because the Israelites living in Transjordan had been reviled as "renegades" (12:1–4). Forty-two thousand Ephraimites were killed by the fords of the Jordan in this civil war (vv 5,6). Thereafter, Jephthah ruled for only six years (v 7).

(9) **Ibzan** (12:8–10). Ibzan was a minor judge from Judah who ruled Israel for seven years.

(10) **Elon** (12:11). A minor judge from Zebulun, Elon ruled Israel for 10 years.

(11) **Abdon** (12:13–15). Abdon was a minor judge from Pirathon, the location of which is uncertain. He ruled for eight years.

(12) **Samson** (13:1–16:31). Samson's greatness in the history of redemption is due to his miraculous birth (13:1–24), his service as a Nazirite (13:7; cf. Nm 6:1–21), the repeated overpowering by the Spirit of the Lord (13:25; 14:6,19; 15:14), the single-handed exploits against the Philistines (Ashkelon, 14:19; the fields, 15:1–6; Ramath Etam, 15:7–17; Gaza, 16:1–3,23–30), and his occasional dependence on the Lord (15:18,19; 16:28–30). However, his personal life was a tragedy because of his weakness for Philistine women (chs 14,16). Having been seduced by Delilah, he was imprisoned at Gaza. He died in the collapse of Dagon's temple, praying that the Lord would permit him to revenge himself (16:28–30). He was buried in his father's tomb in the territory of Dan (v 31).

Epilogue (17–21). The cyclical nature of Israel's existence was without movement. Rest from enemies was always temporary. Israel was not yet ready for dynastic kingship, and whatever one may say of the three years of Abimelech, it was a kingship of the worst sort. Israel vacillated between idolatry and Yahwism. The period of the judges was unstable, marked by petty individualism and provincialism. Yet God remained sovereign in the affairs of his people. The epilogue contains two stories: the story of Micah and the Danite migration (chs 17,18) and the civil war (chs 19–21). The epilogue is bound together by the phrase "In those days Israel had no king; everyone did as he saw fit" (17:6; 18:1; 19:1; 21:25 NIV). The symmetric recurrence (two times in each narrative) emphasizes the anarchy and inability of the tribes to unite together to serve God as a covenant people.

(1) **Micah and the Danites** (17,18). Micah was an Ephraimite who established a shrine and made a Levite from Bethlehem and his own sons to serve as its priests (ch 17). Unable to keep their patrimony, the Danites left to establish themselves at the foot of Mt Hermon. They took the idols and the Levite from Micah's shrine and set up a cultic city at the newly established city of Dan, built on the ruins of Laish (ch 18). Thus, they set up a cultic center that rivaled the tabernacle at Shiloh (18:31).

(2) **The Civil War** (19–21). The people of Gibeah, which belonged to Benjamin, sexually abused the concubine of a Levite so that she died. Like the Levite of chapters 17 and 18, she was from Bethlehem (19:1). Dramatically, the Levite sent pieces of her corpse to all the tribes, which assembled against the Benjaminites because they protected the criminals of Gibeah (19:29–20:19). In the ensuing battle the population of Benjamin was decimated (20:20–48). The 11 tribes gave them 400 virgins taken in a civil war against Jabesh-gilead (21:6–15). These were not enough, however; and because of the threat of the extinction of Benjamin and the vow not to give their daughters in marriage to any Benjaminite, the Israelites devised a plan by which the Benjaminites could take Israelite virgins dancing in the festival at Shiloh (vv 16–22). Benjamin thus was able to rebuild its towns and settlements (v 23).

R.K. HARRISON

See ISRAEL, HISTORY OF; CONQUEST AND ALLOTMENT OF THE LAND; GIDEON; JEPHTAH, JEPHTAE; SAMSON.

Bibliography. R.G. Boling, *Judges*; B.S. Childs, *Introduction to the OT as Scripture*; A.E. Cundall, *Judges*; J.A. Soggin, *Judges: A Commentary*.

Judgment.

Concept in Scripture closely related to the concept of God's justice. In all his relationships God acts justly and morally. Human beings, created by God, are morally structured so that they may positively respond to God's righteous demands in their lives. Divine judgment, involving God's approval or disapproval upon each human act, is a natural consequence of the Creator-creature relationship between God and humanity. Thus judgment, simply defined, is the divine response to human activity. God the Creator must also be God the Judge. Since God is just, he responds with either punishments or rewards to what each person does. One's moral accountability to God, a quality not shared by the rest of creation, is an essential ingredient of being created in God's image. Creation in the divine image meant that God and man could communicate with each other in such a way that all people were able to understand God's moral requirements and willingly respond to them. Among the various positive commands given to men in his original creation—including marriage, the subduing of the earth, and enjoyment of the garden of Eden—was the negative command prohibiting the eating of the fruit from one tree. Defiance of this prohibition carried the threat of death as punishment (Gn 2:16,17). Genesis 3 contains the account of God's first judgment, the one against Adam. He was punished by death since he had not lived within the moral regulations set by God (vv 17–19). In a purely technical sense judgment includes God's approval upon acts which please him; but more frequently judgment is understood negatively in the sense that God punishes those who violate his commands. Since the fall all human activity stands under God's negative judgment (Rom 2:12).

Judgment in This Life. The Christian idea of the atonement, that Christ died for sin in the place of man, depends on the thought that God holds man accountable for his sin. In the atonement Christ, who is sent by God, willingly places himself under God's judgment, and in man's place receives the divine punishment (Gal 3:13). Christ's death for sin may therefore be considered the extreme manifestation of divine judgment. God as judge visits upon the soul of Christ in his crucifixion the total divine judgment against sin.

Through faith, created by the Holy Spirit in the Word, a believer becomes one with Christ and thus escapes divine judgment and is rescued from punishment (Rom 3:22). Those who by faith share in the benefits of Christ's death stand before the divine Judge and receive a verdict of acquittal, and instead of punishment and divine retribution receive a sentence of eternal life. Jesus says of those who believe in him that they have already passed through judgment, have escaped death, and are already sharing in eternal life (Jn 5:24).

Though sins have been atoned for by Christ, each person, believer and unbeliever alike, still suffers certain consequences of his sin here in this life. For every human action there is a divine reaction (Rom 2:6). Paul speaks about the conscience, which carries out a series of judgments even upon the actions of those who do not know the true God (Rom 2:15).

Governments are also manifestations of divine judgment in a more formal sense upon man's public performances of the law. Civil justice, though often corrupted, is a means through which God carries out temporal judgment upon infringement of the law in this life (Rom 13:1,2). Public crimes against society are not the only sins subject to divine judgment.

In addition to the accusations of the conscience against even the most private of sins, each human action carries with it potential reward or punishment. Living within the moral bounds established by God, especially as they are revealed in the Ten Commandments and further explicated in the rest of Scripture, results in certain physical benefits in this life. Living in disregard of the moral law results in penalties and hardships appropriate to the infraction (Gal 6:7,8). For example, refusal to work can result in poverty, and overindulgence can result in poor health. Some activities bring their own penalties. Christians should not conclude that the presence of calamities in a person's life must indicate a specific judgment of God against a particular sin. God can use calamities in the life of a Christian to guide him providentially to the goal of eternal life (1 Pt 4:12,13).

On account of man's sin the creation was subject to a judgment of corruption (Gn 3:17). All of human life participates in a deterioration which is a manifestation of divine judgment against the sin which originated with Adam. God remains sovereign even over the universal corruption and is able to direct and control it for his ultimate purposes (Rom 8:20). Thus he can use calamities for the benefit of the Christian's life (Rom 8:28), but he can also use them to manifest his special wrath on those who persist in deliberate sin and who reject his Son Jesus Christ as the Redeemer from sin.

Judgment in its final and ultimate sense is best understood as the appearance of Jesus Christ on the last day. At that time believers will be sealed in eternal life and unbelievers will be confirmed in their damnation. This final judgment can in certain cases be carried out on certain persons in their lifetime. The cause of the horrible and unchangeable judgment in this life is the persistent rejection of God's offer of salvation. This is the sin against the Holy Spirit (Mt 12:32). Those who may already have fallen under its condemnation are those who have heard God's special message to them and are convinced of its truth, but who nevertheless persist in rejecting this salvation. Pharoah, who recognized Moses as God's prophet and still rejected him and his message, is considered a prime example of a person who has received God's final and ultimate judgment in this life (Ex 10:20). The Jews who saw the miracles of Jesus and rejected his claims to be the Messiah are also considered among those who received God's final judgment while living (Mt 12:22–32).

Through wars and the creation and destruction of nations God carries out judgment collectively against entire peoples. The OT records the rise and fall of nations and of kings. The refusal to acknowledge and worship the true God and to follow his laws eventually and most certainly results in national extinction. The destruction of Nineveh and Israel in the OT and Jerusalem in the NT are clear examples of God's wrath against entire peoples who reject his message of salvation. Public disregard of the moral law must result in national disintegration, which is then frequently compounded by invasion by a foreign nation. The destruction of Sodom and Gomorrah was the direct result of immoral license (Jude 7). Christians who lose their lives in such national catastrophes should not be regarded as having received a divine personal judgment upon their lives.

Last Judgment. The Scriptures speak of a judgment at death and still another one on the last day. At death each person receives God's verdict upon his life (Lk 16:22,23). The Christian does not fear this moment, because he has already been acquitted in Christ Jesus, and at death he is with his Savior in Paradise (Lk 23:43). The unbeliever rightfully fears death. As he has rejected God in this life, so God rejects him in his death forever.

In addition to this individual judgment at death, all nations will appear before Jesus (Mt 25:31,32). The fate of all those who appear before the Judge has already been sealed. The Scriptures teach that the judgment of that last day will be made on the basis of works (Mt 25:31–46). This should not be seen as a denial and contradiction of the evangelical principle that one is saved by faith alone. People enter into a saving relationship with Jesus Christ through faith alone, without works. Faith is known only to God and of itself is not visible to others. The evidence for the presence of faith is works. On the last day Jesus will point to those works as evidence of the presence of faith in Christians.

God's judgments upon people in this life can be of benefit because through these judgments he is calling them to repentance. The judgment of the last day will be final; no one will be permitted to repent or change his mind about God. On that day all will recognize the truthfulness of God's claims in Christ Jesus; but only those who have believed in him and carried out his will in their lives will receive the invitation to enter eternal life (Mt 25:34). As important as God's judgments in this life are, they receive their real importance from God's final day of judgment. Christians must firmly reject any belief that holds that God is now carrying out the final judgment in our lives and that thus there will never really be a final day.

Practical Implications. Christians live a positive and confident life knowing that Jesus has entered under the divine judgment for them and thus they are free from any further divine retribution. At the same time they are aware of God's judgment against all sins, including those of Christians, and that apart from Christ, they would suffer the worst possible divine punishment. They see the evil and calamities of this life as God's continued displeasure with sin. When they come, Christians use them as opportunities for searching their own souls and for repentance. Though they are not aware of the exact date of the last day, they prepare themselves each day for the final judgment.

Conclusion. The concept of judgment covers the entire history of the human race—from the fall to the last day. God as a just God who sees a decisive difference between good and evil has no choice but to carry out judgment upon all people in their daily lives and especially at life's conclusion. God in his grace has sent his Son to suffer the judgment we deserved, and in his mercy delays the final day of judgment so that we can come to repentance by faith in Jesus Christ (2 Pt 3:9). The great concepts of creation, justice, law, salvation, and atonement reach their final climax in the divine judgment of the last day.

DAVID P. SCAER

See JUDGMENT SEAT; SECOND COMING OF CHRIST; JUSTIFICATION; HELL; LAST JUDGMENT; WRATH OF GOD.

Bibliography. J.A. Baird, *The Justice of God in the Teaching of Jesus;* K. Barth, *Church Dogmatics II,* 733–81; D. Bonhoeffer, *Ethics;* R. Bultmann, *Theology of the NT;* L. Morris, *The Biblical Doctrine of Judgment.*

Judgment Seat.

Place before which people will one day stand to give an account of their lives to God.

Old Testament. The NT concept of divine judgment has its roots in the OT. There God is seen as Judge of the whole world, and especially of his own people.

During his intercession for Sodom, Abraham spoke of God as the Judge of all the earth (Gn 18:25). Moses' position as judge over the Israelites was based on the belief that God gave judgments through Moses. A similar relationship existed between God and the judges who led Israel after the conquest of the Promised Land. That understanding of God became explicit in Jephthah's message to the king of Ammon: "The Lord, the Judge, decide this day between the people of Israel and the people of Ammon" (Jgs 11:27). When God called Samuel, he told Samuel he (God) would judge Eli's house.

The concept of God as the Judge of his people is prevalent in the psalms and prophets. In Psalm 9:4 David said of God, "For thou hast maintained my just cause; thou hast sat on the throne giving righteous judgment." He added, "But the Lord sits enthroned for ever;

he has established his throne for judgment; and he judges the world with righteousness, he judges the people with equity" (vv 7,8). Isaiah described a future day when God "shall judge between the nations, and shall decide for many people" (Is 2:4). Joel spoke of God as the judge of the nations: "Let the nations bestir themselves, and come up to the valley of Jehoshaphat; for there I will sit to judge all the nations round about" (Jl 3:12).

New Testament. Statements like those above formed part of the background for the NT understanding of the judgment seat of God or Christ. The image of a judgment seat came from the fact that in the Roman world judgment took place on a platform or tribunal from which a judge would hear and decide cases. Thus most of the NT references to a judgment seat occur when Jesus, or the apostle Paul, was brought before a ruling authority. For example, Pilate sat on his judgment seat when he tried Jesus (Mt 27:19; cf. Jn 19:13; Acts 18:12,16,17; 25:6,10,17).

The two passages in the NT that speak directly of the judgment seat of God or Christ are Romans 14:10 and 2 Corinthians 5:10. In Romans 14:10 Paul addressed the urgent problem of unity within the church, unity based on a loving acceptance of those with different understandings of the effects of faith in a Christian's daily life. Paul urged the Christians, both Jews and Gentiles, to accept one another in spite of differences concerning eating certain foods and observing certain days. All, he reminded them, must eventually stand before the judgment seat of God to give an account of the way they had lived. Further, since God is the proper Judge, Christians should not judge one another.

Again, in 2 Corinthians 5 Paul told the Corinthian Christians why Christians strive to please the Lord: all must appear before the judgment seat of Christ to be recompensed for their deeds.

The judgment seat of Christ or God, therefore, expresses the ultimate accountability of the Christian. This brings to the Christian a very special sense of stewardship before God for the way he or she lives. This is the specific expression for the Christian of the general concept throughout the Bible that God is the Judge and that must ultimately stand before God in the final judgment.

HOBERT K. FARRELL

See JUDGMENT; SECOND COMING OF CHRIST; LAST JUDGMENT; BEMA.

Judith. Daughter of Beeri the Hittite and one of Esau's wives (Gn 26:34). In Genesis 36:2 she is alternately called Oholibamah.

See OHOLIBAMAH.

Julia. Woman greeted by the apostle Paul (Rom 16:15). Her name is coupled with Philologus, who may have been her brother or husband.

Julius. Roman centurion of the Augustan cohort who escorted the apostle Paul and other prisoners from Palestine to Rome (Acts 27:1). Jewish leaders in Jerusalem accused Paul of teaching false doctrine and defiling the temple. Because indecision by two successive Roman governors kept Paul in prison for more than two years, he finally appealed to Caesar.

Julius was a kind man. He allowed Paul to leave the ship in Sidon to be comforted by his friends (Acts 27:3). However, in his eagerness to get his prisoners to Rome, Julius ignored Paul's advice to spend the winter in Fair Havens. Instead, he ordered the ship to sail to Phoenix, another harbor in Crete, which was more suitable to winter in (Acts 27:9–12). During the trip a storm wrecked the ship. The soldiers on board wanted to kill the prisoners for fear of their escaping, but Julius prevented that massacre, ordering all to jump ship and swim to shore. This decision spared Paul's life (Acts 27:42–44). Some scholars have conjectured that Julius was the soldier who stayed with Paul in Rome (Acts 28:16).

Junias, Junia. Jew who, along with Andronicus, was greeted by Paul in his letter to the church in Rome (16:7, KJV Junia). He had some status among the apostles and may have held an office under their direction. He was also a prisoner with Paul at one time for the cause of the gospel.

Juniper. KJV mistranslation for broom, a desert shrub, in 1 Kings 19:4,5; Job 30:4; and Psalm 120:4.

See PLANTS.

Ruins of the bema in the Corinthian agora, where Paul appeared before Gallio (Acts 18).

Remains of a temple of Jupiter (Zeus) in Athens.

Jupiter. Supreme Roman deity, equivalent to Zeus in Greek mythology. He was Saturn's son and Juno's husband and brother. Jupiter (also called Jove) was the god of destiny. His weapon was the thunderbolt; the eagle and the oak and olive trees were considered sacred in his worship. A temple of Jupiter stood in Rome on the Capitoline Hill. During Hadrian's reign (AD 117–138), a temple of Jupiter Capitolinus was erected on the foundation of the Jewish temple ruins in Jerusalem.

As a result of Barnabas and Paul's ministry in Lystra during their first missionary journey, the people of Lystra thought they were Zeus and Hermes (Jupiter and Mercury) come down to visit them (Acts 14:12,13).

Jushab-hesed. One of Zerubbabel's seven sons (1 Chr 3:20). Jushab-hesed means "lovingkindness is returned."

Just. See RIGHTEOUSNESS.

Justification. The act of God in bringing sinners into a new covenant relationship with himself through the forgiveness of sins. Along with such terms as "regeneration" and "reconciliation," it relates to a basic aspect of conversion. It is a declarative act of God by which he establishes persons as righteous; that is, in right and true relationship to himself.

Since the time of the Reformation, when Martin Luther reestablished the doctrine of justification by faith alone as the cornerstone for theological understanding, this term has had special significance in the history of theology. To Luther it represented a rediscovery of Paul and a fundamental counterthrust to medieval Catholicism with its theology of works and indulgences. The doctrine of justification by faith alone affirms the thoroughgoing sinfulness of all persons, their total inability to deal effectively with their own sin, and the gracious provision through the death of Jesus Christ of a complete atonement for sin, to which persons respond in simple trust without any special claims or merit of their own.

The noun "justification" and the verb "to justify" are not used often in Scripture. In the KJV, for example, the verb is found only in the OT, and there fewer than 25 times. In the NT both terms are used only 40 times. The more frequent and more important terms which translate the same Hebrew and Greek words are "righteousness" and "to declare (or make) righteous." Any understanding of justification, therefore, directly involves a biblical understanding of righteousness.

In common Greek, justification and justify are frequently forensic terms; that is, they relate to the law court and the act of acquitting or vindicating someone. It has to do with the innocence or virtue of a person. But more broadly it has to do with the norm of any relationship.

Old Testament. Job knows that he will be vindicated (Jb 13:18). Similarly 1 Kings 8:32 speaks of "vindicating the righteous by rewarding him according to his righteousness" (cf. Lk 10:29.). But the most frequent and most important use has to do with the activity of God.

In the OT righteousness has to do with relationship and the obligations of that relationship. At times one is referred to as righteous because he or she stands in right relationship to another. At other times one is righteous because he or she fulfills certain obligations in a relationship (Gn 38:26). But more important, these terms are used with reference to God, who is viewed as just. He governs with justice (Gn 18:25), and his judgments are true and righteous (Ps 19:9). Both the innocent and the guilty know well the justice of God: the former know they will be vindicated and the latter know his law prevails.

Justification and righteousness have technical significance because of their close association with the saving activity of God on behalf of his covenant people. On various occasions in modern versions these terms are translated "deliverance," "righteous acts," or "triumphs." Thus in Judges 5:11: "To the sound of musicians at the watering places, there they repeat the *triumphs* [righteous acts or saving deeds] of the Lord." Or in Isaiah 46:13: "I bring near my *deliverance*, it is not far off, and my salvation will not tarry." These and other passages show that the righteousness of God is bound up not so much with justice as with his intervention in behalf of his people under the covenant. The righteousness of God or the act of justification is, therefore, to be viewed not primarily in terms of Law but in terms of covenant. The most important expression of this is the example of Abraham, who was reckoned righteous; that is, brought into personal relationship by virtue of his response of faith to the covenant offered by God (Gn 15:6). Abraham could not justify himself, but on the basis of the covenant God established him as righteous. All persons share the helplessness of Abraham. In the sight of God no one shall stand justified (Ps 143:2). "If thou, O Lord, shouldst mark iniquities, Lord, who could stand?" (Ps 130:3). The hope of humanity is that God will remember his covenant. Righteousness is hence a product of the mercy or grace of God, who deals with his people according to his lovingkindness (Is 63:7). Justification is thus derived from the nature of God; it is primarily a religious term, and only secondly ethical.

New Testament. Almost all discussion of justification in the NT is found in the letters of Paul, primarily in those to the Romans and Galatians. In these two letters it is one of the fundamental terms by which Paul seeks to set forth the consequences of the work of Christ for sinful humanity. Justification by faith is set primarily against the background of Jewish legalism and its attempts to make the Law the basis of salvation. Paul regards this as an alien message requiring the strongest condemnation (Gal 1:6–9). The word and work of Christ, embedded in the message that Paul proclaimed, was a reminder that righteousness or justification is the gift of God through the blood (*covenant* blood, Heb 13:20) of Jesus Christ. All this is entirely apart from the Law (Rom 3:21). The Law, in fact, is not capable of leading one to righteousness, nor was it given to bring about righteousness.

Galatians 3:15–25 is especially instructive in understanding the function of the Law, which came 430 years after the covenant by which Abraham was brought into a living, personal relationship with the holy God. Whatever purpose the Law had, it was not given as a means of righteousness. "For if a law had been given which could make alive, then righteousness would indeed be by the law" (Gal 3:21). The atoning work of Christ for the justification of people is to be seen in terms of covenant rather than Law. This is the essential argument of Paul in this section of Galatians; namely, that justification has from the time of Abraham been through faith in the God who keeps covenant and never by the Law. Righteousness is therefore a relational term and is affirmed by one who by faith has been brought into right relationship with God. The Law brings judgment; it confronts one with his incapacity to cope with sin (Acts 13:39; Rom 8:3). Justification then, has its forensic (judicial) dimensions in that it copes with, and represents salvation to, the problem of sin and guilt. The believer is set free from condemnation (Rom 8:1). Yet the fundamental understanding of justification is to be gained in moving away from the Law and judgment to the covenant and grace. The appeal to Abraham in both Romans and Galatians is to show that the covenant has always been the only hope of humanity. God is not man (Hos 11:9), and so he comes in mercy; he keeps covenant, though his covenant people violate it daily.

In Paul's formulation of the gospel God is both just and the one who justifies. Sin demands judgment and must be dealt with. God's pattern of bringing people into personal relationship now stands manifest apart from the Law (Rom 3:21–26) in the ministry and death of Christ, whom God put forth as the atoning agent (v 25). Sin is dealt with directly in the death of the sinless one who became sin for us that we might in him become the righteousness of God (2 Cor 5:21). In his substitutionary death he bears the guilt of all humanity so that by responding in trust mankind might know God in true relationship.

For Paul, then, justification in view of human sinfulness is rooted in the nature of God who alone is able to take initiative in the healing and redeeming of humanity. Justification is by grace alone. Rooted in the nature of God it is also made available through the work of Christ as God's gift. Thus we have the often repeated confession that Christ died "for us" (Rom 5:8; 1 Thes 5:10), or "for our sins" (1 Cor 15:3). The means of appropriation is by faith and faith alone (Rom 3:22; 5:1). This faith is a simple trust in the sufficiency of the work of Christ, a trust by which one freely and wholeheartedly identifies with Christ, loves and embraces his Word, and gives himself to the value system expressed in the kingdom of God. The basic self-consciousness of the justified person is that his right relationship with the living God has nothing to do with merit or achievement. It is from beginning to end a gift of infinite love. His own powerlessness is resolved in the power of the gospel in which God's saving work is revealed (Rom 1:12,17).

The Letter of James is often seen to be in conflict with Paul's teaching on justification by faith apart from works of the Law. In fact, James quotes the same text (Gn 15:6) concerning Abraham and concludes, "You see that a man is justified by works and not by faith alone" (Jas 2:24). Luther even repudiated this letter because it seemed at variance with Paul. But two factors should be observed: (1) Paul and James are faced with two completely opposite crises. Paul is compelled to oppose a legalism which made the Law the basis for righteousness and enabled one to stand justified before God. The legalists were trying to maintain the law of Moses (in particular the obligation of circumcision) for those who would be justified. For these the Law was front and center. James, on the other hand, seeks to cope with an antinomianism which shows no concern for the Law of God and says that faith is enough. For these persons the Law is of no consequence. Paul's opponents would put the Law at the heart of justification, so Paul's response is expressed largely in negative terms: "No one will be justified by works of the law" (Rom 3:20). The opponents of James remove the Law altogether and negate the significance or meaning of works in the name of faith. As a result James speaks positively of the Law in relation to faith.

(2) When Paul and James speak of "works," they speak of different concepts. Paul is speaking of works of the Law; that is, works as an expression of the Law, or what might be called "law-works" (Rom 3:20). James, on the

other hand, never speaks of works of the Law but rather of works that give expression to faith, or what might be called "faith-works." James regards faith without works as dead; that is, as no faith at all (Jas 2:17). For him faith is expressed and perfected by works. Paul and James both affirm that one comes into, and continues in, living relationship to God through faith—apart from the Law but not without the love and obedience that is born of faith.

In the Gospels justification appears in the parable of the Pharisee and the tax collector who went into the temple to pray. The former drew attention to his pious works and moral superiority. The latter, humbled by a deep sense of sin and unworthiness, could only cry for mercy. This man, according to Jesus, went down to his house justified (Lk 18:14). Though this is the only instance of the terminology of justification by faith, the entire ministry of Jesus was among people preoccupied with their own piety and the task of justifying themselves before God, people who set themselves over against sinners and undesirables, people who were so involved in their own works that they were offended by the language of grace and the full pardon of sinners (Lk 7:36–50). Jesus was involved in the same issue which later plagued Paul. Only the humble before God will be exalted (Mt 18:4; 23:12). Only the sinner hears the word of grace (Lk 5:32; 15:7,10; 19:7). The unworthy find healing (Mt 8:8).

Justification (or righteousness) by faith is always to be reaffirmed, for within each person there is the almost inevitable and natural desire to establish personal righteousness, to be able to stand before God on the basis of personal character and piety. But the revival and well-being of the church (note that both Luther and Wesley turned from works to faith upon their study of Romans) is rooted in the understanding that the just live by faith (Rom 1:17; Heb 10:38; 11:7).

ROBERT W. LYON

See FAITH; SANCTIFICATION; LAW, BIBLICAL CONCEPT OF; ADOPTION.

Bibliography. G.C. Berkouwer, *Faith and Justification*; John Calvin, *Institutes*, vol. 3; H. Küng, *Justification*; L. Morris, *The Apostolic Preaching of the Cross*; G.B. Stevens, *The Christian Doctrine of Salvation*.

Justus. 1. Surname for Joseph Barsabbas (Acts 1:23).

See JOSEPH #12.

2. Godly Corinthian man (presumably a convert of Paul), who opened his home to Paul and the Christians after the Jewish synagogue was closed to Paul's preaching (Acts

18:7). There is disagreement among the manuscripts as to the exact form of his name. Various readings are Justus or Titius Justus. He has also been identified as the Gaius of Romans 16:23.

3. Surname of Jesus, a Jewish Christian (Col 4:11).

See JESUS #4.

Juttah. One of the cities of refuge assigned to Aaron's descendants (Jos 21:16). It was in the hill country of Judah's territory and in the district of Maon (Jos 15:55). It has been identified with modern Yatta, about 5½ miles southwest of Hebron.

See CITIES OF REFUGE.

Kk

Kab. Dry measure equaling about a quart, mentioned only in 2 Kings 6:25.

See Weights and Measures.

Kabzeel. City located in the extreme south of Judah's territory adjacent to neighboring Edom (Jos 15:21; also called Jekabzeel in Neh 11:25). Benaiah, one of David's valiant warriors, came from there (2 Sm 23:20; 1 Chr 11:22). The reference in Nehemiah indicates that Judah's tribe returned to this area after the exile. Its exact site is not known, but Khirbet Horah has been suggested.

Kadesh, Kadesh-barnea. Home of the wandering Israelites for nearly 38 years. In the vast area of the Sinai there are two main oases: in the south is Wadi Feran, near the Mountain of Moses (Mt Sinai or Horeb); in the north is Kadesh, or Kadesh-barnea. The former was the place where the Law was given; the latter, the main campsite of the 12 tribes during their exodus from Egypt (Dt 1:46).

In the vicinity of Kadesh-barnea there are

Kadesh-barnea.

four springs: 'Ain Qedeis, 'Ain el-Qudeirat, el-Qoseimeh, and el-Muweilah. 'Ain Qedeis ('Ain Kadesh) is called "Holy Spring"; it was discovered in 1842 by John Rowlands with the help of the local Bedouin tribes; the location was confirmed some years later by the Henry Clay Trumbull expedition. Earlier (1838) Edward Robinson had suggested that 'Ain el-Waibeh was the site of Kadesh-barnea, but this was located in the northern portion of the Arabah, off the route taken by the Israelites, who, when going from Mt Sinai to Kadesh-barnea, passed through the "great and terrible wilderness" (Dt 1:19) rather than along the Arabah.

In addition to being the largest oasis in the northern Sinai, Kadesh-barnea is located near an important crossroad, the road connecting the Gulf of Aqaba with the Mediterranean.

Kadesh-barnea was raided by Chedorlaomer, king of Elam (Gn 14:7, Enmishpat) during the time of Abraham. In this area Hagar was driven from the tent of Sarah, her mistress (Gn 16:14), and here Miriam died and was buried (Nm 20:1). The great contention over water took place here, giving rise to the name Meribah or Meribath-kadesh (Nm 20:2–24; Dt 32:51; Ez 47:19; 48:28, KJV Meribah-kadesh). This was also the scene of Korah's rebellion against the leadership of Moses and Aaron (Nm 16,17). This area would long remain in the memory of the Israelite tribes as the place of their unbelief following the report of the 10 spies and a delay of 38 years before their occupancy of the Promised Land (Ps 95:8–11; cf. Heb 3:7–19).

Recent exploration indicates that the area was occupied by herdsmen during the Middle Bronze Age, corresponding to the time of the patriarchs. Nelson Glueck found evidence indicating that some permanent agricultural settlements were possible. Glueck concluded that "this entire area fanning out east of Kadesh Barnea . . . was an exceedingly important one in the Middle Bronze I–Iron II, and must have been familiar to the Israelites of the Exodus during their periods of encampment at Kadesh Barnea."

Because of the water, pasture, and agricultural lands, plus its proximity to Canaan, the Israelites found this area the best spot in which to spend most of their time prior to entering the Promised Land.

See MERIBAH; WILDERNESS WANDERINGS.

Kadmiel. Head of a Levite family which returned from the exile with Zerubbabel (Ezr 2:40; Neh 7:43; 12:8). Some scholars regard Kadmiel as the ancestor of a family of returnees, but the appearance of his name in the list of those who supervised the temple rebuilding project (Ezr 3:9), participated in sealing the covenant (Neh 10:9), and were prominent in the praise service (Neh 9:4,5; 12:24) leaves little room for doubt that he himself was part of the return.

Kadmonites. Semitic tribe whose land was promised to Abraham's descendants (Gn 15:19). The name of the tribe is the same as the Hebrew adjective "eastern" and suggests that references to people or lands of the east (Gn 25:6; Jgs 8:10; 1 Kgs 4:30; Jb 1:3) may be synonymous with the tribal name.

Kain (Place). Town in the Judean hill country (Jos 15:57, KJV Cain). Its place in the same district as the known cities of Maon, Carmel, Ziph, and Juttah (v 55) favors its identification with Khirbet Yuqim, southwest of Hebron.

Kain (Tribe). Clan name synonymous with the Kenites (Nm 24:22; Jgs 4:11). The name is Hebrew for "spear," suggesting a tribe of metal workers. The nomadic tribe was friendly (1 Sm 15:6) and was eventually absorbed by Judah.

See KENITES.

Kaiwan. Mesopotamian astral deity, called Chiun in the KJV (Am 5:26).

See SAKKUTH.

Kallai. Priest and the head of Sallai's priestly family during the days of Joiakim the high priest (Neh 12:20).

Kamon. City in Gilead where Jair the judge was buried (Jgs 10:5, KJV Camon). While the place has not been identified with certainty, modern Qumran, a small village southeast of the Sea of Galilee, probably reflects the original name, if not the exact location.

Kanah. 1. Brook forming Ephraim's northern border and the southern border of Manasseh's tribe (Jos 16:8; 17:9). It flowed westward, joining the Yarkon about five miles from the Mediterranean just north of the modern city of Tel Aviv (biblical Joppa). It is dry most of the year. Kanah is today called Wadi Qana.

2. City situated along Asher's border (Jos 19:28). It lay about six miles southeast of Tyre on one of the major northeast-southwest routes through northern Galilee. The name may be found on a relief showing the cities Pharaoh Rameses captured in the campaign of his eighth year (c. 1290 BC). Qana (in modern Lebanon) still bears the name and marks the site.

Kanatha. One of the original 10 Greek cities rebuilt by Rome after Pompey's conquest of Palestine and Syria around 63 BC. The region of these cities became known as the Decapolis. Kanatha (also spelled Canatha), positioned about 60 miles east of the Sea of Galilee, formed the easternmost boundary of the Decapolis. Some suggest that the city is identifiable with Kenath of Numbers 32:42 and the subsequent modern town of Qanawat, a short distance northeast of es-Suweideh in the Hauran region.

See DECAPOLIS; KENATH.

Kareah. Father of Jonathan and Johanan (2 Kgs 25:23, KJV Careah). After Jerusalem fell to Nebuchadnezzar's army, his sons joined Gedaliah at Mizpah (Jer 40:8–43:5).

Karka, Karkaa. Unidentified town marking a part of Judah's southern boundary (Jos 15:3, KJV Karkaa). It was located in the southwest section of Palestine between Kadesh-barnea and Wadi el-Arish (Brook Besor).

Karkor. City in the Transjordan where Gideon attacked the armies of the two Midianite kings, Zebah and Zalmunna (Jgs 8:10). Indications of its location are sketchy. Judges 8:11 places it east of Nobah and Jogbehah, which is seven miles northwest of Amman in Jordan. A more feasible site is in the vicinity of ancient Succoth (Tell Deir 'Alla) and Penuel (Tell edh-Dhahab esh-Sherqiyeh), both assigned to Gad's tribe in Gilead.

Karnaim. Town situated along the King's Highway and along one of the northeastern tributaries of the Yarmuk River, 22 miles east of the Sea of Galilee on the Transjordan plateau. The prophet Amos prophesied against Karnaim (also spelled Carnaim), foretelling its impending destruction on account of its wickedness (6:13).

It was the leading town in the area after the decline of its sister city, Ashtaroth, and became the main center of an Assyrian province in the 7th century BC. In 163 BC it was captured by Judas Maccabeus (1 Mc 5:26,43,44). Christian and Jewish tradition believe it to be the home of Job.

Its exact location is disputed. Some identify it with the modern town at Sheikh Sa'd, three miles northeast of Ashtaroth, while others identify it with Ashtaroth itself at Tell 'Ashtarah (cf. Ashteroth-karnaim, Gn 14:5).

See ASHTEROTH-KARNAIM.

Kartah. Levitical city in Zebulun's territory. The list of cities assigned to the Merarite clan of Levites in Joshua 21:34 mentions Kartah, but the parallel passage in 1 Chronicles 6:77 does not. Its site is uncertain.

Kartan. Levitical town assigned to Naphtali (Jos 21:32), called Kiriathaim in 1 Chronicles 6:76. Some have identified it with Khirbet el-Qureiyeh in upper Galilee.

See KIRIATHAIM #2; LEVITICAL CITIES.

Kattath. Town assigned to Zebulun (Jos 19:15), perhaps the same as the Kitron of Judges 1:30. Some have identified it with Khirbet Quteineh.

See KITRON.

Kedar. 1. Second son of Ishmael, Abraham's son (Gn 25:13; 1 Chr 1:29).

2. Tribe or area appearing mainly in the prophetic writings from Solomon to the exile. In Isaiah's prophecy against Arabia (Is 21:13–17) Kedar is mentioned twice (vv 16,17). Along with Arabia, Dedan, and Tema, the Kerarites are threatened with destruction. The "pomp" attributed to them in verse 16 indicates some degree of affluence, and the militaristic tone of verse 17 points to the fact that they were a warring people (see also Ez 27:21). In Jeremiah 49:28 Kedar is linked with Hazor as victims of Nebuchadnezzar's conquests. Although there is no extrabiblical record of Nebuchadnezzar's march on Kedar, Ashurbanipal, the king of Assyria, does mention the conquest of Kedar. That would have been about 650 BC, or a half a century earlier than the Babylonian conquest. Apart from Ashurbanipal's account, the only other ancient extrabiblical reference to Kedar is found on a silver bowl offered to the Arabian goddess Han-'ilat in the Egyptian Delta. There the name is simply "Cain, son of Geshem, king of Kedar," and the date is firmly fixed in the 5th century BC. Geshem is very likely the enemy of Nehemiah (2:19; 6:1–6).

The picture the Bible gives of Kedar is that of a desert nomadic people descended from Ishmael. They were not Yahwists, but are included in the future kingdom of God (cf. Is 42:11; 60:7). Their desert environment limited their work to shepherding and trading. Because of unpredictable water supplies in the desert they were constantly moving—a way of life best handled with tents rather than permanent houses (cf. Ps 120:5; Sg 1:5). For this reason archaeologists have found no site named Kedar. All we can surmise is that the area of Kedar lay to the east and slightly to the south of Israel in what is today the southern part of Jordan. The people of Kedar presumably died out or were assimilated into the surrounding nations.

Kedemah. Son of Ishmael (Gn 25:15) who gave his name to the tribe he fathered (1 Chr 1:31).

Kedemoth. City east of the Jordan, probably located on the upper course of the Arnon River. From the "wilderness of Kedemoth" Moses sent messengers to Sihon, king of Heshbon, asking permission to pass peaceably through his land (Dt 2:26). In the division of the land Kedemoth was given to Reuben's tribe (Jos 13:18) and then set aside as one of the levitical cities for the Merarites (Jos 21:37; 1 Chr 6:79). It may be modern Qasr ez-Za'feran or Khirbet er-Remeil.

See LEVITICAL CITIES.

Kedesh. 1. Town in the Judean Negeb (Jos 15:23); its appearance alongside Adadah (Aroer) militates against its identification with Kadesh-barnea.

2. City of refuge in Upper Galilee, in the territory of Naphtali (Jos 20:7), set apart for the Gershonite clan of Levi (Jos 21:32; 1 Chr 6:76), and the home of Barak (Jgs 4:6). It was conquered by Tiglath-pileser III in 732 BC (2 Kgs 15:29). Jonathan Maccabeus defeated the army of Demetrius there (1 Mc 11:63,73, Kadesh). It is identified with Tell Qadas, 4½ miles northwest of Lake Huleh.

See CITIES OF REFUGE.

3. Levitical city in Issachar (1 Chr 6:72); the parallel passage has Kishion (Jos 21:28). It is perhaps to be identified with Tell Abu Qudeis on the southwest side of the Jezreel Valley between Taanach and Megiddo.

See LEVITICAL CITIES.

Kehelathah. One of the places where the Israelites encamped on their journey from

Egypt to Mt Sinai, located somewhere between Rissah and Mt Shepher (Nm 33:22,23). Its exact site is unknown.

See WILDERNESS WANDERINGS.

Keilah (Person). Caleb's descendant from Judah's tribe, called the Garmite in 1 Chronicles 4:19. Some identify this reference with the city in Judah instead of a person.

Keilah (Place). City assigned to Judah's tribe (Jos 15:44; 1 Chr 4:19), located in the southeast Shephelah near the Philistine border. It is identified with modern Khirbet Qila, 8½ miles northwest of Hebron.

David led a daring expedition to Keilah to deliver it from marauding Philistine bands, who were stealing grain from its threshing floors. He made it his residence for a time and expected to gain the loyalty of its people. However, when it became evident that the men of Keilah were plotting to turn him and his men over to Saul, he retreated into the wilderness of Ziph (1 Sm 23:1–14).

Keilah was reinhabited by Jews after the captivity and was divided into two districts, ruled by Hashabiah and Bavvai. Its rulers were included in the roster of those who participated in rebuilding the Jerusalem wall under Nehemiah (Neh 3:17,18).

Kelaiah, Kelita. Levite mentioned in 1 Esdras 9:23 who had married a foreign wife and pledged to divorce her. In Ezra 10:23 he is also called Kelita (meaning "crippled one"), a name (or nickname) found in Nehemiah 8:7; 10:10 and 1 Esdras 9:48, where he is one who helped Ezra in expounding the Law and who set his seal on Ezra's covenant. It cannot be determined with certainty whether Kelaiah and Kelita are the same individual.

Kemuel. 1. Third son of Nahor; Abraham's brother and the father of Aram (Gn 22:21).

2. Shiphtan's son from Ephraim's tribe; one of 12 men appointed to divide the land among the Israelite tribes (Nm 34:24).

3. Hashabiah's father, a ruler of the Levites during David's reign (1 Chr 27:17).

Kenan. Fourth-generation descendant of Adam (Gn 5:9–14, KJV Cainan; 1 Chr 1:2); alternately called Cainan in Luke's genealogy of Christ (3:37).

See GENEALOGY OF JESUS CHRIST.

Kenath. Town in the Hauran taken by Nobah (Nm 32:42) but later lost to Geshur and Aram (1 Chr 2:23). It was a Canaanite city known from Egyptian execration texts of the 19th and 18th centuries BC and from the conquest by Thutmose III and the Amarna letters. In the Hellenistic period it became one of the cities of the Decapolis; Jewish returnees from Babylon had settled there, and the rabbis considered it a border town of the Promised Land. It was also called Kanatha.

See DECAPOLIS; KANATHA.

Kenaz. Singular form of the name of the Kenizzite tribe, whose land was promised to Abraham's descendants (Gn 15:19). The appearance of three men by this name in the OT may be explained by the spread of the Kenizzite tribe over Edom and southern Judah before the Israelite conquest.

1. Grandson of Esau and chieftain of Edom (Gn 36:11,15,42; 1 Chr 1:36,53).

2. Father of Othniel (Jos 15:17; Jgs 1:13; 3:9,11) and Seraiah (1 Chr 4:13).

3. Caleb's descendant (1 Chr 4:15).

See KENIZZITES.

Kenezite. KJV spelling of Kenizzite in Numbers 32:12 and Joshua 14:6,14.

See KENIZZITES.

Kenites. One of 10 tribes living in Canaan during Abraham's time (Gn 15:19). The Kenites, however, are not included in the parallel statement from Moses' day (Ex 3:17). The apparent reason for this is a more favorable relationship with Israel by that time. "And the descendants of the Kenite, Moses' father-in-law, went up with the people of Judah from the city of palms into the wilderness of Judah, which lies in the Negeb near Arad; and they went and settled with the people" (Jgs 1:26). Some would therefore equate the tribal name Kenite with Midianite. They may rather have been a semi-nomadic subgroup, counted among any with whom they happened to be associated at a given time.

That Israel continued to accord special treatment to the Kenites is clear from 1 Samuel 15:6. When Saul mobilized his army against the Amalekites, he gave a warning before the attack. This kindness seems to reflect the aid given by Hobab, son of Reuel, who were their guide in the wilderness (Nm 10:29–31).

By the time of Barak the judge and Deborah the prophetess there was a branch of the Kenites in Galilee. Judges 4:11 says that "now Heber the Kenite had separated from the Kenites, the descendants of Hobab the father-in-law of Moses, and had pitched his tent as far away as the oak in Zaanannim, which is near Kedesh." This Kedesh was in Galilee, and not the Kadesh-barnea of the Sinai wilderness.

Another indication of the scattered nature

of the Kenite tribe is that they are included among the enemies to be defeated by Israel in the predictions of the mercenary prophet Balaam. This must refer to still another branch, since after referring to the destined destruction of the Amalekites, Balaam declares of some cliff-dwelling Kenites, "Enduring is your dwelling place, and your nest is set in the rock; nevertheless Kain shall be wasted. How long shall Asshur take you away captive?" (Nm 24:21,22). This reference locates at least a portion of the Kenites in Edom and the Wadi Arabah.

Since the name Kenite is closely related to the word for (copper) smith in both Arabic and Aramaic, it may be that this tribe was something of a trade guild of wandering smiths who offered their skills where needed. Nomadic tribes of metal workers were known to have moved about in the ancient Near East from the early 2nd millennium BC. Such artisans are found among the party of Asiatics pictured on the Beni-Hasan tomb in Egypt, dating from the 19th century BC. In modern times at least one Arab tribe of gypsylike traveling smiths or tinkers has followed the trade routes in search of employment.

In light of the biblical information about the Kenites, the major question is the influence this seemingly ubiquitous tribe had on the life and culture of the Hebrews. The least likely suggestion is that Moses was dependent on his Kenite/Midianite father-in-law, Jethro, for making the bronze serpent (Nm 21:4–9). However, it is likely that the Kenites, if indeed expert in metallurgy, may have taught this technology to God's covenant people to help them achieve settled nationhood. More serious is the suggestion that Jethro (also called Reuel), "priest of Midian," was the source of Moses' theology—the monotheistic religion of Jehovah (or Yahweh). This suggestion can be countered from two angles—one biblical and the other historical.

The biblical reference specifically stating that Jehovah was the personal God known to godly men from the earliest generations is Genesis 4:26: "And to Seth, to him also there was born a son: and he called his name Enosh. Then began men to call upon the name of Jehovah" (ASV). Equally significant is the fact that Moses' mother (or ancestress, as some would conclude) bore the name Jochebed, "Jehovah is glory." Obviously, then, Moses did not first hear of Jehovah from his father-in-law during his exile in the wilderness of Midian. The historical evidence indicates that no cultic sites (worship centers) other than the mobile tabernacle were located in Sinai or anywhere south of Beersheba. It was south of that city that the God who earlier revealed himself to the patri-

The wilderness of Sinai, where Moses kept the flock of his father-in-law, Jethro, the ancestor of the Kenites (Jgs 1:16; 4:11).

archs at various localities in the north announced to Moses that he was none other than the God of Abraham, of Isaac, and of Jacob (Ex 3:6). The Israelites never returned to Sinai for worship, even though God had first revealed himself to them there.

Jethro clearly learned of Jehovah through Moses, not vice versa. Those Kenites who became part of the family of God's people did so by adoption, by introduction through Israel's witness into the covenant relationship with the God of Jacob.

Interestingly, 1 Chronicles 2:55 includes the Kenite Hammath, father of the Rechabites, within the genealogy of Judah's tribe, into which they had been assimilated. David also links the Kenites with other inhabitants of southern Judah (1 Sm 27:10). Jeremiah 35 states that the Rechabites preserved the simple nomadic life of their ancestors down to the time of the Babylonian captivity. This, too, conforms to what is known about the nature of the Kenites.   MILTON C. FISHER

Kenizzites. A people related to Kenaz, grandson of Esau (Gn 36:11,15). The Kenizzites were of Edomite stock and resided to the southeast of Judah in the vicinity of the Kenites. They are thought to belong to the pre-Israelite population of Canaan (Gn 15:19). Their territory was to be given to the Israelites along with that of the Kenites, the Amorites, and the Canaanites (Gn 15:19–21).

In Numbers and Joshua, Caleb, the faithful spy, is reckoned to belong to the Kenizzites: "Caleb the son of Jephunneh the Kenizzite and Joshua the son of Nun, for they have wholly followed the Lord" (Nm 32:12, KJV Kenezite; see Jos 14:6,14). According to 1 Chronicles 4:15, Caleb's genealogy is traced back to Judah (1 Chr 4:1). The relationship of Caleb to the Kenizzites is far from clear. Caleb established his patrimony at Kiriath-sepher (Jgs 1:11–13), which is in Judah but which is also situated close to the territory of the Kenizzites. Critical opinion views the Kenizzites as non-Israelites who occupied Hebron, Debir, and the southernmost hill country of the Negeb and became politically incorporated into Judah.

Keren-happuch. Job's third daughter and the sister of Jemimah and Keziah. She was listed as a member of Job's family at the time of his restoration (Jb 42:14).

Kerioth. 1. Town in the Negeb of Judah (Jos 15:25), called Kerioth-hezron. The Hebrew text understands Kerioth and Hezron to be separate towns, the latter being identical to Hazor (Jos 15:23?). The identification with Khirbet el-Qaryatein, about four miles south of Maon (Ma'in), is doubtful, since the latter is in the hill country, not the Negeb.

2. Town in Moab (Jer 48:24,41; Am 2:2, KJV Kirioth). From the Moabite Stone it can be located in the southwest tableland of Moab opposite Ataroth, where a shrine to Chemosh must have been located, probably Khirbet el-Qereiyat. It is not counted among the towns of Reuben and Gad (Nm 34; Jos 13); in other lists it is absent while Ar is mentioned (Is 15,16), which leads scholars to equate Ar with Kerioth.

Kerioth-hezron. Town(s) mentioned in Joshua 15:25.

See KERIOTH #1.

Keros. One of the temple servants whose descendants returned to Jerusalem with Zerubbabel (Ezr 2:44; Neh 7:47).

Kerygma. Basic evangelistic message proclaimed by the earliest Christians. More fully, it is the proclamation of the death, resurrection, and exaltation of Jesus that leads to an evaluation of his person as both Lord and Christ, confronts one with the necessity of repentance, and promises the forgiveness of sins. The kerygma is drawn from two sources: (1) the fragments of pre-Pauline tradition that lie embedded in the writings of the apostle, and (2) the early evangelistic speeches of Peter in the Book of Acts. When these two sources are compared, a single basic message emerges.

The kerygma is essentially the same as the gospel, although the term itself emphasizes the *manner* of delivery somewhat more than the *message* that is being proclaimed. In the ancient world the king made known his decrees by means of a *kerux* (a town crier or her-

ald). This person, who often served as a close confidant of the king, would travel throughout the realm announcing to the people whatever the king wished to make known. It is this note of authoritative declaration that is so appropriately transferred to the evangelizing activities of the primitive church.

Most current discussions of the kerygma, however, center on the content of the apostolic message. In *The Apostolic Preaching and Its Developments* (1936), C.H. Dodd laid the groundwork for all subsequent discussions of the kerygma. Beginning with fragments of early Christian tradition embedded in Paul's letters and then comparing these with the early speeches of Peter in the Book of Acts, Dodd arrived at the outline of an apostolic gospel. The gist of this kerygma is that with the first coming of Christ the prophecies of the OT were fulfilled and the new age was inaugurated. Christ was born of the seed of David. His ministry, death, and resurrection led to his exaltation by God as Head of the new Israel. He will soon return to judge the people and bring the messianic age to its conclusion. For this reason all persons are to repent.

While hailing Dodd's work on the kerygma as plowing new ground, not all have agreed with him at every point. Another evaluation of the same basic material concludes that in simplest outline the kerygma is made up of: (1) a proclamation of the death, resurrection, and exaltation of Jesus, seen as the fulfillment of prophecy and involving human responsibility; (2) the resultant evaluation of Jesus as both Lord and Christ; and (3) a summons to repent and receive forgiveness of sins. However, on the basis of a careful study of the actual texts themselves the kerygma did *not* contain: (1) a declaration of the dawn of the messianic age, (2) any reference to the life and ministry of Jesus (in contrast to his death and resurrection), or (3) a major emphasis on the second advent as part of the evangelistic proclamation. While all of these issues are part of the larger theological presentation of the NT, they do not appear to have been included in the essential apostolic gospel. In any case they are missing from the various texts which provide the source for the kerygma.

It is evident that the resurrection plays the central role in the drama of redemption. The kerygma always focuses on the resurrection. This supernatural act of God in history authenticates the words and works of Jesus and constitutes the basis for the Christian hope of immortality. Without the resurrection, the church would be no more than a group of well-intentioned, religious people who had placed their faith in the superior philosophical and ethical teachings of an unusually fine man. The resurrection is proof positive that Jesus is who he said he was. Only if he is the Son of God can his death provide an appropriate and sufficient sacrifice for human sin. Essentially, the kerygma is a declaration that Christ is risen from the dead, and by that great act God has brought salvation.

When Peter finished his great sermon at Pentecost, the crowd cried, "Brethren, what shall we do?" (Acts 2:37). They could not withstand the logic of the apostle's conclusion that by the resurrection of Jesus, "God has made him both Lord and Christ" (Acts 2:36). Peter responds by admonishing them to repent and be baptized in the name of Jesus Christ for the forgiveness of sins (Acts 2:38). The kerygma is not a dull recital of historical facts but a dynamic confrontation between the Holy Spirit and the sinful heart of man at the point of its basic need. Who can deny that the reality of the resurrection validates the claims of Christ? Who can resist the compelling logic of the resurrection as it leads irresistibly to the conclusion that Jesus of Nazareth is the living Lord? To repent and believe is to enter the kingdom of God. The kerygma has as its ultimate goal not a sophisticated theology but a transformed life. It is the declaration that in Christ the new order of eternal life has already entered into time and history.

See GOSPEL; ACTS OF THE APOSTLES, BOOK OF THE.

Keturah. Second wife of Abraham. It is unclear whether he married her before or after Sarah's death (Gn 25:1). He had six sons with her: Zimran, Jokshan, Medan, Midian, Ishbak, and Shuah (Gn 25:2). Keturah's status was not identical to that of Sarah. She is called a concubine (Gn 25:6, cf. 1 Chr 1:32), and her sons were presented with gifts instead of receiving a share in the inheritance. Keturah's sons were the ancestors of tribes with which Israel came into contact after the conquest, especially Midian and Jokshan's sons Sheba and Dedan (Gn 25:3). As far as can be determined, the tribes settled in the north and central regions of the northern Euphrates as far as the central sections of the Arabian desert. They were merchants (Gn 37) and shepherds (Ex 2:16). They were involved in international trade: "A multitude of camels shall cover you [the land], the young camels of Midian and Ephah; all those from Sheba shall come. They shall bring gold and frankincense, and shall proclaim the praise of the Lord" (Is 60:6). The queen of Sheba, a descendant of Jokshan (Gn 25:3), came to Solomon to initiate trade relations: "She came to Jerusalem with a very great retinue, with camels bearing spices, and

very much gold, and precious stones (1 Kgs 10:2).

See ABRAHAM.

Keys of the Kingdom. Symbolic description of the authority given by Jesus to Peter in Matthew 16:19: "I will give you the keys of the kingdom of heaven, and whatever you bind on earth shall be bound in heaven, and whatever you loose on earth shall be loosed in heaven."

Many ancient peoples believed that heaven and hell were closed by gates to which certain deities and angelic beings had keys. In Greek mythology Pluto kept the key to Hades. Jewish writings near the time of Jesus give God the key to the abode of the dead. In the Book of Revelation John sees Christ holding the keys of Death and Hades (Rv 1:18; see 3:7).

In Matthew's Gospel the keys symbolize the authority to open and shut the kingdom of heaven. In response to Peter's declaration that Jesus is the Christ, the Son of the living God (Mt 16:16), Jesus entrusts authority to "bind" and "loose" to Peter. This authority is later extended to the other disciples (18:18). The words "bind" and "loose" were used by rabbis near the time of Christ to declare someone under a ban ("binding") and relief of the ban ("loosing"). Sometimes this referred to expulsion or reinstatement at a synagogue. At other times binding and loosing indicated consignment to God's judgment or acquittal from it. The "power of the keys" (or binding and loosing) of which Jesus speaks is a spiritual authority like that he gave the disciples in John 20:23: "If you forgive the sins of any, they are forgiven; if you retain the sins of any, they are retained."

The Pharisees and scribes assumed that as teachers of the Law they had power to "shut the kingdom of heaven against men" (Mt 23:13). Yet as "blind guides" they failed to recognize, as Peter had, that Jesus was the one in whom God's kingdom had come. The keys of the kingdom authorized the pronouncement of judgment and the promise of forgiveness—not on human authority, but on the basis of Christ's Word.

See KINGDOM OF GOD (HEAVEN).

Keziah, Kezia. Job's second daughter, born after his restoration (Jb 42:14, KJV Kezia).

Keziz, Valley of. KJV rendering of Emekkeziz, a city allotted to Benjamin's tribe for an inheritance, in Joshua 18:21.

See EMEKKEZIZ.

Kibroth-hattaavah. Location in the wilderness where the Israelites who were slain by plague for craving after the flesh of quails were buried (Nm 11:34,35; 33:16,17; Dt 9:22). It was situated between Mt Sinai and Hazeroth, but its exact site is unknown. The name, meaning "graves of craving," is explained by the account of the quails.

See WILDERNESS WANDERINGS.

Kibzaim. One of several cities in Ephraim given to the levitical family of Kohath after the conquest of Canaan (Jos 21:22). It is probably the same as the Jokmeam of 1 Chronicles 6:68, but it is not to be equated with the Jokmeam (KJV Jokneam) of 1 Kings 4:12. Its exact location is unknown.

Kid. Young goat.

See ANIMALS (GOAT).

Kidney. One of the body parts of sacrificial animals used for offerings to God. The kidneys along with their fat were to be burned on the altar (Ex 29:13; Lv 3:4–15), and represented the blood that the Israelites were not permitted to eat.

In a more figurative sense the kidneys are thought of as the seat of human emotions (Ps 73:21; Prv 23:6) and the rational and moral faculties (Ps 16:7; Jer 12:2). They are closely associated with the "heart" and "soul," standing for one's innermost self-consciousness. The RSV translates the Hebrew word as "mind," "heart," and "soul" in several passages.

As in the OT Jehovah had knowledge of man's inmost thoughts (e.g., Jer 20:12; Pss 7:9; 26:2), so Christ was identified in the Book of Revelation as the one who "searches the minds [reins, KJV] and hearts" (2:23), making an indirect but clear identification of Jesus and Jehovah. This is the only reference to the kidneys in the NT.

Kidron. Valley and stream bed running below the SE wall of Jerusalem and separating the city from the Mt of Olives on the east. It then turns southeast from Jerusalem and follows a winding course to the Dead Sea. The Kidron can be described as a torrent bed that is nearly always dry, since the water course flows only in the rainy season, partly maintained by the two irregular springs Gihon and En-rogel.

The Gihon was the vital water source for the old City of David, and in Hezekiah's day an underground tunnel was cut in the rock to guarantee a water supply in time of siege, thus supplying the pool of Siloam within the city walls.

The term "brook" found in John 18:1 (KJV) would be better translated "winterflow" or "wintercourse," since the original word intends to convey this seasonal character of the creek rather than to suggest a river.

The two most important functions of the Kidron Valley for the city of Jerusalem are military and funerary. The walls of the city have always towered over the valley, and its steepness made it extremely difficult for any attack to succeed from that side. Over the centuries rubble from nearby ruins has raised the floor of the valley. In places the present floor is some 40 feet above earlier historic levels; it is not certain how many ancient caves and tombs must lie below the present surface. The wide space just south of the city, where the Kidron meets and merges with the Tyropean and Hinnom valleys, has always been a favorite spot for the royal gardens, irrigated from the two nearby springs.

Since the 4th century AD, the Kidron has been called "the valley of Jehoshaphat" (Jl 3:12), scene of the judgment of nations at the last day, and this tradition is strong among both Muslims and Jews. Today the sides of the valley are crowded with tombs. Even before the exile it was a popular place for burial (2 Kgs 23:4–12 refers to the graves of the common people and to the dumping of idolatrous refuse there; see also 2 Chr 34:4,5).

The first reference to the Kidron Valley is in 2 Samuel 15:23, where the people and David crossed over toward the desert. This strategic move would give them a way of escape should rebellious Absalom's forces decide to attack the city. The people and the king wept bitterly during this move (vv 23,30) because it had such a depressing significance; David was abandoning Zion without a fight. Later the offensive Shimei was forbidden to cross the Kidron by Solomon (1 Kgs 2:36–38) on pain of death. Josephus mentions that the wicked queen Athaliah was put to death in the Kidron Valley (*Antiq.* 9.7.3), but it is not clear from 2 Kings 11:16 that the horses' entrance to the palace opened onto the Kidron.

The last reference to the Kidron is the occasion of Jesus' crossing it with his disciples on the eve of his betrayal (Jn 18:1, KJV Cedron). The parallels with the crossing of David are interesting, considering the place David holds in the establishment of the biblical symbolism of king and kingdom. Eschatologically, Jeremiah foretells a time when the Kidron will be "sacred to the Lord" (31:38–40), as part of the restoration of Israel (vv 35–37).

See JERUSALEM.

Kiln. Large furnace used in firing pottery (Ex 9:8,10).

See POTTERY.

Kinah. Town in the Negeb of Judah (Jos 15:22), perhaps named after the Kenites who lived in the area (Jgs 1:16). According to a letter discovered at Arad, troops were sent from Kinah to reinforce Ramoth-negeb against an Edomite attack. The ancient name is preserved in Wadi el-Qeini, in the eastern Negeb.

Kine. Cows.

See ANIMALS (CATTLE).

King, Kingship. The word *melek* (king) occurs more than 2000 times in the Hebrew OT. It may refer to God (Ps 95:3) or to human rulers. Generally it designates one invested with ultimate authority and power over his subjects. In the OT, the word *melek* designates the ruler of a tribe ("the kings of Midian," Nm 31:8), a city (Jericho, Ai; cf. Jos 12:9–24, where 31 kings of city-states conquered by the Israelites are listed), a nation (Israel, Judah, Ammon, Moab, Aram), or an international power (such as Egypt, Assyria, Babylonia, or Persia). Other words may also refer to royalty. The Philistines introduced the title *seren* (lord) into Hebrew vocabulary. The 5 Philistine cities were ruled by 5 lords. Another word for an Israelite king was *nāgid* (ruler). Both Saul and David were anointed as ruler (*nāgid*) over Israel (1 Sm 10:1; 2 Sm 7:8). In the NT and the Septuagint, the Greek version of the OT, the word *basileus* has a meaning similar to the Hebrew *melek*. The NT *basileus* refers to secular rulers living in the 1st century, kings of Israel, rulers of the past, and to the great king, Jesus Christ.

The phrase "King of kings" attributed to Jesus (1 Tm 6:15) is a Hebraism meaning supreme or greatest king. For example, in Ezekiel's prediction of the fall of Tyre, Nebuchadnezzar is named the "king of kings" (26:7). The great rulers of Assyria and Babylon introduced this title. Before their time rulers were called either "king" or "great king," as in 2 Kings 18:28: "Hear the word of the great king, the king of Assyria." Later rulers had their titles adjusted to keep up with the expanse of their empires.

Status of Kings in the Ancient Near East. The status of the king differed from country to country, and it changed with the times. The status of the monarchy in Mesopotamia was different from that of the pharaohs in Egypt. Kingship in Israel varied from the surrounding nations. Changes in religious ideas and cultural outlook had an impact on the status of the king. Even in the Bible the kingship of Abimelech varied from that of Saul, and Saul's kingship was different from David's. Nevertheless, the concept of monarchy in the ancient Near East held in common the relation between deity and the king, whether the king was viewed as divine, a representative of God, a son of God, or as the means of God's rule on earth.

Egypt. In Egypt the monarch was considered divine. The gods and the kings became so intertwined that they were fused—gods were kings and kings were gods. Chief among the gods was Amon-Re, who was addressed as "king of the gods" and worshiped in many hymns as "chief of all gods . . . father of the gods, who made mankind . . . the king of Upper and Lower Egypt . . . lord of the gods." Inscriptions refer to the king as "the god" or "the good god." In the Old Kingdom he was a representative of God on earth and was regarded as the only one endowed with immortality. The nobles and servants could hope for a place in the hereafter only by being buried in proximity to the royal tomb. The ancient Egyptians contributed three months out of the year to building royal tombs (pyramids). These people were motivated to quarry, ship, roll, and position huge blocks of stone, that the gods might remember them for their involvement in the preparation of the final resting place of the divine king.

Mesopotamia. The Sumerians held to the coexistence of many gods who together ruled as "king." Chief among them were Anu, the god of heaven; Enlil, the god of heaven and earth; and Enki, the god of the earth. Each of these gods was portrayed as king over a certain realm, and their kingship was recognized by the establishment of shrines and by the composition of hymns, prayers, and ritual texts. With the ascendancy of Marduk, Ashur, Shamesh, Ishtar, and Sin, other gods diminished in importance. Though the supremacy of certain gods might change over the years, the gods remained important in the structure of Mesopotamian society.

In Sumerian culture the kings were the representatives of the gods on earth. Their task was to serve the gods by maintaining the divine laws and by supporting and protecting the shrines. The Sumerian king list begins with the belief that kingship originated with the gods: "When kingship was lowered from heaven, kingship was [first] in Eridu." The early monarchs of Ur (c. 2650 BC) were buried in the royal cemetery with 3 to 74 attendants. The royal funerals resembled those of the Egyptian pharaohs. At this time they were considered gods and took their servants with them to serve in the life hereafter. Divine status did not become a permanent part of the Mesopotamian view of the kingship. The rulers called themselves shepherds, and were originally known as the *en* in Sumerian cul-

The attire of a king.

ture. The *en* was a title given to the highest priest serving the local god. He was the head of the temple cult. Later he was known as the *ensi* (governor) or *lugal* (king), who was charged with the maintenance of the temple. Hence, the kings prided themselves on their building activities, which brought aid from patron gods. Sargon of Agade viewed himself as the "overseer of Ishtar, king of Kish, anointed priest of Anu, king of the country, great *ensi* of Enlil." Hammurabi of Babylon claimed to have built the temples of the gods of Mesopotamia: "The temple é.nam ḫé [House of Abundance] of Adad was built. He constructed the image of the goddess Shala. He built the temple é.tùr.kalam.ma [Fold of the Country] for Anu, Inana and Nana."

The king had an important place in the New Year festival in Babylon. Yearly the king presented himself with the priest before the image of Marduk. Having renewed the signs of royalty, the king humiliated himself before the god. The act was symbolic of the divine order, in which royal status was granted to the king by the god. Upon the completion of these ritu-

als, the priest returned the symbols of royalty to the king; the recoronation of the king was a divine approval on his administration and service as a minister of the god Marduk.

As a shepherd over the people, the ruler protected the rights of the people by introducing and enforcing legal codes. Hammurabi, ruler of Babylon (*c.* 1700 BC), believed himself called by the gods, as he wrote in the prologue to his famous laws: "Anu and Enlil named me to promote the welfare of the people, me, Hammurabi, the devout, god-fearing prince, to cause justice to prevail in the land, to destroy the wicked and the evil that the strong might not oppress the weak." Justice was an outstanding quality of the Mesopotamian king. His calling was to establish justice throughout the kingdom, as Hammurabi claimed to have done: "I understand law and justice in the language of the land, thereby promoting the welfare of the people."

The king fully recognized that as heir to the throne or as a usurper, he could claim the allegiance of the people, thus giving evidence that he had been accepted by the gods. It is for this reason that in Mesopotamia the king stressed the divine grace bestowed upon him as the ruler; Hammurabi claimed: "Marduk commissioned me" and "Hammurabi the shepherd, called by Enlil."

Canaan. It is more difficult to reconstruct the concept of kingship in Canaan. The paucity of original sources, the intermingling of different traditions, and the perpetually changing rule of larger empires do not allow a full understanding of the Canaanite conception of kingship. As important as the Philistines are in the unfolding of the biblical narrative, little is known about their view of kingship. The unified power of the Philistine lords gave rise to the Israelites' desire for a king to lead them into victories. Ahab's sense of kingship may have been modified by the influence of his Phoenician wife, Jezebel.

The Canaanite epics provide some information about the Canaanite monarchy. Kings, like gods, struggled for power. In the legends Baal, Mot, and Yam each have power, but in the conflict for more power one of the gods emerges as the victor. In the Canaanite pantheon El was the "father of the gods" and the "father of mankind." He ruled over the gods and over men, but he also shared his powers with the lesser gods. He may be compared to a patriarch, seated on his throne, extending his authority over kings, the gods, and mankind.

Basically, the Canaanite cities were vassals. The king ruled over a city controlled by Egypt. This local ruler was permitted to continue his kingship if he accepted the conditions imposed on him by the pharaoh. As a vassal, he was responsible to supply whatever was requested: gold, silver, food, manpower, and armies. The pharaohs kept the Canaanite vassals disunited in order to secure their own position in Canaan.

When a city was sufficiently strong to resist the pharaoh, the king of the city enjoyed greater liberties. The kings of Ugarit, situated at a seaport on the Mediterranean Sea, were absolute lords over all citizens and property. Their rule was that of absolute despots. A criminal or a person who fell out of favor might be dispossessed without being able to resort to any legal property rights. The crown was, however, obligated to protect the rights of those who were unable to protect themselves—the widows and orphans.

Kingship in Israel. The Bible begins with the affirmation that God is the Creator (Gn 1:1). The Creator is the great King of all creation. His perfections of kingship are wisdom, power, glory, and fidelity, as witnessed by the harmony in creation. The great King established a relationship with his creation, and he delegates his power to the celestial bodies and to man. The sun, moon, and stars are charged with "ruling" over the day and the night (Gn 1:14–18), and man is entrusted with the rule over God's creation on earth (Gn 1:26,28). The Lord's kingship over man is further expressed by man's service to God (Gn 2:7–22). The great King serves man by fashioning both male and female, in order that they may find joy and happiness together in their service to him. His rule is not totalitarian or selfish. Rather, it is full of love, fidelity, and concern for the well-being of his subjects. He does not "rest" until man is installed in office, endowed with the image of God, and all his needs are fully supplied.

The subsequent development in the history of redemption, therefore, does not result from God's lack of concern for man or because he is a despot. Man's fall and acts of rebellion (Gn 3; 6:1–8; 11:1–9) were revolutionary in nature; man expressed his autonomy over against the great King.

Yet the great King is gracious. He expels Adam and Eve from the garden of Eden, but does not destroy them (Gn 3:24). He bestows on Noah and his descendants his blessings of procreation and provision (Gn 9:1,7). Furthermore, he expects fallen man to continue the exercise of dominion (Gn 9:2,7; "multiply" should be read as "rule," cf. Gn 1:28). The climax of man's attempt at emancipating himself from God's rule is at Babel. At Babel the Lord scattered mankind and permitted the development of nations, languages, and countries (Gn 11:1–9; cf. 10:5,20,31). From this point onward, each nation would be led by its own king, prince, or ruler. From this point onward, there exist two clearly definable kingships: divine and human.

In the establishment of the Abrahamic covenant, God's plan of redemption was temporally limited to Abraham and his descendants. Human government up to this point had been autonomous, rejecting the theocratic rights of the Creator. God chose Abraham as the father of nations; through him and his descendants the messianic rule would be established on earth. In his promises to Abraham, God repeatedly assured him that he would become the father of a mighty nation, to whom God would give the land of Canaan, and that kings would arise from his descendants (Gn 17:6). Abraham accepted the rule of God over his family in the act of circumcision, by which the clan of Abraham was set apart for the service of God (Gn 17:10–14). The ultimate purpose of God's relation with Abraham and his descendants is that God may be King over Israel and that his people will show their acceptance of his rule by their faithful obedience to him (Gn 17:7).

At the heart of the covenant is God's expectation of a response of loyalty to his rule: "I am God Almighty; walk before me, and be blameless" (Ex 17:1b). Abraham and his descendants may exercise their God-given "rule" over the nations by living in fellowship with the great King. Thus the Lord reestablished his dominion over mankind in Abraham. Through Abraham and his descendants he would raise up a "royal nation" to whom the full privileges of rule over his creation would be restored.

From the redemptive-historical perspective, creation and redemption remain intertwined. Through the acts of redemption the Lord reestablishes man's place in harmony with creation. However, the road to rule is the way of testing and suffering, as the patriarchal narratives demonstrate. Abraham, Isaac, and Jacob were severely tested; they lived in hope of the promises of God's blessing and protection on the one hand, while on the other, they suffered famine, warfare, competition, and complications. Abraham proved himself in the eyes of God and man to be father of the faithful (Gn 22:16). Jacob became the father of Israel as he wrestled with the Lord at Peniel and was blessed by his covenant God, who named him *Israel* (Gn 32:28–30). These stories of the rule of God (theocracy) in the lives of people stand in sharp contrast to the stories of the rule of man (autocracy) in Genesis 3–11.

This is the background for the further revelation of God's kingship to Israel in Egypt. In the 10 plagues and in the exodus the Lord revealed the qualities of his kingship: his power to deliver and to vindicate. He is the "divine warrior" who fights for his people, identifying with their lot. At the shore of the Red Sea, Israel joined with Moses in the song celebrating Yahweh's kingship: "The Lord is a warrior; the Lord is his name. The Lord will reign for ever and ever" (Ex 15:3,18 NIV).

Further, the Lord condescended to Israel by making a covenant with them. This covenant was a sovereign administration of grace and promise by which the Lord consecrated a people unto himself by the sanctions of divine law and by his very presence. The connection of covenant, tabernacle, and the sabbath in Exodus 20–31 supports the idea that God's kingship is present with Israel, that they are consecrated to serve him as "a kingdom of priests and a holy nation" (Ex 19:6), and that the "sign" of their consecration, God's kingship, and Israel's royal status is the sabbath (cf. Ex 31:17). Another sign of his kingship is the ark of the covenant (cf. Nm 10:35,36; Ps 132:8).

The nation, having witnessed God's care for them, had to learn that in obedience to God's expectations the theocratic kingdom might become a reality on earth. M.G. Kline views God's covenantal relationship with Israel as sanctions imposed by the great King on his people. In the Sinaitic covenant the theocracy was established. Israel was entrusted with the commandments that they might show themselves to be a theocratic nation, as God revealed to Moses: "You shall be my own possession among all peoples; for all the earth is mine, and you shall be to me a kingdom of priests and a holy nation" (Ex 19:5,6). They were God's elect for the sake of the nations; through Israel's priestly obedience and intercession the whole earth might know the Creator-Redeemer.

The qualities of God's kingship were power, glory, fidelity, wisdom, concern, service, delegation of power to man, blessing and protection, just rule, judgment, vindication, and deliverance. Israel's kingship was to be no different from God's. Their varied and sometimes complex laws taught Israel to distinguish between what is holy and common, clean and unclean, the ways of God and the ways of the nations. The ways of God enhance love, fidelity, justice, peace, harmony, service, concern for others, wise living, defense of the needy, and judgment of the guilty. The ways of the kingdoms of the world all too often promoted selfishness, disregard for justice, anarchy, and despotism.

The Lord also instituted an organizational structure designed to promote his theocratic purposes. In the wilderness Moses and the chosen leaders of Israel (Ex 18:19–26; Nm 11:24,25; cf. Dt 1:15–18) were God's instruments for upholding his kingship in Israel.

Upon Moses' death Joshua took over the theocratic rule. The Lord was with him, as he had been with Moses, and all Israel recognized the continuity of God's rule in Joshua's leadership (Dt 34:9; Jos 3:7; 4:14). Like Moses before his death, Joshua charged the leadership and Israel to persevere in the gracious covenant relationship (Jos 23,24). However, Israel perished because of its greed, immorality, strife, and idolatry. During the period of the judges, each one did what was right in his own eyes (Jgs 17:6; 18:1; 19:1; 21:25). There was no king in the land in those days (Jgs 21:25). The judges were military leaders whom the Lord raised up to deliver his people from their foreign oppressors. God remained King, regardless of the fact that Israel lived as if he were not.

Provision was also made for the rise of kingship in the Law (Dt 17:14–20). However, the institution of monarchic kingship was not practiced until the time of Samuel. The period of the judges demonstrated that apostate Israel was unsuccessful in dealing with the surrounding nations.

The theocratic leadership was restored to Israel by the ministry of Samuel. He was born in a levitical family and served the Lord at the Shiloh tabernacle. He was called to be a prophet—an office which had not been filled since Moses' death (1 Sm 3:20,21). He was recognized as a judge in Israel (1 Sm 7:15). In Samuel the offices of priest, prophet, and king are combined. He is never called king, as his life-style was that of a prophet rather than that of a ruler. The carefully calculated request of the people for a king was a rejection of Samuel's ministry. The people were not satisfied with the spiritual, charismatic leadership of Samuel. In their search for a more dynamic leader they found in the kings of the surrounding nations attractive elements: power, manifestation of glory, and stability. Thus far the tribes had experienced several civil wars that endangered the unity of Israel. It was thought that a king would remedy all of the social and political problems. Though God had foreseen the days of the monarchy in the Law, the people were motivated to introduce the kingship for secular rather than religious reasons: "Now appoint for us a king to govern us like all the nations" (1 Sm 8:5); "we will have a king over us, that we also may be like all nations, and that our king may govern us and go out before us and fight our battles" (v 20). Samuel never accepted the idea of kingship; it was foreign to the theocratic ideal.

The crucial difference between kingship in Israel and in neighboring lands lies in the fact that God endowed the king with his spirit to establish his rule on earth. God rules for his people and his people benefit from his rule; he is their provider, protector, and divine warrior.

Samuel was instrumental in anointing Saul —a sad example of kingship—and David—a good example of kingly rule under God. Saul's kingship revealed a despotic, uncaring attitude and self-aggrandizement. He was intent on establishing his dynasty, while not caring sufficiently for the people of God. Therefore, the Lord rejected his kingship (1 Sm 15:23).

David's kingship, in contrast to Saul's, was in line with God's because it reflected the glory of Yahweh's kingship. David's life and rule are taken up in the two books of Samuel as a commentary on the pros and cons of kingship. Positively, David was a man after God's heart, sought the will of God, repented of his sin, and sought the glory of God. Negatively, David failed in his personal and family life to uphold the high standards of God's Law. Yet God was pleased to choose David's dynasty as the lineage to which Jesus Christ would be related. The prophet Nathan assured David that his dynasty would last: "Your house and your kingdom shall be made sure for ever before me; your throne shall be established for ever" (2 Sm 7:16); but God did not promise that it would be immune from prosecution or banishment.

The outstanding qualities of the kingship of David and Solomon reflect the true theocratic intention: concern for the Lord, for a heart of wisdom and integrity, and for the well-being of God's people. Concern for the Lord found expression in the preparation for and actual building of the temple (cf. Ps 132). Concern for integrity and wisdom is clearly evident, especially in David's response to Nathan's rebuke (2 Sm 12) and in Solomon's request to have a heart of wisdom (1 Kgs 3). Concern for the people comes to expression in their securing the borders against enemies, national unification, and in bringing opportunity for economic growth. The era of David and Solomon represented a true reflection of God's kingship on earth.

The accounts in Kings and Chronicles unfold the history of kingship in Israel and Judah. The good kings followed the examples provided by David and Solomon in securing Jerusalem against foreign invaders, in supplying for the needs of the temple, in having God's people instructed in the Word, and in modeling their rule after the Law of Moses. A good Davidic king loved the Lord, the temple, the Torah, and God's people. He served them as a good shepherd. Evil kings were those who rejected this model of kingship in favor of the pagan models. So Omri and Ahab introduced the Phoenician culture with its Baalism, utterly disregarding the heritage of Israel.

The king received the Spirit of God, which was the spirit of wisdom (cf. 1 Kgs 3:11; Is 11:2). The Spirit of God restored the image of God, given at man's creation but adversely affected by the fall. The Davidic king was treated as a member of God's household, being a "son" of the great King (cf. 2 Sm 7:14–16; Ps 2:6,7). The Davidic king was to be loyal to the great King, Yahweh. He, like Moses and Joshua before him, received his orders directly from the Lord; but unlike Moses, the Word of the Lord was mediated through the prophets. He, like Moses and Joshua, was expected to serve his God and his people.

The prophets spoke of a Messiah who would establish God's kingship on earth. The descendants of David failed to maintain and expand the theocracy. By the 8th and 7th centuries BC it was apparent that even the greatest kings were dwarfed by the stature of David and Solomon. The prophets (Is 9:2–7; 11:1–9; Jer 33:14–16; Ez 34:22–31; Mi 5:2–5) spoke of another king, a descendant of David, who would rule permanently, and by whose rule the reign of God would extend to the ends of the earth. He would put down all opposition to God's rule, remove all enemies, and bring in an era of universal peace and righteousness. The Messiah-king would reveal the perfections of divine rule, as the Spirit of God would be upon him. His kingship would be marked by service to the people of God, so that they would be a well-cared-for flock; he would serve them as their shepherd.

In the coming of Jesus the messianic kingdom is more clearly revealed. He is the king of whom the angels said, "For to you is born this day in the city of David a Savior, who is Christ the Lord" (Lk 2:11). These magnificent words show continuity with the prophetic word. Jesus is the Savior, whose role includes the deliverance from sin, but also from all causes of adversity, evil, and the effects of the curse. His mission pertains to both forgiveness and to the establishment of peace on earth (Lk 1:77–79). In this light we must look at Jesus' ministry of healing, feeding, opposition to the forces of evil, suffering, and teaching as the establishment of God's kingdom on earth. He is the king who serves, fights against the demonic powers, and overcomes. The resurrection marks his victory, and he is crowned with glory by being seated at the right hand of the Father (Acts 2:33–36; cf. 1 Cor 15:25). In being the Savior he is no other than "Christ the Lord." The early apostolic preaching proclaimed that Jesus is the Messiah of God and the Lord. The lordship of Jesus is corollary to his being the Messiah. To those who call on him, he is the Savior-Messiah-Lord (Rom 10:9–15), but to those who reject him, he is the

Divine Warrior, before whom all knees will bow and who will bring in the era of the Father's judgment (cf. Rv 1:12–16; 19:11–21).

Jesus taught his disciples that at his coming in glory he would be seated on his throne and all mankind would pay him obeisance. The enemies of God (the goats) will be cast out from his presence, and the people of God (the sheep) will fully inherit the kingdom (Mt 25:34; cf. vv 31,46). In accordance with Jesus' teaching, the members of his body, the church, are expected to work out the theocratic ideal in their lives, that by their works and faith they may glorify the Father and show that they are his (Jn 17:20–26; cf. Mt 25:33–40). This is the biblical manner of witness which Israel failed to give and which the church is privileged to give; as Paul wrote to Timothy: "I charge you in the presence of God . . . and of Christ Jesus . . . that you keep the commandment without stain or reproach, until the appearing of our Lord Jesus Christ. . . . He who is the blessed and only sovereign, the King of kings, and Lord of lords . . . to him be honor and eternal dominion forever. Amen" (1 Tm 6:14–16). Then follow several instructions as to how the people of God must demonstrate their allegiance to Jesus (vv 17,21). Throughout the Book of Revelation Jesus is viewed as king over the church (4:2,9–11; 5:1,9,10,12,13). At his return his kingship will be established. At this time the enemies of the cross will see whom they have rejected and will bow before the messianic King (1 Cor 15:25–28). Then Jesus "delivers up the kingdom to the God and Father" (1 Cor 15:24); "Amen, Come, Lord Jesus" (Rv 22:20).

WILLEM A. VanGEMEREN

See ISRAEL, HISTORY OF; KINGDOM OF GOD (HEAVEN).

Bibliography. F.M. Cross, *Canaanite Myth and Hebrew Epic;* J.H. Eaton, *Kingship and the Psalms;* H. Frankfort, *Kingship and the Gods;* C.T. Gadd, *Ideas of Divine Rule in the Ancient East;* J. Gray, *The Biblical Doctrine of the Reign of God;* A.M. Hocart, *Kingship;* A.R. Johnson, *Sacred Kingship in Ancient Israel;* S. Mowinckel, *He That Cometh.*

Kingdom of God (Heaven).

The sovereign rule of God, initiated by Christ's earthly ministry and to be consummated when "the kingdom of the world has become the kingdom of our Lord and of his Christ" (Rv 11:15).

According to the testimony of the first three Gospels the proclamation of the kingdom of God was Jesus' central message. Matthew summarizes the Galilean ministry with the words, "And he went about all Galilee, teaching in their synagogues and preaching the gospel of the kingdom and healing every disease and every infirmity among the people" (Mt 4:23). The Sermon on the Mount is concerned with the righteousness that qualifies men to enter the kingdom of God (Mt 5:20). The collection of parables in Mark 4 and Matthew 13 illustrate the "mystery" of the kingdom of God (Mt 13:11; Mk 4:11). The establishment of the Lord's Supper looks forward to the establishing of the kingdom of God (Mt 26:29; Mk 14:25).

The NT reports two different forms of the expression: "the kingdom of God" and "the kingdom of the heavens." The latter is found only in Matthew; but Matthew also has "the kingdom of God" four times (12:28; 19:24; 21:31,43). "The kingdom of the heavens" is a Semitic phrase that would be meaningful to Jews but would clash on the Greek ear. The Jews, out of reverence for God, avoided uttering the divine name, and contemporary literature gives examples of substituting the word "heaven" for God (1 Mc 3:18,50; 4:10; see Lk 15:18). The plural, "heavens," is used because the corresponding Semitic word is in the plural.

The key to an understanding of the kingdom of God is that the basic meaning of the Greek word *basileia*, as of the Hebrew *malkūt*, is rule, reign, dominion. We frequently find in the OT the expression "in the year of the kingdom of . . . ," meaning in the year of the reign of a given king (e.g., 1 Chr 26:31; 2 Chr 3:2; 15:10; Ezr 7:1; 8:1; Est 2:16; Jer 10:7; 52:31). In some places the RSV translates *malkūt* by the word "reign" (2 Chr 29:19; Ezr 4:5,6; Dn 9:2). When we read that Solomon's "kingdom was firmly established" (1 Kgs 2:12), we are to understand that his authority to reign was settled. The kingdom of Saul was turned over to David (1 Chr 12:23); this indicates that the authority which had been Saul's was given to David; and as a result of having received legal authority, David became king. This abstract idea of *malkūt* is evident when it is found in parallelisms with such abstract ideas as power, might, glory, and dominion (Dn 4:34; 7:14).

When *malkūt* is used of God, it almost always refers to his authority or to his rule as the heavenly king. "They shall speak of the glory of thy kingdom, and tell of thy power. . . . Thy kingdom is an everlasting kingdom, and thy dominion endures throughout all generations" (Ps 145;11,13). "The Lord has established his throne in the heavens, and his kingdom rules over all" (Ps 103:19).

However, if a king rules, there must be a realm or sphere over which he reigns. This is also called *malkūt*. "So the realm of Jehoshaphat was quiet, for his God gave him rest round about" (2 Chr 20:30; see Est 3:6; Jer 10:7; Dn 9:1; 11:9).

This same twofold use of *basileia* is found in the NT. In fact, the RSV translates *basileia* by the expression "kingly power" in Luke 23:42 and by "kingship" in John 18:36. When a nobleman went into a far country to get a "kingdom," he went to the governing authority to get appointment as king (Lk 19:12). When Jesus said, "My kingship is not of this world" (Jn 18:36), he does not mean to say that his rule has nothing to do with the world, but that his kingship—his dominion—does not come from man but from God. Therefore he rejects the use of worldly fighting to gain his ends.

This central meaning of *basileia* makes it easy to understand many sayings in the Gospels. In the Lord's Prayer the petition "Thy kingdom come" (Mt 6:10) is a prayer for God to manifest his reign so that his will be done on earth as it is in heaven. When we read that we are "to receive the kingdom of God like a child" (Mk 10:15), we must open our hearts and lives to the rule of God.

Also in the NT are sayings about being *in* the kingdom or of *entering* the kingdom (Mt 8:11; Mk 9:47; 10:23–25; Lk 13:28). There is no philological or theological objection to understanding "the kingdom of God" first as the divine reign or rule and secondly as the sphere of blessing in which that reign is experienced.

Old Testament Background. The expression "the kingdom of God" is not found in the OT, but the idea appears throughout the prophets. God is frequently spoken of as the King, both of Israel (Ex 15:18; Nm 23:21; Dt 33:5; Is 43:15) and of all the earth (2 Kgs 19:15; Pss 29:10; 47:2; 93:1,2; 96:10; 97:1–9; 99:1–4; 145:11–13; Is 6:5; Jer 46:18). Although God is not the earthly King of Israel, other references speak of a day when God shall become King and shall rule over his people (Is 24:23; 33:22; 52:7; Ob 21; Zep 3:15; Zec 14:9–11).

This brief glimpse of the idea of God's kingship provides the outline for the entire OT concept. While God is King over all the earth, he is in a special way King over his people, Israel. God's rule is therefore something realized in Israel's history. However, it is only partially and imperfectly realized. Israel again and again rebelled against the divine sovereignty. Furthermore, Israel was constantly plagued by wars with its pagan neighbors in which it was not always victorious. Again, there are evils in nature and the physical world which often bring suffering to God's people. Therefore, the prophets look forward to a day when God's rule will be fully experienced, not by Israel alone, but by all the world. The main emphasis of the prophets is on the hope, the establishing of God's perfect rule in the world.

The prophets describe the final establishment of God's kingdom in terms of a theophany—a divine visitation. "For behold, the Lord is coming forth out of his place, and will come down and tread upon the high places of the earth. And the mountains will melt under him and the valleys will be cleft, like wax before the fire, like waters poured down a steep place" (Mi 1:3,4). Zechariah foresees a "day of the Lord" when all nations will be gathered in battle against Jerusalem, when "the Lord will go forth and fight against those nations. . . . Then the Lord your God will come, and all the holy ones with him" (Zec 14:3,5). Israel will be "visited by the Lord of hosts" (Is 29:6) and delivered from its enemies. "Behold, your God . . . will come and save you" (Is 35:4). "And he will come to Zion as Redeemer, to those in Jacob who turn from transgression, says the Lord" (Is 59:20). God's coming will also mean judgment. "For behold, the Lord is coming forth out of his place to punish the inhabitants of the earth for their iniquity" (Is 26:21). Isaiah also pictures men hiding in the caves of the rocks and the holes of the ground; they will "go into the clefts of the rocks, and into the tops of the ragged rocks, for fear of the Lord, and for the glory of his majesty, when he ariseth to shake terribly the earth" (Is 2:21 KJV). "For all the earth shall be devoured with the fire of my jealousy" (Zep 3:8 KJV; see Is 63:1–6; 64:1–7; 65:15,16; Zec 14:3). This final coming of God will mean the salvation of the Gentiles as well as of Israel. "Sing and rejoice, O daughter of Zion; for lo, I come and I will dwell in the midst of you, says the Lord. And many nations shall join themselves to the Lord in that day, and shall be my people; and I will dwell in the midst of you" (Zec 2:10,11; cf. Is 66:18–24).

Behind this language is a distinct theology of "the God who comes." It is a fact widely recognized in contemporary OT theology that the God of the OT is not a nature god like the gods of other peoples, but a God of history—a God who visits his people in history to bless or to judge them. God visited Israel in Egypt to deliver them from bondage and to constitute them as his people. The deliverance from Egypt was not merely an act of God; it was an act through which God made himself known and through which Israel was to know and serve God. "I am the Lord, and I will bring you out from under the burdens of the Egyptians, and I will deliver you from their bondage . . . and you shall know that I am the Lord your God" (Ex 6:6,7). God acts in history not only to save his people but to judge them. "Therefore thus I will do to you, O Israel; because I will do this to you, prepare to meet your God, O Israel!" (Am 4:12). The revelation of God as the Judge of his people in historical events is clearly reflected in the description of Israel's historical defeat by the Assyrians in the Day of the Lord (Am 5:18). Israel's history is different from all other history. While God is the Lord of all history, in one particular series of events he has revealed himself as Savior and Judge. This theology of revelation in history is called *Heilsgeschichte*—redemptive history.

Because God has visited his people again and again in their history, he must finally come to them in the future to judge wickedness and to establish his kingdom. Israel's hope is thus rooted in history, or rather in the God who works in history. God will finally break into history in a glorious theophany to establish his rule in all the earth. The source of the kingdom is not history itself, but God.

The Israelites of Amos' day looked for a kingdom which would arise within history and be effected by historical forces. The popular expectation was that of a day of success, blessing, and prosperity for Israel when the glory of David's kingdom would be restored, and Israel would achieve complete victory over its foes. This is the only OT concept of the kingdom that is strictly "this-worldly" and "historical"; but it was not shared by the prophets. In fact, Amos denounces this as a false view. The Day of the Lord will be darkness and not light, judgment and not vindication, wrath and not blessing (Am 5:18–20). The Day of the Lord which Amos announced will first of all be defeat in history by the Assyrians; but beyond this Amos sees an eschatological visitation which will bring a disruption of the physical order—a cosmic catastrophe caused by God himself. The sun will go down at noon shrouding the earth in darkness at midday (8:9). An apocalyptic fire will first devour the sea and then the land (7:4). This is not to be dismissed as poetic exuberance. What Amos seems to envisage is convulsions of nature on something like a cosmic scale. It is global eschatology. Beyond judgment Amos sees the salvation of Israel (9:11–15).

Here are the raw materials of apocalyptic eschatology developed later by both the intertestamental literature and the NT. The evils that affect both the world and mankind, including God's people, are so great that only an apocalyptic (i.e., cosmic) act of God can effect salvation.

While the prophets visualize the kingdom as coming from God, the kingdom is always on earth. The divine irruption into the natural order is not designed to accomplish its destruction but to make way for a new perfect order arising out of the old imperfect one. The prophets do not present a single consistent picture of the new order. Sometimes the new order is described in very this-worldly terms. "The

mountains shall drip sweet wine, and all the hills shall flow with it" (Am 9:13). On the other hand, God will create new heavens and a new earth (Is 65:17; 66:22), where there will be untroubled joy, prosperity, peace, and righteousness. The final visitation of God will mean the redemption of the world, for a redeemed earth is the scene of the kingdom of God. The prophets look forward again and again to the deliverance of creation "from the bondage to decay." The description is often couched in simple physical terms. The wilderness will become fruitful (Is 32:15); the desert will blossom (35:2); sorrow and sighing will flee away (35:10). The burning sands will be cooled and the dry places become springs of water (35:7); peace will return to the animal world so that all injury and destruction is done away (11:9). All this results because the earth becomes full of the knowledge of God (11:9).

Such language is not mere poetry, but reflects a profound theology of creation. Man as creature was made to dwell on the earth, and the earth shares in human destiny. The main point is that creation as such is good, and not a hindrance to true spirituality, as was often true in Greek thought. Redemption always includes redemption of the earth, which then becomes the blessed environment God intended it to be. Salvation does not mean deliverance from creaturehood, for this is not an evil thing but an essential and permanent element of man's true being. Salvation does not mean escape from bodily creaturely existence, as in some Greek thought. On the contrary, ultimate redemption will mean the redemption of the whole person. The emergence of the doctrine of bodily resurrection is a reflection of this theology of creaturehood. The corollary of this is that creation in its entirety must share in the blessing of redemption.

A distinctive element in prophetic eschatology is the tension between history and eschatology. By this is meant that as the prophets looked into the future, they saw an immediate historical judgment and a more remote eschatological visitation. For Amos, the Day of the Lord is both the immediate judgment of Israel by the Assyrians and a final eschatological salvation. Joel sees an imminent historical visitation of drought and locusts, but beyond this he sees the eschatological Day of the Lord. Zephaniah sees an imminent Day of the Lord in some undesignated historical visitation (Zep 1:2–18), but beyond it he sees the salvation of the Gentiles (3:9). The same God who acts in history to bless and judge his people will act at the end of history in an eschatological act of judgment and salvation. The prophets do not sharply distinguish between these two days, for it is one and the same God who is concerned to judge and save his people.

The eschatological hope of the prophets is always an ethical hope. That is to say, the prophets are not interested in the future for its own sake, but only for the impact of the future on the present. The prophetic predictions were given that in light of future judgment and salvation, Israel might be confronted in the present by the will of God. "Prepare to meet your God, O Israel" (Am 4:12) might well be taken as the keynote of all the prophets.

In the Jewish Apocalypses. In NT times there emerged in Judaism certain circles which developed an apocalyptic view of history. They provided such writings as the five parts of 1 Enoch, the Assumption of Moses, 4 Ezra, and the Apocalypse of Baruch. These books are of importance to NT study, for they provide a bridge between the OT and the NT concepts of the kingdom of God.

The apocalypses were written to answer the problems of theodicy (the justice of God). After the days of Ezra, the Law assumed a more important role in the life of the people than before. In prophetic times Israel again and again apostatized from the Law and worshiped foreign gods. The primary message of the prophets was to challenge Israel to get right with God and to turn in repentance to keep the Law. After Ezra and throughout NT times, Israel was obedient to the Law as never before. The Jews abhorred idolatry and faithfully worshiped God. Still the kingdom did not come. Instead came the fearful persecution in the Maccabean times by Antiochus IV Epiphanes, the worldly rule of the Hasmoneans, Pompey and Roman hegemony, and in AD 66–70, the siege and destruction of Jerusalem. Where was God? Why did he not deliver his faithful people? Why did the kingdom not come? The apocalypses were written to answer questions like these.

One of the most important elements in apocalyptic religion is an explicit dualism, expressed as "this age" and "the age to come." The prophets contrasted the present time with the future when the kingdom of God would be established. The apocalyptists radicalized this contrast. Twice we find fragments of this idiom in 1 Enoch. We meet the fully developed idiom in 4 Ezra and the Apocalypse of Baruch (late 1st century AD). "The Most High has made not one age but two" (4 Ez 7:50); "the day of judgment shall be the end of this age and the beginning of the eternal age that is to come" (4 Ez 7:113); "this age the Most High has made for many but the age to come for few" (4 Ez 8:1; see also Apoc Bar 14:13; 15:7; Pirke Aboth 4:1,21,22; 6:4,7). Furthermore, the transition from this age to the age to come can

The southeast corner of the platform of the temple destroyed in AD 70, a destruction that stimulated the writing of some Jewish apocalyptists.

be accomplished only by a cosmic act of God. In the apocryphal Assumption of Moses there is no messianic personage; it is God alone who comes to redeem Israel. In the Similitudes of Enoch the transition is accomplished with the coming of a heavenly, preexistent Son of man. In 4 Ezra we find a conflation of the concepts of Davidic Messiah and the Son of man.

Apocalyptic differs from OT prophetic religion in that it is pessimistic about the present age. It would be wrong to describe the apocalypses as ultimately pessimistic, for their basic message is that in due time God will intervene and save his people. But for the present, as long as this age lasts, he has removed himself from intervening in Israel's affairs. The present age is under the power of evil angelic and demonic forces and is irretrievably evil. God has abandoned this age to evil; salvation can be expected only in the age to come.

The apocalyptists lost completely the tension between history and eschatology. They no longer expected any deliverance in this age. God had in fact become the God of the future, not of the present.

In the dream-visions of Enoch (1 Enoch 83–

90) God faithfully guided Israel throughout its history. Then God withdrew his personal leadership, forsook the temple, and surrendered his people to be torn and devoured. God "remained unmoved, though he saw it, and rejoiced that they were devoured and swallowed and robbed, and left them to be devoured in the hand of all the beasts" (1 Enoch 89:58). After the Babylonian captivity God was conceived to be inactive in history. History was surrendered to evil. All salvation was thrust into the future.

In the Synoptic Gospels. *Dualism.* Jesus' teachings about the kingdom of God embodied the same contrast between the present order and the future age as the prophets, and he expressed it in the idiom "this age and the age to come." This fact is obscured in the KJV, which translates the word for "age" by "world." These are, however, two different concepts. A rich man asked Jesus what he must do to inherit eternal life (Mk 10:17). The context makes it clear that he was asking about eschatological life—the life of the resurrection (Dn 12:2). Jesus speaks of the difficulty of entering the kingdom of God. (The parallel passage in Matthew has both "kingdom of God" and "kingdom of the heaven" [19:23,24], proving that they are interchangeable terms.) In their reaction the disciples ask, "Then who can be saved?" Jesus' answer contrasts the lot of his disciples "in this time" with the "age to come" (Mk 10:29,30) when they would inherit eternal life. It is clear from this passage that in some sense the kingdom of God, the kingdom of the heavens, salvation, and eternal life all belong to the age to come. So far as this saying is concerned, apart from the age to come, God's people will not experience eternal life.

The dualistic terminology also appears in Mark 4:19 in the parable of the sower. "The cares of the age," the concern for security, wealth, recognition, which characterize this age, so oppose the word of the kingdom of God that it can be choked and become unfruitful. The character of this age is hostile to the kingdom of God.

A saying in Luke contrasts "the sons of this age" with "the sons of light" (Lk 16:8). While these expressions have no parallel in the rabbinic writings, we find "the sons of light" contrasted with "the sons of darkness" in the Qumran literature. Although it appears frequently in the synoptic Gospels (Mt 5:14; Lk 22:53), in John the contrast between light and darkness becomes a central theme in Jesus' teaching. In this Lukan saying, this age is in darkness; light belongs to the age to come.

In Luke's account (20:34,35) of Jesus' discussion with the Sadducees about the resurrec-tion, he includes this dualistic terminology: "The sons of this age marry and are given in marriage; but those who are accounted worthy to attain to that age and to the resurrection from the dead" will no longer die but will be imperishable, like the angels. Death belongs to this age; therefore marriage is an absolutely necessary institution. But the age to come will be the age of eternal life when men will no longer die but will enter upon a new level of existence: immortal life.

Matthew alone records the expression "the close of the age." This age will be terminated by the coming of the Son of man (Mt 24:3) and by the judgment of men (13:39–42). Then the righteous will be separated from the wicked (13:49). The same expression occurs in the promise of the risen Jesus assuring his disciples of his presence to the consummation of the age (28:20). It follows that if this age is to come to its consummation, it must be followed by another age—the age to come.

The eschatological kingdom will be inaugurated by an apocalyptic event—the glorious coming of the Son of man. This is made clear by two of the parables about the kingdom of God. In the parable of the tares, "the Son of man will send his angels, and they will gather out of his kingdom all causes of sin and all evildoers, and throw them into the furnace of fire" (Mt 13:41). The parable of the sheep and goats reflects the same eschatology. "When the Son of man comes in his glory," he will sit on his glorious throne to judge the nations, separating the sheep from the goats. The righteous—the sheep—are to "inherit the kingdom prepared for you from the foundation of the world"; and entrance into the kingdom is synonymous with entrance into life (Mt 25:31–46).

The eschatological character of the kingdom of God is seen also in the other two parables of Matthew 25. "The kingdom of heaven shall be compared to ten maidens who took their lamps and went to meet the bridegroom" (v 1). However, five of them were foolish and did not provide an adequate supply of oil for their lamps. Thus they were late for the wedding and were excluded from the wedding feast—a symbol of the eschatological kingdom—while those properly prepared entered the kingdom. In the same way the two faithful servants who had been "faithful over a little" were granted to "enter into the joy of your master" (vv 21,23), while the unfaithful servant was excluded from the kingdom and cast into outer darkness.

Jesus almost never showed any interest in descriptions of the eschatological kingdom, but it is clear that its coming is constantly in his thought. The pure in heart will see God

(Mt 5:8). The harvest will take place and the grain will be gathered into the barn (Mt 13:30,39; Mk 4:29). Jesus frequently used the metaphor of a feast or table fellowship to describe life in the eschatological kingdom. He will drink wine again with his disciples in the kingdom of God. They will eat and drink at Jesus' table in the kingdom (Lk 22:30). People will be gathered from all corners of the earth to sit at table with the OT saints (Mt 8:11,12; Lk 13:29). The consummation is likened to a wedding feast (Mt 22:1–14) and a banquet (Lk 14:16–24). All of these metaphors picture the restoration of communion between God and men which has been broken by sin.

In most of the sayings cited to illustrate the future character of the kingdom, "kingdom" refers to the eschatological order—the eschaton, the age to come. However, when Jesus taught his disciples to pray, "Thy kingdom come" (Mt 6:10), he was not referring to the new eschatological order; he was referring to the kingdom as God's kingly rule, his reign. It is a prayer that God will effectively establish his sovereign rule in the world.

The coming of God's kingdom—God's sovereign rule—will issue in the new order—the eschaton. This will see the end of this age and the inauguration of the age to come.

A further element in the dualism of Jesus' teaching is the role of Satan in this age. Paul characterizes this situation by speaking of Satan as the "god of this age" whose object it is to keep men under his control by holding them in the darkness of unbelief. This dualistic pattern is reflected in Jesus' temptation when Satan showed him all the nations of the world in a moment of time and said, "All this power will I give thee, and the glory of them: for that is delivered unto me; and to whomsoever I will I give it" (Lk 4:6 KJV). Such a saying cannot be taken in an ultimate sense; God forever remains the "king of the ages" (1 Tm 1:17). However, throughout the NT, including the teachings of Jesus, this age is viewed as an age in which Satan has been permitted in the sovereign purpose of God to exercise a tragic sway over humanity. He is referred to as a strongly armed man who guards his house (Mk 3:27). Men must be saved from his power (Mt 6:13; the word "evil" may well be masculine, as the RSV margin notes). He may take possession of the wills of men and cause them to perpetrate monstrous evil, as in the case of Judas' betrayal of Jesus (Lk 22:3). He is eager to bring testings upon Jesus' disciples (Lk 22:31) and constantly aims to frustrate the working of God's kingdom among men (Mt 13:37–39; Mk 4:14,15). Disease may be described as a bondage to Satan (Lk 13:16). Matthew 12:26 speaks of Satan's kingdom as a realm, and the demons who are able to take possession of men are his "angels" (Mt 25:41). The tragedy of those who are outside the sway of God's rule is described by the phrase "sons of the evil one" (Mt 13:38). This does not refer to particular sinfulness but only to the fact that so far as the controlling principle of life is concerned, it is satanic rather than of God.

Only the age to come will witness the destruction of Satan. While no description of the place of punishment occurs in the Gospels as it often does in Jewish literature, there is an eternal fire which is prepared for the devil and his angels (Mt 25:41; cf. Rv 20:10). Reference to this judgment is found in Mark 1:24, when the demons ask Jesus if he has come to destroy them. That there are so few references in the Gospels to the eschatological destruction of the devil is due to the important fact that the center of interest is not the future but the present. Nevertheless, the pattern is clear. Satan is the "god of this age." Until God destroys Satan and his power, the new age cannot come; or better, when the kingdom of God comes, Satan will be destroyed, and this age of evil and death will give way to the age to come and eternal life.

The Kingdom as Present. In his teaching about the kingdom of God as the apocalyptic consummation, Jesus does not differ essentially from the OT prophets. The most distinctive element in Jesus' teaching—indeed, the fact that characterizes his entire mission and message—is the fact that in some real sense of the word, the kingdom of God has come in history in an utterly unexpected way. This sets Jesus' teaching apart from all contemporary Jewish thought.

This is seen first of all in his repeated teaching that his mission is a fulfillment of the OT messianic prophets. Mark summarizes Jesus' message with the words, "The time is fulfilled, and the kingdom of God is at hand; repent, and believe in the gospel" (1:15). This saying can have one of two meanings. It may refer to the imminent coming of the apocalyptic kingdom. Matthew summarizes the message of John the Baptist with nearly the same words: "Repent, for the kingdom of heaven is at hand" (3:2). The Baptist expounds what he means by the approach of the kingdom of God: "His winnowing fork is in his hand, and he will clear his threshing floor and gather his wheat into the granary, but the chaff he will burn with unquenchable fire" (Mt 3:12). John proclaimed an apocalyptic act; "unquenchable fire" can mean no strictly historical event but only an apocalyptic judgment. John expected Jesus to be the one in whom the cosmic event expected by the prophets and apocalyptists would be carried out.

It is possible that this was also Jesus' meaning. However, another interpretation is possible which is better supported by the actual course of his mission: "The time is fulfilled." The messianic promises of the prophets were not only about to be fulfilled; they were actually in process of fulfillment in his mission. In Jesus, God was visiting his people. The hope of the prophets in some real sense was being realized.

The meaning of this can be seen in Luke's introduction of Jesus' ministry. Luke selects an event which occurred in Nazareth later in Jesus' ministry (4:16–21) and places it at the beginning of his Gospel in order to sound this note of fulfillment. Jesus read from Isaiah a promise that looked forward to the messianic salvation: "The Spirit of the Lord is upon me, because he has anointed me to preach the good news to the poor. He has sent me to proclaim release to the captives and recovering of sight to the blind, to set at liberty those who are oppressed, to proclaim the acceptable year of the Lord" (Lk 4:18,19). Then Jesus astonished his audience by the assertion, "Today this scripture has been fulfilled in your hearing" (4:21).

Here was an amazing claim. John the Baptist had announced an apocalyptic visitation of God that would mean the fulfillment of the eschatological hope and the consummation of the messianic age. Jesus proclaimed that the messianic promise was actually being fulfilled in his person. This is no apocalyptic kingdom but a present salvation. In these words Jesus did not proclaim the imminence of the apocalyptic kingdom. Rather, he boldly announced that the kingdom of God had come. The presence of the kingdom was a happening, an event, the gracious action of God. This was no new theology or new idea or new promise; it was a new event in history.

The note of fulfillment is again sounded in Jesus' answer to the question about fasting. "Can the wedding guests fast while the bridegroom is with them? As long as they have the bridegroom with them, they cannot fast" (Mk 2:19). The marriage feast had become a metaphor in Judaism for the messianic consummation. In these words Jesus announced the presence of the messianic time of salvation. It would be a contradiction in terms for the disciples to fast when they were enjoying the blessings of the messianic age. The time of fulfillment had come.

A saying found in different contexts in Matthew and Luke touches this central note of the fulfillment in history of the OT hope: "Blessed are the eyes which see what you see! For I tell you that many prophets and kings desired to see what you see, and did not see it, and to hear what you hear, and did not hear it" (Lk 10:23,24; cf. Mt 13:16,17). Both Matthew and Luke associate this saying with the kingdom of God, and both agree that the hope of former generations has become an object of experience. Many prophets and kings looked forward to something; but they looked in vain, for it did not come to them. What they longed for has now come, and this can be nothing less than the promised messianic salvation.

Fulfillment in history is again asserted in Jesus' answer to John's question about the one who is to come (Mt 11:2,3). "The deeds of the Christ"(Messiah) were not the deeds John had announced. Wicked rulers like Herod were not being judged in fire. Instead, Jesus was helping people, not bringing an apocalyptic kingdom. Jesus replied in words which echo the promise of the messianic salvation in Isaiah 35:5,6: "Go and tell John what you hear and see: the blind receive their sight and the lame walk, lepers are cleansed and the deaf hear, and the dead are raised up, and the poor have the gospel preached to them" (Mt 11:4,5). In these words Jesus claimed that the blessings of the messianic salvation are present. There was indeed reason for John's perplexity, for the fulfillment was not taking place along expected lines. The apocalyptic consummation did not appear to be on the horizon. The point of Jesus' answer was that fulfillment was taking place without the eschatological consummation. Therefore Jesus pronounced a special blessing upon those who were not offended by the character of the messianic fulfillment (Mt 11:6). The fulfillment was indeed taking place, but not the apocalyptic consummation.

The most unambiguous statement of the presence of the kingdom is found in the word about the binding of Satan. One of Jesus' most characteristic acts was the exorcism of demons—deliverance from satanic power. The Pharisees admitted his power but attributed it to Satan. Jesus replied, "If Satan cast out Satan, he is divided against himself; how then will his kingdom stand? . . . But if it is by the Spirit of God that I cast out demons, then the kingdom of God is come unto you" (Mt 12:26, 28). Here the verb has the clear meaning "to have come, to arrive" (Rom 9:30; 2 Cor 10:14; Phil 3:16). Here is a clear affirmation that the kingdom of God has come among men.

In explanation Jesus said, "Or how can one enter a strong man's house and plunder his goods, unless he first binds the strong man? Then indeed he may plunder his house" (Mt 12:29). The strong man is Satan; this "present evil age" (Gal 1:4) is his "house"; his "goods" are demon-possessed men and women. Jesus has invaded the strong man's house to snatch away from him men and women whom he has in his power; and this is the work of the kingdom of God. The kingly reign of God has come into history in the person of Jesus before the apocalyptic consummation when Satan will be destroyed, to render Satan a preliminary defeat. Jesus has already "bound" Satan (i.e., curbed his power). This has been accomplished by the presence of the kingdom of God in the mission of Jesus.

A similar saying is found in Luke 10:18. Jesus had sent a band of his disciples on a preaching mission. Like Jesus, they were to proclaim the nearness of the kingdom of God (Lk 10:9). They too were to exorcise demons. When they returned to Jesus to report their success, Jesus said, "I saw Satan fall like lightning from heaven." This again is metaphorical language which asserts that in the mission of Jesus' disciples as well as in Jesus himself, Satan has fallen from his place of power. Both "binding" and "falling" are metaphors which describe the same truth: the victory of the kingdom of God over Satan.

Here is the element that sets Jesus apart from the OT and from all of contemporary Judaism. The prophets conceived of the kingdom being established by a heavenly supernatural being (Dn 7) or ruled by a powerful Davidic messianic king (Is 9,11). The fulfillment of the messianic hope is everywhere in the prophets an eschatological hope. The same is true of the Jewish writers who despaired of history and cast all hope into the future. The rabbis to be sure had a doctrine of a present kingdom. When a convert turned to Judaism and accepted the Law, he took upon himself the yoke of the kingdom—the divine sovereignty. The daily repetition of the *Shema* with the reading of Deuteronomy 6:4–10 was regarded as repeatedly taking upon oneself the yoke of the sovereignty of God. However, in all this God was not dynamically active. He had given Israel the Law; he was always ready to receive repentant sinners. But assuming the yoke of the Law was a human activity. God will come in his kingdom only at the apocalyptic visitation at the end of the age.

In contrast to all that had gone before him, Jesus proclaimed the kingdom of God as an event taking place in his own person and mission. God had again assumed the initiative; God was acting. No first-century Jew had any idea of the kingdom of God coming into history in the person of an ordinary man—a teacher who was meek and lowly.

The presence of the kingdom is further seen in the fact that the rule of God, present in Jesus, is a gift to be received. This is also true of the kingdom in its eschatological consummation, where the kingdom is freely inherited by the righteous (Mt 25:34). In answer to the young man's question about inheriting eternal life (Mk 10:17), Jesus spoke of entering the kingdom (10:23–24) and receiving the gift of eternal life (10:30) as though they were synonymous. The kingdom is a gift which the Father is pleased to bestow upon the little flock of Jesus' disciples (Lk 12:32).

If God's eschatological rule brings to his people the blessings of that kingdom, and if God's kingdom is his rule invading history before the eschatological consummation, then we may expect God's rule in the present to bring a preliminary blessing to his people. This fact is reflected in numerous sayings. The kingdom is something to be sought here and now (Mt 6:33) and to be received as children receive a gift (Mk 10:15; Lk 18:16,17). Although it is present in an unexpected form, the kingdom of God in Jesus' person is like a hidden treasure or a pearl of great price whose possession outranks all other goods (Mt 13:44–46). The gift of the kingdom is also seen in that the deaf hear, the blind see, lepers are cleansed, and the poor have good news preached to them (Mt 11:5).

The Mystery of the Kingdom. A "mystery" is a divine truth, hidden in the heart of God, but in due time revealed to men (see Rom 16:25,26). The mystery of the kingdom (Mt 13:11; Mk 4:11) is precisely this: that prior to its eschatological consummation, the kingdom has come in an unexpected form in the historical mission of Jesus. This mystery is illustrated in Jesus' parables (Mt 13; Mk 4). Modern scholarship recognizes two critical norms in interpreting the parables. First, a parable is not an allegory but a story taken from daily life, teaching essentially a single truth. Secondly, the parables must be interpreted in the life setting of Jesus' mission.

The parable in Mark 4:26–29 is not a parable of stages of growth but an illustration that "the earth produces of itself" (v 28). The kingdom is God's reign—a supernatural thing, not a human work.

The parable of the four soils (Mt 13:3–9,18–23) does not intend to teach that there are precisely four kinds of hearers of the word of the kingdom. The central truth is that the word of the kingdom must be *received;* otherwise it does not bear fruit. In other words, the kingdom as Jesus proclaimed and embodied it requires a human response to be effective.

The parable of the wheat and weeds (Mt 13:24–30) teaches that the kingdom of God has actually come into history without effecting the eschatological judgment which will separate the good from the bad. Both are to grow together in the world (v 38) until the day of judgment when the eschatological separation will take place.

The parables of the mustard seed and

leaven (Mt 13:31–33) are parables of contrast between present insignificance and future magnificence. The emphasis is not upon how the kingdom progresses from small beginnings. Jesus never spoke of the growth of the reign of God. What is now like a tiny seed—a Galilean prophet and a handful of followers—will one day be like a great tree.

The parables of the treasure and pearl (Mt 13:44–46) teach that this apparently insignificant appearance of the kingdom in Jesus nevertheless merits every effort to attain it.

The parable of the net (Mt 13:47–50) teaches that the movement set up by the presence of the kingdom in Jesus brings together a mixed people. Jesus' disciples even harbored a traitor. There will nevertheless be an eschatological separation.

The Kingdom and the Church. Matthew records a saying of Jesus about his church. Speaking to Peter, Jesus said, "You are Peter, and on this rock I will build my church, and the powers of death shall not prevail against it. I will give you the keys of the kingdom of heaven, and whatever you bind on earth shall be bound in heaven, and whatever you loose on earth shall be loosed in heaven" (Mt 16:18,19). "Church" (*ekklēsia*) in this context is not to be interpreted in light of subsequent history, but against the OT background and in the context of Jesus' mission. *Ekklēsia* is often used in the Septuagint for the assembling of Israel as the people of God (Dt 4:10; 9:10; 10:4; 18:16). Jesus often spoke of people entering or being in the kingdom (Mt 11:11; Lk 16:16; see Mt 21:31; 23:13; cf. Lk 11:52). He calls those who receive the word of the kingdom "the sons of the kingdom" (Mt 13:38); in another place he calls them a "little flock" (Lk 12:32) who are to inherit the eschatological kingdom. By *ekklēsia* Jesus means a new people of God without reference to their structure or organization—a new Israel. In Jesus' day it was his relatively small band of disciples, who were bound together only by loyalty to Jesus.

The church is not the kingdom. The kingdom is the rule of God and the sphere in which his rule is experienced. In this age it is an altogether invisible, spiritual realm (cf. Col 1:13); at the eschatological consummation the sphere of his rule will be universal. The church is the people of the kingdom—those who have received the kingdom of God (Mk 10:15) and thereby have entered into the blessings of God's rule (Mt 11:11). It is the action of God's kingdom—God's rule in Jesus—which creates the church. The church witnesses to the kingdom (Mt 24:14; Lk 10:9). The church is the instrument of the kingdom in the world. As the kingdom worked through Jesus, and then through his commissioned disciples, so the kingdom will continue to work through the successes of his disciples. The church will be in conflict with "the powers of death," but the church will prevail because it is the instrument of the kingdom, the reign of God.

The church is custodian of the kingdom. In rabbinic thought Israel was the custodian of the kingdom of God because to Israel had been committed the Law. The church is to become the custodian of the kingdom (cf. Mt 24:14). The church will thereby be the instrument for the releasing of sins or for their retention (cf. Jn 20:23). The kingdom will be taken away from Israel, the natural "sons of the kingdom" (Mt 8:12), and given to a new people (Mt 21:43; Mk 12:9).

Conclusion. Jesus was an apocalyptist in that his teachings carry the structure of apocalyptic dualism and an age to come to be inaugurated by a divine cosmic event. However, he stands apart from the Jewish writers, but agrees with the prophets, in that his primary concern is not the future for its own sake but the present ethical and spiritual state of the people. Furthermore, he has recovered the tension between history and eschatology. He announced the judgments of God in history, as had the prophets (Mt 11:21–24; 23:38; Mk 12:9; Lk 21:24). A study of the discourse on the Mt of Olives reveals that he blended together in a way we cannot critically dissect the historical fall of Jerusalem (Lk 21:20) and the eschatological antichrist (Mt 24:15). In fact, the whole gospel differs from Jewish apocalyptic in that it conceives of the coming of the eschatological kingdom *only* because the kingdom had first come in history in the person and mission of Jesus.

In the Rest of the New Testament. *John.* In the Gospel of John the concept of eternal life takes the place of the kingdom of God in Jesus' teaching. The kingdom of God is mentioned twice (3:3,5), and it is placed in connection with eternal life. The kingdom of God is here the eschatological kingdom, and eternal life is the life of the kingdom. Thus, as the kingdom of God in the synoptic Gospels is both future and present, so eternal life is both the life of the age to come (12:25) and also a present blessing (3:16, etc.).

Acts. Acts represents the earliest disciples as failing to understand Jesus' message about the kingdom of God as a present spiritual blessing. They gathered together to await the coming of the eschatological kingdom to Israel (1:6). Acts relates that the disciples continued to preach the kingdom of God, but usually it is an eschatological blessing (8:12; 14:22; 19:8; 20:25; 28:23,31). However, the last two references make the kingdom of God synonymous with the gospel about Jesus Christ.

One important theme in Acts is linked to that of the kingdom of God. On the day of Pentecost, Peter announces that God has seated Jesus at his right hand in fulfillment of Psalm 110:1 (Acts 2:33–35). In the psalms this is a prophecy of the enthronement of the Davidic king in Jerusalem. Peter asserts that this prophecy is now fulfilled in the heavenly session of Jesus. Therefore he has been made both Lord and Christ (Messiah). These are interchangeable terms, Lord meaning absolute sovereign, Christ meaning the messianic king.

Paul. Paul carried further this theme of the heavenly rule of Christ, the anointed king. The kingdom is both an eschatological inheritance (1 Cor 6:9; 15:50; Gal 5:21; Eph 5:5; 1 Thes 2:12; 2 Thes 1:5; 2 Tm 4:1,18) and a present blessing into which believers now enter (Rom 14:17; Col 1:13). The key to this is the interchangeable character of lordship and messianic kingship. Jesus is now exalted as Lord over all (Phil 2:11), and even if his lordship is invisible, it will become manifest to all at his second coming. In the same way, he has been enthroned as messianic king by virtue of his resurrection and heavenly session, and he must reign as king "until he has put all his enemies under his feet" (1 Cor 15:25; Eph 1:22). The last enemy to be destroyed is death.

Revelation. The central message of the Revelation to John is the consummation of God's redemptive purpose, when the kingdom of this world becomes the kingdom of our Lord and of his Christ (11:15). Revelation pictures the plight of a persecuted church in a hostile world, but assures the church that Christ has already won a victory over the powers of evil (5:5), by virtue of which he can finally destroy them (19:11–20:14). Again, the last enemy to be destroyed is death (20:13,14). Revelation closes with a highly symbolic picture of the kingdom of God (21,22) when God comes to dwell among his people, and "they shall see his face" (22:4). Thus the NT ends: divine order restored to a disordered world. This is the kingdom of God.

GEORGE E. LADD

See JESUS CHRIST, LIFE AND TEACHING OF; PARABLE; AGE, AGES; APOCALYPTIC.

Bibliography. G.E. Ladd, *Jesus and the Kingdom;* G. Lundström, *The Kingdom of God in the Teaching of Jesus;* A. J. McClain, *The Greatness of the Kingdom;* R. Schnackenburg, *God's Rule and Kingdom;* E.F. Scott, *The Kingdom of God in the NT* and *The Kingdom and the Messiah;* G. Vos, *The Teaching of Jesus Concerning the Kingdom of God and the Church.*

Kings, Books of First and Second.

Books continuing the history of the covenant people as recorded in Joshua, Judges, and the Books of Samuel. The record in Kings begins with the events at the end of David's reign (1 Kgs 1,2). It continues through the reign of Solomon (1 Kgs 2–11); the disruption of the united monarchy (1 Kgs 11,12); the histories of the divided kingdoms (1 Kgs 12–2 Kgs 17); and the history of the surviving kingdom in the south, through its fall in 586 BC and the subsequent kindness shown Jehoiachin by Evil-merodach, king of Babylon, around 561 BC.

Authorship and Date. Kings was originally regarded as one book in the Hebrew canon; the division into two books of approximately equal length appeared first in the Septuagint and finally entered the Hebrew Bible in the 15th century AD.

The book itself is anonymous, and information about its author can only be deduced by examining the concerns and perspectives of the work. The Babylonian Talmud (*Baba Bathra* 15a) attributes Kings to Jeremiah. Although this identification could have arisen from the tendency of later Jewish tradition to assign biblical books to prophetic authors, the theory of origin in prophetic circles fits the evidence quite well. Substantial portions are given to the lives of the prophets: 16 of 47 chapters are devoted to the lives of Elijah and Elisha (1 Kgs 17–2 Kgs 10), and there is considerable interest in other prophetic figures such as Ahijah (1 Kgs 11:29–39; 14:1–16), an unnamed man of God (1 Kgs 13:1–10), and Micaiah (1 Kgs 22:13–28). Possible dependence on Isaiah (2 Kgs 18–20; Is 36–39) and Jeremiah (2 Kgs 24,25; Jer 52) also suggest prophetic origin. The author/compiler also shows intense concern with the efficacy of the prophetic word, frequently calling attention to the fulfillment of words spoken earlier by the prophets.

One might initially think that such a history would be unlikely for a prophet, but the evidence is to the contrary. The prophets were the guardians of the covenant relationship, and are known to have produced accounts used as sources by other biblical historians. The following are among such sources: the acts of Samuel the seer, the acts of Nathan the prophet, the acts of Gad the seer (1 Chr 29:29); the acts of Nathan the prophet, the prophecy of Ahijah the Shilonite, the visions of Iddo the seer (2 Chr 9:29); the chronicles of Shemaiah the prophet and of Iddo the seer (2 Chr 12:15); the annotations of the prophet Iddo (2 Chr 13:22); the acts of Uzziah by Isaiah the prophet (2 Chr 26:22). Add to this the fact that Kings is positioned in the Hebrew canon in the Former Prophets, and a consistent picture of prophetic origin emerges.

The date of the final part of the book must be after the last events recorded. Evil-merodach's kindness toward Jehoiachin (c. 561) is the terminus of the book and therefore fixes the earliest date. Since the work shows no knowledge of the restoration period, a date before 539 is probable. The author's selection of his data to answer the burning theological questions of the exilic community also suggests a date between 561 and 539 BC.

Composition and Contents. The compiler of Kings specifically names three of the sources that he used in his work, and biblical scholars have suggested the presence of a number of other sources which may have been cited. Of course, the sources not mentioned specifically by the compiler are only the speculations of those who have studied his work and can have only varying degrees of probability. The sources both specified and alleged are as follows:

The Book of the Acts of Solomon (1 Kgs 11:41). This source contained additional information about "the rest of the acts of Solomon, all that he did, and his wisdom." Presumably additional materials of a biographical nature were included, specifically accounts similar to the judgment between the two mothers (3:16–28) or the visit of the queen of Sheba (10:1–10). There has been debate as to whether these materials were official court records or nonofficial documents. Some scholars have attempted to isolate further materials within this section by identifying descriptions of the buildings as from temple archives (1 Kgs 6,7) and lists of administrators as from administrative documents (1 Kgs 4,5), but this must remain speculative.

The Book of the Chronicles of the Kings of Israel. This source is mentioned 17 times in Kings, usually in the closing formulas at the end of the account of the reign of a northern king. Some idea of the nature of these chronicles can be derived from looking at the type of information to which the compiler refers his readers. The reader was to go there for more information about "the rest of the acts of Jeroboam, how he warred and how he reigned" (1 Kgs 14:19); "the rest of the acts of Omri . . . and [his] might" (16:27); "the rest of the acts of Ahab, and all that he did, and the ivory house which he built, and all the cities that he built" (22:39); "the rest of the acts of Joash, . . . and [his] might with which he fought against Amaziah king of Judah" (2 Kgs 13:12); "the rest of the acts of Jeroboam, . . . how he fought, and how he recovered for Israel Damascus and Hamath" (2 Kgs 14:28). These passages suggest that this source was the official annals covering the reigns of the kings.

The Book of the Chronicles of the Kings of Judah. This source is mentioned in 15 passages, and as with the kings of Israel, is found in the concluding formulas to the accounts of the reigns. This source was to be consulted for

additional details on individuals' reigns, such as "the acts of Asa, all his might, and all that he did, and the cities which he built" (1 Kgs 15:23); "the acts of Jehoshaphat, and his might that he showed, and how he warred" (22:45); "the deeds of Hezekiah, . . . how he made the pool and the conduit and brought water into the city" (2 Kgs 20:20); "the acts of Manasseh, and all that he did, and the sin that he committed"(21:17).

These sources for the histories of the two kingdoms were probably similar to the annals known from the surrounding cultures, particularly from the reigns of Assyrian kings. They were likely official court histories kept in Samaria and Jerusalem.

In addition to these explicitly mentioned sources, scholars have suggested the compiler drew on other sources that he does not name.

Davidic Court History. Second Samuel 9–20 is often identified as a unit of material in the composition of the Books of Samuel; it is variously called "the court history" or "the succession narrative." Because of similar vocabulary and outlook, 1 Kings 1,2 are often associated with this material from Samuel. The statement of 1 Kings 2:46, "so the kingdom was established in the hand of Solomon," is taken to be the end of this record.

Sources for the House of Ahab. The reigns of individual kings are ordinarily given only brief notices; for example, the father of Ahab, Omri, is given eight verses, even though when judged by political and economic significance he was among the greatest of the northern kings (1 Kgs 16:21–28). However, beginning with the reign of Ahab the record becomes quite expansive, and extensive coverage is given the dynasty of Ahab through the coup by Jehu (1 Kgs 16–2 Kgs 12). The use of the stereotyped formulas for the reigns is suspended in this material, and the existence of other literature used by the compiler is probable. This material is commonly subdivided into further sources for the lives of Elijah and Elisha and the reign of Ahab.

The Elijah section covers material in the following chapters: 1 Kings 17–19, including the feeding by the ravens, the incidents with the widow of Zarephath, the drought, the fire on Carmel, and the revelation of God at Sinai; 1 Kings 21, the affair of Naboth's vineyard; 2 Kings 1, the death of Ahaziah's messengers. The reign of Ahab, which gets so much attention in Kings, is primarily a backdrop for the accounts concerning Elijah.

The Elisha material found in 2 Kings 2–13 may have had an independent literary development from that of the Elijah accounts. It includes the following: 2 Kings 2 (Elisha's succession to the prophetic office, the purifica-

Samaria, where famine and then miraculous relief occurred in Elisha's time (2 Kgs 7).

tion of a spring, the death of mocking children); 2 Kings 3 (on the campaign against Moab); 2 Kings 4 (the widow's oil, the Shunammite woman); 2 Kings 5 (Naaman's leprosy); 2 Kings 6 (the Aramaean attempt to capture Elisha); 2 Kings 7 (the famine in Samaria); 2 Kings 8 (the Shunammite's property, the coup of Hazael); 2 Kings 9 (the anointing of Jehu); 2 Kings 13 (the death of Elisha). No other portion of the OT takes the sheer delight in the miraculous that is seen in the Elisha narratives.

In 1 Kings 16–2 Kings 13 there are additional incidents not directly related to the biographies of Elijah and Elisha; accounts such as the military campaigns of 1 Kings 20:1–34 and further details of Jehu's coup (2 Kings 9:11–10:36) are often attributed to a third source containing accounts of the dynasty of Ahab and his successors. In all three of these possible sources the orientation is toward affairs in the northern kingdom.

Isaiah Source. The account of the reign of Hezekiah contains a section (2 Kgs 18:13–20:19) that is nearly a verbatim citation of material also found in Isaiah (Is 36:1–39:8). The section records the invasion of Sennacherib, the mission of the Rabshakeh, Hezekiah's prayer, Isaiah's prophecy, Hezekiah's illness, the regression of the sun, and the envoys from Merodach-baladan. The material must be regarded as based on the Book of Isaiah or some other source used in both Isaiah and Kings.

A Prophetic Source. Because Kings shows great interest in the prophets and their ministries, various scholars have suggested yet another source was used by the compiler; this would be an independent literary unit containing accounts of the prophets. This source would have contained the records for the material on Ahijah (1 Kgs 11:29–39; 14:1–16), unnamed prophets (1 Kgs 12; 20:35–43), Micaiah (1 Kgs 22:13–28), and other references.

Apart from the sources explicitly mentioned and inferences about their character, the remainder of the sources suggested can have only varying degrees of probability. Considerable scholarly effort has gone into identifying and characterizing such sources, but it remains in the realm of speculation. When considering the sources the compiler may have used, one important caution must be kept in mind. Even if such sources did exist, one cannot have confidence in a reconstruction of the compositional history. Which sources had already been integrated into a larger composition before they were used by the compiler of Kings? We cannot be certain that the life situation out of which these other sources grew has been correctly identified, nor can we know that even the compiler himself was aware of the past history of his sources. Biblical scholarship has expended considerable energy in trying to delineate the past history of the Book of Kings, but it has often been at the neglect of the unity of perspective which is the product of the final compiler(s) in whose hands the book received its canonical form. What is important to understanding the book is not the perspective of its various sources (of which the compiler himself may have been unaware), but the perspective of the book as a whole on the history of the kingdoms. It is the outline which the compiler has imposed on the sources that establishes the teaching of the book; his sources are used in accord with his own purposes, a fact that makes the purposes for which the sources had been prepared largely irrelevant to the teaching of the book in its present form. Exploring possible sources, worthwhile in itself, must not eclipse the message of the book as a whole. This is not to imply that the Books of Kings are simply a compilation of unaltered sources. The writer(s) undoubtedly exercised a measure of selectivity and literary skill in composing the historical narrative.

One compositional technique of the compiler is quite prominent in the histories of the divided kingdoms: this is the use of formulaic introductions and conclusions to the various reigns. The formulas for both kingdoms are quite similar, differing in minor details. For the kings of Judah the full introductory formula is as follows:

(1)   year of accession synchronized with the regnal year of the northern king;
(2)   age of king at his accession;
(3)   length of his reign;
(4)   name of his mother;
(5)   judgment on the character of the reign.

The account of a Judean king's reign is concluded as follows:

(1) a reference to the Chronicles of the Kings of Judah for further information;

(2) a statement regarding the death of the king, including the place of burial;

(3) successor: "And his son reigned in his stead."

The full formula for a Judean king can be seen, for example, in the reign of Rehoboam (1 Kgs 14:21,22,29–31).

The formulas differ slightly for the kings of Israel; the introduction is as follows:

(1) year of succession synchronized with the regnal year of the southern king;

(2) length of his reign;

(3) location of the royal residence;

(4) condemnation for idolatry;

(5) name of the king's father.

The account of an Israelite king's reign ends as follows:

(1) a reference to the Chronicles of the Kings of Israel for further information;

(2) a statement regarding his death;

(3) a statement of the succession of his son, unless a usurper follows.

The full formula for an Israelite king can be seen, for example, in the reign of Baasha (1 Kgs 15:33,34; 16:5,6).

There is some variation in the use of these patterns; but, on the whole, they are consistently followed and provide the basic framework for the history of the divided kingdom. The synchronisms of the reigns provide data for constructing the chronology of the period. The variations in the formulas may reflect the characteristics of the sources the compiler was using or may reflect his own interests. The name of the mother of a Judean king is recorded, but not of an Israelite king, perhaps reflecting concern with a more exact and fuller record of the Davidic succession. The royal residence is presumed to be Jerusalem for the southern kings (though it may be mentioned), but is recorded for the northern kings since it moved several times, from Shechem to Penuel to Tirzah to Samaria. The mention of the king's father for a northern ruler also reflects the frequent change in dynasties there, as opposed to the dynastic stability of Judah, which is reinforced by mentioning the burial of almost all its kings in the city of David.

Kings in Higher Criticism.

The approach taken to the Books of Kings in higher criticism is dominated by the date of the Book of Deuteronomy and the relationship between Deuteronomy and the rest of the "Deuteronomic history" (Joshua through Kings). Higher criticism denies that the date of Deuteronomy could be in the time of Moses. Because of the similar theological perspective in Kings and in the Book of Deuteronomy, higher critics generally date Deuteronomy in one form or another to the time of Josiah's discovery of the law book in the temple (621 BC; 2 Kgs 22). Deuteronomy is then viewed as a pseudonymous work designed to legitimate the reforms of Josiah, and Kings becomes a companion work (along with Joshua through Samuel) viewing history through the eyes of those who produced Deuteronomy in the days of Josiah. The history of the kingdoms on this basis is measured not by standards in the Law of God from the Mosaic period, but by standards which themselves were not propounded until after the events judged by them.

Higher criticism is also much concerned with the redactional history of the books; that is, how many times they were edited to fit earlier theological models before receiving their final canonical shape. Most higher critics suggest at least two redactions, one around 600 BC shortly after the death of Josiah, and the other during the exile. The first of these editions is said to have been primarily concerned with cultic matters, especially with legitimating the centralization of worship in Jerusalem under Josiah. The second editor is regarded as having the task of adding to the previous work material to justify the exile. Some scholars suggest yet a third edition, a "pre-Deuteronomic," that is, pre-Josiah, edition used by the later editors. Perhaps the strongest argument against the validity of this approach is the contradictory results obtained by scholars trying to assign various passages to one or the other editor; the transparent subjectivity and inability to control the evidence is the best refutation.

Another feature of the higher critical approach to the books revolves around the degree to which the author's theology controlled his approach to the evidence. Numerous scholars assert that the writer would falsify the data in order to achieve his desired theological portrayal. An example of this approach would be the golden calves of Jeroboam. Numerous scholars suggest that these were not really images for Yahweh himself, but rather pedestals above which the invisible Yahweh was thought of as standing; therefore they were originally legitimate and only later misunderstood or misrepresented as idols by the compiler of Kings.

Higher critical studies have also evidenced a low regard for the historical trustworthiness of the data reported in Kings. For example, the account of Sennacherib's campaign against Judah (2 Kgs 18,19) is often regarded as a conflation of two separate incidents. In more recent scholarship, however, the trend has been the reverse, toward an increasing confidence in the reliability of the historical data, largely as a result of the continually growing amounts of archaeological materials from Palestine, Mesopotamia, and Egypt.

The chronological framework of the book has been held in particularly low esteem. Kings is seemingly contradicted by other biblical passages (cf. 2 Kgs 25:8 with Jer 52:12; 2 Kgs 25:27 with Jer 52:31) and is even apparently self-contradictory in places (cf. 2 Kgs 8:25 with 9:29; 2 Kgs 1:17 with 3:1 and 8:16). Here too, however, the trend has been reversed. Rather than suggesting the corruption of the text over the centuries of transmission, increasing sophistication in understanding chronological procedures of antiquity has brought rising confidence in the accuracy of the figures, accuracy even to the point of astonishment. Passages once thought contradictory are now viewed as accurate statements based on competing systems of counting regnal years and reckoning the new year.

When Kings is called Deuteronomic history in most literature, it is on the basis of assuming a late date for the book. While there is this liability in the use of the phrase, it nevertheless is an insightful characterization of the compiler's purposes. One need not succumb to the late dating of Deuteronomy to appreciate fully the impact which this Mosaic document had on the compiler of Kings.

Theology and Purpose. The Books of Kings record the history of the covenant people from the end of the reign of David (961 BC) through the fall of the southern kingdom (586 BC). Yet it is not history written in accord with modern expectations for history textbooks. Rather than concentrating on economic, political, and military themes as they shaped the history of the period, the compiler of Kings is motivated by theological concerns.

Evaluation of the theology and purpose of the Books of Kings is made easier by the fact that there is a parallel history for much of Kings found in the Books of Chronicles. By comparing the two accounts, especially where the later Chronicler adds or deletes material found in Kings, the interests of both histories are thrown into clearer relief.

The Books of Kings were composed during the exile, likely between 560 and 539 BC. Jerusalem had been turned into rubble, and there was no longer a throne of David. Those two pillars of the popular theology—the inviolability of the temple and the throne of David (Jer 7:4; 13:13,14; 22:1–9; see 1 Kgs 8:16,29)—had tumbled. If Israel's faith was to survive, the burning questions that had to be answered were "How did it all happen? Can't God keep his promises to David and to Zion? Have the promises failed?" The writer of Kings aims to deal with the bewilderment of the chosen people in response to the disasters of 722 (fall of Samaria) and 586 (fall of Jerusalem). Kings, like the Book of Job, is a theodicy, a justification of the ways of God to men.

In order to answer the question "How did it happen?" the compiler adopts the procedure of recounting the history of the covenant people in light of standards propounded in the Law. For this reason Kings could be called Pentateuchal history, or even more pointedly, Deuteronomic history, for standards propounded only in the Book of Deuteronomy in the Pentateuch are used by the compiler to measure the kingdoms. Among the prominent themes selected from Deuteronomy and applied to the kingdoms are the centralization of worship, the institution of the monarchy, the efficacy of the prophetic word, and the outworking of the covenant curses on disobedience.

Centralization of Worship. The primary concern of the writer is the purity of the worship of the Lord. His major criterion for measuring this purity is the attitude of the kings toward centralization of worship in the Jerusalem temple as opposed to the worship of the Lord elsewhere and the continuation of Canaanite cults mingled with Yahwism at the high places. Centralization of worship at the central shrine is called for in Deuteronomy 12:1–32. Perhaps "centralization of worship" is a misnomer, for worship was always centered around the tabernacle in the periods prior to the temple; the change that is envisaged in Deuteronomy is not the centralizing of worship, but rather the fact that the shrine would no longer be mobile, but stationary. For the kings of the northern kingdom, this criterion becomes virtually a stereotyped formula that "he did that which was evil in the sight of the Lord and walked in the way of Jeroboam son of Nebat, who sinned and made all Israel sin along with him" (1 Kgs 14:16; 15:30; 16:31; 2 Kgs 3:3; 10:31; 13:2,11; 14:24; 15:9,18,24,28; 17:22). The compiler of Kings sees the rival altars with the golden calves at Dan and Bethel as the great sin of which the northern kings never repented (1 Kgs 12:25–13:34). Rejecting the primacy of Jerusalem, these altars became the rod with which to measure the northern kings. All the kings of Israel are condemned by this standard (except for Shallum who reigned but a month, and Hoshea, the last of the northern kings)—even Zimri, the murderer of Elah, who ruled only one week before committing suicide in the flames of his own palace (1 Kgs 16:9–20). For the kings of Judah a different standard is used: their attitude to the high places where heterodox worship was allowed to flourish in the environs of Jerusalem. Only Hezekiah and Josiah receive the compiler's unqualified endorsement for following the ways of David (2 Kgs 18:3; 22:2). Six others are commended for their zeal in suppressing idolatry, though they did not remove the high places (Asa, 1 Kgs 15:9–15; Jehoshaphat, 22:43; Jehoash, 2 Kgs 12:2,3; Amaziah, 14:3,4; Azariah, 15:3,4; Jotham, 15:34,35). The remainder of the Judean kings are condemned for their participation in the high places and their desecration of the temple itself. This one theme is the preeminent motif in the book.

History of the Monarchy. A second prominent interest for the compiler is to trace the history of the monarchy. Deuteronomy 17:14–20 provides for the day when Israel would ask for a king and charges that king with the basic religious responsibility for the people. This provision for a king, again a feature found only in Deuteronomy, becomes the basis for the compiler's intense interest in the history of the monarchy, and particularly the religious fidelity of the kings. David becomes the model of the ideal king, the one by whom the others are measured, the one whose sons "continue long in his kingdom in the midst of Israel" (17:20 NASB; see also 1 Kgs 15:11; 2 Kgs 18:3; 22:2 for following in the ways of David, and 1 Kgs 14:8; 15:3–5; 2 Kgs 14:3; 16:2 for the reverse). The compiler wishes to show that God has been faithful to David even though David's sons were not faithful. While both kingdoms had about the same number of kings, the northern kingdom is marked by repeated dynastic changes and regicide through its 200 years, while the dynasty of David is maintained as a lamp in the south through 350 years (1 Kgs 11:13,32,36; 15:4,5; 2 Kgs 8:19; 19:34; 20:6). It is the disaster that had befallen the house of David, and the consequent doubts about the promises of God, that prompted the compiler to write.

Efficacy of the Prophetic Word. Another reason why Kings can be called Deuteronomic history is its concern with the efficacy of the prophetic word. There are three passages in the Pentateuch that deal with the institution of the prophetic order: Numbers 12:1–8; Deuteronomy 13:1–5; and Deuteronomy 18:14–22. It is only in Deuteronomy 18 that the test of a true prophet is given: that what he has spoken comes about, that his words be fulfilled. Notice the number of instances where the writer calls attention to the fulfillment of the words of the prophets: 2 Samuel 7:13 in 1 Kings 8:20; 1 Kings 11:29–36 in 12:15; 1 Kings 13:1–3 in 2 Kings 23:16–18; 1 Kings 14:6–12 in 14:17,18 and 15:29; 1 Kings 16:1–4 in 16:7,11,12; Joshua 6:26 in 1 Kings 16:34; 1 Kings 22:17 in 22:35–

38; 1 Kings 21:21–29 in 2 Kings 9:7–10,30–37 and 10:10,11,30; 2 Kings 1:6 in 1:17; 2 Kings 21:10 in 24:2; 2 Kings 22:15–20 in 23:30. The writer is concerned to show that the words of the prophets were efficacious, powerful words. His concern with the prophetic order is also seen in the material devoted to Elijah and Elisha and to other prophetic figures.

Fulfillment of the Curses. Another aspect of the compiler's interest in Deuteronomy is seen in his concern to trace the fulfillment of the covenant curses on disobedience. God's covenant with Israel would issue in curses or blessing depending on the obedience of the people; the compiler of Kings sees the curses inflicted on the two kingdoms because of their failure to meet the demands of the covenant. He takes care to show that most of the curses of Deuteronomy 28:15–68 had some historical realization in the life of the people. Moses had warned that disobedience would "bring a nation against you from afar, from the end of the earth, as the eagle swoops down" (Dt 28:49 NASB), and the Assyrians came to Samaria and the Babylonians to Jerusalem. Nations would "besiege you in all your towns, until your high and fortified walls, in which you trusted, come down throughout all your land" (28:52); the siege of Samaria lasted from 724 to 722 BC, and of Jerusalem from 588 to 586 BC. The dire conditions of the siege would drive the people to devouring their own children; women would feed on their afterbirths (28:53–57). It happened to Israel in the siege of Ben-hadad (2 Kgs 6:24–30). Just as the Lord had delighted to prosper and multiply his people, so he would not refrain from destroying them and scattering them among the peoples of the earth (Dt 28:63–67).

In these and other ways the writer of Kings set out to write the history of Israel and Judah to solve a theological dilemma. How was one to reconcile the exile with God's promises to the nation and David? His answer is twofold: (1) the problem was not with God, but with disobedient men; God remains just; (2) the end of the state does not equal the end of the people or the house of David. Here the ending of the book is instructive: Evil-merodach releases Jehoiachin from prison, elevates him above the other kings, and provides his rations (2 Kgs 25:27–30). Even during the exile, though cut down to almost nothing, the house of David still enjoys the favor and blessing of God. God has not abandoned his promises; the people should keep hope.

Other themes in Kings also show the theological motivation underlying the compiler's selection and arrangement of the data, particularly his use of Deuteronomy as a framework for examining the history of the people. Compare the laws governing the observance of Passover in Exodus 12:1–20 and Deuteronomy 16:1–8: whereas the Passover is centered in the family in Exodus, it is celebrated at the sanctuary in Deuteronomy. The writer of Kings is careful to show that the Passover during the reign of Josiah was celebrated in accordance with the requirements of Deuteronomy (2 Kgs 23:21–23). A passage in Deuteronomy is explicitly cited with reference to Amaziah's keeping the law (Dt 24:16 in 2 Kgs 14:6).

Contrast with Chronicles. The interests of Kings are further highlighted when compared with the parallel accounts in Chronicles. While the writer of Kings worked in the aftermath of the destruction of Jerusalem and had to answer the "how and why" questions, the Chronicler is part of the restoration community. Here the burning theological questions were not how and why, but rather, "What continuity do we have with David? Is God still interested in us?" The need is not to account for the exile, but rather to relate the postexilic and the preexilic. The building of the second temple and the ordering of worship there show up in increased detail in Chronicles in any matter pertaining to the former temple. Chronicles is a history of Judah and of the Davidic line, reflecting the fact that it alone survives after the exile. Interesting too are the things omitted from the account by the Chronicler. Since he is not building a case for an indictment, as was done in Samuel and Kings, he is free to omit references to David's sin with Bathsheba (2 Sm 11) or to Solomon's difficulties in gaining the throne (1 Kgs 1,2). Since in his day the northern kingdom had not survived, the Chronicler does not go into detail about the sins of Jeroboam (1 Kgs 13,14). Chronicles is interested more in the affairs of the temple and does not show the marked interest in prophetic matters found in Kings, so that the lives of Elijah and Elisha are omitted (1 Kgs 16–2 Kgs 10). Nor does the Chronicler recite the sins that led to the demise of the northern kingdom (2 Kgs 17:1–18:12). In all these examples one can see the interplay of the historical moment and theological concerns of the people and the compilers. Each compiler has selected and arranged the data in accordance with the concerns and needs of the community in which he was a member; comparing the two accounts throws the interests of each into sharp relief. There is a continuity between the work of these compilers and the task of the Christian church. The church too is to select the data of the history of redemption and to arrange it to meet the needs and issues confronting each generation. While the end product in the case of the church is not authoritative Scripture, as it was with the

compilers of Kings and Chronicles, the task is the same.

Content. The Books of Kings fall into three parts: (1) the reign of Solomon (1 Kgs 1–11); (2) the history of the divided kingdom (1 Kgs 12–2 Kgs 17); (3) the history of the surviving kingdom in Judah (2 Kgs 18–25).

The Reign of Solomon (1 Kgs 1–11). The record begins with an account of the court intrigue surrounding Solomon's accession to the throne, set against the backdrop of the abortive coup by Adonijah (1 Kgs 1). The dying David charges Solomon to obey the commandments of God (2:1–4) and also to take vengeance on his enemies (2:5–9). After David's death Solomon orders the death of Adonijah, Joab, and Shimei, and the banishment of Abiathar, the priest who had supported Adonijah in his bid for the throne (2:13–46). Enemies eliminated, the kingdom was "firmly established in the hands of Solomon" (2:46).

The remainder of Solomon's reign is divided into two parts: Solomon the good, who follows in the ways of his father David (1 Kgs 3–10), and Solomon the bad, whose heart is led astray (1 Kgs 11). While sacrificing at Gibeon, Solomon asks God to give him the gift of wisdom to rule, wisdom promptly demonstrated in the quarrel of two prostitutes about a child (1 Kgs 3). An account is given of the administrative organization of the kingdom and the incomparable wisdom of Solomon (ch 4). The compiler of Kings gives extensive coverage to the preparations (ch 5), building (chs 6,7), and dedication of the temple (ch 8). God appeared to Solomon a second time, reminding him to keep his commandments as David had done (9:1–9); details are given of the king's building and commercial activities (9:10–27). The account of the visit by the queen of Sheba is followed with elaboration of Solomon's splendor (ch 10). But Solomon did not keep God's commands; seduced to pagan worship by his foreign wives, he was not fully devoted to the Lord as David had been (11:4), and God determined to wrest the northern tribes from the rule of his son (11:11–13). As punishment from the hand of God, Solomon faces rebellion among conquered peoples (11:14–25) and within Israel in the person of Jeroboam (11:26–40).

History of the Divided Kingdom (1 Kgs 12–2 Kgs 17). The united monarchy dissolves at the death of Solomon. The northern kingdom (Israel) would exist for about 2 centuries, would be ruled by 20 kings from 9 different dynasties, and would show a history of internal weakness riddled with regicide and usurpation. In contrast, the southern kingdom would last for 3½ centuries and would be ruled by 19 kings of Davidic descent, apart from a short period under the dynastic inter-loper Athaliah.

There had been a long history of independent action and even warfare between the northern and southern tribes prior to David and Solomon, so it is no surprise that the division would take place along the lines that it did. The immediate cause, however, was the unwise severity with which Rehoboam replied to the representatives of the northern tribes while negotiating for the kingship. Jeroboam, the popular hero of the earlier insurrection against Solomon, became king in the north. He immediately erected the rival sanctuaries at Dan and Bethel (1 Kgs 12); these rival altars became the measure by which the kings of Israel were condemned for following in the sins of Jeroboam.

For two generations there would be warfare between Israel and Judah over the border areas in Benjamin claimed by both sides. Fifty years of sporadic fighting on their mutual frontier, interlaced with invasions from the Aramaeans in the north or the Egyptians in the south, would consume the reigns of Jeroboam, Nadab, Baasha, Elah, and Zimri in Israel and Rehoboam, Abijam, and Asa in Judah (1 Kgs 13–16:20).

The accession of Omri in Israel introduced a ruling house that would last for a total of four generations and end the dynastic instability of the northern kingdom. Though Kings gives Omri a scant eight verses (1 Kgs 16:21–28), he was among the greatest of the northern kings, forging alliances with the Phoenicians and Judah; for over a century the Assyrians would call Israel "the house of Omri."

The reign of Omri's successors, Ahab, Ahaziah, and Jehoram, is treated at disproportionate length, taking almost a third of the total book, 16 of 47 chapters (1 Kgs 17–2 Kgs 10). This is due to the fact that the compiler of Kings has incorporated extensive coverage of the lives of Elijah and Elisha, weaving a contrast between good and evil by paralleling the dynasty of Omri with these prophets. Ahab and Jezebel are used as foils for the account of Elijah, so that Ahab becomes a paradigm of the evil king, (e.g., 2 Kgs 21:3).

Because of this preoccupation with the dynasty of Omri and the lives of Elijah and Elisha, the equivalent period in Judah is not given as extensive coverage. During this period the northern kingdom appears to have exercised some hegemony over Judah, as attested by the marriage of an Omride (Athaliah, 2 Kgs 8:18,26) to Jehoram of Judah and the subservient role of Jehoshaphat to Ahab at the battle of Ramoth-gilead (1 Kgs 22). Judah's fortunes declined in this period when Edom revolted against Jehoram (2 Kgs 8:20–22), cost-ing Judah control over the port at Ezion-geber and consequent economic losses, and when Libnah also broke away, loosening Judah's hold on the frontier towns of the coastal plain (cf. 2 Chr 17:11).

In 842 BC Jehu, after being anointed king by a prophet (2 Kgs 9:1–13), leads a coup ending the house of Omri and also killing Ahaziah of Judah (9:14–29). Jehu's purge also brought the death of Jezebel, Ahab's family, members of the family of Ahaziah, and the ministers of Baal (2 Kgs 9:30–10:36). The consequences were severe politically: the murder of the Phoenician princess Jezebel and the king of Judah cost Israel its allies to the north and south.

Jehu's dynasty had the longest succession of any in Israel, including Jehoahaz, Jehoash, Jeroboam II, and Zechariah, a period spanning 90 years. Jehu's murder of Ahaziah of Judah set the stage for the one threat to the continuity of the Davidic dynasty. Queen Athaliah, herself an Omride, seized the throne and attempted a purge of Davidic pretenders. She ruled for six years until the faithful priest Jehoiada staged a countercoup to place the child Joash on the throne of David (2 Kgs 11).

Israel endured a half century of weakness as a result of Jehu's coup, during which the Aramaeans had a free hand, reducing the forces of Jehu's son Jehoahaz to a small army and bodyguard (2 Kgs 13:1–7).

The reemergence of Assyria early in the 9th century gave relief to Israel and Judah. Assyrian armies conquered the Armaeans; and with that threat removed, Israel and Judah enjoyed a dramatic resurgence. Jehoash of Israel, grandson of Jehu, reconquered cities lost to the Aramaeans (2 Kgs 13:25); Elisha died during his reign (13:20). In the south Amaziah reconquered the Edomites (14:7). Amaziah and Jehoash renewed the warfare between the kingdoms, with the north again victorious (14:8–14).

Under Jeroboam II, Israel enjoyed a period of prosperity when the borders of the kingdom reached the same extent as they had under Solomon (14:23–28). Uzziah, his contemporary in Judah, also fortified Jerusalem and undertook a program of offensive operations extending Judah's sway to the south (14:21, 22; 15:1–7).

Yet this resurgence was but a brilliant sunset in the history of the two kingdoms. After the death of Jeroboam II the history is one of successive disasters, culminating in the fall of Israel and the subjugation of Judah to the might of Assyria. The next thirty years in Israel would see four dynasties, three represented by only one king, and repeated regicides as the northern kingdom hastened to its demise. A period of civil war and anarchy would see five kings in just over 10 years (2 Kgs 15). Heavy tribute was paid to Tiglath-pileser III in both the north and south (2 Kgs 15:19,20; 16:7–10). Israel and the Aramaeans forged a coalition to throw back the Assyrians and sought to press Ahaz of Judah into the fight; Ahaz appealed to Tiglath-pileser III for help. The coalition was destroyed, and Israel and Judah became vassals. Hoshea defected as soon as he felt safe, looking to Egypt for help, but it was suicide for the northern kingdom. Shalmaneser V retaliated, and the political history of the state of Israel came to an end (2 Kgs 17:1–23). The area was resettled with other displaced populations (17:24–41).

Just as Israel had faced the Aramaeans and had survived, only to fall to Assyria, so Assyria became the dominant antagonist for Judah, which would outlast Assyria, only to fall to Babylon.

History of the Surviving Kingdom of Judah (2 Kgs 18–25). Ahaz's appeal for Assyrian aid cost him his liberty, and Judah became a vassal of the Assyrian Empire. Illegitimate worship flourished under his rule (2 Kgs 16:1–19).

Ahaz was succeeded by the first of the outstanding reform kings of Judah, Hezekiah. Much of the account of his reign is given to his rebellion against Sennacherib of Assyria: the rebellion, the Assyrian envoys and threats, Isaiah's assurances of deliverance, and the destruction of the Assyrian armies (2 Kgs 18:9–19:37). Hezekiah's illness was averted after a sign and oracle from Isaiah (20:1–11). As part of what appear to be negotiations toward an anti-Assyrian alliance, Hezekiah also entertained envoys from Babylon, a decision that the prophet announced would be costly (20:12–21).

Hezekiah was followed by Manasseh, who ruled longer than any other king of Judah (a total of 55 years). His reign was marked by great apostasy, apostasy so severe that the compiler of Kings regarded his reign as sufficient reason for the exile that was now unavoidable (2 Kgs 21:1–18; cf. 23:26; 24:3,4; Jer 15:1–4). Manasseh in turn was followed by his son Amon, a carbon copy of his father, who ruled only two years before he was deposed by the people (21:19–26).

The second great reform king of Judah, Josiah, followed. In his reign the book of the law was found while the temple was being refurbished; he led the people in a renewal of the covenant and suppressed illegitimate worship (2 Kgs 22:1–23:14). The Assyrian Empire was in rapid decline, so Josiah extended his borders to the north, destroying the altar at Bethel and the high places throughout Samaria (23:15–20). A great Passover celebration was convened in Jerusalem, and further measures were taken to rectify worship (23:21–25). Jo-

siah tried to block Pharaoh Neco's foray to assist Assyria, and he lost his life at Megiddo (23:26–30).

Josiah was the only king of Judah to have three of his sons succeed him. At his death the people put Jehoahaz on the throne, but Neco removed him three months later and took him to Egypt in chains (2 Kgs 23:31–33), replacing him with another son of Josiah, Eliakim, whose name was changed to Jehoiakim (23:34–37). During his reign, Nebuchadnezzar conquered Judah and Jehoiakim became his vassal. Late in his life Jehoiakim rebelled against Nebuchadnezzar; he died leaving his son Jehoiachin to face retaliation from Babylon (24:1–10). Nebuchadnezzar besieged Jerusalem; when the city fell, Jehoiachin, the queen mother, the army, and the leaders of the land were carried away captive. Nebuchadnezzar put Mattaniah, uncle of Jehoiachin and third son of Josiah to be king, on the throne, changing his name to Zedekiah (24:11–17). Nine years later Zedekiah too would rebel against Babylon. Nebuchadnezzar besieged the city for two years and, when it fell, utterly destroyed it. Zedekiah's sons were slain before his eyes, and then his own eyes were put out, and he was taken to Babylon (24:18–25:21). Nebuchadnezzar appointed Gedaliah to rule as governor from nearby Mizpah; he was assassinated, and the conspirators fled to Egypt (25:22–26).

The book concludes by showing that God had not forgotten his promise to David, mentioning that in captivity Jehoiachin enjoyed favor from the hand of Evil-merodach, successor of Nebuchadnezzar (25:27–30).

RAYMOND B. DILLARD

See CHRONICLES, BOOKS OF FIRST AND SECOND; CHRONOLOGY, OLD TESTAMENT; ISRAEL, HISTORY OF; KING, KINGSHIP.

Bibliography. F.W. Farrar, *The First Book of Kings* and *The Second Book of Kings*; J. Gray, *I and II Kings*; C.F. Keil, *The Books of Kings*; J.A. Montgomery and H.S. Gehman, *A Critical and Exegetical Commentary on the Books of Kings*; I.W. Slotki, *Kings I and II*.

King's Dale.

KJV name for the King's Valley near Salem, the city of Melchizedek, in Genesis 14:17.

See KING'S VALLEY.

King's Garden.

Probably an area of the royal estates, situated outside the walls of Jerusalem near the pool of Siloam (2 Kgs 25:4; Jer 39:4; 52:7) in the Kidron Valley, near where the Kidron meets the valley of Hinnom. Upon the return from the exile, Nehemiah set the families to work each building a part of the wall; the "gate of the fountain" is recorded as being near "the pool of Siloam by the king's garden" (Neh 3:15). It is not certain whether the site now called the king's garden outside the walls of modern Jerusalem is the original site or not.

See JERUSALEM.

King's Highway. The trunk route running north-south across the Transjordanian plateau. It appears in the OT only twice, in requests by the Israelites to use this road when passing through Edom (Nm 20:17) and the Amorite kingdom of Heshbon (Nm 21:22). Who the "king" was is not stated. The route may also be called simply "the highway" (Nm 20:19). The northern segment is called "the way of Bashan" (Nm 21:33; Dt 3:1).

This highway connected Damascus with the caravan route running through the Hijaz down to southern Arabia and the rich sources of spices, perfumes, and other exotic products (1 Kgs 10:2; Ez 27:22). Control over it was a key factor in the geopolitics of Israel and its rivals.

The local topography limits the possible lines of march to two parallel routes. A double watershed exists the full length of the Transjordanian plateau. One is created by the shorter streams that bisect the mountains from east to west; they leave a watershed about 13 to 16 miles east of the Jordan Valley. The larger streams, the Yarmuk, Jabbok, Arnon, and Zered, begin some 25 to 30 miles to the east, usually running north before curving westward. The route bypassing them on the east must follow the fringes of the north Arabian desert. Though the latter has an easier course to follow, it passes fewer good water sources and settlements where supplies could

be obtained. The former, on the western watershed, had ample water and was lined with major towns; however, the caravans had to negotiate the steep canyons of the four large wadis.

The earliest record of movement along this route is in Genesis 14. The four kings went from Ashtaroth, the capital of Bashan, to Ham in northern Gilead, then to Shaveh-kiriathaim on the Moabite plateau, and finally to Mt Seir as far as El-paran (Elath?). The patriarchs probably always came this way when traveling to Canaan; Jacob came through Gilead (Gn 31:21) and established a base at Succoth (Gn 33:17) before crossing the Jordan to Canaan (Gn 33:17).

The Israelites were forced to go "by way of the Red [Reed] Sea, to go around the land of Edom" (Nm 21:4) and around Moab by "way of the wilderness of Moab" (Dt 2:8).

See TRAVEL AND TRANSPORTATION.

King's Pool. Reservoir in the king's garden in Jerusalem (Neh 2:14), also called the pool of Shelah (Neh 3:15).

See SILOAM, POOL OF.

King's Valley. Valley near Salem, the city of Melchizedek, where Abraham encountered the king of Sodom and rejected his offer of a morally compromised truce (Gn 14:17, KJV King's Dale); also called the valley of Shaveh (v 17). If Salem is the same site as Jerusalem, the "king's valley" is probably either the Kidron Valley or the valley of Hinnom. This would be the site where Absalom raised a pillar as a monument to himself (2 Sm 18:18).

See JERUSALEM.

Highway sign, pointing travelers in different directions, including the famous King's Highway.

Kir. 1. Mesopotamian city from which the Syrians migrated to Damascus and back to which they were later exiled by the Assyrians (Am 1:5; 9:7). Escape from Kir to Aram paralleled the exodus of the Israelites. It must have been a terribly bitter experience to be deported (by Tiglath-pileser) back to Kir (2 Kgs 16:9). Whether the city actually existed or not is debatable. It could have become a metaphor for enslavement and exile.

2. Fortress usually identified with the ancient capital of Moab. Soldiers from Kir were associated with those from Elam (Is 22:6). Likewise, Kir was paralleled with Ar in Isaiah's lament over Moab (Is 15:1). Kir of Moab, therefore, is probably the same as Kir-hareseth (2 Kgs 3:25, KJV Kir-haraseth; Is 16:7), located at Kerak, 11 miles east of the southern end of the Dead Sea.

See MOAB, MOABITES.

Kir-haraseth, Kir-hareseth, Kir-haresh, Kir-heres. Fortified city often identified with the ancient capital of Moab.

See KIR #2.

Kiriathaim. 1. Town on the Moabite plateau, mentioned in the march of the four kings against the five (Gn 14:5) where the indigenous Emmim were attacked. It was taken by the Israelites from Sihon (Nm 32:37, KJV Kirjathaim) and included in Reuben's inheritance (Jos 13:19). The Moabite Stone records that that Moabite king fortified the place after gaining control of the plateau; in the 7th century BC it was still under Moabite control (Jer 48:1,23; Ez 25:9). Eusebius placed it 10 (Roman) miles west of Medeba. Two identifications have been proposed, either with Khirbet el-Qureiyeh or Qaryat el-Mukhaiyet, six miles northwest and three miles W,NW of Medeba respectively.

2. Levitical town in Naphtali's territory (1 Chr 6:76, KJV Kirjathaim) called Kartan in Joshua 21:32; the latter is probably a dialectical variant. The suggested identification is with Khirbet el-Qurieyeh, northeast of 'Ain Ibl in southern Lebanon.

See LEVITICAL CITIES.

Kiriath-arba. Ancient name of Hebron, near which is the cave of Macpelah, the burial place of the patriarchs (Gn 23:2; Jos 14:15; Jgs 1:10).

See HEBRON (PLACE) #1.

Kiriatharim. Alternate name for Kiriath-jearim in Ezra 2:25.

See KIRIATH-JEARIM.

Kiriath-baal. Alternate name for Kiriath-jearim in Joshua 15:60 and 18:14.

See KIRIATH-JEARIM.

Kiriath-huzoth. Town in Moab to which Balak and Balaam went before going to Bamoth-baal (Nm 22:39, KJV Kirjath-huzoth). Perhaps to be equated with Kiriathaim, but this is uncertain.

Kiriath-jearim. Village on the road from Jerusalem to Tel Aviv, about 10 miles northwest of Jerusalem. Excavations by the French revealed a settlement 7000 years old in which the residents changed from grazing to farming. Its modern name is Abu Ghosh, so named after a family of Arab sheiks who robbed pilgrims en route to Jerusalem until Ibrahim Pasha of Egypt terminated the practice early in the 19th century. The Crusaders mistakenly identified this village as Emmaus, where Jesus revealed himself to two people after his resurrection (Lk 24:13). Because of this they built in the 12th century a church, with massive walls, over the remains of a Roman fort where Titus had stationed his veterans of the Jewish Revolt. The large crypt under the church contains a spring, mentioned in memoirs of the First Crusade as the "Emmaus Spring."

In the time of the judges this village was one of the four cities of the Gibeonites who, under false pretenses, made a mutual defense pact with Joshua and the elders of Israel (Jos 9:3–27). Because it was on the border between Judah and Benjamin, it was integrated into the tribe of Judah (Jos 15:9; 18:14). During the time of Samuel, after the Philistines captured the ark (1 Sm 4:11) and found its possession to be dangerous, they were advised to return it to Israel. This they did; the ark arrived in Beth-shemish, where 70 men who peered into it perished. Because of the danger its presence presented, it was sent on to Kiriath-jearim, where it remained in "the house of Abinadab on the hill" (1 Sm 7:1) for 20 years. One of King David's first official acts after arriving in Jerusalem was to bring the ark from Baalah (Kiriath-jearim) to Obed-edom's house, then on to Jerusalem (2 Sm 6).

Uriah the prophet, who condemned the reign of King Jehoiakim, and was later executed (Jer 26:20–23), was a native of Kiriath-jearim. Among the returnees from the exile were citizens originally from Kiriath-jearim (Ezr 2:25; Neh 7:29).

The long and complicated history of Kiriath-jearim (KJV Kirjath-jearim) is reflected in the multiplicity of its names, and their spellings in various translations. It was known as Baalah (Jos 15:9); Baale-judah (2 Sm 6:2, KJV Baale of Judah); Kiriatharim (Ezr 2:25, KJV Kirjath-arim); Kiriath-baal (Jos 15:60; 18:14, KJV Kirjath-baal); and Kirjath (Jos 18:28 KJV).

Kiriath-sannah. Alternate name for Debir, a Judean city, in Joshua 15:49.

See DEBIR (PLACE) #1.

Kiriath-sepher. Older name for the Judean city Debir in Joshua 15:15.

See DEBIR (PLACE) #1.

Kirioth. KJV alternate spelling of Kerioth, the Moabite city, in Amos 2:2.

See KERIOTH #2.

Kirjath. KJV spelling of Kiriath, an abbreviation of Kiriath-jearim, in Joshua 18:28.

See KIRIATH-JEARIM.

Tomb at Kiriath-jearim, closed by a rolling stone.

Kirjathaim. KJV spelling of Kiriathaim (Nm 32:37; Jos 13:19; 1 Chr 6:76).

See KIRIATHAIM.

Kirjath-arba. KJV form of Kiriath-arba, the ancient name of Hebron.

See HEBRON (PLACE) #1.

Kirjath-arim. KJV form of Kiriatharim, an alternate name for Kiriath-jearim, in Ezra 2:25.

See KIRIATH-JEARIM.

Kirjath-baal. KJV spelling of Kiriath-baal, an alternate name for Kiriath-jearim, in Joshua 15:60 and 18:14.

See KIRIATH-JEARIM.

Kirjath-huzoth. KJV spelling of Kiriath-huzoth, a Moabite town, in Numbers 22:39.

See KIRIATH-HUZOTH.

Kirjath-jearim. KJV spelling of Kiriath-jearim.

See KIRIATH-JEARIM.

Kirjath-sannah. KJV spelling of Kiriath-sannah, in Joshua 15:49.

See DEBIR (PLACE) #1.

Kirjath-sepher. KJV spelling of Kiriath-sepher in Joshua 15:15,16 and Judges 1:11,12.

See DEBIR (PLACE) #1.

Kish. 1. Benjamite of Gibeah, father of King Saul and a man of some position in the community (1 Sm 9:1). His genealogy is traced for four generations, as is that of Elkanah, the father of Samuel, who would anoint Saul king (1 Sm 1:1).

There is some obscurity in the genealogical information about Kish. His father's name is listed as Abiel in 1 Samuel 9:1. If the Kish mentioned in 1 Chronicles 8:30 is the same person, then we must conclude that Abiel was also known as Jeiel. But it may be that this second Kish was an uncle of Saul's father. A further obscurity results from 1 Chronicles 8:33 and 9:39, where Ner, not Abiel, is said to be the father of Kish. Yet in 1 Samuel 14:51 Abiel is said to be the father of two sons whose names were Ner and Kish. The solution probably lies in the assumption of textual corruption in the Chronicles text. The original reading may have been: "Ner was the father of Abner." It is unlikely that Abner, who played such an important role in the Saul stories, would not have been mentioned in this genealogy. Others suggest that Ner in the Chronicles references was an earlier ancestor, probably Abiel's father or grandfather. If that should be the case, then the father-son relationship between Ner and Kish should be taken in an extended sense, as elsewhere in the OT. No other details of Kish's life are available. His grave was in Zela of Benjamin (2 Sm 21:14). The KJV of Acts 13:21 spells his name Cis.

2. Levite, grandson of Merari, Mahli's son and the father of Jerahmeel (1 Chr 23:21,22; 24:29).

3. Abdi's son, another Levite of the family of Merari. He was one of the Levites who assisted Hezekiah in the cleansing of the temple (2 Chr 29:12).

4. Benjamite and the great-grandfather of Mordecai. Mordecai was carried into exile by Nebuchadnezzar in 597 BC (Est 2:5), together with King Jehoiachin and the prophet Ezekiel.

Kishi. Levite of Merari's family whose son Ethan was a singer and musician in the sanctuary during David's reign (1 Chr 6:44). He is also known as Kushaiah in 15:17.

Kishion. City allotted to Issachar's tribe (Jos 19:20) and given to the Gershonite Levites (Jos 21:28, KJV Kishon; 1 Chr 6:72, Kedesh).

See LEVITICAL CITIES.

Kishon. 1. KJV variant of Kishion in Joshua 21:28.

See KISHION.

2. River draining the Valley of Jezreel. It is a mere 25 miles in length but gathers into itself numerous small streams that originate in the hill country to the south and the north along its course. It rises in the north of the Samaritan highlands where the watershed directs some waters north and others west down the Plain of Dothan. Numerous small wadis empty into the main watercourse as it moves northwest down the slopes of the north Samaritan hills into the Plain of Esdraelon. These upper reaches are dry in summer but in winter (the rainy season) can become torrential. From Jenin to the narrow gap at Tell el-Qassis (the "mound of the Priest") the fall is about 250 feet. The course of the river follows the Mt Carmel ridge, and numerous streams join the main stream from the Carmel ranges to the south and the hills of Galilee to the north. Because this region has a much better rainfall than the area of the upper reaches of the river, the Kishon becomes a perennial stream for the last part of its course. It flows for the last six miles of its length beside Mt Carmel and empties into the Mediterranean Sea about two miles north of Haifa. Just before it reaches the sea, it attains a width of 65 feet.

The heavy run-off from the hills, especially at the time of the spring rains, combined with the flat terrain of the Plain of Esdraelon, produced swampy conditions along its course and provided a serious obstacle to transportation in early times. Its middle course has been largely drained in recent years. Because of its irregular flow the Arabs called the stream the Nahr al-Muqatta (the "Cut River").

Two important biblical events took place in the region of the Kishon River. The defeat of Sisera by Barak and Deborah took place here. Canaanite chariots were caught in the swamps of the Kishon and were overcome by the Israelite attack (Jgs 4,5). The river was praised in the Song of Deborah (Jgs 5:21), and the event was recalled in Psalm 83:9, where it is called Kison in the KJV. Later the prophets of Baal, humiliated by Elijah on Mt Carmel, were slain by the banks of the Kishon (1 Kgs 18:40). Some scholars think that "the water of Megiddo" (Jgs 5:19) and "the brook that is before Jokneam" (Jos 19:11) refer to the Kishon. The river is mentioned by the Roman historian Pliny, by Arab writers, and by the Crusaders. In recent years the last part of the river has been deepened and widened so that a channel 984 feet long, 164 feet wide, and 13 feet deep provides an auxiliary harbor for Haifa, especially for fishing vessels.

Kislev. Month in the Hebrew calendar, about mid-November to mid-December; also spelled Chislev or Chisleu.

See CALENDARS, ANCIENT AND MODERN.

Kison. KJV spelling of the river Kishon in Psalm 83:9.

See KISHON #2.

Kiss, Kiss of Peace. Common salutation symbolizing love and fellowship. In the Bible kissing is referred to in a wide variety of contexts. In addition to its ordinary expression among relatives (Gn 29:11; 33:4) its sensual and occasionally wicked side is noted (Sg 1:2; Prv 7:6–13). It is well attested as an act of homage (1 Sm 10:1; Jb 31:27), although such expressions may be heinous in God's sight (1 Kgs 19:18; Hos 13:2). Hypocrisy, even betrayal, may accompany a kiss (Mt 26:48,49).

Five NT texts refer to a "holy kiss," called later in church liturgy a "kiss of peace" (Rom 16:16; 1 Cor 16:20; 2 Cor 13:12; 1 Thes 5:26; 1 Pt 5:14). Peter speaks of a "kiss of love" and mentions peace in conjunction with it. Although the practice is neither described nor limited by Scripture, the kiss was evidently exchanged between Christians as a pledge of brotherly friendship and fidelity (1 Thes 5:25–27).

In the generations following the apostolic era the kiss of peace came to occupy an established place in liturgical worship. In the latter part of the 2nd century Justin Martyr spoke of the exchange of kisses throughout the congregation following the conclusion of prayer. Eventually the church placed the ceremony immediately prior to Holy Communion. Later on the actual kiss was largely replaced by a simple bow. Other variant forms of the practice may still be observed in churches in the Catholic tradition. There are also such practices as kissing the altar and other objects deemed sacred by the worshiper.

The handshake seems to have virtually replaced the biblical kiss as the normative Christian greeting. Regardless of how mutual esteem is shown, true love's expression begins with paying homage to God's Son—by faith "kissing" him (Ps 2:12). All godly displays of brotherly affection must spring from that loving dedication to him.

Kitchen. *See* FAMILY LIFE AND RELATIONS; FOOD AND FOOD PREPARATION; HOMES AND DWELLINGS.

Kite. Bird of prey declared unclean by the Law (Lv 11:14; Dt 14:13).

See BIRDS.

Kithlish. KJV rendering of Chitlish, a Judean city, in Joshua 15:40.

See CHITLISH.

Kitron. City allotted to the tribe of Zebulun from which the Canaanite inhabitants could not be driven out (Jgs 1:30). It has been identified with Kattath (Jos 19:15), Tell el-Far, and Tell Qurdaneh, but its exact location remains uncertain.

See KATTATH.

Kittim. Ancient Hebrew name for the island of Cyprus (Gn 10:4; Dn 11:30).

See CYPRUS.

Kneeling. Position often denoting worship, respect, or submission. A strong knee symbolically implied a man with strength of faith and purpose, and thus bowing the knee indicated submission to a superior. The knee was bowed before a king, a ruler, a governor, or God. Genesis 41:43 describes the people who were kneeling before Pharaoh and Joseph. Kneeling in reverence before the Lord was common (Is 45:23; Rom 14:11; Phil 2:10). In a time of famine, when the Israelites turned away from the Lord, those who remained faithful were described as "all the knees which have not bowed to Baal" (1 Kgs 19:18; Rom 11:4).

As firm knees represented strength, so smiting those knees represented the destruction of that power (Dt 28:35). Isaiah pleaded with the Lord for the strengthening of weak knees (Is 35:3). Weak or feeble knees were terms generally used to show a lack of firmness of faith (Jb 4:4; Heb 12:12), but could sometimes refer to failing health (Ps 109:24). Ezekiel referred to those who had knees as weak as water (Ez 7:17; 21:7).

Kneeling before the Lord was a posture representing worship (Ps 95:6) and also prayer (Dn 6:10). Christ himself knelt to pray in the garden of Gethsemane (Lk 22:41), and Peter, Paul, and Stephen all set the same example (Acts 7:60; 9:40; 20:36; 21:5). Solomon knelt in prayer and supplication before the Lord (1 Kgs 8:54), and even on one occasion had a scaffold built so that he could climb up and be seen by the whole congregation of Israel kneeling before the Lord (2 Chr 6:13).

Some knelt in penitence, as Ezra did at the evening sacrifice (Ezr 9:5), and Peter when begging the Lord's forgiveness for his lack of faith and trust (Lk 5:8). Those who were beseeching the prophet knelt before him as God's representative (2 Kgs 1:13), and many came kneeling and begging the Lord for healing (Mt 17:14; Mk 1:40). Daniel knelt in wonder and awe before an angel (Dn 10:10), and a sign of Belshazzar's fear was the trembling of his knees (Dn 5:6). In the NT a regal and patient Christ is subjected to the taunting and mockery of the soldiers who knelt before him and cried "Hail, King of the Jews" (Mt 27:29; Mk 15:19).

Knife. Small, hand-held, single- or double-edged cutting instrument, usually made of flint or metal.

See TOOLS.

Knowledge. Observation and recognition of objects within the range of one's senses; acquaintance of a personal nature which includes a response of the knower.

The word "know" or "knowledge" occurs more than 1600 times in the Bible. The specific connotation of the word group provides insight into the basic messages of both OT and NT.

In the OT Genesis introduces the concept of "knowledge." The "tree of knowledge of good and evil" is definitely more than intellectual apprehension or insight into moral values. Violation of the specific prohibition introduces the first couple to the intimate acquaintance with the nature of sin.

The Hebrew view of man is one of differentiated totality—heart, soul, and mind are so interrelated that they cannot be separated. "To know" thus involves the whole being and is not simply an action of eye or mind. The heart is sometimes identified as the organ of knowledge (cf. Ps 49:3; Is 6:10). The implication is that knowledge involves both will and emotions. It is in light of this connotation that the OT uses "to know" for sexual intercourse between husband and wife.

The Semitic concept of knowledge is beautifully illustrated in Isaiah 1:3:

The ox knows its owner,
And the ass its master's crib,
But Israel does not know,
My people does not understand.

Israel's failure lies not in ritual behavior, but in refusal to respond in loving obedience to the God who has chosen it. Only the fool refuses to respond to this revelation. Thus the person who does not respond in obedience obviously has an incomplete knowledge of the Lord. "To know God" involves relationship, fellowship, concern, and experience.

The NT continues this basic idea of knowledge and adds some variations of its own. In the Gospel of John the knowledge of God is mediated through Jesus as the Logos. Jesus has perfect knowledge of God's purpose and nature, and reveals it to his followers: "If you had known me, you would have known my Father also; henceforth you know him and have seen him" (14:7). The identification of Jesus' own relationship with the Father as a model for the relationship of the disciples indicates that knowledge signifies a personal relationship which is intimate and mutual.

The definition of eternal life in John 17:3 adds further content to this concept: "And this is eternal life, that they know thee the only true God, and Jesus Christ whom thou hast sent." This concept is vastly different from that of Hellenistic mysticism, in which contemplation and ecstasy are consummated in gradual merging of the knower and God. In John, by contrast, the result of knowledge is the alignment of the will of the knower and the will of God based upon the model of Christ.

Paul also places the revelation of God in Christ as the source of knowledge. God has made known the "mystery of his will" to the one who is "in Christ." The spiritual man is taught by the Spirit of God (1 Cor 2:12–16) and responds to the truth as it is revealed in Jesus Christ. Again there is emphasis on relationship and encounter as essential elements in the concept of knowledge.

Paul is more concerned that God "knows" him (1 Cor 8:3; 13:12; Gal 4:9) than simply to understand God or know about him. Knowledge is only temporary, for love will outlast it (1 Cor 13:8).

Christian knowledge of God obviously is not based simply on observation or speculation, but is the result of experience in Christ. This knowledge is contrasted sharply with natural wisdom, which operates from an incorrect perspective. Paul is quick to point out that the mystery of God's redemptive plan has been made known and there is now no room for ignorance. Knowledge, then, is the whole person standing in relationship with God through Christ.

See REVELATION; TRUTH.

Bibliography. H. Bavinck, *The Philosophy of Revelation*; J.D. Buswell, *A Christian View of Being and Knowing*; J. Orr, *A Christian View of God and the World*.

Koa. People probably living northeast of Babylonia. They are named along with Babylon, Pekod, and Shoa as people who would come against Jerusalem as instruments of God's judgment on Israel (Ez 23:23). They are perhaps identifiable with the Kutu, mentioned frequently in Assyrian inscriptions.

Kohath, Kohathites. Son of Levi (Gn 46:11; Ex 6:16), father of Amram, Izhar, Hebron, and Uzziel (Ex 6:18; Nm 3:19,27; 1 Chr 6:2), and progenitor of the Kohathite branch of levitical families who were responsible for the tabernacle service (Nm 3:31–32). Moses, Aaron, and Miriam were descendants of Kohath (Ex 6:18–20; Nm 26:59; 1 Chr 6:3; 23:13–17).

The three main divisions of the tribe of Levi bore the names of Gershon, Kohath, and Merari, who were traditionally the original sons of Levi (Gn 46:11; Ex 6:16; Nm 3:17; 1 Chr 6:1,16; 23:6). The Kohathites, therefore, were a prominent levitical family. The order of their names in Numbers 4; Joshua 21; 1 Chronicles 6:16; and 2 Chronicles 29:12 indicates that they were assigned a more honorable office than either Gershon or Merari. Their position and responsibilities—whether referred to as "the Kohathites," or "the sons of Kohath"—are noted throughout the early writings of the Hebrews (Ex 6:18; Nm 3:19,27,29,30; 4:2,4,15,18, 34,37; 7:9; 10:21; 26:57; Josh 21:4,5,10,20,26; 1 Chr 6:2,18,22,33,54,61,66,70; 15:5; 23:12; 2 Chr 20:19; 29:12; 34:12).

During the wandering of the Israelites in the desert following their exodus from Egypt, the Kohathites were assigned a position on the southern side of the tabernacle (Nm 3:29). When the tabernacle was moved, they were to carry the ark and other sacred things on their shoulders (7:9). At the time of the building of the tabernacle, a census was taken to determine the number of male Kohathites who would be involved in the service of the Lord (Nm 3:27,28; 4:1-4,34-37).

After the settlement of the tribes in the land of Canaan, the service of the Kohathites appeared to have ended. God, however, specifically stated that they should be cared for in the same manner as the other levitical families. The Kohathites were given numerous cities (Jos 21:4,5,20–26; 1 Chr 6:66–70).

When David became king, he organized the Levites into three divisions (1 Chr 23:6). Heman, who represented the Kohathites, was charged with "the service of song in the house of the Lord" (1 Chr 6:31), and another group of Kohathites was made responsible for the "bread of the presence" each sabbath (9:32). When David brought the ark of the covenant to Jerusalem, Uriel, a Kohathite, was commissioned to supervise its transportation (15:3–5).

During the period of the divided kingdom, the combined forces of the Moabites and Ammonites attacked Judah. King Jehoshaphat admitted his inability to repulse the aggressors and sought the aid of the Lord. The Kohathites led the people in a song of praise, and probably led the army when, the next morning, the king and the fighting men of Judah went out against the invaders (2 Chr 20:19–22).

Two important reform movements characterized the declining years of the kingdom of Judah. The first took place during the reign of Hezekiah (715–686 BC; 2 Kgs 18; 2 Chr 29,30); the second in the reign of Josiah (640–609 BC; 2 Kgs 22,23; 2 Chr 34). The climax of Josiah's reform came in 621 BC with the discovery of the book of the law. In both these movements the Kohathites played an important role. In the reign of Hezekiah they were numbered among those who cleansed the house of the Lord (2 Chr 29:12–16), and in Josiah's time two notable Kohathites were among those appointed to supervise the work of the temple (34:12).

Following the exile, mention is again made of the Kohathites. The paucity of evidence precludes any judgment of the significance of their ministry. In all probability they were numbered among those who attempted to serve the Lord faithfully in the midst of general spiritual decline. The few whose names are forever enshrined in Scripture were appointed to humble offices. In the absence of evidence to the contrary, it may be assumed that they discharged their duties faithfully (1 Chr 9:19,31,32; Ezr 2:42; Neh 12:25).

CYRIL J. BARBER

See TABERNACLE, TEMPLE; PRIESTS AND LEVITES; LEVI, TRIBE OF.

Koine Greek. Type of Greek that was "common" (*koinē*) to the Near Eastern and Mediterranean lands in Roman times. It is the Greek in which the NT was written.

See BIBLICAL LANGUAGES.

Kolaiah. 1. Benjamite; forefather of a family that lived in Jerusalem after the exile (Neh 11:7).

2. Father of Ahab, the false prophet who, along with Zedekiah, prophesied lies in the name of God during Jeremiah's day (Jer 29:21).

Kor. Dry commodity measure equivalent to one homer (about 3.8 to 7.5 bushels).

See WEIGHTS AND MEASURES.

Korah. 1. Third son of Esau by Oholibamah, daughter of Anah (Gn 36:5,14,18; 1 Chr 1:35).

2. Esau's grandson; fifth son of Eliphaz by Adah, daughter of Elon the Hittite (Gn 36:16).

3. Eldest son of Izhar, Kohath's son from Levi's tribe (Ex 6:21,24), who led a rebellion against Moses and Aaron in the wilderness, accusing them of exalting themselves above the assembly of the Lord (Nm 16:1–3). Numbers 16:1 also records a revolt led by two brothers, Dathan and Abiram, and a man named On, all of the tribe of Reuben, who also challenged the authority of Moses. Dathan and Abiram accused Moses of making himself a prince over the people and of failing to lead them into the Promised Land (Nm 16:12–14). The stories of the two rebellions are interwoven in such a way that it is diffi-

cult to separate them. It may be that the two revolts occurred simultaneously.

Moses challenged Korah and his followers to a trial by ordeal. Together with Aaron they were to take censers filled with fire and incense to the tent of meeting the next day; the Lord would then select from among them whoever should be the holy priest before the Lord (16:4–10,15–17). Moses accused Korah and his company of rebelling against God rather than against Aaron (16:11). When the men gathered as Moses had instructed, the glory of the Lord appeared to all the people. The Lord ordered Moses to tell the congregation to separate themselves from the tents of Korah, Dathan, and Abiram (16:19–24). Moses proposed a test to show the source of his authority, but while he was still speaking, the earth opened and swallowed all the rebels, their families, and their possessions. Fire consumed the 250 men who were offering the incense. The rest of the Israelites were terrified and fled from the scene (16:31–35). Numbers 26:11 adds, however, that "the sons of Korah did not die" with the others (Nm 26:58, KJV Korathites).

Then, through Moses, the Lord instructed Eleazar, the son of Aaron, to take the censers of the men who had died and have them made into hammered plates to be used as a covering for the altar; thus they would serve as a reminder to the Israelites that no one who was not a priest and a descendant of Aaron should ever draw near to burn incense before the Lord, lest that person meet the same fate as Korah and his company (16:36–40).

Instead of being convinced that God had vindicated Moses and Aaron, the next day the congregation began complaining that they had killed the Lord's people. For this act of rebellion God threatened to destroy the congregation, and sent a plague among them. Moses interceded and averted complete catastrophe, but not before 14,700 Israelites had died (Nm 16:41–50). The rebellious incident of the Korahites is last mentioned in Jude 11 (KJV Core).

See KORAHITE, KORATHITE.

4. Eldest son of Hebron, included in the genealogy of Caleb (1 Chr 2:43); the reference has been understood as a geographical name, possibly a town in Judah.

5. Aminadab's son and grandson of Kohath, second son of Levi (1 Chr 6:22).

Korahite, Korathite. Member of Levi's tribe, of the division of Kohath (Ex 6:18,21; Nm 16:1). Their ancestor, Izhar, was the father of Moses and Aaron, thus their family position was closest to the priesthood. The rebellion led by Korah, Dathan, and Abiram against Moses and Aaron ended with the death of many members of the Korahite fam-

ily (Nm 16:31–35). Only those who did not participate survived (Nm 16:11). They settled around Hebron in the levitical cities (Nm 26:58, KJV Korathite).

The Korahites were known as temple singers according to the superscriptions of Psalms 42, 44–49, 84, 85, 87, and 88. David put them in charge of the service of song in the house of the Lord after the ark was brought to Jerusalem (1 Chr 6:31–33). They also acted as gatekeepers (1 Chr 9:19; 26:19, KJV Kore) and bakers of sacrificial cakes (1 Chr 9:31). They are mentioned as singers during the celebration of Jehoshaphat's victory over Ammon and Moab (2 Chr 20:19, KJV Korhites).

See KORAH #3.

Kore. 1. Kohathite Levite who, with his brethren, was responsible for the service at the entrance to the "tent of meeting" in David's time (1 Chr 9:19; 26:1).

2. KJV alternate name for Korahite in 1 Chronicles 26:19.

See KORAHITE, KORATHITE.

3. Imnah's son, a Levite who was a keeper of the East Gate in Hezekiah's reign. He had charge of the freewill offerings of the people (2 Chr 31:14).

Korhite. KJV alternate spelling of Korahite, a descendant of Korah, Hebron's son, in 1 Chronicles 12:6.

See KORAH #4.

Koz. 1. Descendant of Judah and possibly an ancestor of the priestly house of Hakkoz (1 Chr 4:8, KJV Coz).

2. KJV rendering of the priestly family of Hakkoz (Ezr 2:61; Neh 3:4,21; 7:63); perhaps identifiable with #1 above.

See HAKKOZ.

Kue. Name of Cilicia in OT times. From there Solomon imported horses (1 Kgs 10:28; 2 Chr 1:16). It included two geographical areas, the plain on the east (Cilicia Pedias) and the mountains on the west (Cilicia Tracheia). It was bounded on the south by the Mediterranean, on the west and northwest by the Taurus ranges, on the northeast by the Anti-Taurus, and on the east by the Amanus.

The Akkadian rulers of the late 3rd millennium, Sargon the Great and his grandson Naram-Sin, claimed to have reached the "cedar forest" and the "mountain of silver," evidently the Amanus and Taurus, respectively. The name of the plain in the Middle Bronze Age was Adaniya; during the Late Bronze Age a kingdom called Kizzuwatna, composed of

Luwian and Hurrian elements, came into being there but was subjugated by the Hittite Empire.

The Iron Age (1st millennium BC) saw the rise of the Neo-Hittite kingdom of Kue; it acted as a middleman, bringing horses down from the north (cf. Ez 27:14). In the 9th century BC Kue joined a coalition of states to resist the aggression of Shalmaneser III (858 BC), who finally conquered Kue in 839–833. When the Assyrians withdrew, Kue was third in importance after Aram-Damascus and Arpad (according to the stela of Zakir, king of Hamath). By the end of the 8th century, Urikki, king of Kue, paid tribute to Tiglath-pileser III (738 BC), and somewhat later Kue was annexed by Assyria. With the death of Sargon (705 BC) all the Assyrian provinces in Cilicia and Anatolia rebelled; Sennacherib did not reconquer them until 695 BC. In spite of pressure from the neighboring Tabal and the tribes of the Khilakku (who later gave the name Cilicia to the plain), Esar-haddon and Ashurbanipal managed to keep their hold on Kue. The Chaldean Nebuchadnezzar conducted campaigns there in 593 and 591 BC. Later, Chaldean kings also controlled it and campaigned against neighboring Lydia. With the fall of Babylon to the Persians, the Khilakku took advantage of the situation to occupy the plain. This brought an end to Kue and the beginning of the classical Cilicia.

See CILICIA.

Kushaiah. Alternate name for Kishi, a Merarite Levite, in 1 Chronicles 15:17.

See KISHI.

Ll

Laadah. Shelah's son and the father of Mareshah from Judah's tribe (1 Chr 4:21).

Laadan. 1. KJV spelling of Ladan, Joshua's ancestor, in 1 Chronicles 7:26.

See LADAN #1.

2. KJV spelling of Ladan, an alternate name for Libni the Gershonite, in 1 Chronicles 23:7 and 26:21.

See LIBNI #1.

Laban (Person). Bethuel's son (Gn 24:24,29), brother of Rebekah (Gn 24:15,29), father of Leah and Rachel (Gn 29:16), and the uncle and father-in-law of Jacob. Laban's forebears lived in Ur, but his father, Bethuel, was called the Aramaean of Paddan-aram and Laban also is referred to as the Aramaean (Syrian; Gn 25:20; cf. Gn 28:5). Their hometown was Haran, which was in Syria and which, like Ur, was a center of the worship of the moon god, Sin or Nanna(r).

When Isaac came of age, Abraham sent his servant, Eliezer, back to Haran to find a wife for Isaac. Laban greeted Eliezer hospitably and made provision for him and his camels (Gn 24:29–33,54). Laban acted as the head of the house; he made the decision concerning Rebekah's marriage to Isaac (24:50,51), and it was to him and his mother that Eliezer made gifts of costly ornaments (24:53).

Laban figures largely in the narrative of his nephew, Jacob, in his quest for a wife. After the deception of Isaac by Rebekah and Jacob, Rebekah feared that Esau would kill Jacob, so she suggested that he flee to her brother, Laban (Gn 27:43); meanwhile she persuaded Isaac that Jacob should go to Haran to find a wife from among their own people. When Jacob arrived in the area of Haran, he met Rachel, the younger daughter of Laban, and was warmly welcomed (29:13). Laban hired Jacob to tend his flocks, and it was agreed that after

seven years of work Jacob would receive Rachel as his wages. At the end of that period Laban substituted Leah, his older daughter. Jacob protested, but the two men finally decided that Jacob should serve another seven years for Rachel.

Both Jacob and Laban were schemers and had serious disputes about wages. Jacob proposed that his wages should be certain of the flocks. When this was accepted, the Lord blessed Jacob and his flocks, and Laban became angry. Jacob claimed that Laban had changed his wages 10 times (31:7,41).

Jacob fled from Haran. Laban pursued him because he was missing his household gods, whose possession made the holder heir to Laban's estate. Rachel had taken them but adroitly concealed them from her father's search.

Laban and Jacob parted after making a covenant of peace and erecting a pillar of stones to serve as a witness between them (Gn 31:46–50).

See JACOB #1.

Laban (Place). Israelite camping place in Sinai (Dt 1:1). Some equate it with the Libnah of Numbers 33:20,21. Proposals for its location have ranged from just south of Rabbath-ammon to the Arabian coast south of Elath. Its site is still unknown.

See WILDERNESS WANDERINGS.

Lachish. Place first mentioned in the Bible in connection with Joshua and the Israelite conquest of Palestine. At that time its king and army were among the coalition of southern Palestinian towns that faced Joshua at Gibeon. After Joshua's victory, he executed the king of Lachish and later took the town itself (Jos 10:26,32). Though David probably brought the town to life again, it gained new signifi-

The mound of Lachish, 30 miles southwest of Jerusalem on the main road from central Palestine to Egypt.

cance when King Rehoboam of Judah (*c.* 920 BC) made it one of his fortified cities to protect the realm against Egyptian and Philistine attacks (2 Chr 11:9). About a century later Amaziah, king of Judah, was killed at Lachish, where he had fled to escape from conspirators (2 Kgs 14:19).

Lachish resisted valiantly when Sennacherib of Assyria invaded in 701 BC, but ultimately fell under furious onslaughts (2 Kgs 18:13–17; Is 36). Reoccupied and rebuilt by the Judeans, it was one of the last outposts of Jerusalem to fall to the Babylonians when Nebuchadnezzar invaded in 588–86 BC and brought the southern kingdom to an end (Jer 34:7). In addition to biblical references, the Egyptian Amarna letters and Assyrian records allude to Lachish.

The location of Lachish was long debated. Originally it was placed at Umm Lakis, then in 1891 at Tell el-Hesi, and finally in 1929 at Tell ed-Duweir, 30 miles southwest of Jerusalem and 15 miles west of Hebron. This last identification has now been confirmed by a variety of indicators. With a summit of 18 acres, the tell is larger than Megiddo, the Jerusalem of David, Debir, or Jericho.

J.L. Starkey launched excavations at the site, leading the Wellcome-Marston Expedition there from 1933 to 1938. After his death C.H. Inge and G.L. Harding continued to dig from 1938 to 1940. Yohanan Aharoni excavated with Israeli teams in 1966 and 1968, and for the last several years David Ussishkin of Tel Aviv University has been leading excavations at the site.

First occupied in about 3000 BC, Lachish came under Egyptian influence during the Egyptian Middle Kingdom from about 2000 to 1800 BC. In the Hyksos period the city evidently was fortified with a glacis (defensive slope in front of a fortification) and a moat. When the Egyptians established their empire after 1600 BC, they conquered Lachish. But two of the Amarna letters sent from Lachish (*c.* 1400) show subsequent weakening of Egyptian power over the city. In the Hyksos

moat the Egyptians built a temple that was twice enlarged before its final destruction. Excavators concluded that the great destruction which ended the Egyptian level of occupation was caused by a Hebrew invasion (dated to 1220 BC). Among the interesting finds of the Egyptian period were five pieces of pottery with alphabetic signs of the Sinaitic type, dating from 1350 to 1200 BC. These contribute to our knowledge of the origin and development of the alphabet.

During the period of the judges Lachish remained virtually uninhabited. David apparently made it an administrative center and built a government house on a platform 105 feet square and 23 feet high.

Excavations confirmed the biblical indication that Rehoboam made Lachish a fortified center. Around the top of the mound he built a mud-brick wall almost 20 feet thick protected by towers; 50 feet down the slope he built a second wall of stone and brick about 13 feet thick and also strengthened with towers. The platform of the government house was extended to a length of 256 feet. It was this city that Sennacherib took in 701 BC, an event he recorded with pictures and inscriptions on the walls of his palace at Nineveh. The great slabs of stone depicting this event now may be seen in the British Museum.

To the period of Sennacherib's invasion dates a mass grave of 1500 bodies uncovered on the mound's northwest slope. This mass burial, which was covered with pig bones, has been interpreted by some as slain defenders buried by the Assyrians after their victory and desecrated with the bones of unclean animals. Others have differing interpretations, such as that the burial was a result of a clearance of the city after Sennacherib's siege and departure.

Apparently the Assyrians held Lachish for some time. Later it reverted to Judean control and was one of the last three cities (along with Azekah and Jerusalem) to stand against Nebuchadnezzar during his final invasion. Dramatic illumination of the final days of Judah came with the discovery of the Lachish letters, 21 inscribed pieces of pottery found in the guardhouse at the city gate. These were addressed by subordinates at military outposts to the commander at Lachish. After Babylonian destruction and a period of abandonment, Lachish was again occupied during the Persian and Seleucid periods, and finally deserted about 150 BC.

HOWARD F. VOS

See LACHISH LETTERS.

Lachish Letters. Collection of letters, sometimes described as "a supplement to Jeremiah," which was J.L. Starkey's most important discovery at Lachish. In 1935 he found 18 ostraca in a guardroom between the outer and inner gates of the city, in a layer of ash deposited by the fire which Nebuchadnezzar kindled when he destroyed the city. Probably the Chaldeans breached the walls late in 589 BC after the olive harvest, since numerous burned olive pits appear in the nearby ruins. Having taken this and other outlying towns, Nebuchadnezzar then laid siege to Jerusalem in January of 588. In 1938 three other letters were found at Lachish. Of uncertain date, these were short and fragmentary. All 21 of these texts were written in black carbon ink with a wood or reed stylus on pieces of broken pottery. The scribes used the Phoenician script, in which classical Hebrew was written.

Nearly all of the 21 documents were letters, and most of them were written by some subordinate officer at an outpost to the commander at Lachish. Unfortunately only seven of the texts are sufficiently legible to make connected sense; on the others only isolated sentences and words can be read. Some of the signs are blotted out and unfamiliar abbreviations and symbols are used. Scholars differ in their interpretations.

One of the most interesting of the letters is No. 4, which says, "We are watching for the fire signals of Lachish, according to all the

The two sides of Letter No. 4 of the Lachish Letters.

signs which my lord has given, for we cannot see [the signals of] Azekah." Jeremiah 34:7 mentions Lachish and Azekah (12 miles northeast of Lachish) as two of the last surviving cities of Judah. Now it would appear that Azekah too has fallen and the Chaldean noose is tightening on the Judean kingdom. However, the signals of Azekah temporarily may not have been visible for climatic or other reasons. It is important to note the external evidence here for the use of fire signals in ancient Israel. The Hebrew word for fire signal is the same as that used in Jeremiah 6:1.

Letter No. 6 alludes to the fact that the princes are weakening the hands of the people. Evidently this refers to some insubordination or defeatism. The text reads: "And behold the words of the princes are not good, but to weaken our hands and to slacken the hands of the men who are informed about them." This is almost identical to the charge which some of the princes lodged against Jeremiah: "For he is weakening the hands of the soldiers who are left in this city, and the hands of all the people, by speaking such words to them" (Jer 38:4).

Letter No. 3 refers to a journey of the Judean army commander to Egypt. Whether he went with an appeal for troops or supplies is not known. This allusion points to the intrigues of the pro-Egyptian party during the reign of Zedekiah. The reason for the present expedition must have been much different from that referred to in Jeremiah 26:20–23. Letter No. 3 also refers to a letter with a warning from a prophet. Efforts to identify this prophet as Uriah or Jeremiah have not been convincing.

Letters 2–6 refer to a defense which a certain Hoshaiah (a name which appears in Jer 42:1; 43:2), the writer of several of the Lachish texts, makes to his superior, Ya'osh. Though the charges are not always clear, they have something to do with reading confidential documents and presumably divulging some of the information contained therein. One scholar has suggested that this collection of letters in the Lachish guardhouse constituted a "file" used in the court martial of Hoshaiah. The guardhouse was not only a military post, but it was located by the gate, where Palestinian trials were held in biblical times.

The Lachish letters have epigraphic, linguistic, and historical value for the Bible scholar. They indicate the kind of language and script the Hebrews were using in the age of Jeremiah, and they give information for textual criticism. They are firsthand documents of the disturbed political and military situation during the months before Nebuchadnezzar's destruction of Jerusalem, when Jeremiah was the leading prophet in Judah. They help to make possible a study of Hebrew proper names in the last days of the monarchy and provide numerous historical references (e.g., No. 20 refers to the ninth year of King Zedekiah).   HOWARD F. VOS

See LETTER WRITING, ANCIENT.

Ladan. 1. Member of Ephraim's tribe who was Joshua's ancestor (1 Chr 7:26, KJV Laadan).

2. Gershonite Levite, named as the head of several families (1 Chr 23:7; 26:21, KJV Laadan). He is also called Libni.

See LIBNI #1.

Lael. Levite of the family of Gershon and father of Eliasaph (Nm 3:24).

Lahad. Jahath's son from Judah's tribe (1 Chr 4:2).

Lahai-roi. KJV form of Beer-lahai-roi, the name of a well mentioned in Genesis 24:62 and 25:11.

See BEER-LAHAI-ROI.

Lahmam. Judahite town in the Shephelah district of Lachish (Jos 15:40), usually identified with modern Khirbet el-Lahm; alternately spelled Lahmas in some versions (NIV, NASB).

Lahmi. Brother of Goliath the Gittite. According to 1 Chronicles 20:5 he was killed by Elhanan. However, 2 Samuel 21:19 says that Elhanan killed Goliath rather than his brother Lahmi. Most interpreters accept the 1 Chronicles passage as the correct reading, the 2 Samuel text being a textual corruption.

Laish (Person). Father of Paltiel (Palti), to whom Saul gave his daughter Michal, who was formerly David's wife (1 Sm 25:44; 2 Sm 3:15,16).

Laish (Place). 1. Early name for the city of Dan (Jgs 18:7,14,27,29).

See DAN (PLACE) #1.

2. KJV spelling of Laishah, a Benjamite town, in Isaiah 10:30.

See LAISHAH.

Laishah. Town in Benjamin mentioned between Gallim and Anathoth (Is 10:30). Its site is possibly Khirbet el-'Isawiyeh if the passage is not restricted to the order of march by the Assyrian troops.

Lake of Fire. Final abode of Satan, his servants, and unrepentant human beings.

This place is mentioned only in Revelation (19:20; 20:10,14,15; 21:8), but its terrible nature is abundantly clear. It is described as a lake of fire or lake of burning sulphur into which are cast (1) the "beast" and his "false prophet" after the Lamb defeats them, (2) Satan after his last rebellion, (3) Death and Hades, and (4) all whose names are not found in the "book of life." It is called the second death, for it is the ultimate separation from God beyond the resurrection and final judgment.

The lake of fire is probably the same place that Jesus calls Gehenna (Mt 10:28; Mk 9:43; Lk 12:5), the "outer darkness" (Mt 8:12; 22:13; 25:30), and "the eternal fire prepared for the devil and his angels" (Mt 25:41; cf. Is 66:24). The imagery is drawn from the fires in the valley of Hinnom outside of Jerusalem and perhaps the stream of fire issuing from God's throne (Is 30:33; Dn 7:10; cf. Is 34:9,10). The picture was known to Jewish as well as Christian writers (Assumption of Moses 10:10; 2 Esdras 7:36). Whatever the image or name, they all point to a place of eternal torment and separation from God where the unrepentant will suffer forever.

See LAST JUDGMENT; GEHENNA.

Lakkum, Lakum. Fortified border town within the territory of Naphtali (Jos 19:33, KJV Lakum). Its site is identifiable with Khirbet el-Mansurah, about three miles southwest of Khirbet Kerak, at the head of Wadi Fejjas.

Lamb. *See* ANIMALS (SHEEP).

Lamb of God. General term used by John the Baptist to show that Christ would fulfill what the OT sacrifices pointed to. John the Baptist uses the expression twice (Jn 1:29,36), adding on the first instance, "who takes away the world's sin!" He does not explain what the term means. In that it is not used by anyone before him, we cannot appeal to established meaning. Christians use the term freely but what do they mean by it? Why would anyone be called "God's Lamb"?

Some maintain that John sees Jesus fulfilling all that the Passover means and that this is a way of referring to the Passover lamb. It is true that the fourth Gospel places the death of Jesus at the time the Passover sacrifices were killed. But "Passover lamb" is a modern expression; not one example of its use is known to occur in antiquity. When people wanted to refer to the animal killed for this sacrifice, they simply called it "the Passover" (as Paul does in 1 Cor 5:7). The Passover victim was not necessarily a lamb; it might be, and often was, a kid. There is no reason for seeing the Passover in this expression.

Other scholars think of Isaiah 53. Sometimes they see the lamb led to the slaughter (v 7) as a way of referring to the Messiah. Sometimes they see a mistranslation of the Hebrew for "the Servant of the Lord." But unless people generally were in the habit of calling the Messiah a "lamb," the first suggestion will not stand up, and there is no evidence for this. Moreover, it is hard to believe that the well-known phrase "the Servant of the Lord" would have been translated by such an unusual expression as "the Lamb of God."

C.H. Dodd makes the interesting suggestion that there is an allusion to the triumphant lamb of the apocalypses. The writers of apocalyptic literature used vivid imagery to reveal their meaning to initiates and to conceal it from outsiders. They sometimes used the lamb as a symbol of a conqueror (cf. the use of the Lamb for the mighty One in Rv). Dodd thinks that John is pointing to Jesus as the Messiah, King of Israel. Many find this view attractive. The royalty it ascribes to Jesus is certainly congenial to John. But against it is the weighty consideration that John is speaking about a Lamb who takes away sin, while the apocalyptic lamb is normally a conqueror. The roles are different. Further, it is not easy to see how non-Jewish readers of the Gospel at the time it was written would have been able to discern the point of apocalyptic imagery.

As Abraham and Isaac climbed the mountain, the lad asked, "Where is the lamb for a burnt offering?" His father replied, "God will provide" (Gn 22:7,8). From this some deduce that John has in mind a Lamb that God will provide. The rabbis made a good deal of "the binding of Isaac" and referred often to the boy's readiness to be sacrificed. But the early Christians do not seem to have done this. It is moreover the case that what God provided proved to be a ram, not a lamb (Gn 22:13). And there is no evidence that anything in this whole transaction was usually referred to by any name resembling "God's lamb."

There are other suggestions. The "gentle lamb" (Jer 11:19), the daily sacrifice in the temple, the scapegoat, and the guilt offering have all been put forward with some confidence. But no one has produced evidence that any of these was ever called "God's lamb."

In the OT most passages referring to a lamb speak of sacrifice (85 out of the total of 96). Combined with a reference to the taking away of sin, it is difficult to see how a reference to sacrificial atonement is to be rejected. Characteristically the lamb in Scripture puts away sin by being sacrificed. "God's Lamb" means

that this provision is made by God himself. A reference to sacrifice seems undeniable, but a connection with any one sacrifice is hard to make. All that the OT sacrifices foreshadowed, Christ perfectly fulfilled. God's Lamb puts sin away finally.

See JOHN, GOSPEL OF; JOHN THE APOSTLE, LIFE AND WRITINGS OF; FEASTS AND FESTIVALS OF ISRAEL; SERVANT OF THE LORD.

Lamech. 1. Methushael's son, a descendant of Cain, and the husband of Adah and Zillah. Lamech's sons by Adah were Jabal, "the father of those who dwell in tents and have cattle," and Jubal, "the father of all those who play the lyre and pipe." A son, Tubal-cain, "the forger of all instruments of bronze and iron," and a daughter, Naamah, were Lamech's children by Zillah (Gn 4:18–22). In the account of beginnings given in the early chapters of Genesis, the sons of Lamech are the first herdsmen, musicians, and metalworkers. His song of vengeance (Gn 4:23,24) is an example of early Hebrew poetry. In the song Lamech declares that he has killed a man for wounding him and compares the act to his forebear Cain's slaying of Abel (cf. Gn 4:8–12). He asserts that "if Cain is avenged sevenfold, truly Lamech seventy-sevenfold." Lamech's song indicates that as civilization became more complex, pride and propensity for violence increased. Jesus' word about forgiving "seventy times seven" (Mt 18:22) stands in sharp contrast to Lamech's example.

2. Methuselah's son, and the father of Noah (Gn 5:25–31; 1 Chr 1:3). When Noah was born, Lamech expressed his hope that the child would bring relief to humanity from the curse placed upon Adam (Gn 5:29; cf. Gn 3:17). His life—777 years—is one of the longest in the listing of those who lived before the flood. Fanciful conversations in old age between Lamech and his father Methuselah are recorded in the Dead Sea Scrolls. Lamech is listed as an ancestor of Jesus in the genealogy recorded in Luke 3:36.

See GENEALOGY OF JESUS CHRIST.

Lamentation. *See* MOURNING.

Lamentations, Book of. Book consisting of five poems that constitute a formal dirge lamenting the fall of Jerusalem. Each poem has a distinct symmetrical pattern. The first (1:1–22) is an elaborate acrostic composed of three-line segments. There are twenty-two segments, each beginning with a different letter of the Hebrew alphabet, proceeding in order from the first to the last. The second poem (2:1–22) is similar except for a transposition of two Hebrew letters. The third poem (3:1–66) is also composed of three-line segments, but each line begins with a different letter of the Hebrew alphabet, rather than only the first line of each segment as in the first two poems. The same Hebrew letters are transposed. The fourth poem (4:1–22) is an acrostic composed of two-line segments. The first line of each segment begins with the appropriate Hebrew letter. The last poem (5:1–22) is not an acrostic, but it contains the same number of letters as the Hebrew alphabet.

The reason for this complex structure is unknown. It has been suggested that it is a device to aid memorization. Another suggestion is that the Hebrews may have seen the alphabet as representing the concept of totality or completeness. This idea derives from the fact that the Hebrew alphabet represented numbers as well as letters. This concept of totality may be reflected in the reference to the first and last letters of the Greek alphabet in Revelation 1:8: "I am the Alpha and the Omega." It is quite possible that the expression of lamentation in the structure of the Hebrew alphabet could have represented the full range of sorrow felt by the author as he pondered the fall of the city of Jerusalem.

Author. The Book of Lamentations has been traditionally ascribed to the prophet Jeremiah. This ascription is supported by the Latin Vulgate and the Septuagint.

The Jeremaic authorship of the book has been questioned by many scholars, however. The chief reasons for this are the different literary styles of the books of Jeremiah and Lamentations and the alleged conflicting viewpoints in the two books.

The literary styles of these books are strikingly different. The prophecies of the Book of Jeremiah are flowing pronouncements that create an impression of spontaneity and are quite unlike the contrived literary structures of Lamentations. But it is somewhat arbitrary to assert that Jeremiah could not have written the Book of Lamentations on the basis of style. The choice of the acrostic form would naturally limit the scope of the writer's freedom and profoundly affect his style. It is clear from 2 Chronicles 35:25 that Jeremiah composed the same type of material as that found in Lamentations. Since the sermons of the Book of Jeremiah were intended for public proclamation, they would naturally have a spontaneity that the Book of Lamentations would not possess. Certainly the sensitive nature reflected in Jeremiah's prophecies characterized the author of Lamentations as well.

Typical of the alleged differences of viewpoint used to deny Jeremaic authorship is the role of the nations in the destruction of Jerusalem. In his prophecy Jeremiah saw the invading Babylonians as a tool of God's punishment, and appealed to the Jews to surrender to the invaders (Jer 38:3,17). The Book of Lamentations seems to make God the direct author of the punishment and sees the enemy nations only as onlookers who will also experience God's wrath (Lam 1:21; 3:59–66). It must be noted, however, that the enemies referred to in Lamentations are not only the Babylonians but all of the hostile powers that threatened Judah and gloated over its destruction (1:21). The assurance that God will judge these enemies is not a denial of the message of the Book of Jeremiah, for it would be artificial for Jeremiah to suppose that the Babylonians, even though they were an instrument of God's anger, were exempt from punishment. Such a concept is at variance with Jeremiah 12:14–17.

A number of phrases used in the Book of Jeremiah are found in Lamentations as well. The expressions "terrors on every side" (Lam 2:22; cf. Jer 6:25; 20:10) and "wormwood" (Lam 3:15,19; cf. Jer 9:15; 23:15) are examples of these. This fact lends support to the concept of Jeremaic authorship of the book.

Other reasons cited for the denial of Jeremaic authorship are the absence of the name of Jeremiah in Lamentations and the position of the book in the Writings, not the Prophets, in the Hebrew Bible. The absence of Jeremiah's name is not a cogent argument against his authorship; there are a significant number of OT books whose authors are not cited. Since the Book of Lamentations is a formal dirge, and is thus unlike the Book of Jeremiah with its numerous autobiographical references, one would not expect personal allusions by the author.

The position of Lamentations in the third division of the Hebrew Bible is sometimes appealed to by those who question Jeremaic authorship. Since Jeremiah is in the second division, it is argued that Lamentations was written too late for it to have been authored by Jeremiah. It should be noted, however, that there is a lack of unity in the early lists of the canonical books in the third division. It is difficult to assign a late date to a book of the third division only because of its inclusion in that division. The early church father Jerome indicated that Lamentations was once on the same scroll with Jeremiah.

Date. If the Book of Lamentations was written by Jeremiah, the time of writing would be shortly after the fall of Jerusalem (586 BC). It is extremely difficult to imagine an author living in later times writing such a poignant lament over Jerusalem's fall.

The vivid descriptions of the suffering endured by the inhabitants of Jerusalem support the possibility that the book was written by an eyewitness to the events.

Background. After many months of siege by the Babylonian armies, Jerusalem fell, and the final deportation of the people of Judah took place. Extrabiblical confirmation of the devastation caused by the Babylonian invasion may be found in the Lachish letters, which record the message from a soldier in the field who indicates that he is watching for the signals of Lachish but cannot see the signals of Azekah (cf. Jer 34:7).

The time preceding Jerusalem's fall was one of internal strife and political intrigue. Jeremiah counseled surrender, while the chauvinistic leaders of Jerusalem tried to encourage the Judahites to fight on against the Babylonian onslaught. The role of Jeremiah in those final events was a tenuous one. His life was threatened, and he suffered numerous imprisonments.

The fall of Jerusalem meant more than ignominious defeat and exile. While these would have been hard to bear, the theological emergency brought about by the event would have been the most difficult thing for believing Jews to comprehend. The fall of the city in which God chose to reveal himself would have signaled the end of God's promises to many people. The OT clearly set forth a glorious future for Jerusalem. It was to be the center of the messianic kingdom in the end time (Mi 4). The destruction of the city would cause many to question the veracity of God's Word. The laments in this book are not only for the suffering that accompanied the fall of the city, but also for the deep spiritual questions posed by its demise.

Purpose and Theological Teaching. A major purpose of the Book of Lamentations was to give expression to the deep grief that Jeremiah felt as a result of Jerusalem's catastrophe. By writing the book he expressed the grief of all the Jews of his time and gave them a vehicle that would give vent to their sorrow.

The book does not contain only lamentation, however, for it expresses hope and comfort as well. Thus another of its purposes was to lift the hearts of the people and point them to God, the source of all comfort. One of the greatest expressions of hope in the book is found in 3:22,23: "The steadfast love of the Lord never ceases, his mercies never come to an end; they are new every morning; great is thy faithfulness."

Perhaps the most important purpose of the book was to explain the theological reason for the catastrophe. The book places the reason for Jerusalem's fall in clear focus and demonstrates what can be learned about God from this. The reason given for Jerusalem's demise

is the sin of the people (1:8,9,14; 4:14). The fall of the city is a vivid illustration of God's justice in not overlooking sin even in those who are his own (1:18). It demonstrates the fact that God may seem like an enemy to his people when they are disobedient (2:5,7). It shows that the catastrophe was not outside the purposes of God (2:17) and vividly describes the results that can come from willful disobedience. But God is envisioned as a God of mercy and faithfulness as well. Even though Jeremiah saw his beloved homeland crumbling about him, there remained one great element of stability: God's loyalty to his promises. Jeremiah knew that this was not the end, for he trusted in the steadfast love of the Lord and learned to wait quietly for God to act in his time (3:22–27).

Content. The first chapter is a lamentation over the captivity of the citizens of Jerusalem and the resultant desolation of the city.

The author alludes to Deuteronomy 28:64,65 at the beginning of the first lamentation (1:3). In that passage Moses warned the people that their disobedience to God would result in their dispersion among the nations, with no resting place. Lamentations 1:3 says that that warning has been realized.

The cause of Israel's misfortune is sin (1:8a). This is a remarkable example of the results of disobedience to God. The dire results of sin permeate this first lamentation in a series of pictures of deep pathos (1:11,12,16,17). In the midst of this suffering Israel confesses that God was in the right (1:18). The righteousness of God involves his acting in integrity. He punishes sin even in his own people.

The first lamentation ends with a prayer in which the people cry out for God's judgment on their enemies (1:21,22). Such imprecations are the OT believer's way of expressing his longing for an end to evil as it was personified in the godless nations.

The second lamentation also concerns the destruction of Jerusalem but places more emphasis on God's judgment. The tone is more strident than in the previous lamentation. Throughout the passage words expressing anger appear (2:1–3,6,7). It is as though the terrible wrath of God evident in the destruction of the city is still vivid in the mind of the writer.

The author lays the blame for God's anger squarely on the false prophets (2:14); but he does not exempt the people from guilt, as is clear from other passages (e.g., 1:5,8). It was the false prophets of the time who failed to warn the people of the results of their sin (2:14). Because of this, destruction came, and the writer can give no comfort to the people (2:13).

The second lamentation begins with a reference to God's "footstool" (2:1), the ark of the covenant. The ark was the focal point of God's revelation of himself. This verse reflects the theological emergency of the time; the writer laments the fact that God has not remembered his "footstool." Even the holy ark, which marked God's presence with his people, has not prevented God from destroying Jerusalem.

The same thought is expressed in verses 6, 7, where the traditional aspects of Israelite worship, as well as the sanctuary, are seen as having been destroyed by God. This important truth demonstrates the viewpoint of the whole book, which sees God as the direct cause of the misfortune.

The third lamentation is very personal. At its conclusion sorrow and complaint pass into a prayer of assurance (3:61–66).

In the first 18 verses of this chapter, the writer describes how the Lord has afflicted him. He refers to God in the third person, not addressing him as Lord until he speaks the words of verse 18. Only after he has poured out his grief in this fashion can he speak the name of the Lord. This poignant grief suddenly changes to an expression of joy. He can affirm the covenant faithfulness of the Lord, and, in the midst of the deepening sorrow, he sees God's mercies as new every morning (3:22–24).

The chapter closes with a sudden burst of assurance (3:58–66), in which the writer affirms his belief that God will vindicate him before his enemies. Only after he meditates on the nature of God's loving-kindness (3:22–27) can he speak these words. The desperate isolation and separation from God expressed in verses 1–17 give way as he affirms God's goodness. Assurance comes as he reflects on the nature and goodness of God.

The fourth lamentation emphasizes the fact that the judgment was well deserved. The author describes the various classes of the population (4:1–16) and indicates how each has been affected by Jerusalem's downfall. Verses 12–20 affirm that the judgment of God is a direct consequence of sin.

This lamentation also becomes a joyous statement of hope (4:21,22) as the writer affirms that God will punish Israel's enemies. Israel's sin will be forgiven, and the guilt of "the daughter of Edom" will be punished. (The "daughter of Edom" undoubtedly stands for all the enemy nations. Edom is used in Isaiah 63:1 in the same fashion.)

This salvation of the nation of Judah will not take place until their guilt is atoned for. It occurs when God conquers the godless nations. This conquest of the nations is an event that takes place in the end time, according to numerous OT and NT passages. It represents the manifestation of God's total sovereignty over his creation.

The last chapter is a poignant prayer in which the author describes the suffering and asks God to restore the fortunes of the people. It begins with a request to God, asking him to consider all that has befallen the people (5:1–18). Part of the ignominy of the captive Jews is that "slaves" rule over them (5:8). This is an apparent reference to the Babylonian captors, who themselves were subject to despotic rule for many decades.

The author's perspective changes in verse 19, where he affirms that the Lord reigns forever. While Jerusalem, the earthly dwelling place of the Lord, has come to an end, the Lord's throne endures forever. Because his throne is everlasting, the author asks, "Why dost thou forget us forever?" (v 20). The question is based on the belief that because God's reign is eternal, he cannot utterly forsake his people. He will restore his kingdom.

The Book of Lamentations is neglected by many Christians. It deserves to be studied more. Its powerful statement concerning the blessings that may come from tragedy is a relevant message in any age, and it is one of the most powerful illustrations of the results of sin to be found in the OT. Its theology is clear and precise, painting a brilliant picture of God's faithfulness against the dark background of the collapse of the city of Zion.

THOMAS E. McCOMISKEY

See JEREMIAH (PERSON) #1; JEREMIAH, BOOK OF.

Bibliography. N.K. Gottwald, *Studies in the Book of Lamentations*; R.K. Harrison, *Jeremiah and Lamentations*; R. Martin-Achard and S. Paul Re'emi, *Amos and Lamentations*; A.S. Peake, *Jeremiah and Lamentations*.

Lamp, Lampstand. Israelite lamps developed from those in general use among the Canaanites in the 2nd millennium BC. Their shape was similar to a shell or saucer with a lip. Lamps of stone, metal, and shells were used, although the majority were of pottery. A multitude of clay lamps, fashioned in a variety of designs, have been excavated in Palestine.

The clay bowl was fashioned first, and the rim was folded over to help contain the oil. A spout was pinched in place at one end, into which the wick would be placed. When the clay had dried, the lamp would be fired to a dull brown shade. Gradually a style with an increasingly sharply pinched lip was developed. The wick was generally made of flax (Is 42:3), although an old piece of linen cloth was sometimes used. Salt could be added to the wick for a brighter flame, and frequently extra wicks were used. This led to the development of multispouted lamps like those found at Tell Dotha from 1200 BC.

Olive oil provided the commonest form of lamp fuel (Ex 25:6; 27:20; Mt 25:3,4), and the average lamp could hold enough oil to burn through the night. Despite this the housewife would have to get up several times to tend the wick and keep her precious lamp lit (Prv 31:18). Tongs were used for extinguishing the flame of a lamp in the tabernacle or temple (Ex 25:38; 37:23; Nm 4:9; 1 Kgs 7:49; Is 6:6). Candles were not known in biblical times, and the translation in the KJV is incorrect.

The saucer lamp, which would have spilled easily, was not suitable for night travel, so a torch was probably used for that purpose (Jgs 7:16–20). In addition, the wick of the open saucer lamp could easily have blown out at night.

Lamps were commonly found in burials along with food offerings. Because the lamp's flame was associated with life, lamps were frequently placed in tombs as a symbol of life being rekindled.

Although a more elaborate "cup-and-saucer" style of lamp was developed in which the flame came from the central area, the saucer lamp remained the most popular. The earliest Hellenistic lamp found in Palestine dates from 630 BC and already shows indications of the later covered model. During the 6th and 5th centuries BC a flat-bottomed, saucer-style lamp was developed.

In the 3rd century BC the more elaborate wheel-made, covered Greek style took precedence. These lamps were often simple in design, rounded, with a central hole for the oil and one in the small spout for the wick.

In the 2nd century BC the wheel-made lamp was replaced by a molded ceramic lamp of finer design with a larger spout. Imported Egyptian lamps of this type have been found in southern Palestine. Multispouted lamps were probably used on festive occasions. From

A saucer lamp.

the same period comes the Hellenistic-influenced bronze lamp of a seated figure holding out a saucer lamp in his hands. At the end of the Hellenistic age the form of lamps deteriorated as the spouts became thick and squat.

Small, round wheel-made lamps of simple design were prevalent in the time of Christ; this would be the type of lamp used by the woman searching the house for her gold coin (Lk 15:8). With wicks trimmed, the lamps of the foolish virgins would probably have lasted approximately five hours, from dark until about midnight (Mt 25:1–12).

Jewish lamps were part of the religious symbolism of the home, probably dating back to the prohibition against lighting a fire on the sabbath (Ex 35:3). References to light abound in Scripture. We read of the eye as a lamp (Mt 6:22,23; Lk 11:34–36) and of Christ as the Light of the world (Mt 5:14–16; Jn 8:12). We are warned to pay attention to teaching as to a light shining in the dark (Prv 6:23; 2 Pt 1:19). Both God and the spirit of man are symbolized as lamps (2 Sm 22:29; Prv 20:27), while in Proverbs 13:9 "lamp" is synonymous with the essence of life itself. Lamps, with or without stands, were also part of the Jewish ritual of death, mourning, and burial.

Lamps representing simple local craftsmanship have been found at sites of the early NT period, along with those of a style reminiscent of the Hellenistic influence and others of purely Roman design.

Ceramic, bronze, or iron lampstands from the period between 1900 and 1000 BC have been excavated, the ceramic stands for saucer lamps probably having been used in sanctuaries. The majority of lampstands, however, seem to have been made of wood. A lampstand figures in the story of Elisha (2 Kgs 4:8–10), where the prophet was provided with a stand, probably of wood, for his sleeping quarters. It could have been a pedestal lamp, or a one-piece lamp and stand common in households.

In Hellenistic times large decorative lampstands were available to the wealthy, and would have been a rare, treasured Palestinian import. The home of a Hellenized Jewish family might have tall, elegant metal stands designed in styles reminiscent of their Phoenician origin. Jesus refers to placing a lamp on a stand so that its light may be seen clearly (Mt 5:15; Mk 4:21; Lk 8:16; 11:33). Household lamps and stands differed greatly from the magnificent lampstand in the temple at Jerusalem, and from the gold lamp which hung in the Jewish temple at Heliopolis in Egypt.

The tabernacle housed an ornate golden lampstand, or menorah. On either side three branches came out from the main central stem, and seven lamps could be lighted in the

Relief on the Arch of Titus in Rome that depicts Romans carrying away the menorah (or golden lampstand) from the temple in Jerusalem in AD 70.

flower-shaped holders. The menorah from the Jerusalem temple is represented in relief on the Arch of Titus in Rome. This particular seven-branched lampstand resembles the 10 that were part of the furnishings of Solomon's temple.

The seven-branched lampstand has been a particular symbol of the Jewish faith from the time of its earliest appearance on a coin in the reign of Antigonus (40–37 BC) up to the present day.   HAZEL W. PERKIN

See FURNITURE; TABERNACLE, TEMPLE.

Lance.   Long, spearlike weapon.

See ARMS AND WARFARE.

Land.   The relationship of man to the land is a prominent theme in the OT. In Genesis the earth with its dry land was created as a place for man to dwell in fellowship with God. Man was given the task of subduing the earth and ruling over the animal creation to satisfy his own needs and to bring glory to his Creator. Subsequent to man's fall into sin he suffered alienation not only from God and his fellows, but also from the land on which he lived. He was driven from the garden of Eden, and the earth became cursed. He was now forced to toil and sweat in order to subdue the earth and provide for his own subsistence because the harvest was choked by thorns and thistles.

After murdering his brother, Cain receives an individual intensification of the land curse as punishment. He is told that the earth will not yield its produce for him even with hard labor, forcing him to wander from one place to another. With no permanent homeland Cain is denied the enjoyment of rest and pros-

perity. Because of sin the important human aspiration for a sense of place is refused to Cain.

After the flood, which was God's judgment on an exceedingly wicked human race, man again provokes God's wrath; the construction of the tower of Babel exalts human might apart from God. God intervenes to confuse the people's language and "scatter them abroad upon the face of the earth." Genesis 1–11 is thus characterized by a sequence of narratives describing land loss with its attendant deprivations as a consequence of sin and rebellion against God.

Land and the Abrahamic Covenant.   In the time of Abraham God intervened in human affairs to provide a special homeland for a select group of people who are set apart unto himself. It is here that the Promised Land theme is introduced in Scripture. God said to Abraham, "Go from your country . . . to the land that I will show you; and I will make of you a great nation" (Gn 12:1,2). This promise to Abraham is enlarged upon in Genesis 12:7; 13:14–18; 15:7–21; 17:7,8. Abraham is told that the land of Canaan is to be the "everlasting possession" of his descendants (Gn 17:8).

The OT narrative then traces Abraham's line of descent through Isaac and Jacob, and tells of the migration of Jacob's family to Egypt, where during approximately four centuries they became a great and numerous people. During this period the promise of possession of the land of Canaan is reiterated (Gn 28:15; 35:11,12; 46:3,4; 50:24) and held before Abraham's descendants as an integral feature of God's covenantal promises.

Land and the Mosaic Covenant.   When God called Moses to lead the Israelites out of

Egypt, he associated Moses' task with the ful-fillment of the promises to the patriarchs: "I have remembered my covenant.... I will take you for my people . . . and I will bring you into the land which I swore to give to Abraham" (Ex 6:5–8). Israel is to be delivered from Egypt for two reasons: first, in order to be established as God's covenant people at Mt Sinai, and second, in order to possess the land promised to their fathers. It is of utmost significance, however, that with the establishment of the Mosaic covenant the continued possession of the land is made dependent on obedience. Should Israel violate the covenantal obligations, it will bring upon itself the covenant curses, the most severe of which is banishment from the Promised Land. God said, "If you walk contrary to me, and will not hearken to me . . . , I will devastate the land . . . and I will scatter you among the nations" (Lv 26:21, 32,33). This does not mean that God will abandon his people and the land totally or forever, because God also promises that when the people repent, "then will I remember my covenant with Jacob . . . and I will remember the land" (Lv 26:42).

The Book of Deuteronomy, which records the renewal of the Sinai covenant in the plains of Moab, reminds the people of Israel that the land is a gift from the Lord (Dt 6:10,11). The land is described as fruitful (Dt 8:7–10; 11:10–12), a place in which Israel will find satisfaction and prosperity. At the same time it is presented as a place in which Israel will be tempted to forget that it has been received as a gift of God's grace (Dt 8:11–17). The land belonged to God, hence his people were only tenants. The kind of ownership that they exercised was inalienable, and every jubilee year all property reverted to the original owners. In the land there is the danger of enticement to turn away from the Lord to other gods (Dt 6:14; 8:19; 11:16). In the land there will be the subtle temptation for the Israelites to shift their sense of security from dependence on the Lord to reliance on the material benefits of landed status. When and if this happens, the Israelites are warned, the result will be expulsion from the land (Dt 28:63,64; 29:25–29) until at some future date repentance would bring restoration (Dt 30:1–16).

This connection between covenantal obedience and continued possession of the land is reemphasized by Joshua subsequent to the conquest and apportionment of the land to the various tribes (Jos 23:14–16). Later, when Israel's security became threatened by the Philistines in the west and the Ammonites in the east, the elders request Samuel to give them a king "like the nations" round about to lead them in battle against their enemies (1 Sm

8:5,20). Here the idea arises that successful land management and defense require a king. Even though this request constituted a rejection of the kingship of Yahweh and a serious breach of covenant (1 Sm 8:6,7), the Lord tells Samuel to give the people a king (1 Sm 8:7–9,22; 12:13). When Saul is inaugurated as king, his role is carefully defined (1 Sm 10:25) so that the exercise of his kingship would in no way detract from or conflict with the continued suzerainty of Yahweh over the nation. Saul and the kings after him are to act as vice-regents for the divine suzerain in their rule of the land and people. The human king is just as much subject to the law of the divine suzerain as any other Israelite (Dt 17:14–20; 1 Sm 12:12–25).

During the reign of King David the promise of land received at least a provisional fulfillment. Although it is true that initial fulfillment occurred when Joshua entered the land, at that time the territory did not extend to the borders promised Abraham (Gn 15:18) and much of the land that was occupied still contained pockets of resistance by the former inhabitants (Jos 13:1–6; Jgs 1). It was not until the time of David that the land was fully possessed as originally promised (2 Sm 8; 1 Kgs 4:21,24).

The responsibility of the king to observe the Law and the connection between covenantal obedience and possession of the land is again made clear when Solomon dedicates the temple (1 Kgs 9:4–9). Disobedience will bring not only expulsion from the land but also the destruction of the temple.

The subsequent history of the divided kingdom era is for the most part a history of covenant abrogation, by the people as well as the kings. The Lord sent repeated warnings through the prophets that such disobedience could only lead to expulsion from the land, but their message fell on deaf ears (Is 6:11,12; Am 5:27; 7:17; Hos 9:17). The occupants of the throne of David repeatedly proved themselves to be unworthy of the office.

As Israel persisted in its evil way Jeremiah announced that Nebuchadnezzar was to be the Lord's agent to drive Israel from the land (Jer 21:2; 22:25; 25:8,9; 27:6; 28:14; 29:21). However, Jeremiah and other prophets also looked beyond the exile to a future restoration and return to the land (Jer 32:6–25). Historically this was accomplished under the rule of Cyrus the Great of Persia (538 BC) and is described in the books of Ezra and Nehemiah.

A difficulty of interpretation arises in finding an adequate fulfillment of certain prophecies of the return (cf. Ez 37:1–28; Am 9:14,15), which envision great prosperity and permanent possession of the land under the rule of a

Davidic king. The intertestamental period does not seem to be a suitable fulfillment for these predictions.

Land and the New Covenant. In the NT the land theme is much less prominent, and seems mostly to be given a spiritual symbolism. The writer of Hebrews suggests that Abraham understood the land promise as something that pointed beyond a merely geographical fulfillment to a higher and far more satisfying heavenly home. Realizing the imperfection and transitory nature of all that this world offers, Abraham looked beyond the temporal fulfillment of the land promise "for a city . . . whose builder and maker is God" (Heb 11:10), and he sought a "better country, that is, a heavenly one" (Heb 11:16). In the NT it appears that Israel's land promise and entrance into Canaan is to be understood as typifying something of the future heavenly rest awaiting God's people (Heb 3,4). Perhaps this explains the OT stress on the connection between Israel's living in obedience to God's Law and their possession of the land. When the Israelites do not typify a condition of holiness, they disqualify themselves from typifying a condition of blessedness, and thus are either denied access to or driven from the land. The NT indicates that it is God's purpose to prepare an eternal homeland for his people where the rule of the divine King is direct and just, and where all things are subject to his will; where death and sin are abolished, and where the needs of his people are completely satisfied (Heb 11:13–16; Rv 21).

The OT land promises have been viewed by some as having only typical significance. In the light of Christ's incarnation any statement of Scripture concerning a future for the land is to be interpreted as fulfilled in a spiritual sense in the church. The church is now the New Israel and heir of the OT promises. Because God's kingdom is now a spiritual reality, it is considered a misunderstanding of the OT to expect yet future fulfillments of the OT prophecies of Israel's return to the land and an establishment of a period of peace and prosperity under the rule of Christ the Son of David (cf. Is 2:1–5; 11:6–11; Ez 37:1–28; Am 9:14,15). To abide in Christ is considered an adequate fulfillment of the physical and geographical promises of the OT economy.

Others, while not denying typical significance for these OT realities, would suggest that the land promises are still operative in the physical and geographical categories in which they were given. It is pointed out that Paul argues in Romans 9–11 that there is yet a future for national Israel. In spite of Israel's history of disobedience, climaxing in the rejection of the Messiah, the election and calling of

God is irrevocable, and Israel is yet to be reingrafted in the olive tree from which it had previously been cut off. Luke says that Jerusalem will be trodden down by the Gentiles until the times of the Gentiles are fulfilled (Lk 21:24), indicating that there is to be a future time when Jerusalem will again be possessed by the Jewish nation. This does not necessarily mean that one must view the present State of Israel as the direct fulfillment of the OT promises of return to the land. The OT indicates that the return will be occasioned by belief (Dt 30:1–16). The present return is in unbelief. At the same time, the remarkable preservation of the Jewish people over the centuries and the recent reestablishment of the nation are perhaps to be understood as anticipations or signs of a future and more complete realization of the OT land promises.

J. ROBERT VANNOY

See JUBILEE YEAR.

Bibliography. Y. Aharoni, *The Land of the Bible*; W.D. Davies, *The Gospel and the Land* and *The Territorial Dimension of Judaism*; G.A. Smith, *A Historical Geography of the Holy Land*.

Landmark. Inscribed stone that denoted a boundary of fields, districts, or nations (Gn 31:51,52). In most Near Eastern countries the removal of a landmark was a serious crime; in Israel it was a violation of the Law of Moses (Dt 19:14; 27:17). Removing landmarks could be represented as changing ancient customs and laws (Prv 22:28; 23:10; cf. Jb 24:2).

See INSCRIPTIONS.

Laodicea, Laodiceans. Largest of three cities in the broad valley area on the borders of Phrygia, Laodicea stood where the Lycus Valley joined the Maeander. Significantly, the western entrance to the city was called the Ephesian Gate. The traveler left the city on the east by the Syrian Gate, for the great road ran to Antioch, where other roads branched to the Euphrates Valley, to Damascus, and to the northeast, where the desert trade routes ran toward the mountains, the Gobi, and the remote lands of the East.

Laodicea was not a natural fortress. The low eminence, on which its Seleucid fortifications stood, might have presented a challenge to invaders, but Laodicea had a serious weakness. The water supply came principally from a vulnerable aqueduct from springs six miles to the north in the direction of Hierapolis. Fragments of the aqueduct can be seen today, the conduit badly narrowed by thick deposits of calcium carbonate. A place with its water so exposed could scarcely stand a determined siege. The double conduit was buried, but was not a secret that could be kept.

cial governorship of Cilicia, and the fact that he cashed drafts in Laodicea shows that the city had outgrown neighboring Colossae and was already a place of financial importance and wealth. One product was a glossy black wool, and the strain of long-haired black sheep bred for the trade were common until the 19th century. The wool was the basis of a textile industry centered in both Colossae and Laodicea. Various types of Laodicean garments are listed in Diocletian's price-fixing edict of AD 300, a copy of which recently came to light from neighboring Aphrodisias.

Laodicea had a medical school. The names of its physicians appear on coins as early as the principate of Augustus. It was probably the medical school of Laodicea that developed the Phrygian eye powder, famous in the ancient world. It is a fair guess that this was the dried mud of the Hierapolis thermal springs, which could be mixed with water to form a kaolin poultice, an effective remedy for inflammation.

It can be readily seen how these features of the city provided the pattern for the scornful imagery of Revelation 3:17,18: "For you say, I am rich, I have prospered, and I need nothing; not knowing that you are wretched, pitiable, poor, blind, and naked. Therefore I counsel you to buy from me gold refined by fire, that you may be rich, and white garments to clothe you and to keep the shame of your nakedness from being seen, and salve to anoint your eyes, that you may see." The black garments exported all over the Mediterranean world, the famous eye ointment, and the city's wealth, form a basis for the writer's stinging reproaches.

The letter may have quoted the very words of a civic inscription. In AD 60 a terrible earthquake "prostrated the city." The phrase is that of Tacitus, who wrote 50 years later. The Roman senate at the time gave large sums to devastated Asian cities in earthquake relief, but the historian records with surprise that Laodicea refused such aid. It rose again, writes Tacitus, "with no help from us." The proud fact would undoubtedly be recorded on stone and would be a theme for orators. Perhaps Jewish bankers aided such finance. It seems likely that there was a large Jewish population, dating from a transfer of Jewish families by Antiochus II (223–187 BC) to Lydia and Phrygia. Two years after the earthquake the governor of Asia refused to allow the annual contribution made by the local Jews to the temple funds in Jerusalem to leave the country. This collection set aside by one section of the community alone, and for one special purpose, is a vivid example of the city's wealth. In AD 79 a large stadium was dedicated

A kudurra (boundary stone) from the time of Nebuchadnezzar I (12th cent. BC). To discourage the removal of such stones, symbols of major deities were inscribed on them.

With the Roman peace Laodicea lost all of its frontier character. Under Rome, the city grew in commercial importance. Cicero traveled that way in 51 BC on his way to the provin-

The ruins of Laodicea.

to Titus, who became emperor that year. A man named Nicostratus, the inscription records, paid the cost "out of his own resources," a phrase oddly echoing both Tacitus and John.

In prosperity men too commonly decay, and the Christian community of the city had become infected with the spirit of the place. If Archippus of Colossae ministered there, a gentle hint in Paul's letter may thus find explanation: "See that you fulfill the ministry which you have received in the Lord" (Col 4:17). That was almost a generation before John wrote his scornful words (Rv 3:14–22), and the church had lost all fervor and passion. The city on the great road may have learned the art of compromise in the school of history, and now it was "neither cold nor hot" (v 15). So, too, was the church that found a place in the same self-confident, easy-going community. "So," the warning continues, "because you are lukewarm, and neither cold nor hot, I will spew you out of my mouth" (v 16). The sharp crudity of the phrase must have shocked the audi-

ence, but it is more than likely that local color again provided the vivid imagery. In any thermal area waters of cold streams mingle with the hot chemical-impregnated effluents of thermal springs. The result is a lukewarm mixture, nauseating in the extreme.

At the head of the Laodicean letter in the Book of Revelation stands a figure girded with authority. He is the "Amen," who brings both a threat and promise. He calls himself "the faithful and true witness" (v 14), words that point to the task of testimony which a self-satisfied group had sadly neglected. Finally, he is "the beginning of God's creation" (v 14). Those words would remind older members of the Laodicean congregation of another letter that was first heard over 20 years before. The letter of Paul to the Colossians was, by the writer's direction (Col 4:16), also read in the church at Laodicea, and in its first chapter was Paul's magnificent and historic exaltation of Christ. No Laodicean could fail to see the link between the two communications and realize that God was calling them back to zeal and dedication in the words from Patmos. They were business folk, proficient in more than one industry; but what they needed was to do business with a strong and demanding Lord, to open their eyes to a commerce where their boasted wealth was trash, and to realize from whom they could draw real gold, buy clothing to cover their shame, and discern true riches. E. M. BLAIKLOCK

See REVELATION, BOOK OF.

Lapis Lazuli. Semiprecious stone (silicate) known for its rich blue color.

See MINERALS, METALS, AND PRECIOUS STONES.

Lappidoth, Lapidoth. Husband of Deborah the prophetess (Jgs 4:4, KJV Lapidoth).

Lapwing. KJV translation for hoopoe, an unclean bird according to the Law, in Leviticus 11:19 and Deuteronomy 14:18.

See BIRDS (HOOPOE).

Lasea. Seaport city on the island of Crete, about 5 miles east of Fair Havens. Paul's ship passed Lasea on its way to Italy (Acts 27:8). Little is known about Lasea; it is probably in ruins near Fair Havens. It may be the same as the Lasos which Pliny the Elder mentions in his *Natural History* (4.12.59). He says it was famous in the ancient world, for its region contained 100 cities and it was one of Crete's most important ports.

Lasha. Place-name, otherwise unknown, used in an ancient description of the southern boundary of the territory occupied by the Canaanites (Gn 10:19). In this passage Lasha is associated with other cities usually located near the southern end of the Dead Sea.

Lasharon. Town in Canaan conquered by Joshua (Jos 12:18). Another early manuscript reads "the king of Aphek in Sharon," perhaps indicating that Lasharon was not the name of a town, but part of a phrase distinguishing this city from the other Apheks mentioned in the Bible.

Last Days. Expression used in Scripture to describe the final period of the world as we now know it. In the OT the last days are anticipated as the age of messianic fulfillment (see Is 2:2; Mi 4:1), and the NT writers regard themselves as living in the last days, the era of the gospel. Thus, for example, Peter explains that the events of the day of Pentecost are the fulfillment of Joel 2:28: "This is what was spoken by the prophet Joel: 'And in the last days it shall be, God declares, that I will pour out my

Spirit upon all flesh' " (Acts 2:16,17); and the author of the letter to the Hebrews declares that God "spoke of old to our fathers by the prophets; but in these last days has spoken to us by a Son" (Heb 1:1,2). The last days, then, are the days of evangelical blessing in which the benefits of the salvation procured by the perfect life, death, resurrection, and glorification of Jesus Christ are freely available throughout the world. They are the days of opportunity for unbelievers to repent and turn to God, and of responsibility for believers to proclaim the gospel message throughout the world.

At the same time, however, the last days are days of testing for the people of God, calling for faithful perseverance in the face of the contempt and hostility of the ungodly. Accordingly, Paul warns Timothy that "in the last days there will come times of stress" (2 Tm 3:1); Peter writes that "scoffers will come in the last days" (2 Pt 3:3); Jude gives a similar admonition: "You must remember, beloved, the predictions of the apostles of our Lord Jesus Christ; they said to you, 'In the last time there will be scoffers, following their own ungodly passions' " (Jude 18). For those who persist in their ungodliness, indeed, these are literally their last days; however prosperous they may appear to be at present, there is no glorious future for them. "You have laid up treasure for the last days," James ironically advises those who are intent on amassing earthly riches (Jas 5:3). So also our Lord gave the solemn warning that "a man's life does not consist in the abundance of his possessions," calling that person a fool "who lays up treasure for himself, and is not rich toward God" (Lk 12:15–21).

Jude 18 indicates that the concept of the "last days" is also conveyed by different but synonymous phraseology ("last time"). This is well illustrated in 1 Peter 1:20, where we read that Christ "was destined before the foundation of the world but was made manifest at the end of the times," that is to say, in the final stage of the sequence of history. The plural "last days" gives the impression of a period of some duration, and the correctness of this impression is confirmed by the fact that this final age has already lasted for many centuries. But in the perspective of eternity it is no more than a short time, and in every generation the end of this final age is always imminent, so much so that John speaks of it as "the last hour." To this the presence of antichrist even within the church of the apostolic period bears witness. "It is the last hour," John says, "and as you have heard that antichrist is coming, so now many antichrists have come; therefore we know that it is the last hour" (1 Jn

2:18). The end of these last days is always at hand, and one day it will certainly come; hence the need, insisted on by Christ, for constant vigilance, in view of the consideration that we know neither the day nor the hour of his return in majesty, the climactic event which will bring these last days to a close (Mt 24:44; 25:13; etc.).

This leads naturally to the further teaching that these last days will have their culmination in "the day": the last days will be terminated by the last day. The use of the term "day" in the singular corresponds in the NT to the concept of the "day of the Lord" familiar in the OT, where it is generally presented as an awful day of final judgment against the unrepentant, but with the implication that it is also the day of the salvation and vindication of God's people (see, e.g., Is 2:12–22; Ez 13:5; Jl 1:15; 2:1,11; Am 5:18–24; Zep 1:7,14). The climax of these last days, and therefore of all history, will be "the day of the Lord," which will overtake the world suddenly (1 Thes 5:2). This last of the last days will be the day of the last judgment for rejecters of the gospel, the purification of our present fallen world, the restoration of the created order, so that in the new heaven and the new earth all God's purposes in creation are brought to fulfillment. Then, at the consummation of our redemption, at last fully conformed to our Redeemer's likeness, we will enter into the enjoyment of his eternal glory (1 Jn 3:2; Rom 8:19–25; Rv 21:1–8).

Moreover, Christians are reminded by the apostle Paul that on this last day, which he calls simply "the Day," the worth of their building upon the one foundation which is Jesus Christ will be revealed; what they have done with their lives will be known. It is not that the security of their salvation in Christ is in any way at stake; rather, it is to measure whether they will meet him with confidence or with shame at his coming (cf. 2 Jn 2:28). "Each man's work will become manifest," Paul writes, "for the Day will disclose it. . . . If the work which any man has built on the foundation survives, he will receive a reward. If any man's work is burned up, he will suffer loss, though he himself will be saved" (1 Cor. 3:13–15).

This last of the last days is followed by the everlasting day of Christ's kingdom when God will be all in all (Phil 3:20,21; 1 Cor 15:28). The last day is also, accordingly, the day of triumph and resurrection, when Christ has promised to raise up everyone who believes in him (Jn 6:39,40,44,54). The last days are like night compared with the glory that will be revealed at Christ's return, so that the end of these last days will also be the beginning of God's unending day. Hence Paul's exhortation to the Christians in Rome: "It is full time now for you to awake from sleep. For salvation is nearer to us now than when we first believed; the night is far gone, the day is at hand. Let us then cast off the works of darkness and put on the armor of light" (Rom 13:11,12). The realization that we are in the last days and that the last day is approaching ought to have a dramatic effect on the quality and intensity of our living here and now: "What sort of persons ought you to be in lives of holiness and godliness, waiting for and hastening the coming of the day of God?" Peter exclaims, adding that in the light of this last of the last days we should be "zealous to be found by our Lord without spot or blemish, and at peace" (2 Pt 3:11–14).

The last days, then, are the days of the gospel of our Lord Jesus Christ. They are preliminary to and preparatory for the last day of final judgment of unbelievers and the dawn of eternal glory for believers. For Christ's faithful followers they are days of joy and blessing, but still days in which the fullness of redemption is awaited. They are days, too, of trial and affliction for the church of Christ. But God has given us the assurance of his Spirit in our hearts, the foretaste which guarantees the full banquet hereafter, the downpayment which pledges the payment in full (2 Cor 1:22; 5:5; Eph 1:14; Rom 8:23). Meanwhile we should be assured with the apostle Paul that the sufferings of these last days are "not worth comparing with the glory that is to be revealed to us" (Rom 8:18). They are days, moreover, of responsibility and opportunity: responsibility because Christians are under orders to proclaim the gospel throughout the world (Mt 28:19,20; Acts 1:8) and all men everywhere are commanded by God to repent (Acts 17:30); opportunity because if these last days seem to be unduly prolonged, if some are tempted to assert mockingly that the day of the Lord will never come, the reason for the apparent delay is the long-suffering of God, "not wishing that any should perish, but that all should reach repentance." Consequently we should "count the forbearance of our Lord as salvation" (2 Pt 3:9, 15).

PHILIP EDGCUMBE HUGHES

See DAY OF THE LORD; SECOND COMING OF CHRIST.

Last Judgment. Time at the end of history when God will judge the deeds of all mankind. In their preaching concerning the Day of the Lord, OT prophets anticipated the time when God would wage war against all wicked nations and establish his rule in the eternal city of Zion (Is 4:2; 11:10; Jer 50:30–32; Jl 2:1,3; 4:9–16; Am 5:18–20; 9:11; Zep 1:7–18). The NT writers continue this theme, restating it in the light of the words and work of Jesus. He has been appointed by God "to be judge of the living and the dead" (Acts 10:42; 17:31). Both believers and unbelievers must appear "before the judgment seat of Christ, so that each one may receive good or evil, according to what he has done in the body" (2 Cor 5:10; cf. Rom 14:10).

The focus of God's judgment is human behavior. Those faithful to the covenant will prosper, but those who are disloyal will perish. The prophet Habakkuk identifies the righteous person as the one who is faithful (Hb 2:4). NT writers state that one will be judged according to whether or not his deeds are pleasing to God (Lk 11:32; 2 Cor 5:10; Rv 20:12). However, the NT also states that no one has met the perfect standards of God. All have sinned and therefore deserve to be punished (Rom 3:9,23). The issue to be determined at the time of judgment is not one's guilt, but rather whether or not one has been acquitted. The NT speaks of this acquittal as justification and reconciliation (Rom 3:21–28; 5:1–21). The means of acquittal is the death and resurrection of Christ; for "as one man's trespass led to condemnation for all men, so one man's act of righteousness leads to acquittal and life for all men" (Rom 5:18). The one who trusts in Christ is not condemned (Jn 3:16–18) and can enter the day of judgment with confidence (1 Jn 4:17). His name is written in the Lamb's book of life (Rv 21:27). The unbeliever must face the day of judgment with no assistance. He will be judged by what is written in the books; that is, by what he has done (Rv 20:11,12).

See JUDGMENT SEAT; DAY OF THE LORD; ESCHATOLOGY; JUDGMENT; LAST DAYS; WRATH OF GOD.

Last Supper. See LORD'S SUPPER, THE.

Last Times. See LAST DAYS.

Latin. Language of the Greco-Roman world. The supremacy of Rome, and the ramifications of its official relations with the people under its control, made the widespread use of Latin, Rome's vernacular, inevitable. This led to a considerable Latin contribution to koinē (common) Greek. From the beginning of the Roman sway in Greece, Roman politics and commerce contributed a constantly increasing number of Latin words to Greek.

Traces of Latin in the NT are, therefore, not surprising. But Latin influence on NT Greek has left its mark mainly upon vocabulary, in the transliterated words and literally translated phrases. Latin was one of the three languages in which the inscription on the cross was written (Lk 23:38 KJV; Jn 19:20). Only in these two passages does the term "Latin" occur in the NT. Latin was the language of Roman law and court procedure. Greek might be allowed but only by favor of the court. This explains why the superscription was written in Latin as well as Greek and Aramaic. Every educated Roman would understand Greek, but Latin was used as the official and military, as well as legal, language. This is reflected in the NT where Latin judicial and military terms occur, along with the names of coins, articles of apparel, utensils, and so on. For example, Latin words are used for farthing, denarius, centurion, colony, guard or watch, legion, towel, parchment, palace, assassin, napkin, and superscription. In addition, over 40 Latin names of persons, titles, and places occur in the NT. Agrippa, Claudius, Caesar, Felix, and Cornelius, are among the better known. Romans 16 reveals that Latin proper names were common among Christians.

In Mark's Gospel more Latin words, apart from proper names, occur than in other NT documents. This is to be expected if the Gospel were indeed written in Rome, but this is by no means established. The occurrence of numerous Latin words in this shortest of the four Gospels is not necessarily evidence of its Roman origin, because they are usually terms which the Roman government would make familiar in all parts of the empire. Also, Latinisms found in Mark's Gospel are also found in the other three Gospels. For example, Matthew uses Latin words for mile, tribute, guard or watch, and to take counsel. Because of the close grammatical affinity between Latin and Greek, the influence of the former upon the grammar of the latter is more difficult to trace.

For over 100 years after the founding of the Christian church Greek dominated over Latin in Christian circles. The providential spread of common Greek made it possible for the church to use one Bible—the Greek OT. To freedmen and slaves, Latin was a foreign, and largely unknown, language. This explains why the earliest traces of a Latin translation of any part of the Scriptures are relatively late.

See BIBLICAL LANGUAGES; ALPHABET.

Latter Days. See LAST DAYS.

Latter Rain. Annual spring rainfall in Palestine from late March to early April, following the citrus harvest and preceding the wheat and barley harvests. The spring rains normally conclude the rainy season until the resumption of the fall (early) rains in October. In Scripture the occurrence or absence of the spring rains was often associated with God's favor or displeasure with Israel (Dt 11:13–17;

Jb 29:23; Prv 16:15; Jer 3:3; Hos 6:3; Jl 2:23; Zec 10:1; Jas 5:7).

See PALESTINE.

Laver. Basin filled with water which the priests used to wash their hands and feet before entering the Holy Place and before returning to serve at the altar (Ex 30:17–21). In Solomon's temple a large laver called the "molten sea" was placed between the altar of burnt offerings in the courtyard and the entrance to the inner temple. This consisted of the large basin and the pedestal on which it sat (Ex 30:18); it was made of bronze or brass, melted and shaped from mirrors of highly polished metal given by Israelite women (Ex 38:8).

In Solomon's temple, in addition to the molten sea (1 Kgs 7:23), there were 10 smaller lavers, 5 on the north and 5 on the south sides of the sanctuary (1 Kgs 7:38,39). Each held 40 baths (320–440 gallons), 1/50 the capacity of the large laver. The lavishly decorated molten sea was used for the ablutions of the priests, while the 10 lavers were no doubt used for the sacrifices (2 Chr 4:6). Later King Ahaz, possibly for religious or financial reasons, severed the lavers from their bases and the sea from its base, placing it on a stone pediment (2 Kgs 16:17). The prophet Jeremiah, during King Jehoiakim's reign, predicted that the molten sea and the bases would be carried into Babylon (Jer 27:19–22), which in fact happened according to Jeremiah 52:17. No mention is made of the 10 small lavers, which were perhaps already melted down and sold.

In Ezekiel's description of the temple to come (chs 40–42) there is no mention of a laver or molten sea. The apostle John, however, in Revelation 4:6 and 15:2 mentions a "sea of glass," perhaps reminiscent of Solomon's molten sea.

See BRONZE SEA; TABERNACLE, TEMPLE.

Law, Biblical Concept of. God's means of consecrating his people to himself. The nature and content of "law" may change, but the goal remains the same: maturity and conformity to the image of God.

Redemptive-Historical Context. When man was created in God's image, he received glory, rule, and provision for his daily sustenance from the Creator-King (Gn 1:27–30). However, in his exalted status as ruler over God's creation on earth, man had to prove his loyalty to the Lord. For this purpose God set up a simple test: the tree of the knowledge of good and evil. Man was prohibited from eating the fruit of that tree (2:17). His disobedience marked him as unfit for fellowship with the great King. He was rebellious and by nature full of treachery, as the subsequent accounts of Cain (4:1–16), the generation of the flood (6:1–13), Ham and Canaan (9:18–26; 10:6–20), and the tower of Babel (11:1–9) demonstrate.

Yet in the midst of all this the Lord graciously called Abraham. He promised to bless him, his seed, and the families of the earth that would join in a common expression of faith (12:2,3; 17:4–7). Abraham responded to God in faith (Gn 15:6), willingly observed the ritual of circumcision as a sign of the covenant (17:10; cf. 21:4), and walked before God with integrity of heart (17:1). Abraham subsequently learned that God had sovereignly and graciously chosen him with the purpose that Abraham's family might distinguish itself from the nations "by doing righteousness and justice" (18:19). The Lord was pleased with his servant Abraham who, though he had not received detailed laws, was a man of integrity. His heart was right with God, so that he willingly did what God commanded.

The father of faith was the father of the faithful; the Lord testified that Abraham "obeyed me and kept my requirements, my commands, my decrees and my laws" (Gn 26:5 NIV). His faith resulted in the fruits of righteousness (Jas 2:21–24).

However, Israel, blessed by the Lord in the increase of descendants, the exodus, the crossing of the Red Sea, and his presence, did not respond to him in faith. They murmured and complained, at Mt Sinai, at Kadesh-barnea,

The Monastery of St. Catherine in the middle of the Sinai desert at the foot of Mt Sinai; it has one of the world's most complete collections of ancient icons.

and in the plains of Moab. They proved themselves to be a rebellious and stiff-necked people (Ex 32:9; 33:3,5; 34:9; Dt 9:6,13). Though they had shown their character, yet the Lord was faithful to Abraham by covenanting himself to them. Israel became his people, his royal priesthood, his holy nation (Ex 19:5,6; Dt 26:18,19). He gave Israel the Ten Commandments, the law, and the covenant, symbolized by the two tablets of the testimony (Ex 32:15,16). Even after Moses had broken them in anger because of the people's idolatrous worship of the golden calf, the Lord renewed his covenant by writing again the words of the covenant (Ex 34:28). On one hand, the context in which the law was given reflects God's grace and forbearance with Israel's sins (Ex 34:6,7) and his determination to use Israel in the unfolding of his plan of redemption for the world. On the other hand, the context reflects Israel's immaturity and stubbornness. Therefore, the Law in the OT has positive and negative purposes.

Law in the Old Testament. The OT has many words for the concept of God's Law. The most general word is *Torah*, which signifies instruction of any kind: religious and secular, written and oral, divine and human. Law in Israel was God's Law, mediated through Moses (Ex 20:19; Dt 5:23–27). Because Israel rejected the direct revelation of God's oracles, the Law was mediated through Moses the servant of God (Jn 1:17).

Synonyms for law are: word (cf. Ex 24:3; 34:27), judgment (cf. Ex 24:3), decree (cf. Lv 10:11; Nm 30:16; Dt 4:1), ordinance (cf. Lv 3:17; Nm 9:12,14; Dt 6:2), command(ment) (cf. Dt 5:28; 6:1,25), precepts (a Hebrew word used only in Psalms; cf. 119:4,15,27,40,45,56,63,69,78,87, 93,94,100,104,110,128,134,141,159,168,173), stipulations, requirements (cf. Dt 4:45; 6:20), precept (a Hebrew term not in the Pentateuch; cf. 1 Kgs 2:3; Pss 19:7; 119:15), or simply the "way(s)" (cf. 1 Kgs 2:3; Pss 18:21; 25:9; 37:34).

These words form a semantic field, and it is far from easy to distinguish clearly between the various forms of laws. Generally "the words" pertain to the duties of man toward God, especially the Ten Commandments (Ex 20:1; 34:28). The "judgments" contain civil regulations and duties to one's fellows and to the social environment (21:1–23:9); these are often in the form of "if . . . then . . . ." In Leviticus and in cultic formulations the word "ordinances" has the technical sense of cultic regulations—the ceremonial laws. However, in other contexts, especially in a series of synonyms for law, it signifies any expectation or regulation. The "commandments" are those regulations given by a higher authority. Though the OT has many words for law, the connotation of one word is often indistinguishable from that of other words, especially in series such as "the decrees and laws" (Dt 4:1,5; 5:1), "the commands, decrees and laws" (6:1), "walk in his ways, and keep his decrees and commands, his laws and requirements, as written in the Law of Moses" (1 Kgs 2:3 NIV).

The motivation for keeping the divine law lies in the acts and presence of the Lord. The prologue to the Decalogue reminds us of God's mighty acts: "I am the Lord your God, who brought you out of the land of Egypt, out of the house of bondage" (Ex 20:2). In the historic acts of Israel's redemption, revelation at Mt Sinai, and consecration of Israel to be his people, he involved himself with Israel as a "father." He adopted Israel to sonship and consecrated them; that is, he declared them holy (Ex 19:6; 31:13; Lv 20:8; 22:32; cf. Rom 9:4). Sometimes the two concepts of redemption and consecration are placed together; but whether they are or not, they are inseparable: "I am the Lord, who makes you holy" (Lv 22:32b NIV). The ground of obedience can be stated simply by an appeal to God's name: "I am Yahweh" (cf. Lv 18:6,21,30; 19:10,14,16,18,28, 30,31,34,36,37). The requisite of practical holiness is also based on the experience of God's presence. The Lord commanded Israel to be holy because he is holy (Lv 11:44,45; 19:2). The "holy one of Israel" dwelt in the midst of his people (Ex 25:8; 29:45; Nm 5:3; 35:34).

How could rebellious Israel grasp what God required, if it were not by precise moral, social, civil, and cultic regulations? The Lord had observed that they did not have "the heart" to serve him as a covenant-loyal people (Dt 5:29). By Israel's very nature it could not develop an adequate moral and cultic system to please God. Because of the people's hardness of heart, God had to reveal (i.e., "spell out") his will.

Israelite Law and the Ancient Near East. Israel's law reflected the practices of its ancient Near Eastern context. Ancient Babylonian law codes (Eshnunna, Hammurabi) show similarities with the biblical codes. The similarities go beyond similarity of cases and include legal formulations (casuistic law). Israelite law is distinct in that it is divine law. Moses is the mediator and not the promulgator of the law, as was the practice of a king who, like Hammurabi, put into force a legal code. The Lord himself gave Israel its laws (cf. Dt 4:5–8). The laws in the ancient Near East dealt with the ordering of society. But Israel's laws were given to regulate every aspect of life: personal, familial, social, and cultic. The laws were to teach Israel to distinguish between holy and profane, between clean and unclean, and between just and unjust.

Old Testament Laws. The legal corpus of the OT is not given in one book or in one section. Moreover, the laws reflect the development from the desert context (Exodus) to the context of the land (Deuteronomy). The OT legal material is complex, full of variations and duplications. It is found in Exodus (chs 20–23; 25–31), Leviticus, Numbers (chs 3–6; 8–10; 15; 18; 19; 28–30), and Deuteronomy (chs 5–26).

The Ten Commandments. The commandments are simply designated as "the words" of God (Ex 20:1). They appear in Exodus 20:1–17 and in Deuteronomy 5:6–21, but minor variations and individual commandments occur in other contexts (e.g., Ex 34:14,17,21; Lv 19:1–18; Dt 27:15,16). As a part of the covenant the commandments were first addressed to Israel; they now form the basis of morality in Christianity. The abiding relevance of the moral law is clear from the NT. Our Lord established his authority as interpreter of all the commandments (Mt 5:17–48; 12:1–8,9–14; 23:23, 24). He summarized the Law in terms of love for God and man (cf. Mt 22:37–40; Mk 12:28–34; Lk 10:27; cf. Rom 13:9; Gal 5:14). Since he is also the Lord of the sabbath, the sabbath cannot be divorced from the other commandments (Mt 12:8). The apostle Paul also upheld the Law, as his "ethics of the spirit" reflects an internalization of the Law of God in the hearts of believers (cf. Rom 8:1–17; 12:1–15:13; 1 Cor 2:6–16; 5:1–8:13; 10:23–11:1; Gal 5:13–6:10; Eph 4:17–6:9; Phil 2:1–18; Col 3:1–4:6; 1 Thes 4:1–12; 5:12–24; 2 Thes 3:6–15; 1 Tm 6:3–10; Ti 3:1–11).

The commandments were written on both sides of the two tablets by the Lord (Ex 32:15,16; cf. 34:28). It is unclear whether or not the tablets were duplicate copies, how the commandments were divided, and how the commandments were numbered. They were kept in the ark of the covenant as a testimony to the covenant (Ex 40:20).

The Book of the Covenant (Ex 20:23–23:19). The purpose of the covenant code was to exemplify and to set into motion the legal machinery by which Israel as a nation could reflect God's concern for justice, love, peace, and the value of life. The laws in the book of the covenant are mainly of the casuistic type. They regulate life in an agricultural society with servants, donkeys, bulls, oxen, sheep, and fields of grain. The regulations pertain to relations with women (including widows), aliens, orphans; to legal concerns (liability, damages, ownership); as well as religious obligations (altar, sabbath). Often the law requires restitution, but restitution is not the rule when human life is involved (Ex 21:12,16,20,22,23,29; 22:2,3), especially when it involves one's family (21:15,17,22–25). The penal code attached to the case-laws makes clear the value of human life, which is protected by the *lex talionis* ("law of retaliation"). The *lex talionis* does not point to a lack of forgiveness under the OT, but was intended to be a legal principle giving coherence and justice to a society. The book of the covenant explicates by means of principles and cases how Israel must live together as a nation embracing the Law of God and applying it *justly* (without discrimination or twisting of rights), *lovingly* (with a concern for the parties involved), and *peaceably*.

The Priestly Law. God's concern for holiness and purity comes to expression in the priestly laws (Ex 25–31; 35–40; Lv 1–27; Nm 4–10). The regulations pertain to the construction of the tabernacle, the consecration and ordination of priests, the offerings and sacrifices, rules of purity, the holy days, and vows.

The tabernacle was set in the middle of Israel's camp in the wilderness. It symbolized the presence of God with his people. The priests and Levites were encamped around the tabernacle to serve and protect God's holiness. All the tribes were situated around the tabernacle; and though the members of the tribes did not have access to all parts of the tabernacle, they had to be ritually clean to live in the camp. Anyone who was ritually defiled (Lv 13:46; Nm 5:1–5) or had sinned grievously was put outside the camp (Lv 24:10–23; Nm 15:32–36). This regulation even included objects that had become defiled (Lv 8:17; 9:11).

By means of prescribed offerings and sacrifices (Lv 1–7; 16; Nm 15:1–31; 28) God assured Israel, individually and corporately, of forgiveness when it had unwittingly sinned. The offerings and sacrifices concretely embodied the purpose of the offerer, whether forgiveness, dedication, or fellowship.

The priests and Levites taught the Law of God (Dt 31:9–13), applied its regulations, and served in courts (Dt 17:8–13).

The Holiness Code (Lv 17–26). The holiness code forms a significant part of the Book of Leviticus. Here Moses addressed all of Israel (cf. 17:2; 18:2; 19:2; 20:2; 21:24; 23:2; 24:2; 25:2; 26:46; 27:2).

The laws are in the form of prohibitions and direct commands. They pertain to the place of sacrifice and the prohibition of eating meat with blood in it (ch 17); the prohibition of sexual relations with specified family members (ch 18; 20:11–21); and regulations promoting godliness, holiness, justice, and love in society (ch 19). The penal code applies penalties to those who sin against the regulations (ch 20; 24:10–23). Chapters 21–24 apply the cultic regulations to the priests and to all Israelites. The institutions of the sabbatical year and the year of jubilee regulate the remission of debts, freedom of people, and restitution of land (ch 25).

The holiness code spells out the qualities required of a holy people: devotion to God (offerings, sacrifices, priests) and love for man (Lv 19:18b) demonstrated in concern for justice, peace, freedom, the value of human life, and a concern for the family. Many of the laws reflect the spirit of the Decalogue (19:3,4,11–13,16–18,30,32).

Both promises and curses are attached to the holiness code (ch 26). The curses predict the exile as a consequence of breaking the laws. But always underlying the laws and penalties is the grace of the Lord, who promises freely to forgive their sins and to renew the broken covenant (26:44,45).

Laws of Deuteronomy. The Deuteronomic laws are explications and new applications of the book of the covenant in view of Israel's new historical situation. Israel was about to enter the Promised Land when Moses outlined to them the Law of God (Dt 1:5). The impersonal element of the book of the covenant is here transformed by personal appeal. Moses strongly appeals to Israel to be loyal to the Lord, the covenant, and the covenantal stipulations. The Deuteronomic laws envision the people in the land of promise, with a central sanctuary (12:5,11,14,18; 14:23; 15:20; 16:5–7,16,21; 17:8; 18:6; 26:2; 31:11) and with a king (17:14–20). The blessings and the curses motivate covenant loyalty (ch 28). However, Israel is also here assured that even if it breaks God's Law, the Lord remains gracious and forgiving.

Purposes of the Law. The Law revealed at Mt Sinai was intended to lead Israel closer to God. Rebellious though they were, God used the Law as his righteous instrument to teach, in a very specific way, what sin is (cf. Rom 5:20; 7:7,8b) and how they should walk on a path which kept them undefiled by sin and holy to the Lord. The Law was the teacher and the keeper of Israel (Gal 3:24). The detailed explications of the laws in all areas of life (work, society, family, cult, and nation) had an important place in God's dealings with Israel. Israel was a nation in a special land, with a theocratic government, and was in need of a legislative corpus. Moreover, Israel's condition at Mt Sinai was such that it could not receive direct revelation. The revelation had to be mediated through Moses. It had to be set forth in detail because Israel had no intuitive grasp of what the revelation of God's holiness, justice, righteousness, love, and forebearance required of them. They had adopted Egyptian ways and had to learn the divine will by revelation. However, Moses and the prophets emphasize that the purpose of the Law is not strict adherence to the Law for its own sake (legalism) or

for a reward (Pharisaism). Keeping the Law is an act of devotion to God, for the sake of God. Our Lord confirmed the purpose of the Law: to establish a dynamic way of life in which one continually seeks God's kingdom and his righteousness (Mt 6:33).

The Law of God is his means of sanctification. He consecrated Israel by an act of grace, and he required Israel to remain holy. Jesus confirmed those uses of the Law whereby one may know his sinfulness and by which he may be driven to Christ. On the cross our Lord carried the penalties of the Law, fulfilled in a greater way the tabernacle/temple presence of God, fulfilled the Father's expectations of atonement, and demonstrated the love of the Father. He, the Son and greater than Moses, gave the essence of the Law in the summary of God's requirements: love of God and love of neighbor (Mt 23:23,24; Lk 11:42–44). Jesus taught that the purpose of obedience is not primarily to receive a reward, but to serve as salt (Mt 5:13) and light (Mt 5:14–16; cf. Eph 4:17–5:20), and to bear fruit (Jn 15:1–17). The purpose of the Law of God is the gradual transformation of the children of God to reflect the image of the Son (Rom 8:29; 2 Cor 3:18; Col 3:10), to be an imitation of the Father (Eph 5:1,2), and to be filled with the Spirit of God (Gal 5:18,22–24). For this purpose Jesus gave us the Beatitudes and the Sermon on the Mount, which summarize the intent of the teaching of Moses and the prophets (Mt 5–7).

The purpose of the Law is to transform regenerate man into maturity. Spiritual maturity is not a privilege that was reserved for believers after Christ; OT saints also walked with God (Enoch, Gn 5:22,24; Noah, Gn 6:9; Abraham, Gn 17:1). These were mature men who lived with integrity in the presence of God (cf. Gn 17:1; Dt 18:13; Pss 15:1,2; 18:26; 101:2,6; 119:80; Prv 11:5).

Maturity, or integrity, is that response to God whereby the believer no longer needs to live by individual stipulations or in fear of mistakes and sins of omission, but delights in doing the Lord's will (Pss 1:2; 112:1). Since the coming of Christ and Pentecost, the Holy Spirit has been poured out on every believer. He has come not only to internalize the Law of God (Jer 31:33), but also to help us develop Christian maturity by giving the fruits of godliness in greater fullness (Gal 5:22–24). Whereas maturity and freedom were experienced by some OT saints, it is God's gift to all his children in Christ (Acts 2:39; 1 Cor 12:13). The purpose is still the same ("so that the man of God may be thoroughly equipped [mature] for every good work," 2 Tm 3:17 NIV; Heb 13:20,21); but the means to accomplish this and the status of the child of God is so much better since Pentecost.

Law and Covenant. Law was incorporated into the covenantal structure (Ex 20–24) at Mt Sinai. The symbol of the Mosaic covenant was the tablets of the covenant, given to Israel through Moses. The covenant may be defined as an administration under which God consecrates his people by divine law. The Law protected the promises of God until the coming of Christ. The Sinaitic covenant stressed the Law as a means to sensitize Israel. The saints in the OT who loved God delighted in his Law as a reflection of his will; saw in it God's fatherly concern for his children to learn to love, to be just and righteous, and to walk humbly before him (cf. Gn 17:1; Mi 6:8). God's goal was to train individuals in Israel to maturity, freedom, and sonship. The mature believer could stand with integrity before God and say,

> For I have kept the ways of the Lord;
> I have not done evil by turning from my
>   God.
> All his laws are before me;
> I have not turned away from his decrees.
> I have been blameless before him
> and have kept myself from sin (Ps 18:21–23
> NIV).

Israel at large rejected God, his covenant, and his laws (Jer 9:2–14; 11:1–13). Therefore, Israel and Judah were exiled (Jer 9:15,16). However, the Lord promised to renew the covenant, to pour out his Spirit, and to internalize the Law, thus leading the humble and righteous in Israel and Judah into a greater position of sonship (Jer 31:31–34; Ez 11:17–20; 16:60–63; 34:25–31; 37:26–28). Postexilic Judaism experienced a greater sense of God's Spirit (Hg 1:14) and presence (Hg 1:13; 2:5). They more readily did the will of God as revealed in his Law. Yet many absolutized law. When our Lord came, he found few of whom it could be said, as it was of Simeon, that he "was righteous and devout . . . and the Holy Spirit was upon him" (Lk 2:25). It was our Lord's purpose to renew the covenant not only with the Jewish people but also with Gentiles; so that having been saved by grace, all in Christ are "God's workmanship, created in Christ Jesus to do good works, which God prepared in advance for us to do" (Eph 2:10 NIV). WILLEM A. VanGEMEREN

See CIVIL LAW AND JUSTICE; CRIMINAL LAW AND PUNISHMENT; HAMMURABI, LAW CODE OF; ISRAEL, RELIGION OF; JUSTIFICATION; TEN COMMANDMENTS, THE; TORAH; TRADITION; CLEANNESS AND UNCLEANNESS, REGULATIONS CONCERNING; ROMANS, LETTER TO THE; GALATIANS, LETTER TO THE.

Bibliography. R.N. Charles, *The Decalogue*; R. de Vaux, *Ancient Israel*, pp 143–63; C.H. Dodd, *Gospel and Law*; J.A. Fitzmyer, *To Advance the Gospel*, pp 186–201; B.N. Kaye and G.J. Wenham, eds., *Law, Morality and the Bible*; E.F. Kevan, *The Evangelical Doctrine of Law*; J.A. Motyer, *The Image of God, Law and Liberty in Biblical Ethics*, and *Law and Life*.

Lawless One. Name Paul used for the antichrist (2 Thes 2:8,9).

See ANTICHRIST.

Lawyer. Term used primarily by Luke in his Gospel in reference to those learned in the Law of Moses.

See SCRIBE.

Laying on of Hands. Phrase used in the Bible to describe a gesture or a ceremonial act. Central to both uses is the notion of power. The hand, particularly the right hand, was often a symbol for power in Bible times (see Ex 15:6; Ps 17:7; 20:6; 44:3).

Laying on of hands was commonly used as an idiom for "arrest," as when the high priest "arrested [literally "laid hands on"] the apostles and put them in the common prison" (Acts 5:18; cf. 2 Kgs 11:16; 2 Chr 23:15; Mt 18:28; Acts 4:3). More important than this usage, however, was the ceremonial act.

To Symbolize Representation or Participation. The laying on of hands was connected with sacrificial procedures. When Aaron and his sons were dedicated to the priesthood, each was required to place his hands on the heads of sacrificial animals, thereby transferring his uncleanness to them (Ex 29:10,15,19). A more elaborate instance of such a ceremonial laying on of hands was when the people of Israel (undoubtedly represented by elders) laid hands on the Levites, who in turn laid their hands on bulls awaiting sacrifice (Nm 8:10,12).

To Symbolize the Bestowal of Blessing. When Israel blessed his two grandsons, Ephraim and Manasseh, the aged patriarch placed his right hand on the younger brother, Ephraim, and his left on Manasseh. The greater power of the right hand may be seen in that Joseph asked his father to change hands. Israel refused because he knew Ephraim would become the greater tribe (Gn 48:19). Jesus blessed the children by placing his hands on them (Mt 19:15).

To Commission People for Important Service. Moses commissioned his successor, Joshua, through a public ritual of the laying on of hands (Nm 27:18–23). That OT ritual was revived in the early church when the apostles commissioned seven deacons (Acts 6:6) and when the prophets and teachers in Antioch commissioned Paul and Barnabas for their mission to Asia Minor (Acts 13:3). The laying on of hands functioned as a recognition of a person's gifts as well as a formal ordination to the Christian ministry (1 Tm 4:14; 5:22; 2 Tm 1:6).

To Symbolize the Bestowal of the Holy Spirit. When the Samaritans accepted the gospel, the Spirit did not immediately fall on them. Peter and John laid their hands on the believers and then they received the Holy Spirit (Acts 8:17). Yet at other times the Spirit came upon believers spontaneously (Acts 2:4; 10:44) or at baptism, a rite with which the laying on of hands was often associated.

To Heal. Laying on of hands was not associated with healing in the OT or in rabbinic tradition. Jesus laid hands on those who were sick while he spoke a word of command to deliver the demon-possessed (Mk 1:31,41; 5:41; 7:33,34; 8:23,25; 9:27). In continuity with Jesus the early church often used the laying on of hands to effect healing (Acts 9:17; 28:8).

DAVID E. AUNE

See ORDAIN, ORDINATION; HEAL, HEALING.

Lazarus. 1. Lazarus the beggar. In one of Jesus' most familiar parables (Lk 16:19–31), he contrasted the earthly circumstances of a beggar named Lazarus with that of a nameless rich man. From the adjective for "rich" in the Latin Vulgate the rich man came to be called in English "Dives." The rich man relished the luxury of his wealth while an ulcerated blind beggar lay at his gate. Jesus said that Lazarus died and went to Abraham's bosom, while Dives suffered everlasting torment.

The parable of Lazarus has been misinterpreted sometimes as a condemnation of wealth instead of a warning against enjoyment of wealth without regard for the poor. It teaches that decisions in the present life determine eternal destiny.

In no other parable did Jesus identify a character by name. Some Bible students have therefore concluded that he was telling a true story. The name's symbolism, however, seems to account for its use, since Lazarus was cast in the role of one "whom God helped." In the Middle Ages the beggar Lazarus was venerated as the patron saint of lepers. Leper hospitals were called lazar-houses.

2. Lazarus of Bethany. Jesus performed the most spectacular of all his miracles (excluding his own resurrection) when he restored Lazarus of Bethany to life four days after death. Lazarus lived with his two sisters, Mary and Martha. They were among Jesus' most intimate friends (Jn 11:3,5,36). On several occasions he visited in their home, which also served as his headquarters during passion week (Mt 21:17; Lk 10:38–42; Jn 11:1–12:11). Lazarus was at the banquet in Jesus' honor when Mary anointed Jesus' feet with costly ointment (Jn 12:1–3).

The raising of Lazarus, climax of the signs in John's Gospel, receives the fullest treatment of Jesus' miracles. It produced three notable results: (1) many Jews in the vicinity of Jerusalem believed in Jesus (Jn 11:45) and some weeks later escorted him into the city (Jn 12:17,18); (2) the Jewish leaders, hardened in their rejection of Jesus, resolved that he must die (Jn 11:53); (3) those leaders also plotted Lazarus' death (Jn 12:10,11). The miracle not only showed Jesus' power over death but set the stage for his own resurrection.

Lead. Heavy, soft, blue-gray metal.

See MINERALS, METALS, AND PRECIOUS STONES.

Leah. Laban's daughter, the wife of Jacob, and the older sister of Rachel.

After deceiving his father, Isaac, into giving him the blessing intended for Esau (Gn 27:5–40), Jacob left home and went to his uncle Laban (27:43; 28:2) in distant Mesopotamia, in order to find a wife (27:46–28:2) and escape the revenge of Esau, who had determined to kill

A tomb, reputed to be that of Lazarus.

him (27:41,42). Here he fell in love with his cousin Rachel and arranged with her father to marry her in exchange for seven years of work (29:17,18). When the time for the wedding feast came, Laban deceived Jacob in an apparent scheme to keep his services for seven more years; he gave Leah instead of Rachel to Jacob on the wedding night (29:21–25). His lame excuse that custom required the giving of the older daughter in marriage before the younger (29:26) was hardly appropriate at that point and certainly should have been explained from the beginning. Leah is described as "weak," perhaps to be understood as "dull-eyed," in contrast with Rachel, who is described as "beautiful and lovely" (29:17).

Jacob's love for Rachel (29:20) induced him to agree to work for another seven years in order to receive her also as his wife. Because of the intense rivalry between the two sisters and Jacob's favoring of Rachel, the Lord blessed Leah with six sons and a daughter (Reuben, Simeon, Levi, Judah, Issachar, Zebulon, Dinah) before Rachel was given any children (29:31–35; 30:1–22). This barrenness became a great burden for Rachel over the years. At one point she bargained with Leah for mandrakes, a plant believed to ensure conception, in exchange for conjugal rights. The result was to increase her sister's advantage, however, because Leah conceived and bore her fifth son, Issachar (30:14–17).

Leah was given the honor of being the mother of the two tribes that played the most significant roles in the history of the nation of Israel. The tribe of Levi became the tribe of the priesthood. The tribe of Judah became the tribe of royalty through which the promised seed (3:15; 12:2,3; 2 Sm 7:16; Mt 1:1) ultimately came in the person of Jesus Christ.

J. ROBERT VANNOY

See JACOB #1.

Leather. Material made of animal hide, used extensively in Bible times for a wide variety of purposes. It was used as clothing in early times (Gn 3:21). At the beginning of the period of the prophets their raiment, made from animal skins, became a means of identifying them (2 Kgs 1:8; Zec 13:4). Elijah's mantle (1 Kgs 19:13,19; 2 Kgs 2:8,13,14) is described in the Greek OT as sheepskin. Animal skins were also used to make shoes (Ez 16:10), girdles (Mt 3:4), and other articles of clothing (Lv 13:48).

Some household utensils were made of leather. The most common was the container for holding liquids such as milk (Jgs 4:19), wine (Mk 2:22), and water (Gn 21:14). Oil, extracted from olives, then purified and refined, was also stored in skins, until required for cooking, toiletry, medicinal purposes, or as fuel for lamps. In all probability leather was used for beds, chairs, and other household articles. There is no reference to leather being used to make tents, but animal skins were employed in the construction of the tabernacle (Ex 25:5; Nm 4:8). Clearly these references are to tanned skins. Their use would ensure that the roof was waterproof.

The Bible is silent concerning the use of leather for making armor or weapons; however, it would be a natural choice for helmets and shields for defense, slings for offense, and quivers to hold arrows. Rubbing oil into the surface of shields, presumably to keep them from becoming brittle and therefore useless, is referred to in 2 Samuel 1:21 and Isaiah 21:5, and points to their being made of leather. A painting in the tomb of an Egyptian nobleman from about 1900 BC supplements the meager knowledge which the Bible provides concerning the use of leather in OT times. In the painting the men wear sandals and the women boots. A skin water bottle is strapped to one man's back. Another, an archer, carries a quiver on his back. The asses are carrying objects which have been identified as two pairs of goatskin bellows.

Leather was used extensively as writing material, but almost wholly in Egypt. There parchment has a very ancient history. No leather documents have been recovered from Assyria or Babylonia, probably because it was used much less extensively there than elsewhere in the ancient East. Elsewhere in the Middle East literary allusions point to its having come into use at a late period. The term "parchment" is not found before the Persian period, while "writer on parchment" does not occur before the early years of the Seleucid period. Papyrus was the chief writing material, but leather documents occurred. According to Pliny the term "parchment" came into use about 160 BC, but the use of prepared skins for writing material was known before 2000 BC in Egypt.

The difference between leather and parchment is that the former is tanned, whereas the latter is produced by treating the skins with solutions of lime, salt, or dyes, scraping off the hair on one side and the flesh on the other, stretching and drying them in a frame, then rubbing them with pumice stone to produce smooth surfaces on both sides. Vellum is fine parchment made from calf or antelope skin; this distinction eventually disappeared. At Rome in the 1st century BC and the 1st and 2nd centuries AD vellum came into restricted use. Not until the 3rd and 4th centuries did vellum prevail, when the celebrated Codex Vaticanus and the Codex Sinaiticus were produced. Whereas the whole Bible could be gathered into a single codex, which is in the form of a modern book with folded sheets, a set of from 30 to 40 rolls of papyrus would be required for the Bible. A palimpsest is vellum from which the original writing has been erased and written upon again.

In the OT leather or skins are not mentioned in connection with writing. Books in roll form are mentioned in Psalm 40:7; Jeremiah 36; and Ezekiel 2:9–3:3; but these were probably papyrus. Before the discovery of the Dead Sea Scrolls the earliest reference to Jews using parchment or leather as writing material is found in Josephus, toward the end of the 1st century AD. However, we now know that around 100 BC parchment was used by Jews. The Talmud requires the Law to be written on skins of clean animals, a regulation that still stands for books to be used in the synagogue, but it is not certain that this points to an ancient tradition.

Some of the Dead Sea Scrolls were written on leather. For example, the great scroll of Isaiah, written about 100 BC, consists of 17 sheets sewn together into a length of almost 23 feet. In 2 Timothy 4:13 the "books" may have been papyrus rolls, while the "parchments" may have been vellum rolls of part of the OT. The autographs of the NT were probably written on papyrus. Certainly John wrote his second letter on papyrus (2 Jn 12) within the last quarter of the 1st century.

Tanning is not mentioned in the OT, but it is implied in Exodus 25:5 and Leviticus 13:48. The possible use of skins of unclean animals and the constant contact with dead bodies made tanning an unclean trade, and was forbidden in the city. However, the preparation of skins for parchment was considered an honorable calling.

J. G. S. S. Thomson

See LETTER WRITING, ANCIENT; WRITING AND BOOKS.

Leaven. Any substance that produces fermentation when added to dough. Leaven may signify the dough already infected by leaven, which was put into the flour so that the leaven could pass through the entire mass before baking; or it may refer to dough that had risen through the influence of the leaven. The early Hebrews apparently depended on a piece of leavened dough for transmission of the leaven; not until much later were the lees of wine used as yeast.

The ancient Israelites regularly ate leavened bread (Hos 7:4), but in the commemoration of the Passover they were forbidden to eat leavened bread or even to have it in their homes during the Passover season (Ex 13:7). This annual observance ensured that the peo-

ple would not forget their hasty exodus from Egypt, when God's command gave no time for the preparation of leavened bread. The people were forced to carry with them their kneading troughs and the dough from which they baked unleavened cakes to sustain them as they journeyed (Ex 12:34–39; Dt 16:3).

Possibly because fermentation implied disintegration and corruption, leaven was excluded from all offerings placed on the altar to be sacrificed to God (Ex 23:18; 34:25). It was also not permitted in meal offerings (Lv 2:11; 6:17). Scripture does not tell us whether or not the showbread was unleavened, but the historian Josephus states that it was leavened (*Antiq.* 3.6.6;10).

Two exceptions to this rule should be noted. Leaven could be used in offerings that were to be eaten by the priests or others. Leavened bread could accompany the peace offering (Lv 7:13), and it was sacrificed at the feast of weeks (Pentecost) because it represented the ordinary daily food that God provided for his people (Lv 23:17).

The slow working of the leaven proved to be a problem during the agricultural stage of Hebrew development, especially during the first busy days of harvest. Unleavened dough therefore became increasingly common for ordinary baking. This practice was encouraged by the growth of the idea that leaven represented decay and corruption, as did other fermented things. This view excluded leaven as inconsistent with the concept of the perfect holiness of God. Plutarch was expressing a longheld belief current also among other peoples when he wrote, "Now leaven is itself the offspring of corruption and corrupts the mass of dough with which it has been mixed." The apostle Paul quotes a similar proverb in 1 Corinthians 5:6 and Galatians 5:9.

The significant thing about leaven is its power, which may symbolize either good or evil. Usually, though not always, leaven was a symbol of evil in rabbinic thought. Jesus refers to leaven in the adverse sense when he uses the word to describe the corrupt doctrine of Pharisees and Sadducees (Mt 16:6,11,12) and of Herod (Mk 8:15). The leaven of the Pharisees is elsewhere identified as hypocrisy (Lk 12:1; cf. Mt 23:28).

Paul applies the same concept to moral corruption, warning that "a little leaven leavens the whole lump" and admonishing his readers to "clean out the old leaven," that is, the vestiges of their unregenerate lives, and to live the Christian life with the "unleavened bread of sincerity and truth" (1 Cor 5:6–8).

On the other hand, Christ uses the concept of leaven's effect upon dough in its good sense to provide his disciples with a brief but memorable parable (Mt 13:33; Lk 13:20,21) illustrating the cumulative, pervasive influence of the kingdom of God on the world.

See FEASTS AND FESTIVALS OF ISRAEL; BREAD; UNLEAVENED BREAD; FOOD AND FOOD PREPARATION.

Lebana, Lebanah. Head of a family that returned to Jerusalem with Zerubbabel following the exile (Ezr 2:45, Lebanah; Neh 7:48).

Lebanon. Region mentioned only in the OT, although its towns, including Tyre and Sidon, are named in the NT. The name Lebanon generally refers to the double range of mountains that commences near Tyre and runs northeast following the Mediterranean coast. The two Lebanon ranges are parallel to one another, Lebanon to the west and Anti-Lebanon to the east. The name Lebanon is derived from the Hebrew root *l-b-n*, meaning "white," which may reflect either the white limestone of the mountains or the snow that lay on the mountains for six months of the year (Jer 18:14).

Geography. At the southern end the Lebanon ranges is a direct continuation of the hills of northern Galilee, with Mt Hermon (Sirion, Senir) very prominent in the Anti-Lebanon range, rising to 2774 feet. The two ranges are divided by a broad valley, the Valley of Lebanon (Jos 11:17) or "the entrance of Hamath" (Nm 34:8), the modern Beqa'a.

In the south the Lebanon range is separated from the Galilee hills by a deep east-west gorge through which the Litani River flows, entering the Mediterranean just north of Tyre. In its upper courses it follows the Beqa'a Valley in a northeasterly direction almost to Baalbek. The Lebanon ridge, about 100 miles long, stretches north to the east-west valley of the Nahr el Kebir and is marked by a series of peaks. In the south are Gebel Rihan, Tomat, and Gebel Niha (ranging from 5350 feet to nearly 6230 feet high) east of Sidon. In the center lie Gebel Baruk, Gebel Kuneiyiseh, and Gebel Sunnin (7220 feet, 6890 feet, and 8530 feet high respectively) east of Beirut. Further north, to the east of Tripoli, lies Qurnet es-Sauda, which reaches 9840 feet, and Qurnet Aruba, about 7320 feet high.

These high mountains trap the rain coming from the Mediterranean, providing both the mountain areas and the coastal strip below with good rainfall; beyond the mountains the rainfall drops. It is along the coastal strip between the mountains and the sea that the Phoenicians flourished and towns like Tyre, Zarephath, Sidon, Berytus (Beirut), Byblos (Gebal), and Tripoli were established. The coastal area has a number of headlands which are extensions of the mountain range. The coastal road had to be cut around or through these spurs. A good example is the headland of Nahr el-Kelb, a little to the north of Beirut.

On the east side of the Lebanon range is the Beqa'a Valley. The Orontes River rises in the north of this valley and flows north to enter the Mediterranean north of ancient Ugarit. This whole valley region was known in classical literature as Coelesyria (Hollow Syria). It was the "breadbasket" of the Romans.

To the east of the Beqa'a Valley is the Anti-Lebanon range, in which the Barada River rises and flows east toward the fertile oasis of Damascus. Mt Hermon in the southern part of the range was known as Sirion by the Phoenicians and Senir by the Amorites (Dt 3:9). Both names are attested in the nonbiblical literature of Assyria, the Hittites, and the Canaanites. In some biblical texts the Promised Land is said to have extended "from the wilderness and Lebanon, and from the River, the river Euphrates, to the western sea" (Dt 11:24; Jos 1:4), a description which prescribes general south-north and east-west limits.

Resources. Lebanon was famous in antiquity for its rich forests of fir and cedar. The coastal areas, the Beqa'a Valley, and the lower slopes of the mountains were suitable for olive trees, fruit trees, and vineyards, as well as some grain crops. One important product came from the sea: a mollusk of the gastropoda class from which a red or purple dye was

A cedar tree in Lebanon.

obtained. The name "Phoenician" derived from the Greek *phoinos*, red-purple. Wool dyed purple was available in Ugarit about 1500 BC. The Phoenicians had a monopoly on this industry for centuries. The people of Israel, who used a great deal of purple dye in their tabernacle furnishings (Ex 26:1,31, etc.) and the garments of their priests (Ex 28:4–6; 39:1,28,29), probably obtained the dye from the Phoenicians.

King Solomon had significant trading relations with Phoenicia. To build the temple in Jerusalem cedar and fir were obtained from Hiram I of Tyre (1 Kgs 5:6,9,14; 7:2; 10:17,21; 2 Chr 2:8,16). Solomon paid for this timber in wheat and olive oil (1 Kgs 5:11). The trees were floated down by sea to a point in Solomon's domain (possibly the Yarkon River just north of Tel Aviv, close to Tell Qasile) and transported from there to Jerusalem. Cedar and fir trees from Lebanon and Anti-Lebanon provided ships for Tyre (Ez 27:5), sacred barges and furniture for Egypt, and timber for building the second temple in Jerusalem (Ezr 3:7).

From the ports of Lebanon the Phoenicians traded with many lands. They mastered the art of shipbuilding, and their ships were used in peace and in war. A vivid picture of the trading activities of traders from Tyre, Sidon, Gebal, and Arvad is given in Ezekiel 27, where the extent and nature of their trade is given in considerable detail.

History. The area became of interest to the Egyptians during the 4th dynasty (c. 2600 BC) when Pharaoh Snofru acquired 40 shiploads of cedar from Lebanon. Byblos fell under Egyptian influence during the 12th dynasty (c. 1980–1800 BC) and Egyptians gave golden ornaments in exchange for cedar. During the 18th dynasty (c. 1552–1306 BC) Egypt conquered Syria, and the records speak regularly of cedar being taken as tribute. Later an envoy of Rameses XI named Wenamon paid dearly for the cedar (c. 1100 BC).

When Egyptian power waned, the Assyrians controlled the area and took vast quantities of cedar as tribute from the days of Tiglath-pileser I (c. 1100 BC) onwards. Nebuchadnezzar and the Babylonian nation likewise controlled Lebanon and took away large quantities of cedar to build temples and palaces. The spoiling of Lebanon's forests was spoken of by Isaiah (14:8) and Habukkuk (2:17). In later centuries Lebanon passed successively under the domination of Persians, Greeks, and Romans.

In NT times the towns of Tyre and Sidon are generally coupled together (Mt 15:21; Mk 3:8; 7:24,31; Lk 6:17; 10:13,14; Acts 12:20), though sometimes they are referred to alone

(Acts 21:3,7). A Greek woman who was a Syrophoenician is referred to in Mark 7:26. Jesus preached in these areas during his ministry. In biblical poetry the tall cedars of Lebanon were a symbol of majesty and strength (Jgs 9:15; 1 Kgs 14:9; Pss 92:12; 104:16; Is 35:2; 60:13). They were also a symbol of earthly pride that would be broken before the wrath of God one day (Ps 29:5; Is 2:13; 10:34; Jer 22:6; Ez 31:3).

JOHN A. THOMPSON

Lebaoth. Town in the Negeb of Judah (Jos 15:32) occupied by the tribe of Simeon under the name Beth-lebaoth (Jos 19:6). The parallel list of Simeonite towns has Beth-biri (KJV Beth-birei) in this place (1 Chr 4:31). The element *beth*, "house of," is undoubtedly original, denoting a place of worship of the goddess of the lions (*lebaoth*); Beth-biri might be another place or just a textual variant typical of the list in 1 Chronicles.

Lebbaeus. Alternate name given to Thaddaeus, one of the 12 disciples, in Matthew 10:3 (KJV only). Most versions omit the name, which comes from a textual variant followed by the KJV translators.

See THADDAEUS, THE APOSTLE.

Lebo-hamath. Town on the Orontes River below Riblah; perhaps the correct reading for the phrase "entrance of Hamath" in numerous OT passages (Nm 34:8; 1 Kgs 8:65; 2 Kgs 14:25; Ez 47:15).

See HAMATH #1.

Lebonah. Town located between Shiloh and Shechem (Jgs 21:19). It is usually identified with modern Lubban, about three miles northwest of Shiloh.

Lecah. Either a person, descendant of the Judahite Er, or an otherwise unknown place in Judah settled by Er, depending on one's understanding of "father" (1 Chr 4:21).

Leech. Blood-sucking, segmented worm, mentioned only in Proverbs 30:15.

See ANIMALS.

Leek. Garden herb (Nm 11:5).

See PLANTS (ONION).

Legion. A unit of the Roman army. In NT times the standard size of the legion was 6000 men, to which some 120 cavalry were added.

Because it represented a large body of men, the word "legion" came to be used symbolically for an indefinitely large number; this use occurs four times in the NT. In the story about the demoniac in the country of the Gerasenes, Jesus asked the man, "What is your name?" and the reply was, "My name is Legion, for we are many" (Mk 5:9,15; Lk 8:30; cf. Mt 12:45; Lk 8:2, which speak of a number of demons possessing a single individual).

The other use of the word is in Matthew 26:53, where at the time of Jesus' arrest one of those with him drew his sword to defend his Master; Jesus forbade such action, saying, "Do you think that I cannot appeal to my Father, and he will at once send me more than twelve legions of angels?" Thus he spoke of the vast number of angels that could be summoned to his aid. However, the armies of heaven were not to be used to do what would have been in opposition to the will of his Father, which Jesus wanted above all things to fulfill.

The word "legion" is never used in the NT in its military sense, but either of the spiritual powers of evil that oppose men (cf. Eph 6:12) or of the spiritual powers that can be summoned to their aid (cf. Heb 1:14).

See ARMS AND WARFARE.

Lehabim. One of several peoples associated with Egypt (Gn 10:13; 1 Chr 1:11). The Lehabim are either an unidentified people near Egypt or, as many scholars hold, probably correctly, identical with the Lubim (Libyans). The latter are often seen in the Bible as fighting in alliance with Egypt (Jer 46:9 Lud; Dn 11:43; Na 3:9), sometimes against Israel, as in the time of Rehoboam (2 Chr 12:3) and Asa (2 Chr 16:8).

Lehem. Obscure Hebrew term in 1 Chronicles 4:22. Following the Hebrew, some understand Jashubi-lehem as a descendant of Judah (KJV) or a place where Joash and Saraph ruled (NIV). Others, changing the Hebrew slightly, translate "returned to Lehem" (RSV), meaning either Bethlehem or some unknown place.

Lehi. Place in Judah where the Philistines assembled to capture Samson (Jgs 15:9). The place was evidently in the hills, and after Samson's victory with a jawbone of an ass for a weapon it was called "the height of the jawbone," that is, Ramath-lehi (v 17). It was apparently near a spring in a crater or depression (v 19). An adjacent cliff was called Etam (v 11). Other than somewhere in the hills behind Beth-shemesh, there is no hint of where to locate (Ramath-) Lehi.

Lemuel. King credited with writing Proverbs 31:1–9. In these verses he sets forth teachings given him by his mother on good government, sex, and wine. Although he has been identified with Solomon, most modern interpreters reject this identification.

Lentils. Pea-like fruit.

See FOOD AND FOOD PREPARATION; PLANTS.

Leopard. *See* ANIMALS.

Leprosy, Leper. Chronic infectious disease caused by *Mycobacterium leprae*, a bacterium similar to the tuberculosis bacillus. The disease is manifested by changes in the skin, mucous membranes, and peripheral nerves. In the skin there are often patches of depigmentation but rarely a total loss of pigment, so a pure white patch of skin is definitely not characteristic of leprosy. Loss of sensation to touch and temperature is frequently associated with the depigmented patches. Thickening of the skin and nodule formation cause the lionlike facial appearance commonly associated with leprosy. Peripheral nerve involvement may cause paralysis of a hand, leg, or face, or it may cause loss of sensation so complete that serious injury or ulceration to an extremity may occur without the afflicted person knowing it. The eyes, ears, and the nose are also frequently involved. An effective though prolonged treatment has been developed, and sometimes spontaneous arrest may occur. The disease is spread through prolonged contact with an individual having leprosy. Children are more susceptible than adults, but in any case the transmissibility is low.

The early history of leprosy is shrouded in uncertainty. Possible references to leprosy have been cited in ancient Egyptian, Babylonian, and Indian writings, but authorities disagree whether the records refer to modern leprosy. This ambiguity in these early records is significant because it limits the help they might give toward our understanding of the meaning of "leprosy" in the OT.

In the Old Testament. Leviticus 13 and 14 contain the most details about what is called "leprosy" in the Scriptures. Careful study of the descriptions of the disease given in these passages strongly suggests that what we now diagnose leprosy is not intended. If a priest today used the criteria given in these verses, he would probably declare many leprosy patients unclean; but he would also pronounce unclean many individuals with a variety of other skin conditions. The disease we call leprosy does not fit the description given in Leviticus. The white hairs referred to so frequently in these verses are not typical of leprosy and may be found in many skin diseases. A white patch of skin is not characteristic of leprosy, nor is the scalp ordinarily affected. A

7- to 14-day period is usually inadequate to observe changes in the disease. If modern leprosy is being described in these verses, it seems strange that the more obvious characteristics of the disease are not mentioned. The bacillus of leprosy has defied attempts by bacteriologists to cultivate it, so leprosy of garments or houses is most unlikely to occur. Therefore the biblical leprosy is not synonymous with modern leprosy. The Hebrew word translated "leprosy" is derived from an Arabic word meaning to strike down or scourge; thus it could be a generic term for serious skin diseases or for signs of defilement on the surface of inanimate objects.

Criteria are given in Leviticus 13:2–8 by which the priest would determine whether a given skin condition was to be regarded as leprosy. Different types of leprosy are described in Leviticus 13:9–59. An ulcer appearing with white skin and hairs was termed chronic leprosy, and the person was declared unclean but without the need of a quarantine period. Another type of leprosy, involving the entire skin, did not make the person unclean. Leprosy coming after the healing of a boil is described in verses 18–23, and after a burn in verses 24–28. In verses 29–39 the description given for leprosy of the scalp and beard is suggestive of a fungus infection. Leprosy in connection with baldness is described in verses 47–59. If "defiling disease" instead of "leprosy" were used in the translation of these verses, as suggested by an eminent leprologist, it would eliminate much confusion and probably convey the true meaning of the original word more accurately.

Ceremonial Purification. The ceremonial purification of one who had recovered from leprosy is described in Leviticus 14:1–32. The first step took place outside the camp, where the priest examined the person to verify his recovery. Then two live birds were taken, along with cedar wood, a piece of scarlet cloth, and hyssop. One bird was killed over an earthen vessel containing fresh running water, and the living bird was dipped in the blood mixed with water and then released. The same blood mixed with water was sprinkled seven times on the healed person. This rite is an expressive symbolization of the healed condition of the individual. The flight of the living bird symbolized the new freedom and liberty entered into by the one previously in a state of living death. The slain bird represented the death that must certainly result from the person's former condition of uncleanness. The blood and water, representing life and purity, were sprinkled upon the healed person, identifying him with the bird that was alive and at liberty. The cedar wood, scarlet cloth, and hyssop were further symbols of life and purity.

After this symbolic purification the individual was required to cleanse himself bodily; and although he could now enter the camp, he still had to remain outside his tent for another seven days.

The second part of the purification rite restored the person to fellowship with God. It began with another bodily cleansing on the eighth day. A male lamb was sacrificed as a trespass offering, and this with a log of oil was used as a wave offering reconsecrating the person to the service of the Lord. Next a lamb was offered in the holy place as a sin offering. Some of the blood of the trespass offering was placed on the tip of the right ear, on the thumb of the right hand, and on the great toe of the right foot of the person to be consecrated, thereby sanctifying the organs of hearing, acting, and walking for God's service, as in the dedication of priests (Lv 8:24). After sprinkling the oil seven times before the Lord in order to consecrate it, the priest put the oil on the same places he had put the blood and poured the remainder on the head, thus making atonement before the Lord.

Students of the OT are generally agreed that leprosy of garments (Lv 13:47–59) and houses (Lv 14:33–53) was probably due to a mold or fungus growth. If a garment was found to have leprosy, it was burned. In the case of a house, an effort was made to eradicate the leprosy, and if that was successful, a ceremonial cleansing was carried out. This rite was similar to the first stage of the ceremonies for a healed person. If the leprosy could not be eliminated, the house was demolished and the remains carried outside the city.

In the New Testament. In the NT there is no description of the disease referred to as leprosy, so again we cannot be certain whether it is the modern disease or not. Modern leprosy was known to the people of that day, but it is doubtful whether they were always able to accurately distinguish it from other skin conditions. The Greek word translated "leprosy" in the NT basically means scaly. The Greeks used it to designate psoriasis-like skin conditions, and they referred to leprosy by the word we translate as "elephantiasis," a word not found in the NT. Confusion concerning the use of the word "leprosy" extends even to the Middle Ages, leaving historians uncertain at times concerning the historical spread of the disease. When we read in the NT that Christ cleansed lepers, we know only that he healed chronic skin conditions considered to be defiling.

The attitude of Christ toward those afflicted with leprosy was in marked contrast to the rabbis of his day. One rabbi would not eat an egg purchased in a street where there was someone with leprosy. Another rabbi threw stones at lepers in order to keep them away. On the other hand, in healing, Christ touched a man with leprosy, thereby demonstrating his power to overcome uncleanness as represented by leprosy (Mt 8:3; Mk 1:41,42; Lk 5:12,13).

See MEDICINE AND MEDICAL PRACTICE; PLAGUE.

Leshem. Alternate name for Laish, the early name for the city of Dan, in Joshua 19:47.

See DAN (PLACE) #1.

Lethech. Dry measure equaling about two to three measures.

See WEIGHTS AND MEASURES.

Letter Writing, Ancient. A communication from a king or high official, usually containing commands, promulgations, or reports. There are letters extant from Arad-Nana, the royal physician, to his master Ashurbanipal on the matter of the monarch's spondylitis and a young prince's eye trouble. The famous Amarna letters are reports and appeals from petty subject princes in Palestine disturbed over the weakness of Pharaoh Akhnaton's foreign policy in the area. There is a tantalizing letter from Tutankhamen's widow to a Hittite king on the subject of a marriage arrangement.

Examples of OT letters are David's deadly letter to Joab about Uriah (2 Sm 11:14,15), Jezebel's equally evil letter over Ahab's forged signature to the elders of Jezreel (1 Kgs 21:8,9), and the Syrian king's letter to the king of Israel about Naaman's leprosy (2 Kgs 5:5–7). All these are reported in the OT record without the customary greetings and the polite forms of address. In Ezra (4:11–23; 5:5–17; 7:11–26), Nehemiah (6:5–7), and Jeremiah, correspondence appears which purports to be the full text. Commonly there is paraphrase, abbreviation, or mere report of content (Neh 2:8; Est 9:20–31).

Official communications in letter form like those noted in the OT are found in the Egyptian papyri. For example, there is the letter of Claudius sent in AD 42 to the turbulent Alexandrians about the Jewish problem in that city. A circular letter of the early 2nd century from the governor of Egypt about the approaching census, and highly relevant to the story of the nativity, is known. The letters of Cicero provide invaluable information on the stormy period which saw the end of senatorial rule and the establishment of the Roman Empire. The letters of Pliny show Roman society at its best at the turn of the 1st century of the Christian era, when the writer was governor of Bithynia, and they give much information

about the first clash between the state and the church.

Ancient correspondence throws vivid light on common life and the mundane occupations of ordinary people in Greco-Roman times and the early Christian centuries in a manner only to be paralleled in the documents of the NT. It provides background, illustration, comment, and sometimes direct historical evidence—as, for example, the letter file of the leader of the second rebellion of the Jews (132–35), Bar Kochba. A cache of Bar Kochba's letters and campaign documents has been discovered in a cave by the Dead Sea. It is strange to read his terse orders. "Whatever Elisha says, do," reads one command. Another orders the arrest of Tahnun Ben Ishmael and the confiscation of his wheat. Another calls for punishment of some who had repaired their homes, in defiance of some scorched-earth policy; it is all very cold, hard, and infinitely pitiable.

Paul observed with some care the forms of polite address common in his day. There is an opening word of salutation, followed by thanksgiving and prayer for the person or company addressed. Then comes the special subject of communication, greetings to friends, and perhaps a closing word of prayer. Here is a 2nd-century letter which shows strikingly the Pauline style in brief:

> Ammonous to her sweetest father, greeting. When I received your letter and recognized that by the will of the gods you were preserved, I rejoiced greatly. And as at the same time an opportunity here presented itself, I am writing you this letter being anxious to pay my respects. Attend as quickly as possible to the matters that are pressing. Whatever the little one asks shall be done. If the bearer of this letter hands over a small basket to you, it is I who sent it. All your friends greet you by name. Celer greets you and all who are with him. I pray for your health.

In subject matter Paul ranges from delicate irony over Corinthian pretensions to stern rebuke for heresy, and from news of friends to some precious books and the warm cloak he left at Troas.

The NT letters continue and adapt a mode of didactic correspondence that can be traced back to Plato and Aristotle, save that the NT writers address themselves to groups or communities (Romans, Corinthians, Galatians, Philippians, Ephesians, Colossians, Thessalonians, Hebrews), to the church at large (the letters of Peter, Jude, James, and John's first epistle), or to individuals or a specific Christian community. The apostolic letter recorded in Acts 15 may have inspired this practice. Revelation 2 and 3 are genuine letters to seven churches on John's Asian circuit and were no doubt understood by those who had the key to their imagery.   E. M. BLAIKLOCK

See WRITING AND BOOKS; LACHISH LETTERS; LIBRARIES, ANCIENT.

Letushim. Second of Dedan's three sons and a descendant of Abraham and Keturah through Jokshan's line (Gn 25:3). Letushim and Leummim (the plural form of the Hebrew names) probably refer to the subsequent tribes founded by Dedan's sons. Some suggest that these tribes eventually settled in northern Arabia.

Leummim. Third of Dedan's three sons and, with Latushim, a descendant of Abraham and Keturah through Jokshan's line (Gn 25:3).

See LETUSHIM.

Levi (Person). 1. Jacob's third son by Leah (Gn 29:34). The etymology of the name is uncertain. Levi's name is associated with the tragedy at Shechem, where the male inhabitants of the city were ruthlessly murdered when Levi and Simeon sought to avenge the violation of their sister Dinah by Shechem the Hivite. Jacob condemned the act and before his death pronounced a judgment on Levi's behavior: "Simeon and Levi are brothers; weapons of violence are their swords. . . . I will divide them in Jacob and scatter them in Israel" (Gn 49:5–7). According to these words Levi's descendants were to be dispersed among the tribes.

The tribe of Levi was composed of the descendants of Levi's three sons: Gershon, Kohath, and Merari. Moses, Aaron, and Miriam traced their genealogy to Kohath (Ex 6:16). The Levites remained faithful to Yahweh at the occasion of the golden calf by Mt Horeb. They were rewarded with the right to special service in and around the tabernacle (Ex 32) and later in the temple.

See LEVI, TRIBE OF.

2. Tax collector in Capernaum (Mk 2:14). Jesus enjoyed a banquet at Levi's house to which other tax collectors had been invited, to the great irritation of some Pharisees (Lk 5:27–32). He may be identified with Matthew, one of the 12 apostles, if the reading "Levi, son of Alphaeus" (Mk 2:14) is maintained. Several Greek manuscripts read "James" instead.

See MATTHEW, THE APOSTLE.

3. Son of Milchi and ancestor of Jesus (Lk 3:24).

See GENEALOGY OF JESUS CHRIST.

4. Son of Simeon and ancestor of Jesus (Lk 3:29).

See GENEALOGY OF JESUS CHRIST.

Levi, Tribe of. Israelite tribe taking its name from the third son of Leah and Jacob (Gn 29:34). The meaning of the name ("attached") is a pun on Leah's position as an unloved wife: now that she has borne three sons to Jacob, surely he will be "attached" to her. Elsewhere, by a similar pun, the tribe of Levi is described as "attached" to Aaron (Nm 18:2). Some have thought this to mean that outsiders could be "attached" to Levi by dedication, like Nazirites. Samuel of Ephraim (1 Sm 1:1) is often given as an example, but 1 Chronicles 6:28 gives him a levitical lineage, and there is no clear evidence in Scripture for such a custom.

Levi appears with Simeon at the treacherous slaughter of the inhabitants of Canaanite Shechem (Gn 34:25–29). This brings Jacob's rebuke at the time (Gn 34:30) and his death-bed curse (Gn 49:5–7), foretelling that the descendants of Levi and Simeon will be scattered throughout Israel. This does not seem a likely background for God's priestly tribe, but so it proved to be; for it was as a priestly tribe that Levi was scattered through Israel, while Simeon merely melted into the desert south of Judah.

At first Levi was apparently a "secular" tribe like any other. True, Moses and Aaron were of Levi (Ex 2:1), but no stress is laid on this. Levi's later position was God's reward for its costly faithfulness when Israel rebelled against God (Ex 32:25–29); this inaugurated the "covenant with Levi" (Nm 18:19). Henceforth the tribe of Levi would be accepted by God instead of Israel's firstborn sons, who belonged to him by the law of "firstfruits" (Nm 3:11–13). Levi, as a tribe, could therefore own no tribal territory: God himself was their inheritance (Nm 18:20). However, they were given 48 villages, with their pasturelands, in which to live (Jos 21:1–42). These included the six cities of refuge (Jos 20:1–9).

Since Levi could not amass wealth, the tribe was to be supported by gifts and tithes (Nm 18:21); like the widow, orphan, and stranger, they were commended to the care of God's people (Dt 14:29). Since they were God's tribe, Joab was unwilling to include Levi in David's census (1 Chr 21:6; cf. Nm 1:49). Naturally, Levi did not serve in war except in a religious capacity (2 Chr 20:21). Their service was that of the meeting tent (Nm 1:50–53) and later, the temple (1 Chr 23:25–32). Within Levi the Bible makes a clear distinction between the high priest (sometimes merely called "the priest," 1 Sm 1:9) who came from one branch of Aaron's family; the rest of the priests, also of particular families; and a mass of subordinate Levites, who had lesser tasks. In early days they packed and moved the portable meeting tent (Nm 1:50,51), among other duties; in later days they apparently served as porters and choristers (1 Chr 16:42). The duties of Levi are summarized in Deuteronomy 33:8–11, where oracular guidance and theological instruction are just as important as their priestly duties. It is therefore no surprise that Jehoshaphat later uses them as teachers of law (2 Chr 17:7–9). Nevertheless, the ordinary Israelite thought of them primarily as priestly (Jgs 17:13).

Later references to the lasting covenant with Levi are found in Jeremiah 33:20–26 and Malachi 3:3–4. Members of the tribe returned from the exile (Ezr 2:36–42), apparently more coming from the priestly than the wider levitical section. Barnabas, in NT days, belonged to the tribe of Levi (Acts 4:36); and indeed among modern Jews, wherever the surname Levy is found, a member of the tribe probably lives on. But to the author of Hebrews, with the coming of the priesthood of Christ, the special position of Levi has lost its meaning (Heb 7:11–14).   R. ALAN COLE

See PRIESTS AND LEVITES.

Leviathan.   Great sea monster or large aquatic reptile (Jb 3:8; Ps 74:14).

See ANIMALS.

Levirate Marriage.   Israelite custom in which a man, upon the death of his brother, marries his brother's widow and raises up children for his brother.

See MARRIAGE, MARRIAGE CUSTOMS.

Levites.   *See* LEVI (PERSON) #1; LEVI, TRIBE OF; PRIESTS AND LEVITES.

Levitical Cities.   Special areas set aside for the tribe of Levi in place of a regular territorial inheritance (Nm 18:20–24; 26:62; Dt 10:9; 18:1,2; Jos 18:7). The Levites were allotted 48 cities, including the 6 cities of refuge (Nm 35:6,7). Each town and a limited zone around it was for the Levites (Nm 35:3–5); their property enjoyed a special status with regard to the laws of redemption (Lv 25:32–34).

Two lists of the levitical cities are given (Jos 21; 1 Chr 26). Thirteen towns were for the priests (Jos 21:4), including the six cities of refuge. In spite of some variation between the two lists, it seems clear that they go back to one original. Thorough study of the list requires careful use of the Greek translations in comparison with the Hebrew text. The towns in the list are nearly all well known from other passages. In fact, only about five of them have no possible identification with a known site of antiquity.

The distribution of the levitical towns tells much about their purpose. They were distributed among the 12 tribes but not usually placed at the tribal centers. Those in Judah and Simeon were actually in the southern hill country, the area where the satellite clans of the Calebites and the Kenizzites had settled. Those in Benjamin were grouped along the southern half of that tribe's inheritance, the part later attached to Judah; the family of Saul was located there. Levitical towns were placed in border areas where garrisons were required—for example, on the eastern desert fringes in Reuben and facing Philistia in Dan. Other key territories were in the plains where Asher, Manasseh, and other Galilean tribes had originally failed to conquer the Canaanite cities (Jgs 1:27,31). Thus, the Levites were assigned places where the special task of controlling strategic areas was necessary. Many of the towns were not taken during the initial conquest and only came under Israelite control in the reign of David.

Though the Levites were not the exclusive residents of any one city (they shared them with other Israelites), they were posted there for specific duties. They tended to the work of the Lord and the service of the king (1 Chr 26:30–32). Collecting tithes (Nm 18:21; Dt 14:28), handling legal and judicial matters (1 Chr 26:29; 2 Chr 17:8; 19:8–10), military garrison duties (1 Chr 26:1–19), and managing the storehouses (1 Chr 26:22) were all levitical responsibilities. Though they served by rotation in the capital (1 Chr 27:1), they also had similar duties the year round in their home districts (1 Chr 26:29–32).

Their loyalty to the house of David caused them to lose their status in the northern kingdom, so most of them joined Judah when the kingdom was split (2 Chr 11:13,14).

There can be no doubt that the list of levitical cities represents a geographical and social reality. There is no need to posit a utopian design in the list. In fact, the geographic distribution of the towns shows that symmetry was not the guiding principle of the arrangement, even though a balance among the 12 tribes is somewhat in evidence.

See CITIES OF REFUGE.

Leviticus, Book of.   Third book of the OT, largely concerned with the duties of the levitical priests.

Author. A traditional alternative title of Leviticus is the Third Book of Moses, which gives proper credit to the man who, humanly speaking, most deserves to be called its author. For though the book never says that Moses wrote down any of the material, it repeat-

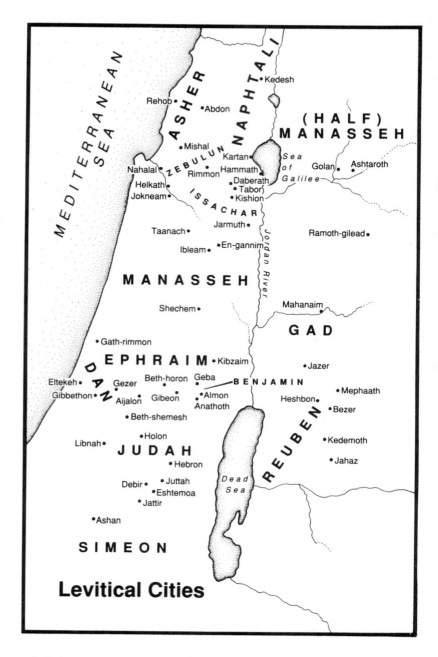

Levitical Cities

edly states that God revealed the contents of Leviticus to Moses. It may be that Leviticus was not put into writing as soon as it was revealed, but there is little to commend the common critical view that it was composed nearly a thousand years after Moses. The spelling and grammar of Leviticus was, like other books of the OT, revised from time to time to make it understandable to later generations of Jewish readers, but that does not mean the essential content of the book was modified.

Date. God revealed some of the laws in Leviticus by speaking to Moses from the tent of meeting, or tabernacle (Lv 1:1). Other laws were revealed on Mt Sinai (26:46). Such statements show that Moses learned the contents of Leviticus after the tabernacle had been built, but before the Israelites left Mt Sinai. This fits in with Exodus 40:17, which says that the tabernacle was erected exactly a year after the Israelites left Egypt. They then spent another month at Sinai, during which time the laws in

Leviticus were given to Moses. Then one month later (Nm 1:1) Moses was commanded to prepare the people to leave Sinai to conquer the Promised Land of Canaan.

It is difficult to give an exact date for the Israelite exodus from Egypt. Dates at the end of the 15th century BC or early in the 13th century are put forward by different scholars. Whichever view is adopted, the origin of Leviticus must be one year later than the exodus. But certainty about the absolute date of Leviticus is unimportant so long as the religious setting of the book is understood.

Background. About 400 years before the exodus God promised Abraham that his descendants would be very numerous and live in the land of Canaan (approximately modern Israel). The family of Abraham multiplied, but as a result of famine they had to go and live in Egypt. Afraid of the Israelites, the rulers of Egypt turned them into slaves.

The Book of Exodus tells how God, acting through Moses, brought the Israelites out of Egypt in a miraculous way. Moses led them to Mt Sinai, where God appeared in fire and smoke on the top of the mountain. Moses went up the mountain, and there God gave him the Ten Commandments and explained various laws. Through these acts God showed that he had chosen the nation of Israel to be his special holy people, different from all the other nations and showing God's character through their behavior (cf. Ex 19:5,6).

God's revelation at Sinai was unique and unrepeatable. But he disclosed to Moses that he wanted to live among the people of Israel permanently. They were therefore told to build a portable royal palace that would be suitable for the divine King of kings. The building of this portable palace, traditionally called the tabernacle, is described in Exodus 35–40. When it was completed, the fire and cloud that had been seen on Mt Sinai appeared over the tabernacle as a sign that God was now dwelling in it (Ex 40:34–38).

Exodus also tells how Moses was told to appoint his brother Aaron and his sons to serve in the tabernacle as priests (Ex 28,29). Unfortunately, before the Israelites even began to build the tabernacle, they made a golden calf under Aaron's leadership and started to worship it instead. Only as a result of Moses' prayers was the whole people spared. The Book of Exodus therefore leaves the reader in suspense. The tabernacle has been built, but no one knows how to worship God in it. Though Aaron and his family are alive, we are left wondering whether they will still be allowed to lead the worship of God after the idolatry of the golden calf. God has been so gracious as to take up residence among Israel,

but how are they to respond? The Book of Leviticus answers these questions.

Purpose and Theology. The Ten Commandments explain briefly and simply how God expects his people to behave. The first four commandments explain our duty toward our neighbor. The Book of Leviticus follows a similar scheme. Chapters 1–17 show how God wanted Israel to worship him, while chapters 18–27 are mainly concerned with how people should behave toward each other. Whereas the Ten Commandments are general and can be applied quite easily to every society, the Book of Leviticus is much more detailed and specifically geared to the special circumstances of ancient Israel. If modern readers are to profit from reading Leviticus, they must look behind the specific regulations to the underlying religious principles which do not change—in other words, to the theology of Leviticus.

Four themes are very important in the theology of Leviticus: (1) the presence of God, (2) holiness, (3) sacrifice, and (4) the Sinai covenant.

The Presence of God. God is always present with Israel in a real way. Sometimes his presence becomes visible in fire and smoke. But even when there is no miraculous sign, God is really present. He is especially near when people worship him and offer sacrifice. The many animal sacrifices mentioned in the book are all brought to the Lord. When the animals are burnt, God is pleased with the smell (1:9). The priests who offer the sacrifices must be especially careful since they come closer to God than other people do. If they are careless in their duties and break God's commands, they may die (10:1,2).

God is present not just in worship but in all the ordinary duties of life. The recurring refrain of the later chapters, "I am the Lord your God" (18:2; 19:3), reminds the Israelites that every aspect of their life—religion (chs 21–24), sex (chs 18, 20), and relations with neighbors (chs 19,25)—matters to God. The behavior of every Israelite must mirror that of God himself (20:7). The fear of God should prompt persons to help the blind, the deaf, the elderly, and the poor. Though such people may have no redress against unfair treatment, God cares what happens to them (19:14,32; 25:17,36,43).

Holiness. "Be holy, for I am holy" (11:44, 45; 19:2; 20:26) could be termed the motto of Leviticus. "Holy," "clean," and "unclean" are common words in this book. God is the supremely holy person in the Bible, and holiness is the distinctive feature of his character. But earthly creatures can become holy too. To become holy a person must be chosen by God and undergo the correct ceremony. Thus, at

Sinai all Israel became a holy nation (Ex 19:6). Leviticus 8,9 explains how Aaron and his sons were ordained priests. This made them more holy than ordinary Israelites and therefore able to approach God and offer sacrifice.

Before anyone could become holy they had to be "clean." Cleanness in Leviticus means more than just being free of dirt, though this idea is included. It means being free of any abnormality. Whenever a person appears to fall short of perfection, he is described as "unclean." Thus, the worst uncleanness is death, the very opposite of perfect life. But bleeding and other discharges and patchy skin diseases can make someone unclean. Animals which move in peculiar ways or have strange habits are also called unclean (chs 11–15).

Holiness and its opposite, uncleanness, can describe behavior as well as outward appearance. To be holy means to obey God and to act like God. Chapters 18–25 explain what holiness means in daily living. It means avoiding illicit sexual relations, caring for the poor, honesty, fairness, and loving your neighbor as yourself. This sort of behavior made Israel different from other peoples. Through their holiness the whole nation was supposed to demonstrate what God was like.

Sacrifice. In practice, unfortunately, the nation and the individuals within it rarely lived up to these ideals of holiness. Even if one did not commit a grievous sin himself, he was always liable to become unclean through contact with someone else, touching a dead animal, or in some other way. To maintain contact with a holy God, Israel's sins and uncleanness had to be removed. This is what the sacrifices were for. They brought the forgiveness of sins and cleansing from uncleanness. Because sin affects relations between God and man in various ways, Leviticus provides four different types of offering to cover the different cases (Lv 1–6), and explains which sacrifices must be offered on which occasion (Lv 7–17). All these rituals served to underline the seriousness of sin and helped preserve peace and fellowship between God and humanity.

The Sinai Covenant. All the laws contained in Leviticus form part of the Sinai covenant. They fill out and apply the principles of the Ten Commandments to the specific circumstances of ancient Israel. But they are more than a set of detailed rules, because they were given as part of the covenant. Three things have to be remembered about this covenant. First, the covenant created a personal relationship. The Lord became Israel's king, and Israel became his special treasure set apart from the other nations of the world. Second, the covenant was based on God's grace. He had made a promise to Abraham and, in saving the people from Egyptian slavery, he demonstrated his faithfulness to his promise and his love for Israel. Israel, in turn, was to show its gratitude for salvation by keeping the Law. In no way did keeping the Law earn them salvation. The Law was given to a redeemed people. Finally, there were promises and threats built into the covenant (Lv 26). When the nation keeps the Law, God promises they will enjoy good harvests, victory over their enemies, and God walking among them as he did in Eden. But if they reject God's laws, terrible calamities will befall them: drought, famine, defeat, and even expulsion from the land God had promised to give them. These covenant curses form the background to the prophets' warnings in later times.

Contents. *Kinds of Sacrifice (Chs 1–7).* These chapters explain how the different kinds of sacrifice were to be offered. Most of these sacrifices also formed part of the regular worship in the tabernacle and later in the temple. But these chapters are concerned with personal offerings made when someone had sinned or made a vow or recovered from an illness. They explain what the offerer must do and what the priest must do; which parts of the animal must be burned, which parts may be eaten by the priest; what is to be done with the blood of the animal.

First, the offerer brought the animal into the outer court of the tabernacle. In the presence of the priest he put his hand on the head of the animal and explained why he was bringing the sacrifice. Then the worshiper killed the animal and chopped it up. The priest then took over. He caught the blood as it ran out of the dying animal and splashed it over the altar, and burned at least some of the animal on the great altar in the court of the tabernacle. These acts were performed with all the animal sacrifices.

The special feature of the burnt offering (Lv 1) was that the whole animal, which had to be unblemished, was burned on the altar. All that the priest received was the skin. This was the most common sacrifice and was offered on many different occasions. In giving the whole animal to God in the sacrifice the worshiper dedicated himself totally to God's service. When someone sinned "he shall lay his hand upon the head of the burnt offering, and it shall be accepted for him to make atonement for him" (1:4).

Chapter 2 deals with the grain offering that always accompanied the burnt offering, but which could also be offered alone. Only part of this offering was burned; the rest was given to the priests to eat. The sacrifices formed an important part of their income.

The peace offering's special feature was that it was the only sacrifice where the offerer was allowed to eat part of the meat (Lv 3). Since in the earliest period Israelites were not permitted to kill animals except for sacrifice (Lv 17), every meal that included meat had to be preceded by a peace offering. Leviticus 7:11–18 mentions three occasions that might prompt a peace-offering "thanksgiving": when someone has something to praise God for or some sin to acknowledge; a vow promising a sacrifice if God will help one out of a difficulty; and a voluntary offering, made just because the person feels like it.

Despite its name, the sin offering (Lv 4) was not the only offering dealing with sin. The other sacrifices also made the forgiveness of sin possible. The special significance of this sacrifice is emphasized by its unusual ritual. Instead of the blood being splashed over the altar, as in the other sacrifices, it was carefully smeared over the horns (corners) of the large altar in the courtyard (4:30) or over the small altar inside the holy place (4:18); once a year the blood was sprinkled over the ark in the Holy of Holies (16:14). Sin makes these different parts of the tabernacle unclean, unfit for the presence of God. And if God is not present in the tabernacle, worship has no point. The blood acts as a spiritual disinfectant making the tabernacle clean and holy again. The sin offering was required whenever a person inadvertently broke one of the commandments or had suffered from a discharge or skin disease that made him unclean for a week or more (chs 12–15).

The guilt offering (5:14–6:7) was for more serious offenses, such as stealing holy property or deliberately using God's name in a false oath. Such an offense was seen as robbing God. Therefore, a ram had to be offered as a sort of repayment. Whereas the poor man could offer just a bird for the other sacrifices, a ram was always required for a guilt offering.

Chapters 6:8–7:38 contain various other regulations about sacrifice, mainly specifying how much of each sacrifice the priests may eat and how much must be burned. One important rule for the layman is that he may not eat any fat or blood or eat sacrificial meat when he is unclean. If he does, he may be "cut off from his people" (7:21–27).

Beginnings of the Priesthood (Chs 8–10). Though Leviticus looks like a law book, because it contains so many regulations, it is really a history book describing the events that occurred about a year after the exodus. These chapters remind us of the true character of the book, for they tell how Moses ordained Aaron and his sons to be priests and how they offered their first sacrifices.

Sheep qualified as sacrificial animals and could be eaten, except for their fat and blood or when the offerer was unclean (Lv 7:21–27).

Awed by the complexity of the ordination rituals, the modern reader may miss the marvel that Aaron should have been appointed high priest. For it was Aaron who had presided over the making of the golden calf and encouraged its worship (Ex 32). Had not Moses interceded for Israel, the whole nation would have been destroyed in the wilderness. Here the gracious forgiveness of God is most clear. Aaron, the chief sinner, is appointed chief mediator between God and the people. In the NT the career of Peter parallels Aaron's in some respect.

The greatness of the high priesthood is symbolized by the richly decorated robes Aaron wears. He and his sons were anointed with oil, and then Moses offered the three most common sacrifices on their behalf. They were confined to the court of the tabernacle for a week, and it seems likely that some of the rituals were repeated each day. By this means they were set apart from the rest of the people and entirely consecrated to their holy office.

By the eighth day the process was complete. Now Aaron and his sons could offer sacrifice. This time, Moses only told them what to do; he did not offer sacrifices himself. Chapter 9 concludes by telling that, after they had offered the sacrifices for themselves and the people, fire came out of the tabernacle to burn up the offerings, thus displaying God's approval of their actions.

After this, 10:1,2 are a surprise. "The sons of Aaron . . . offered unholy fire before the Lord, such as he had not commanded them. And fire came forth from the presence of the Lord and devoured them, and they died before the Lord." We do not know exactly what is meant by unholy fire. What is important is that the priests did something that God had not commanded them. The priests were supposed to set an example of total obedience to God's Word: this is the essence of holiness. Instead, they decided to follow their own plans and the consequences were dire.

"Aaron held his peace" (10:3). He is warned not even to mourn his sons' deaths, lest he be suspected of condoning their sin (vv 6,7). Yet, despite his sons' actions, Aaron and his surviving sons are confirmed as priests. They are reminded that their job is "to distinguish between the holy and the common, and between the unclean and the clean; and you are to teach the people of Israel all the statutes" (vv 10,11). The chapter closes on another note of grace. Although the priests made a mistake in offering one of the sin offerings, God will overlook it on this occasion.

Cleanness and Uncleanness (Chs 11–16). Distinguishing between the unclean and the clean is the theme of chapters 11–15, which prepare for the great Day of Atonement ceremonies of chapter 16. These are designed to cleanse the tabernacle from the uncleannesses of the people of Israel, thereby ensuring that God would continue to dwell among them (16:16,19).

Chapter 11 discusses unclean animals; that is, animals which may not be eaten. Land animals are dealt with first, then fish and birds, and finally various miscellaneous creatures such as locusts and reptiles. To be clean a land animal must have cloven hooves and chew the cud; that covers sheep and cattle but excludes pigs and camels. Fish must have fins and scales to be edible; without them they count as unclean. Birds are clean unless they are birds of prey or scavengers that eat carrion. Insects which resemble birds in having wings and two large legs to hop with—for example, locusts—are clean. Other flying insects are unclean. All squirming creatures which dart hither and thither, such as lizards, are unclean.

The reasons for declaring some animals clean and others unclean has long been a great puzzle. One suggestion is that the unclean animals were used in sacrifice by pagan worshipers or were thought to represent pagan deities. Certainly some unclean animals were used in pagan worship, but so were some clean ones, and that fact makes this explanation unsatisfactory. A second possibility is that the rules were hygienic: the clean animals were safe to eat whereas the unclean were not. There may be some truth in this explanation, but it is not completely adequate, for some clean animals can be harmful while some unclean ones are all right to eat. It also fails to explain why Jesus abolished the distinction between unclean and clean animals.

Unclean animals could not be eaten, but there was no harm in touching them. Israelites could ride camels, for example. However, all dead animals, unless killed for sacrifice, were unclean. Anyone who touched the carcass of a dead creature became unclean himself and therefore could not enter the tabernacle that day (Lv 11:39,40).

The following chapters deal with other conditions that make people unclean. Chapter 12 states that childbirth, or more precisely the bloody discharge that follows childbirth, makes a woman unclean. In OT theology death is the ultimate uncleanness, and conditions that are abnormal or threaten to lead to death are also unclean. When the discharge has ceased, after a fixed period the mother must bring a burnt offering and a sin offering to atone for any sin she may have committed, and to purify the tabernacle which may have been polluted through her uncleanness.

Chapters 13,14 deal with the uncleanness caused by skin diseases. Detailed regulations are given to distinguish between different diseases so that the priests can decide whether a person is unclean or not. If he is unclean, he must live outside the camp until his skin heals up. Traditionally the unclean skin disease has been translated as leprosy. But this is unlikely to be correct, since leprosy was unknown in the Middle East in OT times. Rather, it was any disease that led to the skin peeling off in patches, such as psoriasis. This explains why the disease might spontaneously get better.

If the disease did retreat sufficiently, the sufferer could call the priest, and if the priest was satisfied with the cure, the sufferer could be readmitted to the community after following the rituals prescribed in chapter 14. This also explains what is to be done if patches of mold are found in pieces of cloth or house walls.

Chapter 15 explains how men can become unclean through discharges from their sexual organs, due to gonorrhea or sexual intercourse, while women become unclean through menstruation or a long-term discharge. Part of the purpose of these regulations is to prevent the sacred prostitution that was common in the ancient world. Since sexual intercourse made a person unclean, he could not go to worship immediately afterward. The uncleanness of menstruation should have discouraged men from being overfamiliar with unmarried girls.

The broad scope of these uncleanness regulations meant that nearly every Israelite would be unclean at some time in his or her life. This uncleanness could contaminate God's dwelling place, the tabernacle, making it impossible for him to continue to live there. To avert this catastrophe a Day of Atonement was held once a year. This is the most solemn day in the Jewish calendar, and the ceremonies are described in detail in Leviticus 16.

There are three acts on the Day of Atonement that are described in this chapter. There was first the special sin offering offered by the high priest, in the course of which the outer altar of burnt offering, the incense altar inside the holy place, and finally the ark itself in the Holy of Holies were sprinkled with blood to purify each part of the tabernacle. This was the one occasion in the year when the high priest entered the presence of God in the Holy of Holies, and elaborate precautions were taken to screen the high priest from God's holiness (16:2–4,11–17). There was another public act which pictured the sins of Israel being taken away. A goat was chosen by lot. Then the high priest placed his hands on its head and recited over it the nation's sin. This goat was then led away and driven into a solitary place; in later times it was pushed over a precipice. These actions pictured Israel's sins being carried away, so that they could not disturb the peace between God and man. The third important feature of the Day of Atonement was public prayer and fasting. This showed that sin could not be eliminated without effort, but only through a complete change of heart by every soul in Israel.

Rules for Daily Life (Chs 17–25). Whereas the opening chapters of Leviticus are entirely concerned with the Godward side of religion, the later chapters are more concerned with practical religious duties toward other persons. However, chapter 17 repeats some of the rules about sacrifice and makes one new one: that all sacrifice must be offered in the tabernacle courtyard. This was to prevent people from secretly worshiping heathen gods.

Chapters 18 and 20 spell out the rules governing sexual relations in ancient Israel. Chapter 19 gives further examples of what holiness means in everyday life. Positively it means helping the poor by leaving some grain behind in the fields at harvest time (19:9,10); paying people promptly (19:13); avoiding gossip (19:16); honoring the elderly, helping the immigrant, and being honest in business (19:32–36). But holiness goes beyond deeds and words. It should transform thoughts: "You shall not hate your brother . . . but you shall love your neighbor as yourself" (19:17,18).

Chapters 21 and 22 discuss how the holy men of Israel, the priests, are to demonstrate their holiness in their lives. First, they must avoid approaching dead bodies unless the dead are very close relatives. Second, they must marry women of known moral uprightness. Third, deformed priests—for example, a blind or lame priest—may never offer sacrifices. Here the principle is plain that men who represent God must reflect the perfection of God in normal, healthy bodies. However,

those who are temporarily unclean, through skin disease or a discharge, may resume their duties as soon as their uncleanness is cured.

Chapter 23 lists the main holy days and the sacrifices that had to be offered on each one. Chapter 24 deals with the lamp and special bread kept within the tabernacle. A case of blasphemy that occurred in the wilderness is mentioned. Because the man actually used the sacred name of God in a curse (Yahweh, Jehovah, the Lord) he was sentenced to death.

Chapter 25 deals with the jubilee year. In every society people fall into debt. Today the effects of debt are somewhat cushioned by state welfare payments and bank overdrafts, but ancient societies did not have such aid available. People in debt had to sell off their family land on which they depended for their living, or in more serious situations, they could sell themselves into slavery. Once impoverished in this way it was exceedingly difficult ever to recover one's land or one's freedom. But this law in Leviticus provided an escape. Every 50 years was a jubilee. In this year every slave was released from bondage, and everyone who had sold his land was given it back free. Thus, everyone who fell into debt was given a chance to make a fresh start. Though this law was primarily designed to help the poor, it also served to prevent the accumulation of too much wealth in the hands of a few rich men.

Blessings, Curses, and Vows (Chs 26–27). Chapter 26 contains the blessings and curses that traditionally concluded a covenant. Israel is promised great material and spiritual prosperity if she keeps the Law but is warned that tragedy will befall if she is disobedient.

Chapter 27 is an appendix dealing with vows and other gifts made to God. When a man promises to give something to God, it becomes holy and cannot be retracted unless a suitable payment is made instead. This chapter sets out the rules about such dedications.

Leviticus and the Christian. The laws in Leviticus were given many years before Christ and seem very remote from Christian living in the late 20th century. However, though our circumstances are very different, the basic religious message of Leviticus still is vital and valid today. It is in terms of the sacrifices mentioned in Leviticus that the NT understands the death of Christ. Jesus was the true burnt offering, "the Lamb of God, who takes away the sin of the world" (Jn 1:29). Jesus was the perfect sin offering whose "blood cleanses us from all sin" (1 Jn 1:7). His death has of course made animal sacrifices obsolete, but these old levitical sacrifices show us what Jesus achieved for us.

In other ways too the theology of Leviticus

still applies to the Christian. Christians are still called to "be holy for I am holy" (1 Pt 1:16). As those who ate sacrifices while they were unclean were warned in Leviticus that they would but cut off, so Paul warned the Corinthians that those who partook of the Lord's Supper unworthily would face judgment (1 Cor 11:27–32). Leviticus insists that the priests must be examples of perfect holiness in their behavior; so Christian ministers are expected to be models of Christian virtue (1 Tm 3:1–13).

The practical exhortations to care for the poor, the blind, and the deaf; to be fair and honest; and to be faithful in marriage are just as applicable now as they were 3000 years ago. Our Lord summed up the whole Law and the prophets with a quotation from Deuteronomy 6:5, "You shall love the Lord your God with all your heart," and another from Leviticus 19:18, "You shall love your neighbor as yourself." By studying and meditating on Leviticus, the modern Christian can learn much about the character of God and his will for holy living.　　GORDON J. WENHAM

See MOSES; OFFERINGS AND SACRIFICES; ISRAEL, RELIGION OF; TABERNACLE, TEMPLE; PRIESTS AND LEVITES; AARON.

Bibliography. R.K. Harrison, *Leviticus;* S.H. Kellogg, *The Book of Leviticus;* M. Noth, *Leviticus;* N.H. Snaith, *Leviticus and Numbers;* G.J. Wenham, *The Book of Leviticus.*

Libation.　Ritual of pouring a liquid such as oil or wine upon the ground as a sacrifice.

See OFFERINGS AND SACRIFICES.

Libertines.　Freedmen of Jewish extraction. The only reference to Libertines in the NT is Acts 6:9 (KJV). Most modern versions render this Latin term with the more Anglicized "freedmen" on the assumption that the designation is legal-political, not geographical. The appearance of Libertines with groups from various parts of the empire could be taken to mean that the Libertines were a group from the region of Liberatum in North Africa, at that time under Roman jurisdiction. A more probable understanding, however, is that the people who met in the synagogue of the Libertines in Jerusalem came from Cyrene, Alexandria, Cilicia, and Asia, and together were called Libertines, that is, freedmen. Philo, a Hellenistic Jew of Alexandria, writes about Jews who had been captured during Pompey's conquests and taken to Rome. Later these Jews were set free and settled in various parts of the empire. Tacitus, a Roman historian, remarks that the freed Jews created significant problems for the government.

These Greek-speaking Jews, according to Acts 6:9, worshiped in a synagogue of their own in Jerusalem. They could not speak the Aramaic of their Palestinian counterparts. In 1913 R. Weill found an inscription in Jerusalem relating to a certain Theodotus, son of Vettenos. The inscription refers to a synagogue which fits the description of Acts 6:9. The early church found it necessary to debate its faith with the Libertines of this synagogue. Stephen, a man appointed earlier to deal with problems arising in the Greek-speaking element of the church (Acts 6:1–6), appears as the able exponent of faith in Christ Jesus against the synagogue of the Libertines.

See FREEDMEN.

Liberty.　Quality or state of being free. In the ancient world slavery was universal. The Law of Moses provided that a Hebrew slave serve six years and go free in the seventh (Ex 21:2). This provision of the Law lies behind Jeremiah 34, a passage which makes two things plain: (1) what the Law required was recognized, but (2) many failed to comply with it. But whatever the practice, the Law enshrined the principle of freedom. After each 49 years there was to be a jubilee year when all property would be returned to its original owners and slaves would be freed (Lv 25:8–24; cf. Ez 46:17).

Liberty might be given a slave for other reasons. If his owner destroyed the sight in an eye or knocked a tooth out, the slave must be freed for the loss of his eye or tooth (Ex 21:26,27). In a somewhat gloomy passage Job reflects that in Sheol "the slave is free from his master" (Jb 3:19). In another vein he appreciates the freedom of the wild ass (Jb 39:5).

When the Messiah comes, one of his tasks will be "to proclaim liberty to the captives" (Is 61:1). OT believers thought of this liberty in terms of freedom from foreign domination. But the Messiah is concerned basically with making the spirits of men free. In the same spirit God's people are to practice that fasting that means among other things "to let the oppressed go free" (Is 58:6). Liberty is a way of life before God as well as a state of being free from shackles.

In the NT freedom is sometimes seen as a literal release from captivity. All four Gospels refer to the Jewish custom of having a prisoner set free at Passover and to the release of Barabbas (e.g., Mk 15:6,9,11,15). There are references also to the release of prisoners (e.g., Acts 3:13; 16:35). Not dissimilar is the thought of being freed from illness (Lk 13:12).

There are several passages in which freedom from slavery is in mind. Thus Paul works out his allegory of Hagar and Sarah, making use of the difference between the slave girl and the free woman (Gal 4:22–31). The apostle is bringing out an important truth about the liberty believers enjoy in Christ, and he does so by drawing attention to certain features of literal freedom from slavery.

There are frequent references to slavery as an institution, and the corollary of this is that some men are free. Thus we read, "All men great and small, slave and free, hid themselves" (Rv 6:15 LB; cf. Rv 13:16; 19:18). An interesting aspect of the NT attitude to this important social distinction is that for Christians it is not important whether one is a slave or free. The important thing is that the slave belongs to Christ and in Christ he is free. Paul can write, "For he who was called in the Lord as a slave is a freedman of the Lord. Likewise he who was free when called is a slave of Christ" (1 Cor 7:22). All believers have been bought with the great price of the blood of Christ, and thus all belong to him: they are his slaves. But from another angle, he has liberated them all; they live in real freedom of spirit, whatever their outward circumstances may be. There are worse things than being a slave.

There is dispute about the meaning of 1 Corinthians 7:21. This may be translated, "Were you a slave when called? Never mind. But if you can gain your freedom, avail yourself of the opportunity." More literally the last phrase might be rendered "use it rather," and some scholars hold that this means "use slavery rather." That is to say, they maintain that Paul is saying that the liberty of Christ is so wonderful that slavery does not matter. Do not bother to accept release from being a slave but go on being free in Christ. Paul would then be saying in effect, "Accept your freedom if it is offered. But remember that the freedom Christ gives you is more important." Where Christ is supreme, it matters little to what race one belongs or even whether one is slave or free (Col 3:11). The Lord's recompense is given irrespective of whether one is slave or free (Eph 6:8). From another point of view, Paul can maintain that he is free from all men, but that he has made himself the slave of all so that he might win people for Christ (1 Cor 9:19). From such a point of view being a slave or being free does not matter greatly.

The slavery that matters is the slavery to which Jesus referred when he said, "Truly, truly, I say to you, every one who commits sin is a slave to sin" (Jn 8:34). As Paul put it, such a man is "sold under sin" (Rom 7:14). The trouble is that no one can make a clean break with sin. One may perhaps overcome this or that bad habit. But to get rid of sin altogether is quite another matter, and it is sin that makes the great problems in life. Thus the inability to be rid of it is serious. It means that we are not free. We are slaves. But neither Jesus nor Paul dwells on the fact of slavery. They point us to freedom. Jesus says plainly that people are really free when the Son sets them free (Jn 8:36). Paul exults in the freedom that Jesus Christ brings (Rom 7:24,25). The same idea can be expressed in terms of the truth making men free (Jn 8:32), words which must be understood in light of the fact that Jesus is himself the truth (Jn 14:6). This is not the philosophical concept that error enslaves men while truth has a liberating effect. Truth here is that truth that is associated with Jesus, "the word of the truth, the gospel" (Col 1:5). Paul says, "Now the Lord is the Spirit, and where the Spirit of the Lord is, there is freedom" (2 Cor 3:17).

The NT is insistent that, left to themselves, men cannot defeat sin. And this is a fact of life of which the modern world affords ample proof. We may earnestly desire to do good, but evil is too powerful for us. We cannot do the good we wish to do (Rom 7:21–23). But because of Christ's atoning work the power of sin is broken. "For the law of the Spirit of life in Christ Jesus has set me free from the law of sin and death" (Rom 8:2). This truth is insisted on again and again, and is expressed in a variety of ways.

But there is another freedom that belongs to the Christian, freedom from the Law. There were many in the 1st century who saw the way of salvation as keeping the commandments of God. This was commonly urged among the Jews, and some of the first Christians seem to have taken up the idea from them. After all, it seems so obvious: if we lead good lives, we will be all right with God. The trouble with this position is that we do not lead good lives, for sin is too strong. But there is a further defect; namely, that the way of Law is not the way for which Christ died. This is given special emphasis in Galatians, where Paul argues strongly that salvation is not by way of the Law but by faith (Rom 4; Gal 3). He complains of people "who slipped in to spy out our freedom, which we have in Christ Jesus" (Gal 2:4). He points out that Christ freed us and that we ought not to get caught up in any form of bondage (Gal 5:1).

In one striking passage Paul looks for the whole creation to be liberated from the bondage of decay (Rom 8:21). It will in some way share in the liberty of the glory of God's children. This points to a wonderful destiny for creation. And we should not miss the "glory" that the liberty of God's children means.

There is an obvious temptation to presume on our freedom, since we do nothing to merit our salvation. But we are more than once warned not to misuse our liberty (Rom 6:1–4; Gal 5:13; 1 Pt 2:16). It is important to live as free people, and not make our liberty the means of bringing us into a new form of slavery of our own devising.

LEON L. MORRIS

See SLAVE, SLAVERY.

Libnah. 1. One of the stations at which the Israelites encamped during the wilderness journey. It was situated between Rimmonperez and Rissah (Nm 33:20,21). Its site is unknown.

See WILDERNESS WANDERINGS.

2. Canaanite city-state in southern Palestine, conquered and destroyed by the Israelites under Joshua (Jos 10:29–31; 12:15). It was located within Judah's territory (Jos 15:42), and later given to the Levites for an inheritance (Jos 21:13; 1 Chr 6:57). Its exact location is uncertain.

Three details in the city's subsequent history are noted in Scripture. (1) During the reign of King Jehoram of Judah, at the time of Edom's uprising, Libnah joined in the revolt but was subdued (2 Kgs 8:22; 2 Chr 21:10). (2) After King Sennacherib of Assyria took the city of Lachish, he proceeded to attack Libnah (2 Kgs 19:8; Is 37:8). It was while Sennacherib was besieging Libnah that Isaiah's affirmation to King Hezekiah that a rumor would cause the invading king to interrupt his military campaign against Judah and return to his own land was confirmed (2 Kgs 19:7). (3) The mother of Jehoahaz and Zedekiah, two of Judah's last kings, was a native of Libnah (2 Kgs 23:31; 24:18; Jer 52:1).

Libni. 1. Gershon's son; the grandson of Levi and Shimei's brother (Ex 6:17; Nm 3:18; 1 Chr 6:17,20). He was the father of three sons and the founder of the Libnite family (Nm 3:21). Libni is alternately called Ladan (KJV Laadan) in 1 Chronicles 23:7–9 and 26:21.

2. Mahli's son; the father of Shimei and a descendant of Levi through Merari's line (1 Chr 6:29).

Libnite. Descendant of Libni, Gershon's son, from Levi's tribe (Nm 3:21; 26:58).

See LIBNI #1.

Libraries, Ancient. Collections of records and documents kept in archives attached to temples or private residences such as a palace. Later libraries included books and other materials for reading, study, or reference made available to various classes of users.

China and India. Writing and the preservation of written materials arose and developed in

many places almost simultaneously. One might expect that China, the originator of rag-paper manufacturing and the first nation to invent block printing, might have been a forerunner in the development of libraries. The earliest indication of organized documentary collections there, however, has been traced back no further than the Lu archives (634 BC). From about 600 BC written records seem to have taken on greater importance, though writing and literature were still in the hands of the aristocratic elite. China was, therefore, a latecomer in the development of libraries.

Much Sanscrit material from India has been preserved and translated, but it too is of comparatively recent origin.

Mesopotamia. The oldest known writings are from the libraries of ancient Mesopotamia. Archaeologists have uncovered numerous libraries in the ruins of major Mesopotamian cities of antiquity. They date back to around 3000 BC, when written records began to be kept. Those writings are not lyrical, philosophical, argumentative, or philological; rather, they are manuals of ritual for daily life, such as marriage, burial, the times and seasons of the year, pilgrimages, and vows.

Sumer. Referred to in Scripture as the "land of Shinar" (Gn 10:10; 11:2), ancient Sumer appears to have been the cradle of civilization. Archaeologists have unearthed thousands of clay tablets among temple ruins of ancient Sumer. From these wedge-shaped (cuneiform) tablets comes much current knowledge of that ancient civilization.

In each major city there appears to have been a temple erected in honor of a local deity. Chief among these Sumerian cities were Ur, Akkad, Nippur, and Lagash. The land adjacent to those cities supposedly belonged to the deity and was worked by tenants under longterm leases. This led to the development of commercial contracts and financial record keeping superintended by the local priests. The clay tablets in those temple libraries contain numerous commercial contracts—bills of lading, business accounts, ledgers of private companies, and so on. The documents are replete with "signatures" (i.e., the seals) of contracting parties and witnesses.

In time these libraries included grammatical exercises for young scribes, mathematical texts, medical and astrological treatises, and collections of hymns, prayers, and incantations.

As writing passed into the hands of the wealthy, "libraries" were found in a few private residences, but particularly in the royal palaces.

Babylonia. The Sumerian libraries ultimately fell to the Babylonians. These conquerors, however, failed to profit from the Sumerians' example and had to relearn what had already been taught by experience. Thus, the great lawgiver Hammurabi (1792?–1750? BC) stated that all transactions must be recorded and signed, a practice already 2000 years old.

Notable libraries were developed at Babylonian Mari and Nuzi. Situated at an important caravan junction, Mari contained a temple dedicated to the goddess Ishtar, a ziggurat, and a 300-room palace which dates back to the first dynasty of Babylon (1850?–1750? BC). In the palace area excavators found approximately 20,000 cuneiform tablets. The Mari kings were contemporaries of Hammurabi, and their libraries provide a fascinating account of royal life.

The approximately 4000 clay tablets found in the library of Nuzi probably give a fuller picture of common life in an ancient city than any other single source in the ancient Near East. This find is even more important to the study of the Bible than the information gleaned from the larger collection of tablets at Mari.

Assyria. Whereas the Babylonians occupied the southern section of Mesopotamia, the Assyrian culture developed farther to the north. They produced little native literature, for their economy was essentially a military one. It was not until the reign of Ashurbanipal that an attempt was made to rival Babylon in learning. The Assyrians developed a greater interest in the culture of their predecessors than had the Babylonians, and collected and transcribed information on clay tablets. They even reproduced some of the older tablets with an interlinear translation in Akkadian. These bilingual texts were stored in the palace libraries. This apparently marked the beginning of the large libraries found in the palaces of Sargon II (722–705 BC) and his successors. The palace library he founded at Nineveh was continued by his son Sennacherib and grandson Esar-haddon, and reached its zenith with his great-grandson Ashurbanipal. Ashurbanipal enlarged the palace library holdings, adding vast amounts of information pertaining to the early Mesopotamian civilizations. This library contains tablets covering a wide variety of subjects. Among the most interesting are the hymns to the gods, some of which bear a striking resemblance to the Hebrew psalms, in substance as well as form. Their similarity in expression and feeling is no less remarkable.

The tablets unearthed at Nineveh evidence an advancement in learning. The efficacy of approximately 500 medicinal drugs was known. Such medical knowledge was governed by religious beliefs, including reliance on certain deities. The daily lives of those in the palace seem to have been determined by astrological forecasts and other omens deduced from seemingly insignificant occurrences. The library also contained heroic tales such as the Gilgamesh epic.

Other Near Eastern Lands. *Persia.* In 606 BC the city of Nineveh fell to the Medes and Persians, and the famous library of the Sargon dynasty was broken up and scattered on the floor. There the remains lay until unearthed by Henry Layard in 1845–53.

The Bible contains several interesting references to libraries extant during the Persian domination of the ancient Near East. The first occurs in the Book of Ezra (4:1–24; 5:17; 6:1). When the Jews began to rebuild the temple after their Babylonian exile, their enemies requested that a search be made of the archives in Babylon to see if the Persian king Cyrus had made a decree permitting the rebuilding of the temple (Ezr 4:1–24). The decree was found in the "Royal Archives in Babylon" at Ecbatana (Ezr 5:17; 6:1). Jerome claimed that this "House of Archives" was an official library.

At roughly the same time Esther's uncle, Mordecai, had certain deeds "recorded in the Book of the Chronicles in the presence of the king" (Est 2:23). Then later, when the king was unable to sleep, "he gave orders to bring the book of memorable deeds, the chronicles, and they were read before him" (Est 6:1). Evidently such record keeping was conducted systematically by the Medes and Persians, for toward the end of the Book of Esther (10:2) there is reference to the chronicles of those rulers.

Syria. Another city of antiquity having a large library was Ugarit (modern Ras Shamra). Situated in northern Syria, Ugarit had contact with the Hittites of Asia Minor and with the Egyptians. Like Mari it served as a crossroads between the Mediterranean culture and Mesopotamia. Excavators have discovered numerous royal tombs, two large temples, and a wide variety of artifacts illustrating that international commerce was conducted in the city. The most significant find was the library. This contained material in several Near Eastern languages, including a previously unknown Semitic language that has now come to be known as Ugaritic. Because of Israel's contact with Canaanite culture and the prophetic warnings against idolatry, the Ugaritic materials provide valuable background information highlighting God's concern for his people.

One of the most recent libraries to be uncovered is at Ebla (Tell Mardikh) in northern Syria. Excavation of the site did not arouse interest until 1968, when a statue dedicated to the goddess Ashtar and bearing the name of Ibbit-Lim, King of Ebla, was uncovered. Encouraged by this find, work continued, and in 1974 archaeologists were rewarded by finding 42 tablets in cuneiform script. In 1975, 15,000 more tablets were recovered, and 1600 a year later. The Ebla discoveries are one of the most significant archaeological discoveries of modern times.

The Hebrews. While from a biblical point of view sacred history began with "the book of the generations of Adam" (Gn 5:1), the growth of the OT can be dated from the time of Moses. As early as Israel's victory over Amalek, Moses was commanded to "write this as a memorial in a book" (Ex 17:14). Soon thereafter he was given the Ten Commandments (Ex 20:1–17). These were read to the people (Ex 24:4,7), and later were placed in the ark of the covenant for safekeeping (Ex 40:20; Dt 10:5).

When Moses gave instructions to the Israelites regarding the duties of future kings, he stated that a king was to make a copy of the Law for himself (Dt 17:18,19). From this reference it seems that Moses anticipated that the priests and Levites would be the custodians of the sacred writings (see also Dt 31:24–26; 1 Sm 10:25). Evidently such writings were first kept in the ark, and later in the tabernacle. When the temple was built in Jerusalem, they were undoubtedly transferred there.

When Joshua led the Israelites into the Promised Land and they began their campaign of conquest, one Canaanite city, Kiriath-sepher or Debir, appears repeatedly (Jos 10:38; 11:21; 12:13; 15:15,16). It literally means "Book City." Kiriath-sepher was a royal town in the hill country assigned to Judah's tribe. From its name it appears to have been what we today would call a "university town." Archaeologists have not yet located the site of this early center of learning, but if they do, it may well prove to be a most valuable find.

There were other writings in the annals of God's people that have not been preserved for us. These include "the Book of the Wars of the Lord" (Nm 21:14), "the Book of Jashar" (Jos 10:12,13; KJV "Jasher"), "the story of the prophet Iddo" (2 Chr 13:22), "the Chronicles of Nathan the prophet," and "the Chronicles of Gad the seer" (1 Chr 29:29; see also 2 Chr 33:19). There must also have been genealogical tables, for these take up a considerable portion of 1 Chronicles, are referred to in the books of Ezra and Nehemiah, and probably formed the basis for the genealogy of Christ recorded in the Gospels of Matthew and Luke.

Following the return of the exiles from Babylon in the 5th century, some of the Jews requested that Ezra read to them from "the book of the Law of Moses" (Neh 8:1–8). As a scribe Ezra had in his possession the scrolls containing God's Word, and the people evidently knew this.

Following the close of the OT period (*c.* 300 BC), few libraries can compare in significance and influence with the Dead Sea Scrolls discovered at Qumran in 1947. Hailed as the greatest manuscript discovery of all times, these scrolls, both complete and fragmentary, contain the literature of the Essene sect. The manuscripts were written between 200 BC and AD 50 and include, in addition to the OT (with the exception of Esther), their Manual of Discipline, The Damascus Document, and The War of the Sons of Light and the Sons of Darkness.

Egypt. The oldest hieroglyphic writings now extant came into being approximately 2000 BC. Egyptian temples were centers of literary activity, and to each temple were attached professional scribes who occupied a respected position. Their function was regarded

The Shrine of the Scrolls—the white cupola and the black basalt wall represent the scroll known as The War of the Sons of Light and the Sons of Darkness, one of the scrolls preserved in the shrine.

as a religious one, though the sacred books of Thoth (Egyptian god of wisdom and learning) amounted to a complete encyclopedia of Egyptian religion and science.

In time books were collected not only in the temples but also in the royal tombs. The best known of these libraries dates from the 14th century BC, and both Herodotus and Diodorus Siculus referred to catalogs of books on the wall inscriptions of the "House of Papyrus" at Edfu. The most famous Egyptian libraries, however, were at Thebes, Karnak, and the temple of Denderah. El-Amarna, situated on the east bank of the Nile River about 190 miles south of modern Cairo, occupied a strategic position and engaged in diplomatic correspondence with many of the surrounding nations. Archaeologists and OT scholars have claimed that the Amarna letters are indispensable for understanding Canaan prior to its conquest by the Israelites under Joshua. These letters show that Akkadian was the language of international diplomacy, even though certain Mittani kings sometimes wrote in Hurrian. Furthermore, the grammar and certain glosses in the letters give Semitic philologists insight into pre-Mosaic Canaanite terms and institutions.

As a result of Macedonian conqueror Alexander the Great's expansion eastward, centers of learning sprang up. Following his death (323 BC), when his kingdom was divided among his generals, the Ptolemies brought enlightenment to Egypt. A society of scholars and men of science gathered in their capital. It seems certain that Ptolemy Soter (323–285 BC) had already begun to collect documents, but it was probably not until the reign of Ptolemy Philadelphus (295–246 BC) that libraries were organized and established in separate buildings. Ptolemy Philadelphus secured from different parts of Greece and Asia the most valuable works for his libraries and spared no expense in enriching his collection. His successor, Ptolemy Euergetes, is said to have seized all writings brought into Egypt by foreigners for the benefit of his library, and their owners had to be content with receiving copies of them in exchange. In that way many treasures of Egyptian and even Hebrew literature were preserved by means of translation into Greek.

There were two libraries in Alexandria. The larger one in the Bruchium Quarter was associated with an academy, while the smaller one was in Serapeum. The Serapeum library had a collection of approximately 42,800 volumes or rolls, whereas the Bruchium library possessed 490,000 manuscripts. The first experiments in bibliography appear to have been made in producing catalogs of the Alexandrian libraries.

Tragically, when Julius Caesar set fire to the fleet in the harbor of Alexandria, the flames accidentally extended to the larger library of Bruchium, and it was destroyed.

Greece. Little is known of the public libraries of ancient Greece. Private collections of books appear to have been common. Polycrates, Euclid, Euripides, and Aristotle are known to have been book collectors. Greece, however, does not appear to have developed large libraries, even though many of its best scholars studied in the libraries and the academy of the Ptolemies.

Significant libraries developed in cities that came under Greek influence. Among these were Pergamum and Antioch in Asia Minor.

Rome. The Romans were meticulous record keepers. They maintained archives for official documents, but were slow in establishing libraries. They were far too militaristic and practical a people to devote much attention to literature. It was not until the last century of the Republic that we begin to read of libraries in Rome. However, with the establishment of the *Pax Romana*, it became fashionable for rich people to have extensive book collections. The first public library seems to have been established in Rome around 37 BC, and by the time of Constantine (d. AD 337), there were reported to have been 28 libraries in Rome alone.

Augustus established a notable library next to the temple of Apollo on the Palatine Hill in Rome. From inscriptions that have been unearthed it appears to have consisted of two main divisions, one devoted to Greek literature, and the other to Latin. Unfortunately, a fire in Rome in the reign of Nero destroyed much of the valuable collection.

Augustus' successors did not equal him in their patronage of learning. Nevertheless, they maintained the tradition of forming libraries. Tiberius, Augustus' immediate successor, established a library in his splendid house on the Palatine. Vespasian established a library in the Temple of Peace, erected after the burning of the city under Nero. Domitian restored the libraries that had been destroyed in the fire, procured books from every quarter, and even sent to Alexandria to have copies made. He is also said to have founded the Capitoline Library (though certain historians give the credit to Hadrian). The most famous and important of the imperial libraries, however, was created by Ulpius Trajanus and known as the Ulpian Library. Situated first in the Forum of Trajan, it was afterward removed to the Baths of Diocletian.

From this time onward public libraries flourished. As their number increased, the librarian, who was generally a slave or a freedman, became a recognized public officer.

Little is known of these libraries' methods of cataloging and classification.

Pergamum. The magnificence and renown of the Ptolemies' libraries excited the rivalry of the kings of Pergamum. They vied with the rulers of Egypt in encouraging learning and, in spite of the embargo placed by the Ptolemies on papyrus export, the library of Attali numbered more than 200,000 volumes.

Mark Anthony endeavored to repair the damage done to Egypt by Julius Caesar and promised to give Cleopatra the library from Pergamum. If that presentation ever took place, the collection from Pergamum was probably placed in Bruchium. Unfortunately, that library too was destroyed.

Christian Libraries. Christians traditionally have been book lovers, and the earliest reference to Christian research appears in the prologue of Luke's Gospel. The NT gives evidence that synagogues had their own copies of different scrolls, and perhaps because of that precedent various churches began acquiring copies of the apostles' writings.

The apostle Paul was a lover of books and could think of nothing better to occupy his time in Rome (2 Tm 4:13). Earlier in his ministry he had exhorted young Timothy to "attend to the public reading of Scripture" (1 Tm 4:13), implying that Timothy had the books from which to read. That other people also possessed written materials is evident from Luke 1:1 and Acts 23:26–30.

The work of the apostolic fathers known as the *Didache* and the apologetic literature that came into being in the 2nd century show that a body of Christian literature had grown up in addition to the NT. This was being gathered together and was being used by scholars for different purposes. Ignatius of Antioch speaks of "his archive being Jesus Christ."

Although we have no direct evidence for church libraries at this early period, it is reasonable to believe that they did exist. An inscription on a small Christian edifice in Timgad (Algeria) refers to a bibliotheca, and another inscription on a tomb in a Christian cemetery at Bolsena (Italy) speaks of "a library with books and statues."

In the latter part of the 2nd century AD the church of Alexandria seems to have had a library connected with its catechetical school. Tertullian referred to certain biblical works that were known to him. Clement of Alexandria's writings demonstrate his vast knowledge of literature. And from the writings of Irenaeus there are indications of a library at Lyons (France).

Caesarea (Palestine) became one of the leading centers of Christian learning, and it was there that Origen produced his six-translation OT, the *Hexapla*. Pamphilus accumulated a vast collection of scholarly books, and church historians such as Eusebius and Jerome relied heavily upon these works. Unfortunately, the Roman emperor Diocletian, in his persecution of the Jews, systematically destroyed libraries, and many of the early works perished.

Another center for Christian study was Constantinople (Turkey). However, by the time of Emperor Constantine's death, the number of books there was no more than 7000. When Julian became emperor in 361, he increased the collection considerably, so that by the time of Theodosius in the late 4th century the library possessed approximately 100,000 volumes.

As Christianity and its literature spread, libraries became an organized part of the church. Church libraries in Jerusalem can be traced back as far as the 3rd century. It appears that every church had a collection of books necessary for training converts in Christian doctrine. The largest of these libraries was at Caesarea, where Eusebius had access to more than 30,000 volumes. Augustine, North African bishop of Hippo, bequeathed his books to the church library at Hippo—which escaped destruction by the Vandals.

It would appear, therefore, that among pagans and Christians of antiquity there was a deep regard for written documents. Christians in particular should be proud of their heritage and zealously study the works that have come down to them.   CYRIL J. BARBER

See LETTER WRITING, ANCIENT; WRITING AND BOOKS.

Libya, Libyans. Country to the west of Egypt. Three different Hebrew words are so rendered, but there is some confusion of meaning, partly because of textual uncertainties and partly because classical writers tended to use "Libya" to describe non-Egyptian Africa in general.

From the 12th century BC Libyans served in the armies of Egypt and Ethiopia (2 Chr 12:3; 16:8; Na 3:9, KJV variously Lubims, Lubim). The great invader Shishak himself was of Libyan origin. Ezekiel prophesied that Libya (Hebrew "Cub," KJV Chub) would share in "a time of doom for the nations" (30:3,5), and Libyans are counted among the peoples forced into submission in Daniel 11:43. There is passing reference to the Libyans (Hebrew "Pul") in Isaiah 66:19.

Simon, "a man from Cyrene" in eastern Libya, was forced to carry the cross of Jesus (Mt 27:32; Mk 15:21; Lk 23:26). Libyans are listed among those who thronged Jerusalem on the day of Pentecost (Acts 2:10).

There may also be a connection with the twice-mentioned "Lehabim" (Gn 10:13; 1 Chr 1:11).

Lice. KJV translation for some sort of small insects, probably gnats, the third plague in Egypt (Ex 8:16–18).

See ANIMALS (GNAT).

Life. In biblical perspective, life flows from the living Father through the Son (his agent in creation and redemption) into a world thirsting for "real" life (see Jn 6:57).

The Living Father. The God of Israel, and of Christianity, is before all else "the living God" (Jer 10:10; Jn 5:26; contrast idols, Ps 135:15–17). Men (and God) swore "as the Lord lives," as by an unquestioned certainty (Nm 14:21; 1 Sm 14:39). God, the source of all life (1 Tm 6:13), "inbreathed" man at creation and sustains him continually (Jb 34:14,15). God alone gives life (Gn 17:16; Ex 20:14), and takes it away (Gn 3:22–24; 6:3; Ps 104:29; Lk 12:20).

The sign of life is movement; man is a "lively," animated body; a view modified somewhat in the NT by Greek dualism (Mt 27:50; Lk 8:55). Animals also have this animating "breath-soul" (Hebrew of Gn 1:24; 6:17). Thus all nature is instilled with life deriving from God (Acts 17:24–28).

Life is therefore sacred. The observation that life is "poured out" when blood is shed led to an absolute blood taboo (Gn 9:1–4; Lv 17:14). Blood, "containing" life, is God's; in sacrificial rituals it was thrown against his altar (Ex 24:6), the animal's life being accepted for the life forfeited by sin (Lv 17:11). Shedding of human blood, and adultery, could be atoned for only by capital punishment, as offenses against life's sacredness (Gn 9:5,6; Lv 20:10; Nm 35:33)—hence the concept of life ransomed by life given (Is 53; Mk 10:45).

Reverence for life as God's did not prevent insecurity. Human life is transient as grass, clouds, dew, shadow; there is "no abiding" (1 Chr 29:15; Jb 7:6,9; Jas 4:13–16; 1 Pt 1:24). Long life is desired (Gn 35:29), is preferable to death, and of infinite value (Eccl 9:4–6; Mt 6:25; 16:26), for Sheol houses a ghostly "nonliving," bereft of feeling, hope, or divine help (Ps 88:3–12; contrast Gn 5:24; 2 Kgs 2:11). Suicide was very rare (1 Sm 31:3,4). Later, protests were heard against life ending in nothing (Ps 16:9–11; Is 25:8; 26:19; Dn 12:2,3).

Meanwhile, life may be enhanced, if one so chooses, by loving and serving God (Dt 30:15–20; 1 Pt 3:8–12); by experiences of God's deliverance (Is 38:16); and by divine blessing (Mt 5:3–12). In the intertestamental years arose belief in personal resurrection, the reward of religious struggle (2 Mc 7:9,14,36), of wisdom (Wis of Sol 1:12–15; 3:1–9; 6:15,16), or of holiness (Qumran Community Rule 4:6–8). Pharisees inherited this hope; rabbis often contrasted "this life" with "that of the world to come" (Heb 6:5; 1 Cor 15:19).

Christ Our Life. The overflowing, vibrant quality of life made available in Christ was evident in the authority of his speech and the power of his touch (Mt 9:18; Mk 1:27,41,42; 5:27–29). He is "Author of life" (Acts 3:15, NEB "him who has led the way to life"), constantly advising how to enter into life (Mt 7:14; 25:46; Mk 8:35–37; 9:43–47). And he raised the dead. His own resurrection made him "a life-giving spirit," with the power of "an indestructible life" (Rom 8:2; 1 Cor 15:45; Heb 7:16), so infinitely extending human life's horizons (1 Pt 1:3–5). Jesus is "Christ our life" (Col 3:4), in union with whom we find "newness of life" (Rom 6:4) and are newly created, living henceforth not for ourselves but for him (2 Cor 5:15,17).

John, especially, dwells on Christ as the source of this new quality of life (Jn 3:14–16; 5:21), that of the children of God, reborn from above (1:12; 3:3,5), enjoyed already by knowing God and Christ (5:24; 17:3; 1 Jn 5:11,12), and passing through death as already "eternal" (Jn 10:28; 11:26).

All this is possible because from the beginning "all that came to be was alive with his life" (Jn 1:4 NEB). Thus the life within the Father flows into the world through the Son, who also "has life in himself" and gives it to whom he will (Jn 5:26). He is "the resurrection and the life" (11:25; 14:6), and demonstrates it by restoring life to paralyzed limbs, raising the dead, and conquering death (5:5–9; 11:43; ch 20). Men remain in death only because they will not "come" and "have life" (5:40; cf. 1 Jn 3:14).

So "life indeed" is offered in Christ (1 Tm 6:19). Man truly lives only by God's Word (Mt 4:4); alienated from God he is "dead while he lives" (Lk 9:60; Rom 7:9–11; Eph 2:1–5; 4:18; 1 Tm 5:6). Man may "inherit," "enter" life or reject it; the way is narrow and unfrequented (Mt 7:14; Mk 9:43; 10:17; Acts 13:46; Rom 1:32), but to seek safety at the cost of the soul is profitless (Mk 8:34–37; Jn 12:25). To repent (Acts 11:18), believe (Jn 3:16), be baptized (Rom 6:4) all lead to life, but only through Christ (Jn 20:31; Rom 6:23; 1 Jn 5:11).

This life is lived in trust, the antidote to anxiety (Lk 12:13–21), by faith fastened upon Christ (Gal 2:20) and directed "unto him" (Rom 14:8). To the Christian, "to live is Christ," the flesh or merely human aspect of life firmly subordinated to the Spirit (Rom 8:1–13).

Such life is abundant (Jn 10:10), enlightened (Jn 8:12), free and satisfied (Jn 10:9), victorious (Rom 6:6–14), full of peace and joy (Rom 5:1–11), inexhaustibly refreshed (Jn 4:13,14;

7:37,38), and immortal (Jn 5:24; 1 Cor 15:51–57).

Truly, the gospel consists of "the words of this Life" (Acts 5:20).

R.E.O. WHITE

See ETERNAL LIFE.

Bibliography. J.G. Hoare, *Life in St John's Gospel;* H.D. McDonald, *The Christian View of Man;* H.W. Robinson, *Corporate Personality in Ancient Israel.*

Life, Book of. *See* BOOK OF LIFE.

Life Everlasting. *See* ETERNAL LIFE.

Light. *In the Old Testament.* Light is a many-sided concept in the OT. The term is often used of ordinary, sensible light, but also as a way of communicating spiritual truth. Light was the first thing God created after the heavens and earth (Gn 1:3). God also made individual lights such as the sun, moon, and stars (Gn 1:16). Sometimes light is personified, as when its inaccessibility is indicated by saying that it is impossible to reach the place where it lives (Jb 38:19; cf. Jb 38:24). There are also manufactured light sources such as those used in the tabernacle (Ex 25:37).

Light is a natural symbol for what is pleasant, good, or uplifting, or what is associated with important people and more especially with God. "Light is pleasant," says the preacher (Eccl 11:7). During one of the plagues in Egypt the Egyptians were in thick darkness while the Israelites had light (Ex 10:23). When the Israelites left Egypt, they were led in the wilderness by a pillar of cloud by day and of fire by night (Ex 13:21). The pillar gave them light when their enemies were in darkness (Ex 14:20). In later days Israel remembered that God did not abandon his people even when they sinned; the pillar of fire was always there to show them the right way (Neh 9:19; cf. Neh 9:12; Pss 78:14; 105:39).

Light symbolizes the blessing of the Lord. Job said, "He uncovers the deeps out of darkness, and brings deep darkness to light" (Jb 12:22). In his time of trouble Job recalled the days when God's "lamp shone upon my head, and by his light I walked through darkness" (Jb 29:3). Similarly Eliphaz pictured the happiness that would befall Job if he would take Eliphaz's advice: "You will decide on a matter, and it will be established for you, and light will shine on your ways" (Jb 22:28). Eliphaz's use of that expression shows what it commonly conveyed in his day. The psalmist counted it a blessing when God himself lighted his lamp (Pss 18:28; 118:27; cf. 97:11; 112:4). In Proverbs, "The light of the righteous rejoices, but the lamp of the wicked will be put out" (13:9).

Light is closely linked with God; indeed, God can be said to be light: "The Lord will be your everlasting light, and your God will be your glory" (Is 60:19). The psalmist exulted, "The Lord is my light and my salvation," and proceeded to ask, "whom shall I fear?" (27:1). God is said to be robed with light (Ps 104:2) and light dwells with him (Dn 2:22). Darkness is no problem to God; darkness and light are alike to him (Ps 139:12). The prophet Micah expressed his confidence in terms of light: "Rejoice not over me, O my enemy; when I fall, I shall rise; when I sit in darkness, the Lord will be a light to me. . . . He will bring me forth to the light; I shall behold his deliverance" (Mi 7:8,9). Micah saw God as light and also as bringing his servants into the light. Both are ways of affirming that there is blessing and victory with God, so that a servant of God need never be dismayed.

A king is sometimes identified with light. Thus when the Israelites decided that King David should no longer risk his life on the battlefield they said, "You shall no more go out with us to battle, lest you quench the lamp of Israel" (2 Sm 21:17). This metaphor is carried on with God's promise that David would continue to have a "light" in Jerusalem, which meant that the whole kingdom would not go with Jeroboam (1 Kgs 11:36; cf. 2 Kgs 8:19; 2 Chr 21:7). The king was regarded as the source of illumination for his people, and there may also be some thought that a descendant of David on his throne brings glory to that great king.

God's blessing, described in terms of light, is also related to "the light of his countenance." Something of that expression's meaning is seen from its use in Psalm 4:6: "There are many who say, 'O that we might see some good!' Lift up the light of thy countenance upon us, O Lord!'" The parallelism shows that "good" and the lifting up of the light of God's countenance are much the same. Similarly it was the light of God's countenance that brought victory (Ps 44:3; here it is linked with God's right hand and arm and his delight in his people). Those who walk in the light of God's countenance are blessed (Ps 89:15). There is another side to that expression, for secret sins are set "in the light of thy countenance" (Ps 90:8). There is a close scrutiny from which no one and nothing can escape. But the predominant idea is that of the blessing that follows from God's looking upon his people. On one occasion the phrase is used of a person showing favor to others (Jb 29:24).

An extension of the Lord's blessing is the light God gives to the world through his servants (Is 42:6; 49:6). God's servants can guide others to the revelation and blessing of God.

Light is associated with justice when the Lord says, "A law will go forth from me, and my justice for a light to the peoples" (Is 51:4). Justice means trouble for evildoers: "The light of Israel will become a fire, and his Holy One a flame; and it will burn and devour his thorns and briers in one day" (Is 10:17). God's light in that act of justice is a consuming fire. Sometimes judgment on Israel is expressed as a withdrawal of light: "Woe to you who desire the day of the Lord! Why would you have the day of the Lord? . . . Is not the day of the Lord darkness, and not light, and gloom with no brightness in it?" (Am 5:18,20; cf. Is 13:9,10).

Sometimes light is connected with good behavior: "The path of the righteous is like the light of dawn, which shines brighter and brighter until full day" (Prv 4:18). "For the commandment is a lamp and the teaching a light" (Prv 6:23). In the case of Daniel, light is joined with "understanding and wisdom" to indicate how Daniel surpassed all the Babylonian wise men (Dn 5:11,14). It is a perversion that regards darkness as light and light as darkness (Is 5:20; cf. Jb 17:12).

The OT uses the absence of light as a synonym for disaster. There are those who "grope in the dark without light" (Jb 12:25). Bildad saw the light of the wicked put out in punishment and death (Jb 18:5–17). The wicked will be "thrust from light into darkness, and driven out of the world" (Jb 18:18). In the aftermath of the Babylonian destruction of Jerusalem was the lament, "He has driven and brought me into darkness without any light" (Lam 3:2).

In the New Testament. NT references to light are often figurative. Thus on the Damascus road Saul of Tarsus encountered "a light from heaven" (Acts 9:3; cf. 22:6,9,11; 26:13). Was that light as we know it or something else? Likewise, what quality of light shone in the apostle Peter's cell (Acts 12:7)? The lights that the Philippian jailer called for in another prison were ordinary lamps or torches (Acts 16:29). The light in the heavenly city is not the kind of illumination seen on earth, "for the Lord God will be their light" (Rv 22:5; cf. 21:11,23,24).

The association of God with light is recurrent in the NT. The apostle John wrote that "God is light and in him is no darkness at all" (1 Jn 1:5). The apostle James referred to God as "the Father of lights" (Jas 1:17). Or God may be thought of as living in light, light that no person can approach (1 Tm 6:16; cf. 1 Jn 1:7). Jesus said, "I am the light of the world" (Jn 8:12; 9:5), and "I have come as light into the world, that whoever believes in me may not remain in darkness" (Jn 12:46). Jesus told his followers to believe in the light while it was with them (Jn 12:35). Such passages emphasize that Christ brought a revelation from God, but he was more than a revealer. He was himself that revelation, according to the apostle John (1:1–10). John the Baptist came to bear witness to the light for the purpose of bringing people to believe (Jn 1:7,8). Those who received Jesus, who believed in the light, received "the power to become children of God" (Jn 1:9–12). Sometimes light is used to express the illumination that happens when people come to the knowledge of God and his salvation (Mt 4:16; Lk 2:32; Acts 13:47; 26:18).

Perhaps thinking of a then popular concept of a war between light and darkness, John wrote that the light shines in the darkness and adds that the darkness has not overcome it (Jn 1:5; cf. 1 Jn 2:8). John tells us that "the light has come into the world, and men loved darkness rather than light, because their deeds were evil" (Jn 3:19). To love darkness brings condemnation, now and at the final judgment. John pointed out that evildoers keep away from the light; they do not want their evil exposed. But those who "do the truth" come to the light (Jn 3:20,21). In John's account of the raising of Lazarus, Jesus speaks of the possibility of walking without stumbling in the light of day, but then goes on to the way a man stumbles in the night, "because the light is not in him" (Jn 11:10). The lack of light "in" the man shows that it is a spiritual process with which Jesus is concerned and not with making physical progress by daylight. He who follows Jesus "will have the light of life" (Jn 8:12), which indicates the kind of thing that is in mind.

Those who respond to the light may be characterized as "sons of light" (Jn 12:36). They have thrown in their lot with light rather than darkness. Their allegiance is to the light and their conduct has been shaped by this fact. The concept is not confined to John's Gospel, for we also see it in Luke (16:8). We find it in Paul's affirmation that the Thessalonian Christians "are all sons of light and sons of the day; we are not of the night or of darkness" (1 Thes 5:5). There is a reference to "children of light" (Eph 5:8) and to being "light in the Lord," the latter expression being hard to explain in detail, though the general meaning is clear. Paul gets into a somewhat mixed metaphor when he refers to the "fruit of light" as good conduct (Eph 5:9). A little later his thought is that light shows evil to be the evil thing it is (Eph 5:13). John speaks of walking in the light (1 Jn 1:7) and sees the conduct of the Christian as aptly symbolized by light. He can refer to the way God "called you out of darkness into his marvelous light" (1 Pt 2:9).

This way of looking at the Christian's manner of life reaches its high point in the words of Jesus to his followers: "You are the light of the world" (Mt 5:14), thus applying to them words which are also applied to himself. Of course we are not the world's light in the same sense as he is. When light refers to Christ, there is a reference to him as Savior and not merely one who reveals great truths. When believers are called the light of the world, there is clearly no saving significance in the description. They do not accomplish the world's salvation. But they do point it out. It is their function as redeemed people to live as redeemed people. They are to show the quality of life proper to the people of God and in this way act as light to the people of the world. They are to let their light shine before the world in such a way that people will see their good deeds and so come to praise God (not, be it noted, those who do the deeds, Mt. 5:16). It is important for those in this position to make full use of the light they have. It is tragedy when the light that is in them is darkness (Mt 6:23; Lk 11:35). This metaphor is worked out in a way not congenial to modern men and women, but the basic lesson is clear. We have been illuminated by the light that is Christ, who dwells within his people. If we ignore the illumination he brings us and live like those in the dark, then indeed we are in deep darkness. We are worse than others because we know what light is and what it can mean to us, and have turned away from it. But we need not do this. We are reminded that Jesus said of John the Baptist that the people were ready to rejoice for a period in his light (Jn 5:35). Their response was brief, and they are blamed for not taking John more seriously. But the point is that John's light shone clearly. They knew what he stood for. Paul urges the Romans to put on "the armor of light" (Rom 13:12), a metaphor that points us in the same direction.

Paul asks, "What fellowship has light with darkness?" (2 Cor 6:14). The believer is not to throw in his lot with darkness. He must be constantly on guard, for it is possible for Satan to disguise himself as an angel of light (2 Cor 11:14). This opposition of light and darkness is found in a number of places in antiquity, notably in the Dead Sea Scrolls (one scroll is taken up with "The War of the Sons of Light and the Sons of Darkness"), and some have felt that we must look to such places as the source of the biblical imagery. But this is scarcely necessary. The opposition of light and darkness comes naturally, and can be found in many literatures. We have seen it in the OT and need go no further. It is congenial to the writers of the NT, and it brings out forcefully a variety of important truths.

LEON L. MORRIS

See DARKNESS.

Bibliography. K. Barth, *Church Dogmatics* 4.3.1, 38–165. C.H. Dodd, *The Interpretation of the Fourth Gospel*, pp. 201–4; E.R. Goodenough, *By Light, Light: The Mystic Gospel of Hellenistic Judaism.*

Lign-aloe. KJV translation for aloe in Numbers 24:6.

See PLANTS (ALOE).

Ligure. KJV translation for jacinth in Exodus 28:19 and 39:12.

See MINERALS, METALS, AND PRECIOUS STONES.

Likhi. Shemida's son from Manasseh's tribe (1 Chr 7:19).

Lilith. Night hag referred to in Isaiah 34:14. According to Hebrew mythology Lilith was a female demon.

See BIRDS (OWL, SCOPS).

Lily. See PLANTS.

Lily-work. Design of a lily or lotus used on ancient pillars, inspired by the large water lily found along the Nile. It appeared at the vestibule of Solomon's temple (1 Kgs 7:19,22), around the brim of the "molten sea" basin (1 Kgs 7:26), and in numerous artistic creations of the Assyrians, Persians, and other Near Eastern peoples.

See BRONZE SEA; TABERNACLE, TEMPLE.

Lime. White substance (calcium oxide) obtained by applying heat to materials containing calcium carbonate, such as limestone or shells.

See MINERALS, METALS, AND PRECIOUS STONES.

Linen. Cloth made from flax.

See CLOTH, CLOTH MANUFACTURING.

Lintel. Horizontal beam placed above a doorway, made of either wood or stone. The two upright posts on either side of the door which supported the lintel were called "jambs" or simply "doorposts."

In Exodus 12:11–13, the Israelites are instructed to prepare for the tenth plague, the plague of death, and for the first Passover. After killing a lamb (v 6), the people were to take the blood and "put it on the two door-posts and the lintel of the houses" (v 7).

First Kings 6:31 describes Solomon's building of the temple. The KJV says, "He made doors of olive tree: the lintel and side posts were a fifth part of the wall." The meaning in the Hebrew is a little difficult to determine. The NASB translates it as "the lintel and five-sided doorposts." The NEB replaces the word "lintel" with "pilasters." It may be that the top of the doorway was slanted, formed by beams leaning toward each other (archlike) instead of one horizontal beam.

In Amos 9:1 the KJV has "lintel" whereas the RSV has "capital." The Hebrew word here appears to mean the capital of a column. The same is true in Zephaniah 2:14, where the KJV has "lintels" and the NASB has "tops of her pillars."

See ARCHITECTURE.

Linus. Christian at Rome who joined Paul in sending salutations to Timothy (2 Tm 4:21). According to Irenaeus and Eusebius, the apostles Peter and Paul made a man named Linus bishop of Rome. Eusebius identified him with the Linus referred to by Paul at the end of 2 Timothy and said that he served for 12 years. The *Apostolic Constitutions*, along with other early church documents, also makes this identification.

Lion. *See* ANIMALS.

Litter. Large couch used for carrying dignitaries (Sg 3:7–10; Is 66:20).

See TRAVEL AND TRANSPORTATION.

Liver. Large abdominal organ that performs many functions necessary for life. The

Pink-buff clay model of a liver (from Megiddo).

writer of Proverbs understood the critical nature of the liver when he noted that a dart injury to the liver (RSV entrails) was fatal (Prv 7:23). In most instances in Scripture the liver is mentioned in connection with the description of animal sacrifices (Ex 29:13,22; Lv 3:4, 10,15).

In ancient Babylon sheep liver was occasionally used in fortune-telling; the shape of each small detail of the liver was carefully examined for possible omens. Bronze and baked clay anatomical models of sheep livers have been recovered from archaeology sites dating to the 16th century BC. Evidently this is the use of the liver made by the king of Babylon in Ezekiel 21:21. This use of the sheep liver was popular until the time of the Greeks, and rivaled astrology for many centuries.

Lizard. Small reptile with scaly skin, four legs, and a long tail.

See ANIMALS.

Lo-ammi. Symbolic name, meaning "Not My People" (Hos 1:9), given by the prophet Hosea to his son.

See AMMI.

Loan. Money lent at interest.

See MONEY AND BANKING.

Locust. Various insects known especially for their swarming, mass migration and tremendous destruction of vegetation.

See ANIMALS.

Lod. City on the coastal plain of Palestine. The modern city, called Ludd, is located 10 miles southeast of Tel Aviv. The name of the city first occurs in a list of Canaanite towns which goes back to 1465 BC, to the reign of the Egyptian pharaoh Thutmose III, who supplied the list. The founder of the city is said to have been Shemed, a Benjamite (1 Chr 8:12). It is included in a list of places that were resettled by returning exiles from Babylon (Ezr 2:33; Neh 7:37), and is included in the list of Benjamite settlements (Neh 11:35). The history of the city can be traced continuously from Maccabean times, through the Roman period, including the first and second Jewish wars against the Romans, to the Byzantine and Crusader periods, through to modern times.

In the NT era Jewish sources emphasize the importance of the city, now named Lydda. It had a large market and was noted for the raising of cattle; textile, dyeing, and pottery industries flourished there; it was the seat of a sanhedrin, and famous talmudic scholars taught there. This, then, was the kind of bustling, flourishing community which existed when Peter visited the city and ministered to its Christians (Acts 9:32–35).

Lo-debar. Alternate name for Debir, the Gadite city, in 2 Samuel 9:4 and Amos 6:13.

See DEBIR (PLACE) #2.

Log. Liquid measure mentioned only in Leviticus 14. The log was equal to one-twelfth of a bath or one-half pint.

See WEIGHTS AND MEASURES.

Logos. English transliteration of a Greek term for "word." The term is significant because in John's writings it refers to Jesus. The prologue of John's Gospel (1:1,14) and the beginning of 1 John (1:1) use *logos* to show how Jesus can be God and yet an expression of God in the world. The divine Word took on human form and became a historical personage. Logos is also the title of Christ in the vision of his divine glory (Rv 19:13). Writers outside the NT, such as Philo of Alexandria, used the term but with a different meaning.

See JOHN, GOSPEL OF; WORD.

Loins. Region of the body from the chest to the lower part of the hip; an expression ("out of his loins") for that part of the body which involved procreation (Gn 35:11; 46:26; Ex 1:5; 1 Kgs 8:19; KJV). In most instances the word describes physical features, although occasionally emotion, power, or strength is meant (e.g., Na 2:1). As was the custom of the Hebrews and other Near Eastern peoples, a man would tie up his clothes around the loins before traveling a long distance on foot (Ex 12:11; 1 Kgs 18:46; 2 Kgs 9:1). In the NT girded loins signified that a man was ready for service or heavy battle (Lk 12:35). Metaphorically, girding the loins is a symbolic way of saying that one speaks the truth (Eph 6:14; 1 Pt 1:13 KJV; cf. Is 11:5).

Lois. Maternal grandmother of Timothy (2 Tm 1:5), whose family, including Timothy's mother, Eunice, lived at Lystra (Acts 16:1). Lois was a deeply committed Jew who probably converted to Christianity during Paul's first missionary trip (Acts 14). Paul comments that Timothy had the faith of his grandmother and mother.

Loom. Frame or machine for weaving.

See CLOTH, CLOTH MANUFACTURING.

Lord. Rendering of the Hebrew *'ădōnāy* or of the Greek *kurios*. In Israel both piety and

fear (of transgressing, Ex 20:7) inhibited the correct pronunciation of the sacred consonants of the divine name (probably Yahweh). Instead, the vowel sounds of *'ĕlōhîm* ("God") or *'ădōnāy* ("Lord," from *'ādōn*, ruler, lord, master, husband) were combined with YHWH. This combination is usually translated in the KJV, RV, RSV, NEB, and NIV as "LORD" (in ARV as Jehovah). When *'ădōnāy* itself is used of God, "Lord" is printed. The resulting frequent reminder of God's rule and authority rests ultimately upon his creation and ownership of all things and people (Ps 24:1,2); but as the following verses (7–10) recall, a military application is evident in "the Lord of hosts, the God of the armies of Israel" (1 Sm 17:45; 2 Sm 6:2—the ark being a battle symbol). In other contexts God's total supremacy over nature is emphasized by the title: over earthquake, wind, fire (1 Kgs 19:10–14), stars (Is 40:26), beasts and monsters (Jb 40, 41, note "the Lord"), and primeval chaos (Pss 74:12–14 "King"; 89:8–10 "Lord God of hosts").

The later prophets greatly extended Israel's faith in God as Lord or King of history, directing the affairs of men and nations (1 Kgs 19:15–18; Am 9:7; Is 10:5–9), and as Lord of universal morality (Am 1:3–2:16; Ez 25–32). But especially is God the Lord (Lawgiver and Judge) of Israel; his expressed will represents civil and religious constitution, and demands absolute obedience (Ex 20:2, introducing the commandments). The divine sovereignty was, however, Israel's comfort under oppression and hope for the future, when a triumphant Day of the Lord would right its wrongs, punish its oppressors, and restore its glory (Is 2:2–4,11–12; 34:8; Ez 30:1–5; Jl 2:31–3:1).

In the Septuagint, the regular expression for "Lord/lord/master" is *kurios*, which in the Greek NT also is used of masters, husbands, and rulers (Mt 25:11; Lk 14:21; Acts 25:26; 1 Pt 3:6); of God (Mt 11:25; Heb 8:2); and of pagan gods (1 Cor 8:5). It is used of Jesus as a customary title of respect ("sir," Mt 8:2; 15:25); it also retains its Septuagint associations of faith, reverence, and worship (Mt 3:3; Lk 7:13; Acts 5:14; 9:10; 1 Cor 6:13,14; Heb 2:3; Jas 5:7); it appears in phrases like "the Lord Jesus," "the Lord's day," "the Lord's table," "the Spirit of the Lord" (who is also "Lord," 2 Cor 3:17), "in the Lord," (inheritance), "from the Lord," "light in the Lord," "boast in the Lord." Sometimes it is not clear whether God or Christ is intended (Acts 9:31; 2 Cor 8:21). The title is attributed to Jesus himself in John 13:13,14; in John 20:28 Jesus accepts the title "My Lord and my God!"

In the first Christian sermon Jesus' lordship is made central to salvation (Acts 2:21,36). It appears that the public confession of Jesus as

Lord was the approved focus and expression of Christian faith, and the basis of church membership, in the apostolic church (Acts 16:31; Rom 10:9; 1 Cor 12:3; Phil 2:11). Thus it could become more a formal statement than a sincere expression of belief; hence the warnings in Matthew 7:21 and Luke 6:46.

From the first, such a confession was fraught with meaning. In common usage "lord" reflected the slave system, and implied the absolute power exercised by the master over the purchased slave. So Paul unhesitatingly expounds the moral implications of Christian redemption (1 Cor 6:19,20; 7:22,23). To Jewish minds the title had messianic overtones of kingship and authority (Lk 20:41–44), offending both Jews and Romans. Politically, "Lord" was a title claimed by Caesar; it is significant that the emphatic, insistent form of it, "King of kings and Lord of lords," belongs to the age of Domitian and of the demand for Caesar worship (Rv 17:14; 19:16).

Among Greek-speaking Jews of the dispersion, familiar with the Septuagint, as among Gentiles, for whom "Lord" was the customary title for the many gods of polytheism, the application to Jesus of the epithet belonging to godhead was blasphemous, especially when associated with "Son of God," prayer, praise, total devotion, and hope (Phil 2:9–11; 1 Cor 8:5,6; 1 Thes 4:14–17). On every level, therefore, the adoring tribute given to Jesus was loaded not only with spiritual meaning but with positive and imminent danger.

R.E.O. WHITE

See GOD, NAMES OF; GOD, BEING AND ATTRIBUTES OF; CHRISTOLOGY.

Bibliography. O. Cullmann, *The Earliest Christian Confessions*; R.H. Foller, *The Foundations of NT Christology*; R.J. Knowling, *The Testimony of St Paul to Christ*; W. Kramer, *Christ, Lord, Son of God*; W. Pannenberg, *Jesus— God and Man*; A.E.J. Rawlinson, *The NT Doctrine of the Christ*; H.E.W. Turner, *Jesus: Master and Lord*.

Lord of Hosts. OT name for God found mostly in the prophets. The hosts are the heavenly powers and angels that act at the Lord's command.

See GOD, NAMES OF.

Lord's Day, The. Expression occurring once in the NT (Rv 1:10), where John says, "On the Lord's Day I was in the Spirit" (NIV); synonym for "Sunday" in modern usage.

In the New Testament. The earliest reference to Christian activity on Sunday comes in a brief allusion Paul makes to "the first day of the week" (1 Cor 16:1–4). He instructs individual members of the church in Corinth to remember their poverty-stricken fellow believ-

ers in Jerusalem by setting aside a sum of money each Sunday.

Why Sunday? Obviously the first day of the week had taken on a special significance among Christians in Corinth before Paul wrote this letter (AD 55–56), and he makes it clear that the observance was not merely local (see v 1). There was some special "Sunday event" that would make it easy for Christians to remember their obligations to the poor.

Some have suggested that Sunday was payday at Corinth, so Paul was asking Christians to make the needs of others top priority when they received their wages. It is far more likely, however, that Sunday was the day when special church meetings took place (Paul alludes several times to these in 1 Cor—see, e.g., 5:4; 11:18,20), and that collections were taken on these occasions to meet local needs (cf. 1 Cor 9:7–14). So Paul is saying, "When the collection bag comes round on Sundays, and you are reminded of your local needs, set aside something—privately—for the needs of your brethren in Jerusalem."

There is one further hint in Paul's correspondence with the Corinthians that this "charity reminder" was part of the church's Sunday worship. In 2 Corinthians 9:12 he describes his special collection for the poor in Jerusalem by using a word that has close associations with worship (it is the root of our word "liturgy"). So here is a strong indication that in the churches Paul founded, Sunday was seen as a special day for worshiping God, and that part of this worship focused on meeting the needs of others.

There is a more detailed account of a Christian Sunday meeting in Acts 20:6–12. The all-night service Luke describes there took place in Troas about three years after Paul wrote 1 Corinthians. Luke's main aim is to tell the story of sleepy Eutychus' miraculous recovery, so some of the details of the meeting that would interest us most are missing. Nevertheless, the account is full enough to indicate the kind of things the first Christians did when they met together on Sundays.

The fact that Luke mentions the day of the week at all is significant. Elsewhere he rarely identifies a day, unless it is a sabbath or a special feast. His word for "gathered" (v 7) is important too. It is a semitechnical term the NT uses for Christians gathered together for worship (1 Cor 5:4). So this was not a special meeting convened to hear Paul (who had already been in town six days), but a regular weekly event. The church in Troas may have met daily, like the church in Jerusalem (Acts 2:42,46), but the Sunday meeting was obviously treated as a special occasion.

Luke uses the same word to describe

Paul's preaching (Acts 20:7) that he used earlier for the apostle's preaching ministry in the synagogues at Ephesus and Corinth (Acts 18:4; 19:8). This preserves an interesting link between the Jewish sabbath and the Christian Sunday. When a local church separated from the synagogue, it probably modeled its worship on synagogue practice. Although the three main components of synagogue worship (Scripture reading, teaching, and prayer) are not found together in the few NT accounts of Christian worship, each is separately attested.

The main purpose behind the church's Sunday meeting at Troas, however, was distinctively Christian. It was "to break bread" (Acts 20:7), the NT's term for eating the Lord's Supper (and including, probably, the less formal table fellowship of the love feast—cf. 1 Cor 11:17–34). The Lord's Supper very quickly became a focal point of the early church's Sunday worship. As a memorial of the resurrection and the promise of Christ's presence in the worshiping fellowship, it was an obviously appropriate Christian way of celebrating the first day of the week.

The third clear reference to Sunday in the NT (and the only one which calls it the Lord's Day) takes us from the Turkish mainland to the Aegean island of Patmos, probably about 40 years after Paul's visit to Troas. In Revelation 1:10 John describes how he was worshiping on the Lord's day when he received his great vision. It is just possible that the expression "Lord's day" here means Easter, or even the great day of God's judgment which the OT prophets foretold; but in view of the way later Christian writers used this phrase, it is far more likely to mean simply "Sunday."

The immediate context of Revelation 1:10 makes it clear that John saw Sunday as the Lord's Day because on it Christians expressed together their total commitment to Jesus as Lord and Master (see esp. v 8). It was Jesus' resurrection on the first day of the week that demonstrated his lordship most clearly (see v 18 and Jn 20:25–28). One day the whole world will have to acknowledge that he is "King of kings and Lord of lords" (Rv 19:16; cf. Phil 2:11), but in the meantime it is in the church's worship that his lordship is recognized.

Inevitably this recognition brings Christians into conflict with others who claim mastery over their lives. In John's time non-Christians used the word "Lord" to refer almost exclusively to the Roman emperor. The emperor even had a special day each month when his subjects offered him homage, and John probably had this in mind when he described Sunday in the way he did—the special day of the week when Christians offered homage to *their* Lord and Master, the risen Jesus.

Some have tried to reconstruct the early church's Sunday liturgy from John's descriptions of worship in heaven (see especially 4:2–11; 7:9–17; 15:2–8). It is dangerous to press the details of the Book of Revelation too far, but in general terms John links the worship of the church militant and triumphant. The prayers of Christians on earth mingle with the praise of heaven (5:8; 8:3), and the dominant notes of both are adoration and celebration of Christ's redemptive work (see, e.g., 5:8–10).

Sunday and Sabbath. From these scattered references in the NT it is plain that the first Christians treated Sunday as something special. Above all, it was the *Lord's* day, when they met to celebrate the central fact of their faith, the resurrection of Jesus. It was a day of worship, with the Lord's Supper at its heart. It was an occasion for teaching and fellowship. And it provided an opportunity to do something practical for others by gifts of money.

But was Sunday also treated as a day of rest in NT times? In other words, did the earliest believers observe Sunday as a Christian sabbath? We know that the Roman emperor Constantine commanded his subjects to rest on Sundays (AD 321), but was he recognizing a general Christian conviction based on clear biblical principles—or simply bowing to expediency?

These are difficult questions, and biblical experts are divided in the way they interpret the evidence. Those who see no connection at all between the sabbath and Sunday appeal to Jesus' attitude to sabbath observance, to Paul's teaching on "observing days," and to historical common sense. All three, they argue, point to Sunday as a day for worship but not necessarily a day of rest.

Jesus, they claim, rescinded the fourth commandment (which the NT never quotes) both by his teaching and by his actions. His teaching is typified by Mark 2:27–28, where he claims lordship over the sabbath and says "the sabbath was made for man, not man for the sabbath" (interpreted to mean that if sabbath observance becomes a burden instead of a benefit, we may ignore it without offending God). And though he attended synagogue regularly on the sabbath (Lk 4:16), Jesus' actions showed that he did not consider himself bound by the sabbath law. In particular, he seemed to single out the sabbath day for many of his healing miracles, to show that its day-of-rest regulations held no authority over him. Very few of those cases were emergencies. Most, if not all, could have waited until the next day (Lk 13:14).

Paul, the argument continues, faithfully reflected Jesus' revolutionary approach to the sabbath by teaching his gentile converts that they should not feel bound to observe *any* special days (Gal 4:8–11; Rom 14:5–9). Sabbath regulations "were only temporary rules that ended when Christ came" (Col 2:17). Surely it would have been very difficult for him to write in that way, without even a mention of the Lord's Day, if he had regarded Sunday as the Christian sabbath.

Above all, it is argued, the history of the early church recorded in Acts shows that the first Christians did not—and could not—keep Sunday as a day of rest. If Jewish Christians had attempted to transfer their weekly rest day from the sabbath to Sunday, they would have been persecuted for sabbath-breaking (which, apparently, they were not). And if they had stopped work on both days (a social and economic impossibility for the majority), they would have ended up by breaking the fourth commandment (because it demanded a six-day work week).

Those who see a clear link between sabbath and Sunday, and maintain that Christians should observe Sunday as a day of rest, disagree with the above interpretations of NT teaching. And they lay much heavier stress on the prominent place the sabbath occupies in the OT's account of creation and in the Ten Commandments.

The sabbath, they point out, was not just a piece of Mosaic Law (Ex 20:8–11; Dt 5:12–16) for OT Israel, but a creation ordinance of God, binding on all people at all times in all places. It looks back to God's own rest after creation (Gn 2:2,3), and the fact that he "blessed" it and "declared it holy" implies that man is obliged to imitate his Maker by resting one day in seven. Chapters 1 and 2 of Genesis record four of these creation ordinances. The other three (marriage, family, and work) are reflected and upheld in the NT. It would be very strange if the NT's virtual silence on the fourth should be taken as evidence of its rejection. Indeed, Jesus was surely deliberately endorsing its general and permanent validity when he said "the sabbath was made for man" (Mk 2:27).

This conviction is backed, the argument goes, by the inclusion of the sabbath law in the Ten Commandments. The NT recognizes the abiding significance of the Ten Commandments both by its allusions to them (cf. Mt 5:17–19) and by its direct quotations of the last six (none of the first four is quoted directly, so the sabbath is not unique in that respect). Jesus' and Paul's criticisms relate to the way the sabbath commandment was observed by Jews, not to its redundancy for Christians. Jesus' aim was to expose hypocrisy

and to stress that one of the Law's main purposes was to make time available for helping the needy. Paul wanted to underline the fact that no kind of law observance can make a person right with God.

Jesus' resurrection, the argument concludes, provided the first Christians with all the justification they needed to transfer the permanent significance of the sabbath from the seventh day to the first. Just like the sabbath, the Lord's Day was kept as a day of worship (centered on God's acts of new creation and redemption in Jesus), and—whenever possible—as a day of rest. Separation of worship and rest would never have occurred to a 1st-century Jew (for whom sabbath rest *was* worship).

These, then, are the main arguments for and against observing Sunday as a Christian sabbath. Few of those who deny any necessary connection between Sunday and sabbath would argue that God's creation ordinance to rest is obsolete for Christians. The point at issue is not whether we all need a break from work one day in seven, but whether our duty to God requires us to keep Sunday as that day.

Sunday Observance Today. The absence of detailed directives in the NT for observing Sunday may leave some people today dismayed and bewildered. But in reality it is a striking indication that as Christians we live under the "law of liberty" (Jas 1:25). It is up to the individual Christian to work out a program for Sunday that is right for him or her in God's sight—and not to criticize others who come to different conclusions (Rom 14:1–5).

The NT does, however, give two positive pointers. In the first place, the Lord's Day is a day when Christians should meet together for *worship*. And the glimpses we have of NT worship provide a standard against which we can measure the spirit and content of our own Sunday services. At its heart was exultation in the resurrection of Jesus, expressed in celebration of the Lord's Supper and marked by joy, adoration, and (judging by Acts 20) an absence of clock-watching.

Second, following the spirit of Paul's instruction to the Christians at Corinth, Sunday should be a day for *practical service*. According to Jesus, this was a primary aim of the OT's sabbath law (Mk 3:4). In most churches today more opportunities could be provided for this way of observing Sunday.

Those who see a close link between Sunday and sabbath would add that the Lord's Day should, whenever possible, be a day of rest from routine work. And even those who do not accept such a link may find themselves without very much time for ordinary work on Sundays, if they follow the NT's

"Sunday pointers" to corporate worship and practical service.   DAVID H. FIELD

See SABBATH.

Bibliography. S. Bacchiocchi, *Divine Rest for Human Restlessness* and *From Sabbath to Sunday;* R. Beckwith and W. Stott, *The Christian Sunday;* D.A. Carson, ed, *From Sabbath to Lord's Day;* W. Hodgkins, *Sunday: Christian and Social Significance;* P.K. Jewett, *The Lord's Day;* W. Rordorf, *Sunday.*

Lord's Prayer. Pattern for prayer Jesus gave his followers to use. There are two versions of the Lord's Prayer (Mt 6:9–13; Lk 11:2–4). The former is included in the Sermon on the Mount; the latter is Jesus' response to a disciple's request that he teach them to pray. There are considerable differences between the two versions.

Some scholars devote a good deal of attention to the question of which is the earlier of the two. Generally speaking, they conclude that in most points Luke's is the earlier form. This is largely because it is shorter, and there is no reason why someone should leave out anything in a prayer as short as this, whereas it is easy to see why additions might be made. These scholars usually hold that in some of the wording Matthew is likely to have retained the earlier form.

This approach, however, does not take account of the fact that Jesus seems to have regarded the prayer as a pattern, not as a formula. In Matthew he introduces it with the words, "Pray then like this." If the prayer was seriously meant as a model, it is unlikely that it would be recited only once. On the contrary, it is to be expected that Jesus would have used it on a number of occasions. And if he seriously meant people to pray "in this way" (and not invariably in these words), then variations in the wording are to be expected.

Some recent writers regard the whole prayer as eschatological, as concerned with the end of the world. They take the petition "Thy kingdom come" as central and understand all the other petitions to refer in one way or another to the coming kingdom. The prayer about hallowing the name is then seen as a prayer for the destruction of God's enemies who do not reverence his holiness; that about the bread becomes a petition for the messianic banquet, and so on. But this is to take the words in an unnatural sense. Christians are of course always living in the "last days," and there is no reason why they should not see an application of Jesus' words to the eschatological situation. It seems much more probable, however, that we should understand the prayer with reference to the help we need in our daily lives.

The first person singular pronoun is not used anywhere in the prayer. We say, "Our Father, . . . give us. . . ." This prayer is meant for a community. It may profitably be used by an individual, but it is not meant as an aid to private devotion. It is a prayer to be said by God's people; it is the prayer of the Christian family.

In Matthew the opening words are "Our Father in heaven," whereas Luke has simply "Father." Those who pray like this are members of a family, and they look to God as the Head of the family, one who is bound to them by ties of love. Matthew's "in heaven" brings out something of his dignity, and this is seen also in the petition "Hallowed be thy name" (identical in the two). In antiquity "the name" meant far more than it does to us. In some way it summed up the whole person. Thus this petition is more than a prayer that people will use the name of God reverently rather than blasphemously (though that is important and is included). It looks for people to have a reverent attitude to all that God stands for. They should have a proper humility before God, being ready to honor him as he is in all his holiness. Some hold that the prayer should be understood in the spirit of Ezekiel 36:23: "I will honor my great name that you defiled, and the people of the world shall know I am the Lord." In this view God himself is asked to ensure that his name is honored. But it seems more likely that we have here a prayer that men will come to have a proper reverence for God. A change in the attitude of sinners is in mind, rather than an action of God.

"Thy kingdom come" is the petition that most of all looks for the eschatological activity of God. Christians have always longed for the day when God will overthrow the kingdoms of this earth and when all will become the kingdom of our Lord and of his Christ (Rv 11:15). This is included in the meaning of the petition. But there is another sense in which the kingdom is a present reality, a kingdom that is now in human hearts and lives. This aspect of the kingdom is brought out in the words added in Matthew's version, "Thy will be done on earth as it is in heaven." The servant of God looks for the rule of God to become actual in more and more lives.

In the petition about bread Jesus is concerned with the material necessities of daily life. Jesus' followers are, it is true, not to be anxious about the things they need to eat and to wear (Mt 6:25). But Jesus also taught that they should constantly look to God for such needs to be supplied (Mt 6:32,33). The view that the messianic banquet is in mind does not reckon with the fact that this is regarded as a feast, while it is bread, not some festive food, that is mentioned here. The big problem in this petition is the meaning of the word usually translated "daily." It is an exceedingly rare word, and many scholars think that it was coined by Christians. Since it is impossible to establish its meaning from the way it is used, discussions center on its derivation. The most favored views are those which see it as meaning "daily," "for today," or "for the coming day," "for tomorrow," or "necessary." The traditional understanding, "daily," seems most probable. But however we translate it, the prayer is for the simple and present necessities of life. Jesus is counseling his followers to pray for necessities, not luxuries, and for what is needed now, not a great store for many days to come. By confining the petition to present needs Jesus teaches a day-by-day dependence on God.

The petition about forgiveness differs slightly in the two accounts. In Matthew it is "Forgive us our debts," while Luke has "Forgive us our sins." Without question it is the forgiveness of sins that is in mind, but the Matthean form sees sin as an indebtedness. We owe it to God to live uprightly. He has provided all we need to do this. So when we sin, we become debtors. The sinner has failed to fulfill his obligations, what he "owes." Matthew goes on to say, "as we also have forgiven our debtors," and Luke, "for we ourselves forgive everyone indebted to us." The tense in Matthew indicates that the person praying is not only ready to forgive but has already forgiven those who have sinned against him; in Luke, that he habitually forgives. Further, he does so in the case of every debtor.

In neither form of the prayer is it implied that human forgiveness earns God's forgiveness. The NT makes it clear that God forgives on account of his mercy, shown in Christ's dying for us on the cross. Nothing we do can merit forgiveness. There is also the thought that those who seek forgiveness should show a forgiving spirit. How can we claim the forgiveness of our sins if we do not forgive others who sin against us?

There is dispute as to the precise meaning of the petition traditionally translated "lead us not into temptation." Some favor a rendering like that of the NEB, "do not bring us to the test." The word usually understood as "temptation" does sometimes mean a proving or a testing. But it is the kind of testing that the evil one engages in, testing with a view to failure. It is thus the normal word to be used when temptation is in mind. If the whole prayer is to be understood eschatologically, then "do not bring us to the test" is no doubt the way this petition should be taken. The great testing time that comes with the upsurge of evil in the last days is something from which every Christian naturally shrinks, and the prayer would give expression to this. But it is much more likely that the prayer refers to life here and now. Even so, it may mean "severe trial," and some scholars favor this. They think that Jesus is counseling his followers to pray for a quiet life in which they will not meet serious misfortune. But a prayer to be delivered from temptation is much more likely. Christians know their weakness and readiness to sin, so pray that they may be kept from the temptation to go astray. It is true that God does not tempt people (Jas 1:13). But it is also true that it is important for the believer to avoid evil. One should not see how close to sinning one can come without actually doing it, but should keep as far away from it as possible (cf., e.g., 1 Cor 6:18; 10:14).

Matthew adds, "but deliver us from evil" (as do some manuscripts of Luke). This is a further development of the prayer just offered. There is uncertainty as to whether the last word means "evil" generally or "the evil one." Either meaning is possible. Christians pray that they may not be tempted, and this leads naturally to the thought either that they may not become the prey of evil or that they may be free from the domination of the devil. It is the general thrust of Jesus' teaching that should decide the point, not the precise language used here.

This is where the prayer ends in Luke, and in the oldest manuscripts of Matthew. Few would doubt that here is where the prayer ended in the teaching of our Lord. But many manuscripts, some of them fairly old, add the familiar words, "for thine is the kingdom and the power and the glory for ever" (cf. 1 Chr 29:11). This is the kind of doxology that is often found in prayers in antiquity, both Jewish and Christian. The early Christians used the Lord's Prayer in worship services and doubtless found this a splendid way to end it. In time, what was so acceptable in worship found its way into some of the manuscripts. We may well continue to end the prayer in this way. It is good to remind ourselves that all ultimate sovereignty, power, and glory belong to God for ever. But we should not see this as part of the prayer Jesus taught his followers to use.

It is perhaps surprising that the prayer does not seem to be quoted in the NT (though some scholars discern allusions to it here and there). But it must have been used from the first, and in time it became the characteristic prayer of the Christians. When we use it, we are at one with the followers of Christ through the centuries and throughout the world.

LEON L. MORRIS

See PRAYER; SERMON ON THE MOUNT; WORSHIP.

Bibliography. F. Chase, *The Lord's Prayer in the Early Church*; O.C.J. Hoffmann, *The Lord's Prayer*; J. Jeremias, *The Lord's Prayer*; E. Lohmeyer, *The Lord's Prayer*; W. Lüthi, *The Lord's Prayer*; A.W. Pink, *The Beatitudes and the Lord's Prayer*; H. Thielicke, *Our Heavenly Father*; S. Zodhiates, *The Lord's Prayer*.

Lord's Supper, The. The supper Jesus shared with his disciples a few hours before he was arrested and taken to his trial and death; the ceremony of the bread and wine that Christians have come to call the Lord's Supper (1 Cor 11:20), the breaking of bread (Acts 2:42,46; 20:7), Holy Communion (from the expression of 1 Cor 10:16), the Eucharist (the Greek word for "thanksgiving," see Mk 14:23), or the Mass. The apostle Paul speaks of handing on what he had "received from the Lord" concerning the institution of this supper "on the night when he was betrayed." Like Luke, Paul gives the Lord's command to his disciples, "Do this in remembrance of me" (1 Cor 11:24,25). According to Acts 2, the early Christians from the beginning of the life of the church met regularly for "the breaking of bread."

The Records of the Institution.
The institution of the Lord's Supper is recorded in Matthew 26:26–30; Mark 14:22–26; and Luke 22:14–20. John's Gospel (ch 13) tells of the last supper Jesus shared with his disciples, of his washing the disciples' feet and the teaching associated with that, but does not mention his institution of Holy Communion. Many see the Lord's Supper reflected in the teaching of John 6, following the miracle of the feeding of the 5000 and Jesus' speaking of himself as "the Bread of life," but this is open to question. First Corinthians 11:23–26 gives Paul's version of the institution, which he speaks of as "receiving" and "delivering" to the Corinthian Christians.

In Luke 22:17,18 Jesus is said to have passed the cup to the disciples with the words, "Take this and divide it among yourselves," before taking the bread and giving it to them. In most early manuscripts there is then a second cup after the giving of the bread. This difference of Luke from the other Gospels and from Paul has been variously explained; but whether there are two cups of wine at the supper or a different order in the giving of the bread and the wine, it makes no essential difference to the fact and the meaning of the institution.

The Time of the Institution.
All of the narratives—the three Gospels and 1 Corinthians—speak of the Last Supper when the Eucharist was instituted as taking place a few hours before Jesus' arrest. All four Gospels tell, in this context, of Jesus' words to his disciples, to Judas about his betrayal, and to Peter about the way that he would deny his Master. Matthew (26:17–20), Mark (14:12–17), and Luke (22:7–14) all say clearly that this last supper was prepared by the disciples and kept by Jesus with them as a Passover meal. John speaks of it as happening "before the feast of the Passover," and then says that at the time of the trial of Jesus before Pilate the Jewish leaders "did not enter the praetorium, so that they might not be defiled, but might eat the passover" (Jn 13:1; 18:28).

Various explanations of this difference between John and the other Gospels have been suggested, such as that different groups of the Jews kept the Passover at different times, or that the meal in the upper room was not strictly a Passover but a fellowship meal at the Passover season, or that Jesus deliberately chose for his own special reasons to celebrate the Passover before the normal time. Luke 22:15 gives his words, "I have earnestly desired to eat this passover with you before I suffer." However the differences between the Gospels may be explained, and whenever the gathering around the table took place, it is clear that the Last Supper had the significance of a Passover meal.

Thus there is an inevitable similarity between the celebration of the Passover as a feast of the old covenant and the Lord's Supper as a feast of the new. The former looks back with thankful remembrance to the people's redemption and liberation from Egypt by the act of God, associated with the sacrifice of the Passover lamb. The latter looks back with thankful remembrance to redemption by the act of God through the sacrifice of Christ; as the apostle Paul says, linking the two, "Christ, our Passover lamb, has been sacrificed" (1 Cor 5:7 NIV). In the Jewish keeping of the Passover there was the hope of a new and greater deliverance to come. Jesus, in his words at the last supper (Lk 22:16), spoke of the fulfilling of the Passover "in the kingdom of God." The dimension of hope has a place in the Christian celebration of the Lord's Supper.

Words and Actions of the Institution.
The association of the Last Supper with the Passover points to the importance of the OT background for our understanding of the meaning of the Lord's Supper. This OT background is equally important in understanding the words and actions of Jesus in the upper room.

"This is my body." The actions of Jesus in taking the bread are described similarly in Matthew (26:26), Mark (14:22), Luke (22:19), and 1 Corinthians (11:23,24). Jesus took the bread, gave thanks to God ("blessing" has the same meaning in the biblical context), and broke it. It is noteworthy that the same three actions are described in the records of the feeding of the 5000 and of the 4000 (Mk 6:41; 8:6).

Traditional site of the Last Supper.

What he said, according to all four accounts of the Last Supper, was, "This is my body." Christians in Catholic, Orthodox, and various Protestant traditions have differed in their understanding of the precise meaning of those words. What is clear is that in the taking of the bread there is the realization of Jesus' giving himself, his body to be broken on the cross, his life offered that we, in and through him, might have life. First Corinthians 11:24 gives the words as "This is my body, which is for you," and some early manuscripts have "broken for you."

"Do this in remembrance of me." This specific instruction is found only in Luke 22:19 and 1 Corinthians 11:24. Some have argued that the absence of the words in the other Gospel records indicates that it was not the explicit intention of the Lord that what he did at the Last Supper was to be repeated as a Christian sacrament. Yet all the Gospels were written when the breaking of bread had been a regular practice in the life of the church for years. Matthew and Mark, therefore, may have thought it unnecessary to express Jesus' intention with those words. They were taken for granted.

It must also be said that these words have been interpreted differently in various Christian traditions. Many Protestant Christians have understood them to mean that in the Holy Communion we are to recall with great thankfulness that Christ loved us and gave himself to die for us. In the Roman Catholic Church the word "remembrance" has been understood as a memorial before God, a representing of the sacrifice of Christ before the Father. "This do" has been interpreted as meaning "offer this," and even in the 2nd century Christian writers spoke of the Eucharist as a "sacrifice." Protestant Christians generally have felt the danger of this way of speaking; it can detract from, or even deny, the biblical understanding of the sacrifice of Christ having been offered once and for all, and sufficiently atoning for the sins of the world (cf. Heb 7:27; 9:12). It must be said, however, that many Roman Catholic statements today stress the sufficiency and completeness of Christ's sacrifice on the cross; and many Protestant scholars, while not wishing to introduce a sacrificial understanding of the Lord's Supper, stress that "remembrance" is more than simply calling to mind a past action. In biblical thinking "remembrance" often involves a realization and appropriation in the present of what has been done or what has proved true in the past (e.g., Eccl 12:1; Pss 98:3; 106:45; 112:6; Is 57:11). Then a right human response is the "sacrifice of praise to God" (Heb 13:15) for what Christ has done and for what that means to us today.

"This is my blood of the [new] covenant." When it came to the wine, Jesus took the cup, gave thanks, and handed it to his disciples for them all to drink. In essence the four accounts of the institution agree. Matthew (26:28) and Mark (14:24) give the words of Jesus as "This is my blood of the [new] covenant." Luke 22:20 has "This cup which is poured out for you is the new covenant in my blood," and 1 Corinthians 11:25 is similar to this. This refers back to the ritual of making a covenant with the offering of sacrifice, as the covenant between God and Israel after the exodus (Ex 24:1–8). Implied also is that the prophetic hope of the new covenant (Jer 31:31–34) was fulfilled in Jesus, as Hebrews 8,9 describes.

"Poured out for many for the forgiveness of sins." The meaning of the death of Jesus as sacrifice is linked with the understanding of the Passover and of the covenant. It is also linked with what Isaiah 53 says of the Suffering Servant making himself "an offering for sin" (v 10). Luke 22:37 includes among the words of Jesus in the upper room the statement, "This scripture must be fulfilled in me, 'And he was reckoned with transgressors.'" That verse, Isaiah 53:12, also says, "he poured out his soul to death" and "he bore the sin of many." Mark 14:24 appears to allude to them when Jesus speaks of his blood "poured out for many," and Matthew 26:28 adds "for the forgiveness of sins."

Hope for the Future. All four accounts of the Last Supper associate, though in different ways, a hope for the future with the institution of the Eucharist. In Mark 14:25 it comes in the words of Jesus, "Truly, I say to you, I shall not drink again of the fruit of the vine until that day when I drink it new in the kingdom of God." In Matthew 26:29 that future drinking of the fruit of the vine is said to be "with you in my Father's kingdom." In Luke 22:18 there are similar words, and three verses earlier the statement about fulfilling the Passover "in the kingdom of God." All of these can be understood as the ultimate realization of another hope that both OT and later Jewish apocalyptic writings set forward: the messianic banquet, the feast on the mountain of the Lord of which Isaiah 25:6 speaks. In 1 Corinthians 11:26 that future hope is quite explicitly that of Christ's second coming; for, says the apostle, "As often as you eat this bread and

drink the cup, you proclaim the Lord's death until he comes."

Paul's Teaching. In Paul's teaching as in the Gospels, the Lord's Supper clearly involves the backward look in thankful remembrance for the sacrifice of Christ offered once for all for the sins of the world, the realization of the Lord being with his people in the present, and the look forward in hope. Other aspects of teaching relating to the Eucharist are brought out in 1 Corinthians 10,11. The teaching arises from practical aspects of the situation in the Corinthian church; the need to be aware of the danger of turning back in any way to the worship of idols; and the potential divisions in the Christian fellowship, including that between rich and poor.

Fellowship with Christ. To partake of the bread and to drink of the cup is spoken of as having part with Christ, as indeed sharing in sacrificial meals would mean partaking at "the table of demons" (1 Cor 10:21). "The cup of blessing which we bless, is it not a participation in the blood of Christ? The bread which we break, is it not a participation in the body of Christ?" (1 Cor 10:16). "Participation" is the translation of the Greek word *koinōnia*, so often rendered "fellowship" in NT passages. When the Lord's Supper was celebrated, there must often have been a recalling not only of the last supper on the night before Jesus died, but of his presence with his disciples on the first Easter and his making himself known to them in the breaking of the bread (Lk 24:30–35). They continued to experience that fellowship with him whom they knew to be "the same yesterday and today and for ever" (Heb 13:8).

Feeding on Christ. Of the two Christian sacraments, baptism has a once-for-all nature, while Holy Communion is repeated. The life of Christ has been offered for sins once for all on the cross, and we find life in turning to him—baptism signifies that. At the same time that life is also offered to us constantly for the nourishing of our spiritual lives day by day—of this regular feeding on Christ the Eucharist speaks. First Corinthians 10:3,4 speaks of "supernatural food" and "supernatural drink," and finds in the events at the sea and in the wilderness in the days of Moses foreshadowings of what Christians find in Christ. In Israel the people could eat some of the animal sacrifices offered (1 Cor 10:18); the Lord's Supper was, at least in some sense, the counterpart for Christians (cf. Heb 13:9–12). Christ said, "I am the Bread of life," and, "My flesh is food indeed, and my blood is drink indeed"; thus what we have in John's Gospel (6:35,55) is close to what Paul implies about the Lord's Supper expressing the truth of Christian people feeding their spiritual lives on Christ.

The Unity of Christian People. The Last Supper took place as Jesus met in the upper room with his disciples. Matthew and Mark emphasize their "all" drinking of the cup; Luke gives his words, "divide it among yourselves." Paul draws out more explicitly the significance of their fellowship together: "Because there is one loaf, we, who are many, are one body, for we all partake of the one loaf" (1 Cor 10:17 NIV). Communion with Christ and also communion of disciples with one another are involved. The words of 1 Corinthians 11:29 rebuking "anyone who eats and drinks without recognizing the body of the Lord" (NIV) are probably to be understood as speaking of Christians as "the body" of Christ. At least the context of the chapter is the rebuke of "divisions" when Christians in Corinth met together. "When you meet together, it is not the Lord's Supper that you eat. For in eating, each one goes ahead with his own meal, and one is hungry and another is drunk.... Do you despise the church of God and humiliate those who have nothing?" (1 Cor 11:20–22). In other words, the Lord's Supper is not properly celebrated when Christians who meet are divided among themselves.

The Pledge of Loyalty. Finally, in these chapters in 1 Corinthians the apostle speaks of eating at the Lord's table as indicating allegiance to Christ and not to idols. There can be no compromise. "You cannot drink the cup of the Lord and the cup of demons. You cannot partake at the table of the Lord and the table of demons." That would be to "provoke the Lord to jealousy" (1 Cor 10:21,22). To eat at his table is to be committed to him, identified with his people, and dedicated to the service of his cause in the world.

The Practice of the Early Church. In Acts 2:42, after the record of what happened at Pentecost, it says that "they devoted themselves to the apostles' teaching and fellowship, to the breaking of bread and the prayers." Further, "day by day, attending the temple together and breaking bread in their homes, they partook of food with glad and generous hearts" (Acts 2:46). Two questions are raised about these words and the practice that lay behind them. Do they mean that the Christians simply shared fellowship meals together? Acts 2:46 seems to speak of breaking bread and partaking of food as two separate actions. Moreover Acts 20:7 in speaking of Christians at Troas "on the first day of the week ... gathered together to break bread" seems clearly to allude to a Christian service and not just a meal. From 1 Corinthians 10 and perhaps from the reference to "love feasts" in Jude 12, we may reasonably deduce that a meal in Christian fellowship and the celebration of the Lord's Supper often took place together. A second question is whether the earliest "breaking of bread," as in the Jerusalem church, may have been a different rite from that with the bread and wine, the former recalling the fellowship of the disciples with the risen Lord, the latter especially recalling his sacrificial death. There is no direct evidence to support such a view. The Lord's Supper to which the Gospels bear witness involved the breaking of bread and the sharing of the cup in remembrance of the blood of Christ "poured out for many." We may assume too that the tradition that the apostle Paul received, followed, and passed on to others went back to his earliest years as a Christian, and so involved the breaking of the bread and the sharing of the cup "in remembrance" of Christ, and thus proclaiming the Lord's death until his return.

FRANCIS FOULKES

See MEALS, SIGNIFICANCE OF.

Bibliography. G. Aulén, *Eucharist and Sacrifice;* W. Barclay, *The Lord's Supper;* O. Cullmann, *Early Christian Worship;* A.J.B. Higgins, *The Lord's Supper in the NT;* I.H. Marshall, *Last Supper and Lord's Supper;* R.P. Martin, *Worship in the Early Church;* M. Marty, *The Lord's Supper;* S. McCormick, Jr., *The Lord's Supper, a Biblical Interpretation;* E. Schweizer, *The Lord's Supper According to the NT.*

Lo-ruhamah. Symbolic name, meaning "Not Pitied" (Hos 1:6,8), given by the prophet Hosea to his daughter, indicating God's rejection of Israel.

See RUHAMAH.

Lot. Significant scriptural figure in connection with the destruction of Sodom and the other cities of the plain and as a progenitor of both the Moabites and Ammonites. Like Abraham he was born in Ur. When his father died, he was put in the care of his grandfather Terah, and accompanied him and his uncle Abram to Haran (Gn 11:27–32). After the death of Terah, he joined Abram in the journey to Canaan and subsequently to Egypt and back to Canaan.

By the time the pair returned to Canaan, their flocks and herds were too numerous for them to live together in a single area. Generously, Abram gave Lot his choice of where he would like to settle; Lot chose the fertile plain of the Jordan, which was like a "garden of the Lord" (Gn 13:10) before divine judgment and catastrophe fell on the region. Thus Lot became increasingly involved with and contaminated by the corruption of the cities of the plain and took up his residence in Sodom.

While Lot was living in Sodom, four Mesopotamian kings (probably of small city-states) defeated the kings of the five towns in the area in battle, and in the subsequent plundering carried off Lot and his family and possessions. When word of the loss reached Abram, he

Submerged forest near Jebel Usdum (Sodom); the extreme saltiness of the Dead Sea killed all the vegetation.

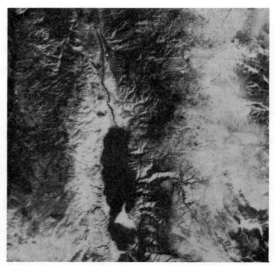

An aerial view of the Dead Sea area, where Lot lived.

launched a rearguard action against the invaders and recovered all the prisoners and the loot at Hobah, north of Damascus (Gn 14).

Subsequently two angelic visitors called on Lot in Sodom to hasten his departure from the doomed city. The homosexual attack on them illustrated the depravity of the city, and Lot's willingness to sacrifice his daughters shows how the corruption of his environment was rubbing off on him. As further evidence of the evil influence, Lot was unwilling to leave Sodom; his future sons-in-law refused to accompany him; and his wife looked back and was turned to a pillar of salt (Gn 19).

The sequel to the story was as sordid as the scene at Lot's door. His daughters, despairing of husbands of their own, got him drunk enough to engage in sexual relations with them. The result was the birth of two sons, Moab and Ben-ammi, ancestors of the Moabites and Ammonites, inveterate enemies of Israel (Gn 19:30–38).

In spite of his waywardness the NT declares that Lot was a "righteous man" (2 Pt 2:7–9), apparently meaning that his faith in God was sufficient to guarantee his salvation. To critics who question the historicity of Lot and the destruction of Sodom, it must be noted that Jesus vouched for both in Luke 17:28,29.

See SODOM AND GOMORRAH.

Lotan. Seir's eldest son (Gn 36:20), and a chief of the native Horite inhabitants of Edom (Gn 36:22,29). Lotan had two sons, Hori and Homan (1 Chr 1:38,39).

Lots, Casting of. Practice common in the OT, less common in the NT prior to Pentecost, and absent in the biblical narrative after Pentecost.

In the Bible the practice was used in a variety of circumstances, including (1) the selection of the scapegoat (Lv 16:8–10); (2) the allocation of the tribal inheritance in the Promised Land (Nm 26:55,56; Jos 14:2; Jgs 1:3; etc.); (3) the determination of the families who had to relocate to give a proper distribution of the populace or of those warriors who had to go to war where only a percentage was required (Jgs 20:9; Neh 11:1); (4) the order of the priests and their duties (1 Chr 24:5–19; Neh 10:34); (5) the determination of an offender (Jos 7:14–18; cf. Prv 18:18).

According to biblical usage lots seem to have been used only when the decision was important and where wisdom or biblical injunctions did not give sufficient guidance. One of the advantages of the casting of lots was the impartiality of the choice. It was held that the Lord directed the lots (Prv 16:33). The method of casting lots is not specified or described and seems to have varied according to the need of the situation (cf. Lv 16:8; Nm 26:55,56; Jgs 20:9).

The practice of casting lots was never condemned by God and in fact on several occasions was sanctioned by him (Lv 16:8; Prv 18:18; Is 34:17). The principle behind the procedure is set forth in Proverbs 16:33, which affirms that the disposition or result of the lot is determined by God; therefore, the theory was that the lot pronounced the will of God.

In the NT the soldiers cast lots over Jesus' garments (Mt 27:35), and the disciples cast lots when they selected Matthias to the apostleship in place of Judas (Acts 1:26). After the outpouring of the Holy Spirit upon the church, the practice of casting lots ceased. Some hold that there was no further need for the practice to continue, as the Holy Spirit guided the church in its decisions.

See URIM AND THUMMIM.

Lotus Bush. Water lily common in the Near East, mentioned only in Job 40:21,22.

See PLANTS.

Love. First and last word in Christian theology and ethics. It is therefore important to understand clearly this exceedingly ambiguous term.

In the Old Testament. Sexual love is frankly recognized in stories of Adam and Eve, Jacob and Rachel, and in the Song of Songs. The Hebrew word can also mean tormenting lust (2 Sm 13:1–15), parental love (Gn 37:4), and both sexual and divine love in one context (Hos 3:1). It is used too of the love of friends (1 Sm 20:17), David's love having some ground in gratitude, Jonathan's in admiration, but with an element of altruistic self-renunciation as the crown prince stepped down for David's sake. For this strong, unselfish love the OT usually employed another word, almost untranslatable, *hesed*, rendered sometimes "loyalty" (2 Sm 22:26 RSV), more often "steadfast love" (Gn 39:21) or "kindness."

The connotation of this significant word is clear in Hosea 2:19,20: "I will betroth you for ever . . . in righteousness . . . justice . . . steadfast love . . . faithfulness"; in Job 6:14,15, where kindness is compared with treachery; and in 1 Samuel 20:8, which speaks of covenanted kindness. This unshakable, steadfast love of God is contrasted with the unpredictable, capricious moods of heathen deities. *Hesed* is not an emotional response to beauty, merit, or kindness, but a moral attitude dedicated to another's good, whether or not that other is lovable, worthy, or responsive (see Dt 7:7–9).

This enduring loyalty, rooted in an unswerving purpose of good, could be stern, determined to discipline a wayward people, as several prophets warned. But God's love does not change. Through exile and failure it persisted with infinite patience, neither condoning evil nor abandoning the evildoers. It has within it kindness, tenderness, and compassion (Pss 86:15; 103:1–18; 136; Hos 11:1–4), but its chief characteristic is an accepted moral obligation for another's welfare, which no ill-desert or want of gratitude will quench.

Nevertheless response was expected. The Law enjoined wholehearted love and gratitude for God's choosing and redeeming Israel (Dt 6:20–25). This was to be shown in worship, and especially in humane treatment of the poor, the defenseless, the resident alien, slaves, widows, and all suffering oppression and cruelty. Hosea similarly expects steadfast love among men to result from the steadfast love of God toward men (6:6; 7:1–7; 10:12,13).

Love for God, and for "your neighbor as yourself" (Lv 19:18) are thus linked in Israel's law and prophecy. While much love of another kind lies within the OT, these are the major points: God's loving initiative, the moral quality of love, and the close relation of love for God with love among men.

In the New Testament. Christianity inherited this strongly moral connotation of love, not always remembered by those who sentimentalize the love ethic.

Agapē. Of Greek words available, *eros* (sexual love) does not occur in the NT; *phileō*, spontaneous natural affection, with more feeling than reason, occurs some 25 times, with *philadelphia* (brotherly love) 5 times, and *philia* (friendship) only in James 4:4; *storgē*, natural affection between kinfolk, appears occasionally in compounds. By far the most frequent word is *agapē*, generally assumed to mean moral goodwill which proceeds from esteem, principle, or duty, rather than attraction or charm. *Agapē* means to love the undeserving, despite disappointment and rejection; the difference between *agapaō* and *phileō* is difficult to sustain in all passages. *Agapē* is especially appropriate for religious love. *Agapē* was long believed to be a Christian coinage, but pagan occurrences have recently been claimed. The verb *agapaō* was frequent in the Greek OT. Though *agapē* has more to do with moral principle than with inclination or liking, it never means the cold religious kindness shown from duty alone, as scriptural examples abundantly prove.

The Synoptic Gospels. Jesus embodied the concept of *hesed* in the all-caring, all-inclusive fatherhood of God, shown toward just and unjust, far exceeding the divine concern for ephemeral grass, falling sparrow, or untoiling lilies of the field. God's sons are freed, by their confidence in the Father's love, from fretful care about material provision and personal safety to seek first God's will and kingdom. This is the Father's world; the Father knows; the Father loves. For the children of a loving Father, life is no struggle for existence but a serenity born of trust in a basically friendly universe.

In a sinful and suffering world divine love will show itself supremely in compassion and healing for the distressed and in redemptive concern for the alienated and the self-despairing. Hence the kingdom Christ proclaimed offered good news to the poor, to captives, the blind, the oppressed (Mt 11:2–5; Lk 4:18); while the attitude of Jesus toward those ostracized, despised, or grieving over sin in some far country of the soul assured them of forgiveness and a welcome return to the Father's house (Lk 15). Such forgiveness was free, its only precondition being readiness to receive it in repentance and faith. Even here, however, the moral clarity of divine love is not obscured. For the obdurate, the unforgiving, the self-righteous, Jesus has only warning of the consequences of sin and the judgment of God (Lk 13:1–5); for the wavering or impulsive, stern discipline and unrelenting standards (Mt 10:34–39; Mk 10:17–22; Lk 9:23–26,57–62).

Moreover, the good news of divine love does impose its own obligation: to love God and to love others as God does (Mt 5:44–48). The first and greatest commandment in God's Law is, "You shall love the Lord your God. . . . And a second is like it, You shall love your neighbor as yourself. On these two commandments depend all the law and the prophets" (Mt 22:35–40, citing Lv 19:18; Dt 6:5).

The first commandment is not identical with, lost in, or only fulfilled through the second; it is separate and primary. What Jesus meant by loving God is indicated by his own habits of public worship, private prayer, absolute obedience; by the requirement "Him only shalt thou serve," not dividing devotion with mammon, hallowing the divine name in daily business by avoiding empty oaths; by his zeal for the Scriptures, his defense of the sabbath, his unshaken trust and frequent thanksgiving (Mt 4:1–11; 5:33–37; 6:1–6,9,24; 7:21; 12:50; 23:16–22; Lk 4:16; 22:42).

Love for one's neighbor is nowhere defined but everywhere illustrated. In the parable of the good Samaritan, "neighbor" is shown to mean anyone near enough to help, and love involves whatever service the neighbor's situation demands. The parable of the sheep and goats shows love feeding the hungry, clothing the naked, visiting with kindness the sick and the imprisoned. In the untiring example of Jesus love heals, teaches, adapts instruction to the hearers by parable and symbolic language, defends those criticized or despised, pronounces forgiveness, comforts the bereaved, befriends the lonely. We are to love others as he has loved us and as we love ourselves, which means "Whatever you wish that men would do to you, do so to them" (Mt 7:12). Such imaginative transfer of self-love does good without expecting return, never returns ill treatment, ensures unfailing courtesy even to the lowliest, sustains thoughtful understanding that tempers judgment.

Nevertheless love deals frankly with human weakness and wickedness. Jesus prays for Peter, but not that he shall be spared temptation; he rebukes disciples, warns Jerusalem and Judas, makes Peter painfully retract his denials, accepts that love may have to lay down its life. Christ's love is no timid meekness, no sentimental mildness, inoffensive and ineffectual, helpless in face of the world's evil. It is a strong determination to seek others' highest good in all circumstances, at any cost. On that simple but demanding principle hang all moral obligation and divine law. To love is enough.

But it is also imperative. To Jesus the outstanding sin was lovelessness, the willful omission of any possible good, passing by on the other side while others suffer, ignoring the destitute at one's gate, withholding forgiveness. Lovelessness was made worse by self-righteousness, censoriousness, the religious insensitivity that ignores another's distress to preserve some petty ritual regulation. At the last, obedience to or neglect of the law of love will determine everyone's eternal destiny (Mt 25:31–46).

Paul. The apostolic church quickly grasped the revolutionary principle that love is enough. Paul's declaration that love fulfills the whole law is almost a quotation from Jesus. His exposition of various commandments against adultery, killing, stealing, and coveting is summarized in loving, because love can do no wrong to a neighbor (Rom 13:8–10). Ephesians 4:25–5:2, where all bitterness, anger, lying, stealing, slander, and malice are to be replaced by tenderness, forgiveness, kindness, among those who by love are made members one of another, makes the same point another way.

Love is, for Paul, "the law of Christ," supreme and sufficient (Gal 5:14; 6:2), and Paul neatly defines what alone "avails" in Christianity as "faith working through love" (Gal 5:6). He insists that the supreme manifestation of the Spirit which Christians should covet is "the more excellent way" of love (1 Cor 12:27–13:13; cf. Rom 5:5; Gal 5:22). Here too he contrasts love with five other expressions of religious zeal much prized at Corinth to show that each is profitless without love (1 Cor 13:1–3). He ends the chapter by comparing love with faith and hope, the other enduring elements of religious experience, and declares love to be the greatest.

Paul's description of love in action includes liberality, acts of mercy, and hospitality; avoidance of revenge; sympathy that weeps; rejoicing with others; sharing of weakness, shame, or need; restoring, supporting, and upbuilding others, giving them all honor, kindness, forgiveness, encouragement; restraining criticism, even of the divisive, overscrupulous "weaker brother"—the list is almost endless. More generally, love is revealed as a quality of activity, of thinking, and of suffering (1 Cor 13:4–8). In brief, love does no harm and omits no good; and it is God's Law.

But for motive Paul appeals beyond duty. To love we owe everything in salvation. God shows his love in that Christ died for us; out of his great love he made us alive in Christ; and in that love we live, by it we conquer, and from it nothing shall separate us (Rom 5:8; 8:32,37–39; 2 Cor 13:14; 2 Thes 2:16; Eph 2:4; Ti 3:4,5). God's love is almost indistinguishable from Christ's. "The love of Christ controls us" reveals the experiential heart of Paul's thinking (Gal 2:20; 2 Cor 5:14; Eph 5:2,25). Our love reflects the love first "poured into our hearts" (Rom 5:5), and is directed toward Christ (1 Cor 7; 16:22; Eph 6:24) and toward others, whom we love for his sake.

The love of God, experienced through Christ, returning in love for God, for Christ, and for his people—such is Christian love as Paul analyzed it.

John. What John later recalled, and reflected upon, forms the crown of biblical teaching about love. For John, love was the foundation of all that had happened—"God so loved the world . . ." (Jn 3:16; 16:27; 17:23). This is how we know love at all: Christ laid down his life for us (1 Jn 3:16). The mutual love of Father, Son, and disciples, must be the fundamental fact in Christianity, because God himself is love (1 Jn 4:8,16).

We know this by the incarnation and by the cross (1 Jn 4:9,10). Thus we know and believe the love God has for us, and that love itself is divine ("of God"). It follows that "he who loves is born of God." "He who does not love does not know God," nor "the message" of the gospel; "is in the darkness," "is not of God," and "remains in death." No one has ever seen God; nevertheless "if we love, . . . God abides in us" and we in God.

God's love is thus prior and original; if we love at all, it is "because he first loved us." Our love is directed first toward God, and John is exceedingly searching in his tests of that Godward love. It demands that we "love not the world," that we "keep his word, . . . his commandments," and that we love our brother. This commandment we received from Christ, "that he who loves God should

love his brother also," for "if God so loved us, we also ought to love one another." Twelve times John stresses the duty of mutual loyalty and love. Indeed, if one closes his heart against his brother, "how does God's love abide in him?"

This emphasis upon the mutual love of Christians has been held a serious limitation of the love Jesus required. "Your brother" appears to have supplanted "your neighbor." In this respect the commandment given in the upper room (Jn 13:34) is "new" compared with that in Matthew 22:39 (citing Lv 19:18), and the circumstances explain why. The night on which Jesus was betrayed was shadowed by the surrounding world's hostility, the imminent crucifixion, and the defection of Judas. All the future depended upon the mutual loyalty of the 11 disciples, standing together under social pressure. By the time of John's letter, new defections had rent the church. A perversion of the gospel called Gnosticism, essentially intellectualist, proud, "giving no heed to love" (Ignatius), had drawn away leaders and adherents (1 Jn 2:19,26). Once again mutual loyalty was all-important, and John wrote expressly to consolidate and maintain the apostolic fellowship (1 Jn 1:3).

However, love for one's brethren does not exclude, but instead leads on to, a wider love (cf. 2 Pt 1:7). John insists that God loved the whole world (Jn 3:16; 1 Jn 2:2; 4:14). Moreover, if love fails within the Christian fellowship, it certainly will not flourish beyond it, but evaporate in mere words (1 Jn 3:18).

In countering the loveless conceit of gnostic Christianity, John's concern was with the basic commandment of love to God and man as at once the criterion and the consummation of true Christian life. He does not, therefore, detail the many-sided expressions of love. For description of love in action, his mind recalls Christ's words about "keeping commandments" and "laying down life" in sacrifice (Jn 15:10,13; 1 Jn 3:16), and he mentions especially love's noticing a brother's need, and so sharing this world's goods (1 Jn 3:17). Terse as these expressions are, they contain the heart of Christian love. John's forthright realism in testing all religious claims ensures that for him love could be no vague sentimentalism.

The Christian ideal can only be socially fulfilled within a disciple band, a divine kingdom, the Father's family, the Christian fellowship. In Scripture love is no abstract idea, conceived to provide a self-explanatory, self-motivating "norm" to resolve the problem in every moral situation. It is rooted in the divine nature, expressed in the coming and death of Christ, experienced in salvation, and so kindled within the saved. Thus it is central, essential, and indispensable, to Christianity. For God is love.

R.E.O. WHITE

See GOD, BEING AND ATTRIBUTES OF; GRACE; MERCY; WRATH OF GOD.

Bibliography. K. Barth, *Church Dogmatics*, 1.2, 371–401; V.P. Furnish, *The Love Command in the NT*; C.S. Lewis, *The Four Loves*; J. Moffat, *Love in the NT*; L. Morris, *Testaments of Love*; A. Nygren, *Agape and Eros*; N. Snaith, *The Distinctive Ideas of the OT*; C. Spicq, *Agape in the NT*, 3 vols.

Lubim. KJV form of Libyan, an inhabitant of Libya, in 2 Chronicles 12:3; 16:8; and Nahum 3:9.

See LIBYA, LIBYANS.

Lucas. KJV alternate spelling of Luke in Philemon 24.

See LUKE (PERSON).

Lucifer. Appellation from a Latin word meaning "light-bearer." The Latin term refers to the planet Venus appearing in the evening and the morning, which is the brightest object in the sky except for the sun and moon. Others have identified it with the crescent moon. It is also said by some to be the planet Jupiter. The Hebrew term, from which the Latin *lucifer* is derived, is found in Isaiah 14:12: "How you have fallen from heaven, O morning star, son of the dawn! You have been cast down to the earth, you who once laid low the nations!" (NIV). The word means the "shining one." It has cognates in Akkadian, Ugaritic, and Arabic. The Septuagint, Targum, and the Vulgate translate it as "morning star," quite fitting in view of the appositional "son of the dawn."

The Hebrew expression was probably never meant to be a name, but has come to be used thus because the verse in which it occurs is applied to Satan. This apparently was done first by two of the church fathers, Tertullian and Origen. However, the popularity of Lucifer as a name for Satan may be attributed to its use in John Milton's *Paradise Lost*.

Some have understood the word in the Hebrew text as being a verb rather than a noun. An example of the term would then be found in Ezekiel 21:12. The word there is parallel to the word "cry," and is translated "wail." In fact the Syriac version renders Isaiah 14:12 with that understanding: "How are you fallen from heaven! Howl in the morning." This meaning is unlikely.

The event recorded in Isaiah 14:12 may be an example of a story quite commonly known in the time of Isaiah. This old Canaanite story concerned the morning star, who had attempted to rise high above the clouds and establish himself on the mountain where the gods assembled, in the uttermost part of the north. He had desired to take the place of the highest god, becoming ruler of the world. His attempts were thwarted, and he was cast into the underworld. This story of the minor star deity aspiring to ascend above the throne of the most high god served, in the purposes of Isaiah, as an excellent analogy to the pride and aspirations of the king of Babylon, the person with whom chapters 13 and 14 are concerned. Isaiah states (14:3,4) that Yahweh, the God of Israel, would give the people relief from the tyranny of their oppressors, and they would take up a taunt song against the king. Although he had sought to be great, he would be brought low; he who sought to be a god would, with his descendants, cease to exist on the earth. Though the Hebrews had no myths, illustrations from familiar gentile mythology often were used to express spiritual truth.

There are many who believe the expression (and surrounding context) refers to Satan. They believe the similarities between Isaiah 14:12, Luke 10:18, and Revelation 12:7–10 warrant this conclusion. However, although the NT passages do speak of Satan's fall, the context of the Isaiah passage describes the defeated king of Babylon. The Babylonian king had desired to be above God, and so fell from heaven. His doom is pictured as already accomplished. Though defeat is certain for Satan, he yet continues his evil acts against God's people. Not until the final judgment (Rv 12–20) will his fate be sealed and his activity stopped. Isaiah, then, is not speaking of Satan in 14:12 but of the proud, and soon to be humiliated, king of Babylon.

See SATAN.

Lucius. 1. Man from Cyrene, listed among the prophets and teachers in Antioch (Acts 13:1). He may have been among the Jewish Christians from Cyprus and Cyrene who preached to the Gentiles in Antioch in face of persecution (Acts 11:19–21). Various attempts have been made to identify him with Luke, the author of Acts, or with the Lucius of Romans 16:21, but these have been unsuccessful.

2. Jewish believer (cf. Rom 9:3) and one of the companions of Paul who sent greetings to those in Rome (Rom 16:21). This casts doubt on Origen's identification of this Lucius with the Luke of the Gospel and Acts, who was most likely a Gentile (Col 4:12–14).

Lud, Ludim. Names occurring in the table of nations in Genesis 10. Ludim is listed as the first son of Mizraim, and Lud is listed as the fourth son of Shem. On the basis of this, it is probably better to consider them as having different ethnic origins. Some, however, have suggested that both names refer to a people of Asia Minor, the Lydians, who are mentioned on Ashurbanipal's inscriptions as *Luddu*.

There is little question that Lud, at least, is to be associated with Lydia as an eponymous ancestor. Josephus makes this identification (*Antiq.* 1.6.4.). Also in Isaiah 66:19, it is listed among other nations of Asia Minor.

Lud is often mentioned in contexts that suggest the men were well known as good soldiers. According to Jeremiah 46:9, they fought with the Egyptians against the Babylonians at the battle of Carchemish in 605 BC. In the lament over Tyre in Ezekiel 27:10, they are listed among others who were mercenaries in the army of Tyre. Perhaps Ezekiel 30:5 is another case of Lydians serving as mercenaries, this time in the Egyptian army. Such military aid to Egypt goes back to the Assyrian period when Gyges sent military aid to Psammetichus of Egypt against the Assyrians.

See LYDIA (PLACE).

Luhith. Moabite city mentioned in connection with the flight of the Moabites to Zoar (Is 15:5). Since it was also listed with Horonaim, it was perhaps situated between these two cities in the southeastern area around the Dead Sea. Its precise location is unknown.

Luke (Person). Faithful companion of the apostle Paul. This is reinforced by the "we" passages in the Acts narrative (16:10–17; 20:5–21:18; 27:1–28:16). The first begins with Paul's Macedonian call and concludes with Paul and Silas' imprisonment in Philippi. The second picks up later on in Philippi and follows through to Jerusalem. The third runs from Caesarea to Rome. It would seem that Luke accompanied Paul at least during a portion of his second and third missionary journeys, as well as his eventful trip to Rome.

We do not know where Luke was born, or about his death. Paul excludes him from the list of his Jewish co-workers (Col 4:14). He seems to exemplify those Gentiles who welcomed the gospel and persisted in the faith. Demas, who is mentioned in connection with Luke, eventually deserted Paul, having "loved this present world" (2 Tm 4:10). The apostle adds "Luke alone is with me" (v 11).

Paul refers to Luke as "the beloved physician" (Col 4:14). He was apparently known and loved by those bonded together in the gentile mission. He appears to have used his gifts unselfishly, and cultivated friendships in the process. Paul anticipates no argument in describing him as "our friend."

Various writers have attempted to demonstrate that Luke and Acts were in fact written by a physician. Much was based on a favorable comparison of the Lucan texts with that of other physicians of antiquity. Other evidence cited includes the interpretation based on synoptic contrasts. For instance, Mark reports on a pathetic woman who suffered greatly and who could not be helped by physicians (Mk 5:26). Luke conversely suggests that she was a hopeless case, as if to defend the medical vocation (Lk 8:43). We can at the least conclude that the narrative in Luke and Acts is quite consistent with being written by a physician, but it is uncertain how much further the evidence can be pressed.

Luke evidently ministered to the apostle Paul's infirmities. We may surmise that his ministry combined the use of such medical skills as he had cultivated with intercessory prayer. This would be consistent with what he records of Jesus' holistic ministry (Lk 4:18,19) and what might be expected of the disciples.

Some have credited Luke with being the first Christian historian. He writes, "Since I myself have carefully investigated everything from the beginning, it seemed good also to me to write an orderly account" (Lk 1:3 NIV).

Luke blends himself into his own narrative. He points us beyond himself to Christ, and to such major figures as Peter and Paul. His literary works remain an impressive memorial to an otherwise little known, but highly cherished member of Paul's inner circle of associates.　　　MORRIS A. INCH

See LUKE, GOSPEL OF; ACTS OF THE APOSTLES, BOOK OF THE.

Luke, Gospel of. Third book of the NT; also the third of the synoptic Gospels (Matthew, Mark, Luke).

Author. Tradition attributes the authorship of the Gospel to the esteemed companion of Paul, Luke the physician (Col 4:14). The Gospel does not identify its author by name, but he is apparently well known in the company of early believers. He had obviously been gathering information for his project for some time. In both Luke and Acts the recipient is identified as Theophilus.

The internal testimony of Acts for Lucan authorship must also be weighed, since there is a close relationship between the two books. In three extensive "we" passages the author reports his presence (Acts 16:10–17; 20:5–21:18; 27:1–28:16). These appear to be excerpts from a travel diary; the last of them places the author in Rome with the apostle Paul. We can by the process of elimination virtually establish Luke as the author. Furthermore, the choice of vocabulary and perspective of Luke is compatible with that of a medical person.

Date, Origin, and Destination. The dating of Luke is debatable. Some argue for a date after AD 70, since Luke 21:20 might suggest it was written after the destruction of Jerusalem. Others suggest a date prior to the death of Paul (AD 64). The latter would readily account for Acts concluding with his ministry in Rome while in prison. A third option, that Luke was written after the decade of the 70s, seems at least likely.

The Gospel may have been written in Rome, but this is by no means certain. Asia Minor and Greece have also been suggested as possibilities. The *Monarchian Prologue to Luke* promotes the latter option, but its reliability is suspect. It was at Rome that Luke could have used the time profitably to put the finishing touches on the third Gospel.

Luke writes to Theophilus. Theophilus ("beloved of God") is probably not, as some suggest, a generic term for all believers. He is a person apparently unfamiliar with the geography of Palestine, for Luke takes care to detail it from time to time. He has a much better grasp of the Greco-Roman world as a whole, for Luke predictably assumes his reader's familiarity with it. Luke also avoids terms that might prove puzzling to a gentile reader, such as "hosanna" in connection with Jesus' triumphant entry into Jerusalem.

In all probability the third Gospel was composed in Rome while Paul awaited trial, on or before AD 64. It was dedicated to the "most excellent Theophilus" (Lk 1:3), as an appropriate custom of the time. He was a prominent Gentile who had become a believer. Luke wants to instruct him (and others) more carefully in the faith.

Background. Jesus lived out his life within an area roughly 50 miles wide and 150 miles long, from Dan in the north to Beersheba in the south. Apart from Jerusalem, the places he is reported to have visited are not important to the secular history of the region. He ignored Sepphoris (the most prominent city in Galilee at the time), Tiberias (dominant port on the Sea of Galilee), Caesarea (Roman capital of Palestine), and Samaria-Sebaste (longtime provincial center)—probably because of their non-Jewish character. He was raised in the humble village of Nazareth, and lived there until about 30 years of age. Capernaum became the center for his Galilean ministry. He passed through Samaria on occasion, and ministered in Perea. He was betrayed and crucified in Jerusalem. He was raised in triumph on the third day.

Luke writes in retrospect. His perspective had shifted during the interim—geographically from Palestine to the Roman Empire, politically from Israel to Rome, socially from Jewish society to pagan, and religiously from the temple to the horizon of Christian mission. It is as if one era were superimposed on the other, so that the significance of the life and ministry of Jesus can be seen for the early church.

Jerusalem rather than Galilee turned out to be the center of outreach for the early church. However, this too would change. While Jerusalem remained a sentimental favorite for the Christian community, other cities began to rival and then surpass it as the focus of Christian activity. Antioch of Syria provided the base for Paul's extensive missionary endeavors. Ephesus proved to be the scene of his most impressive success. Alexandria and Rome were accommodating an increasingly large Christian community. What had once seemed little more than an unpretentious Jewish sect had now become a universal faith.

Purpose and Theological Teaching. Simeon beautifully expresses the redemptive theme of Luke's Gospel when he held Jesus in his arms: "Sovereign Lord, as you have promised, you now dismiss your servant in peace. For my eyes have seen your salvation, which you have prepared in the sight of all people, a light for revelation to the Gentiles and for glory to your people Israel" (Lk 2:29–32). He points to Jesus as the long-anticipated Savior, and offers hope to Gentiles and Jews alike.

Luke weaves the work of the Holy Spirit into the life and ministry of Jesus. Jesus will be conceived by the Holy Spirit (Lk 1:35); the Spirit descends on him at his baptism (3:22); he is led into the desert by the Spirit to be tempted (4:2); he is anointed by the Spirit for his ministry (4:18). The Spirit is, as it were, in the background with regard to Jesus' subsequent labors, but the relationship is understood even when it is not repeated.

Luke accents the experience of messianic joy. The angelic host announced Jesus' birth with the words, "Glory to God in the highest, and on earth peace to men on whom his favor rests" (2:14). Then, as he was approaching Jerusalem, the multitude that accompanied him began to praise God, saying, "Blessed is the king who comes in the name of the Lord! Peace in heaven and glory in the highest!" (19:38).

All this suggests that the redemptive theme in Luke is complex in character. It points to Jesus as the Christ. It invites the favorable response of Gentile no less than Jew. It blends in the empowering of the Holy Spirit for Jesus' ministry and that of his disciples. It emphasizes the joy that accompanies the publication of the gospel. These are simply variations on the one redemptive design of Luke.

Other concerns surface incidentally. Luke's

interest in historical accuracy is one of these. His apologetic burden is another. The critical place he gives to prayer is a third. The list could be extended. Such interests enrich the whole, and invite the reader to investigate topics peripheral to the main theological thrust of the narrative.

Content. *Prologue (1:1–4).* The Gospel begins with a formal prologue. Luke seeks to record in orderly fashion what others had handed down as a legacy of faith. He does so in order to establish the historical credentials of the faith and to assure his readers of their validity.

Nativity and Childhood of Jesus (1:5–2:52). None of the Gospels is strictly speaking a biography of Jesus. But Luke takes a special interest in historical incidents, first with regard to the nativity and childhood narratives. He recounts 10 episodes in all: the annunciation of John the Baptist's birth as the forerunner of Christ; announcement of Jesus' birth to Mary; visit of Mary to Elizabeth; birth of John the Baptist; John the Baptist's time in the wilderness; birth of Jesus; visit of the shepherds; circumcision and naming of Jesus; Jesus' presentation in the temple; and visit to the temple as a youth.

John the Baptist receives considerable attention from the outset. Luke records that it was during the reign of Herod (Herod the Great, 37–4 BC) that Zechariah the priest was ministering in the temple. (Twenty-four platoons of priests served in this capacity for two separate weeks out of the year. The privilege of burning incense was determined by casting lots, and once the priest had done so, he was disqualified from repeating the act.) An angel of the Lord appeared to Zechariah as he was about to burn incense, and announced that he and his wife, Elizabeth, would have a son, whose name should be John. He was to live as a Nazirite (see Nm 6:1–4) and prepare the way for the Messiah. When Zechariah was reluctant to believe (he and Elizabeth were of advanced age), the angel struck him dumb until the time of the promised birth.

We next hear of John in connection with Mary's visit to Elizabeth. The baby leaped within Elizabeth's womb as she heard Mary's greeting (1:4). Luke immediately follows this account with the birth of John the Baptist. Zechariah named the child as he had been directed, received back his speech, and proceeded to prophesy concerning the coming Messiah and the preparatory role his son would play. The child grew and became "strong in spirit," abiding in the wilderness until his public ministry began.

Luke tells the nativity story from the perspective of Mary. The angel Gabriel visits her and announces that she would give birth to the Messiah (1:26–38). She would conceive miraculously by the Holy Spirit. Mary is portrayed as being devoutly submissive to the purposes of God.

The birth is said to have taken place when Quirinius was governor of Syria, and persons had to travel to their ancestral towns to register for a census. Mary gave birth in a Bethlehem stable. Angels announced the birth to shepherds, who left their flocks to observe the child. Mary treasured these things and continued to ponder their significance.

After Mary had observed her 40 days of ritual purification, she went with Joseph to the temple to present Jesus to the Lord (2:21–40). There Simeon and Anna, two elderly and devout persons, recognized the infant as the promised Messiah. Simeon concluded that Jesus would cause many in Israel to fall and rise, and bring deep sorrow to the heart of Mary.

The nativity and childhood narratives close with Jesus' visit to the temple at age 12 to celebrate the Feast of the Passover. Joseph and Mary leave Jesus behind in the temple, supposing that he was among relatives or friends. They retraced their steps, and found him in the temple conversing with the rabbis—listening to them and amazing them with his own understanding. Luke concludes by saying that Jesus "grew in wisdom and stature, and in favor with God and men" (2:52).

Beginning of the Public Ministry (3:1–4:30). Luke next turns to consider those events related to the inauguration of Jesus' ministry. These include the ministry of John the Baptist, the baptism of Jesus, his genealogy, his temptation, and the public announcement in Nazareth. Luke dates the beginning of John the Baptist's ministry in no fewer than six ways: with the terms of office of Tiberius Caesar, Pontius Pilate, Herod Antipas, Philip, Lysanias, and Annas and Caiaphas. John came preaching a baptism of repentance in preparation for the coming of the Messiah. Multitudes came out into the wilderness to hear him and to be baptized by him.

Jesus also came to be baptized. (Luke does not record John's protest that Jesus ought rather to baptize him, or Jesus' insistence, apparently to identify with the people and anticipate his vicarious death on their behalf.) The baptism marked Jesus' entry into public ministry. Luke inserts what may be the genealogical record through Mary, consistent with his earlier efforts to narrate the events from her perspective.

The temptation of Jesus was a probationary test of his messianic ministry. The introduction to two of the temptations, "If you are the

Nazareth, Jesus' hometown and site of a dramatic announcement in the synagogue (Lk 4:18–19).

Son of God," was calculated to make him doubt the words heard at his baptism, "You are my Son" (3:22; 4:3,9). Satan hoped to persuade Jesus to seek to fulfill his calling and yet avoid the cross. Each time Jesus parried the temptation with a quotation from Scripture.

Jesus returned to Galilee and to the synagogue in Nazareth. Here he announced his public ministry in words borrowed from the jubilee observance and associated with the messianic age (4:18,19; Is 61:1,2). They reflected both the religious focus and broad social implications of the ministry to come. The announcement especially held out hope to those who were downtrodden and ostracized by society. When those in attendance challenged his credentials, Jesus replied, "No prophet is accepted in his hometown." And when they would have cast him from the brow of a hill, he passed through their midst and went on his way.

The Galilean Ministry (4:31–9:50). Jesus moved the center of his activity to Capernaum. Luke records a variety of episodes associated with the Galilean ministry that follows. Approximately 30 instances are mentioned. About a third involve some extraordinary occurrence such as healing, exorcism, raising from the dead, or feeding a multitude. These were events associated with the messianic age.

However, it was Jesus' teaching that first seems to have caught the people's attention (Mt 7:29). He did not teach as the rabbis, by drawing upon traditional precedent, but in the authority of his messianic office. Luke weaves into his narrative a considerable amount of Jesus' teaching. There is a fairly extended section on the observance of the sabbath (6:1–11). But it is less prominent than Jesus' sermon "on a level place," with its extended comments concerning blessings and woes, love for enemies, judging others, knowing one by his fruit, and on wise and foolish

builders (6:12–49). Jesus taught by way of parables, and Luke records those of the sower and lamp (8:1–18). In the former instance, the seed represents the Word of God, and the soil the varying preparation to receive the Word. Thereby the disciples might better understand the mixed results of Jesus' ministry and their own. Others would be perplexed by the parables, as "though hearing, they may not understand."

Luke describes the calling of select disciples. He mentions Peter, James, and John, and at a later point Levi (5:1–11,27–32). The former were called from their fishing boats and the latter from his tax booth. All were summoned to follow Christ in his messianic ministry through the Galilean countryside. Later on, when there were 12 disciples, Jesus sends them out to preach the kingdom and heal the sick (9:1–11). No doubt many contributed to the extended ministry. Luke records certain women who traveled with them and were "helping to support them out of their own means" (8:3).

One senses a rising tide of enthusiasm with regard to the Galilean enterprise. It begins with Jesus alone, working in obscurity; it terminates with a faithful band of followers, multitudes hanging on his words, and his name circulated throughout the region. The section peaks with Peter's confession of Jesus as the Christ and the transfiguration of Jesus (9:10–36). The presence of Moses and Elijah represents the Law and prophets as subordinate to the Messiah.

The scene shifts abruptly to the foot of the mount, where the disciples have been ineffective in delivering a demon-possessed boy. Here Jesus points out the need for spiritual resources to accomplish kingdom needs, and thereafter (in response to the disciples' argument over who would be greatest) an appeal to humility.

The Journey Toward Jerusalem (9:51–19:27). Luke next reports Jesus' ministry on the way to Jerusalem. This has sometimes been called the Perean ministry, assuming that much of it took place across the Jordan in the district of Perea. It has also been graphically described as "the road to the cross." The number of incidents are roughly the same as those in the preceding section, although the text is perhaps 25 percent longer.

Opposition is seen building at the outset. Jesus sends messengers ahead to prepare for his arrival at a Samaritan village. But the inhabitants would not welcome him, because he was on the way to Jerusalem. There was bad blood between the Jews and Samaritans. The latter had been settled in the land during the Assyrian occupation, and brought with them foreign religious and social customs—resulting in a syncretism repugnant to the Jews. Certain disciples ask if Jesus would have them bring down fire from heaven on the village, but Jesus rebuked them. He evidenced a more conciliatory spirit.

Luke reintroduces the Samaritans in connection with a story Jesus tells (10:25–37). It seems that a man was attacked by thieves, who left him for dead. First a priest and then a Levite came along, each walking by on the opposite side of the road. Another passed that way, and took pity on the injured stranger. He bound up his wounds and brought him to an inn where he could be cared for at the expense of his benefactor. Jesus adds the detail that the man who stopped to help was a Samaritan. He alone understood that a neighbor is the one we befriend rather than the one who befriends us. (The Samaritans reappear once more in the account of 10 lepers who were healed, of whom only a Samaritan returned to give thanks—17:11–19.)

The story of the good Samaritan suggests the opposition Jesus was encountering from the religious establishment centered in Jerusalem. Even as the crowds increased, Jesus observed: "This is a wicked generation.... The Queen of the South will rise at the judgment with the men of this generation and condemn them, for she came from the ends of the earth to listen to Solomon's wisdom, and now one greater than Solomon is here" (11:29,31). So also will the men of Nineveh stand to condemn the present generation, because they repented at the preaching of Jonah, and now one greater than Jonah is here.

Jesus reserved the severest rebuke for those Pharisees who had come to contest his every move. Jesus and the Pharisees traveled in much the same circles. Some had been sympathetic to his message, but these seem to have been in the minority. Jesus pictures the Pharisees as meticulous legalists (11:37–44). A certain scribe protested that lawyers too were implicated in Jesus' condemnation. Jesus did not leave the matter in doubt: "Woe to you experts in the law, because you have taken away the key to knowledge. You yourselves have not entered, and you have hindered those who were entering" (v 52).

Events were building to a climax. Jesus had prophesied his impending death and subsequent resurrection. His face was set toward Jerusalem. When some solicitous Pharisees warned him of Herod Antipas' plan to have him killed, he refused to be intimidated. "Go tell that fox, 'I will drive out demons and heal people today and tomorrow, and on the third day I will reach my goal'... for surely no prophet can die outside Jerusalem!" (13:32,33).

Jesus labored to prepare the disciples in the short time that remained. Early in this section, he warns them of the cost of discipleship (9:57–62). To the man who refused his invitation to discipleship because he must first bury his parents, Jesus answered, "Let the dead bury their own dead, but you go and proclaim the kingdom of God" (v 60).

The disciples might anticipate that God's grace would be sufficient for this life and that to come. When the 72 returned from their ministry, rejoicing that the demons had been subject to them, Jesus admonished them rather to rejoice in that their names were written in heaven (10:1–18). He added that many prophets and kings had wanted to see what they had seen in their day, and to hear what they heard.

Jesus emphasized the importance of prayer in sustaining the course of discipleship (11:1–13). He encouraged the disciples to ask in anticipation that they would receive; to seek expecting that they would find; and to knock assuming that the door would be open to them. It is the Father's pleasure to give good gifts to his children.

The topics which Jesus chose were pertinent to the occasion. He discussed covetousness, anxiety, trust, and watchfulness (12:13–59). The disciples were to be good stewards of the gifts of God, generous to a fault, not unduly concerned for their own needs, trustful, anticipating the return of the Son of man in glory. They were pilgrims, and a pilgrim needs to travel light in order to make good progress.

Parables abound in this section of the Gospel. They include those of the good Samaritan, mustard seed, yeast, narrow door, invitation to a marriage feast, great banquet, tower builder, the king who goes to war, lost sheep, lost coin, prodigal son, unjust steward, rich man and Lazarus, Pharisee and publican, and 10 minas. These seem to fall characteristically into one of three categories, although perhaps not exclusively so. The one has to do with accepting sinners. (While Scripture reveals that we are all sinners, *sinners* in the synoptic Gospels refers to nonobservant Jews.) A classic instance is the story of the prodigal son (15:11–32).

The second category might be called kingdom parables. They suggest that while the kingdom begins in some relatively insignificant fashion, it will expand to incredible proportions. They also warn that not all that seems a part of the growth is a true extension of the kingdom. These emphases can be recognized by comparing the parables of the mustard seed, yeast, and narrow door (13:18–30).

The third category deals with stewardship. Jesus told one such parable as they neared Jerusalem (19:11–27). It involved a man of noble birth who went to a far country, leaving his servants with 10 minas each (a mina was about a three-month wage for laborers). They were to invest the minas so that the man would have a good profit when he came back. Upon returning, the nobleman called his servants to get an accounting from them. Those who were found faithful in lesser things were given greater opportunity, but one who failed lost even that which he had been given.

There are some especially touching scenes in the Gospel narrative. One shows Jesus welcoming little children (18:15–17). Another describes a rich ruler who inquired of Jesus how he might obtain eternal life (18:18–30). Still another episode concerns a tax collector called Zacchaeus (19:1–10). These help us to gain a better appreciation of Jesus' diversified ministry.

Slowly but surely Jesus had worked his way to Jerusalem. He had met increasing opposition. The cross was just over the horizon. He ministered while time allowed.

Death and Resurrection (19:28–24:53). Luke turns finally to the passion week. First is the triumphant entry of Christ (19:28–44). As those with Jesus came over the crest of the Mt of Olives, they began to praise God for all the miracles they had seen: "Blessed is the king who comes in the name of the Lord! Peace in heaven and glory in the highest!" (v 38). The jubilation of the multitude stands in sharp contrast to Jesus' weeping over an unrepentant city and lamenting the destruction to be visited upon it.

Entering the temple area, Jesus began driving out those who were selling goods there. God's house should be a house of prayer but, Jesus protests, they have made it a den of robbers. He continued to teach daily in the temple precincts, while the religious leaders plotted how to put him to death without inciting the people.

Luke records some of the interchange with the leader and people (20:1–21:38). This includes a challenge to Jesus' authority, the parable of the wicked tenants, the question about paying taxes to Caesar, another question concerning the resurrection, Jesus' question about how to understand the Messiah's Davidic ancestry and lordship, warning against the scribes, comments on the widow's offering, and discourse on the end of the age. This broad range of topics is related to the messianic disputation in progress.

The problem as Luke represents it seems less an intellectual than a moral one. The religious establishment was determined to retain its privileged position at all cost. This Galilean rabbi was a serious threat that had to be eliminated. It was only a matter of waiting for the right opportunity. It appeared when Judas Iscariot offered to betray Jesus (22:1–6).

The last supper and the prayer vigil in Gethsemane intervene between the plot of the leaders and the arrest of Jesus (22:7–46). The Passover celebrated the redemption of Israel from bondage in Egypt. Jesus chose this occasion to anticipate his redemption of sinful humanity by way of the cross. It was to be a continuing memorial meal for the disciples.

From the upper room Jesus and the disciples made their way across the Kidron Valley to the Mt of Olives. Here Jesus prayed in preparation for the crucifixion to follow. The disciples slept, being weary from the heavy demands of those days. Soon Judas appeared to point Jesus out, and the soldiers rushed him away to stand before the high priest. Peter denied Christ, fearing for his own life. Jesus was condemned by the Sanhedrin. (Commentators debate whether this was a formal session of the council of Jewish elders.) He was sent to the Roman governor, Pontius Pilate, then to Herod Antipas, and back again to Pilate. Pilate saw no reason for putting Jesus to death, but the multitude was stirred up to demand his crucifixion. Pilate yielded to their pressure when alternatives seemed to escape him.

Jesus was led away to be crucified. Luke alone mentions those who mourned him (23:27). Jesus warns them rather to mourn for themselves and their children. Here and thereafter we see Jesus' concern for others in the midst of his own agony: those crucifying him, the repentant criminal, and his mother Mary.

Luke records a mixed response to the crucifixion. The people stood watching, as if immobilized by the rush of events. They may have felt helpless to intervene even if disposed to do so. Some of the religious leaders went so far as to mock Jesus; "He saved others; let him save himself if he is the Christ of God, the Chosen One" (23:25). One hardened criminal joined in their derision; the other asked for clemency.

Darkness shrouded the scene. The curtain of the temple was rent, as if to suggest that access was being made available through the shed blood of Christ. Jesus commended his spirit to the Father. He breathed his last. His body was laid in the tomb of Joseph of Arimathea. Women went to prepare spices and perfumes for the interment, but rested on the sabbath in obedience to the commandment.

Early on the first day of the week the women approached the tomb, only to find the stone guarding its entrance rolled away and the body of Jesus missing. Suddenly two figures in gleaming array stood by them. They announced to the frightened women: "He is not here; he has risen!" (24:6). The women re-

A typical 1st-century tomb with a rolling stone such as the one the women found rolled away at Jesus' tomb (Lk 24:2).

turned to report to the apostles. Peter ran to confirm their findings. He discovered the strips of linen laid out as they had been, but with the body absent. He wondered what had happened.

The same day two disciples were going to a village called Emmaus. They were discussing what had happened in Jerusalem when Jesus joined them. They were kept from recognizing him until later on when he broke bread with them. They hurriedly returned to Jerusalem to reassure the fellowship that it was true that the Lord was risen.

While they were still talking, Jesus appeared in their midst. "Look at my hands and my feet. It is I myself! Touch me and see; a ghost does not have flesh and bones, as you see I have" (24:39). Then he helped them understand the implications of what had happened: "This is what is written: The Christ will suffer and rise from the dead on the third day, and repentance and forgiveness of sins will be preached in his name to all nations, beginning at Jerusalem. You are witnesses of these things. I am going to send you what my Father has promised; but stay in the city until you have been clothed with power from on high" (vv 46–49).

Luke concludes his Gospel with an account of the ascension (24:50–53). It was as Jesus blessed them that he was lifted up before their eyes. They worshiped him as the ascended Lord, and returned to Jerusalem with great joy. There they remained in the temple precinct, praising God and anticipating the coming of the Holy Spirit to empower them for witnessing to all the world.

MORRIS A. INCH

See LUKE (PERSON); MATTHEW, GOSPEL OF; MARK, GOSPEL OF; SYNOPTIC GOSPELS; JESUS CHRIST, LIFE AND TEACHING OF; REDACTION CRITICISM; SOURCE CRITICISM.

Bibliography. G.B. Caird, *The Gospel of St Luke*; E. Ellis, *The Gospel of Luke*; J.A. Fitzmyer, *The Gospel According to Luke*, 2 vols; N. Geldenhuys, *Commentary on the Gospel of Luke*; F. Godet, *A Commentary on St Luke's Gospel*; A. Hastings, *Prophet and Witness in Jerusalem*; I.H. Marshall, *The Gospel of Luke*; N.B. Stonehouse, *The Witness of Luke to Christ*; M. Wilcock, *Savior of the World: The Message of Luke's Gospel*.

Lute. Guitarlike musical instrument with strings stretched along a neck and over a sounding box, usually plucked or strummed.

See MUSIC AND MUSICAL INSTRUMENTS (ASOR).

Luz. 1. Original Canaanite name of the city of Bethel (Gn 28:19; 35:6). It was here that Jacob had a vision of God. In recognition of God's presence he called the place "the house of God" (beth-El). Jacob may not have been in the city itself, which might account for the seeming discrepancy in Joshua 16:2. The phrase "from Bethel to Luz" in the description of the border of the land allotted to Joseph (Ephraim and Manasseh) seems to distinguish Bethel from Luz as though they were two different cities. Perhaps the solution is to be found in that originally the name Luz continued to be used of the city, while at the same time the Israelites knew, through tradition, of the place which Jacob had named Bethel outside the city of Luz. According to Joshua 16:2, then, Bethel would be an area lying east of the city of Luz. At the time of conquest (Jgs 1:22–25), or subsequently, the Israelites changed the name of Luz to Bethel.

See BETHEL, BETHELITE (CITY) #1.

2. Hittite city named after Luz in Palestine by one of its inhabitants who migrated to the Hittite region after the Israelites captured his city (Jgs 1:26). Its site is unknown.

Lycaonia. Region in the southern interior of Asia Minor, north of the Taurus Mountains. Prior to Roman occupation it was bordered on the north by Galatia, on the south by Cilicia, on the east by Cappadocia, and on the west by Phrygia and Pisidia. Like many of its neighboring states, Lycaonia was from the time of Alexander the Great ruled by the Seleucids. When the Romans defeated the Seleucids in western Asia Minor (190 BC), Lycaonia was given to the Attalids of Pergamum. It remained under their control until 130 BC, when their king died and their kingdom was dissolved. The area was subsequently administered by the Romans, who attached the northern section of the Lycaonian territory to Galatia, the eastern section to Cappadocia, and the southern section to Cilicia. In AD 37 eastern Lycaonia gained independence from Cappadocia and was known as Lycaonia Antiochiana. By the time of Christ, Lycaonia had essentially been reduced to an ethnic area in southern Galatia and should be considered as such in all NT references.

The territory was situated on a high, barren plateau. The soil was generally of poor quality, though fertile areas existed in the south around the principal cities of Lystra and Derbe. Consequently the primary occupations were the shepherding of sheep and goats, with some agriculture in the south. Lycaonia was bisected by a major trade route between Syria, Ephesus, and Rome.

It is debatable whether Iconium was a city of Lycaonia. Some scholars believe it was the capital and principal city. Others consider it a Phrygian city. The latter position seems to be supported in Acts, where Paul flees Iconium for Lystra and Derbe, "cities of Lycaonia" (14:6)—places where the Lycaonian language was spoken (14:11). It is likely that within the political territory of Galatia there were several ethnic areas and that Paul crossed an ethnic border in an attempt to find safety from the disgruntled Jews of Iconium.

The apostle Paul made three visits to Lycaonia. During his first missionary journey, the preaching of the gospel was very effective and many disciples were made (Acts 14:21,22). In fact, when Paul healed a crippled man in Lystra, the leaders of the pagan cult wished to worship him as a god (Acts 14:11–18). He visited the area again on his second missionary journey. It was here that he met Timothy and asked him to join his company (Acts 16:1–5). A final visit, during his third journey, is indicated by Acts 18:23 (he "went from place to place through the region of Galatia and Phrygia, strengthening all the disciples").

Later Christian inscriptions indicate that by the end of the 3rd century the region of Lycaonia possessed one of the most mature ecclesiastical systems in Asia Minor.

Lycia. Country located in southwest Asia Minor, bounded on the northwest by Caria, on the north by Phrygia and Pisidia, on the northeast by Pamphylia, and on the west, south, and east by the Mediterranean Sea. The geography of the region combines rugged mountainous terrain with fertile valleys formed by the descent of several small rivers to the sea. The mountainous regions produce olives, grapes, and timber, while the valleys are responsible for the production of the area's cultivated grains. At the mouths of the rivers are located the major seaports of the country. Two of these, Patara and Myra, are of interest to students of the NT.

Patara, located in southwest Lycia in the valley of the Xanthus River, was the seat of the oracle of Apollo. Acts 21:1 mentions it as the port where Paul, at the conclusion of his third missionary journey, boarded a ship sailing for Phoenicia (some manuscripts include here an additional stop at Myra). Myra, located in southeast Lycia, is mentioned in Acts 27:5–7 as the port where Paul and Julius, a Roman centurion, boarded an Alexandrian ship bound for Rome. When winds were from the west, it was the practice of Alexandrian grain ships headed for Italy to work north along the shore of Palestine and Syra and west along the southern coast of Asia Minor. This would make the ports of Lycia natural places for ships to harbor in preparation for the final leg of the trip to Italy.

The history of the region is tied closely to that of Asia Minor. Among all the peoples of western Asia Minor, Lycia was alone able to withstand the onslaught of the kings of Lydia. However, in 546 BC it was forced to submit to Persian domination. With the invasion of Alexander the Great in 333 BC, Lycia came under the control of the Ptolemies (308–197 BC) and the Seleucids (197–189 BC). When the Romans defeated Antiochus III at Magnesia (189 BC), Lycia was given to Rhodes, an island off its western coast. Twenty years later Rome granted Lycia the status of an independent state. This status held until AD 43, when Emperor Claudius declared Lycia a Roman province. Under the provincial reorganization of Vespasian in AD 74, it was joined with Pamphylia.

First Maccabees 15:23 gives evidence of a sizable Jewish community in Lycia around 139 BC. The NT provides no evidence of Christians in this area. However, a letter from Lycia written in AD 312 to Emperor Maxim in opposition to Christianity indicates the presence of Christians in this region in the early centuries of the church.

Lydda. NT name for Lod, a town located southwest of Jerusalem in the Shephelah.

See LOD.

Lydia (Person). Gentile woman who was converted under the preaching of Paul in Philippi (Acts 16:14,40). Lydia was a dealer in purple cloth and came from the city of Thyatira in the region of Lydia in western Asia Minor. The description of her as a "worshiper of God" indicates that she was a Gentile who had been attracted to Judaism. After her conversion to Christianity and her baptism, she hosted Paul and Silas during their stay in Philippi.

Lydia (Place). Name designating a geographical area occurring only in 1 Maccabees 8:8, where it refers to a province in western Asia Minor (modern Turkey) bounded on the north by Mysia, on the east by Phrygia, on the south by Caria, and on the west by the Greek cities of Ionia. It is listed among the provinces taken by the conquering Romans from the Syrian king Antiochus the Great and given to Eumenes II, the king of Pergamum, after the battle of Magnesia in 190. The appearance of the word in the KJV in Ezekiel 30:5 is incorrect and has been properly replaced by Ludim in later translations. The text of 1 Maccabees is also problematical, listing India and Media along with Lydia as provinces belonging to Antiochus. These two countries never belonged to Syria, and the text should read Ionia for India and Mysia for Media, which then brings it into accord with the geographical facts and with the text of Livy recounting the same events (*Livy*, 37.56).

The capital of Lydia, Sardis, was considerably inland, and the province never showed any significant maritime development. Sardis has been under excavation since the turn of the century. The temple of Artemis/Cybele has been found, along with a Jewish synagogue and a gymnasium. Although Lydia essentially lost its prominence after the defeat of Croesus, king of Sardis, by Cyrus the Persian in 546 BC and became a satrapy of Persia until Alexander took it in 334 BC, the archaeological remains of Sardis testify to a continuing existence until the 7th century AD.

Herodotus referred to Lydia as a fertile land and to its abundance of silver (*Persian Wars*, 5.49), while Tacitus spoke of the rich countries around Sardis (*Annals* 4.55). According to Herodotus the Lydians "were the first nation to introduce the use of gold and silver coin, and the first who sold goods by retail" (1.94).

The identification of Lydia with Lud or Ludim in the OT is not certain. While Isaiah 66:19 seems to connect Lud with "coastlands afar off," thus offering a fitting description of Lydia from a Palestinian point of view, Jeremiah mentions Lud in connection with the North African countries of Put (Libya) and Ethiopia (46:9). Ezekiel mentions Lud in connection with Put and Persia (27:10), as well as Arabia (30:5). Josephus considered the Lydians to have been founded by Lud (*Antiq*. 1.6.4).

By NT times Lydia had become a part of the Roman province of Asia, having been given to Rome in 133 BC by the Pergamene king Attalus III. Five of the churches to which the Book of Revelation was addressed were in Lydia (Ephesus, Smyrna, Sardis, Philadelphia, and Laodicea).

Lye. Strong alkaline substance (probably potassium carbonate) used for cleaning purposes.

See MINERALS, METALS, AND PRECIOUS STONES.

Ruins at Philadelphia, one of the 5 cities in Lydia that had a church addressed in Revelation (3:7–13).

Lyre. Stringed instrument consisting of a body, crossbar, and sometimes a sounding box.

See MUSIC AND MUSICAL INSTRUMENTS (KATHROS, KINNOR).

Lysanias. Tetrarch of Abilene (the area west of Damascus) in AD 27–28. The Gospel of Luke mentions Lysanias as among those who ruled at the beginning of John the Baptist's ministry (Lk 3:1). This is the only reference to him in the NT.

Josephus mentions a Lysanias who succeeded his father Ptolemaeus as the king of Chalcis. However, he was killed by Mark Antony in 36 BC. Since there is no other known reference to a Lysanias in the writings of antiquity, and since this second Lysanias could not have lived during John the Baptist's lifetime, some biblical scholars assume Luke was inaccurate in his chronology. In defense of Luke other scholars point to a mention in Josephus of "Abila of Lysanias," an area given to Agrippa II by Claudius in AD 53; however, that reference may be to the Lysanias who ruled Chalcis 90 years earlier.

The most conclusive evidence in support of Luke is found in an inscription which records the dedication of a temple at Abila, "for the salvation of the Lords Imperial and their whole household by Nymphaeus, a freedman of Lysanias the tetrarch." The title "Lords Imperial" was bestowed jointly only on Emperor Tiberius and his mother Livia, Augustus' widow. That would fix Lysanias' date between AD 14 (when Tiberius became emperor) and AD 29 (when Livia died). On that basis Luke's chronology may be assumed accurate.

Lysias. *See* CLAUDIUS LYSIAS.

Lystra. City in the region of Lycaonia in the Roman province of Galatia. References to the town in the NT are confined to the Book of Acts. On Paul's first missionary journey, Paul and Barnabas encountered opposition at Iconium and fled to Lystra, Derbe, and the surrounding region (Acts 14:6). While at Lystra, Paul healed a crippled man (v 8). This miracle excited the local crowd to cry out that Barnabas must be Zeus, and that Paul was Hermes (later called by their Latin counterparts Jupiter and Mercury in some English versions) because of his role as chief speaker (vv 9–21).

The town of Lystra was largely inhabited by the remnants of a small Anatolian tribe who spoke their own dialect, attested today by a number of inscriptions found in the area and still spoken as late as the 6th century AD. Evidently the old Anatolian village system prevailed in this market town. Although Roman rule was established there, to judge from a number of Latin inscriptions found in the area, the local farming community still retained many of its native customs.

The Greek deities Zeus and Hermes were worshiped in the area, and archaeological evidence confirms Luke's picture in Acts. One inscription records the dedication to Zeus on a statue of Hermes. Another records a dedication to "Zeus before the town," throwing light on Acts 14:13 with its reference to the priest "of Zeus before the gate."

Geographically Derbe and Lystra both belonged to the same political region, while Iconium lay in another. Lystra was closer to Iconium than to Derbe geographically, commercially, and socially in spite of the political boundary separating them. There was evidently a good deal of communication between the two towns. In Acts 16:1,2 Lystra and Iconium are linked together as places where Timothy was well known and respected.

The site of ancient Lystra (modern Latik) is marked by a mound, Zordula Hüyük, on which the city in Paul's day was located. No excavation of the site has yet been undertaken, but pottery and other artifacts suggest that the site dates to the 3rd millennium BC.

Mm

Maacah, Maachah (Person). Common Hebrew name, often spelled Maachah in the KJV.

1. Last of the four children borne to Nahor, Abraham's brother, by Reumah his concubine (Gn 22:24).

2. Daughter of Talmai, king of Geshur, a wife of David, and Absalom's mother (2 Sm 3:3; 1 Chr 3:2).

3. Achish's father. Achish, king of Gath, housed two of Shimei's slaves during Solomon's reign (1 Kgs 2:39). He is identified with Maoch in 1 Samuel 27:2.

See MAOCH.

4. Daughter of Absalom (Abishalom) (2 Kgs 15:2,10), the wife of Rehoboam, king of Judah (930–913 BC), and the mother of kings Abijah (913–910) and Asa (910–869) of Judah (1 Kgs 15:10; 2 Chr 11:20–22). Later, Asa removed her as queen mother because she had an idol made for Asherah (1 Kgs 15:10–13; 2 Chr 15:16). Maacah is spelled Micaiah (KJV Michaiah) in 2 Chronicles 13:2.

5. Caleb's concubine and the mother of four sons (1 Chr 2:48).

6. Sister of Huppim and Shuppim, the wife of Machir the Manassite and mother of Peresh and Sheresh (1 Chr 7:15,16).

7. Benjamite, the wife of Jeiel, and an ancestress of King Saul (1 Chr 8:29; 9:35).

8. Father of Haman, one of David's mighty warriors (1 Chr 11:43).

9. Father of Shephatiah, chief officer of Simeon's tribe during David's reign (1 Chr 27:16).

Maacah, Maachah (Place). Small kingdom in northern Transjordan. According to Joshua 13:11, the states of Geshur and Maacah were between Gilead and Mt Hermon and they bordered the kingdom of Og, ruler of Bashan (Jos 12:4,5). Its people were reckoned as descendants of Nahor (Gn 22:24) and were the southernmost of the Nahorite tribes. There is a possibility that they appear in the Egyptian Execration texts from the early 2nd millennium BC, but this is not certain.

In the account of the wars of David against the Aramaean alliance of Hanun in northern Transjordan, the hired troops are called the Syrians of Beth-rehob, the Syrians of Zobah, and "the king of Maacah with a thousand men" (2 Sm 10:6). However, the parallel account supplies the reading Aram-maacah and Zobah (1 Chr 19:6, KJV Syria-maachah), though the Samuel text may be more ancient.

See ARAM.

Maachathite, Ma-acathite, Maachathi. People of Maacah who held the territory neighboring the Geshurites and the boundary of land granted to the half tribe of Manasseh (Dt 3:14, KJV Maachathi; Jos 12:5; 13:11). It was taken over by Jair who with his companions were unable to dislodge the Maachathites and Geshurites living among them (Jos 13:13).

From the Maachathites came Eliphelet who joined David's army of "mighty men" (2 Sm 23:34). The parallel passage in 1 Chronicles 11:36 calls him a Mecherathite.

Their unfriendliness persisted throughout Israel's history. When Jerusalem fell to Nebuchadnezzar, Jaazaniah, the son of a Maachathite, sought to join Ishmael, the Ammonite, against Gedaliah whom Nebuchadnezzar had left to govern the city (2 Kgs 25:23; Jer 40:8).

See MAACAH, MAACHAH (PLACE).

Ma-adai. Bani's son, who obeyed Ezra's exhortation to divorce his pagan wife after the exile (Ezr 10:34).

Maadiah. Head of a priestly family who returned to Jerusalem after the exile (Neh 12:5) and whose house was headed by Piltai in the next generation during the days of Joiakim the high priest (v 17 Moadiah). He is perhaps identifiable with the priest Ma-aziah, who set his seal on Ezra's covenant (10:8).

Maai. Priestly musician who participated in the dedication of the rebuilt Jerusalem wall (Neh 12:36).

Maaleh-acrabbim. KJV rendering of "ascent of Akrabbim," a site on Canaan's southern border, in Joshua 15:3.

See AKRABBIM.

Ma'aneh. Unit of measure equivalent to the length of a furrow (20–30 yds).

See WEIGHTS AND MEASURES.

Maarath. One of Judah's cities of inheritance located in the hill country (Jos 15:59); perhaps modern Biet Ummar, seven miles north of Hebron. It may be the same as Maroth, mentioned in Micah 1:12.

Maasai. Priest who returned to Jerusalem with Zerubbabel after the exile (1 Chr 9:12, KJV Maasiai).

Maaseiah. 1. One of the singers appointed by the Levites to accompany David when he brought the ark from Obed-edom's house to Jerusalem (1 Chr 15:18,20).

2. Commander who agreed, along with others, to assist Jehoiada the priest in crowning Joash king (2 Chr 23:1).

3. Officer who served King Uzziah by assisting in the organization of the king's army (2 Chr 26:11).

4. Son of Judah's royal house who was slain when Pekah the king of Israel invaded Judah (2 Chr 28:7).

5. Ruler in Jerusalem whom Josiah appointed to assist in repairing the temple (2 Chr 34:8).

6. 7. 8. Three priests who obeyed Ezra's exhortation to divorce their foreign wives during the postexilic era (Ezr 10:18,21,22).

9. Pahath-moab's son (Ezr 10:30).

10. Father of Azariah, a repairman of the Jerusalem wall (Neh 3:23).

11. Ezra's attendant when he read the Law to the people (Neh 8:4).

12. Levite who, with others, helped the people to understand the Law Ezra read (Neh 8:7).

13. Chief who set his seal on Ezra's covenant under Nehemiah's leadership (Neh 10:25).

14. Judahite chief and the son of Baruch, who lived in Jerusalem with those chosen by lot to inherit the rebuilt city (Neh 11:5). He is

sometimes identified with the Asaiah mentioned in 1 Chronicles 9:5.

15. Masseiah's son from Benjamin's tribe who was chosen to live in Jerusalem (Neh 11:7).

16. Priestly trumpeter at the dedication of the Jerusalem wall (Neh 12:41).

17. Priestly singer at the dedication of the Jerusalem wall (Neh 12:42).

18. Father of Zephaniah the priest. Zephaniah, with Pashhur, was sent to Jeremiah by King Zedekiah to inquire of the Lord concerning the future of Nebuchadnezzar's war against Jerusalem (Jer 21:1,2; 29:25) and to request that Jeremiah pray for Jerusalem (37:3).

19. Father of Zedekiah the false prophet, an opponent of Jeremiah's prophecy about Jerusalem's fall under Nebuchadnezzar's siege (Jer 29:21).

20. KJV form of Mahseiah, Baruch's forefather, in Jeremiah 32:12 and 51:59.

See MAHSEIAH.

21. Keeper of the threshold during Jehoiakim's reign (Jer 35:4).

Maasiai. KJV spelling of Maasai, a postexilic priest, in 1 Chronicles 9:12.

See MAASAI.

Maath. Ancestor of Jesus in Luke's genealogy (3:26).

See GENEALOGY OF JESUS CHRIST.

Maaz. Ram's son from Judah's tribe (1 Chr 2:27).

Ma-aziah. 1. Levite who served in the temple during David's reign (1 Chr 24:18).

2. Levite who set his seal on Ezra's covenant (Neh 10:8); sometimes identified with Maadiah, a postexilic priest (Neh 12:5).

See MAADIAH.

Maccabees, The. Name commonly given to the family who initiated the Jewish revolt in 167 BC, derived from the name of the most renowned brother, Judas Maccabeus.

See JUDAISM.

Mace. Heavy, spiked club used as a weapon.

See ARMS AND WARFARE.

Macedonia. Roman province in NT times, beginning as a kingdom in the 7th century BC. Little is known about the first several centuries of its history, but with the coming to power of the Greek king Philip II (359–336 BC), and especially his son Alexander III (the Great, 336–323 BC), Macedonia became a world power. After Alexander's death, the empire was divided among his successors into several regions, one of them the original Macedonian kingdom. Instability held sway for the next 150 years, and in 167 BC Macedonia came under Roman rule. Initially divided into four districts by the Romans (Acts 16:12 is a possible reference to this division), this territory was made into a Roman province in 14 BC with Thessalonica as its capital. Briefly, from AD 15–44, Macedonia was combined with Achaia and Moesia (other parts of Greece) into one large province; however, in AD 44, the three were again separated. Macedonia's importance continued through the Roman era, and it remained a separate entity down to modern times, though at present no Macedonian state exists.

The Roman province of Macedonia included the northern region of Greece and southern sections of present-day Yugoslavia and Bulgaria. Noted for its gold, silver, timber, and farm lands, the region also served as a land route for trade between Asia and the West. Shortly after the Romans incorporated Macedonia as a province they built the Via Egnatia, a paved road over 500 miles long, running from the Adriatic coast to the Aegean, no doubt traveled by the apostle Paul as he moved through the Macedonian cities of Neapolis, Philippi, Amphipolis, Apollonia, and Thessalonica (Acts 16:11,12; 17:1).

The gospel was introduced to Europe by way of Macedonia when Paul responded to a vision while on his second missionary journey (Acts 16:9–12). Details of that work, centering in Philippi and Thessalonica, are described in Acts 16:11–17:15. On his third journey, though delayed initially (19:21,22), Paul later returned to Macedonia, and again after a stay in Corinth (20:1–3; see 1 Cor 16:5; 2 Cor 1:16 and 2:13 for other references to Macedonian visits).

Macedonian believers played an important part in the collection Paul gathered for the poor in Jerusalem (Rom 15:26; 2 Cor 9:2,4); Paul commended them for their liberality (2 Cor 8:1,2). He also praised them for their example of faith, even in times of adversity (7:5; 1 Thes 1:7), and for their love of others (1 Thes 4:10). Some of the Macedonians worked directly with Paul in carrying out the gospel commission (Acts 19:29; 20:4; 27:2), and he addressed letters to churches in two Macedonian cities, Philippi and Thessalonica.

See GREECE, GREEKS.

Machaerus. Fortified castle where John the Baptist was imprisoned and later beheaded by Herod Antipas (according to Josephus, *Antiq.* 18.5.2). The name does not occur in canonical Scripture nor in the Apocrypha, but it was one of the strongest fortresses in all Palestine, having been built by Alexander Jannaeus (Josephus, *Wars* 7.6.1–4). It was destroyed by Gabinius in the wars of Pompey (*Wars* 1.8.5) but restored and greatly enlarged by Herod the Great, who built a magnificent palace within the enclosure. It was situated east of the Dead Sea at the southern extremity of Perea on a promontory overlooking the Dead Sea. It is identified with the modern M'Khaur.

Matthew (14:3–12) and Mark (6:17–29) report that Herod, upon hearing of the fame of Jesus, attributed his miracle-working power to John the Baptist whom he believed had been restored to life. The confinement of John the Baptist was apparently not so rigorous as to exclude the visit of friends (Mt 11:2,3; Lk 7:18–20). It was from this castle that the Arab wife of Herod, who had been repudiated by him for the sake of Herodias, fled to her father, Aretas, the king of Arabia. This precipitated the war between Herod and Aretas (*Antiq.* 18.5.1) and resulted in the defeat of Herod.

Machbannai, Machbanai. Warrior from Gad's tribe who joined David at Ziklag in his struggle against King Saul (1 Chr 12:13, KJV Machbanai).

Machbenah. Evidently a place-name among the geographical names in the genealogy of Caleb and Judah (1 Chr 2:49). It is followed by Gibea, which is probably the same town mentioned in Joshua 15:57; thus, Machbenah was probably located in the eastern district of the hill country south of Hebron, an area where Calebites were to be expected. The proposal to correct the reading to Cabbon (Jos 15:40) is unsatisfactory since the latter was in the Shephelah.

Machi. Father of Geuel from Gad's tribe. Geuel was one of the 12 spies sent to search out the land of Canaan (Nm 13:15).

Machir. 1. Joseph's grandson and the firstborn son of Manasseh through his Aramaean concubine (Gn 50:23; 1 Chr 7:14). Machir was the father of Gilead and the founder of the Machirite family (Nm 26:29). His descendants dispossessed the Amorites living in the land of Gilead east of the Jordan during the days of Moses (Nm 32:39); later they were assigned this land along with Bashan for an inheritance (Dt 3:15; Jos 17:1,3). In Judges 5:14, the whole tribe of Manasseh is called by this name.

2. Ammiel's son living at Lo-debar, a town east of the Jordan. Machir provided shelter for Mephibosheth (2 Sm 9:4,5) and later, with Shobi and Barzillai, took care of David's do-

mestic needs during his flight from Absalom (2 Sm 17:27).

Machirite. Descendant of Machir, Joseph's grandson from Manasseh's tribe (Nm 26:29).

See MACHIR #1.

Machnadebai. Bani's son, who obeyed Ezra's exhortation to divorce his foreign wife during the postexilic era (Ez 10:40).

Machpelah. Small field of trees and a cave with two chambers near Mamre in the district of Hebron, which was purchased by Abraham as a burial place for Sarah. The seller was Ephron, a Hittite, and the price was 400 shekels of silver (Gn 23:8–19). Later Abraham (25:9), Isaac and Rebekah (49:30,31), and Jacob (50:13) were buried here. The site of the burial place is now covered by a mosque, successor to a building undoubtedly erected by Herod the Great. It seems to be of the same style as the lower courses of the Wailing Wall in Jerusalem. The famous Bordeaux Pilgrim, a 4th-century traveler, describes the beauty of the stone structure enclosing the sepulchers. Many of its dressed stones measure almost 27 feet in length. The sepulchers of Abraham, Isaac, Sarah, and Rebekah are covered with carefully decorated grave clothes. The tombs may be in the original cave underneath the sepulchers. The details of Abraham's purchase of Machpelah, if compared with Hittite laws, support the trustworthiness of the story in Genesis 23. Attention is drawn to the number of the trees, the weighing of silver at the current buyer and seller valuation, and the witnesses at the city gate where the transaction was officially made known. All these details are in accordance with Hittite laws, which would have been forgotten after the time of the patriarchs. Coin was not a circulating medium before 700 BC. The implication that the shekel was a weight and not a coin in the time of Abraham also indicates an early date for the story of the purchase.

During the time of the Crusaders many Christian and Jewish pilgrims were allowed to visit the holy cave. Rabbi Benjamin of Tudela wrote the following words in AD 1163: "If a Jew comes, who gives an additional fee to the keeper of the cave, an iron door is opened, which dates from the times of our forefathers who rest in peace, and with a burning candle in his hand the visitor descends into a first cave which is empty, traverses a second in the same state and at last reaches a third which contains six sepulchers—those of Abraham, Isaac and Jacob, of Sarah, Rebekah and Leah, one opposite the other. A lamp burns in the cave and upon the sepulcher continually, both night and day." Since the time of the Crusaders all entrances to the cave have remained closed. On the outside of the great wall of the holy enclosure "haram," near to the steps of the southern entrance gateway, is a hole in the lowest part of the masonry which probably communicates with the holy cave. Through this hole the Jews of Hebron were accustomed to throw written pieces of paper to the ancient forefathers.

Herodian wall around the Cave of Macpelah in Hebron.

Madai. Third of Japheth's eight sons (Gn 10:2; 1 Chr 1:5).

Madian. KJV spelling of Midian, a geographical region in northwest Arabia, in Acts 7:29.

See MIDIAN, MIDIANITE.

Madmannah (Person). Shaaph's son and a grandson of Caleb (1 Chr 2:49).

Madmannah (Place). Alternate name for Beth-marcaboth, a city in southern Judah, in Joshua 15:31.

See BETH-MARCABOTH.

Madmen. Town in Moab according to Jeremiah's oracle (Jer 48:2). It may be a form created by dittography from an original Dimon, as in the oracle against Moab by Isaiah (Is 15:9). If so, Khirbet Dimneh, seven and one half miles northwest of Kerak at the head of Wadi Beni Hammad, would be a possible site. In any case, there is a word play in the Jeremiah passage between the place-name and the Hebrew word "be silent."

Madmenah. Benjamite town positioned north of Jerusalem along the route taken by the Assyrian army during Sennacherib's military incursion into Judah (c. 701 BC) against King Hezekiah (715–686 BC) and the holy city (Is 10:31). Some suggest that its site is that of modern Shu'fat.

Madon. One of the many Canaanite cities allied against Joshua in a vain attempt to stop the progress of the Israelites into Palestine. A disastrous battle fought at Meron brought these cities under Israelite control (Jos 11:1; 12:19). Madon is probably the modern Qarn Hattin, about five miles from the Sea of Galilee.

Magadan. Locality visited by Jesus after he crossed the Sea of Galilee (Mt 15:39). The correct form was most likely Magdala. The parallel passage in Mark has Dalmanutha (8:10), which is also probably a textual corruption from the plural *Magdaloth*. The only NT reference to this town is in the name of one of the Marys, namely, *Magdalene*. Magadan was known by several names; many Greek sources have Taricheae, "factories for salting fish" (Strabo 16.2.45; Pliny 5.71). Rabbinic sources have Migdal Nunnayah or Migdal Sab'aiyah, "Tower of the Fishes/Dyers." It was el-Mejdel about three miles N,NW of Tiberias, on the southern end of the great plain of Gennesereth, famous for its fertility and year-round tropical climate.

See DALMANUTHA.

Magbish. Town reoccupied after the exile by 156 descendants of its former residents (Ezr 2:30); perhaps to be identified with Khirbet el-Mahbiyeh, near Adullam.

Magdala. KJV place-name used in Matthew 15:39. Recent versions and translations have the name "Magadan." Sources dating from NT times locate the town of Magdala a short distance north of the city of Tiberias on the western shore of the Sea of Galilee.

See DALMANUTHA; MAGADAN.

Magdala, on the shores of the Sea of Galilee.

Magdalene, Mary. Name of one of several Marys who followed Jesus. This Mary was the first to see the risen Christ (Jn 20:11–18).

See MARY #2.

Magdiel. One of the chiefs of Edom (Gn 36:43; 1 Chr 1:54).

Maggot. Fly larvae (Jb 25:6; Is 14:11).
· *See* ANIMALS (FLY).

Magi. Term designating the wise men from the East who came to pay homage to Jesus (Mt 2:1–16).

See WISE MEN.

Magic. Attempt to influence or control people or events through supernatural forces. These forces are called upon by means of ceremonies, the recitation of spells, charms, incantations, and other forms of ritual. Magic was at one time considered to be a practice of unsophisticated primitive cultures only. It was viewed as the attempt of prescientific peoples to control events, the natural causes of which were little understood. Thus it is surprising to see a resurgence of magic in the present age, which is the most technically sophisticated in history.

Some forms of magic are actually nothing more than sleight-of-hand "tricks" used primarily for entertainment. However, there are concepts of magic that seriously attempt to influence and control people and events by using supernatural powers. This serious magic is divided into two distinct categories, according to the goal sought. "Black magic" aims at causing harm and destruction to people or property. "White magic" is intended to benefit someone. Often white magic is used to undo the results of black magic.

Today magic is usually explained in either anthropological or psychological terms. The anthropological view basically holds that magic is used to explain events which are beyond human comprehension. The psychological theories suggest that psychological forces, such as desire and wishing, can lead to wish-fulfillment, and it was the function of the magician to provide a symbolically suggestive setting for the event. It is generally held that magic is related to the cultural development of a people, but it should be noted that many of the historic and contemporary explanations of magic are grounded in an antisupernatural worldview.

The Bible does speak of magic. Some hold that the Bible condemns black magic but condones white magic, as do many other religions. There are a number of terms used in the Bible that might fall into the broad category of magic.

Several of these words are mentioned in Deuteronomy 18:9–14. The use of magical and occult practices by Israel is not permitted. The people of God are instructed to avoid magical practices because God provides them with his personal revelation through his prophets. Human magical practices lead to either false hope or false fear and therefore lead away from the truth of God. Yet while magical practices cannot measure up to the accuracy of God's prophet, the Bible does leave open the possibility that there may be supernatural reality behind some magical practices.

The charms and enchanters of Judah are condemned in clear language in Isaiah 3:1–3, 18–23. In verses 1–3 Judah's confused leadership is in danger of judgment. The people had lost sight of an important distinction between those who claimed the right to give counsel. They grouped together "the judge and the prophet, the diviner and the elder, the captain of fifty and the man of rank, the counselor and the skilful magician and the expert in charms" (vv 2,3). Isaiah 3:20 comments on the wearing of charms by women, and verse 18 mentions discs and crescents.

Magicians are prominent in the OT Book of Exodus, where the magicians of Eygpt contend with Moses. The text does not discount the success of the magicians as mere trickery for they were at least partially successful at first (chs 7,8). But their failures begin to come clear in chapter 8 and continue through chapter 9. The Bible does not flatly deny that there may be certain evil supernatural power at work in the person of the magician. What the Bible does make clear is that this power is not in accord with nor can it defeat the will of God.

The NT addresses the issue of magic in the Book of Acts. When Philip went to Samaria he encountered Simon the Magician. Simon had drawn a great deal of attention to himself: "They gave heed to him, because for such a long time he had amazed them with his magic" (Acts 8:11). Philip's message was believed and people began to be drawn to him.

Simon saw the wonders which Philip was able to perform and thought that these powers were received through the ritual of the laying on of hands. Philip made clear that the wonders of his work could not be purchased, but came through the gracious gift of God to the penitent.

Another important passage is found in Acts 19:11–20. "God did extraordinary miracles by the hands of Paul" (v 11); the source of power responsible for these miracles lay not in trickery or ritualistic use of the name of Jesus. Certain Jewish exorcists thought that they could magically use the name of Jesus in their work (v 13). The result was violent reaction: "The man in whom the evil spirit was leaped on them, mastered all of them, and overpowered them, so that they fled out of that house naked and wounded" (v 16). This passage shows that the power responsible for the apostolic miracles was based upon the personal relationship of the apostle with the Lord Jesus Christ. The result of the above incident is also important; it led the people of Ephesus to make a clear decision between the Word of the Lord and their magical practices: "A number of those who practiced magic arts brought their books together and burned them in the sight of all" (v 19). This dramatic display of the power of God and the need for clear loyalty to him led to further expansion of the gospel. This is an important issue. The display of God's power did not bring attention to Paul but rather drew attention to God's revelation: "So the word of the Lord grew and prevailed mightily" (v 20).

The biblical stand against magic is stated strongly in the last book of the Bible: "But as for the cowardly, the faithless, the polluted, as for murderers, fornicators, sorcerers, idolaters, and all liars, their lot shall be in the lake that burns with fire and sulphur, which is the second death" (Rv 21:8). The biblical view is consistent in its opposition to magic. The Bible does not preclude the possibility that Satan can use magic for evil purposes, and magical practices are condemned because they may lead to false hope or false fear and away from loyalty to God's Word. The Christian hope is based upon the resurrected Lord and the certainty of God's revelation in Scripture. As Christians recognize that the power of their personal relationship to God is sufficient to protect them, they need not fear the power of magic. When John speaks concerning the reality of spirits, not all of which are from God, he says: "Little children, you are of God, and have overcome them; for he who is in you is greater than he who is in the world" (1 Jn 4:4).

PAUL K. McALISTER

See CANAANITE DEITIES AND RELIGION; SORCERY; SOOTHSAYER; OMEN; AMULET; FRONTLET; WISE MEN.

Clay model of a liver, inscribed with cuneiform writing and used by Babylonian diviners about 1600 BC. Some peoples believed that the liver—a bloody organ—was the source of life itself and thus was a reliable means to determine the will of the gods.

Magistrate. Title of a public official who acted as judge and administrator of a given municipality. King Artaxerxes ordered Ezra to select magistrates along with judges to govern the people when they returned to Palestine (Ezr 7:25). This official was one of the officers of Nebuchadnezzar's court invited to the dedication feast (Dn 3:2,3). Luke 12:58 portrayed the magistrate as a ruling authority whose verdict was final.

During the Roman era, each Roman colony was assigned two magistrates (called *duumviri*) who were primarily responsible for judging criminal offenses against the state. Hence, Paul and Silas were brought before the magistrates at Philippi for allegedly advocating customs unacceptable to the Romans (Acts 16:20–38). Before this *duumvir*, they were ordered to be stripped, beaten, and thrown into prison. A chief magistrate was sometimes called a "praetor" (Gk. *stratēgos*), a deferential title given to a leading *duumvir*.

Magnificat. The song of Mary found in Luke 1:46–55. This poem is in the style of the OT psalms, and is strongly reminiscent of the prayer of Hannah in 1 Samuel 2:1–10. At an early date it found a place in Christian worship. It was chanted in the vesper service of the Roman Catholic Church, and was carried over into Lutheran and Anglican usage. From the time of the Renaissance, countless musical settings have been written for this beautiful canticle, both in Latin and in various Western languages.

Magog. Term employed only five times in the Bible, but significant because of its use in the well-known prophetic passages of Ezekiel 38,39 and Revelation 20. In the register of nations in Genesis 10:2 (1 Chr 1:5), Magog was listed among the sons of Japheth, identifying both an individual and the nation that came forth from him. In Ezekiel and Revelation, Magog came to refer either to a land, a people, or both.

Magog is not mentioned in the contemporary literature of biblical times. Therefore, a definition must come primarily from the witness of Scripture, though writers from later times have given additional clues for the identification of the word. Magog was first identified biblically as a son of Japheth (Gn 10:2; 1 Chr 1:5) along with Tubal and Meshech (cf. Ez 38:2). Ezekiel 38:2 associated Magog with the person Gog, indicating that Magog was the land (along with Tubal and Meshech) over which Gog ruled. Ezekiel 39:6 uses the term Magog to speak of the people from the land of Magog. Together, Ezekiel 38 and 39 present an invasion of Israel in the latter days (cf. Ez 38:8,12,16) by Gog and his people from the land of Magog, along with peoples from every corner of the known world (cf. Ez 38:5,6).

Some believe that "Gog" is only a variant of "Magog." Others identify Magog with Lydia, because they equate Gog with Gyges (Gugu), king of Lydia. However, support for such identification is not strong.

Revelation 20:8 depicts Gog and Magog as invading the land of Israel with a great company of nations from every part of the world. It certainly appears that Ezekiel and Revelation had the same event of the latter days in mind. Revelation 20:8 can be understood to identify Gog as Satan and Magog as invading peoples who come with Satan. Some see "Gog and Magog" in Revelation 20:8 as a symbol of a future great battle at the end of the millennium which is similar to the invasion in Ezekiel 38,39, but the terms themselves are not identified specifically. Some see Magog in Revelation 20 as another person along with Gog.

Extrabiblical writings give additional clues. Josephus (*Antiq.* 1.vi.1) equated Magog with the Scythians of the north who lived in the area of present-day Turkey and south-central Russia. Jubilees 7:19; 9:8 refers to Magog as the "northern barbarians." In the OT, Magog is associated with Tubal and Meshech, geographical areas normally believed to lie in the mountainous region between, and south of, the Caspian and Black seas.

The available data argue for the identification of Magog in Ezekiel and Revelation with the northern barbarian hordes (perhaps the area of the Scythians) from the modern geographical region of Turkey and south-central Russia who will invade Israel under the leadership of Gog in the latter days. However, there is no warrant in the Scripture or elsewhere to conjecture that these modern nations are *the* identification of these terms.

Magor-missabib. Name given by Jeremiah to Pashhur, the chief officer in the house of the Lord. Jeremiah did this because Pashhur put him in stocks for prophesying judgment upon Judah (Jer 19:14–20:2). The name Pashhur means "prosperity round about" and was changed to "terror on every side" (Jer 20:3), because Pashhur was to see the horrors of the Babylonian invasion (v 4).

Magpiash. Political leader who signed Ezra's covenant with Nehemiah during the postexilic period (Neh 10:20).

Magus, Simon. Magician mentioned in Acts 8:9.

See SIMON #8.

Mahalab. Reconstructed name of a town in Asher's tribe (Jos 19:29); the Hebrew text has a transposition of the last two consonants, but the town is probably the same as Ahlab and Helbah of Judges 1:31. The correct name is preserved in the Assyrian annals of Sennacherib as Mahalliba; another text has Mahalab. The town is sometimes identified with Khirbet el-Mahalib, northeast of Tyre.

See AHLAB.

Mahalah. KJV rendering of Mahlah, Hammolecheth's son, in 1 Chronicles 7:18.

See MAHLAH #2.

Mahalalel, Mahalaleel. 1. Kenan's son and the father of Jared in Seth's line (Gn 5:12–17; 1 Chr 1:2; KJV Mahalaleel), also mentioned in Luke's genealogy (3:37; RSV Mahalaleel; KJV Maleleel).

See GENEALOGY OF JESUS CHRIST.

2. Perez's son and a postexilic Judahite (Neh 11:4, KJV Mahalaleel).

Mahalath. Musical cue, meaning "sadness," listed in the title of Psalm 53, designating the way in which and/or the melody to which the psalm should be sung.

See MUSIC AND MUSICAL INSTRUMENTS.

Mahalath (Person). 1. Daughter of Ishmael, Nebaioth's sister, Esau's third wife, and Reuel's mother (Gn 28:9); alternately called Basemath (KJV Bashemath) in Genesis 36:3–17.

2. Jerimoth's daughter and King Rehoboam's first wife (2 Chr 11:18).

Mahalath leannoth. Hebrew phrase in the title of Psalm 88, translated "The Suffering of Affliction" (NIV mg); perhaps a familiar ancient melody to which the psalm was performed.

See MUSIC AND MUSICAL INSTRUMENTS.

Mahali. KJV form of Mahli, Merari's son, in Exodus 6:19.

See MAHLI #1.

Mahanaim. Settlement east of the Jordan in Gilead. Jacob met angels there and named the place "God's camp." He divided his household and possessions into two camps (Mahanaim means "two camps" in Hebrew) to keep from losing everything when he confronted Esau (Gn 32:1–8,11).

The city was located along the border between Manasseh and Gad's tribes (Jos 13:26, 30), and was given to the Levites for an inheritance (Jos 21:38; 1 Chr 6:80). After Saul's defeat at Mt Gilboa, Ish-bosheth, his son, fled to Mahanaim to set up a capital in exile. He managed to control much of Israel from there (2 Sm 2:8,12,29) until he was assassinated by Rechab and Baanah (4:5–7). David fled to this city when Absalom rebelled against him. Here he received supplies from Barzillai and some Gileadites (17:24,27). At this city gate he wept as he received the news of Absalom's death. Solomon chose the city for the capital of his seventh district and established Ahinadad as its governor (1 Kgs 4:14).

Biblical references point to a location somewhere along the Jabbok River in central Gilead. Outside of this, the city could have been located virtually anywhere. It was earlier identified with Khirbat al-Makhna, 2½ miles north of Aijalon. Most recent attention, however, has moved to the twin hills of Tulul al-Dhahab on the Jabbok. Aharoni suggests that the western mound of Tulul al-Dhahab is Mahanaim and the eastern mound is Penuel. The site is still unknown.

Mahaneh-dan. Place west of Kiriath-jearim between Zorab and Eshtaol, where the spirit of the Lord began to stir in Samson (Jgs 13:25) and where Dan's tribe encamped on the way to the hill country of Ephraim (18:12).

Maharai. One of David's mighty men and a Zerahite from Netophah in the hill country of Judah. He was appointed commander of a division (24,000 soldiers) during the 10th month of the year (2 Sm 23:28; 1 Chr 11:30; 27:13).

Mahath. 1. Levite, son of Amasai, and ancestor of Heman the temple singer in David's time (1 Chr 6:35).

2. Levite who assisted in the cleansing of the temple during Hezekiah's time (2 Chr 29:12). He was appointed an overseer of "the contributions, the tithes and the dedicated things" (31:13).

Mahavite. Term used in 1 Chronicles 11:46 to designate Eliel, one of David's mighty men. The word was probably added to indicate where he came from to distinguish him from the Eliel in verse 47. The meaning of the term is in doubt.

Mahazioth. One of the 14 sons of Heman the Kohathite, and head of the 23rd course of tabernacle musicians who ministered with cymbals, harps, and lyres (1 Chr 25:4,30).

Maher-shalal-hashbaz. Name of Isaiah's son, meaning "quick to the plunder, swift to the spoil" (NIV mg), which prophetically described the imminent destruction to befall Damascus and Samaria by the hand of the Assyrians (Is 8:1,3).

Mahlah. 1. Manassite and one of Zelophedah's five daughters. She, with her sisters, appealed to Moses to work out an arrangement that would allow them to retain their inheritance in spite of having no brothers (Nm 26:33; 27:1; 36:11; Jos 17:3).

2. Hammolecheth's son from Manasseh's tribe (1 Chr 7:18, KJV Mahalah).

Mahli. 1. Merari's son and Levi's grandson (Ex 6:19, KJV Mahali; Nm 3:20; 1 Chr 6:19,29; 23:21; 24:26,28; Ezr 8:18), and the founder of the Mahlite family (Nm 3:33; 26:58). The Mahlites, along with the other families of Merari, were appointed to carry the frames of the tabernacle and the pillars of the court (Nm 4:29–33).

2. Mushi's son and the nephew of #1 above (1 Chr 6:47; 23:23; 24:30).

Mahlite. Descendant of Mahli, Merari's son from Levi's tribe (Nm 3:33; 26:58).

See MAHLI #1.

Mahlon. Son of Elimelech and Naomi, and Chilion's brother. While with his family in Moab, he married Ruth, the Moabitess. He died in Moab, however, and Ruth later married Boaz (Ru 1:2,5; 4:9,10).

Mahol. Father of three famous wise men (Heman, Calcol, and Darda) during the Solomonic era (970–930 BC; 1 Kgs 4:31).

Mahseiah. Forefather of Baruch (Jer 32:12) and Seraiah (51:59), spelled Maaseiah in the KJV.

Maid, Maiden. Young unmarried woman, often of the servant class. In the OT, five Hebrew words with varying shades of meaning are translated by the English word "maiden."

One of these words is *amah*. Various English translations of this word include "bondmaid," "bondwoman," "handmaid(en)," "maid(en)," "maid servant," "female servant," "female slave," "slave-girl," and "girl."

Another term is *shiphchah*. This Hebrew word is of similar meaning to *amah*. It is translated variously as "handmaid," "maid(en)," "female slave," and "slave girl." Although both *shiphchah* and *amah* refer to female slaves, *shiphchah* seems to infer that a closer relationship existed between the slave and the family to whom she belonged. In the patriarchal story this term is often employed in reference both to female slaves in general and specifically to the concubines who were also slaves to the free wife of their husbands (Gn 16,29,30).

Still another Hebrew term for "maiden" is *bethulah*. This term refers specifically to a virgin, or a young woman of marriageable age (Gn 24:16; Ex 22:16). The OT prophets sometimes used this term figuratively to refer to a city or country as a "virgin" (Jer 31:21; Am 5:2).

Another word, *naarah*, is itself used in several ways in the OT. Often it refers to an unmarried girl (Est 2:4); at other times it is used in speaking of a servant (Est 4:4; Ru 2:23). This same word is the base of the proper name of a woman (Naarah, the wife of Ashhur, in 1 Chr 4:5,6) and of a city in Ephraim near Jericho (Jos 16:7).

For many years controversy has surrounded the meaning of *almah*, the word for maiden used in Isaiah 7:14. The dispute arises because of the varied definitions of the word throughout the OT ("girl," "young woman," "young woman of marriageable age, presumably a virgin"). Only context can accurately determine the meaning of *almah* in any given instance. Looking at Isaiah 7:14 from a NT perspective, *almah* can be seen as a reference to Mary, the mother of Jesus.

Several Greek words are translated as "maiden" in the English NT. The meaning of *korasion* is simply "girl," "little girl," or "maiden" (Mt 9:24,25). Another word, *paidiske*, originally referred to a "young woman" but later came to mean "a female slave," "a servant-maid," or "a servant girl" (Mk 14:66; Lk 12:45). It is a diminutive of *pais* (a Greek word denoting "a young girl," "maiden," or "child") (Lk 8:51,54). *Numphē* is the Greek word meaning "young wife," "bride," and "daughter-in-law" (Lk 12:53; Rv 21:2). *Parthenos* is the usual Greek term for "virgin" and occurs 14 times in the NT. It can refer either to a male (Rv 14:4) or female (Mt 1:23; Acts 21:9) who has never experienced sexual intercourse.

See SLAVE, SLAVERY.

Mail, Coat of. Body armor consisting of small interlaced metal plates sewn onto a leather jacket.

See ARMS AND WARFARE.

Makaz. One of the 12 cities that provided food one month out of the year for King Solomon and his household (1 Kgs 4:9). Situated in northwest Judah, it may be identified with Khirbet el-Mukheizin, south of Ekron.

Makheloth. One of the stopping places of the Israelites on their way to Canaan, situated between Haradah and Tahath (Nm 33:25,26). Its exact location is unknown.

See WILDERNESS WANDERINGS.

Makkedah. One of the Shephelah towns conquered during the southern campaign led by Joshua (Jos 10:10–29; 12:16). It belonged to the same district as Lachish (Jos 15:41). Eusebius placed it eight Roman miles east of Eleutheropolis (Beth-guvrin), which would lead to Beit-Maqdum, a Roman-Byzantine ruin beside the Roman road from Eleutheropolis to Hebron. The biblical site may have been at Khirbet el-Qom about one-half mile to the southwest.

Maktesh. Locality within the topography of Jerusalem (Zep 1:11). Since the word means "mortar," the expression here should refer to some basinlike depression. It is probably the Tyropoeon Valley opposite the temple mount, though the Targum equates it with the Kidron.

Malachi (Person). Author of the last book of the OT (Mal 1:1). The prophet Malachi lived about 500–460 BC. His name means "my angel" or "my messenger" and is so translated in Malachi 3:1 and elsewhere. Apart from the book which bears his name, nothing else is known about him from the Bible. In the apocryphal book of 2 Esdras 1:40 he is identified as "Malachi, who is also called a messenger of the Lord." Rabbinic tradition suggests that Malachi may be another name for Ezra the scribe, although there is no supporting evidence for this identification.

G. LLOYD CARR

See MALACHI, BOOK OF; PROPHET, PROPHETESS.

Malachi, Book of.

Author. The name Malachi means "my messenger" or "messenger of the Lord." Since the word appears in 3:1, some scholars think that it is not a proper name at all and does not provide the name of the author of the book. According to one ancient tradition, the "messenger" was Ezra, the priest responsible for the books of Ezra and Nehemiah. Yet it would be most unusual for the Jews to preserve a prophetic book without explicitly attaching to it the name of the author. All of the other major and minor prophets—including Obadiah—are named after a particular prophet. Moreover, "messenger of the Lord" would be a most appropriate name for a prophet (cf. 2 Chr 36:15,16; Hg 1:13).

Historical Background. During the 5th century BC the struggling Jewish community in Judah was greatly assisted by the return of Ezra and Nehemiah. In 458 BC Ezra was encouraged by King Artaxerxes of Persia to lead a group of exiles back to Jerusalem and to institute religious reform. About 13 years later in 445 BC a high-ranking government official named Nehemiah was allowed to go to Jerusalem to rebuild the city walls, a task he accomplished in 52 days (Neh 6:15). As governor, Nehemiah led the people in a financial reform that provided for the poor and encouraged tithing to support the priests and Levites (5:2–13; 10:35–39). Like Ezra, Nehemiah urged the people to keep the sabbath and avoid intermarrying with pagan neighbors. After a 12-year term, Nehemiah returned to Persia and the spiritual condition of Judah deteriorated. Perhaps discouraged by their lack of political power, tithing became sporadic, the sabbath was not kept, intermarriage was common, and even the priests could not be trusted. When Nehemiah came back to Jerusalem some time later, he had to take firm action to straighten out the situation (13:6–31).

Date. Since Malachi had to deal with the same sins mentioned in Nehemiah 13 (see Mal 1:6–14; 2:14–16; 3:8–11), it is likely that the prophet ministered either during Nehemiah's second term as governor or the years just before his return. The reference to "the governor" in Malachi 1:8 implies that someone other than Nehemiah was in office, so it may be best to place Malachi just after 433 BC, the year Nehemiah had returned to Persia.

Purpose and Theology. Malachi was written to shake the people of Judah from their spiritual lethargy and to warn them that judgment was coming unless they repented. The people doubted God's love (1:2) and justice (2:17) and did not take his commands seriously (1:6; 3:14–18). Yet God was "a great King" (1:14) with a great name that was to be feared even "beyond the border of Israel" (1:5,11). Malachi repeatedly urged both the priests and the people to revere God and give him the honor he deserved. God was Israel's father and creator (2:10), but the nation showed contempt for his name (1:6; 3:5). In response to this contempt, God would send his messenger to announce the day of the Lord (3:1). John the Baptist did call the nation to repentance, and Christ came to cleanse the temple (Jn 2:14,15) and establish the covenant (Mal 3:1,2). Most of the work of refining and purifying will take place at the second coming, however, when Christ returns to purify his people (cf. 3:2–4) and judge the wicked (4:1).

Content. *God's Great Love for Israel (1:1–5).* To introduce the book, Malachi presents a contrast between God's love for Israel and his hatred for Edom. Yet the assertion of God's love is greeted with a strange question: "How have you loved us?" God loved Israel by entering into a covenant with the nation at Mt Sinai, just after he had freed them from the prison of Egypt. He had chosen them as his special people (cf. Gn 12:1–3; Ex 19:5,6), whereas the descendants of Esau were not chosen (cf. Rom 9:10–13). Both Israel and Edom endured invasion and destruction, but only Israel was restored and rebuilt after the exile. The people of Edom were driven from their homeland by the Nabataeans between 550 and 400 BC, and they never regained their territory. Through the judgment of Edom, God demonstrated that he is the great ruler over the nations (1:5) and that he will not forget Israel.

The Unacceptable Sacrifices of the Priests (1:6–14). Although God deserved the honor and reverence of the Israelites, both the people and the priests openly disdained his laws and regulations. Strangely, it was the priests who led the way into disobedience. Sacrifices and offerings were supposed to atone for sin, but the animals offered by the priests only served to pollute or defile the altar (1:7,12). According to Leviticus, animals with defects were unacceptable as sacrifices, but Malachi mentions that the priests were offering "injured, crippled or diseased animals" to the Lord (1:13; cf. 1:8). To emphasize their contempt, the Lord challenges the priests to bring comparable presents to the governor (v 8). Would they dare to insult him in this fashion and face sure rejection? Rather than having the priests continue to bring unfit sacrifices to the altar, the Lord asks them to close the temple doors entirely (v 10). Going through the motions never pleased God, either in ancient times (cf. Is 1:12,13) or modern. By calling the altar and its sacrifices "contemptible" (vv

7,12), the priests were no better than the wicked sons of Eli, whose disregard of the rules for sacrifices sent them to a premature death (cf. 1 Sm 2:15–17).

In sharp contrast to the attitude of the priests stands the emphasis upon God's greatness in verses 11 and 14. God is more powerful than the gods of other nations, and even if Israel's priests and people dishonor the Lord, eventually pure offerings will be brought to God by believing Gentiles. Perhaps these offerings refer to prayer and praise (cf. Ps 19:14; Heb 13:15; Rv 5:8), but others interpret the reference more literally (cf. Is 56:7; 60:7). Peter may be alluding to this verse in connection with the conversion of Cornelius (Acts 10:35).

The Punishment of the Priests (2:1–9). One of the functions of the priests was to pronounce blessings upon the people in the name of God, but their disgraceful behavior turned the blessings into curses (v 2). Because of the priests' sinfulness and the poor condition of the animals, their sacrifices were also worthless, and the entrails of the animals will be spread on their faces as a sign that God holds them in contempt. The disgrace heaped upon the priests differs sharply from the honor enjoyed by Aaron and his descendants. Malachi refers to a "covenant of life and peace" (v 5) made with Levi and more particularly with Aaron's grandson Phinehas, who courageously took action against Jews involved in idolatry and immorality (Nm 25:10–13). In those days the priests revered the Lord "and turned many from sin" (Mal 2:6).

Another responsibility of the priests was to teach the nation the Law handed down by Moses (cf. Lv 10:11). Like prophets, they were messengers of the Lord (Mal 2:7) who were supposed to walk close to the Lord, but now the priests disregarded the Law and were dishonest in handing down judicial decisions (v 9; cf. Lv 19:15).

The Unfaithfulness of the People (2:10–16). In light of the attitude of the priests it is not surprising to discover that the people at large were unfaithful to the Lord. God had formed Israel to be his special people, but the people had broken faith with him. A major factor in their unfaithfulness was intermarriage with foreigners, a sin mentioned in Ezra 9:1,2 and Nehemiah 13:23–29. By marrying pagan women the men of Israel invariably began to worship pagan gods and turn from the Lord. When such intermarriage occurred, it sometimes followed the divorce of an Israelite wife. In verses 14,15 God underscores the sacred commitment that he himself witnesses when two people marry. If that marriage covenant is shattered by divorce, God is deeply displeased (v 16), and it is even more tragic if divorce becomes an excuse to marry a more attractive or appealing foreigner.

The Coming of the Messenger of the Covenant (2:17–3:5). The sins of the priests and the people did not go unnoticed, even though the nation doubted that God would take action (2:17). But the third chapter opens with the announcement that the messenger of the covenant will indeed come to his temple. His way will be prepared by another messenger, a prophecy of John the Baptist, who "cleared the way" for the ministry of Christ (cf. Mt 11:10; Mk 1:2,3). When Christ came, he did reveal his anger when he cleansed the temple (cf. Jn 2:13–17) and denounced the scribes and Pharisees (cf. Jn 9:39), but most of his purifying and refining work awaits the second coming. Some day the priests and Levites will bring acceptable sacrifices, as they did in the days of Moses and Phinehas (cf. vv 3,4 and 2:4,5). Verse 5 broadens the scope of the judgment to include the whole nation, as sorcerers, adulterers, and those who oppress the poor are condemned.

The Benefits of Faithful Tithing (3:6–12). Another specific weakness of postexilic Judah was the failure of the people to bring their tithes to the Lord. Encouraged by Nehemiah, the nation did promise to tithe faithfully (cf. Neh 10:37–39), but apparently their good intentions were short-lived (cf. Neh 13:10,11). According to Malachi 3:8,9, the giving pattern of the nation was so dismal that the people were in effect robbing God and were therefore under a curse. In verses 10–12 Malachi challenges the nation to bring their tithes and then God would pour out his blessing upon them. Just as the opening of the "windows in heaven" meant the end of a famine in 2 Kings 7:2,19, so God promises that their crops will be so abundant that they will run out of storage space. Likewise, Paul challenges believers to give generously to the work of the Lord and discover the overwhelming blessing of God upon their lives (2 Cor 9:6–12). For Israel, renewed prosperity would bring the recognition of the nations that God has blessed them in accord with the promise made to Abraham (Gn 12:2,3; Mal 3:12). The hope of "blessing" in verses 10 and 12 provides welcome relief from the curses mentioned in 1:14; 2:2; 3:9; and 4:6.

The Day of the Lord (3:13–4:6). Faced with the challenge of verses 10–12, the people of Israel responded in two different ways. One group denied that serving God brought any benefit (vv 13–15) while another segment of the nation bowed low before him with deep reverence (vv 16–18). The unbelievers argued that obeying the Lord was useless and that arrogant and evil people were the ones who prospered. In response to their charge Malachi noted that God would remember who the righteous were in the day of judgment. Although all of Israel was included in the promise made to Abraham, only those who genuinely believed would be God's "treasured possession" (3:17; cf. Ex 19:5) and their names will be written in the book of life (cf. 3:16). As for the arrogant and evildoers, the day of the Lord will consume them and they will have no survivors (4:1). Those who revere the Lord will enjoy spiritual and physical health under the blessing and protection of God, who is called the "sun of righteousness" (4:2). Like calves just released from confinement, the righteous will "trample down the wicked" and triumph over them (v 3).

In view of the judgment associated with the day of the Lord, as he concluded the book Malachi urged the people to repent. To do this they needed to heed the Law of Moses and take seriously the decrees and commands given at Mt Sinai (v 4; cf. 3:7). Just as Elijah called on Israel to turn back to God, so a new "Elijah" will preach repentance to a rebellious nation. When John the Baptist prepared the way for Christ (cf. Mal 3:1), he ministered "in the spirit and power of Elijah" and begged the Jews to turn from their sin and humble themselves before God (Lk 1:17). If they refused to listen, the nation faced the prospect of total destruction, the curse placed upon the people of Canaan (cf. Jos 6:17–19) and upon the nation of Edom, whose collapse was described in Malachi 1:2–5.

Herbert M. Wolf

See Israel, History of; Postexilic Period, The; Prophecy; Prophet, Prophetess.

Bibliography. J.G. Baldwin, *Haggai, Zechariah, Malachi*; C.F. Keil, *The Twelve Minor Prophets*, vol 2; G.A. Smith, *The Book of the Twelve Prophets*; C. von Orelli, *The Twelve Minor Prophets*.

Malcam. Sharariam's son from Benjamin's tribe (1 Chr 8:9, KJV Malcham).

Malcham. 1. KJV form of Malcam in 1 Chronicles 8:9.

See Malcam.

2. KJV form of Milcom, an Ammonite god, in Zephaniah 1:5.

See Milcom.

Malchiah. 1. KJV spelling of Malchijah, Gershon's descendant, in 1 Chronicles 6:40.

See Malchijah #1.

2. KJV spelling of Malchijah, Parosh's son, in Ezra 10:25.

See Malchijah #4.

3. KJV spelling of Malchijah, Harim's son, in Ezra 10:31.

See Malchijah #6.

4. KJV spelling of Malchijah, Rechab's son, in Nehemiah 3:14.

See MALICHIJAH #7.

5. KJV spelling of Malchijah the goldsmith in Nehemiah 3:31.

See MALCHIJAH #8.

6. KJV spelling of Malchijah, Ezra's assistant, in Nehemiah 8:4.

See MALCHIJAH #9.

7. KJV spelling of Malchijah, Adaiah's forefather, in Nehemiah 11:12.

See MALCHIJAH #2.

8. Royal prince who owned a cistern in which the prophet Jeremiah was imprisoned (Jer 38:6). Malchiah's son Pashhur (21:1, KJV Melchiah; 38:1) was one of those who, after hearing the harsh prophecies of Jeremiah, appealed to King Zedekiah to put Jeremiah to death. The princes attempted to do so by throwing him into Malchiah's cistern.

Malchiel, Malchielite. Beriah's son, a grandson of Asher (Gn 46:17; 1 Chr 7:31), and the founder of the Malchielite family (Nm 26:45).

Malchijah. 1. Gershon's descendant, appointed by David, along with the rest of his family, to serve as a temple musician (1 Chr 6:40, KJV Malchiah).

2. Priest who served in the time of David (1 Chr 9:12). His descendants were among those who returned to Jerusalem with Zerubbabel (Ezr 2:38; Neh 11:12, KJV Malchiah).

3. Priest in David's reign (1 Chr 24:9); perhaps the same as #2 above.

4. Parosh's son, who obeyed Ezra's exhortation to divorce his pagan wife after the exile (Ezr 10:25, KJV Malchiah).

5. KJV rendering of Hashabiah, another of Parosh's sons, in Ezra 10:25.

See HASHABIAH #9.

6. Harim's son, who obeyed Ezra's exhortation to divorce his pagan wife after the exile (Ezr 10:31, KJV Malchiah). He repaired part of the Jerusalem wall under Nehemiah (Neh 3:11).

7. Rechab's son and the ruler of Beth-haccherem. Under Nehemiah's direction, he repaired the Dung Gate of the Jerusalem wall (Neh 3:14, KJV Malchiah).

8. Goldsmith who worked under Nehemiah's direction to help repair the Jerusalem wall (Neh 3:31, KJV Malchiah).

9. One who stood to Ezra's left during the public reading of the Law (Neh 8:4, KJV Malchiah).

10. Priest who signed Ezra's covenant of faithfulness to God with Nehemiah and others after the exile (Neh 10:3).

11. Participant in the dedication of the rebuilt Jerusalem wall (Neh 12:42).

Malchiram. Son of Jeconiah (Jehoiachin), and a descendant of David (1 Chr 3:18).

Malchishua. King Saul's third son (1 Sm 14:49, KJV Melch-ishua; 1 Chr 8:33; 9:39). He was killed by the Philistines at the battle of Gilboa (1 Sm 31:2, KJV Melchi-shua; 1 Chr 10:2).

Malchus. Name of a slave of the high priest in John 18:10. At the time of Jesus' arrest Peter struck Malchus with a sword, cutting off his right ear. In Matthew 26:51, Mark 14:47, and Luke 22:50,51, no name is given for this person. According to Luke, Jesus immediately healed the wound.

Maleleel. KJV form of Mahalalel, an ancestor of Jesus, in Luke's genealogy (3:37).

See MAHALALEL, MAHALALEEL #1.

Mallothi. One of Heman's 17 children (1 Chr 25:4,5), who became leader of the 19th of 24 divisions of singers for service in the sanctuary during David's reign (25:26).

Mallow. Shrubby plant (Jb 24:24; 30:4).

See PLANTS.

Malluch. 1. Merarite Levite and ancestor of Ethan the singer in Solomon's temple (1 Chr 6:44).

2. Bani's son, whom Ezra required to divorce his foreign wife (Ezr 10:29).

3. Harim's son, whom Ezra required to divorce his foreign wife (Ezr 10:32).

4. Priest who set his seal on Ezra's covenant (Neh 10:4).

5. Another priest who set his seal on Ezra's covenant (Neh 10:27).

6. Priest who returned from the exile with Zerubbabel (Neh 12:2).

Malluchi. Father of a house headed by Jonathan during the days of the high priest Joiakim in the postexilic period (Neh 12:14, KJV Melicu).

Malta. Island in the Mediterranean Sea, south of Sicily. The name Malta occurs only once in the Bible (Acts 28:1, KJV Melita), in connection with the shipwreck which occurred on Paul's voyage to Rome (25:11,12). This voyage was undertaken during the winter, the season in which storms are most likely to be encountered on the Mediterranean. The ship proceeded cautiously, for contrary winds were

St. Paul's Bay, Malta.

blowing (27:4). With difficulty they reached the harbor of Fair Havens on Crete (vv 7,8). In spite of a warning by Paul the decision was made to try to reach the Cretan port of Phoenix, which was more suitable for wintering (vv 9–12).

Caught by a severe storm and driven helplessly by the wind for 14 days, the ship finally neared land during the night. In the morning, the ship tried for the beach but ran aground and was pounded to pieces by the surf. Everyone managed to reach the shore safely. While putting wood on a fire, Paul was bitten by a viper. The natives of the island supposed that he was a desperate criminal whose life was being taken by the bite of a snake. When he did not fall down dead, they radically changed their opinion of him and regarded him as a god (Acts 28:6).

The island of Malta is about 60 miles from Sicily and has an area of 95 square miles. St Paul's Bay marks the traditional site of the shipwreck of Acts. The island is essentially agricultural but production is poor because of the thin calcareous soil. Terracing is practiced in order to utilize the soil to the fullest extent. The island has no rivers and is dependent on rainfall and springs for its water. The climate in general is mild, but in the summer the island is subject to the hot, dust-laden sirocco from the deserts of Libya.

Mammon. Word borrowed from the Aramaic language in the time of Jesus and the early church; also used by Jewish settlers in the community near the Dead Sea. Mammon refers to wealth or property. The Gospel writers wrote the Aramaic word in Greek letters. Some English translations preserve the Greek form of the word in English (KJV, RSV, NASB); others translate it with the words "wealth" or "money" (NEB, TEV, NIV). In Matthew 6:24 and Luke 16:13, "mammon" is personified as a rival to God for the loyalty of the disciple: To which master will obedience be given? In Luke 16:9,11 the term designates material wealth or property. Mammon itself does not carry a negative value, as the parallel phrasing in Luke 16:11 makes clear: "If then you have not been faithful in the unrighteous mammon, who will entrust to you the true riches?"

Mamre (Person). Owner of a parcel of land called "the plain of Mamre." He was an Amorite and is recorded as having two brothers: Aner and Eshcol (Gn 14:13). These became confederates of Abraham when he fought to save his nephew Lot.

Mamre (Place). Important oak grove near which Abraham lived, and named for an Amorite who helped him defeat Chedorlaomer and rescue Lot (Gn 14:13,24). Abraham erected an altar under the oak of Mamre (13:18). Abraham was sitting by the sacred tree when he welcomed three mysterious guests (ch 18). Mamre is also a possible site for the scene of Abrahamic covenant ceremonies (ch 15). Isaac and Jacob also lived there (35:27).

While Mamre is not mentioned in the Bible outside of Genesis, it continued to be an important place of worship and many legends remain about the sacred tree. In the 1st century AD pilgrims journeyed to Mamre for ceremonies venerating the tree. According to Sozomenus (*Hist. Eccl.* 2.4), Jews, Christians, and pagans performed devotions at the site, each in their own way.

In all probability, unorthodox worship was practiced at Mamre. Jerusalem tended to ignore such cults; therefore, it is not mentioned outside of Genesis and even there the location of the site is confused. The oak(s) of Mamre are identified as near Hebron (Gn 13:18) and Machpelah where the patriarchs and their

Ruins at Mamre.

wives were buried (23:17, 19; 25:9; 49:30; 50:13). Eventually, the younger city of Hebron overshadowed the older sanctuary at Mamre.

Mamre has been excavated by archaeologists on a hill 1⅔ miles north of Hebron named Ramet el-Khalil. E.H. Mader cleared a Herodian enclosure wall and a well into which pilgrims threw gifts and money. In the eastern part of the area, Constantine built a basilica with a double narthex indicating that this site remained a place of prayer. It also may have been the site of the infamous "Fair of Terebinthos," where Hadrian sold the captives of the Bar Kochba war (AD 135) into slavery. Pottery from the 9th and 8th centuries BC indicates earlier Israelite occupation.

See ABRAHAM.

Man, Doctrine of.

The study of the origin, nature, and destiny of man. (By "man," generally the generic sense of man as male and female is intended, in accord with regular biblical usage.)

The biblical teaching on man begins with a right notion concerning God. The biblical perspective of anthropology (i.e., the study of man) is centrally displayed in the context of an elevated theology (i.e., the study of God). A high and reverent view of God leads to a noble and dignified view of man, whereas a poorly developed concept of God often produces a distorted perspective on man. Hence, man may be viewed more importantly than he ought, or man may be seen less importantly than is biblical. Either view is sub-biblical. The place to begin a study of man, then, is with a high view of God, his Creator.

His Origin. Against the naturalistic, materialistic theories of origins, the biblical view starts with the assertion that the eternal God has created man, the most significant of all his created works. It is not necessary for one to subscribe to a particular chronological scenario for God's work in the creation of man. Some Christians believe the Bible teaches a closed chronology in Genesis 1 made of 6 literal 24-hour days (cf. Gn 1:5,8,13, etc.), with the stunning, sudden appearance of man coming perhaps just some 6000 years ago (cf. the chronologies associated with but not limited to Archbishop James Ussher, *Annales*, 1650–58). Some who hold this general viewpoint (sometimes called creation science) extend the creation of man to about 10,000 years ago, based on a view of some elasticity in the chronologies of Genesis 5 and 11.

Others believe the texts of Genesis 1 and 2 may be interpreted far more broadly to speak of a most remote antiquity for the creation of man (extending to millions of years). They argue that process (under God's control and direction) may have played a significant role in God's creative work. This viewpoint is best termed progressive creationism, and is to be contrasted with theistic evolution, in which God is usually viewed as initiating the process, but having little involvement once the processes are in motion. In the former approach, the Hebrew term "day" (*yom*) in Genesis 1 may refer to an extended period of time (e.g., the "day-age" theory); the phrasing "an evening and a morning, the *x*th day" may be a literary device to present successive scenes in the creative works of God through the processes of time.

Many Christians find themselves somewhere between a conservative and a broad chronology for man's origin. Yet in spite of individual preferences, one must give assent to God's creative work in producing man in order to think biblically about man. The essence of faith begins in the words, "I believe in God the Father Almighty, Creator of heaven and earth."

Man is not only God's creation, but the pinnacle of his creative effort. Long before modern precision in such things, the ancients were aware of man's anatomical similarities with members of the animal kingdom. Yet despite these similarities, the biblical viewpoint was never to confuse man with animals—man is distinct, the high point of God's creative work, the apex of his handicraft. The progression of the created things in Genesis 1 is climactic; all of God's created work culminated in his fashioning of man.

Sociologically, the distinct behavior characteristics of man include language, toolmaking, and culture. Distinct experiential characteristics include reflective awareness, ethical concern, aesthetic urges, historical awareness, and metaphysical concern. These factors individually and collectively separate man from other forms of animate life. Man is far more than the "naked ape" of some modern evolutionary theories. But sociology alone does not suffice to explain the full nature of man. That is the subject of divine revelation.

While man bears a continuity with God's creation (assumed in the words of Gn 2:7, being fashioned from the dust of the earth), man is also distinct from all that precedes him, as it was into a new creature that God breathed the breath of life so that he became a living being (2:7). The wording of this text deals a blow to the theory of gradualism in the development of man. It was not into one of the developing creatures that God gave an extra boost or a distinctive nature, but into a fully fashioned, yet inanimate creature that he breathed the breath of life. The animating principle of man comes directly as a gift from God.

Man was created by God as male and female (Gn 1:27), meaning that what is said generally of man must be said of both the male and the female, and that the truest picture of what it means to be human will be found in the context of man and woman together. The commands to multiply and exercise sovereignty over the earth were given to both sexes as shared responsibility. Similarly, it is man as male and female that has rebelled against God and bears the consequences of that primeval sin in the postfall world, and man as male and female that Christ came to redeem (cf. Gal 3:28). At the same time, the words male and female denote true distinctions. Many perceived gender differences may be culturally conditioned, yet the prime sexual distinctions between male (Hebrew *zakar*, "the piercer") and female (Hebrew *neqeba*, "the pierced") are divinely intended. It may be too much to argue as did Karl Barth that it was in the male and female relationship that the image of God is to be found; yet the male and female relationship is at least a part of what the image of God means (see Gn 1:27).

The most stunning biblical assertion respecting man is that God made man *in his image*. Of no other creature, not even the angels, is such a statement found. The words "in God's image" in Genesis 1:26–28 are the basis for the psalmist's paraphrase in Psalm 8:5, "for you have made him to lack but little of God" (lit. trans.; "lower than the angels" Septuagint trans.). The meaning of the phrase "the image of God" (Latin, *imago Dei*) has been the subject of much debate. Some have thought the phrase to refer to a physical representation of God, but this is doubtful in that God is spirit (cf. Jn 4:24). Others think the phrase refers to man's personhood, which corresponds to the personality of God (having intellect, sensibilities, and will). Such qualities of man may be found in God's image; however, these varied aspects of personality are also shared by other members of the animal kingdom, and are not unique to the human species.

The basic meaning of the word image (Hebrew *salem*) is "image," "shadow," "representation," or "likeness." The image of God in man reveals God's perspective of man's worth and dignity as a representation or a shadow of himself in the created world. Ancient kings of Assyria were known to have physical images of themselves placed in outlying districts as a reminder to those who might be prone to forget that these areas were a part of the empire. So God has placed in man a shadow of himself, a representation of his presence, in the world that he has made.

This view of God's image in man seems to be confirmed by the immediate context in Genesis 1. Man, created in God's image, is to have dominion over all of God's other works (v 26; see also Ps 8:5). Further, as a representative of the Creator, man is to respond to him. Jesus' assertion of the spirituality of God results in a response of worship in spirit and in truth (Jn 4:21–24).

His Nature. One may tend to think of man in parts, but the biblical emphasis is on man as a whole. Debates continue on the tripartite (threefold) nature of man (cf. 1 Thes 5:23), spirit, soul, and body, as against a bipartite (twofold) nature of man, material and immaterial. Though the Bible does seem to support both positions, the more important issue respecting the nature of man is his unity rather than the number of his parts. Hence, a biblical view of man begins in the assertion that one is a person made up of physical and nonphysical properties. In the words of Karl Barth, the human person is "bodily soul, as he is also besouled body." There is no person in body only (death), nor can one easily think of a bodiless spirit as a person, except in a temporary, transitional state. The Hebrew term *nephesh*, often translated "soul," is best rendered "person" in most contexts (cf. KJV reading of Gn 46:26,27 with RSV). The Hebrew word *ruah* ("breath," "wind," "spirit") and the Greek words *pneuma* ("spirit") and *psyche* ("soul") often speak of the immaterial part of man. This is no less real than the physical. A purely material, physical view of man is frightfully deficient. At the same time, an overemphasis on the spirit and a de-emphasis on the physical is neither realistic nor balanced. One may say, "I am a person whose existence is presently very dependent upon my physical body. But I am more than body, more than flesh. When my body dies, I still live. When my flesh decays, I exist. But one day I shall live in a body again. For the notion of a disembodied spirit is not the full measure of my humanity. God's ideal for me is to live my life in my [new] body. So in hope of the eternal state, 'I believe in the resurrection of the body and life everlasting.' "

One cannot go far in thinking of the nature of man from the biblical vantage point without first facing the problem of the fall. Genesis 3 suggests that unfallen man was immortal, that his powers of sexual reproduction were not originally bound in the pain in childbearing, and that his work was not troubled by reversals in nature. After the fall, however, all was changed: within man himself, between the male and the female, in his interaction with nature, and in his relationship with the Creator.

As a result of the fall man has become profoundly fallen, a fallenness extending to every part of his person. The phrase "total depravity" need not mean that one is as evil as he or she might be, but rather that the results of sin affect one's whole being. At the same time, the image of God in man continues in some way after the fall, providing the divine rationale for salvation (cf. Rom 5). It is essentially because of God's estimation of the intrinsic worth of man that the divine justification of salvation may be maintained.

The old debate between the essential goodness and the evil disposition of man finds its quandry and resolution in the Genesis account: God made man to consciously reflect the dignity and nobility of the Creator; yet man, by his own deliberate rebellion, turned against his Creator and continues, except by God's grace, in the ensuing sin that marks his life. This resultant sin is both a quality of being in the fallen person as well as numerous, continuing acts of pride and selfishness. Though the image of God in man is marred in the post-fall period, it may be stimulated anew by the effective work of the Spirit of God as one comes to newness of life in Christ. This gracious work of God brings personal renewal, restoration of relationships with others, and fellowship with God.

Man, then, was created good by God, has become evil by his own devices, yet in God's power may recapture the good again. The rediscovery of what it means to be fully human as the shadow of God is found in the life of Jesus, whose human life is the new beginning for man. Hence, Jesus is the new Adam; in his model there is a new beginning that replaces the former pattern.

His Destiny. A biblical view of man must include a balanced statement respecting his divine origin, his rebellion against the grace of God, his judgment, and his prospect for redemption in the person of the Savior Jesus with the promise of eternal life. Man has a

beginning and will live forever. This assertion is in stark contrast to naturalistic theories of origins and destinies. One of the most deceptive tendencies of modern thought is the concept "coming to terms with death." People with no thought of God and no hope for eternity are encouraging each other to accept the inevitable decline and demise of their bodies as the natural end to human life. The biblical notion is that death in man is not natural at all.

Death is an acquired trait, not the natural destiny of man. Death may be said of the body, but not of the spirit. The biblical teaching is that while the body dies and decays, the person lives on in hope of a renewed body. Those who have come to know Christ go to be with him when their bodies die (Phil 1:23) and anticipate the resurrection of the body for eternal life to come (1 Cor 15:35–49). Those who die apart from Christ do not cease to exist, but are assigned an eternal existence of conscious knowledge that they are separated from God and have fallen short of their destiny to enjoy his presence forever. The biblical teaching on the destiny of the lost is quite unpalatable for modern man. Even Christians who have generally high views of biblical inspiration may find themselves blanching at the thought of eternal punishment of the wicked. Yet the biblical doctrine of the final judgment of the wicked is as well established as most teachings in the Bible.

One of the most dramatic truths in Scripture respecting the nature of man is to realize that it was for man that God initiated the salvation work that led to the incarnation of the eternal son of God. With the resurrection and ascension of the Lord Jesus Christ, our Savior returned to his eternal position of glory and majesty in heaven, where he forever remains the God-man. As God he shares all the attributes of the Father and the Holy Spirit, and as man, identifies with man. He reveals himself in a physical body, albeit the resurrection body, the first fruits of the resurrection of all who are his. The incarnation, then, brought about an eternal change in deity. Only a very high view of the worth of man could have brought God to such a fundamental change in himself. As the writer to the Hebrews states, "Since the children have flesh and blood, he too shared in their humanity" (Heb 2:14).

The final measure of our humanity is that man was made to worship God and to enjoy him forever. Such thoughts are not attributed to any other created being. Even the angels, who have maintained their perfect state and who worship the Father in conscious bliss, do not have quite the same relationship with God as do redeemed men. "For surely it is not angels he helps, but Abraham's descendants" (Heb 2:16). What is man? In Christ, man is all God means him to be, in majesty and dignity, and in joy before his throne forever.

RONALD B. ALLEN

See IMAGE OF GOD; MAN, NATURAL; MAN, OLD AND NEW.

Bibliography. R.B. Allen, *The Majesty of Man: The Dignity of Being Human;* S.B. Babbage, *Man in Nature and Grace;* G. Carey, *I Believe in Man;* W. Eichrodt, *Man in the OT;* W. Kümmel, *Man in the NT;* J.G. Machen, *The Christian View of Man;* H.D. McDonald, *The Christian View of Man;* J.I. Packer, *Knowing Man;* C.R. Smith, *The Bible Doctrine of Man;* W.D. Stacey, *The Pauline View of Man.*

Man, Natural. Expression occurring in 1 Corinthians 2:14 (RSV mg). The adjective translated there by "natural" is also found in 1 Corinthians 15:44 (twice), 46; James 3:15; and Jude 19. This adjective is related to the Greek noun usually translated "soul." Its meaning, however, is primarily determined by its various contexts, particularly in 1 Corinthians, where all four occurrences are contrasted pointedly with "spiritual," an adjective occurring frequently in the NT, mostly in Paul. In almost every instance it refers to the work of the Holy Spirit. Applied to things, "spiritual" means derived from, or produced by, the Holy Spirit (the Law—Rom 7:14; gifts—1 Cor 12:1; blessings—Eph 1:3; sacrifices—1 Pt 2:5). When it is applied to persons, it means indwelt, motivated, and directed by the Holy Spirit (1 Cor 2:15; 14:37; Gal 6:1). "Natural," then, when contrasted with "spiritual," generally describes what is devoid of or in opposition to the Holy Spirit and his work. In 1 Corinthians 2:14,15 "natural man" is set over against "spiritual man." The significance of this contrast is plain from the emphasis given to the work of the Holy Spirit in revelation (see v 10). This revealing activity is both comprehensive (v 10: "everything, even the depths of God") and exclusive (v 11: "no one comprehends the thoughts of God except the Spirit of God"). Furthermore, only those who have received God's spirit understand what is revealed (v 12); only they grasp what is spoken, not in human wisdom, but in words "taught by the Spirit" (v 13).

Within this context the natural man is one who does not accept the things which come from the spirit of God (1 Cor 2:14). Rather, these things are "foolishness" to him. He cannot understand them because they are "spiritually discerned." This foolishness is the foolishness of unbelief (1:21; cf. vv 18,23), and the discernment lacking is insight produced only by the Holy Spirit. Plainly, Paul has in view someone utterly without and even opposed to the Holy Spirit and God's revealed truth. The

subject of verse 14 is "the man without the Spirit" (NIV), "a man who is unspiritual" (NEB), "the man who isn't a Christian" (LB).

This note of opposition to the Holy Spirit is also clear in other NT uses of "natural." In James 3:15, natural wisdom is also termed "demonic," that is, "inspired by the devil" and is of a piece with jealousy, selfish ambition, arrogance, and lying (vv 14,16), all together in the sharpest conflict with "the wisdom from above" which is "first pure, then peaceable, gentle . . . without uncertainty or insincerity" (vv 15,17). In Jude 19, "scoffers" (see v 18), who cause divisions, are called "worldly people" and then immediately, those who are "devoid of the Spirit."

In these passages the contrast between the spiritual man and the natural man is between the Holy Spirit of God and the sinner in rebellion. Yet in 1 Corinthians 15:44–46, the contrast occurs in a different context of the "body" in death and resurrection. The body of the believer laid in the grave ("sown") is a natural body (v 44a). The body of the believer raised from the dead will be a spiritual body, that is, a body renewed and transformed by the Holy Spirit (Rom 8:11). In verses 44b and 45a, however, the natural body is traced back by appeal to Genesis 2:7 to Adam before the fall, at creation. This shows that biblically what is natural refers to the creation. Originally, as created by God the "natural" was "very good" (Gn 1:31) but subsequently it has been subjected to corruption and death by the sin of man. Therefore, the sinful rebellion of the natural man, measured by the original creation, is thoroughly unnatural and abnormal. The opposing work of the Holy Spirit, now, in Christ, not only removes this abnormality but brings the original purposes of creation to their consummation (Rom 8:19–23; 2 Cor 5:17).

RICHARD B. GAFFIN, JR.

See MAN, DOCTRINE OF; MAN, OLD AND NEW.

Man, Old and New. Biblical terms used to describe the state of man in relation to Christ. Human beings are created in the image of God and are made to have fellowship with him (Gn 1:26,27). God made known to Adam and Eve his will in a specific situation (2:15–17), yet they used the freedom of their will which had been given them to disobey God's law and to enter into open rebellion against him (3:1–7). So God had to punish sinful humanity. The ultimate punishment was eternal, spiritual death.

The human race is dead in sin (Rom 5:12–21; Eph 2:1–3). The sin of Adam and Eve has been passed on to all humanity (original sin). Born with the tendency toward sin (Ps 51:5), as soon as the age of moral responsibility is reached, individuals begin to commit their own sins. Paul, in Romans 3:10–18, assembles a group of OT passages to show that "None is righteous, no, not one."

The Law of God was given as "our custodian until Christ came" (Gal 3:24); that is, condemning all humanity in sin (3:22) and pointing to the way of salvation, one must trust in the mercy and steadfast love of God. Salvation earned by means of the Law is an impossibility (Rom 4:1–25; Gal 3:18). Only Christ the Son of God kept the Law perfectly. All men have broken the Law and are therefore dead in sin. Paul uses the term "old man" to refer to this condition. The old man can keep certain parts of the Law and do various good things. But no old man can ever do enough good things to earn his own salvation. The old man must be made into a new man or he will suffer the consequences of his sin. Only God can bring about that radical change. Human beings can only accept by faith God's gracious gift.

David, in Psalm 51, cries out for God to take away the guilt of his sins. In verse 10 he pleads, "Create in me a clean heart, O God, and put a new and right spirit within me." God promises in Ezekiel 11:19; 18:31; and 36:26 to give repentant sinners a new heart and a new spirit. In Romans 6:5–11 Paul shows how the old nature has been crucified with Christ, so he can conclude, "So you also must consider yourselves dead to sin and alive to God in Christ Jesus" (v 11). In Ephesians 4:22–24 and Colossians 3:9,10 he shows the believer that he has put off the old man and put on the new man, Paul's term for the potential that is man's in Jesus Christ. Jesus speaks of this radical transformation as being born anew—not a second physical birth as Nicodemus thought, but a spiritual birth (Jn 3). And no one can enter the kingdom of God unless he has been born anew "of the Spirit" (v 6). Paul (Rom 8:15; Gal 4:5; Eph 1:5) uses the related concept of adoption. God adopts us into his own family.

Only the grace of God can change the old man into the new man. The old man accepts God's gracious gift by faith, but even that faith is a gift of God (Eph 2:8). The new man becomes a child of God. He does not immediately become perfect. He must fight against sin throughout this life as he strives to come closer and closer to the ideal of perfect holiness. He will attain that perfection only in the resurrection to come (1 Cor 15:42–50), when all things are made new (Rv 21:5).

See MAN, DOCTRINE OF; MAN, NATURAL; REGENERATION; REPENTANCE; CONVERSION; ADAM (PERSON); ETERNAL LIFE.

Man, Son of. *See* SON OF MAN.

Manaen. One of the prophets and teachers in the church at Antioch (Acts 13:1), identified as a close companion of Herod the tetrarch. The name is a Greek form of the Hebrew name Menachem.

Manahath (Person). One of Shobal's five sons (Gn 36:23; 1 Chr 1:40).

Manahath, Manahathite (Place). Evidently a place in the Judean hills near the Benjamite border (1 Chr 8:6). The Manahathites (1 Chr 2:54 and probably v 52 instead of Menuhoth), the people of Manahath, had connections with the Judean and Calebite clans in northern Judea. Its site is apparently that of Malha, three miles southwest of Jerusalem on the northern slope of the Valley of Rephaim.

See MENUHOTH.

Manasseh (Person). 1. Firstborn son of Joseph and his Egyptian wife Asenath (Gn 41:50,51). Manasseh, along with Ephraim his brother, visited their grandfather Jacob on his deathbed. Jacob announced that Manasseh and Ephraim were to be considered his own, not Joseph's, sons (48:5,6), and that Manasseh the firstborn would have descendants not quite as great as those of Ephraim (vv 13–20). This explains why Ephraim and Manasseh (in that order) provided their names for two of the 12 tribes of Israel but Joseph did not, at least in most listings (cf. Rv 7:6, KJV Manasses). Manasseh also founded the Manassite family (Dt 4:43; Jgs 12:4 KJV; 2 Kgs 10:33).

See MANASSEH, TRIBE OF.

2. KJV translation for Moses in Judges 18:30. In Hebrew the two names differ by only one letter. Apparently, an early scribe was offended that this verse connected Moses' grandson with idolatry, so he changed the name to Manasseh to preserve Moses' reputation.

See MOSES.

3. Thirteenth king of Judah (696–642 BC) and Jesus' ancestor (Mt 1:10, KJV Manasses); notorious for his long and wicked reign, described in 2 Kings 21:1–26 and 2 Chronicles 33:1–20. His father was the godly king Hezekiah, and his mother was Hephzibah (2 Kgs 21:1).

At the age of 12, he became co-ruler with his father. In 686 BC, his father died and he became sole monarch at only 23. His 55-year reign (2 Kgs 21:1) is dated from the beginning of his co-regency, so he ruled 11 years as coregent and 44 years as sole king—longer than any other king in Judah or in Israel. Regrettably, he was the most wicked of all the Judean kings, even resorting to a series of murders, presumably to stay in power (21:16; 24:4).

Wall strengthened on Ophel Hill by Manasseh, the most wicked king of Judah.

In addition to murder, among his sins listed in 2 Kings 21:2–9 are: rebuilding the high places for pagan worship; encouraging Baal, sun, moon, and star worship; and burning his son as a child sacrifice (v 6; cf. 23:10; Jer 7:31).

Second Chronicles 33:11–16 indicates that he was taken as a prisoner of war to Babylon, that he genuinely repented there, that God restored him as king, and that he tried to abolish his former pagan practices and to restore proper worship of God alone. Skepticism about this account is not warranted, even though unparalleled in 2 Kings. Surviving Assyrian records twice mention Manasseh, saying that he faithfully provided men to transport timber from Lebanon to Nineveh for the Assyrian king Esar-haddon (681–669 BC) and that he paid tribute to King Ashurbanipal (669–627 BC) after an Assyrian military campaign in Egypt in 667 BC. Though Pharaoh Neco's similar captivity and release is mentioned, Manasseh's is not.

When Manasseh died in 642 BC, at 67, he was buried in his own garden (2 Kgs 21:18) rather than with highly regarded kings like Jehoiada and Hezekiah (2 Chr 24:16; 32:33). His son Amon reverted to his father's wicked practices, but reigned only two years (642–640 BC) before being assassinated. It was his godly grandson Josiah (640–609 BC) who led the people back to true Jehovah worship (2 Kgs 23:4–14), but even his reforms could not avert the judgment promised on account of Manasseh's sins (23:26,27).   JAMES F. BABCOCK

See ISRAEL, HISTORY OF; CHRONOLOGY, OLD TESTAMENT.

4. Pahath-moab's son, who obeyed Ezra's exhortation to divorce his pagan wife after the exile (Ezr 10:30).

5. Hashum's son, who obeyed Ezra's exhortation to divorce his pagan wife after the exile (Ezr 10:33).

Manasseh, Tribe of. Geographically the largest of the 12 tribes of Israel, and unique in having two territories, a half tribe in each. However, isolated from each other by the Jordan River valley, they developed separately. The half tribe west of the Jordan was more important, both in OT and NT times, because it was the main tribe of the northern kingdom of Israel (931–722 BC) and one of the main ancestral stocks of the Samaritans.

Early History.   Its Roots. Its families traced their origins back to Joseph's elder son Manasseh, to Manasseh's son Machir or grandson Gilead, or to later descendants such as Zelophehad and Jair. The chart below shows how the biblical genealogical data (Gn 48:5,6; Nm 26:28–34; Jos 17:1–3; 1 Chr 2:21–23; and 7:14–19, a text corrupted by several copyists' errors) can be harmonized. The mention of Asriel in 1 Chronicles 7:14 seems to be a copyist's mistake; otherwise, the accounts are capable of being reconciled, even if each list preserved different data and none is complete in itself.

Its Size. One year after the exodus, Manasseh had the smallest army (Moses' first census, Nm 1:34,35). On the eve of the conquest of Canaan, after wandering 38 years in the Sinai wilderness and then conquering Transjordan, it had the sixth largest fighting force (2nd census, Nm 26:28–34)—52,700 men.

Its First Settlements. The soldiers of the eastern half tribe of Manasseh settled their families in Gilead which they captured under Moses' leadership from the Amorite king Og (Nm 21:32–35; 32:39–42; Dt 3:1–10, 13–15). Then, under Joshua they crossed the Jordan to help the other tribes conquer Canaan (Nm 32:1–32; Jos 1:12–18). Subsequently the western half tribe received its allotment and began to settle in the central hill country (16:1–4,9; 17:1–18). After the remaining tribes re-

Chart

Manasseh's Descendents

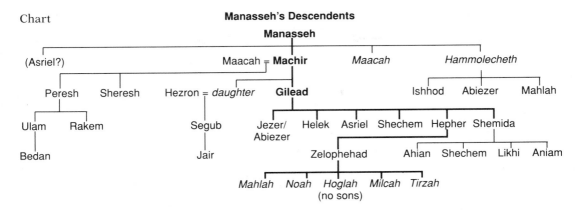

Bold names indicate key people. Daughters are in *italics*. The main line of descent is shown as a thicker line. The symbol = means "married."

ceived their shares of land (vv 18,19), the army from the eastern half tribe returned home (22:1–9). Enroute to their families in Gilead, they helped to build an altar by the Jordan River. This act was intended to preserve national unity, but it nearly started a civil war (vv 10–34).

The Eastern Half Tribe. *Its Territory.* Moses allotted the eastern half tribe nearly 3000 square miles of territory in three geographical regions (northern Gilead, Bashan, and Mt Hermon), but it succeeded in controlling only about 800 square miles—the half of Gilead north of the Jabbok River (and south of the Yarmuk River)—despite successful initial conquests (Nm 32:39–42; Dt 3:12–15; Jos 13:8–13) and gradual northern expansion much later (1 Chr 5:23).

The territory occupied was mostly a high plateau with a mountainous center. It was watered well by rains in winter and by a heavy dew in summer. Olive trees, grape vines, and wheat thrived, and goats and sheep could find adequate pasture on the eastern slopes, which merged gradually into the desert to the east.

People and Places. Prominent citizens of the eastern half tribe included the "judges" Jair and Jephthah (Jgs 10:3–5; 11:6–12) and David's benefactor Barzillai (2 Sm 19:31–39). Principal cities were Jabesh-gilead and Ramoth-gilead, a city of refuge and a levitical city, respectively (originally in Gad, Jos 20:8; 21:38).

The eastern territory was usually called simply "the half tribe of Manasseh" until David (c. 1000–961 BC) made it an administrative district (1 Chr 27:21). Solomon (970–930 BC) divided and incorporated it into two new districts (1 Kgs 4:13,14). Under Jeroboam I (930–909 BC), it joined, on equal terms, with eight other tribes and with the western half tribe, to form a confederacy of 10 tribes—the northern

kingdom of Israel—in 930 BC. Syria and Assyria both held eastern Manasseh temporarily, in the 9th and 8th centuries BC (cf. 2 Kgs 8:12; 10:32,33; 13:7 with 14:25; Am 1:3; cf. 2 Kgs 15:29 with 2 Chr 34:6,7). King Tiglath-pileser III (745–727 BC) of Assyria invaded the area, conquered it, deported its people, and scattered them throughout his empire (1 Chr 5:26; cf. 2 Kgs 15:29) about 10 years before the rest of the northern kingdom fell to the Assyrians in 722 BC. Most of the western Manassites left behind intermarried with the foreigners, began to worship pagan gods, and became ancestors of the Samaritans (17:24–41). Subsequently, the region was known as Gilead and Galaaditis. By NT times the region was partly in the Decapolis and partly in Perea.

JAMES F. BABCOCK

See ISRAEL, HISTORY OF; SAMARIA; SAMARITANS.

Manasses. 1. KJV form of Manasseh, king of Judah, in Matthew 1:10.

See MANASSEH (PERSON) #3.

2. KJV form of Manasseh, one of Israel's 12 tribes, in Revelation 7:6.

See MANASSEH (PERSON) #1; MANASSEH, TRIBE OF.

Manassite. Descendant of Manasseh, Joseph's firstborn son (Dt 4:43; 2 Kgs 10:33).

See MANASSEH (PERSON) #1; MANASSEH, TRIBE OF.

Mandrake. Mediterranean herb believed to have had aphrodisiac properties (Gn 30) and noted for its fragrance (Sg 7:13).

See PLANTS.

Maneh. KJV rendering of mina, a weight, in Ezekiel 45:12.

See WEIGHTS AND MEASURES.

Manger. Feeding trough for domesticated animals. The Greek term for manger is found only four times in the NT. Three of these instances are in the nativity narrative of Luke and are translated with the English word manger (Lk 2:7,12,16). The fourth occurrence, also in Luke's Gospel, is translated manger in the RSV and NEB, but "stall" in the KJV, NIV, and NASB (13:15).

The most common OT equivalent is the Hebrew term translated "crib," or "stall," in Job 39:9, Proverbs 14:4, and Isaiah 1:3. The context of these passages favors the use of the Greek word for manger. In the Septuagint, however, three other Hebrew words are also translated by this same Greek term. They are the Hebrew terms for "a stall," that is, an enclosure for animals (2 Chr 32:28); "a mash" or "fodder" (Jb 6:5); and "pens" or "stalls" (Hb 3:17).

Through a study of modern Middle Eastern customs and biblical archaeology two possible locations of the stable and manger area have been determined. In the home of a poor family, the stable was generally a room adjacent to and slightly lower than the living quarters. The stone manger was either located against one of the wooden walls of the stable or carved from a natural outcropping of rock. The other possible location of the stable was in a cave near the house or in the limestone foundation beneath the living quarters of the house. An example of the first of these was found at the ancient site of Megiddo. At Lachish a cave (c. 1200 BC) which seems to have been used as a stable was discovered beneath the remains of a building.

Traditionally, the manger area in which Jesus was born was a cave stable; it is over such a cave that the present Church of the Nativity was erected. However, the evidence recorded in Luke's Gospel could as easily refer to an area adjacent to a house.

See JESUS CHRIST, LIFE AND TEACHING OF.

Manna. Miraculous food the Lord provided for the Israelites in the desert. It originally appeared in the form of thin flakes, like frost on the ground, around the Israelite camp (Ex 16:14,15). It is compared elsewhere with coriander seed and bdellium, or resin (Nm 11:7). Its taste is said to have been like that of honey or of fresh oil (Ex 16:31; Nm 11:8). Since the experience of taste and color is somewhat subjective, these descriptions do not necessarily conflict. The word comes from the Hebrew *man*, that is, what? When the Israelites saw the manna they asked: "What is it?" (Ex 16:15).

Attempts have been made to link manna with substances discovered by modern travelers in Sinai and Arabia. In early summer (June, July) the tamarisk tree in these regions exudes a sweet-tasting liquid, produced as the result of the activity of a tiny insect. This liquid falls to the ground where it forms small grains which disappear when the sun gets hot. Reference also has been made to an edible lichen which in parts of southwest Asia is used instead of grain in years of famine. Whatever natural causes the manna may have had—and such need not be ruled out by those who seek to honor God's miraculous provision for his people (cf. Ex 14:16,21,31)—the Bible stresses the fact that merely natural causes do not suffice by way of explanation. The regularity, periodicity, and abundance of the manna cannot be explained on any but miraculous grounds. The Israelites were to gather it for one day at a time. Anything collected above that measure was subject to spoiling (16:20). Only the sabbath day was an exception to that rule. Manna was no longer provided after Israel entered Canaan (Jos 5:12). When Israel craved other food besides manna the people were punished with an excess of quail (Nm 11:4–6,18–20). In poetic literature it was called "the grain of heaven" (Ps 78:24; cf. 105:40), and "the bread of angels" (78:25).

The manna served the purpose of teaching Israel complete dependence on the Lord of the covenant (Dt 8:3). By means of this heavenly provision the Lord sought to "test" and to "humble" his people, in order to teach them that life in the full, biblical sense (cf. Gn 2:7b) is obtained when man lives by everything (every word) that proceeds from God's mouth (Dt 8:3,16). Jesus applied this word in its ultimate sense when refusing to yield to the devil's temptation (Mt 4:4; Lk 4:4). Jesus also pointed to himself as the true manna, the bread from heaven, which, when eaten, would nourish man unto life everlasting (cf. Jn 6:25–59 *passim*; esp. 30–35).

A gold pot of manna was preserved in the sanctuary (Ex 16:32–34) in remembrance of the food of the desert journey. Several rabbinic passages speak of the restoration of that pot of manna on the advent of the Messiah. In the NT, the church of Pergamum received the promise that he who overcomes will be given some of the "hidden manna." This is best understood as spoken of the manna in the sense in which Christ understood it in John 6 (cf. Ps 105:40). The hidden manna probably stands for the spiritual gifts to be given to the church triumphant as it enjoys the most intimate communion with Christ.

See WILDERNESS WANDERINGS; PLANTS (ASH).

Manoah. Danite from Zorah whose wife was barren. Through encounters with the angel of the Lord, the couple learned that God was about to give them a son who would judge the Philistines and deliver Israel from its oppression. Manoah later fathered Samson, who fulfilled these promises (Jgs 13; 16:31).

Man of Lawlessness, Man of Sin. Expression used by the apostle Paul of the antichrist in 2 Thessalonians 2:3.

See ANTICHRIST.

Maoch. Father of Achish, the Philistine king of Gath. David sought refuge with this king in order to escape Saul's plots to kill him (1 Sm 27:2).

See MAACAH, MAACHAH (PERSON) #3.

Maon (Place). Chief town in the hill country of Judah (Jos 15:55), about nine miles south of Hebron. David and his men hid in this area while fleeing from Saul (1 Sm 23:24,25), and David's wife Abigail was from this town (25:2,3). It has been identified with modern Tell Ma'in, where pottery was found dating from the time of David.

See MEUNIM, MEUNITE.

Maon, Maonite (Person). Son of Shammai, and Bethzur's father (1 Chr 2:45). He was either the founding father of the people of Bethzur and/or the founder of the city. His descendants are perhaps the Maonites of Judges 10:12.

Mara. Name, meaning "bitter," which Naomi gave to herself when she returned as a widow to Judah from Moab (Ru 1:20).

See NAOMI.

Marah. Spring of water in the wilderness of Etham, the first camping place of the Israelites after crossing the Reed Sea (Ex 15:23; Nm 33:8,9). The accepted identification is with 'Ain Hawarah, a pool of bitter water on the eastern coastal plain of the Gulf of Suez, about 44 miles southeast of Suez, and about 5 miles northwest of 'Ain Gharandel, south of Wadi Amarah (which may preserve an echo of the ancient name).

See WILDERNESS WANDERINGS.

Maralah. KJV rendering of Mareal, a site on Zebulun's western border, in Joshua 19:11.

See MAREAL.

Maranatha. Aramaic expression used by Paul in 1 Corinthians 16:22, meaning either "Our Lord, come!" or "Our Lord has come."

The Linguistic Problem. Quite certainly the use of *maranatha* (cf. *amen* and *abba*) originated in the worship services of early Jewish Christians whose mother tongue was Aramaic. Since Paul wrote in the Greek language, he needed to transliterate (writing the Aramaic phrase with Greek letters), a process which sometimes creates ambiguities. In addition, words were normally not written separately in ancient documents, and because *maranatha* consists of two words, it can be analyzed in different ways.

Most scholars agree that the first word in the phrase is *maran* (or *marana*), meaning "Lord" or more probably "our Lord," and that the second word represents the Aramaic verb "to come." This verb, however, may be taken either as a prayer (imperative *tha* or *etha*, "come!") or as a statement (perfect tense *atha*, "has come"). Five different interpretations are then possible. If the words are considered as a prayer, Paul is praying for either Jesus' spiritual presence, with possible reference to the Lord's Supper, or Jesus' second coming. As a statement, the expression may refer to the incarnation; it may be translated "Our Lord is present," either with reference to the Lord's Supper or to Jesus' more general promise in Matthew 18:20; or it may be translated "Our Lord is coming" (the so-called "prophetic perfect," although some prominent Aramaic scholars argue that this is not really possible).

In support of rendering the expression as a statement is the fact that the Syriac (a form of Aramaic) version of Galatians translates the verb in the perfect tense; further, the early church fathers usually interpreted it the same way. A majority of scholars, however, believe that such an interpretation does not fit the context well. Further, if the phrase is understood as a prayer, it can be related to other passages (Phil 4:5b; 1 Pt 4:7a; esp. Rv 22:20b, which may be a translation of *maranatha*).

Theological Significance. *Paul's View of Jesus' Lordship.* Some scholars of a previous generation argued forcefully that the designation "Lord" was borrowed by Paul from contemporary Hellenistic religions. Paul's use of *maranatha*, however, suggests very strongly that at the earliest stage Christians in Palestine recognized the lordship of Christ.

The Anathema. The fact that *maranatha* occurs immediately after Paul's imprecatory curse (1 Cor 16:22) has led many to the view that the Aramaic expression is part of the curse itself. The KJV rendering ("let him be Anathema Maran-atha") leaves the impression that the two words form a unit, whereas *anathema* is a Greek word meaning "curse" and probably ends the sentence. It is nevertheless quite possible, some modern scholars believe, to relate *maranatha* very closely to the curse, since the prayer for Jesus to come in judgment reinforces the solemnity and reality of Paul's imprecation. Interestingly, a church council in the seventh century anathematizes dissidents with the words "anathema maranatha, let him be condemned at the Lord's coming."

The Lord's Supper. Without necessarily denying the relationship of *maranatha* to Paul's pronouncing a curse, other scholars prefer to emphasize its place in the celebration of the Lord's Supper. Although the context in 1 Corinthians 16 does not clearly suggest such a connection, Paul's discussion of the Eucharist in chapter 11 brings together the note of judgment and the theme of Christ's second coming (vv 26,27). Further, a 2nd-century Christian document, the *Didache*, contains in its description of the Lord's Supper a prayer which ends with the words: "Hosanna to the God of David. If any man is holy, let him come; if any man is not, let him repent. Maranatha. Amen" (10:6).

Marble. See MINERALS, METALS, AND PRECIOUS STONES.

Marcus. KJV alternate spelling of Mark (Col 4:10; Phlm 24; 1 Pt 5:13).

See MARK, JOHN.

Marduk. Supreme Babylonian deity, worshiped as the god of creation and destiny. Marduk (also called Bel) was originally the local city god of Babylon; however, as Babylon increased in power, Marduk achieved preeminence over the whole Mesopotamian pantheon of deities. His rise to supremacy is told in the creation epic Enuma elish, where Marduk is credited with defeating Tiamat, primeval chaos; he then created the heavens and the earth. Zarpanit (Sarpanit) was Marduk's consort and the temple Esagila at Babylon was erected for them. Jeremiah foretold that Marduk would be put to shame for his inability to keep Babylon from destruction (Jer 50:2, NIV, ASV; RSV, KJV Merodach, the Hebrew pronunciation of Marduk).

See BABYLON, BABYLONIA.

Mareal. Town defining part of the western border of the land allotted to Zebulun's tribe for an inheritance. It was positioned between Sarid and Dabbesheth (Jos 19:11, KJV Maralah). Its location is uncertain.

Mareshah (Person). 1. Caleb's firstborn son and the father of Hebron (1 Chr 2:42; based on the Greek text). He is alternately called Mesha in the Hebrew text (RSV mg).

See MESHA (PERSON) #2.

2. Perhaps a Judahite son of Laadah (1 Chr 4:21).

Mareshah (Place). City (Greek, Marisa; Josephus, Marissa) on the road from the coastal plain of Judah toward Hebron and Jerusalem. Remains of Jewish pottery indicate occupation from at least 800 BC. The site is now called Tel es Sandahanna.

At Israel's occupation of Canaan, Mareshah was allotted by Joshua to Judah (Jos 15:44). Later, at the division of the kingdom, Rehoboam fortified it as a protective outpost covering Jerusalem from the southwest, from which many invaders were to approach (2 Chr 11:8). Zerah the Ethiopian, with "a million men and three hundred chariots," penetrated as far as Mareshah and was defeated there by Asa (14:9). In the following reign, that of Jehoshaphat, the prophet Eliezer, born at Mareshah, foretold the destruction of the proud fleet the king had built (20:37).

The prophet Micah, who was born at Moresheth-gath (no longer identified with Mareshah, but on modern biblical maps only 4.5 miles to the north), uttered a moving elegy upon the fate of the regions he knew from boyhood as the Assyrians approached (whether under Sennacherib, 701 BC, or Sargon, 711 BC). Punning upon each familiar place name, he warned Mareshah of a coming "possessor" (Mi 1:15).

Excavation confirms the existence, during Greek rule, of a city on Hellenistic lines, and cave tombs nearby show wall paintings and epitaphs indicating Hellenist and Sidonian influence during the 3rd century BC.

By the time of the Maccabean revolt against Hellenization (167–164 BC), Mareshah was apparently an Edomite stronghold (1 Mc 5:65,66) and the scene of a great Maccabean victory (2 Mc 12:32–38). When at the beginning of the reign of Herod the Great (40 BC), the Parthians, a powerful faction in Persia, overran Syria and Palestine, Mareshah was destroyed (See Josephus *Antiq.* 12.8.6; 14.12.9; 13.9).

Mari. Influential city-state, located in eastern Syria, which became important in the early 2nd millennium BC. It seems to have been settled by Semitic nomads, who adopted the values of city dwellers and progressed so far as to adapt cuneiform to their own Akkadian language.

The importance of this cosmopolitan city, which was an outpost of Sumerian civilization, is highlighted by the fact that it became the capital of an empire extending over a great part of northern Mesopotamia, about 22 miles along the Euphrates River.

Archaeological excavations at Mari yielded a monumental discovery: archives containing over 20,000 documents. These records virtually

Statues of deities from Mari.

rewrite the history of western Asia. In addition to the tablets, a well-preserved palace was also unearthed. Original mural paintings were still intact, as well as some kitchen and bath installations. These artifacts and tablets shed a great deal of light on life during the period from 1810 to 1760 BC.

As one viewed Mari from a distance, a great defensive wall was seen which encircled the city, protecting it from invading forces. One prominent structure rose portentously above the town, probably to an approximate height of 150 feet. This was the ziggurat, a temple tower built in a lofty pyramidal structure with successive stages. One ascended its heights by means of outside staircases, which led to the shrine at the top. There were smaller temples at its base.

Not far away, the royal palace commanded about six acres of land. The palace was constructed of extremely thick walls made of brick covered with clay, rising to a height of 16 feet. An elaborate drainage system was also discovered which effectively carried away rainwater through its bitumen-lined clay pipes, some 30 feet underground. The palace at Mari contained nearly 300 rooms. It was not only the royal residence, but also the center of business, diplomatic services, and military leadership. It even had room to store merchants' goods and military equipment, such as battering-rams and siege towers. The royal court enjoyed such foods as fish, meat, four varieties of

bread, cucumbers, peas, beans, garlic, dates, grapes, and figs. Beverages were beer and wine.

The religious observances involved sacrifices and temple prostitution, which was common in the ancient Near East. In Mari the king had diviners who gave omens for the future by examining the internal organs of sacrificed sheep. One correspondent said: "In the city of Sagaratim, at the monthly sacrifice and my lord's sacrifice, I examined the omens. The left side of the 'finger' was split, the middle 'finger' of the lungs was over to the left. It is a sign of fame. Let my lord be happy." These omens were of definite importance to the kings as affairs of state depended upon the direction of the gods.

The clay tablets of the archives reveal a great deal about the everyday life of the people. Some of the records are bilingual, some literary, but most deal with a period between Jahdun-Lim of Hana, the founder of Mari, to the decline under Zimri-Lim, his son. The city was taken over by Shamshi-Adad, just after the death of Jahdun-Lim. Shamshi-Adad was an Amorite prince, who along with his family has been expelled from their tiny kingdom by Mari. He was committed to revenge and by sheer determination ascended the throne of Assyria in 1814 BC. Whether by Shamshi-Adad's instigation or simple revolt, Jahdun-Lim was killed by his own servants. It was then that Shamshi-Adad made his move. He installed his son Jasmah-Adad as viceroy over Mari, avenging the earlier inequity. Jasmah-Adad—sometimes spelled Yasmah-Adad or Iasmah-Adad—was not all that his father had envisioned. He appeared to lack the strength and determination which had driven his father to power. One of the personal documents discovered in the city chides Jasmah-Adad: "While your brother has won a victory here, you remain there, reclining among women." He is described even more closely by another correspondent: "You remain a child, there is no beard on your chin, and even now, in the ripeness of age, you have not built up a house." It was in this manner that Shamshi-Adad held the reins tightly over his son in the vast Assyrian Empire, governing nearly all of northern Mesopotamia and holding the Tigris and the Euphrates Rivers. Shamshi-Adad was succeeded by his stronger son, Ishme-Dagan, who assured his brother in Mari that his kingdom was secure. The lone surviving prince of Mari, Zimri-Lim, the son of Jahdun-Lim, ousted Jasmah-Adad, however, and began a long reign which ended when Hammurabi pillaged the city.

The recovered information at Mari reveals that the king held court every day, listening to officials and ambassadors presenting affairs of state. He also was called upon to settle certain serious legal disputes. The state religion demanded the daily participation of the king, who visited the temples, officiated at rituals, sacrificed animals, reported to the gods, attended religious feasts, and who was sometimes considered divine. The king also was responsible for regulating the calendar, which necessitated an extra month every three years.

The commercial and economic records indicate that there were metal workers, weavers, fullers, gem cutters, jewellers, painters, perfume makers, boatmen, carpenters; leather workers, fishermen, potters, and masons. Payment for services rendered was largely made in goods, though sometimes in gold or silver. Such commodity payments were corn, wool, clothing, wine, or oil.

See INSCRIPTIONS.

Mariner. *See* TRADES AND OCCUPATIONS (SAILOR).

Marjoram. Small mint growing as high as three feet tall. It was perhaps the "hyssop" of the OT.

See PLANTS (HYSSOP).

Mark, Gospel of. Second book of the NT, probably written by John Mark of Jerusalem some time between AD 60 and 68.

Distinctives. A number of characteristics of Mark set it apart from the other Gospels. For example, a word usually translated "immediately" occurs more than 40 times in Mark and only a dozen times in the rest of the NT. While this feature could be interpreted as a simple "mannerism," consonant with Mark's unpretentious, colloquial style, it certainly adds to the rapid flow of his narrative, which, dwelling more on Jesus' activity than on his discourses (in contrast to Matthew and Luke), shifts from scene to scene with hardly a pause. Since the Gospel is also quite brief (Luke is nearly twice as long), one may wonder whether the author intended for it to be read at a sitting; even if read aloud, this would only take about one and a half hours. At any rate, there can be little doubt that the work conveys a sense of urgency.

Other characteristics, however, prove more significant. Someone unfamiliar with the story of Jesus who happened to read Mark for the first time would no doubt be taken back by its rather abrupt beginning. After a brief clause which stands as a sort of title (1:1), Mark moves on to describe in brief and enigmatic terms the ministry of John the Baptist. Then he introduces Jesus as coming from Nazareth without telling us anything whatever of his earlier life. Furthermore, over one third of the book (including the so-called passion narrative) is devoted to Jesus' last week. These and other factors lend to the work a note of mystery, accentuated by the fact that at various points Mark calls attention to the fear or amazement gripping those who came in contact with Jesus (2:12; 4:41; 5:15,33,42; 6:51; 9:6; and several other passages, esp. the strange words of 10:32). In addition, if one assumes that the Gospel originally ended with 16:8, Mark wished to leave his readers with the same sense of awe that the disciples experienced at Jesus' resurrection.

But how does one account for this fear and amazement? Mark's clear answer is that Jesus, though truly a man, is also divine. Mark underscores, even more than the other Gospels, the humanity of our Lord by calling attention, for example, to his emotions (1:41; 3:5; 8:12; 10:14). His chief emphasis, however, is on the Lord's deity. Indeed, Mark introduces his book by referring to Jesus as "the Son of God" (a phrase omitted in some manuscripts, however), a position that is recognized both by the demons (3:11; 5:7) and by God himself (9:7). What may well be the true climax of the Gospel occurs at 15:39, where Mark writes that a Gentile, a Roman centurion, upon hearing Jesus' death cry exclaimed, "Truly this man was the Son of God!"

Structure. The author organized his Gospel according to a simple plan. The first eight chapters summarize the nature of Christ's public ministry by alternating stories that show his growing popularity with stories that stress the disapproval of the Jewish leaders. This first half of the book, however, while indicating some of the tensions created by Jesus' coming, leave the impression of success and general optimism. A significant shift then strikes the reader toward the end of chapter 8, particularly beginning with verse 31. At Caesarea Philippi, Peter has just confessed that Jesus is the Messiah, and now for the first time Jesus reveals that as Messiah he must die. The disciples become perplexed and discouraged and their pessimism mounts as this thought is brought home to them repeatedly (9:9,31; 10:32–34; 14:17–25). In the end they desert their master (v 50).

Interestingly, this pessimistic note is anticipated in the earlier part of the Gospel at three points: 3:6 (Jesus' enemies plot his death); 6:6a (faithlessness in Nazareth); and 8:21 (lack of understanding in the disciples). Some scholars suggest that Mark used these three verses to indicate the first three divisions of his book. In addition, other scholars note that two healings of blind men (8:22–26; 10:46–52) seem to provide the opening and the conclusion of a section that emphasizes the spiritual blindness of the disciples. One more structural clue is 14:1, which clearly marks out the final section of the Gospel.

Content. Using all of this evidence, one can construct an outline that brings out the development of Mark's narrative by calling attention to six major divisions within its two-fold structure.

> Introduction (1:1–13)
> *Part One: Popularity and Opposition*
> (1) Jesus' authority and the Pharisees' enmity (1:14–3:6)
> (2) The people's response (3:7–6:6a)
> (3) The disciples' misunderstanding (6:6b–8:21)
> *Part Two: Darkness and Death*
> (4) The Messiah's mission and the disciples' blindness (8:22–10:52)
> (5) Final ministry (11:1–13:37)
> (6) The passion narrative (14:1–15:47)
> Conclusion (16:1–8)

Although one can hardly claim that this outline corresponds exactly to the author's original plan (Mark may not have consciously worked out a detailed outline), the sixfold division provides a useful starting point for an interpretive summary of the contents.

Jesus' Authority and the Pharisees' Enmity (1:14–3:6). Immediately after the introductory portion (1:1–13), which describes John the Baptist's ministry as well as Jesus' baptism and temptation, Mark opens the body of the work with a summary statement (vv 14, 15). In these two verses he seems to suggest that Jesus' public ministry, characterized by the proclamation that God's kingdom is about to be inaugurated, was occasioned by John's imprisonment. This is followed by the call of the first disciples (vv 16–20) and then by a complex of stories (vv 21–38), all of which report incidents that took place in Capernaum, apparently within a 24-hour period: synagogue instruction followed by the healing of a demoniac; the healing of Peter's mother-in-law; numerous other healings in the evening; prayer in a lonely place. The statement that Jesus proceeded to expand his ministry throughout the province of Galilee (v 39) is followed by the story of a leper's cure (vv 40–45). Next are found a very important group of incidents (2:1–3:6), all of them focusing on Jesus' conflicts with Jewish leaders: the healing and forgiveness of a paralytic; the call of Levi, whose dinner (attended by Jesus as well as by the hated tax-gatherers) occasioned some disputes, particularly on the issue of fasting; and two significant stories regarding proper behavior on the sabbath.

The People's Response (3:7–6:6a). Mark opens this second section as he opened the first: a summary statement (Jesus' healings by the lake, 3:7–12) followed by the official appointment of 12 apostles (vv 13–19). Then follows a section that focuses on the kinds of charges brought against Jesus by his own family and by the scribes (vv 20–22), leading to a response touching on Satan, on blasphemy against the Holy Spirit, and on what constitutes true membership in his family (vv 23–35). Most of chapter 4 (vv 1–34) is devoted to Jesus' parables of the kingdom—the sower, the seed growing secretly, the mustard seed—and includes statements on the nature and purpose of his teachings (vv 10–12,21–25,33,34). In the evening, Jesus and his disciples set out to cross the Sea of Galilee, leading to the stilling of the storm (4:35–41), the healing of the Gerasene demoniac on the other side of the lake (5:1–20), and, on their return to Capernaum, the healing of a hemorrhaging woman and the raising of Jairus's daughter (vv 21–43). The section concludes with Jesus' visit to his hometown, Nazareth, and the rejection he suffered there (6:1–6a).

The Disciples' Misunderstanding (6:6b–8:21). The third section begins with two introductory passages: the sending out of the 12 (6:6b–13) and the story of John the Baptist's death (vv 14–29). When the disciples return, Jesus determines to seek some rest, but the crowds follow them; Jesus then teaches and feeds the five thousand (vv 30–44) and, after crossing the lake (vv 45–52 which includes Jesus' walk over the water), he performs numerous cures in and around Gennesaret (vv 53–56). Then follows a controversy with the Pharisees regarding the hand-washing ritual (7:1–8), and this incident leads to Christ's assertion of the authority of God's word over human tradition (vv 9–13) and to some general instructions on true purity (vv 14–23). The next several stories describe Jesus' withdrawal from Galilee, first to Tyre, where a gentile woman's daughter is healed (vv 24–30), then to Decapolis, where he cures a deaf-mute (vv 31–37) and feeds a crowd of four thousand (8:1–10). The demand of the Pharisees for a sign (vv 11,12) leads to Jesus' warning against the "leaven" of the Pharisees, a statement misunderstood by the disciples (vv 13–21).

The Messiah's Mission and the Disciples' Blindness (8:22–10:52). Still away from Galilee, but now in the nearby town of Bethsaida, Jesus heals a blind man (8:22–26). He then leads his disciples north toward Caesarea Philippi, which sets the stage for Peter's confession (vv 27–30). This recognition on the part of the disciples (of whom Peter is in effect a representative) leads Jesus to prophesy his death, but Peter's refusal to accept the prophecy calls forth a rebuke and instruction on discipleship (vv 31–38). The failure of the disciples to understand the necessity of Christ's death provides the background for the transfiguration (9:1–8), which assures Peter, John, and James that God's kingdom will indeed come (note v 1); further, the Father himself enjoins them to believe Jesus' prophecy (v 7). After some words about the resurrection and about the coming of Elijah (vv 9–13), Mark relates the healing of a demoniac boy (vv 14–29). Back in Galilee, a second prophecy of Jesus' death (vv 30–32) is followed, sadly, by a trivial discussion among the disciples as to who is the greatest (vv 33–37). Appropriately, one finds some further instructions concerning discipleship (vv 38–50). Mark next writes that Jesus leaves Galilee for the last time and begins his journey toward the south. During this journey Jesus delivers teachings on divorce and on the spiritual privileges of children (10:1–16), then meets the rich young ruler (vv 17–22), an incident that leads to further words on discipleship (vv 23–31). A third prophecy of Jesus' death (vv 32–34) is again followed by selfish behavior on the part of the disciples, in this case an ambitious request from James and John (vv 35–40). The incident produces indignation among the rest of the disciples, thus necessitating another rebuke from their master, who himself came to serve and to die (vv 41–45). The section ends as it began by reporting the cure of a blind man, this time Bartimaeus of Jericho (vv 46–52).

Final Ministry (11:1–13:37). This section seems naturally to divide into three balanced subsections. The first one (11:1–26) includes three events: the triumphal entry, the withering of the fig tree, and the cleansing of the temple. The second subsection (v 27–12:44) is particularly important, for here is found Jesus' final series of controversies with the Jewish leaders. The topics covered are: the source of Jesus' authority (11:27–33), the parable of the wicked husbandmen (12:1–12), the legiti-

macy of Caesar's tax (vv 13–17), the Sadducees' denial of resurrection (vv 18–27), the chief commandment (vv 28–34), and the question regarding David's son (vv 35–37). This subsection ends with a warning against the scribes and with the story of the widow's mite (vv 38–44). The third subsection (ch 13) is devoted completely to the Mt Olive discourse, with its prophecies of destruction (vv 1,2), calamities (vv 3–8), persecutions (vv 9–20), deceivers (vv 21–23), and final vindication (vv 24–27). The discourse ends with various admonitions to keep alert (vv 28–37).

The Passion Narrative (14:1–15:47). This final section, which is introduced by a report of the priests' plot (14:1,2), may be divided into two subsections. The first one relates the events leading up to Jesus' trial (vv 3–52). They include the anointing of Jesus (vv 3–9), Judas' betrayal (vv 10,11), the incidents connected with the last supper (vv 12–31), the scene at Gethsemane (vv 32–42), and the arrest (vv 43–52). The second subsection relates Jesus' trial before the Jews (vv 53–65), Peter's denials (vv 66–72), the trial before Pilate (15:1–15), the crucifixion (vv 16–41), and the burial (vv 42–47).

The Gospel concludes somewhat mysteriously but no less triumphantly with the news that Jesus has risen from the dead (16:1–8). The earliest surviving Greek manuscripts, usually regarded as the most reliable, end at verse 8; the majority of manuscripts, however, include an additional 12 verses that report Jesus' appearances to his disciples.

History of Interpretation. *The Earliest Traditions.* Our most ancient testimony comes from Papias (c. 60–c. 130), author of several expositions of Jesus' teachings, in which he reports various traditions from "the Elder John" (possibly to be identified with the apostle John, although this is by no means certain). At one point Papias states: "The Elder used to say this also: 'Mark became Peter's interpreter and wrote down accurately, though not in order, all that [Peter] remembered concerning the things both said and done by the Lord.' " (This quotation was preserved by the 4th-century writer Eusebius of Caesarea in his *Ecclesiastical History,* 3.39.15). One need not doubt the basic reliability of this statement: Mark, almost surely to be identified with the John Mark of Acts 12:12 (see also 1 Pt 5:13), was a disciple of Peter, and the second Gospel owes its existence, at least in part, to the apostle's reminiscences. It does not follow, however, that one has adequately characterized Mark's work if that is all one says. For instance, Papias' qualification, "though not in order," indicates that Mark did not intend to write a chronological biography. Furthermore,

Hay field on the north shore of the Sea of Galilee, a region that was the site of much of Jesus' ministry.

Papias goes on to comment (according to one interpretation of his ambiguous words) that Mark (or Peter?) adapted the material to the teaching situation and that, therefore, Mark is absolved from any (implied) charges of inaccuracy. It appears that from the earliest times Christians appealed to the purposes and circumstances of Mark's writing in order to account for difficulties in harmonizing the material found in the various Gospels.

Other statements from Christian writers in the 2nd, 3rd, and 4th centuries seem dependent on Papias' testimony, but some additional data they provide may possess independent value. For example, a fairly early document (date uncertain) known as the Anti-Marcionite Prologue asserts that Mark wrote his Gospel somewhere in Italy after Peter's death (in the mid-6os), and this testimony is considered reliable by many scholars. Still, the possibility that Mark composed his work before Peter's martyrdom cannot be ruled out completely.

Generally speaking, it may be said that early writers tended to emphasize the role played by Peter and to ignore the likelihood that Mark may have used additional sources.

16 Centuries of Obscurity. In view of the evidence that Mark recorded the witness of Jesus' most prominent apostle, one might assume that his Gospel would have proved especially popular in the church. The fact is, Christians appear to have paid very little attention to this book. According to H. B. Swete the early fathers had difficulties in forming a clear assessment regarding the distinctive value of Mark's work. Moreover, while numerous commentaries were written during the first five centuries on the other Gospels, no one wrote an exposition of Mark during that period.

It is not difficult, however, to account for this situation. Apart from a detailed comparison of the synoptic Gospels (Matthew, Mark, Luke), any reader would normally gather that *all* of the material in Mark is also found in the other two. Why not then use these two (particularly Matthew, which records fully the Sermon on the Mount), seeing that they give us not only Mark's stories but also a great deal more of Jesus' teachings? The influential theologian Augustine (354–430), not noticing that where Matthew and Mark report the same stories Mark contains the *fuller* account, suggested that Mark simply abbreviated the work of Matthew (who, being an apostle, was by implication more important). Although this conclusion in effect conflicted with the evidence that Mark's material itself went back to another apostle (Peter), Augustine's view was accepted tacitly. As a result, throughout the Middle Ages and into the modern period, Mark continued to occupy a secondary position in the Christian church, an attitude that contrasts sharply with the great importance that contemporary scholars attach to the second Gospel.

It is worthwhile taking note of the providential inclusion of Mark in the Christian canon. The early Christians, in view of their concerns, such as their stress on catechesis by means of the Sermon on the Mount, did not find Mark particularly attractive. Conceivably, they might have reasoned that it was unnecessary to include Mark in their Bible, since all its material could already be found in the other Gospels (besides, the possibility of having *three* Gospels might have attracted those interested in numerical symbolism). But in fact no orthodox Christian ever disputed the place of Mark in the NT, doubtless because of its association with Peter. Ironically, the kinds of historical and exegetical concerns that presently characterize Christians (who are no longer close to the original events) lend Mark a prominence that is hard to overestimate. Thus what may have seemed relatively useless, at least in practice, to the early chuch has become of fundamental importance for us. How do we account for this change?

The 19th Century: Markan Priority. In an article published in 1835, Karl Lachmann (1793–1851) argued that while the synoptic Gospels may appear to be quite different, a comparison of Mark with the other two shows how similar they really are; in fact, he concluded, the order of Mark's narrative is presupposed by Matthew and Luke. From this observation it was only a small step to the view that the Gospel of Mark was the first one to be written and, even more important, that it was actually used by Matthew and Luke. Some contemporary scholars argue that the data can be interpreted differently, but Markan priority is still generally assumed. Furthermore, although researchers have tried to find literary antecedents to the Gospel form, it appears that Mark's work was an innovation—he created a new literary genre, no mean feat for an unpretentious writer.

It is essential to appreciate that this theory was born in the midst of severe attacks against the reliability of the Gospel tradition, with radical scholars doubting that we knew very much at all about the "Jesus of history." Now, however, the possibility—regarded as a practical certainty by the end of the century—that Mark served as the basis for Matthew and Luke catapulted the second Gospel into the arena of research as Christianity's most basic historical document. Interestingly, though, it was not the conservatives (many of whom continued to support Matthean priority), but the early liberals, who became excited about the historical value of Mark: Mark's outline served as the basis for a nonsupernatural, psychological view of Jesus. It soon became clear, however, that the liberal interpretation of Mark was in effect a distortion of that Gospel.

The 20th Century: Renewed Skepticism. The failure of 19th-century, nonevangelical scholarship to demonstrate who the historical Jesus really was had an unfortunate effect. Without abandoning the notion of Markan priority, 20th-century scholars tried to show that even Mark cannot be taken seriously as a historical work. Particularly influential was Wilhelm Wrede (1859–1906), who in 1901 published a work stressing the significance of the so-called "messianic secret" for the composition of the Gospel of Mark. According to Wrede, the early Christians were troubled by the fact that Jesus was not recognized as Messiah during his public ministry. Wrede, who assumed that Jesus himself had no messianic consciousness, argued that Mark invented the following explanation: people failed to recognize that Jesus was the Messiah before his resurrection for the simple reason that he commanded his followers not to publicize that fact. Although this particular interpretation was not generally accepted, Wrede's work persuaded many scholars, especially in Germany, that Mark could no longer be interpreted as a straightforward historical account.

Against this background, German scholarship developed a method of gospel research known as form criticism, according to which attention is focused on small, individual portions (*pericopae*, singular *pericope*) of the narrative. Form critics assume that the Gospel stories and sayings took their *form* as they were transmitted by word of mouth in the first decades of Christianity and that they must have been *adapted* to the needs and circumstances of the time. The task of form criticism, therefore, consists in determining the *development* of each pericope before it found its place in the Gospels. This method can be used with profit even by scholars who have high regard for Mark's historicity. Unfortunately, as the method was developed in the 1920s, the emphasis fell on the arbitrariness with which these pericopae were brought together in the Gospels; in other words, the historical trustworthiness of Mark's outline was thought to be nil. Some radical form critics, particularly Rudolf Bultmann (1884–1976), argued that not only the chronological framework, but the individual stories themselves, were unreliable—the Gospels, he felt, tell more about the view of the early Christians than about what Jesus himself said and did.

Contemporary Scholarship: Mark's Theology. In some respects, form criticism (and broader questions regarding Mark's possible sources) continues to inform the work of most NT scholars. Since the early 1950s, however, the inadequacies of form criticism, when used exclusively, have become increasingly clear. An excessive attention to the individual stories, torn from their literary context, implies that the Gospel writers were dull collectors of tradition. NT scholarship, therefore, has turned its attention to the Gospels as literary compositions, with a view to determining the theological purpose of their authors. This new approach, already anticipated by Wrede and others, has become known as redaction criticism.

A pioneering figure in the application of redaction criticism to the Gospel of Mark is Willi Marxsen. In a work published in 1956 (*Mark the Evangelist*) he argued that some impulse or theological motive must have led Mark to bring together in a coherent fashion the independent units of tradition which had been isolated by form criticism (clearly, redaction critics do not reject form criticism—they assume it and build on it). Marxsen's own formulation of Markan theology has not gained wide assent, but he set the direction of subsequent study. Unfortunately, Marxsen and the leading redaction critics usually take for granted that the presence of theological motives in the Gospel authors discredits the historical worth of their writings. The assumption is invalid. Already in 1944 the evangelical scholar Ned B. Stonehouse had shown that Mark's Gospel cannot be regarded as a historical biography in the modern sense, for the author was primarily an evangelist, proclaiming and interpreting a message. Nevertheless, Stonehouse maintained that Mark's theology *included* the truth of his history, so that "his record cannot be shown to be unhistorical merely by pointing to his presupposition of faith."

Much discussion is going on at present regarding various facets of Mark's message. Why does Mark seem to emphasize the miracle stories? Do these stories reflect Mark's own Christology or is he using them to oppose heretics who overemphasize them? What is the connection between Mark's message and Paul's distinctive theology? And what about the sociological perspective, which may help to illumine the community context giving rise to the Gospel? While no definitive solutions are yet forthcoming, the debate has contributed valuable insights and thus advanced our understanding of the second Gospel.

Author, Date, Provenance. Although the Bible does not tell us who wrote the second Gospel, nor when and where, interpretation of this (or any) book depends to a large extent on one's ability to place it in its proper historical context.

How then does one ascertain these matters? Two kinds of evidence are available, external and internal. External evidence consists of explicit information preserved in ancient documents regarding Mark's Gospel; internal evidence refers to those characteristics of the Gospel itself from which historical information may be deduced. For obvious reasons external evidence is regarded as more "objective" than internal evidence; in particular, the latter requires considerable interpretation. The distinction, however, must not be pressed. On the one hand, the "subjective" factor also enters in when one seeks to evaluate such external evidence as Papias' testimony. On the other hand, a theory based on internal evidence may conceivably account for all the data so persuasively as to outweigh the value of external information. Disagreements among scholars depend precisely on how much relative weight they are willing to give to these two types of data.

An example will help to clarify this methodological issue. A recent and distinguished interpreter, Howard C. Kee, proposes that Mark's Gospel was produced by an apocalyptic community in southern Syria shortly before the destruction of Jerusalem in AD 70. Admittedly, there is no shred of external evidence supporting that theory, yet Kee is persuaded that his interpretation of Mark's contents and characteristics compels ignoring Papias' testimony.

Now it is certainly possible that Kee's view may stand the test of time and win over the world of scholarship. More often than not, however, theories based purely on internal data fail to establish themselves. Indeed, the fact that so many differing views have been proposed regarding Mark suggests that the information drawn from within the Gospel is simply too ambiguous to determine the facts. It therefore seems more reasonable to consider seriously what external evidence exists. If the internal evidence conflicts with it, perhaps ignorance should simply be admitted. However, if the internal evidence supports, or at least is not inconsistent with, Papias' testimony, the latter may be confidently asserted, since it does not have the earmarks of fabrication (e.g., a false tradition probably would have assigned the authorship of the Gospel to a better-known figure).

To begin with, Papias says nothing specific about *when* the Gospel was written. A small minority of scholars date Mark shortly after AD 70. Another minority suggest a date in the 40s on the basis of a papyrus fragment recently discovered in Qumran. (According to José O'Callaghan, the fragment, which has been dated about AD 50, should be identified as Mark 6:52-53. Unfortunately, this fragment contains only 20 letters, nearly half of which cannot be read clearly, so that most scholars are hesitant to accept his identification.) An impressive majority of scholars date Mark in the 60s, with conservatives usually preferring the early years of the decade. Why this preference? If the theory of Markan priority is accepted, then clearly Mark was written before Luke; and since Luke is normally dated by conservatives about AD 62, Mark can be no later than AD 60 or 61. This line of argument, though strong, is not decisive. In the first place, Luke cannot be dated with complete certainty. Second, the view that Matthew and Luke used Mark, while still the working assumption of most scholars, is only a hypothesis, and one that is vigorously opposed by some writers. Third, a tradition going back to the 2nd century (see above) asserts that Mark wrote his Gospel *after* Peter's death, no earlier than AD 64. Fourth, one persuasive view regarding the occasion of this Gospel (see next section) assumes that the Neronian persecution (AD 64) had begun. (According to a different view of the occasion, Mark was written after the beginning of the Jewish revolt in AD 66.) Therefore, while a date in the early 60s remains possible, it does not require commital.

With regard to the authorship of the second Gospel, there seems to be no compelling reason to deny Papias' report that Mark (no doubt the John Mark of Acts 12:12) took down Peter's reminiscences and that these became the basis of his work. Some scholars argue that the Gospel contains geographical inaccuracies (e.g., we have no evidence of a region called Dalmanutha, Mk 8:10) and that a native of Jerusalem such as Mark would have been more reliable in his information. However, the topographical problems in Mark, though real, need not be interpreted as inaccuracies (present ignorance of a place named Dalmanutha is hardly conclusive proof that it did not exist). Furthermore, in other respects (e.g., 14:54,66, 68) the Gospel reveals an impressive knowledge of local details. Many writers also point out bits of information that support a Petrine background, such as the healing of Peter's mother-in-law (1:30,31). In short, the internal evidence, while falling short of proof, does not at all undermine the tradition preserved by Papias. A generation ago, the trustworthiness of Papias' testimony was almost universally accepted. This situation has changed somewhat, but even those scholars who adopt a skeptical attitude toward this tradition concede that it *may* be true.

As attention turns to the provenance of the Gospel, the task becomes more difficult. Tradition going back to the 2nd century asserts what may be already implied by Papias, namely, that Mark wrote his Gospel in Rome. Although some scholars have suggested other possibilities, such as Galilee and Antioch, these have not proved satisfactory. Mark did spend some time in Rome; and some characteristics in the Gospel (such as Latinisms in the Greek and the explanation of Jewish customs, as in 7;3,4), while proving nothing, are certainly consonant with a Roman origin. Furthermore, one persuasive view of the occasion which gave rise to the Gospel assumes a background of persecution in Rome.

Occasion, Purpose, Theology. From the point of view of interpretive method, nothing is more important than the task of providing a coherent picture of the Gospel of Mark *as a whole*. Although it may seem necessary first to solve detailed exegetical problems before attempting the general picture (and there is a measure of truth in that), the fact is that the parts of any book receive their meaning from their relation to the whole. This means that one must constantly hold these two perspectives in tension: one needs to interpret details in the light of the whole book and correct one's view of the whole in the light of the details. However, can one with any confidence determine what gave rise to this Gospel and what the author wished to accomplish?

It is perhaps necessary to point out that no one interpretation will ever account satisfactorily for all the facts; conversely, even the least persuasive interpretations probably contain at least some worthwhile insights. For example, the view was earlier alluded to in passing that Mark may be combatting a heretical sect which stressed the miracles of Jesus and viewed him purely as a divine wonder-worker. Although this view has not gained acceptance as originally formulated, a number of writers do see the Gospel as a theological corrective. Ralph Martin, who links Mark very closely with Paul, suggests that the evangelist is opposing some heretical groups who have distorted Paul's message by placing exclusive stress on Christ as a *heavenly* figure (cf. the views that Paul himself opposes in Colossians). Mark responds to these aberrations by emphasizing, in Martin's words "the paradox of Jesus' earthly life in which suffering and vindication form a two-beat rhythm." Even if one decides that this reconstruction, too, is rather speculative, one may nevertheless retain certain elements in it as valid.

Again, as noted earlier, Kee places emphasis on the apocalyptic background of Mark. Kee and others tie this element to the Jewish revolt of AD 66, but commitment to this particular historical connection is unnecessary to appreciate the great significance of Mark 13 (our Lord's apocalyptic discourse) for those original readers of the Gospel who may have been undergoing persecution.

Perhaps the most satisfactory reconstruction links this Gospel to the Neronian persecution in the mid-6os. Mark, for example, is the only Gospel which records that Jesus, after being driven to the wilderness, found himself in the company of wild animals (1:13). This detail according to William Lane "was filled with special significance for those called to enter the arena where they stood helpless in the presence of wild beasts." This interpretation, while not without difficulties, has the advantage of accounting for most of the available data. First, it is compatible with the strong tradition that assigns the origin of Mark's work to Rome. Second, Mark speaks distinctly to those suffering persecution by introducing them quickly to John's imprisonment and several other details. Third, related to this is Mark's emphasis on discipleship. Christians facing persecution must have been tempted to relax the standards (4:17,19). Fourth, perhaps it is not far-fetched to recall Ralph Martin's viewpoint and suggest that the persecutions may have left Christians wide open to a docetic understanding of Christ (i.e., an exclusive emphasis on Christ's deity, in the light of which the sufferings of his disciples might seem unnecessary). If so, Mark responds by stressing Jesus' humanity, as evinced particularly in his sufferings. Fifth, given this general situation, one can hardly doubt the significance of our Lord's apocalyptic message in chapter 13, intended to encourage the disciples in the midst of their trials by reminding them of the glory to follow. Finally, Mark's clear concern for the gentile mission fits in with the needs of pagan Rome. The suffering Christians cannot afford to forget the unbelieving society in which they live. In the light of this particular responsibility, Mark assures his readers of what even the Roman centurion began to recognize—surely Jesus *is* the Son of God (15:39).   MOISES SILVA

See MARK, JOHN; MARKAN HYPOTHESIS; REDACTION CRITICISM; SOURCE CRITICISM; SYNOPTIC GOSPELS; MATTHEW, GOSPEL OF; LUKE, GOSPEL OF; JESUS CHRIST, LIFE AND TEACHING OF.

Bibliography. J.A. Alexander, *The Gospel According to Mark;* W.C. Allen, *The Gospel According to Saint Mark;* H. Anderson, *The Gospel of Mark;* D.E. Hiebert, *Mark: A Portrait of the Servant;* E. Lohse, *Mark's Witness to Jesus Christ;* V. Taylor, *The Gospel According to St. Mark.*

Mark, John. Son of Mary, an apparently wealthy Christian, probably a widow, whose house was used by the Jerusalem church as a meeting place (Acts 12:12). The Roman name

Mark, used in addition to his Jewish name John, may indicate a Hellenistic background, as may also be suggested by the fact that his cousin Barnabas was a Cypriot who, along with Paul (Saul), supervised the Christian work among Hellenistic Jews in Antioch of Syria (see Col 4:10; Acts 11:19–25).

About the year 46 Barnabas and Paul, who had brought a charitable gift to needy Christians in Jerusalem, took Mark with them as they returned to Antioch (Acts 11:29,30; 12:25). Later, when the Antiochean church sent them off on a missionary journey, Mark became their assistant, a position that probably included teaching responsibilities (13:2–5). Without saying why, Luke reports that Mark soon abandoned the missionary party and returned to Jerusalem (v 13). The reason often given is that Mark's youth and inexperience were no match for the rigors of the journey, but Paul's adamant refusal to take him along on a second journey (15:36–40) suggests a more serious problem. Quite possibly, Mark had reservations about the wisdom of evangelizing Gentiles (such as the Cypriot proconsul, 13:12) without requiring some attachment to Judaism, a problem of conscience over which the early Jewish church continuously agonized (note 11:1–3; 15:5; Gal 2:11–14). After the Jerusalem Council (*c.* AD 49) decreed that gentile Christians need not be circumcised (Acts 15:22–29), Mark may have reconsidered his previous action and decided to cast his lot with Paul. But at this point the apostle may well have doubted the clarity and firmness of the young man's convictions.

Barnabas, who saw things differently, parted company with Paul and returned to Cyprus with Mark. We know nothing of Mark's activities in Cyprus, but approximately 10 years later he is in Rome reconciled to Paul (Col 4:10; Phlm 24; KJV Marcus, assuming that these letters were indeed written from Rome). Subsequently, it appears, he labored with Timothy in Asia Minor (2 Tm 4:11).

Of particular significance is Mark's relationship with the apostle Peter, for a very ancient tradition asserts that Mark was Peter's "interpreter" (perhaps secretary or assistant instructor) and that he wrote down the apostle's reminiscences of Christ. Although some moderns have questioned the accuracy of this report, there is nothing implausible about it. Mark was no doubt well-acquainted with Peter in Jerusalem (note Acts 12:12–17); further, when the apostle writes his first letter from "Babylon," that is Rome, he refers to Mark, who was with him, as his "son" (1 Pt 5:13, KJV Marcus). It is therefore very likely that John Mark was the author of the second Gospel, a document that goes back to Peter's personal witness.

Trees and ruins on Cyprus.

(Many writers believe that Mk 14:51,52 is the author's self-reference and "signature.")

Later, less reliable traditions report that Mark was nicknamed "Stump-fingered," was a founder of Christianity in Alexandria, suffered a martyr's death there, and that his remains were transferred to what is now the famous St Mark's Church in Venice.   MOISES SILVA

See MARK, GOSPEL OF; MARKAN HYPOTHESIS.

Markan Hypothesis. Theory that the Gospel of Mark was the first one to be written and that it (along with a collection of Jesus' sayings, now lost) became the source for the Gospels of Matthew and Luke.

The Gospel of Mark played a relatively unimportant role in the history of the Christian church until the year 1835, when Karl Lachmann (1793–1851) showed that the order of events in Matthew and Luke correspond only to those sections paralleled in Mark; to put it differently, when Matthew and Luke report material absent in Mark, their order does not correspond. Three years later C.H. Weisse

(1801–66) concluded that Mark's Gospel must have provided the chronological framework for the other two synoptic Gospels and that the "sayings material" common to these two (but absent in Mark) had its source in a no-longer extant document, usually designated Q.

The hypothesis did not gain a firm foothold, however, until the work of H.J. Holtzmann (1832–1910). In 1863 Holtzmann published a persuasive work which sought to demonstrate conclusively the priority of Mark. As a result, the second Gospel emerged from relative obscurity to a position of prime importance. The Markan Hypothesis, also known as the Two-Source Theory, has dominated Gospel research in the past century. Some contemporary scholars, however, maintain that the theory rests on fallacious arguments and propose either the priority of Matthew or some other solution. While most NT scholars have not abandoned the Markan hypothesis in principle, a measure of instability characterizes the present situation.

See Source Criticism.

Market, Marketplace.

Place for the buying and selling of goods in antiquity. Generally, the marketplaces of the ancient Near East would be much like the open air bazaars one can still see in any city throughout Israel, Greece, and Turkey.

The marketplace of NT times known as the *agora* was a place for buying and selling goods (Mk 7:4); a place for children to play (Mt 11:16; Lk 7:32); a place for idlers and for men seeking work (Mt 20:3); a place where public events including healings occurred (Mk 6:56); a place where greetings were exchanged (Mt 23:7; Lk

11:43); the center of public life (Acts 17:17) and debate; and a place where trials were held (16:19).

See City.

Mark of the Beast.

Phrase limited to the Book of Revelation; however, the use of the term for "mark" in Ezekiel (9:4–6) supplies the background for the Book of Revelation. In his vision Ezekiel saw the inhabitants of Jerusalem slain for their wickedness, except those upon whom God had put a mark on their foreheads. The mark was one of identification for the purpose of protection.

The usage in the Book of Revelation is quite similar. The idea begins in Revelation 7:3 (though the word does not occur here), where the 144,000 servants of God are sealed on their foreheads to protect them from the coming wrath of God. This sealing is referred to in Revelation 9:4, where it is noted that the demonic locusts of the fifth trumpet are not to harm those with the seal of God.

In Revelation 13 the specific phrase "the mark of the beast" is used. The context is John's vision of the two beasts. The one from the sea (13:1–10) symbolizes the antichrist with political power over the inhabitants of the earth. The beast from the earth (vv 11–18) symbolizes the antichrist's assistant, which is the religious leadership dedicated to securing universal worship of the antichrist. This false religious leader causes all to receive upon their right hand or their forehead the mark (of the antichrist), or the name (cf. 3:12), or the number of the name of the antichrist (13:16, 17). This mark of the beast is necessary for a person to engage in business or economic

Ruins in the agora (marketplace) at Corinth.

transactions involved in physical survival. Perhaps it serves more to identify them for martyrdom (vv 7–10). It stands in sharp contrast to the seal of God marking out the servants of God in chapter 7:1–8 (cf. 14:1). Thus mankind as depicted in this vision is divided into two classes—those belonging to Christ (God) and those belonging to the antichrist (Satan).

Revelation 13:18 is a challenge to the church to have wisdom and to recognize what that mark or number of the beast is. Two things are stated. First, it is of a man or refers to a man. Second, his number is 666.

The interpretation of this number has been discussed at length by biblical scholars without reaching a general consensus. Many think that it was a 1st-century cryptic (Hebrew) reference to Nero. In that context of preliminary fulfillment, it would have simply been an appeal for Christians to recognize the true nature of the godless Nero as having the character of antichrist and to refuse to give him their allegiance. Perhaps this identity indicates that the number or mark of the beast is an expression of one's allegiance to antichrist as expressed in the cult of emperor worship. Thus it would be this activity of worship and not a literal number on one's body that is intended.

When the prophecy is completely fulfilled by the antichrist, believers must be wise and refuse to give their loyalty to him through whatever form or test of allegiance this takes.

The importance of believers' steadfastness is shown in Revelation 14 where the faithful 144,000, with the name of Christ and God on their foreheads, are seen standing victoriously with the Lamb on Mt Zion. On the other hand, the angel warns that those who receive the mark of the beast and worship him will drink the cup of God's wrath (14:9–11). This steadfastness is spoken of as keeping the commandments of God and the faith of Jesus (v 12). A similar vision of those who overcome the beast is given in 15:2–4. Here they are pictured as standing before God singing the song of Moses and the song of the Lamb. Stress falls on their worship of God.

There are three further references in Revelation to the mark of the beast. When the first angel pours out the first bowl of wrath, this falls on those who have the mark of the beast and who worshiped his image (16:2). At the destruction of the beast and the false prophet, the latter is described as deceiving those who received the mark of the beast and worshiped his image (19:20). Finally, those who reign with Christ during the millennium are those who did not worship the beast or receive his mark (20:4).

In sum, the phrase "mark of the beast" or the number 666 is a way of referring to the identity of the followers of the antichrist in the Book of Revelation. Believers are warned not to become a part of those who are deceived, but rather to remain steadfast and faithful to the Lamb and to own his name upon their foreheads.   HOBERT K. FARRELL

See ANTICHRIST; BEAST.

Maroth. City in Palestine, mentioned only by Micah (Mi 1:12). It may be the same as the Maarath in Joshua 15:59; if so, it would be an ancient Canaanite city, part of the inheritance of Judah's tribe.

Marriage, Levirate. *See* MARRIAGE, MARRIAGE CUSTOMS.

Marriage, Marriage Customs. Union between man and woman, sanctified by God as a means of maintaining family life. The idea of marriage was ordained by God in his instruction to Adam that a man should leave his father and mother, and he and his wife should be as one flesh (Gn 2:24). The first actual mention of the word marriage is in Genesis 34:8.

As Hebrew society developed from the nomadic to the agricultural and village stage, the customs involved in marriage became more complex. Ritual functions such as feasts, processions, and dances were added. In the Christian period marriage began to be regarded as a sacrament.

Several forms of marriage are referred to in the OT, the earliest of which seems to be based on a matrilineal principle. Although there appears to be some evidence for this in the Middle Bronze Age and in the early monarchy, it is difficult to be certain about the matter, despite the importance in Egypt, and perhaps elsewhere, of the role of the mother in determining descent.

Jacob remained with the family of Laban because he was working for him until the brideprice had been paid. Laban inferred that the children of the marriage were his children and part of his clan (Gn 31:26,43). At first glance it seems strange that Jacob, having already worked for 14 years for his brides, should remain voluntarily for another 6 years (v 41). He may have been fearful of vengeance from Esau (27:42–45) or he may have felt that his contract with Laban bound him permanently.

Gideon had a concubine who continued to live with her family (Jgs 8:31), and her son considered himself part of his mother's clan (9:1,2). When Samson wished to see his Philistine bride he visited her where she lived with her own clan (15:1,2). It is noteworthy, however, that of these few available examples, Gideon was dealing only with a concubine and Samson with a foreigner. Neither man became part of his wife's family.

Generally, the bride left her parents when she married and went to live with her husband's clan, as Rebekah did (Gn 24:58,59). The phrase "to marry a wife" is from a root meaning to "become master" (Dt 21:13), and the wife frequently treated her husband and referred to him as master.

Hebrew genealogical lists indicate that descent was reckoned through the male line (Gn 5; 10; 36:9–43; Nm 1:1–15; Ru 4:18–22; 1 Chr 1:1–9). The important right of naming a child, indicating power and authority over that child, was exercised almost equally between father and mother in biblical references (cf. Gn 4:1,25,26; 5:29; 35:18; 1 Sm 1:20; 4:21; Is 8:3; Hos 1:4,6,9). Sons were frequently named after their fathers and were identified with them.

The father was the authority figure in the home in a patriarchal society. His wife and children were regarded as his possessions in somewhat the same way as his fields and cattle (Ex 20:17; Dt 5:21). He had the right to sell his daughters (Ex 21:7; Neh 5:5), and even had the power of life and death over his children.

The father was responsible for providing for the family, for ensuring their financial welfare, and for furnishing security for them. Business decisions were generally left to him, though they may possibly have been discussed with his wife. The husband even had to give consent to his wife's promises, otherwise they were invalid (Nm 30:3–16). The ease with which a man could terminate a marriage by divorcing his wife also shows the measure of his authority in the family (Dt 24:1–4; cf. 22:13–21).

A levirate marriage was instituted to preserve a family name and inheritance. When a man died, the responsibility for maintaining his widow and any children that she might have fell upon her husband's closest male relative. The order of responsibility is set out in Deuteronomy 25:5–10. Normally the brother of the deceased husband living with the clan was expected to enter into a levirate marriage with the widow. If she was childless, the firstborn of the new marriage was regarded as a child of the deceased. Levirate marriage was also known to the Canaanites, Assyrians, and Hittites.

The most familiar levirate situation in the OT, although not conforming strictly to the law of Deuteronomy 25, is described in the Book of Ruth. It was essential for Ruth to find some close male relative to marry her so that the family name and property could be preserved. The closest male relative declined the responsibility, feeling that it was a double im-

position not only having to purchase the land and support Ruth, but knowing that the first son would be regarded as his dead brother's child, bearing his name and inheriting the land. It was possible, however, to decline the levirate (Dt 25:5–10; Ru 4:7,8), and in the case of Ruth, Boaz the younger brother agreed to undertake the responsibility (Ru 2:20–4:10).

Tamar, the widow of Er, was promised under the levirate law as the bride of Er's brother Shelah. In some respects a betrothal had the force of a marriage, and when Judah, her father-in-law, suspected that she had had sexual relations with another man when promised to his son, this gave him a reason to condemn Tamar to be burned alive (Gn 38:24).

From an early period it became essential for families to increase in size as a means of maintaining the family property, and also as a source of manpower for military purposes. To this end polygamy was popular, although few men could afford more than two wives. Many, however, had one or more concubines, especially when the wife had not provided her husband with children. Under these conditions Sarah gave her handmaid Hagar to Abraham (Gn 16:3). Jacob married two sisters, Rachel and Leah, and each of them also gave him her maid (30:3–9). Jacob's brother Esau had three wives (26:34; 28:9; 36:1–5). While this practice seems to have been more restricted during the period of the judges and the early monarchy, Gideon is nevertheless reported to have had "many wives," and possibly more than one concubine (Jgs 8:30,31). Vast, polygamous marriages are mentioned in Kings; Solomon had "700 wives, princesses, and 300 concubines" (1 Kgs 11:1–3). The rivalry between wives and children in such households can be imagined, especially if one wife was barren (1 Sm 1:6) or if a particular wife was preferred (Gn 29:30,31; 1 Sm 1:5). Despite this, the rights and dignity of a concubine and her children were firmly upheld in Hebrew society.

The law code of Hammurabi (c. 1700 BC) stated that a husband could only take a second wife if the first was barren, but if his wife provided him with a slave for a concubine, he could not take another wife. A husband could take a concubine even if his wife had provided him with children, but he could not take a second concubine unless the first was barren. In the Assyrian law code (c. 2000 BC) the women of the harem were at an intermediate level between the wife and the concubine, and could be raised to the status of wife.

Despite numerous examples of polygamy cited in the OT, there is no doubt that the vast majority of the Israelites were monogamous. There are no examples given of large polygamous marriages in the families of commoners.

The original instruction to Adam was that a "man . . . cleaves to his wife" (Gn 2:24). Hebrew laws generally imply that a marriage with one wife is the most acceptable form of marriage (Ex 20:17; 21:5; Lv 18:8,16,20; 20:10; Nm 5:12; Dt 5:21). Although this seems to have become the norm by the time of the monarchy, a king such as Solomon did not follow Hebrew traditions in this matter. In the postexilic period marriages were predominantly monogamous, although they were being terminated increasingly by divorce. In the NT period monogamy seems to have been the rule, although persons such as Herod the Great were polygamous. Christ taught that marriage was for the lifetime of the partners, and if a man divorced his wife and married another woman during his previous spouse's lifetime, he committed adultery (Mt 5:27–32).

Marriage generally took place with those who were close to the immediate family circle and it was imperative, therefore, that limits on acceptable consanguinity should be imposed. In patriarchal times a man could marry his half-sister on his father's side (Gn 20:12) and this continued to be the case even under David (2 Sm 13:13), although it was specifically forbidden in Leviticus 20:17. As there is some contradiction between the marriage laws of Deuteronomy and those in the Law of Holiness (Dt 25:5; Lv 18:16), it is possible that there was some modification of the stricter levitical regulations. Marriages between cousins such as Isaac and Rebekah, and Jacob with Rachel and Leah, were common. When a close relative was interested in marriage, it was almost impossible to refuse (Tob 6:13; 7:11,12). Moses was the offspring of a marriage between nephew and aunt (Ex 6:20; Nm 26:59), which would have been forbidden in Leviticus 18:12,13 and 20:19, as would Jacob's marriage with two sisters at the same time (Gn 29:30).

Marriage within the clan or tribe was considered ideal, although marriage with another Israelite family was quite acceptable. Concern was often expressed, however, about marriage with foreigners, as this tended to dilute the strong links with the Hebrew heritage, and could endanger the religion of the covenant people if foreign wives introduced their family members and children to strange gods.

When the Israelites settled in Canaan, many of them married Canaanite women, much to the consternation of those who desired to maintain the purity of the Hebrew religion (1 Kgs 11:4). Such intermarriage was prohibited under Mosaic law (Ex 34:15,16; Dt 7:3,4), although many Israelites ignored these regulations and continued to indulge in mixed marriages. If a woman was captured in war and was prepared to abandon her native country, an exception could be made (Dt 21:10–14). As noted above, Samson married a Philistine woman who remained with her own people, but who received conjugal visits from her husband periodically (Jgs 14:8–20; 15:1,2).

Esau was married to two Hittite women (Gn 26:34) as well as to his cousin; while Joseph, living in Egypt, not surprisingly married an Egyptian (41:45). The wife of Moses was a Midianite (Ex 2:21), while Naomi's two daughters-in-law were Moabites (Ru 1:4). Among David's wives was an Aramaean woman (2 Sm 3:3). Representatives from many neighboring nations were in Solomon's harem, including the daughter of pharaoh, as well as Moabite, Ammonite, Edomite, Sidonian, and Hittite women (1 Kgs 11:1). Jezebel, wife of Ahab, was a Tyrian princess (1 Kgs 16:31) who introduced Baal worship into the northern kingdom. Some Israelite women also married foreigners; for example, Bathsheba, who chose a Hittite husband (2 Sm 11:3), and the mother of Hiram, a bronze worker, who was married to a man from Tyre (1 Kgs 7:13,14).

The danger of intermarriage affecting the purity of Hebrew religion was considered so great that in the postexilic period wholesale divorce was ordered where Jews had married foreign wives (Ezr 9:2; 10:3,16,17). The intent was that the faith should remain pure, even though homes and families were destroyed. Even in NT times, Paul denounced marriage with non-Christians (2 Cor 6:14,15).

It is difficult to estimate at what age young people married. A boy was considered to be a man by his middle teens, and late in Jewish tradition this transition was celebrated by the bar mitzvah, which generally occurred when the boy was 13. It seems most probable that Mahlon and Chilion were still quite young when they died (Ru 1:5,9) from some unspecified illness. At the time of his death, Absalom was about 20, but he had been living in his own house for the previous five years, and may have been married (2 Sm 13:19). In point of fact there were possibly quite different average ages for the marriages of the sons of kings and for other people. Subsequently, minimum ages of 13 for boys and 12 for girls were set.

Normally the young man's parents chose the bride. The resulting discussion about the marriage occurred between the groom's parents and the bride's parents, and often neither of the young people was consulted. It was not essential for the eldest in the family to be married first (Gn 29:26). When Abraham decided that Isaac should be married, a servant was sent to choose a bride from among Abraham's relatives in Mesopotamia. The servant made contact with the bride's brother (24:33–53) and it was only afterwards that Rebekah was asked to give her consent (vv 57,58). If her father had still been alive, it would have been unlikely that her consent would have been asked at all. Caleb arranged the marriage for his daughter (Jos 15:16), as Saul did for Merab (1 Sm 18:17,19,21,27). When Samson wished to marry a Philistine woman, he asked his parents for her (Jgs 14:2,3).

Where a father did not actually choose a bride for his son, he would often guide that choice. Isaac sent Jacob with instructions to marry one of his cousins, and even Esau considered his father's wishes in this matter (Gn 28:8,9). The elder Tobias also recorded his advice to his son on the selection of a bride (Tob 4:12,13). Certainly there is evidence of occasions on which a young man made known his preference (Gn 34:4; Jgs 14:2), or where he simply ignored or rejected his parents' advice (Gn 26:34,35). It was exceptional for the girl to take the initiative, as Saul's daughter Michal did in loving David (1 Sm 18:20).

One of the reasons why the average young man would not have been able to afford more than one wife was the practice of bridewealth, which had to be paid to the bride's father. It was possible to substitute service for the bridewealth (Gn 29:15–30), or the completion of an appointed task (1 Sm 18:25–27). A specific sum is mentioned for the bridewealth in the case of a virgin who had been raped, and who had to be purchased by her seducer. The price was set at 50 shekels, but as this was considered to be a punishment, it is probable that the normal amount was between 10 and 30 shekels (Lv 27:4,5).

At the time of the second temple a virgin bride was considered to be worth 50 shekels, and a widow or divorced woman about half that sum. During this period a virgin bride was normally married in mid-week, so that if her husband found her not to be a virgin, he could bring proof to the court the following day, which would still be in advance of the sabbath. A widow or a divorced woman normally married on the equivalent of a Thursday, giving her two full days with her husband before the sabbath.

Although it might appear that acquiring a wife was a simple exchange of property between father and husband, this was not precisely the case. The Hebrew wife was never considered as a slave. She had a certain position managing her husband's household, and respect was due to her as the mother of his sons.

The bridewealth paid to the father probably reverted to the daughter on his death, or if she happened to be in need when her husband died. Under Assyrian law the bridewealth was paid to the daughter. According to the Code of Hammurabi, the money was paid to the girl's parents, who had to return double the amount if the engagement was broken off. In Hebrew families it also was customary for the groom to bring gifts for the bride and for other members of the family, although it is unlikely that they were always as numerous and elaborate as the gifts described for Rebekah (Gn 24:53). In Babylonian law the bride's father gave the husband gifts, which he could use but not own, and these reverted to the bride if she became a widow or if she was divorced through no fault of her own.

Marriage was a covenant or alliance between two families. It thus united them, and by extending the kinship the overall size of the group was increased. This was important in a society where responsibilities for relatives, however distant, were accepted unhesitatingly. The covenant concept also could have political overtones, as with the marriage between Solomon and the Egyptian princess (1 Kgs 11:1) or Ahab of Israel and Jezebel of Tyre (16:31). The marriage covenant was similar to that which God had with Israel. This is an added argument for supposing that monogamy was the normal form of marriage.

The sealing of the covenant included the transfer of gifts, which would establish the wealth and status of the donor and of the bride (Gn 34:12). In the ancient Near East, the giving of a gift was thought to include a part of the donor, so that the giver was actually offering a portion of himself. The gift which sealed the covenant also established the donor's authority over the bride.

The next stage in the marriage procedure was the betrothal. First mentioned in Exodus 22:16, the term is used several times in Deuteronomy (20:7; 22:23,24). The betrothal had the legal status of a marriage (Dt 28:30; 2 Sm 3:14), and anyone violating a betrothed virgin would be stoned according to the law of Deuteronomy for violating his neighbor's "wife" (Dt 22:23,24). The meaning of a betrothal involved taking possession, in a manner similar to that of receiving tribute. Nevertheless, there remained a distinction between betrothing a woman and taking her to wife (Dt 20:7). During the period of betrothal, the prospective groom was exempt from military service. It was assumed that the betrothal was a formal part of a permanent relationship (Mt 1:18; Lk 1:27; 2:5).

A man who was to marry another's daughter was already regarded as a son-in-law at the time of betrothal (Gn 19:14). Mary, as Joseph's betrothed, was actually considered his wife, although he did not have intercourse with her until after the birth of Jesus. If they followed normal practice, they would not have had sexual relations until after the baby was weaned, usually at the age of three.

Circumcision, as an initiation rite before marriage, dates back to 1500 BC in Palestine and Syria. Probably beginning in Canaan, the Hebrews doubtless continued the rite in Egypt, where it was probably performed at puberty. In the legislation given to Moses at Sinai, the Israelites were ordered to circumcise their male children on the eighth day (Lv 12:3). Circumcision was related to marriage in Genesis 34, and the idea of circumcising Moses' young son, making the father a "bridegroom of blood" (Ex 4:24–26) seems to imply a connection at that period between circumcision and marriage.

The first biblical record of a wedding being celebrated by a feast is in the story of Jacob (Gn 29:22). Bridesmaids are mentioned in the account of Samson's marriage (Jgs 14:10; Ps 45:14).

There was no actual marriage contract recorded until its mention in the Book of Tobit (7:12). This contract was not considered valid until the couple had cohabited for a week (Gn 29:27; Jgs 14:12,18). When Samson left his bride before the end of the seven-day period, the bride's parents considered the marriage void and gave her to another man (Jgs 14:20).

A traditional formula pronounced at a marriage has been found in the Elephantine contracts. The husband made the declaration, "She is my wife and I am her husband, from this day for ever." By the 2nd century AD the declaration was simpler, merely stating: "Thou shalt be my wife."

The wedding was an occasion of great family rejoicing. The special clothing of the bride and groom (Is 61:10; Ez 16:9–13) included for the bride a fine dress often adorned with jewels (Ps 45:14,15; Is 61:10) and other ornaments, while the bridegroom had fine clothing and wore a diadem (Sg 3:11; Is 61:10). The bride wore a veil (Gn 24:65; Sg 4:3), which was removed in the bridal chamber. This would account for Rebekah's need to veil herself in the presence of Isaac, her fiancé (Gn 24:65), and also for the ease with which Laban was able to replace Rachel with Leah on Jacob's wedding night (29:23–25).

One of the main features of the wedding ceremony was the procession of the groom and his friends with tambourines and other musical instruments (Jer 7:34). In later periods the processions of the bride and groom's parties would leave their homes separately, and meet at an agreed-upon location (1 Mc 9:37–39), generally returning to the groom's house for the wedding feast (Mt 22:2). An excuse for rejoicing and indulging in fine food and merriment was welcomed by the Israelites, and the feast could last for 7 days (Gn 29:27; Jgs 14:12) or as long as 14 days (Tob 8:20).

Symbolic ceremonies may sometimes have been included as part of the betrothal or wedding ceremonies, such as Ruth's request that Boaz spread his skirt over her to indicate that he was taking her to wife. Another ritual may have been the ceremonial removal of the bride's girdle by the groom in the nuptial chamber, which was a room or tent specially prepared for the newly married couple. The marriage was normally consummated on the first night (Gn 29:23; Tob 8:1), and the stained linen would be retained as evidence of the bride's virginity.

In contrast to the elaborate procession and feasting of the marriage, divorce was simple. A man could divorce his wife if he found fault with her over any particular matter, and this right was not abolished until the 11th century AD. Divorce was discouraged, however, and gradually the procedure became more complex, being hedged about with a number of deterrents.

If the husband accused his new bride of not being a virgin and the charge was found to be false, she could not be divorced (Dt 22:13–19). If the husband had seduced his wife before their marriage he could not divorce her subsequently (Dt 22:28,29). If the wife was abducted, it was the husband's duty to ransom her. If the wife became deaf and mute, insane, or an alcoholic after the marriage, she could not be divorced.

As the laws regarding divorce became more complex, so the procedure became increasingly expensive. At a later time a lawyer, or sometimes a rabbi, would give advice, especially on such matters as the return of property rightly belonging to the bride or her family.

If a bride was found to have committed adultery, the husband was thought to be entitled to a divorce. This was also the case if he even suspected her of infidelity. He could also divorce his wife if he felt that she had violated normal morality, had become apostate, or had been less than efficient in the management of her household. If a woman refused her husband his conjugal rights for a period of at least one year, she could be divorced. Other grounds for divorcing a wife included insulting behavior to a husband or his relatives, contracting an incurable disease, or refusal to accompany her husband when he moved the domicile to a new area.

In the rabbinic period the wife also had the right to divorce her husband under certain circumstances. In the biblical period the idea of a woman seeking divorce was denounced as being in opposition to Jewish law, and in Mark 10:12 it was considered to be a gentile custom. There is some evidence that women were able to seek divorce in 2nd-century AD Palestine. In the Jewish colony of Elephantine, a writ of divorce was drawn up by the husband (cf. Dt 24:1,3; Is 50:1; Jer 3:8), after which the woman was able to remarry (Dt 24:2).

In the Code of Hammurabi, although the husband could divorce his wife by pronouncing the stated formula, he was still required to pay her compensation. Under Assyrian law no compensation was payable, and the wife could not obtain a divorce. If any form of dowry had been involved in the wedding settlement, this was usually returned to the bride or her family on the couple's divorce.

In general, the status of the wife was low. Despite the fact that she gave advice, managed the household, educated the young children, and worked alongside her husband when necessary, he was still her master, and her role was to obey. She was little more than a servant, although better than a slave, for she could not be sold even though she could be divorced.

In the frequent figurative uses of marriage in the OT, the Hebrew people and God are referred to in terms of bride and bridegroom (Is 62:4,5; Jer 2:2). The desolation which is about to overtake Judah is contrasted by Jeremiah with the celebration of a wedding feast (7:34; 16:9; 25:10). Figurative forms are used again in Hosea, where God rejects the relationship with his wife Israel (Hos 2:2), but is prepared to accept her again if she resumes her faithful practices (vv 19,20).

In the NT, John the Baptist compares his sense of joy with that of a friend of the groom at a wedding (Jn 3:29), while Jesus himself made reference to the wedding preparations in the parable of the wise and foolish virgins (Mt 25:1–12). In the story of the marriage feast (22:1–14) Christ mentions quite incidentally the fact that wedding robes were provided for the guests at such ceremonies. The theme of the Christian church as the bride of Christ occurs in such books as Corinthians, Ephesians, and Revelation.

By the Talmudic period all areas of life, including sexual relations, were subjected strictly to the laws of religion. Marriage was considered a civil contract, not a sacrament. In the early Christian era virginity was considered the most pure state and, therefore, eminently acceptable to God. Thus celibacy after marriage or after the death of a spouse was regarded as the next state in order of preference, with marriage rated as third on this scale. The early church went through a lengthy period of praising celibacy to the detriment of marriage, despite the sanction of marriage by Christ and its acceptance by Paul.　　HAZEL W. PERKIN

See FAMILY LIFE AND RELATIONS; CIRCUMCISION; CRIMINAL LAW AND PUNISHMENT; ADULTERY; DIVORCE; CIVIL LAW AND JUSTICE; SEX, SEXUALITY; VIRGIN; WIDOW; CONCUBINAGE.

Bibliography. D. Atkinson, *To Have and to Hold;* D.S. Bailey, *The Mystery of Love and Marriage;* G.W. Bromiley, *God and Marriage;* R. de Vaux, *Ancient Israel;* A. Edersheim, *Sketches of Jewish Social Life in the Day of Christ;* W.J. Harrington, *The Bible on Matrimony;* K.E. Kirk, *Marriage and Divorce;* H. Thielicke, *The Ethics of Sex.*

Marsena. One of the seven princes of Persia and Media who served Ahasuerus, ranking next to him in authority in the kingdom (Est 1:14).

Marsh Hen. Alternate name for water hen in Leviticus 11:18 and Deuteronomy 14:16.

See BIRDS (WATER HEN).

Mars' Hill. Alternate KJV translation for "Areopagus," the name of a small hill northwest of the Acropolis in Athens and the site of Paul's address to the Athenians (Acts 17:16–34).

See AREOPAGUS.

Martha. Sister of Mary and Lazarus, and friend of Jesus. Martha's family lived in Bethany, a small town on the eastern slope of the Mt of Olives. It is possible that Martha was the wife of Simon the leper.

Luke gives an account of an incident concerning Martha when she was busy preparing and serving food while her sister Mary was listening to Jesus. Martha complained to Jesus that Mary was not helping her; Jesus corrected Martha gently: "Martha, Martha, you are anxious and troubled about many things; one thing is needful. Mary has chosen the good portion, which shall not be taken away from her" (Lk 10:41,42). In saying this, Jesus challenged Martha's anxiousness by pointing out that fellowship with him was life's highest and most rewarding priority.

In John's account of the death and resurrection of Lazarus, it is Martha who, upon Jesus' arrival, goes out to meet him while Mary remains in the house (Jn 11:20). Once again, Martha complains to Jesus, this time saying that if he had come earlier Lazarus would not have died (v 21). When Jesus replied that her brother would rise again, Martha naturally assumed that Jesus was speaking of the future resurrection. Jesus reassured Martha that he in fact was the resurrection and the life and that she must trust in him (vv 23–26). Martha then confessed her belief that Jesus was the Christ (v 27). When Jesus asked that the tomb be opened, Martha protested that the smell would not be pleasant. Jesus replied firmly to

The Church of the Annunciation at Nazareth is one of the largest churches in the Middle East. According to tradition, it stands on the site where Gabriel told Mary she would bear Jesus.

her doubts, "Did I not tell you that if you would believe you would see the glory of God?" (v 40). Jesus then proceeded to raise Lazarus from the dead.

In John 12:1–11 Martha is again serving a meal for Jesus and Lazarus; this time, however, she does not protest Mary's elaborate show of affection for Jesus.

Mary. Popular feminine name among 1st-century Jews, borne by 6 (or 7) women in the NT.

1. Mary, the mother of Jesus. According to the infancy narratives of Matthew and Luke, Mary was a young Jewish virgin, probably from the tribe of Levi (her cousin Elizabeth was a Levite, Lk 1:5,36), who during her engagement to a certain Joseph (of Davidic descent from the tribe of Judah) was discovered to be pregnant. This was due to her submission to the Holy Spirit (Mt 1:18–25; Lk 1:26–38). The couple married and lived first in Nazareth of Galilee, then traveled to Bethlehem (Joseph's hometown) for a census, where Jesus was born (Mt 2:1; Lk 1:5; 2:4,5). Matthew informs us that shortly after the birth the family had to flee to Egypt to escape Herod's wrath (Mt 2:13,14). Later the family resided again in Nazareth (v 23; Lk 2:39).

We have little other information about Mary. She was certainly a concerned mother (as her scolding of Jesus in Lk 2:48 shows), and she later had a high estimate of Jesus' ability (as at the wedding in Cana, Jn 2:1–4, although John does not say what she expected Jesus to do). She had several other sons and daughters to care for, probably as a widow (Mt 13:55 does not name Joseph, probably indicating his death). She appears at the foot of the cross, where Jesus asks "the beloved disciple" to care for her in her grief (Jn 19:25–27; her other

children apparently were not present). After the resurrection she and Jesus' brothers were among the disciples who awaited Pentecost (Acts 1:14). No further mention is made of her.

Luke attributes to Mary the Magnificat, a most famous song of praise (Lk 1:46–55), and she stands as an example of humility and trust in her submission to God's will. She is truly "blessed among women" (Lk 1:42).

See BROTHERS OF JESUS.

2. Mary, the mother of James and Joseph. This woman goes by several names, but in each account she appears among Jesus' faithful female disciples, standing by the cross and witnessing the empty tomb. Matthew calls her "Mary the mother of James and Joseph" or just "the other Mary" (27:56,61; 28:1); Mark names her "Mary the mother of James the younger and of Joses," "Mary the mother of Joses," or "Mary the mother of James" (15:40, 47; 16:1; Lk 24:10—James was probably an apostle; Joseph or Joses was not); in John's Gospel, she is "Mary wife of Clopas" (19:25), though she may possibly be a separate Mary. Tradition has it that this Mary was Jesus' aunt, as Clopas was Joseph's brother (Eusebius, *Ecclesiastical History* 3.11); this tradition is unreliable, however, as its point was to prove that Jesus had no brothers and thus the virgin Mary was perpetually a virgin.

3. Mary Magdalene. We know little about this woman other than that her name indicates that she was from Magdala in Galilee. Somewhere in Galilee she met Jesus, who cast seven demons out of her. She then joined the band of disciples and followed Jesus wherever he went (Lk 8:2), ending up in Jerusalem at the foot of the cross when all the male disciples had fled (Mk 15:40; Jn 19:25). She observed Jesus' burial (Mk 15:47) and witnessed the events surrounding the resurrection. Mat-

thew 28:1; Mark 16:1; and Luke 24:10 group her with the other women who go to the tomb, but John gives her the role of first to discover the resurrection, first to report to the disciples, and first to see the resurrected Christ as she lingers by the tomb weeping after all the others have gone (Jn 20:1,2,11–18). This faithful disciple, however, was not allowed to touch her Lord (Jn 20:17).

4. Mary of Bethany. This Judean Mary was the sister of Martha and Lazarus. We know three facts about her. First, she was such a devoted follower of Jesus that she neglected her household duties to listen to him (Lk 10:38–42; Jesus approved this). Second, she was apparently upset with Jesus when he did not come to heal her brother before he died (Jn 11:20,28–33). Finally, before Jesus died she anointed him with an expensive ointment while he feasted at her home in Bethany (Mt 26:6–13; Mk 14:3–9; Jn 12:1–8—the story in Lk 7:37–50 surely concerns another unnamed woman in Galilee, not Judea).

5. Mary, mother of John Mark. This woman appears only once in Scripture (Acts 12:12). Her house was the meeting place of the persecuted church. Since it was apparently large and she had servants, she was a wealthy woman, probably a widow (since no husband is mentioned). In her house the church prayed for Peter, and Peter came there after being released from prison. Her son John Mark accompanied Paul and probably Peter as well.

6. Mary of Rome. In Romans 16:6 Paul greets a woman in Rome named simply "Mary, who has worked hard among you." At some time she had been in Greece or Asia Minor, perhaps being expelled from Rome with Aquila and Priscilla (Acts 18:2; c. AD 49). While there she had met Paul, perhaps being converted by him, and had worked hard with him in his work of evangelism or caring for the church. By AD 56 (a probable date for the Book of Romans) she had returned to Rome and is distinguished only by the praise Paul here heaps upon her and his other co-workers now living in Rome.   PETER H. DAVIDS

Bibliography. R.E. Brown et al. (eds.), *Mary in the NT*; A. Greeley, *The Mary Myth*; J. McHugh, *The Mother of Jesus in the NT*; H.A. Oberman, *The Virgin Mary in Evangelical Perspective*.

Mary Magdalene. *See* MARY #3.

Masada. Rock fortress on the western shore of the Dead Sea, opposite the Lisan, about 19 miles south of En-gedi and 10½ miles north of Sodom, where the Jewish Zealots made their last stand against the Romans in AD 73. Today

An aerial view of Masada.

it is called in Arabic Qaṣr es-Sebbe and in Hebrew Metsada.

The rock rises some 1400 feet above the Dead Sea, about 2000 feet from north to south, and about 980 feet from east to west, with sheer cliffs on all sides. The top, which slopes gently toward the south and west, is almost flat, about 20 acres in area, or the equivalent of about 2 large city blocks. It is situated about two miles west of the shore of the Dead Sea.

According to Josephus (*War* 7.8–9), this almost impregnable rock was first fortified by Jonathan the high priest, who gave it the name Masada ("mountain stronghold," cf. Jgs 6:2; 1 Sm 23:14, which do not, however, refer to a specific stronghold). The "Jonathan" mentioned by Josephus, long the subject of scholarly debate, is probably to be identified as Alexander Janneus (103–40 BC) on the basis of scores of coins found at Masada. It was Herod the Great who expended a great amount of effort to build and fortify the place, partly out of fear that the Jews might overthrow him and restore the former kings, and partly because he was afraid that Cleopatra would convince Antony to cut him off and give the kingdom of Judea to her.

Present knowledge of Herodian Masada comes not only from Josephus but also from the excavations of Yigael Yadin in 1963–65. The archaeological discoveries confirm many of the statements found in Josephus.

Herod took the stronghold from Helix and installed his family there during the period when he was in Rome to claim his kingdom (40–39 BC). Subsequently he built palaces, a Roman bath, storerooms, an elaborate water-supply system, and a wall. The wall entirely surrounded the top of the rock, a length of 4250 feet, with 30 towers and 8 gates, and was of "casemate" construction, that is, it consisted of an outer and an inner wall, between which were about 110 rooms. The space between the walls was 13½ feet. The water supply consisted of drains from the wadis in the west, designed to collect water in the rainy season, and 12 cisterns in 2 rows on the northwest side of the fortress, having a capacity of 10½ million gallons. A three-tiered palace villa was built in a spectacular location on the northern end of the rock. Other palaces, administrative buildings, and storerooms were located on the top of the rock, at the northern end, at the western side, and in the central region toward the southern end. It is possible that Josephus is correct in reporting that crops were raised, since there is a layer of soil toward the southern end of the rock. The royal buildings contained fine mosaic floors and frescoed walls, and the bath was a typical Roman bath with a caldarium (hot- or steam-room), tepidarium (warm-room), and frigidarium (cold-room). The entire bath-complex was 33 feet by 36 feet with walls 6 feet thick.

When the first Jewish revolt began in AD 66, a number of Zealots led by Menahem took over Masada, which had been occupied by a small Roman garrison. The Zealots made a number of alterations, building a synagogue and two ritual baths and converting the palaces and administrative buildings into living quarters. Coins struck in the 1st, 2nd, 3rd, 4th, and 5th years of the Jewish revolt (i.e., AD 66, 67, 68, 69, and 70) were found, putting the date of the discoveries beyond question. Included in the discoveries were fragments of scrolls, including portions of Leviticus, Deuteronomy, Psalms, the Wisdom of Jesus ben Sirach (Ecclesiasticus), the Book of Jubilees, and a portion containing the words "the song of the sixth sabbath sacrifice on the ninth of the second month." These words, and the calendar system used, connected the scroll with one found in Cave 4 at Qumran. This led Yadin to conclude that some of the Qumran Essenes joined the Zealots in the revolt against Rome, bringing scrolls from Qumran with them to Masada.

After the destruction of Jerusalem (AD 70), the Romans removed all pockets of Jewish resistance until only the fortress of Masada remained. When Flavius Silva became the Roman procurator, he determined to bring to an end the last of the revolt. The Zealots at Masada, 960 in number according to Josephus, were led by Eleazar. Silva surrounded the stronghold with 8 camps and a wall 6 feet thick and 11,400 feet long, with 12 towers at intervals of 240 to 300 feet. The camps could hold about 9000 troops, but it is estimated that Silva had about 15,000 men, including a large number of Jewish prisoners, to mount the siege. It seems obvious that his intent was to prevent a single Zealot from escaping to stir up a new revolt.

There were two routes to Masada, the

The eastern slope of Masada.

"snake path" up the eastern side and a path on the western side. The snake path is tortuous and narrow, requiring about 50 minutes of dangerous climbing. The Zealots had amassed a supply of large boulders near the top, apparently expecting an attack at this point. Silva selected the western approach, ordering his soldiers to build an earthen ramp, about 180 feet in height, about 645 feet in length, and about the same width at the base as the length. It did not quite reach to the top of the fortress, ending about 60 feet below the casemate wall.

By means of a battering ram and missile-catapault, Silva breached the wall, but the Zealots repaired it overnight with timbers and earth. Silva then burned the timbered repair. When Eleazar Ben-Ya'ir saw that the Romans were about to capture Masada, he delivered a stirring speech, given at length (and probably with considerable imagination) in Josephus. Some excerpts may be quoted: "It is still in our power to die bravely, and in a state of freedom. . . . Let our wives die before they are abused, and our children before they have tasted of slavery; and after we have slain them, let us bestow that glorious benefit upon one another mutually, and preserve ourselves in freedom, as an excellent funeral monument for us. But first let us destroy our money and the fortress by fire . . . and let us spare nothing but our provisions, for they will be a testimonial when we are dead that we were not subdued for want of necessaries; but that, according to our original resolution, we have preferred death before slavery."

There was reluctance to perform this mass suicide, and Eleazar had to follow the speech with a second, both shaming them and encouraging them. While he was still speaking, they cut him off and began the bloody work: "The husbands tenderly embraced their wives and took their children into their arms, and gave the longest parting kisses to them, with tears in their eyes." Then the men killed their wives and children, and laid all their possessions in a heap and set fire to them. After that, they chose 10 men by lot to slay the rest, "every one of whom laid himself down by his wife and children on the ground, and threw his arms about them, and they offered their necks" to those chosen to slay them. Finally, the 10 remaining cast lots "that he whose lot it was should first kill the other nine, and after all, should kill himself." Yadin tells of finding 11 ostraca (pottery sherds) each with a single name inscribed on it, which he suggests may have been the means used to select the one to put the others to death. One of the sherds bore the name "ben-Ya'ir," quite likely that of Eleazar ben-Ya'ir.

Storage rooms at Masada.

The plan was carried out almost to the last detail. Two women, however, hid themselves and five children in one of the caverns. The Romans entered the fortress the next day, expecting to meet some kind of resistance, but all they found was silence and the ashes of a great fire—plus vast stores of food in the storehouses. The women who had hidden in the caverns told the story to the Romans.

WILLIAM SANFORD LaSOR

See HEROD, HERODIAN FAMILY; FIRST JEWISH REVOLT; ZEALOT; JUDAISM.

Maschil. KJV rendering of maskil, a musical cue in the titles of numerous psalms.

See MASKIL.

Mash. Aram's fourth son (Gn 10:23), a descendant of Shem. He is called Meshech in 1 Chronicles 1:17.

See MESHECH #2.

Mashal. Alternate spelling of Mishal, a levitical town in Asher, in 1 Chronicles 6:74.

See MISHAL.

Maskil. Hebrew term in the superscriptions of 15 psalms (KJV Maschil); perhaps a musical cue denoting the manner in which the designated psalms were to be performed.

See MUSIC AND MUSICAL INSTRUMENTS.

Mason, Masonry. Worker in and craft of brick and stonework.

See ARCHITECTURE; INDUSTRY AND COMMERCE; TRADES AND OCCUPATIONS.

Masora, Masoretes. Oral tradition concerning the pronunciation and accuracy of the Hebrew text of the OT, and the scholars who were responsible for reducing those traditions to writing.

At the background of the work of the Masoretes lay the efforts of the Sopherim or scribes who, from about 400 BC to AD 200, tried to establish and maintain the true text of the OT. In connection with this effort they made a practice of counting the verses, words, and letters of each Bible book and appending this information in order to give future copyists some standard against which to check the accuracy of their copies. The traditional Hebrew text, called the Masoretic Text, achieved its standard form early in the 2nd century AD. It was based on and substantially agreed with a much earlier textual tradition, as the Dead Sea Scrolls demonstrate. But the text of the scribes or custodians of the Bible was still only consonantal; it had no vowels or accent marks.

The work of the Masoretes picked up where that of the Sopherim left off. They are called Masoretes because they preserved in writing the oral traditions (Masora) concerning the biblical text. These Jewish scholars lived primarily in Tiberias on the western shore of the Sea of Galilee during the period AD 500 to 950. Most prominent among them were the learned Moses ben Asher and his son Aaron; the present text of the Hebrew Bible is based on a ben Asher text.

The Masoretes sought not only to determine the exact text handed down to them but to pass it on to future generations without change. To protect against copyists' errors and alterations, they filled the side margins with all sorts of data concerning how often and where various words and phrases appearing in a given line of the text could be found elsewhere.

The special contribution of the Masoretes was to provide the text with vowels and accent marks. This they achieved with a system of dots and strokes. Their task was not to invent pronunciations but to pass on received or accepted pronunciations and to decide between debatable ones. Of course, the issue was not merely correct pronunciation, because a slight change in vowel pointing or pronunciation would, for instance, turn a noun into a participle.

As the Masoretes sought to vocalize, determine, and protect the true text, they had to engage in a certain amount of textual criticism. But their reverence for the text would not permit making changes in it, so they worked out an ingenious system of editorial notes. Where it appeared to them that a copyist's error had occurred, they left the error written in the text (a *kethib* wording—that which is written) but put vowel markings with it for a preferred wording (*qere*—that which is to be read) and inserted the consonants for that reading in the margin. They also indicated a limited number of words that probably should be omitted altogether.

One of the most interesting of the *qere* readings did not concern a problem of error at all. As early as the 5th century BC Jews began to grow uneasy about pronouncing God's covenant name, properly vocalized as Yahweh. So they substituted the vowel markings for Adonai (Lord), indicating that Adonai was to be uttered instead of Yahweh. This substitute vowel marking of the Masoretes has led to the modern pronunciation of Jehovah (using the vowels of Adonai) and the attitude among devout believers that Yahweh is a concoction of liberal scholars.

The meticulous efforts of the Masoretes and the Sopherim before them resulted in a marvelously successful preservation of the OT text. What the Masoretes passed on to later centuries was meticulously copied by hand until the advent of the printing press. So it may be confidently asserted that, of ancient Near Eastern literature, the OT is unique in the degree of accuracy of preservation.

HOWARD F. VOS

See BIBLE, TEXTUAL CRITICISM OF THE; BIBLICAL CRITICISM, OLD TESTAMENT.

Masoretic Text. *See* MASORA, MASORETES.

Masrekah. Home of an Edomite king named Samlah (Gn 36:36; 1 Chr 1:47). Its location is unknown.

Massa. Ishmael's seventh son and Abraham's grandson (Gn 25:14; 1 Chr 1:30). His descendants inhabited northwestern Arabia. Tiglath-pileser III mentions these people, along with the inhabitants of Tema (cf. Gn 25:15) and others, who were ruled by him and paid tribute to him. The people of Tema probably were descendants of Massa's brother Tema.

Massa forms part of the titles of Proverbs 30:1 and 31:1. The definite article precedes it in 30:1 and can be translated "the burden" or "the oracle." It is frequently used in prophetic passages in the ominous sense of God's impending judgment (Is 13:1; Na 1:1; Hb 1:1). Given these connotations, it is likely that the two superscriptions may refer to the people of northwestern Arabia, as it does in Genesis 25:14.

Massah and Meribah. Two Hebrew words meaning, respectively, "to put to the test" and "to find fault, quarrel." According to Exodus 17:7, after Moses got water from the rock at Rephidim, he called the place by these two names to memorialize the Israelites' "testing" of God's faithful provision.

Massah is mentioned four times (Dt 6:16; 9:22; 33:8; Ps 95:8) as the site of the rebellious rejection of God by the Israelites.

In contrast, Numbers 20:13,24; 27:14; and Deuteronomy 32:51 place Meribah near Kadesh in the wilderness of Zin where Moses struck the rock twice to produce water. Psalm 81:7 and Deuteronomy 33:8 suggest that God was testing the Israelites in these instances.

See MERIBAH.

Master. Word used to translate five different Hebrew words and seven different Greek terms with root meanings of owner (Is 1:3), elder (Dn 1:3), sovereign (1 Pt 2:18), teacher (Lk 6:40), superintendent (5:5), lord (Gn 39:3), sir (Jgs 19:11), rabbi (Mk 9:5), and captain (Acts 27:11); oftentimes used to describe Jesus.

One of the Greek words, *kyrios*, has multiple meanings with important implications for interpretation. It variously means sir or mister (Lk 14:21), master (Mt 6:24), lord (Acts 25:26), and the Lord God (Eph 6:9). Usually the context clearly indicates the specific meaning intended.

Mastic. Small Mediterranean tree which exudes a gum used to make numerous products.

See PLANTS (BALM).

Mathusala. KJV rendering of Methuselah, Enoch's son, in Luke 3:37.

See METHUSELAH.

Matred. Mother of Mehetabel, the wife of King Hadad of Edom (Gn 36:39; 1 Chr 1:50).

Matrites, Matri. Family of Benjamin's tribe. Saul, the first king of Israel, came from this family (1 Sm 10:21, KJV Matri).

Mattan. 1. Priest of Baal killed at the time when Jehoiada the priest had Queen Athaliah killed and Joash placed on the throne of Judah (2 Kgs 11:18; 2 Chr 23:17).

2. Father of Shephatiah, a prince under King Zedekiah and among those who persecuted Jeremiah (Jer 38:1–6).

Mattanah. Place of encampment for Israel following the exodus as the company moved east of the Dead Sea from the Arnon River northward into the territory of Sihon, king of the Amorites (Nm 21:18,19). Its exact location is unknown, but Khirbet el-Medeiyineh on the left bank of Wadi eth-Themed is considered its most likely setting.

Mattaniah. 1. Last king of Judah, whom King Nebuchadnezzar of Babylon enthroned in place of his nephew, Jehoiachin; his name subsequently was changed to Zedekiah (2 Kgs 24:17), and as such he was known in the other references to him in 2 Kings, 2 Chronicles, and Jeremiah.

See ZEDEKIAH #2.

2. Asaph's descendant, named among the Levites living in postexilic Jerusalem (1 Chr 9:15; Neh 11:17,22; 12:8,25,35).

3. Heman's son, who helped lead music in the sanctuary during David's reign (1 Chr 25:4,16).

4. Levite of the sons of Asaph, who was an ancestor of Jahaziel, a messenger of God in the days of King Jehoshaphat (2 Chr 20:14).

5. Another Levite of the sons of Asaph who helped cleanse the temple during King Hezekiah's reign (2 Chr 29:13).

6,7,8,9. Four men of Israel who were exhorted by Ezra to divorce their foreign wives during the postexilic era (Ezr 10:26,27,30,37).

10. One of the gatekeepers at the time of the dedication of the reconstructed wall of Jerusalem in Nehemiah's day (Neh 12:25).

11. Grandfather of Hanan, a treasurer of the temple storehouse in Nehemiah's day (Neh 13:13).

Mattatha. Ancestor of Jesus according to Luke's genealogy (3:31).

See GENEALOGY OF JESUS CHRIST.

Mattathah. KJV spelling of Mattattah, Hashum's son, in Ezra 10:33.

See MATTATTAH.

Mattathias. 1. Member of the priestly family of Joarib (his genealogy can be traced in 1 Mc 2:1 and in Josephus, *Antiq.* 12.6.3). He was a native of Jerusalem who settled in Modein and became the father of the nationalistic leaders, the Maccabeans, who led the Jewish revolt against the Syrians (167 BC). In his attempt to wipe out Judaism and establish Hellenism, Antiochus Epiphanes, king of Syria, outlawed Jewish sacrifices, built pagan altars (including one to Zeus in the temple), and executed anyone who possessed the Law (1 Mc 2:1–49). Mattathias ignited the revolt against this oppression when Greek officers set up a pagan altar at Modein and ordered that sacrifices be offered to heathen gods. Mattathias refused, killed the Jew who volunteered, killed the Greek officer, destroyed the altar, and fled to the hills with a band of followers. He led guerrilla warfare against the Syrians, continued to circumcise children, and made strenuous efforts to preserve the Law. His motto was, "Let everyone who is zealous for the law come after me."

He led the revolt for about a year and died, probably in 167 BC. His last bequest to his sons was, "Obey the ordinance of the law." He was succeeded in military leadership by his son Judas, and the Hasmonean dynasty of priests were his descendants. He is remembered in special Hanukkah prayers because of his zeal in fighting for religious freedom.

See JUDAISM.

2. Amos' son and an ancestor of Jesus according to Luke's genealogy (3:25).

See GENEALOGY OF JESUS CHRIST.

3. Semein's son and an ancestor of Jesus according to Luke's genealogy (3:26).

See GENEALOGY OF JESUS CHRIST.

Mattattah. Hashum's son, who obeyed Ezra's exhortation to divorce his pagan wife after the exile (Ezr 10:33, KJV Mattathah).

Mattenai. 1. Hashum's son, who obeyed Ezra's exhortation to divorce his pagan wife after the exile (Ezr 10:33).

2. Bani's son, who obeyed Ezra's exhortation to divorce his pagan wife after the exile (Ezr 10:33).

3. Head of Joiarib's priestly house during the days of Joiakim the high priest in postexilic Jerusalem (Neh 12:19).

Matthan. Ancestor of Jesus (Mt 1:15); perhaps identifiable with Matthat in Luke 3:24.

See GENEALOGY OF JESUS CHRIST.

Matthat. 1. Ancestor of Jesus (Lk 3:24), perhaps the same as Matthan (Mt 1:15).

2. Ancestor of Jesus (Lk 3:29).

See GENEALOGY OF JESUS CHRIST.

Matthew, Gospel of. First book of the NT. Nowhere does the text of Matthew itself clearly identify the author. Yet, as did the ancient church, we may ascribe authorship to Matthew the apostle.

Matthew wrote to a community of Greek-speaking Jewish Christians, located in a center such as Antioch in Syria. The community was surrounded and beset by Jews hostile to the claims of Jesus and the Christian community. The book may be dated sometime during the 60s.

Purpose. *Apologetics.* Matthew wrote as a Jew for Jews. In Jesus of Nazareth, Matthew contends, the OT reached its appointed goal. Jesus is the Messiah of Israel's expectation. In the opening chapter Matthew identifies him as "the son of David, the son of Abraham" (1:1), indeed as "God with us" (v 23). In later chapters Jesus is revealed as the "Son of Man" of Daniel 7 and the "Suffering Servant" of Isaiah 53. Throughout the book (1:22–27:10) the events of Jesus' life are represented as the "fulfillment" of OT prophecies. He comes to offer Israel salvation from sin (1:21). Nevertheless, the Jews have rejected him as their Messiah, and have thus placed themselves in the most perilous position (11:20–24; 21:33–46). One explanation for Israel's rejection of Jesus is the failure of the Jewish religious leadership to prepare the people for his coming. In the strongest language, Matthew denounces the teachers of the Law and the Pharisees. They have forsaken the word of God in favor of their own traditions (ch 15). Nor have they provided examples that the people could afford to follow (ch 23).

Catechesis. Matthew also wrote as a Christian for Christians. He presents Jesus as a new Moses, indeed as Yahweh incarnate, expounding his own Law for his people (ch 5), now newly constituted around his person under the leadership of the apostles (10:2–4; 16:18,19; 23:8–10). If the Christian church is to function properly, the teaching of Messiah on a host of moral and spiritual issues must be taken with utmost seriousness (chs 5–7,18). To aid this purpose, Matthew takes the form of a theological textbook, a handbook for the church, to instruct the people of God concerning the person and work of Jesus. That these teachings may be more readily and firmly grasped, Matthew presents them in a highly organized and memorable way. To facilitate the learning of the material, he arranges Jesus' teachings in five major discourses (interlocked with narrative portions) in which teachings of the same kind are clustered together (e.g., ch 10 consists of a charge to missionaries, and ch 13 of seven "parables of the kingdom"). Matthew's leading theological themes may be identified as: the *Son* of God (Jesus is Yahweh incarnate, "God with us"); the *kingdom* of God (in Jesus, God is invading history to inaugurate his final rule); the *salvation* of God (as the servant-king, Jesus has come to "save his people from their sins," 1:21); and the *people* of God (Jesus has come to build his church, a redeemed community consisting of both Jews and Gentiles).

Content. *The Coming of the Savior (1:1–2:23).* His name reveals his mission: "Jesus" (1:1) means "Yahweh saves." He is "the son of Abraham" (v 1) who comes to fulfill God's ancient promises to Jews and Gentiles (Gn 12:1–3). He is "Christ [or Messiah] the son of David" (v 1) who comes to inaugurate the kingdom of God (4:17). More than that, as evidenced both by prophecy (vv 22,23) and by the nature of his conception (vv 18,20), he is "God with us"—now come to "save his people from their sins" (v 21). As the son of David, and in accord with prophecy, he is born in Bethlehem (2:1–6). Drawn by the star of Israel's Messiah (cf. Nm 24:17), Gentiles come to worship him (2:1–12). When Herod seeks to destroy him, Jesus finds sanctuary in a gentile land; God's calling his Son from Egypt marks the beginning of a mighty saving work—nothing less than a new exodus under Jesus, the new Moses (vv 13–20). Having been born in the humblest of circumstances, Jesus (the Davidic "branch"), now comes to live in Nazareth (vv 21–23).

The Beginnings of Ministry (3:1–4:25). In face of the judgment that Jesus is about to execute (as evidence of the kingdom's arrival), John the Baptist calls Israel to repentance (3:1–12). Jesus' submission to John's baptism, and the voice from heaven, show him to be a king who serves his subjects by taking their sins upon himself (vv 13–17). Like Israel at the exodus, Jesus is led into the wilderness for a period of testing (4:1). When the devil seeks to turn him away both from God and from his appointed mission, Jesus gains victory by depending upon God and his Word (vv 1–11). Returning to Galilee, Jesus deliberately settles in territory with both Jewish and gentile associations (vv 12–16) and begins a ministry of preaching (like John, he calls for repentance in face of the dawning kingdom), teaching (he calls his first disciples), and healing (vv 17–25).

The Sermon on the Mount (5:1–7:29). Just as Moses ascended Sinai to receive God's Law for Israel, so Jesus—as both the new Moses and as God incarnate—ascends the mountain to set forth his instruction for the citizens of the kingdom of God (5:1,2). He begins with *gospel* (not law), declaring that God shall surely save those who—beset by sin—trust in God's mercy, obey his commands, and long for him to establish his righteous rule in the earth (vv 3–12). Toward that end, disciples are a preservative (salt) and a witness (light) in a sinful society (vv 13–16). As the one who has come not to abolish the Law and the Prophets but to bring them to completion (i.e., to usher in the new age to which the OT pointed, v 17), Jesus calls his disciples to steadfast obedience to God's Law as now expounded by the Lawgiver himself (vv 18–20). God's commands embrace inner desires as well as outward actions, must not be watered down or rationalized, and call for more radical obedience than ever before, now that the end has come (vv 21–48). In their giving, praying, and fasting, disciples are to combat hypocrisy by God-centeredness and self-forgetfulness (6:1–18). The Lord's Prayer (vv 9–13) calls upon God to honor his name by establishing his rule on earth; and to pardon, protect, and provide for his children. Given this prayer, and given the disciples' God-centered view of reality (vv 19–24), there is no cause for anxiety (vv 25–34). Disciples must be discerning without being judgmental (7:1–6), and depend on God for the power needed to love others (vv 7–12). Having completed his

exposition of the Law (5:21–7:12), Jesus now calls would-be disciples to the strict but liberating way of law-keeping (7:13,14), warns against teachers who encourage a lawless life style (vv 15–20), and insists that true disciples do God's will (vv 21–23). Founding one's life on Jesus' teaching means true stability (vv 24–27).

The Authority of Jesus (8:1–9:38). Having given his authority *verbal* expression in teaching (7:28,29), Jesus now gives it *visible* expression in a series of healing miracles, again revealing himself as the servant of Isaiah (8:17). He heals a leper, a centurion's servant, and a bleeding woman by his word (8:1–13; 9:20–22). His touch dispels a fever and raises the dead (8:14,15; 9:23–25). A combination of word and touch cures the blind (9:27–31). As "God with us," Jesus calls for unqualified allegiance (8:18–22). Though lacking even the natural protection enjoyed by animals (v 20), he demonstrates his sovereignty over the natural world—and thus his deity—by calming the storm (vv 23–27). In direct confrontations with demons, he shows his superiority over them (vv 28–34; 9:32,33). Exercising God's own authority, he declares sins forgiven (vv 1–8) and calls sinners to repentance and to discipleship (vv 9–13). Joy over the kingdom's inauguration is mingled with longing for its consummation (vv 14–17). The summary of 9:35–38 echoes 4:23–25, recalls chapters 5–7, and prepares for the next major discourse.

Jesus' Charge to the Missionaries (10:1–42). In response to the prayers that he has commanded, Christ now invests 12 disciples with apostolic authority and sends them out "into his harvest field" (9:37–10:4). The discourse speaks both of the apostles' immediate mission (vv 5–15) and of the church's broader mission (vv 16–42). For now, the apostles are to concentrate on evangelizing Jews (v 6), in preparation for the mission to Gentiles (28:19). The "worthy" are those who welcome the apostles and their message, the "unworthy" those who reject them (vv 11–15). In the broader mission, there is sure to be persecution (vv 16–19,24,25), but this will actually aid the witness (vv 17–23). God will save his faithful missionaries (vv 19–23), but judge those who oppress them and who disown Christ (vv 26–39). A sure reward awaits both the herald and the recipient of the message (vv 37–42).

Christ the Lord (11:1–12:50). The judgment John predicted is already underway; one's stand in the last judgment is now being determined by his response to the words and works of Jesus (11:2–6). Like his herald, Jesus meets with widespread hostility and indifference (vv 7–19). Given the finality of the grace attending his ministry, those who reject him will suffer the severest judgment (vv 20–24). Yet there are others—the lowly, the burdened, the teachable—who learn (by revelation from God the Father and God the Son) that the "Lord of heaven and earth" is also the "gentle and humble" God who comes to give rest to those who trust in him (vv 25–30). As the one who ushers in the new age (12:6), Jesus abrogates OT ceremonial law; but as Lord of the sabbath (v 8), he upholds the fourth commandment (vv 1–8). True rest (11:29) comes to those who keep the Law (cf. 5:17–20) by acts of goodness and mercy (12:7–14), after the manner of God's servant (vv 15–21). Viewing Jesus as the destroyer of the sabbath, the Pharisees ascribe his miraculous powers to Satan (vv 22–24). On the contrary, says Jesus, the rule he is inaugurating is crushing Satan's empire (vv 25–29). To reject this truth in the full awareness of what one is doing is to commit the unforgivable sin against the Holy Spirit (vv 30–32); the words of Jesus' accusers (v 24) expose them as persons destined for condemnation (vv 33–37). The requested sign from heaven will indeed be given, in Jesus' resurrection; but even this sign requires preaching and faith (vv 38–42). And even the experience (and the proper interpretation) of Jesus' exorcising powers, is not so crucial as reception of his teaching and commitment to his person (vv 43–50).

The Parables of the Kingdom (13:1–58). This, the third of Matthew's five great discourses, contains seven parables. In the parable of the sower, four kinds of soil—hard, shallow, cluttered, and fruitful—illustrate the various responses to Jesus' preaching (13:3–9,18–23). As those who have received Jesus' proclamation of the kingdom (4:17), the disciples are given more light; but the crowds must accept that initial proclamation before further light is given (vv 10–17,34,35). In both the parable of the weeds (vv 24–30,36–43) and the parable of the net (vv 47–50), Jesus assures his disciples that the final judgment will separate true believers from false, and warns against hasty, premature judgments (cf. 7:1–5). The parables of the mustard and the yeast (vv 31–33) contrast the smallness of the kingdom's inauguration with the fullness of its consummation. The parables of the hidden treasure and the pearl (vv 44–46) depict the kingdom as a value far surpassing all others (cf. 6:33). Thus illuminated by Jesus, disciples have new treasures to add to their old (vv 51,52). The people of Nazareth, on the contrary, echo the crowds' lack of understanding and the Pharisees' hostility (vv 53–58).

Spiritual Conflict (14:1–16:12). In 14:1–12 the preaching of John exposes the weakness of Herod, and the beheading of John anticipates the crucifixion of Jesus (cf. 17:12). The true king is not Herod, but Jesus. He is sovereign over nature itself (14:13–36)—God incarnate, "God with us," who feeds the hungry multitude in the wilderness (as God once provided manna) and walks upon and calms the sea (whose raging none but God can subdue, Ps 89:9). Peter models Christians' faith, fear, and utter dependence on Jesus (14:28–31). The Pharisees and teachers of the Law appear to worship God but in fact are devoted to their own traditions, which they offer not as supplements but as *rivals* to the Word of God (15:1–9). In verses 10–20 Jesus teaches both that ceremonial law apart from moral law becomes empty ritual, and that the old distinction between clean and unclean foods (Lv 11) is now as obsolete as the distinction between Jews and Gentiles. To underscore the point, Jesus enters pagan territory, heals a Canaanite (vv 21–28) and feeds a gentile multitude (vv 29–39). Pharisees and Sadducees, for all their differences, are united in their opposition to Jesus and in the mancenteredness of their teaching (16:1–12). In the case of the Pharisees, this "teaching" (v 12) manifests itself in the propagation of human traditions (15:1–9), in prideful hypocrisy (6:1–18), and in domination of others (23:4); and in the case of the Sadducees, in the exercise of (and in efforts to safeguard) status, wealth, and power.

The Coming Salvation (16:13–17:27). Going beyond the crowds' respectful but inadequate estimates, Peter confesses Jesus to be "the Christ, the Son of the living God"—a recognition of Jesus' deity granted by divine revelation (16:13–17; cf. 11:25,26). As it is God the Son who possesses and builds the church, Satan and death are victims rather than victors. The word of truth is crucial (16:18,19): Jesus will build his church on Peter, precisely in his capacity as apostolic confessor and representative; and the apostles' prohibiting and granting entry into the church ("binding" and "loosing," respectively) depends upon the prior decision of heaven (i.e., God's revelation of apostolic teaching). In face of Peter's confession and the persistent false notions of messiahship (16:20,23), Jesus now (for the first time) predicts his passion and coming glory (vv 21–28). In anticipation of that glory, Jesus is transfigured before certain disciples; Moses and Elijah (whose experiences on the mountain are here recalled) join God the Father in bearing witness to the unique splendor of God the Son (17:1–8). The latter-day Elijah, far from forestalling Messiah's death, actually foreshadows it (vv 9–13; cf. 14:1–12); Jesus must come to glory through suffering and combatting demonic powers (17:14–18,22,23). Moreover, authority to exorcise demons (cf. 10:1) is no substitute for dependence on God

Olive press at Capernaum, where Jesus was questioned about the temple tax (Mt 17:24–27).

(17:14–21). As Lord of the temple and as Son of the heavenly king, Jesus need not pay the temple tax; yet he freely does so, in the process showing his lordship over nature too (vv 24–27).

Greatness in the Kingdom (18:1–35). In this, the fourth of Matthew's five great discourses, Jesus concentrates on the character and attitudes of church members. He calls upon his followers both to *become* and to *welcome* the lowliest (18:1–5). Leaders especially are enjoined to deal harshly with themselves but gently with those under their care (vv 6–9). Remembering the Father's love for sinners, Christians are to make every effort (both by prayer and by personal initiative) to restore offending brothers, with excommunication being the last resort (vv 10–20). Church members who really understand the Father's amazing grace will never stop offering forgiveness and compassion to those who wrong them (vv 21–35).

Instructions on the Way to Jerusalem (19:1–20:34). Given God's creation ordinances, says Jesus, divorce itself is never *commanded*; it is only *permitted* in face of existent sin—that is, where the marital bond has already been severed through infidelity (19:1–9). As in 5:17–48, Jesus calls his followers to radical obedience (19:10–12). Besides instructing disciples to become like children (18:1–4), Jesus embraces children themselves with his covenantal love (19:13–15). He appeals likewise to the rich young man (vv 16–22); but the man, while faithful to the commands about love of neighbor, is too bound by his wealth to give himself unreservedly to loving God. Yet those who abandon all to follow Jesus will receive wealth untold in the coming kingdom (vv 27–30). The basis for such blessings lies not in human merit but in the astonishing generosity of the gracious God (20:1–16). None—not even the rich—are beyond the power of his grace (19:23–

26). But God offers free salvation only at great cost to himself (20:17–19). Confronting competitiveness and ambition among his followers, Jesus teaches and then shows them (by healing the blind men) that true greatness lies not in lording it over others but in serving them (vv 20–34), as shall be supremely demonstrated in his death as "a ransom for many" (v 28).

Confrontations in Jerusalem (21:1–22:46). As the servant-king (cf. 3:17), and as the Messiah destined for suffering (cf. 16:16–21; 20:28), Jesus enters Jerusalem not upon a war horse but upon a donkey's colt; for he purposes not to declare war on his enemies but to hand himself over to them—and thus achieve his triumph through defeat (21:1–11). As Lord of the temple, he demands that its commerce be halted and that it become (as God ordained) a place of worship for everyone—including the sick, the young, and the alien (vv 12–17; cf. Mk 11:17). He outwits those who refuse to acknowledge the heavenly source of his and John's authority (21:23–27). In dramatic and devastating fashion, first visibly (by cursing the fig tree, vv 18–22) and then verbally (in the three parables of vv 28–22:14), Jesus pronounces judgment upon those Jews who have refused to acknowledge him as Messiah and Son of God. Henceforth the true people of God are those who believe in Jesus (18:6)—whether Jews or Gentiles. He calls upon his people to pledge their supreme allegiance to God without neglecting political responsibility (22:15–22). In the resurrection, what will matter most is one's relationship to God (vv 23–33). Indeed, he who loves God with his whole being and his neighbor as himself, has kept the two foundational commandments of the OT (vv 34–40). Henceforth, submitting to God means rightly recognizing Jesus; he is indeed David's son (Mt 1), but he is supremely David's Lord—the exalted Son of God (vv 41–46; cf. 16:16).

Woes upon the Scribes and Pharisees (23:1–39). Five reasons are stated for Jesus' denunciation of the Jewish religious leaders. First is their hypocrisy: their practice contradicts their teaching (23:1–4), their external purity conceals inner rottenness (vv 25–28), and they appear to champion God's cause but are really enemies of God's servants (vv 29–36). Second is the pride which prompts their hypocrisy (vv 5–12). Third is their exploitation of, and their baleful influence upon, those under their charge (vv 13–15). Fourth is their preoccupation with the minutiae of the Law to the neglect of its weightier matters (vv 16–24). Fifth is their responsibility for the dreadful judgment which the whole nation is about to experience (vv 33–39).

The Coming of the End (24:1–25:46). The introduction to this, the fifth and last of Matthew's great discourses, makes it plain that there is the closest connection (for both Jesus and his disciples) between the coming destruction of Jerusalem and the end of the age (24:1–3). Jesus first characterizes the time between his first advent and his return: There will be natural catastrophes, international warfare, the rise of false messiahs, the persecution of God's people, and the universal proclamation of the gospel of the kingdom (vv 4–14). Then Jesus speaks of the catastrophe that is soon to befall the Jewish nation in particular (as already foretold in 22:7; 23:38), culminating in the destruction of Jerusalem and its temple, AD 70 (24:15–25). Some time thereafter (but after an interval known only to God the Father, v 36), the Son of man will return in great glory, amidst apocalyptic signs, to gather his people (vv 26–31). The present generation will not pass away before judgment falls upon Israel (vv 15–25); so let listeners take heed (vv 32–35). The same warning applies to the more remote coming of the Son of man (vv 36–51): both the certainty of the event, and the uncertainty of its time, call for vigilance and faithfulness in the interval—for that event will bring both salvation and judgment. To drive the lesson home, Jesus tells the parables of the wise and foolish virgins (25:1–13) and the talents (vv 14–30). The concluding parable of the sheep and the goats (vv 31–46) speaks of the urgent necessity of making the right response to the "brothers," that is, the apostles, of Christ; those who feed, clothe, and otherwise care for the messengers of Christ thereby testify to their reception of the apostles' message and their Lord (cf. 10:40–42).

The Road to Golgotha (26:1–27:26). As though in response to Jesus' own prediction, the chief priests and the elders hatch their murderous plot (26:1–5), soon to be aided by Judas (vv 14–16). The anointing at Bethany (vv 6–13) testifies to the extravagance of love and the imminence of death. At the Passover meal (vv 17–30), signalling at what sacrifice the new exodus comes about (cf. 2:15), Jesus interprets his forthcoming death as an atoning sacrifice for the forgiveness of sins (26:26–28; cf. 1:21) and anticipates the day of final victory over sin and death in the consummated kingdom (26:29). Jesus' agony in Gethsemane (vv 36–46) expresses his horror over taking his people's sins upon himself; by a stupendous act of filial obedience he submits his will to the Father, that the Scriptures might be fulfilled (v 54; cf. Is 53). As the servant of God destined to suffer, Jesus resists attempts to thwart his arrest (26:47–56). The Jews' supreme court (the Sanhedrin) and their loftiest religious official (the high priest) condemn Jesus as a blasphemer because he dares to identify himself as "the

Christ, the Son of God" (vv 57–68; cf. 16:16). As though joining the court's repudiation, Peter—in fulfillment of Jesus' prophecy (26:31–35)—disclaims knowledge of Jesus (vv 69–75). Judas' disillusionment finds expression in suicide (27:3–10). The Jews hand Jesus over to Pilate the Roman governor (vv 1,2), he alone having the authority to pronounce the death sentence. Knowing that the charge of blasphemy will carry no weight with Pilate, the Jews now represent Jesus as a threat to Caesar (cf. v 11). In the end, Pilate responds not to specific charges and evidence, but to pressure from the crowd and the threat of riot (vv 11–25). He releases Barabbas and delivers Jesus to be crucified (v 26).

The Death of Jesus (27:27–66). Following his humiliating treatment at the hands of the Roman soldiers, Jesus is led to the place of execution; weakened by the beatings, he requires assistance (27:27–32). He refuses the proffered narcotic so that he might keep his head clear (v 34). His being executed with malefactors (v 38) testifies to the purpose of his death (cf. 1:21). A steady stream of abuse is hurled at him, in blasphemous disregard of the truth of the superscription "This is Jesus the King of the Jews" (vv 37–44). Finally, out of the darkness Jesus utters the cry of dereliction; now is revealed the ultimate horror (that from which his soul shrank in Gethsemane), the sin-bearer's supreme agony—the beloved Son's abandonment by the Father (vv 45–49). Having cried out with a loud voice (cf. Jn 19:30), Jesus dies (27:50). Immediately the saving effects of his death become evident (vv 51–53): Jewish and gentile sinners, now forgiven, have access to the holy God (the veil of the temple is rent asunder); and there is hope of resurrection for those who have died. As at the beginning (2:1–12), Gentiles instead of Jews confess Jesus (27:54; contrast 26:63–65). Joseph's careful attentiveness to Jesus' burial contrasts with the ongoing attempts of the chief priests and Pharisees to resist Jesus' power (27:57–66).

The Triumph of the Savior (28:1–20). Amidst great glory and power and joy, the Savior's victory over death is announced and attested (28:1–7). The risen Jesus appears first to the women who attended him in death (vv 8–10; cf. 27:61; 28:1). The Jews' response to the guards' report signals their growing desperation before irresistible reality (vv 11–15). Meeting with the 11 on the mountain in Galilee (vv 16–20), Jesus the new Moses continues his instructions. He now reveals the evangelistic purpose for which Matthew has been preparing readers from the very threshold of his Gospel. The apostles are to disciple all peoples by baptizing them into the name of the triune

God and by teaching them to obey all that Jesus has commanded. The apostles go forth in the assurance that Jesus—as the Lord—stands over them, and that Jesus—as Immanuel—stands with them, until the very end of the age.

J. KNOX CHAMBLIN

See SYNOPTIC GOSPELS; MARK, GOSPEL OF; LUKE, GOSPEL OF; JESUS CHRIST, LIFE AND TEACHING OF; MATTHEW, THE APOSTLE; SOURCE CRITICISM; REDACTION CRITICISM.

Bibliography. J.A. Alexander, *The Gospel According to Matthew*; M.S. Augsburger, *Matthew*; D. Hill, *The Gospel of Matthew*; A.H. McNeile, *The Gospel According to Matthew*; E. Schweizer, *The Good News According to Matthew*; S.D. Tonssaint, *Behold the King*; R.E.O. White, *The Mind of Matthew*.

Matthew, The Apostle. Jew (his name in Hebrew means "gift of Yahweh"), a tax collector of Capernaum (engaged in taxing fishermen like Peter), whom Jesus called into discipleship (Mt 9:9), and later appointed as one of the 12 apostles (10:3). The early church identified the first book of the NT as "the Gospel according to Matthew."

All three Synoptists place the call of Matthew *after* the healing of the paralytic and Jesus' pronouncement of his right to forgive sins (Mt 9:1–8), and *before* the dinner for "tax collectors and sinners" (vv 10–13), thus identifying Matthew as one of the sinners (v 13) to whom Jesus offers forgiveness.

Matthew's response to Jesus is obedient, decisive, and sacrificial (Lk 5:28). Both Mark (2:14) and Luke (5:27) call the tax collector "Levi" in place of "Matthew" (cf. Mt 9:9). A personal name (Matthew) would be a more natural choice than a tribal name (Levi), for identifying oneself. Mark and Luke locate the dinner "at *his* [Levi's] house" (Mk 2:15; Lk 5:29), but Matthew "in *the* house" (Mt 9:10)—words one might use of his own home.

In all three lists of the 12 apostles (Mt 10:2–4; Mk 3:16–19; Lk 6:14–16), Matthew appears; but Matthew alone speaks of "Matthew the tax collector." Besides distinguishing this Matthew from others, "tax collector" (as Matthew's self-designation) would also recall the life out of which Jesus had called him.

Matthew names the 12 at the point where Jesus sends them forth with the message of the kingdom (Mt 10:1–8). Did Jesus confer the name Matthew upon Levi as a sign of apostleship (cf. 10:2, "Simon, who is called Peter," with 9:9, "a man sitting at the tax collector's booth, called Matthew")? If Matthew is a Christian name, this would help to explain why Levi occurs only in accounts of his call (Mk 2:14; Lk 5:27,29), and Matthew everywhere else.

All three Synoptists number "James son of Alphaeus" among the 12 apostles. As Mark 2:14 identifies Matthew as "Levi son of Alphaeus," it is possible that James and Levi are brothers. Yet this is unlikely; for the evangelists do not make the identification explicit, as they do in the case of Peter and Andrew and the sons of Zebedee.

The "scribe" of Matthew 13:52 is, no doubt, Matthew himself, who as a tax collector had been a secular scribe. Jesus likens him to a person "bringing forth treasures new and old"—the old being those acquired as a tax collector (such as gifts for accuracy and organization), the new being Jesus' teachings "about the kingdom of heaven." As a man doubly equipped, Matthew is now ready for further scribal activity—the writing of the book that bears his name.

Matthew is among those gathered to await the coming of the Holy Spirit (Acts 1:13). The NT records nothing of his activity beyond this point.

J. KNOX CHAMBLIN

See MATTHEW, GOSPEL OF; APOSTLE, APOSTLESHIP.

Matthias. Disciple of Jesus, mentioned by name only in Acts 1:23,26, chosen to take the place of Judas Iscariot.

Shortly after the ascension, Peter voiced the need for another apostle, the stipulations being that the candidate must have been a follower of Jesus from his baptism to his ascension and a witness to his resurrection. The assembly put forward two men who met these criteria: Joseph called Barsabas, surnamed Justus, and Matthias. They then cast lots (some scholars believe they cast ballots). Whatever the method, Matthias was chosen. Later the apostolate was widened to include others such as Paul, Andronicus, and Junias. Scripture never mentions Matthias again, though tradition says that he preached in Judea and was finally stoned to death by the Jews.

See APOSTLE, APOSTLESHIP.

Mattithiah. 1. Levite and Shallum's firstborn son, who was in charge of making the baked cakes that accompanied the offerings in the temple (1 Chr 9:31).

2. Musician appointed by the Levites to play the lyre, along with five others, when the ark was brought to Jerusalem in David's time (1 Chr 15:18,21; 16:5).

3. One of Juduthun's six sons, who was a musician in David's time (1 Chr 25:3,21); perhaps identifiable with #2 above.

4. Nebo's son, who divorced his foreign wife as commanded by Ezra (Ezr 10:43).

5. One who stood to Ezra's right when Ezra read the Law to the people after the exile (Neh 9:4).

Mattock. Agricultural tool used for grubbing or breaking up the soil (1 Sm 13:20,21).

See AGRICULTURE; TOOLS.

Maul. KJV translation for "war club" in Proverbs 25:18.

See ARMS AND WARFARE.

Mazzaroth. Word appearing in Job 38:32 that may refer to a constellation. The Hebrew form is feminine in Job 38:32 and masculine in Job 9:9, where it has usually been thought to refer to the Hyades. Some hold that Mazzaroth refers to the constellation of the Bear while others think it refers to the 12 signs of the zodiac, the Corona Borealis, or the Hyades.

See ASTRONOMY.

Meah, Tower of. KJV translation for "Tower of the Hundred" in Nehemiah 3:1 and 12:39.

See HUNDRED, TOWER OF THE.

Meal Offering. See OFFERINGS AND SACRIFICES.

Meals, Significance of. The meal played a significant role in family, social, and religious life. The evening meal was the time when all family members normally were gathered together, and was thus an important time of fellowship. Providing food for the traveler was both a social and a religious responsibility, while the ideal of a quiet social life was realized by having friends break bread with the family and discuss the problems of the day by the light of small oil lamps. The significance of the meal retains its central focus, both in the Jewish religion with the Passover meal and in Christianity with the celebration of the Lord's Supper.

In the ancient Near East two meals were normally eaten during the day. The first was the noonday meal, usually consumed by laborers in the field and consisting of such items as small cakes or flat loaves, figs or olives, and possibly cheese or curds of goats' milk. This was considered a small meal, eaten for sustenance and refreshment at a time of relaxation and respite from the heat of the sun and the labor of the day (Ru 2:14). Breakfast was considered unnecessary, and biblical references to any such form of early morning meal are very few (Jgs 19:5; Jn 21:12).

Whereas in Egypt the main meal was served at noon, among the Hebrews the evening meal was the most important social occasion of the day. Then the exhausted field workers could return home to relax after their day's work and enjoy the feeling of communal warmth as the family gathered together for their principal meal. This occasion coincided with the arrival of darkness, a time when there was insufficient light for field work to continue.

The laborer's meal consisted of bread or cakes made of hand-ground grain, goats' cheese or curds, vegetables (especially beans, lentils, leeks, and peas, which were popular for the sake of variety although not always plentiful), and figs, olives, raisins, and dates. Meat was usually available, but for the majority was a luxury item. Food was cooked in olive oil, and honey was used for sweetening.

The meal was eaten together by the entire family. There was no separate dining room in the average house, and during the patriarchal period meals were consumed while the family was seated on the floor, a mat often serving as a table (Gn 37:25). Canaanite seating habits were adopted subsequently, and chairs and small tables were used (1 Kgs 13:20; Ps 23:5; Ez 23:41). Eating in the Egyptian fashion in a reclining position became popular, and continued throughout the Roman period. Musical entertainment, dancing, and riddles were sometimes provided on festive occasions for family and guests, since the meal period was the normal time for entertainment in Near Eastern society.

Kings' feasts and banquets were generally on a grand scale. In Egypt at the midday meal, banquets were attended by ladies wearing dresses of gossamer-thin fine linen, with black wigs and perfume cones on their heads and elaborate eye makeup. Couches were placed at low tables for the guests, while the food served consisted of a variety of roasted meats including fowl, along with vegetables and several

A triclinium—in the House of Trebius Valens in Pompeii—at which people recline to eat, as at the Last Supper.

kinds of sweet food. Liberal quantities of beer and wine were drunk in the process of eating. Feasts frequently lasted for several days, like the one recorded in Mesopotamia which continued for 10 days and was attended by 70,000 guests.

The Book of Esther gives insight into 5th-century BC banquet customs. The first banquet lasted for 180 days (Est 1:4), and was followed by two shorter feasts, probably a week long. The first was given for the palace employees, and the second was arranged for the women by the queen (Est 1:5,9). The display was colorful; the location of one feast was the garden of the royal palace, which was decorated with white, green, and blue hangings tied back with cords of linen and purple to silver rings mounted on marble pillars. Gold and silver benches stood on pavements of black, red, white, and yellow marble (Est 1:6).

It was not until the reign of King Solomon (970–930 BC) that Hebrew banquets, like everything else associated with Solomon's wealth and finery, became ostentatious and elaborate. In the 5th century BC, Nehemiah, who provided food for 150 persons, listed his daily food requirements as "one ox, six choice sheep; also fowls . . ." (Neh 5:18).

By NT times a separate upper room often served as a dining room. Guests reclined by leaning on the left elbow so that they were close enough together on their couches to facilitate easy conversation. There was a strict hierarchy to the seating arrangements (cf. Gn 43:33; 1 Sam 9:22; Mt 23:6; Mk 12:39; Lk 14:8) at all formal meals, the "highest" place being that to the right of the servants as they entered the room and the lowest to their left.

Guests washed their hands before and after meals, and normally partook of a form of meat and/or vegetable stew from a common bowl placed in the center of the table. Instead of cutlery, pieces of bread held in the fingers were made into the shape of a small scoop and dipped into the bowl. There would usually be only one main dish requiring preparation, so that the woman who had cooked the meal could partake of it with her guests, thus fulfilling the ideals of community at mealtimes.

On several occasions in the NT Jesus is mentioned as eating meals with disciples and friends. He and his followers were guests at the wedding feast held in Cana of Galilee (Jn 2:1–10), and also at a dinner given by Matthew (Mt 9:10), as well as at another given by Simon the Pharisee (Lk 7:36–50). Jesus also was entertained at dinner somewhat unexpectedly by Zacchaeus (19:6,7). On several occasions Jesus was a guest at a family gathering held at the home of Martha, Mary, and Lazarus in Bethany (10:38–42; Jn 12:2). Following the customs of smaller towns and villages, passers-by may well have called into the house to greet Jesus and perhaps converse with other guests.

There are two important occasions described in Scripture, one involving the old covenant and the other the new, in which meals had a redemptive meaning for the people of God. The first was the institution of the Passover at the time of Israel's departure from Egypt under Moses (Ex 12). This ceremony, which was the initial part of the feast of unleavened bread, required that a male lamb not older than one year was to be sacrificed on the 14th day of the month (v 6) by each of the Israelite households. Some of the blood was to be smeared on the doorposts and lintel of the house, while the meat was to be roasted and eaten along with unleavened bread and a salad of bitter herbs. The salad probably included endive, lettuce, and chicory. Whatever was left over from the feasts was to be burned, and the participants were required to dress for a hurried journey and to eat the meal quickly. The presence of the sacrificial blood protected the members of the various households as God destroyed the firstborn in the land of Egypt (v 13). Because the Passover was meant as a memorial, God ordered it to be observed as a ceremony for all future generations (v 14). The feast of unleavened bread continued for another seven days (Lv 23:6), a period that was observed as a holy assembly during which normal work was forbidden. When the Passover was first instituted, the head of the household was responsible for explaining the meaning of the ceremony that marked the deliverance of the Israelites from slavery in Egypt (Ex 13:8), a tradition that continues in Jewish households when Pesah is celebrated each year. The meal is thus a continual reminder of God's mercy and power in liberating his enslaved people during the days of Moses.

The second meal described in Scripture as having redemptive significance for man is the Lord's Supper (Mt 26:26–30; Mk 14:22–26; Lk 22:17–20). This meal was instituted by Jesus himself, and took place after the Passover rituals had been completed. On that occasion Jesus took unleavened bread, broke it, and distributed it to those eating with him, telling them that it symbolized his body. After this a cup was passed around, and the disciples were instructed to drink from it because the wine represented Jesus' blood of the new covenant that was to be shed for the forgiveness of human sin.

John does not mention this event, and Luke's Gospel has a different order of proceedings from Matthew and Mark. This need only mean that by Christ's time the Passover meal had come to include ceremonies in addition to those prescribed in Exodus 12, or that there was some difference among early Christians in the way the last supper was observed. Whereas some Greek manuscripts of the Gospels speak of the "covenant in Christ's blood," others describe it specifically as the "new covenant." Christ commanded his followers to observe this meal as a reminder of the great deliverance from sin that he had achieved for humanity by his redemptive work on Calvary. In this way the Lord's Supper acquired for the Christian church a saving significance comparable to that which the Passover had for the Israelites in the old covenant era.

The miracle of deliverance from bondage to Egypt is mentioned frequently by poets and prophets alike (Pss 78; 80; 135; Is 10:24; Jer 2:6; 7:25), and in this connection the Passover meal served as a valuable teaching device which kept alive the memory of that mighty divine act. The God who led his people from Egypt was the one who could always give obedient Israel the victory over all oppressive enemies. The fact that God's deliverance was remembered within the specific context of a devotional meal made his redemption a matter of religious belief, not just of historical significance. The Passover was an occasion when liberation from oppression was celebrated, and once the Israelites were settled in Canaan they enjoyed the fulfillment of God's covenantal promises to them. The meal itself was an annual reminder that Israel must also be true to its own responsibilities in the covenant.

In the Gospels the Passover meal is given new significance by becoming the ritual from which the Lord's Supper was derived. Jesus the Messiah proclaims his atoning death for mankind, and commends the ritual that he instituted as a reminder that the cross brings freedom from bondage to sin.

Those who eat Christ's flesh and drink his blood (Jn 6:54–56) will abide in him, while he in turn will possess their lives and give them forgiveness and peace. When first instituted, the Lord's Supper reaffirmed the provisions of liberation contained in Passover by showing that God's Messiah was willing to shed his blood that the world might be redeemed from bondage to sin, and the individual repentant sinner saved from the kind of death reserved for the ungodly.

By the time Paul recorded his account of the last supper (1 Cor 11:23–26), the Passover aspect of the meal had already receded into the background. While there are still certain features in common, such as the ceremonies relating to the bread and the cup, the Lord's Supper has acquired its own distinctive character as a symbol of God's redemption and salvation in Christ. It is a token that the new covenant, long promised by Jeremiah (31:31), has become a reality, and as such it is a source of great joy and strength to the believer.

Paul followed the pattern of instruction regarding the Passover meal in reminding his readers that as often as they followed in a sacramental manner the pattern of breaking bread and drinking wine, they were proclaiming the power inherent in Christ's atoning death. This procedure would be ritually valid and useful until Christ came again, for it depicted him as God's agent of salvation for mankind and the source of grace and spiritual vitality for the individual.

HAZEL W. PERKIN

See FAMILY LIFE AND RELATIONS; FOOD AND FOOD PREPARATION; FEASTS AND FESTIVALS OF ISRAEL; LORD'S SUPPER, THE.

Mearah. Region of Palestine that the Israelites had not possessed (Jos 13:4, NIV Arah). Its location is uncertain. Suggestions include the district of caves (Mearah means "cave") near Sidon called Mughar Jezzin, and the towns Khirbet 'Arah and Mogheiriyeh.

Measure. *See* WEIGHTS AND MEASURES.

Measuring Line. *See* WEIGHTS AND MEASURES.

Measuring Reed. *See* WEIGHTS AND MEASURES.

Meat. *See* FOOD AND FOOD PREPARATION; MEALS, SIGNIFICANCE OF.

Meat Offering. *See* OFFERINGS AND SACRIFICES.

Mebunnai. Alternate name (probably a textual corruption) of Sibbecai, a warrior among David's "mighty men," in 2 Samuel 23:27.

See SIBBECAI, SIBBECHAI.

Mecherathite. Designation for Hepher in 1 Chronicles 11:36. The parallel passage in 2 Samuel 23:34 calls him "the son of the Maachathite" (KJV) or "from Maacah" (RSV).

See MAACAH, MAACHAH (PLACE); MAACHATHITE, MAACATHITE, MAACHATHI.

Meconah. Settlement mentioned beside Ziklag (Neh 11:28, KJV Mekonah) and presumably in the western Negeb. It is missing in most manuscripts of the Greek version.

Medad. Elder of Israel who, with Eldad, prophesied in the wilderness to Joshua's consternation. Moses, however, defended Medad's right to speak in God's name (Nm 11:26,27).

Medan. Third son of Abraham by his second wife, Keturah (Gn 25:2; 1 Chr 1:32).

Medeba. Moabite town in the fertile plain northeast of the Dead Sea, about 25 miles south of Philadelphia (modern Amman). It was situated 6 miles south of Heshbon on the Roman road to Kerak.

Here the Amorites defeated Moab (Nm 21:30). Later Israel defeated Sihon, king of the Amorites, at Medeba and assigned it to Reuben's tribe (Jos 13:9,16). At this place David routed an Aramaean army hired by the Amorites to attack his forces (1 Chr 19:7).

According to the Moabite Stone, the town was once controlled by Omri and Ahab of Israel; however, when Mesha reasserted Moabite dominance in the 8th century BC, he rebuilt Medeba and other Moabite cities. Medeba is named in Isaiah's prophecies against Moab (Is 15:2). In later times Joram and Jehoshaphat made unsuccessful attempts at capturing this city.

In Maccabean times Medeba was the stronghold of the robbers Jambri and his sons. John Maccabeus was seized and killed in this town by this powerful family (1 Mc 9:36–42; Josephus *Antiq.* 13.1.4). John Hyrcanus took the town after a siege lasting six months (*Antiq.* 13.9.9). It was later taken by Janneus, although Hyrcanus II promised to restore it to Aretas, king of Arabis (*Antiq.* 13.15.4; 14.1.4).

During the Byzantine period, the town became quite wealthy. At present, remains of a city wall, numerous churches, and other buildings are extant from this period. A famous mosaic map of ancient Palestine (*c.* AD 560) was found on the floor of one of its ancient basilicas. Originally the map measured 78 feet by 20 feet, but it was partially covered and destroyed by the foundation of a newer church.

Medes, Media, Median. Indo-European speaking people appearing in the highland area of northwest Iran. They were closely related to the Persians, with whom they are often identified or confused by the Greeks, Egyptians, Assyrians, and other writers who referred to all people of the area by the almost generic term "Medes." In fact, the Medes inhabited a defined area in the Zagros Mountains positioned between 3000 and 5000 feet above sea level in a mountainous region divided by valleys. The capital, Ecbatana (now Hamadan), was on the major trade route from Mesopotamia. The elevation provided a temperate summer climate which encouraged the use of Ecbatana as a summer retreat for Persian kings.

As no texts are extant in the Median language relating to the history and culture of the Medes, information must be obtained from references to them in contemporary writings of the Greeks, Neo-Babylonians, and Assyrians. As the Medes and Chaldeans were instrumental in bringing down the Assyrian Empire, it is understandable that they should figure prominently in the Neo-Babylonian texts. Valuable additional information is available from Herodotus, possibly from cuneiform sources.

The Assyrian king Shalmaneser III recorded the activity of the Medes in the area around Ecbatana in the 9th century BC, but historians are uncertain exactly how long before that date they had migrated into the region.

Shalmaneser organized a raid into the plains controlled by the Medes in order to steal herds of the carefully bred horses, the reputation for whose excellence was already deservedly high. Over generations, Assyrian kings continued this type of raid, not only for the purpose of obtaining fresh supplies of horses, but also to ensure the free passage of traders on this major route. During the 8th century BC, Assyrian kings such as Adad-nirari (810–781 BC), Tiglath-pileser III (743 BC), and Sargon II (716 BC), all claim to have conquered Media and the OT records that the Israelites were transported there at the time of Sargon's incursions (2 Kgs 17:6; 18:11).

When Esar-haddon was king of Assyria (681–669 BC), he expected the Medians to acknowledge his overlordship and pay tribute according to their treaty, but, taking advantage of the declining strength of Assyria, the Medians joined forces with the Scythians and Cimmerians in 631 BC. The ebbing strength of the Assyrians was further eroded under a series of attacks led by Phraortes culminating in the fall of Nineveh in 612 BC and of Harran in 610 BC. Under the leadership of Kyaxares of Media, who organized a strong, disciplined army, the Median forces and their allies, having gained control of the major cities, extended their sphere of influence to the northern part of Assyria, negotiating peace with Lydia in 585 BC.

The Elamites, also a people involved in the ebb and flow of the power struggle in the region over the centuries, came into the ascendency in 550 BC when Cyrus of Anshan overcame Astyages. Cyrus was of half-Persian, half-Median ancestry. Ecbatana, capital of Media, was captured, and the entire area was controlled by Elam. Cyrus took on the additional title "King of the Medes." The laws and the heritage of the Medes were incorporated with those of the Persians (Dn 6:8,15). Medians were entrusted with high office in the administration. The Medes and the Persians were referred to in almost synonymous terms (Est 1:19; Dn 8:20). They were also involved in the

Median (left) and Persian (right) guards from Persepolis.

capture of Babylon (Is 13:17; Jer 51:11,28; Dn 6:28). Being of Median heritage (Dn 9:1) Darius, son of Ahasureus, was referred to as "the Mede" (Dn 11:1) from the time he took over as ruler of Babylon. His administration was not altogether peaceful, however, and restlessness led to outright rebellion both in his reign and during that of Darius II (409 BC).

A description of the sumptuous feasting and luxurious appointments of the court apartments are described in the Book of Esther (Est 1:3–7). The Medians subsequently were subjected to the control of the Syrians (Seleucids) and the Parthians. In the NT there is a single combined reference to Parthians, Medes, and Elamites (Acts 2:9), but thereafter Media seems to have become a geographical term,

the people no longer appearing in history as a group in their own right.   HAZEL W. PERKIN

Mediation, Mediator.   An intermediary, go-between, or expert in divine things, not to negotiate agreement or compromise but to approach the deity on behalf of others, and so to convey desired knowledge and reassurance with divine authority.

In the OT.   Job voices longing for such a mediator (only here in Greek OT): "He is not a man, as I am, that I might answer him, that we should come to trial together. There is no umpire [one to arbitrate, NEB] between us, who might lay his hand upon us both" (Jb 9:32,33). "Trial" and "arbitrate" continue the image of chapter 1, where Satan, the accusing attorney (cf. Rom 8:33; Rv 12:9,10), indicts Job before God. Job calls for defending counsel to plead his case (for this legal mediation compare 1 Jn 2:1, following ancient Latin translators and commentators).

More familiar is the mediation of instruction concerning the divine character and will. The Mosaic covenant, the religious constitution of Israel, was given through mediation of angels and of Moses (Ex 20:18–21; Dt 33:2; Acts 7:53; Gal 3:19; contrast Heb 6:13–17, where God, acting alone, "mediated" an oath). The terms of the covenant law were expounded by prophets who "stood in God's council," and by priests who communicated God's mind by oracle, sacred lot, and pronounced blessing (Dt 10:8; 33:8,10; 2 Chr 15:3; Jer 23:10,11,18–22; 31:31–34; Mi 3:11; Mal 2:7).

Most familiar is the liturgical mediation of the priest (whether head of family, people, or tribe; Gn 8:20; 14:18; Ex 3:1), by Moses (24:4–8), or by an appointed class trained in the rituals of worship (28:1). Because of Israel's emphasis upon the holiness of God, sacrificial expiation or "covering" of sin figured largely in priestly mediation. The priest represented before God the people's penitence, confession, and prayers for forgiveness, bearing the tribes' names on shoulders and breastplate, and represented God, in turn, assuring his favor, forgiveness, and protection (see Heb 5:1–4; 7:27–10:11).

Prominent though such mediated experience of God is in the OT, it does not exclude the intimate, unmediated "friendship" with God" of Abraham, Moses, Jeremiah, Hosea, and Psalm 139. Nor does the "official" intercession of the priesthood preclude the personal intercession of Abraham (Gn 18:23–33), Moses (Ex 32:31,32), Samuel (1 Sm 7:5; 12:23), and Job (1:5; 42:7–9). Moreover, sacrificial mediation is already challenged (Pss 40:6–8; 51:16,17; Hos 6:6; Mi 6:6–8). Nevertheless, the religion of the OT may fairly be characterized as mediatorial, and the strength of this conception demonstrates the majesty and holiness of Israel's God.

In the NT. It was natural, therefore, that the mission of Jesus should be described in mediatorial terms, and first as that of a prophet speaking for God to men, "making God known" (Mk 6:15; 8:28). Where applied to Jesus, the actual title mediator refers mainly to his institution of a new covenant, establishing God's new relationship with men (Heb 8:6; 9:15; 12:24). The one other instance is 1 Timothy 2:5, where the unity of God requires a sole, unrivaled mediator, namely Christ.

This last reference mentions Christ's giving himself "a ransom for all." This essentially priestly function is the theme of Hebrews.

Christ as Son of God, divinely appointed, sinless, suffering, tempted, sympathizing and obedient, is uniquely qualified to be high priest of his people. As priest, he offers a perfect sacrifice and ever lives to intercede for those who draw near to God through him. This mediatorial ministry places Jesus "at the right hand of God." His intercession for men is mentioned also in Romans 8:34 (and possibly in 1 Jn 2:1, where ancient Greek commentators, NEB, and other authoritative sources so understand "paraclete," here applied to Jesus). His mediatorial sacrifice is mentioned in Matthew (26:28), John (1:29), Romans (3:25), and 1 John (1:7; 2:2; 4:10).

Still more significant is the insistence, everywhere in the NT, that man's knowledge of God, salvation, and hope are his through Christ alone. Made poor for our sakes, he died and rose "for us"; our peace, access to God, reconciliation, expiation of sin, grace, truth, prayer, and "all spiritual blessings" are "through him," "in him," "through his blood," and "in his name." The purpose of God focuses in him; he mediated at creation and at redemption (Col 1:15,22); in him all the fullness of God dwells, and the face of Christ reveals God's glory. No one knows the Father save the Son and those to whom the Son reveals him; no one comes to the Father but by him; neither is there salvation in any other.

That is mediation, and the fulfillment and end of all mediation. Hebrews opens with the assertion that Christ surpasses all other mediators—angels, Moses, the Aaronic priesthood. His is a timeless priesthood, like Melchizedek's. His sacrifice is unrepeatable, "once for all time," and by it we have been consecrated to God "for all time." The covenant he established between God and man offers better promises, sacrifice, sanctuary, and hope (Heb 7:19; 8:6; 9:1,11–15). Christ's mediation so far excels that it can never be superseded; he is priest without rival and for ever (cf. 1 Tm 2:5).

Without using the priestly analogy, John emphasizes the same truth. The gulf between divine and human has been crossed, decisively and finally, by incarnation. Instead of standing between God and man, Christ unites both within himself by becoming man. Mediating in the beginning at creation, Christ is himself the Word, which from God's side mediates God's mind, embodies God's message, and conveys God's power. No one has seen God at any time, but as unique Son, Jesus "expounds" God. Those who see Christ see the Father, watch his works, and hear his words. From man's side, Jesus prays for the disciples (Jn 17), offers perfect obedience, lays down his life for his flock, and offers the unblemished sacrifice which bears away the sin of the world.

Such incarnation is the perfect mediation, sufficient and final. Two striking sayings appear in John to hint that when men are wholly one with God through Christ, mediation shall have given place to unity: "I do not say to you that I shall pray the Father for you, for the Father himself loves you" (Jn 16:26,27); "[I pray] that they may all be one; even as thou, Father, art in me, and I in thee, that they also may be in us" (17:21).

In the Church. Despite the sufficiency and finality of Christ's continuing mediation, the desire for additional mediators lingered in the church, claiming for martyrs, angels, departed saints, celibates, and supremely for the Virgin Mary, the hearing of prayers, intercession for Christians on earth, and the accumulation of transferable merit for the Christian's benefit. Biblical grounds for this extended mediation were found in the oneness of the church on earth and in heaven, saints in either realm interceding for each other; in allusions to departed souls still praying for others (Lk 16:27, 28; cf. Rv 6:9–11); and especially in the vision of Judas Maccabeus, in which Jeremiah and the high priest Onias, both deceased, invoked blessing on the Jews (2 Mc 15:12; cf. Jer 15:1).

At the same time, John 20:23 was held to show Jesus conferring mediatorial powers of absolution and excommunication upon the apostles and their successors. To these were soon added exclusive powers through the sacraments. This extended mediation was held to complement, not to supplant, that of Christ.

Most Protestants, however, deny the mediation of Mary, angels, departed saints, or the clergy, asserting instead the priesthood of all believers (1 Pt 2:5,9; Rv 1:6; 5:10). This was understood to mean for all Christians the privilege of individual direct access to God (Rom 5:2; Eph 2:18; Heb 10:19–22) and the duty of intercession for others (Rom 15:30; Eph 6:18; Jas 5:6). John 20:23 was held to emphasize the responsibility of all Christians to bring Christ's forgiveness to others by witnessing to the gospel.

With varying clarity, Protestants insist upon the sufficient and final mediation of Christ, who came to show us the Father, died to bring us to God, and ever lives to make intercession for us.

R.E.O. White

See RECONCILIATION.

Bibliography. E. Brunner, *The Mediator*; D. Guthrie, *NT Theology*; P.G. Medd, *The One Mediator*; V. Taylor, *The Names of Jesus*.

Medicine and Medical Practice.

Either the field of knowledge dealing with the diagnosis, treatment, and prevention of diseases, or the actual substances used to diagnose, treat, or prevent disease.

Medicine as a branch of knowledge received little attention from the Hebrew people of OT times, in contrast to the surrounding cultures found in Mesopotamia and Egypt where medical knowledge had a prominent place. Extant in the library of Assyrian king Ashurbanipal are 800 tablets relating to medicine. From these medicine at that time is shown to have been a mixture of religion, divination, and demonology. Their pharmacopeia was extensive and included agents such as aloes, belladonna, cannabis, castor oil, and poppy; others were eccentric such as dog dung and human urine. Surgical operations were performed by some physicians. An unusual method of diagnosis practiced in Babylon was to inspect the liver of a freshly killed animal and compare it with a clay model of a liver from a normal animal. Differences between the two were used to diagnose the condition of the patient. An interesting example of this, and divination, is found in Ezekiel 21:21.

The art of medicine was more advanced in Egypt than in Mesopotamia, depending more upon logic and observation. The Edwin-Smith papyrus is the oldest surgical treatise known. It discusses a variety of fractures, dislocations, wounds, tumors, and ulcers. Adhesive plaster, surgical stitching, and cauterization were used in treatment. The heart was recognized as the center of the circulatory system, and the pulse was observed. The Ebers papyrus deals with problems of internal medicine and their treatment. Enemas were a popular form of therapy, and their *materia medica* contained an assortment of remedies ranging from castor oil to animal fat to hot sand. Other papyri deal with gynecological problems, and contain formularies and many magical incantations. Mummification was a highly developed art; Joseph had his father Jacob embalmed (Gn 50:2).

The outlook of the Hebrew people in OT times toward disease was entirely different from that of their heathen neighbors. They did not believe in the heathen superstitions or gods and, consequently, did not develop a medical knowledge similar to the Egyptians and Babylonians. Instead, the Hebrews regarded sickness as a judgment from God (Ex 15:26; Dt 28:22,35,60,61; Jn 9:2) and recovery also was attributed to God (Ex 15:26; Ps 103:3). In accordance with this philosophy, King Asa's reliance on physicians instead of God is referred to in a reproachful way in 2 Chronicles 16:12. Therefore, while medical treatment was available in Israel, its use and development was less advanced than in neighboring lands.

The most significant contribution the Hebrews gave to medicine was in the hygienic measures outlined in the Law, particularly Leviticus 11–15. While these had primarily a religious significance, they undoubtedly improved the general level of health and physical well-being of the people. The Hebrew priest was not the counterpart of the physician-priest found in other cultures. Although the Hebrew priest was expected to determine what physical conditions rendered a person ceremonially unclean, there is no intimation in Scripture that he treated diseases.

The only surgical operation mentioned in Scripture is circumcision. This was performed by the Hebrews for religious rather than medical purposes, and it was not done by a physician but by the head of the house or someone else (Ex 4:25). In Ezekiel 30:21 reference is made to treating a fracture of the arm by immobilizing and splinting it with a roller bandage.

Obstetrical care was given by women who were experienced midwives (Gn 35:17). In Genesis 38:27–30 there is an account of the birth of twins complicated by a transverse presentation. This is a difficult problem for even the most skilled obstetrician, and the fact that the mother and both babies survived speaks highly for the skill of this midwife. In Exodus 1:15–21 the use of birth stools for delivery is mentioned. This was a device to hold the laboring woman in a position favorable for expulsion of the baby.

In NT times Greek medicine had a dominant influence in the Mediterranean world. Although the practice of medicine was still in a primitive state, Hippocrates and other Greek physicians of his day laid the basis for modern medicine by rejecting magical explanations of diseases and through careful observation attempted to give a rational basis for medical treatment. From Mark 5:26 it is known that physicians were available in Israel. Indeed, the rabbis ordained that every town must have at least one physician, and some rabbis themselves practiced medicine.

Specific medical remedies are occasionally mentioned in the Bible. Mandrakes were used as an aphrodisiac (Gn 30:14; Sg 7:13). When Job was afflicted with generalized boils, he removed the devitalized skin with a piece of pottery and sat in ashes ·(Jb 2:7,8). The ashes would have a drying effect on the draining sores, giving this treatment a rational basis for its use. Jeremiah refers in a rhetorical way to the balm in Gilead, indicating its medicinal use (Jer 8:22; 46:11). The exact nature or use of this balm is not known. When Hezekiah was mortally ill, he was instructed by Isaiah to put a lump of figs on the boil (2 Kgs 20:7). This probably should not be considered a treatment, however, any more than the dipping seven times in the Jordan by Naaman or the application of mud to the eyes of the blind by the Lord. The therapeutic effect of merriment on the mind found in Proverbs 17:22 is in accord with modern mental health.

Medicinal use of wine is recorded several times in Scripture. Its mood-changing ability is alluded to in Proverbs 31:6, and apparently the sour wine offered to the Lord on the cross was intended to ameliorate his suffering through its analgesic property (Jn 19:29). Paul suggests to Timothy that he use a little wine for his stomach and other infirmities (1 Tm 5:23). It is significant that Paul said "a little" because pharmacologists today agree that wine in moderate amounts is an aid to digestion; however, excessive amounts are deleterious to the health in numerous ways. The good Samaritan used oil and wine to treat the wounds of the injured man (Lk 10:34). Because of its alcoholic content, the wine would have an antiseptic action, but at the same time would tend to coagulate the surface of the raw wound and permit bacteria to thrive under the coagulum. The oil, by its emollient effect, would tend to nullify this latter undesirable side effect of wine and would also be soothing due to its coating action. A dressing was then applied, and the patient was taken to a resting place.

In Revelation 3:18 the Laodicean church is admonished to use eye salve. Since Laodicea was famous for a powder used for weak and ailing eyes, this illustration is uniquely appropriate to use in warning this church concerning its lack of spiritual vision.

See DISEASE; PLAGUE; TRADES AND OCCUPATIONS (PHYSICIAN; NURSE).

Mediterranean Sea. Body of water often called the Great Sea bordering Palestine on the west (Nm 34:7; Jos 9:1; Ez 47:10,15); also called "the sea" (Nm 13:29; Jos 16:8; Jon 1:4); "uttermost sea" (Dt 11:24 KJV; RSV western sea); "utmost sea" (Dt 34:2; Jl 2:20 KJV; RSV western sea); "hinder sea" (Zec 14:8 KJV; RSV western sea); "Sea of Joppa" (Ezr 3:7 KJV); and the "sea of the Philistines" (Ex 23:31).

The sea is approximately 2196 miles long from Gibraltar to Lebanon, varies in width from 600 miles to 100 miles, and has a maximum depth of 2 7/10 miles. Its various subdivisions consist of the Adriatic, Aegean, Ionian, Ligurian, and Tyrrhenian seas.

From the Bay of Iskenderun on the north to el-Arish on the south, a distance of about 450 miles, the coastline is rather straight with few deep bays or headlands. Along the Syrian coast as far south as Beirut, the coastline contains rocky formations rising sharply from the water. At Acre the coast recedes, and the land slopes gently upward toward the plain of Esdraelon. South of this the sharp ridge of Mt Carmel projects into the water. From the southern slope of Carmel the Vale of Sharon spreads southward to merge with the plains of Philistia. From there the coast is an almost unbroken curve to the Nile Delta.

Several good harbor areas indented the Syrophoenician coast in antiquity, and the sea played an important role in the development of that region. Byblos was a sea power prior to 1000 BC, and Tyre and Sidon were known for their maritime prowess after 1000 BC. Following their conquest of Palestine under Pompey (63 BC), the Romans made extensive use of the sea and referred to it as "Our Sea."

Although located on the Mediterranean Sea, and having neighbors who were seafaring people, the Israelites never developed any extensive commercial or military use of it. Various reasons have been given for this. First, Israel was a pastoral and agricultural people whose roots were in the soil rather than the sea and who, therefore, looked inland for their development. Second, the primary efforts of Israel in Palestine were directed toward conquest and retention of the lands taken, and this left little time to develop maritime interests. Third, the sea was controlled by Phoenicia, and to a lesser degree by Philistia. From the time of the exodus the Phoenicians had established themselves at points along the coast and formed an essentially maritime confederation extending from the Orontes on the north to Joppa on the south. South of this point, the Philistines controlled the coastline during much of Israel's history. At one time Solomon had a fleet of ships at Ezion-geber on the Red Sea (1 Kgs 9:26,27), and Jehoshaphat also had a fleet in that vicinity (1 Kgs 22:48). Finally, there were no natural harbors along the Israelite-occupied coastline. A few harbors existed such as Ashkelon, Dor, Joppa, and Acco, but the only port to which Israel had access apparently was Joppa during the monarchy. When Solomon was building the temple, lumber from Lebanon was shipped to Joppa and transported to Jerusalem from there.

The NT records one visit by Jesus to the coastal area, when he went to "the district of Tyre and Sidon" (Mt 15:21) and healed the demon-possessed daughter of the Syrophoenician woman. The apostle Paul in his missionary journeys had many contacts with the Mediterranean Sea from Caesarea on the Palestinian coast to Puteoli on the coast of Italy. Under Roman rule, the Mediterranean was widely traveled by merchants, government officials, soldiers, and teachers. Paul and other early Christians took advantage of the Roman roads of land and sea to spread the gospel throughout the world surrounding the Mediterranean.

WAYNE C. HENSLEY

Medium. Person who acts as a channel of communication between human beings and the spirit world.

See MAGIC.

Megiddo, Megiddon. City standing at the southwest edge of the plain of Esdraelon on the main route between Mesopotamia and Egypt. It overlooks the historic route where a pass through the Mt Carmel range led from the plain of Sharon into the plain of Jezreel. This strategic position made Megiddo one of the most important commercial and military centers of Palestine in the 2nd millennium and the early 1st millennium BC. From earliest times the environs have been the scene of major battles. Great military men such as Thutmose III of 15th-century BC Egypt, Napoleon in 1799, and General Allenby during World War I have fought for mastery there.

Biblical References. At the time of the conquest, Joshua defeated the king of Megiddo but did not take the city (Jos 12:21). In the subsequent allotments to the tribes of Israel, Megiddo was assigned to Manasseh, but they could not conquer it from the Canaanites (17:11,12; Jgs 1:27). During the days of the judges, Deborah and Barak defeated the forces of Hazor under the command of Sisera "by the waters of Megiddo" (4:15; 5:19) but did not take the city either. Perhaps David conquered it as part of his program for establishing the kingdom. At any rate, by the time of Solomon, Megiddo served as the headquarters of one of his 12 administrative regions (1 Kgs 4:12). Solomon rebuilt it to serve as one of his chariot and garrison cities (9:15–19).

King Ahaziah of Judah died there (841 BC)

Megiddo—a strategic city captured by Joshua (Jos 12:21)—lies on a major commercial and military route between Gaza and Damascus and was where Allenby's cavalry took the Turks by surprise in 1918.

after being wounded by Jehu while on a visit to the northern kingdom (2 Kgs 9:27). King Josiah of Judah met and intercepted Pharaoh Neco of Egypt (609 BC) at Megiddo in a vain effort to prevent him from going north to aid the Assyrians; he was mortally wounded in the battle (23:29,30). The plain of Megiddo (KJV valley of Megiddon) is referred to in Zechariah's prophecies of restoration for Israel and Jerusalem (12:11). Revelation predicts a great future war that will take place at Armageddon (Har Megiddon, the "mount of Megiddo," Rv 16:16).

History of Megiddo. Excavations demonstrate that Megiddo was first occupied in the 4th millennium BC, but public buildings, temples, and city walls were not constructed until about 3000 BC. Though the city was an important place during subsequent centuries, it did not figure in historical accounts until the 15th century BC when Thutmose III of Egypt won a great victory there after a 7-month siege, and subsequently turned the place into the major Egyptian base in the Jezreel Valley. Thutmose's successor, Amenhotep II, was forced to campaign in the vicinity about 1430; and during the Amarna age, shortly after 1400, the king of Megiddo was having difficulty holding the region for the pharaoh and called for the return of the Egyptian garrison that had been withdrawn.

As already noted, the Hebrews were unable to take the city during the conquest but conquered it by the time of Solomon, when it became a major Hebrew outpost. After the split of the Hebrew kingdom, Shishak of Egypt captured the city in the fifth year of Rehoboam of Judah (926). Subsequently it was an important garrison city of the northern kingdom, especially during the days of Ahab. In 732 BC Tiglath-pileser III of Assyria conquered the northern part of Israel and made Megiddo the capital of the Assyrian province that he constructed.

Perhaps King Josiah of Judah controlled the site briefly in the late 7th century after the decline of Assyria. Destruction of the small unwalled town of the period (found in the excavations) has been connected with Pharaoh Neco's defeat of Josiah there in 609 BC. Subsequently the Persians built a small town there and the place was abandoned about 350 BC.

Archaeological Excavations. Megiddo is now certainly identified with Tell el-Mutesellim, a mound that rises to a height of about 200 feet above the surrounding plain. The top of the mound covered about 15 acres and the slopes about 35 more. Good farmland, a good water supply, and a strategic location attracted settlers for many generations until they built up a deposit of 72 feet of debris.

Excavations at Megiddo began with the efforts of G. Schumacher for the German Society for Oriental Research (1903–05). He dug a trench across the entire mound from north to south, finding in the trench, among other things, two unique tombs thought to belong to the Canaanite royal dynasty and a palace dated to the Israelite period. He also excavated along the walls.

Then in 1925 the Oriental Institute of the University of Chicago began an ambitious project to take the entire mound down to bedrock and make it the real showpiece of modern archaeological technique. They cut down to bedrock on the east side of the tell, where they identified 20 occupational periods, some of which they divided into two phases. In the cut they found at the 13th-century level about 300 fragments of ivory carvings and at the 3000 BC level a Canaanite temple with a circular altar over 25 feet in diameter.

The Chicago team managed to excavate only four levels or strata by the time World War II interrupted them in 1939. Successive directors were Clarence Fisher, P. L. O. Guy, and Gordon Loud. Stratum IV they identified as the Solomonic level. There they uncovered the city gate, the walls, a palace or administrative headquarters, and two stable compounds thought to house about 450 horses.

In 1960–67 Yigael Yadin of the Hebrew University in Jerusalem excavated at Megiddo, modifying conclusions of the Chicago team. He argues that the city wall, the massive city gate, and the palaces in the northern and southern parts of the city belonged to the reign of Solomon. The stables were constructed by Ahab; and the great water system, previously dated to the 12th century, was to be attributed to Solomon and his successors (mostly to Ahab).

Scripture clearly says, however, that Solomon designed this site to house horses and chariots. Perhaps Solomon designed the stable compounds and they were rebuilt by Ahab. James B. Pritchard has advanced the thesis that the buildings identified as stables were not stables at all, and that horses were kept in open enclosures.   HOWARD F. VOS

Megiddo, Waters of. Scene of the battle between Sisera and Barak, mentioned in the victory song of Deborah (Jgs 5:19). It refers to a perennial stream near Megiddo, probably the Wadi el-Lejjun, which drained the basin behind Megiddo.

See MEGIDDO, MEGIDDON.

Megilloth. Plural form of the Hebrew word for scroll. The word occurs several times in

Jeremiah 36, where King Jehoiakim, rejecting the word from God, burned the scroll that the prophet sent to him.

Megilloth is also used collectively of the OT books of Song of Solomon, Ruth, Lamentations, Ecclesiastes, and Esther. These are the "five rolls," which are read by the Jews during the major festivals of the Jewish year: the Song of Solomon at Passover, Ruth at Pentecost (Firstfruits), Lamentations on the anniversary of the destruction of Jerusalem by the Babylonians, Ecclesiastes at the feast of tabernacles, and Esther at Purim.

Mehetabel. 1. Matred's daughter and the wife of Hadar (Gn 36:39; 1 Chr 1:50), king of Edom in pre-Israelite times.

2. Shemaiah's grandfather. Shemaiah was hired by Tobiah and Sanballat to discredit Nehemiah by frightening him into fleeing into the temple (Neh 6:10).

Mehida. Head of a family of temple servants in Ezra's time (Ezr 2:52; Neh 7:54).

Mehir. Chelub's son from Judah's tribe (1 Chr 4:11).

Meholathite. Term used to describe Adriel the son of Barzillai who was the husband of Merab, Saul's eldest daughter (1 Sm 18:19; 2 Sm 21:8). He was probably from Abel-meholah, an important city of Gilead. The marriage of Adriel and Merab was probably a political move by Saul, agreed to by David, who was to have married Merab himself (1 Sm 18:17–19).

Me-huja-el. Irad's son and the father of Methushael in Cain's line (Gn 4:18).

Mehuman. One of the seven chamberlains King Ahasuerus sent to bring Queen Vashti to the royal banquet (Est 1:10).

Mehunim, Mehunims. KJV forms of Meunim and Meunites in Ezra 2:50 and 2 Chronicles 26:7, respectively.

See MEUNIM, MEUNITE.

Me-jarkon. Topographical designation in the description of Dan's inheritance (Jos 19:46). It is probably not a settlement; Jarkon seems to be the name of the river (el-'Awjah) flowing across the coastal plain from the springs at Aphek to the coast four miles north of Joppa. It was a formidable obstacle to north-south travel, but the numerous ancient sites along its banks testify to its importance as an entryway from the sea to the interior of the country.

Mekonah. KJV spelling of Meconah, a Judean city, in Nehemiah 11:28.

See MECONAH.

Melatiah. Descendant of Gideon who helped repair the Jerusalem wall next to the Old Gate during Nehemiah's time (Neh 3:7).

Melchi. 1. Jannai's son according to Luke's genealogy (3:24).

2. Addi's son according to Luke's genealogy (3:28).

See GENEALOGY OF JESUS CHRIST.

Melchiah. KJV spelling of Malchiah, Pashhur's father, in Jeremiah 21:1.

See MALCHIAH #8.

Melchisedec. KJV rendering of Melchizedek, the priest and king of Salem who blessed Abraham, in Hebrews 5–7.

See MELCHIZEDEK.

Melch-ishua. KJV alternate form of Malchishua, King Saul's third son, in 1 Samuel 14:49 and 31:2 (Melchi-shua).

See MALCHISHUA.

Melchizedek. Mysterious biblical personality whose name means "king of righteousness." The historical record about this priest-king is contained in Genesis 14:18–20; Psalm 110:4; and Hebrews 5:10; 6:20; 7:1–17.

In Genesis (*14:18–20*). Chedorlaomer, king of Elam, in conjunction with three other Mesopotamian kings, raided a vassal confederacy of five kings near the shores of the Dead Sea. In the ensuing massacre and rout by the Mesopotamian confederacy, Abraham's nephew Lot and his family and possessions were captured (Gn 14:1–12). Abraham led an attacking force in pursuit of Lot's captors, achieved victory, retrieved the plunder, and secured the release of Lot and his family (vv 13–16).

Upon his return, Abraham was greeted not only by the grateful kings of the Dead Sea confederacy, but also by Melchizedek, king of Salem, who gave Abraham bread and wine along with his blessing as "priest of the most high God" (*El Elyon*) (Gn 14:18). Salem is Jerusalem (cf. Ps 76:2). El Elyon is not the pagan deity of Canaanite worship by the same name but rather the title of the true God who created heaven and earth, an idea foreign to Canaanite religion (cf. Gn 14:22; Pss 7:17; 47:2; 57:2; 78:56). Melchizedek correctly viewed Abraham as worshiping this same God (Gn 14:22) and praised God for giving victory to Abraham (v 20). Abraham identified himself with the worship of the one true God represented by Melchizedek in that he received his gifts and blessing and "gave him a tenth of everything" (v 20), thus recognizing Melchizedek's higher spiritual rank as a patriarchal priest. In contrast, Abraham disassociated himself from Canaanite polytheism by declining gifts from the king of Sodom (vv 21–24).

It is interesting to speculate whether Melchizedek's knowledge of the true God was received by tradition from the past ages closer to the flood, or whether he, like Abraham, had been uprooted from paganism to monotheism by direct divine revelation. It is at least clear from Hebrews 7:3 that his priesthood was isolated and not received through a priestly pedigree.

In Psalms (110:4). In this messianic psalm, David envisioned one greater than himself whom he called "Lord" (v 1; cf. Mk 12:35–37). Thus the perfect messianic king was not an idealization of the present ruler but someone to come. Also he was to be not merely a man but more than this. The Messiah would be the Son of God as well as the son of David. The divine oracle of verse 4 is addressed to the Messiah: "You are a priest for ever after the order of Melchizedek." The significance of this statement is left for the inspired author of the letter to the Hebrews to develop.

In Hebrews (5:6–11; 6:20–7:28). The priesthood of Aaron has been superseded by the superior priesthood of Christ. The superiority of Christ's priesthood is demonstrated by its Melchizedekian character. First, both Christ and Melchizedek are kings of righteousness and kings of peace (Heb 7:1,2). Second, both have a unique priesthood which does not depend on family pedigree (v 3). Third, both abide as "priest continually" (v 3). That the priesthood of Melchizedek is superior to that of Aaron and the levitical priesthood is then demonstrated. Melchizedek was superior to Abraham, the father of Levi, because Melchizedek gave gifts to and blessed Abraham, and received tithes from him (vv 4–10); David predicted the succession of the Melchizedekian priesthood over the levitical priesthood, showing the imperfection of the latter (vv 11–19); the Melchizedekian priesthood of Messiah was confirmed by a divine oath, not true of the levitical priesthood (vv 20–22); and the Melchizedekian priesthood possessed an unchangeable and permanent character (vv 23–25).

The identification of Melchizedek as a theophany, or appearance of the preincarnate Christ in the OT, is sometimes reached on the basis of Hebrews 7:3: "He is without father or mother or genealogy, and has neither beginning of days nor end of life." However, this is simply to be understood in the sense that his priesthood was isolated rather than a contin-

uation of a priestly family line. Melchizedek had a priestly office by special divine appointment, and was thus a type of Jesus Christ in his priesthood. That Melchizedek was one "resembling the Son of God" (v 3) suggests that he was not himself the Son of God. The suggestion that Melchizedek was the patriarch Shem is without real support.

F. DUANE LINDSEY

See HEBREWS, BOOK OF; PRIESTS AND LEVITES.

Melea. Ancestor of Jesus according to Luke's genealogy (3:31).

See GENEALOGY OF JESUS CHRIST.

Melech. Micah's son from Benjamin's tribe (1 Chr 8:35; 9:41).

Melicu. KJV form of Malluchi the priest in Nehemiah 12:14.

See MALLUCHI.

Melita. KJV form of Malta, an island south of Sicily, in Acts 28:1.

See MALTA.

Melkon. Tradition-given name for one of the wise men who brought gifts to Jesus (Mt 2:1,2).

See WISE MEN.

Melon. Generic name for many-seeded fruit of the gourd family.

See FOOD AND FOOD PREPARATION; PLANTS.

Melzar. Steward responsible for the food given to Daniel (Dn 1:11,16). The KJV translates the word as a proper name, but the RSV translates the word as a title. Most likely Melzar is a hebraization of a Babylonian title.

Memorial. Something which keeps remembrance vivid. The ideas represented by the words "remember," "remembrance," and "memorial" are closely connected in common parlance as well as in biblical usage. The Hebrew and Greek words translated as "memorial" in the OT and NT are nominal derivatives of the verbal roots meaning "to remember." It is for this reason one cannot fully grasp the significance of the term "memorial" without first understanding something of the usage and meaning of the term "to remember."

Although "remember" is usually understood as simply recalling to the mind something from the past, and "memorial" as that which serves to preserve the memory of something from the past, there is often another dimension to these terms in biblical usage. In the Bible, the verb "to remember" often represents a broader idea than simply to recall something from the past because it implies and includes resultant action as well. It is not just recalling, but recalling in a way that affects one's present feeling, thought, or action. For example, when it is said in Genesis 8:1 that God "remembered Noah," this does not mean that God merely recalled that Noah was in the ark. It includes this idea to be sure, but more than this it means that God is acting on Noah's behalf. In a similar way, when Genesis 30:22 says that God "remembered Rachel," the meaning is that after a long period of barrenness God is going to answer Rachel's prayer for a child.

One of the most prominent uses of the idea to remember in the OT is the exhortation to the Israelites to remember the mighty acts of the Lord on their behalf in the past (Pss 77:11; 78:7; 105:5). This also means much more than simply recalling events from past history. It means to live in the present in the light of God's past actions. By drawing consequences for the present from the acts of God in the past, Israel's faith is to be strengthened for the challenges and difficulties encountered in the present. Israel's failure to remember in this way repeatedly led to apostasy and disobedience (78:11,42; 106:7,13,21,22).

A brief survey of the usage of the term "memorial" demonstrates that it also often carries this added dimension of meaning. Here one notices in particular its use in connection with the Passover. Exodus 12:14 says that the Passover "shall be for you a memorial day." It is to be an observance which causes the Israelites to live in the present in the light of God's past action in delivering them from sin and bondage in Egypt. This is much more than simply recalling the exodus as a historical occurrence.

In a similar way Joshua 4:7 describes setting up a monument of 12 stones in the midst of the Jordan River as a "memorial" to the miraculous provision for Israel's crossing and entering Canaan. This memorial is to be "for the people of Israel for ever." It is to remind them of God's past deliverance so that they may take courage in their present circumstances.

Another usage of the term is found in connection with the "stones of remembrance" attached to the front of the ephod worn by the high priest (Ex 28:12,29; 39:7). The significance of these stones was that they were to bring the names of the sons of Israel before the Lord. This is not simply in order for the Lord to recall their names, but to assure the Israelites of his present concern for their well-being.

The term "memorial" is used with a somewhat different connotation in connection with

the meal offering in Leviticus 2:2,16. The "memorial of the meal offering" is that portion which the priest offers upon the altar. The remainder is used for the sustenance of the priests themselves. The memorial is that which represents the whole: It does not serve just to remind God of the entire offering, but is viewed as an embodiment of it. A memorial in this sense may be viewed as embodying something of that which it represents.

In the NT the words "memorial" or "remembrance" occur rather infrequently, but in one instance with particular significance. When Jesus instituted the observance of the Lord's Supper, the NT counterpart to the OT Passover, he said, "This is my body which is given for you. Do this in remembrance [or memorial] of me" (Lk 22:19). The Lord's Supper is observed as a remembrance of the suffering and death of Christ. It is much more, however, than simply recalling a historical fact; it is remembering in a way that fills the believer with thanksgiving and determines how he lives and acts in the present.

Memphis. City located about 15 miles southwest of Cairo, once the sprawling capital of Egypt; now for all practical purposes it does not exist.

When the city was founded about 3000 BC, it was known as "White Wall" and was later called Men-nefru-Mine or Menfe in Egyptian. From the latter the Greeks got the name Memphis. Though one Hebrew reference follows the Greek (Hos 9:6), Memphis is commonly called Noph in the OT (Is 19:13; Jer 2:16; 44:1; 46:14,19; Ez 30:13,16); presumably this is a corruption of the middle part of the Egyptian name.

History of Memphis. According to the 5th-century BC Greek historian Herodotus, King Menes founded the city of Memphis and built the temple of Ptah there shortly after unifying the country. Whether or not Menes was a historical person, it is commonly concluded today that shortly after unification of Egypt (c. 3100 BC) a new capital was built on the border between Upper and Lower Egypt. Although the rulers of the first two dynasties after Egypt's unification had come from Thinis, north of Thebes, the fact that they were buried at Saqqara west of Memphis seems to indicate that they made Memphis their capital.

Memphis continued as the capital of Egypt during the Old Kingdom period (c. 2700–2200 BC). And Memphis, or the nearby city of It-Towy, continued as capital during much of the Middle Kingdom (c. 2050–1775).

During the New Kingdom or Empire period (c. 1580–1100), the capital was moved to Thebes. But Memphis was Egypt's second capi-

The Alabaster Sphinx at Memphis (from the period of the New Kingdom).

tal during most of that period, and some rulers lived there because of its central geographical location. Rameses II moved his residence to Tanis in the Delta during the 13th century BC, but built a number of structures at Memphis and engaged in largescale renovation and restoration there. As early as the 16th or 15th century BC, Memphis began to take on a cosmopolitan character. Syrians, Phoenicians, Greeks, and Jews eventually established separate residential quarters there.

Though some decline set in at Memphis during the invasions and uncertainties of the 1st millennium BC, the city remained virtually intact. Even after the founding of Alexandria in the 4th century BC, the city maintained its greatness; some of the Ptolemies were crowned there instead of at the primary capital of Alexandria.

Memphis lost its importance as a religious center after the Christian emperor Theodosius closed its temples and ordered them torn down in the 4th century AD.

Prophecy Against Memphis. As noted above, the only places Memphis is referred to in the OT are in the prophets. Of course Memphis shared in the general condemnation of Egypt, but it was singled out for special attention. Ezekiel declared that God would destroy the idols of the city (Ez 30:13) and bring great distress upon it (v 16). Jeremiah went further, prophesying that Memphis would be utterly destroyed and without inhabitants (Jer 46:19).

Evidently, reasons for this judgment include, first, the punishment that will come on all nations for their sinfulness and idolatry. Second, the prophets condemned the nations surrounding Israel for their animosity and cruelty to the Jews. In the generations before the exodus the Egyptians made their name hated by the Hebrews. After the death of Solomon and the division of the Hebrew kingdom, Shishak of Egypt invaded Palestine in the 5th

year of King Rehoboam and wrought considerable destruction there (926 BC; 1 Kgs 14:25). Then in 609–8 BC Pharaoh Neco held Israel under tribute.

Fulfillment of prophecies against Memphis occurred especially in connection with two major events. The Christian Roman emperor Theodosius (AD 379–95), in his campaign against paganism, ordered destruction of the temples of Memphis and desecration of its statues. Then in the 7th century Muslim monotheists conquered Egypt and likewise tried to obliterate evidences of ancient polytheism. After the Arabs began to build Cairo in 642 Memphis became a quarry for the new city. Gradually the ruins have been carted away until virtually nothing is left. A fallen 40-foot statue of Rameses II, one of his sphinxes, a few column bases, and other minor ruins lie among the palm trees and cornfields at the site. The largest remaining portion sits in a lake because the breaching of the ancient dykes has permitted the place to be inundated.   HOWARD F. VOS

See EGYPT, EGYPTIANS.

Memucan. One of the seven princes of Persia and Media under King Ahasuerus (Est 1:14). He brought charges against Vashti, the Persian queen, who had refused to make a royal appearance which the king had commanded (v 16). Memucan proposed that she be divested of her position and the queenship given to another; the king took his counsel and issued a decree to that effect (v 21). Hence Esther was chosen as queen over Media and Persia.

Menahem. King of Israel who ruled from 752–742 BC. He was the son of Gadi, a name not attested in the OT except in 2 Kings 15:14,17.

Date. It is impossible to say with certainty exactly when Menahem ruled. According to 2 Kings 15:17, he became king in the 39th year of the Judahite king Azariah. However, because Azariah apparently served for some time as a co-regent with his father Amaziah, and his precise dates are difficult to determine, there is some scholarly debate about whether his 39th year would be 752 (Thiele) or 745 (Albright). Second Kings 15:17 also states that Menahem ruled for 10 years. Because Israel was evidently employing an accession-year system of reckoning the length of a king's reign in the time of Menahem, the 10-year figure must be computed as actual years. Accordingly, Menahem would have been on the throne in Israel for roughly 10 years beginning as early as 752 or as late as 745, and this is about as precise as one can get with respect to his date. In this article, Thiele's dates are used for simplicity, and Menahem will be assigned to the decade from 752 to 742.

Political Climate. Regardless of the date chosen as the accession year of Menahem, it is clear that the events of his reign cannot be understood apart from an awareness of the international situation in which Israel existed in the mid-8th century. The reign of Jeroboam II (793–753) had brought stability, great expansion, and prosperity to the nation of Israel. Because both Egypt and Assyria were relatively weak during this period, it was possible for Jeroboam to expand his kingdom by reconquering cities earlier lost to Syria and then to seize control of the international trade routes which thus newly fell within the Israelite borders. The internal sickness which the policies of Jeroboam permitted and fostered were viewed by the prophets Amos and Hosea as evidence of impending doom. Notwithstanding, the death of Jeroboam II provided occasion for more than one faction to envision accession to power of their own man. Menahem gained the throne by murdering Shallum, who himself had assassinated Zechariah the son of Jeroboam (2 Kgs 15:8–10).

After solving this internal crisis among the factions vying for power, Menahem was almost immediately faced with enormous external pressures, for shortly after Menahem became king, a new monarch seized control of Assyria. His name was Tiglath-pileser III, and his policy of imperialistic expansion literally altered the political complexion of the entire Mediterranean world. Menahem was forced to deal directly with him in the course of a campaign westward from Assyria into the Syro-Palestinian region (probably *c*. 743). This was Israel's first contact with the nation by whom she would soon be totally destroyed (722).

The threat posed by the revived and doubly powerful Assyria, along with the internal chaos existing in Israel following the death of Jeroboam, provided the combination which would bring about the total destruction of the nation envisioned by the prophets. Within 12 years of the death of Jeroboam, no fewer than 5 different kings took the throne of Israel, 3 of them (including Menahem) being assassins.

Biblical Evidence. Virtually everything which the OT records about the career of Menahem is contained in a few brief verses in 2 Kings 15. Three important points may be noted from these verses.

First, 2 Kings 15:14 records the assassination of Shallum, which enabled Menahem to seize the throne. Verse 16 then recounts the actions of Menahem against the town of "Tappuah." The entire verse is troublesome, but

may be translated as follows: "Then Menahem attacked Tappuah and everyone who was in her including her surrounding territories from Tirzah [and beyond?]. Because it had not opened [to him], he attacked. All the pregnant women in her he split open." Two things are unusual. First, the actions of Menahem are quite without precedent in Israelite history. Second, the location and identity of the town which Menahem attacked are uncertain. The Hebrew text reads "tipsah," using the spelling of a town normally identified as Thapsacus on the Euphrates. Menahem's reasons for attacking a town this far away from his own territory and interests would be difficult to determine. Accordingly, many scholars have followed the Lucianic version of the Greek Bible which reads the Hebrew letters as if they were "tappuah," a town 14 miles southwest of Menahem's hometown of Tirzah. If this reading is correct, and the textual evidence for it is limited to the one version, the meaning of 2 Kings 15:16 is that Menahem began just outside the boundaries of his hometown (Tirzah) and put to the sword the entire population of a neighboring town (including its citizens who lived outside the city proper) which failed to support his bid to become king.

Second, 2 Kings 15:19,20 provides the biblical view of the way in which Menahem dealt with the Assyrian crisis posed by the campaign of Tiglath-pileser III into the Syro-Palestinian region (*c*. 744). Evidently hoping to persuade the Assyrians to support his claims to the throne in Israel, Menahem levied a stiff tax upon the wealthy citizens of his nation to be used to pay tribute to Tiglath-pileser (called by his Babylonian name "Pul" in v 19). Evidently Menahem hoped this payment would convince the Assyrian king "to confirm the kingdom in his control" (v 19). Politically at least, Menahem appears to have guessed correctly, because the Assyrians withdrew (v 20) and Menahem was left in power.

Finally, the reign of Menahem is introduced (2 Kgs 15:17) and concluded (vv 21,22) by the standard literary forms employed throughout the books of kings. Despite the fact that Menahem was judged to be just as sinful as the original apostate (Jeroboam I) had been, 2 Kings 15:22 appears to attest an unusual fact about his death. Of the last six kings of Israel, only he died a peaceful death; only he was reported to have "slept with his fathers."

See ISRAEL, HISTORY OF; CHRONOLOGY, OLD TESTAMENT.

Menan. KJV form of Menna, an ancestor of Jesus in Luke's genealogy (3:31).

See MENNA.

Mene, Mene, Tekel, Parsin. Mysterious prophetic words in Daniel 5:25 pointing to the judgment of God against Babylon and her king. A decade or so following the death of King Nebuchadnezzar of Babylon (562 BC), a man of lesser moral stature, Belshazzar, became monarch of the empire. The fifth chapter of Daniel tells of a great banquet which Belshazzar made to which a thousand of his nobles and their wives had been invited. Under the influence of wine, Belshazzar ordered his servants to bring the gold and silver vessels taken from the temple in Jerusalem by Nebuchadnezzar a generation earlier. The sacred vessels, kept in storage until then, were distributed to the guests at the feast and sacrilegiously used to offer praise to the gods of Babylon, "gods of gold and silver, bronze, iron, wood, and stone" (Dn 5:4).

In the midst of the revelry, the fingers of a man's hand appeared and wrote upon the plaster of the banquet room wall. The king's composure was altogether shattered by the event and he cried out for someone to interpret the writing. None of his wise men were able, however, to discern the meaning of the words. Finally, the queen proposed a solution to the dilemma: Daniel the prophet—a gifted man in matters such as these—could be summoned to interpret the writing.

Daniel was brought in before the king and immediately rebuked him for his foolish and godless arrogance. His sermon before Belshazzar (Dn 5:17–23) powerfully proclaimed the judgment of God against all sinful pride, a message decisively revealed in the enigmatic words which Daniel then proceeded to interpret.

The words, given in the Aramaic script, are transliterated into English, *Mene, Mene, Tekel, Parsin* (*Upharsin,* KJV). The mystery of the words lay not in the decipherment of the language but in the significance attached to each of the words. Superficially, they simply denoted a series of weights or monetary values. In truth they prophesied the immediate judgment of God against Babylon and its king.

Daniel's explanation of the inscription is recorded in Daniel 5:26,27. *Mene* means "numbered" and its double entry indicated that God had both numbered the days of Belshazzar's kingdom and had reckoned its termination. *Tekel* means "weighed." Applied to Belshazzar, it signified his moral and spiritual inadequacy. He was, as it were, too light to balance out on the scales of God's standard of righteousness. The final participle, *parsin* means "broken" or "divided." Daniel gives the singular form of the word in his interpretation (*peres*). Indicated was the fact that Belshazzar's kingdom was about to be divided be-

tween the Medes and the Persians. There is a bit of word play in that the noun for Persians (*paras*) is virtually the same as the root used here.

Daniel 5:30,31 notes that the words of this prophecy were fulfilled later that evening.

See DANIEL, BOOK OF.

Meni. Pagan god of destiny or luck worshiped by apostate Jews (Is 65:11). The name is rendered destiny in RSV, NASB, NIV; fortune in NEB; and "unto that number" in KJV, reflecting the meaning of the Hebrew word "to count, apportion," as it were, by fate. Meni has been identified with the Arabic god Maniyyat, Babylonian Manu, and Edomite Manat. The reference in Isaiah has to do with preparing meals for pagan deities.

Menna. Ancestor of Jesus according to Luke's genealogy (3:31, KJV Menan).

See GENEALOGY OF JESUS CHRIST.

Menuhoth. People descended from Judah through Shobal, mentioned only in 1 Chronicles 2:52 (rendered Manahethites in NEB, KJV; Manahathites in NIV, NASB). The RSV transliterates the Hebrew word Menuhoth, which derives from the same root as "half of the Manahathites" in verse 54. The dwelling of these people may have been at Nohah (Jgs 20:43), since that place name and the tribe name both mean "resting places" (hence, in KJV "with ease"; NASB "without rest"). Some scholars suggest that Menuhoth is best understood as a place name and identified with the place mentioned in verse 54. The suggested site of Malha, southwest of Jerusalem, is not certain.

See MANAHATH, MANAHATHITE (PLACE).

Meonenim, Plain of. KJV mistranslation for the diviners' oak, a place near Shechem, in Judges 9:37.

See DIVINERS' OAK.

Meonothai. Othniel's son from Judah's tribe (1 Chr 4:13,14).

Mephaath. One of the cities of Reuben's tribe on the plain near Heshbon which was allotted to the Merari family of Levites (Jos 13:18; 21:37; 1 Chr 6:79). Later, it was numbered among Moabite towns during Jeremiah's ministry (Jer 48:21). It has been identified with modern Jawah, six miles south of Ammon.

See LEVITICAL CITIES.

Mephibosheth. 1. Son of Jonathan, David's friend. The original form of the name was undoubtedly Merib-baal (1 Chr 8:34; 9:40), but when the word baal became predominantly associated with the chief male deity of the Canaanite fertility cult it was replaced, in some instances, by the Hebrew word *bosheth* (meaning "shame"). As the grandson of Saul, Mephibosheth was born into a situation of privilege which changed dramatically when the Philistines attacked. Saul, Jonathan, and two of his brothers were killed in the battle on Mt Gilboa (1 Sm 31:1–6). When news of the catastrophe reached the Israelite palace at Jezreel, the five-year-old Mephibosheth was snatched up by his nurse. In a panic scramble for safety, she fell, dropping Mephibosheth, whose legs or ankles were broken. The lack of adequate medical attention meant that, thenceforth, he was completely crippled (2 Sm 4:4). Eventually, he found refuge at Lo-debar in Transjordan, with Machir, who later on befriended David himself (9:4; 17:27). Mephibosheth's uncle, Ish-bosheth (Saul's only surviving son), who had been made Israel's puppet king (2:8–10), was murdered (ch 4). Mephibosheth, although apparently next in succession, appears not to have been considered. When David was established on the throne of a now united kingdom and wished to show kindness to any surviving members of Jonathan's family, he was informed of Mephibosheth's existence by Ziba, once an influential steward in Saul's palace (9:1–13). Summoned to Jerusalem, Mephibosheth was naturally apprehensive, probably fearing that David might want to eliminate all possible rivals (see 19:28). But David's generous nature showed itself in restoring to Mephibosheth all of Saul's original land, with Ziba and his family continuing to manage the estate, and in granting the cripple a permanent place at the royal table.

When Absalom's rebellion broke out, Ziba met the fleeing David and supplied him with welcome provisions, taking the opportunity to curry favor at the expense of his master. Mephibosheth, he suggested, even entertained hopes of gaining the kingdom for himself. David, in the stress of the crisis, was taken in by this unlikely story and promised Ziba all Mephibosheth's property (16:1–4). The civil war over, Mephibosheth himself came to David with clear evidence of his grief at the latter's exile and therefore of Ziba's duplicity. But David, not willing to alienate Ziba and probably grateful for his earlier gift, compromised, dividing the land between the two. Mephibosheth's genuine joy at the king's restoration was such that the loss of his land was of no account in comparison (19:24–30). Later, when seven descendants of Saul were slain to appease the Gibeonites, David's continuing remembrance of Jonathan resulted in Mephibosheth being spared (21:7). Mephibosheth's son, Mica (9:12), became the head of a considerable family (1 Chr 8:35; 9:41).

2. Son of Rizpah, Saul's concubine, unlike his better known namesake, was one of the seven descendants of Saul hanged to appease the Gibeonites, whose ancient treaty with Israel had been violated by Saul, causing a three-year famine (2 Sm 21:8; see Jos 9:3–27). In the sequel (2 Sm 21:10–14), Rizpah's untiring vigil over the corpses prompted David to give them decent burial, together with the remains of Saul and Jonathan, in the family sepulchre.

ARTHUR E. CUNDALL

Merab. Eldest of Saul's two daughters (1 Sm 14:49), who was promised as a wife to David (1 Sm 18:17,18). Saul unexplainedly did not keep the agreement (v 19), instead giving David Michal. Textual and contextual evidence suggests a correction from Michal (Hebrew text) to Merab (RSV) in 2 Samuel 21:8.

Meraiah. Head of Seraiah's priestly family during the priesthood of Joiakim in postexilic Jerusalem (Neh 12:12).

Meraioth. 1. Levite, six to seven generations removed from Aaron (1 Chr 6:6,7; Ezr 7:3).

2. Ahitub's son and the father of Zadok (1 Chr 9:11; Neh 11:11); perhaps identifiable with #1 above, despite differences in genealogy.

3. Priestly house whose head was Helkai during the days of Joiakim in postexilic Jerusalem (Neh 12:15). Its forebear is given as Meremoth (Neh 12:3). Some regard verse 15 as a scribal error and identify the names in verses 3,15 as the same person.

Mt Gilboa, the site of the defeat and death of Saul and Jonathan—Mephibosheth's grandfather and father respectively—an event that had a dramatic effect on Mephibosheth's life (1 Sm 31:1–6).

Merari, Merarite. Transliteration of a Hebrew word meaning "bitter," "bitter drink," or "to be bitter." It means the same in Arabic and Akkadian, but in Ugaritic it means "to strengthen, to bless." Traditionally the word has been understood to be derived from the Hebrew and thus to mean "gall" or "bitterness." But Gordon points out that the Ugaritic root meaning "to strengthen, to bless" is not foreign to the Hebrew way of thinking. When used as a person's name, it probably should be understood to mean "strength" or "blessing." Such an understanding may be preferred in many biblical references.

In the case of Merari, the third son of Levi, this understanding is preferable in noting his importance and that of his family. It is inconsistent for the youngest son to have a name meaning "gall" or "bitterness" and then to have the greatest responsibility and the greatest reward for his service.

The Bible makes numerous references to Merari the son of Levi. He was the youngest of Levi's three sons (Gn 46:11; Ex 6:16,19; Nm 3:17,20,33; 1 Chr 6:1). He was the father of two sons, Mahli and Mushi (Ex 6:19; Nm 3:20), who had the responsibility of carrying the frames (KJV boards), bars, pillars, bases (KJV sockets), vessels, and accessories of the tabernacle (3:36, 37; 4:31–33; 7:8; 10:17; Jos 21:7,34,40). His descendants are known as Merarites. Chronicles makes numerous references to Merari's family as an indication of its importance (1 Chr 6; 9; 15; 23; 26; 2 Chr 29; 34).

See PRIESTS AND LEVITES; LEVI, TRIBE OF.

Merathaim. Name that Jeremiah uses in reference to God's judgment upon Babylon (Jer 50:21). Though it means "double rebellion" or "twofold rebel," it is a word play on the name for southern Babylonia, Marratu. Thus, God says, "Go up against the land, 'Twofold rebel' . . . and utterly destroy it!"

Merchant. See TRADES AND OCCUPATIONS.

Mercurius, Mercury. Roman god.

See HERMES #2.

Mercy. One of the most essential qualities of God (Ex 34:6,7; Dt 4:31; Mi 7:18–20). Specifically it designates that quality in God by which he faithfully keeps his promises and maintains his covenant relationship with his chosen people despite their unworthiness and unfaithfulness (Dt 30:1–6; Is 14:1; Ez 39:25–29; Rom 9:15,16,23; 11:32; Eph 2:4).

The biblical meaning of mercy is exceedingly rich and complicated, as evidenced by the fact that several Hebrew and Greek words are needed to comprehend the many-sided concept. Consequently, there are many synonyms

employed in translation to express the dimensions of meaning involved, such as "kindness," "lovingkindness," "goodness," "grace," "favor," "pity," "compassion," and "steadfast love." Prominent in the concept of mercy is the compassionate disposition to forgive an offender or adversary and to help or spare him in his sorry plight.

Theological Significance. The theological import of the above statements is obvious. At the heart of the concept of mercy is the love of God, which is freely manifested in his gracious saving acts on behalf of those to whom he has pledged himself in covenant relationship. In the OT it was his chosen people Israel whom he elected to be his own and to whom he showed mercy (Ex 33:19; Is 54:10; 63:9). God persistently puts up with his disobedient and wayward people and continuously seeks them out to draw them back to himself. The psalmist describes God as a father who pities his children who reverence and trust him (Ps 103:13). Hosea pictures God as a loving father who looks down from heaven with a yearning heart of compassion upon his rebellious and wayward people (Hos 11; cf. Jer 31:20). He also regards Israel as an unfaithful and adulterous wife whom God loves as a faithful husband in spite of her apostate and sinful condition (Hos 1–3; cf. Is 54:4–8). Isaiah depicts God as a mother who has compassion on the son of her womb (Is 49:15). These pictures reveal God's mercy in rich and different ways. Other dimensions include forgiveness and restoration to favor (2 Kgs 13:23; Is 54:8; Jl 2:18–32; Mi 7:18–20), and deliverance from distress and perils (Neh 9:19–21; Pss 40:11–17; 69:16–36; 79:8,9; Is 49:10).

Because of what Israel as a covenant nation had learned about the steadfast love and faithfulness of God, devout Jews instinctively lifted their voices in petition for divine mercy and forgiveness in times of need, eloquently expressed in the penitential psalms (Pss 6; 32; 38; 51; 102; 130; 143) as well as other OT passages (Ex 34:6; Neh 9:17; Pss 57; 79; 86; 123; Is 33:1–6; Dn 9:3–19; Jl 2:13). It is the remembrance of God's mercy that gives the repentant person the hope and assurance of divine favor and of reconciliation with the offended Lord.

In the NT a very descriptive Greek word is used for Jesus' mercy toward the needy (Mt 9:36; 14:14; 20:34). It expresses his pity and compassion by means of an intense verb literally translated "to be moved in one's bowels." The Hebrews regarded the bowels as the center of the affections, especially that of the most tender kindness. Our Lord is thus described as being fervently moved in his inner feeling of benevolence toward the needy and spontaneously acting to relieve their suffering—to heal (20:34;

Mk 1:41), to raise the dead (Lk 7:13), and to feed the hungry (Mt 15:32).

The OT concept of God's mercy expressed in his faithfulness to the covenant people is found also in the NT (Lk 1:50,54,72,78; Eph 2:4; 1 Tm 1:2; 1 Pt 1:3; 2:10). The most characteristic use of mercy in the NT is that of God's provision of salvation for mankind in Jesus Christ (Rom 11:30–32; Eph 2:4). God is "the Father of mercies" (2 Cor 1:3), which he bestows on those who believe in his Son. It is because he is "so rich in mercy" that he saved those spiritually dead and doomed by their sins—"only by his undeserved favor have we ever been saved . . . all because of what Christ Jesus did" (Eph 2:4–6 LB). It is out of God's mercy that one is forgiven and granted eternal life (1 Tm 1:13–16).

Man's Responsibility to Show Mercy to Others. Because God has freely extended his mercy irrespective of worthiness or faithfulness, men are to respond by showing mercy to others, even though they do not deserve it or seek it. Indeed, men are commanded to be merciful, especially to the poor, the needy, widows, and orphans (Prv 14:21,31; 19:17; Mi 6:8; Zec 7:9–10; Col 3:12). God regards mercy more than the ritual sacrifice (Mt 9:13). In the light of Christ's sacrifice and of the revelation that comes by the inspiration of the Holy Spirit, man's obligation to be merciful toward his fellow men is made clear and vivid. God's mercy in Christ actually puts men under obligation to act toward others as God himself has acted toward them. The Lord made mercy a foundation for his teaching (Mt 5:7; 9:13; 12:7; 23:23; Lk 6:36; 10:37; Jas 3:17). His coming was anticipated and announced in the context of the mercy which would characterize his mission (Lk 1:50,54,72,78).

Members of the Christian church, as participants in the covenant community, are to show compassion and practical concern for each other. They are to give aid and relief, love and comfort to one another as Christ freely gave to them in their need. The apostle James teaches the essential nature of such good works as being of the very essence of genuine faith (Jas 2:14–26). It was the mercy which the good Samaritan had toward the man who was beaten and robbed which was singled out by the Lord for special commendation (Lk 10:36,37). To be full of mercy is a distinguishing virtue of the citizens of the kingdom of heaven (Mt 5:7).

RALPH E. POWELL

See GOD, BEING AND ATTRIBUTES OF; LOVE; GRACE.

Bibliography. W. Eichrodt, *Theology of the OT*, vol 1; N. Glueck, *Hesed in the Bible*; N.H. Snaith, *The Distinctive Ideal of the OT*.

Mercy Seat. Gold slab placed on top of the ark of the covenant with cherubim attached to it on either end, termed the mercy seat in many English versions of the Bible (cf. Ex 25:17–22). The Hebrew word for which "mercy seat" is the translation is technically best rendered as "propitiatory," a term denoting the removal of wrath by the offering of a gift. The significance of this designation is found in the ceremony performed on the Day of Atonement, held once a year, when blood was sprinkled on the mercy seat to make atonement for the sins of the people of Israel (Lv 16). Because of the importance of this covering on the ark and the ceremony associated with it, the Holy of Holies in which the ark was housed in the temple is termed the "room for the mercy seat" in 1 Chronicles 28:11. The term mercy seat came into English use from Luther's German rendering of the Hebrew term, which is difficult to translate appropriately from the Hebrew (cf. NIV "atonement cover").

The mercy seat measured two-and-a-half cubits by one-and-a-half cubits. The cherubim on each end were also made of gold and faced each other with their wings spread upward over the ark. It was in this space above the ark that the Lord's presence with his people was localized in a special sense, and from which the Lord made his commandments known to Moses (Ex 25:22; cf. also Lv 16:2). Because of the close association of the Lord's presence with the space above the ark he is said to be enthroned between the cherubim (1 Sm 4:4; 2 Sm 6:4). The ark itself contained the tables of stone inscribed with the Ten Commandments which summarized the covenantal obligations of the Israelites to their divine King. When the children of Israel fell short of their covenant obligations by sinning against God and breaking his commands, the blood of the sacrifice sprinkled on the mercy seat made atonement for their sin and reconciled them with God.

The propitiatory or mercy seat points forward to Jesus who is termed by Paul (Rom 3:25) the "means of propitiation" through faith in his blood for all who have sinned and fallen short of the glory of God. Here in Romans 3:25 the Greek term translated propitiation is the same Greek word consistently used in the Septuagint and Hebrews 9:5 to translate the Hebrew word for mercy seat in the OT.

See PROPITIATION; ARK OF THE COVENANT; TABERNACLE, TEMPLE.

Mered. Ezrah's son from Judah's tribe, who had two wives. One wife, Bithiah, was the daughter of Pharaoh, and one was a Jewess (1 Chr 4:17,18).

Meremoth. 1. Priest, son of Uriah, grandson of Hakkoz (Ezr 8:33, Neh 3:4,21). The family of

Hakkoz was unable to prove its descent, hence they were excluded from the priesthood. Meremoth appears to be an exception. He weighed silver and gold, a priestly function (Ezr 8:24–30), repaired part of the Jerusalem wall (Neh 3:4,21), and sealed the covenant (10:5).

2. Priest and Bani's son, who severed ties with his foreign wife and children at Ezra's request (Ezr 10:36).

3. Priest who returned from Babylon with Zerubbabel (Neh 12:3) and founded the house of priests called Meraioth in Nehemiah 12:15 (though some identify the two references as the same person).

Meres. One of the seven princes of Persia and Media who acted as personal advisor to King Ahasuerus (Est 1:14).

Meribah. 1. Noun meaning "strife," named for a place at Horeb, near Rephidim (Wadi Feiran), where Israel contended with Moses for water near the beginning of the wilderness wanderings (Ex 17:7). This is the place probably alluded to in Deuteronomy 33:8 and Psalm 95:8, and is alternately called Massah.

2. Another place, near Kadesh-barnea in the wilderness of Zin, where Israel also quarreled with Moses for water, and God again provided it from a rock (Nm 20:13,24; 27:14); alternately called Meribath-kadesh in Deuteronomy 32:51. This episode took place toward the close of the desert wanderings. The waters of Meribah were waters of contention. Here God's anger was provoked against Moses and Aaron because they did not listen to him and sanctify him before Israel. Instead of speaking to the rock as God commanded, Moses, angered at Israel's hardness of heart, struck the rock twice with his rod. The psalmist records that here God tested Israel (81:7), and Israel's subsequent rebellion prodded Moses to sin (106:32). Meribath-kadesh is mentioned as a place on Israel's southern border (Ez 47:19; 48:28).

See MASSAH AND MERIBAH.

Meribath-kadesh, Meribah-kadesh. Alternate names for Kadesh-barnea (Dt 32:51; Ez 47:19; 48:28), a place of lengthy encampment by the Israelites during the wilderness wanderings.

See KADESH, KADESH-BARNEA.

Merib-baal. Original name for Mephibosheth, the handicapped son of Jonathan (1 Chr 8:34; 9:40). The name means "Baal contends" and is displaced by the later name (Mephibosheth, meaning "idol breaker") in 2 Samuel (4:4; 9:6; 17:21). The substitution of bosheth (shame) for baal (lord) was not uncommon

when the term acquired its idolatrous connotation (cf. 2 Sm 11:21).

See MEPHIBOSHETH #1.

Merodach. Hebrew pronunciation of Marduk, the chief Babylonian deity.

See MARDUK.

Merodach-baladan. Name (Berodach-baladan in 2 Kgs 20:12 KJV) meaning "Marduk has given a son!" Second Kings 20:12–19 and Isaiah 39 present a parallel account of Merodach-baladan, son of Baladan, king of Babylon, sending envoys to King Hezekiah of Judah.

Shalmaneser V, king of Assyria, captured Samaria in 722 BC and threatened King Hezekiah in Jerusalem, but died within a year's time. Sargon II succeeded him in 722. At that time Merodach-baladan, living south of Babylon in the land called Bit-iakin, formed an alliance with the Elamites and seized the throne of Babylon, referred to as the second jewel of the Assyrian crown. Sargon II immediately made efforts to regain Babylon as a province in the Assyrian Empire. He must not have been too successful initially for Merodach-baladan reigned over Babylon for 10 years. In 710 Sargon succeeded in defeating him and captured the Babylonian fortresses. Merodach-baladan escaped. After Sargon died in 705, Merodach-baladan, in 703, was able to recapture and hold the throne of Babylon for a short period. It is considered most plausible that during this short reign Merodach-baladan sent envoys to Hezekiah in Jerusalem, as he also is thought to have sent them to Edom, Moab, Ammon, and others, seeking to form an alliance against Assyria. The Arabian desert between Babylon and Palestine made such an alliance ineffective and the new king of Assyria, Sennacherib, thoroughly destroyed Merodach-baladan and then turned to the nations on Palestinian soil.

Isaiah rebuked Hezekiah for receiving the envoys from Babylon, the province which had broken away from the Assyrian Empire and which in a very short time was again forced into the Assyrian Empire. In Isaiah's rebuke lies the prediction that Babylon would become the invading and despoiling nation in the future. Hezekiah, knowing Assyria's power and Babylon's inability to cope with it at that time, felt quite safe as far as Babylon was concerned. "Will there not be peace and security in my lifetime?" (2 Kgs 20:19 NIV).

Merom, Waters of. Site of Joshua's victory over Jabin, king of Hazor, and his allies, mentioned only twice in the Bible (Jos 11:5,7). Jabin's allies included "Jobab, the king of Madon," and kings of Shimron, Achshaph, and "the northern hill country" as well as "those of the lowland" south of the Sea of Galilee. The site of the battle is not clear but a likely place for "the waters of Merom" is near the foot of Har Merom (on modern Israeli maps), or on older maps, Jabel Marun—the highest mountain in Israel (c. 3962 ft.). Near the base of the mountain is the town of Merom, where several roads leading into northern Galilee converge. It is on the road between Hazor and Acco on the coast, hence it was a convenient place for Joshua's enemies to rendezvous. Meron (Merom) is about eight miles southwest of Hazor "as the crow flies." The "waters of Merom" therefore would be the springs which emerge from the mountain to flow down Wadi Leimun into the Sea of Galilee. Merom is mentioned in Egyptian texts of the 2nd millennium BC associated with the campaigns of Thutmose III. The Assyrian monarch Tiglath-pileser III also reported his expedition into this region in 733–732 BC, at the time when he conquered Damascus. The allied forces defeated by Joshua fled northwest, in the direction of Sidon, suggesting an attack by Joshua from the southeast, from the area west of the Sea of Galilee, the natural approach from the south.

Meronothite. Resident of Meronoth, the hometown of Jehdeiah (1 Chr 27:30) and Jadon (Neh 3:17). Its site is unknown.

Meroz. Town in northern Palestine whose inhabitants were cursed for not assisting Deborah and Barak in their war against Sisera and the Canaanites (Jgs 5:23). Its location is uncertain.

Mesech. KJV spelling of Meshech, Noah's grandson, in Psalm 120:5.

See MESHECH #1.

Mesha (Person). 1. King of Moab in the 9th century BC whose name is derived from a root meaning "to save or deliver." According to 2 Kings 3:4,5, Mesha was a sheep breeder who paid heavy tribute to Israel during the time of Ahab, but rebelled after Ahab's death (2 Kgs 1:1). Later Jehoram the son of Ahab joined with Jehoshaphat of Judah and the king of Edom in an attempt to re-establish hegemony over Moab. When the battle went against the Moabites, Mesha took his eldest son and offered him as a human sacrifice upon the wall of the city to the Moabite god Chemosh (3:27).

Further information about Mesha is preserved on the Moabite Stone, a stele erected by Mesha at Dibon to tell of his rule and commemorate his victories. The stone was discovered at Dibon, about 13 miles east of the Dead Sea and a few miles north of the Arnon, in 1868 by German missionary F.A. Klein. After being broken in pieces by Bedouins, the reconstructed monument has been in the Louvre since 1873. In this inscription Mesha says that Omri the king of Israel "oppressed Moab for many days. . . . And his son followed him and he also said 'I will humble Moab.'" Mesha then says he triumphed over Omri's son (Ahab) and mentions various towns he conquered, reaching north in Transjordan from Dibon to the area of Medeba, killing the Israelite inhabitants as he went. There appears to be a discrepancy between the claims of Mesha on the Moabite Stone and the statements of 2 Kings 1:1 and 3:5 concerning the time of Moab's revolt (was it before or after the time of Ahab?). It may be, however, that Mesha revolted twice, once during the time of Ahab as recorded on the Moabite Stone, and once after the death of Ahab as recorded in 2 Kings 1:1; 3:5. Growing awareness of a potential threat from Moab and Mesha may have been one of the reasons why Ahab refortified Jericho, which was just across the Jordan from Medeba, and which previous to this time had remained an open city since the conquest when Joshua pronounced a curse on anyone who would rebuild it (Jos 6:26; 1 Kgs 16:34).

See MOABITE STONE.

2. Caleb's son and the father of Ziph (1 Chr 2:42). The latter part of this verse appears to say that Mesha was the father of Hebron, though the Hebrew text here substitutes the name Mareshah for Mesha. The RSV (following the Septuagint) reads Mareshah in both places.

See MARESHAH (PERSON) #1.

3. Benjamite and one of the sons of Saharaim born by Hodish in the land of Moab (1 Chr 8:9).

Mesha (Place). Place in southern Arabia defining the western boundary of the territory in which the descendants of Joktan settled (Gn 10:30). Its location is unknown. Some suggest that Mesha was a seaport town situated along the eastern shores of the Red Sea in the vicinity of what is modern Yemen; others place it along the Persian Gulf's northwestern banks near the region of Mesene.

Meshach. One of the three companions of the prophet Daniel who was thrown into the fiery furnace (Dn 1:7; 2:49; 3:12–30).

See SHADRACH, MESHACH, AND ABEDNEGO.

Meshech. 1. Son of Japheth and Noah's grandson (Gn 10:2). His descendants are usually mentioned in connection with Tubal, Gog, or Magog (Ps 120:5, KJV Mesech; Ez 27:13; 32:26; 38:2,3; 39:1). They are called Muski in Assyrian records and inhabited the mountains north of Assyria during the reigns of Tiglath-pileser I (1115–1102 BC), Shalmaneser III (859–824), and Sargon (722–705). The people of Meshech are characterized as aggressive and pagan, traders in bronze and slaves with Tyre.

2. Shem's son according to 1 Chronicles 1:17, but rendered Mash in the parallel passage in Genesis 10:23. The latter is generally accepted. Some scholars regard this as a reference to an obscure Aramaean tribe centered around Mt Masius in northern Mesopotamia.

Meshelemiah. Korahite Levite, Kore's son from the house of Asaph, and a gatekeeper of the sanctuary with his sons in the time of David (1 Chr 9:21; 26:1,2,9); alternately called Shelemiah in 1 Chronicles 26:14.

Meshezabel, Meshezabeel. 1. Ancestor of Meshullam who helped repair the Jerusalem wall (Neh 3:4).

2. Political leader who signed Ezra's covenant of faithfulness to God during the postexilic period (Neh 10:21).

3. Father of Pethahiah, an advisor to King Artaxerxes regarding the people in Judah (Neh 11:24).

Meshezabeel is the KJV spelling of Meshezabel.

Meshillemith. Alternate spelling of Meshillemoth in 1 Chronicles 9:12.

See MESHILLEMOTH #2.

Meshillemoth. 1. Father of Berechiah, a chief of Ephraim (2 Chr 28:12).

2. Ancestor of the postexilic priest Amashsai (Neh 11:13); alternately spelled Meshillemith in 1 Chronicles 9:12.

Meshobab. Prince of Simeon's tribe in the days of Hezekiah, who, with 12 other princes, moved to Gedor, dispossessed its pagan people (the Meunim), and settled his family there (1 Chr 4:34).

Meshullam. 1. Forefather of Shaphan, the royal secretary to King Josiah of Judah (2 Kgs 22:3).

2. Zerubbabel's son and a descendant of David (1 Chr 3:19).

3. Gadite leader registered during the reigns of Jotham, king of Judah (950–932 BC), and Jeroboam II, king of Israel (993–953 BC; 1 Chr 5:13).

4. Benjamite and a descendant of Elpaal (1 Chr 8:17).

5. Benjamite and the father of Sallu, a resident in Jerusalem during the postexilic period (1 Chr 9:7; Neh 11:7).

6. Benjamite and the son of Shephatiah, who resided in Jerusalem during the postexilic period (1 Chr 9:8).

7. Priest, the son of Zadok and the father of Hilkiah, whose descendants served in Jerusalem's sanctuary during the postexilic era (1 Chr 9:11; Neh 11:11). He is probably identical with Shallum in 1 Chronicles 6:12,13.

8. Priest, the son of Meshillemith and a forefather of Adaiah. Adaiah served in Jerusalem's sanctuary during the postexilic era (1 Chr 9:12).

9. Kohathite Levite who was appointed to oversee the repair of the temple during King Josiah's reign (2 Chr 34:12).

10. One of the Jewish leaders whom Ezra sent to Iddo at Casiphia to gather Levites and temple servants for the caravan of Jews returning to Palestine from Babylonia (Ezr 8:16).

11. One who opposed Ezra's suggestion that the sons of Israel should divorce the foreign women they had married since returning to Palestine from exile (Ezr 10:15).

12. Bani's son, who was encouraged by Ezra to divorce his foreign wife during the postexilic era (Ezr 10:29).

13. Berechiah's son, who rebuilt the section of the Jerusalem wall opposite the chamber during the days of Nehemiah (Neh 3:4,30). His daughter married Jehohanan, the son of Tobiah the Ammonite (Neh 6:18).

14. Besodeiah's son, who with Joiada repaired the Old Gate in the Jerusalem wall (Neh 3:4).

15. One of the men who stood to Ezra's left when Ezra read the Law to the people (Neh 8:4).

16. One of the priests who set his seal on the covenant of Ezra (Neh 10:7).

17. One of the leaders of Israel who set his seal on the covenant of Ezra (Neh 10:20).

18. Head of Ezra's priestly family during the days of Joiakim, the high priest, in postexilic Jerusalem (Neh 12:13).

19. Head of Ginnethon's priestly family during the days of Joiakim (Neh 12:16).

20. One of the gatekeepers during the days of the high priest Joiakim (Neh 12:25); perhaps identifiable with Shallum in 1 Chronicles 9:17.

21. One of the princes of Judah who participated in the dedication of the Jerusalem wall during the postexilic era (Neh 12:33).

Meshullemeth. Mother of Amon, king of Judah (642–640 BC) and the daughter of Haruz of Jotbah (2 Kgs 21:19).

Mesobaite. KJV spelling of Mezobaite, a title given to Jaasiel, in 1 Chronicles 11:47.

See MEZOBAITE.

Mesopotamia. Name given by the Greeks to the land between the Tigris and Euphrates Rivers, an area today called al-Jazira, "the island," by the Arabs. Mesopotamia, which means literally "between the rivers," is applied to the land between and near those rivers down to the Persian Gulf. Much of it is included in Iraq, but some of it is in Syria, and a small part in Turkey.

Mesopotamia played a significant role in OT history. Much of the tightly compressed account of Genesis 1–11 was centered here. The garden of Eden was situated in this area, for two of the rivers of Genesis 2:10–14 are identified as the Euphrates and the Tigris.

The prehistoric cultures of Mesopotamia are known by the names of type-sites, such as Ubaid, Hassuna, and Halaf. The historical periods also are labeled by the names of various cities which dominated them, such as Ur and Isin-Larsa, or by the names of dynasties established in those places, for example, Ur III.

The southernmost part of Mesopotamia is known as Sumer and was populated by the Sumerians, who had a distinctive culture and a non-Semitic language, which was written in cuneiform script, as were most of the other languages of Mesopotamia. Farther north was the district called Akkad, which was named Agade and had a Semitic population. Still farther north, along the Tigris, was the land which became Assyria, while to the far west was Syria, or Aram, and in between was Mitanni (c. 1400 BC). As portions of Mesopotamia slipped from hand to hand, various sections became parts of different empires, such as Hittite, Assyrian, Babylonian, Persian, Greek or Hellenistic, and Roman.

The sources of the two rivers are in the mountains of Turkey, not far from each other, but their paths diverge. The Euphrates feints toward the southwest as if to empty into the Mediterranean, but then turns toward the south and below Carchemish completes the "big bend" toward the southeast. Its tributaries, which enter from the north, also supported major cities. The Balikh had Haran in its upper reaches, while the Khabur was the location of the site of Tell Halaf. Below the confluence of the Khabur and the Euphrates was the city of Mari, famous for its cuneiform tablets with their interesting political and diplomatic correspondence. Beyond this point, cities were scarce until the Euphrates neared the Tigris.

The Tigris ran a relatively straight course, which probably gave it the name "arrow." The largest city in the north is Mosul, across the river from the remains of Nineveh, marked by the mounds of Kuyunjik and Nebi Yunus ("the prophet Jonah"). In this district there are many important archaeological sites, such as prehistoric Tepe Gawra and Tell Arpachiya, and various Assyrian capitals, such as Ashur (Qalat Sharqat; see Gn 10:11, Asshur, KJV), Nimrud (Bib. Calah, Gn 10:11), and Khorsabad (Dur Sharrukin, "Sargonsburg"). The Assyrian kings Shalmaneser V and Sargon II besieged and captured Samaria (722 BC) and deported its people to the Mesopotamian regions of the Assyrian Empire.

Several streams flow into the Tigris from the northeast: the Great Zab, from the direction of Erbil (Arbela); the Little Zab (near ancient Nuzi and modern Kirkuk); and the Diyala, with mounds like Tell Asmar. In this area the tower of Babel was begun (Gn 11:1–9). It was to Babylon that the conquered Jews were taken by Nebuchadnezzar after the fall of Jerusalem in 586 BC. Here Daniel spent most of his years and from Babylon the Jews returned to Jerusalem. Still farther south and mostly between the rivers were the famous cities Isin, Shuruppak, Umma, Lagash, Larsa, Uruk (Warka, Bib. Erech, Gn 10:10), Ur, and Eridu. The two rivers join near the town of al-Qurnah to form the Shatt el-Arab, which emerges into the Persian Gulf.

In the Hebrew OT the name for Mesopotamia is Aram-naharaim, "Aram of the two rivers." Abraham sent his servant, Eliezer, to Aram-naharaim to find a wife for Isaac (Gn 24:10). In this context it has been suggested that the two rivers were the Euphrates and the Khabur. The account of the adventures of Jacob in this area does not use the term Aram-naharaim, but employs instead the name Paddan-aram, "the field, or garden, of Aram" (28:2).

Balaam, the son of Beor, was from Pethor in Mesopotamia (Dt 23:4). During the period of the judges, Cushan-rishathaim, king of Mesopotamia, oppressed Israel for eight years, but the Lord brought deliverance through Othniel (Jgs 3:8–10).

When the Ammonites expected David to invade their territory because they had insulted his ambassadors, they hired chariotry from Mesopotamia and elsewhere to bolster their forces (1 Chr 19:6).

In the NT Mesopotamia is mentioned only twice. People from Mesopotamia were present on the day of Pentecost (Acts 2:9). Stephen, in his defense before the Sanhedrin, states that Abraham "lived in Mesopotamia, before he lived in Haran" (Acts 7:2; see Gn 11:31).

CARL E. DEVRIES

Messiah. Title derived from the Hebrew, *mashiach*, a verbal adjective meaning anointed one. Along with its NT equivalent, *christos* (Christ), it refers to an act of consecration whereby an individual is set apart to serve God and anointed (smeared or perhaps sprinkled) with oil. The verbal root (*mashach*) conveys this idea as well.

Israel's practice of ceremonially anointing with oil is present in several contexts. Priests were regularly anointed prior to their divinely given service at the altar of sacrifice (Lv 4:3). While there is evidence for a literal anointing of prophets (1 Kgs 19:16) this does not appear to have been a standard practice. The anointing of Saul and David by Samuel established the act as a significant prerequisite for Hebrew kings before they assumed their positions of royal leadership. The king was especially considered to be the Lord's anointed and as such was viewed to hold a secure position before men (1 Sm 12:14; 2 Sm 19:21) and God (Pss 2:2; 20:6). Along with numerous messianic prophecies, these proceedings helped inform the Jews of the anointed one, par excellence, who would eventually come to bring salvation to Israel.

Concluding the 13 articles of Hebraic faith attributed to Moses Maimonides (13th century) is the statement still found in many Hebrew prayer books: "I believe with a perfect heart that the Messiah will come; and although his coming be delayed, I will still wait patiently for his speedy appearance."

Messiah and the Old Testament.

Corporate Jewish hope for the advent of the Messiah developed dynamically from the period of David's reign when it was prophesied that his kingdom would endure to the end of time (2 Sm 7:16). Israel was told that, through David's descendants, his throne would exert a never-ending dominion over all the earth (22:48–51; Jer 33). It is with this aspect of messianic salvation that Jewish minds have been traditionally preoccupied (cf. Acts 1:6). This hope was nurtured even when, some two centuries following the death of Solomon, the truncated northern kingdom of Israel was assimilated by the Assyrians and the house of David drew perilously close to annihilation. With Israel's depressing history of apostate kings culminating in Babylonian supremacy, only a supernaturally supported faith made belief in the promise tenable. During the final two or three centuries of the second commonwealth, a flourishing religious community at Qumran lived in anticipation of "the Coming One's" advent. Their own charismatic figures, "the Teacher of Righteousness" and "the Expounder of the law" were hoped to be God's final witnesses prior to the glorious revelation of the Davidic Messiah. Yet their hopes were shattered in AD 68 when Vespasian's troops overran their encampments and dispersed all of them. Looking for the consolation of Israel (cf. Lk 2:25) yet unsure of the exact character of the redemptive scenario, few within Israel placed much emphasis upon the Gentiles in the grand scheme of things, their status being essentially servile in character (cf. Is 49:6).

Among orthodox rabbis there has never been a lack of conjecture respecting the details of the Messiah's ministry. At one time the rabbis applied no less than 456 passages of Scripture to his person and salvation. Preoccupation with the Messiah is evident in the tractate Sanhedrin (Babylonian Talmud) where passages state that the world was created for him and that all the prophets prophesied of his days (Sanhedrin 98b, 99a). By and large, orthodoxy still retains its time-worn belief in the Messiah's reign in Jerusalem, the rebuilding of the great temple, and the reestablishment of both priesthood and sacrifice. Yet it labors under the wrongly conceived notions of the past, among which are the ideas of multiple messiahs championed in intertestamental literature such as the Psalms of Solomon and 1 Enoch.

While later Judaism points to the Messiah as an eschatological figure who will reign at the end of time, modern Jewish thought has largely jettisoned the traditional notion of a personal Messiah in favor of belief in a messianic age. Prevalent liberal Judaism envisions the world ultimately perfected through the influence of the twin Judaic ideals of justice and compassion. Such conviction, ignoring the plight of fallen man and the teaching of Scripture, substitutes humanistic thinking for miraculous heavenly intervention.

While, humanly speaking, the Messiah's origin is linked firmly to the house of David (2 Sm 7:14; Hos 3:5) one must not imagine the messianic hope to originate at the time of the

The Star (or Shield) of David on the lintels of the synagogue at Capernaum. This six-sided star is the most universally recognized symbol of Judaism.

great Israelite dynasties. In fact, the hope for the Messiah is implicit in the first promise of the establishment of the kingdom of God. Addressed to Satan, Genesis 3:15 declares that God will place hostility between the serpent and the woman until, in the fullness of time, the "seed" of the woman inflicts a fatal blow to the head of the serpent. To those who underestimate the devastating power of sin such a promise seems both unnatural and unnecessary. Along with conventional Judaism, many fail to consider the fall of man seriously and take the Genesis narrative allegorically. The result has been to deny the need of a mediator and thereby stress individual effort as the key to redemption. Yet man has been ruined by sin (Gn 6:5; Jer 17:9); Adam's disobedience brought condemnation to his race (Rom 5:12–21).

The nature of messianic prophecy is progressive; each prophecy casts more light on the subject. This occurs, for example, respecting the concept of the "seed": Messiah is to be born of a woman (Gn 3:15), through the line of Shem (9:26) and specifically through Abraham (22:18). Yet even as late as Genesis 22:18, the "seed" is not clearly presented as a person, since *zerah* (seed) may indicate a singular or plural object. Still less apparent in these early stages of messianic prophecy is the nature of "bruising" which is to occur. Yet the idea of the Messiah being crushed for sin is implicit in the Genesis pronouncement as is the violence associated with that act. The verb *shuph* (to bruise) occurs in rabbinic commentaries describing Moses "grinding" the golden calf until it was fine powder (Ex 32:20). It remains for the prophet Isaiah to give dramatically graphic elaboration to the fact (Is 53:5).

Chief among the messianic prophets, Isaiah gives full range to the axiom that the anointed one must endure extensive suffering. Under the figure, "the Servant of the Lord," four so-called "servant songs" delineate the mission of the future deliverer (Is 42:1–7; 49:1–9; 50:4–11; 52:13–53:12). While it is true that Isaiah does not explicitly link the title "Messiah" with the "Servant of the Lord," identifying both figures as one and the same person is easily verifiable. Both figures are uniquely anointed (61:1); each brings light unto the Gentiles (55:4; cf. 49:6); neither is pretentious in his first appearance (7:14,15; 11:1; cf. 53:1; 42:3); and the title of Davidic "branch" rests upon them both (11:1–4). Equally significant are the dual facts of their humiliation and exaltation (49:7; 52:13–15). Jewish scholars of the early Christian era in the Aramaic Targum on the prophets paraphrase Isaiah 42:1, "Behold my Servant Messiah" and begin Isaiah 53, "Behold my Servant Messiah will prosper." While Cyrus may be

spoken of as "anointed," no final salvific work is attributed to him (45:1,4,5). Israel, although elect and loved by God (41:8), is ill-equipped as God's servant to bring his redeeming work to mankind (42:18). The collapse of David's dynasty points eloquently to Israel's need for an anointed monarch who will heal the apostasy and disobedience which continually characterizes her relationship with God (Ex 33:5; Hos 4:1). More and more, OT history presents Israel's comprehensive moral failure. Her problem, which she shares with mankind, can only be solved by the making of a covenant whose surety and focal point is both personal Savior and sovereign Lord (Jer 23:7; 31:31–34). The advent of such a champion lives in the recorded promise of a shoot from the stump of Jesse's fallen tree who will bring the light of life to God's benighted people (Is 11:1; 9:2).

It is difficult to get away from the idea that the concept of servanthood and lowliness belongs within the sphere of royalty (Zec 9:9). For the Messiah to fill the complementary offices of priest and king finds an incontrovertible foundation (Ps 110:1–4); a suffering priest-king is far less obvious. Some among the Talmudic writers apparently recognized the likelihood that the Messiah would have to suffer. In the Babylonian Talmud, tractate Sanhedrin 98b, the Messiah is said to bear sicknesses and pain. Among the prayers for the day of atonement may be found the words of Eleazar ben Qalir (perhaps as late as AD 1000): "Our righteous Messiah has departed from us; we are horror-stricken, and there is none to justify us. Our iniquities and the yoke of our transgressions he carries, and is wounded for our transgressions. He bears on his shoulders our sins to find pardon for our iniquities. May we be healed by his stripes." In a similar vein Rabbi Eliyya de Vidas writes, "The meaning of 'He was wounded for our transgressions, bruised for our iniquities,' is that since the Messiah bears our iniquities, which produce the effect of His being bruised, it follows that whosoever will not admit that the Messiah thus suffers for our iniquities must endure and suffer for them himself." For all this it is highly doubtful that anyone imagined the Messiah would accomplish his salvational work by means of his own death (cf. Is 53:12). When rabbinic speculation failed to satisfactorily harmonize the paradoxical facts of humiliation and exaltation some hypothesized that God would send a Messiah to suffer as well as a Messiah to reign. Biblically, it is evident that the anointed one's terrible ordeal of suffering is but the necessary prelude to infinite glory. He is pictured not only as a great king (52:13; 53:12) but also as humble (53:2), humiliated

(52:14), rejected (53:3), and bearing the consequences of mankind's rebellion (53:5,6). Yet he is raised up to intercede for, and richly bless his people (53:12). The Messiah, having accomplished that full obedience which Adam and Israel failed to achieve, will bring Israel and the nations back to God (42:18,19; 49:3,6).

The writings of Daniel contain important messianic data. Daniel is unique in that he boldly speaks of "Messiah the Prince" (Dn 9:25), identifies him as the "Son of man" (7:13), and says he suffers (9:26). This statement of the cutting off (i.e., death) of the Messiah makes possible his work of atonement (9:24). The doctrine of a vicarious substitutionary atonement is the only doctrine of atonement found in the Bible (cf. Lv 17:11). Israel understood that to bear sin meant enduring the consequences, or penalty, for sin (cf. Nm 14:33). The same penal substitution is evident in the working principle of the Messiah's atoning sacrifice. He is the victim's substitute to whom is transferred the suffering due the sinner. The penalty having been thus borne vicariously, the suppliant is fully pardoned.

Psalm 22:1 records the plaintive cry of the Messiah bearing man's penalty for sin (cf. Mt 27:46) as he becomes sin on behalf of his people (2 Cor 5:21). Yet his cry, "My God," indicates an intimate relationship which cannot be radically severed. Once again the motif of messianic humiliation prior to great exaltation is in view (Ps 22:27). In the so-called "royal psalms" (e.g., Pss 2,72,110) it is the priestly intercessor who is also ordained to function as monarch and judge.

Jeremiah brings the portrait a step further. The one who will enable man to enter into a salvational covenant with God conveys God's imputed righteousness: the Messiah, God's righteous branch, becomes "the Lord our Righteousness." Paradoxically, under the Law no one could be crucified who was not guilty of sin (Dt 21:22). But at Calvary it is Christ the righteous one who dies, thereby forever undermining any supposed legalistic confidence (21:23; Gal 3:13). More than forgiven, man is deemed righteous in him (Jer 23:7,8).

While the birthplace of the Messiah is well established (Mi 5:2), his deity is a hotly contested matter. Although few in ancient Israel disputed the belief in a superhuman Messiah, it is doubtful that anyone imagined him to be "God with us" in the fullest sense of the expression (cf. Heb 1:3). The Messiah's divinity is not well established but suggested in the OT: compound pronouns representing God (Gn 1:26; 11:7); theophanies through the Angel of the Lord (16:7–13; 18:1–21; 19:1–28; Mal 3:1); the multiple personages in the psalms (Pss 33:6; 45:6,7; 110:1); and the Word of God per-

sonified (Ps 33:4,6; Prv 8:12–31). Divine interrelationships also appear to be at work in Isaiah 48:12,16; 61:1; and 63:8–16.

Messiah and the New Testament. Through the eyes of faith the NT writers discern that he who is the child of supernatural origins (Is 7:14; Mi 5:2) carries the full weight of divinity (Is 9:6; Phil 2:6; Col 1:19). He is veritably the Son of God and worthy to receive the worship of all men (Ps 45:6,7; cf. Heb 1:8,9).

The Jews of 1st-century Palestine knew that messianic promise would be fulfilled in the coming of one like Moses (Dt 18:18). Parallels between Jesus and Moses are abundant. As mediators, innovators, and propagators of new phases of spiritual life for the people, they are unexcelled. Specifically, both are miraculously spared in infancy (Ex 2; Mt 2:13–23); both renounce a royal court for the sake of serving the people of God (Phil 2:5–8; Heb 11:24–28); both exhibit intense compassion for others (Nm 27:17; Mt 9:36); both commune "face to face" with God (Ex 34:29,30; 2 Cor 3:7); and each mediates a covenant of redemption (Dt 29:1; Heb 8:6,7). But, as Luther observes, "Christ is no Moses." In the final analysis Moses is but a household servant; the Messiah is the maker and master of all things (Heb 3:3–6; cf. Jn 1:1,2,18).

Family genealogies are of no little importance in Scripture. Rabbis agreed upon the absolute necessity of the Messiah's Davidic lineage based on Hosea 3:5 and Jeremiah 30:9. The angelic announcement immediately establishes the correct lineage for Jesus (Lk 1:32,33; cf. 2:4), a genealogy which Matthew expands in depth (Mt 1:1–17). The Lukan list, like that of Matthew, sets forth the exclusive kingly retinue verifying Jesus as Messiah (Lk 3:23–38). Although variations occur between the two genealogies there is a firm solidarity emphasizing an ancestry within the unique messianic stock. It is not uncommon to find the omission of one or more generations in a given biblical family chronology. This is true in both OT and NT. For example, six of Aaron's descendants, lacking in Ezra 7:1–5, are given in 1 Chronicles 6:3–14.

Fully aware of the messianic focus of Scripture (Jn 5:46; 8:56), Jesus acknowledges himself to be the Christ on numerous occasions. He accepts the title from blind Bartimaeus (Mk 10:46–48); from the crowds when he enters Jerusalem (Mt 21:9); from the children at the temple (21:15); and in other contexts as well (16:16–18; Mk 14:61,62; Lk 4:21; Jn 4:25,26). He nonetheless warns his disciples not to broadcast his mighty acts as Messiah prior to his resurrection (Mt 17:9; cf. Lk 9:20,21). Owing to the commonly misheld notion that the Messiah's role is primarily that of a political liberator, Jesus actually avoids use of that term and prefers to identify himself as "the Son of Man." Before his revealing use of the title it was by no means assumed that both designations referred to the same person (cf. Mk 14:61,62). Borrowed essentially from Daniel's vision of a heavenly conqueror (Dn 7:13,14), Jesus consistently employs this less known title and fills it with the true character and scope of messianic salvation. Jesus' teaching in this regard enables his disciples to correct their erroneous views concerning his mission (Mt 16:21–23). In the fullness of time they will come to see him not only as Messiah but also as the theme of the entire OT (5:17; Lk 24:27,44; Jn 5:39; cf. Heb 10:7). When Jesus expounds the Scriptures beginning with the Torah (Lk 24:27), he does so as the living exegesis of God, the Word made flesh (Jn 1:14,18). Legitimate messianic exposition is found in a host of texts (which are by no means exhaustive): Psalms 2; 16; 22; 40; 110; Isaiah 7:14; 9:6; 11:1; 40:10,11; 50:6; 52:13–53:12; 61:1; 63:1–6; Jeremiah 23:5,6; 33:14–16; Ezekiel 34:23; 37:25; Daniel 9:24–27; Hosea 11:1; Micah 5:2; Zechariah 9:9; 11:13; 12:10; 13:7; Malachi 3:1; 4:2.

The messiahship of Jesus is firmly proclaimed by all four Evangelists (Mt 1:1; Mk 1:1; Lk 24:26; Jn 20:31). Peter on Pentecost, Philip before the Ethiopian eunuch, and Apollos in open debate all argue convincingly that Jesus is the Messiah (Acts 2:36; 8:35; 28:28). Peter says he was "made" both Lord and Christ (Acts 2:36), signifying that the resurrection rightfully confirms him as such. Similarly, the apostle Paul speaks of Jesus' resurrection as a patent declaration of his inalienable right to the title (Rom 1:4). For the ex-Pharisee and former persecutor of the church, "Jesus the Christ" is the very heart and soul of Paul's preaching. Nothing is worthy to be compared to the glory of the Messiah; everything pales by comparison (Phil 3:5–10). The apostle's all-consuming passion is for others to know the fullness of God in the person of his only Son (Eph 3:14–19). He is "the last Adam" who undertakes both to earn salvation for man and to give himself as the ransom for the sins of his people (Rom 5:12–19).

The Holy Spirit speaks of Jesus with wide-ranging appellatives: Holy One, Judge, Righteous One, King, Son of God, and Lord, but these are not exhaustive. In him all the lines of messianic prediction converge; and he is the touchstone whereby their validity is firmly established. The Lord Jesus Christ is himself the heart and substance of that covenant through which sinful men may be reconciled to a holy God (Is 42:6; Jn 14:6). The message he brings is not a nobler ethical ideal or the necessity for moral improvement; the revelation of the Messiah is that Jesus accepts the Father's horrible judgment in the place of sinful man. That Jesus is the Messiah of Israel, God incarnate, exhaustively fulfills prophecy, type, and symbol—all shadows of his coming. Therefore all should trust in him, the source of all grace, the only abiding treasure (Mt 12:21; Jn 1:16,17; Col 2:3). Anointed as prophet he leads us into all truth (Jn 6:14; 7:16); as priest he intercedes for us (Heb 7:21); and as king he reigns over us (Phil 2:9,10).

When the Jew without the Messiah approaches the OT he may have some valid existential framework for preaching, yet since the OT as an end in itself can never do justice to the vast anticipation of its contents, he is unavoidably frustrated in considering that mighty ruler who brings the covenant to eternal fruition (Jer 31:31–34; Ez 34:25–31; 37:26; Rv 19:10b) and pours out the Spirit on all flesh (Jl 2:28–32). Without the Letter to the Hebrews, the priestly intercessor of Leviticus is veiled in obscure antiquity (Lv 9:7; cf. Heb 5:1–6). Apart from John's apocalypse the new heavens and earth of Isaiah lack substance and definition (Is 65:17; cf. Rv 21:22). As always, however, the personal realization of the Messiah's true identity is not the achievement of personal study and reflection; it is the result of a loving God taking the initiative to reveal himself to the hearts of those he himself has prepared to receive the person of his Son, the Lamb as well as the Lion of the tribe of Judah. STUART D. SACKS

See BRANCH; CHRISTOLOGY; JESUS CHRIST, LIFE AND TEACHINGS OF; SON OF MAN; ATONEMENT; REDEEMER, REDEMPTION; SON OF GOD.

Bibliography. H.L. Ellison, *The Centrality of the Messianic Idea for the OT*; T.W. Manson, *Jesus the Messiah* and *The Servant-Messiah*; S. Mowinckel, *He That Cometh*; H. Ringgren, *The Messiah in the OT*; H.H. Rowley, *The Servant of the Lord*.

Metallurgy. Science and technology of metals.

See INDUSTRY AND COMMERCE; MINERALS, METALS, AND PRECIOUS STONES; TRADES AND OCCUPATIONS (COPPERSMITH, CRAFTSMAN, GOLDSMITH, IRONSMITH, SILVERSMITH, SMITH).

Metheg-ammah. Place (whose name means "Bridle of the Mother City") conquered by David (2 Sm 8:1). Most likely it refers to the Philistine capital, Gath (1 Chr 18:1). The capital city was often referred to as the "mother" city, and surrounding cities as "daughters"; the "bridle" represented control or authority.

Methusael. KJV spelling of Methushael, Mehujael's son, in Genesis 4:18.

See METHUSHAEL.

Methuselah. Son of Enoch, Lamech's father, and the grandfather of Noah through Seth's line (Gn 5:21–27; 1 Chr 1:3). Living 969 years, Methuselah is the oldest recorded person in the Bible. His lineage is included in Luke's genealogy of Christ (3:37, KJV Mathusala).

See GENEALOGY OF JESUS CHRIST.

Methushael. Mehujael's son and the father of Lamech in Cain's line (Gn 4:18, KJV Methusael).

Metretes. In Greek literature a liquid measure equivalent to about 10 gallons.

See WEIGHTS AND MEASURES.

Meunim, Meunite. People living in Edom (Mt Seir, 1 Chr 4:42) who were dispossessed of their rich pasturelands by the Simeonites (v 41). Later, Meunites from Edom attacked Judah's King Jehoshaphat (2 Chr 20:1); later still, King Uzziah of Judah defeated them (26:7, KJV Mehunims). Their original land possession, association with Arabs and Ammonites, and prolonged hostility recall Judges 10:11,12, where "Maonites" are named oppressors of Israel. This word, by Hebrew rules of vocalization, could well become "Meunites," suggesting Maon (Ma'in, Maan) in the Edomite area south of the Dead Sea as their home.

The Meunim are listed among the families of temple servants returning to Jerusalem following the exile (Ezr 2:50, KJV Mehunim; Neh 7:52). However, because ancient enemies seem unlikely temple servants, some suggest that these Meunim were descendants of the Caleb clan within Judah to whom another town named Maon, west of the Dead Sea and south of Hebron, was allotted (Jos 15:20,55; cf. 1 Sm 30:14). First Chronicles 2:45 suggests the city's name became eponymous; "Meunite," like the modern Khirbet Ma'in, could derive from it. This Maon gave David refuge and another wife (1 Sm 23:24–28; 25).

This reconstruction involving two groups, two Maons, and temple servants with very foreign names, is tentative. An alternate view holds that hostile foreigners, formerly captured to become temple slaves (cf. Jos 9:7; Ez 44:6–8), attained freedom during exile and temple-guild status on returning.

See MAON (PLACE).

Mezahab. Matred's father and the grandfather of Mehetabel, the wife of the Edomite king Hadar (or Hadad) (Gn 36:39; 1 Chr 1:50).

Mezobaite. Designation for Jaasiel, one of David's "mighty men" (1 Chr 11:47, KJV Meso-baite). The meaning is unknown, though some suggest "from Zobah."

Miamin. 1. KJV rendering of Mijamin, Parosh's son, in Ezra 10:25.

See MIJAMIN #2.

2. KJV rendering of Mijamin, a postexilic priest, in Nehemiah 12:5.

See MIJAMIN #4.

Mibhar. Warrior among David's mighty men, who were known as "the 30" (1 Chr 11:38).

Mibsam. 1. One of Ishmael's sons and the founder of a tribe named after him (Gn 25:13; 1 Chr 1:29).

2. Shallum's son and the father of Mishma (1 Chr 4:25).

Mibzar. Chief of Edom (Gn 36:42; 1 Chr 1:53). The name means "fortress." Eusebius connects Mibzar with Mabsara, a large town in Edom.

Mica. Common name interchangeable with Micah and probably a contracted form of Micaiah.

1. Mephibosheth's son (Merib-baal). He shared in the fortunes of David's generosity to his father, and in Ziba's treachery. Mica had four sons (2 Sm 9:12, KJV Micha; 1 Chr 8:34,35; 9:40,41, KJV, RSV Micah).

2. Levite and Zichri's son from Asaph's clan, who performed musical service in the temple. He appears to have been one of the exiled priests whose son Mattaniah was among the first group of returning exiles (1 Chr 9:15, KJV Micah; Neh 11:17,22, KJV Micha; 12:35, KJV Michaiah, RSV Micaiah).

3. One who set his seal on Ezra's covenant during the postexilic era (Neh 10:11, KJV Micha).

Micah (Person). 1. Ephraimite judge who had idols made and then hired a Levite to become his priest (Jgs 17;18).

2. Shimei's descendant from Reuben's tribe (1 Chr 5:5).

3. Alternate spelling of Mica, Mephibosheth's son and the great-grandson of King Saul, in 1 Chronicles 8:34,35; 9:40,41.

See MICA #1.

4. KJV spelling of Mica, Zichri's son, in 1 Chronicles 9:15.

See MICA #2.

5. Levite and Uzziel's son from Kohath's clan, whose temple responsibilities included care of the furniture and equipment (1 Chr 23:20; 24:24,25, KJV Michah).

6. Alternate spelling of Micaiah, Achbor's father, in 2 Chronicles 34:20.

See MICAIAH #3.

7. Prophet and author of the OT book that bears his name (Mi 1:1). A native of Moresheth, a town about 21 miles southwest of Jerusalem, Micah prophesied to both northern and southern kingdoms during the reigns of Jotham, Ahaz, and Hezekiah (750–686 BC). According to Micah 1:9, he was still prophesying in 701 BC when the Assyrian armies under Sennacherib (cf. Is 36;37) besieged Jerusalem. About 100 years later, Micah is used as an example of an early prophet who predicted the destruction of Jerusalem (cf. Jer 26:16–19).

See MICAH, BOOK OF; PROPHET, PROPHETESS.

Micah, Book of.

Sixth in the order of the books of the 12 minor prophets.

The first verse of the Book of Micah provides his name, home, dates, the source of his message, and the recipients of his message.

Micah's name was common in ancient Israel. At least seven different individuals in the OT are called Micah or Michaiah. The prophet is mentioned by name only in Micah 1:1 and Jeremiah 26:18 in the OT.

The superscription of Micah (1:1) gives his hometown as Moresheth, which may be identified with the modern village of Tell el Judeideh about 25 miles southwest of Jerusalem on the road from Azekah to Lachish. Moresheth in Micah's time was a frontier village near the Philistine border city of Gath. As a border town Moresheth often took the brunt of enemy attacks on Judah from the south and west (v 15). Such an attack may be reflected in verses 10–16, where 12 towns in southwest Judah are named as being in the path of an invader. Moresheth-gath is ninth in that list. Because Micah lived in this border town, he seems to have developed an international concern with "the peoples" (1:2; 4:1–5,11; 5:7–15; 7:16,17). As a citizen of a small town Micah could identify with peasants and small land holders who were often victims of foreign aggressors and of the politicians and greedy land grabbers in Jerusalem (2:1–4). Although Micah may have left Moresheth to live and preach in Jerusalem, he had very harsh words for cities (1:5,6; 3:12; 4:10; 5:11,14; 6:9).

The date for Micah's ministry (1:1) was sometime during the reigns of three kings of Judah: Jotham (c. 750–732 BC), Ahaz (c. 735–715 BC), and Hezekiah (c. 715–686 BC). The maximum period covered by the reigns of these three kings was over 60 years (750–686 BC), but it is not likely that Micah was active as a prophet during all of that time. Jeremiah dates Micah's ministry in the reign of Hezekiah (Jer 26:18). Some of Micah's oracles seem to predate the fall of Samaria (1:2–7; 6:16), an event that took place in 722 BC. The Assyrians appear to be Israel's primary enemy in Micah's time (5:5,6), a situation that prevailed during the reigns of the three kings listed above. Some striking parallel passages between Micah and Isaiah (Mi 4:1–4; Is 2:2–4) and between Micah and Amos (Mi 6:10,11; Am 8:5,6) make it probable that Micah's ministry was in the last part of the 8th century BC.

Micah 1:1 says that "the word of the Lord" "came" to Micah of Moresheth. Micah was God's spokesman to the people of his day. Micah is not called a prophet in his book. There is no account of God's call for him to be a prophet, but he does claim to be God's witness (v 2). Five times in the book some form of the messenger formula, "thus says the Lord," is used (2:3; 3:5; 4:6; 6:1,9), asserting that the message is from God. Micah, like a true prophet, claims to be "filled with power, with the Spirit of the Lord, . . . to declare to Jacob his transgression and to Israel his sin" (3:8).

Micah's message was a universal message. It was addressed first in a broad sense to "the nations" and to "the whole earth" (1:1) but the focus narrows quickly to the capital cities of Jerusalem and Samaria (v 1; 5:6). Other cities in Judah are the object of one oracle (1:10–16). A group of wealthy land grabbers (2:1), false prophets (2:6–11; 3:5–7), judges, prophets, priests, and dishonest merchants (3:1,11; 6:10–12) are the objects of other messages.

Historical Background. In order to understand the Book of Micah properly one needs a knowledge of the Assyrian crisis in the history of ancient Israel. During the early part of the 8th century BC the northern and southern kingdoms of Israel and Judah experienced a period of peace and prosperity under the long and stable reigns of Jeroboam II (793–753 BC) and Uzziah (792–740 BC). Radical changes in the economic structure occurred within Israel and Judah during this long period. There was a rise of cities and a new wealthy class. Commerce grew enormously. The rich got richer and abused their power over the poor, the priests, and the judges. A class system appeared which struck at the heart of OT covenant religion.

During the reigns of Jeroboam II and Uzziah, Israel and Judah were relatively free from outside intervention. But in 745 BC Tiglath-pileser III became king of Assyria and set out to create an empire. He captured Damascus in 732 BC and made vassals of the small Palestine states of Israel, Judah, and Philistia. Tiglath-pileser III died in 727 BC and was succeeded by Shalmaneser V. In 724 BC Hoshea, the last king of Israel, withheld tribute from Assyria and incurred the wrath of the

Assyrians. Shalmaneser V began his siege of Samaria in 724 BC but the people were not subdued until 722 BC. By that time Sargon II was the king of Assyria. Many of the wealthy and influential people of Samaria were carried into captivity to Assyria (2 Kgs 15:29,30; 17:1–41). Judah did not escape the crisis. Although a fragmentary government of Judean kings was left in Jerusalem by the Assyrians, practically all of their liberties were taken away (2 Kgs 16:10; 17:19). Judah never fully recovered politically nor religiously from the Assyrian crisis.

Purpose and Message. The Book of Micah is made up of about 20 separate sections or oracles. There is a variety of material in the book about different subjects, coming perhaps from different periods. With such variety in the book it is difficult to speak of *the* message of the book. However, certain themes are prominent in the book, the most prominent being judgment. It is coming on Samaria (1:2–6) and on Jerusalem (3:9–12). It is coming on guilty land grabbers (2:3–5), on false prophets, corrupt judges, and hireling priests (3:5–12). Judgment is coming on the cheater, the violent, the liar, and the deceiver (6:9–12). Judgment is coming on the nations (4:11–13; 5:5,6, 8,9,15; 7:16,17). Judgment is due to sin (1:5). Sin takes many forms in Micah ranging from idolatry (1:7; 5:13), to the occult (5:12), to theft (6:11), to lying (6:12), to contempt for parents (7:6), to murder (7:2).

What is Micah's remedy for sin? For the nations it is a knowledge of and obedience to the "ways of God" (4:2). For Israel it is "to do justice, and to love kindness, and to walk humbly with God" (6:8). All of this is possible because God pardons iniquity and is not always angry. He is a God of compasssion who treads iniquities underfoot, casts sins into the depth of the sea, and keeps his covenant with Abraham (7:18–20). Micah caught a glimpse of the future kingdom of God when he saw that a future ruler of Israel would be born in Bethlehem. He would stand and feed his flock in the strength of the Lord. He would provide security because he will be great to the ends of the earth (5:2–4).

Content. Some scholars divide the book into two parts. The first part (chs 1–5) is addressed primarily to the nations, while the second (chs 6,7) is addressed primarily to Israel. The first part ends with a threat of judgment on the nations (5:15) and the second ends with a hymn to the compassion of God. That outline seems too simple, however, and does not cover the diverse materials in the two parts. Other scholars divide the book into three parts: chapters 1–3 (judgment); chapters 4,5 (hope); and chapters 6,7 (judgment and hope).

Again, this outline is too simple because all three sections contain both judgment and hope. Perhaps it is better to divide the book into three parts beginning with chapters 1, 3, and 6. Each of these chapters begins with "hear ye." Each section begins with words of judgment (1:2–2:11; 3:1–12; 6:1–7:6) and ends on a note of hope (2:12,13; 4:1–5:15; 7:7–20). Such an outline can be valuable in attempting to see the book as a whole, but a closer look at each oracle or unit is needed to interpret the book properly. This discussion marks off each of the 20 units by chapter and verse, identifies its literary form, and determines its major motif or theme.

The first unit, "The Lord Is Coming," consists of 1:2–7. Its form is that of a lawsuit and a theophany. The peoples of the world are called to listen to what the Lord will witness against them. He is described as leaving his heavenly temple to come to earth to tread on top of the mountains which melt under him (vv 2–4). God's coming (theophany) is due to the sins of the people. Samaria, the capital of the northern kingdom of Israel, is to be destroyed primarily because of idolatry (vv 5–7).

The second pericope is "The Prophet's Lament" (1:8–16). The prophet sees an enemy army coming from the southwest. Twelve cities are in its path. Desolation, refugees, and hostages are the result. There is a word play on the name of each of the cities except Gath, designed to express the fate of each city. Some of the cities are well known, such as Lachish, Jerusalem, Moresheth-gath, and Adullam. Others cannot be identified. This pericope indicates that even though the first oracle was addressed to the nations and specifically announced the fall of Samaria, Judah was the real concern of Micah.

The third pericope is "Woe to the Wealthy Wicked" (2:1–5). It is a woe oracle, meaning that it is a message of judgment. This time judgment is on a certain group of wealthy men who wickedly devise schemes at night to seize houses and lands from unsuspecting farmers. Micah says their plans will boomerang. Their own lands will be snatched from them.

"Micah and the Wealthy Wicked" is the theme of the fourth section (2:6–11). This passage records a dispute between Micah and those who snatched houses and fields from unsuspecting victims. Micah's wicked listeners could not accept his message of judgment. They found it offensive and commanded him to stop preaching such things. They did not believe that evil would overtake them because they thought God would not do such things (vv 6,7a). But Micah enumerates a number of crimes of these wicked men, such as taking the robes off travelers' backs and driving women and children from their homes (vv 7b–9). Such wicked men follow false prophets (v 11).

The fifth pericope is "A Remnant to be Restored" (2:12,13). The Lord will gather a remnant of his people like sheep in a fold (v 12), then the Lord as their king leads them out through the gate ahead of them (v 13). This section is open to various interpretations. The passage does not indicate the place where the Lord will gather the remnant. Some assume the place is Babylon and take the passage as a reference to the exile. Others believe the place is Jerusalem and relate the incident to refugees fleeing to Jerusalem before Sennacherib's invasion in 701 BC.

The sixth pericope is about "Guilty Rulers" (3:1–4). Micah charges that the heads and leaders of his people act like cannibals. They should know justice but they hate the good and love evil. They will cry to the Lord but he will not hear them.

"Peace Prophets and Micah" is another disputation passage (3:5–8). Micah accuses the false prophets of preaching for money and asserts that they have no vision or message from God. On the other hand, Micah claims to speak in the power and spirit of God.

"Corrupt Leaders and Zion's Fall" is the subject of the eighth pericope (3:9–12). This oracle seems to be a summary of all Micah has been saying to the various groups of leaders in Jerusalem. Because of their sins and crimes Jerusalem and the temple will be destroyed.

"Zion's Future Exaltation" follows immediately the surprising announcement of Zion's fall and the temple's destruction (4:1–5). This oracle of salvation was probably deliberately placed after the previous oracle of judgment to indicate that even though the temple might be destroyed, it would be restored in grander style to be the worship center for all nations. A parallel to this passage is in Isaiah 2:1–4.

"Restoration of a Remnant and Zion" is the subject of the 10th section (4:6–8). The opening phrase "In that day" indicates that this is an eschatological oracle in which the Lord is seen as reigning over his restored flock in Zion.

The next three pericopes (4:9,10; 4:11–13; 5:1–4) all begin with the word "now" and end with an assertion that the present evil situation will be changed for the better. The first of the three is "From Distress to Deliverance" (4:9,10); the second is "From Siege to Victory" (vv 11–13); and the third is "From Helpless Judge to Ideal King" (5:1–4). The last passage in this series is one of the most familiar passages in Micah. It contains the promise of the birth of a new king in Bethlehem who will be great to the ends of the earth.

The 14th section, "Peace and the Overthrow of Assyria" (5:5,6), is followed closely by "The Remnant Among the Peoples" (vv 7–9). The remnant is portrayed as dew on plants and as a lion among sheep. Dew on plants is usually taken to signify a blessing but in 2 Samuel 17:12 it is a metaphor for judgment as a lion is among sheep.

The 16th pericope is "Purge of the Military and False Religions" (5:10–15). The expressions "I will cut off," "throw down," "cause to perish," "root out," and "destroy" suggest radical surgery. It is an oracle on those things that might take the place of God in people's minds.

"God's Lawsuit" (6:1–8) is probably the most familiar passage in Micah. It is one of the great summaries of true religion. The next pericope presents "More Charges and the Sentence" (6:9–16). The further charges are dishonest business practices, lying, and acts of violence. The sentence is a life of futility, frustration, scorn, and destruction.

The 19th pericope in Micah is a "Lament over a Decadent Society" (7:1–6). The prophet begins with a woe because he seems to be the only godly or righteous man left (vv 1,2). He cannot trust anyone. Everyone may be setting a trap for another. People do evil with both hands. Even the members of families rise against each other. Jesus applied the words of 7:6 to his own times (Mt 10:21,35,36).

The last section of Micah (7:7–20) is a prophetic liturgy. It is made up of a psalm of trust (vv 7–10); a prophetic promise of restoration (vv 11–13); a prayer for God to bless Israel and judge their enemies (vv 14–17); and a hymn or a doxology declaring God incomparable in "grace and truth," showing faithfulness to Jacob and steadfast love to Abraham (v 20).

RALPH L. SMITH

See PROPHET, PROPHETESS; PROPHECY; ISRAEL, HISTORY OF.

Bibliography. L.C. Allen, *The Books of Joel, Obadiah, Jonah and Micah;* G.A. Smith, *The Book of the Twelve Prophets;* C. von Orelli, *The Twelve Minor Prophets.*

Micaiah. 1. Prophet and Imlah's son, called by Ahab to forecast the result of projected battles against the Syrians. At first Micaiah mocks him with glad news, then tells the cruel truth. Ahab casts the prophet into prison as a kind of ransom, but the wicked ruler dies in battle just as Micaiah predicted (1 Kgs 22:8; 2 Chr 18:7–25).

2. Father of Achbor, one of the court officials whom King Josiah sent to the prophetess Huldah to get an opinion on the law book that Hilkiah the high priest had found in the temple (2 Kgs 22:12, KJV Michaiah; 2 Chr 34:20, KJV, RSV Micah).

3. Alternate rendering of Maacah, mother of Judah's King Abijah, in 2 Chronicles 13:2.

See MAACAH, MAACHAH (PERSON) #4.

4. Teacher commissioned by King Jehoshaphat to teach the Law of the Lord throughout Judah (2 Chr 17:7, KJV Michaiah).

5. Alternate spelling of Mica, Zichri's son, in Nehemiah 12:35.

See MICA #2.

6. Priest who blew a trumpet at the dedication of the Jerusalem wall (Neh 12:41, KJV Michaiah).

7. Gemariah's son, who reported the words of the Lord to Jewish princes during the reign of King Jehoiakim (Jer 36:11,13, KJV Michaiah).

Micha. 1. KJV spelling of Mica, Mephibosheth's son, in 2 Samuel 9:12.

See MICA #1.

2. KJV spelling of Micah, Uzziel's son, in 1 Chronicles 23:20.

See MICAH (PERSON) #5.

3. KJV spelling of Mica, a Levite, in Nehemiah 10:11.

See MICA #3.

4. KJV spelling of Mica, Mattaniah's son, in Nehemiah 11:17,22.

See MICA #2.

Michael. Name meaning "Who is like God?" used of 10 men in Scripture and also of one who is described as an "archangel."

1. Father of one of the spies sent by Moses into Canaan (Nm 13:13).

2.3. Gadites named in the lists of those who settled in the land of Bashan (1 Chr 5:13,14).

4. Forefather of Asaph, a temple singer in the days of David (1 Chr 6:40).

5. Chief man of Issachar in the temple lists (1 Chr 7:3).

6. Benjamite named in the temple lists (1 Chr 8:16).

7. Man of Manasseh who joined David in Ziklag when he was fleeing from Saul (1 Chr 12:20).

8. Father of Omri, a "top political officer" in the days of David (1 Chr 27:18).

9. Son of King Jehoshaphat of Judah (2 Chr 21:2).

10. Father of Zebadiah, a returnee with Ezra to Jerusalem (Ezr 8:8).

11. Angel in the OT, intertestamental literature, and the NT. In Daniel 10:13 it is said that "the prince of the kingdom of Persia" sought to oppose the purpose of God, but Michael "one of the chief princes," contended against this evil spirit at the Lord's side (Dn 10:21). His conflict on behalf of Israel is referred to further in Daniel 12:1.

In the Book of Enoch Michael is one of four (9:1; 40:9) or of seven (20:1–7) special angels or "archangels." In Enoch, in the War Scroll (of the Dead Sea Scrolls) and in other intertestamental literature, Michael regularly is presented either as the champion of the cause of the righteous or as the patron angel of Israel.

The work known as the Assumption of Moses, which has survived only in an incomplete and corrupt form, seems to be referred to when in the NT Jude (v 9) says: "When the archangel Michael, contending with the devil, disputed about the body of Moses, he did not presume to pronounce a reviling judgment upon him, but said, 'The Lord rebuke you'" (cf. 2 Pt 2:10,11; see also the reference to "the archangel" in 1 Thes 4:16).

The only other reference to Michael in the NT is Revelation 12:7,8, where it is said that "Now war arose in heaven, Michael and his angels fighting against the dragon; and the dragon and his angels fought, but they were defeated and there was no longer any place for them in heaven."

See ANGEL.

Michah. KJV spelling of Micah, Uzziel's son, in 1 Chronicles 24:24,25.

See MICAH (PERSON) #5.

Michaiah. 1. KJV spelling of Micaiah, Achbor's father, in 2 Kings 22:12.

See MICAIAH #2.

2. KJV spelling of Micaiah, the mother of Judah's king Abijah, in 2 Chronicles 13:2.

See MAACAH, MAACHAH (PERSON) #4.

3. KJV spelling of Micaiah, one of King Jehoshaphat's officials, in 2 Chronicles 17:7.

See MICAIAH #4.

4. KJV spelling of Micaiah, an alternate name for Mica, Zichri's son, in Nehemiah 12:35.

See MICA #2.

5. KJV spelling of Micaiah, a postexilic priest, in Nehemiah 12:41.

See MICAIAH #6.

6. KJV spelling of Micaiah, Gemariah's son, in Jeremiah 36:11,13.

See MICAIAH #7.

Michal. Younger daughter of Saul (1 Sm 14:49). She fell in love with David after his defeat of Goliath (18:20). Saul, jealous of David, offered his first daughter, Merab, to David, but the recent victor graciously declined. When Michal's love became known to Saul, he renewed his offer of a wife, providing David produce evidence of killing 100 Philistines, a condition Saul felt would surely lead to David's death (vv 21–29).

David met Saul's condition in double measure and married Michal. Saul's jealousy was only fanned, and he plotted to have David murdered. Michal heard of the plot and assisted in her husband's escape (19:8–17). During David's exile, Saul gave Michal to Palti (25:44).

Following Saul's death, Abner negotiated with David, part of their agreement being the return of Michal to David's household. This was done despite Palti's remorse (2 Sm 3:12–16). But youthful ardor had apparently suffered strain. When David returned with the ark to Jerusalem, dancing before it, Michal voiced her harsh criticism. David's reply was equally severe. Michal would remain childless as punishment for her candidness. (The KJV, using inferior manuscripts, reports Michal as the mother of five sons in 2 Samuel 21:8. Adriel, however, was the husband of Merab, a correction reflected in RSV, NIV, NASB, NEB.)

David's overwhelming popularity should not overshadow the courage and passion displayed by Michal. She let her love be known when women hardly took the initiative in courtship, saved David's life at the risk of her own, was emotionally victimized by her forced marriage and separation from Palti, and voiced her critical convictions against the tide of public opinion.

Michmash, Michmas. Town in southern Mt Ephraim near the edge of the wilderness which descends eastward toward the Jordan Valley. Though it must have been an Israelite settlement in the territory of Benjamin, it is absent from the list of Benjamite towns (Jos 18:21–28). The ancient name is preserved in that of the Arab village of Mukhmas, situated on a narrow ridge to the east of Wadi

The gorge between Michmash and Geba.

Ṣuweiniṭ (valley of Zeboim) overlooking the deep canyon through which it runs. It is about 1½ miles northeast of Geba (Jabaʿ) which stands on the western side of the same valley. A lateral road passed by Michmash to Jericho and a longitudinal road also followed the watershed beside it. The latter route was of only secondary importance but still could serve as an alternate to the main trunk route, the highway west of Bethel.

The town played its best documented role in biblical history during the reign of Saul. When he mustered his troops, part were with him in Michmash while the rest were with Jonathan at Gibeah of Benjamin (1 Sm 13:2). After Jonathan had smitten the Philistine commissioner at Geba, the Philistines came out in force and encamped at Michmash (v 5) since Saul had withdrawn to Gilgal to assemble the rest of his forces. Then he went back to Geba, on the opposite side of the valley from the enemy. Using their base at Michmash (vv 11,16) the Philistines sent out raiding parties north to Ophrah, west to Beth-horon, and southeast along the edge of the valley of Zeboim (vv 17,18); this passage serves to illustrate the value of Michmash as a strategic crossroads.

An outpost south of Michmash was manned by Philistines facing the Israelites on the opposite ridge (1 Sam 13:23). Jonathan went out to the canyon where the two cliffs Bozez (on the side of Michmash) and Seneh (beside Geba) face one another. He and his armor bearer made a surprise attack on the outpost which fled to Michmash. The resultant confusion among the Philistines was taken advantage of by Saul and his troops (14:1–23). The Philistines withdrew under heavy Hebrew harrassment by way of the lateral road via the Aijalon Valley (v 31).

The further importance of Michmash on the secondary longitudinal route is clearly seen in the description of an enemy approach to Jerusalem from the north given in Isaiah 10:27–32, "at Michmash he stores his baggage" (v 28). It would appear that the invading force would have to leave its supplies and noncombat equipment at Michmash before crossing the canyon of Zeboim to continue the march southward. One may perhaps deduce from this passage that Michmash and most of northern Benjamin was at that time (8th century BC) in the hands of Judah although it had not been so during the previous century because the northernmost border fortress of Judah had been established at Geba under King Asa (1 Kgs 15:22) leaving Michmash to the kingdom of Israel under Baasha.

During the return from exile, Michmas (instead of Michmash) was one of the towns resettled (Ezr 2:27; Neh 7:31; 11:31).

The conflict with the Seleucids in the mid-2nd century BC saw Michmas as a residence for Jonathan Maccabee, who seems to have set up his headquarters there for judging the people (1 Mc 9:73; Josephus, *Antiq.* 13.1.6 [34]). He remained there until 152 BC.

Data concerning the Jewish community there are preserved in the Mishna, which praises its wheat. Eusebius (*Onomasticon* 132.3) indicates that there was a large village there.

It would appear that the Moslems in the 7th century AD had set up their own headquarters there soon after their conquest of the land. The name of the Arabic village, Mukhmas, represents a linguistic borrowing based on immediate hearing. If the place had remained isolated, its name would have eventually come into Arabic as Mukmash.

Michmethath, Michmethah. Geographical location (KJV Michmethah) describing part of the boundary dividing the territory assigned to Ephraim (Jos 16:6) and Manasseh's tribes (17:7), situated in the mountains west of the Jordan, midway between the Dead Sea and the Sea of Galilee. Current scholarship tentatively names modern Khirbet Julaijal as the likely site.

Michri. Ancestor of a family that returned to Jerusalem with Zerubbabel after the Babylonian captivity (1 Chr 9:8).

Michtam. KJV rendering of miktam, a musical cue, in the titles of Psalms 16, 56, 57, 58, 59, and 60.

See MIKTAM.

Middin. One of the six cities in the wilderness west of the Dead Sea allotted to Judah's tribe for an inheritance, mentioned between Beth-arabah and Secacah (Jos 15:61). Its location is uncertain.

Midian, Midianite. Person, place, or people, the latter living on the eastern edge of Gilead, Moab, and Edom south into northwest Arabia. They had few, if any, permanent settlements.

Midian and his descendants figure prominently only in the early history of Israel, in connection with Abraham (Gn 25:1-6), Joseph (37:25-36), Moses (Ex 2:15-3:1), Balaam (Nm 22:1-6; 25; 31:1-20), and Gideon (Jgs 6:1-8:28).

Midian was Isaac's younger half-brother, the fourth of six sons born to Keturah, whom Abraham married as an old man (Gn 25:1,2; cf. 23:1,2; 24:67; 1 Chr 1:32). By calling Midian and his full brothers "the sons of Keturah" (Gn 25:4; 1 Chr 1:32,33), the Bible carefully distinguishes them from Isaac, the son of Sarah, who was the one through whom God's promise to Abraham would be fulfilled (Gn 12:1-3; 17:15-21). In fact, Abraham and the Israelites regarded these other sons as having no more inheritance rights than a concubine's sons (25:5,6; 1 Chr 1:31).

Expelled from Abraham's family, for Isaac's sake, they became (semi) nomadic peoples of the deserts east and south of Palestine (Gn 25:5,6).

The Land of Midian. Of uncertain location, Midian is placed far south of Edom on the eastern side of what is today called the Gulf of Aqaba. The Alexandrian geographer Ptolemy (2nd century AD) mentions a city Modiana on the coast and a Madiana 26 miles inland (modern el-Bed') in this region, an identification supported by the Jewish historian Josephus (1st century AD) and the Christian church historian Eusebius (early 4th century).

In early OT times Midian seems to have been the land on the edge of the deserts bordering Gilead, Moab, and Edom south even into eastern Sinai.

In Joseph's day, some Midianite clans must have lived in the northern Transjordanian desert adjacent to Gilead or Bashan, as they were part of an Ishmaelite (cf. Jgs 8:24) caravan traveling the trade route from Damascus across Gilead past Dothan to Egypt (Gn 37:17,25-28,36).

When Moses fled from pharaoh, he settled in Midian and eventually married Zipporah, the daughter of a Midianite priest (Ex 2:15-22). Moses asked his Midianite relative Hobab to act as a guide from Horeb (to Kadesh-barnea, Dt 1:19); Hobab was familiar with the wilderness of Paran (Nm 10:11,12,29-31), even though his own land and relatives were elsewhere (10:30).

In the Balaam episode and its bloody aftermath (Nm 22:31), a substantial group of Midianites appears to have been living on the eastern frontier of Moab. The Moabite king Balak, who was subject to the Amorite king named Sihon (21:26-30; Jer 48:45), discussed the Israelite threat with the elders of Midian (Nm 22:2-4) and a joint delegation was sent to Balaam (vv 5-7). At Acacia in the plains of Moab (22:1; 25:1), an Israelite met and married a Midianite princess (25:6-18; 31:8). The Midianite kings were considered puppet kings of King Sihon (Jos 13:21 NASB). All the indications are that Midianite clans lived nearby, on the borders of Moab. Since Moab is north of Edom, the reference to an Edomite victory over Midian (Gn 36:35) might indicate a northern encroachment by the Midianites on Edomite territory.

The Midianite invasion which Gideon repulsed has all the appearances of an invasion from the east. It would thus appear that while "the land of Midian" is a term that may refer to a territory south of Edom, Midianites were living over a much wider area—on marginal land—east of Moab and Edom and south of Edom into east Sinai and northwest Arabia.

Midianite Society. The Midianites lived more as scattered clans and as a nominally subject people than as an independent country. For instance, one leader, Zur, is called "head of a people of a father's household" (Nm 25:15 NASB), "chief" (Jos 13:21 NASB), and "king," but there were at least five such kings in Moses' time (Nm 31:8), and all five were "princes [vassal-kings] of Sihon" (Jos 13:21 NASB).

Though they are usually presumed to have been mostly nomadic shepherds (as Moses was on Jethro's behalf, Ex 2:16; 3:1) Midianites are also pictured as opportunistic traders (Gn 37:25–36), as camel-riding marauders with substantial livestock (Jgs 6:3–5; 8:21), as middlemen in the gold and frankincense trade north from Sheba in southern Arabia (Is 60:6), and sometimes, by some scholars, as miners, coppersmiths, or tinkers.

The religion and worship of individual Midianites varied considerably. Jethro (Reuel), Moses' father-in-law, was a "priest of Midian" (Ex 2:16; 3:1), but he later identified with the worship of the Lord the God of Israel (Ex 18:1–5; note his confession and priestly ministry, 18:9–12). Although Jethro returned home to his own people (v 27), his son Hobab appears to have stayed for more than a year with the Israelites and became their guide (Nm 10:11; 29–32). On the other hand, the Midianites were so involved in the worship of Baal-peor that they (not the Moabites) were the ones who, at Balaam's counsel, enticed the Israelites into immorality and idolatry (25:1–18; 31:1–20, esp. v 16; cf. 2 Pt 2:13–16; Rv 2:14). In the war that ensued, the Midianites were decimated (Nm 31:7–12). During the period of the judges the Midianites invaded Israel periodically (Jgs 6–8), but were defeated by Gideon and never again threatened Israel (8:11,12,28).

The Later History of Midian. In David's day (c. 1000 BC) an Edomite prince fled to Midian to escape Joab's forces (1 Kgs 11:15–18) and later became the Edomite King Hadad, one of Solomon's main foes (v 14).

Assyrian records from about 732 BC and about 715 BC mention a subject tribe by the name of Haiappu. This may be the same name as Ephah, Midian's eldest son, after whom a tribe would have been named (Gn 25:4). Isaiah confirms that there was a Midianite tribe named Ephah at this time. It would someday come bringing rich offerings from Arabia to Zion to worship the Lord (Is 60:6,7).

By Hellenistic times (c. 300 BC), the Nabataeans controlled Moab, Edom, and Midian. Those Midianites who had survived to that point were probably pushed south into the area usually considered their homeland—the strip of land parallel to the Gulf of Aqaba. Eventually they lost their national identity, leaving only an occasional city name like Modiana (or Madiana) as a reminder that they had once been a great people.

Midian is mentioned one time in the NT (Acts 7:29), where it is spelled Madian in the KJV.

JAMES F. BABCOCK

Midrash. Transliteration into English of a Hebrew word that occurs twice in 2 Chronicles. Second Chronicles 13:22 refers to the literary source which was used for the reign of King Abijah of Judah (913–910 BC) as the "midrash" of the prophet Iddo. Second Chronicles 24:27 mentions, in connection with the reign of King Joash of Judah (835–796 BC), the "midrash" of the book of the kings. Some commentators consider that these references were invented by the author of Chronicles in order to claim authenticity for his work, but most accept them as real works of literature.

Although these are the only times that midrash is mentioned in Chronicles, they do fall into a pattern of appeals to literary sources. For instance, Chronicles often cites "the Book of the Kings of Israel and Judah" or the like (e.g., 2 Chr 16:11; 20:34; 27:7; 33:18). It is probable that the title in 2 Chronicles 24:27 incorporating the term "midrash" is just a variant title of a main source. Again, Chronicles often alludes to various prophetic sources; the otherwise unknown prophet Iddo features also in a work called "the visions of Iddo the seer," in connection with the reign of Jeroboam I of Israel (930–909 BC; 9:29), and also "the chronicles of Shemaiah the prophet and of Iddo the seer," with reference to King Rehoboam of Judah (930–913 BC; 12:15). Here too it is probable that a single prophetic work is labeled with different names.

But what did the term "midrash" mean precisely to the author of Chronicles? The ancient Greek version translated it simply as "book, writing," and it is likely that at this stage it means nothing more than that. The underlying Hebrew verb means to inquire or study, and accordingly the noun could signify "a result of research, a study." Alternatively it may mean "commentary" in the sense of a presentation of history from a certain angle of thought.

Apart from these instances in Chronicles, the other usage of importance for the OT is its meaning as a procedure or product of interpretation of the biblical text, which was eventually incorporated into the Jewish commentaries called Midrashim. In the literature of Qumran, midrash appears in the general sense of "interpretation of the Law." But in later rabbinic literature it became a technical term for a collection of traditional teachings of the rabbis arranged in order of chapter and verse of biblical books. The overall aim of these studies was to apply the ancient text to contemporary circumstances in a variety of ways.

See TALMUD.

Migdal-el. One of the fortified cities belonging to Naphtali's tribe (Jos 19:38). Its site is unknown.

Migdal-gad. Village in Judah which was located in the Shephelah district of Lachish (Jos 15:37). It is perhaps identifiable with Khirbet el-Mejdeleh, southeast of Tell el-Nuweir.

Migdol. Town in the eastern delta of Lower Egypt. In the narrative of the exodus it appears between the place called Pi-ha-hiroth and Baal-zephon (Ex 14:2; Nm 33:7). Some scholars who feel that the exodus route must have taken the Israelites south into the Sinai mountains look for these three sites somewhere near Suez. Others who hold that the Serbonitic Lake is the Reed Sea accept the identification of this Migdol with that mentioned by Jeremiah as the dwelling place of exiled Jews in the 6th century BC (Jer 44:1; 46:14). That place must be identical with the Migdol which represents the north (eastern) extremity of Egypt in juxtaposition to Syene in the far south (Ez 29:10; 30:6). The nonbiblical sources also refer to this Migdol; for example, Papyrus Anastasi 5.19, where it appears in association with Succoth in a message about runaway slaves. It also appears on the wall relief of Seti I as a fortress between Sillo (Sele) and the other northern Sinai forts. The Antonine Itinerary places Magdolo between Pelusium and Sele which would make the equation with Tell el-Heir, 12 1/2 miles north, most likely.

Migron. Site where Saul rested under a pomegranate tree, near Gibeah (1 Sm 14:2); also mentioned as part of the line of march of the Assyrians (Is 10:28). The first reference is to a site south of Michmash, the second is probably north of Michmash. Some scholars, however, try to identify both with the site south of Michmash, though this is doubtful.

Mijamin. 1. Priest who ministered during the time of David (1 Chr 24:9).

2. Parosh's son, who was encouraged by Ezra to divorce his foreign wife during the postexilic period (Ezr 10:25, KJV Miamin).

3. One of the priests who signed Ezra's covenant during the postexilic period (Neh 10:7).

4. Priest who returned to Jerusalem with Zerubbabel after the exile (Neh 12:5, KJV Miamin).

Mikloth. 1. Resident of Gibeon, son of the Benjamite Jeiel, and father of Shimeah (1 Chr 8:32; 9:37,38).

2. Officer in David's army who served under Dodai (1 Chr 27:4) according to some manuscripts. The words "of his course was Mikloth also the ruler" (KJV) are omitted in the RSV.

Mikneiah. Levite of the second order who was a gatekeeper and musician during David's reign (1 Chr 15:18,21).

Miktam. Heading of Psalms 16 and 56–60 (KJV Michtam), possibly also of Hezekiah's recovery psalm, Isaiah 38:9. The precise meaning of the term is uncertain. Its similarity to the Akkadian word "to cover, expiate" suggests the title may mean a psalm of expiation or sin covered. Other suggestions include a psalm of problems or mysteries.

See MUSIC AND MUSICAL INSTRUMENTS.

Milalai. Participant in the dedication of the rebuilt Jerusalem wall (Neh 12:36).

Milcah. 1. Daughter of Haran and half-sister of Nahor who became Nahor's wife (Gn 11:29). She bore Nahor eight sons (22:20–23). Through her son Bethuel she was the grandmother of Rebekah (24:15–47).

2. One of the five daughters of Zelophehad. Because Zelophehad had no sons, his daughters petitioned Moses to allow them to receive their father's inheritance in west Manasseh after their father's death (Nm 26:33; 27:1–11; 36:5–13; Jos 17:3,4).

Milcom. Pagan god of the Ammonites, better known as Molech or Moloch. Solomon built Milcom as a worship site (1 Kgs 11:5,33), which Josiah later tore down (2 Kgs 23:13). Milcom is rendered as "king" in 2 Samuel 12:30 and 1 Chronicles 20:2 (see also Jer 49:1,3; Zep 1:5; KJV Malcham).

See AMMON, AMMONITES; CANAANITE DEITIES AND RELIGION.

Mile. Roman measurement of distance, somewhat shorter than the English mile.

See WEIGHTS AND MEASUREMENTS.

Miletus, Miletum. Important Greek city located at the mouth of the Meander River. It was settled by Crete as early as 1339–1288 BC. Miletus had contact with the Hittite Empire. Her king, in fact, was claimed as a vassal by the Hittite ruler. C. Weickert's excavations (1956 onward) indicate that Miletus, having been destroyed by fire, was later surrounded by a defensive wall (13th century BC). It bears a striking resemblance to the military architecture found in the Hittite new empire of Boğazköy.

Miletus was attacked by Lydia around 650 BC and ruled by a military dynasty headed by Gyges. They still managed, however, to colonize Abydos on the narrows of the Dardenelles. Over 70 cities were founded by Miletus along the Black Sea and its approaches, the most important being Sinope. Miletus became an important city, therefore, in the ancient world. Her traders carried the furniture and woolens for which she was known to many foreign ports.

The city had its own poet, like many other Greek centers, famous in his own time but known today only in a few verses. Phocylides wrote: "A little city on a rock, with order, is better than madness in Nineveh." Again, "all virtue is summed up in justice."

Miletus was also the birthplace of philosophy and scientific speculation. Thales predicted an eclipse in 585 BC, and his disciple, Anaximander, propounded evolution from sea creatures. Much of the city's strength, however, was wasted on bitter civil strife. Two parties, known as the rich and the workers, kept the city torn by inner feuding. Approximately 495 BC the city was sacked by the Persians and never again regained world importance, though it was retaken by Alexander.

Miletus was, of course, well known in NT times, though it was not an important center to early Christianity. The apostle Paul stopped there on the last missionary journey recorded in the Book of Acts (20:15–17). While there, he called for the Ephesian elders and exhorted them to care for the flock in their charge (20:28–35). From Miletus he sailed for Tyre. Second Timothy 4:20 (KJV Miletum) says that Paul left Trophimus in Miletus because he was ill.

Sediment deposited at the mouth of the Meander has greatly changed the contours of Miletus from what they once were. The gulf at the end of the river is nearly filled with silt, and the island of Lade is now only a mound in the marshy land. In fact, the journey from Miletus to Ephesus, which Paul's messenger made, can today be made by land. At the time of its occurrence, however, one had to cross the gulf by boat.

Milk. *See* FOOD AND FOOD PREPARATION.

Mill, Millstone. Implement used in the grinding of grain.

The grinding of grain is an ancient art attested in archaeological excavations in the Middle East from at least the Neolithic period (c. 8300–4500 BC) in the shape of various concave stones with flat grinding pieces accompanying them. These were essentially handmills. Over the centuries improvements in technique took place. But two elements were always necessary, the lower one on which the grain was spread and the upper one which was moved over the surface of the lower one under pressure, to grind the grain into flour. The Hebrew term for mill is grammatically a dual, that is, it refers to two elements.

The earliest mill, the saddle quern, consisted of a rough base stone, slightly concave, and a convex rubbing stone. The base stone varied from 18 to 30 inches across with one end a little thicker than the other. It was known in Hebrew as "the underneath portion" (Jb 41:24). The upper stone, called the "rider portion" (Jgs 9:53; 2 Sm 11:21), varied from 6 to 15 inches in length and was flat on one side and convex on the other. It could be held easily in the hand. Grinding was done by pushing the upper stone backward and forward over the grain, which lay on the lower stone. Clearly only a small quantity of grain could be ground at one time (Gn 18:6).

A second type of handmill consisted of two round stones. The lower one could be either convex or concave on top and the upper one was either concave or convex so as to fit neatly over the lower stone. Some examples of this type of mill have a funnel-shaped hole in the center of the top stone through which grain was poured. The upper mill was turned on the lower one by means of a wooden peg inserted on its outside edge. As the grain was crushed it escaped along the edges of the upper stone. Commonly the stone used was black basalt because its rough and porous surface provided good cutting edges.

The normal type of handmill could be operated by one person but sometimes it seems that two persons were required (Mt 24:41).

So important was the handmill in the life of the people that it was prohibited by law to take a man's millstone as a pledge against the payment of a debt, for this would deprive his family of the means of making flour for bread (Dt 24:6). These stones were heavy enough to kill a man when thrown on his head, as in the case of Abimelech (Jgs 9:53; cf. 2 Sm 11:21).

Normally the grinding of grain was the task of servants (Ex 11:5) or of women (Is 47:2). The noise of grinding could be heard each day in

A large millstone from Capernaum.

every village in Palestine. When that sound ceased the village had come to an end (Jer 25:10).

There seem to have been larger community mills which required animal power. A heavy round stone, perhaps four or five feet in diameter, was rolled on its edge by means of a pole through its center. This pole rotated around a vertical post in much the same way as one finds in some Eastern lands even today. It may have been a large mill of this type which Samson was forced to use to grind grain for the Philistines (Jgs 16:21).

See FOOD AND FOOD PREPARATION; BREAD; AGRICULTURE.

Millennium.

Millennium. Biblical term (taken from the Latin word meaning a thousand) referring to the thousand-year reign of Christ. The primary biblical context for the doctrine of the millennium is found in Revelation 20:1–6 (where the Greek word for a thousand is used five times). The idea of a thousand-year reign is also supported by passages such as Acts 3:19–21 and 1 Corinthians 15:23–26, which speak of a future restoration and reign of Christ. This doctrine, however, is explicitly taught only in the Book of Revelation, resulting in differences of interpretation as well as considerable uncertainty about its importance.

The *a*millennial (*no* millennium, at least of a visible, earthly nature) interpretation stresses the symbolism of Revelation and holds that now, during the present age, Satan is bound and the church is experiencing the millennium. Perhaps the most serious difficulty with the amillennial view is that it interprets the two resurrections of Revelation 20 differently. Though the same Greek word is used for both, the first (v 4) is interpreted as a spiritual resurrection, and the second (v 5) as a physical resurrection, while the passage itself does not indicate that the writer intended a difference of meaning. Hence, the amillennial position is often accused of improperly spiritualizing the meaning of the Bible.

The *post*millennial (Christ will return *after* the millennium) view sees the progress of the gospel as producing the millennium. The essential idea in this interpretation is progress. It may be held that this era of peace is yet future or that it began with the first advent of Christ and is continuing on until the gospel triumphs over the world with the majority being won to Christianity. However, the variant forms of postmillennialism stress that Christ does not return until *after* the millennium. It is not the second coming of Christ and his visible presence that brings about the millennium.

Different from the above two views is the *pre*millennial (Christ returns *before* the millennium) interpretation, which maintains that Christ will return to earth and establish his peaceful reign in a visible and powerful manner.

The premillennialist emphasizes that the visions of the Book of Revelation must be interpreted in a serious and consistent manner, taking into account the flow of thought within the book itself. The scenes are highly symbolical, but have real meaning. The sequence is considered especially crucial for determining the interpretation. First is the return of Christ in chapter 19, followed by the binding of Satan for a thousand years and the first resurrection of the saints to reign with Christ for the thousand years (20:1–6). This in turn is followed by a release of Satan and the battle of those deceived—"Gog and Magog"—against Christ and his people and the final destruction of the devil (vv 7–10). Next, is the account of the final judgment and the last resurrection (vv 11–15), followed by the new heaven and new earth (ch 21).

The premillennialist strongly affirms that this sequence demands that the millennium, the reign of Christ, be understood as a real, future event following Christ's return. None of the variations of amillennialism or postmillennialism that see the millennium in the present church age before Christ returns or even in the future before Christ comes again, adequately accounts for the sequence of events in Revelation.

In addition to the literary argument, there is the theological point that the premillennial position places the real triumph of Christ within history. That is, the victory that the church believes was accomplished through Christ's death on the cross will be made visible to the world and the forces of evil at Christ's return and reign on earth. This is not faith in a merely spiritual or heavenly triumph, but faith that God will genuinely intervene in the course of the world to bring justice and peace.

However, implicit within this is the greatest weakness of the premillennial viewpoint. The Bible does not explain the details of how Christ and his resurrected saints will reign over an earth not yet made new and over nations still living in their natural state. This unresolved problem has led many interpreters to explain Revelation 20 by one of the other interpretations.   HOBERT K. FARRELL

See ESCHATOLOGY; JUDGMENT; RESURRECTION; REVELATION, BOOK OF; SECOND COMING OF CHRIST.

Bibliography. L. Boettner, *The Millennium;* R.G. Clouse, ed., *The Meaning of the Millennium;* A.A. Hoekema, *The Bible and the Future;* J.M. Kik, *An Eschatology of Victory;* J.F. Walvoord, *The Millennial Kingdom.*

Millet. Small-seeded grass grown for food and foliage (Ez 4:9).

See PLANTS.

Millo. 1. Earthen embankment or fortification mentioned in Judges 9:6,20.

See BETH-MILLO.

2. Fortress or embankment mentioned in connection with the construction of the city of David (2 Sm 5:9; 1 Chr 11:8). Solomon apparently either rebuilt or expanded this fortification (1 Kgs 9:15; 11:27).

Two kings of Judah are mentioned in connection with this structure: Joash was slain in "the house of Millo" (2 Kgs 12:20), and Hezekiah strengthened Millo due to the threat of invasion by Sennacherib (2 Chr 32:5).

Mina. Small weight used in the measure of precious metals as well as other substances.

See WEIGHTS AND MEASURES.

Mind. Man's intellectual processes in a narrow sense or, more broadly, the sum total of a man's mental and moral state of being. To the Hebrew way of thinking there is no distinctive terminology for the conception of mind. To the Greek world mind plays a very important role in the understanding of man.

In the OT there was no separate word that could be used for a man's mind. Translators of the English versions have supplied other words (soul, spirit, or heart) as the context dictates. Thus precise distinctions between these terms are hard to define. Generally, one might say that a man in his totality is a soul but he has a spirit and a heart. All of these terms may represent his mind. This means that the widely held distinction between the mind as the seat of thinking and the heart as the seat of feeling is alien to the meaning these terms carry in the OT.

The concept of the soul relates to "person" or "personality." When it refers to the mind the term indicates that the mind is distinct from matter and nearly always dictates more than the reasoning faculty, but includes feelings, interest, and the will (Gn 23:8; Dt 18:6; 28:65; 2 Sm 17:8). In relation to spirit, mind gains much more emotional connotation (Gn 26:35; Prv 29:11). Other times it relates to the thoughts that come from a man's mind (1 Sm 2:35; Ez 11:5; 20:32). Most often in the OT, the underlying conception of mind is that of the heart. The heart is often intended to include the entire inner man and thus often relates especially to the mind (Nm 16:28; 24:13). In these instances it relates primarily to the functions of will and memory (Is 46:8; 65:17; Jer 3:16).

The basic patterns of Hebrew reasoning continue in the Gospel accounts. The conception of mind appears quite rarely. When used, it is mostly in connection with the heart; for example, the imaginations of the heart (Lk 1:51). The only other occurrences of the word "mind" come in the statement of the great commandment: You shall love the Lord your God with all your heart, and with all your soul, and with all your strength, and with all your mind (cf. Mt 22:37; Mk 12:30; Lk 10:27). The Gospel writers are unanimous in their agreement that Jesus added "with all your mind" to Deuteronomy 6:5. In Mark, however, the questioner repeats the command of Jesus but with a word for understanding in place of the word for mind (Mk 12:33). In other places Jesus connects the processes of thinking with the heart (Mt 9:4). He makes the heart the source of the acts of a man (12:34).

With the writings of Paul one moves into the Greek world. Paul understood the mind as distinct from the spirit of man. It possesses the ability to understand and to reason (1 Cor 14:14–19); it is the seat of intelligence. In other places mind is used in a broader sense that includes the entire mental and moral process or state of being of a man (Rom 12:2; Eph 4:23). A man's actions flow from the inclinations of his mind. Whether a man is good or evil depends on the state of his mind.

The state of a man depends upon what or who controls his mind. Romans 8:6,7 speaks of a man's mind being controlled either by the flesh or by the Spirit. The man whose mind is controlled by the flesh is evil. The mind controlled by the Spirit leads to good. Other passages refer to the inclination of a man's mind being controlled by the god of this world (2 Cor 4:4). The temptation of Eve is pictured as a common experience of man, whereby the thoughts of a man are perverted (11:3). This in turn leads to the darkening or ignorance of the entire being and thus actions being controlled by the powers of evil within the world (Eph 4:17–19). A man's ability to learn is connected to the condition of his mind. The man whose mind is controlled by the "god of this world" will have his mind darkened and will not be able to understand the world as it really is (2 Cor 3:14). It is as a veil over one's understanding. On the other hand, Jesus opened the minds of the men who walked the Emmaus road with him so that they might understand the Scriptures (Lk 24:45).

The action of conversion is considered to be a "renewing of the mind" (Rom 12:2; Eph 4:23). In both cases the process is one whereby God takes control of the mind of a man through the Holy Spirit and leads the thoughts of that man into proper channels. Thus the new man is given power to make proper value judgments. He has a new mind with which to make spiritual discernments. He has the mind of Christ (1 Cor 2:15,16). Thus Paul can say that the new man serves God with his mind (Rom 7:25).

DAVID W. WEAD

See MAN, DOCTRINE OF; HEART; SOUL.

Minerals, Metals, and Precious Stones. A

mineral is a naturally occurring substance— normally an ore which must be mined and treated before the metal can be extracted. A *metal* is a chemical element such as iron or copper, which in its pure form is free from contamination by other materials. Metals in a pure form generally do not occur in nature though there are exceptions. A *precious stone* is a naturally occurring substance which, because of its comparative rarity, acquires special value for the manufacture of jewelry and ornaments.

In Palestine mining and smelting are ancient arts, practiced long before the Israelites arrived. The quarrying of suitable stones such as flint for toolmaking goes back to the Stone Age; the quarrying of stone for building is also an ancient craft. In particular, metals, native gold, copper, and meteoric iron were known and used in the Middle East before 4000 BC. From 4000 to 3000 BC native silver became known as well as copper and lead ores. The art of smelting was discovered probably almost by accident, resulting in the production of alloys like bronze. Then the reduction of oxidized iron was discovered. From 3000 to 2000 BC important advances were made. Copper sulfides and tin oxides were reduced to metal, and metallic tin and copper became important items of trade.

In the years 2000 to 1000 BC bellows came into use for furnaces and iron was reduced from its ores and forged. The art of making brass from copper and zinc was discovered

about 1500 BC, but did not become significant till somewhat later. Bronze, known for many centuries, was made sometimes with a high tin content to form speculum for mirrors. By this time the Israelites were settled in the land and the kingdom was established. From 1000 BC to the start of the Christian era, the production of metals, especially iron, greatly expanded. A form of steel was made and used for weapons and tools.

The beginning of the so-called Iron Age in Palestine is dated to about 1200 BC, though iron was known in Anatolia somewhat earlier. By the time of David and Solomon the Israelites had learned many skills in the preparation and working of metals. Under David, Edom with its rich copper and iron deposits was conquered (2 Sm 8:13,14) and there was a lot of activity in the casting of metals in the Jordan Valley (1 Kgs 7:13,14,45,46). In this activity Solomon had the assistance of Hiram, a Phoenician artisan. Israelite tradition associated the origins of metallurgy with Tubal-cain (Gn 4:22), who is said to have forged all kinds of tools out of bronze and iron. Deuteronomy 8:9 refers to the presence of iron and copper in the land to which Israel was going.

Job 28:1–11 gives a remarkable account of mining and a list of metals and precious stones won from the earth: gold, silver, iron, copper, and sapphires (or lapis lazuli). Shafts and tunnels were cut beneath the earth.

Several OT passages refer to the smelting and working of metals. Isaiah found a ready metaphor in the processes of refining metals for God's refining of his people (Is 1:25). Jeremiah also knew about the work of a refiner with his fire and bellows seeking to extract the dross from the ore (Jer 6:29). Ezekiel knew about the fiery blast for the preparation and refinement of silver, copper, iron, lead, and tin (Ez 22:20–22).

While the Israelites eventually undertook their own metalworking processes it is evident from 1 Samuel 13:19–22 that on at least one occasion, in the days of Philistine domination, they were obliged to have their agricultural tools made by their enemies. Similarly, the manufacture of cult vessels for Solomon's temple was supervised by Phoenician artisans (1 Kgs 7:13–50).

Minerals, metals, and precious stones were also important items of trade. Israel was never a land rich in these commodities and was obliged to import a wide variety of them. The visit of the Queen of Sheba was partly diplomatic and partly for trade (1 Kgs 10:2,10,11). Other traders, too, brought precious stones from afar (vv 14,15,22). In the 6th century BC the Phoenicians conducted extensive trade in metals and precious stones (Ez 27:12–16). In

NT times Rome benefited from extensive trade which included gold, silver, precious stones, ivory, bronze, iron, and marble (Rv 18:11–13). These passages provide only a glimpse of the trade in these precious commodities in western Asia in biblical times.

Metals and precious stones featured also among the booty carried off by invaders— notably, but not only, by the Egyptians and Assyrians. Silver, gold, copper, iron, tin, turquoise, precious stones, ores of different kinds, and ivory are recorded on Egyptian and Assyrian booty lists. These items were in constant demand as they were needed for agriculture and making weapons of war, and for the manufacture of jewelry and items of personal adornment.

Minerals. A mineral is an inorganic substance with a definite chemical composition and structure, sometimes occurring alone or sometimes combined with others. Ore refers to any mineral or mineral aggregate containing chemical compounds of metals in sufficient quantity and grade to make the extraction of the metal commercially profitable. The essential element, the metal, occurs in nature as a chemical compound such as a sulfide, an oxide, a carbonate, or some other compound, though the sulfides and oxides are the most common. Minerals exhibit a variety of properties such as color, luster, crystal form, cleavage, fracture, hardness, and density, which help in their identification and exercise control on the commercial and industrial uses of the particular mineral.

Among the black minerals are the iron oxides haematite and limonite, and antimony sulfide (stibnite). The copper minerals are green or blue in color and include the hydrated copper carbonates azurite and malachite, both used for making ornaments and as a source of copper. The mineral is a hydrated magnesium iron phosphate which is found also as a sulfide and was valued for making ornaments. A brilliant blue variety of this mineral was used as a gemstone under the name lapis lazuli.

Silver does occur naturally in a pure form but more often is mixed with lead in a silver-lead ore which is gray and shiny and distinctly crystalline (galena). Tin occurs as a hard brownish-black oxide known as cassiterite. It was comparatively rare in the ancient Middle East but was imported by the Phoenicians from Spain. The mineral from which zinc was prepared, smithsonite, is a white crystalline zinc carbonate often found alongside silver, especially in Greece.

Metals. A metal in its pure form is a chemically pure element with its own fixed physical properties such as density, tensile strength, crystalline structure, melting point, ductility, conductivity, and the like. Metals form alloys with other metals but this process destroys their purity. In both the ancient world and the modern world the alloy is extremely important.

In order to obtain a pure metal the ore in which the metal is contained must be smelted—a process known as metallurgy. In ancient Israel pure metals were widely used, among them gold, silver, iron, and lead; yet alloys such as bronze and brass were more widely used.

Metallurgy and Metal Extraction. While a few metals occur in nature in the pure form, most are embedded in rocks and have to be extracted. Where the metal element exists in the form of a chemical compound such as an oxide, a sulfide, a carbonate, and so on, it must be freed by a complex metallurgical process.

Perhaps as early as 8000 BC native copper was melted and fashioned in molds to form useful objects. More regularly the copper occurs as oxides, sulfides, and carbonates of which there are several, generally blue or green in color. These are widely spread in western Asia and elsewhere. Sulfides are first roasted to drive off much of the sulfur. The roasted sulfur material is then treated in a furnace along with sand and coke when a slag forms, removing iron and other impurities. The slag and copper are poured separately. Bronze was made at first by smelting copper and tin ores together with charcoal, using a forced draft produced by bellows. Later copper and tin previously reduced from their ores were heated together. The copper-zinc alloy, brass, was originally made by heating copper with tin ore and charcoal. But later it was made by mixing copper and zinc which had been reduced from their ores.

Gold occurs naturally and is frequently found in the sands and gravels of streams. Alluvial mining for gold was practiced in Egypt before 4000 BC. The flecks and veins which were found in rocks, however, could only be removed by crushing the rock, grinding it to sand size, and washing the gold out. Egyptian bas-reliefs depict this process in monuments of the first dynasty, about 2900 BC. Sometimes the gold was so deeply embedded in the rock that the crushed rock had to be heated up with lead, salt, and barley bran, which formed a slag with the impurities. After long heating the gold alone remained and could be poured off. By Roman times metallurgists had discovered that mercury could be used to extract gold (and silver). The rock was crushed and mixed with mercury to which the gold adhered. The particles of crushed rock were washed away and the gold was heated. The mercury was driven off as a vapor, condensed, and used again leaving the gold behind.

Meteoric iron was known very early. The iron ores are oxides and carbonates. These are first heated to decompose carbonates and oxidize the sulfides. Then coke is added to produce carbon monoxide which is the reducing agent. Limestone is added to form a slag which removes the silicates. Other processes are needed to produce cast iron, wrought iron, and steel. The method of producing hard wrought iron was discovered by the Hittites of Asia Minor about 1300 BC, and was taken up by the Philistines (1 Sm 13:19,20). At first the iron obtained from simple furnaces was drawn off and hammered to drive out slag (Dt 4:20; 1 Kgs 8:51; Jer 11:4). Later, the addition of carbon produced an early form of steel.

The lead sulfide ore is heated with lime in a flow of air. A slag with rock particles forms. The air is then cut off and the temperature is raised. Finally the lead flows free.

Native silver is known, but more commonly it forms an alloy with lead (galena). By heating in an earthenware vessel exposed to a blast of air, the lead and other impurities are oxidized to a slag and skimmed off (Ez 22:19) leaving the pure molten silver. The OT refers to the mining of silver (Jb 28:1), the refining of the metal (Zec 13:9; Mal 3:3), the melting of scrap metals or jeweler's remnants (Ez 22:20–22), and of multiple refinings in a crucible (Prv 17:3; 27:21) to produce "refined" or "choice" silver (1 Chr 29:4; Ps 12:6; Prv 10:20).

Tin has to be extracted from its oxide. The ore is crushed, washed to remove the crushed rock, then roasted to oxidize the sulfides of iron and copper, and finally heated with coal. The pure metal flows away from the impurities.

Zinc occurs as sulfides and carbonates. The ore is crushed, pulverized, and concentrated by the addition of a small quantity of oil which adheres to the ore. It is then heated to remove sulfur and leave the oxide. Finally the oxide is reduced by heating with powdered coal.

Metals. Athough several OT passages suggest that the science of metallurgy was known in biblical times, comparatively little archaeological evidence is available. The processing plants were small and were used for the treatment of copper and iron. Four furnaces were discovered at Tell Jemmeh near Gaza, probably for iron. Two were found at Ain Shems (Beth Shemesh), one at Tell Qasile near Tel Aviv, and one at Ai for smelting copper. There is evidence of slag heaps in the Jordan Valley, and in the general area of Eilat copper was treated at one time. The archaeological record is far from complete, but the general impres-

sion is that metallic ores were comparatively rare in Palestine; imports must have been considerable. However, numerous molds for casting agricultural and military tools have come to light in excavations. Evidently some refined metal was available locally, but perhaps most of it was imported. The metal was then heated and poured into the appropriate earthenware or pottery mold.

There are many references to metals in the Bible but especially to gold, silver, iron, and lead. While copper was widely used it was normally in the form of its alloys bronze and brass. There are comparatively few references to tin as such though it was used in manufacturing bronze. Similarly zinc, though used in the manufacture of brass, is not mentioned in the Bible.

Gold is referred to hundreds of times in the OT and NT, more frequently than any other metal. It is often mentioned together with silver, and in the majority of cases silver is mentioned first, reflecting a time when gold was less valued.

Gold was used in the manufacture of ornaments for personal use (Gn 24:53; 41:42; Ex 3:22; 11:2; 12:35). Gold was important in worship both in Israel and among the non-Israelites. References to pagan gods occur in several passages (Ex 20:23; 32:2–4; Ps 115:4; Is 2:20; 30:22; 31:7; 40:19; 46:6; Hos 8:4). It seems that the gold was melted down and later engraved so that the replicas could be called both molten images (Ex 32:24) and graven images (v 4). The tabernacle and the temple used a great deal of gold. The wooden ark was covered inside and outside with gold (25:11). Other timber pieces were overlaid with gold (v 11; 1 Kgs 6:20–22,30,etc.).

The vessels and utensils used in the tabernacle and temple were made of "pure gold": the cherubim (Ex 25:18; 37:7), the mercy seat (25:17; 37:6), the candlestick (25:31; Zec 4:2), various vessels (Ex 25:38; 2 Kgs 24:13), chains to carry the ephod (Ex 28:14), and the bells on the high priest's robe (v 34). The high priest's crown, ephod, and breastplate were also of gold (39:2–30). The offerings collected for the manufacture of such articles in the wilderness include golden dishes weighing 120 shekels (Nm 7:86). The more lavishly adorned temple apparently used more gold than the tabernacle (1 Kgs 6:20–28; 1 Chr 29:2–7; 2 Chr 3:4–4:22). The number of specific references to gold in the tabernacle and temple is far too numerous to mention here. The large amount of gold used in the temple was attractive to invaders, who would strip the temple of its gold and carry it off as booty (1 Kgs 14:26; 2 Kgs 16:8; 18:14; 24:13; 25:15; 2 Chr 12:9).

Gold had commercial value. It was imported in Solomon's day and up to 666 talents were brought to Israel annually (1 Kgs 10:14). Hiram of Tyre gave Solomon 120 talents of gold (9:14), possibly as a loan. Certainly Solomon used a lot of gold in the temple (10:16,17). An unusual comment in 1 Kings 10:21 notes that in Solomon's day "it was not considered as anything." Gold was useful, too, for buying off an enemy (2 Kgs 16:8) or simply as tribute (18:14). Evidence of this comes also from the Assyrian annals, where the tribute taken from various lands often included gold.

The possession of gold was not in itself an evil thing but preoccupation with its accumulation was condemned (Jb 28:15–17; Prv 3:14; 8:10,19; 16:16). The possession of wisdom and the knowledge of God was of greater value than the possession of much gold (Pss 19:10; 119:72,127; Prv 20:15). Job rejected trust in gold (Jb 31:24). Gold would not save a man in the day of judgment (Zep 1:18).

In the NT gold was regarded as perishable (Jas 5:3; 1 Pt 1:18) and as an unnecessary burden to carry (Mt 10:9; Acts 3:6). The wearing of a gold ring was certainly no measure of a man's worth (Jas 2:2); indeed, both Paul and Peter forbade it (1 Tm 2:9; 1 Pt 3:3).

The use of gold in itself was no measure of piety. The elders of Revelation 4:4 wore golden crowns, but the great harlot was "bedecked with gold" (Rv 17:4), as was the harlot city Babylon (18:16). By contrast there are some positive statements in the NT about the value of gold (3:18). The wise men brought gold to the infant Jesus as a symbol of his kingly character (Mt 2:11); and the holy city, the new Jerusalem, was a city of gold, clear as glass (Rv 21:18).

In the OT, silver is mentioned in several connections. Being a precious metal, once considered more precious than gold, it was regularly used in commerce for the payments of debts. Small pieces of silver were weighed into a balance against a standard weight. Abraham bought the cave at Machpelah as a burial place for Sarah for 400 shekels of silver and weighed out the "money" according to the weight's current value with the merchant (Gn 23:15,16). Joseph's brothers received 20 pieces of silver in payment for Joseph (37:28), and Benjamin was given a money gift by Joseph in pieces of silver (45:22).

There are other examples of payment in silver for commodities or services (Gn 20:16; Ex 21:32; Lv 27:16; Jos 24:32; Jgs 17:10; 2 Sm 24:24; Neh 7:72; Jb 28:15; Is 7:23; 46:6; Am 2:6; 8:6). Silver was a measure of a man's wealth (Gn 13:2; 24:35; Ex 25:3; Nm 22:18; Dt 7:25; Zep 1:18; Hg 2:8; Zec 6:11). It was regularly taken as booty (Jos 6:19; 7:21; 1 Kgs 15:18). Sometimes the drinking cup of an important man

was made of silver (Gn 44:2). Sometimes, too, a royal crown was made of gold and silver (Zec 6:11). It was important in the manufacture of personal ornaments (Gn 24:53; Ex 3:22; 12:35), and one example is given of ornaments of gold studded with silver (Sg 1:11).

Silver was regularly used among the pagans in the making of idols (Ex 20:23; Dt 29:17; Jgs 17:4; Pss 115:4; 135:15; Is 2:20; 30:22; 31:7; 40:19; Jer 10:4; Dn 2:32,35; Hos 13:2). It had an important place in the tabernacle where it was used to make trumpets (Nm 10:2), sockets to support the boards of the tabernacle (Ex 26:19), hooks and fillets for pillars (27:10,17; 36:24,26), and platters and bowls (Nm 7:13).

Similarly, in Solomon's temple it played an important role (1 Kgs 7:51; 1 Chr 28:15,16; 2 Chr 2:7), and also in the second Jerusalem temple built during the postexilic era (Ezr 8:26,28; Neh 7:71).

The process of refining silver was used as a metaphor for the trying of men's hearts (Ps 66:10; Is 48:10), and the tarnishing and deterioration of silver as a picture of the disintegration of a man's character (Is 1:22; Jer 6:30). God's Word is pictured as "pure" as silver refined and purified in a furnace. Despite silver's great value, wisdom excels it (Job 28:15; Prv 3:14; 8:19; 10:20; 16:16; 22:1; 25:11).

In NT times coins were made of silver, though the metal is not always specified (Mt 22:19; 26:15; 27:3–9; Lk 15:8–10). It is referred to in Matthew 17:24–27 as tax money. In several places silver idols are referred to (Acts 17:29; 19:24; Rv 9:20). It was naturally a sign of wealth (Acts 20:33; 1 Cor 3:12; Rv 18:12).

Native copper is mentioned in Deuteronomy 8:9, though the reference may be to one of its ores. More commonly, biblical references are to brass, the alloy of copper and zinc. However, the chemical analysis of copper-based tools and implements during the Middle and Late Bronze Ages (c. 2000–1200 BC) shows that the material was bronze. References to brass in the KJV are therefore to bronze. This alloy was used a great deal in the tabernacle to make clasps or hooks (Ex 26:11; 36:18), sockets (26:37; 27:10,11,17,18; 36:38; 38:17), various kinds of vessels (27:3; 38:3; 1 Kgs 7:14,45), a laver (Ex 30:18; 38:8; 1 Kgs 7:38), and pillars (Ex 38:17; 1 Kgs 7:16; 2 Kgs 25:13,17). Bronze was used to make items of military equipment like helmets, greaves, coats of armor, and shields (1 Sm 17:5,6,38; 2 Chr 12:10), and musical instruments like trumpets and cymbals (1 Chr 15:19). The metal serpent which Moses set up in the wilderness was made of bronze (Nm 21:9). An altar of bronze is mentioned in 2 Chronicles 4:1. Prisoners were bound in bronze fetters (Jgs 16:21; 2 Kgs 25:7), and bronze was used to cover wooden gates (Ps 107:16).

By NT times, copper in the form of alloys (bronze and brass) was widely used. Bronze coinage was well known and this may be the sense of Matthew 10:9. The widow's mite was a tiny bronze coin, the lepton. Bronze utensils and vessels were well known (Rv 9:20; 18:12). The reference to "sounding brass" (KJV) in 1 Corinthians 13:1 may be to brass which was a bright shining alloy, and was used in musical instruments. In the vision of John in Revelation (1:15; 2:18), the Son of man had feet of fine brass.

The Iron Age began in Palestine about 1200 BC, that is, in the days of the judges, though native iron had been known in Egypt in the predynastic period. Archaeological evidence suggests that the smelting of iron ore was discovered by the Hittites about 1400 BC. The Philistines seem to have introduced iron to Palestine about 1300 BC. In the days of Moses an encounter with the Midianites produced much tribute, among which iron is mentioned (Nm 31:22). When Israel captured Jericho the spoils included iron (Jos 6:24). Manasseh's half tribe also took booty including iron (Jos 22:8). In the days of the judges the Canaanites were equipped with chariots of iron (17:16,18; Jgs 1:19; 4:3).

These early references point to the arrival of iron at the start of the Iron Age. The Philistines enjoyed a local monopoly in its use (1 Sm 13:19–21) and their mighty warrior Goliath was armed with an iron spear (17:7). It was not long, however, before Israel learned the use of iron (2 Sm 12:31; 23:7). Evidently by Solomon's time iron was widely used because builders of the temple were forbidden to use iron tools (1 Kgs 6:7). The false prophet Zedekiah in Ahab's day used horns of iron to thrust toward Syria as he spoke of their defeat (22:11).

The prophet Isaiah in the 8th century BC referred to iron (Is 10:34), and Jeremiah later spoke of the metal in several places (Jer 1:18; 6:28; 11:4; 15:12; 17:1; 28:13,14). Ezekiel made use of an iron plate in one of his symbolic actions (Ez 4:3), referred to iron in his description of smelting (22:18,20), and listed it as a commodity for trade (27:12,19). The prophet Amos spoke of threshing instruments of iron (Am 1:3). Micah used iron as a symbol for military might (Mi 4:13). The Book of Daniel makes several references to it (2:33–35,40–45; 4:15,23; 7:7,19).

By Roman times iron weapons were the regular implements of war. Gates of iron were used to close prisons (Acts 12:10), and in a symbolic usage powerful rulers were said to rule with a rod of iron (Rv 2:27; 9:9; 12:5; 19:15). The term "iron" was used also in some metaphorical expressions. The smelting of iron was a symbol of testing and suffering (Dt 4:20; 1 Kgs 8:51; Jer 11:4; Ez 22:18); a pillar of iron was symbolic of strength (Jer 1:18), and an iron rod of harsh rule (Ps 2:9; Rv 2:27; 12:5; 19:15).

References to lead in the OT are few. It was known as a heavy metal (Ex 15:10). In lists of metals it is mentioned after gold, silver, bronze, iron, and tin (Nm 31:22; Ez 22:18,20). It was used as an agent in the reduction of silver (Jer 6:27–30), and stone inscriptions were sometimes filled with lead (Jb 19:24). As an item of trade lead was collected in Asia Minor and distributed through Tyre (Ez 27:12).

Metaphorically it was a symbol of worthless dross—so regarded because of its use in smelting silver (Ez 22:18,20). Because of its heaviness, it was used to hold down the lids of containers (Zec 5:7,8) and probably was used in plumb lines (Am 7:7,8). Small lead figurines have been found in excavations in Palestine and elsewhere, and the crushed ore galena was used as an eye paint.

References to tin are rare in the OT despite its importance in the manufacture of brass. It was imported into the Middle East by the Phoenicians (Ez 27:12). Its use in smelting is inferred from Isaiah 1:25 and Ezekiel 22:18,20. Numbers 31:22 suggests that Midianite caravans may have carried tin.

Zinc is not mentioned by name in the OT despite its use in the manufacture of brass and in the extraction of silver from crude lead.

Precious Stones. In the ancient world a wide range of materials was used in making objects of adornment. For the most part these were stones, inorganic in nature but with unusual qualities of rarity, beauty, hardness, color, brilliance, and durability. Some organic material such as amber, shell, coral, and pearl were also prized for their aesthetic value; these could be engraved and set in a frame of gold or silver to produce items of beauty for decoration or personal adornment.

In the Bible, jewelry was used by both men and women (Ex 11:2; Is 3:18–21). Items of jewelry were given as presents (Gn 24:22,53) and were regularly seized as spoil in war (2 Chr 20:25). Before coinage came into use jewels were associated with gold and silver as a measure of wealth (21:3) or as a standard of value (Jb 28:16; Prv 3:15).

In the OT a wide variety of jewelry is mentioned—arm bracelets (Gn 24:22,30,47; Ez 16:11), anklet ornaments (Is 3:18,20), necklaces (Gn 41:42), crowns (Zec 9:16), earrings (Gn 24:22), nose rings (Is 3:21), and finger rings (Gn 41:42; Est 3:10). In each case a gold or silver mounting was used to clasp the precious stones. It would seem that the modern art of faceting was not used but the precious stone was rounded, polished, and sometimes engraved. Many of the precious stones valued in antiquity would hardly be classed as precious today, though they might be classified as semiprecious.

A lengthy list of the precious stones used in OT times occurs in Exodus 28:17–20 and 39:10–13, where four rows of three stones, each engraved with the name of one of the 12 tribes of Israel, were set in the high priest's breastplate. Other lists occur in Ezekiel 28:13 and Revelation 21:19–21. It is difficult to properly identify all of these stones, since an accurate translation is not always possible. Some of the differences of translation are indicated in the following list as translated in the RSV: (1) Agate, an oxide of silicon, a type of translucent quartz with layers of different colors (Ex 28:19; 39:12; Is 54:12). (2) Alabaster, a finely granular banded variety of calcium carbonate (gypsum), often white and translucent and widely used in Bible times for ornamental vases, bowls, kohl pots, statues, perfume jars, and so on (Sg 5:15; Mt 26:7; Mk 14:3; Lk 7:37). (3) Amethyst, an oxide of silicon, a purple or violet variety of transparent crystalline quartz (Ex 28:19; 39:12; Rv 21:20). (4) Beryl, a silicate of aluminum (Ex 28:20; 39:13; Sg 5:14; Dn 10:6). It is usually green in color (Rv 21:20), but can be blue, white, or golden and may be either opaque or transparent; the latter variety including the gems emerald and aquamarine. (5) Carbuncle, a silicate of aluminum which may have been a green stone (Septuagint, emerald), especially in Exodus 28:13,17 and 39:10, though in Isaiah 54:12 it is possibly a red stone (see also Ez 28:13). (6) Carnelian (or cornelian), a silicon oxide reddish in color. In translations it is sometimes equated with sardius (Ex 28:17; 39:10; Ez 28:13), a type of deep brown or red quartz (Rv 4:3, KJV sardine stone; 21:20). (7) Chalcedony, translated "agate" in the RSV and NEB (Rv 21:19), is a silicon oxide, a microcrystalline translucent variety of quartz often milky or grayish in color, sometimes having a greenish tint. (8) Chrysolite, an aluminum fluosilicate, yellowish in color (Rv 21:20), probably equivalent to topaz (Ex 28:17) or beryl (Ez 1:16; 10:9; 28:13). (9) Chrysoprase, a nickel-stained apple-green chalcedony widely used in jewelry (Rv 21:20, KJV chrysoprasus). (10) Coral, the hard calcareous skeleton of a variety of marine animals occurring in various colors—red, white, and black. It is not strictly a stone (Jb 28:18; Ez 27:16). The RSV translates coral in Lamentations 4:7, but some red stone is meant. (11) Crystal, a clear, translucent crystalline quartz (Jb 28:18). In Revelation 4:6; 21:11; and 22:1 the Greek word *krystallon* may be rock crystal or even ice. (12) Diamond, a stone of uncertain identification (Ex 28:18;

39:11; Ez 28:13). It may not be the equivalent of the modern diamond. In Jeremiah 17:1, adamant was probably a form of corundum, a very hard substance. (13) Emerald, probably a green stone like the modern emerald (Ex 28:18; 39:11; Ez 27:16; 28:13). The Septuagint suggests a purple stone like a garnet. In the NT *smaragdinos* in Revelation 4:3 and *smaragdos* in Revelation 21:19 suggest an emerald. (14) Jacinth, perhaps a reddish orange zircon or a blue stone such as turquoise (NEB), amethyst, or sapphire (Ex 28:19; 39:12, KJV ligure). In Revelation 21:20 *hyakinthos* is a blue stone. The exact identification is uncertain. (15) Jasper, a compact, opaque, often highly colored crystalline quartz substance (Ex 28:20; 39:13). In the NT the Greek term *iaspis* (Rv 4:3; 21:11,18,19) is a green quartz. (16) Lapis lazuli, a deep blue stone; a compound of sodium, aluminum, calcium, sulphur, and silver containing a mixture of several minerals. It generally has golden flecks of iron pyrites and was widely used for ornamental purposes in the ancient world. It is akin to sapphire. (17) Marble, a limestone crystallized by metamorphism, taking a high polish, durable and suitable for building purposes (1 Chr 29:2; Est 1:6; Rv 18:12). (18) Onyx, a quartz consisting of straight layers or bands which differ in color (Gn 2:12; Ex 25:7; 28:9,20; 38:9,27; 39:6,13; 1 Chr 29:2; Jb 28:16; Ez 28:13). (19) Pearl, a hard smooth substance, white or variously colored, which grows in the shell of various bivalve molluscs. In the NT "pearls" as such are known as ornaments for women (1 Tm 2:9; Rv 17:4), or as items for trade (Rv 18:12,16). The kingdom of heaven is likened to a fine pearl which men seek at great cost (Mt 13:45,46). There is a translation problem in the OT. In Job 28:18a the KJV translates *gabis* as "pearl," but the RSV as "crystal." However, the word *peninim* in Job 28:18b is translated "pearl" in the RSV and as "ruby" in the KJV. Also in Proverbs 3:15; 8:11; 20:15; 31:10; and Lamentations 4:7 the KJV translates *peninim* pearl (or ruby) while the RSV has "jewels" or "costly stones." The meaning of some words cannot be finally determined. (20) Ruby, an uncertain translation of the Hebrew word *peninim* in six places (Jb 28:18b; Prv 3:15; 8:11; 20:15; 31:10; Lam 4:7); the RV translates "ruby" in Isaiah 54:12 and Ezekiel 27:16. This deep red or carmine stone was probably known in the ancient world but there are difficulties in the translation of terms which may refer to it. (21) Sapphire, a deep blue stone (Ex 24:10; 28:18; 39:11; Jb 28:6,16; Sg 5:14; Is 54:11; Lam 4:7; Ez 1:26; 10:1; 28:13), which may have referred at times to lapis lazuli as in Job 28:6 and Revelation 21:19. (22) Sardius, a red or deep brown form of quartz (Ex 28:17; 39:10; Ez 28:13 KJV). It is referred to also in Revelation 4:3 (KJV sardine stone) though in both places the RSV and NEB have "carnelian"/"cornelian." (23) Sardonyx, a form of agate with layers of brown and white (Rv 21:20, KJV, NASB; onyx in RV, NEB, RSV). (24) Topaz, a yellow stone, a fluosilicate of aluminum occurring in crystalline form (Ex 28:17; 39:10; Jb 28:19; Ez 28:13).

JOHN A. THOMPSON

See INDUSTRY AND COMMERCE; TABERNACLE, TEMPLE; TRADES AND OCCUPATIONS (COPPERSMITH; CRAFTSMAN; GOLDSMITH; IRONSMITH; MASON; SILVERSMITH; SMITH; STONECUTTER).

Bibliography. R.J. Forbes, *Metallurgy in Antiquity* and *Studies in Ancient Technology*, 9 vols; H. Hodges, *Technology in the Ancient World*; T.A. Rickard, *Man and Metals*, 2 vols.

Miniamin. 1. Levite who assisted Kore, the son of Imnah, with the distribution of the "contribution reserved for the Lord" among the priests in the cities of Judah (2 Chr 31:14,15).

2. Head of a priestly house during the postexilic era (Neh 12:17).

3. Participant in the dedication of the Jerusalem wall (Neh 12:41).

Minister, Ministry. *See* BISHOP; BODY OF CHRIST; CHRISTIANS, NAMES FOR; CHURCH; DEACON, DEACONESS; ELDER; ORDAIN, ORDINATION; PRESBYTER; PRIESTHOOD; SPIRITUAL GIFTS.

Minni. People mentioned in Jeremiah 51:27 along with Ararat and Ashkenaz as aggressors against Babylon. The Minni first appear in Assyrian inscriptions during the reign of Shalmaneser III (858–824 BC), who pillaged and subdued the people. They lived between Lake Urmia and Lake Van north of Babylon, and are identified with the Mannean people, regularly associated with Urarteans (Ararat) in Assyrian manuscripts. The Minni were restless subjects. They revolted against Assyria in 716 and 715 BC. Further agitation occurred in the reign of Ashurbanipal (669–627 BC). When Nineveh fell to the Babylonians in 612 BC, the Minni disappear from the extrabiblical record.

Minnith. One of the 20 cities conquered by Jephthah in his defeat of the Ammonites (Jgs 11:33). The city was a center for the wheat trade (Ez 27:17, the RSV omits reference to Minnith; cf. 2 Chr 27:5). Its precise location near Hebron is uncertain.

Minstrel. Archaic term for musician (2 Kgs 3:15; Ps 68:25; Mt 9:23 KJV; Rv 18:22).

See MUSIC AND MUSICAL INSTRUMENTS.

Mint. Sweet-smelling herb used in cooking and medicine (Mt 23:23; Lk 11:42).

See PLANTS.

Miphkad, Gate of. KJV translation for Muster Gate, a city gate in northeast Jerusalem, in Nehemiah 3:31.

See MUSTER GATE.

Miracle. Event which may seem contrary to nature and which signifies an act in which God reveals himself to man. The classical definition of miracle assumes that it is contrary to natural law, but this is a misnomer for two reasons. First, many of the miracles of the Bible used nature rather than bypassed it (e.g., the wind which parted the Red Sea, Ex 14:21). Second, there no longer is a concept of "absolute natural laws"; rather, a phenomenon which is not readily explainable (e.g., quasars) may reflect laws with which science is not yet fully conversant. In Scripture the element of faith is crucial; a natural approach cannot prove or disprove the presence of "miracle." The timing and content of the process can be miraculous even though the event may seem natural. The consistent rationalist demonstrates the necessity of faith; he would place any so-called miracle in the category of unexplained phenomena rather than accept it as a pointer to the presence of God's activity in the world. The revelatory significance is also important. In every case God performed the miracle not merely as a "wonder" to inspire awe in man but as a "sign" to draw men to himself.

The Vocabulary of Miracles. In the OT the two main terms are "sign" and "wonder," which often occur together (e.g., nine times in Dt alone, 4:34; 13:1, etc.). More than one Hebrew term is used for "wonder," one referring to it as an act of supernatural power and another to it as beyond man's understanding. On the whole they are used synonymously for God's providential acts within history. The "sign" refers to an act which occurs as a token or pledge of God's control over events and as a revelation of God's presence with his people.

The NT uses the same basic idiom, "signs and wonders," with the same general thrust (cf. Mt 24:24; Mk 13:22; Jn 4:48; Acts 2:43). A third term is that for "power" or miracle, and this becomes the predominant term in the synoptic Gospels. It signifies the mighty act itself by which God is revealed in Christ. A fourth term is "work," which along with sign is preferred in the Gospel of John. This term is used in John to show that in Jesus the work of the Father is revealed. While the terms are often synonymous (the first three terms occur together in Rom 15:19,20; 2 Thes 2:9; Heb 2:4) they at the same time designate three different aspects of miracles. "Signs" point to the theological meaning of miracle as a revelation of God, "power" to the force behind the act, "work" to the person behind it, and "wonder" to its "awesome" effect on the observer.

With respect to the term which best represents this to 20th-century man, none can match "miracle." All of the above translations can do no more than hint at various aspects, but all fail because they mean so many different things in modern idiom. The only one which unambiguously represents the supernatural ramifications is miracle, and recent trends in such translations as the ASV and RSV to replace miracle with related terms seems doomed to failure.

Miracles in the OT. To the Hebrew a miracle was nothing more nor less than an act of God. Therefore, nature herself was a miracle (Jb 5:9,10; Pss 89:6; 106:2) and an act of kindness or victory over one's enemies is so described (Gn 24:12–27; 1 Sm 14:23). The natural order is totally under Yahweh's control, so a miracle was observable not because of its supernatural nature but because of its character as part of the divine revelation. This connection with salvation history is crucial, for Israel at all times tried to guard against a desire for the spectacular. Deuteronomy 13:1–4 warns against accepting a wonder as authenticating a prophet; rather, the authentication must come from the fact that he worships Yahweh.

Miracles in the OT are restricted to critical periods of redemptive history. Many have discussed the act of creation as the first miracle, but in actuality it is not presented as such in the Genesis account. A miracle is signified by its revelatory significance and/or its connection with crucial points in the history of God's people—the exodus, the conquest of Jordan, the battle against the insidious Baal worship of the prophetic period. Creation is characterized by one major theme—a chronicle of the beginnings. The miracles of Genesis—striking blind the inhabitants of Sodom, the flood, Babel—all signify the wrath of God upon those who have turned against him. This is the other side of redemptive history—the judgment of God upon those who are not his people.

The miracles of the exodus account have two foci; the plagues represented the absolute power of Yahweh over the gods of Egypt, and the miracles of the wilderness meant God's absolute care and protection of his people. The plagues are particularly interesting because each one is directed at one of the gods of Egypt and reveals Yahweh as the only potentate. The basic theme is found in Exodus 7:5 and is repeated throughout (cf. 7:17; 8:6,18; 9:14,16,29; 12:12): "The Egyptians shall know that I am Yahweh when I stretch forth my hand upon Egypt." In this regard they were directed not only at the Egyptians but also to the Israelites, who needed to know that their God would vin-

dicate them against the Egyptians. This is borne out in the major miracle, the crossing of the Red Sea. The plagues themselves show a gradual increase in severity and may be organized in a threefold series of three each followed by the culmination in the death of the firstborn son. In each set a purpose clause details the purpose of the three: in the first the theme is the power of Yahweh (7:17, "I am Yahweh"); in the second it is Yahweh's providential involvement in earthly affairs (8:22, "I am the Lord in the midst of the earth"); in the third it is God's revelation of himself ("there is none like me in all the earth," 9:14,16). In each the increasing severity builds the separation between God's people and the Egyptians.

The wilderness miracles are intimately connected to the basic theme of the wandering narratives, the trial of Israel in times of desperate need and God's providential protection of his people when they turn to him. The basic organization of the stories concerns the need itself, which leads to Israel's complaint; this is followed by Moses' intercession and then by God's sovereign intervention. The miracles are interspersed with other stories which tell of God's punishment when their murmuring tried him too far. The parameters are twofold: the promise of provision on the part of God and the necessity of obedience on the part of his people. The miracle functions within both aspects, that is, as privilege which demands responsibility. Israel is being tested as to her faithfulness to the one who provides her needs. The miracle is God's self-revelation regarding his involvement in the needs of his own; Israel must then respond and her response determines her blessing or punishment at the hands of Yahweh.

Miracles are conspicuously absent in the period of the united monarchy. This was a time of self-sufficiency, when God worked through the monarchy and did not intervene directly in the life of the nation. The reason is that Israel's eschatological hopes have been realized and made concrete in the presence of the holy city and the temple. During this harbinger of the kingdom age, God worked within rather than without the nation.

It was different during the prophetic period. In the Elijah-Elisha cycle, miracles were predominant. This was a time of apostasy, and under the reign of Ahab and Jezebel the nation turned to paganism and the worship of Baal. The very existence of the Hebraic religion seemed to be threatened, and so the times called for extraordinary measures. Here the wonderous nature of the miracles is more evident than anywhere else in the OT. There are conscious allusions to the exodus miracles, perhaps looking to Elijah as a new Moses reinstituting the true worship of Yahweh. Parallels are seen in the challenge to the priests of Baal (1 Kgs 18; Ex 7), the revelation of God on Mt Horeb with the wind, earthquake, and fire (1 Kgs 19; Ex 19), and the parting of the Jordan (2 Kgs 2:8,14; Ex 14). Many of the miracles were intended to demonstrate the impotence of Baal, such as the drought, the contest on Mt Carmel, and the miraculous sustenance supplied by God. Again, God's actions within history were part of his self-revelation, the vindication of his messengers, and the punishment of his enemies.

Miracles are infrequent in the writing prophets, perhaps due to the proclamation form of the writings (i.e., they dealt with message rather than deeds). The two major exceptions (apart from the recovery of Hezekiah chronicled in Is 38) are Jonah and Daniel. In Jonah, the miracle is addressed not to the Ninevites but to the Israelites, who are called back to their covenant obligations as the spokesmen of Yahweh. In Daniel the direction is reversed and the situation is the same as that in Exodus or Kings. The miracles are directed to the Babylonians and Persians and have the same foci as the earlier events of the exodus and Elijah-Elisha chronicles, that is, the supremacy of Yahweh over the foreign gods and the vindication of his messengers. This is the third and final time of crisis and illustrates the major theological use of miracles in the OT.

During the intertestamental period it was believed that God no longer spoke directly to his people but rather illuminated them indirectly via the *Bath qol* ("daughter of the voice"), teachers who expounded the OT and interpreted its laws. In the books of the Maccabees, for instance, no miracles or prophecies are mentioned; and prophetic literature, dealing with God's present message to his people was replaced by apocalyptic writings, dealing with God's future manifestation in the coming age. It was believed that prophecies and miracles would return only at the inauguration of the messianic age, when Yahweh would once more intervene directly in world affairs.

The discussion of miracle in books such as the Wisdom of Solomon is clearly related to the past (especially the exodus miracles) and future (the coming age) rather than the present. Even the Essenes of Qumran, who believed that prophecy was reinstituted in their community, relegated miracles to the actual manifestation of God in the coming eschaton. Though they were the people of the end times, the direct, supernatural work of God in history was future.

Miracles in the NT. The presence of the miraculous has a similar purpose in the NT; it has occurred at a crisis point in salvation history to authenticate the presence of God in historical acts. It differs, however, in that it is transcended by the presence of the very Son of God, who himself is the greatest miracle of all. God now has not only acted in history; he has entered history and has turned it to himself. The parallels with the exodus events are obvious and show that the miracles of Jesus paved the way for the entrance of the new covenant in the same way that the exodus miracles prepared for the old.

Jesus' Understanding. Jesus stressed the connection between his miraculous ministry, especially casting out of demons (exorcism), and the coming of the kingdom of God. As in the OT the miracles signify the presence of God, but here it is more direct and also signals the inauguration of his kingdom (Mt 12:28). As such, then, the exorcism miracles mean the binding of Satan and the institution of the reign of God (Mk 3:23–27). At the same time all the miracles signify the dawning of the age of salvation, as expressed in Jesus' inaugural address at Nazareth (Lk 4:18–21, from Is 61:1,2).

Yet these miracles are not automatic signposts to the act of God; they must be interpreted by faith. Jesus was well aware of the presence of other miracles in his day (Mt 12:27) and so stressed the presence of faith in the healing miracles (Mk 5:34; 10:52). This faith must be directed to the presence of God in the event and in Jesus himself. The necessity of faith also helps to understand Jesus' refusal to provide his contemporaries with a "sign" (Mk 8:11,12); miracles could never "prove" the presence of God. For a better understanding of the connection between faith and miracles, it is best to note each Evangelist's individual portrait of the theological use of miracles.

Miracles in Mark. Mark, the first of the four Gospels to be written, has often been called the "action Gospel" because of its emphasis on Jesus' deeds rather than his teaching. This is also true regarding Jesus' miracles, for Mark contains more proportionately than any of the others. R. H. Fuller in his *Interpreting the Miracles* has noted five groups in Mark. The first centers on Jesus' authority over demons (1:21–39). The second concerns Jesus' authority over the Law and conflict with his opponents (1:40–3:6). They result in fame but occasion his refusal to allow his true identity as Son of God to be known. The third group (3:7–30) contains exorcisms and the Beelzebub controversy, centering on his power over Satan. The fourth group (4:35–5:43) contains especially powerful miracles (stilling the storm, the Gadarene demoniac, the raising of

The Miracles of Jesus

	Matthew	Mark	Luke	John
Involving nature				
A. On land				
1. Wine from water				2:1–11
2. Food for 5000	14:15–21	6:35–44	9:12–17	6:5–13
3. Food for 4000	15:32–38	8:1–9		
4. Withered fig tree	21:18–22	11:12–14,20–26		
B. At sea				
1. A catch of fish			5:1–11	
2. A calmed storm	8:18,22–27	4:35–41	8:22–25	
3. Walking on water	14:24–33	6:47–52		6:16–21
4. A coin in a fish	17:24–27			
5. Another catch of fish				21:1–14
Involving people's bodies				
A. Disabilities (overcome)				
1. Another paralytic	9:1–8	2:1–12	5:17–26	
2. A man with a withered hand	12:9–14	3:1–6	6:6–11	
3. A centurion's paralyzed servant	8:5–13		7:1–10	
4. Two blind men	9:27–31			
5. A deaf mute		7:31–37		
6. A blind man at Bethsaida		8:22–26		
7. A man born blind				9:1–41
8. A woman bent over for 18 years			13:10–17	
9. Two other blind men	20:29–34	10:46–52	18:35–43	
10. Malchus and his ear			22:49–51	18:10–11
B. Diseases (healed)				
1. A nobleman's son				4:46–54
2. Peter's mother-in-law	8:14–15	1:29–31	4:38–39	
3. A leper	8:2–4	1:40–45	5:12–16	
4. An invalid at Bethsaida				5:1–16
5. A woman with a blood flow	9:20–22	5:25–34	8:43–48	
6. A Syrophoenician girl	15:21–28	7:24–30		
7. A man with dropsy			14:1–6	
8. Ten lepers			17:11–19	
C. Demons (exorcised)				
1. A demoniac in a synagogue		1:21–28	4:33–37	
2. Two demoniacs	8:28–34	5:1–20	8:26–39	
3. A mute demoniac	9:32–34			
4. A blind and mute demoniac	12:22			
5. Another mute demoniac			11:14–15	
6. A child demoniac	17:14–20	9:14–29	9:37–43	
D. Death (reversed)				
1. A widow's son at Nain			7:11–17	
2. Jairus' daughter	9:18–26	5:22–24,35–43	8:41–21,49–56	
3. Lazarus				11:1–44

Jairus' daughter) and probably center on the disciples, as Jesus thereby reveals to them the meaning of the kingdom and seeks to overcome their own spiritual dullness. The fifth and final group (6:30–8:26) continues the theme of the disciples' misunderstanding and prepares the way for the passion, with the message regarding the bread, blindness, and the judgment of God.

The miracles in Mark center on conflict, first with Jesus' opponents and then with his own disciples. While they are harbingers of God's kingdom, their purpose is to force encounter with Jesus' true significance. They do not show Jesus as a Hellenistic "wonder worker"; in fact they lead only to amazement and then disbelief in those who do not have faith. Jesus' personhood has been hidden and can only be understood in light of the cross. The miracles are not proofs but powers; God does not authenticate himself through them but shows himself to those with eyes to see.

They were therefore manifestations of his compassion for man and not apologetic proofs.

Miracles in Matthew. Matthew's is the teaching Gospel, and in his use of miracles dialogue takes precedence over action. Matthew compresses Mark's narrative in order to make room for didactic material. Therefore, his stress is on the theological implications of faith rather than the results they contain. Matthew's groups of miracles are isometric to teaching passages, in keeping with his general practice of combining narrative portions and organizing them around didactic sections. The first group (chs 8,9) combines miracles from Mark's first, second, and fourth groups and stresses Jesus' significance as the servant of Yahweh who exercises sovereign power and forgives sins. The secondary theme teaches discipleship and shows the awakening faith of the disciples and their involvement in Jesus' ministry. The second group (ch 12) centers on his authority over the Law (the man with the withered hand) and over Satan (the Beelzebub controversy). The third group (chs 14,15) parallels Mark's fifth group but has a different purpose. Rather than conflict and decision, the disciples are seen in positive guise, actively involved in the Master's work. So the disciples become the means by which Jesus' ministry is continued. This is seen especially in Matthew's walking on the water scene (14:22–33), in which Peter's faith is tested (not in Mk).

In conclusion Matthew has continued Mark's emphasis on miracles as establishing Jesus' authority and the inauguration of the kingdom age, but has clarified and expanded it in two directions, that of faith and discipleship. Faith in Matthew is the means of appropriating the power of Jesus (8:13; 9:22; 15:28) and is closely connected to discipleship as the solution to a powerless ministry. Discipleship is the answer to Jesus' call to a radical, sacrificial righteousness which consists of obeying and imitating him. Therefore, the disciples are involved as "learners" (the meaning of "disciple") in his miraculous ministry.

Miracles in Luke. Luke–Acts is remarkable and extremely important because it establishes beyond dispute the early church's belief that it was in absolute continuity with Jesus and was continuing the work of God in the world. Luke's major stress is on salvation history, and so one of his major stylistic methods for showing this direct connection is miraculous deeds. Especially enlightening here is Acts 9:32–42, where in two healing miracles Peter duplicated the Lord's miracles (the paralytic Aeneas, Lk 5:18–26; the raising of Dorcas, Lk 8:49–56).

From this respect also Luke returns to Mark's interest in the deed more than the teaching. However, Luke goes even further than Mark, for the miracles validate Jesus more directly. The first group follows the inaugural address (4:18–22), which itself presents the miraculous deeds as authenticating signposts to Jesus' personhood. They center on Jesus' power and authority (4:31–41) and validate God's power in Jesus (5:17; 8:39) as well as faith in Jesus (seen in the "praise" motif, 5:25; 7:16, etc., but especially in Acts 9:35; 13:12; 19:17). The presence of "fear" at the miracles is man's response to the theophany vindicated before them (Lk 5:26; 7:16; 8:35–37; 24:5). The very call to the disciples occurs in the presence of miracles (5:1–11, at the miraculous catch of fish; vv 27,28, after the healing of the bedridden paralytic).

Therefore Luke views miracles as having redemptive significance. However, this is not contrary to Mark's picture. Luke still avoids picturing Jesus as a mere wonder worker; Jesus still refuses to satisfy people's curiosity for an external sign (Lk 11:29–32; cf. also 9:9), and in the parable of the rich man and Lazarus (16:19–31) he teaches that the unbelieving heart can never be convinced by such events. Nevertheless, they can lead to repentance (10:13–16). Mark views miracles from the standpoint of the unbeliever (they need faith to understand) and so stresses the difficulty of attributing apologetic value to miracles; Luke views them from the standpoint of the saved (as validating the presence of salvation in history) and so stresses the importance of seeing them in the context of God's redemptive plan. For Luke they are seen more directly in an OT fulfillment sense, as showing that Jesus has fulfilled prophecy (Lk 4:18–22; 7:20–22) and through them has directed men to God (note the direction of the praise in 5:26; 7:16; 18:43).

Miracles in John. John is the most directly theological of the evangelists, and miracles are characteristically given a distinctive Johannine coloring. In the Synoptics, miracles are "acts of power" signifying the entrance of God's reign into this world via Jesus; thereby, Jesus establishes Satan's defeat and God's sovereign control of history. John, however, contains no exorcisms and the miracles are seen as "signs." At the same time miracles are part of the larger category of "works" (the other term for miracle used in John), by which Jesus shows the Father's presence in himself (10:32, 37–39; 14:10) and they witness to Jesus as the sent one (5:36; 10:25,38).

John selects only seven "sign miracles" from many others (20:30) and uses them as part of the thematic development in the respective section of each. For instance, changing the water into wine is a messianic act, signifying the outpouring of the kingdom blessing in the ministry of Jesus, the Messiah (ch 2); the multiplication of the loaves builds upon the "bread of life" and points to the messianic banquet as spiritually present in Jesus (ch 6).

The paradoxical nature of miracles in the Synoptics is even greater in John. He gives more stress to the wondrous nature of the events by alluding to such details as the stupendous amount of water changed into wine (2:6, approximately 120 gallons), the distance over which Jesus' healing power works (4:46, almost 20 miles), the time the man of Bethesda had been lame (5:5, 38 years; cf. 9:1 where the man had been born blind); the amount of bread needed to feed the 5000 (6:7, where Philip said 200 denarii or days' wages would not have bought enough); the proof of Lazarus' death (11:39; he had already begun to decay). John has a great interest in the miraculous. Yet at the same time there is even greater stress on the inadequacy of miracles for faith. The miracles as "signs" have saving value and point to the true significance of Jesus but are related to an awakening faith and themselves are insufficient (2:11; 4:50). They have christological force, looking to Jesus' sonship and the Father's authentication of him but are based on the soteriological decision of the individual. As "signs" they contain the very presence of God in Jesus, the spiritual reality of the "sight" and "life" he brings (9:35–38; 11:24–26). Yet their purpose is to divide the audience and confront it with the necessity of decision. Two camps result, those seeking understanding and those considering only the outward aspects. Some refuse to consider the signs and reject them (3:19–21; 11:47–50), while others see them shallowly as mere wonders and fail to see in them the true significance of Jesus (2:23–25; 4:45). On the other hand, some view them with the eye of faith and go on to a realization of his personhood (2:11; 5:36–46; 11:42).

In John the highest faith of all is that which does not need external stimulation (20:29).

Miracles in the Rest of the NT. Apart from Acts, several passages in the NT speak of the value of miracles. Paul in 2 Corinthians 12:12 and Romans 15:18,19 considered them as "sign-gifts" which authenticated the divine authority of the "true apostle." He listed healing and miracles as specific "gifts of the Spirit" in 1 Corinthians 12:9,10. In Galatians 3:5 he considered them evidence for the presence of the Spirit. The author of the letter to the Hebrews in 2:4 said "God bore witness" to the true message of salvation via miracles. Therefore in the apostolic age the miracles of God's servants were seen more directly as authenticating signs of God's action in his messengers. Interestingly, however, in Revelation 13:14; 16:14; and 19:20 we see that the beast has duplicated the signs in order to force men to worship him. So at all times the double-edged nature of miracles is seen; they can only validate when seen through the eyes of faith.

GRANT R. OSBORNE

See SPIRITUAL GIFTS; SIGN.

Bibliography. A.B. Bruce, *The Miraculous Element in the Gospels;* D.S. Cairns, *The Faith That Rebels;* H.H. Farmer, *Are Miracles Possible?;* A.C. Headlam, *The Miracles of the NT;* C.F.D. Moule, *Miracles;* J.B. Mozley, *Eight Lectures on Miracles;* A. Richardson, *The Miracle Stories of the Gospels.*

Miriam. 1. Daughter of Amram and Jochebed and the sister of Aaron and Moses (Ex 15:20; Nm 26:59; 1 Chr 6:3). Miriam first appears in Scripture as a young girl commissioned with the task of watching her infant brother's cradle hidden in the reeds of the Nile River (Ex 2:4), the result of a scheme conceived by her parents (Heb 11:23) to escape the pharaoh's edict that all Hebrew males be drowned at birth (Ex 1:22). Miriam evidences not only courage and concern, but also displays a certain wisdom when her brother is discovered by the Egyptian princess (2:5,6). Taking the initiative, she offers to secure a nurse for the child; and when this plan is accepted, she gets her mother (vv 7,8).

Miriam first appears by name after the crossing of the Red Sea (Ex 15:20). She is given the title of "prophetess" and is, with her brothers, appointed a leader in the nation (Mi 6:4). Following the death of the Egyptian charioteers she leads the women of Israel in an anthem of praise accompanied with dancing and instrumental music (Ex 15:21).

Miriam appears in disgrace after her jealousy of and rebellion against Moses. With Aaron she murmurs against Moses because of his superior influence in the nation and because of his marriage to a Cushite woman (Nm 12:1,2). For this attack against God's chosen spokesman (v 8), she is struck with leprosy (v

The Plain of Tabghaat at the north end of the Sea of Galilee, the traditional site for the feeding of the 5000.

10; Dt 24:9). Moses, however, intercedes on her behalf (Ex 4:6; cf. Nm 12:11;) and she was restored, but only after seven shameful days spent outside the camp while Israel waits to resume its march (Nm 12:14,15). This sad incident is the last recorded event in Miriam's public life. She died near the close of the wilderness wanderings at Kadesh and was buried there (20:1).

2. Son of Mered, descended from Ezra of Judah's tribe (1 Chr 4:17).

Mirmah, Mirma. Son of Shaharaim and Hodesh from Benjamin's tribe (1 Chr 8:10, KJV Mirma).

Mirror. Smooth surface for reflecting images. The word does not occur in the KJV, but the idea is there, translated from the Hebrew or Greek as "glass," "glasses" or "looking glass." Modern translations use the word "mirror."

In the biblical era, mirrors were made of copper, bronze, silver, gold, or electrum. They were highly polished so as to reflect the face as clearly as possible. Glass was in existence but was usually opaque (except Roman glass) and was not used for mirrors until after the biblical period.

The Egyptian Tell el-Amarna tablets from the 14th century BC mention 32 mirrors of polished bronze being sent as a gift from Egypt. A silver mirror is also mentioned.

The Bible first mentions mirrors in the time of Moses in relationship to the building of the tabernacle in the wilderness of Sinai just after the exodus from Egypt (Ex 38:8).

When Alexander the Great spread Greek culture, the use of mirrors became even more widespread in the biblical world. Until that time they were the possession of either court ladies or prostitutes.

Archaeological excavations have unearthed bronze mirrors in Palestine along with various items of women's jewelry and clothes. Most of these date from the postexilic era up through Roman times. The mirrors are usually circular in shape with handles of wood or ivory if they have handles at all.

In Exodus 38:8 Bezaleel made a laver of brass (KJV) "of the looking glasses of the women" for the tabernacle. The RSV says he made the laver of bronze "from" (lit. "with") the "mirrors of the . . . women."

Job 37:18 compares the sky to a "molten looking glass" (KJV) or a "molten mirror" (RSV).

In Isaiah 3:16–26 the Lord is pictured as punishing his people. Because of their pride and seductive ways, God will especially judge the corrupt women of Judah by taking away the things they cherish most, such things as their "rings" (v 21) and "glasses" (v 23) or "hand mirrors" (ASV). The RSV omits the word completely.

In 1 Corinthians 13:12 and James 1:23 the KJV has "glass," but the idea is obviously that of a mirror and the Greek word is so translated in the ASV, RSV, and NASB.

Miscarriage. Spontaneous abortion of a nonviable fetus. It occurs in both human (Jb 3:16; Hos 9:14) and animal (Gn 31:38; Jb 21:10) pregnancies. The major problem is not in being unable to conceive or to become pregnant, but in carrying the pregnancy to full term. The curse of a "miscarrying womb" results in not being able to have children (Hos 9:14) while the blessing of God results in successful pregnancies and long life (Ex 23:26).

The time factor is the key abnormality as indicated by premature delivery or "untimely birth" (Ps 58:8; Jb 3:16). While miscarriages occur for many reasons, Scripture mentions two: improper care (in animals) (Gn 31:38) and trauma to a pregnant woman (Ex 21:22).

Numbers 5 gives the test for an unfaithful wife. If she is guilty of adultery, then her "abdomen will swell and her thigh will waste away" (v 27 NIV) or her "thigh shall rot" (KJV). These phrases are euphemisms for miscarriage.

Paul underscores his inherent unworthiness to be an apostle by comparing himself to an abortion or abnormal birth (1 Cor 15:8).

See BARRENNESS.

Misgab. KJV translation for a place in Moab (Jer 48:1), rendered "the fortress" in the RSV.

Mishael. 1. Uzziel's son (Ex 6:22), who, with his brother Elzaphan, was summoned by Moses to remove the bodies of Nadab and Abihu after they were killed for defiling the altar of the Lord (Lv 10:1–5).

2. One who stood beside Ezra when the Law was read (Neh 8:4).

3. Hebrew name for one of Daniel's companions in Babylon (Dn 1:6), who, with Daniel and two others, remained faithful to God (1:11,19) and was delivered from the fiery furnace into which he had been cast for refusing to obey the king's edict (ch 3). His Babylonian name was Meshach (1:7).

See SHADRACH, MESHACH, AND ABEDNEGO.

Mishal. Levitical town in Asher's territory (Jos 19:26, KJV Misheal; 21:30; 1 Chr 6:74, Mashal).

See LEVITICAL CITIES.

Misham. Elpaal's son from the tribe of Benjamin, who helped to build Ono and Lod with its towns (1 Chr 8:12).

Misheal. KJV spelling of the levitical town Mishal in Joshua 19:26.

See MISHAL.

Mishma. 1. Son of Ishmael, Abraham's grandson, and the father of an Arabian tribe (Gn 25:14; 1 Chr 1:30).

2. Mibsam's son from Simeon's tribe (1 Chr 4:25,26). His omission in Genesis 25 and inclusion in the 1 Chronicles genealogy may indicate either that he was born after Jacob moved his family to Egypt or that he represented an Arabian tribe that affiliated with Simeon when Simeon's tribe expanded to the south (1 Chr 4:38–43).

Mishmannah. Warrior from Gad's tribe who joined David at Ziklag in his struggle against King Saul (1 Chr 12:10).

Mishna. Series of interpretations of the meaning of the Law; according to rabbinic tradition, they were given when Moses received the Law from God on Mt Sinai and were to be passed down in oral form. This "oral tradition" was the "law" to which Jesus referred, for example, in Matthew 15:1–9. By about AD 200, under Rabbi Judah, the work begun by Rabbi Akiba around AD 120 was completed, and the oral tradition was finally written down. This written material is called the Mishna. The word is derived from a verb which means "to repeat something," and reflects the way the material had been repeated orally from teacher to disciple for many generations.

The Mishna is divided into six "orders," each order is divided into sections called "tractates," which in turn are divided into chapters. The orders deal with specific areas of legal concern as follows:

1. *Seeds* is concerned with agricultural laws, and is introduced with a tractate dealing with daily prayers.

2. *Festivals* deals with feasts, fast days, and sabbath regulations.

3. *Women* records marriage and family laws.

4. *Injuries* deals with civil/criminal law and ethical standards.

5. *Holy Things* concerns the ritual laws and the activities of the priesthood.

6. *Purifications* elaborates the laws of ritual purity.

The Mishna, which is essentially a commentary on the OT Law, forms the basis for the Gemara and the Talmud.

See TALMUD; GEMARA.

Bibliography. A. Cohen, *Everyman's Talmud;* H. Danby, *The Mishna;* D. Daube, *The NT and Rabbinic Judaism;* W.D. Davies, *Paul and Rabbinic Judaism;* H.L. Strack, *Introduction to the Talmud and Midrash.*

Mishraite. Descendant of Caleb and a member of Kiriath-jearim's family from Judah's tribe (1 Chr 2:53).

Mispar, Mispereth. One of the men who returned with Zerubbabel to Palestine following the Babylonian captivity (Ezr 2:2, KJV Mizpar); alternately called Mispereth in Nehemiah 7:7.

Misrephoth-Maim. One of the northernmost places to which the Israelites pursued the fleeing Canaanite armies defeated at the waters of Merom (Jos 11:8). Misrephoth-maim, meaning "burning of water," defined part of the boundary of land remaining yet to be possessed by Israel during the days of Joshua (13:6). In all probability, Misrephoth-maim is identical with the cluster of springs at Khirbet el-Musheiriteh near the Mediterranean Sea, 20 miles south of Sidon and 6 miles north of Tyre, at the base of Ras en-Nakurah.

Mite. Small bronze or copper coin worth only a fraction of a cent (Mk 12:42, KJV).

See COINS; MONEY AND BANKING.

Mithkah, Mithcah. One of the temporary camping places of the Israelites during their wilderness wanderings. It was mentioned between Terah and Hashmonah (Nm 33:28,29, KJV Mithcah). Its location is uncertain.

See WILDERNESS WANDERINGS.

Mithnite. Designation for Joshaphat, one of David's mighty warriors (1 Chr 11:43).

Mithredath. 1. Name of the treasurer of King Cyrus of Persia, who was given charge of the sacred vessels to give to the Judean prince Sheshbazzar as the exiles prepared to return to Jerusalem (Ezr 1:8).

2. Persian officer stationed in Samaria who, along with others, wrote a letter to King Artaxerxes of Persia, protesting the restoration of the city and walls of Jerusalem (Ezr 4:7).

A coin—similar to the widow's mite—from the time of Christ.

Mitre. KJV translation for turban, a kind of headdress worn by the high priest of Israel, in Exodus 28:4.

See PRIESTS AND LEVITES.

Mitylene. Main city on the island of Lesbos in the Aegean Sea near the northwestern coast of Asia Minor. Mitylene was a seaport with two harbors. Originally it had been built on a small island separate from Lesbos. In NT times it was connected with the main island by a raised roadway across a narrow stretch of water. Acts 20:14 identifies Mitylene as one of the overnight stopping places where Paul and his traveling companions lodged as they journeyed by ship toward Jerusalem.

Mixed Marriage. Connubial union forbidden between Israelites and Canaanites lest the Hebrews become idolatrous (Dt 7:1–5; cf. 2 Cor 6:14). However, this prohibition was often neglected in the judges (Jgs 3:6) and monarchy periods (2 Sm 11:3; 1 Kgs 11:1–8). No explicit prohibitions were given against marriages with other nationalities (Nm 12:1; Dt 23:7; Ru 1:4). After the exile, marriages to Gentiles were repudiated by Ezra and Nehemiah (Ezr 9:1–4; Neh 13:23–27). Mixed marriages are accepted by many Jews today.

See CIVIL LAW AND JUSTICE; MARRIAGE, MARRIAGE CUSTOMS.

Mizar. Small hill apparently situated in northern Palestine on the Transjordan plateau near Mt Hermon (Ps 42:6).

Mizpah. Name meaning "watch tower" in Hebrew (spelled alternately Mizpeh) used to designate a number of different locations mentioned in the OT and Apocrypha.

1. Place in Gilead where Jacob and Laban made a covenant (Gn 31:49) and set up a heap of stones to mark the borders between their territories.

2. Place referred to as "the land of Mizpah" (Jos 11:3) or the "valley of Mizpah" (v 8) near Mt Hermon and inhabited by the Hivites.

3. Town in Judah near Lachish referred to in Joshua 15:38. Identification is uncertain.

4. Place in the tribal area of Benjamin (Jos 18:26). It was here that the Israelites gathered to war against the tribe of Benjamin (Jgs 20:1; 21:1) after the men of Gibeah had abused and killed the concubine of a visiting Levite. It was here that Samuel called all Israel together to pray for victory over the Philistines (1 Sm 7:5,8). Later Samuel called for an assembly at Mizpah to publicly designate Saul as king and to instruct the people and king in the "manner of the kingdom" (10:17–25). In the time of Asa, Mizpah was a fortified town on the border be-

One of the massive revetments built to strengthen the wall at Mizpah.

tween Israel and Judah (1 Kgs 15:22). After the fall of Jerusalem in 586 BC to the Babylonians, Mizpah became the residence of Gedaliah the governor (2 Kgs 25:23,24; Jer 40:10) who was murdered there by Ishmael of the "royal seed" (Jer 41:3). Two days later Ishmael murdered a company of pilgrims who were going to Jerusalem to bring their offerings at the ruined temple, and he cast their bodies into a cistern which had been constructed centuries earlier by Asa when he had fortified Mizpah (vv 5–9). In the intertestamental period Mizpah continued to be an important religious center. Judas Maccabeus called the people together at Mizpah "because Israel formerly had a place of prayer in Mizpah" (1 Mc 3:46).

It would appear from the biblical data that Mizpah was located to the north of Jerusalem not far from Ramah. Most scholars today identify the site with Tell en Naṣbeh located on a hill about seven and a half miles north of Jerusalem. This identification was suggested as early as 1897 and confirmed by the later excavations of W. F. Bade in 1926–35. Among the findings of Bade was a seal of "Jaazaniah, servant of the king." Bade considered this to be the same person as the official of Gedaliah referred to in 2 Kings 25:23 and Jeremiah 40:8, and thus evidence for identifying Tell en Naṣbeh with Mizpah. Others have preferred to locate Mizpah at Nabi-samwil, about five miles northwest of Jerusalem, largely because of its more strategic location from a military standpoint.

5. Home of Jephthah from which he led the Israelites in battle against the Ammonites, and to which he returned to carry out his vow (Jgs 10,11). This is possibly the same place as the Ramath-mizpeh of Joshua 13:26 and is thought by many to be identified with Khirbat Jal'ad just south of the Jabbok.

6. Town in Moab to which David fled from Saul (1 Sm 22:3).

Mizpar. KJV spelling of Mispar in Ezra 2:2.

See MISPAR, MISPERETH.

Mizpeh. Alternate spelling for Mizpah (Jos 11:3,8; 15:38; 18:26).

See MIZPAH.

Mizraim. Hebrew word for the land of Egypt and/or its people, though some scholars suggest that Mizraim refers either to a site on the Edomite border or in northern Syria. In Genesis 10:6, Mizraim (Egypt) is identified as one of the sons of Ham who settled south of Canaan. Genesis 10:14 and Isaiah 11:11 distinguish Mizraim from Pathrushim, that is, Upper Egypt (the southern half of the United Kingdom of Egypt), but in the majority of the nearly 700 known references to Mizraim, there is no distinction between the two parts of the kingdom, and the term refers simply to the Egyptian territory.

See EGYPT, EGYPTIANS.

Mizzah. Reuel's son and a chief of an Edomite clan (Gn 36:13,17; 1 Chr 1:37).

Mnason. Name of a Christian in Jerusalem (Acts 21:16). He is identified as a native of the island of Cyprus and a disciple of long standing. On their arrival at Jerusalem, Paul and his traveling party were entertained as guests by Mnason.

Moab, Moabites. Name of a small kingdom in central Transjordan and also its inhabitants. The land of Moab was situated on the high plateau immediately east of the Dead Sea; the escarpment of the Jordan Rift formed an effective boundary between Moab and Judah. Moab's northern boundary shifted in accordance with the kingdom's military might, with the Heshbon vicinity forming the northern limit of Moab in periods of strength, and the Arnon River (modern Wadi el-Mujib) functioning as the northern border in times of weakness. The kingdom's eastern boundary was formed by the fringe of the Syrian desert, since the latter demarcated Moab's agricultural zone. On the south, Moab was separated from Edom by the Zered River (modern Wadi el-Hesa). Thus, even at its peak ancient Moab encompassed a relatively small territory, measuring only about 60 miles north south by about 20 miles east west.

Most of Moab is gently rolling tableland that is divided by numerous ravines. Running through the heart of Moab is the King's Highway, a route that probably had military and commercial importance throughout this region's history (Nm 21:21,22; Jgs 11:17). The plateau has always been famous for its abundant pasturage (2 Kgs 3:4), and Moab's soil and climate are quite suitable for growing wheat and barley.

Mountains of Moab, as viewed from the west near the north end of the Dead Sea.

Origin and History. According to Genesis 19:37, the Moabites descended from Moab, the son of Lot and his oldest daughter. Deuteronomy 2:10,11, a passage whose context relates to the Moabites at the time of the Hebrew invasion, says that the pre-Moabite inhabitants of this region were the Emim, but the connection between Lot's descendants, the Emim, and the occupants of Moab at the time of the Hebrew invasion is not identified. There is thus far no specific information concerning the establishment of the Moabite kingdom proper, which existed from around 1300–600 BC. Knowledge of this period of Moabite history and culture is derived from archaeological and textual sources, including Egyptian, Assyrian, and OT texts.

Prior to the Israelites' passage through Transjordan, the Moabites had lost control of the land north of the Arnon and were dominated by Sihon, the Amorite king who ruled at Heshbon (Nm 21:13,26). Having been refused permission to travel through Edom and Moab along the King's Highway, the Hebrews defeated Sihon in one of their most celebrated military campaigns (vv 21–32). Fearing that Israel might conquer his land, King Balak of Moab waged war against the Hebrews (22:6; Jos 24:9) and hired the Mesopotamian diviner, Balaam, to pronounce a curse upon his enemies (Nm 22–24). The tribes of Reuben and Gad settled in Sihon's territory, and the Arnon formed the border between Israel and Moab (ch 32). From the time of the Israelites' apostasy at Shittim onward (ch 25), the Moabite tableland north of the Arnon was a source of contention between Moab and Israel.

Until his assassination by Ehud, the Moabite king Eglon oppressed the Hebrew tribes on both sides of the Jordan (Jgs 3:12–30). By Jephthah's day, northern Moab was once again under Israelite control (11:26). Obviously, as the Book of Ruth indicates, there were also periods in which Moab and Israel lived in peace.

During the reigns of Saul and David, from the late 11th until the mid-10th centuries BC, Moab and Israel were at war, with the latter usually holding the upper hand (1 Sm 14:47; 2 Sm 8:2). Solomon's harem included Moabite women, and he also built a high place for Chemosh, the chief god of the Moabites (1 Kgs 11:1,7). Following the division of the Israelite monarchy in 930 BC, Moab experienced a brief period of independence, but this ended when Omri and Ahab dominated the Moabites and their king Mesha during the 9th century BC. (The famous Moabite Stone, which describes Mesha's conflict with the Omride dynasty, and several shorter texts demonstrate that the language of Moab was closely related to OT Hebrew.) Conflict between Moab and her neighbors (e.g., Israel, Judah, Edom, and, most importantly, Assyria) continued until the Babylonian king Nebuchadnezzar destroyed the Moabite kingdom early in the 6th century BC (Ez 25:8–11). This conflict is documented in the Assyrian literature, which indicates that Moab became an Assyrian vassal in the late 8th century BC, and in the OT (2 Kgs 3; 10:32,33; 13:20; 24:2). Indeed, the enmity between Moab, Israel, and Judah is especially evident in a series of prophetic oracles leveled against the Moabites (Is 15,16; Jer 9:25,26; 48:1–47; Am 2:1–3; Zep 2:8–11). These passages call attention to some of the major towns in ancient Moab (Nebo, Medeba, Heshbon, Dibon, Ar, Kir, and Horonaim).

Following the Babylonian conquest, the region of Moab fell under Persian control and was occupied by various Arab peoples, most notably the Nabataeans. Although a Moabite state was never reestablished, people of Moabite ancestry were recognized in late OT times (Ezr 9:1; Neh 13:1,23), since the postexilic Jewish community was concerned about observing the Law recorded in Deuteronomy 23:3–6. In AD 106, the region of Moab became part of the Roman province of Arabia. Archaeological research has added much to the body of information that relates to Moabite history and culture from the prehistoric through Ottoman periods.

Religion. During the 3rd and 2nd millennia BC, Moabite religion was probably similar to that practiced by the Canaanites, though the religion of Moab eventually developed into a relatively distinct system. Although other deities were worshiped by the Moabites, Chemosh was their national god. The OT refers to the Moabites as "people of Chemosh" (Nm 21:29; Jer 48:46), and the frequent appearance of "Chemosh" in Moabite personal names points to this god's elevated status. In general, the Moabite Stone's dozen references to Chemosh portray him as a god of war who leads his people against their enemies.

Divine guidance and favor were sought, and diviners and oracles were respected (Nm 22–24). A priesthood (Jer 48:7) and sacrificial system (Nm 22:40–23:30; 25:1–5; 2 Kgs 3:27; Jer 48:35) were important aspects of Moabite religion. No Moabite sanctuary has been discovered, but their existence is mentioned in the Moabite Stone and the OT (1 Kgs 11:7,8; 2 Kgs 23:13). Elaborately furnished tombs, like those found at Dibon, point to the Moabites' belief in the afterlife.

GERALD L. MATTINGLY

See CANAANITE DEITIES AND RELIGION; MOABITE STONE.

Moabite Stone. Longest literary source outside the OT dealing with the history of the

The Moabite Stone.

were to act as blessings or offerings for a good harvest. Fortunately, a messenger from the French Consulate had obtained an impression of the writing on the stone. But the "squeeze" began to break apart as the messenger returned to the consulate on horseback. Impressions were also taken of the larger sections when they could be gathered at a later date. Finally many of the other, smaller pieces were located, and the whole stone was put back together as closely as possible. Although parts were missing, the stone did contain a clear description of the history of the Moabites.

The text begins with a dedication to Chemosh, the god of the Moabites. Mesha, the king of the Moabites for 30 years, states that in gratitude for being delivered "from all the kings and letting" him see his "desire over all . . . enemies" he had erected a high place for the god. The place where the stele was found may also have been the location of the high place.

As the text continues, a short sketch of the history of the Moabites appears that can be related to the OT narrative. "Omri, king of Israel," had oppressed Moab for many days for Chemosh was angry with his land [Moab]." Omri's son "succeeded him and he too said, 'I will oppress Moab.' In my [Mesha's] time he said [this] but I triumphed over him and over his house, while Israel has perished for ever." The 40-year domination of Israel over Moab must involve the reigns of Omri (885–874 BC, 1 Kgs 16), his son Ahab (874–853 BC), Ahaziah (853–852), and the first half of Jehoram's reign (852–841). Thus the son mentioned in the text would be Omri's grandson. That would be more consistent with Scripture, which states that Jehoram had tried to destroy Moabite rebels (2 Kgs 3:4–27; to interpret the evidence to say that the stone was done in Ahab's reign would be contrary to 1:1).

The rest of the text describes the victories over the Israelites, Mesha's public works, and the call of the god Chemosh for Mesha to fight the Hauranites.

See INSCRIPTIONS; MOAB, MOABITES.

Moadiah. Head of a family of postexilic priests, whose house was headed by Piltai during the days of Joiakim the high priest (Neh 12:17); alternately called Maadiah in verse 5.

See MAADIAH.

Modius. Dry measure equivalent to about one peck.

See WEIGHTS AND MEASURES.

Moladah. One of the cities belonging to Judah's tribe (Jos 15:26), later assigned to Sim-

region of Palestine and Transjordan during the Iron Age (1300–500 BC). It is a particularly important source for the history of the Moabites, a people who lived in an area east of the Dead Sea. The stone was discovered in the 1860s and has a fairly complete narrative of the reign of Mesha, a Moabite king in the middle of the 9th century BC. When found, the stone itself was a hard slab with rounded top and 39 lines of Hebrew-like writing 3 feet 10 inches high × 2 feet wide × 2½ inches thick).

On August 19, 1868 F. Klein, a German employed by the Church Missionary Society, saw the stele and reported its existence. When the German and French consuls showed an interest in the stone, the Arabs who had discovered it wanted to get the best price that they could from the two governments. The Arabs then began to quarrel among themselves over how much to charge the foreigners, and the dispute became so bitter that one group heated the stone over a fire and then poured water on it, causing the stone to break into pieces. The Arabs then distributed the various pieces among the granaries of the countryside. There they

eon (19:2; 1 Chr 4:28). The people of Judah resettled that area after the exile (Neh 11:26).

Some consider Moladah identical to Malatha which became an Idumean fortress occupied by the Edomites (Josephus, *Antiq.* 18.6.2). Others place it by Jattir, at modern Khureibet el-Waten, as do Jerome and Eusebius. The evidence is, however, too obscure to make certain identification.

Mole, Mole Rat. Small, burrowing rodent (Is 2:20).

See Animals.

Molech. Ammonite god worshiped with human sacrifice (Lv 18:21; Jer 32:35).

See Ammon, Ammonites; Canaanite Deities and Religion.

Molid. Son of Abishur and Abihail from Judah's tribe (1 Chr 2:29).

Moloch. Alternate spelling of Molech, an Ammonite god (Acts 7:43).

See Canaanite Deities and Religion; Ammon, Ammonites.

Molten Sea. Alternate name for the laver in King Solomon's temple in 1 Kings 7:23.

See Bronze Sea; Laver; Tabernacle, Temple.

Money and Banking.
Money. Money was developed as a convenient medium of exchange to supplement and later to replace bartering, although the two systems operated concurrently for many centuries. From the patriarchal period to the present day, wealth has been measured in terms of goods and precious metals, particularly gold and silver, which remain universally acceptable mediums of exchange. Genesis 13:2 describes Abraham as "very rich in cattle, in silver, and in gold."

Wealth in a nomadic or seminomadic society was frequently measured by the number of cattle a person possessed, and because of this, cattle were a readily acceptable and easily valued, if rather large, medium of exchange. The degree to which cattle were commonly recognized as the standard for value, wealth, and exchange is reflected in the Latin form for money, *pecunia*, which is derived directly from *pecus*, meaning "cattle." For religious purposes, taxes or donations paid in cattle were most acceptable, and this not only increased the general recognition for this medium, but also made the temple a repository for large herds of cattle as well as smaller animals and produce, which, if they could not be used directly in the temple rituals, could in

turn be bartered for whatever commodities were required. Perishable foods were less popular for purposes of exchange than animals such as sheep and asses, although timber, wine, and honey were regularly used as a form of currency (1 Sm 8:15; 2 Kgs 3:4; Ez 45:13–16). Both public and private taxes, tribute, and debts of all kinds were settled by this means. Solomon paid Hiram, king of Tyre, in wheat and olive oil for his assistance in the construction of the temple (1 Kgs 5:11), and in the 8th century BC taxes were commonly paid in jars of wine or olive oil. Tribute in the form of sheep and wool is recorded in 2 Kings 3:4.

All the means of exchange mentioned represented goods which could be measured or counted, and attempts were made to establish a standard rate of exchange for them in relation to each other.

Silver was the precious metal most readily available in the ancient Near East and was therefore the one most frequently mentioned in connection with purchases by weight, and at a later period by coin. The first recorded instance in the Bible of silver being used as a medium of exchange occurs in Genesis 20:14–16, where Abraham received a payment of 1000 shekels by weight of silver, as well as animals and slaves. Abraham also purchased the field and cave of Machpelah for 400 shekels of silver (Gn 23:15,16), which according to the custom of the day had to be weighed out in front of the vendor and checked by witnesses (cf. Jer 32:9,10).

As these events occurred about the beginning of the 2nd millennium BC, the term "shekel" would not represent the coin familiar from later periods, but rather a certain weight of silver. At a later time the brothers of Joseph sold him to traveling merchants for 20 shekels of silver (Gn 37:28). Genesis 33:19 mentions another unit of weight for metal in connection with the purchase of a field by Jacob; the term occurs again in Joshua 24:32 and Job 42:11. This unit (Hebrew *qesitah*) may have represented an amount equivalent to the currency value for a lamb.

In time large animals and material objects came to be considered extremely cumbersome as a means of exchange, and metal became increasingly popular. Transportation of large quantities of precious metal remained a problem, however, and a method had to be devised for easy recognition, accessibility, and storage of particular metals of value.

Over the years, fairly uniform shapes were designed for metals used in transactions. Silver could be piled or tied in bundles, as shown in Egyptian bas-reliefs, and the sons of Jacob took advantage of a similar method in transporting the purchase price of the grain they were buying from Egypt (Gn 42:35). About 1500 BC, pieces of metal shaped in the form of ingots, bars, tongues, or heads of animals, were in use, as well as gold discs and rings of gold wire. Perhaps the most popular pieces acceptable as currency were those that had also been designed as jewelry. The valuables listed amongst the spoil of the Midianites included gold chains, bracelets, signet rings, and earrings (Nm 31:50). The bracelets and rings in particular probably represented a standardized weight, and could therefore be used easily as currency. Rebekah received gifts from her fiancé that were in the form of jewelry of specific weight: a gold ring weighing half a shekel and two bracelets weighing 10 gold shekels (Gn 24:22). Job was given a fine ring of gold by a number of relatives, and it is unlikely that they would all have given him the same gift if it did not in fact represent a certain monetary value (Jb 42:11).

The requirement in Deuteronomy 14:25 to "bind up your money" would again imply either thin strips of silver that could be bundled together or rings that could be strung. In either event, transportation would be easier.

The value for weights of silver mentioned in Mosaic times can best be understood in terms of purchasing power. A ram could be bought for two shekels, while fifty shekels was the price of about four bushels of barley (Lv 27:16). In the time of Elisha, during a good year, one and one-half pecks of fine flour or three pecks of barley could be bought for one shekel (2 Kgs 7:16). Needless to say, monetary valuations of this kind would be affected by such economic considerations as supply and demand.

Estimation by eye was an inaccurate means of judging the value of currency, and there is no doubt that cheating was prevalent in the weighing and examination of metal. The weighing, an essential part of every major transaction, was also very time-consuming. In order to ensure the correct value of the weights, which were usually pieces of bronze, iron, or dressed stones, they carried some sort of stamp. Once this practice was generally established, it was a short step to the stamping of the individual pieces of metal, whether tongues, bars, or bracelets, being used as currency. The next logical development was stamping a piece of silver to authenticate its value for purposes of currency. This was the precursor of the coin, which was not known in the ancient Near East prior to the exilic period. Therefore any reference to money before that time indicates bars, bracelets, rings, or other metal objects, stamped or unstamped.

The earliest minted coins came from the kingdom of Lydia in Asia Minor, being credited traditionally to Croesus (560–546 BC), the fabulously wealthy ruler of that land. The coins from Lydia were made of electrum, a natural alloy of silver and gold, and they depicted a lion and a bull. Like most of the early coins, the reverse simply contained a punch mark.

Originally a coin not only represented a value, but its weight was worth the amount of silver or gold of its face value. Thus many of the early coins were slashed heavily by some ancient skeptics, who wished to be sure that the coin was of pure silver and not a less valuable metal coated with silver.

The purity of silver or gold was also a factor in the popularity and acceptance of particular coins. Thus in Greek and Roman times the tetradrachma from Tyre was one of the most widely accepted silver coins because of the purity of its metal content.

The use of coins did not eliminate the necessity for weighing, because the fraudulent clipping of the edges of coins was prevalent from their introduction in the 6th century BC. This particular problem plagued all subsequent issues of coinage, and it was only in the late 18th century in Britain that it was surmounted by a process involving the milling, or reeding, of the edges of the more valuable coins.

In the 6th century BC when the Jews returned from exile in Babylonia, coins were donated for the rebuilding of the temple in Jerusalem, as well as silver and gold in other forms. The gold coin mentioned is a "daric." The term, apparently derived from the name of the great Persian king Darius I (521–486 BC), was in wide current use, and even appears in biblical passages written at a later date but referring to a period before the reign of Darius (cf. 1 Chr 29:7).

Few craftsmen with the skills required for the manufacture of coins would have been available before the 6th century BC, so the earliest gold darics were probably minted at Sardis. The mint itself was taken over by the Persians when they occupied the territory, with production continuing as before.

Western sections of the Persian Empire probably used silver coins more frequently than gold. According to some traditions, coinage developed in Greece at Aegina about the time that the Lydians first adopted the concept. The earliest of these silver coins to be excavated so far dates from the sixth century BC and was minted in northern Greece.

Also in current use were the popular 5th-century BC tetradrachmas from Athens, which had dies on both sides of the coin. These depicted the head of the goddess Athena and the sacred owl.

Although the silver content of many coins in contemporary use was lowered, that of the Athenian tetradrachma remained consistently at its original high standard of purity. This circumstance naturally increased its acceptability, especially in areas caught up in political turmoil where the purity of the local currency was particularly questionable. Because of the stability of the silver content of the coin and the rapidity with which the Greek Empire was expanding, the Athenian tetradrachma was minted and used almost unchanged over a period of 300 years. Many of these coins have been found in hoards all over the eastern Mediterranean.

There is no doubt that by the 4th century BC there was a local mint in Judea, for silver coins imitating the Athenian tetradrachma, but also bearing the legend "Jehud" have been excavated there.

Because of the extent of trade in Greek and Roman times, the coins from the larger centers had a general acceptance in all the Mediterranean coastal areas. They were also favored in the inland areas, especially in those traversed by trading routes or those that were part of a larger empire.

Mints in Gaza, Joppa, and Tyre were established about the end of the 4th century BC to produce local currency. At this period Sidon continued to be an important supplier of silver coins, as it had been since the 5th century BC.

As the Seleucids gained control of Judea in 198 BC, a period of political turmoil commenced when the Syrians tried to hellenize the Jewish people. Resentment toward Greek culture and resistance to all tampering with the traditional Jewish faith increased steadily until it found an outlet in the leadership of Mattathias, father of the Maccabees, who began a guerrilla uprising in 167 BC.

When the fortunes of war shifted temporarily to the Maccabeans, King Antiochus of Syria granted Simon Maccabeus the right to mint his own coins (1 Mc 15:6), but before he could take advantage of this prime symbol of independence the balance of power changed once more. Judea returned to its status as a tributary, and the permission to mint coinage was hastily withdrawn.

Simon's son, John Hyrcanus, succeeded in overcoming the weakened Syrians and declared independence in 129 BC. The small bronze coins minted about 111/110 BC showed a wreath on the obverse bearing the inscription, "Johanan the high priest and the community of the Jews." The reverse displayed a double cornucopia with a poppy head, both of which were Greek symbols of plenty. These were the first genuinely Jewish coins.

With the lack of skilled craftsmen and of a good mint, it is hardly surprising that the resulting coins were simple and unpretentious. In consequence they were quite unlike the elaborate, and often delicate, designs of many contemporary coins.

Meanwhile, silver coins continued to be struck in the Phoenician cities of Tyre and Sidon on the orders of the Seleucids, and they remained the most popular silver coins in everyday use in Palestine until Roman times. Even then they continued to circulate side by side with the Roman coinage.

Banking. Banking as we know it did not exist in the ancient Near East. Nevertheless, many of the services we associate with a modern bank were available for those who required them. These included the provision of a storage area for money, the exchanging of smaller coins for larger denominations, and the changing of international currency for something required for a particular occasion. This could be a Tyrian shekel for the temple poll tax, or change for purchasing something from a merchant.

Being a sacred place, a temple provided an ideal repository for wealth of all kinds, since it was most unlikely to be robbed because of the mystique and superstition surrounding it. As early as the 3rd millennium BC the ziggurat at Ur was fulfilling this role, as well as lending out money at interest by making advances to farmers against the security of their crops. From that time onward, the growth of a rudimentary type of banking system began to be evident. When senior servants of households were sent by their masters on a distant mission, it was normal for them to travel with the equivalent of a letter of credit.

In the time of Hammurabi, receipts were issued for silver held on deposit in the temples, and the receipt itself could also be used as a medium of exchange in a manner similar to that of a dollar bill or a check. Letters of credit, bills of exchange, and promises to pay, as well as checks, were available in ancient

Coins of Pontius Pilate, procurator (AD 30–31), and Tiberius Caesar, emperor (AD 14–37).

Ur, and all were expressed in terms of silver valued against the price of barley. Large Sumerian cities such as Lagash would have had a banking system equally as well-developed as that of Ur, and in Lagash itself financial records are far lengthier than the accounts of the reign of the king. The handling of money by means of a ledger entry appears to have been known at this time. Such a system of bookkeeping may have had some connection with the Babylonian banking center in Aram, from which many fled when the city came under the influence of the Assyrians. In the 8th and 7th centuries BC there was a large Babylonian bank at Nineveh, and much of the precious metal mined at that time throughout the known world was employed in the production of currency. Traveling Aramaeans and Phoenicians brought their own banking techniques with them as they established in Greece a similar system of dealing with money. The result of this activity was that most of the people in the Near East had some rudimentary acquaintance with Mesopotamian techniques for handling financial transactions.

A crisis occurred in fiscal circles in the 5th century BC when coins began to be in short supply. Many of the silver mines had been worked out, and the situation was complicated further by a shortage of labor. Those who already possessed coins, especially the widely accepted Greek tetradrachmas, tended to keep them, and foreigners especially hoarded large quantities of them. In Athens and in most eastern Mediterranean ports, clay facsimilies of coins enjoyed wide circulation.

By the 4th century BC, most financial transactions in Greece were in the hands of temple authorities, public bodies, or private firms. Deposits were accepted, loans were arranged, and business could be conducted between cities on a credit basis without the actual transfer of currency. By Roman times, payment to a bank was an accepted method of discharging a debt.

Like the bank, the money changer charged a fee for exchanging foreign currency. Since every adult male had to pay a temple tax of half a shekel, usually paid in the highly valued silver coins from the mint at Tyre, money changers set up their tables in regional centers to facilitate the collection. At the time of the annual Passover celebration, when Jerusalem was crowded with foreigners who needed to change money, the tables of the money changers were set up in the precincts of the temple.

For those who wished to use silver or gold coins for decorative purposes, one can well imagine that it would be necessary to save the small bronze coins for years to get enough to exchange, again with the help of the money changers, for exactly the right precious coin.

Although a commercial lending system was in operation in Babylon from about 2000 BC, as far as the Israelites were concerned a loan was a form of charity, intended to tide over a farmer during one of the periodic seasons of crop failure. By NT times this idea had changed somewhat, since the debtors referred to in Luke 16:1–8 are either tenants or merchants with goods on credit.

Usury, which in OT times simply meant "interest," was unpopular amongst the Israelites, who considered the practice an unacceptable means of profiting from another's misfortune. Usury is expressly forbidden in Exodus 22:25; Leviticus 25:35–37; and Deuteronomy 23:19,20, although the regulation is relaxed to the extent that it was permissible for a foreigner to be charged interest on a loan. There is no doubt that interest was a regular part of a business transaction under the law code of Hammurabi, and even at an earlier period in Babylonian history, when according to records the interest rates ran as high as 33 percent on food and 20 percent on money.

Like many of the prohibitions in the Pentateuch, when the one forbidding the charging of interest was ignored, it resulted in hardship. Both Ezekiel and Nehemiah attempted to encourage the recognition of the earlier laws, but to little avail (Neh 5:6–13; Ez 18:8,13,17; 22:12). Even sons and daughters could be forced into slavery when holdings were mortgaged, which was directly contrary to the covenantal concept of the Israelites as a free people under God.

By NT times it can be observed that ideas about usury and interest were in process of change. Jesus himself approved of a wise investment as a means of earning income (Mt 25:27; Lk 19:23), but he was concerned about the possibility of excessive rates which could be charged on private loans.

The security for a loan generally consisted of some kind of pledge. Where a small, temporary loan was involved, the pledge could be a personal object (Dt 24:10–13; Jb 24:3), real estate (Neh 5:1–13), or even the word of a guarantor (Prv 6:1–5; 11:15; 20:16). The Law as outlined in Deuteronomy is quite specific about what could or could not be used as security or pledge. No object essential for daily living, such as the upper millstone, could be accepted as a pledge (Dt 24:6). If a man pledged his cloak, it had to be returned to him by nightfall, since it served then as a blanket (Ex 22:26,27; Dt 24:12,13). Moreover, the creditor was not allowed to enter the house to obtain the pledge, but instead had to receive it at the door before witnesses.

A debtor ran the risk of being sold into slavery, and this again violated the concept of covenant freedom. Although a householder and his children may have been sold into slavery on occasions (cf. 2 Kgs 4:1), it is unlikely to have taken place with any degree of frequency. Every seventh year, debts or slavery resulting from money owed were cancelled automatically under the provisions of the Law, and a small respite was given to the debtor (Dt 15:1,2). At the end of a cycle of seven sabbatical years came the jubilee year, when not only were all debts canceled but farm land and village houses which had been sold for various reasons were restored to the original family owner (Lv 25:10). Even in Roman times the jailing of an insolvent debtor was recognized as an unsatisfactory solution to the problem. While Scripture nowhere encourages irresponsible behavior in fiscal or other matters, it recognizes that certain persons will always be close to poverty, either through circumstances of birth, or from sheer inability to handle money in a constructive fashion.

HAZEL W. PERKIN

See COINS; MONEY CHANGER; MINERALS, METALS, AND PRECIOUS STONES; TRADES AND OCCUPATIONS (BANKER); TAX, TAXATION.

Bibliography. F.A. Banks, *Coins of Bible Days;* R. deVaux, *Ancient Israel,* pp 139–42, 164–77; R. Duncan-Jones, *The Economy of the Roman Empire;* G.R. Halliday, *Money Talks About the Bible;* K.A. Jacob, *Coins and Christianity;* F.W. Madden, *History of the Jewish Coinage and of Money in the Old and New Testaments;* H. Mattingly, *Roman Coins;* R.S. Yeoman, *Moneys of the Bible.*

Money Changer. Ancient profession which undertook many of the services performed by the modern banker, particularly in the area of exchanging the currency of one country or province into that of another, or of exchanging small coins for coins of greater value or vice versa. Naturally a fee was charged for such a service.

Coinage as such does not go back beyond the 7th century BC. In earlier periods pieces of silver were weighed out in payment for commodities (Gn 20:16; 37:28; Jgs 17:2). Once the standardized coin was adopted in Asia Minor the idea was copied in other lands, but since coins differed from country to country equivalents had to be worked out by the money changers.

The need for such procedures was particularly important in Palestine, where every adult male Jew had to pay a half-shekel offering (Ex 30:11–16). Jews from various countries who came to pay this sum might bring a variety of types of coinage. Temple authorities had to authorize a coin appropriate for the purpose. This was the silver Tyrian half-shekel or tetradrachma (cf. Mt 17:27, where Peter was told to pay the temple tax for Jesus and himself with the coin he found in the mouth of a fish). The Mishna states (Sheqalim 1:3) that money changers operated in the provinces on the 15th of the month of Adar (the month before the Passover) to collect this tax. Ten days before the Passover the money changers moved to the temple courts to assist Jews from foreign countries.

Jesus encountered the money changers in the temple courtyard when he "cleansed the temple" (Mt 21:12,13; Mk 11:15,16; Lk 19:45,46; Jn 2:13–22). The reason for this action has been a matter of debate. Worshipers needed to procure the half-shekel to pay their tax. But they needed also to purchase birds, animals, or cake offerings in some cases. This wholesale activity in buying and money-changing seemed inappropriate in the temple precincts, which constituted a sacred area (cf. Mk 11:16), although Jesus evidently approved the payment of the temple tax as such (Mt 8:4; 17:24–26; Mk 1:44; Lk 5:14). There is also the possibility that the charge made by money changers and by those who sold sacrificial birds and animals was exorbitant whether for their own profit or for the profit of the temple authorities. Such operations could be carried on at a suitable distance from the sacred area so that the haggling and noise associated with such activities in an eastern setting did not unnecessarily disturb the prayer and the offering of sacrifices carried on in the temple courts (cf. Jer 7:11).

See MONEY AND BANKING; COINS.

Monotheism. Belief that there is only one God. It is distinguished from polytheism, which posits the existence of more than one god; from henotheism, which worships one god without denying the existence of other gods; from atheism, which denies the existence of any god. The three great monotheistic religions of the world are, in their historic order, Judaism, Christianity, and Islam (Muhammadanism).

Definition. If there is only one God, it follows that the Deity is personal, sovereign, infinite, eternal, perfect, and almighty. This is, in fact, what Scripture declares of God in his essential being. It is only in the biblical revelation that we can know clearly and certainly who God is and what he is like. He must be distinct from the world (thus avoiding pantheism) in such a way that he is the only creator and sustainer of the universe and the Lord of history. He is above and beyond his creation (divine transcendence), and yet he enters into time and human affairs (divine immanence).

The biblical doctrine of monotheism is known both through historical events involving "the God who acts" for the salvation of the human race and through his verbal communication as "the God who speaks" to chosen servants for the instruction and edification of those who believe. It is in such dimensions that monotheism embraces the possibility and reality of direct encounter between the eternal and infinite God and the finite, sinful creature. The NT makes it clear that this is accomplished through Jesus Christ.

Biblical Teaching. According to the Bible man was originally a monotheist. No other conclusion is possible from the Genesis records (chs 1–3). Polytheism developed later as a sinful corruption of the pristine belief in one true God, the God of creation, revelation, and redemption. This corruption had set in at least by the time of Abraham, for God's call of Abraham to leave Ur of the Chaldees and journey toward Canaan, the land God had promised him and his posterity, undoubtedly involved a break with the polytheism of his ancestors in the area of Ur (11:31–12:9).

When Abraham reached Canaan, the Promised Land, he and his family found people worshiping a multitude of gods. Each ethnic grouping in Palestine had its own god or many gods (Gn 31:30–35; Jgs 11:24; 1 Sm 5:2–5; 1 Kgs 11:33). In their disobedience, the sons of Abraham were continually losing faith in God and lusting after the gods of the Canaanites or diluting the true worship of God with the heathen practices associated with the worship of the Canaanite gods (Gn 35:2,4; cf. Jos 24:2; 1 Kgs 16:30–33). One of the major roles of the prophets was to call the Jews back to true worship and faith in the one God, "the God of Abraham, the God of Isaac, and the God of Jacob" (Ex 3:6,15,16; cf. 1 Kgs 18:17,18). This reminder of their monotheistic heritage was constantly needed because of the ever-present danger of losing it through contact with the polytheistic beliefs and practices of their idolatrous neighbors. Such reminders were necessary even for leaders like David (1 Sm 26:19), and certainly for Solomon (1 Kgs 11:1–7) and later kings (12:28–32; 2 Kgs 10:31; 22:17).

The early prophets did not clearly delineate a formal doctrine of monotheism; they rather showed the impotence and unreality of the pagan gods (1 Kgs 18:24). It was the 8th-century prophets who asserted a monotheistic faith in the face of a persistent polytheism.

It was not until the time of the exile that the Jews were cured of their idolatrous polytheism when their enemies took away their idols and demonstrated their impotence (Is 46; Ps 115). Then Israel learned that God alone was their refuge and help in the time of trouble, because he only is the true and living God who can save his people when they repent of their sins and obey the divine will.

The NT doctrine of the Trinity is entirely consistent with the concept of monotheism. In the Trinity there are not three gods but one God in three persons. The plurality is in the number of personal distinctions (Father, Son, and Holy Spirit), not in the divine nature—there is a unity of essence in the Trinity. In the first two centuries it was the Ebionites who mistook the church's claim for Christ's essential deity as involving a polytheism which was to overlook or deny Jesus' own claim, "I and my Father are one" (Jn 10:30). The NT and the OT are in perfect agreement regarding the ancient confession: "The Lord our God is one Lord" (Dt 6:4; cf. Mk 12:29; Eph 4:5,6). The Ebionites were wrong, for Christ *is* God, and this confession does not involve polytheism.

Some biblical scholars feel there are data in the OT which express, or at least suggest, a kind of uniplurality in the divine nature, such as the phenomena revealed in connection with "*the* Angel of the Lord" (Gn 16:9,13; 22:11,16; 31:11,13; Ex 3:2,4,5); the plural form for the name of God (Elohim), its use with plural verbs and pronouns (Gn 1:26; 3:22; 11:7; 20:13; 35:7; Is 6:8); the fact that Jehovah distinguishes himself from Jehovah (Gn 19:24; Hos 1:7); God is said to have a Son (Ps 2:7; Prv 30:4); God is distinguished from the Spirit of God (Gn 1:1,2; Is 48:16; 63:7,10); and descriptions of the Messiah as being both one with God and yet distinct from God (Ps 45:6,7; Is 9:6; Mi 5:2; Mal 3:1).

Other biblical scholars, however, resist finding trinitarian ideas in the OT and explain all the above references in ways that take into consideration characteristic Hebrew literary expressions, such as the plural of "majesty," plural forms being employed to indicate special dignity and unlimited greatness. On the other hand, all efforts must be exerted to resist unwarranted attempts to press polytheistic meanings into the data and the Scripture passages referred to above. To read these in the framework of a plurality of gods would do a grave injustice to the natural meaning the writers intended. The plural form of "Elohim," for example, is not a suggestion of polytheism, but expresses the exalted transcendence of God in his manifold fullness and perfection. No devout Jew in OT times would have understood either a trinitarian concept of God or a plurality of gods. If Christians find a basis for the doctrine of the Trinity in the OT it is only because they are reading more developed NT revelational data back into the OT.

The great concern of OT writers was to establish and maintain the unity of God, particularly as against the pagan polytheistic background of the surrounding nations. A prime necessity was that the unity of God should be insisted on. Before there could be any revelation of a doctrine of the Trinity, all dangers of idolatrous polytheism had to be removed.

RALPH E. POWELL

See GOD, BEING AND ATTRIBUTES OF.

Monster. Term designating various creatures of the water.

See ANIMALS (CROCODILE; DRAGON).

Month. *See* CALENDARS, ANCIENT AND MODERN.

Moon. Lesser luminary of the heavens (Gn 1:16). Many Semitic languages use the same word for moon as Hebrew. In three passages (Sg 6:10; Is 24:23; 30:26) the moon is called "The White One," and paired with "The Hot One," the Sun. Another term, "crescent," is used in other languages such as Aramaic and Arabic (perhaps also in Sg 7:3), and "crescent ornaments" (Jgs 8:21,26; Is 3:18) are mentioned.

The moon is nearly always paired in the Scriptures with the sun and often with the stars. Only rarely does the moon appear alone. Even in Psalm 72:7 the moon is not by itself since the sun occurs in verse 5. Likewise, Job 31:26 has moon and "light," the latter apparently being the sun.

In the creation account it is said concerning the functions of the two luminaries: "They will be for signs and seasons, for days and years" (Gn 1:14), that is, "times" are determined by their movements. For this reason, when telling about the mighty deeds of the Lord in creation, the poet says: "Thou hast made the moon to mark the seasons" (Ps 104:19). The ancient Hebrew calendar was lunar (Sir 43:6,7), the months beginning with the new moon, marked by special rituals (Nm 10:10; 28:11–14; 2 Chr 2:4). Two great festivals, Passover and tabernacles, began in mid-month when the moon is full (Lv 23:5,6; Ps 81:3–5; and Lv 23:34, respectively). The seven-day week is a division of the 28-day lunar cycle into logical and convenient units; so the moon may be said to provide the basis for the significance of the number seven. As a corollary, the beginning of the seventh month, the festival of trumpets (Lv 23:24), marked the climax month of the sacred feasts; it also signified the New Year for regnal years and for agriculture (Josephus, *Antiq.* 1.1.3 [81]; Mishna, *Rosh Hashanah* 1:1).

One verse in the creation story speaks of the sun's dominion over the day and the moon's over the night (Gn 1:16; also Ps 136:9 et al.). The moon is also mentioned (alongside the sun) in the general order of creation when the spheres of the universe were established (Jer 31:35). From this the luminaries symbolize the continuity of the world order (Pss 72:5; 89:37,38). The darkening of the moon (and the sun) is a sign of the change of the order in creation in the latter days (Is 13:10; Ez 32:7; Jl 2:10; Hb 3:11; Mt 24:29; Mk 13:24; Rv 6:12; the converse is stated in Is 30:26). Since the moon resembles the sun it also has the power to smite (Ps 121:6) and to influence the growth of crops in the field (Dt 32:14).

The sun, the moon, and 11 stars are the main subject of Joseph's second dream (Gn 37:9). In the Book of Deuteronomy the Israelites were warned against worshiping the moon and the rest of the host of heaven (Dt 4:19; 17:3), but this foreign worship made its inroads into the Judean kingdom (2 Kgs 21:3; 23:4,5; Jer 7:18; 8:2).

Observation of the moon's cycle and movements was deeply rooted in Mesopotamian culture, both for regulating the calendar and for oracular prediction. Appearance of the moon out of its time (during the last days of the month), eclipses, rings around the moon, and similar phenomena were interpreted as clear signs of future events. Certain pivotal days in the lunar cycle, its birth, fullness, and decline, were times of special caution in everyday life requiring special rituals. The moon was thought to have influence over both plant and animal growth as well as the fate of human beings. The god of the new moon, Sin (Ishtar was the goddess of the full moon), was a senior member of the pantheon, and his ritual was prominent especially in Ur and Haran. There is no connection between the moon god and the wilderness of Sin or with Sinai.

The Egyptians also were familiar with the lunar cycle but placed more emphasis on their own calendar of 365 days to the year. The moon was the eye of Horus which was wounded when the moon waned and healed when it was full. The moon was Horus' left eye while the sun was his right. The moon was also a representation of Thoth, god of wisdom.

In south Arabia moon worship was widespread. The moon god appears as an element in many personal names.

Numerous personal names also had the moon god as an element among the West Semitic peoples in the 2nd millennium BC. In Ugaritic poetry a text describes the moon's wedding to Nikkal (the Mesopotamian Ningal, the wife of Sin). There is also a humorous poetic text about a banquet of the gods where the moon god gets drunk and crawls under the table like a dog. However, the moon cult was not prominent at Ugarit and few personal names contain the moon as a divine element. The same may be said for the Phoenicians of the Iron Age. Names with moon as an element are rare. On the other hand, the standard word for month was cognate to the word for moon (contrast Hebrew where the word for month is usually "new [moon]"). A Cilician king, writing in Phoenician, prayed that his own name should be immortalized like the name of the sun and the moon; but this does not of itself prove the presence of moon worship.

In contrast to three places named Beth ("house" or "temple")-shemesh, where sun worship must have existed, only one ancient town is known as Beth-jerach, "House of the Moon," and it is not mentioned in the Bible or sources contemporary with the Canaanite or Israelite societies. It was located by the Chinnereth. The name Jericho is based on the word for moon plus a geographical suffix.

To keep an accurate control over the calendar and the feasts, the new moon was carefully observed seven times during the year in Jerusalem. This assured that the major feasts fell on the proper days. The Sanhedrin would gather early in the morning on the last day of the preceding month and watchmen were posted to observe the moon's first appearance. When the evidence became clear the sacred word was pronounced, and the day became the first of the new month. Fire signals beginning from the Mt of Olives announced the new moon; later they were replaced by messengers because the Samaritans had set up false signals along the way.　　　ANSON F. RAINEY

See CALENDARS, ANCIENT AND MODERN; FEASTS AND FESTIVALS OF ISRAEL; ASTRONOMY.

Moon, New. See CALENDARS, ANCIENT AND MODERN; FEASTS AND FESTIVALS OF ISRAEL; MOON.

Morasthite. KJV designation for the prophet Micah from the name of the town Moresheth (Jer 26:18; Mi 1:1).

See MORESHETH.

Mordecai. 1. Jewish leader during the exile. Our knowledge of Mordecai comes exclusively from the Book of Esther which, according to some rabbinic sources, Mordecai himself wrote. Mordecai's activities are set against the period in which Xerxes (Ahasuerus) reigned over ancient Persia, a vast empire stretching over 127 provinces. Mordecai was a Benjamite descendant of Kish, the father of King Saul. His family were among those Jews who left Palestine during the captivity of Nebuchadnezzar. While his name reveals a Babylonian etymology his heart burned with love for his countrymen who, notwithstanding the decree of Cyrus permitting their return to the Holy Land (538 BC), determined to colonize in dispersion rather than face the hardships of resettling in Palestine.

His remarkable life's drama is intertwined with Hadassah (Esther), his cousin, who became his ward following the death of her parents. Esther's sudden, unexpected exaltation to the position of queen following Vashti's deposition was an essential link to the deliverance of her people; Mordecai's forceful influence upon this beautiful Jewess was another. Behind them both, however, moved their sovereign God whose love for Israel provided protection against the malevolent designs of Xerxes' prime minister, Haman. Haman, the very incarnation of evil, had determined to exterminate the Jews of Persia because of Mordecai's unwillingness to pay him homage. Mordecai, learning of the plot, communicated the matter to Esther by way of Hathach, one of the king's officers. Her initial hesitancy to intervene on behalf of her people was met with her cousin's concise and stern answer:

"Do not think that because you are in the king's house you alone of all the Jews will escape. For if you remain silent at this time, relief and deliverance for the Jews will arise from another place, but you and your father's family will perish. And who knows but that you have come to royal position for such a time as this?" (Est 4:13,14 NIV). Several days elapsed during which Haman erected an enormous gallows upon which to hang Mordecai. On the evening of its completion Xerxes, being unable to sleep, ordered the book containing the record of his reign to be read to him. Upon hearing of the actions of Mordecai in frustrating an earlier assassination attempt against him, he inquired as to what honors Mordecai had received in recognition of his service. Finding he had not been rewarded, Xerxes summoned Haman and asked him what fitting thing should be done for the man the king had purposed to honor. Haman, thinking that he was the object of the king's query, responded with three grand ideas (Est 6:7–9). Ironically, Haman is chosen to carry out his recommendations on behalf of Mordecai. A final touch of irony is seen in the execution of Haman on the very instrument he had prepared for Mordecai.

Following Haman's death, Mordecai and Esther had to act quickly to counteract the irrevocable edict directed against the Jews at Haman's instigation. Xerxes, now solicitous of the Jews' well-being, issued another edict allowing the Jews the freedom both to defend themselves and retaliate against any aggressors. Apparently, the Persian officials to whom Mordecai forwarded this follow-up directive cooperated fully in protecting the Jews from their adversaries, thousands of whom were slain.

Consequently, Mordecai instructed all Jews to celebrate the time of their deliverance annually on the 14th and 15th days of Adar (roughly, March). The name of the festival, *Purim*, is derived from the word *pur* ("lot"), which was cast by Haman to determine the day for the Jews' annihilation.

See ESTHER, BOOK OF.

2. One of the ten leaders who returned with Zerubbabel after the exile (Ezr 2:2; Neh 7:7).

STUART D. SACKS

Moreh, Hill of. Hill close to the Valley of Jezreel, near which the Midianites camped when they were attacked by Gideon (Jgs 7:1). It was probably called by this name because it was the location of a sanctuary where divination was practiced. Its name may imply instruction or divination. It is generally identified with Jebel Nabi Dahi across the valley from Mt Gilboa.

Moreh, Oak of; Plain of. Abraham's first recorded stopping place upon entering Palestine after leaving Mesopotamia. Here he built an altar to God (Gn 12:6). Later, Moses mentioned this place as a geographical landmark to identify the whereabouts of Mt Gerizim and Mt Ebal (Dt 11:30). The KJV improperly reads "plain" of Moreh. The oak of Moreh was located near Shechem.

Moresheth. Micah's hometown (Jer 26:18; Mi 1:1, KJV Morasthite).

See MICAH (PERSON) #7.

Moresheth-gath. Town in the lowland country of Judah included in Micah's lament (Mi 1:14); perhaps the same as Moresheth, Micah's hometown (v 1). The *gath* in Moresheth-gath suggests that the town was in close proximity to the major Philistine city by that name. Its exact location is uncertain. Jerome (a 4th-century church father) suggested that Moresheth-gath was situated a short distance east of Eleutheropolis identifiable with modern Khirbet el-Basel. Another possible site is Tell ej-Judeideh, six miles southeast of Gath.

Moriah. Name used twice in the OT. Abraham was sent to sacrifice his son Isaac in "the land of Moriah" (Gn 22:2). Because in the narrative it is said that the ram was "provided" in the place of Isaac (vv 8,14) when God "appeared" to Abraham, it has been suggested that the form of the name "Moriah" may be connected with this. (The Hebrew verb *ra'a* can have meanings "see," "provide," "appear," and the ending -iah is the shortened form of the name of the Lord which is found in many Hebrew names.)

In 2 Chronicles 3:1 Mt Moriah is the place of Solomon's temple, specifically identified with the threshing floor of Ornan the Jebusite (cf. 2 Sm 24; 1 Chr 21), but not explicitly with the place of Abraham's sacrifice. Some, however, see in the description of the Lord's appearing to David a reminder of his appearing to Abraham there. The Jewish historian Josephus (*Antiq.* 1.13.2, 7.13.4) clearly connects the place of the temple with the place where Isaac was offered up, as does the 2nd-century BC Book of Jubilees (18:13). Samaritan tradition linked Moriah with Mt Gerizim. Muslim tradition connects the Dome of the Rock which stands today on the site of the Jerusalem tem-

The Dome of the Rock, Jerusalem, the site thought by many to be Moriah, where Abraham almost sacrificed his son Isaac.

ple with Abraham's sacrifice of Isaac on the great rock under the dome of the mosque.

See JERUSALEM.

Morning Sacrifice. *See* OFFERINGS AND SACRIFICES.

Morning Star. Literally, the sun (Gn 1:14–18; Jb 38:7; Pss 19:4–6; 110:3); symbolically, a figure of speech which Christ used to describe himself (Rv 22:16). The phrase is closely related to the idea of the "dayspring" (Jb 38:12; Lk 1:78) and the "daystar" (2 Pt 1:19), all of which denote the rising of the sun in the morning. The symbolic application of the phrase to Christ is rooted in the OT (Nm 24:17) where Balaam prophesied, "I see him, but not now; I behold him, but not nigh; a star shall come forth out of Jacob." Having clearly identified "the star" as a person from the family of Jacob, the later prophets develop this theme. Isaiah tells the people of his day to "rise and shine" because "the Lord will rise upon you" (Is 60:1,2). Malachi writes, "For you who fear my name the sun of righteousness shall rise, with healing in its wings" (Mal 4:2). Zechariah, the father of John the Baptist, describes the ministry of his son as that of preparing the way for "the day shall dawn upon us from on high" (Lk 1:78); and we are told that he prepared the way for Christ (Mt 3:3; Mk 1:2,3; Jn 1:6–8,23; cf. Mt 11:7–14; Lk 7:18–28). The identity of the star is settled when Christ says, "I am the morning star" (Rv 22:16). It is another way of saying, "I am the light of the world" (Jn 8:12; 9:5; 12:46). The central concept found in the symbol is that of Christ as light shining in darkness (Lk 2:32; Jn 1:4,7–9; 3:19; 12:35; 2 Cor 4:6; Eph 5:14; 1 Pt 2:9; 1 Jn 2:8; Rv 21:23). With the birth of the Messiah the morning star arose—the gospel light dawned (Is 9:1,2; Mt 4:15,16).

Christ not only describes himself as the morning star but declares that he gives the morning star (Rv 2:28). He bestows his own light upon those who believe in him (Jgs 5:31; Is 60:3; Dn 12:3; Mt 5:14,16; Jn 1:9; Acts 13:47; Eph 5:8; Phil 2:5; 1 Thes 5:5; 1 Jn 1:7). In this sense Peter states that "the morning star [KJV daystar] rises in your hearts" (2 Pt 1:19). Because Christ has come and established his kingdom of light on earth, that light can abide in the minds of humankind.

The phrase then points to Christ's glory, as the source of light, and to his grace in the sharing of light.

Mortar, The. Name given by Zephaniah to a hollow place or depression resembling a mortar in Jerusalem. The "mortar" (Heb. *Maktesh*)

was a place of business whose merchants were soon to grieve for their loss of trade (Zep 1:11). Its location is variously identified with the Phoenician quarter, the Kidron Valley, or the Tyropoeon Valley.

See JERUSALEM.

Moserah, Mosera, Moseroth. Temporary camping place of the Israelites during their wilderness wanderings. It was positioned between Hashmonah and Bene-jaakan (Nm 33:30,31). Later, Aaron died and was buried there (Dt 10:6, KJV Mosera). Moseroth (Nm 33:30,31) is the plural form of Moserah (Dt 10:6). Its exact location is uncertain though it was apparently situated near Mt Hor on Edom's border (cf. Nm 20:23–29).

Moses. Great leader of the Hebrew people who brought them out of bondage in Egypt to the Promised Land in Canaan; also the one who gave them the Law at Mt Sinai that became the basis for their religious faith through the centuries. Focused in this one person are the figures of prophet, priest, lawgiver, judge, intercessor, shepherd, miracle worker, and founder of a nation.

The meaning of his name is uncertain. It has been explained as a Hebrew word meaning "to draw out" (Ex 2:10; cf. 2 Sm 22:17; Ps 18:16). If, however, it is an Egyptian name given him by the daughter of Pharaoh who found him, it is more likely from an Egyptian word for "son" (also found as part of many well-known Egyptian names such as Ahmose, Thutmose, and Rameses). No one else in the OT bears this name.

Without question the greatest figure in the OT (mentioned by name 767 times), his influence also extends to the pages of the NT (where he is mentioned 79 times). The first 40 years of his life were spent in the household of Pharaoh (Acts 7:23), where he was instructed in "all the wisdom of the Egyptians" (v 22). The next 40 years he spent in Midian as a fugitive from the wrath of Pharaoh after killing an Egyptian who was mistreating a Hebrew (vv 23–30). His last 40 years were devoted to leading the Israelites out of bondage in Egypt to the land God had promised to Abraham and his descendants (Gn 12:1–3). He died at the age of 120 after leading the Israelites successfully through 40 years of wandering in the wilderness to the very edge of the Promised Land on the east side of the Jordan River (Dt 34:7). He is one of the great figures in all of history, a man who took a group of slaves and, under inconceivably difficult circumstances, molded them into a nation that has influenced and altered the entire course of history.

Background. The only source of information for the life of Moses is the Bible. Archaeology confirms the credibility of the events associated with Moses, but it has never provided any specific confirmation of his existence or work. His story begins with the arrival in Egypt of Jacob, his sons, and their families during a time of famine in Canaan. Invited by Joseph and welcomed by Pharaoh, the family settled down in northeast Egypt in an area known as Goshen, where they remained for 430 years (Ex 12:40). With the passing of time their numbers grew rapidly so that the land was filled with them (1:7). A new king arose over Egypt who did not know Joseph. The biblical account does not give the name of this pharaoh, and there has never been agreement as to his identity. He has most frequently been identified as Thutmose III (1490–1436 BC), Seti I (1309–1290 BC), or Rameses II (1290–1224 BC). Out of fear that their growing numbers might become a threat to the security of his nation, Pharaoh determined to take measures to reduce their number. He put them to work building the store cities of Pithom and Rameses, but the severity of the work did not diminish them. He next tried to enlist the cooperation of the midwives to destroy the male babies, but they would not carry out his orders. He then ordered his own people to drown the male infants in the Nile River. Against the background of this first-known Jewish persecution, the baby Moses was born.

The First 40 Years—In Egypt. *Birth and Early Life.* A man of the family of Levi named Amram married his father's sister Jochebed (Ex 6:20; cf. 2:1). Their first son, Aaron, three years older than Moses, was born before the command to drown the Hebrew babies was given, as there is no indication that his life was in danger. However, the cruel order was in force when Moses was born, and after three months, when his mother could no longer hide him, she took a basket made of bulrushes and daubed it with bitumen and pitch. She put the baby into the basket and placed it among the reeds along the banks of the river. An older sister, Miriam, stayed near the river to see what would happen. Soon the daughter of Pharaoh (identified by Josephus as Thermuthis and by others as Hatshepsut, but whose actual identity cannot be determined) came to the river to bathe as was her custom, accompanied by her maidens. She discovered the baby, recognized it as one of the Hebrew children, and determined that she would raise the child as her own. Miriam emerged from her hiding place and offered to secure a Hebrew woman to nurse the child, an arrangement that was agreeable to the princess. Miriam took the baby to his own mother who kept him for per-haps two or three years (cf. 1 Sm 1:19–24). Nothing is recorded of those formative years. Whether his mother continued seeing him during his later childhood and young manhood or revealed his true identity to him or taught him the Hebrew faith are matters that can only be speculated about. Moses was instructed in all the wisdom of the Egyptians as would befit a member of the royal household and became "mighty in his words and deeds" (Acts 7:22).

Identification with His Own People. Just when Moses became aware that he was a Hebrew rather than an Egyptian cannot be known, but it is clear that he knew it by the time he was 40 years old. One day he went out to visit his people and to observe their treatment, for the cruel measures taken against them by Pharaoh at the time of Moses' birth had not been lifted. Seeing an Egyptian beating a Hebrew, Moses in great anger killed the Egyptian and buried him. He thought the deed had gone unnoticed until the next day when he encountered two Hebrews fighting with each other. When he tried to act as peacemaker, they both turned on him and accused him of murder: "Who made you a prince and a judge over us? Do you mean to kill me, as you killed the Egyptian?" (Ex 2:14). Acts 7:25 adds: "He supposed that his brethren understood that God was giving them deliverance by his hand." Aware that being a member of Pharaoh's household would not exempt him from punishment now that the deed was known, Moses fled for his life to the land of Midian.

The Second 40 Years—In Midian. *Marriage into the Family of Jethro.* Soon after arriving in Midian, Moses sat down by a well where he observed the seven daughters of the priest of Midian who had come to the well to draw water for their father's flock. Shepherds came and drove them away, but Moses intervened and helped them water their animals. When Jethro (Ex 3:1; also called Reuel, 2:18; Hobab, Nm 10:29) learned what had happened, he invited Moses to stay with his family and gave him Zipporah (which means "bird") as his wife. Two children, Gershom (Ex 2:22) and Eliezer (18:4), were born to Moses and Zipporah during the years in Midian. Forty years passed, and Moses' thoughts about his former life in Egypt must have faded into the past. He could not have foreseen that at his now advanced age of 80, God would soon thrust him back into the midst of the court in Egypt, where he would confront the son of the now-dead pharaoh from whose wrath he had fled with the demand to release the Hebrew people from the bondage they had endured for so many years. God had not

A shepherd with his sheep near Mt Sinai, where Moses tended the flock of his father-in-law, Jethro (Ex 3:1).

forgotten his people and was now ready to deliver them.

Encounter with God at the Burning Bush. One day while Moses was taking care of the flocks of his father-in-law, he led them to Mt Horeb (known also as Sinai) where God appeared to him in a flame of fire out of the midst of a bush that burned, yet was not consumed. Moses approached to observe the strange sight more closely and heard God speak to him out of the bush, "Moses, Moses!" Moses replied, "Here am I," but before he could come any nearer, God said, "Do not come near; put off your shoes from your feet, for the place on which you are standing is holy ground" (Ex 3:5). He further identified himself to Moses as the God of Abraham, Isaac, and Jacob. He assured Moses that he was aware of the cruel afflictions of his people and had heard their cries. Then he told of his plan to send Moses to Egypt to deliver his people from their bondage (v 10).

Faced with a challenge that seemed beyond his capabilities, the aged Moses began making excuses for not accepting the task. To his ex-

cuse, "Who am I that I should go to Pharaoh, and bring the sons of Israel out of Egypt?" God assured Moses that he would be with him (Ex 3:11,12). To his excuse that he would not be able to give an answer if the people asked him the name of the God he represented, God revealed his name in the cryptic statement, " 'I am who I am' . . . say this to the people of Israel, 'I AM has sent me to you' " (vv 13,14). Many interpretations have been proposed for the name. Whatever else it means, it undoubtedly suggests the self-existence and all-sufficiency of God. Moses then argued that the people would not believe him when he told them that God had sent him to deliver them from Egypt. In response God gave him three signs: when he cast his shepherd's rod to the ground, it became a serpent; when he put his hand to his bosom, it became leprous; he was also told that when he would pour water from the Nile upon the ground, it would become blood (4:1–9). Even armed with these powerful evidences of the presence of God with him, Moses raised still another objection, "Oh, my Lord, I am not eloquent . . . I am slow of speech and of tongue" (v 10). God told him that he would teach him what to say but despite such assurance, Moses asked God to send someone else. In anger mingled with compassion, God made Moses' brother Aaron the spokesman, but said his instructions would still be given directly to Moses.

Afterward Moses returned to Jethro but did not tell him about the encounter with God and the divine commission he had received.

Return to Egypt. Moses took his wife and sons and set out for Egypt, telling his father-in-law only that he wanted to go back to Egypt to visit his kinsmen there (Ex 4:18). The biblical account says he put his wife and sons on the same donkey to journey back to Egypt (v 20). The fact that all three rode the same animal indicates that both children were quite young and had not been born in the early years of Moses' marriage. At a lodging place along the way a strange thing happened. The Lord met him and sought to kill him (v 24), apparently because Moses had failed to circumcise the baby before leaving Midian. When Zipporah realized that Moses' life was in danger, she performed the rite herself and said to her husband, "Surely you are a bridegroom of blood to me" (v 25). Whatever else may have been involved in this unusual encounter with God, it was a solemn reminder that the one who was to be the leader of the covenant people must not himself neglect any part of the covenant (Gn 17:10–14).

God told Aaron (who was still in Egypt) to go to the mountain where Moses had encountered God at the burning bush and meet his brother there. Moses told Aaron everything that had happened, and together they went to Egypt, gathered the elders together, and informed them of these matters. When Moses and Aaron performed the signs in the presence of the people, they believed these leaders had been sent by God to deliver them from their affliction (Ex 4:30,31).

The Third 40 Years—From Egypt to Canaan. *The Encounter with Pharaoh.* Soon after his return to Egypt, Moses, accompanied by Aaron, went to Pharaoh and repeated the demands of the Lord, "Let my people go, that they may hold a feast to me in the wilderness" (Ex 5:1). Pharaoh rejected the demand with the observation that he had never heard of this God of Moses. When one realizes that Egyptian kings considered themselves to be gods, the affront to Pharaoh becomes even more acute. Not only did he reject Moses' demands, but he intensified the burdens of the Hebrews. Their work had up until then required them to make brick using straw provided for them, but now Pharaoh said they would have to gather their own straw and still produce the same number of bricks. The Hebrews turned in anguish and anger to Moses and said, "You have made us offensive in the sight of Pharaoh" (v 21). Even Moses could not understand the turn of events and complained bitterly to God, "Why hast thou done evil to this people?" (v 22). God reassured Moses that he would deliver the Hebrews from their bondage, and, moreover, he would bring them into the land he had promised Abraham, Isaac, and Jacob (6:8). He then instructed Moses to return to Pharaoh and repeat the demand to release the Hebrews upon threat of severe reprisal if the demand were ignored.

Ushered again into Pharaoh's presence, Moses repeated his request for release of the Israelites. He attempted to impress Pharaoh by turning his rod into a serpent, but the Egyptian wise men through their secret arts were able to duplicate the miracle so Pharaoh's heart remained hardened and he would not listen to Moses. In rapid succession Moses brought nine plagues upon the land of Egypt to show the omnipotence of God to force the compliance of Pharaoh. These included a plague in which the water of the Nile turned to blood (Ex 7:20–24), frogs (8:1–15), gnats (vv 16–19), flies (vv 20–32), a plague (KJV murrain) on the livestock (9:1–7), boils on the people (vv 8–12), hail (vv 13–35), locusts (10:12–20), and darkness (vv 21–29). During the plagues of the frogs, flies, hail, locusts, and darkness Pharaoh was discomfited and would temporarily relent and agree to Moses' demands, but as soon as the plague was lifted, his heart hardened and he would retract his promise. The outcome of the first nine plagues was terrible devastation of the land of Egypt, but the Israelites were not released. There was yet one more plague in store, the most terrible of all.

The First Passover. God told Moses that there remained one more plague in store for the Egyptians: "All the first-born in the land of Egypt shall die, from the first-born of Pharaoh who sits upon his throne, even to the first-born of the maid-servant who is behind the mill; and all the first-born of the cattle" (Ex 11:5). Furthermore, he assured Moses that the plague would not touch a single household of the Hebrews, "that you may know that the Lord makes a distinction between the Egyptians and Israel" (v 7).

God instructed the people through Moses and Aaron to make their preparations for leaving the land in haste. They were to go to the Egyptians and ask them for their jewels of silver and gold (Ex 11:2,3), a request to which the Egyptians agreed, perhaps out of fear of the Hebrews and in the belief that the gifts would bring about an end of the terrors that had struck the land. The Hebrews were also instructed to prepare a lamb for each family—small families could share—for the last meal to be eaten in the land of Egypt (a rite that became the pattern for the Jewish observance of the Passover for many centuries). Blood of the lamb was to be put on the doorposts and lintels of the houses in which the Passover meal was being eaten that night. The Hebrews were promised that wherever the blood was on the door no harm would come to that household. They were also instructed to prepare unleavened bread. At midnight the death angel of the Lord smote all the firstborn in the land of Egypt, from the firstborn of Pharaoh himself to the lowest captive in a dungeon; not a single house of the Egyptians escaped tragedy. When Pharaoh saw what had happened, he ordered Moses and the people to leave the land at once (12:31,32). The biblical record says that about 600,000 Hebrew men left Egypt. Together with women and children the total would have been in excess of two million people, a grievous blow to the economy and pride of Egypt.

The Exodus from Egypt. The exodus has been called the creative center of the OT. It is certainly the central event of the OT and marks the birth of Israel as a nation. The Jewish people still look back to that event as the great redemptive act of God in history on behalf of his people, much as Christians look upon the cross as the great redemptive act of their faith.

The exact route taken by the Hebrews out of Egypt cannot be determined today, though many solutions have been proposed. They did not take the shortest, most direct route to Canaan (which would have been about a 10-days' journey along the Mediterranean coastline), but set out in the direction of Mt Sinai, where Moses had earlier met God at the burning bush. As a sign that Moses had been sent to deliver the people, God told Moses he would bring them to that same spot, where they would worship God (Ex 3:12). The Hebrews did not forget the request of Joseph to carry his bones with them when they returned to their own land (Gn 50:25; Ex 13:19).

As the people journeyed they were preceded by a pillar of cloud during the day and a pillar of fire at night. The cloud represented the presence of God with his people and guided them along the route they should travel.

Back in Egypt Pharaoh was having second thoughts about letting the Hebrews leave the land and decided to pursue them with his army and bring them back. When the Hebrews saw the approaching cloud of dust and realized that the Egyptian army was pursuing them, they were terrified. The sea lay ahead of them and the Egyptians were behind; there seemed to be no way of escape. The people turned on Moses, blaming him for bringing them out of Egypt. God again assured them that they need not be afraid or do anything to defend themselves. He promised to fight the battle for them and give them victory (Ex 14:14).

The Lord parted the waters of the Sea of Reeds (traditionally but erroneously referred to as the Red Sea) by a strong east wind and allowed the Israelites to pass through the sea on dry ground to the other side.

The Egyptians rushed after the Israelites, following them into the dry bed of the sea, but before they reached the other side, the waters rushed back together, destroying the Egyptian army in the midst of the sea and leaving the Israelites safe on the other side. The people celebrated their great deliverance in song (Ex 15) and then continued their journey. The narrative that follows describes the struggle of the Israelites to survive in the desert—problems of food and water, internal dissension, murmurings against Moses, and battles with enemies. Through all their experiences Moses towers as the unifying force and great spiritual leader.

In spite of having seen God's great act of deliverance so recently, the faith of the Israelites was not strong. Three days later they came to a place where the water was not fit to drink, and they began complaining against Moses. The Lord showed Moses how to purify the water, and the people's needs were satisfied (Ex 15:22–25). When they reached the wilderness of Sin, they complained again, this time because of lack of food. God met their need by supplying manna, a breadlike substance that would serve as their food until they came to Canaan (16:1–21). Later, camped at Rephadim, the people complained again, this time for lack of water. Once again God met their needs by supplying water from the rock at Horeb (17:1–7). The Amalekites attacked them while they were still camped at Rephadim, but God gave a great victory to the Israelites (vv 8–13).

Moses and the people reached Sinai and camped there. Jethro came to visit, bringing Moses' wife and sons. Zipporah had apparently decided to return with her children to stay with her father, rather than to go on to Egypt with Moses. It was a joyful reunion, and Jethro made a burnt offering and sacrifices to God (an act that has evoked the suggestion that Jethro was a true worshiper of God, even as Moses, though nothing is known of his links to the Hebrew faith). When Jethro observed Moses trying to settle all the disputes and problems of the Hebrews unaided, he proposed that Moses delegate responsibility for some of the lesser matters to able men chosen from among the people. Moses accepted the suggestion, and shortly after Jethro returned to his own land. He did not remain at Sinai to participate in the ratification of the covenant (Ex 18:13–27).

Giving of the Law at Sinai. God had kept his promises to Moses. He had delivered the Hebrews from their Egyptian bondage and brought them to the very place where he had commissioned Moses to be their leader. He was now ready to enter into a covenant relationship with Israel. Amidst a spectacular and terrifying scene of lightning, thunder, thick cloud, fire, smoke, and earthquake that has been compared to awesome volcanic activity, God descended to the top of Sinai and called Moses to come up the mountain where he remained 40 days to receive the Law that would become the basis of the covenant.

At Sinai God was revealed as the God who demands exclusive allegiance in all areas of life and at the same time the God who desires personal fellowship with his people.

Apostasy of the People. While Moses tarried on Mt Sinai, the people below became impatient and skeptical about his return so they went to Aaron and asked him to make idols for them to worship. They contributed the gold earrings they were wearing, and Aaron fashioned the gold into the shape of a calf and presented it to them with the words, "These are your gods, O Israel, who brought you up out of the land of Egypt!" (Ex 32:4). The next day they joined in worship of the idol with sacrifices and revelry. God told Moses what was taking place below and angrily declared that he was going to destroy the people but would make a great nation of Moses and his descendants. Moses immediately interceded on behalf of the people, and God's wrath abated. Moses descended the mountain, carrying the two tables of stone on which the Law had been written, but when he entered the camp and saw what was taking place, he could not restrain his anger. He threw the stone tablets to the ground, ground the golden calf to powder, mixed it with water, and forced the people to drink it. He turned angrily to Aaron and demanded an explanation for the great sin that had been committed. Aaron lamely tried to shift the blame by minimizing his own role: "I threw it [the gold] into the fire, and there came out this calf" (v 24). Moses called for volunteers to carry out God's judgment on the people for the great sin they had committed. Men of the tribe of Levi responded and executed about 3000 men. Later they were commended and rewarded (Dt 33:9,10). Moses again interceded for the people, requesting that he be destroyed with the rest if God could not forgive them. God relented and promised Moses that the angel of the Lord would go with them still (Ex 32:34). Then Moses made a special request that he might be allowed to see the glory of the Lord. God instructed Moses to hew out two more tables of stone like the ones he had destroyed and to return to the top of the mountain the next day. There the Lord passed before him and proclaimed his name: "The Lord, the Lord, a God merciful and gracious, slow to anger, and abounding in steadfast love and faithfulness" (34:6). Moses remained on the mountain another 40 days, where he received renewed warnings against idolatry and further instructions from the Lord together with another copy of the Ten Commandments on tablets of stone. When Moses came down from the mountain, he was not aware that the skin of his face shone as a result of talking with God. At first the people were afraid to come near him, but he called them together and repeated all the Lord had said to him on the mountain. Afterward, he covered his face with a veil which he removed only when he went into the presence of the Lord. Paul said the purpose of the veil was to prevent the people from seeing the heavenly light gradually fade from Moses' face (2 Cor 3:13).

The Tabernacle and Establishment of the Priesthood. When Moses went up to the mountain the first time to receive the Law from God, he was instructed to collect materials to be used in the construction of the tabernacle or tent. Gold, silver, bronze, blue and purple and scarlet stuff, fine twined linen,

goats' hair, tanned rams' skins, goatskins, and acacia wood, would be needed, along with oil for the lamps, spices for the anointing oil and for the fragrant incense, onyx stones and stones for setting (Ex 25:3–7). The pattern for construction was also given to him, together with the ritual to be used for the consecration of the priests. A man named Bezalel was put in charge of the construction of the tabernacle assisted by Oholiab (Ex 31:1–6, KJV Aholiab). The tabernacle was portable like a tent so that it could be taken down and moved from place to place as the Hebrews continued their journey toward Canaan.

In addition to giving Moses directions for the tabernacle, God also instructed him concerning the sacrifices that were to be brought: the burnt offering, grain offering, peace offering, sin offering, and guilt offering (Lv 1–7). The solemn ceremony for ordaining Aaron and his sons as priests and for inaugurating the worship practices were performed by Moses (chs 8,9).

Some time after this solemn inauguration of the religious ritual, Nadab and Abihu, two of Aaron's four sons, offered unauthorized fire before the Lord. A fire came out from the Lord and destroyed them. Moses forbade Aaron and his sons Eleazar and Ithamar to express grief because of the sinfulness of the act (Lv 10:1–7). The nature of their sin is difficult to determine, but it surely involved a violation of God's holiness. Therefore, it is appropriate that a large part of the remainder of the Book of Leviticus gives regulations which stress the holy living that God expected from his people. These regulations may be summed up in the words: "You shall be holy: for I the Lord your God am holy" (19:2).

While the people were still encamped in the wilderness of Sinai, God ordered Moses to take a census of them, "every male . . . from twenty years old and upward, all in Israel who are able to go forth to war" (Nm 1:2,3). When the census was completed, it was determined there were 603,550 men. The Levites were counted separately, and there were 22,000 of them.

From Sinai to Kadesh. A year had elapsed from the time the Israelites left Egypt until the census was taken (Nm 9:1). God reminded the people that it was time to observe the Passover, which they did, and a month later they set out from Sinai and came to the wilderness of Paran. Along the way they complained about the unvarying diet of manna and longed for the fish, cucumbers, melons, leeks, onions, and garlic they had eaten in Egypt (11:4–6). In anger God sent quails in abundance, but even while the people were devouring the meat, God sent a great plague that killed many of them. The complaining attitude of the people was shared even by Miriam and Aaron. They began to speak against the Cushite woman Moses had married (12:1,2). It is not certain whether the Cushite was an Ethiopian or another way of referring to Zipporah. If Moses did marry a second time, no mention is made elsewhere in the OT of the marriage. Moses made no reply to the accusations of his brother and sister. It was not necessary, for God intervened in defense of his servant. He smote Miriam with leprosy for her part in speaking against Moses, and when Aaron saw what had happened to Miriam, he acknowledged that they both had sinned (vv 10–12). Miriam's leprosy was removed in response to Moses' fervent intercession.

While the people were encamped at Kadesh (also called Kadesh-barnea, Nm 32:8, etc.) in the wilderness of Paran, Moses sent 12 men into Canaan, one from each tribe, to spy out the land in preparation for the Israelite entry. After 40 days the spies returned and, though they acknowledged that the land was fertile and inviting, 10 of them were afraid of the Canaanite inhabitants and advised against going into the land. Only Joshua and Caleb were willing to go ahead and occupy the territory. The entire congregation joined the protest against going in and determined to choose a new leader and return to Egypt rather than risk death by the sword in Canaan. They threatened to stone Moses and Aaron. At that moment God intervened and would have destroyed all the people on the spot except for the intervention of Moses (13:1–14:19). He declared that if God did not bring the people into Canaan the nations round about would conclude that the God of the Israelites was unable to bring them into the land. Once again God acquiesced to Moses' request to pardon the people but said that none of them 20 years and older who had complained against him would be allowed to enter the land. All the people would wander in the wilderness for 40 years until that generation died, and then their children would be allowed to enter Canaan (14:29–33). When they heard the Lord's sentence upon them, the people quickly decided to lift the sentence of judgment by entering the land at once, but God was not with them, and they suffered a disastrous defeat at the hands of the Amalekites and Canaanites.

Forty Years in the Wilderness. Very little is known about events during the 40 years of wilderness wanderings. In spite of the judgment that had already come upon them, the people did not seem to change their ways. A man named Korah led another rebellion against the authority of Moses and Aaron. God would not listen to the pleas of Moses and Aaron in behalf of these dissidents (Nm 16:22–24), but told the congregation to separate itself from the tents of Korah and his conspirators. While the people watched, the ground split open and swallowed up the rebellious factions together with their households and all their possessions. Though the rest of the Israelites witnessed the fate of the rebels, it did not deter them from again turning on Moses and Aaron, accusing them of killing their kinsmen. At this God told Moses to remove himself from the murmuring congregation in order that he could take vengeance. Though Moses offered atonement for the people's sins, 14,700 died by plague before the punishment was ended. To demonstrate further to the people that Moses was his chosen leader, the Lord instructed Moses to take rods, one for each tribe, and to deposit them in the tent of meeting. God would cause the rod of the man chosen by him to sprout, and so silence the murmurings of the people. The rod belonging to Aaron sprouted and budded and bloomed, but the people only complained more, "We perish, we are undone, we are all undone" (17:12).

As the people neared the end of their years of wilderness wanderings, Miriam died in Ka-

The Jordan Valley near Bethshan, with the Judean hills in the background. It was a glowing report of a rich land that the spies brought to Moses.

desh and was buried there (Nm 20:1). Soon after the people began to complain once more for lack of water. God instructed Moses to speak to a rock that would bring forth water to satisfy the needs of the people. Instead of speaking to the rock, Moses struck it twice with his rod. The water came forth, but God rebuked Moses and Aaron. "Because you did not believe in me, to sanctify me in the eyes of the people of Israel, therefore you shall not bring this assembly into the land which I have given them" (v 12). The nature of the sin is not clear, but Moses and Aaron were apparently taking to themselves honor that belonged to God alone. Because of the sin they were denied the privilege of leading the Israelites into the Promised Land. The punishment may seem too severe for the sin, but it shows that the privileged role of leadership given to Moses and Aaron carried with it an unusual measure of responsibility.

The people then journeyed from Kadesh to Mt Hor on the border of the land of Edom where Aaron died. Moses took his priestly garments from him and gave them to Eleazar, his son, thereby transferring the priestly office (Nm 20:28).

As the people came closer to their destination, resistance on the part of the native population increased. There was a skirmish with the king of Arad and his forces at Hormah, resulting in a victory for Israel (Nm 21:1–3). As they journeyed around Edom, some of the Israelites began speaking against God and Moses because there was no food or water and they were tired of eating manna. This time the Lord sent poisonous snakes among the people, and many of them died of the venomous bites. Those who had not yet been bitten came to Moses, acknowledged their sin, and asked that the serpents be removed from their midst. God instructed Moses to make a serpent of bronze and set it on a pole. If a person bitten by a serpent looked up at the bronze serpent, he would live (vv 8,9).

As the Israelites approached the territory of Sihon, king of the Amorites, they sent messengers asking permission to pass peaceably through his land. Instead of granting the request, Sihon gathered his army together and fought against Israel. He was killed in the battle, and his land and cities were taken and occupied by the Hebrews (Nm 21:21–25).

Arrival at the Jordan River. After their victory over Sihon, the Israelites set out again and encamped in the plains of Moab on the east side of the Jordan River facing Jericho in full view of the Promised Land. The Moabites were terrified by the presence of these people because they had heard what happened to the Amorites. Their king, Balak, hired a magician

named Balaam to curse the Israelites. Three times Balaam attempted to curse them, but each time God turned his words into a blessing (Nm 22–24). Though unable to curse the Israelites, Balaam was responsible for an even greater calamity. He advised the Moabites to entice the Israelites to sacrifice to their gods and bow down to them (25:1–3; 31:16; 2 Pt 2:15; Rv 2:14). While the people were worshiping the Moabite deity, Baal of Peor, God's anger was kindled against them, and he sent a plague that killed 24,000 of their number (Nm 25:9). It was Israel's first encounter with the seductive allurement of licentious idolatry and an ominous foreview of what would happen after they settled down in Canaan. Their continued attraction to idolatry would be their final undoing.

After the plague, God instructed Moses and Eleazar to take another census of the people like the one almost 40 years earlier. A whole generation of Israelites had died in the wilderness, but they had been replaced by an almost equal number, so that now there were 601,730 men 20 years and older who were able to go to war (Nm 26:51). Not a man remained of those who had been counted in the first census except Caleb and Joshua (vv 64,65).

A question concerning the inheritance of the daughters of Zelophehad was brought to Moses for his decision (Nm 27:1–11). Moses took the case before the Lord, who answered that if a man died and had no son his inheritance was to be passed to his daughter, and if there was no daughter, then to his brothers (vv 8,9).

Moses was now drawing near the end of his time as leader of the Israelites. The Lord instructed him to lay hands on Joshua and commission him as the new leader in the sight of Eleazar the priest and all the congregation (Nm 27:12–23). In addition, the Lord gave Moses instructions concerning feasts and offerings and vows (chs 28–30).

God ordered Moses, as his last act as leader, to avenge the Israelites on the Midianites. In that battle, the armies of Israel gained a great victory over the Midianites, killing their kings, their men, and also Balaam. They brought women, children, flocks, cattle, and goods to Moses as spoils of war. Moses was angry when he saw that they had not killed the Midianite women who had enticed them to sin at Peor, and he gave instructions for the soldiers to purify themselves (Nm 31:13–20). Eleazar gave additional instructions for conduct of the Israelite soldiers in time of war (vv 21–24).

The tribes of Reuben and Gad and half the tribe of Manasseh saw the land of Jazer and Gilead and decided that they wanted to settle there instead of beyond the Jordan in Canaan. Their request was granted after they promised Moses that they would participate fully in the task of conquering the land of Canaan (Nm 32).

The Lord gave instructions to Moses concerning the boundaries that would mark the Promised Land and named the men who would divide the land among the tribes (Nm 34). He also ordered that 48 cities be given to the Levites, the priestly tribe, as their portion. Six of these were designated as cities of refuge where murderers could flee so that they would not be killed by those seeking vengeance without having an opportunity to stand before the congregation for judgment (ch 35).

Moses' Death. The Book of Deuteronomy has often been called Moses' valedictory speech to the people for in it Moses is not merely the chief speaker but the only speaker. With the congregation of his people gathered before him, he rehearses all that God has done for them since leaving Sinai, and he reminds them of their failure to enter the Promised Land 38 years earlier (Dt 2:14). He recalls his plea that God would let him cross the Jordan and see the land that was to be the home of the people, but God responded that Moses would only be allowed to view the land from the top of Pisgah. Moses then exhorts the people to obey the statutes and ordinances that have been given to them in order to experience God's blessings in the land. He especially emphasizes the importance of religious instruction in the home (6:4–9) and reviews the laws and statutes that the people should carefully observe (chs 12–26). He warns them of false prophets (ch 13), gives instructions for conduct in war (ch 20), and sets out regulations for divorce (24:1–4). He concludes with a lengthy exhortation to live by the terms of the covenant. He tells the people they will be blessed if they obey God and cursed if they disobey (chs 27–30).

As the day of Moses' death approaches, the Lord orders Moses and Joshua to present themselves at the tent of meeting in order for Joshua to be commissioned as the new leader (Dt 31:14–23). Before his death Moses pronounces a blessing upon all the Israelites (ch 33). Having completed these tasks, Moses goes up from the plains of Moab to Mt Nebo, and to the top of Pisgah. From there God shows him the land promised long ago to Abraham, Isaac, and Jacob—the land that is soon to be the home of the wandering Israelite tribes. Again God tells him that he will not be allowed to cross over the Jordan. Moses died there and God "buried him in the valley in the land of Moab opposite Beth-peor; but no man knows the place of his burial to this day" (34:6). Moses was 120 years

old when he died but "his eye was not dim, nor his natural force abated" (v 7). The Israelites mourned his death for 30 days. The finest tribute to Moses is found in the closing words of the Book of Deuteronomy, "There has not arisen a prophet since in Israel like Moses, whom the Lord knew face to face" (v 10).

Moses in the New Testament. All Jews and Christians in apostolic times considered Moses the author of the Pentateuch. Such expressions as "the Law of Moses" (Lk 2:22), "Moses commanded" (Mt 19:7), "Moses said" (Mk 7:10), "and Moses wrote" (12:19) shows that his name was synonymous with the OT books attributed to him. He is mentioned in the NT more than any other OT figure, a total of 79 times. His role as lawgiver is emphasized more than any other aspect of his life (Mt 8:4; Mk 7:10; Jn 1:17; Acts 15:1). He appears at the transfiguration of Jesus as the representative of OT Law, with Elijah as the representative of OT prophets (Mt 17:1–3).

Moses' role as prophet is also mentioned in the NT. As a prophet he spoke of the coming Messiah and his sufferings (Lk 24:25–27; Acts 3:22). The NT also draws from the life and experiences of Moses to show patterns of life under the new covenant. The nativity story of Jesus parallels the Mosaic story of the infant deliverer being rescued from the evil designs of an earthly despot (Mt 2:13–18). Jesus' proclamation of a new law in his Sermon on the Mount parallels the giving of the Law at Sinai (chs 5–7) and presents Jesus as the authoritative interpreter of the will of God. Contrast between the old Law and the new relationship with God is especially marked in the Book of Galatians. The comparison of Moses with Christ is an important emphasis of the Book of Hebrews (3:5,6; 9:11–22). John contrasted the Law that was given through Moses with the grace and truth that came through Jesus Christ (Jn 1:17). He also contrasted the manna in the wilderness to Jesus as "the bread of life" (6:30–35).

Other references to Moses or to events associated with him include his birth (Acts 7:20; Heb 11:23), the burning bush (Lk 20:37), the magicians of Egypt (2 Tm 3:8), the Passover (Heb 11:28), the exodus (3:16), crossing of the sea (1 Cor 10:2), the covenant sacrifice at Sinai (Mt 26:28), the manna (1 Cor 10:3), the glory on Moses' face (2 Cor 3:7–18), water from the rock (1 Cor 10:4), the brazen serpent (Jn 3:14), and the song of Moses (Rv 15:3).   F. B. HUEY, JR.

See ISRAEL, HISTORY OF; WILDERNESS WANDERINGS; EXODUS, THE; PLAGUES UPON EGYPT; EGYPT, EGYPTIANS; TEN COMMANDMENTS, THE; TABERNACLE, TEMPLE; PRIEST AND LEVITES.

Bibliography. O.T. Allis, *God Spake by Moses;* D.M. Beegle, *Moses the Servant of Yahweh;* J. Bright, *A History of*

Israel, pp 105–26; M. Buber, *Moses*; O. Eissfeldt, "The Exodus and Wanderings," *The Cambridge Ancient History*, vol 2, pt 2 (1975), pp 307–30; J. Finegan, *Let My People Go*; F.B. Meyer, *Moses the Servant of God*.

Moses, Books of. *See* DEUTERONOMY, BOOK OF; EXODUS, BOOK OF; GENESIS, BOOK OF; LEVITICUS, BOOK OF; MOSES; NUMBERS, BOOK OF; PENTATEUCH.

Moses, Law of. *See* COVENANT; DEUTERONOMY, BOOK OF; EXODUS, BOOK OF; ISRAEL, RELIGION OF; LAW, BIBLICAL CONCEPT OF; LEVITICUS, BOOK OF; MOSES.

Moses, Song of. One of two archaic poems: the Blessing of Moses (Dt 33) and the Song of Moses (ch 32). The Song of the Sea (Ex 15) is set at a much earlier period of Moses' life, while these two poems are virtually his "last will and testament."

Moses has already written the Law book as a witness against Israel, should they turn away from God (Dt 31:19). But the Law itself required at least two witnesses to establish any charge (17:6); Moses is now commanded to write down the song as a further witness against Israel (31:19). It is interesting that Moses, like Paul, has no illusions about human nature (v 29; Acts 20:30).

The song is therefore a witness to the greatness and goodness of God, and in particular, his goodness to Israel (Dt 32:10–14). This grace underlines all the more the sinfulness of Israel's response (v 6), which can only call forth the anger of God and consequent punishment (v 19). God will use "natural disasters," wild beasts, and wars, to carry out his purposes. Yet even this is not the end. God, in his grace, will turn his hand against Israel's enemies instead, and rescue his own people (v 36).

This song carries the consistent message of every great prophet of the OT, a message that Psalm 78 expresses in terms of Israel's historical situations. The song outlines the very nature of God, and it is not strange that the song of heaven is "the song of Moses, the servant of God, and the song of the Lamb" (Rv 15:3).

See MOSES.

Moses' Seat. Biblical expression occurring only in Matthew 23:2, where Jesus speaks of the scribes and the Pharisees as having sat down upon the seat of Moses. In biblical times, the seat which one occupied usually indicated the degree of rank or respect one claimed for himself or was to receive from others (Mt 23:6). Sitting on "Moses' seat" referred to a place of dignity and the right to interpret the Mosaic law. The scribes were the successors and the heirs of Moses' authority and were rightfully looked to for pronouncements upon his teaching.

In the context of Matthew 23:2, Jesus does not seem to challenge this right, for he commands his hearers to "practice and observe whatever" the scribes and the Pharisees speak, that is, all they teach which is in accordance with the Law; but he warns the people against doing their works because they do not practice what they speak. On other occasions Jesus condemned their unbiblical traditions relative to the Law of Moses (Mt 15:3–6; 23:4,16–22).

Most High. Ancient name for God (Ps 21:7; Acts 7:48).

See GOD, NAMES OF.

Most Holy Place. Inner room of the tabernacle and temple in which the ark of the covenant was kept.

See TABERNACLE, TEMPLE.

Mote. Term used in the KJV to describe a small particle lodged in the eye of a "brother" (Mt 7:3–5; Lk 6:41,42). More recent translations prefer the term "speck."

Moth. Winged insect noted for its destruction of clothes while it is in the larval stage (Jb 13:28; Mt 6:19,20).

See ANIMALS.

Mount, Mountain. Elevated topographical feature which made a deep impression on people's minds in biblical times. Mountains were connected with fertility (Dt 33:15) and with refuge (Jgs 6:2). In Israel, as in surrounding countries, mountains were places where people expected to meet God. Many significant events in Israel's religion took place on Mt Sinai, or Horeb (see Ex 3:1–4:16; 19–23; 1 Kgs 19:8–18), and Mt Zion became almost as important when David was king (Ps 50:2; Is 2:2–4).

Whereas the Hebrews' neighbors sometimes thought mountains were magical places where their gods actually lived, the Israelites knew that their God lived in heaven and only descended upon the mountain at significant times (Ex 19; cf. 1 Kgs 8:27).

In the NT much of Jesus' activity takes place on mountains. He preached there (Mt 5:1); he retired there to pray (Lk 6:12); and he was transfigured on a mountain (Lk 9:28–36).

See PALESTINE.

Mount Ebal. *See* EBAL, MOUNT.

Mount Gaash. *See* GAASH.

Mount Gerizim. *See* GERIZIM, MOUNT.

Significant Mountains
in Scripture

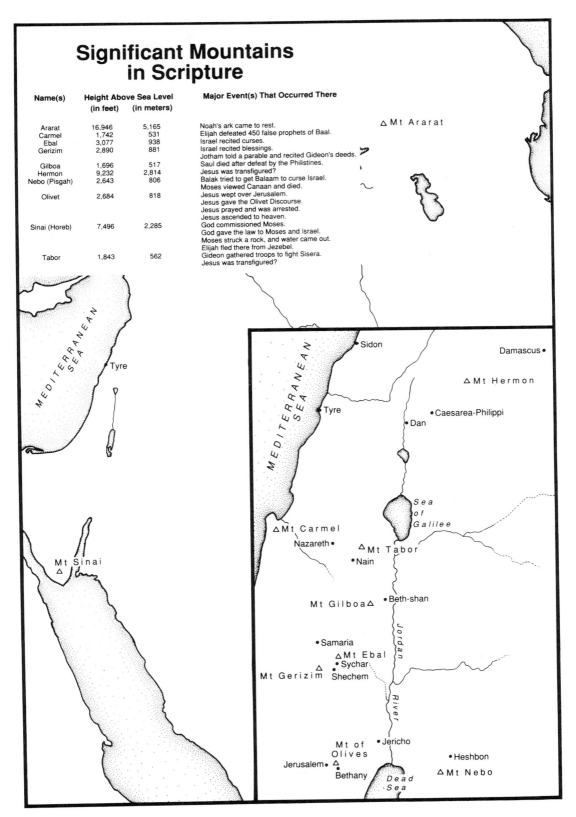

Name(s)	Height Above Sea Level (in feet)	(in meters)	Major Event(s) That Occurred There
Ararat	16,946	5,165	Noah's ark came to rest.
Carmel	1,742	531	Elijah defeated 450 false prophets of Baal.
Ebal	3,077	938	Israel recited curses.
Gerizim	2,890	881	Israel recited blessings.
			Jotham told a parable and recited Gideon's deeds.
Gilboa	1,696	517	Saul died after defeat by the Philistines.
Hermon	9,232	2,814	Jesus was transfigured?
Nebo (Pisgah)	2,643	806	Balak tried to get Balaam to curse Israel.
			Moses viewed Canaan and died.
Olivet	2,684	818	Jesus wept over Jerusalem.
			Jesus gave the Olivet Discourse.
			Jesus prayed and was arrested.
			Jesus ascended to heaven.
Sinai (Horeb)	7,496	2,285	God commissioned Moses.
			God gave the law to Moses and Israel.
			Moses struck a rock, and water came out.
			Elijah fled there from Jezebel.
Tabor	1,843	562	Gideon gathered troops to fight Sisera.
			Jesus was transfigured?

△ Mt Ararat

MEDITERRANEAN SEA

Tyre

Mt Sinai △

Sidon

Damascus •

△ Mt Hermon

• Caesarea-Philippi

Tyre

• Dan

MEDITERRANEAN SEA

Sea of Galilee

△ Mt Carmel

Nazareth •

△ Mt Tabor

• Nain

Mt Gilboa △

• Beth-shan

• Samaria

Jordan River

△ Mt Ebal

• Sychar

Mt Gerizim △

Shechem

• Jericho

Mt of Olives

• Heshbon

Jerusalem • △

Bethany

Dead Sea

△ Mt Nebo

Mount Hermon. *See* HERMON, MOUNT.

Mount Hor. *See* HOR, MOUNT.

Mount Horeb. *See* SINAI, SINA.

Mount Nebo. *See* NEBO, MOUNT.

Mount of Corruption. *See* CORRUPTION, MOUNT OF.

Mount of Olives. *See* OLIVES, MOUNT OF, OLIVET.

Mount of the Amalekites. *See* AMALEKITES, HILL COUNTRY (MOUNT) OF THE.

Mount of the Amorites. *See* AMORITES, HILL COUNTRY (MOUNT) OF THE.

Mount of the Beatitudes. *See* BEATITUDES, MOUNT OF THE.

Mount of the Congregation. *See* ASSEMBLY, MOUNT OF.

Mount Sinai. *See* SINAI, SINA.

Mount Tabor. *See* TABOR, MOUNT.

Mourning. Established ritual for grieving observed by a dead person's relatives and friends. It began with the closing of the eyes of the dead (Gn 46:4), the embracing of the body (50:1), and its preparation for burial. The hot climate necessitated that burial should take place immediately (Acts 5:1–10). But detailed information about burial earlier than NT times (Mt 27:59; Jn 11:44; 19:39,40) is extremely meager. Excavations suggest that the dead were buried fully clothed but not in coffins. The Israelites practiced neither embalming nor cremation but decent burial was essential.

At the news of a death it was customary to tear one's garments (Gn 37:34; 2 Sm 1:11; Jb 1:20), put on sackcloth (2 Sm 3:31), and take off one's shoes (15:30; Mi 1:8) and headdress; a man might cover his beard or veil his face (Ez 24:17,23). Mourners put earth on their heads (Jos 7:6; 1 Sm 4:12; Neh 9:1; Jb 2:12; Ez 27:30) or rolled themselves in the dust (Jb 16:15; Mi 1:10) or sat on a heap of ashes (Est 4:3; Is 58:5; Jer 6:26; Ez 27:30). Such mourning rites as shaving the hair and the beard and making cuts on the body (Jb 1:20; Is 22:12; Jer 16:6; 41:5; 47:5; 48:37; Ez 7:18; Am 8:10), were condemned (Lv 19:27,28; Dt 14:1) because of pagan associations. Mourners refrained from washing and discontinued the use of perfumes (2 Sm 12:20; 14:2).

Fasting was also a mourning rite (1 Sm 31:13; 2 Sm 1:12; 3:27). Neighbors or friends brought mourning bread and the "cup of consolation" to the relatives of the deceased (Jer 16:7; Ez 24:17,22). Food could not be prepared at the house of the dead because death rendered a place unclean. The dead were unclean to the extent that a priest could "profane" himself by taking part in mourning rites, except for his nearest blood relatives (mother, father, son, daughter, brother, and sister provided she was still a virgin; Lv 21:1–4,10,11). It is nowhere indicated that these mourning rites were acts of worship directed toward the dead or constituted a cult for the dead, but were expressions of grief and affection.

At the graveside lamentation for the dead was made (1 Kgs 13:30; Jer 6:26; Am 5:16; 8:10; Zec 12:10) by men and women in separate groups (Zec 12:11–14). These exclamations of sorrow might develop into a rhythmic lament (2 Sm 1:17,19–27; Am 8:10). However, professional mourners, men and women (2 Chr 5:25; Am 5:16), but especially women (Jer 9:16,17, 19), were employed. The Book of Lamentations is a fine example of laments, and is a reminder that among Jews mourning was not always associated with death. It expressed brokenness of spirit for sin, individual and national. National calamity also evoked great lamentation.

These mourning rites were expressive of great grief. But some of them—tearing clothes, wearing sackcloth, disfiguring oneself with dust and ashes, self-mutilation—point to paroxysms of grief, the religious significance of which now escapes us. This was far removed from mourning as an inner feeling or a mood of the mind. It was not just an involuntary outburst of feeling but rather a deliberate, established ritual. When death occurred the Israelite wept because it was customary and seemly. The erection of monuments or memorials was not unknown (2 Sm 18:18), but the average Israelite was too poor for this to be a common practice.

Mourning practices in NT times differed lit-

Mt Tabor.

tle from those described in the OT. Mourning was associated with Christ's second advent (Mt 24:30), with repentance (Jas 4:8–10), with Christ's leaving the 12 (Mt 9:15), with deep spirituality (5:4), as well as with death (Mk 5:38,39; Lk 7:13; Jn 11:33).

True, the overthrow of death by Jesus Christ robbed death of its sting and the grave of its victory (1 Cor 15:54–57), but the Christian still mourns, though not as those who have no hope (1 Thes 4:13; Rv 21:4).

See BURIAL, BURIAL CUSTOMS; FUNERAL CUSTOMS.

Mouse. Small rodent considered unclean by the Law (Lv 11:29).

See ANIMALS.

Moza. 1. Caleb's son by his concubine Ephah (1 Chr 2:46).

2. Zimri's son, the father of Binea and a descendant of Saul and Jonathan (1 Chr 8:36, 37; 9:42,43).

Mozah. Town in the territory assigned to Benjamin's tribe (Jos 18:26); tentatively identified with the village of Qalunyah. It has been suggested that the name is preserved in the modern Khirbet beit Mizza, a small village about four miles northwest of Jerusalem.

Mulberry. Tree with a darkish blue edible berry.

See PLANTS.

Mule. Offspring of a male ass and a female horse (2 Sm 13:29).

See ANIMALS.

Muppim. One of Benjamin's ten sons (Gn 46:21). He is perhaps identifiable with Shephupham (Nm 26:39, KJV Shupham) and Shuppim (1 Chr 7:12).

See SHEPHUPHAM.

Murder, Murderer. *See* CIVIL LAW AND JUSTICE; CRIMINAL LAW AND PUNISHMENT; TEN COMMANDMENTS, THE.

Mushi, Mushite. Son of Merari, the grandson of Levi, and Mahli's brother (Ex 6:19; Nm 3:20; 1 Chr 6:19,47). He was the father of Mahli, Eder, and Jeremoth (1 Chr 23:21,23; 24:26,30) and the founder of the family of Mushites (Nm 3:33; 26:58).

Music and Musical Instruments. A natural expression of man which probably began with speech-singing and developed into songs, which were then accompanied by instru-ments. Music as we know it has become quite complex, a luxury and entertainment; music in antiquity, however, was a functional expression of daily life, work, and worship.

The phrase "sing to the Lord," common to the OT (Ex 15:21; 1 Chr 16:9; Pss 68:32; 96:1,2; Is 42:10; Jer 20:13) was not unique to the Jewish nation. All religions draw on the natural human impulse to sing. The injunction "Sing to the Lord" was a signal for the people to pour out their praise in song.

The Bible, however, is limited in its treatment of music in ancient Israel. Since there was no written musical notation, the primary record of songs sung by the Hebrews is the collection of texts, particularly the psalms, and a few enigmatic musical instructions. The biblical writers were not writing a history of their culture, but of their relationship with God; hence, their comments about music are not critical. Also, the biblical documents cover a long span of history and are grouped according to category rather than in chronological order, thus making it difficult to order the development of musical style with precision. Finally, there is the problem of understanding the biblical descriptions of music and its performance. Only in this century have scholars been able to interpret the information provided in the Bible in terms of oriental music systems.

Music in the Old Testament. The first musician mentioned in the Bible is Jubal, "the father of all those who play the lyre and pipe" (Gn 4:21). The importance of this description of a musician so early in history lies in the equality Jubal is given with his brothers Jabal, the herdsman, and Tubal-cain, the smith. Music making is recognized among the earliest professions of nomadic peoples. The name "Jubal" is believed to be a derivative from the Hebrew word for "ram." The ram's horn (*shophar*) was an early instrument of the Jewish people and was significant in signaling important events.

For the most part, the music described in early biblical history was of a functional nature. Music gained special significance as it became an important part of temple worship. Many of the descriptions of music making in ancient Israel, before David's time, are quite utilitarian. There are accounts of music at times of farewell (Gn 31:27), at times of rejoicing and feasting (Ex 32:17,18; Is 5:12; 24:8,9), at military victories (2 Chr 20:27,28), and for work (Nm 21:17, the song of the well diggers; Is 16:10; Jer 48:33). Most of this music was probably rather crude and primitive in nature, especially the music associated with military advances, which was meant to terrify the enemy (Jgs 7:17–20). The music and dancing that greeted Moses as he descended from the mountain was described first as "fighting in the camp" (Ex 32:17,18).

In the early history of the Jewish people, women played an important part in the performance of music. The image of women dancing and singing for joy accompanied by percussion instruments is repeated several times: Miriam led the women in a hymn of thanksgiving after the deliverance from the Red Sea (Ex 15), Jephthah's daughter welcomed her father in his victory (Jgs 11:34), Deborah joined with Barak in singing a song of victory (Jgs 5), and women hailed David after his defeat of the Philistines (1 Sm 18:6,7). There is little mention of women as musicians following the establishment of the temple in Jerusalem, but there are a few allusions to the fact that women did participate in singing and dancing. The account of the return from exile in Babylon includes both male and female singers (Neh 7:67), confirming that women still took part in musical performance.

As Jerusalem became the religious center of the Hebrew people (950–850 BC), the role of the professional musician became more important. The women's songs became insignificant compared to the pomp and ceremony associated with the temple and the royal court. While the levitical singers took most of the musical responsibility at the temple, the development of antiphonal singing allowed the people to join in on responses in the singing of psalms.

Musical Theory. There are several inherent problems in discussing the theory of OT music. First, the aesthetic standards of oriental music are quite different from those of the West, making it difficult to discuss oriental music in terms that are meaningful to the Western mind. Second, musicologists have had the task of comparing music of the Orient that is known to us with the descriptions of music which is lost. Yet it is largely through comparative musicology that any understanding of the theory of ancient Hebrew music can be found.

In examining OT vocabulary one feature of Jewish music becomes clear—the terms for *vocal* music in the OT greatly outnumber those for *instrumental* music. There are at least a dozen different Hebrew words for the various types of songs, voices, vocal performances, and the like. Most of the instrumental music in both the first and second temple periods was accompaniment to singing. Loud instrumental fanfares and even cymbals were used as signals in the worship service, but singing was given the highest place.

The terms used to describe Western music, such as timbre, melody, harmony, and

rhythm, do not apply to oriental music. However, some correlations can be drawn between Western understanding of these characteristics and theories about ancient Hebrew music.

The timbre (tone quality) of the singing described in the OT is difficult to ascertain. The singing of the Jews has been compared to the early music of Babylonia and Assyria, which was loud and noisy. A general conception of many ancient oriental people was that a god's attention had to be roused by loud praying and singing. Such religious views may have influenced the Jewish attitude toward music (2 Chr 15:12–14), but the words describing music, translated as "loud" or "exceedingly loud," are better thought of as "big" or "great." The singing of the Israelites was undoubtedly more pleasant and refined than that of their neighbors. Most of Hebrew song was accompanied by soft instruments like the lyre and the harp. The aesthetic quality of music described in the OT is quite different from that of occidental music. Western critics usually describe sounds as beautiful or ugly, whereas Hebrew and Greek musicians understood sounds more often as "sweet" or "agreeable" or "strong." Singing, for the Jews, was done to serve and to exalt God, not merely to gain the attention of the gods as with their pagan neighbors.

The concept of melody in ancient oriental music differs from Western modes, scales, and melodic lines. The "tunes" were thematic ideas or kernels sometimes made up of only a few notes. These melodic themes (*makam*) were evidently tetrachordal in nature rather than pentatonic. Each theme was an independent melodic unit of narrow range, not exceeding a fourth or a fifth, rarely including a skip of more than a third, and consisting of intervals different from the Western tempered scale. The basic melodic form was strict, but its embellishment displayed the artistry of the oriental musician. The interpretation of the music by the performer was of paramount importance. Portamento, glissandi, and other ornaments were added to the melodic theme by the performer, especially at the beginning and the end, so that the *makam* would have been beyond easy recognition.

Many of the psalm headings are thought to be *makam*—types popular over a relatively long period of time. The headings would have been indications of the melodies to which the designated psalms were sung. E. Werner has pointed out that this practice of adapting older tunes to new words was an ancient practice, found in the music of the Hittites. This idea was carried through into Western music and even into early music of the church. The levitical singers used specific melodies for specific psalms, and through their training in variation and ornamentation were able to adapt the melodic ideas to the length of each verse. Since the Book of Psalms was written over a long period of time, certain *makam* undoubtedly became obscure. In fact, after Psalm 88, no names appear in the headings to indicate melody. It may have been that the later writers and singers of the psalms were no longer familiar with the earlier *makam* and were allowed to select a proper melody for each poem.

There is much discussion and disagreement about the influence of psalm singing in ancient Israel on early Christian music. The music of the ancient Hebrews for the most part has been lost. But as musicologists have studied the music of the Orient, several Jewish communities have been discovered in Yemen, Babylonia, Persia, Buchara, and other places, that left Israel during the dispersion before the destruction of the second temple. These Jews have lived in fairly complete religious and cultural isolation and carried with them the music of their ancestors. Idelsohn has shown rather clearly that many of the melodies of the Yemenite and Babylonian Jews are closely related to Gregorian chants. This discovery indicates the musical influence of the temple and synagogue on early Christian music.

Harmony was completely unknown to the ancient Israelites. Their music was monophonic, but certainly not simple. Singing was usually accompanied by instruments, and ornamentation provided music of great variety and rich colors.

Even though such rhythmic arts as poetry, music, singing, and dancing were included in the Israelite culture, there is no word in biblical Hebrew for rhythm. The concept of beats or counts is a Western concept. C. Sachs describes the oriental idea of rhythm: "What harmony means to the West, the almost breathless change from tension to relaxation, is in the East provided by rhythm. In avoiding the deadly inertia of evenness, rhythm helps an otherwise autonomous melody to breathe in and out." The rhythm of Hebrew poetry is important in trying to understand musical performance in OT times.

While it would be necessary to have an indepth knowledge of the language to interpret the meter of the poetic lines, a few generalizations that can be made. First, accent is the important element in Hebrew rhythm, not the number of syllables in a line. Meter, regular or irregular, is the main characteristic of Hebrew poetic form. With the exception of the pure narrations and pronouncements of Law, most of the OT could be considered poetic under

this definition. Second, some metrical parts of the OT have a definite folksong quality and were obviously meant to be sung. Most of these examples are found in the early history of the Hebrew people (e.g., Miriam's song of deliverance, Deborah and Barak's song of triumph, etc.). Third, other portions of Scripture, while seemingly nonpoetical, show a fairly regular metric structure and probably were meant to be communicated in a chant form. It is thought that the kind of reading of the Law described in Nehemiah 8:8 was a certain type of speech-melody; this powerful rendering of the text made the people weep (v 9). Fourth, the most examples of evenly shaped poems are found in the Book of Psalms. This poetry shows a regular metric structure that remains relatively unchanged within a section of the poem. This would easily allow the singer to use the variation technique on the *makam* for each phrase. Examples of such poems are Psalms 2,5,10,18,111,112; Proverbs 2,3; Job 6,7; and Deuteronomy 32.

Musical Style and Use. The Jewish people seem to have been especially musical. Of course, they were influenced by other ancient cultures, but there is evidence that they were in demand as musicians by other peoples. According to an Assyrian document, King Hezekiah gave as tribute to King Sennacherib many male and female Jewish musicians. The Babylonians demanded the captive Jews to sing and entertain them (cf. Ps 137:3, "Sing us one of the songs of Zion").

A 7th-century BC relief from the wall of Sennacherib's palace at Nineveh depicting three captive lyre players being watched by an Assyrian guard.

Since the OT's purpose was to narrate the relationship between the Jewish nation and God, most of the references to music deal with its place of worship. However, evidence reveals that there was also a large body of secular musical literature. There may have been guilds of poets and singers early in Jewish history. The kinds of songs recorded in the early part of the OT represent a folklike poetry. The song of thanksgiving to the Lord by Moses and the people of Israel after their escape at the Red Sea is a stirring national song. Many descriptions of the biblical writers reflect the spirit of bardic song. This would be logical as these stories were meant to be passed on. Marching songs (2 Chr 20:27,28), work songs (Is 65:8), and songs of triumph (Jgs 5) also indicate a secular body of music.

Music in Worship. The music of the temple in Jerusalem has been romanticized, and the grandeur of the music and musicians have been set as a standard which moderns could never achieve. However, the "grandeur" of the temple music was completely different from Western contemporary concepts.

The singers and musicians were chosen from the tribe of Levi. King David assembled the Levites for a census. Out of the total of 38,000 over the age of 30, 4000 were chosen as musicians. These 4000 were subsequently given specific jobs. "David and the chiefs of the service also set apart for the service certain of the sons of Asaph, and of Heman, and of Jeduthun, who should prophesy with lyres, with harps, and with cymbals. . . . The number of them along with their brethren, who were trained in singing to the Lord, all who were skilful, was two hundred and eighty-eight" (1 Chr 25:1,7). The singers were further divided into 24 groups of 12 singers, who rotated in participating in the weekday, sabbath, and high holy day services.

According to a later source there were minimum and maximum numbers of singers and instrumentalists required at each service. The minimum number of singers was 12, the maximum was unlimited. There had to be in attendance at least two harps but no more than six, at least two flutes but no more than twelve, a minimum of two trumpets with no maximum, and a minimum of nine lyres with no maximum. There was only one player with a pair of cymbals.

A singer was admitted to the levitical choir at the age of 30 following a 5-year apprenticeship (1 Chr 23:3). Five years is a relatively short time considering the amount of material these singers had to memorize (for there was no notation) and the liturgical ritual they had to master; it is speculated that they actually were in training from childhood. The Levites

lived in villages outside the city wall and may have been actively involved in the musical education of their children (Neh 12:29). The Levites performed other duties connected with the sacred service, but the singers were excused from all other duties "for they were on duty day and night" (1 Chr 9:33). Their skills were an important part of the temple worship, and they were able to devote their entire life to the development of their musical ability. A singer served in the choir for 20 years, from age 30 to 50, and the music was of a high quality due to strict discipline and continuous practice and performance.

From the beginning of Jewish formal worship connected with the tabernacle, music and sound was important. In Exodus 28:34,35 the descriptions of Aaron's robe included bells attached to the lower hem which sounded as he entered the holy place. The first liturgical music mentioned in the OT is found in 2 Samuel 6 in the descriptions of the transfer of the ark: David and the Israelites sang, played instruments, and danced to the glory of the Lord. This music bore little resemblance to the stately ceremony described later in Solomon's temple. In 2 Chronicles 7:6, David is given recognition for inventing the musical instruments used in the temple. In the postexilic era levitical singers are mentioned as the descendants of Asaph, the "singing-master" appointed by David (Ezr 2:41; Neh 7:44; 11:22,23). From passages such as these we have a definite indication that liturgical music and organization stemmed from David's time.

The ceremonies in the Jewish temple were organized around the sacrifice. Singing formed an integral part of the sacrificial service and was necessary to validate the sacrificial action. There were special musical settings for each sacrifice, thus the daily burnt, expiatory, and laudatory offerings and libations had individual liturgies. Particular psalms became associated with certain sacrifices, as well as with certain days of the week. The psalm of the day was intoned as the high priest started to pour out the drink offering. The psalm was divided into three sections, each signaled by the blowing of the trumpets, on which signal the people would prostrate themselves. This is the only time the trumpets were used in the regular services; however, they were used together with the other instruments in orchestral fashion on solemn occasions (2 Chr 5:12, 13; 29:26).

Psalm Titles. The collection of 150 lyric poems known as the Book of Psalms contains the most information on music making in ancient Israel. The Psalter contains not only religious songs, but songs that have their roots in secular or popular songs, such as work songs, love songs, and wedding songs. The majority are songs of praise, thanksgiving, prayer, and repentance. There are also historic odes that relate great national events, for example, Psalm 30, "a song at the dedication of the temple," and Psalm 137, which portrays the sufferings of the Jews in captivity.

The psalms were an important part of all the services of the temple; the Psalter became the liturgical hymnal of the Israelites. Worship included an appointed psalm for each day of the week. On the first day of the week, Psalm 24 was sung in remembrance of the first day of creation. Psalm 48 was sung on the second day, Psalm 82 on the third, Psalm 94 on the fourth, Psalm 81 on the fifth, Psalm 93 on the sixth, and Psalm 92 on the sabbath. After the sacrificial offerings, Psalm 105:1–5 was sung at the morning service and Psalm 96 at the evening service. The Hallel psalms (Pss 113–118,120–136, 146–148) were sung during the offering of the paschal lamb at the Passover feast.

While most of the liturgical music was performed by Levites, texts of the psalms suggest that there was also congregational participation. The forms of music found both in synagogal and ecclesiastical chant had their source in the forms of the poetic text of the psalms. The simplest is the plain psalmody sung by one person (e.g., Pss 3–5,46). In responsorial psalmody the soloist is answered by the choir (e.g., Ps 67:1,2; the soloist sang verse one and the choir answered with verse two). Antiphonal psalmody involves two groups singing alternately (e.g., Ps 103:20–22). The congregation would chant a refrain such as appears in Psalm 80. "Restore us, O God; let thy face shine, that we may be saved!" recurs throughout the psalm.

Even though the synagogue had no altar for sacrifice, psalm singing retained an important place. After the Romans destroyed the temple, the worship heritage of the Jews could have been lost if the customs, including musical customs, had not become an integral part of synagogue worship.

The most enigmatic part of the psalms are the headings that are not part of the poetic text. The first question is whether these should even be considered as superscripts. Greek, Latin, Hebrew, and other ancient languages were written in such a way that the text ran together without any break between chapters or paragraphs. This means that the verses, and even the division of the psalms themselves, were partially determined by copyists, chiefly the Masoretes. There is some question as to which psalms the extrapoetic texts actually belong; they may actually be subscripts instead of superscripts. Sumerian and Babylonian poetry had information such as the name of the author, the musical instrument used for accompaniment, the tune, the purpose, and such listed at the end of the poem. Hence, some of the headings may actually be endings.

The indications at the beginning of a psalm fall into three categories. They are either musical terms giving direction for the actual performance, musical cues designating the tune to which the psalm would be sung, or comments indicating the function of the psalm. These terms have been interpreted in various ways.

Originally these headings may have been marginal notes for the choir leaders. Realizing that these terms were not related to the psalm text proper, early biblical scribes may not have been overly careful with their placement in the text, which may explain some of the discrepancies among the early manuscripts— why certain words are left out in some, and why terms assigned to only a few psalms may have been indicated on more.

All but 50 of the psalms contain a proper name in the heading. These names possibly indicate the author; other commentators, interpreting the preposition appearing before the names to mean "for," think the names are a dedication. Thus the title would be "A Psalm for David," not "A Psalm of David." In most cases this would be more appropriate with the names of Asaph, Heman, Ethan, and especially the sons of Korah, where it would make better sense for the psalm to be written for rather than by the family. Seventy-three psalms have David's name in the heading, hence the common reference to the Psalter as the Psalms of David. Twelve include the name of Asaph, 11 the children of Korah, 2 Solomon, and 1 each contains Moses, Heman, and Ethan.

Musical Terms. Numerous musical terms are included in the superscriptions to cue the kind of instrumental accompaniment, mood, and style of performance.

Alamoth is one of the most controversial terms found in the psalm headings. It appears at the beginning of Psalm 46 and also in 1 Chronicles 15:20. One meaning for the Hebrew word is "maiden," and musicologists interpret this as an instruction that the psalm should be sung in the range of the female singing voice. The reference in Chronicles is to harps in the range of women's voices. This interpretation does not seem to fit Psalm 46, but if we look at the preceding psalm and read the term as a subscript, it becomes logical. Psalm 45 is a song of love, actually a nuptial ode; it would be natural for women to sing the second half (vv 10–17). While there is little mention of women singing in the temple, there is speculation that young boys in training may have sung along with the levitical singers. Also this may be a case where the term appears only once in the modern text, but may have been used more often in the original.

Gittith is a term found in the superscriptions of Psalms 8, 81, and 84. The most common explanation is that it is a collective term for stringed instruments that would have accompanied these psalms.

Mahalath has been left in its original Hebrew form by early translators and is found in the headings of Psalms 53 and 88. It may have roots in the Hebrew *mahaleh* "sickness" or *mahol* "dance," though neither of these words can be related to the psalm texts. Another explanation is a musical one. *Mahalath* may come from the word *halal* meaning "to pierce," implying that the psalm was to be accompanied with pipes.

Maskil (KJV *Maschil*) appears in the headings of 13 psalms (32,42,44,45,52–55,74,78,88,89, 142). It is also found in Psalm 47:8. The term is probably derived from the verb *sakal*, "to have insight or comprehension," but there is no agreement among commentators. By looking at the psalms themselves, their didactic nature and the structure of stanzas and refrains, musicologists conclude the term represents a song of praise, possibly sung by a soloist with participation by the choir.

Menazzeah appears in the heading of 55 psalms. It appears 52 times in the first three books of Psalms (Pss 1–89), not at all in book four (Pss 90–106), and 3 times in book five (Pss 107–150). The most common translation in modern translations is "to the Choirmaster." The word is derived from the Hebrew verb *nazzah*, appearing in 1 Chronicles 23:4 and Ezra 3:8,9 in the sense of "administering." In 1 Chronicles 15:21 the word is found in relation to leading or directing song in the temple. *Menazzeah* relates to the choirmaster and represents the singer chosen to lead the music who probably was involved in rehearsing and instructing. It is now assumed that *menazzeah* indicates the psalm was to be sung partially or entirely by a soloist. This is evidenced by the change in some texts from "I" where the soloist sang, to "we" where the choir or congregation sang. Psalm 5 is an example of a text divided for solo and choral singing: verses 1–3 solo; verses 4–6 choral; verses 7,8 solo; verses 9,10 choral; and verses 11,12 end the psalm with the combined soloist and choir.

Miktam (KJV *Michtam*) is another term which has no clear musical meaning, due mainly to the fact that its etymology is unknown. It occurs in Psalms 16 and 56–60, all of which have a character of lamentation or supplication. In a musical sense, it probably meant that a certain well-known tune was to be selected as the melody of the psalm.

Mizmor is found nowhere else in the Bible; it is included in the superscriptions of 57 psalms. It probably indicated a song accompanied by melodic instruments as opposed to a dance song accompanied by rhythmic instruments.

Neginah appears in the superscriptions of Psalms 4,6,54,55,61,67, and 76. The term *neginah* and its plural *neginoth* are found in Psalm 77:7; Lamentations 5:14; Isaiah 38:20; and Habakkuk 3:19. *Neginah*, from the Hebrew root *naggen* "to touch the strings," instructs that stringed instruments accompany the singing.

Nehiloth is found only in the introduction to Psalm 5. The origin of the word is problematic. It could come from the verb *nahal*, "to possess or inherit," or more feasibly from *hala*, meaning "to pierce." The latter implies the idea of a pierced instrument (the flute or pipe) to be used for accompaniment.

Sheminith appears in Psalms 6 and 12 and also in 1 Chronicles 15:21. The Hebrew word means literally "over the eighth." Some scholars feel it had something to do with an octave, but the Hebrew musical language probably did not include a musical unit divided into eight parts. Other scholars interpret *sheminith* as meaning an eight-stringed instrument. A more logical interpretation comes from examining its use in 1 Chronicles. In 15:20 the instructions are for musicians to play the harps according to *alamoth* and in verse 21 to play the lyres according to *sheminith*. Here the terms *alamoth* and *sheminith* seem to be used in opposition. If *alamoth* implies a register of the female voice, then *sheminith* would imply a lower register. Thus, it may have been an instruction to use a lower pitched instrument for accompaniment.

Ancient Melodies. Many psalms contain headings that are not direct musical references, but are cue words to suggest well-known tunes. They probably refer either to names or the first words of popular secular *makams* whose melodic patterns were used in singing the psalm. Many biblical scholars have tried to find hidden meaning in these headings, but most musicologists believe these are simply references or introductions to melodies.

Aijeleth Shahar, in Psalm 22 (KJV), is translated "according to The Hind of the Dawn" (RSV), and "To the tune of 'The Doe of the Morning'" (NIV).

Al-taschith, in Psalms 57–59,75 (KJV), is translated "according to Do Not Destroy" (RSV).

Jonath-elem-rechokim, in Psalm 56 (KJV), is translated "according to The Dove on the Far-off Terebinths" (RSV), and "To the tune of 'A Dove on Distant Oaks' " (NIV).

Mahalath Leannoth, in Psalm 88, is translated "The Suffering of Affliction" (NIV, mg).

Muth-labben, in Psalm 9, is translated "To the tune of 'The Death of the Son' " (NIV).

Shoshannim, in Psalms 45 and 69 (KJV), is translated "To the tune of 'Lilies' " (NIV).

Shoshannim-eduth, in Psalm 80 (KJV), is translated "To the tune of 'The Lilies of the Covenant' " (NIV).

Shushan Eduth, in Psalm 60, is translated "To the tune of 'The Lily of the Covenant'" (NIV).

These melody types appear only in the first three books of the Psalter, and this may imply that these popular *makam* had fallen into disuse by the time the final books of the Psalter were written. Other *makam*-types had probably become popular, and the authors, realizing the relatively short life of a popular tune, did not include them in the headings of the psalms but left the choice up to the performer.

Psalm Varieties. Some of the notes in the psalm headings are indications of the type or variety of psalm.

Hazkir is found in the headings of Psalms 38 and 70. According to the Targum, this is an indication that the psalm was sung at the sacrificial rite called *askara* and is translated "for a memorial offering."

Lammed appears in the superscription of Psalm 60 in the phrase *le-lammed*, translated "to teach." According to tradition, this was a psalm, though undoubtedly not the only one, taught to young people as part of their education. This is another example of a term which may have been omitted from other psalms in later versions of the Psalter.

Shiggaion is in the heading of Psalm 7 and also in Habakkuk 3:1. The word probably comes from the Hebrew verb *shagah*, "to wander," but may also be connected with the Assyrian liturgical term *shigu*, which represented a plaintive song in several stanzas. Biblical scholars have assumed *shiggaion* (plural *shigionoth*) was a lament or penitential song.

Shir is the simplest word for "song" and was probably used in the headings at an early stage of the Psalter; usually found with *mizmor* (13 times). Fifteen psalms have this heading. It was probably the term for a specific type of praise song, usually performed by the choir.

Shir Hamaalot and *Shir Lamaalot* occur in the headings of Psalms 120–134, which are often referred to as the Psalms of Ascent (KJV Psalms of Degrees). Most explanations offered relate to the fact that the temple was situated on a high ground. Often these 15 psalms are associated with the 15 steps leading from the Court of the Women to the Court of the Israelites, but most contemporary scholars believe the idea of "going up" referred to the pilgrims' journey to Jerusalem to worship at the temple. These psalms are short, with popular appeal, making them appropriate for singing during the journey.

Shir Hanukkat Habayit is found only in the heading of Psalm 30. This phrase tells that the psalm was to be used for the dedication or re-dedication of the house of God.

Shir-yedidot appears only in Psalm 45. It refers to a love song that was probably sung at wedding ceremonies.

Tefillah is a common term for "prayer" and appears in the headings of Psalms 17,90,102, and 142, and also in Habukkuk 3:1. The word probably refers to a specific form of poetic prayer.

Selah is one of the most frequently used, but most enigmatic, terms found in the Book of Psalms. It occurs in 39 psalms, appearing a total of 71 times in the Psalter, 67 times within the text, and 4 times at the end of a psalm. It is most frequent in the first three books. In the first book *selah* appears in 9 psalms; in the second book, 17 psalms; in the third book, 11 psalms. In the 4th book it is not found at all and in the 5th book in only 2 psalms. Thirty-one of these psalms also include the term *menazzeah* in their superscriptions, which implies that they were sung by a soloist and choir. Most commonly *selah* is interpreted as a signal for a break in the singing and possibly for an instrumental interlude. It never appears at the beginning of a psalm but only in the middle of the text or at the end. The regularity of its appearance within a psalm is not consistent, and in only a few instances do these divisions break the psalm into equal sections. Because of the random placement of the term, some scholars believe that, like the headings, *selah* was not always carefully copied into the text. It may have been a note appearing only in the texts of the musicians, which would explain this inconsistency. An explanation of *selah* is found in the talmudic tradition: "Ben Azra clashed the symbal and the Levites broke forth into singing. When they reached a break in the singing they blew upon the trumpets and the people prostrated themselves; at every break there was a blowing of the trumpet and at every blowing of the trumpet a prostration. This was the rite of the daily whole-offering in the service of the House of our God." *Selah* then would be an instruction for the musicians that the singing was to cease and the instrumentalists were to play.

The term *higgaion selah* appears once in Psalm 9:17. The word *higgaion* comes from the root *hagah*, "to murmur, to growl, to produce a low sound." This may have been an instruction for the interlude to be more subdued than a normal *selah*.

Music in the New Testament. *First-Century Influences.*

THE SYNAGOGUE. By the time of Christ, the synagogue had become the chief place of worship for the Jewish people. It began as a place for study of the Law, but gradually became the center of worship for Jews unable to attend the temple. The liturgical service of the temple could not be duplicated in the synagogue as there was no sacrificial rite and the music could not be exactly reproduced as there were no trained levitical singers. Scholars do not agree about the amount of continuity between the music of the temple and the music of the synagogue, but there is evidence that certain musical practices did remain constant between the two places of worship.

Information on the customs and rituals of the synagogue come from talmudic writings. The musical elements of worship in the synagogue were the chanting of Scripture, psalmody, postbiblical prayers, and spiritual songs. The choral singing of the temple was replaced by a single cantor. The cantor was a layman who, according to tradition, had to have the following qualifications: "He had to be well educated, gifted with a sweet voice, of humble personality, recognized by the community, conversant with Scripture and all the prayers; he must not be a rich man, for his prayers should come from his heart." The most important job of the cantor was the cantillation of the Pentateuch and the Prophets. A series of accents and punctuations, forerunners of actual musical notation, were indications for the cantor in the musical interpretation of the Scripture.

Psalm singing was gradually transplanted from the temple to synagogue, which in turn influenced the early Christian church. Through the work of Idelsohn especially, it has been proven that Gregorian psalm tones have their roots in Hebrew psalmody.

GREEK AND ROMAN CULTURES. While both the temple and the synagogue were familiar to the early Christians (Acts 2:46,47; 3:1; 5:42; 9:20; 18:4; etc.), the Greek and Roman cultures also played a major part in shaping the young church. Hellenistic influences by the time of Christ had long been felt in the Middle East, and, while it was strongly opposed by some Jewish leaders, the Greek arts had permeated Jewish culture. Greek philosophers considered music a cathartic force that could lead humans into metaphysical knowledge. This understanding led to the belief that music had a moral substance that could influence man to either good or evil. If this philosophy had to-

tally encompassed Judeo-Christian thought, certainly Paul would have encouraged the use of music in the spread of the gospel. However, Paul's omission of this theory implies that the Judeo-Christian world at that time had rejected the Greek ideal, at least in part.

While the Jewish rabbis considered music an art form for the praise of God, and the Greek philosophers thought of it as a powerful moral force in creation, the Romans considered music mainly as entertainment. The music of the Roman games was neither religious nor philosophic and, from the accounts of witnesses, it was not technically exceptional. In the Roman Empire musicians were given a lower status and looked on as mere entertainers. One reason the early church did not include instrumental music in their worship was in reaction to the debased secular use of instruments by the Romans.

In the NT. The authors of the NT, unlike those of the OT, were not as concerned with ritual or liturgy. The relatively few mentions of music can be divided into five categories.

1. Most references to music are found in the eschatological visions and prophetic passages scattered throughout the NT, but most frequently in the Book of Revelation (also Mt 24:31; 1 Cor 15:52; 1 Thes 4:16; Heb 12:19). Many of these descriptions have a direct association with musical references in the OT (e.g., the use of harps and trumpets and the singing of the Hallelujah). But the value of many of the passages in Revelation comes from their literary style. These doxological and psalmlike passages were probably spontaneous "spiritual songs" composed by the young church (e.g., Rv 5:9,10).

2. One of the few mentions of instruments is the use of flutes at a wake (Mt 9:23).

3. As in the OT, music is associated with feasting and merrymaking (e.g., the return of the prodigal son, Lk 15:25).

4. Five passages mention music metaphorically (Mt 6:2; 11:17; Lk 7:32; 1 Cor 13:1; 14:7,8). The most well-known of these is Paul's celebration of love in 1 Corinthians 13. The denunciation of the gong and cymbals must be understood in light of the attitude of the early Christians toward the music of the Pharisees. Here the signal instruments of the temple were used to represent pompous display of religious pietism. Passages such as 1 Corinthians 14:7,8 have been used as arguments for the supremacy of vocal music in the church, but these references must be understood in the historical context of the supremacy of vocal music in the temple and synagogue, and also in light of the reaction of the early Christians to the pagan Roman use of instrumental music.

5. The passages that mention religious or liturgical music are often more conceptual than literal. Two parallel passages describing the last supper (Mt 26:30; Mk 14:26) mention that Christ and his disciples sang a hymn. This is the only direct account of Jesus singing, but it is probable that when he read in the synagogue he did so in the accepted vocal style (Lk 4:16–20). There is much controversy surrounding the actual events at the last supper, but we can assume that the hymn sung was a traditional Jewish hymn, probably associated with the Passover.

From the account in Acts 16:25 we know that Paul and Silas sang hymns while in jail. Paul gives instruction for music making in 1 Corinthians 14:15,26 in terms of a balance between rationalism and emotion. And, as with all the gifts of the Spirit, Paul asks that singing be done for edification.

In two similar passages (Eph 5:19; Col 3:16) Paul groups together three musical terms—psalms, hymns, and spiritual songs. The singing of psalms was an obvious carryover from the synagogue, and we can assume that the early Christian psalm singing followed the Jewish style. The term for hymns probably refers to poetic texts, possibly modeled after the psalms, but in praise of Christ. Spiritual songs may refer to a spontaneous, ecstatic form of musical prayer, possibly wordless (perhaps related to glossolalia), in a style which was popular in mystical Judaism. These outbursts of song were probably melismatic (sung on one tone) and are perhaps the forerunners of the later Alleluia chant.

Hymnody in the New Testament. It can be assumed that the early Christians composed hymns in praise of Christ. Logically, most of the hymns found in the NT are based on Hebrew poetic psalm forms, but there is Greek and Latin influence also. The hymns from the Gospel of Luke have become well-known canticles adopted by the church: the Magnificat (1:46–55), the Benedictus (vv 68–79), the Gloria (2:14) and the Nunc dimittis (vv 29–32). While patterned after the psalms of the OT, these hymns are full of confidence in the salvation of Christ and in his imminent return. Other christological hymns found in the NT include the prologue to the Gospel of John; Ephesians 2:14–16; Philippians 2:6–11; Colossians 1:15–20; 1 Timothy 3:16; Hebrews 1:3; and 1 Peter 3:18–22. These texts are set apart by their formal poetic structure and their "ardor of enthusiasm."

In Philippians 2:6–11 we find a deviation from the Hebrew poetic structure and spirit. The passage lacks any parallelism between lines, either in poetic reference, length, or accented syllables. While it may have been a hymn of the early church, it could not have been sung in a traditional Jewish psalm *makam*.

Musical Instruments. In contrast to the detailed accounts of liturgical music in the OT, the descriptions of the musical instruments themselves are rather sparse. Because of the injunction of the second commandment, interpreted by the Hebrews as discouraging pictorial representations, there are few drawings of Hebrew instruments. In addition to the instruments used in the temple, the Book of Daniel lists six instruments played in King Nebuchadnezzar's court.

The ancient Hebrew made certain distinctions among the instruments, not on musical, but on ethical grounds. Some instruments were considered "unclean" and were not allowed in temple worship.

Stringed Instruments. The stringed instruments were favored by the Jewish people. In many ancient civilizations the strings were considered the most masculine and noble (e.g., David playing the lyre); the Jews considered them the most suitable for accompaniment in the temple service. The term *minim* is used in Psalm 150:4 to designate the entire family of stringed instruments in the praise of God.

Asor appears three times in the Book of Psalms (33:2; 92:3; 144:9). Although the word derives from a Hebrew root, meaning "ten," the actual description of the instrument remains unclear. The most common theory identifies it with the Phoenician zither having 10 strings; it is perhaps the lute.

Kathros was a stringed instrument included in the list of those played at Nebuchadnezzar's court and was probably a kind of lyre (Dn 3:5,7,10,15).

Kinnor is the most frequently mentioned instrument in the Bible, found in 42 places. It is often called David's Harp and is the most beloved instrument of the Jewish people. We can say with reasonable certainty that it was a lyre and not a harp. The strings, the number of which is not clear, were made of sheep tripe and the sounding box was at the bottom of the instrument. It is not certain whether it was played with a plectrum or with bare hands, but the specific comment that David "played it with his hand" (1 Sm 16:23) may have implied that this was unusual and not the common practice. The biblical descriptions of the sound of the *kinnor* include "pleasant" and "sweet" (Ps 81:2). The *kinnor* was played mainly in worship, but also in celebrations (Is 5:12), for state occasions (1 Sm 10:5; 2 Sm 6:5), and by shepherds (1 Sm 16:16). It remained silent during times of mourning (Is 14:11; Ps 137:2). The term is correctly translated "lyre" in the RSV (except in two places, Ps 150:3; Is

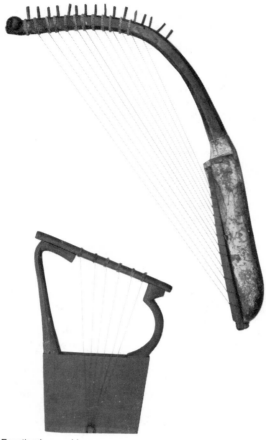

Egyptian lyre and harp.

23:16, where it is rendered "harp" for no apparent reason).

Nebel was another stringed instrument (literally meaning "skin" or "skin bottle") mentioned 27 times in Scripture. Its shape was probably similar to a bottle with the belly-shaped sounding box on the bottom. It definitely belongs to the family of harps (2 Sm 6:5; 1 Kgs 10:12; Neh 12:27; Ps 57:8; Am 5:23) and may have been influenced by similar Egyptian instruments. The *nebel* was probably played without a plectrum and was a larger and louder instrument than the *kinnor*. It is normally translated as harp in most modern English translations (KJV psaltery, viol).

Psantrin or *pesanterin* was a Greek instrument, mentioned in the description of King Nebuchadnezzar's orchestra. It may have resembled a dulcimer, having strings played with hammers (Dn 3:5,7,10,15; RSV mistranslates as "bagpipe").

Sabcha or *sabbeka*, identical with the Greek *sambyke* and the Roman *sambuca*, was a stringed instrument (RSV trigon, KJV sackbut) played in the Babylonian court. It was a tri-angle with four strings, having a high and harsh tone (Dn 3:5,7,10,15).

Wind Instruments. The wind instruments can be divided into two groups, pipes and horns.

Halil is mentioned only six times in the Bible but was referred to frequently by postbiblical writers. This kind of piped instrument was similar to the Greek *aulos* (Mt 9:23; 1 Cor 14:7; Rv 18:22), a primitive oboe, rendered "flute" in many translations. The root word *halal* means "to pierce," thus the meaning "hollow tube." The early pipes were made from reed-like plants. The *halil* had a double-reed mouthpiece and probably produced a shrill and penetrating sound. It was connected with joyful events such as banquets (Is 5:12) and prophetic frenzies (1 Sm 10:5), but its tone was also associated with wailing and mourning (Jer 48:36).

Hatzotzrot was a sort of trumpet. Modern scholars have more information about this horn than many of its ancient Hebrew counterparts. The triumphal arch built by Titus in Rome includes depictions of the captured implements of the temple, among which are two trumpets. The form of these horns may have been influenced by the Israelites' knowledge of Egyptian trumpets. Similar instruments were also known in Assyria, in the Hittite Empire, and in Greece. Moses was commanded to make two silver trumpets (Nm 10:2) and playing these instruments became the exclusive privilege of the descendants of Aaron. These trumpets were made of silver or gold, about a yard long, but narrow, with a pronounced bell. The descendants of the *hatzotzrot* are the herald trumpets. Numbers 10:10 says the trumpets were used "for a memorial before... God." Trumpets and horns were used to signal the gathering of the congregation to the tent of meeting, to sound alarm, to alert the camps to move forward, and to announce when war was at hand. The *hatzotzrot* became an important part of the temple service. There were at least two trumpets in the daily services, but at high holidays the number could be increased indefinitely. "Cornet" is a KJV mistranslation for "horn" (1 Chr 15:28; 2 Chr 15:14; Ps 98:6; Dn 3:5,7,10,15; Hos 5:8).

Mashroqita, considered by modern scholars to be a Pan's Pipe similar to the Greek *syrinx*, this instrument is included in the list of orchestral instruments of King Nebuchadnezzar's court (Dn 3:5,7,10,15).

Shophar is mentioned in the Bible 72 times, more than any other Hebrew instrument. It is the only instrument of ancient Israel which survives in its original form and is still used in Jewish liturgy. The early *shophar* was curved like a ram's horn, but the later form was straight with a bend near the bell of the horn. There is some question whether any of the hornlike instruments can actually be considered musical instruments. The *shophar* could produce two, maybe three tones, and was used for giving signals, not for playing music. It was used in such religious ceremonies as the transfer of the ark (2 Sm 6:15; 1 Chr 15:28), the renewal of the covenant by King Asa (2 Chr 15:14), thanksgiving to God (Ps 98:6; 150:3), and was blown at the new moon and the beginning of the jubilee year. Its secular use included such royal occasions as Absalom's accession to the throne (2 Sm 15:10), Solomon's anointing as king (1 Kgs 1:34), and Jehu's accession to the throne (2 Kgs 9:13).

Sumponia, an uncertain term included in Daniel 3. Many commentators have interpreted it as a bagpipe (RSV), but musicologists strongly argue that at the time of King Nebuchadnezzar there was no such instrument. It has been suggested that *sumponia* was not a musical instrument at all, but signified the playing of the entire ensemble. This could come from the Greek root *symphonia*, meaning "sounding together." The word is also found in Luke 15:25, where it is translated as "music."

Ugab, a more flutelike instrument, is mentioned in Scripture four times (Gn 4:21; Jb 21:12; 30:31; Ps 150:4, KJV mistranslates as "organ"). It is only in Psalm 150 that the *ugab* is connected with a sacred occasion.

Percussion Instruments. Most of the accounts of percussion instruments are found in the early history of the Hebrew people. They were gradually eliminated from the temple orchestra, perhaps because of their association with idolatrous practices.

Mena anim was a loud metal rattle, constructed with a frame carrying loose rings. It is included in a list of instruments in 2 Samuel 6:5 (RSV castanet; KJV mistranslates as "cornet"). It was likely a form of the *sistrum*, an Egyptian instrument.

Pamonim were the bells attached to the lower hem of the priest's garment, described in Exodus 28:33,34 and 39:25,26. They were not loud but indicated the position of the high priest as he entered the sanctuary.

Shalishim, often translated as *sistrum* or *timbrel*, is a kind of rattle. It is not clear whether this term actually refers to a musical instrument. It appears in 1 Samuel 18:6 as part of the reception of King Saul and David after the battle with the Philistines.

Toph or *tof* was an instrument used mainly by women, but there are some indications that men might have played it as well (1 Sm 10:5, KJV tabret; 2 Sm 6:5; 1 Chr 13:8). The mention of this kind of hand drum appears 15 times in the Bible. A wooden or metal hoop was covered with the skin of a ram or wild goat and was played with the hand. It is not clear whether the *toph* had skin on just one side or two. Some commentators have described it as a tambourine or timbrel, but there is no indication that it included jangles. The *toph* was used in merrymaking and was rather loud (Ex 15:20; Ps 81:2).

Zelzelim or *meziltayim* were cymbals. Both of these words come from the Hebrew root *zala*, meaning "to resound" or "to tingle," and the noun forms represent the instrument known as the cymbal. Sometimes these terms are wrongly translated as "castanets." These were the only percussion instruments included in the temple music and were always referred to in a dual form, suggesting a pair of cymbals, but played by one man. Cymbals made of metal were known to most ancient cultures. They appear for the first time in the Bible when the ark was transferred to Jerusalem (2 Sm 6:5; 1 Chr 13:8). Later they were played in the temple by the leaders of the levitical singers (1 Chr 15:19). The function of the cymbals was less musical than liturgical, being used as signals for the singing to begin and between the sections of the psalms. Two different kinds of cymbals are mentioned in Psalm 150, but their difference is not clear, probably involving either size or material.

Implications for Christian Worship. The NT says little about music as a part of Christian worship but, unlike some of the more zealous reformers who interpreted this as an indication that music should not be a part of worship, the NT must be looked at in light of the OT. The apostles were active in temple and synagogue worship and certainly did not abandon the musical forms of Jewish culture. However, the early church, under persecution, was unable to sustain a complicated musical liturgy, since Christians often met in secret and in their homes. The promise of the NT is the fulfillment of the Law: the coming of Jesus, the Son of God. In light of this, Jesus' intention was not to ignore or abandon entirely OT liturgical practices.

It is clear from the Bible that music in itself did not carry any moral implications. The OT prophets often referred to music making in their judgments; however, they were not condemning the music, but the musician. And in 1 Corinthians 13, Paul is not, as some commentators have stated, condemning music, but the idea of pharisaical pietism.

According to the Bible music is an important expression of man and was a functional part of the everyday life of the ancient Hebrews. The OT traces the development of musical complexity and its importance in the worship of God. The God of Jacob did not demand loud noises to attract his attention and the music of the temple became a free expression of the Hebrews in praise of God. The Bible makes it clear that vocal music is most important in the worship life of the church. While the Bible does not condemn instrumental music, the edification of the body of the church through the word is the primary function of church music. According to Paul, music must contribute to the growth of the church in the same way as the gifts of the Spirit.

MARY HOPPER

See CHURCH; FEASTS AND FESTIVALS OF ISRAEL; PSALMS, BOOK OF; SINGERS IN THE TEMPLE; SYNAGOGUE; TABERNACLE, TEMPLE; ISRAEL, RELIGION OF.

Bibliography. P. Gradenwitz, *The Music of Israel: Its Rise and Growth Through 5000 Years;* C.H. Kraeling and L. Mowry, "Music in the Bible," *New Oxford History of Music,* vol 1; C. Sachs, *The History of Musical Instruments* and *The Rise of Music in the Ancient World East and West;* A. Sendrey, *Music in Ancient Israel;* J.A. Smith, "The Ancient Synagogue, the Early Church and Singing," *Music and Letters,* vol 65, pp 1–16; E. Werner, "Music," *Interpreters Dictionary of the Bible,* vol 3, pp 457–76 and *The Sacred Bridge.*

Musician. *See* MUSIC AND MUSICAL INSTRUMENTS; TRADES AND OCCUPATIONS.

Mustard. Herb noted especially for its small seeds (Mt 13:31).

See PLANTS.

Muster Gate. Jerusalem gate located opposite the house of the temple servants and the merchants during the days of Nehemiah (Neh 3:31; KJV Miphkad Gate; NIV Inspection Gate). Its exact location is uncertain. Some suggest that it was a temple gate or a gate in the wall of the old city of David.

See JERUSALEM.

Muth-labben. Hebrew phrase in the title of Psalm 9, translated "To the tune of 'The Death of the Son'" (NIV); perhaps a familiar ancient melody to which the psalm was performed.

See MUSIC AND MUSICAL INSTRUMENTS.

Myra. Port city on the southern coast of Asia Minor in the province of Lycia, identified with the modern Demre in Turkey. According to Acts 27:5,6, Paul and his military escort briefly stopped here to change ships on their journey to Rome where Paul was to stand trial.

Myrrh. Fragrant gum resin obtained from various shrubs.

See PLANTS.

Myrtle. Evergreen shrub with small leaves and scented flowers (Neh 8:15; Is 41:19).

See PLANTS.

Mysia. Region in northwest Asia Minor (modern Turkey). It had a long history, leading up to its annexation into the Roman Empire in 133 BC as part of the province of Asia. For about 150 years before that it had been part of the kingdom of Pergamum. The travel account in Acts 16:7,8 indicates that the apostle Paul passed through this region on his second missionary journey, but did not preach there.

See PERGAMUM, PERGAMOS.

Mystery. Counsel, or secret plan, which God shares only with his people. In most biblical passages it relates to the wise counsel of God in his guidance of history to its destiny. The most specific and significant application of the concept of mystery is to the plan of God regarding the death of Christ. It does not refer to a secret that God is unwilling to tell or to something so obscure that it could not be understood even if told.

The passages in which its theological meaning is most clearly seen (among over 30 occurrences in Scripture) are: Daniel 3:18–28; 4:6 (Septuagint); Matthew 13:11; Mark 4:11; Luke 8:10; Romans 11:25; 16:25; 1 Corinthians 2:7; 4:1; 15:51; Ephesians 1:9; 3:3–6,9–12; Colossians 1:26–29; 2:2; 2 Thessalonians 2:7; 1 Timothy 3:9,16; Revelation 1:20; 10:7; 17:5–18.

In the passages in Daniel, the emphasis is on the revelation that God gave Daniel concerning the content and meaning of King Nebuchadnezzar's dream about the future. It is important to note here that the dream was about what God was going to do; that "no wise man, enchanter, magician or diviner" (2:27) could explain it; and that "there is a God in heaven who reveals mysteries" (v 28).

Scholarly studies in recent years have determined that similar themes are found in other Jewish writings, including the Dead Sea Scrolls. The stress is on the decisions God has made about the future, especially the endtime. The world wrestles with such matters as the problem of evil (i.e., Why, if God is both good and powerful, do people still suffer?). The believer also identifies with these problems, but knows that God has his providential plans and that one day he will make all things clear. The way God will bring vindication for those who are wronged in this world and judgment to those who do wrong is part of the content of the "mystery," and was a major emphasis in the writings around the time of Christ. God controls the affairs of the universe. The nations will eventually fulfill his purposes.

Matthew 13:11; Mark 4:11; and Luke 8:10 are part of the parables of the kingdom. The kingdom itself is related to the final climactic work of God in history. This is seen in some of the imagery of the parables, such as the harvest, which symbolizes future judgment. Therefore the word "mystery" is appropriate and significant here. In the immediate context Jesus is explaining why he uses parables. They both vividly illustrate truth and conceal truth from those who are not receptive to it. Therefore the word "mystery" (plural in Mt and Lk) describes the inner meaning of Jesus' teaching about the kingdom. Those who accept the message will know its meaning; those who do not will lose not only the meaning but apparently also the opportunity to hear and respond to the message of salvation (Mt 13:12–15).

Another aspect of this passage lies in the unasked question as to why, if the Messiah has come, evil still persists in the world. The servants in one of the parables wanted to pull up the weeds, symbolizing evil or evil persons, but were told to allow them to grow until the time of harvest, that is, judgment (Mt 13:24–30). The persistence of evil in the world and the way God will eventually deal with it is one of the "mysteries."

Romans 11:25 occurs in the large section (chs 9–11) that deals with the people of Israel and their future. Once again the issue concerns a present problem and its future resolution. In this case the problem is the unbelief of Israel. The "hardening in part" during the present time is called a "mystery" (11:25). God's purposes will not be thwarted, however, "and so all Israel will be saved" (v 26). This emphasis on the purposes of God is closely intertwined with the concept of the "mystery" and is basic to this entire passage.

Romans 16:25 is broader in its scope, connecting the "revelation of the mystery hidden for long ages past" with Paul's "gospel and the proclamation of Jesus Christ." Here the focus is more closely on the meaning of the death of Christ.

God's "secret wisdom" is mentioned in 1 Corinthians 2:7. The context is the message of the cross that Paul preaches. This message is foolishness to those who consider themselves wise but are lost, and it is the "foolishness" of what is preached that brings salvation to believers (1:18–25). Paul does not attempt to proclaim worldly "wisdom," but he does declare a "message of wisdom" to those who are spiritually mature (2:6). To these he speaks the "secret wisdom," or, literally, "wisdom in a secret" (v 7). This passage clearly connects the basic concept of "mystery" as the counsel of God, with the death of Christ as the means of salvation. It also connects mystery with the process of history ("the rulers of this age" in v 8) and with the sweep of God's purposes from OT times into the future (quoting from Is in v

9). Verse 10 emphasizes the fact that God has indeed revealed these mysteries to us.

In 1 Corinthians 4:1 Paul again speaks from the context of a contrast between God's wisdom and that of the world (3:18–23). He speaks not only of secret things or mysteries but introduces the concept of stewardship. He has been entrusted with the revelation of God's mystery and must be faithful in his ministry of declaring it. This theme will reappear in Ephesians 3:2–6.

Paul returns to the relationship of mystery and the endtime in 1 Corinthians 15:51. The earlier passage (2:9–16) showed that human knowledge cannot possibly anticipate what God has planned, but God has revealed this mystery to believers. A major aspect of this revealed mystery is the way in which the faithful will be brought into the presence of God: "We shall not all sleep, but we shall all be changed—in a flash, in the twinkling of an eye, at the last trumpet" (15:51,52). The other references to mystery in 1 Corinthians occur in the broad context of chapters 12–14 dealing with spiritual gifts, which include receiving divine revelation, so the term "mysteries" in 13:2 and 14:2 is appropriate.

Ephesians opens with a series of statements about God's purpose in history culminating in the universal headship of Christ (1:10). These statements include such terms as "chose," "destined," "will," "purpose," "plan," and "counsel." This is clearly the range of ideas associated with the word "mystery" in ancient Jewish writings and these ideas shed light on Paul's use of the summary expression "And he made known to us the mystery of his will" (v 9).

Part of God's purpose was to form a body of believers, reconciled to himself and to each other through the cross (Eph 2:14–18). In this body, Jewish and gentile believers have been made "members together of one body and sharers together in the promise in Christ Jesus," a new phase of God's revealed plan, which Paul here calls a "mystery" (3:6). As noted above, Paul himself has a responsibility to minister the truth of this "mystery" faithfully (vv 2–5; cf. 1 Cor 4:1–5).

Colossians continues to show Paul's sense of responsibility regarding this "mystery," which is now identified with the "word of God" (1:25–29). Once again there is the idea of the span of history linked with the mystery that is known only by revelation, "the mystery that has been kept hidden for ages and generations, but is now disclosed to the saints" (v 26). As in Ephesians, the church is the locus for the working out of God's mystery, "which is Christ in you [i.e., among you believers], the hope of glory" (v 27). This Christ is proclaimed in wisdom, so that believers may reach mature completion in him (v 28). The Colossian believers are asked to pray for Paul as he preaches this "mystery" (4:3).

It is made clear in 1 Timothy 3:16 that the "mystery of godliness" includes the basic elements associated with the "mystery," such as its manifestation in the world and ultimate vindication. However, this grand plan of God does not unfold without opposition. In connection with the coming of the endtime, Paul again mentions a mystery. This time it is a dark mystery, called the "secret power of lawlessness" (2 Thes 2:7). A similar evil force, "Babylon the Great, the Mother of Prostitutes," is introduced in the Book of Revelation with the word "mystery" (17:5). Perhaps the idea is that there are forces counter to God, whose workings are also impossible for humans to understand. God's truth and power will, however, prevail over these, as he brings his own mystery, his wise counsel, to fulfillment.

Revelation 10:7 declares this fulfillment. The ages of waiting in perplexity, of enduring evil, are over, as the angel announces, "There will be no more delay!" (v 6). The time has finally come when "the mystery of God will be accomplished" (v 7). Note the dynamic quality of the mystery in this context. It is not just static truth, but something that can be "accomplished." This great climax to history is in accord with God's previous revelation "to his servants, the prophets" (v 7b). The mystery then is God's wise counsel, which both guides history and is revealed in its culmination. It expresses God's answer to the problem of evil and the vain opposition by evil powers. It declares the meaning of the central event in history, the death of Christ, and reveals the results of the resurrection in the ultimate transformation of all believers at the coming of Christ.   WALTER L. LIEFELD

Mystery of Iniquity. Phrase used by the apostle Paul to describe a lawless power or force that threatened the world of his day. Better translated "mystery of lawlessness," the expression is found only in 2 Thessalonians 2:7 and must be considered in the light of its context.

Evidently, some members of the church at Thessalonica were convinced that Christ had already returned (2:1,2). In order to counter this belief Paul describes some of the events that must occur before the return of Christ. These events center around the coming of "the man of lawlessness," an evil figure who takes his seat in the temple of Jerusalem and proclaims himself to be God (vv 3,4). Although the man of lawlessness is presently being restrained, the evil that he will perpetrate is already at work (v 6). Paul calls this evil "the mystery of lawlessness."

The term "mystery" is used in Paul's letters to describe either something that has been hidden but is now revealed (Rom 16:25; Eph 3:9; 6:19; Col 1:26) or something too complex for human understanding (1 Cor 13:2; Col 2:2; 4:3). Thus the expression points to the fact that the future work of the lawless one is already a present reality that goes unappreciated by those who naively assume that Christ has returned.

The identity of the man of lawlessness, the restrainer, and the content of the mystery of iniquity have been subject to much debate. Among the suggestions that have been made, the following three predominate:

(1) The mystery of iniquity is the tyranny of the Roman Empire and the man of lawlessness is a future Roman emperor who is being kept from power by the present Roman ruler. In support of this position it can be said that the Jewish apocalypses of Paul's day considered Rome to be the quintessence of evil. In addition, approximately 10 years before the writing of 2 Thessalonians, Caligula, the Roman emperor, ordered his statue to be erected and worshiped in the Jerusalem temple (Josephus, *Antiq.* 18.8.2–6; *War* 2.10.1–5).

(2) The mystery of iniquity is the religion of Judaism and the man of lawlessness is the high priest who is restrained by apostolic preaching. However, it is doubtful that Paul would have considered Judaism in this light (cf. Rom 9:1–5).

(3) Dispensational theology identifies the mystery of iniquity as the whole course of evil, consummated in the figure of the Antichrist (the lawless one) and presently restrained by the Holy Spirit. In such a context, it is difficult to establish a scriptural basis for the Holy Spirit being "taken out of the way" (2 Thes 2:7).

See THESSALONIANS, FIRST LETTER TO THE; THESSALONIANS, SECOND LETTER TO THE; ANTICHRIST; SECOND COMING OF CHRIST; ESCHATOLOGY.

Nn

Naam. Caleb's descendant from Judah's tribe (1 Chr 4:15).

Naamah (Person). 1. Daughter of Zillah and Lamech in the list of Cain's descendants (Gn 4:22).

2. One of Solomon's many wives, an Ammonitess (1 Kgs 14:21,31; 2 Chr 12:13). She was surely responsible in part for Solomon's idolatry. Her son Rehoboam ruled Judah after Solomon's death (1 Kgs 14:21–24).

Naamah (Place). One of the 16 cities located in the Shephelah assigned to Judah's tribe for an inheritance, mentioned between Beth-dagon and Makkedah (Jos 15:41). Its exact site is unknown.

Naaman. 1. Grandson of Benjamin and son of Bela, who gave his name to the Naamite clan (Gn 46:21; Nm 26:38,40; 1 Chr 8:4,7).

2. Commanding general of the army during the reign of Ben-hadad, king of Syria (2 Kgs 5). He was held in honor by the king, evidently for character as well as for military achievements—"but he had leprosy." This did not exclude him from society, as it would have done in Israel (cf. Lv 13,14), but the possibility of a cure suggested by a captive Israelite girl sent Naaman, with Ben-hadad's approval and gifts, to the court of his highly suspicious neighboring monarch (unnamed, but probably Jehoram). Elisha the prophet intervened and prescribed an unlikely mode of healing. The reluctant Naaman followed through because of the good sense of his servants ("If the prophet had told you to do some great thing, would you not have done it?"). Naaman confessed that in Israel is the one true God, and returned home with two mule-loads of earth, perhaps on the assumption that this was a God who could be worshiped only on his own ground (cf. Ex 20:24). Naaman on his homeward journey was overtaken by the grasping Gehazi, an unworthy servant of Elisha, who by false pretenses filched from him gifts of silver and clothing which the prophet had declined. This led to the passing on of Naaman's leprosy to Gehazi and his descendants. A Jewish legend, never authenticated, suggests that it was Naaman who "drew his bow at a venture" and fatally wounded King Ahab (1 Kgs 22:34).

In Luke 4:27 Jesus reminds his synagogue listeners of how Naaman, a non-Israelite, was the only one of his time to be cleansed of leprosy.

Naamathite. Resident of Naameh in northwest Arabia. Zophar, one of Job's friends, was a Naamathite (Jb 2:11; 11:1; 20:1; 42:9).

Naamite. Descendant of Naaman, Bela's son from Benjamin's tribe (Nm 26:40).

See NAAMAN #1.

Naarah (Person). One of Ashhur's two wives, who bore him four sons (1 Chr 4:5,6).

Naarah (Place). City on the eastern border of Ephraim's tribe, just north of Jericho (Jos 16:7, KJV Naarath); alternately called Naaran in 1 Chronicles 7:28. Josephus locates it near Jericho and associates it with abundant water supply in Archelaus' day (*Antiq.* 17.13.1). Some locate Naarah at modern Tell el-Gisr near 'Ain Duq at the foot of the mountains northwest of Jericho. A synagogue dating to the 4th or 5th century AD has been excavated here; it contains a mosaic floor with a zodiac, an ark of the Law, and other figures. Others, less feasibly, suggest Khirbet el-'Ayash as its site.

Naarai. One of David's mighty men (1 Chr 11:37).

Naaran. Alternate name for Naarah, an Ephraimite border town, in 1 Chronicles 7:28.

See NAARAH (PLACE).

Naarath. KJV spelling of Naarah, an Ephraimite border town, in Joshua 16:7.

See NAARAH (PLACE).

Naashon. KJV spelling of Nahshon, Amminadab's son, in Exodus 6:23.

See NAHSHON.

Naasson. KJV form of Nahshon, Amminadab's son, in Matthew 1:4 and Luke 3:32.

See NAHSHON.

Nabal. Wealthy, successful farmer of Maon in the southern wilderness of Judah (1 Sm 25). Unlike his godly forefather, Caleb, Nabal was hard of heart and wicked in all his ways (v 3).

When he enters the story of David, it is sheep-shearing time, which seems to have been a time of festivity and hospitality. Fleeing from Saul, who wanted to kill him, David decided to ask Nabal for a gift, not only to mark the occasion but also because David's presence in the area had served to protect Nabal's flocks (vv 15,16). Nabal refused in a most insulting way, suggesting that David was no better than a runaway slave (vv 10,11).

David decided on revenge. But Abigail, Nabal's quick-witted wife, saved him by bringing David the presents he had asked for and begging him not to stain his record by acting in anger (vv 18–31). David agreed. But when Nabal heard what had happened he was struck down by what appears to have been a stroke, and died 10 days later (vv 37,38).

Nabal, whose name means "fool," stands as a reminder of the deep folly of opposing God. God himself, not David, took revenge (v 39; cf. also Rom 12:17–21).

Nabataeans. Inhabitants of an independent kingdom bordering Judea and existing from 169 BC to AD 106. The reader of the Bible and of standard histories overlooks them for two reasons: their achievements are of recent discovery, and they flourished in a period when other major events, including the life of Christ and the beginning of the church, vastly overshadowed their existence.

The Judeans and Nabataeans of the Hellenistic-Roman era shared borders and politics. The mother of Herod the Great, son of the Idumean ruler Antipater, was herself a Nabataean. Herod fled to Petra, the Nabataean capital, in 40 BC, when the Parthians attacked Jerusalem. Relations between the two kingdoms were strengthened by the marriage in the next generation of Herod Antipas to a daughter of the powerful Nabataean king Aretas IV (9 BC–AD 40); relations soured again due to his divorce to marry his niece and sister-in-law, Herodias.

The NT alludes to the extent of Nabataean influence in the region, when Paul tells of his narrow escape from incarceration following his return from the Arabian desert: "At Damascus, the governor under King Aretas guarded the city . . . in order to seize me, but I was let down in a basket . . . and escaped his hands" (2 Cor 11:32,33).

Nabataean origins are obscure. Their rise to regional power and prosperity contrasts with the ancient tradition that they were once a nomadic Arab tribe without houses or crops,

Ruins of Shivta, a desert city built by the Nabataeans around the time of Jesus.

for they later excelled in the development of water resources and agriculture. Their commercial profiteering by control of caravan routes linking India and south Arabia with the Mediterranean world suggests southern Arabia as their home or training ground. But derivation of "Nabataea" from Nebaioth, son of Ishmael and brother-in-law of Esau (Gn 25:13; 28:9; 36:3), is contested for phonetic reasons.

The best known remains of Nabataean culture are the funerary monuments at Petra. Aramaic inscriptions abound, standardized on coins and dedicatory items, with papyri and ostraca (sherds) revealing a cursive variation which anticipates Arabic script. Adoption of Aramaic language and Syrian deities shows the pragmatism by which they also adapted to their hostile environment. Only their Byzantine heirs approached their ingenuity for capturing precious water to sustain life in an arid region. Caravan travel was enhanced and permanent control thereof made possible only by skillful engineering.

Fascinating descriptions of the hundreds of settlements are given by Nelson Glueck in *The Other Side of the Jordan* (1940) and *Rivers in the (Negeb) Desert* (1956). While the Nabataeans did well in art (pottery and sculpture), architecture, and commercial enterprises, they were unsurpassed in water engineering and dry-climate farming.

The earliest historical reference to the Nabataeans associates them with Antigonus, Alexander's successor in Syria (312 BC). The succession of known kings begins with Aretas I, around 170 BC (2 Mc 5:8). About 100 BC the citizens of Gaza looked to "Aretas (II), king of the Arabs," for aid against Alexander Janneus. Aretas III controlled Damascus (80–70 BC).

The golden age at Petra lasted from 50 BC to AD 70 and included the reigns of Malichus I and Obodas II (period of Herod the Great), Aretas IV, and Malichus II. The rule of Rabbel II marks the end of the Nabataean kingdom. His predecessor, Malichus III, had moved the capital to Bostra, 70 miles east of Galilee. This in turn became the capital of the Roman province of Arabia, following Trajan's conquests, in AD 106. The Nabataeans were absorbed into the population, their distinctive script continuing into the 4th century.

See PETRA.

Naboth. Owner of a vineyard which Ahab, king of Israel, coveted (1 Kgs 21). Ahab's request was perhaps not unreasonable (v 2), and Naboth's refusal may have been a little curt (v 3).

While Ahab sulked, however, Jezebel had two scoundrels accuse Naboth of blasphemy, the greatest crime an Israelite could commit, which was punishable by death (Lv 24:10–23). Two witnesses secured a conviction according to the Law of Moses (Dt 17:6,7). The murder that was carried out had the appearance of being a legal and just execution. A fast was proclaimed and held according to royal instructions. The accusation and trial of Naboth was supervised by the elders of the city, and he was stoned to death in accordance with the law (v 13).

The prophet Elijah, however, knew the real wickedness that lay behind the deed. He faced Ahab with it, and prophesied that he and Jezebel and all their family would be wiped out because of it (vv 19–24).

The words came true. Ahab got a temporary reprieve when he repented (v 29), but was later killed in battle (1 Kgs 22:34–40). The blood of Jezebel was indeed licked up by dogs (2 Kgs 9:36), and the body of Joram, their son, was flung into Naboth's vineyard (2 Kgs 9:25).

Nachon. KJV spelling of Nacon in 2 Samuel 6:6.

See NACON.

Nachor. KJV form of Nahor, Abraham's ancestor, in Joshua 24:2 and Luke 3:34.

See NAHOR (PERSON) #1.

Nacon. Place David passed when he brought the ark from Baale-judah (Kiriath-jearim) to Jerusalem. At the threshing floor of Nacon, Uzzah was struck dead for touching the ark (2 Sm 6:6, KJV Nachon). Hence this place was called Perez-uzzah, meaning "the breaking forth upon Uzzah" (2 Sm 6:8). Nacon is alternately called Chidon in 1 Chronicles 13:9, and Perez-uzzah is spelled Perez-uzza in 1 Chronicles 13:11.

Nabataean pottery.

Nadab. 1. Eldest son of Aaron and Elisheba, the daughter of Amminadab (Ex 6:23; Nm 3:2; 1 Chr 24:1), who, together with his brothers and father, became one of Israel's first priests. He participated in the ratification of the covenant with God on Mt Sinai (Ex 24:1,9) and was ordained to the priesthood (Ex 28:1).

Nadab and his brother Abihu, Aaron's second son, perished offering "strange fire" before the Lord (Lv 10:1,2; Nm 3:4; 1 Chr 24:2). Incense offered in the morning usually preceded the cutting up of the sacrifice. In this case "fire from the Lord devoured them." The offering of "strange fire" does not appear anywhere else in the Bible.

Rabbis have offered various explanations of the offense committed by Nadab and Abihu. Since an admonition against drinking wine in the tent of meeting follows this tragedy (Lv 10:9), an early tradition held that the brothers were drunk. Death was the penalty if a priest were drinking in the tent.

An interesting point arises in the instructions which Moses gave to the grieving father of Nadab and Abihu. Moses exhorted Aaron not to mourn or to interrupt his priestly functions. Since Aaron had been sanctified by the sacred anointing oil, he must continue to serve his God. He was not allowed to go out of the door of the tent "lest he die." Instead, the rest of Israel mourned for Nadab and Abihu (Lv 10:3–7).

2. Son of Jeroboam, whom he succeeded to the throne of Israel (909–908 BC). Nadab ruled two years (1 Kgs 14:20; 15:25), coming to power in the second year of Asa's reign in Judah; he was succeeded in the third year of Asa's reign (15:28). His rule may have been arranged before the death of Jeroboam, for he surely recognized the dangers of the charismatic ideal which continued among the northern tribes. However, Nadab was not successful in stabilizing the kingdom. To gain the acclamation of the army he went into battle against the Philistines at Gibbethon, about two and a half miles southwest of Gezer. Baasha from Issachar, presumably a military officer, assassinated Nadab and all his sons and usurped the throne. So he fulfilled the prophecy predicted by Ahijah the Shilonite (15:29) against the house of Jeroboam.

3. Jerahmeelite, the son of Shammai and grandson of Onam, and the great grandson of Jerahmeel. Nadab in turn had two sons, Seled and Appaim (1 Chr 2:26–30).

4. Son of Jeiel and Maacah, a Gibeonite (1 Chr 8:30; 9:36).

Naggai, Nagge. Ancestor of Jesus according to Luke's genealogy (3:25, KJV Nagge).

See GENEALOGY OF JESUS CHRIST.

Nahalal. City in Zebulun's territory (Jos 19:15, KJV Nahallal), given to the Levites for an inheritance (21:35). Zebulun's tribe was unable to drive the Canaanites from the city, so they forced them into hard labor (Jgs 1:30, KJV Nahalol). The exact location of the city is unknown. Some possible locations include Tell el-Beida, south of modern Nahalal, and Tell en-Nahl, north of the Kishon River and near the southern end of the plain of Acco, near modern Nahalal.

See LEVITICAL CITIES.

Nahaliel. Temporary camping place for the Israelites during their wilderness wanderings, situated east of the Dead Sea in the vicinity of Moab between Mattanah and Bamoth (Nm 21:19). Its exact location is uncertain.

See WILDERNESS WANDERINGS.

Nahallal. KJV spelling of Nahalal, a city of Zebulun, in Joshua 19:15.

See NAHALAL.

Nahalol. Alternate spelling of Nahalal, a city of Zebulun, in Judges 1:30.

See NAHALAL.

Naham. Judahite chief and the brother of Hodiah's wife (1 Chr 4:19).

Nahamani. One of the leading officials who returned with Zerubbabel to Palestine following the exile (Neh 7:7). His name is omitted in the parallel list of returning officials in Ezra 2:2.

Naharai, Nahari. One of David's mighty warriors, who was also Joab's armor bearer. Naharai was from the city of Beroth (2 Sm 23:37, KJV Nahari; 1 Chr 11:39).

Nahash. 1. King of the Ammonites who laid siege to Jabesh-gilead during the days of Saul. The men of the city, offering themselves in servitude, petitioned Nabash to make a treaty with them; he agreed to do so on the condition that he gouge out each one's right eye to shame all of Israel. Given a week's reprieve from his threat, the men of Jabesh organized a secret war plan with Saul and Israel, resulting in the destruction of Nahash's Ammonite army (1 Sm 11:1,2; 12:12). He later honored a reconciliation with David, which his son Hanun, on bad counsel, disregarded (2 Sm 10:2; 1 Chr 19:1,2).

2. Father of Abigail and Zeruiah (2 Sm 17:25). In 1 Chronicles 2:16, Abigail and Zeruiah are listed as the daughters of Jesse and the sisters of David and his brothers. Vari-

ous theories have been offered to resolve this difference. The most feasible suggests that Nahash's wife bore him Abigail and Zeruiah; after his death, his widow married Jesse and subsequently bore David. Others posit that perhaps Nahash was the name of David's mother or another name for Jesse.

3. Father of Shobi from Rabbah, the chief Ammonite city east of the Jordan. Shobi, along with Machir and Barzillai, took care of David's domestic needs during his flight from Absalom (2 Sm 17:27). He is perhaps identifiable with #1 above.

Nahath. 1. Chief of a clan in Edom and Reuel's firstborn son (Gn 36:13,17; 1 Chr 1:37).

2. Levite of the family of Kohath and Elkanah's grandson (1 Chr 6:26).

3. Levite who oversaw the temple in King Hezekiah's reign (2 Chr 31:13).

Nahbi. Son of Vophsi; the head of Naphtali's tribe and one of the 12 spies sent to search out the land of Canaan (Nm 13:14).

Nahor (Person). 1. Abraham's grandfather (Gn 11:22–25; 1 Chr 1:26); also an ancestor of Jesus according to Luke's genealogy (3:34, where some English translations follow the Greek spelling Nachor). The Genesis and 1 Chronicles passages show that Nahor is from Shem's line. Hence, Abraham and his descendants are part of the Semitic family of nations.

See NATIONS.

2. Son of Terah and Abraham's brother (Gn 11:26–29; Jos 24:2). He married Milcah, Haran's daughter, and his family is named in Genesis 22:20–23. Abraham sent his servant to seek a wife for Isaac at Nahor's residence in Mesopotamia (see Gn 24:10, which possibly suggests that it was itself called "Nahor"). There he found Rebekah, Nahor's granddaughter (Gn 24:1–51). Nahor is also named as the father (perhaps grandfather) of Laban, to whom Jacob went when he fled from his brother Esau (Gn 29:5). Both of these texts link Abraham's family with related Semitic people. In Genesis 31:53 God is spoken of as "the God of Abraham and Nahor."

See NAHOR (PLACE).

Nahor (Place). Northwestern Mesopotamian city; home of Rebekah, Isaac's wife, and Nahor, Abraham's brother (Gn 24:10). Nahor is frequently mentioned in the Mari documents (18th century BC) as the town of Nakhur, located near Haran in the Balikh river valley. This city was probably the home of some of the ancient Habiru people. Its site is unknown.

See NAHOR (PERSON) #2.

Nahshon. Amminadab's son; brother of Elisheba and Salmon's father (Ex 6:23, KJV Naashon; 1 Chr 2:10,11). Nashon, the prince of Judah's tribe at the start of Israel's wilderness wanderings (Nm 1:7; 2:3; 10:14), represented his kinsmen at the altar's dedication (Nm 7:12). In Ruth 4:20 he is listed as David's forefather and a descendant of Judah through the line of Perez, and in Matthew and Luke's genealogies as an ancestor of Jesus Christ (Mt 1:4; Lk 3:32; KJV Naasson).

Nahum (Person). 1. A prophet of Judah whose name means "consolation" or "consoler." This name fits his message, as he wrote to encourage the people of Judah while they were being oppressed by the Assyrians (Na 1:1). Other than being the prophet who wrote the Book of Nahum, nothing is known of him except that he came from the village of Elkosh. Its exact location is unknown, but four suggestions have been made. First, it was a town of Alqush, near Mosul on the Tigris River just north of Nineveh. A tradition declares this to be the site of Nahum's tomb, but it is first mentioned by Masius in the 16th century. The tomb and its location have no archaeological confirmation and its authenticity is highly suspect. Second, Jerome recounts a Jewish tradition identifying it with "a village in Galilee called 'Helcesaei'" (Helcesei or Elcesi), and writes: "A very small one, indeed, and containing in its ruins hardly any traces of ancient buildings, but one which is well known to the Jews and was also pointed out to me by my guide." This village is located about 15 miles northwest of the Sea of Galilee. Third, on the northern edge of the Sea of Galilee rest the ruins of Capernaum, meaning "village of Nahum," but there is no proof that this name goes back to the prophet. Finally, some believe it should be identified with Elcesei, near Bet-gabre, about halfway between Gaza and Jerusalem in the territory of Simeon. Internal evidence seems to support this position (Na 1:15).

It is entirely possible that Nahum may have been a member of the northern tribes, but migrated to Judah after the conquest of 722 BC and ministered there.

See NAHUM, BOOK OF; PROPHET, PROPHETESS.

2. Ancestor of Jesus according to Luke's genealogy (3:25, KJV Naum).

DONALD H. LAUNSTEIN

See GENEALOGY OF JESUS CHRIST.

Nahum, Book of. Seventh book in the canonical grouping of the 12 Minor Prophets. Its significance and importance lie in the strategic place it holds in delineating the plan and program of God, in relationship to both Judah and the nations of the world.

Author. Nahum is identified as an "Elkoshite" in the superscription to the book (1:1). The term is somewhat doubtful in meaning but probably refers to a city now unknown. If the term does refer to a geographical location, it may be the village of Elcesi in Judah.

Date. The Book of Nahum deals with the fall of two great cities, Nineveh and Thebes. The fall of Thebes is cited in 3:8–10, and the entire book deals with the destruction of Nineveh, the capital of Assyria, which is yet future. Thebes was destroyed by the Assyrians around 663 BC and Nineveh fell in 612 BC. Within this range of history a number of dates for the composition of Nahum have been suggested. Some scholars prefer a date very close to the fall of Nineveh, perhaps during the time when Assyria was being invaded. However, Assyria's influence extended to Judah at the time of the writing of the book (1:13,15; 2:2), a fact which is hardly consonant with the impending downfall of that nation. Since the influence of Assyria in the western provinces began to decline in the latter half of the 7th century, it is best to place the writing of the book in the middle of the 7th century, subsequent to the destruction of Thebes but before the erosion of Assyrian power in Syro-Palestine.

Scholars who deny the validity of biblical prophecy generally date the book in the period subsequent to the fall of Nineveh.

Background. The extent of Assyrian dominance in the mid-7th century was unparalleled. Never before had Assyrian influence extended so far. The destruction of Thebes brought to an end any significant resistance to Assyria by Egypt, their most powerful foe.

The destruction of Thebes occurred during the reign of Manasseh of Judah (696–642 BC), who was, for all intents and purposes, a vassal of the Assyrians. Assyrian influence in Judah led to the intrusion of non-Yahwistic influences, such as the revival of fertility cults and the worship of Assyrian astral deities (2 Kgs 21:1–9).

Within the structure of Assyria's enormous expansion there were many weaknesses that would bring about the decline and eventual demise of that empire. For one thing, it had overextended itself. The task of keeping hostile captive countries in line, many of which were at vast distances from the capital, became increasingly difficult.

Assyria began to experience internal difficulties, particularly with the Chaldeans, a group of loosely knit tribes who had been absorbed into the Assyrian Empire. Egypt also began to withhold tribute. Numerous border raids by barbarians caused the empire to gradually weaken.

The situation worsened as the internal strife began to burgeon into a major crisis. Finally a coalition of Babylonians, Medes, and Scythians brought about the collapse of Assyria when, after a three-month siege, Nineveh fell in 612.

The site of Nineveh was excavated in 1840 by Henry Layard. The excavation revealed that the city was heavily fortified. Evidence still remains of the moats and bulwarks constructed for its defense. The palace of Sennacherib, with its 71 rooms decorated with artistic works, was also uncovered by Layard. Even though the palace lay buried for millennia, it still revealed the splendor of the days of Nineveh's greatness.

The prophet Nahum predicted that the city would be burned (2:13). In his description of the city, Layard indicated that a great conflagration had destroyed Nineveh. This became evident even when only two small portions of the tell had been explored. The massive gates of the city, which Nahum said would be open to its enemies (3:13), were also burned. The massive sculptures that originally stood by the gate were found buried in debris of earth brick and stones mixed with charcoal.

An important archaeological find is a Babylonian chronicle recording events in the reign of the Babylonian king Nabopolassar (625–605 BC). This chronicle fixes the date of the fall of Nineveh, placing it in the 14th year of Nabopolassar, that is, 612 BC.

Purpose and Theological Teaching. The purpose of the Book of Nahum is to predict the downfall of the Assyrian Empire as prefigured in its capital city, Nineveh. It sets forth the mighty power of God revealed in the arena of history.

At first glance the book may seem to be lacking substantial theological teaching. It is, after all, an extended ode celebrating the downfall of a pagan city. However, when one looks at history from the perspective of a prophet, history becomes the context for the revelation of many of God's attributes.

In chapter 1 the prophet weaves several significant theological themes into his account of the demise of the city. He sets forth the fact that God loves and cares for his own. In 1:7 he describes the Lord as knowing those who take refuge in him. In 1:13 God promises the end of Assyrian oppression of Judah.

God's sovereignty is set forth as well. God is sovereign over the nations that oppose him (1:2). He is sovereign over nature, for the clouds are but the dust of his feet (1:3). God cannot be defied (1:6). He is the sovereign of his people (1:13).

Basic to the theological structure of the book is its affirmation that God is the Lord of history. History is the arena of his activity. God is not merely an abstract concept to the prophet, nor is he a disinterested deity. He brings nations into being and down to defeat. History is not under the control of godless nations or fortuitous events; it is under the control of the Creator.

Nahum points out that God does not deal with people only in wrath. His wrath is revealed against those who oppose him. He deals in tenderness and love with those who find in him a refuge.

Content. *Superscription (1:1).* Like other prophetic books, Nahum begins with a superscription. It attributes the authorship of the book to the prophet Nahum. The first part of the superscription reads "An oracle concerning Nineveh," which indicates the book's content.

The Prophet Considers the Wrath and Might of God (1:2–6). The message of the prophet begins with a descriptive account of a number of attributes of God, specifically his wrath and sovereign power. The statement that God is a jealous God (1:2) is not to be understood as attributing selfish motives to God. Rather, it expresses God's intense devotion and loyalty to those who are his own.

Basic to this section is the affirmation that God takes vengeance on his foes. This theological principle is the basis for Nahum's description of the fall of Nineveh. That Assyria was an enemy of God was made clear in history. The Assyrians were not only an instrument used by God to punish his people, but they were a pagan people who opposed and harassed the Hebrews at every opportunity. Their conquest and exile of the kingdom of Israel was the ultimate manifestation of their opposition to Yahweh. Perhaps it was this dreadful period in Hebrew history that was uppermost in Nahum's mind.

While the Lord does take vengeance on his enemies, he is "slow to anger . . . and the Lord will by no means clear the guilty" (1:3). Even in the case of his enemies God acts in grace, not lashing out in uncontrolled rage but dealing with them in considered anger, giving them time to change their ways. The statement "He will by no means clear the guilty" is an allusion to the great affirmation of God in Exodus 34:6. It is best translated "He will not completely clear the guilty," which affirms that God forgives but often allows the effects of sin to have their course. This is illustrated in the case of David, whose sin with Bathsheba was forgiven, but the child of the union died. The destruction of Nineveh was thus certain to occur, according to the theological principle established by Nahum: God punishes those who oppose him.

The sovereignty of God over the sphere of nature is established in 1:3b–6. It too is the arena in which his awesome power is revealed.

The Fall of Nineveh and the Deliverance of Israel (1:7–15). The prophet now turns to the city of Nineveh in direct address. In verse 11 he speaks of one who comes forth from Assyria plotting evil against the Lord—a reminder of the Rabshakeh, the Assyrian emissary cited in Isaiah 36:14–20 as counseling the people to give in to his demands for surrender.

The words of doom for Nineveh become words of comfort for Judah, for Nahum says that Assyria will afflict them no longer (1:12).

The ultimacy of the destruction of the city is set forth in verses 13–15. No longer would Assyria rise to afflict the Jews. This great truth is celebrated in verse 15, where the prophet encourages the people to return to their worship of God, for they will no longer have Assyria as an enemy.

The Fall of Nineveh (2:1–13). The literary style of Nahum in this section is superb. The fast-moving action, expressed by concise, almost clipped phrasing, lends an atmosphere of excitement and urgency to the description of the collapse of the city. One hears the confused orders of the defenders in the words "Man the ramparts; watch the road, . . . collect all your strength" (2:1).

Nahum seems to describe the rush into the city just moments after the walls had been breached. One sees the flashes of red as shields are brandished (2:3) and hears the crushing sound of the madly dashing chariots (2:4), but the defenders are too late (2:5).

An important part of Nineveh's defensive structure were the moats that surrounded the city. These moats, fed by two rivers in the vicinity, are cited by the prophet in 2:6,8. The gates over these moats were breached (v 6); and even though Nineveh was like a pool of water (v 8), her defenders have been forced to flee from the onslaught.

The language again becomes vivid; punctuated with brisk commands: "Halt; Halt!" (v 8). And the invaders are heard to say, "Plunder the silver, plunder the gold!" Finally the siege is over, and there is only "desolation and ruin" (v 10).

This section closes with a reference to lions (2:11–13). Lions in the OT often stand for the wicked, particularly when the wicked devour the righteous. Assyria was very lionlike in its treatment of the Jews. But God declares that he is against the Assyrians (2:13) and will completely cut them off.

This section, vivid and colorful in its style, contains a deep theological message that should not be overlooked. It affirms God's activity in history and assures the believer that the enemies of God will never ultimately conquer the people of God. For God is almighty, an avenging God who jealously cares for his own.

A Lament for Nineveh (3:1–19). The prophet pronounces "woe" on the city in a lengthy ode celebrating Nineveh's fall. If he seems to get undue satisfaction from Nineveh's destruction, it is not necessarily because he was of a cruel nature. The OT writers had difficulty with the concept of theodicy; they explained the problem of evil not in philosophical or abstract terminology, but in very concrete terms. The godless nations of the world were the personification of evil. When Nineveh fell, the sphere of history witnessed God's conquest of evil in that particular realm. The prophet rejoices in the fact that God has proven himself active in history and victorious over his foes.

In 3:1–7 the prophet speaks of the shame that Nineveh will experience as a result of her fall. He describes one of the causes of Assyria's downfall as her sorceries and harlotries (3:4). This is an evident reference to the idolatrous religion of Assyria. The Assyrian priests were noted for their use of divination and omens. Particularly noteworthy were their attempts to predict the future by observing the motions of the heavenly bodies.

The prophet points to other countries that fell prey to their enemies (3:8–11) and affirms that Assyria is no better than these. He closes by describing the grandeur and might of Nineveh, but he vividly shows how all of that will pass away. Whether it is fortifications (3:12) or extensive trade (3:16) or soldiers (3:17), all will crumble.

The Book of Nahum poses certain problems for the Christian. One wonders how a prophet could rejoice in the carnage of a battle, or how he could take delight in describing the death and destruction of the collapse of the Assyrian empire. But such a view of the book is a caricature. The prophet nowhere delights in the event he describes. He rather predicts with sober certainty the future downfall of the city as revealed to him by God. He does affirm with utmost reverence the fact that God operates in history. This message of comfort is still relevant to the believer today.

THOMAS E. MCCOMISKEY

See NAHUM (PERSON) #1; ISRAEL, HISTORY OF; PROPHECY; PROPHET, PROPHETESS.

Bibliography. R.J. Coggins and S.P. Re'emi, *Nahum, Obadiah, Esther;* A. Halder, *Studies in the Book of Nahum;* W.A. Maier, *The Book of Nahum;* G.A. Smith, *The Book of the Twelve Prophets;* R.L. Smith, *Micah–Malachi;* C. von Orelli, *The Twelve Minor Prophets.*

Nain. Village in southern Galilee near the border of Samaria. It is the location of the miracle in which Jesus brought a dead man back to life (Lk 7:11). The man was the son of a widow who lived in this village.

Naioth. Place where David was given refuge from Saul (1 Sm 19:18–20:1). Here Samuel supervised a group of prophets. According to verses 19 and 23, Naioth was located within Ramah, Samuel's hometown.

The derivation of the term is enigmatic. The word occurs nowhere else in Scripture, and the Hebrew text seems intentionally obscure. The word perhaps stems from a Hebrew root meaning "pastoral abode" or "dwelling place." In 2 Samuel 15:25 another derivative of the Hebrew root refers to the Lord's habitation, leading some to suggest that Naioth is a proper noun referring to a sanctuary in Ramah (see 1 Sm 10:5, where prophets were also associated with a sanctuary). Others conclude that Naioth alludes to a school, cloister, or settlement of prophets, of which Samuel was head. Its exact location is unknown.

Names, Significance of. In biblical times names were given in order to express something about a person, or to express something through him, and not simply to hang a convenient label round his neck. At least six motivations appear in the choice of names:

(1) To record some aspect of a person's birth. Moses was so called by his adoptive mother because he was drawn from the water, the sound of the name recalling a Hebrew verb "to draw out" (Ex 2:10). The circumstances surrounding their births gave Jacob (Gn 25:26) and also Samuel (1 Sm 1:20) their names. In Samuel's case it is interesting to note that his name, meaning "heard by God," records not the offering of prayer but the hearing and answering of it. Something of the deeper and more far-reaching implications of naming is seen in the fact that while the names Jacob and Samuel arise from birth circumstances, they also reveal in advance the person the child will become: Jacob the sneaky opportunist (cf. Gn 27:36), Samuel the man of prayer (1 Sm 7:5–9; 8:6,21; 12:19–23).

(2) To express parental reactions to the birth. Isaac means "laughter" (cf. Gn 17:17; 18:12; 21:3–6). Nabal (1 Sm 25:25), which means "fool," must have been the essence of a mother's prayer—"Let him not be a fool"—though sadly he was! Abimelech (Jgs 8:31) means "My father is king" and may express a secret ambition of Gideon's, at variance with his public testimony (Jgs 8:22,23).

(3) To secure the solidarity of the family. This may explain the proposal to call the baby Zechariah in Luke 1:59.

(4) To reveal the nature of the person, his function, or some other significant thing about

Number of Persons with the Same Name

Alphabetically		Numerically	
Abijah	8	Zechariah	33
Adaiah	8	Azariah	28
Ahijah	10	Shemaiah	28
Amariah	10	Maaseiah	21
Azariah	28	Meshullam	21
Bani	14	Shimei	20
Benaiah	13	Hananiah	15
Berechiah	7	Jonathan	15
Elam	7	Shallum	15
Eleazer	8	Bani	14
Eliel	10	Hashabiah	14
Eliezer	11	Benaiah	13
Elioenai	7	Joel	13
Elishama	7	Joseph	13
Elkanah	8	Seraiah	12
Hanan	10	Zichri	12
Hananiah	15	Eliezer	11
Hashabiah	14	Jehiel	11
Hildiah	8	Malchijah	11
Jehiel	11	Mattaniah	11
Jehohanan	8	Michael	11
Jeiel	8	Ahijah	10
Jeremiah	9	Amariah	10
Jeremoth	8	Eliel	10
Jerimoth	8	Hanan	10
Jeroham	7	Jozabad	10
Joash	8	Nethane(e)l	10
Joel	13	Jeremiah	9
Jonathan	15	Maac(h)ah	9
Joseph	13	Shecaniah	9
Jozabad	10	Shelemiah	9
Judas	7	Shephatiah	9
Maac(h)ah	9	Simon	9
Maaseiah	21	Zebadiah	9
Malchiah	8	Abijah	8
Malchijah	11	Adaiah	8
Mattaniah	11	Eleazer	8
Meshullam	21	Elkanah	8
Micah	7	Hildiah	8
Micaiah	7	Jehohanan	8
Michael	11	Jeremoth	8
Nethane(e)l	10	Jeiel	8
Pedaiah	7	Jerimoth	8
Seraiah	12	Joash	8
Shallum	15	Malchiah	8
Shecaniah	9	Zaccur	8
Shelemiah	9	Berechiah	7
Shelomith	7	Elam	7
Shemaiah	28	Elioenai	7
Shephatiah	9	Elishama	7
Shimei	20	Jeroham	7
Simon	9	Judas	7
Uzzi	7	Micah	7
Zabad	7	Micaiah	7
Zaccur	8	Pedaiah	7
Zebadiah	9	Shelomith	7
Zechariah	33	Uzzi	7
Zichri	12	Zabad	7

him. The preeminent example of this is Jesus (Mt 1:21), named for his saving vocation. Isaiah seems to have seen his own name as significant of his message "the Lord saves" (Is 8:18).

(5) To communicate God's message. Isaiah called his first son Shear-jashub ("a remnant shall return") in order to embody the double-sided thrust of his message: as a result of faithlessness, the people will be reduced to a mere remnant ("only a remnant shall return"); as a result of God's faithfulness, his people will be preserved in life ("a remnant shall indeed return"). He called his second boy Maher-shalal-hashbaz, ("speed-prey-haste-spoil"), indicating the certainty of the imminent onset of a victorious foe. The two boys were "word made flesh"—God's truth for his people embodied before their very eyes.

(6) To establish religious affiliation. All the names in the Bible with the endings -iah or -el (e.g., Jeremiah, Nathanael) are in fact statements with "the Lord" (-iah) or God (-iel) as subject. For example, Adonijah (2 Sm 3:4) means "the Lord is Sovereign"; Nathanael (Jn 1:47) means "God gave." Such names were often chosen in times of religious decline in order to affirm the true faith of the parents.

New Names. The ability of the name to reveal the nature or status of the person who bears it is well illustrated in the biblical practice of giving new names, as when Sarai became Sarah (Gn 17:15). Three motivations are possible:

(1) The new name replaces the old in order to signify the bestowal of powers not hitherto possessed. In this case the new name is equivalent to the experience of regeneration. The childless Abram becomes the "father of a multitude of nations," Abraham (Gn 17:5).

(2) The new name may indicate a new character and status with God, as when Jacob the trickster became Israel the man of power with God (Gn 32:27; Hos 12:3,4); thus also Simon became Peter (Jn 1:42).

(3) The new name may cement a new loyalty in the place of an old. Daniel the captive was given the name Belteshazzar, incorporating the name Bel, one of the gods of Babylon—presumably to turn him from the God of his fathers to that of his captors (Dn 1:7).

The Name of God. In the Book of Genesis, God was known by descriptive labels declaring the ways in which he was known to his people; for example, "the everlasting God" (Gn 21:33; see also 14:18; 16:13; 17:1; 31:13; 33:20). But there was also another label used in Genesis, which appears in most English Bibles as "the Lord" (e.g., Gn 17:1). It was not until the time of Moses that this was revealed as something more than a label: it was a true personal name, Yahweh (Ex 3:13–15). The progress of revelation from Genesis to Exodus is declared in Exodus 6:2,3, which ought to be translated as follows: "I am Yahweh: I showed myself to Abraham, Isaac, and Jacob in the character of God Almighty, but as regards my name Yahweh I did not reveal myself to them." The name "Yahweh" is related to the Hebrew verb meaning "to be actively present" and means "He is actively present." By relating this name to the events which took place at the exodus, the Lord reveals himself as the one actively present to redeem his people and overthrow his foes. This is the central revelation of God in the OT, enshrined in a personal name.

Corresponding to this in the NT, at the very moment when Jesus, by accepting a baptism of repentance for the forgiveness of sins, identifies himself, the sinless one, with sinners, the voice of the Father sounds from heaven declaring Jesus to be the Son, and the Holy Spirit descends in bodily form as a dove (Mt 3:13–17). Once more God has come down to redeem (cf. Ex 3:8; 6:6) and reveals his name—now the final revelation, the name of the Holy Trinity. The incognito of Yahweh has finally been unveiled, not (as is often mistakenly thought) to expose him as God the Father, but as God the Holy Trinity—Father, Son, and Spirit. It is this name which is used in Christian baptism. By sharing his name with us, God first asserts his lordship (cf. 2 Sm 12:26–28); secondly he signifies that he has made us partakers of his nature, a reality whose fullness will come to those with whom Jesus shares his own new name in the City of God (Rv 3:12).

ALEC MOTYER

See GOD, NAMES OF; CHRISTIANS, NAMES FOR.

Naomi. Wife of Elimelech and the mother of Mahlon and Chilion; a member of Judah's tribe, she lived in Bethlehem during the period of the judges. Because of a severe famine in Canaan, Naomi temporarily resettled with her family in the land of Moab, east of the Dead Sea (Ru 1:1,2). Following the death of her husband and two sons in Moab (1:3,5), Naomi returned to Bethlehem with Ruth, her Moabitess daughter-in-law (1:8–22). Upon meeting her friends she told them not to call her Naomi, meaning "pleasant," but Mara, meaning "bitter," for she said, "I went away full, and the Lord has brought me back empty" (1:20,21). Naomi's domestic problems were eventually resolved when Ruth married Boaz, Elimelech's near kin (chs 2–4).

Naphath-dor. Region or town identified with Dor, a site on the Mediterranean coast, in Joshua 12:23 and 1 Kings 4:11.

See DOR.

Naphish. Eleventh of Ishmael's 12 sons (Gn 25:15; 1 Chr 1:31) and the founder of a tribe that later went to war against the tribes of Israel living east of the Jordan (1 Chr 5:19, KJV Nephish).

Naphothdor. Alternate form of Naphathdor, a site on the Mediterranean coast, in Joshua 11:2.

See DOR.

Naphtali (Person). One of Jacob's 12 sons (Gn 35:25; 1 Chr 2:2). He was the 2nd of 2 sons born to Jacob by Bilhah, Rachel's maid. Overjoyed with giving Jacob another son, Rachel named the boy Naphtali, meaning "my wrestling," for her conflict with Leah—"with mighty wrestlings I have wrestled with my sister, and have prevailed" (Gn 30:8). Naphtali eventually moved his family with Jacob to Egypt (Gn 46:24; Ex 1:4). He fathered 4 sons (Nm 26:50; 1 Chr 7:13) and founded one of the 12 tribes of Israel (Nm 1:43).

See NAPHTALI, TRIBE OF.

Naphtali, Mount of. Hill country comprising the majority of Naphtali's territory, in which the town of Kedesh was set apart as a city of refuge (Jos 20:7).

See CITIES OF REFUGE; NAPHTALI, TRIBE OF.

Naphtali, Tribe of. One of the 12 tribes of Israel that migrated from Egypt to Canaan, ultimately settling in northern Canaan in the high country of Galilee.

During the period of the Israelite exodus from Egypt, Naphtali's tribe is mentioned only incidentally. Acting as the leader of the tribe, Ahira, Enan's son (Nm 2:29; 7:28), helped conduct the census of Naphtali (Nm 1:15) as Israel prepared for the prospect of war. The first census records 53,400 men ready for war (Nm 1:42,43), whereas a later census taken near the end of their desert sojourning records 45,400 men capable of battle (Nm 26:48). When Moses sent the 12 spies to search out the land of Canaan, Nahbi, Vophsi's son, represented Naphtali's tribe (Nm 13:14). Other significant activities involving Naphtali's tribe during the wilderness wanderings include: the position of encampment around the tabernacle while in the desert (Nm 2:29); the distribution of the land, in which Pedahel, Ammihud's son, represented Naphtali in the ceremony of choosing lots (Nm 34:28); and the ratification of the covenant at Shechem (Dt 27:13). Finally, like the rest of the tribes, Naphtali was the recipient of a blessing from Moses (Dt 33:23).

The tribal inheritance of Naphtali was located on the eastern side of upper Galilee, bordered on the south by Zebulun and by Asher on the west (Jos 19:34). Within its borders were several levitical cities (Jos 21:6; 1 Chr 6:62) and a city of refuge, Kedesh (Jos 20:7; 1 Chr 6:76). Though they successfully occupied the region, they did not initially drive out the Canaanites (Jgs 1:33). They did, however, subjugate the inhabitants of the Canaanite cities Beth-shemesh and Beth-anath to forced labor. As a result of their location, they were in-

The Jordan River on the eastern border of Naphtali.

minite plateau only to encounter the powerful onslaught of the Syrian army. The other major foreign power to exert its influence in the region of Naphtali was Assyria, particularly during the reign of Tiglath-pileser III. During the rule of Pekah in Israel and Rezon in Syria, this Assyrian monarch came and captured Gilead, Galilee, and Naphtali (2 Kgs 15:29) in 732 BC.

According to the prophet Isaiah (9:1), though the Lord had made Naphtali's land contemptible, he would make it glorious once again. Matthew sees the fulfillment of this prophecy in the person of Christ, who brought the message of God's kingdom to the Jews living in the region of Naphtali's tribe (Mt 4:13,15, KJV Nephthalim; cf. Is 9:1,2). In the Book of Revelation (7:6, KJV Nephthalim), 12,000 members of Naphtali's tribe are included among the sealed multitude of Israel.

GREGORY D. JORDAN

Naphtuhim. Egyptian descendants of Noah through Ham's line (Gn 10:13; 1 Chr 1:11), listed between the Lehabim and Pathrusim tribes. Some scholars suggest that the Naphtuhim were the inhabitants of Middle Egypt, situated between the Libyans of Lower Egypt and the Pathrusim of Upper Egypt. However, the exact site of their ancient settlements is uncertain.

Narcissus (Person). Christian whose household knew the Lord and received greetings from Paul in his letter to Rome (16:11).

Narcissus (Plant). Fragrant plant growing profusely on the plains of Sharon (Is 35:1).

See PLANTS.

Nard. Perennial herb with strong, fragrant roots.

See PLANTS.

Nathan. 1. Son of David by Bathshua (Bathsheba), the third son to be born in Jerusalem (2 Sm 5:14; 1 Chr 3:5; 14:4). Nathan, Solomon's older brother, is featured in the apocalyptic oracle of Zechariah 12:12 and Christ's line of descent via Joseph (Lk 3:31).

See GENEALOGY OF JESUS CHRIST.

2. One of the early prophets and adviser of David. When David's military campaigns were almost completed, he shared with Nathan his desire to erect a suitable dwelling place for God. Nathan's immediate reaction was favorable, but on receiving direct instructions from the Lord, he countermanded his initial approval. He foretells that one of David's sons will build God a house, and that God will establish a house (dynasty) for David through his son, Solomon. The prophecy includes not

volved in some major conflicts with the indigenous population and foreign invaders. The most significant of these was the war with Jabin, king of Hazor. Barak, son of Abinoam, from Kedesh in Naphtali joined Deborah, the prophetess, and together they led the tribes of Zebulun and Naphtali against the Canaanites (Jgs 4,5). Along with the tribes of Asher, Zebulun, and Manasseh, the tribe of Naphtali was also called by Gideon into battle against the Midianites (Jgs 6:35).

During the united monarchy the tribe of Naphtali sent troops to Hebron, demonstrating their support of David's kingship over all of Israel (1 Chr 12:34). Naphtali's continued allegiance to the Davidic dynasty was evidenced in their support of Solomon's administrative system. Ahimaaz of Naphtali's tribe was one of 12 officers who administered the various regional districts for the king; this same Ahimaaz also married Basemath, the daughter of Solomon (1 Kgs 4:15).

The history of the tribe during the divided monarchy is sketchy, and references to Naphtali occur in the contexts of military conflicts. During the reign of Asa in Judah, Baasha, king of Israel, sought to build a fortress at Ramah on the central Benjaminite plateau. Feeling threatened, Asa encouraged Ben-hadad of Syria to attack the northern kingdom. The Syrian monarch complied, and the brunt of his attack was felt by Naphtali's tribe (1 Kgs 15:16–24). Baasha withdrew his troops from the Benja-

only the Davidic line but also the messianic king. Nathan's oracle, therefore, was of vital importance, since it dealt with two great institutions, the temple and the Davidic monarchy (2 Sm 7:1–7; 1 Chr 17:1–15).

During the Ammonite war David, having fathered an illegitimate child, tried to cover his sin by involving the woman's husband, Uriah (2 Sm 11:1–13; 23:39). When this attempt failed, Joab, the general of the army, successfully engineered Uriah's death, whereupon David took Bathsheba openly as his wife (11:14–27). Nathan confronted the king, courageously exposing the enormity of David's crime by a parable which provoked the king's righteous anger and turned the finger of condemnation upon David himself (12:1–9). Nathan foretold the fearful consequences for David's family resulting from his sin and evil example (12:10–12), a prophecy fulfilled in rape, the deaths of three of David's sons, and civil war (2 Sm 13–18; 1 Kgs 1). Bathsheba's child also would not live (2 Sm 12:14).

When David was near death, one of his sons, Adonijah, seized power (1 Kgs 1:1,10). Nathan prompted Bathsheba to remind David of an earlier promise concerning Solomon's succession, supporting her by his own timely intervention (1:10–27). David immediately authorized Solomon's coronation (1:28–53).

Nathan was an important chronicler (1 Chr 29:29; 2 Chr 9:29). With David he played a vital part in developing the musical aspects of temple worship (2 Chr 29:25).

3. Man of Zobah and the father of Igal, one of David's 30 heroes (2 Sm 23:36). He was possibly the Nathan noted as the brother of Joel (1 Chr 11:38).

4. Father of two important court officials (1 Kgs 4:5); probably either the prophet or David's son.

5. Descendant of Judah, in the clan of Jerahmeel, the son of Attai and the father of Zabad (1 Chr 2:36).

6. One of a deputation sent by Ezra to secure levitical reinforcements for the Israelites returning to Jerusalem (Ezr 8:16). Possibly Nathan was among those who covenanted to divorce their foreign wives (10:39); but the name, meaning "gift," was a very common one.

Nathanael.

Jew from Cana of Galilee whom Jesus called to be a disciple (Jn 1:45–50; 21:2). Initially skeptical when Philip described Jesus as the fulfillment of the whole OT (Jn 1:45,46), Nathanael proclaimed Jesus to be the Son of God and the King of Israel (1:49) after an astonishing personal encounter.

The fact that the only NT references to Nathanael occur in the Gospel of John has led some scholars to identify him with several personalities appearing in the synoptic Gospels. Because his call appears with those of Andrew, Peter, and Philip, some have speculated that he was one of the 12, possibly Bartholomew. Three pieces of evidence are cited in support of this position: (1) the name Bartholomew is patronymic (literally "son of Tolmai") and would be accompanied by another name; (2) each of the synoptic lists of the 12 apostles place Bartholomew after Philip (Mt 10:2–4; Mk 3:16–19; Lk 6:14–16) paralleling the call of Nathanael after Philip in John's account; (3) Bartholomew's name does not appear in the fourth Gospel.

A second position identifies Nathanael as James, the son of Alphaeus. According to this view, Jesus' comment in John 1:47 should read "Behold, Israel [not "an Israelite"] indeed, in whom is no guile!" Since Israel is the name God gave to Jacob and the NT form of Jacob is James, John addressed James, the son of Alphaeus, as Nathanael in order to distinguish him from others who had become prominent in the early church.

Two less plausible identifications equate Nathanael with either Matthew or Simon the Cananaean. The first is precariously founded on the similar etymologies of the names, Matthew (gift of Yahweh) and Nathanael (Yahweh has given). The second identifies the two on the basis of the common hometown of Cana. Nathanael was most likely a disciple who was not a member of the 12 and was known only to John. This suggestion conforms to early patristic evidence.

In the fourth Gospel, Nathanael serves as a symbol for the true Jew who overcomes initial skepticism to believe in Christ. This is confirmed by three observations: (1) his initial reaction to Jesus parallels that of others who believed in the Law and the Prophets (7:15,27, 41; 9:41); (2) Jesus' perception of Nathanael under a fig tree (1:48) identifies the latter's devotion to the Torah (In rabbinic literature the proper place to study the Torah is under a fig tree.); (3) Jesus' identification of Nathanael as "an Israelite, in whom is no guile" may be intended to contrast Nathanael with Jacob, the father of the Israelite nation. In Genesis 25–32, Jacob is certainly sly and cunning in his dealings with Esau and Laban. John 1:51 strengthens the ties between Nathanael and Jacob by presenting the imagery of angels ascending and descending reminiscent of Jacob's dream and by locating the event in Galilee close to Bethel and Jabbok, the sites of Jacob's experiences. Nathanael is thus a symbol of the pious Israelite for whom Christ came (v 31). His response typifies what the fourth evangelist understands as the appropriate response of the true Israelite to Jesus—from initial skepticism to faith (cf. Rom 9:6).

See APOSTLE, APOSTLESHIP.

Nathan-melech. Official during King Josiah's reign. Horses for sun worship were kept near his quarters but were removed by Josiah (2 Kgs 23:11).

Nations. Groups formed on the basis of political or social interests or on kinship. Generally the word "nations" implies peoples of the world other than the Hebrews, although it can also include the Jews.

Origins. The Book of Genesis attributes to the three sons of Noah the origin of the various "families" or ethnic groups (about 70 in all) which inhabited the eastern Mediterranean regions (ch 10). The narrative presupposes that each group has its own individual geographical location and language (10:5,20, 31). The story of the tower (ziggurat) of Babel, whose peak was to reach to heaven (ch 11), explains that ethnic groups are separated by language barriers and scattered geographically so that they might not collaborate on presumptuous ventures. (Paul, in his sermon in Athens, assumes that the various nations had a common origin, just as the writer of Genesis did, and accepts as part of the design of God the fact that nations should be separated by geographical boundaries [Acts 17:26].) The prophet Zephaniah looked forward to the day when God would reverse this state of affairs and cause all the nations to speak one language (3:9). The writer of Revelation, in his vision of the new heaven and the new earth, sees these natural boundaries abolished. The nations freely intermingle in the new Jerusalem (Rv 21:22–26).

The distinction between "Israel" and "the nations" is not clear-cut. "Israel" evolved from various ethnic groups, and several of "the nations" traced their origins to prominent figures in the Israelite community. Abraham, the father of the Jewish nation, lived in Ur of the Chaldees in the delta region of the Tigris-Euphrates Valley. With his father he migrated north to Haran, and finally southwest to the land of Canaan (Gn 11:31–12:9). Deuteronomy 26:5 ("a wandering Aramean was my father") suggests Abraham's residence was in the district of Mesopotamia known as Aram-naharaim. When Abraham entered into covenant with God, God gave him the token of the covenant relationship, circumcision. Foreigners purchased as slaves were circumcised, thus including them in the covenant community. When Moses led the Israelites out of Egypt into the wilderness, "a mixed multitude also went up with them" (Ex 12:38), which suggests again that people not biologically related nevertheless identified themselves with the people of Israel.

On the other hand, the nation of Israel did not include all of those physically descended from Abraham. The first son of Abraham, Ishmael, had an Egyptian mother and is the ancestor of the Ishmaelites, bedouins who roamed the southern wilderness region (Gn 16). Of the twin sons born to Isaac and Rebekah, Esau, the firstborn, is the father of the Edomites living in the southeast, traditional enemies of Israel (Gn 25:23; Nm 20:21).

God and the Nations. Scripture presents negative and positive attitudes toward the nations. The nations inhabiting the territory between the Tigris-Euphrates Valley and the Nile River are wicked nations. Therefore, God will take away their land and give it to the descendants of Abraham (Gn 15:16,18–20). Incestuous relationships, adultery, homosexuality, and sexual relationships between men and animals characterize the nations and incur God's displeasure (Lv 18). The nations indulge in the practice of spiritism, augury, witchcraft, and necromancy, and the Hebrews are instructed to avoid such activities (Lv 19:26; 20:6). The nations worship many gods and include in their worship the practice of human sacrifice, often the sacrifice of children, a ritual which God abhors (Lv 20:1–5; 2 Kgs 17:29–34). The prophet Isaiah speaks scathingly of the craftsman who, taking a branch of a tree, uses part of it to kindle a fire and fashions from the remainder a graven image which he then worships (44:12–20). The Baalim and Ashteroth, fertility gods of the Canaanites, were a constant source of temptation to the people of Israel. The message repeated throughout Scripture is that for these reasons God is driving out the nations and is giving their territory to Israel (Ex 34:24; Dt 12:29–31). The prophetic oracles against the nations reinforce this negative attitude (Jer 46–51; Am 1:3–2:3).

However, the Scripture also reflects a more positive attitude toward the nations. As revealed in the Book of Psalms, God is not only concerned about Israel; his eyes keep watch over the nations, and all the earth praises and worships him (Ps 66:1–8). The psalmist prays that God's saving power may be known among all the nations. He affirms that God righteously judges the peoples and guides the nations. All the ends of the earth should fear him (Ps 67:7). The prophet Isaiah declares that the Jerusalem temple is to be a house of prayer for all peoples and that God welcomes the foreigner who comes bearing sacrifices and offering worship (Is 56:6–8). Isaiah's vi-

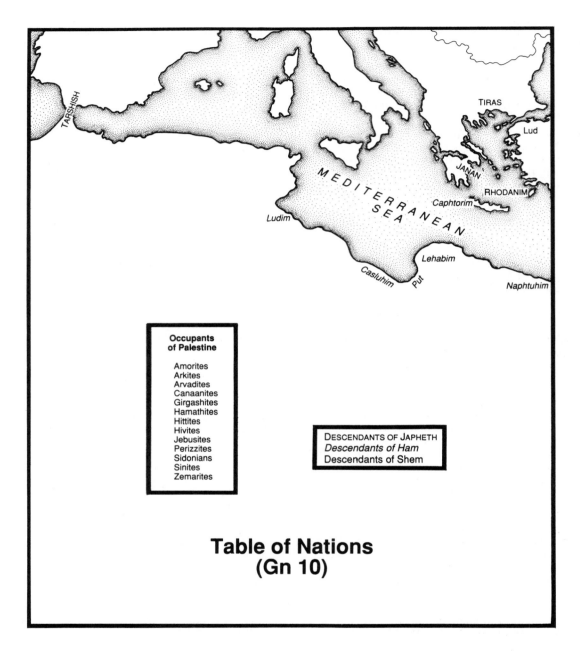

Occupants of Palestine

Amorites
Arkites
Arvadites
Canaanites
Girgashites
Hamathites
Hittites
Hivites
Jebusites
Perizzites
Sidonians
Sinites
Zemarites

DESCENDANTS OF JAPHETH
Descendants of Ham
Descendants of Shem

Table of Nations
(Gn 10)

sion of hope for the latter days pictures people of all nations pouring into Jerusalem to worship the Lord and learn his ways. Instead of nation warring against nation, all will live in peace, ruled by God (Is 2:2–4).

Israel's Separation from the Nations. The earliest traditions of the Hebrews depict them as nomads migrating through territory over which they had no claim and interacting with peoples of differing social, religious, and cultural values. The ancient Hebrews needed to maintain friendly relationships as far as possible with the nations, but the terms of the Mosaic covenant implied that with God's help they would one day conquer them. Consequently the Hebrews tended to regard the nations as potential enemies to be subdued or eliminated. Israel's instinctive dislike of some of the religious practices of the nations, such as the Canaanites' fertility cult, or the Ammonites' child sacrifice rites, nurtured this attitude. However, while a staunch inner core re-

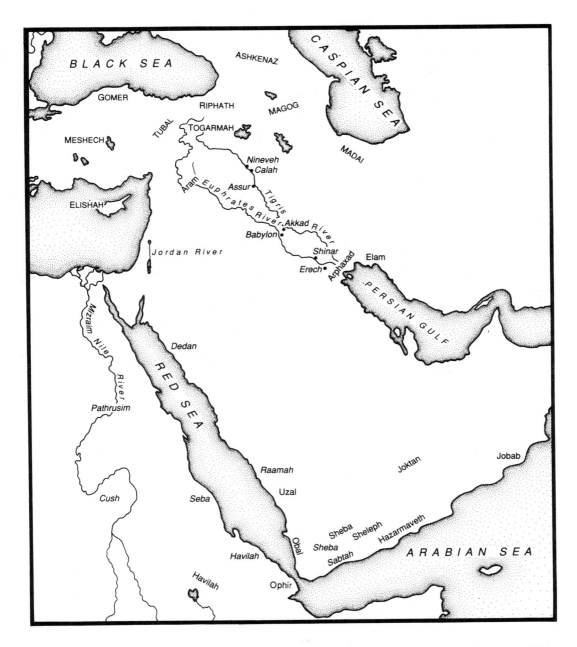

sisted the inroads of the worship of foreign gods and immorality, many of the Israelites found this intriguing and attractive. Consequently, strict prohibitions within the Law forbid the Israelites to participate in the cultural and religious activities of their neighbors. When they conquer the various territories, they are not to make covenant agreements with the nations, but rather they must destroy them, tearing down their cultic shrines and burning their idols. They must not intermarry

with these peoples because to do so would involve a temptation to participate in the worship of foreign gods (Dt 7:1–5).

However, the narratives of conquest and settlement repeatedly make reference to intermarriage and the worship of foreign gods. Solomon, for example, had many foreign wives, each of whom brought to the royal household her own national gods (1 Kgs 11:1–8).

In the early years of the monarchy, Israel conquered the nations and maintained its own political, cultural, and spiritual identity. But as the period of the monarchy comes to an end, Israel is unable to preserve such independence. Assyria and Babylonia prove to be too powerful, and the Jews find themselves taken into exile and scattered among those very nations whose way of life posed such a threat to their own religious and political survival. Indeed, the prophet Jeremiah exhorts them, "Seek the welfare of the city where I have sent you into exile . . . for in its welfare you will find your welfare" (Jer 29:7). Nevertheless the hope never dies that God will restore the fortunes of Israel, gathering the Jews from among the nations and restoring their land to them (Jer 29:14). Although some of the Jews returned to rebuild the temple and resettle the land after the Persian conquest (538 bc), not until the time of Judas Maccabeus did Israel enjoy a brief period of national independence (166–63 bc), never again experienced until the creation of the State of Israel in 1948.

Israel's Mission to the Nations. The emphasis in Scripture on Israel's separation from the nations must not overshadow Israel's mission to the nations. The promise made by God to Abraham is, "By you all the families of the earth shall be blessed" (Gn 12:3, rsv). At the completion of Solomon's temple, the king's dedication prayer includes these words: "When a foreigner . . . comes and prays toward this house, hear thou in heaven . . . that all the people of the earth may know thy name and fear thee, as do thy people Israel" (1 Kgs 8:41–43). The "Servant of God" in Isaiah's prophecy is to be "a covenant to the people, a light to the nations" (Is 42:6). When Daniel saw in his vision the "Ancient of Days" delegating a kingdom to the "Son of Man," clearly this was not the kingdom of the Jews but rather a universal kingdom (Dn 7:14). Zechariah envisages men of all nations joining the Jews as they return to Jerusalem (Zec 8:23).

The Nations in the New Testament. In the Gospels Jesus ministers not only to the Jews but also to the gentile nations in accordance with ancient prophecy (Mt 4:15,16). Jesus teaches in Galilee, a predominantly non-Jewish area, journeys to Tyre and Sidon (Mk 7:24), and travels through the Decapolis (Mk 7:31). He ministers to a Roman centurion (Lk 7:1–10), the widow of Nain (Lk 7:11–17), and a Syrophoenician woman (Mk 7:26). People from Idumea come to observe his miracles (Mk 3:8).

The teaching of Jesus is also wide in scope. The narrative of the great judgment (Mt 25:31–46) depicts all nations gathered before the Son of man, and Jesus commissions the apostles to "make disciples of all nations" (Mt 28:19).

Although the Book of Acts does not overlook the nations' role in the death of Jesus (Acts 4:27) and their role in opposing the ministry of Paul (Acts 26:17), it nevertheless clearly indicates that the church fulfilled its commission to present the gospel to non-Jewish peoples. Peter proclaims the message about Jesus to the household of Cornelius, a Roman soldier of the Italian Cohort (Acts 10). Although the early church resisted the fact that non-Jewish peoples might freely receive the gift of the Spirit, they eventually welcomed this conclusion (Acts 11:1–8; 15:1–29). Paul traveled through Cyprus, Asia Minor, Greece, and Italy, founding or visiting churches which were predominantly gentile. The Book of Acts ends dramatically with Paul preaching the gospel in the city of Rome, the heart of the Roman Empire.

Paul understands Jesus to be the fulfillment of God's promise to Abraham to bless all the nations (Gal 3:14). Peter sees the nations as onlookers surrounding the church. To them the church must bear faithful witness (1 Pt 2:12). The writer of Revelation clearly states that the church consists of men "from every tribe and tongue and people and nation" (Rv 5:9,10; 7:9,10). In his vision of the new Jerusalem, he sees "the glory and honor of the nations" and peace among men (Rv 21:24–26).

E. Margaret Howe

Bibliography. K.N. Clark, *The Gentile Bias and other Essays;* T.R. Glover, *The Conflict of Religions in the Roman Empire;* M. Loane, *Grace and the Gentiles;* G.H.C. MacGregor and A.C. Purdy, *Jew and Greek;* G. Murray, *Five Stages of Greek Religion.*

Natural Man. *See* Man, Natural.

Naum. kjv spelling of Nahum, an ancestor of Jesus (Lk 3:25).

See Nahum (Person) #2.

Nazarene. Native or inhabitant of Nazareth, a NT town in lower Galilee.

Nazareth was Jesus' hometown during the first 30 years of his life. Since the name "Jesus" was a common name among the Jews and since surnames were not used, perhaps the designation "Nazarene" differentiated Jesus of Nazareth from others with the same name (see Greek texts of Mt 27:16,17; Acts 7:45; Col 4:11; and Heb 4:8, where the name Jesus refers to other men), and was not intended to express the degrading tone in Nathanael's remark, "Can anything good come out of Nazareth?" (Jn 1:46).

In the original texts, the designation "Jesus the Nazarene" was used by demons (Mk 1:24; Lk 4:34), the crowd outside Jericho (Mk 10:47; Lk 18:37), a servant girl (Mk 14:67), soldiers (Jn 18:5,7), Pilate (Jn 19:19), the two disciples on the road to Emmaus (Lk 24:19), and the angel at the tomb (Mk 16:6).

The apostles in Acts used the designation to identify Jesus. Peter speaks of Jesus the Nazarene in his sermon on the day of Pentecost (Acts 2:22), and at the temple gate in a subsequent healing (3:6; 4:10). Paul identifies Jesus as such in Acts 26:9.

One hostile reference to the name is Acts 6:14. The false witnesses against Stephen accused him before the Sanhedrin of saying, "This Nazarene, Jesus, will destroy this place [temple] and alter the customs which Moses handed down to us." Another antagonistic reference is Acts 24:5, the only reference to Jesus' followers as Nazarenes. Tertullus accused Paul, saying, "For we have found this man a pestilent fellow, an agitator among all the Jews throughout the world, and a ringleader of the sect of the Nazarenes."

With regard to the name "Nazarene," Matthew 2:23 has always been problematic: "And he went and dwelt in a city called Nazareth, that what was spoken by the prophets might be fulfilled, 'He shall be called a Nazarene.'" No OT prophecy states that the Messiah would be called a Nazarene. Some scholars relate Matthew's reference to Isaiah 11:1, which speaks of the Messiah as a Branch, a Hebrew term derived from the same root as "Nazareth." Others suggest that the OT prophecies concerning the despising and reviling of the Messiah correlate with Matthew 2:23, which should be translated "and he [Joseph] came and dwelt in a city called Nazareth, that what was spoken through the prophets might be fulfilled, because he would be called a Nazarene." The prophecy that Jesus would be scorned and ridiculed was fulfilled when some of his contemporaries called him a Nazarene, from the despised town of Nazareth (Jn 1:46; cf. Mt 13:54; Mk 6:2,3; Lk 4:22).

See NAZARETH.

Nazareth. Village in the Roman province of Galilee, the home of Joseph, Mary, and Jesus. Always small and isolated, Nazareth is not mentioned in the OT, the Apocrypha, intertestamental Jewish writings, or the histories of Josephus. The town lies just north of the plain of Esdraelon in the limestone hills of the southern Lebanon range. It is situated S,SE on 3 sides of a hill. This location forms a sheltered valley with a moderate climate favorable to fruits and wildflowers. Trade routes and roads passed near Nazareth, but the village itself was not on any main road. Nazareth is about 15 miles west of the Sea of Galilee and 20 miles east of the Mediterranean. Jerusalem lies about 70 miles south. Archaeological remains indicate that the ancient town was higher on the western hill than the present

village (cf. Lk 4:29). In the time of Christ, Nazareth, along with the entire region of south Galilee, lay outside the mainstream of Jewish life, providing the background for Nathanael's wry remark to Philip, "Can anything good come out of Nazareth?" (Jn 1:46).

Nazareth is first mentioned in the NT as the home of Mary and Joseph (Lk 1:26,27). Some time after Jesus was born at his parents' ancestral town of Bethlehem, about 80 miles to the south, Mary and Joseph returned to Nazareth (Mt 2:23; Lk 2:39). Jesus grew up there (Lk 2:39,40,51), leaving the village to be baptized by John in the Jordan River (Mk 1:9). When John was arrested, Jesus moved to Capernaum (Mt 4:13). Though Jesus was often identified by his boyhood city as "Jesus of Nazareth" (see Mk 10:47; Jn 18:5,7; Acts 2:22), the NT records only one subsequent visit by Jesus to Nazareth. On this occasion Jesus preached in the synagogue and was rejected by the townspeople (Lk 4:16–30; cf. Mt 13:54–58; Mk 6:1–6). Jesus' followers were also derisively called "Nazarenes" (Acts 24:5).

Nazareth remained a Jewish city until the time of the emperor Constantine (d. AD 327), when it became a sacred place for Christian pilgrims. A large basilica was built in Nazareth about AD 600. Arabs and Crusaders alternately controlled the village until 1517, when it fell to the Turks who forced all Christians to leave. Christians returned in 1620, and the town is an important Christian center in present-day Israel.

See NAZARENE.

Nazirite, Nazarite. Person who was either chosen or consecrated for life or for a set period of time to complete a vow to God. The Nazirite (KJV Nazarite) devoted himself to self-imposed discipline in order to perform some special service.

Israelite tradition viewed the Nazirite as consecrated for life. Samson was the ancient hero of the Nazirites. He was "consecrated to God" through the vow of his mother (Jgs 13:5; 16:17), and remained under that vow to the "day of his death" (Jgs 13:7). As long as Samson's hair was not cut, he was able to receive the "spirit of the Lord" and thereby perform amazing physical feats.

Early Nazirite vows may have been associated with holy-war ceremonies. Combatants were consecrated to God and perhaps wore long hair (Jgs 5:2). The prophet Samuel did not cut his hair because of his mother's vow that no razor would touch his head (1 Sm 1:11; the Septuagint adds that he was not to drink wine). The Nazirite vow of uncut hair was associated with being consecrated to God's ser-

The modern city of Nazareth is one of the largest in Galilee.

vice and was especially common during the charismatic days of Israel's early leaders.

Naziritism developed into a ritual for those who sought to consecrate themselves temporarily to God. During the period of consecration the devotee abstained from drinking wine, allowed his hair to grow, and avoided all contact with dead bodies.

Uncut hair symbolizes strength and life. Perhaps this is the intended meaning of *nazir* when used to describe Joseph in the blessing of Jacob (Gn 49:26) and in the blessing of Moses (Dt 33:16). Vineyards which were not pruned in sabbatical or jubilee years were said to be *nazir*.

In later times, touching or coming in close proximity to a dead body was the most serious offense against the vow. Should anyone die in his presence, a Nazirite became impure. Such a contaminated Nazirite was expected to shave his "defiled head" on the day of cleansing. Next he would bring two young pigeons to the priest who would offer one as a sin offering. And finally he must bring a male lamb for a guilt offering (Nm 6:9–12). Because of this defilement the Nazirite must begin his days of separation again.

At the end of his period of separation, he "desecrated" himself through a ceremony: he offered a sacrifice for sin and a communion sacrifice; he shaved his head and burnt the hair. Thereafter the Nazirite returned to his normal life and could drink wine (Nm 6:13–21).

Paul completed a similar vow at Cenchreae in NT times (Acts 18:18) and again along with four other Nazirites in Jerusalem (Acts 21:23, 24). In the Talmud the period of time for the consecration was usually 30 days. It was customary for the wealthy to aid poor Nazirites in the purchase of their offerings. During the Maccabean period, the Nazirites were unable to complete their rites since the temple was profaned (1 Mc 3:49–51).

Neah. Border town in Zebulun's territory (Jos 19:13), exact site unknown.

Neapolis. Port city of Philippi, identified with modern Kavalla. Neapolis, whose name comes from a Greek word meaning "new city," existed as early as the 5th century BC, and in Roman times was clearly dependent upon the city of Philippi.

After Paul's dream of the man from Macedonia, he left Troas and the continent of Asia for the continent of Europe. The party passed by the island of Samothrace and then came to Neapolis. Thus Neapolis was the first city of Europe visited by Paul (Acts 16:11).

Neariah. 1. One of Shemaiah's 6 sons and a descendant of David (1 Chr 3:22,23).

2. Captain of 500 men of Simeon's tribe who went to Mt Seir, where they destroyed the remnant of the Amalekites and settled their own people in Hezekiah's time (1 Chr 4:42).

Nebai. Political leader who signed Ezra's covenant of faithfulness to God with Nehemiah and others after the exile (Neh 10:19).

Nebaioth, Nebajoth. Firstborn of Ishmael's 12 sons (Gn 25:13; 1 Chr 1:29) whose sister, Mahalath (also called Basemath, cf. Gn 36:3) later married Esau (Gn 28:9). The identification of Nebaioth's descendants is uncertain, though possibly they are the ancestors of the Nabataean Arabian tribe who possessed the land of Edom and parts of the Transjordan as far north as Palmyra (ancient Tadmor). Both the descendants of Nebaioth and Kedar are noted for their superb flocks of sheep (Isa 60:7) and are mentioned in the inscriptions of the Assyrian king Ashurbanipal (7th century BC). Negajoth is the KJV spelling of Nebaioth in Genesis.

Neballat. Town situated in the hills overlooking the southeastern region of the plain of Sharon, settled by Benjaminites after the exile (Neh 11:34). It is identified with modern Beit Nebala, four miles east of Lod and two miles north of Hadid.

Nebat. Ephraimite of Zeredah in the Jordan Valley, a servant to Solomon, and the father of King Jeroboam (1 Kgs 11:26).

Nebo (Deity). Marduk's son and a chief god among the Babylonian pantheon. Nebo (Hebrew spelling; pronounced Nabu in Akkadian) was the patron deity of wisdom, education, and literature. Originally the local city god of Borshippa, Nebo grew in prominence with the rise of the Babylonian Empire. Numerous inscriptions affirm his popularity among the Babylonian and Assyrian kings. At Kalkhi (modern Nimrud), an ancient capital of Assyria, a temple was built and maintained for Nebo and his consort Tashmit. Isaiah ridiculed Nebo for his inability to save even himself from being carried into captivity (Is 46:1).

See BABYLON, BABYLONIA.

Nebo (Person). Forefather of 52 descendants who returned with Zerubbabel to Judah following the exile (Ezr 2:29; Neh 7:33), 6 of whom were encouraged by Ezra to divorce their foreign wives (Ezr 10:43). Some suggest that Nebo refers to a town in Benjamin's tribe from which some inhabitants went into exile to Babylon.

Nebo (Place). 1. City located on the pastoral tablelands of the Transjordan and desired by the sons of Gad and Reuben (Nm 32:3). Reuben was apportioned this town (Nm 32:38; 1 Chr 5:8), but eventually lost it to King Mesha of Moab around 850 BC. Later, Isaiah (15:2) and Jeremiah (48:1,22) predicted Nebo's destruction as part of God's judgment against Moab. Its location is uncertain, though some identify it with Khirbet Ayn Musa.

2. Summit in the Pisgah portion of the Abarim mountain range, situated eight miles east

The springs of Moses in the foreground and Mt Nebo in the distance.

of the Jordan River at the northeastern corner of the Dead Sea, atop which Moses viewed the Promised Land of Canaan before he died (Dt 32:49; 34:16). Its site has been variously identified with Jebel en Neba or with Khirbet el-Mekhaiyet.

See NEBO, MOUNT.

Nebo, Mount. Name of a high mountain on the east side of the Jordan River opposite the city of Jericho. The Israelites encamped near it on the last stage of their journey to the Promised Land (Dt 32:49). The mountain with which Nebo is now identified has two peaks; in the OT the peak of Nebo is called Pisgah (Dt 34:1). From this high vantage point Moses beheld the Promised Land (Dt 34:1–5).

In Jewish legend Jeremiah is said to have buried the ark of the covenant on Mt Nebo (2 Mc 2), but this is entirely spurious. In Byzantine times a Christian church and monastery were built on Mt Nebo to honor the supposed grave of Moses.

Nebuchadnezzar, Nebuchadrezzar. Babylonian king (605–562 BC) who captured and destroyed Jerusalem in 586 BC. He was the son of Nabopolassar and the foremost ruler of the Neo-Babylonian Empire (612–539 BC); his name is alternately spelled Nebuchadrezzar in Jeremiah and Ezekiel.

Nebuchadnezzar states that he conquered all of "Hatti-country," which is a term used for all of Palestine and Syria, including Judah. Jehoiakim had been made king of Judah by Neco (2 Kgs 23:34) and initially submitted to Nebuchadnezzar (24:1; cf. Dn 1:1,2), but three years later rebelled. Jehoiakim died and his son, Jehoiachin, succeeded to the throne (2 Kgs 24:6); however, he reigned for only three months. Nebuchadnezzar came to Jerusalem in 598 BC and took Jehoiachin captive to Babylon (24:10–17). He replaced Jehoiachin with his uncle, Mattaniah, whom he renamed Zedekiah (24:17; 2 Chr 36:10).

Zedekiah rebelled against the king of Babylon (2 Kgs 25:1). Nebuchadnezzar's armies besieged the city of Jerusalem and captured Zedekiah. He was brought to Nebuchadnezzar at Riblah, where Zedekiah's sons were slain before his eyes. He was then blinded, bound, and taken captive to Babylon (25:6,7). The temple was looted and burned, the city walls were dismantled, and the city was plundered and razed (25:9–17). The leading people of the nation were either killed or taken into captivity.

Nebuchadnezzar's military successes were in many respects overshadowed by his building activities in Babylon. The king voiced his pride when he declared: "Is not this great Babylon, which I have built by my mighty power as a royal residence and for the glory of my majesty?" (Dn 4:30). The Hanging Gardens were acclaimed as one of the seven wonders of the ancient world. They were built on terraces in an effort to cure his Median queen of her homesickness for the mountains of her homeland.

The events of the Book of Daniel center on Babylon and Nebuchadnezzar. Daniel was among the captives taken to Babylon in 605 BC. Nebuchadnezzar became aware of Daniel when the king had a dream which none of his occult experts could interpret (ch 2). The Lord gave to Daniel the interpretation of the dream; the human image which the king saw in his dream represented the various governments from the New Babylonian empire to the reign of the Messiah.

Nebuchadnezzar set up a large human statue which was 90 feet high and 9 feet wide. Failure to worship the image would incur death by fire. The three compatriots of Daniel refused and were thrown into a furnace from which the Lord delivered them unhurt (ch 3).

The king had another dream about a great tree that was cut down but later sprouted from the stump (4:4–27). Again the "wise men of Babylon" could not give the interpretation, but Daniel informed the king that the dream prophesied a humbling experience lasting seven years as a consequence of the king's pride (4:28–33).

The remnant of the people in Judah were put under the charge of Gedaliah, the appointed governor. After his treacherous murder, the Jews fled to Egypt. Both Jeremiah (43:8–13; 46:13–24) and Ezekiel (chs 29–32) prophesied that Nebuchadnezzar would invade Egypt. Josephus gives the date as the 23rd year of Nebuchadnezzar (582/581 BC,) but a fragmentary historical inscription dating to the 37th year of Nebuchadnezzar (568/567 BC) indicates that the defeat of Egypt occurred during the reign of Amasis.

CARL E. DeVRIES

See BABYLON, BABYLONIA; DANIEL, BOOK OF.

Nebushazban, Nebushasban. Babylonian officer among those ordered to provide safety for Jeremiah after the Babylonians conquered Jerusalem (Jer 39:13, KJV Nebushasban).

Nebuzaradan. Chief Babylonian official and captain of the bodyguard during Nebuchadnezzar's reign (605–562 BC). Nebuzaradan was one of the officials whom Nebuchadnezzar authorized to oversee Jerusalem and Judah and the deportations of Jewish exiles to Babylon (2 Kgs 25:8–20; Jer 39:9,10; 52:12–30). On the king's orders, he appointed Gedaliah governor of Judah and Jeremiah's guardian (Jer 39:11–13; 41:10; 43:6).

Necklace. See FASHION AND DRESS.

Neco, Necho, Nechoh. Pharaoh of the 26th dynasty of the Saite kings, who succeeded his father, Psammetichus, in 610 BC. Psammetichus had ruled 54 years over Egypt and was instrumental in the renewal of archaic art forms and in the revival of religious fervor. In addition to this Psammetichus had fortified the borders with garrisons and driven the Assyrians beyond the northeast border into Canaan. The alliance of the Babylonians and Medes made Psammetichus realize the potential threat to Egypt's independence, and he allied himself with Assyria, his former enemy.

Neco II fell heir to the accomplishments of his father and to an international political scene out of which he could not easily withdraw. He was allied with a losing power, as Nineveh, Assyria's capital, fell in 612 BC. Neco was called upon to assist the king of Assyria who had retreated to Harran from the Babylonian forces under Nebuchadnezzar. Neco moved his troops through Judah on his way to Carchemish to engage in battle with the Babylonians. As the troops moved through the Megiddo pass, they were ambushed by Judean troops under King Josiah. Neco requested safe passage, but Josiah foolhardily refused. Josiah was killed in the field (2 Kgs 23:29,30; cf. 2 Chr 35:20–25). Neco continued onward to Carchemish. The battle (605 BC) turned out to be a great victory for the young Nebuchadnezzar. Nebuchadnezzar recorded it in glowing terms: "As for the rest of the Egyptian army which had escaped from the defeat . . . the Babylonian troops overtook and defeated them; so that not a single man escaped to that country." The OT briefly observes: "The king of Egypt did not come again out of his land" (2 Kgs 24:7).

Neco strengthened Egypt by a policy of isolation. He made Judah a bumper zone and fortified the borders successfully in order to keep the Babylonians from penetrating into Egypt. He had deposed Jehoahaz, the newly enthroned king of three months, brought him to Riblah in Syria, and later to Egypt (23:33,34). Jehoiakim succeeded to the Davidic throne in Jerusalem and Judah was forced to pay a tribute of 100 talents of silver and a talent of gold (23:33–36). When Judah fell to Babylon, the Judeans considered the Egyptian interest in their survival as vital to Egypt's independence and requested help against Babylonia. The prophet Jeremiah strongly spoke against this dependence on Egypt (46:17–24). Whether Neco risked his forces to penetrate into Judah, a Babylonian province, is not certain. Nebuchadnezzar quickly moved his forces to Judah, exiled Jehoiakim to Babylon, and enthroned Zedekiah (597 BC). Shortly thereafter Neco died (595 BC). His son, Psammetichus II, succeeded him.

See EGYPT, EGYPTIANS; ISRAEL, HISTORY OF; JOSIAH #1.

Necromancer, Necromancy. Practice of communicating with the dead; a practice strictly forbidden by the Law (Dt 18:11).

See MAGIC.

Nedabiah. Son of Jeconiah, king of Judah (1 Chr 3:18).

Needle. Object used in Jesus' lesson about the rich man and entrance into God's kingdom. Following his discussion with the rich young ruler, Jesus told his disciples that "it is easier for a camel to go through the eye of a needle than for a rich man to enter the kingdom of God" (Mt 19:24; Mk 10:25; Lk 18:25). Jesus was not condemning riches or wealth but the change of will and false security that they may engender, as was the case with the

The partially reconstructed ruins of the ancient city of Avdat in the Negeb.

rich young ruler (cf. Mt 19:21,22; Mk 10:21,22; Lk 18:22,23). Entrance into God's kingdom is an act of God not of man. Using the largest land animal in Palestine, Jesus paralleled the absurdity of a camel passing through the eye of a needle with a rich man's attempt to use his position and possessions to gain entrance into heaven. A similar expression is found in rabbinic literature, where the elephant is pictured as passing through the eye of a needle.

Negeb. Southernmost region of Palestine. The name comes from the root "to be dry, parched," although its basic meaning is "south country, south." It is a specific area with no precise geographical boundaries. From north to south, the Negeb covers the area between Beersheba and Kadesh-barnea. From west to east it extends from near the Mediterranean to the Arabah, a distance of some 70 miles.

This is an arid section of the country, with infrequent and limited rainfall. With limited water resources, there was restricted opportunity for agriculture, although in the northern area some grain farming was done on a small scale, with possibly one crop failure every three years. A pastoral economy existed based primarily on the raising of sheep, goats, and camels. Simeon received this territory, including the cities, such as Arad and Rehoboth, in the tribal division of the Promised Land. Later Judah absorbed this tribe. During the monarchy the Israelites pushed into the Negeb. During the reigns of Solomon and Jehoshaphat, there was commercial traffic to and from the port of Ezion-geber on the Gulf of Aqaba. In Greco-Roman times the Nabataeans inhabited the Negeb. Through careful preservation of rainwater, they developed limited agriculture and sustained a number of towns. During NT times the Idumeans controlled the Negeb.

The KJV does not use the term Negeb, but ordinarily translates it as "the south." On the other hand, the RSV, NIV, and NASB regularly use the name for the territory. Abraham was often associated with the Negeb (Gn 12:9; 13:1,2; 20:1). David told Achish, king of Gath, that he had raided "the Negeb of Judah," "the Negeb of Jerahmeelites," and "the Negeb of the Kenites" (1 Sm 27:10), while the Egyptian captured by David stated that the Amalekites had made incursions against "the Negeb of the Cherethites," "the Negeb of Judah," and "the Negeb of Caleb" (1 Sm 30:14).

See PALESTINE; DESERT.

Neginah, Neginoth. Hebrew terms in the superscriptions of Psalms 4,6,54,55,61,67, and 76 (KJV); musical cues, meaning "stringed instruments," describing the kind of musical accompaniment for the performance of the designated psalms.

See MUSIC AND MUSICAL INSTRUMENTS.

Nehelamite. Ancestral name or the geographical designation for Shemaiah the false prophet (Jer 29:24,31,32). Its derivation is unknown. However, etymologically similar to the Hebrew word "dream," perhaps Nehelamite is an epithet coined by Jeremiah to deride Shemaiah, the false prophet, as a dreamer (KJV mg). A less feasible suggestion attempts to identify it with the Transjordanian town of Helam (see 2 Sm 10:16,17).

Nehemiah (Person). Name of three men mentioned in the OT after the period of the exile. The name means "the Lord comforts" and was appropriate for this time of hope and fulfillment.

1. Leader mentioned in a list of Jewish exiles who returned from Babylon with Zerubbabel some time after 538 BC (Ezr 2:2; Neh 7:7).

2. "Ruler of half the district of Beth-zur" who helped rebuild the Jerusalem wall in 444 BC (Neh 3:16).

3. Governor of Judah during the restoration. Originally cupbearer to the Persian king

The Wall of Nehemiah along the eastern edge of the Hill of Ophel in Jerusalem (south of the temple mount).

Artaxerxes I (464–424 BC), Nehemiah pleaded to be sent to Judah to aid his fellow Jews in their difficulties and in particular to rebuild Jerusalem (Neh 1:1–2:8). He was appointed governor of Judah for 12 years.

After inspecting the walls upon his arrival, he realized that their repair was to be his prime task, in order to guarantee the security of the city and also to provide a focal point for the Jewish community scattered throughout Judah. That he was able to marshal support for this project and to complete it attests to his skills in management and administration. He also had a strong personal faith, as his prayers (1:4–11; 2:4) and conviction of divine guidance and help (2:8,18,20) attest. He had to overcome hostility and intimidation from powerful neighboring authorities in Samaria, Ammon, and Arabia (4:1–9; 6:1–14). He also required economic justice (ch 5). A few rich Jews were exploiting a food shortage by exacting high interest from their poorer brothers.

Included in Nehemiah's concern for Jerusalem was a strong interest in the maintenance of temple worship. He was involved in the production of a document in which the Jewish community pledged themselves to support the temple personnel and to provide offerings (10:1,32–39). Clearly he realized that Judah needed at its heart a religious emphasis as well as political stability. These particular religious reforms are linked with those of his second period as governor (ch 13). Other reforms of that period concerned the observance of the sabbath (13:15–22) and the problem of marriages to non-Jews (13:23–27). Nehemiah was a forceful leader (v 25) who used his imperial powers to restore to the settlers a national and religious identity in a period of political and economic weakness. LESLIE C. ALLEN

See NEHEMIAH, BOOK OF; EZRA (PERSON) #1; EZRA, BOOK OF; POSTEXILIC PERIOD, THE.

Nehemiah, Book of.

Background. In 597 BC Nebuchadrezzar of Babylon took away the first exiles from Jerusalem. In 586 BC the Babylonians returned, pillaged and burned the city and its temple, and took an estimated 60,000 to 80,000 Judeans into exile. The expatriates settled in various districts where they enjoyed a measure of freedom. They engaged in agriculture and commerce, and in some instances acquired considerable wealth. The elders continued to function, prophets like Ezekiel ministered amongst the exiles, and resistance to religious apostasy was kept alive in the popular mind.

With the appearance of the Persian king, Cyrus the Great (559–530 BC), the Jewish exiles' future prospects altered dramatically. Cyrus was a civilized and enlightened statesman, and within a short time after his conquest of Babylon he issued an edict (Ezr 1:2–4) which granted the expatriates permission to return to their homeland. Two separate groups of exiles returned to Judah and built a new sanctuary in Jerusalem on the site of Solomon's temple in 516 BC. Then, under King Artaxerxes I (464–424 BC) two separate groups returned from Babylon under Ezra (458 BC) and Nehemiah (445 BC), respectively. From this seed bed there sprang the theocratic people of Judah, the "Jews," dedicated to the Law of God, isolated from foreign influence, and centered in Jerusalem.

Narrative. In the winter of 445 BC the Persian court was in Susa, the ancient capital of Elam (1:1). There Nehemiah occupied a position of honor and influence (2:1). From Jerusalem a company of Judeans arrived, among them Nehemiah's brother, whose description of conditions in Jerusalem horrified and grieved Nehemiah (1:2–4). Four months later and after much prayer, he reached Jerusalem with an armed escort (1:5–2:11). After a three-day inspection of the situation, Nehemiah realized that rebuilding the walls would be his primary task (2:12–3:32).

An outburst of new national spirit caused latent opposition to surface. Sanballat, Tobiah, and Geshem were powerful, resourceful, astute antagonists. Through ridicule and rumors they insinuated that work on the walls was a form of rebellion against the king (2:19; 4:1–3,7–14; 6:1–9). But Nehemiah countered every subterfuge and stratagem with prayer and with an adamant refusal to deviate from his goal. There was also hostility from traitors within the camp (6:10–14,17–19). Despite all opposition, Jerusalem's walls were reconstructed (6:15) and rededicated amid enthusiastic celebration (12:27–43).

The community's response to the reading by Ezra, priest and scribe, of the Law of Moses and to its interpretation by the Levites (8:1–8), was a complex response of sorrow for sin and rejoicing in God (8:9–18); of fasting and prayer (9:1–37); of renewing the covenant (9:38–10:29); and of self-commitment to obey God's commandments, ordinances, and statutes (10:30–39). Chapters 11 and 12 refer to various offices and duties, civil and religious, and the names of the people appointed to them. Then follows the decision to exclude all people of foreign descent from Judaism (13:1–3).

At this juncture Nehemiah traveled to Susa to give an account of his stewardship; a further leave of absence being granted, he returned to Jerusalem to find that serious irregularities were again present. His enemy Tobiah and the priest Eliashib were embroiled (13:4–9); the people failed to provide the Levites with adequate maintenance (13:10–14); the laws of the sabbath were being violated (13:15–22); and Jews were marrying non-Jews (13:23–31). Due to the increase of intermarriage with foreigners, the offspring could not speak Hebrew (13:23–25). The danger of assimilation was halted by enforcing a policy of exclusivism.

The Book of Nehemiah ends rather abruptly with a description of his vigorous and ruthless handling of these deviations from the newly established principles and precepts of Judaism.

Historicity. According to Josephus and other early writers, the books of Ezra and Nehemiah formed one book in the early Hebrew Bible entitled the Book of Ezra. The earliest Hebrew manuscript in which the two books are divided is dated 1448, and modern Hebrew Bibles refer to them as the books of Ezra and Nehemiah. In manuscripts of the Greek OT (Septuagint) they also formed one book. Origen, in the beginning of the 3rd century, is the first to attest to a division. There is general acknowledgement of the genuineness of the personal memoirs of Nehemiah, which constitute a major part of the book.

The historical framework of the book is confirmed by papyri which were discovered between 1898 and 1908 in Elephantine, the name of an island in the upper Nile. Here Psammetichus II (593–588 BC) established a Jewish colony. The Elephantine papyri are well preserved, written in Aramaic, and are the 5th-century BC literary remains of this Jewish colony of the Persian period.

The most important item amongst the papyri is a copy of a letter sent to the Persian governor of Judah in 407 BC. Three years earlier the Jewish temple in Elephantine had been destroyed, which disaster was the occasion of a letter to Jehohanan, the high priest in

Jerusalem (see Neh 12:12,13). Now, in their letter to the governor in Judah they ask permission to rebuild their temple, and add that they have sent a similar request to Delaiah and Shelamiah, the sons of Sanballat (Nehemiah's enemy, 2:10,19; 4:1). The Elephantine papyri reveal that Sanballat was governor of the province of Samaria and that Tobiah was governor of the province of Ammon in Transjordan (2:10,19). Here, then, is evidence that there was in Judah a twofold authority, civil and religious, and that the high priest of 408–407 BC was Jehohanan (12:13). Archaeologists have discovered additional evidence of the historicity of the Book of Nehemiah in the shape of a letter found at Geraza in Egypt from "Tobiah the Governor of Ammon," dealing with affairs in Judah; probably this correspondent was a descendant of the "Tobias the Ammonite" who opposed Nehemiah. Geshem the Arab (6:6) was the Persian appointee to govern northwest Arabia.

Chronology. The question about whether Ezra or Nehemiah came to Jerusalem first has been hotly debated. There is no doubt that Nehemiah arrived in the city in 445 BC. The objections to the view that Ezra came to Jerusalem 13 years earlier, in 458 BC, raise questions concerning historical and textual data which are of such complexity as to preclude discussion of them here. However, achieving an understanding of the spiritual values of the book does not depend on a correct interpretation of the details of chronology. Arguments against the traditional chronology are neither altogether decisive, nor do they dispel the inherent complexities.

Nehemiah the Person. Nehemiah's personal memoirs, which form a considerable portion of the book that bears his name, reveal a man of nobility and piety; compassionate, prudent, and patriotic; a man of generosity and fidelity, political acumen, and religious zeal; of total dedication to God, outstanding organizational ability, and dynamic leadership. At the same time Nehemiah possessed a capacity for ruthlessness when confronting the sin and waywardness of his compatriots (5:1–13) and the intrigues of powerful non-Jewish enemies (13:8,28). Not surprisingly, then, a disspirited and dejected people awoke from their lethargic and apathetic state and responded to Nehemiah's stringent approach to their situation (2:4; 13:14,22,31).

Significance. When the exiles returned to Jerusalem, Judah had neither nationhood nor political status. Only one thing remained to them: their religion; they were the "remnant" of Yahweh's chosen people, from whom would rise the new and glorious Israel. It was this vision that explains Nehemiah's insistence that the Jewish people maintain the purity and exclusiveness of their religious faith and practice in order to rejuvenate their national life and rebuild the city walls (6:15) because this symbolized the racial and the religious purity of the people. He also insisted on separation from paganism, prohibition of marriage with non-Jews (13:23–28), and careful observance of the laws of the sabbath (13:15–22).

It is, therefore, difficult to exaggerate the significance of the Book of Nehemiah. Along with the Book of Ezra it furnishes the only consecutive Hebrew account of that period in Jewish history when the foundations of Judaism, with its inflexible segregation of the Jews and its passionate veneration of the Mosaic law, were laid. Of course Haggai, Zechariah, and Malachi also contribute to knowledge of the period, but Nehemiah, with Ezra, provides a progressive narrative of this epoch. The return from Babylon of the expatriates to Jerusalem constitutes a resumption of the saving purposes of God for his ancient people leading to the advent of Jesus Christ.

The account of the return from Babylon under Nehemiah emphasizes the religious aspect of the community of repatriates in Jerusalem. But other secondary factors should be noted: Nehemiah's preoccupation with Judah's political security and constitutional status to ensure its independence of Samaria; the rebuilding of the city walls; Nehemiah's resettlements of population (7:4; 11:1,2); and his appointment to the governorship of the new province. However, there is no reference in the Book of Nehemiah (or for that matter in Ezra) to a restoration to nationhood under a scion of the House of David, no mention of a Messiah, no allusion to the universal kingdom of God. Nehemiah manifests absolute loyalty to the Persian overlord who, while showing remarkable openness to Nehemiah's request (2:4–9), still continues to levy taxes (5:4,15).

The repatriates retreated behind their city's new walls and congregated around the second temple, completed in 516 BC. "The Book of the Law of Moses" (8:1), recognized by the Persian overlord as the law of the land of Judah, became central to Jewish devotion and worship. Judaism was the product of the restoration, which became both a protective barrier against, and a wall of separation from, the Gentiles. Religious institutions initiated during the Babylonian exile and transplanted to Jerusalem, took deep and firm root: the synagogue where the Law and the Prophets were read and the prayers were offered; the scribes who worked with single-minded devotion; and the Sanhedrin which continued to serve the new theocracy.

The Jewish church of the 3rd century BC

parallels the modern Christian church in that both share the challenge of spiritual reconstruction and renewal essential to God's purposes. Herein lies, in part, the relevance of Nehemiah's reforms, the repentance and obedience essential to moral and spiritual renewal (8:1–10:39).

J.G.S.S. THOMSON

See NEHEMIAH (PERSON) #3; EZRA (PERSON) #1; EZRA, BOOK OF; CHRONOLOGY, OLD TESTAMENT; ISRAEL, HISTORY OF; JUDAISM; POSTEXILIC PERIOD, THE; JEW.

Bibliography. L.W. Batten, *A Critical and Exegetical Commentary on the Books of Ezra and Nehemiah;* L.H. Brockington, *Ezra, Nehemiah, and Esther;* F.C. Fensham, *The Books of Ezra and Nehemiah;* D. Kidner, *Ezra and Nehemiah;* J.M. Myers, *Ezra, Nehemiah;* H.G.M. Williamson, *Ezra, Nehemiah.*

Nehiloth. Hebrew term in the superscription of Psalm 5 (KJV); musical cue, meaning "flutes," describing the kind of musical accompaniment for the performance of the psalm.

See MUSIC AND MUSICAL INSTRUMENTS.

Nehum. One of the men listed in Nehemiah 7:7 who returned with Zerubbabel to Palestine following the Babylonian captivity. His name is alternately spelled Rehum in Ezra 2:2.

See REHUM #1.

Nehushta. Mother of Jehoiachin, king of Judah, who was deported with her son to Babylon (2 Kgs 24:8–15).

Nehushtan. Name given to the bronze serpent that Moses made during the wilderness wanderings. At the time of King Hezekiah's reforms, it was destroyed (2 Kgs 18:4).

See BRONZE SERPENT; WILDERNESS WANDERINGS.

Neiel. Border town in Asher's territory (Jos 19:27). Its site is perhaps identifiable with modern Khirbet Ya'nin, on the east end of the plain of Acco.

Neighbor. Concept apparently limited in the OT period and late Judaism to one's fellow Israelite, or member of the covenant, and extended by Jesus to include anyone encountered in life.

In the Old Testament. Although it is never explicitly limited as such, the prominent connotation of "neighbor" in the OT is that of a fellow member of the covenant community; that is, another Israelite (see Lv 6:1–7; 19; Dt 15:2,3). In Leviticus 19:18, a passage often quoted in the NT, the Israelite is commanded to "love your neighbor as yourself." In 19:34, it is explicitly stated that such love should also be shown to the foreigner (or "sojourner") passing through the land. If "neighbor" (v 18)

implied a more encompassing notion, such as "mankind" or "fellowman," there presumably would have been no need to include the further stipulation in verse 34. "Neighbor" was therefore probably taken to mean one's immediate neighbor, the fellow Israelite.

Within the covenant community, love of neighbor involved certain responsibilities explicitly set forth in the Law. The neighbor was to be treated fairly (Ex 22:5–15; Lv 6:2–7; 19:9–18) and respected (Ex 20:16), as were his belongings (Ex 20:17). To foster such just and merciful relationships within the covenant community, the neighbor was to be thought of as a "brother" (Lv 25:25, Dt 22:1–4). What one did to one's neighbor was to be returned in kind (Lv 24:19–23; Dt 19:11–19).

The grave importance attached to treatment of the neighbor is understandable when seen as part of one's wider relationship with God and was considered something that could affect significantly the divine-human relationship (Lv 6:1–7; 19; 25:17; Dt 24:10–13; Ps 12). Israelites were to treat their neighbors in the same loving way they had themselves been treated by God (Ex 22:21; Lv 25:35–38).

The importance of the neighbor relationship within the covenant community is also demonstrated by the fact that when such responsibilities were ignored, a societal breakdown or national turmoil followed (Dt 28:15–68; Hos 4:1–3; Am 2:6,7). That the Israelites often did neglect love for neighbor, particularly the neighbor in need, is a contributing cause for the divine punishment of the exile (Jer 5:7–9; 7:1–15; 9:2–9; Hos 4:1–3; Am 2:6,7; 5:10–13; 8:4–6). The mere fact that proper love of neighbor was also part of Israel's hope for the Messianic age to come (Jer 31:34; Zec 3:10) also points to its common neglect within the OT covenant community.

In Late Judaism. From the exilic experience, Israel recognized that divine blessing was conditional somewhat on justice and love exercised toward one another (Zec 8:14–17). The identity of the "neighbor" was debatable, however. Several factors suggest that "neighbor" was limited in this period to the fellow Israelite and the proselyte (gentile convert to Judaism). Evidence from rabbinic material excludes Samaritans and the Gentiles living in the land from being considered "neighbors" and thus worthy of love. Within the Jewish Essene community at Qumran, the "neighbor" to be respected and treated fairly was restricted to one's fellow community members. Finally, when Jesus recalls, "You have heard that it was said, 'You shall love your neighbor and hate your enemy'" (Mt 5:43–48), he is quoting only partially from the OT (Lv 19:18—"You shall love your neighbor . . ."). The last phrase (". . . and hate your enemy") reflects the contemporary Jewish feeling toward outsiders; that is, God did not require love toward those considered "enemies" but only toward fellow countrymen.

In the New Testament. Jesus differed dramatically from his Jewish contemporaries by eradicating the limitations on the neighbor to be loved. In contrast to those who would limit love to one's fellow countrymen, Jesus advocated extending the obligation reserved for the neighbor to the enemy as well (Mt 5:43–48) and in so doing, destroyed the distinction between neighbor and enemy altogether.

On another occasion, a scribe asked Jesus what was the greatest commandment given by God (Mk 12:28–31). In response, Jesus cited Deuteronomy 6:5 concerning the nature of God and man's obligation to love God with his entire being: heart, soul, and mind. Of significance is that Jesus did not stop there but linked with this a second commandment to "love your neighbor as yourself" (Lv 19:18). Some scholars suggest that this dramatic and close association of love of God and love of neighbor originated with Jesus. If Jesus did first draw these commands together (see Mt 22:37; Mk 12:29–31), it reveals our Lord's own understanding of the relation of these two obligations: proper love for neighbor derives from love for God and conversely, love for God is inseparable from meeting the needs of a neighbor in love.

The debate in Jesus' time was not over how to properly treat a neighbor but who, in fact, was the neighbor. Jesus is asked this very question by an expert of the Law (Lk 10:29). Jesus had complimented the lawyer for his clear understanding of what was required to inherit eternal life; namely, love of God and love of neighbor. Luke suggests (10:29) that the lawyer asked the further qualifying question in order to "justify himself," that is, justify his actual behavior of limited love toward his fellowman. Jesus chose not to respond directly but through the use of a parable, in this case, the familiar parable of the Good Samaritan (10:30–35). In order to open the lawyer's eyes to the tragic shortsightedness of his question, Jesus related an everyday story of a man traveling the treacherous road from Jerusalem down to Jericho, a road particularly plagued by robbers. The traveler is robbed, stripped, beaten, and left half dead (v 30). To this point, the lawyer might have assumed Jesus was offering an example of who constitutes a "neighbor"—a fellow Jew in need. Jesus proceeds, however, to introduce two figures, a priest and a Levite (10:31,32) who, in an academic discussion, could have argued quite ably on who is the neighbor God calls one to love. The lawyer

would no doubt have anticipated such experts in the Law to act rightly toward the victim. In contrast, the priest and Levite, upon seeing the man in need, respond by "passing by the other side." Unable to determine whether the victim was dead or barely alive (v 30b), and possibly not wanting to risk uncleanness, the experts of the Law pass by, thus violating the greatest of the commandments just identified by the lawyer (10:25–28). Enter a Samaritan, a figure especially despised by the Jews. Viewed as heretics by the Jewish religious authorities, the Samaritans were disqualified in rabbinic circles from being considered a "neighbor" and thus worthy of love. In fact, previous centuries had witnessed the slaughter of many Samaritans by Jewish rulers, and animosity clearly existed between the two peoples (see Jn 4:9). While the lawyer listening to the parable would have expected the priest and Levite to act justly toward the victim, he must have been surprised that a hated Samaritan would show compassion and thus fulfill the greatest commandment. Jesus intentionally spelled out the extent of the Samaritan's compassion (immediate care in dressing wounds, transport to the inn, care for the victim there and extended care in paying for care by others while he is away, 10:34,35) to such a degree that the lawyer would have no doubt as to the genuineness of the Samaritan's love. The irony of the story is that one not considered worthy to be called "neighbor" by Jews was precisely the one who showed himself to be "neighbor" to the victim (10:36,37).

The parable, like the statement in Matthew 5:43–48, reveals Jesus' own understanding of "neighbor" and what "love of neighbor" demands. Jesus sets no limitation on who qualifies as the neighbor commanded by God to be loved.

The forcefulness and power of Jesus' teachings on the love of neighbor and its relationship to one's love for God are demonstrated by a similar emphasis within the early church. Paul on two occasions called the love of neighbor the "fulfillment of the entire law" (Rom 13:8–10; Gal 5:14), while James referred to the same commandment as "the royal law" (Jas 2:8).

DAVID C. CARLSON

See JESUS CHRIST, LIFE AND TEACHING OF; COMMANDMENT, THE NEW; FOREIGNER.

Nekeb. KJV rendering of a town defining the boundary of the territory allotted to Naphtali's tribe for an inheritance, positioned between Za-anannim (or Adami, KJV) and Jabneel (Jos 19:33, RSV Adami-nekeb). Its exact site is uncertain, but it is usually identified with modern Khirbet-ed-Damiyeh.

See ADAMI, ADAMI-NEKEB.

Nekoda. 1. Father of a family of temple servants who returned to Jerusalem following the exile (Ezr 2:48; Neh 7:50).

2. Father of a family of returned exiles who could not prove their Israelite descent (Ezr 2:60; Neh 7:62).

Nemuel. 1. Reubenite and the son of Eliab (Nm 26:9).

2. One of Simeon's sons (Nm 26:12; 1 Chr 4:24), also called Jemuel (Gn 46:10).

See JEMUEL.

Nemuelite. Member of Nemuel's family from Simeon's tribe (Nm 26:12; alternately called Jemuel in Gn 46:10).

See JEMUEL.

Nepheg. 1. Levite of the family of Kohath and the second of Izhar's three sons (Ex 6:21).

2. David's son born to him during his reign in Jerusalem (2 Sm 5:15; 1 Chr 3:7; 14:6).

Nephilim. Early division of the human race, mentioned only twice in the OT (Gn 6:4; Nm 13:33). The Greek translation of the Hebrew Scriptures rendered the name "Nephilim" as "giants," and other versions followed this rendering, including the KJV. Modern translations, however, usually designate them as Nephilim, thus identifying them with the Anakim (Nm 13:33; Dt 2:21) and the Rephaim (Dt 2:20). The latter two were reputed to be large physically, hence the rendering "giants."

The Nephilim are of unknown origin. Some writers have taken the Hebrew verb *naphal*, "to fall," to imply that the Nephilim were "fallen ones," that is, fallen angels who subsequently mated with human women. But Christ taught that angels do not have carnal relationships (Lk 20:34,35), and therefore this view can only be maintained by assuming that Genesis 6:1–4 reflects Greek mythology, in which such unions occurred. The Genesis passage, however, deals with anthropology, not mythology.

The Nephilim were evidently not the "sons of God" and seem to be different also from the "daughters of men." The best classification is with the Anakim and Rephaim as contemporary peoples of unknown origin.

See GIANTS.

Nephish. KJV spelling of Naphish, Ishmael's son (1 Chr 5:19).

See NAPHISH.

Nephisim, Nephishesim. A group of people who returned to Jerusalem with Zerubbabel after the exile, counted among the temple servants (Ezr 2:50, KJV Nephusim; Neh 7:52, KJV Nephishesim, RSV Nephushesim).

Nephthalim. KJV rendering of Naphtali's tribe in Matthew 4:13,15.

See NAPHTALI, TRIBE OF.

Nephtoah, Waters of. Geographical landmark situated between Mt Ephron to the west and the Valley of Hinnom to the east, defining part of the boundary separating the tribes of Judah and Benjamin (Jos 15:9; 18:15). Its site is generally identified with Ain Lifta, three miles northwest of Jerusalem.

Nephushesim. Alternate name for the Nephisim (Neh 7:52).

See NEPHISIM, NEPHISHESIM.

Nephusim. KJV spelling of Nephisim in Ezra 2:50.

See NEPHISIM, NEPHISHESIM.

Nepthalim. KJV rendering of Naphtali's tribe in Revelation 7:6.

See NAPHTALI, TRIBE OF.

Ner. Benjamite, father of Abner, Kish's brother, and the uncle of Saul (1 Sm 14:50; 26:5; 2 Sm 2:8; 1 Kgs 2:32; 1 Chr 26:28). Although Ner's father's name was given as Abiel (1 Sm 14:51), disputed readings put Ner among the sons of Jeiel (1 Chr 8:29,30; 9:35, 36). Elsewhere he is listed as the father of Kish, the father of Saul (1 Chr 8:33; 9:39). Ner was, then, the grandfather or the uncle of Saul, probably the latter. One suggestion is that there were two men called Kish, one of whom was Ner's brother, the other his son. Another is that there were two men called Ner. These speculations demonstrate that genealogical tables were sometimes incomplete or ambiguous.

Nereus. Roman Christian to whom Paul sent greetings in the salutation of his letter to Rome (16:15).

Nergal. Heathen deity worshiped by the men of Cuth after the fall of Israel in 722 BC (2 Kgs 17:30). Nergal, lord of the nether world and associated with the sun god, was the city god of the northern Babylonian city of Cuthah (cf. 2 Kgs 17:24).

See ASSYRIA, ASSYRIANS.

Nergal-sharezer. Babylonian prince who held the title Rabmag. Nergal-sharezer participated with Nebuchadnezzar and the Chal-

The Arch of Titus in Rome, the city in which Nereus lived.

dean army in conquering Jerusalem after a three-year siege from 588 to 586 BC (Jer 39:3) and later entrusted Jeremiah to Gedaliah's care (v 13).

Neri. Ancestor of Jesus in Luke's genealogy (3:27).

See GENEALOGY OF JESUS CHRIST.

Neriah. Father of Baruch the scribe (Jer 32:12,16; 36:4,8) and Seraiah the quartermaster (Jer 51:59), both of whom served Jeremiah the prophet.

Nero. Roman emperor from AD 54 to 68.

See CAESARS, THE.

Netaim. Habitation of the potters who were employed in the king's service (1 Chr 4:23).

Nethanel, Nethaneel. Common OT name spelled Nethaneel in the KJV.

1. Zuar's son and the prince of Issachar's tribe at the start of Israel's wilderness wanderings (Nm 1:8; 2:5; 10:15), who represented his kinsmen at the altar's dedication (7:18,23).

2. Judahite, the fourth son of Jesse and David's brother (1 Chr 2:14).

3. One of the priests assigned to blow a trumpet before the ark in the procession led by David when the ark was moved to Jerusalem (1 Chr 15:24).

4. Levite and the father of Shemaiah, the scribe who recorded the 24 divisions of priests founded during David's reign (1 Chr 24:6).

5. Korahite Levite and Obed-edom's fifth son in David's reign (1 Chr 26:4).

6. One of the princes sent by King Jehoshaphat to teach the Law in the cities of Judah (2 Chr 17:7).

7. One of the levitical chiefs who generously gave animals to the Levites for the celebration of the Passover feast during King Josiah's reign (2 Chr 35:9).

8. Priest and one of Pashhur's six sons who was encouraged by Ezra to divorce his foreign wife during the postexilic era (Ezr 10:22).

9. Head of Jedaiah's priestly family during the days of Joiakim, the high priest, in postexilic Jerusalem (Neh 12:21).

10. One of the priestly musicians who performed at the dedication of the Jerusalem wall during Nehemiah's day (Neh 12:36).

Nethaniah. 1. Elishama's son, father of Ishmael and a member of the royal family of Judah (2 Kgs 25:23,25; Jer 40:8–15; 41:1–18).

2. One of Asaph's 4 sons and the leader of the 5th of 24 divisions of musicians trained for service in the sanctuary during David's reign (1 Chr 25:2,12).

3. One of the Levites sent by King Jehoshaphat of Judah to teach the Law in the cities of Judah (2 Chr 17:8).

4. Shelemiah's son and the father of Jehudi. Jehudi served in the court of King Jehoiakim of Judah (Jer 36:14).

Nethinim. Term appearing only in the books written after Israel's return from exile (1 Chr; Ezr; Neh). Nethinim derives from the verb *nathan*, to give, set apart, dedicate, and means "those given" or "those set apart or dedicated." The Septuagint translates the word *dedomenoi*. Some recent translators have followed Josephus (*Antiq.* 11.5.1) by referring to them as "temple slaves."

Before the exile the Nethinim were active in temple service. First Chronicles 9:2 lists them with the priests and Levites who took possession of their allotted cities. Their listed order, priests, Levites, and Nethinim, suggests their subordinate role to the Levites (see also Neh 7:73; 11:3,20,21). They returned from exile as temple personnel (Ezr 2:43,58; 7:7,24; 8:17, 20; Neh 7:46,60). They had their dwelling in Jerusalem (Ezr 7:7; Neh 3:31; 11:21) and joined in the repair of the walls (Neh 3:26).

The identification of the Nethinim is not absolutely certain. Numbers 31:47 records that the Levites received captives who were assigned the laborious and menial tasks. When the Gibeonites were accepted within Israel as servants, they too were appointed as water carriers and wood choppers for the entire community and the altar of the Lord (Jos 9:9–27). David augmented the number of tabernacle servants by assigning captives taken in war to these duties (Ezr 8:20). At the completion of the temple, the temple services called for more workers, and Solomon added to their number. This new group became known as "Solomon's men." Ezra records that from the

Nethinim, 392 returned from exile to Jerusalem (Ezr 2:58) and performed the work in the rebuilt temple that had been done by their ancestors before the exile.

Considered full members of the restored covenant community, the Nethinim entered into covenant to wholly devote themselves to God (Neh 10:28).

See TABERNACLE, TEMPLE; PRIESTS AND LEVITES.

Netophah, Netophathite.

Home and designation for two of David's 30 mighty men (2 Sm 23:28,29; 1 Chr 11:30; 27:13,15). Seraiah, one of the captains who came to Gedaliah, the governor in Jerusalem after its fall to Babylon in 586 BC, was a Netophathite (2 Kgs 25:23; Jer 40:8). Fifty-six men of Netophah are mentioned as among the exiles who returned from Babylon with Zerubbabel and Joshua (Ezr 2:22).

First Chronicles 9:16 speaks of Levites living "in the villages of the Netophathites," while Nehemiah 12:28 says that temple singers were gathered from the villages surrounding Jerusalem and "from the villages of the Netophathites." Both of these references suggest that Netophah was the name of a district and not just of a town.

The linking of Netophah with Bethlehem (see 1 Chr 2:54; Neh 7:26) indicates that it was in that vicinity. The actual site of Netophah is not known; however, the most probable location is the modern Khirbet Bedd Faluh, 3½

Terraced slopes below Beit Sahur, a suburb of Bethlehem and probably in the vicinity of ancient Netophah.

miles southeast of Bethlehem. Near it is a spring called Ain en-Natuf in which the ancient name of Netophah may be preserved.

Nettle. See PLANTS.

New, Newness.

That the second part of the Bible is called the *New* Testament indicates how fundamental the idea of "new" is to biblical revelation. Many key theological expressions incorporate the idea: new creation (2 Cor 5:17), new birth (Jn 3:3), new man (Eph 2:15; Col 3:10), new commandment (Jn 13:34), new covenant (Jer 31:31), new life (Rom 6:4), and various others.

The Expectation of the New. Immediately after the fall, God speaks a new word of redemption in that he points to the time when the seed of woman shall bruise the head of the serpent (Gn 3:15). All of the OT elation is hence expressed in terms of future expectation of a new condition, a time when nation shall no longer lift up sword against nation (Is 2:4) and when the lion shall lie down with the lamb (Is 11:6). The idea of the new encompasses more than Israel: it involves God's whole creative purpose for all that he has created. Both Isaiah (43:19) and Jeremiah (31:22) speak of the "new thing" to be done in the nation's history.

The totality of the expectation of the *new*, however, is best expressed in Jeremiah and Ezekiel and in the references in the Psalter to the "new song" to be given to the people to sing (e.g., Pss 33:3; 40:3; 149:1; cf., also Is 42:10). Jeremiah speaks of the day when God will make a new covenant with the house of Israel (Jer 31:31–34; cf., Ez 34:25–31; 37:26–28). In contrast with the old, this new covenant will be written upon the heart, that is, it will be internalized. Similarly Ezekiel (36:22–32) tells of the day when God, as an expression of his own holiness (v 23), will cleanse his people and in place of the heart of stone will give a heart of flesh. This will usher in the age of the Spirit and will bring about a new existence, characterized by security and freedom, in which the laws of God are carried out. The supreme feature of this new time is the new spirit within them (Ez 11:19). Joel speaks also of that day when the Spirit of God will be poured out on all flesh (Jl 2:28). Isaiah 65:17 states the promise of "new heavens and a new earth," words which often reflect national circumstances and hopes (for example, after the exile). However, they came to take on new eschatological significance beyond the hope of the nation Israel.

The Coming of the New. One of the most striking parables of Jesus concerns attempts to put old wine into new wineskins (Mk 2:22).

He announced the fullness of time (Mk 1:15). When he read from Isaiah 61 in the synagogue in Nazareth he declared the presence of the Lord's special year, "the acceptable year" (Lk 4:24). When he combines this new word with the casting out of demons, the people express their amazement: "What is this? A new teaching!" (Mk 1:27). The central proclamation of the presence of the kingdom in the word and ministry of Jesus is a declaration that the promised new age has broken into time in powerful ways. Jesus' ministry is one of fulfillment; what has been promised by prophets has begun to take place. John the Baptist had prepared the way for the one who would bestow the promised Spirit. At the Last Supper the cup of wine speaks of the blood of the new covenant (Mk 14:24), by which Jesus meant his atoning death.

The early church expresses this significance in varying metaphors. Through faith in Christ one is born anew (Jn 3:3–7). This "newness of life" is expressed sacramentally through baptism (Rom 6:4). The eucharistic cup is the new covenant through blood (1 Cor 11:25). An extended discourse on the old and new covenants shows that by the shedding of his blood Christ has become mediator of a new covenant (Heb 9:15); by his blood he has opened up a new and living way into the holy place (10:19,20). Paul restates the promise of Ezekiel for a heart of flesh (2 Cor 3:3), after which he gives an account of the ministry of the new covenant in contrast to the old. The church represents the appearance of the new age in the domain of the old.

The one who comes to Christ by faith is declared a new person, a new creation, in whom the old is passed away (2 Cor 5:17; Gal 6:15). Jewish-Gentile hostility disappears in the resulting "new humanity" (Eph 2:15). All other social distinctions (such as male-female, slave-free) pass away in the new humanity created in terms of God's eternal purpose (Col 3:10,11).

The newness of a person in Christ is the foundation for NT ethics (Eph 4:25; Col 3:12). The new commandment (Jn 13:34; 1 Jn 2:8) is not really new (1 Jn 2:7), but now has new possibility and dimension by virtue of the power and pattern of Jesus, the servant Messiah. Though this new life is a gift of God, the *process* of being made new continues. Transformation by the renewing of the mind (Rom 12:2) brings realization of the will of God. Paul finds the inner man being renewed day by day (2 Cor 4:16).

The Realization of the New. As real as the new life of the believer may be, Scripture recognizes a tension between the new age which has come in history, but is not yet fully real-

ized. There is a projection to that time when all things are made new (Rv 21:5). With the end of the old, there is a new heaven and new earth. The new Jerusalem (Rv 21:2) "descends" as the dwelling place of God. The people of God receive a new name (Rv 3:12) as the former things pass away. To the redeemed of the Lord (Rv 14:3), a new song is given, the song of the Lamb slain from the very foundation of creation: "Worthy is the Lamb who was slain, to receive power and wealth and wisdom and might and honor and glory and blessing," and the antiphonal song returns, "To him who sits upon the throne and unto the Lamb be blessing and honor and glory and might for ever and ever."

See REGENERATION; COMMANDMENT, THE NEW; COVENANT, THE NEW; NEW CREATION, NEW CREATURE; NEW HEAVENS AND NEW EARTH; JERUSALEM, THE NEW; MAN, OLD AND NEW.

New Birth. *See* REGENERATION.

New Commandment. Expression used by Jesus (Jn 13:34) to designate his teaching concerning the love of Christians for each other.

See COMMANDMENT, THE NEW.

New Covenant. Expression used by Jesus (Lk 22:20; cf. Jer 31:31) to designate the meaning of his death.

See COVENANT, THE NEW.

New Creation, New Creature. Concept of redemption developed throughout the OT and NT to its final consummation in the second coming of Jesus Christ.

The most fundamental truth of the Bible is that God is the Creator of heaven and earth, who sustains and controls everything (e.g., Gn 1; Pss 33:6–11; 104; Mt 6:25–32). The most basic consideration about man is that he is a creature, made in God's image in order to serve him (Gn 1,2). Accordingly, the Bible's message of salvation is unintelligible apart from what it teaches about God as Creator. The true nature and perversity of man's sin stem from the fact that he "worshiped and served created things rather than the Creator" (Rom 1:25 NIV). God is Redeemer because he is Creator. By the same token, the objects of God's saving activity are his rebellious creatures who, along with the entire created order, are cursed with futility and decay (Gn 3:17,18; Rom 8:20, 21).

In the Old Testament. The tie between creation and salvation is especially prominent in the latter part of Isaiah (40–66). The prophet surveys the grandeur of the final redemption God will accomplish for Israel. Repeatedly the perspective on this promised eschatological deliverance is that God is the Creator of heaven and earth and of Israel in particular (see also the full statement of 40:12–31; e.g., 44:24; 45:18; 48:13; 51:16; 64:8).

In this context, expectation centers on "the new heavens and the new earth" (65:17; 66:22). This reference to the new creation gives the broadest conceivable scope to the eschatological salvation prophesied by Isaiah. God's work of renewal and restoration at the end parallels his work of creation in the beginning (48:12). What God will do in bringing all things to their consummation is of the same order of magnitude as what he did in calling them into existence out of nothing. At the same time, the new creation concept reveals that the end-time salvation promised to Israel has universal and cosmic proportions. The underlying hope is the ultimate entrance of the faithful from among the nations, as well as in Israel, into the bliss of the eternal, new creation order. These themes from Isaiah are taken up and developed by the NT writers, and are integral to their message.

The New Creation and Christ. The NT ties together creation and redemption. Several writers either parallel or in other ways relate the saving work of Christ to his activity at creation (Jn 1:3; Col 1:15–18; Heb 1:2,3; Rv 3:14). What he has done at the end, in "the fulness of time" (Gal 4:4; Eph 1:10), "in these last days" (Heb 1:2), roots in what he did in the beginning. The redemption accomplished by Christ is a work of new creation.

This association of the new creation with Christ's work is unmistakable when Paul designates Christ as the "last Adam" and "second man" (1 Cor 15:45,47; cf. v 22; Rom 5:14). This description has close affinities with "Son of man," a self-designation of Jesus. Paul's use of the last Adam designation is obviously intended to heighten the contrast between Adam and Christ (Rom 1; 1 Cor 15). In antithesis to Adam, who through his disobedience brought into the world sin and the consequent condemnation of death, Christ by his obedience has established righteousness, resulting in justification and life.

Paul discloses something of the full range and implications of the Adam-Christ contrast (1 Cor 15:42–49). He contrasts the believer's present bodily existence, in its weakness and mortality, with the body to be received at the resurrection. He sums up this contrast: the one body is "natural," the other is "spiritual."

Adam and Christ exemplify these two bodies, the natural and the spiritual. At the same time, however, Adam and Christ are brought into view as whole persons. They are the representatives of others (v 48) and heads over con-

trasting orders of life. Adam, the first man, is representative head of the natural earthly order of existence, made subject to corruption and death by his sin (Rom 5:12–19). Christ, the second and last Adam, is the representative head over the spiritual, heavenly order, characterized by life, power, and glory. Ultimately, the contrast in this passage is between two successive world orders, creation and its consummation (new creation), each beginning with an Adam.

Two other points also bear on the new creation gospel of Paul and the other NT writers. First, his own resurrection is when Christ, as the last Adam, became life-giving Spirit (v 45). The controlling emphasis is on the unity between the resurrection of Christ and believers (cf. 1 Cor 15:12–20; Col 1:18). In NT proclamation the resurrection of Christ is the great redemptive counterpart to creation (Rom 4:17). According to the NT, the new creation is a present reality, dating from the resurrection of Christ. Second, in stating that the last Adam became life-giving Spirit, verse 45 points to the unity that exists between the exalted Christ and the Holy Spirit in their saving activity. The Holy Spirit is the power of the new creation (cf. Heb 6:5). Where the Spirit is at work as the gift of the glorified Christ, the new creation is present.

The new creation is the eschatological fulfillment promised and anticipated in the OT. As such it has already been inaugurated and realized by the work of Christ (the last Adam), particularly his death and resurrection, and will be consummated at his return. The interval in between receives its fundamental character from the coexistence of the two creations; the new has begun, while concurrently the old continues to pass away (1 Cor 7:31). The concept of new creation closely parallels that of the kingdom of God, according to the synoptic Gospels the central theme of Jesus' proclamation. Tied to his own person and work in its coming, the kingdom is announced by him as both present (Mt 12:28; 13:11,16,17) and future (Mt 8:11; 25:34). In terms of the two-age distinction, coined by contemporary Judaism to express its eschatological expectations and taken over by Jesus and the early church (e.g., Mt 12:32; Eph 1:21), the new creation is the longed-for "age to come." "New creation" serves to indicate the comprehensive nature of this eschatological reality; redemption involves nothing less than the renewal of all things (Rv 21:5).

The New Creation and the Church. Salvation, according to the NT, is from beginning to end a matter of union with Christ and sharing in all the benefits resulting from his once-for-all redemptive work. Accordingly, because

Christ died and was raised again (2 Cor 5:15), anyone in Christ is already a participant in the new creation order (v 17). The reference is not only personal but cosmic, as seen from the context with its correlative emphasis on the reconciliation and its scope ("all this," v 18; "the world," v 19).

In the only other NT occurrence of the expression "new creation" (Gal 6:15), the perspective is cosmic as well as individual. The new creation, in which neither circumcision nor uncircumcision matters, stands in opposition to the world, to which the believer has been crucified with Christ (v 14; cf. Col 2:20). "When anyone is united to Christ, there is a new world; the old order is gone, and a new order has already begun" (2 Cor 5:17 NEB).

Resurrection is not only a future hope for believers but a present reality; they have already been raised with Christ (Eph 2:5,6; cf. Col 2:12,13; 3:1). Consequently, believers are "created in Christ Jesus for good works" (Eph 2:10). Further, the church is the new covenant reality of "the new man," made up of Israel and the nations (v 15). As such, its members are already being renewed inwardly (2 Cor 4:16) by the Lord-Spirit according to the glorified image of the last Adam (3:18; 4:4,6; cf. Rom 8:29; Eph 4:24; Col 3:10). And they will bear this same image bodily at his return (1 Cor 15:49). The deepest motive for holy living is not gratitude for the forgiveness of sin but the determination of the believer's existence as a new creature. The ethics of the NT are new creation ethics (Rom 12:2; Col 2:20).

The new creation is not only a present reality but a future hope. For the new creation, too, the church lives "by faith, not by sight" (2 Cor 5:7). Reminiscent of Isaiah's expectation, believers are looking to Christ's return for "new heavens and a new earth in which righteousness dwells" and where sin and its effects are nothing more than memories (2 Pt 3:13; Rv 21:1,3,4).

This hope raises the question of the relationship between this final, eternal order and the original creation. The picture of destruction by burning (2 Pt 3:10,12) and some of the images in Revelation 21 and 22 (e.g., no sun, moon, night; cf. 6:12–14) seem to suggest an absolute disjunction. Other passages, however, interpret this imagery. With all the radical differences before and after the resurrection, the natural and spiritual bodies (1 Cor 15:44) are not distinct from each other as bodies. This body, sown in corruption, dishonor, and weakness, will be raised up incorruptible, glorious, and powerful. And what holds true for the believer's body also holds for creation. The anxious longing and groaning of the entire (nonpersonal) creation is not for annihilation, but

that it may be set free from bondage to futility and decay and may share in the glorious freedom of the children of God, which will be revealed in the redemption (resurrection) of the body (Rom 8:19–23). The new creation is not merely a return to conditions in the beginning, but a renewed creation, the consummation of God's purposes set from before the beginning and realized, despite man's sin and its destructive effects, by the redemption in Christ, the last Adam.

RICHARD B. GAFFIN, JR.

See CREATION, DOCTRINE OF; MAN, OLD AND NEW; NEW, NEWNESS; NEW HEAVENS AND NEW EARTH; ADAM (PERSON); ETERNAL LIFE.

New Gate. One of the gates of the temple during Jeremiah's ministry (Jer 26:10; 36:10).

New Heavens and New Earth. Concept first found in the Book of Isaiah. God declares, "For behold, I create new heavens and a new earth; and the former things shall not be remembered or come into mind. . . . For as the new heavens and the new earth which I will make shall remain before me . . . so shall your descendants and your name remain" (Is 66:17,22).

Some scholars think that long before Isaiah's time there existed among many ancient peoples the belief that the end of human history would correspond to its beginning and therefore some sort of universal restoration would take place. The world renewal taught in Scripture regards the event as supernatural and as taking place in a different and higher sphere.

That God is Creator of the heavens and earth is basic to all biblical theology. "Of old thou didst lay the foundation of the earth, and the heavens are the work of thy hands" (Ps 102:25). If God created the heavens and earth, then it is entirely appropriate that, once they have served their purpose, God may do with them what he wishes. "They will all wear out like a garment. Thou changest them like raiment, and they pass away" (Ps 102:26). The same metaphor is found in Isaiah 51:6, which speaks of the earth wearing out like a garment.

The idea of God renewing or transforming his creation is also found among Jewish writings outside of Scripture. The Apocalypse of Ezra, probably written toward the end of the 1st century AD, tells of a future time when God shall "renew his creation" (2 Esd 7:75; cf. the same expression in 2 Bar 32:6). Sometime during the last 2 centuries BC, the writer of the Ethiopic book of Enoch spoke of God transforming both heaven and earth and making them an eternal blessing (1 Enoch 45:4,5).

Scripture gives considerable attention to the passing away of the old order, speaking of a future time when heaven and earth will disappear (Is 34:4; 51:6; Mt 24:35; Rv 21:2). A number of related phrases portray the same idea: "And the world passes away" (1 Jn 2:17); "They [the heavens and earth] will all grow old like a garment" (Heb 1:11; cf. Ps 102:26; Is 51:6); "The heavens will pass away with a loud noise, and the elements will be dissolved with fire, and the earth and the works that are upon it will be burned up" (2 Pt 3:10; cf. Is 34:4). This consummation by fire will take place at the time of final judgment. It will be "the day of God, because of which the heavens will be kindled and dissolved, and the elements will melt with fire!" (2 Pt 3:12).

This judgment, which brings to a close the old order, clears the way for new heavens and a new earth. Peter continues, "But according to his promise we wait for new heavens and a new earth in which righteousness dwells" (2 Pt 3:13). It will be so wonderful that no one will even remember the old (Is 65:17). Peter, preaching in Solomon's Colonnade, says that Jesus will remain in heaven "until the time for establishing all that God spoke by mouth of his holy prophets from of old" (Acts 3:21). This recovery or renewal is eagerly awaited by the created order. Paul writes, "For the creation waits with eager longing for the revealing of the sons of God" (Rom 8:19) because "the creation itself will be set free from its bondage to decay and obtain the glorious liberty of the children of God" (Rom 8:21).

The heaven that will be renewed is not the heaven of God's presence, but the heaven of human existence, the starry expanse which constitutes the universe. In the Book of Revelation we learn that the new Jerusalem comes down from heaven to earth (Rv 21:2,10) and forms the eternal dwelling place of God and his people. The geographic distinction between heaven and earth begins to lose its significance. The new earth will be a place of perfect righteousness (Is 51:6), divine kindness (Is 54:10), an eternal relationship to God (Is 66:22), and total freedom from sin (Rom 8:21).

See HEAVEN; NEW, NEWNESS; NEW CREATION, NEW CREATURE; ESCHATOLOGY; KINGDOM OF GOD (HEAVEN).

New Jerusalem. *See* JERUSALEM, NEW.

New Man. Expression used by the apostle Paul to refer to Jesus Christ and his body, the church (Eph 2:15).

See MAN, OLD AND NEW.

New Moon. Monthly celebration involving cereal offerings, burnt sacrifices, and trumpet blasts.

See FEASTS AND FESTIVALS OF ISRAEL; MOON.

New Testament. *See* BIBLE.

New Testament Canon. *See* BIBLE, CANON OF THE.

New Testament Chronology. *See* CHRONOLOGY, NEW TESTAMENT.

New Testament Theology. *See* BIBLICAL CRITICISM, NEW TESTAMENT; BIBLICAL THEOLOGY; JESUS CHRIST, LIFE AND TEACHING OF; JOHN THE APOSTLE, LIFE AND WRITINGS OF; PAUL, THE APOSTLE; PETER, THE APOSTLE. *See also* EACH INDIVIDUAL NT BOOK FOR A BRIEF STATEMENT ON ITS OWN PARTICULAR THEOLOGICAL TEACHING.

New Year. Ten-day period of penitence which begins the Jewish new year.

See FEASTS AND FESTIVALS OF ISRAEL.

Neziah. Forefather of a family of temple servants who returned to Jerusalem with Zerubbabel following the Babylonian captivity (Ezr 2:54; Neh 7:56).

Nezib. One of the cities in the lowland allotted to Judah for an inheritance (Jos 15:43). Its site is identified with modern Khirbet Beit Nesib, east of Lachish.

Nibhaz. God worshiped by displaced Avites after they were forcibly resettled in Samaria by the Assyrians in 722 BC. They brought the worship of this idol, as well as that of Tartak, with them at that time (2 Kgs 17:31). Although purported to be of Mesopotamian origin, this is not likely because the worshipers were Syrian. The word "Nibhaz" may be a Hebrew corruption of "altar" and hence a reference to a deified altar which was the object of worship.

Nibshan. One of the six cities in the wilderness allotted to Judah for an inheritance (Jos 15:62). Its location is unknown.

Nicodemus. Pharisee and a member of the Sanhedrin mentioned only in John's Gospel (20:30,31). Nicodemus came to Jesus at night, acknowledging him as a teacher sent by God (3:2). He was convinced that Jesus could not perform such things if God were not with him. Following an interchange concerning the need to be born again (v 3), Jesus asked how Nicodemus, a member of the Jewish religious court, could fail to understand such things (v 10). At that time he evidently made no profession of faith, but later did defend Jesus before the Sanhedrin (7:50–52). After Jesus' death, Nicodemus openly assisted Joseph of Arimathea with the burial of his body (19:39–42).

Some scholars suggest that Nicodemus was one of the Jewish leaders who believed in Jesus, but did not confess him openly for fear of excommunication (12:42). Tradition subsequently held that he belonged to the household of faith, as one persuaded to believe through the word and deeds of Jesus, but intimidated by the religious establishment.

See JOHN, GOSPEL OF.

Nicolaitans. Heretical sect in the early church which is mentioned by name twice in the Book of Revelation. The church at Ephesus was commended for hating the works of the Nicolaitans (2:6), and the church at Pergamum was criticized for having some members who held their doctrine (2:15).

Since the specific sins condemned at Pergamum—the eating of food sacrificed to idols and the practice of immorality—were also present at Thyatira (Rv 2:20), it is commonly thought that the woman Jezebel was a leader of the Nicolaitans in that church. In the letter to Pergamum, their sins are equated with the teaching of Balaam (Rv 2:14; cf. Nm 25:1,2; 31:16; 2 Pt 2:15; Jude 11), who advised Balak, the king of the Moabites, to bring about Israel's downfall by inviting them to worship the Moabite gods and engage in intermarriage and the sexual immoralities connected with Moabite religious practices. Thus the Jews would have been separated from God and his protection. In Jewish thought, Balaam was the symbol of all that led men to obscene conduct and the forsaking of God. The ungodly practices at Thyatira are called the "deep things of Satan" (2:24).

The early church was also threatened by the combination of idolatry and immorality so prevalent in the world. The necessity for frequent warning in the NT reveals the gravity of the problem. The Jerusalem council (Acts 15:20) called upon the Gentiles to abstain from eating food that had been offered to idols and sexual immorality. Paul called for a voluntary avoidance of this kind of fare for the sake of those who were weak or immature in the faith (1 Cor 8). He strongly condemned actual participation in idol feasts (1 Cor 10:14–22) as well as fornication in general and temple prostitution in particular (1 Cor 6:12–20).

Who the Nicolaitans were is more difficult to determine. The tendency among the church fathers was to identify them as followers of Nicolaus of Antioch, a gentile convert to the Jewish faith, who had become a Christian and was chosen to be one of the original seven deacons (Acts 6:5). Both Irenaeus and Hippolytus believed that he had fallen from the faith, although Clement claimed that the heretical and immoral Nicolaitans were not actual followers of Nicolaus, but falsely claimed him as their teacher. In any event, there is no direct evidence available.

Since the 19th century it has been common to view the name as a translation into Greek of the Hebrew name Balaam. This is in accord with the allegorical, symbolical nature of Revelation and the apparent linking of the two names in the letter to Pergamum (2:14,15).

Nicolaus, Nicolas. One of the seven men named in Acts 6:5 (KJV Nicolas), who was enlisted for service in the Jerusalem church in its early days. His duty as specified in Acts 6:1–4 was to direct the fair and equal distribution of food. Due to the use of terms in Acts 6:1 ("daily distribution" or "service") and 6:2 ("to distribute at tables" or "to serve"), these seven men traditionally have been called "deacons" (or "servers").

Nicolaus, the last-named in the list, is identified as a proselyte. Thus he was a gentile convert to Judaism before he became a Christian. His name is Greek, and the city of Antioch is mentioned as his home. The NT writings provide no further information about him.

See DEACON, DEACONESS.

Nicopolis. Name meaning "Victory City," a popular choice in the Roman empire when a newly founded city required a name; especially when a newly built town was created to commemorate some military victory in days of warfare.

In his letter to Titus, Paul directs him to leave Crete, where he had been ministering (1:5), and make his way to Nicopolis, where the apostle was working and intended to spend the winter (3:12). Of the nine Nicopolises throughout the empire, Paul almost certainly meant the city situated northwest of the Gulf of Corinth and southeast of the promontory of Epirus.

Octavian founded this city in 31 BC to celebrate his victory over Mark Antony in the great battle of Actium fought nearby. Nicopolis was Greek both in name and constitution. The center of a number of nearby towns, the new Nicopolis was a metropolis, enjoying an independence similar to that of neighboring Athens. Temples, theaters, a stadium, and an aqueduct were built, and games were instituted for the four yearly festivals. Nicopolis' most famous citizen, Epictetus, the Stoic philosopher, lived there around AD 90.

Notwithstanding the enthusiasm with which the citizens of Octavian's "Victory City" observed the anti-Christian cult of emperor worship, Paul made this splendid metropolis and its satellite communities a field of affirmative evangelism.

Niger. Surname of Simeon, one of the leaders in the church at Antioch (Acts 13:1).

See SIMEON (PERSON) #4.

Night. Word in Scripture denoting that time of darkness from dusk until dawn when no light of the sun is visible. For example, Joseph took Mary and Jesus to Egypt by night (Mt 2:14). The shepherds were keeping watch over their flocks at night (Lk 2:8). Nicodemus came to see Jesus at night (Jn 3:2). An angel from the Lord came and opened the prison doors at night in order to let the disciples out (Acts 5:19).

According to Genesis 1, the day-night cycle was instituted by God and "night" was the name given to the period of darkness (Gn 1:5). Later God put the lights in the expanse of the heavens, appointing the sun to rule or dominate the day and the moon, the lesser light, to dominate the night (Gn 1:16,18). The covenant of the Lord is the basis of the regularity of the rotation of day and night.

The night in OT times was apparently divided into three periods or "watches." The latter name originated with the changing of the guard at these times. Gideon's 300 men blew their trumpets and broke their pitchers at the beginning of the middle watch (Jgs 7:19). Although no references in the OT give the limits of these three periods, night was considered to begin at sunset and consequently the periods may have been 6 to 10 PM, 10 PM to 2 AM, and 2 to 6 AM.

Later, according to the Roman calculation of time, night was divided into four watches. Some historians think they began at 9:30 PM, at midnight, at 2:30 AM, and at 5 AM. Others think that the nighttime period between 6 PM and 6 AM was divided equally into four periods, the first beginning at 6 PM, the second at 9 PM, the third at midnight, and the fourth at 3 AM. Mark 13:35 contains the popular designations for these four watches, namely late in the day (early evening), midnight, the cock-crowing, and early in the morning.

Apparently Matthew 14:25 and Mark 6:48 follow the Roman calculation when they locate Jesus' walking on the water at about the fourth watch of the night.

A specialized use of the word "night" along with the word "day" emphasizes the continuance of activity. For example, the man with an unclean spirit is said to have been in the mountains and in the tombs "night and day" (Mk 5:5). Paul refers to his having labored, working night and day, so as not to be a burden to the church (1 Thes 2:9). Later in the same book, he refers to his continuous praying night and day (1 Thes 3:10).

Along with this literal usage of the word "night," there is also a figurative or metaphorical usage. In some references it refers to divine judgment (Mi 3:6; Am 5:8,9). Jesus uses "night" to refer to death (Jn 9:4). Once the night and death comes, time for working is over.

Paul compares this present age, soon to be over, with the night that is almost gone (Rom 13:12). Therefore, he exhorts, "Let us then cast off the works of darkness and put on the armor of the light." Again, Paul speaks of himself and his readers as sons belonging to the light and to the day, not the night and darkness (1 Thes 5:5). In this context he links night with separation from God, sin, intemperance, careless living, and with blindness and ignorance, especially regarding the Lord's return.

See DAY.

Night Hag. Designation for a bird of the wasteland (Is 34:14).

See BIRDS (OWL, SCOPS).

Night Hawk. *See* BIRDS (GOATSUCKER).

Night Monster. Designation for a bird of the wasteland (Is 34:14).

See BIRDS (OWL, SCOPS).

Nile River. Life-stream of Egypt in northeast Africa. Perhaps no other river has been of such importance to the history of the nation through which it flowed. With an attributed length of some 4160 miles, the Nile is the longest river in the world, although its drainage system is ranked 3rd (other sources say 6th) in area (nearly 1,300,000 square miles).

The Names of the River. The origin and meaning of the name Nile are unknown. To the ancient Egyptians the Nile was simply "the river." The Egyptians found it hard to conceive of any river different from the Nile, so when they reached the Euphrates they assumed it was running backwards, since it flowed south instead of north.

Unusual Features. Among the characteristics which distinguish the Nile are its six cataracts, areas where the river has failed to erode a clear channel through hard rock formations. These are numbered from north to south, in order of their discovery by modern explorers. The first cataract is at Aswan in Egypt, near the famous islands of Elephantine and Philae. The other five cataracts lie in the Sudan, with the second just above the city of Wadi Halfa.

Another distinguishing feature of the Nile is that it flows from south to north. This was of importance to Egyptian river transport, for sailing vessels could take advantage of the prevailing north wind for going upstream, while the current propelled travelers downstream.

An additional interesting aspect of the river is that there are no tributaries the last 1500 miles of its length. North of the Atbara, the wadis of the desert provide water only when an occasional desert thunderstorm sends a flash flood racing down the dry beds.

The annual inundation was the foundation of agricultural wealth in Egypt, for the covering of the land by those waters renewed, enriched, and watered the soil. Nilometers were installed at various points along the river to gauge the height of the impending flood. The height of the flood was a critical factor; too little water meant drought, while an abnormally high inundation spelled disaster from flooding.

In the latitude of Memphis, the inundation arrived around July 19th, dating the beginning of the calendar. At that date the Dog Star, Sirius, became visible at sunrise. Since this star was called Sothis, a cycle of chronology (1460 days) called the Sothic cycle developed.

The Egyptian year consisted of 365 days, but the astronomical year was about ¼ of a day longer. This meant that every 4 years there was a divergence of 1 day between the calendar year and the actual year. Therefore, it took 1460 days (365 × 4) to bring about the coincidence of the 2 years.

The Nile River determined the three seasons of about four months each: (1) inundation (mid-July to mid-November); (2) winter (mid-November to mid-March); (3) summer (mid-March to mid-July).

The inundation culminated in late October, softening the soil of the agricultural land for planting.

Course and Tributaries. The Nile has two main streams named for their respective colors, the White Nile and the Blue Nile. These streams owe their existence to the annual rains in equatorial Africa.

The White Nile has its origin in the lake country; Lake Victoria is usually said to be its source, but some geographers pinpoint the source as a little stream which flows into the lake. The only outlet of Lake Victoria is the Victoria Nile, northeast of the lake at Ripon Falls.

The stream goes through Lake Kioga, which is quite shallow, roars down Murchison Falls (120 ft. drop), and flows through Lake Albert. From this point it is known as the Bahr el Jebel, "the river of the mountain." Before reaching Lake No the river traverses the re-gion characterized by masses of thick floating vegetation called the sudd, which often completely block the channel of the river and make travel impossible. This was a chief obstacle for early explorers who were seeking to find the source of the Nile.

A tributary, the Bahr el Ghazal, "the river of the gazelles," enters Lake No and joins the main stream. Below Lake No the river is called the White Nile. Near Malakal, a tributary from the east, the Sobat, flows into the White Nile.

The most important junction of the river is at Khartoum, where the Blue Nile and White Nile are united. At this point one can often clearly see the color difference in the waters of the two rivers. The angle formed by the rivers encloses an area called the Gezira, or "island," an important site for cotton production.

The Blue Nile, only about 850 miles long, originates at Lake Tana in the highlands of Ethiopia. A much more precipitous stream than the White Nile, it too is dependent upon the rainy season in the high country. The White Nile begins its flooding first, but when the onrush of the Blue Nile sets in, it holds in check the water of the White Nile. During flood season the Blue Nile has twice the volume of the White Nile and provides the greater part of the alluvium which built up the soil of Egypt.

To the north of Khartoum is the sixth cataract, the first of the natural barriers. The Atbara, the last tributary of the Nile, enters from the east. The land, called the Island of Meroe, was the capital of the Meroitic kingdom, the Nubian country whose queens were titled Candace (Acts 8).

At the 4th cataract, near Napata, is a group of cemeteries and ruins associated with the Ethiopian or Kushite (25th) dynasty of Egypt. The 18th-dynasty kings penetrated the Sudan to the area of Napata and built temples there, but the later Nubian kings invaded Egypt and assumed control of that country.

Farther downstream is the important archaeological site of Kerma, where the Egyptians maintained a trading post during the Middle Kingdom.

Downstream from the second cataract is the celebrated temple of Abu Simbel, the work of Ramses II, with the smaller temple honoring Nefertari, his wife. These temples were moved to the cliff above their original position before Lake Nasser engulfed the site.

Just above Aswan and the first cataract is the new High Dam and the older Aswan Dam. Between the two dams is the island of Philae, with its well-known temples. At Aswan is the island of Elephantine, with its rich archaeological history, including the evidence of Jewish residents after the time of the fall of Jerusalem to the Babylonians.

A short distance above the Delta lies Cairo and the Giza Pyramids, and farther south are the ruins of Memphis, the first capital of Egypt.

The Delta measures some 125 by 115 miles. Seven ancient streams of the Nile found their way into the sea; but there are only 2 modern ones: the Rosetta on the west, which gave the name to the Rosetta Stone, and the Damietta to the East.

Importance to Egypt. Without the water of the river, life would be impossible in northeast Africa and the civilizations of Egypt could not have come into being. The Greek writers, first Hecataeus and later Herodotus, commented that Egypt is the gift of the Nile. The fertile soil of Egypt, which has produced such abundant crops over so long a span of time, is the alluvium laid down by the river over the course of centuries. Not only was the river the source of the soil itself, but with the annual inundation the Nile fertilized the land by bringing down new alluvium and by depositing organic materials. At the same time, the inundation thoroughly soaked the soil, so that it was possible to produce good crops with a minimum of effort expended on irrigation.

The raising of cattle depended on the river as well, for the prolific vegetation at the river's edge afforded good pasture. A typical scene from daily life shows the cattle being brought across a canal, with close watch for voracious crocodiles.

The Nile also satisfied many personal needs of the people, providing drinking water and a washing place for both the people and their clothing. In ancient times, even members of the royal family came to the river to bathe (See Ex 2:5; possibly 8:20).

The king's children learned to swim in some quiet part of the river. The Nile teemed with fish and waterfowl, and sportfishing (mostly spearfishing) and waterfowling were traditional diversions of the upper classes. Fish and fowl were also regular food, especially for the wealthy. A more hazardous sport, in which nobles traditionally engaged, was the hunting of hippopotami in reed watercraft with harpoons.

The Nile was the primary means of communication with boats plying up and down its channels. Riverboats of large size moved goods from one end to the other. The building of temples, palaces, and tombs throughout the land demanded the moving of granite for hundreds of miles along the river. Even modern man admires the skill of the ancient rivermen in transporting enormous obelisks and great statues from the quarries in the south.

The river was also a feature of the religious life of the Egyptians. The river was deified in the form of the god Hapi, a man who is shown in the various forms of art as having pendulous breasts, and a somewhat corpulent body, probably to represent luxuriant overabundance, along with fish and vegetation from the river.

The Nile and the Bible. The biblical references to the Nile River are naturally found in those parts of the Bible that have to do directly with Egypt, which means that many occur in the Joseph narrative in the latter part of Genesis and in the account of the Israelite bondage in Egypt and subsequent exodus in the early chapters of Exodus.

The first reference to the Nile appears in the mysterious dream of Pharaoh (Gen 41). In his dream the king stood on the riverbank and saw seven well-fed cows, followed by seven lean cows, which came out of the river and devoured the fat cattle (cf. 41:1–4, 17–21). This agrees with grazing practices of ancient Egypt and coincides with the depiction of cattle on the funerary monuments.

During the sojourn in Egypt, when the Israelites multiplied and became a possible threat to Egyptian security, Pharaoh decreed that every Israelite male child should be thrown into the river upon birth (Ex 1:22). This led to the events which marked the early life of Moses. His mother, in order to preserve him from death, hid him for three months at home and then concealed him among the reeds at the edge of the river in a basket made of rushes and waterproofed with bitumen and pitch, materials which were typically Egyptian and easily procured (2:3).

In the providence of God, the daughter of Pharaoh discovered the child when she came with her attendants to the river to bathe (2:5,6). As a result, Moses was brought up in the court of Pharaoh (v 10) and was instructed in all the wisdom of the Egyptians (Acts 7:22), equipping him in part for the divine calling he later received.

After his self-imposed exile, Moses returned to Egypt. The Lord showed his power over natural phenomena and the false gods of Egypt when he gave Moses the power to turn water into blood as a sign of his divine appointment (4:9).

Moses declared the judgments of the Lord at the river (7:15; 8:20). The first plague, the turning of water to blood (7:15–24; 17:5; Ps 78:44), was directed against the river and against the Nile-god, Hapi. The second plague (frogs) was also associated with the river (8:3, 5,9,11), for the swarms of frogs came up out of the river and enveloped the land (cf. Ps 78:45), discrediting the frog-headed goddess, Heket.

Hapi, the god of
the Nile River.

There are few mentions of the Nile in the historical books, for these do not bear many geographical relationships with Egypt. The Assyrian king Sennacherib showed his disdain for Egypt by bragging: "I dried up with the sole of my foot all the streams of Egypt" (2 Kgs 19:24).

There are numerous references to the Nile in the books of prophecy. Isaiah often mentions the Nile, but not always in the same context. In 7:18 Isaiah writes that "the Lord shall hiss for the fly that is in the uttermost part of the rivers of Egypt" (KJV), a statement that Israel would be invaded and humiliated by armies from the Nile. In the "oracle concerning Egypt" (Is 19), the prophet foresees both evil and good for the land of the Nile. Egypt will suffer severe drought for "the waters of the Nile will be dried up, and the river will be parched and dry" (v 5); "and the branches of Egypt's Nile will diminish and dry up" (v 6). The natural vegetation and sown crops along the river will be destroyed (vv 6,7), while the fishermen will lament (v 8). These dire prospects are offset by the prediction of final blessing for Egypt.

In the burden of Tyre (Is 23) the revenue of the Sidonian merchants was "the harvest of the Nile" (v 3), indicating the importance of agricultural produce in the Nile valley. In verse 10, Tyre casts off all restraint and is told to "overflow your land like the Nile," for the Lord is bringing the pride of Tyre to an end.

Jeremiah also predicted a severe defeat for Egypt and speaks of Egypt, "rising like the Nile, like rivers whose waters surge" (46:7,8).

The prophecy of Ezekiel concerning Egypt (ch 29) singles out Pharaoh, king of Egypt, and describes him in figures of speech drawn from the Nile. He is described as "the great dragon that lies in the midst of his streams" (v 3), a reference to the mighty crocodile. Pharaoh boasts, "My Nile is my own" (v 3, cf. v 9), but the Lord said that he would put hooks into the king's jaws and draw him out of the water of his streams with all of the fish sticking to his scales (v 4). The king and the fish of the streams will perish in the wilderness (v 5). Because of the proud boasts of the king, the Lord declares that he is against him and his streams and that Egypt will become a desolation and a waste (v 10).

Amos describes the northern kingdom of Israel as being tossed about, and sinking again, "like the Nile of Egypt" (7:8; 9:5).

Finally, Zechariah speaks of an ingathering of Israel by the Lord and comments that in this process "all the depths of the Nile [will be] dried up" (10:11).

Although the prophetic references to the Nile primarily deal with severe judgments, the prophets looked forward to a time beyond judgment to eventual blessing for this land of the Nile.   CARL E. DEVRIES

See EGYPT, EGYPTIANS.

Nimrah. Alternate rendering of Beth-nimrah, a city in Moab, in Numbers 32:3.

See BETH-NIMRAH.

Nimrim, Waters of. One of the places in the southern extremity of Moab denounced by Isaiah (15:6) and Jeremiah (48:34) in their oracles of judgment against the nation. The waters of Nimrim were spring-fed freshwater streams originating in the Transjordanian hills, following a northwesterly track down into the Arabah Valley, and eventually emptying into the southeast corner of the Dead Sea. The region surrounding the streams was evidently well known for its lush vegetation (see Is 15:6). This watercourse is probably identifiable with the modern Wadi en-Numeirah positioned about eight miles north of the Brook Zered.

Nimrod. Cush's son and grandson of Ham the son of Noah (Gn 10:8; 1 Chr 1:10). He is described as "the first man of might on earth" and "a mighty hunter" (Gn 10:8,9). Nimrod was the first to establish a great empire and was a well-known hunter. Tradition makes him ruler over Babylon and Akkad in southern Mesopotamia, and over Nineveh in Assyria. The phrase "land of Nimrod" seems to be synonymous with Assyria (Mi 5:6).

The OT references to Nimrod indicate that in ancient tradition he was a man of indomitable personality, possessing extraordinary talents and powers. Some scholars identify him with a Mesopotamian king who united Assyria and Babylon in the 13th century BC. This conflicts with the statement connecting him with Cush the son of Ham and pointing to an association with the south of Egypt where Cush was located (Gn 10:8).

The name and fame of Nimrod have a secure place in Talmudic Judaism and in Islamic tradition. In the former he personifies both rebellion against God and military might in the earth. In rabbinic tradition, the Tower of Babel (Gn 11:1–9) is "the house of Nimrod" where idolatry was practiced and divine homage offered to Nimrod. In Islam, Nimrod persecutes Abraham and has him thrown into a fiery furnace.

Nimshi. Father of Jehoshaphat and grandfather of Jehu, king of Israel (1 Kgs 19:16; 2 Kgs 9:2–20; 2 Chr 22:7).

Nineveh (Nineve), Ninevite. One of the capitals of the Assyrian empire and at the

Winged human-headed bull from Nineveh.

1553

height of that empire one of the great cities of the world. Nineveh was situated in what is now northern Iraq and is represented today by the mounds of Kouyunjik and Nebi Yunus to the east of the Tigris River and opposite the main part of the city of Mosul.

The larger mound, Kouyunjik, to the northwest (approximately a mile in area and some 90 feet in height above the plain), is separated from Nebi Yunus by the Khosr River. A village, a cemetery, and a mosque said to contain the tomb of Jonah occupy Nebi Yunus, preventing extensive archaeological work.

Nineveh's surrounding brick wall, 7 ½ miles long with 15 gates (of which 5 have been excavated) was guarded by the colossal stone bulls which typify Assyrian city architecture of this period.

History. The occupation of the site dates to prehistoric times (c. 4500 BC), in agreement with the record of the founding of the city in Genesis 10. Materials from the various early cultures (Hassuna, Samarra, Halaf, Ubaid) have been found at Nineveh.

Sargon of Akkad (mid-24th century BC) was acquainted with Nineveh, which flourished during his time. A record from the reign of a later king, Shamsi-Adad I (c. 1800 BC), relates that a son of Sargon, Manishtusu, restored the temple of Ishtar at Nineveh.

Ishtar (Inanna), the goddess of love and war, was a fitting deity for the rapacious and warlike Assyrians. Many other deities were worshiped at Nineveh and gates of the city were named after them. The Assyrians worshiped at the temple of Nabu, the god of writing and of arts and sciences, who reflects the Assyrian interest in records, literature, and sculpture in relief and in the round.

Shamsi-Adad I and Hammurabi also restored the temple of Ishtar at Nineveh. Shalmaneser I and Tukulti-Ninurta I enlarged and strengthened the city, and other rulers built their palaces here—Tiglath-pileser I, Ashurnasirpal II (883–859 BC), and Sargon II (722–705 BC). But Sennacherib (705–681 BC) made Nineveh the capital and went to great lengths to beautify the city. In addition to his famous palace, he undertook many projects, rebuilding the city walls, creating parks, making botanical and zoological collections, and constructing aqueducts to bring water for the city from 30 miles away. To Nineveh came the tribute which the conquering Assyrians exacted from the nations, including Israel and Judah, which fell victim to their awesome armies.

After the assassination of Sennacherib, his son and successor, Esar-haddon (681–669 BC), captured Nineveh from the hands of rebels. He built a palace at Nineveh and had another at Calah, where he spent most of his time.

Esar-haddon's son, Ashurbanipal (669–633 BC), made his residence at Nineveh, where he had been educated and trained in sports and military skills. He was somewhat of an antiquarian and mastered the reading of Akkadian and Sumerian. In his palace was housed the famous library of such importance for the study of Assyriology. The temple of Nabu contained a library dating at least to the time of Sargon II, but the royal library of Ashurbanipal far surpassed it in size and importance. Sargon and his successors had collected many tablets, but Ashurbanipal sent scribes all over Assyria and Babylonia to gather and to copy tablets, so that tens of thousands of tablets accumulated. Like the library of Nippur, the Nineveh collection covers a great range of materials: business accounts, letters, royal records, historical documents, lexicographical lists and bilingual texts, legends, myths and various other kinds of religious inscriptions, such as hymns, prayers, and lists of deities and temples. Among the tablets were 7 that preserved a Babylonian creation story and 12 which bore the epic of Gilgamesh, with a version of the flood. Other writings which sometimes are cited as parallels to Bible accounts include the story of Adapa, with the lost opportunity to achieve immortality, and the legend of Etana, a shepherd who ascended to heaven.

Ashurbanipal was also well known for his wars and for his cruelty. The palace relief showing a peaceful banquet scene also displays the severed head of an Elamite leader hanging in a tree.

In the later years of the aging king and after his demise, the vassal kingdoms rebelled. Babylon became independent and joined with the Medes to take Ashur and Calah in 614 BC. Cyaxares the Mede, Nabopolassar of Babylon, and a Scythian force laid siege to Nineveh in 612 BC; the city fell and King Sinshariskun (Sardanapalus) perished in its flames.

Although a Ninevite remnant under Ashuruballit held out at Harran until 609 BC, Nineveh had been destroyed: the divine predictions of the Hebrew prophets had their complete fulfillment.

Nineveh and the Bible. Six books of the OT refer to the city of Nineveh. In Genesis the only mention of Nineveh appears in the table of nations (Gn 10), which states that Nimrod went out from the land of Shinar to Assyria and built Nineveh, Rehoboth, Calah, and Resen between Nineveh and Calah (vv 11,12; the KJV attributes this building to Asshur).

The tribute paid by Menahem (2 Kgs 15:19,20) and the spoil taken at the fall of Samaria (Is 8:4) were brought to Nineveh. To this city also came the tribute which Sennacherib received from Hezekiah (2 Kgs 14–16).

Among the scenes commemorated in the reliefs found in Sennacherib's palace at Nineveh is the depiction of the siege and capture of Lachish (cf. 2 Kgs 19:8). Sennacherib is shown on a throne, with suppliant captives before him. The siege itself is shown in progress, with archers and battering-rams on the attack, while defenders on the walls use bows and arrows and firebrands to repulse the onslaught. From one gate people are emerging with bundles on their backs as if in surrender or flight. At the lower right three naked men have been impaled on poles.

On the prism at the Oriental Institute of the University of Chicago and on the Taylor Prism at the British Museum there is Sennacherib's account of this invasion of Judah. Since the Assyrians did not take Jerusalem, Sennacherib had to be content with boasting: "As to Hezekiah the Jew, he did not submit to my yoke. I laid siege to 46 of his strong cities, walled forts and to the countless small villages in their vicinity, and conquered them.... Himself I made a prisoner in Jerusalem, his royal residence, like a bird in a cage."

The Assyrian kings associated with Nineveh played an important part in the history of Israel, but the name Nineveh occurs only once in the historical books of the Bible. Second Kings 19:36 states that after the loss of 185,000 soldiers at the hand of the angel of the Lord, Sennacherib "went home, and dwelt in Nineveh." There, in 681 BC he was murdered by his sons in the temple of Nisroch (Ninurta?; cf. 2 Kgs 19:37; 2 Chr 32:21; Is 37:38).

There are many references to Nineveh in the Book of Jonah, for the prophet was expressly sent to that city to warn it of impending judgment. Nineveh is called "that great city" (1:2; 3:2) and it is described as "an exceeding great city of three days' journey" (3:3). Nineveh must include more than the area represented by the mounds of Kouyunjik and Nebi Yunus. Some commentators believe that Nineveh takes in other cities associated with it, including the "Assyrian triangle," the angle of land between the Tigris and the Great Zab Rivers, reaching from Khorsabad in the north to Nimrud in the south.

The Lord speaks of "that great city, in which there are more than 120,000 persons who do not know their right hand from their left" (4:11). Some writers interpret this statement as indicating the number of innocent children in the city and therefore arrive at a total population of some 600,000 for greater Nineveh. However, it is more reasonable to conclude that the entire population is meant

and that the descriptive clause relates to the utter spiritual darkness of the Ninevites.

Jonah preached a message of judgment and destruction, but the repentance of the city brought about its deliverance (3:6–10). Nahum declared the final downfall of the city in language that is vivid and stirring. Zephaniah also foretold the doom of Nineveh and prophesied that it would be a desolation, a place for flocks to lie down, as even the casual visitor to the site would note (Zep 2:13–15).

Nineveh was destroyed by a coalition of Babylonians, Medes, and Scythians. The devastation of the city was overwhelming and complete and within several centuries the very location of the city was forgotten. Xenophon and the Greek armies retreated past the site in 401 BC without realizing it. In the 2nd century AD the Greek satirist Lucian commented: "Nineveh is so completely destroyed that it is no longer possible to say where it stood. Not a single trace of it remains."

The only NT references to Nineveh in the Gospels also have to do with judgment. Jesus asserted, in response to a demand from the scribes and Pharisees, that an evil generation looks for a sign; as Jonah had been a sign to the Ninevites, so Jesus would be a sign to his generation (Mt 12:38–40; Lk 11:29–31). He went on to declare that the people of Nineveh would rise at the judgment with his generation and condemn it, for the Ninevites repented at the preaching of Jonah. Now one greater than Jonah had come (Mt 12:41; Lk 11:32, KJV Nineve).   CARL E. DeVRIES

See ASSYRIA, ASSYRIANS; HAMMURABI, LAW CODE OF.

Nippur. City in ancient Mesopotamia (modern Iraq), and a center of religious, commercial, and literary activity. Although the city is not mentioned in the Bible, either as Nippur or under any other name, the discoveries made at Nippur in the course of archaeological investigation are important for the OT scholar. Many cuneiform tablets found at the site bear parallels to OT accounts, provide material which illustrates the biblical narrative, or otherwise shed light on the OT text or background.

Many deities were worshiped at Nippur, but its primary god was Enlil, the storm god, who was known to the Semites as Bel, or Baal. Enlil was also called "the king of heaven and earth," "the king of the lands," and the "father" and "king of the gods." His temple, Ekur ("House of the Mountain"), was an important religious structure. Pilgrimages were made to Nippur, much as today Muslims journey to Mecca.

The ruins of Nippur, called Nuffar today,

are about 100 miles south of Baghdad and 60 miles southeast of Babylon, between the remains of Shuruppak and Kish, ancient cities which are named in the Sumerian king list and associated with the flood. Nuffar consists of a number of mounds, which average about 50 to 60 feet above the plain. The tallest of these, at the northeast corner and some 95 feet high, is called Bint el Amir, "the Princess" (literally "the daughter of the ruler"). This marked the location of the ziggurat, or temple-tower characteristic of cities in Mesopotamia. The temple of Enlil was situated nearby. The triangular mound known as "Tablet Hill" from the quantity of cuneiform tablets found there, was the location of the residences of the priests, the temple library, and the school.

The site represents many levels of occupation and has provided much knowledge of the architecture and art of a long sequence of civilizations, down to and including Arabic times. An abundance of ceramic materials and of small objects contribute to the understanding of the daily life and interests of the peoples of various ages and cultures.

Perhaps most important is the mass of inscriptional material, especially thousands of tablets, which afford in particular a knowledge of a vast Sumerian literature of the 2nd and 3rd millennia BC. Many of the tablets were found in duplicate, a fact which enabled scholars to piece together stories that were found on broken ones.

An early Sumerian story of the flood is among the interesting literary legacy of Nippur. The flood story from Mesopotamia is often referred to as the Gilgamesh epic, for it is part of the tale of the adventure of Gilgamesh, a legendary king of Uruk. The Gilgamesh epic was written in Akkadian, a Semitic language, and is said to date from around the beginning of the 2nd millennium BC. Most of the Akkadian texts come from the library of Ashurbanipal at Nineveh, but some have been found at Hittite Boghazköy and at Amarna in Egypt.

These early flood stories have many interesting parallels to the biblical account, but the differences also are remarkable. The contrast between the gross polytheism of Mesopotamia and the clear monotheism of the Bible is especially striking. Both the Mesopotamian legends and the biblical account go back to an original event, but the Mesopotamian version was corrupted by priests and historians who were responsible for the writing and copying of the texts.

In the Sumerian writings from Nippur there also is an allusion to creation by the deities, a theme which likewise is paralleled by other creation stories from the Mesopotamian area and by the biblical account.

In addition to myths, legends, and epics (sometimes a reflection of actual events, as in the creation and flood), there were law codes, hymns and other religious writings, proverbs, letters, royal inscriptions, commercial records, and syllabaries.

Sumerian poetry, like much poetry of the ancient Near East, shows the characteristics of parallelism, whether synonymous or antithetic, in which, particularly in proverbs, the same idea or its opposite is expressed in a couplet.

Since the temples of any Mesopotamian city received many offerings and dues in kind, many economic texts may be found among the tablets. Many of these are dull and repetitive, but are of value for the study of the economic history of a site. Records from the 5th century BC include a group of more than 700 tablets dealing with the transactions of a firm of Babylonian bankers and businessmen. Since one of the responsibilities of the company was to collect taxes in the area for the Persian government, the records of the firm give the names of taxpayers. Among these are a number of Hebrew names, indicating that many Jews of the exile had settled in this area and had followed the admonition of Jeremiah to seek the peace of the city of exile, to pray for it, and to continue to reside there for 70 years (Jer 29:1–14).

The city of Nippur was connected to Babylon by a navigable canal which in Babylonian was called Kabaru and in the Bible is named Chebar. The prophet Ezekiel, who was taken to Babylonia in captivity with King Jehoiachin of Judah in 597 BC, mentions that he saw visions of God while he was with the captives by the "river of Chebar" (Ez 1:1,3), placing the exiled Jews at or near Nippur.

At the end of the 70-year period, Israelites returned to Judah from the Babylonian captivity, but many stayed in the place of exile. A number of bowls from the excavations at Nippur bore Hebrew inscriptions, indicating that Jews continued to live in Nippur for many centuries after that time.

CARL E. DEVRIES

See MESOPOTAMIA.

Nisan. Babylonian name for a Hebrew month (Neh 2:1; Est 3:7).

See CALENDARS, ANCIENT AND MODERN.

Nisroch. God of King Sennacherib, in whose temple at Nineveh the king was assassinated by Adrammelech and Sharezer, his sons (2 Kgs 19:37; Is 37:38). Nisroch was the city god of Nineveh, the chief capital of the Assyr-

Nisroch—from the northwest palace at Nimrud.

ian Empire; he was perhaps identical with the Assyrian god Nusku.

See ASSYRIA, ASSYRIANS.

No. KJV form of Thebes in Nahum 3:8.

See THEBES.

Noadiah. 1. Binnui's son and one of the two Levites present when the temple treasure that was brought back to Jerusalem by Ezra was weighed and recorded (Ezr 8:33).

2. Prophetess who, along with Tobiah, Sanballat, and some false prophets, attempted to intimidate Nehemiah when he was engaged in rebuilding Jerusalem's walls after the exile (Neh 6:14).

Noah. 1. Son of Lamech and the grandson of Methuselah, a descendant of Seth, third son of Adam (Gn 5:3–29). "He will comfort us," said Lamech, giving his son a name evidently derived from that Hebrew verb, "in the labor and painful toil of our hands caused by the ground the Lord has cursed."

Determined to destroy creation because of rampant wickedness (cf Mt 24:37–39; Lk 17:26,27; KJV Noe), God made an exception of Noah, a man righteous in his sight and blameless before men (6:3–9). Following God's precise instructions, Noah constructed an ark into which went only eight people—Noah and his wife, and his three sons and their wives—and all kinds of creatures in pairs. They were thus protected from the ensuing deluge in which all other living things perished (6:14–8:19). Noah's survival made him the second father of mankind.

When they emerged from the ark, Noah built an altar and sacrificed burnt offerings which pleased God, who promised that the flood would never be repeated or the sequence of the seasons disrupted, despite man's sin (8:20–9:17).

Noah had withstood mighty temptations but, whether through carelessness or old age, he became drunk. Family members reacted differently, and were judged accordingly. Shem and Japheth received blessing. Ham received no blessing, but his son Canaan was cursed (9:20–27). Noah was 950 years old when he died, 350 years after the flood.

Noah, Daniel, and Job, because of "their righteousness," are cited as the only individuals who would be spared God's punishment on a sinful nation (Ez 14:12–14,19,20), in the context of the much more dreadful divine judgment directed at Jerusalem.

The Letter to the Hebrews commends Noah who by faith, holy fear, and world-rejection became the heir of righteousness (11:7), and 2 Peter 2:5 calls him "a preacher of righteousness." First Peter 3:19,20 refers to "the spirits in prison who disobeyed long ago when God waited patiently in the days of Noah while the ark was being built."

See FLOOD, THE; FLOOD MYTHS;

2. Daughter of Zelophehad of Manasseh's tribe (Nm 26:33). When their father died without a son, she and her four sisters successfully petitioned for a change in the law that would protect their inheritance rights (Nm 27:1–11; cf. Jos 17:3–6). They were, however, restricted to marrying within their own tribe (Nm 36:1–12).

J.D. DOUGLAS

No-Amon. Alternate reading for No, the Hebrew name for Thebes, capital of upper Egypt (Na 3:8).

See THEBES.

Nob. City located on the eastern slopes of Mt Scopus opposite the Mt of Olives and northeast of Jerusalem. An important religious center, eighty-six priests resided there, as well as the ephod (1 Sm 22:13–20). Nob was the central sanctuary in which the priests served who had fled from Shiloh when the Philistines destroyed the sanctuary there.

The episode of David and the priests of Nob (1 Sm 21:2–7) attests the antiquity of the details of the table and the bread of the presence (Ex 37:10–16). Jesus cites David's hunger as a just reason for breaking the ritual laws govern-

ing sabbath observance (Mk 2:23–28). David, fleeing from Saul and needing food, went into the sanctuary at Nob and took the loaves laid out each sabbath as an offering to the Lord.

Ahimelech, a descendant of Eli and leader of the priests of Nob, gave the showbread to David, along with the sword with which Goliath had been slain. This incensed Saul, who ordered the murder of Ahimelech and the massacre of all the priests and citizens of Nob (1 Sm 22:6–23), an act which sealed the fate of the king. Abiathar, a priest who evaded the massacre, played a prominent role in the reign of David until Solomon eventually removed him from his position (1 Kgs 2:26,27). The phrase "where God was worshiped" may refer to the sanctuary at Nob (2 Sm 15:32).

Nobah (Person). Manassite who conquered and settled the town of Kenath, east of the Jordan, and subsequently renamed it after himself (Nm 32:42).

Nobah (Place). 1. Town east of the Jordan, previously named Kenath, allotted to Nobah the Manassite for an inheritance, at which time he called it Nobah after his own name (Nm 32:42). Nobah is perhaps also identifiable with Kanatha, the easternmost city of the Decapolis during the Roman era.

See DECAPOLIS; KANATHA.

2. Place near the Gadite town of Josbehah east of the Jordan, near which Gideon ambushed the Midianites (Jgs 8:11). Its site is unknown.

Nod. Land east of Eden to which Cain went after he murdered his brother Abel (Gn 4:16). The location of Nod is undetermined.

Nodab. Forefather of an Arabian tribe that joined forces with the Hagarites to fight against the tribes of Israel who were living east of the Jordan (1 Chr 5:19). Though not included in the list of Ishmael's sons (cf. Gn 25:13–15), he was perhaps a distant relation.

Noe. KJV rendering of Noah in Matthew 24:37,38 and Luke 3:36; 17:26,27.

See NOAH #1.

Nogah. One of 13 sons of David born in Jerusalem after David established his kingdom (1 Chr 3:7; 14:6).

Nohah (Person). Fourth son of Benjamin (1 Chr 8:2).

Nohah (Place). Place west of Gibeah in Benjamin's territory (Jgs 20:43). Other translations consider "Nohah" (meaning quiet) an adverb and translate it accordingly, "with ease" (KJV), because no town by that name is known.

Non. KJV form of Nun, Joshua's father, in 1 Chronicles 7:27.

See NUN.

Noph. KJV translation of the Hebrew word for Memphis (Egypt).

See MEMPHIS.

Nophah. Place delineating the boundaries between Israel and the Moabites and Amorites (Nm 21:30). Some equate Nophah with the Nobah of Judges 8:11.

North, North Country. Cardinal point on a compass opposite the south, often having the connotation of "dark," perhaps because the north side is often in shadow. In biblical literature, notably in the books of Joshua and Ezekiel, the term "north" is used frequently to designate direction, whether of tribal boundaries or of a temple.

An enemy from the "north" is mentioned at least 40 times in the prophecies of Jeremiah, Ezekiel, Daniel, and Zechariah. During the time of the exile (Jeremiah and Ezekiel) it referred to invaders who came from the East, pushed westward north of the Syrian desert, and then turned south to invade Judah from the north. Hence they were viewed as invading from the "north country"; this latter phrase occurs at least 10 times in Jeremiah and Zechariah.

Jerusalem is vulnerable only from the north. The topography of the country is such that seldom in history has any invader conquered the holy city from any direction except from the northern approach. The city was protected by deep valleys on each of the other three sides. In biblical times only the Egyptians and the Philistines threatened Jerusalem from the west; even the Philistines, during the time of Saul, were successful only in the areas north of Jerusalem. In Daniel the "king of the north" doubtless refers to Syrian forces in mortal combat with the "king of the south" (Egypt).

Northeaster. Name given to the stormy wind of Acts 27:14, encountered by Paul on his journey to Rome. Against his advice, the ship weighed anchor from a harbor near Lasea. Their course was "close in" along the Cretan coast, as a gentle breeze encouraged them along. Probably no further than nine miles out, a sudden squall threatened their tiny craft. Luke calls it a typhoon (KJV "tempestu-ous wind"), its name being Euroclydon, meaning "the southwest wind, that stirs up waves."

Not My People. Symbolic name given by the prophet Hosea to his third son (Hos 1:9) as a warning of the coming judgment of God upon Israel.

See AMMI.

Not Pitied. Symbolic name given by the prophet Hosea to his daughter (Hos 1:6,8) as a warning of the coming judgment of God upon Israel.

See RUHAMAH.

Numbers and Numerology. Individual numbers do have a symbolic as well as a literal sense in the Bible. In Daniel and to a lesser extent in Revelation, there is a developed system of numerology where interrelated systems of numbers are used in a definite pattern.

Traditionally, conservative Christians have been suspicious of numerology because of its unwise use by groups of Christians who see theological symbolism in every number in the OT, even the most factual. This view was inherited from mystical, pre-Christian Jewish groups, and later carried to extremes by the Kabbalists. There are certain radical groups who claim to be able to establish the original text of the Bible, either by simply counting the alphabetical letters in the different verses, or by assigning to each letter a numerical value and then totalling the amounts.

Expression of Numbers. Hebrew, and indeed any other Semitic language, has a simple but adequate system of numeration. One is an adjective. After that, the numerals are nouns, in parallel masculine and feminine forms, although the masculine is used with the feminine noun and vice versa. Ordinal numbers (first, second, third, etc.) exist alongside cardinal numbers (one, two, three), but, as in most languages, the second set can be used instead of the first ("day two" instead of "second day"). From 10 to 19, there is one composite form built like English "thirteen" ("three-ten"), but "twenty" is literally "tens" (the plural of "ten"). Thirty, forty, and so on, are literally, "threes," "fours" (the plural of the words "three" and "four," respectively) and so on, up to a hundred, which is a new word. There are also separate words for "thousand" and for "ten thousand," as in Greek, Chinese, and many other languages. Larger numbers must be expressed by multiples of these ("ten thousand times ten thousand" and "thousands of thousands"), suggesting that large figures, rarely needed for small populations and tiny kingdoms, were expressed approximately. Hebrew has not only a singular and plural, but also a dual form, to express two of any thing (two hundred, two thousand). Fractions (a half, a third, a tenth, etc.) could be expressed, and multiplication, division, addition, and subtraction were used. Indeed, instances of all four operations can be found in the Bible. The Hebrew mathematical system was basically part of the larger western Asian mathematical system, of which we know a great deal from Mesopotamia and Egypt. These countries of course used a more highly developed mathematical system than Israel; had Israel ever needed to make use of advanced mathematics, they were certainly available. For instance, the building of Solomon's temple must have demanded very exact calculations by the Phoenician craftsmen.

Ways of Writing Numerals. In the Bible, numbers are always written out in words, as on the famous Moabite Stone and the Siloam Inscription. But every nation in the ancient world could also express numbers by using figures or ciphers of various kinds (like our 1,2,3). These appear often on ancient tablets and other similar archaeological objects both from Israel and surrounding countries. Some scholars believe that such signs may have been used in the earliest manuscripts of the OT, and that perhaps confusion or corruption of these signs in the original text has led to apparent contradictions in the recording of numbers in the present text. Certainly a few cases can be explained in this way. Because of this danger of error, in later days numbers were normally written out in full, in words, where confusion, although still possible, was not nearly so likely. An additional way of writing numbers, known both to the Hebrews and Greeks, was the use of consecutive letters of the alphabet instead of consecutive numerals (as if we used A for 1, B for 2, etc.). This system, in wide use by NT times, is the usual system in modern Hebrew and has the advantage that numerical combinations can be pronounced by inserting arbitrary vowels, thus making artificial words. For example, if the number of the beast (Rv 13:18), 666, is expressed in alphabetical letters, it can spell out the consonants of "Nero Caesar," although other names are possible, especially if the variant reading 616 is used. However, this system of recording numbers still has potential for error (e.g., if one letter of the alphabet is hastily written for another, or mistaken for another in reading). Some of the anomalies and apparent inconsistencies of biblical numbers in the present text have been attributed to this cause.

On the other hand, an indiscriminate dependence on this system can produce names from numbers anywhere in Scripture. For instance, the 318 servants of Abraham (Gn 14:14, a circumstantial detail which seems perfectly literal) can be transformed into a cryptic reference either to Eliezer, Abraham's servant, or to the Torah, or by a similar manipulation, a reference to Christ and his cross.

Problems of Large Numbers. Even allowing for all these possibilities, there remain certain problems connected with large numbers, particularly in the OT. The most obvious is that of the 10 long-lived patriarchs, whose ages are recorded in Genesis 5. Different figures (varying by whole centuries) are recorded for their ages in the Hebrew text, the Samaritan text, and the earliest Greek translation (known as the Septuagint), but all figures are very large. Some interpret these figures literally, and point out that there is a steady reduction from the ages attained by these patriarchs to the more modest 120 years allotted to man in Noah's time (Gn 6:3) and the 70 years accepted later as the human life span (Ps 90:10). This would correspond to the progressive spiritual deterioration of mankind after the fall, from the perfect state of Adam to the present condition. Whatever the explanation of the figures, there is no doubt that this is the theological intent of the Bible.

The Hebrews counted to the base of 10 although they did not use a full decimal system. The Sumerians counted to the base of 60. Therefore, some early manuscript confusion may have resulted when all numbers were reduced to the base of 10.

The large number of Israelites who left Egypt is also problematic. If there were actually 600,000 fighting men (Nm 1:46), this would correspond to a whole nation of some two million or more. Possibly the word translated "thousand" means "clan," or even "clan chief." Six hundred "clan units" would clearly be a much smaller total body, whatever its exact size. Of course God could have maintained any number of people in the desert. The evidence of archaeology as to the population of Canaan both before and after the Israelite onslaught seems to support a lower number. The same principle might explain the large numbers given for the fighting men of the various Israelite tribes, and the huge totals for Israel and Judah's military strength given at later times in the historical books of the OT. Forty thousand may be a stock figure (e.g., Jgs 5:8) for a military levy, and is certainly used frequently in the OT. As mentioned, large numbers on this scale do not occur in the NT with the exception of the Book of Revelation, where some are certainly used symbolically (e.g., "thousands of thousands").

To the ordinary Bible reader, perhaps one

of the biggest problems is the different numbers recorded in Chronicles and Kings, when the same incidents are being described. Manuscript errors, or confusion of numbers written by signs or single letters of the alphabet, may account for numerous individual inconsistencies, but not for wholesale differences, particularly as the figures in Chronicles are consistently much larger. These very large round numbers may have symbolic significance, and may not be intended to be taken in their literal sense at all. Indeed, since the Jews had before them the Book of Kings and the Book of Chronicles at the same time, they can hardly have taken both sets of numbers literally themselves.

Counting by Generations. One of the problems of the OT is that of the dating of events. Even with an exact number system, there is no absolute fixed point from which to reckon. Later Jews and Christians counted from the presumed date of the creation. Not until after the time of David and Solomon are both internal reference between the comparative dates of kings of Judah and Israel and external reference to monarchs outside Israel used. This open-endedness accounts for the vague period of "forty years" used so often in the OT (e.g., the Book of Judges) for any long but indeterminate period of time, almost certainly corresponding to a generation (Hebrew *dōr*). Counting by generations is specific in some places in the Bible, and may be implicit in others. For instance, Abraham's descendants are to return to Canaan "in the fourth generation" (Gn 15:16), and the genealogy of Christ is neatly constructed on a pattern of three groups of fourteen generations (Mt 1:17), rather than on periods of years. Wherever people use and recite genealogies, such counting by generations is natural. But Abraham's descendants also return to Canaan approximately four centuries later (Gal 3:17), and therefore the word "generation" sometimes stands for 100 years. The Hebrew word for "generation" may mean 120 years (Gn 6:3). Usually, the ancient Hebrews used vague phrases like "in those days," or "after those days," or "the days are coming," which expressed past, present, and future without any specific mention of number. In other words, the Bible writers were more concerned with theology than with mathematics.

Approximate Use of Numbers. In the OT, Israel's 40 years in the desert is a good example of the approximate use of numbers (Nm 14:33). In the NT, Jesus is in the wilderness 40 days during the temptation (Mt 4:2), and there are 40 days between his resurrection and ascension (Acts 1:3). Moses is 40 years old at his call (Acts 7:23), apparently lived 40 years in Midian (Ex 7:7), and spent 40 years leading Israel out of Egypt and through the desert (Dt 34:7), for he is said to be 120 years old at his death. However, two generations of 40 years is the normal maximum for a healthy man (Ps 90:10), and even this is often shortened to 70 years by the rigors of life. Seventy is also used at times in this approximate sense.

Sequential numbers in a rising scale can also be used as an approximation in Hebrew as in English. Because Hebrew poetry delights in parallelism, one line of verse will often contain a particular number, and the next line the number immediately above it (e.g., Prv 6:16), with no great stress on the actual numbers. An interesting example of this is that the Hebrew for "previously" is literally "yesterday and three days ago," where the thought is vague past time (Ex 4:10). Similarly, "tomorrow" and "the third day" (Hos 6:2), while the sense may be quite literal, may also be used of indefinite future time.

Inclusive Enumeration. Many languages, including both Hebrew and Chinese, count numbers and days by the marker at each end, counting inclusively, not exclusively. Therefore in the NT, Friday evening till Sunday morning can be described as "three days" (Mk 8:31). This system probably rose from the counting of animals or objects, where counting is inclusive. Presumably, this would create problems in adding or subtracting periods of time, although not in either counting or weighing objects, the primary use of numbers.

Symbolic Use of Numbers. In Scripture, seven symbolizes completeness or perfection. On the seventh day God rests from his labors and creation is finished (Gn 2:2). Pharaoh in his dream sees seven cattle coming from the Nile (Gn 41:2). Samson's sacred Nazirite locks are braided in seven plaits (Jgs 16:13). Seven devils left Mary of Magdala, signifying the totality of her previous possession by Satan (Lk 8:2); "seven other devils" will enter the purified but vacant life of a man (Mt 12:45). However, on the positive side, there are the seven spirits of God (Rv 3:1). In the seventh year the Hebrew slave is to be freed (Ex 21:2), having completed his time of captivity and service. Every seventh year is a sabbatical year (Lv 25:4). Seven times seven reiterates the sense of completeness. In the year of Jubilee (the 50th year), all land is freed and returns to the original owners (Lv 25:10). Pentecost, the Feast of Weeks, is seven-times-seven days after Passover. "Seventy," which is literally "sevens" in Hebrew, strengthens the concept of perfection. There are 70 elders (Ex 24:1) in Israel, and the Lord sends 70 disciples on a mission (Lk 10:1). Israel was exiled to Babylon for 70 years (Jer 25:12) to complete its punishment. "Seventy times seven" (Mt 18:22) reiterates this still further. The Lord was not giving Peter a mathematical number of times that he should forgive Andrew, but insisting on limitless forgiveness for a brother's sin.

"Three" may well share in this meaning of completion or perfection, although not so forcibly (2 Kgs 13:18). Many things happen "on the third day" (Hos 6:2). Jonah spent three days in the stomach of the fish (Mt 12:40), and the Lord rose again on the third day (1 Cor 15:4). David is offered a choice of divine punishments—three years; three months; three days (2 Sm 24:13). For the Christian, "three" takes on a far deeper significance as the number of the Persons of the Trinity. The three Persons are clearly expressed for instance, in the Great Commission (Mt 28:19) and in the Pauline "grace" (2 Cor 13:1). Many echoes of this threefold expression are in the NT, and many anticipations of it in the OT, of which the thrice-repeated "Holy" in Isaiah 6:3 is the most famous.

Some scholars see four as another symbol of completeness (four winds of heaven, Dn 7:2; four horsemen, Rv 6:1–7; four living creatures around the throne of God, Rv 4:6). Five is certainly used in an indefinite sense as a small number (Is 19:18; 30:17). Nor do eight or nine seem to have any special significance, although, like other numbers, they may be used in a factual sense to describe any of God's activities (nine plagues on Egypt, Ex 7–10). "Ten" does have significance because of the Ten Commandments (Ex 20:1–17), but not any special symbolism earlier in the Bible. If anything, "ten" is elsewhere used in a vague way. Laban changes Jacob's wages 10 times (Gn 31:7); Daniel and his friends are 10 times better than all other students (Dn 1:20); 10 times over, the Jewish settlers will be warned of impending enemy attacks (Neh 4:12).

Eleven appears to have no special biblical significance, but 12 certainly has. The clearest proof of this is the existence of the 12 tribes in Israel. In Revelation 7:4–8, where it is mathematically important that the number of tribes be limited to 12, the tribe of Dan is altogether omitted on account of Dan's sin of idolatry (Jgs 18:14–20). Some have compared the number 12 with the 12 months of the year, as symbolizing completion, but, if so, the Bible gives no hint of it. Ishmael's descendants were also divided into 12 clans (Gn 17:20), so that the number 12 was apparently significant outside Israel as well. In the NT Christ chose 12 apostles (Mt 10:1–4). The link with the number of tribes is made specific when Christ tells the apostles that they will sit on 12 thrones, judging the 12 tribes (Mt 19:28). However, it is interesting that, after the election and appointment of Matthias (Acts 1:26), the Christian church apparently made no subsequent efforts to maintain the number of apostles. Like "seven times seven," "twelve times twelve" increases the force of the number. When this is further multiplied by a thousand, the figure becomes the 144,000 redeemed (Rv 7:4), who were sealed "out of all the tribes of Israel."

Thousand and ten thousand are sometimes used symbolically to denote vague but large numbers. So "ten thousand times ten thousand" and "thousands of thousands" (Rv 5:11) are attempts to express the inexpressible. Typical of the Bible, these vast numbers, which can be used to teach the joy and wonder of heaven, can also be used to show the awfulness of the wrath of God. Those armies that carry out the punishment of God on sinful mankind are "twice ten thousand times ten thousand" (Rv 9:16).

Exact Statistics. As distinct from the metaphorical use of numbers to denote completion, immensity, and the like, numbers in Hebrew were often used to give exact tallies or measurements. Such usage is only known to us from clay tablets and ostraca (broken pieces of potsherd engraved in ink, used as rough notebooks). However, ascertaining exactly what the text was in its earliest form and what that text means is difficult.

An example is the number of the sons of Jeconiah among the inhabitants of Bethshemesh. They were struck down by the Lord because of their failure to rejoice with the others when God's ark returned to Israel from the Philistine country (1 Sm 6:19). The Greek text reads "seventy"; the later Hebrew manuscripts add "fifty thousand." But, as Bethshemesh itself was only a small frontier town, and the "sons of Jeconiah" was presumably only one clan among several, the smaller number is obviously the original, and the large addition due to some later manuscript confusion.

A good rule in trying to decide whether a number is statistical or impressionistic is whether or not it is a small number, and whether or not it is an unusual number for which there is no obvious theological explanation. When the men of Ai killed some 36 Israelites at the first assault on the city (Jos 7:5), the smallness of the number is evidence that this is a vividly remembered factual detail. Similarly, in the case of the number of Abraham's 318 retainers (Gn 14:14) or the catch of 153 fish after the resurrection (Jn 21:11), the numbers, though large, are not round numbers but unusual combinations, and are obviously meant in a literal or statistical sense. Irrelevant details like this have a habit of remaining in the memory, and are the best guarantee of the trustworthiness of the narrative.

Numerology Proper. Numerology is the deliberate and systematic use of numbers as symbols, not in isolation but as part of a close-knit schematic system of figures. Often they are used to explain the developments of past history, and sometimes to map out and to predict the future. Frequently, but not always, numerology is associated with a division of time into epochs or ages.

Numerology may be said to be an extended application of the metaphorical significance of numbers (seven, forty, etc.) already discussed. In the Bible, this systematization of numbers always goes with a strong sense of the sovereignty of God, his control over human history, and a belief in his ongoing purpose and its triumphant conclusion.

Perhaps the first clear instance of numerology in the Bible is 1 Kings 6:1, where Solomon began to build the temple 480 years after the exodus, a period 4 times 10 times 12, or 4 times 120, the ideal lifespan of man in early days (Gn 6:3). First Chronicles 6:3–8 gives 12 generations of men (presumably 40 years each) to cover the same period, so "twelve generations" is probably the real basis for the computation, rather than any exact year-by-year tally. A tally would have been impossible in the days of the judges and unlikely before the monarchy. David was the first to establish an official scribe or recorder to keep daily annals in Israel (2 Sm 8:16,17), as was common in the great kingdoms from far earlier times. Such Israelite annals are later mentioned as sources of the books of the kings (2 Kgs 14:18). The number 480 is probably a rough approximation rather than exact and denotes the end of one of God's epochs. Twelve generations express the completion of one stage of God's plan, as the thrice-repeated "fourteen generations" do in the genealogy of Christ (Mt 1:2–17). The "four hundred years" of Israel's oppression in Egypt probably falls into the same category (Gn 15:13) and perhaps even the "four hundred and thirty years" of Galatians 3:17, though this may be an exact statistical count, based on recorded ages of patriarchs.

When Jeremiah prophesies an exile of 70 years for Judah (Jer 25:11; 29:10), it is not only a historical prediction which was literally fulfilled, but also a symbol of completeness; Judah's punishment is complete (cf. Is 40:2). Isaiah (23:15) had made a similar prophecy of a 70-year punishment for Tyre, and Ezekiel (29:11–13) prophesied a 40-year "exile" for Egypt. When these 70 years are regarded as sabbatical years, where the land must lie untilled to compensate for the 7 times 70 years of sin before, then true numerology begins (2 Chr 36:21). Here numerology is used only as an explanation of past and present, but it can also be used to explain the future, especially in the Book of Daniel.

Daniel (9:2) refers to the literal 70 years of the exile as foretold by Jeremiah. In Daniel 9:24, this has been extended to 70 weeks of years (490 years) applied to the distant future. Daniel 9:25 sees 69 of these (483 years) as elapsing before Messiah appears. Presumably, the last week of the 70 is therefore thought of as the time of his activity. However this may be interpreted in terms of actual dates, it must be harmonized with 9:26, where the Messiah is "cut off" after 62 weeks of years (434 years). The difficulty lies in establishing the starting-point for this long period. This is an example of an elaborate numerology, embracing centuries of history, all ultimately based on the 70 years of Jeremiah. According to biblical principles this can have both an "immediate" fulfillment in the return from exile, and a "prophetic" fulfillment in the far distant future in connection with the coming of Christ.

The other major example of extended numerology in Daniel is in connection with the "time, times, and half a time" (7:25). This must stand for three and a half "times," that is, half of seven "times." Thus it refers either to three and a half years (half a "week" of years) or three and a half "weeks" of years (cf. "seven times" in 4:16, where "seven years" is clearly meant). Whatever may be its ultimate prophetic fulfillment in Christ, the "initial" or "partial" fulfillment is the roughly three and a half years of bitter persecution of God's people by Antiochus Epiphanes (167–164 BC). This figure of three and a half years reappears in Revelation 11:2 ("forty-two months"), and 12:14 ("a time, and times, and half a time"), to describe the period of Rome's persecution of the Christian church. The figure had possibly become a symbol of any bitter but limited persecution. The "two thousand three hundred evenings and mornings" of Daniel 8:14 may mean 1150 days, which is approximately the same length of time.

A complex system of numerology, arranging and explaining the past within mathematical terms, also arranges the future on a similar plan, so that the future is seen to be a further projection of the patterns of the past. This pattern of numerology was followed extensively in the intertestamental period, and in the apocalyptic literature that continued well into the Christian period. But no real place is found for numerology in the NT, apart from the few isolated instances mentioned. The probable reason is that the "fullness of time" has arrived (Gal 4:4), and that Messiah has already come. The details of his birth, life, death, and resurrection have already passed into recorded Christian history. There is still a looking forward to the end, but the date of the end is hidden in the foreknowledge of God, and not even known to the Messiah himself in his earthly life (Mt 24:36). Speculation as to its date is therefore discouraged (Jn 21:22).

Even within the Book of Revelation, while there is a plethora of symbolic numbers, there is no new numerology that is not directly derived from the OT, usually from the Book of Daniel. Such numerology is designed to set the event in the OT framework of God's planning and timing and is an assertion that the new event will be a "fulfillment" of the old event.

The three and a half years of Daniel 7:25 reappear in Revelation 11 in the form of "forty-two months," the time when the heathen will trample down Jerusalem (Rv 11:2). The 1,290 days of Daniel 12:11 reappear here (in the slightly different form of 1,260 days) as the time that God's two witnesses will prophesy (Rv 11:3). The 42 months reappear in 13:5 as the period that the wild beast will be allowed to blaspheme. While the "thousand years" of 20:6 is not derived from Daniel at all, the metaphorical use of "thousand" is familiar to the OT. The closest direct parallel is in Deuteronomy 7:9, where God's covenant will be kept with a "thousand generations" to come.　　　　　　　　　　R. Alan Cole

Numbers, Book of. Fourth book of the English Bible. Its title is the English translation of the Latin Vulgate title, *Numeri.* The book takes this name from the fact that several rosters of various kinds are recorded in the book, specifically, the two army musters in chapters 1 and 26, the tribal camp and march arrangements in chapter 2, and the levitical censuses in chapters 3 and 4.

Author. The question of the authorship of Numbers is part of the larger question of the authorship of the Pentateuch. Until the appearance of the higher critical documentary theories of Eichhorn (1823), Hupfield (1853), Graf (1865), and Wellhausen (1878), the Mosaic authorship of the Pentateuch was almost universally held by both Jews and Christians alike. This time-honored tradition is supported by the Pentateuch itself (e.g., Ex 17:14; 24:4; 34:27; Nm 33:2; Dt 31:9,24), the rest of the OT (e.g., Jos 23:6; Jgs 3:4; Mal 4:4), Jesus' teaching (e.g., Jn 5:46,47), and the rest of the NT (e.g., Acts 28:23; Rom 10:19; 1 Cor 9:9). Although discrepancies in the Pentateuch were widely and openly acknowledged, nevertheless Moses, the 15th-century BC lawgiver, was affirmed as the primary author of the Pentateuchal literature. Payne believes that Scripture defines three levels of Mosaicity within these books: (1) parts actually written down by Moses (e.g., Nm

33:3–49; cf. v 2); (2) parts composed by Moses, though not necessarily written down by him (e.g., Dt 33:2–29; [perhaps written by inspired "officers" of Nm 11:16 which the Septuagint translates "scribes"]); and (3) parts historically authentic and springing from the Mosaic period and incorporated under Mosaic instruction (e.g., Nm 12:3; Dt 34). Once these parts are recognized, it is possible to affirm the over-all Mosaic superintendence of the Pentateuch as a whole, explaining at the same time the fact that portions of the Pentateuch are written in the third person about Moses.

Historical and Archaeological Background. *The Sinai Peninsula (1:1–21:9).* The historical and archaeological background of Numbers begins primarily in the geographical region of the Sinai Peninsula of the mid-2nd millennium BC.

The Sinai Peninsula is in the shape of an inverted triangle with the base on the north. It is approximately 240 miles long from north to south and 175 miles wide at the northern base, with an area of approximately 22,000 square miles. It is bounded on the north by the Mediterranean Sea and the southern border of Canaan, on the west by the Bitter Lakes and the Gulf of Suez, and on the east by the Arabah and the Gulf of Aqaba. Beginning in the north at the Mediterranean coast and moving south, for about 15 miles the soil is sandy. South of

Bible lands from Egypt to Syria, with the Sinai Peninsula in the center—the area in which Israel lived and wandered for 40 years.

this coastal plain is a high plateau (Et-Tih) of gravel and limestone (2000–2500 feet above sea level), stretching south into the peninsula for approximately 150 miles. Rising above the plateau at this point is a granite mountain formation with peaks up to 8000 feet above sea level. In this mountainous region at the apex of the peninsular triangle, Jebel Musa (7363 feet high), the traditional site where Israel camped before Mt Sinai and Moses received the Law, rises above the plain.

The peninsula itself is comprised of 5 wildernesses. In the north and immediately east of the land of Goshen is the approximately 40-mile-wide wilderness of Shur, which runs past the River of Egypt (Wadi el-Arish) to the region of Kadesh-barnea and northeast to Beersheba. East of this region is the wilderness of Zin, extending east from the wilderness of Shur to the southern tip of the Dead Sea. Kadesh-barnea is located on its southern border (20:1; 33:36). South of the wilderness of Shur is the wilderness of Etham, and east of this wilderness in the east central region of Sinai is the wilderness of Paran, referred to by Moses as the "great and terrible wilderness" (Dt 1:19). Kadesh-barnea is on the northern border of this territory (Nm 13:26). In this area the Israelites spent 38 of their 40 years of "wandering." Southwest of the wilderness of Paran, on the western slopes of the peninsula, not far from the granite mountains standing in the southern apex of the triangle is the wilderness of Sin.

While the region is generally desolate and barren, it is not impassable or incapable of sustaining travelers. Wells and springs dot both the western and eastern borders at reasonable distances from each other. The water table is fairly close to ground level, making the digging of wells possible (Nm 20:17; 21:16–18). The limestone rocks are also capable of holding great amounts of water (Nm 20:11). Vegetation is sparse except around the more permanent streams where vegetation and date palms flourish (cf. Wadi Feiran). The rainy season in winter is approximately 20 days. Quail (Nm 11:31,32) are known to migrate across the peninsula to Europe in the spring.

Few site locations in the Numbers 33 list of encampments are known since at least some were named by the Israelites themselves in relation to events that occurred in their travels (11:1–3,31–34; 20:13; 21:3), and no sedentary population was left behind to perpetuate the name of the site. However, Kadesh-barnea (13:26) is almost certainly 'Ain Qudeirat or 'Ain Kudeis; Ezion-geber (33:35) is certainly located at the northern tip of the Gulf of Aqaba; and Mt Hor (33:38) is perhaps the holy mountain near the Wadi Harunia. Jotbathah (33:33)

may be Tabeh, on the western shore of the Gulf of Aqaba about seven miles southwest of Elath. The "way to the Red Sea" (14:25; 21:4; Dt 1:40; 2:1) is doubtless an ancient route in the Arabah region toward the Gulf of Aqaba.

Amalekites and Canaanites (14:25,43–45; 24:20). The Amalekites were descendants of Amalek, son of Eliphaz and grandson of Esau (Gn 36:12,16). They were generally a nomadic people. In the Sinai Peninsula they were the first to war against Israel at Rephidim (cf. 24:20), perhaps the Wadi Refayid in southwest Sinai (Ex 17:8–16), before Israel reached Horeb. A year later, the Amalekites settled in the hills and valleys north of Kadesh-barnea. In league with the Canaanites, the inhabitants of Palestine, they blocked the effort of Israel to invade the land of promise from the south and "pursued them, even to Hormah" (14:45). Israel's will to wage war appears to have been completely broken for years to come.

Edom (20:14–21; 21:4,10,11). Edom, or Seir (24:18), is the territory south of the Dead Sea occupied by Esau's descendants. Stretching from its northern border at the Wadi Zered (21:12), which flowed into the Dead Sea at its southern tip, 100 miles south to the Gulf of Aqaba, it occupied both sides of the Arabah, with Kadesh-barnea again standing on the edge of its western border (20:16), giving it a land area of approximately 4000 square miles. It is a rugged mountain region with peaks rising to 3500 feet. The "king's highway" (20:17, 19), an ancient trade route from Damascus through the Transjordan to the Gulf of Aqaba, passed through its territory and major cities, Bozrah and Leman. While Edom was not fertile, it did have cultivatable areas (20:17,19).

During Israel's march to the Transjordan region, Edom refused to let Israel journey directly east from Kadesh through its territory but forced Israel to move southeast into and up the Arabah (21:4,11). In spite of this hostility to God's people, Israel was forbidden to attack (Dt 2:2–8) or to hate the Edomites (Dt 23:7), and so Edom was spared from destruction during the conquest of the land. The area was later conquered by David (2 Sm 8:13,14) according to Balaam's prophecy (Nm 24:18).

Arad (21:1–3). Arad was a south Canaanite settlement in the Negeb. Its king, after fighting against Israel and taking some captives, was later defeated at Hormah.

Moab (21:11–15; 22:1–24:25). Moab, occupied by the descendants of Lot (Gn 19:37), is the territory east of the Dead Sea lying primarily between the Wadi Arnon (Nm 21:13) and the Wadi Zered with a land area of approximately 1400 square miles.

In the Late Middle Bronze Age, the Moabites had overflowed their main plateau and had extended well to the north of the Arnon all the way to the northern end of the Dead Sea (21:20). At the time of the events recorded in Numbers, however, the Amorites occupied the area from Arnon all the way north to the Wadi Jabbok (21:13,21–24), having earlier taken this land from Moab (21:26–30). The Moabite kingdom was highly organized, with agriculture and livestock, splendid buildings, distinctive pottery, and strong fortifications around her borders. Its god was Chemosh (21:29).

Balak, king of Moab during the period of the conquest, in league with Midian, hired Balaam to curse Israel (chs 22–24). When this failed, the two heathen powers sought to neutralize Israel by luring the people of God into the worship of Chemosh and into idolatory (25:1,2). In the war that ensued, Israel defeated Midian (31:1–18), but by God's express command (Dt 2:9–13) spared Moab. But as Balaam had prophesied earlier (24:17), David in the 11th century warred against and defeated Moab (2 Sm 8:2,13,14).

Amorites (21:21–35). The Amorites, the people who had occupied northern Moabite territory (21:25–30), were descendants of Canaan (Gn 10:16) who had scattered throughout the hill country on both sides of the Jordan River. Heshbon was their capital city. Both Sihon of Heshbon and Og of Bashan were Amorite kings (Dt 3:8; 4:47).

As for Bashan (21:33–35; cf. Dt 1:4; 3:1–12), it is the fertile grazing region (32:1–5) east of the Sea of Chinnereth (Galilee) whose northern border extended to Mt Hermon and whose southern border, while normally the river Yarmuk, in the Mosaic Age was the Wadi Jabbok (Jos 12:4,5; note "half of Gilead to the boundary of Sihon king of Heshbon," i.e., as far south as Jabbok, Nm 21:24). Its land area covered approximately 5000 square miles. Its major cities were Ashtaroth, Edrei, and Golan. After the conquest of the land this territory fell to the half tribe of Manasseh, with Gad occupying southern Gilead and Reuben the region south to the Wadi Arnon.

Midian (25:16–18; 31:1–54). The Midianites, descendants of Abraham through the concubine Keturah (Gn 25:2), were desert dwellers in Transjordan from Moab to the region south of Edom. The elders of Moab and Midian cooperated in hiring Balaam to curse Israel (22:4–7). Later, when that effort proved fruitless, the Midianites, again with Moab, led Israel into idolatry and immorality (25:1–6,14,15). Cozbi, the Midianite woman who was executed for her wickedness (25:8), was the daughter of Zur, one of the five Midianite kings confederate with the Amorite king Sihon

(Jos 13:21) who were later killed in Israel's holy war against Midian (31:8). This war with Midian apparently broke the back of any remaining Amorite resistance, for Joshua 13:15–23 clearly intimates that as a result the tribe of Reuben occupied this territory.

Purpose. Numbers serves a twofold purpose. First, as a historical book it contains the account of Israel's fortunes from Mt Sinai to the plains of Moab on the eve of the conquest of Canaan—that almost 40-year period spent in the wilderness of Sinai and in Transjordan (1447/46–1407/6 BC). While recounting Israel's many failures and God's many faithfulnesses, it depicts Moses, Israel's leader, in all of his greatness and in all of his weakness. The two army musters (chs 1 and 26) introduce the "acts" of the main drama of its history: the first in preparation for entering the land, which failed due to Israel's unbelief; the second, after the death of the entire generation that left Egypt, in preparation for the successful invasion of Canaan under Joshua's leadership.

Second, in line with Paul's general belief that "whatever was written in former days was written for our instruction, that by steadfastness and by the encouragement of the scriptures we might have hope" (Rom 15:4), and in keeping with his specific teaching that "these things [that befell Israel in the wilderness] happened to them as a warning, but they were written for our instruction, upon whom the end of the ages has come" (1 Cor 10:11), Numbers serves a doctrinal, typical, and hortatory purpose (cf. 1 Cor 10:12). Historical events are divinely invested with spiritual truths, thereby becoming object lessons for the Christian.

Content. *Chapter 1.* The Lord commanded Moses to register (1:18) the men able to go to war (vv 2,3). The total number of soldiers in Israel was 603,550 (v 46). The Levites were not numbered in this muster (vv 47–54), since they were to be set apart for special service pertaining to the tabernacle.

Chapter 2. The Lord instructed Moses concerning the arrangement of the tribes while encamped and on the march. With the tabernacle in the center of the camp, Judah, Issachar, and Zebulun, totaling 186,400 (v 9), were to camp on the east; Reuben, Simeon, and Gad, totaling 151,450 (v 16), were to camp on the south; Ephraim, Manasseh, and Benjamin, totaling 108,100 (v 24), were to camp on the west; and Dan, Asher, and Naphtali, totaling 157,600 (v 31), were to camp on the north.

On the march, Judah's east group (v 9) was to set out first, followed by Reuben's south group (v 16). The Levites with the tabernacle were to follow (v 17). Then Ephraim's west group (v 24) was to follow the Levites, with Dan's north group (v 31) bringing up the rear. This means that the Levites were flanked by two groups, before and behind.

Chapter 3. Aaron, the great-grandson of Levi through Kohath (Ex 6:16–20), and his descendants were designated to serve as priests at the tabernacle (vv 2,3). The remaining descendants of Levi, from the families of Gershon, Kohath, and Merari, were to serve the Aaronic line at the tabernacle (vv 5–10). The Gershonites were responsible for the tabernacle coverings, hangings, and screens (vv 25,26); the Kohathites were responsible for the "furniture" in the tabernacle (v 31); and the Merarites were responsible for the frames, bars, and foundations for the tabernacle (vv 36,37).

God instructed Moses to number the three levitical families. Gershon's descendants, totaling 7500 (v 22), were to camp on the west, between the western group of tribes and the tabernacle. Kohath's descendants, totaling 8300 (v 28), were to camp on the south, between the southern group of tribes and the tabernacle. Merari's descendants, totaling 6200 (v 34), were to camp on the north, between the northern group of tribes and the tabernacle. Moses and the Aaronic family were to camp on the east, between the eastern group of tribes and the tabernacle (v 38). Both in camp and on the march, then, the tabernacle was in the midst of Israel.

After the census of Israel's firstborn males disclosed 273 more male babies than Levites (vv 40–46), and since the Levites were a ransom for Israelite males on a one-to-one basis, the 273 additional male children had to be ransomed by atonement money (vv 46–51).

Chapter 4. God instructed Moses that only Levites between the ages of 30 and 50 were to serve at the tabernacle. A census disclosed that there were 2750 Kohathites (v 36), 2630 Gershonites (v 40), and 3200 Merarites (v 44), making a total of 8580 (v 48) who were eligible to serve the Aaronic priests.

God further ordered the Aaronic priests, when the tabernacle was being dismantled for the march, to cover all the tabernacle "furniture" before the Kohathites even looked at them (v 20) lest the Kohathites, either looking at or touching them (v 15), should die (vv 15,20).

Chapter 5. For ceremonial purposes, God demanded that lepers, those with a bodily discharge, and those who had touched the dead, must be put outside the camp until they were purified (vv 1–4).

Furthermore, God instructed those making restitution for a wrongdoing, if the wronged person was no longer alive, to give the restitution price to a priest (vv 5–10).

Finally, if a woman was suspected by her husband of infidelity but there was no evidence of such, the woman was to undergo a trial by water ordeal to relieve the man of his suspicions. The priest was to give her holy water with dust from the floor of the tabernacle in it to drink. If she was guilty, the water by divine direction would cause her pain, make her abdomen swell, and her thigh waste away (vv 11–31).

Chapter 6. Laws pertaining to the Nazirite were given next. A Nazirite was a person who determined to take a vow to separate himself wholly to the Lord. To dramatize this separation, the Nazirite was to drink no intoxicating beverage, let the hair grow long, and touch no dead body (vv 3–6). Should he defile himself, he was to follow prescribed rules for ceremonial cleansing (vv 9–12). When his vow had run its course, he was to follow prescribed rules for terminating his vow (vv 13–21).

Finally, God instructed the Aaronic priesthood concerning the blessing they were to pronounce upon the Israelite worshiper (vv 22–27).

Chapter 7. The leaders in Israel brought six wagons and twelve oxen for use in the transfer of the tabernacle (7:3). Moses gave two wagons and four oxen to the Gershonites (v 7), and four wagons and eight oxen to the Merarites (v 8). (The Kohathites were to carry the "furniture" of the tabernacle on their shoulders, v 9.) For twelve consecutive days, to consecrate the altar after it was anointed (vv 10,88), the tribal leaders, in the order of march (cf. ch 2), brought similar offerings. God demonstrated his pleasure with this gesture by speaking to Moses from the mercy seat (v 89).

Chapter 8. God granted the prerogative to light the seven-lamped lampstand to the Aaronic priests (vv 1–4).

Following divine instructions, Moses and Aaron consecrated the Levites to the service of the tabernacle by means of a purification ceremony (vv 5–22).

Chapter 9:1–14. For the benefit of the worshiper who was ceremonially unclean or away on a journey at the time of the Passover, God granted permission to observe the Passover a month later (v 8; see also ch 27).

Chapters 9:15–10:10. God gave final instructions to the people before their departure from Sinai. They were to prepare for march when they saw the cloud ascending from the tabernacle, and they were to stop at the place where the cloud settled down (9:15–23). The people were to assemble at the tabernacle if two silver trumpets were blown; only the leaders were to come if one was blown; and at the blast of a military alarm, the several groups of tribes were to prepare for immediate march (10:1–10).

Chapters 10:11–14:45. The next section recounts the march from Sinai to Kadesh-barnea, a period of time approximately one and a half to two months in length (cf. 10:11; 13:20). Almost immediately the people began to complain as they passed through the "great and terrible wilderness" of Paran (Dt 1:19), angering the Lord at Taberah (11:1–3) and at Kibroth-hattaavah (11:4–35; Pss 78:26–31; 106: 13–15). Miriam and Aaron challenged Moses' sole right to speak for God to the people, which resulted in temporary leprosy as Miriam's punishment, doubtless the leader in the provocation. Through Moses' intercession, the two were forgiven (ch 12). Out of this event, however, came the remarkable description of Moses' relationship to God as a unique means of revelation (vv 6–8).

From Paran (Kadesh-barnea) Moses dispatched the spies to survey the land (ch 13). Deuteronomy 1:22 suggests that the plan to spy out the land originated with the people, with Moses at God's behest, acquiescing. At the end of 40 days, they returned. Only Caleb and Joshua urged the people to advance to the conquest; the other 10 spies spoke of foes too formidable for them to defeat. The people, greatly discouraged, attempted to stone Caleb and Joshua (14:10), and were prevented from doing so only by the sudden appearance of the glory cloud at the tabernacle. God swore in his wrath (14:21; cf. Heb 3:7–4:10) that, with the exception of Caleb and Joshua, none of that generation would enter the land of promise (14:21–35). He then struck down the 10 unbelieving spies (14:37). Presumptuously and in spite of God's express command to the contrary (Dt 1:42), Israel attempted to advance on the land, leaving Moses and the ark of the covenant in the camp. They were challenged by the Amalekites and Canaanites who "chased you as bees do and beat you down in Seir as far as Hormah" (Dt 1:44).

Israel remained in this general area with tribal families fanning out over the wilderness and settling around springs and oases (Dt 1:46). Chapters 15:1–21:20 relate the account of the 38 years of wilderness wandering. Much of this time was probably spent around Kadesh-barnea (Dt 1:46).

Chapter 15. Further priestly legislation was given (vv 1–21). Also, the procedure to be followed when an Israelite committed a sin deliberately and defiantly was spelled out in terms of excommunication: there was no atonement for such an attitude (vv 22–31). A sabbath violater was executed (vv 32–36), perhaps as

an illustration of the foregoing legislation. Finally, to assist them in obeying God's laws, the Israelites were instructed to tie blue cord tassels to their outer garments as reminders (vv 37–41).

Chapter 16. Korah challenged Aaron's high priesthood and Dathan, Abiram, and On challenged Moses' leadership (vv 1–14). God, at Moses' word, opened up the earth and swallowed the offenders (v 32; cf. Dt 9:6; Ps 106:16–18). Korah is regarded in the NT (Jude 11) as a classic example of a rebellious malcontent.

Numbers 26:11 states that Korah's young children did not perish with him. Perhaps they became the ancestors of the "sons of Korah," the sacred musicians of the temple who composed 12 Korahite psalms (Pss 42–49,84, 85,87,88).

Chapter 17. God then instructed the leaders of each tribe to bring rods, 12 in all, to write the names of the tribes upon them (with Aaron's name on Levi's rod), and to deposit them in the tabernacle. The following day, Aaron's rod had sprouted with blossoms and ripe almonds, thus vindicating Aaron's special high-priestly status.

Chapters 18,19. Further priestly legislation was given. In 18:1–7, the full responsibility for the priestly service was given to the Aaronic priests—a very natural consequence of the preceding chapter. The Levites were to assist the Aaronic order (v 6). Since the tribe of Levi received no land inheritance, they were to be supported from the offerings of the people (vv 8–20).

In 19:1–22 instructions concerning the "water for impurity" designed to remove ceremonial impurity was given. When an Israelite became ceremonially unclean through contact with death (vv 11–16), God required that he be purified from his "sin" (vv 9,17) by the sprinkling of this specially prepared water upon him.

Chapter 20. With Israel once again at Kadesh on the southern border of the wilderness of Zin in the first month of the 40th year of wandering, Miriam died and was buried (v 1). According to the encampment list in chapter 33, 18 encampments may have occurred for Israel since the nation had last been at this site (cf. 33:18–36).

At this time the nation complained once again because there was little water (v 2). Moses, at God's instruction, brought forth water from a rock (vv 8–11); but because of a gross infraction by Moses and Aaron on this occasion, God announced that they would not be permitted to lead Israel in the conquest of the land (vv 12,23,24).

The chapter closes with Edom refusing Israel passage across its territory (vv 14–21) and

Arad.

Aaron dying on Mt Hor on the border of Edom (vv 22–29) in the 5th month of the 40th year (33:38). Eleazar, Aaron's son, assumed the office of high priest.

Chapter 21. After a quick victory over Arad (vv 1–3), Israel started south to encircle Edom. Becoming impatient with God and with Moses, the people expressed their disgust with God's provision of manna. The Lord sent poisonous snakes to the camp, causing many to die. But at God's command, Moses fashioned a snake out of bronze and placed it atop a standard. All who looked to the bronze snake survived (vv 4–10). The bronze snake was preserved and later was destroyed by Hezekiah, the symbol having become by his time an idol (2 Kgs 18:4). Later still, Jesus drew an analogy between these wicked sinners looking to the bronze snake and being delivered and men looking to him by faith and being saved (Jn 3:14,15).

Leaving that fateful place, Israel journeyed into and up the Arabah, crossed the Wadi Zered in an eastern swing around Moab, finally crossing the Arnon into Amorite territory. Journeying north, they camped at Pisgah (vv 10–20).

At this point the conquest of the Transjordan begins. In quick succession Israel defeated Sihon of Heshbon (vv 21–31) and Og of Bashan (vv 33–35) and settled in the plains of Moab (22:1). This encampment was the scene for the remainder of the activities of Numbers, Deuteronomy, and Joshua 1–3. In a real sense, one can say the wilderness wanderings were now over.

Here is the place, then, to summarize the spiritual condition of Israel on the eve of the conquest of Canaan. Numbers makes it quite evident that the entire generation that left Egypt, with the exception of Joshua and Caleb, were to die in the wilderness because of its apostasy (cf. Am 5:25), unbelief, and general failure to keep covenant with God. None of the generation of male children born in the wilderness had been circumcised (Jos 5:2–9). Psalm 90 underscores Israel as the recipient of God's wrath in the wilderness. It is in this pitiable spiritual condition that Israel arrived on the plains of Moab.

Chapters 22–24. Balak, king of Moab, frightened by Israel's presence, joined with Midian to hire Balaam, the false prophet, to curse Israel. For gain, Balaam agreed (2 Pt 2:15; Jude 11), but God prevented him rather to bless Israel in his four oracular utterances (23:7–10,18–24; 24:3–9,15–19) and to predict destruction of Moab, Edom, Amalek (24:20), the Kenites (24:21), and Asshur (24:24). With that, Balak and Balaam separated. Balaam in collusion with Midian agreed to counsel Israel to commit idolatry and immorality (31:16). And so, where Balak failed to turn the Lord against Israel, Balaam succeeded (ch 25).

Chapter 25. Israel sinned against God by idolatrous and immoral acts with the people of Moab (vv 1–3). In carrying out the command of God to destroy the reprobate Israelites, Phinehas killed Zimri and Cozbi, the latter being a daughter of one of the five kings of Midian (vv 4–14). This event provided the occasion for God to declare a holy war against Midian (vv 16–18; cf. ch 31).

Chapter 26. The Lord commanded Moses to take a muster of the men of the second generation who were capable of warring against Israel's enemies. The total number came to 601,730 (v 51), a reduction of 1820 men from the first muster. With a smaller force than the first generation Israel conquered Canaan, clearly indicating that Israel could have spared itself the years of wandering if only the nation had obeyed God 38 years before at Kadesh.

The Levites totaled 23,000 males a month old and upward (vv 57–62).

Chapter 27. At the request of the daughters of Zelophehad (cf. 26:33) that they be granted the right to inherit their father's possessions since he had no sons, the Lord agreed that they could, using the occasion to give further laws of inheritance (vv 1–11).

Reminded that he would soon die in Abarim, Moses requested that God appoint his successor. God selected Joshua and Moses commissioned him (vv 12–23).

Chapters 28,29. Further priestly legislation regarding offerings for various occasions was given.

Chapter 30. God instructed Moses to inform the people concerning vows. When a man made a vow, it was inviolable (v 2); but if a woman made a vow, the man (father, husband) responsible for her could nullify it if he felt that it was rash (vv 1–16).

Chapter 31. The account of the holy war declared against Midian in 25:16–18 is given. With Phinehas accompanying 12,000 warriors,

Israel defeated Midian, killing Balaam along with the five kings and many male adults of Midian (31:1–8). The Midianite women and children were taken captive, but Moses commanded that all the male children and the nonvirgin women be killed (vv 9–18). One must not conclude that this war meant the end of Midian as such, for Midian later proved a formidable foe of Israel in the time of the judges (Jgs 6).

After the battle, the warriors were instructed to purify themselves, their clothing, and the booty from the war before coming into the camp (vv 19–24). Furthermore, they were instructed to divide the booty in half and to contribute one-fifth of one percent of their half to the high priest ("the Lord's tribute"). The other half was divided among the people who had remained in camp, after the Levites received a 2 percent contribution (vv 25–31).

Verses 32–47 give the tally of the booty after its division into two parts and the amount that was given from each part to Eleazar and the Levites. The tally is said by some to be too high to be authentic, but there is no evidence that disputes the recorded figures.

In thanksgiving to God because no Israelite had been killed in the war (v 49) and to make atonement for themselves (v 50), the army officers brought a special offering of gold trinkets to Moses and Eleazar, which was placed in the tabernacle as a memorial (vv 48–54).

Chapter 32. At their request and on the condition that they aid the other tribes in the conquest of Canaan, Reuben, Gad, and the half-tribe of Manasseh were allotted the Transjordan region.

Moses earnestly besought the Lord to change his mind about not permitting him to enter the land of promise (Dt 3:23–27). God's reply was curt: "Let it suffice you; speak no more to me of this matter" (Dt 3:26).

Chapter 33. At God's command, Moses kept a written record of Israel's itinerary from Egypt to the plains of Moab. Here is biblical evidence of the Mosaic authorship of Numbers.

Chapter 34. The boundaries of the Promised Land were now given. The southern boundary would run from the southern tip of the Dead Sea, south of Kadesh-barnea up to the River of Egypt (Wadi el-Arish), and on to the Mediterranean Sea (34:3–5). The western boundary would be the coastline of the Mediterranean Sea itself (v 6). The northern boundary, not realized until the times of David and Solomon (2 Sm 8:3–12; 1 Kgs 8:65), was to extend from the Mediterranean Sea east to Hamath, at the head of the Orontes River (vv 7–9). The eastern boundary was to be practically on a vertical line, with the Jordan Valley run-

ning north to the northern boundary (vv 10–12). The nine and a half tribes were to divide this area among themselves (vv 13–15).

The Lord then selected the men who were to bear the responsibility of dividing the land of Canaan among the western tribes after the conquest (vv 16–29).

Chapter 35. God next instructed Israel to give 48 cities throughout the land on both sides of the Jordan to the Levites for a permanent possession (vv 1–8), since that tribe was not included in the land allotments to the other tribes. The number of cities each tribe was to give was to be determined by its size (v 8). Six of the levitical cities, three on each side of the Jordan, were to be designated "cities of refuge" for the manslayer (v 6; cf. Jos 20).

Legislation concerning the manslayer follows (vv 9–34). If the slayer committed murder, the kinsman avenger had the right to fulfill his role as executioner (vv 16–21). If, however, the killing was unintentional, the manslayer was to flee to the nearest city of refuge for a trial. If found innocent of murder, he was assigned to remain within the city of refuge until the death of the high priest. If he left the city before then, the kinsman avenger was permitted to execute him (vv 22–34). Apparently the death of the high priest, anointed as he was with the holy oil (v 25), was an expiation for the manslayer.

Chapter 36. Basing their question on the earlier law established in chapter 27, the leaders from Manasseh asked whether an heiress should be allowed to marry outside her tribe, with the accompanying transfer of property from one tribe to another that would ensue. God directed that an heiress would have to marry within her tribe (vv 1–12).

The last verse of the book refers to all the laws given in the plains of Moab (26:1–36:12; cf. Lv 27:34).

Teaching. God is revealed as the unchangingly faithful God of the covenant (23:19). This faithfulness to his covenant required that he both guide and care for his people and punish their sins against him. But no impediment was so great that God's design to bring his people to the land of promise was thwarted (11:23).

Both by his wrathful reaction to Israel's sin and by the numerous priestly laws, God highlights his awful holiness. The legislation expressly teaches that the man who approaches God must be clean. Even to look with unholy eyes upon the holiness of God meant death (4:20).

His sovereignty over all of life is evident from the attention he displays over even the minutest aspects of life. The phrase, "And the Lord said unto Moses," occurs over 50 times, and the words that follow in each case deal with all kinds of matters.

As the God of the covenant, God's "christological" character is also apparent. God's blessing and faithfulness reflect the christological motif. Finally, Moses' prophetic leadership (Acts 7:37,38) and intercessory ministry (e.g., 11:2; 12:13; 14:19), in the Aaronic priesthood (e.g., 16), in the animal sacrifices (cf. 19:9; Heb 9:13), and in the symbols (the manna, the water, the bronze snake) foreshadow the future Christ.

In Israel's responses to God the people depict all of human sinfulness and faithlessness. Israel's wanderings illustrate the results of unbelief. The punishments of Israel prove the maxim of Numbers 32:23: "Be sure your sin will find you out." Numbers forcefully teaches that safety and blessing are to be found only in trust in the Lord. Only he is capable of bringing men and women to the place of rest (Heb 4:9).   ROBERT L. REYMOND

See GENESIS, BOOK OF; EXODUS, BOOK OF; LEVITICUS, BOOK OF; DEUTERONOMY, BOOK OF; MOSES; DOCUMENTARY HYPOTHESIS; WILDERNESS WANDERINGS.

Bibliography. P.J. Budd, *Numbers*; M. Noth, *Numbers*; N.H. Snaith, *Leviticus and Numbers*; R.A. Watson, *The Book of Numbers*; G.J. Wenham, *Numbers*.

Nun. Ephramite, Elishama's son, and the father of Joshua, the great leader of Israel (Ex 33:11; Nm 11:28; Dt 1:38; Jos 1:1; Jgs 2:8, etc.), also called Non (1 Chr 7:27, KJV).

Nurse. *See* TRADES AND OCCUPATIONS.

Nut. *See* FOOD AND FOOD PREPARATION; PLANTS (ALMOND; PISTACHIO).

Nuzi. Town in northeastern Mesopotamia, about nine miles southwest of present-day Kirkuk. In ancient times the site was called Gasur, but the modern name is Yorgan Tepe. Excavations at Yorgan Tepe were carried out from 1925 to 1931 by an expedition of a number of cooperating archaeologists who made many interesting finds. But Yorgan Tepe is best known for its clay tablets which primarily deal with business transactions.

In the 3rd millennium BC the population of Gasur was largely Semitic, but by the middle of the 2nd millennium the inhabitants were Hurrians, and the name of the city had been changed from Gasur to Nuzi. The Hurrians are identified as the Horites of the Bible (cf. Gn 14:6; 36:20,21; Dt 2:12,22).

Many clay tablets of the 3rd millennium BC were unearthed, including one tablet inscribed with a map regarded as the oldest map in the world. The records also show that installment buying was practiced even then.

In the 15th to 14 centuries BC, Hurrian scribes wrote thousands of clay tablets, mostly in the Babylonian language. These records provide much information about Near Eastern customs and legal practices, and shed light on the patriarchal period of the Bible.

The following examples may serve as illustrations of possible relationships between Nuzi and the Bible. In Nuzi a childless wife could give her handmaid to her husband, so that the maid could bear children in the name of the wife. This practice was followed by Sarai, who gave her maid, Hagar, to her husband Abram (Gn 16:1–4); by Rachel, who gave Bilhah to Jacob (Gn 30:1–8); and by Leah, who gave Zilpah to Jacob (Gn 31:9–13). In such a case the father had a responsibility to rear the child as the offspring of his legal wife, and the wife could not drive away the child. According to this rule, Sarai had no right to drive out Hagar's son, Ishmael (cf. Gn 16:4–6).

In Nuzi there was a law against the sale of property outside one's own family. Several schemes were employed to circumvent this prohibition, including adoption and the exchange of property. In return for a guarantee of lifelong care and burial costs, a wealthy landowner would have himself "adopted" by landholding peasants so that he received their property. The records indicate that the very same man could be adopted by 300 or 400 peasants. A couple without children could legally adopt someone to provide for them in their old age and for their burial. The adopted person would be the heir to the property of his adopting parents; this may have been the relationship between Abram and his servant Eliezer (Gn 15:2). One could also exchange property of little value for valuable property. In some instances the difference in value could be made up in money. At Nuzi a man named Tehip-tilla sold his inheritance rights in a grove to his brother, Kurpazah, in exchange for three sheep, paralleling Esau's sale of his birthright to Jacob for a serving of stew (Gn 25:27–34).

In Nuzi an oral will or blessing given on one's deathbed was legally binding and irrevocable. A man named Huya was lying on his sickbed at the point of death. He took the hand of his son, Tarmiya, and gave to him a woman, Sululi-Ishtar, to be his wife. Tarmiya's two brothers challenged his claim in court but the court recognized the validity of Tarmiya's case. Although Jacob obtained the blessing of his blind and aged father by deception, Isaac had to stand by what he had done (Gn 27:33).

The Nuzi tablets also indicate that the person who had possession of the teraphim, or household gods, was the heir to the property of the owner of the idols. For this reason Rachel took the teraphim of her father Laban (Gn 31:19), who was very disturbed over their disappearance (Gn 31:30–35).

Another case of adoption parallels the relationship between Jacob and Laban. Nashwi adopted Wullu and gave his daughter, Nuhuya, to him in marriage. If Wullu married another wife, he would have to forfeit the property he had received from Nashwi. Laban also made Jacob covenant that he would not take a wife other than Laban's two daughters, Leah and Rachel (Gn 31:50).

CARL E. DeVRIES

See INSCRIPTIONS.

Nympha, Nymphas. Christian woman living in Laodicea (or perhaps Colossae), in whose house believers gathered for worship. Paul sent greetings to her and the church (Col 4:15, KJV Nymphas).

Oo

Oak. *See* PLANTS.

Oak, Diviners'. Tree near Shechem (Jgs 9:37).

See DIVINERS' OAK.

Oak of Meonenim. Tree near Shechem (Jgs 9:37).

See DIVINERS' OAK.

Oak of the Pillar. Sacred meeting place in Shechem where the citizens of that city and the inhabitants of Beth-millo made Abimelech king (Jgs 9:6, KJV Plain of the Pillar). It is perhaps identifiable with the "Oak of Moreh."

See MOREH, OAK OF; PLAIN OF.

Oak of Weeping. Tree near Bethel under which Deborah, Rebekah's nurse, was buried, (Gn 35:8), hence called "Allon-bacuth," meaning "Oak of Weeping." Its exact location is unknown.

Oak of Za-anannim. Site regarded as a border point in the territory of Naphtali (Jos 19:33; Jgs 4:11).

See ZA-ANANNIM.

Oaks of Mamre. Site associated with Abraham and Isaac (Gn 13:18).

See MAMRE (PLACE).

Oath. Solemn vow or promise to fulfill a pledge. There are two terms in Hebrew that mean "oath": 'ālâ and šebû'â. The latter, more general term meant in ancient times to enter into a solemn (even magic) relationship with the number seven, although ancient connections are lost. Even so, when Abraham and Abimelech entered into an oath at Beersheba (the well of seven, or the well of the oath), Abraham set aside seven ewe lambs as a witness to the fact that he had dug a well (Gn 21:22–31). The former term, 'ālâ, often translated "oath," properly means "curse." At times the two terms are used together (Nm 5:21; Neh 10:29; Dn 9:11). Any breach of one's undertaking affirmed by an oath would be attended by a curse. The Lord affirmed that he had established a covenant and a curse with Israel, that is, a breach of covenant would be followed by a curse (Dt 29:14).

An oath was taken to confirm an agreement or, in a political situation, to confirm a treaty. Both in Israel and among its neighbors, God (or the gods) would act as the guarantor(s) of the agreement and his name (or names) was invoked for this purpose. When Jacob and Laban made an agreement, they erected a heap of stones as a witness and declared, "The God of Abraham and the God of Nahor, the God of their father, judge between us" (Gn 31:53). If either party transgressed the terms, it was a heinous sin. For this reason one of the Ten Commandments dealt with empty affirmations: "You shall not take the name of the Lord your God in vain; for the Lord will not hold him guiltless who takes his name in vain" (Ex 20:7). The people of Israel were forbidden to swear their oaths by false gods (Jer 12:16; Am 8:14). To breach an international treaty where the oath was taken in the Lord's name merited death (Ez 17:16,17). It was one of the complaints of Hosea that the people of his day swore falsely when they made a covenant (Hos 10:4). Judgment would attend such wanton disregard of the solemnity of an oath. Certain civil situations in Israel called for an oath (Ex 22:10,11; Lv 5:1; 6:3; Nm 5:11–28). This practice provided a pattern for the Israelite covenantal oath of allegiance between God and his people.

Christ taught that oaths were binding (Mt

5:33). In the kingdom of God oaths would become unnecessary (Mt 5:34–37). At his trial before Caiaphas, Jesus heard an imprecatory oath from the high priest (Mt 26:63–65), and Paul swore by an oath on occasion (2 Cor 1:23; Gal 1:20). God himself was bound by his own oath (Heb 6:13–18) to keep his promise to the patriarchs (Gn 50:24; Pss 89:19–37,49; 110:1–4).

See Covenant; Vow.

Obadiah (Person). 1. Governor of Ahab's house (1 Kgs 18:3–16). Elijah met him after the years of drought and requested Obadiah to bring Ahab to him, while both Ahab and Obadiah were looking for water and grass (1 Kgs 18:5). Obadiah was an important officer in charge of Ahab's house (v 3). Unlike his master, Obadiah was faithful to the Lord, as he hid 500 prophets in caves and provided them with food and drink (v 4).

2. Descendant of David (1 Chr 3:21).

3. Descendant of Izrahiah from Issachar's tribe (1 Chr 7:3).

4. Azel's son and a descendant of King Saul from Benjamin's tribe (1 Chr 8:38; 9:44).

5. Son of Shemaiah, who was among the first Levites returning from exile to Jerusalem. He lived in one of the villages of the Netophathites (1 Chr 9:16). He is called Abda in Nehemiah 11:17.

See Abda.

6. Gadite who joined David at his stronghold in the wilderness. He was a mighty warrior, able to handle shield and spear, and was extremely fast (1 Chr 12:8,9).

7. Father of Ishmiah, commander over the forces of Zebulun (1 Chr 27:19).

8. Prince of Judah in Jehoshaphat's time (2 Chr 17:7). He joined four other officers and the Levites in teaching the Law throughout the cities of Judah.

9. Levite overseer in Josiah's time (2 Chr 34:12), in charge of the repair of the temple.

10. Son of Jehiel (Ez 8:9), who joined Ezra in his journey from Babylon to Jerusalem, leading 128 men with him.

11. Priest who signed Ezra's covenant (Neh 10:5).

12. Gatekeeper, and Levite charged with the oversight the storehouses by the gates in the days of Joiakim, son of Jeshua (Neh 12:25,26).

13. Prophet who prophesied against Edom, which had rejoiced at the Babylonian victories in Jerusalem in 597 BC. Obadiah described the behavior of the Edomites (vv 11–14) in his prophecy, the shortest book in the OT, and predicted God's judgment on Edom (vv 2–10,15).

See Obadiah, Book of; Prophet, Prophetess.

Obadiah, Book of. Fourth book of the Minor Prophets, having a noble name meaning "Servant of Yahweh"; shortest book in the OT.

Author. Practically nothing is known about Obadiah the prophet. Not even the name of his father or his home region is given in the superscription (v 1).

Historical Background. It would seem likely that Obadiah came from Judah because he expresses deep concern over the inroads made into his land by the Edomites in the day of Judah's destruction (v 12). He probably had his vision concerning Edom (v 1) shortly after the fall of Jerusalem and the devastation of Judah by Nebuchadnezzar in 586 BC. It is unlikely that the Edomites heard this prophecy composed for a home audience, possibly during the early exile period. We have only limited information about the land of Edom during the Iron II period although archaeological data have become available in recent years. A few important sites have been excavated, including Tawilan, which was occupied from the 8th to the 6th centuries BC. Nebuchadnezzar may have invaded Edom in 582 BC, although no certain reference to such an invasion exists. The Babylonian king Nabonidus stayed at Teima for several years, and the town of Tell el Kheleifeh near the Gulf of Aqaba flourished early in the century. However, Edom entered a period of decline in the 6th century BC, due to interference from its trading partners from Arabia and the south, such as Teima and Dedan.

Content. Edom's fall is announced (vv 1–4) by the prophet. Evidently a coalition of neighboring Arab tribes was conspiring to attack Edom, which added weight to his message (v 1). Little did these tribes know that their planned assault on Edom was part of the divine plan.

Edom's destruction is declared (vv 2–9) and its actual downfall is described (vv 2–4). Edom, strong and safe in the rocky bastion in the high mountains (v 3), would be brought low (v 4). Edom's overthrow would be complete (vv 5,6). As thieves and marauders ravage a place by night, so Edom would be stripped, houses and vineyards plundered. Edom would know no merciful alleviation as sometimes happens when robbers raid a house. Even allies would prove treacherous (v 7), confederates would deceive, and guests would set snares. Taken by surprise, Edom would fall an easy prey. When the day of Edom's doom came, the famous wise men (v 8) would be destroyed and soldiers demoralized and slaughtered (v 9).

Edom's wrongdoing is spelled out (vv 10–14,15b). Edom showed ill will toward Judah on the day when the Babylonians attacked.

Rather than helping Judah, Edom stood aloof and behaved like one of Judah's foes (vv 10,11). To make matters worse Edom gloated over Judah's misfortune, jeered at the people (v 12), and laid hands on their property (v 13). Edom collaborated with Babylon, cutting off Judah's refugees from escape and handing them over to Judah's enemies. Such deeds would return to Edom (vv 14,15b).

On the Day of the Lord (vv 15a,16–21) guilty Edom would be caught up in the wider scale of God's judgment on all nations. Beyond the day of disaster endured by Jerusalem in 586 BC stood another day, a day of vindication and judgment in Israel's favor.

Positively, the remnant of Judah (vv 17,21) would be preserved, the sacred site, Mt Zion, would be rehabilitated, and the Edomites would come under the control of the remnant of Israel. Like a fire, Israel would consume the stubble of Edom (v 18) and regain their lost territories (vv 19,20).

Theologically, the prophecy stresses divine sovereignty in the midst of the cruel invasion of Judah's restricted sovereignty. The Lord of history works out his purposes in the midst of past and present events. As Lord of the future he would visit Israel's foes, and his foes, with judgment in the Day of the Lord. Zion would be reestablished as the proud capital of a glorious nation, freed from pagan defilement for ever.   JOHN A. THOMPSON

See PROPHET, PROPHETESS; PROPHECY; ISRAEL, HISTORY OF.

Bibliography. L.C. Allen, *The Books of Joel, Obadiah, Jonah, and Micah*; R.J. Coggins and S.L. Re'emi, *Nahum, Obadiah, Esther*; G.A. Smith, *The Book of the Twelve Prophets*; C. von Orelli, *The Twelve Minor Prophets*.

Obal. Alternate spelling of Ebal, Joktan's descendant, in Genesis 10:28.

See EBAL #2.

Obed. 1. Ruth and Boaz's first child, listed among the ancestors of Jesus (Ru 4:17,21,22; 1 Chr 2:12; Mt 1:5; Lk 3:32).

See GENEALOGY OF JESUS CHRIST.

2. Jerameelite and Ephlal's son (1 Chr 2:37,38).

3. One of David's mighty men (1 Chr 11:47).

4. Shemaiah's son and an able leader who ruled his father's house (1 Chr 26:6,7).

5. Father of Azariah, a captain of Jehoiada (2 Chr 23:1).

Obed-edom. 1. Man in whose care David placed the ark of the covenant when he was transferring it from Gibeah to Jerusalem (2 Sm 6:10–12; 1 Chr 13:5–14). He is called a "Gittite," which indicates that his birthplace was Gath. This was not the Philistine city of Gath but the levitical town in the territory of Dan known as Gath-rimmon (Jos 19:45). It is likely that Obed-edom was a Levite and therefore qualified to care for the ark of the covenant. Uzzah's rash action in steadying the ark when the oxen stumbled brought upon him immediate death. David's consternation and fear at this turn of events led him to reconsider his intention of bringing the ark to Jerusalem. Apparently Obed-edom's home was nearby and it was convenient to leave the ark in his care. When David was informed after three months that the Lord had greatly blessed Obed-edom, he realized that the judgment which fell on Uzzah was incurred because the ark was carried contrary to the method prescribed in the Law (Nm 4:15; 7:9) and not because of the Lord's anger with him. He ordered that the ark be taken from Obed-edom's home and carried to Jerusalem in the proper manner (1 Chr 15:25–28). Apparently Obed-edom was rewarded for his faithful service by being appointed a gatekeeper for the ark in Jerusalem (1 Chr 15:24; 26:4,8,15). Some scholars believe that Obed-edom the gatekeeper was a man other than the one referred to above.

2. Levitical musician who ministered before the ark (1 Chr 15:21; 16:5; 16:38). He was the son of Jeduthun, one of David's chief singers. Some scholars also believe that the musician and singer were different men.

3. Levitical guardian of the sacred vessels of the temple taken hostage by Joash (2 Chr 25:24).

Obedience. Act or instance of submitting to the restraint or command of an authority; compliance with the demands or requests of someone or something over us. The general words for obedience in both Hebrew and Greek refer to hearing or hearkening to a superior authority. Another major Greek word includes the idea of submission to authority in the sense of arranging or ordering oneself under someone in a place of command. A third Greek word suggests obedience that is a result more of persuasion than of submission.

Obedience to God and human authorities is an obligation stressed in both the OT and NT. Abraham was additionally blessed on one occasion because he obeyed God in offering Isaac on the altar (Gn 22:18; cf. Gn 26:5). God's continued blessing upon Israel by virtue of the Sinai covenant was contingent upon their obeying his voice and keeping his covenant (Ex 19:5). On the verge of entering Canaan, Moses placed before Israel a blessing and a curse, the former if they listened to and obeyed the commandments of the Lord and the latter if they did not (Dt 11:22–28).

Deuteronomy warns that the penalty for stubborn and rebellious children is, first of all, chastisement, and then death by stoning if they persistently refuse to listen (Dt 21:18–21).

One evidence that a person is a child of God is continued obedience to the commandments of God (1 Jn 2:3–5). Jesus said that those who love him would keep his commandments (Jn 14:15). And Peter, speaking of Christians, calls them "obedient children" (1 Pt 1:14; see also Heb 5:9; 11:8).

Christians are to render obedience to a variety of people: believers to the Lord (Jn 14:21–24; 15:10), wives to their own husbands (Eph 5:22,24; Col 3:18; Ti 2:5; 1 Pt 3:1,5), children to their parents (Eph 6:1; Col 3:20), citizens to their government officials (Rom 13:1–7; Ti 3:1; 1 Pt 2:13,14), and servants to their masters (Eph 6:5; Col 3:22; Ti 2:9; 1 Pt 2:18).

However, in spite of the strong stress on obedience in the Bible, such obedience is never made the grounds for justification before God. Paul declares, "For by grace you have been saved through faith; and that not of yourselves; it is the gift of God; not of works, lest any man should boast. For we are his workmanship, created in Christ Jesus unto good works" (Eph 2:8–10 KJV). Paul goes on to encourage believers to "be careful to engage in good deeds" (Ti 3:14). So, too, James speaks of works of obedience logically flowing from faith (2:14–26). Such obedience is the fulfillment of Paul's command for Christians to continue working out their salvation (Phil 2:12).

In both the OT and the NT, obedience on the part of believers stands as the supreme test of faith in God. Consequently, Samuel says to Saul after his disobedience in sparing the king of Amalek and some animals, "Has the Lord as great delight in burnt offerings and sacrifices, as in obeying the voice of the Lord? Behold, to obey is better than sacrifice, and to hearken than the fat of rams. For rebellion is as the sin of divination, and stubbornness is as iniquity and idolatry" (1 Sm 15:22,23a).

James strongly emphasizes that faith without works is dead (Jas 2:14–18). Jesus himself, on the night of his betrayal, emphasized by repetition, that love for him is measured by obedience to his commandments (Jn 14:15,21,23,24; 15:10). He underscored this by asserting that his own love for the Father was evidenced by his obeying the Father's commands (14:31).

The Bible mentions many people whose obedience to God comes from their faith and love for him (see Heb 11). For example, Abel believed God and offered a more excellent sacrifice (Heb 11:4); Noah put his faith in God's word and prepared an ark (11:7); by faith Abra-ham left Ur at God's direction, not knowing his destination (11:8); Moses put his faith in God and refused the privileges of being called Pharaoh's son, choosing rather to identify with Israel, God's people (11:24,25). The greatest example of obedience based on trust in God is Jesus Christ himself. Paul writes that Jesus emptied himself, taking the form of a bond-servant, and "humbled himself and became obedient unto death, even death on a cross" (Phil 2:7,8).

Obil. Ishmaelite steward of King David's camels (1 Chr 27:30).

Oblation. *See* OFFERINGS AND SACRIFICES.

Oboth. Temporary camping place of the Israelites during their wilderness wanderings, mentioned between Punon and Iye-abarim (Nm 21:10,11; 33:43,44). Although its exact location is uncertain, some have attempted to identify it with 'Ain el-Weiba, 33 miles south of the Dead Sea in the Arabah Valley.

See WILDERNESS WANDERINGS.

Occupations. *See* TRADES AND OCCUPATIONS.

Ochran, Ocran. Father of Pagiel, the leader of Asher's tribe during the wilderness journeys (Nm 1:13; 2:27; 7:72,77; 10:26; KJV Ocran).

Offend, Offense. Words used two ways in the Bible: doing what is wrong oneself, or causing someone else to do wrong or to stumble.

Doing Wrong. In both the Hebrew of the OT and the Greek of the NT there are several words for sin or wrongdoing having a variety of different translations. With the word "offend" or "offense," the accent is on the sin being against a person or against the law, an offense against either God or man.

Sin is fundamentally an offense against God. For example the people of Edom had "grievously offended" in taking vengeance on Judah and so the hand of the Lord was against them in judgment (Ez 25:12,13). Israel "offended" in their worship of Baal (Hos 13:1). The breaking of God's Law is spoken of as an "offense committed" (Dt 19:15; cf. Dt 22:26; 25:2). In the NT James (2:10; 3:2) speaks of offenses against God and against his Law.

There are many passages in the Bible addressing one man's offense against another, for example, Abraham's against Abimelech (Gn 20:9), or Pharaoh's chief butler and chief baker against their master (Gn 40:1). Sometimes it is an alleged offense and no actual wrong has been done (e.g., Gn 31:36; 2 Kgs 18:14; Jer 37:18). Paul in his defense before the

Roman governor Festus said, "Neither against the law of the Jews, nor against the temple, nor against Caesar have I offended at all" (Acts 25:8).

Finally, the Bible speaks about dealing with real offenses against God and man. Offenses should be acknowledged and confessed (Hos 5:15). One's proper resolution before God is, "I will not offend any more" (Jb 34:31). One needs to "make amends for offenses" (Eccl 10:4) and to forgive the offenses of others (Prv 17:9; 19:11). Jesus Christ died for our offenses (Rom 4:25; 5:15–21), so that in turning to him there is forgiveness for all sins.

Causing Another to Sin. The noun "offense" and the verb "offend" are also used in reference to a person being caused to stumble or to do what is wrong. There are three ways in which this may happen:

(1) There may be something in the individual which causes him or her to stumble. Jesus expresses the seriousness of this, and, though speaking metaphorically, indicates the strenuous steps of prevention (Mt 5:29–30; 18:8–9).

(2) There may be something in a person that causes offense to others. Jesus says, "Woe unto the world because of offences! for it must needs be that offences come; but woe to that man by whom the offence cometh!" (Mt 18:7 KJV). There are, in fact, many NT passages which insist on living so as not to cause others to stumble (Rom 16:17). The apostle Paul says, "Do not, for the sake of food, destroy the work of God. Everything is indeed clean, but it is wrong for any one to make others fall by what he eats; it is right not to eat meat or drink wine or do anything that makes your brother stumble" (Rom 14:20,21; cf. 1 Cor 10:32; 2 Cor 6:3).

However, people may be offended at the truth through no fault of the person who presents it. Isaiah speaks of God as "a stone of offense, and a rock of stumbling to both houses of Israel" (8:14) in that people would not always accept his demands and the way of faith in him. The NT takes these same words and applies them to the offense of the gospel of Christ (Rom 9:32,33; 1 Pt 2:8). In the time of his ministry there were those who were offended at Jesus, at his lowly birth (Mt 13:57), at what he said and did (Mt 15:12) or because of the cost of following him (Mt 13:21). Even disciples were capable of being offended and turning aside (Jn 6:61). In the end all were offended and fled from him (Mt 26:31,56). Finally the apostle Paul spoke of the offense in the preaching of the cross of Christ. He could have chosen to preach a popular message and avoided persecution, a "message that doesn't offend anyone" (Gal 5:11 LB). He chose rather to preach the cross even though it was "a

stumbling block to Jews and folly to Gentiles" (1 Cor 1:23).

See SIN.

Offerings and Sacrifices. Major ritual expressions of religious life with accompanying rites, such as libations, effusions, and sacred meals. The ideology expressed in Israel's ritual complex made its religion unique in the ancient Near East. The concepts of OT ritual also underlie NT theology with regard to sin and reconciliation to God through the atoning death of Jesus Christ.

Performance and Order of Sacrifices. The main source for a description of the correct performance of sacrificial ritual is the opening section of Leviticus (chs 1–7). It consists of two separate parts. The first (Lv 1:1–6:7) is didactic, dealing with two categories of sacrifice: those of a "pleasing odor," namely, the burnt, the grain (2:1–16), and the peace offerings (3:1–17); and the expiatory sacrifices, namely, the sin (4:1–5:13) and the guilt or trespass offerings (5:14–6:7). Attention is paid to the minute details of each ritual, and they are grouped according to their logical or conceptual associations.

The grain (or cereal) offering follows the burnt offering because it always accompanied it in actual practice (Nm 15:1–21; chs 28–29); it also went with the peace offering (Lv 7:12–14; Nm 15:3,4). Special emphasis is placed on burning the inward parts on the altar to make a "pleasing odor to the Lord" (Lv 1:9,17; 2:2,9,12; 3:5,11,16). When the Lord "smelled the pleasing odor" (Gn 8:21) it was a sign of divine favor; refusal indicated God's displeasure (Lv 26:31). The officiating priest evidently knew how to read the signs and would tell the offerer whether his sacrifice had been accepted (1 Sm 26:19; cf. Am 5:21–23).

The sin and guilt offerings were expiatory (Lv 4:1–7,20). The situations requiring such offerings are listed, and special emphasis is laid on the handling of the blood in the ritual.

The second major section in this passage (Lv 6:8–7:38) stresses the administrative details for the various offerings. This section consists of a series of "instructions" for each type of offering pertaining to the distribution of the sacrificial materials. Some went to the priest(s), some to the offerer, and others were burned on the altar or disposed of outside the camp. Those sacrifices designated as "most holy" were to be eaten only by qualified members of the priesthood (Lv 2:3,10; 10:12–17; 14:13; Nm 18:9).

The burnt offering is discussed first because it was entirely consumed on the altar (and thus not eaten by anyone). After it follows the sacrifices distributed to the officiants (Lv 6:17,

Ruins of a large altar at Dan.

25,29; 7:1,6), and at the end come the peace offerings, a significant portion of which was returned to the offerer.

The order in which the sacrifices are treated in this passage also corresponds to their relative frequency in the rituals of the sacred calendar (Nm 28,29; 2 Chr 31:3; Ez 45:17a). This would be particularly important for the priests and Levites on duty at the temple because they were responsible for the logistics of the daily sacrificial ritual, especially on the high holidays; management of the temple storehouse was a formidable task (1 Chr 23:28–32; 26:15,20,22; 2 Chr 13:10,11; 30:3–19; 34:9–11).

Each section concerning a particular offering concludes with the logistic or administrative details peculiar to it. There then follows a summary of the matters treated thus far (Lv 7:7–10), and the section concludes with a treat-

ment of the peace offerings (7:11–36). The latter did not play a role in the sacred calendar except during the Feast of Weeks (23:19,20); on all other occasions peace offerings were purely voluntary sacrifices and thus not subject to any fixed bookkeeping.

In other biblical contexts the sacrifices are listed according to the same "bookkeeping" or "administrative" order: burnt, cereal, and drink; sin (or guilt); and sometimes peace offerings. An example is the roster of donations made by the tribal leaders for dedication of the altar (Nm 7). The information is organized like an everyday ledger from the temple storehouse; the summary classifies the animals as burnt, sin, and peace offerings (7:87, 88) in accordance with the respective entries from each donor (7:15–17). The levitical scribe had two purposes for such a record: to credit the offerers and to record the treasures and food supplies coming in. Much of the foodstuffs being given as offerings were actually apportioned to the officiating priests (18:8–11; 2 Chr 31:4–19).

When prescriptions were made as to the type and number of offerings to be brought (e.g., Nm 15:24), the "bookkeeping" order is generally followed. This was true of the calendarial sacrifices; burnt and cereal offerings and libations were listed followed by a sin offering for each of the following: New Moon (Nm 28:11–15), each day of Passover (28:19–22), the Festival of Weeks (Lv 23:18,19; 28:27–30), Trumpets (29:2–5), Day of Atonement (29:8–11a) and each day of the Feast of Tabernacles (29:12–16a).

For sacrifices required in specific cases, the instructions as to what offerings to bring follow this sequence (e.g., the purification of a woman after giving birth, Lv 12:6,8). Note also the offerings given at the successful termination of a Nazirite vow; the Nazirite brought burnt, sin, and peace offerings (with some special cereal offerings, Nm 6:14,15). However the priest conducted the actual ritual according to a different order; the sin offering was made first, followed by the burnt offering, and finally the peace offering (Nm 6:16,17). In the case of an incomplete vow the first step was to offer a sin and then a burnt offering to renew the vow (6:11). The reconsecration of the Nazirite's head required a separate guilt offering—a distinct ritual act (6:12).

The description of the offerings made by the prince of Israel in the latter days presents the same contrast between the two orders of sacrifices. On festival holidays the prince brought burnt, cereal, and drink offerings but he offered them as sin, cereal, burnt, and peace offerings (Ez 45:17). This second order of sacrifices in which the sin offering precedes the burnt offering was also followed in the re-dedication of the altar (Ez 43:18–27).

The same "procedural" sequence of sacrifices appears in other instances: the purification of the leper—guilt and sin offerings (14:19) followed by a burnt offering (Lv 14:12–20); the man with a discharge—sin and burnt offerings (15:15); likewise the woman with a discharge (15:30). The same order is followed for the sacrifices on the Day of Atonement (16:3–6,11,15,24).

The Book of Leviticus furnishes two examples of the proper order in which sacrifices were offered. One is the ordination of Aaron and his sons (Ex 29; Lv 8). The sin offering came first and then the burnt offering (Ex 29:10–18; Lv 8:14–21). The focal point in this ritual was the sacrifice of ordination or literally "installation," a special form of peace offering (Ex 29:19–34; Lv 8:22–29). The second passage is the formal inauguration of the sacrificial system at the tabernacle (Lv 9). The sacrifices for Aaron were sin and burnt offerings followed by those for the people: sin, burnt, cereal, and peace offerings (9:7–22).

The same sequence is followed at the cleansing and restoration of the temple in Jerusalem conducted by King Hezekiah (2 Chr 29:20–36). A great sin offering was first (vv 20–24), followed by the burnt offerings accompanied by music and song (vv 25–30). Then the king proclaimed that the people had committed themselves to the Lord (v 31); in this new state of purity they could now share in the sacrifices of devotion (burnt offerings) and thanksgiving (peace offerings) (vv 31–35).

The procedural order of the sacrifices embodies the OT ideology of how God may be approached. First, atonement for sin had to be made and then total consecration of self; these are symbolized by the sin and/or guilt offerings and the burnt and cereal offerings, respectively. When these conditions were met, the offerer could express his continued devotion by more burnt offerings and also take part in the fellowship sacrifices (peace offerings) in which he himself got a large portion of the slaughtered animal (to share with his friends and the poor in his community; Dt 12:17–19).

Description of Sacrifices. The ensuing description of the different types of sacrifice will treat them in accordance with the "procedural" order, that is, as symbolic stages in one's approach to God.

Expiation. These two offerings were required for making atonement for sins and trespasses. (1) Sin offering (Lv 4:1–35; 6:24–30). Different animals were specified in accordance with the rank of the offerer. A high priest had to bring a young bull (Lv 4:3), as did the congregation as a whole (v 14) except when the matter was a ritual infraction (Nm 15:24). A ruler would bring a male goat (Lv 4:25) but a commoner could provide a female goat (Lv 4:28; Nm 15:27) or a lamb (Lv 4:32). If he were indigent, he could offer two turtledoves or two young pigeons (one of which would be a burnt offering; Lv 5:7), or if he was extremely poor he might even substitute a tenth of an ephah of fine flour (Lv 5:11–13; cf. Heb 9:22).

The offerer brought the animal to the entrance of the temple court and laid his hand on it (Lv 4:4). He did not confess his sin in this act because the animal was not being sent away (cf. the goat for Azazel, Lv 16:21); rather, he was identifying himself with the sacrifice. The offerer also had to slay the animal on the north side of the altar (Lv 4:24,29; see also 1:11). The animals were never slaughtered on the altar proper.

The officiating priest collected the blood; when it was a bull for himself or for the congregation, he sprinkled some of the blood before the veil inside the temple (Lv 4:5–7) and put some on the horns of the incense altar (vv 16–18). On the Day of Atonement he brought the sacrificial blood for himself and for the people into the Holy of Holies (16:14,15). From all other animals, the blood was applied to the horns of the altar of burnt offering (4:7,18); the blood of fowl was sprinkled on the side of the altar (5:9). Finally, the remaining blood from any offering was poured or drained out at the base of the altar (4:7).

The choicest of the internal organs, namely, the fatty tissue over and on the entrails, the two kidneys and their fat, and the appendage to the liver, were all offered to the Lord on the altar (4:8–10). The carcass and the other entrails were burned outside the camp when it was a bull for the priest or for the people (vv 11,12,21). This was also true of the bull for the ordination of the priests (Ex 29:10–14; Lv 8:14–17). Otherwise, the priest who conducted the rites received the edible flesh as his portion. He had to eat it within the temple area and its preparation was governed by very strict rules of ritual purity (Lv 6:25–30; cf. 10:16–20). A sin offering of one male goat was presented at each of the sacred holidays: the New Moon (Nm 28:15), each day of Passover (vv 22–24), the Festival of Weeks (v 30), and of Trumpets (29:5), the Day of Atonement (v 11), and each day of the Feast of Tabernacles (vv 16,19). The high priest also offered a bull for himself and then sacrificed one of the two goats on the Day of Atonement. Certain purification rites required lesser sin offerings, namely, lambs or birds: childbirth (Lv 12:6–8), cleansing from leprosy (14:12–14,19,22,31), and abscesses and hemorrhages (15:14,15,29,30)

A bull adorned for sacrifice by a Roman.

or after defilement while under a vow (Nm 6:10,11).

(2) Guilt offering (Lv 5:14–6:7; 7:1–7). The guilt or trespass offering was a special kind of sin offering (cf. Lv 5:7) required whenever someone had been denied his rightful due. Reparation of the valued amount that had been defrauded had to be made plus a fine of one-fifth (5:16; 6:5). The animal was usually a ram (5:15,18; 6:6). The cleansed leper and the defiled Nazirite had to bring a male lamb (14:12,21; Nm 6:12). The offerer apparently handled the sacrifice as he would a sin offering, but the priest had to sprinkle the blood around the altar (Lv 5:12). Viscera were burned on the altar as usual (7:3–5). Some of the blood was then applied to the tip of the cleansed leper's right ear and to his right thumb and big toe (14:14). Again the priest received most of the animal's flesh for food (7:6,7; 14:13). A guilt offering was required whenever another party had suffered some loss. Ritual infractions, such as eating the "holy things" without proper authorization (5:14–19; 22:14), called for payment of the sum that should have gone to the Lord plus the fine

of one-fifth which went to the priest (5:16; 2 Kgs 12:16). The leper belongs in this category, since during the time of his infection he was unable to render service to God (14:12–18). The same applies to the Nazirite who had suffered defilement while he was set apart to God by the vow; thus a guilt offering was required (Nm 6:12). Violation of another person's property rights could only be expiated by the guilt offering and its additional one-fifth. Such matters included cheating on deposits or security, robbery or oppression, failing to report the find of some lost property, or false swearing or failing to testify (Lv 6:1–5). Intercourse with a betrothed slave girl was also a violation of property rights (19:20–22). If the offended party was no longer living and had no surviving kinsmen, the payment went to the priest (Nm 5:5–10).

Effectiveness. Ritual infractions called for sin and guilt offerings (Lv 4:14,16; 5:2,3; 22:14; Nm 15:22–29). Ritual acts in the OT were expressions of faith and devotion, reflecting a universal human tendency to substitute the outward act for the proper heart attitude (Hos 6:6). All sins committed "inadvertantly" could be atoned for by sacrifice (Lv 4:2,13,22,27; 5:14) but only after the offender had realized his guilt (Lv 4:13,14; cf. 5:17; 14:23,28; Nm 15:24). Other consciously committed offenses that could be atoned for were acts of shady dealing (Lv 6:1–5; cf. Ex 22:7–15) and failure to follow the rules of testimony (Lv 5:1,4). However, sins of the "upraised hand" (Nm 15:30,31) could not be expiated by sacrifice. All offenses warranting the death penalty would fall in this category. Generally, they can be seen as violations of the Decalogue: for example, the second commandment—idolatry (Lv 20:2; Dt 13:6; 17:2–7), sacrificing children to Molech (Lv 20:3), witchcraft and false prophesy (Ex 22:18; Lv 20:6,27; Dt 13:5; 18:20; 1 Sm 28:9); the third—blasphemy (Lv 24:14,16,23; 1 Kgs 21:10); the fourth—violating the sabbath (Ex 31:14; 35:2; Nm 15:32–36); the fifth—striking or reviling a parent (Ex 21:15,17); the sixth—murder (Lv 24:17,21) and kidnapping (Ex 21:16); the seventh—adultery (Lv 20:10; Dt 22:22), incestuous and unnatural sexual relations (Ex 22:19; Lv 18:29; 20:11,14), unchastity (Lv 21:9; Dt 22:23), and rape (Dt 22:25); and the ninth—false witness in capital court cases (Dt 19:16, 19). One precedent case is given with regard to violation of the sabbath (Nm 15:32–36) requiring an explicit oracle for the punishment to be imposed. The death penalty was exacted whenever desecration of the sabbath represented a rejection by the offender of the covenant (Ex 20:8–11; Dt 5:12–15; cf. Ex 31:12–17).

Laws against violations of the ritual calendar and related rules are probably extensions of this concept in that disregard for the sacrificial system implied rejection of the covenant which itself was instituted by a sacrifice (Ex 24:3–8). Such violations were: nonobservance of (Nm 9:13) or eating leavened bread during (Ex 12:15,19) the Passover; failing to observe the Day of Atonement (Lv 23:29,30); eating blood (Lv 7:27; 17:14) or the choice viscera of the sacrifices (Lv 7:25); failure to slaughter burnt or peace offerings at the proper sanctuary (Lv 17:4,9); eating sacrifices while unclean (Lv 7:20,21; 22:3,4); eating the leftovers from a peace offering after the time limit had expired (Lv 19:8); touching holy things unlawfully (Nm 4:15,18,20); polluting the sanctuary by being unclean (Nm 19:13,20); misuse of the sacred ointment (Ex 30;32,33) or perfume (Ex 30:38).

The second test case for "high-handed sin" was Korah's rebellion and the people's subsequent bitterness (Nm 16). The offense was so great that atonement could not be made by a sin offering; however, by intercession, symbolized in the burning of incense, expiation was achieved (vv 46,47). In the same manner Moses had interceded for the people and gained at least partial atonement for the sin of the golden calf (Ex 32:11–13,30–35).

Forgiveness would be granted to anyone with a "broken and contrite heart" even when the offenses (murder and adultry) were too heinous for ritual atonement (Ps 51:1,16,17; 2 Sm 12:13). When Isaiah and his people were too defiled by moral uncleanness to deserve sacrificial cleansing (Is 6:5; cf. 1:10–17), their guilt could still be removed and the sin atoned for by prayer and intercession (Is 6:6,7). In summary, the sin and guilt offerings were effective for less serious violations against the eighth and ninth commandments and for some ritual infractions, but in every instance the offender had to be fully conscious of his responsibility and had to make reparation when required. For greater sins against the Ten Commandments no ritual would help; nevertheless, forgiveness could be obtained on condition of sincere repentance.

Consecration Offerings. These rituals usually come to mind when one hears the word "offering." They represent acts of personal commitment that must accompany the repentance expressed in the sin and guilt offerings. They were also a prerequisite for the fellowship or communal sacrifices that might follow.

(1) Burnt offerings (Lv 1:3–17; 6:8–13). The burnt offering could be a bull (1:3–5), a sheep (v 10), or a bird (v 14). The offerer presented the animal, laid his hand on it, and slew it on the north side of the altar (vv 3–5,11). The bird was simply given to the priest (v 15). The latter collected the blood, presented it before God, and then sprinkled it around the altar (vv 5,11). When the offering was a bird, he wrung off its head and drained the blood at the side of the altar (v 15). Though the slaughtering and sprinkling of the blood relates the burnt offering to the expiatory sacrifices of the previous section, the main emphasis here is on slaying the animal, washing its unclean parts, and then carefully arranging all of the pieces on the altar (vv 6–9,12,13). All of this was then consumed on the altar as "a pleasing odor" to the Lord. Only the skin of the animal went to the priest (Lv 7:8). Since burnt offerings were offered morning and evening, a good supply of wood by the altar was necessary. The officiating priest, dressed in proper garments, had to keep the fire burning continuously (Lv 6:8–13).

Burnt offerings played a prominent role in the sacrifices of the ritual calendar. The "continual burnt offering" was made twice a day, a male lamb morning and evening (Ex 29:38–42; Nm 28:1–8). Two additional lambs were sacrificed each sabbath (Nm 28:9,10).

Except for these daily offerings, a sin offering of one goat was usually made along with the burnt offerings on these holidays. For the New Moon at the beginning of each month, two young bulls, one ram, and seven male lambs were offered (Nm 28:11–14). The same were required for each day of the Passover festival (vv 19–24) and again on the Feast of Weeks (vv 26–29). On the festival of Trumpets and the Day of Atonement the requirement was one bull, one ram, and seven lambs (29:2–4,8).

The great Feast of Tabernacles was characterized by a series of elaborate burnt offerings, plus one goat per day as a sin offering. On the first day 13 young bulls, two rams, and 14 male lambs were offered (29:12–16).

Each successive day the number of bulls was decreased by one until on the seventh day there were only seven (the rams and lambs remained the same; 29:17–25). On the eighth day the animals required for Trumpets and Atonement were offered, namely, one bull, one ram, and seven lambs (vv 35–38). Certain rituals of purification also required burnt offerings in addition to sin offerings: after childbirth (Lv 12:6–8), abscesses (15:14,15) and discharges (15:29,30), or after defilement while under a Nazirite vow (Nm 6:10,11). Though it is not stated that cereal offerings were required in these cases, they certainly were for the cleansing from leprosy (Lv 14:10,19,20,22,31) and the completion of the Nazirite vow (Nm 6:14,16).

(2) Cereal offering (Lv 2; 6:14–23). The Hebrew term referring to this particular offering means "gift," or "offering," including animals (Gn 4:3–5; Jgs 6:18; 1 Sm 2:17). But in the specific sacrificial context it signifies a combination of fine flour, olive oil, and frankincense that could be made up in the form of baked loaves, wafers, or morsels. The offering of firstfruits was to be "crushed new grain from fresh ears" (Lv 2:14). No leaven or honey was permitted (v:11) on the cakes although those same commodities could be accepted as a firstfruits offering (v 12). They would not go to the altar but were given to the priest. The offerer had to bring the prepared loaves or wafers to the temple. The priest would burn one handful on the altar as its "memorial portion" (Lv 2:2), keeping the remainder for his own food (6:16; 7:9). But when the priest was making a cereal offering on his own behalf, he burnt it all on the altar (6:22,23).

A cereal offering was usually given with every burnt offering, especially those pertaining to the sacred calendar (Nm 28,29). The amounts of flour and oil were set according to the animal being sacrificed: three-tenths of an ephah of flour and one-half a hin of oil for a bull, two-tenths ephah and one-third hin for a ram, and one-tenth ephah plus one hin for a lamb (Nm 15:2–10). Other happy occasions for a cereal offering included the cleansing of a leper (Lv 14:10,20,21,31; unspecified quantity for a bird) and the successful consummation of a Nazirite vow (Nm 6:5,13). Though not specifically mentioned, a cereal offering was probably made when a woman was being cleansed after childbirth (Lv 12:6–8), or when someone had been freed of abscesses (15:14,15) or discharges (vv 29,30). However, their omission in these cases may have been intentional; no cereal offering accompanied the burnt offerings of the high priest and the people in the Day of Atonement ritual (Lv 16:3,5,24).

Peace offerings were invariably followed by cereal offerings (Lv 7:12–14; Nm 15:4). The priest received one of each pair of cakes or wafers. The remainder was returned to the offerer to be eaten with the flesh of the sacrificial animal at a place of his choice.

A special case where such offering was used was the one-tenth of an ephah of barley meal required in the jealousy ritual. It was to have no oil or frankinsence (Nm 5:15,18,25,26). A very poor individual was permitted to bring one-tenth of an ephah of fine flour without oil or frankincense as a sin offering (Lv 5:11–13).

(3) Drink offering (Nm 15:1–10). The standard libation was one-fourth of a hin of wine for a lamb, one-third for a ram, and one-half for a bull. The wine (Ex 29:40), also called "strong drink" (Nm 28:7), is probably an intentional substitute for the blood used by other nations (Ps 16:4). The libation was classed as a "pleasing odor" offering (Nm 15:7). As with the burnt offering, the entire drink offering was expended; nothing was given to the priest (28:7).

Drink offerings accompanied the daily offering (Ex 29:40,41; Nm 28:7) and the sabbath offering (Nm 28:9) as well as the New Moon festival (v 14). Reference is also made to them in connection with the second and following days of the Feast of Tabernacles (29:18,21); for the first day their absence is probably unintentional (vv 12–16). The same might hold true for the Passover, Firstfruits, and Feast of Trumpets (Nm 28:16–29:11; cf. Ez 45:11). A libation was required for the rites concluding a Nazirite vow (Nm 6:17) but not for cleansing a leper (Lv 14:10–20).

Fellowship Offerings. These sacrifices expressed a desire on the part of the offerer, and generally are not imposed by regulations except for the Nazirite (Nm 6:17) and the Feast of Tabernacles (29:39–40). An offerer who had already fulfilled the ritual requirements for atonement and personal consecration was permitted to make a fellowship offering. Burnt offerings often accompanied the fellowship sacrifices as a further expression of devotion.

(1) Peace offering (Lv 3; 7:11–36; Am 5:22). This is the basic class of all fellowship or communal offerings; the others are simply subclasses of the peace offering. In terms of holiness, or restrictedness, they were not so rigidly confined as the other offerings. Animals from the herd or flock, male or female (Lv 3:1,6,12), were permitted. The usual stipulation of freedom from blemish was in force except in the case of the free-will offering, in which the animal could have one limb longer than the other (22:23). Unleavened cakes were also required, at least for the thank (Lv 7:12,13) and votive (Nm 6:15,17,19) offerings. Each of these three types will be discussed with their special features.

The first part of the ritual, the presentation and laying on of the hand, were identical to those of the other sacrifices. However, the animal was slaughtered at the door of the sanctuary courtyard and not on the north side of the altar (Lv 3:1,2,7,8,12,13; 7:29,30). The priest collected the blood and tossed it against the altar as he did with the burnt offering (3:2,8,13). The choice viscera were offered up as a "pleasing odor" (vv 3–5,6–11,14–16).

The priest also received a certain portion of the offering. He was allowed to eat it in any ritually clean place and to share it with his family (Lv 7:14, 30–36; Nm 6:20), in contrast to his portion of other sacrifices which he had to eat somewhere in the temple compound (Nm 18:10,11). He received one of the cakes and the breast as a wave offering and the right thigh as a contribution from the offerer. This latter is the so-called "heave offering"; the technical term developed from a root signifying "to be high" and meaning "that which is lifted up." The heave offering did not really represent a special kind of ritual ceremony.

The ritual act of peace offering culminated with a fellowship meal. Except for those parts burnt on the altar or given to the priest, the body of the animal was returned to the man who offered it. He had to prepare it as a communal meal for himself, for his family, and for the Levite in his community (Dt 12:12,18,19). This would have to be at the official sanctuary (12:6,7,11,12,15–19,26; cf. 1 Sm 1:3,4) and the participants had to observe very strict rules of purity (Lv 7:19–21; 19:5–8). It may be contrasted with the ritual slaughtering of animals for a banquet that was permitted at any local altar (Dt 12:16,20–22). The flesh of the thank offering had to be eaten on the same day of the sacrifice (Lv 7:15), while that of the votive or freewill offerings could be finished off on the following day (vv 16–18). Whatever remained then had to be burned before the time limit expired.

Only three times is there a specific demand for a peace offering: in the Feast of Weeks (Lv 23:19,20), upon completion of a Nazirite vow (Nm 6:17–20), and at the installation of the priesthood. Other public ritual occasions included the inauguration of the temple (1 Kgs 8:63; 2 Chr 7:5). Events on a national level that evoked the peace offering were the successful conclusion of a military campaign (1 Sm 11:15), the end of a famine or pestilence (2 Sm 24:25), confirmation of a candidate to the throne (1 Kgs 1:9,19), or a time of religious revival (2 Chr 29:31–36). On the local level they were offered at the annual family reunion (1 Sm 20:6) or other festive occasions such as the harvest of the firstfruits (Ex 22:29–31; 1 Sm 9:11–13,22–24; 16:4,5).

(2) Wave offering. The first portion of the peace offering was "waved" before the Lord to signify that the priest was eating it as a representative of God (the actual motion evidently resembled the wielding of a saw or a staff, Is 10:15). The same technical term, "wave offering," was also used for other kinds of offering: precious metals donated for making the cultic artifacts (Ex 35:22; 38:29) and the guilt offering of the cleansed leper (Lv 14:12).

(3) Freewill offering. These gifts, brought to the holy convocations which took place three times per year (Ex 23:16; 34:20; Dt 16:10,16,17; 2 Chr 35:8; Ezr 3:5), were voluntary (Lv 7:16; 22:18,21,23; 23:28; Nm 15:3; 29:39; Dt 12:6,17). Like the votive offering, the freewill offering could be a burnt rather than a peace offering (Lv 22:17–24; Ez 46:12). If it were the latter, the flesh could be eaten on the second day but must be burned before the third (Lv 7:16,17). Unlike some other peace offerings the animal being sacrificed could have one limb longer than the other (22:23).

(4) Installation offering. This Hebrew term refers to the settings of precious stones (Ex 25:7; 35:9,27; 1 Chr 29:2), so "installation" seems an appropriate translation. It had to do with "filling the hand," a ritual act that consecrated someone to divine service (Ex 28:41; cf. Ex 32:29) and required ritual purity and spiritual devotion (2 Chr 29:31).

The details of the original ceremony at the installation of the first priest is described in two passages (Ex 29:19–34; Lv 8:22–32). Moses himself functioned as the officiant, since Aaron and his sons could not conduct their own ordination. He presented the ram of consecration and the priests laid their hands on it. Then Moses slew it and treated the blood in a special way: he applied it to the tip of the right ear, thumb, and big toe of each candidate. The rest was splashed around the altar. The wave offering also received special treatment. The choice viscera, three of the cereal offerings, and the right thigh were all placed in the hands of the novitiates and waved before the Lord, after which they were burned together on the altar as a "pleasing odor." Though Moses was not given the thigh, he was allowed to take the breast, which he waved himself. Finally the anointing oil, mixed with blood from the altar, was sprinkled on the candidates and their garments. After this they were permitted to eat the remaining flesh of the ordination offering which they had boiled at the entrance to the tabernacle courtyard. Like the other sacrifices in this category, none was allowed to remain till the following day.

ANSON F. RAINEY

See FEASTS AND FESTIVALS OF ISRAEL; ATONEMENT; ISRAEL, RELIGION OF; TABERNACLE, TEMPLE; CLEANNESS AND UNCLEANNESS, REGULATIONS CONCERNING.

Bibliography. M.F.C. Bourdillon and M. Fortes, eds., *Sacrifice;* A.B. Davidson, *The Theology of the OT,* pp 306–356; R. de Vaux, *Ancient Israel,* pp 415–456, and *Studies in OT Sacrifice;* G.B. Gray, *Sacrifice in the OT;* F.D. Kidner, *Sacrifice in the OT;* J.H. Kurtz, *Sacrificial Worship of the OT;* G.F. Oehler, *Theology of the OT,* pp 261–323; F.M. Young, *Sacrifice and the Death of Christ.*

Officers in the Church. See BISHOP; DEACON, DEACONESS; ELDER; PASTOR; PRESBYTER; SPIRITUAL GIFTS.

Og. King whose fame partly came from his being a giant. He alone "was left of the remnant of the Rephaim [giants KJV]; behold, his bedstead was a bedstead of iron.... Nine cubits was its length, and four cubits its breadth" (Dt 3:11).

Og, king of Bashan, fell before Joshua's assault immediately after the defeat of King Sihon the Amorite (Nm 21:33–35). Bashan lay along the northern part of the Transjordan. Og's land stretched northeast from the lower course of the Jarmuk (Yarmouk) River, and lofty mountain ranges protected him on the east from scorching desert winds.

Og and his people had several settlements, primarily Ashtaroth and Edrei (Jos 13:12).

Og had fortified his land with 60 walled cities and was probably overconfident before Moses' army. Moses completely destroyed the populace of those cities; he spared only the livestock and the spoils of war (Dt 3:5,6).

Three tribes of Israel found the Transjordan particularly suitable for grazing their herds. So at the defeat of Sihon and Og, Moses assigned the newly won lands to the tribes of Gad, Reuben, and half of Manasseh (Nm 32:33; Jos 12:4–6).

Ohad. Simeon's son (Gn 46:10; Ex 6:15), whose name does not appear in the list of Numbers 26:12–14.

Ohel. Descendant of Jehoiakim and King David (1 Chr 3:20).

Oholah, Oholibah. Names given to the northern kingdom (KJV Aholah), with its capital at Samaria, and to the southern kingdom (KJV Aholibah), with its capital at Jerusalem, respectively, by Ezekiel in his allegory depicting the unfaithfulness of God's people (ch 23). The daughters of one woman, Israel, God had adopted as his own. The names characterized the basic attitude of each of the twin kingdoms toward God and his worship. Samaria (Oholah) had her own tent and had invented her own centers of worship; Jerusalem (Oholibah) prided herself in being the custodian of the temple (vv 1–4).

Rather than being true to the Lord, Samaria had committed spiritual adultery. Not being content with her spiritual infidelity in wooing the gods of Egypt, she had lusted after the idols of Assyria and the worldly attractions that the Neo-Assyrian culture held out before her. Both courses of action are adequately documented by archaeological discoveries from the ancient Near East, such as Jehu's act of homage as portrayed on the Black Obelisk of King Shalmaneser III of Assyria (859–824 BC). Samaria's conduct had been judged by God; her newfound desire had proved to be her destruction, God giving her over into the hands of the Assyrian conqueror (vv 5–10).

Far from learning from Israel's example, Judah had not only courted Assyria and its idolatry (e.g., 2 Kgs 16:10–18) but had added to her affections the Neo-Babylonian Empire (e.g., 2 Kgs 20:14–18) and then had turned once again to Egypt (e.g., Jer 37; 46), her earlier lover (Ez 23:11–21). Therefore, God would sorely punish her at the hands of the Babylonians, and she would know the just judgment of God (vv 22–35).

Ezekiel closes his allegory with a rehearsal of God's charges against the two kingdoms (vv 36–42). God's people were doubly guilty. Not being content with their apostasy, they had gone so far as to profane the sanctuary of God and his sabbath by entering the temple with hands bloodied in the sacrifice of their own children in pagan rites. He then reiterates God's certain judgment against spiritual infidelity. God's dealing with Oholah and Oholibah was a lesson for all people that a holy God will not countenance unfaithfulness in any form (vv 43–49).

Oholiab. Man assigned by Moses to assist Bezalel, the master craftsman, in the construction and ornamentation of the tabernacle. Son of Ahisamach and member of Dan's tribe, Oholiab was specifically noted as a designer and embroiderer. Along with Bezalel, he taught the skills necessary for the construction of the tabernacle (Ex 31:6; 35:34; 36:1,2; 38:23; KJV Aholiab).

Oholibamah. 1. Esau's wife, the daughter of Anah the Hivite (Gn 36:2,5,14,18,25; KJV Aholibamah), who bore to him Jeush, Jalam, and Korah before Esau left Canaan for Seir.

The absence of her name from the other lists of Esau's wives (see Gn 26:34; 28:9) has occasioned a great deal of discussion. The considerable variation in these lists may indicate either a confusion in the scribal transmission or may point to the use of alternate names, gained either at marriage or as a result of some memorable event in the women's lives. Whether or not she is identified with Judith, as some have suggested, doubtless the scriptural observation that she was "a source of grief to Isaac and Rebekah" is true (Gn 26:34, 35 NIV).

2. Edomite clan chieftain descended from Esau (Gn 36:41; 1 Chr 1:52; KJV Aholibamah).

Oil. Substance most commonly produced from the olive berry, although the word could also apply to oil of myrrh (Est 2:12). Oil was used primarily in cooking, but additionally as a cosmetic for anointing the body, for medicinal purposes, as a source of light, for the anointing of kings and priests, and in religious offerings.

The growth of olive trees was widespread, and the Israelites took advantage of this major crop to establish a thriving trade in oil with Tyre and Egypt. Like precious metals and animals, oil became an established medium of exchange. Solomon used it as part of the payment to Hiram for construction expenses connected with the temple (1 Kgs 5:11; Ez 27:17).

Because oil was essential for everyday life, it was an effective and acceptable medium of barter. Oil was used in the preparation of most food (1 Kgs 17:12–16). The common cake or patty of grain which formed the basis of the noon meal would be cooked on a griddle with a little oil.

As a cosmetic, oil was used for anointing the body after a bath (Ru 3:3; 2 Sm 12:20). It was frequently used on festive occasions, and at Egyptian banquets the heads of both the guests and the female entertainers were anointed. In the NT, the anointing of the sick is mentioned (Jas 5:14). Olive oil could also be taken internally as a medicine for the relief of gastric disorders. It had a soothing effect and was also used as a mild laxative. It was applied externally as an ointment for bruises, burns, cuts, and abrasions (Is 1:6; Mk 6:13; Lk 10:34).

As soon as the sun set, the only source of light was the oil lamp. Often the small porta-ble one could be placed easily on a shelf, but in large homes, palaces, synagogues or temples, the lamp could rest on a tall metal base like a standard lamp. The wick of flax (Is 42:3) or hemp was placed in the oil which gave out a flame until extinguished or the supply of fuel ran out. Torches were used in the streets both to light the way and for additional security. They added immeasurably to the festive atmosphere of evening processions. Torches were an essential part of the wedding procession, and normally those carrying the torches brought a spare quantity of oil in a container in case there was a delay and their supply was exhausted. This scene is vividly portrayed in Jesus' parable of the wise and foolish virgins (Mt 25:1–13).

In other ceremonial events, oil had a special meaning when used for the anointing of kings (1 Sm 10:1; 1 Kgs 1:39) and priests (Ex 29:7). It was symbolic of the office and of the recognition by God of his blessing on the office holder.

Quantities of oil were used in the temple. It was donated as part of the firstfruit offering (Ex 22:29) and was also subject to tithing (Dt 12:17). Oil was frequently used for the ceremonial aspect of temple life or as part of the offering. The meal offering was mixed with oil (Lv 8:26; Nm 7:19), and the oil in the lamp which burned in the sanctuary constantly needed replenishing (Lv 24:2). The daily sacrifice required the use of oil (Ex 29:40), although the sin offering (Lv 5:11) and the jealousy offering (Nm 5:15) specifically did not use oil.

A pestle and mortar or a stone press pressed oil from the olives (Ex 27:20). Where the latter was used, the pulp initially produced by the press was often trodden out or subjected to further extensive pressing. Stone presses were set up to process the quantities of berries available at the Mt of Olives. The word for oil press was *gatt-šemen*, hence the name Garden of Gethsemane.

Stone press for making olive oil.

Oil was symbolically associated with joy, festivity, ceremony, honor, light, and health (both spiritual and physical), while its absence spelled sorrow (Jl 1:10), and the withdrawal of all that is good in life. HAZEL W. PERKIN

See FOOD AND FOOD PREPARATION; MEDICINE AND MEDICAL PRACTICE; PLANTS (OLIVE, OLIVE TREE); ANOINT, ANOINTED; OINTMENT.

Oil, Anointing. See ANOINT, ANOINTED.

Oil Tree. Small tree bearing an olive-like fruit that yields a medicinal oil.

See PLANTS.

Ointment. Various preparations, generally of a spicy nature with an oil base. In Palestine olive oil was the chief base of ointments and was itself considered an ointment. The OT does not distinguish between "oil" and "ointment." In Egypt and Mesopotamia numerous vegetable oils and animal fats formed the basis of ointments. Among the vegetable oils some of the more important include castor oil, sesame oil, linseed oil, radish oil, colocynth oil, and oil from various nuts.

Ointments played an important and visible role in antiquity. In the hot and dry climate of the Near East, ointments gave a measure of protection. Widespread medicinal uses, soothing qualities, and effectiveness in masking odors made the use of ointments a virtual necessity among all classes. Lack of ointments occasioned a strike among Egyptian workers at the Theban necropolis in the days of Ramses III (c. 1183–1152 BC). The fact that Hezekiah included ointments within his treasury (2 Kgs 20:13) illustrates the value of these preparations.

The preparation of ointments was not restricted to any group except in the case of the holy anointing oil (Ex 30:33). However, the OT mentions apothecaries or perfumers (1 Sm 8:13; 2 Chr 16:14), artisans who were organized into guilds (Neh 3:8).

In general, ointments were made by boiling aromatic substances in oil (cf. Jb 41:31). Perfumed ointments were combinations of certain raw materials with specially prepared oil. In the OT, qualifying terms such as "fragrant" (Sg 1:3) or "precious" (Eccl 7:1) signify perfumed oils. Ointments could be stored in a variety of vessels, but flasks made of alabaster were preferred. An alabaster jar held the expensive ointment with which Mary anointed Jesus in Bethany (Mk 14:3).

Ointments had a variety of uses. Among the Semites in particular, ointments acquired important associations. Aaron, his sons, the tabernacle and its furnishings were all consecrated by holy anointing oil. This compound consisted of myrrh, cinnamon, calamus, and cassia mixed with olive oil (Ex 30:23–25). Kings and prophets were anointed, but not with the holy anointing oil mixture.

As a cosmetic, perfumed ointments controlled unpleasant odors. Applications were made to the body (2 Sm 12:20), clothing (Ps 45:8), or personal objects (Prv 7:17). Women utilized ointments for cleansing the skin and enhancing the attractiveness of their skin (Est 2:12). The fragrance of certain ointments attracted the attention of the opposite sex (Sg 4:10). Not surprisingly, the Song of Solomon has several references to fragrant ointments.

The use of ointments to refresh and soothe guests was a mark of hospitality in the ancient Near East. Cones of ointment placed on the heads of guests and allowed to drip down over the body were used by the Egyptians (cf. Ps 133:2). As a sign of respect and honor the head of a guest was anointed with oil. Jesus chided a Pharisee who neglected this traditional mark of hospitality (Lk 7:37–40). Mary anointed Jesus with a costly flask of nard, a fragrant ointment obtained from the roots of an aromatic herb from India (Mk 14:3).

Ointments were used in the burial process. The Egyptians utilized ointments extensively in mummification. In the NT a corpse would be washed (Acts 9:37) and anointed with ointments (Mk 16:1). The body was wrapped in linen garments with spices and ointments (Jn 19:40; Lk 23:56). Both the Jews and Romans utilized nard for burials. A mixture of myrrh and aloes was used in connection with the burial of Jesus.

Medicinal uses of ointment were frequent. Oil was applied to wounds (Lk 10:34). Balm, probably an aromatic gum, had well-known medicinal uses and is associated with Gilead (Jer 8:22). Balm was an item of export from Palestine (Gn 37:25; Ez 27:17). Biblical reference is made to a famous eye ointment produced and exported by the city of Laodicea (Rv 3:18). Ointments formed an important commodity of merchants in the Roman period (Rv 18:13).

Anointing with oil came to be associated with gladness and joy (Ps 45:7; Is 61:3). Thus one was to refrain from anointing during times of mourning (2 Sm 14:2). The lack of oil for anointing was viewed as a judgment (Mi 6:15). Shields were anointed with oil to make them supple and possibly to help deflect projectiles (2 Sm 1:21). WILLIAM B. TOLAR

See OIL; MEDICINE AND MEDICAL PRACTICE; PLANTS (OLIVE, OLIVE TREE).

Old Gate. Jerusalem gate repaired by Joiada and Meshullam under Nehemiah's supervision (Neh 3:6), and subsequently mentioned in the northerly route traveled by one of the companies of celebrants during the Jerusalem wall's dedication (12:39). The Old Gate was located in the city's northern wall between the Fish Gate (3:3) and the Broad Wall (v 8).

See JERUSALEM.

Old Man. See MAN, OLD AND NEW.

Old Testament. See BIBLE.

Old Testament Canon. See BIBLE, CANON OF THE.

Old Testament Chronology. See CHRONOLOGY, OLD TESTAMENT.

Old Testament Quotations in the New Testament. See QUOTATIONS OF THE OLD TESTAMENT IN THE NEW TESTAMENT.

Old Testament Theology. See FEASTS AND FESTIVALS OF ISRAEL; GOD, BEING AND ATTRIBUTES OF; GOD, NAMES OF; ISRAEL, RELIGION OF; JUDAISM; LAW, BIBLICAL CONCEPT OF; MEDIATION, MEDIATOR; MESSIAH; OFFERINGS AND SACRIFICES; PRIESTHOOD; PRIESTS AND LEVITES; PROPHECY; TABERNACLE, TEMPLE. See also each individual OT book for a brief statement on its own particular theological teaching.

Olive, Olive Tree. See AGRICULTURE; FOOD AND FOOD PREPARATION; PLANTS.

Olives, Mount of, Olivet. Prominent north-south ridge in the Judean mountains lying due east of Jerusalem and the Kidron Valley. Three summits with two intervening valleys distinguish the mountain. The northern summit is Mt Scopus. To its south is a small saddle through which the ancient Roman road to Jericho passed. The central hill is the traditional Mt of Olives (2684 ft) standing across from the temple platform (the *Haram esh-*

The Mt of Olives.

Sherif). Here Constantine built the great Church of the Ascension dedicated to his mother Helena. Another saddle to the south contains the modern road to Bethany. The southern hill, overlooking Jebusite Jerusalem and the city of David, is called the Mt of Offense since here Solomon built temples for his foreign wives. Beneath it is the Arab village of Silwan and the confluence of the Kidron and Hinnom valleys.

The Mt of Olives gained its name from its extensive olive groves which were renowned in antiquity (Zec 14:4; Mk 11:1). Its western face collects rainfall from the Mediterranean which together with decomposed limestone makes for fertile orchards. The eastern side on the other hand marks the boundary of the arid Judean wilderness. Bethany and Bethphage are two NT villages hugging these eastern slopes.

In the OT the Mt of Olives is first mentioned when David flees from Absalom's conspiracy. He departs from Jerusalem, climbs the Mt of Olives in the east, and continues on toward the rift valley (2 Sm 15:30). Solomon chose this mountain for the construction of "high places" for the foreign deities of Sidon, Moab (1 Kgs 11:7) and Ammon—each of which were later destroyed by Josiah (2 Kgs 23:13). Ezekiel (11:23) records the vision of the glory of God departing from the temple and resting on the Mt of Olives. The most famous description appears in Zechariah's apocalyptic vision (14:1–5): "On that day [the Lord] shall stand on the Mount of Olives which lies before Jerusalem on the east; and the Mount of Olives shall be split in two from east to west by a very wide valley."

Later Jewish interest in the mountain is recorded in the Mishna. The burning of the red heifer was an elaborate ceremony on the Mt of Olives (Nm 19:1–10). In addition, since the mountain was clearly visible from the east, it was used as a signal station to indicate the new moon.

In the NT Jesus appears at the Mt of Olives during passion week. The only exceptions are the Bethany stories when Jesus visits Mary and Martha (Lk 10:38–42) and Lazarus (Jn 11:17–44). On his triumphant entry to Jerusalem, Jesus came from Jericho, crossed the mountain from the east, and then descended into the Kidron Valley (Mk 11:1–10). On his descent he paused and wept over the city (Lk 19:41–44).

During his final week Jesus taught on the Mt of Olives (Mk 13) and spent his evenings there (Lk 21:37; although this may refer to Bethany). Following the last supper, Jesus came to this mountain for prayer (Mk 14:26). In a garden near an olive oil press ("Gethsemane"), he was arrested (Mk 14:32). The final event of Christ on earth, his ascension, was viewed from the mount by his followers (Acts 1:12).

The Mt of Olives quickly became a center of Christian devotion. In the Byzantine era the mountain had 24 churches with vast numbers of monks and nuns. Constantine's church dominated the summit, celebrating Christ's ascension. In the 4th century it had even become the customary burial site for Jerusalem's bishops.

Jews and Muslims likewise revere the site because it will be the place of judgment. According to the Talmud, the righteous will be resurrected between Jerusalem and the Mt of Olives. This explains the vast Muslim and Jewish cemeteries especially on the west slope of the Mt of Olives. Christian, Jew, and Muslim alike view the Mt of Olives as one focal point on the final Day of the Lord.

GARY M. BURGE

Olympas. Member of the church in Rome to whom Paul sends personal greetings (Rom 16:15).

Omar. Second son of Eliphaz, grandson of Esau and the great-grandson of Abraham (Gn 36:11,15; 1 Chr 1:36); an Edomite clan chief.

Omega. English spelling of the name of the last letter of the Greek alphabet.

See ALPHA AND OMEGA.

Omen. Natural sign or occurrence prefiguring the outcome of a future event. Augury was listed among the abominable pagan practices forbidden to Israel (Dt 18:10). Balaam, upon seeing that the Lord was pleased with his blessings on Israel, did not seek omens as he normally did (Nm 24:1). The men of Syria looked for an omen to see if King Ahab of Israel (874–853 BC) would be favorably disposed to release the Syrian king Ben-hadad from captivity (1 Kgs 20:33). Isaiah reveals the Lord as one "who frustrates the omens of liars, and makes fools of diviners" (44:25).

See MAGIC; SORCERY.

Omer. Measuring unit used in gathering manna (Ex 16:16,18,22,36).

See WEIGHTS AND MEASURES.

Omnipotence. God's unlimited authority to bring into existence or cause to happen whatsoever he wills.

See GOD, BEING AND ATTRIBUTES OF.

Omnipresence. Aspect of God's infinity in which he transcends the limitations of space and is present in all places at all times.

See GOD, BEING AND ATTRIBUTES OF.

Omniscience. God's infinite knowledge and understanding of things past, present, and future.

See GOD, BEING AND ATTRIBUTES OF.

Omri. 1. King of Israel who first appears in Scripture as general of the army during the reign of Elah, king of Israel. In 885 BC Elah sent Omri to besiege the Philistine fortress of Gibbethon. During the siege Zimri, another military leader, launched a coup against Elah, killed him, and immediately wiped out all Elah's male relatives. When Omri heard of the assassination, he had the army declare him king and marched to the capital at Tirzah to deal with Zimri. When Zimri saw that the siege of Tirzah was going to be successful, he set fire to the king's palace and died in the flames after only seven days on the throne.

But Omri's rule over Israel was not yet established. Tibni seized control of part of the state and held it for about 4 years. Finally Omri was able to crush Tibni and extend his power over all Israel. He established Israel's 4th ruling dynasty, which was destined to continue through 3 more generations after his own. His reign lasted a total of 12 years (885–874), including the years of sovereignty disputed with Tibni.

International Developments. To the northeast of Israel, the Aramaeans of Syria were building a strong state with its capital at Damascus. A few years before Omri took the throne, Asa of Judah had sought the help of Syria against Baasha of Israel. Soon Syria would become a threat to both Hebrew kingdoms.

Farther east, Assyria was growing in strength under the leadership of Ashurnasirpal II (883–859 BC), the founder of the empire. He marched into Phoenicia, but Israel was spared Assyrian attack until the days of Omri's son Ahab.

Omri's Reign. Since the purpose of Scripture is not to provide a political, military, or even social history of Israel or the countries surrounding it, administrations of the kings of Israel and Judah are often very briefly treated. For a fuller picture it is necessary to turn to nonbiblical sources. From Assyrian records it is evident that Omri must have been an impressive ruler. Generations later Assyrians still spoke of Israel as the "land of Omri."

Perceptive leader that he was, Omri recognized that the nation needed a capital that was centrally located and militarily defensible. He settled on the site of Samaria, the third and most significant capital of the realm (Shechem and Tirzah had previously served as capitals). Located 7 miles northwest of Shechem on the main road leading to Galilee and Phoenicia, it perched on a free-standing hill which rose some 300 to 400 feet above the surrounding plain. Thus it could be quite easily defended; it had a prosperous hinterland to supply it with food and taxes; and it was conveniently located on a main road. Omri bought the hill from Shemer and named the city after its owner. Then he leveled the top of the hill and began the palace compound, which originally measured 160 feet square. He built a 33-foot thick wall around the summit of the hill.

Omri's expansionist activities are not mentioned in 1 Kings, but Scripture is supplemented by discovery of the Moabite Stone in 1868 at Dibon, east of the Jordan River. On this stela, Mesha, king of Moab tells that Omri conquered Moab. Israel had continued to subjugate the land in the days of Ahab, but during his days Mesha successfully rebelled against Israel (2 Kgs 3:4). That Omri could mount a successful war against Moab soon after becoming king shows that he was a capable ruler, because previously the kingdom of Israel had been greatly weakened by insurrection and political instability.

Omri also reestablished the friendly relations with Phoenicia that had been initiated in the days of David and Solomon. Presumably he made a full alliance with King Ethbaal of Tyre and then sealed it with the marriage of his son Ahab to the Phoenician princess Jezebel. Such an alliance would have been mutually beneficial, for it would have brought cedar, beautifully crafted goods, and Phoenician architectural or technical expertise to Israel; and it would have provided Israelite grain and olive oil to Phoenicia. Moreover, it would have linked their forces against the threat of the rising power of Assyria.

This pact was destined to corrupt Israel, however, for it brought Baal worship into the land. Probably this is what the writer of Kings had in mind when he said that Omri "did worse" than the other kings of Israel before him (1 Kgs 16:25) while walking in the idolatrous ways of Jeroboam. Baal worship was regarded as more degrading than the calf worship Jeroboam had introduced. Omri, and his son Ahab after him, subscribed to both.

The relations between Israel and Syria during Omri's reign are not entirely clear. First Kings 20:34 refers to a pact between Ahab and Ben-hadad of Syria. During the discussion about the pact, Ben-hadad talks about cities which his father took from Ahab's father. That would seem to imply a war between the two states in Omri's day which ended in a significant defeat for Israel. But commentators argue that Omri was too strong and successful to have suffered such a defeat. They suggest that "father" here should be understood in the common Semitic sense of "predecessor." The Hebrew "father" in this instance could then refer to Jeroboam as the one who lost to Syria. Further, this interpretation suggests that "Samaria" in 1 Kings 20:34 refers to the kingdom of Israel as the place where trade concessions were granted. "Samaria" was often used synonymously with "northern kingdom." Samaria was not yet built in the days of Jeroboam, and was only under construction in Omri's day.

Omri was one of the most powerful kings of Israel, building its new capital, winning the state a reputation for prowess, and setting a course for future kings to follow. But unfortunately that course was morally corrupt; the introduction of Baal worship was one of the terrible results of Omri's alliance with Tyre.

HOWARD F. VOS

See ISRAEL, HISTORY OF; CHRONOLOGY, OLD TESTAMENT.

2. One of Becher's sons from Benjamin's tribe (1 Chr 7:8).

3. Descendant of Perez, son of Judah (1 Chr 9:4).

4. Son of Michael, prince of the tribe of Issachar during David's reign (1 Chr 27:18).

On (Person). Reubenite, Peleth's son who joined Korah's rebellion against Moses and Aaron in the wilderness (Nm 16:1).

On (Place). Hebrew name for Heliopolis, an Egyptian city (Gn 41:45,50; 46:20).

See HELIOPOLIS.

Onam. 1. Grandson of Seir and Shobal's fifth son (Gn 36:23; 1 Chr 1:40).

2. Son of Jerahmeel and Atarah, the father of a clan in Judah (1 Chr 2:26–28).

Onan. Second son of Judah and a Canaanitess named Shua (Gn 38:4–10; 46:12; Nm 26:19; 1 Chr 2:3). Judah forced him to enter into a levirate marriage with Tamar, the wife of his deceased brother, Er. Er and Tamar had no children. Onan refused to have children by Tamar, knowing that they would be heirs to his brother's estate. As a result of Onan's refusal to raise up descendants for his brother, the Lord punished him with death (Gn 38:8–10).

Onesimus. Slave on behalf of whom Paul wrote the Letter to Philemon. A slave of Philemon, he had run away from his master and robbed him. He is also mentioned with Tychicus as a bearer of the Letter to the Colossians (Col 4:9), indicating that he came from that region. Paul becomes acquainted with him, converts him, and they develop a close friendship (Phlm 10). Paul wishes that he might keep Onesimus with him during his imprisonment because he had been faithful to him (in Greek, Onesimus means "useful"). However, Paul returns the slave to his master, confident that the runaway slave will be received by his former owner as a Christian brother and that Philemon will charge any wrong that Onesimus has done to Paul's account.

Onesimus is sometimes identified with a bishop mentioned by Ignatius in his letter to the Ephesians, although this is not probable. Others try to identify him with Onesiphorus mentioned in 2 Timothy 1:16–18.

See PHILEMON, LETTER TO.

Onesiphorus. Christian who took care of Paul during his confinement in Ephesus. After Paul's transfer to Rome, Onesiphorus eagerly sought him out and ministered to him there (2 Tm 1:16). In the salutation of his second letter to Timothy, Paul sent greetings to Onesiphorus and his household (4:19).

Onion. See FOOD AND FOOD PREPARATION; PLANTS.

Only Begotten. Phrase deeply entrenched in Christian language as descriptive of Jesus. The word traditionally translated "only-begotten" does not carry the idea of birth at all. Literally it means "only one of its kind," "unique." This can be readily seen in the way it is used in the NT and in the Septuagint (the Greek translation of the OT).

The word appears nine times in the NT, but only five of these occurrences, all from the Johannine writings, make reference to Jesus. Three of the other occurrences are of an *only* son or daughter (Lk 7:12; 8:42; 9:38; cf. Jdg 11:34 in the Septuagint). Because of its frequent use for an only child, the word often conveys the idea of something especially favored or precious. The remaining non-Johannine reference, Hebrews 11:17, is to Isaac as Abraham's "favored" or "unique" son. Isaac was not Abraham's "only-begotten" since he had other children, but Isaac was his favored and unique son fulfilling God's promise. In the Septuagint for Psalm 22:20 and 35:17 the psalmist in his plea for deliverance even uses this word of his own soul as that which is of great value. The Hebrew word that stands behind each of these OT texts also means "only" and does not carry any idea of birth.

Where the word is used of Jesus, its meaning is likewise not "only-begotten" but "only" or "unique." The word is used with "son" and should be understood as God's *only* Son, indicating both God's favor toward him and his uniqueness (Jn 3:16,18; 1 Jn 4:9). The statement at the baptism and transfiguration of Jesus in the Synoptics ("This is my beloved son . . .") expresses virtually the same idea. In fact, the word "beloved" is used in the Septuagint as an equivalent to the word "only" to translate the same Hebrew word. In John 1:14 the word "only" is used by itself to stress that the incarnate Word comes as a unique one from the Father. The final reference (Jn 1:18) is especially interesting because of the fact that some texts read "the only son" while others read "the only God." Because scribes could easily have written "only son" due to their familiarity with the other texts in John and because of the superiority of the texts that read "only God," this latter reading is preferred. The attitude expressed toward the incarnate Word is the highest possible. No one has ever seen God, but the unique (or only) God who is in the bosom of the father has revealed him.

The phrase "only-begotten" is not an accurate translation and should not be used in any of the nine passages. This phrase is derived from the Latin Vulgate (a translation of the Bible from about the 5th century which has been quite influential on other translations) and reflects certain theological debates about the person of Christ. While the language of the Word being born of God is present in the 2nd century, the most notable occurrence of this language is the creed from the Council of Nicaea in AD 325. This creed speaks of the Son of God as begotten of the Father, unique—that is, from the substance of the Father—God from God, light from light, true God from true God, begotten not made, of one substance with the Father. This creed was the result of the rejection of the heresy that the Son of God was the first created being. Ultimately the phrase "begotten not made" leads to what theologians call the doctrine of the eternal generation of the Son. It is an attempt to say that the Son is derived from the Father but that he is eternal with the Father. However, this discussion is an attempt to explain the mystery of the Trinity and goes far beyond the biblical text. Whether there is any biblical passage that speaks of the Son being born from the Father is doubtful at best. The use of Psalm 2:7 in Acts 13:33; Hebrews 1:5; and 5:5 ("You are my son, today I have begotten you") refers to the resurrection and exaltation of Christ. The use of "firstborn" (Rom 8:29; Col 1:15,18; Heb 1:6) stresses sovereignty rather than birth. The only text that possibly points to the idea of the

Son's being born from the Father is 1 John 5:18, but the meaning of the words "the one having been born from God" is debated both because of a textual variant and because of the grammar. The words may refer to Christians instead of the Son.

"Only-begotten" is an incorrect translation. The idea being stressed is the uniqueness of Jesus' relation to the Father.

KLYNE R. SNODGRASS

See CHRISTOLOGY; GOD, BEING AND ATTRIBUTES OF.

Ono. Benjamite town built by Shemed (1 Chr 8:12). Some of its inhabitants returned to Palestine with Zerubbabel following the exile (Ezr 2:33; Neh 7:37). Its location was variously known as the plain of Ono (Neh 6:2) or as the valley of craftsmen (11:35). Ono is identified with Kefr 'Ana, seven miles southeast of Joppa.

Onycha. One of the sweet spices used in the sacred incense of the tabernacle (Ex 30:34). Its identification is uncertain. Some suggest that onycha was derived from the shell of a certain mussel found in India which exuded a musk-like fragrance when burned.

See PLANTS.

Onyx. Semiprecious stone used on the breastplate of the high priest (Ex 28:9).

See MINERALS, METALS, AND PRECIOUS STONES.

Ophel. 1. Hill or mound in Samaria where Elisha's house stood (2 Kgs 5:24).

2. Fortification in the southeast portion of ancient Jerusalem high above the slopes of the Brook Kidron strengthened by Jotham (2 Chr 27:3) and Manasseh (2 Chr 33:14). Isaiah describes the destruction of such a fortress when prophesying the judgment of God upon Jerusalem (Is 32:14). After the exile the temple servants lived there and repaired its walls (Neh 3:26,27; 11:21). Josephus states that it was near

The Hill of Ophel (also called the City of David), on the west side of the Kidron Valley.

the temple. Archaeological excavations at the traditional site in Jerusalem reveal fortifications dating from pre-Israelite times to the Maccabean period.

Ophir (Person). Joktan's son and a descendant of Shem through Arpachshad's line (Gn 10:29; 1 Chr 1:23).

Ophir (Place). Place to which Solomon sent a fleet of merchant ships to bring back gold and all sorts of precious and exotic products. The location of Ophir is not certain; most place it in southwest Arabia. There may be a relationship between the place and the man named Ophir, who appears in the table of nations as a son of Joktan (Gn 10:29; cf. 1 Chr 1:23), a descendant of Shem. The names of Joktan and his sons are connected with the southern and western parts of Arabia.

First Kings 9:26–28 reports that Solomon built a fleet of merchant ships at Ezion-geber, which was near Eloth on the Gulf of Aqaba. Hiram, king of Tyre, provided seamen to accompany those of Solomon. This expedition returned with 420 talents of gold for Solomon. First Kings 10:11 adds that the fleet of Hiram "brought from Ophir a very great amount of almug wood and precious stones."

Later, Jehoshaphat built "ships of Tarshish" to go to Ophir for gold, but the ships were wrecked at Ezion-geber. Then Ahaziah, the son of Ahab of Israel, offered to send his men with the seamen of Judah, but Jehoshaphat refused (see 1 Kgs 22:48,49).

The premier product of Ophir was fine gold. Eliphaz the Temanite comments that the Almighty should be one's gold rather than the gold of Ophir (Jb 22:24). Job himself declares that wisdom cannot be valued in "the fine gold of Ophir" (Jb 28:16). In his description of the glories of the king, the psalmist states, "at your right hand stands the queen in gold of Ophir" (Ps 45:9). Isaiah prophesies that in the day of the Lord the Lord will "make men more rare than fine gold, and mankind than the gold of Ophir" (13:12).

Some suggest that the ships of Tarshish mentioned (1 Kgs 10:22) were those ships that went to Ophir and returned every three years with "gold, silver, ivory, apes, and peacocks [or baboons]." Traders brought the products, some from as far away as India, to the ports of Ophir where Solomon's representatives bought them.

Ophni. Village allotted to Benjamin after Israel had taken possession of Palestine (Jos 18:24). Its precise location is unknown, but some early writers suggest the town of Gophna (modern Jifna) on the highway from Samaria to Jerusalem, a day's march north of Gibeah. This identification assumes that the boundary of Benjamin turned north near Bethel on the northern boundary. The modern Jifna is located three miles northwest of Bethel.

Ophrah (Person). Meonothai's son from Judah's tribe (1 Chr 4:14).

Ophrah (Place). 1. City in Benjamin toward which Philistine raiders turned shortly before their battle against Saul at Michmash (Jos 18:23; 1 Sm 13:17). It is probably identical to Ephraim (2 Sm 13:23; 2 Chr 13:19 Ephron; Jn 11:54). Ophrah is usually identified with the modern et-Taiyibeh, five miles north of Michmash and four miles northwest of Bethel.

2. City in Manasseh owned by Gideon's father, Joash the Abiezrite, and Gideon's home (Jgs 6:9). There the angel appeared to Gideon, commissioning him as God's agent of relief from the Midianites (6:12–24). Gideon demanded that the angel identify himself before he would seriously regard the summons. The angel did so with a fire and instantaneous disappearance. Gideon subsequently destroyed the area's pagan gods, angering the neighbors and precipitating a confrontation (6:28–35). Gideon's original militia was reduced to 300 men by divine command, and this courageous band routed the Midianites. Following the spectacular victory, Gideon was nominated for kingship, but he refused. Strangely, he constructed an idol from the spoils of battle (8:22–28) before which Israel "played the harlot." The idol at Ophrah became a snare to Gideon and his family. Gideon died at Ophrah, an old man (8:29–32). His son, Abimelech, ambitious for power, slaughtered his sibling rivals at Ophrah; only one of the 70, Jotham, escaped (9:1–6).

Oracle. Divine revelation communicated through God's spokesperson (prophet, priest, or king), usually pronouncing blessing, instruction or judgment. Contrary to Balak's request for Balaam to curse Israel, Balaam spoke an oracle of blessing instead (Nm 24:3–16). God instructed Moses through "living oracles" (Acts 7:38), and entrusted them with the Jewish people (Rom 3:2). The Book of Proverbs records two oracles of wisdom: one given by Agur, Jakeh's son (30:1; RSV mg), and the other by King Lemuel (31:1; RSV mg). Oracles of judgment were uttered against kings Joram of Israel (2 Kgs 9:25) and Joash of Judah (2 Chr 24:27). The prophets often delivered them against wicked nations: Isaiah (Babylon 13:1; 21:1; Damascus 17:1; Egypt 19:1; Jerusalem 22:1; Moab 15:1; Philistia 14:28; Tyre 23:1); Nahum (Nineveh 1:1); Habakkuk (Judah 1:1); and Malachi (Israel 1:1). Sometimes "oracles false and misleading" were given by false prophets (Lam 2:14).

See PROPHECY.

Ordination. The act of officially investing someone with religious authority. However, older translations of Scripture speak of God's "ordaining" burnt offerings, a place for Israel, moon and stars, strength from babes, human government, good works for believers to fulfill, and much else. Christ "ordained" support

Ruins of the temple of Apollo at Delphi, the location of the famous Greek oracle.

for preachers; a king "ordained" a feast, the Jews a festival; Paul "ordained" a practice (1 Cor 7:17). Among numerous other "ordinances" are civil laws, institutions of worship, the Passover, priests' portions, legal documents, specifications for the temple, and pious customs. In several instances, the RSV retains the word, elsewhere freely substituting "appointed," "instituted," "made," "established," "commanded," and the like. In current usage, the words "ordination" and "ordain" are applied to persons, signifying selection and appointment to God's service. Christ himself is said to be ordained judge (Acts 10:42), and Paul, a preacher and apostle (1 Tm 2:7).

In Israel and Judaism. Throughout the OT, emphasis falls upon God's choosing and appointing whom he will. Priestly functions passed very early from the head of each household to the divinely chosen tribe of Levi (Dt 33:8–11; Jgs 17:13). Through all subsequent clan rivalries—"Zadokite," "Aaronic," "Hasmonean"—this claim to inherited privilege persisted. Divine appointment through Levi was traced back to Moses (Ex 4:14; 28:41; 29:9), claimed for the Ephraimite Samuel (1 Chr 6:28), and still celebrated by Sirach (45:6–22, c. 180 BC). As the Book of Hebrews states (5:1,4), no one takes the honor upon himself; he is "called by God, as Aaron was," by birth into an inherited status.

The first Levites were presented at the tabernacle in the presence of the people, and acknowledged by "the laying on of hands" (Nm 8:10,14–18). Similarly, Moses received instructions for the week-long consecration of Aaron and his sons, with elaborate sacrifices (including a "ram of ordination"), vestments, anointing, and ritual (Ex 29; Lv 8). In both cases, the careful preservation of these detailed instructions suggests that the ceremonies were retained, to some degree, in later years, though no repetition is recorded.

Alongside the priests there existed establishments of recognized prophets, or prophetic communities, sometimes with royal patronage (1 Sm 10:5; 1 Kgs 1:9,10; 18:17–19; 20:35; 22:5–28; 2 Kgs 2:3,5,7; 23:2). The line of prophecy was also traced back to earliest days (see Gn 20:7; Dt 34:10; Jgs 4:4; Jer 7:25). The phrase "sons of the prophets," and an obscure hint in Jeremiah 35:4, may imply that prophecy, like priesthood, was sometimes hereditary, but the manner of appointment and installation is unknown. The outstanding prophets were frequently opposed to the prophetic "schools" (Am 7:14; Elijah, 1 Kgs 17; Micaiah, 1 Kgs 22:5–28; Jeremiah, Jer 27:14–16; ch 28). Such men were appointed by direct divine call, with no recorded installation (1 Kgs 17:1; 21:17; Is 6; Jer 1; Am 7:15), though by God's instruction

Elisha was called and anointed by Elijah (1 Kgs 19:16; cf. Is 61:1). Authentication of the prophet's message lay not in appropriate installation ceremonies, but in its self-evident truth; in the case of predictions, in their fulfillment (1 Kgs 22:13,14,26–28; Jer 28:5–9).

By NT times the priest's functions were mainly liturgical and political. The teaching and spiritual leadership of the people fell to scribes and Pharisees, the former trained experts in sacred Law, the latter a lay society devoted to observance of the Law. The only scriptural references to their official appointment and social standing are in criticisms made of Jesus and later of the apostles for teaching or preaching without such status and training (Mt 13:53–55; Acts 4:13).

In the Church. Christian ordination is also a matter of divine choice. Neither Jesus, nor any disciple, came from the professional religious classes. In ordaining the 12, Jesus "called to him those whom he desired," later insisting, "You did not choose me, but I chose you and appointed you" (Mk 3:13,14; Jn 15:16). The selection of Matthias rested upon prayer and "the divine lot" (Acts 1:24–26). Paul contended that he had been "set apart" before he was born, and did not receive his apostleship from or through men (Gal 1:1,15). Paul and Barnabas were commissioned by direction of the Spirit during worship, probably through a Christian prophet. They were "sent out by the Holy Spirit" (Acts 13:1–4). Similarly, Timothy was first chosen as assistant to Paul by "prophetic utterances which pointed to" him (1 Tm 1:18; 4:14).

At Corinth, various ministries of speaking, teaching, healing and administration were directly conferred as "gifts of the Spirit," who "apportions as he wills" (1 Cor 12:8–11,28; cf. Eph 4:11). Elders of the church at Ephesus were made guardians of the flock by the Holy Spirit (Acts 20:28). The divine prerogative is everywhere clear: any attempt to obtain the privilege of ministry by personal initiative and unworthy means meets with sharpest condemnation (Acts 8:18–24).

On the other hand, the assembled church "put forward" Barsabbas and Matthias before submitting the final choice to God (Acts 1:15, 23). The "body of the disciples" chose the seven servers, then presented them to the apostles (Acts 6:2–6). An assembled church, at the Spirit's command, commissioned and "sent . . . off" Paul and Barnabas (Acts 13:3). Paul and Barnabas themselves appointed elders (Acts 14:23), as Titus is instructed to do (Ti 1:5), and probably Timothy also (1 Tm 5:22; this may refer to restoring backsliders, but the context suggests a warning against hasty appointments, to avoid subsequent scandal).

Elders at Lystra and Iconium, obeying a Christian prophet, laid hands upon Timothy, with Paul (1 Tm 4:14; 2 Tm 1:6); Luke's account rests the choice of Timothy upon his being "well spoken of by the brethren" (Acts 16:1–3). By the time letters were written to Timothy and Titus, elaborate lists of qualifications required of church leaders, and some training for their work, have replaced "the gifts of the Spirit" as the basis of appointment (1 Tm 3:1–13; 2 Tm 2:2). This indication of divine choice through human agency complements ordination with the equally scriptural conception of the priesthood of all believers, the whole church called and equipped for ministry (Eph 4:12; 1 Pt 2:5,9; Rv 1:5,6).

The forms of this human participation in ordination include, beside prayer, fasting, and casting lots (Acts 1:26; 6:6; 13:2,3; 14:23), sometimes "selection-by-hands" (*cheirotonein*, originally "election by raising hands," later "selection by pointing to"; cf. 2 Cor 8:19; Acts 14:23), and sometimes selection by group choice (Acts 1:15,23; 6:2–5; 13:3; 16:2; 1 Tm 4:14). The characteristic expression of the church's approval and support was, however, the laying on of hands. This ancient gesture had many meanings—conferring blessing (Gn 48:14,15), commissioning and investing with authority (Nm 27:18–23), self-identification with a sacrifice (Ex 29:10), transfer of guilt (Lv 16:21), healing (Lk 4:40; Acts 9:17; 28:8), and sympathy (Mk 1:41).

By no means confined to ordination, the gesture was so familiar that Jesus was asked for it (Mt 9:18; 19:13). New members were welcomed into the Sanhedrin with this simple act of identification with others, and sometimes into the church likewise, especially where any question of their valid reception might arise (Acts 8:12–17; 19:6). On these two occasions only, the laying on of hands is associated with the reception of the Spirit, never in connection with appointment to ministry (Acts 6:6; 13:3; 1 Tm 4:14; 5:22; 2 Tm 1:6). Certainly, Paul, Barnabas, and the servers had already received the Spirit (Acts 6:3; 9:17; 11:24; Rom 8:9; 1 Cor 12:3,13). It would be hard to suppose that the unspecified "gift" which Timothy received, and is not to neglect but to "stir up," is the Holy Spirit. This he was given at Pentecost, and apparently at Corinth, without laying on of hands. Nor is Christ's bestowal of the Spirit on the Eleven (Jn 20:22,23) anywhere cited in relation to ordination.

Another later conception, that of a continuing "hereditary" ministry defined as "apostolic succession," finds scriptural support only in OT priesthood, and possibly in the ordination of elders by Paul and Barnabas following their own commissioning. Further, any idea that ordination itself invests with authority needs to be very carefully defined (despite Nm 27:18–23), in view of Christ's warning against the personal exercise of authority in the kingdom of God (Mt 23:8–12; Mk 10:42–44). The only fitting response to ordination in the ordinand is humility (note 2 Cor 1:24; Eph 3:7,8; 1 Pt 5:2,3).

Nevertheless, those whom Christ commissions are promised his presence and power to the end of the age (Mt 28:18–20). The dedication of one's life and gifts to a sincerely felt call to ministry cannot go unrewarded (Heb 6:10). The prayers and encouragement of fellow Christians, however expressed, will become increasingly precious (Eph 6:18–20). Ordination cannot make a minister; but within NT terms, to have been so privileged brings welcome reassurance in times of despondency.

R.E.O. White

See FOREORDINATION.

Oreb. One of two Midianite chieftains (the other being Zeeb) put to death by men from Ephraim's tribe (Jgs 7:25). The occasion for this execution was Gideon's surprise attack on the Midianite encampment at the hill of Moreh in the Valley of Jezreel. The Midianites' line of retreat eastward required them to re-cross the Jordan River. Gideon sent word to the Ephraimites to seize the fording places on the river to prevent the Midianites from escaping. The Ephraimites, following the orders, intercepted a contingent of fleeing Midianites including the prominent leaders Oreb and Zeeb. They beheaded these two leaders and sent their heads as a war prize to Gideon, who was then pursuing the Midianites on the east side of the Jordan (Jgs 8:3).

The locations where these men were executed were afterward known by their names—"the rock of Oreb" and "the wine press of Zeeb." Some scholars suggest that the place names were conferred upon the unknown Midianite chieftains. This is less likely. At present these locations cannot be identified with certainty but the general area near the junction of Wadi Fariah and the Jordan River best fits the biblical description.

During Israel's later history, the deaths of Oreb and Zeeb were recognized as a great triumph of God over the enemies of his people. The psalmist implores God to overthrow the nobles among Israel's current enemies just as he did the Midianite chieftains (Ps 83:11). The Lord, speaking through his prophet Isaiah, pledged that the Assyrians would be overthrown "like the slaughter of Midian at the rock of Oreb" (9:4; 10:26), implying that the earlier victory amounted to more than the capture of two leaders. It was an important and strategic defeat of the Midianite invasion force.

Oreb, Rock of. Place where the Ephraimites killed the Midianite chieftain Oreb (Jgs 7:25; Is 10:26).

See OREB.

Oren. Descendant of Judah and the third son of Jerahmeel (1 Chr 2:25).

Organ. KJV mistranslation for pipe in Genesis 4:21; Job 21:12; 30:31; and Psalm 150:4.

See MUSIC AND MUSICAL INSTRUMENTS (UGAB).

Orion. Septuagint name for a constellation widely believed to resemble a giant hunter, belted or fettered, around whom various legends grew—in Greece, that he had been banished to the sky for foolish boasting; in Semitic lands, for foolishly asserting his strength against God (the Hebrew means both "sturdy" and "fool"). Job 9:9 mentions the "making" of Orion among the great, unsearchable things God does in nature (cf. Am 5:8). God challenges Job to attempt what only God could do—loose Orion's fetters (38:31,32). The real significance of the question lies in the Pleiades ushering in the spring and Orion the winter, that is, "Can you change the seasons which God has ordained?"

See PLEIADES.

Ornan. Alternate rendering of Araunah, the Jebusite, in 1 Chronicles 21:15.

See ARAUNAH.

Orontes. River of the great Rift Valley, flowing northward from the watershed and reaching the Mediterranean at Seleucia Pieria, the harbor city for Antioch. The Orontes never provided Syria with an economic backbone such as the Nile gave Egypt or the Tigris-Euphrates gave Mesopotamia.

The countries which form the Fertile Crescent include Syria, which powerfully affected Israel's history, principally through the cities that stood on the Orontes; for example, the city of "Hamath the great" (Am 6:2) on the Orontes against which Solomon fought (2 Chr 8:3,4) and which Jeroboam II much later recovered for Israel (2 Kgs 14:28). When Samaria fell to Assyria, Sargon deported its inhabitants and replaced them with people from Hamath (2 Kgs 17:24,30). The inscriptions of Shalmaneser III say that Ahab of Samaria fought in the battle of Qarqar on the Orontes in 854 BC. Jehoahaz of Judah was summoned by Pharaoh

Neco to Riblah on the Orontes (2 Kgs 23:30), an event that Jeremiah mourned in a dirge (22:10). At Riblah, Nebuchadnezzar had Zedekiah blinded and led in chains to Babylon (2 Kgs 25:20).

Near the bay at which the Orontes enters the Mediterranean, Antioch was built in 300 BC and became the third largest city in the Roman Empire. Here a Christian church was founded (Acts 11:19,20). Revival there stimulated the apostles in Jerusalem to send Barnabas to assess the situation (vv 21–24). He recognized that a man of the highest spiritual caliber was required in Antioch, and he persuaded Paul to join him there (vv 25,26). The church in Antioch was a concerned, caring fellowship (vv 17–30) which eventually became the seedbed of Christianity's world mission (Acts 13:1–3).

Orpah. Woman of Moab who married Chilion (Ru 1:1–14), son of Elimelech and Naomi. After her husband and sons died, Naomi decided to return to Judah. Both Orpah and Ruth resolved to go with Naomi, but at Naomi's urging Orpah remained in her homeland.

See RUTH, BOOK OF.

Orphan. Word coming from a Hebrew root meaning "to be alone" or "bereaved," often rendered as "fatherless." The idea describes any person who is without legal standing in the covenant community of Israel, who is unprotected or needy, and who is especially exposed to oppression, as well as one bereft of one or both earthly parents (cf. Lam 5:3).

Since God has a special concern for the fatherless (Ex 22:22–24; Dt 10:18; Pss 10:14,18; 27:10; 68:5; 146:9; Is 1:17; Hos 14:3), OT legislation made special provision for them by protecting their rights of inheritance (Nm 27:7–11; Dt 24:17; Prv 23:10); ensuring their freedom to glean the fields and vineyards (Dt 24:19–21); allowing their participation in the great annual feasts (Dt 16:11,14); and allotting them a portion of the tithe crops collected every three years (Dt 14:29; 26:12). Strong condemnation awaits those who oppress them (Dt 24:17; 27:19; Mal 3:5).

While the orphans of Israel were sometimes aided by friends and relatives (Jb 29:12; 31:17), there was general failure to meet the requirements of the Law as is witnessed by the accusations of the inspired writers (Jb 6:27; 22:9; 24:3,9; Ps 94:6; Is 1:23; 10:2; Jer 5:28; Ez 22:7). Consequently the prophets never tire of pleading the orphan's cause (Jer 7:6; 22:3; Zec 7:10).

The word is used only twice in the NT; once in a general sense to describe those who are "desolate" or "comfortless" (Jn 14:18), and once in the specific sense to describe the "fatherless" (Jas 1:27). In the spirit of an OT prophet, James declares that true religion involves the care of orphans.

Oshea. KJV form of Hoshea, the alternate name for Joshua, in Numbers 13:8,16.

See JOSHUA (PERSON) #1.

Osiris. See EGYPT, EGYPTIANS.

Osnapper. Biblical name for the Assyrian king Ashurbanipal (Ezr 4:10).

See ASHURBANIPAL; ASSYRIA, ASSYRIANS.

Osprey. Large predatory bird, also known as the black vulture, considered unclean (Lv 11:13; Dt 14:12).

See BIRDS (VULTURE, BLACK).

Ossifrage. Largest of the vulture family, also known as the bearded vulture, considered unclean (Lv 11:13; Dt 14:12; KJV).

See BIRDS (LAMMERGEIER).

Ostraca. Inscribed pieces of pottery.

See INSCRIPTIONS; POTSHERD; POTTERY; WRITING AND BOOKS.

Ostrich. See BIRDS.

Othni. Levite; Shemaiah's son and a gatekeeper in Solomon's temple (1 Chr 26:7).

Othniel. Judge of Israel, mentioned as the son of Kenaz and Caleb's nephew (or perhaps brother), who delivered Israel from the tyranny of Cushan-rishathaim, and who earlier distinguished himself by capturing Debir (Jos 15:15–17; Jgs 1:11–13; 3:8–11).

At Caleb's prompting (promising his daughter Achsah to anyone who could conquer Debir), Othniel took Kiriath-sepher (Debir) and received Achsah for his wife. When Caleb gave her and her land as a present, Achsah asked for a water source and was given "the upper springs and the lower springs" (Jos 15:19; Jgs 1:15).

Later, Othniel delivered the Israelites from the oppressive Cushan-rishathaim, king of Mesopotamia (Aram-naharaim), whom the Israelites had served for eight years on account of their sin (Jgs 3:7). When the people cried for relief, the Lord raised up Othniel. Delivering them, he was described as someone that the "Spirit of the Lord came upon" (v 10). The effects of his work as judge lasted for a generation (vv 9–11).

See JUDGES, BOOK OF.

Outward Man. Part of a person outwardly observed. Used in contrast with "inner man," the term is not to be confused with other terms, both biblical and extrabiblical, such as "old man and new man," "natural man and spiritual man," "body and soul." Near Eastern and particulary Semitic thinking dealt in wholes instead of dichotomies, so the inner and outward man were viewed as parts of a whole rather than as irreconcilable opposites.

Although the phrase appears only in 2 Corinthians 4:16 ("outer nature" RSV) similar terms, such as "outward appearance," are found elsewhere in Scripture (1 Sm 16:7; Mt 23:27,28; 2 Cor 10:7). From the biblical perspective, appearance should correspond to that which is inside a person. The Talmud says, "A scribe whose inner man does not correspond to the outer is no scribe."

See MAN, DOCTRINE OF; INNER MAN.

Oven. See FOOD AND FOOD PREPARATION.

Ovens, Tower of the. Structure in the Jerusalem wall restored by Nehemiah and his workmen after the exile (Neh 3:11; 12:38; KJV, tower of the furnaces). Malchijah, son of Harim, and Hasshub, son of Pahath-moab, are named as its builders. The tower was likely a defensive work on the northwest section of the wall, named for its proximity to nearby baking ovens.

See JERUSALEM.

Overseer. Word appearing 12 times in the OT (KJV) and once in the NT. The NIV uses it at least six times in the NT to translate the word *episkopos*, which is derived from "peer" or "watch over." In the OT "overseer" is used to translate three words, which literally mean (1) to visit with authority, (2) to be the preeminent one, or (3) to be the head writer.

Joseph was given authority to watch over and administer all aspects of Potiphar's house (Gn 39:4,5), advising Pharaoh to appoint 50 men to regulate and watch over the abundant harvest for 7 years (41:34). Solomon appointed 3600 overseers ("supervisors" NASB) to make the people work (2 Chr 2:18). In Josiah's time of temple renovation there were overseers over all the workmen in every job (2 Chr 34:13,17). Nehemiah appointed men to oversee the rebuilding of the wall (Neh 11:9,14), to oversee the Levites (Neh 11:22), and to be in charge of the levitical singers (12:42).

The word "overseer" speaks of one or many to represent the highest person of authority and to exercise authority over whatever was designated. Included in this authoritative oversight was the idea of watching, directing, and protecting the master's interests. The NT carries these ideas also in regard to men appointed to serve the church on behalf of Jesus Christ (Acts 20:28; Phil 1:1; 1 Tm 3:1,2; Ti 1:7). Jesus Christ is the great Overseer (1 Pt 2:25).

See BISHOP; ELDER.

Owl.   See BIRDS.

Ox.   See ANIMALS (CATTLE).

Ozem.   1. Sixth son of Jesse and a descendant of Hezron (1 Chr 2:15).

2. Fourth son of Jerahmeel by his first wife (1 Chr 2:25).

Ozias.   KJV rendering of Uzziah, king of Judah in Matthew 1:8,9.

See UZZIAH #1.

Ozni, Oznite.   Alternate names for Ezbon and his descendants (Nm 26:16).

See EZBON #1.

Pp

Paarai. One of David's mighty men, said to be from Arba, in Judah (2 Sm 23:35); perhaps the same as Naarai the son of Ezbai (1 Chr 11:37).

Pace (Measure). Linear measure equivalent to the average distance of a man's stride, or about one yard.

See WEIGHTS AND MEASURES.

Paddan, Padan, Paddan-aram, Padan-aram. Northwestern Mesopotamian district whose name means, "Field of Aram," distinguishing this flatland from the mountainous regions to the north and east. Paddan-aram (KJV Padan-aram) is alternately called Paddan (KJV Padan) in Genesis 48:7, the "land of Aram" in Hosea 12:12, and Aram-naharaim (Gn 24:10; RV mg., RSV Mesopotamia), meaning "Aram of the two rivers." The two rivers probably referred to the Euphrates and Khabur Rivers, between which this tract of land was situated.

Haran was the chief city of this district, playing an important part during the patriarchal period. Upon his father's death in Haran, Abraham left Paddan-aram for Canaan (Gn 11:32; 12:4,5). Later, Isaac received Rebekah his wife from among Abraham's relatives at Nahor (i.e., Haran), and Jacob found refuge from Esau (Gn 27:43), married two of Laban's daughters (28:2–7), fathered 11 sons (35:26; 46:15), and grew prosperous (31:18) in Paddan-aram.

See ARAM-NAHARAIM.

Padon. Forefather of a family of temple servants who returned with Zerubbabel to Palestine following the Babylonian captivity (Ezr 2:44; Neh 7:47).

Pagiel. Ochran's son from Asher's tribe, who was appointed by Moses to help number the people in the wilderness. He also served as leader of his tribe during that time (Nm 1:13; 2:27; 7:72,77; 10:26).

Pahath-moab. Head of a family of Israelites that returned with Zerubbabel to Palestine after the Babylonian captivity (Ezr 2:6; Neh 7:11). Other members of his family, about 200 men, came with Ezra (Ezr 8:4). After the return, certain of his sons were included among the Israelites having foreign wives, who vowed to sever the relationship according to Jewish law (Ezr 10:30). Hashub, Pahath-moab's son, helped rebuild the Jerusalem wall and the tower of furnaces in Nehemiah's day (Neh 3:11). Pahath-moab, called a chief of the people, set his seal on Ezra's covenant (Neh 10:14).

Pai. Alternate form of Pau, an Edomite city, in 1 Chronicles 1:50.

See PAU.

Palal. Uzai's son, who helped rebuild the Jerusalem wall in Nehemiah's day (Neh 3:25).

Palestina. KJV rendering of Philistia, a country along the southwest coast of Canaan, in Exodus 15:14 and Isaiah 14:29,31.

See PHILISTIA, PHILISTINES.

Palestine. Country on the eastern shore of the Mediterranean Sea, also known as Canaan and Israel.

Palestine was situated at the west end of the Fertile Crescent, that arching stretch of highly productive land that ran from the Persian Gulf through Mesopotamia and Syria to Egypt. Palestine lay in a unique position, for it constituted a land bridge between Mesopotamia and Egypt, the two primary cultural centers of the ancient Near East. It also served,

The western wall of Jerusalem. Palal and Hashub (Pahath-Moab's son) were among the many who helped rebuild Jerusalem's walls (Neh 3:11,25).

therefore, as a connection between the continents of Asia and Africa and as a continental link between Africa and Europe. Trade moved by well-defined routes as goods were brought into the Fertile Crescent from as far as northern Europe, India, and south of Egypt. The same roads were followed by prospective conquerors as they moved their armies from area to area in quest of power and wealth.

It was the land promised by God to Abraham and his descendants, the homeland of God's chosen people, and the geographical scene for much of biblical history. It has become a land sacred to three great world religions, Judaism, Christianity, and Islam. Physically, Palestine is a kind of microcosm. In a stretch of 150 miles one can find almost every kind of climate and terrain known on the earth. It has fertile plains, sand-swept deserts, rocky wastes, forests, mountains, lakes, and rivers. With such a variety in so small an area, the land provides sharp contrasts. In the north, Mt Hermon stands perpetually snow-capped at an altitude of about 9100 feet, while a scant 100 miles distant in the subtropical depression of the Jordan Valley is the Dead Sea, representing the deepest spot on the earth.

Name. This land has been known by many names over its long history. Ironically, the country which in most minds is associated with Israel came to be known as Palestine after the inveterate enemies of Israel, the Philistines. The country seems to have been named after the maritime region, perhaps because this was the area which most foreigners contacted. So the land was called Canaan and later named after Philistia. In the table of nations, Canaan is said to have extended from Sidon in the north toward Gerar as far as Gaza and east toward the Cities of the Plain (Gn 10:19). The name Canaan appears in the Bible; the first occurrence of the name as that of a country or region is in Genesis 11:31. It appears in the Amarna Letters and in the historical records of the Egyptian 19th dynasty. In the Akkadian of the Amarna Tablets and the Hurrian the name is transliterated Kinahhu, which has been associated with Phoenicia.

After the Israelite conquest of Canaan the country was known as the land of Israel (1 Sm 13:19; 1 Chr 22:2). With the division of the kingdom in the reign of Rehoboam (930 BC), the name Israel went with the northern kingdom and the southern kingdom was known as Judah and, later, Judea.

Herodotus regarded Palestine as part of Syria, and for many centuries it was known under the name of Syria. Josephus says that the area from Gaza to Egypt was referred to as Palestine by the Greeks. The Romans named the land Palaestina, from which the English Palestine is derived. During the Crusades the country was called the Holy Land, a name used even today. With World War I, the Balfour Declaration, and the British mandate, the name Palestine was again applied.

Territory. The earliest reference to the extent of Palestine appears in the promise of the land to Abraham and to his descendants (Gn 15:18–21). Here the borders are given as the River of Egypt (Wadi el-Arish) in the southwest to the Euphrates River in the northeast. It is further defined in terms of the peoples who occupied it at that time, 10 in all, including the Kenites, the Kenizzites, the Kadmonites, the Hittites, the Perizzites, the Rephaim, the Amorites, the Canaanites, the Girgashites, and the Jebusites. In Genesis 17:8 the land is called simply "all the land of Canaan."

The Lord gave more detailed directions to Moses concerning the borders of the land that Israel was to occupy (Nm 34:1–12). The southern boundary was to be from the River of Egypt to the south of Kadesh-barnea and along the wilderness of Zin to the southern extremity of the Dead Sea. The western boundary was the Mediterranean, the northern border was set at the entrance to Hamath, and the eastern limit was the Jordan River and the Dead Sea.

The extent of the land is spelled out somewhat more generally in Deuteronomy 1:7,8. Just prior to the death of Moses, the Lord showed him the land from Mt Nebo (from "the top of Pisgah") (Dt 34:1–4). In this case many elements of the description are geographical features.

The country is described in more detail in the account of the division of the land among the tribes (Jos 13:1–19:51). This territory ran from Kadesh-barnea in the portion of Simeon in the south to the town of Ijon in Naphtali's tribal allotment in the north. The limits of Israel also included the allotments east of the Jordan which had been given to Reuben, Gad, and half-Manasseh from the Arnon River in the south to the region of Mt Hermon (Jos 13:8–13), although this territory was not part of Palestine proper.

The greatest extent of the Promised Land is seen in the Lord's declaration to Moses that he would set the bounds of Israel from the Red Sea to the Sea of the Philistines (Mediterranean) and from the wilderness to the Euphrates River (Ex 23:31). Historically, during the period of the judges and the reign of Saul, Israel did not conquer the land that had been given to the tribes in the division under Joshua. The military strength of David and the diplomacy of Solomon enabled them to achieve a marked expansion of Israelite rule. David defeated Hadadezer, king of Zobah, and thus pushed his northern frontier to the Euphrates River; he defeated Syria, Ammon, Moab, Edom, and Amalek, enlarging the kingdom also to the east and south (2 Sm 8:1–14; 1 Chr 18:1–13). Solomon had a fleet of merchant ships stationed at Ezion-geber on the Gulf of Aqaba. He also engaged in copper mining activities in that area.

The expression "from Dan to Beer-sheba" (*c.* 150 mi) appears in the historical books as a designation of the extent of the territory of Israel. The breadth of the land, from the Mediterranean to the Jordan, measured from about 28 to 70 miles, an average of about 40 miles in width.

Climate. It has been said that the climate of Palestine is more varied than that of any other area of comparable size in the world. Generally, the climate may be described as temperate; at Jerusalem, for example, the temperature extremes range from 26° to 107° and the average annual rainfall is about 20 inches. The coastal plain is warmer and has been compared to the east coast of Florida. The average annual temperature at Jaffa (Joppa) is 67°. The Jordan Valley in the area of the Dead Sea is subtropical; in summer its temperatures may reach 120°.

Rainfall is seasonal, with rain coming in the cooler months of the year as the prevailing west wind brings moisture over the comparatively colder land area, much like the "lake effect" snows of the Great Lakes region of the United States. The rainy season extends from October to April. Within this time the Israelites singled out two periods (Jer 5:24; Jl 2:23), the former rain and the latter rain, with the former rain occurring in the months of October and November and the latter rain falling in March and April. The coastal area receives about 28 inches of rain annually while the average for the country in general is said to be 22 to 24 inches.

Snow is somewhat rare, but it does occur (cf. 2 Sm 23:20; Ps 147:16). About once in 15 years it snows enough to block the highways. From time to time there are hailstorms, some of which have caused damage to crops and even killed animals (Is 30:30; Ps 18:12,13; on effects of hail in Egypt, see Ex 9:18–34).

Winds are important in Palestine. In the heat of summer the winds from the sea provide cooling. Even in ancient times the residences of rulers were situated so as to take advantage of this effect. The south wind brings scorching heat in summer (Jb 37:17; Lk 12:55) and with the east wind comes stifling heat and dust (Is 27:8; Ez 17:10; 19:12). Winds also accompany rain (1 Kgs 18:45) and are sometimes very destructive (Jb 1:19). Stormy winds come too with hail and snow (Ps 148:8; Is 28:2).

The fauna and flora of Palestine demonstrate a diversity which parallels that of the climate.

Geography. For purposes of description, the land of Palestine may be conveniently divided into five longitudinal sections: I. the Maritime or Coastal Plain; II. the Shephelah; III. the Western Plateau; IV. the Arabah, or Jordan Valley; and V. the Eastern Plateau or Transjordan. These divisions are based essentially on differences in elevation, but other geographic elements also serve to mark their limits or otherwise distinguish them.

The Maritime or Coastal Plain may be divided into three separate plains from south to north: the Plain of Philistia; the Plain of Sharon; and the Plain of Acre. All along the Palestinian coast there is not an adequate harbor. Herod the Great built a port at Caesarea, from which Paul set sail as a prisoner bound for Rome.

(1) The Plain of Philistia begins with the Wadi el-Arish or River of Egypt and extends north to the Nahr el-Auja, about 5 miles north of Joppa. This plain is about 70 miles long and reaches its greatest width in the latitude of Gaza, where it measures about 30 miles. Along the Mediterranean there were dunes of sand, but for the most part this area was very fertile and admirably suited for the production of grain. The region was also important for commerce, since along it lay the most important trade routes linking Asia and Africa, with Gaza as an important center for land trade. The Philistines dominated the plain and also part of the Shephelah and other districts of Palestine. The Philistine Pentapolis (Gaza, Ashkelon, Ashdod, Gath, and Ekron) formed a defensive league of cities, for the roads, which were an advantage for commerce, were a disadvantage militarily because armies of various nations used them repeatedly. The city of Joppa was known in both OT and NT times (e.g., Jon 1:3; Acts 9:36–43).

(2) The Plain of Sharon is not sharply demarcated from the Philistine plain and was probably under Philistine control, but the OT recognizes it as a separate entity (cf. Sg 2:1; Is 65:10). The plain extends north to Mt Carmel. On the coast are the town of Dor, which is mentioned in the Tale of Wenamon, and the city of Caesarea, where Herod the Great did much building.

Six styles of fans used in ancient times to relieve the summer heat.

(3) Beyond the promontory of Carmel lies a bay, on which was situated the city named Ptolemais (Acts 21:7), later known as Acre, and finally as Accho. Here a narrow plain stretches some 20 miles to the Ladder of Tyre (Ras en-Nakurah). The Kishon River (Jgs 4:7,13; 1 Kgs 18:40) flows through this plain to the sea.

The Shephelah constitutes a kind of "midlands," intermediate between the lowlands of the coastal plain and the highlands of the Western Plateau, with an elevation of about 500 to 1000 feet and a width of only a few miles. It is said to extend from about the Valley of Ajalon to Beersheba. These low hills are cut through by four principal passes which give access to the Western Plateau: the Valley of Ajalon (Wadi Selman), where Joshua commanded the sun and the moon to stand still (Jos 10:12); the Valley of Sorek (Wadi es-Sarar), where Samson became involved with Delilah (Jgs 16:4); the Valley of Elath, where David defeated Goliath (1 Sm 17:2); and the Valley of Zephathah, which begins near Beit Jibrin and debouches into the Plain of Philistia near Ashdod.

The valleys of the Shephelah produced grain crops, while the hills were well suited for grapes and olives. The region was very important strategically, because it afforded approaches to Jerusalem.

The Western Plateau or Hill Country ranges from 1000 to 4000 feet in elevation and covers some 150 miles from Lebanon to Beersheba. It may also be divided into three areas: Galilee, Samaria, and Judea.

(1) Galilee may be regarded as two parts, Upper Galilee (2000–4000 ft) and Lower Galilee (below 2000 ft). The area was agricultural and pastoral, like much of Palestine, and was open to invasion. The highways which traversed Galilee made it a cosmopolitan district, so that Isaiah 9:1 calls it "Galilee of the nations." Among its cities were Nazareth, Cana, Capernaum, Tiberias, and Chorazin, towns Jesus frequented and which entered into his preaching. The Western Plateau is interrupted by the Plain of Esdraelon.

(2) Samaria was also suitable for crops and pasture. The brothers of Joseph were grazing their flocks in the Plain of Dothan when Joseph visited them and became the victim of their conspiracy (Gn 37:17). In Samaria there was the Plain of Moreh, the city of Shechem, the mountains Ebal and Gerizim, the capital of the northern kingdom (Samaria), and the home of the Samaritan people, a mixed group with whom the Jews had no dealings (Jn 4:9).

(3) Judea has an elevation of about 2000–3500 feet and reaches some 60 miles from Bethel to Beersheba. The city of Jerusalem stands at an elevation of 2654 feet, surrounded by mountains and valleys which served as part of its defense system (Ps 125:2). This was the heart of the nation, for from the time of David onward the capital was here, and more important, the ark of the covenant had been brought here during David's reign. As the Lord had long foretold, Jerusalem had become the center of his worship; here Solomon built the temple, one of the greatest structures ever made.

Toward the east, the land of Judea falls off dramatically to the Jordan Valley. This means that much of the rainfall that falls on the heights runs off very quickly in the steep wadis or valleys and in the tangle of rocks that make up the Wilderness of Judea, which skirts the Dead Sea.

Judea had its famous cities—Bethlehem, Hebron, Beersheba—all rich with biblical history. Beyond Beersheba to the south was the vast sweep of the Negeb.

The Arabah or Jordan Valley presents the extremes of height and depth. Mt Hermon (Jebel esh-Sheikh) rises to 9166 feet, while the surface of the Dead Sea lies 1296 feet below sea level, and at its deepest part the sea plunges another 1300 feet.

(1) The North Arabah or Upper Jordan Valley. The Jordan River has four sources, all near Mt Hermon. From west to east these are the Nahr (River) Bareighit, the Nahr Hasbani, the Nahr el-Leddan, and the Nahr Banias. The latter two provide most of the water of the Jordan. The Leddan begins near the ancient city of Dan (Tell el-Qadi). Banias is named after an old shrine of the pagan god Pan. Caesarea Philippi was located here (Mt 16:13; Mk 8:27).

The Jordan flows through what was Lake Huleh, now partly drained and designated as a wildlife refuge. Two miles below the Huleh basin is the Bridge of Jacob's Daughters, by which the old road to Damascus crossed the river. The Jordan then flows into a gorge some 1200 feet deep.

(2) The Sea of Galilee, about 10 miles from Huleh, has an elevation of −685 feet. It measures 15 by 8 miles, with a maximum depth of 750 feet. The shape of the lake gave it the OT name, Chinnereth ("harp") (Nm 34:11; Jos 13:27). In the NT it was also called the Lake of Gennesaret (Lk 5:1) and the Sea of Tiberias (Jn 6:1; 21:1).

On its northwest shore was the site of Capernaum; on the west were Magdala, the home of Mary Magdalene, and Tiberias. To the northeast was the location of Bethsaida, where the feeding of the 5000 took place (Lk 9:10). At the southwest was the district of the Gerasenes (Gadarenes), where Jesus healed the demoniac (Mk 5:1–13).

(3) The Middle Arabah, or Ghor. The name

The Huleh Valley, as seen across a manmade pond at the north end of the valley.

Jordan means "descender"; in the 60 miles (in a straight line) from the outlet of the Sea of Galilee to the northern end of the Dead Sea there is a fall of more than 600 feet, or 10 feet per mile. The river flows in a series of S-curves or zigzags, so that its actual course between Galilee and the Dead Sea covers some 200 miles.

This stretch of the Jordan Valley is known as the Ghor, or Rift. Six miles below the Sea of Galilee the Yarmuk River enters from the east. Some smaller streams empty into the Jordan, but the next river of consequence is the Jabbok (Gn 32:22). Just south of the Sea of Galilee the Ghor is about 4 miles wide; near Beth-shan it reaches 7 miles; beyond that for some 15 miles the mountains close in on the river on both sides, narrowing the valley to 2 to 3 miles; near Jericho it broadens to about 12 miles. Normally the river is 90 to 100 feet wide, but it spreads out greatly when in flood. This flood-plain is named the Zor in Arabic; it is covered with nearly impenetrable thickets called the "jungle" of the Jordan (Jer 12:5).

Jericho was situated 10 miles northwest of the Dead Sea. Near the Allenby Bridge is the traditional site of the baptism of Jesus.

(4) The Dead Sea is unique. Its surface is the deepest point on the face of the earth and its waters are of tremendous wealth. In the OT it is known as the Salt Sea (Gn 14:3; Nm 34:12; Jos 12:3) and the Sea of Arabah (Jos 12:3). Josephus calls it Lake Asphaltitis.

This body of water 46 miles long, 10 miles wide, and 1300 feet deep consists of about 25 percent mineral matter, making it a chemical deposit of great value. In addition to the flow of the Jordan, the Dead Sea receives the water of other streams, such as the Arnon River on the east. Much of the runoff of the seasonal rains also finds its way into the Salt Sea. Temperatures in the valley may reach 120 degrees in summer; with the extreme humidity the climate is very debilitating and almost unbear-able. It is estimated that the daily evaporation from the sea is 6 to 8 million tons.

At the northwestern end of the lake is the site of Khirbet Qumran, the source of the Dead Sea Scrolls. Farther south on the eastern shore is the Herodian fortress of Masada, the scene of the heroic resistance of the Jews against the Romans. On the eastern side is the fortress of Machaerus, where John the Baptist was beheaded (Mt 14:10,11). The five Cities of the Plain, with Sodom and Gomorrah best known, were located at the southern end of the Dead Sea.

(5) The Southern Arabah, mostly a barren wilderness, extends from the Dead Sea to the Gulf of Aqaba, a distance of 150 miles. There is a gradual ascent from the Dead Sea to a watershed just west of Petra. Near the tip of the Gulf of Aqaba were the ports of Elath (mod Eilat) and Ezion-geber.

The Eastern Plateau, or Transjordan, was not named as part of the land of promise, but it was taken by the tribes of Reuben, Gad, and half-Manasseh. The region is better supplied with water than the Western Plateau and has perennial streams, such as the Yarmuk, Jabbok, and Arnon. A principal north road was the King's Highway, followed by the Israelites during the exodus (Nm 21:22) and probably also the route taken by the invading kings of Genesis 14.

The northern section of Transjordan was known as Bashan, noted for its cattle (Ps 22:12; Ez 39:18) and for its oak trees (Is 2:13; Zec 11:2). Among its cities were Golan, Edrei, and Ashteroth-karnaim. Its southern boundary was the Yarmuk River.

Gilead, famed for its balm (Gn 37:25; Jer 8:22), was often mentioned in the OT (e.g., Dt 3:10–16; Jgs 11). It extended from the Yarmuk River to the city of Heshbon. This area was heavily forested in David's time (cf. 2 Sm 18:8).

From the Yarmuk to the Arnon was the land of Perea. Here were found some of the

The Yarmuk River.

cities of the Decapolis, like Pella, Gadara, and Gerasa. South of the Arnon was the country of the Moabites, who were related to Lot (Gn 19:37).

In Palestine proper, there were two important divisions: the Plain of Esdraelon and the Negeb. The Plain of Esdraelon, often associated prophetically with Armageddon, lies between Galilee and Samaria. This is one of the most fertile areas of Palestine and also was the scene of numerous battles. The plain was guarded by fortress cities on its southern side (Megiddo, Ibleam, and Taanach). In the OT the Valley of Jezreel was not regarded as a part of Esdraelon but as the valley between the hill of Moreh and Mt Gilboa. At the eastern end was the stronghold of Beth-shan.

In the extreme south of the land is the wilderness area called the Negeb, or South Country. This begins in the region of Beersheba and extends roughly to Kadesh-barnea. A district of infrequent and irregular rainfall, its agriculture is restricted, although a nomadic pastoral life has been widely practiced. Its population has been sparse and its cities few. In Nabataean times (Greco-Roman period) a number of cities existed and prospered by careful storage of the limited rainfall. CARL E. DeVRIES

See JORDAN RIVER; NEGEB; SHEPHELAH; TRANSJORDAN; ARABAH; DEAD SEA; GALILEE, SEA OF; DECAPOLIS; CONQUEST AND ALLOTMENT OF THE LAND.

Bibliography. Y. Aharoni, *The Land of the Bible;* D. Baly, *The Geography of the Bible;* L.H. Grollenberg, *Atlas of the Bible;* J.H. Kitchen, *Holy Fields;* E.G. Kraeling (ed.), *Rand McNally Historical Atlas of the Holy Land;* G.A. Smith, *The Historical Geography of the Holy Land;* G.A. Turner, *Historical Geography of the Holy Land;* G.E. Wright and F.V. Filson, *The Westminster Historical Atlas to the Bible.*

Pallu, Palluite. Reuben's son, father of Eliab (Gn 46:9, KJV Phallu; Ex 6:14; Nm 26:8; 1 Chr 5:3) and the founder of the Palluite family (Nm 26:5).

Palm. *See* PLANTS.

Palm and Handbreath. *See* WEIGHTS AND MEASURES.

Palmerworm. *See* ANIMALS (LOCUST).

Palm Trees, City of. Designation for Jericho in Deuteronomy 34:3 and 2 Chronicles 28:15.

See JERICHO.

Palsy. *See* PARALYSIS, PARALYTIC.

Palti. 1. One of the 12 spies Moses sent to explore the land of Canaan before the Israelite conquest. Palti represented Benjamin's tribe (Nm 13:9).

2. Laish's son, to whom King Saul gave Michal, his daughter and David's wife, after the break between Saul and David (1 Sm 25:44, KJV Phalti). Michal was recovered from him and returned to David (2 Sm 3:15); in that reference he is called Paltiel (KJV Phaltiel).

Paltiel. 1. Son of Azzan and a leader of Issachar's tribe (Nm 34:26). He was appointed by Eleazar and Joshua to assist in the distribution of the land west of the Jordan River among the 10 tribes to whom it was given.

2. Alternate rendering of Palti, Laish's son, in 2 Samuel 3:15.

See PALTI #2.

Paltite, The. Designation for Helez, one of David's mighty men (2 Sm 23:26). He lived in Beth-palet. In 1 Chronicles 11:27 he is called a "Pelonite."

See BETH-PELET.

Pamphylia. Coastal region on the southern shore of Asia Minor (Turkey) stretching 80 miles from Lycia on the west to Cilicia on the east, and about 20 miles wide from the sea coast to the Taurus Mountains. Being little more than a narrow coastal plain with an unpleasantly hot and humid climate, this province never produced any important cities. This, combined with its general inaccessibility lying as it did deep at the north end of the bay of Adalia and separated from the rest of inland Asia by a rugged mountain range, made it a haven for pirates. In 102 BC the Roman senate established patrol stations on the coasts of Pamphylia and western Cilicia to police the area, but no effective control was established until 67 BC, when Pompey was given unlimited resources to clean up the Mediterranean.

Some have doubted the accuracy of Luke's designation of Pamphylia as a separate province from Lycia (Acts 27:5) because of an apparent contradiction by the early Roman historian Dio Cassius (60:17) who stated that Claudius combined Pamphylia and Lycia into one imperial province in AD 43. However, an inscription from Pamphylia establishes that it remained an independent province for a while longer, was eventually connected with Galatia to the north, and finally was united to Lycia about AD 74 by the Roman emperor Vespasian. Therefore, when Paul traveled through the region on his first missionary journey (Acts 13:13; 14:24; 15:38) it is correctly referred to by Luke as Pamphylia.

There was evidently a Jewish population in the province because Luke names Pamphylia among 15 countries from which Jews came to Jerusalem to the feast of Pentecost (Acts 2:10). Arguments are not convincing that Pamphylia could not have possessed any significant numbers of Christians because it and Lycia are not mentioned in 1 Peter 1:1, which seems to sum up the whole of Asia Minor. The date of the writing of 1 Peter is not known, but if it was written during the period from AD 43 to 74, when Pamphylia was considered a part of Galatia, Pamphylia would be included in that designation. Peter may also have considered Lycia in the broad designation of Galatia because his introduction mentions only the larger political divisions of Asia Minor. Nevertheless it must be noted that Paul apparently had little success in the Pamphylian city of Perga because there is no statement of opposition to him there or of any converts being made, and he did not revisit the province on his second journey even though his plan was to "return and visit the brethren in every city where we proclaimed the work of the Lord" (Acts 15:36). Perhaps Paul's separation from Barnabas was the reason for this, and it may be that Barnabas and John Mark visited Pamphylia after Cyprus (Acts 15:37–41).

Whatever relation Paul's "thorn in the flesh" (2 Cor 12:7) may have had to his short stay in Perga of Pamphylia (Acts 13:14) is purely conjectural. Equally involved might have been the unexpected departure of John Mark (Acts 13:13). Whatever the reason, Paul left Perga without preaching there and only did so on his return through the area from Pisidia (14:25). There is no record of his ever having visited the area again.

See ANATOLIA; ASIA.

Pannag. KJV rendering of millet (Ez 27:17), an annual grass whose seeds are used in making bread.

See PLANTS (MILLET).

Paper. *See* WRITING AND BOOKS.

Paphos. Originally a Phoenician settlement in southwest Cyprus. "Old Paphos" was supplemented by a Greek settlement, "New Paphos," some 10 miles distant, becoming the administrative center when Cyprus became a senatorial province of Rome in 22 BC. The combined city was famous for its temple, dedicated originally to the Syrian goddess Astarte, worshiped (according to Tacitus) with ancient Phoenician rites involving anointing of a conical (meteorite?) stone. The Greeks identified her with Aphrodite, claiming she sprang from the sea.

Strangely, Luke's record (Acts 13:6–12) omits reference to this pagan shrine, concentrating upon Paul's confrontation with the proconsul, and with Elymas, a Jewish "false prophet" and "magician," probably soothsayer and astrologer to the governor. Here the Christian world mission beyond Palestine began, and Paul adopted the gentile form of his name. Here, too, Paul first offered the gospel to a Roman official—another "Paul"—and found him "intelligent," eager "to hear the Word," "astounded at the teaching," and a believer; this was a significant precedent for most of Paul's subsequent relationships with Roman officials.

At Paphos Paul first met vigorous opposition to the gospel from Elymas, fearful for his own position with the proconsul. Here Paul performed his first recorded miracle, a strangely unattractive, punitive one, accompanied by somewhat violent condemnation, and apparently never repeated. Mercifully, Elymas' blindness was only "for a time"; Bede remarks that Paul remembered how blindness had contributed to his own conversion.

Here, too, Mark reached the limit of his missionary vision. Cyprus had a large Jewish population (Acts 4:36; 13:5 note plural; Col 4:10), and was a natural mission field. Leaving Paphos for mainly gentile Pamphylia was an unexpected extension, geographically and mentally. After some disagreement Mark left, as soon as the ship landed at Perga (Acts 13:13; 15:38).

R.E.O. WHITE

Papyrus. Ancient Egyptian writing material derived from the papyrus plant.

See PLANTS; WRITING AND BOOKS.

Parable.
Introduction. An understanding of parables is essential if one is to understand the teaching of Jesus, since the parables make up approximately 35 percent of his recorded sayings. At no point are the vitality, relevance, and appropriateness of his teaching so clear as they are in his parables. While the parable form is not unique to Jesus, he was certainly a master at using parables as a way of teaching. The parables are not merely illustrations for Jesus' preaching; they *are* the preaching, at least to a great extent. Nor are they simple stories; they have been truly described as both "works of art" and "weapons of warfare." How one interprets the parables is not as easy a task as one might think. The way one understands the nature of a parable and the essence of Jesus' message obviously will determine the method and content of interpretation.

History of Interpretation of the Parables. A great deal of insight can be obtained by following the course of treatment the parables have received over the centuries. Not surprisingly, they have been subjected to radically different approaches, but the questions that underlie all interpretations are: (1) How much of the parable is really significant? (all the details or only one point?) (2) What is the meaning of the parable in the teaching of Jesus? (3) Of what relevance is the parable to the interpreter?

The Allegorizing Approach. From the 2nd century even to the present many people have allegorized the parables. In effect they have said that every detail in the account is significant and that the meaning and relevance of a parable are to be found in the way it portrays Christian theology. This method, often identified as the Alexandrian school of interpretation, is best illustrated by a classic example that comes from Augustine (354–430), the 4th-century scholar who despite his allegorizing was a great theologian. His interpretation of the parable of the Good Samaritan views Christ as the Good Samaritan, the oil as the comfort of good hope, the animal as the flesh of the incarnation, the inn as the church, and the innkeeper as the apostle Paul (to say nothing of the other details). Obviously this interpretation has nothing in common with Jesus' intention but rather reads into the story preconceived ideas of the interpreter. Such an approach can even sound good theologically, but it prohibits the hearing of the Word of God. Medieval interpreters went even further than the allegorizing approach by finding multiple meanings in the text. Usually four were listed: (1) the literal meaning; (2) an allegorical meaning relating to Christian theology; (3) a moral meaning giving direction for daily life; (4) a heavenly meaning indicating something about future life.

Not all of the church was dominated by such allegorizing interpretations. The school of Antioch was known for its commonsense approach to hearing the text. However, its influence was limited when compared to the Alexandrian school and, apart from notable exceptions, most of the church's efforts at understanding the parables over the centuries have involved allegorizing.

The Approach of Adolph Jülicher (1867–1938). Jülicher was a German scholar who published two volumes on the parables toward the end of the 19th century. His major contribution was the wholesale rejection of allegorizing as a means of interpreting the parables. In his reaction against allegorizing Jülicher went to the opposite extreme to say that a parable of Jesus has only one point of contact between the story and the fact being portrayed. He believed this one point alone is important in interpretation and it will usually be a general religious statement. Jülicher went so far as to say that not only was allegorizing wrong but that Jesus did not use allegories, since they tend to hide rather than reveal. He said that any allegory appearing in the NT comes from the writers of the Gospels rather than Jesus. Jülicher was correct to reject allegorizing (making an allegory of what was not intended to be allegory) but the rejection of allegory itself as a legitimate means of communication for Jesus is unfounded.

The Historical Approach. Twentieth-century study of the parables, particularly the work of C.H. Dodd (1884–1973) and Joachim Jeremias, has rightly emphasized the historical context in which the parables were originally told. Focus is placed on cultural factors that help in understanding the details of the parables and on the context of Jesus' original preaching about the kingdom of God. Usually this approach has assumed that the 1st-century church changed the original thrust of some of the parables to meet her own needs and consequently various procedures have been proposed to recover the original intent. It is true that the parables have been shaped, edited,

and collected in units by the Gospel writers (note, e.g., Matthew's collection of 8 parables in chs 13:1–52). Also, the aim of an interpreter should be to hear the parables as they were originally intended by Jesus and as his original audience heard them. The attempt to go behind the Gospel accounts, however, is a very delicate task and some of the procedures proposed for doing so need to be questioned. Notice must be taken of the way each of the Gospel writers has used his material, but the extent to which one can go behind the Gospels is limited.

Modern Trends in Parable Research. In the past two decades a number of attempts to interpret the parables have suggested new avenues of approach. Basically these new approaches have been somewhat dissatisfied with (although appreciative of) both Jülicher and the historical approach in that both limit the impact of the parables on today's reader. Jülicher reduced Jesus' teaching to pious moralisms, and the historical approach tended to focus on 2000 years ago while ignoring both the artistic and psychological features of the parables. Consequently, numerous attempts have been made to convey the same impact the parables had for the original hearers to today's hearers. Increasingly less focus is placed on the historical meaning of the parables and more emphasis is placed on their artistic, existential, and poetic effect. Jesus' parables are regarded as works of art that can be regarded as open-ended as far as meaning is concerned. A parable then would have an original meaning and the potential for a series of further possible meanings.

While the original meaning would provide some control for reinterpretation, these approaches are not bound by the author's intention. The latest of these attempts is structuralism, which tries to plot the unconscious structure inherent in a story and, in comparing it to similar structures, derive meaning from it. A great deal can be learned from these modern approaches, especially from their concern to make sure that the parables speak to our day with their original vitality. However, there is also the danger of abusing the parables in a way similar to earlier mistreatments. Those allegorizing the parables in the history of the church were not bound by the meaning of Jesus and found their own meaning. Modern interpreters, too, can find their own meaning, and even though the explanations may sound convincing (as no doubt Augustine's did to his hearers) they will not be a communication of the Word of God. If God and his ways are revealed by Jesus, then we err if we do not hear his parables as they were intended in their original context. There is indeed a dynamic interaction between the text and the interpreter, but the interpreter is brought to a moment of truth most effectively when the Spirit confronts him or her with the parable as Jesus intended it for his hearers.

Consequently, a great deal can be learned from the history of interpretation of the parables. With Jülicher one must reject allegorizing the parables into pictures that Jesus did not intend. A historical approach emphasizes the cultural background and the context in Jesus' ministry. With the more recent attempts (but avoiding their extremes), one must allow the parables to speak with all their original vigor to our own day.

The Meaning of "Parable."

The usual definition of a parable as "a heavenly story with an earthly meaning" will not suffice for understanding Jesus' parables. Nor are parables merely comparisons or illustrations of what Jesus wanted to say. The situation is much more complex with regard to the biblical meaning of the word "parable." In fact, one must distinguish between three uses of the word "parable" in biblical studies.

First, one should be aware that the Greek word for parable and its Hebrew counterpart are both broad terms and can be used for anything from a proverb to a full-blown allegory including a riddle, a dark saying, an illustration, a contrast, or a story. For example, the Greek word for parable is used in Luke 4:23 with reference to the saying "Physician, heal yourself" and most translations render it as "proverb." In Mark 3:23 "parables" is used with reference to the riddles Jesus asks the scribes, such as "How can Satan cast out Satan?" Similarly Mark 13:28 uses "parable" of a simple illustration. In Luke 18:2–5 the unjust judge is *contrasted* with God who brings justice quickly. If one compares the Hebrew OT and the Septuagint (an ancient Greek translation of the OT), the word for parable is used most frequently with reference to a proverb or dark saying. The broad meaning of parable, then, can refer to any unusual or striking speech, any dark saying intended to stimulate thought. When the word "parable" occurs in the biblical text, one must allow for this broad meaning.

Second, "parable" can be used of any story with two levels of meaning (literal and figurative) which functions as religious and ethical speech.

Third, "parable" can be used technically in modern studies to distinguish it from other types of stories such as similitude, exemplary story, and allegory. In this case a parable is a fictitious story which narrates a particular event and is usually told in the past tense (e.g., the Parable of the Lost Son). A similitude, however, is a comparison which relates a typical or recurring event in real life and is usually told in the present tense (e.g., Mt 13:31,32). An exemplary story is not a comparison at all; rather it presents character traits as either positive or negative examples to be imitated or avoided. Usually four exemplary stories are identified: The Good Samaritan (Lk 10:30–35); The Rich Fool (Lk 12:16–20); The Rich Man and Lazarus (Lk 16:19–31); and The Pharisee and the Tax Collector (Lk 18:10–13).

Allegory is the most difficult to define and has caused considerable debate. Usually allegory is defined as "a series of related metaphors." A metaphor is an implied comparison that does not use "like" or "as." This definition is used broadly, but it is not entirely satisfactory for two reasons: (1) It does not indicate whether obscurity is an essential element in allegory. Some view allegory as needing to be decoded and as being understandable only to a select few. If, however, the allegory uses customary metaphors that all would understand, it would not be obscure. (2) It does not specify how much of the story is important as related metaphors. If there were only two or three related metaphors, would the story be an allegory? At the other extreme, do minor details in the story (such as the three levels of harvest in the Parable of the Sower) have significance? An example of an allegory would be the Parable of the Sower.

This raises the problem of the difference between a parable and an allegory, a frequently debated issue. On definitions one and two above, allegory is included in parable, but on definition three a distinction is made between them because a parable is not a series of related metaphors. The details of the story of the Lost Son (the swine, the far country, etc.) do not stand for something else as they would if they were in an allegory but rather convey in dramatic terms the depths to which the son had sunk. However, a parable is *not* thereby limited to one point of comparison between the story and the fact being portrayed (as Jülicher argued). There may be several items that need to be mentioned from a particular parable. The Parable of the Lost Son emphasizes the rejoicing that takes place at repentance (note the repetition of this theme in Lk 15:24,32), but the receptivity of the father obviously parallels the grace of God and the younger and elder sons reflect sinners and religious authorities, respectively. The distinction between parable and allegory is vague at best and will vary, depending on what definitions are assigned the terms. One should note that what can be said about parable usually can also be said about allegory.

The discussion of allegory raises a further

question: Did Jesus use allegories? Jülicher argued that allegories were too complex for Jesus (even though they appear in the OT) and attributed allegorical interpretations such as the interpretation of the Parable of the Sower and allegories such as the Parable of the Wicked Tenants to the writers of the Gospels. Jülicher's influence has been so great that in many modern approaches to the parables any part of a parable that seems allegorical is eliminated as an addition by the early church. Allegorizing is wrong, but allegory itself is a perfectly legitimate and effective means of communication. Not only does allegory appear in the OT (note Ez 17:3–10 and the interpretation that follows), but it is frequent in rabbinic parables. Each story needs to be analyzed on its own merits, but there is nothing to prevent the use of allegory by Jesus.

The discussion of the meaning of "parable" has proven to be somewhat involved and has necessarily led into other issues. As long as the complexity of the term in the biblical use is remembered, one can avoid serious pitfalls in interpretation.

The purpose of parables and a description of their characteristics will assist understanding. The parables focus on God and his kingdom and in doing so reveal what kind of God he is, by what principles he works, and what he expects of humanity. Because of the focus on the kingdom, some of the parables reveal many aspects of Jesus' mission as well (note the Parable of the Wicked Tenants in Mt 21:33–39 and pars).

The following characteristics of parables should be observed: (1) Parables are usually concise and symmetrical. Items are presented in twos or threes with an economy of words. Unnecessary people, motives, and details are usually omitted. (2) The features in the story are taken from everyday life, and the metaphors used are frequently common enough so that they set up a context for understanding. For example, the discussion of an owner and his vineyard would naturally make hearers think of God and his people because of the OT use of those images. (3) Even though the parables speak in terms of everyday life, often they contain elements of surprise or hyperbole (an exaggeration used as a figure of speech). The Parable of the Good Samaritan (Lk 10:30–35) introduces a Samaritan in the story where one would probably expect a layperson. The Parable of the Unforgiving Servant (Mt 18:23–34) puts the debt of the first servant at 10 million dollars, an unbelievable sum in that day. (4) Parables require their hearers to pass judgment on the events of the story and having done so to realize that they must make a similar judgment in their own lives. The classic

example is the parable of Nathan to David (2 Sm 12:1–7), where David judges the man in the story as worthy of death and then is told that he is the man. Because they force one to decide, to come to a moment of truth, parables force their hearers to live in the present without resting on the laurels of the past or waiting for the future. The parables are the result of a mind that sees truth in concrete pictures rather than abstractions, and they teach that truth in such a compelling manner that the hearer cannot escape it.

Guidelines for Interpreting the Parables. Interpreting the parables is not easy, but certain guidelines can be presented that will avoid past errors and make sane interpretation possible.

1. *Analyze the parable thoroughly.* Note the characters and movement of the story, its climax, and the repetition of key words or ideas. If it appears in more than one Gospel, do a comparative analysis of the various accounts to note both similarities and differences. Care should be taken to avoid making too simplistic a conclusion about which account is earliest. The criteria by which some scholars argue for the priority of Mark's account (or even the apocryphal Gospel of Thomas) are questionable at best and are susceptible to being used just as easily to argue that one of the other accounts is earliest.

2. *Listen to the parable without any preconceptions as to its form or its meaning.* Attempt to hear the parable as if sitting at the feet of Jesus without knowing the parable, its meaning, and Christian theology. While it is impossible for a modern reader to become a 1st-century Jewish hearer, it is imperative that a parable be interpreted in its original context and in the way its author originally intended it to be understood.

3. *Look for help in the surrounding context but realize that the original context for many of the parables has not been preserved.* Often the parables appear where they do in the Gospels because of the arrangement of the Gospel writers. However, the wholesale rejection of the conclusions and interpretations of the parables by some scholars cannot be accepted. A comparison of the OT and rabbinic parables will show that these items are regularly part of the story.

4. *Notice features in the parable that reflect the life and thinking of the 1st-century world.* An understanding of cultural and religious factors and an awareness of OT ideas reflected in a parable will greatly assist in its interpretation. Obviously one cannot interpret the parables without some sensitivity to the nature of the life that they reflect.

5. *Note how the parable fits into the purpose*

and plan of the entire book. If the parable is present in the other Gospels, note its location and how it has been shaped to fit into the purpose of each Gospel writer.

6. *Determine as explicitly as possible the message of the parable in the teaching of Jesus.* There may be several points that need to be made in a given parable as was indicated above for the Parable of the Lost Son. There may be legitimate secondary features in the parable, but be careful not to push the story too far. One should exercise caution since it is easy to violate a parable's intention. No one would want to suggest that God has tormentors on the basis of the Parable of the Unforgiving Servant (see Mt 18:34); rather this verse points up the seriousness of the sin and its judgment. However, some people wrongly overemphasize minor features of other parables. If one will interpret the parable as a whole in keeping with its original intention such errors will be minimized.

7. *Note where the teaching of the parable conforms to the teaching of Jesus elsewhere.* Jesus' nonparabolic teaching may provide the key for or strengthen the interpretation of a parable.

8. *Give due emphasis to the "rule of end stress."* Usually the climax and the most important part of a parable comes at its conclusion. Consequently, the focus of the interpretation should be there as well. Often the end of the parable will include the theme of reversal. As elsewhere in the teaching of Jesus, his statement on a given topic is often the exact reverse of what others say or expect. (Note Mt 10:39 and pars: "The one finding his life loses it and the one losing his life for my sake finds it.") The Parable of the Workers in the Vineyard tells of those who receive less than they expected and closes with a classic reversal statement: "the last shall be first and the first last" (Mt 20:16; cf. 19:30). Note the reversal in Matthew 21:31 at the end of the Parable of the Two Sons (Mt 21:28–30). After the religious authorities have made a judgment on the basis of the parable, the reversal is accomplished as they are told that the tax collectors and whores are going into the kingdom of God before them (vv 31–32).

9. *Determine what principles are present in the parable that reveal the nature of God, his kingdom, the way he deals with humanity, or what he expects of humanity.* These principles will be of particular relevance for 20th-century persons, and the parable will remain as one of the most effective means of communicating them to modern society.

The Reason Jesus Taught in Parables. There is little doubt that Jesus taught in parables because they are both interesting and compelling and therefore one of the most effective means of communicating. When one reads Mark 4:10–12, however, it seems that Jesus taught in parables in order to *keep* people from understanding so that they would not turn and be forgiven. It seems as well that there is a mystery that is given to the "in" group and that the "out" group is prohibited from learning. This text is one of the most difficult in the NT and requires careful attention in order to avoid misunderstanding. Some, in fact, have suggested that this is Mark's understanding of parables and not Jesus'. Others have pointed to the agreement between the OT quotation in Mark and the Targum (an Aramaic paraphrase of the OT used in the synagogue) and have tried to explain the statement in Mark as a misunderstanding of the Targum. The agreement between the Targum and Mark is noteworthy, but neither of these suggestions is satisfactory. Several factors about this context need to be considered.

In Mark 4:1–9 Jesus is teaching the crowd from a boat. In verses 10–20 he is alone with the 12 and *other disciples* who are asking questions. Verses 21–32 do not give indication of either place or hearers, and verses 33,34 are a summary statement. But in verses 35,36 Jesus is in the boat dispersing the crowds, the same scene as verses 1–9! Obviously chapter 4 has been arranged by Mark as a context for giving the essence of Jesus' teaching in parables. Verses 2 and 10 both speak of parables in the plural although the Parable of the Sower is the only parable mentioned. The tense of the verbs in verses 10 and 11 indicates that certain disciples with the 12 were *customarily* asking about the parables and Jesus was explaining them. The theme of the whole chapter is on *hearing* Jesus' teaching about the kingdom of God. (Note the repetition of "hear" in 4:3,9, 15,16,18,20,23, and especially 24, "Take heed what you hear.") The Parable of the Sower is a parable about response, really hearing the Word of God. Where the parable is heard, and additional information is sought, additional teaching and explanation are given. That there is no hard and fast "in" group or "out" group can be seen from Mark 8:17–21, where the same language of blind eyes and nonhearing ears is used of the disciples. It should be emphasized that the words of 4:12 are derived from Isaiah 6:9,10, where in response to Isaiah's volunteering to proclaim God's message he is told to go and tell the people to hear and not understand as if God did not want them to repent. Obviously, however, God wanted repentance. These words were told to Isaiah because of the difficulty of his task and the hardness of heart of the people. The words express the response Isaiah would find. The quotation of this passage in Mark 4:12 (with pars in Mt 13:14,15 and Lk 8:10) expresses that the response Isaiah received is paralleled in Jesus' experience. In Matthew 13 these words come at the point where Jesus turns from the public to the private teaching of his disciples. John 12:40 uses Isaiah 6:10 at precisely the same point, the end of the public ministry, to indicate the lack of reception of Jesus' message and the hardness of heart of the people. (Note that Is 6:9,10 is also quoted in Acts 28:26,27 to express the same themes for Paul's ministry to the Jews.)

An additional fact important for consideration is the meaning of the term "mystery." Rather than being that which is not known or understood as the word is used today, the biblical use of this word is usually for that which has been revealed by God and would not have been known had God not revealed it. The content of the mystery is not explained here, but from Jesus' teaching on the kingdom elsewhere it probably refers to the fact that the kingdom is present in Jesus' own words and actions.

The other factor crucial for understanding this passage is that the word "parable" in biblical usage has a broad meaning referring to any striking speech or dark saying intended to stimulate thought. Jesus did not "spoon feed" his hearers, rather he taught in such a way as to bring about response and where there was response he gave additional teaching. No doubt there were some things told in parables that were not said openly. Note, for example, the Parable of the Wicked Tenants in Matthew 21:33–39 and parallels with its devastating indictment of the religious authorities. But even when things are not said openly, the parable still is understood, as is clear from the reaction of the religious authorities to this parable (Mt 21:45,46).

The correctness of this understanding of Mark 4:10–12 can be verified by two discussions later in the chapter. In verse 22 Jesus says, "Nothing is hidden except in order that it should be made plain," and this seems to express the motive for teaching in parables. They do not prevent understanding; rather Jesus' teaching is "hidden" in parables in order to reveal. Verses 33,34 provide a summary of the whole approach to parables: "With many such parables he was speaking the word to them even as they were *able to hear*. Without parables he was not speaking to them; alone with his own disciples he was explaining all things."

Consequently, it is not merely that parables are interesting, poetic, and arresting—as important as those characteristics are. In addition, parables stimulate thought and bring about response—if hardness of heart does not prevent it. It is as if Jesus were saying, "If you cannot hear what I am saying, I will reveal my thought in parables." Where there is response to this initial teaching, additional information is given.

The Distribution of the Parables. Before noticing the location of the parables in the NT, one should be aware that parables also occur in the OT. Usually nine OT parables are listed: the Parable of Nathan to David about the ewe lamb (2 Sm 12:1–7); the Parable of the Two Brothers and the Avenger of Blood (2 Sm 14:1–11); The Escaped Prisoner (1 Kgs 20:35–40); The Vineyard (Is 5:1–7); The Eagles and the Vine (Ez 17:2–10); The Lion Whelps (Ez 19:2–9); The Vine (Ez 19:10–14); The Forest Fire (Ez 20:45–49); The Seething Pot (Ez 24:3–5). In addition, Judges 9:7–15 records the fable of the trees, and 2 Kings 14:9 contains the fable of the thistle and the cedar. (A fable is a story in which plants and animals talk and behave as humans.)

Parables also occur frequently in the writings of ancient Jewish rabbis. In fact, many of the parables of the rabbis are similar to the ones told by Jesus and show that parables were common in ancient Jewish culture. There is one significant difference between Jesus' parables and those of the rabbis. The latter nearly always told parables in order to explain an OT text, but Jesus rarely uses parables in this way (although his parables may reflect OT ideas or on occasion conclude with an OT quotation).

In the NT the word "parable" does not occur outside the synoptic Gospels (Mt, Mk, Lk) except for Hebrews 9:9 and 11:19 where the word means a "figure" or "type." Often it is said that there are no parables in John, which is true if one understands "parable" in the sense of a story as in definitions 2 and 3 above. If, however, one includes the broad meaning of parable, then certain passages in John qualify, such as the allegory of the vine in John 15 or the image of the good shepherd in John 10. Also in the broad meaning, there are several parables in Mark, but most of them are short comparisons (Mk 2:17). Only 4 parables in Mark are stories (according to definitions 2 and 3 above), 3 of which are in chapter 4: the parables of the Sower, the Seed Growing Secretly, and the Mustard Seed. The remaining story parable in Mark is The Wicked Tenants in 12:1–9. Most of the parables then obviously appear in Matthew and Luke, both of which also contain the parables in Mark except for that of the Seed Growing Secretly. Matthew has collected 8 parables on the kingdom in chapter 13. Most of the other parables in Matthew appear in chapters 18

(The Lost Sheep and The Unforgiving Servant), 20 (The Workers in the Vineyard), 21 (The Two Sons and The Wicked Tenants), 22 (The Great Banquet), and 25 (The Ten Virgins and The Talents). Luke has more parables than any of the other Gospels, and most of them are collected in chapters 10–20. In most cases the parables are grouped according to a common theme. Luke 12 contains sayings and parables dealing with trust, anxiety, and final reckoning. Chapter 14 contains incidents, sayings, and parables related to feasts. Chapter 15 is made up of 3 parables of lostness (Lost Sheep, Coin, and Son). Chapter 16 is composed of parables and sayings dealing with the use and abuse of wealth, and chapter 18 begins with 2 parables relating to prayer (The Unjust Judge, and The Pharisee and Tax Collector). The total number of parables is debated because there is disagreement about whether some passages should be called parables, but usually somewhere between 60 and 65 is the number given for the total of Jesus'

recorded parables. Obviously the number depends on how broad a definition of parable is accepted.

A Summary of Jesus' Teaching in Parables. Most of Jesus' parables either directly or indirectly relate to the kingdom of God (or its synonym "the kingdom of heaven" in Mt). With "kingdom of God" Jesus was not referring to a political or geographical entity over which God was King but to the rule of God in fulfillment of the OT promises, the fact that God was actively ruling over and for his people. A great deal of debate has taken place over the intent of Jesus' proclamation about the kingdom. Some have argued that Jesus' preaching focused on a future kingdom that God would establish shortly. Others countered by stressing the emphasis on the presence of the kingdom in Jesus' ministry. Reasonable consensus has been achieved in recognizing that the solution is not in an either-or direction but in affirming that Jesus proclaimed the kingdom as both present and future. In

The Parables of Jesus

	Luke	Matthew	Mark
New cloth on old coat	5:36	9:16	2:21
New wine in used wineskins	5:37–38	9:17	2:22
Houses on rock and on sand	6:47–49	7:24–27	
The moneylender	7:41–43		
Sower and soils	8:5–8	13:3–8	4:3–8
Lamp under a bowl	8:16; 11:33	5:14–15	4:21–22
The Good Samaritan	10:30–37		
Friend in need	11:5–8		
Rich fool	12:16–21		
Watchful servants	12:35–40		
Faithful servant	12:42–48	24:45–51	
Unfruitful fig tree	13:6–9		
Mustard seed	13:18–19	13:31–32	4:30–32
Yeast	13:20–21	13:33	
Best places at a wedding banquet	14:7–14		
Great banquet and reluctant guests	14:16–24		
Cost of being a disciple	14:28–33		
Lost sheep	15:4–6	18:12–13	
Lost coin	15:8–10		
Lost son	15:11–32		
Shrewd manager	16:1–8		
Rich man and Lazarus	16:19–31		
Master and servant	17:7–10		
Persistent widow	18:2–5		
Pharisee and tax collector	18:10–14		
Pounds	19:12–27		
Tenants	20:9–16	21:33–41	12:1–9
Fig tree	21:29–32	24:32–33	13:28–29
Weeds		13:24–30	
Hidden treasure		13:44	
Pearl		13:45–46	
Net		13:47–48	
Unmerciful servant		18:23–34	
Workers in the vineyard		20:1–16	
Two sons		21:28–31	
Wedding banquet and garment		22:2–14	
Ten virgins		25:1–13	
Talents		25:14–30	
Sheep and goats		25:31–36	
Growing seed			4:26–29

fulfillment of the OT promises, God's active rule was inaugurated in a new and decisive way in the words and deeds of Jesus in order to defeat evil and establish justice and righteousness. This activity of God was present in Jesus' ministry as is evident by such passages as Matthew 12:28 ("But if I by the Spirit of God cast out demons then is the kingdom of God come upon you"). (See also Mt 11:2–15; 13:16–17; Lk 17:21.) At the same time Jesus' expectation of a future consummation of the OT promises, a time of ultimate blessing from God, is also evident in such passages as Matthew 8:11 ("And I tell you, many will come from the east and the west and shall sit at table with Abraham and Isaac and Jacob in the kingdom of heaven"). (See also Mt 24:4–31; 26:29; Lk 17:22–37.) Any discussion of Jesus' teaching on eschatology (the study of last things) or of the NT teaching on eschatology as a whole should include the emphasis on both present and future. The kingdom or rule of God has already broken in decisively in Jesus' ministry and will be brought to completion at a later time.

This same dual emphasis is reflected in the parables. The "seed" of the kingdom has already been sown. It receives both positive and negative responses, but an abundant harvest is assured. (Note the parables of the Sower and the Weeds in Matthew 13.) The proclamation of the kingdom has been given and requires radical action as can be seen in the parables of the Hidden Treasure and the Pearl (Mt 13). The Parable of the Strong Man (Mt 12:29 and pars) shows that Satan has been bound and his "house" is being spoiled by the ministry of Jesus. Several parables emphasize the growth of the kingdom from its small, inauspicious beginnings to a large and wide-reaching effect. (Note the parables of the Mustard Seed and of the Yeast in Mt 13.) Other parables stress the presence of the kingdom by assuming the operation of God's grace to accept sinners. Note the parables of the Workers in the Vineyard (Mt 20) and of the Two Sons with its emphasis on tax collectors and whores who are entering (present tense) the kingdom of heaven before the religious authorities (Mt 21). Still others carry the motif of the present kingdom by focusing on the celebration of God's people either generally or for the return of the lost. Note the feast parables in Luke 14 and the parables of the lost being found in Luke 15. The parables of the Weeds and of the Net (Mt 13) emphasize the presence of the kingdom even when external circumstances appear to deny the fact. They warn that people should not be misled because judgment and separation are not presently taking place.

At the same time numerous parables reflect the expectation of a future time when judgment takes place and the kingdom comes in its fullness. The Parable of the Fig Tree (Mk 13:28–29) is one of the most explicit in pointing to something that is still future (even though there is considerable debate about the time and fulfillment being discussed). Numerous parables point to the idea of judgment by telling of a king or master who returns to assess the activity of his servants. Note the Parable of the Talents in Matthew 25:14–30 (with its near par in Lk 19:12–27) or the collection of parabolic sayings in Luke 12:35–48 that focus on faithful and unfaithful servants and are applied to the time of the coming of the Son of Man. The Parable of the Ten Virgins in Matthew 25:1–12 and that of the Shut Door in Luke 13:24–27 also point to the expectation of a future kingdom.

This dual emphasis on the present and future aspects of the kingdom leads to other subjects that appear frequently in the parables, notably the conflict with the religious authorities and the call for an ethic suitable for the kingdom. The fact that Jesus is proclaiming the presence of the kingdom in his own ministry, the acceptance of sinners, and a righteousness that exceeds that of the religious authorities places him continually at odds with the Jewish leaders. It is here that his parables especially are "weapons of warfare." The parables of the Two Sons (Mt 21:28–30), the Good Samaritan (Lk 10:30–35), the Lost Sheep and Coin, especially the Lost Son (Lk 15), and the Pharisee and the Tax Collector (Lk 18:10–13) all stand as strong indictments of the attitudes and practices present among Jewish leaders of Jesus' day. An even stronger indictment comes in the Parable of the Wicked Tenants (Mt 21:33–39; Mk 12:1–9; Lk 20:9–16), which makes the authorities so angry that they want to arrest Jesus. Care should be taken not to assume that Jesus implies the rejection of Israel or that the kingdom has been taken from Israel. Even though the Parable of the Barren Fig Tree points to the unfruitfulness of Israel (Lk 13:6–9), Israel is not outrightly rejected. The passage that many have interpreted as the removal of the kingdom from Israel is Matthew 21:43, but this passage is clearly addressed to the religious authorities and not the people of Israel as a whole. As Paul argues strongly in Romans 9–11, God does not reject his people.

Obviously, the parables that speak against the religious authorities carry with them strong ethical messages as well. One cannot read the Parable of the Good Samaritan without realizing that the love for one's neighbor called for in the OT is a love so radical that it knows no limits or boundaries. This call of obedience to God is a continual theme in the parables. The Parable of the Wise and Foolish Builders (Mt 7:24–27; Lk 6:46–49) refers to those who hear Jesus' words and do them as opposed to those who hear and do not obey. The little parable in Luke 17:7–9 stresses that after we have done all that is commanded we should say, "We are unworthy servants; we have only done what was our duty." The Parable of the Unforgiving Servant (Mt 18:23–34) shows that the love and mercy of God toward his people is to be reflected by his people toward others. The most frequent theme in the area of ethics is faithfulness. All of the parables referring to an absentee owner call for faithfulness. In the Parable of the Talents (Mt 25:14–30) faithfulness is the criterion used for judging the servants. It is saying occasional or past obedience is not sufficient. One is required to live continually in the present because of the coming kingdom. The parables do not ask "What have you done?" but "What kind of person are you?" The answer to that question will determine whether real obedience is given.

An additional theme related to ethics is the use and abuse of wealth. The Parable of the Rich Fool in Luke 12:16–20 emphasizes that life does not consist in the abundance of possessions. The man is a fool because he has focused his life on material "things" rather than on his relation to God. The Parable of the Rich Man and Lazarus also shows further abuse of wealth and carries with it condemnation for the neglect of the poor. Several other parables breathe a concern for the poor even though they do not deal with the theme of riches. Note the Parable of the Unjust Judge in Luke 18:2–5 and the Parable of the Unforgiving Servant in Matthew 18:23–34. The ultimate challenge to obedience and concern for the poor is expressed in the Parable of the Sheep and Goats in Matthew 25:32–46, in which eternal judgment is made on the basis of whether one has responded to the needs of the poor!

The last theme that will be mentioned is prayer. The Parable of the Pharisee and the Tax Collector (Lk 18:10–13) indicate wrong and right attitudes in prayer. The other parables that relate to prayer focus on the God who answers prayer, rather than on how one should pray. It is true that the introduction of the Parable of the Unjust Judge (Lk 18:1–8) mentions not tiring in prayer, but the point of the parable is that God is *not* like the unjust judge; rather, as verse 8 indicates, he will bring justice for his people *quickly*. Similarly the Parable of the Friend at Midnight seems to indicate that if a friend will respond to a request, how much more will God respond (note Lk 11:5–8,13).

Other themes are present in the parables, but like the ones mentioned they reveal what God is like, how he acts, and what he expects of his people. Like the Sermon on the Mount, the parables of Jesus are frequently disconcerting. They confront and force reconsideration of our thinking, but where proper attention is given to their message they create new lives by bringing God's vitality and reality to our existence. KLYNE R. SNODGRASS

See JESUS CHRIST, LIFE AND TEACHING OF; KINGDOM OF GOD (HEAVEN).

Bibliography. W. Arnot, *Parables of Our Lord;* C.H. Dodd, *The Parables of the Kingdom;* A.M. Hunter, *Interpreting the Parables;* J. Jeremias, *The Parables of Jesus;* S.J. Kistemaker, *The Parables of Jesus;* R.H. Stein, *An Introduction to the Parables of Jesus.*

Paraclete. Transliteration of a Greek word meaning "one who is called to someone's aid" or "one who advocates another." Thus the term may be used technically for a lawyer. More generally the word denotes one who acts in another's behalf as a mediator, an intercessor, or a comforter. In 1 John 2:1 Christ is called a paraclete as he represents people to God. This function is akin to his ministry as high priest (cf. Heb 7:25–28).

The most numerous uses of paraclete come in John's Gospel, all referring to the work of the Holy Spirit (Jn 14:16,26; 15:26; 16:13). In these passages Jesus declares that the Holy Spirit will come from the Father when he departs. The paraclete, also called "the Spirit of truth," will lead them into all truth and aid them in their ability to recall correctly Jesus' message. He is to become their special replacement for the departed Lord.

See HOLY SPIRIT.

Paradise. "Garden of God." The Hebrews originally used a word which they applied not only to ordinary gardens but also to God's garden in Eden (Gn 2,3; Is 51:3; Ez 28:13). Comparatively late in their history, they adapted from the Persian language the word which afterwards became "paradise"; it appears three times in the OT referring to a park or orchard (Neh 2:8; Eccl 2:5; Sg 4:13). Later still, when the OT was translated into Greek, there was a Greek form of the same word, and the translators used it extensively for "garden"; for Greek-speaking Jews, the garden of Genesis 2 became *paradeisos*.

The idea of the original Persian word was that of an enclosure or walled garden. It referred particularly to the royal parks of the Persian kings and this was how the Greeks came to know it. Both ideas fit well with the Hebrews' picture of a garden where the Lord God walked (Gn 3:8) and from which his subjects could be excluded (Gn 3:24). Further important features of the Genesis paradise were its fruit trees and its rivers.

By NT times this picture of God's garden had developed in various ways, which are paralleled, not unexpectedly, in the folk-beliefs of many nations. Like the Golden Age of Greek and Roman mythology, paradise was first of all something belonging to the remote past. But the Jews came to believe that it still existed in some undiscoverable place; like the Elysian Fields, it was inhabited by the deserving dead. Then, with ever more elaborate descriptions of its glories, they wrote of its eventual reappearance at the end of this age.

Thus, in the idea of paradise converge all myths of another world, past, present, and future, where death and evil have no place. The NT witnesses to the truth which is at the core of all such beliefs. Paradise is the place into which, as an actual but otherworldly reality, Paul was once mysteriously "caught up" during his lifetime (2 Cor 12:3). It is also the place where the penitent thief on the cross was promised he would be, with Christ, immediately after his death (Lk 23:43). The third and last NT reference, a similar promise (Rv 2:7), tells us in addition that paradise is where the tree of life grows, and so identifies it both with the original world of Genesis 2 and with the future world of Revelation 22, complete with the life-giving tree and river, the encircling wall, and the presence of the King.

See HEAVEN; NEW HEAVENS AND NEW EARTH.

Paradox. Form of expression which seems to be either self-contradictory or absurd, but which at another level expresses fundamental truth. It is often employed to get hearers to think at a deeper and more critical level. It may often be closely related to hyperbole, an exaggerated statement, except that for the paradox there is an apparent element of contradiction, which arrests attention and almost demands consideration.

In the ministry of Jesus one finds it in such expressions as grown persons being born again. "Can a man enter a second time into his mother's womb," Nicodemus asks, "and be born?" (Jn 3:4) Or again in response to the attempts of rich men to enter the kingdom Jesus says that it is easier for a camel to go through the eye of a needle (an impossibility) than for a rich man to enter the kingdom (Mk 10:25). The point is not to focus on the literal statement or take it word for word, but to understand its essential purpose. In this instance it is a form of "shock treatment" to force the wealthy to see how their attitudes toward wealth have excluded them from the kingdom.

Much of the use of paradox in Jesus' ministry has to do with his attempts to show that the perspective, or value system, of the kingdom represents a complete reversal of the values by which people live. Whosoever will lose his life will find it (Mt 10:39). The last shall be first, and the first last (Lk 13:30). Whoever would be greatest of all must be servant of all (Mk 10:43; Lk 22:26). Indeed, the servant ministry of Jesus himself underscores this great reversal of the kingdom. After washing the feet of the disciples Jesus says, "You call me teacher and master, and rightly so. And if I, your master and teacher, wash your feet, you ought also to do the same" (Jn 13:13,14).

Paradox also enters Christian expression when one attempts to speak of God in the language of men. Thus God is "before all time." Even "God in flesh" is paradoxical, yet profoundly true. People inevitably and of necessity speak of God in terms of their own experience, yet God cannot be limited by such experience or language, for he is infinitely greater. Hence language is a limited instrument for speaking of him who is not limited.

Parah. City belonging to Benjamin's inheritance (Jos 18:23). It is undoubtedly Khirbet el-Farah, approximately 5½ miles northeast of Jerusalem.

Paralysis, Paralytic. Symptom of an organic disease of the central nervous system affecting the temporary or permanent loss of sensation and/or voluntary muscle control. This degenerative condition was usually incurable. A few cases of paralysis (palsy) are mentioned in the NT, all of which occur in connection with Christ's healing ministry.

Paralytics were included in the group of ailing people seeking Jesus' healing in Galilee (Mt 4:24), numbered among the sick at Bethesda in Jerusalem (Jn 5:3), and represented among those cured by Philip in Samaria (Acts 8:7). The paralyzed servant of the centurion was described by Luke as very sick and at the point of death (Lk 7:2). This man was probably victimized by an often fatal form of paralysis which begins in the legs and spreads rapidly upward through the rest of the body. The paralytic at Capernaum was most likely ailing from paraplegia, a paralysis of the lower half of the body (Mt 9:2,6; Mk 2:3–10; Lk 5:18,24). This disease may have been brought on by an injury at birth or by damage to the spinal cord. Perhaps Aeneas, whom Peter healed at Lydda, also suffered from paraplegia (Acts 9:33).

See DISEASE; MEDICINE AND MEDICAL PRACTICE.

Paran. Desert region in the northeast Sinai Peninsula west of the Arabah (Rift Valley). The settlement of Kadesh-barnea is its northernmost limit. Some scholars identify the great Et-Tih plateau of the central Sinai as a part of this wilderness. It is difficult, however, to fix the southern and western limits with precision from the biblical evidence.

The wilderness of Paran is a wild, arid expanse of tableland, mountains, gorges, and wadis. The lack of water and vegetation made it a most inhospitable place and a stark contrast to the land flowing with milk and honey which was promised to Israel.

This wilderness became the home of Ishmael (Gn 21:21). The nation of Israel camped there on the way from Egypt to Canaan (Nm 10:12; 12:16). From Kadesh-barnea at the northern edge of the wilderness, Moses sent spies to reconnoiter the Promised Land (Nm 13:3,26).

David is said to have led his band of men to this region after the death of Samuel to be out of the range of King Saul (1 Sm 25:1). A textual problem emerges at this point. The Greek translation of 1 Samuel 25:1 reads "wilderness of Maon." This was probably the reading of the original Hebrew manuscript. The wilderness of Maon was the mountainous area around the village of Maon just south of Hebron, where David had sought refuge previously (1 Sm 23:24,25) and where Nabak lived. It is unlikely that David would have traveled so far to the south as to reach the wilderness of Paran. There he would not have had contact with Nabal's shepherds. It is probable that a copyist accidentally substituted Paran for Maon.

El-paran (Gn 14:6) is the name of a location, perhaps an oasis near the head of the Gulf of Aqaba, which marked the limit of Chedorlaomer's conquest of Edom. It was "on the border of the wilderness" (of Paran) and situated on the caravan route to Egypt. This is probably the Paran of Deuteronomy 1:1. Hadad the Edomite passed through this location on his way from Edom to Egypt (1 Kgs 11:18).

Mt Paran should not be considered as an actual mountain or range of mountains (Dt 33:2; Hb 3:3). In both instances it serves as a poetic allusion to the appearance of God's power and majesty at Mt Sinai.

See PALESTINE; SINAI, SINA; WILDERNESS WANDERINGS.

Parapet. Protective barrier around the circumference of house roofs. The parapet was required by the Law (Dt 22:8) since flat roofs were widely used (Jos 2:6; Jgs 16:27; 1 Sm 9:25; Is 22:1). Construction of a parapet would relieve the dweller from liability should a person fall from the roof.

See HOMES AND DWELLINGS; ARCHITECTURE.

Parbar. Room or uncovered area of the courtyard in the temple complex (1 Chr 26:18).

See TABERNACLE, TEMPLE.

Parchment. *See* WRITING AND BOOKS.

Pardon. *See* FORGIVENESS.

Parent. *See* FAMILY LIFE AND RELATIONS.

Parmashta. One of the 10 sons of Haman slain by the Jews (Est 9:9).

Parmenas. One of the 7 men "full of the Spirit and of wisdom" chosen by the Jerusalem church to minister to the widows (Acts 6:5).

Parnach. Elizaphan's father from Zebulun's tribe (Nm 34:25).

Parosh. Head of a family that returned to Jerusalem with Zerubbabel after the Babylonian exile (Ezr 2:3; 8:3, KJV Pharosh; Neh 7:8). One of his descendants, Pedaiah, participated in rebuilding the Jerusalem wall (Neh 3:25); other descendants are mentioned as having taken foreign wives (Ezr 10:25).

Parousia. Transliteration of a Greek word meaning "presence," "arrival," "appearance," or "coming." While it is used often with reference to men (1 Cor 16:17; 2 Cor 7:6; 10:10; Phil 1:26; 2:12) and once with reference to the antichrist (2 Thes 2:9), the word is employed most frequently with reference to Christ (Mt 24:3,27, 37,39; 1 Cor 15:23; 1 Thes 2:19; 3:13; 4:15; 5:23; 2 Thes 2:1,8). Consequently, the Parousia has come to denote the second coming of Christ at the end of the ages.

Paul, who was probably responsible for the technical emphasis on Christ's return, while rejecting all attempts to calculate the time (1 Thes 5:1,2; 2 Thes 2:2,3; cf. Mt 24:4–36), nonetheless paints a vivid picture of the Parousia (1 Thes 4:13–18; 2 Thes 1:7–2:8; see also 1 Cor 15:20–28,50–55). According to his teaching, it will be a personal, visible, sudden, and glorious coming (1 Cor 15:23; 1 Thes 2:19; 3:13; 4:15–17). Though apparently he felt he and his readers would experience Christ's return (1 Thes 4:15; cf. Rom 8:23; 13:11), his approaching martyrdom caused him to moderate his thinking (Phil 1:23). James, also sensing the delay in Christ's return, calls for patience (Jas 5:7,8). Peter, too, cautions against allowing the delay to create doubt (2 Pt 3:8–10). The message is not myth (2 Pt 1:16), and scoffers will be silenced (2 Pt 3:3,4). John encourages consistent faith lest the believer be put to shame at his coming (1 Jn 2:28).

See SECOND COMING OF CHRIST; ESCHATOLOGY.

Parshandatha. One of the 10 sons of Haman slain by the Jews (Est 9:7).

Parsin. Aramaic word interpreted as "divided" (Dn 5:25,28).

See MENE, MENE, TEKEL, PARSIN.

Parthia, Parthians. Land (roughly corresponding to modern Iran) lying beyond the eastern boundaries of the Roman Empire, and so almost outside the world of the NT.

It is included, however, in maps of the OT world, which generally encompass eastern territory. Many Jews deported from Palestine after the Assyrian and Babylonian invasions were living in this area when in the 6th century BC it became part of the vast Persian Empire of Cyrus, and thousands stayed on in spite of Cyrus' offer of repatriation. Two centuries afterwards that empire was conquered by Alexander the Great, but 100 years later several parts of it, including Parthia, threw off the yoke of his successors and became independent.

Parthia eventually became a great empire, stretching from the Euphrates to the Indus. In the NT period, even mighty Rome regarded it as a potential threat. The first confrontation between the two powers actually resulted in a defeat for the Romans (at Carrhae, the biblical Haran, in 53 BC). Only in the 2nd century AD did the balance shift, and even then, though twice annexed, Parthia twice recovered its independence. It fell eventually in AD 226, not to the Romans, but to a neo-Persian coup within its own borders.

Wealthy because of their position astride Asian trade routes, and militarily strong because of their famous mounted bowmen, who won many a battle by apparently retreating and then shooting at the pursuing enemy (hence the phrase parting, or "Parthian," shot), the Parthians seem also to have been a tolerant people. A large Jewish community continued to live among them, and at the time of Pentecost (Acts 2) their province of Babylonia had, curiously, a Jewish governor. More important, Jews from Parthia, and possibly also Parthian converts to Judaism ("proselytes"), were in Jerusalem on that epoch-making day (Acts 2:9). By them the gospel may have been taken, within weeks of the resurrection, well on its way to India.

Partridge. See BIRDS.

Paruah. Father of Jehoshaphat from Issachar's tribe. Jehoshaphat was appointed to provide food for King Solomon and his household one month out of the year (1 Kgs 4:7,17).

Parvaim. Geographical area from which Solomon obtained gold for use in the temple (2 Chr 3:6). According to rabbinic sources the gold had a reddish hue, and was used to make the vessel with which the high priest removed the ashes from the altar of burnt offering on the Day of Atonement. Parvaim was probably located in Arabia.

Pasach. Japhlet's son from Asher's tribe (1 Chr 7:33).

Pas-dammim. Alternate form of Ephes-dammim, a place in Judah's tribe, in 1 Chronicles 11:13.

See EPHES-DAMMIM.

Paseah. 1. Eshton's son, the brother of Beth-rapha and a descendant of Chelub from Judah's tribe. Paseah was mentioned as one of the men of Recah (1 Chr 4:12).

2. Ancestor of a family of temple servants who returned to Palestine with Zerubbabel after the Babylonian captivity (Ezr 2:49; Neh 7:51, KJV Phaseah).

3. Joiada's father. Joiada, along with Meshullam, repaired the Old Gate of Jerusalem under Nehemiah's direction during the post-exilic period (Neh 3:6).

Pashhur, Pashur. Common OT name, spelled Pashur in the KJV.

1. Forefather of a family of priests who returned to Jerusalem with Zerubbabel after the exile (Ezr 2:38; Neh 7:41). He was perhaps also the son of Malchijah and the grandfather of Adaiah the priest. Adaiah served in the sanctuary during the postexilic period (1 Chr 9:12). Six of Pashhur's sons were encouraged by Ezra to divorce their foreign wives (Ezr 10:22).

2. One of the priests who with Nehemiah set his seal on the covenant of Ezra (Neh 10:3).

3. Immer's son and the priest and chief officer of the sanctuary during the reign of King Zedekiah of Judah (597–586 BC). Frustrated with Jeremiah's predictions of doom for Jerusalem, Pashhur beat him and had him put in stocks at the temple's Benjamin Gate. Upon his release, Jeremiah exposed Pashhur's false prophecies and foretold his exile and death in Babylon (Jer 20:1–6).

4. Son of Malchijah and perhaps the grandson of King Zedekiah of Judah (597–586 BC; Jer 21:1; 38:1; cf. 38:6). The king sent Pashhur, with Zephaniah the priest, to Jeremiah re-

questing that he ask the Lord to deal favorably with Judah. It was in his father's cistern that Jeremiah was imprisoned (Jer 38:6).

5. Father of Gedaliah. Gedaliah with Shephatiah, Jucal, and Pashhur opposed Jeremiah and attempted to kill him by imprisoning him in Malchiah's cistern (Jer 38:1).

Passover. Important Jewish festival celebrating Israel's redemption from Egypt.

See FEASTS AND FESTIVALS OF ISRAEL; MEALS, SIGNIFICANCE OF.

Pastor. Word literally meaning "shepherd," used in both the OT and NT in a figurative sense for rulers and leaders. Of the 12 times the word is used in the NT as a metaphor for "leader," it is translated as "pastor" only in Ephesians 4:11 (KJV, RSV, NIV, TEV, ASV).

The NT imagery comes from an OT and Palestinian background. In the Jewish economy, the shepherd who tended a flock of sheep or goats held a responsible position. Great flocks had to be moved from place to place, and it was necessary that they be guarded from wild animals and robbers. Because of the fundamental role of shepherding in the ancient world, the word "shepherd" became a common term for a ruler. The kings of Assyria, Babylon, and Egypt were often referred to as shepherds who protected their people. This imagery formed the background for the OT, where the same usage is found. God is pictured as the shepherd of Israel, concerned for every aspect of his people's welfare. Rulers and leaders of the people are often referred to as shepherds (cf., e.g., Nm 27:17; 1 Kgs 22:17; Jer 10:21; 12:10; 22:22; 23:1,2).

By the time of Jeremiah, "shepherd" begins to be used as a title for the coming Messiah. God himself undertakes to provide for his flock (Jer 23:3; 31:10; Ez 34:11–22) and promises to provide faithful shepherds who are concerned for his people (Jer 3:15; 23:4). He explicitly promises that he will be their God and will set the Messianic Son of David as shepherd over them (Ez 34:23,24).

The OT imagery continues in the NT. God is pictured as a shepherd concerned for his sheep (Lk 15:4–7), and Jesus refers to himself as the promised Messianic Shepherd (Mt 10:16; 25:32; Mk 14:27; Jn 10:1–30; cf. Heb 13:20; 1 Pt 2:25). Ephesians 4:11 (LB) speaks of leaders of the church as shepherds or pastors, and this usage continued in the early church and down until the present day. Paul says they are special people given to the church by God to care "for God's people as a shepherd does his sheep, leading and teaching them in the ways of God."

Pastors and teachers together formed a group which complemented the work of apostles, prophets, and evangelists. The titles "bishop" and "elder" refer to the same office in the NT (cf. Acts 20:17,28; Ti 1:5,7), and "pastor" seems to be practically synonymous with them, as shown by Jesus being referred to as "the Shepherd and Bishop of your souls" (1 Pt 2:25 KJV). The verb "to shepherd" is used to describe the work of local church leaders (Jn 21:16; Acts 20:28; 1 Pt 5:2), and often the congregation is called a flock. It is the pastor's responsibility to build up the body of Christ by watching over the congregation (Acts 20:28; Heb 13:7) and countering false teaching (Acts 20:29,30). More detailed information regarding the duties and responsibilities of pastors is found in Paul's letters to Timothy and Titus, which have come to be called the "pastoral letters."

See BISHOP; ELDER; DEACON, DEACONESS; PRESBYTER; SPIRITUAL GIFTS.

Pastoral Letters. Descriptive phrase used in modern biblical study to designate the letters known as 1 and 2 Timothy and Titus. In Christian tradition these three writings have been grouped together since the 2nd century. They are addressed to individuals rather than to churches. The benediction at the end of each letter assumes a group of readers, however. In general, the letters offer advice to their recipients about church order, false doctrine, leadership standards, and pastoral oversight of church life.

See TIMOTHY, FIRST LETTER TO; TIMOTHY, SECOND LETTER TO; TITUS, LETTER TO; PAUL, THE APOSTLE.

Patara. Seaport of the ancient region of Lycia, now located in modern Turkey. The ancient city, one of the largest and most prosperous of the region, was a center of trade and commerce. A temple to Apollo stood in Patara. Remains of a theater and baths can still be seen. Prevailing winds made Patara a convenient place for ships to begin their voyages to the eastern Mediterranean. The apostle Paul changed ships at Patara on his final journey to Jerusalem (Acts 21:1,2).

Pathros. Region mentioned five times in the Hebrew OT and only in the Prophets (Is 11:11; Jer 44:1,15; Ez 29:14; 30:14). Each time it occurs in conjunction with a city in lower Egypt (Noph=Memphis or Zoan=Tanis) in connection with Egypt. The Hebrew (*Pathros*) and the Greek (*pathoure*) words are borrowings of the Egyptian *pa to resy* ("the Southern Land"—the exact pronunciation is uncertain). Egyptologists believe that the Hebrew form is a corruption of *Pethoris* or *Pethores*.

Esar-haddon claimed to be king of Muṣur (Heb: Misrayim for Egypt), Paturisi (Pathros), and Kūsi (Heb: Kush, Cush). The sequence in Isaiah 11:11 (NIV) follows the threefold division of the Assyrian text, "In that day the Lord will reach out his hand a second time to reclaim the remnant that is left of his people from Assyria, from Lower Egypt [KJV Egypt], from Upper Egypt [KJV Pathros], from Cush, from Elam, from Babylonia, from Hamath and from the islands of the sea." Both texts suggest that *Misrayim* is to be equated with Lower and Middle Egypt and *Pathros* is the region south of it up to the border of Cush (i.e., Upper Egypt). According to Ezekiel 29:14, Pathros is the original home of the Egyptians. The prophets spoke about God's judgment on Pathros, "I will lay Pathros waste, set fire to Zoan and inflict punishment on Thebes" (Ez 30:14 NIV). After the exile, Jews migrated to Egypt and some settled in Pathros. Jeremiah warned that God's judgment on Egypt was to come and that they would not escape it: "This word came to Jeremiah concerning all the Jews living in Lower Egypt—in Migdol, Tahpanhes and Memphis—and in Upper Egypt [KJV Pathros]: This is what the Lord Almighty, the God of Israel, says: You saw the great disaster I brought on Jerusalem and on all the towns of Judah. Today they lie deserted and in ruins" (Jer 44:1,2; cf. v 15 NIV).

Pathrusim. Inhabitants of Pathros, a region of southern Egypt (Gn 10:14; 1 Chr 1:12).

See PATHROS.

Patience. Ability to take a great deal of punishment from evil people or circumstances without losing one's temper, without becoming irritated and angry, or without taking vengeance. It includes the capacity to bear pain or trials without complaint, the ability to forbear under severe provocation, and the self-control which keeps one from acting rashly even though suffering opposition or adversity.

The usual Hebrew expression for patience is related to the verb "to be long" and involves the idea of being long to get riled or slow to become angry. Two different Greek words are translated by KJV translators with the word "patience." One of the words has the idea of "remaining firm under" tests and trials and is better translated "endurance" or "steadfastness." The other Greek word is related to the above Hebrew meaning and refers to patience as "long-spiritedness" or "calmness of spirit" even though under severe provocation to lose one's temper.

The great biblical illustration of patience in operation is God himself. Several passages speak of him, in conjunction with other gracious attributes, as "slow to anger." In a context which stresses Israel's rebellion and provocation of God, he is contrasted as a God who is forgiving, gracious, compassionate, slow to anger, and abounding in lovingkindness (Neh 9:17). The psalmist declares, "Thou, O Lord, art a God merciful and gracious, slow to anger and abounding in steadfast love and faithfulness" (Ps 86:15; see also Ex 34:6; Nm 14:18; Ps 103:8; Jl 2:13; Jon 4:2). In addition, the virtue of a patient spirit on the part of mankind is extolled in the OT, especially in Proverbs (14:29; 15:18; 16:32; 25:15; see also Eccl 7:8).

The NT also stresses the patience of the Lord. It is God's kindness, forbearance and patience that lead people to repentance (Rom 2:4). This attribute of God is seen clearly in his patient enduring of Pharaoh who fitted himself for destruction (Rom 9:22). God was patient in holding off the flood for the sinners of Noah's day while the ark was being built, thereby giving more time for repentance (1 Pt 3:20). Probably the greatest of the NT references to God's patience is in 2 Peter 3:9. The delay in Christ's return is not an indication of slowness on God's part, says Peter, but of his long-suffering, not being willing that anyone should perish. A specific reference to Jesus Christ's patience is made by Paul who claimed that, in his case, Jesus was able to demonstrate perfect patience (1 Tm 1:16).

Patience then, which is an attribute of our God and of our Lord Jesus Christ, is also to characterize each Christian. Paul's prayer for the Colossians is that they might demonstrate this quality (Col 1:11). It is one of the fruits of the Spirit (Gal 5:22), an attribute of love (1 Cor 13:4), and a virtue (Col 3:12; see also 2 Tm 3:10). In addition, Christians are exhorted to be patient (1 Thes 5:14). If we are not, we will be treated as the slave in the parable which Jesus told. This slave pleaded with his lord, to whom he owed a great sum, for patience, promising to pay all. The lord was patient and forgave all the debt, until he found out that the slave had refused to show the same patience to a fellow servant who owed him a pittance in comparison (Mt 18:26–29).

In some contexts, the word "patience" takes on the more general meaning of waiting long and expectantly for something. The farmer waits patiently for the crop to come (Jas 5:7b). Abraham waited patiently for God's promise to give him the land of Canaan to be fulfilled and died without seeing what was promised, although still believing (Heb 6:15; 11:39). Finally, all Christians are commanded

The Isle of Patmos.

to be longsuffering until the coming of the Lord (Jas 5:7a).

See FRUIT OF THE SPIRIT.

Patmos. Small island in the Aegean Sea, located about 35 miles west of the city of Miletus off the coast of Asia Minor. Patmos is about 10 miles long and 6 miles wide at its northern end, and consists of rocky volcanic hills.

In Revelation 1:9 John says that he was on the island of Patmos "on account of the word of God and the testimony of Jesus." He also indicates that he is a fellow participant in their "tribulations." The Roman historian Tacitus informs us that the Romans used some of the Aegean islands as places of banishment and exile during the 1st century (*Annals*, 3:68;4:30;15:71). Thus the language of the author and the evidence of Tacitus, joined to Christian traditions from the 2nd and 3rd centuries about John's banishment, support the likelihood that Patmos was a place of exile or political confinement.

In a time when the Asian churches were undergoing persecution, John wrote to them from this island. He addressed each of seven churches by means of a letter of encouragement and warning. The series of letters is followed by the author's account of the divinely sent vision of impending judgment which "must soon take place" (Rv 22:6). Patmos, then, was the location from which this NT writing originated.

Patriarchs, Period of the. Period of time during which the biblical fathers of Israel lived. The Bible tells of long-lived patriarchs before the flood (Gn 1–5); of Noah (Gn 6–9); and of a line of patriarchs after the flood (Gn 10,11). However, the word in the narrower sense usually refers to Abraham, Isaac, and Jacob (Gn 12–36), with the addition of Joseph (Gn 37–50).

Date. Exact dating of the patriarchs is difficult because, apart from the kings mentioned in Genesis 14:1,2, we do not have any fixed ex-

ternal point of reference from which to calculate. While this chapter does refer to historical persons and places, we cannot identify with certainty any one of the kings. The Italian excavators of Tell Mardikh (ancient Ebla) have reported finding the names of the "Cities of the Plain" of Genesis 14:2 (whose destruction is reported in Gn 19) and even the name of one of their kings on the clay tablets excavated. These clay tablets seem to date from well before 2000 BC, which is too early for Abraham; all that they would prove is that the cities were in existence long before his time. What we can say is that the patriarchs must have belonged to the Middle Bronze Age, probably early in the 2nd millennium BC, and that this was the general period of the Amorite "drift" into Palestine from the north and the west. The most usual modern view is that the Amorite migration was in two "waves," the earlier one being seminomadic (like Abraham's friends, Aner, Eshcol, and Mamre, Gn 14:13) and the second and later wave, probably from Syria in the north, being urbanizers and settlers (the group usually described as "the Amorites" in the catalog of the various races in Canaan, e.g., Ex 3:8). The society of the time of the patriarchs has been described as "dimorphic," or twofold. On the one hand, there were the city communities, while on the other were open village settlements and seminomadic tribes that at times were loosely grouped around the towns, and at times drifted away from them. It is against this sort of background that we must imagine the patriarchs. Joseph of course lived in the fully settled world of Egypt, but Scripture does not give us the name of the pharaoh of his day.

Parallels. While we have no direct historical references to the patriarchs outside the Bible, we do have much material illustrating their culture and customs. Texts from the Amorite culture of Mari, a Mesopotamian town of the 19th century BC, and texts from the Hurrian city of Nuzi (also in Mesopotamia) and the north Canaanite city of Ugarit (15th–13th centuries BC) are the best known. Excavations have shown that at least some of the names in Abraham's family tree also appear as the names of "clan villages" in the general area of Haran. Personal names similar in form to those of the patriarchs occur widely among Semitic-speaking peoples during this millennium and the next. The whole general impression is therefore that the patriarchal stories are set against a strongly historical background, even if we cannot pinpoint the men themselves at any one particular moment of history.

Range. For such an early period, and seeing that it is really only the chronicle of one family, the patriarchal history has a remarkable geographic and climatic range, covering many hundreds of miles of varied country. It begins at Ur, an old Sumerian city on the Persian Gulf at one extreme end of the "Fertile Crescent." Then the center of interest moves far to the northwest, to Haran on the Balikh River, between the Tigris and the Euphrates Rivers in their upper courses. Then the action sweeps far southwest to Palestine; but twice the interest moves back to Haran, and twice it goes into the Egyptian delta. This is truly history on a wide canvas. Even when in Palestine, there is no fixed quiet center of life. The patriarchs are endlessly on the move, backwards and forwards, mostly along the north-south mountain spine, but sometimes also in the coastal plain and even in Transjordan. Nor is there steady development; some groups slip away from the seminomadic life to join the city cultures (like Lot in Gn 13:12) while others melt back into the desert or semidesert (like Ishmael in Gn 25:18, or Esau in Gn 36:6–8). Yet always at the center the life of the patriarchs goes on. What was this life, and what is its theological message for us today?

Importance. It is impossible to exaggerate the importance of the place of the patriarchs in God's gradually unfolding plan of redemption. The process that is to culminate in the coming of Christ begins with Abraham (Jn 8:56). This is not, of course, to deny that in a more general sense, God's plan of salvation begins to unfold in the opening chapters of Genesis. But, in a more special way, God's particular revelation begins with the call of Abraham (Gn 12:1–3) and continues, with ever increasing clarity, through the lives of the other patriarchs. It is no accident that the Bible speaks of God as the God of Abraham, Isaac, and Jacob, even at the moment when a further revelation is about to be made to Moses (Ex 3:6). This is because the revelation made to the earlier patriarchs is the foundation of all that follows; indeed, we in the New Covenant look back to Abraham as our "father" too (Rom 4:16).   R. Alan Cole

See Chronology, Old Testament; Israel, History of; Abraham; Isaac; Jacob #1; Joseph #1.

Patrimony. Inheritance from a father or ancestor (Dt 18:8).

See Heir; Inheritance.

Patrobas. One of the Christians in Rome to whom Paul sent greetings (Rom 16:14).

Pau. City located in Edom, in which King Hadar reigned (Gn 36:39); alternately called Pai in 1 Chronicles 1:50.

Paul, The Apostle.   Known as Saul of Tarsus before his conversion to Christianity and the most influential leader in the early days of the Christian church. Through his missionary journeys to Asia Minor and Europe, Paul was the primary instrument in the expansion of the gospel to the Gentiles. Moreover, his letters to various churches and individuals contain the most thorough and deliberate theological formulations of the NT.

Most of the biographical material available comes from the Book of Acts. Though modern critics question the reliability of this narrative, there is every good reason to use it as the basis for outlining Paul's life. Moreover, the teachings of Paul, as set forth in his letters, are best summarized within the historical framework provided by the Acts narrative.

Background and Conversion. *Date of Birth.* Little is known of Paul's life prior to the events discussed in Acts. He is first mentioned in chapter 7 in connection with the execution of Stephen. According to verse 58, "the witnesses laid their clothes at the feet of a young man named Saul." The term "young man" probably indicates someone in his 20s, though this is uncertain.

The events mentioned in Acts 7 may have occurred as early as AD 31 if Jesus' death took place during the Passover of AD 30. On the other hand, if Jesus' death is dated in the year 33 then those events could have taken place no earlier than 34, but no later than 37. (Second Cor 11:32,33 states that when Paul escaped from Damascus that city was being ruled by the Nabataean king Aretas, who died in the year 40. Since, according to Gal 1:17,18, Paul left Damascus three years after his conversion, the year 37 must be regarded as the latest possible date for Stephen's death.)

Using the year 34 as an approximate date for the time when Saul is described as a "young man," and assuming that Saul was no older than 30 years at that time, then it can be concluded his birth took place no earlier than AD 4. And since it is very unlikely that he was younger than 20, AD 14 can be set as the latest possible date for his birth. This conclusion is supported by the knowledge that Paul studied under the famous Gamaliel I (Acts 22:3), who according to some scholars became a member of the Sanhedrin about AD 20. If Paul was 15 years old when he entered the school, the range of AD 4–14 for his birth fits all the information available. So it can be said with a degree of accuracy that Saul was born in the city of Tarsus about AD 9, but any estimates about his age should allow a leeway of 5 years either way.

Upbringing.   The city of Tarsus was a major population center in the province of Cilicia

Paul, The Apostle

A scene from Asia Minor, the location of Paul's birth (Tarsus) and much of his ministry.

in the southeastern region of Asia Minor. Lying on a significant commercial route, Tarsus felt the influence of current cultural movements, particularly Stoic philosophy. It is difficult to determine to what extent Greek thought affected Paul as a child. There is a possibility that his family had become "Hellenized"–after all, Paul was born a Roman citizen (it is not know how his father or ancestors acquired citizenship, though military or other notable service is a strong possibility); accordingly, he was given not only a Hebrew name (*Shaul*) but also a Roman cognomen (*Paulus*, though some have argued that he adopted this Roman name at a later point). At any rate, the fact that in his letters he shows great ease in relating to Gentiles suggests that he obtained a Greek education while in Tarsus.

On the other hand, he describes himself as one "circumcised on the eighth day, of the people of Israel, of the tribe of Benjamin, a Hebrew born of Hebrews" (Phil 3:5), and such a characterization, particularly the last phrase, perhaps served to distinguish him from those Jews in the Dispersion who freely adopted Greek ways. Moreover, according to Acts 22:3, he was actually brought up in Jerusalem (possibly in his sister's house, cf. Acts 23:16), and some scholars infer from that statement that Paul was brought up in a totally Jewish environment from earliest childhood.

It is worthwhile pointing out that Gamaliel is represented in later rabbinic literature as a teacher who had considerable appreciation for Greek culture. Besides, soon after his conversion, Paul spent at least 10 years ministering in Tarsus and its environs (cf. Acts 9:30; Gal 1:21; 2:1; see below). These questions are interesting for more than historical reasons. One of the most basic issues debated among modern interpreters of Paul is whether he should be viewed primarily as a Greek or as a Hebrew. The latter position has, with good reason, become more and more prominent, but the strong Hellenistic elements that formed part

of the apostle's total character should not be overlooked.

From Pharisaism to Christianity. In addition to the statement in Philippians 3:5, Paul makes some biographical comments in Galatians 1:13,14: "For you have heard of my previous way of life in Judaism, how intensely I persecuted the church of God and tried to destroy it. I was advancing in Judaism beyond many Jews of my own age and was extremely zealous for the traditions of my fathers." It is clear that Paul had made a total religious commitment to his Pharisaic heritage. But what precisely did that mean? The difficulty in answering that question arises from two problems. One is the issue of how 1st-century Pharisaism should be characterized; the other is the debate that has raged over the relation between Paul's religious background and his conversion to Christianity.

The first issue may be dealt with briefly. Paul's own statement in Galatians 1:14 provides an important key, namely, his reference to "the traditions of my fathers." That phrase is equivalent to "the traditions of the elders," used by the Pharisees to criticize Jesus' conduct (Mk 7:5). It refers to the rabbinic "oral law," a body of legal biblical interpretation that played an authoritative role among the Pharisees. Unfortunately, much of that interpretation was characterized by a tendency to relax the stringency of God's commands, and the Pharisees were often in danger of thinking that they had satisfied the divine requirements (cf. esp. Mt 5:20,48; Lk 19:9–14). This religious background is clearly reflected in Philippians 3:9, where Paul, obviously referring to his pre-Christian experience, speaks of "a righteousness of my own that comes from the law."

This fact leads naturally to the second difficulty: how do we relate Paul's background to his conversion? Some scholars have argued forcefully that Protestants have interpreted Paul's conversion in the light of Martin Luther's experience. This reading, they add, is quite misleading, for there is no evidence that Paul was moved to embrace Christianity out of a sense of guilt. In fact, they say the term "conversion" should not even be used since Paul himself speaks rather of a "call" (e.g., Gal 1:15).

There are some valid insights in the charge that Protestantism has placed too much emphasis on "the introspective conscience of the West" (so Krister Stendahl), but it would be a serious mistake to suggest that Luther and the Reformers misunderstood Paul's experience at a fundamental level. Part of the debate focuses on the meaning of Romans 7:7–25, especially such a statement as the following: "Once I was alive apart from law; but when the commandment came, sin sprang to life and I died" (v 9). Whether this and subsequent verses should be understood as biographical or not is a question that has divided exegetes for a long time.

However, the significance of Philippians 3 is clear. In verse 6 of that chapter Paul characterizes his pre-Christian life as "blameless" with reference to legal obedience. Since he can hardly mean that he was (or had earlier thought he was) free from sin, the statement reflects the same attitude expressed by the Pharisee in the parable of Luke 18:9–14, namely, religious self-satisfaction and a lack of sense for the need to cry out for divine mercy. Whether Paul went through a period of guilt (comparable to Luther's) before he surrendered to the claims of the gospel is not known. What matters is that he came to view the knowledge of Jesus Christ as incomparably superior to what he had earlier known. In the light of the gospel, his previous advantages and accomplishments, great as they were, could only be regarded as rubbish (Phil 3:7,8).

With regard to Paul's pre-Christian attitude to the gospel, one thing is certain—he was opposed to it with his whole heart. In his apostolic letters he speaks of his previous hatred for the church (e.g., Gal 1:13; Phil 3:6). Paul does not say explicitly why he felt this way, but there are some hints. In 1 Corinthians 1:23, for example, he speaks of the crucifixion of Christ as a stumbling block to the Jews; and in Galatians 3:13 he quotes Deuteronomy 21:23 ("Cursed is everyone who is hung on a tree") as evidence that Christ, by dying on the cross, became a curse for us. It seems reasonable to infer that Paul, along with many other Jews, viewed the preaching of the gospel as blasphemy. How could these Christians regard as Messiah (God's anointed) a lowly man who suffered a criminal's death and received the divine curse itself? Not surprisingly, this theme would become a basic one in Paul's own proclamation of the gospel.

At any rate, Paul did become a Christian, and thanks to the Book of Acts we are well informed regarding this event. According to chapter 8, not only did he give approval to Stephen's stoning, but soon after that he "began to destroy the church. Going from house to house, he dragged off men and women and put them in prison" (vv 1,3). Not satisfied, he decided to pursue the disciples as far away as Damascus. The sequel is familiar to all Bible students. As he and his traveling party approached Damascus, a light flashed and a voice said to him, "Saul, Saul, why do you persecute me?" The One speaking identified himself as "Jesus, whom you are persecuting"

The street called "straight" (Acts 9:11) in Damascus.

(Acts 9:1–5; cf. also 22:4–8 and more fully 26:9–18). Unable to see anything, he followed the Lord's instructions and waited in Damascus. Ananias, a disciple, was sent to speak to Paul, restore his sight, and baptize him (Acts 9:6–19).

Early Ministry. *Damascus.* To the surprise of everyone who had heard of Paul's enmity toward the church, the new apostle began to preach the gospel vigorously and convincingly. According to Galatians 1:17,18, Paul spent some three years in Damascus and its environs. His ministry, however, eventually drew opposition and he had to escape from Damascus. Upon his return to Jerusalem, the Christians at first could not bring themselves to trust the one who had earlier persecuted them so fiercely, but Barnabas, a highly respected leader in the church, made it possible for Paul to receive a hearing (Acts 9:23–27).

Jerusalem. At once he resumed his preaching, and the Acts narrative gives us a significant clue regarding the distinctiveness of Paul's ministry. According to 9:29 Paul "talked and debated with the Grecian Jews, but they tried to kill him." The significance of this statement is that it draws a suggestive parallel between Paul's preaching and Stephen's ministry. The story that describes Stephen's selection as a deacon is set in the context of conflicts within the church between Greek-speaking, partially Hellenized Jews and those who spoke Hebrew or Aramaic (Acts 6:1; the latter were natives of Palestine and probably stricter in their observance of the Jewish ceremonies). Since Stephen himself belonged to the Greek-speaking community, this is where he took his ministry; indeed, he spoke powerfully as he presented the gospel to the Jews of Cyrene, Alexandria, and other foreign places (vv 8,9).

To judge by the Jews' subsequent accusations (that he spoke against the temple and the OT customs, vv 11–14), it seems that an important theme in Stephen's preaching was the newness of the gospel message and therefore the secondary importance of the Jewish traditions. This is probably the best explanation for the violent reaction of the Jews against him. Up to this point, the Jewish leaders, though annoyed by the preaching of the apostles, put up with it (see esp. Acts 5:27–40). Now, however, that preaching may have taken a new twist that threatened in a fundamental way the Jewish establishment. So significant was this turn of events that it led to Stephen's death and the persecution of the Christians.

It can be said that, in a very important sense, Paul took up Stephen's mantle. Bible students have long recognized that Luke, as he wrote the Book of Acts, appears to picture Stephen as a precursor of the great apostle to the Gentiles. More recently, scholars have become increasingly aware of the significance of this connection in the light of the serious Jewish-Gentile conflicts experienced by the early church. During its first years the Christian church was totally Jewish and it was taken for granted that it would remain so. In spite of persecution from their countrymen, it does not seem to have occurred to the early Christians that the gospel might affect their evaluation of Jewish observances. They continued to circumcise their boys, to attend the sacrifices at the temple, to keep the sabbath, to make Nazirite vows, to avoid association with Gentiles, and so on.

Probably because of his Hellenistic background, Stephen was apparently one of the first Christian leaders to raise questions about these matters. Perhaps reflecting Jesus' own remarks about the transitory character of the temple (cf. Jn 2:19; 4:21–24), Stephen challenged his hearers' assumptions in clear terms (Acts 7:44–53). Paul too had a Hellenistic background, and one wonders whether his earlier enmity toward Stephen may have been occasioned in part by fear that Stephen was possibly correct. Whether guilt over Stephen's death played a part in Paul's conversion—and in his later decision to take up the ministry to Hellenistic Jews—is much too speculative.

What matters is that Paul did in fact pick up where Stephen had left off. This ministry once again aroused the ire of the Jews, and so the believers in Jerusalem, concerned for Paul's life and no doubt fearing that a new wave of persecution might be unleashed, sent the apostle off to Tarsus (Acts 9:30). According to Galatians 1:18–24, Paul's stay in Jerusalem had lasted only two weeks, and most of the Christians there and in the outlying areas had no personal acquaintance with him. Subsequent events suggest strongly that from the beginning of his ministry Paul's distinctive interests and emphases created special tensions. While it would be an exaggeration to say that the Jerusalem church was opposed to him (note esp. Gal 1:24), it is certain that some individuals and groups entertained doubts about his ministry. The Christians in Judea had no desire to break off their ties with Judaism, and preachers like Paul who emphasized the antithesis between it and the gospel could easily be perceived as troublemakers or worse.

Tarsus and Antioch. The time Paul spent in Tarsus and other parts of Cilicia must be regarded as "dark years" in his ministry, since virtually nothing is known about his activities during this period. Luke gives us no information in Acts, and the casual reader might infer that this was a relatively brief period. In Galatians 2:1, however, Paul says that 14 years elapsed from the time of his conversion (or possibly from the time he was sent off to Tarsus) to the time of an important meeting with the Jerusalem apostles. The identification of this visit to Jerusalem is a major point of controversy among scholars, but even if the earliest possible date for it is taken, the year AD 46, it appears that Paul spent at the very least 9 years in Tarsus before he became a prominent figure in the early church. It has been suggested that some of the experiences listed by Paul in 2 Corinthians 11:23–27 (perhaps also the revelations mentioned in 12:1–10) may have taken place during these "dark years," but even if this thesis is correct, there are little more than generalities to back it up. It is a most intriguing fact that the great apostle to the Gentiles spent the first decade of his ministry in relative obscurity, virtually unknown by the vibrant early church in Jerusalem.

At least one leader in the Jerusalem church, however, had not forgotten Paul. Barnabas—himself a Hellenistic Jew from Cyprus—was sent by the church to Antioch of Syria, a large metropolitan center in the Middle East and the third largest city in the Roman Empire. The Christians in Jerusalem had heard that the gospel was being preached with great success in Antioch. Some of them probably were concerned about reports that this evangelistic effort had been extended to the "Greeks," and this represented quite an innovation.

Some time earlier Peter had by revelation brought the gospel to Cornelius, a "God-fearer," that is, a Gentile who was sympathetic to Judaism and probably attended the synagogue services but who was not willing to adopt Judaism completely. The Christians who accompanied Peter were astonished to find out that a non-Jew was granted the gift of the Holy Spirit (Acts 10:44–46), and when the church in Jerusalem heard about his visiting a Gentile, Peter was under considerable pressure to explain his actions (11:1,3). His explanation satisfied the church (see v 18), but obviously not everyone was happy.

In any case, the news that Antiochene Gentiles (presumably "God-fearers" too, though there is some disagreement about this) were being received into the church suggested that some supervision might be required. The Jerusalem leaders wisely chose Barnabas, no doubt because he, like some of the "evangelists" in Antioch, was from Cyprus; certainly someone was needed who enjoyed the confidence of both parties. Barnabas was greatly encouraged by what he saw in Antioch (Acts 11:22–24). The work was so large and promising that he traveled to nearby Tarsus and persuaded Paul to help him with this work. "So for a whole year Barnabas and Saul met with the church and taught great numbers of people" (Acts 11:26).

Because of the great famine of AD 46, predicted by the prophet Agabus, the Christians in Antioch sent a gift to Jerusalem by the hand of Barnabas and Paul (Acts 11:27–30). According to some scholars, this "famine visit" is to be identified with that related by Paul in Galatians 2:1–10. In any case, Barnabas and Paul returned to Antioch, taking along with them John Mark, Barnabas's cousin (Acts 12:25).

Ministry in Asia Minor and Syria. *First Missionary Journey.*

Beginning with chapter 13, the Book of Acts focuses almost exclusively on the missionary work of Paul. Under direct divine guidance, the church in Antioch sent him and Barnabas, with Mark as helper, to spread the gospel abroad. Sailing from the port city of Seleucia, they traveled to Cyprus, Barnabas' home country. When they reached the city of Paphos, a significant event took place: the proconsul Sergius Paulus, after witnessing the miraculous blinding of a sorcerer, responded to the preaching of the gospel. It is at this point in the narrative (Acts 13:9) that Luke tells us for the first time that Saul was also called Paul. Some have thought that Paul adopted this name as a result of this incident and in honor of the proconsul Sergius Paulus,

but Luke certainly does not say that, and it seems unlikely anyway (Paul would almost surely have been given a Roman name at birth.)

The significance of this information should be tied to the fact that, while up to this point Luke has referred to the party as "Barnabas and Saul," from now on he uses the expression "Paul and his companions" (v 13) or "Paul and Barnabas" (v 43, etc.; the only real exception is 15:12). There appears to have been, therefore, not merely a name change, but a shift of leadership, and possibly a change in the party's missionary strategy. It has been suggested, with good reason, that the conversion of Sergius Paulus signaled a fundamentally new development. Prior to this incident, the reception of Gentiles into the church seems to have been limited to "God-fearers," that is, individuals who already had a point of contact with Jewish tradition. Quite possibly, the proconsul's conversion was the first instance of a Gentile who was received as part of God's people *without the intermediary role of the synagogue*.

This seems so natural to modern Christians that it is difficult to appreciate how shocking it must have sounded to Jewish ears. Indeed, it may well be that this *theological* problem (and not merely homesickness!) is what led Mark to abandon the missionary party and return to Jerusalem (Acts 13:13; this would also help to explain why Paul was so adamantly opposed to taking Mark again at a later point, 15:36–40). Whether this interpretation of the evidence is valid or not, the fact is that Paul plays a prominent role in the subsequent narrative, and that the distinctiveness of his ministry lay in his vigorous presentation of the gospel to Gentiles in spite of Jewish opposition.

An immediate example of this is in connection with the party's arrival in Antioch of Pisidia (inland in Asia Minor). Paul and Barnabas preached the gospel in the Jewish synagogue there and received a positive response (Acts 13:42,43), but their success led to Jewish enmity and a word of judgment had to be pronounced: "We had to speak the word of God to you first. Since you reject it and do not consider yourselves worthy of eternal life, we now turn to the Gentiles" (v 46). Great success among the Gentiles led to further and more vigorous persecution and so they moved on to Iconium, where the same pattern developed. After visiting two other nearby cities (Lystra and Derbe), they retraced their steps, strengthening and encouraging the believers. Eventually they returned to their "headquarters" in Antioch of Syria, where they stayed for "a long time" (Acts 14:28).

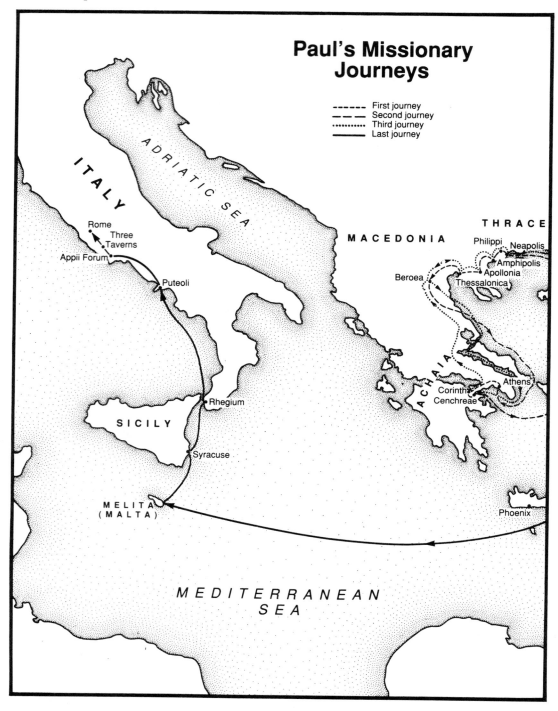

Paul's Missionary Journeys

- - - - - First journey
- - - Second journey
··········· Third journey
——— Last journey

ADRIATIC SEA

ITALY

THRACE

MACEDONIA

Rome
Three
Taverns
Appii Forum

Philippi
Neapolis
Amphipolis
Apollonia
Thessalonica

Beroea

Puteoli

Athens

Rhegium

ACHAIA

SICILY

Corinth
Cenchreae

Syracuse

MELITA
(MALTA)

Phoenix

MEDITERRANEAN
SEA

The Apostolic Council. Chapter 15 of Acts plays a key role in the narrative, since it relates what was perhaps the most important event in early church history, the great Apostolic Council in Jerusalem (AD 49). Some of the Jewish Christians who were quite unhappy with the way in which Gentiles were being freely received as believers traveled to Antioch of Syria and demanded that they become Jews by submitting to circumcision (v 1). This led to intense debate and the church, no doubt deeply troubled, commissioned Paul and Bar-

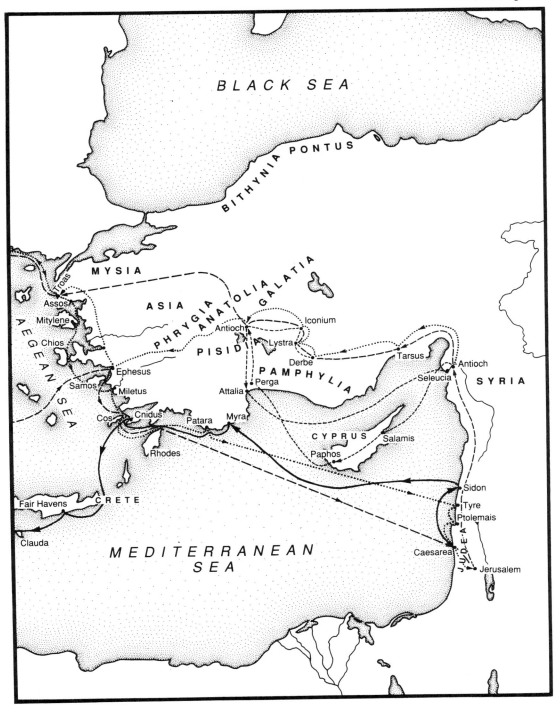

nabas to visit Jerusalem and discuss the matter with the apostles and elders there.

An apparently formal meeting was called and the missionaries reported on their activities. This report led to a lengthy discussion on the question whether Gentiles should be expected to become Jewish. If this is the same meeting to which Paul refers in Galatians 2:1–10, the Gentile Titus became a test case, with the Judaizers arguing that he ought to be circumcised. Paul's description in that passage suggests that the great "apostles of the circumcision," James, Peter, and John, may have at first been impressed by the Judaizers' arguments. Finally, however, Peter stood up and, reflecting on his experience with Cornelius, argued that the Gentiles' salvation comes through grace and not by fulfilling the Jewish ceremonies (Acts 15:7–11). At that point Barnabas and Paul gave further testimony to the mighty works of God among the Gentiles (that Barnabas is mentioned first in v 12 may reflect his prominence in that particular setting).

Having no doubt perceived a growing sense of unanimity in the council, James (who was apparently regarded as the leader of the Jerusalem church) appealed to a prophecy regarding the Gentiles in Amos 9:11,12 and concluded that no unnecessary obstacles should be placed before believing Gentiles (Acts 15:13–21). The council drafted a letter that was taken to Antioch by Paul and Barnabas along with two men from Jerusalem, Judas Barsabbas and Silas. The letter in effect rejected the Judaizers' view that Gentiles must be circumcised; instead, it simply requested that gentile Christians abstain from certain practices that were offensive to the Jews. This decision was a source of great joy and encouragement for the believers in Antioch (vv 22–30).

It is difficult to grasp fully what a magnanimous decision this was and what a fundamental role it played in the development of early church history. The churches in Jerusalem and Judea were under great pressure to do nothing that might infuriate the unbelieving Jews; indeed, to accept Gentiles as part of the church could easily be interpreted as apostasy. Nevertheless, they were willing to suffer the consequences of their action for the sake of preserving the great principle of salvation by grace.

This great event had a major significance therefore for Paul's ministry. His concern to preach a gospel of freedom now received the support of "the pillars of the church," who gave him and Barnabas the right hand of fellowship and commended them to preach among the Gentiles (Gal 2:7–9). However, the Judaizers who were so soundly defeated at the Council of Jerusalem were not all necessarily submissive to this decision. Eventually they would take more positive steps to undermine the work of the apostle.

Conflict in Antioch. It should also be noted that in spite of the significant agreement reached at the council, not all of the leaders saw the issues as clearly as Paul did. Evidence for this appears in an incident that perhaps took place soon after the council (though scholars are not agreed on this matter). According to Galatians 2:11–14, Peter visited Antioch and took it upon himself to eat with the Christian Gentiles. It could be argued that this move went beyond what the council had required. The council's decision seemed to suggest that Christian Jews would continue practicing their customs and that Gentiles need not follow them. It did not address the question of table fellowship, however. If a Jew wanted to preserve Jewish practices, he would not be able to have this kind of fellowship with Gentiles; on the other hand, refusing to commune in this way with them implied a lack of acceptance. Accordingly, Peter chose the more generous option.

Unfortunately, when certain strict Jews from Jerusalem came to Antioch, it seems that Peter felt ashamed of how they might interpret his actions and therefore withdrew from the Gentiles. This decision influenced other believers, even Barnabas himself. Paul, however, saw clearly that this turn of events was a blatant denial of the very principle upon which the council had agreed. By their actions, Peter and the others were in effect telling the Gentiles that they must become Jews—otherwise they would always remain second-class citizens. Not surprisingly, the apostle proceeded to rebuke Peter publicly. There is possibly a summary of the contents of Paul's rebuke in Galatians 2:15–21. Here Paul affirms that the Law itself, by its teachings and effects, leads us to die to the Law so that we might live to God by faith in Christ. If we suggest in any way that the righteousness required by God can be obtained by our own obedience to the Law, then we are in effect saying that Christ died in vain.

Asia Minor Revisited. What is usually called Paul's "second missionary journey" began perhaps a few months after the Council of Jerusalem. After the dispute with Barnabas over the advisability of taking along Mark, Paul chose as his new companion Silas, who no doubt had strongly supported the council's decision. Traveling on land, the party went through Cilicia, surely visiting Tarsus, then on to the cities of Derbe and Lystra, where churches had been established earlier. In Lystra, Paul was apparently impressed with a young man named Timothy who had never been circumcised even though his mother was Jewish. Paul wanted to take him along and, in order to avoid unnecessary conflicts with Jews (who might consider Timothy an apostate), he had Timothy circumcised (Acts 16:1–3). Luke makes a point of telling about this, perhaps to make clear that Paul had no objections whatever to a Jew retaining his cultural identity; he also states, for example, that some years later Paul himself took on a Jewish vow (18:18).

Ministry in Macedonia and Achaia. Philippi. Paul's travels eventually took him to the port city of Troas, on the western coast of Asia Minor. Here he had the well-known vision of a Macedonian asking him, "Come over to Macedonia and help us" (16:9). At this point in the narrative the author of Acts begins to refer to the missionary party, not as "Paul and his companions," but rather as "we" (v 10). It appears therefore that Luke joined the party in Troas (indeed, some speculate that he was the Macedonian who appeared in Paul's vision) and that he accompanied them to Philippi, Paul's first major stop in what is now called Europe.

Since the author drops the "we" in describing Paul's departure from Philippi, it may well be that Luke was left in charge of the new Christian congregation in that city. That congregation consisted of Lydia and other influential women (such as Euodia and Syntyche, Phil 4:2,3), and their faithful support of the apostle's labor stands as one of the most beautiful examples of Christian commitment in the pages of the NT (cf. 2 Cor 8:1–5; Phil 4:14–19).

Paul's stay in Philippi was cut short on account of his having exorcised a divining spirit from a slave girl. The girl's owners had profited considerably from her fortune-telling, so when they "realized that their hope of making money was gone" they accused Paul and Silas of "throwing our city into an uproar by advocating customs unlawful for us Romans to accept or practice" (Acts 16:19–21). The two men were severely flogged, put in prison, and fastened in the stocks.

Miraculously, about midnight, while they were singing hymns, an earthquake shook the prison, the doors were opened, and all the chains came loose. When the jailer woke up, he assumed that the prisoners had escaped and, to save his honor, prepared to kill himself. Paul assured him, however, that no one had escaped. The jailer, acknowledging the evidence of God's work in the ministry of the apostle, asked how he could be saved. "Believe in the Lord Jesus," they replied, "and you will be saved—you and your household" (Acts 16:31).

Thessalonica, Beroea, Athens. The next morning the city officials decided to release Paul and Silas, but now Paul accused them of punishing Roman citizens without due process. Alarmed, the officials apologized and requested them to leave. Soon after that they traveled west to the capital of Macedonia, Thessalonica. Following the usual pattern, Paul spoke powerfully to the Jews, some of whom were persuaded by his preaching. The majority, however, were angered and started a riot. They accused Paul and Silas of political sedition against Caesar (Acts 17:6,7), precipitating their flight south to Beroea. As soon as the Thessalonian Jews heard of this they went to Beroea as well. The agitation was such that the believers took Paul to the coast, boarded a ship with him, and headed for Athens.

According to 1 Thessalonians 3:1,2, Timothy must have joined Paul in Athens soon after this. The apostle, however, was intensely concerned about the welfare of the Thessalonians, whom he had left after only a few weeks of ministry (1 Thes 2:17–20; cf. Acts 17:2). Unfortunately, as he says, Satan prevented him from returning to the church, a remark that may allude to some recurrent physical ailment. (Cf. 2 Cor 12:7,8; Gal 4:13–15. On the slim basis of Acts 23:1–5 and Gal 6:11, some have argued that Paul suffered from an eye disease. Perhaps better is the suggestion that he contracted malaria when he reached Asia Minor in his first journey, but this too is speculative.) At any rate, Paul decided to send Timothy back to Thessalonica. His form of expression in 1 Thessalonians 2:17–3:10 suggests strongly that this was a period of great loneliness and stress for him (note also 1 Cor 2:3, in which Paul tells the church in Corinth that he first came to them, right after his experiences in Athens, "in weakness and fear, and with much trembling").

All that Luke says in his narrative of Acts 17:16–34 is that Paul was distressed to witness the idolatry of the city, preached to both Jews and God-fearers, and began to dispute with the city's philosophers. Their interest piqued, the philosophers brought Paul to a formal meeting of the Areopagus, where he challenged their idolatry and proclaimed the only God as the one who commands people to repent, because he will judge everyone through Jesus, whom he raised from the dead (vv 22–31). Paul's reference to the resurrection was more than they could take, however, and they dismissed him, some courteously, others mockingly.

Corinth. During this time Paul had been anxiously waiting for Timothy's return and for news of the situation in Thessalonica. Perhaps discouraged, he left Athens and traveled to Corinth, a very busy commercial center in the province of Achaia. Some time later Timothy and Silas joined Paul in Corinth.

Timothy's report was very encouraging. The Thessalonians, in spite of many trials, had remained strong in their faith. At the same time, it appears that some opponents of Paul had accused him of being a charlatan, a fly-by-night philosopher who had stayed in Thessalonica just long enough to cause trouble and make a profit. In addition, some of the believers, having misunderstood Paul's teaching concerning the return of Christ, were very depressed that friends and relatives had died prior to this great event. They wondered if this meant they were lost. Others in the congregation, sure that Jesus' return was near, thought it unnecessary to continue working and were making themselves a burden.

Immediately, Paul sat down to write a letter to these believers. It is quite likely that 1 Thessalonians is the earliest of Paul's letters (many prominent scholars, however, believe that Galatians is even earlier). The thrust of this letter is generally positive. He does however defend himself against the apparent charges of dishonesty (cf. 2:1–12). He encourages them in their difficult times of trial (2:13–16; 3:2–10), reminds them of their need for sanctification (4:1–12), and clarifies the doctrines associated with the second coming of Christ (4:13–5:11).

Soon after, while Paul was still in Corinth, he found it necessary to write a second letter to the Thessalonians. Perhaps some of the believers had further misunderstood Paul's teaching; perhaps a false letter had been circulated (2 Thes 2:2). In any case, 2 Thessalonians gives further instruction regarding the end times as well as more severe warnings to those who remain idle (2 Thes 3:6–15).

Although Luke says nothing about this correspondence, he does give some interesting information regarding Paul's ministry in Corinth, which lasted more than 18 months (Acts 8:11,18). With the support of an influential Christian couple, Aquila and Priscilla, Paul preached in the synagogue until, as usual, Jewish opposition forced him to focus his ministry on Gentiles. It seems clear that the Christian congregation in Corinth, composed of both Jews and Gentiles, flourished dramatically (cf. vv 8–10). Luke also mentions that at one point the Jews brought Paul to trial.

Nothing came of this, but the incident is of some importance because Luke identifies the proconsul as Gallio (vv 12–17), whose name is otherwise attested. According to an inscription, Gallio served as proconsul of the province of Achaia beginning in the year 51 (possibly 52), and thus Paul's second missionary journey can be dated with relative precision as covering the years 50–52 (it began no earlier than 49 and it ended no later than 53), that is, when Paul was in his early 40s.

Third Missionary Journey. *Ministry in Ephesus.*

On his way back to Antioch, Paul stopped to visit the great port city of Ephesus, on the southwestern coast of Asia Minor. The apostle was no doubt impressed with the potential of this metropolitan center for the spread of the gospel and he determined to return (Acts 18:18–21). It is not know how long it was before Paul set out on his third mission-ary journey (Luke merely tells us that he spent "some time in Antioch," v 23). For this trip Paul appears to have followed the same route he had traveled on the previous journey, except instead of heading northwest to Troas he went to Ephesus, as he had planned (18:23; 19:1).

His stay in Ephesus was long, productive, and stormy. As usual, he began to preach in the synagogue; as usual, opposition drove him away (19:8,9). His ministry lasted for more than two years and the gospel spread throughout the large province of Asia (v 10). Luke also relates two major incidents: an exorcism that led to many conversions (vv 13–17) and a riot provoked by craftsmen (vv 23–40). The latter, who fashioned shrines for the goddess Artemis, were losing money as a result of Paul's success. Paul was not directly affected by the uproar. Luke may have emphasized the incident as evidence that officials could find nothing legally wrong with Paul's activities.

The Corinthian Problem. Some important events took place, however, that Luke does not mention at all. Paul had sent, perhaps at the beginning of this journey, a letter to the Corinthian Christians in which he warned them of associating with disobedient believers (1 Cor 5:9). He had also mentioned to this church that he was raising a collection for the poor in Jerusalem (1 Cor 16:1). While in Ephesus, however, Paul received reports that the church in Corinth was experiencing severe problems, particularly divisions within the congregation (1 Cor 1:11,12). Immorality, disruptions in the worship services, confusions about the resurrection, and several other evils threatened the spiritual life of this church. Moreover, the church itself had written a letter to Paul requesting instruction about such matters as marriage and divorce, meat offered to idols, spiritual gifts, and the method Paul was using for his collection (1 Cor 7:1; 8:1; 12:1; 16:1).

The apostle was confronted with a massive task, and his long first letter to the Corinthians was his attempt to deal with the problem. It appears that the church as a whole did not respond positively to this letter. Encouraged by a certain false apostle who opposed Paul, the members resisted the apostle's authority. Paul found it necessary to pay a "painful visit" to Corinth (not recorded in Acts, but alluded to in 2 Cor 2:1; cf. 13:1). This too was unsuccessful, so Paul sent Titus as his representative. It is probable that Titus carried with him a written ultimatum (the "sorrowful letter" mentioned in 2 Cor 2:4 and 7:8, though some scholars believe these verses refer to 1 Cor). In any case, Paul instructed Titus to attempt to resolve the problem and to meet him in Troas (cf. 2 Cor 2:12,13).

The Galatian Problem. During this difficult time in Ephesus, Paul was also facing one of the most serious challenges to his ministry. Reports from the churches in Galatia (Iconium, Lystra, Derbe) indicated that Judaizers had visited these Christians and largely persuaded them that Paul, who had received his teaching and authority from the Jerusalem apostles (James, Peter, John), was a renegade who could not be trusted. Quite impressed by the Judaizers' arguments, the Galatians listened to their claim that Gentiles ought to be circumcised and observe the Jewish rites.

Paul, deeply disturbed by these reports, feared that the Galatian churches were at the point of committing apostasy: adopting the Judaizers' position meant abandoning the freedom of the gospel, salvation by grace (Gal 1:6–9; 2:15–21; 3:1–5; 4:8–11; 5:2–4). Accordingly, his Letter to the Galatians is full of polemics, with some very harsh statements against the false teachers (esp. 5:7–12). In it he denies absolutely that he received his gospel from the other apostles, for it came to him as a revelation from God himself (1:11–17); he also argues very carefully that the true heirs of Abraham are not those who are his physical descendants but those who, whether Jews or Gentiles, believe in God's promise as Abraham himself believed (3:7–29). Unfortunately, there is no evidence of how these churches responded to Paul's letter, though the apostle's expression of confidence (e.g., 5:10) indicates that they would have recognized the truth of his message.

(It should be pointed out that many conservative scholars do not think it possible that the Letter to the Galatians could have been written as late as the third missionary journey. In their opinion, the letter was written many years earlier, prior to the Apostolic Council of Jerusalem, usually dated in the year 49. If this early date is correct, there is reason to believe that the Galatians did repent of their error, for Paul continued to visit those churches in his subsequent journeys.)

Travel to Corinth. When Paul finally left Ephesus he went to Troas and was distressed not to find Titus there (2 Cor 2:12,13). Concerned that perhaps Titus had met more trouble in Corinth, Paul continued on to Macedonia, probably to the city of Philippi (cf. Acts 20:1). There he did meet Titus, who reported with great joy that the Corinthians had finally come around (2 Cor 7:5–7,13–16). To be sure, not everything was in order. There seemed to be some hesitation, for example, with regard to supporting the collection Paul was raising. More seriously, a few individuals in the church continued to resist Paul's authority, and their opposition had to be dealt with.

In preparation for his upcoming visit to Corinth, therefore, Paul wrote 2 Corinthians from Macedonia. In this letter he expresses considerable joy at the response of the church, explains the nature of his ministry (3:1–5:21), encourages the congregation to give generously for the poor in Jerusalem (chs 8,9), and argues vigorously against the "super-apostles" who oppose him (chs 10–13). All indications are that the response to 2 Corinthians was positive. Later Paul mentioned, for example, that the believers in Achaia (the province where Corinth was located) "were pleased to make a contribution for the poor among the saints in Jerusalem" (Rom 15:26). Another indirect piece of evidence is that during his three-month stay in Corinth (cf. Acts 20:2,3) Paul wrote the great Letter to the Romans. The character of this letter—it is the lengthiest and the most carefully reasoned-out of his writings—suggests strongly that Paul enjoyed a period of relative calm in which he was able to formulate in coherent fashion his most important theological concerns.

The Letter to the Romans. The fact that Romans is so clearly theological in character has led most interpreters to ignore the historical occasion of the letter. It is important to remember, however, that during the third journey Paul had been dealing in a painful and personal way with the very issues that Romans carefully expounds. Moreover, the letter itself indicates that the apostle was anticipating controversy in the near future, upon his arrival at Jerusalem. In 15:30–32 Paul urges

Inscribed sherds from Corinth, where Paul stayed 3 months and founded a church.

the believers in Rome to "struggle" in prayer with regard to this visit to Jerusalem. Paul was concerned not only about the unbelieving Jews, but also about Jewish believers who might question or even oppose his work among the Gentiles and who therefore might be reluctant to accept the offering he was bringing to them.

The apostle realized that when he met the Jerusalem church he would be faced with the same objections that had been thrown at him by the Judaizers during his third journey. The calm that he was enjoying in Corinth provided him with the opportunity to gather his thoughts and to formulate in a clear and organized way his answer to those objections. Under divine inspiration, therefore, he wrote a letter that may be viewed as a systematic response to the criticisms raised by Jews against what he called *his* gospel, that is, his distinctive presentation to the Gentiles.

After emphasizing the sin of both Jews and Gentiles (1:18–3:20), Paul states briefly the essence of his preaching in 3:21–24—free justification, apart from the Law, to those who believe in Jesus Christ. But a Jew might object that this renders God unjust: how can a just God simply acquit the guilty? Paul's answer is that God has not overlooked sin but condemned it by offering Christ as the atoning sacrifice (vv 25,26). Again, it may be objected that God revealed his salvation to Abraham and that obedience to the sign of circumcision was part of the divine covenant. But Paul responds that Abraham was accounted righteous when he *believed*, and this happened while Abraham was still uncircumcised (4:9–12). Similarly, the charge that Paul's preaching encouraged sinful behavior ("if obedience to the law is not necessary for salvation, Gentiles will conclude that they might as well continue sinning") is one that the apostle answers with a three-chapter-long discussion of sanctification: those who have been justified freely have also been sanctified, they have broken their bond to sin and walk according to the Spirit (6:1–4,15–18; 7:4–6; 8:1–8).

Most important is Paul's handling of the unbelief of Israel in chapters 9–11. Though many view this section of the letter as parenthetical or otherwise unrelated to the previous chapters, it is more likely the very heart of the letter, for no Jewish objection to the gospel was so powerful as their claim that, if Paul's preaching were true, then surely God's own people would recognize it as such. The fact that the Jewish nation as a whole rejected the gospel, they claimed, could only mean one of two things: either the gospel is not true or else God's promise has failed and his people have been rejected. Yet the apostle gives us a third

option. God's word has *not* failed—it is simply that being a descendant of Abraham does not make one automatically part of God's people (Rom 9:6). Earlier in the letter he had affirmed that a true Jew is one who is circumcised, not in the flesh, but in the heart (2:28,29); and that the true child of Abraham is one who, whether circumcised or not, follows in the steps of Abraham's faith (4:11,12; note the earlier discussion of Gal). Chapter 9 picks up this emphasis, relating it to God's purpose of election (v 11), the OT concept of the remnant (v 27), the sin of the Israelites (10:16), and God's future plans (11:25–36).

If Paul, by writing this letter, was rehearsing his upcoming "defense" in Jerusalem, why would he send the letter to Rome? Paul had for some time wanted to visit Rome, the capital of the Roman Empire (cf. Acts 19:21). He intended to fulfill those wishes as soon as he had delivered the offering to the saints in Judea (Rom 15:23–25,28,32). It is likely, however, that the church in Rome had some awareness of the criticisms that had been raised against Paul. In fact, this church too was experiencing some Jewish-Gentile tensions of its own (cf. Rom 11:13–21 and the debate over eating meat in ch 14). Therefore, the best way for Paul to introduce himself to the Roman Christians was by giving them a clear exposition of "his" gospel (cf. 2:16) in the context of the controversies that surrounded him.

Travel to Jerusalem. Picking up the Acts narrative at 20:3, Paul left Corinth and retraced his steps through Macedonia. He and those accompanying him stopped in Troas for a week (20:6–11), then sailed on to the island of Miletus, where the elders from nearby Ephesus came to hear a farewell from the apostle (vv 13–38). To them he mentioned that the Holy Spirit had warned him of hardships he would have to face in Jerusalem (v 23). Indeed, as the party landed in Palestine, some of the brethren in Tyre pleaded with Paul not to go to Jerusalem; the scene repeated itself in Caesarea after the prophet Agabus prophesied that Paul would be imprisoned (Acts 21:4,10–12). Paul was persuaded, however, that he must fulfill his mission, and he was more than ready to suffer in the name of Christ (v 13).

Upon his arrival in Jerusalem, he was met by James and the elders, who informed Paul that thousands of Jewish believers had questions about his methods and wondered whether in fact Paul was leading Jews to abandon Judaism. They suggested that Paul give evidence of his own obedience to the Law by joining four men who had made a vow and by paying for the expenses involved (21:17–24). Paul was quite willing to do this. Unfortunately, some Jews from the area around Ephesus recognized Paul and incited the crowds in the temple to riot (vv 27–30). When the Roman troops arrived on the scene, Paul was given the opportunity to speak to the crowds. He gave a ringing affirmation of his Christian faith, but as soon as he mentioned that God had commissioned him to go to the Gentiles (22:21) the crowds became unruly again.

Imprisonment and Death. *Caesarea.* The next day Paul was brought before the Jewish Sanhedrin; on this occasion he made an issue of his belief in the resurrection, and as a result members of the Sanhedrin began to argue vigorously among themselves. (The Sadducees opposed this doctrine while the Pharisees accepted it.) The dispute led to violence and Paul was taken to the barracks (23:6–10); the following night, having been apprised of a Jewish plot to kill Paul, the commander dispatched him to Caesarea, the official residence of the Roman governor, Felix (23:12–35).

Within a week Felix gave audience to the Jewish accusers and listened both to their complaints and to Paul's defense, but he refused to make a judgment in the hopes of receiving a bribe. As a result Paul remained imprisoned in Caesarea for two years, until the governor was replaced by Porcius Festus (24:1–27). The most likely date for this change in administration is the year 59. Paul's imprisonment in Caesarea, therefore, is usually dated about 57–59; this means that the third missionary journey would have spanned the period from 53 to 57.

Soon after Festus became governor, the Jews urged him to send Paul to Jerusalem to be tried. Paul protested, however, and, exercising his right as a Roman citizen, demanded to be tried by the emperor himself (Acts 25:1–12). Festus consulted with King Agrippa, who asked to hear Paul. Luke records a lengthy defense by Paul in chapter 26; Agrippa's judgment was that "this man could have been set free, if he had not appealed to Caesar" (v 32).

To Rome. Luke also documents quite carefully the trip to Rome, including the shipwreck and the stay on the island of Malta (27:1–28:10). Upon his arrival in Rome, Paul asked to see the Jewish leaders, to whom he gave an account of his situation. They were at first receptive and Paul presented the gospel to them. While some believed, most apparently objected, for the apostle reminded them of Isaiah's mission to blind the eyes of the people and then concluded, "Therefore I want you to know that God's salvation has been sent to the Gentiles and they will listen!" (28:17–28). The Book of Acts somewhat abruptly comes to an end with the information that Paul stayed under house arrest for two years and that he continued to preach boldly and without hindrance (vv 30,31).

Traditionally, this two-year period is regarded as the setting for the so-called prison letters—Ephesians, Philippians, Colossians, and Philemon. Many modern scholars question this opinion and prefer to view either Caesarea or Ephesus as the place from which these letters (some or all of them) were written. It is doubtful if a definitive solution to this problem will ever be reached, but there is no compelling reason to abandon the traditional view.

Apart from Philemon, which was written to deal with the very specific problem of the runaway slave Onesimus, the prison letters are characterized by an emphasis on the *present* enjoyment of heavenly blessings ("realized eschatology"; see esp. Eph 1:3,13,14; 2:4–7; Phil 1:6; 3:20; Col 3:1–4). In addition, Ephesians and Colossians are similar in their treatment of the unity of the church as the body of Christ (Eph 1:22,23; 4:15,16; Col 1:18,24; 2:19). Philippians, perhaps best known for its "Christ-hymn" (2:6–11), is an important source for Paul's teaching on joy, suffering, and sanctification (1:9–11,21,27–30; 2:12,13; 3:12–14; 4:4–9).

Last Years. The evidence gathered from outside of Acts is not at all clear as to whether or not Paul was released from his imprisonment. If the Letter to the Philippians was written during this period, it can be inferred that Paul had some concern that he might be executed (cf. Phil 1:19–24; 2:17). On the other hand, he sounds rather confident that he will be released and will be able to see the Philippians again (1:25,26; cf. also Phlm 22).

Conservative scholars have argued that Paul was indeed released after two years, since the charges against him were groundless; that he possibly traveled to Spain as he had hoped (Rom 15:24,28); that he returned to the east, visiting Crete (Ti 1:5), Ephesus and Macedonia (1 Tm 1:3), Miletus and Corinth (2 Tm 4:20), Troas (2 Tm 4:13), and Nicopolis (on the western coast of the Greek mainland, Ti 3:12); that he wrote 1 Timothy and Titus during this period of freedom; that finally he was imprisoned again after AD 64 (the year of the great fire in Rome, which led to the Neronian persecution of Christians); that he wrote 2 Timothy during this second imprisonment in Rome; and that he was decapitated under Nero between the years 65 and 67. Most likely, Paul was not yet 60 years old when he became a martyr for the faith.

This reconstruction of events is somewhat speculative, but it seems to account for the data more clearly than other suggestions. However, even if Paul was indeed released after the imprisonment described in Acts 28, it must be emphasized that almost nothing is known about his activities after such a release. In

Mamertine prison in Rome, where, according to tradition, both Paul and Peter were imprisoned.

other words, the real significance of Paul's ministry must be deduced from the material actually found in the Book of Acts and in the major Pauline letters. God in his wisdom had determined that Paul would be "my chosen instrument to carry my name before the Gentiles and their kings and before the people of Israel. I will show him how much he must suffer for my name" (Acts 9:15,16). The evidence is clear: Paul was obedient to the heavenly vision (26:19), and his ministry made possible the spread of the gospel to the ends of the earth.   MOISES SILVA

See JUDAISM; PHARISEES; HELLENISTIC JUDAISM; BARNABAS; STEPHEN; ACTS OF THE APOSTLES, BOOK OF THE; JUDAIZERS; JERUSALEM COUNCIL; AREOPAGUS; SILAS; TIMOTHY, TIMOTHEUS (PERSON); TITUS (PERSON) #1; ROMANS, LETTER TO THE; CORINTHIANS, FIRST LETTER TO THE; CORINTHIANS, SECOND LETTER TO THE; GALATIANS, LETTER TO THE; EPHESIANS, LETTER TO THE; PHILIPPIANS, LETTER TO THE; COLOSSIANS, LETTER TO THE; THESSALONIANS, FIRST LETTER TO THE; THESSALONIANS, SECOND LETTER TO THE; TIMOTHY, FIRST LETTER TO; TIMOTHY, SECOND LETTER TO; TITUS, LETTER TO; PHILEMON, LETTER TO; PASTORAL LETTERS; APOSTLE, APOSTLESHIP.

Bibliography. G. Bornkamm, *Paul*; F.F. Bruce, *Paul: Apostle of the Heart Set Free*; W.D. Davies, *Paul and Rabbinic Judaism*; J.W. Drane, *Paul: Libertine or Legalist?*; M. Grant, *Saint Paul*; R.N. Longenecker, *Paul, Apostle of Liberty*; J.G. Machen, *The Origin of Paul's Religion*; J. Munck, *Paul and the Salvation of Mankind*; H.N. Ridderbos, *Paul: An Outline of His Theology*; D.E.H. Whiteley, *The Theology of St. Paul*.

Paulus, Sergius. *See* SERGIUS PAULUS.

Pavement.
Term occurring 10 times in the Bible, usually alluding to the stone floor of the temple(s). Particular interest focuses on the reference in John 19:13 to the "pavement" on which Jesus stood trial before Pilate. It was at the decisive moment of the Roman phase of the trial of Jesus when "Pilate had Jesus brought out, and seated himself on the chair

of judgment at a place called the Pavement, in Hebrew Gabbatha" (Jn 19:13 JB). This verse has played an important role in determining the location of Jesus' trial. Most scholars now locate this "pavement" where Pilate's "judgment seat" was placed under the present street level in Jerusalem at the site of Herod's fortress Antonia. This enormous stone pavement consists of large blocks of limestone, excavated in the 1930s by Pere Vincent. It now lies under the convent of the Dames of Zion on the Via Dolorosa in East Jerusalem.

Dominican scholars in Jerusalem are among those who believe this pavement to have been adjacent to Herod's palace which lay in the Upper City, south of the Jaffa Gate. This seems the more likely site, all things considered. No such pavement has been discovered there but it may still lay beneath the surface, awaiting further excavation.

Peace.
Total well-being, prosperity, and security associated with God's presence among his people. Linked in the OT with the covenant, the presence of peace, as God's gift, was conditional upon Israel's obedience. In prophetic material, true peace is part of the end-time hope of God's salvation. In the NT, this longed-for peace is understood as having come in Christ and able to be experienced by faith.

In the OT. Shalōm, the most prominent OT term for "peace," held a wide range of connotations (wholeness, health, security, well-being, and salvation) and could apply to an equally wide range of contexts: the state of the individual (Ps 37:37; Prv 3:2; Is 32:17), the relationship of man to man (Gn 34:21; Jos 9:15) or nation to nation (e.g., absence of conflict—Dt 2:26; Jos 10:21; 1 Kgs 5:12; Ps 122:6,7), and the relationship of God and man (Ps 85:8; Jer 16:5).

The presence of *shalōm* in any of these contexts was not considered ultimately as the outcome of human endeavor, but as a gift or blessing of God (Lv 26:6; 1 Kgs 2:33; Jb 25:2; Pss 29:11; 85:8; Is 45:7). It is not surprising, therefore, to find "peace" tied closely to the OT notion of covenant. *Shalōm* was the desired state of harmony and communion between the two covenant partners (God and man—Nm 6:26; cf. Is 54:10), its presence signifying God's blessing in the covenant relationship (Mal 2:5; cf. Nm 25:12), and its absence signifying the breakdown of that relationship due to Israel's disobedience and unrighteousness (Jer 16:5, 10–13; cf. Ps 85:9–11; Is 32:17).

Shalōm becomes a pivotal term in the prophetic writings. It was the "false" prophets who, forgetting the conditions for national well-being within the covenant relationship, assumed God's loyalty to Israel (Ps 89) would guarantee political peace forever (Jer 6:14; 8:15; Ez 13:10,16; Mi 3:5). Against such popular but false security, the preexilic prophets proclaimed the coming judgment precisely as a loss of this *shalōm* due to Israel's persistent disobedience and unrighteousness (Is 48:18; Jer 14:13–16; 16:5,10–13; 28; Mi 3:4,9–12).

The prophets did, however, point beyond the crises of exile and subsequent setbacks to a time when *shalōm*, characterized by prosperity and well-being (Is 45:7; Ez 34:25,26), absence of conflict (Is 2:2–4; 32:15–20; Ez 34:28–31; cf. Hos 2:18), right relations (Is 11:1–5; Mi 4:1–4; Zec 8:9–13), restoration of harmony in nature (Is 11:6–9; cf. Ez 47:1–12), and salvation (Is 52:7; 60:17; Ez 34:30,31; 37:26–28) would again return. Often this eschatological (or end time) expectation of peace in the OT was associated with a messianic figure, as in Isaiah 9:6 where the future Messiah is termed the "Prince of Peace." Moreover, his reign would be one of "peace" not only for Israel, but would extend throughout the whole earth (Zec 9:9,10). The OT ends with this hope of peace still unrealized in its full sense.

In the NT. The Greek term for "peace" used predominantly in the NT is *irēnē*, a word expanded from its classical Greek connotation of "rest" to include the various connotations of *shalōm* discussed above. As with *shalōm*, *eirēnē* could be used as a greeting or farewell (as in "peace be with you"—Lk 10:5; Gal 6:16; Jas 2:16; cf. Jn 20:19), or could signify the cessation of conflict (national—Lk 14:32; Acts 12:20; or interpersonal—Rom 14:19; Eph 4:3), or the presence of domestic tranquility (cf. 1 Cor 7:15).

The chief issue concerns how Jesus incorporated the OT hope for the eschatological peace of God into his ministry. In the "benedictus" of Zechariah (Lk 1:67–69), the coming of Jesus as the Messiah is expected to "guide our feet into the way of peace" (Lk 1:79). So also the angelic testimony to the shepherds proclaims Jesus as the bringer of God's peace to men (Lk 2:14). That is, Jesus as the Messiah would usher in God's reign of peace, that time of salvation longed for since the days of the prophets. Jesus' self-understanding as expressed in the fourth Gospel corresponds to this association. This long-expected peace of God is Jesus' "farewell gift" to the disciples (Jn 14:27), that which the disciples are given with the indwelling Holy Spirit (Jn 20:19–22; cf. Mk 4:39) now that Jesus has won his victory on the cross and reigns in power in heaven.

The nature of this gift of peace brought by Jesus may be easier to explain by stating what it is not. It is not an end to tension, an absence of warfare, domestic tranquility, nor anything like the worldly estimation of peace (Lk 12:51–53; Jn 14:27; 16:32,33). Its presence may, on the contrary, actually disturb existing relations, being a dividing "sword" in familial relations (Mt 10:34–37). Jesus' gift of peace is, in reality, the character and mood of the new covenant of his blood which reconciles God to man (Rom 5:1; Col 1:20) and forms the basis of subsequent reconciliation between men under Christ (Eph 2:14–22).

The early church understood "peace" in this same way as the final, end-time salvation of God given already through Jesus Christ (cf. Phil 4:7,9). Peter preached the "peace with God through Jesus, the Messiah" (Acts 10:36,37 LB), while Paul similarly preached Jesus as "our Peace," bringing near through him those formerly far away from God (Eph 2:13,14; 6:15; cf. Heb 7:2).

This peculiarly Christian understanding of "peace" (the Jewish hope of God's future peace believed to be a present reality through Christ) altered the content of the common greeting, "go in peace," as it was taken up in the Christian community. In Paul's common "grace and peace" greeting (1 Cor 1:3; 2 Cor 1:2; Gal 1:3; Eph 1:2, etc.; cf. also 1 Pt 1:2; 2 Jn 3; Jude 2; Rv 1:4), it is no longer a mere "wish" for peace which Paul extends to his readers, but is a reminder of the messianic gifts available in the present time through Christ to the man of faith. In accord with this, Jesus is described as "peace" itself (Eph 2:14), while God, too, because of his act of reconciliation through Christ is known as a "God of peace" (Phil 4:9; Col 3:15).

This gift of peace or reconciliation with God, made available through Christ, places an ethical demand on the Christian; it calls for the exercises of "peace" (as reconciliation between persons) within the church. Peace, as a fruit of the Spirit (Gal 5:22), is to be the goal of the Christian's dealings with others (Rom 12:18; 14:19; Heb 12:14, etc.), that which marks one's identity as a "child of God" (Mt 5:9).

DAVID C. CARLSON

See FRUIT OF THE SPIRIT.

Peace Offering. *See* OFFERINGS AND SACRIFICES.

Peacock. *See* BIRDS.

Pearl. Word appearing only once in the OT (Jb 28:18). The reference to a reddish stone in Lamentations 4:7 may be to the pink pearl found in the Red Sea.

By the NT period the pearl was a prized piece of feminine jewelry (1 Tm 2:9), an item of trade (Mt 13:45,46; Rv 18:12–16), and an object of high price. Christians were discouraged from the display of pearls (Rv 17:4).

Being familiar objects, pearls were frequently used by Christ as an illustration. A fine pearl was an object of such great value that a man might sell all his accumulated wealth to purchase it (Mt 13:45,46), but a pearl, used figuratively for the word of the Lord, would not be cast before swine (Mt 7:6). The gates of New Jerusalem (Rv 21:21) were probably mother-of-pearl.

See MINERALS, METALS, AND PRECIOUS STONES; FASHION AND DRESS.

Pedahel. Ammihud's son from Naphtali's tribe, appointed to work with Joshua and Eleazar in distributing Canaanite territory west of the Jordan River among the Israelites (Nm 34:28).

Pedahzur. Gamaliel's father from Manasseh's tribe (Nm 1:10; 2:20; 7:54,59; 10:23).

Pedaiah. 1. Maternal grandfather of Judah's King Jehoiakim. Pedaiah was from Rumah (2 Kgs 23:36).

2. Jeconiah's third son (1 Chr 3:18,19).

3. Joel's father from the half-tribe of Manasseh (1 Chr 27:20).

4. Parosh's son, who worked with the temple servants living on Ophel to repair the Jerusalem wall to a point opposite the Water Gate (Neh 3:25).

5. One who stood beside Ezra during the public reading of the Law (Neh 8:4).

6. Kolaiah's son and Joed's father (Neh 11:7). He was a member of Benjamin's tribe and lived in Jerusalem after the return from exile.

7. Levite appointed by Nehemiah as treasurer of the storehouse to distribute grain, wine, and oil to the priests who served in the temple (Neh 13:13).

Pekah. Name meaning "he has opened (the eyes)." It is an abbreviated form of Pekahiah, "Yahweh has opened (the eyes)." The name has been found on a fragment of an 8th-century BC wine jar from Hazor stratum V, the level destroyed by Tiglath-pileser in 734 BC. It is thought that this is a reference to Pekah and to a kind of wine. It is likely that the usurper Pekah, one of Pekahiah's officers, was so eager to ensure his position as king that he deliberately assumed the name of his predecessor. Moreover, Isaiah refers to him as the "son of Remaliah," almost scornfully, to indicate his nonroyal descent, but when Isaiah refers to his heathen ally he uses the specific name "Rezin, the king of Syria" (Is 7:4–9; 8:6).

Accession to the Throne. Pekah, son of Remaliah, is described as "an officer" of Peka-

hiah, the third man in a chariot apart from the driver and the warrior. He was the shield and armor bearer of the warrior. In time the term came to signify a royal aide-de-camp.

The account of Pekahiah's murder has been somewhat obscured because of the difficulty in understanding the terms Argob and Arieh (2 Kgs 15:25). Some translators and commentators have thought these referred to persons, whereas others have held these are place names. Some scholars radically alter the text here and eliminate the troublesome words by claiming they were a scribal mistake or emendation. A key seems to have been found by comparing them with the Ugaritic. The terms mean "eagle" and "lion," respectively. Thus Pekahiah was murdered "near the eagle and the lion." It is suggested that this means he was put to death near the guardian sphinxes of his palace. Such sphinxes were a common motif in ancient eastern palaces and were duplicated on ivory plaques erected in the gateway. This interpretation seems very plausible as it avoids critical emendation and solves the major problems in the text.

Date. The solution to the length of Pekah's reign is not an easy one. Second Kings 15:27 clearly states that he reigned 20 years over Israel. Most historians have dated Menahem's payment of tribute to the Assyrians in 738 BC, although Thiele claims it could be dated as early as 743. The fall of Samaria was in 722. Pekahiah reigned 2 years (2 Kgs 15:23)

Cuneiform tablet from Ugarit containing a private legal action.

and Hoshea reigned 9 years in Samaria (2 Kgs 17:1). The total number of years required for the reigns of Pekahiah, Pekah, and Hoshea is 31. If Menahem's tribute took place in 743 and he died that same year, the combined regencies of the last 3 kings of Israel would require a date of 712 for the fall of Samaria which is impossible. Adjustments have usually been made by reducing Pekah's reign, but to do so implies a low view of biblical numbers. Co-regency could supply a solution to the problem.

Political Significance. The brilliant Tiglath-pileser III, leading the kingdom of Assyria to prominence, appeared on Israel's border. Menahem "deemed it wise under the circumstances to become tributary to him." Apparently Pekahiah, Menahem's successor, could not appease the Assyrians during his short reign. The conciliatory efforts of Menahem and Pekahiah may well have prompted the Syrians to conspire with Pekah, the army officer, to gain control of the throne of Samaria in order to present a united military front against Assyrian encroachment. Once Samaria was under control, the Syrians led by Rezin, Israel ruled by Pekah, and several Transjordanian kingdoms formed a powerful alliance.

In time Pekah and Rezin began to pressure the kingdom of Judah in order to induce it to join their alliance against the impending Assyrian attack. Jotham resisted their invitations and fortified the Judean hill country. Jotham's son, Ahaz, continued his father's policy of non-cooperation with the Samaria-Damascus coalition. Pekah and Rezin invaded Judah with the intent of taking Jerusalem and placing "the son of Tabeel" on the throne of Judah in Ahaz's place (Is 7:1–6). He presumably was a son of Uzziah or Jotham by a princess of Tabeel. Although the actual siege of Jerusalem was unsuccessful, Pekah and Rezin inflicted severe casualties upon Ahaz's army. In one day of battle they killed 120,000 men of Judah and carried away 200,000 captives including women and children. However, the prophet Oded prophesied in Samaria before the army. He urged the leaders of Samaria to return the captives. Apparently there still remained a measure of piety in Israel, for the leaders heeded the prophetic word and sent the captives back to Jericho (2 Chr 28:8–15).

Rezin's revolt against Assyria brought a quick response from Tiglath-pileser who laid siege to Damascus in 734 BC. The city fell in 732 BC. Another detachment of the Assyrian army descended on the upper districts of Syria and Samaria. Second Kings 15:29 lists the districts and cities that were overrun. They included Gilead (regions beyond Jordan), Naphtali (regions lying to the west of the lakes of Galilee and Merom), and all Galilee as far south as the plain of Esdraelon and the valley of Jezreel. Isaiah refers to this lost tribal territory (9:1–7). From this Assyrian-controlled region the messianic ruler would arise and give light to "those who dwelt in a land of deep darkness" (Is 9:2). Thus Pekah's kingdom was reduced to a third of its original size by the Assyrian campaign of 734–732 BC.

Death. In 732 a palace conspiracy led by Hoshea plotted the assassination of Pekah. He was put to death in the coup d'etat and the throne was usurped by Hoshea. The annals of Tiglath-pileser III claim that the Samaritans overthrew Pekah and that Tiglath-pileser placed Hoshea upon the throne in his place. There are two possibilities: (1) Hoshea may have aspired to the throne of Samaria independent of Assyrian political power and in opposition to Tiglath-pileser. (2) Hoshea may have been the willing tool of Tiglath-pileser, who desired to eliminate the troublesome Pekah and control the area with his own appointee. Hoshea later revolted against Assyrian domination (2 Kgs 17:4). The second alternative seems reasonable as it harmonizes the biblical record with Tiglath-pileser's Annals.

Spiritual Influence. The author of Kings evaluates the reign of Pekah as follows: "And he did what was evil in the sight of the Lord; he did not depart from the sins of Jeroboam the son of Nebat, which he made Israel to sin" (2 Kgs 15:28). It is likely that he continued the calf worship at the shrines at Dan and Bethel. The continuation of the apostasy during successive regencies was the cause for the judgment that befell the northern kingdom. Pekah is the last king of Israel given such an evaluation.   GERARD VAN GRONINGEN

See ISRAEL, HISTORY OF; CHRONOLOGY, OLD TESTAMENT.

Pekahiah. Son of Menahem, king of Israel. Pekahiah (meaning, "Yahweh has opened [his eyes]") was among the 20 kings who ruled Israel from Samaria following its decline consequent to the fracture of the Solomonic monarchy in the 10th century BC. The brief account in the Bible concerning him (2 Kgs 15:22–26) points to the godlessness of his life ("he did what was evil in the eyes of the Lord," 2 Kgs 15:24). His sin, like that of his father's, was linked to the false worship of Jeroboam who built shrines at Dan and Bethel to rival worship in the temple at Jerusalem. Such religious activity threatened the true worship of God by attempting to fuse biblical concepts with the fertility cult of Baal, a movement sharply denounced by the word of God (1 Kgs 13:1–5). Like many of Israel's kings, Pekahiah ruled briefly, being assassinated in the 2nd year of his reign. The chief instigator of the plot against him, a captain named Pekah, took 50 men of Gilead and slew the king, along with 2 aides, in the citadel of the royal palace at Samaria. His successor, Pekah, was regrettably as evil as Pekahiah and received the condemnation of Scripture typical of virtually all the Israelite kings: "he did what was evil in the sight of the Lord" (2 Kgs 15:28). During the final years of Pekah's 20-year reign, Tiglathpileser mounted the forces of Assyria and made extensive inroads into Palestine, occupying all the territory of Naphtali and deporting its people to Assyria. Pekah was finally assassinated by Hoshea, Israel's last king before the conquest of Samaria and the deportation of its inhabitants by the Assyrian king Shalmaneser (722 BC).

See ISRAEL, HISTORY OF; CHRONOLOGY, OLD TESTAMENT.

Pekod. Place mentioned as the location of an Aramaean tribe living in southern Babylonia between Babylon and Elam and more exactly on the eastern bank of the Lower Tigris by modern Kut-el-Amara and the confluence of the Kerkha (Jer 50:21; Ez 23:23). Tiglathpileser III (745–727), Sargon II (722–705), and Sennacherib (705–681) subjugated the population and exacted tribute of horses, cattle, and sheep from Pekod.

Pelaiah. 1. Elioenai's son and a remote descendant of David (1 Chr 3:24).

2. Levite who helped Ezra expound the Law to the people following its public reading (Neh 8:7; 10:10).

Pelaliah. Forefather of Adaiah, a priest living in Jerusalem during Ezra's day (Neh 11:12).

Pelatiah. 1. Hananiah's son, in a list of King Solomon's descendants (1 Chr 3:21).

2. Military leader among the Simeonites who helped destroy an Amalekite remnant at Mt Seir during Hezekiah's reign (1 Chr 4:42).

3. Political leader who signed Ezra's covenant of faithfulness to God with Nehemiah and others after the exile (Neh 10:22).

4. Benaiah's son and one of the two princes seen by Ezekiel in a vision of judgment, identified by the Spirit of the Lord as one who devises wickedness and gives wicked counsel in the city (Ez 11:1,2,13).

Peleg. Son of Eber and the father of Reu (Gn 10:25; 11:16–19; 1 Chr 1:19,25; Lk 3:35, KJV Phalec) in whose day the earth was divided

(Peleg means division or water course). Precisely what the division refers to is still debated. Suggestions include: (1) the geographical and linguistic dispersion following the Tower of Babel fiasco (Gn 11:1–9), (2) dispersion of Noah's descendants, (3) separation of the people of Arpachshad from Joktanide Arabs (Gn 10:24–29), (4) the division of land by irrigation canals (the term is so used in Is 30:25; 32:2; Jb 29:6; 38:25). Peleg lived four generations after Shem (five in the Lukan account). Origin of the name is usually traced to the city of Phalga, north of the junction of the Euphrates and Khabur Rivers.

See GENEALOGY OF JESUS CHRIST.

Pelet. 1. Jahdai's son from Judah's tribe (1 Chr 2:47).

2. Warrior from Benjamin's tribe who joined David at Ziklag in his struggle against King Saul. Pelet was one of David's ambidextrous archers and slingers (1 Chr 12:2,3).

Peleth. 1. On's father from Reuben's tribe (Nm 16:1).

2. Jonathan's son and a Jerahmeelite from Judah's tribe (1 Chr 2:33).

Pelethites. Bodyguards of David, and loyal mercenaries during the king's political setbacks. They are always associated with the Cherethites, and both are believed to be of Philistine stock with Crete as their place of origin (Caphtor, home of the Philistines, generally taken to be Crete, Am 9:7). The Pelethites accompanied David when he fled Jerusalem under threat from Absalom's forces (2 Sm 15:18) and fought for David in the rebellion of Sheba (2 Sm 20:7). Their leader, Benaiah, supported Solomon's claim to David's throne against the ambitions of Adonijah, and the presence of the Pelethites at Solomon's anointing surely contributed to Adonijah's demise (1 Kgs 1:38,44). Mercenaries from the Aegean were common.

Pelican. See BIRDS.

Pella. City located east of the Jordan River in the Decapolis region. There is no reference to this city in the Bible, but records show that it was an important Canaanite city, influenced by Egypt and later by Greece and Rome. During the Jewish revolt against Rome (AD 66–70), Pella became a refuge for many Christians and a center for the early church.

See DECAPOLIS.

Pelonite. Designation given to two of David's mighty men, Helez and Ahijah (1 Chr 11:27,36; 27:10). No source for the designation is known, which has led some scholars to consider it a textual corruption. In 2 Samuel 23:26, Helez is called a Paltite, and Ahijah is probably identical to Eliam the Gilonite in 2 Samuel 23:34. The latter are preferred over "Pelonite" in both cases. Others suggest that Pelonite is derived from the town Beth-pelet (see Jos 15:27; Neh 11:26).

Pelusium. City known for its flax and wine, but also a strategic fortified town on Egypt's Mediterranean coast, situated on the trade route between Egypt and Mesopotamia (Ez 30:15,16). Today the site is called Tell Farama and is located about 20 miles southeast of Port Said. The Hebrew OT uses the old Egyptian name for the town, *Sin* meaning "fortress." Some English translations of the OT (e.g., KJV) use this English name. When the Greeks controlled Egypt they renamed the town Pelusium, "the muddy city," apparently confusing the Egyptian name with a similar Egyptian word *sin* meaning "mud" or "clay." In Ezekiel it is called "the stronghold of Egypt" because it provided a defense against the ever present danger of attack from the north.

Pen. *See* WRITING AND BOOKS.

Pence. KJV form of denarius in Matthew 18:28; Mark 14:5; Luke 7:41; 10:35; and John 12:5.

See COINS; MONEY AND BANKING.

Peniel. Alternate form of Penuel, the Palestinian city where Jacob wrestled with the "angel" of God, in Genesis 32:30.

See PENUEL (PLACE).

Peninnah. One of Elkanah's two wives, the other and more favored being Hannah (1 Sm 1:2–6). Peninnah's fortune in bearing children was the source of much domestic friction for the childless Hannah, especially at the time of the annual sacrifice at Shiloh. Rabbinic tradition positively explains Peninnah's taunts as attempts to provoke Hannah into pregnancy, but the biblical record portrays the women as rivals.

Penknife. Iron tool used to sharpen reed pens, cut papyrus, and carve letters in stone. It is mentioned by name only in Jeremiah 36:23, but referred to elsewhere as a pen or tool of iron (Jb 19:24; Jer 17:1). Another reference may be found in Isaiah 8:1 (KJV "a man's pen," RSV "in common characters," NASB "in ordinary letters," NEB "in common writing"). The Hebrew word in Isaiah 8:1 is translated as a graving tool in Exodus 32:4.

See WRITING AND BOOKS.

Penny. 1. KJV translation of denarius (Mt 20:2,9,10,13; 22:19; Mk 12:15; Lk 20:24; Rv 6:6).

2. RSV translation of the Roman assarion, equivalent to one-sixteenth of the denarius (Mt 10:29; Lk 12:6).

3. RSV translation of the Roman quadrans equivalent to one-fourth of the assarion, or one sixty-fourth of the denarius (Mt 5:26; Mk 12:42).

See COINS; MONEY AND BANKING.

Pentateuch. Word formed by two Greek words, *pente*, "five," and *teuchos*, "book" and commonly used to refer to the first five books of the OT (Genesis, Exodus, Leviticus, Numbers, Deuteronomy). This portion of God's Word was written by the prophet Moses (Ex 17:14; 24:4; 34:27; Nm 33:1,2; Dt 31:9,22) and constitutes the foundation upon which all other Scripture rests. The Pentateuch begins with the creation of the universe and records God's dealings with mankind in the Garden of Eden, his preparation of a seed-bearing line (the patriarchal stories), and the formation of the nation Israel. A substantial portion of the Pentateuch consists of laws governing the religious and civil life of the theocratic nation.

See GENESIS, BOOK OF; EXODUS, BOOK OF; LEVITICUS, BOOK OF; NUMBERS, BOOK OF; DEUTERONOMY, BOOK OF; DOCUMENTARY HYPOTHESIS; TORAH.

Pentecost. Word derived from the Greek word *pentēkostē* (fiftieth) which stood for the festival celebrated on the 50th day after Passover. In the OT this festival, called *Shavuoth* (Weeks) in Judaism, is referred to as the Feast of Weeks (Ex 34:22; Dt 16:10) because it occurs 7 weeks after Passover. Other names include "the Feast of Harvest" (Ex 23:16) because of its relationship with harvest season and "the Day of First Fruits" (Nm 28:26) because two loaves of newly ground grain were presented before the Lord. This latter name, however, should be distinguished from the offering of first fruits at the beginning of the harvest season as mentioned in Leviticus 23:9–14.

The Feast of Weeks was one of three OT pilgrimage festivals when individuals were to appear before the Lord with gifts and offerings (Ex 23:14–17). The festival was primarily a harvest festival and celebrated the end of the barley harvest and the beginning of the wheat harvest. Traditionally, grain harvest extended from Passover, when the first grain was cut (Dt 16:9) around mid-April, to Pentecost which marked its conclusion in mid-June. Josephus' statement that Pentecost was called "closing" illustrates this understanding (*Antiq.* 3.10.6).

Each year the priest waved a sheaf of newly harvested grain before the Lord on the day after the sabbath during the Festival of Unleavened Bread (the period of 7 days following Passover). The people then counted 50 days from the offering of that first sheaf of grain until the day after the seventh sabbath to observe the Feast of Weeks (Lv 23:11). On this day 2 loaves made of 2/10 of an ephah of flour and baked with yeast were waved before the Lord (Lv 23:17) and freewill offerings were encouraged (Dt 16:10). In addition to the agricultural produce which represented thanksgiving for God's blessing, during harvest burnt offerings of various animals were prescribed (Lv 23:18; Nm 28:27). This harvest festival was a time of great rejoicing and a holy assembly when no work was to be done (Lv 23:21; Dt 16:11). Observance of the Feast of Weeks during Solomon's time (2 Chr 8:13) is the only OT reference outside of the Pentateuch, for Ezekiel makes no mention of it in his calendar for future festivals (Ez 45,46).

Pentecost is first mentioned in the NT as the occasion for the outpouring of the Holy Spirit upon the disciples of Christ, an event which many theologians understand as marking the beginning of the church (Acts 2:1). Since this was a required festival Jews had gathered from great distances to observe Pentecost in Jerusalem, making it an appropriate time for God's work. On two occasions Paul takes into consideration the Festival of Pentecost when anticipating his travels. In the first instance he writes to the Corinthians about delaying his visit to them until after Pentecost (1 Cor 16:8) while later he is desirous of traveling to Jerusalem in time for Pentecost (Acts 20:16).

Judaism today celebrates the giving of the Law at Sinai on Shavuot in addition to aspects of the harvest. After the destruction of the temple in AD 70 this association, which was supported from Exodus 19:1, where it is stated that the Law was given three months after the first Passover, became stronger and is now a central part of the festival. In addition to readings from the Pentateuch, the Book of Ruth is read because of its harvest background. Much later in Judaism this festival came to commemorate the anniversary of David's death so the Psalms are read as well.

Christians annually celebrate Pentecost on a designated Sunday on the assumption that 50 days from Passover to the Feast of Weeks were counted until the day after the seventh sabbath (our Sunday) as prescribed by Leviticus 23:15,16. According to some Jewish interpreters, however, the sabbath of Leviticus was not the sabbath day but the holy day of Passover which fell on a different day each year. Following this view, which was supported by the Pharisees, the Feast of Weeks was observed on a different day each year rather than the day after the seventh sabbath. While the early church celebrated God's gift of the Holy Spirit on Pentecost, in time it became a popular occasion for baptisms. The white dress of the candidates gave rise to the name Whitsunday (White Sunday) in Christian tradition.

See FEASTS AND FESTIVALS OF ISRAEL.

Penuel (Person). 1. Descendant (possibly son) of Hur and father (in the sense of progenitor) of Gedor from Judah's tribe (1 Chr 4:4).

2. Shashak's son from Benjamin's tribe (1 Chr 8:25).

Penuel (Place). Name given to the place near the Jabbok River where Jacob strove all night with God (Gn 32:31); alternately called Peniel in verse 30. During the period of the judges Gideon destroyed the tower of Penuel and killed the men of the city for refusing to join him in war against the Midianites (Jgs 8:8,9,17). Later, King Jeroboam rebuilt the town (1 Kgs 12:25). It was positioned near Succoth east of the Jordan River, though its exact location remains uncertain.

People of the East. Tribes located east and northeast of Canaan, many of them overtly hostile to the Jews. Genesis 29:1 provides the first reference to these peoples. Jacob, enroute to Haran, crossed through territory designated as "the land of the people of the east."

The comprehensiveness of the term is evident in the way it is used to refer to nomads (Ez 25:10) or Mesopotamians (1 Kgs 4:30). The term also occurs in association with specific tribes, such as the Amalekites (Jgs 6:3), Ammonites (Ez 25:4), Edomites (Is 11:14), Kedarites (Jer 49:28), Midianites (Jgs 6:33), and Moabites (Ez 25:10).

The most distinguished OT personality linked to the term is the patriarch Job, who is called the greatest man among all the people of the east (Jb 1:3). Job's homeland, the land of Uz, was probably in the vicinity of Edom to the southeast of the Dead Sea. This being the case, his link to the people of Israel may be more spiritual than genealogical.

People of the Land. OT phrase also known by its Hebrew transliteration, 'Am-Ha'arez. In a generic sense, the 'Am-Ha'arez referred to a political or ethnic group of people, such as the Hittite sons of Heth (Gn 23:7), the Egyptians (Gn 42:6), the Israelites (Ex 5:5), the nations of Canaan (Nm 13:28; Neh 9:24), and the Ammonites (Nm 21:34). With the expansion of Israel as a nation, this expression was used to define the general class of people who were not part of the upper religious and political levels of society (2 Kgs 11:14–20; 25:3; 2 Chr 33:25; Jer 52:25). During the postexilic period, the mixed race of Jews who had intermarried with heathen peoples were called the people of the land and mostly shunned by Ezra and his followers (Ezr 4:4; 10:2,11; Neh 10:28–31). Later rabbinic Judaism labeled the Jewish people who were unwilling or unable to observe the whole Law as the 'Am-Ha'arez.

See Judaism.

Peoples. *See* Nations.

Peor. Contraction for the Canaanite god of Baal-peor, or for the place itself (Nm 25:3,5; 23:28).

See Baal-peor; Canaanite Deities and Religion.

Peor (Place). 1. Mountain east of Jordan and north of the Dead Sea where Balak led Balaam in a final effort to evoke a curse on Israel (Nm 23:28). The camp of Israel at Shittim was visible from the site (Nm 24:2). There Israel initiated a sexual orgy with the Moabite women, and worshiped Baal (Nm 25:1–13). The exact location of the mountain is not certain, though Eusebius and Jerome place it opposite Jericho on the way to Heshbon. It is thus believed to be near Mt Nebo in the Abarim range.

2. Place cited in the Septuagint in Joshua 15:59, but not in Hebrew manuscripts. It is identified as the modern Khirbet Faghur, southwest of Bethlehem.

Perazim, Mount. Mountain mentioned in Isaiah 28:21, apparently near Baal-perazim, the "Baal of Breaches," where David defeated the Philistines. From the context of 2 Samuel 5:20, this battleground was evidently located in the Valley of Rephaim, southwest of Jerusalem.

Perdition. Term used eight times in the KJV NT to express the eternal dimension of the destruction of life and self. In Philippians 1:28, "perdition" is the opposite of "salvation." Hebrews 10:39 contrasts it with "preserving one's soul." Second Peter 3:7 links perdition with the day of judgment, while 1 Timothy 6:9 has both present and future in view. "Son of Perdition" is a label affirming the destiny of the betrayer Judas (Jn 17:12) and of the antichrist (2 Thes 3:2). In Revelation 17:8,11 perdition designates the final abode of the beast. Revelation 19:20 and 20:10 identify this abode as the "lake of fire," a place of everlasting torment.

"Perdition" occurs four times in the RSV (Jn 17:12; 2 Thes 2:3; Rv 17:8,11) and twice in the OT (2 Sm 22:5; Ps 18:4). In the latter, the parallel lines of Hebrew poetry show that perdition is the equivalent of death.

See Lake of Fire; Antichrist; Judgment; Death.

Perea. Term not occurring in the NT except in the 4th-century manuscript, Codex Sinaiticus, where it appears in Luke 6:17, and is treated as a variant reading by most editions of the Greek NT. It was used in the 1st century AD by Josephus to refer to the region "beyond the Jordan" (he derived the word Perea from the Greek "beyond"). The geographical location of the area is therefore best understood from Josephus' *War of the Jews* (3.3.3). "Now the length of Perea is from Macherus to Pella, and its breadth from Philadelphia to Jordan; its northern parts are bounded by Pella, as we have already said, as well as its western with Jordan; the land of Moab is its southern border, and its eastern limits reach to Arabia, and Silbonitis, and besides to Philadelphene and Gerasa." Gadara is called "the metropolis of Perea," by Josephus because it was a "place of strength" and because "many of the citizens of Gadara were rich men" (*War* 4.7.3). This Gadara is not to be confused with the Gadara of the Decapolis, modern Um Qeis, but is to be identified with Tell Gadura about 15 miles northwest of modern Amman, Jordan.

The Decapolis is separated from Perea in Matthew 4:25, where it is listed among the various sections of Palestine from which people came to hear Jesus. Perea is here called the region "beyond the Jordan" and is so designated also in Mark 3:8. In one place Matthew refers to Perea as "the region of Judea beyond the Jordan" (19:1), which is perplexing because politically Perea was never a part of Judea, belonging to the jurisdiction not of Archelaeus but of Herod Antipas, who also controlled Galilee. The parallel passage in Mark 10:1 reads: "the region of Judah *and* beyond the Jordan." Perhaps Matthew is using the phrase to refer to that part of Perea which, though politically not a part of Judea, was Jewish in population. In his *Natural History* (AD 77) Pliny spoke of Perea as a place "separated from the *other parts* of Judaea by the River Jordan" (5.70), and the "*rest* of Judea" as being divided into 10 local government areas, as though he considered Perea to be a part of Judea. However, this may be a mistaken assumption as Pliny's knowledge of the immediate area is somewhat questionable; in the same context he erroneously asserts that the Dead Sea is "more than 100 miles long and fully 75 miles wide at its widest part" (*Nat. Hist.* 5.72), whereas in reality it is less than 50 miles long and only 11 miles wide.

The area was well known and often mentioned in the OT by the phrase "beyond the Jordan" (Nm 22:1; Dt 1:1,5), and was occupied in its southern portion by the two Israelite tribes, Gad and Reuben (Jos 1:12–14). Stretching from the Brook Cherith in the north almost to the Arnon River in the south, Perea was virtually synonymous with OT Gilead (Jos 22:9; Jgs 5:17).

It seems to have been an important district in the decades before the birth of Christ (Hellenistic Period) when Jewish (Maccabean) leaders controlled it after 124 BC. Under Roman rule it was given to Herod the Great until his death in 4 BC, when it passed according to his will into the hands of his son Herod Antipas, along with Galilee. Because the area was beautiful and productive, and had trees noted for their medicinal balm (Jer 8:22; 46:11) it was always well populated and supported numerous well-known cities such as Pella, Madeba, Jabesh-gilead, Succoth, Penuel, and Gerasa (modern Jerash). Herod Antipas even had a fort named Macherus in the southern extremities of Perea, where he imprisoned John the Baptist and had him put to death (Josephus, *Antiq.* 18.5.2).

It was customary for Jews traveling back and forth from Galilee to Judea to cross the Jordan into Perea in order to avoid contact with the Samaritans. Before his death, John the Baptist had been baptizing in Bethany beyond the Jordan when he announced Jesus as the Lamb of God (Jn 1:28,29) and Jesus returned here during his ministry once when he was being severely persecuted (Jn 10:40).

Peres. Singular form of Parsin meaning "divided" (Dn 5:28).

See MENE, MENE, TEKEL, PARSIN.

Peresh. Son of Maachah and Machir from Manasseh's tribe, and the grandson of King Manasseh (1 Chr 7:16).

Perez, Perezite. Son of Judah whose name is derived from a Hebrew word meaning "he who bursts forth"; his name refers to the manner in which he unexpectedly came first from Tamar's womb before his twin brother Zerah (Gn 38:29). He fathered two sons, Hezron and Hamul, and became the ancestral head of the Perezite family (Gn 46:12; Nm 26:20,21; 1 Chr 2:4,5; 4:1). The KJV and the Apocrypha translate the name variously as Pharez, Phares, and Pharzite. Through the descent of his son Hezron he became the ancestor of David and Jesus Christ (Ru 4:18–22; Mt 1:3; Lk 3:33). The esteem which this clan enjoyed in the tribe of Judah is evidenced by the blessing pronounced upon it by the men of Bethlehem (Ru 4:12). A descendant named Jashobeam commanded David's captains for the first month of each year (1 Chr 27:2,3). Upon the return from captivity in Babylon, 468 Perezites were chosen to live in Jerusalem (1 Chr 9:4; Neh 11:4,6).

Perez-uzza, Perez-uzzah. Alternate names given to the site associated with the threshing floor of Nacon in 1 Chronicles 13:11 and 2 Samuel 6:8, respectively.

See NACON.

Perfume. Term covering a wide range of materials prepared from ground up minerals, vegetable oils, and roots, which were used from the earliest times to enhance one's personal appearance or to produce pleasing fragrances both for secular and religious purposes. The Bible mentions a wide variety of perfumes such as aloes, balm, balsam, bdellium, cassia, cinnamon, frankincense, gum, myrrh, nard, sweet cane, spice, ointment, and so on. There must have been a vigorous perfume trade with such lands as Arabia (frankincense, myrrh), India (aloes, nard), Ceylon (cinnamon), Persia (the spice galbanum), and Somaliland (frankincense). In the Bible there are several references to those who traded in these items, for example, the Arabian (Ishmaelite) merchants who took Joseph to Egypt (Gn 37:25), the caravans of the Queen of Sheba (1 Kgs 10:10), and the traders of Sheba and Raamah who brought spices to Tyre (Ez 27:22).

There are several biblical references to those who prepared perfumes. Thus Bezalel prepared holy anointing oil and sacred incense for the tabernacle (Ex 37:29). The holy anointing oil was a mixture of four constituents (Ex 30:22–25): myrrh, cinnamon, aromatic cane, and cassia mixed in olive oil. Samuel warned the people that a king would turn the women of the land into perfume-makers (1 Sm 8:13). In postexilic times some priests were charged with the mixing of perfumes for incense (1 Chr 9:30) and a perfumer is mentioned among those who built Nehemiah's wall (Neh 3:8).

Modern excavation has produced tangible evidence of a variety of cosmetic vessels and appliances, although strangely enough little is said in the Bible about these (Is 3:20; Mt 26:7; Mk 14:3; Lk 7:37). The reference to alabaster containers gains support from their use in Egypt and from archaeology. The ancient town sites of Palestine have yielded numerous small decorated cosmetic bowls often made of alabaster, small bottles for scents and oils, and palettes for mixing cosmetics. Some of these items are imports from lands like Egypt.

There was a wide range of uses for the various perfumes, whether powders or oils. Perfumed oils were regularly used to anoint the body in order to soothe sun-dried skin (Ru 3:3; 2 Sm 12:20). On one occasion King Ahaz clothed, fed, and anointed men who returned home from captivity (2 Chr 28:15). The rich in the land could afford the "finest oils" (Am 6:6) although such extravagance could be costly (Prv 21:17). This biblical picture is corroborated by evidence from Egypt and Mesopotamia. In particular, there was a lavish use of oils and ointments in the royal palaces of the East.

The use of paints to enhance personal appearance was common. The areas around the eyes and the eyebrows were darkened with black galena (lead sulfide). Queen Jezebel was given to this practice (2 Kgs 9:30) and harlots "enlarged the eyes" with eyepaint (Jer 4:30; Ez 23:40).

Ointments and oils of various kinds which gave off a pleasing fragrance were regularly used. The Song of Songs has many references to such ointments (1:3), some of which are specifically named: spikenard (1:12; 4:13,14), myrrh (1:13; 3:6; 4:6; 5:1,5,13), frankincense (3:6; 4:6), spices (5:13; 6:2; 8:14), henna (1:14; 4:13), fragrant powders (3:6), saffron (4:14), calamus and cinnamon (4:14). But there are references in other parts of the Bible to perfumes and ointments of various kinds (1 Kgs 10:2,10; 2 Kgs 20:13; Prv 27:9; Is 3:24).

Perfumes were put on clothes (Ps 45:8; Sg 4:11) and sprinkled on couches (Prv 7:17). Perfumes and spices also played an important role in the burial of the dead. They were used in embalming (Gn 50:2,3,26) and were sprinkled on the bier or burned in the fire at some funerals (2 Chr 16:14). Nicodemus brought a mixture of myrrh and aloes to be used in wrapping the body of Jesus (Jn 19:39,40). In the funeral of Herod the Great 500 slaves carried the spices (Josephus, *Antiq.* 17.8.3).

Besides the personal use of such materials, there was a wide range of oils, perfumes, and incense used in worship. A holy anointing oil was used to anoint the tabernacle and its furnishings and the Aaronic priests at their induction (Ex 30:22–25; Ps 133). An interesting prescription for the sacred incense to be prepared by the perfumer is given in Exodus 30:34,35. The items listed are well known both in Israel and in other parts of the ancient East. The NT contains a number of figurative references. Christ gave himself as a fragrant offering to God (Eph 5:2). The gifts of the Philippians to Paul were described as a fragrant offering (Phil 4:18) and the prayers of the saints are described as bowls of incense (Rv 5:8).

A clearer understanding of the character and use of the perfumes of the Bible comes from a comparative study of similar usages in neighboring countries. This is available in their literature and in excavations.

See FASHION AND DRESS; OINTMENT; OIL; TRADES AND OCCUPATIONS (PERFUMER).

Perfumer.   Pharmacist.

See TRADES AND OCCUPATIONS.

Perga.   City probably of very early Greek origin and the religious capital of ancient Pamphylia. In the 2nd century BC the Romans overthrew a Syrian garrison there, and thereafter the city apparently had a substantial degree of independence from external control.

On their first missionary journey Paul and his colleagues passed through the city on their way to Pisidian Antioch. The Acts of the Apostles reports no preaching activity on that occasion, but notes only that it was at Perga that

Ruins at Perga.

John Mark left his companions and returned to Jerusalem (13:13,14).

If we assume that Luke would have recorded the fact that Paul had preached during this visit, we can only speculate why he did not do so. The presence nearby of a renowned temple of Artemis, an Anatolian nature goddess, would surely have challenged rather than deterred him. The apostle may have been ill (some commentators suggest a possible connection with the reference in Gal 4:13), but in that case we might have expected Barnabas to have taken his place. It has been suggested that at this point the group had disagreed about outreach to and acceptance of Gentiles, and that it was his differences with Paul (and perhaps his resentment at the latter's leadership) that precipitated John Mark's departure.

On the homeward journey, however, Paul and Barnabas "preached the word in Perga" before going on down to Attalia, where they took a ship to Antioch (Acts 14:25,26). The results from that preaching are not known, but it is evident that Christianity did not flourish in Perga as it did in other cities of Asia Minor.

J.D. Douglas

Pergamum, Pergamos. City just north of the Caicus River, in the southern part of Mysia (eastern Turkey), and one of the greatest cultural centers of the Hellenistic era. The early geographer Strabo (63 BC–AD 24?) called the area around Pergamum the richest land in Mysia. It is mentioned only twice in the Bible (Rv 1:11; 2:12; KJV Pergamos), both times referring to one of the seven churches of Asia to which the last book of the NT was written.

The province of Mysia was combined with Lydia and Caria to form the Roman district of Asia, comprising the western portion of modern Turkey. Pergamum lies less than 20 miles inland from the sea and about 3 miles north of the Caicus River on a large conical hill, 1000 feet high, which is sandwiched between 2 smaller streams that flow into the Caicus, the Selinus on the west and the Cetius on the east. This natural position of strength combined with its religious significance as a temple site made it a desirable place to store wealth. Lysimachus, one of Alexander the Great's generals, deposited an enormous sum of money here (9000 talents) which was later used by Pergamene kings to create the glory of Pergamum. Although coins were minted in Pergamum before 400 BC, it was not a great city until long after the death of Alexander.

The splendor of Pergamum began with Attalus I (241–197 BC) who took the title of king and founded the Attalic dynasty. His wealth, success in battle (defeating the Gauls who moved into Galatia in 278 BC), and his judicial alliance with the rising power of Rome contributed to his ability to embellish his kingdom with Hellenistic culture, adorning it with temples, theaters, a library, and other public buildings.

He was succeeded by his son Eumenes II who, because of his help in Rome's conquest of the Seleucid kingdom of Syria, was given in 189 all Seleucid territory northwest of the Tarus mountains, thus extending the Pergamene kingdom from the Tarus to the Dardanelles. Under Eumenes (197–159), Pergamum attained the height of its power and glory. He expanded the library to 200,000 volumes (Strabo, 609) thus rivaling the great one at Alexandria, and among other building programs constructed the Altar of Zeus which stood on a hill 800 feet above the city and could be seen for miles. It is tempting to see this altar as the place "where Satan's throne is" (Rv 2:13), especially since Pergamum was the chief center of worship for four of the greatest pagan deities—Zeus, Athena, Dionysus, and Asclepius. However, it may be that the author is referring to the fact that Pergamum was the center of emperor worship in Asia at that time.

The last king of the Attalic dynasty, Attalus III, died without leaving an heir in 133 BC. In his will he gave all of his kingdom to Rome with the exception of Pergamum and other Greek cities which were given freedom as independent administrative units and were exempt from tribute. In order to reduce its obligation to police the distant parts of the new territory, the Roman consul bequeathed the easternmost territory of Phrygia to Pontus and Cappadocia. Thus the newly created Roman province of Asia was smaller than the Pergamene Empire had been. Even though after 120 BC Phrygia was reclaimed by the Roman senate (upon the death of Mithridates, king of Pontus), it was not actually incorporated into Asia until 85. At that time, the Roman provincial unit was again roughly comparable in size to the old Pergamene kingdom.

Pergamum was built across the centuries in three separate areas. The upper city on top of the mountain was the northernmost area and was largely the domain of the royal family, the nobility, and the military commanders. It had an air of officialdom. The middle city, further south and lower down the mountain, contained the part of the city visited by the common people, and included sportsfields for the youth and temples frequented by those of less education. These facilities were not controlled directly by the city and the priesthood, and the general citizenship of Pergamum had unrestricted access to them. The third area, across the Selinus River to the southwest, contained

The upper and middle cities of Pergamum.

the famous Asclepian of Pergamum, a center for the healing arts containing a medical school which produced the celebrated physician Galen. Here the god Asclepius was worshiped in a cylindrical temple, which was a small replica of the famed Pantheon built in Rome some 20 years earlier (AD 130). There was also a lovely fountain, theater, pool, medical building, library, and various temples, the striking remains of which may still be seen.

The references in Revelation 2:12–15 to the Nicolaitans and those who hold the doctrine of Balaam probably refers to the extensive influence of the immoral and idolatrous worship of Dionysus and Aphrodite, which was especially offensive to the known Jewish population (Josephus, *Antiq.* 14.10.22) as well as to true Christians. Pliny (*Nat Hist* 5.30) considered Pergamum to be the most distinguished city of Asia, and as such it would have been the natural place for emperor worship. The reference to the martyrdom of Antipas, "my faithful witness" (Rv 2:13), can easily be understood in the light of the Jewish and Christian refusal to worship the emperor in this city.

Because of the extensive manufacture of writing material from sheepskin in Pergamum, the name parchment (pergamena) was given to the product.   JOHN R. McRAY

Perida. Alternate rendering of Peruda, the ancestor of a family of servants that returned to Jerusalem after the exile, in Nehemiah 7:57.

See PERUDA.

Perizzite. One of several population segments occupying the land of Palestine prior and subsequent to the Israelite conquest (Gn 15:20; Ex 3:8,17; 23:23; 33:2; 34:11; Dt 7:1; 20:17; Jos 3:10; 9:1; 11:3; 12:8; 24:11; 1 Kgs 9:20; 2 Chr 8:7; Ezr 9:1; Neh 9:8). The enumeration of these peoples throughout the OT serves a variety of purposes, none of which is strictly historical or geographical. It serves to inform the reader that, no matter how numerous, the doom of these people is sure when God's time

has come (Gn 15:20; Ex 3:8). At other times they are mentioned to illustrate the hostility of the enemies of God and of the people of God against Israel's onward march into the land promised to them by the Lord (Jos 9:1; 11:3; 24:11). But they are also portrayed as conquered and reduced to servile labor (Jos 12:8; 1 Kgs 9:20). In the postexilic period they continue to be a threat to the purity of life of the covenant community recently settled in the land of their fathers (Ezr 9:1), even though it is acknowledged by that same community that the Lord of the covenant had given the land in which they dwelt to the Israelites (Neh 9:8).

There are a few instances where the word "Perizzites" occurs in conjunction with "Canaanites" (Gn 13:7; 34:30; Jgs 1:4,5), and in one instance it is combined with "Rephaites" (Jos 17:15). The name "Pirizzi" also occurs once in the tablets of El Amarna.

The exact identity of the Perizzites has thus far remained obscure. In a few instances, those in which the name occurs in conjuction with "Canaanites," it seems to refer to one of the major components of Canaan's population. Some have even suggested that the Perizzites were the pre-Canaanite population of Palestine, in view of the omission of them in the list of Genesis 10:10. But this cannot be proven.

Others have attempted to read this name as an appellative meaning "inhabitants of unwalled villages." This view finds some support in another Hebrew word: *perazoth*, "unwalled villages" (Est 9:19; Ez 38:11; Zec 2:4; cf. also *perazi*, "open country," Dt 3:5; 1 Sm 6:18). But the fact that the name occurs so frequently among other peoples whose identity is known to a certain extent should caution against such an approach.

Several commentators, instead of regarding the Perizzites as one of the major components of Canaan's population, have sought to localize them, either in the vicinity of Bethel (cf. Gn 13:7) or of Shechem (Gn 34:30), or in the territory of Judah (Jgs 1:4,5). But these locales are by no means contiguous. The reference to the Rephaim in Joshua 17:13 has prompted the suggestion that the Perizzites belonged to the Transjordan region, but this does not follow either from the immediate context or from the use of the word "Rephaim" elsewhere.

See CANAAN, CANAANITES.

Persecution. Infliction of suffering, injury, or death on another. The Bible begins with the persecution of the righteous by the unrighteous (Gn 4:3–7 "regard for Abel"; Mt 23:35; Heb 11:4). The Wisdom of Solomon (2:12–20) dramatically illustrates the envy and guilt that prompt such persecution. Lot's experience likewise illustrates the suffering involved in refusing to conform to popular behavior (Gn 19:9; 2 Pt 2:7,8). The ill-treatment of Israel in Egypt, like her later oppression by the Philistines, Midianites, and others, had economic and political grounds. Persecution for religious reasons, of those who refused the royal policy of syncretism and official tolerance of injustice and pagan immoralities, becomes frequent from Elijah's period onward (1 Kgs 19:10). Later prophets, as spokesmen of uncompromising truth and the claims of divine Law in face of social evils, suffered severely at the hands of the ruling classes, so that persecution became, in Jewish eyes, the hallmark of the true prophet (2 Chr 36:15,16; Mt 5:12; 23:29–37; Acts 7:52; Heb 11:32–38).

Daniel's stories illustrate persecution during the exile. On the return under foreign rule, strict Jews ("saints," "holy ones," "the poor righteous") sought to preserve the nation's identity and religion amid alien pressures and the compromises of lax Jews anxious for accommodation and prosperity (1 Mc 1:11–15; 2:42–48). The result was the social oppression and harassment which made the repeated pleas for vindication and divine intervention, in such psalms as 10, 69, 140, and 149, painfully relevant in postexilic worship. This persecution reached a horrifying climax of cruelty during the Maccabean age, provoking armed resistance in response (2 Mc 6, 7; Heb 11:35–38).

Thus, despite her confidence in God's sovereignty and "protection," Israel learned that right does not always prosper in God's world, that faithfulness to truth does not ensure immunity from suffering, sacrifice, or martyrdom.

This acceptance of the high cost of righteousness was inherited by Christianity. Jesus repeatedly warned of persecution, even within households, and urged "armed" preparation for it, promising the Spirit's assistance at judicial examinations (Mt 5:11,12; 10:16–23,34–36; 23:34; Lk 6:26; 22:35,36). Jesus was deeply angered by the murder of John the Baptist by Herod (Lk 23:9), and foresaw his own fate. Because he criticized the legalism and nationalism of the Pharisees, and the compromises of the Sadducees to protect their own privileges (Jn 11:47–50); because he disappointed both the militarist and the miraculous hopes centered upon the Messiah by the common people, Jesus knew he would be rejected. His call to discipleship came to include warnings of danger, reviling, slander, accusation, flogging, arraignment before courts, hatred, and death. He frankly invited followers to prepare for crucifixion, as the only way to life and the kingdom (Mt 16:21,24–26; 20:17–19,21,22; Mk 10:29, 30; Jn 15:18–25; 16:1–4). Jesus was killed on the charges of subverting the nation, forbidding Roman tax payment, claiming to be king (Lk 23:2).

The first persecution of the church by Jewish authorities was provoked mainly by Peter's accusations concerning the murder of the Messiah. As apostolic influence increased, official action came to include imprisonment and beating (Acts 5:17,40). The powerful advocacy of the Hellenist Stephen provoked a Jewish mob to stone him (Acts 6,7), the signal for "a great persecution," scattering most Christians from Jerusalem. The conversion of the arch-persecutor, Saul of Tarsus, marked a resounding victory over opposition, and Herod's sudden death just after attacking the church "to please the Jews," was another (Acts 12:1–3,20–24).

As Christianity moved into the Gentile world, a new cause of Jewish persecution arose from disturbances in the synagogues (Acts 13:44,45,50; 14:1–6,19; 17:1,5,13; 18:4–6,12). The healing of the slave girl at Philippi led to a brief imprisonment (Acts 16:19–24); at Ephesus, the effect of Christian preaching on the trade of idol makers occasioned a dangerous threat, which the authorities averted (Acts 19:23–41). Twice warned of persecution, Paul was arrested at Jewish instigation, with more than 40 men involved in a plot to ambush him (Acts 21:4,5,10–15,27–36; 23:12–15). The Book of Acts closes with Paul awaiting trial before Caesar (28:30,31).

Throughout this period persecution of Christians was sporadic, local, and mainly Jewish, provoked by envy of the church's missionary success. Officially, Christianity, as a Jewish sect (Acts 24:5,14), shared the state's legal recognition won by the Jews. Thus Paul received Roman protection at Paphos, Philippi, Corinth, Ephesus, and Jerusalem from governors Felix and Festus and their adviser Herod Agrippa, and from the centurion conveying him to Rome. This explains Paul's confident appeal to Caesar; an imperial acquittal would ensure Christianity freedom from harassment throughout the empire.

Paul's attitude to persecution included regretful remembrance of his own persecuting days (Acts 22:4; 26:9–11; Gal 1:22–24), deliberate acceptance of risks in obedience to Christ (Acts 20:22–24; 21:13), continual warning that tribulation is inseparable from discipleship (Acts 14:22; Rom 5:3; 12:12; 1 Thes 3:4), and assurance that in every form of tribulation, Christians are more than conquerors (Rom 8:35–37).

Almost certainly, Paul was beheaded during fierce persecution at Rome following the fire for which the Christians were blamed. Christians were often accused of "atheism" (rejecting polytheism), of appealing only to slave classes, of "scandalous" love feasts, and unsociable, austere behavior (cf. Jn 15:19), making them a popular target for blame during public disasters.

About this time, Peter warned Christians in the East of the danger confronting the church. For a little while, "various trials" (cf. Heb 10:32–34) only prove the genuineness of faith. Slander should be answered by blameless living. Honor should be paid to the authorities. Suffering for righteousness should be accepted without fear. Let Christians prepare respectful defense, with consciences clear of blame. If they suffer for doing right, remember that Christ did too—for them. Thus they must "arm themselves" for suffering, not be surprised at persecution as "something strange." They are sharing Christ's sufferings. His final word is "Stand fast!" (1 Pt *passim*).

Mark, too, is thought to have written at this time for the benefit of the suffering Roman church. His Gospel dwells upon Christ's conflict, its causes and forms, and vividly portrays Christ's own heroic death. Like Peter, Mark meets persecution by pointing back to the suffering Lord.

Somewhat later, Christianity was exposed as an "illegal religion," no longer a protected sect of Judaism, by the introduction into synagogue services of a prayer against "Nazarenes" which Christians could not offer. Thereafter, the church was liable to official suppression. Rome readily incorporated old, national religions into state rituals for the sake of imperial unity, but she resisted new, nonconformist movements, especially those with secret meetings (as for the Eucharist), as politically dangerous (cf. Acts 17:6,7).

Towards the end of the century, faced with a growing church and political unrest, the state required public "worship" of "the genius of Rome" alongside any other religious rites, and in Domitian's reign (AD 81–96) this became worship of the living emperor, with elaborate temples and an official priesthood. When Christians refused, acknowledging Jesus alone as divine Lord, official, and increasingly barbaric, persecution began.

It is probable that Revelation reflects this situation (Rv 1:9; 2:13; 6:9; 13; 19:2). So the Bible ends as it began, with persecution of the people of God.   R. E. O. WHITE

See AFFLICTION; TRIBULATION.

Bibliography. W.H.C. Frend, *Martyrdom and Persecution in the Early Church*; H. Musurillo, *The Acts of the Christian Martyrs: Texts and Translations*; A.A. Trites, *The NT Concept of Witness*; W.C. Weinrich, *Spirit and Martyrdom*; H.B. Workman, *Persecution in the Early Church*.

Perseverance. Action or condition of steadfastness. OT Israel waited generations for ful-

fillment of promises which many believers never lived to see (Heb 11:1,13,21,22,39). The promise to Abraham sustained hope for centuries before Canaan was possessed. The lesson of the wilderness journey, when the waning of initial zeal prevented the people from entering the Promised Land, was never forgotten (Heb 3:16–19). Prophets looked constantly beyond failure and tragedy to distant horizons and nourished a patient faith (Jer 32:1–15; Hos 3:4,5; Jl 2:28,29; Hb 2:1–3; Dn 7; 12:11–13— "Blessed is he who waits . . .").

The NT everywhere urges similar perseverance. Among several Greek expressions, the usual word, *proskartereō*, has the root meaning "to attend continually, adhere steadfastly" (Mk 3:9; Acts 8:13; 10:7; Rom 13:6), and is variously translated "devoted," "continued," "constant," "(be) steadfast."

This persistent patience is called for in prayer (eight times, Lk 18:1–8; Col 4:2); in well doing (five times, Rom 2:7; Gal 6:9); in Christian teaching (four times, Acts 2:42; 2 Tm 3:14); in "holding fast" (repeatedly, to the Lord, the Head, our confidence, the word, our confession, eternal life, "what we have"); in affliction (2 Thes 1:4); in grace (Acts 13:43; 2 Cor 6:1); in faith (Acts 14:22; Col 1:23); in divine love (Jn 15:9; Jude 21); and quite generally "standing firm" (seven times, 1 Cor 16:13; 2 Thes 2:15); "abiding in Christ" (Jn 15:4–10; 1 Jn 2:28); "running with patience" (Heb 6:12; 12:1); "not falling away . . . failing to inherit" (Heb 3:12; 4:1–10); "watching with perseverance" (Eph 6:18) and "zealous to confirm our call and election" (2 Pt 1:10).

The failure in perseverance of Judas, Demas, and Hymenaeus must be kept in mind, and the dread possibility of neglecting so great a salvation (Heb 2:3), being disqualified (1 Cor 9:27), falling while we think we stand (1 Cor 10:12), and committing apostasy (Heb 6:1–8). For, as the Master said, "He who endures to the end will be saved" (Mt 10:22; 24:13).

Such extraordinary emphasis cannot be accidental. The pressures of pagan society, the danger of persecution, emotional reaction after a wonderful initial experience, and the apparent implication of "instant salvation," made it imperative for Christians to understand that "by your endurance you will gain your lives" (Lk 21:19; Rom 5:3; Col 1:11).

Yet Scripture never implies that perseverance depends entirely upon human effort. In the OT, the redeeming purpose of God is unswerving; God's covenant stands, though it needs to be renewed (Jer 31:31–34); divine love (*hesed*) connotes changeless loyalty; God "will never fail nor forsake" for "his own name's sake." The NT assurance is that Christ will

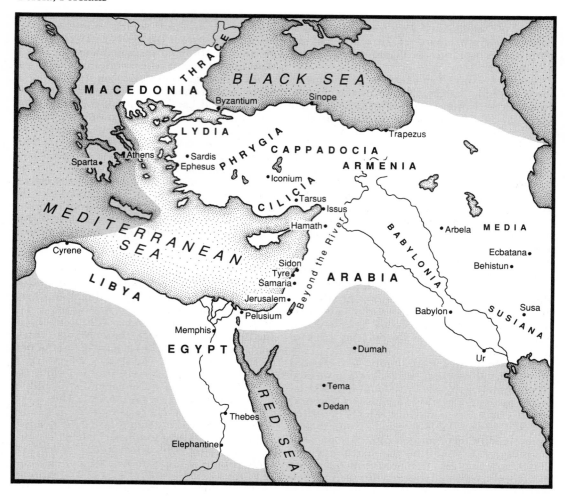

raise his own at the last day—none shall pluck them from his hand or the Father's. Christ will keep us from falling. God is faithful, who works in us to will and work for his good pleasure, and will not allow us to be tempted beyond our strength. Nothing, in heaven or earth, present or future, shall separate us from divine love. We are already sealed by the Holy Spirit as a guarantee of eternal salvation, and kept by the power of God unto salvation still to be revealed.

This scriptural tension between exhortation and assurance gives rise to debate between those who hold to the eternal, unchangeable salvation of every believer, and those who concede that salvation is all of God but *not* despite man's God-given freedom. The intellectual paradox is resolved only in the spiritual experience of utter dependence that yet knows itself fully responsible for seeking and accepting divine assistance.

R.E.O. WHITE

See BACKSLIDING; ASSURANCE.

Persia, Persians. Country laying just to the east of Mesopotamia (modern Iraq) and covering virtually the same territory as present-day Iran. It was known in ancient times by various forms of Fars or Pars, which came down to us as Persia. It continued to be known as Persia until 1935, when its name was changed to Iran. The official modern language of the country is Persian, an Indo-European language written in Arabic characters.

Geography and Climate. Persia served as a geographical link between inner Asia and the plateau of Asia Minor. It has been described as a triangle set between two depressions, the Persian Gulf on the south and the Caspian Sea to the north. The sides of the triangle are made up of mountain ranges which enclose an area of desert. On the west the Zagros Mountains run northwest-southeast, with many fertile valleys which are suitable for agriculture. Severe summer heat requires that animals be taken to cooler elevations during that season, so much of the population is nomadic.

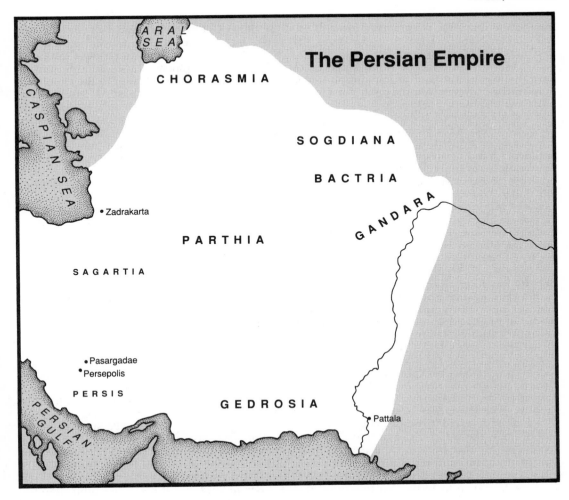

On the north is the Elburz range, with Mt Devavend reaching a height of more than 19,000 feet. The most heavily populated area of Persia is Azerbaijan, which, because of routes leading from various northern points, was one of the most accessible parts of the country and therefore had to be protected by strong fortifications.

Farther east the Elburz becomes the mountains of Khorasan, which also afford easy passage into the country. This district, which has been called the "granary of Iran," has been susceptible to foreign invasion over the centuries. On the south, the third side of the triangle, is another mountain range, the Makran.

Within these ranges is a saline depression, the southern part of which has been regarded as more arid than the Gobi Desert.

One of the important sections of the country was actually an extension of the Mesopotamian plain; this was known in ancient times as Susiana and now is called Khuzistan. Here the capital, Susa, was situated. Adjoining it to

the north is a mountain spur which was the location of Luristan, famous for its bronzes. Another plain, near the Caspian Sea, is tropical in climate; because of heavy rainfall it produces an abundance and variety of food.

Lacking a river like the Nile or the Tigris-Euphrates system and having no regular seasonal rains as in Palestine, the agriculture of Persia is dependent on irrigation. Rainfall varies dramatically from one region to another and the climate differs markedly with the topography.

In antiquity the lower mountains were heavily forested with many kinds of trees sought for building by the Sumerian kings of Mesopotamia. Alabaster, marble, lapis lazuli, carnelian, and turquoise were used from early times. Iron, copper, tin, and lead were found here. In modern times the oil resources of Iran have been widely exploited.

Prehistory and History. The Medes are a people about whom relatively little is known. They were pictured in Assyrian reliefs. It was the Median Cyaxares who teamed up with the Babylonian Nabopolassar to bring about the destruction of Nineveh in 612 BC.

In the 7th century BC a small kingdom of Persians was established at Parsumash under Achaemenes, after whom the great Persian dynasty was named. Teispes (675–640 BC), the son and successor of Achaemenes, was under the domination of the Medes, who were gathering forces to overthrow Assyria. Trouble for the Medes freed Teispes from their control and the weakness of Elam enabled him to gain the province of Parsa (modern Fars). The Assyrians under Ashurbanipal put an end to the nation of Elam and came into contact with the Persians under Cyrus I, son of Teispes.

Cambyses, son of Cyrus, married the daughter of the Median king, Astyges; their son, Cyrus II the Great (559–530 BC), built a great palace complex for himself at Pasargadae. The Babylonian king, Nabonidus, allied himself with Cyrus against the Medes. Cyrus fought and defeated his grandfather, Astyges, and made the Median capital, Ecbatana, "place of assembly" (Hamadan), his own capital and set up his archives there (cf. Ezr 6:2).

Cyrus, and later Darius, exhibited an attitude of benevolence and generosity toward defeated enemies, a policy which sometimes worked to the disadvantage of the Persians. A capable military leader, Cyrus invaded Asia Minor and defeated Croesus, king of Lydia, and brought the Greek cities of that area into subjection. He then solidified his eastern frontier. In 539 BC he captured Babylon with virtually no resistance and decreed that the exiled Jews could return to Jerusalem to rebuild the temple (Ezr 1:1–4).

The son of Cyrus, Cambyses II (529–522 BC), conquered Egypt. Upon his suicide the empire nearly disintegrated. Cambyses was succeeded by Darius I the Great (521–486 BC), the son of Hystaspis, satrap of Parthia. Darius put down the internal revolts and consolidated the empire. For efficient administration of his vast empire, he created 20 provinces or satrapies, each under a satrap or "protector of the kingdom." Other offices were instituted to check on the activities of the satraps. Darius changed the principal capital from Pasargadae to Persepolis where his building activities were continued by later Achaemenid kings to make a tremendous palace complex. He was a follower of Zoroaster and a worshiper of Ahura Mazda, as were Xerxes and Artaxerxes.

The early victory of Darius over the rebels is commemorated on the famous rock of Bisitun (Behistun). This memorial took the form of reliefs and a long cuneiform inscription in three languages, Persian, Elamite, and Akkadian. A copy of these records was made by Henry C. Rawlinson in 1855 at considerable risk, for the monument was difficult to approach, situated some 500 feet above the plain. This accomplishment played a large part in the deciphering of languages in the cuneiform script. During the later part of Darius' reign he suffered defeat at the hands of the Greeks at Marathon (491 BC). Upon his death Darius was buried in a rock-cut tomb at Naqsh-i-Rustam, a short distance northeast of Persepolis. This was a memorial consisting of reliefs and a trilingual inscription which lauds his person and reign. Later kings were buried in tombs cut in the same cliff.

Darius was succeeded by his son, Khshayarsha, better known as Xerxes (485–465 BC). An inscription at Persepolis lists the nations subject to him at the time of his accession and confirms his devotion to Ahura Mazda. During his rule the Persian fleet was defeated at Salamis (480 BC).

Artaxerxes I Longimanus (Artakhshathra, 464–424 BC) was followed by Darius II (423–405), Artaxerxes II Mnemon (404–359), Artaxerxes III Ochus (358–338), Arses (337–336), and finally Darius III (335–331).

The loss of the empire has been attributed to the cowardice of Darius III, whose armies were defeated by Alexander the Great at Issus in 333 BC and ultimately at Gaugamela, near modern Erbil (Arbela) in 331 BC. Upon the death of Alexander in 323 BC Persia became the lot of Seleucus, one of his generals. Persian sources say little of the period between Darius III and the beginnings of Sassanian rule in the early 3rd century AD.

Persia and the Bible. The biblical references to Persia occur in the later period of OT history and in the writings of the prophets who ministered during that time. The earliest mention is the reference to Cyrus in Isaiah 44:28–45:1, a passage which has confounded scholars who have felt that the foreknowledge of the Lord could not be so precise. This predictive prophecy was given to Isaiah by God more than 150 years before Cyrus captured Babylon and decreed the return of the captive Jews to Jerusalem.

The chronological notations in Daniel, Ezra, Nehemiah, Zechariah, Haggai, and Esther enable us to set chronological markers with some degree of certainty. The first year of Cyrus (Ezr 1:1) may be fixed at 538 BC. The rebuilding of the temple met with opposition from enemies of the Jews in the time of Cyrus and Darius (Ezr 4). In the reign of Artaxerxes a letter of complaint was written to the king, with the result that building on the temple was forced to halt (Ezr 4:23,24).

It was at this time that the prophets Haggai and Zechariah encouraged the Jews and urged the completion of the temple. Haggai 1:1 places the message of that prophet on the first day of the sixth month of the second year of Darius I, which translates into August 29, 520 BC. Similarly, Zechariah 1:1 is dated to the eighth month of the same year, that is, October/November 520 BC. The letter which was sent to Darius concerning the decree for rebuilding the temple (Ezr 5:6–17) brought about a search of the royal archives that Cyrus had set up at Ecbatana (cf. Ezr 6:1,2). The finding of the decree of Cyrus enabled the Jews to complete the temple project, which was finished on March 12, 515 BC (the third day of the month Adar in the sixth year of Darius, Ezr 6:15).

The work of Nehemiah occurred in the reign of Artaxerxes I Longimanus. Nehemiah's request that he be allowed to return to Jerusalem to rebuild the wall was made in the month of Nisan in the 20th year of Artaxerxes (Neh 2:1, April/May 445 BC). This building project also met with strong opposition. The date is generally confirmed by a letter from the 17th year of Darius II (408 BC) and found among the Elephantine papyri in Egypt. Two personal names found in Nehemiah also occur in this letter: the sons of Sanballat, Nehemiah's most virulent enemy (cf. Neh 2:19; 4:1–8), and Johanan the grandson of Eliashib, who was high priest at Jerusalem when Nehemiah arrived there (Neh 3:1). Another letter among these papyri grants Persian authority to the Jews at Elephantine to celebrate the Passover according to their custom.

The Book of Esther is set in the time of King Ahashuerus, who is Xerxes, referred to in Ezra 4:6 between Darius and Artaxerxes. The Hebrew Ahashuerus represents Khshayarsha, which the Greeks gave as Xerxes. On the other hand, the Septuagint has Artaxerxes and Josephus names Artaxerxes as the king of the Book of Esther. Esther provides a number of details of the life and customs of Persian royalty.

Persia figures in the prophecies of Ezekiel, where Persia is named among the armies of Tyre (27:10). It is also listed as an ally of Gog in the invasion of Israel (Ez 38:5). The recorded history in Daniel refers to Persia (10:1; cf. 5:31; ch 6; 11:1), as do the prophecies of that book (8:20; 11:2; cf. 2:32,39; 7:5; 8:3,4).

CARL E. DEVRIES

See POSTEXILIC PERIOD, THE.

Persis. Christian woman in Rome to whom Paul sent greetings (Rom 16:12).

Peruda. Head of a family of Solomon's servants (Ezr 2:55); alternately called Perida in Nehemiah 7:57. His descendants formed part of the remnant of Israel which returned to Jerusalem after the exile (1 Esd 5:33).

Pestilence. Derivation of a Hebrew word referring to a contagious epidemic disease of devastating proportions. Pestilence is never portrayed in the Bible as an aimless, naturally occurring phenomenon. It is always regarded as a judgment or punishment sent by God. Only once is it used to denote a disease of cattle and there it is usually translated "murrain" in the KJV (Ex 9:3).

Pestilence was one form of chastisement which was to be brought upon Israel for neglect of her covenant obligations (Lv 26:25; Dt 28:21). This is the reason for the frequent use of the word by both Jeremiah and Ezekiel. These prophets were prosecuting God's covenant lawsuit against his people. The sentence had been determined and they announced that its infliction was impending. For this reason pestilence almost always occurs as part of a list of scourges such as the formula "sword, famine and pestilence" used throughout Jeremiah's prophecy (14:12, etc.). Because pestilence is a punishment for sin, it is not applied indiscriminately upon all. The one who remains faithful will be protected from its effects (Ps 91:1–3). The enemies of Israel could also be objects of this form of judgment (Ps 78:50; Ez 28:23; 38:22).

Pestilence is not identical with plague in the OT. Plague often denotes such diseases as bubonic plague, measles, and smallpox whereas pestilence might refer to cholera, typhus, typhoid and dysentery—diseases often afflicting a city under siege. There is some overlap in the terms however. The death of 70,000 Israelites after David's census is an example of the severity and virulence of this form of divine chastisement (2 Sm 24:13,15).

The Greek word *loimos* occurs three times in the NT. In Acts 24:5 Tertullus used this term as a derogatory description of Paul—"a pestilent fellow." Jesus predicted that the destruction of the temple would be preceded by several judgments, including pestilence or plague (Mt 24:7; Lk 21:11).

See DISEASE; PLAGUE.

Peter, First Letter of.

Author. The author says he is the apostle Peter (1:1), a witness of Christ's sufferings (5:1)—thus one of the original apostles chosen by Jesus (Mk 3:14–19) as authoritative spokesmen. Also known as Simon and Cephas, Peter probably saw and felt Jesus' last hours of suffering more keenly than any of the other apostles (Mk 14:54) because he had denied Jesus three times (Mk 14:66–72). In 1 Peter the sufferings of Jesus are mentioned at least four times (1:11; 2:23; 4:1; 5:1).

Peter was known as the apostle to the Jews

just as Paul was the apostle to the Gentiles (Gal 2:7). Since Peter was a traveling missionary (1 Cor 1:12; 9:5), he could have actually visited the Asia Minor churches to whom this letter was sent.

That Peter had been with Jesus during his earthly ministry may help account for the strong influence of Jesus' teaching in 1 Peter. Except for James, 1 Peter probably echoes more of Jesus' words than any other NT letter (see 1:3,23 = John 3:3,7; 1:4 = Lk 12:33; 1:8 = Jn 20:29; 1:10–12 = Lk 24:25–27; 1:13 = Lk 12:35; 1:22 [4:8] = Jn 13:34 [15:12]; 2:4,7 = Mk 12:10 [Mt 21:42]; 2:12 = Mt 5:16; 2:19,20 = Lk 6:32–35; 2:25 = Jn 10:11,14; 3:9 = Lk 6:27,28; 4:13 = Mt 5:12; 5:3 = Lk 22:24–27; 5:5,6 = Lk 14:11 [18:14]).

Some scholars think that the Greek of this letter is too good to have been written by a former fisherman whose native language was Aramaic; that the doctrine is too much like Paul's to have been written by an apostle whose position was different from Paul's; and that someone wrote the letter after Peter's death and used his name to give apostolic weight to it.

Other scholars answer that if the author wanted to give authority to a letter whose teaching resembles Paul's, he would have used Paul's name, not Peter's; that most Galileans probably learned Greek as well as Aramaic early in life; and that there is no evidence that the teaching of Peter and Paul fundamentally differed. When Paul rebuked Peter (Gal 2:11–14) it was due to a temporary lapse in conduct, not a basic disagreement in teaching. Besides, some key doctrines of Paul are missing from 1 Peter (e.g., justification) and those similar to Paul's were the common possession of all the early churches. We may reasonably conclude that the apostle Peter wrote this letter.

Destination, Origin, Date. *Destination.* The people to whom 1 Peter is addressed lived in Pontus, Galatia, Cappadocia, Asia, and Bithynia. These Roman provinces covered all but the southernmost part of Asia Minor, the bulk of modern Turkey.

Christianity may have been brought back by pilgrim Jews converted in Jerusalem on the day of Pentecost (cf. Acts 2:9). More likely, these churches included some founded by Paul on his first and second missionary journeys, and others by unknown missionaries. Peter does not include himself among "those who have preached the gospel to you" (1:12).

Whether the readers were Christian Jews or converted pagan Gentiles is not known. First Peter 1:1 reads: "To God's elect, strangers in the world, scattered. . . ." That the readers are in some sense exiles is confirmed by 1:17 and 2:11. These verses could refer to a literal exile of Jews outside of Palestine, or a spiritual exile of all believers on earth because their true home is in heaven. No one denies that there was (and is) a literal Jewish dispersion (Diaspora). Peter, viewing the church as the true Israel (cf. Gal 6:16; Rom 2:29; Phil 3:3), may simply have transferred the language of exile from the nation Israel onto the church. The phrase used by Peter in 2:11 is almost identical to the one in Hebrews 11:13 (cf. Gn 23:4; Ps 39:12).

Against the view that construes the dispersion of 1:1 as Christians (Jew and Gentile), rather than Jews only, one may argue that Peter was specifically the apostle to the Jews (Gal 2:7), and that the use of so much OT in 1 Peter demands a Jewish readership. But there is evidence that Peter did not restrict his ministry to Jews (Gal 2:12; 1 Cor 1:12) and the use of the OT is not surprising even if the readers were not Jews, because so many gentile God-fearers (like Cornelius, Acts 10:2) were fa-

Aqueduct near Pisidian Antioch, part of the area to which Peter wrote (1 Pt 1:1).

miliar with the OT. Paul, too, uses the OT heavily when writing to Gentiles (Gal).

Whether the readers were Jews or mainly Gentiles is decided by several texts that reflect the pagan background of the readers. Peter says in 2:10 that his readers were once "not a people," a reference to Hosea 2:23 (cf. Rom 9:25). Then in 4:3 Peter describes their past "debauchery, lust, drunkenness, orgies, carousing and detestable idolatry." This does not describe unbelieving Jews, whose problem was not gross immorality, but hypocrisy and legalism. Thus the recipients of this letter were mainly gentile Christians in Asia Minor, characterized as aliens and strangers in the world.

Origin. Most scholars think 1 Peter was written from Rome. The clue is found in 5:13: "She who is in Babylon, chosen together with you, sends you her greetings." Babylon (which had come to symbolize a big, powerful, evil city) was substituted as a kind of code name for Rome in much early Christian literature (e.g., Rv 14:8; 16:19; 17:5; 18:2,10,21; 2 Bar 10:1,2; 11:1; 67:7; Sib Oracles 5:143, 159f).

Date. The date of 1 Peter is probably AD 64 or 65 (see next section).

Background Material. While other NT writings refer now and then to Christian suffering, 1 Peter is preoccupied with it. How Christians should conduct themselves when abused is often discussed (1:3–7; 2:12,20–23; 3:13–17; 4:12–19; 5:9,10). Official state persecution is not clearly affirmed; abuses seem to be the common lot of all Christians everywhere (5:9). Cruel masters may sometimes abuse their Christian servants (2:18–20); Christian wives may have to endure harsh, unbelieving husbands (3:1–6); and, in general, people are on the lookout to revile Christians as wrongdoers (2:12; 3:9,16; 4:15,16).

Even though no official state persecution is in view, the letter apparently indicates that there is something worse on the horizon (4:12–19). Peter seems to sense that the present tension between believers and their society could flare into something much worse.

Early church tradition says that Peter was crucified in Rome during Nero's persecution and there is no good reason to doubt it. Moreover, since 1 Peter was written from Rome, and since 4:12,17 implies an impending crisis like the one that struck the Christians in Rome in AD 65, we may suppose that this letter was written not long before Nero began to oppress the Christians in Rome. According to the historian Tacitus, Nero blamed the Christians for burning Rome, in order to squelch the rumor that he himself had done it so that he could build a greater city. His relentless persecution of Christians had not yet broken out when 1 Peter was written (cf. 2:14; 3:13), but Peter may have seen it coming and may have wanted to prepare the churches outside Rome, should the holocaust reach them too. Nero's persecution apparently did not affect the Christians in the provinces outside Rome, but that does not diminish the value of Peter's letter, because mostly it deals with how Christians should relate to their society and how they should respond when abuse and suffering come.

If this is a correct picture of the background of 1 Peter, its date would be the early to mid-60s, since the fire of Rome broke out on July 19, AD 64, and the persecution occurred later that year or in the spring of 65. The impending persecution in which Peter would die elicited the clearest apostolic expression of how to suffer unashamedly for the glory of God (3:16).

Purpose and Theological Teaching. The main purpose of 1 Peter is to exhort Christians to conduct themselves among fellow-believers (3:8; 5:1–7), but especially in non-Christian society (2:12), testifying clearly to their hope in Christ (3:1,15), to the glory of God. The letter aims also to help Christians understand and endure the abuses that often come from relationships with non-Christians (1:6,7; 2:12;18–25; 3:9,14–17; 4:1–5,12–19; 5:8–10).

Peter's exhortation is based on the good news of God's salvation through the death, resurrection, and second coming of Christ. God is merciful (1:3; 2:10), "the God of all grace" (5:10), and his people stand in this grace (4:10; 5:12) and hope in its ultimate display at Christ's coming (1:13). God foreknew and determined (1:2,20; 2:8) a plan of redemption by which to create a holy people for his own possession (2:9,10). Accordingly, Christ was sent into the world to accomplish this redemption for the sake of God's elect (1:20). Although he was "chosen and precious" to God, he was "rejected by men" (2:4) who did not believe him (2:7). But his sufferings (1:11; 4:1,13; 5:1) were not a meaningless tragedy; they were for the sake of his people (2:21,24; 3:18), to redeem them with his "precious blood" from their "empty way of life" (1:18,19).

Put to death in the flesh, he was "made alive by the Spirit" (3:18), raised from the dead and glorified (1:21; 2:7), and holds the place of authority at God's right hand (3:22).

Further still, we must try to explain the link between the good news of God's saving activity and our good conduct. The good news must be proclaimed if it is to change anybody's life. This proclamation happens in the power of God's Holy Spirit (1:12). It is not merely a "newscast" but is "the living and abiding word of God" (1:23; 4:11), by which God calls his people into being and summons them "out of darkness and into his wonderful light" (2:9; 1:15), "to his eternal glory in Christ" (5:10).

This change is described in 1 Peter as a "new birth" (1:3,23); what distinguishes a new-born person is the "living hope" that he has in Christ (1:3,13).

This hope, grounded in Christ's resurrection and his sure return, transforms behavior (1:13–15). No longer will we have to seek satisfaction and fulfillment in harmful, unloving ways, but by entrusting our souls to a faithful Creator (4:19; 5:7), we can endure unjust suffering patiently (2:20), not return evil for evil (3:9), and seek to extend the mercy of God to others in doing good (2:12,15; 3:11,16; 4:19).

Lively Christian hope does not lead us *out* of non-Christian society but rather changes our behavior *in* it. Christians are addressed as citizens of the state (2:13–17), as slaves of cruel masters (2:18–25), and as wives of unbelieving husbands (3:1–6). By living as new and hopeful persons *in* the institutions of society, men see our good deeds and give glory to our Father in heaven (2:12; Mt 5:16).

Content. *1:1,2.* This section describes "God's elect," their election defined by three prepositional phrases.

First, it accords with the foreknowledge of God. This means more than that God knew ahead of time whom he would elect. As in 1:20, foreknowledge probably also includes God's purpose (cf. Am 3:2; Acts 2:23; Rom 8:28–30; 11:2; 1 Cor 8:3; Gal 4:9).

Second, the election is "by the sanctifying work of the Spirit." "Election" here is the Spirit's effectual call that transfers a person from darkness into light (2:9). In Ephesians 1:4 election was before the foundation of the world.

Third, our election is "for obedience to Jesus Christ and sprinkling by his blood." The latter probably refers to the moral effect of Christ's death in purifying our conscience and our behavior as we trust in him (see Heb 9:13,14).

Thus the elect people of God: have their origin in the eternal, purposive foreknowledge of God; owe their call and conversion to the work of the Holy Spirit; and have as their goal in life obedience to God (cf. 1:14).

1:3–12. This section describes how tremendously valuable salvation is—a vast inheritance absolutely perfect, never diminishing in beauty or worth (v 4), the goal of our faith (v 9), the basis of inexpressible joy (vv 6,8). Searched into and desired by the holy prophets of old, it is so amazing even angels long to peer into it (vv 10–12).

It originates in the great mercy of God, and was made available to men through the resurrection of Jesus from the dead (v 3). Even though a *future* inheritance is "ready to be revealed in the last time" (v 5), it offers many *present* spiritual benefits for those who trust in Christ. Another is the promise of God's present power to cause the believer to persevere in faith (v 5). This does not mean Christians escape hardship; it may be "necessary" that they suffer (v 6). If so they should not grumble but see suffering as a refining fire for their good as it burns away false dependencies and leaves only the pure gold of genuine faith (v 7). So suffering may be an important preparation for the full experience of salvation, since it is faith alone which will be blessed in the end.

Faith is not the same as sight, for believers have never seen Jesus, yet trust him and love him (v 8). There are good grounds for hope (3:15), founded mainly on the resurrection of Jesus (1:3)—a real historical event.

1:13–25. Peter now gives a command: hope fully in the grace coming to you at the revelation of Christ (v 13); lead a new life of obedience to God (vv 14,15). Hope is an intense desire for something and a confidence that it will come. So Peter is commanding the churches to *desire* Christ strongly and be assured of his glory and his coming. Thus, believers must use their minds and keep clearheaded (sober) about what is truly valuable in life (v 13).

This strong hope changes behavior by replacing our former "evil desires," held in ignorance of what is truly desirable and satisfying (v 14). Full hope in Christ always results in holiness of life. If we delight in being God's children (v 14), we will surely imitate our Father (vv 15,16; cf. Lv 19:2).

But there is another motivation for good conduct: fear of God who judges each one according to his work (v 17). Yet Peter in verse 17 motivates with fear and in verses 18,19 assures us that we have been redeemed from our futile conduct with the precious blood of Christ. We are saved by faith (vv 9,21), not by good works. Probably Peter means us to fear God's displeasure with unbelief. When it says he will judge our works, it probably means that he will look for evidences of obedient, loving conduct which is the sure sign of hope and faith. If we are lacking in this, fear of his judgment should drive us back to God's mercy where we can have peace and joy which in turn lead to love.

This love is commanded toward believers in verse 22. Hope is not mentioned in verses 22–25, but it is implied when Peter says we are born anew through the *abiding* Word of God. Since "the word of the Lord stands forever" (1:25 = Is 40:6–8), those whose life depends on it will abide forever too (cf. 1 Jn 2:15–17). Having this security, we can gladly love our brothers earnestly from the heart (v 22).

2:1–10. This passage is filled with OT quotations and imagery (2:3 = Ps 34:8; 2:4,7 = Ps 118:22; 2:6 = Is 28:16; 2:8 = Is 8:14; 2:9 = Ex 19:5,6; Is 9:2; 43:20,21; 2:10 = Hos 2:23). Verses 9 and 10 indicate that Peter pictures the Christian church as a new Israel. He probably sees the experience of the church in the world as an *exile* like the Jewish Babylonian exile (1:1,17; 2:11), and considers conversion as a kind of *exodus* out of the darkness of an old futile life into God's light like the Jewish exodus out of Egypt.

Verses 6–8 show that Jesus is a precious jewel for some but a stumbling stone for unbelievers. Behind that stands God's inscrutable predestination (v 8). Those who trust him are chosen (v 9; cf. 1:1), as a royal priesthood (see below on 2:5), as a nation having God's own holy character (cf. 1:14,15), and as a people cherished as God's special possession. All of this is due not to our merit but to God's mercy (v 10).

Verses 1–3 are again a command—to desire the kindness of Christ which we have tasted through the milk of the Word and so grow stronger in faith or to hope fully in the grace of Christ.

Verses 4,5 are a complex, mixed metaphor which pictures Christ as a living stone and the church both as a spiritual house of stones and as a priesthood. The church is, on the one hand, a dwelling place for God (cf. 1 Cor 3:16; Eph 2:21,22), and, on the other, a group of ministers at that dwelling who offer God the sacrifices of obedience (cf. Rom 12:1,2).

2:11,12. This is the central concern of the letter. Since Christians are exiles in this world, they must not share the same desires as unbelievers. Such fleshly desires are ephemeral (1:24,25) and destroy the soul that follows them. Instead, God's new people should devote themselves to good deeds even though people may slander them, for this will ultimately cause people to glorify God. The sequence, again, is: changed desires, changed behavior, God glorified (cf. Mt 5:16).

2:13–17. There is a sense in which Christians should be subject to every human creature (2:13,18; 3:1, cf. "lowliness" in 3:8,9,16; 5:3,6). They are to "show proper respect to everyone" (2:14). That Christ died for sinners is a very humbling truth which forbids Christians to be arrogant or to think that they do not owe others love (cf. Rom 13:8–10). Rather, they are adjured to count others better than themselves (Mk 10:44; Phil 2:3).

Peter declares, then, that believers should be subject to the king and to the civil authorities under him. They should positively devote themselves to doing good so that those who say Christianity makes no difference in life will be silenced.

However, subjection to the state is not absolute, for Christians are first and foremost slaves of God (v 16). It is out of freedom that they acknowledge the propriety of a God-ordained state to preserve orderly life. Because Christians serve God first, and the king is merely God's creature, subjection to him is a subjection "for the Lord's sake," not the king's sake.

2:18–25 (cf. Rom 13:1–7). Christian slaves have consciences oriented toward and shaped by God (v 19). They also have experienced his grace, and are here told to rely on it by enduring unjust suffering patiently. They are not to strike back: they were called to live this way because Jesus suffered *for them* and because he suffered *as an example.* Verses 21–23 describe the example. Verses 24,25 describe the atonement and its effects. That is, Jesus not only modeled the life of nonretaliation but enabled his followers to live this way by dying *for* them that they might "live for righteousness" (v 24). Only when Christians are secure and content in the hope Christ achieved *for them* can they have the freedom and inclination to follow his costly example. When believers are tempted to take vengeance into their own hands they should recall that even Jesus "entrusted himself to him who judges justly" (v 23), to the one who said, "It is mine to avenge; I will repay" (Rom 12:19,20).

3:1–7. Here are six verses for wives and one for husbands. How shall a believing wife win her unbelieving husband (v 1)? Peter warns against preoccupation with making the body more attractive (v 3). Instead, he stresses the adornment of the heart with a meek and tranquil spirit (v 4), accompanied by pure, loving conduct (v 2), which may win the husband "without talk" (v 1). This is not a call to mindless subservience but to poise, to free and confident service in love. The wife is not to be afraid even of an abusive husband (v 6). But how? By following Sarah's example of *hoping* in God (v 5). So it is seen as hope again which transforms life and enables believers to be subject to every creature. The wife is bound first to the Lord and only secondarily to her husband. Like the slave the Christian wife will use her God-oriented conscience (2:16) to decide when, for Christ's sake, she cannot follow the lead of her man. Some scholars argue that the idea of women being subject to their husbands merely reflects a patriarchal culture and should be abandoned. Others argue that it reflects profound, valuable, God-given differences between maleness and femaleness which are preserved and enhanced in a loving relationship of headship and subjection, or initiation and response (see also Eph 5:21–33; Col 3:18,19).

Husbands are admonished in verse 7 to bring their relationships to their wives into conformity with natural and revealed truth. The *natural* truth is that women are weaker. This does not mean that they are inferior mentally or emotionally. It is a simple statement of observed fact: women's bodies are not as strong as men's. In a culture without all kinds of automatic devices, physical strength was much more crucial for survival and comfort than it is today. So the man is urged to use his superior strength for the sake of his wife.

The *revealed* truth is that the wife is a "fellow-heir of the gracious gift of life," to be honored and respected.

3:8–12. This concludes the section 2:13–3:12 and admonishes the whole church first to love the brotherhood (v 8) and then to love the hostile outsider (vv 9–12). Verse 9 recalls Jesus' behavior (2:23) and his commands (Lk 6:27–36). Not only are Christians to endure abuse patiently (2:19,20); they are also to react positively and "bless" those who revile (v 9). To bless means to wish well and turn the wish into a prayer. Believers' real desire for their enemies is that they be converted and come to share in the blessing that the Christian will inherit (3:1,9). Psalm 34:12–16 is brought in to support the logic of verse 9. If Christians want to inherit the blessing of salvation 1:4,5; 3:9) they must bless those who revile them. This does not mean they *earn* their salvation, but that salvation is the goal of faith (1:9) and true faith always makes a person loving.

3:13–17. Peter still seems to be optimistic that when Christians do good they will not be harmed for it (v 13). Nevertheless, it may be God's will that Christians suffer for doing good (v 17) and that is far better than suffering for doing evil. It is better not only because they ought never do evil, but also because they are "blessed" when they suffer for righteousness' sake (v 14 cf. 4:14; Mt 5:10–12). So instead of being afraid of men, believers should fear displeasing Christ and so be at peace in his faithfulness (cf. vv 14,15 with Is 8:12,13). Thus consciences will be clear and believers will be freed so that when they explain the ground of their hope even their demeanor will bear witness to its truth (cf. v 15 with 1:3). The Christians' abusers may be put to shame (v 16) and be won (3:1) and give glory to God (2:12).

3:18–22. Similar to 2:21–25 and 1:18–21, this unit grounds Peter's call for innocent and patient suffering. Since Christ died once for all for mankind's sins and thus freed all from guilt and opened a way into the fellowship of the merciful God, believers should be able to bear unjust suffering meekly. Refusing to bear undeserved suffering would be a mark of unbelief in the all-faithful Creator (4:19) who cares for his children and wants to bear their anxieties for them (5:7).

Just as in the days of Noah only a few were saved (cf. 3:1,20; 4:17) so now only a few are being saved in Peter's hostile generation through baptism (vv 18–21). Their encouragement is heightened by the reference to Christ's victorious subjection of the wicked "angels, authorities and powers" (v 22).

Peter defines very carefully in what sense he means that baptism saves; not by the cleansing function of the water, but rather by the "pledge of a good conscience toward God . . . by the resurrection of Jesus Christ" (v 21).

4:1–6. Christians should not live according to merely human desires, but according to the will of God (cf. 1:14; 2:1,2,11,12,15). This will mean a break with the behavior of their unbelieving friends and will probably result in being slandered (v 4). But this should not cause believers to avenge themselves, for God will take care of judgment (v 5).

Believers are commanded (v 1): "Since Christ suffered in his body, arm yourselves also with the same attitude, because he who has suffered in his body is done with sin." Some have taken this to mean that through a process of suffering we are increasingly sanctified; however, if suffering here refers to dying (as the parallel with 3:18 and the "therefore" of 4:1 suggest), then probably verse 1 is to be understood along the lines of Romans 6:6, 10,11.

Verse 6 is difficult. Some think it refers to the same preaching referred to in 3:19. Another, perhaps preferable, interpretation is that there is no preaching to the dead here but rather a preaching of the gospel to those who afterwards died. That is, those who heard the gospel, believed, and then died, did not hear the gospel in vain. For the purpose of the preaching was that, while from a merely human standpoint these believers have been judged in the flesh (i.e., have died), from the divine standpoint they live in the spirit. The purpose of verse 6 is thus a great encouragement to live by God's will even when former friends scorn the Christian hope by pointing out how even Christians die.

4:7–11. Activity among believers in the church is again the theme here. Peter saw contemporary events as the beginning of the end (4:7,17). This gave an earnestness to his exhortation that believers keep their minds clear and sober (cf. 1:13) for prayer.

By steadily drawing upon God in prayer, Christians find the help they need to love each other and to overlook many offensive things (cf. Eph 4:1–3). This love should manifest itself in joyful hospitality, especially important in times of persecution (v 9), and should move believers to use all their varied gifts and talents to build each other up in faith (v 10). Two examples are given: speaking and ministering (the work of the preacher and the work of the deacon). Most important is the goal of speaking and ministering and how to reach that goal. The goal is "that in all things God may be praised" (v 11). This may be done by recognizing that he gives the strength for service and the words for edifying speech.

4:12–19. Here the situation of suffering and bearing reproach for being Christians is again in view. The prospect of a "painful trial" (v 12) is impending (cf. 1:6,7). Peter sees these sufferings (probably from hostile associates rather than official state persecution) as God's judgment on the world, beginning with the church (vv 17,18; cf. Prv 11:31). But God's judgment on the church is not punitive but purgative (v 14; 1:6,7).

Peter gives a reminder that suffering is normal Christian experience (v 19; 3:14; Acts 14:22; 1 Thes 3:3) and that Christ himself was so mistreated (2:21–25; Mt 10:25). Entrust your soul to a faithful Creator (v 19). Do not be ashamed (v 16), but rejoice (v 13; cf. Rom 5:3–5; Jas 1:2,3). Do not suffer as a wrongdoer (v 15), but persevere in doing good (v 19; 2:15; 3:11,17). Finally—the result of all the rest—glorify God (v 16).

When believers respond to suffering in this way they are blessed (v 14), for God manifests himself to them in an intimate and reassuring way. There is also the promise that if they endure suffering for Christ joyfully then they will have the consummation of that joy at his second coming (v 13; cf. Mk 8:38; Rom 8:17).

5:1–7. Again (as in 3:8; 4:7–11) Peter treats relations within the church. He tells the elders how to be good shepherds of the flock (vv 1–4); tells the younger people how to treat their elders (v 5); and tells everyone to be humble toward each other.

Without humility, love and unity are impossible (Eph 4:1–3). Peter reminds believers that God opposes the proud but gives grace to the lowly (v 5; cf. Mt 23:12; Jas 4:6), whom he will exalt in the age to come (v 6; cf. Lk 14:11; 18:14; Jas 4:10). Most important, God invites his people to throw all their anxieties on him because he cares for them (v 7; cf. Ps 55:22; Mt 6:25–30).

The young people who are thus made humble will be subject to their elders and respect them (v 5). The elders who are thus made hum-ble will not lord it over the flock (v 3) or be greedy or begrudging in their service (v 2), but will lead the flock by a humble example. Thus life within the church will be a stimulus for subjection and love outside the church.

5:8–11. Peter returns to his concern with suffering. Suffering is the universal lot of believers (v 9; cf. 4:12). Although willed in one sense by God (1:6; 3:17; 4:19), it is used by Satan to try to destroy their faith. So Peter appeals to the church to be wakeful and sober (v 8; 1:13; 4:7) so that they can resist the lion by faith.

5:12–14. In conclusion, Peter describes his "brief" writing as an exhortation and a testimony concerning the true grace of God. So the letter is not a call for hard labor for God; rather it is a call to recognize, enjoy, and live by the hard labor that God graciously has exerted and will exert for his children. The letter was delivered by Silvanus (probably the same as Silvanus in Acts 16:25; 1 Thes 1:1; 2 Thes 1:1). It was written from Rome, and greetings were sent from Mark (probably the Gospel writer and former missionary companion of Paul, Acts 13:13; 15:37; 2 Tm 4:11) and the whole church. Peter's last word is to invoke peace upon the churches and to urge them to keep the affection warm among themselves.

JOHN PIPER

See AFFLICTION; SPIRITS IN PRISON; PETER, THE APOSTLE.

Bibliography. F.W. Beare, *The First Epistle of Peter;* J.H. Elliott, *A Home for the Homeless;* J.N.D. Kelly, *A Commentary on the Epistles of Peter and Jude;* J. Lillie, *Lectures on First and Second Peter;* J.R. Lumby, *The Epistle of St. Peter;* E.G. Selwyn, *The First Epistle of St. Peter.*

Peter, Second Letter of.

Author. The author is clearly identified in 1:1 as Simon Peter, one of the 12 apostles chosen by Jesus. However, two things should be noted. First, its style differs markedly from 1 Peter. Second, because 2 Peter is obviously a later work (see Date below) and incorporates Jude in abstract, it is possible that a trusted co-worker (e.g., John Mark) put together Peter's final concerns along with an abstract of Jude after Peter's death. Thus 2 Peter is the final words of Peter, a type of posthumous testament directing the church in the post-apostolic age.

Date, Origin, Destination. Tradition holds that Peter was martyred about AD 64 in Rome. If that is so, this work was probably written in Rome before AD 70 (before his last teaching was forgotten) and after AD 60 (the earliest date when Peter might have known Paul's letters). Furthermore, it was written after Jude, for 2 Peter 2 incorporates a shortened form of Jude. The Roman place of origin also accounts for 1 Clement's apparent knowledge of 2 Peter in AD 96, the earliest use of the letter. If 3:1 refers to the same churches mentioned in 1 Peter, then the letter is destined for northeastern Asia Minor. The group of churches includes some to which Paul wrote letters (3:15).

Background. Peter probably never visited the churches of northeastern Asia Minor, but while in Rome heard of their persecution and wrote them a letter of encouragement (1 Pt). But in a context of many attractive libertine cults, the church was constantly in danger from within as well as from without, as internal leaders corrupted moral teaching. While 2 Peter is written to churches in Asia Minor, Corinth in Greece certainly had similar problems and Romans 6 may show that Paul was aware of a like misuse of his teaching that had reached Rome. Paul's declaration that Christians are free from the Law (see Gal 3–5) always carried the danger that instead of yielding to the Spirit, people would yield to their fallen desires, ignoring Paul's warning that those who did such things would not inherit the kingdom of God. This tendency in the early church seems to lie behind 2 Peter.

Purpose and Theology. As 1:12–15 makes clear, the letter is a testament, a final reminder of truth written in the face of the divisions caused by false teachers. It is one final attempt to stabilize the church.

Three main theological themes stand out: (1) a call to Christian virtue and faithfulness to the apostolic tradition on which the church had been founded; (2) a basing of this call on the exalted status of Jesus Christ and his return in judgment, making all other goals of life irrelevant; and (3) an apocalyptic denunciation of those who had compromised with the world and were therefore living with a sub-Christian ethic.

Content. *Greeting (1:1,2).* The greeting stresses both the authority of Peter and of his teaching by using the title "apostle," and solidarity with his readers by including the word "servant" and mentioning "a faith of equal standing" with respect to the readers. Furthermore, the theme of moral purity comes out in the citation of "the righteousness" of God in which Christians stand.

Call to Virtue (1:3–21). God has already acted to call Christians to himself. He has by sovereign grace given them all that is needed to truly live in a godly manner. And he has set fantastic promises before them. They must not allow themselves to be caught again in the moral morass of the world, for it was God's purpose in saving them to enable them to escape from this trap. Instead they should become like Christ ("participate in the divine nature") and must therefore grow in Christian virtue. If they fail in this growth they miss

God's promises, but zealousness to move forward will confirm their election and their future in heaven (1:3–11).

Peter is about to die, as Jesus predicted (cf. Jn 21:18,19). The purpose of this letter is to encourage his readers once more to moral steadfastness. Peter's encouragement is important for two reasons: first because he was truly an eyewitness of Christ's glory (i.e., the transfiguration, an event that must have deeply impressed Peter, but is cited here because it revealed the glory, power, and authority of Jesus and bound OT and NT together). Unlike the false teachers, his tradition is based on what God really did, not in mere speculation. Second, his experience confirms OT prophecy. Like Peter and his followers in the apostolic tradition, the OT prophets were inspired by the Holy Spirit. Thus the Spirit alone gives the true interpretation, and the idiosyncratic interpretations of the false teachers are therefore wrong (1:12–21).

Denunciation of False Teachers (2:1–22). Christians need to be encouraged to stand firm in virtue because there are false teachers in the church who are twisting the OT Scriptures to support their own behavior. One cannot be sure exactly who these teachers were, but some of their actions are clear. First, they were libertine in their morals, probably twisting Paul's teaching on freedom from the Law to support their actions (cf. 3:15; 1 Cor 6:12–20 shows a similar problem in Corinth). Second, they were forming groups loyal to themselves, exploiting these people and leading them into sin (cf. 1 Cor 1–3 for another example of building splinter groups). Third, they were teaching about angelic and demonic powers, some of which they were cursing, which revealed a general disrespect for authority (2:10; cf. Col 2:8). Fourth, while ultimately sectarian, they were still celebrating the Lord's Supper (which at that time was still a common meal, as it would be for another century) with the church and thus defiling the whole celebration (2:13).

Peter's great concern is that these people are sectarian ("destructive heresies" refers to groups split from the church, not to doctrinal differences, which is the meaning "heresy" took centuries later). These teachers form groups marked by their immoral behavior. They thus deny the authority of Christ, even though he once bought them out of sin. They deny Christ by rejecting his clear teaching against greed and immorality, and lead others in their wake, making the whole Christian faith disreputable before the world. Their motivation is greed, and their predicted destiny is judgment, although it might not be apparent to those unfamiliar with the Scriptures (i.e., it is "of old") (2:1–3 = Jude 4,17–19).

This judgment is sure, as OT examples of the judgment of immoral persons (along with the salvation of the righteous) show, for example, of angels (Gn 6:1–4), of the people of Noah's day (Gn 6:5–22), and of Sodom (Gn 18,19). In each case God delivered the few righteous individuals even though he severely judged the evil majority; this encourages the readers to be righteous like Noah and Lot. Furthermore, the readers might identify with Lot in their own distress at the immorality going on in their church (2:4–10 = Jude 6,7).

Like those judged in the OT, these false teachers are both proud and ignorant, cursing spiritual powers they do not really understand (probably demonic powers, for Peter is following Jude who draws in turn on a tradition from the Assumption of Moses). Even angels, who know far more than these teachers do and are more powerful, are not so disrespectful. Even Satan is to be spoken of with respect according to Scripture. The teachers are not only proud, but are also immoral and greedy, even at the Lord's Table ("reveling in their pleasures while they feast with you," NIV). They claim to teach freedom, but are themselves ensnared in desire, so their words are empty. Their teaching seems impressive, but it is all sound and wind. Teaching without spiritual power and a godly life is worthless. Because they have returned to evil after once experiencing freedom from sin in Christ, they are worse off than if they had never heard the gospel. They are like dogs (cf. Prv 26:11) or like pigs (2:11–22 = Jude 8–13).

Warning of Coming Judgment (3:1–16). Both the OT and Jesus himself speak of coming judgment. The false teachers may scoff at the idea, but the story of Noah shows that God does eventually judge. God judged the world in Genesis by water (the very water from which he once separated land in Gn 1); he will do so again, but this time by fire (3:1–7).

Judgment has not yet fallen because God is wonderfully patient; time does not have the same meaning for him as for humans. The scoffing of the false teachers simply reveals their ignorance of God. And they also do not know God's motives for his seeming delay, that is, that God wants to forgive people, not condemn them. He takes no pleasure in sending people to hell, but wills that everyone be saved; not everyone, however, will accept God's offer, and eventually his judgment will come and the universe will be burned. All that is now visible is transitory (3:8–10).

Therefore Christians ought to live holy lives, preparing for the new and permanent world God has promised them, instead of indulging in the desires of this temporary, perishing world as the false teachers do (3:11–16 = Jude 20,21).

Closing (3:17,18). Therefore Christians must be on guard against such false teaching. Instead of copying the life of the false teachers, they are to imitate the life of Jesus. A doxology to Christ ends the letter.

PETER H. DAVIDS

See PETER, THE APOSTLE.

Bibliography. R.J. Bauckham, *Jude, 2 Peter*; J.N.D. Kelly, *A Commentary on the Epistles of Peter and Jude*; J. Lillie, *Lectures on First and Second Peter*; D.M. Lloyd-Jones, *2 Peter*; J.B. Mayor, *The Epistle of St. Jude and the Second Epistle of St. Peter.*

Peter, The Apostle. One of Jesus' 12 disciples who rose to preeminence both among the disciples during Jesus' ministry and among the apostles afterwards. There are actually four forms of his name in the NT: the Hebrew/Greek Simeon/Simon and the Aramaic/Greek Cephas/Petros. His given name was Simon bar-Jonah (Mt 16:17; cf. Jn 1:42), "Simon the son of John," which was common Semitic nomenclature. It is most likely that "Simon" was not merely the Greek equivalent of "Simeon" but that, having his home in bilingual Galilee, "Simon" was the alternate form which he used in dealings with Gentiles. In fact, it was quite common for a cosmopolitan Jew to employ 3 forms of his name depending on the occasion: Aramaic, Latin, and Greek. The double name "Simon Peter" (or "Simon called Peter") demonstrates that the second name was a later addition, similar to "Jesus, the Christ." The number of times that the Aramaic equivalent "Cephas" is used (once in Jn, 4 times each in Gal and 1 Cor) and its translation into the Greek (not common with proper names) indicates the importance of the secondary name. Both Aramaic and Greek forms mean "the rock," an obvious indication of Peter's stature in the early church (see below on Mt 16:18). It is obvious that he was called "Simon" throughout Jesus' ministry but came to be known as "Peter" more and more in the apostolic age. For example, Paul never uses the patronym, not even in the form of the double name "Simon Peter," but always uses "Peter" (twice) or "Cephas" (8 times); and the Petrine letters use "Peter" (1 Pt 1:1) or "Simon Peter" (2 Pt 1:1). Acts uses "Peter" 42 times, "Simon Peter" 4 times, and "Simon" only 9 times.

His Background. As previously stated, Peter was raised in Galilee. John 1:44 says that the home of Andrew (his brother) and Peter was Bethsaida, the whereabouts of which is difficult to place archaeologically. Yet John 12:21 places Bethsaida in Galilee; however, it is possible that John is reflecting the popular

Ruins of the house of Peter in Capernaum.

use of the term "Galilee" rather than the legally correct one. Peter and Andrew had a fishing business centered in Capernaum (Mk 1:21,29), and perhaps were partners with James and John (Lk 5:10). It is also likely that they intermittently continued in their business while disciples, as indicated by the fishing scene in John 21:1–8. Some scholars doubt the authenticity of this account, calling it a doublet of Luke 5:1–11, the "fishers of men" account. However, on both linguistic and critical grounds, the differences are sufficient to argue for two separate episodes. Whether or not Peter continued in his business during the apostolic age is nearly impossible to say with certainty, but it may be surmised on the basis of the common practice in the 1st century that it is likely (e.g., Paul's tentmaking).

One difficulty with this is the series of statements saying "We have left everything and followed you" (Mt 19:27; Mk 10:28; Lk 18:28). The majority of interpreters have given this an absolute sense of "sold" or "left" their businesses. However, Luke 18:28 occurs in the context of leaving their homes but is obviously not meant in an absolute sense. It seems most likely that the disciples did leave their businesses to follow Christ, but kept the tools of their trade and returned to them when necessary (Jn 21; Paul in Acts).

They certainly did not abandon their families, as evidenced by Peter, who returned to his home at the end of each tour. The NT says that Peter was married. In Mark 1:29–31 and parallels Jesus heals Peter's mother-in-law, who perhaps was living with him, of a fever. In fact, it is possible that his home became Jesus' headquarters in Galilee (Mt 8:14 may indicate that Jesus dwelt there). First Corinthians 9:5 says that Peter, along with the other married apostles, often took his wife with him on his missionary journeys. Later tradition discusses his children (Clement of Alexandria; Stromateis 3.6.52) and states that Peter was present at the martyrdom of his wife (Eusebius, *Eccles. Hist.*, 3.30.2).

Peter's Conversion and Call. Peter's brother, Andrew, was a disciple of John the Baptist (Jn 1:35–40). This follows the witness of John in 1:29–34 and is the second stage of John's discipleship drama in chapter 1, that is, after bearing witness John the Baptist now sends his own followers to Jesus. Andrew and the unnamed disciple (perhaps Philip as in v 43 or the "beloved disciple," whom many identify with John) then "follow" Jesus (a term used often in the Gospel of John for discipleship) and answer his call. The next day Andrew follows the Baptist's example and finds his brother Simon, saying "We have found the Messiah" (v 41). Peter's conversion is presupposed in verse 42, where Simon is brought to Jesus by Andrew and there given a new name.

There are three separate episodes in the Gospels in which Simon is called and these overlap with three episodes in which he is given the name "Cephas" (Peter = rock) by Jesus. This certainly shows how important it was for the early church. In fact, many commentators note this theological stress and assert that it spawned separate traditions rather than having been based upon separate historical events. The problem is that while the four Gospels agree that Peter was called early in Jesus' ministry, they differ with respect to the exact time. John, as we have seen, locates the event in Judea where John the Baptist was baptizing. The identification of Jesus as Messiah and the renaming of Simon, which in the Synoptics occurs together at Caesarea Philippi, are placed here at the very beginning of Jesus' ministry. Some scholars think that Johannine drama has led the fourth Evangelist to combine the synoptic call and the Caesarea Philippi confession and to insert the scenario at the very outset of Jesus' ministry.

The synoptic Gospels have two ordination scenes. The first takes place at the Sea of Galilee (Mt 4:18–22; Mk 1:16–20). Jesus is walking along the shore and sees Peter and Andrew along with James and John casting their nets into the sea. At this time he calls them to become "fishers of men." Luke then expands this into a fishing scene (5:1–11), in which the disciples have fished all night and caught nothing, but at the command of Jesus lower their nets and catch an amount of fish so great that the boat starts to sink. The episode concludes exactly like the Markan abbreviated form: Jesus says that from now on they will be "catching men" and as a result they "leave everything and follow Him."

The second synoptic episode involving Peter's call (and his new name) is the official choice of the 12 upon the mountain (Mk 3:13–19 and pars); in the list of the names we have "Simon, to whom he gave the name Peter." The final occurrence dealing with Peter's new name is found in Matthew 16:17–19, in connection with Peter's confession at Caesarea Philippi.

As can readily be seen, it is somewhat difficult to harmonize these episodes properly. Were there three different episodes in which Simon was called (Mk 1:20; 3:16; Jn 1:42) and three separate incidents in which he was given the name Cephas/Peter (Mt 16:17; Mk 3:16; Jn 1:42)? It is attractive to assume that one single event, which happened at some indeterminate time toward the beginning of Jesus' ministry, was later expanded into these diverse traditions. However, a closer examination of the Gospel data does not necessitate such a conclusion. John 1:35–42 is not an institutional scene which connotes an official "call." Rather, it describes the first encounter with Jesus and realization regarding his significance. The "renaming" is in the future tense and looks to a later event. Moreover, John deliberately omits most of the crucial events in Jesus' life (the baptism, the choice of the 12, the transfiguration, the words of institution at the Last Supper, Gethsemane) and replaces them with highly theological scenes which teach the spiritual significance of the events. This is what he has done here.

The same is true of the first synoptic call, that is, the fishing scene. Again, there is no hint of official ordination to office but rather a proleptic or prophetic hint of future ministry. This is especially true of the highly theological scene in Luke, which promises abundant results. Again in all three accounts the future tense is employed: "I will make you fishers of men" (Mt and Mk)/"You will be catching men" (Lk). The "call" in Mark 1:20 and Matthew 1:21 and the reaction ("leaving" all behind and "following" Jesus) is the opening gambit which is finalized in the actual institutional scene in Mark 3:13–19 and parallels. The wording does not indicate that these two episodes are doublets, for the actual appointment of the disciples occurs in the second passage. A differentiation must be made between the original call to one segment (who became the so-called "inner circle" of the 12) and the final choice of all the disciples. It might be noted in passing the call of Levi (Matthew) in Mark 2:14 and parallels and the later "call" and sending of the 12 on their preaching mission in Mark 6 and parallels. All of these are separate but connected aspects of the road to discipleship in general and of Peter's development in particular.

Peter's Place Among the Twelve. The prominence of Simon Peter in the Gospels and Acts cannot be disputed. While some have attempted to attribute this to his leadership role in the later church, there is no basis for that in the text of the NT. From the very beginning Simon attained preeminence above the others. In the lists of the 12 just mentioned, Simon's name always appears first, and Matthew 10:2 prefaces his name with "first." Moreover, the Twelve are often designated "Peter and those with him" (Mk 1:36; Lk 8:45; 9:32).

Throughout the accounts Peter acted and spoke on behalf of the other disciples. At the transfiguration it is Peter who wanted to erect tents (Mk 9:5) and he alone had sufficient faith to attempt walking on the water (Mt 14:28–31). It is Peter who asks the Lord to explain his teaching on forgiveness (Mt 18:21) and parables (Mt 15:15; Lk 12:41) and who speaks the disciples' minds in Matthew 19:27, "Behold, we have left everything and followed you; what's in it for us?" (author's translation). In two synoptic accounts one Gospel has the disciples asking a question while the parallel has Peter asking the question (Mk 7:17; cf. Mt 15:15; 21:20; cf. Mk 11:21). The collectors of the temple tax come to Peter as leader of the group (Mt 17:24). As a member of the inner circle (with James and John, possibly Andrew in Mk 13:3) he was often alone with Jesus (at the raising of Jairus' daughter, Mk 5:37 and pars; at the transfiguration, Mk 9:2 and pars; at Gethsemane, Mk 14:33 = Mt 26:37). Jesus asks Peter and John to prepare the Passover meal in Luke 22:8, and in Mark 14:37 (= Mt 26:40) he directs his rebuke to Peter as representing the others ("Could you not keep watch one hour?"). Finally, the message of the angel at the tomb as recorded in Mark 16:7 says, "Go tell the disciples and Peter. . . ." Certainly Peter held a very special place among the Twelve.

This was especially evident in the Caesarea Philippi episode (Mk 8:27–33 and pars). It was Peter whose confession became the high point of the Gospel accounts: "You are the Christ (Luke adds 'of God,' Matthew 'the son of the living God')." After Jesus then interpreted this in terms of the suffering Son of Man, Peter rebuked him, and in Mark's description Jesus then turned, gazed at all the disciples, and said to Peter, "Get behind me, Satan, for you are not thinking the things of God but of men." This was obviously directed at them all through Peter.

The portrait of Peter that comes through all four accounts pictures him as impulsive, often rash; he is the first to act and speak his mind and was typified by his enthusiasm for everything in which he had a part. At the sight of Jesus walking on the water, Peter asked that the Lord "command" him to do the same, and then immediately leaped out of the boat and began doing just that. At the transfiguration, while the others were awed into silence by the appearance of Moses and Elijah, Peter the man of action (and ego) said, "If you wish, *I* will make three booths [tabernacles] here" (Mt 17:4; Mk 9:5 and Lk 9:33 have "let us make"). Mark and Luke both add that Peter did not know what he was saying. Peter's unguarded and unthinking tendency to protest Jesus' statements is seen not only at Caesarea Philippi but also at the foot-washing scene in John 13:4–11 when he said, "You will never ever wash my feet"; and then after Jesus' strong retort, "If I do not wash you, you have no part with me," he reversed himself completely, stating, "Lord, not my feet only, but also my hands and head" (vv 8,9). Finally, in the tableau on the race to the tomb (Jn 20:2–10), the beloved disciple, reaching the tomb first, paused while Peter immediately and impulsively entered it. Peter was certainly one who "rushed in where angels fear to tread." However, this very trait aligns him with all humanity and may be one of the major reasons why he becomes the representative disciple throughout the Gospels.

Peter the Rock. The key to the significance of Simon Peter is obviously the controversial addendum to the Caesarea Philippi episode, found only in Matthew 16:17–19. Due to its stress on the "church," which is found only here and in 18:17 in the Gospels, many believe that this saying is incompatible with Jewish ideas regarding the community of the people of God and therefore was a later creation of

A source of the Jordan River in Caesarea Philippi, where Peter made his famous confession about Jesus' deity and messiahship.

the early church. This, however, is unnecessary for several reasons: (1) Qumran called the community itself the "rock" and a rabbinic saying called Abraham a "rock" upon which God could build the world. (2) The institutionalism found here is not at all non-Jewish in its orientation, for the theology of the righteous remnant, an OT idea, would explain the presence of authority in the disciples. (3) The concept of the "church" has a definite OT background in the concept of the messianic community and in the Jewish development of the synagogue. (4) Jesus certainly prepared for an interim period between his death and parousia (return); this is found in his parables, the Sermon on the Mount, the Olivet Discourse, and so on. (5) The passage itself contains several semitisms (Jewish rather than Greek phrasing) which shows at the least that it derives from the very earliest period and gives it the ring of authenticity.

There have been many interpretations of Matthew 16:18 through history: (1) It refers to Peter as the "rock" or first bishop of the church. This of course was the Roman Catholic interpretation from the 3rd century on and was employed as a proof text for apostolic succession. This is not hinted at anywhere in the context or even in the epistles; it was not a 1st-century concept. (2) The majority of Protestants since the Reformation have taken this to be a reference to Peter's faith statement rather than to Peter himself, but this neglects the wordplay, which is even more pronounced in Aramaic. (3) An alternative has been to take "this rock" as a reference to Jesus himself, but that is fanciful and is hardly justified by the context. In conclusion, "this rock" is almost certainly a reference to Peter.

First, Peter was to become the foundation upon which Christ would build his church, a position which is clearly attested in Acts. This does not mean that Peter had an authority above the other apostles. Paul's rebuke of Peter in Galatians 2:11–14 demonstrates that he was not above them, and at the Jerusalem Council in Acts 15 it is James who has the position of leadership. Second, Peter is seen not merely as an individual but as the representative of the disciples. This view is coming to increasing prominence today. It recognizes the Jewish concept of "corporate identity," in which the leader was "identified" with the "corporate" body (e.g., the king or high priest representing the nation before God); and is in keeping with Matthew 18:18–20, which passes on the same authority given Peter to the church (note esp. 16:19b = 18:18, the "binding and loosing" authority). In this view Peter as the rock becomes the first of the building blocks upon which Christ, the chief cornerstone (to continue the metaphor), will build his church.

First, verse 18b says "the gates of Hades will not overpower it." The "gates of Hades" is a common Jewish euphemism for death's inevitable and irrevocable power, but at the same time "overpower" is too strong a term for death by itself. The whole must be interpreted in light of other passages on the power of Satan, seen here in the guise of the power of death. It was a common apocalyptic concept that Satan would continue to rule this realm until the parousia, and this saying belongs in this category. Jesus is saying that Satan will not be triumphant over the church and his sphere of operations, death, will be defeated (cf. 1 Cor 15:26,54,55). The church would undergo persecution and martyrdom but throughout the church would be triumphant.

Second, verse 19a promises, "I will give you (singular) the keys of the kingdom," another statement used of apostolic succession by the medieval church. Again, this must be understood in light of corporate identity; Peter, as the preeminent figure in the early church, here embodies the community in his leadership. The "keys of the kingdom" are in direct contrast to the "gates of Hades" (cf. Rv 1:18, "the keys of death and Hades" and Rv 3:7, the "keys of David"), and this follows the imagery of the building seen in the "rock" upon which Christ will "build" his church. Here Peter is given the "keys" which will unlock the power of the "kingdom" in building God's community, the church. The future "will give" undoubtedly points to the postresurrection period, when that power was unleashed and the church erected.

Gospel Portraits of Peter. Traditionally, it has been common to assert that the synoptic Gospels are consistent in their picture of Peter's role and that only John diverges from the common pattern. However, with the emergence of biblical theology as a discipline and the new stress on the Evangelists as theologians as well as historians, a new understanding of Peter as representative has come to the fore. This is especially seen in the highly significant Roman Catholic-Protestant symposium on Peter, the results of which have been chronicled in R.E. Brown, K.P. Donfried, and J. Reumann, eds., *Peter in the NT* (Minneapolis: Augsburg, 1973).

Mark has often been said to have written the "Gospel of Peter," that is, to have been the scribe who recorded Peter's teaching on the life of Christ. While that is probably an overstatement, one cannot deny the centrality of Peter in Mark. He is prominent in no less than 15 separate episodes and appears as the

spokesman for the whole group. Mark gives the failure of the disciples greater stress than any other Evangelist; it is part of his overall theological purpose. Several writers have noted recently that Mark's so-called "messianic secret" theme can better be described as a "messianic misunderstanding." That is, Mark shows how the disciples continually failed to recognize the true significance of Jesus and so misinterpreted his teachings. Therefore Peter becomes the quintessential disciple in his weaknesses—failing to understand Jesus' true purpose (1:35–38), rebuking Jesus (8:32), speaking without knowledge and out of fear (9:6), swearing allegiance then denying the Lord (14:29,31,66–72), falling asleep at the critical hour (14:37). This must be coupled with the resurrection message to tell "the disciples and Peter," which hints at the reinstatement of Peter and the others. In conclusion, Mark shows Peter as failing in his own strength but victorious through the power of the risen One, a magnificent study of true discipleship.

Matthew has a slightly different emphasis. Peter's human failure is still seen and he is the spokesman and representative of true discipleship, but Matthew develops this latter theme. He tones down Mark's suggestions of ignorance and hardness and stresses the process of spiritual growth. Peter is seen as the leader of those who grow in their realization of Jesus' significance and by their imitation of and obedience to Christ respond to his call. It is Peter whose questions lead to further understanding (15:15; 18:21), whose faith causes him to walk on the water (14:28–31), whose confession of Jesus not only as Messiah but also as "Son of the Living God" leads to Jesus' remarkable benediction regarding Peter's future authority (16:16–19; see above), he who is the representative of the people of God submitting to government in the temple tax episode (17:24–27). Nevertheless, Matthew does not gloss over Peter's weaknesses; he is still referred to as one "of little faith" (14:31) and as "Satan" (16:23). In both cases, however, Peter is seen as one who is growing in discipleship. The true disciple's faith can be fearless one moment and faulty the next (14:28–31), and a declaration of faith can be followed by ignorance (16:17–23), but in all cases the power of Christ is available to transcend and strengthen those on the path to discipleship.

Luke goes further than Matthew in modifying Mark's portrait of Peter. He continues the leadership role but omits such negative scenes as Peter's rebuke at Caesarea Philippi (9:18–22) and the centrality of Peter in the Gethsemane failure (22:45,46). Also, he mellows Peter's denial by prefacing it with Jesus' prayer that

Peter's faith not fail and that he strengthen the others after he has "turned again" to God (22:31,32). This plus the later stress on the resurrection appearance to Peter (24:34), the only Gospel reference to such (cf. 1 Cor 15:4,5), shows that Luke places even greater stress on Peter's reinstatement. Luke is definitely building a bridge to Peter's role in Acts as both leader and succorer of the church. As is the case with the whole picture of the disciples in the Gospel of Luke, Peter becomes the connecting link between the ministry of Jesus and the mission of the church.

John contains the most unique schema of the four Evangelists. The unprecedented factor here is the interaction between Peter and the beloved disciple (hereafter BD) in several scenes found only in John; while it is debated in higher critical circles, the traditional identification of the BD is the apostle John. As a control, the many scenes where Peter appears by himself must be noted first. John 1:40–42, where Simon is called, has already been noted. To that we will add 6:67–69, where Peter confesses Jesus as "the Holy One of God" in contrast to the many "disciples" who desert Jesus. Jesus' prediction of Peter's denial and the denial itself (13:36–38; 18:17,18,25–27) is given a slightly modified twist by the great separation between the two (unlike the Synoptics); a dramatic contrast is also drawn between Peter's failure and the majestic dignity of Jesus before Annas (18:19–24). An interesting story (18:10,11) is the one in which Peter cuts off the ear of Malchus, the servant of the high priest. This continues the synoptic portrait of Peter's impulsive nature and adds to his human weaknesses. These episodes, together with the foot washing scene (13:6–11), show that Peter is also given a representative role as the spokesman for the disciples in the Gospel of John. In fact when one adds the reinstatement episode (21:15–17), with its emphasis on Peter's pastoral authority (perhaps reminiscent of the shepherd imagery in 10:1–18), Peter's authority is more clearly seen in John than in any other Gospel except Matthew. Many critics regard chapter 21 as a later addendum by a different editor. While we must agree that it was added later (20:30,31 is an obvious conclusion to the original Gospel), it is not necessary to posit a different author. Stylistic and thematic considerations are in sufficient continuity with the Gospel as a whole to allow one to posit the same author.

The scenes with the BD add a unique element. They all occur in the passion and resurrection narratives and each involves a vivid interplay between the two. In 13:23–26 Peter asks the BD, who is "reclining on Jesus' bosom," to query Jesus with respect to his prediction regarding the betrayal. In 20:2–10 the two race to the tomb, with the BD arriving first, then pausing at the entrance. Peter impulsively enters first; then the BD joins him, and only of the latter does it say he "saw and believed" in contrast to the others, who "did not understand" (vv 8,9). At the miraculous catch of fish in 21:7, it is the BD who recognizes Jesus but Peter who spontaneously dives into the sea to get to Jesus. Finally, in 21:18–23 Peter's martyrdom is predicted and then he is contrasted to the BD, who will not suffer martyrdom. The key to this last scene is the discipleship command, "Follow me," which occurs twice (vv 19,22) and links the two.

The question here is John's purpose in these scenes. Most today concede that there is no sense of rivalry or predominence of one over the other. In fact, it is exactly this which typifies each of the scenes, culminating in the portrayal of 21:18–23—both Peter and the BD are authoritative witnesses (note 19:35, which, if it reflects a link between the BD and the evangelist, shows that the "true witness" theme is the major motif with regard to the BD). In conclusion, the preeminence of Peter is enhanced rather than disparaged in the fourth Gospel's juxtaposition of the BD with Peter.

Peter the Apostle. Two events led to the new Peter who appears in Acts: his reinstatement (Jn 21:15–17) and the resurrection appearance of the Lord, which is never described but alluded to in Luke 24:34 and 1 Corinthians 15:5. Peter's denial was certainly proof that he was not yet able to assume his predicted position as the "rock" of the church. Both Luke and Paul seem to state that the risen Lord appeared to Simon Peter before the others, which would be fitting in light of his preeminence in the early church. During the Palestinian era, the 15-year period prior to the gentile mission, Peter was the leading figure. The others mentioned in Acts 1–12—John, who is with Peter in the temple (3:1), prison (4:13), and Samaria (8:14); Stephen, whose revolutionary preaching led to his martyrdom (chs 6,7); Philip, who proclaimed the gospel in Samaria and to the Ethiopian eunuch (ch 8); Barnabas, official delegate to Antioch (11:20–30); Paul, miraculous convert and witness (9:1–30; 11:25–30; 12:25); and James, the first apostolic martyr (12:2)—are all secondary to Peter, the dominant director of church policy. It is he who proposes the choice of the 12th disciple (1:15–17), who proclaims the gospel at Pentecost (2:14–40), who utters the healing word (3:6), who defends the gospel before the Sanhedrin (4:8–12, 19,20; 5:29–32). The episode regarding Ananias and Sapphira is particularly poignant, for here Peter functions as the avenging angel of Yahweh; nowhere is his authority more evident. This authority also surfaces in the scene at Samaria concerning the attempt of Simon the Sorcerer to buy the charismatic power (8:18–24). Again, it is Peter whose influence commands the situation. In these two incidents we certainly see the "binding and loosing" jurisdiction (cf. Mt 16:19) exhibited in Peter.

Yet Peter and the church still came under the strictures of their Jewish heritage. The evidence points to a Jewish proselyte self-consciousness on the part of the early church. They viewed themselves as the righteous remnant, living in the age of messianic fulfillment, but still conducted their evangelism as Jewish particularists: Gentiles could only be converted through Judaism. Two events altered this: first, the Hellenistic Jewish branch of the church rebelled against the Hebrew Christians, which resulted in the appointment of the Seven and a change in the orthodox policy of the Palestinian church. This then led to a new preaching ministry, first by Stephen, whose insights ended in his martyrdom and the dispersal of the Hellenistic branch in chapter 8; then by Philip and others, who extended the gospel even further, to the Samaritans and God-fearers. As a further result, Peter and John came to Samaria (8:14), the next significant step toward the gentile mission. Thus ended the centrality of Jerusalem in the unfolding story.

The miracles of Peter at Lydda (curing the paralytic) and Joppa (raising the dead woman) in 9:32–42 are probably intended to parallel miracles of Jesus (Lk 5:18–26; 8:49–56). This is a major theme in Acts: Jesus' life and ministry are paralleled and continued in the work of the Spirit through the church. Again Peter is seen in a representative role (note the fact that in Acts Paul also has this representative role).

The new relationships are extended in two further scenes. First, Peter stays with "Simon, a tanner," in Joppa, an unclean trade; no pious Jew would knowingly have social contact with a tanner. Even more importantly, God teaches Peter through a dream (10:10–16) that the old dichotomy between clean and unclean has been broken. This then leads Peter to the home of an uncircumcised Gentile, the most serious social taboo for the Jew, and subsequent events force Peter to admit Gentiles into the church without demanding Jewish proselyte requirements. The serious consequences of this are seen in the debate which ensued in Jerusalem (11:2,3) and later at the Council (15:1–21). The centrality of this event is demonstrated in the extent to which Luke reproduces Peter's speech, which seemed to be a repetition of chapter 10 but is meant to highlight

Excavations at Joppa, where Peter raised Dorcas from the dead.

this crucial episode. Often forgotten is the fact that for Luke the gentile mission begins with Peter, not Paul. He is the one upon whom the salvific act of God descends; and as the leader of the church, he was the first important witness to it.

The persecution of Herod Agrippa (12:1–4) was likely due to the furor which this free intercourse with Gentiles caused; and it ended the period of Peter's leadership in Jerusalem. The Jews were greatly offended by the new Christians; and according to Luke in Acts, the idyllic period of popularity, in which the common people supported the church, effectively ceased at this time. Peter's miraculous release and the dramatic scene at Mary's house typified the special place of Peter, but the momentum shifts. Peter is forced to flee Jerusalem, and in the interim James rises to leadership (12:17); at the Jerusalem Council it is the latter who has the chair and presents the council's decision (15:6–29).

The exact relationship between Peter and the other disciples, especially James, John, and the apostle Paul, cannot be ascertained. The evidence is too vague. Many have thought that indeed there were no truly universal leaders, for the early church was too diverse. However, that is unlikely, and Luke's portrayal in Acts parallels Paul's statement in Galatians 2:8 that Peter was the apostle par excellence to the "circumcised" and Paul to the "Gentiles."

They were the universal leaders, while James became the local leader of the Jerusalem eldership. However, neither Peter nor Paul had dominical status similar to that of later popes, that is, neither was the absolute spokesman of the church and above criticism. So-called emissaries from James could have such an influence on Peter that he would hypocritically change his behavior before Gentiles (Gal 2:12), and Paul could rebuke Peter publically for doing so (Gal 2:11–14). Paul never claimed authority over the other disciples and even sought their approval and "right hand of fellowship" for his ministry to the Gentiles (Gal 2:1–10).

Peter's Future Ministry. There is little hard evidence for Peter's other movements. It seems as though Peter gradually turned from leadership to missionary work. However, this is an oversimplification. It is most likely that, like Paul, he combined the two. The presence of a "Cephas party" at Corinth (1 Cor 1:12; 3:22) may indicate that Peter had spent some time there. This is made even more likely when Paul uses Peter as the main example for taking one's wife on missionary expeditions (1 Cor 9:5). The "Cephas party" probably consisted of those who were converted under his ministry; it is probable that they were Jewish Christians who opposed the "Paul party."

The first letter of Peter was sent to churches in northern Asia Minor: the provinces of Pontus, Galatia, Cappadocia, Asia, and Bithynia. The problem here is that there is no hint that Peter had been there and no personal notations in the epistle to demonstrate his acquaintance with these churches. However, it does show that he was very interested in them. In fact, some believe that the reason Paul was not allowed into this district (Acts 16:7,8) was that Peter was already ministering there. In short, the question of Peter's involvement in Asia Minor must remain an open one.

There is no final NT evidence that Peter went to Rome. First Peter 5:13 says that the epistle was sent from "Babylon"; it is doubtful that this was the literal Babylon, because there is no tradition that Peter ever went there, and Babylon was sparsely populated. It is probably a cryptic reference to Rome, the "Babylon of the West." It is most likely that the "Babylon" of Revelation is also a symbol of Rome and one could also consult other Jewish works of that period (e.g., Apocalypse of Baruch 11:1, 4 Esdras 28:31, Sibylline Oracles 5.159). This would fit the strong tradition in the early church that Peter did indeed minister there.

There are four early external witnesses. John 21:18 mentions the martyrdom of Peter but does not give any hint as to the place. First Clement was written at the end of the 1st century and reports the martyrdom of Peter and Paul among others. While 5:4 testifies only to the fact and not the place of Peter's martyrdom, a study of two aspects favors Rome—the reference to a "great multitude" of martyrdoms, which best fits the Neronian persecution; and the phrase "glorious example among us," which shows that the people of Clement's own church (Rome) were involved. Ignatius' letter to the Romans (4:3) also testifies generally to the martyrdom of Peter and Paul, and again the context favors Rome as the place. He says, "I did not command you as did Peter and Paul," which shows that they had ministries in Rome. The Ascension of Isaiah 4:2,3, a Jewish Christian work of the same period, speaks of Beliar (probably Nero) who martyrs "one of the Twelve," almost certainly Peter. Therefore the earliest evidence does not explicitly point to Rome as the place of Peter's death, but that is the most likely hypothesis.

Definite statements to that effect appear toward the end of the 2nd century. Dionysius, bishop of Corinth, in a letter dated approximately AD 170 (preserved in Eusebius' *Eccles. Hist.* 2.25.8) says that Peter and Paul taught together in Italy. At the end of that century Irenaeus says (*Adversus Haereses* 3.1–3) that Peter and Paul preached in Rome, and Tertullian in the same general period adds that Peter was martyred "like . . . the Lord" (Scorpiace 15). Clement of Alexandria and Origen both allude to Peter's presence in Rome and the latter adds that he was "crucified head-downwards" (Eusebius, *Eccles. Hist.* 2.15.2; 3.1.2), a tradition which many see supported in John 21:18, "when you grow old, you will *stretch out your hands*, and someone else will . . . bring you where you do not want to go." The Presbyter Gaius of Rome early in the 3rd century discusses the "trophies" or burial places at "Vatican Hill or the Highway to Ostia," an important reference to the historical development of the legend.

The fact that Paul's Epistle to the Romans (c. AD 55) does not mention Peter, tells us that he could not have gone there earlier than that. If 1 Peter was written during the Neronian persecution, as those who hold to Petrine authorship believe, he must have gone there sometime in the late 50s or early 60s. Of course, the extent of his ministry in Rome also cannot be known. Some indeed have posited that he had little or no extensive stay in Rome. The facts as they can be recovered point to certain tentative conclusions: Peter did have some type of ministry in Rome, though the extent of it cannot be known. However, it is doubtful, in light of the early testimony to his preaching ministry there, that he was merely passing through Rome when caught in Nero's pogrom. Therefore he most likely spent the last years of his life in Rome and there suffered martyrdom under Nero, perhaps the reverse crucifixion as tradition states.

The Location of the Burial. There has been a vigorous debate regarding the exact location of Peter's tomb, mostly on the basis of sectarian interests. Only the archaeological ramifications will be discussed here. Constantine, on the basis of the tradition recorded by Gaius, built a church on Vatican Hill to commemorate Peter's grave. In 1939 excavations under the altar of St. Peter's discovered a memorial similar to Gaius' "trophy," and Pope Paul VI in 1968 went so far as to announce that Peter's actual bones had been found in a marble chest uncovered in an ancient wall under the church. Neither, of course, is conclusive and the latter has especially been challenged.

Other locations have been proposed from time to time. The most frequently cited is the graffiti which contain invocations to Peter and Paul in the catacombs of St. Sebastian on the Appian Way. This accords with the tradition stemming from the 4th century (the Depositio Martyrum *et al.*), which connects Peter with the catacombs and Paul with the Highway to Ostia. On this basis some have posited that Peter's remains were transferred from Vatican Hill to the catacombs during the terrible persecution under Vespasian around AD 258. However, there are too many difficulties with this hypothesis to accord it any degree of probability at all. Finally, an ossuary inscription from the Mt of Olives reading "Simeon bar Jonah" has resulted in the theory that he was buried in that place. Again, however, this is too inadequate (there were probably many with that name) to support such a conclusion. In short, the best data would point to a burial near Vatican Hill, but the precise or even probable site cannot be established with existing evidence.

Simon Peter, along with Paul, was a leading figure in the early church. His impact has been tragically dimmed by the acrimonious debates of Roman Catholic-Protestant circles, but the biblical evidence is clear. He was the leading disciple of Jesus and indeed the "rock" who provided the foundation for the church. As the representative disciple, his enthusiasm and even his weaknesses have made him the supreme example of the developing disciple, one who through the power of the risen Lord rises above his faults to become a towering figure on the church scene.

GRANT R. OSBORNE

See PETER, FIRST LETTER OF; PETER, SECOND LETTER OF; APOSTLE, APOSTLESHIP.

Bibliography. K. Aland, *Saints and Sinners*, pp 33–36; F.F. Bruce, *Peter, Stephen, James, and John;* O. Cullmann, *Peter: Disciple, Apostle, Martyr;* F.J. Foakes-Jackson, *Peter: Prince of Apostles;* C.A. Glover, *With the Twelve;* E.G. Goodspeed, *The Twelve;* E. Kirschbaum, *The Tombs of St. Peter and St. Paul;* D.W. O'Connor, *Peter in Rome.*

Pethahiah. 1. Levite and ancestor of one of the postexilic priestly families (1 Chr 24:16).

2. Levite who obeyed Ezra's exhortation to divorce his pagan wife after the exile (Ezr 10:23).

3. Levite who assisted Ezra at the Feast of Tabernacles (Neh 9:5).

4. Meshezabel's son from Judah's tribe, who served as an adviser to the Persian king (Neh 11:24).

Pethor. Hometown of Baalam (Nm 22:5). Pethor is located in Upper Mesopotamia at the confluence of the Sajur River and the Euphrates. In Deuteronomy the location of Pethor is specified in these words: "because they [the Moabites] hired against you Balaam the son of Beor from Pethor of Mesopotamia, to curse you" (Dt 23:4). Pethor is identified with Pi-it/tiru of the inscriptions of Shalmaneser III (859–824 BC) as a site on the Sajur River. The city was known according to the inscriptions as Pethor by the Hittites (i.e., Syrians or Aramaeans), whereas the Assyrian name was Ana-Asshur-utīr-aṣbat ("I settled it again for Asshur"), commemorating the victory of Tiglath-pileser I (1116–1077 BC). The city went from Assyrian control to Aramaean dominion, was taken again by Shalmaneser, and resettled with Assyrians.

Pethuel. Father of the prophet Joel (Jl 1:1).

Petra. Capital of the Nabataeans, who first appear in history in 312 BC. These people were of Arab origin, though their ancestry is uncertain. They occupied the old land of Edom and made Petra their capital. Petra lay in an impressive valley about 1000 yards wide among the mountains of western Edom, some 60 miles north of Aqaba. The only access to the valley is through a narrow gorge called the Siq. On all sides massive cliffs of reddish sandstone arise. Today ruins of many temples, houses, tombs, and other structures hewn out of the reddish sandstone remain. A Roman basilica and theater are still to be seen. The place continued through Roman times and later had a Christian church and a bishop. It fell into ruins during the days of the Moslem conquest in the 7th century AD.

Petra is not known biblically but has been identified, tentatively, with Sela (es-Sela'), a site 2½ miles northwest of Bozrah (Buseira) since the 3rd century BC (see Septuagint: 2 Kgs

The treasury at Petra.

14:7; Ob 3). Eusebius identified Petra with Rekem; the Nabataeans called it Raqmu. The only Edomite remains found at Petra are on the top of a high mountain outcrop standing independently of Petra, Umm el-Biyyara. In recent times the Iron Age site es-Sela' seems to suit the biblical and postbiblical evidence (2 Kgs 14:7, KJV Selah; Is 16:1). The "rock" of Judges 1:36 and Isaiah 42:11 is of uncertain identity.

Peullethai, Peulthai. Obed-edom's son, who was a Levite gatekeeper in the sanctuary during David's reign (1 Chr 26:5, KJV Peulthai).

Phalec. KJV rendering of Peleg, a descendant of Shem and an ancestor of Jesus, in Luke 3:35.

See PELEG.

Phallu. KJV spelling of Pallu, Reuben's second son, in Genesis 46:9.

See PALLU, PALLUITE.

Phalti. KJV spelling of Palti, Laish's son, in 1 Samuel 25:44.

See PALTI #2.

Phaltiel. KJV spelling of Paltiel, an alternate name for Palti, Laish's son, in 2 Samuel 3:15.

See PALTI #2.

Phanuel. Father of Anna, the prophetess. Anna prophesied in connection with the presentation of the infant Jesus at the temple (Lk 2:36).

Pharaoh. Ruler over Egypt also known as "the King of Upper and Lower Egypt." He lived in a palace known as the "great house," which was the symbol of his authority. The Egyptian word for the palace was applied to the kings of the New Kingdom (c. 1550–1070 BC). As king, the pharaoh personified the rule of the gods over Egypt. The 18th and 19th dynasties frequently employed the term "pharaoh" without further giving the actual name of the pharaoh.

The title is not used officially. Rather, it is

A monastery at Petra.

Pharaohs Referred to in Scripture

Name and/or Significant Events in His Life	Scripture Passage(s)
1. The pharaoh who discovered Abraham's lie about Sarah	Gn 12:15–20
2. The pharaoh at the time of Joseph	Gn 37:36; 39–50; Acts 7:10,13
3. The pharaoh of the oppression	Ex 1:8–14
4. The pharaoh who tried to kill Moses	Ex 2:15,23
5. The pharaoh of the exodus	Ex 5–12; Rom 9:17
6. The pharaoh who took Gezer and gave it to his daughter when she married Solomon	1 Kgs 9:16; cf. 3:1; 7:8; 9:24; 11:1
7. The pharaoh who granted asylum to Hadad of Edom and gave him his wife's sister in marriage	1 Kgs 11:14–22
8. Shishak (940–915 BC), the pharaoh who granted asylum to Jeroboam and later invaded Palestine	1 Kgs 11:40; 14:25–26; 2 Chr 12:1–9
9. So (727–720 BC), the pharaoh to whom Hoshea—just before revolting against the Assyrians—sent messengers	2 Kgs 17:4
10. Tirhakah (689–664 BC), the pharaoh who is called the king of Ethiopia	2 Kgs 19:9; Is 37:9
11. Neco (610–594 BC), the pharaoh who (a) defeated and killed Josiah at Megiddo, (b) put Jehoiakim on the throne instead of Jehoahaz, and (c) was defeated by Nebuchadnezzar at Carchemish	2 Kgs 23:29–35; 24:7; 2 Chr 35:20–24; 36:1–4; Jer 46:2
12. Hophra (589–570 BC), a pharaoh who, according to Jeremiah and Ezekiel, would be defeated by his enemies	Jer 43:9; 44:30; 46:17,25; 47:1; Ez 29:1–3; 30:21,22,25; 31:1–2,18; 32:1–2,31–32

a popular designation for the king. In the OT the title is used to refer to men who lived in different historical periods. They were representatives of various dynasties. The use of the royal designation without the name was sufficient for the period in which the pharaoh ruled or for people who were acquainted with the pharaoh. However, for us it is often difficult to ascertain who the pharaoh is and what dynasty he represented.

In the OT the title pharaoh appears by itself (Gn 12:15), with the additional description "king of Egypt" (Dt 7:8), and the name of the pharaoh, such as Neco (2 Kgs 23:29). The use of the title pharaoh in Genesis may be anachronistic in that Moses in covering the events of the patriarchs in relation to Egypt used the commonly accepted term "pharaoh" even though the title was not in use at the time of the patriarchs (cf. Gn 12:15–20; 37:36).

The pharaoh was considered to be a representative of the gods Ra and Amun on earth. They upheld the divine order in Egypt and were supportive of the temples. The position of the pharaoh as civil and religious head of state gave him unique authority. Unlike his counterparts in the surrounding nations, the authority of the Egyptian king was not easily upset by insurrection.

It remains difficult to identify the pharaohs during the period of the patriarchs. Abraham and Joseph had dealings with the pharaohs of the Middle Kingdom and the Second Intermediate period. Also the issue of the pharaoh of the oppression of the Israelites and of the exodus is not satisfactorily resolved. Those who hold the early date of the exodus see Thutmose III as the pharaoh who did not know

Joseph and began the oppression of the Israelites in Egypt (Ex 1:8). In this view Amenphis II (c. 1440 BC), who succeeded Thutmose upon his death (Ex 2:23), is the pharaoh of the exodus. Another view posits the oppression to have begun under the 18th dynasty and to have continued until the 19th dynasty. In this view Rameses II is the pharaoh of the exodus (c. 1290 BC). During the united monarchy Israel's position as an international power grew. David subdued the nations on Israel's border zones. When Joab took Edom, an Edomite prince, Hadad, fled to Egypt to find protection at pharaoh's court. The 21st dynasty ruled in Egypt during David's time and it may be that Pharaoh Siamun welcomed Hadad as a political weapon to be used against the growing strength of Israel (1 Kgs 11:14–22). Pharaoh Siamun is possibly also to be identified with the pharaoh who made an incursion into the Philistine coastland, conquering Gezer to be given as dowry to Solomon at the marriage of his daughter to Solomon (1 Kgs 3:1,2). At the collapse of Israel's unity, Pharaoh Shishak (Shishong I) of the 22nd dynasty made a campaign against Judah and Israel, and took much booty with him (1 Kgs 14:25,26). After the exile of the northern kingdom, which hoped in vain for help from Egypt against the Assyrians (2 Kgs 17:4), Tirhakah made an unsuccessful attempt to defeat the Assyrians. Pharaoh Neco defeated the Judean forces at Megiddo, killing King Josiah in action (2 Kgs 23:29). The last king of Judah (Zedekiah) also hoped in vain for help from Egypt, where Pharaoh Hophra of the 26th dynasty ruled. The prophet spoke harshly against the king of Egypt. Ezekiel wrote: "Thus says the Lord

God: 'Behold I am against you, Pharaoh king of Egypt.... It [Egypt] will be the lowest of the kingdoms; and it will never again lift itself up above the nations. And I shall make them so small that they will not rule over the nations' " (Ez 29:3,15). Under the Persian regime the power of the pharaohs dwindled in fulfillment of the prophetic word.

See EGYPT, EGYPTIANS.

Pharaoh Hophra. Fourth king of the 26th dynasty (Egypt), he ruled 589–570 BC (Jer 44:30).

See HOPHRA.

Pharaoh-necho, Pharaoh-nechoh, Pharaoh-neco. Alternate names for Neco, pharaoh of the 26th dynasty (Egypt), who ruled 609–594 BC (2 Kgs 23:29).

See NECO, NECHO, NECHOH.

Pharaoh's Daughter. 1. Egyptian princess who rescued the infant Moses and adopted him as her own son (Ex 2:5–10; Acts 7:21; Heb 11:24). If one accepts an early date for the exodus, this foster mother of Moses could have been Hatshepsut. Some scholars who accept a later date for the exodus believe the pharaoh of the oppression was Rameses II; if so, this princess may have been the daughter of Seti I or the daughter of a pharaoh of the later 18th dynasty. It is likely that she was born to a concubine from a royal harem near the region of Goshen.

2. One of the two wives of Mered (a descendant of Caleb) who gave birth to three children (1 Chr 4:17). Her name ("daughter of the Lord") implies that she was converted to the worship of Israel's God. It is not known which pharaoh was her father.

3. Princess whom Solomon married in order to seal an alliance with Egypt. Her father was probably Siamun (978–959 BC). He gave to Solomon the town of Gezer as a marriage dowry (1 Kgs 3:1; 9:16; 11:1). Solomon built her a palace in Jerusalem because he would not have her live in David's house (1 Kgs 7:8; 9:24; 2 Chr 8:11).

Phares, Pharez. KJV forms of Perez, Judah's elder son by Tamar.

See PEREZ, PEREZITE.

Pharisees. Religious sect active in Palestine during the NT period. The Pharisees are consistently depicted in the Gospels as Jesus' antagonists. It is commonly held that the Pharisees represented mainstream Judaism early in the 1st century and that they were characterized by a variety of morally objectionable features. Accordingly, most Bible dictionaries and similar works of reference depict the Pharisees as greedy, hypocritical, lacking in a sense of justice, overly concerned with fulfilling the literal details of the Law, and insensitive to the spiritual significance of the OT. These and other characteristics are furthermore viewed as giving shape to Judaism more generally.

There are several problems with this common perception of Pharisaic Judaism. In the first place, the Gospels themselves give some important information that appears inconsistent with this view. Second, the primary documents of rabbinic Judaism (such as the Mishna, the Talmud, and the Midrashim) are positive and praiseworthy. Third, it has become increasingly clear, especially since the discovery of the Dead Sea Scrolls, that prior to AD 70 the Pharisees constituted only a small movement in a highly diversified society; whatever their popularity and influence, they can hardly be taken as representative of Judaism in general.

These three factors, especially in the context of contemporary ecumenical efforts between Christians and Jews, have led many to play down the negative picture of the Pharisees that we find in the Gospels. Conservative Christians, understandably, wonder whether these developments undermine the authority of the Scriptures and more particularly the teachings of Jesus. A reliable description of the Pharisees requires that our Lord's assessment of these Jewish leaders be taken with utmost seriousness; after all, the distinctive elements of the doctrine of salvation in the Gospels is formulated in conscious opposition to Pharisaic practice. On the other hand, we cannot assume that the church's traditional view of the Pharisees is necessarily correct at every point; a genuine effort must be made to understand whatever evidence is available to us.

Origin. The origins of the Pharisees are obscure. According to Jewish tradition, Pharisaic (= rabbinic) Judaism can be traced back to Ezra and the beginnings of the scribal movement in the 5th century BC. At the opposite extreme, a few scholars argue that, since there are no explicit references to the Pharisees in historical documents prior to the 2nd century BC, Pharisaism appeared suddenly after the Maccabean revolt (167 BC). Many specialists take the position that perhaps as early as the 3rd century BC (e.g., The Wisdom of Joshua ben Sirach, also known as Ecclesiasticus) one can find evidence of an incipient form of Pharisaism. It may well be, moreover, that the intellectual pursuits associated with the work of the scribes did have something to do with the development of the Pharisees. It is also probable that prior to the Maccabean revolt some distinctive Pharisaic concerns appeared in connection with the development of the Hasidim ("the faithful ones," traditionalists who opposed Greek influence in Jewish society). According to a popular and reasonable interpretation, the Hasidim became disillusioned with the Maccabean rulers, whose conduct violated Jewish sensibilities in several respects. Some of the Hasidim separated themselves from the nation and developed into nonconformist sects, such as that of the Essenes. Those who remained tried to exert their influence on Jewish life and developed into the sect of the Pharisees.

The Pharisees no doubt played a significant role in Jewish affairs during the next century, even though at times they had little political clout. By NT times they were widely recognized as religious leaders. Josephus, who tells us that he belonged to this sect, wrote toward the end of the 1st century that the Pharisees were "extremely influential among the townsfolk; and all prayers and sacred rites of divine worship are performed according to their exposition. This is the great tribute that the inhabitants of the cities, by practising the highest ideal both in their way of living and in their discourse, have paid to the excellence of the Pharisees" (*Antiq.* 18.15). We cannot determine whether this description applies to the period before AD 70, but the evidence of the Gospels themselves confirms it to some extent. For example, the parable of the publican and the Pharisee (Lk 18:9–14), while it condemns the Pharisee, makes sense only if we appreciate the role reversal it announces: the wicked publican, not *the one generally regarded as righteous*, goes home justified.

If the Pharisees were "the slaves of lust, and avarice, and pride," as one Bible dictionary puts it, one could not very well account for the fact that large portions of the population viewed them as great moral examples. It is true, of course, that some of our Lord's criticisms (particularly in Mt 23) call into question the integrity and moral standards of the scribes and Pharisees. We should keep in mind, however, that the *main thrust* of Jesus' condemnation lies in a different direction. Moreover, we must recognize that not all Pharisees were alike. Jesus himself commended one wise Pharisee (Mk 12:34; cf. also Nicodemus' actions, Jn 7:50,51), while the rabbinic literature warns against the pride and ostentation of some Pharisees. It is reasonable to conclude that Jesus' criticisms were not intended to describe all (perhaps not even most) Pharisees; rather, they were informal generalizations that served as warnings. After all,

self-importance was a temptation to which Pharisees, because of their standing, were particularly susceptible.

Basic Characteristics. It cannot be possible to give an accurate characterization of the Pharisees, since scholars disagree sharply concerning their fundamental distinctiveness. Some stress the notion of "separateness," partly on the basis of the supposed etymology of the name (from Hebrew *parush*, "separated one," though other suggestions have been made). A more carefully nuanced viewpoint calls attention to the Pharisees' concern with ritual purity (cf. Mk 7:1–4); some of the evidence indicates that the Pharisees wished to apply the priestly rituals to the people generally (this factor may help to explain the relative ease with which the Pharisees adapted to the absence of the temple and its sacrifices after AD 70). Still another position sees the Pharisees as the scholar class: the close connection between them and the scribes (experts in the Law) gives credence to this view, as does the fact that much of the later rabbinic literature reflects an intellectual pursuit, particularly in its detailed logical argumentations regarding the meaning and application of the Torah.

These various approaches are not mutually exclusive. Moreover, there appears to be widespread agreement about one theological conviction that was foundational to Pharisaism, namely, their commitment to the notion of a twofold law, the Written Torah (the OT, principally the Pentateuch) and the Oral Torah (the traditions handed down through many generations of rabbis). This is certainly one feature that distinguished them from the Sadducees (cf. Josephus, *Antiq.* 13.297–98). The latter accepted only the authority of the books of Moses and argued strongly that the importance which the Pharisees attached to oral traditions represented an unjustifiable innovation. These traditions, which sought to regulate the lives of the people before God, became more and more detailed over the course of time and were eventually brought together and written down as a single document, the Mishna (dated *c.* AD 210). Somewhere in its development the view arose that the Oral Law itself had been given by God to Moses and thus shared divine authority with the Scriptures.

A careful look at the NT helps in understanding that this feature more than anything else explains the nature of the conflict between the Pharisaic viewpoint and the message of the gospel. The apostle Paul, for example, stresses the distinctiveness of his apostolic preaching by contrasting it to "the traditions of the fathers" which he zealously pursued in his youth (Gal 1:14). Especially instructive is the key passage in Mark 7, where it is written that the Pharisees complained to Jesus, "Why don't your disciples live according to the tradition of the elders instead of eating their food with 'unclean' hands?" (v 5). Christ's reply counters their criticism with a serious indictment: "You have let go of the commands of God and are holding on to the traditions of men. . . . Thus you nullify the word of God by your tradition that you have handed down" (vv 8,13; cf. Mt 15:1–6).

The importance the Pharisees attributed to their interpretations of the Law compromised the authority of God's own revelation. To make matters worse, the genius of those interpretations was to distort the doctrine of grace by relaxing the divine standards. The very example used by Jesus in Mark 7:10–12 indicates that a rabbinic regulation—the Corban—made it possible for people to ignore the fifth commandment and feel justified in so doing. Though we often think of the Pharisees as very strict and "legalistic," in an important sense their legal enactments made it easier for people to "obey" the Law. A prominent Jewish scholar believes that the Pharisees, in contrast to the idealistic prophets of the OT, appreciated the weaknesses of human nature and adjusted the impossibly high standards of the Law so as to take into account the realities of life. This insight is what made it possible for Pharisaic Judaism to survive the catastrophes of AD 70.

The Pharisaic regulations were numerous and aggravating, but at least they could be fulfilled. Those who followed scrupulously the rabbinic traditions were in danger of concluding that their conduct satisfied God's demands (cf. Paul's description of his own preconversion attitude, Phil 3:6). And a muted sense of one's sin goes hand in hand with a false sense of spiritual security; the need to depend on God's mercy no longer appears crucial. This is of course the point of the parable of the publican and the Pharisee (Lk 18:9–14). In contrast, Jesus calls for a much higher righteousness than that of the Pharisees: "Be perfect, as your Father in heaven is perfect" (Mt 5:20,48).

MOISES SILVA

See SADDUCEES; TALMUD; JUDAISM; JEW; TORAH; TRADITION; TRADITION, ORAL; ESSENES.

Bibliography. I. Abrahams, *Studies in Pharisaism and the Gospels*; L. Baeck, *The Pharisees*; J. Bonsirven, *Palestinian Judaism in the Time of Jesus Christ*; J. Bowker, *Jesus and the Pharisees*; W.D. Davies, *Introduction to Pharisaism*; J. Finkelstein, *The Pharisees*, 2 vols.; M. Hengel, *Judaism and Hellenism*, 2 vols; J. Neusner, *From Politics to Piety: The Emergence of Pharisaic Judaism*; M. Simon, *Jewish Sects at the Time of Jesus*; R.T. Travers Herford, *The Pharisees*.

Pharosh. KJV spelling of Parosh, the ancestor of a postexilic family, in Ezra 8:3.

See PAROSH.

Pharpar. One of two rivers named by Naaman as in or near Damascus (2 Kgs 5:12). Its exact identity is uncertain. One tradition identifies it with the Taura, one of seven waterways branching off the Barada River, which flows through Damascus. Another identifies it with the Awaj, a river originating in the eastern foothills of Mt Hermon and flowing south of Damascus by some 10 miles. In its early going, its course is steep and swift. The Awaj swells during the spring because of the melting of the snows on Mt Hermon, and subsides as the heat of the summer sets in. The river accounts for the good productivity of the southern Damascan plain, and flows much more rapidly than the sluggish Jordan.

Pharzite. KJV form of Perezite, a member of Perez's family, in Numbers 26:20.

See PEREZ, PEREZITE.

Phaseah. KJV spelling of Paseah, the head of a family of temple servants, in Nehemiah 7:51.

See PASEAH #2.

Phebe. KJV spelling of Phoebe, a Christian woman, in Romans 16:1.

See PHOEBE.

Phenice. 1. KJV form of Phoenicia, the country on the east Mediterranean coast and north of Palestine, in Acts 11:19 and 15:3.

See PHOENICIA, PHOENICIAN.

2. KJV form of Phoenix, a harbor along Crete's southern coastline, in Acts 27:12.

See PHOENIX.

Phenicia. KJV spelling of Phoenicia in Acts 21:2.

See PHOENICIA, PHOENICIAN.

Phicol, Phichol. Commander of Abimelech's army, mentioned in connection with his ruler's treaty negotiations with Abraham and Isaac (Gn 21:22,32; 26:26, KJV Phichol). The presence of an army commander was in stark contrast to Abraham's relatively more vulnerable position, but the adversaries acknowledged the superior power of Abraham's God and thus sought peaceful coexistence with him.

Philadelphia. 1. City of the Decapolis. It is not mentioned in any NT writing. Located on the plateau about 25 miles east of the Jordan River, the city had formerly been known as Rabbah, or Rabbath-amman. The modern capital of the Hashemite kingdom of Jordan, Amman, now occupies this site. About the mid-

Ruins at Philadelphia, a city in Asia Minor that had a church addressed in Revelation (3:7–13).

dle of the 3rd century BC Ptolemy Philadelphus of Egypt captured the city and renamed it after himself.

In 63 BC Palestine came under Roman domination. Pompey, the Roman general who conquered the region, reorganized the territory. He established a league of 10 self-governing cities or city-states. Most of these were located on the eastern side of the Jordan River. Philadelphia was the southernmost and Damascus the northernmost of the 10. In the Gospels this territory is referred to as "the Decapolis."

See DECAPOLIS.

2. City in western Asia Minor. It was one of the seven Asian cities to which the author of the Book of Revelation addressed letters, mentioned in 1:11 and 3:7–13.

This city was founded about 140 BC by Attalus II of the city of Pergamum. He intended that it would serve as a center for the spread of Greek culture throughout the region, especially to the people of Phrygia. It was situated on a fertile plain which brought it prosperity in the form of vineyards and wine production. Attalus II was also known as "Philadelphus"; the name of the city was derived from this royal nickname.

Asian Philadelphia was heavily damaged by an earthquake in the year AD 17. For the purpose of rebuilding it was granted disaster aid by the Roman emperor Tiberius.

When John wrote from Patmos near the end of the 1st century, the churches of western Asia were undergoing persecution. The church in Philadelphia was one of them. This church was enduring the persecution faithfully, and the letter to it (Rv 3:7–13) contains no words of reproach or warning. It consists entirely of encouragement and promise.

Some years later, the Christian bishop and martyr, Ignatius of Antioch, also wrote a letter to the church in Philadelphia. He expressed appreciation for his recent visit with them, and encouraged them in Christian unity.

Philemon (Person). Christian known only from the letter addressed to him by the apostle Paul. He is mentioned nowhere else in the NT. From Colossians 4:17 it is clear that Archippus, mentioned along with Philemon in the letter (and perhaps his son), was a man of Colossae. Although Paul had never visited that city (Col 2:1), he obviously knew Philemon well. He addressed him as "our beloved fellow worker" (Phlm 1); perhaps Philemon had been a colleague during Paul's three-year mission in Ephesus (Acts 19:8–10; 20:31), and Paul knew that he could appeal to him on behalf of his runaway slave, Onesimus.

See PHILEMON, LETTER TO.

Philemon, Letter to.

Author. In keeping with his custom and with the contemporary canons of the epistolary genre, the apostle Paul identifies himself as the author of this letter. He says that he is a prisoner at the time of writing (vv 9,10,13,23) because of his witness to Jesus Christ.

Origin. It is difficult to ascertain the location of Paul's imprisonment at the time of writing. Of Caesarea, Ephesus, or Rome, either of the latter locations seems to correspond to the data available in this epistle and in Colossians with which it is closely related (Col 4:7–14; cf. Phlm 23,24). The mention of Mark and Luke as Paul's companions favor Rome as the point of origin of the letter (v 24). However, the relative proximity of Ephesus to Colossae where Philemon resided (about 100 miles) and the announcement of Paul's forthcoming visit to Colossae (v 22) suggest Ephesus as the place of confinement. Although an Ephesian imprisonment is not explicitly mentioned in the Book of Acts, the account of Paul's missionary endeavors in that city make it clear that he met with considerable opposition (Acts 20:19), which Paul describes in terms that could imply a time spent in prison (1 Cor 15:32; 2 Cor 1:8–10).

Recipient. This document is often improperly viewed as a personal note from Paul to Philemon, his convert and friend, church leader in Colossae, and slave owner. In reality, the epistle is addressed to Philemon, to Apphia (presumably Philemon's wife), to Archippus, and to the congregation of believers that met in Philemon's house (vv 1,2). Greetings are sent by the medium of the epistle on behalf of Epaphras, Mark, Aristarchus, Demas, and Luke, who represent together an impressive contingent of church leaders (vv 23,24). Paul's purpose in mentioning them is to make Philemon realize that his response to Paul's plea will not be a private decision, but one for which he will be accountable to the community of believers of which he is a part. In the body of Christ, matters that pertain to relationships of believers among themselves are of concern to the whole community. Such matters may not be treated as private issues since they necessarily affect the well-being of the entire church (Mt 18:15–20).

The epistle makes it clear that a warm bond of brotherly love existed between Paul and Philemon. The apostle calls Philemon his "beloved fellow worker" (v 1); he commends him in effusive terms for Philemon's involvement in the missionary enterprise (vv 5–7); he appeals to him on the basis of love (v 9); he evokes their sharing a common partnership (v 17); he gently reminds Philemon that he owes his salvation to Paul (v 19) and trusts him to do what is requested of him and even more (v 21).

Circumstance. The object of Paul's letter pertains to a third party, Onesimus, the runaway slave of Philemon. After having committed some indiscretion not revealed in the letter (v 18), the slave had escaped and, having traveled to the big city, he had sought anonymity among the heterogeneous groups of people that form the underclass of any metropolis. Through providential circumstances that remain shrouded in mystery, the fugitive slave

had come under Paul's influence; he had been converted by him (v 10), had endeared himself to Paul's heart (v 12), and had become involved with him in the work of the gospel to the extent that Paul would have been glad to keep him in his service as his "faithful and dear brother" (v 13; Col 4:9).

Paul knew that, had he kept Onesimus at his side as a co-worker, Philemon would have been compelled to assent to his decision (vv 13,14). However, Paul decided to use the ambiguous situation that had developed as the occasion to make Philemon think through the implications of his faith on slavery, and to cause him to free Onesimus and elevate him to the status of brother, not only in a spiritual sense ("in the Lord") but also in regard to his civil status ("in the flesh," v 16). That Philemon acceded to Paul's request and granted freedom to Onesimus is attested by the preservation of this document. Had Philemon rejected Paul's request, he would have destroyed the letter in order to erase from human memory what would have become incriminating evidence of his recalcitrance.

An intriguing postscript has been added to this story by the discovery of the repeated references to an elderly bishop named Onesimus who led the church at Ephesus in the early part of the 2nd century, according to Ignatius' letter to the Ephesians. The identification of the bishop with Philemon's slave is suggested by the use in Ignatius' letter of Paul's play on words with the name of Onesimus in verses 11 and 20 (Onesimus means "useful" or "beneficial"). Should this be the case, it is conceivable that the former slave was the individual who collected the Pauline letters that were eventually integrated into the NT canon, including the letter to Philemon.

Purpose. The purpose of Paul's letter to Philemon was to dramatize the incongruity of the institution of slavery with Christianity and thus obtain the release of Onesimus. There is no evidence in the epistle that Paul was worried about Philemon inflicting upon Onesimus the harsh punishments that were prescribed by Roman law for runaway slaves. However, Paul was concerned that Onesimus not be reinstated as slave but that he be received as a full-fledged member of Philemon's family, and that he be treated with at least the same deference and dignity that might have been extended to Paul himself (vv 17,21).

Teaching. Among the many teachings contained in this small epistle, three deserve special mention.

First, the letter bears witness to the revolutionary challenge brought by the gospel to the sin-laden institutions of society. As such, it constitutes a condemnation of the practice of slavery. Jesus had denied his followers the right to own or control other human beings. Within the Christian community, mastery or leadership was to be exercised in servanthood from the bottom of the social ladder rather than hierarchically along lines of authority (Mk 10:42–45). As a result, class differences had become irrelevant among Christians. In Christ, there was neither slave nor free but all were one in him (Gal 3:28). Enslaved Christians who could obtain their freedom were to avail themselves of the opportunity (1 Cor 7:21), and those who were free were to avoid becoming slaves of men (1 Cor 7:23; Gal 5:1). Conversely, Christian slave owners were to act as servants to their slaves (Eph 6:9a), and all Christians were to be servants to one another (Gal 5:13). Consequently, Philemon was to receive Onesimus "no longer as a slave" (v 16).

Second, if adherence to the gospel prohibits a conservative maintenance of the status quo, it also rules out its violent overthrow. The revolutionary temper of the gospel is expressed in a posture of servanthood rather than in militant hostility. Onesimus was advised by Paul to demonstrate this theology of liberation by returning in submission to Philemon so as to allow the Holy Spirit to effect radical change in their relationship. The employment of Satan's methods to achieve kingdom results rules out divine intervention and results in increased oppression.

Finally, the epistle provides a masterful model of inspired churchmanship. The situation that had developed between Philemon and Onesimus required the mediation of an advocate who could command the respect of the former in order to speak successfully on behalf of the latter. To win his case, Paul used the psychology of commendation (vv 4–7); he emphasized his own self-sacrificial suffering for the sake of the gospel (v 9); he played on Philemon's good will (v 14); he appealed to personal bonds of friendship (vv 17,20); he offered to assume responsibility for losses incurred (v 18); he reminded Philemon of his own indebtedness to Paul (v 19), and announced a forthcoming encounter that might have caused embarrassment had Philemon demurred at his request (v 22). Paul's approach is personal and pastoral, friendly but fervent. It exhibits a perfect balance of firmness and finesse. It demonstrates how genuine Christian leadership is to be exercised through persuasion and entreatment rather than by heavy-handed authoritarian impositions.

Although it is one of the shortest documents in the Bible, the Letter to Philemon stands as a timeless monument to the dignity and equality conferred by Christ on all humans regardless of rank, gender, class, or status. It also offers Christians a mandate and a methodology to pursue effective social reform.

See PAUL, THE APOSTLE; PHILEMON (PERSON).

Bibliography. F.F. Bruce, *The Epistles to the Colossians, to Philemon, and to the Ephesians;* J. Knox, *Philemon: Among the Letters of Paul;* J.B. Lightfoot, *St. Paul's Epistles to the Colossians and to Philemon;* R.P. Martin, *Colossians and Philemon;* C.F.D. Moule, *The Epistles to the Colossians and to Philemon;* L.B. Radford, *The Epistle to the Colossians and the Epistle to Philemon.*

Philetus. False teacher who, along with his companion Hymenaeus, held an erroneous view of the resurrection of believers—that the resurrection had already happened (2 Tm 2:17; cf. v 11).

Philip. 1. Apostle whose name is placed fifth in each of the lists of the 12 after the two pairs of brothers, Simon Peter and Andrew, and James and John (Mt 10:3; Mk 3:18; Lk 6:14). John says that when John the Baptist bore witness to Jesus with the words, "Behold, the Lamb of God!", two of his disciples began to follow Jesus, and that one of these two was Andrew, who then declared to his brother Simon Peter, "We have found the Messiah!", and brought him to Jesus. (The other unnamed disciple was quite probably John himself, the writer of this account.) On the next day Jesus went to Galilee and there found Philip and addressed the call to him, "Follow me." John adds that Philip was from Bethsaida. Philip in turn found Nathanael and told him, "We have found him of whom Moses in the law and also the prophets wrote," and invited Nathanael, who was skeptical that any good could come out of Nazareth, to come and see for himself (Jn 1:35–51). From this is concluded that Philip was one of the first to follow Jesus and that he lost no time in persuading others to do the same.

Like the other apostles, however, he still had much to learn about the person and the power of Christ. Hence the testing question of Jesus to him on the occasion of the feeding of the 5000. "How are we to buy bread, so that these people may eat?"; and his puzzled response that even if they had 200 denarii (i.e., a large sum, roughly a person's wages for half a year) it would not buy enough bread for each one to be given just a little to eat. The miracle that followed taught him that the feeding of this multitude presented no problem to the One who is the Lord of all creation (Jn 6:5–7). Philip's next appearance is in Jerusalem after Christ's triumphal entry into the city, when "some Greeks" (i.e., Greek-speaking non-Jews) approached him with the request, "Sir, we wish to see Jesus." Philip informs Andrew and together they bring them to Jesus (Jn 12:20–

22). This perhaps indicates that Philip was a person whom others found readily approachable, and also that he spoke Greek. In the upper room, prior to his arrest and trial, Jesus took the opportunity to impart further instruction to Philip, who had said, "Lord, show us the Father, and we will be satisfied." Philip hoped perhaps, in all devoutness, for the privilege of some special revelation (reminiscent of the request of Moses, Ex 33:18); but Jesus teaches him that he himself, the incarnate Son, is the all-sufficient revelation of the Father to mankind (Jn 14:8–31).

There is a tendency to confuse the apostle with the evangelist (see below) of the same name. It seems probable, however, that after preaching in various parts he settled in Hierapolis, a city of the Roman province of Asia, and died there, though whether his was a natural or a martyr's death is uncertain.

See APOSTLE, APOSTLESHIP.

2. Hellenistic Jew and one of the seven men appointed by the church in Jerusalem to supervise the daily ministry of succor to the impoverished widows of the Christian community. They all, including Philip, had Greek names, and one of them, Nicolaus, was a proselyte (i.e., not a Jew by birth). Whether or not they were regarded as deacons in the technical sense is not absolutely clear from the account; this occasion has, however, been generally accepted as the origin of the order of the diaconate (Acts 6:1–7). Of the seven, Stephen and Philip are the only ones of whom we have any further record in the NT. They are described as "men of good repute, full of the Spirit and of wisdom" (v 3). That Philip became known as "the evangelist" is apparent from Acts 21:8. The designation was well deserved, for when the Jerusalem Christians were scattered by the persecution led by Saul of Tarsus, Philip went to a city of Samaria and proclaimed the gospel with such power there that a great number of the populace joyfully turned to Christ (Acts 8:1–8). In the midst of this spectacular work, Philip was divinely instructed to leave Samaria and go down to the desert area in the southern part of the country. Humanly speaking, for him to turn away from the multitudes who were so eagerly responding to his preaching and to go to the uninhabited territory in the south must have seemed incomprehensible and even foolish. Yet Philip showed himself not only sensitive but also obedient to the will of God and followed this guidance without question. In the desert he found not a crowd but a single person to whom to minister, an important Ethiopian court official who had visited Jerusalem and was now returning to Africa. The wisdom of God in directing Philip to this place was fully vindicated,

for the Ethiopian was reading Isaiah 53, the great gospel chapter of the OT. Philip gave him the good news that this and the other prophecies of the OT were fulfilled in Jesus Christ. The Ethiopian subsequently believed and was baptized and went on his way rejoicing (Acts 8:25–40). The conversion of this one person meant not only that Philip was the first to proclaim the gospel to a Gentile, but also that the gospel was taken by this Ethiopian courtier to the continent of Africa. The prevailing nationalistic pride of the Jews was such that they despised the Samaritans and regarded the Gentiles as unclean; but Philip, by his eager preaching of Christ first to the Samaritans and then to the Ethiopian, reflected the way in which the gospel penetrated social barriers and dissolved racial prejudices and demonstrated that the grace of God in Christ Jesus is freely available to all. Subsequently, Philip made his home in the coastal town of Caesarea. There he hospitably entertained Paul and Luke when they were enroute to Jerusalem at the conclusion of the apostle's third missionary journey. Luke tells us that Philip had four unmarried daughters who prophesied (Acts 21:8,9). Not long after this, when Paul was in custody in Caesarea for two years, the kindness and friendship of Philip must have meant much to him (Acts 23:31–35; 24:23,27).

3. Son of Herod the Great and Cleopatra and half-brother of Antipas, whose mother was Malthace. He is called Herod in Luke 3:1. The latter was tetrarch of Perea and Galilee from 4 BC to AD 39; Philip was tetrarch of Ituraea and Trachonitis (plus certain other territories) to the northeast of Galilee for 37 years (4 BC to AD 33). His wife was his niece Salome who danced for the head of John the Baptist (Mt 14:3–12; Mk 6:17–29).

See HEROD, HERODIAN FAMILY.

4. Son of Herod the Great and Mariamne and husband of Salome's mother Herodias, who left him to become the mistress of his half-brother Herod Antipas. It was for this immoral relationship that John the Baptist rebuked Herod and was later imprisoned and beheaded (Mt 14:3–12; Mk 6:17–29; Lk 3:19,20).

PHILIP EDGCUMBE HUGHES

Philippi. Minor village of Thrace (known in antiquity as "The Springs" [Krenides]) until about 357 BC when the father of Alexander the Great, Philip II of Macedon, conquered the site and rebuilt it. He gave the village his name ("Philip's City"), fortified it as a military stronghold in subduing the area, and exploited the nearby gold mines. Two hundred years later in the Roman era it became a chief city of one of the four Roman districts into which Macedonia was divided. But because it

The theater at Philippi.

was about 10 miles inland from the port of Neapolis, its growth was limited. Nearby Amphipolis (southwest) was the center of Roman government.

Philippi gained worldwide fame in 42 BC when the imperial armies of Antony and Octavian defeated the Republican generals Brutus and Cassius (the assassins of Julius Caesar). The victory opened the way for the emergence of the Roman Empire under the rule of Octavian (Augustus).

Veterans from the war of 42 BC and other battles commonly settled in Philippi. When Paul came to the city it still reflected its Latin/military heritage. Situated on the Ignatian Way it was one stop on that great military highway connecting the Adriatic with the Aegean. It possessed a distinct civic pride inasmuch as it was a Roman colony (enjoying numerous privileges such as tax exemptions), promoted Latin as its official language, and hosted numerous Roman citizens. Its government was modeled on the municipal constitution of Rome (its leader bearing Roman titles throughout) and the people lived as if they were indeed located in Italy. As Luke records in Acts 16:21, the citizens viewed themselves as "Romans."

Paul visited the city on his second missionary tour and years later wrote one letter to the church. The account of Acts gives detailed attention to Paul's visit. The narrative frequently refers to the city's Roman heritage: not only does Paul successfully employ his Roman citizenship in his defense (16:36), but the city magistrates bear the dignified Latin title *Praetor* (given in its Gk translation, *strategos*, 16:20,22,38). There appears to have been a small Jewish community here. The church began with believing Jewish women who met outside the city because there was no synagogue. Later they convened in the home of an important woman convert named Lydia (16:14,15,40).

Some have suggested that Luke may have had a special interest in Philippi. This is explained not only by his careful attention to the city, but by the "we" sections of Acts. The first "we" section (when Luke joins Paul) begins and ends at Philippi (16:10,40). This suggests that Luke stayed behind in the city after Paul's departure. Then on the third tour Luke joins Paul again when the apostle passes through Philippi (20:6).

Archaeological evidence of Christianity has been found at the ruins of Philippi (modern Filibedjik). Christian epitaphs and Latin crosses may stem from the 2nd to the 4th centuries. In addition, two large basilicas (5th or 6th centuries) have been uncovered.

Philippians, Letter to the.

Author. Philippians is like 2 Corinthians, Colossians, 1 and 2 Thessalonians, and Philemon in that Paul shared its authorship with Timothy. The appearance of Timothy's name at the start of these letters, however, probably does not mean that he had any greater part in their composition than perhaps to act as Paul's secretary.

Distinction. Philippi had the distinction of being a Roman colony (Acts 16:12), a privilege accorded to only a few cities outside Italy. Some 90 years before the gospel arrived there (c. AD 50; Acts 16:12–40), it had been greatly expanded by large numbers of Roman soldiers, who were settled there by their commanding officers. As a consequence the town acquired its coveted status as a "colony," which meant that for all intents and purposes its citizens were treated as if they lived in Italy, and the town had a fully Roman administration. Paul alludes to this status in 3:20, where he teaches that Christians likewise are citizens of another city, the heavenly one, while yet resident elsewhere. It was a rich and busy place, one of the main centers of life in Macedonia, and consequently was "home" to the adherents of many different religions, from both east and west. There was a strong Jewish community there, as well as pagans of many sorts, and this has all left its mark on the letter.

Date and Origin. While it is clear that Paul is writing from prison (1:12,13), it is not clear where he is imprisoned. The most likely possibility is Rome, in which case the date would be around AD 62, but some have felt that all the journeys implied in 4:14 and 2:25–26 make such a distant place unlikely (the Philippians hear that Paul is in prison and send a gift by Epaphroditus; Epaphroditus hears in Rome that the Philippians have heard that he has been ill). So the alternatives of Ephesus (c. AD 55) and Caesarea (c. AD 58) have been proposed. We know that Paul was imprisoned in

Caesarea (Acts 23:33–35), but the greeting "from those of Caesar's household" is difficult to explain if it was written there, in spite of the coincidence of name. Ephesus is certainly near enough to Philippi for plenty of interchange, but no imprisonment is recorded in the account of Paul's ministry there in Acts. So we would have to assume that Luke's account in Acts 19 is not complete, and perhaps that Paul was placed in protective custody at the time of the riot (see esp. Acts 19:30,31). But such an imprisonment could hardly have led Paul to wonder whether his time "to depart and be with Christ" had now come (1:23). At the time of writing, he was clearly facing a capital charge.

The traditional location seems the most satisfactory, especially when one reflects that Paul was imprisoned in Rome for at least two years (Acts 28:30), and that it took about three weeks to travel from Rome to Philippi.

Theology. In a sense Paul's imprisonment is not just a background "fact," but lies at the heart of the letter's message. In his imprisonment, he is experiencing the "abasement" that he mentions in 4:12, using there the same word used in 2:8 to describe the self-humbling of Christ unto death. The pattern of the ministry of Jesus described in the great "hymn" of 2:6–11—humiliation followed by glorification—becomes the pattern of Paul's own life and of the vision he holds out before the Philippians. So alongside abasement and suffering, joy is the other great theme of the letter. Within suffering and self-sacrifice, true joy is born: in fact Philippians could justly be titled, "The Epistle of Joy." Other prominent themes include the gospel, the Day of the Lord, and, in addition to the famous "hymn" in chapter 2, a comparison of Paul's Jewish past with his present Christian experience (3:4–16).

Content. *Greeting and Opening Prayer (1:1–11).* In the opening paragraph of his letter, Paul presents the themes which will be uppermost in his mind throughout. His personal warmth toward the Philippians is immediately striking: "I have you in my heart . . . I long for all of you" (vv 7,8), and this thought of outgoing and suffering love undergirds the whole letter. It is notable too that the letter begins and ends with the themes of "grace" and of "the saints" (1:1,2; 4:21–23). The condescending grace of Christ, which reaches out to sinful man and transforms him, separating him from the world, occupies Paul throughout. "The saints" are the ones who, touched by that grace, are transformed in heart and mind, so that their love abounds "more and more in knowledge and depth of insight" (v 9).

Two more great themes appear here. The Greek word *phroneō*, "to think," is used more in Philippians than in any other letter of Paul, no fewer than 9 times (as against 7 in Romans). Unfortunately, it is not uniformly translated in the English versions, and so it is hard for the English reader to notice its repeated appearance and the emphasis on the right use of the mind which goes with it. But for Paul this is vital: the way we think is at the heart of the Christian life—and in these opening verses he makes it clear that the love he feels for the Philippians is actually the Christian way of thinking about them (v 7: literally, "It is right for me to think this way about you"). This leads naturally to another emphasis—growth. For the Christian mind does not appear overnight: it develops, "abounds more and more" (v 9), and needs to be worked at. So Paul prays that this mind may grow, giving the Philippians powers of discernment which will transform their character and prepare them for "the day of Christ" (vv 10,11; cf. v 6).

Finally, we note in this opening prayer the twin emphases on the gospel and on fellowship—linked in Paul's prayer of thanksgiving for the Philippians' "partnership in the gospel" (v 5; cf. v 7)—and also the introduction of the great theme of joy (v 4). All three are vital to the whole letter.

Paul and His Imprisonment: Christ Exalted! (1:12–26). Paul writes about his own situation to present the heart of his message. For when he writes, "For me to live is Christ" (v 21), he means more than that his every waking moment is taken up by fellowship with his Lord and service for him. He means also that, in his own person and experience, he displays Christ and "lives" him. Later he will say, "Whatever you have learned or received or heard from me, or seen in me—put it into practice" (4:9). Few Christian ministers would dare make such a claim today! Yet Paul believed that, as an apostle of Christ, it was his privilege not just to speak on Christ's behalf, but also to live out Christ's life in his own person, even if that meant suffering and humiliation.

There are two historical difficulties here. First, it is hard to reconstruct the situation to which Paul refers in verses 12–18. The church in Rome (if that is where he is) was clearly divided about his imprisonment, some believers actually being glad that he was behind bars. It seems as though they were prompted by his imprisonment to get on with preaching their own version of the gospel. Far from being upset by this, Paul is delighted! "What does it matter?" he asks (v 18). Whether by friend or foe, Christ is being proclaimed in a new way as a result of his imprisonment (v 14). He was normally quick to defend the purity of the Word proclaimed, so these "rivals" of Paul cannot have been too "unsound."

The other historical difficulty surrounds verses 19–26. At one moment Paul seems not to know what the outcome of his imprisonment will be (vv 19–21). Yet he then suggests that he can "choose" whether to live or die (v 22), and finally tells the Philippians that he is sure he will "remain" (v 25). The best explanation is that Paul believed he had received a personal assurance from the Holy Spirit that his imprisonment would not end with his execution.

At any rate, his attitude about his own death is most moving. He expects "deliverance . . . whether by life or by death" (vv 19,20), and has an unshakeable confidence that to die is "better by far" (v 23), because it means being "with Christ." The section ends wonderfully—on the note of joy.

The Life Worthy of the Gospel (1:27–2:18). This section ends with "joy" just as the last did, and its whole message is summed up in the opening exhortation of verse 27. Paul wants the Philippians to be people in whom there is no gap between profession and practice, in whom the gospel believed is the gospel lived. The section falls into four portions, which might be entitled as follows: (1) 1:27–30: the worthy life in a hostile world; (2) 2:1–4: the worthy life in Christian fellowship; (3) 2:5–11: the gospel which inspires us; (4) 2:12–18: priorities for lives worthy of the gospel.

Paul refuses to let the Philippians feel that he is worse off than they. "You are going through the same struggle you saw I had, and now hear that I still have," he writes (1:30). For suffering at the hands of a hostile world is part and parcel of Christian discipleship. If we profess to believe a gospel about One who, though equal with God, left aside the glory of heaven and submitted not just to incarnation but also to a horrible death (2:6–8), then we must think of suffering not as an unfortunate necessity, but as a privilege! "It has been granted to you [as part of God's grace to you] on behalf of Christ . . . to suffer for him" (1:29).

The essential quality which they will need, in order to face successfully the hostility of the world, is unity. They must "stand firm in one spirit, contending as one man for the faith of the gospel" (1:27), and believing one gospel will produce a united front against the world—and not a purely defensive front, either. The theme of unity continues into chapter 2, where Paul turns to life within the fellowship (2:1–4)—as if to say that external unity before the world will not be possible unless their hearts and minds are truly united in one love, spirit, and purpose (2:2), whatever their outward situation. Such a unity will only come if there is "tenderness and compassion" (2:1) among them. The lovely progression in

verse 1 reaches a climax with this phrase—and that in turn leads into the famous "hymn" in 2:6–11. Such tenderness will not find its home in their hearts unless they believe the gospel about which the hymn sings.

Whether 2:6–11 was in fact a real hymn, sung in the context of early Christian worship, is now impossible to know for sure. Certainly Paul's language here takes on a hymnic quality, though it is not in poetic form. Many scholars have held that Paul did not write these verses himself, but is quoting a well-known piece of liturgy. All one can say for certain is that his language changes in style, and he expresses here ideas which are unique in his writings (and for that reason hard to interpret!).

The hymn blends in with its context beautifully, and in fact forms the core of the whole letter. For we see here how the experience of imprisonment and deliverance, and of suffering and joy, is an entering into the experience of Jesus himself—who died and rose, was humbled and glorified.

Two Worthy Examples and Friends (2:19–30). Paul again writes about his own situation and plans, but as before this section is not just concerned with practical arrangements. On the face of it, he is simply explaining why he is sending the letter by the hand of Epaphroditus instead of Timothy. But actually he is holding them up as practical examples of the life lived by the gospel, about which he has just written. Timothy "takes a genuine interest in your welfare" (v 20), because, unlike "everyone else," he does not seek his own interests but those of Jesus Christ (v 21). He lives the gospel! He is committed to "the work of the gospel" (v 22). And Epaphroditus is the same, though in a different way. His union with Jesus is expressed not so much in his self-giving service for the gospel and his fellow-saints, as in the illness which he suffered and the pains of separation which he endured. Like Jesus, he put his life on the line (v 30), and like Jesus he was restored to life again (v 27). Now he is to be restored to his beloved Philippians, and the *joy* which they will experience together will be a further outworking of the gospel.

Pressing Forward and Standing Firm (3:1–4:1). This section also begins and ends on the note of joy (3:1; 4:1)—not accidentally. The way of the cross which Paul describes is also the way of joy (cf. Heb 12:2). It begins and ends also with the address "my brothers," and this too is not accidental, for once again in this passage Paul writes about himself, and once again the underlying thought is that his experience is typical, and that his readers should expect and seek to see the same pattern in their lives. "Join with others in following my example, brothers," he writes (v 17), having held up Timothy and Epaphroditus as examples in 2:19–30, Paul now does the same with himself.

The tone seems to change dramatically in 3:2, as Paul turns to warn the Philippians against "those dogs," who are probably the same as those to whom he refers in 1:28, "those who oppose you." There, he was much concerned about the inner foundation of the Philippians' stand against them, so he did not specify who they were. But now he examines them more closely, in order to show the Philippians that the Christian life entails a complete reversal of the values held by their opponents.

It seems that they are Jews, the sort in Acts 17:5 who opposed Paul's ministry in nearby Thessalonica. They believe that they are God's chosen race, but Paul thinks that is "confidence in the flesh" (v 4). They think that they know the way of righteousness—it is the way of rigorous and disciplined obedience to God's Law in every detail of life; but Paul thinks that is to seek "a righteousness of one's own" (v 9), having nothing to do with the righteousness that God wants to give. The true way to be God's people, he movingly insists, is the way of self-renunciation, so that all he previously held dear as a Jew came to be seen as "rubbish" (v 8), considered "loss for the sake of Christ" (v 7). The only way to attain righteousness is through faith in Christ (v 9): for you must "become like him in his death" if you are to "know the power of his resurrection" (v 10). For Paul, dying with Christ meant not just suffering imprisonment and many other indignities for Christ's sake, but also renouncing all the prized possessions which his Judaism had given him.

It is easy to see how not just Jews but also Jewish Christians were suspicious about Paul. But for him salvation is first and last Christ, and anything that takes its place must be cast aside. To place one's confidence in a Jewish heritage is "to think the things of this earth" (v 19); to place confidence in Christ is to set one's heart on a heavenly city and to expect to be taken there (vv 20,21).

Thinking, Rejoicing, Sharing . . . (4:2–23). Again the tone changes suddenly (both at 4:2 and at 4:10), so much so that some scholars have suggested that Philippians was compiled by an editor out of originally distinct letters. But such a view misunderstands the way Paul's mind moves, and the way in which there can be a hidden link which only becomes clear on careful reflection.

When Paul turns in 4:2 to address Euodia and Syntyche, he is not really changing the subject. The link with the last section is the same as that between 1:27–30 and the first

paragraph in chapter 2: how can Christians expect to be able to hold their own in the face of "enemies of the cross of Christ" (3:18) if they are disunited and at odds with each other? For if there is just one gospel, disharmony between Christians means that the gospel is not having its full effect. So Euodia and Syntyche are urged (literally) to "think the same thing in the Lord" (v 2), and are then reminded of how they once found a wonderful unity in "striving side by side in the cause of the gospel" (v 3).

The "agreement" which Paul urges them to come to does not mean complete identity of opinions on all subjects. It means a oneness of heart in a common love for Christ and the gospel; and in the rest of the letter Paul spells out what this oneness means in practice—both what it should mean and what it has meant for the Philippians. The use of the mind is vital, and in verses 4–9 Paul holds out a picture of the Christian life in which careful and intelligent prayer (vv 6,7) and the deliberate directing of the mind toward "whatever is true . . ." (v 8) will produce a life marked by the two qualities of peace and joy, whatever the circumstances (v 7 balances v 9b, and v 4 stands at the head of the whole paragraph).

That leads into the final paragraph, in which Paul gives thanks that, in spite of the disharmony evident in one part of the Philippian church, nevertheless the church as a whole has already displayed this true Christian "mind." For they have shown their oneness with Paul in the cause of the gospel by sending him a gift by Epaphroditus. "You have shared in my troubles," Paul writes (v 14), and our thoughts go back again to the hymn in 2:6–11. From the gospel about the One who came from heaven to bear our burdens comes this mutual sharing—and so does Paul's wonderful attitude to his circumstances: "I know how to be humbled [the same word as in 2:8], and I know how to abound . . ." (v 12). Joined to that Christ, we do not anxiously seek provision for our needs (v 17; cf. v 6), but share with him and with others whatever humiliation and exaltation he sends, confident that "my God will meet all your needs according to his glorious riches in Christ Jesus" (v 19).

STEPHEN MOTYER

See PAUL, THE APOSTLE; PHILIPPI.

Bibliography. D. Guthrie, *Epistles from Prison*; G.F. Hawthorne, *Philippians*; J.H. Michael, *The Epistle of Paul to the Philippians*; J.J. Müller, *The Epistles of Paul to the Philippians and to Philemon*; A. Plummer, *A Commentary on St. Paul's Epistle to the Philippians*; R. Rainy, *The Epistle to the Philippians*.

Philistia, Philistines. Small, aggressive country situated in southwestern Palestine, along the Mediterranean coast (also called Palestina in KJV Ex 15:14; Is 14:29,31); Aegean people who settled on the maritime plain of Canaan.

Sources. Most of the knowledge of the Philistines comes from the Bible, the monuments and records of Egypt, and the archaeological excavations of Philistine cities. The biblical information centers in the historical books, but there are references to the Philistines in the prophets and psalms as well. The historical records of Egyptian kings tell of their contacts with the Philistines. Other Egyptian written sources include the Amarna Letters, the Story of the Capture of Joppa, The Tale of a Mohar, The Harris Papyrus I, and the Adventures of Wen-Amon. Paintings and reliefs of Philistines are found in the Theban necropolis and particularly in the temple of Rameses III at Medinet Habu.

Many excavations have been made in Philistine cities, from the work of R.A.S. Macalister to the more recent excavations, those at Ashdod, Tel Mor (Tell Murra), Tell Qasile, and most recently, Askelon.

Territory. Strictly speaking, Philistia is that part of the maritime plain that is called the Plain of Philistia, extending from the Wadi el-Arish (River of Egypt) in the south some 70 miles north to the Nahr el-Aujah, 5 miles north of Joppa. Near Gaza the plain reaches its greatest width, about 30 miles. There are sand dunes near the shore, but most of the area is very fertile and produces an abundance of grain (cf. Jgs 15:1–5) and fruit.

The main highway between the East and Egypt lay along the coast. This was of commercial advantage for the Philistines, but it left them open to foreign invasion. God did not lead Israel from Egypt to Canaan by this shortest route through the land of the Philistines, for he did not want them to encounter fierce fighting from the Philistines, (or perhaps from an Egyptian garrison stationed there) so soon (Ex 13:17). Apparently the Philistines had little to fear from the Egyptians, for some scholars think that the Egyptians had a hand in locating the Philistines in Palestine.

From this constricted area the Philistines soon felt a necessity to expand. The passes through the Shephelah provided natural access to the hill country of Israel. They established outposts in Israelite territory, and at the time of the battle in which Saul and his sons were slain they exercised control over the city of Beth-shan (1 Sm 31:10).

The People. The origin of the Philistines is still not certain. The Bible states that the Philistines came from Caphtor (Dt 2:23; Jer 47:4; Am 9:7), which is generally regarded as Crete,

although some scholars place it in Asia Minor. The attire of the Philistines, as shown at Medinet Habu, is like that of Cretans, especially the headdress. The name of the Cherethites has been equated with Cretans, for the names have the same consonantal base, *c*, *r*, and *t*. The Cherethites were apparently a Philistine subgroup who lived in the Negeb not far from Ziklag, David's home among the Philistines (cf. 1 Sm 30:14). The Cherethites and the Pelethites were among David's bodyguards, along with 600 Gittites (men from Gath) (cf. 2 Sm 15:19; 20:7,23; 1 Chr 18:17).

The name "Philistines" is recognizable in several languages. In Hebrew they are known as the Pelishtim, which translated into English as Philistines. In the Egyptian sources they are listed among the Sea Peoples and are called the Peleset or Peleste. They are best known for their part in the invasion of Egypt by the Sea Peoples, who were vanquished by Rameses III in a land and sea battle in the Delta. Detailed scenes of this fighting are shown in deep sunk relief on the north exterior wall of the temple of Rameses III at Medinet Habu, opposite Luxor. These depictions give some idea of the attire and arma-

Relief on the wall of the temple at Medinet Habu that depicts two Philistine prisoners being brought to Rameses III.

ment of the Philistines, who are easily identified by their headdress, which was made of feathers (or reeds?).

These people settled along the coast of Palestine after their defeat by Rameses, but it is possible that some stayed in Canaan on their way to Egypt. Possibly an earlier migration to Palestine occurred, perhaps before the time of the patriarchs.

Language. The language of the Philistines is unknown; they left no inscriptions or other records. A few possible signs on seals from Ashdod may be Philistine writing, but these signs have not as yet been deciphered.

Government. Philistia had no single ruler over their entire land; the cities were independent, so they operated as city-states. The heads of these cities were not called kings, but were spoken of in the Bible as "lords" (e.g., 1 Sm 5:11; 6:12; 29:2), and there were five of them, corresponding to the five major cities which comprised the Philistine Pentapolis: Gaza, Ashkelon, Ashdod, Gath, and Ekron (1 Sm 6:17; cf. Jer 25:20). The people had a voice in matters that related to them, for example, the return of the ark of the covenant (1 Sm 5:6–12), but the great decisions were made by majority vote of the five lords. While David and his men were living at Ziklag, the Philistines planned a big military campaign against Israel. David was subject to Achish, king of Gath, who asked David to join forces with the Philistines against Israel. David agreed to this, but when the Philistine lords found that David was present, they complained and voted him out (1 Sm 29:1–11).

Material Culture. An aggressive and militant people, the Philistines also had the advantage of superior weapons, for they used iron and exercised a monopoly on iron-making in the area. Their control over Israel allowed them to prohibit blacksmithing in Israel, forcing the Israelites to go to the Philistines even for sharpening tools (1 Sm 13:19–22). The Israelites were so poorly armed that only Saul and Jonathan had a sword or a spear (1 Sm 13:22). Facilities for smelting iron have been found at Ashdod, Tell Qasile, Tell Jemmeh, and Tel Mor. It has been suggested that similar equipment found at Deir 'Alla in Transjordan may be the work of Philistines.

The Medinet Habu reliefs show the Philistines armed with spears and long straight swords, with large round shields for protection. They had three-man chariots with six-spoked wheels and transported people by means of solid two-wheel carts pulled by four oxen. Their ships were rigged with a square sail, like those of the Egyptians, and had a duck-shaped prow, which possibly was used for ramming enemy vessels.

Private dwellings, as at Ashdod, were made of mud brick and had several rooms. One house had a large court with two column bases of stone, reminiscent of the temple of Dagon at Gaza (cf. Jgs 16:26–30).

The greatest amount of information concerning the material culture of the Philistines comes from the pottery, which was distinctive and homogeneous. The earliest Philistine pottery at Ashdod had fish designs and other decorative motifs which resemble Cypriot ware. Decorations included several bands of designs, with metopes of geometric pattern. Paintings of birds were common, particularly the preening bird, with one wing raised and the head turned back. Interesting pottery forms included kraters (large, wide-mouthed bowls with two handles) and single-handled beer jugs with strainer spouts.

Religion and Ritual Objects. Whatever gods the Philistines brought with them seem to have been abandoned relatively early in favor of Canaanite deities. A primary Philistine god mentioned in the Bible is Dagon, a grain god. Temples to Dagon have been found at Ras Shamra (Ugarit) and Mari. The Bible refers to a temple of Dagon at Gaza (Jgs 16:23–30) and another at Ashdod (1 Sm 5:1–5).

The excavation of the University Museum of the University of Pennsylvania at Tell el-Husn (Beth-shan, Beth-shean) unearthed two temples of 11th-century date. Possibly the southern temple is that of Dagon (1 Chr 10:10) and the northern temple the House of Ashtaroth (1 Sm 31:10). Ashtaroth was not a Philistine deity, but one borrowed from the Canaanites. Ekron had a god named Baal-zebub (2 Kgs 1:2,3; Mt 2:24; Mk 3:22), who is equated with Beelzebul.

At Tell Qasile there was a Philistine temple with two pillars in the holy place, suggestive of the Gaza temple. This temple contained many objects associated with the cult, including a bird-shaped vessel and an incense altar. In houses and small shrines in Ashdod there were numerous clay figurines, both male and female, regarded as a pair of deities. There was also a strange ritual object of clay called an "Ashdoda," best described as a four-legged chair, whose back becomes the stylized upper part of a nude goddess. Another pottery form of religious use was the kernos, which is a hollow ring vase with attached miniature vessels and figurines of heads of animals and birds.

Burial Customs. A form of Philistine grave found at Tell Sharuhen was of Mycenean type, with a stairway leading to a rectangular room, which had the middle excavated so as to form two benches, one on either side, on which the deceased and the grave furnishings were placed. Some have suggested that the coffins—clay anthropoid sarcophagi, with the arms, hands, and the facial features modelled in realistic fashion—found at Philistine sites were of Philistine origin, reflecting Egyptian influence; however, more recent scholarship attributes them to an Egyptian source. A related form of coffin, but with the very stylistic modeling is labelled "grotesque."

Philistines and the Bible. The various forms of Philistine and Philistia appear almost 300 times in the OT, mostly in the books of Judges and Samuel. The earliest occurrence is in Genesis 10:14, where it is said that the Philistines came from the Casluhim, an unidentified people related to the Caphtorim (cf. 1 Chr 1:12).

In the patriarchal age it is said that both Abraham and Isaac had contacts with the Philistines at Gerar, in parallel incidents involving their wives (Gn 20,26). Here, however, the Philistines are not on the coast but at Gerar and as far east as Beersheba (Gn 26:33). In both references the king of Gerar is called Abimelech, a good Semitic name. It has been suggested that the Philistines of that time were an earlier migration from Crete, but this has not been demonstrated.

After the Israelite conquest of Canaan, the Philistines began to exercise superiority over the Israelites. Apostasy came early in Israel and the Lord used the Philistines to chasten his people. Shamgar delivered Israel by killing 600 Philistines with an ox goad (Jgs 3:31). The account of Samson has many touches of Philistine life (Jgs 13:1–16:31). This record demonstrates that there was intermarriage between Israelites and Philistines, contrary to the OT law.

Warfare between Israel and the Philistines is reported in 1 Samuel 4:1, when the Israelites were camped at Ebenezer and the Philistines at Aphek. The Philistines won that round and captured the ark of the covenant (1 Sm 4:17), which they returned after seven months because the Lord sent plagues upon them (1 Sm 5:1–6:21). Later, when Samuel had become leader, the Philistines attacked Israel at Mizpah, but God gave the victory to Israel. On this occasion Samuel set up a memorial stone and named it Ebenezer ("Stone of Help," 7:12). The Philistines did not invade Israel again during the lifetime of Samuel, and Israel recovered cities that had been taken by the Philistines (1 Sm 7:14).

The greatest activity of the Philistines in Israelite territory came during the reign of Saul, Israel's first king. More than 80 references to the Philistines are related to that period. The Philistines established outposts or garrisons in various parts of Israel (cf. 1 Sm 10:5; 13:3). Jonathan defeated the garrison at Geba (1 Sm 13:3); his exploit related in 1 Samuel 14:1–15 led to a rout of the Philistines.

Reconstructed 11th-century BC Philistine residence at Tell Qasile.

A confrontation of the Philistine and Israelite armies took place in the valley of Elah, where the Philistines challenged Israel to provide an opponent to meet their champion, Goliath, in single combat (1 Sm 17:1–11). The young shepherd, David, killed Goliath; David became a hero, but Saul's jealousy made David a hunted man. In the course of dodging Saul's army, David's men rescued the town of Keilah from the Philistines (1 Sm 23:1–5). Eventually David sought political asylum with Achish, king of Gath, who gave him the town of Ziklag, from which David made raids in the Negeb (1 Sm 27).

When the Philistines were preparing for war against Israel, Achish asked David to join the Philistine forces and David agreed. The lords of the Philistines voted down this participation, for they feared that David would turn against them (1 Sm 28:1,2; 29:1–11). In the ensuing battle Saul and his sons were killed on Mt Gilboa by the Philistines (1 Sm 31:1–7). The Philistines cut off Saul's head, placed his armor in the temple of Ashtaroth in Bethshan, and hung his body on the wall of that city (1 Sm 31:8–11).

When the Philistines learned that David had become king, they made an effort to destroy him, but he defeated them "from Geba to Gezer" (2 Sm 5:17–25). David broke the Philistine power and although they again attempted war against Israel they met with no success (2 Sm 21:15–21).

Uzziah warred against the Philistines; he broke down the walls of Gath, Jabneh, and Ashdod and built cities in Philistia (2 Chr 26:6,7). In the reign of Ahaz, the Philistines invaded the Shephelah and the Negeb and captured a number of cities (2 Chr 28:18). Hezekiah fought against the Philistines as far as Gaza (2 Kgs 18:8).

References to the Philistines in the prophets are relatively few, although Jeremiah devotes a short chapter to the Philistines (47), dated "before Pharaoh smote Gaza." The Philistines were gradually assimilated into Canaanite culture and they disappeared from the pages of the Bible and from secular history, leaving the name Palestine as a monument to their presence.

Bibliography. T.K. Dothan, *The Philistines and Their Material Culture*; E.E. Hindson, *The Philistines and the OT*; K.A. Kitchen, "The Philistines" in D.J. Wiseman (ed.), *Peoples of OT Times*, pp 53–78; R.A.S. Macalister, *The Philistines, Their History and Civilization*; T.C. Mitchell, 1967, "Philistia," in D.W. Thomas (ed.), *Archaeology and OT Study*; N.K. Sandars, *The Sea Peoples: Warriors of the Ancient Mediterranean, 1250–1150*.

Philo Judaeus. Hellenistic Jewish philosopher (*c.* 25 BC–*c.* AD 40) whose thought represents the first major confrontation of biblical faith with Greek thought. Son of a prominent Alexandrian family, Philo was educated both in the Jewish faith and in Greek philosophy and culture. Of the events of his life we know little, except that in AD 40 he headed a delegation from the Jewish community in Alexandria to the emperor Caligula in Rome.

The Jewish community in Alexandria was thoroughly Hellenized. Even the Scriptures were read in the Greek translation called the Septuagint. In spite of the fact that these Jews were living and participating in Greek culture, they remained orthodox. Philo was no exception. On the one hand, he carefully observed the Mosaic law and held that it is the infallibly revealed will of God both for God's chosen people, the Jews, and for Gentiles. On the other hand, Philo was Greek. He probably knew Hebrew only imperfectly and received a liberal education under Greek tutors. He held the Pentateuch to be most authoritative, but read it in Greek translation. Because he held that the Septuagint was divinely inspired, Philo did not refer to the original Hebrew text.

To understand Philo's work it must be recognized that the need to come to terms with Greek culture stemmed not merely from practical necessity but also from the fact that Judaism is a missionary religion. Jews could not simply turn their backs on the Greek world, for the prophets had called Israel to be a light to the Gentiles. From his studies Philo was also convinced that there is much that is true in Greek philosophy. Consequently, he was anxious to find some way of correlating and harmonizing biblical-revealed truth with the teachings of the philosophers.

The method Philo used to harmonize Scripture with the teachings of the philosophers was allegorical interpretation. This method of interpretation had been practiced by many before Philo and others followed his example. Through the use of this method Genesis could be read as a contemporary myth about the human condition and man's search for salvation, rather than as an ancient and somewhat crude legend. The proper reading of the text gives not ancient history and geography, but philosophical and moral truth. According to Philo, Moses, both because he was divinely instructed and because he had attained the summit of philosophy, did not resort to mythical fictions, as poets and sophists do; but he was able to make ideas visible. By using allegorical interpretation, Philo found in the historical narrative and ceremonial law an inward, spiritual meaning which incorporates the truth he found in Greek thought.

In general one can say that in dealing with the conception of God, Philo approaches Greek views critically and rejects what is opposed to Scripture. However, in dealing with the structure and composition of the world, Scripture is quite vague and so Philo feels free to adopt whatever seems most reasonable in the philosophers. He holds that God is the source of both the Mosaic law and the truths of Greek philosophy. The human mind is made in the image of the divine Logos, and so it has some capacity to receive and discover truths about realities beyond the sensible.

Among the philosophers, Philo found Plato's view closest to the truth. God existed from eternity without a world, and after he made the world he continued to exist above and beyond it. God is the active cause, and this world is passive, incapable of life and motion by itself, but a most perfect masterpiece when set in motion, shaped, and quickened by God. Moreover, God does not neglect his creation, but cares for it and preserves it. This care is called providence. While the Greeks had spoken of a universal providence which preserves natural processes, for Philo providence acquires a new meaning. It is God's care for individual beings, so that it includes the power to suspend the laws of nature.

God is One, but the source of all multiplicity. He is immutable and self-sufficient, and hence does not need the world. Creation has its source in his Goodness. Plato was right in affirming that the Father and Maker of all is good, and because of this does not grudge a share in his own excellent nature.

Although Moses says that the world was created in six days, God must be thought of as doing all things simultaneously. The account of six days serves to show that there is order in things. The visible world was created out of nonbeing from nothing. All the available matter was used in creation, so the world is unique. The world was created by God's will, and it may be imperishable. Philo thinks that Plato followed Moses in holding that the world is created. The world is created through the Logos.

In the doctrine of the Logos the way in which Philo is both dependent upon and yet critical of the philosophers is evident. Plato had affirmed that there are eternal ideas to which the Craftsman or Maker looks when forming the world. Philo could not accept this position, because God alone is eternal. He harmonizes the two views by affirming that from eternity the ideas existed as thoughts of God, but they became a fully formed, intelligible world only when God willed to create the visible world. The universe of the ideas which has no location other than the divine reason is the pattern according to which the sensible world is made.

The Logos is much more than just the instrument by which the visible world was made. It is also described as "the idea of ideas," the first-begotten Son of the uncreated Father and "second God," the archetype of human reason, and "the man of God." The Logos is the vital power which holds together the entire hierarchy of created beings. As God's viceroy he mediates revelation to the created order. He stands on the frontier between Creator and creature. He is the high priest who intercedes with God on behalf of mortals. He appeared in the burning bush and dwelt in Moses. Some think that the Logos is God, but he is really God's *image*. While one can be quite certain that the Logos was not a person for Philo, the exact status of this power in relation to God is by no means clear. Various aspects of this teaching were taken up by Christian thinkers, most notably the teaching that the Logos is the instrument by which God creates the world.

About the origins of this view much less is known. It appears that the notion of the Logos was current in Hellenistic Judaism. Its function in Philo's thought seems to indicate that it is philosophical considerations rather than biblical ones which were most significant in his teaching. As such Philo's Logos speculations are a stage toward the development of a view of levels of being in God, a development which culminated in Plotinus. It has been claimed that the Word or Logos of the prologue of John's Gospel was derived in some sense from Philo's position, but this now seems unlikely.

While the heavenly bodies are living creatures endowed with mind and not susceptible of evil, man is of a mixed nature, liable to contraries. He can be both wise and foolish, just and unjust, and so on. God made all good things by himself, but man, because he is liable to both good and evil, God made with the aid of fellow-workers. This is why we are told by Moses that God said, "Let us make man." In the case of man, then, being created involves a fall. Here also there are two steps in creation. First, there is man created after the divine image, and this is an idea or type, an object of thought only, incorporeal, neither male nor female and by nature incorruptible (Gn 1:26). Later, Scripture says that "God formed man by taking clay from the earth, and breathed into him the breath of life" (Gn 2:7). This man became an object of sense perception, consisting of body and soul, man or woman, by nature mortal. Woman became for man the beginning of blameworthy life. When man and woman saw each other, desire was set up, and this desire produced bodily pleasure. This pleasure is the beginning of wrongs and violation of law. The garden of Eden is also meant to be taken symbolically rather than literally. There never have been trees of life or of understanding, nor is it likely that any will ever appear on earth. The tree of life signifies reverence toward God; the tree of knowledge of good and evil signifies moral prudence.

One sees in Philo, then, a tendency toward dualism, in which spirit is good and matter evil, a tendency derived from Platonism and read into the OT. This leads Philo to agree with the Stoics that the only good is the good of the soul. God gives the world to use, not to possess. To rise to the eternal world of mind, a man must suppress all responses to the sensible world. In general, Philo tends in his ethic toward a world-denying asceticism.

The only temple worthy of God is a pure soul. True religion consists in inner devotion, rather than externals. In this life the soul is a pilgrim, like Abraham or like the Israelites wandering in the desert. Through spiritual self-discipline the soul comes to realize that the body is a major obstacle to perfection. The goal is the vision of God, "drawing near to God who has drawn the mind to himself." God is knowable by the mind, but he is unknowable in himself. We can know only *that* he is, not *what* he is. For Philo the soul in its search for perfection ultimately comes to discover that it must cease to rely on itself and must acknowledge that virtue is a gift of God. The man who has discovered his own limitations comes to know God and his own dependence upon God. In connection with this theme of grace Philo speaks of ecstasy, symbolized by Moses in the ritual of the high priest entering the Holy of Holies.

Philo's greatest influence was on Christian writers. Hellenistic Judaism became less significant as the Judaism of the rabbis became the norm during the next two centuries. By contrast 2nd- and 3rd-century Christians had much in common with Philo. Parts of his work were translated into Latin and Armenian. Clement and Origin among the Greek fathers and Ambrose among the Latin fathers were especially indebted to him.

ARVIN G. VOS

See HELLENISTIC JUDAISM; JUDAISM; ALLEGORY; ALEXANDRIA.

Bibliography. N. Bentwich, *Philo-Judaeus of Alexandria;* E. Caird, *The Evolution of Theology in the Greek Philosophers,* 2, 184–209; J. Drummond, *Philo Judaeus,* 2 vols.; E.R. Goodenough, *An Introduction to Philo Judaeus;* J. La Porte, *Eucharistia in Philo;* R. Williamson, *Philo and the Epistle to the Hebrews;* H.A. Wolfson, *Philo,* 2 vols.

Philologus. Early Christian acquaintance or friend of the apostle Paul to whom he sent greetings (Rom 16:15). In the series of greetings, he is paired with a woman named Julia.

Philosophy. Logically disciplined, self-critical inquiry into the basic questions of life. "Philosophy" itself means "love of wisdom." This "love" treasures pursuing, discovering, and analyzing and justifying wisdom. Although the word "philosophy" appears only once in the Bible, both Judaism and Christianity were considered philosophies in the Hellenistic world. In fact, from their very earliest encounters with Jewish scholars in Alexandria in the 3rd century BC, Greek philosophers referred to the Jews as a "philosophical race." Biblical religion is philosophical because, unlike Greek religion, it makes holistic claims about the nature of reality and it sets out concrete values that can guide community life and individual decisions.

In the only explicit use of the word "philosophy" in the Bible (Col 2:8–10), a point of contrast is made between pagan and Christian philosophy. Paul wants the Colossians to develop philosophy according to Christ, not according to empty deceit, human tradition, or "the elemental spirits of the universe." In contrast to empty philosophy based on pagan deceit and human tradition, Christ is himself the fullness of deity dwelling bodily—a sound foundation for wisdom and philosophy. In contrast to the mere "elemental spirits," Christ himself is the "head of all rule and authority,"

the greatest source of truth and justice. The discipline of philosophy is not condemned, for the alternative to deceit and human tradition is "philosophy. . . according to Christ."

As a discipline, philosophy developed in Greece only after the OT was complete, so it could not have been mentioned in the OT. Nevertheless, the biblical Wisdom Literature serves a function quite similar to some philosophical writings. It provides either proverbial instruction for wholesome living (esp. Prv), or inquiry into the puzzles of human existence (esp. Jb and Eccl).

Some characteristics of biblical revelation are shared with the pagan philosophy of its time. For example, the idea of "conversion" was an assumed pattern in the Hellenistic world of the NT, for to change one's philosophy meant to adopt a new form of life. Moreover, the literary form of an "epistle" was developed by philosophers prior to the NT. Plato and Isocrates started the practice of using letters to defend doctrines or ways of life.

Also, a concern for practical life questions was central to philosophy at the time of the NT; to learn a philosophy came to mean to acquire the art of living well. Furthermore, to be a philosopher meant to be someone who is interested in the question of "God," however one understood that question. The NT world was ripe for guidance in right living and in knowing God.

Two specific philosophies are mentioned in the NT: Epicureanism and Stoicism (Acts 17:18). Epicureans followed the teachings of Epicurus (342?–270 BC), an Athenian philosopher who had taught practical ways of achieving a pleasant life through moderate behavior and stable human relationships. He believed that human beings are merely material objects produced by chance combinations of atoms—small, indestructible material pieces.

Stoics also emphasized moderate living, but they believed that there is an ultimate purpose in the world. This purposefulness is established by an all-pervading substance called "Logos" or reason. However, like Epicureans, Stoics were materialists, believing all things to be made of matter including humans, the divine, and the Logos (which they sometimes treated as God).

In Athens, Paul may have also encountered the "academic skeptics." These philosophers emphasized the fallibility and finitude of human understanding to the point of withholding judgment whenever possible. However, they knew they had to make daily personal decisions, and they remained very curious about other people's ideas. In fact, "all the Athenians and the foreigners who lived there" at the time of Paul's visit seemed to

Ruins at Bethel, where Phinehas promised that Israel would defeat Benjamin.

sustain a high level of curiosity about new ideas (Acts 17:21)—providing a mentally lively atmosphere.

It was only appropriate for Paul to present the gospel to these curious minds, and he was convincing enough to win some converts. He established a common ground by agreeing with ideas from two Greek philosophers: ancient Epimenides (6th century BC), "In him we live and move and have our being"; and Cleanthes the Stoic (3rd century BC), "We are his offspring." Nevertheless, Paul inevitably offended most of his philosophic listeners by defending the uniqueness of a particular man, Christ, and by claiming that he had been resurrected from the dead—a claim that contradicted these philosophers' materialist resignation to the finality of death. Clearly, Christianity entailed a dramatically different "philosophy."

That difference is evident in many biblical passages, especially the first chapter of John. This Gospel starts off with language that would attract Stoics' attention and approval: the "Logos" is external, divine, the cause of all order, and the source of human understanding (Jn 1:1–4). Moreover, John takes pains not to offend defenders either of the main theories of knowledge (empiricist or rationalist) by making his own writing clearly ambiguous on the disputed point. On the one hand, Stoics and Epicureans, both of whom saw experience as the primary source of knowledge, would read "That was the true light which, coming into

the world, enlightens every person" (Jn 1:9). On the other hand, Platonists and Neoplatonists, both of whom claimed inborn mental content to be the primary source of knowledge, would read the same text as "that was the true light which enlightens every person when coming into the world." Both interpretations are grammatically justified, and both leave the central Christian claim unambiguous: The Word is the light that brings truth to all people—whether through experience or through inborn mental content.

Instead of taking sides on this epistemological issue, John writes five more verses before he offends all the ancient philosophical schools equally by asserting the central Christian doctrine of the incarnation: "The Word became flesh and dwelt among us" (Jn 1:14). The unique revelation of grace and truth in Christ remains the cornerstone of Christian philosophy.

PAUL H. DE VRIES

See EPICUREANS; STOICS, STOICISM.

Bibliography. G. Clark, *A Christian View of Man and Things*; W. Cordvan, *Handmaid to Theology*; J. Orr, *The Christian View of God and the World*; H.A. Wolfson, *The Philosophy of the Church Fathers*, vol. 4.

Phinehas. 1. Eleazer's son, grandson of Aaron (Ex 6:25), and Abishua's father (1 Chr 6:4,50). During the high priesthood of Eleazer, Phinehas had charge over the keepers of the tabernacle (1 Chr 9:20), as did Eleazer his father when Aaron served as chief priest (cf. Nm

3:32). Phinehas, grieved by Israel's sin with Baal of Peor at Shittim, slew an Israelite man and a Midianite woman for their licentious behavior in Israel's midst (Nm 25:7). Following this act, the Lord turned his wrath from Israel and made a covenant of peace with Phinehas, a "covenant of a perpetual priesthood" for him and his descendants (Nm 25:11,13); his deed was "reckoned to him as righteousness from generation to generation for ever" (Ps 106:30). Save for the brief interval when Eli acted as high priest (cf. 1 Sm chs 1–3; 14:3), Phinehas and his posterity officiated the high priestly position until the destruction of the Jerusalem temple by the Romans in AD 70. Following the Baal of Peor incident, he joined Israel in defeating the Midianites in war (Nm 31:6).

After taking possession of the land of Canaan, Phinehas was given the town of Gibeah in the hill country of Ephraim for an inheritance (Jos 24:33). He was sent with a small delegation of Israelite leaders to question the building of an altar on the west bank of the Jordan River by the tribes of Israel living east of the Jordan (Jos 22:13,30–32). Later, at Bethel, Phinehas promised Israel victory over Benjamin's tribe in battle (Jgs 20:28). His descendants, Ezra the scribe (Ezr 7:5) and Gershom (Ezr 8:2), returned with their families to Jerusalem following the exile.

2. One of Eli's two sons, who served as a priest at Shiloh (1 Sm 1:3). Phinehas was a despicable priest, who along with Hophni his brother, profaned the offered sacrifices (2:12–17) and the sanctuary (2:22), and scorned Eli (2:25). His death was foretold to his father by a man of God (2:34). In a subsequent war with the Philistines, Phinehas was killed on the same day his wife bore him a son, named Ichabod (4:11,17,19; 14:3).

3. Eleazer's father. Eleazer helped Meremoth and the Levites, Jozabad and Noadiah, take inventory of the temple's precious metals and vessels during the postexilic era (Ezr 8:33).

Phlegon. Christian in Rome to whom Paul sent greetings (Rom 16:14).

Phoebe. Christian woman of the church at Cenchrea, the eastern port for the city of Corinth. In Romans 16:1,2 (KJV Phebe), Paul commends Phoebe to the recipients of the letter on the basis of her valuable service to other Christians. He asks that they give her whatever assistance she needs.

The term "deacon" is applied to Phoebe. It probably designates an "office" as in Philippians 1:1, although it may mean "minister" in the same sense that Paul uses it elsewhere of himself and others (1 Cor 3:5; 2 Cor 3:6; 6:4).

Phoenicia, Phoenician. Group of city-states that occupied a strip of the Syrian coastal plain at the foot of the Lebanon Mountains, also spelled Phenice, Phenicia. At their height these states extended from Carmel in the south to Arvad in the north, a distance of less than 200 miles. Nowhere is the Phoenician plain more than 4 miles wide. It is misleading to call it a plain, because it is cut into pockets of plains by mountain spurs and rivers or rivulets. In these fertile plains rose independent city-states; so Phoenicia was neither a political nor a geographical unity.

Bereft of good natural ports, the Phoenicians were forced to build their own. Fortunately they had abundant supplies of magnificent cedar on the western slopes of the Lebanon Mountains, which they dominated. Thus they had good ship timber and an important source of revenue in a wood-starved region of the world. Offshore grew some of the finest dye-producing murex (sea snails) of the Mediterranean, making possible quality textiles and dye stuffs. These two sources of income were supplemented by superior industrial production in metal and glassware and the transport of the goods of other peoples in Phoenician ships. With the passage of time Phoenician colonies grew up along their trade routes. Prominent among them was Carthage.

Phoenicia and the Bible. Phoenicia first became involved in biblical history shortly after 1000 BC when David obtained from Hiram I of Tyre some of the much-coveted cedars of Lebanon for construction of his palace. Solomon also bought cedar from Hiram for his palace and the temple. He hired Phoenician craftsmen for building the temple, constructing fortifications at strategic centers, and a major port facility at Ezion-geber on the Gulf of Aqaba, an arm of the Red Sea. Phoenician architectural design was employed in various Hebrew building projects in Solomon's day, and Phoenician shipbuilding expertise made possible Solomon's merchant marine. Phoenician sailors manned the ships after they were launched (see esp. 1 Kgs 9:10–28).

During the first half of the 9th century BC Phoenician impact on Israel was largely religious. Then Jezebel, a princess from Tyre, married Ahab and introduced Baal worship to the northern kingdom.

More than a century later Phoenicia was the subject of prophetic condemnation. Isaiah (before 700 BC, see ch 23) and Ezekiel (about 600 BC, see 26:2–19; 28:21–23) hurled predictions of suffering and destruction at both Tyre and Sidon.

Phoenician medallions.

In NT times the apostle Paul spent a week at Tyre with a group of Christians on his return to Jerusalem at the end of his third missionary journey (Acts 21:2–7).

Phoenicia's Cultural and Historical Significance. As the finest mariners of the ancient world, the Phoenicians dominated the Mediterranean during the first half of the 1st millennium BC, and the Aegean Sea for much of that time. As intrepid seafarers, they not only shipped products but also transmitted ideas and processes and engaged in much cultural cross-fertilization.

Though there is no evidence that the Phoenicians invented the alphabet, they disseminated it so widely that it became known as the Phoenician alphabet. Especially important was their transmission of it to the Greeks (at least by 750 BC), who then added vowels and passed it on to the Western world.

The Phoenicians also planted colonies in numerous places in the western Mediterranean, notably during the 8th century BC. Most powerful of these colonies was Carthage, which at its height controlled the western part of north Africa, much of Spain, and numerous Mediterra-

nean islands, and which almost brought Rome to her knees during the 3rd century BC.

Furthermore, the Phoenicians developed advanced techniques in metal working; and some scholars believe the Egyptians and possibly even Aegean peoples derived some of their processes from the Phoenicians. Though they may not have invented glass-making, as many ancient authors claim, they certainly contributed much to its development and the spread of its knowledge in the ancient world. The Phoenicians exported quantities of purple dye or dyed cloth and their famous cedars, as already noted. Cedars of Lebanon found their way not only to Palestine but also to Egypt, Mesopotamia, and far-away Iran.

Of all Phoenician exports, most severely censured in Scripture was Baal worship, which found its way into the kingdom of Israel through the marriage of Jezebel to Ahab and into the kingdom of Judah through the marriage of their daughter Athaliah to Jehoram.

Phoenician Religion. Less is known about Phoenician religion than that of most other peoples of antiquity. This is primarily because the Phoenicians' own literature has not been preserved. One cannot be sure that information from ancient Ugarit in nearby Syria correctly reflects religious practices and beliefs of the Phoenician cities. Nor should it be assumed that the religion of Phoenicia's colonies was transported without modification from the mother country. Unfortunately, what the OT says about Canaanite religion does not differentiate the beliefs or practices of individual Phoenician cities. The following information has been gleaned almost exclusively from Phoenician sources.

Several general names appeared in Phoenician religion. *El* was both the Semitic word for god and a specific god who was head of the pantheon. *Baal* simply means "lord" but it also applies to the son of El. *Baalat* means "lady" but it often designated a specific deity as the Baalat of Gebal or Byblos. *Milk* (Hebrew, *melek*) was a "king" or "ruler" but it might form part of a name of a deity such as *Melqart* ("ruler of the city"), chief god of Tyre.

As in the Greek city-states, Phoenician cities had patron deities that were not necessarily the head of the pantheon. On the female side there was really only one deity worshiped in all the cities, the mother and fertility goddess Ashtart or Astarte (Heb. Ashtoreth), the Babylonian Ishtar. She was regarded as the genetrix of the gods and man as well as plants. Promiscuity characterized her conduct and religious prostitution was carried on in her name.

Baalat Gebal, who symbolized fertility and thus corresponded to Astarte, was the preeminent deity of Byblos, but Adonis was also very

Phoenician idol, typical of the patron deities of Phoenician cities.

important. As the young god who died and was resurrected, he was linked to the annual death and rebirth of vegetation.

Astarte was also predominant in the pantheon of Sidon, as is demonstrated by numerous inscriptions, temples built in her honor, and the fact that kings and queens called themselves her priests. The male deity most involved in Sidonian life was *Eshmun*, thought to correspond to Adonis in function. By the Greeks he was identified as Asklepios, god of healing.

The chief god of Tyre was *Melqart*, the Baal or lord of Tyre. Since an annual feast of resurrection was celebrated in his honor, he was equated with Eshmun of Sidon and Adonis of yblos. The Greeks identified Melqart with Heracles or Hercules. When Tyre came to domi-

nate the other Phoenician cities, Melqart rose to a place of prominence in their pantheons. Melqart would have been the Baal introduced to Israel in the days of Ahab, who married Jezebel of Tyre. The main female deity of Tyre was Astarte. Hiram built temples at Tyre to both Melqart and Astarte, and Solomon brought the worship of Astarte (Ashtoreth) to Jerusalem in his day (1 Kgs 11:5). Her shrine remained to plague the Jews until the reform of Josiah late in the 7th century BC (2 Kgs 23:13). No doubt Elijah's mocking that Baal might be asleep and needed to be awakened referred to his function as a god of nature and his involvement with the annual death and rebirth of nature (1 Kgs 18:27–30).

The places for worship of Baal were either high places in the hills (consisting of an altar and a stone pillar representing the Baal; and a tree or pole representing Astarte) or stone enclosures with an altar, a stone pillar, and a tree. Sometimes they were covered temple buildings. Sacrifices consisted of animals and vegetables, and in times of great disaster, of human beings. Great religious festivals were held in observance of the god's connection with the rhythm of the seasons. When he and nature died there were mourning, funeral rites, and perhaps self-torture. The spring festival, which celebrated his resurrection and new life in nature and which sought fertility of nature, commonly was accompanied by sacramental prostitution. The idolatry, human sacrifice, and sexual promiscuity connected with Baal worship brought upon it God's special condemnation.

History of Phoenicia. Though peoples of Mediterranean stock occupied Lebanon by about 4000 BC, there was no significant political or cultural development in the area until after 3000 BC, when the Canaanites arrived. Canaanite (Hamitic) culture and ethnic stock were diluted by an Amorite (Semitic) invasion of Phoenicia, Syria, and Palestine about 2000 BC. Subsequently, Semites became dominant in the area.

Long before the Semites arrived, Egyptians established commercial contacts with Phoenicia. During the Old Kingdom (c. 2700–2200 BC) Egyptians seem virtually to have controlled Byblos, about 25 miles north of Beirut. It was the main port through which Phoenician timber moved to Egypt and Egyptian papyrus and influences entered Phoenicia.

Though Egyptian influence slipped during Egypt's First Intermediate Period (2200–2050 BC), it was fully restored during the Middle Kingdom. In fact, some like to speak of much of Phoenicia falling within an Egyptian Middle Empire at this time (2050–1800), but others feel that Egypt's control was only economic. Subsequently the Hyksos dominated the whole eastern end of the Mediterranean.

During the Egyptian Empire period (c. 1580–1100 BC) the Egyptians at first effectively controlled the cities of Phoenicia, even stationing garrisons in them. But during the latter part of the period, Egyptians and Hittites fought for the mastery of Phoenicia. By 1100 BC both Egyptians and Hittite empires had come to an end and Phoenicia entered a period of independence.

During the next two centuries Tyre built her power and established a hegemony over the other Phoenician cities. Of special significance in this rise to power were the efforts of Hiram I. At the same time the Hebrew united monarchy was building, and the two powers reached out to each other in ventures of mutual advantage.

Conditions changed in the 9th century. In 868 BC Ashurnasirpal of Assyria forced the Phoenician states to pay tribute, and their freedom was lost again. But under the Assyrians the Phoenicians prospered and planted numerous colonies in the west. By the end of the 8th century Isaiah could wax eloquent about the prosperity of Tyre (Is 23:3–8).

But as time wore on, the Phoenicians grew restless under increasing Assyrian restriction of liberties. About 678 BC Sidon led a revolt against Esar-haddon of Assyria which turned out to be a total failure. The furious Assyrians killed or carried off captive most of the inhabitants and leveled the city of Sidon, thus intimidating all the Phoenicians. But Assyrian power subsequently diminished and Tyre became independent about 625 BC. Her greatness largely remained and Ezekiel penned a remarkable description of her attainments (Ez 27).

After Nebuchadnezzar of Babylon destroyed Jerusalem in 586 BC, he turned his attention to Phoenicia, easily conquering the rebuilt Sidon but requiring 13 years to subjugate Tyre. At that time he took only the mainland city of Tyre, however. The island city was safe because Nebuchadnezzar had no fleet. The greatness of Tyre was gone; the mainland city was never rebuilt.

When Cyrus the Great conquered the Babylonian Empire in 539 BC, the Phoenicians were absorbed peacefully. But about two centuries later they participated in a rebellion against the Persians. When the Persian army stood before Sidon in 352 BC and the inhabitants faced the destruction of their homes and the prospect of being sold into slavery, they set fire to their homes and perished with them. It is said that 40,000 died in the conflagration. The other Phoenician cities had no heart to continue the rebellion.

When Alexander the Great came through Phoenicia in 332 BC, most of the cities welcomed release from Persian rule and opened their gates to him. Tyre did not, however, and was totally destroyed after a 7-month siege. When the city was rebuilt, it was populated with immigrants from Asia Minor and had little ethnic connection with the earlier period. Phoenician maritime supremacy was forever broken.

Subsequently Phoenicia passed under the control of the Ptolemies (286 BC), the Seleucids (198 BC), and the Romans (64 BC). During the Roman period Phoenicia was part of the province of Syria and enjoyed new prosperity during the Pax Romana (the Roman peace) of the first two centuries of the Christian era. By that time it was largely Hellenized and its former Semitic character was gone.

See Canaanite Deities and Religion.

Bibliography. D.B. Harden, *The Phoenicians;* S. Moscati, *The World of the Phoenicians;* J.I.S. Whitaker, *Motya, A Phoenician Colony in Sicily.*

Phoenix. Harbor town on the southern coast of Crete where Paul and his shipmates hoped to spend the winter during their voyage to Rome (Acts 27:12, KJV Phenice). Phoenix was situated west of Fair Havens near the island of Cauda. Against Paul's better judgment, his ship was ordered to leave the bay of Fair Havens and sail westward to Phoenix. While enroute to this harbor town, Paul's ship was struck by a powerful gale from the northeast. This wind drove the ship southwest past the island of Cauda and threatened to push it across the Mediterranean Sea into the treacherous north African shoals of Syrtis Major (Acts 27:9–17).

Though the exact location of Phoenix is not certain, historical records indicate that its site is located on Cape Mouros, a peninsula extending from Crete's southern coastline. This region of Crete was known for its temperate weather and mild temperatures year around. Luke's description of Phoenix as "looking northeast and southeast" (Acts 27:12) suggests that the harbor town of Loutro on the eastern shore of Cape Mouros is the place of ancient Phoenix. Loutro has a deep harbor and faces northeast and southeast. However a literal rendering of Acts 27:12 in the Greek text pictures the harbor of Phoenix as facing "northwest and southwest" (RSV mg). This reading identifies Phoinika, a town on the western edge of Cape Mouros, as the location of Phoenix. In antiquity, this deep harbor was apparently accessible to ships and afforded protection from the winter winds. The name Phoenix is retained in Phoinika.

Phrygia. Area in western Turkey on the Anatolian plateau, the boundaries of which cannot be defined precisely. The Phrygians were originally Europeans, called Phryges by the Greeks, who crossed the Hellespont from Macedonia and Thrace and settled here. This migration followed the general pattern of invasions from Europe into this section of Asia Minor. The Phrygians formed a powerful confederacy that flourished between the downfall of the Hittite and the rise of the Lydian empires, that is, between the 7th and the 13th centuries before Christ.

Their religious capital was at "Midas City," now modern Yazilikaya, about 150 miles southwest of Ankara. This "city of Midas" consisted of an acropolis, defended by a wall with towers, and a lower city. Within a large cave was a spring, approached by steps cut in the rock, which supplied water for the upper and lower cities. The famous tomb or monument of King Midas has a Phrygian inscription which mentions the goddess "Mida," identified with Cybele the mother goddess, considered to be the mythical mother of the king. French archaeologists in 1948–49 discovered remains which indicate that the city was destroyed in the 6th century BC, rebuilt about a century later, and finally destroyed in the 3rd century BC.

The capital of ancient Phrygia was Gordium, which lies about 37 miles east and south of Ankara, the modern capital of Turkey. Ancient Gordium was built on an Early Bronze Age site and by the 8th century BC was the chief city of Phrygia. The capital passed through many vicissitudes before being overrun by the Cimmerians (684 BC), then by the Lydians, then by the Persians (546 BC), later by the Macedonians, and finally by the Romans. According to an old legend the one who could

untie the "Gordian Knot," which bound a chariot, would rule all of Asia. Alexander the Great cut the knot with his sword (or removed a peg and untied it).

These people were said to be warlike and very emotional. Their chief goddess was Cybele. She later became the fertility goddess of all Anatolia. Orgiastic rites were performed in her honor leading to sensuality intended to facilitate reproduction among humans, animals, and crops. When the Ionians and the Greeks settled in Miletus and Ephesus, Cybele was transformed into Artemis, the Greek goddess of fertility, whose temple in Ephesus was one of the Seven Wonders of the World. Her image originally was a black meteorite stone (cf. Acts 19:35). She became the consort of Adonis, a vegetation god, and their fertility rites were common throughout the Middle East. This goddess was imported into Rome and a temple in her honor was built on the Capitoline Hill soon after the organization of the empire.

Gallic tribes invaded the region some three centuries prior to Paul. This changed the demographic situation with the result that the political, geographical, and ethnic divisions did not always coincide. What was formerly Phrygia became known as Galatia because of the new inhabitants. Yet the old names persisted. Today it is impossible to differentiate between ethnic and geographic divisions. Politics also played a decisive role in changing boundaries.

Jews were encouraged to settle in this area by the Syrian kings. They were an important part of society and their synagogues were to be found in every major city. Paul passed near this area on his way from Lycaonia to Troas (Acts 16:6) after bypassing "the region of Phrygia and Galatia, having been forbidden

A view looking north along the archaeologists' tram tracks on the main street of Hierapolis, a city in Phrygia.

by the Holy Spirit to speak the word of God in Asia" (Acts 16:6). The gospel probably came to this area from the pilgrims who went to Jerusalem and heard Peter preach. There, in astonishment, they heard each in their own native language, "Parthians and Medes and Elamites and residents of Mesopotamia, Judea. . . Phrygia and Pamphylia . . . the mighty works of God" (Acts 2:8–11). Some were converted and went home to spread the good news.

That Christianity made early inroads and received a wide following here is indicated by the fact that in the middle of the 2nd century Montanus, a zealous leader of the church, arose and called the church back to the primitive dynamism that characterized Pentecost. Thus arose the sect of Montanism in which the leader was sometimes viewed as the incarnation of the Holy Spirit; but, in its best light, the movement is seen as a return to primitive Christianity and a protest against the increasing formalism among the churches. By the 3rd century the entire region was almost entirely Christian according to Eusebius.

The fact that the Christian gospel could transform a wildly emotional people like the inhabitants of Phrygia is eloquent testimonial to the fact that it is "the power of God unto salvation, to everyone that believes." More powerful than the march of conquering armies was the quiet leaven of the Christian message challenging entrenched prejudices and traditions of the past "days of their ignorance."

GEORGE A. TURNER

Phurah. KJV spelling of Purah, Gideon's servant, in Judges 7:10,11.

See PURAH.

Phut. 1. KJV spelling of Put, Ham's third son, in Genesis 10:6.

See PUT (PERSON).

2. KJV spelling of Put, a region close to Egypt along the Mediterranean Sea, in Ezekiel 27:10.

See PUT (PLACE).

Phuvah. KJV spelling of Puvah, Issachar's son, in Genesis 46:13.

See PUVAH.

Phygelus, Phygellus. Asian Christian, who along with others, "turned away" from the author of the letter (2 Tm 1:15, KJV Phygellus). Phygelus is mentioned with Hermogenes, also otherwise unknown.

Phylactery. Small prayer case containing Scripture passages worn at times of prayer by pious Jews. Orthodox Jewish males wear two small black leather cubes or boxes, with Scripture inside, at the time of prayer.

In its original form the phylactery was probably not a box containing Scripture but a strip of parchment on which four passages from the OT were written in Hebrew. The passages were Exodus 13:1–10; 11–16; Deuteronomy 6:4–9; and 11:13–21. The Deuteronomy 6:4–9 passage contains the "Shema"—the confession of God being one Lord. All four passages contain the idea that God is commanding the people to bind his ordinances and commandments upon their hands and have them as "frontlets" between their eyes. Some Jews took this literally and began wearing portions of their Scriptures on their foreheads and on their hands. Other Jews took the command more figuratively or spiritually and did not actually wear them. Exactly when they began to do this is not agreed upon by scholars. There is an explicit mention of the practice as early as 100 BC in a Jewish nonbiblical document. It is thought by some to have begun as early as the 4th century BC but by others even centuries earlier.

In Matthew 23:5 Jesus condemned the scribes and Pharisees for, among other things, making "broad their phylacteries." The context of the passage is Jesus' condemnation of ostentation in religion. Apparently the broad phylactery would impress others with how religious the wearer was. It was evidence of pride, pretence, and hypocrisy in religion.

See FRONTLET; AMULET.

Physician. *See* MEDICINE AND MEDICAL PRACTICE; TRADES AND OCCUPATIONS.

Pibeseth. City mentioned together with Thebes, Memphis, and On in Ezekiel's oracle about Egypt's fall (30:17). In Egyptian the name is translated "house of the goddess Bastet." Bastet was first represented as a woman with the head of a lioness, and in later periods by the head of a cat. In Greek it was known as *Boubastis* (or Bubastis). The city of Boubastis was extensively described by Herodotus. It was located on the right shore of the Old Tanite branch of the Nile, also known as the Branch of Boubastis. Boubastis is the present Tell Basta. Archaeological excavations in 1866–67 unearthed evidence that it is a very old city, dating from the Old Kingdom. It was not until Shishak I, the founder of the 22nd (Libyan) dynasty that Pibeseth became the capital. Hence the dynasty is also known as the dynasty of Boubastis. The 23rd dynasty kept Boubastis as the capital. It served about two centuries as the capital (c. 950–750 BC). The city was destroyed around 350 BC by Persian forces.

Pig

Pig. *See* ANIMALS.

Pigeon. *See* BIRDS.

Pi-hahiroth. Stopping place of the Israelites on their journey from Egypt to the Promised Land (Ex 14:2). It was here that the pursuing Egyptians overtook them (Ex 14:9), which led to the deliverance at the Red Sea, where Israel went through on dry ground but the Egyptians were drowned. Israel never forgot how the Lord had saved them. The precise location of Pi-hahiroth is uncertain, as with Baal-zephon and Migdol, also mentioned as being in the same vicinity. After the Israelites had departed from Egypt, they camped first at Succoth in Goshen, and then at Etham (Nm 33:6). After Pi-hahiroth (v 7) they journeyed three days to Marah and Elim, thought to be on the east shore of the Gulf of Suez, en route to Sinai. It seems that Pi-hahiroth was on the northeast border of Egypt, possibly on the west shore of the Bitter Lakes. Israel did not travel by the expected route of the Way of the Philistines, but southeast by the desert route (cf. Ex 13:17,18), eventually linking up with the old Egyptian road to the copper and turquoise mines of Sinai.

The Hahiroth of Numbers 33:8 is clearly Pi-hahiroth in abbreviated form, as appears in the Samaritan Pentateuch.

See WILDERNESS WANDERINGS.

Pilate, Pontius. Appointed by Tiberius as the fifth prefect of Judea, and who served in that capacity from AD 26–36. He appears prominently in the trial narratives of the Gospels as the Roman governor who authorized Jesus' crucifixion. In addition he appears in a variety of extrabiblical sources as a dispassionate administrator who relentlessly pursued Roman authority in Judea.

Tacitus (*Annals* 15.44) mentions Pilate in connection with the crucifixion of Jesus but adds little to the Gospel account. Josephus, on the other hand, provides three narratives. First, he describes Pilate's arrival as the new prefect (*War* 2.9.2; *Antiq.* 18.3.1; cf. Eusebius, *Hist.* 2.6). Offending Jewish law, Pilate brought ensigns to Jerusalem which bore the image of Caesar. A large gathering of Jews then came to Caesarea in protest, fasting there for five days. Pilate called in troops to dismiss them but he learned his first lesson about Jewish intransigence. The Jews were ready to die rather than tolerate the ensigns. Soon thereafter Pilate relented.

A second incident occurred when Pilate appropriated temple funds in order to construct a 35-mile aqueduct for Jerusalem (*War* 2.9.4;

Antiq. 18.3.2). Again there was a major protest. Pilate ordered his soldiers to dress in tunics and so disguised infiltrate the crowds. At his command, the troops used clubs to beat the offenders and many Jews were killed. Josephus records the horror with which Jerusalem perceived the affair.

Finally, Josephus records the story of Pilate's dismissal (*Antiq.* 18.4.1–2). In AD 36 a Samaritan false prophet (pretending to be the *Taheb*, or Samaritan messiah) promised to show his followers sacred vessels hidden by Moses on Mt Gerizim. Pilate sent a heavily armed contingent of footmen and cavalry which intercepted the pilgrims and slaughtered most of them. The Samaritans complained to Vitellius, the prefect of Syria, whereupon Pilate was ordered to report to the emperor Tiberius. Another prefect, Marcellus, was then sent by Rome as Pilate's replacement.

Philo records yet another event (*Leg. to Caius*, 299–305). While extolling the liberal policies of Tiberius toward Judaism he cites a negative example in Pontius Pilate. The prefect had erected gilded shields in Herod's former palace in Jerusalem which bore the name of the emperor. Refusing to hear Jewish complaints, the sons of Herod appealed to Tiberius who ordered Pilate to transfer the shields to the temple of Augustus in Caesarea. The similarities with the parallel story in Josephus have led many scholars to believe that Philo is merely recounting another version of the same event.

Luke mentions a minor incident which contributes to this same portrait. In Luke 13:1 some Jews tell Jesus about the Galileans whose blood Pilate had mixed with their sacrifices. While this story is not corroborated by any other witness, still, it conforms to the accounts of Philo and Josephus. In fact, Luke adds another detail of interest in his trial narrative. In Luke 23:12 he says that prior to the crucifixion of Jesus, Herod Antipas (in Galilee) and Pilate "had been at enmity with each other." This may have stemmed not simply from Pilate's usual antagonism, but particularly from the Galilean incident.

Pilate's role in the death of Jesus is recorded in each Gospel (Mt 27:2; Mk 15:1; Lk 23:1; Jn 18:29) and was remembered as a historical datum in the preaching of the later church (Acts 3:13; 4:27; 13:28; 1 Tm 6:13; Ignatius: *Mg* 11; *Tr* 9:1; *Sm* 1; and the *Gospel of Peter*, 1:1; 2:3–5; 8:29; 31; 11:43; 45; 49). In order to secure the conviction and death of Jesus, Caiaphas and the Sanhedrin brought their charges to Pilate. While the accusations now took on a political flavor to evoke the governor's interest, he still could find no grounds for condemnation. In the end, Pilate is unexpectedly accommodating and Jesus is killed. Why would Pilate act in behalf of the Sanhedrin? Two answers are possible. First, there may have been collusion between Caiaphas and Pilate that stemmed from a longstanding relationship and conterminous reign. Ten of Caiaphas' 18 years in power were under Pilate and when the prefect was dismissed in AD 36, Caiphas was simultaneously removed. Second, if Jesus' trial occurred in AD 33, Pilate may have been concerned about his impeachment. He had originally been appointed by Sejanus (prefect of the praetorians in Rome who had appointed men to colonial office under Tiberius) but in the autumn of AD 31 Sejanus died. This explains why a Jewish delegation could report directly to Tiberius during the votive shield incident. Hence the charge recorded in John 19:12 ("if you release this man, you are not Caesar's friend") would have had genuine power over Pilate. Pilate perceived his jeopardy and was anxious to pacify the Jews and please the emperor. This may help to explain an inscription recently found in Caesarea bearing the name of both Pilate and Tiberius in connection with the dedication of a building or temple to the emperor.

The history of Pilate after his dismissal in AD 36 is unknown. However, many postapostolic legends flourished and concentrated on one feature of the passion story. The Synoptics and particularly John show Pilate's repeated verdict of Jesus' innocence. In Matthew 27:19, Pilate's wife has an ominous dream about Jesus' conviction and she warns her husband. Pilate tries to have Jesus released, but the crowd cries for Barabbas. Matthew even records that Pilate washed his hands (27:24,25),

A pool built by Pontius Pilate.

declaring his own innocence in this. And finally, John says that Pilate refused to alter the title over the cross (19:19–22). These accounts clearly exonerate Pilate and place full blame for Jesus' death on the Jews. Critics, to be sure, have been quick to identify these as legendary accretions. Nevertheless, the later church fully redeemed Pilate's image. For instance, the apocryphal *Acts of Pilate* recounts the trial showing that Pilate's decision was forced upon him. Colorful embellishments bring home the point: when Jesus enters Pilate's praetorium, the imperial standards miraculously bow down. Tertullian even speaks of Pilate as a "Christian at heart" and contributes to the legendary conversion of both Pilate and his wife (who later gains the name Procula). Eusebius reports that Pilate ultimately committed suicide during the reign of the emperor Caligula, AD 37–41 (*Hist.* 2.7).

GARY M. BURGE

Pildash. Sixth son of Nahor and Milcah and nephew of Abraham. He is mentioned immediately following the repeated announcement of God's promise that Abraham's descendants will be too numerous to count (Gn 22:22).

Pilha, Pileha. Political leader who set his seal on Ezra's covenant during the postexilic era (Neh 10:24, KJV Pileha).

Pillar of Fire and Cloud. One of the most frequent modes of God appearing to man in the OT; a visual manifestation of the presence of God common in the narratives of the exodus, Sinai covenant, the wilderness wanderings, and the dedication of the temple. The Bible refers to this phenomenon in a variety of ways: the pillar of cloud and of fire (Ex 14:24); pillar of cloud (Ex 33:9,10; Nm 14:14); pillar of fire (Ex 13:21; Nm 14:14); cloud (Ex 40:34,35; Dt 1:33); fire (Dt 1:33; 4:12). Though the Bible itself does not use this designation, the cloud and associated theophanies are often called the "Shekinah glory" or simply "the Shekinah," terms which have entered Christian theology from rabbinic literature. The Bible also alludes to the cloud theophany in a number of passages where the characteristic terms designating it are not present.

The dominant theological motif associated with the pillar of cloud and fire is the "Immanuel concept"; it represents an incipient fulfillment of God's purpose to be with his image-bearers, a desire which was interrupted by the fall into sin. Because the radiance and splendor of God are so overwhelming, because no man can look on him and live (Ex 33:17–23; Jn 1:18; 6:46; 1 Tm 6:15,16), that splendor is concealed within the cloud to protect man from his presence (Ex 16:10; 19:16–20; 24:15–17; Pss 18:11,12; 97:2,3).

The cloud theophany is associated with a variety of functions; common to all of them is that it is a visible expression of the presence of God. The cloud filled the tabernacle and was there day and night as a witness to the presence of God (Ex 40:34–38); God appeared in the cloud on the day of atonement (Lv 16:2). God's acceptance of the temple built as his dwelling is shown when the cloud comes at the dedication (1 Kgs 8:10,11; 2 Chr 5:13,14).

The cloud was also a protection for Israel. At its first appearance in the events of the exodus, the cloud positions itself between the armies of Egypt and Israel, engulfing the Egyptians in darkness on the one side while lighting the way with its fire for Israel on the other (Ex 14:19,20). The psalmist recalls how God "spread out a cloud as a covering, and a fire to give light at night" (Ps 105:39).

The pillar also served as Israel's guide during the exodus and wandering in the wilderness. "By day the Lord went ahead of them in a pillar of cloud to guide them on their way and by night in a pillar of fire to give them light, so they could travel by day or night. Neither the pillar of cloud by day nor the pillar of fire by night left its place in front of the people" (Ex 13:21,22). "Whenever the cloud lifted from above the Tent, the Israelites set out; wherever the cloud settled, the Israelites encamped" (Nm 9:17; see vv 15–23). In spite of the sins of the people, the Lord God "went ahead of you on your journey, in fire by night and in a cloud by day, to search out places for you to camp and to show you the way you should go" (Dt 1:33). Subsequent generations would recount how God was guide by day and night (Neh 9:12,19; Ps 78:14).

The cloud also had an oracular function (Ps 99:7). Not only did God speak from the cloud at Sinai (Ex 19:9,16; 34:1–25; Dt 4:11,12; 5:22), he also spoke from there when Israel rebelled (Ex 16:10; Nm 14:10; 16:42,43), when Aaron and Miriam had a quarrel with Moses (Nm 12:1–15), and when the 70 elders were appointed (Nm 11:25). Only Moses had this ready access to the very words of God. When Moses went into the tabernacle, "the pillar of cloud would come down and stay at the entrance. . . . The Lord would speak to Moses face to face, as a man speaks with his friend" (Ex 33:9–11). At the death of Moses the Lord appears in the pillar at the tent and speaks of the coming apostasy of the nation (Dt 31:14–29).

Other theophanies having the features of cloud, fire, and light or some combination should probably be associated with the pillar of fire and cloud. The similarity of the language in Deuteronomy 32:10,11 and Genesis

1:2 suggests that the cloud theophany is also intended in the creation account. The smoking brazier and blazing torch of Abraham's dream reflect the fire of the pillar (Gn 15:8–21; see Is 31:9). The flame of the burning bush is the same flame that would surround Sinai at the giving of the Law (Ex 3; 19:16–19). Ezekiel saw an immense cloud with flashing lightning and surrounded by a brilliant light (Ez 1:4); when he looked inside the cloud, he saw flame, creatures in the service of God, the throne of God, and the awesome presence of the One who sat upon it and spoke (Ez 1:5–28). Ezekiel also had a vision of the glory of God leaving the temple, and later a vision of its return (Ez 10; 43).

During his vision of the glory cloud, Ezekiel saw within it the chariot of God moving on wheels within wheels (Ez 1:15–21; see Dn 7:9). God is elsewhere in the OT also depicted as riding within or upon clouds (Dt 33:26; Ps 18:10–12; 68:4,33,34; 104:3; Is 19:1). The Canaanite god Baal was a weather god, and he is called in the texts from Ugarit "the rider on the clouds." Though there is some question about the verse, that same epithet appears to be applied to the Lord in Psalm 68:4.

In Daniel's vision of the Ancient of Days, he sees one "like a son of man coming with the clouds of heaven" to receive authority, glory, and power (Dn 7:13). The phrase "son of man" becomes Jesus' favorite self-designation in the Gospels. At the transfiguration when he reveals his own glory, the clouds envelop him (Mt 17:5; Mk 9:7; Lk 9:34). At his ascension he is received into the clouds, and angels remind the apostles of his promise to return in the same way (Acts 1:9–11; see Mt 24:30; Mk 13:26; Lk 21:27; Rv 1:7).

From his vantage point in the 8th century, Isaiah looked to a day when the glory cloud would not be above one little room in the temple or tabernacle, but it would become a canopy "over all of Mount Zion . . . a cloud of smoke by day and a glow of flaming fire by night . . . a shelter and shade from the heat of the day, and a refuge and hiding place from the storm and rain" (Is 4:5,6). In the New Jerusalem of Revelation the whole city is infused with the glory of God (Rv 21,22); the pillar is not localized over the one room but has transformed the entire city.   RAYMOND B. DILLARD

See THEOPHANY; SHEKINAH; GLORY.

Piltai. Priest and head of Modiah's house during the days of Joiakim the high priest in the postexilic period (Neh 12:17).

Pim. Weight measurement equivalent to about two-thirds of a shekel.

See WEIGHTS AND MEASURES.

Pine Tree. *See* PLANTS.

Pinon. One of the "chiefs," descended from Esau (Gn 36:41; 1 Chr 1:52).

Pipe. *See* MUSIC AND MUSICAL INSTRUMENTS (MASHROQITA; UGAB).

Piram. King of Jarmuth, a Canaanite city located southwest of Jerusalem. After joining an alliance with four Amorite kings against Joshua, Piram, along with the other kings, was defeated and slain (Jos 10:3).

Pirathon, Pirathonite. Home of Abdon, one of the minor judges (Jgs 12:13,15). It is described as being "in the land of Ephraim, in the hill country of the Amalekites." This may indicate that it originally belonged to the Amalekites, or that it was seized by them during one of their invasions. Some manuscripts of the Septuagint read "in the hill country of Ephraim, in the land of Shaalim," which is the reading accepted by the Jerusalem Bible. Benaiah, one of David's mighty men, is called a Pirathonite (2 Sm 23:30; 1 Chr 11:31; 27:14). It is generally identified with Fer'ata, situated on a high rock six miles southwest of Samaria. Some have identified it with a fortress at the head of the Wadi Far'ah, while others have suggested it was Fer'on, due west of Samaria.

Pisgah, Mount. Mountain located at the northeast end of the Dead Sea near the ancient city of Jericho. Balak took Balaam to the top of Pisgah (Nm 23:14), and Moses was told to go to its summit to view the Promised Land (Dt 3:27). Later, Moses returned to the top of Pisgah to die (Dt 34:1). Pisgah's slopes border the Dead Sea or Sea of the Arabah (Dt 3:17; 4:49; Jos 12:3; 13:20). The KJV sometimes refers to these slopes as "Ashdoth-pisgah." Many scholars identify Mt Pisgah with modern Ras es-Siyaghah, just north of Mt Nebo.

See NEBO, MOUNT.

Pishon. First of four divisions of the river that flowed out of the garden of Eden (Gn 2:11, KJV Pison). Suggestions for its identity include the Rion, the Indus, the Ganges, a canal connecting the Tigris and Euphrates, and a symbol of the Milky Way. No consensus exists on Pishon's identity. Leupold suggests that the flood so altered the area's topography that the Pishon will likely never be identified.

Pisidia. Region included in the Roman province of Galatia at the time of the visit of Paul and Barnabas about AD 48.

It is north of the Taurus mountain range which parallels the coastline of Cilicia and Pamphylia. Separated from these coastal provinces by the mountain range, it lies in the central plateau of Anatolia about 3600 feet above sea level. The territory includes the foothills of the Taurus range and measures about 400 feet long and 165 feet wide. It was joined by the large province of Asia on the west, by Galatia on the north, and by Lycaonia on the east. The inhabitants of the mountainous terrain were predatory tribesmen who were subjugated with great difficulty over a period of years by the Selucids and later by the Romans. To assist in controlling these tribes, the city of Antioch was founded by Seleucus I Nicator (312–280 BC). Concern with security led Amyntas of Galatia to strengthen the city (c. 26 BC). At his death in 25 BC Pisidia was absorbed into the province of Galatia. Augustus undertook the final phase of pacification of the populace by founding five cities in addition to Antioch: Crimma, Comana, Olbase, Parlais, and Lystra, all linked to Antioch by military roads. An inscription, discovered in 1912, indicates that Quirinius (cf. Lk 2:2) was administrator of the district and responsible to Augustus. Its capital, Antioch, was on the main road between Ephesus to the west and Derbe and Tarsus to the east. It was primarily a Roman colony and included a sizeable Jewish community, introduced by the Seleucids for the purpose of trade.

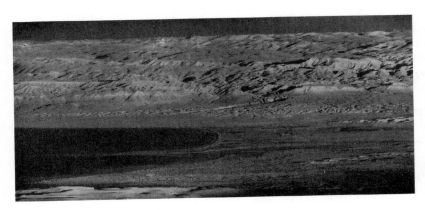

Infrared telephoto view of the Promised Land (Judea) from Mt Nebo (including the north end of the Dead Sea in the center of the photograph).

In AD 74 southern Pisidia was severed by Vespasian from the province of Galatia and transferred to the principality of Lysia-Pamphylia, while the northern section remained in Galatia. The entire area became nominally Christian at the time of Constantine.

About AD 297 Diocletian reorganized the area and Pisidia was included in the Dioecesis Asiana. Urbanization was accompanied by the conversion of the mountain tribes to Christianity.

Paul and Barnabas passed through the country at least twice (Acts 13:14; 14:24) in the journey between Perga and Derbe. It was in Antioch of Pisidia that one of the most important decisions in the history of Christianity missionary strategy was made and announced. After being rebuffed by a majority of his Jewish audience, accompanied by a more cordial response from the Gentiles, Paul and Barnabas announced, "Since you thrust it [the Word of God] from you, and judge yourselves unworthy of eternal life, behold, we turn to the Gentiles" (Acts 13:46). Henceforth the strategy of Paul and his associates was oriented more specifically to the non-Jewish peoples, thus making Christianity a world religion, rather than another Jewish sect.

Pison. KJV translation for the Pishon River in Genesis 2:11.

See PISHON.

Pispa, Pispah. Jether's son from Asher's tribe (1 Chr 7:38, KJV Pispah).

Pistachio. *See* FOOD AND FOOD PREPARATION; PLANTS.

Pit. Word used frequently in the OT to denote the grave, the abode of the dead, or Sheol, that is, a shadowy existence which the living feared as cutting them off from light, joy, and vitality. Godly men abhorred it because it seemed to negate their fellowship with God: Hezekiah (Is 38:17,18), Job (17:13–16; 33:22), and the psalmists (28:1; 30:3; 55:23; 88:4,6). Rarely did the OT saint rise to the insight of resurrection which came with the gospel.

See BOTTOMLESS PIT; DEAD, ABODE OF THE; DEATH; SHEOL.

Pitch. *See* ASPHALT; BITUMEN.

Pitcher. *See* POTTERY.

Pithom. One of the store-cities (along with Raamses) built by the Israelites during their Egyptian captivity (Ex 1:11). There has been considerable debate among Egyptologists for over a century as to the identification of these sites. The identification of Raamses is fairly well established as being associated with Pi-rameses, the capital of Pharaoh Rameses II (1290–1224 BC). A number of ancient sites have been suggested as Raamses, but Tanis in the northeastern Delta for many years was the assumed location. However, Qantir in the same general region is the more likely spot.

Pithom is derived from the Egyptian phrase meaning "House of (the god) Atum." This would have been a temple dedicated to the worship of the solar deity Atum. The Israelites would have been involved in building the storage facilities of the temple. Storage facilities from the mortuary temple of Rameses II in Thebes are well-preserved, long rectangular structures with arched roofs. They were built side by side and covered a significant portion of the mortuary complex. This gives us a fairly accurate picture of the sort of structures for which the Israelites were forced to provide bricks.

While the etymology of Pithom is known, its location continues to be a subject of scholarly discussion. The two sites most frequently associated with Pithom are Tell er-Retabeh and Tell el-Maskhutah, both located in the Wadi Tumilat which extends eastward from the Nile Delta to Lake Timsah. Excavations have taken place at both sites in recent years, and both tells have yielded evidence for the presence of Asiatics from Palestine and Syria. Since there might be a link between the Arabic name Maskhutah and Hebrew Succoth (mentioned in Ex 12:37 as a stopping-off point on the route of the exodus), Tell-er Retabeh is now thought to be the best possible location for Pithom and Maskhutah would be Succoth. Further excavation at Retabeh may yield the necessary evidence to confirm the identity.

See EGYPT, EGYPTIANS; RAMESES (PLACE).

Pithon. Benjamite, Michah's son and a descendant of Jonathan (1 Chr 8:35; 9:41).

Plague. Word used to refer to a disease, disaster, or pestilence. Although there is a specific disease known as plague, the term "plague" as used in Scripture is not restricted to a single disease (1 Kgs 8:37; Lk 7:21). Plague can indicate an epidemic disease or refer to widespread calamity like the 10 plagues of Egypt (Ex 7–12). Plague can also be used in connection with a single person's disease (Mk 5:29,34).

There is no question in the Hebrew or NT mind that plagues are part of the judgment God sends to individuals, families, and nations. God himself threatens to send plagues to the Israelites in proportion to their sins (Lv 26:21) and takes full responsibility for the Egyptian plagues (Jos 24:5). The OT plagues demonstrated God's control over the processes of nature just as do Christ's miracles in the NT.

At one point in the history of Israel, the Philistines won a battle and captured the ark of God (1 Sm 4:10,11). When the ark was kept at Ashdod, however, God showed his power by allowing a fatal disease characterized by swellings or tumors to be prevalent (1 Sm 5:6). The Philistines sent the ark on to Gath, but people of all ages began to have buboes ("emerods") in the region of the groin (1 Sm 5:9). A similar occurrence at the next city, Ekron, resulted in many deaths (1 Sm 5:12).

Finally after seven months, the Philistines decided to return the ark of God to Israel along with a trespass offering of five golden rats ("mice") and five golden swollen lymph nodes ("emerods") (1 Sm 6:1-4). The selection of this unusual offering was made because the Philistine diviners associated the swarms of rodents which marred the land with the plague that was upon them (1 Sm 6:5).

The first Israelite village to receive the ark of God from the Philistines was punished with the same disease for looking into it (1 Sm 6:19). The epidemic in Beth-shemesh left 50,070 men dead. Assuming bubonic plague was the means the Lord used to teach the Philistines and the Israelites a spiritual lesson, then this episode is probably the first recorded example of biological warfare, although admittedly unintentional.

See EXODUS, BOOK OF; PESTILENCE; DISEASE; PLAGUES UPON EGYPT.

Plagues upon Egypt. Unprecedented series of disasters striking Egypt, probably culminating in the spring or early summer (*c.* 1400 BC). They struck particularly the Nile delta, although apparently not affecting the area called Goshen. These disasters were of such magnitude that the Egyptians from their earliest history could recall nothing like them (Ex 9:24).

The Plagues. The plagues are described in Exodus 7–11. At first sight one might imagine that the plagues took place in succession within a few weeks, but casual notes of time (e.g., 7:25; 9:31,32) as well as the nature of some of the plagues would suggest that several months may well have been involved. Taken in order, the plagues were: the turning of the water into blood (7:20), so that the fish died and the water stank. Next came a plague of frogs (8:6); even after their death, the land

was strewn with piles of their bodies (8:14). Next came a plague of lice (8:17), or possibly gnats, sandflies, or mosquitoes. The exact sense of the word is not clear, but it obviously means some small irritant creature. After that came "swarms," presumably of flies (8:24). Again, the meaning is not quite clear: later Jewish tradition made it swarms of wild beasts, but flies is a much more likely sense. Then some sort of cattle plague struck (9:3), affecting the domestic animals. After that came boils on humans (9:9), boils that erupted into painful blisters and vesicles, apparently irritating rather than fatal. Hail followed (9:18), so severe that nothing like it had been seen before—hail associated with thunder and lightning (9:24). This was so heavy it could be fatal (9:19), and naturally did great harm to the early crops of Egypt (9:31). After that came the locusts in vast numbers (10:13)—again on an unparalleled scale. Then came three days of complete darkness (10:22) which brought Egyptian life to a standstill. Finally all the firstborn of the Egyptians died (12:29), from Pharaoh's household down to the lowliest homes in the land.

First, of course, all the plagues are seen in the Bible as successive judgments of God. Normally, each is preceded by a warning from Moses, which is disregarded by Pharaoh, and then each is lifted as a result of temporary repentance on the part of Pharaoh. But it is also clear that the plagues gradually increase in severity and intensity, until the climax comes in the death of the firstborn: with that, even Pharaoh is broken. The first plagues represent discomfort rather than danger for the Egyptians: then their animals and crops are struck down; finally death takes the firstborn, the flower of the nation.

There are certain common features that run through the account of the plagues. At first, Pharaoh's magicians try to belittle the plagues, and the signs that precede them, by producing similar effects themselves (7:11,12; 8:7). This is an interesting warning that miracles may be produced from various sources, and that this sort of sign is therefore not important in itself. But the time comes when the magicians are beaten (8:18) and can no longer compete; even they admit that this is God's hand (8:19). Their discomfiture goes further, told with robust Israelite humor. When the plague of boils comes, the magicians cannot even present themselves before Pharaoh, so bad is their condition. After that, the magicians disappear from the story.

Another motif which becomes increasingly clear as the account of the plagues continues, is the increasing emphasis on the way in which God's people, living in Goshen, were delivered from the plagues that affected the Egyptians. It could be assumed anyway that, as Goshen was not on the Nile, the water that turned to blood and the plague of frogs and mosquitoes might affect them less. But in the case of the later swarms of flies (8:22), the cattle plague (9:4) the hail (9:26), and the darkness (10:23), we are specifically told that Israel was spared; in the case of the death of the firstborn, the Lord "passed over" Israelite homes.

At first, to take another aspect, it seems as if the hearts of all the Egyptians are just as hard as that of Pharaoh (7:13). Yet as the story goes on, his own people keep urging him to yield to God. They are the forerunners of the gentile "god-fearers" of later generations, of those in the OT who, although heathen, would yet glorify God. The magicians admit God's role in the plague of lice (8:19). Pharaoh's servants who heeded God's Word brought their servants and cattle indoors before the great hailstorms, and thus escaped loss and death (9:20). Only the unbelieving suffered. Finally, Pharaoh's own servants exhort him to let Israel go, bluntly telling him that the land is being ruined by his stubbornness (10:7); at this point, God's judgments have achieved their effect.

Pharaoh and the Plagues. Pharaoh's reaction to God's Word is remarkable. The question of the hardness of his heart need not be entered into here except to say that Scripture describes it in three ways, obviously with no sense of any contradiction involved. In 7:3 it speaks of God hardening Pharaoh's heart; 7:14 has the neutral statement that Pharaoh's heart was hardened; and 8:15 has Pharaoh hardening his own heart. Obviously, these all refer to the same process, which must be taken into account in any explanation. Furthermore, Paul must be allowed to have the last word on the matter (Rom 9:18).

But, within this theological framework, there is quite a movement, not merely a succession of shallow repentances designed to secure the removal of the plague, and then a renewed stubbornness, calling down a fresh judgment. There is also a typically Asian bargaining session between Pharaoh and Moses. After Pharaoh's broken promises to let the people go (8:8), he tries to bargain: the people should sacrifice to God in Egypt, without going at all (8:25); only the men should go (10:11); they should all go, but leave their flocks and herds as hostages (10:24). But there can be no bargaining of this sort in response to the call of God, as Pharaoh was to learn. After the death of the firstborn, he was glad to see the Israelites leave (12:31–33).

In this sense, the whole story of the plagues is a struggle. It has sometimes been seen as the struggle of the prototype prophet, Moses, (Dt 18:15) against the prototype king, Pharaoh: but, while it may be that, it is far more. It is the struggle of Moses, the servant of God, against the magicians. It is the struggle of Moses against mighty Pharaoh or rather, the confrontation of Pharaoh by God, in the form of the word brought by his servant. At the deepest level, it is a victory won by God over the false gods of Egypt. This gives to many of the stories their peculiar relish, which may escape us at first. For the Nile is the god Hapi; Hept the frog is a god of fertility and childbirth; Ra the sun (outraged by the darkness) is a god; Hat-hot had the form of a heifer, and Apis that

Hat-hot (Hathor, or Hathar), the cow goddess of Egypt.

Apis, the bull god of Egypt.

of a bull; the flying hornet symbolized Egypt; and Pharaoh himself was a god. Yet all were helpless before the God of Israel (Col 2:15).

The Nature of the Plagues. It is not known how God brought about the plagues, and some may think it vain even to ask, since God is free to use whatever means he pleases. Yet the statement that God turned back the waters of the "Reed Sea" by a strong east wind (Ex 14:21) indicates that God could use natural means to bring about his will. The Hebrew concept of "miracle" was not the same as the modern one, which usually regards miracles as "supernatural," and sees all else as "natural," and thus as nonmiraculous. The Hebrews, however, regarded everything in nature as the work of God; it was only that in certain instances he had acted more "wonderfully" (perhaps one would say more "obviously") than others. There is thus nothing in any way rationalistic in saying that on this occasion God may have sent a series of "natural" disasters (the sort of disasters to which Egypt was geographically prone), but so heightened and in such rapid succession that they constituted a miracle.

Most of the explanations of this sort assume a year of unusual climatic conditions, and in particular, a variation in the annual rise of the Nile. For instance, either an exceptionally low rise of the Nile (leading to red and muddy water) or an exceptionally high rise of the Nile (bringing down red earth from the Ethiopian highlands) have been suggested as explanations of the first plague. If one feels that the description "turned into blood" would be satisfied by thick blood-colored water, then either would be satisfactory. Another attractive suggestion is the multiplication of red plankton in the water. This phenomenon is fairly common across the world, especially in tropical and subtropical areas. This would make the likeness to blood much closer. In either of these cases, death of fish in foul water, and migration of frogs from the river would be understandable. If the Nile was flooding more widely than usual, the plague of frogs would be even more understandable. Some have seen the sudden death of the frogs as due to some type of internal anthrax; and, with piles of stinking frogs' bodies in the fields, the way was wide open both for the carriers of the plagues (flies, etc.) and the plagues that followed.

The next plague, for instance, was one of mosquitoes, sandflies, or possibly lice. At least the first and the last are potent carriers of disease, and all three would cause irritant sores by their bites. The flooding of the stagnant waters of the Nile would give perfect breeding conditions for mosquitoes in particular. The suggestion that the word means "lice," and that these multiplied because of the shortage of water, seems farfetched and unnecessary.

If we are right in assuming that the swarms that followed were swarms of flies, then everything would fit into a divine pattern. Piles of dead frogs, piles of rubbish strewn over the land by the flood (including, no doubt, raw sewage), foul and muddied Nile waters—this would be a prime breeding place for flies. Further, Jewish interpreters suggest that the flies in question were biting or stinging flies (like our "gadflies" or "horseflies"). Perhaps these were the agents of the disease of the cattle. Modern interpreters have suggested a particular type of fly, still known in the area, which multiplies very rapidly amid rotting vegetation. The flies and the dust (9:9) between them could have produced that dreaded tropical scourge, "prickly heat," easily becoming infected.

Again, in the providence of God, if the Israelites were not in the Delta area, nor actually living along the Nile itself, but concentrated in the Wadi Tumilat to the east, they would be spared these plagues, a fact that did not escape Pharaoh's notice (9:7). The miracle thus lay in God's overruling providence, using his world and its geographic and climatic conditions to do his work of judgment on the stubborn-hearted.

Hail, accompanied by violent thunderstorms (this seems to be the meaning of the Bible text, with its possible mention of "fireballs," 9:24) would be easily explicable (although rare in Egypt), especially in the "funnel" conditions of the Nile valley, surrounded by hot dry desert on either side. As to the severity of the hail (more common in Palestine) there are biblical parallels (Jos 10:11). With this plague there is a valuable note of time, given incidentally (9:31–32) in connection with the crops destroyed by the hail.

In the case of the plague of locusts, God's use of natural means is made plain in the text, where an "east wind" brings them and a "sea wind" takes them away (10:13,19). The "plague" here is both the enormous number of the locusts (see Jl 1:1–12 for another illustration of this scourge) and the timing of their arrival. There are many other places in the OT where the precision of God's time clock is shown and where indeed the miraculous element lies in the timing of the event.

The locusts may have darkened the land with their numbers (Ex 10:15), but that was nothing compared with the three days of darkness that followed. Most commentators are agreed that this is the dreaded *khamsin*, the hot desert wind bringing dust storms or sandstorms that fill the sky, and may last for days without respite. If the red earth from the Ethiopian highlands had been brought down by the flood waters of the Nile and deposited widely over the land, some commentators have suggested that it was whipped into the air by this wind, thus giving an even darker pall over the land.

In the case of the last plague, the death of the firstborn, we have no indication of what, if any, particular disease was used by God. Everything from the common Western phenomenon of "cot-deaths" (apparently arising from a vitamin deficiency), through poliomyelitis, to typhus or famine fever, has been suggested. Here, however, Scripture gives us no clue, so we must be content to remain ignorant. What can be said is that the Egyptians suffered, but the Israelites did not. After this plague, they were free. Henceforth, it was their glad knowledge that none of "the plagues of Egypt" would strike them as God's people (15:26). It was their unshakable belief that these plagues were God's judgment, a punishment on stubborn Pharaoh, but the means of their salvation. Therefore, the plagues are not only a warning to us, but an encouragement.

R. ALAN COLE

See EXODUS, BOOK OF; EGYPT, EGYPTIANS; MOSES; PLAGUE.

Plain of the Pillar.
KJV for "oak of the pillar," a sacred tree at Shechem, in Judges 9:6.

See OAK OF THE PILLAR.

Plain of Zaanannim.
KJV translation for "Oak of Za-anannim," a border site for Naphtali's tribe, in Joshua 19:33.

See ZA-ANANNIM.

Plane Tree.
Large spreading tree having a wide trunk and scaly bark, indigenous to Palestine.

See PLANTS.

Plants.
Introduction.
The Holy Land provides a great variety of plant habitats within a short distance, perhaps as great a variety as anywhere in the world.

Identifying biblical plants has always been a difficult task, partly because people continue to identify the biblical elm, sycamore, lily, rose, and vine with modern plants, and also because they assume that all the plants now growing in the Holy Land were there in ancient biblical days, or that the plants referred to in the Bible are still to be found there today. Unfortunately, many plants now quite common in the Holy Land were not there in bibli-

cal days. Many plants that once grew in abundance in the Holy Land are now extinct. Some have been driven out by foreign invaders; others have been exterminated or nearly exterminated by overcultivation of the land, the destruction of forests, and the resulting changes in climatic and other environmental conditions. At one time the Holy Land was a land of palm trees with the date palm as abundant and characteristic there as it was in Egypt, but today the date palm is much less common. Similarly in antiquity the towering cedars clothed the slopes of Lebanon and other mountain ranges. Now the few remaining specimens must be carefully fenced in to protect them against trampling and the ravages of goats.

Plants of the Bible.
Acacia (*Acacia tortilis* and *A. seyal*). Any tree or shrub of the mimosa family of plants growing in warm regions. The plant referred to in the KJV as "shittah" (singular) or "shittim" (plural) is undoubtedly the acacia tree, the only timber tree of any considerable size in the Arabian desert. It is essentially a tree of barren regions seemingly able to flourish in dry lands where no other tree can grow. *Acacia tortilis* is by far the largest and most common tree in the desert in which the Israelites wandered for 40 years. It is especially conspicuous on Mt Sinai and was probably the species used for the tabernacle furnishings. *A. seyal* is less common, at least today. It can grow as high as 25 feet, and bears yellow flowers on twisted branches. The wood is close grained, heavy and hard, orange-brown in color, and much valued in cabinet work. The ancient Egyptians clamped shut mummy coffins with acacia wood.

In the OT, the word "Shittim" is used as a place name, probably because of the abundance of acacias at those places (Nm 25:1; Jos 2:1; 3:1; Jl 3:18; Mi 6:5). The reference in Isaiah 41:19 may be to another tree, perhaps the box tree.

Acanthus (*Acanthus syriacus*). The acanthus, perhaps referred to in Job 30:7 and Zephaniah 2:9, is a perennial thistle-like herb or small shrub about three feet tall, and is a common weed in all Eastern countries. It has been used since time immemorial as a model for the leaf or scroll decorations in art.

Algum (*Pterocarpus santalinus*). Almug or algum was the precious wood imported by King Solomon and used in making the pillars for the house of the Lord and for making harps and psalteries (1 Kgs 10:11,12). This timber was brought by sea from Ophir to Ezion-geber, near Elath. Modern authorities suggest that Ophir was either in Arabia, India, or West Africa near Mozambique. If the wood came from India it was probably the red sandalwood, *Pterocarpus santalina*, a large leguminous tree with hard heavy red wood which takes a fine polish.

The reference in 2 Chronicles 2:8 is probably not to this tree but to the juniper (*Juniperus excelsa Bieb*).

Almond (Amygdalus communis). The almond is a peach-like tree with saw-toothed pointed leaves and gray bark. It grows to a height of 10 to 25 feet. It blooms very early in the year; its Hebrew name has its roots in "watch for." The flowers are large, sometimes pink and sometimes white, and appear before the leaves. When the Israelites were encamped in the barren desert of Sinai where no almonds grow they adopted them as models for ornamenting the cups of the golden lamp stands (Ex 25:33–36; 37:19,20). To the Jews it was a welcome harbinger of spring (Jer 1:11).

The almond is highly valued in the Orient because it furnishes a very pleasant oil. The "hazel" of Genesis 30:37 (KJV) is actually the almond and not the true hazel. The name "Luz" (Gn 35:6) probably refers to a locality in which there was an abundance of almond trees.

Aloe (Aloe succotrina, Aquilaria agallocha). Chiefly African, lily-like plant of the genus *Aloes*, certain species of which yield a drug and a fiber. Aloe is an aromatic substance mentioned in the Bible together with myrrh, balm, and other fragrant plants (Ps 45:8; Prv 7:17; Sg 4:14; Jn 19:39). Most commentators believe these passages refer to two different plants. The OT plant is likely to have been *Aquilaria agallocha*, the eaglewood, a large tree growing up to 120 feet tall with a trunk 12 feet in circumference. It is native to northern India, Malaya, and Indochina. The decaying wood is highly fragrant, and as such is highly valued as perfume and incense, and for fumigation.

The aloe of John 19:39 is believed to be the true aloe, *Aloe succotrina*, the juice of which was used by the Egyptians in embalming. Its smell, however, is not very agreeable, and it has a bitter taste. It is sometimes used by veterinarians as a horse medicine. The drug is manufactured principally from the pulp of the fleshy leaves. The plant is a native of the island of Socotra off the coast of East Africa at the mouth of the Red Sea.

Apricot (Prunus armeniaca). Yellow-orange peach-like edible fruit native to western Asia and Africa, and the tree producing it. While domesticated apple trees are now found in the Holy Land no wild specimens have ever been found there, although wild apple trees are found in areas nearby. The fruit of the wild apple tree is not very attractive being both small and acidic. Hence, scriptural references are most probably to the apricot. It is abundant in the Holy Land and probably has been

so since early biblical times. The tree is a round-headed reddish-barked tree growing 30 feet tall (Prv 25:11; Sg 2:3,5; 7:8; 8:5; Jl 1:12). This tree (Hebrew *tappuch*) also gave its name to several places and also to a descendant of Caleb (Jos 15:53; 17:8; 1 Chr 2:43).

Ash (Alhagi maurorum, Fraxinus ornus, Tamarix mannifera). There are several ash trees found in the Near East. One of these, the prickly alhagi, *Alhagi maurorum*, is a member of the pea family. It is a low, many-stemmed, much-branched shrub growing about three feet tall with somewhat hairy twigs and pea-like flowers. The plant grows in waste places from Syria through the Holy Land to Stony Arabia and the Sinai. During the heat of the day leaves exude a sweet, gummy substance which hardens in the air and is collected by shaking the bushes over a spread-out cloth.

The manna tamarisk, *Tamarix mannifera*, is a multibranched shrub or a small tree 9 to 15 feet tall with rigid branches that drop off and tiny pink flowers. It is found on deserts from the Holy Land to Stony Arabia and the Sinai. At certain seasons of the year its tender stems are punctured by a small scale insect, and from these punctures a honey-like liquid exudes which quickly hardens and drops from the tree.

The flowering or manna ash, *Fraxinus ornus*, is a tree which grows from 15 to 50 feet tall. The fruits are very similar to those produced by our species of ash. It too secretes a "manna" which is exuded in the form of flakes, ("flake manna") or fragments ("common manna"), or as a viscid mass ("fat manna").

The ash of Isaiah 44:14 (KJV) is believed to be the Aleppo pine.

Aspen (Populus euphratica or P. tremula). Any of several trees of the genus *Populus* with leaves attached by flattened leafstalks so that they tremble or "quake" in the wind. The tree mentioned in 2 Samuel 5:23,24 and 1 Chronicles 14:14,15 (both KJV; balsam, RSV) is probably not the mulberry tree but rather the aspen. Mulberry leaves are soft-textured and are borne on a firm round leaf stem or petiole; for that reason they do not make a rustling sound when stirred by the breeze. Of several possible species the Euphrates popular or balsa tree, *Populus euphratica*, is the most likely. This tree is from 30 to 45 feet tall with spreading branches, growing along rivers and on stream banks throughout the area from Syria through the Holy Land to Stony Arabia, especially in the Jordan Valley. The trembling aspen, *P. tremula*, has also been suggested. It has a whitish-gray bark and its leaves tremble in the slightest breeze.

The references in Leviticus 23:40; Psalm 137:2; and Isaiah 7:2 are also believed by scholars to refer to the Euphrates poplar. The tree referred to in Psalm 137:2 is definitely not the weeping willow *Salix babylonica*, which is of Chinese origin. The reference may be to the Euphrates poplar.

It is possible that the place named "Baca" in Psalm 84:6 refers to the aspen, the valley perhaps being a place where there was an abundance of aspen trees.

Balm (*Balanites aegyptiaca, Pistacia lentiscus, Commiphora opobalsamum*). An oily aromatic resin exuded by chiefly tropical trees and shrubs and used medicinally; trees and shrubs producing this substance. References in Genesis 37:25; Jeremiah 8:22; 46:11; and 51:8 are believed to be either the Jericho balsam, *Balanites aegyptiaca*, or the lentisk or mastic tree, *Pistacia lentiscus*. The Jericho balsam is very common in Egypt, North Africa, the plains of Jericho, and the hot plains bordering on the Dead Sea. It is a small desert-loving plant, 9 to 15 feet tall with slender thorny branches and small clusters of green flowers. Its fruits are pounded and boiled to extract an oil which is said to possess medicinal and healing properties. An intoxicating drink is also made from the fruit by fermentation.

The lentisk or mastic tree is native to the Holy Land, and the reference in Genesis 43:11 is probably to this plant, since the implication is that this is a native product of the Holy Land unknown in Egypt at the time. This tree is a shrubby or bushy tree 3 to 10 feet tall with evergreen leaves. The "balm" is a fragrant gummy exudation of the sap secured by making incisions in the stems and branches usually in August. The best grades are in the form of yellow-white translucent tears or drops; they are employed in medicine as an astringent and aromatic. The poorer grades are used extensively as a varnish. Children in the East use it as chewing gum. The Greeks make a liquor flavored with this material from grape skins and call it "mastiche." The tree is native to southern Europe and the Middle East.

References to spices in 1 Kings 10:10; 2 Kings 20:13; Song of Solomon 3:6; Isaiah 39:2; and Ezekiel 27:17 are believed to be the balm of Gilead, *Commiphora opobalsamum*, which in spite of its name is not a native of Gilead or even of the Holy Land, but is indigenous to Arabia, especially the mountainous regions of Yemen. The trees were still in existence on the plain of Jericho at the time of the Roman conquest. The Roman conquerors carried branches to Rome as trophies of their victory over the Jews.

This tree is a small, stiff-branched evergreen tree seldom more than 15 feet high with straggling branches. The "balm" is obtained by making incisions in the stem and branches of the tree. The sap soon hardens into small irregular nodules which are collected. Gum is also procured from green and ripe fruit.

See MYRRH.

Barley (*Hordeum distichon*). A cereal grass bearing bearded flower spikes and edible seeds. The common barley, *Hordeum distichon*, the winter barley, *H. hexastichon*, and the spring barley, *H. vulgare*, have been cultivated in temperate regions of the world since time immemorial and today still constitute one of the principal grain foods of man. Barley and wheat were the two staple cereal crops of Egypt and the Holy Land. Barley being less expensive was mostly used for feeding cattle, although it was also used by itself or mixed with wheat and other seed as food for man (Ez 4:9–12). Barley is mentioned in the Bible over 30 times, either as a plant growing in the fields or in reference to products made from it such as barley meal, barley bread, barley cakes, and barley loaves.

Barley is sown anytime between November and March. The green ears are boiled and served with milk forming a dish frequently eaten in Egypt. The barley harvest takes place in March or April in Palestine depending on the locality. It ripens about a month earlier than wheat in Egypt: the plague of hail destroyed Pharaoh's barley but not his wheat (Ex 9:22–35).

Barley was so well known in ancient times that it supplied a unit of linear measure, 2 barley corns making a "finger breadth," 16 "a hand breadth," 24 a "span," and 48 a "cubit."

As the common food of the poor, barley was also regarded as a symbol of poverty and cheapness or worthlessness (Hos 3:2). This also explains the use of a small amount of barley meal instead of wheat meal in the jealousy offerings described in Numbers 5:15, indicating to the people the low regard in which the implicated parties were held. It explains too the force of the exclamation of shocked insult in Ezekiel 13:19. Present-day bedouins refer to their enemies as "cakes of barley bread" to indicate their utter scorn for them. This helps us interpret the dream of Gideon in Judges 7:13–15: Gideon was a very poor and humble man of the type who would most certainly have been scornfully referred to as a "cake of barley bread" by the haughty Midianites.

Bdellium (*Commiphora africana*). Aromatic gum resin similar to myrrh, produced by various trees of the genus *Commiphora* of Africa and western Asia. The reference in Genesis 2:12 and Numbers 11:7 to bdellium is believed by most scholars today to refer to a gum resin, obtained from a shrub *Commiphora africana* that grows in south Arabia and northeastern

Africa. The resin is yellowish, transparent and fragrant, and looks like a pearl.

Bean (Faba vulgaris). The references in 2 Samuel 17:27,28 and Ezekiel 4:9 are generally regarded as referring to the broad bean, *Faba vulgaris*. This species, an annual plant, is thought originally to have grown in northern Persia, but it was extensively cultivated in western Asia in very early times as a food plant. Beans have been found in the mummy coffins of Egyptian tombs, and were also cultivated by the Greeks and Romans.

Beans were held in disrepute in classical times; they were thought to cause nightmares and insanity. To dream of beans presaged trouble. Hippocrates believed that eating beans was injurious to the vision.

Beans were sown in November and ripened at the time of the spring wheat harvest. They were cut with scythes and then prepared for market. Second Samuel 17:28 and Daniel 1:12,16 may refer to beans or beans mixed with lentils.

Bitter Herbs (Cichorium endivia, Taraxacum officinale, Lactuca sativa, Centaurea sp., Silybum marianum). The "bitter herbs" of Exodus 12:8 and Numbers 9:11 seem to have been plants like endive, *Cichorium endivia*, the common chicory, *Cichorium intybus*, lettuce, *Lactuca sativa*, or the common dandelion, *Taraxacum officinale*. These are all weedy plants common in modern Egypt and western Asia, and are still eaten by people living there. Endive is native to India, and it may have been known in Egypt at the time of the exodus. There is some question as to whether the common chicory was known in Egypt at that time. The leaves of the ordinary garden lettuce are intensely bitter when bleached. This is also true of the common dandelion. Others suggest that the bitter herbs were derived from thorns and thistles.

Boxthorn, European (Lycium europaeum). Various often thorny shrubs, some species of which bear purplish flowers and brightly colored berries. The reference in Judges 9:14,15 is believed to be to the European boxthorn or desert-thorn, *Lycium europaeum*. It is a thorny shrub 6 to 12 feet tall with clustered leaves and small violet flowers eventually producing small globular red berries. It is native to and common throughout the Holy Land, especially in the region from Lebanon to the Dead Sea. It is frequently used for hedges.

Box Tree (Buxus longifolia). The long-leaved box tree is a hardy evergreen tree found in the mountainous regions of the northern part of the Holy Land, the Galilean hills, and Lebanon. It grows to a height of about 20 feet with a slender trunk seldom more than 6 or 8 inches in diameter. Its wood is very hard

A bramble bush.

and takes a fine polish. It is valued for all purposes where hardness is required, such as wood carving, turnery, and the manufacture of combs, spoons, and mathematical instruments. Writing tablets were also made of this wood. It was cultivated by the Romans for its hard wood which they inlaid with ivory for cabinets and jewel caskets. Scriptural references include Isaiah 41:19 and 60:13 (both KJV; myrtle RSV).

Bramble (Rubus sanctus, R. ulmifolius). The Palestinian bramble, *Rubus sanctus* and the closely related elmleaf bramble, *R. ulmifolius*, are prickly evergreen shrubs which spread by means of suckers. The stems and young shoots are covered with a characteristic bloom or whitish powder and short hairs. The prickles are strong, erect and hairy. The flowers are white, pink, rose, or purple in color and the fruit is round and black. The Palestine bramble grows mostly near water while the elmleaf bramble is common in thickets in Lebanon and Palestine.

Not all references to brambles are believed to refer to these two species. The bramble of Judges 9:14,15 may be the European boxthorn, *Lycium europaeum*, that of Isaiah 34:13 may be the Syrian thistle (*Notobasis syriaca*) and the spotted golden thistle (*Scolymus maculatus*), the "brier" of Micah 7:4 may be *Solanum sodomeum*, and the "briers" of Ezekiel 2:6 and 28:24 may be prickly butchers-broom, *Ruscus aculeatus*.

See THISTLE, THORN.

Broom (Retama raetam). A shrub native to Eurasia. The word translated "juniper" in the KJV has nothing to do with the true junipers but refers rather to a species of broom, known as the white broom, *Retama raetam*. Its branches are longer and flexible, forming an erect, dense bush 3 to 12 feet tall. The leaves are small and sparse, yet it forms an agreeable shade in a desert region. The white pea-like flowers are sweet and very fragrant and are borne in clusters along the twigs. It is a beautiful shrub which grows in the desert regions of Palestine, Syria, and Persia. In desert areas it is in many places the only bush that affords any shade (1 Kgs 19:4,5).

In Numbers 33:18,19 "Rithmah" ("place of broom") probably refers to the abundance of these plants at that locality. The "coals" of broom (Ps 120:4) refer to the extensive use of white broom wood in the making of charcoal.

The "juniper roots" of Job 30:4 are not the roots of either the juniper or white broom. The roots of the latter are very nauseous and could not be eaten in the manner described by Job. Job's "juniper roots" were probably an edible parasitic plant, *Cynomorium coccineum*. This plant grows in salt marshes and maritime sands. It is frequently eaten in times of food scarcity and at one time was highly prized for its supposed medicinal value in the treatment of dysentery.

Buckthorn (Rhamnus palaestina). The Palestinian buckthorn, *Rhamnus palaestina*, is a shrub or small tree attaining a height of 3 to 6 feet with velvety, thorny branches, evergreen leaves, and clusters of small flowers blooming in March or April. It grows in thickets and on hillsides from Syria and Lebanon through the Holy Land to Stony Arabia and the Sinai.

Bush (Acacia nilotica, Loranthus acaciae). Low, branching, woody plant, usually smaller than a tree. There are differences of opinion in regard to the bush out of which the Lord appeared to Moses (Ex 3:2–4). Many believed that the event was a miraculous one. Others seek some natural explanation and believe that the burning bush may have been the crimson-flowered mistletoe or acacia strap flower, *Loranthus acaciae*, which grows in great profusion as a partial parasite on the various acacia shrubs such as the thorny acacia, *Acacia nilotica*, in the Holy Land and Sinai. When in full bloom, the mistletoe imparts to the shrub or tree the appearance of being on fire because its brilliant flame-colored blossoms stand out against the green foliage and yellow flowers of the host plants.

Buttercup (Ranunculus asiaticus). The Persian buttercup, *Ranunculus asiaticus*, is one of the flowers or grasses of the field (Mt 6:28–30). It is a showy plant blooming in all brilliant colors except blue with double flowers sometimes measuring 2 inches across. It has fleshy roots which resemble small dahlia tubers.

Calamus (Acornus calamus, Andropogon aromaticus). A plant, or its aromatic root; any of a variety of tropical Asiatic palms. One of the plants that grew in Solomon's garden (Sg 4:14). It was possibly also among the substances ordered by the Lord for the holy anointment of the tabernacle (Ex 30:23 KJV), and is mentioned as one of the products in the markets of Tyre (Ez 27:19). The sweet flag, *Acornus calamus*, and the beardgrass, *Andropogon aromaticus*, have been suggested as the plants from which calamus came. The sweet flag is highly aromatic and grows in Europe and Asia, but it is not known in the Holy Land. Indigenous to India, beardgrass is highly odoriferous when bruised, and is believed to have furnished the calamus of the Bible. It yields an oil known as ginger-grass oil.

Camel's Thorn (Alhagi camelorum). There is no reference to the Camel's Thorn in the OT or NT, but there is an allusion to a plant "aspalathus" in Ecclesiasticus 24:15. Botanists believe that this is a reference to the Camel's Thorn, *Alhagi camelorum*, a many-stemmed, multi-branched shrub which is covered with sharp spines. The reference obviously is to some sweet-smelling plant. Aspalathus was also used for thickening ointments.

Cane (Saccharum officinarum). It is believed that there were two species of sugar cane indigenous to and growing wild in the Holy Land. One of these, *Saccharum sara*, is known to be only from Lebanon. The other native species is *S. biflorum*, which grows on the banks of ditches and streams from Syria and Lebanon through the Holy Land south to Stony Arabia and the Sinai. This may be the wild cane familiar to the Jews. Most authorities, however, believe that the "sweet cane" of Isaiah 43:24 was the true sugar cane, *S. officinarum*. This plant is thought to have originated in the tropics of the eastern hemisphere. It has been cultivated by man since time immemorial and is not now known in the wild state anywhere. It is a tall, stout perennial grass, maize-like in aspect with many jointed stems and a large plume-like terminal cluster of flowers. It does not bloom in the Holy Land although it is widely cultivated there. Although the art of making sugar from this plant was probably unknown to the Jews, the canes would nevertheless be highly esteemed for sweetening food and drinks and for chewing as a confection. The references to the River Kanah (Jos 16:8) and to the village or city of Kanah (Jos 19:28) are possibly to places named after this plant or a wild variety which perhaps grew abundantly along the river or in the village.

Caper Plant (*Capparis sincula*). Spiny, trailing shrub of Mediterranean region; the flower bud of this shrub. The word "desire" in Ecclesiastes 12:5 may actually refer to the caper berry. The common caper or caper berry, *Capparis sicula*, grows profusely in Syria, Lebanon, the Holy Land, and in the mountain valleys of Sinai. The plant may sometimes grow upright, but more generally spreads itself weakly over the ground like a vine, covering rocks, ruins, and old walls like ivy. The young flower buds, pickled in vinegar, were used by the ancients as a condiment for meat. The berries were also used in cooking.

The peculiar suitability of this plant to a description of man's old age depends both upon the structure of the caper fruit and its stimulating nature, exciting both hunger and thirst and thus strengthening the appetite which in old age has a tendency to become sluggish. To say "the caper berry shall fail" indicated that even the stimulating effect of the caper was unable to excite the appetite of an old man any longer. The fruit hangs on stalks and the over-ripe berry is thought to be suggestive of the drooping head of an old man bowed low by the weight of many years.

Other references in Scripture to the caper plant may include Exodus 12:22; Leviticus 14:6; Numbers 19:18; 1 Kings 4:33; Psalms 51:7; John 19:29; and Hebrews 9:19. In these references the "hyssop" of the KJV is thought to be the caper. A number of scholars point out that the caper is found in lower Egypt where Moses commanded the children of Israel to use the hyssop for sprinkling the blood of the sacrificial lamb onto the lintels and door posts of their houses, so that the destroying angel would pass them by. It occurs also in the Sinai desert, where it was to be used in the ceremonial cleaning of the leper. It is found on the ruined walls of Jerusalem, where Solomon spoke of seeing the hyssop that springs out of the wall (1 Kgs 4:33). It has always been considered to possess the implied cleansing properties.

See Sorghum.

Carob Tree (*Ceratonia siliqua*). Evergreen of the Mediterranean region having edible pods. Scholars generally agree that the pods of the carob or locust tree, *Ceratonia siliqua*, were the "husks" of Jesus' parable of the prodigal son (Lk 15:16). The carob is an attractive evergreen leguminous tree that is very common throughout the Holy Land, Syria, and Egypt. The pods are most abundant in April and May, and contain numerous pea-like seeds embedded in an agreeably flavored mucilaginous sweetish pulp. The pods are also used abundantly now as they were in antiquity for feeding cattle, horses, and pigs. In time of scarcity, they are used as human food and perhaps even regularly by the very poor. When completely ripe, the pods are full of a sweet dark-colored palatable honey-like syrup, and the Arabs eat them today with considerable relish, considering their flavor to be like that of manna. The carob is frequently mentioned in the Talmud as a source of good food for domestic animals. The seeds of the carob were formerly employed as a standard of weight and are the source of the term "carat." Some commentators suggest that the "locust" eaten by John the Baptist (Mt 3:4) were not insects but the fruit of the carob tree.

Cassia (*Cinnamomum cassia, Saussurea lappa*). Tree of tropical Asia with bark similar but inferior to cinnamon. The "cassia" of Exodus 30:24 and Ezekiel 27:19 is the cassia bark tree, *Cinnamomum cassia*. In Psalm 45:8 the reference seems to be to the Indian orris, *Saussurea lappa*.

The cassia and other Indian spices were apparently secured by Moses and Solomon through trade, the cassia bark probably coming from Ceylon. Cassia and cinnamon, although native to Ceylon, the Malabar coast, Malaysia, and the East Indies, were probably known in the Holy Land and Egypt from early days. The spices are secured from the inner bark of the tree. Cassia bark has always been considered inferior to that of the true cinnamon, being coarser and more pungent. It is often used to adulterate cinnamon. The buds may also be added to food as a seasoning. The smaller leaves and pods are sometimes used medicinally.

The Indian orris is a composite from the Himalaya Mountains of Kashmir. Its fragrant roots are gathered in great quantities and shipped to Bombay and then to ports on the Persian Gulf and Red Sea. It is employed medicinally and also as an aphrodisiac; its chief use is in perfume.

Castor Oil Plant (*Ricinus communis*). Large plant, native to tropical Africa and Asia, cultivated for ornamental reasons and for extraction of oil from its seeds. The gourd of Jonah 4:6,7 was probably the ordinary castor bean, *Ricinus communis*, which provided Jonah with shade and was later attacked by a "worm" so that it withered and died. The castor bean is a tender shrub, growing 3 to 12 or more feet tall with huge leaves that resemble the outstretched human hand. The castor bean plant is found in waste places especially near water in both Lebanon and the

The cedar of Lebanon.

Holy Land and often is cultivated. In hot climates it becomes tree-like and affords a dense shade by the abundance of its huge umbrella-like leaves. It is known in the Orient for the rapidity of its growth. The oil extracted from the seeds of the castor bean was used by the Jews in ceremonial rites, and is mentioned among the five kinds of oil which rabbinical tradition sanctioned for such use. The seeds themselves are poisonous when eaten.

Cedar (*Cedrus libani*). Any of several coniferous evergreen trees of the genus native to the Old World. With few exceptions the references to "cedar" are to the well-known cedar of Lebanon, *Cedrus libani*. This is a noble tree, the tallest and most massive with which the Israelites were acquainted. It grows quite rapidly, attaining a height of up to 120 feet with a trunk diameter of as much as 8 feet. In Solomon's day these trees were obviously abundant on the mountains of Lebanon, but now because of excessive lumbering and the grazing of goats, they are very rare. The cedar of Lebanon was held in high esteem not only for its vigor, beauty, and age but also for the fragrance and remarkable lasting qualities of the wood. It was employed to symbolize grandeur, might, majesty, dignity, lofty stature, and wide expansion. References in Ezekiel 17:3,22–24 and 31:3–18 beautifully illustrate how these lofty kings of the forest were used by the prophet to symbolize and typify worldly strength, power, and glory.

The frequent references in Samuel, Kings, and Chronicles show that the wood of the cedar of Lebanon was preferred above all other wood for building purposes. This was because of its tremendous size, remarkable durability, and beautiful fragrance. King Solomon, Hiram, Cyrus, the kings of Assyria, and the rulers of all neighboring countries plundered the mountain heights of Lebanon for this wood with which to embellish their palaces. Planks and perhaps masts for the great fleet maintained at Tyre were made of this wood as were Solomon's palanquins or sedans (his "chariots"). The temple begun by David and completed by Solomon was constructed of this wood. Solomon drafted 30,000 Israelites who went to Lebanon in shifts to aid King Hiram and his slaves; they all but destroyed these beautiful forests.

Several passages may not refer to the cedar of Lebanon but to some other tree. These include Numbers 19:6; 24:6; Leviticus 14:4,6–8,49–52; Ezekiel 27:5; and 31:8. The Pentateuch passages may refer to the Phoenician juniper, *Sabina phoenica*, and the Ezekiel passages to the Aleppo pine, *Pinus halepensis* (q.v.).

Cinnamon (*Cinnamomum zeylanicum*). Two varieties of trees of this genus, native to tropical Asia, with aromatic bark which, when ground, is used as a spice. The cinnamon of Exodus 30:23; Proverbs 7:17; Song of Solomon 4:14; and Revelation 18:13 is undoubtedly *Cinnamomum zeylanicum*. The tree is a rather low-growing one, never getting more than 30 feet high with a smooth ash-colored bark and widespread branches and white flowers. Its shiny, beautifully veined evergreen leaves grow about 9 inches long and 2 inches wide.

The cinnamon of commerce is taken from the inner bark peeled from trees 4 to 5 years old; in hilly country the trees must grow a few years longer before they can be stripped. The finest grade of cinnamon comes from younger branches. Incisions are made lengthwise with a sharp knife on both sides of the branch, and the bark is then removed in the form of a hollow cylinder. These cylinder sticks or "quills" are tied into bundles of about one pound each. The cinnamon is gathered in the same way as cassia bark, but it is far superior to it in quality.

The Jews always regarded cinnamon as a deliciously fragrant substance and valued it highly as a spice and a perfume. It was one of the principal ingredients used in the manufacture of the precious ointments or "holy oil" which Moses was commanded to use in the tabernacle for anointing the sacred vessels and officiating priests. It was undoubtedly very costly and precious.

Citron Tree (*Tetraclinis articulata*). Tree native to Asia bearing lemonlike fruit with a thick, fragrant rind. The "thyine wood" of Revelation 18:12 (KJV) refers to the wood of the sandarac tree, *Tetraclinis articulata*. It is a conifer closely related to the arborvitae. It seldom exceeds a height of 30 feet and has hard, dark-colored, durable fragrant wood which takes a fine polish. The wood was one of the most highly prized woods of the ancients, who employed it extensively for cabinet work. It was commonly referred to as being worth its weight in gold. The wood, owing to its resinous properties, is slow to decay and remains practically uninjured by insects.

Coriander (Coriandrum sativum). The references in Exodus 16:31 and Numbers 11:7 are clearly to the common coriander plant, *Coriandrum sativum.* This is an annual herb, 16 to 20 inches tall, with slender round stems, white or reddish flowers, deeply cut leaves, and a heavy odor. The seeds are pearl-like, about 1/4 inch in diameter, quite aromatic, and employed chiefly in confectionary. They are also used medicinally. The coriander was found quite commonly growing along with grain in cultivated fields throughout the Holy Land. It grows wild in Egypt and was used by the ancients both as a condiment and as a medicine. The leaves are quite aromatic and are used in soups and for flavoring puddings, curries, and wines. The coriander is still used today as a spice by the Arabs. In Scripture it is mentioned only in connection with manna which was said to resemble coriander seeds in size, shape, and color.

Cotton (Gossypium herbaceum). Any of various plants or shrubs of this genus grown in warm climates for the soft white fiber attached to their seeds and the oil from these seeds. The "green" of the KJV in Esther 1:6 is undoubtedly a reference to the Levant cotton, *Gossypium herbaceum,* which was cultivated since time immemorial in the Far East. Alexander the Great brought it back from India. It is probable that the Jews became acquainted with cotton during the period of their Persian captivity under King Ahasuerus.

Cotton is grown as an annual but in its native habitat it is a perennial, growing to become an erect, freely branching shrub as much as 6 feet tall. The flowers are large, showy, and yellow with a purple center, fading to pink or red. The fruit or "boll" splits open when fully ripe and a mass of fine white or golden brown filaments is extruded. The seeds are attached to these cotton filaments or fibers. After the seeds are removed the fibers are woven into thread.

Cucumber (Cucumis chate, C. sativus). The cucumber is an annual climbing or trailing vine, the origin of which is unknown. It has been cultivated in all the warm countries of the Old World since prehistoric times. Cucumbers are usually eaten raw; a cucumber and a barley cake or some other kind of bread often constitute a meal. The reference to "a lodge in a garden of cucumbers" (Is 1:8) refers to the crudely built small house or lodge often set up in Palestinian cucumber fields and vineyards.

The cucumber was cultivated extensively in Egypt in ancient times, and along with fish, melons, leeks, onions, and garlic formed the common diet of the land; both the Israelites and the Egyptian masses subsisted on it. The Israelites apparently became quite attached to this diet during their 400-year sojourn in Egypt (Nm 11:5).

Cummin (Cuminum cyminum). The references in Isaiah 28:25,27 and Matthew 23:23 are clearly to the cummin, *Cuminum cyminum,* a common annual plant of the carrot family said to be native to Egypt and the region of the eastern Mediterranean. It has long been cultivated for its powerfully aromatic and pungent seeds which are similar to caraway seeds but larger. They do not have as agreeable a taste as caraway seeds but nevertheless were used extensively as a flavor or spice and sometimes were even mixed with flour in making bread. Cummin was also used medicinally and as a condiment with fish and meats.

Cummin was included only by inference in the Mosaic law governing tithing; hence the charge of Jesus that the scribes and Pharisees punctiliously tithed mint, anise, and cummin but overlooked and ignored more important matters such as justice, mercy, and trustworthiness.

Cypress (Cupressus sempervirens horizontalis). The cypress is a massive tall-growing evergreen with scale-like leaves and is widely distributed in the mountainous regions of the Bible lands. On Mt Lebanon and Mt Hermon it grows together with the cedar and oak. Its usual height is 50 to 60 feet but it may grow as tall as 80 feet. The cones are rounded and smaller than most pine cones. Cypress wood is very hard and durable and was employed by the ancients in the manufacture of idols. It is said to have been used extensively in ship building by the Phoenicians, Cretans, and Greeks. There is general agreement that the "gopher wood" of Genesis 6:14 is cypress because the wood is very durable. The ancient Egyptians used it for making coffins.

It is believed that the references in Isaiah 41:19 and 60:13 to fir trees are references to cypress. The algum trees of 2 Chronicles 2:8 are likely cypress logs.

Darnel Grass (Lolium temulentum). It is generally agreed that the "tares" of the KJV (Mt 13:24–30) are the annual or bearded darnel grass, *Lolium temulentum.* Darnel grass is a strong grass closely resembling wheat or rye in appearance. The seeds are much smaller than those of wheat or rye but it is extremely difficult to distinguish it from wheat or rye in its early stages. If it is not eradicated early but

The anise bush.

is left until the time of harvest, it is cut down with the wheat and subsequently very difficult to separate. The seeds are poisonous, either due to some chemicals naturally present or because of a fungus that grows within the seeds. Theophrastus and other early Greek writers were well acquainted with the poisonous effects of the darnel, and the plant is sometimes referred to as the drunken darnel. It is also said to cause blindness.

Dill (Anethum graveolens). Dill is a weedy annual plant resembling parsley and fennel, 12 to 20 inches tall with yellow flowers. The reference in Matthew 23:23 (KJV) to anise is probably a reference to the dill. This plant is widely cultivated for seeds which are aromatic and carminative. It is also used for flavoring vegetables (especially pickles) and in medicine. Dill water is obtained from the seeds by distillation and provides an oil used medicinally. It is cultivated in the Holy Land.

Ebony (Diospyros ebenaster, D. ebenum, D. melanoxylon). Chiefly tropical tree of southern Asia with hard, dark-colored heartwood. Ebony comes from the date plum or date tree, *Diospyros ebenaster* and *D. melanoxylon*, of India and is quite different from the date palm. It was sent by Phoenician ships across the Ara-

bian Sea and up the Red Sea to the market in Tyre from which it was carried overland by camel caravans. The outer wood of these trees is white and soft, but when old the interior wood becomes hard, black, heavy, and durable and still constitutes most of the costly ebony of commerce. Ebony takes on a fine polish and is highly valued for cabinet work, turnery, the manufacture of fancy ornamental articles and instruments, and as a veneer for other woods.

Ezekiel mentions ivory and ebony together (27:15). Ebony was and still is frequently inlaid with ivory with which it contrasts so strikingly in color.

Another source of ebony is *D. ebenum* which comes from Ceylon.

Fig, Fig Tree (Ficus carica). Any of several trees or shrubs of this genus, native to the Mediterranean region; its edible fruit. The common fig, mentioned some 60 times, is one of the most important Bible plants. Its leaves are spoken of first in Genesis 3:7. The fig is generally regarded as native to southwestern Asia and Syria, but already in early times was also cultivated extensively in Egypt and the Holy Land where it was one of the principal foods. First Samuel 25:18 states that a part of the present sent by Abigail to David consisted of 200 cakes of figs.

The fig tree is still common in the Holy Land both in the wild and cultivated form. In addition to the extensive fig orchards it is quite common to find one or more fig trees in an individual's private garden (2 Kgs 18:31; Mi 4:4). In favorable situations it grows as a tree of 20 or 30 feet in height. When standing singly it often forms a conspicuous object in the landscape (Mk 11:13). Its trunk may measure 2 to 3 feet in diameter. Trees of this sort are often seen overshadowing wells. It is frequently planted in the corners of vineyards even today, as in NT times (Lk 13:6–9).

The fig tree has a very peculiar type of fruit called a syconium, which is actually a very much enlarged and fleshy receptacle. It is pollinated by a wasp without which it cannot set its fruit; this was discovered when it was first transplanted in California. Normally two crops of figs are produced each year; the first or winter figs ripening in June, the second or summer figs being produced on the new wood in August or September. Often when the summer figs are just starting some ripe winter figs may still be found on the tree half hidden by foliage.

The fig puts out its earliest fruit buds before its leaves, the former in February and the latter in April or May; when the leaves are out the fruit ought to be ripe (Mt 21:19).

Whenever the prophets of old berated the

people for their wickedness, they always threatened that the vine and the fig crops would be destroyed and when they held out the promise of great rewards, they said that the vine and fig crop would be restored (Jer 8:13; Hos 2:12; Jl 1:7,12; Mi 4:4; Zec 3:10).

Figs are used medicinally in the East and are commonly employed as a remedy for boils and other skin eruptions (2 Kgs 20:7).

In addition to the Hebrew and Greek words for the fig and the fig tree, there are four words referring to different stages or conditions of the fruit. The word used in Jeremiah 8:13 refers to the fig fruit; in Song of Solomon 2:13 the word used refers to the green or unripened fruit which remains on the tree through the winter. The word used in Hosea 9:10 and elsewhere refers to the first ripe or early fig, and the word used in 1 Samuel 25:18; 2 Kings 20:7; and elsewhere speaks of a cake of dried figs, the main product of the tree kept for winter use.

The word "Bethphage" mentioned in the NT signifies literally a "house of green figs" probably because it was in a dark ravine where figs did not ripen.

Fir Tree (*Abies cilicica*). Various evergreen trees of this genus with flat needles and erect cones. In all probability most of the references in Scripture to the fir are references to the pine, cypress, or juniper. The only true fir (*Abies cilicica*) in the Holy Land grows in the higher parts of Lebanon and the mountains northward. It attains a height of from 30 to 75 feet and is widely cultivated. Other references to the fir are to the Aleppo pine.

Flax (*Linum usitatissimum*). Any of several plants of this genus, one particularly being widely cultivated for the linseed oil from its seeds and the fine textile fibers from its stems. Flax is the oldest known of the textile fibers. Cotton is identified only once in the Bible (Est 1:6). There is no mention of any other fiber plant being cultivated in Egypt or the Holy Land in biblical days, and for that reason it is believed that linen was the material out of which clothes other than woolen ones were made. Linen was also used for domestic purposes such as towels (Jn 13:4,5), napkins (Jn 11:44), girdles and undergarments (Is 3:23; Mk 14:51), nets (Is 19:8,9), and measuring lines (Ez 40:3). Flax was an important crop in Egypt and was known and used in the Holy Land before the arrival of the Israelites (Jos 2:6). It was woven into garments by the ancient Egyptians and wrapped around mummies. The Greeks and the Hebrews also employed it for the winding sheets of the dead (Mt 27:59; Mk 15:46; Lk 23:53). The priests serving in the temple were to wear nothing but linen clothes, and a mixed cloth of wool and flax together

was strictly forbidden to the Jews (Lv 19:19; Dt 22:11).

At least three kinds of linen were used in biblical times, and apparently there were particular uses for each kind. Ordinary linen of coarsest texture is mentioned in Leviticus 6:10; Ezekiel 9:2; Daniel 10:5; and Revelation 15:6. The second type of linen of superior quality is mentioned in Exodus 26:1 and 39:27. A third type of linen of finest texture and high cost is mentioned in 1 Chronicles 15:27; Esther 8:15; and Revelation 19:8.

The common flax plant grows from 1 to 4 feet tall with a simple, slender, wire-like stem and numerous small, pale, lance-like, green leaves. The failure of the flax crop is listed as one of God's punishments (Hos 2:9). The manufacture of linen from flax fibers was a domestic industry of Jewish women (Prv 31:13,19), ranging from ordinary clothing to the robes and aprons worn by the priest and temple attendants. Linen was also used for wicks in lamps (Is 42:3).

Flax capsules are often called "bolls" and the expression in Exodus 9:31 (KJV) means that it had reached maturity. When the bolls were ripe, the flax plants were harvested and tied into bundles or sheaves. These were then immersed in water for several weeks which caused them to "ret" (i.e., the fibers separate from the nonfibrous portion of the stems). The bundles were then opened and the retted stems spread out to dry (Jos 2:6), after which they were combed or hackled to remove the fibers. The fibers are from one to three feet long and are of great tensile strength and durability.

Flower. The word "flower" is used several times in Scripture. Sometimes the context makes it possible to identify a particular flower, though this is not always the case. In Isaiah 28:4 the glorious beauty of Ephraim is described as nothing but a "fading flower," and in Job 14:2 man's life span on this earth is described as "a flower." Since the Jews were close to the soil and its products, it was natural that preachers, prophets, and writers would draw on plants to illustrate their statements. The more common the plant the more likely it would be that all members of the audience would be acquainted with it and therefore appreciate the reference. Thus it seems "flower" ordinarily referred to a number of common plants in the area.

Forest. Dense growth of trees, with other plants, covering a large area. There are many references to "forest" or "forests" in the Bible. Where these terms are used in connection with a definitely identified area or locality, the botanical character of the forest may readily be inferred. Often the terms are used very generally, (e.g., Ps 50:10). The concept imparted in such cases is that of a wooded land and not of a particular kind of tree. In Jeremiah 46:23 the "forest" to be cut down is that of Egypt and, furthermore, of the limited part of the country with which the Jews were acquainted. In such cases it might be possible to identify the type of tree most common in the locality.

Frankincense (Boswellia sp.). Aromatic genus resin used chiefly as incense. Frankincense is obtained from three species of a single genus of plants which grow in southern Arabia, Ethiopia, Somaliland, India, and the East Indies. The trees are large in size, related to the turpentine or terebinth tree, and to those which produce balsam and myrrh. The gum has a bitter taste and gives off a strong odor in the form of a volatile oil when warmed or burned. It is obtained by successive incisions in the bark of the trunk and in the branches of living trees. The first incision yields the purest and whitest gum while that obtained from later incisions is spotted with yellow or red. It is believed that the Hebrews imported all their frankincense from Arabia, especially from the region about Sheba.

Frankincense is mentioned 21 times in the Bible (e.g., Ex 30:34; 1 Chr 9:29; Neh 13:9; Sg 3:6; 4:6,14; Mt 2:11; Rv 18:13), and was probably employed almost exclusively in the sacrificial services of the tabernacle and temple until the time of Solomon. It has always been the most important incense resin in the world.

Fruit. The terms "fruit" and "fruits" occur frequently throughout the Scripture. In many cases the reference is clearly to the fig, grape, or olive, the three most important fruits of the Holy Land. In Song of Solomon 4:16 there is a reference to fruits cultivated by Solomon in his garden. It is generally believed that his gardens were a sort of combined herbarium and arboretum containing plants from all parts of the then-known world.

In Deuteronomy 26:2 there is a reference to the "first fruits," the basis for tithing. The first fruits of the land included the products of all plants cultivated by a man, not only the plants themselves—cereal grains, figs, olives, and the like—but also the wine made from grapes. The precious fruits referred to in Deuteronomy 33:14 probably included the same items. The word "fruit" is often used in the figurative sense, as in Galatians 5:22.

The references in Matthew 3:10; 12:33; Luke 3:8,9; and Romans 1:13 to good fruit and corrupt fruit are apparently to the fig which under favorable conditions will produce delicious fruits and in other circumstances will yield only hard and inedible fruit. The references in Amos 8:1,2 to a basket of summer fruit

and in Isaiah 28:4 to hasty fruit are also references to the fig.

Galbanum (Ferula galbaniflua). Galbanum is a malodorous yellowish or brownish gum resin containing the chemical substance umbelliferone, obtained from several species of plants related to the fennel, native to Syria and Persia. The gum is a natural exudation of the stem or is obtained by making a transverse incision in the young stem a few inches above the ground. The milky juice soon hardens and forms one of the kinds of commercial galbanum. Its odor is strongly balsamic, pungent, and disagreeable when burned. Galbanum was one of the ingredients used to form the "holy incense" (Ex 30:34).

Gourd, Wild (Citrullus colocynthis). There has been considerable difference of opinion regarding the meaning of the words translated "wild gourds" (2 Kgs 4:39) or "gall" (Dt 29:18; 32:32; Ps 69:21; Jer 8:14; 9:15; 23:15; Lam 3:5,19; Am 6:12; Mt 27:34; Acts 8:23). Most scholars today believe the plant referred to was the colocynth, *Citrullus colocynthis*, a cucumber-like vine which trails on the ground or climbs over shrubs and fences. The fruit contains a soft spongy pulp which is intensely bitter and poisonous, a strong cathartic.

The colocynth is common in western Asia and in the entire Mediterranean region. In the Holy Land it is found in the dry sandy flats around the Mediterranean Sea, the Red Sea, and the Dead Sea, and on the plains of Engedi, Beersheba, Jericho, Jaffa, and Sidon. It has been suggested that the vine of Sodom (Dt 32:32) is the colocynth, and that the gall referred to above is derived from the colocynth. Throughout Scripture it is used as a symbol of bitter calamity. A number of scholars have translated the knops of 1 Kings 6:18 and 7:24 as "gourds."

Some have suggested the globe cucumber, *Cucumis prophetarum*, as the plant of Elisha's miracle. However, the fruits of this vine are ordinarily less than an inch in diameter and are covered with prickles. Though bitter they are not poisonous and for these reasons this plant does not seem to fit the story in 2 Kings. It has also been suggested that the plant involved may have been the squirting cucumber, *Ecballium elaterium*, common throughout the region. Since its fruits are covered with prickles and spines, it seems unlikely that it would be collected for food.

Grass (Gramineae). Various plants of this family, usually having narrow leaves, hollow jointed stems, and spikes or clusters of small flowers. The word "grass" occurs over 60 times in the Bible, in many cases being used figuratively. Because its green herbage fades rapidly and withers under the parching heat of the sun, it afforded the biblical writers a ready symbol of the fleeting nature of human fame and fortune. In many cases the word probably refers to all tender green herbaceous plants, rather than to grasses in particular.

The word used in Genesis 1:11 (KJV) is probably the nearest equivalent of our "grass" as distinguished from "herbs." The "grass" of the field (Mt 6:30; Lk 12:28) probably refers to the lily, as does the "flower of the field" mentioned in Isaiah 40:6–8.

The grass of Genesis 41:2,18; Job 8:11 and Hosea 13:15 may be either the papyrus or the reed. The references in Proverbs 27:25 and Isaiah 15:6 to hay seems to be to the stems of tall grasses.

There are about 460 different kinds of grasses found in the Holy Land. The six grasses most abundant in Bible times were *Aegilops variabilis, Alopecurus anthoxanthoides, Avena sterilis, Eragrostis megastachya, Nardurus orientalis,* and *Polypogon monspeliensis.* All of these were native grasses quite common to the Holy Land, and were undoubtedly familiar to both OT and NT writers. Grasses have elongated leaves with parallel veins. They produce grain fruits which contain a food reserve and an embryo, the sperm.

Hedge (Rhamnus palaestina, Balanites aegyptiaca, Lycium europaeum). Row of closely planted shrubs or low-growing trees forming a fence or boundary. A number of plants were used to provide hedges in Bible times. One of these was the Palestine buckthorn, *Rhamnus palaestina.* This plant is a shrub or a small tree growing from 3 to 6 feet tall with velvety thorny branches, evergreen leaves, and clusters of small flowers blooming in March and April. It grows in thickets and on hillsides from Syria through the Holy Land to Stony Arabia and the Sinai. The Jericho balsam, *Balanites aegyptiaca,* and the European boxthorn, *Lycium europaeum,* are also prickly shrubs widely used as hedges in the Holy Land and may be the plants referred to in Proverbs 15:19 (KJV) and Hosea 2:6. Another possibility is one of the hawthorns, *Crataegus,* of which there are five species native to the Holy Land. The hawthorn has spines and small red fruit about the size of a cherry which has an apple flavor.

Henna (Lawsonia inermis). Tree or shrub of Asia and northern Africa with fragrant reddish or white flowers and leaves from which a reddish dye is made. The plant referred to in Song of Solomon 1:14 and 4:13 and translated as "camphire" (KJV) is believed by scholars today to refer to the henna plant, *Lawsonia inermis.* The true camphor is a Chinese plant, and it is doubtful that it was known in Asia Minor in Solomon's time. The henna is a na-

tive of northern India and grows wild in the Sudan, Egypt, Arabia, Syria, Lebanon, and the Holy Land. It grows from 4 to 12 feet tall, and its scent is similar to that of roses.

Henna leaves are dried, crushed into a powder, mixed with water and made into a paste that has been used since time immemorial as a cosmetic. A number of mummies have been found decorated with henna. Henna was used to provide a bright yellow, orange, or red color to the fingernails, toenails, the tips of the fingers, the palms of the hand, and the soles of the feet of young girls. Men also used it for coloring their beards and the manes and tails of horses. The dye had to be renewed once every two or three weeks. This use of henna as a cosmetic was common in Egypt at the time the children of Israel were there as slaves; they were undoubtedly familiar with it. The provision in Deuteronomy 21:11,12 suggests that the use of henna was frowned on as something pagan.

Holm Tree (Ilex aquifolium). The Holm tree or holly occurs only in the mountains of Syria. It has been suggested that this is the tree referred to in Isaiah 44:14 and in the apocryphal book of Susannah. It is more likely that the tree referred to is the Holm oak, *Quercus ilex,* which is common from the coasts of Syria to Judea. This tree is an evergreen which grows to a height of 60 feet.

Hyacinth (Hyacinthus orientalis). The lily referred to in Song of Solomon 2:1,2,16; 4:5; and 6:2–4 may well be the garden hyacinth, *Hyacinthus orientalis.* It is native to and very common in the fields and rocky places in the Holy Land, Lebanon, and northward. Its flowers in the wild form are always deep blue and very fragrant.

See LILY.

Hyssop (Origanum maru). Woody plant native to Asia with spikes of small blue flowers and aromatic leaves used as a condiment and in perfumery. There is little agreement among botanists as to the exact identity of the biblical "hyssop." Some have suggested *Hyssopus officinalis,* the well-known garden herb now called "hyssop." However, this plant is not native either to the Holy Land or Egypt, being found only in southern Europe. Moreover, it does not fit the requirements of the biblical plant.

The "hyssop" of the OT is likely the Syrian or Egyptian marjoram, *Orignum maru.* It is referred to in Exodus 12:22; Leviticus 14:4, 6,52; Numbers 19:6,18; 1 Kings 4:33; Psalm 51:7; and Hebrews 9:19. The marjorams are mints growing under favorable conditions 1½ to 3 feet tall but more often are dwarfed when growing in rock crevices and walls (cf. 1 Kgs 4:33). An aromatic substance is obtained from the crushed and dried leaves. If gathered together in a bunch with leaves and flowers, the hairy stems of the marjoram would hold a liquid very well and would make an excellent sprinkler.

The hyssop of the crucifixion passages in the NT (Jn 19:29) is probably the sorghum.

Ivy (*Hedera helix*). The English ivy is a high-climbing evergreen vine which spreads over rocks and walls by means of numerous short adhesive aerial rootlets growing along the stems and branches. Apparently it is this plant that is referred to in 2 Maccabees 6:7.

Juniper (*Juniperus* sp.). Variety of evergreen tree or shrub. The plant referred to in Jeremiah 17:6 and 48:6 and translated in the KJV "heath" is probably the savin or juniper. The Phoenician juniper, *Juniperus phoenicia*, is found in the hills and rocky places of Stony Arabia. The savin juniper, *J. sabina*, is common throughout the deserts, plains, and rocky places of Syria and Palestine. These references are to the brown-berried cedar, or sharp cedar, *J. oxycedrus*. It is ordinarily a hemispheric or prostrate shrub, though in especially favorable habitats it may attain a height of 15 to 20 feet. The species is common in the mountainous regions of Syria, Lebanon, the Anti-Lebanon, Galilee, Gilead, and Bashan, often inhabiting the most barren and rocky parts of the desert or lonely cracks and inaccessible fissures of rocky cliffs. This fits very well with the reference in Jeremiah.

The common juniper, *J. communis*, has also been suggested as a common shrub of the desert places.

Some have suggested that the cedarwood of Leviticus 14:4–6 and Numbers 19:6 is actually the wood of the brown-berried juniper or the Phoenician juniper.

Laurel or Sweet Bay (*Laurus nobilis*). Shrub or tree native to the Mediterranean region. While the reference in Psalm 37:35 may be to the cedar of Lebanon, most scholars refer the "green bay tree" of the psalmist to the sweet bay, *Laurus nobilis*, a native of the Holy Land, inhabiting thickets and woods from the coast to the middle montane zone. It is an evergreen tree attaining a height from 40 to 60 feet. The flowers of the green bay tree are small and greenish-white and the fruit is a one-seeded black berry about the size of a small grape. The leaves are thick, lance-shaped, and glossy. From an early period the bay has symbolized prosperity, authority, and success.

Even though the tree is abundant on Mt Carmel and around Hebron, it is generally not common in the Holy Land. Its leaves are still used as a condiment and its fruit, leaves, and bark have long been used in medicine.

Lentil (*Lens esculenta*). The lentil plant to which Genesis 25:29–34; 2 Samuel 17:27–29; 23:11; and Ezekiel 4:9 refer is a small erect annual vetch-like plant with slender stems and tendril-bearing leaves. It produces small, white, violet-striped flowers with flat, pea-like pods in which the lentils are borne. There are three or four kinds of lentils, all highly regarded in the countries in which they are grown. Lentils are still widely cultivated in Egypt and the Holy Land for their nutritious seeds. A fairly good bread may be made from lentils and barley; this kind of bread is quite common in parts of Egypt where it is widely eaten by the poor.

The barley of 1 Chronicles 11:13 may be a mistranslation for lentil (see also 2 Sm 23:11).

Lily (*Lilium* sp., *Anemone coronaria*, *Anthemis palaestina*, *Nymphaea alba*, *Gladiolus byzantinus*). Any of various plants of the genus *Lilium* having large, variously colored, trumphet-shaped flowers; and related plants. The lily is one of the most famous of all the plants in the Bible, but it is also one about which there has been considerable difference of opinion. It seems probable that several kinds of plants, perhaps five or six, are called lilies in the KJV. Most authorities regard the Palestine anemone and wind flower, *Anemone coronaria*, as the "lily of the field" which surpassed Solomon in all his glory. These flowers are found in every part of the Holy Land in profusion; the most common forms are scarlet or yellow but the Palestine anemone may also be blue, purple, rose, or white in color. The flower attains a diameter of 2¾ inches.

An alternative suggestion is the Palestinian chamomile, *Anthemis palaestina*, a common white daisy-like plant. The chamomile is gathered like dry grass and "cast into the furnace" when it dries up.

Another proposed plant is *Lilium chalcedonicum*, the scarlet or Martagon lily. The statement in Song of Solomon 5:13—"his lips like lilies"—would better fit this plant than the Palestine anemone. The reference is apparently to a rare plant of exceptional beauty. The scarlet lily is rare in the Holy Land; indeed some botanists doubt that it occurs there.

The references in 1 Kings 7:19,22,26 and 2 Chronicles 4:5 are probably to the water lily, *Nymphaea alba*, which served as the pattern. The water lily is quite common in Europe and also in the Holy Land and northern Africa.

Still others suggest that the references to lilies are to one of the gladiolas, *Gladiolus byzantinus*, whose purple color would match Solomon's robe.

The place named Susa (Neh 1:1; Est 1:2) may refer to the fact that lilies were very common around palaces. It has also been suggested that the title of two of the psalms, Psalm 45 ("Shoshannim") and Psalm 60 ("Shushan Eduth") refers to lilies.

Lotus Bush (*Zizyphus lotus*). The "shady trees" of Job 40:21,22 may be the lotus bush of the Middle East, *Zizyphus lotus*, a shrub or low tree which grows to a height of about 5 feet with smooth, zig-zag, whitish branches.

Other commentators believe that the shady trees of Job are large-leafed trees such as the plane tree, *Platanus orientalis*, or the Oleander, *Nerium oleander*. This suggestion is based on the assumption that the animal described in Job 40 is the hippopotamus, and it seems unlikely that the hippopotamus would live under a lotus bush or even be found in places where this shrub grows. These individuals regard the plane tree or the oleander as more likely.

Mallow (*Atriplex* sp.). The Hebrew word used in Job 30:4 implies saltiness, and for this reason botanists believe that it refers to one of the species of the saltwort or orach. Twenty-one species of saltwort occur in the Holy Land, almost all of which are common and could well meet the requirements of the text. *A. halimus* is the species usually suggested, a strong-growing bushy shrub related to the spinach, 1 to 3 feet tall with small inconspicuous flowers. It is abundant on the shores of the Mediterranean and in the region about the Dead Sea where it may attain a height of 5 to 10 feet.

Some botanists believe the plant referred to is one of the true mallows, *Malva*. These are soft and mucilaginous, not unwholesome, and they may well have been gathered and eaten in times of scarcity.

Mandrake (*Mandragora officinarum*). The mandrake or love apple is a stemless herbaceous perennial related to the nightshade, potato, and tomato. It has a large, beet-like, often forked tap root from the top of which arise many dark leaves about a foot long and 4 inches wide. The plant is slightly poisonous, and the thick tap roots have some resemblance in shape to the lower parts of the human body. For this reason certain aphrodisiac properties were ascribed to it (cf. Gn 30:14–16).

The love apple was a common plant in deserted fields throughout the Holy Land. It is native to the entire Mediterranean region, southern Europe, and Asia Minor. Because neither the flowers nor the fruit of the mandrake "give a smell," either pleasant or unpleasant, the reference in Song of Solomon 7:13 may be to the citron, or to the common edible field mushroom, *Agaricus campestris*.

Melon (*Cucumis melo*, *Citrullus vulgaris*). Any of several varieties of these two related vines having a hard rind and juicy flesh. The melons of Numbers 11:5 may be either the muskmelon, *Cucumis melo*, or the watermelon, *Citrullus vulgaris*. It may be that both fruits are referred to. The muskmelon is perhaps native to Egypt; in any case it has been cultivated in Egypt since antiquity. Its fruit is said to grow to a large size in hot countries and is very refreshing.

The watermelon is believed to be a native of tropical central Africa and has also been cultivated in Egypt since before the dawn of recorded history. It is now extensively cultivated in the Holy Land, especially on the plain between Haifa and Jaffa. It served the Egyptians for food, drink, and medicine; indeed it was the only means of relief poor people had from fevers.

Millet (*Panicum miliaceum*). A grass grown in Eurasia for its edible seed. Millet seeds are the smallest of all the grass seeds cultivated as food by man, but are produced profusely. Millet is an annual grass seldom more than 2 feet tall. The small seeds of the millet are used on cakes and eaten uncooked by the poor of the land. A bread made out of millet (Ez 4:9) would not be especially tasty. The pannag of Ezekiel 27:17 (KJV) is probably a reference to millet.

Mint (*Mentha* sp.). Any of various plants of this family with aromatic foliage which is processed for flavoring. Quite a few mints are common in the Holy Land, but the horse mint, *Mentha longifolia*, is probably the one referred to in Matthew 23:23 and Luke 11:42; the horse mint is found throughout Palestine and Syria, and is still commonly planted at Aleppo. It is a much larger plant than ordinary garden mints, attaining a height of 3 or more feet. Mints were employed by the ancient Hebrews, Greeks, and Romans for flavoring, as a carminative in medicine, and as a condiment in cooking.

Mulberry (*Morus nigra*). Any tree of this family, some bearing dark purple fruit and one bearing white fruit, having leaves used as food for silkworms. The sycamine tree of Luke 17:6 is evidently the black mulberry, *Morus nigra*. Originally native to northern Persia, it is now cultivated throughout the Middle East for its delicious fruit. The Chinese or Indian species, *M. alba*, was until recently widely cultivated in Syria and the Holy Land but is not indigenous. Silk evidently was not known to the Jews until late in their history. The reference in Ezekiel 16:10,13 seems to be to silk. In Revelation 18:12 silk was one of the valuable commodities in Babylon.

The tree to which Jesus referred was undoubtedly the black mulberry, a low-growing, thick-crowned, stiff-branched tree standing from 24 to 35 feet tall, though rarely more than 30 feet tall. The mulberry trees of 2 Samuel 5:23,24 and 1 Chronicles 14:15 (all KJV) are now thought to have been aspens.

Mustard (Brassica nigra, B. arvensis). Various plants of this genus native to Eurasia, some of which are cultivated for their edible seeds. While there is considerable controversy as to the identity of the "mustard" of Matthew 13:31,32; 17:20; Mark 4:31; Luke 13:19; and 17:6, it is generally thought to be the ordinary black mustard, *Brassica nigra.* This plant is extensively cultivated for its seeds, which are not only ground up to produce the mustard of commerce but also yield a useful oil.

The mustard our Lord referred to may be the charlock or wild mustard, *B. arvensis,* which normally grows from 1 to 3 feet tall. Some have suggested that it was actually *Salvadora persica,* found in thickets around the Dead Sea. The plant has a pleasant aromatic taste resembling that of mustard, and if taken in considerable quantity will produce an irritation of the nose and eyes similar to that of mustard. However, this plant does not grow as far north as Galilee and the fruits are rather large and stony, thus hardly fitting the description of the parable.

While the seeds of the mustard are not the smallest known, they were probably the smallest familiar to the common people who comprised Jesus' audience in Galilee.

Myrrh (Commiphora myrrha, C. kataf). Shrub or tree exuding an aromatic gum resin used in perfume and incense. Most of the references in Scripture to myrrh are to *Commiphora myrrha,* although *C. kataf* may also be involved since it grows in the same region and is similar. The two trees are native to Arabia, Ethiopia, and the Somali coast to east Africa. They yield a gummy exudation which constitutes most of the myrrh of commerce. Both species are low, scrubby, thick- and stiff-branched thorny shrubs or small trees which grow in rocky places especially on limestone hills. The wood and bark are strongly odorous and a gum exudes naturally from the stems and branches. It is bitter and slightly pungent to the taste and not at all palatable, but for a time was esteemed in medicine as an astringent tonic. In the Orient it is highly regarded as an aromatic substance, perfume, and medicine. The ancient Egyptians burned it in their temples and embalmed their dead with it; the Jews also used it for embalming (Jn 19:39). The Hebrews also held it in high regard as a perfume (Ps 45:8).

Myrtle (Myrtus communis). The myrtle tree, *Myrtus communis,* is common in the Holy Land and in Lebanon, especially around Bethlehem, Hebron, and the slopes of Mt Carmel and Mt Tabor. It is native to western Asia and in good environments grows into a small ever-green tree 20 to 30 feet tall. More often, however, it is a straggling bush 1½ to 4 feet tall. Its wood is very hard and mottled, often knotty, and is highly valued in turnery. A fragrant oil is also produced from the myrtle.

In the Bible myrtle is referred to chiefly as a symbol of God's generosity. Branches of myrtle trees were included among those which Nehemiah ordered to be gathered for the Feast of Tabernacles (Neh 8:15). The myrtle was symbolic not only of peace but also of justice. Hadassah, the original name of Esther, was very similar to the Hebrew word for myrtle.

Narcissus (Narcissus tazetta). Widely cultivated plant of this family with narrow leaves and usually white or yellow flowers with a cup- or trumpet-shaped crown. The polyanthus narcissus, *Narcissus tazetta,* appears to be the plant referred to in Isaiah 35:1. The authors of the KJV confused the showy fruits of the rose called "hips" with the Hebrew word for "bulb" which appears in this text. This narcissus grows abundantly on the plains of Sharon and elsewhere in Palestine. Being sweet-smelling, it is a great favorite.

Nard (Nardostachys jatamansi). The nard is a perennial herb with strong, pleasantly scented roots. It is native to high altitudes in the Himalayas, and its range extends from there into western Asia. The roots and spike-like wooly young stems are dried before the leaves unfold and are used for making perfume. It is still used in India as a perfume for the hair, and there is every reason to believe that the spikenard of Scripture (Sg 1:12; 4:13,14; Mk 14:3; Jn 12:3) came originally from India. Because of the long distance from which it had to be imported it would be understandably expensive. The best spikenard ointment was commonly imported in sealed boxes of alabaster, which were stored and opened only on very special occasions.

Nettle (Urtica sp.). Plant of this genus having toothed leaves covered with hairs that exude a stinging flush. Four species of nettle are found in the Holy Land; the common or great nettle *Urtica dioica,* the Roman nettle, *U. pilulifera,* the small nettle, *U. urens,* and *U. caudata* which is similar to the small nettle. Some nettles attain a height of 5 to 6 feet. They are common pests of waste places and fields. They are often seen occupying ground that was once cultivated but has since been neglected (Is 34:13; Hos 9:6). The irritant of nettles is formic acid, the same substance as in a bee sting. The nettles of Job 30:7 and Zephaniah 2:9 were probably the acanthus and those of Proverbs 24:31 were probably the charlock.

See MUSTARD.

Nutmeg Flower (Nigella sativa). The "fitches"

of Isaiah 28:25,27 are probably the nutmeg flower, *Nigella sativa*, an annual plant of the buttercup family. The plant grows wild in southern Europe, Syria, Egypt, north Africa, and other Mediterranean lands where it is extensively cultivated for its strongly pungent, pepper-like aromatic seeds. These are sprinkled over some kinds of bread and cakes in the Orient and are used for flavoring curries and other dishes in the Holy Land and Egypt. Cummin and nutmeg flowers are still gathered in the Holy Land in the same way described by Isaiah. If a wheel passes over these plants, they are crushed and the valuable carminative oil wasted. To avoid this the seeds are beaten out with a staff or flail. Being more easily detached, the cummin seeds can be harvested by being beaten with a short rod, but the nutmeg flowers require a longer and stronger staff or flail.

The word "fitches" suggests that these were vetches, species of the genus *Vicia*, but today it is generally agreed that this identification is incorrect.

Oak (*Quercus* sp.). At least five species of oaks are found in Palestine. One of these is the kermes oak, *Quercus coccifera*, the host of the insect, *Coccus ilicis*, which produces the scarlet dye used in coloring linen and wool (Gn 38:28,30; Ex 25:4; 26:1; 28:33; 35:23; 39:24; Lv 14:4,6,51,52; Nm 19:6; 2 Chr 2:7,14; 3:14; Is 1:18; Heb 9:19; Rv 18:12). The kermes oak grows from 6 to 35 feet tall and is found in the mountainous regions of Syria, Lebanon, and the Holy Land. The insect from which the scarlet dye is prepared is a scale insect which covers the young branches in white fluffy masses. The tint produced is crimson rather than scarlet.

A second oak is the valonia oak, *Q. aegilops*, perhaps the oak of Isaiah 2:13 and 44:14. It is common in the middle montane zones and probably was abundant in the area around Bashan. The oak of Genesis 35:4,8 is thought to have been the holm oak, *Q. ilex*, an evergreen oak which grows to a height of 60 feet. Still another oak is *Q. lusitanica*, the cypress oak, a small deciduous tree seldom more than 20 feet tall. It is valued for the galls produced on its leaves and twigs through the activity of small insects. These galls or "oak apples" were important articles of trade used for tanning leather, dyeing, and ink making. The very large acorns of this tree were sometimes eaten. *Q. palaestina*, Abraham's oak, is another Holy Land species. The word translated "plain" (KJV) in Genesis 12:6; 13:18; 14:13; and 18:1, should probably be translated "oak." When it grows alone the kermes oak often becomes a large tree. It was regularly planted by tombs in the East. The oak was always respected and even venerated in biblical times for its large size and strength, and great men were usually buried in its shade.

Some commentators suggest that the "oaks" mentioned in Judges 6:11; 2 Samuel 18:9,10; and Amos 2:9 were actually terebinths. However, today it is generally thought that it was really an oak on which Absalom was hanged. The battlefield on the mountains east of the Jordan was always celebrated for its great oaks.

The many references to "groves" in the OT, usually in connection with the worship of Baal or other heathen gods (Ex 34:13; Dt 16:21; Jgs 3:7; 1 Kgs 14:23; 18:19; 2 Kgs 17:16, all KJV), were probably groves of sacred oak trees.

Oil Tree, Oleaster (*Elaeagnus angustifolia*). Small Eurasian tree with oblong silvery leaves, greenish flowers, and olive-like fruit. There is question as to which tree is referred to when 1 Kings 6:23,31–33 and 1 Chronicles 27:28 refer to "olive trees." The same word occurs in Isaiah 41:19 and Micah 6:7. The plant referred to is probably the narrow-leaved oleaster, *Elaeagnus angustifolia*, a small stiff-branched tree or graceful shrub growing from 15 to 20 feet tall, common in all parts of the Holy Land except in the Jordan Valley. At one time it was particularly common on Mt Tabor and at Hebron and Samaria. The wood is hard and fine-grained and therefore well suited for carving of images and figures. The oil which it yields is a rather inferior type used in medication but not for food; this may be the oil of Micah 6:7. The word translated "pine branches" in Nehemiah 8:15 (KJV) is the same word used to refer to the oleaster, and apparently it is to this plant and not to the pine that Nehemiah is referring.

Oleander (*Nerium oleander*). Any poisonous evergreen shrub of this genus growing in warm climates. One of the suggestions for the plants identified as "roses" in various translations is the oleander. Two references in the Book of Ecclesiasticus (Ecclus 24:14; 39:13) are probably to the oleander, *Nerium oleander*. This plant, originally native to the East Indies, has been cultivated throughout the warm regions of the world for centuries. It flourishes in the Holy Land today and forms dense thickets in some parts of the Jordan Valley. It is usually a shrub from 3 to 12 feet tall. Every part of the plant is dangerously poisonous.

Olive, Olive Tree (*Olea europaea*). Old world semitropical evergreen tree bearing edible fruit. The olive, *Olea europaea*, was unquestionably one of the most valuable trees known to the Jews. There are innumerable references to it in Scripture as well as to olive oil, which was used for anointing. The tree is quite common in the Holy Land, and in many places it

Olive trees in the Garden of Gethsemane.

is the only tree of any substantial size. The branches of the wild olive are rather stiff and spinescent, and the typical cultivated tree is a multibranched evergreen, 20 or more feet tall with a gnarled trunk and smooth ash-colored bark. The leaves are leathery and the flowers are small, yellow or white. The fruits are large, black or violet, ripening in September, and it is the outer fleshy parts of the fruit which yield the valuable olive oil of commerce. Thirty-one percent of the ripe fruit is oil. The ripe fruit is eaten raw as is the green unripe fruit. The wood of the trunk and limbs is hard, rich yellow or amber in color, and fine-grained, often handsomely variegated. It is still used today for the finest cabinet work and turnery. The tree grows very slowly but it attains a great age. It is difficult to kill the olive tree by cutting it down because new sprouts are sent up from the root and all around the margins of the old stump, often forming a grove of two to five trunks, all from a single root which originally supported only one tree.

As an emblem of sovereignty olive oil was used in coronations. The oil was also employed in sacrificial offerings, as fuel for lamps, a tonic for the hair and skin, and medicinally in surgical operations. The fruit was normally gathered by shaking or beating the tree, but a few fruits were always left on the boughs for the poor, the stranger, the orphan, and the widow. The olive requires grafting; ungrafted suckers produce small, worthless fruits (Rom 11:17–25).

There is also some question about the identification of the "olive branches" and "olive tree" of Nehemiah 8:15 and 1 Kings 6:23,33.

Some have claimed that both passages refer to the oleaster. Since the cherubim of 1 Kings were 18 feet high and the spread of each wing was 9 feet, it can be assumed that they would have been made of numerous pieces of wood joined together. In either case a number of pieces would have to be used, but in the case of the oleaster the number needed would be larger than in the case of the olive.

Onion (*Allium* sp.). The onions referred to in Numbers 11:5 are undoubtedly *Allium cepa*, the Egyptian onion, which is made up of a compact coated bulb formed of layers consisting of broad fleshy bases of closely overlapping leaves. The leaves are slender and hollow. The entire plant has a characteristic pungent taste and odor. It has been cultivated in Egypt since time immemorial and was used extensively as food in the days of Moses, as it still is in Egypt and Palestine today. Ancient writers wrote glowingly of the excellence of the Egyptian onions, and in view of these accounts it is not difficult to understand why the Israelites in a moment of rebellion and dissatisfaction remembered them and even longed to return to Egypt for them.

Closely related to the onion is the garlic, *A. sativum*. The common garlic is a hardy, bulbous perennial plant which is cultivated in Europe, western Asia, and Egypt. The leaves are narrow, flat, and ribbon-like. It is extremely popular with people of the Mediterranean region. It has been much used in cooking and is often eaten raw on slices of bread. The bulb has a characteristic strong scent and pungent flavor and is composed of a number of small bulblets called "cloves," which are closely crowded together and are the usual means of reproduction. The stem bears an umbrella-like cluster of pinkish flowers and miniature bulbs called bulblets. Another variety of garlic is *A. ascalonicum*. It is milder in taste than the common garlic and occurs wild as well as cultivated. Its common name is the shallot.

Still another one of the onions is the leek, *A. porrum*. The bulb of the leek differs from that of the onion and garlic in being slender, cylindrical, and more than 6 inches in length. The flavor resembles that of the onion but is more pungent. The leaves are eaten as a relish or are cooked in soups. The bulbs are cut into small pieces and employed as seasoning for meat. The leek is still a favorite food of the Jews and is common to the Egyptian diet. Because the leek has always been the food of the poor in the Orient, it has come to be regarded as a symbol of humility.

The reference in Numbers 11:5 may not be to the true leek but to the fenugreek, *Trigonella foenumgraecum*, common in Egypt. It is a three-leaved, clover-like annual with small yellow flowers. The seeds are mucilaginous and strongly aromatic. They are eaten boiled or raw and mixed with honey.

Onycha (Custus sp., *Styrex benzoin).* The word translated "Onycha" in Exodus 30:34 and listed in Ecclesiasticus 24:15, probably refers to two substances, one a plant product and the other an animal product. "Onycha" may be identical with ladanum, a gum resin derived from species of rock rose, *Cistus* sp. The ladanum of commerce is a soft, dark brown or black viscid gummy exudation from the stems and leaves of these plants. It is collected during the heat of the day by drawing leather thongs or some woven material to which the gum adheres over the bushes. It sometimes adheres copiously to the beards of goats which browse among the bushes and it is combed out of their beards and thus collected. The gum has a fragrant odor and a bitter taste. At one time it was used in medicine but now is only employed in perfumery and plasters.

Others regard the onycha as the gum resin known as benzoin and derived from *Styrax benzoin*. This tree is native to the East Indies, and it is doubtful whether trade extended that far east in early biblical days.

The animal source of onycha is a mollusk of the genus *Strombus*.

Orange (Citrus sinensis., C. vulgaris). The fruit of any of several varieties of evergreen trees grown in tropical and subtropical regions. Some have suggested that the "apples of gold" in Proverbs 25:11 are oranges, *Citrus sinensis;* however, it is doubtful whether this fruit was cultivated in Palestine in Solomon's time. Another suggestion has been the Seville

The date palm.

or bitter orange, *C. vulgaris,* but this is not native to Palestine.

Palm (Phoenix dactylifera). The palm tree of the Bible is undoubtedly the date palm, *Phoenix dactylifera.* At one time it was as characteristic of the Holy Land as it is still today of Egypt. It is characterized by a branchless, tapering stem of up to 80 feet or more in height and a large terminal cluster of feathery leaves, each 6 to 9 or more feet long. Because of its height and unusual structure, it was natural that it should be used as a form of ornamentation in oriental architecture. The stem and leaves were favorite subjects of architectural embellishment. The immense branch-like leaves which are referred to as branches in the Bible were symbols of triumph and were used on occasions of great rejoicing (Jn 12:13; Rv 7:9). The large leaves are still used to cover the roofs and sides of houses and to give solidity to reed fences. Mats, baskets, and even dishes are made of them. Small leaves are used as dusters and the wood of the trunk is used for timber. Rope is made from the web-like integument in the crown. The fruit, borne in an immense drooping cluster which may weigh from 30 to 50 pounds, is the chief food of many natives of Arabia and north Africa. A single tree may yield up to 200 pounds of dates a year. They may be dried for future use.

A liquor is secured by piercing the flower whereupon a syrupy liquid exudes which is made into an intoxicating beverage, perhaps the "strong drink" of the Bible as distinct from wine (Lv 10:9; Nm 6:3; Dt 14:26; 29:6; Jgs 13:14; Prv 20:1; Is 5:11; 24:9; 28:7; Mi 2:11; Lk 1:15). Possibly this syrupy exudate was the "honey" of Genesis 43:11; 1 Samuel 14:25; Psalm 19:10; Proverbs 24:13; 25:16; 27:7; Song of Solomon 4:11; Isaiah 7:15; and Revelation 10:9.

The date palm was a symbol of grace and elegance to the Jews. The name Tamar (2 Sm 13:1), is derived from the Hebrew word for the date palm and is an allusion to a woman's graceful upright carriage. A coin issued at the time of Judas Maccabaeus (175 BC) bears the figure of a palm.

Palms require a great deal of careful cultivation, and it is probably owing to a lack of this cultivation that they died. It takes about 30 years for them to reach full maturity and they usually live a total of about 200 years; however, the last period is one of gradual decline.

Many places in the Bible are identified by the abundance of date palms (e.g., Jericho, Hazazon-tamar, Baal-tamar, Bethany).

Papyrus (*Cyperus papyrus*). The Egyptian bulrush or papyrus, *Cyperus papyrus*, (Ex 2:3,5; Jb 8:11; Is 18:2; 19:6,7; 35:7; 58:5), has smooth 3-sided stems ordinarily attaining a height of 8 to 10 feet but sometimes even 16 feet and the thickness of 2 to 3 inches at the base with a large tuft of florets at the end. The papyrus formerly grew in great abundance along the banks of the Nile, forming what was almost a dense jungle. Today it is practically extinct in lower Egypt, although it is still found along the White Nile and in the Sudan. The papyrus still grows in parts of the Holy Land, especially around the north end of the plain of Galilee and the Huleh swamps.

In addition to being used for making small vessels to float in water (Ex 2:3), for mats, and

Papyrus.

for various other domestic purposes, it is best known as the source of ancient paper. In manufacturing paper from papyrus the stems of the plant were first peeled and the pitch then cut longitudinally into thin slices which were laid side by side. These were then sprinkled with water and pressed to unite the whole into one piece. The sheet was then dried and cut into pieces of the required size. In the better grades of papyrus paper, several layers of stem slices were laid crosswise on each other.

The pale fawn-colored tassel-like inflorescences at the summit of the stems were used to adorn Egyptian temples and to crown the statues of gods. They were also worn as crowns by famous men and national heroes.

Pine Tree (*Pinus brutia, P. halepensis*). Various evergreen trees of this family with needle-shaped leaves in clusters and bearing cones. While there is considerable confusion surrounding the conifers of the Bible, it seems apparent that pines are referred to in such passages as Leviticus 23:40; Nehemiah 8:15; Isaiah 41:19; and 60:13. One of the Holy Land pines is the Brutian pine, *Pinus brutia*, a mountain-inhabiting species of the northern regions of Palestine. It attains a height of 10 to 35 feet with a rather diffuse growth and branches in whorls.

Another of the pines is the Aleppo pine, *Pinus halepensis*. Most of the instances of the occurrence of "fir" or "fir tree" in the KJV probably refer to the Aleppo pine (2 Sm 6:5; 1 Kgs 5:8,10; 6:34; 2 Kgs 19:23; 2 Chr 2:8; Ps 104:17; Sg 1:17; Is 14:8; 37:24; 55:13; 60:13; Ez 27:5; 31:8; Hos 14:8; Na 2:3; Zec 11:2). It grows from 9 to 60 feet tall with diffuse ascending branches and yellowish or brownish branchlets. The Aleppo pine is a native of the Mediterranean area and is abundant on the dry hills of the Holy Land and Lebanon. Its wood is said to be scarcely inferior to that of the cedar of Lebanon. The "ash" of Isaiah 44:14 (KJV) may be the Aleppo pine. This tree is believed to have grown in Lebanon along with the famed cedars. Its timber was used for flooring, ceiling, and doors in Solomon's temple, the rafters of ship decks, and for musical instruments (especially harps and lutes).

Pistachio (*Pistacia terebinthus, P. vera*). The Palestine terebinth, *Pistacia terebinthus*, is a large deciduous tree with straggling boughs. In the winter without its leaves it looks much like the oak. It grows from 12 to 25 feet tall. Every part of the tree contains a fragrant resinous juice. It is common on the lower slopes of the hills throughout Syria, Lebanon, Palestine, and Stony Arabia, generally growing as a solitary tree and found mostly in localities too warm or too dry for the oak which it generally replaces. Since it is native to Gilead, it is quite probable that its resinous juice formed part of the spicery that the Ismaelites carried to Egypt from Gilead (Gn 37:25). It is this tree that is referred to in Genesis 18:8, "He stood by them under the tree"; Isaiah 6:13 (KJV), "a teil tree"; and Hosea 4:13 (KJV), "elms." It is also believed that the Valley of Elah (1 Sm 17:2,19) received its name from the terebinth trees growing there.

The nuts of Genesis 43:11 are apparently pistachio nuts from the pistachio tree, *Pistacia vera*. It attains a height of 10 to 30 feet with a spreading top. It is found wild in many rocky parts of Lebanon and the Holy Land. The nut has a light-colored shell and the kernel has a sweet delicate flavor much relished wherever it grows.

The proper name Betonim in Joshua 13:26 may refer to the abundance of pistachio trees in that locality.

Plane Tree (Platanus orientalis). Any of several trees of this family with bell-shaped fruit clusters and usually an outer bark that flakes off in patches or strips. The references in Genesis 30:37 and Ezekiel 31:8 are apparently not to the chestnut tree which is not indigenous to Palestine, but to the oriental plane tree, *Platanus orientalis.* Some think that the pine of Isaiah 41:19 and the cedar of Isaiah 44:14 also refer to the plane tree, although this seems doubtful.

The plane tree is a massive tree 60 or more feet tall with a trunk often of vast circumference, sometimes as much as 40 feet. The outer bark peels off in sheets or scales thus exposing a smooth whitish or yellowish inner bark. The tree is common throughout Lebanon, Syria, and the Holy Land, growing even in subalpine regions. However, it is primarily a tree of the plains and low lands, growing on the edges of streams and lakes and in marshy places.

The Hebrew word for this tree is derived from a root meaning "nakedness." This seems to refer to the fact that the outer bark of the plane tree regularly falls off in layers or small strips leaving the trunk and larger branches quite smooth and thus "naked."

Pomegranate (Punica granatum). The pomegranate is usually a small bush-like tree but may occasionally become a large branching shrub or small tree reaching a height of 20 to 30 feet. The branches are often thorny. The showy bell-like flowers are usually scarlet, though sometimes yellow or white. The globular fruit is as large as an orange or medium-size apple. It has a hard rind of a bright red or yellowish color when ripe and is surmounted by the dry sepals which resemble a crown. The fruit itself is a crimson juicy pulp in which many red seeds are imbedded. The flowers of the pomegranate undoubtedly served as

Pomegranates.

a pattern for the golden bells referred to in Exodus 28:33,34 and 39:24–26, and the open flowers of 1 Kings 6:32. The erect calyx lobes on the fruit served as a model for crowns of kings.

The pomegranate is native to Asia, but it has been cultivated since prehistoric times and is now quite common in the Holy Land, in Egypt, and along the shores of the Mediterranean. It is listed as one of the pleasant fruits of Egypt (Nm 20:5), and one of the promised blessings of the Holy Land (Dt 8:8). The pulp of the fruit has been used extensively since the days of Solomon for making cooling drinks and sherbets, and it is also eaten raw. The astringent rind of the unripe fruit yields a red dye which has been used in medicine and for tanning red Morocco leather. A spiced wine is made from pomegranate juice (Sg 8:2). The soft seeds are eaten, sprinkled with sugar, or dried as a confection. It is probable that the proper names of the towns Remmon and Rimmon in Numbers, Joshua, and Judges refer to the abundance of pomegranates at these localities.

Poplar (Populus euphratica, P. alba). Fast-growing deciduous tree of the same genus as the aspen and cottonwood. The KJV references in 2 Samuel 5:23,24 and 1 Chronicles 14:14,15 to mulberry trees are more probably to the Euphrates popular or aspen, *Populus euphratica*. This tree grows to a height of 30 to 45 feet with spreading branches. The Euphrates aspen is found only on rivers and stream banks throughout the area from Syria through the Holy Land to Stony Arabia. It is especially common in the Jordan Valley.

The "willows" of Leviticus 23:40 may also be a reference to the Euphrates poplar; this suggestion is also made with regard to the "willow" of Psalm 137:2.

There is some question as to whether "the valley of Baca" in Psalm 84:6 refers to the aspen or not; it may well allude to the abundance of these trees at that place. The noise made by a "driven leaf" (Lv 26:36) may apply to the aspen because of its flattened leafstalk.

The white poplar, *Populus alba,* is common in wet places in Syria, Lebanon, the Holy Land, and Sinai. It attains a height of 30 to 60 feet with spreading branches. Some suggest that the altars of various pagan religions were usually erected on the top of a hill and in the shade of a poplar grove. Perhaps instead of "altars of brick" in Isaiah 65:3 the text should read "burning incense under the white poplars." Hosea 4:13 states that pagan altars were built in the shadow of oaks, poplars, and terebinths. It is also suggested that Hosea 14:5 does not refer to Lebanon, but rather states "strikes roots down like a poplar." It is, of course, well known that poplar roots grow rapidly toward any water in the vicinity.

The reference in Genesis 30:37 to branches is believed to be to the white poplar.

Quince (Cydonia oblonga). Tree native to western Asia, having white flowers and apple-like fruit which is edible when cooked. Some believe that the "apples" of the OT were quinces, *Cydonia oblonga.* The quince tree is quite common in the Holy Land, though chiefly as a cultivated tree. It may occur wild in the northern parts of Syria. It is native to northern Persia and Asia Minor. The fruit is yellowish and highly fragrant, and it is the fragrance that caused it to be held in high regard by the ancients. However, it is not sweet to the taste and therefore does not fit such passages as Song of Solomon 2:3,5. Most commentators think that the fruit referred to is the apricot.

Reed (Juncus sp., Scirpus sp., Typha angustata, Arundo donax). Numerous species of the rush and bulrush grow in the Holy Land. There are at least 21 varieties of rushes. The common soft rush or bog rush, *Juncus effusus,* is found in wet places even in the Sinai and other deserts. The sea or hard rush, *J. maritimus,* is found in damp places throughout the Holy Land and even in Sinai.

At least 15 kinds of bulrushes, *Scirpus,* are known in the Holy Land. The cluster-headed club rush, *Scirpus holoschoenus,* is common in damp places throughout the Holy Land to the Sinai. The lake club rush or tall bulrush, *S. lacustris,* is found in swamps and ditches throughout northern Africa to the Dead Sea. The sea club rush or salt marsh club rush, *S. maritimus,* is found in ditches and swamps in many places of the Holy Land. Any of these species may be the one referred to in Job 8:11; Isaiah 9:14; and 19:6,15.

The reference in Genesis 41:2 to the feeding of cattle in the meadow seems to be to the tall reed, *Arundo donax,* which grows 18 or more feet in height. This plant is also known as the Persian reed and is common throughout the Holy Land, Syria, and the Sinai peninsula. It is a gigantic grass which may have a stem diameter of 2 or 3 inches at the base and is terminated by a plume of white flowers similar to those of the sugar cane or pampas grass. The plant was used for many purposes by the ancients: for walking sticks, fishing rods, measuring rods, and musical pipes. It is therefore quite possible that the "reed" of Matthew 27:48 and Mark 15:36 was a carpenter's reed or measuring rod.

The reference in 2 Kings 18:21 to the stem of a broken reed piercing a man's hand calls attention to the well-known fact that the culms of all stout bamboo-like grasses break into many thin, sharp-pointed slivers which can pierce skin.

The bruised reed of Isaiah 42:3 may be the cattail, *Typha latifolia,* but it seems more likely to be *A. donax,* the bulrush. The "reed shaken by the wind" of Matthew 11:7 may be the common reed, *Phragmites communis,* but it too is more likely to be the bulrush. It is also believed that the bulrush is the "staff of the bruised reed" to which Sennacherib compared the power of Egypt in 2 Kings 18:21 and Ezekiel 29:6,7.

There is no general agreement regarding the "reed" of the NT (Mt 27:29; Mk 15:19). Many have suggested the cattail, *Typha latifolia.* However, while cattails are said to be common along the streams of the Holy Land, they would hardly have been in flower or fruit in March or April when the mock trial of Jesus took place. The Palestinian species all bloom in July and August.

See also PAPYRUS; SORGHUM.

Rue (Rute chalepensis, R. graveolens). Aromatic Eurasian plant with evergreen leaves that yield an acrid, volatile oil once used in medicine. There is little question as to the correctness of the translation of "rue" in Luke 11:42, but there is some doubt as to the exact species. Most writers think that it was the common rue, *Rute graveolens,* a perennial shrubby plant with erect stems 2 to 3 feet tall and deeply cut leaves. A very strong odor emanates from the foliage. This species is native to the Mediterranean region and is said to grow wild in the Holy Land, especially on Mt Tabor.

Others suggest that the rue of Luke 11:42 was the African rue, *R. chalepensis,* which is very similar to the common rue but has less deeply divided leaves. It is common on the hillsides and in thickets of northern Syria, Lebanon, the Holy Land, and Sinai. It is quite possible that both species were used and even cultivated by the Jews in biblical days. The fact that it was tithed in the time of the NT implies that it was a cultivated plant; earlier it apparently grew wild.

Rue was very highly thought of by the ancients as a medicinal, supposed to prevent dizziness, dumbness, epilepsy, eye inflammations, insanity, and the "evil eye." Rue was also used for seasoning dishes.

Rush (Butomus umbellatus). Generic term for any of various grass-like marsh plants having pliant, hollow, or pithy stems. There is considerable uncertainty about the identification of the plant referred to in Genesis 41:2 translated in the KJV as "meadow," and in Job 8:11 as "flag." Since it is mentioned along with the papyrus in the Job passage it seems that it refers to a specific kind of plant rather than to an aggregate of plants in a meadow. From the description in Genesis as being a plant on which Pharaoh's cattle might feed along the banks of the Nile and yet not the papyrus, it may refer to the flowering rush or water gladiola, *Butomus umbellatus*, which flourishes both in Egypt and in the Holy Land along with the papyrus. It is a showy aquatic or bog plant growing from horizontal root stocks with a cylindrical stalk over-topping the leaves. The reference may also be to the tall reed, *Arundo donax.*

See REED.

Saffron (Crocus sativus). Saffron, referred to in Song of Solomon 4:14, is the product of several species of *Crocus*, especially of the blue-flowered saffron crocus, *C. sativus*, which is native to Greece and Asia Minor. The commercial product consists of the stigma and upper portions of the style, the top parts of the flower ovary, which are collected shortly after the flower opens. It requires at least 4000 stigmas to make an ounce of saffron. After being gathered, the stigmas are dried in the sun, pounded, and made into small cakes. Saffron is used principally as a yellow dye and also as a fruit coloring for curries and stews. In spring many parts of the Holy Land are brilliant with the white, pink, purple, lilac, blue, or orange-yellow flowers of some 14 or 15 species of crocus, several of which yield saffron. The ancients are said to have scattered saffron on the floors of their theaters mixed with wine and to have used it extensively during wedding ceremonies. It is still employed to lend color to confections, liquors, and varnishes.

Another entirely different kind of dye-producing plant, *Carthamus tinctorius*, called carthamine, bastard saffron, or safflower, is a member of the thistle family. Its red florets yield a dye used extensively for coloring silk, in cooking, and for adulterating genuine saffron. It is an annual spiny plant 3 to 4½ feet tall, native to Syria and Egypt. In Egypt the grave clothes of mummies were dyed with this

material, and it is quite possible that this plant may also have been the saffron of the Bible.

Sage (Salvia judaica). The Judean sage, *Salvia judaica*, grows to 3 feet tall in the mountains and hills of Palestine. Its stems are four-angled, stiff, and rough. The plant grows from Syria south through Nazareth, Hebron, Tiberius, Samaria, and Judea.

This plant is the origin of the seven-branched lampstand of Exodus 37:17,18, which is known as the Menorah, the traditional Jewish symbol. The inflorescence of the plant when pressed flat has almost exactly the same shape and form of the seven-branched candlestick with its central spike and three pairs of side branches each bending upward and inward in a symmetrical fashion. On each branch of the plant's inflorescence are whorls of buds which perhaps give the idea for the "knops" or "knobs" on the biblical golden candlesticks.

Shrub. Shrubs are low-growing, multi-branched woody plants. A tree has a single main stem or at best a very few main stems. A bush or shrub has a great many main stems. Both shrubs and trees provide wood for fires. In some cases the shrub referred to can be identified with a fair degree of accuracy, but in most cases identifying the particular plant is a hopeless task.

The shrub of Genesis 21:15 is in all probability the tamarisk.

Sorghum (Sorghum vulgare). Old World grass, several varieties of which are cultivated as grain and forage and processed into syrup. Considerable controversy has surrounded the identification of the reed or hyssop to which the sponge of vinegar of the crucifixion story was attached (Mt 27:48; Mk 15:36; Jn 19:29). One suggestion is that it was the stem of the tall reed, *Arundo donax.* It seems unlikely that it was the true hyssop, *Origanum maru*, since it has a very weak stem. Many commentators think that it is the dhura, or common sorghum, *Sorghum volgare*, which is also known as durra, Indian millet, yellow milo, or Jerusalem corn. It is a medium-to-stout annual maize-like grass commonly growing to the height of at least 6 feet in Egypt and the Holy Land and attaining an even greater height elsewhere. The thick pith is dry and not sweet as is the sugar cane. The grains are quite large and often collected, roasted and eaten. They may also be used to make a coarse bread. One stalk may furnish a meal for an entire family.

It is possible that this is the "parched grain" which Boaz gave to Ruth (Ru 2:14) and it may also be the corn which Joseph sent to his brethren.

See also WHEAT.

Spelt (*Triticum aestivum*). Hardy member of the wheat family. The rye of Exodus 9:32 and Isaiah 28:25 (KJV) as well as the fitches of Ezekiel 4:9 are thought to be the spelt, *Triticum aestivum*. Spelt is a hard-grained species of wheat with loose ears and grains triangular in cross-section, and was the most common form of wheat in early times. It has a stouter stem than wheat and strong spikes of grain. Bread made of its flour is much inferior to that made from wheat, but spelt will thrive well in almost any kind of soil and will yield a crop on land that is totally unfit for wheat. The ancients preferred it to barley for bread.

True rye, *Secale cereale*, grows in colder and more northern countries and was almost unknown in Egypt and the Holy Land.

Spice (*Commiphora opobalsamum*). Any of various aromatic and pungent vegetable substances used as flavorings. The references to spices in 1 Kings 10:10; 2 Kings 20:13; and Isaiah 39:2, to the powders of the merchants in Song of Solomon 3:6, and to balm in Ezekiel 27:17 are thought to be to the balm of Gilead, *Commiphora opobalsamum*. Contrary to the popular name it is not native to Gilead or even to Palestine but is indigenous to Arabia. It was cultivated in the Holy Land at the time of Solomon, particularly around the city of Jericho, and it has been suggested that the trees there grew from seeds brought by the Queen of Sheba as a part of her gift of "spices."

The balm of Gilead is a small stiff-branched evergreen tree seldom more than 15 feet tall with straggling branches and white flowers borne in clusters of three. The balm or balsam is a gum which is obtained by making incisions in the stem and branches of the tree. The gum is also procured from the green and ripe fruit.

Spicery (*Astragalus gummifer.*, *A. tragacantha*). The species collectively. A number of suggestions have been made for the source of the spicery of Genesis 37:25 (KJV) and the spices of Genesis 43:11 (KJV); 2 Kings 20:13; Song of Solomon 4:10,14; 5:1,13; 6:2; 8:2,14; and Isaiah 39:2. One suggestion has been the gum tragacanth, *Astragalus tragantha* and *A. gummifer*. These are native to dry, subalpine regions and fit these passages quite well. The reference in Song of Solomon 8:14 to mountains of spice implies the kind of spice-producing plant which grows naturally in mountainous areas. The reference in Song of Solomon 5:13 and 6:2 to "beds of spices" suggests herbaceous or low-growing plants, rather than tree forms such as cinnamon or cassia and fits the gum tragacanth.

Storax Tree (*Styrax officinalis*). Various trees of this genus yielding an aromatic resin.

Today it is thought that the storax of Exodus 30:34 was derived from the storax tree, *Styrax officinalis*. It is an irregularly stiff-branched shrub or small tree 9 to 20 feet tall. This tree is abundant on low hills and rocky places from Lebanon through the Holy Land. Its gum is obtained by making incisions in the stems and branches. It is highly perfumed and is still prized today as a perfume.

Sycamore (*Ficus sycomorus*). Tree of northeastern Africa and adjacent Asia related to the fig. The word translated sycamore in 1 Kings 10:27; 1 Chronicles 27:28; 2 Chronicles 1:15; 9:27; Psalm 78:47; Isaiah 9:10; Amos 7:14; and Luke 19:4 undoubtedly refers to the well-known sycamore fig, *Ficus sycomorus*, which is also known as the mulberry fig or fig-mulberry. It should not be confused with the common "sycamore" of the North American continent, which is actually a plane tree. The sycamore fig of the Bible is a strong-growing, robust, wide-spreading tree growing 30 to 40 feet tall and sometimes attaining a trunk circumference of 20 or more feet with a crown 120 feet in diameter. It is a tree which is easily climbed and is frequently planted along roadsides, which accounts for the reference in Luke 19:4. It produces an abundant amount of fruit in clusters on all parts of the tree, on both young and old branches and even on the trunk itself. It is very similar to the common fig, only smaller and much inferior in quality. In David's day it was so valuable that he appointed a special overseer for the sycamore trees (1 Chr 27:28).

The tree is evergreen, unlike the common fig, and produces fruit several times a year. It is essentially a lowland tree and will not survive the unfavorable weather of mountainous regions (Ps 78:47).

It is thought that Amos was not a gatherer of sycamore fruit but rather a dresser of sycamore trees. It was customary for growers of the sycamore fig to pare or scrape off a part of the center of the fruit or to make a puncture with the fingernail or sharp pointed instrument three or four days before gathering when the fruit was about an inch long. Unless this is done the fruit will secrete a quantity of watery juice and will not ripen.

Tamarisk (*Tamarix* sp.). The references in Genesis 21:33; 1 Samuel 22:6 and 31:13 seem to be to the tamarisk. These trees or shrubs are small and fast-growing with a durable wood. They are abundant in deserts, dunes, and salt marshes. *Tamarix aphylla* is leafless and has small white flowers. These trees or shrubs often provide a soothing touch of green foliage and a promise of cooling shade to the traveler. Beersheba, where Abraham planted the tamarisk, is a region troubled with droughts which would make the cultivation of most other kinds of trees very impractical. In the very desolate portions of the desert of Shur, the stunted bushes of the desert species of tamarisk still grow in abundance, and it was probably under one of these that the despairing Hagar cast Ishmael, the child of her blighted hopes. Tamarisks are able to survive because they either have small scale-like leaves which lose little moisture by transpiration, or no leaves at all. The larger of the tamarisks are valued for their wood in a region where wood is scarce. The wood was used for building purposes and also as a source of an excellent type of charcoal.

Terebinth (Pistacia terebinthus). The Palestine terebinth or turpentine tree, *Pistacia terebinthus*, is a large deciduous tree with straggling boughs much like an oak when in the winter leafless condition. It grows from 12 to 25 feet tall and has red fruit. Every part of the tree contains a fragrant resinous juice. It is common on the lower slopes of hills throughout Syria, Lebanon, the Holy Land, and Stony Arabia. It was venerated like the oak in ancient times because it is a tree of considerable size and longevity.

Incisions in the stem and branches yield the so-called Chios, or Cyprus turpentine of commerce. Since it is native to Gilead it may be that its resinous juice formed part of the "spicery" which the Israelites carried into Egypt from Gilead (Gn 37:25).

In Genesis 18:8 the tree referred to is probably the terebinth, though it may have been oak. The teil tree of Isaiah 6:13 is apparently the terebinth as are the elms of Hosea 4:13.

The valley of Elah referred to in 1 Samuel 17:2,19 received its name from the terebinth trees growing there. "Elah" was also used as a personal name (Gn 36:41 and 1 Kgs 16:8 probably refer to the fragrance and value of the tree).

Thistle, Thorn (Lycium europaeum, Solanum incanum, Centaurea sp., Notobasis syriaca, Scolymus maculatus, Ruscus aculeatus, Agrostemma githago, Paliurus spina-christi, Zizyphus spina-christi). There are some 22 different Hebrew and Greek words used in Scripture to refer to spiny or prickly shrubs or weeds, and these are translated as bramble, briar, cockle, thorn, and thistle. At the present time there are about 125 species of thorns and thistles that grow in the Holy Land.

The bramble in the allegory of Judges 9:14,15 is believed to refer to the European boxthorn or desert-thorn, *Lycium europaeum*. This plant is a thorny shrub 6 to 12 feet tall with clustered leaves and small violet flowers. Eventually it produces small globular red berries. It is native to and common throughout

A thistle.

the Holy Land, especially from Lebanon to the Dead Sea. It is frequently used for hedges.

The general consensus is that the "briers" of Isaiah 10:17; 55:13; Micah 7:4; and Hebrews 6:8 are the Palestine nightshade, *Solanum incanum*, or "Jericho potato." It is a coarse stiff-branched shrubby plant growing from 1½ to 4 or 5 feet tall. The fruit is a handsome yellow berry about an inch in diameter, which when ripe bursts to emit what appears to be smoke and ashes. This characteristic of the fruit has caused the plant to be known as the apple of Sodom, an allusion to the destruction of Sodom and Gomorrah.

The thistles of Genesis 3:17,18; 2 Kings 14:9; 2 Chronicles 25:18; Hosea 10:8; and Matthew 7:16 as well as the thorns of Matthew 13:7 and Hebrews 6:8 are thought to be one of the species of the thistle, *Centaurea*. At present some 125 species of thistles grow in the Holy Land. Of these the most common are the true star-thistle, *Centaurea calcitrapa*, the dwarf centaury, *C. verutum*, the Iberian centaury, *C. iberica* and the lady's thistle, *Silybum marianum*. Some thistles attain a height of 5 or 6 feet. Thistles are characteristic of an area which is uncultivated and neglected. Many have beautiful flowers but all are covered with sharp spines.

There are two references either to the Syrian thistle, *Notobasis syriaca*, or the spotted golden thistle, *Scolymus maculatus*. The Syrian thistle is a spiny herb with erect stems and grows to 3 feet tall. It has purple heads of flowers underneath and floral leaves that are modified into sharp spines. It is very common in fields and along roadsides throughout the Holy Land. Perhaps Job 31:40 and Isaiah 34:13 refer to this plant and to the spotted golden thistle. The latter is a spiny herb about 3 feet tall with white-margined leaves and terminal heads of yellow flowers. It is also common in fields and waste places throughout the Holy Land.

The references in Ezekiel 2:6 to "briers" and Ezekiel 28:24 to a "pricking brier" may be to the prickly butchers-broom or knee-holly, *Ruscus aculeatus*. The plant is common in rocky woods in the northern regions of the Holy Land especially around Mt Tabor and Mt Carmel.

The cockle of Job 31:40 (KJV; foul weeds, RSV) perhaps refers to the corn cockle, *Agrostemma githago*. This plant is common in grain fields throughout the Holy Land. It is a strong-growing and very troublesome weed in grain fields growing from 1 to 3 feet tall.

Many commentators think that the "thorns" out of which the crown of thorns (Mt 27:29; Jn 19:2) was made were from the Christ-thorn, *Paliurus spina-christi*. This belief has lead to its specific name; the Christ-thorn is a spiny plant which ordinarily grows as a straggling shrub 3 to 9 feet tall. The flexible branches are armed at the base of each leaf with a pair of unequal, very stiff, sharp spines. The unusual pliable texture of the young branches renders it particularly easy to plait into a crown-like wreath.

The thorns of Judges 8:7; Isaiah 7:19; 9:18; 55:13; and Matthew 7:16 may refer to the Syrian Christ-thorn, *Zizyphus spina-christi*, a shrub or small tree 9 to 15 feet tall sometimes growing into a 40-foot tree with smooth white branches bearing a pair of stout unequal recurved spines at the back of each leaf. It has also been suggested that this was the plant from which our Lord's crown of thorns was plaited because there is some question as to whether the Christ-thorn, *Paliurus*, grew around Jerusalem, where *Zizyphus* does. However, it is taller than the Christ-thorn.

See also ACANTHUS; BRAMBLE; BUCKTHORN.

Tree. A tree is a woody plant with a single or very small number of main branches as opposed to a shrub which has a great many main branches. In Deuteronomy 20:19,20 the Israelites were forbidden to destroy in war trees which bore an edible fruit; other trees could be destroyed and could be used for lumber. In Job 14:7–9 reference is made to a tree which when cut down is able to sprout from adventitious buds around the margins of the stump. Olive trees and willows have this property.

In many passages of Scripture the term "tree" is employed in an allegorical sense (Is 56:3; 61:3). Even in these cases writers may have had a definite kind of tree in mind.

One kind of tree, for instance, may have suggested the concept of a "dry tree," possibly a species of tamarisk. The reference in Mark 8:24 to "men as trees walking" is not a reference to a particular kind of tree but to the general outline of an erect slender tree seen indistinctly and dimly through a fog. The cypress might well fit this description.

Tulip (Tulipa montana, T. sharonensis). Any of several bulbous plants of this family native to Asia. The Rose of Sharon in the Song of Solomon 2:1 may be the mountain tulip, *Tulipa montana*, or the closely related Sharon tulip, *T. sharonensis*. The former is an attractive plant which grows from a bulb and has leaves that are often wavy-margined. The species is common in the mountainous regions of Syria, Lebanon, and the Anti-Lebanon. It is primarily a mountainous species. The Sharon tulip, *T. sharonensis*, is found in sandy places on the Sharon coastal plains.

Tumbleweed (Gundelia tournefortii, Anastatica hierochuntica). The references in Psalm 83:13 to "whirling dust" and in Isaiah 17:13 to "wheel" or "rolling thing" (KJV) (tumbleweed NIV) seem to be to the Palestinian tumbleweed, *Gundelia tournefortii*, a member of the thistle family. It is a prickly herb with milky juice. It rolls over the land and gathers in tremendous heaps in hollows.

Another of the Palestinian tumbleweeds, *Anastatica hierochuntica* has also been suggested. This is a member of the mushroom family and grows abundantly around Jericho and in the Mediterranean region of the Holy Land. The branches bear small leaves and small white flowers; when the seeds have matured the stems become dry and hardened, forming a globe or hollow ball. Through the force of the wind pressing against it in time the ball breaks off at ground level and is blown about. As it lands on a wet spot, the dry globe expands and in that way resembles a resurrection plant.

Vegetable. Scriptural references to vegetables are probably, in most cases, to the dried leguminous seeds of beans and lentils.

Vine (Vitis vinifera). Any plant with a flexible stem that climbs, twines, or creeps along a surface or support. The common grape vine, *Vitis vinifera*, is mentioned throughout the Bi-

A vineyard.

ble. The fruitful vine (Ez 17:5–10) and "the vine brought out of Egypt" (Ps 80:8) were symbolic of the Jewish people. Jesus compares himself to the true vine of which his disciples were the branches (Jn 15:1–6). The grape vine was held in high regard by the Israelites. It was cultivated by the ancient Egyptians, as is evident from paintings and representations on their tombs. It is the first cultivated plant recorded in the Bible and is thought to have originated in the hilly regions of Armenia. The Promised Land was described as a land of wheat and barley, of vines and fig trees and pomegranates (Dt 8:8). It is apparent that the vine was cultivated very early in the Holy Land, not only from the numerous scriptural references but also from the numerous remains of old wine presses found cut in rocks of that country.

The grape vine of the old world sometimes assumes the characteristics of a tree with stems up to a foot and a half in diameter, the branches then being trained on a trellis and bearing bunches of grapes 10 to 12 pounds in weight, with the individual grapes the size of small plums. Bunches have been produced weighing as much as 26 pounds. The vines of the Holy Land were always renowned both for the luxuriance of their growth and for the immense clusters of grapes they produced. Thus it does not seem improbable that the spies sent to the Promised Land should have employed a pole to transport some of the clusters home (Nm 13:23,24).

The "raisins" of 1 Samuel 25:18 and 1 Chronicles 12:40 were merely dried grapes, as they are today. The productiveness of the grape vines in the famous valley of Eshcol (literally "grapes") was well known.

The ancient Hebrews probably allowed their vines to trail on the ground or over rocks and walls. Later they used supports and trellises. The time of vintage was a season of great festivity and usually commenced in September. The finest grapes were saved for eating and kept in flat open wicker baskets; these were also the source of dried raisins. The rest of the harvest was carried to the large stone wine presses dug or hewn out of the rocky soil. There the treaders pressed out the juices.

The wild grape, *Vitis orientalis*, is referred to in Isaiah 5:2–4; Jeremiah 2:21; and Ezekiel 15:2–6. It is known as the native wild fox grape and has small, black, very acidic berries about the size of currants with little juice. It also lacks tendrils. The plant grows wild in rocky places and hedges in the Mediterranean area.

Walnut (Juglans regia). Any of several trees of this genus having round sticky fruit enclosing an edible nut. The reference in Song of Solomon 6:11 to "nuts" is thought to refer to the Persian or common walnut, *Juglans regia*. The tree is believed to have been indigenous to northern Persia, but it is actually found wild in many parts of northern India, eastward as far as China, and westward through Persia. At the time of Solomon it was widely cultivated for its fruit throughout the Orient. Perhaps Solomon's garden of nuts was a part of his extensive gardens at Etham, six miles from Jerusalem.

The Persian walnut tree attains a height of 30 feet or more with a hemispheric crown. It produces dense shade. An oil is extracted from it which is only slightly inferior to olive oil and is used extensively for soap manufacturing in Europe. It is this tree which has been introduced into England and is known as the English walnut. Its fine shade, fragrant leaves and delicious fruit doubtless made it a favorite in Solomon's garden. Today it is probably the most important commercial nut.

Water Lily (Nymphaea sp.). Any of numerous aquatic plants of this genus with floating leaves and showy flowers. The carved lily ornamentation of 1 Kings 7:19,22,26 and 2 Chronicles 4:5 was probably patterned after the flowers of the water lily. Few flowers can equal the Egyptian lotus or water lily, *Nymphaea lotus*, in beauty. It looks very much like a large white rose and at one time floated in profusion on the waters of the Nile.

The common European white water lily, *N. alba*, was also familiar to the children of Israel. It grows not only in Europe but also in the Holy Land and North Africa. It is, however, not as common in Egypt as is the white lotus.

Another water lily with which the Israelites were probably familiar is the blue lotus, *N. caerulea*. Its leaves are 12 to 16 inches across and it has light blue flowers which are 3 to 6 inches in diameter.

Wheat (Triticum aestivum, T. compositum). Various cereal grasses of this family widely cultivated for its edible grain. Five kinds of wheat are native to and still wild in the Holy Land and at least eight others are cultivated there today; probably most if not all were known in Bible times. The wild varieties were probably more abundant then than they are today. Among these are the einkorn, *T. monococcum*, the thaoudar, *T. thaoudar*, and the wild emmer, *T. dicoccoides*. The composite wheat, *T. compositum*, with its branched spikes, often bearing as many as seven heads per stalk, is definitely referred to in Genesis 41:5–57. It is depicted on numerous Egyptian monuments and on inscriptions and is still commonly seen in the Nile delta where it is known as "mummy wheat." It is also cultivated in the Holy Land.

The most frequently mentioned wheat of the Bible is undoubtedly the commonly cultivated summer and winter wheat, *Triticum aestivum*. It is an abundant annual grass cultivated in Egypt and other eastern lands since earliest times. The exact place of its origin is unknown. Grains of wheat have been found in the most ancient Egyptian tombs and in the remains of prehistoric lake dwellings in Switzerland. It was certainly the chief grain of Mesopotamia in Jacob's time (Gn 30:14).

In ancient times Babylon, Assyria, and the Holy Land were known for the excellent quality of their wheat (Ps 81:16; 147:14), but they were all frequently subject to droughts resulting in widespread famine (Gn 12:10; 41:57). The Holy Land at one time exported wheat (Ez 27:17; Am 8:5).

Wheat is still "trodden out" by oxen (Dt 25:4), pressed out by a wooden wheel (Is 28:28), or threshed with a flail (1 Chr 21:20–23; Is 41:15,16), and then winnowed with a fan and sifted. The time of wheat harvest is from the end of April well into June, depending upon the latitude, soil, and altitude, and still marks the definite division of the year in oriental lands. Dates are often reckoned as so many days or weeks before or after the "wheat harvest" (cf. Gn 30:14).

Wheat was the main constituent of the "corn" of the Bible. Corn is mentioned some 71 times in the Scriptures. Wheat fields are known even today in the old world as "corn fields," and "parched corn" is used as food in modern Palestine. This is prepared by picking ears that are not too ripe, tying them in small parcels and roasting them over a blazing fire of dried grass and thorn bushes until the chaff is mostly burned off. The grain is then rubbed between the hands.

Corn in biblical days often included a mixture of peas, beans, lentils, cummin, barley, millet, and spelt, but wheat was always its main constituent. Egypt was a great grain-producing country, and Abram (Gn 12:10) and Joseph's brothers (Gn 42) naturally turned to Egypt for wheat when famine visited Canaan.

Wheat crops today may be expected to yield about twentyfold of what was sown. In ancient times when the land was much more fertile the yield was far greater. In good soil certain strains of *T. aestivum* will sometimes even today produce ears or heads with 60 or even 100 grains each.

Wheat seeds were planted in the winter by the Hebrews and were either sown broadcast and then plowed in or trampled by cattle (Is 32:20), or more rarely were painstakingly planted in rows to insure healthier and huskier plants (Is 28:25). Wheat and spelt in antiquity were not planted until well after the barley was planted. This accounts for the story of the hail destroying Pharaoh's barley but not his wheat and spelt, since only the former had grown (Ex 9:32).

The mills, millstones, granaries, and threshing floors mentioned in the Bible all refer to equipment employed in processing grain to produce flour. The fine flour of which the showbread loaves were made (Lv 24:5) was unquestionably wheat flour. Wheat intended for home consumption was often stored in the central part of the house; this explains the story told in 2 Samuel 4:6. It was also sometimes stored in dry wells (2 Sm 17:19).

Wormwood (Artemisia judaica, A. herba-alba). Wormwood is a general name given to a group of woody plants with a strong aromatic odor. Wormwood plants have a strong bitter taste, and their young shoots and branch tips furnish the "wormwood" of commerce. Its bitter taste accounts for its being spoken of with gall as being symbolic of bitter calamity and sorrow (Prv 5:4; Jer 9:15; 23:15; Lam 3:15,19). *Artemisia herba-alba* is the com-

Millstone and oven at a bakery.

mon species of wormwood in the Holy Land today. It is strongly aromatic, smelling like camphor, and bitter. *A. judaica* occurs only in the Sinai.

Absinthe is made from species of this group. It first leads to greater activity and pleasant sensations and fills the mind with grandiose ideas (Lam 3:15). The habitual use of it, however, brings on a stupor and gradual diminution of intellectual faculties, ending in delirium and even death. Perhaps the hemlock of Amos 6:12 was wormwood.

JOHN W. KLOTZ

Bibliography. D.A. Anderson, *All the Trees and Woody Plants of the Bible*; H.N. and A.L. Moldenke, *Plants of the Bible*; A.I. Perold, *Treatise on Viticulture*; W.E. Shewell-Cooper, *Plants and Fruits of the Bible*; L. Untermeyer, *Plants of the Bible*; W. Walker, *All the Plants of the Bible*.

Pledge. *See* MONEY AND BANKING.

Pleiades. Name of a constellation in the eastern sky composed of six bright and many other less visible stars. Telescopic photography has captured the appearance of these stars as being strung together by currents of matter. Job is asked a question which reflects this phenomenon: "Can you bind the chains of the Pleiades . . . ?" (Jb 38:31). This translation is not in agreement with the KJV, but is a proper rendering of the Hebrew.

Plow, Plowman, Plowshare. *See* AGRICULTURE; TOOLS; TRADES AND OCCUPATIONS (FARMER).

Plumline, Plummet. *See* TOOLS.

Pochereth-Hazzebaim, Pochereth of Zebaim. Head of a family of Solomon's servants who returned from the exile with Zerubbabel (Ezr 2:57; Neh 7:59). The KJV renders the name Pochereth of Zebaim, making the latter part a place name.

Poetry, Biblical. The OT contains all that we know of the poetry of Israel, and what we have occupies an important place in that literature. It was presumably well known throughout the ancient Near East, for its fame had spread even to Babylon (Ps 137:4). Much of the OT is poetic in spirit and structure—a feature of the prophetic writings as well as the poetic literature. In the former are found passages of elevated poetry, studded with brilliant gems of imagery. The movement is rhythmical, with meter, parallelism, and strophic arrangement, as in the poetry books.

The RV of the Bible first rendered a great service to English readers by printing OT poetry in parallel lines. Where this is not done in the prophetic literature, the poetic quality of these books is obscured. Note that besides the OT books recognized as poetry—the Psalms, Job, Lamentations, Song of Songs, and Proverbs—Ecclesiastes and the prophets consist of prose and poetry. The historical books also contain fine examples of poetry.

The Hebrew language was an ideal instrument for expressing poetic speech. Its simplicity of form combined intensity of feeling and pictorial power, and allowed great play of imagination. Figures, metaphors, and hyperboles are extremely common. In its powerful imagery the genius of Hebrew poetry comes to finest expression. Here it lays heaven and earth, and the wonders of the natural world, under tribute.

The normal unit of Hebrew verse is the couplet of two parallel lines. But this is not the only grouping of lines in Hebrew poetry. Units of three (Ps 1:1; 5:11; 45:1,2), four (Ps 1:3; 55:21; Prv 27:15,16), five (Ps 6:6,7; Prv 24:23–25), six (Ps 99:1–3; Prv 30:21–23), and even larger combinations of parallel lines occur.

As far as can be determined meter is absent from biblical poetry. Certainly there is little concern for the careful meter which marks classic Greek and Latin as well as much of English poetry. Rhyme also is so rare as to be almost nonexistent; except in wailing songs or laments (Jer 9:18–20; Lam 1–4). This is called lamentation meter, where the verse is in two parts.

On the other hand, Hebrew poetry is rhythmical—one of its distinguishing features. Its rhythm recurs with stressed and unstressed syllables in relatively regular succession. There are usually three or four accents or beats to a line, but the rhythmic unit is not uniform. Rhythm in Hebrew poetry, however, is not confined to the balance of accent or beat in a line. The meaning of the words and their position in the line are also significant—a feature called parallelism. This distinguishing characteristic was first clearly recognized by Dr. Robert Lowth, who in 1753 developed the principle of parallelism.

He distinguished three types. The first is *synonymous parallelism*, where the thought expressed in the first part of the verse is repeated in the second part, in different but equivalent terms (Ps 2:4; 19:1; 36:1,2; 103:11,12; Prv 3:13–18). The second is *antithetic parallelism*, where the thought in the first part of the verse is contrasted with its opposite in the second (Ps 1:6; 19:8,9; Prv 10:1–4,16,18; 13:9). The third is *synthetic parallelism*, where the idea expressed in the first line of a verse is developed and completed in the following lines (Ps 1:1; 3:5,6; 18:8–10; Prv 26:3). There are more complicated forms of parallelism but these three are most common.

Another characteristic of biblical poetry is the use of the letters of the Hebrew alphabet. Psalms in which verses are linked together by this means are called acrostic. Today, an acrostic is formed by taking a name and beginning the successive lines of the short poem with the letters that make up the name. The Hebrews took only the alphabet and arranged the lines of the poem according to the succession of the letters.

Each line of a psalm may begin with a different letter, as in Psalm 25. Or each of the stanzas may begin with the same letter until all 22 letters of the alphabet are exhausted, as in Psalm 119. However, this psalm, which is the most conspicuous example of a Hebrew acrostic poem, is quite complicated in its arrangement. Not only does each stanza begin with a letter, but each of the eight lines of every stanza begins with the same letter; so that eight alphabetic arrangements move through the psalm in parallel lines. Other elaborate acrostics are Psalms 9, 10, 34, 37, 111, 112, and 145.

The first four chapters of Lamentations also follow an acrostic arrangement. This example of acrostic arrangement is less noticeable to the English reader because the names of the Hebrew letters do not mark the beginning of the stanzas. In Lamentations 3 each letter of the alphabet begins three successive lines numbered as verses. Another acrostic occurs in Proverbs 31:10–31. It is an alphabetic description of the virtuous woman.

Another poetic device giving unity to a poem and marking its divisions is the refrain. Psalm 136 is an outstanding example of this arrangement. The refrain is "his love endures forever" and is used to conclude every verse.

The foregoing references to the external features of Hebrew poetry indicate no general agreement as to the nature of OT poetry. Parallelism or rhythmic balance of thought is not uniquely a feature of Hebraic poetry. For example, texts from Ras-Shamra, in northwest Syria, dated from around 1400 BC, exhibit extraordinary resemblances in style and language to the poetic books of the OT. In the Ras-Shamra texts reappears the parallelism of Hebrew poetry; it occurs also in Babylonian and Egyptian poems.

The meter of Hebraic poetry is dependent on accentuation; the unit is the couplet, in which the members may be of equal or varying length. Couplets are often arranged into strophes. The fundamental category of Hebrew poetry is the song or lyric. The song was accompanied by music (Gn 31:27; Ex 15:20; 1 Chr 25:6; Is 23:16; 30:29; Am 6:5), and could be associated with dance (Ex 15:20,21).

Apart from its poetic significance, parallelism can be useful in interpreting Scripture. The pairing of similar thoughts can aid in the correct exegesis of an ambiguous word or phrase. Psalm 33:6 is a simple example. In the second line of the verse the word "breath" parallels the Hebrew for "word" in the first line, by which the heavens were made (see also Ps 87:11). This reminds the interpreter of Holy Scripture that one must be able to use the aids which history, archaeology, and grammar provide in order to discover what literary forms the writers used. This applies particularly to Hebrew poetry when it occurs in the historical and prophetical books. Poetic imagery is not to be interpreted as if it were prose.

Some complete poems in the OT are embedded in the narrative books, and represent various types of Hebrew poems. The first recorded poem in the Bible is a battle song (Gn 4:23,24). Other famous examples of this type are the Song of Moses (Ex 15:1–18) and the Song of Deborah (Jgs 5:1–31). Then there is the Taunt Song (Nm 21:27–30), the Song of the Well (Nm 21:17,18), and the Song of Blessing. Of this latter type well-known examples are the Blessing of Jacob (Gn 49:1–27), the Blessing of Moses (Dt 33:1–29) and the four Blessings of Balaam (Nm 23:7–10; 23:18–24; 24:3–9; 24:15–25). There are also laments for the dead (2 Sm 1:19–27), and didactic poems which warn against improvidence (Prv 6:6–11) and drunkenness (Prv 23:29–35). Common throughout all of these various types of poems is religious emotion and fervor. The Songs of Moses and Deborah praise God as the giver of victory.

Most poems of distinctively religious fervor characterize the worship of the sanctuary. The psalms are religious poems sung with musical accompaniment. Many are private prayers, while others were composed for public worship, especially hymns of thanksgiving sung at the tabernacle or temple. It is in the Psalter that the soaring spirit of Hebrew poetry rises to a level never achieved by Israel's pagan neighbors; for the Hebrew worshiped God in spirit and in truth, and as he did so he was giving expression to a personal experience of the living God in his soul.

The internal qualities of Hebrew poetry are in part influenced by the age, social conditions, and environment in which the writers lived. Although the OT is of divine authorship it also comes within the scope of literature, and should be appreciated as such. Though the Holy Spirit inspired the message of the Hebrew writers, their individual writing styles remain clearly evident. Using simple and vivid diction, figures of speech, and literary devices, each poet expressed a wealth of religious thought, experience, and emotion; simile, metaphor, allegory, hyperbole, personification, irony, and wordplay all variously enhanced each writer's pattern of thinking. Hebrew poetry is the expression of the poet's human spirit, and it is the literature of revelation—the Word of God to humankind.

The NT has only a few poetical sections, and these are confessedly Hebraic in character. Probably the NT contains very little poetry because Christianity found the Hebrew Psalter adequate for its devotional purposes. All the writers of the NT were Jews, save Luke; yet he, curiously enough, is the one who has preserved for us the greater part of the poems: the Magnificat (Lk 1:46–55), the Benedictus (Lk 1:68–79), and the Nunc Dimittis (Lk 2:29–32). These poems are strongly Hebraic in form, character, and content.

As might be expected, the nature of Christian worship, the outpouring of the Holy Spirit, the joy of God's salvation, and the close connection between the worship of the earliest disciples and that of the Jews, all contributed to inspire the formation and use of Christian hymns.

This is proved by incidental references in the NT: Acts 16:25; 1 Corinthians 14:15,26; Ephesians 5:19; Colossians 3:16; and James 5:13. One should note, too, ascriptions of praise (Jude 24,25), and passages where rhythm is prominent (1 Cor 13; 15:54–57; Phil 2:5–11). The introduction of hymns of praise in the Book of Revelation, for example, in 5:12–14, probably points to their use by the early church. Ephesians 5:14 and 1 Timothy 3:16 probably contain fragments of hymns. It comes as a surprise to learn that parallelism, so common in OT poetry, is present in some forms of the teaching of Christ. For example, the Beatitudes (Mt 5:3–12) are an illustration of synthetic parallelism (where the second line of each verse completes the meaning of the first line). There is also a definite rhythmic quality in Matthew 11:28–30.

J. G. S. S. THOMSON

See BIBLE, INTERPRETATION OF THE; WISDOM, WISDOM LITERATURE; MUSIC AND MUSICAL INSTRUMENTS; JOB, BOOK OF; PSALMS, BOOK OF; PROVERBS, BOOK OF; SONG OF SOLOMON; ECCLESIASTES, BOOK OF; LAMENTATIONS, BOOK OF.

Bibliography. C.F. Burney, *The Poetry of Our Lord*; F.M. Cross and D.N. Freedman, *Studies in Ancient Yahwistic Poetry*; G.B. Gray, *The Forms of Hebrew Poetry*; J.L. Kugel, *The Idea of Hebrew Poetry*; T.H. Robinson, *The Poetry of the OT*; P.W. Skehan (ed.), *Studies in Israelite Poetry and Wisdom*.

Pollux. Son of Zeus and Castor's twin brother in Greek mythology. The twin brothers (Acts 28:11) are also called the Dioscuri.

See DIOSCURI.

Polygamy. *See* MARRIAGE, MARRIAGE CUSTOMS.

Pomegranate. *See* PLANTS.

Pontius Pilate. *See* PILATE, PONTIUS.

Pontus. Roman province in northeastern Asia Minor, located along the southern coast of the Black Sea. Galatia, Cappadocia, and Armenia bordered Pontus. About 1000 BC the first Greeks started to colonize the southeastern coast of the Black Sea, founding Sinope and Trebizond. Here Xenophon and his men reached the sea after their great eastern adventure. The famous geographer Strabo, to whom is owed knowledge of the ancient history of

Pontus, was born in the inland city of Amasia. Mithradates Eupator, king of Amasia, was, according to the Romans, the most formidable enemy the Republic ever encountered. He waged three wars against the Romans until his final defeat by Pompey around 60 BC.

Aquila, the tentmaker, whose wife Priscilla was a helpful co-worker of the apostle Paul, was born in Pontus. Unlike Paul, however, he was not a Roman citizen; hence, he was subject to the edict of Claudius and expelled from Rome because he was a Jew (Acts 18:2; 22:25–28).

The Christians who were resident there in Peter's day (1 Pt 1:1) were probably converts of those who returned from Jerusalem after the first Pentecost when Peter spoke (Acts 2:9).

Pools of Solomon. *See* SOLOMON, POOLS OF.

Poor, The.

Poverty as a Bad Thing. At times the Bible gives a very simple explanation of why people are rich or poor. If a man delights in the Law of the Lord, "wealth and riches are in his house"; "in all that he does, he prospers" (Ps 1:3; 112:3). With regard to Israel in OT days, these ideas are not quite as naive as they might seem. There is indeed a connection between sin and poverty. Israelite society was built on rules laid down by God, and if there was poverty in it, that must mean that somewhere the rules were being broken. The prophets often denounce those sins of men which impoverish their neighbors (Is 10:1,2; Jer 22:13; Ez 22:29; Am 2:6; 5:11,12; 8:4–6; Mi 2:2).

Whether a man's poverty was due to his own sin or to someone else's, the OT saw it as an evil to be combated, and the law made many provisions for the relief of it (e.g., Ex 22:21–27; Lv 19:9,10; Dt 15:1–15; 24:10–22). God cared for the needy, and expected his people to do the same.

During the period between the Testaments, that care continued to be exercised within Jewish communities scattered round the Mediterranean, and it was in due course taken up as a practical responsibility by the Christian church (Acts 11:29; 24:17; Rom 15:26; 1 Cor 16:1; Gal 2:10; Jas 2:15,16; 1 Jn 3:17); for Christians also, the giving of alms was a duty plainly expected by their Lord (Mt 6:2–4; Lk 12:33). It was not really a primitive communism that the early church practiced, for had they renounced personal possessions, they could not have done what they in fact did—namely, to *give* in cash or in kind *"as any had need"* (Acts 2:45; 4:35; emphasis added).

Poverty, then, although it provides the wealthy with a chance to show the virtue of generosity, is in itself (in the NT as in the OT) a bad thing. It is therefore quite appropriate for Scripture to use wealth, its opposite, as a metaphor for something good—in fact, for the supreme good—"the unsearchable riches of Christ" (Eph 3:8; see 2 Cor 6:10; 8:9).

Poverty as a Good Thing. As we can see, there is a certain sense in which righteousness will make a man prosperous and sin will make him poor. But ordinary life is more complicated than that. Psalms 1 and 112, referred to above, show only one side of the matter. What about "the prosperity of the wicked" (Ps 73:3) and its corollary, the man who is righteous yet poor? The answer of Scripture (e.g., Ps 37, 49,73; see Jb 21) is of course that the wealth of bad men is a fleeting thing, and that the righteous, though poor in worldly goods, have spiritual riches.

This thought—that so far from being prosperous, the good man may often be poor—is sometimes curiously inverted. The righteous may be poor, but Scripture sometimes appears to reckon that to be poor is to be righteous. Of course it is not automatically so (Prv 30:8,9), but such references are frequent enough, especially in the psalms (e.g., 9:18; 10:14; 12:5; 34:6; 35:10; 74:19), to deserve careful consideration. And on reflection they are not so strange. As God is specially concerned about the poor, so the poor may be specially concerned about God, for two good reasons. If there is poverty in Israel, it is because those with power are misusing it; so the poor will claim God's help first because it is his rule which is being flouted, and he must vindicate himself, and secondly, because in the circumstances there is no one else to turn to. In this way "poor" becomes almost a technical term. "The poor" are the humble, and the humble are the godly (Ps 10:17; 14:5,6; 37:11; Zep 3:12,13). Just as being rich can foster self-indulgence, self-confidence, pride, and the despising and oppression of one's fellows, so being poor should encourage the opposite virtues.

Instead of being an evil to be shunned, poverty thus becomes an ideal to be sought. Following the OT use of "the poor" and "the pious" as almost interchangeable terms, personal property was renounced by many Jews during the period between the Testaments. Among them were the sect of the Essenes, and the related community which was set up at Qumran near the Dead Sea. The latter actually called themselves "The Poor." This tradition continued into NT times. Possibly "the poor" at Jerusalem means a definite group within the church there (or even the Jerusalem church as a whole; Rom 15:26; Gal 2:10). Certainly there emerged later a Jewish-Christian sect called the "Ebionites" (from a Hebrew word for "poor").

The NT teaches clearly, of course, that what really matters is the attitude of the heart. It is quite possible to be poor yet grasping, or rich yet generous. Even so, with the OT background outlined above, the general sense of these words in the Gospels is that rich = bad, poor = good. On the one hand, the Sadducees are rich in worldly wealth and the Pharisees in spiritual pride, and men of property are selfish, foolish, and in grave spiritual peril (Mk 10:23; Lk 12:13–21; 16:19–31). On the other hand, it is devout and simple folk like Jesus's own family and friends who generally represent the poor.

In truth, therefore, the two versions of the first beatitude amount to the same thing. Matthew's has the depth: "Blessed are the poor in spirit" (5:3). But Luke's has the breadth. When he says simply "Blessed are you poor" (6:20), he means those who in their need—in *any* kind of need—turn to the Lord (6:17–20). It is to bring the gospel to such people that Christ has come into the world (Mt 11:5; Lk 4:18).

Christ himself embodies the same ideal, showing in his earthly life what it means to have nothing to fall back on except his Father's loving care (Mt 8:20), and finally allowing himself to be deprived even of life (Phil 2:5–8). In this way both lines of teaching converge on a passage mentioned earlier: "Though he was rich, yet for your sake he became poor, so that by his poverty you might become rich" (2 Cor 8:9). Our helpless poverty is an evil from which he comes to rescue us; his deliberately chosen poverty is the glorious means by which he does so.

MICHAEL J. WILCOCK

See RICHES; WEALTH; RIGHTEOUSNESS; WAGES; ALMS.

Poplar. See PLANTS.

Poratha. One of the 10 sons of Haman slain by the Jews (Est 9:8).

Porch. Court associated with the temple or palace. In the KJV it is the translation of several Hebrew words. In 1 Kings 7 and Ezekiel 40 the KJV has the most occurrences of porch as a part of the temple. The porch separated the Holy Place from the rest of the world. By means of several steps one would enter into the porch, which was elevated above the surrounding area. Both the steps and the elevation emphasized the separation of the temple. On both sides of the entrance to the porch stood the supporting pillars, the Jachin and the Boaz. In the NT the KJV has porch for *proaulion* and *stoa* ("portico"). The stoa was a roofed portico supported by pillars. Solomon's portico was the famous collonaded porch around the temple area facing the temple (cf. Jn 10:23; Acts 3:11; 5:12).

See ARCHITECTURE; TABERNACLE, TEMPLE.

Porcius Festus. See FESTUS, PORCIUS.

Porcupine. See ANIMALS.

Porphyry. See MINERALS, METALS, AND PRECIOUS STONES.

Porter. KJV rendering of gatekeeper.

See TRADES AND OCCUPATIONS (GATEKEEPER).

Portico, Solomon's. See PORCH; TABERNACLE, TEMPLE.

Possession, Demon. See DEMON, DEMON POSSESSION.

Postexilic Period, The.

The Biblical Perspective. The books that specifically cover the history of the postexilic or Persian period (539–c. 331) are Ezra, Nehemiah, Haggai, and Zechariah. These cover a period of over a century, only a portion of which is dealt with in detail, as the following table shows:

Books of Postexilic Times

Ezra 1:1–4:6,24	538–536
Ezra 5:1–6:22, Hg, Zec	520–515
Ezra 7–10	458
Ezra 4:7–23	c. 447
Neh 1:1–13:3	445–433
Neh 13:4–31	c. 431

The general religious level of the period immediately prior to the arrival of Ezra is illustrated in the Book of Malachi, where the hypocrisy blatantly practiced in the temple is attacked. Some scholars believe that the Book of Joel may have originated as late as 400 (others favor a 9th-century date), but there is no certain evidence. Joel views a massive infestation by swarms of locusts as God's judgment, a forerunner of the day of the Lord, and calls the nation and its priesthood to prayer and repentance.

The Collapse of the Babylonian Empire. This occurred with dramatic suddenness, largely because of internal resistance to the policies of the last Babylonian king, Nabonidus (555–539). His neglect of the traditional Babylonian deity, Marduk, in favor of the moon god, Sin, was particularly resented. Nabonidus lived in Taima during the last decade of his reign, refusing to enter Babylon where his son Belshazzar, ruled as virtual king, as noted in Daniel 5. Babylon fell to the

Persians in October 538 and the entire empire passed into their control.

The Policy of Persia. This is well documented through contemporary inscriptions, notably the record of Cyrus, the first king of the Persian Empire (559–530), in the "Cyrus Cylinder." A new phase in the relationship of conqueror to conquered peoples opened up, which contrasted with the policy of the Assyrian and Babylonian empires of crushing any opposition by massive force. Cyrus and his successors followed a conciliatory line, allowing exiled groups to return home, encouraging local faiths, posing as the champions of the territorial deities, and allowing local autonomy except where Persian interests were affected adversely. Doubtless the cost of this operation, although considerable, was infinitesimal compared with that of keeping rebellious subjects under constant subjection.

The Effects upon the Jews. The new enlightened policy is reflected in the decree of Cyrus, dated 538 (Ezr 1:1) and preserved in two versions. The first (Ezr 1:1–4) is clearly the official proclamation, while the second (Ezr 6:3–5) is a more prosaic memorandum dealing with building specifications, a record of Cyrus' commitment stored in the official archives (Ezr 6:1,2). The critical tendency to question the narrative in Ezra 1, especially on the score of the favorable references to the God of Israel and the vast financial support promised, has been nullified by the archaeological evidence, which shows an identical policy elsewhere. The Cyrus Cylinder, for example, notes "the gods who live within them [i.e., the cities] I returned to their places. . . . All of their inhabitants I collected and restored to their dwelling places." There is also a conciliatory reference to "Marduk, the great Lord" in the same source, and a similar reference to Sin, the moon god, in an inscription at Ur.

In Judah itself there is no evidence for any warfare in this period, which suggests that the Persian takeover of the area was nonviolent.

Judah was incorporated into the fifth Persian province, which included the entire area "west of the Euphrates River" (Ezra 7:21 LB). It was no more than a minor subdistrict, governed through Samaria.

The Return from Exile. The continuance of a large Jewish community in Babylonia shows that not all the Jews responded to the invitation to return to their homeland, probably because of the prosperity acquired in exile. But 42,360 dedicated Jews (Ezr 2:64) braved the challenge of a 4-month 900-mile journey under Sheshbazzar (Ezr 1:8), the officially appointed leader, and Zerubbabel his nephew (Ezr 3:2), who was probably the one to whom the Jews looked as leader. With great enthusiasm the Jews rebuilt the altar of sacrifice and resumed the observance of the traditional feasts (Ezr 3:1–6), revealing both a sense of stewardship (Ezr 2:68,69) and careful attention to the requirements of the Law (Ezr 3:2,4, etc.). Soon after, work on the second temple commenced, the materials and master craftsmen being imported from Tyre and Sidon (Ezr 3:7–9; cf. 1 Kgs 5). When the foundations were laid the worshipers were doubtless aware that they were fulfilling God's promise through Jeremiah (Ezr 3:10,11; cf. Jer. 33:10,11). But their high hopes were quickly dashed: there was opposition from neighboring areas (Ezr 4:4,5); selfishness in giving their own accommodations a higher priority than the Lord's house (Hg 1:2–4,9); and a series of crop failures which further reduced morale (Hg 1:6,10,11; 2:17).

Work on the temple was not resumed until Haggai and Zechariah appeared in 520. They encouraged Zerubbabel and Joshua the high priest, rebuked the people for their apathy and selfishness, and promised God's presence and blessing upon the temple project (Hg 1:12–2:9). Zechariah's preaching went beyond the building of the temple, including the rebuilding of Jerusalem itself (Zec 2:1–5) and its world reputation (Zec 2:1–5,11,12; 8:22). The

The Three Returns from Exile

	First Return	Second Return	Third Return
Scripture	Ezra 1–6	Ezra 7–10	Nehemiah 1–2
Date	538 B.C.	458 B.C.	445 B.C.
King of Persia	Cyrus	Artaxerxes	Artaxerxes
Leader of Return	Zerubbabel	Ezra	Nehemiah
Leader's Tribe and Ancestry	Judah (through David and Jehoiakin)	Levi (through Aaron, Phinehas, Zadok)	
Leader's Role	governor	priest	governor
Number	49,897	1,774	armed escort
Other Leaders at the Time	Joshua the priest; Haggai, Zechariah	Nehemiah, Malachi	Ezra, Malachi
Result	Temple built	Law taught People separated	Jerusalem's walls rebuilt

two leaders were addressed in ways which anticipated the Messiah (Hg 2:21–23; Zec 6:10–14). But the Persian king Darius (521–486 BC) was not alarmed when the rebuilding operation was reported to him (Ezr 5:1–6:13) and allowed the work to continue. In February 515 it was dedicated (Ezr 6:14–16). The Jewish community again had a focal point for its religion but the political situation remained difficult, with no real security in a still shattered city.

The Return of Ezra. The traditional date of Ezra's return is 458, surmising that the king Artaxerxes noted in Ezra 7:7 was Artaxerxes I Longimanus (464–424) and not Artaxerxes II Mnemen (404–359). Some scholars, allowing that Ezra and Nehemiah were contemporary but believing that Nehemiah preceded Ezra, suggest that a tens unit has dropped out in Ezra 7:7, and that the date should be the 27th (438) or 37th year (428). While this is plausible, there remains strong support for the traditional view. It accords with the order of the two books in the OT and requires no textual emendation. It also accounts for the section in Ezra 4:7–23 where, in the reign of Artaxerxes, an abortive effort was made by a recently returned group to rebuild the wall of Jerusalem. Nehemiah 1:1–4 suggests that this was regarded as important and its abrupt termination, by a decree of the king, caused Nehemiah great distress. The probability is that Ezra, recently returned, realized that little could be done in the way of major religious reformation until Jerusalem was secure, but in attempting to rebuild the wall he exceeded his mandate and was not able to function adequately until Nehemiah arrived, when the new security of Jerusalem allowed the great Law-reading ceremony of Nehemiah 8:1–12 to take place.

Ezra's ministry concerned the promulgation of the Law of Moses, the Pentateuch, which had long been extant in its final form by this time. Ezra 7 shows that Artaxerxes was following the traditional Persian policy of encouraging good relationships with his subject peoples. Ezra's appointment (7:12) was to a state office; it has frequently been paraphrased as "Secretary of State for Jewish religious affairs." Ezra himself was possibly responsible for the terms of reference, favorable to the Jews, in Artaxerxes' letter (Ezr 7:12–26). His appointment, covering the whole area west of the Euphrates (7:21), included the Samaritans, which accounts for their bitterness in referring to him subsequently as "Ezra the accursed."

The first crisis which confronted Ezra on his return concerned mixed marriages (Ezr 9:10). This was to prove a recurring problem, probably because of the low number of females who returned from captivity. Nehemiah had to deal twice with the same situation (Neh 10:28–30; 13:23–28). It is noteworthy that Ezra did not exercise his Persian-backed authority, preferring to rely solely on a moral and spiritual appeal, which, in the event, proved effective (Ezr 10).

Nehemiah's Return and Ministry. The approach to Nehemiah by Hanani and others (Neh 1:1–3) could hardly have been connected with the Babylonian destruction of Jerusalem in 586, 140 years before. Nehemiah would have known about that and his grief (Neh 1:4) would have been inexplicable. Almost certainly, these men had traveled as far as they had to inform Nehemiah of the complete failure of a recent attempt to rebuild the wall, recorded in Ezr 4:7–23, and to seek his mediation before the very king who had authorized the decree which compelled work on the wall to cease. A friend in high places was vital, and Nehemiah, a trusted and influential member of the court (Neh 1:11), was approached for this delicate and dangerous task. Nehemiah 1:4–2:8 shows how well he prepared for and seized his opportunity. His appointment as the governor of Judah (Neh 5:14) involved the removal of this area from the control of the governor of Samaria, which accounts for the unrelenting hostility of Sanballat (Neh 2:19; 4:1, etc.). The evidence of Nehemiah 3 suggests that the extent of Judah at this time was limited, probably not reaching as far north as Bethel or as far south as Hebron. Nehemiah was faced with opposition which included ridicule (Neh 2:19; 4:1–3), armed force (Neh 4:8,11), discouragement (Neh 4:10), internal economic problems (Neh 5:1–18), intrigue (Neh 6:1,2), intimidation, and blackmail (Neh 6:5–14). In spite of this the wall was completed in the incredibly brief period of 52 days (Neh 6:15). (Archaeological investigation under Kathleen Kenyon demonstrated that Nehemiah deliberately restricted the perimeter of the city wall.) Aware through his nocturnal reconnaissance (Neh 2:11–15) of the difficulty of building on the steep eastern slopes of Mt Ophel, where the debris from the Babylonian destruction and the neglect of one and a half centuries had accumulated, he built on the easier line along the ridge of the mountain in this sector.

In addition to this monumental achievement, Nehemiah completely reorganized the social and economic life of Jerusalem, dealing with alienated mortgages, excessive interest rates (Neh 5:1–13), mixed marriages (Neh 10:30; 13:23–30), sabbath observance (Neh 10:31; 13:15–21), and temple supplies (Neh 10:32–40; 13:10–13). Almost certainly, it was this political and economic security which allowed Ezra, who arrived 13 years earlier, to proceed with his great religious reformation based on the Law. Nehemiah's book, usually called the "Nehemiah Memoirs," was probably presented by him in the temple as a "votive offering" (as indicated by the form of Neh 5:19; 13:14,22,31).

The Emergence of Judaism. The reforms of Ezra and Nehemiah, in their distinct but complementary fields, brought much-needed security to Judah. Jewish religion and politics from this point on was dominated by their influence. The origins of Judaism must, however, be seen as predating both Ezra and Nehemiah. In particular, the collapse of a temple-dominated cult when Jerusalem was destroyed in 586, and the period of the exile, were decisive. The Jews who survived, under the leadership of prophets like Ezekiel, viewed the national calamity as God's righteous judgment. They had forsaken the covenant and were in grave danger of vanishing as a distinguishable group. Their survival is largely due to the fact that they rediscovered their identity as the covenant community which marked them off from other nations and called for a measure of separation. The symbols of the covenant, sabbath observance and circumcision, and the need for ritual cleanness gave outward expression to this particularism. In the immediate postexilic period this distinction was frequently blurred, especially because of the prevalence of mixed marriages and the lack of an authoritative code which could act as a uniting bond. Nehemiah's wall and the measures against intermarriage introduced by both Ezra and Nehemiah provided a quasiphysical security against intrusion by the heathen. But such factors required a more positive impetus if the small Jewish community was to survive, and it was here that Ezra's contribution was decisive. The law book which formed the basis of his reforms was not new in either its content or form. Although often neglected, it had been the law code for centuries and was evidently the basis of appeal of the great classical prophets. Now, however, it became more than a collection of laws. It was accepted as a manual of instruction covering every area of life. Strict adherence to it, and to the oral and literary interpretations of its contents which gradually developed, was required. The Jews became the people of the Book. There was both weakness and strength in this movement. The weakness is clearly seen in the unlovely features of later Judaism, when an unduly literalistic emphasis threatened to destroy the spirit of the Law. The strength is perhaps best seen in the Maccabean crisis in the early 2nd century BC, when the Jewish faith faced the challenge of an attractive and apparently all-powerful Hellenism. It is a great tribute to successive generations of unknown teachers of the Law that Judaism was sufficiently strong, integrated, and organized to surmount this crisis. Ezra and, to a lesser extent, Nehemiah, can hardly be blamed for the regrettable features of the Judaism that emerged later. Without their contribution, it is difficult to envisage how the Jewish faith could have survived. The small, defenseless group, surrounded by hostile powers, with no political independence or adequate spiritual cohesion, would surely have been engulfed. Ezra's reputation in Jewish circles in the intertestamental period, which regarded him virtually as a second Moses (cf. 2 Esd 14), was well founded.

The Remainder of the Persian Period. Persian control, which probably centered on Lachish, was traditionally mild, except where her interests were directly threatened. There is no evidence of any major discontent in Judah, which enjoyed a considerable degree of autonomy. The Phoenician revolt of 351, which took Artaxerxes III (359–338) three years to subdue, was the only serious disturbance in the area. While Artaxerxes deported some Jews to Hyrcania, southeast of the Caspian Sea, that was probably a precautionary measure, and Judah does not appear to have been greatly involved in the revolt. The Jerusalem priests were allowed to mint their own coinage and levy a temple tax. Under the wider influence of the Persian Empire, Hebrew gradually fell out of popular usage as a spoken language, being replaced by Aramaic. As the international stature of Greece increased so the influence of Hellenism began to be felt, even in Judah.

The Jews of the Dispersion. *In Egypt.* Jewish mercenaries were in Egypt as garrison troops before the fall of Judah in 586 and subsequent events sent a further flood of refugees southwards (Jer 43:5–7). Major archaeological discoveries at Elephantine, near the modern Aswan, have illumined the conditions under which a Jewish community, numbering about 350, lived. The documents, mainly private contracts, date from 495–399 BC. They show that the religion of these Jews was markedly syncretistic, with Anath, the so-called Queen of Heaven (cf. Jer 7:18; 44:15–19) being worshiped as the wife of Israel's God. One document, usually referred to as the Passover Papyrus and dated 419 BC, indicates that Jerusalem was regarded by the Persians as the official center for the Jewish religion, which harmonizes with Ezra's commission (Ezr 7).

Of principal interest to the historian is the correspondence between the Elephantine Jews and the Persian governor concerning the temple. This was destroyed in 410 in a riot spearheaded by Egyptian priests who may have objected to the offering of animal sacrifices but were probably motivated by jealousy. The Persians, understandably, kept a tighter reign on the Egyptians. For instance, when Cambyses invaded Egypt (525 BC) he destroyed the Egyptian temple but spared the Jewish one at Elephantine. The Jerusalem authorities pointedly ignored the pleas from Elephantine, probably an indication of the disfavor with which they viewed its religious deviations. When permission to rebuild the temple was finally granted through the mediation of Samaria and Bagoas, the Persian governor, animal sacrifices were specifically excluded, possibly in deference to either the Egyptians or the Jerusalem priests, or both. The correspondence with Samaria was with the two sons of Sanballat, Delaiah and Shelemiah, suggesting that Sanballat, Nehemiah's old adversary, was no longer the real power.

The community at Elephantine must not be regarded as typical. But it may be assumed that there were other such tightly knit Jewish communities that occasionally faced local opposition and looked to Jerusalem for leadership, while allowing themselves considerable freedom in modifying its strict Judaism. The correspondence also illustrates the tolerant Persian patronage of local religions.

In Babylonia. A considerable community of Jews elected to remain in Babylonia. Archaeological evidence suggests that many of them prospered, since there is a high incidence of Jewish names occurring in business transactions of various kinds. There were also close and continuing links between them and Jerusalem. Ezra's appeal for levitical reinforcements, addressed to a group at Casiphia (Ezr 8:15–20), suggests that the Jewish community in Babylonia was extremely well-organized. The Book of Esther also witnesses to the dispersion of Jews throughout this area of the Persian Empire during the reign of Ahasuerus, who is usually regarded as Xerxes I (485–465). The deliverance of the Jews from their oppressors, as recorded in Esther, was celebrated subsequently as the Feast of Purim.

In Antioch. As elsewhere, the Jewish community was a closely knit group, respected and tolerated for the stable contribution it made to the economic life of the city. As in Egypt, the Jews enjoyed special privileges and displayed great enthusiasm in their proselytising.

Other Religious Features of the Postexilic Period. *The Decline of Prophecy.* There were three main reasons for this:

1. The prophetic movement as a whole became discredited after Jerusalem fell in 586.

The large number of popular cult prophets who foretold a sudden end to the Babylonian oppression (e.g., Jer 28:1–4) were proved decisively wrong. The suspicion which henceforth attached to prophecy was increased further in the Persian period, when large numbers of itinerant "prophets" of various religions traveled widely. Zechariah 13:2–6 shows the stern measures advocated against such "false prophets and fortune tellers."

2. There was a markedly different historical situation. The chastened remnant which survived had turned away from the blatant apostasy which characterized the preexilic period, so that the prophetic condemnation was not required with the same urgency. The temple and its cult and the Law had acquired a new prominence and postexilic prophecy generally was concerned either with the rebuilding of the temple (e.g., Haggai and Zechariah) or the purification of its cult (e.g., Malachi). Once this goal had been realized, the role of the prophet was diminished. Another historical factor was the relatively large number of priests who returned from captivity, doubtless encouraged by the prospect of serving in the rebuilt temple. The main need at this time was for the priest, revealing God's will on the basis of the Law.

3. There was an increasing stress on the transcendence of God, caused partly by an emphasis upon priestly mediation through the cult and partly by a fear of God which resulted from the recent judgment. The apocalyptic movement, with its emphasis on angelic intermediaries between man and a transcendent God, encouraged this tendency. Correspondingly, the prophetic appeal for a personal, moral walk with God weakened.

The Rise of the Synagogue. Some type of local worship, independent of the temple and its sacrifices, must have developed in captivity, with the Law increasingly occupying a dominant position. Later on the prophetic books were read and expounded but the primary stress was always on the Law. This mode of worship later took root in the homeland, and the synagogue gradually developed into the focal point of the community, social and educative as well as spiritual. It facilitated the worldwide continuance and expansion of the Jewish faith, independent of Jerusalem.

The Extent of Persian Religious Influence. This has often been overexaggerated. The high ethical tone of the Jewish faith was established long before the Persian period, and the development of Judaism as a "book religion" was due to the pressures of a historical situation, not in imitation of Zoroastrianism, the official Persian religion. Similarly a highly developed eschatology, including a belief in the resurrection, had an indigenous origin. Possibly in two realms only, the language and thought forms of apocalypticism and the remarkable development of angelology in the postexilic period, was the Persian influence. But this was peripheral to the mainstream of Israel's unique religious heritage.

The Samaritans. The rivalry between north and south of the preexilic period increased rather than diminished in the Persian period. The returned exiles in 538 refused the offer of help from the local residents (Ezr 4:1–5), who doubtless included the Samaritans, probably realizing that the offer was more a device to infiltrate and control the temple rebuilding operation. Ezra's mission, centered on Jerusalem but including Samaria within its scope (Ezr 7:25,26), was deeply resented, and Nehemiah's appointment as governor of Jerusalem meant that it was again politically independent of Samaria. The flames of bitter division were thus fanned by racial, religious, historical, and political considerations, and by the time of Ezra and Nehemiah the rift was complete and virtually unbridgeable. But a total break was unlikely until the Greek period (c.331 BC), since Jerusalem was recognized by the Persians as the official center for the Jewish faith. ARTHUR E. CUNDALL

See EZRA, BOOK OF; NEHEMIAH, BOOK OF; ISRAEL, HISTORY OF; CHRONOLOGY, OLD TESTAMENT; HAGGAI, BOOK OF; ZECHARIAH, BOOK OF; JUDAISM; DIASPORA OF THE JEWS; SAMARITANS; JEW.

Pot. *See* POTTERY.

Potiphar. Officer who purchased Joseph when he arrived in Egypt after being sold by his brothers to the Ishmaelites/Midianites (Gn 37:36; 39:1). The word translated "officer" is derived from an Akkadian word for a court official. By the 1st millennium the meaning eunuch was attached to the term; hence, the NEB has eunuch in Genesis 37:36 following the Septuagint tradition. But most English versions are correct in rendering it "officer" or "official." Little, if anything, is known of eunuchs in Egypt, and certainly they played no role in Pharaoh's court in the 2nd millennium BC.

A second title held by Potiphar was "captain of the guard," which seems to be a Semitic expression for an Egyptian title rather than a transliteration of an Egyptian phrase. This same title is applied to Nebuzardan, Nebuchadnezzar's general (see 2 Kgs 25:8,11, 20; Jer 39:9–11). The Egyptian counterpart to this title suggests that this officer was an instructor for retainers, who were attached to the king. The titles indicate that Potiphar was

a man of some importance and status. His purchase of a Semitic slave to serve as a domestic is in keeping with the practice of Egyptians from 1800 BC onward.

The name Potiphar seems to be a transliteration of the Egyptian name, meaning "he whom Pre [the sun god] has given." This name formula is known in Egypt beginning around the 13th century BC.

When falsely accused of trying to seduce Potiphar's wife, Joseph is placed in prison (Gn 39:20). Some think that Potiphar as "captain of the guard" would have been the warden. But Genesis 39:21 tells us that the "keeper of the prison" was impressed with Joseph's abilities (something Potiphar had already learned—cf. Gn 39:2–6), and so gave him special responsibilities. The warden's discovery of Joseph's talents while in prison suggests that he was a different man.

See EGYPT, EGYPTIANS; JOSEPH #1.

Potiphera, Potipherah. Priest of On whose daughter, Asenath, was given to Joseph as his wife by Pharaoh (Gn 41:45,50; 46:20; KJV Potipherah). On (or Heliopolis) was the center of the sun god cult, and Potiphera was likely a high ranking priest in the cult. His name, which means "he whom Pre [the sun god] has given," does not appear in Egyptian records until the 10th century BC, a fact employed by those who prefer a late date for the Book of Genesis. Yet the name is known from the 13th century (the time of Moses), and its full form may be a modernization of a name common in Joseph's era (c. 1780–1570 BC).

See EGYPT, EGYPTIANS; JOSEPH #1.

Potsherd. Pieces of broken pottery used in OT times to carry hot coals or dip water, as lids for storage containers or cooking kettles, as a medium for written communication, or to add grit to waterproofing compounds. Job used sherds to scrape himself (2:8) and as a symbol for mythical might (41:30). The symbolic importance of sherds is clear in Psalm 22:15; Isaiah 30:14; 45:9 (KJV); and Ezekiel 23:34.

See POTTERY; WRITING AND BOOKS.

Potsherd Gate. Gate in the south section of the preexilic Jerusalem wall. It led to the Valley of Hinnom and to the Potter's Field. Potters could dispose of sherds there, hence its name. Some identify it with the Dung Gate, and the KJV (relating the term to the Hebrew word for sun), renders it "East Gate" (Jer 19:2).

See JERUSALEM.

Pottage. Red-colored vegetable stew commonly served in the OT (Hg 2:12). Pottage was made of lentils, herbs, onions, and sometimes meat. Its aroma proved strong enough to shift a birthright from Esau to Jacob (Gn 25:29–34). Elisha's disciples relished its nourishment (2 Kgs 4:38–41).

See Food and Food Preparation.

Potter. *See* Pottery; Trades and Occupations.

Potter's Field. Name of a burial ground outside Jerusalem (Mt 27:7,10).

See Blood, Field of.

Pottery.

Introduction. There are many references to the potter and his work in the Bible. Typical are the following: "O house of Israel, can I not do with you as this potter has done? says the Lord. Behold, like the clay in the potter's hand, so are you in my hand . . ." (Jer 18:6); "Thou hast made me of clay; and wilt thou turn me to dust again?" (Jb 10:9); "O Lord . . . we are the clay, and thou art our potter; we are all the work of thy hand" (Is 64:8). In the creation story God is portrayed as a potter making man from the ground (Gn 2:7). His absolute sovereignty in the election of Israel is argued by Paul (Rom 9:20,21) from an illustration used by Isaiah (45:9) about a potter: "Does the clay say to the potter, 'What are you making?' Does your work say, 'He has no hands'?" (NIV). Jeremiah graphically prophesied the destruction of Jerusalem by breaking a potter's earthen flask into so many pieces that it could not be restored (19:11). The Jews, at the time of the destruction, though precious in God's sight, were "reckoned as earthen pots, the work of a potter's hands!" (Lam

A Sumerian steatite bowl, carved with human figures and animals (from Khafajah, in central Iraq, *c.* 2700).

4:2)—an expression of their human frailty; they could be easily broken and destroyed.

A broken pottery vessel in the ancient world was considered so worthless that the pieces were swept aside or thrown out the window and a new one made. The potter's art was widely known and vessels were readily available at a cheap price. People normally did not transport their vessels when they moved. It was easier to make or buy new ones than to try to carry them, especially the larger ones. Broken pieces, however, were not without some use. Job scraped the secretion from his sores with a potsherd, which is a broken piece of pottery (2:8). At a much later time, potsherds were used to write notes on and were called ostraca. The psalmist spoke of his strength as having dried up like a potsherd (22:15), a reference to the lack of moisture in a dried and fired pottery vessel. The eventual defeat of polytheistic and idolatrous pagan nations is described as vessels of pottery being dashed to the ground and broken by the righteous (Ps 2:9; Rv 2:27).

History and Development. The first pottery was made by hand, molded into the desired shape and dried in the sun. There are no records describing the work of the ancient potter and his or her place in society, although the walls of tombs and palaces in Egypt abound with pictures of potters at work and a great deal can be learned by observing the activities portrayed. The first potters are thought to have been women who out of necessity tried to produce vessels to use in the preparation of food while the men were out trying to bring in the food. This still seems to be the pattern in places like Africa, Anatolia, Kurdistan, and the southwestern United States. Eventually the making of pottery became a profession, apparently practiced by certain people in a large village and often by itinerant craftsmen moving from village to village making pottery to meet the demand and then moving on.

The discovery that moved pottery making from an occasional activity of a housewife to that of a profession was the invention of the potter's wheel. The speed with which vessels could then be made industrialized the craft and it eventually became an exclusively male occupation, although there is evidence that people continued to make some vessels at home. Until the discovery of the potter's wheel the techniques of making pots by laying coils of clay, one on top of the other, was the predominant method used, especially for large vessels. The first potter's wheel found in excavations in the lands of the Bible come from Ur in Sumer around 3500 to 3000 BC. It may have been developed in emerging urban settlements due to a greater market for pottery. Jeremiah speaks of a potter's workshop in the 6th century BC: "So I went down to the potter's house, and there he was working at his wheel. And the vessel he was making of clay was spoiled in the potter's hand" (18:3,4). There is evidence in Greece of large workshops in the Classical period employing more than 50 workers.

Clay must be spun at least 100 revolutions a minute to create the centrifugal force necessary to "throw" the vessel. The oldest wheels were made of two stones, a lower one with a hole in the center and an upper one with a protrusion that fits into the lower hole allowing the upper stone to be turned. The upper stone with a larger board attached to it on which the vessel rested was undoubtedly turned by an apprentice. By the Hellenistic period, after 300 BC, the foot wheel was invented. Existence of foot wheels much earlier, as early as the 4th millennium BC, has been argued but not clearly demonstrated.

Another technique used in ancient pottery making was the molds. Molds were carved out of soft stone or made from clay for use in mass production of the same kind of vessel. Lamp molds are rather common in museums of the Middle East from the Hellenistic and Roman periods. Small oil lamps were made in two parts in the molds, upper half and lower half, and then fused together before firing. Herodian lamps also had spatulated spouts that were formed independently of the other two parts.

Archaeological Importance. Clay is found virtually everywhere on the earth, a fact which contributes to its widespread use in simultaneously developing cultures. This, in turn, has been a major contributing factor to the growing importance of pottery making in the study of ancient civilizations through archaeology—especially in the Mediterannean world.

Because clay is so abundant and widespread and because it was so cheaply and easily turned into pottery, ancient people tended to leave that pottery behind when they moved to a new location. Furthermore, because the clay, once fired, was virtually indestructible it remained for millennia in exactly the same condition as it was when it was left behind. It is not affected by burial in the earth. Due to these factors modern archaeology has developed a technique of dating ancient cultures based on ceramic remains.

Sir Flinders Petrie, while working in Egypt, noticed that in tombs, palaces, and temples which could be dated from hieroglyphic inscriptions on the walls, there were pottery vessels that differed in style from one time period to another. For example, vessels characteristic of the Bronze Age were different from those characteristic of the Iron Age. Later, in 1890, when Petrie was working at Tell Hesi in southern Israel, he discovered that distinct layers of occupational debris called strata, could be distinguished like layers of cake, and that each layer successively lower was successively earlier. He also noted that the pottery was not only different from layer to layer but was similar to the pottery he had seen in Egypt which he could date. By carefully recording these changes in form, Petrie worked out a chronology that has become the foundation of dating excavations in a part of the world where little else remains by which dates may be determined. This technique was further refined by W.F. Albright at Tell Beit Mirsim, also in southern Israel, in 1926–32, and is continually being upgraded by scores of excavations every year all over the Middle East. There are still gaps in the typology established and uncertainties regarding the transition from one cultural period to another, but general patterns are emerging with increasing clarity and this technique remains a preferred method of establishing chronology in Middle Eastern excavations.

Differences in the form as well as the content of ancient pottery help in determining not only the date but the locality from which the pottery's clay originated. Technical means are now available by which we are able to locate the general area and sometimes the very quarry from which certain kinds of clay have come. Generally speaking, the pottery of Bible lands gradually became better with the passing of the centuries. There were occasional exceptions to this rule, however, and some Bronze Age vessels were lovelier and better made than some of those in the Iron Age. Vessels from Egypt and Greece or Cyprus tended to be nicer than those made in Israel, Jordan, and Syria. There was also a difference in the vessels depending upon the nature of their intended use. Pottery used for routine purposes was often rougher than that which is intended for special purposes. Economics was undoubtedly the reason. Ancient "crystal and china" were rare and expensive, just as today.

For vessels that required greater asthetic quality a technique was developed of painting the pot with a mixture of fine clay and water just before firing to produce a smooth pleasing surface (slip). Burnishing was another technique used on ancient pottery, consisting of rubbing the vessel with a stone before firing which caused a lovely gloss on the vessel. Usually this was done along with the application of slip and together they helped prevent the loss of liquids through the pores of the clay. Some of the most beautiful pottery found in the Mediterranean world are of this type— terra sigillata, both eastern and western, Cyp-

A painted Corinthian vase.

riot Red Slip, African Red Slip, Egyptian Red Slip, and Arretine Ware.

Although glaze was known in Egypt, probably as far back as the 5th millennium BC, it was not common in Syria/Palestine (modern Israel, Jordan, Lebanon, and Syria) until the Arab (Moslem) periods, beginning in the 7th or 8th centuries. Glaze is a thin glossy coat on the outside of vessels. It is made of the same minerals as clay—silica and alumina—to which soda or lead has been added. When heated to a certain temperature the solution melts, forming a glass-like appearance, and can be produced in several colors. Glazes are known from the Hellenistic and Roman periods but became prominent in Moslem pottery.

An average ancient home would have within it large amphorae and pithoi to hold liquids such as wine or water. These were pointed on the bottom and designed originally to lie against the slope of a ship's hull while being transported. In homes of the common people they were partially set into the ground and leaned against the wall. In taverns in Pompeii and Herculaneum they were stored in wooden racks. Large open-mouthed jars would be partially buried into the ground to keep the liquid contained in them cool. Also, grains of various kinds could be kept in these, some of which were four feet in height and three feet wide. Smaller water decanters holding a quart or more were commonly used. Globular jugs were used to serve wine, having spouts that prevented spilling the precious liquid. Round canteens, with handles on either shoulder, were used to carry water on a journey. Bowls and dishes were common in various sizes and depths in ancient homes but as yet no pottery cups or flat plates have been found. Large mouth dishes known as kraters were used for drinking. Cooking was done in medium-sized (about one gallon) pots with rounded bottoms which would sit easily in the fire or in a dug-out place in the floor after being taken from the fire. They also had two looped handles, which allowed them to be hung over the fire.

The amount of diversity in both size and shape of ancient pottery is truly remarkable. Vessels were painted in classical Greece with vivid descriptions of religion, sex, warfare, and community life. Earlier vessels of Minoan and Mycenean cultures contain beautiful artwork in the form of plants, animals, and marine life, as well as geometric design. From earliest times in the Middle East, variations in design were created by the use of dark and light shades of slip painted or poured randomly on vessels. There seems to be an inherent desire in people to beautify the implements with which they work.

JOHN R. MCRAY

See INDUSTRY AND COMMERCE; INSCRIPTIONS; ARCHAEOLOGY; TRADES AND OCCUPATIONS; ARCHAEOLOGY AND THE BIBLE; BRICK, BRICKKILN.

Bibliography. W.F. Albright, *The Archaeology of Palestine;* R.B.K. Amiran, *Ancient Pottery of the Holy Land;* J.L. Kelso, *Ceramic Vocabulary of the OT;* N. Lapp, *Palestinian Ceramic Chronology,* 200 BC–AD 70.

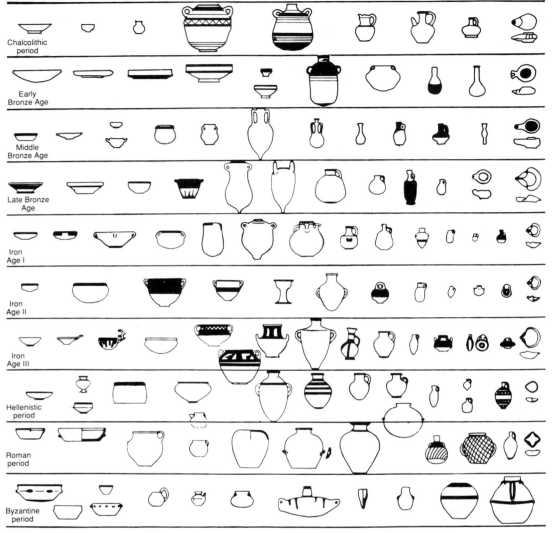

Ten periods of pottery, showing a variety of shapes and sizes.

Pound. *See* WEIGHTS AND MEASURES.

Power. Ability to do things, by virtue of strength, skill, resources, or authorization. In the Hebrew of the OT and the Greek of the NT there are several different words used for power. What the Bible says about power may be subsumed under four headings: (1) the un-limited power of God; (2) the limited power God gives to his creatures; (3) the power of God seen in Jesus Christ; (4) the power of God (by the Holy Spirit) in the lives of his people.

The Unlimited Power of God. God is al-mighty and all other power is derived from him and subject to him. Much that the Bible says is summed up in the words of 1 Chroni-cles 29:11–12 addressed to God in praise: "Thine, O Lord, is the greatness, and the power, and the glory, and the victory, and the majesty; for all that is in the heavens and in the earth is thine; thine is the kingdom, O Lord . . . thou rulest over all. In thy hand are power and might; and in thy hand it is to make great and to give strength to all." Using human terms the OT often speaks of God's "mighty hand" and his "outstretched arm," both being used for the power of God in action (Ex 6:6; 7:4; Ps 44:2,3). His power is seen in creation (Ps 65:6; Is 40:26; Jer 10:12; 27:5), in his rule over the world (2 Chr 20:6), in his acts of salvation and judgment (Ex 15:6; Dt 26:8) and in all that he does for his people (Ps 111:6).

The NT as well as the OT speaks of the mighty power of God. Ephesians 1:19 speaks of "the immeasurable greatness of his power" and the words of Jesus in Matthew 26:64 show that the word could be substituted for the very name of God when he said that the Son of man would be seen "seated at the right hand of Power."

The Limited Power God Gives to His Creatures. Animals have power, as is particularly evident in the wild ox, the horse, and the lion (Jb 39:11,19; Prv 30:30). There is power in wind and storm, thunder and lightning. Power is given to men: physical strength (Jgs 16:5,6), power to fight (Jgs 6:12), and the power to do good and the power to do harm (Gn 31:29; Prv 3:27; Mi 2:1). Rulers have God-given power and authority (Rom 13:1). The Bible also speaks of the power of angels (2 Pt 2:11) and of spiritual beings known as "principalities and powers." Certain powers are given to Satan (see Jb 1:6–12; 2:1–6). Sin, evil, and death are allowed to have some power over men (Hos 13:14; Lk 22:53; Rom 3:9). All of these, however, have only limited power and God is able to give his people strength to conquer all these powers when arrayed against them. He can save them from the power of animals (Dn 6:27; Lk 10:19) and from the power of men over them. To Pilate Jesus said, "You would have no power over me unless it had been given you from above"(Jn 19:11). He is able to deliver men from the power of sin and death, from Satan and from all the spiritual forces of evil (2 Cor 10:4; Eph 6:10–18). The "ruler of this world" could ultimately have no power over Christ (Jn 14:30) and so cannot have power over those who rely on him.

The Power of God Seen in Jesus Christ. The Gospels bear frequent witness to the power of Christ and in the preaching in the Acts of the Apostles reference is made similarly to this. Power was shown in his miracles (Mt 11:20; Acts 2:22), in his work of healing and exorcism (Lk 4:36; 5:17; 6:19; Acts 10:38). Power is shown supremely in his resurrection. Jesus speaks of his power to give up his life and power to take it again (Jn 10:18), but the NT speaks most frequently of the power of God the Father shown in the raising of his Son from the dead (Rom 1:4; Eph 1:19,20). In the end he will be seen coming "on the clouds of heaven with power and great glory" (Mt 24:30). With regard to his human life on earth, however, it may be noted in the light of what follows that he lived and did his mighty works in the power of the Holy Spirit (Lk 4:14; Acts 10:38).

The Power of God in the Lives of His People. In the OT it is often said that by the power of God the weak are made strong. "He gives power to the faint, and to him who has no might he increases strength" (Is 40:29) so that they "go from strength to strength" (Ps 84:7; see also Ps 68:35; 138:3). We read in particular of his power being given to prophets (Mi 3:8) and kings (1 Sm 2:10; Ps 21:1) and it is said that in an outstanding way power will be given to the Messiah (Is 9:6; 11:2; Mi 5:4), but to all God's people power is offered that they may live for him and serve him (Is 49:5). When we turn to the NT we read of the gospel itself as "the power of God for salvation to every one who has faith" (Rom 1:16). "To all who received" Jesus Christ "who believed in his name, he gave power to become children of God" (Jn 1:12). In that life as children of God power is received from the Holy Spirit (Acts 6:8), inner strength to live in his service (Eph 3:16), power to be his witnesses (Lk 24:49; Acts 1:8), power to endure suffering (2 Tm 1:8), power that enables for ministry (Eph 3:7), power in the face of weakness (2 Cor 12:9), power through prayer (Jas 5:16), and power to be kept from evil (1 Pt 1:5). Those who do great things in the service of Christ do not do them in their own strength (Acts 3:12); he sent out his disciples confident only in the assurance that all things are under his authority and that they would have the power of his unfailing presence with them (Mt 28:18–20).

FRANCIS FOULKES

See PRINCIPALITIES AND POWERS; GOD, BEING AND ATTRIBUTES OF.

Powers. *See* PRINCIPALITIES AND POWERS.

Praetorium, Praetorian Guard. Term which appears in the Greek NT in Mark 15:16; Matthew 27:27; John 18:28,33; 19:9; Acts 23:35; and Philippians 1:13. It is a Latin word borrowed from the usage of the Romans who dominated the Mediterranean world in NT times. It was used primarily in military and governmental affairs. Originally it designated the tent of the general (*praetor*) in a military encampment. The meaning was extended to include the residence of a governor or other Roman official as, for example, that of Pontius Pilate, the procurator of Judea. In looser usage the term may also have referred to a part of the residence, for instance, the barracks of the soldiers.

In English translations of the NT, the variety of terms used by translators indicates the uncertainty about the specific reference. The general reference to the headquarters of the Roman representative and military force is clear, however. In the Gospels of Matthew and Mark, the praetorium is the location of the Roman soldiers' mocking of Jesus after his appearance before Pilate. Mark also calls this place a "palace" (RSV) or "courtyard" (NEB; TEV). In the Gospel of John the "praetorium" is the place within which Pilate examines Jesus about the charges brought against him. He goes outside the praetorium to meet with the accusers who brought the charges.

Within Jerusalem, two locations are possible for Pilate's headquarters. One is the fortress known as the Tower of Antonia at the northwest corner of the temple area. The other is the old palace of Herod the Great, in the western part of the city. Either one could have served as the praetorium, but the Gospel sources identify neither by name or description.

In Acts 23:35, on the other hand, the praetorium in which Paul is held in Caesarea pending the arrival of his accusers is called "Herod's praetorium." This probably means that the procurator Felix (and his predecessors) had taken over the old official residence of King Herod as their coastal headquarters.

The location of Paul's imprisonment at the time he wrote to the Philippians is not clear. His mention of the "praetorium" in Philippians 1:13 suggests some center of Roman government. The phrase "the whole praetorium," however, indicates that in this context he is referring to the personnel, rather than to a building or a place. Recent translations reflect this meaning: "the whole Praetorian Guard" (RSV); "all at the headquarters" (NEB); "the whole palace guard" (NIV).

Praise. Honor, commendation, and worship.

To Whom Praise Is Offered. The one Lord who is God over all is alone worthy of praise. Frequently the OT stresses that the praise due him is not to be offered to other gods or to idols of any kind (e.g., Is 42:8). There is a place for the commendation of men and women for their qualities of life and their right actions (Prv 31:28–31; 1 Pt 2:14). Ultimately, however, they should seek the praise and commendation of God (Rom 2:29), not the praise of their fellows (Mt 6:1–6; Jn 12:43), that others may be led to glorify God for whatever good is found in them (Mt 5:16). Frequently the Bible speaks of praising "the name" of God (e.g., Ps 149:3), meaning that he is to be praised for all that he is and has revealed himself to be. The often repeated word "Hallelujah" is simply the Hebrew equivalent of "Praise the Lord."

By Whom Praise Is Offered. God is praised perfectly by his angels in heaven (Ps 103:20; 148:2). They caroled their praise when Jesus was born (Lk 2:13,14), and the Book of Revelation (e.g., 7:11,12) speaks about their continual praise in heaven. All creation praises God in the sense that it shows his greatness as Creator (Ps 19:1–6). Psalm 148 lists sun, moon and stars, fire and hail, snow, rain, wind and weather, mountains and hills, fruit trees and cedars, wild animals, cattle, snakes and birds, as praising God together. Heaven and earth are spoken of as involved in the praise of God (Ps 89:5; 96:11; 98:4). The Psalter closes with the words, "Let everything that breathes praise the Lord!" (Ps 150:6). In the OT we read of the special role of priests and Levites (Ps 135:19,20) and of the temple singers (2 Chr 20:21) and of those who, like Miriam (Ex 15:20) and David (2 Sm 6:14), led others in God's praise. But it was the duty of all God's people to praise him and their praise was intended, moreover, to lead the gentile nations to know and to praise him (Ps 67:2,3). The NT has this same emphasis (Rom 15:7–12) and it stresses that God's gifts are given to his people to be used to his praise and glory (Eph 1:6,12,14). It is by a life of righteousness as well as by word of mouth that men are to praise him (Phil 1:11). The redeemed people of God are appointed to show forth the praises of him who has called them "out of the darkness into his marvelous light" (1 Pt 2:9). The last book of the NT presents the praise of God in heaven where the four living creatures (representing all creation) and the 24 elders (representing the people of God under the old and new covenants) unite in worship, adoring the mighty God who created them and the Lamb of God who redeemed them (Rv 4,5).

When God Is to Be Praised. In the OT there were times of special praise, sabbaths, new moons, and festivals. In Psalm 119:164 the psalmist says, "seven times a day I praise thee for thy righteous ordinances." "From the rising of the sun to its setting the name of the Lord is to be praised!" is the exhortation of Psalm 113:3. Psalm 145:1 says, "I will extol thee, my God and King, and bless thy name for ever and ever." A dedication to a life of praise is expressed in Psalm 146:2: "I will praise the Lord as long as I live; I will sing praises to my God while I have being." In the NT, likewise, there are special times of praise, but the whole of the Christian's life is intended to be devoted, in word and action, to the praise of God.

Where Praise Is to Be Offered. In the OT the temple (and thus "Zion" or "Jerusalem" where the temple was located) had a special place in the purpose of God: his people should praise him there. Psalm 102:21 pictures people declaring "in Zion the name of the Lord, and in Jerusalem his praise." People are to praise God publicly before the congregation and before the leaders of the nation (Ps 107:32), but they may also do so alone. For the whole of life is to be praise. Thus praise can come from unexpected places. Godly men and women can "sing for joy on their couches" (Ps 149:5). Paul and Silas can sing praises to God in a Philippian prison (Acts 16:25).

How God Is to Be Praised. As there is no limit to time or place, so there is no limit to the ways in which God may be praised. He may be praised with singing (Ps 47:7), with dancing (Ps 149:3), or with instruments of music (Ps 144:9; 150:3–5). The Psalter provides us with many songs of praise and others are scattered throughout the OT. The NT speaks of "psalms and hymns and spiritual songs" (Col 3:16; see also Eph 5:19) and examples of Christian songs of praise are probably to be seen in Ephesians 5:14; Philippians 2:6–11; 1 Timothy 1:17; and 2 Timothy 2:11–13.

Why God Is to Be Praised. Creation provides reason for the praise of God (Ps 8:3), as does his preserving love and care (Ps 21:4) and the fact that he is a prayer-answering God (Ps 116:1). His redeeming work leads his people to worship him (Ex 15:1,2). Some of the psalms (e.g., 107) list many reasons why he should be praised. With the coming of the Lord Jesus Christ there is a fresh outburst of praise because the Messiah, the Savior, has come to his people (Lk 2:11). All that he did by his life, death, and resurrection calls for praise. But ultimately praise will be made perfect when in the end God is seen to reign victorious over all. Thus John speaks in the Book of Revelation (19:6) of hearing "what seemed to be the voice of a great multitude, like the sound of many waters and like the sound of mighty thunderpeals, crying 'Hallelujah!' For the Lord our God the Almighty reigns."

FRANCIS FOULKES

See WORSHIP; TABERNACLE, TEMPLE; PRAYER.

Prayer. The addressing and petitioning of God. Prayer to a god or gods is a feature of many, if not all, religions, but here attention will be restricted to the biblical teaching and some of its implications. A classic definition of Christian prayer is "an offering up of our desires unto God, for things agreeable to his will, in the name of Christ, with confession of our sins, and thankful acknowledgement of his mercies" (Westminster Shorter Catechism). Christian prayer is the end product of a long process of change and development in God's relation to men, as a survey of the biblical data shows.

Prayer in the OT. Newly created man, made for fellowship with God, "walked with God." Sin broke this intimate, direct relationship. Nevertheless, when the Lord formed his gracious covenant with Abraham (Gn 15) the relationship between the covenant partners was also direct, at least by comparison with what was to follow. Abraham's prayer for Sodom and Gomorrah (Gn 18) is a striking combination of boldness and persistence, and a recognition of his own smallness and inferiority compared to God. The same could be said about Jacob's wrestling with the angel at Peniel (Gn 32). But boldness and directness is not to be confused with familiarity. Biblical prayer is shot through with a recognition of the distance between the Creator and the creature, of human sin and of God's grace. The basis of a person's approach to God in prayer is never simply "man's search for God" but God's gracious initiative, the establishing of the covenant, and the promise of help and deliverance on the basis of that covenant. It is this covenant relationship that gives the *warrant* for prayer. Thus in patriarchal times prayer was conjoined with sacrifice and obedience.

The reestablishing of the national consciousness of Israel at the time of their deliverance from Egypt marks another phase in the biblical development. Moses is not only the political leader of Israel but their divinely appointed mediator and intercessor with the Lord. Repeatedly he "pleads the name of the Lord" in the face of the human uncertainties of the wilderness journey and his own people's unbelief and disobedience. "Pleading the name of Jehovah" is not to be thought of as an incantation, but as a reminder to God of who he has revealed himself to be. (God's revelation of himself to Moses at the burning bush is fundamental to an understanding of this). In this revelation of himself God has made promises to his people, and in prayer Moses holds God to these promises. Moses was by no means the only intercessor. Aaron, Samuel, Solomon, and Hezekiah were among those who interceded for the people.

With the formation of the priesthood and the establishment of the ritual worship of the tabernacle and later the temple, the worship of God seems to be characterized by distance. There is little indication that the people personally prayed to God and with the exception of Deuteronomy 26:1–15 there is nothing about prayer in all the instructions for worship given to the people. However, there is indication in the psalms that sacrifice and prayer would be coupled together (Ps 50:7–15; 55:14). Many of the psalms are remarkable for the way in which personal perplexities are acknowledged, leading to "arguing with God" and an ultimate resolution of the conflict (e.g., Ps 73).

The prophets were men who prayed, and it seems that God's Word came to them in prayer (Is 6:5–13; 37:1–4; Jer 11:20–23). Jeremiah's ministry was characterized by times of conflict in prayer (18:19–23; 20:7–18) as well as

Remains of the prayer room in
the synagogue at Chorazin.

more settled times of fellowship with God
(10:23–25; 12:1–4; 14:7–9; 15:15–18). At the exile, with the establishment of the synagogue,
corporate prayer became an element in Jewish
worship. God's face was sought in prayer (Ps
53:1; 100:2), while after the exile there is an
emphasis on spontaneity in prayer, and on the
need for devotion to be more than mechanical
and routine (Neh 2:4; 4:4,9).

Prayer in the NT. The NT's teaching on
prayer is dominated by Christ's own example
and teaching. His dependence on his Father
in his mediatorial work expresses itself in repeated prayer, culminating in his high-
priestly prayer (Jn 17) and the agony of Gethsemane with the prayer from the cross. Yet
Christ is explicit in describing his relationship to his Father as a unique one (Jn 20:17).
His teaching on prayer, particularly in the
Sermon on the Mount, is to be understood as
contrasting with current Jewish practices, not
with OT ideals. Prayer is an expression of sincere desire. It is not to inform God of matters
that he would otherwise be ignorant of, and
the validity of prayer is not affected by length
or repetitiveness. Private prayer is to be dis-
creet, secret (Mt 6:5–15).

The parables are another important source
of Christ's teaching, emphasizing persistence
in prayer (Lk 18:1–8), simplicity and humility
(Lk 18:10–14), and tenacity (Lk 11:5–8). A third
source of teaching is the Lord's Prayer. Once
again there is the blend of directness ("Our
Father") and distance ("Who art in heaven.
Hallowed be thy name"). The requests given
in the Lord's Prayer are concerned first with
God, his kingdom and his glory, and then with
the disciples' needs for forgiveness and for
daily support and deliverance. Occasionally it
seems from our Lord's teaching that anything
that is prayed for will, without restriction, be
granted. But such teaching ought to be understood in the light of Christ's overall teaching
about prayer ("Thy kingdom come. Thy will
be done in earth, as it is in heaven").

Christ stated that when the Holy Spirit, the
Comforter, came the disciples would pray to
the Father in the name of Christ (Jn 16:23–25).
Accordingly we find that after the coming of
the Spirit on the Day of Pentecost the early
church is characterized by prayer (Acts 2:42)
under the leadership of the apostles (Acts 6:4).
The church praises God for the gift of his Son
and his Spirit and petitions God in times of
difficulty (Acts 4:24; 12:5,12).

It is in Paul's writings that the theology of
prayer is most fully developed. The NT believer is a son, not only a servant. The Spirit
who, as a result of Christ's triumph, has come
to the church is the Spirit of adoption, enabling the Christian to come to God as his Father, with all his needs. Prominent among
these needs, in the mind of the apostle, are a
deepening of faith in Christ, love for God, and
a growing appreciation of God's love in turn
(Eph 3:14–19). Prayer is a part of the Christian's armor against satanic attack (Eph 6:18),
the effective ministry of the Word of God depends on the prayers of God's people (Eph
6:18,19), and the Christian is enjoined to pray
for all sorts of things, with thanksgiving (Phil
4:6), and so to be free from anxiety. Paul's own
example in prayer is as instructive as the
teaching he gives.

The Christian's prayer is rooted, objec-
tively, in Christ's intercession; subjectively, in

the enabling of the Holy Spirit. The church is a kingdom of priests, offering spiritual sacrifices of praise and thanksgiving (Heb 13:15; 1 Pt 2:5), but Christ is the "great High Priest." This thought is developed fully in Hebrews. Because of Christ's human sympathy, the power of his intercessory work (i.e., the triumph of his atonement) and his superiority over the old Aaronic priesthood, the church is encouraged to come to God ("the throne of grace") boldly, to find grace when it is needed (Heb 4:14–16; 9:24; 10:19–23). Prayer and obedience are linked both in the case of Christ, who learned obedience by the things that he suffered (Heb 5:7,8), and in the case of the church (Heb 10:21–25).

The priesthood of the OT, although ordained by God, was of purely symbolic significance. The OT high priest could no more effectively intercede for the people than the blood of bulls and goats could take away their sins (Heb 10:4). Further, nowhere in either the OT or NT is there any encouragement to pray to individuals other than God. Nowhere in Scripture is it suggested that there is any other mediator between God and men except Christ (1 Tm 2:5).

The Elements of Prayer. Although prayer is, typically, an unself-conscious activity in which the person praying devotes himself to God, it is possible to distinguish various elements in prayer, as will be apparent from the discussion of the biblical data. *Praise* involves the recognition of who God is and what he does. It is "giving God the glory," not in the sense of adding to his glory, which would be impossible, but of willingly (and where appropriate, publicly) recognizing God as God. Typical expressions of such praise are to be found in the psalms (Ps 148,150). When the recognition of God's goodness is in respect of what he has done for the one who prays, or for others, then the prayer is one of *thanksgiving*, for life itself, for the use and beauty of the physical universe, for Christ and his benefits ("Thanks be to God for his inexpressible gift," 2 Cor 9:15), and for specific answers to prayer. *Confession* of sin recognizes the holiness of God and his supreme moral authority, together with the personal responsibility of the one making the confession. Confession thus involves the vindicating or justifying of God, and an explicit and unreserved recognition of sin, both as it takes its rise in sinful motives and dispositions, and as it finds outward expression. Psalm 51, David's confession of sin regarding Bathsheba, is the classic biblical instance of a prayer of confession. *Petition* can be thought of as it concerns the one praying, and also as it concerns others, when it is *intercession*. Scripture never regards prayer for one-

self as sinful or ethically improper, as can be seen from the pattern of prayer given in the Lord's Prayer. Prayer for others is an obvious expression of love for one's neighbor which is fundamental to biblical ethics.

Difficulties in Prayer. How creatures are able to petition God, and to receive answers to their prayers, is a mystery that Scripture does not theorize about, but asserts as fact. Thus petitionary prayer is central to biblical religion. Yet the possibility of petitionary prayer has presented difficulties for many. Why does God answer some prayers and not others? And, more fundamentally, how is God able to answer any prayers at all?

In attempting to answer the first question it is necessary to bear in mind that prayer is not to be thought of in mechanical terms. Prayer involves a personal relationship with God. So the reason why God answers one prayer and not another has nothing to do with volume or length of prayers in themselves. Because prayer involves a personal relationship with God, sincerity and unaffectedness in that relationship are of paramount importance. As already noted, there must be no hypocrisy or mere formalism in prayer. Length of prayer may be an indication of strength of desire, or it may not. Scripture contains examples of both long and short prayers.

Assuming sincerity, the most fundamental factor is the relationship between the one who prays and the express will of God. The only warrant for praying at all is that God commands it and desires it, and the only warrant for praying for some particular thing rather than for some other thing is that God wills it, or may will it. A knowledge of the will of God as it is revealed in Scripture is basic to a proper understanding of petitionary prayer and to proper conduct in prayer.

It is necessary to distinguish between those matters that God has declared that he will unfailingly grant upon true prayer being made and those matters that he may grant upon true prayer being made. The guide for prayer is not the petitioner's own needs, either real or imaginary, nor his feelings or state of mind when he prays, nor his or others' speculations about the future. The guide is Scripture alone. And the Scriptures distinguish between those things a person may pray for that are desirable or good in themselves and yet that are not for every believer's highest good, and those things that concern redemption. For instance, health or wealth, or a particular career, though each is desirable and lawful, may nevertheless not be best, in the wisdom of God, for a particular individual at a particular time. Paul's "thorn in the flesh" (2 Cor 12:7–9) and the death of the child of David and Bathsheba (2 Sm 12:15–23) are examples of unanswered prayer. So although health or wealth may be sincerely and warrantably prayed for, yet God in his wisdom and sovereignty may decline to grant these things, they not being included in that particular array of things that are working together for the good of the believer concerned (Rom 8:28).

By contrast, the blessings of redemption—such as forgiveness of sins, sanctification, and strength and wisdom for the fulfilling of duties—are always given to those who truly pray for them (Ps 84:11; Lk 11:13; Jn 6:37; 1 Thes 4:3; Jas 1:5). Even such unqualified or unconditional blessings may come after apparent delay, or from an unexpected source, and allowance for factors such as these must be made when judging whether or not prayer has been answered. An important part of petitioning God is the discipline of conforming desires to the revealed will and the ongoing providence of God. In this sense prayer is educative for the believer. "Not my will, but thine be done" is the concern of the sincere petitioner. The exercise of faith in prayer to God is seen in submission to the express will of God. Otherwise faith becomes presumption, and humility becomes arrogance.

Behind the question, Why does God answer some prayers and not others? there is a deeper difficulty. How can God answer prayers at all? This question is usually prompted either by theological or scientific convictions. How can petitionary prayer be efficacious if God knows (and has ordained) all that is to take place in the future? Or, how can petitionary prayer be efficacious if the physical universe is governed by exceptionless regularities? These difficulties can both be expressed as follows: how can petitionary prayer be effective in a situation in which the outcome is already ordained or determined? Or, how can God intervene in answer to prayer if there are physical laws that govern the whole of the natural order? In answering these questions it is necessary to see that the objections behind petitionary prayer are, if valid, also objections to any kind of human activity whatsoever. If petitionary prayer is rendered impossible by God's sovereignty, then so are such basic activities as walking and talking. For if God has already ordained the future, what use is there in doing anything?

There has been a tendency since the 18th-century Enlightenment, particularly through the influence of deism and of Immanuel Kant (d. 1804), to restrict prayer to acts of passive acceptance of and acquiescence to the divine will. In the words of Albrecht Ritschl (d. 1889) "prayer is the expression of humility and patience, and the means of confirming oneself in these virtues." This restricted view of prayer is taken because petitionary prayer is thought to be inconsistent with the universal reign of law and because to ask for things for oneself is judged to be unethical and impious.

But views of this kind rest on a radical misunderstanding. The biblical portrayal of God is not of one who has set a mechanical universe in motion, but of one who knows the end from the beginning and who, upholding all things by his power, works these things according to the counsel of his own will (Is 46:9,10; Heb 1:3; Eph 1:11). To do this God uses human activities such as walking, talking, and praying. In the overall providence of God prayer is one means among many by which God has chosen to reach his ordained purposes. He has ordained the ends and the petitionary prayers of believers as one of the means to those ends. In Ezekiel the Lord promises a new heart and a new heritage to the people, yet desires to be prayed to for these things (Ez 36:33–38). As the hymn writer Joseph Hart quaintly but concisely puts it:

> Prayer was appointed to convey
> The blessings God designs to give.

But what of those occasions on which God is said to "repent" of the carrying out of an expressed threat or promise? (Ex 32:14; 2 Sm 24:16; 1 Chr 21:15; Jer 26:19; Jon 3:10). Are such expressions consistent with his unchanging character and will? Do they not convey the impression that petitionary prayer can actually change the will of God? Can God be sincere in telling King Hezekiah that he will not recover and then, shortly afterward, bringing about Hezekiah's recovery in answer to prayer? (2 Kgs 20; Is 38). Did God intend Hezekiah to recover, or not? The most satisfactory way of approaching this problem is to bear in mind that in Scripture the warrant of any prayer is God's promise. When God says "Hezekiah will not recover," a condition such as "unless prayer is made for his recovery" is to be understood. So what God intends is the recovery of Hezekiah upon prayer being made for him, knowing that the prayer will be made. In other words, in his wisdom God is willing to grant certain things upon persistent prayer being made for them, and the assertion "Hezekiah will not recover" is intended to elicit that believing prayer that God has ordained as a means to the recovery of Hezekiah. There is nothing here that is inconsistent with either God's changelessness or his eternal foreknowledge of all events, or with the efficacy of petitionary prayer.

If it is asked, "Why does God go to such lengths?" we must look for an answer in two directions. One part of the answer is the educative function of prayer—to teach his children their entire dependence on him for all their good. The other part of the answer is to be found in God's sovereignty, in the day-to-day and moment-to-moment dependence of his people upon him.

The alternative to this view, that petitionary prayer does change God's will, is fraught with difficulties. It represents God as having continually to adjust his will to the desires of his creatures, and it implies that God does not know what is going to happen in his universe until people petition him and he decides what to do in the light of their requests.

The difficulties raised by views of scientific law do not seem to be different in principle from those just discussed. It is argued that natural science presents us with a view of the universe as totally "closed," totally subject to law-like operations. How, it is asked, can prayer be genuinely efficacious in such circumstances? For example, how can a person's health be restored in answer to prayer when the causes of sickness and health are solely physical? These questions neglect the fact that from a theistic standpoint physical laws are simply human accounts of observed regularities. On a theistic view of physical nature, God ordains not only the laws of nature (to which scientific laws are approximations) but also the actual course of events occurring in accordance with these laws. The ultimate cause of things is not the operation of natural forces and the occurrence of certain chance events "in the beginning," but the creative will of God, who ordains both the law-like regularities and, should he choose to do so, exceptions to these. So that science presents no problems for petitionary prayer not already present in theological discussions about it.

It must be stressed that the duty to pray does not depend in any way on being able finally to solve all the difficulties associated with prayer. According to Scripture the duty and privilege of prayer is founded on the command of God to pray.

Motives for Prayer. In the broadest terms the motive for prayer is the fact that God commands it. More particularly, the motives for prayer are the glory of God and the good of the one who prays and of those for whom he prays. These ends are not in conflict since the biblical picture is of God being glorified in the blessing of his people (Eph 1:6). More particularly still Scripture provides us with many different motives for prayer which throw light on the character of prayer itself. In the case of petitionary prayer prominent among these motives is the need for forgiveness of sins (1 Jn 1:8,9), freedom from anxiety (Phil 4:6,7), deliv-

erance from temptation (Mt 26:41) and the provision of temporal needs (Mt 6:11). Undergirding all of these is the recognition that men depend upon God for all good things. Undoubtedly one of the reasons why prayer has such a prominent position in biblical religion is that it brings the recognition of this dependence into prominent focus.

Prayer and Worship. Prayer is both a private and a congregational activity. It is an integral part of church worship for the essence of worship—God being addressed as "Thou"—cannot be conceived apart from prayer. So worship cannot be scriptural unless prayer is included.

This does not mean simply that prayer ought to be an ingredient in worship, but that the structure which the Christian gospel gives to services of worship is impossible to achieve without prayer. This structure might be expressed as: Sin—Grace—Faith. Worship starts from the recognition of sin and need (hence, prayers of confession of sin), proceeding to an awareness of God's provision of forgiveness, righteousness, and new life in Christ, in turn leading to the response of faith (prayer and praise for pardon, thanksgiving to God for his "unspeakable gift," and intercession to God for that grace for others). So not only is prayer an element in gospel-worship, that worship is shapeless without prayer.

Christians and churches have divided over the question of whether or not prayers must have a set, word-for-word form. There are those who have argued that the use of fixed liturgical forms makes for formalism, deadness, and inflexibility in the face of changing circumstances and sudden needs, and a "quenching of the Spirit." Others have argued that fixed liturgical forms ensure that worship is truly communal, and that such forms minimize the risk of clumsy or eccentric leadership in worship. But the question ought not to be settled merely in terms of the expediencies of worship, much less of church custom and tradition. One question is whether the Bible *requires* such fixed prayers. An examination of the OT reveals mandatory strict liturgical patterns, while an examination of the NT reveals no such structure. Every example of prayer is of extempore prayers, with the possible exception of the Lord's Prayer. But even in the case of the Lord's Prayer it can be argued that the Lord was indicating a pattern for prayer, not providing a formal liturgy. A further and more fundamental question is: Is the authority of Scripture such that whatever is not expressly commanded is forbidden? The different answers that have been given to this question have implications not only for the practice of congregational prayer but for the doctrine of the church and indeed for the whole of theological discussion.

Historically, the controversy between written versus extempore prayers has become most acute and vexing when fixed forms of prayer have been legally enacted, thus violating the consciences of many who, though perhaps agreeing that fixed prayers were occasionally permissible, could not agree that they were mandatory. The most famous and far-reaching of these conflicts occurred in England in the 1660s. In 1662 hundreds of English ministers were ejected from their churches for refusing to agree to the legally imposed Book of Common Prayer. This event, together with the previous migration of Puritan congregations to America, has had far-reaching implications for the organization of prayer in public worship, as well as for much else.

In her worship during the present era the church occupies an in-between situation. The kingdom of God is initiated but not consummated. The church looks back with thankfulness to what God has done in Christ and forward to what he will yet do. Her petition is: Thy kingdom come. When the kingdoms of this world have become the kingdom of our Lord, and of his Christ (Rv 11:15), when death has been swallowed up in victory (1 Cor 15:54) such petitions will cease. Petition will dissolve into ascriptions of praise.

PAUL HELM

See PRAISE; WORSHIP; LORD'S PRAYER.

Bibliography. P.R. Baelz, *Prayer and Providence*; D.G. Bloesch, *The Struggle of Prayer*; F.H. Chase, *The Lord's Prayer in the Early Church*; F.D. Coggan, *The Prayers of the NT*; P.T. Forsyth, *The Soul of Prayer*; O. Hallesby, *Prayer*; F. Heiler, *Prayer*; J.G.S.S. Thomson, *The Praying Christ*; G.P. Wiles, *Paul's Intercessory Prayers*.

Prayer, Lord's. *See* LORD'S PRAYER.

Precious Stones. *See* MINERALS, METALS, AND PRECIOUS STONES.

Predestination. *See* ELECT, ELECTION; FOREORDINATION.

Preparation Day. Term used in Scripture for the day before the sabbath. Each of the Gospels refers to a day that it calls "the Preparation" (Mt 27:62; Mk 15:42; Lk 23:54; Jn 19:14,31,42), Mark calling it "the day before the sabbath." The Jews did not have specific names for the days (preferring to speak of "the first [second, etc.] day of the week." But the Sabbath was distinctive, and the previous day was used to prepare for this weekly day of rest and worship. Thus what we call "Friday" the Jews called "Preparation." What was "prepared" is not said. But as no work could be done on the sabbath, preparations had to be made for food and other necessities.

"The Preparation of the Passover" (Jn 19:14) is often understood to mean "Passover-eve," the day before Passover, just as "the Preparation" means the day before the sabbath. There appears, however, to be no specific extrabiblical examples of the day before Passover being called "the Preparation" or "the Preparation of the Passover."

Presbyter. NT term referring to an elder in the church. Following the OT pattern of synagogues governed by a council of elders, the church of the NT had officers (*presbuteroi*, "older persons") whose task was to "tend the flock of God that is in your charge" (1 Pt 5:2). Thus they were called to "labor in preaching and teaching" (1 Tm 5:17); visit, pray over, and anoint the sick (Js 5:14); administer famine relief (Acts 11:29,30); and generally oversee the affairs of the church (Acts 15:4; 16:4). There is evidence to suggest that all elders were of equal status and that the terms "presbyter" and "bishop" were at first used interchangeably (Acts 20:17,28; Phil 1:1; Ti 1:5,7).

In the 2nd century, however, the presiding presbyter gradually emerged as a distinctive figure with a position of preeminence and as in some sense the source of authority. As the years passed, the designation "presbyter" was contracted to that of "priest," and in churches of the episcopal order it remains so today. It is significant, nevertheless, that the NT nowhere links priestly functions with the office of presbyter. With the spread and development of Christianity, the priest became a powerful figure. With eucharistic theology there grew up unbiblical accretions. These were exposed and rejected when the Reformers triumphed in the 16th century and stressed the priesthood of all believers. In Protestantism priests became ministers, pastors, or (in more modern times) clergymen. In non-Roman Episcopal churches, "priest" is found again today. Even where it is interpreted differently from Roman usage, most evangelical Anglicans refuse to use it. In Presbyterian and similar churches the elders (whether teaching or ruling) are still officially called presbyters, and all are of equal status.

See ELDER; BISHOP; DEACON, DEACONESS; PASTOR; SPIRITUAL GIFTS.

Presence, Bread of the. *See* BREAD OF THE PRESENCE.

Presence of God, The.

Introduction. Since God is spirit and invisible, the means he uses to reveal his presence will always be inadequate. In this sense

Mt Sinai, where God's presence was dramatically emphasized in the lives of Moses and Elijah (Ex 29:43; 1 Kgs 19:11–13).

the God of the Bible is a hidden God, but a hidden God who makes himself known. He appears in nature, particularly in catastrophic forces—fire, lightning, and earthquake (1 Kgs 19:11–13). He also appears in human form (Gn 18; 32:22–32). So God, who cannot be seen, chose means to reveal himself which harmonize his transcendence and his nearness.

The OT. *The Angel of the Lord.* The angel of the Lord was God's emissary and Israel's special helper, although it is not said that the same angel is meant in every instance (Ex 14:19; 23:20; 33:2). Hagar insists, after the angel vanishes, that she had seen God himself (Gn 16:13); and in Jacob's experience the angel identifies himself with God (Gn 31:11,13); while in Genesis 21:18; 22:11; Numbers 22:35, the "I" of deity signified God's presence in the angel. There is also oscillation between God and the angel in Exodus 12:23 and Genesis 48:15,16. Here God was temporarily incarnating himself within the quasihuman form of the angel, assuring his own that he was immediately present with them, yet harmonizing his transcendent majesty and his immanent energy. Note that the angel's role is always beneficent, and he functions only by virtue of God's free decision.

The Glory of God. Glory is what God possesses in his own right, a visible extension of his nature, a "concrete" form of his divine presence. The heavens are a visible form of God's presence (Pss 8; 19:1–6; 136:5), for they are his glory. The glory which appeared to Israel as devouring fire on Sinai (Ex 29:43) filled the tabernacle (Ex 40:34–38). By it God consecrated the tabernacle as the place of his presence. In Isaiah 6 the glory appears as the normal expression of the divine presence. In Ezekiel the glory is identical with God (9:3,4). Throughout the OT the glory of God is the transcendent God making his presence and nearness visible to his own.

The Face of God. In the OT "presence" is used to represent the Hebrew word for "face";

and when "face" is conjoined with a preposition it means "in the presence of." In Genesis 32:30 Jacob saw God "face to face." A man's personality and character are made visible on his face. In this sense a man's face is the man. So, "the angel of his presence [face]" (Is 63:9) may mean "the angel who is his face," since the prophet may have intended the identification. The face of God is the revelation of the grace of God. So, when he hides his face he is withholding his grace. But when he makes his face shine (Ps 31:16) there are blessing and victory (Ps 44:3). The face of God, then, is the presence of God (Ex 33:14) who delivers Israel (Dt 4:37; Is 63:9). To pray to God in a holy place was to "seek God's face" (Ps 24:6), his personal presence. Indeed, this sums up temple worship and private prayer in Israel (Ps 63:1–3; 100:2). The blessing of God consisted in his face shining upon them (Nm 6:25; Ps 80:3,7,19).

The Name of God. Among Semites the equation of the name and the person was a common idea. So also the name of God was an interchangeable term for God himself, a symbol of his activity in revelation. The linking of man's worship of God with the divine name of God was the medium of his operation (Ps 44:5; 89:24; Is 30:27); a designation for the power of God which radiates help and energy universally. God could act by his name. The angel of the Lord's authority and power functioned because God's name was in him (Ex 23:20,21). As bearer of the divine name he made real the hidden presence of God. The temple was the dwelling place of the name (1 Kgs 11:36), not only because God's name was invoked there but because God's presence, God himself, dwelt there.

The Spirit of God. In the Holy Spirit the transcendent God draws near to his people. The Spirit is the medium through whom God's presence becomes real among his own (Is 63:11–14; Zec 7:12) and by whom God's gifts and powers operate among them (2 Chr 15:1; 20:14; 24:20; Zec 4:6; 6:1–8). The Spirit was the presence and power of God with his people, God himself acting in accordance with his essential nature. The sinner cannot be in the presence of God without the aid of God's Holy Spirit; to be deprived of the Holy Spirit is to be deprived of God's presence (Ps 51:11). Without the Spirit communion between God and man is not possible.

The Place of God's Presence. With such emphasis on the presence of God, the conviction that God's presence was localized is very prominent. The presence of God made Israel the people of God. Without it they would cease to be such. The tabernacle was "the tent of reunion" (Ex 27:21) where God met his people

(Ex 40:34–38; see also 33:7–23). The ark of God was where God was enthroned upon the cherubim (1 Sm 4:4). The ark guaranteed the presence of God (Nm 10:35; 1 Sm 4:3). In 1 Kings 8:27 the immanental and the transcendental views of God are perfectly balanced. The "person" of God dwelt within the sanctuary (1 Kgs 8:28,29). In Ezekiel's vision of the glory returned to the temple after the exile, Jerusalem's name was "Jehovah is there" (Ez 48:35); and Daniel in distant Babylon prayed toward Jerusalem (Dn 6:10).

The NT. In the NT a new mode of God's presence is revealed. It is in Jesus Christ the incarnate Word that God is present among his own. He revealed the name of God to men (Jn 1:14–18; 17:6,26). This he did through his whole life's work, as well as his word. His revelation of the name of God was expressed in the name of Jesus ("The Lord is Salvation") itself; and in the person of Jesus the function of the name of God found fulfillment. Christ was the new temple (Jn 2:21; 1:14; Col 2:9). He was the locus of the tabernacling presence of God. But that was only a first installment of the unveiling of God's presence. Christ's crucifixion was the hour of divine glory (Jn 12:23–33). In the Crucified, faith discerns the presence of God and the glory of God shining in his face (2 Cor 4:4,6).

But the church now constitutes the temple of God in the NT. Christianity is essentially the religion of the presence of God and of communion with God. The body of Christ, "the spiritual temple" (Eph 2:22), made of "living stones" (1 Pt 2:5), is the depository of the presence and glory of God; and is infinitely greater than the old, the veil of whose Holy of Holies was rent at the moment of Christ's dying on the cross (Mt 27:50,51).

And now even the individual Christian is a temple of God (1 Cor 3:16,17; 6:19; 2 Cor 6:16). God is especially present in the Christian's heart; there God reigns for there is his kingdom; there he is worshiped for there his glory and his presence have consecrated the heart into a temple. Taken together Colossians 1:19; 2:9; John 14:23 sum up the whole biblical theme of God's indwelling presence.

J. G. S. S. THOMSON

See GOD, BEING AND ATTRIBUTES OF.

Pride. A reasonable or justifiable self-respect; or improper and excessive self-esteem known as conceit or arrogance. The apostle Paul expresses a positive kind of pride when speaking of confidence in Christians (2 Cor 7:4) or of strength in the Lord (2 Cor 12:5,9). However, it is the latter sinful meaning of pride which most frequently appears in the Bible, both in the OT and the NT.

The 10 Hebrew and 2 Greek words generally used for pride refer to being high or exalted in attitude, the opposite of the virtue of humility, which is so often praised and rewarded by God. One other Greek word refers to a person's being puffed up or inflated with pride or egotism. The idea is that one gives the impression of substance but is really filled only with air (see, e.g., 1 Cor 5:2; 8:1; 13:4; Col 2:18).

Pride is basically a sin of attitude and of the heart and spirit. Hence one reads, "Haughty eyes and a proud heart, the lamp of the wicked, are sin" (Prv 21:4). Ecclesiastes 7:8 speaks of "proud in spirit" and the psalmist declares, "O Lord, my heart is not proud, or my eyes haughty" (Ps 131:1 NASB). Pride is cited in the two lists of the most glaring sins in the Bible. Along with the sins for which God is going to judge the Gentiles, one finds insolence, arrogance, and boasting (Rom 1:30). Included with the sins that will be prevalent in the last days, Paul includes boasting, arrogance, and conceit (2 Tm 3:2,4).

As so many of the sins of attitude, pride cannot remain internalized. It can infect one's speech; and boasting is one way by which this sin can appear in one's speaking (see the passages referred to above and also Mal 3:13). Pride can also appear in the way one looks at another person. Hence the Scriptures speak of "haughty eyes" in Proverbs 6:17, or, as some translators render it, "a proud look." The psalmist speaks of a person with "haughty looks and arrogant heart" as one he cannot endure (Ps 101:5; see also Prv 30:13.) Pride may also take the ugly form of contemptible treatment of others (Prv 21:24). One of the illustrations of this in the Bible is the way in which the Pharisees and other Jewish leaders treated and spoke of those beneath their social level (e.g., Mt 23:6–12; Jn 9:34). They especially despised tax collectors and sinners.

Outstanding examples of proud people can be found in both Testaments. Pride was the downfall of King Uzziah who, because of this sin, dared to offer incense on the altar of incense and was smitten with leprosy as his punishment from God (2 Chr 26:16). Hezekiah, after his healing by the Lord, became proud of heart and brought wrath upon himself, Judah, and Jerusalem (2 Chr 32:25,26). The Pharisee in the temple, praying and comparing himself with the humble tax collector, is another example (Lk 18:9–14). Herod's refusal to give God the glory for his greatness brought judgment from God and he was eaten by worms and died for his sin of pride (Acts 12:21–23). In fact, Ezekiel 28, which describes the pride of the leader of Tyre, is taken by many biblical scholars to refer, in a deeper sense, to the fall of Satan back in the beginning.

Pride cannot only bring the downfall of individuals but also of nations. This was the sin which is specifically mentioned as leading to other sins and which ultimately brought about the removal of both Israel and Judah from the land of Canaan (Is 3:16; 5:15; Ez 16:50; Hos 13:6; Zep 3:11). It is also the specific sin which brought about the downfalls of the king of Assyria (Is 10:12,33) and the king of Moab (Jer 48:29). Because of its deadliness, Israel is specifically warned against pride and the tendency to forget God which so often stems from it (Dt 8:14).

In the light of the preceding, it is no surprise to read that pride is one of the seven things which the Lord hates (Prv 6:17). It is also said by two different writers that "God opposes the proud but gives grace to the humble" (see Jas 4:6 and 1 Pt 5:5; see also Prv 3:34 and 18:12, to which James and Peter may be referring.) The words of Mary, the mother of Jesus, in her hymn of praise to God may summarize the attitude of God and the Bible toward pride: "[God] has done mighty deeds with His arm; He has scattered [those who were] proud in the thoughts of their heart. He has brought down rulers from [their] thrones and exalted those who were humble" (Lk 1:51,52 NASB).

See BOAST; SIN.

Priest, High. *See* PRIESTS AND LEVITES.

Priesthood. Office or function of a priest; the condition of being a priest. The modern word "priest" (in French *prêtre* and in German *priester*) is used of a clergyman in Episcopalian churches (Roman, Orthodox, and Anglican). It is also used in the description of the whole church as "a royal priesthood" (1 Pt 2:9). To ascertain how this usage arose and to see what priesthood means it is necessary to look briefly at both biblical and theological developments.

OT. In the covenant made between God and Israel, the whole people is seen as a "kingdom of priests" and thus a holy people (Ex 19:6). Within this context, specific priestly activities belonged to three orders—high priest, priest, and Levite. Priests were male descendants of Aaron (Nm 3:10) and Levites were male members of the tribe of Levi. The chief functions of the priesthood were in the temple. They looked after the ceremonial vessels and performed the sacrifices. In doing their duties they dressed in special, symbolic vestments. They were also teachers, passing on the sacred traditions of the nation. This included such matters as medical information (Lv 13–15). The high priest was the spiritual head of Israel and he had special functions, for example, entering the Holy of Holies on the Day of Atonement (Lv 16). The Levites assisted the priests and served the congregation in the temple. They sang the psalms, kept the temple courts clean, helped to prepare certain sacrifices and offerings, and also had a teaching function.

Through this threefold order, the priesthood of the nation was exercised. By it the people offered worship to God, made intercessions and petitions, and learned of God's will. Thus what occurred in the worship of every pious home as the head of the house guided his family occurred in a larger and ceremonial way in the temple.

NT. It is remarkable that the term "priest" is never used in the NT of a minister or order in the church. Certainly the usage with reference to Judaism and paganism continues (Acts 4:1,6; 14:13) but it is never introduced into the church. The Letter to the Hebrews presents the OT priesthood as fulfilled in Jesus Christ. First of all, he has been appointed high priest by God himself (5:4–6). Yet it is a superior priesthood to that of Aaron (7:1–28). Second, being totally sympathetic to the needs of sinful people and tempted in all points like them, he was without sin (4:15; 7:26). Third, instead of offering animal sacrifices to take away sin, he offered himself, as the sinless lamb, to take away sin. This was a perfect atonement (7:27; 9:24–28; 10:10–19).

Not only was the OT sacrificial system fulfilled, it was also finished by the unique, unrepeatable, and unlimited sacrifice of Christ. Having risen from the dead he is a priest forever (7:17) and he remains the same "yesterday and today and for ever" (13:8). Part of his high priesthood is to offer intercession for his people (7:25). He is the mediator of a new and better covenant (7:22; 8:6; 9:15). Only through him are sinful human beings able to enter the holy presence of God and be accepted as children of God (Jn 14:6; 2 Cor 5:18–20; 1 Tm 2:5). Therefore, whatever priesthood Christians have they have only in and through Christ, their High Priest and Mediator.

The NT describes believers as "a royal priesthood, to offer spiritual sacrifices acceptable to God through Jesus Christ" (1 Pt 2:5); "priests to his God and Father" (Rv 1:6); "a kingdom and priests to our God" (Rv 5:10); "priests of God and of Christ, and they shall reign with him a thousand years" (Rv 20:6). Such statements as these are reflected in Exodus 19:6: "You shall be my kingdom of priests, my holy nation" (see also Ps 132:9,16; Is 61:6). Obviously the idea has its roots in the OT and is given through Christ a new and larger content in the NT.

What, then, does the priesthood of all believers mean in the NT? The high priesthood of Christ may be defined as his complete dedication and obedience to God, his Father, and unlimited compassion for his fellow human beings. At the center is his sacrificial death on the cross. On this basis and in union with him, the priesthood of Christians is their sacrificial obedience to God; this involves spiritual worship and love of God and compassionate activity and prayer for their fellow human beings. Paul wrote: "Present your bodies as a living sacrifice, holy and acceptable to God, which is your spiritual worship" (Rom 12:1). Each Christian offers his whole body to Christ and each local church offers itself wholly to Christ: and Christ offers his whole body (the church) to God the Father. Thus, in and by Christ, the priesthood of believers is exercised and made effectual. In the hearts of believers is the indwelling Spirit and it is in his power that acceptable service and worship is offered. Christ is the pattern of priesthood as well as being high priest.

The Nature of Priesthood.

The concrete content of priesthood may be put in the following way:

1. Direct access to God. By faith all Christians approach God directly and personally (Rom 5:2; Eph 2:18) through Christ.

2. Offering spiritual sacrifices to God. The whole life of the Christian is to be a service of love—"a fragrant offering, a sacrifice acceptable and pleasing to God" (Phil 4:18). All work, activity, prayer, and praise is to be offered to God.

3. Declaring the gospel. By word and deed Christians are to reveal the love of God in Christ. They are to "declare the wonderful deeds of him who called you out of darkness into his marvelous light" (1 Pt 2:9), and they are to make sure that even pagans can recognize their behavior as good (1 Pt 2:12).

4. Worshiping as a local church. "Supplications, prayer, intercessions, and thanksgivings" are to be made for all persons (1 Tm 2:1). The sacraments of baptism and the Lord's Supper are to be administered on behalf of the whole church as the community serves God and extends his kingdom.

In summary, it may be said that priesthood is an activity and function which is best viewed in a collective sense as belonging to the whole body of Christians, though including of necessity the individual Christian life of service. Its full meaning is negated if it is seen only in individualist terms—*my* access to God, *my* right to interpret the Bible, and *my* ability to discern God's will.   PETER TOON

See PRIESTS AND LEVITES; TABERNACLE, TEMPLE; WORSHIP; OFFERINGS AND SACRIFICES.

Priests and Levites.

Introduction.

There were three basic classes of religious personnel in ancient Israel: prophets, wise men, and priests and Levites. The classical prophets fulfilled a vocation, but were not professionals; they were not paid for their task and functioned only in response to the particular call of God. The wise men were involved in government and education; some of their duties were secular, though they were also involved in moral education. The priests and Levites fulfilled a variety of essentially religious duties and were equivalent approximately to the clergy in modern times. They were professional men and were supported for their full-time religious work.

The role of the priesthood may be seen most clearly in the context of Israelite religion as a whole. At the heart of religion was a relationship with God; to be an Israelite or a Jew was to know and maintain a continuous relationship with the living God. This relationship found its outward expression in a variety of contexts: the covenant, the temple, worship, and every facet of daily life. Thus religion, understood as a relationship, had two perspectives, the relationship with God and that with fellow human beings; it had both a personal and a communal dimension to it. The priests were the guardians and servants of this life of relationship, which was at the heart of OT religion; all their functions can best be understood within the context of a relationship between God and Israel. The prophets, too, were servants of the covenant relationship. While the priests functioned as the normal servants of religion, the prophets' role was more that of calling a delinquent people back to the relationship with God in times of crisis.

In the OT, there are frequent references to both priests and Levites; in a number of biblical texts, however, the distinction is not clear (see, e.g., Dt 18:1–8). From the scholarly point of view, the precise relationship between priests and Levites is a continuing problem which has not yet been fully resolved. In general terms, only the sons of Aaron were to assume the role of priests; all other Levites would have religious functions, though technically they would not be priests. While this distinction is clear in most biblical texts, in others there is lack of certainty and clarity. It is clear, however, that *priests* (Levites descended from Aaron) and *Levites* (other than the descendants of Aaron) all had professional religious duties to perform. The precise nature of those duties varied from time to time in the course of Israel's history.

The Origins of the Priesthood.

The priesthood in Israel began during the time of Moses and Aaron, but antecedents to the Hebrew priesthood and the context in which it began occur in Genesis.

The Background to Priesthood. Genesis refers to "priests" a number of times, though they are all non-Hebrew priests. Potiphera, an Egyptian priest of On, had a daughter called Asenath who married Joseph (Gn 41:45); he is indicative of the presence of priests in most religions of the ancient Near East. Egyptian priests possessed land and received a stipend from the pharaoh (Gn 47:22,26). There is also a reference to a priest called Melchizedek (Gn 14:18), whose theological significance emerges more clearly in the NT. In Genesis, Melchizedek is described as a priest-king; he ruled Salem during Abram's time and was a "priest of the God of Highest Heaven." Little more is known of him, other than the words of his blessing of Abram (Gn 14:19,20).

Although there are no explicit references to Hebrew priests in Genesis, several passages illustrate the need for a priesthood and anticipate the later activity of the priests. The need for priesthood may be seen from the time of Adam; Adam's sin caused a disruption in the relationship between man and God and thus demonstrated the need of a mediator between the separated parties. The priests in OT times were to serve in the role of mediator. The awareness of the broken relationship may be seen at many other points in the narrative of Genesis, particularly in passages describing offerings and sacrifices. Noah built an altar and made offerings to God after the flood (Gn 8:20). Abram engaged in sacrifice in the formation of his covenant with God (Gn 15:9,10), and Jacob, too, offered sacrifices (Gn 31:54). In all these instances, the heads of families functioned as priests, though they are not named priests; they stood before God, as representatives of their people, and sought to establish and maintain that relationship with God which is the foundation of human existence. When the religion of the patriarchs, which was based on the family unit, developed into the religion of a nation, Israel, there arose at the same time the need for a formal and professional priesthood.

The Mosaic Establishment. The transition from patriarchal religion to the religion of Israel took place in the time of Moses. The exodus from Egypt was not only the liberation of a group of Hebrew slaves, but the birth of the nation of Israel. The nation that was born in the exodus was given its constitution in the covenant of Sinai. The Law of this covenant established the foundations and origins of Israelite priesthood. It provides insight into the three basic categories to be considered: (a) the high priest; (b) the priests; and (c) the Levites.

(a) *The High Priest.* Any large and complex organization requires a head or leader, and this was true also of the Hebrew priesthood (though in its early days it was a small organization). The covenant was established through Moses, the prophet, through whom God gave the offer and substance of the covenant relationship; religious life within the covenant was to be the primary responsibility of Aaron, who was the first and chief priest.

In the earliest days of Israel's priesthood, it is probable that the chief priest's office was relatively informal; he was chief or leader among his fellow priests. He had a title, but it was essentially a description of his work: "the greatest priest among his brethren" (the literal sense of Lv 21:10). The office was significant, nevertheless, and involved a special ritual of investiture, special clothing, and certain special responsibilities. While the high priest's duties were similar in principle to those of other priests, he had certain exclusive responsibilities. To some extent, his duties were administrative, pertaining to all the priests of whom he had charge. But his position was more weighty than that of an administrator; just as all priests were the servants and guardians of the covenant relationship, the high priest was chief servant and chief guardian. In his hands rested spiritual responsibility for the entire people of God, and therein lay the true honor and gravity of his position.

This spiritual seniority of the high priest is seen most clearly in certain tasks he undertook within Israel's life of worship. The clearest example may be seen in the annual observation of the Day of Atonement (Yom Kippur). On that day alone, the high priest entered the Holy of Holies and, standing before the "mercy seat," he sought God's forgiveness and mercy for the whole nation of Israel (Lv 16:1–9). It is in that ceremony that Israel's covenant faith is seen most clearly. Israel's religion was one of relationship with a holy God, and human evil disrupted that relationship. While all worship and sacrifices throughout the year were concerned with the continuation of the relationship, the Day of Atonement was the most solemn day of the year in which the attention of all the people focused upon the meaning of their existence. Life only held meaning if the relationship with God could be maintained; the high priest had the great honor and heavy burden of seeking God's mercy for all Israel.

The investiture, or ordination, of the high priest, and of Aaron, the first holder of the office, illustrates further the nature of the office. The ordination service lasted for a full week, and is described in detail in Exodus 29 and Leviticus 8. The service was a joint service, involving not only the ordination of Aaron as high priest, but also of his sons as priests. It was held at the entrance to the tabernacle in the presence of all the Israelites who assembled for the occasion. The ordination involved a number of symbolic activities, all indicating the nature and gravity of the occasion. The persons to be ordained were washed with water, symbolizing the necessity of purity in those who were to serve God as high priest and as priests. They were then robed in special garments. They were anointed with oil (as was the tabernacle itself), signifying separation (being set aside) for divine service. Certain sacrifices (a bull and two rams) and offerings were made, in which the persons being ordained participated; they signified the confession and atonement for sins in those about to be ordained, thanksgiving to God, and consecration to the service of God. The dominant theme running through the entire seven-day service of ordination is that of the holiness and dedication required of Aaron and his sons in order to serve God properly, for they were being ordained into the service (Ex 29:44) of a God who is holy. The service itself was conducted by Moses, and although Moses is not normally referred to as a priest, it may be that his role in ordaining the high priest and first priests accounts for the single designation of him as a "priest" (Ps 99:6).

The special clothing to be worn by the high priest Aaron and his successors was also symbolic of the nature and gravity of the office. The basic garment was a coat of checkered design. Upon this was placed the robe of the ephod, a simple blue tunic with a hole for the head to go through; the skirts of the robe had attached to them, in an alternating design, representations of pomegranates (made of blue, purple, and scarlet material) and golden bells, which were heard when the high priest entered the Holy of Holies. Above the robe of the ephod came the ephod itself, skillfully made from gold, blue, purple, and scarlet materials, with finely twined linen. The ephod was suspended by two shoulder pieces, in which were inserted two onyx stones; on each of the stones six names of the tribes of Israel were engraved. The breastpiece, made of the same materials as the ephod, was a square pouch attached to the ephod by means of cords from the four gold rings at each corner. Four rows of precious stones were attached to the pouch, with three different stones per row representing the 12 tribes of Israel individually. The inside of the pouch contained the Urim and Thummim; although there cannot be absolute certainty on the nature of these objects, they were the means by which God expressed his will to his people through the high priest.

(They may have been two flat stones, with the equivalent of "yes" [thummim] and "no" [urim] inscribed on them.) Around his waist, the high priest wore a girdle, or belt, embroidered with fine needlework. He wore a turban, and attached to the front of the turban by blue lace was a gold plate or "crown," on which were inscribed the words "Holy to the Lord."

The special clothing worn by the high priest was symbolic of the nature and importance of his office; although all the symbolism cannot be determined, some of it is made clear in the biblical text. There are three particular themes in the symbolism. The first is beauty. The sense of beauty emerges from the quality and design of all the items of clothing, together with the use of color and precious stones. But beauty is dominant in the breastplate; the Hebrew word, translated approximately as "breastplate," has as its basic sense "beauty" or "excellence." The clothing symbolizes beauty, while beauty describes the office; the two other themes associated with the symbolism bring out the excellence of the office.

The second theme is the role of the priest as representative of Israel before God. This essential dimension of the office of the high priest is explicitly identified in the names of the tribes of Israel in the two onyx stones in the ephod, and in the 12 precious stones attached to the breastplate. The high priest enters God's presence to seek deliverance from God's judgment (the breastplate is identified with judgment; Ex 28:15) for his people and in order to keep the people constantly in God's remembrance (Ex 28:12), as symbolized by the two onyx stones. The third theme is the role of the high priest as the representative of God to Israel. This dimension of the office is seen in the Urim and Thummim, kept in the breastpiece, by means of which God made known his will to Israel. The high priest, Aaron, fully robed, was a splendid figure, and the splendor of his garments indicated the magnificence of the office with which he had been entrusted.

The high priesthood was to be passed on within the family (for the high priest was expected to be a married man), although in later history, the practice was not always adhered to. On Aaron's death, the office passed to Eleazar, one of his four sons.

(b) *The Priests.* Priests took office not as the result of a particular vocation, but by virtue of priestly descent. Thus the first priests were the four sons of Aaron: Nadab, Abihu, Eleazar, and Ithamar; these four were ordained at the same time that Aaron was ordained high priest (Ex 28:1). Like him, they had special clothing, which was basically similar, though it lacked the distinctive garments of the high

A depiction of an OT priest.

priest (the special ephod, the breastpiece, and the crown). The priesthood would be passed down through their sons.

The sanctity of the priestly office was such that it was preserved from degeneration through specific laws. A man must be a descendant of Aaron to be a priest, but he was also required to meet a variety of other qualifications. He would not marry a divorcée or a former prostitute (Lv 21:7). If he was afflicted by certain kinds of disease or congenital defects, he was barred from priestly office (e.g., blindness, lameness, mutilation, being a hunchback or dwarf; Lv 21:16–23). The principle involved was similar to that applying to animals used in sacrifice—only those free from defect or blemish were suitable for divine service.

In the earliest days of the priesthood there is some information provided in the biblical text concerning the specific duties of the priests. Eleazar had overall responsibility for the tabernacle and its offerings (Nm 4:16), assisted Moses in a number of duties, such as numbering the people and dividing the land (Nm 26:1,2; 32:2), and later served as an adviser to Joshua. Ithamar was responsible for the construction of the tabernacle (Ex 38:21) and supervised the families of the Gershonites and Merarites (Nm 4:28–33). Nadab and Abihu, however, died soon after their ordina-

tion as a result of a sinful act in their priestly duties (Lv 10:1–7), which may have been related in part to drunkenness (Lv 10:8,9).

Priestly duties, in general, fell into three areas (Dt 33:8–10). First, they were responsible in conjunction with the high priest for declaring God's will to the people. Second, they had responsibilities in religious education; they were to teach to Israel God's ordinances and Law (Torah; Dt 33:10). Third, they were to be the servants of the tabernacle, participating in Israel's sacrifices and worship. There were a number of other duties which may have fallen to them, which they would have shared with the Levites in general.

The priests, along with all other Levites, did not hold any land, as did the other Israelite tribes. Their task was to be entirely in the direct service to God. The absence of land, however, meant that they could not support and feed themselves as could other men and women. Consequently, the law specified that they could be supported for their services by the people as a whole. They were to receive, from worshipers, portions of animals that were brought to the tabernacle, corn, wine, oil, and wool.

(c) *The Levites.* This term includes the priests, in a broad sense, for the sons of Aaron belonged to the tribe of Levi. For practical purposes, however, the Levites were those of the tribe other than the priests. The Levites also functioned in the service of the tabernacle, though they had a subordinate position. They, too, were professional men and were paid in money and in kind for their services. Though they did not inherit tribal territory of their own, there were a number of cities set aside for their use (Nm 35:1–8) and pasturelands were designated outside those cities for their livestock.

The Levites were divided into three principal families, the descendants of Kohath, Gershon, and Merari, respectively (Nm 4). Each of these families had particular responsibilities with respect to the care and transport of the tabernacle. The sons of Kohath carried the tabernacle furniture (after it had been covered by the priests), the sons of Gershon cared for the coverings and screens, and the sons of Merari carried and erected the tabernacle's frame. The priests, by contrast, were responsible for the transportation of the ark of the covenant. The role of each Levite, as servant of the tabernacle, was restricted; he undertook his professional duties between the ages of 25 and 50 (Nm 8:24–26).

Although many of the duties of the Levites were of a mundane nature, they also had a very significant religious role. The Law required that all the firstborn, including firstborn sons, be given to God, recalling the slaying of the firstborn at the exodus from Egypt. The Levites' role in religion was that of being accepted by God in the place of the firstborn sons of Israel (Nm 3:11–13); their cattle, too, were accepted in place of the Israelites' firstborn cattle. In the census taken in the time of Moses, the firstborn Israelites exceeded the number of the Levites and a five-shekel redemption fee had to be paid into the priestly coffers for each person in excess (Nm 3:40–51). The representative and substitutionary nature of the Levites can be seen in Israelite religion. Like the priests, they played a part in the larger activity of mediation between God and Israel.

The law of Deuteronomy specifies a number of duties which may have fallen upon both priests and Levites (though the texts are ambiguous). These duties included participation in the activity of the law courts as judges, perhaps with special reference to religious crimes (Dt 17:8,9), taking care of the book of the law (Dt 17:18), controlling the lives and health of lepers (Dt 24:8), and participating directly in the conduct of covenant renewal ceremonies (Dt 27:9).

The History of the Institution. In theory, the covenant Law of Moses determined the nature and course of the offices of priests and Levites for the future history of Israel. In practice, however, changing historical circumstances and changes in the shape of Israel's religion and culture altered the shape of the priesthood and the role of the Levites from time to time. And even more significantly, the persons who held the offices shaped them and their effectiveness through their faithfulness or unfaithfulness.

The Priesthood Before the Monarchy. In the years between the time of Moses and the establishment of the monarchy under Saul and David, the religion of Israel went through a time of laxity and uncertainty, which was to affect the priesthood and the Levites as it did all other parts of national life. It is not possible to write a complete history of the priesthood during this time; a number of general details emerge from the sources which indicate the state of affairs, and a few specific accounts give information about particular people.

In the time of Joshua, the priests continued to undertake their important task of carrying the ark of the covenant. The Levites assisted in the division and allocation of the newly acquired land among the Israelite tribes. In Joshua 21, there is a detailed list of the allocation of cities to both priests and Levites, in fulfillment of the earlier legislation. In the days of the settlement, beyond the conquest, there is some evidence that the Levites took over the priestly duty of transporting the ark (1 Sm 6:15; 2 Sm 15:24).

The writer of the Book of Judges has recorded two stories which illuminate the lives of particular Levites. The first, the story of Micah (Jgs 17,18), describes the establishment of a local shrine in which Micah's son was appointed as a priest (though he was not of Levite or Aaronic descent). Later, Micah hired an itinerant Levite to function as a priest in his shrine, though subsequently that Levite was persuaded to serve the tribe of Dan as a priest. It is difficult to fit the details of this story into the theoretical model of priests and Levites, though the story may illustrate the confused state of Israel's religion at the time. What is particularly significant is that the role of the Levite-priest was primarily oracular (Jgs 18:5, 6). The second story in Judges is the rather horrifying account of a Levite and his concubine (Jgs 19). The story illustrates the moral decline and lack of law and order in Israel at the time, but it sheds little light on the role of the Levites.

More information is provided about the priesthood during the 11th century BC, immediately before the establishment of the monarchy. The tabernacle (by now probably a semipermanent structure) and the ark of the covenant were located in Shiloh. The priest in charge of the sanctuary in Shiloh was Eli, who may have been a descendant of Aaron's son, Ithamar. His two sons, Hophni and Phinehas, also served as priests, indicating that the principle of family descent was still operative with respect to the priesthood. But although Eli was a faithful priest, his two sons sadly abused the office.

The precise role of Samuel in this period is unclear. He was primarily a judge and a prophet, but it is difficult to determine whether he was also a priest. In the historical narratives, he is not called a priest, though Psalm 99:6 might be interpreted to indicate his priestly office. There are a number of passages, however, which indicate that he acted like a priest. For example, he offered sacrifices (1 Sm 7:9–10); as a young man he served in the sanctuary of Shiloh and wore an ephod (1 Sm 2). Furthermore, one of the biblical genealogies implies priestly descent (1 Chr 6:23–30). Nevertheless, he is not normally identified as a priest and the introduction to his story refers to him as an Ephraimite, by descent from his father (1 Sm 1:1), not a Levite. If the priest is perceived as a permanent servant of the sanctuary, as was Eli, then it is clear that Samuel was not a priest. But the priestly role of Samuel may perhaps be related to the fact that his mother "lent" him to God (1 Sm 1:28) while he was still a boy.

The Priesthood During the Time of David and Solomon. Several radical changes took place during the reign of David and Solomon; these were a result, primarily, of the establishment of a permanent temple in Jerusalem and the installation of the ark of the covenant there. During the time of Saul, the first king of Israel, the social structure was essentially the same as it had been in the time of the judges. Saul, as king, was a military leader, but his relationship to religion and the priesthood was not clearly determined.

David changed the situation in many important respects. After his capture of the city of Jerusalem, he made that place the political and religious capital of his nation. The religious centrality of Jerusalem was assured by moving the ark of the covenant there, together with the tabernacle. Jerusalem now became the permanent location of the ark, and therefore the permanent center of religion; at the same time, the various regional shrines, which had developed in the premonarchical period, were gradually eliminated.

These changes had numerous implications for the priesthood and the Levites. During David's reign, there were two principal priests, Abiathar and Zadok. Abiathar, a former priest of Nob, had joined David before his rise to power; he appears to have been a descendant of Eli, and through him of Ithamar, one of Aaron's sons. Zadok's background is less clear, though his lineage appears to go back to Aaron's other son, Eleazar. These two priests are always named together in the texts describing David's reign, and Zadok is always mentioned before Abiathar. Although neither is explicitly identified as high priest in the ancient texts, there is some evidence to suggest that Abiathar functioned as high priest (1 Kgs 2:35); in NT times, he is identified as such (Mk 2:26). Zadok, during David's reign, may have been particularly responsible for the care of the ark of the covenant (2 Sm 15:24–25). These two priests had a significant position in David's royal establishment; they may also have shared overall responsibility for the priests, whose lives were now centered on the Jerusalem temple.

Much of David's time was focused upon the preparations for building a permanent temple for God. In the preparation for the temple, and in its completion during the reign of King Solomon, the new activities of the Levites may be seen. (The construction of a permanent temple automatically removed their former responsibilities related to the care and transportation of the tabernacle.) Large numbers of Levites were employed as laborers in the actual building of the temple. Others found new tasks in the worship of God in the tabernacle during David's reign and in the temple upon its completion. To the Levites, and especially Herman, Asaph, and Ethan, was given primary responsibility for the music of worship; this involved not only singing, but also the playing of a variety of instruments in the temple's orchestra or band. The Levites had also a variety of other tasks; they worked as gatekeepers at the sanctuary, assisted the priests in the preparation of sacrifices, kept the sanctuary clean, and some functioned as general administrative and legal officers (1 Chr 23:1–32). Other Levites functioned as bankers, with primary responsibility for the temple treasuries (1 Chr 26:20–28).

Following David's death, there was a dispute over the royal succession, from which Solomon emerged as the new king. During his reign, the temple was brought to its completion and the regular worship of the nation was conducted there. In the matter of succession, however, Abiathar had supported a losing candidate, and when Solomon was made king, he lost his important office in the royal court. During Solomon's reign, the control of the priesthood passed into the hands of Zadok.

The Priesthood During the Divided Monarchy. The great empire, which had been built by David and maintained by Solomon, collapsed after Solomon's death; from the ruins, two new and relatively insignificant states emerged. The southern kingdom, Judah, retained Jerusalem as its capital and the temple as its center of worship. The northern kingdom, Israel, located its first capital at Shechem, from where it was later moved to Tirzah.

In the southern state of Judah, the priests and Levites continued to function normally within the Jerusalem temple. The office of high priest continued to be passed on by descent within the family of Zadok, who had held office in Solomon's reign; the continuity of office in this family was to be retained down into the time of the second temple, when the Zadokite succession was interrupted about 171 BC. Nevertheless, for all the continuity of religion in Jerusalem, all was not well with religion in Judah, neither during the reign of its first king, Rehoboam, nor during the reigns of his successors. During Rehoboam's reign, there was a decline in religion and also in the priesthood, when popular forms of religion were introduced as a result of foreign influence (1 Kgs 14:22–24). The history of the southern kingdom was marked by periods of religious decline followed by reform, often as a result of the activities of the prophets. The role of the priesthood was all too rarely one of spiritual leadership, and the priests themselves were often the subject of criticism by the prophets (e.g., Jer 2:8,26).

The northern kingdom, whose first king was Jeroboam I, inevitably had to introduce some radical changes in religion. Jeroboam could not recognize the temple of Jerusalem, partly because it lay outside his state and partly because it was intimately associated with the royal line of David. Jeroboam established two principal shrines in his kingdom, both of which were to retain importance during the relatively short life of the northern kingdom (200 years). The first was at Bethel, in the southern part of his kingdom near the border with Judah (it was only about 12 miles north of Jerusalem). The second shrine, or sanctuary, was at Dan, in the far northern part of his kingdom.

Both these sanctuaries had ancient associations with the Hebrew traditions. Bethel is referred to as early as the time of Abram (Gn 12:8) and the sanctuary at Dan is known from the history of the judges (Jgs 18). There may indeed have been priests and Levites still residing in these two places, descendants of the former servants of the sanctuaries. But Jeroboam established a nonlevitical priesthood to serve in these sanctuaries, and in various smaller shrines or "high places," thereby cutting off the religious tradition of the northern state even more radically from that of Judah. The royal sanctuary at Bethel, so close to the Jerusalem temple, may have been set up in deliberate "competition" with the Judean sanctuary.

The history of the priesthood in the northern kingdom is no more impressive than that of Judah. Many of the prophets, including Amos, Hosea, and Jeremiah, condemned the northern sanctuaries and their priests. Hosea was forceful in his condemnation: "As marauders lie in ambush for a man, so do bands of priests; they murder on the road to Shechem, committing shameful crimes" (Hos 6:9 NIV). Those to whom the spiritual lives of the chosen people had been entrusted only rarely lived up to their responsibilities.

Priests and Levites During and After the Exile. The northern kingdom came to its end in 722 BC, defeated by the armies of Assyria, but religious life continued in Judah for a while longer. Eventually, the end of the southern state came about 586 BC; the defeat of the state by the Babylonians was accompanied by the destruction of Jerusalem and its temple (Lam 2:20). The Babylonian commander took Seraiah, the high priest, and Zephanaiah, his assistant, to Riblah, along with other officials; there they were executed (2 Kgs 25:18–21). Then a policy of exile was established by the Babylonians; the most important and influential people of Judah were deported to Babylon, while the less significant were allowed to remain, for they were unlikely to cause trouble. Of those exiled from Judah, many may have been priests (Jer 29:1), for they were men of influence. By way of contrast, it seems likely that a much smaller number of Levites was exiled, reflecting perhaps their inferior social position.

In the city of Jerusalem there was little normal religious life during the years of the exile; the altar had been destroyed and was not restored until after the exile. No doubt some kind of activity continued, but it was an impoverished form of religion. Most of the priests were in exile in Babylon, but they could not function, for there was no temple or sanctuary. Ezekiel implies that God himself was the only "sanctuary" for the exiles (Ez 11:16). Not until the return from exile and the restoration of Jerusalem and its temple could the normal functions of priests and Levites resume.

When the Babylonian Empire was defeated, the new Persian conquerors instituted a policy whereby the Hebrew exiles could return to their homeland. Of those returning, 4289 are designated as priests and members of priestly families, while only 341 were Levites (Ezr 2:36–42); the imbalance probably reflects the imbalance in the number of those exiled initially. Under Joshua (Jeshua), the priest, and Zerubbabel work began on the restoration. The priests played a significant role in the first year of the return, in the restoration of the altar in Jerusalem, so that sacrifice and worship to God could resume. Once the altar had been restored, the work began on the temple itself in the second year of the return. In this work, both the priests and the Levites were involved, and the laying of new foundations for the temple began. When the foundation had been laid, both priests, in their vestments, and Levites, in their role as singers and musicians, participated in the ceremony of dedication (Ezr 3:8–13). Again, when the temple had been rebuilt, both priests and Levites participated in the ceremony of dedication (Ezr 6:16–18). The restoration, however, was concerned with more than buildings; it involved a moral and religious component. Though priests and Levites helped in this task, they were also affected by it. Many, for example, had married foreign wives (Ezr 9:1), and thus had to conform to Ezra's reform laws.

To some extent, the priests and Levites resumed their normal duties in the worship of the postexilic period. The priests were engaged in the conduct of the temple worship. The Levites assisted, as temple servants (Neh 11:3), as treasurers and collectors of tithes (Neh 10:37–39), and as instructors or teachers of the Law of God (Neh 8:7–9). Nevertheless, the history of the priesthood after the exile is not free of blemish; there are few more powerful condemnations of the abuse of the priestly office than that delivered by the prophet Malachi (1:6–2:9). Malachi catalogues a list of priestly evils reminiscent of the evil priests who lived during the time of the monarchy.

The office of high priest continued after the exile among the descendants of Zadok, being held first by Joshua (Hg 1:1). The different political circumstances, however, changed the nature of the high priestly office. Whereas in the days of the monarchy, the high priest was subservient to the king, there was no king, in the proper sense, after the exile. From a political perspective, the Jews were members of a province or colony; for practical purposes, they were a community based upon a common religion. The high priest was no longer subject to the secular authority of a Jewish king, but his religious authority was considerable, and in some ways his functions were similar to those of a king in pre-exilic times.

The Priesthood in the Maccabean Period. During the 2nd century BC, some changes took place in the priesthood, particularly with respect to the office of high priest, which marked the end of the OT era and set the background for the NT period. Judea, in the 2nd century, was ruled by the Seleucid kings, who had inherited a portion of the massive Greek Empire established by Alexander the Great. The Judean province was controlled internally under the high priesthood, whose authority was received from the Seleucid kings.

For the first three decades of the 2nd century BC, the high priesthood remained with the Zadokite line of descent; the high priests were members of the (Zadokite) Oniad family; Onias III (198–174 BC); Jason, brother of Onias III (174–171 BC). It was in the period of Jason that there began a series of events which would terminate the Zadokite tradition.

Onias III had opposed the Hellenization policy of Antiochus IV (Epiphanes), which threatened to undermine the Jewish faith. Antiochus replaced Onias by Jason, who in effect purchased the high priesthood from the Seleucid king. In purchasing the priestly office, Jason had set a dangerous precedent; although he was of Zadokite descent, his act implied that the office could be bought, and that descent was not vital. The opponents of Jason, the Tobiads, were able to remove him from office and have their own candidate, Menelaus (who was not a Zadokite), appointed in his place. This act resulted in a civil war between those supporting Jason and those supporting Menelaus, and the war in turn culminated in ruthless repressive measures by Antiochus Epiphanes; there were massacres in Jerusalem and

the temple was desecrated (167 BC). The desecration of the temple led to the Maccabean revolt, as a result of which the Jews regained their independence for a short time. Menelaus retained the office of high priest until 161 BC and was succeeded by Alcimus (161–159 BC).

There then followed a period during which there was no high priest for seven years. The political climate, however, was such that it became unlikely that the Zadokite line would ever regain the high priesthood, which had been established in the time of King Solomon. The Maccabean Jonathan gained control of Jerusalem and in 152 BC, with the approval of the Seleucid king, he was formally invested with the high priest's robes of office. He was succeeded as high priest and ruler by Simon in 143 BC, who also held the office with the approval of the Seleucids (Demetrius II). But in the third year of his reign (140 BC), the high priesthood of Simon received public approval in a great religious assembly, and the family of Simon became "high priest forever" (1 Mc 14:41–47). That event marked the real termination of the Zadokite tradition and the foundation of the Hasmonean line.

The establishment of the high priestly office outside the Zadokite line did not go without challenge. It is probable that a sect within Judaism, now known as the Essenes, was born in reaction to the high priesthood of Simon. The Essenes, better known for the Dead Sea Scrolls which have survived into the 20th century, appear to have been founded by a Zadokite priest who rejected the authenticity and authority of Simon. Thus, in a limited sense, the Zadokite priests continued to survive.

The Priesthood in NT Times. In the early NT period, both priests and Levites continued to function within the Jewish religion. Zacharias, father of John the Baptist, was a priest belonging to the division of "Abijah" (Lk 1:5) and his wife was also of priestly descent. When Zacharias was visited by an angel, he was engaged at the time in priestly duties in the Jerusalem temple; various divisions of priests took responsibility for the temple services for a period of time and then returned to their homes (Lk 1:23) as another division took over. The distinction between priests and Levites is also maintained in the NT (Jn 1:19) and appears in Jesus' parable concerning the good Samaritan (Lk 10:31,32). Both priests and Levites were among the earliest converts to Christianity; Barnabas was a Levite from Cyprus (Acts 4:36) and several priests responded to the proclamation of the gospel (Acts 6:7).

The office of high priest is frequently referred to in the NT. Several high priests are named, the plurality of current and former holders of the office reflecting the nature of the position as an essentially political appointment as distinct from its oldest definition, that of an office passing from father to son on the death of the father. The two most significant high priests in the NT are those who held office during the lifetime of Jesus. Annas was high priest about AD 6–15, but even after he ceased to hold the office formally, he continued to exert considerable influence through his son-in-law, the high priest Caiaphas (c. AD 18–36). Both were significant figures in the trial of Jesus. At a later date, Ananias, son of Nedebaeus, was high priest (c. AD 47–58) and president of the Sanhedrin during the time in which Paul was brought to trial.

The priesthood held considerable authority in NT times. Most internal and religious matters in the Roman province of Judea were within the authority of the Sanhedrin, which functioned as a kind of provincial government, though its powers were limited in certain matters by Rome. Its membership included the ruling and former high priests and a large number of Sadducees, many of whom belonged to influential priestly families. This priestly influence in the Sanhedrin was indicative of the important role of the temple in Jewish life during the 1st century AD.

In AD 70, following the destruction of the temple in Jerusalem, a radical change came about in the significance of the priesthood in Judaism. The end of the temple removed in effect the purpose for the existence of the priesthood. Although the priesthood continued after a fashion until the Bar Kochba rebellion in AD 135, its days were numbered after AD 70. Since the end of the 1st century AD, Judaism has developed without priests and its course down to the present century has been charted by the rabbis, the spiritual descendants of the Pharisees.

Priests in the Biblical World. The idea and practice of priesthood are by no means distinctive or unique in biblical religion. In the civilizations of the ancient Near East, there were priestly classes in the Sumerian, Hittite, and Egyptian religions and Zoroastrianism in the Persian Empire, to name a few. There were also priests in religious cults in Syria and Palestine, and in these areas even the terminology for priests is identical with that of the OT. In NT times, there were priests in several of the religions existing within the Roman Empire; in Acts, a priest of Jupiter is referred to, who was a resident of Lystra. Almost all religions have some concept of priesthood, so that the existence of priests and Levites in biblical religion is not surprising.

The roles of the priests and Levites are closely paralleled by priestly roles in other reli-

A Sumerian priest from Tell Asmar.

gions. For example, in Assyrian and Babylonian religion, the priests were divided into a variety of classes, each with different religious functions. Some had administrative or supervisory roles, some functioned in the context of worship and sacrifice, some specialized in singing and music, some were diviners, and others practiced magic. Very often groups of priests with special functions occurred in an organization, a kind of guild, which traced its origin to a forefather or patriarch in ancient times. The priests wore special robes and distinctive hats; for certain types of expiation ceremonies, they donned purple robes. Thus the general category of priests in Assyria and Babylonia undertook the same duties as did both priests and Levites in Israel. The commonality of priesthood in the ancient world, however, is such that it is probably not possible to trace precisely the historical antecedents of the Israelite priesthood.

For the common ground between priesthood in the OT and the ancient Near East, there were nevertheless differences. There was one major and principal distinction, from which all other distinctions followed. The priests and Levites of Israel served the God of Israel; theirs was a monotheistic faith, serving a single, unitary, and omnipotent God. In this, they differed from their fellow priests in other cultures, who served the variety of gods and goddesses in the many pantheons of Near Eastern religions. Other differences flowed from the nature of this God; thus, priests could not practice magic (the manipulation of divine power for personal use), for it was prohibited by the God of Israel. Just as many features of biblical religion had precise parallels in other religions, such was also the case with the priestly office; the radical differences emerge only when a careful comparison is undertaken of the differences between God and the gods.

Theological Significance of Priesthood. *The OT.* The priests and Levites were servants of God and, from a different perspective, servants of the covenant. Both the human and divine aspects of their service can be seen in the covenant context. As servants of God, they represented God's principal purpose in this world, namely, the well-being of his chosen people; the people would only experience that well-being if their relationship with God was maintained. As servants of Israel, they undertook specific responsibilities and leadership with respect to that which is most central in human life, the worshipful life of relationship to God.

From these comments, it is clear that the priests and Levites possessed the role of mediation between God and Israel. In significant ways, they represented each member of the covenant before the other member. The need for a mediator was partly practical. In the days of the patriarchs and family religion, there had been no formal priesthood, for the family unit was small. But Israel was an entire nation, bound to God in covenant; the existence of priests and Levites recognized the human need for so large a community to set aside a group of people whose permanent task was to watch over and care for the relationship with God. The need for mediation, however, was also based upon a particular understanding of the nature of God. Although God was Father, he was also an awesome and holy being. His holiness was such that he could not lightly be approached by the ordinary man and woman. The priests and Levites thus assumed the grave task of approaching God on behalf of the people as a whole.

For all the necessary aspects of priesthood, there was also a sense in which it was unnecessary. The patriarchs had no priests. In the exile, there were priests but they could not function as such; the exiles lived without the normal services of a priest. In the Psalms, the many individual hymns and laments indicate that it was possible for the ordinary individual to approach God directly without the aid of a priest. Likewise, the role of the great

prophets indicates that it was possible for God to speak to his people directly, without the mediation of a priest.

Nevertheless, the existence of a priesthood provides a fundamental insight into the nature of religion. Religion is a relationship with the living God. Yet human beings are aware of a gap, or sense of distance, between themselves and God. It seems almost presumptuous for sinful man to attempt to bridge that gap in his own right. Yet a priest could take steps to bridge that gap, not because priests were innately better than other men or women, but precisely because that was the task to which *God*, in his mercy, had appointed them. Thus, from an OT perspective, the existence of a priesthood is not evidence of the genius of the founders of Israelite religion; rather, it is evidence of the mercy of God toward his people.

There is one further vital theological dimension to priesthood in the OT. It is that the role of the priests as servants of Israel was parallel to the role of Israel as servant to all nations. God addressed to Israel some words of remarkable privilege in the formation of the Sinai covenant: "And you shall be to me a kingdom of priests and a holy nation" (Ex 19:6). Just as the Israelites had need of a priest to represent them before God, so too the nations of the world required a priest to represent them. From a Christian perspective, this priestly role of Israel as a whole is to be understood partially in the meaning of Jesus Christ for the world.

The NT. To a very limited extent, the OT theology of priesthood continues into the time of the church. The earliest Jewish Christians did not automatically renounce their ties with the worship of the Jerusalem temple (Acts 3:1; 21:26); in that sense, they continued to worship through the mediacy of the temple priesthood, though the destruction of the temple in AD 70 brought to an end that possibility. In reality, however, their understanding of priesthood had undergone a radical change through the illumination of the gospel. Central to the proclamation of the gospel was that God had provided a mediator in the person of Jesus Christ. What had formerly been undertaken, in a limited fashion, by priests and Levites on a continuing basis, had now been fully achieved in the death and resurrection of Jesus Christ on a permanent basis.

Although this theme of the mediatory role of Jesus Christ penetrates the entire gospel, it is given its fullest expression in the Letter to the Hebrews. Therein, the writer elaborates upon the whole tradition of priests and Levites to demonstrate the fulfillment and consummation in the gospel. But the focal point of the epistle is the office of high priest; Jesus is the full and final High Priest of the new covenant who achieved that mediation with God (Heb 2:17) which used to be sought annually on the Day of Atonement. Jesus was not a high priest in the tradition of Aaron, or Zadok, which would have identified him with the old covenant. Jesus was designated by God "after the order of Melchizedek" (Heb 6:20), for "he is without father or mother or genealogy, and has neither beginning of days nor end of life, but resembling the Son of God he continues a priest for ever" (Heb 7:3). The eternality of the high priesthood of Jesus eclipsed the temporality of the priesthood in the OT.

But there is a final dimension to the concept of priesthood in the NT which is of vital significance. It is the concept of all Christians belonging to the priesthood. Peter indicates that Christians are "a royal priesthood, a holy nation, God's own people" (1 Pt 2:9). But the conception of all Christians as priests does not mean that they no longer need priests as in OT times, though that is true; they have a High Priest in the person of Jesus Christ. More than that, it implies that all Christians must be priests to the world at large. Just as Israel, the community of the old covenant, was called upon to be a nation of priests on behalf of all nations, so Christians, citizens of the new covenant, are called upon to be priests representing all mankind before God—and so before all mankind. PETER C. CRAIGIE

See PRIESTHOOD; OFFERINGS AND SACRIFICES; TABERNACLE, TEMPLE; WORSHIP; PRAYER; FEASTS AND FESTIVALS OF ISRAEL; AARON; LEVI, TRIBE OF; LEVITICAL CITIES; ISRAEL, RELIGION OF.

Bibliography. A. Cody, *A History of the OT Priesthood;* R. de Vaux, *Ancient Israel,* 344–405; W. Eichrodt, *Theology of the OT,* 1: 392–436; G.B. Gray, *Sacrifice in the OT;* J. Jeremias, *Jerusalem in the Time of Jesus;* G. Oehler, *Theology of the OT,* 200–217.

Primogeniture. Word not found in the Bible; derived from the Greek translation of the Hebrew word for firstborn. Primogeniture refers specifically to the exclusive right of inheritance which belonged to the firstborn male. If the firstborn died, the next oldest living male did not receive that exclusive right; neither did a female if she were the firstborn, nor the firstborn if he was born of a concubine or of a slave woman (e.g., Gn 21:10). That the Scriptures attached much importance to the rights of the firstborn (primogeniture) can be seen in the distinction drawn between the firstborn and other sons (Gn 10:15; 25:13; 36:15), the double portion to be given to the firstborn (Dt 21:17), as well as the paternal blessing given to them (Gn 21:1–14; 27:1–28; 48:18).

Primogeniture was recognized by non-Israelites also. In parts of ancient Babylonia, according to private legal documents, the first-born son enjoyed special inheritance privileges. This was also the case in Nuzi and Egypt. There is evidence, however, from extant records, that exceptions could be made if the family patriarch chose to do so.

It is of interest that God, in electing and placing Israelite sons in strategic roles of service, did not adhere to the principle of primogeniture in each case. Jacob was chosen instead of firstborn Esau (Mt 1:2,3); David, the seventh son, was chosen king (1 Sm 16:6–12). Jesus Christ, the only begotten Son of God, is spoken of as the One Who inherits all of the Father's kingdom.

See FIRSTBORN; BIRTHRIGHT.

Principalities and Powers. Phrase, familiarized by the KJV, occurring several times in Paul's writings, and expressed by means of three Greek synonyms. The concept of principalities is signified by *exousia* and *archai,* while powers is represented by *dynamis.* In the NT, *exousia* describes the power inherent in authority as something confirmed by or derived from a position of prominence. There is nothing evil about this kind of authority and, on the contrary, it is essentially right both morally and spiritually (Mt 21:23). It thus applies most appropriately to the authority of the Messiah (Mt 9:6; Mk 2:10), of the apostles (2 Cor 10:8; 13:10), and of human government (cf. Mt 8:9; Lk 20:20). *Archai* has several meanings, but occurs 12 times in the sense of command, rule, or sovereignty, 9 of which (Rom 8:38; 1 Cor 15:24; Eph 1:21; 3:10; 6:12; Col 1:16; 2:10,15; Ti 3:1) appear in Paul's letters. Finally *dynamis,* a common word for power, denotes the ability or strength to achieve an impressive goal (Mt 25:15; Acts 3:12).

By using the expression "principalities and powers," Paul is referring to the hierarchy of supernatural agencies such as angelic beings who worship and serve the Creator of the universe. Some commentators have divided this hierarchy into five categories, namely thrones, principalities, powers, authorities, and dominions. This conclusion, however, can only be arrived at by general inference, since there is nothing in Scripture that points directly to such distinct groups. In using the phrase, Paul is expressing the cosmic lordship of Jesus in as colorful and dramatic a manner as possible.

The entire host of heaven, he says, stands in admiration of Christ's bride, the church (Eph 1:10), because such a splendid creation has been raised from the humblest of origins by his atoning death. Yet the host of angelic beings in heaven is also God's creation, and like the Christian church has experienced its own agonies as a result of some primeval conflict between sin and righteousness (cf. Lk 10:18).

In giving Jesus a name above every other name, which all forms of creation whether good or bad would acknowledge as superior in power to any other name (Rom 14:11; Phil 2:10), Paul was demonstrating the supreme lordship of Christ. As their Creator, the heavenly hosts were his subjects, acknowledging him with the church as Lord of the universe. This affirmation was important for the Colossians, whose theology had apparently been tainted by unbiblical speculation (Col 2:8). The truth is that in the incarnate Jesus there resided all the fullness of God, and this is transmitted to believers when they are totally committed through repentance and faith to Christ as Lord. This mighty Savior is the one who bears all authority in heaven and on earth.

See HEAVENLIES, THE.

H.W. PERKIN

Prisca. KJV rendering of Priscilla, Aquila's wife, in 2 Timothy 4:19.

See PRISCILLA AND AQUILA.

Priscilla and Aquila. Christian couple who were friends and possibly converts of the apostle Paul during his ministry at Corinth (Acts 18:1–3). They are always mentioned together in the NT. Priscilla's personal character or her role in the church may account for her name coming before her husband's in four out of six references (Acts 18:18,26; Rom 16:3; 2 Tim 4:19).

Aquila was a Jew and a native of Pontus in Asia Minor. He had been expelled from Rome by the AD 49 edict of Claudius (Acts 18:2). Suetonius records that the emperor "banished from Rome all the Jews, who were continually making disturbances at the instigation of one Chrestus." From Rome, Aquila and Priscilla went to Corinth, where Paul (on his second missionary journey) met them. There they lived together and worked at the same trade of making tents. After such close association with Paul, they were able to instruct even the learned Apollos, a Jewish teacher who then became a Christian (Acts 18:24–28). Both were Paul's loyal friends and trusted co-workers (Rom 16:3,4). When he left Corinth they accompanied him and remained at Ephesus when he returned to Syria (Acts 18:18,19). When Paul wrote the first letter to Corinth they were still at Ephesus, where their home was used as a place for Christians to gather (1 Cor 16:19). Since the decree of Claudius was temporary, Priscilla and Aquila were again in Rome when Paul wrote to the Roman Christians (Rom 16:3). When the second letter to Timothy was written, they were again in Ephesus (2 Tm 4:19).

Prison, Court of the. KJV rendering of "Court of the Guard," an open court where the prophet Jeremiah was kept prisoner, in Jeremiah 32:2.

See GUARD, COURT OF THE.

Prison, Spirits in. *See* SPIRITS IN PRISON.

Prison Gate. KJV rendering of "Gate of the Guard," a gate in Jerusalem possibly in the palace complex, in Nehemiah 12:39.

See GUARD, GATE OF THE.

Prochorus. One of the 7 men appointed by the 12 in Jerusalem for service in the early days of the church (Acts 6:5). They were to oversee the fair distribution of food in the

Shops in the agora (market-place) of Corinth, like the ones in which Paul and Aquila and Priscilla worked.

Christian community. Two of the 7, Stephen and Philip, proclaimed the gospel (Acts 6–8).

See DEACON, DEACONESS.

Proconsul. Governor (KJV deputy) appointed by the senate of Rome to govern a province. From the time of Augustus, the Roman senate appointed governors to administer certain of the Roman senatorial provinces, provinces considered secure enough that no army was kept in them. Proconsuls were appointed for the period of one year between a time when they were *praetor* and the time when they became consul of Rome. They are to be distinguished from procurators who were appointed by the emperor to rule imperial provinces for an indefinite period. We meet two proconsuls in the Book of Acts: Sergius Paulus of Cyprus (Acts 13:7–12) and Gallio of Achaia (Acts 18:12–17).

See GALLIO; GALLIO INSCRIPTION; SERGIUS PAULUS.

Procurator. Financial officer of Rome usually from the equestrian rank whose responsibilities included the supervision and collection of imperial revenues in an assigned province. In Judea and other lesser provinces of the Roman Empire, the procurator acted at times as the governor of that region. He not only managed financial affairs but also exercised judicial and military authority and was primarily responsible for keeping peace in his jurisdiction. The NT mentions three Roman procurators: Pontius Pilate (AD 26–36; Mt 27; Jn 18,19), Antonius Felix (AD 52–59; Acts 23:24–25:14), and Porcius Festus (AD 59–62; Acts 24:27–26:32). These administrators were held accountable and subordinate to the governor of Syria.

See PILATE, PONTIUS; FESTUS, PORCIUS; FELIX, ANTONIUS.

Promise. Declaration by one person to another that something will or will not be done, giving the person to whom it is made the right to expect the performance of whatever has been specified.

Types of Promise. In biblical usage there are scattered examples of promises which men give either to their fellow man (e.g., Nm 22:17; Est 4:7) or to God (e.g., Neh 5:12), but far more significant are the promises which God gives to man. These divine promises are absolutely trustworthy because the One who gives them is "not man, that he should lie" (Nm 23:19; Ti 1:2; Heb 10:23; 11:11), and he is totally able to perform that which he has promised (Rom 4:21).

Divine promises in Scripture assure their recipients of many spiritual and temporal benefits, including sonship (2 Cor 6:16–7:1), forgiveness of sin (1 Jn 1:9), answer to prayer (Lk 11:9), deliverance from temptations (1 Cor 10:13), sustaining grace for difficult times (2 Cor 12:9), provision for all needs (Phil 4:10), reward for obedience (Jas 1:12), and eternal life (Lk 18:29,30; Jn 3:16; Rom 6:22,23). God's promises are certain and sure, but participation in their blessing often requires that certain conditions on which they are predicated be met. Divine promises also are not always guarantees of blessing. Indeed, there are promises which announce the certainty of judgment on those who "do not know God and . . . do not obey the gospel of our Lord Jesus" (2 Thes 1:8,9).

In addition to the promises of God which have subjective and individual application to many different people in widely different times and places, there are a great many promises which pertain to the programmatic unfolding of God's plan of redemption in a grand procession of historical events. These promises have neither repeated applications nor conditional natures. In such cases promise becomes nearly synonomous with prophecy, and promises of this type along with their subsequent fulfillment are intricately intertwined in the entire fabric of redemptive history.

Terminology. Even though the basis for viewing the promise-fulfillment theme as one of the most important in all of Scripture is rooted primarily in the narratives of the OT, it is striking that there is no single term in the Hebrew language which corresponds to the English idea of promise. Instead of any one technical term, Hebrew utilizes a variety of rather ordinary words to convey the idea of promise in certain specific contexts. These include "to speak" (Ex 12:25; Dt 6:3; 9:28; Jos 23:15; 2 Sm 7:28); "to say" (Nm 14:40; 2 Kgs 8:19; Ps 77:8); "to swear" (Gn 26:3; 1 Chr 16:15–18; Neh 9:15). When these words occur with God as the subject and God's people as the ones to whom certain assurances are given, they are properly understood as conveying the idea of promise, and hence the common English translation "promise."

In the NT the Greek verbal and noun form of "promise" occurs more than 40 times. With the exception of Acts 23:21 the reference is always to the promises of God to man. This is in marked contrast with usage in extrabiblical Greek literature, where there are many examples of promises between men, but only one known example of a promise by a god.

Promise in the OT. The highlights of the promise theme in the OT can be seen in the promise of what is often termed the protevangelium (i.e., the first announcement of the gospel) given to Adam and Eve in the Garden of

Eden immediately after the fall into sin (Gn 3:15), and the subsequent promises of the Abrahamic (Gn 12,15,17), Davidic (2 Sm 7), and new covenants (Jer 31).

The Protevangelium. Genesis 3:15b says: "I will put enmity between you and the woman, and between your seed and her seed; he will bruise your head, and you shall bruise his heel." This statement is a promise that at some future time the offspring of the woman will crush Satan. The offspring of the woman is individualized in the "he" of the last phrase. "He" shall strike you (i.e., Satan) on the head, although Satan will inflict a wound on the offspring of the woman. Here then is the promise which gives Adam and Eve as well as their descendants the basis to expect the eventual destruction of their adversary Satan through the offspring of the person whom he seduced.

The Promise to Abraham. In Genesis 12:1–3,7 Abraham is told to leave his people and country, and to go to a land which the Lord would show to him. God in turn promises him that: (1) his offspring would become a great nation; (2) he would be blessed and his name made great; (3) through him other nations would be blessed; and (4) the land of Canaan would be given to his descendants. Of particular significance among these promises given to Abraham is that through his offspring he will bless many nations. This promise is repeated five times in the Book of Genesis (12:3; 18:18; 22:18; 26:4; 28:14), and points back to the promise of Genesis 3:15 as well as forward to Christ and the salvation which he secures.

The Promise to David. In 2 Samuel 7 God gave a promise to King David that his dynasty would endure forever (v 16; Ps 89:34–37). It is with this Davidic covenant that the promised line which had previously run from Adam through Seth, Shem, Abraham, Isaac, Jacob, and Judah is now narrowed to the royal line of the house of David. David is to be the ancestor of the Messiah-king to come (Ps 89:3,27–37). David thus becomes a central figure in redemptive history. Jesus Christ is referred to as the son of David, the son of Abraham (Mt 1:1).

The Promise of a New Covenant. In Jeremiah 31:31–37 it is promised that in future days the Lord will make a new covenant with the house of Israel and the house of Judah. The content of this new covenant reemphasizes and extends the basic promises of the former covenant: "I will be their God, and they shall be my people" (v 33b), and "I will forgive their iniquity, and I will remember their sin no more" (v 34b). It would appear then that the "new covenant" of Jeremiah is to be viewed as a restatement of the same basic promises included in the Abrahamic and Davidic covenants, but under the new cov-

enant administration the ceremonies and ordinances of the Mosaic covenant are phased out because the one pictured in symbol and type in these observances has appeared in the flesh (Heb 9:11,12).

The new covenant was inaugurated with the first advent of Christ and believers in Christ are now recipients by the Holy Spirit of the blessings of that new covenant (Heb 8:6–13), although complete and final realization of these blessings in all their fullness awaits the return of Christ, the complete establishment of his kingdom in its outward and final form, and the blessedness of life in the new heavens and new earth. In the intervening time God's people live in a time in which some of the benefits of the age to come are a present reality, but the fullness of the new age is yet future.

Promise in the NT. NT writers refer to the OT promises in a way which indicates that they did not view these promises as separate and isolated assertions, but rather as individual manifestations of a unitary promise which is ultimately fulfilled in Christ (see Lk 1:54, 55,69–73; Acts 13:23,32,33; 26:6,7; 2 Cor 1:20). Jesus is the fulfillment of the promises made to the patriarchs and David, and these promises are accordingly to be viewed as having a single focal point in him.

In the books of Galatians and Ephesians Paul develops this idea in more detail, saying to the gentile Christians that "you were at that time separate from Christ, alienated from the commonwealth of Israel, and strangers to the covenants of promise" (Eph 2:11,12). Yet when these Gentiles come to Christ they are made "heirs together with Israel, members together of one body, and sharers together in the promise in Christ Jesus" (Eph 3:6 NIV). In fact Paul says that Gentiles who trust in Christ are incorporated into the seed of Abraham and are thus "heirs according to the promise" (Gal 3:29), and he even goes so far as to equate the gospel with the promise given to Abraham when he states, "The Scripture foresaw that God would justify the Gentiles by faith, and announced the gospel in advance to Abraham: 'All nations will be blessed through you'" (Gal 3:8 NIV).

These and other NT texts establish the close connection between the coming of Christ and the fulfillment of the promise. The promises of God find their point of convergence in Christ and all that he accomplished and will yet accomplish for his people.

One further aspect of the promise particularly emphasized in the NT concerns the coming of the Holy Spirit. Paul refers to believers as sealed with the promised Holy Spirit (Eph 1:13), and as receiving the promise of the

Spirit (Gal 3:14). The gift of the Holy Spirit is not only the fulfillment of an OT promise (Is 32:15; Ez 36:27; Jl 2:28), and that of Christ himself (Lk 24:49; Jn 14:16,20; Acts 1:4), but it is also itself a promise of something yet future. Paul speaks of the Holy Spirit's presence within the believer as a "guarantee of our inheritance" (Eph 1:14; 2 Cor 1:22; 5:5). The Holy Spirit is the "firstfruit" of future glory (Rom 8:23). In Galatians 3 Paul links the gift of the Holy Spirit with faith in Christ as the means of the Spirit's reception, for Christ is the one who sends the Spirit (Acts 2:33) to those who by faith have become the true descendants of Abraham and heirs of the promise (Gal 3:29; Acts 2:38,39).

One final aspect of the promise theme in the NT concerns the assurance of Christ's second advent and the establishment of the new heavens and the new earth (cf. Jn 14:1–3; 2 Pt 3:4,9,13).　　　　　　　J. ROBERT VANNOY

See GOD, BEING AND ATTRIBUTES OF; GOD, NAMES OF; COVENANT; PROPHECY; PROPHET, PROPHETESS; HOPE.

Prophecy. Term, along with its English cognates ("prophet," "to prophesy," "prophetism," and "prophetic"), derived from a group of Greek words which, in pagan Greek, mean "speak forth," "proclaim," "announce." In biblical Greek, however, these terms always carry the connotation of speaking, proclaiming, or announcing something under the influence of divine inspiration.

Prophecy in the OT. *The Nature of Prophecy.* Prophecy is closely associated with divination; both are means for determining the future or the unknown or for ascertaining the will of God on particular occasions. The methods used for divination, however, sharply differ from those used in prophecy.

Divination can be defined as the art or science of determining the unknown or the future through the careful observation and interpretation of some aspect of nature or human life. Some of the more typical forms of divination, all of which are referred to in the OT, are necromancy (consultation with the dead), oneiromancy (the interpretation of dreams), kleromancy (the casting of lots), astrology (the interpretation of the movement of celestial bodies), and hepatoscopy (the interpretation of the liver of sacrificial animals).

Most forms of divination are expressly forbidden in the OT (Dt 18:9–14; 2 Kgs 23:24). The two kinds of divination not expressly forbidden and which are frequently found in the OT are kleromancy and oneiromancy. The presuppositions for the use of kleromancy are stated in Proverbs 16:33: "The lot is cast into the lap,

but the decision is wholly from the Lord." The casting of lots occurs frequently in the OT (Jos 7:14; 1 Sm 10:20–21; 16:8–10; cf. Acts 1:26), and the Urim and Thummim used by the priests were apparently a kind of divination by lot (1 Sm 14:41,42). Some divination is based on observing and interpreting natural phenomena (astrology, hepatoscopy), while other forms of divination are based on man-made phenomena (kleromancy). Divination, then, consists of technical skill combined with a knowledge of interpretative lore.

Prophecy, on the other hand, sometimes called oracular divination, or intuitive divination, is based on the direct inspiration of the prophet, either through trance or vision or by direct, unmediated revelation.

Modes of Prophetic Inspiration. One of the clearest and most significant statements on the nature of prophetic inspiration in the OT is found in Numbers 12:6–8:

> And he [Yahweh] said, 'Hear my words: If there is a prophet among you, I the Lord make myself known to him in a vision, I speak with him in a dream. Not so with my servant Moses; he is entrusted with all my house. With him I speak mouth to mouth, clearly, and not in dark speech; and he beholds the form of the Lord.'

Several important insights into the nature of prophetic inspiration are found in this passage: (1) The prophetic gift of Moses was unique in that he alone received revelations directly from God. (2) Ordinarily, prophetic revelation was received through the medium of a dream or a vision. (3) The meaning of prophetic revelation is not always completely clear; prophecy is sometimes ambiguous.

Moses claimed to be a prophet (Dt 18:15), a claim confirmed by God (Dt 18:18), and reiterated by the author of the closing section of Deuteronomy (34:10–12):

> And there has not arisen a prophet since in Israel like Moses, whom the Lord knew face to face, none like him for all the signs and wonders which the Lord sent him to do in the land of Egypt, to Pharaoh and to all his servants and to all his land, and for all the mighty power and all the great and terrible deeds which Moses wrought in the sight of all Israel.

Again the unique relationship between Moses and God is stressed, and an entirely new element is added: the signs and wonders which Moses performed are considered part of his prophetic role. The Israelite prophet, of which Moses was the outstanding example, was not only one who spoke the words of God by divine inspiration, but also one who could perform mighty deeds by divine power.

Further insight into the nature of prophetic revelation is found in Deut 18:18: "I [God] will raise up for them a prophet like you [Moses] from among their brethren; and I will put my words in his mouth, and he shall speak to them all that I command him." While this passage is of interest because Jesus was identified as "the prophet like Moses" who came in fulfillment of this prediction (Acts 3:22; 7:37), the more immediate historical reference is to the succession of prophets which guided Israel from Joshua to Malachi. The phrase "I will put my words in his mouth" refers to the process of divine inspiration and is reminiscent of the common OT prophetic formula "the word of the Lord came to [such and such a prophet]" (1 Kgs 19:9; 1 Sm 15:10; 2 Sm 24:11; Jon 1:1; Hg 1:1; 2:1,20; Zec 7:1,8; 8:1; etc.). A true prophet is one who speaks (or repeats) all that God has told him (cf. Ex 7:12; 4:16, where Aaron functions as Moses' "prophet" before Pharaoh).

The primary modes of prophetic inspiration, then, are direct encounter, dreams, and visions. The prophetic inspiration of Moses is unique and without parallel in the history of Israelite prophecy. This unique inspiration of Moses gives exceptional status to the Pentateuch, a status reflected in the central role assigned to it in Judaism.

Dreams were a commonly recognized mode of inspiration throughout the ancient world, though they were more highly regarded in Greece than in ancient Israel. Revelatory dreams in the Bible fall into two major categories: (1) dreams whose meaning is self-evident, and (2) symbolic dreams which usually require the expertise of an interpreter of dreams. Both types normally involve both visual and auditory elements. In those dreams whose meaning is self-evident, normally a supernatural being (God or an angel) appears to the dreamer and speaks to him or her in a straightforward manner. Typical examples of such dream revelations are found in Genesis 20:3,6,7; 31:11–13; 31:24; 1 Kings 3:5–15; Matthew 1:20–23; 2:13,19–20; Acts 27:23,24. Genesis 20:3 is an excellent example: "But God came to Abimelech in a dream by night, and said to him, 'Behold, you are a dead man, because of the woman whom you have taken; for she is a man's wife.'"

More frequently, revelatory dreams have symbolic elements which require interpretation. The two great dream interpreters of the OT are Joseph and Daniel; the latter is clearly a prophet. The two symbolic dreams which Joseph himself dreamed (Gn 37:5–11) had sufficiently self-evident meaning that his brothers and father were able to interpret them immediately. More complex were the dreams of the butler and baker (Gn 40:1–19) and of Pharaoh (Gn 41:1–36) which Joseph was able to interpret with the help of God. Similarly, Daniel was enabled to interpret the dreams of Nebuchadnezzar (Dn 2:25–45; 4:4–27). The skill in interpreting such dreams was attributed by both Joseph and Daniel, not to their own cunning, but to God (Gn 40:8; 41:16,25; Dn 2:27–30; cf. 4:9).

While dreams are used almost interchangeably with visions in referring to modes of prophetic inspiration (Jl 2:28), in actual fact dreams do not occupy a significant role in the prophetic revelations of any of the OT prophets with the exception of Daniel. Jeremiah attacked false prophets who claimed to have received prophetic revelations in that way (Jer 23:27,28,32; 29:8,9). Jeremiah, like Deuteronomy, places a higher value on more direct forms of prophetic inspiration, as we see in Jeremiah 23:28: "Let the prophet who has a dream tell the dream, but let him who has my word speak my word faithfully. What has straw in common with wheat? says the Lord." Like Deuteronomy 18:18, Jeremiah favors that kind of prophetic inspiration whereby God puts his Word in the mouth of his prophet.

One of the most characteristic modes of prophetic inspiration was the vision (Nm 12:6; 24:4,16; Hos 12:10). The revelatory visions experienced by the classical (canonical) prophets were not limited to visual phenomena alone, but also included the auditory dimension as well. In Isaiah 1:1, the author describes his entire prophetic book as a "vision": "The vision of Isaiah the son of Amoz, which he saw concerning Judah and Jerusalem in the days of Uzziah, Jotham, Ahaz, and Hezekiah, kings of Judah." Yet in the very next verse, Isaiah tells the heavens and earth to listen, "for the Lord has spoken." Again, in Amos 1:1, "The *words* of Amos, who was among the shepherds of Tekoa, which he *saw* concerning Israel."

The intimate connection between Israelite prophecy and revelatory visions is indicated by the older term "seer," once used for the functionary later called a "prophet" (1 Sm 9:9). The term "seer" refers to one who "sees" that which is hidden to others. The terms seer and prophet were virtual synonyms (Am 7:12). Samuel was called a seer (1 Sm 9:11,18,19; 1 Chr 9:22; 26:28; 29:29), as was Gad (2 Sm 24:11, where he is called "the prophet, David's seer"; 1 Chr 21:9) and Amos (Am 7:12).

An important aspect of the prophetic visionary experience is the prophet's participation in the heavenly council. In Jeremiah's condemnation of false prophets he says, "But if they had stood in my council, then they would have proclaimed my words to my people" (Jer 23:22), and again, "For who among them has stood in the council of the Lord, to perceive and to hear his word?" (Jer 23:18). These statements imply that the true prophet has, through visionary experience, been present at the council of God where he could hear God's Word. The heavenly council referred to in such passages as Genesis 1:26; and Job 1:6–12; 2:1–6, is depicted as a gathering of angelic and other supernatural beings before the throne of God, at which the events which will occur on earth are discussed.

This kind of visionary prophetic experience is described by Micaiah ben Imlah, a 9th-century prophet active during the reign of Ahab, king of Israel, in 1 Kings 22:19–23:

> And Micaiah said, "Therefore hear the word of the Lord: I saw the Lord sitting on his throne, and all the host of heaven standing beside him on his right hand and on his left; and the Lord said, 'Who will entice Ahab, that he may go up and fall at Ramoth-gilead?' And one said one thing, and another said another. Then a spirit came forward and stood before the Lord, saying, 'I will entice him.' And the Lord said to him 'By what means?' And he said, 'I will go forth, and will be a lying spirit in the mouth of all his prophets.' And he said, 'You are to entice him, and you shall succeed; go forth and do so.'"

In this rare explanation of prophetic visionary experience, it appears that the prophet is present and overhears the deliberations at the heavenly council (cf. Is 6:1–5; 2 Cor 12:2–4; Rv 4:1); this is the source of his authentic word from God. More often than not, however, no reference is made to the nature of the prophetic revelation, apart from such vague phrases as "the word of the Lord came to. . . ." In such instances, a visionary experience is presupposed.

Types of OT Prophets. (1) Ecstatic Prophets. All prophecy, whether biblical or not, presupposes that the prophet either possessed or is possessed by a personal supernatural power. The external behavioral manifestations of this possession can exhibit great variety.

The prophetic phenomenon generally designated "ecstatic" prophecy appears to have existed in Canaan prior to the arrival of the Hebrew tribes in the 13th century BC. The first reference to ecstatic prophecy in Israel occurs in 1 Samuel 10:5–13 (11th century BC), and it still persists at least down to the 6th century BC (Jer 29:26). Israelite ecstatic prophecy seems to have been more prevalent in the premonarchic and early monarchic period; after the 8th century BC, there is little evidence to suggest that it continued to be a widespread phenomenon.

The ecstatic prophet achieves a trance-like state by self-induced means. The most common devices used to achieve a state of ecstasy were musical instruments, such as the harp, tambourine, flute, and lyre (1 Sm 10:5). Among the prophets of Baal, self-flagellation was another means of inducing ecstasy (1 Kgs 18:28,29).

This kind of prophetic ecstasy was usually practiced by groups of prophets (1 Sm 10:5), and such ecstasy was contagious. When Saul met a band of such prophets, the Spirit of God came upon him and he too began to prophesy (1 Sm 10:10–13), a phenomenon which occurred repeatedly to various messengers sent by Saul on a later occasion (1 Sm 19:20–22). Then Saul also prophesied and his ecstatic behavior is described in 1 Samuel 19:24: "And he too stripped off his clothes, and he too prophesied before Samuel, and lay naked all that day and all that night." When Elisha was asked to prophesy for King Jehoram of Israel, he first requested a minstrel. "And when the minstrel played, the power of the Lord came upon him" (2 Kgs 3:15).

Ecstatic prophets were usually members of prophetic associations, called "sons of the prophets" (2 Kgs 2:3,5,7,15; 1 Kgs 20:35; Am 7:14). These prophetic associations were presided over by leaders such as Samuel (1 Sm 19:20,24) and Elisha (2 Kgs 4:38; 6:22), who may have borne the title "father" (2 Kgs 2:12; 6:21; 13:14).

Ecstatic prophets were closely connected with cultic worship (1 Sm 9:19; 10:5). Frequently groups of such prophets were in the employ of rulers where they functioned as court prophets. These court prophets seem to have made regular use of magical divination; rather than use their prophetic gifts to foresee the future, they tried to influence its outcome (Nm 22:5,6; 1 Kgs 18:19; 22:10–12; 2 Kgs 3:15). Zedekiah ben Chenaanah used mimetic magic in an attempt to secure victory for Ahab (1 Kgs 22:11): "And Zedekiah the son of Chenaanah made for himself horns of iron, and said, 'Thus says the Lord, 'With these you shall push the Syrians until they are destroyed.'"

Ecstatic prophets, then, could be cult prophets, court prophets, or free practitioners of the prophetic arts. The two distinctive marks of the ecstatic prophet were (1) the use and control of prophetic ecstasy, or trance, and (2) the ability to deliver oracles, either upon request, or less commonly, upon one's own initiative. They were frequently consulted by persons who wished to "inquire of the Lord" about lost property (1 Sm 9:3–10), the outcome of military engagements (1 Kgs 22:6), or the result of illness (2 Kgs 1:2), etc.

There were rather large groups of ecstatic prophets; 450 prophets of Baal and 400 prophets of Asherah were maintained by Jezebel (1 Kgs 18:19), a group of 50 followed Elisha (2 Kgs 2:7), and Obadiah had concealed 100 prophets of the Lord from Jezebel (1 Kgs 18:3,4).

(2) Cult Prophets. Throughout Israelite history, numbers of prophets were associated with particular sanctuaries and holy places, especially the temple in Jerusalem. A cult prophet was one who functioned as part of the religious personnel at a sanctuary and whose livelihood was earned in that way.

Free prophets, though they frequently chose to associate with the religious life of certain holy places and may even have used liturgical forms as vehicles for their prophetic proclamations, were not, according to strict definition, cult prophets. Isaiah's commissioning vision occurred in the temple in Jerusalem (Is 6:1–13). Amos, though a native of Judah, went to the Israelite sanctuary at Bethel to prophesy (Am 7:10–13). Jeremiah was closely associated with the temple in Jerusalem and its priestly and prophetic staff (Jer 28:1,5). In spite of these associations, neither Isaiah, Amos, nor Jeremiah can be regarded as cult prophets.

The association of prophecy with the religious cult was a heritage of ecstatic prophecy in the premonarchical period. Samuel was both priest and prophet (1 Sm 2:18–20; 3:1,19–21) in the 11th century, just as Ezekiel was in the 6th century (Ez 1:3).

In 1 Chronicles 25:1–8 we find that a large staff of prophets was associated with the temple, and that they would prophesy "with lyres, with harps, and with cymbals" (1 Chr 25:1). The use of musical instruments is not to produce an ecstatic state, as in 1 Samuel 10:5, but rather for the purpose of providing musical accompaniment for the chanting or singing of prophecy. The greater portion of OT prophecy which has survived is in poetic form. Recent studies have determined that all or portions of many psalms may have originated with cult prophets (Pss 2,6,12,20,21,31,45, 50,60,72,75,81,82,85,87,89,91,95,108,110).

Several of the canonical prophets appear to have been cult prophets; these include Nahum, Joel, and Malachi. The great interest in the rebuilding of the temple by the prophets Haggai and Zechariah has led many to regard them also as cult prophets.

Many of the false prophets who were opposed by Jeremiah and Ezekiel appear to have been cult functionaries associated with the temple in Jerusalem. Though certainly all cult prophets were not false prophets, the temptation must have been great to prophesy in accordance with the wishes of both the temple authorities and the king. Many cult prophets succumbed to this temptation. The message of the cult prophets appears to have consistently promised salvation (Jer 23:16,17; Ez 13:10–12), whereas the free prophets, such as Isaiah, Jeremiah, and Amos, were primarily known for their rebukes and proclamations of judgment. The distinction between true and false prophets was a difficult problem in ancient Israel. Several criteria were developed in order to evaluate prophets and prophecy: (1) prophecy must be in continuity with the customs and traditions of Israel as enshrined in the Torah (Dt 13:1–5; 18:20; Is 8:20; cf. Rom 12:6); (2) the prophet must speak only that which the Lord commands (Dt 18:20); and (3) true prophecy will be historically verified (Dt 18:21–22; Jer 28:8,9).

(3) Free Prophets. The majority of classical (canonical) OT prophets, with the exceptions mentioned above under the section on "cult prophets," were free prophets. Free prophets were those who were not cult functionaries and whose livelihood was not earned by the exercise of their prophetic gifts; in addition, free prophets were conscious of having been commissioned by God to perform the prophetic task. There is no evidence to suggest that cult prophets experienced a prophetic commission.

The first of the free prophets who was also a writing prophet was Amos of Tekoa, whose ministry was exercised during the decade following 760 BC in Israel. Yet free prophecy had historical roots in the premonarchic period.

Samuel, Elijah, and Elisha are examples of an earlier type of prophet which, though occasionally associated with various cultic activities, nevertheless exhibits the basic characteristics of free prophecy: (1) uninhibited movement, (2) deliverance of unsolicited prophetic oracles, and (3) oracles characterized by invective and pronouncements of judgment.

The free prophets were in no sense innovators or revolutionaries, but were rather primarily concerned to call Israel back to the customs and traditions in the Torah that they had violated or neglected. These prophets became particularly active when gross violations of the covenant became evident. In consequence, their proclamations were characterized more by invective, censure, predictions of doom, and the call to return to former ways than by the announcement of salvation and bliss. The free prophets were not exclusively prophets of doom, for not infrequently their messages to Israel were tempered with promises of ultimate salvation and restoration.

While cult prophets could rely on their office and position within the religious establishment to provide the necessary authority and legitimation for their prophetic pronouncements, the free prophets had no such secure position. The free prophets, consequently, depended not on the authority derived from the religious establishment, but rather on a direct commission from God. Divine commissions were also associated with some of the predecessors of the free prophets, such as Moses (Ex 3:1–4:17), Samuel (1 Sm 3:2–14), and Elisha (2 Kgs 2:9–14).

There are two basic types of prophetic commission in the OT. One type is that of a narrative call by God to a particular individual whose objections to the call are gradually overcome in a dialogue between himself and God. The classical example of this type of prophetic commission is found in Jeremiah 1:4–10:

> Now the word of the Lord came to me saying, 'Before I formed you in the womb I knew you, and before you were born I consecrated you; I appointed you a prophet to the nations.' Then I said, 'Ah, Lord God! Behold, I do not know how to speak, for I am only a youth.' But the Lord said to me . . . [etc.]

Similar prophetic commissions including such dialogues are associated with the calls of Moses (Ex 3:1–4:17) and Gideon (Jgs 6:11–17).

The second major form of prophetic commission is the "Throne Vision," of which the outstanding example is Isaiah 6:1–13:

> In the year that King Uzziah died I saw the Lord sitting upon a throne, high and lifted up; and his train filled the temple. . . . And I heard the voice of the Lord saying, 'Whom shall I send, and who will go for us?' Then I said, 'Here am I! Send me.' And he said, 'Go, and say to this people. . . .

Here we have an account of the visionary presence of a prophet in the heavenly council; in this case, however, the prophet participates in the deliberations and thereby receives a prophetic commission. Though few free prophets have left accounts of their divine commissions, most of them appear to have been conscious of having been "sent" by God (Is 48:16; Hos 8:1; Am 7:14,15). According to Jeremiah, false prophets did not receive such divine commissions (Jer 23:21,32; 28:15).

All OT prophets are ecstatic prophets in the sense that they are possessed by the Spirit of God and thereby enabled to speak the words of God. Yet there are vastly different behaviors associated with various types of Israelite prophecy. Two kinds of prophetic ecstasy have been suggested in order to differentiate the behavior of ecstatic prophets from that of the free prophets: absorption ecstasy and concentration ecstasy. In absorption ecstasy, the prophet loses control of himself, while in concentration ecstasy the prophet retains full use of his rational powers, yet experiences prophetic inspiration.

Anathoth—a levitical city 2.5 miles northeast of Jerusalem—was the birthplace of Jeremiah, the "weeping prophet."

The Message of the Prophets. (1) The Form of the Message. The most common introductory formula for prophetic oracles in the OT is the phrase "Thus says the Lord," which occurs hundreds of times in prophetic contexts. This formula clearly implies that the pronouncement so introduced is not the word of the prophet who utters the oracle, but of the God of Israel who delivered his Word to his prophet. The use of this formula also reiterates the prophet's sense of divine commission. In oracles which are introduced in this manner, God speaks in the first person. In fact, virtually all Israelite prophetic utterance is formulated as the direct speech of the God of Israel.

The introductory formula "thus says the Lord" has been appropriately designated as a messenger formula. An example of the secular use of the messenger formula is found in Genesis 32:3,4:

> And Jacob sent messengers before him to Esau his brother in the land of Seir, the country of Edom, instructing them, 'Thus you shall say to my lord Esau: Thus says your servant Jacob. . . .

Other examples are found in Numbers 22:15, 16; Judges 11:14,15; 1 Kings 2:30; 20:2,3. However, the use of such a formula in prophetic speech does not guarantee the divine origin of the oracle (Jer 23:31). Other formulas characteristic of prophetic speech include "Hear the word of the Lord," another introductory formula (Is 1:10; 28:14; Jer 2:4; 10:1; 19:3; 22:2; Ez 6:3; 20:47; Hos 4:1; Am 7:16), and "the Lord has spoken," or "I the Lord have spoken," a concluding formula (Is 21:17; 22:25; 24:3; 25:8; 40:5; the phrase is particularly favored by Ezekiel: 5:13,15,17; 17:21, etc.).

The classical prophets used many literary forms in which to express their oracles. Two of the more widely used forms of prophetic speech are the judgment speech and the oracle of salvation. The judgment speech is composed of at least two central elements, the speech of rebuke or invective, and the pronouncement of judgment. Second Kings 1:3,4 will serve as an example of the judgment speech:

(1) Introductory Word:
But the angel of the Lord said to Elijah the Tishbite, 'Arise, go up to meet the messengers of the King of Samaria, and say to them.

(2) Speech of Rebuke:
'Is it because there is no God in Israel that you are going to inquire of Baalzebub the god of Ekron?'

(3) Pronouncement of Judgment:
Now therefore thus says the Lord, 'You shall not come down from the bed to which you have gone, but you shall surely die.'

(4) Concluding Comments:
So Elijah went.

The second common prophetic speech form is the oracle of salvation, of which Isaiah 41:8-13 will serve as an example:

(1) Recitation of God's Past Dealings with Israel:
But you, Israel, my servant, Jacob, whom I have chosen, the offspring of Abraham, my friend; you whom I took from the ends of the earth, and called from its farthest corners, saying to you, 'You are my servant, I have chosen you and not cast you off. . .';

(2) Promise of Salvation:
Fear not, for I am with you, be not dismayed, for I am your God; I will strengthen you, I will help you, I will uphold you with my victorious right hand.

(3) Description of the Results of God's Saving Act:
Behold, all who are incensed against you shall be put to shame and confounded . . .

(4) Basis for God's Action:
For I, the Lord your God, hold your right hand; it is I who say to you, 'Fear not, I will help you.'

Other fixed forms of prophetic speech include the prophecy of salvation (Is 43:14-21), the proclamation of salvation (Is 41:17-20; 42:14-17; 43:16-21; 49:7-12), and the woe oracle (Is 5:8-10; 10:1-4; Am 5:18-24; 6:1-7; Mi 2:1-5).

(2) The Content of the Message. The common adage that OT prophets were not "foretellers" but "forth-tellers," is not strictly correct. All of the classical (canonical) prophets predict the future. Such prediction, however, is based not on human curiosity of what the future will hold, but is rather rooted in the future consequences of past or present violations of the covenant, or on a future act of deliverance which will provide hope for a discouraged people. Most of the prophetic speeches that have been preserved in the OT were originally delivered as public proclamations or sermons. Most of these prophetic proclamations were evoked by the iniquity and apostasy of Israel. Hosea and Jeremiah condemned Israel because she had broken the covenant (Jer 11:2,3; Hos 8:1).

The preexilic prophets freely criticized the religious cult as it was practiced in their day (Is 1:11-17; Jer 6:20; 11:14,15; 14:12; cf. 7:21-26; Hos 6:6; 8:13; Am 2:6-8; 3:4; 5:21-27; Mi 6:6-8). Amos 5:21-24 is a typically anticultic diatribe:

I hate, I despise your feasts, and I take no delight in your solemn assemblies. Even though you offer me your burnt offerings and cereal offerings, I will not accept them, and the peace offerings of your fatted beasts I will not look upon . . . But let justice roll down like waters, and righteousness like an ever-flowing stream.

In considering the anticultic stance of many of the prophets, several points should be borne in mind: (1) In the preexilic period particularly, the religious cult was periodically invaded by pagan customs and practices. (2) The self-righteousness engendered by the formal observance of cultic ritual combined with an avoidance of the moral demands of the Torah was the primary focus of prophetic criticism. (3) The term mishpat ("commandment") is frequently used by the prophets for that which Israel has violated; yet the mishpatim ("commandments") in the Torah include both ritual obligations as well as moral demands; the OT makes no distinction between ritual and moral law.

The prophets are frequently associated with social justice and social reform, and these elements were unquestionably an important dimension of their message. Amos denounced the rich who afflicted the poor (2:6-8; 4:1; 5:11; 8:4-6). He railed against sexual immorality (2:6-8) and against those who take bribes (5:12). Hosea provides a list of prevalent vices including lying, killing, stealing, adultery, and idolatry (4:2). Idolatry is a particular target for his denunciations (8:5; 11:2). The background for such heated denunciations of Israel's behavior is God's unquenchable love for Israel (Is 43:4; Jer 31:3; Hos 3:1; 11:1,4; 14:4; Mal 1:2), which is inseparable from his election of Israel (Is 43:1; Jer 33:24; Ez 20:5; Hos 3:1–5). The close association of God's love for and election of Israel is seen in Hosea 11:1, a passage whose messianic dimensions were seen by Matthew (2:15):

"When Israel was a child I loved him, and out of Egypt have I called my son." Since God's love and election were historically revealed to Israel through the event of the exodus, the phrase "out of Egypt," is fraught with salvific overtones. The extent of Israel's rebellion occasionally moved the prophets to speak of a new exodus, with the implication that the extent of the iniquity of God's people necessitated a new and striking renewal of the original exodus event (Is 43:1–7,14–21).

The classical prophets were concerned not only with the transgressions of Israel and the historical judgment that would inevitably follow, but also with the achievement of a final future time of bliss. If eschatology is defined as an account of those final events which will occur before, during, and after the cessation of the old order (or, old age), and the institution by God of the new order, then the message of many of the canonical prophets is thoroughly eschatological.

One such eschatological concept is that of the Day of the Lord. The concept of the Day of the Lord first appears in Amos, where the emphasis lies on the disaster which will befall Israel on that day. Amos' emphasis on disaster notwithstanding, the Day of the Lord is a conception which had both salvific as well as judgmental overtones for Israel. While the disaster which will occur in the Day of the Lord can be viewed in terms of a literal historical fulfillment in the tragic events of 722 BC (the fall of Samaria) and 586 BC (the fall of Judah), there are nevertheless features of these predictions which transcend historical fulfillment and reach toward eschatological fulfillment.

Since the dominant message of the prophets centers on the theme of judgment, the Day of the Lord is primarily conceptualized as a day of divine judgment (Is 2:12–22; Ob 15; Zep 1:7–18; 2:1–3; 3:8). In spite of these proclamations of judgment, ultimately the prophets predicted the return of Israel from exile (Jer 29:10–14; 30:3 Ob 19–21; Mi 7:8–20). Though Israel will suffer for her general rebellion against the covenant, yet a remnant will be preserved (Is 10:20–22; 11:10–16; 28:5; 37:4; Am 9:8; Zep 2:3; 3:12,13).

Since the Israelite conception of "salva-

tion" was largely temporal in its dimensions, it included such blessings as length of life, fruitfulness of the womb and field, peace and victory over one's enemies, the abundance of water, and so on. In harmony with this conception of salvation, the future age is conceived in precisely those terms, as in Amos 9:13,15:

Behold, the days are coming, says the Lord, when the plowman shall overtake the reaper and the treader of grapes him who sows the seed; the mountains shall drip sweet wine, and the hills shall flow with it. . . . I will plant them upon their land, and they shall never again be plucked up out of the land which I have given them, says the Lord your God.

The prophets envisaged the ideal future using the imagery from those golden ages of the past which were appropriate precursors of the eschaton. When Isaiah envisioned the virtual domestication and peaceful association of wolf and lamb, cow and bear (Is 11:6–9; 65:25), he derived this imagery from the Eden traditions which described the perfect relationship between man, beast, and the world prior to the fall. Similarly, for Israel of the latter days to be leaderless would be an anomaly, yet what would that future leader be like? David himself, or someone very much like him, would return and inaugurate a golden era reminiscent of the great Davidic and Solomonic period. According to Ezekiel 34:23,24:

And I will set up over them one shepherd, my servant David, and he shall feed them and be their shepherd. And I, the Lord, will be their God, and my servant David shall be prince among them; I, the Lord, have spoken.

The covenant of God with David was not a conditional covenant, but rather one which was absolutely inviolable (2 Sm 7:4–17; Ps 89; Jer 33:19–22) and it was with this knowledge that the prophets could look forward confidently to a restoration of the Davidic throne (Jer 17:24–26; 23:5,6; 33:14,15). Though there are very few explicitly messianic passages in the canonical prophets, this longing for an ideal king modeled after David forms the basis for all later messianic expectation.

The Decline of Prophecy. Postexilic prophecy flourished for nearly a century-and-a-half before many changes resulted in its apparent extinction. One such change was the marked decline in the prestige of prophecy, exemplified by these words of Zechariah (13:2–6):

And on that day, says the Lord of hosts, . . . I will remove from the land the prophets and the unclean spirit. And if any one again appears as a prophet, his father and mother who bore him will say to him, 'You shall not live, for you speak lies in the name of the Lord.' . . . On that day every prophet will be ashamed of his vision when he prophesies.

This decline in the prestige of prophecy was at least partially occasioned by the multiplication of false prophets, and the basic inability of Jews to distinguish the true from the false.

Another factor which resulted in the cessation of prophecy was the consciousness on the part of official circles in Judaism that the Spirit of prophecy had been taken from Israel (1 Mc 4:46; 9:27; 2 Bar 85:3). The later rabbis expressed the opinion that the Spirit of prophecy ceased with the activity of the prophets Haggai, Zechariah (both late 6th century BC), and Malachi (mid-5th century BC?). At least part of the reason for this belief in the cessation of the authentic prophetic voice in Israel was in order to elevate the sanctity of the prophetic canon of Scripture, which must have taken fixed form some time after the composition of Malachi.

A third reason for the decline of prophecy was the gradual transformation of prophecy into the scribal phenomenon of apocalyptic. Apocalypticism is known only through the medium of the apocalypse, a particular genre of early Jewish literature. Apocalypticism is characterized primarily by a very pessimistic outlook. While the prophets looked forward to the action of God in history to restore Israel and bring about ideal, Edenic conditions, apocalypticism expected that only after a cataclysmic intervention of God whereby history would be brought to an end and the world recreated for the habitation of the righteous. Another characteristic feature of apocalypticism is its view of revelation as a mystery in need of interpretation. One of the central features of prophetic revelation in the OT is its very directness and immediate comprehensibility. In apocalyptic literature, even within the OT itself, where it has its beginnings, the indirectness and obscurity of divine revelation is emphasized. In such 6th-century prophets as Daniel and Zechariah, the dreams and visions that they experience are not comprehensible apart from the intervention of an interpreting angel (Dn 7–12; Zec 1:7–21; 4:1–6:8). Revelation had become a mystery which required the expertise and wisdom of the scribe.

Prophecy in Intertestamental Judaism.
The apocalyptic tendencies which are evident in a number of postexilic prophetic books (Daniel, Joel, and Zechariah) came to full flower in the Greco-Roman period (332 BC–AD 135) in Palestine. With the completion of the prophetic canon of the Jewish Scriptures by at least the 3rd century BC, more recent prophetic writings would hardly be widely accepted, particularly in view of the decline in prestige of prophecy. Nevertheless, scores of apocalypses were written. These compositions were not sent out under the names of their actual authors, but were falsely attributed to such ancient Israelite worthies as Adam, Enoch, Moses, Baruch, and Ezra. Apocalyptic literature, with the exception of the biblical apocalypses of Daniel and Revelation, were all written under false names in order to enhance the value of the composition.

While official circles within Judaism may have regarded the Spirit of prophecy as absent from Israel, the views of the apocalyptists were quite different. The degree of inspiration which they claimed indicates that they placed their compositions on a par with the Mosaic revelation (1 Enoch 91:1; 93:1; Life AE 29:2; 2 Enoch 22:4–12; Jub 1; 2 Bar 59). For these authors, "prophetic" inspiration was a living reality. In the apocalypse of 2 Esdras (c. AD 80), the author (pretending to be the biblical Ezra) claims that the Jewish Scriptures have been entirely destroyed by fire. God then gives Ezra a fiery potion to drink, and for 40 days thereafter, with the assistance of 5 secretaries, he is inspired to rewrite the 24 lost canonical books and 70 additional ones. The 24 books, God tells him, are for both the worthy and the unworthy to read, while the additional 70 books (undoubtedly current apocalyptic literature) must be reserved for the wise alone (2 Esd 14:45–47). The Ezra of this apocalypse is regarded as the last of all the prophets (2 Esd 12:42), and the inspiration he claims is simply astonishing.

Unlike the biblical prophets, who addressed all Israel, apocalyptists direct their revelations only to a select few (2 Esd 12:37,38):

> Therefore write all these things that you have seen in a book, and put it in a hidden place; and you shall teach them to the wise among your people, whose hearts you know are able to comprehend and keep these secrets.

The canonization of the biblical prophets by the 1st century BC resulted in a further development in the notion of prophecy as the interpretation of mysteries. The Jewish Scriptures themselves came to be regarded as repositories of divinely concealed mysteries which required the expertise of an inspired interpreter. This view is clearly reflected in the literature produced by the Qumran community, an apocalyptic sect within Judaism which flourished from the 1st century BC to about AD 66. In the Habakkuk Commentary 7:1–4, produced by this sect, we read:

> And God told Habakkuk to write down the things which will come to pass in the last generation, but the consummation of time He made not known to him. And as for that which He said, 'That he may read it easily that reads it' [Hab 2:2 b], the explanation of

this concerns the Teacher of Righteousness to whom God made known all the Mysteries of the words of His servants the prophets.

A final development in the notion of prophecy in the intertestamental period is that prophecy came to be regarded as an eschatological phenomenon, that is, as a feature of the last days. The Teacher of Righteousness of the Qumran community and his followers used charismatic interpretation to learn what Habakkuk and other prophets had to say about the days in which the interpreters themselves lived, which they regarded as the last days. In the OT prophets, a number of passages reveal that the outpouring of the Spirit of God was an event that was expected to occur at the end of time (Is 44:3; Ez 36:26,27; 37:14; 39:29; Jl 2:28). The Qumran community believed that the Spirit had been poured out upon them as a sign indicating that the end was about to occur.

The eschatological nature of prophecy in the intertestamental period is also indicated by a number of messiahs and messianic movements which occurred during the 1st century BC and the 1st century AD. Most of these messiahs also made prophetic claims (Acts 5:36,37; 21:38). In addition, such 1st-century Jewish figures as Josephus and Philo appear to have regarded themselves as prophets.

Prophecy in the NT. In contrast to the few self-proclaimed prophets of which we have knowledge during the intertestamental period, early Christianity began with a flurry of prophetic activity which lasted well into the 2nd century AD. Jesus, his disciples and followers, and the early Christians were convinced that the times in which they lived were times in which OT prophecy was being fulfilled (Mk 1:14,15; Acts 2:16–21; Rom 16:25–27; 1 Cor 10:11). Yet this era was not only one of fulfillment, but also of the renewal of the prophetic gift.

John the Baptist. John the Baptist is remembered in the NT primarily as the forerunner of Jesus whose coming was predicted by Malachi (4:5–6; Mt 11:14). Yet in his own right, John proclaimed the imminent judgment of God with a flair of denunciation and rebuke reminiscent of the invective of the OT prophets. John's costume, consisting of a hairy cloak and a leather girdle (Mk 1:6), was reminiscent of the typical garb of OT prophets (1 Kgs 19:19; 2 Kgs 1:8; 2:13,14; Zec 13:4). John was widely regarded as a prophet (Mt 14:5; 17:10–13; Mk 9:11–13; 11:32; Lk 1:76; 7:26). Luke reports, in a style reminiscent of OT prophetic narratives, that "the word of God came to John" (Lk 3:2; cf. Jn 1:1; 3:1; Mi 1:1; Zep 1:1; Hg 1:1; 2:1; Zec 1:1). Two short prophetic speeches have been preserved in Matthew 3:7–10 (Lk 3:7–9) and Mark 1:7–8 (Mt 3:11,12; Lk 3:15–18). In the first speech, John denounces those of his generation who have transgressed the covenant Law and exhorts them to change their manner of life. In the second speech, John predicts the coming of the Mighty One, Jesus (Mt 3:11; Mk 1:7; Lk 3:16; Jn 1:15,27,30; Acts 13:25). John's style, however, is not precisely that of the OT prophets. His pronouncements are made on his own authority; never does he resort to formulas such as "thus says the Lord," or present his prophetic utterances as if they were speeches made by God. Yet, in spite of these differences, John is appropriately regarded as the last representative of the OT prophetic tradition (Mt 11:13; Lk 16:16).

Jesus of Nazareth. Jesus was popularly regarded as a prophet (Mt 16:14; 21:10,11; Mk 6:14,15; 8:28; Lk 7:16,39; 9:8,19; Jn 6:14; 7:40,52). This assessment was based as much on the mighty deeds which Jesus performed as on his prophetic speeches and predictions. Though Jesus nowhere claimed prophetic status directly, that claim is implicit in Mark 6:4 (Mt 13:57; Lk 4:24): "A prophet is not without honor except in his own country," and Luke 13:33: "Nevertheless I must go on my way today and tomorrow and the day following; for it cannot be that a prophet should perish away from Jerusalem." In Acts, Jesus is regarded as "the prophet like Moses" predicted in Deuteronomy 18:18 (Acts 3:22; 7:37). Matthew presents Jesus as the New Moses, but does not particularly emphasize his prophetic role. John, however, like Luke, emphasizes Jesus' role as the eschatological Mosaic prophet (Jn 7:40; 4:19; 6:14,15).

While the Gospels and Acts reflect the notion that Jesus was a prophet, they also emphasize the fact that he was much more than a prophet. Nevertheless, the notion of prophetism was sufficiently important in early Judaism that Jesus' recognition as a prophet is very significant. There are no less than 13 reasons for regarding Jesus as a prophet in the OT tradition: (1) The sovereign authority of Jesus' teaching (Mk 1:27), a feature underlined by his use of the introductory formula "(Amen) I say to you," is reminiscent of that claimed by OT prophets with their use of such formulas as "thus says the Lord." (2) The poetic character of many of Jesus' sayings is unlike contemporary rabbinic teaching, but similar to the poetic rhetoric of the OT prophets. (3) Jesus experienced visions (Lk 10:18) like the ancient prophets. (4) Jesus, like the prophets, made many predictions (Mt 23:38; Mk 13:2; 14:58; Lk 13:35; etc.). (5) Like the OT prophets, Jesus performed symbolic acts (such as the cleansing of the temple, the entry into Jerusalem, and the Last Supper). (6) Jesus, like the prophets, when necessary rejected the formal observance of religious ritual and emphasized the moral and spiritual dimensions of obedience to God. (7) Jesus announced the imminent arrival of the kingdom of God, an eschatological proclamation similar to those made by the prophets. (8) Like the OT prophets, Jesus functioned as a preacher of repentance. (9) Jesus, like many of the prophets, was conscious of a special calling of God (Mt 15:24; Mk 8:31; 9:37; 14:36; Lk 4:18–26). (10) Jesus, like the prophets, received divine revelation through intimate communion with God (Mt 11:27; Lk 10:22). (11) Like the prophets, Jesus represented God; to obey him was to obey God, to reject him was to reject God (Mk 9:37; cf. 2 Sm 7:7; Ez 33:30–33). (12) Like the prophets, Jesus was conscious of a mission to all Israel (Mt 15:24; 19:28; Lk 22:30). (13) Like many of the prophets, Jesus not only announced the Word of God, he also participated in its fulfillment.

Like John the Baptist, but unlike the OT prophets, Jesus never used the prophetic messenger formula "thus says the Lord." However, Jesus' distinctive use of the solemn formula "(Amen) I say unto you," to introduce many of his sayings does underline the authority of the speaker. Jesus did, however, use a number of forms of speech reminiscent of prophetism. One distinctive expression is "who among you," or "which man among you" (Mt 7:9,10/Lk 11:11,12; Mt 12:11/Lk 14:5; Lk 17:7–10; 11:5–8; 15:4–7,8–10; 14:28–30,31–32; Mt 6:27/Lk 12:25). While there are no rabbinic parallels to this expression used by Jesus, it was used by several OT prophets (Is 42:23; 50:10; Hg 2:3).

Again, Jesus frequently used a form of speech which has been labeled the "eschatological correlative." An example is Luke 11:30: "For *as* Jonah became a sign to the men of Nineveh, *so* will the Son of man be to this generation." The first line relates to an event of the past or present, while the second, in the future tense, compares it to an eschatological event, hence the designation "eschatological correlative." This pattern occurs with such frequency in OT prophecy that it must be considered the source of Jesus' own use of this form of speech (Is 10:11; 24:13; 41:25; 66:13; Jer 31:28; 32:42; 42:18; Ez 20:36; 22:20; 34:12; 3:12; Ob 15).

Another characteristic form of speech used by Jesus, and which can be considered prophetic, is the two-part structure of many of his sayings. The first line concerns the present situation, while the second line relates to the future eschatological activity of God. A typical example of this form of speech, which is closely related to the eschatological correla-

tive, is found in Matthew 5:7: "Blessed are the merciful/ for they shall obtain mercy." A more complex example is found in Mark 8:38: "For whoever is ashamed of me and of my words in this adulterous and sinful generation,/ of him will the Son of man also be ashamed, when he comes in the glory of his father with the holy angels."

Among the many prophetic predictions of Jesus are the following: (1) Predictions of the imminent arrival of the kingdom of God (Mk 1:15/Mt 10:7,8; Mt 10:23; 23:39; Mk 9:1; 13:28–29). (2) Predictions of the destruction of Jerusalem and the temple (Mk 14:58/Mt 26:61; Mk 15:29/Mt 27:40; Jn 2:19–21; Mk 13:2/Mt 24:2/Lk 21:6; Lk 13:34,35/Mt 23:37–39). One of the more striking of these predictions is that found in Luke 19:41–44:

> And when he [Jesus] drew near and saw the city he wept over it, saying, 'Would that even today you knew the things that make for peace! But now they are hid from your eyes. For the days shall come upon you, when your enemies will cast up a bank about you and surround you, and hem you in on every side, and dash you to the ground, you and your children with you, and they will not leave one stone upon another in you; because you did not know the time of your visitation.

This prediction was literally fulfilled when the Romans destroyed Jerusalem in AD 70. (3) Predictions of the coming of the Son of man (Mk 8:38/Mt 16:27/Lk 9:26; Mt 10:32–33/Lk 12:8–9; Mk 13:26,27; 14:62; Lk 11:30/Mt 12:40; Lk 17:24/Mt 24:27; Lk 17:26/Mt 24:37–39; Mt 13:40,41;

The Dome of the Rock, a site of fulfilled prophecy—the death of Jesus and the destruction of the temple.

10:23). (4) The longest prophetic section in the Gospels is the eschatological discourse of Jesus in Mark 13:1–32 (Mt 24:1–36; Lk 21:5–33), in which a number of predictions concerning the destruction of Jerusalem and end of the age are woven into a lengthy discourse to the disciples.

Early Christian Prophecy. 1. Prophecy as an Eschatological Gift. The beginning of prophetic activity in early Christianity, according to Acts, coincided with the outpouring of the Holy Spirit upon the earliest Christians on the Day of Pentecost (Acts 2:1–21). Peter's Pentecost sermon views the outpouring of the Spirit together with the resultant prophetic activity (in early Judaism, the Spirit of God was primarily thought of as the Spirit of prophecy) as the fulfillment of the prediction made in Joel 2:28,29 (as quoted in Acts 2:16–18):

> But this is what was spoken by the prophet Joel: 'And in the last days it shall be, God declares, that I will pour out my Spirit upon all flesh and your sons and your daughters shall prophesy, and your young men shall see visions, and your old men shall dream dreams; yea, and on my menservants and my maidservants in those days I will pour out my Spirit; and they shall prophesy.

It is clear that the phenomenon of speaking in tongues is regarded as an essentially prophetic activity (Acts 2:4,17; 19:6; cf. 16:7). Further, since the Spirit has been poured out upon all early Christians (that Spirit being a Spirit of prophecy), all are actual or potential prophets. Since this event was expected by Joel in the last days, its fulfillment must be regarded as an eschatological event. Therefore, unlike its OT counterpart, NT prophecy is essentially an eschatological gift. The prevalence of prophecy in early Christianity was itself a sign of the presence of the last days. One general early Christian view seems to be that since all Christians share the Spirit of God (Rom 8:9–11,23; 1 Cor 3:16; Gal 3:2–5; Heb 6:4; 1 Thes 4:8), then all are potentially (even if not actually) prophets; we have seen this view expressed in Peter's Pentecost sermon in Acts 2. Yet there were also particular individuals who appear to have possessed a particular gift for prophesying, and it is these who are customarily designated as "prophets." According to 1 Corinthians 12:28 (see also Rom 12:6; Eph 4:11): "And God has appointed in the church first apostles, second prophets, third teachers. . . . " Further, the names of several early Christian prophets have been preserved. These include Agabus (Acts 11:27,28; 21:10,11), Judas and Silas (Acts 15:32), Barnabas, Simeon Niger, Lucius of Cyrene, Manaen, and Paul (Acts 13:1), and the four virgin daughters of Philip the Evangelist (Acts 21:8,9). John, the author of Revelation, was certainly a prophet (Rv 1:3; 22:9,18), though he never directly assumes that title. In Revelation 2:20 John provides us with a cryptic designation for a prophetess of Thyatira whom he calls "Jezebel" and regards as a false prophetess. A few more names of 2nd-century prophets have been preserved in various Christian writers, but little or nothing is known about them. The title "prophet" was claimed by no one in early Christianity whose writings have survived, or about whom we have substantial information. John the Baptist, Jesus, Paul, and John did not claim the title, though it is clear that all functioned as prophets.

2. The Role of the Christian Prophet. Christian prophets were leaders in early Christian communities (1 Cor 12:28; Eph 4:11), yet this leadership was not administrative, but rather took place primarily within the framework of the gatherings of Christians for worship (Acts 13:1–3; 11:27,28; 1 Cor 12–14; Rv 1:10). Since it was within the framework of Christian worship that the Spirit of God was particularly active and evident, prophecy was a major means whereby God communicated with his people. In many respects the roles of apostle, prophet, and teacher overlapped one another. Apostles such as Peter (Acts 4:8) and Paul (Acts 13:1) were prophets as well as teachers. Apostles, in fact, seem to have possessed all of the charisms granted to the church. Prophets also functioned as teachers (1 Cor 14:3,4,19,31), though unlike teachers their words came with immediate divine authority. The primary role of teachers was to expound the meaning of the OT and of the traditions stemming from Jesus. Prophets, like apostles and teachers, did not hold offices in local communities like bishops, elders, and deacons. Rather they were chosen, not by individual congregations, but by divine commission and so were honored and accepted in all local communities.

Early Christian prophets were both itinerant and settled, though itinerant prophets seem to have been more prevalent in Syria-Palestine and Asia Minor than in the European churches. A group of prophets including Agabus traveled from Jerusalem to Antioch, according to Acts 11:27–30. Later, Agabus traveled from Jerusalem to Caesarea to deliver a prophetic warning to Paul (Acts 21:8–11). Judas and Silas, both prophets (Acts 15:32), carried a letter from the apostles and elders in Jerusalem to the Christian church in Antioch (Acts 15:22–35); they appear to have been specially selected for that mission because of their prophetic status. The prophet John addressed seven different communities in Asia Minor (Rv 2,3), and it is probable that he was personally acquainted with each community,

The Roman theater at Caesarea, the city where Agabus the prophet warned Paul not to go to Jerusalem (Acts 21:8–11).

probably through past visits. On the other hand, many prophets seem to have remain settled in their communities and to have exercised their prophetic gifts only locally (1 Cor 12–14).

3. The Function of Prophecy. According to Paul, the central purpose of prophecy (as of all other spiritual gifts) was that of building up or edifying the church. According to 1 Corinthians 14:3, "On the other hand, he who prophesies speaks to men for their upbuilding and encouragement and consolation." Again, in 1 Corinthians 14:4, Paul states that "he who prophesies edifies the church." Paul discussed the subject of spiritual gifts, particularly speaking in tongues and prophecy, at great length because the Corinthians had placed an excessive emphasis on speaking in tongues. Paul did not object to speaking in tongues in principle (1 Cor 14:18,39), but only to the extent that since it was generally incomprehensible, the church could not be edified. Prophecy, which consisted of comprehensible speech inspired by the Spirit, contributed to the mutual edification, encouragement, and consolation of all present (1 Cor 14:20–25,39). A similar emphasis on the function of prophecy as a means of exhorting and strengthening believers is found in Acts. In Acts 15:32, we read, "And Judas and Silas, who were themselves prophets, *exhorted* the brethren with many words and *strengthened* them." An emphasis on exhortation and encouragement as prophetic activities is found throughout Acts (2:40; 9:31; 11:23; 14:22; 16:40; 20:1,2). This hortatory, or paraenetic, function of Christian prophecy is an element virtually unique to Christian prophecy. In general, ethical exhortation is almost totally absent from the messages of the OT prophets, and it is rarely found in Jewish apocalyptic. However, a strong element of ethical exhortation is found in the preaching of John the Baptist, Jesus, and early Christianity.

4. The Content of Christian Prophecy. The fact that the central function of Christian prophecy is paraenesis, or ethical exhortation and encouragement, tells us very little about the content of such prophecy. Prophetic utterance occasionally provided divine guidance in making important decisions in early Christianity. Through a prophetic utterance, Paul and Barnabas were selected for a particular mission (Acts 13:1–3; cf. 1 Tm 1:18; 4:14). Probably through prophetic utterance, Paul and Timothy were forbidden to preach the gospel in Asia (Acts 16:6), and they were similarly forbidden by the Spirit of Jesus to go into Bithynia (Acts 16:7). Perhaps the most frequent use of prophecy is the prediction of the future. Agabus predicted a universal famine (Acts 11:28) and the imminent arrest of Paul (Acts 21:11). Other prophets had also predicted his impending imprisonment (Acts 20:23). The prophecies contained in the Revelation of John are all oriented toward the future events which will gradually unfold in the last days. Yet the purpose of John's elaborate prophecy is not to satisfy the curiosity of his audience, but rather to comfort and encourage them in the midst of the persecution and testing which they were undergoing.

5. The Form of Christian Prophecy. Unlike the prophets of the OT, Christian prophets did not always present their message in the form of a direct speech of God or Jesus. Consequently, the messenger formula is rarely used. It does occur, however, in a prophetic speech of Agabus in Acts 21:11: "Thus says the Holy Spirit, 'So shall the Jews at Jerusalem bind the man who owns this girdle and deliver him into the hands of the Gentiles.'" The prophetic letters of Revelation 2,3 are all written

in the first person, and the speaker is the risen Jesus. Each of the letters also concludes with the formula "He who has ears to hear, let him hear what the Spirit says to the churches" (Rv 2:7,11,17,29; 3:6,13,22). Apart from these rare occurrences of introductory formulas to prophetic speech, there are few if any formal indicators of the presence of prophetic speech in early Christian literature.

6. The Decline of Christian Prophecy. Though Christian prophets appear until the middle of the 2nd century AD, they are increasingly regarded as heretical. As in the postexilic era of Israelite history, false prophets abounded, and the defenses against them were weak. Prophecy declined primarily because its central role, that of ethical exhortation and consolation of Christians, was scarcely unique, and was quickly taken over by other functionaries in early Christian communities. Further, the gradual formation of the NT canon of Scripture made the necessity of direct prophetic inspiration less important than in the early days of the church. The prophets are gone, but "the encouragement of the Scriptures" (Rom 15:4) remains. DAVID E. AUNE

See PROPHET, FALSE; PROPHET, PROPHETESS; VISION; DREAMS; ISRAEL, RELIGION OF; ORACLE; PROMISE.

Bibliography. W.J. Beecher, *The Prophets and the Promise*; M. Buber, *The Prophetic Faith*; A.B. Davidson, *OT Prophecy*; W. Eichrodt, *Theology of the OT*, 1:289–391; E.E. Ellis, *Prophecy and Hermeneutic in Early Christianity*; A. Heschel, *The Prophets*; D. Hill, *NT Prophecy*; Y. Kaufmann, *The Religion of Israel*, 343–446; D.L. Peterson, *The Roles of Israel's Prophets*; T.H. Robinson, *Prophecy and the Prophets in Ancient Israel*; H.H. Rowley (ed.), *Studies in OT Prophecy*; G. von Rad, *OT Theology*, vol 2.

Prophet, False.

Spokesman, herald, or messenger falsely speaking for, or on behalf of, someone else. The false prophet was often motivated not by loyalty to God, but by a desire for popularity. This was the main difference between Jeremiah and his contemporaries. While Jeremiah was foretelling doom (Jer 4:19), the false prophets were assuring the people of peace when war was at hand (6:14; 8:11). The people preferred it that way saying, "Prophesy not to us what is right; speak to us smooth things, prophesy illusions . . ." (Is 30:10).

The false prophet's message frequently appealed to national pride—Israel was God's people, God's temple was in their midst, hence all would be well (Jer 7:10). Jeremiah, however, warned them not to be fooled into thinking that just because they had the temple they would never suffer (vv 12–15). Such confrontation between the prophet of God and the national cult is exemplified in Amos' encounter with Amaziah the priest of Bethel, who accused Amos of conspiring against Israel (Am 7:10–13). Yet Amos was proved right when the northern kingdom fell to the Assyrians in 722 BC and the Jews were taken into exile. Here we have a classic example of the prophet's function as "seer," that is, one who warns against approaching disaster in the name of God.

The message of the false prophet was usually spurred by self-interest and given to please the people. It was not necessarily his intention to speak falsely, yet when spoken with wrong motivation his message was often in error. This sometimes means that even a true prophet could become false and occasionally a false prophet could be used of God for the right purpose. For example, Moses acted as a false prophet by striking the rock twice at the waters of Meribah (Nm 20:11,12), while Balaam, a non-Israelite—whom God entrusted with a vision—found himself in the difficult position of having to please Balak, who had hired him, and the God of Israel, who spoke to him (Nm 22,23). A fascinating story is told in 1 Kings 13 of two nameless prophets—one true and the other false—who abruptly change roles when the lying prophet speaks truth and the true prophet by disobedience is proven false. In the case of Jeremiah in confrontation with Hananiah, the son of Azzur, the two prophets meet in the temple before the priests and the people to pitch prophecy against prophecy. Hananiah was proved false, though he appeared as a legitimate "prophet from Gibeon" (Jer 28:1). He prophesied the very thing the people in Jerusalem wanted to hear, namely the imminent fall of Babylon; subsequent events, however, proved this thinking wishful. We may therefore say that false prophecy is self-centered, wrongly motivated, and detached from reality.

The concept of the false prophet is carried over into the NT. Our Lord warns against those who disguise themselves as harmless sheep but are in fact wolves ready for the kill. Jesus cautions his disciples saying, "Not every one who says to me, 'Lord, Lord,' shall enter the kingdom of heaven"—the way to identify a person is by the kind of fruit he produces; only a good tree produces good fruit (Mt 7:15–21). The warning is repeated in Matthew 24:11. False Christs will also arise trying to deceive God's elect (v 24).

The early church must have been plagued by such "pseudo-prophets" for the apostolic letters further warn against such men (cf. 2 Pt 2:1; 1 Jn 4:1). In the context of these letters "prophets" and "teachers" are interchangeable, though the original text speaks of them as "false prophets." Though pretending to be Christians, they are deceptive teachers because their instruction is perverse. These people even perform miracles, but with the help of evil spirits, not the Spirit of Christ (cf. Rv 13:11–15).

False prophets, fraudulent spirits, and wrong teaching is a recurrent problem in the church. Believers should constantly stand guard against those who cleverly lie about the truth (cf. Eph 4:14–16); careful to discern the spirits whether they be from the evil one or from God (1 Cor 12:10,11). We are told not to believe everyone who claims that his message is from God, but to "test" the spirits to see whether their message be from the Holy Spirit and in agreement with the Spirit of Christ, the Son of God (cf. 1 Jn 4:1–3).

JAKOB JOCZ

See ANTICHRIST; PROPHECY; PROPHET, PROPHETESS; FALSE CHRISTS.

Prophet, Prophetess.

Introduction. When Jesus raised the widow's son from the dead, the onlookers responded by saying that "A great prophet has arisen among us!" and "God has visited his people!" (Lk 7:16; cf. Mk 6:15; 8:28). In Jewish religious thought, the most vivid and formative religious happenings found their focus in the call and ministry of a prophet, through whom God made known his Word and himself to his people. In their appraisal of Jesus the people were in fact more correct than they knew, for in him God had in reality visited them and he, though so much more than a prophet, was in fact the crown and climax of the prophetic order predicted by Moses (Dt 18:15–19).

The Titles and History of the Prophets. The main words used to describe such individuals in the OT are "prophet" (e.g., Jgs 6:8), "man of God" (e.g., 2 Kgs 4:9) and "seer"—the latter word doing duty for two distinct but synonymous words in the Hebrew lying behind our English translations (e.g., 1 Sm 9:9; 2 Sm 24:11).

The word translated "prophet" seems to have the idea "called" as its first emphasis: God takes the initiative, selects, summons, and sends the prophet (e.g., Jer 1:4,5; 7:25; Am 7:14). "Man of God" speaks of the relationship into which the prophet is brought by his call: he is now "God's man" and is recognized as belonging to him (2 Kgs 4:9). "Seer" indicates the new and remarkable powers of perception granted to the prophet. In Hebrew as in English the ordinary verb "to see" is used also of understanding ("I see what you mean") and of the power of perception into the nature and meaning of things ("He sees things very clearly"); in the case of the prophets, their powers of "perception" were raised far above normal as the Lord inspired them to become vehicles of his message.

The line of great prophets upon whose shoulders the story of the OT moves forward began with Moses, who is recognized as the prophet *par excellence* (Dt 34:10). This was a correct perception, for all the distinctive marks of a prophet began in the experience of Moses: the call (Ex 3:1–4:17; cf. Is 6; Jer 1:4–19; Ez 1–3; Hos 1:2; Am 7:14,15; etc.), the awareness of the importance of historical events as the acts of God in which he confirms his word (Ex 3:12; 4:21–23), ethical and social concern (Ex 2:11–13), and championship of the helpless (Ex 2:17).

But the comment in Deuteronomy 34:10 not only looks back to the greatness of Moses, but on to the coming of a prophet like Moses. This accords with his own prediction (Dt 18:15–19), which undoubtedly anticipates a single, great individual prophet. Moses makes a striking comparison with himself: the coming prophet will fill just such a role as Moses filled at Mt Sinai (Dt 18:16). On that occasion Moses acted as the prophetic mediator of the voice of God in a unique sense, for at Sinai God fashioned the old covenant into its completed form. In expecting a prophet cast in this mold, Moses was therefore looking forward to another covenant-mediator, to Jesus Christ himself.

But the forward, expectant look which Moses thus inculcated into his people was fulfilled in a fuller way, which Deuteronomy 18:20–22 does little more than hint at: as well as the coming great prophet there would also be other prophets (see vv 21,22). The expectation of the great prophet was kept alive as God kept sending prophets to his people: in each case, such a prophet was known to be true by his likeness to Moses; in each case he would be viewed with excitement by genuine believers to see whether he was the great one come at last. Seen in this light we can understand the excitement of the people who saw Jesus raise the dead (Lk 7:16).

The prophetic line stemming from Moses had its share of such unknowns as the prophet of Judges 6:8, but from the earliest post-Mosaic times the real leadership of the people frequently lay in prophetic hands: Deborah (Jgs 4:4), Samuel (1 Sm 3:20), Elijah (1 Kgs 17:1). Even in the case of those whose leadership was less dramatically obvious, the decisive word which shaped events was the word of the prophet (e.g., 2 Kgs 22:12–20), a word which even the most influential kings ignored at their peril (e.g., Is 7:9).

The OT mentions the existence of prophetic groups, sometimes called "schools." Elisha clearly had such a group under his instruction (2 Kgs 6:1), and "sons of the prophets" (e.g., 2 Kgs 2:3,5; Am 7:14) probably refers to "prophet in training" under the care of a master prophet. "Guilds" would be a better description of the groups in 1 Samuel 10:5,6,10,11. Such groups enjoyed an enthusiastic ecstatic worship of the Lord, touched with a marked activity of the Spirit of God, but at the heart of their devotion was "prophecy," that is, a declaration of the truth about God himself. The extravagant behavior of Saul in this connection (1 Sm 19:24) happened to a man far gone in some form of dementia, and must not be taken as typical of the ecstatic groups. After this early period the prophetic groups seem to have diminished in significance (at least judging by the disappearance of plain references similar to those in 1 Sm), and the gradual change of things from ecstasy to a more direct ministry of the Word could well lie behind the comment in 1 Samuel 9:9.

Inspiration. The spirit of the Lord whose inspiration lay behind the activities of the ecstatic groups (1 Sm 10:6,10; 19:20,23) was active in all the prophets, and the claim to divine inspiration is plainly registered from time to time (e.g., 1 Kgs 22:24; Neh 9:30; Hos 9:7; Jl 2:28,29; Mi 3:8; cf. 1 Chr 12:18; 2 Chr 15:1; 20:14; 24:20). The upshot of this inspiring activity of the Spirit was what can justly be called a miracle: chosen men, without in any way ceasing to be men, spoke with the very words of God (cf. 2 Pt 1:21). The OT never involves itself in the question how this could have been brought about; it contents itself with illustrating the reality.

Jeremiah claims that the hand of God was laid on his mouth, putting the words of God into his lips (Jer 1:9); Ezekiel records how he was made to eat a scroll, by which means he received the words the Lord had written, and was thus enabled to speak what the Lord called "my words" (Ez 2:7–4:4). The miracle is stated in a nutshell at the beginning of Amos (1:1,3): "The words of Amos . . . Thus saith the Lord"—Amos remains Amos and the words are truly his; Amos has been divinely called to be a prophet (7:14) and the words are the Lord's.

The first time the word "prophet" appears in the OT it is used of Abraham as a man of prayer (Gn 20:7; cf. Jer 7:10; 11:14; 14:11), that is, a person brought into communion with God. Amos claimed such an experience of fellowship for prophets (Am 3:7, literally "He opens his fellowship to his servants the prophets"); Jeremiah uses the same word when he claims that true prophets stand in the "council" (or "counsel" or "fellowship") of the Lord (Jer 23:18,22). It is a biblical truth that the nearer a man comes to God, and the more he reflects the likeness of God, and the more he hears and obeys the divine Word, the more he becomes truly human (i.e., man "in the image

of God," man as God made and intended him to be). God brought his servants the prophets into a unique reality of fellowship and closeness with himself, with the blessed result that their characteristic cry "Thus says the Lord" meant exactly what it claimed.

True and False Prophets. The Lord is given to testing his people with adversity in order to establish their hearts (e.g., Dt 8:2,3). In connection with their supreme privilege of hearing the Word of God through the prophets no exception was made: the area of privilege was the arena of testing (Dt 13:3,4) to see if they truly loved his truth. But when he tests, the Lord in mercy opens doors of escape (cf. 1 Cor 10:13), and it was so in relation to false prophecy: He allowed his people to know how to test what they heard so as to hold fast to what is good (1 Thes 5:19–21).

The first test was doctrinal. In Deuteronomy 13 the motive of the false prophet was to draw the people away from the God who had revealed himself in the exodus (Dt 13:2,5–7, 10). Notwithstanding that the word of the false prophet might be supported by apparent signs and wonders (Dt 13:1,2) it was to be refused—not simply because it introduced novelty (Dt 13:2,6) but because that novelty contradicted the revelation of the Lord at the exodus (Dt 13:5,10). The first test was thus doctrinal and required in the people of God knowledge—knowledge of the truth whereby they could, by comparison, recognize error.

The second test was practical and required patience. It is stated in Deuteronomy 18:21,22: the Word of the Lord always comes to pass. This requires patience because as Deuteronomy 13:1,2 indicates, a false word may be supported by an apparent spiritual proof. The call of Deuteronomy 18:21,22 is a call for patience: should there be any real doubt whether a prophetic word is true or false, wait for the confirmatory turn of events.

The third test is moral and calls for watchful discernment. Jeremiah, of all the prophets, was most afflicted in his spirit by the presence of false prophets and gave the longest and most sustained consideration to the problem (Jer 23:9–40). His answer is striking and challenging: the false prophet will be found out as a man of unholy life (Jer 23:11,13,14) whose message has no note of moral rebuke, but rather encourages men in their sin (Jer 23:16, 17,21,22; cf. the contrasting message of the true, vv 18–20).

The Function of the Prophet. It is sometimes said that prophets are not *foretellers* but *forthtellers*. As far as the OT is concerned, however, the prophets are forthtellers (declaring the truth about God) by being foretellers (predicting what God will do). Prediction is neither an occasional nor a marginal activity in the OT; it is the way the prophet went about his work, under the inspiration of God. Not only the actual evidence of the books of the prophets, wherein the gaze is uniformly forward, supports this contention but also a key passage like Deuteronomy 18:9–15, which explains the function of the prophet in Israel: the surrounding nations are revealed as probing into the future by means of a variety of fortune-telling techniques (vv 10,11); these things are forbidden to Israel on the ground of being abominable to the Lord (v 12); Israel's distinctiveness is maintained in that the nations probe the future by diviners, whereas the Lord gives Israel a prophet (vv 13–15). Elisha (2 Kgs 4:27) is surprised when foreknowledge is denied him; Amos teaches that foreknowledge is the privilege of the prophets in their fellowship with God (Am 3:7). But prediction in Israel was totally unlike prognostication among the nations, for in no way was it motivated by a mere curiosity about the future.

First, biblical prediction arose out of the needs of the present. In Isaiah 39 it is the faithless commitment of Hezekiah to rely for security on a military understanding with Babylon that prompts Isaiah to announce the future Babylonian captivity. Isaiah does not snatch the name "Babylon" out of thin air; it is given to him within the situation in which he was called to minister. Second, prediction aimed

The ruins of Babylon, which, before it fell, took Judah captive, as Isaiah had announced.

at giving that sort of knowledge of the future was to result in moral reformation in the present. How often the moral exhortations of the prophets find their explanation in what the Lord is about to do (e.g., Is 31:6,7; Am 5:6). Third, the predicted course of events was aimed at stabilizing the faith of the true believer in dark times (see e.g., how Is 9:1–7; 11:1–16; 40:1–3 have the effect of lifting the eyes out of the immediately preceding grim tragedy to the coming glory, thus giving faith the strength of sure hope).

Methods of Communication. In foretelling the prophets were forthtelling, proclaiming the wonderful works of God (cf. the definition of prophecy in Acts 2:11,17). For the most part, this proclamation was by direct word of mouth, by verbal preaching. The prophets were men of the word. They believed their words (which were God's words) were far more than a sound addressed from one person to another; the word was really like a messenger sent by God (Is 55:11) endowed with all the divine efficacy of the creative word of Genesis 1:3 (cf. Ps 33:6). Sometimes the efficacy of the word was enhanced by being embodied in a sign or symbolic action (e.g., Jer 13:1–11; 19:1–15; Ez 4:1–17; 24:15–24), or identified intimately with a person (Is 7:3; cf. 10:21; 8:1–4). Such things had, of course, the effect of visual aids whereby the word would be made clearer to those present, being seen as well as heard. But it would seem that the intention of the symbolic action (sometimes called an "acted oracle") was not so much to make understanding easier but to give more power and effect to the word as it was sent like a messenger into that situation. This is the conclusion to be drawn from 2 Kings 13:14–19 where the extent to which the king "embodied" the word in action determined the extent to which the word would prove effective in bringing events to pass.

The final embodiment of the words of the prophets was in the books which have, by the rich providence of God, been preserved. Jeremiah 36 may be taken as an object lesson in the fact that the prophets took the time and trouble to record their spoken messages in writing: there was stress on careful word by word dictation (vv 6,17,18). But the actual literary form of the messages themselves tells the same tale. What we find in the books of the prophets cannot be the preached form of their words, but rather the studied wording in which they preserved (and filed away) their sermons. It stands to reason that men who were conscious of communicating the very words of God would see to it that those words were not lost. We may take it for granted that every prophet preserved a written record of his ministry. Whether each of the named prophets was himself directly responsible for the final form of his book we are not told and have no way of knowing: the careful way in which the books of Isaiah or Amos, for example, are arranged is best suited by assuming that the author was also his own editor; the freedom with which the oracles of Jeremiah are arranged in defiance of chronological order, makes one wonder if anyone but Jeremiah would have taken such liberties. It is usually assumed that the final arrangement of the books of the prophets was a fairly long process, attended to by the continuing circles of disciples of the prophet in question, but there is no evidence for the continuing existence of such circles of disciples, or of their engaging in the editorial and expansionist work often attributed to them. The books are best considered as the last and greatest acted oracles of the prophets, embodying their message in visible, enduring form and blessing the succeeding ages of the church with the imperishable Word of God. ALEC MOTYER

See PROPHECY; PROPHET, FALSE; ISRAEL, RELIGION OF.

Bibliography. W.J. Beecher, *The Prophets and the Promise;* H.E. Freeman, *An Introduction to the Old Prophets;* A. Herschel, *The Prophets;* A.R. Johnson, *The Cultic Prophet in Ancient Israel;* D.L. Peterson, *The Roles of Israel's Prophets;* L.J. Wood, *The Prophets of Israel;* E.J. Young, *My Servants the Prophets.*

Propitiation. Turning away of anger by the offering of a gift. The word was often used by the pagans in antiquity, for they thought of their gods as unpredictable beings, liable to become angry with their worshipers for any trifle. When disaster struck it was often thought that a god was angry and was therefore punishing his worshipers. The remedy was to offer a sacrifice without delay. A well-chosen offering would appease the god and put him in a good mood again. This process was called propitiation.

Understandably, some modern theologians have reacted against using the term in reference to the God of the Bible. They do not see him as one who can be bribed to be favorable, so they reject the whole idea. When they come to the term in the Greek NT they translate it by "expiation," or some equivalent term which lacks any reference to anger, an unjustified avoidance because, in the first place, the Greek term for propitiation occurs in some important biblical passages (Rom 3:25; Heb 2:17; 1 Jn 2:2; 4:10). In the second place, the idea of the wrath of God is found throughout the Bible. It must be taken into account in the way sin is forgiven.

The idea that God cannot be angry is found neither in the OT nor the NT. It is neither Jewish nor Christian. It is an idea that comes from the Greek philosophers. They thought of their gods as aloof and passionless beings, too lofty by far to be interested in the deeds of little men. But the Bible states that God loves men with a pure and boundless love. It says that because he loves his people so greatly he is not indifferent when they soil his creation with sin and bring misery into the lives of those he loves. Clearly, in those circumstances he is angry. Whenever his children sin they draw down upon themselves the anger of God. Of course, his anger is not an irrational lack of self-control as it so often is with humans. His anger is the settled opposition of his holy nature to everything that is evil.

Such opposition to sin cannot be dismissed with a wave of the hand. It requires something much more substantial. And the Bible states that it was only the cross that did this. Jesus is "the propitiation for our sins; and not for ours only, but also for the sins of the whole world" (1 Jn 2:2 KJV). This is not the only way of looking at the cross, but it is an important way. If God's anger is real, then it must be taken into account in the way that sin, which caused that wrath, is dealt with. When the NT says "propitiation," then, it means that Jesus' death on the cross for the sins of mankind put away God's wrath against his people once and for all.

See ATONEMENT; WRATH OF GOD; EXPIATION.

Bibliography. C.H. Dodd, *The Bible and the Greeks;* L. Morris, *The Apostolic Preaching of the Cross;* R.V.G. Tasker, *The Biblical Doctrine of the Wrath of God.*

Proselyte. Gentile who signified his wish to convert to Judaism by being circumcised, baptized, and offering a sacrifice in the temple.

OT. Foreigners who resided on some fairly permanent basis in Palestine in OT times were encouraged to become integrated into the full religious life of Israel through circumcision (Ex 12:48). The "proselytizing," or bringing into the covenant community of willing Gentiles, occurred most predominantly in the Diaspora, that is, the Jewish communities outside Palestine. Jews, living in most areas of the known world due to exile, commercial, or military reasons, naturally carried their religious faith and practice with them. This Jewish way of life, particularly its monotheistic faith in an invisible Creator not worshiped through images together with its high ethical standards, was attractive to many of the surrounding Gentiles accustomed to polytheism. The result was that many Gentiles attached themselves in varying degrees to the Jewish faith through the life of the synagogue (see Is 56:1–8; Mal

1:11). Extrabiblical Jewish (Philo, Josephus) and Roman sources (e.g., Horace, Seneca, Tacitus) reveal that Jews (particularly those in the Diaspora) carried on in the centuries immediately preceding the life of Christ and then on into the early NT era a quite aggressive mission to Gentiles (see Mt 23:15).

The more zealous of those attracted to Judaism at this time became full members of the Jewish community through a rite involving three elements: circumcision (if male), a baptism representing a break with pagan background, and an offering in the temple at Jerusalem. Termed "proselytes," these converts were considered true Jews in the sense of being obligated to follow the entire OT Law. The legal rights of such gentile converts were somewhat limited although their everyday life did not differ greatly from that of Jews by birth.

There were other Gentiles who admired the monotheism and moral superiority of Judaism and were attracted to synagogue life but did not desire to take such a final step as circumcision. These were termed "God-fearers" (see Acts 10:22; 13:16,26) or "devout" ones (10:2; 17:4,17), and were regarded favorably by some Jews, particularly of the Diaspora, but were disregarded by others as no better than Gentiles.

NT. Some proselytes responded to the preaching of the gospel and were welcomed into the early church (Acts 2:10,11; 6:5; 13:43). The early church was divided, however, on what to require of the "God-fearer" who, hearing Christian missionaries preaching in the synagogues of the Diaspora, wished to respond to the gospel. Many of the Jewish Christians from Jerusalem felt that for salvation, interested God-fearers should be circumcised and follow OT Law in addition to faith in Christ. These Jewish Christians were in fact known as the "party of the circumcision" and attempted to influence the widening church mission to the Gentiles in this direction (Acts 11:2; 15:1–5; Gal 2:12). Following his experience with the God-fearer Cornelius and seeing the power of God fall upon this gentile family (Acts 10:1–11:18), Peter became convinced circumcision was not a divine requirement for the salvation of God-fearers (10:44–48; 11:15–18). It was Paul, however, who most aggressively preached the gospel to God-fearers and other interested Gentiles (Acts 13:16,26,48; 16:14; 17:4, 17; 18:7) and fought for salvation on the basis of faith in Christ alone (Gal 3:11; 5:2–6). The disagreement climaxed at the Council of Jerusalem (*c.* AD 48–49) where the leadership of the early church judged in favor of Paul's position, ruling circumcision unimportant for the salvation of Gentiles (Acts 15). Incorporation of Gentiles into the Christian church became conditional solely upon faith in Christ and baptism.

DAVID C. CARLSON

See DIASPORA OF THE JEWS; JEW; GOD-FEARER.

Prostitute, Prostitution. *See* HARLOT.

Proverbs, Book of.
Authorship. While there is an underlying unity of thought in the Book of Proverbs there is no question of unity of authorship, since the writers of the seven or more sections into which the book is divided, are, in most cases, clearly noted.

1:1–9:18. There is a division of opinion as to whether the opening verse refers to the Solomonic authorship of the entire section, or whether it simply underscores the name of the main contributor to the book. It is objected that the man who wrote so carefully about the danger of promiscuous relationships with immoral women, one of the main themes of this section, is not likely to be Solomon, who failed significantly in the matter of mixed marriages (1 Kgs 11:1–8). There are evident flaws in such an argument: one may be capable of giving excellent advice without necessarily having the strength of character to follow it oneself; and there is surely a distinction between the seductive prostitutes or adulteresses of 5:1–21; 6:20–35; 7:1–22 and Solomon's polygamous but respectable relationships. However, the question of authorship is probably best left open. Those who question the Solomonic origin of this section regard 1:2–7 as setting out the purpose of the whole book. 1:8–9:18 is a series of 13 practical discourses on wisdom, lovingly and honestly given as by a father to a son. This provides an indispensable foundation for the more popular proverbial teaching in the remainder of the book.

10:1–22:16. Solomon is specifically noted as the author or compiler of this main section of Proverbs. The probability that he played a major part in the production of the Book of Proverbs finds strong support in the historical books. Soon after his coronation he was endowed with the spirit of wisdom, in response to his request (1 Kgs 3:5–14). The incident concerning the two prostitutes (1 Kgs 3:16–28) provided public proof of this. His universal reputation, especially in connection with proverbial wisdom, is attested in 1 Kings 4:29–34 and in the visit of the Queen of Sheba (1 Kgs 10:1–13).

22:17–24:22. The title "the words of the wise" (22:17) is incorporated into the opening verse of this section. But an evident difference of style, replacing the simple, one-verse proverb by a more discursive approach which deals with a subject over several verses, *and* the title of the next section, "These *also* are sayings of the wise" (24:23), strongly suggest the independence of this collection. Of major interest is the remarkably close parallel between 22:17–23:11 and the Egyptian book of Amenemope, which has been dated variously between the 13th and 7th centuries BC. Scholars have detected as many as 30 connections between the two. Most incline to the view that this section in Proverbs is an adaptation of an Egyptian original, such selection and modification being entirely congruous with the doctrine of inspiration. However, a minority of scholars, including several prominent Egyptologists, argue persuasively on the basis of grammatical structure that Amenemope is derived from a Hebrew original.

25:1–29:27. Basic Solomonic material has here been edited and incorporated by "the men of Hezekiah king of Judah" (25:1). The tendency to group proverbs dealing with specific subjects is well illustrated, for example, the relationship between a king and his subjects (25:2–7); the lazy man (26:13–16) and the mischief-maker (26:17–27). Solomon and Hezekiah were frequently linked together in Jewish thought (e.g., 2 Chr 30:26) and rabbinic tradition in fact credited Hezekiah with the production of both Proverbs and the Book of Ecclesiastes. The national prestige during the reigns of both kings would have been conducive to literary pursuits.

30:1–33. Nothing is known of Agur, his father Jakeh of Massa, or the two other characters mentioned, Ithiel and Ucal. According to Genesis 25:14 Massa was one of the 12 princes of Ishmael, and it is likely that Agur came from north Arabia, an area traditionally renowned for its wisdom. The pattern which he uses, "three things . . . no four" (30:18,21,29– the actual numbers may vary) is possibly derived from the teaching technique of "the wise" (cf. Am 1:3,6,9, etc.).

31:1–9. Lemuel, the author of this section, also came from Massa, but apart from this is otherwise unknown. The inclusion of wisdom sayings from sources outside Israel illustrates the international connections of the wisdom movement during the period of the monarchy.

31:10–31. It is possible that Lemuel's authorship includes this superb acrostic poem on the ideal wife; its inspiration may have come from his mother, like the earlier section. But the pattern of life would fit more easily into the context of a prosperous, agricultural community in Palestine rather than in an Arabian nomadic or seminomadic community. For this reason most scholars regard the poem as anonymous.

Date. The larger part of the book may, with confidence, be ascribed to Solomon (*c.*

970–930 BC), but the considerable contribution of Hezekiah and his men rules out a date for the completion of the book before 700 BC. The inclusion of sections by non-Israelites, like Agur and Lemuel, is more likely in the preexilic period, with its wider international interests, than in the more particularistic atmosphere of postexilic Judaism. Probably the final, sophisticated acrostic poem was the last section to be included, but there is nothing in the book that demands a date later than the early 7th century. In rabbinic tradition Proverbs was invariably grouped with Psalms and the Book of Job in the third section of the Jewish canon, the Writings or Holy Books. While the content of the Writings was not authoritatively finalized until the end of the 1st century AD, it is likely that Proverbs was accepted as inspired long before this, as witnessed by its inclusion in the Septuagint, the principal Greek translation. The order in our English versions may have been influenced by the rabbinic tradition which linked the books of Job, Psalms, and Proverbs with Moses, David, and Hezekiah, respectively.

Background. The Book of Proverbs is included in the OT corpus of books known as the wisdom literature. This corpus is further represented in Scripture by the books of Job and Ecclesiastes and certain of the psalms (e.g., Ps 1,37,73,119, etc.). Proverbs represents one major class of this literature. Individual proverbs contain sharp, practical applications of wisdom covering many facets of life. The other major class, Job and Ecclesiastes, consider one major problem, or a group of interrelated problems, in monologue or dialogue form.

In the ancient Near East, wisdom was originally connected with all skills, manual as well as intellectual, and was considered to be the gift of the gods. Gradually it acquired a dominantly intellectual significance, particularly in a cultic setting, in such magical or semimagical arts as exorcism. A moral element also developed, indicating that quality of life, or explanation of the problems of life, was believed to derive from the gods. A wide range of wisdom literature from Egypt, Canaan, and Mesopotamia, of the two basic types noted in the preceding paragraph, has survived, making it possible to see its Hebrew counterpart against this background. There is no slavish duplication, however, and the spirit of the Hebrew wisdom literature is markedly superior to anything comparable in the ancient world. This was due principally to the strong religious foundation in Israel, where wisdom's first step was to trust and reverence the Lord (Pr 1:7).

When Israel emerged historically as a nation in the Mosaic period, it was in a world where individuals or groups of "the wise" al-

The mound of Tekoa, where there was a wise woman (2 Sm 14:2).

ready existed. Israel shared this inheritance, with both men and women being involved, as witnessed by the wise women of Tekoa and Abel in Beth-maacah (2 Sm 14:2; 20:16) and the professional military or civic court counselors Ahithophel and Hushai (2 Sm 15:1,2,31; 16:15–19). As the institutional forms of Israel's religion developed during the monarchy, three classes of officials attached to the sanctuary are seen: the priests, who made known the will of God on the basis of the Mosaic law or by the use of the divine oracle, Urim and Thummim (Dt 33:8–11); the cult prophets, who professed to declare God's will either by direct oracle or through dreams (Jer 23:21–32) and who were often at variance with the canonical prophets; and the wise, who related the law to the detailed requirements and problems of everyday life. Passages like Isaiah 29:14; Jeremiah 8:9; and 18:18 show that this third group was operating in Judah by the 8th and 7th centuries BC. The transition from the earlier "secular" counselors to cultic functionaries was doubtless due to the way in which Israel's religion increasingly integrated all aspects of life. Proverbs shows this group at its best, and the life of uprightness, diligence, honesty, and self-control which it advocates sets a standard of morality which accords with the Law on which it was based.

It is probable that many proverbs predate the emergence of a class of the wise. Most communities develop their own collections of short, witty sayings which express practical wisdom and form a store of primitive philosophy. Solomon's part in giving definitive shape to Israel's proverbs (1 Kgs 4:32) has already been noted. The antithetic form of Hebrew poetry, where the parallelism of the second line allows either a sharp contrast (as generally in Prv 10–15) or further support (i.e., synony-

mous parallelism, as in chs 16–22) is an ideal medium for the proverb. When the class of "the wise" developed, this popular wisdom became part of their provenance. If it be objected that the wisdom of Proverbs is hardly religious and out of harmony with the spirit of the rest of the OT, it must be pointed out that it was never meant to be taken in isolation. The whole wisdom movement was erected on the sure foundation of Israel's historically based faith, and the incorporation of Proverbs into the nation's religious life, and ultimately into the Scriptures, testifies to the fact that matters of everyday conduct and relationships *are* matters of concern to the God of Israel— and to ourselves. Wisdom is sometimes personified in the wisdom literature. A good example of this is Proverbs 8:1–9:6. While this will be dealt with more fully, it should be noted that some scholars have set a late date on this section, because of the personification. This is done with other biblical passages like Job 28, where Persian or Greek influence is alleged. This is not a necessary explanation, as the personification of qualities such as truth and righteousness is found in the ancient Near East at least a millennium before the time of Solomon. Wisdom, being one of the main attributes of the Egyptian and Mesopotamian deities, was an obvious candidate for personification. But the real significance of 8:1–9:6 is best seen in connection with the immoral women of the surrounding sections (7:1–27; 9:13–18) and not in isolation.

Purpose and Theological Teaching. *The Close Relationship Between Religion and Everyday Life.* While the general tone of Proverbs is dominantly rational, the importance of reverencing and trusting the Lord is stressed throughout the book (1:7; 2:5; 3:7; 8:13, etc.). This "fear of the Lord" is one of the main definitions of religion in the OT, the other being "the knowledge of God" stressed especially by Hosea and Jeremiah (Hos 4:1; Jer 9:24). *Both* are found in parallel in Proverbs 2:5 and 9:10. Far from there being an unbridgeable gap between religion and the secular world, Proverbs shows the results, in noble character and harmonious, happy homes, when the whole of life is brought under God's control. A danger exists when the moral elements are taken in isolation from the religious foundation which is assumed throughout. Then the pursuit for happiness or success can become selfish, inward looking, and ultimately self-defeating.

Proverbs and the Prophetic Movement. There are many similarities between Proverbs and the prophets, including: a down-to-earth realism; a championing of the poor and underprivileged groups (e.g., 14:31); a realization of the inefficacy of sacrifice apart from morality

(15:8; 21:27); and an emphasis on the individual, which was sometimes overlooked because of the strong sense of corporate identity within the covenant community. Jeremiah and Ezekiel, especially, restated strongly the theme of individual responsibility (Jer 31:29, 30; Ez 18). But there is a vital difference which Proverbs shares with the remainder of biblical wisdom literature, namely, the absence of any clear, historical reference to Israel's election and covenant relationship with God. This was the consistent point of appeal of the great preexilic prophets. Similarly, Jerusalem and its king temple theology are not mentioned, although the wisdom movement, especially as reflected in Proverbs, flourished under the patronage of the Davidic monarchy. The explanation of this, in the fact that the wisdom movement was developed on the already existing foundation of a covenant people, has been noted previously. Nevertheless, the absence of any obvious allusion to these fundamental facts is remarkable. Even the name, "Israel," does not occur. This has lent strength to the view that Proverbs is the clearest and most comprehensive manual of *universal*, practical ethics existing in the ancient world. An educated contemporary Egyptian would have found Proverbs readily comprehensible and uplifting, and although this was not its primary purpose, the book still has a strong appeal to the moral non-Christian.

Proverbs and the Historical Books. Proverbs shares with the historical books an emphasis on retribution and reward (2:22; 3:9,10; 10:27–30) which is sometimes called "Deuteronomic" because its clearest statement is found in the fifth book of Moses (e.g., Dt 28). This doctrine could be perverted into an invariable equation: the righteous are *always* rewarded and the wicked are *always* punished, a view against which Job (Jb 21:7–34) and Jeremiah (Jer 12:1–4) protested strongly. It could also result in a hypocritical, self-seeking approach; I *want* the blessings promised (e.g., Prv 3:9,10), therefore I will "honor" God in the matter of tithes. This substitution of an outward show for the inward dynamic of love, gratitude, and faith was often the curse of Israel's formalized religion. However, the principle itself—that those who honor God and live in cooperation with him and his laws, are generally those who are God-blessed (not necessarily in material terms)—is a sound scriptural one, and the authors of Proverbs must not be blamed for the perversions which arose subsequently. Later wisdom writers modified the view that vindication or punishment were necessarily in this life, their faith reaching to an ultimate judgment in the afterlife (e.g., Jb 19:25–27; Eccl 3:17; 12:14; Dn 12:2,3).

Content. 1:1–7 sets out the purpose of the wisdom movement in Israel and part of verse 2, "how to act in every circumstance," could well be a subtitle of the whole book. The question of the authorship of this section has already been discussed, but there is certainly nothing incongruous about a Solomonic origin. In the earlier part of his reign, Solomon showed a deep longing for that wisdom required to govern his people rightly (1 Kgs 3:7–9), and there is the earnest desire here that his subjects might have a similar understanding. Verses 1–6 form one sentence in Hebrew and include no fewer than 11 different aspects of wisdom. The first of them, "wisdom," occurs 37 times in Proverbs and indicates an informed, skillful use of knowledge. It is only by taking the first step of trust in and reverence for the Lord that a person can enter into wisdom. Morality is not situational, or an absolute in itself; it requires an unchanging point of reference which can only be found in God. In a consideration of the individual proverbs, many of them mundane, it is well to bear in mind that the foundation of the moral life has, at the outset, been clearly defined.

1:8–9:18 is composed of 13 distinct lessons on wisdom, most of which are introduced by "My son" or something similar. The final lesson (8:1–9:18) is given by Wisdom herself. This method indicates the warm, personal relationship between the teacher and his pupils, who, in the ancient Near East, would be exclusively male. A similar style is found in both Egyptian and Mesopotamian wisdom literature and could well have been adopted by Solomon, who, in the humility and God-fearing concern for the national well-being of his earlier years, would have been a teacher *par excellence*.

(1) Lesson 1 (1:8–33). Avoid evil companions. Three voices are raised: the specious voice of those who promise quick gains by violence (10–14); the wise man himself (15–19), reinforcing the advice of parents patiently given over the years (8,9), advocating a clean break with violent men, themselves doomed to a violent end; Wisdom (20–33), whose appeal is not furtive, but open, and who seeks to bestow, not ill-gotten gains, but her own spirit of wisdom (23). Tragically for Israel, she rejected both Wisdom's gentle pleading and the prophets' forthright, "Thus said the Lord," meriting fully the inevitable judgment (29–33).

(2) Lesson 2 (2:1–22). The rewards of wisdom. While wisdom is ultimately God-given (6) it must be sought with an intensity of desire which characterized the psalmist (2–4; cf. Ps 63:1). There is no contradiction here, but a paradox which underlines the fact that God's gifts are not given lightly, but to those who, by their attitude of heart and will, merit them.

The benefits of wisdom outlined (7–22) have both negative and positive, material and spiritual elements. The peril of associating with immoral women, which is referred to so frequently in Proverbs, is mentioned for the first time (16–19).

(3) Lesson 3 (3:1–10). Complete trust in God will be rewarded. For the Jew there was always the temptation to try to ensure blessing by an outward show of religion, and as we have noted, verses 9,10 *could* be misinterpreted. But the context stresses the requirement of heart loyalty and obedience (1–8). "God first" (6) is the fundamental need; without it an individual or a nation is impoverished (cf. Hg 1:1–11).

(4) Lesson 4 (3:11–20). One of the main themes in the later sections of Proverbs is the necessity for discipline, including chastisement when necessary, in the father-son relationship, which itself reflects the God-man relationship (11,12; cf. Heb 12:5–11). The other theme here is the praise of Wisdom and the benefits it bestows, anticipating 8:11–32 and foreshadowing the person and work of Christ himself.

(5) Lesson 5 (3:21–35). The two-fold goal of "wisdom . . . and common sense" (21) will result in safety (23–26) and guard against unwise acts (27–32). But the underlying security is found in verse 26, "the Lord is with you."

(6) Lesson 6 (4:1–9). Here the teacher gives his own testimony and shows that he is drawing on the accumulated wisdom of an earlier generation (1–6). There is an emphasis upon determination, with the will resolutely set to gain wisdom, as the verbs in verses 5,7–9 show.

(7) Lesson 7 (4:10–19). An equal determination is necessary to keep clear of evil men and their pursuits (14–17). Note the graphic description, both beautiful and frightening, of the two ways (18,19).

(8) Lesson 8 (4:20–27). The single-minded pursuit of righteousness and its corollary, the avoidance of every kind of evil (cf. 1 Thes 5:22) involves our hearing (20), memories (21), hearts (21,23), sight (25), and wills (26,27). It means total commitment to God.

(9) Lesson 9 (5:1–23). In blunt language that cannot possibly be misunderstood, the perils of sexual prostitution and the wisdom of faithfulness within the marriage relationship are underscored. In sexual relationships there can be no purely private morality; others are necessarily involved, and God is more than a concerned spectator (21). Harlotry was clearly widespread at this time, although technically, the penalty for it was death (Dt 22:20–24).

(10) Lesson 10 (6:1–19). First (1–5), there is straightforward advice about the need to avoid rash pledges. If foolish enough to be already involved, the sensible thing is to swallow one's pride and extricate oneself as soon as possible. The second lesson, to emulate the ants in their diligent preparation for future need (6–11), anticipates the contrasting attention later given to the sluggard (22:13; 26:13–16). The third lesson describes in detail the slick, deceitful "con-man," violent when crossed (12–19). He is to be avoided.

(11) Lesson 11 (6:20–35) returns to the subject of illicit sexual relationships, showing God's attitude to this particular form of sin. The wounded husband, too, will prove a formidable adversary should he discover such a liaison (33–35), and the effect upon the adulterer himself will be utterly disastrous (26–32). Happy the parents whose persistent wise counsel is taken to heart (20–24).

(12) Lesson 12 (7:1–27) gives a graphic illustration of the wiles of a prostitute. Speciously, the pleasures she offers appear alluring, enhanced by the element of risk, but in fact the night's adventure invariably proves to be "the road to hell" (27). With great daring, the writer advocates the universal "sweetheart." Wisdom, whose words, the commandments of God, will keep her "lover" in the testing time of temptation (Ps 119:9).

(13) Lesson 13 (8:1–9:18). Wisdom's direct appeal. In contrast to the smooth-tongued, deadly seductress of chapter 7 and the brazen, loud-mouthed prostitute of 9:13–18, there are two complementary pictures of Wisdom. The first, in 8:1–36, is one of the most remarkable examples of personification in the OT. Wisdom seeks, not the ruin of one but the welfare of all and so frequents the most heavily trafficked area for her universal appeal (1–5). Wisdom and integrity, righteous conduct and frankness are seen as inseparable (6–13). But there remains an emphasis on the blessings which result from the quest for wisdom (14–21). Kings, judges, and rulers are dependent on her, and success of the most desirable kind is her gift to her followers. Verses 22–31 are virtually a theological explanation for the pre-eminence of Wisdom, showing her close association with God's creative activity. Understandably, many Christians have seen in these verses an anticipation of Christ himself. The NT sees Christ as the answer to two of the most vital religious issues: how does God approach mankind, and how did he create the world? Here the answer is—by Wisdom. The connection may be carried into the next section (33–36), where Wisdom, like Christ in the NT, is seen as the one absolutely essential and desirable thing.

So Wisdom, in this chapter, reaches its highest expression in Proverbs. Yet it is brought down to earth, appealing to men at the crossroads of humanity and it is manifestly the supreme good from which all that is desirable and worthwhile flows. By Wisdom God and his standards are made tangible, which contrasts with the priestly and apocalyptic tendencies in the postexilic period which made God remote from man.

In the second picture of Wisdom (9:1–6), she is seen as a gracious, generous hostess, offering a banquet which issues in life (cf. our Lord's parable, Lk 14:15–24). A further contrast with the immoral woman in 13–18 notes, pointedly, that the latter's guests end up in hell. A series of proverbs on the contrast between the wise and foolish (7–12) come between the two pictures. They show how teachable the wise man is, in contrast to the fool. Once more the true foundation of life is clearly defined (10).

10:1–22:16. The collected proverbs of Solomon. Probably the 375 proverbs in this section were selected from the 3000 for which Solomon is credited (1 Kgs 4:32). Each verse is a unit, with a contrast or a comparison between its two lines. There are understandable repetitions (e.g., 14:12; 16:25), almost inevitable in a large collection of this kind. The sound common sense of the proverbial sayings, each of which has been proved in experience, is evident, but one must allow for varying levels; some appear rather mundane and close to worldly wisdom. But taken as a whole, they provide a practical guide, sanctioned by God, for everyday life. Again, it must be stressed that the religious life, based on the Law and the covenant relationship, is assumed, so there is little of theological significance, except that God is vitally concerned with the minute details of life, and religious issues are not entirely bypassed (e.g., 10:27,29; 14:27; 15:16,33; 18:10). This section in Proverbs cannot be read quickly; each verse demands a pause to allow its point to penetrate the mind.

The Hebrew word for proverb is itself many-sided. It is used of Balaam's message (Nm 23:7) and of Job's defense of himself (Jb 27:1–29:1); in Psalm 44:14 it is translated "byword" and in Isaiah 14:4 it has the meaning of "taunt." In Proverbs it is a striking, epigrammatic expression of some aspect of practical wisdom by example, warning, or precept. Since there is no systematic arrangement of the proverbs, the most helpful way of approach into this section may be by a consideration of the principal themes. It would be a valuable study to collate the references to each subject.

(1) The rewards of the righteous and the end of the ungodly (10:2,7,16,27–30; 11:3–9).

(2) The fool. The three Hebrew words translated "fool" can all have the sense of stubborn rebelliousness as well as dullness of intellect, so "rebel" is often an apt rendering. The fool is a sorrow to his parents and a menace to society. His mind is completely closed to reason and his unbridled words cause untold damage. In his case correction is pointless; he is beyond hope.

(3) The simple. The reference here is to the large, uncommitted group, neither fools nor yet numbered amongst the wise, but those who are open to the gentle persuasion of concerned wisdom teachers. The main appeal of the section is to this group rather than to the wise and prudent who have already "graduated."

(4) The lazy is often contrasted with the industrious (e.g., 10:4,5) and is mercilessly satirized for his apathy and weak excuses.

(5) The power of words. They can wound or heal (12:18). The stress on honest speech in contrast with deceitful, thoughtless words is well illustrated in the same chapter (e.g., 12:6,13,14, 17,19,22).

(6) Wisdom, inevitably, is a recurring theme. Chapter 13 shows how it may be derived from parents (1), the Scriptures (13) the class of the wise (14) and good company (20).

(7) Justice. The stress on this echoes the great prophets and doubtless mirrors the contemporary scene. In particular bribery is condemned (17:8,23; 18:16), as are false witnesses (19:5,9,28) while open-mindedness is commended (18:17).

(8) Neighborliness. Fair-weather "friends" are often referred to (e.g., 19:4,6,7) and contrasted with the constancy and faithfulness of the true friend (17:17; 18:24).

(9) Riches and poverty are approached in a variety of ways, but always with an emphasis on moral and spiritual rather than merely material prosperity (e.g., 21:6; 22:1,4). Care for the poor is frequently demanded (21:13) and with the highest of motives (22:2).

(10) Family life. There is an attractive picture of an ideal family, with its industrious husband, an understanding wife who is a blessing to him (12:4; 14:1; 18:22; 19:14), and obedient children, disciplined when necessary by punishment (13:24; 19:18; 23:13,14).

22:17–24:22. More wise advice. While the subjects considered and the general outlook are unchanged, the proverbs in this section are generally longer and there is an evident attempt to group together proverbs dealing with particular subjects, for example, the perils of strong drink (23:29–35). The religious motive of the editor of this section is evident; he writes that men may "Trust in the Lord" (22:19). The connections with the Egyptian Wisdom book of Amenemope has already been considered; the Egyptian version is longer and contains many verses not paralleled in Proverbs.

24:23–34. Additional proverbs. This may be viewed as a supplement to the previous section dealing further with the subjects of justice, wise business policy, slander, and laziness. The humorous but pointed proverb of the lazy man's field is the longest in the book.

25:1–29:27. Additional Solomonic proverbs. From the many Solomonic proverbs not included in the main collection (10:1–22:16) the aides of Hezekiah (715–686) selected and edited a further group. Again, there is evidence of an effort to group interrelated proverbs, for example, the place of the king (25:2–7); unwise litigation (25:8–10); the fool (26:1–12); laziness (26:13–16); the trouble-maker (26:17–27), etc.

30:1–33. The wisdom of Agur. The humility of the wise man in the presence of an all-wise God emerges clearly in Agur's introduction (1–4), a passage paralleled in Job 38,39. His teaching method was apparently to confront his students with a number of examples of a point under discussion, the "two . . . three . . . four" method, indicating that the catalogue was not complete and encouraging them to add further illustrations from their own experience. Agur was evidently in close and perceptive touch with life at every level.

31:1–9. The wisdom of Lemuel, derived from his mother, deals yet again with sexual relationships, the perils of intoxication, and the need to champion the poor and oppressed. Lemuel's name, meaning "belonging to God," probably tells us still more about his mother.

31:10–31. The ideal wife. Every verse of this poem, which was possibly anonymous, begins with a successive letter of the Hebrew alphabet, a device which often signified completeness. Coming at the end of Proverbs, a book which pulls no punches when dealing with the subject of the immoral woman, it gives, in antithesis, a refreshing picture of a cultured, well-to-do housewife and mother, providing an enlightening insight into several facets of contemporary life. As elsewhere in the book, her underlying relationship to God (30) results in desirable virtues which include trustworthiness (11), immense application (13–19,24,27), charity (19,20), foresight (21,25), wisdom, and kindness (26).   ARTHUR E. CUNDALL

See POETRY, BIBLICAL; WISDOM, WISDOM LITERATURE; SOLOMON (PERSON).

Bibliography. F.H. Horton, *The Book of Proverbs;* D. Kidner, *Proverbs;* W. McKane, *Proverbs;* W.G. Plaut, *The Book of Proverbs;* R.B.Y. Scott, *Proverbs—Ecclesiastes;* R.N. Whybray, *The Book of Proverbs; Wisdom in Proverbs;* J.G. Williams, *Those Who Ponder Proverbs.*

Providence. God's activity throughout history in providing for the needs of human beings, especially those who follow him in faith.

Significance of Providence. Providence occurs because God cares about the universe and everyone in it. All through the centuries of human existence there have been those who took great comfort in the fact of providence. It means realizing at certain places in life that God has been there before. It is the evidence that God has not left this planet alone in the vast universe or forgotten for a moment the human situation. God visits, touches, communicates, controls, and intervenes, coming before and between man and his needs. Providence is ground for thankfulness.

Counterfeit Concepts of Providence. The fact that the nonbelieving world has so many erroneous ideas about providence proves that this is an immensely realistic issue. At the heart of every nonbiblical proposal about providence is the denial of the personhood of God. In its place stands some cold principle or force, dominating man and clashing with his humanity. It may be all-pervasive or local. It may be rational or irrational, consistent or arbitrary. False providences include:

(1) *Fate.* Countless numbers of people have believed themselves to be trapped by a sometimes fickle and always foreboding fate. "As fate would have it . . . ," they say.

(2) *Luck.* Life is indeed fortuitous at times. Optimists speak of "fortune," or less solemnly of "luck." But, then, since this is all so impersonal, fortunetellers arose, and someone dreamed up "lady luck."

(3) *Serendipity.* This is the term used by the one who takes credit for unintentional discoveries of good things along the way in life. But he refuses to acknowledge God was there before him and does not give thanks.

(4) *History.* Some Marxist propagandists have championed their cause by saying, "History is on our side." They are appealing to a supposed inevitability of future events beyond their power to effect or non-Communists to hold back. "History" in such a statement appears to have taken on a divine dimension. Likewise when American leaders have affirmed a "manifest destiny" for the United States to be the superior power in the western hemisphere or in the world at large, the same kind of reasoning is employed.

(5) *Progress.* The development of science and technology, education and social evolution, and territorial conquests have made some men believers in progress as something more than what is seen. Until the two great world wars there was the illusion of a relentless momentum pushing upward and onward

forever. In some respects progress is but providence by another name, but not to the degree that man grabs the glory that belongs to God.

(6) *Nature.* Men like Ralph Waldo Emerson and Henry David Thoreau of 19th-century New England attributed to "nature" the gifts of providence. Nature is abstract. It was but a short step to personalize it as "mother nature."

(7) *Natural selection* and *the survival of the fittest.* Charles Darwin's classic on biological evolution, *The Origin of the Species,* appeared in 1859. It popularized two relatively new theories. For millions of people the mysterious decisions behind "natural selection" intrigued the thoughtful more than matters of providence. And the idea that "the fit survive" necessarily makes providence altogether unnecessary.

(8) *Know-how* or *applied science.* Many people suspect that the human race is sufficient in itself to make all things happen whether good or bad. Hybrids have been developed that can feed the world, if man so chooses (and the weather cooperates). The efforts of thousands of men can bring rocks back from the moon and produce photographs of the earth. There are even computer banks of data for those seeking proper dates and mates. The scientific journals afford much know-how for those eager to take life into their own hands. But when one's "own understanding" is substituted for the God of all providence, the excitement of being in the world with God is traded for being quite alone.

These counterfeit views compete with the idea of God's providence. Of course, they cannot all be true. Nor can they satisfy the inquirer whose personhood calls insistently for a personal providence that reflects a knowledge of his individual needs and uniqueness. Only the Christian doctrine of providence provides that.

Biblical Meaning of Providence. Providence is basically *God's provision for the needs of men on time.* The classic statement is found in Abraham's confession of faith in his life's most difficult test. He was under the duress of God's command to provide something he could not afford—his son in sacrifice. He struggled with the dilemma of losing his son or losing God's friendship. In answer to Isaac's question about a sacrifice for God, Abraham exclaimed, "God himself will provide the lamb for the burnt offering, my son" (Gn 22:8 NIV). The word *providence* means literally "to see before," and therefore by implication to do something about the situation. In this case, there was already upon Mt Moriah a suitable sacrifice, "a ram, caught in a thicket by his horns" (Gn 22:13). The unbelieving analysis of

Near the upper center is the Dome of the Rock, the Mt Moriah where providence was so important in Abraham's life.

that situation would understand only that through an ordinary process an animal had become entangled in dense underbrush, and coincidentally Abraham and Isaac happened to arrive on the scene. But to believing Abraham who was led for three days toward that one point in time and space in desperate need of a *divine* provision, it was altogether clear to him that God, by whatever process, had stationed the ram at the place of sacrifice for his use. "Provision" and "providence" are coordinately related to their verbal root, *provide,* and are essentially and etymologically the same. However, they are theologically distinguished in usage by providence's having come to mean in most all cases *divine provision* on the basis of foresight. Abraham was so moved by the whole experience of divine providence that he named that mountain with a new name celebrating God's providence—a name that lasted for at least half a millennium. Using two Hebrew words, he called the mountain (in a literal translation) "the Lord will see" [my need, and provide in the future as he did once here].

The great text on providence in the NT is also set in a context of sacrifice pleasing to God. Paul had reason to commend the Philippians' sacrificial support of his missionary work. To them he stated his unbounded confidence in the providential intervention of God: "And my God will supply every need of yours according to his riches in glory in Christ Jesus" (Phil 4:19). The sacrifice of Christ Jesus for us confirms the doctrine of providence with a most reasonable certitude. What God required of Abraham and did not exact (his son), he required of himself and did exact two millennia later. It is God's nature to supply, to foresee man's need and to provide for him.

Providence and the Nature of God. Immediately following his reassuring words to the Philippians about the treasury of providence ("his riches in glory"—Phil 4:19), the apostle Paul wrote a doxology to God "our Father" (Phil 4:20). Providence is appropriately pictured in the fatherhood of God. His fatherhood is the attribute, and providence the act that expresses it. Fathers provide and guide. Fathers construct conditions of opportunity for children without crowding their freedom. They exercise governance in a context of caring. Providence, therefore, as an activity of God flows naturally from the moral nature of God. If one begins to list those attributes inherent in his perfect fatherhood, it becomes necessary to list them all, if that were possible, for providence expresses the concern of God's whole personality.

General and Special Providence. God's immensely complex preparations for this earth with life-support systems exhibits one dimension of general providence. Ages ago, for instance, God caused organic matter to be amassed into peat bogs and to undergo a slow transformation so that modern man might be able to burn coal today for heat and electricity. In addition, God's general providence is appropriately conceived as restating the doctrine of *preservation.* Theologians speak of God's creation and preservation of the natural order. Despite the curse of God that permitted disorders in nature and death as the consequence of man's sin, preservation is dominant over disintegration, however difficult life may be in the world. God is in control and sustains natural life, although indirectly and mediately in a fallen world.

When large groups of people are in view, one also can speak of general providence, for God rules over all. Sovereignty over nations and the universe as a whole is basic to God's dispensing to humanity his provisions in wholesale quantities. If sovereignty pertains to what God *permits* in history, providence pertains to all the good he *provides* within historical processes.

The earth is no amusement park where every ride has its fixed circuit. Men move about on the earth with freedom, and it is special providence concentrated upon the people of God that makes their lives individually meaningful and exciting. Thinking of his whole situation in life the psalmist sang: "Thou dost beset me behind and before, and layest thy hand upon me" (Ps 139:5). Once one begins like the psalmist to catalog the special providence of God, it becomes a massive undertaking, because he meets God wherever he has been, where he is going, and in a thousand ways.

Biblical Instances of Providence. Even seemingly minor books of the Bible like Esther and Philemon substantiate the theology of providence. God provided Esther with information not even known by the Persian officials (Est 2:21–23) in order to preserve ultimately the Jewish people in a foreign land

as God's purposes were being worked out. Among the Gentiles, Onesimus, Philemon's slave, was providentially directed to the apostle Paul hundreds of miles away. Paul was able to meet his spiritual need, and he in turn became "useful," the meaning of his name, to Paul (Phlm 11).

Joseph's experiences in Egypt have been cited as a classic demonstration of providence (Gn 37:1–47:25). God was properly credited with turning the tragedy of his youth into the triumph of his maturity. The more protracted the series of events in the course of turning an evil act (as the betrayal of Joseph by his brothers) into a good thing for all concerned (as Joseph's being the natural savior of the Near East, alias agricultural minister of Egypt), the more beautiful God's providence is seen to be.

In order to straighten out Jonah's course and concepts, God supplied one of the largest of all creatures and one of the smallest to cross his paths. Both the great fish and worm were used by God providentially without disordering their natural instincts or habitats (Jon 1:17–2:10; 4:7).

The same Roman government that ordered the execution of Jesus was used providentially by God to spare the life of Paul four times in the closing decade of his life: at Corinth (Acts 18:12–17), outside the temple gate in Jerusalem (Acts 21:32–36), at the Sanhedrin (Acts 23:10), and from a Jewish plot on his life (Acts 23:12–35).

Practical Applications. (1) For some gamblers the need to win—the subconscious desire for providence—is a need greater felt than that for the money itself. Those believers who truly understand the extent to which God has provided for them past, present, and future will not fall into that temptation.

(2) Providence guarantees that there is built into every temptation a way of escape (1 Cor 10:13).

(3) One of the most staggering thoughts you can imagine is this. You will only meet in your lifetime far less than one-hundredth of one percent of all the people in your generation, and you will really get to know by face and name only a much smaller fraction. One has to live with the fact that he will never meet in this life hundreds of millions of interesting people. Providence becomes one's consolation: you will meet certain ones whom God brings across your path (e.g., Gn 14:18–20; 24:15; 29:4–12; Ex 2:5,6; 1 Sm 9:17; 25:23,24; 1 Kgs 18:7; Acts 21:16).

(4) The truth of providence takes the chance out of chance for God's people. That is, "The lot is cast into the lap, but the decision is wholly from the Lord" (Prv 16:33). The casting of lots was used to single out Jonathan when

King Saul's word had been unknowingly violated (1 Sm 14:24–45). The infant church, having two equally well-qualified candidates for one important office, affirmed their belief in providence by prayer *and* the drawing of straws (Acts 1:21–26).

(5) Astrology with its supposed influences on human characters and events is a poor counterfeit for biblical providence.

(6) The eye of faith recognizes God's timely interventions which other eyes fail to see.

(7) The proper response to providence is thanksgiving to the personal God. Confession of luck denies providence.

WILLIAM GRAHAM MacDONALD

See GOD, BEING AND ATTRIBUTES OF; FOREORDINATION.

Bibliography. G.C. Berkouwer, *The Providence of God;* W. Eichrodt, *Theology of the OT,* 2:167–185.

Pruning Hook. *See* TOOLS.

Psalms, Book of. Poems sung to musical accompaniment, originally the harp. The alternative title, the Psalter, refers to a collection of songs sung to harp accompaniment. The English title, therefore, broadly defines the form employed, whereas the Hebrew title of the book, "Praises" or "Book of Praises," suggests the content.

Author. *The Evidence of the Titles.* The Hebrew Bible credits David with 73 psalms, compared with 84 in the Septuagint and 85 in the Latin Vulgate. Asaph and Korah, the leaders of the levitical singing groups, are connected with 12 and 11 psalms, respectively (although Ps 43 is almost certainly to be attributed to Korah also). Two psalms are ascribed to Solomon (72; 127), one to Moses (90), and one to Ethan (89), while Heman shares the credit for one psalm with the sons of Korah (88). The remainder are sometimes called "orphan psalms" because of their anonymity.

The preposition "of" found in the titles, for example, "A Psalm of David" usually indicates authorship. But in the case of groups such as the sons of Asaph or Korah it may simply indicate the psalms which were included in their repertoire. Less plausible is the suggestion that it may also be rendered "for the use of," for example, some of the "Psalms of David" might be "for the use of" the Davidic king on some cultic occasion.

The Historical Allusions in the Titles. Many of the titles refer to specific events in the life of David (e.g., Pss 3,7,18,30,34,51, etc.). While the view that the majority of psalms were written in the postexilic period, which would mean that the historical references were valueless, is rarely voiced now, some scholars still regard them with scepticism. But there is evidence that the titles were added at an early date. When the psalms were translated into Greek there appears to have been some difficulty in translating the titles, possibly because of their antiquity. Further, if the historical references were added at a late date, there is no reason why plausible backgrounds could not have been supplied for all the Davidic psalms, instead of only a few. Moreover, the apparent disparity between the title and the actual content of some psalms (e.g., Ps 30) indicates that the titles were supplied by those who *knew* a connection which would never have suggested itself to a later editor. Admittedly, there are minor discrepancies between the titles and the references in the historical books, for example, in Psalm 34 David acts the madman before Abimelech, whereas in 1 Samuel it is before Achisch. But probably Abimelech was the general name (like "Pharaoh" for the kings of Egypt) for all the Philistine kings (e.g., Gn 21:32; 26:26).

Evidence of authorship and historical background in the titles, therefore, may be taken as a reasonably reliable guide. But the internal difficulties, together with the freedom exercised by successive translators into Greek, Syriac, and Latin indicates that they were not regarded as inspired.

The Case for Davidic Authorship. (1) The authenticity of David's lament over Saul and Jonathan (2 Sm 1:19–27) is generally accepted. This indicates a deeply poetic spirit and a generous temperament which prepares us to accept those psalms ascribed to David which evidence similar characteristics. "The last words of David" is another Davidic poem in the historical books (2 Sm 23:1–7).

(2) David had a reputation as a skillful musician at Saul's court (1 Sm 16:16–18). Amos comments on his inventiveness as a musician (Am 6:5), while the Chronicler repeatedly stresses his contribution to the musical aspect of the temple cultus (e.g., 1 Chr 6:31; 16:7; Ezr 3:10). The Jewish historian, Josephus, declared that "David composed songs and hymns to God in varied meters." The probability is that David, as well as amassing materials and preparing the plans for Solomon's temple, also gave definitive attention to the temple worship. This is his place in Jewish tradition as Moses is identified with the Law.

(3) The early monarchy, with a freshly secured independence, national prestige, and a new prosperity, would most likely be a time of artistic creativity. David was at the heart of this movement.

(4) There is a close correspondence between David's career as described in the historical books and certain of the psalms, for example, his sin concerning Bathsheba and Uriah (2 Sm

11:2–12:25) and Psalm 51, as witnessed in the title. David's lapses and genuine repentance, as well as the varied aspects of his career—shepherd, fugitive, warrior, and so on—find expression in many of the psalms attributed to him. The correspondence between the David of the psalms and the David of the historical books is close, especially in the display of strong faith in God.

(5) Although some scholars believe that when "David" is mentioned in the NT it is simply as a reference to the Book of Psalms and not an ascription of authorship, a straightforward interpretation of the NT text strengthens the case for Davidic authorship. David is specifically named as the author of various psalms in Matthew 22:41–45; Acts 1:16; 2:25,34; Romans 4:6; 11:9.

(6) In conclusion, while it would be unwise to contend that every psalm attributed to David was actually written by him, a few may have been composed on the pattern of accepted Davidic psalms or for succeeding Davidic kings, there is strong support for the view that the substantial nucleus of the Psalter is Davidic. Moreover, it is probable that some of the anonymous psalms were the work of the "sweet psalmist of Israel" (2 Sm 23:1). Hebrews 4:7 refers one of these, Psalm 95, to David (see also Acts 4:25 and Ps 2).

Date. Increasingly, modern scholarship accepts an early dating for the psalms, although Engnell's contention that probably only one psalm (137) is postexilic may be too extreme. The study of psalmody in Egypt, Mesopotamia, and neighboring Canaan, as well as the realization that many poems embedded in the early books (e.g., Ex 15; Dt 32, 33; Jgs 5) predated David, increase the disposition to accept David's traditional contribution to the music and poetry of Israel's cultus. In particular, the material from Canaanite Ugarit, where the structure and form of psalms connects with 120 of Israel's psalms, is noteworthy. Julius Wellhausen's once-accepted maxim, "The Book of Psalms is the hymn-book of the second Temple," is completely outmoded. It *may* be true, but most of the psalms formed the hymn book of Israel in the period of the monarchy.

General assent may be given to Mowinckel's assertion that "The classical age of psalmography is the period of the monarchy." Psalm 137 is clearly exilic, and Psalms 107:2,3; 126:1 allude to the return from captivity. Psalms 44,79 are probably, but not conclusively, postexilic. Some scholars regard Psalm 74 as the latest psalm, its historical references (3–9) being thought to connect with the Maccabean period in the early 2nd century BC. But the destruction of Jerusalem in 586 BC is quite as suitable; historical dogmatism is unwise, as

there may have been other, unrecorded catastrophes in the postexilic period. The Book of Psalms was probably the product of a considerable period of growth. The incidence of Davidic psalms in the first section indicates that it was completed early, possibly toward the end of David's reign. The remainder of the process of compilation is difficult to reconstruct, but the fact that the titles, with their allusion to authors, events, and musical directions, become less frequent in the two final collections (90–150) lends support to the probability that the collections were combined chronologically in the sequence in which they are found today. Traditionally, Ezra is credited with the final grouping and editing of the psalms, a hypothesis which appears reasonable in the light of his vital contribution to the systematic reshaping of the national religious life. In any case, the process was completed before the translation of the Psalter into Greek (the Septuagint) at the end of the 3rd century BC, since the traditional order is found there. General, but not complete support comes also from the evidence of the Dead Sea Scrolls. At some point minor dislocations occurred. Psalms 9 and 10 may have originally formed one psalm (as in the Septuagint), and there is a strong case for combining Psalms 42 and 43. Less convincing is the view that Psalms 114 and 115 should be linked, or that Psalm 19 combines two distinct psalms (1–6; 7–14).

Background. *The Cultic Connection of the Psalms.* (1) Musical directions. As the Book of Psalms lies before us, its connection with the cult is apparent. Fifty-five psalms are addressed to the Choirmaster, and, as we have noted, 23 or 24 are linked with the 2 main guilds of levitical singers, Asaph and Korah. The musical instruments, such as stringed instruments (Ps 32:2) and flutes (Ps 5) are noted.

Cave 4 at Qumran. The Dead Sea Scrolls help confirm the order of the biblical psalms.

Probably other terms concern musical directions: Selah, which occurs 71 times, may indicate a pause or crescendo; Higgaion (Ps 9:16) may recommend a meditative attitude; while seemingly obscure references like "The Hind of the Dawn" (Ps 22), "Lilies" (Pss 45, 80) and "The Dove on Far-off Terebinths" (Ps 56) may indicate the tunes to which the psalms were to be sung. The precise meaning of other terms such as "Shiggaion" (Ps 7) or "Alamoth" (conjecturally a choir of ladies, Ps 46) may also be in the realm of musical directions.

(2) Connections with specific aspects of the cult. Certain psalms connect with particular aspects of the cult, such as the "memorial offering" (Pss 38, 70); "A Song for the Sabbath" (Ps 92), and "A psalm for the thank offering" (Ps 100). Others show internal evidence of such connections. For instance, the second section of Psalm 22 (22–31) appears to be associated with a vow-offering (25) following the answer to the psalmist's desperate plea in the first section (1–21). There is public testimony "before the congregation" (22,25) and probably participation in a communal, sacrificial meal (26).

(3) Definition of adversity. One other factor, namely, the stereotyped way in which distress, in its various forms, is recorded, suggests a communal use of psalms which may have originated as individual prayers. Rarely is the actual predicament of the psalmist made clear; instead a series of metaphors or similes is employed, including: assaults by wild animals (Pss 22:12,13,16; 59:6,7); the elemental forces of nature, such as waves and billows (Ps 42:7); the snares and pit-traps of the hunter (Pss 7:15; 57:6; 91:3); references to weapons (Pss 57:4; 91:5); and enemies (Pss 17:9; 55:18), who may, of course, be literal as well as metaphorical. Note the series of vivid similes in Psalm 102:3–11. Such psalms are readily usable by others whose distressed circumstances may, in fact, be vastly different.

(4) Structure of the Book of Psalms. The Psalter, possibly in conscious imitation of the five books of Moses in the Law, is divided into five sections (1–41; 42–72; 73–89; 90–106; 107–150), separated by four doxologies (41:13; 72:18,19; 89:52; 106:48). While the editorial comment in Psalm 72:20 notes that the psalms of David were ended, Davidic psalms are found later in the book (Pss 86, 101, 103, etc.) suggesting that at least some of these sections circulated independently until their inclusion in the final collection. Such independence is further indicated by the duplications in the various sections (e.g., Ps 14 and 53; 40:13–17 and 70) and by the use of different names for God, who is usually referred to as "Lord" in the first collection and as "God" in the second.

(5) Canonicity. In the various recensions of the third section of the Hebrew canon, the Writings or Holy Books, the Book of Psalms is almost invariably placed first. It was clearly regarded as the most important book in this section, and in Luke 24:44, "Psalms" is synonymous with "Writings" as its title. While the canonicity of all the contents of the Writings was not finalized until the end of the 1st century AD, it is likely that the Book of Psalms was accepted as inspired long before this, probably by 300 BC.

It must not be inferred that all the psalms had their origin in the cultic life of the community, but the sanctuary *was* the focal point of Israel's worship for the greater part of the OT period. Prayer was possible elsewhere, but whenever practicable, it was customary for the worshiper to present his petitions at the main sanctuary. And thanksgiving in ancient Israel was almost invariably connected with a thank-offering, vow-offering, or free-will offering. The psalms could have been composed by individuals, like David, who had the requisite technical ability, and it must be appreciated that poetry, an unfamiliar medium to most Western civilizations, was the natural way for the ancient oriental to express his emotions. Or the individual could have engaged a member of the levitical guilds of musicians to frame either his supplication or thanksgiving. Gradually, a comprehensive collection of psalms would be available for the use of individuals, the congregation, and even the entire nation in any conceivable situation. Once finalized, this collection served not only the subsequent needs of Israel but the devotional requirements of successive generations of Christians. Whatever the origin of an individual psalm, each has finally been incorporated in a cultic setting and it may be assumed that the best of Israel's psalmody has thus been preserved.

Purpose and Theological Teaching. *The Doctrine of God.* In both adversity and prosperity the psalmists indicate a strong faith in God and a clear conception of his attributes. He is seen in personal relationships with individuals within the covenant community. Understandably, anthropomorphisms (ascribing human characteristics to nonhuman things) abound, with references to God's voice, words, ears, eyes, face, or hands and fingers. No exception needs to be taken to this. Anthropomorphisms of this kind are, in fact, widely used by 20th-century Christians. Their great value is that they make God real to the worshiper. How else could man describe God except in terms of his own understanding? The only viable alternative is probably the vague mysticism of pantheism. Describing God's interaction with man in terms of human categories involves no compulsion to accept that he is merely "glorified man."

The monotheism of the psalms emerges clearly in Psalms 115:3–8; 135:15–18; 139. God is viewed as the Creator (Pss 8:3; 89:11; 95:3–5), with references to the creation mythology of surrounding nations (e.g., Ps 89:10) serving merely as illustrations of his almighty creative power. He is proclaimed as the Lord of history (Pss 44, 78, 80, 81, 105, 106) and as the sovereign controller of nature (Pss 18:7; 19:1–6; 65:8–13; 105:26–42; 135:5–7). The psalmists never tired of celebrating God's absolute greatness, which nowhere appears as a barrier to the reality of fellowship which his worshipers might enjoy with him.

The Doctrine of Man. The Psalter is a "God-centered" book, but man has a worthy place, in spite of the vast gulf between him and his Creator (Pss 8:3,4; 145:3,4) and the limitation of his earthly life (Ps 90:9,10). In the will of God he occupies a responsible, mediating position; creaturely, but with authority over all other created beings (Ps 8:5–8). The relationship with a righteous God is endangered by sin (Ps 106) but God is gracious and long-suffering (Ps 103), faithful and forgiving (Ps 130). While references to the sacrificial system are not lacking (Pss 20:3; 50:8,9), the emphasis is upon a personal religion that demands obedience and a surrendered heart (Ps 40:6–8). Psalm 51 indicates a depth of sin with which the sacrificial system was totally inadequate to cope; the psalmist could only cast himself, in total penitence upon God's mercy. Man's moral obligations (Pss 15; 24:3–5) and loyalty to the Law (Pss 19:7–11; 119) are fully accepted. Throughout, there is the revelation of a strong personal relationship which encourages prayer and praise and invites trust.

The Afterlife. The traditional Hebrew view of Sheol as the abode of the departed, without distinction, where all but mere existence has perished, is evidenced. The chief complaint of the devout man was that, in Sheol, all meaningful relationship with God ceased (Pss 6:5; 88:10–12). Increasingly, however, it was recognized that, since God was almighty, even Sheol was not exempt from his reach (Ps 139:8). Added to this was the preciousness and strength of fellowship with God which, faith demanded, *surely* could not be terminated even by death. Psalms 16:9–11; 49:15; 73:23–26 well illustrate this tendency. The Psalter, therefore, witnesses to an important transitional phase in Israel's belief, without reaching a developed doctrine of a personal resurrection.

Universalism. Passages like Psalms 9:11; 47:1,2,7–9; 66:8; 67; 117:1 calling upon all nations to acknowledge and praise God, show an awareness of his sovereignty over all nations. But this universalism does not appear to involve any desire to convert the heathen nations and, indeed, it is balanced by strong particularistic elements. God's covenant relationship with his people and his mighty deeds on their behalf are the chief items for which the praise of all nations is summoned (Pss 47:3,4; 66:8,9; 98:3; 126:2). As elsewhere in the OT the role of Israel is passive; her continued existence witnesses to God's faithfulness and brings glory to him.

Abiding Value. Whatever the emotion of the psalmists, be it bitter complaint, anguished lament, or joyous exultation, all the psalms reflect one or other of the many aspects of communion with God. The reader may look "into the heart of all the saints" (Luther) as they faced life's experiences in the awareness of a God who was all-seeing, all-knowing, and all-powerful. The strength of that personal relationship with God which typified OT worship at its best is exemplified here, and the many echoes of the psalms elsewhere in Israel's literature show how powerful was the influence of these testimonies of the faithful. The fact that, almost invariably, little specific detail is given of the psalmists' actual conditions has made it easier for the Psalter to become the universal hymn book and devotional treasury of God's people, in both public and private worship, until and including the present day. Modern life, materially, is vastly different from that of ancient Israel, but God remains unchanged and so do the basic needs of the human heart. The Holy Spirit, therefore, can still use this spiritual treasury as a means of revelation and communication between God and man. Few books in the Bible have exercised so profound an influence or been so widely used.

Main Characteristics of Hebrew Poetry.
Word Structure. In Hebrew poetry little corresponds with Western concepts of rhyme and meter. Every line contains between 2 and 4 words, each of which is accented in a regular manner in relationship to its main tone syllable, thus forming a type of rudimentary meter. The commonest "meter" has 3 such words (or word units, since a single Hebrew word, when translated, may form a short sentence in English) in the first line and 3 in the second and is termed 3+3 meter. Other variants are 2+2, 3+2, and 3+3+3. Such variants are also found in the poetry of contemporary Canaan and Babylon. Occasionally a change of meter may occur within a psalm.

Parallelism. The most obvious feature of Hebrew poetry is that the unit is not a verse or a single line but a balanced couplet, with a short pause between the lines and a more definite pause at the end of each couplet. The main types of parallelism are:

(1) Synonymous. Here the lines, repeating the same thought, reinforce one another (e.g., Pss 1:2,5; 49:1; 61:1; 83:14).

(2) Antithetic, where there is a contrast of some kind between the two lines (e.g., Pss 1:6; 37:9; 90:6).

(3) Synthetic, where the second line completes or supplements the thought of the first (e.g., Ps 3:4).

(4) Climactic or stair-like parallelism, where part of the first line is repeated, the thought then being carried forward an extra step. Sometimes a triplet, as an alternative to the couplet, utilizes this method (e.g., Ps 29: 1,2; cf. 96:7,8).

Other types are sometimes listed, but most of these are merely variants of numbers 1–3.

Acrostic Poems. In these, each verse begins with a successive letter of the Hebrew alphabet (which contains 22 letters). Psalms 9,10,25, 34,37,111,112,145 employ this method, while Psalm 119 contains 22 eight-verse sections, every verse in each separate section beginning with the appropriate letter of the alphabet. This method, in Western thought, had often been branded as artificial, but there is evidence to show that it was used to suggest the idea of completeness. Moreover, poetry was a much more natural form of expression to the oriental, especially where emotion was involved, than to the average modern westerner.

Content. *Introduction.* Until relatively recent times the customary approach to the Psalter was to consider the title and content of each psalm individually, seeking to establish a reasonable historical situation for each. The work of Hermann Gunkel in the earlier part of this century constituted a watershed. Many have followed his views, with or without modifications; some have rejected them, but almost all have felt compelled to make some reference to his monumental contribution. Gunkel's view was that the psalms, most of which were regarded as free compositions, were nevertheless composed with the background of the cult where the various types were established by tradition. He claimed to detect five principal categories: Hymns, Communal Laments, Royal Psalms, Individual Laments, and Individual Songs of Thanksgiving. Supplementing these were a number of minor types, chief of which were Songs of Pilgrimage, Communal Songs of Thanksgiving, Wisdom Psalms, and Cultic and Prophetic Liturgies. He also wisely provided a "Miscellaneous Group" for psalms which could not be neatly categorized. The great value of Gunkel's work was that the psalms were viewed, not merely as literary works, but as arising in definite life situations,

thus capturing the moods and emotions of the individual psalmists. Subsequent scholarship has tended to emphasize the cultic connections of the psalms, sometimes in a rather limited way. For example, it has been held (e.g., by Sigmund Mowinckel and Arthur Weiser) that most of the psalms were linked with one of Israel's major feasts, Tabernacles, the background of which is regarded as closely corresponding with the New Year Festival in Canaan and Babylon. This theory will be dealt with later. Nowadays, a recognition of the wide range of religious experience within any particular category has led to a less rigid approach to classification. The following broad divisions may be distinguished:

Psalms of Praise. The Hebrew title, "Praises," defines accurately a large part of the contents of the book. Each of the first four sections concludes with a doxology, while the fifth section concludes with five psalms, each of which begins and ends with one or two "Hallelujahs." The last of these, Psalm 150, sounds the call to total praise. God is to be praised for his being, for his great acts in creation, nature, and history on both the individual and the communal level.

(1) Individual praise. In comparison with the number of individual laments, there are relatively few psalms in this category. Those normally included are Psalms 9, 18, 32, 34, 116, and 138. This may, in part, be due to the universal tendency to complain rather than to express thanks, but a number of the laments do, in fact, include the note of thanksgiving for the anticipated deliverance, and, in addition, the normal round of congregational thanksgiving would allow the individual to express his personal praise. However, it was customary in the temple cult to give a verbal act of thanksgiving before the whole assembly whenever a vow-offering or a thank-offering was made. Such public testimony, and the communal meal associated with this type of sacrifice, is indicated in Psalms 22:22–26; 66:13–20; 116: 17–19. The inclusion of such opportunities for personal praise and testimony in the structure of the temple cult must have added warmth and significance to worship. Each act of deliverance and every experience of God's mercy became part of salvation history, which was a cumulative, ongoing concept, not simply a recital of God's deeds in earlier centuries.

(2) General communal praise. This is sometimes entitled "Hymns" or "descriptive praise," its main feature being that, not being linked to a particular act of deliverance, it could be used repeatedly in various cultic settings. God is usually referred to in the third person, not directly. Psalm 103 may be taken as representative of this group. It begins and

ends with individual references (1–5,22b), but the central section (esp vv 6–14) shows that the psalmist was part of a worshiping community. There is first of all the imperative call to praise God for the full range of his mercy to each individual, including physical and spiritual deliverance and his sustaining and satisfying grace. Then the focus changes to his great works in history (6,7) which forms a natural basis for the recital of those gracious qualities revealed so consistently during the course of the national history, especially his tender, fatherly care (8–14). The frailty of man contrasts with God's constancy (15–18) and his rule, being universal and absolute (19), merits the praise of all things, living and inanimate, in heaven and on earth (19–22). There is, however, a great number of possible variations in the way in which God is celebrated, as Psalms 113 and 136, which come within this class, illustrate.

(3) Specific communal praise. Occasionally termed "declarative praise," this type of psalm connects with a particular outstanding evidence of God's mercy and would most naturally follow soon after the event itself. Deliverance from an enemy provides the occasion for most of the psalms in this category (e.g., Ps 124, 129). Psalm 66:8–12, now the nucleus of an expanded recital of God's goodness, was possibly once complete in itself. Psalms 46–48 may form a trilogy connected with the remarkable deliverance of Jerusalem from Sennacherib's Assyrians in 701 BC (2 Kgs 18:17–19:37). Psalm 67 was probably composed in gratitude for a particular harvest. It is easy to see how psalms of this type could, in the process of time, acquire a more general usage.

(4) Praise for the God of nature. In the earlier part of Israel's history such a stress was placed on a God omnipotent in history that there was, almost inevitably, a lack of emphasis on God's sovereignty in nature. It has even been alleged that, until the 8th century BC, Israel had *no* view of God as Creator, which would have made her unique in the ancient world. Certainly there is no such lack of awareness in the psalms. The first part of Psalm 19:1–6 pictures the praise of God sounding from the heavens; Psalm 29 celebrates him as the God of the thunderstorm which, sweeping in from the Mediterranean near Lebanon, pursues its awe-inspiring path southward into the wilderness of Kadesh, with the result that "in his temple" (the created world?) all are praising, "Glory, glory to the Lord" (9); his sovereignty and self-sufficiency in this world are celebrated in Psalm 50:10–12; he is the God of growth and harvest (Ps 65:9–13); in Psalm 104, often called the "Hymn of Creation," he sustains and supplies everything on the earth and

in the seas and is the absolute Lord of all life (29,30). There is no confusion between God and his creation; even the seemingly permanent heaven and earth will perish but "you go on forever" (Ps 102:25–27). Nature's role is to proclaim the glory of God (Ps 19:1) and to praise him (Ps 148). Man sees himself as insignificant when set against those forces of nature which are themselves dwarfed by God, hence the awareness of the immeasurable gulf between God and man which the former has bridged by his grace (Ps 8).

(5) Praise for God's kingship. A relatively small group of psalms (Pss 47, 93, 96–99) celebrate the kingship of God in a way which goes beyond the ascription of praise noted in the foregoing groups. They are marked by acclamation, both by shouting and clapping, when God "ascends," presumably the reference is to his throne (Ps 47:1–5; cf. 99:1,2). "The Lord reigns" (Pss 93:1; 97:1; 99:1) is the frequent cry, and the nature of his reign is extolled (Ps 99:4,5). Gunkel described these psalms as "eschatological songs of Yahweh's enthronement" but it was one of his successors, Mowinckel, who, developing Gunkel's work, formulated a theory, which, resting on the "Enthronement Psalms" (a group of about 40, including those noted above) has been associated with the view popularly known as "Sacral Kingship." Mowinckel held that in Jerusalem during the Davidic monarchy, in conjunction with the Autumn New Year Festival, Jehovah's enthronement as the universal King was celebrated as the highlight of the cultic year. He regarded the normal translation of the recurring phrase, "The Lord is King!", as incorrect and held that it should be rendered, "The Lord *has become* King." In this theory, which rests heavily on Babylonian evidence and on late rabbinic tradition, the New Year Festival was the time when God renewed every aspect of his rule, reenacting his creative triumph over the primeval powers of chaos. There is considerable divergence among the advocates of this theory concerning the details of this "Accession Festival," but there is general agreement that a ritual drama portraying the conflict between God and the enemies of Israel culminated in a procession where the ark of the covenant, symbolizing God's presence, was carried in triumph to the temple, where it was again placed in its customary position. The main purpose of this procedure was that God, being acclaimed afresh as universal Lord, would grant his favor upon the year which followed. His covenant with the reigning Davidic king, as his vice-regent, would be renewed. This festival, with its notes of optimism and victory, may have been the original "Day of the Lord" (Am 5:18) which

later, disillusioned generations projected into the future.

Most of the biblical evidence brought forward in support of this theory is drawn from the psalms. It has come under critical scrutiny on many major issues:

It rests heavily on the annual Babylonian Accession Festival and on somewhat scanty Canaanite evidence. Similarities in time and procedure are stressed more than the noticeable differences. There was considerable divergence in attitudes toward the monarchy throughout the ancient Near East. Whenever a king claimed to be the representative or embodiment of the deity it would be natural for him to act as a divine substitute, but this was not always the case in Mesopotamia. In Israel the attitude to the king was vastly different from any other region, due to the insistence that God was the real King of his people. The Davidic king was no more than the "first among equals," in no way divine, although God's son by adoption. Moreover, any view that David took over the idea of "sacral kingship" from Jebusite Jerusalem which he captured faces the difficulty that David appears consistently concerned to uphold the traditional values of Israel and not to alienate his own religious leaders.

Apart from psalms, there is no clear biblical evidence of what is conceived to be the principal feast of preexilic Israel. Another similar difficulty is accounting for the overall failure of the Davidic monarchy with this theory's glowing background of faith and practice.

Many of the non-Israelite texts used in support are admittedly difficult; yet frequently a dogmatic interpretation, in the interests of the theory, is set upon them. Further, a literary connection cannot establish actual dependence; for instance, God, in the psalms, is sometimes described in terms which are paralleled by the references to Baal in the Ugaritic texts (e.g., 68:4,33), but his unique being is not thereby compromised.

The fundamental objection is not concerning the person of the king in relation to his contemporary counterparts, but concerning God when compared with the nature deities of the ancient world. Throughout the area the Autumn New Year Festival was linked with the end of the summer drought and the onset of the autumn rains. The mythology corresponding to this, envisaged a nature god (e.g., Baal in Canaan or Tammuz in Mesopotamia) who died in midsummer, descended into the underworld, but was revived at the Autumn Festival, with the encouragement of the correct cultic procedures. Thus the dormant forces of nature were stimulated for the ensuing agricultural year. There can be no question of Israel's

God dying and rising again, therefore no question of his reenthronement. He could not be equated with other gods. This objection is so weighty that the proponents of the theory now accept that, in Israel, any connection with death-resurrection and fertility have been eliminated.

It is reasonable to insist that, accepting Israel's high view of the sovereignty of God, references to his rule could hardly be confined to one festival in the year! But how can we differentiate between a once-a-year cultic use and any noncultic use of the expression "The Lord reigns!"?

Although the views of sacral kingship and an Accession Festival have come under warranted criticism, it is still possible that the New Year was the time when Israel was reminded of the kingship of God. The use of these accession psalms at this time of the year in the liturgy of the synagogue may connect with their usage in the preexilic Jerusalem temple, since traditions are notoriously tenacious. It is to be expected also that the Davidic covenant would be celebrated at some point, and a time link with ceremonies connected with the monarchy amongst Israel's neighbors is reasonable. The views of H.J. Kraus appear more acceptable in this light. He accepts the observance of Tabernacles, linked with the exodus and wilderness wanderings and thus a historically based feast, not merely a harvest festival. But when the Davidic dynasty was established, then, in his view, Tabernacles became the feast when God's unchanging sovereignty was reflected in the continued rule of his vice-regent. It was not a case of the human king taking God's place but rather the king evidencing God's enduring covenantal relationship. The Festival would therefore develop naturally out of God's choice of David and his successors, as a distinctively Hebrew celebration. While such theories retain a conjectural element however, there is no doubt that praise to God for his eternal kingship was a marked feature of the psalms.

Psalms Concerning the Davidic King. In view of the prominence given to the king in the preceding section, it would be wise to consider next this group, often called the Royal Psalms. Psalms 2, 18, 20, 21, 45, 61, 72, 89, 101, 110, 132, and 144 are usually included. They do not form a literary category, since psalms of various types are included, but they all have some reference to the king, the nature of his rule, and his relationship to God. Since the Davidic monarchy was terminated in 586 BC, these psalms, almost certainly, were composed before that date. The language in these psalms could be interpreted in support of the view of sacral kingship noted earlier; for example, Psalm 45, a royal marriage psalm, contains the assertion "Your divine throne endures for ever and ever" (45:6). But this is best understood in terms of the throne being regarded as the Lord's, occupied by the king as his representative. Similarly Psalm 2:7, "You are my Son," probably implies no more than a sonship by adoption, while Psalm 110:1, "Sit at my right hand," indicates the privileges and prerogatives which the king enjoys as God's vice-regent. The balance of the OT evidence concerning the king shows that the monarchy in Israel was qualified by the nature of God's covenantal relationship with his people; the king did not enjoy the absolutism claimed by most of the rulers of surrounding kingdoms.

Nevertheless, the king *did* play a vital role; indeed, there is strong evidence to suggest that the Sinaitic covenant was subordinate to the Davidic covenant during the dynasty of the Davidic kings. The blessings of God's rule were mediated *through* his reigning representative. Psalm 72, for instance, which may have been composed as a coronation oracle, speaks of the benefits resulting from that righteous government which adequately reflects the role of God. This placed great responsibility upon the kings, who, with few exceptions, sadly disappointed the hopes of the pious in Israel.

But the underlying hope itself persisted, being projected into the future, and thus forming the basis of the Messianic hope, a remarkable feature of Israel's history. The monarchy, which was a brief interlude (1020? BC–586 BC) and which ultimately was a failure, nevertheless gave definition to the imperishable hope that God's righteous rule would ultimately be established through the man of his choice. Indeed, the word *Messiah*, meaning "anointed," has often been limited to the promises which link directly with the Davidic king. A broader interpretation is desirable, including all references which foreshadow Christ in the fourfold aspect of his mission, King, Prophet, Priest, and Servant. However, most of the so-called Royal Psalms could be re-categorized Messianic Psalms, and were interpreted as such in the early Christian church, as witnessed in Christ's general statement that the psalmists wrote of him (Lk 24:44) and by particular NT quotations. The main psalms concerned, and the NT references are:

1. Psalm 2 (Acts 13:33; Heb 1:5; 5:5), while linked with the Davidic king, nevertheless speaks of a universal vindication and rule (8,9) which far transcended even David's rule. Further, the picture of the Davidic king, anointed (2) to rule on the earth as the representative of God who is enthroned in heaven (4), strongly suggests Christ's mediating, incarnate ministry.

2. Psalm 45 (Heb 1:8,9), a marriage psalm for one of the Davidic kings, possibly Solomon, speaks not only of a permanence and quality of rule, but in the most obvious translation of verse 6, addresses him, "Your divine throne, endures for ever and ever." The writer to the Hebrews clearly accepted this interpretation and used it in contradistinction to the exalted status of even the angels, reinforcing it with two other quotations from the psalms which originally applied to God (Ps 97:7; 102:25–27; cf. Heb 1:6,10–12).

3. Psalm 110 (Mt 22:43–45; Acts 2:34,35; Heb 1:13; 5:5–10; 6:20; 7:21) is the most frequently quoted messianic psalm. The language, speaking of the privileges, universal victory and continuing priesthood of David and his successors, would be considered hyperbolic and possibly misleading but for its fulfillment in "great David's greater Son." In contrast to the angels who are privileged to stand in God's presence (Lk 1:19), Christ the Son sits in the place of power and authority (Heb 1:13).

4. Psalm 132 (Acts 2:30). Other psalms which could also be designated messianic but are not specifically included among the Royal Psalms are: Psalm 8 (1 Cor 15:27); Psalm 40 (Heb 10:5–10); Psalm 72, with its idealized picture of the nature, consequences, and extent of the rule of God's representative; Psalm 118:22, 23 and the "Passion Psalms," which will be considered separately.

Zion Psalms. This group could have been classified as a subsection of Communal Praise, but due to the close connection, historically, between God's choice of the house of David and Jerusalem (Pss 78:68–72; 132:11–13) and their subsequent interrelated fortunes, we consider them at this point. There was a biting satire in the request of the Babylonians to the refugees of a shattered city to "Sing us one of the songs of Zion!" (Ps 137:4 NIV), but it witnesses to the existence of such a collection. Praise of Zion was, in fact, almost synonymous with the praise of the Lord who dwelt there. Jerusalem's continued survival, in spite of its vicissitudes, was ample demonstration of God's enduring greatness (Pss 48:11–14) and peculiar affection for the city which housed his temple (Ps 87:1–3). Psalms 48, 76, 84, 87, and 122 are the main psalms in this category, but the theme itself appears widely throughout the psalms (e.g., 102:16; 125:1; 126:1–3; 133:3; 147:2, etc.). The basis of the NT concept of a heavenly Jerusalem, the spiritual home of the regenerate of all nations, finds its origin in this concept, especially in Psalm 87.

Laments. These are associated with specific occasions of distress and are of two types:

1. National. The prophetic and historical books give several examples of the kind of oc-

casion, such as drought, locust infestation, or enemy attack, which could prompt national laments, and also the inward and outward attitudes which accompanied them (e.g., Jgs 20:23,26; Jer 14:1–12; 36:9; Jl 1:13,14; 2:12,15–17; Jon 3:5). There is a regular structure in the 10 or so psalms of this class: the distressing situation is first described; God is petitioned to come to the aid of his people, often with the reminder of his past mercies for Israel; finally, there is often an expression of confidence that God would heed their cry. Israel's adversaries are clearly in mind in Psalm 14, 44, 60, 74, 80, and 83, and possibly Psalms 58, 106, and 125 reflect situations less critical.

2. **Individual.** There are so many of this type (approximately 50) that it is frequently described as "the backbone of the psalter." Their most obvious features are the sharpness of complaint and the bitterness of attack upon those responsible. As in the national laments, there is often complaint against God, especially for his lack of attention or his tardiness in intervening. The basic components of this type are almost identical to the national laments, except that often they conclude with the avowal to praise God which anticipates deliverance (e.g., Ps 13:5,6). Frequently, the lament is accompanied by the thanksgiving consequent upon the deliverance sought and experienced, as illustrated in the two sections of Psalms 22:1–21; 22–31 and 28:1–5;6–9. As noted earlier, this possibly indicates the cultic connection of the psalms, further suggested by the fact that the reason for the distress of the supplicant is rarely indicated, being described symbolically by the forces and creatures of nature and by analogies drawn from hunting or military conflict. This latter fact undoubtedly facilitated the universal use of the psalms.

A special problem concerning this class arose in the context of OT scholarship and almost as rapidly faded into insignificance. For some decades early in the 20th century, it was questioned whether the "I" of these psalms was truly individual or rather the personification of Israel or the king speaking representatively. This view, an expression of the awareness of the solidarity of Israel as a people with a "corporate personality" has now been generally abandoned. Both personal and corporate features were clearly evidenced in Israel. However, it is possible that in a few cases the "I" could be representative, for example, in Psalm 102, where the apparently strong individualism of the earlier section (1–11) progresses to petition concerned with national issues (12–28). The psalmist may have been the king, speaking on behalf of Israel on some cultic occasion.

Three subsections of this group call for particular comment:

a) **Imprecatory Psalms.** Approximately 20 psalms contain passionate pleas for the overthrow of the wicked in language which is often shocking to those illuminated by Christ's example and teaching (e.g., Pss 35:4–8; 41:10; 69:22–28; 109:6–20; 137:7–9). Any instant condemnation of this attitude must, however, be tempered by certain relevant considerations:

1. The cry for vengeance was not purely personal; it was firmly believed that God's honor was at stake (e.g., Ps 109:21). In an age where there was a less-developed view of an afterlife it was axiomatic that rewards and punishments, resulting from obedience or disobedience to God, must be observable within the sphere of this life. Whenever this was not apparent it would seem that no righteous God existed, and the name of God was dishonored (e.g., Ps 73:10). This burning desire for the eradication of evil and evil men sprang from a consciousness of a moral God and virtually demanded the triumph of truth.

2. The poetic, oriental attitude is naturally prone to the extreme language of hyperbole, a feature not confined to the psalms (e.g., Neh 4:4,5; Jer 20:14–18; Am 7:17). Such language is startling; indeed, part of its function was probably to startle, to express and promote a sense of outrage.

In the pre-Christian period, therefore, such outbursts were not completely unjustifiable. But in the light of the fuller revelation in the NT such an attitude cannot now be condoned. The Christian is to love as Christ loved (Jn 13:34); to pray for his enemies and to forgive them (Mt 5:38–48; Col 3:13). The theme of judgment continues into the NT and is indeed heightened there, since Christ's coming has left man without excuse (Jn 16:8–11), but there can be no place for purely private vengeance.

b) **Passion Psalms.** The four psalms in this group (Pss 16, 22, 40, 69; some scholars would also include Pss 102, 109) may also be regarded as messianic. They connect with that line of OT prophecy which interprets the Messiah's ministry in terms of the Suffering Servant who features prominently in Isaiah (e.g., Is 42:1–9; 52:13–53:12). Of these four, Psalm 22 is the most remarkable. Its content formed at least part of Christ's consciousness when he was on the cross (22:1; cf. Mt 27:46) and other connections with the crucifixion scene are noteworthy (e.g., 22:6–8;14–18). Two further considerations are even more significant: there is no suggestion of any awareness of sin; the suffering of the psalmist appears completely unjustified; there is no imprecatory element, even in the face of bitter persecution. This connects with the sinless Christ (2 Cor

5:21), who could even pray for his executioners (Lk 23:34). Psalm 16:10 anticipates the triumph of the incorruptible Christ over the grave (cf. Acts 2:24–31). Psalm 40:6–8 foreshadows the incarnation and self-giving redemptive work of Christ (Heb 10:5–10). Psalm 69 refers to the isolation resulting from a commitment to God's cause (69:8,9) and anticipates the part played by Judas in what was fundamentally God's work in Christ (69:25,26; cf. Ps 109:8; Is 53:10; Acts 1:20).

c) Penitential Psalms. Psalms 32, 38, 51, 130 are the clearest examples, although, tradition-ally, the church has also included Psalms 6, 102, 143, where there is no explicit confession of sin. However, a point made earlier may weaken this last qualification. In an age when adversity in its various forms was seen as God's judgment for wrongdoing, the admis-sion of distress was tantamount to a confes-sion of guilt. In the four main examples there is an intensity of feeling and a deep sense of the enormity of sin in God's sight, although, as elsewhere, there is no indication of specific sin, even in Psalm 51, which is surely to be connected with David's sin against Bathsheba (2 Sm 11,12). Significantly, David bypasses the sacrificial system, which was totally ineffica-cious in his case, casting himself entirely on the mercy of God (Ps 51:1,16). The burden of unconfessed sin is clearly revealed in Psalm 32 and sin's searing corrupting effect in Psalm 38. In Psalm 130 an originally individual lament has been augmented by two verses (7,8) to adapt it for national use.

Wisdom Psalms. While it is accepted that prophets, priests, and wise men all functioned at the major sanctuaries, some overlap in their modes of expression is to be expected. Proverbial forms are not infrequently found in the psalms (Pss 37:5,8,16,21,22; 111:10; 127:1–5). Psalm 1, probably an introduction to the whole Psalter, contrasts the diverging paths of the righteous and ungodly (cf. Ps 112), while Psalms 127 and 128 concentrate on the bless-ings which attend the godly. Psalm 133 is writ-ten in praise of unity. The problem of explain-ing the sufferings of a righteous man and the apparent prosperity of evil men, dealt with in the wisdom literature in the Book of Job and in the prophets also (e.g., Jer 12:1–4), is taken up in Psalms 37, 49, and 73. The divine perspec-tive, which a man may share in the sanctuary, and the preciousness of the fellowship which the godly enjoy with God, outweighing all other considerations, are the means by which the psalmist is lifted out of his depression in Psalm 73.

The historical psalms should be included in this category, since they underscore the les-sons arising from the favored nation's often

Sheep, the subject of part of the familiar Psalm 23.

bitter experience. It is apparent that Israel de-lighted in the recital of salvation history. The main psalms, and the periods covered are: Psalm 78, from the exodus to the establish-ment of the Davidic monarchy (note the de-clared intention to teach in vv 1–4); Psalm 105, from Abraham to the conquest of Canaan; Psalm 106, from Egypt to the judges; Psalm 136, from the creation to the Promised Land.

Psalms of Trust. While some of these may also be classified as laments, the dominant fea-ture of this group is the serene trust in God revealed, which makes them particularly suit-able for devotional use. Many begin with an affirmation of gratitude to and affection for God. Psalms 23 and 27 are the outstanding ex-amples of this type, which could also include Psalms 11, 16, 62, 116, 131, and 138.

Other Minor Groups. The liturgical struc-ture of Psalm 136 draws attention to a group of psalms which clearly connect with the cultus. A similar antiphonal element appears in Psalm 15, often called a "liturgy of prepara-tion for worship," and in Psalm 24, which may have been associated with a procession to the temple on a festival occasion. Psalm 84 is evi-dently a Pilgrim Psalm, while the Songs of As-cent (Pss 120–134) were probably also con-nected with the thrice-yearly pilgrimages to Jerusalem for the Feasts of Passover, Weeks, and Tabernacles.

The difficulties in any precise categoriza-tion of psalms are obvious; many refuse to fall neatly into one group, hence the occasional overlap. What is clearly evident is a pulsating, vital religious life which has found its clearest expression in the Book of Psalms. To say that it expresses the worship and devotion of the ordinary man is a simplification; kings and priests, wise men and prophets all contributed to this remarkable collection. Yet there re-mains the truth that, in God's sight, all men, regardless of human achievement or privilege, are "ordinary," for all are sinners on the one level of need dependent wholly on his grace and goodness. So, the worshiping community of ancient Israel, and the saints of every succeeding generation, in the vastness of their diversity, have nevertheless found the expression of their own hearts' condition, desires, and devotion in this unique treasury.

ARTHUR E. CUNDALL

See POETRY, BIBLICAL; DAVID; MESSIAH; MUSIC AND MUSICAL INSTRUMENTS; TABERNACLE, TEMPLE; SINGERS IN THE TEMPLE; WISDOM, WISDOM LITERATURE.

Bibliography. G.S. Gunn, *God in the Psalms*; J.H. Hayes, *Understanding the Psalms*; J.A. Lamb, *The Psalms in Christian Worship*; A. Maclaren, *The Book of Psalms*, 3 vols; H. Ringgren, *The Faith of the Psalmists*; N.H. Snaith, *Hymns of the Temple*; *Studies in the Psalter*; C.H. Spurgeon, *The Treasury of David*; C. Westermann, *The Praise of God in the Psalms*; R.E.O. White, *A Christian Handbook to the Psalms*.

Psalm Titles. Superscriptions to numerous psalms.

See MUSIC AND MUSICAL INSTRUMENTS; PSALMS, BOOK OF.

Psaltery. KJV rendering of harp.

See MUSIC AND MUSICAL INSTRUMENTS (NEBEL).

"P" Source. Name used by the proponents of the Documentary Hypothesis (a critical theory that attributes the five books of Moses to several authors and redactors) for those portions of the Pentateuch supposedly derived from the Priestly Code. The Priestly Code was a collection of priestly writings detailing the functions of the priesthood as practiced in postexilic Judah during the fifth century BC.

See DOCUMENTARY HYPOTHESIS.

Ptolemais. Alternate name for Acco, a city in northern Palestine, in Acts 21:7.

See ACCO, ACCHO.

Pua. KJV form of Puvah, Issachar's son, in Numbers 26:23.

See PUVAH.

Puah. 1. One of two Hebrew midwives Egypt ordered by Pharaoh to kill Hebrew males at birth. However, she feared God and did not carry out the order (Ex 1:15).

2. Father of Tola, a judge of Israel (Jgs 10:1).

3. Alternate form of Puvah, Issachar's son, in 1 Chronicles 7:1.

See PUVAH.

Publican. KJV translation for "tax collector."

See TRADES AND OCCUPATIONS (TAX COLLECTOR).

Publius. Name of a resident of the island of Malta, mentioned in Acts 28:7,8. He hosted Paul and others briefly after a shipwreck had stranded them on the island as they journeyed to Rome. Publius bore a title which indicated that he was an important official on Malta at the time. His ailing father was healed by Paul during the visit.

Pudens. Companion of Paul mentioned in 2 Timothy 4:21. At the close of the letter his personal greetings are communicated to the recipient. Three other companions, who also send greetings, are named: Eubulus, Linus, and Claudia.

Puhite. KJV spelling of Puthite, a member of a family of Judah's tribe, in 1 Chronicles 2:53.

See PUTHITE.

Pul. 1. Name given to Tiglath-pileser, the Assyrian ruler (745–727 BC), when he became king of Babylon (729–727; 2 Kgs 15:19; 1 Chr 5:26). The meaning of the name is unknown, and Assyrian manuscripts do not mention it, suggesting to some scholars that Pul was Tiglath-pileser's original name.

See TIGLATH-PILESER.

2. African people mentioned only in Isaiah 66:19 (KJV). Their connection with Tarshish and Lud has strongly suggested that Pul is a copyist's error for Put (RSV), a people related to the Egyptians and possibly a subculture of Libyans.

See PUT (PERSON).

Pulse. KJV translation of a Hebrew word perhaps better rendered as vegetable (Dn 1:12,16). Not wishing to defile themselves with the king's food, Daniel and his friends requested permission to live on a diet of vegetables and water. The Hebrew word translated as vegetable literally refers to "things sown" and probably includes any kind of edible seed.

See PLANTS.

Punishment, Everlasting. See HELL.

Punishments. See CRIMINAL LAW AND PUNISHMENT.

Punite. Member of a family in Issachar's tribe headed by Puvah (Nm 26:23).

See PUVAH.

Punon. Town identified with the modern Feiran, lying on the eastern side of the Arabah in the hill country of Edom. Punon lay conveniently on the road from Edom through the Negeb to Egypt. It enjoyed an abundant supply of water and the presence of copper. Punon became an ancient smelting center of copper (c. 2000 BC), which was mined in the vicinity or was imported to Punon. When the Israelites passed by Punon on their way into Transjordan (Nm 33:42,43), Punon was at a low point in her industrial history. Remains of slag heaps abound in the vicinity. Archaeological evidence indicates that Punon was an extensive settlement at the time of the patriarchs (Middle Bronze Age) and that after a period of 500 years of no settled occupation, it was resettled around 1300 BC. The mining and smelting operations lasted till 700 BC, and were not renewed until the Nabataeans. Eusebius reports that Christian martyrs worked in the mines along with criminals at Punon. In the Byzantine period the Christians built a basilica and monastery. An inscription bearing the name of Bishop Theodore (c. 587/8) was found in the monastery.

Pur. Hebrew word, meaning "lot," from which the name of the Jewish festival Purim celebrating their deliverance from Haman was derived (Est 3:7; 9:24,26).

See FEASTS AND FESTIVALS OF ISRAEL.

Purah. Gideon's servant, who accompanied his master on a secret night visit to the Midianite camp where they were encouraged by the Lord (Jgs 7:10,11, KJV Phurah).

Purification. See CLEANNESS AND UNCLEANNESS, REGULATIONS CONCERNING.

Purim. Hebrew name, meaning "lots," for the Jewish festival celebrating their deliverance from Haman (Est 9:26–32).

See FEASTS AND FESTIVALS OF ISRAEL.

Purple. Highly prized dye extracted from sea snails. Purple was used for dyeing fabrics in the tabernacle and making the clothes of wealthy people (Ex 25:4; Jgs 8:26).

See ANIMALS (SNAIL); COLOR; FASHION AND DRESS.

Put (Person). Third of Ham's four sons, who most likely settled in northern Africa and is perhaps the forefather of the peoples of Egypt and Libya (Gn 10:6; KJV Phut; 1 Chr 1:8).

See PUT (PLACE).

Put (Place). Ancient nation, descended from a man of the same name. It is commonly identified as Libya, although it has been argued that it was the Punt of Egyptian records, somewhere along the northeast coast of Africa, perhaps Somalia. Its association with Egypt, Cush, and Canaan and the usage of the name in the OT make the Libyan location probable. In the OT the Libyan people are called Lubim, a name which always appears in the plural.

Ancient Libya was situated to the west of Egypt, the site of modern Libya, on the Mediterranean coast of North Africa. The Egyptians distinguished several groups of Libyans. The Tjehenu, who inhabited the coastal region, were primarily herdsmen. They were represented in Egyptian art as having long hair and wearing only a belt and a penis-sheath. They were listed among the Nine Bows—the nine traditional enemies of Egypt. The Tjemehu were nomads and were physically different from other African ethnic groups in that they had blond hair and blue eyes. Their relationships with Egypt date back to the Old Kingdom and from time to time they tried to make their way into Egypt. The Libu (after whom the country was named) and the Meshwesh (western Libyans) are described as fair-skinned, tattooed, and with long leather garments.

The Egyptians had commercial and military contacts with Libya throughout its history. The Libyans periodically attempted to penetrate Egypt from the northwest. From the Middle Kingdom there is the story of Sinuhe (c. 2000 BC), which begins with the death of Amenemhet I, while his son, Senusert (Sesostris) was fighting the Libyans in the western Delta. Later, Libyans did infiltrate the delta, but Seti I and Ramses II kept them under control. The Stela of Merneptah (c. 1224–c. 1214 BC), which mentions Israel, is largely devoted to Egypt's victory over the Libyans. Ramses III drove them out of the western Delta in connection with his victorious land and sea struggles with the Sea Peoples.

Eventually Libyans gained control of Egypt and made up the 22nd (Bubastite) dynasty (c. 946–c. 720 BC) and 23rd (Tanitic) dynasty (c. 792–c. 720 BC). Their kings bore foreign names like Sheshonk (the Shishak of the OT, 1 Kgs 11:40; 14:25; 2 Chr 12:2–9), Osorkon, and Takelot.

The first occurrence of Put in the Bible is in the table of nations (Gn 10), where Put is listed as a son of Ham, along with Cush (Nubia, Ethiopia), Egypt, and Canaan (Gn 10:6, KJV Phut; cf. 1 Chr 1:8).

Jeremiah 46 speaks of the battle of Carchemish and refers to the warriors of Ethiopia (Cush) and Put, "who handle the shield," among the hosts of Egypt (v 9). Ezekiel names Persia, Lud, and Put as being in the army of Tyre (Ez 27:10 KJV Phut). Nahum mentioned "Put and the Libyans" among the allies of Thebes who were unable to stop the onslaught of the Assyrians against Egypt (Na 3:9). Daniel predicts that the Antichrist will have the Libyans, Egypt, Cush, and others in submission (Dn 11:43).

In Isaiah 66:19 the Hebrew text reads "Pul,"

while the Greek version gives "Put," which most of the English translations follow. Here Put is listed between Tarashish and Lud in a list of nations that will be told of the glory of God.

Similarly, in Ezekiel 30:5 the Hebrew has "Cub" and the Greek "Put." Since Put appears earlier in the verse, the RSV, NIV, and NASB retain the reading Put in that instance, but translate the second Put (Cub) as "Libya." The AV translates the earlier Put as "Libya" and gives the transliteration "Chub" later in the verse.

In the records of King Xerxes of Persia (485–465 BC), Libya is listed among the nations subject to Xerxes.

Puteoli. Italian seaport town on the Bay of Naples. It was a normal stopping place for seafaring travelers and cargo going to Rome. Paul, following his landing at Rhegium, resided with Christians in Puteoli for seven days before he was taken to Rome (Acts 28:13). The modern city is called Pozzuoli.

Puthite. Family of Judah's tribe from Kiriath-jearim mentioned only in 1 Chronicles 2:53 (KJV Puhite).

Putiel. Father of Eleazer's wife and the grandfather of Phinehas (Ex 6:25).

Puvah. Issachar's son, who went with Jacob and his household to Egypt where they sought refuge from the severe famine in Palestine (Gn 46:13, KJV Phuvah). Puvah founded the Punite family (Nm 26:23, KJV Pua), and is alternately called Puah in 1 Chronicles 7:1.

Pygarg. KJV translation for antelope in Deuteronomy 14:5.

See ANIMALS (ANTELOPE).

Pyramids. See EGYPT, EGYPTIANS.

Pyrrhus. Father of Sopater of Beroea, who, with others, accompanied Paul on his return trip through Macedonia (Acts 20:4).

Qq

Qesitah. Weight unit of uncertain value.

See WEIGHTS AND MEASURES.

Qoheleth. Hebrew title for the Book of Ecclesiastes, meaning "the preacher." Derived from a word meaning "to call an assembly," it came to mean "to address an assembly." The author of the book calls himself Qoheleth in numerous passages.

See ECCLESIASTES, BOOK OF.

Quail. See BIRDS.

Quart. See WEIGHTS AND MEASURES.

Quartus. Christian who joined the apostle Paul in sending greetings to the church in Rome (16:23).

Quartz. See MINERALS, METALS, AND PRECIOUS STONES.

Quaternion. KJV translation for "squad" in Acts 12:4.

See ARMS AND WARFARE.

Queen, Queen Mother. Word used to describe a reigning monarch, a queen consort, or a queen mother. The Queen of Sheba became the epitome of wealth at the time of her visit to the luxurious court of King Solomon (1 Kgs 10:1; Mt 12:42; Lk 11:31) when she arrived with a large retinue, and camels bearing gold, jewels, and spices. Candace, Queen of Ethiopia, is mentioned when a eunuch, a senior minister in her court, is converted by Philip while on a visit to Jerusalem (Acts 8:27).

In Jewish history, Athaliah, thinking that she had murdered all rival claimants to the throne within the royal family, reigned for six years (2 Kgs 11:3), and Salome Alexandra succeeded her husband Alexander Janneus from 76–67 BC. A queen consort normally played a minor role, although Bathsheba (1 Kgs 1:15–31), who was determined to ensure the succession of her son, and Jezebel (1 Kgs 21), who plotted the false accusation leading to the death of Naboth, are notable exceptions. The powerful role was that of queen mother. She not only ruled over the royal household, but was held in respect both by the court and by the monarch (cf. Ex 20:12). Her requests were unlikely to be denied (1 Kgs 2:20). As the mother of the king, she was unique, whereas his wives might share their position with several others. Maacah, queen mother of Abijam, even retained her authority during much of her grandson's reign (1 Kgs 15:2,10,13; 2 Chr 15:16). The queen mother was crowned (Jer 13:18), and Bathsheba, powerful enough as queen, was seated at the right hand of King Solomon when she became queen mother (1 Kgs 2:19).

See ISRAEL, HISTORY OF.

Queen of Heaven. Goddess mentioned by Jeremiah in his denunciations of Judah's idolatry (Jer 7:18, 44:17–19,25). The women of Judah were especially involved. In an earlier prophecy he observes that "the children gather wood, the fathers kindle fire, and the women knead the dough, to make cakes for the queen of heaven." After the destruction and depopulation of Jerusalem in 586 BC, a group of exiles fled to Egypt, carrying Jeremiah with them. There he again condemned the idolatry which had brought this disaster. This provoked a sharp reaction from the men and their wives. In the recent catastrophe they had seemingly vowed to return to the worship of the queen of heaven. They claimed that since they had given up this worship, presumably during the reforms of Josiah, nothing but trouble had befallen the nation—the complete reversal of Jeremiah's affirmation. To this, the prophet's response was that if this was their attitude nothing remained to be said. He delivered them over to their reprobate mind, asserting that in Egypt, among the Jews that settled there, true worship would become extinct, so that even the name of the Lord would not be heard (44:25–28).

The goddess is generally identified with Ishtar, a Babylonian deity associated with the planet Venus, whose worship was probably imported into Judah during Manasseh's reign. Through the preaching of the prophets and the reforms of Josiah it largely died out, but must still have been cherished secretly, possibly among the women of the royal court.

See CANAANITE DEITIES AND RELIGION.

Quirinius.
Roman governor of Syria at the time of Jesus' birth (Lk 2:2). According to the Roman historian Tacitus (*Annals* 3.48), Publius Sulpicius Quirinius was elected consul of Syria in 12 BC. Around 7 BC he was appointed, along with Varus, legatus or governor of Syria. His duties concentrated on military and foreign affairs, while Varus concerned himself with civil matters. Quirinius' first administration as governor lasted several years during which time he led a successful expedition against the Homonadenses, an unruly group of rebel mountaineers who lived in the Cilician province of Asia Minor, and superintended in his region the empire-wide census decreed by Caesar Augustus. Luke records that Jesus' birth took place at the time of this first enrollment "when Quirinius was governor of Syria" (Lk 2:2, KJV Cyrenius, original Latin name later modified to Quirinius in Greek), and according to Matthew, during the days of King Herod the Great (2:1)—presumably in 4 BC.

Quirinius became rector to Gaius Caesar in 1 BC and married Aemilia Ledipa in AD 2, whom he subsequently divorced. In AD 6, he was reappointed legatus of Syria, perhaps serv-

Pottery from the Herodian period, when Cyrenius (Quirinius) was governor of Syria.

ing in this position for a couple of years. In this second administration Quirinius again supervised a census of Judea. However, the second census was not administered according to Jewish custom as the first, but taxed the Jews as a subservient people to the Roman state, thus causing Jewish opposition and rebellion toward Rome. This is probably the census referred to by the Jewish historian Josephus (*Antiq.* 17.13.5) and Gamaliel in his speech (Acts 5:37). The remainder of Quirinius' career was probably spent in Rome where he died at an advanced age (*c.* AD 21).

See CENSUS; CHRONOLOGY, NEW TESTAMENT.

Qumran.
Ancient Jewish religious community near the site where the Dead Sea Scrolls were found in 1947.

See DEAD SEA SCROLLS; ESSENES; JUDAISM.

Quotations of the Old Testament in the New Testament.
One of the most complex problems in interpreting the Bible is in understanding how NT writers quote the OT. Obviously nothing is so formative and authoritative for the NT writers as Scripture. However, the way that they use OT passages often seems strange to modern readers. The use of OT quotations is important in the discussion of the relation and unity of the Testaments, which is a central theological issue. Despite the fact that there is great diversity as well as unity between the Testaments, the church cannot tolerate the attempt to devalue or reject the OT.

This conclusion is obvious if sufficient attention is given to the amount of the OT embedded in the NT. The OT has provided the words and ideas for much of the NT. Unless one has a Bible that prints OT quotations in bold print, this may not be easily seen, for the NT writers often weave the OT words into their own without indicating they are borrowing from the OT. One Bible that does use bold print for NT passages that explicitly use OT words reveals that there are over 400 such texts. Almost half of these are introduced by a statement like "Scripture says" to draw attention to the fact that the authority and thought of the OT is being implemented. For the others, however, the OT words are woven into the fabric of the author's own statement.

In addition to the over 400 passages consciously using the explicit words of an OT text, there are well over 1000 places where there is an allusion to an OT text, event, or person. The difference between a quotation and an allusion is sometimes debated for particular texts, but usually the distinction is that in a quotation the author consciously uses the words of an OT passage whereas with an allusion he has the texts in mind but is not consciously trying to use the words.

Quotations are easy to identify if there is an introductory formula such as "Scripture says" (as in Rom 10:11; cf. Is 28:16). Where there is no introductory formula it is easy to overlook explicit quotations (Rom 10:13; cf. Jl 2:32).

The allusions are, of course, harder still to recognize, but they often provide the key to interpretation. For example, John 1:14–18 with its mention of glory, grace, and truth, Moses, and the fact that no one has seen God is much more easily and profoundly understood in connection with Exodus 33:17–34:8, where the glory of God and his grace and truth are revealed to Moses. The author is showing that a much more complete revelation of God is given in Jesus than was given Moses in the account recorded in Exodus.

In addition, significant light is shed on many NT passages from OT passages with similar ideas and words even where the NT author may not have been consciously alluding to those texts (e.g. Mt 16:19; Is 22:22). What was behind the author's thinking is not certain, but in such cases the OT reflects the thinking, the culture, and language of the NT period.

Distribution of Old Testament Quotations.

Particular insight can be gained by noticing where and how the NT writers used the OT. The books that show the most dependence on the OT are Matthew, John, Romans, Hebrews, 1 Peter, and Revelation. Such a statement can be misleading, however, because the writers have different methods.

Matthew quotes or consciously reflects the wording of OT passages about 62 times, almost half of which have an introductory formula. The Book of Revelation, on the other hand, never quotes the OT and never has an introductory formula but is probably more dependent on the OT than any other NT book. The Book of Hebrews quotes or consciously reflects the OT about 59 times, again half of which have an introductory formula, but the Gospel of John does so only 18 times, nearly always with an introductory formula. However, the allusions to the OT are present on virtually every page of John's Gospel, so much so that some scholars have argued that he has modeled his account on the exodus narrative, the Jewish feasts, or OT persons and images. Paul's Letter to the Romans uses the OT 54 times (about ¾ of which have introductory formulas), but nowhere else so frequently (e.g., 1 Cor 16 times, Gal 11 times, Phil one time, 1 Thes one time).

In addition to the indication that Philippians and 1 Thessalonians use the OT only once each, some other books make explicit use of the OT rarely or never. Colossians, Titus, Philemon, and the Johannine letters do not use the OT at all; 2 Timothy and Jude use the OT only once; while 2 Peter and 1 Timothy make use of it twice.

The important point is to realize that the OT is used most frequently in circumstances where the audience is familiar with the OT or where the OT is essential for describing the events relating to Christ and the church. The books using the OT most frequently (Mt, Jn, Rom, Heb, 1 Pt, Rv) either stem from or are addressed to a Jewish context or, as in the case of Romans and John, deal specifically with the relation of Jews and Christians. The Gospels generally, including Mark and Luke, make rather extensive use of the OT because the language of the OT is necessary to convey the identity and importance of Jesus in the purposes of God. Similarly 1 Peter uses the OT frequently because the author is trying to convey to his persecuted audience that they are the people of God and the inheritors of the promises of God.

Difficulties in Interpretation.

Often when people think of quotations of the OT in the NT they think only in terms of prophecy. Some have been guilty of counting up the OT statements that the NT applies to Christ and the church and viewing these OT texts as predictions that prove Jesus is the Messiah and has performed God's promised work. Such a procedure is filled with problems because it is too simplistic and does not do justice to either the OT or to the way the NT uses it. Indeed the early church used the OT to show that Jesus fulfilled the promises of God and did God's work, but the use the church made of the OT was quite varied and much of it cannot be classified as predictive prophecy. Prophecy itself is too complex to be limited to predictive thinking. Some of the most obvious examples of the difficulties appear in Matthew's Gospel although they are by no means confined there. Matthew 2:15—"Out of Egypt I called my son"—is a quotation of Hosea 11:1, but in Hosea these words do not refer to the Messiah. They refer to the nation of Israel. Similarly Matthew 2:18 quotes Jeremiah 31:15 ("A voice was heard in Ramah, weeping and great mourning, Rachel weeping for her children, and refusing to be comforted, because they are no more") as fulfilled in the slaughter of the innocent babies in Bethlehem, but in Jeremiah the weeping is over the destruction of Jerusalem. John 12:40 views Isaiah 6:10 as fulfilled in Jesus' ministry, but this verse deals with the call of Isaiah and is not a prediction concerning the ministry of the Messiah. The examples could be multiplied but these should be sufficient to illustrate the problem. For this reason the NT writers have often been accused of twisting the Scriptures, but this charge is as simplistic as the thought that all prophecy is predictive and in fact springs from the same error. Therefore, any attempt to understand the use of the OT in the NT will have to deal with the variety of ways in which the OT is used and with the methods employed by the NT writers.

There are other difficulties that are encountered as well. Sometimes the NT writer will indicate that some fact related to Christ is a fulfillment of the OT but the explicit text which he had in mind cannot be identified. For example, John 7:38 introduces the words "Out of his heart shall flow rivers of living water" with the statement "as Scripture has said." No OT text reads this way. Possibly the allusion is to the rock that provided water in the wilderness (Ex 17:1), or to the waters that flowed from the new temple (Zec 14:8) or, more generally, it is a reference to Isaiah 58:11. Similarly, the difficulty in determining the OT text behind the prophecy that Christ will be called a Nazarene (Mt 2:23) is notorious. Probably the reference is to Isaiah 11:1 and the Hebrew word there translated as "branch," but the connection is not easily made and is not certain. A third example of this kind of difficulty is in 1 Corinthians 14:34, where Paul indicates that women should be in submission just as the Law says, but there is no OT text expressing this idea. His statement is probably to be understood as a summary rather than a quotation or allusion. Similarly on a few occasions an OT text is seemingly attributed to the wrong OT book. In Mark 1:2,3 an OT quotation is attributed to Isaiah but the quotation is really a conflation (or mixing) of Exodus 23:20, Malachi 3:1, and Isaiah 40:3. Matthew 27:9,10 quotes a passage which is said to be from Jeremiah when really it is dependent on Zechariah 11:13 and might best be described as a summary of Zechariah 11:12,13 with certain words included from Jeremiah 32:6–9. These two examples do not create a major problem, however, for the determination of the origin of the words may be due to their use in collections of quotations from various prophets, in which case the more prominent prophets would be used to designate origin.

The wording of the quotations of the OT text does not always conform to the modern form of the OT. Just as today there are numerous translations of the Bible, when the NT was being written there were various forms of the OT text. With regard to the Hebrew text (for the OT was written mostly in Hebrew), there were different traditions. Such differences in the Hebrew traditions would have been relatively small. Because of the increasing importance of Aramaic after the Babylonian captivity and of Greek after the conquests of Alexander the

Great, the OT was also known and used in both these languages when the NT was being written. In fact, the Jews found it necessary in their synagogue services after reading the Hebrew OT to paraphrase the reading in Aramaic so all could understand. These paraphrases were later written down and are known as Targums. The Greek translation of the OT that stems from the 3rd century BC is known as the Septuagint, but there were also other Greek translations in use. This being the case, the wording of a NT quotation is not identical in every detail to the text of the Hebrew OT.

Added to the fact that there were various forms of the text known in 1st-century Palestine is the complicating factor that NT writers often did not intend to quote the OT exactly. The use of formal quotation marks is a modern device, and ancient writers were not so taken by technical precision. They were more concerned with the intention of a text and consequently might copy or quote it verbatim, quote it from memory, use or adapt part of a verse, or even change certain words as they borrowed the verse to express their points. (The NT writers often use the OT words describing God's actions in the past to explain what he has done in their time.) The importance of any differences between the NT quotation and the OT depends on the use to which the quotation is put and the degree to which the use is dependent on textual differences.

Some examples should illustrate the nature of these difficulties. Ephesians 4:8 quotes Psalm 68:18. Whereas the Hebrew and Septuagint read, "You ascended to the heights, you lead captivity captive, you received gifts among mankind," Ephesians records the verse as "After he ascended into the heights, *he* led captivity captive; he *gave* gifts to men." Paul is stressing that Christ has given grace to people for ministry. Has he adapted the wording of the OT to make his point or is he aware of a text that read "*he gave* gifts"? Some versions do have this reading. In fact the Targum understands this verse as Moses giving the words of the law to the children of men, and Paul may well be adapting this understanding to the new revelation that has come in Christ.

Matthew 1:23 quotes Isaiah 7:14, but as is well known, there are distinct differences between the Hebrew text and the wording in Matthew. The Hebrew reads "Behold the young woman will become pregnant and will bear a son and you will call his name Immanuel," whereas Matthew's text records "Behold, the *virgin* will become pregnant and will bear a son, and *they* will call his name Immanuel." The Septuagint does have the specific word "virgin," like Matthew, but is not the source of Matthew's quotation since other differences exist. Some have argued that the change from "you will call" to "they will call" was made by Matthew when he applied the words to Jesus. However, there are several traditions known for this part of the quotation and partial support for the reading in Matthew is provided by the text of Isaiah found among the Dead Sea Scrolls.

Romans 11:26,27 is a conflation of Isaiah 49:20,21 and part of Isaiah 27:9, but there are important differences. One of these is that the OT has "the redeemer will come to Zion," whereas Romans has "the deliverer will come *from* Zion." The change to "from Zion" could indicate that Paul had a different textual tradition, could be the result of an intentional change by Paul, or, more probably, could reflect the wording of Psalm 14:7.

An awareness of the difficulties involved in the quotations of the OT by the NT writers will prohibit a simplistic approach and will prevent hasty conclusions. Care to ask not only which text was used but also which form of the text was used and how is obviously essential in any serious study. In addition it is necessary to allow for the possibility that the NT writers knew forms of a text that are now lost.

The Methods of the New Testament Writers. The methods used by the NT writers were not unique to them. Many of these methods were also employed in 1st-century Judaism. In fact both the technique used in quoting and the understanding of the OT text itself in many cases are paralleled in Judaism. For example from the standpoint of technique used in quoting, the same kinds of formula introductions are used in the Dead Sea Scrolls, the rabbinic writings, and elsewhere. The rabbinic technique of "pearl stringing," that is, of applying verses from various parts of the OT (the Law, the prophets, the writings) to a subject, can be seen especially in Paul's writings (note Rom 9:12–19 or 11:8–10). Somewhat related is the practice of using quotations that all contain a key word or key words (note 1 Pt 2:6–8, which draws together quotations using the word "stone," or Rom 15:9–12, which joins OT verses referring to the "nations").

The methods used in the NT to interpret an OT text are also displayed in Judaism. Some passages interpret the OT "literally," such as Jesus' replies during temptation (see the quotations of Dt 8:3; 6:16; 6:13; in Mt 4:3–10), his teachings on marriage based on Genesis 2:24 (Mt 19:5), or Paul's use of Habakkuk 2:4 (Rom 1:17) or Genesis 15:6 (Rom 4:3–9). Many such examples could be given. With regard to prophecy, some of these statements are fulfilled in a "literal" or "direct" way in keeping with the

A jar and other items discovered at Qumran, where the Dead Sea Scrolls were found.

intention of the OT (e.g., Mi 5:2 Bethlehem as the birthplace of the Messiah; Mt 2:4–6). Jeremiah 31:31–34, the promise of the new covenant, is viewed as directly fulfilled in Christ (Heb 8:7–13). The prophecy of Joel 2:28–32 concerning the pouring out of the Spirit of the Lord is directly fulfilled in the Pentecost event (Acts 2:17–21), but the changing of the sun to darkness and the moon to blood are certainly not understood literally in connection with this event.

A different method of interpretation is based on the concept of *corporate solidarity*. This technical expression is an attempt to convey the idea that the individuals among God's people are not merely individuals; they are part of a larger whole. Consequently what is said about the individual can apply to the whole and vice versa. This is the reason the Servant of the Lord in Isaiah is seen both as the nation (44:1) and as an individual (52:13–53:12). Also the king is sometimes viewed as representative of the nation. The easiest places to see the concept of corporate solidarity are in the effect of the sin of Achan on all the people (Jos 7:1–26) or the sin of David in numbering the people (1 Chr 21:3–8).

Correspondence in history is not so much a method of interpretation as it is a way of thinking about God. It assumes that the things that happen to God's people are the things that have happened to previous generations and that God is faithful and operates in the present as he has in the past. Consequently, the trials and deliverance of God's people are often expressed with words borrowed from the previous accounts of God's people. Isaiah describes the anticipated deliverance in terms of a second exodus (11:15,16). Ezekiel describes the king set up over the people in terms of a second David (Ez 37:25). In the NT, Revelation 22 describes the new heavens and the new earth in terms of the garden of Eden (Gn 2,3). Sometimes this technique is described as "typology," but this term has been used for so many questionable interpretations that it is misleading. The most important thing about this concept is that it is a view of God and his working among his people.

With these two concepts the way that the OT is quoted in the NT can be understood. The conviction that Jesus was the promised deliverer and that the last days had dawned in his ministry are evident everywhere. The quotation of Hosea 11:1 can be used in Matthew 2:15 because of corporate solidarity and correspondence in history. What was said of the nation is true of the one who is its representative and there is correspondence in their respective histories. Jeremiah 31:15 can be used in Matthew 2:18 because of correspondence in history and especially because Jeremiah looked forward to God's intention for Israel and prophesied a new covenant (31:17,31–34). Matthew saw not only the correspondence in history but believed that in Jesus this promised salvation had been granted. John 12:40 can quote Isaiah 6:10 of Jesus' ministry, not because he twists the meaning of the OT text, but because he saw that what had happened with God's messenger before happened again and even *ultimately* in Jesus' ministry. The instances of such correspondences in history are numerous.

There are other texts where there seems to be an *actualization* of the OT text. Some quotations seem to be "lived out" in the ministry of Jesus. Because of their conviction about Jesus and his kingdom, the NT writers often saw certain OT texts as appropriated and made alive by Jesus. Psalm 118:22 was not intended as a prophecy of the Messiah but Jesus saw it as descriptive of his ministry (Mt 21:42) and the early church saw this verse as actualized in his death and resurrection (Acts 4:11). Isaiah 53 is another text that the NT views as actualized in Jesus' ministry (see Acts 8:32–35 and 1 Pt 2:22–25). Some Christians would view Psalm 22 as a prophecy of the crucifixion of Jesus, but it seems instead to be the lament of a righteous OT sufferer. Through correspondence in history, and because Christians saw so much of the psalmist's plight actualized in Jesus' crucifixion, the psalm became the easiest way to describe what once again had happened to God's righteous sufferer. The words of Isaiah 40:3 describe the ministry of John the Baptist (Mt 3:3). Jews had come to see this verse as a prophecy of God's end-time salvation, and the early church saw John the Baptist fulfilling this forerunner's task. Luke made this identification (3:4–6), but he applied the same role to Jesus' disciples (9:52; 10:1). This seems to be a further example of actualization and correspondence in history. In other places the church has applied to Christians ideas that were previously understood of Christ (e.g., the stone image in 1 Pt 2:4,5; the ministry of the suffering servant in Acts 13:46,47).

The most convenient term to describe the way the OT is "fulfilled" in Christ is to say that the OT finds its climax in Jesus. Even where actual quotations are not involved, the OT ideas such as prophet, priest, or king are climaxed in him as the ideal and embodiment of all the OT models. He could tell religious authorities that "One greater than Solomon is here" (Mt 12:42) or "One greater than the temple is here" (Mt 12:6). Those passages involving correspondence in history or actualization also lead to the conviction that he is the climax of the OT Scriptures.

Some Christian scholars would describe the interpretation of the OT by the NT writers somewhat differently. Rather than stressing corporate solidarity, correspondence in history, or actualization, these scholars would de-emphasize the importance of the meaning of the OT writer. The focus would be placed on God's meaning which might go well beyond the human author's intention. Without doubt, the OT writers did not see the final outworking of their writing, and indeed the OT is viewed differently after Christ. However, the attempt to focus on a meaning in God's purposes that was unknown to the human author does not do justice to the fact that the OT has primary reference to Israel in her particular historical circumstances. Also this approach places all the emphasis on a particular view of inspiration and does not deal with the methods of interpretation used by the NT writers. However, these methods were in use among various Jewish groups and were not uniquely Christian.

The same methods of interpretation were used in Judaism, but many of the interpretations of specific OT texts were traditional. Certain OT verses are used as they are in the NT because that is the way the verses had come to be understood in Judaism. Therefore, the NT usage often reflects its Jewish heritage or a dialogue with Jews or Jewish Christians. Deuteronomy 18:15 is clearly not intended messianically in its original context since it refers to prophets generally who will communicate God's Word to his people. Later, probably because of the influence of Deuteronomy 34:10, this verse became the basis of the expectation that one day a final prophet would arise who would give God's revelation for the end time. Acts 3:22,23 and 7:37 see Deuteronomy 18:15 as climaxed in Jesus, but the NT has not suddenly established a new messianic meaning for the verse. This understanding of the verse is present in several sections of Judaism. Isaiah 28:16 is not messianic in its original context, but various parts of Judaism understood the verse to be speaking of the last days. The early church merely said "Indeed, we have found the foundation of the last days in Jesus Christ, our risen Lord," and used Isaiah 28:16 in a variety of ways to explain the Christ event (see Rom 9:32,33; Eph 2:20; 1 Pt 2:4–8). The understanding of Isaiah 40:3 as relating to the coming of salvation in the final days was also part of the common heritage of Judaism. No doubt many uses of the OT by the NT writers were due to the new insight of Jesus or of his disciples after the resurrection, but their use of Scripture reflects the fact that they were partakers of a living tradition.

The Purposes of the Use of the Old Testament.
The variety of methods of interpretation and application of the OT parallels the fact that the OT was used for a variety of purposes. People tend to think only in terms of the use of the OT to show that Jesus was the Messiah, but there are a number of other uses with a variety of goals. Many OT texts are used to show Jesus is the Messiah, the fulfillment of the OT promises (Lk 4:16–21). Without lessening the fulfillment emphasis, however, other verses are applied to Jesus for other purposes: to evangelize (Acts 8:32–35); to demonstrate or convince (Acts 13:33–35); to rebuke (Mk 7:6,7; Rom 11:7–10); and to worship (Phil 2:10,11). On the other hand, many quotations of the OT in the NT are not directly related to the Messiah. OT passages are adapted to provide a word from God on some aspect of life or ethics. For example, Jesus used Genesis 2:24 to substantiate his teaching on divorce as he attempted to deal with the issues raised by the civil regulation of divorce (Dt 24:1; Mt 19:1–12). The stress on the OT commandments shows their importance for Christians (Mt 19:16–22; Rom 13:8–10). Often OT statements deal with specific problems. The problem of pride at Corinth is solved by the quotation of Jeremiah 9:24 ("Let the one boasting, boast in the Lord," 1 Cor 1:31). First Peter 3:19–22 incorporates Psalm 34:12–16 as ethical instructions and 3:14,15 borrows Isaiah 8:12,13 to address the fear of suffering. The spiritual armor in Ephesians 6:14–17 is derived largely from OT passages. Such examples are so numerous that there can be no doubt that the OT is used to describe Christian existence. In fact nearly every subject discussed in the NT is presented somewhere via OT terms and quotations. Frequently OT passages are used to describe the church as God's end-time community. Hosea 2:23 is used to show that those who formerly were not God's people now are (Rom 9:25,26; 1 Pt 2:10). Several OT texts contribute to the description of the church in 1 Peter 2:9. OT texts which speak of the word of God describe the apostles' preaching (Rom 10:8; 1 Pt 1:24,25). OT quotations describe the sinful condition of humanity (Rom 3:10–20). Salvation is explained through OT concepts and symbols and is based on OT statements (Jn 6:31–33; Gal 3:6–13). The words of Daniel describe the second coming (7:13,14; Mt 24:30). Even the worship of early Christians was expressed through use of the OT (see Acts 4:24; Rom 11:34,35).

Understanding the Use of the Old Testament in the New Testament.
The description of the use of the OT in the NT has pointed to the frequency of use, the difficulties encountered, and the variety of methods and purposes employed. A concluding list of suggestions for understanding the use of the OT follows: (1) Identify if possible which OT text is being employed. (2) Compare the wording of the NT and the OT passages. If there are significant differences, assistance may be required from scholarly studies before drawing conclusions. (3) Determine the original intention of the OT text in its context. (4) Determine how the NT uses the OT text. Identify both the method by which the OT text is appropriated and the purpose for which it is employed. (5) Identify the teaching of both OT and NT texts for Christian understanding.

While the use of the OT in the NT is complex, no subject is more important or rewarding for a faith that speaks of itself and its founder as the fulfillment and climax of God's Word in the OT.

KLYNE R. SNODGRASS

See BIBLE, INTERPRETATION OF THE.

Bibliography. F.F. Bruce, *This Is That;* C.H. Dodd, *The OT in the New;* E.E. Ellis, *Paul's Use of the OT;* R.T. France, *Jesus and the OT;* A.T. Hanson, *Jesus Christ in the OT;* R.L. Longenecker, *Biblical Exegesis in the Apostolic Period;* R.V.G. Tasker, *The OT in the NT.*

Rr

Raamah, Raama. One of Cush's five sons and a descendant of Noah through Ham's line. He was the father of Sheba and Dedan (Gn 10:7; 1 Chr 1:9, Raama). Ezekiel 27:22 mentions the people of Sheba and Raamah trading spices and precious stones with the merchants of Tyre. Raamah's name was later given to a town perhaps identifiable with Ma'in in southwest Arabia.

Raamiah. One who returned with Zerubbabel to Palestine following the Babylonian captivity (Neh 7:7). Raamiah is alternately spelled Reelaiah in Ezra 2:2. The correct form of the word is uncertain.

See Reelaiah.

Raamses. Alternate spelling of Rameses, an Egyptian city, in Exodus 1:11.

See Rameses (Place).

Rabbah. One of the towns in the hill country assigned to Judah's tribe for an inheritance (Jos 15:60). Its location is uncertain. Some identify it with Rubute, mentioned in the Amarna tablets, or Khirbet Bir al-Hilu, a recently discovered town near Jerusalem.

Rabbah of the Ammonites. Capital of the ancient Ammonite kingdom. Located near the sources of the Jabbok River, it stood about 25 miles east of the Jordan and lay astride the main caravan route leading from Damascus south along the length of the Transjordanian plateau. This road was also known as the King's Highway (Nm 20:17; 21:22). Modern Amman, the capital of Jordan, with its population of some 635,000, covers the ancient city. During the 3rd century BC, Ptolemy II Philadelphus of Egypt rebuilt the city and renamed it Philadelphia. After the Romans took Palestine in 63 BC, the city became part of the Decapolis,

and after AD 106 was part of the Roman province of Arabia.

Rabbah first appears in Scripture as the place where the great iron bedstead of Og, king of Bashan, was kept (Dt 3:11, KJV Rabbath of the children of Ammon). When Transjordan was divided among the tribes of Gad, Reuben, and the half tribe of Manasseh, the territory of Gad extended to the vicinity of Rabbah but did not include it (Jos 13:25).

Rabbah figured most significantly in Scripture during David's reign. Then Joab laid siege to the city, and during the battle Uriah the Hittite lost his life by the specific command of the king (2 Sm 11:1; 12:26–29). At that time the city was built in two parts—the lower city or "city of waters" (2 Sm 12:27) and the upper or "royal city" (2 Sm 12:26). Joab took the lower city and perhaps gained control of the water supply, and then waited for David to come and complete the conquest (2 Sm 12:27–28). After a thorough sack of Rabbah, David did not station troops in the city but left it under the control of the Ammonites who became vassals of Israel.

About 250 years later Amos pronounced judgment on the then prosperous city (1:13,14). When Nebuchadnezzar stopped at Rabbah during his invasion of Transjordan, it was a significant place (Jer 49:2,3). Baalis, king of the Ammonites, later plotted the attack on Jerusalem which resulted in the death of Gedaliah, the Babylonian governor of Judea, and the exile of Jeremiah into Egypt at Rabbah (Jer 40:14).

Since modern Amman covers ancient Rabbah, no excavation of the ancient city is possible. The Roman theater stands in the center of the city with seating for 6000 people. Dilapidated remains of an odeion or music hall and a fountain, also of the Roman period, stand nearby. Everything visible on the ancient citadel is Roman, Byzantine, or Arab, except at the northeast corner, where part of the Iron Age town wall is still exposed. The Roman temple at the southwest corner of the citadel was dedicated to Hercules.

See PHILADELPHIA #1; DECAPOLIS.

Rabbi. Title of respect, meaning "my great one," or "my superior one," used in Jesus' day for Jewish religious teachers.

According to Matthew 23:7, "rabbi" was evidently used as a common title of address for the Jewish scribes and Pharisees; however, in the NT it is most commonly used as a title of respectful address when others were speaking to Jesus. It was used by Nathanael (Jn 1:49), by Peter and Andrew (Jn 1:38), by Nicodemus (Jn 3:2), by the disciples as a group (Jn 9:2; 11:8), and by a crowd generally (Jn 6:25). Mary Magdalene (Mk 10:51) and blind Bartimaeus (Jn 20:16) both use the longer form, "rabboni," to address Jesus directly, thus indicating even more profound respect than the use of the mere title, "rabbi." By the time of the writing of John's Gospel, the title "rabbi" meant "teacher"; and this John says explicitly in 1:38 and implicitly in 3:2.

Jesus condemns the scribes and the Pharisees for their evident pride displayed in their love of being greeted in the marketplaces and their insistence on having men call them "rabbi" (Mt 23:7,8). Jesus prohibited the use of the title for his own disciples, saying, "You are not to be called Rabbi." However, Jesus' prohibition was more against seeking to be called this and insisting on it than the mere legitimate possession of the title itself. In fact, several people did use the title of Jesus in a reverent way and they were not in any way rebuked.

Rabbith. Town defining the border of Issachar (Jos 19:20) and perhaps identifiable with the levitical town called Daberath (Jos 19:12; 21:28; 1 Chr 6:72). Its site is near Mt Tabor at modern Debuyiyeh.

See DABERATH.

Rabboni. Variant of rabbi in Mark 10:51 and John 20:16.

See RABBI.

Rab-mag. Title given to a certain Babylonian officer, Nergel-sharezer, who was in charge of Jeremiah's safety during the fall of Jerusalem (Jer 39:3,13). The meaning of the title is uncertain.

Rabsaris. Title of a high-ranking Assyrian and Babylonian court official, usually a eunuch and sometimes supervisor of the royal harem. A rabsaris was part of the Assyrian delegation (2 Kgs 18:17), a judge at the gate (Jer 39:3), the official who released Jeremiah from prison (Jer 39:13), and one of Nebuchadnezzar's officials (Dn 1:3,7).

Rabshakeh. High Assyrian official, originally a cupbearer or chamberlain, but later a powerful palace official. The Rabshakeh was the emissary of Sennacherib, who insultingly demanded that Hezekiah and Jerusalem abandon their reliance on both Egypt and God and surrender to Assyria. Hezekiah refused; Rabshakeh returned to find his king at war against Libnah (2 Kgs 18:17–37; 19:4,8; Is 36:2–22; 37:4,8).

Raca. Derogatory expression used by Jews of the 1st century to show open contempt for another. *Raca* is derived from an Aramaic and Hebrew term meaning empty or worthless. Literally meaning "empty headed," *raca* probably insinuates an intellectual stupidity or inferiority rather than a moral deficiency. In the OT it is comparable to the worthless lot that Abimelech hired to follow him (Jgs 9:4), the idle men who gathered around Jephthah (Jgs 11:3), and the scoundrels who joined up with Jeroboam (2 Chr 13:7). Michal accuses David of acting like "one of the vulgar fellows [*raca*]" who "shamelessly uncovers himself!" (2 Sm 6:20). Rabbinic literature used this term to describe an immoral, untrained person.

Jesus warned against calling a brother "*Raca!*" (Mt 5:22). According to Jesus, the perpetrator of the insult was to be judged by the highest court of the land and punished by its severest penalty. The commandment against murder (Ex 20:13) not only prohibited the deed itself but also the thoughts of unrighteous anger and expressions of unwarranted contempt for one's fellow man. Jesus was not literally enacting new civil law but emphasizing the moral offense of these slanders against God.

Racal. One of the towns in southern Judah in which David distributed the spoils taken from the defeated Amalekites (1 Sm 30:29, KJV Rachal). The city is named Carmel in the Septuagint.

Rachab. KJV form of Rahab in Matthew 1:5.

See RAHAB (PERSON).

Rachal. KJV form of Racal, a Judean town, in 1 Samuel 30:29.

See RACAL.

Rachel. Beautiful younger daughter of Laban; she was the favorite wife and cousin of the patriarch Jacob. He first met her as he arrived at Paddan-aram in Haran. There he assisted her by attending to the needs of Rachel's father's sheep, removing a stone from the mouth of a well in order to water them (Gn 29:10). Jacob loved Rachel exceedingly and agreed to work seven years for Laban in return for her hand in marriage. His seven years' service seemed like only a few days because of his great love for her. Laban deceptively reneged on his bargain, however, and required Jacob to marry Leah, his older, less attractive daughter, before finally giving him Rachel for his wife (vv 22–27). Unlike Leah, Rachel was barren in the early years of her marriage to Jacob (30:1). Consequently she gave her servant, Bilhah, to Jacob in order to have children. Thus by following this commonly accepted ancient custom, Dan and Naphtali were born. In time, Rachel herself conceived and bore Joseph (vv 22–25). After this, Jacob took his wives, children, and possessions away from Haran. Unknown to him, Rachel had taken Laban's household gods, something she cleverly concealed when Laban overtook Jacob's caravan to search for them (31:4–34). Her actions, while dishonest, were probably prompted by Laban's unscrupulous dealings with Jacob; possession of these "gods" could prove invaluable in settling any questions of inheritance.

Somewhere between Bethel and Bethlehem Rachel died while giving birth to Benjamin (35:16,19). Jacob set up a pillar over her tomb there (v 20), a landmark known even in the days of Saul (1 Sm 10:2). Rachel and Leah are highly regarded as those who built up the house of Israel (Ru 4:11). In Jeremiah 31:15 (KJV Rahel), Rachel is pictured as crying for her children being carried off into captivity. Later, Matthew recalls Jeremiah's words in describing Herod's slaughter of the male infants (Mt 2:18).

See JACOB #1.

Rachel's Tomb. Landmark set up by Jacob at the site of Rachel's grave (Gn 35:19,20) which was still in existence at the time of Samuel (1 Sm 10:2). Two persisting traditions make its original location still questionable. The older tradition locates the tomb near Bethlehem, south of Jerusalem (Gn 35:19; 48:7; Mt 2:18). This option has won the impressive historical support of Josephus, Eusebius, Jerome, Origen, and the Talmudists. At this site the Crusaders erected a monument during the Middle Ages. Additional restoration and construction was undertaken in 1841 by Moses Montefiori. A domed roof was added, supported by four pillars, at the end of the 18th century. The tomb became part of a Moslem cemetery during the Jordanian occupation, but following the Six-Day War in June, 1967, the tomb was refurbished by the Israeli government and adapted to mass pilgrimage.

A second site has been suggested by S.H. Hooke. He argues that Ephrath (Gn 35:19) was on the northern border of Benjamin, 10 miles north of Jerusalem (1 Sm 10:2; Jer 31:15), near ancient Bethel.

Rachel's tomb is the first recorded instance of a sepulchral monument. A picture of the tomb is a common decorative piece in Jewish homes throughout the world.

Raddai. Fifth of Jesse's seven sons and the brother of David from Judah's tribe (1 Chr 2:14).

Building over the traditional site of Rachel's tomb near Bethlehem.

Ragau. KJV rendering of Reu, Peleg's son, in Luke 3:35.

See REU.

Raguel. KJV spelling of Reuel, an alternate name for Jethro, Moses' father-in-law, in Numbers 10:20.

See JETHRO.

Rahab (Person).   Heroine of the battle of Jericho (Jos 2–6). Soon after Moses' death, God told Joshua that he and the people were to cross the Jordan and occupy the land of promise. Before the crossing, however, Joshua sent two spies into the land to reconnoiter the opposition, in particular the fortified city of Jericho. Upon entering the city, the spies found their way quickly to Rahab's house, which was perhaps an inn and/or a brothel. She apparently was a prostitute.

News of the arrival of spies was not long in reaching the king of Jericho, who quite naturally demanded that Rahab divulge their whereabouts. She cleverly admitted seeing them, but insisted that they had left the city at nightfall. Actually, the spies were hiding under stalks of flax on the roof of her house. When the king's search party left Jericho to hunt the spies, Rahab confessed to the spies the reason for her complicity with the Israelites' cause. She feared the God of the Jews, believing that he would surely give them victory. "For the Lord your God is God in heaven above and on the earth below" (Jos 2:11 NIV).

For her help, the spies agreed to save Rahab and her family. The sign was to be a cord of scarlet thread hanging from her window, the same avenue the spies used to escape the city. Rahab and her family were indeed the only survivors of the subsequent battle. They were led to safety on Joshua's command by the very men Rahab had saved.

Jewish tradition added to the biblical account the notion that Rahab married Joshua after converting to faith in God, that her progeny included eight priests and prophets, including Jeremiah. She was supposedly a most beautiful woman who had become a prostitute at the early age of 10, but whose subsequent record exonerated her. A variant to the tradition holds that Rahab was not a prostitute at all, but an innkeeper, a suggestion advanced by the Targum's euphemistic rendering of prostitute as innkeeper. Rahab (KJV Rachab) became the wife of Salmon and mother of Boaz, and thus an ancestor of Jesus (Mt 1:5).

Rahab is listed, along with Moses, David, Samson, and Samuel, as an example of faith

Excavations at Jericho reveal what may be the oldest city on earth; the circular tower is part of the Jericho city wall before the time of Joshua.

(Heb 11). Her deed is an example of good works and justification (Jas 2:25).

See CONQUEST AND ALLOTMENT OF THE LAND; JOSHUA, BOOK OF.

Rahab.   Mythological sea monster that poetically represented Egypt (Ps 87:4). "For Egypt's help is worthless and empty, therefore I have called her 'Rahab who sits still' " (Is 30:7). The biblical writers, with Israel's crossing of the Red Sea and the Egyptian army's subsequent drowning (cf. Is 51:10), portray God as waging war against this monster and cruelly defeating it: "By his understanding he smote Rahab" (Job 26:12); "Thou didst crush Rahab like a carcass" (Ps 89:10); and the prophet Isaiah's lament, "Was it not thou that didst cut Rahab in pieces, that didst pierce the dragon?" (51:9).

See EGYPT, EGYPTIANS.

Raham.   Son of Shema, Jorkeam's father and a descendant of Judah (1 Chr 2:44).

Rahel.   KJV spelling of Rachel, Jacob's wife, in Jeremiah 31:15.

See RACHEL.

Rain.   *See* PALESTINE.

Rainbow. Sign of God's covenant with Noah following the flood (Gn 9:8–17). The normal Hebrew word for "war bow" is used. Jewish tradition interpreted this as a symbol that God's anger had ceased since the rainbow pointed downward, just as an antagonist lowers his bow to declare peace. To the biblical account the rabbis added the notion that the rainbow was created at evening on the sixth day of creation, and that it did not appear during the lifetime of a saint whose good life was sufficient to preserve the world from destruction. To gaze directly at a rainbow risked injury, since the bow was a reflection of the glory of the Lord. A prescribed blessing was to be recited on seeing a rainbow: "Blessed are Thou O Lord Our God, King of the Universe, Who remembers the Covenant, is faithful to the Covenant, and keeps His promise."

In the NT, the rainbow forms part of the heavenly vision (Rev 4:3; 10:1).

See FLOOD, THE; FLOOD MYTHS.

Raisin. Staple food in biblical lands made by drying grapes on housetops. Raisins were used as gifts (1 Sm 25:18; 2 Sm 16:1–3), sometimes offered to false gods (Hos 3:1), and considered a source of nourishment (1 Sm 30:12; 1 Chr 12:40).

See FOOD AND FOOD PREPARATION.

Raisin-cake. Culinary delicacy of ancient peoples (Is 16:7). The cakes resisted deterioration and thus were useful for soldiers and travelers (2 Sm 6:19). They were used as cultic offerings (Hos 3:1) and sometimes served as aphrodisiacs (Sg 2:5).

See FOOD AND FOOD PREPARATION.

Rakem. Manasseh's grandson (1 Chr 7:16).

Rakkath. One of 19 cities allotted to Naphtali's tribe for an inheritance (Jos 19:35). The city served as a buffer against military attack on the western shore of the Sea of Galilee. Jewish tradition identifies Rakkath with Tiberias, but modern scholars prefer its location at either Khirbet el-Quneitireh or Tell Eklatiyah.

Rakkon. One of the cities assigned to Dan's tribe (Jos 19:46). It is identified today with Tell er-Ragguat, one and a half miles north of the mouth of the Yorkon River.

Ram. *See* ANIMALS (SHEEP).

Ram (Person). 1. Ancestor of King David (Ru 4:19; 1 Chr 2:9,10), listed in Matthew's genealogy of Christ (1:3,4, KJV Aram; called Arni in Lk 3:33).

See GENEALOGY OF JESUS CHRIST.

2. Jerahmeel's eldest son (1 Chr 2:25,27), and perhaps the nephew of #1 above.

3. Head of the family of Elihu, one of Job's friends (Jb 32:2).

Rama. KJV spelling of Ramah, a Benjamite city, in Matthew 2:18.

See RAMAH #1.

Ramah. 1. One of the cities located in the territory allotted to Benjamin's tribe for an inheritance, listed between Gibeon and Beeroth (Jos 18:25). In the proximity of this town, Rachel, Jacob's wife was buried (Mt 2:18, KJV Rama; cf. Gn 35:16–21; Jer 31:15). Ramah, positioned near Bethel, was the place where Deborah judged Israel (Jgs 4:5). This city was a temporary resting place for a Levite and his concubine traveling north from Bethlehem (Jgs 19:13).

During the period of the divided kingdom (930–722 BC), King Baasha of Israel (908–886 BC) fortified Ramah. From Ramah, Baasha was able to prevent an invasion of King Asa's (910–869 BC) Judean army. Baasha later abandoned the city and hurried his army north to repulse a Syrian offensive led by King Ben-hadad I (c. 885 BC). Asa dismantled Ramah's military fortifications, using the material to build the towns of Geba and Mizpah (1 Kgs 15:17–22; 2 Chr 16:1–6).

The cities of Geba, Ramah, and Gibeah formed the route taken by the Assyrian army during Sennacherib's military incursion into Judah (c. 701 BC) against King Hezekiah and Jerusalem (Is 10:29). Later King Nebuchadnezzar used Ramah as a place of detainment for the Jews being deported to Babylon. Here Nebuzaradan, the captain of the guard, released Jeremiah from among the captives (Jer 40:1).

Following the Babylonian captivity, inhabitants of Ramah returned with Zerubbabel to Palestine and rebuilt this city (Ezr 2:26; Neh 7:30). Some suggest that the postexilic town of Ramah was another Benjamite town located further west near the coastal plain (Neh 11:33). The site of Ramah is identified with the modern village of er-Ram, five miles north of Jerusalem.

2. City in the Negeb marking the southern extremity of the territory allotted to the tribe of Simeon within Judah's inheritance (Jos 19:8); also called Ramoth of the Negeb (1 Sm 30:27) and Baalath-beer (Jos 19:8; cf. 1 Chr 4:33).

See BAALATH-BEER.

3. Town defining the boundary of the territory assigned to Asher's tribe for an inheritance, mentioned between Sidon and Tyre (Jos 19:29). Its location is uncertain.

4. One of 19 fortified cities given to Naphtali's tribe for a possession, mentioned between Adamah and Hazor (Jos 19:36). Its location is identifiable with the modern town of er-Rameh, about 11 miles northwest of the Sea of Galilee.

5. Home of Samuel's parents Elkanah and Hannah, the birthplace of Samuel (1 Sm 1:19; 2:11), and later his home (7:17; 16:13). Samuel judged Israel from Ramah, Bethel, Gilgal, and Mizpah (7:17). Saul first met Samuel at this city (9:6–10). Here the elders of Israel petitioned Samuel to appoint a king for them (8:4) and later this city provided David a place of refuge from King Saul (19:18–20:1). Samuel was buried at Ramah (25:1; 28:3). Ramah is alternately called Ramathaim-zophim in 1 Samuel 1:1. Its location is uncertain. Some identify Ramah with: er-Ram, 5 miles north of Jerusalem; Nebi Samwil, 7 miles north of Jerusalem; Ramallah, 12 miles north of Jerusalem; and Beit Rama, 13 miles northeast of Lydda.

6. Abbreviated name for Ramoth-gilead (2 Kgs 8:29; 2 Chr 22:6).

See RAMOTH-GILEAD.

Ramah of the Negeb. Alternate name for Baaleth-beer, a town in Simeon's territory, in Joshua 19:8.

See BAALATH-BEER.

Ramath of the South. KJV rendering of Ramah of the Negeb, an alternate name for Baalath-beer, in Joshua 19:8.

See BAALATH-BEER.

Ramathaim-zophim. Alternate name for Ramah, Samuel's hometown, in 1 Samuel 1:1.

See RAMAH #5.

Ramathite. Inhabitant of Ramah (1 Chr 27:27), though which Ramah is uncertain.

Ramath-lehi. Place where Samson routed the Philistines with an ass's jawbone (Jgs 15:17).

See LEHI.

Ramath-mizpeh. Alternate name for Mizpah, a town in Gad's territory, in Joshua 13:26.

See MIZPAH #4.

Rameses (Person). Name of 11 kings of the 19th and 20th Egyptian dynasties (also spelled Ramses). Rameses II reigned for some 67 years (dates vary from *c.* 1292–1225 to 1279–1212 BC). He was known as "Rameses the Great," mostly because of his extensive building activities, such as his mortuary temple at Thebes (the

The statues of Rameses II at Luxor.

Ramasseum), the rock-cut temple of Abu Simbel in Nubia, and his additions to the temples of Karnak and Luxor. Pictured on his temple walls as a great military leader, he fought with the Hittites at Kadesh on the Orontes, where, because of a serious tactical blunder on his part, he nearly lost his life. The battle was at best a draw, but he depicted it as an Egyptian victory in the Ramasseum and Abu Simbel. His treaty with the Hittites is the earliest known international nonaggression pact. He has often been suggested as the pharaoh of the oppression (Ex 1:8–11), but this is improbable.

Rameses III (*c.* 1195–1124 BC), of the 20th dynasty, saved Egypt from an invasion by the Sea Peoples in a land and sea battle in the Nile Delta. He built a large mortuary temple complex and royal residence in the Theban area, at Medinet Habu. On the northern exterior wall of the temple area are the first known representations of a naval battle. Among the captives are the Peleset, who are believed to be Philistines. The exterior walls also bear excellent reliefs of lion and wild bull hunts. From late in the reign of Rameses III comes the famous Harris Papyrus, which lists the benefactions of the king to Amon. Because of withheld wages in kind, workers in the royal necropolis went on strike. Similar strikes occurred in the times of Rameses IX and X. From the end of the reign of Rameses III come records of the court trial of a harem conspiracy in which Rameses III apparently was killed.

The other Ramessides were minor rulers who played no great part in history. The instability of the country is further illustrated by widespread looting of the royal tombs. A complicated and dubious investigation of these robberies was conducted in the reign of Rameses IX.

See EGYPT, EGYPTIANS.

Rameses (Place). Place (also called Ra'amses or Ramses) mentioned with Pithom in Exodus 1:11 (KJV Raamses) as one of the locations where the Hebrews were engaged in a building program for the pharaoh. Here they were afflicted with heavy burdens by the pharaoh's officers. In due course they escaped their oppression and set out for the Promised Land (Ex 12:37; Nm 33:3). The identification of this place and the period is important for establishing the date of the exodus from Egypt.

The great Rameses II (c. 1290–1224 BC) built extensively in the east Delta region. The ambitious pharaoh determined to add a center of his own creation, using as a nucleus the old family seat of Avaris where his father had built a summer palace. On the north side of Avaris, he built a majestic palace which he named Pi-ramesse. The location of its site is much debated, having been variously located at Pelusim (on the Mediterranean Sea), and at Tanis (or Zoan). This latter suggestion is now rejected since the stonework was reused material taken from elsewhere and not original. However, 19 miles south of Tanis near the town of Qantir, considerable remains of a palace commenced by Seti I with an adjacent glazing factory, dwellings of princes and high officials, and traces of a temple and public audience halls are now recognized as the site of Ra'amses (Pi-ramesse). The old Hyksos center was destroyed when these foreigners were expelled early in the 18th dynasty (c. 1552–1306 BC). The place was then abandoned but later rebuilt under the 19th dynasty. Rameses II lav-

ishly adorned his father's palace and established nearby a marshalling place for his chariots, a mustering place for his infantry, and a mooring place for his armies.

See EGYPT, EGYPTIANS; PITHOM.

Ramiah. Pharosh's son, who obeyed Ezra's exhortation to divorce his foreign wife after the exile (Ezr 10:25).

Ramoth (Person). KJV (RSV mg) form of Jeremoth, Bani's son, in Ezra 10:29.

See JEREMOTH #8.

Ramoth (Place). 1. Abbreviated form of Ramoth-gilead.

See RAMOTH-GILEAD.

2. Alternate name for Baalath-beer, the city in the Negeb, in 1 Samuel 30:27.

See BAALATH-BEER.

3. Alternate name (or textual corruption) of Jarmuth, a levitical city, in 1 Chronicles 6:73.

See JARMUTH #2.

Ramoth-gilead. City lying in the Transjordan area of Gilead and probably identifiable with Tell Ramith, although the site of Tell el-Husn has also been suggested. Initially biblical references refer to Ramoth in Gilead (Dt 4:43; Jos 20:8; 21:38) while later it is called Ramoth-gilead. Combined names were used to avoid confusion with cities of the same name in other locations.

Ramoth-gilead, a possession of the tribe of Gad, first appears in the biblical narrative as one of three Transjordan cities of refuge (Dt 4:43) later included in the six cities of refuge for all Israel (Jos 20:8). It was allotted to the Merarites as one of 48 levitical cities (Jos 21:38), and was most likely located along the King's Highway which transversed that area.

During the time of Solomon, Ramoth-gilead enjoyed a place of prominence as the central city in his sixth administrative district and residence of Ben-geber, chief officer of that district (1 Kgs 4:13). After the division of the kingdom, this border town was taken by the Aramaeans and became a site of contention between Israel and Aram. King Ahab's final battle began with his desire to retake Ramoth-gilead. In seeking to convince his ally Jehoshaphat, king of Judah, to support him in this maneuver he produced many prophets who spoke favorable and victorious words to the king (1 Kgs 22; 2 Chr 18). Unconvinced, Jehoshaphat inquired of the word of the Lord through Micaiah, a prophet of the Lord, who warned of impending disaster. The message was ignored and Ahab was killed at Ramoth-gilead. Ahab's son, Joram, also fought with Aram here and was wounded in battle (2 Kgs 8:29; 2 Chr 22:6; also called Ramah). Shortly thereafter, Elisha sent one of the sons of the prophets to Ramoth-gilead, where he anointed Jehu to be king over Israel (2 Kgs 9:1–14).

See LEVITICAL CITIES; CITIES OF REFUGE.

Ramoth of the Negeb. Alternate name for Baalath-beer, an unknown site in Simeon's territory, in 1 Samuel 30:27.

See BAALATH-BEER.

Ramses. Alternate form of the Egyptian Rameses of the 19th and 20th dynasties.

See RAMESES (PERSON).

Ram's Horn. Primitive musical instrument made from animal horn (Jos 6:4–6,13).

See MUSIC AND MUSICAL INSTRUMENTS (SHOPHAR).

Ransom. Price for redeeming or liberating slaves, captives, property, or life. Jesus describes his entire ministry as one of service in giving his life "as a ransom for many" (Mt 20:28; Mk 10:45). Hence "ransom" is closely linked to such terms as "redemption" and "salvation," to the satisfaction Christ made in atonement for sin.

In the Old Testament. In the OT God provided various regulations for his covenant people whereby life and property could be "redeemed," "bought back," or "set free" by payment of ransom (cf. Lv 25–27). Ransom involved a price paid as a substitute for that which was redeemed or set free.

The OT uses three different Hebrew words for ransom or redemption. Only when there is a clear indication of the payment of a price are these terms translated by "ransom," but even when another term, such as "redemption," is used in English translation, a ransom price is usually implied.

One of the Hebrew terms (*kopher*) means "a cover" or a "covering" which was made in place of life or punishment. A ransom could be paid to redeem the life of the owner of an ox that had gored a person to death (Ex 21:30). A half-shekel ransom price was required by God for each Israelite at census taking to prevent a plague (30:12), and this "atonement money" (v 16) was an offering to the Lord for use in the tabernacle service. A murderer could not be ransomed, and anyone who found safety in a city of refuge could not be taken back by ransom (Nm 35:31,32). It is impossible to avoid death by paying a ransom (Ps 49:7–9). God ransomed Israel from captivity (Is 43:3,4; see also Prv 13:8; 21:18; Jb 33:24; 36:18). In a few instances the term takes on the meaning of a "bribe" or "hush-money" (1 Sm 12:3; Prv 6:35; Am 5:12).

A second Hebrew word-family for "ransom" and "redemption" is related to *goel*. *Goel*, meaning a "reclaimant" or "redeemer," derives from the root meaning of the Hebrew term "to restore, repair, deliver, rescue." The term refers to God's family-law regulations which place various obligations on a relative or kinsman (Lv 25:25–55). The kinsman had the right and duty of redeeming by ransom any family property that a person was compelled to sell (vv 25–34; Ru 4:4,6); of ransoming a relative who was compelled by poverty to sell himself as a slave to a stranger or sojourner (Lv 25:47–55); and of acting as avenger of the blood of a dead relative, thus enforcing the claim for satisfaction for shedding his blood (Nm 35:19–27; Jos 20:3–5). The kinsman was also obligated to marry the wife of a dead brother who had died without leaving children so that the kinsman might raise up seed and the brother's name not be forgotten in Israel (Ru 3:9–13; 4:1–12). In a general sense the *goel* was a "vindicator" or "redeemer"; a familiar example is Job's cry for God to vindicate him (Jb 19:25). In the highest sense, God is the kinsman and *goel* of Israel, redeeming them from the bondage of Egypt (Ex 6:5–7), from captivity in Babylon, and from distress in general (*goel* occurs 13 times in Is 40–46). Thus Israel is called "the ransomed of the Lord" (Is 35:10), having been "redeemed without money" (52:3). In such contexts, however, the cost is indicated in terms of God's might and power, his "outstretched arm" and his "great acts of judgment" (Ex 6:6).

The OT uses a third Hebrew word (*pidyôn*) from the area of commercial law for ransom or payment. Since God spared the firstborn in Israel at the time of the Passover, "the first offspring of every womb" belonged to God and the oldest male was redeemed by ransom (Ex 13:12–15; 34:20; Lv 27:27; Nm 18:15–17). Later the entire tribe of Levi was set aside as priestly substitutes for the firstborn. Since there were 273 more firstborn than Levites, a payment of five shekels was paid in ransom for each (Nm 3:40–46). This term was also used for the price paid to ransom a slave from slavery (Dt 15:15; 24:18); a slave concubine could also be ransomed (Ex 21:8–11; Lv 19:20). God motivates these provisions by his own ransoming of Israel as slaves in Egypt (Dt 15:15; 24:18). This Hebrew term is also applied to God's deliverance of Israel from Egypt (cf. also Dt 7:8; 9:26; 13:5; 2 Sm 7:23; 1 Chr 17:21; Ps 78:42) and from Babylonian captivity (Is 35:10; 51:11). Sometimes God ransoms without reference to a specific occasion (Hos 7:13; cf. Dt 21:8; Neh 1:10; Is 1:27; Jer 31:11). God also ransoms from "the power of the grave" (Hos 13:14), from iniquities (Ps

130:8), and from troubles (Ps 25:22). This deliverance always implies some sort of payment or cost, such as "the mighty power" or "strong hand" of God needed for the redemption.

In the New Testament. In the NT there is just one family of words used for ransom. The term basically means "to loose" or "to set free," and refers to releasing, redeeming, or liberating on payment of the ransom price, to redemption, deliverance, or liberation, and to the one who does these things. The translation "ransom" is restricted to approximately eight instances where there is a clear reference to the payment of some sort of price. The translators of the Septuagint restricted their use of this Greek word to those instances where the three Hebrew terms clearly meant ransom payment.

The most important occurrence in the NT is Jesus' description of his death "as a ransom for many" (Mt 20:28; Mk 10:45). Three features stand out in Jesus' words: his service is one of ransom, his self-sacrifice is the ransom price, and his ransom is substitutionary in character, "a ransom for many" (1 Tm 2:6). Jesus Christ "gave himself for us to redeem [ransom] us from all iniquity" (Ti 2:14). The ransom price was "the precious blood of Christ" who was "a lamb without blemish or spot" (1 Pt 1:18,19), thus linking Christ's self-sacrifice to the sacrifices of the OT as pointing to Christ. "The blood of goats and calves" was not able to save, but "an eternal redemption" was obtained by Christ's blood (Heb 9:12). The great price of Christ's ransom is contrasted with "perishable things such as silver or gold" (1 Pt 1:18; cf. Is 52:3). Paul motivates his readers by reminding them that they were bought with a price (1 Cor 6:20; 7:23). The grandest display of love is revealed in the fact that "Jesus Christ laid down his life for us"; that is why "we ought to lay down our lives for our brothers" (1 Jn 3:16; cf. Jn 10:14–18; 15:13; Heb 10:3–18). In heaven the redeemed sing the new song to the one who "was slain and by thy blood didst ransom men for God" (Rv 5:9; cf. 14:3,4).

Theories of Ransom. Origen (c. 185–254), a theologian of Alexandria, maintained that the ransom was paid to the devil. Origen's form of the theory was that Christ cheated the devil by escaping through his resurrection.

Although Jesus Christ defeated Satan and liberates believers from Satan's bondage, Scripture does not indicate that the ransom was paid to him. God was wronged by human sin, yet he showed his great love in providing redemption (Jn 3:16). God declared man guilty for his sin and imposed the death penalty for human transgression. Thus Scripture indicates that the ransom was really directed by Christ to the Father. The biblical references to Jesus'

life as a ransom are echoed in the satisfaction views of the atonement.

Anselm of Canterbury in 1098 developed the satisfaction view of the atonement, emphasizing that the honor of God required satisfaction for man's sin. Later satisfaction views emphasized the justice of God in requiring payment (ransom) for the just demands of the Law and for the removal of the curse of the Law (death). "In him we have redemption through his blood, the forgiveness of our trespasses" (Eph 1:7,14; Col 1:14). Paul emphasizes the justice of God which was met so that he would be just in justifying sinners who believe (Rom 3:23–26). Reformed theology most consistently emphasizes the ransom in connection with the satisfaction of God's justice in Christ's atonement. Without the term "ransom," the same implications are carried in such condensed expressions as "Christ died for our sins" (1 Cor 15:3). The ransom terminology also appears in the eschatological passages referring to the completion of the redemptive process already begun in the lives of believers (Lk 21:28; Rom 8:23; 1 Cor 1:30; Eph 4:30; Heb 11:35).

FRED H. KLOOSTER

See ATONEMENT; REDEEMER, REDEMPTION.

Rapha. 1. Benjamin's fifth son (1 Chr 8:2). His name is omitted in the earlier list of Genesis 46:21.

2. KJV spelling of Raphah, an alternate name for Rephaiah, Bine-a's son, in 1 Chronicles 8:37.
See REPHAIAH #4.

Raphah. Alternate form of Rephaiah, Bine-a's son, in 1 Chronicles 8:37.

See REPHAIAH #4.

Raphanah. One of the original 10 Greek cities rebuilt by Rome after Pompey's conquest of Palestine and Syria around 63 BC. Raphanah (also spelled Raphana) was situated in the Decapolis region.

See DECAPOLIS.

Raphu. Benjamite and the father of Palti, one of the 12 spies sent to search out the land of Canaan (Nm 13:9).

Ras Shamra. Modern name for the mound on which the ancient city of Ugarit once stood.

See UGARIT.

Raven. *See* BIRDS.

Ravenous Bird. KJV translation for "birds of prey" in Isaiah 46:11 and Ezekiel 39:4.

See BIRDS (KITE; VULTURE; VULTURE, GRIFFON).

Remains of a pool in the palace at Ras Shamra.

Reaia. KJV spelling of Reaiah, Micah's son, in 1 Chronicles 5:5.

See REAIAH #2.

Reaiah. 1. Shobal's son and the father of Jahath from the tribe of Judah (1 Chr 4:2), perhaps identifiable with Haroeh (1 Chr 2:52).

2. Reubenite, Micah's son and the father of Baal (1 Chr 5:5, KJV Reaia).

3. Head or founder of a family of temple servants who returned with Zerubbabel from captivity in Babylon (Ezr 2:47; Neh 7:50).

Reaper, Reaping. *See* AGRICULTURE; TRADES AND OCCUPATIONS (FARMER).

Reba. One of the five Midianite kings killed by Moses at the Lord's command for seducing the Israelite settlers to idol worship (Nm 31:8; Jos 13:21).

Rebekah, Rebecca. Daughter of Bethuel and the wife of the patriarch Isaac. Her name appears 31 times in Genesis (primarily chs 24–27) and once in Romans 9:10. The same Hebrew letters spell "stall" and refer to stall-fed cattle as opposed to pastured cattle. Her name might be translated therefore as "well-fed" or "choice."

Rebekah's father was Bethuel, who, in turn, was the son of Milcah and Nahor, Abraham's brother (Gn 22:20–23). Abraham was her great uncle and eventually, of course, her father-in-law. Laban, the father of Leah and Rachel, was her brother. Thus her son Jacob married his two cousins, who were sisters.

Genesis 24 is the account of the successful search by Abraham's servant for a wife for Isaac. He went to Aram-naharaim (northwest Mesopotamia) in obedience to Abraham, who did not want his son to marry a local Canaanite. In answer to the servant's prayer, Rebekah not only gave a drink to the man but also watered his camels. After a certain amount of hospitality was extended and payment was made, Rebekah willingly went to meet her new husband.

Like his father before him, Isaac lied to a king of the Philistines, Abimelech, about his relationship to his wife (26:7–11).

Rebekah bore twins, Esau and Jacob (25:20–27). She preferred Jacob, the younger, over Esau and was a party to the deception of her husband in securing the right of the firstborn for Jacob. Disguising Jacob to feel, look, and smell like Esau the outdoorsman was her idea. She also prepared Isaac's favorite dish in order to facilitate the event (27:5–17).

The Scripture records little more of her life, but does report that she was buried next to her husband in the cave of Machpelah near Mamre (49:31).

See ISAAC.

Recah. Town in Judah occupied by Eshton, Bethrapha, Paseah, Tehinnah, Irnahash, and their families (1 Chr 4:12, KJV Rechah). Its location is unknown.

Rechab. 1. Rimmon's son who, with his brother Baanach, commanded bands of raiders under Saul's son Ish-bosheth. Hoping to please David, they killed Ish-bosheth. David, however, angered with this killing, had the two put to death (2 Sm 4:1–3,5–12).

2. Father of Jehonadab (or Jonadab), the violent supporter of Jehu who killed Ahab's supporters in Samaria (2 Kgs 10:15–27). Jeremiah refers to the followers and descendants of Rechab as Rechabites. These were nomadic people who lived by Jonadab's command that his descendants not drink wine, live in houses, sow seed, or plant vineyards. Jeremiah applauded the Rechabites' loyalty to their forebear, contrasting them with Judah and Jerusalem's unfaithfulness to God. Jeremiah predicted doom for Judah and Jerusalem, but promised that the Rechabites would be preserved (Jer 35:1–19).

Rechabite. Descendants of Rechab, Jonadab's father (Jer 35:2–18).

See RECHAB #2.

Rechah. KJV spelling of Recah, a Judean town, in 1 Chronicles 4:12.

See RECAH.

Reconciliation. Restoration of friendly relationships and of peace where before there had been hostility and alienation. Ordinarily it also includes the removal of the offense which caused the disruption of peace and harmony. This was especially so in the relation of God with humanity, when Christ removed the enmity existing between God and mankind by his vicarious sacrifice. The Scripture speaks first of Christ's meritorious, substitutionary death in effecting reconciliation of God with sinners; of sinners appropriating this free gift by faith; the promised forgiveness and salvation that become the sinners' possession by grace; and, finally, reconciliation to God (Rom 5:10; 2 Cor 5:19; Eph 2:16).

The term *katalassein* (Rom 5:10; and 2 Cor 5:19) signifies first of all the reconciliation of God with the world, expressing God's initial change of heart toward sinners. The problem is not rightly addressed by questioning whether the unchanging God ever changes his mind; the situation rather is one where an altered relationship now exists between God and sinners by Christ's interposing sacrifice on behalf of fallen mankind. The point of the reconciliation is that God for Christ's sake now feels toward sinners as though they had never offended him. The reconciliation is complete and perfect, covering mankind both extensively and intensively, that is, all sinners and all sin. The cause of rupture between God and sinners has now been healed, a truth wholly independent of humanity's mood or attitude. While sinners were still the objects of God's just wrath, Christ, in full harmony with the gracious will of his heavenly Father, interposed himself for their sakes, for the restoration of harmony. So basic is this truth that without objective reconciliation there is no thought of salvation, of regeneration, of faith, of Christian life. The initiative in reconciliation, moreover, is all on God's side; through his Word, the gospel, God reveals to sinners that he is fully reconciled with them because of Christ.

Self-evidently, then, the vicarious atonement or redemption of Christ underlies God's reconciling activity. Reconciliation took place not by God's exercise of divine fiat or decree of power, but through Christ interposing himself as the people's surrogate or substitute before the Law's condemnation. Thus the vicarious atonement is the key to understanding reconciliation as scripturally conceived and taught. Christ "became sin for us"; he clothed himself, not with holiness (which was his proper attribute), but with the garments of unrighteousness, and assumed the full obligations of the Law, perfectly fulfilling it, and fully bearing the guilt and punishment. Sins and guilt were laid on him; his righteousness attained under the Law was imputed to mankind. Martin Luther underscores the significance of the words "for us" as used in Galatians 3:13 (cf. Is 53:4–7; Mt 20:28; 2 Cor 5:21; Gal 4:4,5; 1 Pt 3:18) and presses home the point that Christ has for the sake of all people "become the greatest transgressor, murderer, adulterer, thief, rebel, blas-

phemer, etc., that ever was or could be in all the world." And were this not the wonderful truth and were people in their misguided pride to try "to turn away this reproach from Christ, that he should be called a curse or execration," then they would have to "bear them, and in them die and be damned" (*Luther's Works*, vol. 26, 277ff.).

The human predicament simply and precisely was the human inability to change or rectify in any way the broken, hostile relationship existing between humanity and God. Christ was the bridge. To carry out his substitutionary mission was the purpose of his incarnation. His sacrificial suffering and death, sealed by his triumphant resurrection, achieved mankind's redemption (Rom 4:25). Christ suffered death not as the common lot of all people, but as the wages of sin.

His vicarious satisfaction for all sins is the central teaching of the Scripture. Everything literally depends upon the fact that the turning point for humanity came from God who was working out reconciliation with the world through Christ. This is not simply an imagined or piously conceived idea, something presented as true by deeply concerned and thoughtful people, but a reality that happened (Is 53:6; 2 Cor 5:21; Heb 9:12,14; 1 Pt 1:19). It was God's solution for the grievous, hostile state that existed between a righteous, angry God and sinful, offending people. Even now God's punitive justice and wrath continue against all sin and all sinners (Ps 5:5; Eph 2:3). But the true wonder of God's indescribable mercy and grace toward sinners is this fact: that "God was in Christ reconciling the world unto himself" (2 Cor 5:19).

Whatever difficulty people might have in seeing wrath and love in God at the same time must finally be resolved by viewing the desperate human situation itself, not by trying to probe into God's own holy nature (Rom 11:33–36; 1 Tm 6:16). The problem of resolving or harmonizing wrath and love in God is directly connected with rightly distinguishing between Law and gospel. What lies beyond the power of human dialect is directly addressed and resolved in the harmonious activity of God in the history of mankind. God addresses human need through Law and gospel.

If critics of God's saving activity declare God's method of reconciling the world to himself unworthy, or as lacking in ethical virtue, or as in some way insufficient or deficient, the fact must nonetheless stand that the Scripture speaks of the altered judicial situation now existing between God and sinners as resulting from Christ's work, the imputation of sin upon him, and the imputation of his righteousness upon sinners. Moreover, Scripture never loses sight of the sweeping extent of Christ's work, the atonement for the sins of all people (Jn 3:16; 1 Jn 2:2). Christ is the sinners' shield from and before the just wrath of God. Nor was it merely by God's accepting it as sufficient that Christ's atonement availed; it was in fact and in truth the adequate and full payment (Mt 20:28; Rom 3:25; Heb 7:26–28; 1 Tm 2:6; 1 Jn 2:2).

The gospel, therefore, is the message, or *kerygma*, which informs the sinner of God's reconciliation with sinners through Christ and powerfully persuades the sinner to accept this truth in faith, or as the apostle Paul puts it, "be reconciled to God" (2 Cor 5:20). The church is to proclaim this saving gospel, for God has entrusted to us "the message of reconciliation" (2 Cor 5:19). The objective reconciliation of the world, therefore, has its counterpart in the subjective reconciliation of sinners by faith. Thus faith justifies by laying hold of the objective fact of what Christ achieved for sinners by his cross. Faith is a good work, too, particularly because it is accompanied by Christian obedience to the Word and will of God. Faith is also the source and beginning point in the renewal of life that follows after faith in the Christian life, as Christ dwells in and motivates his followers. Reconciliation thus precedes faith; it is an accomplished work of God, the content of the gospel which Christ's followers are to carry to the world (Mt 28:19). Faith does not bring it about in any way but receives it. The peace of God which passes all understanding (Phil 4:7) comes not by the sinner's subduing the enmity within his heart but by Christ's having abolished in his holy flesh the enmity of the Law which was against sinners (Eph 2:14,15; Col 2:14). By the sinner's "faith in his blood," he has peace, righteousness, access before God, hope, and strength in every trial (Rom 5:1–11).

When this great objective truth of God's reconciliation with sinners—the gospel available for acceptance by faith—is altered or cut down, the result is always the same. People seek to reconcile God through some sort of self-transformation, self-redemption, works-righteousness. Such pseudoreconciliation is doomed to fail and to fall under God's judgment.

EUGENE F. A. KLUG

See ATONEMENT; MAN, OLD AND NEW.

Bibliography. R.J. Banks, ed., *Reconciliation and Hope;* J. Denney, *The Christian Doctrine of Reconciliation;* J.A. Fitzmyer, *To Advance the Gospel,* pp 162–85; R.P. Martin, *Reconciliation;* L. Morris, *The Apostolic Preaching of the Cross;* V. Taylor, *Forgiveness and Reconciliation.*

Recorder. High public official and perhaps the keeper of the official records (2 Sm 8:16; 2 Kgs 18:18).

See TRADES AND OCCUPATIONS.

Red. *See* COLOR.

Redaction Criticism. A method of biblical interpretation that originated in Germany and has come into prominence since World War II. Although not without application to parts of the OT, in particular the Samuel-Kings-Chronicles corpus, it has been applied primarily in NT studies and especially in the study of the Gospels and portions of Acts.

A redactor is by definition one who puts a literary work in publishable or final form, that is, an editor. Redaction criticism is thus an attempt to discover the distinctive contribution of a biblical writer to the final form of the information he records. All four Gospel writers, for example, had access to much of the same data regarding Jesus' life and teachings. Nevertheless, the Gospels stress different aspects of Jesus' ministry and reactions to him, and report similar incidents but with varying, at times even contrasting emphases. Each writer's work, even granting that it was Spirit-led and without error, reflects his own outlook, purpose in writing, and individual personal knowledge of and experience with Jesus. He interpreted the sources and other data available to him, putting his own distinctive twist on them. Redaction criticism scrutinizes this distinctive contribution.

Redaction criticism generally builds upon but goes beyond two earlier interpretive methods often applied to NT documents. First, source criticism sought to determine the (usually) written sources which lay behind the biblical texts (see, e.g., Lk 1:1–4). Next, form criticism was concerned with the original shape of Gospel material in its oral form and how early church life might have affected the formation of individual portions (pericopes) of each Gospel.

The Rise of Redaction Criticism. The beginning of redaction criticism is generally traced to three scholars in Germany. Willi Marxsen's work on Mark (1956), Günther Bornkamm's on Matthew (1940s–50s), and Hans Conzelmann's on Luke (1953) were each ground-breaking in going beyond the form-critical methods of their predecessors. No longer was the stress on individual pericopes and their presumed oral development and transmission. Now the attempt was made to note each Gospel writer's individual emphasis in order to highlight the particular message he sought to convey in his work as a whole. Although many of the underlying assumptions of the first redaction critics were hardly compatible with an evangelical theological outlook (e.g., it was common for the historical accuracy of the Gospels to be radically doubted, especially when they treated theological themes), their contribution has set the tone for all redaction-critical study since. Today, while some skeptical scholars maintain that redaction criticism has turned "the balance in the two hundred odd years struggle over the nature of the gospels—historical versus religious—in favor of the latter" (W. Kelber), evangelical scholars, for whom the historical integrity of Scripture is not in doubt, take advantage of redaction criticism's helpful features without necessarily endorsing the skepticism of some of its practitioners.

Redaction criticism of a sort has long been practiced even by evangelical interpreters. "Redaction criticism" in a narrow sense refers to successors of German form criticism, but in a broader sense "it covers all those works, whatever their date or country of origin, in which the evangelists are not treated as mere compilers, but as authors with a point of view or even a theology of their own" (G. B. Caird). Ned Stonehouse (1902–62), a Westminster Seminary professor, was practicing redaction criticism in the broad sense in the late 1930s, while England's William Alexander expressed similar insights much earlier: "There was lodged in the memory of the original Apostles and disciples a treasury of recollections. The works, the discourses, the personality of Jesus Christ, were there in abundant fulness. As time passed, and a written record of those momentous years became necessary, the evangelists selected such actions and sayings as brought out certain aspects of the Lord's ministry, purpose, character, and teaching. Each Gospel is arranged round one centre, or at least round a few central points" (*The Leading Ideas of the Gospels*, 1892).

Redaction Criticism Today. Among non-evangelicals, redaction criticism is typically carried on under the assumption that the Gospel accounts contradict one another, that much of the Gospel material was fabricated by the writer to advance some point or doctrine, that the Gospels are really indifferent to the historicity of that which they recount, and that in general "a Gospel does not portray the history of the ministry of Jesus from A.D. 27–30 . . . but the history of Christian experience in any and every age" (N. Perrin). For this reason many evangelicals rightly point out the need for caution in taking up redaction-critical methods.

While some evangelical scholars have caused consternation in recent years by a use of redaction criticism that seemed to compromise a high view of Scripture, and while others eschew redaction criticism altogether because of its perceived misuse, many evangelical interpreters find it a helpful tool. Used alone its benefits are admittedly limited; but in conjunction with other methods it can yield useful results. When a writer's special focus and emphasis on a large scale are delineated, this knowledge can in turn inform and enhance understanding of the smaller components of the document.

R. Gruenler's conclusion regarding redaction criticism in the Gospels would be endorsed by many today. "The evangelist is not a creator, for the original creator, speaker, and doer of the gospel story is Jesus himself; but as subcreator the evangelist reflects the original light of Jesus' field of force through the prism of his own self-understanding as well as that of his audience" (*New Approaches to Jesus and the Gospels*). Redaction criticism employed with care, methodological self-awareness, and a commitment to Scripture's integrity will continue to serve as a much-used instrument for many evangelical NT scholars. Even those who are suspicious of it will need to stay abreast of its findings.

Weaknesses and Strengths. If redaction criticism is to be used judiciously, it must be aware of such potential dangers as undue skepticism regarding the historical veracity of NT documents; an unjustifiable assumption that where NT writers speak of theological or religious matters, they abandon concern for historical facts; and the demonstrated limitations of source and form criticism, which redaction criticism unavoidably inherits to some extent. There is the temptation to couple aspects of redaction criticism to new forms of literary criticism which disregard sources underlying the document being interpreted. Redaction criticism proper is only fruitful where the sort of alteration or modification the redactor is making to or on his sources can be clearly seen. Other dangers include an overoptimism that the redaction critic is able to pinpoint the precise reason why a certain change is made and what the implication for the change is; a dogmatism regarding the order of writing of the four Gospels; and a confusion between the results of applying redaction criticism, which may illuminate how a text took on its final form, and the results of rightly apprehending the message of the text itself, which goes beyond what redaction criticism theorizes (often cogently) to what God's Word is actually saying.

Strengths of a balanced application of redaction criticism include a recognition that Gospel (and other biblical) writers were not faceless, anonymous compilers of tradition but author-proclaimers in their own right; a discovery of the unique outlook and burden which informs the whole and thus the parts of a document; and a recognition of the differences between various Gospel accounts and therefore encouragement to furnish a plausible explanation of them. Also included are a realization of the necessity and fruitfulness of close comparative study of the Gospels and other portions of Scripture that duplicate or parallel each other; an appreciation for the theological perspective that characterizes a document in its literary unity; and an understanding of NT documents as part of a distinctive 1st-century milieu and process of composition.

The use of redaction criticism can contribute much to the understanding of Scripture, especially the Gospels. However, as with every interpretive method, it must be applied responsibly so as to preserve both the historicity and integrity of the text.

ROBERT W. YARBROUGH

See FORM CRITICISM; BIBLICAL CRITICISM, NEW TESTAMENT; DEMYTHOLOGIZATION; SYNOPTIC GOSPELS; MATTHEW, BOOK OF; MARK, BOOK OF; LUKE, BOOK OF; DOCUMENTARY HYPOTHESIS; SOURCE CRITICISM; TRADITION CRITICISM; MARKAN HYPOTHESIS.

Bibliography. D. Carson, *Redaction Criticism: The Nature of an Interpretive Tool;* W. Kelber, "Redaction Criticism: On the Nature and Exposition of the Gospels," *Perspectives in Religious Studies* 6 (1979): 4–16; N. Perrin, *What Is Redaction Criticism?;* S. Smalley, "Redaction Criticism," in *NT Interpretation,* ed. I.H. Marshall.

Redeemer, Redemption.

English words derived from a Latin root meaning "to buy back," thus meaning the liberation of any possession, object, or person, usually by payment of a ransom. In Greek the root word means "to loose" and so to free. The term is used of freeing from chains, slavery, or prison. In the theological context, the term "redemption" indicates a freeing from the slavery of sin, the ransom or price paid for freedom. This thought is indicated in the Gospels, which speak of Christ who came "to give his life as a ransom for many" (Mt 20:28; Mk 10:45).

Old Testament Words. For a full understanding of the concept of redemption, it is necessary to look at the OT. There are three different words used in Hebrew, depending on the particular situation, which convey the idea of redemption. The meaning of these redemptive terms rests on legal, social, and religious customs which are foreign to modern culture. An understanding of the culture is needed for an understanding of the terminology and its use.

The first term used for redemption has a legal context. The verb *pādāh* is used when an animal substitutes (or redeems) a person or another animal. The noun derived from the root means the *ransom* or price paid. In the Greek language this term is generally translated by the verb *luō*, which means "to loose." The noun derived from this term, *lutron*, is the price paid for loosing or freeing, hence, the ransom.

When a living being, person or animal, requires redemption, the substitution must be made, or price paid, otherwise the being involved is killed (Ex 13:13; 34:20). However, there is evidence that this rule was not always strictly followed (Ex 21:8; Jb 6:23).

The concept of redemption had special significance for the firstborn. The firstborn male, both man and beast, belonged to God. In theory the firstborn was sacrificed to him. This was done in the case of many animals, but the human firstborn and some animals were redeemed (Ex 13:13; 34:20; Nm 18:15,16). In the redemption of the firstborn son, an animal was substituted, although later a sum of money was paid (Nm 18:16). Unclean animals were redeemed by substitutions of a sacrificial animal or put to death (Ex 13:13; 34:20; Nm 18:15).

A special case was the animal or person promised to the Lord. Such a one was sacrificed without exception. The Lord made no allowance for the redemption of persons or animals so dedicated.

However, in the case of King Saul and his son an exception was made (1 Sm 14:24–46). Saul had placed a curse on anyone eating on the day of a particular battle. When he learned that his son, Jonathan, had (unknowingly) violated his edict, he still ordered him put to death. The people intervened and redeemed Jonathan by substituting an animal sacrifice in his place.

The second term involved is the Hebrew root *gāʾal*, which is used primarily in relation to family rules and obligations, the laws governing family property rights and duties. For example, should a piece of property be lost to a family member, the next-of-kin had both the right and the obligation to redeem this property. This right of redemption protected the family inheritance. The noun derived from this root is equivalent to the English root *redemption*, and the person who buys back the property is the *goel* or redeemer.

Gibeah—Saul's early home and his headquarters for fighting the Philistines—was located 3 miles south of Michmash, where the battle occurred during which Jonathan fell under his father's curse but was redeemed by the people.

An Israelite who was forced to sell himself into slavery to pay his debts could be redeemed by a near relative or even by himself (Lv 25:47–49). Land might also be redeemed in the same fashion (vv 25–28; Jer 32:6–9).

The right of redemption extended also to persons in special circumstances. The obligation of a man to marry his brother's widow is well known. In the Book of Ruth, the right of redemption is extended to a distant relative. In this story, Boaz redeemed not only the property but Ruth as well, and she became his wife (Ru 3:13; 4:1–6).

The third term used in Hebrew is the root verb *kāpar*, which means "to cover." From this root comes the terms meaning to cover sin, atone, or expiate. The noun derived, *kōpher*, means the price paid to cover sin, when the term is used in the religious sense.

The term is used to mean the payment made for any life which has become forfeit. A good illustration is the price paid by the owner of an ox which had gored a person to death. Under the law the owner's life was forfeited, but he could redeem himself by paying the required *ransom* (Ex 21:28–32).

All three terms are translated by the same Greek verb, *luō*, meaning "to loose." *Lutron* (ransom) is used for all three terms on occasion. This indicates that while the Hebrews used different words for different situations, the same essential meaning of *redemption* is involved in all situations. The concept of redeeming or freeing is of primary concern.

God as Redeemer. In the OT the object of God's redemption is generally the people as a whole, or nation, rather than individuals.

The beginning of this concept of national redemption is seen in God's freeing the people from slavery in Egypt. Though they were in bondage, their God ransomed them (Ex 6:6; Dt 15:15).

As indicated by the terms used for redeeming or ransoming, the payment of a set price or the substitution of another life was involved.

When the redemptive concept is applied to God as the subject, he delivers—without the payment of a price—by his might or power. "Say therefore to the people of Israel, 'I am the Lord, and I will bring you out from under the burdens of the Egyptians, and I will deliver you from their bondage, and I will redeem you with an outstretched arm and with great acts of judgment' " (Ex 6:6; Dt 15:15).

The same thought is carried forward in other times of need and deliverance, such as the time of the exile. God is the national deliverer (e.g., Is 29:22; 35:10; 43:1; 44:22; Jer 31:11).

Again there is no suggestion that God paid a price to free his people. God redeems by his own power. "For thus says the Lord, 'You were sold for nothing, and you shall be redeemed without money' " (Is 52:3). When Cyrus let the people free, it was again without payment of a price (Is 45:13).

The prophet emphasizes that when God judged Israel and allowed his people to be taken captive as punishment for their sins, they are freed again by divine power once their guilt has been expiated and their sins covered.

In the Christian community, especially in the early centuries of the church, there arose the idea that a ransom price was needed to pay for sins. In fact it was often taught that the sinner was, in effect, held captive by Satan. Christ's death was the ransom price paid by God to Satan to free sinful people. This teaching is not supported by Scripture. The death of Christ is an atonement or expiation made for sin, but this does not mean that his death was a price paid to anyone. God is not pictured anywhere in Scripture as getting into such a commercial transaction with Satan. The redeeming work of the cross must always lie within the realm of divine mystery.

Redemption and Messiah. In the OT redemption is closely linked with the messianic hope. From the time of the exodus on, God is revealed as a deliverer. The hope of redemption is very strong during the captivity. The prophets constantly spoke of God as redeemer or deliverer. This hope was fulfilled ultimately through God's anointed one or Messiah who would be of the line of David (Isa 9:1–6; 11:1–9; Jer 23:5,6).

The messianic hope grew stronger during periods of exile and persecution. In fact during the long centuries of persecution, this hope of a messianic deliverer was stronger than ever. This period, generally called the intertestamental period, lasted about four centuries and extended from the last of the prophets until the time of John the Baptist and Jesus.

Redemption and Jesus Christ. Christians believe that in Jesus the Christ (or Jesus the Messiah), we see the fulfillment of the OT redemptive concept. The redemptive image is very evident in the Gospels. John the Baptist depicted Jesus of Nazareth as the fulfillment of God's redemptive kingdom (Mt 3:12) and hence, the Messiah of Israel. Jesus, the Son of man, came to give himself as a ransom for many (Mt 20:28; Mk 10:45). The work of the Messiah was vicarious and substitutionary.

The same thought occurs especially in the writings of Paul. Christ is the sin offering to the Father (Rom 3:25). Redemption is by the giving of his life (Acts 20:28) for a purchased people (1 Pt 2:9; also 1 Cor 7:22–24; 2 Cor 5:14–17). These are all words, or expressions, used to present the central idea of redemption or atonement. Jesus Christ is the one who in himself, fulfilled the redemption concept of Scripture and by his sacrifice provided for the redemption of sinners.

The concept of redemption has deep meaning for God's people. In the OT it illustrates the truth that God is the Savior of his covenant people. Although Israel fell into sin by denying God's Law, God did not destroy them, but restored them to favor upon repentance.

In the prophets, especially, God's redemptive work was to be completed through the Messiah and his redemptive sacrifice. The followers of Jesus believed that he was the Messiah who would provide redemption for the whole world. Coupled with the idea of redemption is the motivating force of divine love as the basis for restoration (Jn 3:16). The one who believes will be freed from the bondage of sin and find favor again with his redeeming God. WARREN C. YOUNG

See ATONEMENT; RANSOM; CRUCIFIXION; OFFERINGS AND SACRIFICES; SALVATION; MESSIAH; REPENTANCE; CONVERSION.

Bibliography. S. Lyonnet and L. Sabourin, *Sin, Redemption, and Sacrifice;* L. Morris, *The Apostolic Preaching of the Cross;* J. Murray, *Redemption—Accomplished and Applied;* L.J. Sherril, *Guilt and Redemption;* B.B. Warfield, *The Plan of Salvation.*

Red Heifer. *See* ANIMALS (CATTLE).

Red Sea.
Arm of the Indian Ocean, extending to the northwest and lying between the continents of Africa and Asia. It is a long, narrow body of water, some 1,450 miles long and averaging 180 miles in width. It is flanked on the east by the Arabian peninsula, while its African shore includes Egypt, the Sudan, Eritrea, and Ethiopia. At the northwest the peninsula of Sinai juts into the sea, with the Gulf of Suez on the west and the Gulf of Aqaba on the east. At the northwestern end of the Gulf of Suez is the city of Suez and the water connection with the Mediterranean Sea via the Suez Canal. At the tip of the Gulf of Aqaba is the Israeli port of Eilat and the sole Jordanian port, Aqaba. The waters of this sea are extremely rich in aquatic life and the fish and other animal life from the Red Sea could provide much of the food needs for this part of the world. There are few cities, few good roads, and little arable land adjoining the Red Sea.

In the Hebrew OT the Red Sea is called the "Sea of Reeds, or Rushes," but English translations ordinarily give "Red Sea," which is the name used by secular writers. In the NT the only references to the Red Sea by that name are in the defense of Stephen before the council (Acts 7:36) and in the "heroes of faith" chapter (Heb 11:29). It is also referred to twice simply as "the sea" (1 Cor 10:1,2).

The crossing of the Red Sea by the Israelites at the time of the exodus is one of the most celebrated events of Hebrew history and has been memorialized by the Jewish people to the present time. The place of this crossing is much debated, but wherever it occurred it is evident that the water was too deep to wade across and the distance too far to swim. Yet it was deep enough to cover all the Egyptian army and wide enough to drown all of their number. Confronted by the sea and closely pursued by the crack troops and skilled chariotry of the best army in the world at that time, the Israelites were delivered by the direct intervention of the Lord, who used an east wind to make a channel for their passage upon the bed of the sea, answering even before they called (see Ex 14:10–31).

When the Lord overwhelmed the Egyptian forces in the sea, the deliverance of the Israelites from the Egyptian threat was complete. This victory was celebrated by songs (Ex 15:1–21) and was often recalled in accounts of the Lord's works in behalf of Israel (e.g., Jos 4:23; 24:6,7; Pss 106:7–9,22; 136:13–15). Even the people of Jericho heard of what God did at the Red Sea and fear fell upon them (Jos 2:9,10). In the NT the passage through the Red Sea is cited as an act of faith (Heb 11:29).

The route taken by Israel paralleled the eastern shore of the Gulf of Suez for some distance. After they left Elim they camped beside the sea (Nm 33:9–11), before turning inland to head for Mt Sinai.

From Sinai they headed northeast, paralleling the Gulf of Aqaba as closely as possible and certainly touching the Red Sea at Ezion-geber (Nm 33:35). Following their failure to enter Canaan from Kadesh-barnea and their defeat at Hormah, they turned south to the point at which Mt Seir approaches the Gulf of Aqaba (cf. Dt 2:8).

The southernmost border of the Promised Land is indicated as the Red Sea (Ex 23:31). Solomon's kingdom extended to the Gulf of Aqaba, for at Ezion-geber near Eloth he built a fleet of ships which went to Ophir, from which gold and other precious and exotic commodities were brought (1 Kgs 9:26–28; cf. 2 Chr 8:17,18). Later Jehoshaphat attempted to do the same, but his ships were wrecked at Ezion-geber (1 Kgs 22:48; 2 Chr 20:36,37).

See EXODUS, THE; EXODUS, BOOK OF.

Reed.
Tall grass that grows in damp places and beside bodies of water.

See PLANTS; WEIGHTS AND MEASURES.

Reeds, Sea of. Hebrew designation for the body of water crossed by the Israelites during the exodus from Egypt.

See EXODUS; THE RED SEA.

Reelaiah. Head of a family that returned to Jerusalem with Zerubbabel after the exile (Ezr 2:2); alternately called Raamiah (Neh 7:7).

See RAAMIAH.

Refuge, Cities of. *See* CITIES OF REFUGE.

Regem. Jahdai's son and a descendant of Caleb (1 Chr 2:47).

Regem-melech. One of the delegation sent to inquire whether fasting to commemorate the temple destruction should continue (Zec 7:2). The name may refer to a person or could be a title meaning "friend of the king."

Regeneration. Inner cleansing and renewal of the human nature by the Holy Spirit. Mankind's spiritual condition is transformed from a disposition of sin to one of a new relationship with God (Ti 3:5). Regeneration involves both moral restoration and the reception of new life. The idea of regeneration is expressed as rebirth—being born again (Jn 3:3–7). This new birth suggests the newness of life in Christ. The process of regeneration is not brought about by human righteousness but by the gracious act of God (Eph 2:8,9).

See ATONEMENT; REDEEMER, REDEMPTION; SALVATION; REPENTANCE; CONVERSION.

Rehabiah. Levite, son of Eliezer the priest and Moses' grandson (1 Chr 23:17; 24:21; 26:25).

Rehob (Person). 1. King of Zobah whose son, Hadadezer, was defeated by David at the Euphrates River (2 Sm 8:3,12).

2. One of the Levites who set his seal on Ezra's covenant (Neh 10:11).

Rehob (Place). 1. Northernmost territory explored by the Israelite spies prior to occupation of Canaan (Nm 13:21). It agrees with the location of Beth-rehob (Jgs 18:28) and is mentioned with Zobah and Maacah as an opponent of David in the Ammonite war (2 Sm 10:6–8).

See also ARAM.

2. Two cities belonging to Asher's tribe (Jos 19:28,30). One was given to the levitical family of Gershon (Jos 21:31) and became a city of refuge (1 Chr 6:75). The other remained in Canaanite hands (Jgs 1:31). Some scholars identify the references as one city. Its site is unknown.

See CITIES OF REFUGE; LEVITICAL CITIES.

Rehoboam. King (930–913 BC, KJV Roboam, Mt 1:7) especially remembered for his part in perpetuating the split of the Hebrew kingdom and for being the first king of the separate kingdom of Judah.

Split of the Kingdom. When Solomon died (930 BC), his son Rehoboam ascended the throne. Perhaps as a concession to the Ephraimites, who often seemed to have been piqued at their inferior status, Rehoboam agreed to hold his coronation in their town of Shechem instead of Jerusalem, a traditional place of meeting on which "all Israel" could agree (1 Kgs 12:1).

At the conclave, leaders of the northern tribes accompanied by Jeroboam approached the new king for concessions. Jeroboam, an official under Solomon's administration who had fled to Egypt when Solomon suspected him of treason, had returned to Israel to assume a position of leadership. Jeroboam was destined to be the ruler of Israel because of Solomon's apostasy (1 Kgs 11). Solomon's numerous building projects and his ostentation seem to have bankrupted the kingdom, resulting in an intolerable tax burden. Especially objectionable was forced labor on various projects. (See 1 Kgs 12:4; 2 Chr 10:4.) The populace sought relief from high taxes.

The new king asked for a three-day grace period in which to study the request. Advisers from Solomon's administration counseled concessions; the younger men urged no moderation but an even greater tax burden. Following the advice of his peers, Rehoboam arrogantly threatened even higher taxes. The restless northern tribes broke away to establish a separate kingdom under the leadership of Jeroboam. Judah and Benjamin were the only tribes loyal to Rehoboam.

The separate existence of the northern kingdom was not a new development. After Saul's death the north had gone its own way while David ruled in Hebron. Some 30 years later, it had briefly supported Sheba in a revolt against David. Now under the leadership of Jeroboam, the rupture was to become permanent.

Not accepting the apparent success of the secession, Rehoboam sent his tribute-master or treasurer, Adoram, to try to heal the division. North Israelite partisans stoned him to death, and Jeroboam and his party fled to Jerusalem. Rehoboam immediately tried to subjugate the rebellious tribes. Raising a force of 180,000 men from Judah and Benjamin, he prepared to march north, but the prophet Shemaiah brought word from God to abandon the project since the breakup of the kingdom was part of the judgment of God on Israel for the sinfulness of the nation during Solomon's reign. Rehoboam promptly abandoned his military efforts, but intermittent military skirmishes plagued the relations of Rehoboam and Jeroboam throughout their reigns (1 Kgs 14:30).

Reign of Rehoboam. In the face of constant threat of attack, Rehoboam set about to fortify his kingdom. He built extensive fortifications with adequate supplies of weapons and food at Bethlehem, Etam, Tekoa, Bethzur, Shoco, Adullam, Gath, Maresha, Ziph, Adoraim, Lachish, Azekah, Zorah, Aijalon, and Hebron.

Military preparedness was supplemented by spiritual underpinning. As a result of the establishment of a new apostate religion in the northern kingdom, priests and Levites streamed to the south, where they greatly strengthened the spiritual fiber of the realm. Apparently they helped to maintain the stability of Judah for "three years" (2 Chr 10:17).

However, the people built high places and pagan sanctuaries throughout the land. They began to engage in the corrupt religious practices of the heathen nations around them, including homosexuality (1 Kgs 14:22–24).

Soon Rehoboam "forsook the law of the Lord, and all Israel with him" (2 Chr 12:1). Rehoboam was the son of Solomon, a preoccupied father who himself grew increasingly lax about spiritual things. Rehoboam's mother was Naamah, a pagan Ammonite princess who presumably lacked any spiritual perception (1 Kgs 14:21). His father's example of keeping a harem and having numerous children likewise had an impact on him. Rehoboam had 18 wives, 60 concubines, 28 sons, and 60 daughters. He spent a considerable amount of time providing living arrangements for them in the fortified cities of Judah (2 Chr 11:21–23).

At length the apostasy of Judah became so great that God brought judgment on the nation in the form of a foreign invasion. In the fifth year of Rehoboam (c. 926 BC), Shishak I (Sheshonk I) of Egypt invaded Palestine with 1,200 chariots and 60,000 men (1 Kgs 14:25; 2 Chr 12:2,3).

After Shishak's initial successes, the prophet Shemaiah made it clear to the king and the nobility that the invasion was direct punishment for their sinful ways. When they repented of their waywardness, God promised to moderate their punishment. They were subjected to either a heavy tribute or a plundering of their cities. The national treasury and the temple treasury were emptied to satisfy the demands of the Egyptians.

Shishak's invasion continued into the northern kingdom, for his inscription in the temple of Karnak at Luxor tells of his conquest of 156 towns in the two kingdoms. Only a fraction of the names listed can be identified.

Rehoboam's repentance was only temporary. Scripture implies that his latter years were characterized by evil (2 Chr 12:14), and that his son and successor Abijam "walked in all the sins which his father did before him" (1 Kgs 15:3). Probably the sins of his father would not have been condemned if Rehoboam's last 12 years had been a good example to his maturing son.

Rehoboam was 41 when he ascended the throne, and he reigned for 17 years. He designated as his successor Abijam, son of his favorite wife Maachah.

HOWARD F. VOS

See ISRAEL, HISTORY OF; CHRONOLOGY, OLD TESTAMENT; GENEALOGY OF JESUS CHRIST.

Rehoboth. 1. KJV name for Rehoboth-ir, a city built by Nimrod, in Genesis 10:11.

See REHOBOTH-IR.

2. Site of the third well dug by Isaac (Gn 26:22). This time Abimelech and the herdsmen of Gerar did not lay claim to it, and Isaac named the well "broad places" or "room." The well was located about 20 miles southwest of Beersheba.

3. Home of Shaul (KJV, NEB Saul), an Edomite ruler (Gn 36:37; 1 Chr 1:48). The place is identified as "on the river," a frequent biblical reference to the Euphrates. But the distance separating Edom and the Euphrates has caused doubt as to whether the Euphrates is meant in these verses (NASB, RSV insert "Euphrates" into the text).

Rehoboth-ir. Name meaning "broad places of the city." It was the second city built by Nimrod the hunter (KJV Asshur) in Assyria (Gn 10:11, KJV Rehoboth). Opinion differs as to whether it was a distinct municipality (a suburb of Nineveh) or, since the name of the town is not mentioned in Assyrian literature, open squares or broad streets within Nineveh itself.

Rehum. 1. One of the 12 Jewish leaders who returned from captivity with Zerubbabel (Ezr 2:2; Neh 7:7 where "Nehum" is apparently a copyist's error).

See NEHUM.

2. Persian commander who, with Shimshai the scribe, wrote to Artaxerxes I complaining of the Jews' temple rebuilding project and promising dire consequences should the project be completed. The king's response halted construction until the second year of Darius' reign (Ezr 4:8–23).

3. Levite identified as Bani's son, who helped repair the Jerusalem wall under Nehemiah's direction (Neh 3:17).

4. Leader who set his seal on Ezra's covenant (Neh 10:25).

Carved on a wall at Karnak is the likeness of Shishak I, who invaded Palestine in the 5th year of Rehoboam.

5. Priest who **accompanied** Zerubbabel (Neh 12:3), called Harim (v 15).

See HARIM #5.

Rei. Officer who supported Solomon when Adonijah attempted to become king near the end of David's reign (1 Kgs 1:8).

Rekem (Person). 1. Prince or king of Midian killed with his four accomplices in a battle waged by Moses at the Lord's command (Nm 31:8; Jos 13:21). Israelites living in the vicinity of Rekem's dominion had been seduced to the worship of Baal-peor.

2. Son of Hebron, a descendant of Caleb, and Shammai's father (1 Chr 2:43,44).

Rekem (Place). One of 26 cities assigned to Benjamin's tribe for an inheritance (Jos 18:27). Its location is uncertain.

Remaliah. Father of King Pekah of Israel (737–732 BC). Pekah, through treachery, claimed Israel's throne (2 Kgs 15:25–37) and later terrorized Jerusalem (Is 7:1–9).

Remeth. Border town in Issachar's territory (Jos 19:21), and probably the same as Ramoth (1 Chr 6:73), also called Jarmuth.

See JARMUTH #2.

Remmon. KJV form of En-rimmon, a town in Simeon's territory, in Joshua 19:7.

See EN-RIMMON.

Remmon-methoar. KJV translation for "Rimmon it bends toward Neah," in Joshua 19:13.

See RIMMON (PLACE) #2.

Remnant. Group of people who survive a catastrophe brought about by God, ordinarily in judgment for sin. This group becomes the nucleus for the continuation of mankind or the people of God; the future existence of the larger group focuses in this purified, holy remnant that has undergone and survived the judgment of God. The remnant concept is found in all periods of redemptive history where catastrophe—be it natural disaster, disease, warfare, or other instruments—threatens the continuity of God's purposes. From the creation account to the NT, the concept is progressively sharpened.

The remnant motif is not unique to the Bible among the literatures of the ancient Near East; the same theme is found in the myths, legends, prayers, hymns, and other literary genres in Sumerian, Akkadian, Hittite, Ugaritic, and Egyptian cultures. Stories of survival from threats to the existence of the individual, family, clan, tribe, army, nation, or mankind as a whole are recounted in these literatures as well, for example, in the extrabiblical flood stories. In some respects the sharing of the motif is the natural result of a common human concern with the preservation of life in the face of mortal threat or the need to explain a disaster in terms of the acts of the gods. Only in the Bible is the remnant motif organically brought into relation with the ongoing history of redemption in a unified and recapitulatory fashion.

The Problem. The theological problem which the remnant concept addresses is the tension between the grace and promises of God over against his holiness and just judgment of sin. God has chosen, created, and called a people for himself and has promised to them his unfailing grace and favor. The remnant motif addresses the tension between God's grace and his judgment by presenting a distinction between the true and false people of God and between the present and future people of God. The holy, pure, and true people of God will survive his judgment on sin as a faithful remnant and will become the nucleus of a renewed, chosen people. The purposes of God are not frustrated but are effected among that true and renewed people.

The concept is one which cuts in two directions. On the one hand, depending on the imminent expectation of the biblical author, it may emphasize judgment, that God is on the verge of destroying his people because of their sin; the remnant itself may even be threatened because the contemplated judgment is so severe. On the other hand, the fact that a remnant survives emphasizes both the grace of God, his favor shown to those he has kept safe, and the dawning of a new age and a new community, which inherits the promises of God as it springs from that remnant.

Old Testament. *Prior to the Patriarchal Period.* The first passage exhibiting the remnant concept is the account of the fall into sin. Though there is no actual loss of life or numerical reduction, the judgment of God threatens the continued existence of mankind (Gn 2:15, 16; 3:4). Judgment is averted by God's grace, and Adam and Eve become the nucleus of humanity; the hopes of the future are focused in their offspring (3:16,20; 4:1). God's purposes for mankind will not be frustrated but will be realized through the seed of the woman.

The flood narrative is more specific. Because of the wickedness of mankind God determines to blot out all life, but a righteous man who was blameless before God, together with his family, receives God's favor (6:8,9; Heb 11:7). Only Noah and those with him in the ark survived the judgment of God (Gn 7:23). The continued existence of mankind focuses in the fruitfulness and increase of his sons (9:1), introducing a new age and a new covenant (vv 8–17). God's purpose remains the same and will be realized in the seed of Noah (v 26).

From the Patriarchal Period to the Monarchy. Not all passages contributing to the development of the remnant motif involve the threat of universal judgment. The sins of the twin cities of Sodom and Gomorrah were so grievous that God determined to destroy them. For the sake of his servant Abraham (Gn 18:16–19; 19:29) and because of Lot's righteousness (2 Pt 2:8), God spared Lot and his two daughters. Abraham's negotiations with God to spare the entire city if 50, and finally even 10, righteous persons could be found there (18:22–33) emphasize again that the righteous escape judgment. God will not sweep away the righteous with the wicked (v 22); even when they hesitate, he is merciful and leads them out of the city (19:16,29).

The story of Joseph is the literary bridge from the children of Jacob, a family in Canaan (46:26,27), to the thousands of children of Israel at the time of the exodus. The dominant theological motif in the story is the preservation of the patriarch's family in the face of mortal threat from famine. God sent Joseph into Egypt to save lives and to preserve for his family a remnant (45:6,7). What Joseph's brothers had done intending harm, God had done intending good, the saving of many lives (50:19,20). Once again the purposes of God are not thwarted but will be realized in these survivors from the threat of extinction.

Obedience to the commands of God and trust in his promises are at issue when the spies return from reconnoitering Canaan (Nm 13,14). Representatives from all the tribes had explored the land; in spite of their agreement about its excellence, all but two of the spies reported that the land could not be taken (13:26–33). Because of their grumbling, God announced his intention to destroy them all and to recreate a greater nation from his faithful servant Moses (14:10–12). After Moses intercedes on behalf of the people, the Lord relents: Instead of destruction for all, only Joshua and Caleb would enter the promised inheritance because of their faithful report. The people would remain in the wilderness 40 years until all died except these two (14:20–35). The transgressors would die, but the faithful remnant would receive the promise.

The Law, too, stipulates that faithfulness is required to retain possession of the land. Disobedience would bring disease, defeat in war, drought, crop failure, attack by wild animals, death by sword and famine, cannibalism, destruction of cities, and exile into enemy lands (Lv 26:1–39). But for those who were left, those who confess their sins and repent—the remnant—God will keep his covenant with them, restore them to their land (vv 40–45), and realize his purpose in them.

From the Monarchy to the Exile. Even in the apostate northern kingdom the Lord keeps his faithful remnant. At the end of a three-year drought in punishment for sins in the northern kingdom (1 Kgs 17:1; 18:1) and after the victory over the priests of Baal at Mt Carmel, Elijah goes to Mt Sinai, fleeing for his life from Jezebel (1 Kgs 19). There he lamented that Israel had given itself totally to false worship and that he alone was left of the faithful (19:10,14). God replied by instructing him to anoint Jehu as king and Elisha as his prophetic successor. Jehu and Elisha would destroy the apostate, while God preserved for himself the 7000 who had not bowed the knee to Baal (vv 15–18). The faithful remnant would be spared destruction.

The preexilic prophets emphasize the smallness of the remnant that will survive the destruction under Assyria and Babylon. Amos addressed those whose confidence in the inviolability of the promises of God led them to ignore his holiness. He warned of great judgment which would threaten even the remnant itself. God would destroy the sinful kingdom, though not totally (9:8). All sinners among the people would die, and even those who were left would be killed; Israel is like grain in a sieve, and not one kernel escapes (vv 1,8). God will bring an enemy against Israel; what is left of it will be like what the shepherd finds after the lion's attack—only a piece of an ear and some bones (3:12). Its armies will be decimated (5:3). Amos' warnings about judgment to come are a call to repentance, to "hate evil, love good, and maintain justice" so that the Lord will "have mercy on the remnant of Joseph" (5:14,15). Transgressors will be punished, but the righteous will enjoy his promises.

Isaiah, too, speaks of the smallness of the remnant. Israel is left "like a shelter in a vineyard, a hut in a melon field" only narrowly avoiding the fate of Sodom and Gomorrah (1:8,9). It is left like a pole on a hilltop (30:17), like the stump of a felled tree (6:13). When the reaper gathers his harvest, Israel is the gleanings that are left, the few olives that remain in the top of the tree (17:4–6). But from the stump of that felled tree will spring new life (6:11–13). Those who survive in Jerusalem will be holy, and the Lord will bring a new shoot from the stump of Jesse, a righteous servant (the Branch) who will bring the remnant of the people of God from many nations (4:2,3; 11:1–16). After God has purged away the iniquity of the people, Jerusalem will be known as the "city of righteousness, the faithful city" (1:21–26). Isaiah names his sons in terms of his prophetic expectations: Maher-shalal-hash-baz ("quick to the plunder, swift to the spoil") testified to the certainty of coming judgment, while Shear-yashub ("a remnant will return") spoke of his future confidence. Isaiah and his sons were portents to Israel of the intent of God (8:16–18). Israel will be cut down because the Lord has decreed destruction on the land, but a remnant will return, those who truly "lean on the Lord" (10:20–23). The remnant will take root and be a fruitful people (37:30–32).

In the latter chapters (40–66), Isaiah contemplates the postexilic community. The so-called "servant songs" in these chapters are brought into direct relationship with the remnant motif. The faithful remnant arises from a period of judgment and can therefore be called a "suffering servant." God would make "little Israel" strong again while he destroys her enemies (41:8–14). The Lord's servant will be righteous and will bring justice to the nations (42:1–9). Though Israel would be plunder for the nations (43:22–25), yet God will bring people from the ends of the earth to be his witnesses, his servants (43:5–13). Where once the land was parched, the Lord will bring water; his Spirit will be poured on the offspring of the servant of the Lord, and they will flourish like grass in a meadow (44:3,4). The surviving faithful servant who has undergone judgment becomes the hope for the future people (53:10–12). The people of God will be tested in the furnace of affliction but not forsaken (48:9–11). Isaiah individualizes this servant: he is born of a woman and is called "Israel," and he comes to restore the tribes of Jacob, to bring back Israel (ch 49). Israel has sinned, but the remnant/servant is faithful and obedient (ch 50).

Micah, a contemporary of Isaiah, also announces the coming judgment on Israel and Judah (1:1–16; 2:1–11; 4:9–11; 6:1–16; 7:1–6). Those whose confidence in the inviolability of Zion allows them to think the city cannot be touched will see Zion plowed like a field, Jerusalem a heap of rubble, and the temple hill a mound overgrown with thickets (3:12). Yet mixed in with these stern warnings of impending destruction are the promises of a faithful remnant led by a righteous king (2:12,13). The nations will flow to Jerusalem, and the Lord will rule over them in Zion (4:1–8). Their king will come from Bethlehem (5:1–5). Though Israel is trampled underfoot, the day for rebuilding will come, and the Gentiles will come to Jerusalem from the ends of the earth (7:1–12). God will pardon the sins of the remnant (vv 18–20).

Zephaniah, whose prophecy is devoted almost solely to the coming Day of the Lord, that great day of judgment, yet speaks of a day when Jerusalem will no longer be put to shame, when sin is removed from the city, and there are left "the meek and humble, who trust in the name of the Lord" (3:11,12). These survivors are a pure people: "The remnant of Israel will do no wrong; they will speak no lies, nor will deceit be found in their mouths" (v 13).

During the Exile. From his vantage among the exiles by the Chebar River (Ez 1:1), Ezekiel too is concerned about the future remnant and the promises of restoration. In a vision (ch 9), he sees a scribe pass through the city of Jerusalem placing a mark on the foreheads of all who grieved for the sins committed in the city. Behind the scribe came a group of warriors slaying the population—"old men, young men, maidens, women and children"—all who did not have the mark on their foreheads. Fearing the destruction of all the people, Ezekiel calls out, "O Lord, will you destroy the entire remnant of Israel?" Immediately thereafter he sees the glory cloud—the visible presence of God in the midst of his people—rise and depart from the temple (ch 10). Ezekiel prophesies judgment on the leaders of Israel, and Pelatiah (whose name means "escape") dies, prompting Ezekiel to ask again, "O Lord, will you destroy the entire remnant of Israel?" (11:13). The Lord will gather his people and restore them to their land as a pure people free of idolatry (vv 14–21). Though their sins were great, there would

yet be mercy and restoration for a purified nation. The glory cloud that Ezekiel saw departing from the temple will return to a new temple (ch 43). The people will no longer stray from God (14:11) but will enjoy a new and everlasting covenant (16:60–62). Ezekiel recalls the remnant motif as it applied to the wilderness community after the exodus: many will leave the land of bondage, and the rebellious will die along the way, not entering Israel (20:35–38). God will gather his flock, and they will have "one shepherd, my servant David" (34:20–24). God will remove their hearts of stone, give them hearts of flesh, and put his Spirit in them (36:24–32). Though Israel appears dead and incapable of living again, yet God will speak to these dry bones and bring them to life (37:1–14).

After the Exile. The biblical authors of the restoration period view their community as the restored remnant. Haggai addresses sermons to "the whole remnant of the people" (1:12; 2:2). Zechariah's first night vision asks when God will fulfill his promises to the remnant (Zec 1:7–17); God promises that he will yet return to the city. He says, "I will not deal with the remnant of this people as I did in the past" (8:11). God is jealous for Zion (8:3); his glorious presence will return (1:16,17; 2:10; 8:3). What may seem incredible to the remnant of the people, the Lord will do (8:6). Where once God purposed destruction for Jerusalem, now he intends only good (vv 14,15), but the people must be holy and keep the Law (vv 16–19).

Ezra regards the restoration community as the remnant (9:8,13–15). Nehemiah's mission to Jerusalem was prompted after his inquiry "about the Jewish remnant that survived the exile" (Neh 1:2).

Though the restoration community and their prophets and leaders looked at themselves as the remnant, yet a problem remained: the prophets had spoken of a remnant that would be a holy people, righteous and blameless before God. The restoration community itself fell short. The problem of sin remained. In one of his night visions Zechariah sees a scroll of the law hovering over the city pronouncing a sentence on those who sin against God and their fellow men and women. Behind this scroll came a measuring basket containing the figure of a woman representing the iniquity of the people throughout the land; two winged figures carry that basket to Babylon (Zec 5). Sin is still found in Israel, and must be taken to the place of judgment. Ezra too sees the anomaly of sin in the remnant. At the end of a lengthy prayer of praise and confession of sin (9:1–15), he asks if the people continue their sin, "would you not be angry enough to destroy us, leaving us no remnant or survivor? O Lord God of Israel, you are righteous! We are left this day as a remnant, yet here we are before you in our guilt, and because of it, not one of us can stand in your presence."

The restoration prophets see themselves as the remnant community, but one that falls short. Sin remains in Israel; the period of judgment and refining in the exile had not produced a pure people, an Israel wholly faithful to the commands of God.

New Testament. *As Applied to Christ.* All the features of the remnant concept are transferred to Jesus Christ. Jesus becomes the embodiment of Israel, the faithful servant (Is 41:8,9; 42:1; 44:1,2; 49:1–7; 50:10; 52:13; 53:11). Unlike the remnant of the restoration period, he committed no sin (Is 53:9; 1 Pt 2:22). He alone could undergo the judgment of God and survive. On the cross he endured exile from the Father (Mt 27:46; Mk 15:34), and on the third day he enjoyed restoration at the beginning of a new age as the nucleus of the people of God. In him the basic theological problem of the tension between the grace and justice of God is resolved.

Having survived judgment, he becomes the focus of the hopes for the continued existence of the people of God in a new kingdom, a new Israel. As the founder of that new Israel, he summons the "little flock" that will receive the kingdom (Dan 7:22,27; Lk 12:32), and he appoints judges for the 12 tribes of Israel in the new age (Mt 19:28; Lk 22:30). Other sheep will join this Jewish fold (Jn 10:16). The church is viewed as the Israel of that new age (Gal 6:16), the 12 tribes (Jas 1:1), "a chosen race, a royal priesthood, a holy nation, God's own people" (1 Pt 2:9).

As Applied to the Church. The remnant concept is alluded to often in the NT as a warning to the church. Peter frequently refers to the relevance of the flood narrative for the church. Only a few were saved from the waters of the flood (1 Pt 3:20–22). False teachers are warned that God judged the angels that disobeyed, destroyed the ancient world with a flood, and rained fire on Sodom and Gomorrah; the righteous were saved while the unrighteous are held for the day of judgment (2 Pt 2:4–10). Those who say that the Day of the Lord will never come should be warned by the flood (3:3–13).

Paul also draws on the remnant motif as a warning to the church. The Israel of the wilderness generation—though they were the ones God had redeemed from Egypt—were the objects of his displeasure. Their experience warns the church against idolatry, sexual immorality, and complaining (1 Cor 10:1–10). What happened to them was an example, written down

Sodom, referred to by Peter in his warning to false teachers (2 Pt 2:6–8).

as a warning because the fulfillment of the ages has come (v 11). RAYMOND B. DILLARD

See SERVANT OF THE LORD; MESSIAH.

Bibliography. G.F. Hasel, *The Remnant;* J. Jocz, *A Theology of Election;* P. Richardson, *Israel and the Apostolic Church.*

Remphan. KJV form of Rephan, a pagan deity, in Acts 7:43.

See REPHAN.

Repentance. Literally a change of mind, not about individual plans, intentions, or beliefs, but rather a change in the whole personality from a sinful course of action to God. Such a change is sometimes referred to as "evangelical repentance," since it arises out of the proclamation of God's grace to the sinner and the correlative work of the Holy Spirit in the new birth (Jn 3:5–8). Such a change is the fruit of Christ's victory over death—a gift bestowed as a result of his exaltation to his Father's right hand as Prince and Savior (Acts 5:31).

Such repentance accompanies saving faith in Christ (Acts 20:21). It is inconsistent and unintelligible to suppose that anyone might exercise faith in Christ as the divine Savior from sin who is not aware and repentant of his own sin. Repentance is such an important aspect of conversion that it is often stressed rather than saving faith, as when Christ said that there is joy in heaven among the angels over one sinner that repents (Lk 15:7). The apostles described the conversion of the Gentiles to Christ as God granting them "repentance unto life" (Acts 11:18). Evangelical repentance and faith in Christ are in fact inseparable, though a convert may be aware of one aspect more than another.

Such penitence is not an isolated act but a disposition of the mind, providing a spur for behavior (including acts of reparation where appropriate, Lk 19:8) which is in accordance with God's declared will. Recognition of daily sins and shortcomings provides the occasion for renewed acts of penitence and for fresh exercises of faith in Christ. One of the deepest and most noteworthy expressions of such penitence is David's account of his adultery with Bathsheba (Ps 51). Whole churches are, on occasion, called upon to repent (Rv 2:5). Second Corinthians 7 contains an interesting and full description of such corporate repentance involving the elements of sorrow for sin and a determined resolve to forsake old sinful ways and to behave properly. While repentance is often accompanied by deep feelings, it is not equivalent to such feelings but is rooted in convictions about the sinner's own need before a holy God.

Besides such "evangelical repentance" Scripture records many other cases of repentance, such as those of Pharaoh (Ex 9:27), Saul (1 Sm 24:16–18), and Judas Iscariot (Mt 27:3), which are not the result of an awareness of God's mercy to sinners but rather arise from a fear of unpleasant consequences and a desire to avoid them, unaccompanied by any true change in character or outlook.

Both John the Baptist (Mt 3:2; Mk 1:4) and Christ (Mk 1:15) were preachers of repentance, calling not the righteous but sinners. And in accordance with the Great Commission (Lk 24:44–49), the apostles continued such preaching, beginning with Peter's preaching on the day of Pentecost (Acts 2), with noteworthy results (v 41).

According to the Roman Catholic Church, the sacrament of penance includes the elements of contrition, confession, and satisfaction, and the priest is required to pronounce absolution. But according to the NT, the linking of penitence both to a sacramental framework and to absolution by a human priest are unknown and are inconsistent with the need for the sinner to turn personally to God in penitence and receive absolution through Christ the only mediator (1 Tm 2:5), the great High Priest of his people.

Frequently in the OT God is said to repent, for instance in his treatment of Nineveh during Jonah's prophetic ministry there (Jon 3:10). Such an attribution is not to be understood as denoting either personal sorrow on God's part or a change in his eternal purpose, but rather a change in or an updating of his announced purpose and in his relations with men as they themselves change. Such a way of describing God's relation to his creatures is one of many in which, as Calvin and others have stressed, God "accommodates himself" to human capacities by the way in which he presents himself in Scripture.

See Conversion; Regeneration; Salvation; Confession; Forgiveness.

Paul Helm

Bibliography. W.D. Chamberlain, *The Meaning of Repentance;* J. Jeremias, *NT Theology,* vol 1, pp 152–58.

Rephael. Shemaiah's son and a temple gatekeeper in David's time (1 Chr 26:7,8).

Rephah. Resheph's father from Ephraim's tribe (1 Chr 7:25).

Rephaiah. 1. Jeshaiah's son and a descendant of Solomon (1 Chr 3:21).

2. Ishi's son and a captain from Simeon's tribe who led 500 Israelites to destroy the Amalekites at Mt Seir (1 Chr 4:42,43).

3. Tola's son and a warrior from Issachar's tribe in the days of David (1 Chr 7:1,2).

4. Son of Bine-a and Eleasah, a descendant of Saul (1 Chr 9:43); also called Raphah in 1 Chronicles 8:37 (KJV Rapha).

5. Hur's son, who worked on the Jerusalem wall during the days of Nehemiah (Neh 3:9).

Rephaim. 1. A mighty people tall in stature living in Palestine during the days of Abraham. The Rephaim, along with the Zuzim, Emim, and Horite peoples, were defeated by Chedorlaomer and his allied armies (Gn 14:5). They were one of nine nations living in Palestine at the time when the Lord promised to give the land to Abraham's descendants (15:20). The ancient Rephaim were called the Emim by the Moabites and the Zamzummin by the Ammonites; they were comparable in size and number to the giant Anakim (Dt 2:11,20). Og, king of Bashan, represented the last of the Rephaim. He was later killed and his kingdom dispossessed by the Israelites under Moses (Dt 3:11; Jos 12:4; 13:12). Perhaps the giants among the Philistines were descendants of the Rephaim (2 Sm 21; 1 Chr 20).

See GIANTS.

2. Shades or departed spirits whose dwelling place was the habitation of Sheol (Prv 2:18; 9:18; 21:16). The Rephaim of the underworld suffered anguish (Jb 26:5) and were separated from God (Ps 88:10–12) and living people (Is 26:14). Their immaterial being bore a weakened shadow-like resemblance to their former corporeality (Is 14:9).

See INTERMEDIATE STATE.

Rephaim, Valley of. Geographical landmark forming part of the common boundary of the tribes of Judah and Benjamin (KJV the valley of the giants in Jos 15:8; 18:16), a broad valley in the southwestern outskirts of Jerusalem thought to be frequented by giants like the Anakim and the Nephilim. During David's reign, after hearing that he had been anointed king, the Philistine armies came up from the coast to search for him and on two occasions spread out in the valley of Rephaim (2 Sm 5:18,22; 1 Chr 14:9). This valley joined the Wadi Serar which led down to the Philistine coast, and was a fertile area where grain was grown (Is 17:5).

Rephan. Pagan deity mentioned by Stephen in Acts 7:43 (KJV Remphan; NASB Rompha) when he cited the text of Amos 5:26 to portray the paganism of the wandering Israelites. Stephen was quoting from the Septuagint, whose translators had taken *kaiwan* (NASB *kiyyun;* KJV *chiun*) to refer to the Assyrian god of Saturn, or perhaps to the Egyptian Saturn god Repa. Some scholars argue that Amos 5:26 is a general reference to the Israelites' wilderness paganism and names no ancient deities at all.

See KAIWAN.

Rephidim. Camping place of Israel in the wilderness of Paran following their exodus from Egypt. Exodus 17:1 lists Rephidim as Israel's stopping place after the wilderness of Sin; Numbers 33:14,15, however, specifies that after the wilderness of Sin, they camped at Dophkah and Alush then Rephidim before they journeyed on to the Sinai wilderness.

Several incidents occurred at Rephidim during the wilderness travels of Israel. Upon arriving at Rephidim, the Israelites learned that there was no water to drink. The thirsty, disgruntled people complained to Moses. In reply, Moses struck a rock in Horeb with his staff according to the Lord's instruction and water issued forth to satisfy the nation; Moses, however, named Rephidim Massah (meaning testing) and Meribah (meaning quarreling) because of Israel's doubt of the Lord's presence and provision (Ex 17:1–7). Rephidim was the site near which the Israelites led by Joshua engaged the Amalekites in battle. The Lord promised to grant Israel victory as long as Moses kept his hands in the air. With the assistance of Hur and Aaron, Moses held up his hands for the duration of the day, and the Israelites prevailed over the Amalekites (vv 8–16). This place was perhaps also the desert setting where Moses was visited by Jethro his father-in-law (ch 18).

The location of Rephidim is uncertain. Some suggest Wadi Refayid in southwest Sinai. Others variously place it near modern Jebel Musa at Wadi Feiran or at Wadi es-Sheykh.

See WILDERNESS WANDERINGS.

Reptile. See ANIMAL (ADDER; ASP; GECKO; LIZARD; SERPENT; SKINK).

Resen. City built by Nimrod between Nineveh and Calah (Gn 10:12). It was part of the complex known as "the great city," and could have been a suburb of Nineveh. Some interpreters suggest it was a waterwork between Nineveh and Calah.

Resheph. Rephah's son, a descendant of Ephraim and an ancestor of Joshua, son of Nun (1 Chr 7:25).

Respect of Persons. Scriptural expression generally used in a negative sense of partiality or favoritism shown to persons. In Hebrew, the expression refers literally to "the lifting up of the face" of another person (2 Chr 19:7), while in the Greek it means "to receive the face" of someone or to accept his external appearance as the real thing and to make an evaluation on that basis.

Because respect of persons or partiality is used biblically in this sense, the Bible declares several times that God is never guilty of such partiality. Paul clearly states in a universal context that God does not show partiality or respect of persons in his judgment of the works of individuals (Rom 2:1–16). God's impartiality is made the basis for Paul's command to Christian masters to treat their slaves fairly since there is no favoritism with God, their own great Master in heaven (Eph 6:9). Paul uses this attribute of God to encourage the Christian slave to serve his master wholeheartedly, since he will be repaid by his impartial God in heaven (Col 3:25; cf. 1 Pt 1:17).

Because of these references to God's fairness in refusing to respect persons, God's people are not to pervert justice by showing partiality to the poor or favoritism to the great, but they are to be fair in their evaluation of cases when required to make such judgments (Lv 19:15). They are not to corrupt justice by showing respect of persons because of the fear of man (Dt 1:17) or because of bribery (16:18–20; see also 2 Chr 19:7; Prv 24:23; 28:21).

The favoring of the rich and the slighting, even the humiliating, of the poor on the basis of external appearance is expressly forbidden in the NT (Jas 2:1–13).

Rest. Freedom from work or activity. The source of the Christian doctrine of rest is the rest of God himself, who, after completing the work of creation in six days, "rested on the seventh day from all his work which he had done" (Gn 2:2). This provides the basis for the Hebrew sabbath as the weekly seventh day of rest (*sabbath* is the Hebrew term for rest), which is presented as an ordinance of creation. The fourth commandment enjoins the consecration of the sabbath day to God and the limitation of labor to six days precisely because God made all things in six days and rested the seventh day: "therefore the Lord blessed the sabbath day and hallowed it" (Ex 20:8–11).

The concept of rest, however, was not just past (creation) and present (weekly) but also future. This future aspect received symbolic expression in the Israelites' pilgrimage under the leadership of Moses through the wilderness from the bondage of Egypt to the rest of the Promised Land. That rest was attained under Joshua, who led them into the land and settled them there (see Jos 23,24). But God's rest is something which transcends any earthly and temporal experience. Abraham, whom God had first brought to the land of promise (Gn 12), not only lived by faith but also died in faith, knowing that the promise of perfect rest and an everlasting inheritance has its fulfillment not here but hereafter, and perceiving that the earthly territory pointed beyond itself to the reality of "a better country, that is, a heavenly one" (Heb 11:8–16).

The 40 years of restless wandering in the wilderness meant that the whole adult generation that set out with Moses perished without entering the Promised Land. This was a judgment they brought on themselves by their ingratitude and rebelliousness (Nm 14:26–35). Centuries later God warned their descendants against the danger of following this example of hard-heartedness and reaping a similar consequence of not entering his rest: "Today, when you hear his voice, do not harden your hearts" (Ps 95:7–11). The author of Hebrews cites this passage (3:7,8; 4:7) as evidence that God's rest is not a matter of past history, but that "the promise of entering his rest remains." The word "today" indicates that the day of grace is not closed: "For if Joshua had given them rest, God would not speak later of another day. So then, there remains a sabbath rest for the people of God" (Heb 3:7–4:11).

It is *God's* rest into which all persons are encouraged to enter. The weekly day of rest is a reminder and a reflection of that rest. The rest of the Israelites in the Promised Land after their wilderness wanderings is a symbol of God's eternal rest which his people are to share. The rest that Christ gives to those who come to him (Mt 11:28) is a foretaste and a guarantee of the divine rest that awaits them. The rest after death of believers who have fallen asleep in Christ—"Blessed are the dead who die in the Lord. . . . They rest from their labors" (Rv 14:13)—is a blissful intensification of the reality of this experience. But the completion of this rest in its inexpressible fullness will take place at the return of Christ, when at last all who are his will be fully conformed to his likeness (1 Jn 3:2), salvation will be consummated as they are clothed with imperishable, glorified bodies (2 Cor 5), and the renewed order of creation in which righteousness dwells will be established (2 Pt 3:13).

This coming of Christ will be the climactic point of all history and the moment of the entry of God's people into the full and unending enjoyment of his rest. The completion of the redemption purchased by Christ at the cross will mean rest and freedom from all sin, and this in turn will mean rest and freedom from all sorrow, pain, suffering, persecution, frustration, injustice, and death (Rv 7:9–17; 21:1–7). The rest of mankind, moreover, will involve the rest of God's whole creation as it is brought to the perfection of that glorious destiny for which it was intended from the very beginning (cf. Rom 8:19–25).

Rest is not synonymous with inactivity. What God rested from was the work of creation. He continues constantly to be active, however, in providentially sustaining all that he has created and in the work both of righteous judgment and gracious salvation. Jesus Christ, indeed, in his incarnation, life, death, rising, and glorification is precisely God in action (2 Cor 5:19). Hence the assertion of Jesus: "My Father is working still, and I am working" (Jn 5:17). What the Christian will rest from is the struggle against the forces of evil and the afflictions by which this present life is marred. The rest into which the Christian will enter will not be a state of uneventful inertia. God himself is dynamic, not static, and so also is his rest.

Consequently, all that a Christian rests from simply sets him free to be active ceaselessly and joyfully in the service of God, the Creator and Redeemer. In perfect harmony with all God's works and in complete fulfillment, Christians exultantly praise and serve the Triune God. Joy will be full, without possibility of improvement or deficiency (cf. Rv 4:8–11; 5:8–14; 7:9–12). Such will be the rest without end of that eternal sabbath which has a morning but no evening. "Let us therefore strive to enter that rest!" (Heb 4:11).

PHILIP EDGCUMBE HUGHES

See SABBATH; LORD'S DAY, THE; HEAVEN.

Resurrection.   Act of being raised from the dead, used in the Bible with three different meanings. It refers to miraculous raisings of the dead back to earthly life, such as when Elijah raised a boy (1 Kgs 17:8–24); Elisha raised the Shunammite's son (2 Kgs 4:18–37); Jesus raised both Jairus' daughter (Mk 5:35–43) and Lazarus (Jn 11:17–44); Peter raised Dorcas (Acts 9:36–42); and Paul raised Eutychus (Acts 20:9–12). There is no hint that these resuscitations would prevent future death. It also refers to the eschatological resurrection at the end of time for punishment or reward (Jn 5:29; cf. Rv 20:5,6). Finally, resurrection refers frequently to the resurrection of Jesus Christ.

Resurrection and the Greeks.   Greek dualism, the separation of body from soul, was not conducive to the acceptance of resurrection, with the exception of some miracle-story resuscitations.

Instead of a doctrine of resurrection, the Greeks developed a doctrine of the immortality of the soul. The body was thought to be a disposable physical outer garment, whereas the soul was related to the immortal forms and sustained from age to age. The Greek cyclical view of time lent itself to the development of a sophisticated view of the transmigration of the soul from body to body.

Whether the Athenians misunderstood Paul or not, their reaction to Paul's preaching of Jesus and the resurrection (Acts 17:16–32) is quite compatible with Greek thought. The idea of a genuine resurrection from the dead to an immortal state, whether for persons in general or a specific person like Jesus, was foreign to Greek philosophy.

Resurrection in the Old Testament and Judaism.   The concept of resurrection developed slowly in Israel. Life and death were related to physical existence in this world. Death

meant leaving this world and entering a shadowy existence known as Sheol, the place of the *rephaim* or shades (Is 14:10), a place of hopelessness (Jb 7:9,10; 2 Sm 12:23). The tragedy of Sheol was that a person was cut off from fellowship with God. At that stage of Israel's thought, there seemed little hope for resurrection (Pss 6:4,5; 88:10–12).

But in the midst of hopelessness concerning a personal future, Israel developed a sense of faithfulness to God. In spite of the fact that the future was not clear, Job cried helplessly, "If a man dies, will he live again?" (14:14). As Job sought for the seemingly impossible, the difficult passage in 19:25,26 at least suggests that in the reality of a living redeemer (*goel*) there might be an answer. Likewise, the hymns of Israel began to affirm something more universal about God's presence in such statements as, "If I make my bed in Sheol, thou art *there*!" (Ps 139:8).

While some would argue that Hosea 6:1–3 suggests a resurrection, it is more likely that to Israel it seemed like a promise of God's continuing care, even when it experienced defeat at the hands of its enemies. Whether Paul saw in the third-day statement of Hosea a reference to Jesus is difficult to assess. This passage, along with texts like the dry bones of Ezekiel (ch 37), focus primarily on giving Israel hope in spite of defeat, but they may have become part of a developing sense in Israel that after death there should be something more.

In Daniel 12:2, however, there is a sure reference to the resurrection of the dead. Indeed, the text announced a twofold resurrection of Jews: some to eternal life and some to eternal contempt. But there was no general resurrection of all people suggested by this text.

The Enoch and Elijah stories pose other issues concerning the afterlife. The Enoch story, though brief (Gn 5:23–31), is intriguing because Enoch was seventh in the generations from Adam, and in walking with God, he lived a year of (365) years. In the intertestamental period and in Hebrews 11:5, the idea that "God took him" was viewed as a translation of Enoch to heaven. Enoch (48:10) is even quoted in Jude 6. Also in the Elijah-Elisha cycle, the transference of power is indicated by Elisha witnessing the translation of Elijah. Elijah went up by means of a whirlwind to heaven (2 Kgs 2:1,11). While neither the Enoch nor Elijah story asserts the resurrection, both stories undoubtedly contributed to the development of the concept of a postresurrectional life.

In the intertestamental period, views began to solidify. The theologically staunch conservative Sadducees would have nothing to do with the new ideas of resurrection and the afterlife.

They continued to argue that there was no resurrection in Moses, that life pertained to this earthly realm, and that the future hope was experienced through one's children (Sir 46:12, etc.). Sheol, the place of the dead, was devoid of relationship with God and was a place of hapless existence (Sir 10:11; 14:16; 18:28; etc.). The Sadducean opinion of the resurrection is generally well known to Christians because of the encounter between Jesus and the Sadducees when they sought to ensnare him concerning the wife of seven brothers. Jesus rejected their views of the resurrection, of God, and of the Scripture as inadequate (Mk 12:18–27). The this-worldly, politically compromising Sadducees, however, ceased to exist with the fall of Jerusalem and the loss of their temple power base.

The Pharisees, along with the Essenes and their Qumran brethren, adopted a resurrectional stance. A twofold pattern of resurrection was suggested by the famous eschatological passages of 2 Esdras 7 and the Apocalypse of Baruch 50–51. Both texts may be as late as the 1st century AD. In the Similitudes of 1 Enoch, the righteous Jews could generally expect resurrection but not the wicked (46,51,62). But elsewhere in Enoch there is a hint that some wicked may be raised for judgment (22,67,90). The resurrection of the righteous in these texts would generally be linked to a spiritual type body, yet in 2 Maccabees 7,14ff., the view seems less developed and more physical. The Qumran covenanters who took up the spiritual war against the sons of darkness, like the Pharisees, expected a resurrection in the great Day of the Lord.

While in Judaism there was a growing sense of an eschatological day of resurrection and reckoning, there was no hint anywhere of a resurrection of the Messiah. Such an idea had to await the historical reality of Jesus.

The Resurrection of Jesus Christ.

The resurrection of Christ is the central point of Christianity. So important was the resurrection for Paul that he hinged both preaching and faith upon its validity. He considered that a Christianity without the resurrection would be empty and meaningless (1 Cor 15:12–19). Indeed, the resurrection for him was the unveiling of God's messianic power in Jesus (Rom 1:4).

The resurrection of Christ was the presupposition behind other texts of the NT as well. Rebirth to a living hope is based upon the resurrection (1 Pt 1:3). It is the foundation for witness and fellowship with God because the living Lord has been seen and touched (1 Jn 1:1–4). It is the bedrock thesis for ministry and apostleship (Acts 1:21–25). The exalted Christ who sits at the right hand of God is the key to understanding the call to perseverance in Hebrews (1:3; 8:1). And the victorious Lamb standing in spite of the fact that he was slain is the premise of the victorious expectation in Revelation (5:6). The Gospels likewise would hardly have been good news if they did not conclude with Christ's resurrection.

The Resurrection Accounts and Scholarly Debate.

While the resurrection of Jesus Christ is critical to the very essence of Christianity, it has been the subject of considerable debate. Scholars have frequently noted the variations which are present in the accounts. How many and who were the women at the tomb? Was/ were there one (Mk, Mt) or two (Lk, Jn) angels/ men at the tomb? Did the women come to anoint the body (Mk, Lk) or to see the tomb (Mt)? Did the man/angel state "He is going before you *into Galilee*" (Mk, Mt) or "Remember how he said . . . when he was still *in Galilee*" (Lk)? Did the women say nothing to anyone because of fear (Mk) or did they report to the disciples (Mt)? What was the order of the appearances and did they take place in Jerusalem (Lk, Jn 20), or in Galilee (Mt, Jn 21), or in both places? Can the appearances be harmonized? What kind of body did Jesus possess? These and many other questions have been the watershed for a great deal of contemporary scholarly debate.

Many of these questions were not first discovered by recent scholars. Tatian in the 2nd century sought to remove the questions by composing his *Diatessaron* (harmony) in hopes that Christians would accept his work as a variant-free substitute for the Gospels. Although Christians liked the harmony, they continued to transmit faithfully the Gospels, because they believed that in them, by divine inspiration, God had provided a powerful witness concerning his Son. Many today still try the way of harmonization in an effort to deal with the minutia of historical questions, but they usually miss the uniqueness of each testimony. Others emphasize the differences and speculate on the Gospel constructs, but the fact of the resurrection usually becomes lost in the details of these human constructs. Both are attempts at protecting the essence of faith and reason in different ways.

The Empty Tomb. Some scholars think that Paul did not speak of an empty tomb because the tradition was in error and was late. Yet for a trained Pharisee, body speaks of a tomb, and there would be no resurrection without a body (cf. 1 Cor 15:35–57 on bodies, death, and change).

On the other hand, the tomb was empty. The body could have been stolen by the disciples (already suggested by Mt 28:13), but then one needs to explain the church on the basis of

A garden tomb.

fraud. The Jews could have stolen the body or the disciples could have mistaken the tomb, but then the body would soon have been produced by the enemies. Jesus could have lapsed into a swoon, reviving later in the cold tomb, but then the result would hardly have inspired the power of the Christian church. These explanations are all rationalistic attempts based upon a preconception that an actual resurrection of Jesus could not have happened.

In spite of the material differences and while the Gospel writers have used a great deal of common material in their tomb stories, they themselves refrained from employing the tomb as a basis for resurrection faith. With the exception of John 20:8, the tomb engendered surprise and fear. Indeed, it seemed to be an idle tale (Lk 24:11). It is not the tomb stories but the appearances that gave rise to faith.

The Appearances. Unlike the tomb stories, there is little commonality of material in the appearances. Yet the appearances are the basis for faith that the unbelievable happened. An enemy like Paul was converted into a zealous apostle (Acts 9:1–22; 1 Cor 15:18). A fearful fisherman like Peter abandoned his nets (Jn 21). A doubter like Thomas uttered early Christianity's greatest confession (Jn 20:24–28). And two weary travelers to Emmaus found new zeal to return quickly to Jerusalem and share about their encounter with the risen Jesus (Lk 24:13–35).

Scholars have debated the nature of these appearances. Starting from Paul's list of ap-

pearances (1 Cor 15:5–8), some have argued that all appearances are of the same nature, and since the Damascus road appearance to Paul recorded in Acts seems to have been of a spiritual nature (9:1–9; cf. 22:6–11; 26:12–19), then all the appearances must have been similar. Statements that the risen Jesus was touchable (Mt 28:9; Lk 24:39; Jn 20:27) and that he ate food (Lk 24:41–43) are rejected as later accretions to an earlier vision-type tradition. This type of argument is based on presuppositions of consistency and noncorporeality, and minimizes the self-confessed irregularity by Paul of his own experience (1 Cor 15:8).

Another theory was based on the division between the Jesus of history and the Christ of faith. The resurrection according to this view was not to be regarded as a fact of history but as an experience of the faith of the disciples. The issue, however, is that the NT witnesses are not testifying to what God accomplished in them but how God acted in Jesus. While these two may be related, Paul defined the encounter with Christ in terms of salvation, transformation, and being "in Christ." He would hardly have agreed to call the experiences of encountering Christ the resurrection.

Resurrection and Gnosticism. Gnostic eschatology is indebted to the Greek view of immortality and involves the shedding of the bodily husk in the spiritual ascent of the devotee to the Pleroma or Gnostic heaven. Because of the way Gnostics use words, the *Gospel of Philip* is a helpful window for understanding the Gnostic twisting of ideas. There it is argued that "those who say that the Lord died first and

[then] arose are in error; because he first arose and [then] died. If anyone does not attain the resurrection first, will he not die?" (56:15–19). The concept of resurrection is deeschatologized and defined not in terms of a truly future expectation of resurrection, but in terms of a realized spiritual awakening in this world. The *Gospel of Philip* is also useful in perceiving why in 2 Timothy 2:17–19 the criticism was so severe against Hymenaeus and Philetus for holding that the resurrection was past. Clearly, realized eschatology was rejected in the Pauline community and by the church when it appeared in Gnosticism. And it should continue to be rejected by the church in the 20th century.

Resurrection in General. Paul looked for the Day of the Lord when the dead in Christ would be raised and those who were still alive would join the dead in final victory (1 Thes 4:15–18). There was no doubt in his mind that this resurrection was a glorious expectation, that it involved some type of a personalized body, and that this body would not be physical but spiritual (1 Cor 15:35–44). Paul did not speak of two resurrections as do the Johannine texts (e.g., Jn 5:29) but merely of the resurrection to life. Perhaps the Revelation of John provides the best clue in understanding NT thought on this issue when it refers to the blessing of being part of the first resurrection (20:5,6). Although in Revelation the term *resurrection* is not used in connection with judgment, the appearance at the judgment seat and the verdict of the second death in the lake of fire indicate that a resurrection to judgment will hardly be of the same essence as resurrection to life.

GERALD L. BORCHERT

See SECOND COMING OF CHRIST; DEAD, ABODE OF THE; ESCHATOLOGY.

Bibliography. J. Alsup, *The Post Resurrection Appearance Stories of the Gospel Tradition;* E. Bode, *The Gospel Account of the Women's Visit to the Tomb of Jesus;* R.C. Brown, *The Virginal Conception and Bodily Resurrection of Jesus;* O. Cullmann, *Immortality of the Soul or Resurrection of the Dead;* R. Fuller, *The Formation of the Resurrection Narratives;* M.J. Harris, *Raised Immortal;* G.E. Ladd, *I Believe in the Resurrection of Jesus;* W. Marxen, *The Resurrection of Jesus of Nazareth;* C.F.D. Moule, *The Significance of the Message of the Resurrection for Faith in Jesus Christ;* H. von Campenhausen, *Tradition and Life in the Church,* pp 42–90.

Reu. Peleg's son, the father of Serug, and a descendant of Shem (Gn 11:18–21; 1 Chr 1:25), listed in Luke's genealogy of Christ (3:35, KJV Ragau).

See GENEALOGY OF JESUS CHRIST.

Reuben (Person). Eldest son of Jacob and Leah (Gn 29:32; 46:8) and forefather of one of the 12 tribes of Israel. Reuben was involved in the mandrake incident (30:14) and had sexual relations with Bilhah, his father's concubine (35:22). But he emerges into full adulthood as one of the more honorable of Jacob's sons. Reuben objected to the plot to kill Joseph and planned to rescue him from the pit (37:22–35). He moralized about the brothers' imprisonment in Egypt (42:22) and guaranteed the safety of Benjamin at immense risk to his own family (v 37). Yet at Jacob's pronouncement of blessing, Reuben is declared unstable and his birthright forfeited (49:3,4). He fathered four sons (1 Chr 5:3).

See REUBEN (PLACE); REUBEN, TRIBE OF.

Reuben (Place). Territory east of the Jordan given to Reuben's tribe on the condition that they assist in taking Canaan west of the Jordan (Nm 32). Moses agreed to the Reubenites' request for lands suitable for cattle grazing. The area was bordered on the south by the Arnon River, on the north and east by the wadi of Heshbon and the Ammonite kingdom, and on the west by the Jordan and Dead Sea. Reubenites dwelt there until taken into captivity by Tiglath-pileser III of Assyria around 732 BC.

See REUBEN (PERSON); REUBEN, TRIBE OF.

Reuben, Tribe of. Tribe descended from Reuben, the eldest of Jacob's sons (Gn 29:32). The tribe of Reuben usually receives the place of honor in lists of the tribes, being named first (Nm 13:4). Similarly, in lists of the two-and-a-half tribes residing east of Jordan, Reuben is always mentioned first (Jos 1:12), though Gad seems to have held a larger portion.

Because of Reuben's sin (Gn 35:22), his father prophesied that his preeminence among his brothers would disappear (49:4). In spite of the prayer of Deuteronomy 33:6, this disaster did overtake the tribe in later years. In desert days, Reuben's tribal chief appears with all the others (Nm 1:5), and a spy goes forth from Reuben as with the other tribes (13:4). Reuben has his special place in camping and marching (2:10). Only the spies of Ephraim (Joshua) and Judah (Caleb) are faithful (14:6), but Reuben appears no worse than his brother tribes: all were equal in unbelief.

The revolt of Dathan and Abiram, men of Reuben, against the authority of Moses (16:1) and possibly against the special position of Levi may be significant. Reuben may be claiming his old primacy, forfeited by sin (Gn 49:3,4). The attempt failed, and God's judgment was a signal lesson (Nm 16:33).

Reuben was rich in herds of cattle (Nm 32:1), and presumably a powerful tribe. Reuben, Gad, and the half-tribe of Manasseh ask to remain in the richly timbered and well-watered lands to the east of Jordan, recently conquered from Sihon, the Amorite king, and Og, the ruler of Bashan (v 33). This selfish request (for it would involve no sharing in the hard fighting across the Jordan) was rightly denounced by Moses (vv 6,7), perhaps as another example of the traditional instability of Reuben (Gn 49:3,4).

However, on the promise of the two-and-a-half tribes to bear the brunt of the fighting for their brothers in the west, their request was granted (Nm 32:20). They were evidently good soldiers, and Joshua sent them home at the end of the campaign (Jos 22:1–5). Although living east of the Jordan, and separated from their brethren by what was sometimes an insuperable natural obstacle, they had no desire to form an independent state. They showed this by building a great memorial altar at the spot where they crossed the Jordan on their way home (Jos 22:10). Fearing that this was a second rebellion, the other tribes mustered at once to compel unity by force (Jos 22:12). So important was religious unity that they were prepared to encourage the two-and-a-half tribes to migrate to the west bank, where there would be neither reason nor temptation for such secession (v 19). However, bloodshed between brother-tribes was averted on this occasion by lack of rashness and patient explanation (vv 22–29). Their action, indeed, was seen as praiseworthy, not culpable (v 31).

Reuben does not appear again until the time of Deborah the prophetess. When the clans of Israel rallied to God's call under Barak to fight Sisera the Canaanite, Reuben did not respond. The wording suggests that Reuben once again was influenced by material possessions, as the tribe had been in the days of the conquest, when, because of their cattle, they chose the lush lands of Transjordan rather than the rugged hills of Canaan (Nm 32:5). The easy shepherd's life appealed more to them than warfare on the slopes of Mt Tabor (Jgs 5:16). Also the wording suggests long inconclusive discussions—or even perhaps great protestations of bravery and fidelity to God's cause—that finally led to nothing (Jgs 5:15). Reuben had not changed: the tribe, like its ancestor, was still "unstable as water" (Gn 49:4).

Reuben's tribal lands, to the southeast of Gad, were probably overrun and occupied by the Moabites at a later date. Certainly the whole area to the east of Jordan was an area of contention between Israel and Aram later (1 Kgs 22:3). Finally, Transjordan with the north of Israel was one of the first areas overrun and devastated by the Assyrians (2 Kgs 15:29). Although Ezekiel, in his vision, allowed a symbolic strip of territory north of Judah for Reuben (Ez 48:6), it could only have been a small remnant, if any, that returned from the exile of the northern kingdom. Indeed, although Reuben finds his place in the list of the redeemed in Revelation (Rv 7:5), no man of Reuben plays a part in the NT.

R. ALAN COLE

Reubenite. Descendant of Reuben, Jacob's son (Nm 26:7; Jos 1:12).

See REUBEN, TRIBE OF.

Reuel. 1. Son of Esau by his wife Basemath (Gn 36:4,10), and the father of four sons: Nahath, Serah, Shammah, and Mizzah (vv 13,17).

2. Priest of Midian who gave his daughter to Moses for a wife. He is perhaps the same person as #1 above, and identical to Jethro (Ex 2:18; cf. 3:1). He is also called Raguel in Numbers 10:29.

See JETHRO.

3. Alternate spelling of Deuel, Eliasaph's father, in Numbers 2:14.

See DEUEL.

4. Ancestor of Meshullam in Benjamin's tribe (1 Chr 9:8).

Reumah. Nahor's concubine (Gn 22:24). Her four sons became the ancestors of the Aramaean tribes living north of Damascus.

Revelation. Term from the Latin *revelatio*, referring to either the act of revealing or making known, or the thing which is revealed. In theology it designates God's own self-disclosure or manifesting of himself, or things concerning himself and the world; it may also mean the word itself, oral or written, which bears such revelation. The equivalent NT terms are *apokalupsis* (apocalypse), which means unveiling, uncovering, or making someone or something known. It can also mean the word itself which reveals. The Greek word *phanerōsis* is virtually synonymous, though usually with the nuance of a clear, readily discernible presentation.

Rationalistic philosophy (René Descartes, Immanuel Kant, J.G. Fichte, F.W.J. Von Schelling, G.W.F. Hegel) finds in human reason the sole source for whatever shape revelation takes or is, acknowledging only natural religion and denying the reality of all supernatural divine revelation. A rationalist may at times admit the possibility of supernatural religion, but holds divine intervention to be nonessential to religion.

Christian theology, on the other hand, is committed to the idea that the principle of knowledge is the Word of God, specifically the Scripture, despite the severe critique of higher criticism against any claim that the Scripture affords a secure, reliable, and independent base for theological truth. Modern critical theology has declared its support for what it calls "scientific theology," for the "sure" judgments of natural science and the supposed improbability of all supernatural happenings. This has forced the Scripture, as the inspired Word of God, out of its authoritative normative position. What the Scripture contains is not the account of *what actually happened,* or *what God actually said or did,* but merely the early church's confession of faith as to what 1st-century followers of Christ supposed or contrived to have happened. The Bible, therefore, is not unique in its divine origin; it is only the unique product of early religious searchings and strivings.

Christian theology, on the other hand, asserts, on the basis of the scriptural text and the confirming mighty acts of God, that divine revelation is the first, last, and only source for the theological task; that without such firm base all theological discussion becomes aimless, indeed futile. The mere consent of the primitive church cannot be the basis or source for Christian faith. People have knowledge of God because of God's initiative and activity. God is always the initiator and author of revelation; men are the recipients. God discloses what otherwise would be unknown; he uncovers what would otherwise be hidden (Dt 29:29, Gal 1:12; Eph 3:3).

General Revelation. God draws back the veil in a twofold manner. There is first of all what has come to be called *general revelation.* God reveals himself in nature, in history, and in all people as made in his image. The association of God's revelation with nature, by which people have an intuitive knowledge of God's existence, is of long standing and is a truth supported throughout Scripture, OT (Pss 10:11; 14:1; 19:1) and NT (Acts 14:17; 17:22–29; Rom 1:19–21). That there is a God, that God is the Creator with almighty power, that God deals justly as the supreme Judge, or rules as the "Wholly Other" over his creatures—these things are known and recognized by all people. Thus the fact of God, that God *is,* is undeniable. When people do so, as is the case with the atheist, it is a forced effort against an inner conviction worked by nature itself. Paul could expect concurrence from the Athenians when he asserted that it is in God, the one and only true God, that all people live and move and have their being (Acts 17:28). Because of the natural knowledge of God (for this reason the Scholastics, like Thomas Aquinas, termed it natural theology in distinction from that which was revealed by God directly), which confronts man on every side in the sum of created things and

created laws of nature, Paul can say that men are "very religious" (Acts 17:22). It is not a case of identifying God and nature, but rather of recognizing that the natural knowledge of God is deeply ingrained in humanity's own nature and in the natural realm.

Natural knowledge of God, however, has its limitations, and is inadequate. Because it confronts the individual with the fact of God's existence, the individual consequently engages in religious practice and asks some of the ultimate questions concerning the source, reason, and end of his or her own existence. But the tragic thing is, as the apostle Paul writes (Rom 1:18–2:16), that since the fall people turn knowledge of God into perverse practices, worshiping not him, but images, creatures, or created things. Thus sinners drift further from God and satisfy themselves with foolish answers for the ultimate questions of existence. Because of a tendency to distort and twist this natural knowledge, the Swiss theologian Karl Barth, with others, denied that this should be called revelation at all. According to Barth, revelation effects a confrontation with God within the individual. But this was an explanation widely disputed. Emil Brunner opposed Barth sharply on this point, arguing that, if general revelation be denied, people could no longer be held accountable or responsible before God.

Martin Luther recognized the validity of natural knowledge of God. For Luther God was not sought behind his creation, or merely inferred in an abstract way from the creation, but rather the wonders in the natural realm were among the "veils" or "masks" of God whereby he made himself known. They are not mere starting points to forming ideas about God, but represent God on the stage where he himself has the principal part or plays the chief role. Distortions of these natural evidences, Luther held, do not negate the validity of God's revelation. Although fragmentary, incomplete, and often distorted, general or natural revelation is a genuinely valid disclosure by God of his majesty and power in the created realm (Rom 1:18–32).

Special Revelation. To know God from his revelation in nature, however, still leaves him and his gracious purposes completely unknown. The gracious, loving heart of God intends the salvation of all people. By special revelation God purposes to share this with mankind in various ways. Mankind would know nothing at all of God's messianic purposes in Christ, had God not revealed his heart and purposes throughout Scripture. Before the fall this intercourse between the Creator and man was direct and apparently uninterrupted. With the earliest patriarchs like Adam, Noah, and others, God's revelation came by means of articulate language used in a supernatural way, thus directly spoken (Gn 3:14–19; 6:13–21; 7:1–4; 12:1–3). At other times his revelation came through various means, as the Angel of the Lord appeared at Abram's tent (Gn 18:1–15), in the burning bush (Ex 3:1–22), the cleft in the rock (Ex 34:6,7), or the fire and cloud over Mt Sinai for Moses and the people of Israel (Ex 19). On the holy mountain God spoke and made known his mind and heart through his special servant Moses. At times dreams and visions, either waking or sleeping (e.g., the case of young Samuel, 1 Sm 3:1–14), were used by God with his chosen prophets. Through inner prompting God moved his prophets, later also the apostles, to speak and write his thoughts and words to humanity. Mighty acts of God on behalf of his people, like the exodus, the crossing of the Red Sea, the 40 years in the wilderness with the accompanying miraculous sustaining of the people there, were carefully and rightly interpreted by God through his prophets. By inner, immediate illumination of their hearts and minds by God, the prophets and apostles spoke his Word as he gave them utterance (Jer 1:4–19; 1 Cor 2:13; 1 Thes 2:13; 2 Pt 1:16–21). The zenith of God's revelation was the coming in flesh of his beloved Son, Jesus Christ (Jn 1:14–18; Gal 4:4,5; Heb 1,2). Jesus' revelation of the Father and the Father's gracious will toward all people was direct, accurate, and preeminent (Jn 14).

God not merely illuminated the hearts and minds of his prophets and apostles to speak his Word, but in specific instances also inspired them to record in writing the thoughts, words, and promises that he wanted revealed and retained for all time. The sacred collection of writings forms a remarkably harmonious and unified whole by which God reveals his thoughts and purposes toward humanity. For this writing the prophets and apostles were prompted not only to recount certain historical events and happenings but also what God revealed for special communication. Revelation and inspiration are necessary companions in God's disclosing of himself and his will, and at some places simply coalesce into his gracious giving of his Word. They may differ in that, while revelation has to do with the divine illumination (given by God in various ways) whereby prophets and apostles knew God and the things of God, inspiration is that divine agency employed by God in the recording of his Word. Thus inspiration's focal point is first of all the written text; revelation's focal point is the information or disclosure God gives of himself and his purposes. By virtue of its inspiration by God, Scripture is rightly known and respected as God's revelation for people today, proclaiming the two great doctrines of Law (God's will) and gospel (God's saving promises in Christ) (Jn 20:21).

In Modern Theology. Currently neoorthodoxy has cast doubt upon the Bible as God's revelation to men. In turn neoorthodoxy has led a reaction against liberal theology's concentration on the immanence of God, available to the insights and perceptions of the human mind. According to liberal theology, there is no need for special revelation, since God can be comprehended and apprehended through inner illumination. To Karl Barth, once a liberal himself, that was misplaced optimism in man's essential nature. Man, he said, was a sinner, desperately in need of God's help in bridging the gap between himself as a sinful creature and the transcendent Lord and Creator. This God did in Christ. To Barth, Jesus in the strict sense is the only valid revelation. Barth was so narrow in this that he defined other mighty acts for man's salvation, like the virgin birth, even the resurrection of Christ, as *signs* of revelation, but not revelation in themselves. So also the Bible! It was merely a written record or witness to the revelation itself, and, therefore, must not be identified as revelation. For Barth the Bible was merely a record where we confront the human attempts to repeat and reproduce God's mighty acts by recounting them in human words and thoughts, according to human situations. It was misdirected honor to call the Bible revelation. Emil Brunner agreed, stating that revelation cannot be either book or doctrine, but only God himself. Thus revelation is something that really goes on in man, illumination within the questing heart; it is the "Word of God," specifically Christ, coming directly to the heart of man (so Barth); the "personal encounter" (so Brunner); the "I-thou relationship" (so Friedrich Gogarten 1887–1967); the "kerygma" which leads to self-realization and authentic existence (so Rudolf Bultmann 1884–1976); the "word event," or faith *of* Jesus rather than *in* Jesus (so Gerhard Ebeling and Ernst Fuchs). In each case there is rejection of the Bible, or its propositional truths, or its doctrines as revelation, and a corresponding elevating of the personal encounter of the believer with God as the only genuine revelation or revelatory happening prompted by God. This also implied that there could be no revelation where it is not received or where man fails to encounter God.

Needless to say, this is a strange bifurcation of God's gracious purposes in his revelation, particularly as recorded in the inspired prophetic and apostolic Word. God took the initiative to make himself, his judgments against sin and unrighteousness, his mercy and grace in Christ, known in this way. This Word remains his sacred revelation, whether received by people or not. But God's loving purpose is that all people shall hear him as he discloses himself in his Word, embrace him in faith and trust, and finally be saved by faith in the Savior.

Modern theologians express such narrow obsession with revelation as pertaining only to an individual's personal encounter with God, and such denigrating of revelatory truths and the Bible itself because they maintain the presuppositional stance against the Bible as the truly inspired Word of God. The Bible accounts for itself as the product of human authors who wrote under divine inspiration. Modern theology, however, admits only that it is a thoroughly human record of God's mighty acts. There is grave inconsistency when liberal theologians speak, on the one hand, of God's mighty acts and, on the other hand, reject God's mighty act in entrusting mankind with his Word, the Bible. There is no other Christ save the Christ of Scripture; and no other Scripture than that which the Lord Jesus Christ gave and attests. To him all Scripture gives witness (Jn 10:35; 5:39; Acts 10:43; 18:28; 1 Cor 15:3).

EUGENE F. A. KLUG

See BIBLE, INSPIRATION OF THE; BIBLE, AUTHORITY OF THE.

Bibliography. G.C. Berkouwer, *General Revelation;* E. Brunner, *Revelation and Reason;* B.A. Demarest, *General Revelation;* C.F.H. Henry, *God, Revelation, and Authority,* 6 vols; J. Orr, *Revelation and Inspiration;* E.F. Scott, *The NT Idea of Revelation;* B.B. Warfield, *Revelation and Inspiration.*

Revelation, Book of.

Author. The earliest witnesses ascribe Revelation to John the apostle, the son of Zebedee. Dionysius, the distinguished bishop of Alexandria and student of Origen (d. *c.* 264), was the first within the church to question its apostolic authorship. From the time of Dionysius, the apostolic origin of the book was disputed in the East until Athanasius of Alexandria (d. 373) turned the tide toward its acceptance. In the West, the book was widely accepted and was included in all the principal lists of canonical books from at least the middle of the 2nd century on.

From the internal evidence, the following things can be said about John as the author with some confidence.

He calls himself John (1:4,9; 22:8). This is most likely not a pseudonym but rather the name of a person well known among the Asian churches.

This John identifies himself as a prophet (1:3; 22:6–10,18,19) who was in exile because of his prophetic witness (1:9). As such, he speaks to the churches with great authority.

His use of the OT and Targums makes it virtually certain that he was a Palestinian Jew, steeped in the ritual of the temple and synagogue. He may also have been a priest.

The authorship of Revelation is admittedly problematic. However, early and widespread testimony attributes the book to the apostle John, and no convincing argument has been advanced against this view.

Date, Origin, Destination. Only two dates for Revelation have received serious support. An early date, shortly after the reign of Nero (54–68), is allegedly supported by references in the book to the persecution of Christians, to the *Nero redivivus* myth (a revived Nero would be the reincarnation of the evil genius of the whole Roman Empire), to the imperial cult (ch 13), and to the temple (ch 11), which was destroyed in AD 70.

The alternate and more generally accepted date rests primarily on the early witness of Irenaeus, who stated that the apostle John "saw the revelation . . . at the close of Domitian's reign" (AD 81–96).

The origin of the book is clearly identified with Patmos, one of the Sporades Islands, located about 37 miles southwest of Miletus, in the Icarian Sea (1:9). John was apparently exiled on the island due to religious and/or government persecutions arising from his witness to Jesus (1:9).

Likewise the recipients are clearly the seven historic churches in the Roman province of Asia (modern western Turkey): Ephesus, Smyrna, Pergamum, Thyatira, Sardis, Philadelphia, and Laodicea (1:4,11; 2:1, etc.).

Background. The Book of Revelation differs from the other NT writings, not in doctrine but in literary genre and subject matter. It is a book of prophecy (1:3; 22:7,18,19) that contains both warning and consolation—announcements of future judgment and blessing—communicated by means of symbols and visions.

The language and imagery were not as strange to 1st-century readers as they are today. Therefore, familiarity with the prophetic books of the OT (especially Dn and Ez) will help the reader grasp the message of the Apocalypse.

While the symbolic and visionary mode of presentation creates ambiguity and frustration for many, it actually lends to the description of unseen realities a poignancy and clarity unattainable by any other method. Such language can trigger a variety of ideas, associations, existential involvement, and mystical responses that the straight prose found in most of the NT cannot achieve.

The letters to the churches indicate that five of the seven were in serious trouble. The major problem seemed to be disloyalty to Christ; this may indicate that the major thrust of Revelation is not sociopolitical but theological. John is more concerned with countering the heresy that was creeping into the churches toward the close of the 1st century than with addressing the political situation. This heresy seems to have been a type of Gnostic teaching.

Revelation is also commonly viewed as belonging to the body of nonbiblical Jewish writings known as apocalyptic literature. The name for this type of literature is derived from the Greek word for "revelation," *apokalypsis*. The extrabiblical apocalyptic books were written in the period from 200 BC to AD 200. Although numerous similarities exist, these are also some clear differences.

Much more important than the Jewish apocalyptic sources is the debt John owes to the eschatological teaching of Jesus, such as the Olivet discourse (Mt 24,25; Mk 13; Lk 21). Four traditional ways of understanding Revelation 4–22 have emerged in the history of the church.

Futurist. This view holds that, with the exception of chapters 1–3, all the visions in Revelation relate to a period immediately preceding and following the second advent of Christ at the end of the age. The beasts (chs 13,17) are identified with the future antichrist, who will appear at the last moment in world history and will be defeated by Christ in his second coming to judge the world and to establish his earthly millennial kingdom.

Variations of this view were held by the earliest expositors, such as Justin Martyr (d. 164), Irenaeus (d. *c*. 195), Hippolytus (d. 236), and Victorinus (d. *c*. 303). This futurist approach has enjoyed a revival since the 19th century and is widely held among evangelicals today.

Historicist. As the word implies, this view sees in Revelation a prophetic survey of history. It originated with Joachim of Floris (d. 1202), a monastic who claimed to have received on Easter night a special vision that revealed to him God's plan for the ages. He assigned a day-year value to the 1260 days of the Apocalypse. In his scheme, the book is a prophecy of the events of Western history from the time of the apostles until Joachim's own time. In the various schemes that developed as this method was applied to history, one element became common: the antichrist and Babylon were connected with Rome and the papacy. Later, Luther, Calvin, and other Reformers came to adopt this view.

Preterist. According to this view, Revelation deals with the time of its author; the main contents of chapters 4–22 are thus viewed as describing events wholly limited to John's own day. The beasts (ch 13) are identified as imperial Rome and the imperial priesthood. This is the view held by many contemporary scholars.

Idealist. This method of interpreting Revelation sees it as being basically poetic, symbolic, and spiritual in nature. Thus Revelation does not predict any specific historical events at all; on the contrary, it sets forth timeless truths concerning the battle between good and evil that continues throughout the church age. As a system of interpretation, it is more recent than the other three schools.

Revelation is unique in its use of the OT. Of the 404 verses of the Apocalypse, 278 contain references to the Jewish Scriptures. John refers frequently to Isaiah, Jeremiah, Ezekiel, and Daniel, and also repeatedly to Exodus, Deuteronomy, and the Psalms.

Purpose and Teaching. "In form it is an epistle, containing an apocalyptic prophecy; in spirit and inner purpose, it is a pastoral" (Swete). As a prophet, John is called to separate true from false belief—to expose the failures of the congregations in Asia. He desires to encourage authentic Christian discipleship by explaining Christian suffering and martyrdom in the light of the victory over evil won by Jesus' death and resurrection. John is concerned to show that the martyrs (e.g., Antipas, 2:13) will be vindicated. He discloses the end both of evil and of those who follow the beast (19:20,21; 20:10,15) and describes the ultimate victory of the Lamb and of those who follow him.

Content. The main contents of Revelation are arranged in series of seven, some explicit, some implied: seven churches (chs 2,3), seven seals (chs 6,7), seven trumpets (chs 8–11), seven bowls (chs 16–18), seven last things (chs 19–22). It is also possible to divide the contents around four key visions: (1) the vision of the Son of man among the seven churches (chs 1–3); (2) the vision of the seven-sealed scroll, the seven trumpets, and the seven bowls (4:1–19:10); (3) the vision of the return of Christ and the consummation of this age (19:11–20:15); and (4) the vision of the new heaven and new earth (21,22).

John's Introduction (1:1–8). The first three chapters of Revelation form a unit and are comparatively easy to understand. They are the most familiar and contain an introduction to the whole book (1:1–8); the first vision: the Son of man among the seven lampstands (vv 9–20); and the letters or messages to the seven churches in Asia (2:1–3:22).

The first eight verses introduce the whole book. They are freighted with theological content and detail. After a brief preface (vv 1–3), John addresses the book to the seven churches of Asia in an expanded ancient letter form (vv 4–8).

The Son of Man Among the Lampstands (1:9–3:22). After a brief indication of the historical situation that occasioned it (1:9–11), John describes his vision of "someone, like a son of man," walking among seven golden lampstands (vv 12–16). The person identifies

Carving in the synagogue at Capernaum that depicts the menorah (7-branched lampstand used in the tabernacle and temple). John saw 7 golden lampstands that represented the 7 churches addressed in Revelation (1:11–13,20).

cases (Sardis and Laodicea) the assessment proves totally negative. The enemy of Christ's churches is the deceiver, Satan, who seeks to undermine the churches' loyalty to Christ (2:10,24).

(4) Following his assessment of the churches' accomplishments, the speaker pronounces his verdict on their condition in such words as "You have forsaken your first love" (2:4) or "You are dead" (3:1). Two letters contain no favorable verdict (Smyrna, Philadelphia) and two no word of commendation (Sardis, Laodicea). In the letters all derelictions are viewed as forms of inner betrayals of a prior relation to Christ.

(5) To correct or alert each congregation, Jesus issues a penetrating command. These commands further expose the exact nature of the self-deception involved.

(6) Each letter contains the general exhortation: "He who has an ear, let him hear what the Spirit says to the churches." The words of the Spirit are the words of Christ (cf. 19:10).

(7) Finally, each letter contains a promise of reward to the victor. Each is eschatological and correlates with the last two chapters of the book. Furthermore, the promises are echoes of Genesis 2,3: What was lost by Adam in Eden is more than regained by Christ. We are probably to understand the seven promises as different facets that combine to make up one great promise to believers: wherever Christ is, there will the "overcomers" be.

The Seven-Sealed Scroll (4:1–8:1). In view of the elaborate use of imagery and visions from 4:1 through the end of Revelation and the question of how this material relates to chapters 1–3, it is not surprising that commentators differ widely in their treatment of these chapters.

(1) The Throne, the Scroll, and the Lamb (4:1–5:14). Chapters 4–5 form one vision consisting of two parts: the throne (ch 4) and the Lamb and the scroll (ch 5). Actually, the throne vision (chs 4,5) and the breaking of all seven seals (chs 6–8:1) form a single, continuous vision and should not be separated; indeed, the throne vision should be viewed as dominating the entire vision of the seven-sealed scroll, and, for that matter, the rest of the book (cf. 14:1; 22:3).

A new view of God's majesty and power (throne) is disclosed to John so that he can understand the events on earth that relate to the seven-sealed vision (4:1–11; cf. 1 Kgs 22:19). For the first time in Revelation, the reader is introduced to the frequent interchange between heaven and earth found in the remainder of the book. What happens on earth has its inseparable heavenly counterpart.

Chapter 5 is part of the vision that begins

himself as the exalted Lord, Jesus Christ (vv 17,18), and then explains the meaning of the symbolic vision (vv 19,20). Finally, the Lord addresses a rather detailed and specific message to each of the seven churches in Asia (2:1–3:22).

The Letters to the Seven Churches (2:1–3:22). These seven churches contained typical or representative qualities of both obedience and disobedience that are a constant reminder to all churches throughout every age (cf. 2:7,11, 17,29; 3:6,13,22; esp. 2:23). Their order (1:11; 2:1–3:22) reflects the natural ancient travel circuit beginning at Ephesus and arriving finally at Laodicea.

Each message generally follows a common literary plan consisting of seven parts:

(1) The addressee is given first, following a common pattern in all seven letters: "To the angel of the church in Ephesus write."

(2) Then the speaker is mentioned. In each case, some part of the great vision of Christ and of his self-identification (1:12–20) is repeated as the speaker identifies himself; for example, "These are the words of him who holds the seven stars in his right hand and walks among the seven golden lampstands" (2:1; cf. 1:13,16).

(3) Next, the knowledge of the speaker is given. He knows intimately the works of the churches and the reality of their loyalty to him, despite outward appearances. In two

with chapter 4 and continues through the opening of the seven seals (6:1–8:1; cf. introduction to ch 4). The movement of the whole scene focuses on the slain Lamb as he takes the scroll from the hand of the One on the throne. The culminating emphasis is on the worthiness of the Lamb to receive worship because of his death.

(2) Opening of the First Six Seals (6:1–17). The opening of the seals continues the vision begun in chapters 4 and 5. Now the scene shifts to events on earth. The scroll itself involves the rest of Revelation and has to do with the consummation of the mystery of all things, the goal or end of history for both the overcomers and the worshipers of the beast.

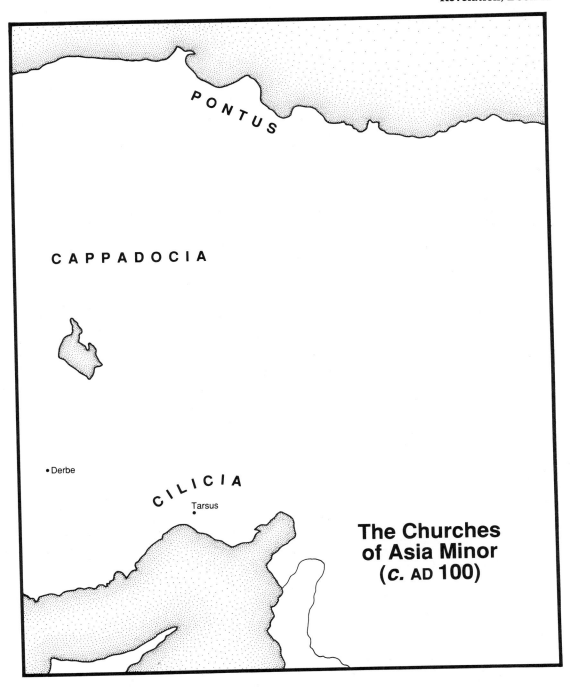

The Churches of Asia Minor (*c.* AD 100)

The writer tentatively suggests that the seals represent events preparatory to the final consummation. Whether these events come immediately before the end or whether they represent general conditions that will prevail throughout the period preceding the end is a more difficult question.

The seals closely parallel the signs of the approaching end times spoken of in Jesus' Olivet discourse (Mt 24:1–35; Mk 13:1–37; Lk 21:5–33). This parallel to major parts of Revelation is too striking to be ignored. Thus the seals would correspond to the "beginning of birth pains" in the Olivet discourse. The events are similar to those occuring under the trumpets (8:2–11:19) and bowls (15:1–16:21), but should not be confused with those later and more severe judgments.

(3) First Interlude: The 144,000 Israelites and the White-Robed Multitude (7:1–17). The change in tone from the subject matter in the sixth seal as well as the delay until 8:1 in opening the seventh seal indicate that chapter 7 is a true interlude. John first sees the angels who will unleash destruction on the earth restrained until the 144,000 servants of God from every tribe of Israel are sealed (vv 1–8). Then he sees an innumerable multitude clothed in white standing before the throne of God; these are identified as those who have come out of the "great tribulation" (vv 9–17).

Some separate the two groups into Jews and Gentiles at large, while others see the two groups as one viewed from different perspectives.

(4) The Opening of the Seventh Seal (8:1). After the interlude (ch 7) the final seal is opened, and silence for half an hour occurs in heaven either solemnly to prepare for judgment on earth or to hear the cries of the martyrs on earth (cf. 6:10).

The First Six Trumpets (8:2–11:14). After a preparatory scene in heaven (8:2–5), the six trumpets are blown in succession (8:6–9:19), followed again by an interlude (10:1–11:14).

(1) The First Six Trumpets (8:6–9:21). Opinion differs but it may be best to see the first five seals as preceding chronologically the events of the trumpets and bowls. But the sixth seal enters into the period of the outpouring of God's wrath that is enacted in the trumpet and bowl judgments (6:12–17). The trumpet judgments, thus, occur during the seventh seal, and the bowl judgments (16:1–21) during the seventh trumpet's sounding. Therefore, there is some overlapping, but also sequence and advancement, between the seals, trumpets, and bowls.

As in the seals, there is a discernible literary pattern in the unfolding of the trumpets. The first four trumpets are separated from the last three, which are called "woes" (8:13; 9:12; 11:14) and are generally reminiscent of the plagues in the Book of Exodus.

The last three trumpets are emphasized and are called also "woes" (8:13) because they are so severe. The first of these involves an unusual plague of locusts (9:1–11) and the second a plague of scorpion-like creatures (9:13–19). Both of these plagues can best be seen as demonic hordes (cf. 9:1,11).

(2) The Second Interlude: The Little Book and the Two Witnesses (10:1–11:14). The chief import of chapter 10 seems to be a confirmation of John's prophetic call, as verse 11 indicates: "You must prophesy again about many peoples, nations, languages and kings." More specifically, the contents of the little scroll

(book) may include chapters 11, 12, and 13 of the book.

Chapter 11 is notoriously difficult. It includes a reference to measuring the temple, the altar, the worshipers, and to the trampling down of the Holy City for 42 months (vv 1,2), as well as the description of the two prophet–witnesses who are killed and raised to life (vv 3–13).

Opinions vary considerably here from a reference to the restored Jewish nation and the prophets Moses and Elijah revived to seeing the temple as the true church being protected by God during the tribulation and the two witnesses representing the whole faithful church under persecution.

The Seventh Trumpet (11:15–14:20). The seventh trumpet sounds, and in heaven loud voices proclaim the final triumph of God and Christ over the world. The theme is the kingdom of God and Christ—a dual kingdom, eternal in its duration. The image suggests the transference of the world empire that, once dominated by a usurping power, has now at length passed into the hands of its true Owner and King. The announcement of the reign of the King is made here, but the final breaking of the enemies' hold over the world does not occur till the return of Christ (19:11–21).

(1) The Woman and the Dragon (12:1–17). In this chapter there are three main figures: the woman, the child, and the dragon. There are also three scenes: the birth of the child (vv 1–6), the expulsion of the dragon (vv 7–12), and the dragon's attack on the woman and her children (vv 13–17).

Since the context indicates that the woman under attack represents a continuous entity from the birth of Christ until at least John's day or later, her identity in the author's mind must be the believing covenant-messianic community.

The woman is in the throes of childbirth (v 2). The emphasis is on her pain and suffering, both physical and spiritual. The meaning of her anguish is that the faithful messianic community has been suffering as a prelude to the coming of the Messiah himself and of the new age (Is 26:17; 66:7,8; Mi 4:10; 5:3).

(2) The Two Beasts (13:1–18). Turning from the inner dynamics of the struggle (ch 12), chapter 13 shifts to the actual earthly instruments of this assault against God's people—namely, the two dragon-energized beasts. The activities of the two beasts constitute the way the dragon carries out his final attempts to wage war on the seed of the woman (12:17).

The dragon and the first beast enter into a conspiracy to seduce the whole world into worshiping the beast. The conspirators summon yet a third figure to their aid—the beast from the earth, who must be sufficiently similar to the Lamb to entice even the followers of Jesus. As the battle progresses, the dragon's deception becomes more and more subtle. Thus the readers are called on to discern the criteria that will enable them to separate the lamblike beast from the Lamb himself (cf. 13:11 with 14:1).

(3) The Harvest of the Earth (14:1–20). The two previous chapters have prepared Christians for the reality that, as the end draws near, they will be harassed and sacrificed like sheep. This section shows that their sacrifice is not meaningless. In chapter 7 the 144,000 were merely sealed; here, however, they are seen as already delivered. When the floods have passed, Mt Zion appears high above the waters; the Lamb is on the throne of glory, surrounded by the trimphant songs of his own; the gracious presence of God fills the universe.

Chapter 14 briefly answers two pressing questions: What becomes of those who refuse to receive the mark of the beast and are killed (vv 1–5)? What happens to the beast and his servants (vv 6–20)?

The Seven Bowls (15:1–19:10). The inclusive series of bowl judgments constitutes the "third woe," announced in 11:14 as "coming soon" (see comments on 11:14). These last plagues take place "immediately after the distress of those days" referred to by Jesus in the Olivet discourse and may well be the fulfillment of his apolcalyptic words: "The sun will be darkened, and the moon will not give its light; the stars will fall from the sky, and the heavenly bodies will be shaken" (Mt 24:29).

(1) Preparation: The Seven Angels with the Seven Last Plagues (15:1–8). Chapter 15 is related to the OT account of the exodus and is strongly suggestive of the liturgical tradition of the ancient synagogue. The chapter has two main visions: the first portrays the victors who have emerged triumphant from the great ordeal (vv 2–4); the second relates the emergence from the heavenly temple of the seven angels clothed in white and gold who hold the seven bowls of the last plagues (vv 5–8).

(2) The Pouring Out of the Bowl Judgments (16:1–21). These occur in rapid succession with only a brief pause for a dialogue between the third angel and the altar, accentuating the justice of God's punishments (vv 5–7). This rapid succession is probably due to John's desire to give a telescopic view of the first six bowls and to hasten then on to the seventh, where the far more interesting judgment on Babylon occurs, of which the author will give a detailed account. The final three plagues are social and spiritual in their effect and shift from nature to humanity.

(3) The Prostitute and the Beast (17:1–18). To a majority of modern exegetes, Babylon represents the city of Rome. The beast stands for the Roman Empire as a whole, including its subject provinces and peoples.

However, it is not sufficient simply to identify Babylon with Rome. For that matter, Babylon cannot be confined to any one historical manifestation, past or future; it has multiple equivalents (cf. 11:8). Babylon is found wherever there is satanic deception. Babylon is better understood here as the archetypal head of all entrenched worldly resistance to God. Babylon is a transhistorical reality that includes idolatrous kingdoms as diverse as Sodom, Egypt, Babylon, Tyre, Nineveh, and Rome. Babylon is an eschatological symbol of satanic deception and power; it is a divine mystery that can never be wholly reducible to empirical earthly institutions. Babylon represents the total culture of the world apart from God, while the divine system is depicted by the New Jerusalem. Rome is simply one manifestation of the total system.

(4) The Fall of Babylon the Great (18:1–24). Chapter 18 contains the description of the previously announced "judgment" (NIV, punishment) of the prostitute (17:1). Under the imagery of the destruction of a great commercial city, John describes the final overthrow of the great prostitute, Babylon.

(5) Thanksgiving for the Destruction of Babylon (19:1–5). In stark contrast to the laments of Babylon's consorts, the heavenly choirs burst forth in a great liturgy of celebration to God.

(6) The Marriage of the Lamb (19:6–10). Finally, the cycle of praise is completed with the reverberating sounds of another great multitude (v 6): the great redeemed throng (cf. 7:9). They utter the final great Hallel in words reminiscent of the great royal psalms (93:1; 97:1; 99:1).

The Vision of the Return of Christ and the Consummation of the Age (19:11–20:15). (1) The First and Second Last Things: The Rider on the White Horse and the Destruction of the Beast (19:11–21). In one sense, this vision (vv 11–21), which depicts the return of Christ and the final overthrow of the beast, may be viewed as the climax of the previous section (vv 1–10), or as the first of a final series of seven last things—namely, the return of Christ; the defeat of the beast; the binding of Satan; the millennium; the release and final end of Satan; the last judgment; and the new heaven, the new earth, and the new Jerusalem.

Although Satan has been dealt a death blow at the cross (cf. Jn 12:31; 16:11), he nevertheless continues to promulgate evil and deception during this present age (cf. Eph 2:2; 1 Thes 3:5; 1 Pt 5:8,9; Rv 2:10). Yet he is a deposed ruler who is now under the sovereign

Ruins of a theater at Laodicea, with Hierapolis visible in the distance. The overcomers were promised regal rights (3:21) such as will be experienced when Christ returns for the 1000-year reign with those who have part in the first resurrection (Rev 20:4,6).

authority of Christ, but who for a "little time" is allowed to continue his evil until God's purposes are finished. In this scene of the overthrow of the beast, his kings, and their armies, John shows us the ultimate and swift destruction of these evil powers by the King of kings and Lord of lords. They have met their Master in this final and utterly real confrontation (vv 17–21).

(2) The Third and Fourth Last Things: The Binding of Satan and the Millennium (20:1–6). The millennium has been called one of the most controversial and intriguing questions of eschatology. The main problem is whether the reference to a millennium (from the Latin *mille*, thousand; *annus* or *ennus*, year) indicates an earthly historical reign of peace that will manifest itself at the close of this present age, or whether the whole passage is symbolic of some present experience of Christians or some future nonhistorical reality. The former view is called premillennial, the latter is amillennial.

The binding of Satan removes his deceptive activities from the earth (vv 1–3) during the time the martyred saints are resurrected and rule with Christ (vv 4–6).

(3) The Fifth Last Thing: The Release and Final End of Satan (20:7–10). In Ezekiel 38,39, Gog refers to the prince of a host of pagan invaders from the North, especially the Scythian hordes from the distant land of Magog. In Revelation, however, the names are symbolic of the final enemies of Christ duped by Satan into attacking the community of the saints. The change in meaning has occurred historically through the frequent use in rabbinic circles of the terms "Gog and Magog" to symbolically refer to the "nations" of Psalm 2 who are in rebellion against God and his Messiah.

(4) The Sixth Last Thing: The Great White Throne Judgment (20:11–15). The language of poetic imagery captures the fading character of everything that is of the world (1 Jn 2:17). Now the only reality is God seated on the throne of judgment, before whom all must appear (Heb 9:27). His verdict alone is holy and righteous (expressed symbolically by the "white" throne). This vision declares that even though it may have seemed that the course of earth's history ran contrary to his holy will, no single day or hour in the world's drama has ever detracted from the absolute sovereignty of God.

(5) The Seventh Last Thing: The New Heaven and the New Earth and the New Jerusalem (21:1–22:5). John discloses a theology in stone and gold as pure as glass and color. Archetypal images abound. The church is called the bride (21:2). God gives the thirsty "to drink without cost from the spring of the water of life" (21:6). Completeness is implied in the number 12 and its multiples (21:12–14,16,17,21) and fullness in the cubical shape of the city (21:16). Colorful jewels abound, as do references to light and the glory of God (21:11,18–21,23,25; 22:5). There is the "river of the water of life" (22:1) and the "tree of life" (22:2). The "sea" is gone (21:1).

Allusions to the OT abound. Most of John's imagery in this chapter reflects Isaiah 60,65 and Ezekiel 40–48. John weaves Isaiah's vision of the New Jerusalem together with Ezekiel's vision of the new temple. The multiple OT promises converging in John's mind seem to indicate that he viewed the New Jerusalem as the fulfillment of all these strands of prophecy. There are also allusions to Genesis 1–3: the absence of death and suffering, the dwelling of God with men as in Eden, the tree of life, the removal of the curse. Creation is restored to its pristine character.

The connection of this vision with the promises to the overcomers in the letters to the seven churches (chs 2,3) is significant. For example, to the overcomers at Ephesus was granted the right to the tree of life (2:7; cf. 22:2); at Thyatira, the right to rule the nations (2:26; cf. 22:5); at Philadelphia, the name of the city of God, the New Jerusalem (3:12; cf. 21:2,9–27). In a sense, a strand from every major section of the Apocalypse appears in chapters 21, 22.

John's Conclusion (22:6–21). With consummate artistry, the notes of the introit (1:1–8) are sounded again in the conclusion: the book ends with the voices of the angel, Jesus, the Spirit, the bride, and, finally, John (v 20).

ALAN F. JOHNSON

See APOCALYPTIC; DANIEL, BOOK OF; ESCHATOLOGY; JOHN THE APOSTLE, LIFE AND WRITINGS OF.

Bibliography. I.T. Beckwith, *The Apocalypse of John*; G.B. Caird, *The Revelation of St John the Divine*; H. Hailey, *Revelation*; W. Hendriksen, *More Than Conquerors*; M. Kiddle, *The Revelation of St John*; G.E. Ladd, *A Commentary on the Revelation of John*; H. Lilje, *The Last Book of the Bible*; W. Milligan, *The Book of Revelation*; R.H. Mounce, *The Book of Revelation*; C.A. Scott, *The Book of the Revelation*; H.B. Swete, *The Apocalypse of St. John*; M.C. Tenney, *Interpreting Revelation*; J.F. Walvoord, *The Revelation of Jesus Christ*.

Revenge, Revenger. *See* AVENGER OF BLOOD.

Reward. Recompense for good or evil; most often it suggests a benefit or favorable compensation. Both good and evil are rewarded or punished, and man's responsibility and accountability are involved in an ethical sense. Related terms such as wages, hire, recompense, or requital are a part of the broader concept. In this fullest sense, the operation of reward ranges from the consequences resulting from dealings between people to God's compensation for obedience or disobedience, from the consequences of actions felt in this life to divine recompense in the life to come.

To Greek and Hebrew minds the concept of reward suggested the ideal of wholeness of an action, the completion of a deed. Just as work was completed for a man in the payment of wages, so it was assumed that an action naturally carried certain results, either reward or punishment. The overtones of commercial transactions were not absent, as when the reward is referred to as "wages." Thus Paul says "the wages of sin is death" (Rom 6:23). The idea involves an equal return commensurate with the action performed.

The biblical conception of reward was both ethical and religious. The covenant of God made with Israel was evidence of God's loving favor; it promised good things to Israel on the condition of their obedience to God's commands. Disobedience was a violation of the covenant and would bring disaster and death. Deuteronomy 28 spells out the blessings that obedience would bring and also the national disasters that would come upon Israel if they did not observe what was right and good in the sight of the Lord (see also Lv 26). In the period of the wilderness wanderings, failure to obey on the part of the people and their leaders brought suffering and death. The history of the judges and the kings was written in terms of reward for faithfulness and punishment for sin and idolatry. Earthly victory and the national welfare depended on obedience and faithfulness to the Lord (Jos 1:7–9; cf. Jgs 2).

This national pattern of reward and punishment was also applied to the individual life. The good life was assured on the basis of obedience and discipline. The wisdom of Israel identified the good life with the blessing of God. The first psalm portrays the fortunes of a wise, pious man in contrast to the ungodly fool. Proverbs clearly pictures a man as bearing the consequences of his own actions. "He who digs a pit will fall into it; and a stone will come back upon him who starts it rolling" (Prv 26:27). Jeremiah pictures life as being out of order if the good should be repaid with evil (Jer 18:20).

Those who had been wronged were usually responsible for bringing the wrongdoer to judgment and for carrying out the sentence. Individual laws with their punishments were given immediately following the Ten Commandments (Ex 21, 22; Dt 19–24). Provision was also made in cases where an individual was not able to avenge himself (e.g., for murder), but needed to rely on another to "avenge his blood" (Nm 35:19–27; Dt 19:1–10; Jos 20:5–9). In such cases an individual's close relative would pursue the wrongdoer to the city of refuge where a trial would take place. If the verdict was guilty of murder out of hatred, the elders of the city of refuge would deliver the guilty party to the relative, who would then take his life. The OT law was "life for life, eye for eye, tooth for tooth, hand for hand, foot for foot" (Dt 19:21).

In cases where a vindication could not be rendered, the offended person increasingly looked upon God to become his avenger. In this sense, God is called the Redeemer of the one who had been wronged, and his redemption involved the punishment of the one who had done wrong as well as the salvation of the wronged.

Similarly in a national sense, Israel believed that God would punish its enemies on the Day of the Lord. This day would be a day of national salvation when God would intervene militarily to vindicate the Israelites over their enemies who had done wrong. The prophet Amos began a transformation of this concept so that Israel was led to see its own national destruction in terms of God's punishment of the nation for its sins (Am 5:18–20). When the intervention of God seemed more and more distant, the prophets proclaimed the Day of the Lord as the final judgment of God at which time the good would be rewarded and the evil would be punished (Jl 2:1–11; Zep 1:2–2:15).

The pattern of reward and punishment was not always carried out. The Jews believed that God would be a merciful, forgiving God. Forgiveness involved the removal of the punishment for sin. "He does not deal with us according to our sins, nor requite us according to our iniquities (Ps 103:10).

The writer of Ecclesiastes found that life did not work out so neatly and that the doctrine of retribution did not always apply in the span of an individual life. There is a somewhat cynical note when the righteous suffer and the wicked prosper. Job's friends took the position that his sickness is the result of some hidden sin. Job maintains his integrity, and for him the answer lies outside the pattern of strict reward for righteousness and punishment for evil. In the outcome Job is rewarded for his good life.

In Jesus' day Judaism had changed significantly. The legal system of the judges had been replaced with Roman law. But Judaism had no hesitation about recognizing the merit of good works and in exhorting people to accumulate a store of merit on a basis of which God would bless them (Tob 4:7–10; Ecclus 51:30; 2 Mc 5:15,16). The Pharisees especially believed that accurate and conscientious observance of the Law would oblige God to recompense them for their performances. The individual who did much was to expect reward from God, while every transgression entailed its corresponding recompense for evil. What was not repaid in this life would be a part of future reward.

Reward was a significant part of Jesus' teaching, especially in the Sermon on the Mount (Mt 5–7). The Beatitudes proclaimed that the blessing of God would come upon all people who exhibited certain characteristics and related what the result of these characteristics would be (Mt 5:1–12). The individual who acts to receive the praise of others shall receive that and nothing more, but the one whose motives call him to please God shall be rewarded by God (Mt 6:1,4,6,18). However, Jesus sharply curbed this idea when he taught the parable of the laborers (Mt 20:1–16). Here each was paid the same amount no matter how long he had worked. Jesus calls us to work for motives higher than reward. In the discourse on the good shepherd, the hireling who only works for wages is contrasted with the shepherd who is willing to lay down his life for the sheep (Jn 10:11–14). The servant who had only done his duty deserves no reward (Lk 17:9–10).

Beginning with Paul, the idea of reward especially as it relates to salvation is seen in a drastically different light. No longer is salvation considered to be the result of an individual having done more good than evil in life. Salvation is an act of divine favor which no one can earn (Rom 4:4). Salvation is not earned but given by a loving, beneficent God. The idea of reward does not disappear. Reward results from good done after salvation is attained. First Corinthians 3:8–14 teaches that the quality of a person's works will be examined and rewarded, but that salvation does not hinge upon good works. However, works do have an important place in eternal destiny (Col 3:24; Rv 14:13).

With the state assuming the role of enforcer of the law, no longer does the individual have the right to exercise vengeance. Vengeance becomes the prerogative of God (Rom 12:19; Heb 10:30). The state becomes God's minister to carry out God's function as avenger of wrong in this present age (Rom 13:1–7). But God's punishment of wrong is not limited to the action of the civil authorities. He also acts to darken the human mind as a result of sin (Rom 1:18–32; 2 Pt 2:13–15). The Bible is clear that those who do evil will also reap eternal consequences of that which they have done (Gal 6:7,8; Rv 11:18; 22:12).   DAVID W. WEAD

See JUDGMENT; CROWN.

Rezeph. City destroyed by the Assyrians. It was mentioned in a derisive letter sent from Sennacherib, king of Assyria, to King Hezekiah of Judah. Rezeph was listed along with the conquered cities of Gozan and Haran and the sons of Eden in Telassar. The Assyrian king was reminding Hezekiah that just as the local deities of these cities were not able to protect them from Assyrian conquest, so neither could Hezekiah's God preserve Jerusalem (2 Kgs 19:12; Is 37:12). Rezeph was a notable Assyrian city, known for its commerce and governing seat. It was brought into the Assyrian empire well over a century before Hezekiah's confrontation with Sennacherib. It is perhaps identifiable with the modern Syrian city of Resafa.

Rezia. KJV spelling of Rizia, Ulla's son, in 1 Chronicles 7:39.

See RIZIA.

Rezin. 1. Syrian monarch who ruled in Damascus during the earlier part of Isaiah's prophetic ministry and the last years the northern 10 tribes existed as a nation. Rezin was used by God to humble both Israel and Judah because they had forsaken him and rejected his covenant (2 Chr 28:5,6).

Rezin was born in the town of Bit-hadara near Damascus in the land of Syria (also called Aram). Upon his accession to the throne, the Syrian people (also called Aramaeans) re-asserted their independence from Israel's domination. During this period, Assyria was strengthening itself and expanding its empire throughout the Near East. Along with King Menahem of Israel, Rezin was forced to pay tribute to the Assyrian monarch Tiglath-pileser III in 738 BC. The heavy burden of vassalage to the Assyrians generated anti-Assyrian senti-ment among the Syrian and neighboring peo-ple. During this time Rezin seems to have helped Pekah in his successful coup to seize the throne of Israel. Immediately upon his acces-sion to the throne, Pekah formed an anti-Assyrian coalition with Rezin. They soon real-ized that successful resistance against Assyria required a larger alliance. They invited King Ahaz of Judah to join their coalition, but Ahaz adamantly refused. With the intention of plac-ing an Aramaean of Davidic lineage upon the throne of Judah in order to effect a broader Syrian-Israelite alliance, Rezin and Pekah joined in an attack on Judah. They inflicted heavy casualties upon the southern kingdom. Rezin took advantage of his operations in south-ern Palestine to move further south and cap-ture the port of Elath. He ceded possession of the port to the Edomites (2 Kgs 16:6). In spite of winning most battles, Rezin and Pekah were unsuccessful in their attempt to take Jerusalem and replace Ahaz (2 Chr 28:5–15; Is 7:1–9). Dur-ing these dark days for Judah, Isaiah brought an encouraging word to the people. He prophe-sied the imminent destruction of Israel (Ephra-im) and Damascus by Assyria (Is 7:1–9; 8:1–8). So certain was the destruction of these king-doms that he referred to their two kings as "stubs of smoldering firebrands" about to be extinguished (7:4). Disregarding Isaiah's proph-ecy, Ahaz sent a large sum of money to Tiglath-pileser III, hoping to induce him to come to Judah's aid.

Rezin and Pekah moved their forces to the north to prepare for the impending Assyrian invasion. Tiglath-pileser attacked in 733 BC and captured much of the area of Galilee. He then turned his attention to Damascus, to which Rezin had fled. Assyrian records refer to Rezin as a "caged bird" in besieged Damas-cus. When Damascus fell in 732 BC, Rezin was executed and many citizens of Damascus were exiled. Samaria, the capital city of Israel, fell to the Assyrians in 722 BC. Damascus and the nation of Syria became an Assyrian province. Rezin thus was the last Syrian king to reign in Damascus.

See ISRAEL, HISTORY OF; ISAIAH (PERSON); SYRIA, SYRIANS.

2. Father of some of the temple servants who served in postexilic times (Ezr 2:48; Neh 7:50).

Rezon. Son of Eliada, who set himself up as ruler of Damascus and Syria following David's slaying of Hadadezer, king of Zobah. Rezon was a God-appointed adversary who despised Israel and was a constant problem to Solomon during his reign (1 Kgs 11:23–25).

Rhegium. Important Italian harbor visited by Paul in his journey to Rome (Acts 28:13). From Malta, Paul's ship traveled north to the Sicilian capital of Syracuse; then in the ab-sence of a south wind they may have tacked into the Strait of Messina, finding good har-bor at Rhegium. Another south wind carried them from Rhegium to Puteoli in the Bay of Naples—the ship's destination, since Puteoli was southern Italy's chief port, receiving the great Alexandrian grain vessels.

The Strait of Messina was well known to every Roman navigator. Passage here was nec-essary in order to gain access to Italy's west coast; but its obstacles were numerous. Ob-structions, shallows, and the narrow width (*c.* seven miles from Rhegium to Messina) forced ships to stay at Rhegium until an adequate south wind arose.

The name "Rhegium" (modern Reggio or Reggio di Calabria) may have come from a Greek verb, meaning "to tear" or "rend." Sic-ily, it seemed, had been "torn from the main-land" and Rhegium was the nearest Italian port.

Rhesa. Descendant of Zerubbabel and an an-cestor of Jesus Christ (Lk 3:27).

See GENEALOGY OF JESUS CHRIST.

Rhoda. Maid in the home of Mary the mother of John Mark in Jerusalem. Rhoda re-ported to those in the house that Peter was standing outside the door. Since they were un-aware of his release from prison, the others at first did not believe her report (Acts 12:13–15).

Rhodes. Port of call on Paul's return trip to Jerusalem from his third missionary journey (Acts 21:1). The mention of Rhodes in Genesis 10:4; Ezekiel 27:15; and 1 Chronicles 1:7 is not based on the Hebrew text of the OT, but on its Greek translation. The island of Rhodes, an area of more than 500 square miles, is situated near the southeast coast of modern Turkey.

In Paul's time the island had long been an important establishment of Dorian Greek culture, with several cities. Rhodes, the capital, lay on the busiest ancient sea route between the ports of Italy and the province of Asia to the west, and those of Syria and Egypt to the east. It was distinguished for its natural harbor and public works. Rhodes was a prominent center of business, and supplied most of the precedents for Roman law of the sea. The 2nd century BC marked the height of its political power, which included control of most of Caria and Lycia on the mainland of Asia Minor. Roman power first deprived Rhodes of its commerical domination, and during the Roman civil wars of the 1st century BC, it was reduced politically to little more than a provincial town in the Roman Empire.

To celebrate a military victory in 280 BC, the city of Rhodes erected near the harbor an immense bronze statue of the Greek sun god, 121 feet tall—about the height of the Statue of Liberty. It was 12 years in the making, and soon after its completion an earthquake broke it off at the knees (224 BC). But the fragmented ruins remained as a curiosity until the Arab occupation of the island in the 7th century. This "Colossus of Rhodes" was included in some ancient lists of wonders of the world. Since the Middle Ages it has sometimes been erroneously described as straddling the harbor entrance, though this would have been physically impossible.

Ribai. Benjamite of Gibeah and the father of Ittai, one of David's mighty men (2 Sm 23:29; 1 Chr 11:31).

Riblah. 1. Town along the Orontes River located some 35 miles northeast of Baalbek, identifiable with modern Ribleh in Syria. Riblah was well situated topographically for military operations, especially when the great powers of Egypt and Mesopotamia were crossing the northern part of the Fertile Crescent. The Egyptians are mentioned in Scripture as the first people that troubled this town. After the death of King Josiah in his battle with the Egyptian pharaoh Neco, Jehoahaz was made king. Neco did not approve of the election. So the pharaoh imprisoned Jehoahaz at Riblah and made Eliakim (Jehoiakim), Jehoahaz's brother, king of Judah (2 Kgs 23:33).

After the defeat of Neco at Carchemish in 605 BC, Nebuchadnezzar of Babylon took control of the area, making Riblah his headquarters for his South-Syria and Palestine dominions. When Zedekiah, king of Judah, opposed Nebuchadnezzar, the Babylonians captured him and imprisoned him at Riblah, where the king "passed sentence upon him" (2 Kgs 25:6; Jer 39:5,6; 52:9,10). Consequently, many of Zedekiah's sons were killed at Riblah and

Zedekiah was bound and taken to Babylon (2 Kgs 25:20,21; Jer 52:26,27).

Riblah is also called Diblah (ASV) and Diblath (KJV) in Ezekiel 6:14.

2. Town defining part of the eastern boundary of Israel, located east of Ain (Nm 34:11). Its exact location is unknown, though probably not identifiable with #1 above.

Riches. Wealth measured in money, or the amount of property owned—whether land and buildings (Is 5:8–10), livestock (1 Sm 25:2,3), or slaves (1 Sm 8:11–18). Great riches brought great influence and power, as the Hebrew word for "wealth" implies.

The Bible seems to speak with two voices on the subject of riches, sometimes describing material wealth as a sign of God's blessing and approval (e.g., Gn 24:35), at other times virtually identifying the rich with the wicked (e.g., Ps 37:7,16). Jesus, in particular, is very stern in his denunciations of the wealthy. "How hard it will be for those who have riches to enter the kingdom of God!" (Mk 10:23).

God made all things for people to enjoy (1 Tm 6:17). That is why being rich is a matter for thanksgiving, not embarrassment. Every possession that a person can possibly own comes from the Creator (Ps 24:1), so all wealth can rightly be counted as a blessing from God. It was in this spirit that Abraham's servant could say, "The Lord has greatly blessed my master" (Gn 24:35) and David could pray to God, "Riches and honor came from thee" (1 Chr 29:12). Even when wealth is earned by hard work, the Bible reminds its readers that both their talents and their resources are God-given. Jesus illustrates this important lesson in the parables of the 10 talents (Mt 25:14–30) and the 10 minas (Lk 19:11–26).

Nowhere, then, does the Bible say that having possessions and becoming wealthy are things that are wrong in themselves. There would be no point in the Ten Commandments' ban on stealing and envy if it was wrong for God's people to own anything at all. Jesus himself never taught that it was sinful to be rich.

Some have tried to show from the life-style of the early church that Christians ought to live without private possessions or personal wealth of any kind. "No one said that any of the things which he possessed was his own," Luke tells us: "they had everything in common" (Acts 4:32). This example of sacrifice is a challenge to all Christians, especially the affluent, but it does not teach that private ownership is wrong. The terrible fate of Ananias and Sapphira makes that clear (Acts 5:1–11).

The OT is particularly positive in its attitude to wealth. "All hard work brings a profit,

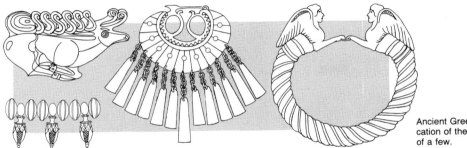

Ancient Greek jewelry, an indication of the personal wealth of a few.

but mere talk leads only to poverty" (Prv 14:23). But the Book of Proverbs also paints in the darker side of the biblical picture. Riches may be a blessing, say the wise, but they can also lead to broken relationships and personal disaster (Prv 18:23; 22:16).

These practical warnings anticipate Jesus' teaching about the dangers of becoming rich. Affluence, he taught, can destroy peace (Mt 6:24–34), blind people to the needs of others (Lk 16:19–31), stand between individuals and the gateway to eternal life (Mk 10:17–27), and even bring God's judgment (Lk 12:16–21). He told his disciples not to accumulate personal wealth (Mt 6:19), and praised those who gave up their possessions (Mt 19:29).

These strong words suggest that Jesus was against wealth, but his sharp warnings are not in fact directed against riches in themselves. What he condemns is the wrong attitudes many people have toward acquiring wealth, and the wrong ways in which they use it. Longing for riches, not having them, chokes the spiritual life like weeds in a field of grain (Mt 13:22). The greedy desire to have more doomed the unforgiving servant (Mt 18:23–35). And the rich man's selfishness, not his wealth, sealed his fate (Lk 16:19–26). Paul captures the main lesson in these parables exactly when he writes to Timothy, "For the *love* of money is the root of all evils" (1 Tm 6:10).

The greatest danger of all arises when riches gain the mastery in a person's life. The whole Bible warns against this idolatrous attitude to material things (e.g., Dt 8:17,18; Lk 14:15–24). Satan tempted Jesus to put material wealth and power in God's place (Mt 4:8,9), and Jesus delivers the clearest warning against making money into a master (Mt 6:24). In this light Jesus instructs the rich young ruler to sell everything (Mk 10:17–22). Here was a wealthy man who had allowed his possessions to possess him. Jesus' aim was to make him recognize his bondage so he could escape from his self-made prison. The fact that he turned away from Jesus demonstrates the powerful pull of riches.

These blunt warnings are the most striking aspect of Jesus' teaching on wealth. But along-side his exposure of wrong attitudes he was careful to sketch in the outline of right attitudes. Those who recognize that they are God's trustees (not owners) of their possessions, he taught, will find many valuable outlets for their riches in the Lord's service (Lk 12:42–44). Instead of coming between him and them, their possessions (great or small) can be used as aids to worship (Lk 21:1–4; 25:50–53; Jn 12:1–7). Instead of making them tight-fisted, their riches will allow them to express neighbor-love in many practical ways (2 Cor 8:2). And instead of having their inward peace ruined by anxious greed, they will find the secret of serenity in an increasing sense of dependence on their heavenly Giver (Lk 12:29–31; 1 Tm 6:17).

According to the Bible, then, the morality of riches depends entirely on personal attitudes. And nowhere does this come out more powerfully than in the frequent comparisons Scripture draws between material and spiritual wealth. Those who make material riches their goal in life have wrong values. However wealthy they may appear, they are poverty-stricken in God's sight (Mt 16:26; Rv 3:17). In his view, the truly rich are those whose main aim in life is to serve him as King (Mt 13:44–46). Their wealth lies in the currency of faith and good works (1 Tm 6:18; Jas 2:5)—a heavenly bank balance which no one can steal and nothing can erode. "For where your treasure is, there will your heart be also" (Mt 6:19–21).

DAVID H. FIELD

See MONEY AND BANKING; POOR, THE; WEALTH; WAGES.

Riddle. Word puzzle widely used and esteemed in the ancient world, both as an everyday amusement and as a test of wisdom at a more serious level. The point of a riddle was the discovery of a concealed meaning. Riddles, therefore, may be broadly distinguished from fables, which, like Jotham's celebrated plant fable (Jgs 9:7–15), contained an easily discerned significance. Obviously, there is an intermediate area where there is no sharp differentiation. For instance, Ezekiel's riddle (Ez 17) has sometimes been classified as a plant fable. Isaiah's "song of the vineyard," although not termed a riddle, is in the same general category, with the middle set out in 5:1–6 and its solution immediately following (Is 5:7; cf. Ez 15). Ezekiel acquired a certain reputation in this area (Ez 20:49).

Samson's riddle at his wedding feast is the best-known biblical riddle (Jgs 14). Probably it was a form of diversion used on such occasions (vv 12,13). The riddle took the form of a couplet:

"Out of the eater, something to eat;
out of the strong, something sweet" (NIV).

Samson's "thirty young men" threatened his betrothed, who wheedled the secret from him:

"What is sweeter than honey?
What is stronger than a lion?" (NIV).

Some scholars suggest that both the riddle and its answer may have been proverbial before this particular occasion.

Solomon's wisdom was demonstrated in his ability to answer the "hard questions" (lit. "riddles") of the Queen of Sheba (1 Kgs 10:1–4). His reputation for this kind of wisdom is further demonstrated by Ben Sira: "Your soul covered the earth, and you filled it with parables and riddles" (Ecclus 47.15).

Josephus notes a contest of wits between Solomon and Hiram, with riddles being exchanged. Solomon won the earlier exchanges, but Hiram finally outwitted him by enlisting outside help (*Antiq.* 8.5.5). Such wisdom to solve riddles was, understandably, claimed by Israel's wise men (e.g., Ps 49:4; Prv 1:6). In Daniel 8:23,24 there is the apocalyptic vision of "an angry king" who "shall rise to power with great shrewdness and intelligence" (lit. "one who understands riddles"). Daniel himself possessed the same ability to "interpret dreams, explain riddles, and solve problems" (Dn 5:12). Israel's traditions were at least partly enshrined, as a means of revelation, in "dark sayings (lit. "riddles") from of old" (Ps 78:2).

In the NT riddles figure infrequently. The various "hard sayings" of Jesus (e.g., Jn 6:60) are difficult to accept and are equally as hard to understand. Possibly the only true riddle is the number of the beast, 666 (Rv 13:18). Various attempts have been made to identify a person, after the pattern of numerical references in contemporary literature. Of these the emperor Nero is the most plausible candidate.

Right, Right Hand. Sense of "being straight"; terms used to describe that which is just or righteous (cf. Gn 18:25).

Figuratively speaking, God's right hand is the means whereby victories are obtained for the people of God (Pss 17:7; 98:1); it is also an instrument of punishment for the ungodly (Hb 2:16). While the right hand of man is impotent to save (Jb 40:14), God's right hand sustains his children in the hour of need (Ps 139:10). Furthermore, God promises to strengthen the right hand of the person he purposes to help (Is 41:13).

To be at the right hand of God is to occupy a place of the choicest blessings (Ps 16:11); it is the place where the Lord Jesus Christ now reigns in glory and intercedes for those he has redeemed (Rom 8:34).

To offer the right hand of fellowship is to extend the warmest and most accepting type of comradeship and is commonly practiced in the church (Gal 2:9). Giving the right hand as the sign of a pledge also has a biblical antecedent (2 Kgs 10:15).

Although the left hand is often linked to blessings (Prv 3:16), it may also be associated with treachery or other undesirable activity (Eccl 10:2).

See HAND; LAYING ON OF HANDS.

Righteousness. Conformity to a certain set of expectations, which vary from role to role. Righteousness is fulfillment of the expectations in any relationship, whether with God or other people. It is applicable at all levels of society, and is relevant in every area of life. Therefore, righteousness denotes the fulfilled expectations in relationships between man and wife, parents and children, fellow citizens, employer and employee, merchant and customers, ruler and citizens, and God and man. Depending on the fulfillment of one's expectations, an individual could be called righteous and his or her acts and speech could be designated as righteous. The opposite of righteous is "evil," "wicked," or "wrong" (cf. Ps 1:6; Zep 3:5). Righteousness is the fiber which holds society, religion, and family together. Righteousness enhances the welfare of the community. A godly (not "pious" in the modern sense) person was called "righteous" (*ṣaddîq*). The *ṣaddîq* was a person of wisdom, whose "righteousness" brought joy to his family (Prv 23:22–25), to his city (Prv 11:10), and to the people of God (Prv 29:2).

In Israel the concept of righteousness transformed all of life, both religious and secular. Israel had been called into existence as a separate nation through which Yahweh was to witness to the nations concerning his universal rule, his nature, and his expectations of life on earth. This meant that Israel required a revelation from God so that they might learn his will and be instructed in maintaining a relationship with him. The quality of a person's relationship with God is directly linked to his relationship with his fellowman. God is righteous (2 Chr 12:6; Ps 7;9; 103:17; Zep 3:5; Zec 8:8). The righteousness of the Lord is a dynamic concept, since it describes his acts on behalf of his people and also the nature of his relationship with them.

Righteousness is an attribute which stems from a covenantal relationship. Israel received the revelation of God's creative acts, transmitting the glorious acts of God's salvation from Egypt, and the gift of the land of Canaan as expressions of his "righteousness." All of God's acts are righteous (cf. Dt 32:4; Jgs 5:11; Ps 103:6), and God's people rejoiced in the righteous acts of God (Ps 89:16). In creation, God's rule over the nations, and his acts of salvation, Israel perceived the ordering and design of God's manifold relations to this world and to his people. The fidelity of God to his creatures and particularly to his chosen people was an expression of his righteousness. Because of this revelation, Israel's conception of history was a linear, progressive unfolding of God's plan. By grace Israel had received a place in his order, and they could never claim that their own righteousness had contributed to their inclusion in the history of salvation (cf. Dt 9:5,6). The continuation of God's ordering (governance) is seen in his saving acts on behalf of his covenant people. His acts in creation and in salvation are righteous in that they are the working out of his glorious ordering of his kingdom purposes for the earth (Ps 11; cf. 2 Pt 3:13).

Not only is God righteous, revealing his righteousness in his mighty acts, but he also expects righteousness of others, who are to reflect the nature of their Creator. The expected response to God's rule is in the form of righteousness, that is, conformity to his rule and will. In this basic sense, Noah is called "righteous" because he walked with God and showed integrity in comparison to his contemporaries (Gn 6:9). After humanity's fall and acts of rebellion culminating in the flood and the dispersion at Babel, God renewed his relationship with humanity in Abraham and his descendants. Abraham was righteous because he ordered his life by the revealed will of God (Gn 15:6; cf. 17:1b; 18:19; 26:5).

The Lord revealed to Israel more clearly how they were to relate to him and to each other. The Law in Israel was for the purpose of helping the people of God to live in conformity to the will of God. The person who was devoted to the service of God in worship and life was called righteous (cf. Mal 3:18). Thus, righteousness is a state of integrity in relation to God and one's fellowman, expressing itself in

one's acts and speech. Even as the Lord is righteous in his creative, sustaining, and salvific acts, so people are expected to act and speak in such a way that righteousness is evident and is advanced (Hos 10:12).

Yahweh, the Righteous One, freely established the covenant with Israel, lovingly redeemed them, and graciously promised to be their God and the God of their children. The covenant relationship was not dependent on Israel's righteousness, past, present, or future. In order to secure the outworking of his plan, he chose David and his descendants to lead God's people into righteousness. The Law was an impersonal instrument which found its complement, as in the days of Moses and Joshua, in a righteous leader, by whom righteousness was to be advanced.

The king in Israel was expected to lead God's people in righteousness. As God's appointed theocratic ruler, he reflected the glory and majesty of God. However, the king had another related responsibility. He was to protect the divine order and create a sphere in which God's people would be encouraged to do God's will so that the blessings of God would be assured. To this end David exhorted Solomon, "Show yourself a man, and observe what the Lord your God requires" (1 Kgs 2:2,3). Solomon's prayer (Ps 72) was for righteousness so that he might rule Israel righteously, the righteous might flourish, and the nation might enjoy God's blessing. "The mountains will bring prosperity to the people, the hills the fruit of righteousness" (vv 1–7).

The hope for an era characterized by righteousness was rooted in the prophetic revelation of the messianic rule and the establishment of God's kingdom (Is 11:1–9), whose rule will extend to the nations (vv 10–16) and last forever (9:7). Isaiah develops the revelation of the glorious, victorious entrance of the kingdom of God in a most exquisite way, when his enemies will be subdued, and his people will be gathered together and will live in a state of peace in his presence. The acts of restoration, extending from Israel's return from exile till the final coming of the external kingdom are, in his prophetic purview, the demonstration of God's righteous acts. He forgives, restores, remains faithful, loves, elects, and sends his Spirit to renew his people and to bestow on them all the benefits of the renewed covenant relationship. Both Jews and Gentiles will be the recipients of his righteous acts (Is 45:8,23; 46:13; 48:18; 51:5,8,16; 56:1; 59:14,17; 60:17; 61:10,11). In the new era "then will all your people be righteous and they will possess the land forever" (60:21), and the Lord will clothe his people with "garments of salvation" and "a robe of righteousness" (61:10).

Out of concern for the salvation of his people and the establishment of his everlasting kingdom, God revealed his righteousness in the sending of his beloved Son. The coming of Christ marks an era of renewal of his relationship with man, the renewal of the covenant and renewal of his kingdom on earth. The older covenant was mediated by Moses; the covenant was renewed by the Son of God, who came "to fulfill all righteousness" (Mt 3:15). The message of Jesus is consistent with the OT in the close identification of God's kingdom with his righteousness (Mt 6:33; 13:43; cf. Rom 14:17; 1 Cor 6:9). Jesus also taught that God expects all people to live in harmony with his will (Mt 7:21), rather than being mere imitators of other people's righteousness (Mt 5:20). Jesus is God's final revelation of what he requires of individuals to enter the kingdom and to live righteously. By repentance, faith in Christ, and following the Messiah, each person is again shown how to enter the kingdom. The law of the kingdom is freshly interpreted by Jesus in the Beatitudes and the Sermon on the Mount (Mt 5:1–7:27) with the intent not to set the OT revelation aside, but to confirm it.

Jesus taught that legal righteousness was never intended as an end in itself. The righteous live by faith and walk with God in the footsteps of Jesus and in communion with the Holy Spirit. For Paul, too, righteousness was not a legalistic system (Rom 9:30; 10:5; Phil 3:6; Gal 2:21).

The apostle Paul develops most extensively the doctrine of righteousness when he distinguishes the righteousness of people from the righteousness of God. First, righteousness is forensic. Individuals cannot attain to righteousness, but receive it as a gift from God (Rom 3:21–5:21). There is no righteousness apart from Jesus Christ. In the proclamation of the gospel of Jesus, "righteousness from God is revealed, a righteousness that is by faith from first to last" (Rom 1:17; cf. Hab 2:4). Therefore the Father requires acceptance of his Son as his appointed means of justification (Rom 3:25,26; 5:9). Righteousness carries a forensic significance in that God declares people to be righteous (Rom 8:33,34; 2 Cor 3:9; 11:15). God pardons sins, is reconciled with sinners, and grants his peace to them (Rom 5:1,9–11; Eph 2:14,15,17).

Second, righteousness is a relational term. Those who have been declared righteous enjoy a new relationship. They are "sons of God" by adoption.

Third, righteousness is a dynamic expression for newness of life. The Father relates to his children righteously and expects them to relate righteously to him. Righteousness as a dynamic quality expresses itself in the newness of life in the Spirit, which is freely given to those who have been justified (Rom 8:9–11). The way of righteousness manifests itself in love (Gal 5:22–26; Jas 3:17,18).

Fourth, righteousness is also an expression of hope, since the righteous acts of God stretch from creation to the new creation in Jesus Christ. Paul defines hope as the eager anticipation of righteousness (Gal 5:5), that is, the era of restoration of which Isaiah spoke. The fullness of righteousness will be manifest at the coming of our Lord Jesus, when all those who have been justified will also be glorified (Rom 8:30). The goal of salvation history moves toward the final glorious manifestation of God's kingdom, when all creation will be renewed in "righteousness," that is, conforming in every aspect to God's plan in Jesus Christ (Rom 5:17,21; 2 Pt 3:13).   WILLEM A. VANGEMEREN

See LAW, BIBLICAL CONCEPT OF; ISRAEL, RELIGION OF; GOD, BEING AND ATTRIBUTES OF; SANCTIFICATION; JUSTIFICATION.

Bibliography. J.A. Baird, *The Justice of God in the Teaching of Jesus*; H. Bavinck, *The Doctrine of God*; G. Rupp, *The Righteousness of God*; N.H. Snaith, *The Distinctive Ideas of the OT*, pp 51–78.

Rimmon (Person). 1. Benjamite of Beeroth, whose two sons, Baanah and Rechab, assassinated Ish-bosheth (2 Sm 4:2,5,9).

2. Deity revered by the Syrians of Damascus, whose temple was frequented by Naaman, captain of the Syrian army and his master (2 Kgs 5:18).

See SYRIA, SYRIANS.

Rimmon (Place). 1. Alternate name for En-rimmon, a town in southern Judah, in Joshua 15:32 and 1 Chronicles 4:32.

See EN-RIMMON.

2. Town in the territory allotted to Zebulun's tribe for an inheritance (Jos 19:13, KJV Remmon-methoar); alternately called Dimnah in Joshua 21:35.

3. Large cave about 12½ miles north of Jerusalem and 2½ miles south of biblical Ephraim (modern Taiyiba), also called the Rock of Rimmon. Six hundred refugees from the city of Gibeah found shelter in the cave for 4 months (Jgs 20:45,47; 21:13).

Rimmon, Rock of. Large cave north of Jerusalem (Jgs 20:45,47; 21:13).

See RIMMON (PLACE) #3.

Rimmon-perez, Rimmon-parez. Temporary camping place of the Israelites during their wilderness wanderings, mentioned between Rithmah and Libnah (Nm 33:19,20, KJV Rimmon-parez). Its location is unknown.

See WILDERNESS WANDERINGS.

Ring. *See* FASHION AND DRESS.

Rinnah. Shimon's son from Judah's tribe (1 Chr 4:20).

Riphath. Gomer's son and the brother of Ashkenaz and Togarmah, non-Semitic descendants of Noah through Japheth's line (Gn 10:3). First Chronicles 1:6, a parallel passage, reads Diphath instead of Riphath, undoubtedly a later copyist's misspelling that was never corrected.

Rissah. Stopping place for Israel in the wilderness between Libnah and Kehelathah (Nm 33:21,22). Its site is unknown.

See WILDERNESS WANDERINGS.

Rithmah. Stopping place for Israel in the wilderness between Hazeroth and Rimmon-perez (Nm 33:18,19). Its site is unknown.

See WILDERNESS WANDERINGS.

River of Egypt. 1. Alternate name for the Nile River in Genesis 15:18.

See NILE RIVER; SHIHOR.

2. Alternate name for the Brook of Egypt.

See BROOK OF EGYPT.

River of the Wilderness. KJV reading for an unidentifiable brook in the Arabah in Amos 6:14; called Brook of the Arabah in the RSV.

See BROOK OF THE ARABAH.

Rizia. Capable leader and mighty warrior, Ulla's son from Asher's tribe (1 Chr 7:39, KJV Rezia).

Rizpah. Daughter of Aiah and a concubine of Saul. She bore two sons, Armoni and Mephibosheth, to Saul. In a dispute between Ish-bosheth and Abner, Ish-bosheth accused Abner of having relations with Rizpah, suggesting an attempt to gain a royal claimant to Saul's throne. Infuriated at this apparent false accusation, Abner vowed to assist David in defeating Saul and to make David king of Israel (2 Sm 3:7). During the reign of David, Rizpah's two sons, along with five other sons of Saul, were killed by the Gibeonites as reparation for Saul's unwarranted slaughter of the sons of Gibeon. Rizpah courageously protected her sons' exposed bodies from natural predators until they were buried by David (2 Sm 21:8–11).

Robber, Robbery. *See* CRIMINAL LAW AND PUNISHMENT.

Robe. *See* FASHION AND DRESS.

Roboam. KJV rendering of Rehoboam, Solomon's son, in Matthew 1:7.

See REHOBOAM.

Rock Badger. *See* ANIMALS (BADGER).

Rodanim. Fourth son of Javan and a descendant of Noah through Japheth's line (1 Chr 1:7). An alternate spelling in Genesis 10:4 reads Dodanim, possibly a copyist's error. Both words probably refer to the Greek peoples of Rhodes and its neighboring islands in the Aegean Sea.

Roe, Roebuck. *See* ANIMALS (DEER; GAZELLE).

Rogelim. Home of Barzillai the Gileadite, who served David at Mahanaim, where David sought refuge from Absalom (2 Sm 17:27; 19:31). Rogelim was situated in the highlands east of the Jordan River. Its location is not known.

Rohgah. Shemer's firstborn son from Asher's tribe (1 Chr 7:34).

Romamti-ezer. Heman's son and a musician appointed by King David to serve in the sanctuary (1 Chr 25:4,31).

Romans, Letter to the.

Author. Romans is written in the first person (1:5,10, etc.) and is clearly from the pen of the apostle Paul. The actual transcription of the letter, however, was done by Tertius (16:22), who acted as Paul's amanuensis. The letter's authenticity has never been disputed by reputable scholarship, liberal or conservative, and Romans stands at the head of virtually every ancient list or collection of Pauline letters.

Date, Origin, and Destination. The destination of the letter is stated to be Rome (1:7). The composition of the Roman church is not clear. Paul speaks at times directly to Jews: "I am speaking to those who know the law" (7:1), "if you call yourself a Jew and rely on the law" (2:17), "we Jews" (3:9). And at times he speaks directly to gentile readers: "Now I am speaking to you Gentiles" (11:13), "the rest of the Gentiles" (1:13). The arguments in chapters 1–3 and 9–11 clearly presuppose both Jewish and gentile readers. It is probably best, therefore, to think of a mixed congregation in the empire's capital city as recipients of this

Inside the Colosseum in Rome.

masterpiece on God's role in bringing salvation to the Gentiles through the efforts of the Jews.

Relevant to this observation is the question of whether there could be Jews in the church in Rome at the time of the composition of this letter since Claudius had expelled the Jews from Rome in AD 49 (Acts 18:2). Recent numismatic evidence has established a new date for the accession of Festus as procurator of Judea—AD 56. Since Paul appeared before him at the end of a two-year imprisonment in Caesarea (Acts 24:27), Paul must have ended his third missionary journey in the early summer of AD 54 (Pentecost; Acts 21:16). In the months prior to this he was in Greece (Acts 20:2), where he probably wrote the Roman letter expressing his intent to visit as soon as he had delivered the contribution to Jerusalem (Rom 15:28). This was not Paul's intent during his earlier visit to Corinth on his second missionary journey, so Romans must have been written during this later visit.

That Paul was in Corinth at the time of the writing seems clear from his reference to Erastus in 16:23 as the treasurer of the city. An inscription in the stone pavement beside the large theater in Corinth states that it was laid by Erastus, the city treasurer, in appreciation for his election. This could hardly be coincidental. Erastus evidently remained in Corinth because it is mentioned as his home (2 Tm 4:20). Furthermore, Paul refers to Gaius as his host at the time he wrote Romans (16:23), probably the same Gaius who lived in Corinth (1 Cor 1:14).

We know that Claudius, who expelled the Jews from Rome in AD 49, reigned from 41 till his death in 54. If Romans was written from Corinth in 54, the Jews might have been allowed to return by this time. On the other hand, Christian Jews possibly were not expelled from Rome, and Priscilla and Aquila were converted after arriving in Corinth (Acts 18:2). In either case there may have been Jews in the church in Rome as early as 54.

Background. In a previous visit to Corinth, during his second missionary journey, Paul established the church there and remained in the city for 18 months (Acts 18:1,11). His arrival coincided with the arrival of Priscilla and Aquila, who had recently come from Rome. At the end of his 18-month stay, Paul was brought before the newly appointed proconsul, Gallio (v 12), whose arrival can be dated from the Gallio inscription found at Delphi to the spring of 51. Thus Paul arrived in Corinth in the winter of 49.

Leaving the city, he returned to Antioch, gave a report on his work, and set out on his last journey to collect the contribution for Jerusalem from the gentile churches (Rom 15:25–29), which he had previously prepared them to give (1 Cor 16:1; 2 Cor 9:5). Continued problems in Corinth (1 Cor 1:11; 7:1) necessitated his return to the city (Acts 20:3), at which time he wrote Romans. It is clear from the last two chapters of the letter that he planned to take the contribution to Jerusalem almost immediately and from there go on to Rome (Rom 15:23,24). The occasion for the letter, therefore, is to alert the Romans to his coming so that they can assist him in his journey to Spain (vv 24,28). Rome was the only church other than Colossae which Paul did not establish. His letter does not reflect awareness of specific problems in the membership there, dealing rather with broader themes helpful to any church.

Purpose and Theological Teaching. In addition to the purposes already stated above, Paul intended to lay out before the Roman church the means by which the righteousness of God was made known to the Gentiles through the Jews, who had been created through Abraham for this purpose. Paul himself had been commissioned as an apostle for the specific purpose of bringing the Gentiles into the kingdom and considered this to be his priestly service for which his appointment constituted him a "priestly servant," just as Jesus was a servant to the Jews (15:8,15,16). The conversion of the Gentiles was his "offering" to God (15:16). The collection for the saints (i.e., Jewish Christians) in Jerusalem, given by Gentiles who were in greater poverty than the recipients ("extreme poverty" 2 Cor 8:2), would be a strong theological affirmation of the validity of Paul's apostleship. The contribution therefore not a benevolent gesture, coming from the wealthy to the poor, since those who gave were in worse shape than those who received. It was rather an indication that Paul's work among Gentiles had been accepted by the Jerusalem church and freed Paul to leave the eastern Mediterranean and move on to the west (Rom 15:23). The Gentiles should make such a contribution not because they could afford it, but in order impressively to demonstrate their gratitude for what Jews had sacrificially brought to them—the gospel. And if the Jewish Christians would accept it, this would impressively demonstrate that the promise to Abraham had been fulfilled and the Jews had truly become a blessing to the Gentiles. The Gentiles would now be fellow citizens, fellow partakers of the promise (Eph 2:19; 3:6).

Paul writes to clarify this teaching for the Romans. The theme running throughout the book is that both Jew and Gentile had fallen short of God's glory and stood in need of atonement (3:21–31). God's righteousness has not been revealed only to the Jew. God is not God only to the Jews but to the Gentiles as well, since there is only one God (v 29). He will justify the Jews on the basis of the saving work of Christ at Calvary and the Gentiles on the basis of that same act of faithfulness to Abraham's promise (v 30). Their common faith gives them access to this grace (5:2). The gospel is thus to the Jew first and also to the Greek (1:16).

Content. The thematic statement of the first eight chapters of the letter is set forth in 1:16,17: "He who through faith is righteous shall live." This quotation from Habakkuk (2:4) sets Paul's teaching on faith over against that of the OT on works. Thus he affirms the fact that his teaching on faith is not new but is squarely rooted in the OT prophets. What was new was not Paul's emphasis that Jews would be a "light to the Gentiles," since Isaiah had already foretold that quite clearly (42:6; 49:6), but that the Gentiles would be fellow citizens with the Jews (Eph 3:5,6). They would not have to become proselytes to Judaism in order to be acceptable to God, as some Jewish Christians demanded (Acts 15:1). This was the mystery of which Paul spoke in Ephesians (3:6).

The first eight chapters are built around this theme. Chapters 1–4 deal with the phrase "He who through faith is righteous," showing that the words of Habakkuk apply to both Gentile and Jew. The first three chapters demonstrate that Jew and Gentile are under sin and that the atonement of Christ is applicable to both (3:21,22). The fourth chapter demonstrates Abraham as the father of Gentiles as well as Jews, because he is the spiritual father of believing Israel just as he is of believing Gentiles. Then in chapters 5–8, Paul deals with the latter part of the theme: "he who through faith is righteous *shall live.*" Whether Jew or Gentile, the person who accepts the righteous acts of God on Calvary through Christ will live free from the wrath of God (ch 5), the power of sin (i.e., Satan, ch 6), the enslaving power of the Law (ch 7), and the power of death (ch 8).

In chapters 9–11, Paul discusses the relation

of Israel according to the flesh, physical Jews, to the future purpose of God, concluding that God has not cast off his people who were Israelites descended from Abraham (11:1,2). He can regraft them back into the tree from which they have been cut off if they will accept Christ as Messiah (11:23).

Then in his closing section, characteristic of Paul's method of following theological discussions with pragmatic applications, he discusses the implications of the first 11 chapters for everyday Christian living (chs 12–16), closing the book with a reminder of the importance of the "offering of the Gentiles" through his own ministry (ch 15).

The first chapter argues that the pagan gentile world was in a state of rebellion against God and the wrath of God had been revealed against their ungodliness (1:18). Even though God had given sufficient revelation of his monotheistic existence to them in the world of nature, they had nevertheless become polytheistic and idolatrous with all the attendant moral degradation (v 20). Thus, three times Paul emphasizes that God gave them up to their lusts (v 24), to dishonorable passions (v 26), and to a base mind and improper conduct (v 28). The meaning is that he passed over their sins (3:25), overlooked their spiritual ignorance of his true existence (Acts 17:30), and did not put a stop to such idolatry (Acts 7:42).

The Jews fared little better because even though they had received the Law of Moses containing a revelation of the will of God for their nation, they had not kept that Law (2:17–29). Even the Gentiles had those among them who "did by nature the things contained in the law" and were acceptable because their consciences were pure (vv 14,15). For a Jew, keeping the Law was insufficient unless he did so as a spiritual conviction, not as a mere legal requirement (v 29). God-fearing Gentiles who kept the essence of the Law were a model for condemnation of the Jews who did not (vv 14,27). How-

ever, the faithlessness of the chosen nation did not nullify the faithfulness of God to the fulfillment of the promise to Abraham (3:3). Although the Jew had every advantage over the Gentile, he was no better off because both had given themselves over to the power of sin (3:1,9). The situation now was: "all have sinned [both Jew and Gentile] and fall short of the glory of God" (3:23).

God had therefore set Christ forward as atonement for the sins of the world (3:21–31). The righteousness of God (equal revelation of himself in a saving way to Jew and Gentile) had been manifested apart from the Law, through the "faith of Christ" (3:22; i.e., the faithfulness of Christ to the promise) and was available to Gentile as well as Jew on the basis of personal faith. On the other hand, if this righteousness were available only through the performances of the Law, as good and holy as it was (7:12), then God was a God of Jews only and not of Gentiles, because the Law was given to the Jews (3:29). But God is also the God of Gentiles and justifies the Jew on the basis of Christ's faithfulness and the Gentile on the basis of that same faithful act. Christ died for all who believe in him (3:30). Thus God's righteousness was manifested through Christ's faithfulness (3:3,22) and provides the basis of salvation for everyone who believes (5:9).

Several times in the fourth chapter Paul insists that Abraham was the father of the Jews and of the Gentiles (vv 11,12,16–18). Christ's faithfulness to the promise to Abraham that all nations (Gentiles) would be blessed through his seed (the descendants of Isaac) enabled Abraham to become the father of all nations, that is, of all who believe (v 11).

Having laid this broad theological base, Paul then argues that the impact of this justification or righteousness was that all believers experience salvation from the wrath of God and thereby experience peace (5:1,9). Sin entered the world through the first transgressors, Adam and Eve, and passed unto all people (v 12). Justification, however, was brought by the second Adam, Christ, whose declaration of God's righteousness to all people at Calvary and the empty tomb provided the basis for salvation to those who believe and receive the abundance of that grace (vv 16–18).

The function of the Law was not to save the Jew. It was added because of transgressions (Gal 3:19) and served to intensify the awareness of sin, present in all people, to the point of transgression of Law (Rom 5:20). Sin used the Law to deceive and destroy those who tried to keep it (7:11). Paul had known what it was to covet before the Law entered his life, but when he became subject to the dictates and penalties of the Law at age 12 or 13, the commandment

An altar at the Temple of Apollo in Greece, indicative of the polytheism to which Paul alludes (Rom 1).

against covetousness became even more demanding and destroyed him (v 11). It became "sinful beyond measure" (v 13). After the Law entered one's life, the penalty for its disobedience was fully applicable. Now if Paul committed adultery, he would be stoned to death. Sin had been intensified to transgression of Law. This very fact caused the need for greater grace, because where sin abounded, grace abounded all the more (5:20). But it would be a gross perversion of what it means to live free from wrath, Law, sin, and death to argue that one should therefore continue in sin that grace may abound (6:1). Paul argues that those who have been justified and saved by Christ have died to the power of sin, which no longer has enslaving power (vv 2, 6). The key thought here is that sin (i.e., Satan—sin personified) cannot exercise dominion over the believer (vv 9,14); it cannot reign over him (v 12) and make him its slave (vv 17,20). Paul writes: "Now that you have been set free from sin and have become slaves of God" (v 22), the legalism of law keeping "cannot hold us captive (7:6). Here Paul spoke to Jews who lived under the Law but kept it in a legalistic way. In such cases sin found opportunity in the commandment and killed them (7:11). There was nothing wrong with the Law (v 12), but Satan used its divisive tendencies and its partitioning effects to encourage the Jew to hide behind its legal requirements and restrict God's concern to the Jews alone, and in the process nationalized God. Paul reminded them that God was a God of Gentiles as well (3:29), and therefore justification could not be based on any nationalistic principle, valid for Israel only. The principle of justification would have to be broad enough for all people to accept. That principle would have to be faith. Paul felt that Christianity was Judaism internationalized. Israel had become enslaved to its own sense of nationalism through law keeping and made God a God of Jews only (3:29).

In addition to being made free from wrath, the Law, and sin, those who have been justified by faith (both Christ's and their own) have been freed from death, and God will give life to their mortal bodies through his Spirit (8:2,11). If they live according to the flesh they will die, but if by the Spirit they will live (v 13). Not even death will be able to separate them from the love of Christ (v 38). The Spirit leads them and helps in their human infirmity, praying and interceding for them just as Christ does (vv 14,26,34).

Paul does not discuss the pragmatic application of these theological principles until chapter 12. The reason is that a serious problem of theodicy confronts Paul which must be dealt with at precisely this point in his thinking. His entire argument hinges on the fact that everything which has happened in God's redemptive history has been due to God's faithfulness to the promise he gave to Abraham and his descendants. Paul's gospel was no innovation. As Jesus had said, "Salvation is from the Jews" (Jn 4:22). The entire OT is a witness to this fact. How is it that they, of all people on earth, with the history of God's personal involvement with them, could have rejected the Promised One? Chapters 9–11 labor with this important question.

Paul's answer is fourfold. First, it was God's purpose by election. He chose Israel knowing what would happen in the future. These were physical Jews, Israelites, who enjoyed all the special relationships to God that an elect people could experience: sonship, glory, covenants, the law, worship, the promises, the patriarchs, and Christ (9:1–5). God had elected them just as he had chosen Jacob over Esau before either was born, just as he had hardened the heart of Pharaoh, just as the potter molds the clay into the vessel he desires (vv 6–26). It had nothing to do with their character or inherent worth; it was strictly a matter of God's purpose for them (v 11). There is no injustice on God's part in making this choice because it was necessary in order for God to show his power through them so that his name might be proclaimed in all the earth (vv 14,17). He had chosen Israel to serve his purposes just as he had chosen Pharaoh and Jacob and Moses; their salvation was a matter of faith (Heb 11). After all, only a remnant of Israel ever really believed (9:27–29).

Second, Paul argues that Israel, in rejecting the Messiah and his gospel, is following a precedent that appears repeatedly throughout history (9:30–10:21). The Jews did not seek righteousness by faith, and thus never found it. They based their righteousness on the Law and thus stumbled over their own Messiah (9:30–33).

Third, he argues that since a "remnant" of Israel has already believed the gospel it is a clear indication that Israel as a whole will yet do so (11:1–16,26). So, even though he says that God has rejected Israel, he argues that God has not rejected them finally and irrevocably (vv 1,15). He has broken them off the cultivated branch of the Abrahamic promise, but he has not rejected his people (vv 2,17). The elect (remnant) obtained what it sought, but the rest were hardened for a period of time (vv 7,25) until they could be provoked to jealousy by the Gentiles' inclusion into the kingdom (vv 11–14). So Israel's alienation is not necessarily final.

Fourth, Paul argues that since Israel's rejection has been such a blessing for the inclusion of the Gentiles, the scenario of their conver-

of the Gentiles, the scenario of their conversion in large numbers would be like a resurrection from the dead (vv 12,15). This argument runs throughout the rest of the chapter (vv 17–36). The Gentiles should not be haughty because Israel stumbled so as to make their inclusion possible (vv 17–19). Israel did not stumble just so they could fall (11:11); their fall was a blessing to Gentiles and was a part of the purpose of God. And God, who broke them off for their unbelief, will be able to regraft them back into the tree from which they were cut off, "if they do not persist in their unbelief" (v 23).

Just as a "fulness" of Gentiles will be saved by the temporary hardening of Israel (v 25), so a "fulness" of Jews will be saved by being provoked to jealousy through the Gentiles' acceptance (vv 11–14). Together they will become "all Israel" (v 26). In anticipation of this, Paul views his work among Gentiles as an effort to provoke Jews to righteous and saving jealousy by converting Gentiles to Christ in order to save "some" of his "fellow Jews" (v 14).

Chapters 12–16 deal with the pragmatic implications of Paul's impressive arguments. Thus the chapter begins with "I appeal to you therefore . . ." (12:1). What follows is a lengthy list of Christian virtues and responsibilities. Paul frequently includes advice in his letters so as to assist the young converts in their transition from paganism into the Judeo-Christian ethical and moral value system. He often even modifies some behavior patterns among Jewish converts. Chapter 13 discusses the important relationship that should exist between Christians in the capital city of the Roman Empire and their government officials. They should recognize that civil government is, as such, ordained by God and has a right to exist even if those who hold the offices are corrupt. They are God's servants to execute wrath on the disobedient (13:4). Chapter 14 encourages Christians to live without influencing others to violate their own consciences through imitating the activities of other Christians whose advanced knowledge of right and wrong has given them a greater deal of freedom in spiritual matters. Nor should those with weaker consciences try to restrict others who have found this precious freedom. Mutual love and respect is the mark of a true disciple of Christ. Chapter 15 contains Paul's travel plans and his understanding of his role as a priestly minister to Gentiles, offering their conversion to God symbolically on the altar at Jerusalem in the form of a large collection of money taken up among gentile churches. Chapter 16 closes typically with greetings and commendations from various individuals. Twenty-seven people are to be greeted in Paul's name in Rome.

JOHN R. McRAY

See PAUL, THE APOSTLE.

Bibliography. K. Barth, *The Epistle to the Romans;* F. Godet, *Commentary on St Paul's Epistle to the Romans;* W. Hendriksen, *Romans,* 2 vols; C. Hodge, *Commentary on the Epistle to the Romans;* E. Käsemann, *Commentary on Romans;* H.C.G. Moule, *The Epistle to the Romans;* W.R. Newell, *Romans Verse by Verse;* W.G.T. Shedd, *Commentary on Romans.*

Rome, City of.

City in Italy founded, according to tradition, in 753 BC on 7 hills some 15 miles from the mouth of the Tiber River. The 7 hills were outcrops of rock which formed where the Latin plain fell away into the Tiber bed. It was of no biblical interest until NT times. There are 9 references to the city in the NT (Acts 2:10; 18:2; 19:21; 23:11; 28:14,16; Rom 1:7,15; 2 Tm 1:17), but Paul's sojourn there and his letter to the Roman Christians, written probably from Corinth between AD 57 and 59, make the imperial city of considerable interest to Bible readers.

History. In the 2nd millennium BC, Indo-European migrants moved into Europe and settled in the Italian peninsula. One group settled around the mouth of the Tiber River. A vigorous and more cultured group, the Etruscans from Asia Minor, occupied central Italy. At the time of Rome's emergence in the 8th century BC, the population of the Italian peninsula was mixed. The Latin-speaking enclave which settled toward the mouth of the Tiber were agriculturalists. The scattered groups formed leagues and communities to defend themselves against raiders. They built stockades on the hills to protect families and flocks while fighting off the raiders. From such beginnings Rome emerged as a dominant center with its focal point in the area of the seven hills (the Palatine, the Capitoline, the Aventine, the Caelian, the Esquiline, the Viminal, and the Quirinal). Traditionally these hills were held to be seven in number; in fact, there were more than seven, although some were simply flat-topped spurs. The Tiber River wound in a large S-curve between the hills. At one point it divided to form an island where it was shallow enough to ford. The town that grew up here was linked by road, north to the Etruscans, south to the Greek trading cities, west to the coast, and inland to the tribal areas on the highlands. Knowledge of early Rome is based largely on archaeological evidence from the remains of the simple forts and numerous burial sites in the area.

Rome developed politically in a remarkable fashion over the next 1000 years. The loose association of the original chieftains who comprised the earliest "senate" gave place to domination by Etruscan kings who seem to have trained the people in discipline and obedience. They constructed numerous works, draining the forum area and making it a social, commercial, industrial, and political center and building a temple for Jupiter, Juno, and Minerva on the Capitoline Hill as a common shrine for all the people. When the kings became autocratic, the Latin population rebelled, expelled the alien kings, and developed a horror of royal rule so that a republic was established in 510 BC. During the period of the kings, the city was surrounded by a strong wall, the Servian Wall, with a number of gates. Fragments of this wall are still visible. The establishment of the republic marked the beginning of Rome's remarkable expansion to a world empire. The population which was now spread out over the hills and valleys, despite the tribal differences, united and solved political problems without bloodshed.

Strictly speaking, the term "republican" should not be understood in any modern sense as indicating a kind of democracy. Rather, the ancient families (patricians) dominated the senate and constituted an oligarchy of blood, wealth, and experience. This arrangement was useful for Rome at that time. The small city-state soon broke out of its confined area, overcame the Etruscans, and dominated the Greek cities to the south. The Romans then looked further afield. In 273 BC they made a treaty with the Ptolemies of Egypt. Before long they expanded into North Africa, overcame the Carthaginians, pressed on into Spain, and developed ambitions to occupy the Middle East as well. Rome's many conquests brought enormous wealth.

With geographical expansion came social changes in Italy. During the 2nd century BC, rich landowners bought out the small independent farmers, who subsequently drifted into the captial landless and unemployed, seeking a place in Rome where wealth, entertainment, vice, and opportunity abounded. Huge overcrowded tenement houses appeared which constituted creeping slums. Alongside squalor there was evidence of vast wealth from Rome's conquests in distant lands. In the capital, many fine buildings appeared. Pompey, who subdued and organized the East, did much to adorn the great capital.

The next stage in Rome's political development came when the senate, the governing body of the republic, proved unable to control its more radical and violent members. As their political ambitions increased, aspiring leaders sought to gain popular support by granting privileges to the people without the concurrence of the senate. Civil strife broke out and plagued the last century of the republic. Military victories beyond Rome gave power to the generals. In the civil wars that followed, constitutional questions were decided by the power of the sword. Marius, Sulla, Pompey, Crassus, Julius Caesar, Antony, and Octavian were the real political force in the land.

By 27 BC, Octavian emerged supreme and was given the title Augustus. Theoretically a dual government existed between the senate and Augustus, the emperor, but a weak senate allowed the emperor to become the virtual ruler. As a result peace reigned at home and abroad until well into the 2nd century AD. The emperors of the 1st century AD cover the period of the life of Jesus and of the emerging church, and several are mentioned in the NT—Augustus (Lk 2:1), Tiberius (Lk 3:1), Claudius (Acts 11:28; 18:2), and Nero (Acts 25:10–12; 27:24; 2 Tm 4:16,17).

The city of Rome was the capital of the empire and the home of the emperor, senators, administrators, military personnel, and priests. Augustus, the first of the emperors whose leadership and diplomatic endeavors gave peace to Rome after two civil wars and a century of strife, gave attention to the restoration and adornment of the city. He boasted that he found Rome built of brick and left it built of marble. His efforts at restoring Rome's ancient religious commitment led to the building of many temples. On the Palatine hill Augustus united several houses already there into a palace for his own residence. A new and sumptuous temple of Apollo surrounded by colonnades in which the emperor housed a large library was erected near the palace. The palace itself overlooked an imposing group of new marble buildings in the valley floor below, a fine basilica-business hall, a senate house, a temple of the Divine Julius, a marble speakers' platform, two impressive new forums, the forum of Caesar and the forum of Augustus. Later emperors added to this splendor. Beyond the central forum area in the course of the 1st century, the palaces of Tiberius and Caligula, various baths, arches, theaters, the Circus Maximus, and the Circus Nero were built. The whole was enclosed by a wall built outside the old rampart of Servius. Several aqueducts brought water into the city, and significant roads from north, south, east, and west converged on the central city area.

Christians in Rome. It was to this magnificent city that Paul came under escort in March AD 59. He found a Christian church already established. Indeed, he had already communicated with the Christians in his letter to the Romans early in 55. There was a considerable Jewish colony in Rome in the 1st century AD, descended from the large number of Jewish slaves brought to the city by Pompey after the capture of Jerusalem in 63. The emperor Claudius expelled Jews from Rome in AD 49, possibly when Jesus was proclaimed as Messiah in

The Colosseum in Rome, where many Christians died as martyrs.

the synagogue. Who the preachers were is not known, but they were probably Christian travelers and traders. Paul's Letter to the Romans was his exposition to the gentile churches which had come into existence independently of him. His first known contact with the people of Rome was when he met Aquila and Priscilla at Corinth (Acts 18:2). This couple was expelled from Rome in the time of Claudius. Later Paul hoped to visit Rome (Acts 19:21) on his way to Spain (Rom 15:24). In his salutation he mentioned a considerable circle of Christians in Rome (Rom 16). The references to households in several places (Rom 16:5,10,11,14,15) suggests that these were the basis of the Roman Christian church. During his captivity, Paul was a prisoner of the Roman authorities, but was able to meet the local leaders of the Jews, explain his experiences to them, and expound the gospel to them in person (Acts 28:16–31).

In the Book of Revelation Rome is given a sinister significance. By the end of the 1st century AD, Rome had already drunk the "blood of the martyrs of Jesus" (Rv 17:6), a reference to early martyrs.   JOHN A. THOMPSON

See CAESARS, THE.

Bibliography. J. Carcopino, *Daily Life in Ancient Rome;* T. Frank, *A History of Rome;* T.R. Holmes, *The Roman Republic,* 3 vols; T. Mommsen, *The History of Rome,* 5 vols; M.P. Nilsson, *Imperial Rome;* M. Rostovtzeff, *A History of the Ancient World,* vol 2, *Rome;* and *Out of the Past of Greece and Rome.*

Root of Jesse. *See* JESSE, ROOT OF.

Rose. *See* PLANTS (OLEANDER; TULIP).

Rosh. 1. Seventh of Benjamin's 10 sons (Gn 46:21).

2. Northern nation from the people of Magog often identified with Russia. The RSV rendering of Ezekiel 38:3 and 39:1, "the land of Magog, the chief prince of Meshech and Tu-

bal," might better be translated "the land of Magog, the prince of Rosh, Meshech and Tubal" (KJV mg).

Ruby. *See* MINERALS, METALS, AND PRECIOUS STONES.

Rue. Perennial shrub whose leaves were used for medicinal purposes (Lk 11:42).

See PLANTS.

Rufus. Latin name for two men in the NT.
1. One of the sons of Simon of Cyrene (Mk 15:21).
2. Christian to whom Paul sends greetings, adding a special endearing comment about his mother (Rom 16:13). He is perhaps the same as #1 above.

Ruhamah. One of two symbolic names showing God's altered perspective toward Israel from one of hostility to one of mercy. God's attitude of displeasure was symbolized by the name Lo-ruhamah (meaning, "not pitied"), which Hosea named his daughter. God was withdrawing his compassion on Israel because of their great sin (Hos 1:6,8). His new attitude of mercy was portrayed by the name Ruhamah (meaning "having obtained pity"), revealing God's revived spirit of compassion that was to be poured out on Israel (Hos 2:1,23).

Ruler. *See* TRADES AND OCCUPATIONS.

Ruler of the Synagogue. Senior official in the synagogue of NT times. It is generally understood that there was only one such official in any one synagogue.

His function was to take care of the physical arrangements for the services of worship, the maintenance of the building and fabric, and to determine who would be called to read from the Law and the prophets or to conduct the prayers. The office was sometimes held for a specified period, sometimes for life.

The NT refers to this official on four different occasions. Jairus apparently was the ruler of the synagogue at Capernaum. When his daughter was ill, he went to Jesus for help, and Jesus raised her from the dead (Mt 9:18–26; Mk 5:21–43; Lk 8:41–56). Luke 13:14 records the hostility of another ruler of the synagogue who objected to Jesus healing on the sabbath after teaching in that synagogue.

On his missionary journeys Paul generally began his ministry in each place he visited by going to the synagogue. At Pisidian Antioch (Acts 13:15), the rulers of the synagogue welcomed and encouraged him to preach the gospel and to return again the following week. Crispus, the ruler of the synagogue at Corinth, was converted (Acts 18:8), and later Sosthenes (Crispus' successor) was beaten by the mob after the Jews had made an abortive charge against Paul before Gallio, the governor of Achaia.

See SYNAGOGUE.

Rumah. Home of Pedaiah, the father of Zebidah, Jehoiakim's mother (2 Kgs 23:36). Some identify it with Arumah, near Shechem (cf. Jgs 9:41) or with Khirbet el-Rumah in Galilee.

Rush. KJV form of reed in Job 8:11 and Isaiah 9:14.

See PLANTS.

Ruth (Person). Moabitess and the widow of Mahlon, the son of Naomi and Elimelech, who were Ephrathites from Bethlehem living in Moab because of a severe famine in Judah. Upon the death of Elimelech and Naomi's two sons, Naomi returned to Bethlehem with her daughter-in-law Ruth during the time of the barley harvest (Ru 1:4–22). While gleaning in the barley fields of Boaz, Ruth found favor in his eyes (2:2–22). She later married Boaz, when he, serving as nearest kin to the childless Naomi, purchased Naomi's estate to keep it within the family (4:5–13). Ruth is mentioned in Matthew's genealogy of Christ as the mother of Obed and the great-grandmother of David (Mt 1:5).

See RUTH, BOOK OF; GENEALOGY OF JESUS CHRIST.

Ruth, Book of.

Author and Data. The author of the book is unknown. The question of authorship has particular connection with the date of writing, and a few clues provide at least an "educated guess." The book must have been written sometime after the beginning of David's reign. The reference of 4:18–22, which pertains to the historical significance of Ruth as David's great-grandmother, bears this out. Since foreign marriages were not approved in the Book of Ruth, it scarcely could have been written during the period in which Solomon began his policy of foreign marriages. Also, David's close friendship with Moab might have prompted someone in his kingdom to write the book, thus presenting objective rationale for David's actions (see 1 Sm 22:3–5). Consequently the author may have been someone close to David, possibly Samuel, Nathan, or Abiathar.

This view is not without its critics, however. Some scholars consider the opening statement, "in the days when the judges ruled," to demonstrate the late composition of the book. However, such a phrase need not refer to an extensive period. In today's world one might use a similar phrase in reference to conditions at the beginning of the 20th century. The dates of the judges probably comprise a period of about 300 years, beginning with the judgeship of Othniel and concluding with that of Samson, though Samuel also served as a judge. If the genealogical information is complete in 4:18–22, the events took place during the life of David's great-grandfather and mark the birth of his grandfather. Allowing a 35-year generation span, the events would have taken place somewhere about the turn of the 11th century BC, or about 100 years before David's birth.

Purpose. The book's purpose is closely related to its date of composition. Assuming an early date, that is, one close to David's lifetime, its principal thrust must be the authentication of the Davidic line. The book may be considered as a justification for including the godly Moabitess in the nation of Israel.

Content. *Introduction (1:1–5).* Driven by famine, Elimelech, his wife Naomi, and two sons, Mahlon and Chilion, cross the Jordan to stay for a period of time in Moab where there was sufficient provision. The two sons, after marrying Moabite women, die, and their father dies as well. Naomi is left a widow with two foreign daughters-in-law.

Return to Bethlehem (1:6–22). Hearing reports from Bethlehem that the famine had ended, Naomi makes preparations to return. Both of her daughters-in-law, Orpah and Ruth, accompany her for at least a portion of the journey. Probably thinking of the problems which might be encountered by them as foreigners in Judah, Naomi strongly urges the girls to stay in their own land. Both of the young widows refuse, but Naomi presents the facts. First, she is not pregnant, so the chance of a younger brother fulfilling the levirate responsibility is not imminent. Second, she has no prospects of remarriage and consequently no prospect of further children. Then, she also notes that even if the first two conditions were met immediately, the possibility of their waiting was impossible. Orpah is persuaded and kisses her mother-in-law good-bye.

But Ruth "clung to her" (NEB). The verb, having the connotation of being glued to something, is the same verb used of marriage (Gn 2:24). Ruth demonstrates her serious intentions by making five commitments. In essence, Ruth renounces her former life in order to gain a life which she considers of greater value. At this point, she is contrasted with Naomi, who had encouraged both of them to return to Moab and its gods (1:15). But Ruth decides to follow the God of Israel and his laws. Ruth's appeal to the God of Israel was more than equal to Naomi's pleas, and the two of them return together.

Their arrival in Bethlehem is traumatic for Naomi. Having left Bethlehem with a husband and two sons, she returns empty. She tells her friends to call her "Mara" (bitter). But she has returned at a propitious time, the beginning of the harvest season.

Reaping in the Fields of Boaz (2:1–23). The first verse of the chapter provides the setting for the narrative which follows, introducing Boaz, a wealthy relative of Elimelech.

Ruth volunteers to glean the fields, to follow the reapers and pick up the insignificant amounts left behind. Gleaners were also permitted to harvest the grain in the corners of the fields, a provision for the poor contained in Yahweh's Law (Lv 19:9,10).

She happens to come to the field of Boaz. As he visits this field, he notices Ruth, inquires about her, and learns her identity. His overseer reports that she has industriously worked the fields from early morning until that time. Boaz, attracted to her because of her loyalty and concern for Naomi, graciously makes additional provision for her. She is given a favored position in reaping, directly behind the main body of reapers. Further, she is to receive water which has been drawn for her by the young men—an unorthodox arrangement.

Ruth, falling before Boaz in a gesture of great humility and respect, asks why as a foreigner she should be accorded such favor. Boaz gives two reasons, her kindness to her mother-in-law, and her spiritual insight which led her to seek after Israel's God, "under whose wings you have come to take refuge" (NEB).

She is also given a place at the reapers' table and, upon Boaz's orders, returns to the fields—this time to reap from the unharvested grain. At the end of the day she returns home to Naomi and tells her of the day's events. Naomi informs Ruth that Boaz has the right of redemption. Ruth returns to his fields until the end of the harvest season.

Relying upon the Kinsman (3:1–18). Naomi advises Ruth with regard to approaching Boaz as a *goel*, or kinsman-redeemer.

The plan suggested by Naomi seems peculiar, yet some thoughts may give a certain colouring to it. (1) Naomi seems to have believed that Boaz was the nearest kinsman, being ignorant of the yet nearer one (v 12). Consequently, according to Israelite law (Dt 25:5ff.), it would be the duty of Boaz to marry Ruth to raise up seed to the dead. (2) The general tone

of Naomi's character is clearly shown in this book to be that of a God-fearing woman, so that it is certain that, however curious in its external form, there can be nothing counselled here which really is repugnant to God's law, or shocking to a virtuous man such as Boaz, otherwise Naomi would simply have been most completely frustrating her own purpose. (3) Her knowledge by long intimacy of Ruth's character, and doubtless also of that of Boaz by report, would enable her to feel sure that no ill effects could accrue (Sinker, *Ellicott's Commentary on the Whole Bible, Ruth*, p 283).

His response to Ruth's actions demonstrates his gentlemanly concerns for her. He explains the situation of not being the nearest kinsman, but promises that he will take care of the necessary procedures the next day. Protecting her reputation, Boaz sends her home before daylight. Naomi, wise in these matters, succinctly predicts of Boaz, "He will not rest until he has settled the matter today" (NEB).

Redeeming the Inheritance (4:1–21). Boaz goes to the place of business, the city gate. The city gate area comprised the forum of the city where the public affairs of the city were discussed. Boaz indicates that he wishes to discuss a matter of business with the nearer kinsman. Ten of the city elders act as witnesses. Beginning with the property matter, Boaz inquires whether this nearer kinsman is willing to acquire the property for Naomi, including the traditional stipulation, "On the day when you acquire the field from Naomi, you also acquire Ruth the Moabitess, the dead man's wife" (NEB). The nearer kinsman is unwilling because to marry Ruth would inevitably cost him some financial loss, since he would have to divide his own property with any son of his born to Ruth. Thus he relinquishes his rights by the custom of taking off his shoe. Significantly the shoe was symbolic of the land rights which belonged to the inheritance. So Boaz takes the part of the kinsman-redeemer.

The marriage of Boaz and Ruth produces a son who, under Israel's laws, is reckoned as Naomi's child and heir.

Teaching. The Book of Ruth traces the lineage of David to the Messiah. The completion of that line is in Matthew 1 and finds its focus in Jesus.

A second teaching is the beauty of God's grace. A foreigner, even a Moabitess, can be linked with Israel's blessing.

Theologically, the concept of kinsman-redeemer as a type of Messiah is clearly evident. He must be a blood relative, have the ability to purchase, be willing to buy the inheritance, and be willing to marry the widow of the deceased kinsman.

And finally, the love which Ruth shows be-

comes a pattern of devotion, a woman of whom it was said to Naomi, "your daughter-in-law who loves you is better to you than seven sons."
RICHARD I. MCNEELY

Bibliography. A.E. Cundall and L. Morris, *Judges and Ruth;* G. Gerleman, *Ruth;* R.M. Halo, *The Theology of the Book of Ruth;* A.R.S. Kennedy, *The Book of Ruth;* C. Lattey, *The Book of Ruth.*

Rye. KJV rendering of spelt, a common form of wheat in Bible times, in Exodus 9:32.

See FOOD AND FOOD PREPARATION; PLANTS (SPELT).

Ss

Sabachthani. One of the final words of Jesus on the cross, "a cry of dereliction" (Mt 27:46; Mk 15:34).

See ELI, ELI, LAMA SABACHTHANI.

Sabaoth. Hebrew word meaning "hosts" or "army," as in the expression "Lord of hosts."

See GOD, NAMES OF.

Sabbath. Derivation of a Hebrew word which means "cease" or "desist." The sabbath was a day (from Friday evening until Saturday evening in Jesus' time) when all ordinary work stopped. The Scriptures relate that God gave his people the sabbath as an opportunity to serve him, and as a reminder of two great truths in the Bible—creation and redemption.

OT. The creation note is first sounded in Genesis 2:2,3. God "ceased" his work in creation after six days and then "blessed" the seventh day and "declared it holy."

In the fourth commandment (Ex 20:8–11) God's "blessing" and "setting aside" of the seventh day after creation (the words used are the same as those in Gn) form the basis of his demand that man should observe the seventh day as "a day of Sabbath rest before the Lord your God."

The idea of God resting from his work is a startling one. It comes across even more vividly in Exodus 31:17, where the Lord tells Moses how he "was refreshed" by his day of rest. This picture of the Creator as a manual laborer is one the Bible often paints. No doubt it is presented in vividly human terms in Exodus to reinforce the fundamental sabbath lesson that man must follow the pattern his Creator has set for him. One day's rest in seven is a built-in "creation necessity" for individuals, families, households—and even animals (20:10).

The sabbath's setting in the biblical account of creation implies that it is one of those OT standards which are meant for all men, and not just for Israel. The inclusion of the sabbath law in the Ten Commandments underlines this important truth. The Decalogue occupied a special place in OT law. Alone of all God's instructions, it was spoken by his audible voice (Ex 19:25; 20:1), written by his finger (31:18), and placed in the tabernacle ark at the heart of Israel's worship (25:16). The NT, too, confirms the strong impression that the Decalogue as a whole embodies principles which are permanently valid for all men in all places at all times. Whether or not Sunday is recognized as the Christian sabbath, one is obliged to accept the central principle of this biblical teaching as far as the sabbath is concerned. God's instructions require man to observe a regular weekly break from work.

If the sabbath principle is built so securely into God's creation plan, one might expect to find signs of its ancient observance on a worldwide scale. Although understandably scant, some evidence of this exists, particularly in the widespread acceptance of a seven-day week. There are, for example, intriguing references to ancient Babylonian taboos on the seventh day, and to a monthly festival in Babylon called "sabattu." Their connection with the biblical sabbath is very tenuous (certainly not strong enough to justify suggestions that the Jews adopted their sabbath from Babylon), but they do provide pointers, from a very early period of human history, to man's recognition of the seventh day as something special.

Even in the OT itself, there is only one clear reference to sabbath observance prior to the Ten Commandments—in Exodus 16:22–30, where the Israelites gather twice as much manna as usual on the sixth day of the week and are told not to look for any on the following day because "the Lord has given you the seventh day as a day of Sabbath rest." From the people's puzzlement (which probably accounts for their disobedience, v 27; if their disobedience had been deliberate and clear-sighted, they probably would have been severely punished—cf. 31:15), it seems that sabbath observance had fallen into disuse. This would have been the natural outcome of Israel's long years of forced labor in Egypt.

It cannot be ascertained that the patriarchs observed the sabbath regularly before the people settled in Egypt, but it is likely that they did, in spite of the Bible's silence. There are plenty of pointers to a seven-day week in early times (see, e.g., Gn 50:10), and the sabbath would have provided opportunities for those acts of worship which took place (e.g., 12:8; 26:25).

To discover more about the way God marked out the sabbath day at creation, and how he intended man to observe it thereafter, one must explore the meaning of the words "bless" and "declare holy" (or "set aside") which occur in both the creation story and the Ten Commandments (Gn 2:3; Ex 20:11). In brief, "bless" is the language of giving, while "declare holy" is the language of claiming. When something is blessed by God, it becomes a vehicle of his generous giving and an expression of his warm concern. When God declares something holy, he claims it for himself, taking it out of ordinary circulation (whether it is a place, a day, or an animal for sacrifice) and declaring it special.

This provides a clue to God's intention in requiring man to observe the sabbath. Freed from time-consuming everyday work, man should accept the seventh day as a blessing from his Creator (using it to recall all God's goodness in creation and to praise him for it), and recognize the claim it makes on his life. As a day "set aside," the sabbath is a reminder that all time is the Creator's gift—a fact man acknowledges when he consciously gives back to God part of what is his anyway.

This, then, is the first note the OT strikes in its teaching on the sabbath. In recognition of his Creator, and of the way he is made as a creature, man should stop work one day in seven. Any attempt to work a seven-day week is therefore an affront to humanity as well as disobedience to God.

Significantly, the second main strand of the Bible's sabbath teaching—that of redemption—also features in a list of the Ten Commandments. The sabbath law (already noted in 20:8–11) reappears in Deuteronomy 5:12–15, but here a different reason is attached to its observance: "You shall remember that you were a servant in the land of Egypt, and the Lord your God brought you out thence with a mighty hand and an outstretched arm" (v 15).

The differences between these two accounts of the fourth commandment are important. The first (Ex 20) is addressed, *through* Israel, to all men as created beings. The second (Dt 5) is directed *to* Israel as God's redeemed people. So the sabbath is God's signpost, pointing not only to his goodness toward all men as their Creator, but also to his mercy toward his chosen people as their Redeemer.

The OT itself uses this "sign" language of the sabbath in Exodus 31:12–17. "The Sabbath," God instructs Moses, "is a sign between me and you throughout your generations . . . for ever between me and the people of Israel" (cf. Ez 20:12).

After man had spoiled his relationship with God by falling into sin (Gn 3), God himself set about repairing the damage. He began by saving Noah from the flood, and by selecting first a man (Abraham) and then a nation (Israel) to convey his redeeming love to the world. Each stage in the redemption story was marked by a covenant sign. In Noah's case it was the rainbow and in Abraham's circumcision (Gn 9:8–13; 17:1–14). And what better symbol of God's covenant relationship with Israel, as a perpetual reminder of his redeeming love, than the sabbath? The annual celebration of the Passover would act as a powerful reminder of the exodus, of course, but the weekly sabbath would underscore God's covenant mercy in giving his people rest from slavery in Egypt.

There is one other significant point in Deuteronomy's version of the sabbath commandment that must not be missed. The prohibition of all work on the sabbath day is followed by an explanatory note—"that your manservant and your maidservant may rest as well as you" (Dt 5:14). Practical concern for others is a feature of all the OT's covenant teaching (see, e.g., 12:12; 16:11). So God's loving concern for Israel in her Egyptian slavery must be matched by the Israelite family's loving concern for those who served them. The sabbath offered an ideal outlet for the practical expression of that concern. Jesus was especially keen to rescue this humanitarian side of sabbath observance from the mass of callous regulations which threatened to suffocate it in his day (see, e.g., Mk 3:1–5).

The OT's provision for a "sabbatical year" develops this humanitarian theme further (see Ex 23:10–12; Lv 25:1–7; Dt 15:1–11; also the regulations for the "year of jubilee" in Lv 25:8–55). Every seventh year the land was to "lie fallow before the Lord, uncultivated" (Lv 25:4 LB). It needed a regular rest just as much as the people it sustained, but the primary purpose of this law was clearly philanthropic and benevolent: "let the poor among the people harvest any volunteer crop that may come up; leave the rest for the animals to enjoy." Deuteronomy 15:1–11 extends the same humanitarian principle into the world of commerce. The sabbatical year must see the cancelling of all debts within God's redeemed community. "Every creditor shall release what he has lent to his neighbor; he shall not exact it of his neighbor, his brother" (v 2). For the tight-fisted who might be tempted to refuse a loan if the sabbatical year was imminent, the law added a warning and a promise. "If you refuse to make the loan and the needy man cries out to the Lord, it will be counted against you as a sin. You must lend him what he needs, and don't moan about it either! For the Lord will prosper you in everything you do because of this!" (vv 9,10 LB).

Observing the sabbatical year was obviously a great test of the people's obedience to God and of their willingness to depend on him for their livelihood. Sometimes the temptation to turn a blind eye was too strong (Lv 26:34, 35). But history testifies to Israel's courage in observing the letter of this law on many occasions, despite threats of invasion and famine. Both Alexander the Great and the Romans excused Jews from paying taxes every seventh year in recognition of the depth of their religious convictions.

Returning from the seventh year to the seventh day, the OT law codes go to considerable lengths to buttress the sabbath ban on work by defining what may and may not be done by God's people on the sabbath day. The prohibitions were not meant to rule out activity of any kind. Their aim was to stop regular, everyday work—because if God had "set aside" the sabbath (Ex 20:11), the most obvious way of profaning it was to treat it just like any other day. So when the nation was in the desert, it was enough to say "stay where he is" (16:29 NIV). But with a more settled life in view, the rule had to be spelled out in specific terms that the farmer (34:21), the salesman (Jer 17:27), and even the housewife (Ex 35:2,3) would understand.

The details may seem trivial, but obedience to the sabbath law was seen as the main test of the people's allegiance to the Lord. It was made quite clear that willful disobedience was a capital offense (Ex 35:2), and the fate of the man found gathering wood in defiance of sabbath regulations showed that this was no idle threat (Nm 15:32–36).

On the positive side, the Law also laid down rules and guidelines for the liturgical observance of the sabbath day. The 12 loaves of the "showbread" (the OT version of the prayer, "Give us this day our daily bread") were to be replaced every sabbath in the tabernacle, and special sacrifices offered (Lv 24:5–8; Nm 28:9,10). Above all, the sabbath provided "a day for sacred assembly" for all the people (Lv 23:3).

Hemmed in by so many rules and regulations (and with the death penalty overhanging all), the sabbath easily could have become a day of fear, a day when the people were more afraid of committing an offense than worshiping the Lord and enjoying a weekly rest. This, however, was never the case. The sabbath was intended to be a blessing, not a burden. Above everything else, it was a weekly sign that the Lord loved his people and wanted to draw them into an ever closer relationship with himself. Those who valued that relationship enjoyed the sabbath, calling it "a delight" and "honorable" (Is 58:13,14). Those on the cold fringes of the community, like the eunuch and the gentile outsider, were warmed on the sabbath as they were drawn into the center of God's love (56:1–7).

Nowhere does the OT express its sheer joy in sabbath worship more exuberantly than in Psalm 92, which has the title *A Song for the Sabbath*. "For thou, O Lord, hast made me glad by thy work; at the works of thy hands I sing for joy" (v 4).

The later prophets, were, however, far from blind to the darker side of human nature. They knew that a great deal of sabbath observance was a sham. Many people treated the sabbath day more as holiday than holy day, an opportunity for self-indulgence rather than delighting in the Lord (Is 58:13). Some greedy tradesmen found its restrictions an annoying irritant (Am 8:5).

As God's spokesmen, the prophets did not shrink from exposing such neglect and abuse (even in the best ecclesiastical circles—Ez 22:26). Those who go through the motions of sabbath worship with unrepentant hearts nauseate the Lord, cries Isaiah (Is 1:10–15). As a symptom of rebellion against God, Jerusalem's sabbath-breaking will bring destruction on the city, thunders Jeremiah (Jer 17:27). The Lord has been very forbearing with his people, warns Ezekiel, but prolonged neglect of his sabbath makes judgment a certainty (Ez 20:12–24).

When the ax of judgment fell (in the exile to Babylon, 586 BC), the surviving remnant of the nation took the lesson to heart. Sabbath-keeping was one of the few distinctive marks faithful Jews could keep in a foreign land, so it assumed extra significance. At the prompting of prophets like Ezekiel, who set out rules for sabbath worship in the rebuilt temple at Jerusalem (Ez 44:24; 45:17; 46:3), and under the leadership of men like Nehemiah, the returning exiles were more careful than their predecessors in observing the sabbath day (Neh 10:31; 13:15–22).

Between the Testaments. The sabbath day has a twofold significance in the OT. It points to God's blessings in creation, calling all men to respect their Maker's instructions by observing one day's rest from work in seven, and it points to God's mercy in redemption, as a special sign of his covenant relationship with the people of Israel. Generally speaking, Jewish writers who lived outside Palestine (so-called Hellenists) stressed the creation aspect of this sabbath teaching, while those who lived and wrote in the Holy Land itself (the Palestinians) placed far more emphasis on the special relationship between the Lord and Israel the sabbath signified. Some Palestinian Pharisees, for example, denied that the sabbath had any relevance for gentiles at all; while the Hellenist writer Philo described the sabbath day as "the birthday of the world" and "the festival not of a single city or country but of the universe."

It is in the Palestinian literature of this period that one finds the elaborate directions about sabbath observance which aroused so much controversy in NT times. Two tractates of the Mishna are devoted exclusively to these sabbath rules and regulations. Their main purpose is to define work (one tractate does so under 39 headings) in an attempt to show every Israelite what is and is not permitted on the sabbath. Unfortunately, though well intended, this led to such hairsplitting complexities and evasions that ecclesiastical lawyers often differed among themselves in their interpretations—with the inevitable result that the main purpose of the sabbath became lost beneath a mass of legalistic detail. The rabbis themselves were aware of how much they were adding to the straightforward teaching of the OT. As one of them put it, "The rules about the sabbath . . . are as mountains hanging by a hair, for Scripture is scanty and the rules many."

Nevertheless, in spite of the weight of the rule books, the positive notes of joy and celebration never quite disappeared from sabbath observance. Two of the family's main duties on the sabbath day, according to the rabbis, were to praise God and to enjoy the best food and drink in the home.

NT. Jesus' confrontations with the Jewish religious leaders over sabbath observance are well known. It is strange that the accusation of sabbath breaking was not pressed at his trial. Possibly it was because the Pharisees disagreed so much among themselves that they could not have made such a charge stick.

Jesus, however, never saw himself as a sabbath-breaker. He went to synagogue regularly on the sabbath day (Lk 4:16). He read the lesson, preached, and taught (Mk 1:21; Lk 13:10). He clearly accepted the principle that the sabbath was an appropriate day for worship.

His point of collision with the Pharisees was the point at which their tradition departed from biblical teaching. He made this clear when he defended his disciples by appealing to Scripture, after they had been accused of breaking sabbath tradition by walking through grain fields and breaking off heads of wheat (which fell in the category of "harvesting" according to the Pharisees; Mk 2:23–26). He followed this up with a remark that took his hearers straight back to God's creation purpose for the sabbath: "The Sabbath was made for man, not man for the Sabbath" (Mk 2:27).

Rabbinic tradition had exalted the institution above the people it was meant to serve. By making it an end in itself, the Pharisees had effectively robbed the sabbath of one of its main purposes. Jesus' words must have sounded uncomfortably familiar in his opponents' ears. A famous rabbi had once said, "The Sabbath is given over to you, but you are not given over to the Sabbath." By "you" the rabbi meant "you Israelites" (to the exclusion of everyone else). Jesus, by giving this well-known saying with its important half-truth a new twist, recalled the Creator's purpose in instituting the sabbath. It was given as a blessing to *all* mankind, not just to the Jewish nation.

More than anything else, Jesus' sabbath healings put him on a collision course with rabbinic restrictions. The OT does not forbid cures on the sabbath day, but the rabbis labeled all healing as work which must always be avoided on the sabbath unless life was at risk. Jesus fearlessly exposed the callousness and absurd inconsistencies to which this attitude led. How, he asked, could it be right to circumcise a baby or lead an animal to water on the sabbath day (which tradition allowed), but wrong to heal a chronically handicapped woman and a crippled man—even if their lives were not in immediate danger (Lk 13:10–17; Jn 7:21–24)? The sabbath, he taught, was a particularly appropriate day for acts of mercy (Mk 3:4,5). If tradition said otherwise, it was high time to get back to the Bible (Mt 12:7).

In stressing the aptness of healing on the sabbath, Jesus was reminding his disciples and opponents that the sabbath was a sign of redemption. The same God who had broken the enemy's power in Egypt, and commanded his people to remember that great act of mercy by observing the sabbath (Dt 5:15), was now breaking Satan's grip on people's lives through Jesus' healing miracles (Lk 13:16).

Jesus went one vital step further than that. He claimed that the sabbath, God's great redemption sign-post, was pointing straight at

Inscription on a column from the ruins of the synagogue at Capernaum.

him! He, the man from heaven, was Lord of the sabbath (Mk 2:28; cf. Mt 12:5–8). The great OT Scriptures which forecast the good news of man's redemption in the language of sabbatical release had reached their fulfillment in him, the redeemer of the world (Lk 4:16–21). Just as God kept working, despite his creation rest, to sustain the world in his mercy, so Jesus would continue to teach and to heal on the sabbath day (Jn 5:2–17). But one day his redemptive work would be complete, and then the sabbath's purpose as a sign of redemption would be accomplished.

Living on the other side of Jesus' death and resurrection, Paul was quick to grasp the significance of both for sabbath observance. As the Creator's directive to all mankind, the principle of sabbath rest was obviously still relevant. As an opportunity and stimulus for worship, the sabbath was still important, but already giving way to Sunday, especially in

churches where Gentiles were in the majority. But as a pointer to redemption and as a necessity for salvation, the rules and regulations of OT Law (together with their embellishments in rabbinic tradition) were clearly redundant.

Paul does not go so far as to ban all observance of the Jewish sabbath. Indeed, he attended many sabbath synagogue services himself in his evangelistic travels (see, e.g., Acts 13:14–16). Jewish Christians who insisted on keeping up their sabbath practices were free to do so, provided they respected the opinions of those who differed (Rom 14:5,6,13). But any suggestion that observing the Jewish calendar was a necessity for full salvation must be resisted as a relapse into slavery from the glorious freedom which Jesus had brought (Gal 4:8–11). For "these are only a shadow of what is to come; but the substance belongs to Christ" (Col 2:17).

It is left to the writer of the letter to the

Hebrews to explain just how the twin biblical "sabbath themes" of *creation* and *redemption* find their joint fulfillment in Christ. He does so by linking together the ideas of God's rest after creation and his redemptive act in bringing Israel to her "rest" in Canaan; and by showing how both relate to the present and future rest that Christians can and do enjoy in Jesus (Heb 4:1–11).

God intends all his people to share his rest—that is his promise (Heb 4:1). He showed this intention clearly when he brought Israel to the Promised Land, but that did not mark the complete fulfillment of his promise (v 8). The "full, complete rest still waiting for the people of God" (v 9 LB) is in heaven. "Christ has already entered there. He is resting from his work, just as God did after the creation" (v 10 LB). And because of his redeeming work he invites all those who believe in him to share that same "sabbath rest" now (v 9).

So here, finally, the two main strands of biblical teaching on the sabbath meet. The promised fulfillment in heaven does not, of course, necessarily rule out the idea of a Christian sabbath that can be observed in the world here and now as a pledge of the "real thing" (Col 2:17) still to come. But Hebrews' main concern is to challenge its readers to continuing faith and complete obedience. "Let us therefore strive to enter that rest, that no one fall by the same sort of disobedience" (Heb 4:11).   DAVID H. FIELD

See TEN COMMANDMENTS, THE; LORD'S DAY, THE; SABBATH DAY'S JOURNEY.

Bibliography. N.E. Andreasen, *The OT Sabbath;* N.E. Andreasen, *Rest and Redemption;* S. Bacchiocchi, *From Sabbath to Sunday;* N.A. Barach, *A History of the Sabbath;* R. de Vaux, *Ancient Israel;* S. Goldman, *Guide to the Sabbath;* A.J. Heschel, *The Sabbath;* A.E. Millgram, *Sabbath: The Day of Delight.*

Sabbath, Covert for the. Covered place in the court of the temple reserved for the king who stood there with his attendants on a sabbath or feast day (2 Kgs 16:18 KJV; RSV covered way). Ahaz, king of Judah (735–715 BC) tore it down for fear of Tiglath-pileser, king of Assyria. It is not known why.

Sabbath Day's Journey. Regulation derived from Jewish literature limiting travel on the sabbath. The prohibition against work on the sabbath was interpreted to exclude inordinate travel (Ex 16:27–30): "Everyone is to stay where he is on the seventh day; no one is to go out" (v 29). One was permitted no more than 2000 cubits (1000–1200 yds). This was determined by the distance between the ark and the people following it (Jos 3:4) or from the pasture lands to the Levitical cities (Nm 35:4,5). Thus,

in the former instance, one would not go further to worship or in the latter to pasture an animal. The only biblical reference describes the distance from the Mt of Olives to Jerusalem as "a Sabbath day's walk" (Acts 1:12).

The rabbis invented ways to at least double the distance. One could establish his home 2000 cubits away by carrying food sufficient for two meals: one to be eaten and the other to be buried—thereby to mark a temporary domicile. He might alternately fix his gaze upon a location 2000 cubits away as his legal home for the sabbath. He could, separately or in conjunction with a preceding modification, view the entire town as his home and so figure the sabbath day's journey from the village limits.

See SABBATH.

Sabbatical Year. Last year of the seven-year cycle established for keeping time in the Mosaic law.

See CALENDARS, ANCIENT AND MODERN; FEASTS AND FESTIVALS OF ISRAEL; LEVITICUS, BOOK OF.

Sabeans. Inhabitants of Sheba, a country in southwest Arabia. The Sabeans were noted as men of stature (Is 45:14), as a nation far off (Jl 3:8), and for their murder and theft of Job's servants and property (Jb 1:15).

See SHEBA (PLACE) #2.

Sabtah, Sabta. One of Cush's five sons and a descendant of Noah through Ham's line (Gn 10:7); alternately spelled Sabta in 1 Chronicles 1:9. Sabtah presumably settled along the southern coast of Arabia, where several cities bear his name.

Sabteca, Sabtecha. One of Cush's five sons and a descendant of Noah through Ham's line (Gn 10:7; 1 Chr 1:9; KJV Sabtecha). Sabteca undoubtedly settled in Arabia, but the exact location remains unknown.

Sachar, Sacar. 1. Hararite and Ahiam's father. Sachar was one of David's mighty men (1 Chr 11:35, KJV Sacar). In a parallel account he is alternately called Sharar the Hararite (2 Sm 23:33).

2. Korahite and one of Obed-edom's eight sons. Sachar and his brothers were listed among the families of gatekeepers (1 Chr 26:4, KJV Sacar).

Sachia. Son of Shaharaim and Hodesh from Benjamin's tribe (1 Chr 8:10, KJV Shachia).

Sackbut. KJV rendering of trigon, a triangular-shaped harp, in Daniel 3:5,7,10,15.

See MUSIC AND MUSICAL INSTRUMENTS (SABCHA).

Sackcloth. Poor quality material or a garment of goat hair usually worn as a symbol of mourning, but also worn by some prophets and captives.

Sackcloth was coarse and probably dark in color (Is 50:3; Rv 6:12). The shape of the garment is disputed. Two views are prominent. One view is that the garment was rectangular, sewn on both sides and one end with spaces left for the head and arms. This shape resembles the grain sack used by Joseph's brothers in Egypt (Gn 42:25,27,35) and the worn sacks used by the Gibeonites (Jos 9:4; cf. Lv 11:32). A second view is that sackcloth was a small garment resembling a loin cloth. Asiatic captives are pictured in such garb. The Hebrew practices of girding the loins with sackcloth (2 Sm 3:31; Is 15:3; 22:12; Jer 4:8) and the placing of sackcloth on the loins (Gn 37:34; 1 Kgs 20:31; Jer 48:37) support this view, though more than one type of garment could have been made from sackcloth. Sackcloth was associated primarily with mourning (Gn 37:34; 1 Kgs 21:27; Lam 2:10). National (Neh 9:1; 2 Kgs 6:30; Jon 3:8; Is 37:1) as well as personal crises constituted times for the wearing of sackcloth. Kings (1 Kgs 21:27; 2 Kgs 6:30), priests (Jl 1:13), elders (Lam 2:10), prophets (Is 20:2; Zec 13:4), and cattle (Jon 3:8) all wore sackcloth. Sackcloth was found on the penitent (Neh 9:1; Jer 6:26; cf. Mt 11:21) though such usage was not restricted to Israel (Is 15:3; Jer 49:3; Ez 27:31; Jon 3:5). The physical characteristics of the material made it suitable attire for times of danger, grief, personal and national crisis, and distress. It has been suggested that the coarse fabric produced physical discomfort and was used to inflict self-punishment on the wearer. There is no evidence, however, to support this position.

See MOURNING; BURIAL, BURIAL CUSTOMS.

Sacrifice. *See* ATONEMENT; OFFERINGS AND SACRIFICES.

Sadducees. Jewish party cited 14 times in the NT, not referred to in the OT. In the Gospel narrative they first appear together with Pharisees at John's baptism. He addressed them as "sons of snakes" and challenged them by asking, "Who said that you could escape the coming wrath of God?" He demanded that they show repentance in their lives and that they not make the idle boast that they were sons of Abraham (Mt 3:7–10). Later the Sadducees came along with some Pharisees to "test" Jesus, asking him to "show them a sign from heaven" (16:1). Jesus told his disciples, "Take heed and beware of the leaven of the Pharisees and Sadducees," and this is explained further as their "teaching" (vv 6,11,12).

A great difference begins to emerge between Pharisees and Sadducees in Matthew 22:23–33 (cf. Mk 12:18–27; Lk 20:27–38). The Sadducees who, like others, wanted to embarrass Jesus with their questions, came with a trick question that showed their doubts concerning the resurrection of the dead. The Sadducees are described in this context as those "who say there is no resurrection after death." They cited the case of a woman who had seven brothers as her husbands in succession. "Whose wife will she be in the resurrection?" they asked, implying that because of such a problem the resurrection could not be a reality. Jesus answered by speaking of the "error" of their view "caused by [their] ignorance of the Scriptures and of God's power."

In the early days of the church in Jerusalem "the priests and the captain of the temple police and the Sadducees" became "annoyed because they were teaching the people and proclaiming in Jesus the resurrection from the dead" (Acts 4:1,2). They thus seem to have led the opposition to the apostles and their preaching. Later "the high priest rose up and all who were with him, that is, the party of the Sadducees, and filled with jealousy they arrested the apostles and put them in the common prison" (5:17). The only other reference to them in the NT is in Acts 23:6–8 in the record of Paul's trial before the Jewish Sanhedrin. On that occasion Paul deliberately acted in such a way so "dissension arose between the Pharisees and the Sadducees; and the assembly was divided. For the Sadducees say that there is no resurrection, nor angel, nor spirit; but Pharisees acknowledge them all."

Thus from these NT passages one realizes something of the basic tenets of the Sadducees, of their prominence among the high priestly families, and of the cleavage between Pharisees and Sadducees.

Josephus, the Jewish historian who wrote in the closing years of the 1st century AD, adds to the information in the NT about this party. He says that the Sadducees, in contrast to the Pharisees and Essenes, gave no place to the overruling providence of God, but emphasized that all that happens to us is the result of the good or evil that we do (*Antiq.* 13.5.9; *War* 2.8.14). Josephus, in a way comparable to the NT, speaks of the Sadducees' rejection of "the immortal duration of the soul, and the punishments and rewards in Hades" (*War* 2.8.14). "Souls die with the bodies" was what they said (*Antiq.* 18.1.4). Early Christian writers—Hippolytus, Origen, and Jerome—said that the Sadducees accepted only the Pentateuch and not the other OT books. It would seem, however, that they were not opposed to other OT books as a whole (though it is doubtful whether they accepted books such as Daniel with its clear statement of the resurrection of the dead), but rather that they opposed the legal regulations introduced by the Pharisees and were saying that only the OT Law should be considered mandatory. In this, as in their stand against belief in angels and in life after death, they appear to have regarded the Pharisees as innovators and themselves as conservatives.

The other main source of knowledge about the Sadducees is the Mishna, the collection of the teaching of the rabbis put down in writing in the 2nd century AD. The Sadducees opposed many of the detailed regulations that the Pharisees sought to impose on the people (Parah 3.3,7). It also indicates that they had a greater tendency to compromise with the ways of the Gentiles than other Jewish parties (Niddah 4.2).

A number of suggestions have been made as to the origin of the name. First, it has been connected with the Hebrew word for "righteous," (saddik). This is difficult from an etymological point of view, as there would have been a change from i to u in the word. Nor is there reason to think that they made such a claim to be the "righteous ones."

Second, the name has been connected with Zadok (sometimes written Saddouk in Greek), a priest in the days of David (2 Sm 8:17; 15:24–29) who anointed Solomon (1 Kgs 1:32–39) and in his reign became chief priest (2:35). He is said to have descended from Eleazar, the son of Aaron (1 Chr 6:3–8), and Zadokite priests seem to have been responsible for priestly duties in the temple until the exile. In the blueprints for the restoration of the worship of the temple (Ez 40–48), it is the Zadokite priesthood that is again given charge to minister as "Levitical priests" (44:15,16; 48:11,12). After the exile we read of Joshua (Jeshua) the son of Jehozadak as high priest (Hg 1:1) and his lineage was traced back to Zadok (1 Chr 6:15). The significance of the Zadokite priesthood continues to be stressed in writings of the early 2nd century BC, but it is by no means clear that the Sadducees made a stand for the Zadokite priesthood. It may be added that the double d in the word is not readily explained by this view of Sadducean origins.

Third, a late rabbinic tradition is that the Sadducees took their name from another Zadok who lived in the 2nd century BC. There is little to commend this view.

Finally, the British NT scholar, T.W. Manson, has suggested that their name is to be connected with the Greek word syndikoi, meaning "members of the council," thus marking out the Sadducees as councilors under the Hasmonean rulers, essentially lay people rather than priests.

The first historical knowledge of the Sadducees is in the time of Jonathan Maccabeus, who led the Jewish struggle against the Seleucids from 160 to 143 BC. Josephus (Antiq. 13.5.9) says that they were a party at this time and then, when John Hyrcanus was head of the Jewish state (135–104 BC), he tells of strife between the Pharisees and the Sadducees (Antiq. 13.10.6). It is possible that the Sadducees stood in some sense for the Zadokite priesthood or for the claim that the Jerusalem priesthood of their day was Zadokite in origin, but this is far from clear. Josephus says that the Sadducees had the rich on their side while the Pharisees had a following among the common people. In the days of Salome Alexandra (76–67 BC) the Pharisees were in the ascendancy, but when later Judea became a Roman province and Roman governors began to put one high priest down and raise another up, it appears that most of the high priests were from high-born Sadducean families. While they could temporize with the Romans these Sadducean families had power and influence in the land. As hostilities developed between the Jews and their Roman overlords, the influence of the Sadducees declined, and after the fall of Jerusalem to the Romans in AD 70, the Sadducees fade from history.

FRANCIS FOULKES

See PHARISEES; JUDAISM; ESSENES.

Bibliography. J.W. Lightley, *Jewish Sects and Parties in the Time of Christ*; M. Simon, *Jewish Sects at the Time of Jesus*; M. Stone, *Scriptures, Sects, and Visions*; S. Zeitlin, *The Sadducees and the Pharisees*.

Sadoc. KJV form of Zadok, an ancestor of Christ, in Matthew 1:14.

See ZADOK #9.

Saffron. *See* PLANTS.

Sage. Plant growing three feet tall and indigenous to Palestine. When pressed flat, the inflorescence of this plant provides the pattern for the seven-branched lampstand used by the Jews (Ex 37:17,18).

See PLANTS.

Sailor. *See* TRADES AND OCCUPATIONS; TRAVEL AND TRANSPORTATION.

Saint. *See* CHRISTIANS, NAMES FOR.

Sakkuth. Name of the Babylonian Saturn, an astral deity in Mesopotamian religion (Am 5:26; NASB Sikkuth). Some suggest that sakkuth reflects a corruption of *sukkah*, meaning "shrine" (NIV) or "tabernacle" (KJV) within which an image would be placed.

See KAIWAN.

Sala. 1. Alternate name for Salmon, Boaz's father, in Luke 3:32.

See SALMON (PERSON).

2. KJV rendering of Shelah, Eber's father, in Luke 3:35.

See SHELAH #1.

Salah. KJV form of Shelah, Eber's father, in Genesis 10:24 and 11:12–15.

See SHELAH #1.

Salamis. Seaport on the eastern shore of Cyprus where Barnabas and Saul landed near the beginning of their first missionary journey. Here they "proclaimed the word of God in the synagogues of the Jews" (Acts 13:5). Tradition states that the city was 1000 years old when the missionaries arrived, having been found by Teucer after his return from the Trojan war.

Recently archaeologists have found evidence of Mycenaen residence centuries earlier. For centuries it was a major seaport, shipping copper, timber, ceramics, and agricultural products to Europe, Africa, and Asia. The Ptolemies encouraged Jews to settle there, hence the "synagogues of the Jews" in which Barnabas and Saul presented the good news. Barnabas' tomb is at nearby Ali Barnaba monastery (discovered in AD 477).

After the destruction of the city by Hadrian and by earthquakes in AD 332 and 342, it was rebuilt by the Byzantine emperor Constantius II (AD 336–361). Prior to AD 332 Salamis had the largest Jewish community on the island. Afterwards it apparently contained the largest Christian community, as it became the metropolitan see of the island.

After the destruction of the city by the Saracens in AD 647 the harbor silted up and the site was abandoned. During the centuries of Ottoman dominance the harbor was replaced by the port of Famagusta.

Excavation of the site of Salamis reveals Roman baths, a Roman villa, a granite forum, the Basilica, the Agora, and the Temple of Zeus. Portions of the city wall and ancient harbor have also been identified. The most impressive remains are at the north end and are called the "Marble Forum." This vast complex includes remains of the gymnasium of the Greco-Roman period, the great hall, and baths from the early Byzantine period. The main forum or market measured 750 by 180 feet in dimension, surrounded by large Corinthian columns. The basilica or church building is the largest known on the island. It was apparently built after Constantius II had renamed the city Constantia. The large Christian community which once flourished here bears witness to the pioneering work of Barnabas and Saul.

Salathiel. KJV alternate spelling of Shealtiel, King Jehoiachin's son, in 1 Chronicles 3:17; Matthew 1:12; and Luke 3:27.

See SHEALTIEL.

Salecah, Salcah, Salchah. City or district that formed the northeastern extremity of the Amorite kingdom of Og in Bashan, east of the

Ruins of the forum in Salamis.

Jordan River. Salecah (variously spelled Salcah and Salchah in the KJV) was located near the city of Edrei (Jos 12:5). The Israelites gained possession of this city when they defeated Og (Dt 3:10). Later Salecah was included in the land received by Gad's tribe for an inheritance (Jos 13:11; 1 Chr 5:11). The city is identifiable with the modern town of Salkhad.

Salem. City from which the priest-king Melchizedek came (Gn 14:18; Ps 76:2; Heb 7:11,2). Salem is believed to be an ancient name of Jerusalem.

See JERUSALEM.

Salim. Familiar location near Aenon on the west side of the Jordan River. Aenon was known for its many springs and was used by John as a place for baptism (Jn 3:23). Its location is not certain. Some agree with Eusebius (an early church father) that its location was about seven miles south of Scythopolis (Bethshan) in the Decapolis region. Others suggest that the Salim east of Nablus near Shechem in Samaria or perhaps the Wadi Saleim, six miles northeast of Jerusalem, was its location.

Sallai. 1. One of 928 Benjaminites who lived in the city of Jerusalem during the postexilic period (Neh 11:8).

2. Levitical household in the postexilic period during the days of Joiakim, the high priest (Neh 12:20); perhaps the same as Sallu in Nehemiah 12:7.

See SALLU #2.

Sallu. 1. Son of Meshullam and a Benjamite, who resided in the city of Jerusalem during the postexilic period (1 Chr 9:7; Neh 11:7).

2. Levitical priest who returned to Jerusalem with Zerubbabel following the Babylonian captivity (Neh 12:7). The Sallai mentioned in Nehemiah 12:20 is thought to be a variant spelling of Sallu.

Salma. Hur's son of Caleb's family. He is considered the founding father of Bethlehem (1 Chr 2:11,51,54).

Salmon (Person). Nahshon's son and an ancestor of David from Judah's tribe. Salmon fathered Boaz by Rahab (Ru 4:20,21) and is listed in Matthew's genealogy as a forefather of Jesus Christ (1:4,5); his name is alternately spelled Sala in Luke's genealogy (3:32).

See GENEALOGY OF JESUS CHRIST.

Salmon (Place). KJV spelling of Zalmon, a mountain in Bashan, in Psalm 68:14.

See ZALMON (PLACE).

Salmone. The wife of Zebedee and the mother of James and John (Mt 27:56). She ministered to Jesus on his prolonged Galilean tour, was present at the crucifixion, and later brought spices to anoint Jesus' body on the morning of his resurrection (Mk 15:40; 16:1; where she is called Salome).

See SALOME #1.

Salome. Name deriving from the Hebrew greeting *salom* (peace), with the additional letter being a Greek suffix.

1. Woman who followed Jesus and was perhaps Mary's sister and the mother of James and John. In Mark 15:40, the evangelist describes the women who stood at the foot of the cross, and names three of them: Mary Magdalene, Mary the mother of James the lesser and of Joses, and Salome. Similarly, when describing the women who arrived at the tomb at dawn, Mark recounts that Mary Magdalene, Mary the mother of James, and Salome had brought spices to anoint the body (16:1). Matthew speaks of two women named Mary, and the mother of the sons of Zebedee (Salmone), who could have been Salome, while John describes the sister of Mary the mother of Jesus. If Mary's sister was Salome, and she and the mother of the sons of Zebedee were one and the same, then James and John, the sons of Zebedee, were cousins of Jesus.

See SALMONE.

2. Daughter of Herodias, from her first marriage to Herod Philip. Although not specifically named in Mark 6:22 or Matthew 14:6, she is traditionally believed to be the girl whose dancing so pleased Herod that he promised her on oath anything she asked for up to half his kingdom. Prompted by her mother, she demanded the head of John the Baptist.

Salt. *See* MINERALS, METALS, AND PRECIOUS STONES.

Salt, City of. City in Judah (Jos 15:62).

See CITY OF SALT.

Salt, Covenant of. *See* COVENANT OF SALT.

Salt, Valley of. Valley in the southern vicinity of the Dead Sea. The Valley of Salt was the scene of two major military campaigns recorded in the OT. Initially, it was where David made a name for himself by routing the Edomite army (2 Sm 8:13). Abishai, one of David's mighty men, was credited with killing 18,000 Edomites there (1 Chr 18:12). Later, King Amaziah of Judah defeated the Edomite army in this valley and captured Sela, an

Edomite stronghold in the nearby hill country (2 Kgs 14:7; 2 Chr 25:11).

The location of the Valley of Salt is not altogether certain. Some identify it with Wadi el-Milh (meaning salt) east of Beersheba in Judah. A more probable suggestion is with es-Sebkha, a lifeless saline plain south of the Dead Sea positioned in the Arabah leading to the hill country of Edom.

Salt Sea. *See* DEAD SEA.

Saltwort. Family of bushy shrubs of which numerous species can be found along the coasts of the Mediterranean Sea.

See PLANTS (MALLOW).

Salu. Zimri's father from Simeon's tribe. Zimri, head of his father's household, was slain by Phinehas (Nm 25:14).

Salvation. One of the central messages of the Bible. Scripture reveals God but it also reveals his plan for the human race, that of salvation. In that sense, salvation is the theme of both the OT and NT. Because of the progressive nature of revelation man sees different aspects of God's plan, but the kernel truth of salvation is present throughout the writings of the Bible. God is a God of salvation desiring that all humankind repent and be saved (Ez 18:32; 1 Tm 2:3,4).

In the OT. The concept of salvation is represented by various terms and situations in both Testaments. Among several Hebrew words which mean "deliver" or "save," the Hebrew verb *yasha'* and derivatives are most frequently translated by English versions as "save" or "salvation." Frequency in the English Bible depends upon the version considered. For example, in the OT "salvation" is found in the NIV 80 times, RSV 90 times, NASB 111 times, and KJV 119 times. Salvation is not used as a technical term in the OT and is predicated of both individuals and God. Leaders like Samson (Jgs 13:5) or David (2 Sm 8:6) are used of the Lord to bring deliverance to God's people.

Israel's concept of salvation was rooted in the historical experience of the exodus. This momentous occasion was an opportunity to witness "the salvation of the Lord" (Ex 14:13) firsthand. Poets (Ps 106:8) and prophets (Is 43:3; Hos 13:4) later reiterated God's salvation when recalling the exodus experience. Israel's understanding of salvation was worked out in historical instances like Sennacherib's attack on Jerusalem in 701 BC, when the Lord declared that he would save the city for his name's sake (2 Kgs 19:34; cf. 18:30,35). Israel's opportunity to see God's salvation through various leaders and sit-

uations corroborated this understanding of God as the God of salvation.

Israel's response to God's deliverance was primarily praise, as evidenced so often in the psalms (i.e., Ps 3:8; 9:14; 21:1) and earlier poetic passages (Ex 15:2; Dt 32:15; 1 Sm 2:1). In addition, they directed petitions and pleas for help to the Lord for his salvation—whether from enemies (Ps 35:3; 38:22), sickness (69:29), or battle (140:7; 144:10,11)—and, in faith, expected his deliverance (35:9; 65:5). The expected salvation of the Lord was for the righteous (24:5; 37:39; 70:4; 85:9) and, in turn, motivated them to proclaim God's righteousness and salvation.

The prophets emphasized the eschatological aspect of salvation. God's ability to save was revealed by his great works in the past which thus promoted the anticipation of his work of deliverance in the future. This future hope was for the nation of Israel (Is 45:17) but anticipated universal dimensions (49:6). The prophets looked forward to deliverance and return from exile in Babylon (49:25,26; Jer 46:27; Ez 36:29); yet they also spoke of an abiding future salvation (Is 45:17; 51:6–8). The messianic hope is indicated in passages which speak of an individual who will bring God's salvation. Isaiah speaks of the Servant who brings salvation to the ends of the earth (49:6) while Jeremiah writes of deliverance by God's righteous Branch (23:5,6). The mention of the king who brings salvation in Zechariah 9:9 reflects this messianic theme and is applied to Jesus Christ in Matthew 21:4,5.

Israel understood salvation to be God's work—they saw his deliverance, cried unto the Lord for help, trusted him for it, and praised him in response. The song of salvation in Isaiah 12:2, taken from the exodus experience (Ex 15:2) and echoed in the psalms (Ps 118:14), is a beautiful example of that expression: "The Lord, the Lord, is my strength and my song; he has become my salvation" (NIV).

In the NT. In classical Greek the verb *sōzō* "to save" and noun *sōtēria* "salvation" are used for the concept of "rescue," "deliverance" or "salvation," and even "well-being" or "health." The Septuagint most frequently uses *sōzō* to render the Hebrew *yasha'* ("to save") and the NT primarily employs *sōzō* and its derivatives for the idea of salvation.

These Greek terms are generally used theologically in the NT, but examples of nontheological usage occur. In Acts 27 these words refer to the threat and deliverance of the soldiers, sailors, and prisoners from shipwreck (vv 20,31) as well as their well-being (v 34).

In the Gospels "salvation" is clearly connected with the OT concept of salvation and applied to the coming of Christ in Zechariah's prophecy (Lk 1:69,71; cf. Ps 106:10; 132:17) and

Simeon's hymn of praise (Lk 2:30). While *sōtēria* does not occur frequently in the Gospels, the concept of salvation is implied in Jesus' statement about entrance into the kingdom of God (Mt 19:24–26) and his miracles of healing (Lk 17:19; 18:42).

Paul especially brings out the universality of God's offer of salvation in his writings (Rom 1:16; Ti 2:11). His desire was for Jews to be saved (Rom 10:1) though he primarily preached the message of salvation to the Gentiles (Rom 11:11–13).

The NT teaches that salvation has its source in Jesus Christ (2 Tm 2:10; Heb 5:9) who is the "author" and mediator of salvation (2:10; 7:25). Salvation is God's work (1 Thes 5:9) and is offered by his grace (Eph 2:8,9). The message of salvation is contained in the Scriptures (2 Tm 3:15) and is carried by those who proclaim the word of truth (Eph 1:13). Correct response is repentance (2 Cor 7:10) and faith (2 Tm 3:15; 1 Pt 1:9). This was the preaching of the early church as it proclaimed Jesus the means of salvation (Acts 4:12; 13:23–26; 16:30,31).

Within the Scriptures there are many other terms associated with the concept of salvation. The new birth speaks of being made alive in Christ ("born again," Jn 3:3). Justification envisions one's legal standing before God, while redemption speaks more of the means of salvation—the payment of a price to bring one back to God. Reconciliation speaks of a change in relationship and propitiation, which evokes the OT sacrificial system, and points to the turning away of God's wrath. These terms and others share some common ground with the biblical concept of salvation but all point to the person and work of Jesus Christ the Savior.

ROBERT D. SPENDER

See KINGDOM OF GOD (HEAVEN); MESSIAH; CRUCIFIXION; JUSTIFICATION; RECONCILIATION; ATONEMENT; REDEEMER, REDEMPTION; CONVERSION; REPENTANCE; ETERNAL LIFE.

Bibliography. E.M.B. Green, *The Meaning of Salvation;* E. Kevan, *Salvation;* H.R. Mackintosh, *The Christian Experience of Forgiveness;* H.D. McDonald, *Salvation;* U. Simon, *Theology of Salvation;* C. R. Smith, *The Bible Doctrine of Salvation;* G.B. Stevens, *The Christian Doctrine of Salvation.*

Samaria. Capital of the northern kingdom of Israel, identified with the hill on which the village of Sebasṭieh is located.

The hill was purchased by Omri from Shemer, the clan who had occupied it. He built his new capital there (1 Kgs 16:24). A village was evidently there dating at least from the 10th or perhaps the 11th century BC. It became the center of the revived kingdom and enjoyed the new prestige of the Omride dynasty. But it was also subject to siege; Ben-hadad of Syria (Aram-Damascus) came up

The mound of Samaria.

against it with an alliance of 32 kings (1 Kgs 20) but the Israelites succeeded in driving them off (vv 1–21). Under Ahab's son Joram, Ben-hadad came again (2 Kgs 6:24–7:20) and almost conquered the city with a lengthy siege.

After a series of wars and the coup d'etat by Jehu which resulted in the slaughter of the priests of Baal in Samaria (2 Kgs 10:18–28), the city returned to Yahwism under Jehu's descendants. Nevertheless, the Asherah cult remained in Samaria under Jehoahaz (13:6). Syria continued to have the upper hand militarily (13:7).

During the 8th century the balance changed in Israel's favor (2 Kgs 13:14–25) and under Jeroboam II Samaria enjoyed great prosperity (14:23–28; Am 3:10,15; 4:1; 6:1,4–6). In the late 8th century the internal strife in Israel (ch 15) left the kingdom open to subjection by the Assyrians (vv 29–31). Finally, after Galilee, Transjordan, and perhaps the coastal plain were already detached, Samaria fell to Sargon II (18:9–12). During the ensuing decades foreign exiles were transported there.

In the Persian period (6th through 4th centuries), Samaria was the center of an administrative district governed by a dynasty of rulers whose names included several Sanballats (e.g., Neh 2:10 et al.), usually every other generation. The resultant Samaritan population considered itself part of Israel but were rejected by the Judeans (Ezr 4:1–3). They were consulted, however, by the Jews of Elephantine when help was needed to rebuild the temple in Egypt.

When Alexander the Great came to the Levant in 331 BC the Samaritans at first curried his favor (Josephus, *Antiq.* 11.8.4) but later they murdered his governor (Curtius, 4.8.9–10). Their leaders evidently took refuge in the Wadi Dalieh cave where they were trapped with their personal documents (papyri) and suffocated. Macedonian colonists were settled there.

Samaria was taken by Hyrcanus in 108–107 BC (*Antiq.* 13.10.2; *War* 1.2.7), who destroyed the city. It was rebuilt by Pompey, and further restored by Gabinius. King Herod changed the name of the city to Sebastia in honor of Caesar Augustus (Sebastos) and built a large temple to him there. At Sebastia Herod entertained Agrippa, killed his wife Mariamne, and strangled his sons. During the first Jewish war the Sebastenes went over to the Romans.

Two archaeological expeditions worked at Samaria: the Harvard project in 1908–10; and the joint Harvard, Palestine Exploration Fund, British School of Archaeology in Jerusalem, and Hebrew University in 1931–35. They uncovered the ruins of ancient Samaria/Sebastia on the hill of the village Sebaṣtieh. This hill stands in the center of a basin widely separated from the surrounding ridges which look down upon it (Am 3:9).

The stratigraphy is very complicated due to repeated rebuilding of the site. The royal acropolis, surrounded by an impressive casemate wall of ashlar masonry, was found, including storehouses and other important structures. On bedrock were pits containing sherds of the pre-Omride period (10th–9th centuries BC).

Among the important finds were a collection of ivories showing strong Egyptian influence via Phoenician artistic tradition. The Samaria octraca were potsherds denoting shipments of wine and oil to important people in the capital city; sometimes the manager of the local estate who sent the shipment is mentioned. The texts fall into two groups, those of years 9 and 10 and those of year 15, respectively. They may derive from the 15-year reign of one king or they may stem from two different reigns. They came from the fill under the floor of the storehouse and must date to the early or mid-8th century BC.

Buildings of the later periods include massive fortifications from the Macedonian city, the foundation and altar of Herod's temple to Augustus and temple to the goddess Kore, a residential quarter, a colonnaded street, a stadium, theater, basilica, and other structures. A medieval monastery commemorating the tra-

Round Hellenistic tower at the western entrance to Samaria.

dition that John the Baptist's head was buried there was also found.

Due to the population changes which brought Macedonian and later other veterans under Herod as colonists, the Semitic name disappeared and the Greco-Roman Sebastia survived in the name of the Arabic village, Sebaṣṭieh.   ANSON F. RAINEY

See ISRAEL, HISTORY OF; SAMARITANS; JUDAISM.

Samaritans. Schismatic monotheistic group similar in theology to the Jews. The group resided north of Judea and south of Galilee in hostile tension with its Jewish neighbors. Jesus' attitude toward this despised group radically contrasted with contemporary sentiment.

Origins of the Sect. It is difficult to determine precisely when the Samaritan sect arose and when the final break with Judaism occurred. The OT conception of the origin of the Samaritan sect is that they stemmed from repopulated foreign peoples whose worship of God was only a veneer for underlying idolatry. According to 2 Kings 17, the Samaritan sect arose from the exchange of peoples following Israel's defeat by Assyria in 722 BC. Removing the Israelites from the land, the king of Assyria repopulated the area with conquered peoples from Babylon, Cuthah, and various other nations (v 24).

The Samaritans offer a vastly different interpretation of their origin. They claim descent from the Jewish tribes of Ephraim and Manasseh (see Jn 4:12), and hold that the exile of Israelites in 722 BC by Assyria was neither full-scale nor permanent. To account for the mutual hostility that developed between their group and the Jews, the Samaritan version holds that the Jews were guilty of apostasy, setting up heretical sanctuaries during the time of Eli, rather than staying with the only holy place on Mt Gerizim. The Samaritans therefore considered themselves true Israelites in descent and worship.

From Assyrian records of this period, an exchange of population is in fact affirmed for the northern kingdom, but apparently a total deportation was not carried out (see 2 Chr 34:9). This would suggest that there were two elements in the land; first, the native Israelite remnant not exiled; and second, the foreign exiles who were gradually won over to the faith of the native residents, although syncretism no doubt existed during the early period of assimilation.

Relations Between the Samaritans and the Jews. The history of relations between the Samaritans, situated in the north around Mt Gerizim (their holy mountain), Shechem, and Samaria, and Jewish populations in Judea and then later in Galilee is one of fluctuating tensions. The ancient tension between the northern and southern kingdoms was revived with the return of exiles to Jerusalem under the Persian ruler Cyrus' edict (*c.* 538 BC). The entire southern area was at the time being governed from Samaria in the north by Sanballet, a native ruler of Palestine under Persian authority. The return of exiles to Jerusalem, particularly with their intentions of rebuilding the Jerusalem temple, posed an obvious political threat to his leadership in the north (Ezr 4:7–24; Neh 4:1–9).

Opposition was at first politically motivated, but became religious as well when sometime later, possibly the 4th century BC (toward the end of Persian or beginning of Greek rule), a rival temple was erected on Mt Gerizim. An example of Jewish hostility toward the Samaritans about this time comes from Ecclesiastes 50:25,26 (written approximately 200 BC), where the Samaritans are placed below the Edomites and Philistines in esteem and are termed a "foolish people" (cf. Test. Levi 7:2).

Jewish regard for the Samaritans was not enhanced by their lack of resistance to Antiochus Epiphanes' campaign (*c.* 167 BC) to promote Hellenistic worship in the area. While part of the Jewish community resisted the transforming of the Jerusalem temple to a temple for Zeus (1 Mc 1:62–64) and eventually followed the Maccabees in revolt (2:42,43), sources suggest that the Samaritans did not (see 6:2).

Poor relations came to a climax during the brief period of Jewish independence under the Hasmoneans, when the Jewish ruler, John Hyrcanus, marched against Shechem and Samaria, conquering and destroying the Samaritan temple on Mt Gerizim (*c.* 128 BC).

Under Herod the Great, Samaria's fortunes improved, although animosity still continued between the Samaritans and Jews in Judea and Galilee. Holding the Jerusalem temple to be a false cultic center and excluded from the inner courts by the Jerusalem authorities, a group of Samaritans desecrated the Jerusalem temple in approximately AD 6 by spreading human bones within the temple porches and sanctuary during Passover. Hostility toward Galilean Jews traveling through Samaria on the way to Jerusalem for various feasts was also not uncommon (Lk 9:51–53), with the massacre of a group of such Galilean pilgrims occurring in Samaria in approximately AD 52.

This animosity continued in Jesus' day. Both groups excluded the other from their respective cultic centers, the Jerusalem temple and the Samaritan temple on Mt Gerizim. The Samaritans, for example, were forbidden access to the inner courts of the temple and offerings they might give were accepted as from Gentiles. Thus, although probably more accurately defined as "schismatics," it appears Samaritans were in practice treated as Gentiles. All marriage between the groups was therefore forbidden and social intercourse was greatly restricted (Jn 4:9). With such proscribed separation, it is not surprising that any interaction between the two groups was strained. The mere term "Samaritan" was one of contempt on the lips of Jews (8:48) and among some scribes it possibly would not even be uttered (see the apparent circumlocution in Lk 10:37). The disciples' reaction to the Samaritan refusal of lodging (9:51–55) is a good example of the animosity felt by Jews for Samaritans at the time.

Although there is less evidence for similar attitudes from the Samaritan side, we can assume they existed. It is probable to speculate, therefore, that the Samaritan shunning of hospitality in Lk 9:51–55 was not uncommon toward other Jews whose "face was set toward Jerusalem."

Samaritan Beliefs. The main beliefs of the Samaritans demonstrate both the close affinities as well as obvious divergencies from mainstream Judaism. They held in common with Judaism a strong monotheistic faith in the God of Abraham, Isaac, and Jacob. In contrast, however, there was an elevating of Mt Gerizim in the north as the only holy place for sacrifice, based on several divergent passages in Deuteronomy and Exodus in the Samaritan text. Mt Gerizim came to be identified with the site of Abel's first altar (Gn 4:4), the site of Noah's sacrifice after the flood (8:20), the meeting place of Abraham and Melchizedek (14:18), the site of Isaac's intended sacrifice (ch 22), and many other associations.

The Samaritans held only the first five biblical books (Pentateuch) to be inspired and based their dogma and practice exclusively on these books. Such a narrow canon not only determined the direction of Samaritan theology, but further separated them from contemporary Jewish thought. Moses, for example, becomes in Samaritan thought an even more exalted figure than in Judaism. He was considered not only the chief prophet, but in later thought was described as the choicest of men, pre-existing from creation, interceding with God for Israel, and being to man "the light of the world." The messianic hope of Samaritan theology also reflects this narrow canon. A Messiah from the house of David could not be anticipated, as no evidence for such could be found in the Pentateuch. Rather, the Samaritans awaited a "prophet like Moses" based on Deuteronomy 18:15–18. This anticipated prophet was also designated the "Taheb," the Restorer, for he would in the last days restore proper cultic worship on Mt Gerizim and bring the worship of the heathen to that site.

It is clear, therefore, that it was primarily the claim of supremacy for Mt Gerizim that separated this group theologically and culturally from their Jewish neighbors.

Jesus and the Samaritans. The common Jewish perspective on Samaritans as being nearly gentile was evidently held to some extent by Jesus as well. Jesus refers to the Samaritan leper as "this foreigner" (Lk 17:18) and prohibits his disciples, during their commissioning, from taking the message of the kingdom's nearness to either the Samaritans or the Gentiles (Mt 10:5).

Yet the overwhelming evidence in the Gospels is that Jesus' attitude toward the Samaritans differed radically from that of his Jewish contemporaries. When his disciples display the usual Jewish animosity in asking to have the "fire of judgment" rain down upon the inhospitable Samaritans, Jesus "rebuked them" (Lk 9:55). Moreover, he did not refuse to heal the Samaritan leper, but honored him as the only one of the 10 who remembered to give glory to God (17:11–19). So also in the parable of the good Samaritan (10:30–37), Jesus clearly breaks through the traditional prejudices in portraying the despised Samaritan, not the respected Jewish priest or Levite, as the true neighbor to the man in need. Here as elsewhere, Jesus, in confronting his audience with God's demand, breaks through traditional definitions of "righteous" and "outcast."

What Jesus implied in words concerning the Samaritans, he equally practiced in personal interactions with them. John 4:4–43 not only records the fascinating exchange between Jesus and the Samaritan woman, but also Jesus' subsequent two-day stay in the town of Sychar, a Samaritan city. Here we see Jesus not only risking ritual uncleanness by contact with the Samaritan woman at the well (v 7–9), but also offering the gift of salvation to her (v 10) and the entire Samaritan town (vv 39–41). Through Jesus' knowledge of her marital life (vv 16–18), the woman concludes he must be a "prophet." Remembering that the Samaritans were expecting a "prophet like Moses" in the last days, it is possible that the woman is wondering if Jesus is their long-awaited prophetic Messiah (vv 19,25,26). Jesus not only breaks through the rigid animosity of Jews to Samaritans by doing the unthinkable in staying with this despised people, but accepts their faith in him as "Messiah" (v 26) and "Savior of the world" (v 42). Here, as with his association with the outcasts of Jewish society, Jesus redefines righteousness not according to descent or religious practice, but according to faith in himself. In so doing, he shatters the racial and cultural distinctions of his day and lays the foundation for the gospel's subsequent spread to the entire gentile world.

Samaria in the Mission of the Early Church. In the great commission given at the ascension, Jesus, in parting, requests his disciples to remember Samaria in the spread of the gospel (Acts 1:8), and the missionary activity of the early church did indeed include this region. When, following the martyrdom of Stephen, many Christians were forced to leave Jerusalem (8:1), one such Christian, Philip, spread the gospel in the city of Samaria (v 5). The response was so great to the miracles performed that Peter and John were sent representing the apostles in Jerusalem to investigate and to confirm the presence of the Holy Spirit among them. Evidence from the second century AD suggests, however, that the Samaritans did not to any enduring extent respond to the gospel. A small remnant of the Samaritan sect continues to exist to this day around Mt Gerizim (Shechem) and in various cities in Israel.

DAVID C. CARLSON

See ISRAEL, HISTORY OF; JUDAISM; POSTEXILIC PERIOD, THE; SAMARIA.

Bibliography. R.J. Coggins, *Samaritans and Jews;* J. MacDonald, *The Theology of the Samaritans;* J.A. Montgomery, *The Samaritans;* J.D. Purvis, "The Samaritan Problem" in B. Halpern and J. Levenson (eds.), *Traditions in Transformation,* pp. 323–350.

Samgar-nebo. Babylonian prince who took part with Nebuchadnezzar and the Chaldean army in conquering Jerusalem after a three-year siege from 588–586 BC (Jer 39:3).

Samlah. King of the Edomites from the town of Masrekah. Samlah came to power before any king ruled in Israel (Gn 36:36,37; 1 Chr 1:47,48).

Samos. Small Greek island located off the coast of Asia Minor in the Aegean Sea near

Fields near the border of Galilee and Samaria. The Jews had "no dealings" with the Samaritans (Jn 4:9), but Jesus did—and that with a woman who had an unsavory past.

the promontory of Trogyllium. This Ionian island was positioned southwest of Ephesus and northwest of Miletus. In Paul's day, it was a prosperous commercial center and considered autonomous by Rome. In his wish to bypass Ephesus, Paul anchored near Samos on his journey to Jerusalem at the close of his third missionary journey. Paul's stay at Samos was mentioned between stops at Chios and Miletus (Acts 20:15).

Samothrace, Samothracia. Island in the northeastern part of the Aegean Sea off the coast of the Roman province of Thrace. It was named Samothrace or "Samos of Thrace" to distinguish it from the other Samos (cf. Acts 20:15) which was also in the Aegean Sea but a little southwest of Ephesus. Samothrace was about halfway between Troas and Neapolis, the seaport of Philippi.

This island was the stopping place for the apostle Paul on his way from Troas to Neapolis on his second missionary journey (Acts 16:11). It is not clear whether Paul landed on the island or his boat only anchored off its coast before sailing for Neapolis the next day. The usual anchorage was on the north side of the island since boats were thereby protected from the southeast wind. Apparently, Paul's voyage from Troas to Neapolis via Samothrace was made with a fair wind behind the boat because it took two days. Returning, it took five days (see 20:6).

Samothrace is a very mountainous island with its central peak the highest point in the northern part of the Aegean, apparently second in height only to Mt Athos on the mainland. The island has always been, in clear weather, an ancient landmark for sailors sailing between Troas and Neapolis. It is about 20 miles in circumference.

Samson. Manoah's son, from Dan's tribe. His mother, whose name is not given in the Bible, was barren. The angel of the Lord announced to her that she would have a son, who was to be a Nazirite all of his life (i.e., he was not to drink wine or strong drink, not to eat anything ceremonially unclean, and no razor was to touch his head, Nm 6:1–6). She was also told that he would begin to deliver Israel from the Philistines, who had subjugated them for 40 years (Jgs 13:1–5). She reported this to her husband, Manoah, who lived at Zorah in Dan. Manoah prayed concerning this angelic visit. The angel of the Lord appeared again and gave instructions about the child who was to be born. Manoah made a burnt offering and the angel of the Lord ascended to heaven in the smoke. Manoah feared that they would die, for he now realized that they had

seen God (v 22). The child was born and the Lord blessed him as he grew. The Spirit of the Lord moved upon him in Mahaneh-dan (v 25).

Samson went to Timnah and saw a Philistine woman whom he wished to marry. The Lord was seeking an opportunity against the Philistines and in Samson's case these occasions came through Philistine women. When he and his parents went to Timnah to arrange the marriage, a lion came out of the vineyards and Samson, upon whom the Spirit of the Lord came mightily, tore the lion in half. Later he found that a swarm of bees had made honey in the carcass of the lion (Jgs 14:2–9).

Samson made a feast at Timnah, as was the custom, and told the Philistine men a riddle which involved the lion and the honey. A wager was made on the riddle and the Philistines prevailed upon his wife to learn the answer and disclose it to them. When they came up with the answer, Samson knew what had happened, so he went out and killed 30 Philistine men to pay for his bet (Jgs 14:19). Samson went home and his father-in-law gave Samson's wife to Samson's best man (vv 10–20).

When Samson returned to see his wife, he was not allowed to visit her, so he took 300 foxes, tied them in pairs tail-to-tail, fixed a torch to each pair, and turned them loose in the grain fields of the Philistines, so that the shocks and standing grain were burned. Consequently the Philistines came and burned his wife and her father; Samson went out and slaughtered many of them (Jgs 15:1–8).

The Philistines now came against Judah and the people of Judah bound Samson with new ropes to turn him over to the Philistines. When they came to Lehi, where the Philistines were camped, the Spirit of the Lord came on him mightily. He snapped the ropes, seized the jawbone of a donkey, and killed 1000 Philistines; he was very thirsty and cried to the Lord, so God opened a spring of water at Lehi (Jgs 15:9–20).

Samson's weakness for Philistine women continued to create trouble for both him and the Philistines. He went down to Gaza, where he became involved with a prostitute (Jgs 16:1). The men of the city learned that he was there and plotted to kill him at dawn, but he arose at midnight and walked off with the doors, posts, and bar of the city gate and put them on top of the hill before Hebron (vv 2,3).

Then he found Delilah, from the Valley of Sorek. The Philistines enlisted her by bribery to find out the source of his strength (Jgs 16:4,5). She kept pestering him so he told her that if they bound him with seven fresh bowstrings he would be as weak as other men. So she bound him and cried, "The Philistines are upon you." He easily broke the bowstrings. In response to her continued questions, he kept lying to her about the secret of his strength. In succession, she bound him with new ropes (v 11) and seven locks of his hair woven together and attached to a loom (v 13). Finally she wore him down and he told her the truth. If someone shaved his head and broke his Nazirite vow his strength would be gone (v 17). While Samson slept with his head on her knees, she called a barber, who shaved off his hair. This time when she cried "The Philistines are upon you," the Philistines seized him, gouged out his eyes, and took him to Gaza.

At Gaza, Samson was bound with bronze fetters and forced to grind at a mill, during which time his hair began to grow again. At a time when the Philistines were having a great festival at the temple of their god, Dagon, they celebrated their victory over Samson and asked that he be brought so they could mock him. Some 3000 people watched while Samson entertained them. At his request, Samson was placed between the two pillars supporting the temple. He asked the Lord for strength and pushed against the pillars, so that the entire building collapsed. Samson died with the Philistines as he had requested, but he killed more Philistines in this final act than he had previously (Jgs 16:1–30).

Samson's family came to retrieve his body and they buried him between Zorah and Eshtaol in the tomb of his father, Manoah. He had served as "judge," or leader, of Israel for 20 years (Jgs 16:31).   CARL E. DeVRIES

See JUDGES, BOOK OF; ISRAEL, HISTORY OF.

Samuel (Person). Last of the judges, his name means "name of God," or "His name is El" (El: God of strength and power). The play on words in 1 Samuel 1:20 (cf. Ex 2:10) is not intended to be an explanation of the meaning of Samuel's name; Hannah's words recall only her prayer and the circumstances surrounding her son's birth.

Place in History. Samuel was the last of the judges (1 Sm 7:6,15–17) and the first of the prophets (3:20; Acts 3:24; 13:20). He also anointed Saul (1 Sm 10:1,17–25; 11:12–15), and David (16:12,13) as king.

Personal History. Samuel's parents were a devout couple who went annually to the sanctuary at Shiloh (1 Sm 1:3). His father, Elkanah, was a Levite (1 Chr 6:26, KJV Shemuel in v 33) resident in Ramah, territory of Ephraim. His mother, Hannah, was unable to bear children; Elkanah had a second wife, Peninnah.

On a visit to Shiloh, Hannah prayed in the sanctuary (1 Sm 1:6–11), vowing that, if the Lord would give her a son, she would dedicate

him as a Nazirite (Nm 6:1–21) to God's service for life. The Lord heard Hannah's prayer and granted her request. She had no other children until after Samuel's dedication.

When Samuel was presented to Eli and began his service in the sanctuary, he bowed before the Lord and "worshiped the Lord there" (1 Sm 1:28). Three ingredients—a feeling of worth, a knowledge of his parents' love (cf. 2:19), and a sense of purpose—laid the foundation of his personality and his future accomplishments.

Further proof of Samuel's valuable early training is evidenced in 1 Samuel 2:12–17. Eli's sons had followed the licentious practices of the pagan religions about them. Eli was old, indulgent, and powerless to restrain them. Samuel neither developed irreverence for Eli nor followed his sons in the path of evil.

God determined to judge Eli and his house for their sins. Special communication from God was infrequent (1 Sm 3:1). When God announced his purpose to Samuel (vv 4–18), Samuel responded with reverence and respect (v 19). His personal and spiritual growth indicated that he had been marked out as the future prophet of the Lord (v 20). Samuel treated each new revelation of the Lord in an appropriate way.

When everyone did what was right in his own eyes (cf. Jgs 17:6; 21:25), God invariably allowed an adjacent nation to serve as his instrument to chasten his people, until a judge arose to deliver them. When the Philistines again invaded the land (1 Sm 4–6), the Israelites mustered their army at Ebenezer, only to be defeated. Believing that the ark of the covenant would guarantee success, they sent to Shiloh for it. The next day the Israelites were again defeated and the ark captured. When this news reached Eli, he fell from his stool and died (vv 12–18).

Twenty years elapsed before Samuel's name is mentioned again (1 Sm 7:2b,3). Evidently, following the destruction of Shiloh (cf. Jer 7:12,14,26; 26:6,9; Ps 78:60), he lived in Ramah, and went on annual preaching missions that included Bethel, Gilgal, and Mizpah, "judging" the people in these places (cf. Dt 16:18–22; 17:8–13).

Samuel probably also founded "schools of the prophets" during this period. Such schools had been established at Bethel (1 Sm 10:5; 2 Kgs 2:3), Gilgal (2 Kgs 4:38), Ramah (1 Sm 19:20), and elsewhere (2 Kgs 2:5), perhaps as a natural outgrowth of Samuel's ministry.

After a 20-year ministry, Samuel thought it timely to move toward spiritual and national unification. He convened a meeting at Mizpah (1 Sm 7). There, with a symbolic rite expressive of deep humiliation and in keeping with the libations of a treaty, the Israelites poured out water on the ground, fasted, and prayed.

The Philistines mistook the nature of the convocation and decided to attack the defenseless worshipers, who entreated Samuel to pray for them. He offered a sacrifice and the Lord sent a violent thunderstorm, causing the invaders to flee in panic. The pursuing Israelites won a significant victory at Ebenezer (1 Sm 7:12), thus ending the Philistine invasions.

In Samuel's declining years, the elders rejected him in favor of a king (1 Sm 8). Following earnest prayer, he received new direction from the Lord, acceded to their request, and later anointed Saul prince over God's people (10:1). Samuel then summoned the Israelites to Mizpah, God's choice was made official, and Saul was hailed as king (vv 17–26). Following Saul's victory over Nahash (ch 11), Samuel at Gilgal confirmed Saul's kingship (vv 12–14). Thereafter Samuel retired to Ramah to train men to carry on his ministry.

Samuel twice had to reprove Saul, first for impatience and disobedience (1 Sm 13:5–14), and then for disobeying the express command of the Lord (15:20–23) who now rejected him as king. Samuel was then sent to the home of Jesse in Bethlehem, where he anointed David as the chosen one of the Lord (16:1–13).

In 1 Samuel 25:1 is a very brief account of Samuel's passing, where all Israel gathered together and mourned for him. He was buried in Ramah.

The only subsequent mention of Samuel is in 1 Samuel 28. Summoned by the witch of Endor at Saul's request, Samuel announced that on the following day Saul and his sons would die in battle (vv 4–19).

Character. Samuel overcame many problems through piety, perseverance, dedication to the service of the Lord, and patriotism. His overriding concern was for the good of his people. Wise and courageous, he boldly rebuked king, elders, and people when necessary, always from the sure ground of the revealed will of God.

While Samuel served as judge and priest, he was preeminently a prophet. Through his ministry the spiritual life of the Israelites improved. In inaugurating the monarchy, he led the people from tribal disunity to national solidarity. He appointed gatekeepers to the tent of meeting (1 Chr 9:17–26), organized observance of the Passover so memorably that it was still spoken about in Josiah's day (2 Chr 35:18), committed the "manner of the kingdom" to writing (1 Sm 10:25), and penned "the Chronicles of Samuel the seer" (1 Chr 29:29). A man of prayer (1 Sm 15:11; Ps 99:6), he well deserves a

place among the great men of faith (Heb 11:32).   CYRIL J. BARBER

See SAMUEL, BOOKS OF FIRST AND SECOND.

Samuel, Books of First and Second.

Name, Authorship, and Date. First and Second Samuel derive their name from the individual whom God used to establish kingship in Israel. Samuel is the most prominent figure in the early narratives of 1 Samuel. His key role in leading the nation of Israel through the transition from the period of the judges to that of the monarchy warrants the use of his name as the title for the book.

These books, however, have not always been so designated, nor was the material originally divided into two books. As far as is known the Septuagint (the Greek translation of the OT dating from the 3rd century BC) translators were the first to separate the material of Samuel into two books (they made a similar division in the material of Kings). The Hebrew original of these books was written, as is characteristic of Hebrew, with symbols only for consonants and none for vowels. When translated into Greek, it was necessary to use symbols for both vowels and consonants, thus greatly lengthening the manuscript. Presumably the practical consideration of the length of the scroll was the cause for dividing the material of both Samuel and Kings into two books (scrolls) instead of retaining just one. The Septuagint translators, recognizing the continuity of content and emphasis in Samuel and Kings, designated what is now known as 1,2 Samuel as "The First and Second Books of Kingdoms" and then designated what now is known as 1,2 Kings as "The Third and Fourth Books of Kingdoms." The Latin Vulgate (the Latin translation of the Bible prepared by Jerome in the late 4th century AD) slightly modified the Septuagint titles to "First, Second, Third, and Fourth Kings." These titles were utilized all through the Middle Ages and were modified into our present titles by the Protestant Reformers in the 16th century AD in agreement with Jewish rabbinic tradition. The Reformers, however, retained the division into two books, and this has been followed in modern English versions as well.

Even though Samuel is prominent in the early part of the book, and the book bears his name in our English versions, it is clear that he is not the author of the entirety of 1,2 Samuel. Samuel's death is recorded in 1 Samuel 25:1 prior to the time of the accession of David to the throne in place of Saul. Who wrote the material of 1,2 Samuel if it was not Samuel? On the basis of the statement in 1 Chronicles 29:29, it has been suggested by some that Samuel composed the early narratives of the book and that his work was later supplemented by the writings of the prophets Nathan and Gad. Others have suggested one of David's contemporaries, such as Ahima-az (2 Sm 15:27,36; 17:17), Hushai (15:32; 16:16), or Zabud (1 Kgs 4:5). Presumably these men would have had access to the writings of Samuel, Nathan, and Gad as well as to other sources (see, e.g., 2 Sm 1:18, the Book of Jashar) pertaining to the life and reigns of Saul and David. Who the real author was, however, cannot be determined from available evidence. Whoever it was, it seems to be clear that he lived after the death of Solomon and the division of the kingdom in 930 BC (see references to "Israel in Judah" in 1 Sm 11:8; 17:52; 18:16; 2 Sm 5:5; 24:1–9; and "kings of Judah" in 1 Sm 27:6).

Purpose and Theological Teaching. The theme which binds the narratives of 1,2 Samuel together is that of kingship and covenant. Although the author himself never specifically formulates his purpose for writing the book, reflection on its content suggests that the author intends to describe this period of Israel's history in a way which demonstrates that kingship as requested by the people was a denial of the covenant; kingship as instituted by Samuel was compatible with the covenant; kingship as practiced by Saul failed to correspond to the covenantal ideal; and kingship as practiced by David was an imperfect but true representation of the ideal of the covenantal king.

It has often been pointed out that there is ambivalence in the description of the establishment of kingship in Israel (1 Sm 8–12) because in some places it seems to be suggested that kingship is improper for Israel, while in other places it seems to be suggested that kingship was God's will for his people. Resolution to this tension is provided in 1 Samuel 12, when Samuel inaugurates Saul as Israel's first king in the context of a covenant renewal ceremony by which Israel renews its allegiance to the Lord. Here it becomes clear that kingship in itself was not wrong for Israel; God desired Israel to have a king. But kingship of the type Israel desired (as the nations round about) and for the reasons she wanted a king (to give a sense of national security, and lead her to victory in battle) involved a denial of the Lord as her ultimate sovereign. Samuel defined the role of the king in Israel and presented Saul to the people in a ceremony in which at the same time they renewed their allegiance to the Lord. The monarchy in Israel was first established in a form which was compatible with the covenant. The king in Israel was to be subject to the Law of the Lord as every other citizen of the nation, and to the word of the prophet as well. From this perspective the author depicts the reign of Saul as failing to cor-

respond to the covenantal requirements, while the reign of David, although imperfect, reflects the covenantal ideal.

When one considers the prominence which kingship assumes in the Scriptures in connection with the rise of messianic expectation, it is certainly important to understand the circumstances and conceptual considerations associated with the origin of the institution. It is in 1,2 Samuel that the expression the "anointed of the Lord" is first used and it is thus in the books of Samuel that the messianic idea finds its roots.

There are at least two other important advances in the history of redemption that are recorded in 1,2 Samuel. The first of these is that in the narratives of David's conquests the land promise, initially given to Abraham and repeated to succeeding generations, finds an incipient fulfillment. It is in the time of David that Israel's borders are extended from Egypt to the Euphrates as had been promised. A second event of major significance for the remainder of the Bible is David's selection of Jerusalem to be the political and religious center of Israel. The narratives of 1,2 Samuel are thus foundational for much of what follows in biblical revelation and the progress of redemptive history.

Content. *Samuel (1 Sm 1–7).* (1) Samuel's youth (1 Sm 1–3). The birth of Samuel is narrated in 1:1–28. God granted the request of Hannah for a son after a long period of barrenness. She named her son Samuel (a wordplay on the Hebrew expression "heard of God"), and dedicated him to the service of the Lord with Eli the priest at the tabernacle in Shiloh. Hannah's beautiful song of praise to God who hears and answers prayer (2:1–10) exalts the sovereignty of God and prophetically anticipates not only the establishment of kingship in Israel but ultimately the highest fulfillment of the royal office in Christ himself (v 10). The evil practices of the sons of the priest Eli are described in verses 11–26. These men not only used their office for personal gain (vv 12–17), but also committed immoral acts with the women serving at the entrance to the tabernacle (v 22). Although Eli rebuked his sons (vv 22–25), his warnings were too little and too late. It was in this loose environment that Samuel grew up (vv 18–21,26). In verses 27–36 an unnamed prophet pronounced judgment on Eli and his priestly line. The prediction of the imminent death of Hophni and Phinehas, Eli's sons, was fulfilled when the Philistines took the ark and destroyed the tabernacle at Shiloh (4:11; Jer 7:14). In 1 Samuel 3:1–4:1a Samuel is called to be a prophet and he too is given a message of judgment for the house of Eli (3:11–14). As the reliability of Samuel's words are attested it is

Ruins of a building at Shiloh, the town where Hannah earnestly prayed for a son. Her prayer was answered in the birth of Samuel; he later served the Lord there.

recognized by the people that he was a true prophet of the Lord (3:19–4:1a).

(2) The loss and return of the ark (1 Sm 4–6). In a battle with the Philistines the prophecy of 2:27–36 and 3:11–14 was partially fulfilled. The Israelites were defeated, the ark was taken, and Hophni and Phinehas were killed. Upon hearing the report of these calamities Eli also died (4:17,18). The Philistines placed the ark of the Lord in the temple of their god Dagon in Ashdod (5:1,2); however, when the idol of Dagon broke in pieces and fell before the ark and a plague broke out in Ashdod, the ark was moved to Gath; when the plague broke out in Gath it was moved to Ekron; when the plague erupted in Ekron the Philistines were compelled to return the ark to Israel—it was placed on a cart pulled by two nursing cows. These cows left their penned up calves and headed for the Israelite border and the town of Beth-shemesh (6:1–21). In all this the Lord demonstrated that although he would not be manipulated by his own people when they thought carrying the ark into battle would automatically guarantee victory for them, at the same time he would not let the Philistines think that the victory over the Israelites and the capture of the ark signified the superiority of their god Dagon.

(3) The defeat of the Philistines (1 Sm 7). Twenty years went by (v 2). Samuel assured the people of deliverance from Philistine oppression if they would confess their sin and turn from the worship of Baals and Ashtaroths (v 3). He called for a national assembly at Mizpah (v 5) to renew allegiance to the Lord. While the Israelites were assembled the Philistines attacked and the Lord gave the Israelites a miraculous victory (vv 10,11), demonstrating that obedience to covenant obligations would insure national security (see Ex 23:22; Dt 20:1–4).

Kingship Established in Israel (1 Sm 8–12). (1) The people request a king (1 Sm 8:1–22). In Samuel's old age the elders of the nation approached him and requested that he give them a king. Samuel immediately perceived that their request entailed a rejection of the Lord who was their king (v 7), because the people desired a king "like the other nations" (vv 5,20) as a symbol of national unity and military security (v 20). Nevertheless, the Lord told Samuel to give the people a king (vv 7,9,22). At the same time, however, he told Samuel to warn the people concerning what having a king "like the nations" would mean (vv 9–18). The warning, descriptive of the practices of contemporary Canaanite kings, fell on deaf ears (v 19) and the people persisted in their desire for a king.

(2) Samuel privately anoints Saul (1 Sm 9:1–10:16). The narrative of Saul's search for the lost donkeys of his father and his encounter with Samuel in the process of his search is given to explain how Samuel and Saul first met, and how the Lord indicated to Samuel who the person was that he was to anoint as Israel's first king (9:16,17). After Samuel privately anointed Saul (10:1) he was given three signs to confirm that his new calling was of the Lord (vv 2–7).

(3) Saul publicly chosen by lot at Mizpah (1 Sm 10:17–27). After the private designation and anointing of Saul to be king (9:1–10:16) Samuel convened a national assembly at Mizpah to make the Lord's choice known to the people (10:20–24) and to define the king's task (v 25). Again at this assembly Samuel emphasized that the people had rejected the Lord in requesting a king because they sought a king for the wrong reasons and failed to recognize the Lord's past faithfulness in delivering them from their enemies (vv 18,19). But again it was clear that the time for kingship in Israel had

come and it was the Lord's desire to give the people a king. Samuel's explanation of the "regulations of the kingship" (v 25) was an important step in resolving the tension between Israel's sin in desiring a king on the one hand, and the Lord's intent to give them a king on the other. This document, which was preserved at the tabernacle, probably contained an enlarged version of the "law of the king" in Deuteronomy 17:14–20 and spelled out regulations governing the role of the king in Israel for the benefit of both the king and the people. This document undoubtedly clearly distinguished Israelite kingship from that of the kings of the surrounding nations.

(4) Saul leads Israel to victory over the Ammonites (1 Sm 11:1–13). When Nahash, king of the Ammonites, attacked Jabesh-gilead, a town east of the Jordan in the territory of Manasseh, Saul left his farm work (vv 4,5) to lead a volunteer army (vv 6–8) in support of the inhabitants of Jabesh-gilead. The victory over the Ammonites under Saul's leadership (v 11) placed another seal of divine approval on his selection to be king. Saul attributed the victory to the Lord rather than his own military strategies (v 13).

(5) Saul inaugurated as king (1 Sm 11:14–12:25). The victory at Jabesh-gilead prompted Samuel to call for a national assembly at Gilgal to "renew the kingdom" (11:14) and "make Saul king" (v 15). At the Gilgal assembly Samuel led the people in confessing the sin of their initial request for a king (12:13,19) and in renewing their allegiance to the Lord (vv 14,15,24). In the context of this covenant renewal ceremony Saul was formally inaugurated in his office as king. By inaugurating Saul in this manner, Samuel effectively provided for covenantal continuity in the transition from the period of the judges to that of the monarchy. There was no inherent conflict between kingship in Israel and recognition of the Lord's continued sovereignty over the nation if both the people and the king would continue to fear and serve the Lord.

Saul Rejected as King (1 Sm 13–15). (1) Saul's disobedience (1 Sm 13:1–22). When Saul was threatened with an imminent attack from the Philistines, he gathered troops at Gilgal and awaited Samuel as he had been instructed (10:8; 13:8). When it appeared that Samuel would not come within the prearranged time, Saul became impatient and offered a sacrifice himself without waiting for Samuel's arrival (13:9). Just as the sacrifice was completed, Samuel appeared and rebuked Saul for not keeping the commandment of the Lord (v 13). In disobeying Samuel's previous instruction Saul had violated a fundamental requirement of his office. The king in Israel

was always to be subject to the Law and the Word of the Lord through his prophets. Saul was seriously mistaken in thinking he could strengthen Israel's hand against the Philistines by sacrifice to the Lord when this was done in violation of the Lord's specific command. Samuel told Saul that because of his disobedience his dynasty would not endure (v 14).

(2) Jonathan's victory (1 Sm 13:23–14:52). Saul's son Jonathan and Jonathan's armor bearer skillfully and courageously attacked a Philistine outpost killing about 20 men (14:8–14). The Lord used this defeat along with an earthquake to bring panic to the entire Philistine force (v 15). In the meantime Saul sought divine guidance on whether to join the fray with his own forces. When the Lord's answer did not come immediately, Saul concluded that waiting for the Lord's word might jeopardize his military advantage (v 19). Here again he demonstrated that he trusted more in his own insight than in waiting upon the Lord. Saul further damaged his own stature in the eyes of his troops by pronouncing a foolish curse on any who would eat food before the battle was won. This nearly cost Jonathan his life (vv 24,43,44); he was spared only because of the intervention of the troops in his defense (v 45).

(3) Saul rejected as king (1 Sm 15:1–35). Saul was commanded by the Lord through Samuel to attack the Amalekites and totally destroy them, sparing neither human nor animal life (vv 1–3). The Amalekites had previously attempted to destroy Israel shortly after their exodus from Egypt while journeying to Sinai to enter into covenant with the Lord (Ex 17:8–16; Dt 25:17–19). Saul disobeyed the Lord in sparing the best of the animals for sacrifice and in sparing Agag the Amalekite king. The Lord sent Samuel again to rebuke Saul for his disobedience. Samuel charged Saul with rebellion against the Lord and told him that because he had rejected the word of the Lord, the Lord had rejected him as king (1 Sm 23).

Saul and David (1 Sm 16–2 Sm 1:27). (1) Samuel anoints David (1 Sm 16:1–13). The Lord instructed Samuel to go to the house of Jesse in Bethlehem to anoint one of his sons to be king in place of Saul (v 1). By divine leading Jesse's youngest son, David, was shown to be the one whom the Lord had chosen (v 12). When Samuel anointed him as king, the Spirit of the Lord came upon him in power (v 13).

(2) David in the service of Saul (1 Sm 16:14–17:58). When Saul became plagued by an evil spirit his attendants sought a harpist whose music would soothe his troubled disposition (16:16). David was the one chosen for this purpose (vv 18–23). The position at the

court, however, was not permanent (17:15), and David divided his time between the court and his home duties. In due time the Philistines led by the giant Goliath encamped against the Israelites. Goliath challenged any Israelite who dared to meet him in individual combat (vv 8–10). No Israelite ventured to accept his challenge (v 11) until David, who was visiting the camp of the Israelite forces to bring food to his brothers, heard the challenge and responded in the strength and power of the Lord (vv 37,45–47). The Lord gave David a great victory because he acknowledged that "the battle is the Lord's" (v 47).

(3) *Saul's hatred toward David* (1 Sm 18:1–19:24). In the aftermath of David's victory over Goliath, Jonathan, Saul's son, pledged loyalty to David in a covenant of friendship. As David achieved further successes in leading Israel's armies, and as his public acclaim grew, Saul began to fear that David was a threat to his throne (18:14–16,28–30). An intense hatred toward David arose in Saul and he made several attempts on David's life (18:17,25; 19:1,10). David was finally forced to flee and sought refuge with Samuel at Ramah (19:18). When Saul and three of his messengers went to Ramah to apprehend David, they were so overcome by the Spirit of God that they were incapable of fulfilling their mission (vv 20–24).

(4) *David and Jonathan* (1 Sm 20:1–42). David's absence from the royal table at the new moon festival provoked Saul to again threaten David's life (vv 30,31). Jonathan, however, met with David at a prearranged place to inform him of the danger and say good-bye (v 42). Jonathan and David again pledged themselves to mutual loyalty and kindness (vv 13–16,42). In the encounter it is clear that both men knew that David, not Jonathan, would be the successor to Saul on the throne of Israel (vv 13–15).

(5) *David at Nob* (1 Sm 21:1–9). In his flight David went to the priest Ahimelech at Nob and, indicating he was on a secret mission for Saul, asked for bread and for the sword of Goliath, both of which were given him. One of Saul's servants, Doeg the Edomite, who was at Nob observed the transaction.

(6) *David at Gath* (1 Sm 21:10–15). David then went into Philistine territory to King Achish at Gath. When his identity was discovered he feigned insanity in order to escape.

(7) *David at Adullam* (1 Sm 22:1–5). From Gath David went to the cave of Adullam where he was joined by about 400 supporters. He took his parents to Moab for their own protection and then returned to the Forest of Hereth in Judah.

(8) *Saul kills the priests at Nob* (1 Sm 22:6–23). Doeg the Edomite reported to Saul that Ahimelech the priest had given assistance to David. At Saul's command Doeg massacred all the priests at Nob except for Abiathar, who escaped with the high priestly ephod and joined David.

(9) *David at Keilah* (1 Sm 23:1–13). David and his men delivered the citizens of Keilah from Philistine raiders, but were forced to leave the city when it was apparent that its unthankful inhabitants were prepared to hand David over to Saul.

(10) *David in the Desert of Ziph* (1 Sm 23:14–29). While David was in the Desert of Ziph, he was encouraged by a visit from Jonathan who again pledged to him his loyalty. Although the Ziphites promised to aid Saul in capturing David, a Philistine attack forced Saul to abandon his attempt to apprehend him.

(11) *David spares Saul's life* (1 Sm 24:1–22). While hiding deep in a cave at En-gedi, David was unexpectedly provided the opportunity to take Saul's life when Saul relieved himself at the entrance to the cave. Nevertheless because Saul was "the anointed of the Lord" David spared his life and shamed him into confessing his own wickedness by showing Saul a piece of his robe that he had cut off while Saul was in the entrance to the cave.

(12) *David, Nabal, and Abigail* (1 Sm 25:1–44). David was badly mistreated by a sheepherder named Nabal; he was deterred, however, from foolishly taking the man's life by the discerning words of Nabal's wife, Abigail. Shortly after this incident Nabal died, and David took Abigail as his wife.

(13) *David spares Saul's life a second time* (1 Sm 26:1–25). For a second time the Ziphites joined Saul in attempting to capture David. While Saul and his men were sleeping, David and Abishai crept into their camp and took Saul's spear and water jug. On the next day David was again able to demonstrate to Saul that he did not seek to wrest the kingship from his hands.

(14) *David among the Philistines* (1 Sm 27:1–12). David eventually became weary of hiding from Saul in Israelite territory and in a time of discouragement he went again to Philistia to seek refuge beyond Saul's reach. Ingratiating himself with Achish, a Philistine ruler, he was given the town of Ziklag as a place for himself and his men to reside. From Ziklag David raided various tribes inhabiting the area south of Philistia, but deceived Achish into thinking he was raiding the territory of Judah.

(15) *Saul and the medium of Endor* (1 Sm 28:1–25). The Philistines again gathered an army to fight Israel, and Saul, terrified and seemingly anticipating an imminent defeat, vainly sought for some word from the Lord

concerning the outcome of the battle. When this was denied he went in disguise to a medium at Endor and requested her to bring up to him the spirit of Samuel. Saul is told by this spirit that Israel will be defeated and that he and his sons will die in the upcoming battle. This prediction is viewed by some as divine revelation by means of Samuel's departed spirit, and by others as the result of a limited satanic knowledge of the future by means of an evil spirit representing itself as the spirit of Samuel.

(16) The Philistines mistrust David (1 Sm 29:1–11). Although Achish desired David to join the Philistine army in its battle with Israel, the other Philistine commanders mistrusted him and forced Achish to send David and his men back to Ziklag. This turn of events rescued David from a serious dilemma created by his apparent friendship with Achish.

(17) David defeats the Amalekites (1 Sm 30:1–31). Upon returning to Ziklag, David discovered that in his absence the city had been raided and burned by the Amalekites and that their wives, children and cattle had been taken captive. After inquiring of the Lord through Abiathar the priest, David and his men went in pursuit of the Amalekites and recovered all they had taken, and more. He divided the plunder among his troops and sent gifts from it to various towns in Judah.

(18) The death of Saul and his sons (1 Sm 31:1–2 Sm 1:27). As had been predicted, the battle with the Philistines ended in a disastrous defeat for Israel in which Saul took his own life after being seriously wounded, and Jonathan as well as two other sons of Saul were killed. David mourned for Saul and Jonathan and exalted their memory in his tribute to them recorded in 2 Samuel 1:19–27.

David (2 Sm 2–24). (1) David anointed king over Judah (2 Sm 2:1–7). Subsequent to Saul's death, the Lord instructed David to go to Hebron where the tribe of Judah anointed him as their king.

(2) David, Ish-bosheth, and Abner (2 Sm 2:8–4:12). Although David became king over Judah, the remaining tribes under the influence of Abner, commander of Saul's army, recognized Ish-bosheth as Saul's successor (2:8–10). Ish-bosheth was a son of Saul who had survived the battle with the Philistines. Conflict quickly broke out between the men of David led by Joab and the men of Ish-bosheth led by Abner. In this conflict Asahel, Joab's brother, was slain by Abner (vv 12–30). As David grew stronger and Ish-bosheth weaker, Abner shifted his allegiance from Ish-bosheth to David (3:1–21). Joab, however, avenged the blood of his brother Asahel by murdering Abner under the pretense of negotiating with him (vv 22–38). Al-

though David detested this act, mourned for Abner, and cursed Joab (v 39), the crime was not punished until early in the reign of Solomon (see 1 Kgs 2:5,6,29–34). Shortly afterwards Ish-bosheth was slain by two soldiers who brought his head to David at Hebron, expecting to be rewarded (2 Samuel 4:1–8). David, however, had them both put to death (v 12). The only male survivor of Saul's line was the crippled son of Jonathan named Mephibosheth (v 4).

(3) David king over all Israel (2 Sm 5). After Ish-bosheth's death David was made king over all the tribes at Hebron (vv 1–4). One of David's first acts as king was to capture the fortress of Zion from the Jebusites. David established Zion as his capital and built a palace there for his residence (vv 6–12).

(4) The ark brought to Jerusalem (2 Sm 6). Recognizing the importance of the ark as a symbol of God's presence with his people, David determined that it should be brought to Jerusalem from the obscurity of the house of Abinadab in Kiriath-jearim where it had remained throughout the entirety of Saul's reign. Violation of prescriptions for handling the ark led to the death of Uzzah, one of Abinadab's sons, and delayed the ark's conveyance to Jerusalem for three months (vv 3–11). In a second attempt David led a joyful procession into the city of Jerusalem where the ark was placed in a tent that had been prepared for it (vv 12–17).

(5) David, Nathan, and the temple (2 Sm 7). It soon became David's desire to build a temple to house the ark and provide a center for Israel's worship of the Lord (v 1). The Lord told David through Nathan the prophet that he was not to build the Lord a house (temple), but that the Lord would build him a house (a dynasty) that would endure forever (vv 5–16). Here the line of the promised seed is narrowed to the house of David within the tribe of Judah. This promise finds its fulfillment in the birth of Jesus, who was the "son of David, the son of Abraham" (see Mt 1:1). It would be the task of Solomon, David's son, to construct the temple (2 Sm 7:13).

(6) David's victories (2 Sm 8). David was able to defeat numerous surrounding peoples, to extend Israel's borders, and to establish a time of prosperity and rest for the nation.

(7) David and Mephibosheth (2 Sm 9). Remembering his covenant with Jonathan (see 1 Sm 18:1–3; 20:13–16,42), David inquired concerning survivors of the house of Saul to whom he could show kindness. When Mephibosheth was sought out, David brought him to the court to enjoy the honor of eating at the king's table.

(8) David and Bathsheba (2 Sm 10–12). During a war with the Ammonites, David commit-

ted adultery with the wife of one of his soldiers, Uriah the Hittite. When Bathsheba became pregnant David arranged for Uriah's murder. These sinful acts provoked God's wrath (12:10–12) and David experienced the bitter fruits of his misconduct during the remainder of his life.

(9) Amnon, Absalom, and Tamar (2 Sm 13). David's oldest son, Amnon, feigned sickness in order to arrange for his half-sister, Tamar, to care for him. When Tamar refused Amnon's sexual advances to her, he raped her. This incident enraged Tamar's full brother Absalom, who determined to avenge his sister by killing Amnon. Absalom waited two years and then arranged for the murder of Amnon during the festivities of the time of sheep shearing. He then fled to Geshur, a small city-state in Syria, where his maternal grandfather was king.

(10) David and Absalom (2 Sm 14–19). Absalom remained in exile for three years until Joab arranged for his return by securing a renunciation of blood revenge from David through his response to a fabricated story told by a woman from Tekoa (14:1–27). Upon Absalom's return, however, David refused to see him for two years, until they were finally reconciled (vv 28–33). In this whole episode David sidestepped the issues of repentance and justice and took no effective disciplinary action. In the meantime Absalom conspired to wrest the throne from David his father by attempting to discredit his administration of justice, and by seeking to win the favor of the people and members of David's court. After four years Absalom proclaimed himself king in Hebron and gathered sufficient military strength to force his father to flee from Jerusalem (ch 15). Failure to immediately pursue after David led to the defeat of Absalom's forces and to Absalom's own death at the hand of Joab, David's commander (16:15–18:18). David mourned for his son Absalom (19:1–8), but was able to return to Jerusalem and to reestablish his government (vv 9–43). David disciplined Joab for killing Absalom by replacing him as commander of his troops with Amasa (v 13).

(11) Rebellion of Sheba (2 Sm 20). In the unsettled conditions immediately after David's return to Jerusalem another abortive revolt was attempted by Sheba of the tribe of Benjamin. Joab, in defiance of David's disciplinary action, killed Amasa, pursued after Sheba, and crushed his revolt.

(12) David and the Gibeonites (2 Sm 21:1–14). At some unspecified time during David's reign the land suffered a three-year famine. It was revealed to David by the Lord that the famine was due to Saul's violation of an Israelite treaty with the Gibeonites (see Jos 9:15,18–26). This offense was atoned for by giving seven descendants of Saul to the Gibeonites for execution.

(13) David and the Philistines (2 Sm 21:15–22). In this pericope four episodes of heroic accomplishments by David's mighty men against the Philistines are recounted.

(14) David's song of praise (2 Sm 22). In a beautiful song of praise David described his deliverance from his enemies (vv 4–30) and the help with which the Lord sustained him (vv 31–51). The same song occurs with minor variations in Psalm 18.

(15) David's last words (2 Sm 23:1–7). In a

The Dome of the Rock, built on the site of Araunah's threshing floor.

brief statement David acknowledges the work of God's Spirit in enabling him to speak God's word, and confesses his confidence in the realization of the Lord's promise to him and his dynasty.

(16) David's mighty men (2 Sm 23:8–39). This pericope contains a list of 37 of David's warriors and a description of some of their accomplishments.

(17) The census and David's punishment (2 Sm 24:1–25). David's decision to take a census of his fighting men reflected an improper trust in military-political organization and power. The Lord judged him by sending a plague on the land in which many of the people died. At the word of the Lord through Gad the prophet, David built an altar on the threshing floor of Araunah, which was later to become the site of the temple (see 2 Ch 3:1). The Lord responded to David's sacrifices and prayers on behalf of the people and the plague was stopped.

J. ROBERT VANNOY

See SAMUEL (PERSON); SAUL #2; ISRAEL, HISTORY OF; DAVID.

Bibliography. W.G. Blaikie, *The First Book of Samuel;* W.G. Blaikie, *The Second Book of Samuel;* H.W. Hertzberg, *I & II Samuel: A Commentary;* C.F. Keil and F. Delitzsch, *Biblical Commentary on the Books of Samuel;* R.W. Klein, *I Samuel;* P.K. McCarter, Jr., *I Samuel;* H.P. Smith, *A Critical and Exegetical Commentary on the Books of Samuel.*

Sanballat. Leading political official of Samaria residing at Beth-horon in Ephraim. In a letter from Elephantine of Egypt, Sanballat was named as the governor of Samaria in 407 BC. Sanballat along with Tobiah the Ammonite and Geshem the Arab were adversaries of Nehemiah, furiously trying to prevent him from rebuilding the walls of Jerusalem during the postexilic period (Neh 2:10,19; 4:1,7; 6:1–14; 13:28). The Judean province was probably included under Samaritan rule since its defeat by Babylon under Nebuchadnezzar in 586 BC. Nehemiah's determination to rebuild the walls of Jerusalem was in essence an assertion of Judean independence from Sanballat and Samaritan control.

Sanctification. Term meaning being made holy, or purified, it is used broadly of the whole Christian experience, though most theologians prefer to use it in a restricted sense to distinguish it from related terms, such as regeneration, justification, and glorification.

Definition. A comprehensive definition of santification by the New Hampshire Baptist Confession (1833) states: "We believe that Sanctification is the process by which, according to the will of God, we are made partakers of his holiness; that it is a progressive work; that it is begun in regeneration; and that it is carried on in the hearts of believers by the presence and power of the Holy Spirit, the Sealer and Comforter, in the continual use of the appointed means—especially the Word of God, self-examination, self-denial, watchfulness, and prayer" (Article X).

This definition helps us to distinguish sanctification from regeneration in that the latter speaks of the *inception* of the Christian life; but sanctification is thus also distinguished from glorification which focuses on the *consummation* of God's work in the believer. Put quite simply, then, regeneration refers to the beginning, sanctification to the middle, and glorification to the end in the "order of salvation."

The distinction between sanctification and justification, on the other hand, calls for more detailed attention, both because it is somewhat subtle and even more fundamental. In the first place, justification, like regeneration, refers (though not exclusively) to the beginning of the Christian experience, whereas the above definition emphasizes the *progressive* character of sanctification. Second, justification refers to a *judicial* act of God whereby believers are at once absolved of all their guilt and accounted legally righteous, whereas sanctification, like regeneration and glorification, calls attention to the transforming power of the Holy Spirit upon the character of God's children.

This distinction played an important role at the time of the Reformation. The Roman Catholic Church, in the opinion of the Reformers, confused these two doctrines by insisting that justification "is not remission of sins merely, but also the sanctification and renewal of the inward man" (Decrees of the Council of Trent, Sixth Session, 1547, ch. VII). In contrast, the Reformers emphasized that the two doctrines, although inseparable, must be distinguished. Calvin argued that, to be sure, these two elements of God's saving act cannot be torn into parts any more than Christ can be torn. "Whomever, therefore, God receives into grace, on them he at the same time bestows the spirit of adoption, by whose power he remakes them to his own image. But if the brightness of the sun cannot be separated from its heat, shall we therefore say that the earth is warmed by its light, or lighted by its heat?" (*Institutes of the Christian Religion*, 3.11.6, tr. F. L. Battles). In short, then, justification is a once-for-all, declarative act of God as Judge, whereas sanctification is a progressive change in the character of the person justified (this distinction, too, is qualified below).

One more element in the definition requires comment, namely, the statement that "we are made partakers of his holiness." A complete survey of what the Bible has to say about sanctification is not possible here, since practically the whole of Scripture addresses this issue in one way or another. One central theme in that teaching, however, must be emphasized: "You shall be holy as I am holy" (Lv 11:45; 1 Pt 1:16; cf. Mt 5:48). According to the Westminster Shorter Catechism (1647), by sanctification "we are renewed in the whole man after the image of God" (Question 34; see Col 3:10). Nothing can be more crucial to our view of sanctification than this truth. The standard of holiness is complete conformity to Christ's image (Rom 8:29); anything less than that is a lowering of the scriptural standard and thus a dilution of the doctrine. The definition above, however, implies that Christ is more than our pattern: he himself provides his holiness for those united with him—he *is* our sanctification (1 Cor 1:30).

Definitive Sanctification. The *progressive* nature of our sanctification is explicit in many passages, particularly Paul's statement that Christians are transformed "from glory to glory" into the Lord's image (2 Cor 3:18; see also Rom 12:1,2; Phil 3:14; Heb 6:1; 2 Pt 3:18). Moreover, the numerous commands found in Scripture imply that the Christian experiences growth.

At the same time, however, a number of expressions in Scripture force qualification of the previous statements. For example, Paul frequently refers to Christians as "saints," that is, "holy ones" (Rom 1:7; Eph 1:1; etc.), and this language suggests that sanctification is already the possession of believers. In fact, Paul specifically says that the Corinthian Christians "have been sanctified" (1 Cor 1:2), and he even coordinates sanctification with washing (= regeneration?) and justification as though all three elements had taken place at the same time (6:11). Perhaps more impressive is the apostle's declaration that Christians have *died* to sin (Rom 6:2). One can hardly think of a more powerful figure than death, suggesting as it does a permanent, irrevocable dissolution of the believer's relationship with sin; indeed, Paul goes on to declare that sin will no longer master us (v 14).

It goes without saying, of course, that these passages do not teach absolute perfection for every Christian upon conversion. Such an interpretation would bring us into conflict with the clear teaching of Scripture as a whole. Furthermore, one should note that the Corinthian "saints" were marked by woeful immaturity (1 Cor 3:1–3; 6:8; 11:17–22, etc.).

How then should these passages be interpreted? Some writers have suggested that Paul is speaking of "potential" sanctification; that is, although our relationship with sin has not been *actually* severed, God has given us what we need for that to take place. There is an element of truth in this formulation, but it

hardly does justice, by itself, to the force of Paul's language. Coming somewhat closer to an adequate explanation is to speak of "positional" sanctification. According to this view, Paul is only speaking in *judicial* terms regarding our status before God. One should certainly recognize a judicial element in Paul's discussion (Rom 6:7 uses the word "justified"), but if that is all that is said, then it suggests that Romans 6 simply restates the doctrine of justification—a very doubtful conclusion. Much more satisfactory is the view of John Murray, who argues that Paul's teaching contains both a judicial element—God has executed judgment on sin with a view to man's deliverance—and an actual, experiential reference. One may indeed say that for *all* Christians "there is a once-for-all definitive and irreversible breach with the realm in which sin reigns" (*Collected Writings*, vol. 2, p. 229).

What all of this means is that the earlier statements need modifying by introducing a new distinction between *definitive* and *progressive* sanctification. At first sight the distinction may appear unnecesssary or unhelpful. Someone might argue that "definitive sanctification" looks too much like justification because of its judicial character (particularly since justification already includes the imputation of Christ's righteousness to the believer) and too much like regeneration, which already seems to account for the initial renewal of the individual's character. Nevertheless, there are good grounds for accepting the distinction, which impresses upon one the multifaceted richness of God's redemptive work on behalf of believers. In particular, to recognize the truth of definitive sanctification provides a fundamentally important perspective on both the relationship of Christ's work to the believer's experience, and the nature of that experience itself.

The first of these two issues relates to Paul's statement that man has died *with Christ* (Rom 6:8). What could that possibly mean? Paul is here making clear reference to a past, objective, nonrepeatable event: Christ's own death and resurrection. Further, he writes that Christians (even though not yet born when Christ died) participated in that redemptive-historical event. Whatever intellectual difficulties may arise from such unusual statements, the clarity of Paul's language cannot be compromised: by virtue of man's corporate union with Christ, man was directly involved with him in his death and resurrection. It seems unnecessary, however, to think exclusively in such historical terms, for Paul is also appealing to the subjective experience of the Christian; what Christ accomplished with his death and resurrection the Holy Spirit applies to believers at their conversion (note Eph 2:4–7). The significance of this point is that Christ's redemptive work is as clearly linked to man's sanctification as it is to man's justification. People need to become sensitive to the power of this truth. Just as the atonement obtained man's forgiveness, *so did it accomplish man's sanctification,* both of which blessings are appropriated at once through faith.

In the second place, however, it should be noted that to recognize the truth of definitive sanctification is to apprehend a new and glorious dimension in the believer's experience itself. If it is true that Christians *actually* severed their relationship with sin, that sin *has* been dethroned in their lives, then they may be certain of ultimate victory, no matter how discouraging or even hopeless some of their failures may appear (Phil 1:6). Indeed, it should be understood that progressive sanctification itself is built on definitive sanctification; in other words, that the *commands* to an obedient walk have their ground on the *fact* that one has been made obedient. Theologians often speak of the Christian tension between the "already" and the "not yet." While that tension accounts for much spiritual frustration, it also provides all the necessary encouragement: if Christ has truly destroyed the power of sin over men, then men hardly have an excuse to sin. "Set your minds on things above, not on earthly things. *For* you died, and your life is now hidden with Christ in God" (Col 3:2,3 NIV).

Progressive Sanctification. *Historical Survey.* Although all Christian groups recognize the need to become transformed by the renewing of the mind (Rom 12:2), considerable differences are found among them regarding specific issues. The Reformers, generally speaking, held to what some call a "pessimistic" view of personal sanctification. This perspective is clearly reflected in the Westminster Confession of Faith (1647), which states that sanctification "is imperfect in this life; there abideth still some remnants of corruption in every part, whence ariseth a continual and irreconcilable war" within the believer (XIII.ii). Although the confession goes on to emphasize the overcoming power of the Spirit, some Christians believe that its basic thrust obscures the need and possibility of spiritual victory.

To some extent, the teachings of John Wesley (1703–91) may be viewed as a reaction to the usual Calvinistic and Lutheran formulations. Strongly influenced by the Pietistic movement of his day, Wesley paid much attention to the experiential side of Christianity and eventually formulated, though not with great consistency, the doctrine that "entire sanctification" is possible in this life. During the 19th

century, interest in the possibility of perfection (not understood in an absolute sense, however) spread to many Christian circles. According to some, perfection resulted from the eradication of sin; according to others, spiritual victory was gained by counteracting the sin that remains even in the Christian's heart. The latter approach became characteristic of the so-called Victorious Life Movement. These various "perfectionist" groups were subjected to a searching criticism by the Princeton theologian, Benjamin B. Warfield (1851–1921). The debate has continued, though not as vigorously, during this century.

The Agency in Sanctification. Much of the controversy focuses on the human role in sanctification. While all Christians agree that holiness would be impossible without God's help, it is difficult to define precisely how that truth affects one's own activity. In the Roman Catholic tradition so much stress has been placed on the cleansing power of baptism and on the meritorious character of good works that one may rightly question whether the significance of divine grace is not thereby ignored. (A similar criticism can be leveled at certain strands of Arminian theology.) At the other extreme stand some exponents of the Victorious Life Movement, whose stress on "let go and let God" (a slogan that has some value if properly used) sometimes suggest that believers remain completely passive in sanctification.

No passage of Scripture is more relevant to this issue than Philippians 2:12,13, where Paul juxtaposes the command for one to work out one's own salvation with the declaration that it is God who provides the spiritual strength necessary for the task. It may be tempting to emphasize the first part of the statement so as to ignore the fundamental significance of the second; or else to become so arrested by Paul's stress (here and elsewhere) on divine grace that the weight of personal responsibility is overlooked. The apostle, however, appears to have deliberately and carefully preserved a fine balance between these two truths.

Sanctification requires discipline, concentration, and effort, as is clear by the many exhortations of Scripture, especially those where the Christian life is described with such figures as running and fighting (1 Cor 9:24–27; Eph 6:10–17). On the other hand, men must always resist the temptation to assume that they in effect sanctify themselves, that spiritual power comes from within them and that they may therefore rely on their own strength. This is a difficult tension, though no more puzzling than the paradox of prayer ("Why pray when God, who knows our needs and who is all-wise and sovereign, will always do what is best anyway?"). Yet perhaps the real "secret" of holiness consists precisely in learning to keep that balance: relying thoroughly on *God* as the true agent in sanctification while faithfully discharging one's *personal* responsibility. "The horse is made ready for the day of battle, but victory rests with the Lord" (Prv 21:31).

The "How" of Sanctification. Even if one agrees that God alone is the author of sanctification and yet that one must remain active in it, many questions remain as to the actual process involved. Only a few of these questions can be treated here.

For example, does God's work consist only in providing the power to *suppress* one's evil impulses or does the Holy Spirit actually *eliminate* (by gradual "eradication") those impulses? The final answer to this question will depend largely on one's understanding of man's nature, but some preliminary comments may be in order. One may argue that the notion of suppression or counteraction by itself does not do justice to the strong scriptural statements on the *transformation* which the Christian undergoes (Rom 12:2; 2 Cor 3:18; Col 3:10). The doctrine of definitive sanctification suggests instead that the Spirit begins at conversion an actual renewal of the Christian's nature. Acceptance of this viewpoint, however, does not rule out the need for suppression. To begin with, godly and mature Christians testify to the presence of old desires. Further, one dares not suggest (as might be tempting if the aspect of elimination is overstressed) that one's evil actions are wholly uncontrollable, on the grounds that the Spirit has not yet sufficiently altered the source of those actions. It would appear, then, that a judicious balance is needed between these two aspects of the doctrine.

Second, considerable disagreement surrounds the question of the place of God's *Law* in sanctification, and here again a decision is not possible apart from a detailed study of much broader issues. Briefly, however, some theologians, particularly those in the Lutheran tradition, have been greatly concerned with the danger of confusing law and gospel and thus reintroducing legalism into the Christian life. Now one ought most surely to heed this warning: Christians have been absolutely freed from the enslaving power of the Law (Gal 3:13,23–25), so that obedience to God cannot find its motive in a spirit of terror and servility but must arise from a heart full of confidence, love, and gratitude. Nevertheless, God's Law is but an expression of his will, which one is certainly required to perform (Mt 7:21; Mk 3:35); further, it must be remembered that the Gospels and the Letters are full of specific commands. Christ's work was not intended to displace the divine Law but rather to write it

within men's hearts so that men might walk according to God's statutes (Jer 31:31–34; Ez 36:26,27). Even the Lutheran standards recognize the so-called "third use of the Law," namely, that although believers have been "set free from the curse and constraint of the Law, they are not, nevertheless, in that account without Law, inasmuch as the Son of God redeemed them for the very reason that they might meditate on the Law of God day and night, and continually exercise themselves in the keeping thereof" (The Formula of Concord, 1576, Article VI).

A third issue concerns whether or not sanctification is tied to a *crisis* (or a series of crises) in the Christian experience. It is generally admitted that the Scriptures do *not* explicitly teach the doctrine of a "second blessing," although some passages, it is claimed, do allow for such a teaching or one very similar (note J. Sidlow Baxter, *His Deeper Work Within Us*, reprinted in *Christian Holiness: Restudied and Restated*). The testimony of many Christian leaders is used to support this view, but opponents argue that evidence is lacking of a similar experience in the lives of many others. Although the doctrine of a "second blessing" raises some serious theological problems, one may gladly recognize that spiritual crises (and in some cases one major crisis) form an important part in the experience of most, if not all, Christians. It seems unnecessary, however, to affirm that some such crisis is a prerequisite of true sanctification or to suggest that *gradual* growth does not play a fundamental role in it.

Finally, the function of the *church* in the process of sanctification may be briefly noted. It is very easy to think of Christian holiness in exclusively individualistic terms. Yet the preaching of God's Word, baptism, the celebration of the Lord's Supper, the acts of corporate prayer, and the fellowship and exhortation of the Christian community—all of these elements are indispensable to biblical sanctification. According to Paul, the maturity that belongs to the fullness of Christ comes about by the mutual strengthening of each part of the body (Eph 4:11–16).

The Extent and Time of Sanctification. All Christians agree that the ultimate goal of sanctification is moral perfection (Phil 1:6; 1 Thes 5:23), but differences exist regarding *when* perfection may be received, whether during this life or at death. Much (but not all) of the discussion centers on Romans 7:14–25. Does that passage describe the frustrations that all Christians should expect in this life? Theologians in the Wesleyan tradition affirm that Romans 8, not Romans 7, constitutes the model, so that "entire sanctification" may indeed be experienced before death (see G. A. Turner, *The Vision*

Which Transforms). They do not mean by this absolute sinlessness, but rather a genuine deliverance from *conscious* sinning (a theme which is also frequent in the Victorious Life Movement). Critics argue that such "perfection" can only be had by a lowering of God's absolute standard; and, to be sure, it cannot be forgotten that unqualified conformity to Christ is the goal from which one must never deviate.

The theological disagreement regarding this issue should not be played down as unimportant. Nevertheless, one occassionally receives the impression that the difference between some writers is largely one of semantics. In other words, they agree basically on the extent to which sanctification is possible in the present life but disagree as to whether the expressions "entire" and "perfect" are appropriate to describe it. Perhaps the disagreement is one of attitude. One writer feels that Christians are not sufficiently sensitive to the greatness of sin and to the holiness of God and so his basic approach is "pessimistic." Another writer feels burdened by the dangers of spiritual defeatism and so he presents an "optimistic" picture. More than likely both kinds of emphases are needed to prevent imbalance. It may even be worth considering whether Paul himself intended to describe every Christian's experience from two different perspectives in Romans 7 and 8.

Summary. It seems significant that most of this discussion has focused on the tensions present in the doctrine of sanctification. It has been necessary to give due weight both to the objective-historic perspective and to the subjective-experiential, the judicial and the transforming, the definitive and the progressive; it has been necessary to recognize both the divine agency and the human task, the elimination of sin and its suppression, freedom from the Law and submission to it, the individual and the corporate concerns, the pessimistic and the optimistic outlooks.

No doubt these "paradoxes" are an important reason why Christians have disagreed on this fundamental doctrine. Is it possible that the whole program of Christian sanctification can be reduced to the goal of learning to keep all these tensions in balance? One may say, without exaggeration, that perhaps all perversions of the doctrine have resulted from a failure to do precisely that. MOISES SILVA

See HOLINESS; JUSTIFICATION; SPIRITUAL GIFTS; FAITH.

Bibliography. G.C. Berkouwer, *Faith and Sanctification;* R.N. Flew, *The Idea of Perfection in Christian Theology;* P.T. Forsyth, *Christian Perfection;* W.E. Hulme, *The Dynamics of Sanctification;* R. Lovelace, *Dynamics of Spiritual Life;* D.C. Needham, *Birthright;* A.W. Pink, *Sanctification;* W. Romaine, *The Life, Walk and Triumph of Faith;* J.C. Ryle, *Holiness.*

Sanctuary. Translation of two Hebrew words, *kodesh* and *mikdosh*, both of which are derived from the verb "to be clean" and/or "to be holy." It appears approximately 60 times in Exodus, Leviticus, and Numbers where the building, moving, and initial use of the tabernacle is reported. Places of revelation, sacrifice, and worship are referred to in Deuteronomy but not by the term *sanctuary*. The term appears over 60 times in Ezekiel, Daniel, and postexilic writings because of the importance the sanctuary had in the life of Israel during and after the exile.

Sanctuary refers to the place where God appeared and/or dwelt as indicated by the presence of the ark. God's Word was kept there and issued forth from it. There God's people gathered for sacrifice, for hearing the covenant word, for worship and prayer, and for the celebration of the major feasts.

The patriarchs had places of worship (Gn 26:24,25; 28:16–22) but no actual sanctuary. The first reference to sanctuary (Ex 15:17) speaks of it as a symbol of God's dwelling among his people and ruling over them from within it. The tabernacle, moved from place to place, was the central sanctuary until the time when Solomon built the temple in Jerusalem. It must be emphatically stressed that God's people were to have one central sanctuary (Dt 12:4–7; 16:5–8). More than one sanctuary was permitted so they could, without long-distance traveling, gather for eating and worship (12:15–25). The one and the same God, however, was to be worshiped at these various places. But the Israelites also made use of pagan sanctuaries, which was considered an abomination (vv 1–3,29,30).

The NT refers to the OT sanctuary as a type of a foreshadowing of God's eternal dwelling with and among his people (Heb 8:6; 9:1–14).

See TABERNACLE, TEMPLE.

Sandal. *See* FASHION AND DRESS.

Sand Lizard. *See* ANIMALS (SKINK).

Sanhedrin. Supreme judicial council of Judaism with 71 members, located in Jerusalem. It figures prominently in the passion narrative of the Gospels during Jesus' trial and appears again in Acts as the judicial court which investigates and persecutes the growing Christian church.

History. The history of the Sanhedrin is difficult to reconstruct. Jewish tradition recorded in the Mishna views it as originating with Moses and his council of 70, but this is doubtful (Mishna tractate *Sanhedrin* 1:6; cf. Nm 11:16). These were probably informal gatherings of tribal elders (1 Kgs 8:1; 2 Kgs 23:1).

The likely origin of the Sanhedrin is to be found in the postexilic period, when those who reorganized Israel without a king made the ancient ruling families the basis of authority. The legislative assembly that emerged was a union of the nobility of the land and the priestly aristocracy (see Ezr 5:5; Neh 2:16). The influence of this council increased due to the relative freedom enjoyed under the Persians.

The advent of Hellenism in Israel in the 4th century BC affirmed this government. Hellenistic cities commonly possessed democratic assemblies and a council. Jerusalem hosted an aristocratic council which was given its appropriate Greek title, *Gerousia*. This council is first noted by Josephus, who records the decree of Antiochus III after his seizure of Jerusalem (*Antiq.* 12.3.3). Yet even though the political climate shifted drastically, the council still remained in force. Judas Maccabeus expelled the old line of elders and installed another hereditary rulership stemming from the Hasmonean families. Thus the Gerousia continued as a council of the nobility. But in the 1st century BC, as the tensions between Sadducees and Pharisees were pulling apart the fabric of Judaism, the council underwent a transformation. From the time of Alexandra (76–67 BC), scribes of Pharisee persuasion entered the council. Thereafter the Gerousia consisted of a compromise: aristocratic nobility on the one hand (both lay and priestly) and the popular Pharisees on the other.

The Romans left the council intact but more carefully defined the limits of its jurisdiction. As Judaism lost its self-government, the council lost much legislative and political power. Rome appointed the true powers of the land. For instance, Herod the Great began his rule in severe conflict with the old aristocracy, and in the end executed most of the Sanhedrin members (*Antiq.* 14.9.4). The prefects appointed the high priests and, as a symbol of control, from AD 6–36 they kept the priests' vestments in the Antonia fortress.

The name "Sanhedrin" [Gk. *sunedrion*, from *sun*, together; plus *hedra*, seat] occurs for the first time in the reign of Herod the Great (*Antiq.* 14.9.3–5). This is the term used throughout the NT (22 times) along with "the elders" (Lk 22:66; Acts 22:5) and "gerousia" (Acts 5:21). The Mishna provides still more titles: The Great Tribunal (*San* 11:2), the Great Sanhedrin (*San* 1:6), and the Sanhedrin of the 71 (*Shebuoth* 2:2).

After the great war of AD 70 when the final vestiges of Jewish autonomy were destroyed by Rome, the Sanhedrin reconvened in Jamnia. Its power, however, was only theoretical (addressing religious issues primarily) and the Romans gave it little consideration.

Character. Little is known about the procedure for admission into the Sanhedrin, but because the council had aristocratic roots (and was probably not truly democratic) appointments were probably made from among the priests, leading scribes, and lay nobility. The Mishna stipulates that the sole test of membership was rabbinic learning along with true Israelite descent (*San* 4:4). The council had 71 members (*San* 1:6) divided into the following three categories: the high priests, the elders, and the scribes.

The High Priests. Usually from Sadducean backgrounds, these were the most powerful men of the Sanhedrin. Some scholars believe that they comprised an executive council of 10 wealthy and distinguished citizens on the pattern of several Greek and Roman cities. Tiberias in Galilee, for instance, was ruled by such a board (*Life*, 13, 57) and Josephus can refer to a body of "the ten foremost men" (*Antiq.* 20.8.11; cf. Acts 4:6). One was the captain of the temple who supervised temple proceedings and was commander of the temple guard (5:24,26). Others served as treasurers who controlled the wages of priests and workers and monitored the vast amount of money coming through the temple. Income came from sacrifices and market taxes and the payroll included as many as 18,000 men during Herod's reconstruction of the temple. There was a president of the Sanhedrin who also headed this council and was called "The High Priest" (*Antiq.* 20.10.5; *Apion* 2:23). In the NT he is a leading figure: Caiaphas ruled in Jesus' day (Mt 26:3) and Ananias in Paul's day (Acts 23:2). In Luke 3:2 and Acts 4:6, Annas is termed a high priest, but his title is emeritus, since his reign ended in AD 15.

The Elders. This was a major category and represented the priestly and financial aristocracy in Judea. Distinguished laymen, such as Joseph of Arimathea (Mk 15:43), shared the conservative views of the Sadducees and gave the assembly the diversity of a modern parliament.

The Scribes. These were the most recent members of the Sanhedrin. Mostly Pharisees, they were professional lawyers trained in theology, jurisprudence, and philosophy. They were organized in guilds and often followed celebrated teachers. One famous Sanhedrin scribe, Gamaliel, appears in the NT (Acts 5:34) and was the rabbinic scholar who instructed Paul (22:3).

In Jesus' Day. The domain of the Sanhedrin was formally restricted to Judea, but there was a *defacto* influence that affected Galilee and even Damascus (cf. Acts 9:2; 22:5). The council was chiefly concerned to arbitrate matters of Jewish law when disagreements arose (*San* 11:2). In all cases, its decision was final.

It prosecuted charges of blasphemy, as in the cases of Jesus (Mt 26:65) and Stephen (Acts 6:12–14), and participated in criminal justice as well.

It is still undecided whether or not the Sanhedrin had the power of capital punishment. Philo seems to indicate that violations to the temple could be prosecuted in the Roman period (*Leg. to Caius*, 39). This may explain the deaths of Stephen (Acts 7:58–60) and James (*Antiq.* 20.9.1). At any rate Gentiles caught trespassing the temple precincts were warned about an automatic death penalty. On the other hand, the NT and the Talmud disagree with this. In the trial of Jesus the authorities are compelled to involve Pilate who alone can put Jesus to death (Jn 18:31). According to the Talmud, the Sanhedrin lost this privilege "forty years before the destruction of the temple" (Jer Talmud, *Sanhedrin*, I 18a, 34; VII 24b).

Judicial Procedure. Despite the serious irregularities of Jesus' trial, the formal procedures of Sanhedrin law describe a court that was fair and exceedingly concerned about the miscarriage of justice. Unfortunately, the procedural notes in the Mishna only address guidelines for lesser courts (Sanhedrins with 23 members), but it can be reasonably conjectured that similar rules applied to the Great Sanhedrin of 71. In sections four and five of the Mishna tractate *Sanhedrin*, these guidelines are carefully set forth.

The Sanhedrin sat in semicircular rows so that members could view one another. Two clerks sat at either end taking notes and recording votes. Facing the assembly sat three rows of students who were usually disciples of leading scribes. The accused stood in the middle facing the elders. He was required to show abject humility: he was dressed in a black robe as if in mourning and wore his hair dishevelled (*Antiq.* 14.9.4). After questioning, he was dismissed and deliberations were private.

The procedures for capital cases illustrate the concern for fairness. The defense would be heard first and then the accusations. An elder who had spoken *for* the defense could not then speak against the accused. Students could only speak *for* but never *against* the accused (but in noncapital cases they could do either). Members stood to vote, beginning with the youngest. Aquittal required a simple majority, but condemnation demanded a majority of two.

In noncapital cases the trial was heard during the daytime and the verdict could be given at night. In capital cases, both trial and verdict were during the day and thus open to more public scrutiny. In noncapital cases any verdict could be reached the same day. In capital cases, the verdict of guilt (which was immediately followed by execution) had to be postponed one day because its consequences were irreversible. Hence these trials were not to be held on the eve of the sabbath or a festival day (*San* 4:1).

The trial of Jesus as recorded in the Gospels shows many departures from the usual pattern of Sanhedrin justice. Certainly dominant personalities or interest groups might be able to abbreviate or avoid altogether the usual procedures. If the trial narratives in the Gospels are exhaustive, it seems clear that a miscarriage of justice is evidenced in Jesus' arrest, interrogation, and death.   GARY M. BURGE

See HELLENISTIC JUDAISM; JUDAISM; COURTS AND TRIALS; JERUSALEM COUNCIL.

Sansannah. One of 29 cities at the southern extremity of the land inherited by the sons of Judah (Jos 15:31). It is possibly the same city as Hazar-susah mentioned in a parallel description of the territory allotted to Simeon within Judah's inheritance (19:5).

Saph. Descendant of the giants, slain by Sibbechai the Hushathite (one of David's warriors) at Gad in a battle between Israel and Philistia (2 Sm 21:18); alternately called Sippai (1 Chr 20:4).

Saphir. KJV spelling of Shaphir, a place mentioned in Micah 1:11.

See SHAPHIR.

Sapphira. Member of the Jerusalem church and wife of Ananias (Acts 5:1).

See ANANIAS #3.

Sapphire. *See* MINERALS, METALS, AND PRECIOUS STONES.

Sara. KJV rendering of Sarah, Abraham's wife, in Hebrews 1:11 and 1 Peter 3:6.

See SARAH #1.

Sarah. 1. Wife of Abraham whose name was originally Sarai (Gn 11:29). Her name was changed to Sarah (princess) when she was promised that she would bear a son and become the mother of nations and kings (17:15,16). Sarah was both the wife and half sister of Abraham (20:12).

Sarah accompanied Abraham in his journey from Ur of the Chaldees to Haran and eventually into the land of Canaan (Gn 11:31; 12:5). She remained barren for much of her marriage (v 30). When God promised Abraham that he would make of him a great nation (12:2) and that the land of Canaan would be given to his seed (v 7), Sarah was still barren.

After 10 years had passed (cf. Gn 12:4; 16:16) and Sarah continued without children, she gave her Egyptian slave Hagar to Abraham as a concubine. Hagar conceived and bore a son, Ishmael (16:3,4). God promised that a nation would come from Ishmael (17:20), but indicated that he was not to be the child of the promise (v 21). Sarah herself was to be the mother of this child (vv 19–21; 18:10–14) even though she laughed when the birth was predicted. The fulfillment of this prediction took place with the birth of Isaac (21:2,3) when Sarah was 90 years old, 25 years after the original promise of a seed to Abraham (17:17; 21:5).

When famine forced Abraham and Sarah to journey down into Egypt shortly after their entrance into Canaan, Sarah was represented to the Egyptians as Abraham's sister. This resulted in Sarah's being taken into the harem of Pharaoh because of her great beauty (Gn 12:11,14), and Abraham's being well treated and rewarded by the Egyptians instead of being killed. God intervened to protect the marriage of Abraham and Sarah by plaguing the house of Pharaoh to force Sarah's release. A similar tactic was followed by Abraham and Sarah on another occasion in Gerar (ch 20), where she was taken into the household of Abimmelech the king of Gerar. Again God protected Sarah, preserved her as the mother of the promised seed, and prevented any suspicion or doubt concerning who was the father of Isaac. Significantly Isaac was born not long after this incident (21:1–5), his birth having been promised about a year earlier (17:21; 18:10–14).

Sarah died at the age of 127 and was buried in the cave at Machpelah which Abraham had purchased from Ephron the Hittite (Gn 23).

Apart from the Book of Genesis, Sarah is referred to in the OT only in Isaiah 51:2. Reference is made to her in the NT in Romans 4:19; 9:9; Hebrews 11:11 (KJV Sara); 1 Peter 3:6 (KJV Sara) and Galatians 4:21–31, although in the Galatians text she is not mentioned by name.

See BARRENNESS; ABRAHAM; PATRIARCHS, PERIOD OF THE.

2. KJV spelling of Serah, Asher's daughter, in Numbers 26:46.

See SERAH.

Sarai. Original name for Sarah, Abraham's wife (Gn 11:29).

See SARAH #1.

Saraph. Shelah's son from Judah's tribe. Saraph ruled in Moab and later returned to Lehem. Lehem may refer either to his own countrymen or to a geographical location. The reading of the Hebrew text is unclear (1 Chr 4:22).

An American expedition in the 1910s set upright some Roman columns at the temple of Artemis in Sardis, one of the largest Greek temples yet excavated.

Sardine Stone. KJV form of carnelian in Revelation 4:3.

See MINERALS, METALS, AND PRECIOUS STONES.

Sardis. Important city in the Roman province of Asia, once the capital of the ancient kingdom of Lydia. It lay astride great highways linking it to the coastal regions to the west and to eastern Asia Minor. It was a cultural, religious, and commercial center. Under King Croesus (c. 560–547/6 BC) its wealth became legendary. In his day gold and silver coinage came into use. The geography and topography of Sardis were advantageous. The Pactolus River lay on its eastern side and flowed eventually into the Hermus River. The broad ridge of Mt Tmolus springing from the central plateau dominates the Hermus Valley to its north and a series of steep spurs jut out into the plain, offering almost impregnable strongholds. Sardis lay on one of these. The site of Sardis proper lay 1500 feet above the plain and assumed a position of great importance from the earliest days of the Lydian kingdom (13th century BC), although it was occupied in earlier times; the lower city spread to the valley floor. The king lived in the great acropolis which became a place of refuge in time of war.

Under Croesus, Lydia reached its peak, bringing Greek colonies to the west like Ephesus and Smyrna under its control. However, the Persian ruler Cyrus besieged the city, and captured it by scaling the cliffs of the citadel under cover of darkness. In 334 BC the city surrendered to Alexander the Great, who left a garrison on the acropolis. Following Alexander's death, Sardis changed hands several times. It was controlled first by Antigonus, then by the Seleucid rulers, and then by Pergamum which had broken away from the Seleucids. When Antiochus III (231–187 BC) sought to restore the city to his rule the lower city was burned (216 BC) and the citadel entered (214 BC). After the defeat of Antiochus III by Pergamum and the Romans, Sardis was placed under Pergamum's jurisdiction until 133 BC. Later it became a Roman administrative center and, although enjoying considerable prosperity during the first three centuries AD, it never again held the prominence of earlier centuries. It was overlooked in AD 26 when the cities of Asia Minor vied with one another for the honor of building a second temple for the Caesar cult. A great earthquake destroyed the city in AD 17 and Emperor Tiberius assisted in its rebuilding on the valley floor. Christianity took root here before the end of the first century, and later included a bishopric. The NT letter to "the angel of the church in Sardis" (Rv 1:11; 3:1–6) gives insight into the condition of the church at that time. After the Arab invasion of AD 716 the city declined. Today the small village of Sart preserves its name.

Extensive excavations in recent years have identified many Roman public buildings: a theater, a temple of Artemis, a gymnasium, and an impressive late Jewish synagogue, suggesting that it became an important center for the Jewish Diaspora.

Sardite. KJV form of Seredite, a member of Sered's family, in Numbers 26:26.

See SERED, SEREDITE.

Sardius. KJV form of carnelian in Ezekiel 28:13.

See MINERALS, METALS, AND PRECIOUS STONES.

Sardonyx. KJV form of onyx in Revelation 21:20.

See MINERALS, METALS, AND PRECIOUS STONES.

Sarepta. KJV form of Zarephath, a Phoenician town, in Luke 4:26.

See ZAREPHATH.

Sargon. Assyrian monarch from 722–705 BC whose military campaigns are historically

Statue of a guardian deity from the palace of Sargon II (722–705 BC) at Khorsabad, Iraq.

well documented. Excavations have revealed his palace at what was probably Nineveh as well as an incompleted palace at Khorsabad. Sargon II bore the name of an illustrious conqueror who lived and fought some 1500 years earlier (Sargon I of Agade). His true identity has not been easily discerned. Previous generations, thinking that his name was an "alias," incorrectly identified him as Shalmaneser V (727–722 BC), Sennacherib (705–681 BC), or Esar-haddon (699–681 BC).

The only place in the Bible where Sargon is specifically mentioned is Isaiah 20:1. Despite warnings of the prophet Isaiah against placing any trust in Egypt (10:9), Judah was moving contrary to her best interests by considering just such an alliance. But in 713 BC, the Philistine city of Ashdod rebelled against Assyria thereby instigating a campaign by the forces of Sargon against this strategically important metropolis. A man named Yamani sought to secure support from Egypt, Ethiopia, and even Judah, in mounting an effective coalition against the might of Sargon. However, in 711 BC Ashdod was subjugated by Sargon's army under his delegated official "the Tartan" (20:1). Egypt failed to rally behind Ashdod when the Assyrians laid siege to it and the Ethiopians actually handed Yamani over to the Assyrian host. Sargon's successful quelling of the uprising at Ashdod removed any false hopes the Judahites might have been nurturing with regard to a winning alliance against Assyria. Judah was left unscathed by the Assyrians and in a better position to realistically evaluate herself. Sargon's activities thus served to reinforce the warning of Isaiah that trusting in the arm of flesh would ultimately bring nothing but disillusionment.

Sargon finished the task of conquering Samaria, begun by his predecessor, Shalmaneser V. Apparently, Shalmaneser V had besieged the northern kingdom of Israel for three years (2 Kgs 17:5,6) and had virtually completed that campaign when he died. While other military victories earmark the public life of Sargon, many of his battles were indecisive. A large part of his reign was spent suppressing rebellions and handling major domestic problems. He was finally killed on the battlefield in a remote area known as Tabal. Even before his untimely death, Sargon's popularity at home had diminished, perhaps owing to his adoption of a conciliatory attitude toward Babylonia. Sargon's son, Sennacherib, succeeded him in 705 BC.

See ASSYRIA, ASSYRIANS.

Sarid. Town located in the region of Zebulun near its southern border, situated between Maralah to the west and Chisloth-tabor to the east (Jos 19:10,12). Some suggest that this town is the same as Tell Shadud—a town near the Valley of Jezreel.

Saron. KJV spelling of Sharon, the large coastal plain in northern Palestine, in Acts 9:35.

See SHARON #1.

Sarsechim. Personal name or title of an official who participated with Nebuchadnezzar and the Chaldean army in conquering Jerusalem. Some have questioned the present word division of the Babylonian names in Jeremiah 39:3. Perhaps Sarsechim Rabsaris is identifiable with Nebushazban Rabsaris in Jeremiah 39:13.

See NEBUSHAZBAN, NEBUSHASBAN.

Saruch. KJV rendering of Serug, an ancestor of Jesus, in Luke 3:35.

See SERUG.

Satan. Spirit being who opposes God and seeks to frustrate his plans and lead his people into rebellion.

Satan is seldom mentioned in the OT. The roots of the later idea are expressed in the image of the great monster God subdues (probably in creating the world as in Babylonian creation stories, called Rahab or Leviathan, Is 27:1, Jb 9:13), in the story of "the serpent" who tempts Eve (Gn 3:1), and in the picture of an angel who acts as the heavenly prosecutor (Jb 1:6–12; 2:1–7; Zec 3:1,2). Only this last being is called "the satan" or "the accuser," and there is nothing in the context to indicate that the angel is evil (although in Zechariah God's grace overturns the valid accusation). It is not until the late OT period that Satan appears as a tempter: in 1 Chronicles 21:1, the story of 2 Samuel 24:1 is retold with Satan (used for the first time as a proper name) substituted for God and pictured as an evil figure. The OT, then, has no developed doctrine of Satan, but contains the raw material from which the later doctrine came. (Some people see Lucifer of Is 14:12 as a reference to Satan, but the context is clearly referring to the king of Babylon; it is therefore unlikely that any reference to Satan is intended.)

The Jews further developed the idea of Satan during the intertestamental period, also calling him Belial, Mastema, and Sammael. Three differing conceptions appear. First, the Satan of the OT reappears in the roles of tempting people, of accusing them in heaven before God, and of hindering God's saving plan (Jubilees 11:5; 17:16; As Moses 17; 1 Enoch 40:7). Second, the Dead Sea Scrolls present Satan (Belial) as the leader of the evil forces and attacker of the righteous. This development was probably influenced by the evil god of Zoroastrian religion, but unlike the Zoroastrian idea the scrolls never present two gods, but one God who has created *both* Belial *and* the Prince of Light (who is sure to win in the end for God is with him). Third, Satan is often identified with stories in the OT from which his name was originally absent: he lusted after Eve and therefore caused the fall

(Wis Sol 2:24), he controls the angels who fell in Genesis 6:1–4 (Jubilees 10:5–8; 19:28), or he is a fallen angel himself (2 Enoch 29:4). We see, then, a coming together of scattered OT ideas and themes under the title of Satan.

The NT does have a developed doctrine of Satan, and he comes with a whole list of names: Satan (Hebrew for "accuser"), devil (the Greek translation of Satan), Beliar, Beelzebul, the Adversary, the Dragon, the Enemy, the Serpent, the Tester, and the Wicked One. Satan is pictured as the ruler of a host of angels (Mt 25:41) and the controller of the world (Lk 4:6; Acts 26:18; 2 Cor 4:4), who especially governs all who are not Christians (Mk 4:15; Jn 8:44; Acts 13:10; Col 1:13). He is opposed to God and seeks to alienate all men from God; therefore he is a specially dangerous foe of Christians (Lk 8:33; 1 Cor 7:5; 1 Pt 5:8) who must steadfastly resist him and see through his cunning (2 Cor 2:11; Eph 6:11; Jas 4:7). Satan works his evil will by tempting persons (Jn 13:2; Acts 5:3), by hindering God's workers (1 Thes 2:18), by accusing Christians before God (Rv 12:10), and by controlling the evil persons who resist the gospel, (Rv 2:9,13 esp. the anti-Christ, 2 Thes 2:9; Rv 13:2).

Most importantly, however, the NT teaches us that this being who has been evil from the beginning (1 Jn 3:8) has now been bound and cast out of heaven through the ministry of Jesus (Lk 10:18; Rv 12). While Satan is still a dangerous enemy, Jesus himself prays for us and has given us the powerful weapons of prayer, faith, and his blood. Satan can still cause physical illness when allowed by God (2 Cor 12:7) and persons can be delivered over to him for chastening (1 Cor 5:5; 1 Tm 1:20), but that can be for our good in God's providence. Satan's end is sure (Rom 16:20; Rv 20:10).

See LUCIFER; ANGEL; DEMON, DEMON POSSESSION.

Bibliography. E. Langton, *Satan: A Portrait*; E. Lewis, *The Creator and the Adversary*; D.W. Pentecost, *Your Adversary the Devil*; W. Robinson, *The Devil and God*; J.B. Russell, *The Devil*; J.B. Russell, *Satan: The Early Christian Tradition*; F.A. Tatford, *The Prince of Darkness*.

Saton. Dry commodity measure equivalent to the OT seah equaling about one peck.

See WEIGHTS AND MEASURES.

Satrap. Governor who held jurisdiction over a number of provinces within the king's domain. This official represented the authority of the king in both civil and military matters, and supplied the means for maintaining the king's sovereignty over the whole empire. Satraps were listed among the high ranking officers of the Babylonian and Persian empires (Ezr 8:36; Est 3:12; 9:3 Dn 3:2,3,27; 6:1–7).

Satyr. Creature of uncertain identification, possibly referring to a demon, a goat, or a deity that resembles a goat.

See ANIMALS (GOAT).

Saul. Name meaning "asked", with the implication being "asked *of God.*" A name with a usage extending far back into prebiblical times, it is attested in third millennium texts from Tell Mardikh in Syria (ancient Ebla), and appears also to have been used in the second millennium in the city of Ugarit on the coast of Syria.

The name is also fairly common in the OT; in addition to the conventional spelling, it is sometimes spelled *Shaul* in English versions. Apart from King Saul, the most famous bearer of the name, three other persons called Saul are referred to in the OT, though little is known about them.

1. Saul, king of Edom, is mentioned in an ancient list of kings who ruled Edom (in Transjordan) in pre-Israelite times (Gn 36:37,38; 1 Chr 1:48,49; RSV Shaul) He is described as coming from "Rehoboth on the river"; although "the river" usually refers to the Euphrates, in this text it probably refers to a small river in the vicinity of Edom.

2. Saul, King of Israel, is the best known and documented person with this name in the OT. He was a member of the tribe of Benjamin, one of the smallest of the Israelite tribes, whose territory was located just north of the Canaanite city of Jerusalem. His father was Kish, son of Abiel, though little is known of him. Saul was born in Gibeah, a small town just a few miles north of Jerusalem in the hill country, and apart from his travels and military expeditions, Gibeah was Saul's hometown for his entire life. He was a married man with one wife, Ahinoam, and five children, three sons and two daughters. His best-known son, Jonathan, later served him in a senior military capacity; all Saul's sons died with him in battle (1 Sm 31:2). Of his

The mound of Gibeah, Saul's hometown.

two daughters, the best-known is Michal, the younger daughter, who married David.

The Soldier. Saul lived during a very critical period in the history of the Israelite tribes. Though the dates cannot be determined with any certainty, he lived during the latter half of the 11th century BC and probably ruled as king from about 1020–1000 BC. Before he became king, the Israelite tribes were on the verge of military collapse. The Philistines, a powerful military people, had settled along the Mediterranean coast; they were well established on the coast and planned to move eastward and take control of Palestine as a whole. In order to do this, they first had to eliminate the Israelites, who were settled in the hill country on the west of the Jordan, and also in Transjordan. The absence of any strong and permanent military authority among the Israelites meant that the Philistines were a grave military threat to the continued existence of Israel.

The immediate crisis, which was to contribute to Saul's rise to power, was a crushing defeat of the Israelite army by the Philistines at Ebenezer, in the vicinity of Aphek. The victory gave the Philistines more or less complete control of Israelite territories lying to the west of the Jordan; they attempted to maintain that control by establishing military garrisons throughout the country which they had captured. Israel, weakened by the Philistine defeat, became vulnerable to enemies on other borders. The nation of Ammon, situated to the east of the Israelites' land in Transjordan, attacked and laid siege to the town of Jabesh (1 Sm 11:1). Saul, summoning an army of volunteers, delivered the inhabitants of Jabesh and defeated the Ammonites. It was after this event that Saul became king. He had already been anointed a prince or leader among the people by Samuel; after his military success at Jabesh, he assumed the office formally at the sanctuary in Gilgal (v 15).

The defeat of the Ammonites provided a significant boost to Israelite morale, but it did not significantly change the military crisis and threat posed by the Philistines. Indeed, the location of Saul's appointment to kingship is significant. Gilgal, in the Jordan Valley near Jericho, was chosen partly because the earlier shrine of Shiloh was held by the Philistines. Gilgal was in one of the few areas remaining outside Philistine control. Hence, if Saul's kingship was to mean anything, he had to address the Philistine problem immediately; if he did not, there would be no Israel to rule.

Saul acted promptly. Although the precise historical details are difficult to reconstruct, a general view of Saul's anti-Philistine campaign is provided in the biblical text. He attacked garrisons at Gibeah, and later at Michmash, about four miles northeast of Gibeah. He had great success at Michmash, thanks in part to the military aid of his son Jonathan. The Philistines were routed and retreated from that portion of the hill country. Saul established his military base in his hometown, Gibeah, and built a citadel there.

In the years that followed this initial campaign against the Philistines, Saul was constantly engaged in other military activities. He continued to fight with enemies on his eastern borders, particularly Ammon and Moab, to the east of the Dead Sea (1 Sm 14:47). He engaged in a major campaign on the southern border with the old enemies of the Israelites, the Amalekites (ch 15); in this, too, he was successful. And throughout all this, he had to keep constant watch on Philistine activity on his western border.

Saul was faced with an extraordinarily difficult task as military commander. His home ground had the advantage of being reasonably easy to protect, for most of it was mountainous countryside. But he was surrounded on all four sides by enemies who wanted his land, he had inadequate weapons (for Philistines controlled the supply of iron), he had no large standing army, he had inadequate communication systems, and he did not have the wholehearted support of all the Israelites. For several years, he was relatively successful against almost impossible odds, but eventually his military genius failed.

The Philistines assembled a large army in the vicinity of Aphek, but instead of attacking Saul's mountain territory directly, the army moved northward and then began to penetrate Israelite territory at a weak point in the vicinity of Jezreel. Saul attempted to gather an adequate military force to meet the Philistine threat, but was unable to do so. With inadequate preparation and insufficient forces, he prepared for battle at Mt Gilboa; he should never have entered that battle, for it could not have been won. His sons were killed on the battlefield, and Saul, rather than fall into the hands of the Philistines, committed suicide.

From a military perspective, Saul had become king at a time of crisis; he had averted disaster and gained some respite for his country. But the battle in which he died was a disaster for Israel; the country he left behind after his death was in worse straits than it had been on his assumption of power.

The King. If Saul had a difficult task as Israel's military commander, he had an even more difficult task as Israel's king. Before Saul's time, there had been no king in Israel. The absence of any form of monarchy in Israel was largely a religious matter. God was the one and only true King of Israel; he was the one who reigned (Ex 15:18) and was Head of state. Consequently, although there had been single, powerful rulers in Israel's earlier history (Moses, Joshua, and certain judges), nobody had assumed the title or office of king, for it was thought that that would in some way undermine the central position of God as King.

It was sheer necessity which forced a monarchy upon Israel. It was not because of any plot on Saul's part, nor was it the result of any radical change in religious thinking. It was a necessity created by the constant military threat of the Philistines. A brief external threat could have been met by a temporary ruler, a judge. But a permanent and serious threat to Israel's existence could not be coped with by such temporary measures. If Israel was to survive as a nation (and it very nearly did not), it needed a central military government with recognized authority over the various tribes which constituted the nation of Israel.

Thus the kingdom was established and Saul became the first king, facing incredible difficulties. Since there had never been a kingdom before in Israel, there were no precedents. What were his responsibilities? Primarily, they were military, for that was why the monarchy had been established; in this area, Saul was successful in the early years of his reign. But apart from his military responsibilities, King Saul faced an enormously difficult task. Given the nature of Hebrew theology, it was inevitable that many Israelites were opposed to the idea of kingship from the very beginning. Indeed, Samuel, who was instrumental in the initial anointing of Saul and then in the formal coronation, appears to have been ambiguous in his attitudes toward the kingship, and later toward Saul himself. Furthermore, nobody had specified precisely what it was that the leader could do. He was a soldier; that much was clear. But did he also have religious responsibilities? Though the judgment of history upon Saul is often harsh, it is wise to recall the difficulty of the task he undertook. The military problems alone would have been more than sufficient for most great men; Saul also had to fashion the new role of king.

In practical matters, Saul's leadership was modest and praiseworthy. He sought none of the pomp and splendor of many oriental kings. He had a small court, located in his military stronghold of Gibeah; there is little evidence that it was characterized by great wealth. For practical purposes, he had no standing army; he had only a few men close to him, in particular his son Jonathan and his general Abner. He also sought out young men of promise, like David. By way of contrast, Saul's court was rustic and feudal in comparison to the later splendor of David and Solomon.

But Saul, as national leader, ran into difficulties with Samuel, who had appointed him and had influenced Israel prior to his kingship. While the responsibility for the trouble may lie primarily with Saul, Samuel himself did not appear to have been particularly supportive and helpful. On one occasion, Saul was roundly criticized and condemned by Samuel for assuming the priestly role of offering sacrifices in the absence of Samuel at Gilgal (1 Sm 13:8–15). The judgment was no doubt deserved, though one can perceive Saul's dilemma. Did the king have a priestly role or not? The issue had not been made clear and the judgment assumed he did not. Furthermore, Saul was at the time in a state of crisis; he had waited seven days for Samuel to turn up, and as each day passed his army was reduced by deserters, so Saul acted. Perhaps he may not be excused, but his actions may easily be understood, and the incident itself is indicative of the difficulty of being a nation's first king. Again, after the Amalekite war, Saul was subject to divine condemnation from Samuel.

Saul was Israel's first king, but not its greatest. Yet no criticism of Saul's leadership should be so harsh as to wipe out his strengths. He faced extraordinary difficulties and for a while was successful. Few other men could have done what he did. Ultimately, he died in failure, yet his achievements might have been better remembered if he had been succeeded by any other leader than David. David's gifts and competence were so magnificent and unusual that Saul's modest achievements paled and only his failure is remembered.

The Man. The writers of the OT have presented the story of Saul in a fascinating manner. While some OT characters remain shadowy figures, Saul stands out, with all his strengths and weaknesses, as a fully human figure. He was, in many ways, a great man, but there were also flaws in his personality which emerged more and more in the later years of his life.

Born of a wealthy father, Saul is described as being both tall and handsome (1 Sm 9:1,2). He was a man of immense courage and part of his military success was rooted in his fearlessness. In his early years as king, Saul is portrayed as a man whose basic instincts were generous; he was kind and loyal to his friends and did not easily carry a grudge or hatred toward those who opposed him (11:12,13). But the real strength of Saul in his early days lay in his relationship to God. For all his natural gifts and abilities, Saul became king as a result of divine appointment (10:1) and because the "Spirit of the Lord" came upon him (v 6).

Yet in his later life, a change came over Saul which transformed him into a tragic, pitiable person. The many incidents in Saul's relationship to the young David provide insight into the transformation. Once a friend, then perceived as an enemy, David became the object of Saul's unfounded suspicions and irrational jealousy. Saul's periods of sanity became punctuated by periods of depression and paranoia. The paranoia affected his rational thought; much of the time which should have been spent directed toward the Philistine threat was diverted toward the pursuit of David.

The biblical writers describe this change as the departure of the Spirit of God from Saul, and its replacement in the form of an evil spirit (1 Sm 16:14). Many modern writers have interpreted this as the onset of a form of mental illness, perhaps manic depression, the alternation between active and lucid periods, followed by intense depression and paranoia, in Saul's case accompanied by homicidal tendencies. But there is a certain danger in psychoanalyzing the figures of ancient history, principally because the literary sources are rarely adequate to the task. The biblical writers indicated a theological basis for the change in Saul: the Spirit of God had departed from him. From a simple human perspective, the man was not equal to the enormity of the task before him. Overcome by its complexity, and lagging in the faith of the one who appointed him to such awesome responsibility, Saul ended his days in tragedy.

Yet there was one bright moment at the end. Saul's dead body was decapitated by the victorious Philistines and suspended as a warning from the walls of Beth-shan (1 Sm 31:9,10). The men of Jabesh, whom Saul had rescued from defeat and death many years earlier, came to Beth-shan, and at great personal risk removed the bodies of Saul and his sons from the wall. They took them back to Jabesh, burned the bodies, and buried the ashes. A man is not completely bad who has friends willing to risk their own lives in order to give his corpse a decent burial.

See DAVID; ISRAEL, HISTORY OF.

3. Saul, mentioned in the NT, whose name was changed to Paul (Acts 13:9).

See PAUL, THE APOSTLE.   PETER C. CRAIGIE

Savior. One who delivers or rescues. The term "savior" is most frequently applied to God and Jesus Christ in the Bible. The understanding of Jesus as Savior is a key truth in appropriating the biblical message.

Versions of the English Bible use "savior" in the OT to translate various forms of the Hebrew *yāshā'* which means "to save," "to deliver," or "to rescue." Most frequently it is used to translate the participle of the verb *mōshīa'*, meaning "the one who saves" hence "savior." In the KJV, RSV, and NASB, the word "savior" is found 13 or 14 times, depending upon the version, consistently translating the Hebrew participle *mōshīa'*. The NIV uses the word "savior" 31 times in the OT, with the additional references being found in the psalms where the other versions translate "salvation." All four of these versions, however, translate the Hebrew participle as "deliverer" in Judges 3:9,15, where it refers to specific judges.

The basic understanding of the term "savior" as one who delivers or rescues is illustrated in Deuteronomy 22:27, where the Law anticipated a situation when no deliverer was near in a time of need. *Mōshīa'*, is also used for individuals, as both Othniel and Ehud are called "deliverers" (Jgs 3:9,15) and Nehemiah 9:27 speaks of the judges collectively as deliverers sent by God. Second Kings 13:5 reports that

Beth-shan, where the Philistines hung the bodies of Saul and his sons.

the Lord gave Israel a savior in reference to their deliverance from the Aramaeans. Some have identified this deliverer with King Jeroboam II of Judah, others with a foreign king, quite often Zakir of Hamath, but the text does not clearly indicate who this savior might have been. The point of the text is that *God* sent this deliverer for his people. The majority of references in the OT refer to God himself as Israel's Savior and even when other individuals are so termed it is clearly stated that God sent them or raised them up.

Israel understood that God was their Savior and declared this in songs of praise (Ps 17:7; 106:21) and cries of help (Jer 14:8). David writes of God: "He is my stronghold, my refuge and my savior" (2 Sm 22:3 NIV). Quite often the psalmists refer to the Lord as their "help" or "salvation" (Ps 27:9; 38:22; 42:5,11; 65:5; 68:19; 79:9; 85:4; 89:26; all rendered "Savior" by the NIV), which further underscores this understanding.

The exodus was undoubtedly the greatest example of deliverance for Israel and undergirded their knowledge of God as the Savior. The psalmist, in remembrance of Israel's sin (making a golden calf), proclaims that: "They forgot God, their Savior, who had done great things in Egypt" (Ps 106:21; cf. Is 63:11; Hos 13:4). In Isaiah, where "savior" is a frequent title for God, the term is used to emphasize his uniqueness. God alone is seen as Savior in contrast to foreign gods and idols: "I, even I, am the Lord, and apart from me there is no savior, I have revealed and saved and proclaimed—I, and not some foreign god among you" (Is 43:11,12 NIV). Isaiah further states that God would show himself as savior by the future blessing and restoration of Israel (Is 49:26; 60:16). The designation *savior* is not directly applied to the Messiah in the OT, but a passage like Zechariah 9:9 indicates that salvation would be an aspect of God's anointed one.

Several apocryphal books use the term *savior* for God, some in lofty titles like "everlasting savior" (Bar 4:22) or "the eternal savior of Israel" (3 Mc 7:16). This later usage also illustrates the idea of God as the one who is able to save Israel.

The Greek literature uses *sōtēr* ("savior," "deliverer" from the verb *sōzō* "to save," "to rescue") for both gods and humans. For example, at one point Herodotus refers to the Athenians as the "saviors" of Greece (*Persian Wars* 7.139.5). In the Septuagint *sōtēr* ("savior") is used to render various forms of the Hebrew *yāshā'* ("to save").

Sōtēr occurs 24 times in the NT and is exclusively applied to God and Jesus Christ; to God 8 times and to Christ 16 times. Out of the 24 NT occurrences of *sōtēr*, 10 are in the Letters and 5 in 2 Peter.

Dependence upon the OT can be seen in Luke 1:47, where Mary praises God as savior in her hymn of praise. Jesus' name (Greek for Joshua) means "the Lord is salvation" and was given in anticipation of his function as the Savior (Mt 1:21). As the Savior, Jesus completes God's plan for a promised deliverer (Acts 13:23; Ti 3:4), provides redemption for mankind (Ti 2:13,14), and is the hope of the believer (Phil 3:20,21). Inherent in the term *savior* is the concept of one who saves or delivers from danger to a position of safety. Jesus has delivered the believer from sin and death unto immortality and life (2 Tm 1:10).

While Jesus never refers to himself as savior (*sōtēr*), he is announced as such by the angels at his birth (Lk 2:11), confessed as such by those who heard his words (Jn 4:42), and proclaimed as Savior by the early church (Acts 5:31; 13:23). Salvation is central to the very mission of Jesus (Lk 19:10). Paul teaches that Christ is the Savior of the church in the present (Eph 5:23) and future (Phil 3:20).

Savior as a title is applied to God in the Pastorals and Jude 25 clearly represents God as Savior of all persons (1 Tm 2:3; 4:10). The Pastorals also clearly designate Jesus as Savior (2 Tm 1:10; Ti 3:6), in some instances in close association with God (Ti 2:13; 3:4–6). This emphasis upon God and Jesus Christ as Savior in the Pastorals has been taken by some to be a teaching against Gnostic influences.

Savior is used as a title for Jesus Christ five times in 2 Peter and John in his first letter refers to the sending of Jesus as Savior by the Father for the world (1 Jn 4:14). This message of Jesus Christ the Savior was the witness of the disciples of Christ (2 Tm 1:10,11; 1 Jn 4:14) and is the message of the church of Jesus Christ today.   ROBERT D. SPENDER

See SALVATION; REDEEMER, REDEMPTION.

Saw.   *See* TOOLS.

Scab.   *See* SORE.

Scall.   KJV rendering for an eruption, a skin rash, in Leviticus 13:30–37 and 14:54.

See SORE.

Scapegoat.   Goat that, on the day of atonement, is sent into the wilderness, symbolically bearing away the sins of the people (Lv 16).

See ATONEMENT, DAY OF.

Scarab.   Type of signet ring modeled after the scarab beetle, developed in ancient Egypt.

See SEAL.

Scarlet. *See* COLOR.

Scepter. Long staff with an ornamental head and other decorations used to represent royal authority; a shorter staff was used as a battle mace to symbolize royal military power. It is of more than passing interest that those two ideas are also conveyed by the Bible when the word *scepter* appears in a passage. The scepter of royal authority is referred to in Genesis 49:10, indicating that Judah's descendants would exercise royal authority (so also in Ps 45:6, two times, and quoted in Heb 1:8). Amos (1:5,8) refers to the royal authority of the kings of Syria and Philistia and Zechariah (10:11) to that of Egypt. King Ahasuerus held out this type of scepter to Esther (Est 4:11; 5:2; 8;4). The scepter of royal military power is referred to in Numbers 24:17 in reference to the coming messianic king. In Isaiah 14:5 it refers to the means by which Babylon exercised its oppressive military power that was to be destroyed by God. Ezekiel 19:11,14 uses *scepter* to refer to the authority, power, and dominion which Israel lost and was not able to regain. In Psalm 2:9 and Isaiah 30:31 some recent translations (e.g., NIV) have *scepter*, not *rod of iron*, to indicate divine power. Some scholars have suggested that the rod of discipline in Proverbs 22:15 should read *scepter;* this suggests that *scepter* would refer to parental authority to be exercised for the proper training of children.

Sceva. Father of seven sons and a Jewish chief priest in Ephesus at the time of Paul's visit on his third missionary journey. Sceva's sons attempted to imitate Paul's exorcism of evil spirits in the name of Jesus. Their exorcisms failed, and their authority was not recognized; they consequently were attacked and harmed by the evil spirits they tried to rebuke (Acts 19:14).

School. *See* EDUCATION.

Schoolmaster. KJV rendering of custodian in Galatians 3:24,25.

> *See* EDUCATION; TRADES AND OCCUPATIONS (CUSTODIAN).

Scorpion. *See* ANIMALS.

Scourge. *See* CRIMINAL LAW AND PUNISHMENT.

Screech Owl. *See* BIRDS (OWL, BARN; OWL, SCOPS).

Scribe. Reference in early OT times to those employed for their ability to transcribe infor-

mation. After the exile, scribes are a class of scholars who teach, copy, and interpret the Jewish Law for the people. They appear in the Gospels primarily as opponents of Jesus.

Scribes in Preexilic Times. The ability to read and write was not very widespread in ancient Israel and professional secretaries were needed in the various aspects of public life. This appears to be the earliest biblical notion of the term *scribe* and has no particular religious connotation. Scribes were employed to keep accounts or transcribe legal information (Jer 32:12), military data (2 Chr 26:11), other public documents (Jgs 8:14; Is 50:1), or personal correspondence (Jer 36:18). These secretaries were essential to royal administrations, and there is frequent mention of a chief scribe who functioned as a court recorder (1 Kgs 4:3; 2 Chr 24:11), advisor (2 Sm 8:16,17; 2 Kgs 18:18; 22:12; 1 Chr 27:32; Is 36:3), and financial overseer (2 Kgs 22:3,4). Secretaries or scribes were associated with the priesthood as well, serving as recorders for temple affairs (1 Chr 24:6; 2 Chr 34:13,15).

Scribes in Postexilic Times. With the restoration under Ezra–Nehemiah, the term *scribe* begins to be associated more narrowly with those who gathered together, studied, and interpreted the Torah (Jewish Law). They became in essence a separate profession of teachers (although unpaid), able to preserve accurately the Law of Moses and interpret it to meet conditions in postexilic times. In this initial period, Ezra himself appears as the ideal scribe, "learned in matters of the commandments of the Lord and his statutes for Israel" (Ezr 7:11) because he had "set his heart to study the law of the Lord, and to do it, and to teach his statutes and ordinances to Israel" (v 10). In Ecclesiasticus 38:24,33, and 39:1–11, the scribe is portrayed as one who, because of his diligent study of the Law, the prophets, and writings (38:34; 39:1), is able to penetrate the hidden meanings of texts (39:2,3) and thus is able to serve as judge and counsel for the affairs of the people and state (38:33; 39:4–8). Because of his absolutely invaluable place in a society governed by the Torah, the scribe is worthy of praise and veneration throughout succeeding generations (39:9).

By the 2nd century BC the scribes were a fairly distinct class in Jewish society. They appear as such during the Maccabean wars, acting as a negotiating body with the rival Syrians (1 Mc 7:12). It is also significant that from this time forward, the history of the scribe in Jewish life is closely linked with the rise of the Pharisees. Although there were apparently some scribes affiliated with the rival Sadducean party, the lay party of the Pharisees with its absolute devotion to the Law (including the oral law) became the primary religio-political affiliation for the scribes (see the close connection in the NT, Mt 5:20; 12:38; 15:1; Mk 7:5; Lk 6:7).

Training and Status Within the Community. The training of scribes initially occurred within priestly family-based guilds which guaranteed the regulation and perpetuation of this now vital responsibility (1 Chr 2:55). Later, scribal training in the Law became open to members of all classes, with the eventual result, by Jesus' time, of scribes from nonpriestly families being far more numerous and influential. Training in the Law began at an early age under the personal supervision of a teacher (rabbi), who instructed in all matters of the Law and its interpretation for present needs. Because the written Law of Moses could not possibly speak directly to conditions in postexilic times, the oral interpretation and application of the written law to meet such current needs was a significant contribution by the scribes. Such "oral law" promulgated by them was regarded as equal to the written and equally binding for those desiring to please God (see Mk 7:6–13).

This important function, lying at the very heart of Jewish life, accounts for the participation of the scribes in the Sanhedrin. The Sanhedrin, in order to make legal decisions in keeping with the Law, obviously needed the presence of those most knowledgeable about the minutest details of the Torah and the principles governing its application to new circumstances. The scribes, consequently, were the only members outside the aristocratic high priests and elders to be represented in this Jewish supreme court (Mt 26:57; Mk 14:43,53; Lk 22:66; Acts 23:9).

Being the authoritative instructors of the Law both within the temple (Lk 2:46) and within the various synagogues of Judea and Galilee (Lk 5:17), as well as prominent members of the Sanhedrin, the scribes were greatly respected within the Jewish community. They wore special robes (Mk 12:38) with memorial fringes (Mt 23:5) at the bottom, pencases possibly from the girdle (Ez 9:2), and phylacteries or "prayer boxes" hanging from the arms (Mt 23:5). Such attire made their presence obvious and occasioned the rising or bowing of the common people when they passed (Mk 12:38).

They were addressed with respect as "rabbi" or "master" (Mt 23:7) and were given the place of honor at worship as well as at social affairs (Mt 23:2; Mk 12:39; Lk 20:46). Indeed, the high regard the Jews held for their scribes is testified by the fact that such teachers of the Law were buried alongside the purported tombs of the patriarchs and prophets.

Jesus and the Scribes. The scribes appear predominantly in the ministry of Jesus as those concerned with the circumspectness of legal observance. Luke refers to the scribes as "lawyers," describing their chief function as interpreters of the Jewish Law in a way readily comprehensible to his gentile audience. It is often found, therefore, that the scribes were critical members of Jesus' audience, accusing him of violating the Law on numerous occasions: in forgiving sins (Mt 9:1–3; Lk 5:17–26), in breaking their notion of sabbath observance through work (Lk 6:1,2) and healing (Lk 6:6–11), in not following their accepted ceremonial washings (Mk 7:2–5), and in ignoring their practice of fasting (Lk 5:33–39). Not surprisingly, they especially disapproved of Jesus' practice of mixing with the unclean and outcasts of Jewish society (Mk 2:16,17; Lk 15:1,2). In a similar light, they are not unfrequently found posing questions concerning the Law for the purpose of tricking Jesus (Mk 7:1; 12:28,35; Lk 11:53; Jn 8:3). In a similar fashion, they demanded that Jesus make his identity clear (Mt 12:38) and reveal the source of his authority to perform miracles (Mk 3:22; Lk 20:1–4).

Although there is evidence that a minority of the scribes accepted Jesus (Mt 8:19; 13:52; Mk 12:32; Jn 3:1), their primary attitude toward Jesus was one of hostility. As previously suggested, this was partly due to Jesus' differing expression of fidelity to the Mosaic law and his openness toward the outcasts. It was also partly due to the rising popularity of Jesus among the people, which posed a threat to their own authority (Mt 7:29) and to the safety of the city (21:15; Mk 11:18).

Certainly another major contributing factor of their opposition to Jesus was his open exposure of their hypocrisy and corruption. In his rebukes of the scribes and the Pharisees, Jesus openly accused them of catering to public approval (Mt 23:5–7; Mk 12:38,39; Lk 11:43) and, while appearing outwardly correct and holy, being inwardly utterly corrupt (Mt 23:25–28; Lk 11:39–41). Jesus also attacked the principle of oral law promulgated by the scribes, which they demanded the people to follow. Jesus charged that the oral law was a "heavy burden" which led the people astray and which the scribes themselves did not even bother to follow (Mt 23:2–4,13–22; Lk 11:46). While emphasizing the minor points of the Law, the scribes were also guilty of ignoring the weightier concerns of justice, mercy, and faith (Mt 23:23,24; Mk 12:40; Lk 11:42). Furthermore, contrary to being the descendants of the prophets, as the scribes held themselves to be, the scribes, Jesus claimed, would have killed the prophets if they had lived in their day (Mt

23:29–36; Lk 20:9–19). Those hoping to see the kingdom of heaven would, Jesus suggested, have to surpass this kind of "righteousness" practiced by the scribes (Mt 5:20).

It is not surprising to find, therefore, the scribes anxious to get rid of Jesus (Mk 14:1; Lk 11:53). His more flexible interpretation of the Law posed a clear threat to their position and authority within the community. The scribes joined forces with their normal opponents (the high priesthood) to engineer Jesus' arrest (Mk 14:43). When Jesus appeared before them and the rest of the Sanhedrin, they worked with the other leaders to construct a case against him worthy of death (Mt 26:57–66). When taking Jesus before Herod, they stood by and shouted their accusations with the others (Lk 23:10). Finally, they participated with other members of the Sanhedrin in mocking Jesus on the cross, demanding that Jesus save himself by coming down from the cross to "inspire their faith" (Mt 27:41–43).

Prior to the destruction of Jerusalem in AD 70, the scribes continued with the other elements of the Sanhedrin to oppose the early Christian church, and brought about Stephen's martyrdom (Acts 6:12–14).   DAVID C. CARLSON

See JUDAISM; PHARISEES.

Scripture.   Name given to the holy writings of any religious group. These are usually gathered into an authorized collection or canon to which final appeal in religious questions is made. Scriptural writings comprise a large portion of the world's great literature. Different religions define the authority of their scriptures in varied ways, but devout members of most religious groups generally regard their scriptures as in some way different and more sacred than other writings. Among the sacred scriptures of other religions are the Vedas and Upanishads of the Hindus, the Theravada of the Buddhists, and the Qur'an of the Muslims. Christians recognize the Jewish scriptures—Torah, Prophets, and Writings—as Scripture, along with the four Gospels, 21 Epistles, the Book of Acts, and the Revelation. Some Christians also recognize the Apocrypha as Scripture. Christians call their book of scripture the Holy Bible.

See BIBLE, CANON OF THE; BIBLE.

Scroll.   *See* WRITING AND BOOKS.

Scrolls, Dead Sea.   *See* DEAD SEA SCROLLS.

Sculpture.   *See* ART.

Scurvy.   Term used three times in the Bible (Lv 21:20; 22:22; KJV; Dt 28:27). In none of the instances does it refer to the modern disease by the same name which results from severe vitamin C deficiency.

In the Leviticus passages, "scurvy" is found in the sequence "...scurvy, or scabbed...." This phrase is translated "festering or running sores" in the NIV. Scurvy indicates a wet or draining lesion, while scabbed refers to a dry or scaly skin sore.

These terms could be describing a wide variety of skin diseases and it would be impossible to diagnose them today. The important concept in each verse is that both the priests (Lv 21:20) and animals used for burnt offerings (22:22) had to be healthy physical specimens without blemish. In this respect, they are OT types of Christ.

Scurvy was also one of the skin diseases with which the Lord would smite Israel for their disobedience.

See DISEASE; MEDICINE AND MEDICAL PRACTICE.

Sea, Dead.   *See* DEAD SEA.

Sea, Molten.   Alternate name for the laver in King Solomon's temple (1 Kgs 7:23).

See LAVER; BRONZE SEA; TABERNACLE, TEMPLE.

Sea, Red,   *See* RED SEA.

Sea, The Great.   *See* MEDITERRANEAN SEA.

Sea Gull.   *See* BIRDS.

Seah.   Unit of dry measure mentioned twice in the Bible (Gn 18:6; 1 Kgs 18:32, both NIV).

See WEIGHTS AND MEASURES.

Seal.   Small engraved object widely used in the ancient Near East to produce an image in soft clay.
     Origin. The exact origin of seals cannot be determined. It has been claimed that the cylinder seal preceded the invention of writing. The first seal probably developed from the amulet, whose purpose was to give protection to its wearer or to ward off evil. At one time a seal was believed to have some kind of magical protective power that would bring a curse or harm to the unauthorized person who dared to break it to obtain the contents it protected. Primitive seals were little more than tiny clay spools scratched with twigs to produce simple designs or figures. Glyptic art (the technical name for engraving or carving of seals on gems) flourished in the ancient Near East from the 4th millennium BC down to the end of the Persian period in the 4th century BC.

Types of Seals. *Stamp Seals.* Seals were produced in many shapes and sizes, the earliest being the stamp seal, a flat engraved gem or bead which produced a copy of itself by pressing it against soft clay. It was superceded about 3000 BC in Mesopotamia by the cylinder seal and began to be used again only at the end of the 8th century BC; by Hellenistic times it had replaced the cylinder seal altogether.

Cylinder Seals. The cylinder seal first appeared in Mesopotamia before 3000 BC and became the most widely used kind of seal until the middle of the 1st millennium BC. Its use in Egypt is evidence of very early Mesopotamian cultural influence upon Egypt; however, it was soon replaced there by the scarab seal, which was better adapted for sealing papyrus documents.

Symbols or designs were carved on the outside of the cylinder which left their imprint when the seal was rolled over the wet clay. Some of the earliest symbols used were geometric designs or representations of some magical symbol. Later seals depicted everything from mythology (deities seated conversing with each other, receiving worshipers in audience, riding in a boat or chariot, or fighting an enemy) to scenes from everyday life (hunting, marriage, banqueting, feeding animals, fighting wild beasts, offering sacrifices to the deity, war, leading prisoners away) and representations of animals, flowers, and birds. Writing (e.g., the owner's name or a declaration of loyalty to a god or king) began to appear on seals in the 3rd millennium BC. Because of the great number and variety of seals that have been found, they are invaluable for what they reveal about ancient peoples—how they dressed, their hairstyles, furniture, utensils, and religious beliefs.

Seals were made from a variety of materials, including shells, baked clay, limestone, lapis lazuli, gold, silver, onyx, serpentine, marble, aragonite, opal, amethyst, jasper, quartz crystal, chalcedony, carnelian, ivory, hematite, jade, glass (rare and of a late period), terra-cotta, obsidian, agate, glazed pottery, and wood. Stones from which seals were cut were carefully chosen, as some were considered "unlucky." Stones that were readily available were ordinarily used, though lapis lazuli was imported from Persia, Afghanistan, and India and shells from the Persian Gulf.

Earlier seals of soft materials such as shell and marble were easily cut with flint, but as harder materials such as quartz and agate began to be used, a harder cutting tool was required. Coarse corundum was probably used for this purpose, and the earlier seals were all incised by hand. The Egyptians are credited with making tools for engraving that were later used in Assyria. Holes that pierced the cylinders were probably made by a copper tool, used with emery, and revolved by the aid of a bow string, or simply rolled by hand. Some designs produced by these tools were so crude that they are almost unrecognizable, but many were extremely well done. It is quite possible that engraving tools were eventually revolved by wheel that was worked by foot, like the potter's wheel (Jer 18:1–4).

Seals were so widely used and have been unearthed in such quantity in the ancient Near East that they can be dated within a century or two of their origin, though sometimes it is difficult to determine the exact period or country of origin. Herodotus observed that every Babylonian gentleman "carries a seal and a walking stick" (Book I, 195). The seal was suspended by a cord about the neck or the wrist or attached to some part of the owner's clothing (cf. Gn 38:18; 41:42; Sg 8:6; Jer 22:24). Graves have been found with cylinders tied to the wrists of the skeletons.

Scarab. The scarab, a kind of stamp seal, soon replaced the cylinder seal in Egypt because it was better adapted to sealing documents of papyrus, the principal Egyptian writing material. The scarab was shaped like the dung beetle (*Scarabaeus sacer*), which was venerated in Egypt as the emblem of resurrection and continued existence. The Egyptians noted the similarity between the sun rolling across the sky like a great ball and the beetle laying its eggs in animal droppings which it rolled into a ball. They believed that their sun god Ra, who at dawn was Khepera, took the form of a beetle at noon. From this belief the symbol of the beetle evolved as an emblem of eternal life; therefore, it was only natural that the scarab should become the most distinctive form of Egyptian seal. It was usually made from stea-schist, fibrous steatite, or schist, but sometimes from quartz, carnelian, jasper, black obsidian, or limestone. It bore symbols or designs cut in the scarab (called cartouches) and was often coated with glaze. It was set in a seal ring on a swivel or mounted in fixed fashion and was frequently used as a person's signature. The signet ring Pharaoh gave to Joseph (Gn 41:42; cf. Est 3:10,12) was undoubtedly a scarab that served as Joseph's authority for transacting royal business. Every pharaoh had his own distinctive scarab. Cartouches of the principal pharaohs have been identified so that when found in excavations of ancient cities or in tombs (often wrapped in the bandages of the mummy), scarabs have been invaluable for dating these archaeological discoveries. Soldiers and traders carried scarabs to the entire Mediterranean and Mesopotamian regions.

Jar Handle Seal. Another type of seal was the jar handle seal. Cloth was placed over the neck of a bottle, soft clay was smeared on top of the binding cord, and then the seal was pressed into the wet clay. The unbroken seal showed that the merchandise had not been opened before delivery. In Judea the seal was impressed on jar handles as evidence of ownership. Some jar handle stamps were probably trademarks of pottery factories; some bear private names (perhaps the owner of the factory). The so-called royal jar handle stamps contain either a four-winged or two-winged symbol and a short inscription consisting of two lines. The line above reads "belonging to the king" and the lower line contains the name of a city, probably where the jar was made.

Uses. Functional Uses. Since they first developed from an amulet, seals continued to serve as protection. An unbroken seal proved that the contents had not been tampered with, whether on a document, a granary door, or a wine jar. The lion's den into which Daniel was cast was sealed with the king's signet and those of his nobles (Dn 6:17). Jesus' tomb was secured by sealing the stone (Mt 27:66). The seal also served as a mark of ownership or as a trademark (e.g., placed on pottery before firing). It was also used to validate documents (letters, bills of sale, government documents, etc.). Jezebel wrote letters in her husband's name and sealed them with his seal, thus bringing about the death of Naboth (1 Kgs 21:8–13). Jeremiah sealed a deed of purchase when he bought a kinsman's land (Jer 32:10–14). An edict with the Persian king's seal could not be revoked (Est 8:8).

Symbolical Use. Symbolical use of the seal is found both in nonbiblical and biblical literature. A Babylonian prayer says, "Like a seal may my sins be torn away." The OT says, "Seal the teaching among my disciples" (Is 8:16); "My sister . . . a fountain sealed" (Sg 4:12). Zerubbabel was told he would become God's signet ring (Hg 2:23); the earth took shape like clay pressed by a signet ring (Jb 38:14); "seal both vision and prophet" (Dn 9:24; see also Gn 38:18,25; Jb 9:7; 14:17; 37:7; Is 29:11; Dn 12:4).

The NT makes frequent symbolical use of the seal: John 3:33; 6:27; Romans 4:11 (circumcision, a seal of the righteousness of faith); 1 Corinthians 9:2 ("seal of my apostleship"); 2 Corinthians 1:22; Ephesians 1:13; 4:30 ("sealed for the day of redemption"); 2 Timothy 2:19; and especially the Book of Revelation (5:1,2,5,9; 6:1–12; 7:2–8; 8:1; 9:4; 10:4; 22:10).

F. B. HUEY, JR.

See ARCHAEOLOGY; INSCRIPTIONS; POTTERY.

Sea Monster. KJV rendering of jackal in Lamentations 4:3.

See ANIMALS (DRAGON; JACKAL).

Sea of Chinnereth, Chinneroth. Early names for the Sea of Galilee.

See GALILEE, SEA OF.

Sea of Galilee. *See* GALILEE, SEA OF.

Sea of Reeds. Hebrew designation for the body of water crossed by the Israelites during the exodus from Egypt.

See EXODUS, THE; RED SEA.

Sea of the Arabah. *See* DEAD SEA.

Sea of Tiberias. Alternate name for the Sea of Galilee in John 6:1 and 21:1.

See GALILEE, SEA OF.

Seat, Moses'. *See* MOSES' SEAT.

Seba. Semitic people descended from Cush (Gn 10:7; 1 Chr 1:9; Is 43:3).

See SABEANS.

Sebam. City located on the pastoral tablelands of the Transjordan and desired by the sons of Gad and Reuben (Nm 32:3, KJV She-

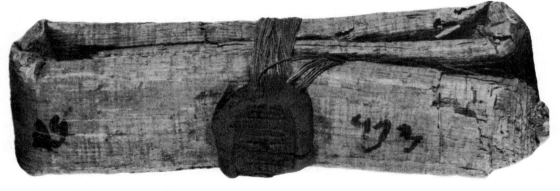

A sealed contract from Elephantine, Egypt.

bam). Reuben was apportioned this area (Jos 13:19), but eventually lost it to the marauding Moabites. This city was known for its vineyards (Is 16:8,9; Jer 48:32). Sebam is alternately called Sibmah in the Hebrew text (cf. Nm 32:38, KJV Shibmah; Jos 13:19; Is 16:8,9; Jer 48:32).

Sebat. KJV spelling of Shebat, the Hebrew month extending from about mid-January to about mid-February, in Zechariah 1:7.

See CALENDARS, ANCIENT AND MODERN.

Secacah. One of six cities situated in the wilderness region immediately west of the Dead Sea in the Valley of Achor and included in the territory allotted to Judah, mentioned between Middin and Nibshan (Jos 15:61). Its location is perhaps three miles southwest of Khirbet Qumran at the modern town of Khirbet es-Samrah.

Sechu. KJV spelling of Secu in 1 Samuel 19:22.

See SECU.

Second Adam, The. Analogy that compares and contrasts the first man with the one he is seen to typify, the Lord Jesus Christ. Two essential passages develop the idea, which basically states that, while Adam's historically-rooted sin caused horrible consequences for the human race, the perfect work of Jesus Christ provided the complete remedy for mankind's resultant condition (Rom 5:12–21; 1 Cor 15:22,45–49). Fundamental to this assertion is Paul's recognition that Adam's sin was committed representatively, that is, he acted not only for himself but also for all his posterity (Rom 5:12; 1 Cor 15:22). As the Scriptures clearly indicate, each person carries the stain and shame of that original rebellion (Ps 51:5; Is 53:6; Rom 5:18,19).

God's great redemption may be appreciated by carefully observing several points of correspondence between Adam and Christ. Both were sons of God by virtue of their unique origins (Lk 3:22,38). Notwithstanding, the first Adam failed in obedient sonship, plunging his progeny headlong into destruction. His sin caused both physical and spiritual death to reign in the lives of all men (Rom 5:17,18). Although Adam failed to represent man acceptably before God, Jesus Christ succeeded in fulfilling all the demands of his Father's absolute standards for righteousness. Moreover, as the Lord from heaven, he graciously and powerfully conveys the benefits of his saving righteousness to others (Rom 3:24,25; 5:15–21). As God the Father joins men to the person of his

Son, he accomplishes a radical transformation in their lineage and affections (2 Cor 5:17). It is this union with Christ, made possible by God's free and unmerited favor, which nullifies the negative effects of Adam's sin and works justifying righteousness in those whose faith is directed to the final Adam as their living Savior and Lord.

See TYPE, TYPOLOGY; CHRISTOLOGY; ADAM (PERSON).

Second Coming of Christ. Doctrine of Christian faith concerning the consummation of Christ's saving work upon his return to earth.

Terms Used. The doctrine is expressed by verbs such as *come, descend, appear,* and *is revealed,* with Christ as the subject ("I will come again," Jn 14:3; "the Lord himself will descend," 1 Thes 4:16; "when he appears," 1 Jn 2:28; 3:2; "the day when the Son of man is revealed," Lk 17:30; "when the Lord Jesus is revealed from heaven," 2 Thes 1:7), or *send,* with Christ as the object and God as the subject ("that he may send the Christ appointed for you," Acts 3:20). It is expressed also by a variety of nouns, principally by *coming* (which is the regular translation of the Greek word *parousia,* meaning presence, visit, arrival, advent, esp. of a royal or distinguished person), also by *appearing* (as in 2 Tm 4:8; Ti 2:13), *revealing,* or *revelation* (1 Cor 1:7). These different verbs and nouns point to the same event but highlight different aspects of it, especially the manifestation of God's glory in Christ when he comes.

The time of this event is repeatedly referred to as "the Day," sometimes absolutely (as in Rom 13:12; 1 Cor 3:13; Heb 10:25), more often with a qualification, such as "the day of Christ" (Phil 1:10; 2:16), "the day of the Lord" (1 Thes 5:2; 2 Thes 2:2), "the day of the Lord Jesus" (1 Cor 5:5; 2 Cor 1:14), "the day of Jesus Christ" (Phil 1:6), "the day of our Lord Jesus Christ" (1 Cor 1:8), and "the day of God" (2 Pt 3:12). When such expressions are used, there is often some reference to the judgment to be passed at the coming of Christ: his day is "the day of judgment" (1 Jn 4:17, etc.) or "the day of wrath" (Rom 2:5)—"that day when ... God judges the secrets of men by Christ Jesus" (v 16). For the hard-pressed people of God, however, it is "the day of redemption" (Eph 4:30).

In some evangelical circles today a technical term widely used with regard to the second coming is *rapture.* This is the noun corresponding to the verb used in 1 Thessalonians 4:17, where those believers who are still alive at the coming of Christ are described as being "caught up" together with their resurrected fellow Christians to meet him "in the air." This rapture or translation is an incident in the second coming, not something distinct from it. (It may be relevant to note that the verb of 1 Thes 4:17 is used in 2 Cor 12:2,3 to denote Paul's mysterious experience of being "caught up" into the third heaven or Paradise).

Difference of interpretation about the time relation of the second coming to other end-time events or epochs has led to the emergence of distinct schools of eschatological thought. This is especially so as regards its relation to the 1000-year period of Revelation 20:2–7 (if that period is indeed an end-time epoch).

The NT Evidence. That the second coming of Christ was an essential element in the gospel as preached in the apostolic age is clear from one of the earliest, if not absolutely the earliest, of the NT documents. Writing to his converts in Thessalonica (cf. Acts 17:1–9) a few weeks after they first heard and believed the gospel, Paul reminds them how they had "turned to God from idols, to serve a living and true God, and to wait for his Son from heaven, whom he raised from the dead, Jesus who delivers us from the wrath to come" (1 Thes 1:9,10). Here Jesus' expected deliverance of his people from end-time judgment is put on the same plane as his historical resurrection; the Christian way of life embraces both serving God and waiting for Christ. This note of waiting for Christ is repeated and amplified several times in this short letter.

A few years later Paul uses similar language when writing to his converts in Corinth (cf. Acts 18:1–18): "you are not lacking in any spiritual gift, as you wait for the revealing of our Lord Jesus Christ" (1 Cor 1:7). And in what may have been his last letter he speaks of "the crown of righteousness" which the Lord will award him "on that Day, and not only to me," he adds, "but also to all who have loved his appearing" (2 Tm 4:8). To love his appearing and to wait for him are two different ways of expressing the same attitude.

Nor is Paul the only NT writer to use this kind of language. The writer to the Hebrews encourages his readers with the assurance that in a little while "the coming one shall come and shall not tarry" (Heb 10:37). James says that "the coming of the Lord is at hand" (Jas 5:8). Peter speaks of the time "when the chief Shepherd is manifested" (1 Pt 5:4). The Revelation to John ends with the risen Lord's promise, "Surely I am coming soon," and the church's response, "Amen. Come, Lord Jesus!" (Rv 22:20).

·The record of Acts begins with the angels' assurance at the ascension of Christ that "this Jesus, who was taken up from you into heaven, will come in the same way as you saw him go into heaven" (Acts 1:11). The summaries of apostolic addresses which the book contains make repeated references to Jesus as "the one ordained by God to be judge of the living and the dead" (10:42; cf. 17:31).

The origin of this entrenched belief and proclamation is found in the teaching of Jesus before his death. In the synoptic Gospels appears ample reference to the coming event, if one accepts that the Son of man mentioned so frequently by Jesus is to be identified with Jesus himself. On "the day when the Son of man is revealed" (Lk 17:30) he will come "in clouds with great power and glory" (Mk 13:26). This language is derived from the OT, especially from Daniel's vision in which "one like a son of man" is brought "with the clouds of heaven" to receive everlasting dominion from the Ancient of Days (Dn 7:13,14). A cloud or clouds regularly enveloped the divine glory in the OT (as in Ex 40:34; 1 Kgs 8:10,11); their mention in connection with the coming of the Son of man indicates that, when he comes, the glory of God will be manifested in him. The Son of man discharged his earthly ministry "in weakness"; thanks to his victory on the cross he discharges his present ministry "in power" (cf. Mk 9:1), and this power will be consummated at his revelation from heaven. His revelation from heaven will bring judgment to the ungodly and rewards to his followers: "every one who acknowledges me before men, the Son of man also will acknowledge before the angels of God" (Lk 12:8); but "whoever is ashamed of me and of my words in this adulterous and sinful generation, of him will the Son of man also be ashamed, when he comes in the glory of his Father with the holy angels" (Mk 8:38), for "then he will repay every one for what he has done" (Mt 16:27).

Jesus' last reference to this consummation was made at his trial before the Jewish authorities when, asked by the high priest to say whether or not he was "the Christ, the Son of the Blessed," he replied, "I am; and you will see the Son of man seated at the right hand of Power, and coming with the clouds of heaven" (Mk 14:62).

It may be that the NT points to a succession of partial comings of the Son of man, but these in turn point to the final coming. As in the OT age, so too in the Christian era can one recognize outstanding days of the Lord in which his judgment of evil and vindication of righteousness are signally displayed. The early church recognized one such "day of the Lord" or "coming of the Son of man" in the destruction of the temple and city of Jerusalem in AD 70—an event which took place within a generation of Jesus' prediction of it (Mk 13:30)—but even while predicting that judgment was relatively near, he

Mt Scopus, the north extension of the Mt of Olives, where Titus camped in AD 70 before he captured and destroyed Jerusalem and the temple, fulfilling Christ's prediction.

went on to speak of his final coming, on a day and hour of which no one knew (v 32).

While the synoptic Gospels stress the public and earth-shaking aspect of Jesus' coming, the Gospel of John dwells on its inward and personal aspects. The action of the Son in raising the dead for life or judgment does indeed find a place in this Gospel (5:25–29); but in the upper room the promise of his return is intended to comfort his bewildered disciples: "when I go and prepare a place for you, I will come again and will take you to myself, that where I am you may be also" (14:3). The possibility that one or more of them might remain on earth until he comes is mentioned, but no positive statement is made one way or the other (21:22,23).

In this Gospel also one can trace references to anticipatory comings of Christ. When, for example, John says in 14:18, "I will not leave you desolate [orphans]; I will come to you," the immediate context suggests that he is speaking of his coming in the person of the Spirit, the "other Counselor." But this cannot be identified with his coming again to take them to himself; it is a preliminary visitation to that final coming.

The second coming of Christ is specially associated in the NT with his activity in resurrection and judgment.

Resurrection. In 1 Thessalonians, written not more than 20 years after the death and resurrection of Christ, his coming again is presented by way of comfort and encouragement to those whose Christian friends have died. Paul had been compelled to leave Thessalonica before he had time to give his converts there as much teaching as they required, and when some of their number died shortly after his departure, their friends wondered if they would suffer some serious disadvantage at the second coming, in contrast to those who would still be alive to greet the returning Lord. No, says Paul, "those who have fallen asleep" will suffer no disadvantage; on the contrary, the first thing to happen when "the Lord himself will descend from heaven" is that "the dead in Christ will rise"; only after that will those who survive until then be caught away to join them and be for ever "with the Lord" (4:15–17).

Fuller information on the same subject is given in 1 Corinthians, written about five years later. There the coming resurrection of believers is the full harvest which was inaugurated by the resurrection of Christ: "Christ the first fruits, then at his coming those who belong to Christ" (15:23). An additional revelation is imparted: not only will each believer who has died be raised in a "spiritual body" (v 44); those who are still alive will be "changed" so as to conform to the conditions of the resurrection age. For dead and living believers alike it holds that "as we have borne the image of the man of dust (that is, Adam; cf. Gn 2:7), we shall also bear the image of the man of heaven" (i.e., the risen Christ; 1 Cor 15:49).

To the same effect Paul writes, a few years later still, in Philippians 3:20,21, that from heaven "we await a Savior, the Lord Jesus Christ, who will change our lowly body to be like his glorious body."

A deeper unfolding of what this will involve is made in Romans 8:18–23, where the resurrection of the people of Christ, their investiture with his risen glory, carries with it the renewal of all creation: creation, at present subject to change and decay (cf. Gn 3:17,18), "waits with eager longing for the revealing of the sons of God," because then it will obtain a share of their "glorious liberty."

Judgment. The association of judgment with the second coming arises in Jesus' teaching in the Gospels. The association is equally plain in the epistles of the NT. Paul in particular puts the subject on a personal level. He forbids premature judgment of fellow Christians: "do not pronounce judgment before the time, before the Lord comes" (1 Cor 4:5). The Lord will conduct an investigation which will bring to light the hidden motives of the heart such as no earthly court can penetrate, without the knowledge of which judgment must remain a blunt tool. Paul knew that his own apostolic work would be assessed on "the day of Christ" (Phil 2:16), and he expected that the chief criterion in that assessment would be the quality of his converts. So he writes to the Thessalonians: "For what is our hope or joy or crown of boasting before our Lord Jesus at his coming? Is it not you?" (1 Thes 2:19).

Elsewhere Paul urges his converts to bear in mind that they, with himself, must appear before the tribunal variously called "the judgment seat of God," to whom "each of us must give account of himself" (Rom 14:10,12), or "the judgment seat of Christ," where each will "receive good or evil, according to what he has done in the body" (2 Cor 5:10). It seems clear that this judgment is to take place at the second coming of Christ, who will then "judge the living and the dead" (2 Tm 4:1). Because Paul is writing to Christians, he tends to concentrate on the judgment or assessment which *they* will undergo at the Lord's return. But in writing to the persecuted members of the church in Thessalonica, he makes it plain that the same coming will bring relief from their afflictions to them and retribution to their persecutors (2 Thes 1:6–10). The outstanding act of retribution will be visited on the "man of lawlessness," the incarnation of evil and rebellion against God, for "the Lord Jesus will slay him with the breath of his mouth and destroy him by his appearing and his coming" (2:3–8). This language echoes that used in Isaiah 11:4 of the expected Prince of the house of David, who "shall smite the earth with the rod of his mouth, and with the breath of his lips he shall slay the wicked."

More generally, the apostolic statement that God "has fixed a day on which he will judge the world in righteousness by a man whom he has appointed" (Acts 17:31)—the day being self-evidently that of Christ's return—implies that it is the second coming of Christ that will give effect to the OT prophecies of the new age when God "will judge the world with righteousness, and the peoples with his truth" (Ps 96:13; cf. 98:9).

Its Meaning for Church and World. From the earliest days when Christians began to confess their faith in a commonly accepted form of words, the second coming of Christ has been one of its basic articles. For example, the Apostles' Creed (which is based on the 2nd-century baptismal confession of the church in Rome) devotes its central section to a recital of the saving acts of Christ, "who was conceived by the Holy Spirit, born of the Virgin Mary, suffered under Pontius Pilate, was crucified, dead and buried; he descended into hades; the third day he rose again from the dead; he ascended into heaven, and sits at the right hand of God the Father Almighty; from thence he shall come to judge the living and the dead." Most of these acts are expressed in the past tense, one in the present, and one in the future; but the act expressed in the future tense is held to be as factual as those which have taken place in the past. Jesus' coming to judge the living and the dead does not occupy a different plane of reality from his suffering under Pilate. The series of his saving acts is incomplete without this consummating act which still lies in the future; those which have taken place already provide the guarantee that this also will take place.

The Nicene Creed (AD 325 and 451), which is based on the baptismal confession of the church in Caesarea, enumerates the same saving events in somewhat fuller language, concluding them with the words: "and he shall come again with glory to judge both the living and the dead; of whose kingdom shall be no end."

The second coming of Christ consummates his saving work. It is to this event that Paul refers when he says that "salvation is nearer to us now than when we first believed" (Rom 13:11). The writer to the Hebrews similarly assures his readers that Christ "will appear a second time . . . to save those who are eagerly waiting for him" (9:28). This final salvation of God—or we might say (using a different idiom) the consummation of his kingdom—was inaugurated by the ministry, death, and resurrection of Christ but will be manifested in full by his coming again.

Because of an inevitably changing perspective, the second coming is no doubt envisioned rather differently by most Christians today than it was by their predecessors in the primitive church. If Christians of the first generation assumed that theirs was the generation that would witness the second coming, those of later generations have learned to be more cautious. It is for man's spiritual health that it is not known when the Lord will come. In the words of the 18th-century German commentator Johann Albrecht Bengel, "each separate generation, living at this or that time, occupies during its own life-span the place of those who are to be alive when the Lord comes." Each Christian generation, therefore, should live as though it might be the last one, while bearing in mind that Christians in the remote future may look back on the first 2000 years AD as the early period of church history. The second coming of Christ remains the hope of his people, as it is also the hope of the world (without the world's necessarily being aware of this); but its timing is not of the essence of the hope.

If one asks what, in that case, is to be made of the NT assurance that the Lord is at hand, an answer may be found in a sermon entitled "Waiting for Christ" by the 19th-century English preacher John Henry Newman. He pointed out that, before Christ's first coming, the course of time ran straight toward that event, but that since then the course of time runs alongside his second coming, on its brink. If it ran straight toward it, it would immediately run into it; but as it is, the great event is always at hand throughout the present era. The course of time will one day merge in the presence or *parousia* of Christ. If reckoned in terms of the succession of years, final salvation is nearer now than when Christians first believed; but personally, Christ is not nearer now than he was in NT times, and he is as near now as he will be when he returns.

There are times when the partition between his presence now and his coming *parousia* becomes paper thin; one day it will disappear completely and this mortal life will be swallowed up in the eternal order.

In the meantime, the real presence of the Lord at his table is a promise and foretaste of his presence when he comes in glory. At his table his people "proclaim the Lord's death until he comes" (1 Cor 11:26). In the early days of the church Christians reminded one another of this in the Aramaic invocation *Maranatha*, "Our Lord, come!" (16:22). With this invocation the communion service appears to have been regularly concluded; as is gathered from the document called the *Didache* or *Teaching of the Twelve Apostles* (a primitive manual of church order dating about AD 100). The corresponding Greek invocation, "Amen. Come, Lord Jesus!" appears in Revelation 22:20 as the church's response to her Lord's assurance: "Surely I am coming soon."

There are other moments of such conscious nearness to the presence of Christ that something like absorption into it is experienced. For each believer the partition disappears in the moment of death; at the last advent it will disappear on a universal scale.

Not only in personal experience but at various junctures in world history it has seemed to some Christians that the second coming of Christ must be just about to break in. A particularly fierce imperial persecution in AD 202, the collapse of the Roman Empire in the West in the 5th century, the fall of Constantinople to the Turks 1000 years later, the French Revolution (AD 1789 onwards) and its aftermath in the Napoleonic wars, not to speak of events in the 20th century, have stimulated expectations of this kind. The fact that these crises have passed without Christ's personal return does not mean that those who cherished such expectations were entirely wrong; these and similar crises may be recognized as anticipatory "days of the Lord" or even "comings of the Son of man," just as, for example, the fall of Jerusalem in AD 70 was so recognized.

Again, the numerical notes of time in Daniel and Revelation have been studied and reinterpreted, with a zeal and ingenuity which might have been more profitably employed, in order to calculate the probable date of the second advent. The dates suggested have regularly come and gone without any fulfillment of these calculations; they were so artificially determined that they cannot for the most part

be recognized as even anticipatory "days of the Lord."

In the NT and in historical theology the *parousia* of Christ has been presented not only as the hope of the believer but also as the hope of the world. Paul appears to link it, too, with the ultimate salvation of Israel when, adapting OT prophecies, he speaks of the deliverer who "will come from Zion" and "banish ungodliness from Jacob" (Rom 11:26)—if it is the heavenly Zion that he has in mind. The NT interpretation of the "one like a son of man" whose eternal dominion replaces that of warring empires based on force (Dn 7:13,14) points to the universal establishment of the peaceful reign of Christ, as does the vision of the seer of Patmos in which "the kingdom of the world has become the kingdom of our Lord and of his Christ, and he shall reign for ever and ever" (Rv 11:15). John's favorite acclamation of God in three tenses as the one "who is and who was and who is to come" (cf. 1:4,8) is reduced to two tenses: "who art and who wast" (11:17). He is no longer the one "who is to come"; he has come.   F. F. BRUCE

See ESCHATOLOGY; JUDGMENT; APOCALYPTIC; JUDGMENT SEAT; REVELATION, BOOK OF; TRIBULATION; LAST JUDGMENT; MILLENNIUM; AGE, AGES; DAY OF THE LORD; LAST DAYS; RESURRECTION; WRATH OF GOD.

Bibliography. G.R. Beasley-Murray, *Jesus and the Future;* G.C. Berkouwer, *The Return of Christ;* T.F. Glasson, *The Second Advent;* G.E. Ladd, *The Blessed Hope;* R. Pache, *The Return of Jesus Christ;* D.W. Pentecost, *Things to Come;* A. Reese, *The Coming Advent of Christ;* G. Vos, *The Pauline Eschatology.*

Second Death, The. *See* DEATH, THE SECOND.

Second Temple, Period of the. Time interval from the dedication of the rebuilt Jerusalem temple in 516 BC to its destruction by the Romans in AD 70.

See JUDAISM.

Secu. Town or topographical landmark where Saul stopped to ask the whereabouts of Samuel and David, located between Gibeah and Ramah. It was especially noted for its large well—a natural place to go for information (1 Sm 19:22, KJV Sechu). Its location is unknown.

Secundus. Fellow Thessalonian and traveling companion of Aristarchus. Secundus accompanied Paul on his third missionary journey through Macedonia and Greece and awaited him at Troas in Asia Minor (Acts 20:4). It is not known whether Secundus remained at Troas or went with Paul on his final trip to Jerusalem.

Seer. *See* PROPHECY; PROPHET, PROPHETESS.

Segub. 1. Youngest son of Hiel the Bethelite. Hiel rebuilt Jericho during the reign of King Ahab of Israel. His violation of Joshua's curse against anyone rebuilding the city (Jos 6:26) cost him his oldest and youngest sons. Segub was killed while rebuilding the city gates (1 Kgs 16:34).

2. Son borne to Hezron by the daughter of Machir, the father of Gilead. Segub was the father of Jair (1 Chr 2:21,22).

Seir (Person). Father of seven sons and a descendant of Abraham through Esau's line. Originally a Horite tribe dwelling in the land of Edom, this nation was first dispossessed by but later intermarried with Esau's descendants. Perhaps for this reason Seir and his offspring were included in the genealogies of Abraham (Gn 36:20,21; 1 Chr 1:38).

Seir (Place). 1. Mountain range of Edom extending from the Dead Sea southward to the Gulf of Aqaba. Mt Seir was bordered by the great valley of Arabah on the west and desert on the east. Seir is the modern Jebel esh-Shera'.

Seir was formerly inhabited by the Horites, whose defeat to King Chedorlaomer was recorded in Genesis 14:6. The Horites were later dispossessed from this region by Esau (Dt 2:12); however, a remnant of Horite chiefs were listed among the descendants of Esau living in Seir (Gn 36:20–30). Given by the Lord as an inheritance to Esau (Jos 24:4), the Israelites were warned not to provoke the sons of Esau to war as they passed through Seir on their wilderness travels (Dt 2:1–8). During Israel's occupation of Palestine, they were drawn into a number of battles against the people of Seir: a band of Simeonites destroyed the Amalekites dwelling in Mt Seir and resettled it with their own people (1 Chr 4:42); Jehoshaphat king of Judah (872–848 BC) gained an incredible victory over the allied armies of Ammon, Moab, and Seir (2 Chr 20:10–23); King Amaziah of Judah (796–767 BC) routed an army from Seir in the Valley of Salt (25:11–14); and the prophet Ezekiel pronounced a curse of destruction on the inhabitants of Seir for their antagonism against Israel (Ez 35:1–15).

See EDOM, EDOMITES.

2. Place defining part of the northern boundary of the land assigned to Judah's tribe (Jos 15:10). It was positioned west of Kiriath-jearim and northeast of Beth-shemesh. Mt Seir is perhaps the ridge on which the modern town of Saris is built.

Seirah, Seirath. Place where Ehud sought refuge after murdering Eglon, the king of Moab, and from where he summoned Israel to war against the Moabites (Jgs 3:26, KJV Seirath). It is unclear whether Seirah refers to a city or to a topographical landmark; however, it does appear that it was located in the hill country of Ephraim.

Sela, Selah. 1. Unidentified site on the border of the Amorites (Jgs 1:36).

2. Edomite stronghold (2 Kgs 14:7, KJV Selah). On this site the Nabataean city of Petra was built.

See PETRA.

3. Unidentified place mentioned in Isaiah's prophecy against Moab (Is 16:1).

Selah (Music). Musical notation, perhaps designating a pause in performance, occurring over 70 times in psalm texts and in Habakkuk 3:3,9,13.

See MUSIC AND MUSICAL INSTRUMENTS; PSALMS, BOOK OF.

Sela-hammahle-koth. Cliff in the wilderness of Maon, meaning "the Rock of Escape." Saul, in his desire to kill David, attempted to catch him in the steep-ravined mountains of Judah, where David had fled. Saul's attentions were diverted by a Philistine raid, thus enabling David to escape (1 Sm 23:28). The Wadi el-Malaqi, about eight miles E,NE of Maon is a suggested location for this cliff.

Seled. Nadab's son from Judah's tribe (1 Chr 2:30).

Seleucia. Name of several ancient Middle Eastern cities, all founded by Seleucus I, Nicator (312–281 BC). The most important is Seleucia in Syria on the northeast corner of the Mediterranean, five miles north of the mouth of the Orontes River and 15 miles from Antioch, for which it was the port. Built by Seleucus I in 301 BC and strongly fortified to guard his capital from the west, it changed hands several times in the disputes between the Seleucid rulers in Syria and the Ptolemies of Egypt (Dn 11:7–9; 1 Mc 11:8–19). In 109 BC the Seleucid ruler, having shaken free of the Ptolemies, granted freedom to the city, and the privilege of coining money. When the Romans appeared in the east Pompey conferred the status of "free city" on Seleucia. However, he broke the power of the Seleucids and formed the Roman province of Syria with the free city of Seleucia as a port of entry to the east. Its fine natural harbor and artificial defenses were improved.

In NT times Seleucia remained a free city, and harbored Rome's Syrian fleet. Barnabas, Saul, and John Mark sailed from here on their first missionary journey (Acts 13:4) and returned to Antioch via Seleucia (14:26). Later, on Paul's second missionary journey, Paul and Silas (15:40,41) and Barnabas and Mark (v 39) again set out from Seleucia. The city was undoubtedly an attractive place with many public buildings, a temple, and an amphitheater cut out of a cliff. The site awaits thorough archaeological investigation.

Seller. See TRADES AND OCCUPATIONS (MERCHANT).

Sem. KJV form of Shem, Noah's son, in Luke 3:36.

See SHEM.

Semachiah. Korathite Levite, Shemaiah's son and a gatekeeper in the temple (1 Chr 26:7).

Semein, Semei. Descendant of Josech and an ancestor of Jesus Christ (Lk 3:26, KJV Semei).

See GENEALOGY OF JESUS CHRIST.

Senaah. Father of a family of Israelites that returned with Zerubbabel to Palestine following the exile (Ezr 2:35; Neh 7:38). They helped Nehemiah rebuild part of the Jerusalem wall (3:3). Some suggest that Senaah refers to a town or district; however, no evidence for such has been found. Hassenaah is an alternate spelling of Senaah in Nehemiah 3:3; Hassenuah is a possible variant for Senaah (1 Chr 9:7; Neh 11:9).

See HASSENUAH.

Senate, Senator. See SANHEDRIN; TRADES AND OCCUPATIONS.

Seneh. Name of one of the two rocky crags at a pass across the Wadi es-Suweinit over which Jonathan and his armor bearer crossed in their skirmish against the Philistines. The crag opposite Seneh was called Bozez and faced the town of Michmash to the north. Seneh was visible to the town of Geba to the south (1 Sm 14:4).

Senir. Amorite name for Mt Hermon in Deuteronomy 3:9 and Song of Solomon 4:8.

See HERMON, MOUNT.

Sennacherib. King of the Assyrian empire from 705–681 BC. His name, meaning "sin has replaced brothers," may refer to a specific family situation by means of which he, a younger son of Sargon II, came to succeed his father. Before the death of his father, Sennacherib acted as military governor of the northern provinces of the Assyrian Empire. He was successful in quelling unrest in those areas. When Sargon II was assassinated in 705 BC, Sennacherib lost no time in claiming the throne.

As king of Assyria, he was a bold administrator. He was soon known to be a just and tolerant man. Sennacherib is usually known as a military man—for thus the biblical account speaks of him. Extra-biblical sources indicate that while he was conducting military campaigns he also developed a strong rule at home and, employing slave labor acquired through his military victories, he did much building in Nineveh, his capital city. Many of the decorations of his palace, as well as inscriptions he prepared, are housed in museums today.

Shortly after Sennacherib became king he was confronted by rebellion in the eastern and western provinces. It is at this point that the biblical record refers to Sennacherib. Judah was a vassal state of Assyria. It is likely that Merodach-baladan in Babylon and Hezekiah, king of Judah, joined in this insurrection (2 Kgs 18:8; cf. 20:12).

Sennacherib was ready for the challenge from Babylon and Palestine. In 703 BC he first led his forces to Kish near Babylon where he defeated Merodach-baladan's army and then captured the city of Babylon itself. Turning west in 701 BC, Sennacherib led his armies against the Palestinian alliance headed by Hezekiah. He captured the cities of Tyre and Sidon and then continued his campaign southward. Several of the Philistine cities submitted before the Assyrian onslaught but Ashkelon, Beth-dagon and Joppa resisted and were captured and plundered. The leaders of the city of Ekron were put to death by being skinned alive because they had delivered up their pro-Assyrian king to Hezekiah. Sennacherib then turned to Judah. He besieged the Judean city of Lachish and captured 46 other towns, taking 200,150 Jewish captives. Hezekiah began to realize his desperate situation as Sennacherib's military victories came one after the other, so he sent tribute to Sennacherib at Lachish. The tribute amounted to 300 talents of silver and 30 talents of gold (2 Kgs 18:13–16). From his camp at Lachish, Sennacherib sent envoys to Jerusalem to demoralize the city inhabitants by asking "On what do you rest this confidence of yours? Do you think that mere words are strategy and power for war?" (vv 19,20). In their effort to convince Jerusalem that it should surrender, the Assyrians referred to Hezekiah's removal of altars and places of worship, an act which was considered an affront to the God the

Lachish besieged by Sennacherib, as portrayed in his palace at Nineveh.

Judeans worshiped and on whom they relied for victory who would not aid a people led by an idol-breaking king as Hezekiah.

It is unclear whether Sennacherib conducted one or two military campaigns into the southern areas of Palestine. Some OT scholars maintain that 2 Kings 18:13–16 describes Sennacherib's military campaign of 701 BC whereas 18:17–19:37 is thought to refer to a later campaign Sennacherib carried out from 689–686 BC. Extrabiblical sources favor the two-campaign view.

While Sennacherib was threatening Jerusalem, Tirhakah, the Ethiopian king of Egypt, led his army to Libnah. Sennacherib was able to defeat this Egyptian force. He then turned his full attention to Jerusalem again. (2 Kgs 19:15–19). Isaiah was sent by God to inform Hezekiah that the mocking Sennacherib would be humbled and Jerusalem would be spared for David's sake (vv 20–34). The Lord's word was fulfilled. Sennacherib's plans to take Jerusalem by siege had to be abandoned when 185,000 of his troops died of a miraculous plague.

Sennacherib returned to Nineveh, the capital city of Assyria. He was murdered in the temple of Nisroch by Adrammelech and Sharezer, two of his sons. A third son, Esar-haddon succeeded him upon the throne of Assyria.

See ASSYRIA, ASSYRIANS.

Sentry. *See* ARMS AND WARFARE; TRADES AND OCCUPATIONS (SOLDIER).

Senuah. KJV form of Hassenuah in Nehemiah 11:9.

See HASSENUAH.

Seorim. Levite and the head of the fourth of 24 divisions of priests formed during David's reign (1 Chr 24:8).

Separation, Water of. KJV translation of "the water for impurity," a water denoting cleansing from sin or impurity, in Numbers 19:9,13,20,21; 31:23.

See CLEANNESS AND UNCLEANNESS, REGULATIONS CONCERNING.

Sephar. Geographical landmark defining one of the boundaries of the territory settled by the sons of Joktan (Gn 10:30). Undoubtedly located in southern Arabia, Sephar is most often identified with one of two towns bearing the Arabic name Zafar: the seaport town in central Yemen's Hadhramaut province or the site in southern Yemen, once the capital of the Himyarites.

Sepharad. Place of exile for the Jews of Jerusalem (Ob 20). Its location is not certain; however, good evidence is available to support Sardis, the capital of Lydia, in Asia Minor as the place of captivity. Other less feasible suggestions are Saparda in eastern Assyria where Sargon transported Jews; and Spain, as mentioned in the Targum of Jonathan.

Sepharvaim, Sepharvite. One of five cities whose inhabitants were transported to Samaria after the fall of Israel to Sargon II, king of Assyria in 722 BC (2 Kgs 17:24). The Sepharvites were remembered for their abominable practice of offering their children as burnt sacrifices to their gods Adrammelech and Anammelech (v 31). In a taunting message to King Hezekiah of Judah (715–686 BC), King Sennacherib of Assyria (705–681 BC) warned that as the gods and kings of Sepharvaim were not able to prevent her fall to the Assyrians so too it would be with Jerusalem and Hezekiah's God (18:34; Is 36:19; 37:13). The location of Sepharvaim is uncertain. It was probably identifiable with the Syrian city of Sibraim near Damascus (Ez 47:16). A less credible suggestion identifies Sepharvaim with the Babylonian city of Sippara along the Euphrates River.

Septuagint. *See* APOCRYPHA, OLD AND NEW TESTAMENT; BIBLE, CANON OF THE; BIBLICAL LANGUAGES.

Sepulcher. *See* BURIAL, BURIAL CUSTOMS.

Serah. Asher's daughter (Gn 46:17; Nm 26:46, KJV Sarah; 1 Chr 7:30).

Seraiah. 1. Royal secretary of King David (2 Sm 8:17); alternately called Sheva in 2 Samuel 20:25, Shisha in 1 Kings 4:3, and Shavsha in 1 Chronicles 18:16.

2. Chief priest in Jerusalem at the time of its destruction by the Babylonians in 586 BC. He was taken by Nebuzaradan, the captain of the guard, to Nebuchadnezzar at Riblah where he was put to death (2 Kgs 25:18; Jer 52:24). 1 Chronicles 6:14 records Seraiah as the son of Azariah, the father of Jehozadak and a descendant of Levi through Aaron's line.

3. Son of Tanhumeth the Netophathite and one of the captains of the Judean forces who sought clemency from Nebuchadnezzar under Gedaliah (2 Kgs 25:23; Jer 40:8).

4. Judahite, the son of Kenaz, the brother of Othniel and Joab's father (1 Chr 4:13,14).

5. Simeonite, the son of Asiel and Joshibiah's father (1 Chr 4:35).

6. One of the men who returned with Zerubbabel to Judah following the exile (Ezr 2:2); called Azariah in Nehemiah 7:7.
See AZARIAH #23.

7. Father of Ezra the scribe. Ezra returned to Jerusalem during the reign of King Artaxerxes I of Persia (464–424 BC; Ezr 7:1). He is perhaps identical with #2 above, in which case Jehozadak would be Ezra's brother.

8. One of the priests who set his seal on the covenant of Ezra (Neh 10:2).

9. Son of Hilkiah and a priest living in Jerusalem during the postexilic era (Neh 11:11); called Azariah in 1 Chronicles 9:11.
See AZARIAH #10.

10. One of the leaders of the priests who returned with Zerubbabel and Jeshua to Judah after the exile (Neh 12:1). His house in the

next generation was headed by Meraiah (v 12). He is perhaps identical with #6 above.

11. Son of Azriel who, with Jerahmeel and Shelemiah, was ordered by King Jehoiakim of Judah (609–598 BC) to capture Baruch and Jeremiah (Jer 36:26).

12. Son of Neriah and the official who accompanied King Zedekiah of Judah (597–586 BC) to Babylon. Seraiah was to relay Jeremiah's message against Babylon (Jer 51:59,61).

Seraph, Seraphim. Angelic beings mentioned only twice in the Bible, both occurrences in the same chapter of Isaiah (6:2,6). The word *seraphim* is plural in number, but it is impossible to say from Isaiah's vision just how many he saw. The prophet spoke of them as though they were quite familiar spiritual beings, which seems a little curious since they are not mentioned elsewhere.

Isaiah described each seraph as having six wings: two shielded the face, two covered the feet, and the remaining pair enabled the seraph to fly.

In the vision the seraphim expressed their thoughts in words which Isaiah understood and reported, but this fact need not be taken to imply that the beings were partly human in form. The most that can be said from the available evidence is that they were exalted spiritual entities who were occupied constantly in the praise and worship of God, and seem to have had delegated to them certain powers by which forgiveness and divine grace could be mediated. This was appropriate for beings who attended the throne of God, the seat of supreme power.

The meaning of seraph is uncertain. Some scholars think that it came from the root "to burn," while others argue for some such meaning as "aristocrat" or "nobleman." One theory associated the seraphim with the fiery serpents (*seraphim*) which afflicted the Israelites in the wilderness, and the bronze serpent set up on a pole (Nm 21:6–9), but this is based upon very questionable etymology.

One proposed identification is with a six-winged creature holding a snake in each hand, carved on a relief from Tell Halaf in Mesopotamia. This figure may have been a representation of the mythological scorpion-men mentioned in the Gilgamesh Epic as guardians of certain sacred mountains.

Some scholars have regarded the seraphim as equivalent to the griffins that were thought to function as guardians by the ancient Babylonians, but there is little evidence to support this view. Equally improbable is the suggestion that there was a connection between certain snake cults in the ancient Near East and the seraphim, if only because the serpent was an accursed species to the Hebrews.

Most probably the seraphim were an order of celestial beings comparable in nature to the cherubim, and engaged in a somewhat similar form of service around the divine throne.

See ANGEL; CHERUB, CHERUBIM.

Sered, Seredite. One of Zebulun's sons (Gn 46:14) and the father of the Seredite family (Nm 26:26, KJV Sardite).

Sergius Paulus. Proconsul of Cyprus, described as a "man of intelligence" (Acts 13:7). Paul and Barnabas on their first missionary journey evangelized the Cyprian city of Paphos, Sergius Paulus' residence. Here they met the Jewish false prophet and sorcerer named Bar-Jesus (or Elymas), who strongly opposed their gospel message before the proconsul. Paul, however, rebuked Elymas and cursed him with blindness. When Sergius Paulus witnessed what had happened he believed, "for he was astonished at the teaching of the Lord" (v 12). Thus he became the first recorded convert on Paul's first missionary journey.

It is here that we find the transition from the name Saul to that of Paul. Origen and many since his time believe that Paul made the change at this point in honor of his famous convert.

Sermon on the Mount. See BEATITUDES, THE; JESUS CHRIST, LIFE AND TEACHING OF.

Serpent. See ANIMALS.

Serpent, Bronze. See BRONZE SERPENT.

Serpent's Stone. Place where Adonijah, the son of David, sacrificed sheep and oxen and attempted to secretly set himself up as king (1 Kgs 1:9). The serpent's stone was located near En-rogel, a spring in the Kidron Valley located just south of Jerusalem. Some suggest that this stone was named for the large stone conduits nearby that emptied into the pool of Siloam; a steep rock formation; or perhaps for a cultic shrine with the serpent used as its emblem. The Stone of Zoheleth is the English equivalent for the Hebrew term preferred by some versions.

Serug. Reu's son from Shem's line (Gn 11:20–23), Abraham's forefather and an ancestor of Jesus Christ (Lk 3:35, KJV Saruch).

See GENEALOGY OF JESUS CHRIST.

Servant. See CHRISTIANS, NAMES FOR; TRADES AND OCCUPATIONS.

Servant of the Lord. Grand title applied to a variety of persons in the Bible. The basic term, *servant*, covers a range of meanings. Used some 800 times in the OT alone, servant refers to a slave (with less stigma than in most recent history), to an officer close to the king, or to the chosen leader of God's people.

Isaiah 41:8,9 defines this highest servanthood as something granted by God's grace: "But you, O Israel, my servant, Jacob whom I have chosen, . . . I took you . . . I called you. I said, 'You are my servant.'" This title is thus applicable to heroes of faith and action—to patriarchs (Gn 26:24; Ez 28:25; 37:25; including Jb 1:8; 2:3; 42:7,8), Moses (Ex 14:31; 1 Kgs 8:53,56; and elsewhere), David (2 Sm 7:26–29; Jer 33:21,22,26; Ez 37:24) and his descendants (as Hezekiah, Eliakim, Zerubbabel—Hg 2:23), the prophets of Jehovah (2 Kgs 10:10; 14:25), and other faithful Israelites such as Joshua and Caleb (Nm 14:24; Jos 24:29; Jgs 2:8).

Prophets other than Isaiah employ this term, but only Zechariah joins him in giving an apparently messianic prediction under this name. Zechariah 3:8 says, "Listen, O high priest Joshua and your associates . . . men symbolic of things to come: I am going to bring my servant, the Branch." Some would see Zerubbabel as the individual in view here (cf. Zec 6:12.); however, the use of "Branch" is decidedly messianic in Isaiah (11:1) and Jeremiah (33:15).

The servant of the Lord in specialized biblical usage points to Messiah, at the same time alluding to Isaiah's central message. Though he, with others, employs *servant* with a range of significations, he composed some passages known as the Servant Songs. These distinctive sections of his bok are distinguishable in content, but they cannot be extracted from the surrounding context without disrupting the flow of prophecy. Isaiah's focus is on the future Messiah-servant.

None can question the NT's unanimous messianic interpretation of Isaiah's servant, nor its application of this understanding to Jesus Christ. The more debatable issue is how to discern a definitive messianic intent in Isaiah's prophecy itself. Most are agreed that Duhm's 1892 commentary on Isaiah correctly highlighted four servant songs: 42:1–4; 49:1–6; 50:4–9; and 52:13–53:12. The last of these is "foolproof," but some would include verses 5–7 in chapter 42, verse 7 in 49, and 10,11 in 50. Should one add Isaiah 61:1, cited by Jesus Christ himself at Nazareth (Lk 4:16–21)?

Though the title *servant* is not repeated here, the theme is unmistakable.

Since Isaiah 49:3 addresses Israel as "my servant," some scholars read a *collective* idea into all the songs. Others find a *cultic* significance, comparing the Babylonian Tammuz myth. Various *individualistic* views suggest some unknown contemporary of Isaiah (or "Deutero-Isaiah"), a choice from known historical figures (e.g., Jeremiah, Cyrus, Zerubbabel, or the prophet himself), or the coming Messiah. The latter was the predominant Christian view until the end of the last century. The *synthetic* interpretation is an attempt to understand a development, progressing from a collective figure to a clear individualization in the fourth song. The movement is personification to person, corporate personality to messianic Savior.

Isaiah sets the stage for the Messiah-servant's appearance by introducing Immanuel in chapter 7, divine Prince in 9, and the Branch in 11. The shock to Israel of a suffering servant-king is eased in this series of songs, where their own corporate struggles (Is 49:4) typify Israel's (and the world's) redeemer. Oscillation between nation (or remnant) and individual is between type and ideal anti-type. Franz Delitzsch suggests a pyramid, with national Israel as the broad base (42:19), spiritual Israel in the center (41:8-10), and Messiah at the apex.

A "servant Christology" pervades Acts (3:13, 26; 4:27,30), and 1 Peter, with numerous allusions in the Gospels. Jesus himself quotes Isaiah 53 explicitly only in Luke 22:37, but he seems to allude to it in Mark 10:45; 14:24; and possibly 9:12. Peter not only emphasizes vicarious, redemptive suffering (1 Pt 2:21-25; 3:18) but seems to highlight the theme of Isaiah 53 in summing up OT prophecy (1:11) as predicting "the sufferings of Christ and the glories that would follow." Paul includes these elements (1 Cor 15:3; Phil 2:6-11; cf. Rom 4:25; 5:19; 2 Cor 5:21), and John's "Lamb of God" title derives from Isaiah 53:7 no less than from the entire sacrificial system.

MILTON C. FISHER

See CHRISTOLOGY.

Bibliography. H.L. Ellison, The Servant of Jehovah; M.D. Hooker, *Jesus and the Servant*; T.W. Manson, *The Servant-Messiah*; C.R. North, *The Suffering Servant in Deutero-Isaiah*; H.H. Rowley, *The Servant of the Lord and Other Essays*; W. Zimmerli and J. Jeremias, *The Servant of God*.

Servitor. KJV rendering of servant in 2 Kings 4:43.

See TRADES AND OCCUPATIONS (SERVANT).

Seth. Third son of Adam and Eve, replacing Abel whom Cain murdered (Gn 4:25). He appears as the firstborn son of Adam in the genealogies of Genesis 5:3-8; 1 Chronicles 1:1 (KJV Sheth); and Luke 3:38. It was through Seth's line that Jesus was born. Seth was the father of Enosh and lived 912 years.

See GENEALOGY OF JESUS CHRIST.

Sethur. Asherite, Michael's son and one of the 12 spies sent by Moses to search out the land of Canaan (Nm 13:13).

Seven. *See* NUMBERS AND NUMEROLOGY.

Seven Last Words, The. Recorded words of Jesus between the time he was crucified and the time he died. These seven sentences are not found in any one Gospel. Instead, the first two and the seventh occur only in Luke, the third, fifth, and sixth only in John, and the fourth in both Matthew and Mark. The order is traditional; because no Gospel records them all, it is uncertain in which order they really came. Also unknown is whether Jesus said other things from the cross or whether the seven sayings are summaries of longer statements, but considering the trauma of crucifixion it would not be surprising if this were all he said.

"Father, forgive them; for they know not what they do" (Lk 23:34).

This is the only one of the seven last words whose genuineness is questioned, for several of the best Greek manuscripts do not contain it. Even if an element of doubt exists (the evidence is fairly evenly balanced), it certainly fits what is known of Jesus and his love, whether or not Luke originally recorded it. Just a few verses before, Jesus showed more concern for others than for himself (Lk 19:41; 22:50,51; 23:28). Jesus lived his own teaching and prayed for those who were torturing him (6:27,28)—no greater impulse for mankind to go and do likewise could be given. Certainly the soldiers and Jewish leaders were not totally unaware of what they were doing (cf. Acts 3:17), but in that they did not know the *real* import of their action they were ignorant. For Christians, the request "Father, forgive" is more important than the reason, as Stephen recognized when he paraphrased it at his own martyrdom (Acts 7:60). In the end, forgiveness demands no reason; it is grace.

"Truly, I say to you, today you will be with me in Paradise" (Lk 23:43).

Luke does not record this statement to teach about the abode of the dead but to express the response of God to faith. One criminal quite understandably joins with the jeering crowd and gets only silence (Lk 23:40), but the other quite remarkably recognizes not only the innocence of Jesus but also that the cross was only a prelude to the crown (vv 40–42). Peter could acclaim Jesus in the midst of his miracles, but this man did it in the midst of his suffering. The response of God to such mighty faith is declared quite simply: "You might expect your sins to damn you, but instead the mercy you asked for is granted. Through faith you will share that bright future you see coming to me." Here again is grace, asked for and received; Jesus did not forget others in the hour of his death.

"Woman, behold your son! . . . Behold, your mother!" (Jn 19:26,27).

Jesus has already cared for both enemies and a new convert. Now he turns to set his own house in order. John pictures Jesus as fully in control of the situation, and at this point that control is obvious as he calmly cares for his mother instead of focusing on his own suffering. Mary was also suffering as the "sword" pierced her heart (Lk 2:35). Jesus, now much more her Lord than her son, remembers his natural as well as his spiritual relationships. It is not known why Jesus' brothers were not around to care for Mary, or why they missed the Passover festival. It also is unknown why the beloved disciple was chosen, but perhaps the choice fell on him because he was there at Calvary, he was trustworthy, and he was a native of Judea, not a Galilean, and owned a house nearby to which he could take Mary.

"My God, my God, why hast thou forsaken me?" (Mt 27:46; Mk 15:34).

It is now hours later than the first three words, deep in the darkness that covered Calvary for the last three hours. Suddenly Jesus cries out the first words of Psalm 22. Mark records them in Jesus' native language, Aramaic, while Matthew changes them to Hebrew. The meaning of the cry (called the cry of dereliction) has been variously explained as an expression of human feeling, a statement of disappointment that God did not deliver him, an expression of separation from God because he was bearing sin, or a citation of the whole psalm with its triumphal ending being intended. Although the full depth of this cry is a mystery known only to Jesus and his Father, it is probable that, because the psalm is a cry to God for vindication, Jesus is here asking for that. He cries to God to show that he is truly God's chosen one, and the cry is partially answered in the resurrection and completely in the second coming.

"I thirst" (Jn 19:28).

At the beginning of the crucifixion Jesus was offered a drugged wine as a soporific to deaden the pain of crucifixion. He refused it (Mt 27:34;

Mk 15:23). Now, severely dehydrated, Jesus accepts the soldiers' sour wine (Jn 19:29) which would sharpen his senses for his final cry. He needed it, for he had been hanging there six hours. Perhaps at no place in the life of Jesus do we see his full humanity quite so clearly as here. For Jesus this was a very human act, but John sees it as a fulfillment of Psalm 22:15 (and perhaps 69:21).

"It is finished" (Jn 19:30).

John completes the crucifixion account with this simple statement (a single word in Greek). The sentence naturally reveals relief and satisfaction that the pain and agony are over, that death will soon release him, but John's context gives the word a deeper meaning. For John, Jesus controls the whole crucifixion. He said that no one could take his life (Jn 10:18; 19:10,11); so here, knowing that he has totally completed the will of the Father, he voluntarily lays his life down. His sovereignty shines through. What is finished, then, is not simply his dying, nor his life *per se*, nor the work of redemption, but the total reason for his being in the world. The last act of obedience has been accomplished; the last scripture has been fulfilled. Jesus proclaims his life "finished," and exits from the stage until the resurrection begins a new act.

"Father, into thy hands I commit my spirit" (Lk 23:46).

Luke has a different picture of the end than John and the other evangelists. Matthew and Mark report only "a great cry" after the cry of dereliction, ending on a dark note. John ends with the completed work. Luke, who reports no feeling of forsakenness, ends by telling us the great cry was a quotation of Psalm 31:5 (cf. Stephen in Acts 7:59). The quotation is prefaced by "Father," the familiar "Abba," a form of address characteristic of Jesus. His relationship to God is unbroken to the end. Jesus is not leaping into the dark or fighting against the unknown, but placing himself in death into the hands of the same Father he has served in life. Thus this saying serves as a model for the dying Christian as Psalm 31 did for the dying Jew.

The seven last words have a deep pastoral content which has captured the imagination of the church. Many forms for Christian meditation focus on these words. They have been celebrated in liturgy (especially Good Friday liturgies). They have been put to music (e.g., Heinrich Schütz in the 1700s). They have been an example of Christian behavior and a basis for passion theology (particularly the fourth). Thus they form an invaluable part of church tradition.

PETER H. DAVIDS

See ELI, ELI, LAMA SABACHTHANI; CRUCIFIXION.

Seventy Weeks, Daniel's. Expression occurring only in Daniel 9:24. It is the central point in a short passage (vv 24–27) which has been described by one modern commentator as "one of the most difficult in all the OT." Part of the difficulty of the expression relates to the interpretation of the passage as a whole; another part relates to the meaning of the Hebrew word which is rendered in English as "weeks."

The basic sense of the word is a "period of seven"; thus the normal sense is "week" or "seven days." This common usage of the word can be seen in Daniel 10:2,3. The word can also mean "a period of seven years"; if taken in this sense, it would be best to translate it as "sevens" and 70 "sevens" would be 490 years. But the word is definitely ambiguous and it is wise to recognize the ambiguity before positing too rigid an interpretation. Both the numbers 7 and 70 indicate a certain roundness or completeness in Hebrew thought. Seven is not only the number of days in a week, but also the number of years in a sabbatical cycle. And 70 is used, in both OT and NT, of groups of people; it is, for example, the number of disciples sent out by Jesus during his earthly ministry (Lk 10:1). These and other factors indicate that the numbers 7 and 70 may have symbolic significance.

The Text: Daniel 9:24–27. At the beginning of chapter 9, Daniel is engaged in prayer to God. During his prayer, he has a vision in which the angel Gabriel appears to him and addresses him. The words in the passage under discussion are thus all explicitly identified as the words of Gabriel to Daniel; in this sense, the words are direct revelation from God to Daniel through the intermediary of an angel. The fact that words are spoken by an angel and perceived in a vision requires an element of care with respect to interpretation; in the other visions perceived by Daniel, there is powerful symbolism.

Central to the revelation in the vision is a period of time which, taken as a whole, is designated "seventy sevens," "seventy weeks," or "seventy weeks or years" (RSV). The whole period breaks down into three component parts: first, "seven sevens" or "seven weeks" (v 25); second, "sixty-two sevens" or "sixty-two weeks" (v 25); and third, "one seven" or "one week," which is divided into halves (v 27). The substance of the whole period, together with its sub-periods, is summarized on the basis of the text in the following table.

The basic difficulty in understanding all the details of the text compounds the difficulty of the interpretation of the passage as a whole. There are three chief problems in interpretation. First, should the word "sevens" be

The Seventy Weeks

Seventy sevens/weeks (Dn 9:24): the whole period

(a) *Negative aims:*	(b) *Positive aims:*
(i) to end transgression	(i) to bring righteousness
(ii) to end sin	(ii) to seal vision and prophecy
(iii) to atone for iniquity	(iii) to anoint a holy one

1. *Seven sevens/weeks* (v 25)
   Time specified: (a) *from* "the going forth of the word to restore and build Jerusalem"
   (b) *to* "the coming of an anointed one"

2. *Sixty-two sevens/weeks* (v 25)
   (a) Jerusalem rebuilt
   (b) time of trouble

3. *One seven/week* (vv 26,27)
   (a) the anointed one cut off
   (b) People of evil prince destroy city and sanctuary
   (c) people make "strong covenant"
   (d) War, desolation, and the end

4. *Half seven/week:* sacrifice and offering cease

interpreted symbolically, or as representing literally "weeks of years" (groups of seven years)? Second, what is the historical starting point for the interpretation of the "seventy sevens/weeks"? It is specified in verse 25 as "the time the command is given to rebuild Jerusalem"; historically, the time that the rebuilding commenced can be specified, but it is not known exactly when the command was given. Third, is the vision, or prophecy, messianic? Or does it have more limited historical perspective? The reference to the "Anointed One" (v 25, literally messiah) certainly implies a messianic interpretation, but it should be recalled that Cyrus is also identified as messiah/ "anointed one" in the OT (Is 45:1).

Interpretations of the "Seventy Weeks." The difficulties noted above have contributed to the multitude of interpretations set forth concerning the "seventy weeks." The three most common interpretations can be summarized as follows.

The first regards the entire passage, in historical terms, as referring to events from the beginning of the exile to the middle of the 2nd century BC; this interpretation is non-messianic. Chronologically, it can be represented as follows:

1. 7 weeks/49 years = 587–538 BC
   (Exile)
2. 62 weeks/434 years = c. 588–171 BC
   (Persian/Greek period)
3. 1 week/7 years = 171–165 BC
   (Antiochus IV)

This interpretation is sometimes advocated from a prophetic perspective; that is, future history was revealed to Daniel in the 6th century BC. More commonly, however, this is the interpretation of those who believe the Book of Daniel was written between 171–165 BC. Thus, from a theological perspective, the vision represents an understanding of past history and a conviction that God is in control of history, despite apparent disasters and chaos.

A second approach to interpretation is to see the passage as messianic in significance, and to attempt to calculate the "weeks of years" literally in relation to messianic events. This kind of interpretation perceives the first "seven weeks" to relate to the rebuilding and restoration of Jerusalem (c. 445–396 BC). The "sixty-two weeks" (434 years, c. 396 BC–AD 38) would culminate in the arrival of the Messiah in Jerusalem and his death a week later. Then, according to this interpretation, there would be a gap (namely, the present age) before the beginning of the "seventieth week," which still lies in the future from our contemporary perspective.

The third interpretation, which is also messianic, differs from the second in that it takes the "weeks" as symbolic periods of time, rather than precise periods of seven years each. Though the details of this type of interpretation differ enormously, a typical approach might be as follows in broad outline. The first period of seven weeks specifies the period of time from Cyrus to the coming of the Messiah (Christ). The second period, 62 weeks, refers to the time since that advent of the Messiah (the present age). The final week, or period, lies still in the future.

In summary, there will continue to be differences of opinion in the future about the significance of the "seventy weeks." It is not too fruitful to argue *ad infinitum* over the calculations. The greatest significance of the text lies in the absolute conviction of the writer that human history, past, present and future, lies ultimately within the control of God, who is infinite.   PETER C. CRAIGIE

Sex, Sexuality. Unlike some religious and philosophical systems, the Bible takes a very positive view of human sexuality. According to the OT's account of creation, it was God himself who made people sexual beings. Being male or female is part of what it means to be created in the image of God (Gn 1:26–28). Above everything else, therefore, sexuality is a precious aspect of what a person *is*, not merely a description of what he or she *does*.

In line with this positive approach, the OT sees nothing embarrassing in the bodily differences between the sexes (Gn 2:25) and nothing shameful in physical expressions of love-making (Prv 5:18,19; Eccl 9:9). The Song of Songs, in particular, is a most beautiful love poem. Its powerful language should not be so spiritualized that the physical passion it describes is stripped of its delight and candor.

Paul strikes the same positive note in his letters to Corinth and to Timothy at Ephesus. Sexual vice was rampant in both these cities. Partly as a reaction to this, a negative, ascetic attitude was threatening to take control in the life of Christians. Marriage was being decried (1 Tm 4:3) and married couples were abandoning intercourse in the belief that this would help them to become more spiritually mature (cf. 1 Cor 7:5). There were even some men who thought that it was "good for a man not to marry" (1 Cor 7:1 NIV).

Paul has no hesitation in branding such attitudes as heretical. Recalling his readers to the message of Genesis, he encourages them to receive God's gifts thankfully (1 Tm 4:3–5). Husbands and wives, he writes, are mutually obliged to express their love for one another in sexual intercourse (1 Cor 7:3,4). Physical love-making in marriage is as much part of what it means to "honor God with your body" as refusing to go to bed with a prostitute (cf. 1 Cor 6:15,20).

As well as telling us that sexuality is the result of the Creator's initiative, the Bible also sets out its two main purposes in human life as God has planned it. Most obviously, God made sex for *procreation* (Gn 1:28). Here we have the basis for family life, something the Scriptures strongly affirm. Salvation on Passover night in Egypt was by families (Ex 12:3), and in early NT times whole households came to salvation in Christ together (e.g., Acts 16:29–34). In days when the focus of interest in the Western world is on the prevention of births, it is salutary to note the Bible's insistence that having children is a special blessing for which married couples should be thankful to God (cf. Gn 24:60).

God's second main purpose in creating man and woman as sexual beings is given even greater prominence in the Bible. Sex is for *relationship* as well as procreation. Genesis 2 describes how God made woman to fill man's relationship vacuum (vv 18–24). The chief reference is to the institution of marriage, as the NT explains (Mt 19:4–6; Eph 5:31–33). But the way key words and phrases from this passage are used in the rest of the OT makes it clear that sexuality has a major role to play in cementing a broad spectrum of human relationships. The phrase "bone of my bones and flesh of my flesh" (Gn 2:23), for example, is not reserved to describe a married couple's intimacy alone. It is also used to express close relationships within the extended family (cf. Jgs 9:2) and even the fierce loyalty a nation felt toward its leader (2 Sm 5:1).

Here is a powerful indicator that the relational purpose of human sexuality embraces far more than physical intercourse. In this broad sense, being male or being female is a God-given aid to making all sorts of relationships—including some not normally thought of as "sexual" at all.

The Bible does not, of course, ignore the darker side of human nature. Having described the goodness of sex in the Creator's perfect plan, Genesis goes on to explain how man's disobedience to God spoiled sex, just as it spoiled every other aspect of human life.

Nudity became a matter of embarrassment and fear, as men and women eyed each other as sex objects instead of as people with physical differences (Gn 3:7–10). On the relational side, trust and tenderness gave way to betrayal and harshness (vv 12,16). Here lies the root cause of all the discrimination and abuse which fuel modern feminist protests. And procreation was spoiled too, as the marvelous experience of childbirth was marred by unnecessary pain and distress (v 16).

This is the context in which the Bible's ban on extramarital intercourse should be read. The veto itself is clear. It covers homosexual practice (Lv 18:22; Rom 1:26,27; 1 Cor 6:9,10; 1 Tm 1:9,10), adultery (Ex 20:14), and premarital sex (1 Cor 6:18; 1 Thes 4:3). Even the thought of such things (as distinct from the temptation to think about them) is wrong, according to Jesus (Mt 5:27,28).

The Bible does not usually pause to back up its prohibitions with arguments, but on the rare occasions when it does expand its veto on extramarital intercourse, the reasons given are highly instructive. There is no appeal to consequences (these things are wrong because they result in disease and unwanted babies) or even to motives (these things are wrong if they are done in an unloving spirit). All extramarital sex is wrong *in itself*, simply because "the body is not meant for sexual immorality" and "he who sins sexually sins against his own body" (1 Cor 6:13,18). In other words, coitus between two unmarried people is a subhuman act, because sexual intercourse is a unique kind of body language which the Creator has designed to express and seal that special, exclusive, lifelong relationship between a man and a woman which the Bible labels "marriage."

The Bible's advice to anyone caught up in sexual temptation is practical. When Joseph was invited by another man's wife to go to bed with her, "he left his cloak in her hand and ran out of the house" (Gn 39:12). And Paul tells his Christian readers to follow Joseph's good example (1 Cor 6:18; 2 Tm 2:22).

This is an acknowledgment of the power of the normal person's sex drive, not a counsel of despair. The power of the Holy Spirit, Paul taught, gives any believer the strength to win the war against sexual temptation. He knew Christians who had found the Spirit's power to gain self-control and conquer the most deeply ingrained habits (1 Cor 6:9–11; Gal 5:22,23; 2 Tm 1:7).

The Bible's guideline for conduct in a morally legitimate sexual relationship is *agapē* love. Again, it is Paul who spells it out most clearly in his teaching on relationships within marriage. Unlike other kinds of loving, *agapē* puts God first and others before self (Eph 5:21–33; cf. Gal 5:13). And this focus on *agapē* destroys the modern assumption that love is a meaningless term outside the context of physical, sexual experience. Jesus called all Christians—single as well as married—to live lives of *agapē* love (Jn 15:12). He never got married himself, but he epitomized *agapē* when he gave his life, in love, for others on the cross (1 Jn 4:9,10).

Finally, there is a strong hint in the NT that God is going to end human sexuality just as he began it. There will be no marriage, Jesus taught, in heaven (Mt 22:30). That is an unlikely but fitting climax to the Bible's teaching on sex and sexuality. When there is no more death, the need to procreate will be over. And when relationships are perfectly loving, there will no longer be any need for a sexual prop to support them. So both of God's main purposes for human sexuality will be perfectly fulfilled in eternity.

DAVID H. FIELD

See MAN, DOCTRINE OF; MARRIAGE, MARRIAGE CUSTOMS; WOMAN, DOCTRINE OF; FAMILY LIFE AND RELATIONS; DIVORCE; VIRGIN.

Bibliography. V.A. Demant, *An Exposition of Christian Sex Ethics*; O.A. Piper, *The Biblical View of Sex and Marriage*; C. G. Scorer, *The Bible and Sex Ethics Today*; H. Thielicke, *The Ethics of Sex*; M.O. Vincent, *God, Sex, and You*.

Shaalbim, Shaalabbin, Shaalbon, Shaalbonite.

Amorite city assigned to Dan's tribe for an inheritance, mentioned between Irshemesh and Aijalon (Jos 19:42, Shaalabbin). The Danites, however, were unable to defeat the Amorites and take possession of the city. When the house of Joseph grew strong, the Ephraimites conquered Shaalbim and reduced the Amorites to forced labor (Jgs 1:35). Later Shaalbim along with the cities of Makaz, Bethshemesh, and Elonbeth-hanan made up Solomon's second administrative district (1 Kgs 4:9). Eliahba the Shaalbonite was one of David's 30 mighty men (2 Sm 23:32; 1 Chr 11:33). Shaalbon is perhaps the same city as Shaalbim. The modern town of Selbit is a suggested site for Shaalbim.

Shaalim. Region within the land of Ephraim or Benjamin where Saul searched for his father's asses (1 Sm 9:4, KJV Shalim). Its exact location is uncertain.

Shaaph. 1. Jahdai's sixth son, included in the genealogy of Caleb, Jerahmeel's brother (1 Chr 2:47).

2. Caleb's son, the brother of Jerahmeel, by Maacah his concubine, and the father of Madmannah (1 Chr 2:49).

Shaaraim. 1. One of 14 cities in the lowland region of the territory allotted to Judah's tribe for an inheritance, listed between Azekah and Adithaim (Jos 15:36, KJV Sharaim). Shaaraim was the direction in which the fleeing Philistines tried to escape from the pursuing Israelites following David's slaying of Goliath (1 Sm 17:52). Its site is perhaps located in the vicinity of the Wadi es-Sant near Azekah.

2. One of 14 cities where the sons of Shimer, a descendant of Simon, dwelt until David's reign (1 Chr 4:31). It is possibly the same city as Sharuhen (Jos 19:6), mentioned in a parallel passage, and Shilhim located in the southern portion of Judah near Edom's border (15:32).

Shaashgaz. Eunuch of King Ahasuerus, in charge of the concubines (Est 2:14).

Shabbethai. 1. Levite who opposed Ezra's suggestion that the sons of Israel should divorce the foreign women they had married upon returning to Palestine from exile (Ezr 10:15). He explained the Law to the people at Ezra's reading (Neh 8:7).

2. One of the chiefs of the Levites who oversaw the outside work of the sanctuary during the postexilic period (Neh 11:16). He is perhaps identical with #1 above.

Shachia. KJV spelling of Sachia, Shaharaim's son, in 1 Chronicles 8:10.

See SACHIA.

Shaddai. Part of the Hebrew name "El Shaddai," for God, meaning "God Almighty" (Ps 68:14).

See GOD, NAMES OF.

Shadrach, Meshach, and Abednego. Babylonian names of three Hebrew youths, Hananiah, Mishael, and Azariah, who along with Daniel and others were taken to Babylon as hostages by Nebuchadnezzar in 605 BC (2 Kgs 24:1; Dn 1:1–4). They may have been of royal descent (2 Kgs 20:18; Is 39:7) and their presence in Babylon guaranteed the good behavior of the Judean king Jehoiakim. Desiring to grace his court with intelligent and handsome men and to provide able administrators for his kingdom, Nebuchadnezzar directed that certain of the Judean hostages be selected for special training. Among those chosen were Daniel and "his three friends." Their Hebrew names, each of which exalted Jehovah, were changed to Babylonian names whose meanings are not clear but may have been intended to honor a Babylonian god. Thus Hananiah ("The Lord is gracious") was changed to Shadrach ("Command of Aku"—the Sumerian moon god). Mishael ("Who is what God is") was changed to Meshach ("Who is what Aku is"), and Azariah ("The Lord has helped") was changed to Abednego ("Servant of Nabu"—the Babylonian god of wisdom). Also Daniel ("My judge is God") was changed to Belteshazzar ("Bel protects"—the chief Babylonian god). These young men underwent a three-year course of instruction in the languages and literature of the Chaldeans, the learned men of Babylon. This instruction would have included the Aramaic, Akkadian, and Sumerian languages; cuneiform writing; and perhaps also astronomy, mathematics, history, and agriculture.

Nebuchadnezzar provided food for this academy. The four Hebrew youths refused to defile themselves with it because it likely had been sacrificed to one or more of the pagan gods. It had not been properly prepared, therefore, and was unfit for Jewish consumption (cf. Ex 34:15; Lv 17:10–14). Fearing the king's displeasure should the young scholars appear undernourished, the chief eunuch expressed his concern to Daniel. Daniel proposed a substitute diet of vegetables to be tested for 10 days. At the end of that period, the four Hebrew youths appeared healthier than their colleagues and were allowed to continue their diet. When the course of their instruction was completed, the four stood out from the rest because of their academic excellence and superior competence in every area of knowledge. Their intellectual superiority had been bestowed upon them by God but the very nature of their faith in the true God enabled them to see through the futile superstitions of the pagan culture in which they lived.

Apparently these four young men joined the ranks of the "wise men of Babylon" (Dn 2:12–49). When the enchanters, sorcerers, and wise men of Babylon were unable to tell Nebuchadnezzar the nature and interpretation of a dream, he lashed out at them in a fitful rage and ordered them all put to death. Daniel appealed to the king and their lives were spared when the dream and its interpretation were made known to him in a vision. Later Shadrach, Meshach, and Abednego refused to comply with the king's command to prostrate themselves before an enormous golden image which Nebuchadnezzar had erected (ch 3). Confronted by Nebuchadnezzar and threatened with terrible punishment for their intransigence, they replied that their trust was fully in the Lord. A blazing furnace was stoked so that the heat was far more intense than usual, for the immediate execution of the faithful Hebrews. The Lord was with his faithful servants and preserved their lives by sending his angel to protect them in the furnace. In the end it was Nebuchadnezzar who had to acknowledge that his own kingdom and power could not compare to the power of the true God.

See DANIEL, BOOK OF.

Shagee, Shage. Hararite and Jonathan's father (1 Chr 11:34, KJV Shage). Jonathan was one of David's mighty men.

Shaharaim. Benjamite living in Moab, father of nine sons, who sent away two of his three wives (1 Chr 8:8).

Shahazumah, Shahazimah. Town situated between Tabor and Beth-shemesh on the border of the land allotted to Issachar's tribe for an inheritance (Jos 19:22, KJV Shahazimah). Its location is unknown.

Shalem. Mistranslation for a town near the city of Shechem to which Jacob traveled (Gn 33:18). It is not to be confused with Salem, the residence of Melchizedek (14:18). A better reading would translate Shalem, meaning "safe," as the description of Jacob's journey: "Now Jacob came safely to the city of Shechem."

Shalim. KJV spelling of Shaalim in 1 Samuel 9:4.

See SHAALIM.

Shalishah, Shalisha. One of the regions, mentioned between the hill country of Ephraim and the district of Shaalim, through which Saul traveled in search of his father's lost asses (1 Sm 9:4, KJV Shalisha). Its specific location is uncertain, though most likely in the land of Ephraim.

Shallecheth, Gate of. Gate located on the western side of the temple, which was guarded by Shuppim and Hosah (1 Chr 26:16). Some have speculated that it was a refuse door. This is inconsistent, however, with the refuse door located on the eastern side by the Kidron Valley.

See TABERNACLE, TEMPLE.

Shallum. 1. Son of Jabesh and Israel's 16th king (752 BC). In a conspiracy against King Zechariah, Shallum murdered the monarch at Ibleam and declared himself ruler of Israel during the 39th year of King Uzziah's reign in Judah (792–740 BC). However, in like manner, he was killed at the hands of Gadi after ruling for only one month (2 Kgs 15:10–15).

See ISRAEL, HISTORY OF; CHRONOLOGY, OLD TESTAMENT.

2. Son of Tikvah (alternately spelled Tokhath, see 2 Chr 34:22), who was keeper of the wardrobe and the husband of Huldah the prophetess, living in Jerusalem during the days of King Josiah (640–609 BC; 2 Kgs 22:14).

3. Sismai's son and the father of Jekamiah from Judah's tribe (1 Chr 2:40,41).

4. Alternate name for Jehoahaz, the youngest of King Josiah's four sons and later Judah's 17th king, in 1 Chronicles 3:15 and Jeremiah 22:11.

See JEHOAHAZ #2.

5. Shaul's son, Simeon's grandson, and the father of Mibsam (1 Chr 4:25).

6. Alternate name for Meshullam, Zadok's son and Ezra's forefather, in 1 Chronicles 6:12,13 and Ezra 7:2.

See MESHULLAM #7.

7. Alternate name for Shillem, the youngest of Naphtali's four sons, in 1 Chronicles 7:13.

See SHILLEM, SHILLEMITE.

8. Alternate name for Meshullam, Kore's son and chief of the gatekeepers (1 Chr 9:17,19,31; Ezr 2:42; Neh 7:45).

See MESHULLAM #20.

9. Ephraimite and the father of Jehizkiah (2 Chr 28:12).

10. One of the Levitical gatekeepers who was encouraged by Ezra to divorce his foreign wife during the postexilic era (Ezr 10:24).

11. One of the descendants of Binnui who was encouraged by Ezra to divorce his foreign wife (Ezr 10:42).

12. Hallohesh's son and a ruler of Jerusalem who, along with his daughters, repaired the section of city wall next to the Tower of the Ovens (Neh 3:12).

13. Colhozeh's son and ruler of the Mizpah district, who rebuilt the Fountain Gate and "the wall of the Pool of Shelah of the king's garden, as far as the stairs that go down from the City of David" (Neh 3:15, KJV Shallun).

14. Uncle of Hanamel and Jeremiah, who sold to the latter his field at Anathoth during King Zedekiah's reign (597–586 BC; Jer 32:7). He is perhaps identifiable with #2 above.

15. Maaseiah's father. Maaseiah, keeper of the threshold, owned a chamber in the sanctuary during Jehoiakim's reign (609–598 BC; Jer 35:4; cf. 52:24).

Shallun. KJV spelling of Shallum, Colhozeh's son, in Nehemiah 3:15.

See SHALLUM #13.

Shalmai. Alternate rendering of Shamlai in Ezra 2:46 (KJV) and Nehemiah 7:48.

See SHAMLAI.

Shalman. Unknown conqueror whose brutal destruction of Beth-arbel was descriptive of Israel's approaching judgment (Hos 10:14). Several suggestions as to the identification of Shalman are Salamanu, the king of Moab who paid tribute to Tiglath-pileser of Assyria; one of the Shalmaneser kings of Assyria; or Shalmah, a north Arabian tribe that invaded the Negeb.

Shalmaneser. Name of several Assyrian rulers, two of whom had direct contact with the people of Israel. However, only the latter is known by name in the Bible.

1. Shalmaneser I (1274–1245 BC), the first king of this name, was active in the days when Israel was emerging as a significant group in Palestine. He had no direct contact with Israel.

2. Shalmaneser II (1030–1019 BC) was roughly contemporary with King Saul, but he had no contact with Israel.

3. Shalmaneser III (859–824 BC) had the first significant contact with Israel. This ruler made frequent raids into the lands west of Assyria during his reign. In his annals, he left accounts of his exploits and gave lists of small kingdoms he overwhelmed. From time to time these kingdoms formed coalitions to resist the Assyrian advance. Early in his reign he overwhelmed a north Syrian coalition. In the year 853 BC he encountered a south Syrian coalition led by Irhuleni of Hamath and Hadadezer of Damascus at Qarqar (Karkara). A notable ally on that occasion was Ahab the Israelite (874–853 BC) who, according to the annals of Shalmaneser, provided 2000 chariots and 10,000 foot soldiers for the battle. Shalmaneser claimed to have won this battle, but the fact that he did not return to the west for three years suggests that his forces were severely defeated. In fact, rulers to the west returned to their own local struggles during those years (cf. 1 Kgs. 16:29; 20:20; 22:1).

Another significant entry in the annals of Shalmaneser III is his reference to a campaign against Syria in 841 BC in which he claimed to have defeated Hazael of Damascus (1 Kgs 19:15–18). He did not capture Damascus but moved further west to the region of Lebanon, where he received tribute from "Jehu, son of Omri." The black obelisk on which he recorded these events portrays Jehu, the king of Israel (842–814 BC), on his knees submitting to Shal-

The Black Obelisk of Shalmaneser III.

maneser while Israelites bear assorted booty to present to the king. This event is not mentioned in the Bible. Another interesting entry in his annals is the reference to Hazael as "a commoner" (lit. son of nobody) who "seized the throne." It is clear from 2 Kings 8:7–15 that the story of Hazael's usurpation of the throne of Damascus from Ben-hadad was also known in Israel.

4. Shalmaneser IV (782–772 BC) had no contact with Israel. He ruled Assyria during a period of decline. His successor Tiglath-pileser III (745–727 BC) was an exceedingly vigorous and able ruler who conducted campaigns in Syria and further west from 743 BC onwards and made several contacts with Israel (2 Kgs 15:17–29).

5. Shalmaneser V (727–722 BC) was able to

bring Hoshea, the last king of Israel (732–723 BC), under his control (2 Kgs 17:3). Hoshea failed to pay his annual tribute in his seventh regnal year and was visited by Shalmaneser V who placed Samaria, the capital of Israel, under siege. The king of Egypt was implicated in this treachery in some way (v 3), for he gave encouragement to Hoshea in his rebellious intentions. The siege of Samaria lasted for three years (v 5), and in Hoshea's ninth year the city fell. The biblical record seems to attribute the fall of the city to Shalmaneser (vv 3–6). Unfortunately there are no extant records for the reign of Shalmaneser V, and the capture of Samaria was claimed by Shalmaneser's son Sargon II (721–705 BC) in his own annals as an important event in his accession year. However, the Assyrian Eponym List refers to the siege of Samaria as a reprisal for Hoshea's failure to pay tribute and seems to belong to the years 725–723 BC. The Babylonian Chronicle, in a reference to Shalmaneser's reign, states that he "broke [the resistance] of the city of Shamara in." There is some doubt about whether this refers to Samaria. Certainly verse 6 does not introduce a new name into the record, and it is likely that the "king of Assyria" referred to is Shalmaneser V (cf 18:9–12). It is possible that Sargon usurped the throne during the last stages of the siege of Samaria or that Shalmaneser V died or was murdered during the siege, so that Sargon continued the campaign and brought it to a successful conclusion.   JOHN A. THOMPSON

See ASSYRIA, ASSYRIANS.

Shama. One of the mighty men of David's army, son of Hotham the Aroerite and the brother of Jeiel (1 Chr 11:44).

Shamariah. KJV spelling of Shemariah, King Rehoboam's son, in 2 Chronicles 11:19.

See SHEMARIAH #2.

Shamed. KJV spelling of Shemed, one of Elpaal's sons, in 1 Chronicles 8:12.

See SHEMED.

Shamer. 1. KJV spelling of Shemer, Bani's son, in 1 Chronicles 6:46.

See SHEMER #2.

2. KJV spelling of Shemer, Heber's son, in 1 Chronicles 7:34.

See SHEMER #3.

Shamgar. Son of Anath from Beth-anath. Two brief references in the OT (Jgs 3:31; 5:6) tell us little of the man except for his one major exploit: the killing of 600 Philistines with an oxgoad. How such a feat was performed is not recorded. The oxgoad could

have had a sharpened metal tip, and may have been used as a spear. The timing of the reference indicates that his deeds took place early in the period of Philistine settlement in Canaan. Judges 5:6 would place him prior to the battle of Kishon (c. 1125 BC). If indeed responsible for the deaths of 600 Philistines, his exploits would have brought some respite to the Israelites. It is not known whether he himself was an Israelite or a Canaanite.

Suggestions have been made that Shamgar was Ben-anath, a sea captain from Syria and the son-in-law of Rameses II, or that the oxgoad described in the event was the name of a ship. Both theories seem unlikely.

See JUDGES, BOOK OF.

Shamhuth. Alternate form of Shammah the Izrahite in 1 Chronicles 27:8.

See SHAMMAH #4.

Shamir (Person). Micah's son from Levi's tribe (1 Chr 24:24).

Shamir (Place). 1. One of the 11 towns in the hill country allotted to Judah. First in the list of towns, Shamir is followed by Jattir (Jos 15:48). Its location is perhaps at el-Bireh, about 12 miles W,SW of Hebron.

2. Town where Tola the judge lived and was later buried. Shamir was in the land of Ephraim (Jgs 10:1,2). Its location is unknown.

Shamlai. Father of a family of temple servants returning to the land of Canaan with Zerubbabel after the Babylonian captivity; alternately spelled Shalmai in Ezra 2:46 (KJV) and Nehemiah 7:48.

Shamma. Zophah's son from Asher's tribe (1 Chr 7:37).

Shammah. 1. One of Reuel's four sons, the grandson of Esau and a chief in the land of Edom (Gn 36:13,17; 1 Chr 1:37).

2. Third-born of Jesse's eight sons, the brother of David and the father of Jonathan and Jonadab (1 Sm 16:9; 17:13). Shammah is alternately called Shimea in 1 Chronicles 2:13 (KJV Shimma) and 20:7, Shimeah in 2 Samuel 13:3, and Shimei in 21:21 (KJV Shimeah).

3. Son of Agee the Hararite and one of the elite among David's mighty men. He was renowned for his valiant stand against the Philistines at Lehi (2 Sm 23:11).

4. Harodite and one of David's 30 valiant warriors. He was listed between Elhanan and Elika (2 Sm 23:25). The parallel passage of 1 Chronicles 11:27 reads Shammoth, the plural form of Shammah. Shamhuth the Irahite, the

commander of a division of David's soldiers, is perhaps also the same man (27:8).

5. Hararite and one of David's mighty men, listed between Jonathan and Ahiam (2 Sm 23:33).

Shammai. 1. Onam's son, brother of Jada and the father of Nadab and Abishur from Judah's tribe (1 Chr 2:28,32).

2. Rekem's son and the father of Mahon from Caleb's house (1 Chr 2:44,45).

3. Mered's son by Bithiah, Pharaoh's daughter, and a descendant of Caleb (1 Chr 4:17).

4. Prominent rabbi whose life spanned the period 50 BC to AD 30. His name is most frequently coupled with that of his equally famous contemporary, Hillel, who was president of the Sanhedrin while Shammai was vice-president. Shammai had the reputation for being strict and rigid in his application of the Law and severely literal in his interpretation of the Scriptures, while Hillel was more liberal and humane in applying the Law and more imaginative in the use of the Scriptures. Shammai was renowned for his hatred of Roman domination and tried to forbid Jewish people from buying food or drink from Gentiles.

Two schools of interpretation followed these two contemporaries—"the house of Shammai" and "the house of Hillel"—continuing to the time of the compilation of the Mishna, though the house of Hillel seems to have gradually gained ascendancy over the house of Shammai. The debates and conversations between the two rabbis or the two schools are recorded in the Mishna and the Talmud, relating to such matters as offerings, priestly dues, tithes, levitical cleanness and uncleanness, the observance of the sabbath, marriage, and divorce.

Of greatest interest from the NT point of view is the probability that when it is said in Matthew 19:3 (cf. Mk 10:2) that "Pharisees came up to him [Jesus] and tested him by asking, 'Is it lawful to divorce one's wife for any cause?'" they wanted to see whether he would side with the school of Shammai or the school of Hillel. The Shammai school would allow divorce only for what was morally shameful while the school of Hillel allowed a husband to divorce his wife for a variety of lesser reasons.

Not all of Shammai's interpretations, however, were rigid, and the Mishna quotes as a celebrated dictum of his: "Make your study of the Law a matter of established regularity; say little and do much; and receive all men with a friendly countenance."

See HILLEL; JUDAISM; PHARISEES; TALMUD.

Shammoth. Alternate form of Shammah the Harodite in 1 Chronicles 11:27.

See SHAMMAH #4.

Shammua. 1. Reubenite, Zaccur's son and one of the 12 spies sent by Moses to search out the land of Canaan (Nm 13:4).

2. Alternate name for Shimea, David's son, in 2 Samuel 5:14 and 1 Chronicles 14:4.

See SHIMEA #2.

3. Alternate name for Shemaiah, Galal's son, in Nehemiah 11:17.

See SHEMAIAH #6.

4. Head of a family that returned to Jerusalem with Zerubbabel after the Babylonian exile and who set his seal on Ezra's covenant (Neh 12:18).

Shammuah. KJV spelling of Shammua, an alternate name for Shimea, David's son, in 2 Samuel 5:14.

See SHIMEA #2.

Shamsherai. Jeroham's son and a chief in Benjamin's tribe (1 Chr 8:26).

Shapham. Leader in Gad's tribe (1 Chr 5:12). He is believed to have lived in Bashan and served during the days of Jotham, king of Judah (v 17).

Shaphan. 1. Son of Azaliah and the father of Ahikam, Elasah, and Gemariah. He and his household favored Josiah's reforms, supported the prophet Jeremiah, and complied with Babylonian hegemony.

Shaphan served as the royal secretary to Josiah, king of Judah (640–609 BC). He read the book of the Law to the king after it was found by the high priest Hilkiah in the sanctuary of Jerusalem. Later Josiah sent him with a small delegation to hear the words of the prophetess Huldah (2 Kgs 22:3–14; 2 Chr 34:8–20).

Shaphan's sons were mentioned among the political leaders of Judah during the days of its desolation by Nebuchadnezzar and Babylon (605–586 BC). Ahikam assisted with the repair of the sanctuary and protected Jeremiah from the men who sought his death during the reign of King Jehoiakim (609–598 BC; 2 Kgs 22:12; Jer 26:24). Elasah delivered a message from King Zedekiah of Judah (597–586 BC) to Nebuchadnezzar in Babylon (Jer 29:3). Gemariah was the prince of Judah from whose chamber Baruch read the scroll of Jeremiah to the people (36:10–12).

Shaphan was the grandfather of Micaiah (Jer 36:11–13) and Gedaliah. Gedaliah was appointed governor of Judah by Nebuchadnezzar (2 Kgs 25:22; Jer 40:5–11) and ordered to protect Jeremiah (Jer 39:14). Gedaliah was later murdered by a mob led by Ishmael (Jer 41:2).

2. Father of Jaazaniah and, in Ezekiel's vi-

sion, a leader of idolatrous practices in Israel (Ez 8:11).

Shaphat. 1. Simeonite, Hori's son and one of the 12 spies sent by Moses to search out the land of Canaan (Nm 13:5).

2. Father of the prophet Elisha from the town of Abel-meholah (1 Kgs 19:16,19; 2 Kgs 3:11; 6:31).

3. Youngest of Shemaiah's six sons from Judah's tribe and a descendant of David (1 Chr 3:22).

4. Gadite chief in Bashan, a region west of the Jordan River (1 Chr 5:12).

5. Adlai's son and a member of King David's staff. Shaphat had charge of David's cattle in the valleys (1 Chr 27:29).

Shapher. KJV form of Shepher, the name of an unidentified mountain, in Numbers 33:23, 24.

See SHEPHER, MOUNT.

Shaphir. One of the towns spoken against by Micah the prophet (Mi 1:11, KJV Saphir). Its exact location is not certain. Eusebius (a 4th-century church historian) suggested that it was a village positioned between the cities of Eleutheropolis and Ashkelon, placing Shaphir in Philistine territory. If this is correct, perhaps Shaphir is identifiable with one of three villages known as es-Suwafir near the city of Ashdod. Another possible site is Khirbet el-Kom, situated west of Hebron in the hill country of Judah.

Sharai. One of Binnui's sons who was encouraged by Ezra to divorce his foreign wife during the postexilic era (Ezr 10:40).

Sharaim. KJV spelling of Shaaraim, a city in Judah's territory, in Joshua 15:36.

See SHAARAIM #1.

Sharar. Alternate name for Sachar, Ahiram's father, in 2 Samuel 23:33.

See SACHAR, SACAR #1.

Sharezer. 1. One of the sons of Sennacherib, the king of Assyria. In 681 BC he, along with his brother, Adrammelech, killed Sennacherib while he was praying in the house of Nisroch (2 Kgs 19:37; Is 37:38).

2. One who was sent from Bethel to inquire from the priests and prophets in postexilic Jerusalem as to whether or not the mourning and feasting in commemoration of the destruction of the temple should be confined to the fifth month of that year. The temple was nearing its restoration and so there was some ques-

tion about the commemoration on the part of the populace at Bethel (Zec 7:2, KJV Sherezer).

Sharon. Section of the plain on the Mediterranean coast of Israel. It extends from Joppa in the south to the Crocodile River, which serves as the northern border and separates it from the Plain of Dor. The largest of the northern coastal plains, it is 34 miles from north to south and 10 miles wide. Its shore is straight and consists of beach and cliffs. There are no natural harbors along the coast, so the plain had no large trading ports. The Via Maris, a major north/south trading route, skirted the eastern edge of the plain.

Five streams or wadis cross the Sharon Plain: Nahal Tanninim (Crocodile River), Nahal Hadera, Nahal Alexander, Nahal Poleg, and Nahal Yarqon. These streams drain water from the Samaritan hills and empty into the Mediterranean. Until recent times the streams formed extensive swamps which were infested with malaria-carrying mosquitoes. Sharon also has sand dune hills which rise to an elevation of 180 feet above sea level in the central part of the plain. In biblical times the elevated areas of the Sharon were covered with oak trees. The combination of swamps, sand dunes, and forests made the area almost impenetrable. The plain was granted to Manasseh's tribe by Joshua (Jos 17); but it was not effectively controlled by Israel until the time of David (1 Chr 27:29) and even then it was only used for pasturage.

In the Book of Isaiah the Sharon is ranked with the regions of Carmel and Lebanon for its fertility and luxuriance (33:9; 35:2). It seems, however, that the area was somewhat exotic to the Hebrew mind which regarded the rugged, rocky terrain of the central hill country as normative. When Isaiah speaks of the final restoration, he refers to the Sharon pastures as the place for flocks (65:10).

At the time of the exile it was depopulated, but more than 700 men from the towns of Lod, Hadid, and Ono returned from captivity and probably resettled in those towns in the plain (Ezr 2:33; Neh 7:37).

The "rose of Sharon" (Sg 2:1) may have been one of several varieties of red flowering plants which grow in the plain. The beauty of the rose is contrasted with the dense bramble-like underbrush characteristic of the plain.

In NT times Herod built the lavish city of Caesarea, named in honor of Caesar Augustus, in the northern part of the plain. He constructed a breakwater to the north and south of the city to form an artificial harbor. This allowed Caesarea to become a major maritime trading center. It was at Caesarea that Pilate resided in the governor's residence. Paul used this port as a point of departure on his way to

Tarsus (Acts 9:30). The centurion Cornelius lived there. Paul landed at the city when returning from his second and third missionary journeys. He was imprisoned there for two years. Lydda was also a plain city. Peter visited the Christian community residing in it. When Peter healed Aeneas, it is recorded that all those who lived at Lydda and Sharon turned to the Lord (v 35, KJV Saaron).

2. Place perhaps identical with the town of Lasharon in Joshua 12:18.

See LASHARON.

3. Area east of the Jordan called "the pasture lands of Sharon" in 1 Chronicles 5:16.

Sharonite. Designation for Shitrai, a royal steward in charge of David's flocks in the plain of Sharon (1 Chr 27:29).

Sharuhen. Alternate name for Shaaraim, a city in Simeon's territory, in Joshua 19:6.

See SHAARAIM #2.

Shashai. Binnui's son, who was encouraged by Ezra to divorce his foreign wife during the postexilic era (Ezr 10:40).

Shashak. Benjamite, Elpaal's son and the father of 11 sons (1 Chr 8:14,25).

Shaul. 1. Alternate name for Saul, an Edomite king, in Genesis 36:37,38 and 1 Chronicles 1:48,49.

See SAUL #1.

2. Son of Simeon by a Canaanite woman (Gn 46:10; Ex 6:15; 1 Chr 4:24) and head of the Shaulite family (Nm 26:13).

3. Levite and Uzziah's son from the house of Kohath (1 Chr 6:24).

Shaulite. Descendant of Shaul from Simeon's tribe (Nm 26:13).

See SHAUL #2.

Shaveh, Valley of. Alternate name for the King's Valley near Jerusalem in Genesis 14:17.

See KING'S VALLEY.

Shaveh-kiriathaim. Plain east of the Dead Sea near the city of Kiriathaim and occupied by the people of Emim. The Emimites in Shaveh-kiriathaim are listed with a number of other tribes and nations which King Chedorlaomer and his allies defeated (Gn 14:5). This plain was later inherited by the sons of Reuben.

Shavsha. Alternate name for Seraiah, the secretary to King David, in 1 Chronicles 18:16.

See SERAIAH #1.

Sheal. One of Bani's sons who was told by Ezra to divorce his foreign wife (Ezr 10:29).

Shealtiel. Son of King Jeconiah (Jehoiachin) of Judah (598–597 BC) and the father of Zerubbabel. Zerubbabel led the Jews back to Palestine and there ruled as governor of Judah during the postexilic period (Ezr 3:2; 5:2; Neh 12:1; Hg 1:1,12,14). In the genealogies of Christ, Shealtiel is variously mentioned as the son of Jeconiah (Mt 1:12) and as the son of Neri (Lk 3:27). In 1 Chronicles 3:17–19, Shealtiel appears to be the grandfather or perhaps the uncle of Zerubbabel. One probable solution is that Shealtiel was the son of Neri and the heir apparent to the throne of Jeconiah and, at Shealtiel's death, Zerubbabel was next in succession. Salatheil is the KJV spelling of Shealtiel (1 Chr 3:17; Mt 1:12; Lk 3:27).

Sheariah. One of Azel's six sons, a descendant of Jonathan, son of King Saul, from Benjamin's tribe (1 Chr 8:38; 9:44).

Shearing House. KJV translation for Betheked, a place on the road between Jezreel and Samaria, in 2 Kings 10:12,14.

See BETH-EKED.

Shear-jashub. Isaiah's son whose name, meaning "a remnant shall return," symbolized the prophecy that, although Israel and Judah would be destroyed, a remnant would be saved and later return (Is 7:3).

Sheba (Person). 1. Son of Raamah, the brother of Dedan and a descendant of Noah through Ham's line (Gn 10:7; 1 Chr 1:9).

2. One of the 13 sons of Joktan and a descendant of Noah through Shem's line (Gn 10:28; 1 Chr 1:22).

3. Son of Jokshan, the brother of Dedan and the grandson of Abraham and Keturah (Gn 25:3; 1 Chr 1:32).

4. Benjamite and the son of Bichri. After the death of Absalom, Sheba incited Israel to rebel against David. Under the command of Joab, the revolt was subdued and Sheba was beheaded at Abel-beth-maacah (2 Sm 20:1–22).

5. One of the Gadite leaders ruling in Bashan, registered during the reigns of Jotham king of Judah (750–732 BC) and Jeroboam II king of Israel (793–753 BC).

Sheba (Place). 1. One of 13 cities assigned to Simeon's tribe within the southern portion of Judah's inheritance. Sheba was named between Beersheba and Moladah (Jos 19:2). Its identity and location are uncertain. Some suggest that Sheba is a later copying mistake and should read Shema (cf. Jos 15:26). Others identify it with Tell es-Saba' near Beersheba.

2. Territory located in southwestern Arabia known also as the kingdom of Saba'. The Sabeans were of Semitic descent and governed by a priest-king ruler from the royal city of Ma'rib. During the Solomonic era (970–930 BC), the Queen of Sheba traveled to Jerusalem to see Solomon's riches and to test his wisdom with riddles. Solomon exceeded her expectations on both counts (1 Kgs 10:1–13; 2 Chr 9:1–12).

The Sabeans were a merchant people holding trade relations with Israel and other countries as far east as India. Rich in spices, precious stones and agricultural commodities, the people of Sheba established a network of overland and sea routes to trade their wares (Ps 72:10,15; Is 60:6; Jer 6:20; Ez 27:22,23). Numerous inscriptions have been found attesting to the Sabean civilization in southern Arabia and their travels.

Sheba, Queen of. *See* SHEBA (PLACE) #2.

Shebah. KJV rendering of Shibah, a well near Beersheba, in Genesis 26:33.

See SHIBAH.

Shebam. KJV spelling of Sebam, a city in Reuben's territory, in Numbers 32:3.

See SEBAM.

Shebaniah. 1. One of the seven priests assigned to blow a trumpet before the ark of God in the procession led by David when the ark was moved to Jerusalem (1 Chr 15:24).

2. One of the Levites who led the people in worship following Ezra's reading of the Law (Neh 9:4,5) and who set his seal on the covenant of Ezra (10:10).

3. Head of a priestly family who set his seal on the covenant of Ezra (Neh 10:4; 12:14) and perhaps the same person as Shecaniah in Nehemiah 12:3.

See SHECANIAH #9.

4. Another Levite who set his seal on the covenant of Ezra (Neh 10:12).

Shebarim. Location between Ai and Jericho to which the men of Ai pursued the fleeing Israelites. This region was evidently situated near the place of descent from the hill country to the lowlands (Jos 7:5). Shebarim means "breaches" or "ruins" and might possibly refer to the rough, rocky conditions that would characterize the region at the top of a steep mountain slope. Its location is unknown.

Shebat. Name of the Hebrew month extending from about mid-January to about mid-February in Zechariah 1:7.

See CALENDARS, ANCIENT AND MODERN.

Sheber. Caleb's son by his concubine Maacah (1 Chr 2:48).

Shebna, Shebnah. Eighth-century official of the kingdom of Judah. The name "Shebna," alternately spelled "Shebnah," is Aramaic in form and has been interpreted to mean "return please [O Lord]," relating it to either a fuller spelling (Shebaniah) or to a Semitic root meaning "youthful."

Because of the Aramaic spelling, some have argued that Shebnah was of foreign birth. The appearance of the name, however, on several contemporary Palestinian inscriptions (e.g., from Lachish) may make such a view unnecessary.

Two major passages mention Shebnah by name: Isaiah 22:15–25 and 2 Kings 18:17–19:7. The unlikelihood of two men with the same name, both holding high-ranking positions in the Judahite government in the same general time period, has caused most scholars to argue that the two passages in Isaiah and 2 Kings refer to a single individual. Against this it may be noted that the name itself was quite common and that the office held by the Shebna in each passage is different.

Of greater significance than the identity of Shebna is the fact that the oracle in Isaiah 22 cannot be dated with assurance. In verse 15, Shebna carries the title *ha-soken*, a difficult Hebrew word to translate, but probably the reflection of a commonly known official title in Assyrian political structure. In Assyrian government the office was that of treasurer, but Shebna is also titled "the one who is in charge of the [king's] household" (v 15). This second title carried great authority and probably means that Shebna was second only to the king in rank.

Because of his arrogance in building an ostentatious tomb for himself and because of excessive pride in his position and importance, Shebna was denounced by the prophet Isaiah. In fact, the prophet even predicted that Shebna would go into exile and die in a foreign country (Is 22:18). But the verses immediately following this prediction speak merely of Shebna's demotion and his replacement by Eliakim. There is no simple explanation for these two apparently contrasting statements which stand together in Isaiah.

On the contrary, the events described in 2 Kings 18:17–19:7 (cf. the parallel account in Is 37) are clearly traceable to the year 701 BC and the invasion of Sennacherib. If the Shebna described in this story is the same person denounced by Isaiah in the passage just discussed, as seems likely, the date of the prophetic denouncement must be placed sometime earlier than 701.

In 701, the Assyrian ruler Sennacherib captured virtually all of the cities of Judah and clearly had his heart set on the capture of Jerusalem. King Hezekiah of Judah sent three official representatives to negotiate with the invading Assyrians: Joah, Eliakim, and Shebna. At this time, Eliakim was titled "the one who is in charge of the [king's] household (2 Kgs 18:18) and Shebna held the rank of *sopher*, an important position, probably equal to that of a secretary of state, but not as high in rank as that of "the one who is in charge of the [king's] household."

So again, if the Shebna in Isaiah 22 is the same person mentioned in 2 Kings 18 and 19, then the demotion part of the prophet's prediction had taken place by the year 701 BC. Concerning the death of Shebna the biblical record is silent.

As Shebna and other governmental officials might have expected, Isaiah responded to the specific threat posed in 701 in characteristic fashion (see Is 37:33–35). Whether Shebna was singled out for special attention by the prophet again is not known. But in addition to his arrogance and pride described in Isaiah 22, no doubt his deep involvement in a government whose policies were pro-Egyptian, and which so easily overlooked the dimension of the spiritual, evoked the opposition of Isaiah.

Shebuel. 1. Gershon's son and Moses' grandson from Levi's tribe (1 Chr 23:15,16); father of Jehdeiah (1 Chr 24:20, Shubael). He was the chief officer in charge of the treasuries (1 Chr 26:24).

2. Levite, Heman's son and a musician in the tabernacle (1 Chr 25:4,20, Shubael).

Shecaniah, Shechaniah. Common OT name, frequently spelled Shechaniah (#'s 3–9) in the KJV.

1. Descendant of David through the line of Zerubbabel living in postexilic Palestine (1 Chr 3:21,22).

2. Levite and the head of the 10th of 24 divisions of priests formed during the reign of David (1 Chr 24:11).

3. One of six priests serving under Kore during the reign of King Hezekiah of Judah (715–686 BC). Shecaniah assisted with the distribution of the temple offerings among his fellow priests living in the priestly cities (2 Chr 31:15).

4. Father of Hattush. Hattush returned with Ezra to Judah following the Babylonian captivity during the reign of King Artaxerxes I of Persia (464–424 BC; Ezr 8:3).

5. Son of Jahaziel who returned with Ezra to Judah during the reign of King Artaxerxes I of Persia (Ezr 8:5).

6. Son of Jehiel in the house of Elam, who urged Ezra to command the sons of Israel to divorce the foreign women they had married since returning to Judah from exile (Ezr 10:2).

7. Father of Shemaiah. Shemaiah, the keeper of the East Gate, helped Nehemiah rebuild a section of the Jerusalem wall (Neh 3:29).

8. Father-in-law of Tobiah the Ammonite and the son of Arah (Neh 6:18).

9. Head of a priestly family that returned to Judah with Zerubbabel following the exile (Neh 12:3). Shecaniah is perhaps identical with Shebaniah in verse 14.

See SHEBANIAH #3.

Shechem (Person). 1. Son of Hamor the Hivite. He raped Dinah, the daughter of Jacob, and was later killed along with his father and all the males of his town by Simeon and Levi (Gn 34; Jos 24:32).

2. One of Gilead's six sons, a descendant of Joseph through Manasseh's line, and the founder of the Shechemite family (Nm 26:31; Jos 17:2).

3. One of Shemida's four sons from Manasseh's tribe (1 Chr 7:19).

Shechem (Place). Town in the center of western Palestine, near the watershed which separates the waters that flow to the Jordan from those that descend to the Mediterranean. The site is 40 miles north of Jerusalem at the eastern entrance to the pass between Mt Ebal and Mt Gerizim. The ancient town stood on the lower southeastern slope or shoulder of Mt Ebal, hence the meaning of the name (Shechem = shoulder). Samaria, later capital of Israel, lay about eight miles to the northwest by road. Although strategically located—the town controlled all roads through the central hill country of Palestine—it was without natural defenses, and required extensive fortifications.

Identified with Tell Balâta, Shechem stood a mile or two east of modern Nablus and near Jacob's well. In fact, many identify Sychar (Jn 4:5) with Shechem; these scholars argue that, because only consonants were written in Hebrew and related languages, a scribe may have erroneously substituted a final "r" for an "m." The KJV of Acts 7:16 spells the name Sychem, and in Genesis 12:6 the KJV renders the name as Sichem.

Biblical References. Shechem first appears in the Bible as the initial campsite of Abram after he entered Canaan from Mesopotamia.

There God promised him the land of Canaan and Abram built his first altar in the land (Gn 12:6,7). After Jacob's 20-year sojourn in northern Mesopotamia at Paddan-aram, he returned to Shechem and bought a piece of land. By this time the place was already a walled city with a gate (34:20,24). After the defilement of their sister Dinah, Simeon and Levi massacred Shechem's male population in revenge (v 25). Years later when the patriarchal family was living in the Hebron area, Joseph went to Shechem to look for his brothers (37:12–14).

After the conquest, the ceremony of antiphonal blessing and cursing on Mt Gerizim and Mt Ebal, respectively, was fulfilled in the vicinity of Shechem (Jos 8:30–35; cf. Dt 27:11–13). In the division and settlement of the land, Shechem became one of the cities of refuge (Jos 20:7; 21:21) and one of the 48 Levitical cities (21:21). Here Joshua delivered his farewell address (24:1,25), and the bones of Joseph were buried on the land Jacob had bought there (v 32).

During the unsettled days of the judges, Gideon's son Abimelech set himself up as king of Israel there, at first with the support of the inhabitants. But a later revolt against him resulted in destruction of the city (Jgs 9:1–7,23–57). Rehoboam was crowned there just before the split of the kingdom (1 Kgs 12:1), and Jeroboam, first king of the northern kingdom, rebuilt the city and made it the first capital of the kingdom (v 25).

History and Archaeology. Tell Balâta was first identified as the site of ancient Shechem by the German scholar Hermann Thiersch in 1903. Subsequent excavations were conducted by Ernst Sellin, G. Welter, and others on behalf of the German Society for Scientific Research in 1913–14, 1926–28, 1932, and 1934. More recently the Drew-McCormick-Harvard Expedi-

tion excavated there in 1956, 1957, 1960, 1962, 1964, 1966, 1968, and 1969, under the leadership of G. Ernest Wright, Lawrence E. Toombs, and Edward F. Campbell, Jr.

Excavations reveal that the earliest settlement at the site dates back to the 4th millennium BC but the first significant settlement occurred during the first half of the 2nd millennium and was the work of Amorites or Hyksos. The Hyksos surrounded the city with an immense sloping embankment about 80 feet wide and 20 feet high, upon which they built a brick wall. There was a two-entry gate on the east side and a three-entry gate on the northwest. On the acropolis they built what has been interpreted as a fortress temple, which was rebuilt several times and finally destroyed by the Egyptians in about 1550 BC.

About a century later the Canaanites rebuilt Shechem on a smaller scale. A new fortress temple was built on the ruins of the old one and measured 53 feet wide and 41 feet deep, with an entrance on the long side. It had three sacred standing stones next to an altar in the open court. This temple is believed to be the house of Baal-berith destroyed by Abimelech about 1150 BC (Jgs 9:3,4,46), and its sacred area was never rebuilt. Before that, however, there is no archaeological evidence of destruction for some 300 years, confirming the biblical indication that the Hebrews did not take the city at the time of the conquest and that the inhabitants lived peaceably among the Hebrews.

Evidently Solomon rebuilt Shechem as a provincial capital but it suffered great destruction late in the 10th century, probably at the hands of Shishak of Egypt when he invaded Palestine in 926 BC (1 Kgs 14:25). Shortly thereafter Jeroboam I refortified the city and made it the capital of the kingdom of Israel. Either he or a successor built a government ware-

The fortress temple at Shechem, with its white sacred pillar just left of the center in the foreground.

house on the ruins of the temple. Israelite Shechem met its end at the hands of the Assyrian king Shalmaneser V in 724 BC, just before the destruction of Samaria, and the town was virtually uninhabited for about 400 years.

In the 4th century, Alexander the Great established a camp on the site for his soldiers, and subsequently the Samaritans moved from Samaria and settled there. They built their temple on Mt Gerizim. John Hyrcanus destroyed Shechem for the last time either in 128 or 107 BC. His violent opposition to the Samaritans also involved destruction of their temple on Mt Gerizim and of Samaria at the same time. The Roman emperor Vespasian in AD 72 built the Neapolis ("new city," of which modern Nablus is a corruption) west of Tell Balâta. The modern village of Balâta is south of the tell.　　　　　　　　　　HOWARD F. VOS

Shechem, Tower of. Fortress erected on the acropolis of Shechem, housing the temple of Baal-berith and situated inside the city walls. The city of Shechem was located in the hill country of the tribe of Ephraim near Mt Gerizim.

The tower of Shechem served as the citadel to which the leaders of Shechem fled from the onslaught of Abimelech. They sought refuge in the inner chamber of the temple of Baal-berith; Abimelech, however, set the upper parts of the inner chamber on fire, killing all the men and women housed within (Jgs 9:46–49).

The remnants of the tower of Shechem have been found within the ancient town of Shechem at Tell Balâta, a short distance northeast of modern Nablus in central Palestine. Modern excavations show that the tower of Shechem was used as a temple and a fortress.

Shechemite. Descendant of Shechem, Gilead's son from Manasseh's tribe (Nm 26:31).

See SHECHEM (PERSON) #2.

Shedeur. Elizur's father. Elizur represented Reuben's tribe in Moses' census of the men capable of bearing arms (Nm 1:5; 2:10; 10:18), and in the dedication of the altar (7:30–35).

Sheep. *See* ANIMALS.

Sheep Breeder. *See* TRADES AND OCCUPATIONS (SHEPHERD).

Sheep Gate, Sheep Market. Jerusalem gate repaired by Eliashib and the priests under Nehemiah's supervision during the postexilic era (Neh 3:1,32; 12:39). It was positioned east of the Fish Gate by the Tower of the Hundred, near the pool of Bethesda (Bethsaida) and a

short distance from the modern St. Stephen's Gate. The KJV translation of sheep market in John 5:2 (from the Greek word meaning "sheep") is more accurately rendered Sheep Gate (RSV).

See JERUSALEM.

Sheepshearer. *See* TRADES AND OCCUPATIONS (SHEPHERD).

Sheerah. Daughter or granddaughter of Ephraim. Her offspring built lower and upper Beth-horon and Uzzen-sheerah, named after her (1 Chr 7:24, KJV Sherah).

Shehariah. Jehoram's son and a chief of Benjamin's tribe in Jerusalem after the exile (1 Chr 8:26).

Shekel. Weight, and later also a coin.

See COINS; WEIGHTS AND MEASURES.

Shekinah. Transliteration of a Hebrew word meaning "the one who dwells" or "that which dwells." The term enters Christian theology from its use in the Targums and rabbinic literature to describe the immanent presence in the world of the transcendent Deity. Although the word is not itself used in either Testament, it clearly originates in OT passages which describe God as *dwelling* among a people or in a particular place (Gn 9:27; Ex 25:8; 29:45,46; Nm 5:3; 1 Kgs 6:13; Ps 68:16,18; 74:2; Is 8:18; Ez 43:7–9; Jl 3:17,21; Zec 2:10,11); God, whose dwelling is in heaven, also dwells on earth. In its narrower uses the term is applied to the "shekinah glory," the visible pillar of fire and smoke that dwelled in the midst of Israel at Sinai (Ex 19:16–18), in the wilderness (40:34–38), and in the temple (1 Kgs 6:13; 8:10–13; 2 Chr 6:1,2).

The rabbinic sources used the term more widely than with specific reference to this OT phenomenon alone. In the Targums "shekinah," "glory of God," and "word of God" are used synonymously. Shekinah became a comprehensive term for any form of the presence of God; it could be used as a designation for God or as a circumlocution for references to the face or hand of God. Only in the later rabbinic sources does the Shekinah become a separate entity created by God as an intermediary between God and man.

The NT frequently alludes to the concept of the Shekinah, even though the term itself is not used. God's presence in the NT is frequently associated with light and glory (Lk 2:9; 9:29; Acts 9:3–6; 22:6–11; 26:12–16; 2 Pt 1:16–18). John's Gospel emphasizes both the concept of glory and of dwelling. When the word became flesh, he dwelled among men who beheld his glory (Jn 1:14). The Spirit of God remained on him (v 32) and would be with his followers forever (14:16). He would abide in those who abide in Jesus (15:4–10). The same themes of dwelling in Christ and of his dwelling in his people occur repeatedly also in John's letters (1 Jn 2:6,14,24,27,28; 3:6,14,15,24; 2 Jn 9).

Paul also identifies Christ as the Shekinah of God. All the fullness of the godhead dwells in him bodily (Col 1:19; 2:9). The dwelling of Christ in the church constitutes the saints as the people of God (1:15–23). Paul's message was the "gospel of the glory of Christ," for God had caused light to shine to give "knowledge of the glory of God in the face of Christ" (2 Cor 4:4–6 NIV). Finally, the writer of Hebrews sees Christ as "the radiance of God's glory and the exact representation of his nature" (Heb 1:3 NIV).

See GLORY; THEOPHANY; PILLAR OF FIRE AND CLOUD.

Shelah. 1. Arpachshad's son and the father of Eber (Gn 10:24; 11:12–15; KJV Salah; 1 Chr 1:18). Shelah is listed in Luke's genealogy of Christ as the son of Cainan (3:35, KJV Sala); Cainan is omitted in the Hebrew text.

See GENEALOGY OF JESUS CHRIST.

2. Judah's third son by Bathshua the Canaanitess. He was born at Chezib, a small town in Judah (Gn 38:5; 1 Chr 2:3). Shelah founded the Shelanite family (Nm 26:20).

Shelah, Pool of. Reservoir in the King's Garden in Jerusalem (Neh 3:15).

See SILOAM, POOL OF.

Shelanite. Descendant of Shelah, Judah's son (Nm 26:20).

See SHELAH #2.

Shelemiah. 1. Korahite from the tribe of Levi and a gatekeeper who was chosen by lot to guard the east gate of the sanctuary during David's reign (1 Chr 26:14); also named Meshelemiah (9:21; 26:1,2).

See MESHELEMIAH.

2,3. Two of Bani's sons, who were encouraged to divorce their foreign wives during Ezra's postexilic reforms in Israel (Ezr 10:39,41).

4. Father of Hananiah. Hananiah repaired a section of the Jerusalem wall under Nehemiah (Neh 3:30).

5. Priest and one of the three men appointed by Nehemiah as the treasurers of the temple in Jerusalem. Their task was to oversee the distribution of the tithes among their fellow priests (Neh 13:13).

6. Son of Cushi, the father of Nethaniah, and a forefather of Jehudi (Jer 36:14).

7. Son of Abdeel who, with Jerahmeel and Seraiah, was commanded by King Jehoiakim of Judah (609–598 BC) to seize Baruch and Jeremiah (Jer 36:26).

8. Father of Jehucal (Jer 37:3), alternately spelled Jucal in 38:1.

9. Son of Hananiah and the father of Irijah. Irijah arrested Jeremiah for apparently deserting to the Babylonians (Jer 37:13).

Sheleph. Joktan's son and the founder of an Arabian tribe living in Yemen (Gn 10:26; 1 Chr 1:20).

Shelesh. Helem's son and a chief of Asher's tribe (1 Chr 7:35).

Shelomi. Ahihud's father. Ahihud represented Asher's tribe in the division of the land of Canaan among Israel's 10 tribes west of the Jordan (Nm 34:27).

Shelomith. 1. Dibri's daughter and the mother of a man from Dan's tribe who blasphemed the Lord's name, for which he was subsequently stoned to death (Lv 24:11).

2. Sister of Meshullam and Hananiah, all of whom were descendants of David (1 Chr 3:19).

3. KJV spelling of Shelomoth, Shimei's son, in 1 Chronicles 23:9.

See SHELOMOTH #1.

4. Alternate spelling of Shelomoth, Izhar's son, in 1 Chronicles 23:18.

See SHELOMOTH #2.

5. KJV spelling of Shelomoth, Zichri's son, in 1 Chronicles 26:25–28.

See SHELOMOTH #3.

6. Son of Rehoboam and Maachah (2 Chr 11:20).

7. One of Ezra's companions (Ezr 8:10).

Shelomoth. 1. Gershonite Levite and one of Shimei's sons serving in the sanctuary during David's reign (1 Chr 23:9, KJV Shelomith).

2. Levite and priest from the family of Izhar during David's reign (1 Chr 23:18, Shelomith; 24:22).

3. Zichri's son, who was in charge of the royal treasuries during David's reign (1 Chr 26:25–28, KJV Shelomith).

Shelumiel. Simeonite, Zurishaddai's son and one of the leaders who assisted Moses in taking a census of Israel in the wilderness (Nm 1:6; 2:12; 7:36,41; 10:19). He is the forefather of the apocryphal Judith (Jth 8:1, where his name is Salamiel and his father's Sarasadai).

Shem. Eldest son of Noah (Gn 5:32; 6:10; 7:13; 9:18,23,26,27; 11:10; 1 Chr 1:4,17–27; Lk

3:36) and the ancestor of the Semitic peoples (Gn 10:1,21–31). Shem lived 600 years (cf. 11:10,11). In Hebrew Shem means "name," perhaps implying that Noah expected this son's name to become great.

After their deliverance from the great flood, Shem and Japheth acted with respect and dignity toward their drunken father Noah, on an occasion when their brother Ham dishonored him (Gn 9:20–29). Because of this act, Noah later pronounced a curse on Canaan, the son of Ham, and a blessing on both Shem and Japheth: "Blessed by the Lord my God be Shem; and let Canaan be his slave. God enlarge Japheth, and let him dwell in the tents of Shem" (vv 26,27).

In Genesis 11:10–27, the line of descent for the promised seed which was to crush Satan (3:15; 5:1–32) is traced through Shem to Abraham, and ultimately through Judah and David to Christ (cf. Lk 3:36, KJV Sem). The blessing of Noah on Shem is thus to be taken as an indication that the line of Shem will be the line through which the seed of Genesis 3:15 will come. This is the first time in the Bible that God is called the God of some particular individual or group of people. The statement that Canaan would be a servant to Shem was fulfilled centuries later when the Israelites descended from Shem entered the land of Canaan and subdued the inhabitants of the land (cf. 1 Kgs 9:20,21).

Noah also said that Japheth would be enlarged and dwell in the tents of Shem (Gn 9:27), the latter of which would seem to imply sustenance and protection. After Japheth would be greatly increased in numbers, the Japhethites would be brought into connection with Shem and would share in the blessings and promises of the Semitic faith. Many see fulfillment of this prophecy in the opening of the gospel to the Gentiles during the NT era of the establishment of the church.

In the table of nations recorded in Genesis 10, five descendants of Shem are mentioned (Elam, Asshur, Arphachshad, Lud, and Aram; v 22) and from whom 21 additional descendants are listed. Receiving particular emphasis among these descendants is Eber from the line of Arphachshad (vv 21,24), whose line is traced to Abraham in 11:16–27.

See Abraham; Noah #1; Nations; Genealogy of Jesus Christ.

Shema (Person). 1. Judahite, Hebron's son and a descendant of Caleb (1 Chr 2:43,44).

2. Reubenite, and Joel's son (1 Chr 5:8). He is perhaps identifiable with Shemaiah or Shimei in verse 4.

3. Benjamite, and head of a family in Aija-lon, who helped defeat the inhabitants of Gath (1 Chr 8:13; alternately called Shimei in v 21, KJV Shimhi).

4. Levite who explained to the people passages from the Law read by Ezra (Neh 8:4).

Shema (Place). One of the 29 cities located near the border of Edom in the southern extremity of the land inherited by Judah, mentioned between the cities of Amam and Moladah (Jos 15:26). In Joshua 19:2, Sheba was one of 13 cities assigned to Simeon's tribe within the southern portion of Judah's inheritance. Named between the towns of Beersheba and Moladah, possibly a later copyist mistook Sheba for Shema. Its location is unknown.

Shema, The. The declaration "Hear, O Israel, Yahweh our God is one Yahweh" (Dt 6:4). *Shema* comes from the first Hebrew word of the verse, *sh'ma,* "hear". Verses 4–9 make up the whole of this foundational biblical truth. While several translations of verse 4 are grammatically correct, the Lord's words in Mark 12:29 correspond most closely to the one given above. Religious Jews recite the Shema three times daily as part of their devotional life; no Sabbath worship is conducted in the synagogue without its proclamation.

Within the Shema is found both a fundamental doctrinal truth and a resultant obligation. There is an urgency connected to the teaching: the word *sh'ma* demands that the hearer respond with his total being to the fact and demands of this essential revelation.

With regard to the teaching pertaining to the nature of God, the word "one" (*echad*) designates a compound unity rather than an absolute singular. While the eminent medieval Jewish theologian, Maimonedes, insisted that God was *yachid* (an absolute singular), the OT does not use this word to define God's nature. The compound singular word for "one" first occurs in Genesis 2:24 where a man and woman, though separate entities, are seen to be one (*echad*) in marriage. Understandably, Jesus could freely quote Deuteronomy 6:4 without infringing upon the truth of his own deity. It is important for Christians to recognize that the doctrine of the Trinity is by no means in conflict with the vigorous monotheism of the Shema.

Although the Shema teaches that God is a unity within himself, its primary thrust affirms the absolute uniqueness of Yahweh: there simply are no gods in addition to him. Jesus reiterated this when he said, "He is one, and there is none other but he" (Mk 12:32). The OT refers to the false idols as *elilim* ("good-for-nothing-ones"). Israel's deliverance from Egypt enabled the people to personally experience the fact that no heathen god could be compared to Yahweh; there were simply no gods like the Lord (Ex 15:11).

This being the case, man is obligated to love the sole deity with all of his heart, soul, and strength (Dt 6:5). Moses clearly taught that to acknowledge other deities is both a grievous sin against the Lord and a denial of the unique covenant of redemption (4:23,24; 17:2–5).

While the entire message of the Scripture is built upon the Shema (cf. Mk 12:29,30), the Bible leaves no doubt that man is unable to love God in the way he should. Because of his fallen, sinful nature, man's heart is desperately corrupt (Jer 17:9). It was altogether fitting and necessary, therefore, that the Son of God should obey the demands of the Shema on behalf of fallen man. The all-encompassing love for God required by the Law found perfect expression in our representative before the Father, the sinless Messiah.

Having fulfilled God's requirements on man's behalf, Jesus enables his disciples to relate to the Shema in a vital and meaningful way. Moses wrote of a time when God, having circumcised the hearts of his people, would enable them to love him with all their hearts (Dt 30:6). Under the provisions of the new covenant and spiritual rebirth, an inward change of heart makes the Shema a delight and not a burden.

See DEUTERONOMY, BOOK OF.

Shemaah. Father of Ahiezer and Joash, two bowmen who joined David at Ziklag (1 Chr 12:3).

Shemaiah. 1. Prophet during the reign of Rehoboam, king of Judah (930–913 BC). He warned the king not to go to war against Jeroboam and the 10 northern tribes of Israel (1 Kgs 12:22; 2 Chr 11:2). Five years later he spoke words of comfort to a repentant Rehoboam and people of Judah (2 Chr 12:5–7). Shemaiah chronicled the life of Rehoboam in a book that has since been lost (v 15).

2. Son of Shecaniah, the father of six sons and a descendant of David through Rehoboam's line (1 Chr 3:22).

3. Simeonite, father of Shimri and an ancestor of Jehu (1 Chr 4:37).

4. Reubenite and a son of Joel (1 Chr 5:4).

5. Merarite Levite and the son of Hasshub who returned to Jerusalem after the exile (1 Chr 9:14). He was made a leader in the work of the temple during the days of Nehemiah (Neh 11:15).

6. Son of Galal and the father of Obadiah, a Levite who returned to Jerusalem following the Babylonian captivity (1 Chr 9:16); called Shammua in Nehemiah 11:17.

7. Levite and the leader of his father Elizaphan's house. Shemaiah was summoned by David to help carry the ark from Obed-edom's house to Jerusalem (1 Chr 15:8–11).

8. Son of Nethanel and the Levitical scribe who recorded the 24 divisions of the priests during David's reign in Israel (1000–961 BC; 1 Chr 24:6).

9. Oldest of Obed-edom's eight sons and the father of gifted sons who served as the gatekeepers of the south gate and storehouse of the sanctuary during David's reign (1 Chr 26:4–7).

10. One of the Levites sent by King Jehoshaphat of Judah (872–848 BC) to teach the Law in the cities of Judah (2 Chr 17:8).

11. Son of Jeduthun and Uzziel's brother, who was among the Levites chosen by King Hezekiah of Judah (715–686 BC) to cleanse the house of the Lord (2 Chr 29:14).

12. One of the Levites assisting Kore with the distribution of the offerings among his fellow priests living in the priestly cities of Judah during the days of King Hezekiah (2 Chr 31:15).

13. One of the Levitical chiefs who generously gave animals to the Levites for the celebration of the Passover feast during King Josiah's reign (640–609 BC; 2 Chr 35:9).

14. Son of Adonikam who returned with Ezra to Judah after the exile during the reign of King Artaxerxes I of Persia (464–424 BC; Ezr 8:13).

15. One of the Jewish leaders whom Ezra sent to Iddo at Casiphia to gather Levites and temple servants for the caravan of Jews returning to Palestine from Babylon (Ezr 8:16).

16. Priest and one of Harim's five sons who was encouraged by Ezra to divorce his foreign wife during the postexilic era (Ezr 10:21).

17. Son of another Harim who was encouraged by Ezra to divorce his foreign wife (Ezr 10:31).

18. Son of Shecaniah and the keeper of the East Gate who repaired a section of the Jerusalem wall under Nehemiah's direction (Neh 3:29).

19. Son of Delaiah and a false prophet hired by Tobiah and Sanballat to frighten Nehemiah and hinder him from rebuilding the Jerusalem wall (Neh 6:10).

20. One of the priests who set his seal on the covenant of Ezra (Neh 10:8).

21. One of the leaders of the priests who returned with Zerubbabel and Jeshua to Judah after the exile (Neh 12:6), whose house in the next generation was headed by Jehonathan (v 18).

22. One of the princes of Judah who partici-

pated in the dedication of the Jerusalem wall during the postexilic period (Neh 12:34).

23. Son of Mattaniah, grandfather of Zechariah, and a descendant of Asaph. Zechariah was one of the priests who played a trumpet at the dedication of the Jerusalem wall (Neh 12:35).

24. 25. Two priestly musicians who performed at the dedication of the Jerusalem wall (Neh 12:36,42).

26. Father of Uriah the prophet from Kiriath-jearim. Like Jeremiah his contemporary, Uriah spoke words of doom against Jerusalem and Judah during the reign of King Jehoiakim of Judah (609–598 BC), who deplored Uriah's message and eventually had him killed (Jer 26:20).

27. Nehelamite and a Jew deported to Babylon by Nebuchadnezzar, from where he opposed Jeremiah. He sent letters to the priests in Jerusalem which criticized Jeremiah for predicting a long captivity for Judah. Jeremiah exposed Shemaiah as a false prophet and foretold that he and his descendants would not live to see the return to Palestine (Jer 29:24–32).

28. Father of Delaiah, a prince of Judah during the reign of King Jehoiakim (Jer 36:12).

Shemariah. 1. Warrior from the tribe of Benjamin who joined David at Ziklag in his struggle against King Saul. Shemariah was one of David's ambidextrous archers and slingers (1 Chr 12:5).

2. One of Rehoboam's sons (2 Chr 11:19, KJV Shamariah).

3. Harim's son, who obeyed Ezra's exhortation to divorce his foreign wife after the exile (Ezr 10:32).

4. Binnui's son, who obeyed Ezra's exhortation to divorce his foreign wife (Ezr 10:41).

Shemeber. King of Zeboiim, who joined a confederacy with four other kings in rebellion against Chedorlaomer and his allies. Abraham rescued Lot from captivity after Shemeber, along with Sodom and Gomorrah, was defeated (Gn 14:2).

Shemed. Elpaal's son and a descendant of Benjamin through Shaharaim's line. Shemed rebuilt the towns of Ono and Lod after the Babylonian exile (1 Chr 8:12, KJV Shamed).

Shemer. 1.Owner of the hill of Samaria, which Omri, king of Israel, bought as the site of his new capital city and named after Shemer (1 Kgs 16:24).

2. Merarite Levite, Mahli's son and the father of Bani; he was a temple singer during David's reign (1 Chr 6:46, KJV Shamer).

The ruins of the forum of Herod's Samaria, the city bought from and named after Shemer.

3. Asherite, Heber's son and a leader among his people (1 Chr 7:34, KJV Shamer; alternately called Shomer in v 32).

Shemida, Shemidah, Shemidaite. Father of the family of Shemidaites (Nm 26:32) in Manasseh's tribe (Jos 17:2; 1 Chr 7:19, KJV Shemidah).

Sheminith. Obscure Hebrew term, meaning "the eighth," in 1 Chronicles 15:21 and the superscriptions of Psalms 6 and 12, whose function as a musical cue or instrument is uncertain.

See MUSIC AND MUSICAL INSTRUMENTS.

Shemiramoth. 1. One of the Levites whom David commanded to play the harp when the ark of God was brought from the house of Obed-edom to Jerusalem (1 Chr 15:18,20), and who retained a permanent position under Asaph as one of the "ministers before the ark of the Lord" (16:4,5).

2. Levite commissioned by Jehoshaphat to teach the Law "through all the cities of Judah" (2 Chr 17:8).

Shemuel. 1. Ammihud's son and the representative of Simeon's tribe in the division of the land of Canaan among Israel's 10 tribes west of the Jordan (Nm 34:20).

2. KJV rendering of Samuel, Elkanah's son, in 1 Chronicles 6:33.

See SAMUEL (PERSON).

3. Tola's son and chief in Issachar's tribe (1 Chr 7:2).

Shen. KJV form of Jeshanah, a town near which the prophet Samuel set up the Ebenezer stone, in 1 Samuel 7:12.

See JESHANAH.

Shenazzar, Shenazar. Fourth son of Jeconiah (Jehoiachin), captive king of Judah (1 Chr 3:18, KJV Shenazar).

Shenir. KJV alternate spelling of Senir, the Amorite name for Mt Hermon, in Deuteronomy 3:9 and Song of Solomon 4:8.

See HERMON, MOUNT.

Sheol. Hebrew term of uncertain etymology. In ordinary usage it means ravine, chasm, underworld, or world of the dead. In the OT it is the place where the dead have their abode, a hollow space underneath the earth where the dead are gathered in. Synonyms for Sheol are pit, death, and destruction (Abaddon). Sheol is a place of shadows and utter silence. Here all existence is in suspense, yet it is not a nonplace like utopia, but rather a place where life is no more. It is described as the Land of Forgetfulness. Those who dwell there cannot praise God (Ps 88:10–12). In Revelation it is called the "bottomless pit" presided over by Abaddon, the prince of the pit (9:11).

It is not, however, a place where God is entirely absent; there can be no escape from God even in Sheol (Ps 139:8). This omnipresence of God is graphically described in Job: "Sheol is naked before God, and Abaddon has no covering" (26:6). A similar thought is expressed in Proverbs: "Sheol and Abaddon lie open before the Lord, how much more the hearts of men!" (15:11). In both texts Sheol and Abaddon are used interchangeably (parallelism). Abaddon means literally "destruction," but in Revelation is used as a personal name.

In the Bible death is not a natural occurrence. It violates the principle of life which is a gift from God. Sheol is therefore not only a place of rest but also of punishment. Korah and his associates who instigated rebellion against Moses were swallowed up by the open pit and perished in Sheol (Num 16:30–33). Fear of death is natural to man; Sheol therefore serves as a symbol of the journey without return (Ps 39:13). King Hezekiah of Judah laments on his sick-bed: "In the noontide of my days I must depart; I am consigned to the gates of Sheol for the rest of my years" (Is 38:10).

Sheol as conceived in the OT differs from the later doctrine of Hell in that it is the place where all the dead are gathered indiscriminately, both the good and the bad, the saints and the sinners. To die means to be joined to those who have gone before. When a Jew dies he is "gathered unto his people" (cf. Gn 25:8,17; 35:29; 49:29; etc.). Beyond Sheol there seemed to be no hope (cf. Eccl 9:10). The utter despondency of death is expressed pathetically in the Book of Job: "before I go whence I shall not return, to the land of gloom and deep darkness, the land of gloom and chaos where light is as darkness" (10:21,22). Yet this is not Job's last word. He also knows of the power of God which reaches beyond the grave: "For I know that my Redeemer lives, . . . and after my skin has been thus destroyed, then from my flesh I shall see God" (19:25,26). Unfortunately, the text is not entirely clear and other readings are possible (cf. mg.). Yet it manifests the triumph of faith which trusts God beyond the grave. There are two other texts which clearly convey faith in life after death. Isaiah 26:19 reads: "The dead shall live, their bodies shall rise. O dwellers in the dust, awake and sing for joy! For thy dew is a dew of light, and on the land of the shades thou wilt let it fall." The text in Daniel is equally explicit: "And many of those who sleep in the dust of the earth shall awake, some to everlasting life, and some to shame and everlasting contempt" (12:2; cf. v 13). Here we already meet a moral distinction between the dead and their ultimate destiny: "And those who are wise shall shine like the brightness of the firmament; and those who turn many to righteousness, like the stars for ever and ever" (v 3). For the godless there is no future. Isaiah's poem of taunt against the king of Babylon expresses the transience of human pomp. The ultimate end of those who act as if they were God will be of all flesh: "maggots are the bed beneath you, and worms are your covering" (Is 14:11). The higher the presumption the greater the fall: "But you are brought down to Sheol, to the depths of the Pit" (v 15).

The idea that the dead abide in the underworld persists in the OT. The incident in the case of Saul with the medium of Endor (1 Sm 28:11) is a good illustration. Samuel is brought "up out of the earth" to be consulted by the king at a time of crisis. Such necromancy was strictly prohibited both by the Law of Moses (Dt 18:9–11) and by the king himself (cf. 1 Sm 28:3,9). Apparently, those in the underworld, though separated from the living, were held to be familiar with the affairs of men.

In the NT Sheol is translated into Greek as *Hades*. Another term in frequent use is *Gehenna*. Both these terms are usually rendered in English as hell (cf. Lk 16:23 and mg.).

Gehenna is a geographical location near Jerusalem. It refers to the Valley of Hinnom ("lamentation"?) where in ancient days child sacrifices were offered to Molech (cf. 2 Chr 28:3). In later times it was used as a dump for burning the city refuse. In the popular mind Gehenna acquired a sinister meaning as a place for future punishment. The NT uses Hades and Gehenna interchangeably to indicate the destiny of those who lead godless lives (cf. Mt 5:22; 10:28; 11:23; 16:18; 23:15,33; Jas 3:6).

The Christian confession of faith states, in accordance with NT teaching, that Jesus descended into hell (Hades). The source for this clause in the creed is 1 Peter 3:18–20; 4:6. But there are also hints of Jesus' descent in Romans 10:7 and Ephesians 4:9. Although 1 Peter specifically refers to those who have perished at the time of the flood as the reason for Jesus' descent, theologically speaking it indicates that the victory of the cross and resurrection extends as far as hell itself. In fact, according to Revelation, Jesus holds in his hands the key of hell and death (1:18). Because Jesus conquered death, hell is no more for those who belong to him. Both hell and death are thrown into the lake of fire (20:14). The believers' names are henceforth written in the Book of Life (v 15).

JAKOB JOCZ

See DEAD, ABODE OF THE; HADES; HELL; DEATH; INTERMEDIATE STATE.

Shepham. One of the places used by Moses to establish the eastern border of the Promised Land, mentioned between Hazar-enan, which marked the northeastern corner of the land, and Riblah (Nm 34:10,11). Its specific location is unknown.

Shephathiah. Alternate KJV spelling of Shephatiah, Meshullam's father, in 1 Chronicles 9:8.

See SHEPHATIAH #2.

Shephatiah. 1. One of six sons born to David during his seven-year reign at Hebron. Shephatiah's mother was Abital, one of David's wives (2 Sm 3:4; 1 Chr 3:3).

2. Benjamite and the father of Meshullam, a returnee to Jerusalem after the Babylonian captivity (1 Chr 9:8, KJV Shephathiah).

3. Haruphite from Benjamin's tribe and one of the men of military prowess who came to David's support at Ziklag (1 Chr 12:5).

4. Son of Maacah and chief official of the Simeonites during David's reign (1 Chr 27:16).

5. One of the seven sons of King Jehoshaphat of Judah (872–848 BC) and the brother of Jehoram who became sole regent (853–841 BC) at his father's death (2 Chr 21:2).

6. Forefather of 372 descendants who returned with Zerubbabel to Judah following the exile (Ezr 2:4; Neh 7:9). Later, 81 members of Shephatiah's house accompanied Ezra back to Palestine during the reign of King Artaxerxes I of Persia (464–424 BC; Ezr 8:8).

7. Founder of a household of Solomon's servants that returned with Zerubbabel to Judah after the Babylonian captivity (Ezr 2:57; Neh 7:59).

8. Descendant of Perez and an ancestor of a Judahite family living in Jerusalem during the postexilic period (Neh 11:4).

9. Son of Mattan and a prince of Judah during the reign of King Zedekiah (597–586 BC). Annoyed with Jeremiah's prophecies of doom for Jerusalem, Shephatiah (with Gedaliah, Jucal, and Pashhur) sought to put him to death. With Zedekiah's permission, they hoped to achieve their ends by imprisoning Jeremiah in a cistern (Jer 38:1).

Shephelah. Longitudinal geographical division of Palestine, situated between the Mediterranean coastal plain and the western plateau, or Judean highlands (1 Kgs 10:27; 1 Chr 27:28; 2 Chr 1:15; 9:27; 26:10; 28:18; Jer 17:26; 32:44, 33:13; Ob 1:19). The term is derived from a root meaning "to be or become low," so the Shephelah is hills, as contrasted with mountains. The KJV translates the word as "valley"; the NASB gives "lowland"; in the NIV it is "western foothills," which is the most accurate translation (cf. Jos 9:1; 11:2,16).

The Shephelah is only a few miles wide, but it extends from Carmel in the north to Beersheba in the south, a distance of some 70 miles.

The area was important agriculturally, for its valleys produced good grain crops and its hills supported vineyards and olive groves. It was also of strategic significance, for the valleys which passed through it gave access to the central plateau and Jerusalem. For that reason strong fortified cities were built to protect the approaches to the capital. Among these were lower Beth-horon, Gezer, Beth-shemesh, Azekah, Lachish, and Debir (Kirjath-sepher) (cf. 1 Kgs 9:15–19).

See PALESTINE.

Shepher, Mount. Temporary camping place for the Israelites during their wilderness wanderings. Mt Shepher was located between Kehelathah and Haradah (Nm 33:23,24, KJV Shapher) Its location is unknown.

See WILDERNESS WANDERINGS.

Shepherd. See TRADES AND OCCUPATIONS.

Shepho, Shephi. One of Shobal's five sons and a descendant of Seir the Horite. Shepho is listed in the genealogy of Abraham through Esau's contact with the nation (Gn 36:23); his name is alternately spelled Shephi (1 Chr 1:40).

Shephupham. Benjamin's fourth son and the father of the Shuphamite family (Nm 26:39, KJV Shupham). In the corresponding genealogy of Benjamin (1 Chr 7:12) he is called Shuppim, appearing as Benjamin's great-grandson.

See SHUPPIM #1.

Shephuphan. Bela's son from Benjamin's tribe. Bela was the firstborn of Benjamin's sons (1 Chr 8:5). The exact position of Shephuphan in Benjamin's genealogy is unclear.

See SHEPHUPHAM.

Sherah. KJV spelling of Sheerah in 1 Chronicles 7:24.

See SHEERAH.

Sherebiah. 1. Levite, a descendant of Mahli. Sherebiah, described as a man of understanding, was sent with 18 of his sons and brothers as a priest for the temple at Jerusalem following the exile (Ezr 8:18; Neh 12:8). During the return journey, he was one of 12 chief priests appointed to guard the silver, gold, and vessels presented for temple use (Ezr 8:24).

2. One who helped the people understand the Law read by Ezra (Neh 8:7), and among the Levites who stood on the stairs leading the praise service (9:4,5). Later, he set his seal on Ezra's covenant (10:12).

3. One of the chiefs of the Levites who led the songs of praise and thanksgiving (Neh 12:24).

Scholars disagree as to whether the above references refer to three men or to one man.

Sheresh. Machir's son and the brother of Peresh from Manasseh's tribe (1 Chr 7:16).

Sherezer. KJV form of Sharezer in Zechariah 7:2.

See SHAREZER #2.

Sheshach. Term that is probably a cryptic name for "Babel" (Babylon) found in Jeremiah 25:26 and 51:41.

Sheshai. Descendant of Anak who was at Hebron when the 12 spies searched out the land of Canaan (Nm 13:22); he was defeated and displaced by Israel (Jos 15:14; Jgs 1:10).

Sheshan. Descendant of Judah through Jerahmeel, whose family line is traced in 1 Chronicles 2:25–41 to Elishama, evidently a contemporary of the writer. In verse 31 Sheshan's son Ahlai is named, but verse 34 says that Sheshan had no sons. Perhaps two men of the same name are denoted here, or Ahlai

may be identical with Attai (v 35), Sheshan's grandson.

Sheshbazzar. Jewish leader who found favor with Cyrus the Great, king of Persia. In the first year of his reign Cyrus issued a decree that the temple in Jerusalem should be rebuilt (Ezr 1:1–4; cf. 6:1–5). He appointed Sheshbazzar governor of Judah (5:14) and handed over to him the gold and silver vessels which Nebuchadnezzar had carried off when he took Jerusalem (1:7–9; cf. 5:14,15). Sheshbazzar fulfilled this commission by taking the vessels to Jerusalem with the returning exiles (1:9) and beginning the restoration of the temple (5:16).

Sheshbazzar is mentioned in the Bible only four times, all in the Book of Ezra (1:8,9; 5:14,16). For many years it was commonly held that Sheshbazzar was another name for Zerubbabel. Both were of the royal line; Sheshbazzar is called "the prince of Judah," which may mean that he was heir apparent to the throne. Since his genealogy is not given, he may be represented in that listing by some other name, either Zerubbabel or Shenazzar (1 Chr 3:18,19). In the record of people who returned to Jerusalem, Sheshbazzar's name does not appear. The name of Zerubbabel is at the head of this list, where one would expect Sheshbazzar's to be; both were governors of the province of Judah. Zerubbabel is associated with the laying of the foundation of the temple (Ezr 3:8–11), but that work is attributed to Sheshbazzar in 5:16, in accordance with chapter 1. It is evident that the name Sheshbazzar is found only in connection with the Persians, for chapter 1 relates his dealings with Cyrus and in chapter 5 the two occurrences of his name are in a letter written by the Persian official, Tattenai. One may conclude that the Persians knew him as Sheshbazzar but the Jews called him Zerubbabel. Both names are Akkadian, so there is no parallel here to the renaming of Jewish captives in Babylon (Dn 1:7).

Objections to this identification have been raised and it has been proposed that the name of Shenazzar (1 Chr 3:18), the son of King Jehoiachin and uncle of Zerubbabel, is a variant spelling of Sheshbazzar. It is argued that Ezra 5:6,17 is not intelligible unless Sheshbazzar was dead at the time of writing, but this argument is not clear. The exact identification of Sheshbazzar remains uncertain.

Sheth. 1. Reference to the sons of Moab, who were the cause of tumult and war to Israel (Nm 24:17).

2. KJV spelling of Seth, Adam's son, in 1 Chronicles 1:1.

See SETH.

Shethar. One of Ahasuerus's seven counselors who, when Queen Vashti defied the king's command, advised him to deprive her of her title and to seek a new queen, as an example of domestic discipline (Est 1:14).

Shethar-bozenai, Shethar-boznai. Persian official (KJV Shethar-boznai) in a province west of the Euphrates River, who joined with Tattenai and his colleagues in writing a letter to Darius Hystaspis, king of Persia, protesting the rebuilding of the temple and walls of Jerusalem under Zerubbabel (Ezr 5:3,6). Darius warned them not to interfere with Zerubbabel's work and they obeyed him (6:6,13). Shethar-bozenai is perhaps identical to the Shethar mentioned in Esther 1:14.

Sheva. 1. Scribe or personal secretary of David (2 Sm 20:25). He is called by various names elsewhere.

See SERAIAH #1.

2. Caleb's son in the family of Hezron from Judah's tribe and the father of Machbena and Gibea (1 Chr 2:49).

Shewbread. KJV rendering of showbread.

See BREAD OF THE PRESENCE.

Shibah. Name of the fourth well dug by Isaac's servants, so named for the covenant made between Isaac and Abimelech, king of Gerar. The city at the location of the well was called Beersheba (Gn 26:33, KJV Shebah).

Shibboleth. Term used by Jephthah to detect the Ephraimites at the banks of the Jordan River (Jgs 12:6). After the battle many Ephraimites tried to escape by crossing the Jordan and returning to their own land. When each of them came to the river he was asked by one of Jephthah's soldiers to say "shibboleth." An Ephraimite could not pronounce the word with the same accent as Jephthah's men and was thus discovered and immediately slain.

The exact problem in pronunciation is not known. Two possibilities exist. First, the Ephraimites had no sound comparable to "sh." Thus they pronounced "sh" as "s" ("shibboleth" becoming "sibboleth"). Second, the Gileadites pronounced "sh" as "th," a sound which was unknown to the Ephraimites who pronounced it as "s." Thus "shibboleth" was pronounced "thibboleth" by the Gileadites and "sibboleth" by the Ephraimites. At any rate this story is evidence that some differences in dialect did exist between the two groups.

Shibmah. KJV form of Sibmah, an alternate name for Sebam, a city in Reuben's territory, in Numbers 32:38.

See SEBAM.

Shicron. KJV form of Shikkeron, a city in Judah's tribe, in Joshua 15:11.

See SHIKKERON.

Shield, Shield Bearer. Protective armor and the soldier or servant who carried the shield and weapons of a warrior.

See ARMS AND WARFARE; TRADES AND OCCUPATIONS (SOLDIER).

Shiggaion, Shigionoth. Hebrew words in the titles of Psalm 7 and Habakkuk 3, respectively, perhaps denoting a hymn, a psalm of distress, or a psalm accompanied with instruments.

See MUSIC AND MUSICAL INSTRUMENTS.

Shihon. KJV rendering of Shion, a town in Issachar's territory, in Joshua 19:19.

See SHION.

Shihor. Body of water in Egypt. The name is Egyptian (KJV Sihor) and is given as a boundary of the land to be possessed by the Hebrews (Jos 13:3). First Chronicles 13:5 refers to Shihor as the southwestern limit of Israelite settlement in the time of David. Isaiah speaks of grain from the region of Shihor as a source of income for the city of Sidon (Is 23:3). Jeremiah describes Shihor as "the waters of the Nile" (Jer 2:18, KJV waters of Sihon). Some believe that the Shihor was the easternmost branch of the Nile delta. Others identify the Shihor with the Wadi el-Arish, 90 miles east of the Suez Canal. Still others identify it with the Brook (or River) of Egypt, a body of water whose precise location cannot be determined with certainty.

See BROOK OF EGYPT; NILE RIVER.

Shihor-libnath. Place defining the southern boundary of Asher's tribe (Jos 19:26). Some have identified it with the Nhar ez-Zerqa (Crocodile River) which flows into the Mediterranean Sea about six miles south of Dor.

Shikkeron. Town near the Mediterranean Sea on the northern border of the land allotted to Judah's tribe for an inheritance, mentioned between Ekron and Mt Baalah (Jos 15:11, KJV Shicron). Its locality is uncertain, though perhaps identifiable with Tell el-Ful.

Shilhi. Grandfather of King Jehoshaphat of Judah (1 Kgs 22:42; 2 Chr 20:31).

Shilhim. Alternate name for Shaaraim, a town in southern Judah, in Joshua 15:32.

See SHAARAIM #2.

Shillem, Shillemite. Fourth son of Naphtali (Gn 46:24), and father of the Shillemites (Nm 26:49); alternately called Shallum in 1 Chronicles 7:13.

Shiloah. Name of an aqueduct in Jerusalem (Is 8:6).

See SILOAM, POOL OF.

Shiloh. Town identified with Tell Seilun located 10 miles northeast of Bethel, 12 miles southeast of Shechem, and 3 miles east of the road between Shechem and Jerusalem, precisely fitting the description of its location in Judges 21:19. In addition to the continuity of the name of the site and its fitting the biblical requirements for location, excavation results agree with the history of Shiloh as far as it is known from the Bible and confirm the identification.

The town is not mentioned in any prebiblical sources. Excavations show that Shiloh flourished as a fortified town in the early 2nd millennium (Middle Bronze II).

The site was abandoned and resettled in the early Israelite period. The Bible provides no information as to how the site passed into Israelite hands. Joshua established the tabernacle there (Jos 18:1), and Shiloh became the center of religious life during the period of the judges. There Joshua cast lots to apportion the inheritance of land to seven of the tribes (18:1–19:51) and to designate the Levitical cities (21:1–42). A dispute regarding an altar erected by the two-and-a-half tribes that settled in Transjordan was settled at Shiloh (22:9–34). Some Benjamites abducted women from there during a religious festival (Jgs 21). Elkanah and Hannah often traveled to the tabernacle at Shiloh, where Hannah vowed to give her child to the service of the Lord (1 Sm 1:3,9,24). The sons of Eli who ministered there had dis-

honored their office and were rejected, so the Lord appeared to Samuel (2:14; 3:21). When the ark was taken from Shiloh to battle, news of its loss to the Philistines reached Eli and brought about his death (4:1–18). The ark was never returned to Shiloh; the psalmist records that God had "abandoned the tabernacle of Shiloh, the tent he had set up among men" (Ps 78:60 NIV).

Some scholars associate the fact that the ark was not returned to Shiloh but to Kiriathjearim with an assumed destruction under the Philistines around 1050 BC. Over 400 years later Jeremiah does use the destruction of Shiloh as a model for what he prophesied would happen to Jerusalem (Jer 7:12–14; 26:6–9). Many authorities regard Jeremiah as speaking of the assumed Philistine destruction, but this cannot be certain. Preliminary reports from the excavations in 1926 and 1929 had indicated a major destruction in the Iron I period (c. 1050) and that the site was not inhabited thereafter. However, a reexamination of the materials and supplementary excavations in 1963 require the revision of these earlier reports. The 1963 excavations indicate that there was no comprehensive destruction in the Iron I period, and that the site continued to flourish into Iron II, the period of the divided monarchy. The biblical data also support the continued existence of the site during this period. The wife of Jeroboam (930–909 BC) went to Shiloh to inquire about the outcome of her husband's illness (1 Kgs 14:2,4); she inquired of Ahijah "the Shilonite" who had prophesied Jeroboam's kingship (11:29; 12:15; 15:29; 2 Chr 9:29; 10:15). The town would presumably have suffered some destruction at the time of the fall of the northern kingdom in 722 BC. The sudden scarcity of ceramic remains in the Iron III period suggests that the site was largely abandoned around 600 BC. After the destruction of the temple in 586 BC people came from Shiloh to offer sacrifices in Jerusalem (Jer 41:5). Shilonites were also among the first returnees from the Babylonian captivity (1 Chr 9:5).

Excavators found no traces of any permanent temple or shrine on the summit of the site where it would have been expected; however, portions of the summit were cleared to bedrock during reconstruction in the Roman period. It is also possible that the tabernacle was kept outside the city, as seen in the setting of a religious festival in the surrounding vineyards (Jgs 21). A portable shrine like the tabernacle may not have left any traces.

The site was resettled around 300 BC and flourished through the Roman period. It is mentioned by Eusebius, Jerome, and in Talmudic sources. It lost much of its importance after the Islamic conquests.

Tel Shiloh.

The transliteration of a Hebrew word in Genesis 49:10 was taken as a messianic name by the translators of the KJV: "The sceptre shall not depart from Judah, nor a lawgiver from between his feet, until Shiloh come; and unto him shall the gathering of the people be."

The dominant nonmessianic interpretation of the verse understands the term *Shiloh* as a reference to the city of that name which was so prominent during the period of the judges; the last clause of the verse is translated "until he comes to Shiloh." The basic objection to this approach is historical: Judah does not come into prominence until the monarchy when Shiloh was no longer an important center. Shiloh plays no particular role in the history of Judah to whom Genesis 49:8–12 was spoken.

Messianic interpretations associate this verse with the Davidic kingship and/or the Christ. Christian tradition since the Reformation has for the most part understood the word as a messianic proper name, as reflected in the translation of the clause in the KJV. This approach has a questionable origin: it first appears in a fanciful part of the Talmud (Sanhedrin, 98b) where groups of students are arguing the merits of their teachers, each group seeking to associate the name of its teacher with some title or aspect of the Messiah. One group taught by Rabbi Shelah used this word in Genesis 49:10 to associate their teacher's name with the Messiah. When Talmudic materials were receiving attention from Christian scholars 1000 years later, the word *shiloh* appears as a messianic name in the Great Bible of 1539; this tradition was followed in Christian translations for several centuries. Another objection to taking *shiloh* as a messianic name is the fact that this name or title is not developed as such in the rest of the Bible.

Luther and Calvin viewed the word as derived from a Hebrew word they translated as "son." This interpretation is forced: the word in question is not the same as the word *shiloh*, and its more precise meaning is "embryo."

Others associate the word with a Hebrew term meaning "be at ease, at rest" and translate the word as "rest-bringer." The basic objection here is also the fact that this title is not further developed in the messianic expectation of the Bible.

Some commentators and translations divide the word in two, and translate it "as long as tribute comes to him" or "until tribute comes to him." This approach is followed in the GNB, the NEB, and the NAB. Others identify the word *shiloh* as a Hebrew equivalent to a term in cognate languages meaning "ruler, prince." The translation would read "until his ruler comes."

The ancient translations (Septuagint, Pesh-itta, and Targums) understood the word *shiloh* as meaning "he to whom they belong." This translation also has the support of Ezekiel 21:27; Ezekiel appears to be alluding to Genesis 49:10 and paraphrases the last clause "until he comes to whom it rightfully belongs" (NIV). Commentators and translations following this interpretation usually also understand the word translated "lawgiver" as "lawgiver's staff," so that the entire verse would read as follows: "The scepter will not depart from Judah, nor the lawgiver's staff from between his feet, until he comes to whom they belong." This approach is taken in the JB and the NIV.

There are difficulties with these and other approaches taken to the word *shiloh* in Genesis 49:10; while a degree of uncertainty remains about the precise force of the term, the immediate context (v 9) is brought into association with the Messiah in the NT (Rv 5:5).

RAYMOND B. DILLARD

Shiloni. KJV form of Shilonite in Nehemiah 11:5.

See SHILONITE #2.

Shilonite. 1. Inhabitant of Shiloh, the hometown of Abijah the prophet (1 Kgs 11:29; 12:15; 15:29; 2 Chr 9:29; 10:15).

See SHILOH.

2. Hometown of the forefather of a family of exiles that returned to Jerusalem following the Babylonian captivity (1 Chr 9:5; Neh 11:5, KJV Shiloni). This place is probably the same as #1 above.

See SHILOH.

Shilshah. Zophah's son and a chief of Asher's tribe (1 Chr 7:37).

Shimea. 1. Alternate name for Shammah, Jesse's third son, in 1 Chronicles 2:13 and 20:7.

See SHAMMAH #2.

2. David's son borne to him by Bathsheba during his reign in Jerusalem (1 Chr 3:5). He is called Shammua in 2 Samuel 5:14 (KJV Shammuah) and 1 Chronicles 14:4.

3. Uzzah's son, the father of Haggiah and a descendant of Levi through Merari's line (1 Chr 6:30).

4. Gershonite Levite, Michael's son, the father of Berechiah, and the grandfather of Asaph. Asaph, with Heman and Ethan, was appointed by David to lead the musicians before the sanctuary (1 Chr 6:39).

Shimeah. 1. Alternate name for Shammah, David's brother, in 2 Samuel 13:3,32.

See SHAMMAH #2.

2. Mikloth's son and the grandson of Jeiel

from Benjamin's tribe (1 Chr 8:32); called Shimeam in 1 Chronicles 9:38.

Shimeam. Alternate spelling of Shimeah, Mikloth's son, in 1 Chronicles 9:38.

See SHIMEAH #2.

Shimeath. Ammonitess mother (2 Chr 24:26) or perhaps father (2 Kgs 12:21) of one of the royal servants who conspired against and murdered King Jehoash of Judah (835–796 BC).

Shimeathite. One of three families of scribes living at Jabez in Judah. They were perhaps Kenites and descendants of Hammath (1 Chr 2:55). Their history is not certain. The Shimeathites may be identified with one of the nomadic Kenite tribes that settled with the Amalekites in southern Palestine during Saul's reign in Israel (1020–1000 BC).

Shimei. 1. Son of Gershon, the grandson of Levi, and the brother of Libni (Ex 6:17, KJV Shimi; Nm 3:18; 1 Chr 6:17). He was the father of four sons and the founder of the Shimeite family (Nm 3:21, KJV Shimite; 1 Chr 23:7,10).

2. Benjamite, and the son of Gera from the house of Saul. He met King David at the village of Behurim during the king's journey from Jerusalem to Mahanaim. Here Shimei bitterly opposed David, cursing him for the ruin of Saul's house (2 Sm 16:5–13). Later, Shimei repented of his shameful behavior, entreated David's forgiveness, and received the king's pardon (19:16–23). After David's death, King Solomon ordered Shimei to settle in Jerusalem and never to leave the city for any reason. Shimei disobeyed the decree and was killed (1 Kgs 2:8,36–44).

3. Brother of David and the father of Jonathan (2 Sm 21:21); alternately called Shammah in 1 Samuel 16:9.

See SHAMMAH #2.

4. One of David's court officials who did not support Adonijah's attempt to set himself up as king (1 Kgs 1:8).

5. Benjamite, the son of Ela and one of King Solomon's officials who oversaw the royal household (1 Kgs 4:18); perhaps identical with #4 above.

6. Judahite, the son of Pedaiah, the brother of Zerubbabel, and a descendant of David through Solomon's line (1 Chr 3:19).

7. Simeonite, the son of Zaccur and the father of 16 sons and 6 daughters (1 Chr 4:26,27).

8. Reubenite, the son of Gog and the father of Micah (1 Chr 5:4).

9. Son of Libni, the father of Uzzah, and a descendant of Levi through Marari's line (1 Chr 6:29).

10 Gershonite Levite, the son of Jahath, the father of Zimmah, and an ancestor of Asaph who served as a leader of the musicians in the sanctuary during David's reign (1 Chr 6:42).

11. Benjamite, the father of nine sons and a head of his father's house (1 Chr 8:21); alternately called Shema in verse 13.

See SHEMA (PERSON) #3.

12. Gershonite Levite, and the father of three sons in the house of Ladan (1 Chr 23:9).

13. Son of Jeduthun and the leader of the 10th of 24 divisions of musicians trained for service in the sanctuary during David's reign (1 Chr 25:3,17).

14. Ramathite, and a member of King David's staff who had charge of David's vineyards (1 Chr 27:27).

15. Son of Heman, the brother of Jehuel, and one of the Levites selected to cleanse the house of the Lord during King Hezekiah's reign (715–686 BC; 2 Chr 29:14).

16. Levite, and the brother of Conaniah appointed by King Hezekiah of Judah to oversee the administration of the temple contributions in Jerusalem (2 Chr 31:12,13).

17, 18, 19. Three men, a Levite, Hashum's son, and Binnui's son, who were encouraged by Ezra to divorce their foreign wives during the postexilic era (Ezr 10:23,33,38).

Shimeite. 1. Family of Levites founded by Shimei, Gershon's son (Nm 3:21; 1 Chr 23:7,10).

See SHIMEI #1.

2. Family of Benjamites founded by Shimei, Kish's son (Zec 12:13).

Shimeon. Harim's fifth son, who was encouraged by Ezra to divorce his foreign wife whom he had married during the postexilic era (Ezr 10:31).

Shimhi. KJV form of Shimei, an alternate name for Shema, in 1 Chronicles 8:21.

See SHEMA (PERSON) #3.

The Kidron Valley, beyond which Solomon forbade Shimei to go.

Shimi. KJV spelling of Shimei, Gershon's son, in Exodus 6:17.

See SHIMEI #1.

Shimite. KJV spelling of Shimeite in Numbers 3:21.

See SHIMEI #1.

Shimma. KJV spelling of Shimea, an alternate name for Shammah, Jesse's son, in 1 Chronicles 2:13.

See SHAMMAH #2.

Shimon. Head of a Judahite family (1 Chr 4:20).

Shimrath. Shimei's son from Benjamin's tribe (1 Chr 8:21).

Shimri. 1. Simeonite, Shemaiah's son and the father of Jedaiah (1 Chr 4:37).
2. Father of Jediael (and perhaps Joha), two of David's mighty men (1 Chr 11:45).
3. Merarite Levite, Hosah's son and a temple gatekeeper during David's reign (1 Chr 26:10, KJV Simri).
4. Levite, of the family of Elizaphan, who assisted in Hezekiah's temple reforms (2 Chr 29:13).

Shimrith. Moabitess mother of Jehozabad, a royal servant, who along with Zabad conspired against and murdered King Jehoash of Judah (2 Chr 24:26). She is alternately called Shomer in 2 Kings 12:21; Shimrith is the feminine form of Shomer.

See SHOMER #1.

Shimron (Place). Canaanite town whose king joined the confederacy of King Jabin of Hazor in unsuccessful resistance to the Israelites under Joshua (Jos 11:1). Its site is uncertain, though it was in Zebulun's territory (19:15).

Shimron, Shimrom (Person). Issachar's fourth son (Gn 46:13; 1 Chr 7:1, KJV Shimrom) and the founder of the Shimronite family (Nm 26:24).

Shimronite. Family founded by Shimron, Issachar's son (Nm 26:24).

See SHIMRON, SHIMROM (PERSON).

Shimron-meron. Canaanite city destroyed by Joshua on his northern military campaign in Palestine. The king of Shimron-meron was one of 31 kings defeated by Joshua (Jos 12:20). This king was perhaps one of the northern kings summoned by Jabin, king of Hazor, to combine forces in an attempt to defeat Joshua (11:1). In all probability Shimron-meron was one of the 12 cities included in the territory allotted to Zebulun for an inheritance (19:15).

Shimshai. Persian government official whose territory included Palestine. With another official (Rehum), he wrote a letter to Artaxerxes opposing the rebuilding of the temple by the Jews returned from exile (Ezr 4:8,9). He succeeded in halting the rebuilding project (vv 17–23).

Shinab. King of Admah, who joined an alliance with four neighboring rulers against King Chedorlaomer. Chedorlaomer defeated this confederation of kings in the Valley of Siddim—the southern region of the Dead Sea (Gn 14:2).

Shinar. Name for a district of Babylonia mentioned exclusively in the Bible. The "Plain of Shinar" comprised the region approximately from modern Baghdad to the Persian Gulf. In the ancient world this was the region of Sumer (south) and Akkad (north), which later became generally known as Babylonia (Dn 1:2). The etymology of the term has proven difficult since it fails to appear outside the Bible. Any derivation from the name *Sumer* seems doubtful. This has led some to speculate that Shinar should be found in Syria since there are parallels with the western Semitic *Sangar* and the Akkadian *Sanhar*. But the biblical location is consistent and specific.

The renowned cities of Erech, Akkad, and Babel (Babylon) all were in Shinar as a part of the kingdom of Nimrod, son of Cush (Gn 10:10). Genesis 11:2 also mentions Shinar in connection with the Tower of Babel. And in Genesis 14:1,9 we read about Amraphel, "king of Shinar," who was part of an eastern league in war with Abraham and the residents of Transjordan. The region also appears in Joshua 7:21 as the origin of the mantle which Achan coveted. Shinar's identification with a district of Babylon becomes clear in Israel's exile. Shinar is the destination of Nebuchadnezzar's new subjects (Dn 1:2) and the place of Israel's later rescue (Is 11:11; cf. Zec 5:11).

See BABYLON, BABYLONIA.

Shion. One of 16 cities in the territory allotted to Issachar's tribe for an inheritance, mentioned between Hapharaim and Anaharath (Jos 19:19; KJV Shihon). Its location is unknown.

Shiphi. Ziza's father and a prince in Simeon's tribe (1 Chr 4:37).

Shiphmite. Designation for Zabdi (1 Chr 27:27). He may have come from Shepham or Siphmoth.

See ZABDI #3.

Shiphrah. One of two Hebrew midwives who refused to kill Hebrew male infants at Pharaoh's command (Ex 1:15).

Shiphtan. Father of Kemuel, a prince of Ephraim appointed by Joshua to help divide the land among Israel's 10 tribes west of the Jordan (Nm 34:24).

Shipmaster. *See* TRADES AND OCCUPATIONS (SAILOR).

Ships and Shipping. *See* TRAVEL AND TRANSPORTATION.

Shirt. *See* FASHION AND DRESS.

Shisha. Alternate name for Seraiah, King David's scribe, in 1 Kings 4:3.

See SERAIAH #1.

Shishak. Egyptian pharaoh, descendant of a powerful family of Libyan chieftains, and founder of Egypt's 22nd Dynasty. His Egyptian name was Sheshonk. He was a contemporary of Solomon, Jeroboam, and Rehoboam. His regnal years are variously given as 940–915 BC or 935–914 BC.

During Solomon's reign, he afforded asylum to Jeroboam, Solomon's servant and subsequent adversary, who escaped to Egypt to avoid being killed by his lord against whom he had rebelled (1 Kgs 11:40). Since Jeroboam was to set up the northern kingdom after Solomon's death—an event used by God to punish his people for Solomon's sin—Shishak's readiness to harbor the fugitive rebel plays a part in God's design to bring about his purposes.

God used Shishak a second time to further his plans. When Judah under Rehoboam became sinful and engaged in idolatrous practices, allowing male shrine prostitutes to operate in the land (a practice not to be equated with the phenomenon of homosexuality as presently known), God used Shishak's invasion of Palestine to punish his people. This invasion took place in the fifth year of Rehoboam's reign (1 Kgs 14:25; cf. 2 Chr 12:2–9). A great number of Judean towns were taken, but God spared Jerusalem from being captured, when the princes and the king showed repentance and humbled themselves (2 Chr 12:7). However, Shishak did show his mastery in Jerusalem by plundering both temple and royal palace and carrying off the gold shields that Solomon had made. Although the biblical account focuses on Shishak's invasion of the Judean area only, extra-biblical data indicate that he also invaded the territory of Jeroboam, to whom he had previously given refuge.

The discovery of a triumphal inscription prepared by Shishak for the temple at Karnak (ancient Thebes) is also of great significance for biblical history. This inscription contains the names of many towns Shishak claims to have captured on his raids into the Asian region. Some of these in Egyptian orthography correspond to names in the Hebrew language. Two dozen can be identified with certainty, affording valuable outside confirmation of biblical geography and history. Additional evidence of Shishak's raid into Palestine was found at Megiddo (north central area of Palestine) where a fragment of a triumphal stele erected by the pharaoh has been located. Those assisting him on his Asian raids were the Lubim and the Sukkiim of Libyan origin and the Ethiopians.

Shishak's expedition has been used as a means of reconstructing some of the biblical chronology. Some scholars have maintained that Shishak was the pharaoh whose daughter was given in marriage to Solomon (1 Kgs 3:1), but this is not proven and is disputed by others.

See SOLOMON (PERSON); ISRAEL, HISTORY OF; JEROBOAM; REHOBOAM; EGYPT, EGYPTIANS.

Shitrai. David's chief shepherd in charge of his flocks in Sharon (1 Chr 27:29).

Bracelets of gold for the son of Shishak I (c. 930 BC).

Shittah Tree. KJV rendering of acacia, a common desert tree, in Isaiah 41:19.

See PLANTS (ACACIA).

Shittim (Place). Site on the plains of Moab where the Israelites made their final Transjordan encampment after defeating Sihon and Og (Nm 22:21–35) and prior to their crossing of the Jordan (25:1). According to Numbers 33:49 this camp was near "the Jordan from Beth-jeshimoth as far as Abel-shittim." Here Abel-shittim appears to be the full name of the place, while Shittim is the more common abbreviated toponym.

Archaeologists have suggested its identification with both Tell Kefrein (an area seven miles north and six miles east of the Dead Sea and opposite Jericho) and Tell el-Hammam (an elevated fortress about one-and-a-half miles east of Tell-Kefrein). Those favoring Tell Kefrein argue that the eight-mile wide and 15-mile long area on the plains of Moab would have been well suited for accommodating the host of Israel; while those who prefer Tell el-Hammam stress its strategic location on a hill at the base of the Moabite plateau commanding the outlet of Wadi el-Kefrein.

Here Balak of Moab attempted to thwart the Israelite penetration of Canaan by hiring Balaam to curse the people of God (Nm 22–24), and later, apparently incited by Balaam's counsel, Israel "played the harlot" with women from Midian and Moab (25:1–5; cf. 31:15,16). Israel's apostasy, participating in idolatrous rites and engaging in ritual prostitution, was punished by Yahweh with the plague of Baal-peor (25:6–9; cf. 1 Cor 10:6–8). Moses and Eleazar organized a census of the tribes while encamped at Shittim and here Joshua was publicly proclaimed as Moses' successor (Nm 27:18–22). Finally, Joshua dispatched two spies from Shittim to reconnoiter Jericho (Jos 2:1) and the Israelites prepared for the river crossing by breaking camp at Shittim and traveling to the Jordan (3:1).

Outside the Hexateuch the place name Shittim occurs only in Joel 3:18 and Micah 6:5. The reference to the "valley of Shittim" or "wadi of the acacias" seems to be a symbol of barren aridity transformed into well-watered land when Yahweh restores his people in the eschaton, not a literal geographical location. Micah charges the people to remember "what happened from Shittim to Gilgal," no doubt a reference to the crossing of the Jordan and the covenant promise of a land ultimately realized, as he recites the "saving acts" of Yahweh on their behalf. The RSV rendering of Hosea 5:2, "And they have made deep the pit of Shittim," has no manuscript support and is better translated "and the rebels are entrenched in deceitfulness."

Abel-shittim means "meadow of the acacias." Shittim wood or lumber from the acacia tree was an important building material for the tabernacle and its furniture, including the ark of the covenant (Ex 25–27,30,35–38).

A. E. HILL

Shittim Wood. KJV rendering of acacia wood in Exodus 26:15, etc.

See PLANTS (ACACIA).

Shiza. Reubenite and the father of Adina, one of David's select warriors (1 Chr 11:42).

Shoa. Assyrian prince and people listed with the Babylonians, Chaldeans, and other Assyrian tribes, who were used by the Lord to punish Judah (Ez 23:23). The historical background of this Assyrian prince and his people is unknown.

Shobab. 1. Second of David's four sons by Bathsheba (2 Sm 5:14; 1 Chr 3:5; 14:4).
2. Caleb's son by his wife Azubah (1 Chr 2:18).

Shobach. Commander of the army of Hadadezer, king of Zobah, who led the Ammonite-Syrian campaign against Israel. David's army killed Shobach and so completely destroyed his forces that the Ammonite-Syrian alliance was broken, and the kingdoms that were tributary to Hadadezer became subject to David (2 Sm 10:16,18). He is also called Shophach in 1 Chronicles 19:16,18.

Shobai. Ancestor of a group of people that returned to Jerusalem with Zerubbabel after the Babylonian exile (Ezr 2:42; Neh 7:45).

Shobal. 1. One of the seven sons of Seir the Horite in Edom (Gn 36:20; 1 Chr 1:38). Shobal became the father of five sons (Gn 36:23; 1 Chr 1:40) and a chief among the Horites (Gn 36:29).
2. Hur's son, the father of Haroeh, and the founder of the families of Kiriath-jearim (1 Chr 2:50,52).
3. One of Judah's five sons and the father of Reaiah (1 Chr 4:1,2), and perhaps the same as #2 above.

Shobek. Leader who signed Ezra's covenant of faithfulness to God during the postexilic era (Neh 10:24).

Shobi. Ammonite prince, son of King Nahash, who, along with Machir of Lo-debar and Barzillai of Rogelim, generously supplied David with food and equipment at Mahanaim during Absalom's rebellion (2 Sm 17:27).

Shocho, Shochoh, Shoco. KJV variant spellings of Socoh.

See SOCOH #1.

Shoe. *See* FASHION AND DRESS.

Shoham. Merarite Levite, and Jaaziah's son in David's reign (1 Chr 24:27).

Shomer. 1. Father (2 Kgs 12:21), or perhaps the Moabite mother (2 Chr 24:26), of Jehozabad, a royal servant, who with Jozacar (Zabad?), conspired against and murdered Jehoash, king of Judah. Shimrith is the feminine form of Shomer.

See SHIMRITH.

2. Alternate name for Shemer, Heber's son, in 1 Chronicles 7:32.

See SHEMER #3.

Shophach. Alternate form of Shobach in 1 Chronicles 19:16,18.

See SHOBACH.

Shophan. Part of the name Atroth-shophan which the KJV translates as two towns in Numbers 32:35.

See ATROTH-SHOPHAN.

Shophar. Primitive musical instrument made from animal horn.

See MUSIC AND MUSICAL INSTRUMENTS.

Shoshannim, Shoshannim-eduth. Hebrew word and phrase in the superscriptions of Psalms 45, 69, and 80 (KJV), translated "according to Lilies" (RSV); perhaps a familiar ancient melody to which the psalms were performed.

See MUSIC AND MUSICAL INSTRUMENTS.

Showbread. Bread that was kept in the holy place of the temple (2 Chr 2:4).

See BREAD OF THE PRESENCE.

Shrub. *See* PLANTS.

Shua. 1. Canaanite whose daughter Judah took for a wife. She bore Judah three sons: Er, Onan, and Shelah (Gn 38:2,12; KJV Shuah).

See BATH-SHUA #1.

2. Asherite, Heber's daughter and the sister of Japhlet, Shomer, and Hotham (1 Chr 7:32).

Shuah. 1. One of six sons borne to Abraham by Keturah (Gn 25:2; 1 Chr 1:32). He was per-

haps the forefather of the Shuhite Arab tribe which dwelt near the land of Uz (Jb 2:11).

2. KJV spelling of Shua, Judah's father-in-law, in Genesis 38:2,12.

See SHUA #1.

3. KJV spelling of Shuhah, Chelub's brother, in 1 Chronicles 4:11.

See SHUHAH.

Shual (Person). Zopah's son and a leader in Asher's tribe (1 Chr 7:36).

Shual (Place). Region that included the town of Ophrah and was perhaps situated in the territory of Benjamin and Ephraim. The land of Shual was the direction taken by one of the invading companies of Philistines, camped at Michmash during Saul's reign (1 Sm 13:17). Shual was located to the north of Michmash.

Shubael. 1. Alternate form of Shebuel, Gershon's son, in 1 Chronicles 24:20.

See SHEBUEL #1.

2. Alternate form of Shebuel, Heman's son, in 1 Chronicles 25:20.

See SHEBUEL #2.

Shuhah. Chelub's brother from Judah's tribe (1 Chr 4:11; KJV Shuah).

Shuham, Shuhamite. Alternate name for Hushim, Dan's son, and his descendant in Numbers 26:42,43.

See HUSHIM #1.

Shuhite. Arab tribe, apparently descended from Shuah, the son of Abraham by Keturah. It was located near the land of Uz. Bildad, one of the three friends of Job, is identified as a Shuhite (Jb 2:11; 8:1; 18:1; 25:1; 42:9).

Shulammite, Shulamite. Name or title of Solomon's lover in his Song (6:13; KJV Shulamite). Her identity is not certain. Some suggest that Shulammite refers to a woman from the city of Shunem. Her designation as Shunammite was perhaps changed to Shulammite for its similarity in sound to Solomon's Hebrew name. Shunem was situated in the land of Issachar near Mt Gilboa (1 Sm 28:4). It was from this city that Abishag the beautiful Shunammite woman was called to nurse King David in his later years (1 Kgs 1:1–4,15; 2:17–22). It is possible that Abishag became the beloved Shulammite maiden of Solomon's song.

See SHUNEM.

Shumathite. Family of Judah, descended from Shobal of Kiriath-jearim. Shobal was the son of Hur from Caleb's line (1 Chr 2:53).

Shunammite. Inhabitant of Shunem; hometown of Abishag (1 Kgs 1:3,15).

See SHUNEM.

Shunem. Village of Issachar's tribe (Jos 19:18) strategically located in the Jezreel Valley. Shunem (modern Sulem) is about three-and-a-half miles north of Jezreel, situated on the outer hills of Mt Moreh. Both Shunem and Jezreel guard the eastern approach to the Jezreel Valley from Beth-shan through the Valley of Harod. This strategic location explains the appearance of Shunem on city lists of various foreign invaders: Thutmose III (15 centry BC); the Amarna letters (15 century BC) which mention it in conjunction with Megiddo; and the 10th-century record at Karnak of the Egyptian Shishak who listed Shunem's importance. Preliminary archaeological surveys of the site evidence occupation from the Middle Bronze Age to the Islamic era.

The Philistines used Shunem to launch their siege of the Israelite forces at Jezreel (1 Sm 28–31). Because Shunem was on a well-used route, Elijah frequented the town and even resided there (2 Kgs 4:8). Later Elijah raised a woman's son from death (vv 32–37). During the latter years of the reign of David a beautiful woman from Shunem named Abishag was summoned to care for the ailing king (1 Kgs 1:3,15). After David's death Abishag appears in the story of the rivalry between Adonijah (David's eldest son) and Solomon. Adonijah requests Abishag for his own once Solomon gains the throne, but the king views his brother's interest as presumption—and a possible attempt at his throne (2:13–25).

See ABISHAG; SHULAMMITE, SHULAMITE.

Shuni, Shunite. Third of Gad's seven sons (Gn 46:16) and the founder of the Shunite family (Nm 26:15).

Shupham, Shuphamite. Benjamin's son and descendant. Shupham is the KJV spelling of Shephupham in Numbers 26:39.

See SHEPHUPHAM.

Shuppim. 1. Son of Ir and a great-grandson of Benjamin (1 Chr 7:12,15). Shuppim is perhaps a shortened form of Shephupham, mentioned in Numbers 26:39 as the son of Benjamin.

See SHEPHUPHAM.

2. Levite gatekeeper, who with Hosah, watched the gate of Shallecheth on the western side of Jerusalem (1 Chr 26:16). Shuppim is probably a later addition by a copyist who absentmindedly repeated the last word of 1 Chronicles 26:15 to form this name.

Shur. Wilderness region located in the Sinai peninsula east of Egypt's Nile delta and west of the Negeb. In antiquity, a caravan route passed through this region from Egypt to Palestine. It was perhaps along this route that the Angel of the Lord found Hagar (Gn 16:7). Abraham lived for a time between Shur and Kadesh (20:1) and it was part of the territory occupied by the Ishmaelites (25:18). After crossing the Red Sea, Moses led Israel on a three-day trek through this arid wasteland (Ex 15:22). King Saul of Israel (1020–1000 BC) conquered the Amalekites in the vicinity of Shur (1 Sm 15:7), and later David (1000–961 BC) defeated the Geshurites, Girzites, and Amalekites here (27:8). The wilderness of Etham in Numbers 33:8 is identical with the wilderness of Shur.

See SINAI, SINA; WILDERNESS WANDERINGS.

Shushan. KJV form of Susa, the Persian capital.

See SUSA.

Shushan Eduth. Hebrew phrase in the superscription of Psalm 60, translated "To the tune of 'The Lilies of the Covenant'" (NIV), perhaps a familiar ancient melody to which the psalm was performed.

See MUSIC AND MUSICAL INSTRUMENTS.

Shuthelah. 1. Ephraim's son, the brother of Becher and Tahan, and the father of Eran and Bered. He founded the Shuthelahite family and was the ancestor of Joshua, the son of Nun (Nm 26:35; KJV Shuthalhite; 1 Chr 7:20,27).

2. Zabad's son from Ephraim's tribe (1 Chr 7:21).

Shuthelahite, Shuthalhite. Descendant of Shuthelah, Ephraim's son (Nm 26:35; KJV Shuthalhite).

See SHUTHELAH #1.

Sia, Siaha. Ancestor of a group of temple assistants that returned to Jerusalem with Zerubbabel following the exile (Neh 7:47); alternately spelled Siaha in Ezra 2:44.

Sibbecai, Sibbechai. Zerahite from the town of Hushah and one of David's "mighty men" (1 Chr 11:29; 20:4; KJV Sibbechai; 27:11). He is credited with killing the giant Saph when Israel fought Philistia at Gob (2 Sm 21:18; KJV Sibbechai). In 2 Samuel 23:27, he is called Mebunnai, probably a later erroneous reading of the original.

Sibboleth. Spelling of the Gileadite password as mispronounced by the Ephraimites (Jgs 12:6).

See SHIBBOLETH.

Sibmah. Alternate rendering of Sebam, a city in Reuben's territory, in Numbers 32:38; Joshua 13:19; etc..

See SEBAM.

Sibraim. Geographical landmark between Damascus and Hamath, marking the northern boundary of Israel (Ez 47:16). Its exact location is unknown.

Sichem. KJV form of Shechem in Genesis 12:6.

See SHECHEM (PLACE).

Sickle. *See* TOOLS.

Sickness. *See* DISEASE; MEDICINE AND MEDICAL PRACTICE; PLAGUE.

Siddim, Valley of. Location of the battle between four kings from Mesopotamia and five allied kings living near the Dead Sea (Gn 14:3,8,10; KJV vale of Siddim). The precise location of the battle in the vicinity of the Dead Sea has proven impossible to determine; one is left with conjectures. The valley is described as "full of bitumen pits" (Gn 14:10; KJV slimepits). This description fits well the areas adjacent to the Salt or Dead Sea.

The account in Genesis describes an important military campaign believed to have occurred in the Middle Bronze Age (c. 1900 BC) which would place it at the time of Abraham. The kings mentioned in the coalition from the East are unknown, since the alleged link of Amraphel with Hammurabi is now considered untenable. These four allies came south from Damascus and conquered a series of cities, including Karnaim, Ham, and the Horites in Mt Seir, as far south as the Gulf of Elat. They then turned northwest to Kadesh-barnea and from there northeast toward the Dead Sea. This seems to be the locality where they met resistance from the coalition of the kings of Sodom, Gomorrah, Admah, Zeboiim, and Zoar (Gn 14:2–9) south of the Dead Sea.

The reference to "bitumen pits" further substantiates this locale since the Greek name of the Salt Sea was the Asphaltis Sea, and pieces of bitumen have been reported in its waters. Archaeological surveys have verified settlements in this area during the early Canaanite period.

At one point between the Dead Sea and the Gulf of Elat the floor of the Arabah, or Rift Valley, is 250 feet above sea level, while the Dead Sea is over 1200 feet below sea level. It is not unlikely that the armies were joined in battle on higher ground. As the local armies fell back before the invaders, some fled to the mountains, either east or west, while others fleeing north encountered the soft asphalt pits (Gn 14:10). It is widely believed that the area of the Dead Sea south of the Lisan peninsula was once dry ground and that the cities of Sodom and Gomorrah lie beneath the waters which now cover this entire area. Remains have recently been recovered near the edge of the Lisan peninsula.

Sidon (Person). Canaan's firstborn son; Canaan was the son of Ham and grandson of Noah (Gn 10:15,19; 1 Chr 1:13). Sidon founded a city (bearing his name) that set the northern boundary of the land of Canaan and later played a dominant role in Palestinian history.

See SIDON, SIDONIAN (PLACE).

Sidon, Sidonian (Place). City on the Phoenician coast, between Beirut and Tyre; frequently called Zidon in the KJV. The present town, Saida, is not regarded as a direct continuation of the ancient city, but a development of post-Crusader times. The names Sidon and Sidonian appear 38 times in the OT and Sidon occurs 12 times in the NT.

Sidon harbor, with the ruins of a maritime castle.

The relative antiquity of Byblos (Gebal, Jebeil), Tyre, and Sidon may be determined by the table of nations (Gn 10), which names Sidon as the firstborn son of Canaan (v 15), who was a son of Ham (v 6). The territory of the Canaanites extended from Sidon to Gaza and east to the Cities of the Plain (cf. v 19).

Sidon is situated 22 miles north of Tyre, with which it is often associated (e.g., Is 23:1,2; Jer 47:4; Mt 11:21,22); both were much concerned with commerce and industry. Sidon was built on a headland that jutted into the sea toward the southwest. It had two harbors, the northern one having inner and outer ports. Sidon was also a center for the manufacture of the purple dye made from the *Murex* shellfish.

Archaeological work in Sidon has been hampered because the present city is built largely over the ancient remains; the site has been used as a convenient source of stone for building. Casual digging unearthed the Egyptian sarcophagus of Eshmunazar II, king of Sidon (5th century BC). Excavations in the royal necropolei produced the so-called "Sarcophagus of Alexander," executed with an exquisitely painted high relief of Greek style (late 4th century BC) and a number of anthropoid sarcophagi, including that of King Tabnit, father of Eshmunazar II.

Many gods were worshiped at Sidon. The chief male deity was Eshmun, a god of healing, to whom a large temple had been built. The principal goddess was Astarte, who was well known throughout Palestine in the Israelite period. Jezebel, the wicked wife of Ahab, king of Israel, was the daughter of Ethbaal, king of Sidon. She fostered the worship of Baal and Ashtoreth in Israel (cf. 1 Kgs 16:31–33).

References to Sidon in secular literature are numerous. In the Amarna letters, the Sidonian king, Zimrida, is accused by Rib-Addi, king of Byblos, and Abi-Milki, king of Tyre, of disloyalty to the pharaoh. Zimrida protested his innocence, but it is evident that the charge was true. The city suffered two complete destructions by Esar-haddon, king of Assyria (880–869 BC), and by the Persian ruler, Artaxerxes, in 531 BC. The Babylonians, Persians, Greeks, Romans, and others left their mark on Sidon.

The Bible mentions Sidon several times in connection with the conquest of Palestine. Joshua defeated the northern confederation under Jabin, king of Hazor, and pursued the enemy as far as "Great Sidon" (Jos 11:8). Joshua also stated that the land of Israel included all of Lebanon, "even all the Sidonians" (Jos 13:4–6). The tribal allotment of Asher extended as far north as "Sidon the Great" (Jos 19:28), but Asher did not drive out the inhabitants of Sidon (Jgs 1:31).

The gods of Sidon are listed among the foreign deities that Israel served (Jgs 10:6); David's census included Sidon and Tyre (2 Sm 24:6,7); and during a famine in the time of Ahab, the prophet Elijah was sent to live at the home of a widow in Zarephath (Sarepta) "which belongs to Sidon" (1 Kgs 17:9; Lk 4:25,26). Sidon is referred to often by the Hebrew prophets (Is 23:2,4,12; Jer 25:22; 27:3; 47:4; Ez 27:8; Jl 3:4; Zec 9:2).

In the NT, Jesus healed the daughter of a woman of that area (Mt 15:21–28). People came from as far away as Tyre and Sidon to hear Jesus and to be healed by him (Lk 6:17). On Paul's voyage to Rome to appear before Caesar, the ship made its first stop at Sidon, where the centurion, Julius, allowed Paul to go ashore to visit friends (Acts 27:3).

Siege. *See* ARMS AND WARFARE.

Sign. Word connoting a visible event intended to convey meaning beyond that which is normally perceived in the outward appearance of the event.

In the Old Testament. In a few instances in the OT, "sign" refers to the observances of heavenly bodies probably in an astrological sense (Gn 1:14; Jer 10:2), or to the "signs and wonders" as marks of the miraculous actions of God within the history of the world (Dt 4:34; 6:22; Neh 9:10; Ps 105:27; Jer 32:20). On other occasions it is used as an insignia of the Mosaic covenant. Thus the wearing of the Law on the wrist and forehead and the keeping of the sabbath are considered signs of the relationship between Israel and God (Dt 6:8; 11:18; Ez 20:12,20).

The most numerous and significant usages of "sign" appear in relation to the OT prophetic ministry. Beginning with Moses, signs are used to confirm that God has spoken to the prophet. Thus when Moses receives the message of deliverance that he is to bear to the children of Israel in Egypt and the pharaoh, he is given two signs: his staff is changed into a serpent and his hand is afflicted with leprosy (Ex 4:1–8). They are to show that Moses has not merely been dreaming and that his message is the Word of God and not his own invention. The prophet receives the message from the Lord, the message is proclaimed, and the message is then confirmed by a sign that may or may not be related to the message. A late psalm laments that with the passing of the prophets there are also no longer signs given from the Lord (Ps 74:9).

Sign and wonders were also used by false prophets. After a sign had been given and had come to pass, the leaders of Israel were to examine the message of the prophet to see if it led the people away from the true worship of

God. If it did, the prophet who had given the sign was to be put to death (Dt 13:1–5).

The character of the sign varies, and often is miraculous. Some of the great miracles of the OT are prophetic signs, for example, the moving of the shadow back up the steps of Hezekiah's palace to confirm Isaiah's prediction that the king would recover from what was a mortal illness (2 Kgs 20:8,9; Is 38:22). Often the sign is predictive only, and the people can know whether the prophet has spoken the truth by whether or not the event comes to pass, for example, the prophet's foretelling the death of both of Eli's sons on the same day (1 Sm 2:34; see also 14:10; 2 Kgs 19:29; Is 37:30). Sometimes the sign was carefully timed and the recipient was told that the appearance of the sign would show when to act to fulfill the prophetic message (1 Sm 10:7–9). At other times the events predicted were acted out in the life of the prophet. These symbolic actions demonstrated the truth of the prophet's message, for example, Isaiah's nakedness for three years to demonstrate the fate of those who preached trust in Egypt's power (Is 20:3; see also Ez 4:3).

The Hebrew concept of the sign differed from the Greek view. In the Greek religions the sign came first in the form of an event, dream, or vision. Then a prophet or augur was called to make an interpretation. This occurs twice in the OT, when Israel was living in a foreign environment. Joseph's interpretation of the dreams of the butler, baker, and the pharaoh (Gn 40:1–41:26) and Daniel's interpretation of the dreams of Nebuchadnezzar and of the handwriting on Belshazzar's wall follow the Greek pattern (Dn 2:1–45; 5:1–28). In the case of the handwriting on the wall, for example, the sign is an event; the mysterious hand comes and brings the message from God that no one can interpret. When Daniel is called to interpret the sign, the special wisdom he has been given by God enables him to read the message hidden in the sign.

In the New Testament. The NT occurrences are much like those in the OT. There are references to heavenly signs that will occur as indications of the end of time, and those with special knowledge will understand that the end is drawing near (Mt 24:3,30; Mk 13:4,22; Lk 21:11,25). These apocalyptic signs have no astrological connotations as in the OT. There is also mention of the sign as the seal of the covenant between God and Israel in reference to circumcision in Romans 4:11.

As in the OT the chief NT uses of sign are confirmations of the message given by God, and this message comes through the apostolic community to the church. Thus there is great emphasis on the way God confirms the message of the apostles through their ability to perform signs and wonders (Acts 2:43; 4:30; 5:12; 8:13; 14:3; Rom 15:19; Heb 2:4).

In Matthew, Mark, and Luke, Jesus' miracles are not called signs. Only in Acts 2:22 does Peter proclaim that Jesus' message was attested by the signs he performed. Rather, Jesus' miracles are seen as acts of divine power and mercy. When the Jews ask for a sign, they are consistently refused with the promise that the only sign they will receive is the sign of Jonah (Mt 12:38,39; 16:1; Mk 8:11,12; Lk 11:29, 30), a sign that refers to the death and resurrection of the Christ. As Jonah was in the belly of the whale for three days and three nights, so will the Son of man be in the heart of the earth for three days (Mt 12:40).

In the Gospel of John, however, the miracles of Jesus are seen in a strikingly different light and are considered signs. Beginning with the changing of water into wine (2:1–11), the miracles are called signs and are intended to lead those who see them to faith (v 23). Jesus even laments that the people will not believe unless they see signs (4:48). John's purpose in writing his Gospel is to present the signs of Jesus so that those who come to faith may do so through seeing these signs (20:30). The signs in the Gospel are expressly chosen because they lend themselves to the development of true faith.

In the Gospel of John the miracles of Jesus confirm the teaching of Jesus. In the synoptic Gospels the miracles are seen as acts of mercy and divine power. In John they are carefully selected to demonstrate what Jesus has to tell the world about himself. In this respect they are a bit like the symbolic actions of Isaiah and Ezekiel in that the action of the speaker dramatizes the message. After Jesus feeds the 5000 with the five loaves of bread and the two fishes, he announces in the synagogue at Capernaum, "I am the bread of life which came down from heaven" (6:51). He tells them not to labor for the bread of this world that perishes. In much the same way the healing of the man born blind is bound up with Jesus' teaching that he is the light of the world (9:5). The resurrection of Lazarus is tied to Jesus' teaching that he is the resurrection and the life (11:25). In John's Gospel the signs are not only a demonstration of divine power but also a revelation of Jesus' divine character. In addition to confirming his divine message, they also proclaim his personhood and mission.

See MIRACLE; TYPE, TYPOLOGY.

Signet. *See* SEAL.

Sihon. King of the Amorites who ruled in Heshbon, about 14 miles east of the north end of the Dead Sea. His defeat by Israel under Moses, together with that of Og, king of Bashan, is frequently mentioned in OT prose and poetry, in narrative, parenesis, and song (Dt 1:4; 2:26–37; 4:46; 29:7; 31:4; Jos 2:10; 9:10; 12:2–6; 13:10–12). In the eyes of the sacred writers this dual defeat is so significant that it can be ranked with the exodus as one of the singular manifestations of God's saving intervention on behalf on his people (Pss 135:11; 136:19,20), and as evidence of his everlasting love for them. In the postexilic period this event is recalled in prayer as a pleading ground for God's continuing mercy to the returned exiles (Neh 9:22).

Before Israel's arrival in Transjordan, Sihon had conquered Moab's territory as far south as the Arnon River (Nm 21:26). This conquest gives rise to a piece of ancient poetry that is incorporated into sacred Scripture (vv 27–30). Sihon's realm extends from the Arnon on the south to the Jabbok on the north, with the Jordan as its western boundary. It also includes the Jordan Valley as far as the Sea of Chinneroth (Jos 12:2,3), comprising part of the region known as Gilead. On the east it extends toward the desert and touches on Ammonite land.

Sihon's refusal to grant Israel passage through his domain is similar to that of Edom (cf. Nm 21:23 with 20:20). However, Sihon exhibits overt hostility toward Israel. This poses a serious threat to fulfillment of the promise made to Abraham. It endangers the very continuation of the people of the promise. Sihon's hostility proceeds from his own willful intent (Nm 21:23), but Scripture also views it from the divine perspective of making Sihon's spirit stubborn (Dt 2:30; cf. also Jos 11:20 for the Canaanites in general).

Sihon is defeated and killed at Jahaz and his country occupied by Israel. Subsequently, it is distributed to the tribes of Gad and Reuben (cf. Nm 32:33–38; Jos 13:10).

Sihor. KJV form of Shihor, a body of water in northeast Egypt, in Joshua 13:3; Isaiah 23:3; and Jeremiah 2:18.

See SHIHOR.

Sikkuth. NASB spelling of Sakkuth, a Mesopotamian astral deity, in Amos 5:26.

See SAKKUTH.

Silas. Respected leader in the Jerusalem church, also called Silvanus (2 Cor 1:19; 1 Thes 1:1; 2 Thes 1:1; 1 Pet 5:12). "Silas" is most likely the Aramaic form of the Hebrew name "Saul," which when given a Latin form became *Silouanos* (Silvanus). Silas thus carried two names, one Latin and one shorter Semitic version. The name was known in the Hellenistic era and appears in various sepulcher inscriptions. Luke employs the name Silas as he narrates the history of the Jerusalem church in Acts. Paul and Peter make reference to the Roman name in their epistles.

Silas is introduced in Acts 15:22 as a distinguished delegate (a prophet, v 32) who conveys to Antioch the decree of the Jerusalem Council. A minority of manuscripts include 15:34, indicating that he remains in Antioch because shortly thereafter he joins Paul on his second missionary tour (Acts 15:40). His service as a prophet may be evident in Acts 16:6, when the Spirit redirects the company through Asia. Silas' name appears eight times within the second tour (16:19,25,29; 17:4,10,14,15; 18:5) as he accompanies Paul through the hardships suffered at Philippi, Thessalonica, and Beroea. When Paul is safely ushered out of Macedonia by the Beroean Christians (17:14), Silas remains behind with Timothy to oversee the work already begun in the region. Later in Corinth (Acts 18:5) Silas and Timothy rejoin Paul. Their report no doubt prompts Paul to correspond with the church at Thessalonica. This explains Silas' name in the prescript of both 1 and 2 Thessalonians.

It seems clear that Silas is well known to the Corinthians. Not only does he stay in the city with Paul for a year and a half (Acts 18:11) but it may be conjectured that he stays behind in Corinth after the dispute before Gallio. Paul, on his final tour, writes to Corinth from Ephesus and mentions Silas again (2 Cor 1:19), reminding the Corinthians of the earlier ministry among them. According to one early tradition Silas became the Bishop of Corinth.

The subsequent history of Silas is obscure. Some believe Silas was a respected Christian scribe. Silas' involvement in 1 and 2 Thessalonians is often mentioned, pointing to Paul's sustained use of the first person plural. Some scholars find resemblances among 1 and 2 Thessalonians, the decree of Acts 15, and 1 Peter, where Silas is mentioned as a scribe (1 Pt 5:12). This latter association with Peter is intriguing and has led to the speculation that Silas ultimately joined Peter and ministered in North Asia.

Silk. Fine, delicate thread extracted from the cocoon of the silkworm. Originating in China, silk may have been introduced into Palestine as early as the Solomonic period (970–930 BC), or perhaps not until the conquests of Alexander the Great (336–323 BC). A fine silken fabric was apparently included in the fashionable attire of Jerusalem (Ez 16:10–13). Revelation 18:12 lists silk as a valuable trade commodity of Babylon (Rome).

See CLOTH, CLOTH MANUFACTURING.

Silla. Geographical landmark defining the whereabouts of "the house of Millo," the place of King Joash's murder (2 Kgs 12:20). Its exact location is unknown, though it was probably in the vicinity of Jerusalem.

Siloah. KJV rendering of Shelah, an alternate name for the Pool of Siloam, in Nehemiah 3:15.

See SILOAM, POOL OF.

Siloam, Pool of. Pool mentioned in John 9. Jesus, after anointing with clay the eyes of a blind man, directed him to go and wash in the pool. The man obeyed; he washed and came back with his sight fully restored.

The Pool of Siloam of NT days marked the emergence of Hezekiah's tunnel, dug during the threat of the Assyrian invasion about 700 BC. This tunnel is S shaped and is described both in 2 Kings 20:20 and 2 Chronicles 32:2–4. Archaeologists found inside the tunnel the so-called Siloam inscription, consisting of Hebrew letters chiseled into the side of the tunnel indicating the progress and the meeting of

The Pool of Siloam.

the workmen. This inscription has since been removed and is now in the museum in Istanbul. The ancient Hebrew reads:

"When the tunnel was driven through . . . each man toward his fellow, and while there were still three cubits to be cut through—the voice of a man calling to his fellow. . . . And when the tunnel was driven through, the quarrymen hewed, each toward his fellow, axe against axe; and the water flowed from the spring toward the reservoir for 1200 cubits, and the height of the rock above the heads of the quarrymen was 100 cubits."

The purpose of the pool originally was to bring water inside the city walls and deny it to invaders of Jerusalem. It flowed through the temple mount to the inner part of the city where it was accessible to the residents. Water from Spring Gihon flows through the tunnel, emerges at the pool (also called the King's Pool in Neh 2:14 and the pool of Shelah in 3:15; KJV Pool of Siloah), continues down the valley through the ancient area of the king's gardens, reenters the Kidron Valley and makes its way toward the Dead Sea south of the Essene site at Qumran. The Spring Gihon, the only natural source of water in Jerusalem, is a copious perennial stream. This, together with a rugged terrain, explains the strength of Jerusalem and the reason why it has been chosen for a place of habitation since the early Bronze Age. Siloam now lies outside the old city of Jerusalem. The pool today measures 50 feet long and 5 feet wide and lies 16 steps below street level. A Byzantine church stood over the pool until it was destroyed by the Persians in AD 614.

See AQUEDUCT.

Siloam, Tower of. Edifice that collapsed killing 18 people. Jesus compared those killed by the fallen tower to the rest of the people living in Jerusalem (Lk 13:4,5). Though nothing is known of this tower, it seems reasonable to conclude that it was situated in Jerusalem. Perhaps it can be identified with the great tower built by Nehemiah on the wall of Ophel (2 Chr 27:3; Neh 3:26,27) or with one of the towers built on the wall of Jerusalem near the Pool of Siloam.

See JERUSALEM.

Siloam Inscription. Hebrew inscription in the Siloam Tunnel, also known as Hezekiah's tunnel, which marked the progress of the tunnel as it was being built.

See SILOAM, POOL OF.

Siloam Tunnel. Conduit, also known as Hezekiah's tunnel, built by Hezekiah at the time of the Assyrian invasion to bring water into Jerusalem (2 Kgs 20:20; 2 Chr 32:2–4).

See SILOAM, POOL OF.

Silvanus. Latin name for Silas, a companion of Paul and Peter (2 Cor 1:19; 1 Thes 1:1; 2 Thes 1:1; 1 Pt 5:12).

See SILAS.

Silver. *See* COINS; MINERALS, METALS, AND PRECIOUS STONES; MONEY AND BANKING.

Silverling. KJV rendering of shekel in Isaiah 7:23.

See COINS.

Silversmith. *See* INDUSTRY AND COMMERCE; TRADES AND OCCUPATIONS.

Simeon (Person). 1. Second of the 12 sons of Jacob (Gn 35:23; 1 Chr 2:1) and the second son borne to him by Leah (Gn 29:33). Simeon fathered six sons (Ex 6:15) and settled his family in Eygpt with Jacob and his brothers (1:2). He was the founder of the Simeonites (Nm 26:12–14) and one of the 12 tribes of Israel (1:23). He is remembered most for his vengeance on the men of Shechem because of Dinah's rape (Gn 34:25).

See SIMEON, TRIBE OF.

2. Pious Jew living in Jerusalem who was assured that he would not die before he saw the promised Messiah. Led by the Holy Spirit to the temple, Simeon met Mary and Joseph there, held Jesus in his arms, and prophesied about the Messiah's coming work (Lk 2:25–35).

3. Ancestor of Jesus in Luke's genealogy (3:30).

See GENEALOGY OF JESUS CHRIST.

4. One of five prophets and teachers mentioned in Acts 13:1 who was serving in the church of Antioch. Simeon was surnamed Niger and was perhaps from Africa. Symeon is a better reading of the Greek in this text.

5. Reference to Simon Peter in Acts 15:14.

See PETER, THE APOSTLE.

Simeon, Tribe of. One of the 12 tribes of Israel descended from Jacob's second son. Because of Simeon's evil deed at Shechem, Jacob foretold that Simeon's descendants would be dispersed among the other tribes of Israel (Gn 49:7).

According to the Book of Joshua, Simeon's inheritance was included in Judah's territory (Jos 19:1,9). Judges 1:3 points to a very close bond between the tribes of Simeon and Judah—they march and fight together as brothers to establish themselves in Canaan. In addition, the list of Levitical towns included Simeon's with Judah's (Jos 21:9–16). Inevitably, then, the Simeonites were linked to the kingdom of Judah throughout the period of the monarchy, and its tribal destiny was tied to that of the southern division of the divided monarchy. However, in spite of their minor inheritance within Judah's tribe, the Simeonites were able to preserve to some extent their own tribal identity, unity, and traditions, as indicated by the keeping of genealogical records, even to the days of Hezekiah, king of Judah (1 Chr 4:24–42).

During Hezekiah's reign, Simeonites took possession of and settled the Arab areas of Seir (1 Chr 4:24–43) and perhaps the hill country of Ephraim (2 Chr 15:9). Although Simeon was Jacob's second oldest son, his progeny never achieved a position of prominence in Israel, before or after the conquest and occupation of Canaan. For example, the tribe apparently provided no judges, and the Song of Deborah contains no references to this group (see Jgs 5). According to 1 Chronicles 4:28–33, Simeon's tribe settled in the southern extremes of Canaan (called the Negeb in Hebrew)—an extensive region, consisting largely of dry, parched land, but with an annual rainfall and perennial springs, that ensured fertility in the early summer. This explains why Simeon's territory is also called "the Negeb of Judah," a phrase that serves to differentiate it from other racial groups occupying parts of southern Canaan (1 Sm 27:10; 30:14; 2 Sm 24:7).

Among the place-names mentioned in Simeon's territory the term "hazar" occurs (e.g., Hazar-shual, Jos 19:3; Hazarsusah, 19:5), which, in Hebrew, means a small settlement without boundary walls (see Lv 25:31; Neh 12:29), typical of settlements in the Negeb region. In such villages, shepherd communities managed to subsist, and seminomadic groups could find temporary shelter (Gn 25:16; Is 42:11; Jer 49:33). Allotted this kind of territory for an inheritance, Simeon's tribe was probably content to follow pastoral pursuits, and wandered over the wide open spaces of the Negeb in search of grazing land for their livestock.

This roving, pastoral life in the endless search for pasture involved Simeon's tribe in constant confrontations and hostilities with both desert and border tribes, who were engaged in the same interminable quest. This belligerence is hinted at in Jacob's blessing in Genesis 49:5–7; and later during Hezekiah's reign, Simeonite families were in conflict with the Meunites and the Amalekites in the Gerar district, wandering with their flocks over the Negeb of Judah as far as Mt Seir (1 Chr 4:24–43).

The genealogies of the Simeonites reveal a certain amount of intermarriage with other Israelite tribes and, indeed, with non-Israelites as well. Shaul, Simeon's son, is the "son of a Canaanite woman" (Gn 46:10; Ex 6:15). Two of Simeon's sons (1 Chr 4:25) bear names of Ishmael's sons (Gn 25:13,14; 1 Chr 1:29,30); Jamin (Gn 46:10; Ex 6:15) is a descendant of Ram (1 Chr 2:27). Numbers 25:6–8 suggests ties between the Simeonites and Midianites.

In the NT, Simeon's tribe appears in the seventh place on the list of the sealed (Rv 7:7).

Simeonite. Member of Simeon's tribe (Nm 26:14; Jos 21:4).

See SIMEON (PERSON) #1; SIMEON, TRIBE OF.

Simon. Greek form of a Hebrew/Aramaic name meaning "God has heard."

1. Son of Jona (Mt 16:17) or John (Jn 1:42), Andrew's brother (v 40), and surnamed Cephas and Peter (respectively Aramaic and Greek, for *rock*, v 42) by Jesus. A fisherman of Bethsaida (Mk 1:16; Jn 1:44), he became an apostle of Jesus' and author of two NT letters bearing his name.

See PETER, THE APOSTLE.

2. Brother of Jesus, named with other brothers (James, Joses or Joseph, and Judas) by the people of Jesus' own country who took offense at the Lord's claims and works (Mt 13:55; Mk 6:3).

3. Leper, perhaps cured by Jesus, in whose house at Bethany Jesus and his disciples were eating when a woman poured an alabaster flask of very costly ointment on the Lord's head. Over the disciples' objections against the waste of what could have been sold to support the poor, Jesus commended the act as a beautiful thing (Mt 26:6–13; Mk 14:3–9). From John 12:1–8 it appears that Simon's house was also the house of Mary, Martha, and Lazarus; but their relationship to Simon is uncertain.

4. Man of Cyrene, a district of North Africa, whom the Romans forced to carry Jesus' cross (Mt 27:32; Mk 15:21; Lk 23:26). He was the father of Alexander and Rufus (Mk 15:21; cf. Rom 16:13).

5. Apostle of Jesus called a Zealot (Lk 6:15; KJV Zelotes), presumably because of prior association either with the party of political extremists by that name, who adopted terrorism to oppose the Roman occupation of Palestine, or with one of a number of Jewish groups noted for their zeal for the Law. In Matthew 10:4 and Mark 3:18 he is designated as the "Cananaean"—from the Aramaic word for *zealot*. He is mentioned again in Acts 1:13, as one of the 11 apostles in Jerusalem after Jesus' ascension. Otherwise the NT is silent about him.

6. Pharisee whose treatment of Jesus evoked the parable of the two debtors (Lk 7:36–50). He invited Jesus to eat at his house, but withheld

The house of Simon the tanner in Joppa.

courtesies customary for guests, and disapproved of Jesus' acceptance of a "sinner"—the woman who wet the Lord's feet with her tears, dried them with her hair, and anointed them with ointment from an alabaster flask. Jesus' parable contrasted the woman's act of loving and repentant faith with Simon's unloving and self-righteous skepticism.

7. Father of Judas Iscariot, the disciple who betrayed Jesus in Gethsemane (Jn 6:71; 13:2, 26; cf. 12:4 KJV).

8. Magician (often called Simon Magus) of great repute in Samaria. Impressed by the signs and miracles performed by Philip the deacon, he joined the crowd of baptized believers. He offered Peter and John money in exchange for the gift of the Holy Spirit, provoking Peter's emphatic rebuke (Acts 8:9–24). From the association of this incident with his name, the English word *simony*, is derived, denoting the sale or purchase of church positions, or any profiteering from sacred things.

9. Tanner of Joppa. Peter lodged "for many days" at his house (Acts 9:43; 10:6,17,32). On Simon's housetop Peter experienced the vision of a great sheet let down from heaven, containing animals and birds prohibited as food in Jewish law. Upon Peter's refusal of an invitation to "kill and eat," the voice from heaven said: "What God has cleansed, you must not call common" (10:15). Peter later recognized this vision as his preparation for consenting to preach the gospel to the Gentiles (vv 28,29). The fact that Simon was a tanner may bear on this theme, since the tanner's necessary contact with dead bodies made him ceremonially unclean in Jewish law (Lv 11:39,40).

Simon Magus. Sorcerer of Samaria apparently converted by Philip (Acts 8:9–24).

See SIMON #8.

Simon of Cyrene. Man who was ordered to carry Jesus' cross on the road to Golgotha (Mt 27:32, pars).

See SIMON #4.

Simon Peter. See PETER, THE APOSTLE.

Simon the Canaanean. One of Jesus' disciples (Mt 10:4; Mk 3:18); also called Simon the Zealot in Luke 6:15 and Acts 1:13.

See SIMON #5.

Simon the Zealot. One of Jesus' disciples (Luke 6:15; Acts 1:13); also known as Simon the Canaanean in Matthew 10:4 and Mark 3:18.

See SIMON #5.

Simri. KJV spelling of Shimri, Hosah's son, in 1 Chronicles 26:10.

See SHIMRI #3.

Sin. Evildoing seen in religious perspective, not only against humanity, society, others, or oneself, but against God. The concept of God, therefore, gives to the idea of sin its many-sided meaning. Other gods, conceived as capricious and characterless, exercised unlimited power in unbridled behavior; they engendered no such sense of sin as did Israel's one God, holy, righteous, and utterly good. This religious conception of wrongdoing with the terminology it created, persists into the NT.

Israel's God sets the ideal, the standard for human behavior, and the most frequent biblical words for sin (Heb *ḥāṭāʾ*; Gk *hamartēma*) meant originally "to miss the mark, fail in duty" (Rom 3:23). As Lawgiver, God sets limits to man's freedom; another frequent term (Heb *ʿābar*; Gk *parabasis*) describes sin as transgression, overstepping those set limits. Similar terms are *pešaʿ* (Heb) (rebellion, transgression); *ʾāšam* (Heb) (trespassing upon God's kingly prerogative, incurring guilt); *paraptōma* (Gk) (a false step out of the appointed way, trespass on forbidden ground).

"Iniquity" often translates *ʿāôn* (Heb) (perverseness, wrongness), for which the nearest NT equivalent is *anomia* (Gk, lawlessness), *paranomia* (Gk) (law-breaking), rejecting divine rule; *rāšaʿ* (Heb), also, means "lawless, unruly." Hosea sets Israel's "adulterous" sin in contrast with God's faithful love: such sin is falseness, bad faith, *maʿal* (Heb). God's holiness is outraged by sin, which explains *ḥālāl* (Heb) (to desecrate), *tôʿēbâ* (Heb) (abomination, abhorrence). God being devoted to the right, sin is *ʿewel* (Heb), *adikias* (Gk) (unrighteousness; for description cf. Ez 18:5–9). Sin against religion itself is *asebia* (Gk) (ungodliness, impiety, with-

holding due reverence). Sin is spoken of as debt, an unpaid obligation to God, who is good (Mt 6:12).

These examples indicate the essential nature and variety of sin in Scripture, but any impression that sin is a merely religious concern would be false. Since in Israel God owned land, nation, and neighbor, every social crime—adultery, oppression, injustice, theft, cruelty, inhumanity, neglect of the poor—is also sin (Ex 20:12–17; Dt *passim*; Jb 31; Is 1:12–20; Am 1:3–2:16). This socio-religious concept of evildoing was almost unknown outside Israel.

Yet this social emphasis did not obscure sin's individual origin and responsibility. Genesis traces evil to deliberate misuse of God-given freedom in disobedience of a single limiting prohibition, allurement, deceit, and evil persuasion assisting. Ezekiel insists eloquently upon individual responsibility against traditional theories of corporate guilt (Ez 18). Following Jeremiah, he urges the need for a cleansed, renewed inner life if outward behavior is to be reformed; the divine Law must become a motive force within personality if sin is to be overcome (Jer 31:29–34; Ez 36:24–29).

Psalm 51 offers a keen analysis of the inner meaning of sin. By affirming "in sin did my mother conceive me" the psalmist emphasizes that from the first moment of his life he has been sinful. His whole personality needs "purging"; he is defiled, needing to be "trodden in the wash." False in his inward being, broken, unclean, foolish, guilty, weak, he is deeply aware that sin is aimed directly at God whatever wrong is done to others. It is judged by God, cuts one off from God's presence (Is 59:2), and silences praise.

Ritual sacrifices offer no solution. Only a broken, contrite heart can prepare for God's own cleansing, truth, and wisdom, the blotting out of iniquities, the gift of a clean heart, and a steadfast, holy, and obedient spirit. The only hope, the sole ground of appeal, lies in God's steadfast love and abundant mercy, nor will that plea be rejected. In spite of its rigorous view of sin, the OT also contains gracious assurance of forgiveness (Ps 103:8–14 Is 1:18; 55:6,7).

After that masterpiece of spiritual perceptiveness, the Wisdom school's insistence that sin is folly seems true but superficial. The later ascription of most evil to demonic invasion of human lives traces sin back to a cosmic struggle between light and darkness, good and evil, God and the "prince of this world," a conception familiar in Qumran literature and the NT. The obvious danger of undermining individual responsibility was countered by insisting that, under God's control, demons invaded only those who offered opportunity. Some rabbis emphasized instead the duality within man, the "evil impulse" and the "good impulse" in each man from Adam onward—"Every man has been the Adam of his own soul" (2 Bar 54:19).

Jesus' teachings on the subject of sin took up the gracious offer of divine forgiveness and renewal, not only proclaiming with authority "your sins are forgiven," but showing by many acts of compassion and social recognition that he came to be the friend of sinners, calling to repentance, restoring their hope and dignity (Mt 9:1–13; 11:19; Lk 15; 19:1–10). His parables show he knew what men were like.

Jesus says little of the origin of sin, except to trace it to the human heart and will (Mt 6:22,23; 7:17–19; 18:7; Mk 7:20–23; Lk 13:34), but he significantly redefines sin's scope. Where the Law could assess only men's acts, Jesus shows that anger, contempt, lust, hardness of heart, and deceitfulness are also sinful, even if their expression is frustrated. He emphasizes sins of neglect, good left undone, the barren tree, the unused talent, the priest ignoring the injured, and the love never shown (Mt 25:41–46). He especially condemns sins against love—unbrotherliness, implacable hostility, selfishness, insensitivity (Lk 12:16–21; 16:19–31); self-righteousness, and spiritual blindness (Mt 23:16–26; Mk 3:22–30); and sins against truth—hypocrisy, ostentatious piety (Mt 6:1–6; 23:2). He condemns, too, sin against the love of God, that will not trust his goodness, revere his name, or love him wholly (Mt 5:33–35; 6:9,10,25–33; 22:35–38; Jn 5:42). In such attitudes Jesus sees a deeper alienation from God than in sins of the flesh.

Jesus could speak of sin as sickness (Mk 2:17) and sometimes as folly (Lk 12:20), yet no one ever treated sin more seriously, as the description of the prodigal's despair and five parables of judgment clearly show. Nevertheless, Jesus declares that fallen man is redeemable with God's help (Lk 7:36–50).

In the earliest training of converts, assumed within the apostolic writings, it is possible to trace (esp. in Rom 13:1–7; Eph 5:21–6:9; Col 3:18–4:1; 1 Pt 2:13–3:8), an emphasis upon subordination, within home, church, and society, which is consonant with the basic biblical idea of sin as self-will, "lawlessness," the assertion of human free will against God who gave it. Salvation must therefore involve submission.

Paul argues strongly, from observation and from Scripture, that "all have sinned" (Rom 1–3). To him, sin is a force, a power, a "law" ruling within men (Rom 5:21; 7:23; 8:2; 1 Cor 15:56), allied with ignorance (Eph 4:17–19), producing all manner of evil behavior, hardening of conscience, disintegrating personality (Rom 7:21–24), alienating them from God, and subjecting them to death (Rom 5:10; 6:23; Eph 2:1–5,12; Col 1:21). Man is helpless to reform himself (Rom 7:24).

Paul's explanation of this desperate universal condition is variously interpreted. Some find in Romans 5:12–21 that Adam's sin is the source of all sin; others, that it is the "similitude" (KJV) of all sin (as the parallel with Adam in Rom 7:9–11 might confirm). The difference of interpretation turns upon a point of Greek grammar. As a Pharisee, Paul would have held to the "evil impulse" explanation, possibly with the thought of "every man his own Adam." Certainly Paul never questioned man's full responsibility for his sinful condition.

The solution, for Paul, lies in Christ's expiation for sin, the believer's death in unity with Christ to sin, self, and the world, and the invasive power of the Holy Spirit tranforming life from within, making each person a new creature and sanctifying the renewed personality into the likeness of Christ (Rom 3:21–26; 5:6–9; 6; 8:1–4,28,29; 2 Cor 5:14–21). The same faith that accepts Christ's death for human sin binds believers to die with him to sin; and that union with Christ also achieves the moral resurrection into newness of life in which sin's power is broken. Such death to the past (repentance) and laying hold of the risen Christ by the Spirit (faith) brings divine forgiveness, peace, renewal, and joy.

John's Gospel assumes sinful man's need, the sacrifice of Christ the Lamb to bear away the sin of the world, and the offer of light and life in Christ. The new note is an emphasis on sin that refuses to accept the salvation provided in Christ, by the love of God for the world—the refusal to believe. It is for loving darkness, rejecting light, refusing to "see" Christ the Savior, that man is judged already (Jn 3:16–21).

Against Gnosticism's claim that for advanced Christians "sin does not matter," 1 John affirms 15 reasons why sin cannot be tolerated in the Christian life and emphasizes again that sin is equally want of truth and lack of love (3:3–10). Yet God forgives the penitent, Christ atones and intercedes (1:7–2:2).

R.E.O. White

See IDOLS, IDOLATRY; JUSTIFICATION; PRIDE; SANCTIFICATION; SIN UNTO DEATH; UNPARDONABLE SIN, THE; FLESH.

Bibliography. M.B. Ahern, *The Problem of Evil*; K. Barth, *Church Dogmatics*, III,3, 289–368; G.C. Berkouwer, *Sin*; E. Brunner, *Man in Revolt*; D. Daube, *Sin, Ignorance and Forgiveness in the Bible*; A. Farrer, *Love Almighty and Ills Unlimited*; J.S. Feinberg, *Theologies and Evil*; C.S. Lewis, *The Problem of Pain*; P. Schoonenberg, *Man and Sin*; R. Smith, *The Bible Doctrine of Sin*; F.R. Tennant, *The Concept of Sin*; N.P. Williams, *The Ideas of the Fall and Original Sin*.

Sin (City).   Hebrew name for an Egyptian city named Pelusium (Ez 30:15,16 KJV).

See PELUSIUM.

Sin, Man of.   KJV translation for "man of lawlessness," an expression used by Paul of the antichrist in 2 Thessalonians 2:3.

See ANTICHRIST.

Sin, Wilderness of.   Arid, sandy region in the southwestern part of the Sinai peninsula, described in the Bible as being "between Elim and Sinai" (Ex 16:1). It is mentioned only four times in the Bible (16:1; 17:1; Nm 33:11,12) in itineraries of the exodus from Egypt.

It is difficult to identify Sinaitic sites with certainty, for many of the place-names appear to have been coined by the Israelites spontaneously and often are based on events that occurred at those sites. These names have not been retained in modern Arabic, as is sometimes the case with city names in the Palestinian region. Furthermore, the maps published by recent surveys do not usually give names of geographical features such as plains, although wells, springs, and wadis ordinarily are identified by their current Arabic names. The wilderness of Sin lies to the southeast of Elim, which generally is regarded as the Wadi Gharandel.

According to the passage in Numbers, the next halting place of the Israelites after leaving the wilderness of Sin was Dophkah and the following encampment was at Alush (Nm 33:11–14). Neither of these places can be identified with certainty, although Serabit el-Khadem has been suggested for Dophkah. Serabit el-Khadem was the site of Egyptian mining for copper and turquoise and the location of the proto-Sinaitic inscriptions.

Acccording to Exodus 17:1, the next stopping place after the wilderness of Sin is Rephidim. This itinerary omits some of the lesser stops and concentrates on those encampments on which some comment is given. Clearly, the wilderness of Sin was between Elim and Rephidim, but the location of Rephidim is not certain. G.E. Wright regards the Wadi Refayid as Rephidim, probably on the basis of the similarity of the names.

There are also several suggestions concerning the identity of the wilderness of Sin. It has been proposed that it is the Debbet er-Ramleh, "plain of sand," which lies at the base of Gebel et-Tih in the Sinai peninsula. Another, which is more probable, is the sandy plain of el-Markha, close to the Gulf of Suez, about midway between the city of Suez and the tip of the Sinai peninsula.

Exodus 16 relates the events that occurred while the migrating Israelites were in the wilderness. Here they protested bitterly against Moses and Aaron, complaining that they were better off in Egypt, for there they had plenty to eat, while here they were the victims of their leaders, who had brought them into the wilderness to die of hunger (vv 2,3). In this instance the Lord responded by sending them manna for food. This is described as "a fine flake-like thing, as fine as hoarfrost" (v 4) and "like coriander seed, white, and the taste of it was like wafers made with honey" (v 31). When the people first saw the manna on the ground, they asked, "What is it?" and this question in Hebrew became the name by which it has been known ever since. Manna continued to serve as sustenance for the full 40 years of the wilderness wandering.

See WILDERNESS WANDERINGS; SINAI, SINA.

Sinai, Sina.   Name of the mountain where God met Moses and gave him the Ten Commandments and the rest of the Law. The name applies not only to the mountain itself but to the desert around it (e.g., Lv 7:38) and to the entire peninsula embraced by the two arms of the Red Sea known as the Gulf of Suez and the Gulf of Aqaba (or Elath).

The name is probably related to Sin (wilderness of) and may even be an alternate spelling (cf. Ex 16:1; 17:1; Nm 33:11,12). Sin is one name of the ancient moon god which desert dwellers worshiped. The mountain is also called Horeb, mostly in Deuteronomy (see also 1 Kgs 8:9; 19:8; 2 Chr 5:10; Ps 106:19; Mal 4:4).

The traditional location of Mt Sinai is among the mountains at the southern end of the Sinai peninsula. Since at least the 4th century Christians have venerated Jebel Musa (Mt Moses in Arabic) as the site where God molded the families of Jacob into the nation of Israel. A Greek Orthodox monastery of Saint Catherine at the base of the 7500 foot peak has been there for over 1500 years. Other candidates for the holy mountain have been the nearby Jebel Katerina (8670 feet) and Jebel Serbal (6800 feet). Some scholars prefer a northern location near Kadesh-barnea while others argue for a volcanic mountain across the gulf to the east in ancient Midian or Arabia (Ex 3:1; Gal 4:25).

Most references to Sinai are in Exodus (13 times), Leviticus (5 times), and Numbers (12 times) for these are the books that report the giving of the Law and the two-year encampment of the Israelites on the plains adjacent to the mountain. Exodus 19 and 34 especially are replete with references because these are the chapters that describe the encounters between Moses and Yahweh on the two occasions when the Law was actually given.

In both the OT and NT Sinai came to repre-

Mt Sinai, with the monastery of St Catherine at its base.

instruments (1 Chr 15:16). At the beginning of Solomon's reign, 4000 of the 38,000 priests were "praising the Lord" with their instruments (1 Chr 23:3–5). Heman and his sons sang in the worship services with cymbals, harps, and lyres, and the number of those trained for singing to the Lord totaled 228 (1 Chr 25:6,7). Lots were cast among them allowing for 24 orders of 12 each, who took their turn providing music.

At the dedication of the first temple, the levitical singers, Asaph, Heman, and Jeduthun, along with their kinsmen musicians, "made themselves heard with one voice" in their worship on the glorious occasion (2 Chr 5:11–14). When the foundation of the second temple was laid, the levitical singers, sons of Asaph, also sang in a choir, along with orchestral instruments (Ezr 3:10,11), and later when the city wall was dedicated by Ezra and Nehemiah, the choir was divided into two and the singing appears to be responsive or antiphonal (Neh 12:27–47). The Mishna has numerous references to choirs and musical instruments in the second temple period, but after its destruction, the melodies were lost. Perhaps some of the ancient synagogue music dates back to the hymnody of the second temple.

See MUSIC AND MUSICAL INSTRUMENTS; TABERNACLE, TEMPLE.

Sinim, Land of. KJV rendering of Syene, an Egyptian town, in Isaiah 49:12.

See SYENE.

Sinite. Canaanite tribe, possibly located in northern Lebanon, whose ancestry is traced to Canaan, Ham's son (Gn 10:17; 1 Chr 1:15).

Sin Offering. *See* OFFERINGS AND SACRIFICES.

Sin unto Death. Sin mentioned in 1 John 5:16; John discourages prayer for those who sin in this way. Identifying such irremediable behavior is a complex manner. Inasmuch as all sin deserves the wrath of God, John can hardly be distinguishing between venial and mortal sin as elaborated in Roman Catholic theology. He may have in mind those sins that cause the physical death of offenders (Acts 5:1–11; 1 Cor 11:30) and thereby prohibits prayers for the dead. Perhaps he is thinking of high-handed, presumptuous sin or the unforgivable sin against the Holy Spirit (Nm 15:30,31; Mt 12:32; Heb 10:26,27). Reference may be to those who decisively turn their backs upon the truth as well as those false teachers who deceive the church (Heb 6:4–6; 2 Jn 7–9). It is doubtful that John is referring to genuine Christians when he thinks of those who sin unto death. Notwithstanding, it is

sent the place where God came down to his people. In the blessing of Moses (Dt 33:2), the song of Deborah (Jgs 5:5), Psalm 68 (vv 8,17), the confession of the Levites in the time of Nehemiah (Neh 9:13), and the speech of Stephen (Acts 7:30,38; KJV Sina) Sinai was remembered as the scene of that momentous encounter. Paul in Galatians 4:21–26 spells out an allegory in which Mt Sinai represents the old covenant, slavery, and the present city of Jerusalem.

See SIN, WILDERNESS OF; WILDERNESS WANDERINGS; PARAN; SHUR; ZIN, WILDERNESS OF; TEN COMMANDMENTS, THE.

Singer. *See* MUSIC AND MUSICAL INSTRUMENTS; SINGERS IN THE TEMPLE; TRADES AND OCCUPATIONS.

Singers in the Temple. Trained musicians serving in worship appearing during the time of David and Solomon. Prior to this date, not much is known of the production of music and its use. Miriam led women in singing and dancing after the defeat of the Egyptians at the Red Sea (Ex 15:20,21). When Jephthah returned from battle, his daughter met him, leading women in dance and timbrels (Jgs 11:34). Music also was employed by the school of the prophets (1 Sm 10:5).

At David's instructions, the chief of the Levites was to appoint the musicians, and Heman, Asaph, and Ethan and certain of their families became the official singers at the tabernacle worship, raising sounds of joy with their

certain that prayer may not be expected to bring healing grace for some types of sin.

See Sin; Blasphemy Against the Holy Spirit.

Sion. 1. KJV designation for Mt Hermon in Deuteronomy 4:48.

See Hermon, Mount.

2. KJV form of Zion in Psalm 65:1 and in the NT.

See Zion.

Siphmoth. Town in southern Judah to which David gave part of the spoils of his victory over the Amalekites because its residents had aided him in his flight from Saul (1 Sm 30:28). Its location is uncertain.

Sippai. Alternate form of Saph, a descendant of the giants, in 1 Chronicles 20:4.

See Saph.

Sirah. Well or cistern where Joab's messengers intercepted Abner as he returned from pledging allegiance to David in Hebron (2 Sm 3:26). Its site is probably the same as the present 'Ain Sarah, located about one and a half miles northwest of Hebron.

Sirion. Sidonian name for Mt Hermon (Dt 3:9; 4:48; Ps 29:6; Jer 18:14).

See Hermon, Mount.

Sisamai. KJV spelling of Sismai, Eleasah's son, in 1 Chronicles 2:40.

See Sismai.

Sisera. 1. Commander of the army of Jabin, king of Canaan. Sisera resided in Harosheth-hagoyim from where he oppressed northern Israel for 20 years. His army, strengthened by 900 iron chariots, was routed at the swollen river of Kishon near Megiddo under the leadership of Barak and Deborah. Having fled the battlefield, Sisera was killed by the hand of Jael, the wife of Heber the Kenite, in the hill country overlooking the Jordan Valley (Jgs 4; 1 Sm 12:9). The events of this battle were remembered in the Song of Deborah (Jgs 5:19–30) and Psalm 83:9.

See Judges, Book of.

2. Forefather of a family of temple servants that returned with Zerubbabel to Palestine following the Babylonian captivity (Ezr 2:53; Neh 7:55).

Sismai. Eleasah's son and the father of Shallum; a Judahite from the house of Hezron and Jerahmeel's line (1 Chr 2:40; KJV Sisamai).

Sister. *See* Family Life and Relations.

Sistrum. Ancient percussion instrument consisting of a thin metal frame with numerous metal rods or loops that jingle when shaken, translated as "castanet" (RSV) in 2 Samuel 6:5.

See Music and Musical Instruments (Mena 'anim; Shalishim).

Sithri. Kohathite Levite and Uzziel's third son. Sithri was the cousin of Aaron and Moses (Ex 6:22; KJV Zithri).

Sitnah. Well dug by Isaac's servants in the region of Gerar, receiving its name (meaning "enmity") from a dispute between Isaac's servants and the herdsmen of the region. Its location was possibly near Rehoboth (Gn 26:21).

Sivan. Name of a Hebrew month, perhaps of Babylonian origin (Est 8:9).

See Calendars, Ancient and Modern.

Six Hundred Sixty-six. Number of the beast of the earth envisioned in the Book of Revelation (13:18).

See Antichrist; Mark of the Beast.

Skink. NIV rendering of sand lizard, an unclean animal, in Leviticus 11:30.

See Animals.

Skirt. *See* Fashion and Dress.

Skull, Place of the. Place in Jerusalem where Jesus was crucified (Mt 27:33; Mk 15:22; Jn 19:17). Golgotha is the Greek transliteration of the Aramaic word for skull.

See Golgotha.

Slave, Slavery. Person owned as property by another, and the relationship that bound the owner and the slave. Slavery was widespread in the ancient Near East, although the economy was not dependent upon it. By Roman times slavery was so extensive that in the early Christian period one out of every two people was a slave. From at least 3000 BC captives in war were the primary source of slaves (Gn 14:21; Nm 31:9; Dt 20:14; Jgs 5:30; 1 Sm 4:9; 2 Kgs 5:2; 2 Chr 28:8).

Slaves could be purchased locally from other owners, or from foreign traveling merchants who sold slaves along with cloth, bronzeware, and other goods (Jl 3:4–8). Joseph was sold by Midianites and Ishmaelites to an Egyptian (Gn 37:36; 39:1) in this manner. Debt was the basic cause for many families being reduced to slavery; an entire family could be subject to slavery (2 Kgs 4:1; Neh 5:5–8). The law code of Hammurabi stipulated a maximum of three years of slavery for the family (Section 117), as opposed to a maximum of six years under Hebrew law (Dt 15:18). Voluntary slavery was widespread as a means of escape from abject poverty and starvation (Lv 25:47,48). Selling a kidnapped person into slavery, the crime of Joseph's brothers (Gn 37:27,28), was a capital offense under the law code of Hammurabi (Section 14) and the Mosaic law (Ex 21:11; Dt 24:7).

In Sumerian society slaves had legal rights, could borrow money, and engage in business. As the normal price for a slave was probably less than that for a strong donkey, the slave always had the hope that he could save sufficient money to purchase his freedom. Slaves performed tedious labor on farms and in households, though some gifted individuals occupied executive positions in households. Despite provisions in ancient law, the release of slaves was not always honored on schedule. A Hebrew who voluntarily entered slavery was normally released the next jubilee year, and theoretically in Israel no Hebrew could be enslaved for life (Ex 21:2; Lv 25:10,13; Dt 15:12–14).

The Israelites made a deliberate attempt to safeguard the slave from brutality by a master or overseer. By law a maimed slave must be released (Ex 21:26,27). The few Hebrew slaves in a household frequently toiled alongside their masters in the fields, and they and household slaves often had a reasonable and secure existence, compared with the threat of starvation and destitution of the poorest free men.

In Greek and especially in Roman times, when the number of slaves increased dramatically, household slaves remained the best treated. Many became servants and confidants; some even established good businesses to their own and their masters' benefit.

Information from Ur, Nuzi, and the Book of Genesis shows that where a wife was childless, the female slave could bear the master's child (Gn 16:2–4). Legally a Hebrew master could agree to marry a young female slave, have his own son marry her, or establish her as a concubine. If subsequently she was discarded, or the agreement was not fulfilled, she would be released from her slavery (Ex 21:7–11). Conquered people were required to perform forced labor for the state (2 Sm 12:31; 1 Kgs 9:15,22,23), including the Israelites themselves in Lebanon (1 Kgs 5:13–18). Temple slaves recruited from the same source included Midianites (Nm 31:28,30,47) and Gibeonites (Jos 9:23–25), and the practice continued through the reigns of David and Solomon (Ezr 2:58; 8:20). Nehemiah records that foreign slaves helped make repairs on the walls of Jerusalem (Neh 3:26,31).

The NT attitude toward slavery indicates that the status of the slave was more like that of a servant and that the institution of slavery generally was declining. There was no strong opposition to slavery from Jesus or the apostles, but an admonition that slaves and servants should serve their masters faithfully and that masters should treat their slaves humanely and fairly (Eph 6:9; Col 4:1; 1 Tm 6:2; Phlm 16). Frequently masters and servants as a household became Christians (Acts 16:31,32), and worked together to the glory of God (Eph 6:5–8; Col 3:22).

See BOND, BONDAGE; LIBERTY; CHRISTIANS, NAMES FOR.

Bibliography. A.G. Barrios, *Ancient Israel: Its Life and Institutions;* R.H. Barrow, *Slavery in the Roman Empire;* W.W. Buckland, *The Roman Law of Slavery;* R. de Vaux, *Ancient Israel,* pp. 80–90; M.I. Finley (ed.), *Slavery in Classical Antiquity;* I. Mendelsohn, *Slavery in the Ancient Near East;* W.L. Westermaann, *The Slave Systems of Greek and Roman Antiquity;* T. Wiedemann, *Greek and Roman Slavery.*

Slime. KJV rendering of asphalt or bitumen in Genesis 11:3 and Exodus 2:3.

See ASPHALT; BITUMEN.

Slime Pits. KJV rendering of asphalt pits or bitumen pits, found in the valley of Siddim (Gn 14:10).

See SIDDIM, VALLEY OF.

Sling, Slinger. Weapon of war used to fire stones or lead pellets, and the thrower.

See ARMS AND WARFARE; TRADES AND OCCUPATIONS (SOLDIER).

Smith. Worker in metals; a blacksmith.

See INDUSTRY AND COMMERCE; TRADES AND OCCUPATIONS.

Smyrna. One of the seven churches of the Book of Revelation (Rv 1:11; 2:8–11). It is the modern Izmir, located in Turkey.

Smyrna was inhabited at least 3000 years before Christ. The Aeolian Greeks were replaced by the Ionians. The city, along with Miletus and Ephesus to the south, flourished under Ionian dominance. The city was conquered by the Lydians whose capital was Sardis. The site was left in ruins for nearly two centuries until its refounding by Alexander the Great in 334 BC at a site further south along the gulf. Although built through the energy of the Seleucids the city recognized the coming dominance of Pergamum and entered into an alliance with its king. Later, with remarkable foresight, she transferred her allegiance to Rome and in 195 BC built a temple in which Rome was worshiped as a deity. As a reward for Smyrna's early commitment to the rising Roman influence the city prospered under Roman rule, partly as a rival to Pergamum and partly as a rival to the prosperous island of Rhodes. Because they had been an ally of the Romans, both on land and sea, the people of Smyrna thought it would be to their credit to build in AD 26 another temple in which the Roman emperor would be honored. This city became the seat of the caesar-cult which afflicted the church so seriously during the latter half of the first century.

Revelation 2:8 speaks of the city as being "dead and then alive," a possible reference to the period of 300 years when it lay devastated until revived by Alexander and the Macedonians. Ancient writers, including Appollonius and Aristides, spoke of Smyrna as having the "crown of life" (v 10), a reference to the hilltop behind the city which symbolized a statue with its crown on top and its feet at the seashore. At the time the Apocalypse was written the infant church was undergoing persecution. The reference to the "synagogue of Satan" (v 9) and to the devil putting them in prison reflects (v 10) the tribulation probably experienced under the Roman emperor Domitian (c. AD 95). It became a crime punishable by death to refuse to worship the image of the Roman emperor as "lord." Many Christians were compelled to choose between "Caesar is Lord" (and life) or "Jesus is Lord" (and physical death).

See REVELATION, BOOK OF.

Snail. *See* ANIMALS.

Snake. *See* ANIMALS (ADDER; ASP; SERPENT).

So. A king of Egypt, mentioned once in Scripture (2 Kgs 17:4), with whom Hoshea, king of Israel, sought an alliance. This rebellious move, in part, prompted Shalmaneser V of Assyria to imprison Hoshea (v 5). It is difficult to identify So with any of the rulers of Egypt who are named in extrabiblical sources.

Soap. Cleansing agent extracted from a number of alkali-bearing plants. The alkali was gathered from the ashes of the burned plants and formed into a detergent. Saltwort, soapwort, and glasswort were alkali–bearing plants indigenous to western Asia and known to the ancient Hebrews. Soap was used primarily for cleansing purposes. In Jeremiah 2:22 soap is used to clean the body and in Malachi 3:2, to wash clothes.

Socho. KJV form of Soco, Heber's descendant, in 1 Chronicles 4:18.

See SOCO #2.

Sochoh. KJV form of Socoh, a town in Sharon, in 1 Kings 4:10.

See SOCOH #3.

Social Customs in Bible Times. *See* AGRICULTURE; BURIAL, BURIAL CUSTOMS; CIVIL LAW AND JUSTICE; CRIMINAL LAW AND PUNISHMENT; COURTS AND TRIALS; FAMILY LIFE AND RELATIONS; FASHION AND DRESS; FEASTS AND FESTIVALS OF ISRAEL; FOOD AND FOOD PREPARATION; FURNITURE; HOMES AND DWELLINGS; INDUSTRY AND COMMERCE; MARRIAGE, MARRIAGE CUSTOMS; MEDICINE AND MEDICAL PRACTICE; MONEY AND BANKING; MUSIC AND MUSICAL INSTRUMENTS; OFFERINGS AND SACRIFICES; TOOLS; TRADES AND OCCUPATIONS; TRAVEL AND TRANSPORTATION; EDUCATION; WAGES; CLEANNESS AND UNCLEANNESS, REGULATIONS CONCERNING; DIETARY LAWS; INHERITANCE; SLAVE, SLAVERY.

Soco. 1. One of 14 cities located in the Shephelah of the territory allotted to Judah's tribe, mentioned between the towns of Adullam and Azekah (Jos 15:35). Soco was situated near the place where David killed Goliath during Saul's reign over Israel (1 Sm 17:1). Later this city was fortified by King Rehoboam of Judah (2 Chr 11:7) and was one of 15 cities eventually taken by the Philistines from King Ahaz of Judah (28:18).

See SOCOH #1.

2. City in Solomon's third administrative district under the charge of Ben-hesed (1 Kgs 4:10). In 1 Chronicles 4:18 (KJV Socho), Soco possibly refers to either a personal offspring of Heber or to a town he founded in southern Judah.

See SOCOH #2.

Socoh. 1. Town in the northernmost district of the Shephelah where it appears between Adullam and Azekah (Jos 15:35). Jerome, in his Latin translation of Eusebius' *Onomasticon* (157:18–20), states that there were two settlements, one on the mountain and another on the plain. The description fits exactly the situation at Khirbet esh-Shuweikeh, a Roman-Byzantine site on the southern edge of the Vale of Elah; just beside it to the east is a lofty mound with heavy fortifications from the Israelite period called Khirbet 'Abbad. Given this location, one sees that Socoh guarded the junction between two wadis that join to form the Vale of Elah, a passageway to the central hill country, to Bethlehem or Hebron, respectively. This situation provides the background for 1 Samuel 17:1 (KJV Shochoh); the Philistines lined up their troops beside Socoh and extended toward Azekah. The Israelites were on the opposite ridge with the creek bed of the Vale of Elah in between.

Rehoboam included Socoh in his network of fortifications designed to place forces on the main lines of communication throughout his kingdom (2 Chr 11:7; KJV Shoco). The town apparently remained in Judah's hands from the 10th to the 8th century BC when the Philistines, moving against Ahaz, took it and several other key towns on the approach routes (28:18; KJV Shocho). King Hezekiah must have regained his control over it because Socoh is one of the key towns mentioned on royal seal impressions on wine jars from his reign. Surface surveys of Khirbet 'Abbad have produced many examples of these stamped jar handles, but none with the name Socoh.

2. Town in the southernmost district of the Judean hill region (Jos 15:48). The reference to Socoh (Soco) in 1 Chronicles 4:18 in the genealogy of the sons of Caleb is evidently to this same place since the Calebites were located in the southern hill country of Judah. It is identifiable with Khirbet Shuweikeh just to the east of Dhahariyeh.

3. Town in the Sharon Plain listed once in the Bible but well known from nonbiblical sources. It is listed thrice in Egyptian records, especially the topographical list of Thutmose III (no. 67) where it comes after Aphek and before Yaham. The former is at Ras el'Ain (Rosh Ha'Ayin) by the springs of the Jarqon River; the latter must be located at Khirbet Yamma on the eastern edge of the Sharon Plain. Socoh is mentioned in similar geographical context in the Annals of Amenhotep II. Thus, it was a key town on the highway passing along the western edge of the mountains of Samaria in the 15th century BC. It comes again in an identical position in the topographical list of Pharaoh Shishak (no. 38) from the late 10th century BC.

The town conquered by Shishak was that mentioned in 1 Kings 4:10 (KJV Sochoh) as being in Solomon's third administrative district, which comprised "the land of Hepher" and other sub-districts in the Sharon Plain.

All of these texts point to this Socoh as the ancient name of present-day Khirbet Shuweiket er-Ras, just to the north of Tul-Karem. Between Aphek and Socoh there were no good water sources along the road, so these two towns mark the principal way stations in the southern Sharon Plain.

Sodi. Father of Gaddiel, one of the 12 spies sent by Moses to search out the land of Canaan (Nm 13:10).

Sodom, Sea of. Alternate name for the Dead Sea.

See DEAD SEA.

Sodom, Vine of. *See* PLANTS (GOURD, WILD).

Sodoma. KJV alternate spelling of Sodom in Romans 9:29.

See SODOM AND GOMORRAH.

Sodom and Gomorrah. Two of the "cities of the plain [valley]" referred to in Genesis 13:12. There were five cities, Sodom, Gomorrah, Admah, Zeboiim, and Bela (14:2), all situated in the Valley of Siddim (i.e., the Salt Sea) according to verse 3. Of these, Sodom is mentioned most frequently in Genesis—36 times in all—of which 16 references are to Sodom alone. Sodom became known in biblical literature as the supreme example of a wicked city, and its destruction (19:24) was used as a warning of judgment on those who sin against God in other biblical writings (Dt 29:23; Is 1:9,10; Jer 23:14; 49:18; Lam 4:6; Am 4:11; Zep 2:9). The story of Sodom's destruction found its place also in the NT (Mt 10:15; Mk 6:11; Lk 10:12; 17:29; Rom 9:29 KJV Sodoma; 2 Pt 2:6; Jude 7; Rv 11:8).

The basic story of Sodom and Gomorrah occurs in Genesis 18 and 19 although the biblical interest in the city begins in chapter 13 with the decision of Lot, Abraham's nephew, to settle in the Jordan Valley in the vicinity of Sodom (vv 10–13), among people who were "wicked, great sinners against the Lord" (v 13). It becomes clear (19:4,5) that one of Sodom's most grievous sins was sexual perversion, especially homosexuality. Lot's offer of his virgin daughters to the men of Sodom to turn their attention away from his heavenly visitors is an indication of the demoralizing influence of the city (v 8). The prophet Ezekiel (16:49) lists pride, prosperous complacency, and "abomination" as the sins of Sodom.

Four rulers from the East descended on the region of Sodom and Gomorrah some time after Lot settled there and subdued the area. They returned 14 years later to quell a rebellion (Gn 14:1–5). Among their captives was Lot, who was (subsequently) rescued by Abraham (vv 12–16). The evil of Sodom and Gomorrah was so great that the Lord determined to destroy them. Abraham pleaded for mercy for them if 10 righteous men could be found (18:20–33). The two heavenly visitors who went from Abraham to Sodom found Lot sitting in the gate of Sodom (19:1), revealed God's intentions to him, and persuaded Lot and his wife and two daughters to flee the city. Then the Lord rained brimstone and fire on Sodom and Gomorrah (vv 24,25). The next morning Abraham saw the smoke from the destroyed cities rising like the smoke of a furnace (v 28).

Several questions are posed by this story. First, no conclusive archaeological evidence of these cities has been found. Existing geographical and topographical data point to the southern end of the Dead Sea. One widely held and plausible view is that the cities were engulfed by the waters of the Dead Sea as they crept slowly south. Several wadis descend from the mountains of Moab on the eastern side of the Dead Sea and there is archaeological evidence of considerable settlement along these wadis as late as the Early Bronze IV period which ended about 2100 BC. There may have been towns at the point where these wadis entered the low-lying and probably swampy areas.

Another question concerns the manner of destruction of these towns. Some aspects of the story suggest earthquake activity, accompanied by the release and ignition of natural gases associated with oil deposits in the area. Again, however, this is conjecture.

Nor is it possible to provide an exact date for the destruction. Some writers have associated it with the termination of the occupation of sites to the east of the Dead Sea like Bah edh Dhra. The Bible places the destruction in the time of Abraham, but there is also great uncertainty about the exact date of Abraham. However, the theological signficiance of the story, namely, divine judgment on wicked men in any age, is clear.

See CITIES OF THE VALLEY, CITIES OF THE PLAIN.

Sojourner. *See* FOREIGNER.

Soldier. *See* ARMS AND WARFARE; TRADES AND OCCUPATIONS.

Solomon (Person). Third king over Israel, the second son of David and Bathsheba, who reigned some 40 years (970–930 BC). His alternative name was Jedidiah, "beloved of the Lord."

Ascension to the Throne. Once Amnon and Absalom were no longer in competition for the throne, the two most likely remaining candidates were Solomon and Adonijah, although the kingship had been assured to the former (1 Chr 22:9,10). Near the end of David's life, Adonijah contested the choice of Solomon and took steps to become king; with the help of Joab, general of the army, and Abiathar the priest, he was proclaimed the monarch. Solomon was not invited and neither were Nathan the prophet and Benaiah of the mighty men. Nathan brought word of this plot to Bathsheba who in turn quizzed David as to his intentions. David then ordered Solomon to be proclaimed king over Israel; he was anointed by Zadok amidst the blowing of the trumpets and the shout of the people: "Long live King Solomon."

Adonijah realized his claim had collapsed and asked for mercy, promising to be faithful to the new king.

Quickly, Solomon moved to establish his hold on the government (1 Kgs 1,2). When Adonijah asked to marry Abishag, David's companion in his old age (1:1–4), Solomon refused, and ordered his death because of possible claims to the throne (2:22–25). In addition, because Abiathar had joined with Adonijah, he was removed from his service as priest and sent back to Anathoth. Joab fled to the altar, and there took hold of its horns and refused to let go. The king ordered his death at the hand of Benaiah who then became commander-in-chief of the armies. Another contender, Shimei, of the house of Saul, was also executed.

One of Solomon's earliest recorded acts as king was to go to the high place at Gibeon and sacrifice 1000 burnt offerings. On the following night, the Lord appeared to the king in a dream, asking as to his fondest wish. Solomon asked for wisdom to judge Israel and God was pleased with the request (1 Kgs 3). Israel's king was given his wish, along with the gifts of long life, riches, and fame. In time Israel held Solomon in high esteem for the wisdom God gave him.

Solomon's Achievements. *The Government.* David's efforts had brought about a union of the 12 tribes, but Solomon established an organized state with many officials to help him (1 Kgs 4). The entire country was divided into 12 major districts, and each district was to ensure the provisions of the king's court for one month each year. The system was equitable and designed to distribute the tax burden over the entire country.

Solomon the Builder. One of Solomon's earliest building attempts was to construct the temple. David had it on his heart to build the temple, but this task was left to Solomon, the man of peace. Hiram, king of Tyre, provided cedar trees from Mt Lebanon for the temple (1 Kgs 5:1–12), and in return he was given an appropriate amount of food. In order to provide the necessary labor for these building projects, the Canaanites became slaves (9:20,21). Israelis likewise were compelled to work in groups of 10,000 on every third month (5:13–18; 2 Chr 2:17,18). The workers for the temple alone comprised 80,000 stone cutters, 70,000 common laborers, and 3600 foremen.

It took seven years to finish the temple, which by modern comparison was a rather small building: 90 feet long, 30 feet wide, and 45 feet high. Nevertheless, the gold covering for both walls and furniture made it quite expensive.

In the 11th year of Solomon's reign, the dedication of the temple was celebrated in a

The pillars of Solomon
at Eilat.

great convocation (1 Kgs 6:38). The presence of the Lord filled the temple, and Solomon then offered his great dedicatory prayer (8:23–53), marking it as one of the great peaks of his devotion to the Lord. Afterward, he offered up 22,000 oxen and 120,000 sheep, as well as other offerings (vv 62–66), and the people were full of joy because David had so great a successor.

Solomon built other buildings: the House of the Forest of Lebanon; the Hall of Pillars; a Hall for his Throne; and a house for the daughter of Pharaoh (1 Kgs 7:2–8). Thirteen years were involved in the building of his own house, large enough to take care of his wives and concubines as well as the servants. A great fortress was also built, Millo, used to protect the temple (9:24), as well as other store and fortified cities.

Trade with Other Nations. The king had an agreement with Hiram, king of Tyre, to pay yearly for cedar trees, stone cutters, and other buildings; 125,000 bushels of wheat; and 115,000 gallons of olive oil (1 Kgs 5:11 NIV). In addition, Hiram received 20 cities in Galilee

The ruins of Solomon's stables at Megiddo.

Solomon, Pools of. Water-storage pools, whose construction tradition attributes to Solomon. Solomon did make pools for watering his vineyards, gardens, parks, and orchards (Eccl 2:4–6), but their location is uncertain.

The so-called pools of Solomon are situated in the Valley of Etham, about 10 miles south of Jerusalem and a little south of Bethlehem. The three reservoirs, which are somewhat rectangular in shape, are placed consecutively at successive levels. They vary in size, with the

to cover all indebtedness. Contrary to the instruction not to trade in horses (Dt 17:16), Solomon bought horses and chariots from the Egyptians and some of these in turn were sold to the Hittites and Aramaeans at a profit (1 Kgs 10:28,29).

Furthermore, Solomon carried on trade on the high seas. Ships built at shipyards at Ezion-geber, sailed to points on the Red Sea and Indian Ocean. Once in three years, the mariners collected gold, ivory, and peacocks; from Ophir, the traders brought back 420 talents of gold, a considerable fortune.

Solomon's Wisdom. Solomon wrote 3000 proverbs and 1005 songs (1 Kgs 4:32); most of the Book of Proverbs is attributed to him (25:1), as well as Ecclesiastes, Song of Solomon, and Psalms 72 and 127. His obituary notice mentions his literary accomplishments in the book of the acts of Solomon (1 Kgs 11:41).

The Queen of Sheba came to see and hear if the fame and wisdom of Solomn was correct. After viewing all he had in Jerusalem and hearing his wisdom, her final response was a blessing to the Lord God of Israel who raised up such a wise person to sit upon such a magnificent throne (1 Kgs 10).

Solomon's Fall. Solomon made many misjudgments during his reign, and one of them was his excessive taxation of the people. His worst blunder was adding more and more wives to his harem, accommodating their religious preferences with pagan shrines (1 Kgs 11:1–8). The Lord plagued Solomon, permitting Israel to be attacked on all sides. Although the kingdom was not withdrawn from Solomon, his son experienced its division. There is no record that Solomon repented, but it is quite possible that the Book of Ecclesiastes does reveal his realization of his wrong decisions.   LOUIS GOLDBERG

See ISRAEL, HISTORY OF; CHRONOLOGY, OLD TESTAMENT; KING, KINGSHIP; SONG OF SOLOMON; ECCLESIASTES, BOOK OF; PROVERBS, BOOK OF; WISDOM, WISDOM LITERATURE.

The three pools of Solomon.

highest the smallest and the lowest the largest. The lower pool is 582 feet long, 148 to 207 feet wide, and 50 feet deep. The small pool is also the most shallow, having a depth of only 15 feet. The estimated capacity of all three is about 40,000,000 gallons.

The pools are partly rock-cut and in part built of masonry; they are connected by conduits, and the lower end of the biggest pool serves as a dam. The water is supplied by springs and run-off rain water.

An aqueduct of Roman date, known as the "lower aqueduct," ingeniously carries water from these storage basins to the Bahr el-Kebir, "the great sea," under the temple area in Jerusalem.

See AQUEDUCT.

Solomon, Song of. *See* SONG OF SOLOMON.

Solomon's Porch. Part of the outer court of Herod's temple (Jn 10:23; Acts 3:11; 5:12).

See TABERNACLE, TEMPLE.

Son. *See* FAMILY LIFE AND RELATIONS; GENEALOGY; SON OF GOD.

Song. *See* MUSIC AND MUSICAL INSTRUMENTS.

Song of Ascents, Song of Degrees. Title given to each of the Psalms from 120 to 134. Perhaps these psalms were sung by pilgrims journeying up to Jerusalem for the major feasts.

See MUSIC AND MUSICAL INSTRUMENTS; PSALMS, BOOK OF.

Song of Solomon. Short OT book (eight chapters) containing only poetry. Its beautiful poetic passages describe the many dimensions of human love; there is little in this book that is explicitly religious. In addition to the popular title, the book is sometimes referred to as the "Song of Songs"; this is the most literal translation of the short title of the book in the original language and means "the best of all possible songs." Some writers also entitle the book "Canticles"; this title is based on the name of the Latin version of the book, *Canticum Canticorum.*

Author. There is an old opinion within the Jewish and Christian traditions that King Solomon (*c.* 970–930 BC) wrote the Song of Songs. This view is based on one of several possible translations of the first verse of the Song: "Solomon's Song of Songs" (1:1 NIV). This view could be correct, though there cannot be absolute certainty, for the last words of the verse in the original language could be translated in various ways. An English translation which preserves the ambiguity of the original would be: "The Song of Songs, which is Solomon's" (KJV); the last words could mean that Solomon was author, but equally they could indicate that the song was "dedicated to Solomon" or "written for Solomon." As is often the case with the OT writings, authorship cannot be known with absolute certainty.

Date. It follows that if the authorship is uncertain, there must also be uncertainty concerning the date at which the song was written. If Solomon were the author, it would have been written during the latter half of the 10th century BC. If he were not the author, then the song would probably have been written at a later date, but the contents indicate that the song must have been written and completed at some point during the Hebrew monarchy (before 586 BC). For those who do not accept Solomon as author, the precise date will depend to some extent upon the theory that is adopted concerning the interpretation of the song. If the song is in fact an anthology of Israelite love poetry, then the many poems which make up the song would have been written at different dates and gathered together into a single volume toward the end of the Hebrew monarchy.

Purpose and Theological Teaching. The purpose and teaching of this book cannot be established clearly unless first an approach to its interpretation has been determined. There are two major difficulties in interpretation. First, the song appears to be secular in its present form and God's name does not appear; the only exception to this statement is in 8:6, where some English versions translate the text to show God's name, though the original text uses the name in an unusual (adjectival) sense. The second problem is that, taken at face value, the song contains only the secular poetry of human love. What is the theological significance of love poetry? These and other difficulties have led to a multitude of different interpretations of the song. A brief survey of some of the most significant interpretations will clarify not only the problem of understanding the book, but also its content and meaning.

The Song as an Allegory. One of the oldest interpretations of the song sees it as an allegory. This view was held by both Jewish and Christian scholars from an early date. The description of human love in the song is an allegory of the love between Christ and the church. Augustine of Hippo (354–430) believed that the marriage referred to in the song was an allegory of the marriage between Christ and the church.

This theory was important for a long time. It influenced the translators of the KJV. They added chapter headings to their translations as an aid to readers in understanding the Bible. For example, at the beginning of the first chapter of the Song of Solomon, they wrote: "1. The Church's love unto Christ. 5. She confesseth her deformity, 7. and prayeth to be directed to his flock." It is important to stress, however, that the Hebrew text does not mention Christ or the church. The notes represent the understanding of the translators, not the content of the original Hebrew.

The Song as a Drama. The view that the song is a drama is also an old one. Those who hold this theory begin by noting that there are several speakers or actors. Perhaps, then, the song is the script of an ancient dramatic play.

This theory has some strong points. In the manuscript of an ancient Greek translation of the OT, headings have been added to the Song of Solomon which identify the speakers. The cast includes bride, bridegroom, and companions. However, the headings were probably not a part of the original Hebrew text. They reflect the interpretation of the early Greek translators.

There is a further difficulty with this theory. There is no clear evidence that drama was a form of art used by the Hebrews. Although drama was common among the Greeks, it does not appear to have been employed in the Near East. It is possible to suggest a slight variation to the drama theory. Perhaps the Song of Solomon is not a drama, but simply dramatic poetry, similar to the Book of Job. This possibility is more plausible, but it too has difficulties. A story or plot would be expected for either drama or dramatic poetry, but it is not clear that there is a story.

According to one interpretation, the story might go as follows. The song tells the story of true love. A maiden was in love with a shepherd lad. King Solomon, however, fell in love with a maiden and took her to his palace. There he tried to win her love with beautiful words, but failed. She remained faithful to the shepherd lad whom she loved. Failing to win her, Solomon released her and allowed her to return to her true lover. The story is beautiful and simple, but it is not easy to see in the text, without added headings and explanations. Other interpreters have discerned a quite different story in the Song of Solomon. In conclusion, it is not absolutely clear that there is a single story being told.

The Song and the Fertility Cult. Some modern scholars claim that the origin of the Song of Solomon is to be found in the fertility cults of the ancient Near East. In ancient fertility cults there was great emphasis on the fertility of the land, which would be seen in bountiful harvests. The cults were designed to ensure that the land remained fertile. They were accompanied by a mythology describing the gods responsible for fertility. This mythology included love poetry about the gods and the poetry has some similarity to the Song of Solomon.

The theory might go like this: originally the Hebrews also had a fertility cult. The Song of Solomon contains the love poetry associated with that cult. Later, the mythological references were omitted, so that the present song looks like secular love poetry.

The main difficulty with this theory is the lack of any firm evidence. There is no reference to God or any other gods in the Song of Solomon. There is no reference to a fertility cult or any other kind of cult. If the theory has some validity to it, the evidence no longer exists. So the question still remains.

The Song as an Anthology. This last, most probable theory of interpretation involves two basic principles. First, the song is to be interpreted literally; it is what it seems to be, human love poetry. Second, the Song of Solomon is an anthology, not a single piece of poetry. Just as the Book of Psalms contains songs, hymns, and prayers from many different periods of Israel's history, so too the Song of Solomon contains poetry from different periods and different authors. The common theme joining all the passages together is human love. Opinions differ concerning where one song ends and the next begins. There may be as many as 29 songs in the book, some consisting of only one verse and others much longer.

If the Song of Solomon is primarily an anthology of the poetry of human love, what is its significance as a biblical book? What are its theological implications? First, the presence of the song in the Bible provides a valuable insight concerning human love. The love between a man and a woman is a noble and beautiful thing; it is a gift of God. It is characterized by a certain mystery and cannot be bought. But because human love is a beautiful and noble thing, it can easily be debased. In the modern world, the Song of Solomon provides a proper perspective and a balanced view of human love. Further, a high value of human love is essential. Since human love and marriage are employed in the Bible as an analogy of God's love for humanity, love in itself must be good and pure.

Returning to the interpretation of the song as an allegory, perhaps it was not written originally as an allegory of God's love for mankind, or Christ's love for the church. Nevertheless, the Bible as a whole provides the legitimacy of interpreting it as an allegory. From a historical perspective, the Song of Songs was included in the canon of Scripture largely on the basis of the Jewish allegorical interpretation of it. Thus the joy and beauty of love which are described in the song, even its sadness and longing, illumine the relationship of love between God and all human beings which is at the heart of the Christian faith.

The mistake made by some of the older allegorical interpreters of the song was not that they read into the book an allegory of God's love for mankind; rather, it was that they failed to see beauty or wonder in the human love which formed the basis of the allegory. If human love (romantic and sexual love) were debased and unclean, then there is no sense in which it could form the foundation for teaching concerning God's love for mankind. One requires a high view of human love in order to perceive the true theological depths of the Song of Solomon.

Contents. *The Woman Sings Her Love Song (1:2–7).* In each of the songs, the reader is like an eavesdropper listening to the words of love spoken, sometimes privately and sometimes to the beloved one. The opening song is a song of praise, rejoicing in love and delighting in a particular loved one: "Let him kiss me with the kisses of his mouth—for your love is more delightful than wine" (v 2). This song, as many others, is characterized by a country setting, here highlighted by a contrast with the city. The young woman is from the country and tanned from working in the open air; it makes her self-conscious among the city women of Jerusalem (vv 5,6). But love overpowers self-consciousness, and it is in the country that she will meet her lover (v 7).

The King Converses with the Woman (1:8–2:7). In this passage, both the man and the woman are talking, though it is not a conversation in the normal sense. They are talking *about* each other, rather than *to* each other, and the beauty of both the man and the woman emerges, not in an abstract sense, but through the eyes of the beholder. Though beauty may perhaps be defined in an abstract sense, the beauty perceived by lovers is of a different kind; it is rooted in the lover's perception of the loved one and in the relationship of love which acts like a lens to focus that perception.

A Song of Springtime (2:8–13). This beautiful song describes the young maiden watching her beloved come to her. He calls her to join him in the countryside, where the winter has passed and the new life of spring can be seen in the land. The beauty of young love is here likened to the blossoming forth of fresh life and fragrance that characterizes Palestine in spring.

The Woman Searches for Her Loved One (2:14–3:5). Now the woman sings and a new dimension of her love emerges from the words of her song. Love is full when the partners are together, but separation creates sorrow and loneliness. The words of the maiden evoke the desperation of separated lovers, a desperation that could only be dissipated when she held her lover again and would not let him go (3:4).

The King's Wedding Procession (3:6–11). The song begins with a description of the approach of the royal wedding procession, a litter surrounded by men of war. The king approaches the city for his wedding, and the young girls of the city go out to greet him. The song can be compared with Psalm 45, another wedding song.

The Woman's Beauty, Like a Garden (4:1–5:1). In sumptuous language, the man describes his maiden's beauty. To the modern reader, the language is sometimes strange: "your neck is like a tower of David" (4:4)! But the strangeness lies principally in unfamiliarity with the setting. Much of the language here draws upon the imagery of nature and wildlife, which can be appreciated by all. Again, beauty is not described merely as something aesthetic, for it is intimately tied to the relationship of love: "How delightful is your love, my sister, my bride! How much more pleasing is your love than wine" (4:10). And again, the maiden's beauty is not simply to be admired; it is to be given to the beloved. So when the man stops his words of adoration, the woman offers herself to him (v 16) and he accepts (5:1).

The Woman Speaks of Her Beloved (5:2–6:3). In this song, the woman is talking with other women, and the man is not present. In her words, there is a change from the words expressing a sense of loneliness and separation (5:4–8) to a resurgence of delight as she contemplates her loved one. The sorrow of separation from her beloved is dispelled as she recounts to them the handsomeness of her man (vv 10–16).

The Man Speaks of His Loved One's Beauty (6:4–7:9). This long passage may contain more than a single song; there are words from the man, the maiden, and the female companions. The principal theme is further description by the man of his beloved's beauty (6:4–10; 7:1–9), a theme already known from an earlier passage (4:1–5:1). Each part of the maiden's body is filled with exquisite beauty in the eyes of the one who loves her.

The Woman and the Man Reflect upon Love (7:10–8:14). Both partners speak in this complex passage, which may contain a number of short love songs. While some parts are difficult to interpret (esp. 8:8–14), other verses reveal in the most profound language the meaning of love. Love, that most powerful of all human relationships, creates a sense of mutual belonging and mutual possession: "I belong to my lover, and his desire is for me" (7:10). And later, the girl speaks of love with words which convey one of the most powerful understandings of love in the entire Bible, "for love is as strong as death, . . . Many waters cannot quench love; rivers cannot wash it away. If one were to give all the wealth of his house for love, it would be utterly scorned" (8:6,7).

Summary. Though the allegorical interpretation of these words of love is left to the reader, there are some principles of interpretation which may help in the task. The approach to interpretation is helped if the purpose is kept in mind. The purpose of the book, from an allegorical perspective, is to enable an understanding both of God's love for humanity and the manner in which humans may love God. But how does one love a God who, in a literal sense, is invisible and intangible? The Song of Solomon suggests that human love provides one way of understanding God's love for man and man's love for God. As one begins to perceive human love, one may learn of divine love from that experience. It is the tragedy of many human lives that, for a variety of reasons, they never experience the fullness of human love. So how can human love illuminate divine love? It is here that the role of literature may be perceived. It is the peculiar genius of the poet that through his words he may create an awareness of certain realities and emotions in the experience of his readers. Those who have not experienced profound human love, or do not presently experience it, may nevertheless know it and feel it through reflection on the words of the poetry of love.

Thus the Song of Songs first recreates for the reader the diverse faces of human love, its beauty, joy, sadness, and sometimes grief. From the sense of wonder which emerges from perceiving human love, then gradually there emerges a deeper understanding of what it means that God loves humanity, and what it may mean for men to love God. On this note, it is wise to add a postscript to the Song of Solomon. The words of the girl reveal an extraordinary truth: "love is as strong as death" (8:6); but in the NT, Jesus added something to that in his crucifixion: love is stronger than death. Eventually, God's love goes beyond the possibility of any mere allegory.   PETER C. CRAIGIE

See SOLOMON (PERSON).

Bibliography. G.L. Carr, *The Song of Solomon;* R. Gordis, *The Song of Songs;* M. Jastrow, *The Song of Songs;* H.G. Schonfeld, *The Song of Songs;* L. Waterman, *The Song of Songs.*

Song of Songs.   See SONG OF SOLOMON.

Son of God.   Term used to express the deity of Jesus of Nazareth as the one, only begotten Son of God.

Jesus' unique sonship is antithetical to concepts of sonship popular in the ancient world. In Hellenism, people believed a man could be a "son of the gods" in many ways: in mythology, by cohabitation of a god with a woman whose offspring was imagined to be superhuman; in politics, by giving generals and emperors high honors in the cult of Roman emperor worship; in medicine, by calling a doctor "son of Asclepius"; and eventually by ascribing to anyone with mysterious powers or qualities the title or reputation of "divine man."

In the OT, certain men before the days of Noah (Gn 6:1–4) and "the angels" (including Satan, Jb 1:6; 2:1, and other heavenly beings, Ps 29:1; 82:6; 89:6 RSV margin) are called "sons of God." Israel as a people was the chosen son of God. This corporate sonship became the basis of Israel's redemption from Egypt: "Israel is my first-born son" (Ex 4:22; cf. Jer 31:9). Corporate sonship was the context for focus on personal sonship in the divine sanction of David as king: "I will be his father, and he will be my son" (2 Sm 7:14). David's "adoptive" sonship was by divine decree: "I will proclaim the decree . . . 'You are my son; today I have become your Father" (Ps 2:7); and it was the prophetic prototype of the "essential" sonship of Jesus, David's royal son (Mt 3:17; Mk 1:11; Lk 3:22; Acts 13:33; Heb 1:5; 5:5). Other messianic prophecies ascribe divine names to the Davidic messiah: "Immanuel" (Is 7:13,14) and "Mighty God, Everlasting Father" (9:6,7). These are fulfilled in Jesus (Mt 1:23; 21:4–10; 22:41–45).

The NT has a striking fullness in the revelation of Jesus as the Son of God. In the Gospels, as G. Vos (*The Self-Disclosure of Jesus*) showed, this truth is uniquely revealed with the use of the term "Son of God" in four distinctive senses.

First is *covenant sonship*, which focuses on the fact that Jesus lived his earthly life in a positive religious relationship to God as his heavenly Father. In this respect Jesus shares sonship with all the children of God, for to his covenant people God gives this identity: "You are the sons of the Lord your God" (Dt 14:1). Jesus' life exhibited a perfect relation to God and example for humanity in that he could both pray "My Father" (Mt 26:39) and also teach men to pray "Our Father" (6:9). As covenant children men share the same Father with the Lord Jesus, which means he is man's covenant brother: "For whoever does the will of my Father in heaven is my brother and sister" (12:50). Further, Jesus taught covenant obedience by paying the temple tax (17:24–27) to show that he and Peter, as sons of God, were free to serve their heavenly Father in the expected manner.

Second is *nativity sonship*. The nativity of Jesus is traced to the direct, spiritual paternity of God. Jesus is the Son of God because his incarnation and birth into the human race was by conception of the Holy Spirit, as the Apostles Creed confesses. In Matthew, Jesus' conception "is of the Holy Spirit" (1:20). He is to be named "Jesus" (meaning Yahweh is salvation) "because he will save his people from their sins" (v 21); and "Immanuel" (God with us) because he is himself the Son of God in human flesh (v 23). In Luke, Jesus' conception was by the Holy Spirit and the power of the Most High (vv 31,35); so Jesus will be called "the Son of the Most High" (v 32) and "the Son of God" (v 35). If the father of Jesus was the man Joseph, he would be called "Jesus, the son of Joseph." Luke's teaching clearly means that since the Spirit of God was the father of Jesus, this son of the virgin Mary is properly called "Jesus, the Son of God."

Third is *messianic sonship*. Jesus is the Father's son and representative whose earthly mission is to establish the kingdom of God. At his baptism, he began his mission with the Father's coronation: "This is my beloved Son, with whom I am well pleased" (Mt 3:17; cf. Ps 2:7). With a similar word from heaven at his transfiguration (Lk 9:35), Jesus went to the cross, his victory, and throne (Jn 12:32; 18:36; 19:7,19; Heb 1:3). As messianic Son, Jesus perfectly completed the redeeming work given him to do by his Father. The other messianic titles "Son of Man" and "Son of David" focus attention on the messianic work he came to accomplish; the former on his passion, resurrection, and second coming (Mk 9:31; 10:45; 14:62), the latter on his ministry of mercy and healing (Mt 9:27; 12:23; 20:30; 22:42). Frequently, the demoniacs identified him publicly: "You are the Son of God!" (Lk 4:41) and were silenced by Jesus for their public outcry.

Finally is *personal sonship*. Jesus' personal sonship is revealed in Peter's confession, "You are the Christ, the Son of the living God" (Mt 16:16) and in Jesus' identification of himself at his trial: "Are you the Christ, the Son of the Blessed One? . . . I am, said Jesus" (Mk 14:61,62). In both instances, the issue is his personal being or essence, his essential identity. In Matthew 11:27, Jesus had claimed unity of knowledge and oneness with the Father: "No one knows the Son except the Father, and no one knows the Father except the Son." Matthew attributes the trinitarian baptismal formula, "in the name of the Father and of the Son and of the Holy Spirit," to Jesus himself (28:19).

In John's Gospel, Jesus claimed the oneness of personal essence with God the Father: "I and the Father are one" (10:30; 14:11; 15:24). He claimed to be sent from the Father's heavenly home (8:16; 14:2,12,24) into the world to do the will of the Father for the salvation of mankind (17:1–12). John further teaches that Jesus, as the Word (Logos) of God, was already with God in the beginning, before the creation of the world, and was himself the creator (1:1–4). He became a real human being so that the glory of the one and only Son, who came from the Father (v 14) was revealed in him. He is "God the only Son, who is at the Father's side" (v 18). This "only begottenness" doctrine means that Jesus is from all eternity the Son of God. He is preexistent (3:17; 11:27; 1 Jn 3:8; 4:9–14). Jesus and the Father even share the same name: "your name-the name you gave

Ruins of the synagogue at Capernaum, the city where demons cried out that Jesus was the Christ, the Son of God (Lk 4:41).

me" (Jn 17:11), for God had given his own name Yahweh to his Son when he required him to be named Jesus, meaning Yahweh saves. In 1 John 4 and 5, belief in Jesus as the incarnate Son of God is essential for salvation; disbelief is of the antichrist.

Paul teaches the essential, ontological sonship of Jesus not as an isolated fact, but in the context of his redemptive work. It was as "his Son" that Jesus took human nature (Rom 1:3) and as "the Son of God" that he was resurrected and enthroned in power (Mt 28:18; Rom 1:4; 1 Cor 15:28). Jesus' incarnation was "God . . . sending his own Son" (Rom 8:3; Gal 4:4) for man's redemption "through the death of his Son" (Rom 5:10; 8:29,32). So believers have "fellowship with his Son Jesus Christ our Lord" (1 Cor 1:9), and live by faith in "the Son of God" (Gal 2:20). Paul's first preaching was "that Jesus is the Son of God" (Acts 9:20), later expounded in the light of Psalm 2:7 (see Acts 13:33).

In Hebrews, Jesus is "the Son" who is God's "firstborn" and personal "heir," who is creator and sustainer of the universe, and who is the "radiance of God's glory" (1:2–9; 3:6; 5:5). As the Son, he is the final and eternal high priest who ascended to heaven and whose mediatorial work remains perfect forever (4:14; 6:6; 7:3,28).

In Revelation 2:18,27, Jesus reveals himself as the Son of God, to whom his Father gave authority to rule and judge the nations.

Early Christian confessions have as a primary element that Jesus is the Son of God, the only begotten of the Father, the second person of the Trinity.   JAMES C. DEYOUNG

See CHRISTOLOGY; JESUS CHRIST, LIFE AND TEACHING OF; MESSIAH; SON OF MAN.

Bibliography. O. Cullman, *The Christology of the NT;* R.H. Fuller, *The Foundations of NT Christology;* M. Hengel, *The Son of God;* W. Kramer, *Christ, Lord, Son of God.*

Son of Man. Messianic title used by Jesus to express his heavenly origin, earthly mission, and glorious future coming. It does not refer merely to his human nature or humanity, as some church fathers or contemporary scholars believe. Rather, it reflects on the heavenly origin and divine dignity of Jesus, on the mystery of his manifestation in human form, and on his earthly mission which involved suffering and death but which issued in heavenly glory to be followed by eschatological vindication.

The background of the term "Son of man" is to be found in the OT. The Book of Ezekiel is the general source, since this prophet used "Son of man" 90 times as a cryptic, indirect reference to himself. For example, God ad-

dresses him, "Son of man, stand up on your feet and I will speak to you." (2:1). Jesus' use of the term "Son of Man" and numerous themes from Ezekiel suggest his desire to identify himself as the eschatological prophet who, like Ezekiel (ch 4,7,10,22,40–48), had the last word about the destruction of Jerusalem and the restoration of the kingdom of God to Israel (Mt 23,24; Acts 1:6–8).

The specific source of the term is Daniel 7:13,14, with its vision of one "like a son of man" who "comes with the clouds" into the presence of "the Ancient of Days" who gives him the universal and eternal kingdom of God. Jesus repeatedly quoted parts of this text in teaching about his second coming (Mt 16:27; 19:28; 24:30; 25:31; 26:64). Clearly, Jesus understood this passage as a prophetic portrayal of his own person: his incarnation, ascension, and inheritance of the kingdom of God.

In the Gospels, the term "Son of man" is used by Jesus some 80 times as a mysterious, indirect way of speaking about himself (Mt, 32 times; Mk, 14; Lk, 26; Jn, 10). In all these texts, Jesus is always the speaker, and no one ever addresses him as "Son of Man." In some texts the reference is cryptic enough for some interpreters to insist that Jesus is speaking about another person. Such uncertainty is recorded in only one text in John, where the crowd asks Jesus, "Who is this 'Son of Man'?" (12:34). In most texts, the identification is clear; in some it is explicit: "Who do men say that the Son of Man is?" . . . "Who do you say that I am?" (Mt 16:13,15). The conclusion generally drawn is that Jesus used the term as a messianic title for himself, so that he could speak modestly about his person and mission, yet convey the exalted content he wished to reveal about himself. He could do this with considerable originality because the term was not fraught with popular misconceptions concerning messiahship.

The term occurs only four other times in the NT. In Acts 7:56, Stephen says, "I see heaven open and the Son of Man standing at the right hand of God." Hebrews 2:6 quotes Psalm 8:4 as applying to Jesus. Finally, Revelation 1:13 and 14:14 record visions of someone "like a son of man" who is undoubtedly the glorified Jesus.

In the synoptic Gospels, the first theme in Jesus' self-revelation with his use of the title "Son of man" concerns his coming to earth to accomplish his messianic mission.

A general comparison of Jesus' present earthly condition with that of his previous heavenly glory is expressed in the logia: "Foxes have holes and birds of the air have nests, but the Son of Man has no place to lay his head" (Mt 8:20; Lk 9:58). Some scholars believe this text refers merely to the poverty of his earthly situation. It is too simplistic for Jesus to mean that, unlike birds and foxes, he accepts the lifestyle of a drifting vagabond. This logia really means that the Son of Man gave up his heavenly home to suffer all the humiliations of his earthly ministry (Phil 2:5–11).

Some interpret Matthew 11:19 and Luke 7:34 to be a mere comparison of John the Baptist as an ascetic, with Jesus as the Son of Man who "came eating and drinking." This view is entirely too earthbound, because even John was a heaven-sent messenger (Lk 3:2; Jn 1:6). Thus the "coming" of the Son of Man ought to be seen as an allusion to his heavenly origin and to his mission in this sinful world.

Jesus uses the title to claim divine prerogatives, saying, "the Son of Man is Lord of the sabbath" (Mt 12:8; Mk 2:28; Lk 6:5). The sabbath, a divine institution, may not be revised by ordinary men. But, since Jesus is the Son of Man from heaven, he is free to rule as Lord even of the sabbath, because he alone is in filial harmony with the same Lord who instituted the sabbath (Gn 2:2; Ex 20:8–11). Indeed, the Lord of the sabbath is also the creator of all things (Jn 1:3,10).

After healing the paralytic at Capernaum, Jesus claimed that he as "the Son of Man has authority on earth to forgive sins" (Mt 9:6; Mk 2:10; Lk 5:24). Previously, forgiveness of sins came from heaven and from God; but now forgiveness comes from Capernaum and is given by Jesus.

This group of texts clearly reveals the heavenly origin and divine authority of Jesus for his earthly mission.

A second aspect of Jesus' use of the "Son of Man" title concerns his suffering, death, and glorious resurrection as the mysterious method he would use to fulfill his earthly mission as the Son of Man.

Jesus began expounding this passion theme after Peter confessed him to be Messiah and Son of God (Mt 16:16). Jesus' prediction of his passion as the Son of Man begins in Mark 8:31,32, and is repeated in several other texts. The Gospels expand the theme to include his suffering of mockery and scourging (Mt 17:12; 20:18; Mk 8:31; Lk 9:22), betrayal by Judas (Mt 17:22; 26:24; Mk 14:21,41), rejection by the Jewish leaders (Mt 20:18), death by gentile crucifixion (Mt 20:19; Mk 9:12,31; 10:33), burial for three days (Mt 12:40; Lk 11:30), and resurrection after three days (Mt 17:22,23; Mk 8:31).

In the famous ransom text, "the Son of Man did not come to be served, but to serve, and to give his life as a ransom for many" (Mt 20:28; Mk 10:45), Jesus teaches that his death was a vicarious sacrifice for the salvation of his people. This idea of substitutionary atonement is a new element in the Son of Man material and

derives from Jesus' understanding of himself as the suffering servant of the Lord (Is 53).

Jesus also used the "Son of Man" title to teach about his second coming. As the eschatological Son of Man, Jesus will return to earth from heaven in the glory of his Father with the angels (Mt 16:27; Mk 8:38; Lk 9:26). First, he will be seated at the right hand of God, and then he will come again (Mt 26:64; Mk 14:62; Lk 22:69), with the clouds (Mt 24:30; Mk 13:26; Lk 21:27). This coming will be unexpected (Mt 24:27; Lk 12:40), like a flash of lightning or the flood of Noah (Mt 24:37; Lk 17:24). His coming will be for the gathering of the elect, the judgment of all the nations of the earth (Mt 19:28; 25:32), and the restoration of final righteousness in the world (Mt 19:28; 25:46).

In these passages, Jesus' focus shifts from the provisional victory in his passion and resurrection to the final victory of the Son of Man at his second coming from heaven. Here again, the dramatic emphasis is on the heavenly origin and divine prerogatives of the Son of Man. This man Jesus, the Son of Man, will be the final judge (cf. Acts 17:31).

The Gospel of John has its own distinctive material concerning the Son of Man. The angels ascend and descend on the Son of Man (1:51), probably signifying that he is a preexistent person who has come from heaven (3:13; 6:62). His being lifted up (by crucifixion) will bring about eternal life for all who believe in him (3:14). The Son of Man (3:14) is also the Son of God (v 16), his Son (v 17), and God's one and only Son (v 18). The Father has given authority to raise the dead and to judge the world to his Son, the Son of Man (5:25,27). The Son of Man gives food that endures unto eternal life; this food is his flesh and blood (6:53). Jesus' passion is the hour of the lifting up and glorification of the Son of Man (8:28; 9:35; 12:23,34; 13:31). In John's Gospel, the "Son of Man" title is equivalent to the title "Son of God." It reveals his divinity, preexistence, heavenly origin, and divine prerogatives: it affirms his present earthly condition for revelation and passion, and his future eschatological glory.   JAMES C. DEYOUNG

See CHRISTOLOGY; JESUS CHRIST, LIFE AND TEACHING OF; MESSIAH; SON OF GOD.

Bibliography. C.K. Barrett, *Jesus and the Gospel Tradition*; F.H. Borsch, *The Son of Man in Myth and History*; O. Cullmann, *The Christology of the NT*; F. Hahn, *The Titles of Jesus in Christology*; A.J.B. Higgins, *Jesus and the Son of Man*; T.W. Manson, *The Teaching of Jesus*; H. Tödt, *The Son of Man in the Synoptic Tradition*.

Sons of God. Expression common to both OT and NT, perhaps designating either angelic or earthy beings.

The first occurrence of the term in Genesis

6:1,2 helps define an ill-advised union between Sethites (sons of God) and morally corrupted daughters of Adam (Cainites). These intermarriages between the chosen line of Seth and the seed of the ungodly world contributed to an ever-increasing wickedness (v 5). Although angelic beings are not indicated by the Genesis 6 passage, such is doubtless the meaning in several sections of Job (1:6; 2:1; 38:7). In the psalms, these heavenly creatures are called "sons of the mighty" (Pss 29:1; 89:6).

At one stage of Hebrew history the Israelite judges were called "children of the most High" because they exercised divine power over life and death (Ps 82:6). More significant, however, is that usage which denotes a special covenantal relationship between God and his people. Collective Israel is God's son because of the adoptive, redeeming love of God (Ex 4:22). That sonship is particularly evident in the ideal Davidic king who both rules (Ps 2:7) and represents his people as their deliverer (Hos 11:1; cf. Mt 2:15). Through the work of God in Christ the children of God not only receive the title of sonship (Dt 14:1) but also manifest attributes commensurate with their position in Christ (Jer 31:31–34).

From a biblical perspective children were generally expected to possess the character of their fathers. "Children of iniquity" (Hos 10:9) or "children of Belial" (Dt 13:13) described sons of ethically poor substance. "Children of God," on the other hand, referred to those who bore something of the nature of their heavenly Father. Christ, being by very nature God, is the Son of God *par excellence*. Those who trust in the Son of God have received the divine life of God (Jn 1:12) and actually partake of him through spiritual rebirth (2 Cor 5:17). Furthermore they have become heirs of God through adoption into his family (Rom 8:15). This is a distinct privilege and one that is totally the product of grace (Eph 2:8,9). A full appreciation of the greatness of God's gift of sonship should motivate all his children to submit to the leadership of the Holy Spirit (Rom 8:14).

See CHRISTIANS, NAMES FOR.

Sons of the Prophets. "Band of prophets" whom Saul met (1 Sm 10:5,6,10–13) and forerunners of the "schools," "guilds," or "sons of the prophets," which flourished under Israel's earlier kings. Jezebel persecuted those defending the worship of Jehovah, and established rival "schools" to propagate worship of Baal and Asherah (1 Kgs 18:19–29; 22:6). Ahab's steward, Obadiah, sheltered two companies of 50 prophets of Jehovah in caves with provisions (18:4). Use of music, frenzied actions, and mystic excitement conferring "second sight" and hearing (1 Sm 10:5; 19:24; 1 Kgs 18:28,29; 22:17; cf. 2 Kgs 6:17) indicate communities of ecstatics, whose abnormal mental states were commonly associated with "possession," or mental derangement, until events confirmed their prophecies. Hence Amos' indignant protest (7:14).

First Kings 22:5–28 illustrates the political danger of such royal guilds, and the emergence of individual spokesmen, claiming spontaneous inspiration. First Kings 20:35–43 shows another individual, acting strangely yet recognizable as a true prophet. From 2 Kings 2:3,5,7,15–18; 4:1,38,42–44; 5:21–23; and 6:1, we learn that groups persisted, however, at Bethel (about 50) and Gilgal (about 100), both famous shrines, at Jericho, and elsewhere, doubtless offering counsel and instruction. The common meals, the need for extended premises, and the receiving of public support by way of firstfruits and other gifts all suggest a monastic type of life, though marriage and private dwellings are mentioned. Elisha visited Gilgal, apparently teaching ("sons . . . sitting before him"), and attended the new building at Jordan, exercising an almost paternal oversight.

Second Kings 9:1–13 illustrates the lingering association of ecstatics with madness, combined with swift obedience when prophetic inspiration is recognized and also the political significance of the whole movement. But the future lay with the individual poets, statesmen, visionaries, and martyrs, called prophets.

R. E. O. WHITE

See PROPHECY; PROPHET, PROPHETESS.

Sons of Thunder. Translation of the word "Boanerges," the surname given by Jesus to James and John (Mk 3:17).

See BOANERGES.

Soothsayer. One who foretells events; a pagan practice, soothsaying was forbidden in Israel (Dt 18:10,14). In Scripture, soothsaying was practiced by Balaam, Beor's son (Jos 13:22) and King Manasseh of Judah (2 Kgs 21:6; 2 Chr 33:6); Jacob's house was likened to the soothsayers of Philistia (Is 2:6); its practitioners were listed among the false prophets of Judah (Jer 27:9). During the NT times it was the source of a lucrative trade in Philippi (Acts 16:16).

See MAGIC; SORCERY.

Sop. Thin piece of bread, dipped into a common dish and used as a spoon (Jn 13:26; RSV morsel).

See FEASTS AND FESTIVALS OF ISRAEL; LORD'S SUPPER, THE; MEALS, SIGNIFICANCE OF.

Sopater. Man from the church at Beroea who, with others, accompanied Paul to Jerusalem to deliver the offering collected by the gentile churches for the Jewish Christians who were suffering privation (Acts 20:4). Sopater is perhaps identical to Sosipater, the kinsman of Paul who sent greetings to the church at Rome (Rom 16:21).

Sophereth. Alternate form of Hassophereth, the name of a postexilic levitical family, in Nehemiah 7:57.

See HASSOPHERETH.

Sorcery. Practice whose adherents claim to have supernatural powers and knowledge; the ability to foretell the future and to summon evil spirits through charms and magical spells. Sorcerers were present in the high courts of Egypt (Ex 7:11), Assyria (Na 3:4), and Babylonia (Dn 2:2). Sorcery was forbidden in Israel (Dt 18:10) and was punishable by death (Ex 22:18); however, Israel later entrusted herself to sorcerers (2 Kgs 17:17; 2 Chr 33:6; Mi 5:12), provoking God's wrath against her (Is 57:3; Mal 3:5). Paul included it in a list of sinful works (Gal 5:20) and the Book of Revelation condemned its practitioners to the lake of fire (21:8) and to eternal separation from the righteous (22:15).

See MAGIC.

Sore. Any localized abnormality of the skin. It must be a well-demarcated skin abnormality with a definite border between the inflammed or abnormal skin and the normal skin. Even the person "covered with sores" from head to toe has some normal skin between each of the sores. As such, "sore" is a broad term encompassing all the following types of skin abnormalities: scall, scab, rising, emerod, plague, and scar. Scall, used 13 times in the KJV in Leviticus 13,14, is best translated "itch." Scab appears nine times in the KJV—in four instances it means "rash" (Lv 13:2,7,8; 14:56); in five cases it means "festering sore" (13:6; 21:20; 22:22; Dt 28:27; Is 3:17). "Rising" (Lv 13:2; 14:56 KJV) refers to large soft swellings of the skin, most commonly seen in abscesses. Emerod (KJV) appearing in Deuteronomy 28:27 and 1 Samuel 5:6–6:17 may designate some abnormal growth of tissue (i.e., tumor, NIV) or skin erosion (i.e., ulcer, RSV). Plague indicates a rash (Lv 13). Scar is used only in the NIV and refers to the abnormal tissue which occurs following a boil (13:23) or a burn (v 28).

The KJV uses the word "sore" in translating 32 different Hebrew or Greek words to mean "extremely," a nonmedical use: "and Hezekiah wept sore" (2 Kgs 20:3) or "sore afraid" (Ez 27:35).

There are four medical meanings to the word sore as used in the KJV. On two occasions the term refers to wounds (Jb 5:18; Ps 38:11). In Solomon's prayer, sores refers to afflictions or disasters (2 Chr 6:28,29). In the section dealing with instructions to the priest on how to evaluate skin diseases, some sores are called leprosy (Lv 13). Finally, there are three references to people who are covered with open, draining, ugly sores indicating a most repulsive situation (Is 1:6; Lk 16:20,21; Rv 16:2).

See DISEASE; MEDICINE AND MEDICAL PRACTICE; PLAGUE.

Sorek, Valley of. Valley in which Delilah lived (Jgs 16:4). It began in the hill country of Judah, about 13 miles W,SW of Jerusalem, and took a northwesterly course to the Mediterranean Sea. It is identifiable with the Wadi es-Sarar. The Danites attempted to settle this area, but were driven out by the Philistines in the region by the Mediterranean. The town of Zorah, Samson's birthplace, was near the head of the Valley of Sorek, which provided the setting for his intrigues and the concentration of his activities as judge.

Sorghum. Medium to stout annual grass growing over six feet tall and perhaps the "hyssop" to which the sponge of vinegar was attached during the crucifixion (Mt 27:48; Mk 15:36; Jn 19:29).

See PLANTS.

Sosipater. Jewish Christian who joined Paul, Timothy, Lucius, and Jason in sending greetings to the church at Rome (Rom 16:21).

The Valley of Sorek, west of Jerusalem.

Sosthenes. 1. Leader of the synagogue in Corinth who brought legal action against Paul before Gallio, proconsul of Achaia. Upon hearing Gallio's dismissal of the Jewish accusations against Paul, a mob, possibly of Greeks, seized Sosthenes and beat him (Acts 18:17).

2. Christian brother and companion of Paul, known to the Christians at Corinth and mentioned by Paul in 1 Corinthians 1:1.

It is uncertain whether these two men named Sosthenes refer to the same person.

Sotai. Head of a family of temple servants that returned to Jerusalem with Zerubbabel following the exile (Ezr 2:55; Neh 7:57).

Soul. Term translating the Greek word *psychē* and the Hebrew *nepeš*.

The Greek philosopher Plato (4th century BC) perceived the soul as the eternal element in man: whereas the body perishes at death, the soul is indestructible. At death the soul enters another body; if it has been wicked in this life, it may be sent into an inferior human being, or even an animal or bird. By means of transmigration from one body to another, the soul is eventually purged of evil. In the early centuries of the Christian era, Gnosticism also taught that the body was the prison house of the soul. Redemption comes to those initiated into the Gnostic secrets, leading to the release of the soul from the body.

Biblical thought about the soul is different. In the OT the soul signifies that which is vital to man in the broadest sense. The Hebrew and Greek words for soul often can be translated as "life"; occasionally they can be used for the life of creatures (Gen 1:20; Lv 11:10). "Soul for soul" means "life for life" (Ex 21:23). Blood is said to be the seat of life, for when blood is shed death ensues (Gn 9:4–6; Lv 17:11,14; Dt 12:23). In legal writings a soul means the person concerned in a particular law (e.g., Lv 4:2; 5:1,2,4,15). When people were counted, they were counted as souls, that is, persons (Ex 1:5; Dt 10:22).

In a narrower sense the soul denotes man in his varied emotions and inner powers. Man is called to love God with all his heart and soul (Dt 13:3). Within the soul lies the desire for food (12:20,21), the lust of the flesh (Jer 2:24), and the thirst for murder and revenge (Ps 27:12). The soul is said to weep (Jb 30:16; Ps 119:28), and to be exercised in patience (Jb 6:11). Knowledge and understanding (Ps 139:14), thought (1 Sm 20:3), love (1 Sm 18:1), and memory (Lam 3:20) all originate in the soul. Here the soul comes close to what today would be called the self, one's person, personality, or ego.

There is no suggestion in the OT of the transmigration of the soul as an immaterial, immortal entity. Man is a unity of body and soul—terms which describe not so much two separate entities in man as the one man from different standpoints. Hence, in the description of man's creation in Genesis 2:7, the phrase "a living soul" (KJV) is better translated as "a living being." The thought is not that man became a "soul," for clearly he had a body. The use of the word in the original draws attention to the vital aspect of man as "a living being." The Hebrew view of the unity of man may help to explain why man in the OT had only a shadowy view of life after death, for it would be difficult to conceive how man could exist without a body (Pss 16:10; 49:15; 88:3–12). Where hope of an after-life exists, it is not because of the intrinsic character of the soul itself (as in Plato). It is grounded in confidence in the God who has power over death and the belief that communion with him cannot be broken even by death (Ex 3:6; 32:39; 1 Sm 2:6; Jb 19:25,26; Pss 16:10,11; 73:24,25; Is 25:8; 26:19; Dn 12:2; Hos 6:1–3; 13:14).

In the NT the word for soul (*psychē*) has a range of meanings similar to that of the OT. Often it is synonymous with life itself. Followers of Jesus are said to have risked their lives for his sake (Acts 15:26; cf. Jn 13:37; Rom 16:4; Phil 2:30). As the Son of Man, Jesus came not to be served, but to serve and to give his life as a ransom for many (Mt 20:28; Mk 10:45). As the Good Shepherd, he lays down his life for the sheep (Jn 10:14,17,18). In Luke 14:26 the condition of discipleship is to hate one's soul, that is, to be willing to deny oneself to the point of losing one's life for Christ's sake (cf. Lk 9:23; Rv 12:11). In Luke 12:19 the rich man addresses his soul, that is, himself. But the soul can indicate the essential self of a man with its desire for life and well-being.

Frequently "soul" can mean "person" (Acts 2:43; 3:23; 7:14; 27:22; Rom 2:9; 13:1; 1 Pt 3:20). The expression "every living soul" (Rv 16:3 KJV; cf. 8:9) reflects the vital aspect of living beings (cf. Gn 2:7). In his teaching on the resurrection Paul contrasts the merely physical aspect of the soul with the resurrection body. "Thus it is written, 'The first man Adam became a living being'; the last Adam [Christ] became a life-giving spirit" (1 Cor 15:45). In the following verses Paul goes on to contrast the resurrection body with the natural body. It is clear that Paul is talking neither about the immortality of the soul nor of the resuscitation of corpses to the state in which they were at death. The resurrection body will be a new kind of body. "Just as we have borne the image of the man of dust, we shall also bear the image of the man of heaven" (v 49).

As in the OT the soul can denote not only

the vital aspect of the person on the physical level, but it can also connote one's emotional energies. It denotes man himself, the seat of his emotions, man in his inmost being. Jesus could speak of his soul being crushed (Mt 26:38; Mk 14:34; cf. Ps 42:6). In Matthew 11:29 Jesus promises rest to the souls of those who come to him. Here as elsewhere "soul" denotes the essential person (cf. Lk 2:35; 2 Cor 1:23; 2 Thes 2:8; 3 Jn 2).

Several passages place the soul alongside the spirit. Luke 1:46 is probably a case of Hebrew poetic parallelism which expresses the same idea in two different ways. Both terms denote Mary as a person to the depths of her being. Similarly in Hebrews 4:12, dividing the soul and the spirit is a graphic way of saying how the Word of God probes the inmost recesses of our being. The prayer in 1 Thessalonians 5:23—that the readers may be kept sound and blameless in spirit, soul, and body—is a way of speaking of man on the level of his mind, will, emotions, and physical needs. Here soul probably suggests physical existence, as in Genesis 2:7 and 1 Corinthians 2:14, whereas spirit may imply the higher or "spiritual" side of life.

In other passages the emotions, the will, and even the mind come to the fore, though in each case there is the accompanying idea of man in his inmost being. Man is to love God with all his soul (Mt 22:37; Mk 12:30; Lk 2:27; cf. Dt 6:5). The expression "from the soul" (Eph 6:6; Col 3:23) means "from the heart," with all one's being. In Philippians 1:27 believers are called to be of one mind (cf. Acts 4:32; 14:2). Passages that speak of the soul in relation to salvation include Matthew 10:28; Luke 12:5; Hebrews 6:19; 10:39; 12:3; 13:7; James 1:21; 5:20; 1 Peter 1:9,22; 2:25; 4:19; and Revelation 6:9; 20:4. Such passages speak of the soul either to stress the essential human being, as distinct from the physical body, or to express man's continued existence with God prior to the resurrection. Jesus' promise to the penitent criminal (Lk 23:43; see 2 Cor 5:8; Phil 1:21,23; 1 Thes 4:14) gives assurance of abiding in his presence without, however, using the word "soul."

In quotations from the OT "my soul" is another way of saying "I." Thus God speaks of his soul, thereby summing up all that characterizes God in his love, holiness, wrath, and faithfulness (Mt 12:18, cf. Is 42:1; Heb 10:38, cf. Hb 2:4).

COLIN BROWN

See MAN, DOCTRINE OF; SPIRIT.

Bibliography. G.C. Berkouwer, *Man: The Image of God;* R. Bultmann, *Theology of the NT;* A.B. Come, *Human Spirit and Holy Spirit;* O. Cullmann, *Immortality of the Soul or Resurrection of the Dead?;* H.W. Robinson, *The Christian Doctrine of Man.*

Source Criticism. The attempt to explain the extensive duplications and disagreements among the Gospels through an examination of their literary histories and sources.

Problem. The puzzle that is especially acute for Matthew, Mark, and Luke. They are termed "synoptic" (Gk. *syn-optikos,* "viewed together") Gospels because they have so much in common. For example, 93 percent of Mark is found paralleled in Matthew and Luke; on the other hand, merely 8 percent or 9 percent of John is found in the other three Gospels. Therefore, the problem rests with the Synoptics and its study is often termed the synoptic problem. Its chief task is unraveling the mystery of why the synoptic Gospels have so much overlapping material. Were they each dependent on the same source or were they interdependent? Are they independent of each other or was there borrowing? A close look at any synopsis (an arrangement of the Gospels showing parallel accounts) illustrates the problem well.

The early church was not unaware of the problem. Gospel harmonies such as Tatian's *Diatessaron* (AD 170) provided syntheses. The popular view defended by Augustine, however, was that the NT sequence reflected a literary history: Matthew was the earliest Gospel, Mark was his abbreviator, and Luke was dependent on both. This might be illustrated thus:

It was not until the 18th and 19th centuries that critical scholarship challenged this solution. It was generally agreed that all three Synoptics were mutually dependent on something earlier. Hence:

Sources

MT   MK   LK

For some (e.g., Herder, Westcott) an oral Gospel was being tapped. Others thought of written tracts or fragments. Still others such as Lessing suggested an old Aramaic Gospel ("The Gospel of the Nazarenes")—a short "pregospel" (or *Urevangelium*). This shows that a documentary solution involving literary borrowing was forming and would soon find a consensus. Unfortunately all evidence for these pre-Gospel sources has been lost.

Methods of Interpretation. The numerous synoptic coincidences—seen especially in the Greek text—soon compelled scholars to look within the Gospels themselves for a solution. Perhaps the Synoptics were not independent witnesses to something original, but dependent on one another.

The Priority of Matthew. The first scholar to attempt this solution was J.J. Griesbach

(1745–1812). Rather than harmonize the Gospels, Griesbach printed the Gospels in parallel columns in order to make scientific comparisons possible. For him the antiquity of Matthew could be defended, but Mark had to be seen as the abbreviator of both Matthew and Luke. Hence:

MT.
↓ ＼
LK→MK

Today this is a minority viewpoint but it still has its passionate defenders (e.g., W.R. Farmer).

The Priority of Mark. Karl Lachmann (1793–1851) not only edited the first critical edition of the Greek NT in 1831, but four years later made a breakthrough in the synoptic problem by analyzing the *order of events* in each Gospel. Lachmann found the following: when Matthew and Luke use Mark, the sequence of these events in their Gospels is the same. When they interrupt Mark's outline with new materials, their method of arrangement completely diverges. This suggested that Matthew and Luke were indeed using Mark (or an early form of Mark) and other sources, but not each other.

This new emphasis on Mark was developed by many (H. Weisse, 1801–66; H. Holtzmann, 1832–1910; B. Weiss, 1827–1918) and given its classic form by B.H. Streeter (1874–1937) in his book, *The Four Gospels: A Study of Origins* (1924). The arguments for Mark's priority are numerous: (1) *Subject matter.* Much of Mark is found in Matthew and Luke. Of Mark's 661 verses, 601 are found in the other two Synoptics (or, of Mark's 11,078 words, Matthew has 8555 of them and Luke has 6737). Good explanations are available showing why Matthew and Luke omitted these few Markan units (see Kümmel, 1975, 56f). (2) *Sequence.* Lachmann observes that there is no case in which Matthew and Luke fully agree in the way in which they diverge from Mark (see Kümmel's tables, 58f). (3) *Literary characteristics.* There are elements of Mark's style which suggest that Mark is the more primitive account. First, Mark's narratives are abbreviated in Matthew and Luke to make the pericope more concise (see Mk 1:32/Mt 8:16; Mk 6:39/Mt 14:19); for example, Matthew 9:2 ("Jesus saw their faith") makes little sense unless we read Mark 2:4 which Matthew omitted. Second, Mark's rugged style is modified and/or improved by Matthew and Luke. Thus the correct title for Herod is given in Matthew 14:1 (cf. Mk 6:14) and the improper Greek term for pallet used by Mark (*krabbaton*, 2:4) is changed by both Matthew and Luke. Further, historic presents in Mark (151) are reduced to 21 in Matthew and one in Luke, and many of Mark's redundant negatives and awkward con-

structions are removed. Of Mark's eight Aramaic words, Matthew contains only one and Luke none. Third, substantive changes improve the content of Mark. Embarrassing statements (Mk 6:5) and even the failure of the disciples (Mk 4:13; cf. Mt 13:18; Lk 8:11; also Mk 4:40/Mt 8:26/Lk 8:25) are modified. The confession of Peter at Caesarea Philippi ("You are the Christ," Mk 8:29) is expanded in Matthew 16:16 and Luke 9:20. Together these data have a cumulative force and have led most scholars to accept the antiquity of Mark.

The Case for Q. What do we make of the material common to Matthew and Luke which is not found in Mark? Griesbach could explain this by Matthew and Luke's use of each other. Now it is argued that another written source was used by Matthew and Luke alongside of Mark. This source is called "Q" from the German word *Quelle* (source). The following categories suggest Q's existence: (1) *Agreements.* Numerous corresponding verses (about 250) show such precise parallels (see Mt 3:7–10/Lk 3:7–9; Mt 7:7–11/Lk 11:9–13) and close similarities (Mt 10:26–33/Lk 12:2–9) as to urge a common document. (2) *Sequence.* If the sequence of Q sayings in Matthew and Luke are compared, the order in which they are used has a surprising number of parallels (although there are variations). This does not refer to the point where each has interrupted Mark's outline (cf. Lachmann), but instead to the mere sequence of Q sayings. (3) *Doublets.* This is decisive for many. A doublet is when a saying of Jesus occurs twice in Matthew or Luke—one source being clearly from Mark while the other is not. These include narratives (the sending of the disciples, Lk 9:1–6; 10:1,2 with Mk 6:7–13/Mt 9:35–37) and sayings (Mt 13:12/Mk 4:25/Lk 8:18 with Mt 25:29/Lk 19:26). Q is thus a written source consisting chiefly of sayings with little narrative. (On the other hand, if Luke knew Matthew as A.M. Farrer has argued, then the hypothetical source "Q" disappears.)

The Four-Source Hypothesis. The sources of the Synoptics are now postulated with some certainty. Matthew and Luke were dependent on Mark and Q. But B.H. Streeter also points to the independent materials contained in Matthew and Luke which might represent other primitive sources. This might be illustrated thus:

MK   Q
M↘↓ ✕ ↓↙L
MT   LK

Thus Matthew employed Mark, Q, and his own sources (M= about 300 verses or 42% of Mt), and Luke used Mark, Q, and his own sources (L= about 520 verses or 59% of Lk). The size of "L" has led some to argue for yet another homogenous source for Luke, namely proto-

Luke, which might be another ancient text (see Martin, 1975, 1:151–156).

Assessment. While there seems to be a general consensus in favor of the four- (or two-) source hypothesis, extensive debate surrounds its particulars. Many even challenge its basic assumptions. For instance, why does Luke omit Mark 6:45–8:26 (Luke's so-called "great omission")? Streeter explained that Luke possessed a damaged copy of Mark. Others have said that Luke used an early, shorter form of Mark (*Urmarkus*) and that a later editorial hand added the debated section to the Second Gospel. But there is no evidence whatsoever for this. Moreover, it runs the danger of adapting the data to the theory rather than the other way around.

While the conclusion of Markan priority seems assured, the continued disagreement over details may indicate that source criticism has reached its limitations. The literary history of the Synoptics may have been extremely complex. Each Gospel may have gone through numerous recensions at its earliest stage. If this is so then only the broadest outline of literary dependence is obtainable.

The conclusions of source criticism have become basic to any critical study of the Gospels today. Its use, however, must be seen in a much larger theological context. Scholars are endeavoring to get behind the Gospel tradition *as a feature of the quest for the Jesus of history.* Ancient traditions are deemed more reliable: hence sources such as Mark, Q—even proto-Luke—are valued due to their antiquity. Thus the conclusions of source criticism are presupposed in redaction criticism (the study of how the evangelists themselves shaped these ancient traditions as editors) and form criticism (the history of the tradition prior to its written stage).

Fundamental to Christian faith is some certainty concerning the historical traditions within the Gospels. Source criticism helpfully shows how the evangelists used primitive sources in their work (see Lk 1:1–4). However it would be misguided to disparage a portion of the Gospel *when no source can be determined* (Wenham, 1977, 145f). Source criticism effectively illustrates literary dependence, but has severe limitations when used to affirm historical certainty. A completely independent pericope, for instance, in Matthew might theoretically bear a greater antiquity than Mark or Q. At least in this example the source critic is incapable of making an objective historical judgment on it. GARY M. BURGE

See FORM CRITICISM; MARKAN HYPOTHESIS; DOCU-MENTARY HYPOTHESIS; REDACTION CRITICISM; TRADI-TION CRITICISM; SYNOPTIC GOSPELS; MATTHEW, GOSPEL OF; MARK, GOSPEL OF; LUKE, GOSPEL OF; BIBLICAL CRITICISM; NEW TESTAMENT; DEMYTHOLOGIZATION.

Bibliography. W.R. Farmer, *The Synoptic Problem: A Critical Analysis;* D. Guthrie, *NT Introduction;* W.G. Kümmel, *NT Introduction;* R.P. Martin, *NT Foundations,* 2 vols; S. Neill, *The Interpretation of the NT 1861–1961;* B.H. Streeter, *The Four Gospels: A Study of Origins;* D. Wenham, "Source Criticism," in I.H. Marshall, ed., *NT Interpretation.*

Spain. Name of the most westerly peninsula in southwestern Europe. Biblical references to the peninsula note the role of Phoenicians whose far-flung Carthaginian Empire reached into Spain. The Romans expelled the Carthaginians from Spain as early as 206 BC, but they did not conquer the local tribes until 25 BC. Only by then had the Romans "gained control of the whole region" (1 Mc 8:3).

The Phoenician traders of Tyre extended their commercial empire to Spain or historic Iberia as early as 1100 BC. From Carthage on the North African coast, which was a center of the Phoenician Empire, a series of colonial thrusts followed the trading contacts. The Carthaginians during the flourishing of their republic established many settlements on the Spanish coast. These included Carthago Nova (now Cartagena) and Malacca (now Malaga). Later they took Tartessus and absorbed much of the peninsula into their empire. From this base in Spain the Carthaginians sought to expand their empire into Europe. The Romans met the Carthaginian challenge. After beating Hannibal back in his attack on Italy in the Second Punic War (218–201 BC), the Romans extended security by onslaughts toward Carthagians on the Spanish peninsula. Finally, under Augustus the Romans made Spain part of the empire. At that time the Romans built a magnificent road system circling and crossing the whole Spanish peninsula.

Roman civilization had a deep and lasting influence on Spain. Three emperors, Trajan, Hadrian, and the first Theodosius, were born in Spain. Several scholars and writers of note in Roman culture came from Spain. These included the two Senecas, Martial, Prudentius, Lucan, Quintilian, Pomponius, and Mela. In the apostle Paul's scheme for reaching the uttermost regions of the civilized world with the good news of Jesus Christ, he probably realized the potential of converts in Spain.

The chief evidence that Paul included Spain in his strategic planning is in Romans 15:24,28. In that letter Paul clearly sets forth his message to Romans and Gentiles throughout the empire. To follow up on the letter he planned to visit Rome and then make his way to Spain. Testimony of Paul actually visiting Spain comes only from a vague reference after his death. Clement of Rome, an early Christian writer at the end of the 1st century AD, stated that Paul went to "the limits of the West" (Eph 1:5). Although most Romans considered Spain as the western limit of their empire, this vague phrase does not give sufficient evidence for a Pauline visit. Yet clearly Paul saw Spain as a strategic place for mission work, and he or others that he designated planted the Christian church in Spain during the 1st century AD. That Spanish church has had both a tortuous and glorious history.

Span. Hand measurement equaling one-half cubit (Ex 28:16; 39:9).

See WEIGHTS AND MEASURES.

Sparrow. See BIRDS.

Spear, Spearman. See ARMS AND WARFARE; TRADES AND OCCUPATIONS (SOLDIER).

Spelt. Hard-grained species of wheat that flourishes in various kinds of soils; hence, it was popular grain among the ancients (Ex 9:32; Ez 4:9).

See PLANTS.

Spice, Spicery. See PLANTS.

Spider. See ANIMALS.

Spikenard. Perennial herb with strong, pleasant-smelling roots.

See PLANTS (NARD).

Spin, Spinner, Spinning. See CLOTH, CLOTH MANUFACTURING; TRADES AND OCCUPATIONS.

Spirit. Designation for that aspect of existence, human or otherwise, which is noncorporeal and immaterial. Its Latin derivation (as with the Heb and Gk words in the Bible) denotes blowing or breathing (Jb 41:16 air; Is 25:4, etc.) In Judges 8:3 the heavy breathing sense of "spirit" describes anger and resentment. So the noun *spiritus* signifies breath, vigor, courage, and (more metaphysically) life or soul. Spirit most essentially defines the life principle, especially in man—infused by deity (Zec 12:1), and it is often used synonymously with "soul." As distinguished from body, it is the inner consciousness, the thinking, planning, motivating intelligence; hence it often refers to one's "frame of mind"—tendency toward enthusiasm or depression, courage or fear, and the like.

The highest evidence of the transcendence of spirit over the physical aspects of existence is in reference to God. "God is a spirit" (Jn 4:24). Spirit can also describe created beings other than human—good or evil angels (1 Sm 16:14); lying (1 Kgs 22:21–23) demonic beings. The Sadducees' denial of resurrection, angels, and spirit are linked together by Luke in Acts 23:8. Dissociation of spirit from flesh is scriptural, but not to be confused with dualistic cosmologies, such as in Eastern religions or the Judaic sect at Qumran, setting in opposition a spirit of light and a spirit of darkness. God's communion with his own is Spirit to spirit (Rom 8:16; 1 Cor 2:10–16).

The term "spirit" is applied to God in 35 percent of its OT occurrence, while soul is so used only 3 percent. In fact, since "spirit" signifies wind in 113 of its 389 OT instances, its 136 references to God exceed those to man, false gods, or bad spirits individually. In Isaiah 31:3 the antithesis between flesh and spirit (as also Gn 6:1–8) is not metaphysical, but one of principle, contrasting God's spiritual strength with man's physical weakness (cf. Christ's remark in Gethsemane, Mt 26:41).

From the standpoint of theology, the Bible is slow to isolate the spirit aspect of man's makeup. In Genesis spirit occurs only twice with reference to humans: the pharaoh's spirit was troubled after his dreams (Gn 41:8) and Jacob's spirit revived when he saw the carts Joseph sent from Egypt (45:27). Exodus adds little, speaking only of the Israelites' anguish of spirit (6:9), of a spirit of wisdom imparted by God for designing the priests' garments (28:3), and of persons with a willing spirit supplying gold for the tabernacle (35:21). "Familiar spirits" are associated with soothsayers (Lv 20:27; 1 Sm 28), the latter narrating Saul's recourse to the medium at Endor. In this instance the spirit (or "spirits") of Samuel is described as ascending from the ground, the Hebrew word meaning "God" or "gods" (as usually translated). But it is in the poetic books, Job, Psalms, Proverbs, and Ecclesiastes, that we begin to get the more metaphysical and psychological uses of spirit. Here life, personhood, and immortality come into focus.

A clear case of the parallel (synonymous) use of soul and spirit (as in Jb 7:11; Is 26:9, etc.) is in Mary's *Magnificat*. She says, "My soul magnifies the Lord, and my spirit has rejoiced in God my Savior" (Lk 1:46,47, NKJV). Rather than divide the two as "parts," some have suggested man *has* a spirit, he *is* a soul. (First Jn 4:1, however, unless referring to external influences, seems to employ spirit as synonymous with *person*.) Usually spirit indicates the vitalizing, energizing, empowering agent. In John 3:5–8; Romans 8:3–16, Galatians 4:21–5:26, etc., the flesh versus spirit distinction is between man's will and power, doing what he chooses apart from God, as against the life, will, and power given by God's Spirit, enabling us to do his will. Similarly, in 2 Kings 2:9–15, the spirit of Elijah is said to rest upon Elisha.

Loss of the spirit spells death (Lk 23:46; Jas 2:26), while eternal spiritual life is generated through Christ's spirit-word (Jn 6:63). Remarkably, 1 Corinthians 5:5 speaks of destruction of the flesh for salvation of the spirit. Only 1 Thessalonians 5:23 implies a tripartite design for mankind, in Paul's all-inclusive manner of speaking; and the other suggestive text, Hebrews 4:12, is apparently hyperbolic—performance of the impossible by God's incisive written Word.

Scripture commonly uses spirit to indicate some attribute or disposition—various talents, abilities, attitudes, and influences, as have been alluded to above. Deuteronomy 34:9 speaks of a "spirit of wisdom," and spirit is translated "mind" (NIV) or "thoughts" (NASB) in Ezekiel 11:5.

MILTON C. FISHER

See GOD, BEING AND ATTRIBUTES OF; MAN, DOCTRINE OF; SOUL.

Bibliography. G.C. Berkouwer, *Man, The Image of God;* E. deW. Burton, *Spirit, Soul, and Flesh;* W.P. Dickson, *St. Paul's Use of the Terms Flesh and Spirit;* P.K. Jewett, *Man as Male and Female;* R. Jewett, *Paul's Anthropological Terms;* W.G. Kümmel, *Man in the NT.*

Spirit, Holy. *See* HOLY SPIRIT.

Spirit, Unclean. *See* DEMON, DEMON POSSESSION.

Spirits, Discerning of. *See* SPIRITUAL GIFTS.

Spirits in Prison. Term used in 1 Peter 3:18–20a. There is little agreement among scholars as to *what* "spirits in prison" really refers to or *why* Jesus would have gone to preach to them. Martin Luther confessed that verse 19 "is an amazing text and as dark as any in the New Testament and I am not sure I know what St. Peter means." Because there is so much disagreement and uncertainty, several possible interpretations are presented here.

First, many commentators take "spirits in prison" to refer to the disembodied spirits of the people who disobeyed the preaching of Noah and are now in Sheol or Hades—the place of the departed unbelievers. Some think Christ preached the gospel to them so that they could believe and be saved (though there is little, if any, support in the NT that a person who dies as an unbeliever can get a second chance). Others think that Christ simply proclaimed his victory over Satan and made

known the blessings which these spirits once for all rejected.

Second, other commentators argue that the "spirits in prison" are not human spirits but rather are the same supernatural beings referred to in 1 Peter 3:22—the evil angels, authorities, and powers. They are related to the "sons of God" in Genesis 6:1–4. In support of this, they argue that the proclamation to these spirits is not before, but after, Jesus' resurrection and so is probably not a *descent* to the dead but an *ascent* to the "heavenly places" (cf. Eph 6:12) where the rebellious spiritual powers dwell. Furthermore, in the pre-Christian Jewish book of 1 Enoch, Enoch is pictured as proclaiming doom to the apostate angels. So Christ is seen as the new Enoch declaring to the "spirits in prison" his victory on the cross and their final defeat.

Finally, still others have suggested that the preaching of Christ was neither to supernatural spiritual beings nor to the departed spirits in Hades. Rather the preaching took place in the days of Noah and was addressed to Noah's contemporaries who because they disobeyed are *now* in prison. In other words the Spirit of Christ, referred to in 1 Peter 1:11, and which existed before the incarnation, inspired Noah to preach to the people. In this interpretation there is no "descent into Hell" and no declaration to the fallen angels. The text simply says that Christ in his spiritual dimension preached in the days of Noah.

Each of these interpretations could have relevance in the context of 1 Peter. The first interpretation would mean that, because Christ's redemption is made available even to the disobedient generation of Noah's time, then surely one should seek to bear witness to one's own hostile generation and win them. The second interpretation would mean that, because Christ has proclaimed to the evil powers their defeat and his victory, one should be confident and resist those powers, firm in one's faith (5:9). Finally, the third interpretation would mean that, even though Christ himself preached to Noah's generation, nevertheless only a few—namely, eight souls—were saved in the ark. This is an example of how believers are only a few in a hostile society; however, one must not be discouraged because Christ is at work and believers are saved, even though few in number.

See PETER, FIRST LETTER OF.

Spiritual Gifts. Phrase regularly used to translate two Greek words, *charismata* and *pneumatika* (the plural forms of *charisma* and *pneumatikon*). Both words are almost exclusively Pauline within the biblical writings;

Biblical Lists of Spiritual Gifts

Rom 12:6–8	1 Cor 12:8–10	1 Cor 12:28	1 Cor 12:29–30	Eph 4:11	1 Pet 4:11
prophecy	prophecy	prophets	prophets	prophets	
ministry					ministry
teaching		teachers	teachers	pastor-teachers	
exhortation					
giving					
ruling		governments			
showing mercy					
	word of wisdom				
	word of knowledge				
	faith				
	healing	gifts of healing	healing		
	miracles	miracles	miracles		
	discerning of spirits				
	tongues	tongues	tongues		
	interpretation		interpretation		
		apostles	apostles	apostles	
		helps			
				evangelists	
					speaking

elsewhere in the NT they appear only in 1 Peter 2:5 and 4:10. Other writers, of course, mention phenomena that fall within Paul's definition of "spiritual gifts," but for specific teaching on the subject one must depend on Paul first and foremost.

Both words are derived from more familiar words, *charis* (grace) and *pneuma* (spirit). Both have similar senses—*charisma* meaning "expression or manifestation or embodiment of grace," *pneumatikon* meaning "expression or manifestation or embodiment of Spirit." Their range of application, however, is somewhat different.

Charisma denotes God's saving action in Christ (Rom 5:15–16) and the gift of eternal life (6:23). More generally, in Romans 11:29 it probably refers to the series of gracious acts on behalf of Israel whereby God made Israel's calling and election sure. In 2 Corinthians 1:11 it probably refers to a particular action of God that brought Paul deliverance from deadly peril. Otherwise the reference seems to be to divine grace as mediated through individuals, with Paul presumably thinking of the sort of utterances and deeds that he illustrates in Romans 12:6–8 and 1 Corinthians, 12:8–10 (so in Rom 1:11; 1 Cor 1:7; 7:7; 12:4,9,28,29,30; similarly 1 Pt 4:10). There is some dispute over 1 Corinthians 7:7. It is unlikely, however, that Paul regards marriage as a "spiritual gift"; possibly he thinks of the celibate state as a "spiritual gift"; but more probably he thinks of the "spiritual gift" as that enabling "not to touch a woman" (v 1), to refrain from sexual relationships for a season for the purpose of prayer (v 5) or for some act of ministry.

Pneumatikon has a wider range of usage. It is more properly an adjective and so de-

scribes various things (and people) as "spiritual," as manifesting the Spirit, or serving as the instrument of the Spirit—thus some particular word or act (Rom 1:11), the Law (7:14), the manna, water from the rock, and the rock itself in the wilderness wanderings of Israel (1 Cor 10:3,4), the resurrection body (15:44,46), unspecified blessings "in the heavenly places" (Eph 1:3), particular insights into the divine will (Col 1:9), and songs in worship (Eph 5:19; Col 3:16). As a plural noun it can be used of individuals ("the spiritual ones" 1 Cor 2:13,15; 14:37; Gal 6:1) or of things ("the spirituals," "spiritual gifts," Rom 15:27; 1 Cor 2:13; 9:11; 12:1; 14:1, even "spiritual powers in heaven," Eph 6:12).

From this brief survey a more precise definition of "spiritual gifts" can be made. Whatever thing, event, or individual serves as an instrument of the Spirit, or manifests the Spirit, or embodies the Spirit is a spiritual gift (*pneumatikon*). Whatever event, word, or action is a concrete expression of grace or serves as a means of grace is a spiritual gift (*charisma*). *Pneumatikon* is the more general word, *charisma* more specific. Moreover, *charisma* is probably Paul's own word (Rom 1:11; 12:6; 1 Cor 7:7; 12:4) in preference to the more ambiguous *pneumatikon*, which seems to have been popular with those causing difficulty for Paul in Corinth (1 Cor 2:13–3:4; 14:37; 15:44–46). Consequently, attention will focus in what follows on *charisma*. Not forgetting those passages where Paul uses this word in broader terms for the direct act of God (Rom 5:15,16; 6:23; 11:29; 2 Cor 1:11), concentration will be on the passages where Paul speaks in more precise terms of particular manifestations of grace mediated through one individual to others, "spiritual gifts" in this the narrower sense of *charisma*.

The lists of *charismata* (Rom 12; 1 Cor 12; Eph 4; 1 Pt 4) are the obvious starting point, because they provide the clearest indications of what Paul would include within the range of spiritual gifts. For the sake of clarity in analysis they are most simply divided into four groups—revelation, miracles, leadership, and service.

Gifts of Revelation. *Knowledge and Wisdom.* The first two gifts mentioned in 1 Corinthians 12:8 are "utterance of wisdom" and "utterance of knowledge." Paul mentions wisdom and knowledge first presumably because the Corinthians made so much of them, as is clear from 1:17–2:13; 8; 13:2,8. Paul clearly thinks they have the wrong idea of wisdom, understanding it as rhetorical skill or eloquence (1:17,19,20; 2:1,4,5), or as a this-worldly sophistication (1:20,22;2:5,6,13; 3:19). The wisdom by which believers should live is the wisdom of God, the wisdom expressed in God's plan to achieve salvation through Christ, that is, through the crucifixion of Christ and the proclamation of the crucified Christ (1:20–25,30; 2:6–8). In other words, Christian wisdom is rooted in the recognition that God's saving purposes center on the crucified Messiah and stem from the experience of that saving power (2:4,5). Lest his readers think of divine wisdom as something that they possess and can use at will, Paul narrows his description of the spiritual gift to "*utterance* of wisdom" (12:8). That is to say, the gift is not wisdom itself but the utterance that mediates the recognition and experience of God's saving purpose to others (2:4–7,13).

Similarly, the Corinthians laid claim to "knowledge," presumably understood as an insight into the relation between themselves and the spiritual realm that enabled them to disregard idols as irrelevant to their spiritual health (8:1–6; cf. 13:2). Paul seems to accept this insight of "knowledge" (8:5), but he warns his readers that the true index of spiritual health is not "knowledge" but concern for one's brother in the faith (vv 7–13)—"'knowledge' puffs up, but love builds up" (v 1). Elsewhere "knowledge" for Paul seems to overlap largely in meaning with "wisdom," as knowledge or experiential awareness of God's grace in Christ (2:12; 2 Cor 2:14; Eph 1:17–23; 3:19; Phil 3:8; Col 2:3). As with wisdom so with knowledge; Paul seems to take care to specify the spiritual gift as "utterance of knowledge" (1 Cor 12:8). Once given the knowledge, one can of course claim to "have it" (8:1,10), but the *charisma* as such for Paul is the utterance that first brings that insight into God's purpose and the cosmos to the hearer.

Insofar as these two gifts are distinct and insofar as their meaning is determined by the contexts of 1 Corinthians 1,2 and 8, "utterance of wisdom" may be more an evangelistic gift and "utterance of knowledge" more a teaching gift. Much of the preaching and teaching of Jesus and the earliest apostles could be described as charismata in these terms.

Prophecy. Paul clearly understands prophecy not merely as bold speech making critical comment on current issues but as *inspired* speech—like prophecy of old, as words given to the speaker to speak by divine compulsion (cf. Jer 20:9; Am 3:8; 7:14). Though it comes sixth in the list of 1 Corinthians 12:8–10, prophecy is (next to apostleship, 1 Cor 12:28) clearly the most important gift for Paul (Rom 12:6; 1 Cor 14:1; 1 Thes 5:19,20; cf. Eph 2:20; 4:11; 1 Pt 4:11). This was presumably for several reasons.

First, it was *the* mark of the outpouring of the Spirit in the "last days" (Jl 2:28; Acts 2:16–18). The widespread experience of prophecy among the earliest Christians was therefore proof that the climax to God's salvation history was already in train. Unlike glossolalia, prophecy spoke to mind as well as spirit (1 Cor 14:1–33). In other words, it addressed the whole man, expressing the wholeness of God's saving power, thus preventing the believer from setting rational and spiritual against each other. Thus, consequently it built up the church more than any other gift, ministering both encouragement and consolation (vv 3,31), bringing new revelation (vv 6,26,30)—of guidance for life or of God's plan of salvation confirming the believers in their faith and converting the unbelievers (vv 22–25).

Discernment of Spirits. Not properly a gift of inspired utterance, it nevertheless has to be included here, since Paul sometimes associates it with prophecy (1 Cor 12:10; 14:29; 1 Thes 5:20,21). Claims of inspired speaking were no proof that the words were from God (1 Cor 12:3). Those who have also received the Spirit have the responsibility of evaluating the utterance as to its source and significance (2:12,13; 14:29; also 1 Jn 4:1–3); they must test the charisma and hold only to that which is good, rejecting what is bad (1 Thes 5:19–22). In other words, this gift is not independent of prophecy; it serves as a check on it. To put it the other way round, prophecy is not independent of discernment of spirits. Prophecy is a community gift, and the gift of prophecy is only complete when the community has tested and approved the message of God in it.

Glossolalia and Interpretation of Tongues. Like prophecy and discernment of spirits these last two members of the 1 Corinthians 12:8–10 list hang together, the latter providing a check on the former lest it be abused in the

Ruins at Corinth, the city where the church had to be corrected by Paul regarding spiritual gifts.

ecstasy of inspiration. That glossolalia (speaking in tongues) was experienced in ecstasy at Corinth seems clear from the picture of uncritical enthusiasm and confusion that emerges from Paul's rebukes (12:2,3; 14:12,23,27–28,33, 40). Similarly, ecstasy is implied in Acts (2:4, 6,13; 10:44–46; 19:6).

Paul values glossolalia, not as ecstatic speech, but as a quieter, less abandoned gift (1 Cor 14:28), particularly in his own private worship (v 18). He seems to think of glossolalia rather as language: the word "tongue" certainly implies this, and "interpretation of tongues" could equally well be rendered "translation of languages." However, the language is not that of men (as in Acts 2:6–11); it is rather the language of angels (1 Cor 13:1), whereby the believer speaks to God (14:2). Paul values it as such, as enabling a different level of communication with God ("praying with the Spirit"—vv 4–7; cf. Rom 8:26,27). In the assembly, however, he would prefer that the gift was restrained and only manifested if a subsequent utterance in the vernacular (interpretation of tongues) enabled the worshiping assembly to share in the individual glossolalist's blessing (1 Cor 14:19, 27,28).

Other forms of inspired utterance mentioned by Paul include preaching (1 Cor 2:4–5; Eph 6:17; 1 Thes 1:5; cf. Jn 16:8–11; Acts 4:8; 13:9; 1 Pt 1:12), teaching (Rom 12:7; 1 Cor 14:6,26; Col 3:16), exhortation (Rom 12:8); "the Paraclete" could be called "the Exhorter" (Jn 14:16,26; 15:26; 16:7), singing (1 Cor 14:15,26; Eph 5:18,19; Col 3:16), and prayer (Rom 8:15, 16,26,27; 1 Cor 11:4,5; 14:15; Eph 6:18; cf. Jude 20).

Gifts of Healing and Power. In 1 Corinthians 12:6 Paul describes *all* spiritual gifts as "actions of divine energy." This power aspect of *charismata* is, however, most clearly seen in healings and miracles.

Faith. The third gift mentioned in 1 Corinthians 12:8–10 is faith. As is generally recognized Paul would be referring here to justifying faith, which is the mark of all believers (by definition), but must have in mind more concentrated *experiences* of faith, particularly surges of confidence wherein the believer is enabled to trust God in a particular situation or for a particular event (faith "to remove mountains"—13:2). Hence it is a *charisma* given only to some (12:9). Hence too its association with healings and miracles in this list. It was a gift widely experienced in and through the ministry of Jesus and of the earliest churches (e.g., Mt 8:10; 15:28; Mk 5:36–42; 9:23–27; Acts 3:6–8; 14:9–10).

Healings. Fourth in the list of 1 Corinthians 12:8–10 is "gifts of healings" (v 9; also vv 28,30). The plural form implies that Paul does not have in mind some general power on which the healer could draw to deal with all sorts of diseases; rather, the *charisma* is the actual healing itself, with a different *charisma* for each different healing. In this way Paul once again underlines how necessary it is for the would-be healer to rely on God's gracious power to be bestowed afresh through him in each instance. Such healings were, of course, a feature of Jesus' ministry and of the early mission.

Miracles. Fifth comes "workings of power, miracles" (1 Cor 12:10,28,29). Note again the plural form. Paul gives first-hand testimony that such miracles were a feature of his own ministry (Rom 15:19; 2 Cor 12:12; Gal 3:5; cf. Heb 2:4). What he has in mind is presumably distinct from healings. Perhaps he thinks of exorcisms, though demon possession does not feature prominently in his thought (cf. 1 Cor 10:20,21; Eph 2:2). Or we may think of the wider range of miracles recorded in the Gospels and Acts, including "nature" miracles and miracles of judgment (e.g., Mk 6:35–52; 11:12–14,20; Acts 5:1–11; 19:11,12).

Gifts of Leadership. *Apostleship.* Apostles receive first mention in the lists of spiritual gifts (1 Cor. 12:28; Eph. 4:11). Since these gifts are bestowed by the risen Christ through the Spirit, it is probable that at the beginning of the apostolic age these men who had been appointed by Jesus and trained by him were now regarded as possessing a second investiture to mark the new and permanent phase of their work for which the earlier phase had been a preparation. They became the foundation of the church in a sense secondary only to that of Christ himself (Eph. 2:20).

The duties of the apostles were preaching, teaching, and administration. Their preaching rested on their association with Christ and the instruction received from him and it included their witness to his resurrection (Acts 1:22). Their converts passed immediately under their instruction (Acts 2:42), which presumably consisted largely of their recollection of the teaching of Jesus, augmented by revelations of the Spirit (Eph. 3:5). In the area of administration their functions were varied. Broadly speaking, they were responsible for the life and welfare of the Christian community. Undoubtedly they took the lead in worship as the death of Christ was memorialized in the Lord's Supper. They administered the common fund to which believers contributed for the help of needy brethren (Acts 4:37), until this task became burdensome and was shifted to men specially chosen for this responsibility (Acts 6:1–6). Discipline was in their hands (Acts 5:1–11). As the church grew and spread abroad, the apostles devoted more and more attention to the oversight of these scattered groups of believers (Acts 8:14; 9:32). At times the gift of the Holy Spirit was mediated through them (Acts 8:15–17). The supernatural powers which they had exercised when the Lord was among them, such as the exorcism of demons and the healing of the sick, continued to be tokens of their divine authority (Acts 5:12; 2 Cor. 12:12). They took the lead in the determination of vexing problems which faced the church, associating the elders with themselves as an expression of democratic procedure (Acts 15:6; cf. 6:3).

Teaching. Clearly related to, but carefully distinguished from, the gift of prophecy is the gift of teaching (1 Cor. 12:28–29; Rom. 12:7). The prophet was a preacher of the word; the teacher explained what the prophet proclaimed, reduced it to statements of doctrine, and applied it to the situation in which the church lived and witnessed. The teacher would offer systematic instruction (2 Tim. 2:2) to the local churches. In Ephesians 4:11 Paul adds the idea of pastor to that of teacher, because no one is able to communicate effectively (teach) without loving those who are being instructed (pastor). Likewise, to be an effective pastor, one must also be a teacher.

Governments or Administration (1 Cor. 12:28; cf. Rom. 12:8). The early church's organization was still fluid. Official offices had not been established, nor were duly appointed officials yet ruling the churches. It was necessary, therefore, that certain members should receive and exercise the gift of ruling or governing the local assembly of believers. This gift would take the form of sound advice and wise judgment in directing church affairs. Gradually, of course, this gift of guiding and ruling in church affairs would come to be identified so closely with certain individuals that they would begin to assume responsibilities of a quasipermanent nature. They would become recognized officials in the church, fulfilling well-defined duties in the administration of the Christian community. At the beginning, however, it was acknowledged that some Christians had received the

gift of ruling and had liberty to exercise it. In addition to administration, practical matters in the conduct of public worship would require wisdom and foresight, and here again those who had recognizably received the gift of ruling would be expected to legislate.

Exhortation (Rom. 12:8). The possessor of the gift of exhortation would fulfill a ministry closely allied with that of the Christian prophet and teacher. The difference between them would be found in the more personal approach of the former. If his exhortations were to succeed, they would have to be given in the persuasive power of love, understanding, and sympathy. His aim would be to win Christians to a higher way of life and to a deeper self-dedication to Christ. The Spirit, therefore, who bestowed the gift of exhortation would with the gift communicate spiritual persuasiveness and winsomeness.

Evangelism. Another gift to the church is the ability to do evangelism. Timothy is called an evangelist in 2 Timothy 4:5, as is Philip, one of the seven, in Acts 21:8. The task of preaching the gospel, although theoretically everyone's responsibility, is entrusted specifically to certain individuals by the Holy Spirit. They are to exercise their ministry in the full realization that the power comes from God, making faddish and manipulative techniques not only unnecessary but wrong. When such are present, it is a clear indication that the Spirit is absent. Converts from the evangelist's ministry are to be funneled into the church, where they are to be built up by those exercising the other gifts.

Gifts of Service. Just as Paul calls all spiritual gifts "actions of divine energy" (1 Cor 12:6), so he calls them all "acts of service" (v 5). A word or deed is only to be regarded as a spiritual gift when it both manifests divine grace and serves others. Paul sometimes speaks of such acts of ministry without specifying what he has in mind (Rom 12:7; 1 Cor 16:15; cf. 1 Pt 4:11); but the lists do mention four service gifts.

The Gift of Helpers (1 Cor. 12:28). What spiritual gift was signified by "helper" may be gathered from Acts 20:35, where Paul exhorts the Ephesian elders to labor "to help the weak" and constantly to remember the Lord's own words, "It is more blessed to give than to receive." Paul supports this exhortation from his own example. The early church seems to have had a special concern for the needy among her members, and those who helped the indigent were considered to have been endowed by the Spirit for this ministry. It is not impossible that the office of elder originated in the gift of government or rule. By the same token, the office or duty of deacon may have originated in this gift of helpers. The deacon was one who ministered to the needy (Acts 6:1–6).

Service (Gr., *diakonia*). Service is called a gift in Rom. 12:7. This term is used in a number of ways in the NT, from a generalized idea of ministry (2 Cor. 5:18, where Paul's preaching is called a ministry of reconciliation) to a specific office or task (1 Tim. 1:12). It is difficult to know exactly how Paul means it here. It is perhaps a generalized gift of power to anyone exercising a specific function in the church.

Contributing. Paul speaks of contributing as a gift (Rom. 12:8). All are to give to the needs of the church, its ministry, and the poor, but a special gift enables some to make joyous sacrifice in this area. Paul adds that this gift should be exercised "without grudging" or "in liberality."

Acts of Mercy (Rom. 12:8). Merciful acts are to be performed with cheerfulness under the guidance of the Spirit. It might be wondered why such a noble act would require charismatic endowment, but the circumstances of the time explain it. To render aid was dangerous. Such identification with other Christians in need branded one as a Christian as well, opening up the possibility of persecution.

Such gifts would of course be manifested regularly by particular individuals. Just as he who manifested the gift of prophecy regularly came to be recognized as a prophet (1 Cor 12:28; 14:29–32; Eph 2:20; 3:5; 4:11; cf. Acts 11:27,28; 13:1,2; 15:32; 21:9), and as he who manifested the gift of teaching regularly came to be recognized as a teacher (1 Cor 12:28; Gal 6:6; Eph 4:11; cf. Acts 13:1; Jas 3:1), so those who regularly manifested particular gifts of service would probably be recognized as deacons ("servers"—Rom 16:1; Eph 6:21; Phil 1:1; Col 1:7; 4:7; 1 Thes 3:2; 1 Tm 3:8,12; 4:6). Similarly "overseer" (bishop) was probably a name first given to one who regularly manifested gifts of counsel and leadership (Phil 1:1; 1 Tm 3:2; Ti 1:7).

Characteristics of Charismata. For Paul (the one who gave Christianity the concept of *charisma*), a spiritual gift is essentially an act of God's Spirit, a concrete manifestation in word or deed of God's grace through an individual for the benefit of others.

In its basic sense a spiritual gift is a specific act of God, and this remains true even when it is mediated through any individual. This means that no one can hope to manifest such a gift except in conscious openness to and dependence on God. By extension Paul can speak of individuals "having, possessing" certain spiritual gifts (Rom 12:6; 1 Cor 7:7; 12:30), but this is presumably just shorthand for their being so open to God's grace that grace regularly or constantly manifests itself through them in particular ways. Such language no more means that the *charisma* is an ability at the individual's command than does the similar talk of "having the Spirit" (Rom 8:9,23). It is true, however, that in 1 Timothy 4:14 and 2 Timothy 1:6 this basic sense is beginning to be left behind.

A spiritual gift is any event, word, or action that embodies and expresses God's grace. In this sense sacraments can be "means of grace" (though they are never called this in the NT), as are many other utterances and actions as well. In recognizing this, one can recognize too that the lists of gifts (e.g., Rom 12:6–8; 1 Cor 12:8–10) are neither definitive nor exhaustive, simply typical manifestations of the Spirit (or those with which readers were most familiar or on which they needed some advice). The degree of overlap between these various lists shows that Paul was not concerned to specify a precisely defined catalogue; he simply selected a number of activities and utterances through which he saw the grace of God manifesting itself in his churches.

It is important to grasp that Paul saw all Christians as charismatics. Whoever "has" the Spirit, that is, is open to and being led by the Spirit (Rom 8:9,14), will inevitably manifest the grace of God in some way and should also be open to the Spirit's power coming to expression in particular words and deeds within the community of the Spirit. For Paul, the church is the body of Christ. The functions of that body's members are exemplified by the spiritual gifts (12:4–6; 1 Cor 12:14–30). Unless the individual is functioning charismatically, he is not functioning as a member of the body. The Spirit's gifts are the living movements of Christ's body. As the body is many different members functioning as one body, so the unity of the church grows out of the diverse functions (gifts) of its members. It follows that a spiritual gift is given primarily with the community in view. It is given "for the common good" (1 Cor 12:7). That is why a selfish, loveless clutching after *charismata* is wrong and futile (13:1–3). A spiritual gift is never one's to use as one wants for one's own benefit (except perhaps glossolalia, but that is why Paul gives it lower value). It is given to one only in the sense that God chooses to act through one for others. More precisely, it is given only through one to the community, and one benefits only as the community benefits. The spiritual health and edification of the individual is inextricably bound up with the health and well-being of the whole body (12:14–26; Eph 4:16).

From Paul to the Present. There is no clear indication that Paul expected the cessation of spiritual gifts prior to the return of

Christ, though some see 1 Corinthians 13:8–10 as teaching that certain gifts were only for the early church; but "the complete, the perfect" to which he refers there seems to refer to the consummation at Christ's return. Indeed, on the definition of *charisma* as any word or act that manifests and mediates grace to another one may say that spiritual gifts have never been absent.

But on a narrower understanding of spiritual gifts, which focuses attention on the more striking manifestations of prophecy, glossolalia, and healing, it is true that they seem to have disappeared from the mainstream of the church's life by the middle of the 3rd century. The late ending to Mark (16:17), Justin Martyr, Irenaeus, and Tertullian all testify to the continuing experience of such gifts before then, but in the 4th century Chrysostom and Augustine of Hippo seem to think of them as belonging to the past. This was in large part due to the increasing institutionalization of the church, in the course of which *chrismation* (anointing with oil) progressively replaced *charismata* as the sign of the Spirit; the body of Christ came to be conceived as a hierarchical structure, and the phrase "gifts of the Spirit" was referred more frequently to Isaiah 11:2. Over the centuries there were successive claims that one or more of the more striking gifts had been restored—most notably by the early Montanists (second century), Joachim of Fiore (1132?– 1202), many of the Anabaptists, and the early Quakers—but such claimants were usually either pushed to the fringes of Christianity or persecuted outright. Orthodoxy's fear of enthusiastic excess and abuse of ecclesiastical authority were too often justified in the event.

More recently events have taken a different turn. Renewed interest in spiritual gifts, particularly healing and glossolalia, at the end of the 19th century heralded the emergence of Pentecostalism in the 20th century. With the acceptance of Pentecostalism as a third or fourth main stream of Christianity (beside Orthodoxy, Catholicism, and Protestantism), and charismatic renewal within the older denominations, the charismatic dimension of Christian life and worship has steadily gained recognition, not least among Catholics. It remains to be seen whether the dynamism of charismatic order and worship can be held together with the conservatism of institution and tradition in fruitful interaction.

See HOLY SPIRIT; TONGUES, SPEAKING IN; BAPTISM OF THE SPIRIT.

Bibliography. F.D. Bruner, *A Theology of the Holy Spirit*; M. Griffiths, *Grace-Gifts*; A.A. Hoekema, *Tongues and Spirit Baptism*; L. Morris, *Spirit of the Living God*; H.W. Robinson, *The Christian Experience of the Holy Spirit*; J.R. Williams, *The Gift of the Holy Spirit Today*.

Spirituality. *See* SANCTIFICATION.

Sponge. *See* ANIMALS.

Sprinkling of Blood. *See* OFFERINGS AND SACRIFICES.

Stachys. Christian in Rome to whom Paul sent greetings, calling him "my beloved" (Rom 16:9).

Stacte. One of the fragrant spices used by Moses to make the incense offering (Ex 30:34).

See PLANTS (BALM; SPICE; STORAX TREE).

Stadium. Greek unit of linear measure equivalent to about 200 yards (Mt 14:24).

See WEIGHTS AND MEASURES.

Stag. *See* ANIMALS (DEER).

Stairs of the City of David. Staircase cut into a rock wall and located in the southern section of the City of David. These stairs are mentioned in Nehemiah's account of the restoration of Jerusalem (Neh 3:15; 12:37). Such stairs have been found in this region of Jerusalem.

See JERUSALEM.

Stallion. *See* ANIMALS (HORSE).

Star. *See* ASTRONOMY.

Star in the East. Star that guided the magi to the infant Jesus (Mt 2:2,7,9,10). The magi were residents of some Eastern land (possibly Parthia, Babylon, or Arabia) who came to Herod explaining that they had seen the star of the King of the Jews in their homeland. Herod directed the men to Bethlehem (2:8), but the star guided them to the place of Jesus' birth (vv 9,10).

Numerous theories have been advanced to explain this phenomenon. In the 17th century Johannes Keppler suggested that the explosion of a distant star (supernova) would emit extraordinary light. While many such explosions are recorded each year (few visible to the naked eye), none are known from the time of Christ. The ancients were fascinated with comets. Halley's comet was first sighted and recorded in 240 BC and, if calculated at 77-year intervals, would have appeared in Judea in 12–11 BC. This, however, significantly antedates Jesus' birth; moreover, comets were usually associated with catastrophies in the ancient world. That the ancients practiced astrology, plotting the constellations and the course of the planets, is well known. Rare planetary conjunctions were studied and interpreted. For instance, in 7 BC Jupiter and Saturn came together in the zodiac constellation of Pisces (this occurs every 257 years). According to this view Jupiter was associated with the world ruler, Saturn with the region of Syria-Palestine, and Pisces with the last days. Despite the fact that medieval Judaism held a messianic interpretation of this conjunction (even seeking the Messiah's coming in 1464), it is difficult to know what 1st-century Parthians or Jews believed.

First-century readers—Jewish or Greek—would not have been surprised to read about a new star presaging the birth of Jesus. In Matthew 2:2 "in the east" might mean "at its rising." In other words, the wise men had witnessed a new star and interpreted it as hallmarking some new event. In Greco-Roman society the heavens often foretold or explained historical events (e.g., the founding of Rome, the birth of Augustus, etc.). Judaism likewise emphasized stars: Josephus recorded astral phenomena during the fall of Jerusalem in AD 70. Moreover, rabbis swept up the imagery of the Balaam story in Numbers 24:17 (see esp. Nm 24:17, LXX) and symbolized their messianic expectations in a star. This was also common at Qumran (CD 7:19f; 1QM 11:6; cf. T.Levi 18:3; Rv 22:16). Similarly coins struck after the onset of the revolt of Simon bar Kochba ("son of a star") bore a star.

See ASTRONOMY.

Stater. Common coin in Jesus' day (Mt 17:27).

See COINS.

Stealing. *See* CRIMINAL LAW AND PUNISHMENT; TEN COMMANDMENTS, THE.

Steer. *See* ANIMALS (CATTLE).

Stephanas. Christian convert at Corinth. He and his household were evidently Paul's first converts in Achaia. The members of Stephanas' family were some of the few Corinthian believers personally baptized by Paul. Stephanas and his kin were praised for their devotion and service to the Corinthian church. Stephanas, with Fortunatus and Achaicus, visited Paul at Ephesus in Asia Minor. Their mission probably included bringing aid for Paul's personal needs and seeking his advice for resolving the problems in the Corinthian church. Undoubtedly Paul wrote and sent his first letter to the Corinthian church with this little delegation when they returned to Corinth (1 Cor 1:16; 16:15,17).

Stephen. Important figure and first martyr of the apostolic church. For Luke, Stephen represents the growing Hellenistic interest of certain members in the early Jerusalem church. In addition, Stephen's major speech (Acts 7:1–53) serves as a critique of traditional Judaism and suggests evangelization beyond Judea.

In Acts 6 Luke abruptly introduces a division in the early church. The community consisted of two Jewish groups described as "Hebrews" and "Hellenists." These terms no doubt indicate cultural and linguistic divisions: Jews who had emerged from either Aramaic or Greek-speaking synagogues. Stephen was one of seven deacons nominated to serve the needs of the Hellenists. Yet even in his introduction it is evident that his importance stands out; he alone is described as "full of faith and of the Holy Spirit" (v 5). After their commission Stephen is mentioned again as "full of grace and power," doing "great wonders and signs among the people" (v 8).

Stephen's efforts included preaching, which placed him in contention with the Hellenistic synagogues of Jerusalem (Acts 6:9). As his subsequent speech before the Sanhedrin indicates, Stephen propounded a radical abrogation of the ancestral customs of Judaism and the temple cult. Luke's account of his arrest and interrogation (vv 10–15) is intended to evoke memories of Jesus' trial. While capital punishment was reserved for the Roman governor once Judea had become a province, offenses against the temple still could be prosecuted by the Sanhedrin. The interrogation opens with the same incriminating charges ("this man speaks against this holy place and the law"; "destroy this place and change the customs of Moses"); Stephen's verbal defense confirms what the Sanhedrin viewed as blasphemy. In the end, Stephen's execution by stoning is pursued with a vengeance (7:54–60). As the first martyr of the church, Stephen models Jesus even in death. He commits his Spirit to Jesus (as Christ had done to the Father, Lk 23:46) and dies asking forgiveness for his prosecutors (v 34).

The speech in Acts 7 provides us not merely with Stephen's defense, but serves Luke's broader interests as he explains the dissemination of the gospel abroad (1:8). It is the longest speech in Acts and appears at a pivotal place in apostolic history. Stephen provides a critical recital of biblical history and argues that the major pillars upon which Judaism rested were in jeopardy. Indeed these were the tenets which made Judaism exclusivistic: they offended Jews in the diaspora and were inhibiting the church's mission.

Stephen explains that the land of Israel is not the only locus of God's revelation. In various settings and cultures (Egypt, Mesopotamia) God has addressed his people. Second, the temple in which the Jews took pride was not a divine invention—Solomon's temple was contrary to the earlier tabernacle in the wilderness. Finally, the Torah (in which religious security was sought) is used as the source of criticism, chronicling Israel's consistent disobedience. Indeed these same Scriptures announced the "coming of the righteous one" whom Israel crucified.

The implications of the speech are vital. God is free to move beyond the national/religious boundaries of Judaism. The exclusivistic outlook of Judaism is artificial. God's work is dynamic. And if Stephen's conclusions are correct, the Jewish church ought to be free to take the gospel beyond Judea.

Stephen's martyrdom introduced a major persecution in Jerusalem (Acts 8:1–3). One disciple named Philip, however, understood the consequences of Stephen's thoughts. He made an unprecedented evangelistic move into Samaria. Shortly thereafter, the followers of Stephen moved north to Phoenicia and Antioch, bearing the gospel to the gentile world (11:19).

Steward. One in charge of domestic duties.

See TRADES AND OCCUPATIONS (CHAMBERLAIN).

Stocks. Common form of punishment and confinement in Bible times (2 Chr 16:10; Acts 16:24).

See CRIMINAL LAW AND PUNISHMENT.

Stoics, Stoicism. A widespread Greek and Roman philosophy, well represented in Paul's audience at Athens (Acts 17:16–34). The apostle was probably familiar with it, for it had begun in Athens around 300 BC, with Zeno's teaching in the "stoa" (porches) of public buildings, and had spread throughout the Greco-Roman world. It was known, for example, at Tarsus and on the island of Cyprus, so that Paul would normally have encountered Stoics earlier in his journeys and possibly even in his hometown. The scope and power of its influence are indicated by the fact that the Roman emperor Marcus Aurelius (d. AD 180) was himself a Stoic, some of whose philosophical writings have survived.

The earliest Stoics were primarily concerned with cosmology, that is, the study of nature's origin and its laws. They were materialists, who held that all things both come from the one basic element of fire and will eventually return thereto in a vast cosmic conflagration. They therefore had a cyclical view of cosmic history, such that one universe after another arises and is destroyed. Both the orderliness of things as we know them, and this cyclical pattern of history, were ascribed to the organizing and sustaining power of a pervasive force known as the *Logos* that is sometimes regarded as divine. Its laws were the laws of nature to which all creatures must conform. It gives to all things their essential nature and so gives life and reason to men. In fact the Logos is in man, taking the form of the human soul. Hence, to live according to reason is to live according to the natural order of things, and this is good. Conscious obedience to natural law liberates a man from fear and concern about external circumstances over which he has no control, but which are still ruled by nature's laws. The good life, then, is one in which reason, not passion, rules, and peace of mind and harmony with nature consequently prevail.

Later Roman Stoics sometimes refer to the Logos as divine providence, but they concentrated on ethical and political matters without dwelling on the cosmology of their Athenian predecessors. They valued universal human brotherhood and world citizenship over divisive loyalties; hence some of them repudiated family life and other institutional alignments. In any case, in the natural order of things all men together come under the common rule of reason. The Roman philosopher-statesman Cicero (106–43 BC) developed an ethical and political theory in which both morality and law are based on natural law rather than on expediency or utilitarian considerations.

Stoic ideas proved attractive to Christians because of apparent similarities between the Stoic logos and the Logos of John 1:1–18, and between the idea of natural law and the Law of God. But in his *City of God*, Augustine of Hippo (354–430) criticized Cicero's natural law theory for assuming that men are ruled by what they know rather than by what they love: even so he adapted other aspects of the theory for his own Christian purposes. Moreover, some have seen the language of Stoic cosmology in Peter's reference to a fiery apocalypse (2 Pt 3:7–10). Perhaps more significant is Paul's apparent agreement that the natural order of things embodies moral law, as in his verdict that homosexual behavior is contrary to nature (Rom 1:26,27). For the Bible teaches that this is a moral universe governed by divine providence; God's Law is written into the created nature of man.

Paul's address at Athens may be understood against this background, if he was indeed familiar with Stoic philosophy. He preached a God who made the world, gave it order, and gives men life; a God who is Lord over all nations of men so that they must live within the framework of his Law, but a God also who is both Judge and Savior. The Stoics could not altogether agree with this last idea for, while they might regard whatever happened as the work of providence, their cyclical view of history conflicted with Paul's claim that all history is moving in linear fashion towards its culmination. The last straw for them was Paul's mention of the resurrection; for they were materialists whose god was an organizing force within nature rather than a transcendent personal being acting in ways forbidden by nature's orderly cycle of life and death. For them, death was a rationally inevitable fate to be accepted with equanimity, though ultimately without hope.

See EPICUREANS; PHILOSOPHY.

Bibliography. E.R. Bevan, *Stoics and Skeptics;* W.K.C. Guthrie, *A History of Greek Philosophy,* 3 vols; P.P. Hallie, *Encyclopedia of Philosophy,* vol. 8; F.H. Sandbach, *The Stoics;* E. Zeller, *Outlines of the History of Greek Philosophy;* E. Zeller, *The Stoics, Epicureans, and Sceptics.*

Stone. *See* MINERALS, METALS, AND PRECIOUS STONES.

Stonecutter. *See* TRADES AND OCCUPATIONS.

Stoning. *See* CRIMINAL LAW AND PUNISHMENT.

Storax Tree. Small, stiff-branched tree from which stacte was extracted for making incense (Ex 30:34).

See PLANTS; SWEET STORAX.

Stork. *See* BIRDS.

Straight Street. Street in Damascus where Paul lodged after his vision of Jesus and where, in the house of Judas, he was baptized by Ananias and recovered his eyesight (Acts 9:11). The street is called "Straight," no doubt, because unlike many others this one was straight. It still is, though on an elevation about 15 feet higher than the original thoroughfare; it is called by this same name (Rue Droite). It runs east and west, on the south boundary of the Christian quarter. The "house of Judas" is no longer there, but in a lane off the eastern end of Straight Street is the "house of Ananias." At the easterly terminus is the monumental stone gateway from the Roman period now called Bab esh Sharqi. South of this gate there is on the old city wall a building called St Paul's Chapel, commemorating the site where Paul was lowered over the wall in a basket to escape his enemies (Acts 9:25; 2 Cor 11:33).

See DAMASCUS.

Stranger. *See* FOREIGNER.

Strange Vine. KJV rendering of wild vine in Jeremiah 2:21.

See PLANTS (VINE).

Strangle, Strangling. One of four practices from which the early gentile Christians were asked to abstain out of respect for their Jewish brethren. Jewish law prohibited the eating of any meat from which the animal's blood was not fully drained at the time of slaughtering. The Jerusalem Council requested the early church to observe this practice in order to keep peace between Jewish and gentile Christians (Acts 15:20,29; 21:25).

Strangulation was also one of four forms of capital punishment administered by the Jewish law courts. Though it was not mentioned as a method of punishment in the Bible, strangulation was later adopted by rabbinic Judaism as the mode of execution for any crime deserving the death penalty not mentioned in connection with burning, stoning, or decapitation in the Pentateuch.

See CRIMINAL LAW AND PUNISHMENT.

Stream of Egypt. KJV designation for the Brook of Egypt in Isaiah 27:12.

See BROOK OF EGYPT.

Stringed Instrument. *See* MUSIC AND MUSICAL INSTRUMENTS.

Strong Drink. Any intoxicating liquor. It was forbidden to Levites who were entering the tent of meeting (Lv 10:9); to those taking the Nazirite vow (Nm 6:3; Jgs 13:4–14); to kings and rulers (Prv 31:4); and to John the Baptist (Lk 1:15). The writer of Proverbs 20:1 suggests that the wise man does not become intoxicated by it. Isaiah pronounces woe on those addicted to it (5:11,22). Strong drink was used as a libation in the levitical sacrifice (Nm 28:7) and was permitted in the menu of the feast at the time of tithing (Dt 14:26).

See WINE.

Stumbling Block. Term used both literally and figuratively to refer to anything which might cause one to stumble.

The phrase is used literally in Leviticus 19:14, where the people of Israel are admonished not to "put a stumbling block before the blind," but to "fear the Lord your God." An isolated figurative use occurs in Jeremiah 6:21, where God promises to put a stumbling block before the people of Israel if they do not heed his warnings.

The most common OT usage, however, is found in Ezekiel where the phrase is used to refer to idols and idolatry: "Son of man, these men have taken their idols into their hearts, and set the stumbling block of their iniquity before their faces; should I let myself be inquired of at all by them?" (14:3; also 7:19; 44:12).

In the NT the term essentially retains its Hebraic meaning. Even so, the phrase is employed figuratively to speak of the difficulties encountered by many Jews in believing Jesus to be the Son of God: "But we preach Christ crucified, a stumbling block to Jews and folly to Gentiles" (1 Cor 1:23; see also Rom 9:31,32). In Romans 11:11,12, Paul says that this resistance is actually part of God's plan to spread his riches to the world. Apparently Paul does not see this as a final exclusion of the Jews from God's purposes but rather hopes for their eventual inclusion.

Finally, 1 Corinthians 8:9 uses stumbling block to speak of some practices that might in themselves be appropriate but might also have the unintended effect of offending a weaker brother (see also Rom 14:13).

Stylus. Instrument used for writing characters on clay tablets (Jb 19:24; Jer 17:1; NASB).

See WRITING AND BOOKS.

Suah. Zophah's son, who was a leader in his father's household and a mighty warrior in Asher's tribe (1 Chr 7:36).

Sucathite. Family of scribes living at Jabez of Judah and descendants of the Kenites (1 Chr 2:55; KJV Suchathite).

Succoth. 1. Town in the Jordan Valley listed along with other towns in the inheritance of Gad (Jos 13:27). It is located in the fertile valley called Ghaur Abu 'Udeidah, known in the Bible as the Valley of Succoth (Ps 60:6; 108:7) and comprising the central por-

tion of the Jordan Valley on the eastern side, between the Wadi Rejeb and the Jabbok.

The place is mentioned for the first time in the account of Jacob's meeting with Esau, which occurred just south of Penuel. Jacob went from the meeting to Succoth and built booths for his cattle, which is given as the explanation for the name of the settlement (Gn 33:17). From Succoth, Jacob crossed the Jordan into Canaan (v 18).

The men of Succoth refused to give food to Gideon and his men when they were pursuing the Midianites (Jgs 8:5–9). Upon his return, Gideon made a point of punishing the elders of Succoth (vv 13–17). The form of social organization reflected in this passage has suggested that the population was not Israelite at the time of Gideon's visitation.

Finally, Succoth is mentioned with regard to Solomon's building projects. The metal casting for the important fixtures and implements of the temple were cast in the area between Succoth and Zarethan (1 Kgs 7:46; 2 Chr 4:17). It is possible that Succoth of the monarchial period was destroyed by Shishak of Egypt.

It has been proposed that the place name occurs in two other passages: as the staging area for David's forces in the battle with Ammon when the ark and the army were "dwelling in *booths (sukkoth)*" (2 Sm 11:11), and as the staging area for Ben-hadad's troops in his war against Samaria (1 Kgs 20:12,16).

Numerous sites in the immediate vicinity of the Jabbok have been proposed for Succoth. The Jerusalem Talmud (Sheviith 38 d) makes the equation of Succoth with Tar'alah; the latter place (which may appear in another rabbinic source as Dar'alah) is now Tell Deir 'Allah. In spite of some reservations on the part of the excavator, H. J. Franken, the identifica-

The site of ancient Succoth.

tion of Succoth with Tell Deir 'Allah still seems the most likely.

2. Town in Egypt mentioned as the first station of the Israelites in their exodus from Egypt (Ex 12:37; 13:20; Nm 33:5,6); it appears between Rameses and Etham.

Egyptian sources, texts of the Anastasi collection, refer to a place which is most likely the same as biblical Succoth. An Edomite tribe is recorded as bringing their herds in from the desert to pasture them in the delta, passing by the strongpoint at *T*kw (Papyrus Anastasi VI, 54). The military garrison there was commanded by a "commander of (archer)-troops and the fort was named after Pharaoh Mernephta (Papyrus Anastasi, VI, 55).

Scholarly opinion usually places Succoth (*T*kw) at Tell el-Maskhuta, a site near the mouth of the Wadi Tumeilat. The main period represented archaeologically in that site is much later according to recent excavations. The question of the exact geographical identification remains open but the linguistic equation of the Hebrew and the Egyptian names seems highly probable. Like neighboring Selle, Succoth evidently had a Semitic rather than an Egyptian name in the New Kingdom Period.

Succoth-benoth. Deity and shrine worshiped by Babylonians settled in Samaria by Assyria after the fall of Israel in 722 BC (2 Kgs 17:30). Various opinions exist as to the specific understanding of Succoth-benoth. Some suggest that it refers to a place of prostitution honoring a Babylonian deity or to a small structure housing female idols. Others suggest it refers to Sarpanitu, the consort of Marduk (a Babylonian deity), or to Marduk himself.

Suchathite. KJV spelling of Sucathite, a family of scribes, in 1 Chronicles 2:55.

See SUCATHITE.

Suffering. *See* AFFLICTION.

Suffering Servant. *See* SERVANT OF THE LORD, THE.

Sukkiim, Sukkiims. One of three peoples who joined forces with King Shishak of Egypt and entered Palestine to wage war against King Rehoboam of Judah (930–913 BC). The Sukkiim are mentioned with the Libyans and the Ethiopians (2 Chr 12:3; KJV Sukkiims). They were probably a Libyan people.

Sulfur. *See* BRIMSTONE; MINERALS, METALS, AND PRECIOUS STONES.

Sun. A creation of God appointed as one of the great lights in the heavens, "to rule over

the day" (Gn 1:14,15). The new day begins with its setting and the daily sacrifices were offered in accordance with its position: the first burnt offering with its rising (Ex 29:39; Nm 28:4). The hours of the day in rabbinic Judaism vary with the length of the solar day throughout the year.

The months in the Israelite year were determined by the moon, but the fact that the major festivals fell in the fall (Trumpets, Atonement, Tabernacles) and the spring (Passover) show that account was taken of the solar year. The Gezer calendar has 12 months according to the agricultural activities of the solar year. The Jewish calendar is based on a 19-year cycle in which extra months are added to seven of the years thus harmonizing the lunar and solar cycles. Silence in the Bible about this system has led scholars to assume the intercalation of a 13th month was a late innovation. However, Aramaic documents from the Jewish colony at Elephantine show that in the 5th century BC the Jews there were using the 19-year cycle in their reckonings. It is probable that the monarchies of Judah and Israel were using a system of intercalation even though documentary evidence is lacking.

Rabbinic Judaism recognizes four seasons while the OT usually mentions only two, "seedtime and harvest, cold and heat, summer and winter" (Gn 8:22). The four seasons are marked by phases of the sun. The fall (called *Stav*, a word originally meaning rainy season, rain; Sg 2:11) begins with the equinox; the winter (*Horeph*) begins with the winter solstice (c. Dec 22); the spring (*Aviv*) begins with the spring equinox (Mar 21); and the summer (*qaiṣ*) begins with the summer solstice (Jun 22). Recently, a temple was discovered at Beersheba, dating to the Hasmonean period (125 BC) which was oriented toward the sunrise of the summer solstice. A temple at Lachish with a similar ground plan and date seems to be oriented toward the winter solstice. The Arad temple from monarchial times faced almost due east, probably toward the equinox sunrise; such was probably the case with the Jerusalem temple.

The sun also plays a role in Hebrew poetic imagery. It was said to have a habitation (Hb 3:11), a tent set up by the Lord out of which he comes like a bridegroom (Ps 19:4,5). The sun is a symbol of constancy (72:5,17), of the Law (19:7), of the presence of God (84:11), and of beauty (Sg 6:10).

A time of chaos and wrath upon the earth will be marked by the darkening of the sun (Is 13:10; Ez 32:7; Jl 2:10,31; 3:15; Zep 1:15; Mt 24:29; Rv 8:12). This is obviously an allusion to an eclipse, something viewed with terror by the ancients. The sun's turning pale may also be derived from the effect of the sirocco, when sand storms and hazy clouds often darken the sky. On the other hand, the day of the Lord's victory will be characterized by the sun's shining sevenfold brighter than at present (Is 30:26).

Life in this temporal world is that which is "under the sun" according to Qoheleth (Eccl 1:3,9,14; 2:11) That is not a late Greek concept but rather is known from 5th-century Phoenician inscriptions.

The sun was worshiped in Mesopotamia under the Sumerian name Utu and the Semitic name Shamash. It was a male deity, the god of law and justice. King Hammurabi claimed to have received his code of laws from Shamash. He had cult places in northern and southern Mesopotamia and in Asshur, capital of Assyria. In the pantheon he was son of the moon goddess Nanna-Sin and the brother of Inanna-Ishtar.

In Egypt the sun was honored as a world deity. His principal name was Re but he was also identified with Horus of the Horizon. The kings of Egypt were considered to be his sons. He was the king of the gods and in the days of the Middle Kingdom (first half of the 2nd millennium BC) he was identified with the national god, Amon. The religious reform of Pharaoh Amenhotep IV (Akhnaton) brought an exclusive emphasis on the worship of the sun disk, called Aton, at the expense of the Amon cult and all other deities.

Anatolia had more than one solar deity, especially the sun goddess of Arinna and a sun god of the daytime.

The peoples of the Levant knew the sun as both a male and female deity. Most languages preserve the common Semitic name Shamash, for example, among the Amorites, Aramaeans, and Hebrews. However, some Northwest Semitic dialects have a variant form, Shapash. Personal names attest the presence of this deity in the Levantine pantheon from the second millennium BC, but there is no doubt that it was worshiped much earlier.

In Ugaritic literature, the sun is Shapash, a female "luminary of the gods," as she is called. She plays a minor but interesting role in the literary texts. She helps 'Anat look for Baal and when he is found she loads him on 'Anat's shoulder. When news comes of Baal's death at the hands of Mot (god of death), the sun becomes livid, a reference to the pale sky of a winter sirocco.

Shamash/Shemesh is known as an element in place-names from the Middle and Late Bronze ages. Biblical towns such as Bethshemesh, "house of the sun," testify to pre-Israelite shrines for sun worship in the north (Jos 19:38), center (v 22), and south (v 41, Ir-shemesh).

Sun worship in ancient Israel was not one of the dominant forms like the Baal cult, but it did find its way into the life of the people. Like all foreign religious practices it was forbidden (Dt 4:19 et al.), but it was a common temptation (Jb 31:26,27) for the individual to adore the sun and the moon.

The cult of the sun received special emphasis under Manasseh (2 Kgs 21:3,5). It is a subject of controversy whether or not this was a political act expressing his subservience to Assyria. Such does not seem to be the case; Asshur, the national deity of Assyria, was not really a solar deity though the sun disk was a frequent Assyrian symbol. Manasseh's immediate successors continued the sun cult (Jer 8:2), and even after the stringent reforms of King Josiah (2 Kgs 23:5) some traces of sun worship survived on the popular level (Ez 8:16). Except for the place names mentioned above, the main references to sun worship are from the 7th century BC. Special reference is made to models of horses and chariots displayed at the entrance to the Jerusalem temple (2 Kgs 23:11). One is reminded of the usual view among neighboring countries that the sun rode a chariot across the sky.

The subjection of the sun as a purely created being to the God of Israel stands behind such passages as the song by Joshua about the sun's standing still to give victory to the forces of Israel in battle (Jos 10:12,13).

Royal emblems on jar handles from the end of the 8th century BC have been interpreted as representations of a winged sun disk but the design is not very clear. The symbolism of this design is unknown; it seems to have replaced the winged scarab of the other royal seals and was itself replaced later by a neutral rosetta design.

ANSON F. RAINEY

See CALENDARS, ANCIENT AND MODERN; ASTRONOMY; MOON; DAY.

Sun, City of the. Phrase in Isaiah 19:18; generally taken as a reference to Heliopolis.

See HELIOPOLIS.

Sun, Worship of the. See SUN.

Sunday. See LORD'S DAY, THE.

Sun Dial. Instrument used for telling time installed by King Ahaz of Judah (737–715 BC) in the royal palace of Jerusalem. Some suggest that this time indicator was not a sundial but a stairway. The time of day was determined by the position of the shadow of some object cast on the stairs. At Isaiah's command, the Lord miraculously caused the shadow to recede 10 steps, divinely confirming to King Hezekiah of

Judah (715–686 BC) that he would recover from his illness, live 15 more years, and be delivered from the Assyrian threat (2 Kgs 20:11; Is 38:8).

Suph. Region mentioned in Deuteronomy 1:1 to help identify the place from which Moses gave his Deuteronomic addresses. The text records the place as "beyond the Jordan in the wilderness, in the Arabah over against Suph." The exact location of Suph is uncertain. It may refer to the region of Suphah (cf. Nm 4:14), east of the Jordan River, or perhaps to the Gulf of Aqaba (cf. Dt 1:1 KJV), the northeastern branch of the Red Sea.

Suphah. Place east of the Jordan in the land of Moab (Nm 21:14); translated as "Red Sea" by the KJV. Its exact identification is uncertain.

See WAHEB.

Supper. *See* FAMILY LIFE AND RELATIONS; FOOD AND FOOD PREPARATION.

Supper, Lord's. *See* LORD'S SUPPER, THE.

Supplication. *See* PRAYER.

Sur, Gate of. Gate in Jerusalem linking the king's palace to the temple. It is mentioned in 2 Kings 11:6 in connection with the enthronement of Jehoash over Judah and the murder of Athaliah. Its parallel passage in 2 Chronicles 23:5 reads the "Gate of the Foundation," revealing perhaps a corruption within the Hebrew text.

See JERUSALEM.

Surgery. *See* MEDICINE AND MEDICAL PRACTICE.

Susa. Capital of the non-Semitic people and district of Elam. Susa (modern Shūsh, KJV Shushan) is located in southwest Iran, about 150 miles north of the Persian Gulf and due east of

An aerial view of Susa.

the well-known city of Babylon. French archaeologists have been excavating the site since 1884, discovering that it was occupied as long ago as about 4000 BC. Its importance in the OT derives mainly from the fact that it was incorporated into the Persian Empire founded by Cyrus in 550 BC. It became a royal city along with Ecbatana (the other main city in Elam), Babylon, and Persepolis. This was the great period of importance for Susa, although it had known an earlier golden age in the 12th century BC. (The first copy found of the law code of Hammurabi was discovered at Susa, dated in the 12th century BC.)

The center of Persian Susa was an acropolis or citadel which rose above the city as a rectangular platform surrounded by a massive wall. This was the royal quarter within which the palace stood. The palace was the winter residence of the Persian kings.

Nehemiah was a cupbearer at the palace of Susa in the reign of Artaxerxes I (Neh 1:1,11; 2:1). In Esther 1:2 and 2:8 the young Jewess Esther was introduced to the court of King Ahasuerus, who was evidently the Persian king Xerxes (485–465 BC). Most of the action of the narrative of the book takes place in Susa (cf. 3:15; 8:14,15; 9:6–18).

In Ezra 4:9 mention is made of the Susa of an earlier period. "The men of Susa" (KJV Susanchites) are included in a list of people who were deported to the west from their homelands by "Osnappar," the Assyrian king Ashurbanipal (669–633 BC).

According to Daniel 8:2, the place of Daniel's vision is Susa. Probably Daniel is not to be regarded as having been there literally, but rather he was spiritually transported there in the vision. Chronologically Daniel's vision is set at the end of the Babylonian period just before the Persian conquest (8:1; cf. 7:1). At this time Susa controlled the Medians and was not subject to Babylon. The reference in 8:27 to his performing his duties for the king shortly after the vision implies that Daniel received it at a place within the Babylonian sphere of influence. The visionary transportation to Media corresponds well to the mention of Media in verse 20. It was presumably the reference to Susa that gave rise to the still current Muslim tradition that Daniel was buried there.

See PERSIA, PERSIANS.

Susanchite. KJV translation for "men of Susa" in Ezra 4:9.

See SUSA.

Susanna. One of the women who ministered to Jesus out of her own resources (Lk 8:3).

Susi. Gaddi's father from Manasseh's tribe. Gaddi was one of the 12 spies sent to search out the land of Canaan (Nm 13:11).

Swallow. *See* BIRDS.

Swan. *See* BIRDS.

Sweet Cane. *See* PLANTS (CANE).

Sweet Storax. Small stiff-branched tree from which stacte was extracted for making incense (Ex 30:34).

> *See* PLANTS (STORAX TREE).

Swine. *See* ANIMALS (PIG).

Sword, Swordsman. *See* ARMS AND WARFARE; TRADES AND OCCUPATIONS (SOLDIER).

Sycamine. Black mulberry tree, valued for its fruit (Lk 17:6).

> *See* PLANTS (MULBERRY).

Sycamore. Large, spreading tree bearing a figlike fruit (1 Kgs 10:27; Lk 19:4).

> *See* PLANTS.

Sychar. Town in Samaria, mentioned in the Bible only in John 4:5. Generally the name has been taken as a variant form of the Greek transliteration of the Hebrew name *Shechem.* Many scholars favor an identification with the present-day village of Askar, which is located at the southeast foot of Mt Ebal, about one-half mile north of Jacob's well. Excavations appear to favor the Shechem identification, which was proposed by Jerome. The Babylonian Talmud refers to a place called Sichar or Suchar, but its location is not known.

Sychar is said to be "near the field that Jacob gave to his son Joseph" (Jn 4:5). The record of the giving of this parcel of land is recorded in Genesis 48:22. When Jacob had concluded the blessing of Joseph's two sons, Manasseh and Ephraim, he told Joseph that he had given to him rather than to his brothers "one mountain slope which I took from the hand of the Amorites with my sword and with my bow." The Hebrew word translated "slope" is the word for shoulder and the name of the city of Shechem. It was on this piece of property that Joseph was buried (Jos 24:32). This passage also states that Jacob bought the ground "from the sons of Hamor the father of Shechem for a hundred pieces of silver" (cf. Gn 33:19; Acts 7:16).

The account of Jesus' visit to Sychar in John 4 is important. Jesus came to Sychar because of a spiritual, not geographical, imperative (v 4). One of the objectives of this mission was to break down barriers: the hostility between the racially pure Jew and the mongrel Samaritan (v 9); the social restrictions between men and women (v 27); the societal separation between the ritually clean and the morally impure (this woman was ostracized; she came to the well alone and at an unusual time, v 6). The conversation between Jesus and the woman is instructive as to personal witness. The spiritual discernment and compassion of Jesus are evident. When the woman received the testimony of his identity as the Messiah, she too became a witness, hesitant and perhaps uncertain, but effective (vv 28–30). At Sychar the disciples received instruction concerning priority, time, work, and rewards (vv 31–38).

Sychar, with Mt Gerizim
in the background.

The new believers among the Samaritans asked Jesus to stay with them, so he remained for two days and many more believed in him (vv 39–41).

Sychem. KJV form of Shechem in Acts 7:16.

See SHECHEM (PLACE).

Syene. Southern Egyptian village (modern Aswan) demarcating Egypt's border with Ethiopia. The Hebrew form possibly derives from a word for "market" or "trading center," reflecting the importance of the outpost as a place of commerce. The remote location of Syene (KJV Land of Sinim) made it a useful geographical reference for designating the full span of Egypt's borders. "From Migdol to Syene" (Ez 29:10; 30:6) describes Egypt from northern delta to southern border (cf. Israel's description, "From Dan to Beersheba," 1 Sm 3:20; 1 Kgs 4:25). Syene was located on the east bank of the Nile just north of the first cataract. While valued by the Egyptians as a source of granite, Syene's fate was closely tied to Elephantine Island nearby. Elephantine was South Egypt's administrative center and was well fortified against attack. It was at Elephantine that Jews fleeing Judea in 587 BC found refuge and formed a colony.

Synagogue. Transliteration of the Greek word *synagōgē,* meaning "a gathering together." It is used more than 50 times in the NT, mostly for the religious gathering places of Jewish communities in Palestine and throughout the dispersion. The word *synagōgē* is usually the Greek rendering of Hebrew words in the OT that speak of the assembling or assembly of the people. Only in one place is the word "synagogue" used in some English translations of the OT (Ps 74:8 KJV). Psalm 74 speaks essentially of the destruction of the temple, and probably verse 8 is probably better translated "every place where God was worshiped in the land" (NIV). It is doubtful whether the synagogue had been developed at the time when the psalm was written.

Origins and Early History. It is unknown just how or when the synagogue as an institution first began. One can imagine the situation in Jerusalem after the destruction of the temple by the Babylonians in 586 BC. The people who remained in and around the city who wanted to keep true to their faith, would have felt the need to meet for worship, where they would continue to teach the Law and the message of the prophets. Some think, therefore, that synagogues may have had their origin in such a situation. Jewish people in the various places of the dispersion would have been aware of a similar need. Jewish elders met together with Ezekiel in exile in Babylon (Ez 8:1; 14:1; 20:1). Yet there is no positive evidence of actual synagogues at this early stage. In Nehemiah 8:1–8 the postexilic community gathered in Jerusalem and "Ezra the scribe . . . the priest" brought the Law, read it from a "wooden pulpit," "gave the sense so that the people understood the reading" and, as "Ezra blessed the Lord," "the people bowed their heads and worshiped." These were the basic elements of what came to be synagogue worship. The first undisputed evidence of a synagogue comes from Egypt in the 3rd century BC. From the 1st century BC onwards the evidence of synagogues is abundant.

Synagogues in NT Times. The Gospels give the impression of many synagogues existing throughout Palestine. Jesus frequently taught in synagogues (e.g., Mt 4:23; 9:35), especially in relation to his Galilean ministry but

Column supporting the upper section of the synagogue at Chorazin.

probably in Judea as well. In John 18:20 are the words of Jesus in his trial before the high priest: "I have spoken openly in the world; I have always taught in synagogues and in the temple, where all Jews come together."

The Acts of the Apostles refers to synagogues in Jerusalem (6:9), Damascus (9:2), Cyprus (13:5), the Roman province of Galatia (13:14; 14:1), Macedonia and Greece (17:1,10,17; 18:4), and Ephesus in the province of Asia (19:8). Paul made it his practice to go directly to the synagogue and to preach there as long as he was given freedom to do so.

Synagogue Worship. The Gospels and the Acts of the Apostles give abundant evidence for the meeting of Jewish people on the sabbath to worship in the synagogue. People also met for worship on the 2nd and 5th days of the week. Luke provides us with the earliest description of a synagogue service. The Mishna states that the pattern of the synagogue service involved: the confession of faith, the Shema, which included Deuteronomy 6:4–9; 11:13–21; and Numbers 15:37–41; prayer (such as the Eighteen Benedictions); Scripture reading (the reading of the Law was basic, see Acts 15:21, and was read according to a 3-year cycle; the prophets were also read, but more at random); interpretation (as the knowledge of biblical Hebrew diminished in Palestine, an Aramaic translation of the Scriptures was presented after the reading in Hebrew, and in the dispersion a Greek translation); address (following the reading anyone suitably qualified might address the people, as Jesus and the apostle Paul often did) and blessing.

Judicial Functions. Administration of justice was also part of the work of the synagogue. Offenders against the Law and those whose actions were held to be contrary to Jewish religion were brought before the elders of the synagogue. They might, under extreme circumstances, excommunicate an offender (see Jn 9:22,34,35; 12:42) or have him scourged. Jesus warned his disciples to be prepared to face either possibility (Mt 10:17; Jn 16:2). Saul, as persecutor of the Christians, had "letters to the synagogues at Damascus," giving authority to arrest Christians and "bring them bound to Jerusalem" (Acts 9:2). In Acts 22:19 he speaks of causing them to be both beaten and imprisoned. Paul himself received the 39 lashes that were administered in the synagogues (2 Cor 11:24).

Teaching of the Law. The reading of the Law was of central significance in synagogue worship. The teaching of the Law to people generally, and especially to children, was intimately associated with the synagogue. Either the synagogue building or a school was used.

Organization. The NT refers in particular (e.g., Mk 5:22; Lk 13:14; Acts 18:8,17) to two appointments in the synagogue: the "ruler of the synagogue" who was responsible for order and for selection of the Scripture reader, and an attendant (Lk 4:20) who brought out and put away the Scripture scrolls and also inflicted corporal punishment. Later on there was a person appointed as leader of the prayers.

Architecture. In structure the temple seems to have been taken as a model for the synagogue. It was built when possible on high ground, and often constructed so that the people could sit facing the direction of Jerusalem. There was a portable chest for the scrolls of the Law and the Prophets, and a platform for the reading of the Scriptures and for preaching. Men and women sat apart. Jesus spoke of the way the scribes loved the "chief seats" facing the people (Mk 12:39). Many synagogues had ornamentation of vine leaves, seven-branched candlesticks, the paschal lamb, and the pot of manna. Early synagogues also had a genizah, which was a cellar or attic where worn scrolls were put, because, as they bore the name of God, they were too sacred to be destroyed.

FRANCIS FOULKES

See JUDAISM; RULER OF THE SYNAGOGUE.

Bibliography. C.W. Dugmore, *The Influence of the Synagogue upon the Divine Office;* J. Gutman, *The Dura-Europos Synagogue;* L.A. Hoffman, *The Canonization of the Synagogue Service;* L.I. Levine (ed.), *Ancient Synagogues Revealed;* I. Levy, *The Synagogue: Its History and Function;* W.O.E. Oesterley and G.H. Box, *The Religion and Worship of the Synagogue;* E.L. Sukenik, *Ancient Synagogues in Palestine and Greece.*

Synoptic Gospels.

Term applied to Matthew, Mark, and Luke because they see the ministry of Jesus from generally the same point of view, which is quite different from that of the Gospel of John.

The similarities among these three Gospels include their use of a common outline: introduction; ministry of John the Baptist and the baptism and temptation of Jesus; greater Galilean ministry; journey and ministry through Samaria, Perea, and rural Judea; and passion week, death, and resurrection of Jesus in Jerusalem. They also record the same emphasis in the teaching of Jesus—the presence, nature, and implementation of the kingdom of God. Furthermore, these three Gospels relate much of the same material, usually in the same order, and often with similar or identical words.

In addition to similarities there are also striking differences between Matthew, Mark, and Luke. These fall into the same general categories as do the similarities—outline, material, organization, and wording. Matthew and Luke also have considerable common material not found in Mark which, save for the healing of the centurion's slave, is composed exclusively of words and teachings of Jesus. Each Gospel also contains accounts and teachings that are unique. The result is a rich diversity within the synoptic unity which provides portrayals of Jesus from a variety of viewpoints. Matthew emphasizes Jesus' Jewishness and the continuity of his person and work with the OT. Mark's fast-moving account presents Jesus as a man of action, the Son of God who was a servant among men. Luke, in exquisite Greek literary style, seems to address cultured Gentiles and shows Jesus as a friend of disadvantaged groups.

Attempts to account for *both* the similarities and differences within these Gospels constitute the "synoptic problem." Solutions have been sought in many ways. As early as the 2nd century Tatian combined the four accounts into one; additional "harmonies" of the Gospel accounts have been continually produced. Since the 17th century scholars have attempted to account for the similarities and differences by examining the stages through which the Gospel material is assumed to have passed before coming into its present form. Form criticism attempts to identify the influences from the period of oral transmission; source or literary criticism considers the alleged written documents from which the evangelists drew information; redaction (or editorial) criticism seeks to determine the nature of purposes and personalities of the final editor-authors upon the accounts of the activities and teachings of Jesus. Other suggestions have called attention to the adaptation of material for a specific audience, the similarities between the synoptic accounts of Jesus' teachings and the parallel accounts of those of the Jewish rabbis in the Talmud, and more. No completely satisfactory solution to the synoptic problem is at hand. The fact remains that the Scriptures present Jesus in various perspectives; the conscientious reader must seek the divine purpose of both the similarities and the differences of these proclamations of "the good news of Jesus Christ, the Son of God" (Mk 1:1).

J. JULIUS SCOTT, JR.

See MATTHEW, GOSPEL OF; MARK, GOSPEL OF; LUKE, GOSPEL OF; SOURCE CRITICISM; REDACTION CRITICISM; FORM CRITICISM; GOSPEL.

Bibliography. W.R. Farmer, *The Synoptic Problem;* K.F. Nickle, *The Synoptic Gospels;* J.H. Ropes, *The Synoptic Gospels;* W. Sanday (ed.), *Studies in the Synoptic Problem;* E.F. Scott, *The Validity of the Gospel Record;* B.H. Streeter, *The Four Gospels;* V. Taylor, *The Formation of the Gospel Tradition;* B.F. Westcott, *Introduction to the Study of the Gospels.*

Synoptic Problem. *See* SYNOPTIC GOSPELS.

Syntyche. Woman encouraged by Paul to reconcile her differences with Euodia. Syntyche worked with Paul in proclaiming the gospel and evidently held a position of leadership in the Philippian church (Phil 4:2).

Syracuse. Town on the east coast of Sicily and the island's most important city. Here Paul's ship, on which he traveled to Rome as a prisoner, made a 3-day stop following his shipwreck and 3-month stay in Malta (Acts 28:12). Syracuse had a fine harbor and was a natural port of call for a ship sailing from Malta through the straits of Messina between Sicily and Italy en route to Rome.

In the 8th century BC Syracuse became a Greek colony, founded by Archias of Corinth. During the 5th century it grew to great power and influence, and was second only to Carthage as the most prominent city of the western Mediterranean. It played a significant role in the struggle between Rome and Carthage in the 3rd century, and was captured by Rome in 212 BC. Caesar Augustus settled Syracuse in 21 BC, making it a Roman colony (cf. Philippi). It is not stated in Acts 28 that Paul found Christians there, but later evidence from its catacombs indicates the existence of a church.

Syria, Syrians. Terms used in the Septuagint and in some English translations to render the names *Aram, Aramaeans.*

Geography. The area occupied by the Syrians (Aramaeans) was approximately the same as that occupied by the modern states of Syria and Lebanon, though not until Roman times was there a geographical entity known as Syria, one of the Roman provinces. The Aramaeans (Syrians) comprised a variety of small states such as Damascus, Bit-adini, Yahan, Bit-agusi, Hattina, Ya'di (Sam'al), Hamath, Zobah, Tob, Maacah, Beth-rehob, and others.

The region contains important mountains.

Pillars of the temple of Jupiter at Baalbek, Lebanon.

To the west lies the high Lebanon and Anti-Lebanon ranges between which flow, in the south, the upper waters of the Jordan River and the Litani River while in the north the Orontes River takes its rise and flows north. In the northwest lie the Amanus mountains. To the extreme south the Djabel Druze, a large volcanic outcrop, is situated. No other high mountains occur although there are some moderately high areas north and southwest of Palmyra. Around Damascus there exists a fine oasis fed by the Barada River, which rises in the Anti-Lebanon Mountains, and various smaller streams to the east and north of the city. To the east lies the Euphrates River, which has provided irrigation over the centuries. Several of the small Aramaean kingdoms were found in the neighborhood of the river and its tributaries. The whole region is bounded on the south by desert which merges into the Arabian desert. Cultivation of crops has been carried on over the centuries in the region of the rivers.

History of the Aramaeans. According to the table of nations in Genesis 10:22,23 the Aramaeans were a Semitic group, descendants of Shem. Another genealogy in chapter 22:20,21 makes Aram a descendant of Nahor. According to Amos 9:7 the Aramaeans (Syrians) came from Kir which is linked with Elam in Isaiah 22:66. The exile of the Aramaeans to Kir (2 Kgs 16:9; Am 1:5) may suggest they were to go back to their original home. The precise origins of this group of people are, however, lost in antiquity. When they emerged clearly into history they were settled round the central Euphrates from which they were spread out east, west, and north. Accepting the biblical record about the patriarchs, the Aramaeans were established in upper Mesopotamia in the first part of the 2nd millennium BC. Bethuel and Laban were known as Aramaeans (Gn 25:20; 28:1–7); the home of Bethuel was in Paddan-aram (25:20). The prophet Hosea recalls the tradition by noting that Jacob fled to "the field of Aram" (Hos 12:12) or "Aram-naharaim" (Aram of the two rivers) which was the northern part of Mesopotamia between the Euphrates and Tigris. It is of some interest that the first oppressor of Israel in the days of the judges (Jgs 3:8,10), about 1200 BC, was Cushan-rishathaim from Aram-naharaim. The stone heap set up as a witness to the agreement between Jacob and Laban (Gn 31:47) was named in Hebrew *Galeed* (Gilead). The Aramaic equivalent is added—*Yegar sahadutha* (Jegarsahadutha). In the credal confession in Deuteronomy 26:5 the Israelite who brought his first fruits confessed, "My father [probably Jacob] was a wandering Aramaean."

The name Aram occurs on an inscription of Naram-sin of Akkad as early as the 22nd century BC. In about 2000 BC documents from Drehem, a city on the Lower Tigris, mention Aram as a personal name. Aram occurs as a personal name in the Mari texts (18th century BC), Alalakh tablets (17th century BC), and from Ugarit (14th century BC). The name occurs in a geographical list of Amenophis III (c. 1403–1364 BC) and also on an Egyptian frontier report from the days of Merenptah (c. 1220 BC). None of these references provides much detail. Important texts from the days of Tiglath-pileser I of Assyria (1116–1076 BC) refer to the Ahlame-armaya. Evidently the Ahlame were the same as the Aramaeans. If that is so, the Ahlame were known in the Persian Gulf area in the early 14th century BC. There is some variation in the use of the name because the successor to Tiglath-pileser I, Ashur-bel-kala, refers to both Ahlame and Aramaeans. Perhaps they were related nomadic groups.

Probably the best early evidence is that of Tiglath-pileser I. In his annals of his 4th year (1112 BC) he speaks of a campaign among the Ahlame-armaya on the Middle Euphrates and the sacking of 6 Aramaean villages in the Mt Bishri area. These Aramaeans offered resistance to the Assyrians who mounted many campaigns into their area. Clearly the Aramaeans were already settled in the area to the southeast of the big bend in the Euphrates at that time. They were in the region of Mt Lebanon, in the area of Tadmor, south along the Euphrates to Anat in the land of Sutu, and as far south as Rapiqu not far from Babylon. They even penetrated into Assyria proper and an Aramaean usurper even seized the throne of Babylon.

Certainly by the end of the 2nd millennium BC and at the beginning of the 1st millennium BC (i.e., in the years just before and just after 1000 BC), a group of Aramaean states appeared—Bit-adini (Beth-eden of Am 1:5), Bit-bahyan (capital Gozan, 2 Kgs 17:6), Bit-halupe on the lower Habur River, Laqe, Hindan, and Sahu on the Middle Euphrates, Bit-zamani further north in northern Mesopotamia, while the states of Bit-amukkani, Bit-dakuri and Bit-yakin appeared in the lower Euphrates area. The Aramaeans of upper Mesopotamia became important in biblical history. Two states in particular were important for the people of Israel—Aram-zobah in the days of David and Aram-damascus from the days of Solomon onwards.

By about 1100 BC the Aramaean tribes had spread throughout Syria and had expanded into northern Transjordan, where they came into conflict with the Israelites. In this southwestern area of Syria the kingdom of Zobah became a focal point for several small Aramaean states called "the kings of Zobah" (1 Sm 14:47). A famous leader of this group was Hadadezer ben Rehob (2 Sm 8:3). Hadadezer seems to have amalgamated a small kingdom (Beth-rehob) with Zobah to the north of it. At his peak Hadedezer embraced several vassals such as Damascus, Maacah, and Tob (10:6). He could not conquer Hamath to the north (8:9,10), although he had some influence in Ammon (10:6). King David of Israel encountered Hadadezer during the early years of the 10th century BC. David was victorious over the Aramaean and Ammonite forces (vv 6–8; 1 Chr 19:6–8). Later the Israelites had another success at Helam (2 Sm 10:15,16; 1 Chr 19:16–19) and finally David's army penetrated deep into central Syria so that he was able to bring back a considerable quantity of booty (2 Sm 8:3,4; 1 Chr 18:3,4). Though this ended the Zobah coalition, the power of the Aramaeans was by no means at an end. Aram-damascus replaced Aram-zobah as the dominant power on Israel's northeastern border. This kingdom was founded in the last days of Solomon by Rezon ben Eliadah who had fled from Hadadezer king of Zobah and become leader of a marauding band and occupied Damascus. He became an opponent of Solomon (1 Kgs 11:23–25). During the 9th and 8th centuries BC Aram-damascus became the most important Aramaean state in Syria until it was finally destroyed by Assyria.

Events in Israel and Judah had some bearing on Damascus. After the death of Solomon, when the formerly united kingdom became divided into Judah and Israel, tension arose between the two small states. War broke out between Baasha of Israel and Asa of Judah in the years 890–880 BC. Damascus saw a way to exploit both parties. Asa induced Ben-hadad, son of Tab-rimmon, the son of Hezion, to support him. Tab-rimmon was once an ally of Asa's father Abijah of Judah. Soon after Ben-hadad of Damascus allied with Baasha of Israel and subsequently a military pact was proposed between Ben-hadad and Judah (1 Kgs 15:20), which led to a war in which Ben-hadad seized areas in eastern Galilee from Israel, "Ijon, Dan, Abel-beth-maachah, and all Chinneroth, with all the land of Napthali." Clearly the Aramaeans of Damascus and their ruler Ben-hadad were gaining control over Israel. Lands in Transjordan changed hands several times. The successors of Omri of Israel, namely Ahab, Ahaziah, Jehoram, Jehu, Jehoahaz, and Jehoash had many conflicts with Damascus. Ahab fought Ben-hadad and his 32 allies who besieged Samaria (20:1–21), but Israel defeated him. A second time Ben-hadad entered Israelite territory and reached Aphek, but was again defeated and captured (vv 23–30). As a consequence of his defeat and for the

price of his release he was obliged to make bazaars available in Damascus for Israelite trade (v 34). After three years of peace between Israel and Damascus hostilities broke out again and resulted in a battle in the region of Ramoth-gilead in which Ahab was killed (22:1–38).

In the intervening years it seems likely that Damascus and Israel forgot their private dispute to join a defensive coalition which opposed the Assyrians under Shalmaneser III (859–825 BC). On the Orontes an indecisive battle (of Qarqar) was fought. Assyria did not return to aggressive campaigns for five years; however, Assyria's momentary weakness gave Israel and Damascus the chance to fight their third war. Hazael replaced Ben-hadad (2 Kgs 8:7–15) and clashed with Ahab's son Joram at Ramoth-gilead (vv 25–29). The western alliance against Assyria was over and in the years 841 and 838 BC Shalmaneser III defeated Aram-damascus, destroying plantations and orchards and pressing on south to areas around Galilee. He followed this up by occupying Israelite territory east of the Jordan (10:32,33). He even raided western Israel (13:7, 22) in the days of Jehoahaz and reached the borders of Judah, which was forced to pay heavy tribute (12:17,18); many atrocities were committed by the Aramaeans in Gilead (Am 1:3–5). Israel was saved from further hostile Aramaean acts when Adad-nirari III came to the throne of Assyria and renewed campaigns against the Aramaeans in Syria in 805–802 BC, primarily against Damascus. This man was the "savior" of Israel referred to in 2 Kings 13:5. Relieved of Aramaean attacks, Joash king of Israel was able to win back lands in Transjordan lost by his father Jehoahaz (vv 24,25). Jeroboam II (793–753 BC) pressed his advantage and freed all of Transjordan and even extended Israelite territory toward Hamath (14:25,28). The Aramaeans were nearing dissolution although Rezin, a vassal of the Assyrian Tiglath-pilezer III (745–727 BC), annexed Transjordan as far south as Ramoth-gilead and even reached Elath on the Red Sea (16:6), thus threatening Judah. Judah's King Ahaz appealed to Tiglath-pileser for help. He responded and crushed Aram-damascus in 733–732 BC (v 9), dividing its lands into several provinces. The prophets of Judah spoke about the judgment on Aram-damascus (Is 17:1–3; Jer 49:23–27; Am 1:3–5).

Syria After the Collapse of the Aramaean Kingdoms. After the collapse of Aram-damascus in 733–732 BC the political character of the whole region changed. Over the centuries that followed and on into Christian times the region passed under the control of several great powers and no independent Aramaean state survived. When Assyria collapsed in 612–609 BC the region came under Babylonian control, but only for a comparatively short period. With the rise of Cyrus the Persian, the Syrian region was quickly overrun by Persian armies. Palestine, Asia Minor, and Egypt were absorbed into the Persian Empire at the same time. The Persians divided their domains into a series of large provinces called *satrapies* (a *satrap* was a protector of the kingdom), each of which was divided into smaller areas. Governors were appointed to control both the large satrapy and the small provinces. Thus Darius I (521–486 BC) had 23 *satrapies*, although these were reorganized from time to time. Most of Syria fell into the *satrapy* of "Beyond the River" along with the Palestine area (Ezr 4:11, 5:6; 6:6). By that time the ancient Aramaean kingdoms had been amalgamated with larger units and were absorbed politically and culturally into these newer political entities.

The next significant political change which affected the region came with the appearance of Philip of Macedon in 360 BC. His son Alexander the Great (336–323 BC) consolidated Greek power throughout western Asia and as far as the borders of India. On his death in 323 BC at the age of 33, the control of western Asia passed to Alexander's generals. After a settling down period General Seleucus I (312–280 BC) controlled the southern half of Asia Minor, the region of Syria, Mesopotamia, and eastward to the borders of India. Syria thus fell under the influence of Hellenist rulers, the Seleucids, who founded a new capital at Antioch.

Further west Rome was rising to power and cast her eyes eastward. It was General Pompey who overcame Mithridates, the young king of Pontus, and moved to crush the remnants of the kingdom of the Seleucids. The western parts of Syria were formed into a Roman province in 64 BC. Pompey finally moved into Palestine, which came under Roman control in 63 BC.

A few years earlier, through Roman policy, Damascus had become the capital of an independent Nabataean kingdom (85 BC) under Aretas III. When the Romans conquered Syria, Damascus came under a Nabataean governor. At the time of Paul's conversion, there were many Jews living in Damascus as well as a Christian group (9:2; 22:5,6,10,11; 26:12). It was on that occasion that Paul was lowered over the wall in a basket to escape from the Jews who plotted to kill him (9:23,24). The city was under a governor of King Aretas the Nabataean (2 Cor 11:32). The Jewish community at Damascus was only one of many Jewish groups in Syria at the time. The Roman emperor

Trajan (AD 98–117) later joined Damascus to the Roman province of Syria.

The Roman province of Syria included Cilicia, a strip of territory in the southeastern corner of Asia Minor. The northern boundary reached to the Euphrates River. The boundary then swung south well to the east of Damascus and then turned west about half-way down the Dead Sea and continued west to the Mediterranean Sea. Syria was bound to the west by the Mediterranean up the the Gulf of Alexandretta where it turned west. The province of Syria and Silicia (Acts 15:23,41; Gal 1:21) was governed by an imperial legate (*legatus*) who commanded a strong force of legionary troops. One such governor, Quirinius, governed Syria at the time of the census of Caesar Augustus which brought Joseph and Mary to Bethlehem for the birth of Jesus (Lk 2:2).

In the following centuries the population of Damascus was christianized and Christianity spread throughout the Roman province of Syria, giving rise to the Old Syrian Church which remains to this day. It has left a remarkable legacy of Christian literature written in Syriac (Aramaic). The old Aramaic language remained though a modified alphabet was used to write it.

A further important political change took place in western Asia in the days of the emperor Constantine (AD 323–337). In the closing years of his reign he built his capital on the Bosphorus at the ancient Greek town of Byzantium and named it Constantinople (AD 330–334). Within a generation after Constantinople was founded the Roman Empire had, in fact if not in name, become two states and they were never more than temporarily united again. This act gave the eastern Roman Empire wonderful vitality and enabled it to survive almost unparalleled calamities and to outlive many kingdoms. The Byzantine Empire made possible the survival of the Christian church in the East of which the church in Syria formed a part. It was the rise of Islam in the 7th century AD which brought about a considerable weakening of the church although it has never been completely destroyed. Scattered communities of Aramaic-speaking people still survive in parts of Syria and numerous remains of Christian churches have been brought to light as a result of modern archaeological work.

Language and Culture. Aramaic was the language of the Aramaeans, of which numerous inscriptions have been discovered. The Aramaic script was adapted for use by the Israelites and the language became the international language for diplomacy and administration all over the Near East. It was the *lingua franca* of

Bibliography. S. Moscati, *Ancient Semitic Civilizations;* S. Moscati, *The Face of the Ancient Orient;* A.T. Olmstead, *History of Palestine and Syria;* M.F. Unger, *Israel and the Arameans of Damascus;* D.J. Wiseman (ed.), *People of OT Times.*

Syria-maachah. KJV rendering of Aram-maachah in 1 Chronicles 19:6.

See MAACAH, MAACHAH (PLACE).

Syrophoenicia. Homeland of the Greek woman who approached Jesus in the region of Tyre and Sidon and pleaded with him to cast a demon out of her daughter (Mk 7:26). The region of Phoenicia was located in the Roman province of Syria. Perhaps the designation of Syrophoenicia was used so as not to confuse this woman's country with the Phoenicia of North Africa called Libyphoenicia. In a parallel passage, this woman is identified as a Canaanite, a name which Phoenicians called themselves (Mt 15:22).

Syrtis. Two bodies of water on the northern coast of Africa dreaded by ancient mariners. The larger was known as Syrtis Major and the smaller as Syrtis Minor. The former was the water to which Paul and his shipmates were dangerously drifting. After leaving the island of Crete on Paul's voyage to Rome, a furious northeasterly wind crossed their course, threatening to push their ship southwestward across the Mediterranean into Syrtis Major (Acts 27:17; KJV Quicksands).

Syrtis Major, now called the Gulf of Sidra, indents the coast of Libya and stretches 275 miles from the town of Misratah to the city of Banghazi. Syrtis Minor, now known as the Gulf of Gabes, is an indenture into the eastern coast of Tunisia. These bodies of water were feared for their quick shifting sands which produced unpredictable shoals and hazardous tides and currents.

Wheatfields in Syria, with Mt Hermon (snowcapped in July) in the background.

the Persian period from Egypt to India and was widely spoken in Palestine in Jesus' day. The words "talitha cumi" (Mk 5:41) and "maranatha" (1 Cor 16:22) are Aramaic.

Excavations in many sites have provided a good idea of the Aramaean architecture, sculpture, pottery, and other arts. The religion of the Aramaeans was polytheistic. The people adopted many foreign deities as well. The principal Aramaean deity was the ancient west Semitic storm god Hadad. In the days of Ahaz of Judah the Damascus cult was forced on the people of Jerusalem when an altar based on a Damascus model was placed in the temple (2 Kgs 16:10–13). Aramaeans exiled to Samaria by the Assyrian ruler Sargon brought foreign Aramaean cults with them (17:24–34).

Through the centuries that followed the disappearance of the Aramaean states the Aramaic language has survived. The Christian form of Aramaic, Syriac, has left behind a vast legacy of literature, histories, theologies, commentaries, treatises, and translations, which have been carefully preserved in ancient monastic libraries particularly in northern Syria, northern Iraq, and southern Turkey.

JOHN A. THOMPSON

Tt

Taanach. One of the Canaanite fortress cities bordering the Plain of Esdraelon and the Valley of Jezreel, including Jokneam, Megiddo, Ibleam, and Beth-shan.

The modern site, about five miles southeast of Megiddo, retains the ancient name, Tell Taanak. Excavations reveal a 14th-century BC wall made of huge, irregularly shaped rocks, with smaller stones set in the chinks, along with ruins of a local king's palace. Some 40 cuneiform tablets of 15th–14th-century BC date were unearthed, and from a later period brick houses possibly of Israelite construction. A terra cotta incense altar was found in a house of Israelite date. Possibly from the Solomonic period, a pillared building resembles the structures of Megiddo and Hazor, which have been regarded as stables for Solomon's horses.

The name Taanach appears in many Egyptian records, including the list of the cities captured by the great conqueror, Thutmose III. Taanach is associated with Megiddo in one of the Amarna Letters. Taken by Sheshonk (Shishak) in his invasion of Israel in the fifth year of Rehoboam, Taanach appears between Shunem and Megiddo in the victor's reliefs at Karnak.

Taanach is first mentioned in the Bible in a list of kings conquered by the Israelites on the west side of the Jordan (Jos 12:21). In the tribal division of Palestine, Manasseh received Taanach (Jos 17:11) which was also named as a levitical city (Jos 21:25, KJV Tanach). Manasseh, however, was not able to capture Taanach or any of the other strong cities in its inheritance (Jgs 1:27).

After the defeat of Sisera, Deborah and Barak sang a song in which it was said that the fighting took place at "Taanach, by the waters of Megiddo" (Jgs 5:19). In the time of Solomon, Taanach was one of the towns mentioned in the enumeration of the administrative districts responsible for supplying monthly provisions for the king's household (1 Kgs 4:12).

The last mention of Taanach in the Bible is in a genealogical list (1 Chr 7:29), where the city is said to have belonged to Ephraim, "along the borders of the Manassites."

Taanath-shiloh. City on the northeast border of the territory allotted to Ephraim's tribe for an inheritance, positioned between Michmethath and Janoah (Jos 16:6). Its suggested location is at the modern site of Khirbet Ta'nah el-Foqua.

Tabbaoth. Ancestor of a family of temple servants that returned to Jerusalem with Zerubbabel after the exile (Ezr 2:43; Neh 7:46).

Tabbath. Town on the outskirts of Abel-meholah on the east side of the Jordan River in the hill country of Gilead, to which Gideon and his small army chased the fleeing Midianites (Jgs 7:22).

Tabeel, Tabeal. 1. Ruler in Samaria who, with his associates, wrote a letter to King Artaxerxes I of Persia (464–424 BC) protesting Zerubbabel's rebuilding of the Jerusalem wall (Ezr 4:7).

2. Father of the man whom King Pekah of Israel and King Rezin of Syria wanted to put on the throne of Jerusalem after they conquered it and subdued Ahaz, king of Judah (735–715 BC; Is 7:6, KJV Tabeal).

Taberah. Temporary stopping place for Israel in the wilderness of Paran, listed with Massah and Kibroth-hattaavah as places where Israel complained against the Lord. Taberah was named for the fire that God used to judge the grumbling Israelites (Nm 11:3; Dt 9:22). Its location is unknown.

See WILDERNESS WANDERINGS.

Tabernacle, Temple. Place of worship, the house of God.

Introduction. The tabernacle was the precursor of the temple during most of the period between the formation of Israel, at Sinai, and its final establishment in the Promised Land in the early period of the monarchy. A portable sanctuary in keeping with the demand for easy mobility, it was the symbol of God's presence with his people, and, therefore, of his availability, as well as a place where his will was communicated. At an early period it was anticipated that, when peace and security had been secured, a permanent national shrine would be established (Dt 12:10,11). This was not realized until the time of Solomon, when the temple was erected (2 Sm 7:10–13; 1 Kgs 5:1–5). History, as well as the similarities in construction and underlying theology, illustrate the close connection between the tabernacle and temple.

Tabernacle. Terminology. Several words and descriptive phrases are used:

(1) "Sacred temple" (Ex 25:8) or "sanctuary" (Lv 10:17,18) derive from the verb "to be holy."

(2) "The tent" occurs 19 times and is also found in expressions such as "the tent of the testimony" (Nm 9:15), "the tent of the Lord" (1 Kgs 2:28–30), "the house of the tent" (1 Chr 9: 23), and "the tent of meeting" (e.g., Ex 33:7). The last name appears approximately 130 times. The word involves the concept of meeting by appointment and designates the tabernacle as the place where God met with Moses and his people to make known his will.

(3) "Tabernacle of habitation" comes from the verb "to dwell." In Exodus 25:9 it indicates the whole tabernacle, but in Exodus 26:1 it refers to the inner structure which included the holy place and the Holy of Holies. A variant of this is "the tabernacle of the testimony" (Ex 38:21) which, with other expressions like "the tent of the testimony," stresses the presence of the two tables of the Law.

(4) "The house of the Lord" (Ex 23:19).

Historical Background. The three-part construction of the tabernacle and temple, allowing a general area and two restricted areas, was not unique. In any developed religion which included an organized priesthood there would be three main levels of approach: for all members of the community; for the priests generally; and for the chief religious leaders, an inner sanctuary, conceived as the dwelling place of the deity. Excavations of heathen sanctuaries in Palestine and Syria in the pre-Israelite period have revealed this type of divided sanctuary.

There is also widespread evidence of the use of portable, often complex, prefabricated

Tabernacle

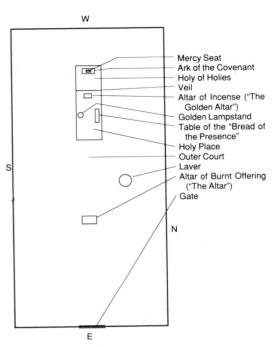

structures during the 2nd millennium BC, usually as either staterooms for kings and other high dignitaries or sanctuaries. Rulers of settled communities used these structures when traveling to other areas within their kingdoms (e.g., Egypt, and to a lesser extent, Canaan). Also nomadic or seminomadic peoples, such as the Midianites, used portable sanctuaries. In pre-Mosaic Egypt, craftsmen used techniques similar to those used in the construction of the tabernacle.

The Tabernacle and Its Furniture. The materials used (Ex 25:1–7; 35:5–9) included items ranging from precious to common materials. An important principle was established, namely, anything offered to the Lord must be voluntary. The three metals are mentioned in descending order of importance, gold alone being employed in the principal sanctuary furnishings. The total amount of metals used was approximately one ton of gold, three of copper, and four of silver (38:24–31). The relatively large amount of silver came from the offering (30:11–16), which augmented the silver and gold already given by the Egyptians (12:15). The fine-twined linen was made from high-grade flax.

The furniture of the Holy of Holies (25:10–22; 37:1–9). Significantly, in God's building specifications, the starting point was the furniture of the inner sanctuary. In the actual construction, this furniture was made after the tabernacle itself, presumably so that it could be immediately and adequately housed (25:9–27:19; cf. 36:8–37:28).

The first item listed was the ark, a wooden box, sheathed in gold, approximately 3¾ feet long, with a width and height of 2¼ feet. The supreme symbol of the covenant relationship between God and Israel, it was often called "the ark of the covenant of the Lord" (Dt 10:8). Unlike contemporary arks in some neighboring countries, it contained no representation of the deity, only the Ten Commandments (Ex 25:16), a jar of manna (Ex 16:33), and Aaron's rod (Nm 17:10)—all symbolic of various aspects of God's provision (see Heb 9:4).

The ark was transported by two poles which passed through rings attached to each lower corner (Ex 25:13–15). These poles left in place would project underneath the veil into the holy place, serving as a reminder of the presence of the unseen ark.

Resting upon the ark was the mercy seat, a rectangular slab of solid gold, to which were attached two cherubim. The inward-looking cherubim and the mercy seat formed a throne for the invisible God (Ex 25:22), who is frequently described as enthroned above or upon the cherubim (Pss 80:1; 99:1). The noun "mercy seat" comes from a verb meaning to make atonement. The mercy seat was sprinkled with blood at the climax of the annual Day of Atonement (Lv 16:14). The fact that the ark was placed *under* the mercy seat (Ex 25:21) signifies that the Law was under God's protection and explains the references to the ark as his footstool (e.g, Ps 132:7). Like the cherubim in the garden of Eden (Gn 3:24), those in the Holy of Holies probably had a similar protective function. In the ancient world, symbolic winged creatures like the cherubim were frequently placed as guardians of thrones and important buildings.

The furniture of the holy place (Ex 25:23–40; 37:10–28). Like the ark, the portable table of the "Bread of Presence" (Ex 25:30) was made of acacia wood overlaid with gold. It was marginally smaller, with a length of 3 feet, a width of 1½ feet and a height of 2¼ feet. The various auxiliary vessels and implements are detailed (v 29); presumably the dishes would be used for carrying the bread. Each sabbath day 12 specially prepared loaves, symbolizing God's provision for the 12 tribes of Israel, were placed in two rows on the table (Lv 24:5–9), which stood on the north side of the holy place (Ex 40:22). The use of the pitchers and flagons is not specified; possibly they were connected with the wine-offering.

On the south side was the seven-branched golden lampstand (Ex 25:31–39; 37:17–24; 40:24). The most impressive item of furniture in the holy place, it was, like the cherubim and the mercy seat, made of pure gold. Six golden branches, three on either side, extended from a central shaft, and the whole lampstand was ornamented with almond flowers. From the biblical evidence it is not clear whether the lampstand gave continuous illumination (Ex 27:20; Lv 24:2) or night light only (1 Sm 3:3 in most versions). Leviticus 24:4 strongly supports the former, and the reference in 1 Samuel probably reflects the laxity which had crept in during the period of the judges. In Scripture, the golden lampstand symbolizes the continuing witness of the covenant community (Zec 4:1–7; Rv 2:1). The precise attention to the smallest detail is well illustrated in the listing of the supplementary items, all made of pure gold, required for the servicing of the lamps. Without this precise attention, the light would soon grow dim, and the sanctuary itself be defiled by carbon deposits (Ex 25:38). Moreover, only the best quality olive oil was used, thus ensuring the brightest possible light (27:20).

The altar of incense (30:1–10) may have been deliberately played down to give greater prominence to the sacrificial altar in the outer court, which is frequently referred to as "*the* altar" (vv 18,20). In order to distinguish the altar of incense from the bronze altar of sacrifice, it was called "the golden altar" (40:5). The altar of incense was located in the holy place, immediately opposite the ark but just outside the veil, between the table of the "Bread of the Presence" and the lampstand (vv 1–5,20–27). Made of acacia wood overlaid with gold, it was 18 inches square and 3 feet high, with horns and a golden molding around the four sides. Like the ark, it was made readily portable by the provision of rings and carrying poles. The altar was used for the offering of incense every morning and evening and for anointing the horns for the yearly atonement (30:7,8). The incense from a special recipe was forbidden for secular use (vv 34–38). Originally, incense indicated something that ascended from a sacrifice, a pleasing aroma to God. Incense acknowledged God in worship (Mal 1:11), and at an early date signified the prayers of the godly (Ps 141:2). It also concealed God from human eyes (Lv 16:13).

The Tabernacle Proper. This was fundamentally a tent structure supported on a rigid framework. As with most of the other items, a triplication of detail underlines the importance of the tabernacle project. The specifications are given in Exodus 26, the construction in Exodus 36:8–38, and the final erection in Exodus 40:16–19. The overall dimensions were approximately 45 feet long, 15 feet wide, and 15 feet high.

The basic framework was a series of upright supports, each 15 feet high and 2¼ feet wide and each standing on two silver bases (Ex 26:15–25). Formerly scholars thought that these supports or frames were solid planks of acacia wood, but most modern scholars accept that each comprised two upright sides connected by horizontal pieces like a ladder. Such sections would be considerably stronger, would keep their shape better, and would allow a view of the beautiful inner layer of curtains from within the sanctuary. On the south and north sides were 20 such frames, with 6 more at the western end. In addition, on the western side were two corner pieces to which all the walls were attached by clasps (vv 23–25). A series of bars, which passed through gold rings attached to each upright frame, provided further security and alignment (vv 26–29). There were five such bars on each of the three sides. The central one on both south and north sides extended the entire length; the other four probably extended half way, so that each frame was effectively secured by three bars. All the wooden sections were sheathed in gold.

Over this framework several layers of coverings formed the top, sides, and back of the tabernacle. The first layer of 10 linen curtains was dyed blue, purple, and scarlet, and embroidered with cherubim (26:1–6; 36:8–13). Each measured 42 feet by 6 feet. Pairs joined along their length formed five sets of curtains. The two large curtains were themselves attached with 50 golden clasps which passed through a similar number of loops in each. A few scholars suggest that the curtains were suspended over a ridge pole, which would prevent any sagging due to their considerable weight. But nowhere is a ridge pole mentioned, nor any supporting pillar, which would need to be higher than the rest of the structure. Probably the curtains were stretched over the structure like a tablecloth. Possibly bars attached across the top to take the weight and give extra strength, but they are not mentioned.

Eleven curtains or tarpaulins of goat hair, each 45 feet by 6 feet, form the next layer. These were divided into two sets by joining together five and six curtains respectively and were linked together using a similar method as the under curtain, except that bronze clasps instead of gold were used. The extra length of the goat-hair tarpaulins provided an overlap to protect the under curtain, and the larger tarpaulin overlapped at both the front and the rear of the tabernacle (26:9,12).

Two further layers ensured complete weatherproofing, one of rams' skins dyed red and one of goat skins (v 14).

A veil made of the same material as the undercurtaining divided the sanctuary and hung under the golden clasps which joined the two curtains, supported by four pillars of acacia wood plated with gold and resting in silver bases (vv 31–33). The cherubim on both the veil and the curtains were symbolic guardians of the sanctuary. The positioning of the veil made the Holy of Holies a perfect cube of 15 feet. The layers of overlapping material and the attention given to the joints emphasizes the darkness of the innermost shrine. God was surrounded by darkness, carefully isolated from any unauthorized sight (Ps 97:2). The holy place occupied an area 30 feet by 15 feet, exactly twice the area of the Holy of Holies. A screen made from the same fabric as the main curtain stood between the holy place and the outer court and hung from golden hooks on five posts of acacia wood, overlaid with gold and resting on bronze sockets (Ex 36:36,37). There is no mention of embroidered seraphim on this section, which formed the tabernacle's eastern wall.

The tabernacle, while probably having a somewhat squat appearance suggestive of strength, could be easily dismantled, transported, and assembled. By the standards of that age, it was a fit dwelling place for God, using the best human skills and the highest quality materials.

The Outer Court and Its Furnishings. The court of the tabernacle was a rectangle 150 feet long on the north and south sides and 75 feet wide on the east and west (27:9–18; 38:9–19). The tabernacle itself was at the western end. Curtains of fine-twined linen 7½ feet high screened the entire tabernacle area. In the eastern section, there was a central entrance, 30 feet wide. An embroidered curtain of the same height screened this doorway, which was probably recessed to facilitate entrance on either side. Silver rods supported all the curtains. These rods passed through silver hooks attached to the silver-plated posts which rested on bronze bases (38:17).

The altar of burnt offering (27:1–8; 38:1–7), at the eastern end of the court adjacent to the entrance (40:29), was a reminder that there could be no approach to God except by the place of sacrifice. Seven feet square and 4½ feet high, it was small in comparison to the gigantic altar in Solomon's temple (2 Chr 4:1). Basically it was a hollow wooden framework overlaid with bronze, light enough to be carried on bronze-plated poles which passed through bronze rings at each corner. The grating (Ex 27:5) was probably inside the altar at the middle, although some scholars believe that it extended around the lower, outer sides of the altar, to provide draft and to allow the sacrificial blood to flow to the base of the

Temples

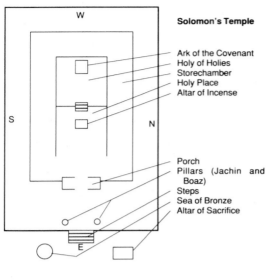

Solomon's Temple

Ark of the Covenant
Holy of Holies
Storechamber
Holy Place
Altar of Incense

Porch
Pillars (Jachin and Boaz)
Steps
Sea of Bronze
Altar of Sacrifice

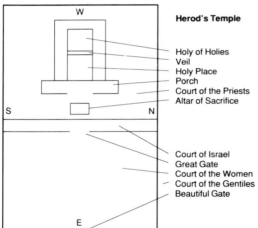

Herod's Temple

Holy of Holies
Veil
Holy Place
Porch
Court of the Priests
Altar of Sacrifice

Court of Israel
Great Gate
Court of the Women
Court of the Gentiles
Beautiful Gate

altar. The horns, possibly symbolizing the sacrificial victims, could be used to tether the animals about to be sacrificed. In Israel, a person could claim sanctuary by clinging to the horns of the altar (e.g., 1 Kgs 1:50), with the possible symbolism that he was offering himself as a sacrifice to God and so claiming his protection. The lower part of the altar may have been partly filled with earth to absorb the blood (Ex 20:24). All the accessories, ash buckets, shovels for removing the ashes and filling the base with earth, basins for the blood, carcass hooks, and fire pans were bronze (Ex 27:3).

No specifications concerning the size of the laver have survived (Ex 30:17–20; 38:8). It was made from the mirrors of the women who

served at the entrance to the court. The laver stood between the altar of sacrifice and the tabernacle. Failure to wash at the laver prior to ministering was punishable by death, a solemn reminder of the need for cleanliness and obedience before undertaking any task for God. The bronze pedestal may have been merely a support for the laver, but possibly incorporated a lower basin in which the priests could wash their feet.

The Construction and Consecration of the Tabernacle. The God-given specification required skills beyond the range of Moses and Aaron. Prominent in the construction were Bezalel and Oholiab (Ex 31:1–11), with a large supporting force of "experts" (v 6), who, presumably, learned their craftsmanship in Egypt. In a remarkable community effort, the Israelites, probably chastened in spirit following the incident of the golden calf (32:1–33:6), gave so generously that the flow of gifts had to be checked (35:20–24; 36:4–7). In addition, many gave of their special skills (35:25–29). To combat any danger of an excessive enthusiasm trespassing upon the rest-day, strict Sabbath observance was particularly stressed (31:12–17; 35:2,3).

When all the items had been completed and placed in position (40:1–33), every piece except the mercy seat and the cherubim was anointed with special oil (31:22–33; 40:9–11) and symbolically consecrated for its particular function. Moses' total obedience in all details of the tabernacle project is heavily underlined (40:16,19,23,25,27,29,32). The great climax came when the glory of the Lord filled the tabernacle (v 34). He was in the midst of his people, and thereafter the cloud by day and fire by night provided reassurance concerning his presence and guidance (vv 36–38). Yet there could be no laxity in approaching him, and even Moses was excluded from the Holy of Holies. The tabernacle was erected exactly one year after the deliverance from Egypt and a mere nine months after the Sinai revelation (vv 1,17).

Thereafter, when Israel camped, the Levites surrounded the tabernacle on three sides, with the families of Moses and Aaron occupying the remaining eastern side (Nm 3:14–38). This prevented any unauthorized intrusion into the sacred area. When the tabernacle was moved, the dismantlement was carefully regulated (Nm 4:5–15). The Kohathites were responsible for transporting the more sacred items, using the carrying poles (vv 5–20); the Gershonites dealt with all the soft furnishings, the altar of sacrifice, and its accessories (vv 21–28); and the Merarites carried the hard furnishings such as the frames, bars, and bases (vv 4:29–32). Even on the march the tabernacle remained central, with six tribes preceding and the remaining six following (Nm 2).

Problems Involving the Tabernacle. Critical scholarship frequently asserts that the tabernacle was a postexilic, imaginative reconstruction of Solomon's temple. The basic presuppositions of this view are that religion developed gradually in Israel and that nothing as complex as the Mosaic legislation could have existed in the 2nd millennium BC; and that writing was not in widespread use until the 9th century BC, so that anything purporting to be from an earlier period is suspect.

However, archaeological excavation has revealed that writing was common long before the period of Moses. The religions of the ancient Near East in the earliest part of the 2nd millennium were extremely well developed. In ancient Israel there is the strongest possible tradition of a religious covenant between the nation and the Lord, and of an ark which was the symbol of his presence in the midst of his people. The sanctuary housed the ark and served as a focal point of national life and worship. Such a central sanctuary must be an adequate structure.

Although great detail is given, certain other facts and specifications are not given, such as the thickness of the mercy seat and side frames, the size of the cherubim, and the dimensions of the two outer layers of skins. Also, the construction of the sacrificial altar of wood overlaid with bronze so as to enable it to withstand intense heat is not clear. However, the records are not the actual blueprints, with every single fact in place. The outworking of the plans would depend on the craftsmanship of the workmen, with some initiative left to the master craftsmen, Bezalel and Oholiab.

The objection that the Israelites would not have possessed the skills necessary to construct the tabernacle and its furnishings rests upon ignorance of the kinds of occupation they had held as slaves. Probably a reasonable range of skills had been acquired, and a small number of craftsmen could readily supervise a larger workforce. The time factor is also not vital. Given a powerful enough incentive, provided by the the exodus and the encounter with God at Sinai, a period of 6 to 8 months would be adequate. Another objection, dependent on reducing the number of those involved in the Exodus (cf. Nm 1; 26), is that the weight of gold, silver, bronze, and other raw materials could not have been provided by so small a company. It would be a problem if the Israelites were as few as 2000, as some have conjectured. But scholars who interpret the figures in Numbers in the light of other biblical evidence suggest a total between 100,000 and 140,000. Much depends on how much the Israelites received from the Egyptians (Ex 12:35,36).

There is an alleged disparity between the elaborate tabernacle and the simple "tent for meeting with God" (Ex 33:7,11). Unlike the centrally situated tabernacle, this tent, it is alleged, was pitched outside the encampment. However, the Tent of Meeting existed before the tabernacle and was its simpler precursor. Second, the narrative of Exodus 33:7-11 is clearly connected with the incident of the golden calf (32:1-33:6). The tent outside the camp was not customary, but rather a punishment for Israel's sin. The centrality of the symbol of God's presence was meaningless when the nation disobeyed him. Once the tabernacle was built it was often called the tent of meeting.

The Central Sanctuary in the Pre-Solomonic Period.
For about 38 years the Israelites remained at Kadesh-barnea, on the southern threshold of the Promised Land. Because of the nation's disobedience and the breaking of the covenant relationship with God, the covenant sign of circumcision was not practiced during this period (Jos 5:2-9), and the whole sacrificial system was probably in abeyance (Am 5:25). In the early stages of the conquest, the tabernacle was located at the base camp at Gilgal, near Jericho (4:19; 5:10; 9:6; 10:6,43). Later on, when the central highlands had been occupied, the tabernacle was probably transferred there. Although the exact location is not clear, it was probably sited successively at Shiloh (18:1,10; 22:9,12; Jgs 18:31), Shechem (Jos 24), Mizpah (Jgs 20:1), and Bethel (Jgs 20:18,26). Its essential mobility allowed transference to the most convenient location according to the national situation. Finally it was moved back to Shiloh. By the time of Samuel, the sanctuary at Shiloh, called a temple, appears as a more permanent structure with doors (1 Sm 1:9; 3:3,15). Probably this building had replaced the earlier tabernacle, which, with the passing of many years and the wear and tear of many moves, had deteriorated. In any case, this structure at Shiloh was almost certainly destroyed by the Philistines after the double defeat of Israel at Aphek, when the ark was used in an attempt to compel God to fight for his people (1 Sm 4:1-11). Archaeology attests a destruction of Shiloh about 1050 BC which accords with Scripture. This recalls a catastrophic judgment on Shiloh during the judges period, an event Jeremiah foresaw as a pattern of God's inevitable judgment upon the temple (Ps 78:59-64; Jer 7:12-14; 26:6,9). Whether by natural decay or by the ravages of war, it is unlikely that the Mosaic tabernacle survived beyond this period. The later references to a tabernacle at Nob (1 Sm 21:1-6) and

Gibeon (1 Chr 16:39; 20:29) probably refer to a substitute sanctuary which itself eventually became old in relation to the tent at Jerusalem to which David brought the ark (2 Sm 7:17). The Gibeonite shrine continued to be used until the time of Solomon (1 Kgs 3:4,5), but some of the precious furniture surviving from the Mosaic tabernacle was transferred to the temple at Jerusalem (1 Kgs 8:4).

Temple. *Background.* David's capture of Jerusalem (2 Sm 5:6–9) and his designation of it as the nation's capital is one of the great master-strokes of history. Occupied by the Jebusites, it was a pocket of neutral territory between the northern and southern sections of David's united kingdom and politically acceptable to both. Jerusalem was then established as the national religious center by returning the ark, which had been largely neglected since its capture by the Philistines (2 Sm 6:1–17). Henceforth, God's choices of both David and Zion were insolubly linked (Ps 78:67–72).

David's impulse to build an adequate dwelling place for Israel's God was initially approved by Nathan the prophet (2 Sm 7:1–3). But God revealed otherwise to Nathan, who conveyed the divine purpose to David (vv 4–17). In a significant word play, David was informed that, while he was not to build a house (temple) for God, his son would, and moreover, God would build a house (dynasty) for David. The reason David was not allowed to build a temple was the numerous wars during his reign (1 Kgs 5:3; 1 Chr 22:7,8; 28:3). David was not blamed for the bloodshed of these wars; they were in fact necessary to complete the conquest and to establish peace (Dt 12:10,11). Nevertheless, David enthusiastically amassed most of the necessary finances and materials and drew up the blueprints for the temple (1 Chr 22:3–5,14; 28:2,11–19).

David also purchased the temple site where the plague, which had decimated Israel because of his sinful pride in taking a national census, was averted (2 Sm 24). Fittingly, therefore, the temple stood where God's grace and mercy had been revealed. The cost of the actual threshing floor, a relatively small area, was 50 silver shekels (v 24), but the chronicler probably links in the subsequent purchase for 600 gold shekels of the far larger area needed for the whole temple complex (1 Chr 21:25).

Solomon's Temple. Date. Construction work commenced in Solomon's 4th year, about 959 BC, and took 7 years to complete (1 Kgs 6:1,38). Although Solomon's palace took 13 years to complete, everything necessary for the temple, including the workers, had been prepared by David (1 Chr 28:21). The temple evidently had first priority among Solomon's building schemes.

Superintendents and workforce. The principal architect for the bronze furnishings was Hiram, the son of a Tyrian metal craftsman by his Israelite wife (1 Kgs 7:13,14). Cedar in Lebanon was felled and transported by the skilled woodsmen of another Hiram, king of Tyre, Solomon's ally (5:5–9). Thirty thousand Israelites, divided into three groups, were drafted to assist at Lebanon. Each group was on duty for one month in three (v 13). In addition, Solomon conscripted 153,600 foreigners resident in Israel to provide a self-contained group of loggers and their supervisors (2 Chr 2:17,18, cf. 1 Kgs 9:15–23). Possibly the men from Gebal, with their specialized skills, formed yet another group (1 Kgs 5:18). It was obviously a national project of immense size and effort. In order to preserve the sanctity of the site and to eliminate as much noise as possible, most of the masonry and carpentry was done beforehand (v 18; 6:7).

Description. As in the case of the tabernacle there are a few unrevealed details; for example, what use, if any was made of the area 15 feet high immediately above the Holy of Holies (1 Kgs 6:2,16). But the general detail is sufficiently clear to make a reasonably accurate reconstruction, assisted by supplementary detail from Ezekiel's temple, which was broadly based on his knowledge of the Jerusalem temple (Ez 40–48).

The side rooms probably rested on a separate foundation or platform from the temple itself (1 Kgs 6:5,10; cf. Ez 41:9) and were arranged in 3 stories each 7½ feet high, extending around the whole building except the porch side. Each successive story was 1½ feet wider than the one below, these dimensions coinciding with the thickness, decreasing with height, of the side walls of the holy place. The ground floor rooms were 7½ feet wide; the first story 9 feet and the second 10½ feet. Access to the upper stories was possibly by winding staircases (1 Kgs 6:8). There is some uncertainty concerning the location of the entrances; there may have been one on either side, but only one is mentioned (2 Kgs 6:8). As in Ezekiel's temple (Ez 40:17,28) there were two adjacent courts, an inner and an outer (1 Kgs 6:36; 7:12; cf. 2 Kgs 23:12; 4:9), but no dimensions are given for these. The inner court, or "court for the priests," being proximate to the temple itself, was also called "the upper court" (2 Chr 4:9; Jer 36:10). The wall of the inner court was made of three courses of hewn stone held together by a layer of cedar beams (1 Kgs 6:36), and the doors of both courts were sheathed in bronze (2 Chr 4:9). The palace buildings were within the outer court area, probably with a private passageway between the palace and the temple which was later closed during the reign of Ahaz (1 Kgs 4:9,12; 2 Kgs 16:18).

The temple itself was 90 feet long, 30 feet wide, and 45 feet high (1 Kgs 6:2), with a porch or vestibule 15 feet deep stretching across the width. Probably the vestibule was on the east end of the temple, thus corresponding with the orientation of Ezekiel's temple (Ez 43:1; 44:1). The larger part of the main sanctuary, next to the porch, formed the holy place, which was 60 feet long (1 Kgs 6:17). Beyond this was the innermost sanctuary, the Holy of Holies, which was a perfect cube of 30 feet (v 20). All the interior walls were panelled with cedar decorated with flower patterns, cherubim, and palm trees (vv 18,29), so that no masonry was visible. The walls of both inner and outer sanctuaries were overlaid with pure gold (vv 20,21). Some scholars suggest that the golden decoration was inlaid, on the basis that a sheath of gold would spoil the natural beauty of the wood carving. The floor was made of cypress planks (v 15). Narrow windows set high in the walls above the level of the three-storied outer chambers provided light in the holy place (v 4). The ceiling was panelled with beams and planks of cedar (v 9). No detail is given about the exterior roofing but probably the contemporary technique was employed, using a wooden, lattice-like framework into which a waterproof, limestone plaster was packed and rolled.

The outer porch was simply an open space, since no doors are mentioned. Access into the holy place was by double doors, both hinged to fold back on themselves, made of cypress and decorated in exactly the same way as the interior walls (vv 33–35). The doorposts were made of olive wood. Within the holy place was the altar of incense made of cedar overlaid with gold which was probably placed centrally before the Holy of Holies (vv 20,22; cf. Ez 41:21,22). Also in the holy place were a table for the "Bread of the Presence of God," 10 lampstands, arranged in 2 groups of 5 on either side, and various utensils required for maintaining the priestly duties (1 Kgs 7:48–50). All these were made or overlaid with gold. The 10 tables, arranged 5 on each side, were presumably for the utensils and accessories (2 Chr 4:8).

Between the holy place and the Holy of Holies was a double door made of olive wood, carved with cherubim, palm trees, and flower patterns and overlaid with gold. Inside these doors, veiling still further the Holy of Holies, was a blue, purple, and crimson curtain, made of the finest fabrics and ornamented with cherubim (2 Chr 3:14).

As noted, the Holy of Holies was 30 feet high, involving a difference of 15 feet from the

The Dome of the Spirit, which probably stands over the Holy of Holies in the temple.

height of the whole building. Since there is no mention of any steps leading from the holy place into the Holy of Holies, they were probably on the same level, with an unused space above the Holy of Holies. However, archaeological evidence, dating from widely separated periods in the 1st millennium BC, includes flights of stairs leading to the raised innermost sanctuaries of heathen temples, and some scholars reconstruct the Jerusalem temple in this light.

In the Holy of Holies were 2 cherubim, each 15 feet high and made of olive wood covered with gold (1 Kgs 6:23–28). Each wing measured 7½ feet. A wing of each touched the side walls; the other wings met at the center of the room. The impression of a divine throne was considerably less in the tabernacle, where a wing of each cherubim fused into the mercy seat above the ark (Ex 25:17–22). In Solomon's temple, the ark of the Covenant was placed below the forward-facing cherubim, the symbolic protectors. The ark, the only major item surviving from the Mosaic tabernacle, still contained tablets of the law, but the pot of manna and Aaron's rod were missing (1 Kgs 8:9).

Immediately outside the temple and on either side of the vestibule were 2 hollow bronze pillars (1 Kgs 7:15–20; 2 Chr 3:15–17). According to the Book of Kings, these pillars were 27 feet high, with a circumference of 18 feet. The metal itself was about 4 inches thick. The pillars were surmounted by bronze, lily-shaped capitals 7½ feet high and 6 feet wide, intricately adorned with a chain latticework which supported 2 rows of pomegranates. The total weight must have been enormous, but their size is attested to by Jeremiah, who notes that the Babylonians had to break them in pieces before transporting them to Babylon (Jer

52:17,21–23). The function of these pillars and the significance of their names, Jachin and Boaz, have been much disputed. In view of their size, they probably were not incense altars. In other ancient Near Eastern countries, freestanding pillars or obelisks near a sanctuary have been interpreted as dynastic or religious symbols, indicating the support given by the deity to the monarchy or priesthood. The fact that the traditional place of the Davidic king on important occasions was "beside the pillar" (2 Kgs 11:14; 23:3) suggests that in Solomon's temple the pillars were dynastic symbols, signifying that the Davidic monarchy, being under divine protection, would endure as long as the temple itself. Their names could be derived from the first letters of the verses inscribed on each, and appropriate verses might be "the Lord will establish thy throne for ever and ever" and "in the strength of the Lord shall the king rejoice." Certainly the Jerusalem temple and the Davidic dynasty were bound together inextricably in Israel's tradition (e.g., Ps 132:11–18).

The bronze altar of sacrifice is not listed in the specifications of 1 Kings 7. However, it is mentioned in the temple dedication and subsequently (1 Kgs 8:22,54,64; 9:25) and clearly stood in the inner court. Its dimensions were 30 feet square and 15 feet high. In view of its weight, it was probably cast in sections at Solomon's foundry in the Jordan Rift valley (2 Chr 4:17,18) and then transported to the actual temple site for assembly.

Probably the most striking article in the inner court was the "molten sea," a huge, round tank made of bronze 4 inches thick, 7½ feet high and 15 feet in diameter (1 Kgs 7:23–26). Its rim flared out like a lily (2 Chr 4:2–5). The tank was supported by 12 bronze oxen, 4 on each side, and had 2 rows of decoration, possibly gourds or pomegranates, under the brim. Its capacity was between 10,000 and 12,000 gallons. The bronze sea may have had a cosmic significance, with reference to the pagan mythology of creation in which, prior to creation, conflict existed between the sea monster of chaos and the god of order. The many references elsewhere in the OT to Leviathan and Rahab (e.g., Jb 41:1; Ps 104:26; Is 30:7; 51:9) all derive from the same creation epic. Since these references are in the most strongly monotheistic books, there is no question of a belief in the existence of these mythical creatures. Rather, they serve as illustrations to highlight God's almighty power in his creation and continued rule. The bronze sea in Solomon's temple possibly has similar theological significance, stressing that the powers ascribed to false deities belonged exclusively to the Lord. However, there were obvious dangers to the average Israelite in any accommodation to heathen mythology, and the oxen or bulls, the chief sexual symbol of the Canaanite fertility cult, would heighten this. There are ominous connections with the worship of the golden calf (Ex 32) and the calf-images of Jeroboam I (1 Kgs 12:28–30). The bronze sea had a humble, practical purpose, the priestly ablutions (2 Chr 4:6). Presumably this would involve a platform of sorts, for the brim of this vast basin would be about 15 feet above ground level.

Hiram also constructed 10 large lavers, mounted on moveable stands and disposed in 2 groups of 5, on the north and south sides of the inner court (1 Kgs 7:27–39). Basically the stands were bronze boxes, 6 feet square and 4½ feet high with a nine-inch rim around the top edge. Each corner was attached to braced posts to which the axles were fixed. The four-spoked wheels were 27 inches high. Into each stand there fitted a laver containing approximately 220 gallons of water, used for washing sacrificial animals (2 Chr 4:6). Probably each was adjacent to one of the 10 tables which would be used to flay and otherwise prepare the sacrifices (v 8). Supplementary items such as pots, shovels, and basins, all made of bronze, were also manufactured (1 Kgs 7:40,45).

The Dedication of the Temple (1 Kgs 8; 2 Chr 5:2–7:10). Eleven months elapsed between the completion of the temple and its dedication (1 Kgs 6:38; 8:2), during which time the major items of furniture were set in place. The dedication itself took place in the 7th month, presumably in connection with the Feast of Tabernacles and the Day of Atonement (Lv 23:23–36). The ark of the covenant was brought into its final resting place (1 Kgs 8:3,4), but the inner court proved inadequate for the vast numbers of beasts sacrificed (1 Kgs 8:62–64; 2 Chr 7:7).

The temple employed the most sophisticated building techniques of the age, and no expense had been spared in construction, ornamentation, or equipment. Yet Solomon readily confessed its utter inadequacy to house the eternal God (1 Kgs 8:27). His prayer also underlines Israel's propensity to forsake the Lord, contrasting it with a God, who, though a just judge, was also merciful and faithful. The climax of the proceedings came when fire from heaven consumed the sacrifices and the Shekinah glory filled the temple.

Worship in the Solomonic Temple. Israelite worship was carefully structured, so, although there is little direct evidence of actual temple worship during the period of the monarchy, it followed the same basic pattern as that laid down in the Pentateuch. The festivals of Passover, Weeks, and Tabernacles were observed, as well as the daily and monthly sacrificial routine and the presentation of tithes and firstfruits. The tradition that David organized the musical aspects of worship in the projected temple is strong (1 Chr 25; Ezr 3:10). A nucleus of over 70 Davidic psalms provided the basis for the Book of Psalms. Almost all of the psalms were composed during the pre-exilic period and have a definable place in the temple cult, which became the focal point of national and personal religion. As well as the recitation of God's gracious deeds for the whole nation (Pss 105, 106), there was opportunity for the individual to testify to the gathered congregation when he presented his vow, freewill, or thank offering (e.g., Ps 22:22–31). Temple worship must have been colorful, meaningful, and uplifting.

At the autumn New Year Festival, the king, as the visible deputy of the invisible God, played an important part in an annual celebration of God's continued sovereign rule. Not all scholars accept this, while others go to the other extreme in theories of sacred kingship that seek to equate the Davidic kings with the priest-kings of surrounding nations. The realization that God was the true King of his people limited Israel's monarchy (Jgs 8:23). The king's role in the cult was strictly limited (e.g., 1 Kgs 12:32–13:3; 2 Chr 26:16–21). However, the king participated in an annual renewal of the Davidic covenant celebrating God's rule through his vice-gerent. Certainly the Lord's choice of Jerusalem and of the Davidic kings was celebrated together (Ps 78:67–72), and the temple was often viewed as a royal chapel, although public access was unrestricted.

The Jerusalem national shrine was a strong conservative influence in the centuries which followed. The increasing ascendency of the Zadokites among the priests strengthened the part played by a well-organized priesthood in maintaining the purity of the cult. There were dangers, however. The first sprang from a tendency to view God as localized in the impressive new temple, in spite of Solomon's perception (1 Kgs 8:27). Linked with this, God's choice of Jerusalem and his approval of the temple project led to the belief that whatever happened to the rest of the country, God would never allow the city which housed his temple to fall. Therefore, proximity to the building itself ensured safety. Jeremiah sought to demolish this superstitious faith in a building, rather than in God himself (Jer 7:4–14). Finally, a Phoenician element in the bronze furnishings of the temple, while no apparent problem in the early period, would become more influential when Canaanite influences penetrated. Eventually the more sensuous and degrading aspects of the Canaanite nature

cult, as well as the worship of the sun, infiltrated the temple (2 Kgs 23:6,7,11).

The History of the Temple. Like most ancient shrines, the temple became a treasury for national wealth and as such was often the target for attack. Shishak of Egypt plundered it within five years of Solomon's death (1 Kgs 14:25–28). Shortly afterward King Asa (910–869 BC) depleted its gold and silver treasures to buy Syrian help against his oppressor, Baasha (908–886 BC), king of Israel (15:16–19). Joash, the king of Judah (835–796 BC), who was concealed in the temple from the vicious Athaliah during his minority (2 Kgs 11), made provision for its repair after protesting the priests' embezzlement of gifts (12:4–16). But after the death of Jehoiada, the high priest, Joash himself was adversely influenced by his nobles (2 Chr 24:15–19). As punishment for his apostasy, the Lord allowed the Syrians to attack, and Joash used the temple treasures to buy them off (2 Kgs 12:17,18). Hardly had provision for replacements been made when Jehoash of Israel (798–782 BC), having shattered the arrogant pride of Amaziah of Judah (796–767 BC), again stripped the temple (14:8–14). Uzziah (792–740 BC) entered the holy place to burn incense. The king was punished for this by being smitten with leprosy (2 Chr 26:16–21). His son, Jotham (750–732 BC), built a new gate for the temple (2 Kgs 15:35). The next king, Ahaz (735–715 BC), was completely subservient to the Assyrians, using the resources of the temple to enlist their initial support (16:7–9). Possibly under constraint from Assyria, Ahaz replaced the altar of sacrifice in the inner court by one copied from an Assyrian original, and officiated at it personally, like a priest-king of the surrounding nations (vv 10–16). He also partially dismantled the 10 moveable water tanks, and replaced the 10 bronze oxen which supported the great sea by stone pedestals, presumably as a financial measure to help pay the annual tribute to Assyria (v 17). His personal authority within the temple was symbolically weakened, due to direct Assyrian pressure, by the removal of the private way connecting palace and temple (v 18).

Hezekiah (715–786 BC), one of the great reforming kings, thoroughly renovated the temple and restored worship after it had fallen into disuse during the closing years of Ahaz (2 Chr 29:1–19; 31:9–21). The miraculous deliverance from Sennacherib, king of Assyria, occurred after Hezekiah had spread out before the Lord in the temple the insulting, arrogant letter from the Assyrians (2 Kgs 19:14). However, this deliverance had an unfortunate aftermath, in that the lie arose that God was not concerned for his people but only for the city which housed his temple, therefore Jerusalem would never be taken. This dogma of Jerusalem's inviolability was exploded by Jeremiah (Jer 7:4–15). Manasseh (696–642 BC) completely reversed his father's policy, introducing the practices of Canaanite and Mesopotamian worship into the temple (2 Kgs 21:3–7). His conversion experience, which probably occurred late in his reign and resulted in certain reform measures in the temple (2 Chr 33:12–19), was not far-reaching enough to escape the final judgment that his reign was the dark spot of Judah's history (2 Kgs 21:10–16).

Manasseh's grandson, Josiah (640–609 BC), was the second great reforming king. He organized the repair of the temple in 622 BC, during which the lost book of the Law, almost certainly the Book of Deuteronomy, was discovered (2 Kgs 22:3–13). As a result, Josiah's reformation gained a new dimension and sense of urgency (22:14–23:3). The reformation included a thorough purge of all idolatrous elements from the temple (23:4–7,11,12) and the restoration of the traditional festivals (e.g., vv 21–23). Sadly, however, Josiah's reformation died with him, and Judah's downward slide continued under the apostate Jehoiakim (609–598 BC). Jeremiah preached his famous Temple Sermon foretelling its destruction (Jer 7:1–8:3; 26:1–19), which alienated him from the religious leaders. In Nebuchadnezzar's reprisal raid following Jehoiakim's rebellion in 601 BC (2 Kgs 24:1), Jerusalem was captured (597 BC) and many of the temple treasures were transported to Babylon (2 Chr 24:7). The temple itself appears to have escaped damage, but when Judah again rebelled under Zedekiah (597–586 BC) the temple was demolished (2 Kgs 25:8–10). The remaining temple treasures were taken away (vv 13–17). To the Babylonians, the sacking of the temple indicated the superiority of their gods, but Jeremiah declared that the temple vessels would be returned in God's time (Jer 27:21,22), a prophecy which was remarkably fulfilled (Ezr 1:7–11). No more is heard of the major items (Jer 3:16).

Attempts at Reconstruction. While the general detail of the temple complex is reasonably clear, a number of problems confront any attempt at reconstruction, since the biblical detail is not an exact construction blueprint. For instance, no detail is given of the thickness of the walls, or whether there was a wall, as well as doors, between the holy place and the Holy of Holies. The Holy of Holies may have been raised above the holy place and reached by a flight of steps, as in other contemporary temple architecture. The pillars Jachin and Boaz could have been part of the structure or free-standing. No detail is given of the roofing or of the eastern facade. The means of access to the side chambers is not clear, nor are the construction details of the altar of sacrifice. How were the stone walls of the courts and vestibules bound together by the cedar beams (1 Kgs 6:36; 7:12)? Archaeology has been of limited help in solving these problems, since most excavated temples have been destroyed to foundation level. However, many attempts at reconstruction have been made. The earlier ones suffered from an overelaboration drawn from the architecture of later civilizations, and failed to reproduce the rugged simplicity of Palestinian/Syrian architecture.

Zerubbabel's Temple. Construction. Although devasted, the temple site still remained as a place of pilgrimage during the exile (Jer 41:4,5). In 538 BC the Persian king, Cyrus, in pursuance of a liberal policy diametrically opposed to that of the earlier empires,

Steps (from Christ's time) leading to the temple mount.

permitted the Jews to return from exile and authorized the rebuilding of the temple and its financing from the Persian treasury. The decree of authorization has been preserved in two forms: the general proclamation (Ezr 1:2–4), and a more prosaic memorandum in the national archives indicating the main temple specifications and the amount of promised Persian help (6:1–5). Probably only a minority of the Jews opted to leave the relative comforts of Mesopotamia for the dangers of a long journey to their desolated homeland. But 42,360 dedicated individuals and their servants (2:64, 65) responded under the leadership of Sheshbazzar (1:8,11; 5:14–16) and Zerubbabel (2:2; 3:2,8; 4:2, etc.). With great enthusiasm the altar was rebuilt on the temple site and the traditional pattern of worship reestablished (3:1–6). Soon after, utilizing the grant from Persia as well as their own freewill gifts (2:68,69; 3:7), the Jews began to plan the second temple and lay its foundations (3:7–13). The initial impetus quickly died as a result of local opposition (4:1–4,24), selfish preoccupation, and crop failures (Hg 1:2–11). In 520 BC (Ezr 4:24; Hg 1:1; Zec 1:1), inspired by the prophets Haggai and Zechariah, the Jews under Zerubbabel and Joshua the high priest commenced rebuilding. Work continued in spite of official suspicion, if not direct opposition, and the temple was completed and dedicated in 515 BC (Ezr 5:1–6:22).

Little is known of Zerubbabel's temple. The inference that it was vastly inferior to Solomon's temple (Hg 2:3) relates to an early stage in the building operation. In fact, the second temple stood for over 500 years. The dimensions noted in Ezra 6:3 are incomplete, but the new temple was about the same size as its predecessor and was probably built on the same foundation. The construction technique appears to have followed the method of the original, with courses of timber providing a framework for sections of masonry (v 4). Clearly, there was auxiliary accommodation, probably like the side-rooms of Solomon's temple (Ezr 8:29; Neh 12:44; 13:4,5). If Persian aid was forthcoming as promised (Ezr 6:8–12), the second temple was a more splendid, substantial structure than is generally supposed.

Later history. Several references in the Apocrypha, Pseudepigrapha, rabbinic writings, and the historian Josephus help to illumine the history of the temple and give more detail on its structure and furnishings. Josephus, quoting from Hecateus of Abdera (4th century BC) states that the temple was a large building in an enclosure about 500 feet by 150 feet, surrounded by a stone wall, with an altar of unhewn stones the same size as Solomon's bronze altar (2 Chr 4:1). Within the sanctuary was a golden altar of incense and a lamp-stand, the flame of which burnt continually. The Letter of Aristeas has been dated variously from about 200 BC to AD 33, so it could relate to Herod's temple, not Zerubbabel's. He tells of rich gifts given by the Egyptian king, Ptolemy Philadelphus (285–246 BC), of fortified walls around the temple over 100 feet high, and of a perpetual spring in the temple courts, no evidence for which has been discovered. Josephus also notes considerable support from Antiochus III (223–187 BC) when the Seleucids displaced the Ptolemies as masters of Jerusalem. This included finance for repairs and further building and an inscription barring foreigners from the inner courts of the temple. Ben Sirach, early in the 2nd century BC, commended Simon, the son of Onias the high priest, for his work in fortifying and repairing the temple area. First Maccabees provides valuable evidence of the fate of the temple during the oppression under Antiochus IV Epiphanes (175–164 BC). It recounts the defilement of the altar of burnt offering and the plundering of the golden lampstand, altar of incense, table of offering, the veil as well as other treasures. When the temple was recaptured and restored, the victorious Maccabees replaced the items taken by the Seleucids, except for the altar of sacrifice, which was considered so polluted that it was dismantled and replaced by a new one constructed of unhewn stone. Clearly the temple area was used as a fortress, both in opposition to the Seleucid garrison which was maintained in Jerusalem in the Maccabean period, and in the conflicts of the later Hasmonean period. When Pompey captured Jerusalem about 63 BC, he entered the temple to assert his authority but took no plunder, thus showing his respect for it. The history of Zerubbabel's temple closed when Herod, having carefully preserved it from any major damage when he gained control of Jerusalem with Roman aid in 37 BC, began to dismantle it about 21 BC in preparation for the construction of his own grand temple.

Herod's Temple. Construction. Apart from over 100 references in the NT, our main sources of information about Herod's temple are the Jewish historian, Josephus, and Middoth, a section of the Jewish rabbinic writings. There are considerable differences in detail between the two, which rules out any dogmatic interpretation in attempted reconstructions. Since Josephus was contemporary with the temple (he was born about AD 37 and died early in the 2nd century), he is probably more reliable than Middoth, which, dating from about AD 150, appears to exaggerate occasionally. Archaeological research has been helpful in determining the positions of the outer walls and gates.

Herod's motive in building his temple was political rather than religious. As an Idumaean, he wished to placate his Jewish subjects by constructing a sanctuary as magnificent as Solomon's. Possible fears that the site might be profaned, or that the existing temple might be demolished and never rebuilt, were allayed by the training of 1000 priests as masons and the amassing of materials before the work commenced. Herod's temple followed the tripartite plan of its predecessors, although its porch was much larger. It was built in the contemporary Greco-Roman architectural style and must therefore be regarded as distinct from Zerubbabel's temple. Work began in 20 BC and while the main sanctuary was quickly erected (it was in full operation within 10 years), the total project was not completed until AD 64, only 6 years before it was destroyed by the Romans.

Herod first prepared the site by clearing and levelling an area approximately 500 yards from north to south and about 325 yards from east to west. This involved cutting away sections of rock in some areas and building up with rubble in others. Considerable sections of the enclosing wall, constructed of stone blocks averaging about 15 feet long by 4 feet high, still survive. Some of the stones in the corners of the south wall weigh up to 70 tons.

The sanctuary itself had exactly the same dimensions as Solomon's temple, divided into the holy place, which was 60 feet long, 30 feet wide, and 60 feet high and the Holy of Holies, which was 30 feet square. There was no furniture within the Holy of Holies, which was separated by a veil from the holy place. The holy place contained the 7 branch lampstand, the table for the Bread of the Presence, and the incense altar. The main divergence from Solomon's Temple was the imposing porch, 150 feet in width and height. Outside was a doorway approximately 30 feet wide by 40 feet high, with an inner doorway about half that size leading into the sanctuary. By allowing empty rooms over the Holy of Holies and the holy place, there was a uniform roof height of 150 feet. Golden spikes on the roof discouraged birds from alighting and defiling the structure. Like its predecessors, the temple was orientated toward the east and was surrounded on the other sides by 3 stories of rooms rising to a height of 60 feet. The stone used was the local white stone, cut in huge blocks and highly polished.

Access to the porch was by a flight of 12 steps from the Court of the Priests. Centrally placed before the porch and 33 feet away was the altar of sacrifice. Made of unhewn stone, it was a multilevelled construction 15 feet high and about 48 feet square at its base. Male Israelites were allowed into this area once a year, during the Feast of Tabernacles, to walk around the altar of sacrifice. Otherwise, they were restricted to the Court of Israel. To the east of the Court of Israel and separated from it by a flight of 15 steps and by the ornate Great Gate, made of Corinthian bronze, was the Court of the Women. Here the offertory chests for temple expenses were located (Mk 12:41–44). The next court was the large, lower, outer Court of the Gentiles, which surrounded the inner courts and was separated from them by a balustrade and a series of warning notices. Two of these have been excavated, written in Latin and Greek and forbidding trespass by Gentiles into the inner areas on pain of death. This outer court was widely used. Immediately inside its walls was a portico, supported by four rows of columns almost 40 feet high on the south side (the Royal Porch), and 2 rows on the other sides, the eastern portico known as Solomon's porch (Jn 10:23; Acts 3:11; 5:12). In the royal court were the stalls of the moneychangers and merchants, the areas where the Sanhedrin met, and where Christ and the scribes taught and debated (Mk 11:27; Lk 2:46; 19:47; Jn 10:23, etc.). Here, too, the infant church met before it was rejected by a hostile Judaism (Acts 3:11; 5:12). Just to the northwest of the temple enclosure was the Fortress of Antonia, where the Roman governor resided while in Jerusalem, and where a Roman garrison was on hand to deal with disturbances (Acts 21:31–40). Overlooking the temple area, it was separated from it by a wide moat. The high priest's vestments were stored in the fortress as a symbol of Roman authority. Access to the Court of Gentiles was by 4 gates in the west wall; 2 in the south wall, where the ground fell away steeply into the valley, a site often identified as the pinnacle of the temple (Mt 4:5; Lk 4:9); and 1 gate in each of the east and north walls.

Archaeological data. On its east, south, and west sides, the present Moslem complex (the Haram esh-Sharif) obviously adheres closely to the lines of the Herodian temple. The circumference of the Herodian site was considerably smaller. Its north wall was probably sited just north of the present Golden Gate, as indicated by a deviation in the east wall at that point. The Golden Gate dates from Byzantine times, but is probably at the same place as a Herodian gate. In the southeast corner, impressive remains of Herodian masonry form a major tourist attraction, with 14 courses above and 21 courses below the present ground level. Two of the 3 walled-up gates in the present south wall, the so-called Triple Gate and Double Gate because of the number of arched entrances, probably correspond with

The Triple Gate to the temple in Jerusalem.

the two gates noted in Middoth and Josephus. Below the south wall was a "plaza" or open space where worshipers could gather before entering the temple area via a broad monumental staircase and the Double Gate. Remains of large cisterns just south of this area served the needs of the large number of pilgrims. The famous Robinson's Arch, in the west wall, near the southwest corner, is now known to have been part of an impressive stairway leading up to the temple area from a street which ran alongside the west wall. A tower surmounted the structure at the southwest corner, and a Hebrew inscription "to the place of trumpeting" found in debris nearby, suggests that this was the place where the trumpet was sounded to announce the Sabbath. A little to the north of Robinson's Arch is the walled-up Barclay's Gate, below the present Gate of the Moors. North of Barclay's Gate is the Wailing Wall, with masonry dating from the Herodian period surmounted by Arab and Turkish stonework. Beyond this, and adjacent to the main modern gate, the Gate of the Chain, are a series of underground vaults and Wilson's Arch. This was probably the connecting route between Herod's palace and the temple. In the west wall north of Wilson's Arch is evidence of two more gates. The southernmost of these, Warren's Gate, was, like Barclay's Gate, at street level, considerably lower than the others.

Attempts at reconstruction. As noted earlier, the considerable differences between Josephus and Middoth make this difficult, and some attempts have failed to appreciate that the Herodian site was not identical in size to the present Haram. The positioning of Herod's temple in relation to the sacred rock in the Dome of the Rock is also uncertain. Most modern Bible atlases, such as the Westminster Historical Atlas of the Bible (1956) and the Oxford Bible Atlas (1974), contain ground plans based on sound archaeological evidence. But since all trace of the central temple buildings has been lost, the precise detail of one of the ancient world's most spectacularly beautiful buildings remains uncertain.

Theological Significance of the Tabernacle and Temple. *Significance in the OT.* The center of worship. The tabernacle functioned as the focal point of the tribal confederation, with Jerusalem as its natural successor, particularly after David brought the ark of the covenant to the newly designated capital (2 Sm 6). In spite of the attempt of Jeroboam I, the first king of the northern kingdom, to divert attention from Jerusalem by establishing shrines at Bethel and Dan (1 Kgs 12:26–30), Jerusalem never lost its preeminence. Naturally both Hezekiah and Josiah sought to extend their reformation into the area of the northern tribes (2 Chr 30:1–12; 34:6,7), and Jerusalem was a pilgrimage center for those areas even after its destruction (Jer 41:5). The prophets foretold its destiny as the focal point of universal worship (Is 2:1–4).

God's dwelling place among his people. God's presence, symbolized in the Shekinah glory and the pillar of cloud, was associated with the tent of meeting (Ex 33:9–11), with the tabernacle (40:34–38), and finally with the temple (1 Kgs 8:10,11). The paradox is that while God is completely unrestricted, the temple was "a place for you to live forever" (1 Kgs 8:13,27). God had chosen Zion, as he had chosen David (Pss 68:15–18; 76:2; 78:67–72), so the temple was regarded as his house (Pss 27:4; 42:4; 84:1–4, etc.). The prophets, accepting this divine election, viewed Jerusalem as the springboard of God's judgment (Am 1:2;

Robinson's Arch, in the southwest corner of the temple area.

Mi 4:1–4). Almost all postexilic prophecy was concerned with rebuilding the temple (Hg and Zec) or re-establishing a pure worship there (Mal). The tension between God's transcendence and his immanence was lessened by the fact that no representation of him was made, the cloud and thick darkness of the Holy of Holies suggesting an inscrutability as well as a revelation. Possibly too, the concept of God "putting his name" in the place of his choice (Dt 12:5,11; 1 Kgs 8:17,29) guarded against any notion that he was contained physically within the sanctuary.

The idealized symbol of restoration. Ezekiel's detailed description of the ideal temple (Ez 40–48) was not used as the blueprint for Zerubbabel's temple. In fact, since Ezekiel must have been familiar with Solomon's temple before his deportation in 597 BC, his description is of greater help in determining uncertain details of the first temple. Ezekiel's concern was to show the nature of a pure, totally loyal worship, safeguarded from all contamination. This worship would allow the glory of God, which had departed from the corrupted Solomon's temple (9:3; 10:4,18,19; 11:22,23), to return so that Jerusalem could again be named "the Lord is there" (43:1–5; 48:35). This thought, linked with Ezekiel's vital concept of God's Spirit indwelling his faithful worshipers (36:24–28), anticipated the NT teaching of the believer as a temple. Finally, the prophecy of Zechariah 6:11–15, originally related to the high priest Joshua, encouraged the eschatological expectation of a messianic king, the builder of a perfect temple (Mt 16:18; Jn 2:21).

Significance in the NT. Christ and the temple. Christ showed considerable respect for the temple. When he was 12 years old he entered into the rabbinic discussions in its porticoes and described it as his Father's house (Lk 2:41–50). To him "the house of God" was indwelt by God (Mt 12:4; 23:21). Although he twice cleansed it in righteous anger (Mt 21:12,13; Jn 2:13–16), he wept over the impending destruction of the city (Lk 19:41–44). He often taught there, but he was greater than the temple (Mt 12:6; Lk 19:47). When his presentation to Jerusalem as the predicted Messiah was rejected, in spite of attendant miracles, he foretold its inevitable destruction (Mt 21:9–15; 24:1,2). For a brief period after Pentecost the early church used the temple as its meeting place, until mounting opposition drove believers from Jerusalem (Acts 5:12,21,42; 8:1).

The church as the temple. Paul looked upon the church as Abraham's children, the spiritual Israel, a called covenant community, the new Jerusalem, and a temple indwelt by God (Rom 4; 1 Cor 3:16,17; 2 Cor 6:16–18; Gal 3; 4:21–31;

Eph 2:18–22). The corollary of this was purity, which included the individual Christian indwelt by the Holy Spirit (1 Cor 6:19,20; 2 Cor 7:1), and unity, with earth-bound distinctions no longer valid (Gal 3:27–29; Eph 2:11–18).

The typology of the tabernacle and temple. The Letter to the Hebrews, addressed to Christian Jews who were in danger of reverting to Judaism, draws out the complete superiority of the new covenant in comparison with the obsolete old covenant (8:19). Christ's priesthood is seen as immeasurably superior to the Aaronic priesthood (4:14–5:10; 7:1–8:4). In comparison with the new "Temple in Heaven," the Mosaic tabernacle was "a mere earthly model" (8:2,5). The description of the tabernacle furniture introduces a statement of the functions of the Aaronic priesthood, underlining its limited efficacy in contrast to Christ's perfect mediation (9:1–18). The perfect access and complete confidence of the believer to enter the Holy of Holies, that is, the immediate presence of God, is valued above the tabernacle and temple, which are "copies of the heavenly things" (9:23; 10:19–22).

The temple in John's revelation. John dispenses with any material temple in his vision of the ultimate spiritual community, although he continues to use the imagery of Jerusalem and Mt Zion (3:12; 14:1; 21:2,10,22). Three interrelated ideas dominate. First is the concept of the martyr church, whose faithful members in God's temple surmount the spiritual Zion as the material temple did ancient Jerusalem (3:12; 14:1). This temple grows gradually as the number of martyrs increases (6:11). Another aspect is the temple as the place of judgment (11:19; 14:15; 15:5–16:1). Finally, any temple in the new age is unnecessary, "for its temple is the Lord God the Almighty and the Lamb" (21:22). The ultimate state would be God's dwelling with men (v 3). The cube-like proportions of the city may even suggest the immediate presence of God in the Holy of Holies (v 16). All lesser types fade away in the glorious reality of God's supremacy (1 Cor 15:28) and the realization of perfect unity of the completed church (cf. Eph 2:20–22).

ARTHUR E. CUNDALL

See ARK OF THE COVENANT; FEASTS AND FESTIVALS OF ISRAEL; PRIESTS AND LEVITES; OFFERINGS AND SACRIFICES; BREAD OF THE PRESENCE; CLEANNESS AND UNCLEANNESS, REGULATIONS CONCERNING; DAVID; SOLOMON (PERSON); MERCY SEAT; ISRAEL, RELIGION OF; SANCTUARY; SINGERS IN THE TEMPLE; JUDAISM; FIRST JEWISH REVOLT; ALTAR.

Bibliography. R.E. Clements, *God and Temple;* A. Cole, *The New Temple;* R. de Vaux, *Ancient Israel,* pp 274–344; A. Edersheim, *The Temple: Its Ministry and Services;* D.W. Gooding, *The Account of the Tabernacle;* M. Haran, *Temples and Temple Service in Ancient Israel;* A. Parrot, *The Temple of Jerusalem.*

Tabernacles, Feast of. One of the three great festivals of Israel, celebrating the completion of the agricultural year. The Jews built booths or tabernacles (temporary shelters) to commemorate their deliverance from Egypt by the hand of God (Lv 23:33–43).

See FEASTS AND FESTIVALS OF ISRAEL.

Tabitha. Aramaic name meaning "gazelle"; the name in Greek is Dorcas (Acts 9:36,40).

See DORCAS.

Table. *See* FURNITURE.

Table of Showbread. Piece of furniture in the tabernacle and temple upon which was the Bread of the Presence (Ex 25:23–30).

See BREAD OF THE PRESENCE; TABERNACLE, TEMPLE.

Tablet. *See* WRITING AND BOOKS.

Tabor, Mount. Important hill in lower Galilee located in the northeast area of the Jezreel Valley (often called the Chesulloth Valley). About six miles east of Nazareth, Tabor rises abruptly from the valley floor. Appearing more prominent than its height would indicate (1929 feet), it became an important geographical reference point in antiquity. It de-fined the western boundary of Issachar's tribe (Jos 19:22) and was a useful navigation tool on the international coastal highway (the Via Maris) which passed through Megiddo in Galilee en route to Hazor. Its prominence invited comparison with Mt Hermon far to the north (Ps 89:12; cf. Jer 46:18).

In the OT, Mt Tabor is mentioned in the Book of Judges when Deborah and Barak fight Sisera, the commander of a Canaanite army from Hazor (Jgs 4:1–24). Barak's troops from the nearby tribes of Naphtali and Zebulun meet on Mt Tabor and at Deborah's command launch a successful campaign against Sisera. Later in the same book Mt Tabor is named as the place where Gideon finally confronts the Midianite kings, Zebah and Zalmunna, who had slain his brothers (8:18).

Strategically located, Tabor's moderately sized top, less than a half mile square, was easily fortified. During the OT Kingdom Period, shrines may have been located there (see Hos 5:1), but by the Hellenistic era fortifications were built. The Ptolemies strengthened it, and by the time of Antiochus III (218 BC), Tabor may have become the administrative center of the Jezreel Valley. The Roman era witnessed various conflicts on Mt Tabor. In the major Jewish war of AD 66, Josephus fortified the hill with a large wall which is still

The churches and other buildings on Mt Tabor.

visible. Since the 4th century Mt Tabor has been identified as the site of Jesus' transfiguration (Mk 9:2–13). This is uncertain, however, since the NT fails to mention Mt Tabor by name. Helena, the mother of Constantine, was convinced that the transfiguration did take place here and in AD 326 built a church on the site. Other shrines, monasteries, and churches graced the hill until the 12th century, when everything was destroyed by the Arab conqueror Saladin. Today a Greek orthodox monastery and a Latin basilica dating from the 19th century can be seen on the mountain.

Tabor, Oak of; Plain of. Place near Bethel and perhaps in Benjamin's tribe where Saul was to meet three men (1 Sm 10:3; KJV Plain of Tabor). This encounter was the second of four signs given to Saul to confirm his appointment as king.

Tabret. KJV rendering of tambourine in Genesis 31:27 and 1 Samuel 10:5, and timbrel in 1 Samuel 18:6; Job 17:6; Isaiah 5:12; 24:8; 30:32; and Jeremiah 31:4.

See MUSIC AND MUSICAL INSTRUMENTS (TOPH).

Tabrimmon, Tabrimon. Hezion's son and the father of Benhadad I, king of Syria (1 Kgs 15:18, KJV Tabrimon).

Tachmonite. KJV form of Tahchemonite, designation for one of David's mighty men, in 2 Samuel 23:8.

See TAHCHEMONITE.

Tadmor. Ancient city whose name appears only once in the Bible (2 Chr 8:4), in a list of Solomon's achievements. Solomon built or rebuilt a number of cities, including store-cities and cities for his horses and chariots. Among the cities mentioned is "Tadmor in the wilderness." Tadmor, situated some 140 miles northeast of Damascus, is mentioned in the records of the Assyrian king Tiglath-pileser I (c. 1114–c. 1076 BC).

In Greek and Roman times the city was known as Palmyra, whose ruins may be seen today. The oasis city was an important stopping place on the caravan route, and therefore could have been of much value to Solomon in his extensive trading ventures. It gained its greatest prominence during the reign of Queen Zenobia. The Roman Aurelian destroyed it in AD 273. Though rebuilt, it never regained its former position.

In 1 Kings 9:15–25 there is a parallel list of building activities of Solomon. Verse 18 lists "Tamar in the wilderness, in the land of Judah" (RSV). Tamar ("palm tree") has been iden-

tified as 'Ain Hosb, or as 'Ain el Arus, farther north, and presently called 'Ain Tamar.

Although the passages are parallel and similar, they are not identical. The Chronicles account mentions Hamath in Syria (2 Chr 8:4) and building in Lebanon (v 6), possibly Tadmor (Palmyra) is intended. The statement in 1 Kings seems to favor Tamar in Judah. (The NIV reads "Tadmor" in both passages, while the RSV and NASB give "Tamar" in Kings and "Tadmor" in Chronicles.)

See TAMAR (PLACE).

Tahan. 1. Ephraim's son and the father of the Tahanite family (Nm 26:35).

2. Telah's son and a descendant of Ephraim (1 Chr 7:25).

Tahanite. Descendant of Tahan from Ephraim's tribe (Nm 26:35).

See TAHAN #1.

Tahapanes. KJV alternate spelling of Tahpanhes, an Egyptian city, in Jeremiah 2:16.

See TAHPANHES.

Tahash. Son of Nahor and Reumah his concubine; Abraham's brother (Gn 22:24, KJV Thahash).

Tahath (Person). 1. Son of Assir and a descendant of Levi through Kohath's line. He was an ancestor of Heman, one of David's musicians, and the father of Uriel and Zephaniah (1 Chr 6:24,37).

2. Ephraimite, the son of Bered and the father of Eleadah (1 Chr 7:20).

3. Ephraimite, the son of Eleadah and the father of Zabad (1 Chr 7:20).

Tahath (Place). Temporary camping place for the Israelites during their wilderness wanderings, mentioned between Makheloth and Terah (Nm 33:26,27). Its location is unknown.

See WILDERNESS WANDERINGS.

Tahchemonite. Identification of Joshebbasshebeth (also called Jashobeam in 1 Chr 11:11), one of David's mighty men (2 Sm 23:8, KJV Tachmonite). This word probably refers to the Hachmonite of 1 Chronicles 11:11, revealing a possible error in copying where the Hebrew letter "h" was confused for a "t."

See HACHMONITE.

Tahpanhes. Important Egyptian center in the eastern Delta. Listed with Memphis (KJV Noph) among Israel's enemies (Jer 2:16, KJV Tahapanes) it is the place to which Jews fled after the murder of Gedaliah in 586 BC when Jeremiah was taken to Egypt (43:7–9; 44:1; 46:14). Ezekiel prophesied doom against this city (alternately spelled Tehaphnehes in 30:18). It is linked to Baal-zephon in the phrase "Baal-zephon and the gods of Tahpanhes" (cf. Ex 14:2).

Today the site is identified with Tell Dephneh (Defenneh) 26 miles S,SW of Port Said. Flinders Petrie found little evidence of occupation here before the time of Psammethicus I (664–610 BC), who established a fortress at the site and left a garrison of Greek mercenaries. "Pharaoh's palace in Tahpanhes," where Jeremiah buried stones as a promise of Nebuchadnezzar's invasion (Jer 43:9), has been identified with the fortress of Psammethicus. A fragmentary Neo-Babylonian text of the 37th year of Nebuchadnezzar refers to operations against Pharaoh Amasis and a Greek garrison.

Tahpenes. Egyptian queen who lived during the reigns of David (1000–961 BC) and Solomon (970–930 BC). Pharaoh gave her sister to Hadad the Edomite in marriage. Tahpenes' sister bore to Hadad a son named Genubath (1 Kgs 11:19,20).

Tahrea. Alternate form of Tarea, a descendant of King Saul, in 1 Chronicles 9:41.

See TAREA.

Tahtim-hodshi. One of the towns polled in David's census of Israel. Tahtim-hodshi (KJV) is listed between Gilead and Dan-jaan (2 Sm 24:6). Possibly this town is identical to the northern city of Kadesh (RSV) in the land of the Hittites.

Talent. Unit of measure used in weighing gold or silver (Mt 25:14–30).

See COINS; WEIGHTS AND MEASURES.

Talitha Cumi. Aramaic words spoken by Jesus and retained by Mark in his Gospel (Mk 5:41). Jairus, a synagogue official in the Galilean region, called on Jesus to heal his sick daughter; however, she died before Jesus arrived. Coming to the girl, Jesus took her hand and said "Talitha cumi," meaning "Little girl, arise." "Talitha" is a term of affection meaning "lamb" or "youth." "Cumi" is a command to rise up, translated by Mark as "I say to you, arise!"

Mark shows originality in his Gospel by the inclusion of Aramaic phrases attributed to Jesus (3:17; 5:41; 7:11,34; 11:9,10; 14:36; 15:22,34). Matthew retains only one Aramaic phrase (Golgotha, 27:33) and Luke keeps none. Some suggest that Mark kept these original words to impress upon his gentile readers the miracle that Jesus performed. Perhaps a better explanation is that Mark wanted to preserve the actual words of Jesus, especially on more significant occasions.

Talmai. 1. Son of Anak and brother of Ahiman and Sheshai. Talmai and his people were observed by the 12 Israelite spies when they searched out the land (Nm 13:22). Later Caleb successfully defeated Talmai and his brothers, who were living in Hebron (Jos 15:14; Jgs 1:10).

2. Son of Ammihud and father of Maacah. Maacah bore to David Absalom, his third son (2 Sm 3:3; 1 Chr 3:2). Absalom eventually sought refuge in Talmai's small kingdom of Geshur after murdering Amnon (2 Sm 13:37).

Talmon. Head of a Levite family who served as temple gatekeepers (1 Chr 9:17). His descendants returned from the exile with Zerubbabel and served as gatekeepers in the rebuilt temple (Ezr 2:42; Neh 7:45; 11:19; 12:25).

Talmud. Word meaning "to study," "to learn." It is a body of literature in Hebrew and Aramaic, covering interpretations of legal portions of the OT, progressive establishment of traditional materials, and addition of a body of wise counsel from many rabbinical sources, spanning a time period from shortly after Ezra at about 400 BC until approximately the AD 500s.

Origin and Development of the Oral Law. The traditional Jews believe that a second law was given to Moses in addition to the first or written word, and that this second one was given orally, and handed down from generation to generation in oral form. The Talmud itself makes this claim for an early origin and *Pirke Aboth* 1:1 states that it is attributed to Moses. Other scholars do not agree on this origin of the oral law and insist that it had its beginning and development after Ezra. For example, there is no mention by the preexilic prophets concerning a lapse from the oral law, but the messages of the prophets abound in warnings about abandoning the written revelation given to Moses, thereby indicating the absence of a body of oral tradition prior to the Babylonian exile.

In the period succeeding Ezra ("a scribe skilled in the law of Moses," Ezr 7:6) teacher succeeded teacher in synagogues and schools, and their understanding of the OT was treasured and memorized. Across the centuries many memorizing devices were employed to learn and remember the growing mass of opinions and interpretation, but eventually not even the best memory could retain all the available materials. It was finally necessary to compile a summary of all the essential teachings of preceding generations, and also to facilitate access for future generations to the immense treasure of thought, religious feeling, and wisdom for guidance and inspiration. The compilation is known as the Talmud, the basic repository of the oral law. Jewish people regard it as second to the Scriptures. A literature recognized as the genius of a national and religious creation, it has a profound influence upon the development of the Jewish world view.

Need for an Oral Law. With cessation of the postexilic prophets and with the continual development of the complexity of life in Israel and its relationships to the outer world, there arose a need for further elaboration of the laws of the Pentateuch. Those who returned from Babylon saw this need of providing for Israel's obedience to the law of Moses. The oral law at first was intended to be helpful so that people could obey the written word of God.

The oral law contained in the Talmud has a twofold function. There is an interpretation of the written law. According to the rabbis, this is necessary since the oral law makes it possible to observe the written law. Without the former it would be impossible to observe the latter. A good example is work as indicated by the biblical sabbath law. Everyone knew that work was not done on the sabbath. The rabbis contend however that it took the oral law to define what was meant by work, and if this meaning was not present then the biblical injunction would not be helpful at all.

But there also came eventually the emphasis that the oral law modifies and seeks to adapt the written law to fit new conditions and circumstances. The argument is that the oral law makes the written law a viable document from generation to generation. Without this oral law, the written law would become obsolete. Therefore, the oral law is necessary for observance of prohibitions as well as for stressing what is good Jewish devotion and loyalty.

Every generation must face new social, political, and economic conditions which make necessary a different application of the word of God. The word of God cannot be changed in order to accommodate personal desires or interpret new problems in different ages. Something of this is apparent in the 1st century AD, when Jesus referred to men's traditions and the word of God (Mk 7:9–13).

Basic Antecedents to the Talmud. One of the earliest means for teaching oral law was a running commentary, or Midrash ("to expound"), of the biblical text. If the teaching handled the legal portions of the OT, then it was referred to as Midrash Halakah (the latter emphasized a way by which one walks or lives). When treating nonlegal, ethical, or devotional portions of the OT, then the opinions and understanding was called Midrash Haggadah ("narration"). Ezra and his trained associates were using the method of Midrash upon the occasion of the completion of the Jerusalem wall in 444 BC when they "explained the law to the people while the people remained in their place. And they read from the book, from the law of God, translating to give the sense so that they understood the reading" (Neh 8:7,8 NASB). This kind of oral Midrash is the method followed by generations of teachers after Ezra, when the religious leaders were known as Soferim ("bookmen," or "scribes"), until about 200 BC. Sometimes referred to as the "Great Synagogue," these scholars provided teaching to "hedge" the revealed moral and ceremonial word so that Israel would never stray into idolatry or ignorance again. The Soferim were succeeded by the Hasidim ("pious ones") who tried to maintain a high level of religious devotion. In turn, the Hasidim were succeeded by the Pharisees ("separated ones") at about 128 BC. Each of these groups contributed to the Midrash method. This material continued to increase and was transmitted orally.

In the period from about 270 BC to the end of the 1st century BC, five pairs (zugot) of teachers appeared of whom the last and greatest were Shammai and Hillel. The Zugot were responsible for a new method of teaching, developing oral law without reference to the Scriptures. This method allowed the study of numerous subjects without being tied to the sequence of biblical materials. By the end of the 1st century BC, Midrash Halakah was so cumbersome that any further expansion of oral law proceeded without reference to the sequence of Scripture. However, the defenders of the oral law claim that even in this new approach every oral teaching can be traced to some biblical base. Succeeding generations learned these materials through continuous repetition. Therefore, the new method was called Mishna ("repetition"), and the teachers of the Mishna were known as Tannaim ("those who handed down orally").

Both Midrash and Mishna existed side by side in ensuing generations. There came a time, however, when it was necessary to codify the oral law covered by Mishna since this too became cumbersome to learn as a body of material. In the later period of the Tannaim, Rabbi Akiba (d. under the Hadrian persecution in AD 135), had already collected much of the Mishna teaching and put it into some kind of order. His disciple Rabbi Meir (AD 110–175) continued this development which in turn became the working model for Rabbi Judah HaNasi (AD 135–217). This latter teacher, held in highest esteem by the schools of his day, chose the most significant material for Jewish life and action, covering the periods of *Soferim, Hasidim, Zugot,* and *Tannaim* up to his own day, as the basis for his work, entitled *Mishna.* Widely recognized as definitive of the oral law in that period, it became the basis of instruction and provided the materials for further study, research, and commentary. The *Mishna* of HaNasi appears in a combination of early and later Hebrew with some Aramaic and the language is known as a postbiblical or Mishnaic Hebrew.

What was codified by Judah HaNasi obviously did not cover all the existing materials. Other teachers had their collections which included many materials HaNasi did not use for his *Mishna.* Subsequent study and research used the extra works—for example, *Tosefta* ("additions") and *Baraita* (single lines of oral law)—in Israel's schools along with the existing *Mishna.* The scholars of the period following HaNasi were known as *Amoraim* ("speakers," between AD 200–500). The *Amoraim* commented on the *Mishna,* using the materials omitted by the *Mishna,* and continued to develop oral law, or *halakot* (legal judgments), to fit new conditions of life. Many *Haggadah* as well as *Midrash* sources were also used. All of this intellectual activity, put into writing, came to be known as *Gemara* ("completion") and the combination of *Gemara* and *Mishna* constitute the Talmud.

Division of Mishna and Talmud. The *Mishna* and Talmud are divided into six orders. Each order in turn is divided into tractates; the total number of tractates is 63. The tractates are subdivided into chapters. When references are made to material in the Talmud, they are designated by tractate, followed either by chapter and verse for the *Mishna,* or by page number and letters a–d for *Gemara.* The Orders are: 1) *Zeraim* ("seeds"), which treat the laws of agriculture; 2) *Moed* ("feasts"), the regulations of the sabbath and other yearly festivals; 3) *Nashim* ("women"), laws concerning women, marriage, and divorce; 4) *Nezikin* ("damages"), regulations of the civil and criminal law codes; 5) *Kodashim* ("consecrated things"), laws that treat the temple observances and sacrificial rites; and 6) *Toharoth* ("purifications"), laws of levitical purity.

The Intent of the Terms. *Halakah* refers to the legal material of the Talmud while *Haggadah* had in mind the areas of ethics and religious practices. In the latter homilies, moral emphases, statements of wisdom, the stories of Israel of both historical, prophetic, and legend, and even statements concerning the sciences of medicine, astronomy, botany, geometry, and so forth. But the sole purpose of the *Haggadah* was not merely to engage in secular studies by themselves, but to inspire and move a people to righteousness as indicated by the *Halakah.*

The Talmud Versions. Two active schools were present during the period of the *Amoraim* in Israel and Babylon. The two sets of scholars worked with the *Mishna* of Judah

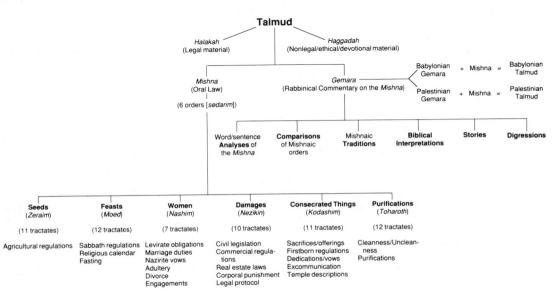

HaNasi as well as with the material that HaNasi omitted. By providing their own commentaries on these materials, they produced two versions of the *Gemara,* and therefore two versions of the Talmud.

One is the *Yerushalmi* or Jerusalemite of the land of Israel. Sometimes referred to as the "Talmud of the Children of the West," the language is western Aramaic. As a result of the persecutions which Jewish people suffered in the 2nd, 3rd, and 4th centuries, this *Gemara* is shorter than the Babylonian version. One main scholar who probably laid the groundwork for this Talmud was Rabbi Yohanan ben Nappaha (d. AD 279). A prominent disciple of Judah HaNasi, he founded the academy at Tiberias which became an important center of the development of this Talmud. In this version there is only *Gemara* for the first four Orders of the *Mishna,* and the work does not have the completeness and smooth reading as its sister version of Babylon. While this Talmud is therefore subordinate to that of the Babylonian, it is extremely interesting since it provides a *Halakah* in direct succession to the *Mishna* in the homeland of Jewish people, and the *Haggadah* provides insight as to Jewish life in Israel. It was completed shortly before the closing of the Tiberias school when the Jewish patriarchate ended about AD 425.

The other version, known as the Babylonian, is written in eastern Aramaic. It is three times as long as the Jerusalem and is the most definitive for belief and practice. Each *Gemara* was not developed without interchange and interrelation of ideas between both sets of leaders in Israel and Babylon. The Israel schools were responsible for the initial training of the leaders in Babylon. Two well-known Babylonians were disciples of Judah HaNasi, Rav Abba (d. AD 247) and Mer Samuel (d. AD 254). When they completed their training in Israel, they returned and founded schools in Babylon. Under the guidance of these two the serious work of traditional development began. Other scholars followed suit and the rabbis of Babylon produced their *Gemara.* One-third of the contents of the Babylonian *Gemara* matches the *Haggadah* and reflects much of the secular and religious knowledge of that day.

Influence and Persecution. The Talmud was finished at a time when in the western world Jewish people turned inward as a result of pressure and persecution. These traditional materials were therefore instrumental in influencing a dispersed people and became even more important to the succeeding generations. Jewish preservation, both as a people and as a religion, was due in large part to the Talmud. In times of stress and danger, Jewish people found in the pages of the Talmud their solace, from which they could draw religious inspiration and guidance. It was a retreat where they could forget the world around them, but also where they would find religious strength to endure pressures. In a number of instances the Talmud did exert a profound influence on the church of the Middle Ages, and this in turn helped to prepare for the Renaissance of the 1200s and 1300s.

On the other hand, the Talmud did incur animosity from a number of sources. Astute leaders, both pagan and gentile Christians, recognized the supreme importance that *Mishna* and *Gemara* played in the belief and practice of the Jewish people. Jewish leaders in Israel were not able to quietly do a definitive work on their *Gemara.* The Middle Ages had a notorious record of hatred for this work. Especially in the period from 1200–1500, many copies of the Talmud were burned publicly with the idea that this would deter further study by Jewish people. The Babylonian Talmud in particular was censored by the church and passages, thought to be offensive to Christianity, were deleted altogether. This persecution has continued even to modern times where it is believed that all misdeeds committed by Jews against non-Jews could be directly traced to the teachings of the Talmud. The obvious desire in the modern period was to encourage anti-Semitism. Translations of the Talmud have helped to dispel the false charges of those who have wrongly maligned the Talmud and thereby the Jewish people.

Present Significance of the Talmud. The Talmud across the centuries occupied an important place in Jewish education and was the principal text of study. Jewish academies and schools studied the completed Talmud. At an early age, Jewish youth began study, and this emphasis continued in the more advanced program of instruction in the *Yeshivot* (seminary equivalents). This distinctive feature of study, spanning the Middle Ages to the modern period, reached the point where the knowledge of the Talmud was considered better than that of the Scriptures. However, the Jewish humanist Enlightenment movement in the 1800s, no doubt resulting from attacks on the validity of the OT by critical scholars in the continental church in Europe, appealed to great numbers of Jewish people who could find little help in the Talmud for the secular world view of the 19th century. At the same time however, the Talmud was the mainstay of the religiously oriented Jew who sought by *Halakah* to meet the new demands of a modern world.

With the rise of the State of Israel there appeared a greater interest in the Talmud, even where it had been previously neglected. More and more Jewish schools outside of Israel and the schools in Israel include it as a course of study. In Israel in particular, many laws which had become obsolete with the fall of Israel in AD 70 are now beginning to find application, for example, in agriculture, and the Talmud is providing more light and guidance. Even in situations where the laws of the Talmud would not directly apply the Talmud provides applicable guidelines, for example, in observance of Jewish festivals, marriage laws, virtues of compassion and benevolence, and hatred for injustice in society, that reflect biblical and Jewish values.

The Christian can also benefit from the Talmud since it provides insights into life, beliefs, and religious practices of the 1st century AD. The Gospel accounts find parallels in the Talmud. Not unexpectedly, the Gospels reflect a Jewish world and culture, and therefore the Talmud provides an indispensible background. The *Mishna* in particular provides a great deal of knowledge as to temple life and practices. There is also an opportunity to observe ancient Jewish insights into scriptural exegesis and practice. LOUIS GOLDBERG

See JUDAISM; MIDRASH; MISHNA; GEMARA; TRADITION, ORAL; LAW, BIBLICAL CONCEPT OF; SHAMMAI #4; TORAH; HILLEL #2; PHARISEES; HELLENISTIC JUDAISM; JOHANAN BEN ZAKKAI; HAGGADAH; HALAKAH; AKIBA, RABBI; HALLEL; TRADITION.

Bibliography. M. Adler, *The World of the Talmud;* B.Z. Bokser, *The Wisdom of the Talmud;* A. Cohen, *Everyman's Talmud;* H. Danby, *The Mishna;* R.T. Herford, *Christianity in Talmud and Midrash;* A.J. Kolatch, *Who's Who in the Talmud;* C.G. Montefiore and H. Loewe, *A Rabbinic Anthology;* S. Schechter, *Aspects of Rabbinic Theology;* H.L. Strack, *Introduction to the Talmud and Midrash.*

Tamah. KJV spelling of Temah in Nehemiah 7:55.

See TEMAH.

Tamar (Person). 1. Wife of Er, the firstborn son of Judah by Bath-shua, the Canaanitess. Later, as a widow, Tamar bore two sons to Judah named Perez and Zebed (Gn 38:6–24; 1 Chr 2:4). Tamar preserved the line of Judah through Perez (Ru 4:12), and her name is recorded in the genealogy of Christ (Mt 1:3, KJV Thamar).

See GENEALOGY OF JESUS CHRIST.

2. Sister of Absalom and the daughter of David by his wife Maacah, the Geshurite. Through deceit, Tamar was seduced by Amnon, her half-brother. In vengeance, Absalom her full brother had Amnon murdered at Baal-hazor (2 Sm 13; 1 Chr 3:9).

3. Daughter of Absalom who was noted for her beauty. She perhaps married Uriel of Gibeah and became the mother of Maacah (2 Sm 14:27).

Tamar (Place). City located southwest of the Dead Sea in Judah's tribe. It was one of the places built up by Solomon in his extensive campaign to increase the might and grandeur of the Hebrew empire and was carefully fortified to safeguard the important trade route between the Elath seaport and southern Arabia (1 Kgs 9:18).

In 2 Chronicles 8:4–6, a parallel list of Solomon's building enterprise, the text reads Tadmor (v 4) instead of Tamar. Hence, some scholars have identified Tamar with Tadmor, an affluent mercantile center northeast of Damascus. Others view the cities as two distinct places, since the parallel readings are not identical and Tamar is said to be in "the land" (presumably Judah; 1 Kgs 9:18). The latter identify Tamar with the place mentioned by Ezekiel, a town on the eastern border of Israel's promised southern extremity (47:18,19; 48:28). Its site is located between Elath and Hebron at modern Kurnub.

See TADMOR.

Tamarisk. Small, mainly desert tree with small flowers (Gn 21:33).

See PLANTS.

Tambourine. Percussion instrument consisting of a shallow one-headed drum with small metal discs attached on the side which jingle when the instrument is tapped or shaken (1 Sm 10:5).

See MUSIC AND MUSICAL INSTRUMENTS (TOPH).

Tammuz. Chief Sumerian deity whose name derived from the Sumerian *dumuzi*. He is the god of fertility, of vegetation and agriculture, of death and resurrection, and the patron of shepherds. The son and consort of Ashtar (Inanna), Tammuz represented the annual vegetation cycle of death during the heat of summer and the rebirth of life with the coming of the fall and spring rains, as mythically recounted in the Akkadian poem, "Inanna's Descent into the Netherworld." This rejuvenation of life and defeat of death was annually celebrated during the Babylonian New Year Festival. In the OT, the prophet Ezekiel sees in a vision women weeping for Tammuz at the north gate of the temple, descriptive of coming desecrations of the Lord's house (8:14).

In subsequent cultures following the Sumerian civilization (3rd millennium BC), the Tammuz cult was carried on; it was undoubtedly embodied in the worship of Marduk of Babylon, Ashur of Assyria, Baal of Canaan, Attis of Phrygia, and Adonis of Syria (Aram) and Greece. Numerous liturgies and dirges have been found detailing Tammuz worship in ancient Mesopotamian culture. During the post-exilic era, the fourth month of the Hebrew calendar was named Tammuz.

See CALENDARS, ANCIENT AND MODERN.

Tanach. KJV spelling of Taanach, a levitical town, in Joshua 21:25.

See TAANACH.

Tanhumeth. Seraiah's father from the town of Netophah in Judah. Seraiah captained an army of Netophathite men, who served under Gedaliah during the Babylonian suzerainty (2 Kgs 25:23; Jer 40:8).

Tannaim. Teachers of the oral law mentioned in the *Mishna* during the period beginning with the students of Shammai and Hillel in AD 10 and ending with the pupils of Judah HaNasi I in AD 220.

See TALMUD.

Tanner, Tanning. Worker and process of changing hide into leather (Acts 9:43).

See TRADES AND OCCUPATIONS.

Taphath. Solomon's daughter and the wife of Ben-abinadab, Solomon's officer in Naphath-or (1 Kgs 4:11).

Tappuah (Person). Hebron's son and a descendant of Caleb from Judah's tribe (1 Chr 2:43).

Tappuah (Place). 1. One of 14 cities located in the Shephelah assigned to Judah's tribe for an inheritance, mentioned between En-gannim and Enam (Jos 15:34). This locality is not to be mistaken for the land of Tappuah in Manasseh (17:8) or the town of Beth-tappuah at Hebron (15:53). Perhaps this was the town formerly ruled by the Canaanite king (12:17). Its location is unknown.

2. City situated in the hill country of Palestine defining part of the northern boundary of the territory allotted to Ephraim's tribe for an inheritance. From Tappuah the northern border ran westward to Kanah Brook then followed its course to the Mediterranean Sea (16:8). The land of Tappuah was a district within the territory given to the tribe of Manasseh; however, the city of Tappuah, located on the border of Manasseh, belonged to the Ephraimites (17:8). The land of Tappuah is unknown. The city of En-tappuah (v 7) is possibly the same as Tappuah (also called Tephon in 1 Mc 9:50). The site for this city is perhaps eight miles southwest of Shechem (Nablus)

and twenty-five miles northwest of Jerusalem at Sheikh Abu Zarad.

Tarah. KJV spelling of Terah, one of the stopping places during the wilderness journey, in Numbers 33:27,28.

See TERAH (PLACE).

Taralah. One of 26 cities in the land assigned to Benjamin's tribe for an inheritance, listed between Irpeel and Zelah (Jos 18:27). Taralah was possibly situated to the northwest of Jerusalem, though its present site is unknown.

Tarea. Micah's son, Benjamite, and a descendant of King Saul (1 Chr 8:35); alternately called Tahrea in 1 Chronicles 9:41.

Tares. KJV rendering of weeds in Matthew 13:25–30.

See PLANTS (DARNEL GRASS).

Tarpelites. KJV rendering of "officials" in Ezra 4:9. Its precise meaning is uncertain but possibly is a Persian title or an ethnic name.

Tarshish (Person). 1. One of Javan's four sons and a descendant of Noah through Japheth's line (1 Chr 1:7).

2. Sixth of Bilham's seven sons. He was a capable leader in Benjamin's tribe and numbered among those able to go to war (1 Chr 7:10, KJV Tharshish).

3. One of the seven princes of Persia and Media. These men had personal access to King Ashasuerus's presence and positions of honor second only to the king himself (Est 1:14).

Tarshish (Place). Place regarded as distant from Israel. Many countries have been proposed as the site for Tarshish, from Sardinia to Great Britain. The most commonly accepted identification is Spain, where the name Tartessus hints at Tarshish.

Tarshish is listed as a son of Javan (Greece) (Gn 10:4) with brothers Elishah (Cyprus?) and Kittim (Rome), which seems to locate it in the Mediterranean world (cf. 1 Chr 1:7).

The Phoenicians, who were great sea voyagers, are often associated with Tarshish. Solomon used the sailors of Hiram, king of Tyre, for his fleet (cf. 2 Chr 9:21). They used sailing vessels that were called Tarshish ships (1 Kgs 10:22; 22:48, KJV Tharshish); apparently they were a distinctive type used to journey to that place or were typical of Tarshish (Ps 48:7; Is 2:16; 23:1-14). Jehoshaphat also attempted to engage in such trading ventures, but his ships wrecked (2 Chr 20:36,37).

In his prophecy against Tyre (Is 23), Isaiah mentions Tarshish four times. With their commercial enterprises, Tyre and Tarshish had much in common (e.g., v 10 calls Tyre a "daughter of Tarshish").

The ships of Tarshish will return to Israel the distant Israelites with their treasures, because of the name of the Lord (Is 60:9). Tarshish is listed among the distant peoples to whom the glory of the Lord will be declared (Is 66:19).

Jeremiah refers to "beaten silver" from Tarshish as material for making idols (Jer 10:9).

In his long prophecy against Tyre, Ezekiel comments on the trade between Tarshish and Tyre (27:12). Tarshish exchanged silver, iron, tin, and lead for Tyre's wares. He also states that ships of Tarshish carried Tyrian merchandise (v 25).

The most famous reference to Tarshish in the Bible is in the account of Jonah, who attempted to flee to Tarshish to escape doing the will of God (Jon 1:3; 4:2).

Tarsus. Birthplace and hometown of Saul (Paul) and the capital and chief city of the Roman province of Cilicia in Asia Minor. The city is mentioned only five times in the Bible, always in the Book of Acts. After Saul's conversion, the Lord directed Ananias to visit Saul; Ananias was told to ask for "a man of Tarsus named Saul" (9:11). Then when Saul returned to Jerusalem and a plot against his life was discovered, the Christians sent him to Tarsus (9:30). When Barnabas was serving in Syrian Antioch and needed help, he went to Tarsus to get Saul to work with him (11:25). On the occasion of Paul's rescue from the Jewish mob in the temple, the Roman tribune was concerned with Paul's identity. Paul identified himself: "I am a Jew, from Tarsus in Cilicia, a citizen of no mean city" (21:39). In the defense he made before that angry multitude, speaking in Hebrew, he declared, "I am a Jew, born at Tarsus in Cilicia" (22:3).

Tarsus was situated on the Cydnus River, some 12 miles upstream from the Mediterranean. The plain on which the city was built was very fertile, composed of alluvium carried down from the Taurus Mountains by the Cydnus and several other streams.

Although the river was navigable by small boats as far as Tarsus, the overland trade routes were the most important. Asia Minor was interlaced with roads long before the Romans came into the area. From the east there were two main routes, one of which began in northern Mesopotamia and went on to Carchemish or Aleppo, across the Amanus Pass. The other ran from Nineveh through Malatya and Antioch to the Syrian Gates. These two routes converged near Caesarea, some 50 miles east of Tarsus. During the Roman Empire "the Old Way to the East" ended at Babylon; coming westward it reached Aleppo, Syrian Antioch, Adana, Tarsus, the Cilician Gates, Derbe, Lystra, Iconium, Pisidian Antioch, Hierapolis, Colossae, Laodicea, Ephesus, Smyrna, and Troas, most of which are well known from the writings of Paul and from the Apocalypse.

The Cilician Gates were the narrow pass through which the travelers, traders, and armies of many ages funneled through the Taurus Mountains. About 35 miles north of Tarsus, this short defile saw the passage of the Hittite forces, the hosts of Persia, the 10,000 of Xenophon, and the armies of Alexander the Great on their way to defeat Darius at Issus.

Tarsus was an educational center; the university of Tarsus was famous for its scholarship and Strabo indicated that Tarsus surpassed Athens, Alexandria, and other cities as a seat of learning. The university offered instruction in a wide range of studies; one of its specializations was the philosophy known as Stoicism, with which Paul was familiar. Although Paul does not say that he attended this institution, it has often been suggested that he studied there.

Historically, Tarsus is mentioned on the Black Obelisk of Shalmaneser III (858–824 BC) and also appears in the *Anabasis* of Xenophon

A portion of Cleopatra's Arch at Tarsus.

(*c.* 400 BC). Pompey made Cilicia a Roman province in 64 BC and it was a free city from the time of Augustus. Plutarch even reported a voyage made to Tarsus by Cleopatra.

Also of interest in connection with Paul is the fact that Tarsus was a center of tent-making, a vocation in which Paul had been trained (cf. Acts 18:3). The goats of the cold, snow-swept Taurus Mountains produced long hair which was made into a fabric particularly well-suited for tents.

Tarsus has been described as "the heart of the Greco-Roman world" and "a meeting place of East and West." From such an environment a man like Saul of Tarsus, at home with Greek and Roman culture and educated at the feet of Gamaliel, was singularly equipped to bring the gospel to the Jew first and also to the Greek.

See PAUL, THE APOSTLE.

Tartak. Deity worshiped by the Avvites in Samaria (2 Kgs 17:31). This deity may be a union of the deities Athtar and Anath, and thus a fertility god.

See SYRIA, SYRIANS.

Tartan. Highest-ranking Assyrian official, second in command only to the king himself. He was the commander in chief of the Assyrian army. Sargon II, king of Assyria (722–705 BC), ordered his commander to subdue and capture the Philistine city of Ashdod (Is 20:1). The tartan was one of three officials whom King Sennacherib of Assyria (705–681 BC) posted over the Assyrian army sent from Lachish to Jerusalem to confront King Hezekiah of Judah (715–687 BC). The commanders of Sargon II and Sennacherib were probably not the same person.

Taskmaster. *See* SLAVE, SLAVERY; TRADES AND OCCUPATIONS.

Tattenai, Tatnai. Persian governor of a province west of the Euphrates River, who opposed the rebuilding of the Jerusalem temple and walls under Zerubbabel during the postexilic period (Ezr 5:3,6; 6:6,13, KJV Tatnai).

Tax, Taxation. Amount of money or goods that was extracted by the powerful nations from those whom they subjected. It commonly consisted of gold, silver, animals, produce, or forced labor. Taxes were also levied on the people both by their ruler and by the priesthood to pay for the maintenance of the temple. The term "tribute" is first used in Genesis 49:15, and in Numbers 31:28 the spoils of battle were divided up to include a tribute or levy for the priesthood. For the Hebrews this temple tribute was originally a voluntary "freewill offering to the Lord" (Dt 16:10), but later became a prescribed tax (Mt 17:24).

Even in 2500 BC in Lagash, taxes were imposed on most facets of life, from the means of earning a livelihood to marriage, divorce, and death. Like many ancient peoples, the Sumerians believed that the land belonged to the god and his representative the king, and that therefore a rent or levy was payable to the owner.

In Egypt, Joseph exacted a burdensome 20 percent tax in grain during the seven years of plenty, which alleviated the food shortages during the subsequent seven years of famine (Gn 41:25–42:5). The tax on the crops was facilitated because in Egypt the ownership of the land was vested in the ruler.

Warrior kings, such as David, were able to maintain a healthy treasury without taxing their own people. The Canaanites and neighboring conquered peoples contributed great wealth to the treasury (2 Sm 8:6–14; 1 Chr 27:25–31), one list of which included silver, gold, bronze, 1700 horsemen, and 20,000 foot soldiers. Forced labor was often required by David and his successors of aliens who remained within the boundaries of the Israelite kingdom (Jos 16:10; 17:13; Jgs 1:28).

Israel was probably first taxed during Solomon's reign. In this more stable period, income came from tribute but not from booty. To maintain the grandeur of the court and the extensive building program, Solomon divided Israel into 12 areas under an officer, each of whom provided food and support for the king and his household for one month per year (1 Kgs 4:7). Solomon also derived considerable income from levying custom duties on trading caravans that passed regularly through his kingdom. In addition to all of this, both foreigners and native Israelites were subject to forced labor for major building projects, especially for the temple (1 Kgs 5:13; 9:20,21; 2 Chr 8:7,8). Handles from 10-gallon jars have been excavated, bearing a Hebrew stamp "to the king," indicating that they formed part of a levy in kind (2 Chr 2:10).

Jehoshaphat was equally successful in taxing the people at home (2 Chr 17:5) and maintaining the tribute from abroad, including silver and gold from the Philistines and 7700 rams and 7700 he-goats from the Arabs (18:11, 12). As the power of the surrounding empires increased, Judah found itself forced to pay tribute in turn. Sennacherib, king of Assyria, required 300 talents of silver and 30 talents of gold, which necessitated the depletion of the gold from the temple doors (2 Kgs 18:14–16). Approximately a century later, Pharaoh Neco required 100 talents of silver and a talent of gold from Judah (23:33), and shortly thereafter Nebuchadnezzar removed all the treasure from the temple and the royal palace, together with 10,000 captives, all the craftsmen, and 1000 smiths, leaving few in Jerusalem except the poor (24:13–16).

A definite, regular, organized tax system was instituted by the Persians, whose satraps, ruling each province, were required to make payment of fixed sums into the royal treasury (Est 10:1). Tax exemption was introduced by Artaxerxes I, who stated that levies should not be collected from priests, Levites, or any others occupied in any way with the service of the temple (Ezr 7:24). An additional tax was required for the maintenance of the governor's household, and consisted of food, wine, and 40 shekels of silver (Neh 5:14,15). As governor, Nehemiah did not claim this allowance of food (v 18) because he considered the taxes already burdensome, causing the mortgaging of fields, vineyards, and houses "for the king's tax" (vv 3,4). Simultaneously a levy was imposed upon the Jews for the rebuilding of the walls of Jerusalem (4:6). Darius was politically astute enough to encourage the rebuilding of the temple and to allow the Jews to use some of the royal tax money for this purpose (Ezr 6:7–10).

Under the Seleucids, the Ptolemies, and subsequently the Romans, there was a change in the collection of taxes whereby the office of tax collector was sold to the highest bidder, who in turn extracted the maximum payment from the people and built up his own wealth from the surplus generated. At times the Jews were paying tithes for the maintenance of the temple, in addition to taxes of as much as one-third of the grain and half of the fruit grown. Excise, sales, and poll taxes were also collected.

After the extortionate level of tax imposed by Pompey, Julius Caesar reduced the amount paid by the Jews and exempted them from all payment in the sabbatical year. The provinces were considered booty by the Romans, and were plundered physically by the army and financially by the tax collectors. In imperial times there was greater regulation of the tax system. An income tax was imposed on produce from the field and from artisans and tradesmen, as well as a poll tax, port duties, sales taxes, an auction tax, and an estate duty.

In addition to the taxes paid to foreign powers, all Jews worldwide who were 20 years of age and older (Ex 30:11–16) were assessed a half-shekel per person annually as a tax to support the temple in Jerusalem (Mt 17:24), a tax which continued to be levied even after the destruction of the temple in AD 70. Jesus was questioned on the validity of this tax (v 25), as well as the lawfulness of payment of taxes to Rome (22:17; Mk 12:14,15; Lk 20:22). Despite Jesus' famous reply (Mt 22:21; Mk 12:17; Lk 20:25) he was still accused before Pilate of "forbidding us to give tribute to Caesar" (Lk 23:2). The early church also reinforced the legality of taxation as a legitimate responsibility required of all people (Rom 13:5–7).

HAZEL W. PERKIN

See MONEY AND BANKING.

Bibliography. A. Bailey, *Daily Life in Bible Times;* S.W. Baron, *A Social and Religious History of the Jews,* 8 vols; W.E. Caldwell and M.F. Gyles, *The Ancient World,* 3rd ed; H. Daniel-Rops, *Daily Life in Palestine at the Time of Christ;* H. Jagersma, *A History of Israel in the OT Period;* J.B. Pritchard, *Ancient Near Eastern Texts.*

Tax Collector. *See* TAX, TAXATION; TRADES AND OCCUPATIONS.

Teacher. *See* EDUCATION; TRADES AND OCCUPATIONS.

Tebah. Oldest son of Abraham's brother Nahor (Gn 22:24). His mother was Reumah, Nahor's concubine.

Tebaliah. Hosah's son, Merarite Levite, and a temple gatekeeper who served during the postexilic period (1 Chr 26:11).

Tebeth. Month in the Hebrew calendar corresponding to about mid-December to mid-January (Est 2:16).

See CALENDARS, ANCIENT AND MODERN.

Tehaphnehes. Alternate spelling of Tahpanhes, an Egyptian city, in Ezekiel 30:18.

See TAHPANHES.

Tehinnah. Forefather of the people of Irnahash in Judah's tribe (1 Chr 4:12).

Teil. KJV rendering of terebinth in Isaiah 6:13.

See PLANTS (TEREBINTH).

Tekel. Aramaic word interpreted as "weighed" in Daniel 5:25,27.

See MENE, MENE, TEKEL, PARSIN.

Tekoa, Tekoah, Tekoite. City about six miles south, southeast of Bethlehem on the edge of the Judean desert and its residents. Tekoa may also be the name of a person, the son of Ashur of Judah's tribe; "father" could mean founder or leader of Tekoa (1 Chr 2:24; 4:5). Tekoa does not appear on the list of cities given to Judah (Jos 15). Today the unexcavated site is marked by Khirbet et-Tequ‘ (meaning ruins of Tekoa in Arabic). A nearby village still bears the ancient name whose meaning is uncertain.

Tekoa is located on the high ground between two watersheds both of which flow eastward to the Dead Sea. The southern slopes climb off to the upper reaches of the Nahal Arugot which eventually comes out at En-gedi. The northern slopes are drained by the Nahal Darga. The ridge between them is the Ascent (or Pass) of Ziz (2 Chr 20:16). Because Tekoa lies between the desert and the town on the marginal land just east of the main north-south watershed, the area around it came to be known as the Desert of Tekoa (2 Chr 20:20), a part of the larger Desert of Judea. Tekoa marks the border where farming gives way to herding, explaining why Amos, a native of Tekoa, had two dimensions to his preprophetic career: a herdsman and a dresser of sycamore trees (Am 1:1; 7:14).

Apart from incidental references to people who came from Tekoa (Amos—Am 1:1; Ikkesh—2 Sm 23:26; 1 Chr 11:28; 27:9; and certain builders on the postexilic wall of Jerusalem—Neh 3:5,27), two noteworthy OT events involved Tekoa.

The record of 2 Samuel 14 (KJV Tekoah) tells of the return of Absalom to Jerusalem and to his father David. It was Joab's idea to recruit a "wise woman" from Tekoa to fabricate a story about her sons which had marked resemblances to recent events in David's family, namely, one brother murdered another brother, and the life of the killer was now in danger of clan revenge. Even though David discovered the ruse, the episode still prompted him to return Absalom to the capital city. Whether Tekoa was a repository for wisdom or whether it was quite incidental that such a woman was found there for Joab's purpose is a moot question.

The second incident occurred about 850 BC during the reign of the Judean king Jehosha-phat. Second Chronicles 20:1–28 records the invasion of the Moabites, Ammonites, and Meunites. They probably forded the Dead Sea at the Lisan, the peninsula that points from the east side toward Masada, marched northward along the western shore, turned left at En-gedi, and climbed steeply north and west toward Jerusalem. (Rehoboam, the first king in Judah after the division of the kingdom in 930 BC, had fortified a number of cities on his border. Tekoa was one of these.)

After prayer the word of the Lord came through the prophet Jahaziel. He indicated that Jehoshaphat should march out and "see the deliverance the Lord will give" (v 17). Somewhere between Tekoa and the "end of the gorge in the Desert of Jeruel" (cf. v 1) some unspecified disaster befell the invaders so that they ended up fighting and killing each other. The soldiers of Judah only gathered the plunder.

In an oracle predicting the siege of Judah, Jeremiah (6:1) makes a pun with the phrase, "Sound the trumpet in Tekoa." The Hebrew word for "sound" is spelled with the same consonants (but not vowels) as Tekoa.

ROBERT L. ALDEN

Telabib. Village on the river Chebar where Ezekiel visited the Babylonian exiles (Ez 3:15). Although the exact location of the site is unknown, it was probably in the delta region of southern Babylonia. The Chebar was likely an irrigation canal which enhanced the fertility of the surrounding soil; hence, the name Tela-bib ("hill of corn").

Telah. Resheph's son, father of Tahan, and an ancestor of Joshua, the son of Nun, from Ephraim's tribe (1 Chr 7:25).

Telaim. Place where Saul organized Israel's army in preparation for war with the Amalekites (1 Sm 15:4). Telaim is perhaps identifiable with Telem, a city situated near Edom's border in the southern extremity of the territory allotted to Judah's tribe for an inheritance (Jos 15:24). Its site is unknown.

Telassar. Principal city of the people of Eden who were conquered by Sennacherib of Assyria (2 Kgs 19:12, KJV Thelasar; Is 37:12). The conquest is mentioned in the Rabshekah's taunt that the Lord would similarly be unable to protect Jerusalem. Though a town Til-asshuri is mentioned frequently in ancient records, its location has not been identified.

Telem (Person). One of the gatekeepers who was encouraged by Ezra to divorce his foreign wife (Ezr 10:24).

Children with a sheep at the ruins of Tekoa.

Telem (Place). Alternate name of the city Telaim in 1 Samuel 15:4.

See TELAIM.

Tel-harsha, Tel-haresha, Tel-harsa. One of the Babylonian villages from which some returning exiles could not establish their genealogy (Ezr 2:59, KJV Tel-harsa; Neh 7:61, KJV Tel-haresha). Its precise location is uncertain, though it is likely near the Persian Gulf in the lowland region of Babylonia.

Tell. Arabic word (Heb *tel*) meaning an artificial mound composed of many layers of occupational debris, representing the ruins of successive cities, roughly like layers of a cake. The unraveling of the strata, or building levels, is one of the biggest challenges of the field archaeologist. The levels are dated primarily by the pottery found in them. The basis for pottery chronology and for stratigraphic archaeology in Palestine was laid by W.M. Flinders Petrie in six weeks of exploration at Tell el Hesi in 1890. This site in southwest Palestine had its layers conveniently exposed by a watercourse which ran along one side of the mound.

Usually tells bear Arabic names, which sometimes have interesting or amusing names. Tell el Ful (Gibeah), the hometown of King Saul, means "the mound of the beans." Tell Beit Mirsim translates into "the mound of the house of the fast camel driver." Other modern names preserve the identity of ancient sites; for example, Tell Taanak is biblical Taanach; Tell Jezer is biblical Gezer.

There are numerous references to tells in the Bible, although in English tell may appear as "mound, heap, or heap of ruins." The Lord commanded Israel that a city which practiced abomination should be burned and "be a heap for ever, it shall not be built again" (Dt 13:16). Joshua 11:13 states that Israel burned none of the cities that stood on mounds, except Hazor. Joshua burned Ai and made it "a heap of ruins for ever" (8:28). In speaking of restoration in the land of Israel, Jeremiah declares: "the city shall be rebuilt upon its mound, and the palace shall stand where it used to be" (30:18). In a prophecy against the Ammonites Jeremiah said that Rabbah "shall become a desolate mound" (49:2). Ezekiel reports that he went to the Israelite exiles in Tel-abib in Babylonia, by the River Chebar (3:15).

Several other place names compounded with the element "tel" are mentioned in the Bible. Among the exiles who returned to Jerusalem from the Babylonian captivity were those from Tel-melah ("the mound of salt") and Tel-harsha (Ezr 2:59; Neh 7:61).

See ARCHAEOLOGY; ARCHAEOLOGY IN THE BIBLE; POTTERY.

Tell Beit Mirsim. Archaeological site 12 miles southwest of Hebron generally identified with biblical Debir (Jos 11:21; 15:15; Jgs 1:11). Excavations during the years 1926–32 revealed occupation beginning with Early Bronze IV (2300 BC) culture and extending, with some interruptions, well into the Israelite period. While some have questioned the connection between Tell Beit Mirsim and Debir, most scholars have accepted the identification. Other scholars have argued that Khirbet Rabud, which was excavated in 1968–69, better fits the details of the biblical text. Tell Beit Mirsim does appear, however, to have been a major settlement that meets the description of Debir as a district capital, levitical city, and a military fortress, having been fortified both by David and later by Asa.

See DEBIR.

Tell El-amarna. *See* AMARNA TABLETS.

Tel-melah. One of the Babylonian towns situated in the vicinity of the Chebar River near the city of Nippur from which exiles, who were unable to establish their Israelite descent, returned to Palestine with Zerubbabel following the Babylonian captivity (Ezr 2:59; Neh 7:61). Its exact location is unknown.

Tema. Ninth son of Ishmael who became chief of a powerful nomadic tribe in the north Arabian wilderness (Gn 25:15; 1 Chr 1:30; Jer 25:23). The descendants of Tema were primarily caravan traders who controlled access to important routes across the desert (Jb 6:19). Tema was also associated with the territory and a town they occupied, the town being generally identified with Teima', an oasis located 400 miles north of Medinah and 40 miles south of Dumah. Teima' was located on an ancient caravan route that connected the Persian Gulf with the Gulf of Aqabah. In prophetic literature, Tema is mentioned with Dedan and Buz as Arabian oases which would not escape God's judgment (Is 21:14; Jer 25:23). The Jeremiah passage contains an obscure indication that Dedan, Team, and Buz were those who "cut the corners of their hair" (RSV; NIV—"all who are in distant places"). The practice of cutting the corners of the hair would distinguish them from the Jews, who left the corners of their hair uncut (Lv 19:27). Like uncircumcision, the practice would identify the men of Tema as pagans.

Temah. Forefather of a family of temple servants that returned with Zerubbabel to Jerusalem following the exile (Ezr 2:53, KJV Thamah; Neh 7:55, KJV Tamah).

Teman, Temani, Temanite. One of the chiefs of the Edomites and Eliphaz's firstborn son (Gn 36:11,15; 36:42; 1 Chr 1:36,53). He was likely either the founder or chief of the Edomite city of Teman.

In the prophetic writings, Teman seems to have been considered the principal city of Edom and is often used as a poetic parallel for the entire land of Edom (Jer 49:7,20; Am 1:12; Ob 9). Since Teman means "south" it is likely that Teman was located in the far south of Edom; however, its precise location remains unknown. The residents of Teman (Temanites; Gn 36:34, KJV Temani; 1 Chr 1:45) were evidently well known for their wisdom (Jer 49:7; Ob 9). This reputation may well derive from Eliphaz the Temanite, who was one of Job's counselors (Jb 2:11; 4:1; 15:1; 22:1; 42:7,9).

Temeni. Ashhur's son by his wife Naarah, and a descendant of Caleb (1 Chr 4:6).

Temple, The. See TABERNACLE, TEMPLE.

Temple Servants. See NETHINIM.

Tempter. See SATAN.

Ten Commandments, The. List of commands given by God to Moses. The Ten Commandments are stated twice in the OT; first in the Book of Exodus (20:2–17), in a passage describing God's gift of the commandments to Israel, and secondly in Deuteronomy (5:6–21), in the context of a covenant renewal ceremony. Moses reminds his people of the substance and meaning of the commandments, as they renew their covenant allegiance to God. In the original language, the Commandments are called the "Ten Words" (from which comes the name Decalogue). According to the biblical text, they are "words," or laws, spoken by God, not the result of human legislative process. The commandments are said to have been written on two tablets. This does not mean that five commandments were written on each tablet; rather, all 10 were written on each tablet, the first tablet belonging to God the lawgiver, the second tablet belonging to Israel the recipient. The commandments pertain to two basic areas of human living; the first five concern relationships with God, the last five, relationships between human beings. The commandments were given first to Israel in the making of the covenant at Mt Sinai, shortly after the exodus from Egypt. Though the date of the Sinai covenant cannot be fixed with certainty, it was probably around 1290 BC. In order to understand the commandments, it is necessary first to understand the context in which they were given.

The Context of the Commandments. The commandments are inseparable from the covenant. The making of a covenant between God and Israel at Sinai was the formation of a particular relationship. God made certain commitments to Israel and in return imposed certain obligations upon Israel. Although Israel's obligations are expressed in detail in a mass of precise legal material, they are given their most precise and succinct expression in the Ten Commandments. The commandments set down the most fundamental principles of all Hebrew law, and the detailed laws contained in the Pentateuch are for the most part applications of the principles to particular situations. Thus, the role of the Ten Commandments in ancient Israel was to give direction to a relationship. They were not to be obeyed simply for the sake of obedience, as though obedience accumulated some kind of credit. Rather, they were to be obeyed in order to discover that life in which the fullness and richness of a relationship with God.

The commandments in ancient Israel were not an ethical code or compilation of advice on the fundamentals of morality. The covenant was between God and a nation; the commandments were directed toward the life of that nation and its citizens. Consequently, the initial role of the commandments was similar to that of criminal law in a modern state. Israel was a theocracy, a state whose king was God (Dt 33:5). The commandments provided guidance to the citizens of that state. In addition, to break a commandment was to commit a crime against the state and the ruler of that state, God. Thus the penalties were severe, for the breaking of the commandments threatened the covenant relationship and the continued existence of the state. This state context is important for understanding the commandments in their initial form.

The Meaning of the Commandments. The commandments begin with a preface (Ex 20:2; Dt 5:6) which identifies the lawgiver, God, who gave the commandments to a people with whom he already had a relationship. The lawgiver is the God of the exodus, who redeemed his people from slavery and granted them freedom. The preface is vital, for it indicates that God's gift of Law was preceded by an act of love and grace. The commandments were given to a people who had been redeemed; they were not given in order to achieve redemption. There are some variations in the manner of numbering the commandments. According to some systems, the preface is identified with the first commandment. It seems preferable, however, to understand the opening words as a preface to all ten commandments. In the notes on the Ten

Commandments which follow, there is first an explanation of the original meaning, then some indication of the contemporary meaning.

The Prohibition of Gods Other than the Lord (Ex 20:3; Dt 5:7). The first commandment is in negative form and expressly prohibits the Israelites engaging in the worship of foreign deities. The significance of the commandment lies in the nature of the covenant. The essence of the covenant was a relationship, and the essence of relationship, from the biblical perspective, is faithfulness. God's faithfulness to his people had already been demonstrated in the exodus, as indicated in the preface to the commandments. In turn, God required of his people, more than anything else, a faithfulness in their relationship with him. Thus, though the commandment is stated negatively, it is full of positive implications. And its position as first of the ten is significant, for this commandment establishes a principle which is particularly prominent in the social commandments (six through ten). The contemporary significance of the commandment is in the context of faithfulness in relationship. At the heart of human life, there must be a relationship with God. Anything in life which disrupts that primary relationship breaks the commandment. Foreign "gods" are thus persons, or even things, that would disrupt the primacy of the relationship with God.

The Prohibition of Images (Ex 20:4–6; Dt 5:8–10). The possibility of worshiping gods other than the Lord has been eliminated in the first commandment. Thus the second commandment prohibits the Israelites from making images of the Lord. To make an image of God, in the shape or form of anything in this world, is to reduce the Creator to something less than his creation and to worship the created, instead of the Creator. The temptation for Israel to worship God in the form of an image must have been enormous, for images and idols occurred in all the religions of the ancient Near East. But the God of Israel was a transcendent and infinite being, and could not be reduced to the limitations of an image or form within creation. Any such reduction of God would be so radical a misunderstanding, that the "god" worshiped would no longer be the God of the universe. In the modern world, the shape of the temptation has changed. Few are tempted to take power tools and shape from wood an image of God. Nevertheless, the commandment is still applicable and the danger against which it guards is always present. A person can construct an image of God with words, creating an image of God no less fixed or rigid than the image of wood or stone. Although not prohibited from using words about God, if the words and personal understanding

of them acquire a rigid structure, then an image forms. To worship God in the form of a word-image is to break the commandment. God is transcendent and infinite, always greater than any words a creature can use of him. The second commandment thus guards the ultimate greatness and mystery of God.

The Prohibition Against the Improper Use of God's Name (Ex 20:7; Dt 5:11). There is a popular understanding that the third commandment prohibits bad language or blasphemy; however, it is concerned with the use of God's name. God had granted to Israel an extraordinary privilege; he had revealed to them his personal name. The name, in Hebrew, is represented by four letters, YHWH, which are variously rendered in English Bibles as LORD, Yahweh, or Jehovah. The knowledge of the divine name was a privilege, for it meant that Israel did not worship an anonymous and distant deity, but a being with a personal name. Yet the privilege was accompanied by the danger that the knowledge of God's personal name could be abused. In ancient Near Eastern religions, magic was a common practice. Magic involved the use of a god's name, which was believed to control a god's power, in certain kinds of activity designed to harness it for human purposes. Thus the kind of activity which is prohibited by the third commandment is magic, namely, attempting to control God's power, through his name, for a personal and worthless purpose. God may give, but must not be manipulated or controlled. Within Christianity, the name of God is equally important. Through God's name is access to God in prayer. The abuse of the privilege of prayer, involving calling upon the name of God for some selfish or worthless purpose or swearing falsely by it, is tantamount to the magic of the ancient world. In both, God's name is abused and the third commandment is broken. Positively, the third commandment is a reminder of the enormous privilege of knowing God's name, a privilege not to be taken lightly or abused.

The Observation of the Sabbath (Ex 20:8–11; Dt 5:12–15). This commandment, once again, has no parallels in ancient Near Eastern religions; furthermore, it is the first of the commandments to be expressed in a positive form. While most of life was characterized by work, the seventh day was to be set aside. Work was to cease and the day was to be kept holy. The holiness of the day is related to the reason for its establishment. Two reasons are given, and though at first they appear different, there is a common theme linking them. In the first version of the commandment (Ex 20:11), the sabbath is kept in commemoration of creation; God created in six days and rested on the seventh day. In the second version (Dt 5:15), the sabbath is observed in commemoration of the exodus from Egypt. The theme linking the two versions is creation: God not only created the world, but also "created" his people, Israel, in redeeming them from Egyptian slavery. Thus, every seventh day throughout the passage of time, the Hebrew people were to reflect upon creation; in so doing, they were reflecting upon the meaning of their existence. For most of Christianity, the concept of "sabbath" has been moved from the seventh to the first day of the week, namely Sunday. The move is related to a change in Christian thought, which is identified in the resurrection of Jesus Christ on a Sunday morning. The change is appropriate, for Christians now reflect each Sunday, or "sabbath," on a third act of divine creation, namely the "new creation" which is established in the resurrection of Jesus Christ from the dead.

The Honor Due to Parents (Ex 20:12; Dt 5:16). The fifth commandment forms a bridge between the first four, concerned primarily with God, and the last five, concerned primarily with human relationships. On first reading, it appears to be concerned with family relationships only: children are to honor their parents. Although the commandment establishes a principle of honor or respect in family relationships, it is probably also related to the responsibility of parents to instruct their children in the faith of the covenant (Dt 6:7), so that the religion could be passed on from one generation to another. But instruction in the faith required an attitude of honor and respect from those who were being instructed. Thus, the fifth commandment is not only concerned with family harmony, but also with the transmission of faith in God throughout subsequent generations. With the fifth commandment, there is little need to convert its meaning into contemporary relevance. At a time in which so much education is undertaken beyond the confines of the family unit, the commandment serves a solemn reminder, not only of the need for harmonious family life, but also of the responsibilities of religious education which rest upon both parents and children.

The Prohibition of Murder (Ex 20:13; Dt 5:17). The wording of this commandment simply prohibits "killing"; the meaning of the word, however, implies the prohibition of murder. The word used in the commandment is not related primarily to killing in warfare or to capital punishment, both of which are dealt with in other portions of the Mosaic law. The word could be used to designate both murder and manslaughter. Since manslaughter involves accidental killing, it cannot be sensibly prohibited; it, too, is dealt with in other legis-

lation (Dt 19:1–13). Thus, the sixth commandment prohibits murder, the taking of another person's life for personal and selfish gain. Stated positively, the sixth commandment preserves for each member of the covenant community the right to live. In the modern world, a similar statute prohibiting murder exists in almost all legal codes, having become a part of state law, in addition to purely religious or moral law. Jesus, however, pointed to the deeper meaning implicit in the commandment. It is not only the act, but also the sentiment underlying the act, which is evil (Mt 5:21,22).

The Prohibition of Adultery (Ex 20:14; Dt 5:18). The act of adultery is fundamentally an act of unfaithfulness. One, or both, persons in an adulterous act are being unfaithful to another person, or persons. Of all such crimes, the worst is that which signifies unfaithfulness. It is for this reason that adultery is included in the Ten Commandments, while other sins or crimes pertaining to sexuality are not included. Thus the seventh commandment is the social parallel to the first commandment. Just as the first commandment requires absolute faithfulness in the relationship with the one God, so the seventh requires a similar relationship of faithfulness within the covenant of marriage. The relevance of the commandment is apparent, but again, Jesus points to the implications of the commandment for the mental life (Mt 5:27,28).

The Prohibition of Theft (Ex 20:15; Dt 5:19). The eighth commandment establishes a principle within the covenant community concerning possessions and property; a person had a right to certain things, which could not be violated by a fellow citizen for his or her personal advantage. But while the commandment is concerned with property, its most fundamental concern is human liberty. The worst form of theft is "manstealing" (somewhat equivalent to modern kidnaping); that is, taking a person (presumably by force) and selling him or her into slavery. The crime and the related law are stated more fully in Deuteronomy 24:7. The commandment is thus not only concerned with the preservation of private property, but is more fundamentally concerned with the preservation of human liberty, freedom from such things as slavery and exile. It prohibits a person from manipulating or exploiting the lives of others for personal gain. Just as the sixth commandment prohibits murder, so the eighth prohibits what might be called "social murder," that is, the cutting off of a man or woman from a life of freedom within the community of God's people.

The Prohibition of False Witnessing (Ex 20:16; Dt 5:20). The commandment is not a general prohibition against lies. The wording of the original commandment sets it firmly in the context of Israel's legal system. It prohibits perjury, or the giving of false testimony within the proceedings of the law court. Thus, it establishes a principle of truthfulness and carries implications with respect to false statements in any context. Within any nation, the courts of law must be able to operate on the basis of true information. If law is not based on truth and righteousness, then the very foundations of life and liberty are undermined. If legal testimony is true, there can be no miscarriage of justice; if it is false, the most fundamental of human liberties are lost. Thus, the commandment sought to preserve the integrity of Israel's legal system while guarding against encroachments on personal liberties. The principle is maintained in most modern legal systems, for example, in the taking of an oath before giving evidence in court. But in the last resort, the commandment points to the essential nature of truthfulness in all interpersonal relationships.

The Prohibition of Coveting (Ex 20:17; Dt 5:21). The tenth commandment is curious in its initial context. It prohibits the coveting, or desiring, of persons or things belonging to a neighbor (that is, a fellow Israelite). To find such a commandment in a code of criminal law is unusual. The first nine commandments prohibited acts, and a criminal act can be followed by prosecution and legal process if detected. But the tenth commandment, in contrast, prohibits *desires*, or covetous feelings. Under human law, it is not possible to prosecute upon the basis of desire, since proof would be impossible. While the crime involved in the tenth commandment could not be prosecuted within the limitations of the Hebrew system, it was known, nevertheless, by God, the "Chief Judge." The genius of the commandment lies in its therapeutic nature. It is not enough merely to deal with crime once it has been committed; the law must also attempt to attack the roots of crime. The root of almost all evil and crime lies within the self, in the desires of the individual. Thus evil desires are prohibited. If covetous desires are gradually eliminated, then natural desires may be directed toward God.

The Principle of the Commandments. The relevance of each commandment is understood in the underlying principle of the whole Decalogue. The principle of the whole is the principle of love, the heart of Israel's religion. God loved Israel and called them in love. In return, he imposed one commandment upon Israel which superseded all others: "You shall love the Lord your God with all your heart, and with all your soul, and with all your might" (Dt 6:5). That is the central commandment of Israel's religion. How to love the invisible, intangible God is partly explained in the Decalogue. For the person who loves God, the Ten Commandments provide guidance; they point to a way of life which, if lived, reflects love for God and leads to a deeper experience of God's love. Therefore, the Ten Commandments continue to be a central part of Christianity. Jesus repeated the commandment to love from Deuteronomy 6:5 and he called it "the great and first commandment" (Mt 22:37,38). Consequently, the Ten Commandments still serve as a guide within Christianity by pointing to one way in which love may be expressed for God and the love of God may be experienced. PETER C. CRAIGIE

See CIVIL LAW AND JUSTICE; LAW, BIBLICAL CONCEPT OF.

Bibliography. R.H. Charles, *The Decalogue*; E. Nielsen, *The Ten Commandments in New Perspective*; G. Oehler, *Theology of the OT*, pp 182–191; H. Schultz, *OT Theology*, 2 vols; J.J. Stamm and M.E. Andrew, *The Ten Commandments in Recent Research*; Th.C. Vriezen, *An Outline of OT Theology*.

Tent, Tentmaker. See HOMES AND DWELLINGS; TRADES AND OCCUPATIONS.

Tent of Meeting. Designation for the tabernacle (Ex 28:43).

See TABERNACLE, TEMPLE.

Terah (Person). Father of Abram (Abraham), Nahor, and Haran (Gn 11:26, 1 Chr 1:26; Lk 3:34, KJV Thara). Though Abram is listed first among his sons, it is likely that Abram was not the oldest. Terah lived 70 years fathering Abram, Nahor, and Terah (Gn 11:26). Stephen reports in the NT, however, that Abram left Haran after the death of his father, at which time Abram was 75 years old (Gn 12:4; Acts 7:4). This synchronism suggests that Terah was at least 130 when Abram was born. Joshua reports that Terah was one of the fathers who "lived of old beyond the Euphrates" (Jos 24:2). Terah initiated the trip to Canaan, though he failed to go beyond Haran (Gn 11:31,32). Abram was commanded there to leave his family and proceed to Canaan (12:1).

See GENEALOGY OF JESUS CHRIST; ABRAHAM.

Terah (Place). One of the stopping places of the Israelites during their wilderness wanderings, listed between Tahath and Mithkah (Nm 33:27,28, KJV Tarah). Its site is unknown.

See WILDERNESS WANDERINGS.

Teraphim. Idols which were generally associated with pagan magical rites. In the OT, the term is often translated "household gods," indicative of talismans which were kept in family shrines (Gn 31:19,34). These were the idols that Rachel stole from her father and which occasioned Laban's angry pursuit (vv 17–55). Many have postulated that Laban's anger reflects a Nuzian tradition where ownership of the household gods conferred inheritance rights to the owner. It is more likely that Rachel stole the teraphim simply to insure good luck and safety.

Teraphim are also mentioned in connection with Micah's attempt to establish a private priesthood (Jgs 17:5). When the Danites moved to Laish, they stole Micah's teraphim and ephod for oracular use (Jgs 18:14–20,31). Teraphim were typically small idols but on occasion could be life-size as well. David escaped from Saul when Michal placed a teraphim in his bed as a dummy (1 Sm 19:13,16). During Israel's kingdom period, teraphim continued to be used in heretical cultic practices. Josiah attempted to rid the country of teraphim, wizards, and mediums, but his reforms appear to have been temporary (2 Kgs 23:24). The prophets regularly condemned the oracular use of teraphim, identifying them with heathen abominations (Ez 21:21; Hos 3:4; Zec 10:2).

See IDOLS, IDOLATRY.

Terebinth. Large deciduous tree, also called the turpentine tree (Is 6:13; Hos 4:13).

See PLANTS.

Teresh. One of two chamberlains who guarded the chambers of King Ahasuerus. When the two planned to kill the king, Mordecai discovered their plot and informed Esther, who in turn told the king. The guards were hanged (Es 2:21; 6:2).

Tertius. Amaneunsis (secretary) of the Book of Romans for Paul (16:22). Since his name is a common Roman name, he was probably Roman and known by the recipients of the letter. The supposition that Tertius is the same person as Silas because their names had similar meanings in Latin and Hebrew lacks any biblical or traditional evidence.

Tertullus. Prosecuting attorney chosen by the Sanhedrin to lead in the trial of Paul before Felix, Roman procurator of Judea (Acts 24:1–2). It is not clear whether Tertullus was a Roman, Greek, or Jew. The chief arguments that he was a Jew come from references to "our law" and to the mention that Lysias had taken Paul from "our hands." However, whether these words represent Tertullus or his clients is questionable. In addition some of the most ancient textual authorities omit both segments of the text. From the speed with which the Jews were able to bring him forward, he was probably a professional attorney who practiced law regularly in the Roman court. His speech (Acts 24:2–8) begins with a word of flattery for Felix. Then he proceeds to charge Paul with being a public nuisance, a disturber of the peace, and a leader of the sect of the Nazarenes. All of these were serious charges in Roman law.

Testament. English word translated from the Greek signifying the covenantal administrations of God: that prior to Christ being the "Old Testament" and that under Christ the "New Testament."

The Greek word, generally meaning "last will and testament," contains certain legal characteristics which have important theological implications. First, a testament was not an agreement between parties (especially equals), but rather was exercised solely by the testator. Second, the testament became effective upon the death of the testator. Third, the testament was irrevocable.

When the OT was translated into Greek, the translators had the option of two words to translate the Hebrew word for covenant. One term carries the idea of a mutual agreement and this often between equals. Since this would blur the divine initiative in God's covenantal dealings with the patriarchs and with Israel, the other word was used. It connoted the self-determined action of the sovereign in making the covenant. The NT writers saw in the word testament an additional significance. As a testament became valid at the death of the testator, the benefits of the new covenant have come to believers after the crucifixion and the death of the Christ (Heb 9:15–22; cf. 1 Cor 11:25; Lk 22:20, KJV).

See COVENANT; COVENANT, THE NEW.

Tetragrammaton. Term referring to the four consonants of one of the primary Hebrew names for God (fr. Gk *tetra*, "four," and *gramma*, "a letter of the alphabet"). These letters are the Hebrew equivalents of English Y (or J), H, W, and H. The most widely accepted meaning of the name is "the one who is, that is, the absolute and unchangeable one" (F. Brown, S.R. Driver, and C.A. Briggs, *A Hebrew and English Lexicon of the Old Testament*, p 218.) This is the name which the Lord revealed to Moses (Ex 3:15; cf. vv 13,14; Jn 8:56–58). This name, which appears in the Ten Commandments, the Jews were not to take in vain (Ex 20:2,7). The Jews therefore regarded the name as so holy that they would not pronounce it, but read instead *Adonai*, "Lord."

Originally the text was written only with consonants, but when the scholars called Masoretes added the vowel points, they inserted the vowels for Adonai as a reminder not to read the sacred name. Non-Hebraists combined the vowels of Adonai with the consonants of JHWH, producing a new form, "Jehovah," which does not exist in the Hebrew language. The correct pronunciation of the name must have been Yahweh, but most translations render it LORD, using capital letters to distinguish it from other words or names which have that meaning.

See GOD, NAMES OF.

Tetrarch. Title of a class of Roman provincial officials. Tetrarchs were tributary princes who were not deemed important enough to be designated kings. The title was used in the Roman provinces of Thessaly, Galatia, and Syria. The origin of the title appears to have come from governors who ruled over a fourth part of a region or country, as was the case in Syria following the death of Herod the Great. By NT times, the etymological significance had diminished, however, so that the title merely designated secondary princes. Three tetrarchs are mentioned in the Bible. Luke reports that Herod (Antipas) was the tetrarch of Galilee, Philip was the tetrarch of Ituraea and Trachonitus, and Lysanius was the tetrarch of Abilene (Lk 3:1). Of these, only Herod is mentioned elsewhere in the Bible (Mt 14:1; Lk 3:19; 9:7; Acts 13:1). Herod's greater significance is also indicated by the fact that he is also referred to as "king" by his Jewish subjects (Mt 14:9; Mk 6:14).

Thaddaeus, The Apostle. One of the 12 original apostles according to the lists in Mark 3:18 and Matthew 10:3 (KJV, "Lebbaeus, whose surname was Thaddaeus"). It is quite likely that this is the same person as Judas son of James (not Iscariot) in Luke 6:16 and Acts 1:13.

See APOSTLE, APOSTLESHIP.

Thahash. KJV spelling of Tahash, Reumah's son, in Genesis 22:24.

See TAHASH.

Thamah. KJV alternate form of Temah in Ezra 2:53.

See TEMAH.

Thamar. KJV spelling of Tamar, Judah's firstborn son by Bath-shua, in Matthew 1:3.

See TAMAR (PERSON) #1.

Thank Offering. *See* OFFERINGS AND SACRIFICES.

Thanksgiving. *See* GRATITUDE.

Thara. KJV form of Terah, Abraham's father, in Luke 3:34.

See TERAH (PERSON).

Tharshish. 1. KJV alternate spelling of Tarshish, a port city, in 1 Kings 10:22 and 22:48.

See TARSHISH (PLACE).

2. KJV spelling of Tarshish, Bilham's son, in 1 Chronicles 7:10.

See TARSHISH (PERSON) #2.

Theater. A flat semi-circular orchestra surrounded by an open-air auditorium which originated in the 6th to 5th century BC. A chorus and actors performed in the orchestra and

A theater at Pompeii.

the audience sat on the raised hillside before them. The earliest drama was tragedy, which celebrated the deeds of the god Dionysus and began with a sacrifice on the altar in the orchestra. Later, comedy developed.

The Golden Age of Athens (c. 450 BC) proved to be also the golden age of Greek drama; Sophocles, Euripides, and Aeschylus wrote their dramas then. At that time audiences sat on the ground or on the wooden seats of the Theater of Dionysus in Athens, located on the south slope of the acropolis. During the 4th century BC theaters in Greece were equipped with stone seats arranged in concentric tiers against a concave hillside, and the orchestra was paved.

By the 2nd–1st centuries BC great stone theaters were being built all over the Hellenistic East, and by that time a raised stage was constructed against the straight side of the semicircle of the orchestra. Action was now transferred to the stage. The auditorium of the typical theater henceforth consisted of three great bands of seats which were divided into great wedges by the stairways that gave access to the seating. The elaborate stage was built in stone and had dressing and storage rooms. The orchestra was always paved.

Although initially the theater was intended for dramatic events, it came to be used for a variety of public meetings because it was one of the largest structures. For example, the great theater in Ephesus held about 25,000; the Theater of Dionysus in Athens, about 17,000; and the south theater in Jerash of the Decapolis, about 5,000.

The theater should be distinguished from the odeion, which was shaped like a theater but was roofed, held only 1000 or 2000, and was used primarily for musical events. It should also be distinguished from the amphitheater, which was a free-standing structure in stone, like the Colosseum of Rome and the arena of Verona, with an oval arena surrounded by concentric tiers of seats and used for gladiatorial combats, wild beast hunts, and other such events. Only occasionally, as at Salamis in Cyprus and Caesarea in Palestine, were theaters free-standing stone structures; almost always they were built into the side of a hill.

By NT times, theaters were built in Greco-Roman towns all over the Mediterranean world. They even made their appearance in Palestine, as a result of the Hellenizing activities of Herod the Great, who constructed Greek-style theaters in Samaria, Caesarea, and Jerusalem.

Only one theater, that of Ephesus, figures specifically in the NT (Acts 19:29–41). Apparently the theater at Caesarea also was in-volved with the NT narrative, however, because Josephus (*Antiq.* 19.8.2) mentions it in reference to the events of Acts 12:20–23.

See ARCHITECTURE.

Thebes. City appearing in the OT as No, or No-Amon. "No" means *city* and is equivalent to the Egyptian *Waset* or Greek *Thebes*. No-Amon means "city of Amon." Thebes appears only in the prophetic Scriptures of the OT and only in a context of judgment (Jer 46:25; Ez 30:14–16; Na 3:8). Thebes would suffer judgment and loss of population, but would not be utterly destroyed. These prophecies were fulfilled in ancient times when Cambyses of Persia marched through in 525 BC and when the Roman Cornelius Gallus punished the city for a revolt in 30 BC.

Thebes was the capital of Egypt during most of the Empire period (c. 1570–1100 BC) when the Hebrews were in bondage in the land and when the exodus took place. By that time Amon had become the chief god, and the Pharaohs lavished their wealth on the great temples of Amon at Thebes, hoping for the god's help in overcoming their enemies.

The city of the living in ancient Thebes was located on the east bank of the Nile, the side of the rising sun; and the city of the dead (the necropolis) was located on the west bank, the side of the setting sun. The city of the living had an estimated population of nearly one million at its height. When Strabo visited the city in 24 BC, he said that the extent of its ruins was about nine miles.

The modern city of Luxor occupies the site of ancient Thebes. There are two massive complexes on the east bank of the Nile: the area around the great Karnak temple in the north, and the area around the Luxor temple in the south. Even the ruins of the great temples are magnificent.

The temple of Luxor is a compound 858 feet long, built primarily by Amenhotep III, with a magnificent addition by Ramses II and a small chapel commissioned by Alexander the Great. To give some idea of its impressive nature, before the entrance pylon of Ramses II were four seated figures (two of which remain) of the king, each 76 feet high. The colonnade of Amenhotep III consists of seven pairs of papyrus columns 53 feet high. Leading from the temple of Luxor to the temple of Karnak was an avenue of ram-headed sphinxes two miles long.

The temple of Karnak was even more grand than that of Luxor; both were dedicated to the god Amon. The temple of Karnak was actually a complex of temples involving some of the best efforts of rulers from the Middle King-

A wall painting from Thebes that portrays five musicians.

dom to the last centuries BC. Dominating the temple is the great hypostyle hall of Seti I and his son Ramses II. This forest of 134 sandstone columns covers an area of about 66,000 square feet. The central avenue has 12 columns with open papyrus capitals which soar to a height of 70 feet, making them the tallest columns in the world. The shorter columns in the hall are 53 feet high.

On the west bank of the Nile stand the great mortuary temples of Ramses III at Medinet Habu, the Rameseum of Ramses II, Hatshepsut's great temple at Deir el Bahri, and the Colossi of Memnon (Amenhotep III) before what was Amenhotep's temple. The Valley of the Kings (with Tutankhamon's tomb), the Valley of the Queens, and the Valley of the Nobles are also located there. All these temples and tombs have important paintings and inscriptions on their walls.

Thebez. City where Abimelech was killed when "a certain woman" dropped a millstone on him (Jgs 9:50). Abimelech had attacked Thebez after burning down the Tower of Shechem but had failed to capture the fortress within the city. After being critically injured by the millstone, Abimelech ordered his armor bearer to kill him lest it be said that he had been killed by a woman (v 54). The incident was recalled somewhat ironically in David's words concerning the death of Uriah the Hittite (2 Sm 11:21). Thebez was located about 11 miles northeast of Shechem, traditionally identified with modern Tabas.

Thelasar. KJV alternate form of Telassar in 2 Kings 19:12.

See TELASSAR.

Theocracy. Form of government which acknowledges God alone as the highest political authority, whether or not he is represented by a human ruler such as a king. Thus Deuteronomy 17:14–20 argues that a human king rules only as one designated for kingship by the Lord.

In ancient Israel, the concept of theocratic government developed through several historical stages. A fundamental theological conception of the sons of Israel in Egypt involved the belief that Yahweh, their special God, cared enough about their plight to become personally involved in redeeming them from slavery and establishing them in freedom from all earthly rulers (specifically the pharaoh). They would then be able to serve him alone (see Ex 3:7–10; 8:1; 9:1, etc.). It is necessary to remember that the conditions of oppression described in Exodus were everyday features in the life of Egyptian peasants. Living under the rulership of the pharaoh as a peasant implied oppression, unreasonable work assignments, loss of freedom and self-respect, and many other things. By contrast, life under the rulership of Yahweh came to signify freedom, justice, and equality.

Upon arriving in Canaan, the young tribes encountered a system of kingship widely different from the Egyptian model but equally opprobrious. Ancient Canaanite rulers normally owned the city-state that they governed, and rented out at least some of the land to their subjects. But the Israelites who occupied Canaan under Joshua were meant to be free inhabitants of the territory allotted to them and subservient to God alone.

In the period of the judges, the idea of theocracy continued to be expressed consistently and explicitly. The various groups comprising the "sons of Israel" were not welded together into a unified body by any external political structure. Rather, acceptance of the rulership of Yahweh alone continued to function as the foundational unifying element. Thus Gideon, when asked by some to accept kingship, could say in words acceptable to virtually all Israelites, "The Lord shall rule over you" (Jgs 8:23).

In this period, human leadership became necessary from time to time as threats arose to one or more of the tribes. These judges were regularly described as "raised up" for the specific task of averting immediate danger, but more specifically to lead the people back to the Lord (Jgs 2:16). But no judge was believed to have brought victory to Israel by means of his personal abilities. Yahweh alone was credited with having won the battle; hence he deserved and received the fealty of Israel.

Samuel bridges the time of the judges and the new era of monarchy in Israel. Philistine social and military pressure was confronting the Israelite theocratic government with a challenge of enormous proportions. For roughly 200 years preceding Samuel, Israelites and Philistines had co-existed, if not peaceably, at least short of open warfare. During the career of Samuel, however, the Philistines inaugurated a policy of open aggression toward Israel aimed at conquest and expansion. The tribal confederacy, which for years had successfully defended one or more tribal groups, now appeared incapable of resisting the Philistines. A new governmental structure had clearly become necessary. In the minds of many influential Israelites, only a kingdom headed by a king could enable Israel to survive (see 1 Sm 8:5,19,20).

At this point the concept of theocracy received a severe test. Politically and militarily, a king appeared to be a wise and necessary choice. But the tradition of charismatic rule was deeply ingrained. Samuel viewed the desire for a king as rejection of the rulership of Yahweh (8:10–18; 10:19). On the other hand, he also appears to have received a prophetic word concerning Saul and the willingness of God to have him anointed as king (9:27–10:1).

In addition to his prophetic anointing, Saul also received a designation from "the spirit of God" (11:6) which closely paralleled the experiences of earlier judges. A third ingredient to Saul's claim to kingship was added when the people acclaimed him following a military victory over the Ammonites (v 15).

Apart from the clarity of the biblical tradition that two opinions of kingship were represented among Israelites, clearly God chose the king and revealed his choice through his messenger-prophet.

It was on this basis that the prophet Samuel retained the right to renounce Saul in the face of his spiritual failures (13:14; 15:23,26). This prophetic prerogative endured throughout the era of the monarchy, as the examples of Solomon (1 Kgs 11:29–31), Jeroboam (14:5–14), Baasha (16:1–4), Ahab (21:17–22), and others show.

The theocratic concepts of Ezekiel (40–48), in which God would rule his people through the Zadokite priesthood, began to be implemented through the work of Haggai and Zechariah in 520 BC. This was a particularly important feature of postexilic life and imparted a distinctive character to the Judean community. The work of Ezra made the theocracy normative for Judaism, and thereafter the priesthood exercised an important role in national life. Although the people were subjected to human rule under the Seleucids, they looked for the true king, a descendant of David. This man, the Messiah, would be the peaceful prince who would redeem Israel and bring the ancient covenantal values of justice, righteousness, and equity to fruition.

See KING, KINGSHIP.

Theophany. An appearance or manifestation of God; a compound word derived from the Greek noun for God and the Greek verb "to appear."

In its broadest meaning the term has been applied to many forms of divine revelation in both Testaments, whether occurring in a vision or dream or in normally perceptible realities such as unusual natural phenomena, appearances of the Deity in human form in the OT, or the incarnation of Christ in the NT. The use of the term theophany is restricted here to manifestations of God in temporary forms perceptible to the external senses, and thereby excludes divine manifestations in dreams or visions and the incarnation of Christ.

Theophany is regarded as one of the means by which God's special revelation comes to man. God's special revelation may be divided into two basic forms, that of word and deed. God's revelatory deeds may be further divided into the categories of theophany and miracle. A theophany is then a form of divine revelation in which God's presence is made visible and recognizable to man. God therefore reveals himself not only by word and miracle, by prophecies and signs, but also by making his presence perceptible to men.

Occurrences. *The Angel of the Lord.* The most important form of divine manifestation in the OT is the "Angel of the Lord" or the "Angel of God." This remarkable angel, who is clearly distinguished from angels in general and who both represents himself as deity as well as distinguishing himself from God, appears to Hagar (Gn 16:7), to Abraham and Lot (18; 19; 22:11,12), to Jacob (32:29–31; cf. Hos 12:4,5), to Moses (Ex 3:2–6), to Balaam (Nm 22:22), to Joshua (Jos 5:14,15), to Gideon (Jgs 6:11–14), to Manoah and his wife (Jgs 13), and to David (1 Chr 21:15,18,27). He goes before the Israelites to lead them out of the land of Egypt (Ex 13:21; 14:19), and he remonstrates with the Israelites when they disobey God after settling in the land of Canaan (Jgs 2:1–4).

A study of these passages reveals that the Angel of the Lord appeared in human form (cf. Gn 18:2,22; Heb 13:2) and performed normal human functions (Gn 32:24; Nm 22:23,31), yet he was an awe-inspiring figure (Gn 32:30; Jgs 6:22; 13:22) exhibiting divine attributes and prerogatives including predicting the future (Gn 16:10–12), forgiving sin (Ex 23:21), and receiving worship (Ex 3:5; Jg 13:9–20). The title Angel of the Lord is particularly striking because it is used in many of these passages interchangeably with the terms Yahweh (Jehovah) and God in such a way as to leave little doubt that the angel is a manifestation of God himself. Nevertheless, at the same time the angel and God clearly are not equated because the angel often refers to God in the third person.

Divine Manifestations in the OT Where the Precise Form Is Not Specified. There are a number of passages in the OT where God speaks or acts in the presence of human witnesses, but where no clear indication is given of the precise form of the divine manifestation. Possibly in some of these passages anthropomorphic language is utilized, or God speaks directly to the consciousness of the individual rather than by externally audible language. Nevertheless in most of the following passages some form of theophany probably took place.

Genesis 2:15,16 states that "The Lord God *took* the man and put him in the garden of Eden to work it. And the Lord God *commanded* the man...." Genesis 3:8 states that "the man and his wife heard the *sound* of the Lord God as he was *walking* in the garden in the cool of the day, and they hid from the Lord God" (NIV). The implication of the latter verse is that Adam and Eve heard the footsteps of God, that God appeared in the garden in some sense-perceptible form. Exactly what form is not described, but presumably it was a human form. (Other passages which suggest some form of theophany are Genesis 3:9–19,21; 4:9–15; 6:12–21; 7:1–4; 8:15–17; 9:1–17.)

In Genesis 12:1–3,7 God calls Abraham to leave his own country and his father's house and to go to a land the Lord would show him. In verse 7 the Lord "appeared to Abram." This is the first time in the Bible that this expression is used, and it clearly implies that the Lord came to Abraham in some sense-perceptible form (cf. Acts 7:2,3). The OT records similar occurrences of manifestations of God in some unspecified form to Isaac (Gn 26:2,24), to Jacob (Gn 35:1,9,13), to Moses (Ex 4:24–26), and to Samuel (1 Sm 3:10).

The Pillar of Cloud and Fire. When Israel departed from Egypt the Lord himself went before them in a pillar of cloud to guide them on their way during the day, and a pillar of fire to give them light and direction at night (Ex 13:21,22; 14:19,24; Nm 14:14; Neh 9:12,19; Ps 99:7). On certain occasions the pillar of cloud descended to the tent of meeting where God entered into verbal communication with Moses, Joshua, Aaron, and Miriam (Ex 33:7–11; Nm 12:5; Dt 31:15). From the cloud God spoke to Moses on Mt Sinai (Ex 24:15–18; 34:5). In God's initial appearance at Sinai, his presence was indicated by thunderings, lightnings, fire, smoke, and the sound of a trumpet as well as a thick cloud (Ex 19:16,18). The pillar of cloud and fire, along with the other heightened forms of natural phenomena at Sinai, are clearly to be understood as sense-perceptible representations of God's presence with his people.

Shekinah Glory. A visible manifestation of the majesty of God, apparently in the form of a radiant light, is often referred to as the Shekinah glory, that is the glory of God which dwells (Shekinah) among his people. Israel was told that when the tabernacle was set up God would come to "dwell among the Israelites and be their God" (Ex 29:44,45). The Lord had brought his people out of Egypt so that he might dwell in their midst. This great event occurred when "the cloud covered the tent of meeting, and the glory of the Lord filled the tabernacle. Moses could not enter the tent of meeting, because the cloud had settled upon it, and the glory of the Lord filled the tabernacle" (Ex 40:34,35). Previously when Moses had received the Law on the mountain at Sinai we are told that "the glory of the Lord settled on Mount Sinai ... to the Israelites the glory of the Lord looked like a consuming fire on the top of the mountain" (24:16–18). After God's displeasure with his people because of their worship of the golden calf, Moses requested the Lord to show him his glory. The Lord agreed, but told him that "when my glory passes by, I will put you in a cleft in the rock and cover you with my hand until I have passed by. Then I will remove my hand and you will see my back; but my face must not be seen" (33:22). Later when Solomon completed the temple, "the glory of the Lord filled the temple" (1 Kgs 8:11; 2 Chr 5:13,14). At the time of the Babylonian captivity Ezekiel saw in a vision that the glory of the Lord went up from Jerusalem (Ez 11:22,23), only to return at some future time when God himself establishes his kingdom and comes to dwell in the midst of his people forever (Ez 43:1-9).

Theological Significance. Theophanies served to forcibly impress upon God's people the existence and sovereignty of God as well as to assure them of God's presence with and concern for his people. Those forms of theophany which utilized some heightened form of natural phenomena conveyed a sense of the awesome majesty and power of God who is to be approached only with reverence and humility according to divinely prescribed procedures.

Theophany is frequently associated with divine revelation in verbalized form. Here the human-form theophanies are of particular significance, where the theophany is the means to the divine communication. The "Angel of the Lord" theophanies are linked with major advances in redemptive history including the establishment of the Abrahamic and Mosaic covenants, the entrance into the Promised Land, and the selection of the site for the Solomonic temple.

The human-form theophanies in the OT are often referred to as Christophanies on the basis that these appearances of God are best explained as pre-incarnate manifestations of the Second Person of the Trinity. These appearances thus anticipate the incarnation of Christ and provide an OT glimpse into the triune nature of the Godhead.   J. ROBERT VANNOY

See ANGEL OF THE LORD; SHEKINAH; PILLAR OF FIRE AND CLOUD; GLORY; ANGEL.

Theophilus. 1. Person to whom the books of Luke and Acts are addressed (Lk 1:3; Acts 1:1). Since Theophilus can be translated "lover of God" or "loved of God," many have suggested that Theophilus is a title rather than a proper name and that it designates the general audience of the books. However, the use of such generic titles is contrary to ordinary NT practice. Furthermore, the adjective "most excellent" generally designates an individual, particularly one of high rank. Paul refers to Festus as "most excellent," just as Claudius Lysias and Tertullus address Felix (Acts 23:26; 24:2; 26:25). Though Theophilus may well have had some noble standing, it is difficult to speculate what his position might have been.

2. Jewish high priest who was the son of Annas, the brother-in-law of Caiaphas, and the brother of Jonathan. The Roman prefect Vittelius installed him as high priest succeeding Jonathan in AD 37. He served until he was deposed by Herod Agrippa in AD 41 and was likely the high priest who gave Paul the au-

thority to persecute the Christians. He is not mentioned by name in the NT.

Thessalonians, First Letter to the.

Authorship. The names of Paul, Silvanus, and Timothy stand at the head of this letter, and, as with other letters of Paul, his colleagues may have had some share in the writing of the letter. Often the plural pronouns "we" and "us" are retained, but "I, Paul" (2:18) and the singular pronoun in other places (see 3:5; 5:27) show that the letter was essentially Paul's. From the 19th century a few scholars have questioned the Pauline authorship of the epistle, but without convincing reasons. The issues dealt with in this letter are manifestly issues faced by a church in the earliest stages of its existence. In the light of differences of expression between this and other Pauline letters, some have suggested that Silvanus or Timothy may have had a significant part in writing it, but that is uncertain. The early church had no doubts about the authorship of the letter.

Date, Origin, and Destination. The letter is addressed specifically to "the church of the Thessalonians" (1:1). According to Acts 17:1-9, Paul, with Silas (Silvanus) and Timothy, in the course of their missionary work in the Roman province of Macedonia, came from Philippi to Thessalonica. He went first, as was his custom, to the synagogue, and for three sabbaths explained and proved from the Scriptures that the Christ should suffer and rise from the dead, asserting that Jesus was the Christ. Some Jews believed and "a great many of the devout Greeks and not a few of the leading women." When the Jews stirred up opposition, Paul and his colleagues had to leave Thessalonica.

Probably the actual time spent in Thessalonica was a good deal more than three weeks. In this letter Paul speaks of working for his support so as not to burden the Thessalonians (2:9). References concerning his actions and attitudes among them imply a longer time, and Philippians 4:16 speaks of the Philippian Christians twice sending help to Paul in Thessalonica.

With Silas, and presumably Timothy, Paul went on to Beroea (Acts 17:10), and his colleagues stayed there when Paul proceeded to Athens (v 15). Timothy came to Paul at Athens, but then, concerned for the Thessalonian Christians, Paul was "willing to be left behind at Athens alone" (1 Thes 3:1) and sent Timothy to them. He returned from Thessalonica with good news (vv 6-10), in the light of which Paul wrote this letter.

Acts 18:5 speaks of Timothy and Silas coming back from Macedonia to the apostle in Corinth. It was probably from Corinth, in the early part of his 18-month stay, that Paul wrote this letter. Since his work in Corinth can be approximately dated, this epistle was probably written early in the year 50, in all likelihood about a year after the first preaching of the gospel in Thessalonica.

Purpose. Timothy's report of the situation in Thessalonica motivated Paul to write this letter. Possibly Timothy brought a letter from the Thessalonians. The way Paul introduces some of the subjects about which he writes suggests this: "concerning love of the brethren" (4:9), "concerning those who are asleep" (4:13), "as to the times and the seasons" (5:1; cf. 1 Cor 7:1,25; 8:1; 12:1; 16:1,12). The following were involved in Paul's purpose in writing:

(1) He wanted to commend the Thessalonian Christians for their faith and devotion which was widely known as an example to others (1:7–10).

(2) He realized that the persecution he had faced in Thessalonica had continued for those he left behind, and he wanted to encourage them to stand fast (2:13–16). He had feared for them, but was delighted by the news of their steadfastness (3:1–10).

(3) There were those who had been misrepresenting the apostle in Thessalonica, perhaps the Jews who had initiated opposition to him when he was there (Acts 17:5). They probably said that he was only a religious charlatan who had turned them away from their religion to his new faith, and they would never see him again. So the apostle reminded them of his methods and attitudes among them (2:1–12) and told of his desires and plans to see them again (vv 17,18).

(4) It was necessary also to urge the Thessalonian Christians to live true to Christian standards, especially in the matter of sexual morality (4:1–8). Other matters concerning their way of life and their relationships within the Christian fellowship also needed attention (4:9–12; 5:12–22).

(5) Another major concern was to deal with the misconceptions of the Thessalonian Christians regarding those who had died and the second coming of the Lord (4:13–18). In relation to the future hope there was also the question of "the times and the seasons," and Paul repeated the teaching he had given when among them (5:1–11).

(6) There may also have been a danger of disunity that led the apostle to emphasize the fellowship of all believers (5:27), to urge them not to disparage any spiritual gifts (vv 19–21), and not to fail in respecting their leaders (v 12).

Content. *Thanksgiving for the Thessalonians' Response to the Gospel (1:2–10).* Paul can pray with gratitude that in their lives the fruits of faith, love, and hope are evident. The gospel had come to them in the power of the Holy Spirit, backed by the lives of its messengers. Even though receiving the gospel had involved suffering, their faith was an example to the Christians of the Roman provinces of Macedonia and Achaia. The Thessalonians had turned to the living God from idols, indicating that most of the believers were Gentiles rather than Jews, and had found in Christ their salvation and their hope.

Paul's Defense of His Ministry in Thessalonica (2:1–12). Because of false accusations made about him, Paul found it necessary to defend his ministry. He had come from an experience of persecution in Philippi and had to face "great opposition" in Thessalonica. There was no guile in his trying to persuade them of the gospel's truth. That gospel was entrusted to him by God, and his one desire was to communicate it to them in all integrity.

Their Acceptance of the Gospel (2:13–16). The Thessalonians had accepted the gospel as "the word of God" and had suffered at the hands of their own people. Such persecutors must indeed face the righteous judgment of God.

Paul's Continuing Concern for Them (2:17–20). If Paul's accusers were saying that the Thessalonians would never see him again, he could give the assurance that he had often wanted to return, but had been prevented. Perhaps in saying "Satan hindered us," he refers to Jason being compelled to promise the authorities that Paul would leave the city and not return (Acts 17:9). In any case the Thessalonian Christians are his "glory and joy." His delight will be for them to stand "before our Lord Jesus Christ at his coming."

Timothy's Mission (3:1–5). Fearful for the Thessalonian Christians facing persecution, Paul was willing to be left alone in the work of the gospel in Athens (see Acts 17:16–34) and sent Timothy to encourage and support them in all their "afflictions." Paul reiterated that Christians must always be prepared to face suffering.

The Good News That Timothy Brought (3:6–10). Paul himself had continued to have "distress and affliction" in the gospel's cause, but the news of their faith and love had revived his spirit and given him great cause for thanksgiving to God. He was praying that he might see them again and strengthen them further in faith.

Paul's Prayer (3:11–13). Paul's prayer was that God might return him to his friends in Thessalonica, and that they might overflow with love and be established in holiness of life, so as to appear "unblamable . . . before our

God and Father, at the coming of our Lord Jesus with all his saints."

Exhortation to Purity of Life (4:1–8). Holiness, not immorality, and sanctification, not uncleanness, are the Christian's calling. Paul stresses this by saying that living in a contrary way demonstrated disregard for the Holy Spirit. Christian standards must be utterly different from the prevailing standards among the "heathen who know not God." For example, sexual relationships must not be determined by "lust," but expressed "in holiness and honor" within the bonds of marriage.

Practical Exhortation (4:9–12). The Christian duty of mutual love had been demonstrated in Thessalonica, but Paul asked that it be shown in increasing measure. Perhaps because some had been unduly excited by the hope of the second coming of Christ, he then exhorted them to live quietly and work for their living, and neither be dependent on others for support nor fail to command the respect of those who were not Christians.

Paul's Response to the Concern for Those Who Had Died Since They Became Believers (4:13–18). The apostle now turns to this matter of special concern about which the Thessalonians may have written. They need not grieve as those without hope over their loved ones who had died. Those who are alive and those who have died will share together in the joy and triumph of the Lord's return. Those who have died "will rise first"; those who are alive on earth will be caught up to meet their Master; then together, living and departed, "shall always be with the Lord." With that assurance they can "comfort one another."

Living in Readiness for the Lord's Coming (5:1–11). Perhaps further questions had been asked about "the times and the seasons" in relation to the second coming. They are not given to know the time. The Lord will come unexpectedly like "a thief in the night." What matters, therefore, is that Christians should never be complacent, but ready at all times, living as "children of the day," that, waking or sleeping, "we might live with him." To this end these Thessalonians are urged to continue to encourage one another.

Other Christian Duties (5:12–22). In the last main section of the letter the Thessalonian Christians are urged to respect their leaders and to acknowledge their oversight; to live at peace, in unity; to do and encourage all that is good. The will of God for the Christian life is constant joy, prayer, and praise. The Holy Spirit is not to be quenched, the gift of prophecy not to be despised, but all things claiming to be of God must be tested, so that the good can be embraced and the evil rejected.

Conclusion (5:23–28). The final prayer of the letter is for their holiness of life, that they may stand "blameless at the coming of our Lord Jesus Christ." "Pray for us" is the apostle's plea. Greetings are to be passed on and the letter read to "all the brethren." Then, with the prayer for grace with which the letter began, it is brought to a close.

FRANCIS FOULKES

See PAUL, THE APOSTLE; SECOND COMING OF CHRIST; THESSALONIANS, SECOND LETTER TO THE; THESSALONICA; ESCHATOLOGY; DAY OF THE LORD.

Bibliography. J. Denney, *The Epistles to the Thessalonians;* J. Eadie, *Commentary on the Epistles to the Thessalonians;* C. Ellicott, *Commentary on Epistles to the Thessalonians;* J.E. Frame, *A Critical and Exegetical Commentary on the Epistles of St. Paul to the Thessalonians;* I.H. Marshall, *1 and 2 Thessalonians;* G. Milligan, *St. Paul's Epistles to the Thessalonians.*

Thessalonians, Second Letter to the.

Authorship. This letter, like 1 Thessalonians, begins with the names of Paul, Silvanus, and Timothy, and like that letter often retains the plural pronouns "we" and "us," but also has the singular "I" (e.g., 2:5). The end of the letter reads: "I, Paul, write this greeting with my own hand. This is the mark in every letter of mine; it is the way I write" (3:17).

Nevertheless some scholars have questioned Paul's authorship, mostly because of the difference between the teaching about the future this letter and that in 1 Thessalonians. It is also argued that there is a difference of tone and expression between the two letters, and yet the difference of subject matter from 1 Thessalonians could best be explained by a person writing in Paul's name consciously imitating 1 Thessalonians. In the light of the words of 3:17, the letter would have to be seen as a blatant forgery. However, the early church did not question Paul's authorship.

Date, Origin, and Destination. In the first verse, exactly as in 1 Thessalonians, the letter is addressed "to the church of the Thessalonians," but unlike 1 Thessalonians, this letter provides us with no other personal details of the movements of Paul and his colleagues. Thus there is no direct evidence of the date and place of the letter.

Just as the difference between the teaching of this epistle from that of 1 Thessalonians has led some to question its Pauline authorship, so it has led others to a variety of explanations for its date and destination. These include:

It was written much later than 1 Thessalonians. This is improbable because both Silvanus and Timothy were still with Paul.

It was written earlier than 1 Thessalonians. In 2:15, however, there is a reference to a letter written previously to Thessalonica, and the early church from the 2nd century certainly called this 2 Thessalonians.

It was written to Jewish Christians in Thessalonica, while 1 Thessalonians was written to gentile Christians. This, however, is most unlikely, as the apostle who had such concern for the unity of all Christians in one place (e.g., 1 Cor 1–3) and especially for the unity of Jewish and gentile Christians (see Eph 2:11–22) could hardly have done such a thing.

It was written to Christians in a different place (Beroea or Philippi), and then came to be in the hands of the Thessalonian Christians. There is no evidence to support the idea that the letter was sent anywhere but to Thessalonica.

When this epistle was written, Paul had the same colleagues with him (1:1). Probably a short time after writing 1 Thessalonians, Paul heard of further problems being faced by the Christians in Thessalonica, and, in his concern for them, he wrote this second letter.

Purpose and Teaching. There were three main concerns in the mind of the apostle Paul as he wrote this letter.

As in all his letters, he wanted to encourage his readers to stand firm in their faith (2:15). He could thank God for his work in their lives (1:3; 2:13), evidenced by their faith, love, and steadfastness in the face of persecutions (1:4). Paul assured them of the righting of wrongs in the ultimate judgment of God. Their task was to glorify the name of Jesus by their lives; then at his coming he would be glorified "in his saints," his faithful people (1:5–12).

There was false teaching, even purportedly from Paul, that "the day of the Lord has come" (2:2). The apostle rejected that by saying that certain things must take place prior to the second coming. There must be a still greater manifestation of evil in the person of one called "the man of lawlessness" or "the son of perdition." This one will reject all true worship, show signs and wonders, and proclaim himself to be God. At present there is a restraining influence. The time will come, however, when "the lawless one will be revealed." Then the Lord himself will come and "the lawless one" will be conquered and destroyed. This teaching (vv 1–12) is similar to that in the Gospels about antichrist or antichrists, claiming to be Christ, deceiving people by signs and wonders (Mt 24:5,23–26; Mk 13:5,6,20–23). In 1 Thessalonians the fact that the time of the Lord's coming is unknown and believers must be ready for him at any time is stressed. Here, in opposition to the idea that the Lord had already come, those things which must take place before the Lord's coming are emphasized. The two aspects of Christian teaching about the future are found side by side in the Gospels where Jesus teaches about the future (Mt 24; Mk 13; Lk 21).

Finally, the problem of laziness in the Christian community (referred to in 1 Thes 4:11; 5:14) remained, and probably had increased. Paul had to refer again to the example that he and his colleagues had given, working with their own hands when they might have been dependent on those to whom they brought the gospel. Paul had a simple dictum that he applied, "If any one will not work, let him not eat!" (3:10).

Content. *Thanksgiving for Their Christian Lives (1:3,4).* God can be praised and they commended for their growing faith, their increasing love, and their endurance of persecution.

The reversal in God's judgment of the present roles of persecutors and persecuted (1:5–10). Now the Thessalonian Christians are having to suffer, but their persecutors must face the just judgment of God at the coming of the Lord Jesus "with his mighty angels." Those who reject the knowledge of God and the salvation offered in the gospel must "suffer the punishment of eternal destruction." His people will experience that glory of his coming and will realize that they have not believed or suffered in vain.

Prayer That the Lord Jesus Will Be Glorified (1:11,12). This is Paul's prayer for the Thessalonian Christians, a life worthy of their calling, the fulfilling of their resolves, and, by the grace of God, the name of Christ glorified.

The Things That Must Precede the Second Coming of Christ (2:1–12). Paul deals with the false teaching that the day of the Lord had already come. The Christian hope is expressed simply as "the coming of our Lord Jesus Christ," and "our assembling to meet him." Before this event, however, there must be the revealing of "the man of lawlessness," otherwise called the antichrist (though it may be noted that the NT also speaks of "antichrists" and "the spirit of antichrist"—1 Jn 2:18; 4:3). What is meant when Paul speaks of the one "who now restrains the mystery of lawlessness," but later will be taken away is unclear. From the time of the 2nd-century writer Tertullian, many have understood the restraining force to be the Roman Empire of Paul's era, though some understand "the man of lawlessness" as the later persecuting Roman emperor, Nero. Some have understood the restraining factor as the preaching of the gospel, others as a supernatural being, like the angel who restrains Satan (Rv 20). However this may be, Christians must be prepared for a supreme manifestation of evil "with pretended signs and wonders" by which many—will be deceived. The coming of Christ will mean the overthrow of evil and the judgment of those who oppose the truth and take pleasure in unrighteousness.

Renewed Thanksgiving, Encouragement, and Prayer (2:13–17). Subsequent to the discussion of the power of evil in people's lives, Paul gives thanks for the work of the Spirit of God in the lives of the Thessalonian Christians. They are encouraged to continue in all that the apostle has taught them, when present with them or by letter. Paul's prayer is that God, as the great Giver of comfort and hope, will "establish them in every good work and word."

Prayers One for Another (3:1–5). Paul expresses his need of their prayers, that God may continue to prosper the word he preaches and deliver him from evil men. His Christian readers, for their part, can be assured of God's faithfulness. Paul's prayer for them is that, as they continue in the things in which they have been taught, they will be directed "to the love of God and the steadfastness of Christ."

Warning Against Disorderliness and Idleness (3:6–15). Another of Paul's special purposes in writing is to stress that there is no place for idleness in the lives of Christians. He has taught this and given them an example. Christian people are "to do their work in quietness," "earn their own living," and "not be weary in well doing." There should be no associating with those who reject this teaching; they should be admonished as brothers but not treated as enemies.

Conclusion (3:16–18). With the prayer for grace and peace (the opening greeting in 1:2), and with Paul's personal signature, the letter closes. When Paul speaks of writing with his own hand in verse 17, it may mean that up to that point he dictated his letter to some one else (cf. 1 Cor 16:21; Col 4:18). FRANCIS FOULKES

See PAUL, THE APOSTLE; SECOND COMING OF CHRIST; THESSALONIANS, FIRST LETTER TO THE; THESSALONICA; ESCHATOLOGY; DAY OF THE LORD.

Bibliography. J. Denney, *The Epistles to the Thessalonians*; J. Eadie, *Commentary on the Epistles to the Thessalonians*; C. Ellicott, *Commentary on Epistles to the Thessalonians*; J.E. Frame, *A Critical and Exegetical Commentary on the Epistles of St. Paul to the Thessalonians*; I.H. Marshall, *1 and 2 Thessalonians*; G. Milligan, *St. Paul's Epistles to the Thessalonians*.

Thessalonica. Chief city of Macedonia and the seat of Roman administration in the century before Christ. In addition to a magnificent harbor Thessalonica had the good fortune of being located on the overland route from Italy to the East. This famous highway, called the Egnatian Way, ran directly through the city. Two Roman arches, the Vardar Gate and the Arch of Galerius, marked the western and eastern boundaries.

According to Strabo, a famous Greek geographer, Thessalonica was founded in 315 BC by the Macedonian general Cassander, who named it after his wife, the daughter of Philip and stepsister of Alexander the Great. It was settled by refugees from a large number of towns in the same region which had been destroyed in war. When Macedonia was divided into four districts (167 BC), Thessalonica was made the capital of the second division. Its influence continued to expand when the area became a Roman province. In the second civil war between Caesar and Pompey (42 BC) Thessalonica remained loyal to Anthony and Octavian and was rewarded by receiving the status of a free city. This gift of autonomy allowed the city to appoint its own magistrates, who were given the unusual title of politarchs. The historical accuracy of Luke is seen in the fact that while the term politarch does not appear in earlier Greek literature it is used in Acts 17:6,8 and has been found on an inscription on the Vardar Gate and in other inscriptions from the area. At the beginning of the 1st century Thessalonica had a council of five politarchs. Cicero, a Roman statesman who lived shortly before the time of Christ, spent seven months in exile at Thessalonica.

The church at Thessalonica was founded by Paul on his second missionary journey (Acts 17:1–4). At Troas the apostle had been directed in a vision to cross over the Aegean Sea to Macedonia. After ministering at Philippi, where he was beaten and jailed, Paul's Roman citizenship secured his release and he traveled on to Thessalonica. On the Sabbath Paul went into the synagogue and reasoned with his Jewish brethren that Jesus was the Christ. Some were persuaded along with a number of God-fearing Greeks and quite a few prominent women (Acts 17:4).

Paul's success stirred the jealousy of the Jews, who gathered some rabble from the marketplace and started a riot. They rushed the house of Jason where Paul was staying, but when they were unable to find the apostle, they dragged his host and some other brethren before the city officials. They claimed that Paul was guilty of defying Caesar's decrees because he taught another king called Jesus. That very night Paul slipped out of town and made his way to Beroea (Acts 17:5–10). The hostility of the Thessalonian Jews toward Paul is seen in the fact that when they learned that he was preaching at Beroea they followed him there and stirred up the crowds against him (Acts 17:13).

Our basic knowledge of the church at Thessalonica comes from two letters by Paul from Corinth at a slightly later date. These early letters of the apostle supply an important insight into the life of a 1st-century Macedonian congregation which was primarily gentile. Paul probably passed through Thessalonica on at least two other occasions (coming and going from Greece on his third journey). In the centuries that followed, the city remained as one of the major strongholds of Christianity. It won the epithet, "The Orthodox City." ROBERT H. MOUNCE

See PAUL, THE APOSTLE; THESSALONIANS, FIRST LETTER TO THE; THESSALONIANS, SECOND LETTER TO THE.

Theudas. Rebel referred to by Gamaliel in his speech before the Sanhedrin as an example of the fact that false messiahs would fall without their intervention (Acts 5:36). Theudas evidently led an unsuccessful rebellion against Rome in which he and 400 others were killed. A chronological difficulty is created by the fact that Josephus reports a rebellion led by Theudas during the reign of Claudius (*c.* AD 44), 7 to 10 years *after* Gamaliel's speech. While critics have offered this apparent anachronism as evidence that Luke (or some later editor) was in error, several other solutions are possible. Possibly the error is in Josephus' report rather than Luke's, or two different individuals named Theudas are intended. During the final years of Herod the Great several rebellions occurred, one of which may have been instigated by Theudas. It has been suggested (without any direct evidence) that Herod's slave Simon may have adopted the name Theudas when he gained freedom and subsequently rebelled against Herod. While the identity of Theudas remains unknown, this fact does not necessarily discredit the historical accuracy of Luke's narrative.

Thimnathah. KJV form of Timnah, a city on the northern border of Judah's tribe, in Joshua 19:43.

See TIMNAH (PLACE) #1.

This Age, Age to Come. *See* AGE, AGES.

Thistle. *See* PLANTS.

Thomas, The Apostle. One of the 12 apostles whose name appears in all four Gospel traditions. The name is a transliteration of an Aramaic word meaning "twin" and appears in the NT as *thōmas*. Among Greek Christians there was a tendency to use the Hellenistic name Didymus (*didumos*, "twin"), and this name appears three times in the fourth Gospel (11:16; 20:24; 21:2). There is ample evidence from Koine papyri that the name Didymus was well known in the NT era.

Thomas appears in each synoptic list of apostles (Mt 10:3; Mk 3:18; Lk 6:15; cf. Acts 1:13) but plays no further role. His celebrated appearance in the fourth Gospel is interesting, however, since John does not even provide an exhaustive list of apostles. Here Thomas expresses the despair of the final approach to Jerusalem (11:16) and presses Jesus to explain his words of departure in the upper room (14:5). In the Gospel's closing scenes is the familiar episode in which Thomas doubts the Lord's resurrection (20:24) and then is given compelling proof (vv 26–28). Thomas even appears in the Johannine epilogue (21:2) with Peter fishing in Galilee.

The postapostolic era witnessed a renewed interest in Thomas. The Syrian tradition (cf. Gospel and Acts of Thomas) refers to him as Judas the Twin, a tradition attested in Syriac manuscripts at John 14:22. Here is the apocryphal belief that Thomas was the twin brother of Jesus. Along with Matthew and Philip he is commanded to record the discourses of Jesus for the church.

Two texts from Nag Hammadi bear tribute to this apostle as well. Here the full text of the Gospel of Thomas records 114 "secret sayings which the living Jesus spoke" and which Thomas preserved. "The Book of Thomas the Contender/Athlete" provides a gnostic revelatory dialogue with the apostle.

The gnostic Acts of Thomas (extant in both Greek and Syriac) says that Jesus and Thomas were twins (sharing similar appearances and destinies) and that the apostle obtained secret teachings. This apocryphal account even explains Thomas' fate. Against his wishes Thomas traveled to India under the command of the Lord. There he was martyred with spears by the hand of an Indian king. He was raised up and his empty tomb took on magical properties. Today in St. Thomas, India, Christians assert that they descend from the apostle. GARY M. BURGE

See APOSTLE, APOSTLESHIP.

Thorn. *See* PLANTS (THISTLE, THORN).

Three Taverns. Way station where the brethren came to meet Paul when he arrived in Rome (Acts 28:15). It was on the Appian Way located at milepost 33 (30.5 English miles). The Forum of Appius is 10 miles further south along the same road. Three Taverns was near modern Cisterna at an important junction between the Appian Way and the road from Antium to Norba and was thus a common meeting place for travelers.

Thresher, Threshing, Threshing Floor. *See* AGRICULTURE; TRADES AND OCCUPATIONS (FARMER).

Throne. Elevated, ceremonial chair, its height symbolized the importance and the authority of the person seated on it. With the widespread use of the word "throne" the term

The throne of Tutankhamen, its back depicting the king and his wife under the sun disk (Aton).

ple, a priest (1 Sm 4:13,18), a ruler (Ps 94:20), a military officer (Jer 1:15), a favored guest (2 Kgs 4:10); although it is principally used for a king's chair from which he discharged his royal duties. The OT refers to thrones of foreign kings (Ex 11:5; Jer 43:10; Jon 3:6), but particular emphasis is on the throne of Israel, especially on the throne of David.

The God of Israel is described metaphorically as sitting upon a throne (Is 66:1). The vision of God seated on a throne as seen in prophetic visions is described by Micaiah (1 Kgs 22:19), Isaiah (6:1–3), Ezekiel (1:4–28; 10:1), and Daniel (7:9,10). Later, Ezekiel's vision of the throne of God was of major significance in Jewish "throne mysticism." In Revelation 4 the throne of God is flanked by the 24 thrones of the elders, surrounded by an emerald rainbow and 7 torches, with a crystal sea in front, and 4 living creatures on each side. Usually, God's throne is spoken of as being in heaven (Ps 11:4; Mt 5:34), but Jerusalem (Jer 3:17), the temple (Ez 43:7), or the nation Israel (Jer 14:21) may be called the throne of God. The throne of God may have been associated with the ark of the covenant in Israelite thought (2 Sm 6:2; Jer 3:16,17; Ez 43:7; see also Nm 10:35,36). Both God's throne and David's are judgment seats (Ps 9:4; Is 9:7; 16:5; see also Mt 25:31; Lk 22:30). The concept of Messiah's throne is rare in the OT (Is 9:7; Jer 17:25) but common in the NT (Lk 1:32; Acts 2:30, etc.).

Thummim. *See* URIM AND THUMMIM.

Thunder, Sons of. Translation of the word "Boanerges," the surname given by Jesus to James and John (Mk 3:17).

See BOANERGES.

Thutmose. *See* EGYPT, EGYPTIANS.

Thyatira. One of the seven churches of the Apocalypse. The city was founded by the Lydian kingdom and later captured by Seleucus, Alexander's general. It then served as a border settlement to preserve his kingdom from Lysimacus, his rival to the west.

After the kingdom of Pergamum was founded (282 BC), Thyatira became the borderline between Pergamum and the Syrians. The city was without natural defenses. It was not built on a hill and therefore was subject to repeated invasions. The strength of the city lay largely in its strategic location and also upon the fertility of the area surrounding it. Its inhabitants were descendants of Macedonian soldiers and retained much of their ancestors' militancy. They made formidable defenders of the city.

came to symbolize kingship, and became equivalent in meaning to the kingdom itself. When Pharaoh elevated Joseph to the status and office of viceroy, he emphasized "only with respect to the throne shall I be superior to you" (Gn 41:40). The establishment of David as king of Israel was equivalent to the establishment of the throne of David (2 Sm 3:10). To occupy the throne indicated the succession to the kingship (1 Kgs 1:46).

Only one throne is described in detail in the OT, the throne of Solomon (1 Kgs 10:18–20; 2 Chr 9:17–19). The description, combined with the representation of thrones on ancient monuments, gives an idea of the appearance of the throne of Israel. An elevated seat with six steps leading up to it, the throne was partly made of ivory and overlaid with gold. The throne had a backrest and arms; alongside it were statues of lions and six similar statues on either side of the steps. Although not mentioned in the OT's description, a footstool was an indispensable part of the throne (Is 66:1).

The Hebrew term *kisseh* is used of a seat of honor for any distinguished person: for exam-

When Rome defeated Antiochus in 189 BC, Thyatira was incorporated into the kingdom of Pergamum, Rome's ally. Peace and prosperity followed. Under the Roman emperor Claudius (AD 41–54), Thyatira rose to new prominence and was permitted to issue its own coins. The emperor Hadrian included this city in his Middle East itinerary (AD 134), a hint of the importance of Thyatira in the 2nd century AD.

Prosperity attracted many Jews to this area. Among the commercial activities of the city were textiles and bronze armor. The armorers were in a guild, like the silversmiths in Ephesus. A coin from the city reveals a smith hammering a helmet on an anvil, a reminder that in the letter to Thyatira the Son of God has eyes that glow like fire and his feet like white-hot metal (Rv 2:18). On the coin the coppersmith is the god Hephaestus. The first known Christian convert in Europe was a businesswoman from Thyatira named Lydia (Acts 16:14,15,40). She specialized in the costly purple garments which were exported from Thyatira to Macedonia. Here the purple dye, from the madder root, offered a much cheaper cloth to compete with costlier garments dyed with the expensive murex dye from Phoenicia.

In the message to the church in Thyatira, the members are commended for their love, faith, service, and endurance (Rv 2:19). But the influence of paganism is still reflected in the sharp rebuke of those who tolerate the heresy of which "Jezebel" was the leader. Their temptation was similar to that of the Corinthian believers who were uncertain about eating food that had been dedicated to idols (1 Cor 8:1–13). The trade guilds held periodic festivals in which food offered to idols was consumed. This was sometimes accompanied by licentious rites in which religion and sex were mingled. This church was condemned for the accommodation to these pagan practices. Immorality was so rife among the pagans that the early church, with its uncompromising attitude toward unchastity, stood in constant tension with the mores of the community. Superstition and devil worship were apparently a great temptation as well. The "deep things of Satan" (Rv 2:24) is probably an allusion to one of the gnostic sects which stressed "depth" and carried on secret rites in which only initiates participated. So serious was the temptation that the best hope was for survival of the remnant, hence the exhortation "only hold fast what you have, until I come" (Rv 2:25).

The main dangers to the church of Thyatira were indifference (as at Laodicea), legalism (as in Galatia), asceticism (as at Colossae), and lawlessness (as at Thyatira). The young church at Thyatira was especially vulnerable to false doctrine, especially if it catered to the "lust of the flesh" and was promoted by an influential leader like "Jezebel."

See REVELATION, BOOK OF.

Thyine. KJV translation for "scented wood" in Revelation 18:12. Thyine was a dark-colored, fragrant, and valuable wood used for making furniture.

See PLANTS (CITRON TREE).

Tiberias. City midway along the western shores of Lake Galilee, built about AD 20 by Herod Antipas, Herod the Great's son and the tetrarch of Galilee and Perea (4 BC–AD 39), who named the town in honor of the emperor Tiberius. The name is preserved in the modern town Tabariyeh. The site became his new capital after abandoning Sepphoris, which he built in 4 BC. The location of Tiberias had several advantages: it lay just below a rocky projection above the lake, a natural acropolis which offered good protection; it was a center where roads from north, south, and west met, allowing Herod to move readily to various parts of his domain; and famous warm springs lay a little to the south, which were known to

Tiberias, with the Golan Heights across the Sea of Galilee.

the Roman writer Pliny the Elder, who spoke of their health-giving qualities. Herod built a lakeside palace, feeling secure in the knowledge that a naturally fortified acropolis lay behind him. From there he would have enjoyed a superb panorama which took in the whole of Galilee at a glance.

During the building of the town, a necropolis was discovered, which led to the Jewish banishment of the site, although a number of Jewish centers bordered the Sea of Galilee, especially to the north of Tiberias at Magdala, Capernaum, Bethsaida, and others. The town was subsequently settled by a heterogeneous company of Gentiles, some of whom were brought forcibly to the place by Herod, poor, slaves, and others quite well off. By offering good houses and land to all, Herod assembled a sizable population (Josephus *Antiq.* 18.2.3). According to the Gospels, Jesus never went there, probably in deference to Jewish scruples about the pollution caused by corpses. The town is mentioned only once in the NT (Jn 6:23), where boats came from Tiberias following the episode of the feeding of the 5000. The Sea of Tiberias, that is, Lake Galilee, is referred to in John 6:1 and 21:1.

The gentile residents of Tiberias held Jewish sympathies when the revolt against the Romans broke out in AD 65. The palace on the acropolis was subsequently destroyed and the defenses of the city were strengthened by the Roman forces. Tiberias persisted in a pro-Jewish policy throughout the great Jewish revolt. However, when General Vespasian laid siege to towns in the area, Tiberias surrendered. The emperor Nero had placed the Galilean towns of Tiberias, Tarichaea, and Bethsaida-julias with 14 villages under Herod Agrippa II, a puppet king (AD 48–100, Acts 25:13–27), so that Tiberias remained under Jewish rule until AD 100 though it was no longer a capital. After Jerusalem fell in AD 135 during the second Jewish revolt, Tiberias became a strong Jewish center and was recognized as one of the four sacred sites of Palestine. The Sanhedrin moved here from Sepphoris in AD 150 and soon established schools for rabbinic study. The Mishna and the Palestinian Talmud were edited in Tiberias in the 3rd and 5th centuries AD.

Tiberias, Sea of. Alternate name for the Sea of Galilee in John 6:1 and 21:1.

See GALILEE, SEA OF.

Tiberius. Roman emperor (AD 14–37) during Jesus' earthly ministry.

See CAESARS, THE.

Tibhath. City of King Hadadezer from which David received a large quantity of bronze as booty (2 Sm 8:8, Betah; 1 Chr 18:8). Hadadezer was the king of Zobah which is located in the region of Hamath in Syria, so the location of Tibhath was likely in that region. The spelling difference between 1 Chronicles and the parallel passage in 2 Samuel is probably the result of a copyist inadvertently transposing the first two letters. A further transmission problem comes in the reporting of the booty from the battle. First Chronicles reports 1000 chariots and 7000 horsemen (18:4), while 2 Samuel records simply 1700 horsemen.

Tibni. Ginath's son, who competed with Omri to be king of Israel after Zimri's assassination of Elah. The subsequent coup ended with Zimri's suicide (1 Kgs 16:21,22). Tibni ruled over half of Israel from 885–880 BC before Omri defeated him in a civil war.

See ISRAEL, HISTORY OF.

Tidal. King of Goiim who fought with Chedorlaomer's confederation against Sodom (Gn 14:1,9). There are large differences of opinion concerning the identity of Tidal (Septuagint Thurgal). Some have suggested that "Thurgal" is correct and the phrase means "great chief of the nations" (i.e., chief of large bands of nomads). Others argue a Hittite connection, linking Tidal with Tudhaliya, a common Hittite throne name (i.e., Tudhaliya, son of Hattusilis), while yet others posit a Babylonian connection with the name Tudhula. The first alternative is weakened by the fact that the name Thurgal is linked to a Hamitic dialect, while "goiim" (the nations) is Semitic. The Hittite alternative suffers from a lack of direct attestation, while a Babylonian connection would create severe chronological difficulties. Therefore, the precise identification remains uncertain.

Tiglath-pileser. Name of three Assyrian kings, the most important of whom was Tiglath-pileser III (745–727 BC). The name means "my trust is in the son of the temple Esharra," and appears in various forms (cf. 2 Kgs 15:29; also called Tilgath-pilneser in 1 Chr 5:6; 2 Chr 28:20).

Tiglath-pileser I (1115–1077 BC) was the son of Ashur-resh-ishi. Having gained independence from Babylonian overlordship, Tiglath-pileser consolidated his hold over the territory newly acquired in his father's reign, maintaining control and guarding against counterattacks from the former occupiers. A large displaced group of Musku (OT Mesech; Greek Phrygians) invading Asia Minor were routed by Tiglath-pileser, who then sent an expedition to the Syrian coastal cities where he established trade links. Contact was also made with Egypt, and the pharaoh sent a crocodile as a gift. Security brought increased trade and prosperity, and a large temple-building program was undertaken.

Tiglath-pileser II (c. 967–935 BC) was a weak king who ruled Assyria during a period of decline. Although he was able to maintain some degree of internal control, he was powerless to prevent outside peoples from encroaching upon Assyrian territory. In particular the Arameans took advantage of Assyrian weakness to occupy large areas of land, and an Aramean ruler named Kapara built a palace at Guzana (the Gozan of 2 Kgs 17:6). Some of the Arameans who occupied the area have been identified from inscriptions found at the site. This period was of particular importance for the emergence of the Aramean Empire.

Tiglath-pileser III (745–727 BC) ascended the throne at a time when he could stem and reverse another decline in Assyrian fortunes. Although not directly in line for the throne, he was probably of royal descent. On occasion he used the name Pul (2 Kgs 15:19; 1 Chr 5:26), which may have been his real name as opposed to his throne name.

Tiglath-pileser III was a strong, able, resourceful king whose reign is remarkable for the rapid extension of Assyrian boundaries and for the peaceful administration of the newly acquired territories. He assisted Babylon by defeating the Arameans, and by his diplomacy retained Babylonian support while he concentrated his military efforts elsewhere. On the death of the vassal king Nabu-nasir of Babylon in 734 BC, Tiglath-pileser gained the support of some of the tribes and finally forced the submission of Marduk-apla-iddina (the Merodach-baladan of Is 39:1). According to the Babylonian Chronicle, he used the name Pul when acceding to the throne of Babylon himself in 729 BC. He was the first Assyrian king on the throne of Babylon for 500 years.

During a campaign in northern Syria in 743 BC, Tiglath-pileser marched against the city-states controlled by Barduri of Urartu (Armenia). While engaged in a three-year siege of Arpad, he received tribute from the rulers of Carchemish, Hamath, Tyre, Byblos, and Damascus. Menahem of Syria also paid Tiglath-pileser 1000 talents of silver collected from wealthy Israelites (2 Kgs 15:19,20). Meanwhile the Aramean states in south Syria fell under the control of Azariah of Judah, who died shortly afterward (2 Kgs 15:7). The Phoenician seaports, probably feeling the economic loss from the disruption of their former trade with Egypt and resenting the burden of Assyrian taxes and administration, revolted against Tiglath-pileser, who marched west to the attack in 734 BC.

Ashkelon and Gaza were severely damaged, and heavy tribute was paid to the invader. Statues of Tiglath-pileser, including a large golden statue, were erected in local temples to mark his victory. He also received tribute from the city of Damascus, as well as from Ammon, Edom, Moab, and Jehoahaz of Judah (2 Chr 28:19–21). When Judah was raided by a combined force from Damascus and Israel, which also included Edomites and Philistines, Assyria sent no help (2 Chr 28:17,18). Not until Jerusalem was besieged did Assyrian troops attacked Damascus, and the besiegers were forced to turn their attention away from Jerusalem toward the new threat (2 Kgs 16:5–9).

When Damascus fell to the Assyrians in 732 BC, Metenna of Tyre also capitulated. Many towns and villages in Israel were destroyed, and their peoples taken captive to Mesopotamia. Tiglath-pileser claims to have replaced Pekah on the throne of Israel with Hoshea, and he may even have been responsible for plotting the murder of the former (2 Kgs 15:30).

As an administrator, Tiglath-pileser III followed the pattern of Tiglath-pileser I, who adhered to a policy of sending war captives in vast numbers to populate other areas of newly acquired territory, thus helping to destroy resurgent nationalism. Captive Israelites are mentioned amongst the people settled in Ullubu (Bitlis). The deportations also provided a massive mobile labor force which in one year alone was estimated to number 154,000.

The established system of Assyrian provincial administration was extended further when officials sent to newly conquered cities not only acted as tax collectors and administrators but also as valuable sources of intelligence on the local area.

The authority of individual provincial governors was limited during this period, and the local officials concentrated upon setting up an efficient system for the collecting of taxes, most of which were in kind.

That Assyrian taxes formed an undue burden for the people is unlikely. Whether they were paying taxes to their own people or to a foreign ruler made little difference if the tax was collected equitably.

As the central administration kept a close watch on the local officials, it is unlikely that large amounts of extra tax were collected to line the pockets of Assyrian officials. In all their duties the authority of these persons was backed by contingents of the Assyrian army. Peace and security under the reign of Tiglath-pileser III brought trade and commerce.

Stone relief that depicts Tiglath-pileser III at Ashtaroth.

In Babylonia, Tiglath-pileser continued the policy which had already proved successful—siding with the cities against the rulers of rebellious local tribes. In Calah he built himself a palace, which was the first to be constructed in the area according to a style newly introduced from Syria.

His reign, which was marked by a vast increase in territory coupled with a firm and able administration, also had long-term effects far beyond Assyria's immediate borders. The expansion into Syria and Palestine was bound to lead eventually to conflict with Egypt when that country wished once again to mount a more aggressive foreign policy. Tiglath-pileser was the father of Shalmaneser V (727–722 BC). HAZEL W. PERKIN

See ASSYRIA, ASSYRIANS.

Tigris River. One of the two major rivers that drains the Mesopotamian plain. Unlike the Euphrates, it is seldom mentioned in the Bible. In the description of the Garden of Eden, it is listed as the third of the four rivers that flowed out of the river that watered the garden (Gn 2:14, KJV Hiddekel). Unfortunately, this reference provides little help concerning the location of Eden. The river is not mentioned again until Daniel 10:4 (KJV Hiddekel), where Daniel referred to it as the "great river." Nahum is likely referring to the Tigris when he describes the opening of the river gates of Nineveh during the Babylonian siege (Na 2:6).

When its two principal tributaries are included, the length of the Tigris is 1146 miles. Its primary source, a mountain lake called Golenjik, is only two or three miles from the channel of the Euphrates. As is the case with most of the rivers of the region, the flow of the Tigris varies considerably during the year. Flood season begins in early March with its peak in early to mid-May. Though the river is generally navigable, historical records suggest that the river never had great commercial significance. However, it did gain political significance during the period of Assyrian dominance. Nineveh, Asshur, and Calah were all located on the banks of the Tigris. Unfortunately for the Assyrians, the Tigris never proved to be a formidable natural barrier and thus failed to protect the empire from its enemies.

Tikvah. 1. Harhas' son, father of Shallum, and the father-in-law of Huldah the prophetess (2 Kgs 22:14); alternately called Tokhath in 2 Chronicles 34:22 (KJV Tikvath).

2. Father of Jahzeiah, one of the four individuals on record as opposing the divorcing of foreign wives as commanded by Ezra (Ezr 10:15).

Tikvath. KJV spelling of Tokhath, an alternate name for Tikvah, Harhas' son, in 2 Chronicles 34:22.

See TIKVAH #1.

Tilgath-pilneser. Alternate spelling of the Assyrian king Tiglath-pileser III's name in 1 Chronicles 5:6,26 and 2 Chronicles 28:20.

See TIGLATH-PILESER.

Tiller. See AGRICULTURE; TRADES AND OCCUPATIONS (FARMER).

Tilon. Shimon's son from Judah's tribe (1 Chr 4:20).

Timaeus. Father of Bartimaeus, the blind beggar whose sight Jesus restored near the gateway leading from Jericho (Mk 10:46).

Timbrel. Small hand drum.

See MUSIC AND MUSICAL INSTRUMENTS (SHALISHIM; TOPH).

Timna. 1. Daughter of Seir, sister of Lotan, and a native Horite inhabitant of Edom (Gn 36:22; 1 Chr 1:39). She was a concubine to Eliphaz, Esau's son, and the mother of Amalek (Gn 36:12).

2. Edomite chief (Gn 36:40; 1 Chr 1:51, KJV Timnah; 1 Chr 1:36). This name may refer either to the name of the ancestor of the Edom-

ite clan or to the geographical area occupied by the clan.

Timnah (Person). KJV spelling of Timna, an Edomite chief, in Genesis 36:40 and 1 Chronicles 1:51.

See TIMNA #2.

Timnah (Place). 1. One of the cities on the northern boundary of Judah's inheritance, located between Beth-shemesh and Ekron (Jos 15:10). This is the likely site of Judah's affair with Tamar, which resulted in the birth of Perez and Zerah (Gn 38:12–14, KJV Timnath). A frontier town between Judah and Philistia, Timnah was the place where Samson had his first marital difficulties with one of the daughters of the Philistines (Jgs 14:1,2,5, KJV Timnath; 15:6, KJV Timnite). The town evidently changed hands frequently between the Israelites and the Philistines. Apparently Israel did achieve control of Timnah during the conquest (cf. Jos 19:43, KJV Thimnathah), but it was under Philistine control by the time of Samson (Jgs 14:1). Ahaz recaptured Timnah (c. 730 BC) from the Philistines (2 Chr 28:18). Assyrian records reveal that Sennacherib (701 BC) defeated the Philistines at Tamna (likely Timnah) before he attacked Ekron. Timnah is likely the same as modern Tibneh.

2. One of the cities of the southern hill country that was part of the inheritance of Judah (Jos 15:57). It is possible that this is the site of Judah's misadventures with Tamar (Gn 38:12, 14; and perhaps the same as #1 above).

Timnath. KJV spelling of Timnah, a town in northern Judah, in Genesis 38:12–14 and Judges 14:1,2,5.

See TIMNAH (PLACE) #1.

Timnath-heres, Timnath-serah. The city that Joshua, the son of Nun, asked for and which was given to him as his inheritance when the land was divided among the tribes of Israel (Jos 19:49,50; here the name is given as Timnath-serah). Joshua rebuilt the city and settled there. When Joshua died, he was buried on the property located "in the hill country of Ephraim, north of the mountain of Gaash" (Jos 24:30). Judges 2:9 gives the same location, but these geographical notations are too indefinite to determine the precise location of the city. Possibly the site is represented by Khirbet Tibneh, which is about 17 miles north, northwest of Jerusalem and nearly the same distance S,SW of Nablus (Shechem).

In the Judges passage, however, the name is Timnath-heres, which means "territory, or portion, of the sun," thus seeming to associate the city with an older form of sun-worship, as may also be the case with the city of Beth-shmesh ("house of the sun").

There are several possible explanations of the different names. The place could have had two names, with the second element of the names made up of the same three Hebrew consonants but in a different order. This would be a remarkable coincidence, but possible. Timnath-serah would mean something like "territory of excess." Palestinian towns often bore more than one name, usually at different times (cf. Bethel [earlier Luz, Gn 35:6]; Dan [Leshem, Jos 19:47]; Hebron [Kiriath-arba, Gn 23:2]). Or if the correct name was Timnath-heres, it could have been deliberately changed by a scribe to avoid any reference to the worship of the sun. Whichever name is original, the other may be explained as an unintentional transposition made by a copyist so that the positions of several letters were exchanged.

Timnite. Inhabitant from the town of Timnah in northern Judah (Jgs 15:6).

See TIMNAH (PLACE) #1.

Timon. One of the seven men of the Jerusalem church "of good repute, full of the Spirit and of wisdom" appointed to minister to the widows (Acts 6:5).

Timothy, First Letter to. First and 2 Timothy and Titus, known as the pastoral letters, were written to two young pastors and deal with pastoral problems in the churches of Ephesus and Crete.

Authorship of the Pastoral Letters. All three letters name Paul as the author in the first verses. Paul's name is the only one assigned as author in the tradition of the early church since the time of Irenaeus (c. AD 185). Throughout the letters are many personal references to the life of Paul which constitute strong evidence that he was truly the author.

However, many scholars object to Pauline authorship on the following grounds.

The Greek vocabulary contains a large number of words that are not found in the other Pauline letters. The subject matter in these letters is also different. Here the author is dealing with the more technical matters of church organization and discipline—a preacher writing to other preachers. Paul was a highly educated man, with a large vocabulary at his disposal. None of the words peculiar to the pastoral letters would have been beyond Paul's own vocabulary. Because Paul regularly used scribes, possibly some of the unusual words came from them.

Another objection is that there are notes

about Paul's journeys that will not fit into the journeys described in the Book of Acts. To believe that Paul wrote the pastorals and did the things described in them, he must have been released from the Roman imprisonment and then traveled to Crete, Ephesus, and Macedonia. These later journeys may not have been mentioned in Acts because the writer of Acts may have intended to conclude simply with Paul's imprisonment in Rome. There is some legal evidence that Paul would automatically have been released after two years, if he had not been convicted by that time.

Some scholars contend that the advanced development of the church described in the pastorals proves a date later than the life of Paul. Elders, bishops, and deacons are mentioned. However, elders existed in OT times and bishops, as officers within local churches, are almost certainly the same as elders. In addition, Paul refers to deacons elsewhere in his letters, such as Philippians 1:1.

Most conservative scholars and many others as well believe very strongly that Paul did write all three of the pastoral letters. Of course, the Holy Spirit could have chosen and inspired someone else, but the positive evidence is much stonger that he did choose the apostle Paul.

Date. Assuming that Paul wrote the pastorals, 1 Timothy would have been written after his release from the first Roman imprisonment, about AD 61, and before his second Roman imprisonment, somewhere between 64 and 67, the date of the death of Nero. As to the place, Paul left Timothy in Ephesus and then went on to Macedonia (1 Tm 1:3), where he may have written 1 Timothy. The letter was, of course, written to Timothy at Ephesus (1:3).

Historical Background. Paul left Timothy in charge of the church at Ephesus (1:3). Paul wanted to go to the province of Asia, of which Ephesus was the chief city, on his second missionary journey, but the Spirit did not allow him to do so. He went on to Macedonia and Greece (Acts 16:6). He briefly visited Ephesus as he was completing his second journey (Acts 18:19,20). Then on his third journey he made Ephesus the center of his activity and spent three years there (Acts 19:1–20:1). From his first Roman imprisonment he wrote his letter to the Ephesians. Only a few years later he wrote 1 Timothy to Timothy at Ephesus.

Theology. In general we can say that the theology of 1 Timothy is thoroughly consistent with that of the other Pauline letters and of the NT as a whole. The sovereignty and love of God are clearly presented time and again throughout the letter. Jesus is always presented as truly God as well as man. Salvation is by faith in God through Christ. The Law will not save a person, because all people have broken it. Yet the Law is good, and is God's guide for the saved person in living a life pleasing to God.

The church occupies a large place in the letter. All Christians should be a part of the church. They gain much from the church for the development of Christian character, and they can serve God far more effectively in the church than apart from it. The church needs organization to do its work effectively. And the church must strive always to avoid heresy and to teach the truths of the gospel.

Specifically, the letter is full of encouragement and good advice from the old pastor to the young pastor, his beloved child in the faith.

Content.   *Salutation (1:1,2).*   The author names himself, Paul, and describes himself as an apostle, chosen and given his authority by God the Father and his Son, Christ Jesus. Paul has the right to speak words of authority to the young pastor and to the church.

The letter is written to Timothy, Paul's beloved spiritual child to whom Paul sends his triple greeting—grace, mercy, and peace from God.

Heretical Theology (1:3–20).   One of the reasons Paul left Timothy in Ephesus was that he wanted him to "charge certain persons not to teach any different doctrine" (1:3). Paul believed that what a person believed was as important as what he did. The heresy here is described as an early form of the Gnostic heresy, a most dangerous heresy with which the church contended for centuries.

These early Gnostics claimed to have a deeper insight into truth than the average Christian. They separated God as Spirit from man as matter. For Gnostics the bridge between the two was innumerable angels of various ranks, emanations, aeons, and such, rather than the one mediator, Jesus Christ. They argued about myths and fables. They sought salvation by finding favor with an endless chain of angels rather than by accepting God's salvation by faith. They had strange views of the law which identified sins. But only the grace of God can save sinners, as Paul himself knew well.

Correct Worship in the Church (2:1–15).   "I urge that supplications, prayers, intercessions, and thanksgivings be made for all men" (2:1). Prayer is an exceedingly important part of the worship of the Christian church. Paul emphasizes the importance of special prayer for persons in high places of authority in the state (even though the state was the Roman Empire with Nero as its emperor). Paul had taught this clearly in Romans 13, and Jesus had told his disciples to render unto Caesar the things that belonged to him (Mt 22:17).

Christian men and women should pray to God, lifting up holy hands to him, hands free from sin and anger and resentment.

"Also that women should adorn themselves modestly and sensibly in seemly apparel, not with braided hair or gold or pearls or costly attire but by good deeds, as befits women who profess religion" (2:9,10).

Paul then goes on to say, "I permit no woman to teach or to have authority over men" (2:12). Christian churches are still arguing among themselves about the place of women in the church. The place of women has changed greatly in many ways, though in other ways there are still differences between the sexes. At this time, Paul did not allow women to teach men or occupy official positions of authority over men.

Correct Organization in the Church (3:1–5:25). "The saying is sure: If any one aspires to the office of bishop, he desires a noble task" (3:1). In all the pastorals the bishop is clearly an officer within a local church rather than an official over a group of churches, such as the office of episcopal bishop developed in the early 2nd century. And in the light of Titus 1:4–6, where Paul passed directly from elders to bishops, most scholars believe that Paul used the two terms interchangeably. Timothy himself would be the closest thing to a modern pastor in the church, and there were elders (bishops) and deacons assisting him in governing the church.

To be an elder in the church is a worthy aspiration. But a person must have high qualifications to be elected to such a responsible position. He should be respected by other members of the church and by those outside the church. Most of the qualifications are quite clear, but several of them deserve some attention.

"Now a bishop must be above reproach, the husband of one wife" (3:2). The Greek says literally, "a man of one woman." That would clearly prohibit polygamy and eliminate a man who was unfaithful to his wife. It would probably neither eliminate a man who had been divorced and remarried nor a bachelor who had never had a wife. The church should insist that its official leaders conform to a high view of sexual morality.

The elder should be able to discipline his own family life if he is to exert discipline in the church.

The RSV says that he should not be a drunkard. Paul does not demand total abstinence, but he clearly demands that an elder not be a person under the domination of strong drink.

A person occupying the high office of elder

should not be a new Christian (lit. a neophyte), lest this go to his head and keep him from being a good elder.

All in all, only a person of excellent character should be elected to the high office of elder, or bishop, in the church.

Then Paul goes on to the office of deacon: "Deacons likewise must be serious, not double-tongued" (3:8). The qualifications for the deacons are virtually the same as those for elders. Before being elected as deacons, they should have experience in church work. First Timothy 3:11 applies the same qualifications for women where the text may refer to female deacons as well as to wives of deacons. Verse 12 continues with the qualifications of deacons in general.

Paul tells Timothy that he hopes to come to see him and the church soon, but he is writing the letter to help him with the problems of selecting church leaders until he comes. He recognizes the difficulty of living a good Christian life, but Christ can help him succeed. He goes on to describe Christ in words which many scholars think were taken from an early hymn of adoration to Christ (3:16).

In chapter 4 Paul emphasizes for Timothy his duties as pastor of the church, especially in his relation to the heretics in the church. Paul called his times "the last times," in which heretics were to be expected.

Some of the Gnostic heretics taught a false kind of asceticism, forbidding marriage and the eating of various foods. But God has given these things to be used and appreciated to God's glory. Timothy's pastoral duty was to teach his people God's truths and not to allow himself to be caught up in arguing about the heretics' "godless and silly myths" (4:7). Paul urged Timothy to keep his spirit fit by constant spiritual exercise, which was even more important than exercise of the body.

Paul recognized that Timothy was a young man, and that some of the older Christians might be tempted to look down upon his youth. Timothy should strive even harder to deserve their admiration—"in speech and conduct, in love, in faith, in purity" (4:12). Because God has called Timothy and the church has ordained him by the laying on of hands, Timothy should strive to live up to these high responsibilities.

Paul gives Timothy very practical advice as to how a young preacher should deal with the different age and sex groups in the church. He should treat the older men as his own father, the older women as his mother, the younger men as his brothers, and the younger women as his sisters—adding significantly, "in all purity" (5:2).

Paul deals in a very practical way with the

problem of charity in the life of the church (5:3–16). He deals especially with the problem of widows. At that time, when few women could work and before the days of insurance and social security, women who had lost their husbands were in a hopeless situation. The early church developed a roll for widows that would enable it to minister to their needs. Various kinds of practical problems having arisen, Paul gave some advice about their solution. Younger widows were to be encouraged to marry again and get new husbands to support them. Able families should recognize their responsibility to take care of their own needy ones. The church, then, would have the responsibility of taking care of the older widows who have no families to take care of them. The church, with its charitable obligations, must use its limited means responsibly, wisely, and fairly so that the greatest possible good can result.

Even in the early church, pastors were paid for their work. Paul says that they "be considered worthy of double honor" (5:17), and goes on to quote the OT as his authority for this command.

Even ancient church leaders were not perfect, and their imperfections needed to be dealt with. There were those who enjoyed gossip and criticism against their leaders. Those criticisms should be rejected unless they could be conclusively proven true. In that case, formal discipline should be exercised without partiality.

Church leaders should not be chosen or ordained too quickly. Their sins should not be overlooked, or it will seem as if they are being approved. Timothy himself was warned to keep himself free from sin.

First Timothy 5:23 is a problem to many Christians. Some of the early Christians evidently believed in total abstinence from alcohol; at least the ascetic branch of the Gnostic heresy did. But Paul definitely advised Timothy to use a little wine "for the sake of your stomach and your frequent ailments." At least the medicinal use of wine is approved here. The total approach of a Christian to alcohol is far more complex than what is taught in this one verse.

The section ends with another treatment of the sins of church leaders (5:24,25). When the sins are clear, the sinner must be disciplined by the church. At times sins are not evident to men, but God knows them and will deal with them. Conversely the same is true about the many good deeds of the leaders.

Some Practical Teaching About the Christian Life (6:1–21). Slavery was a recognized institution in those days. Christian slaves should be good slaves, and Christian masters should be good masters. After many centuries, Christian principles would bring slavery to an end, but it would have been impossible for Paul or anyone else at that time to lead a crusade for the abolition of slavery.

Timothy is urged again to avoid the teaching of the heretics but to be faithful in teaching the positive truths of the gospel.

Two sections (6:6–10;17–19) deal with the Christian's attitude toward wealth. Here Paul follows closely the teachings of Jesus. Money can be made into a false god and bring all kinds of evil to the church member. But it can also be used in the service of God and be changed into treasure in heaven.

Finally, in two sections (6:11–16,20,21), Paul encourages Timothy to strive to do his very best to be truly God's man. He should fight a good fight as a soldier of God. This life will often be hard, but Timothy should keep his eyes fixed on the second coming of the glorious Christ.

The letter closes with a brief benediction, "Grace be with you."   SAMUEL CARTLEDGE

See PAUL, THE APOSTLE; TIMOTHY, SECOND LETTER TO; TITUS, LETTER TO.

Bibliography. J.H. Bernard, *The Pastoral Epistles;* P. Fairbairn, *Commentary on the Pastoral Epistles;* W. Henriksen, *Exposition of the Pastoral Epistles;* J.N.D. Kelly, *The Pastoral Epistles;* G.W. Knight, *The Faithful Sayings in the Pastoral Letters;* A. Plummer, *The Pastoral Epistles.*

Timothy, Second Letter to.

Authorship. Many of those who deny the Pauline authorship of the pastoral letter recognize that 2 Timothy contains some true Pauline fragments in the numerous personal references in the letter. But the evidence in favor of the Pauline authorship is much stronger than the evidence against it. (See the authorship of the pastoral letters under *Timothy, First Letter to,* for a full discussion of the authorship of all three pastoral letters.)

Place and Date of Writing. "That is why I am suffering as I am" (1:12 NIV) lets us know that Paul was in prison when he wrote; 1:15–18 tells specifically of his being in Rome and how Onesiphorus was faithful to him when others from the province of Asia had deserted him. Second Timothy 2:9 again refers to his being in jail for his preaching the gospel. Toward the end of the letter, starting at 4:6, Paul refers to his experience in prison and that he has no hope for a release. Second Timothy is a type of last will and testament of the apostle. Early, trustworthy tradition purports that Paul was martyred in Rome under Nero. Rome, then, was the place from which 2 Timothy was written.

The letter was written to Timothy in Ephesus, as is made plain throughout the letter.

Ruins of the forum in Rome.

As to the year in which it was written, two dates are possible. The year 64 AD was the date of the great fire in Rome. Nero tried to shift responsibility for the fire to the Christians. Possibly Paul was martyred at that time. Nero himself died in AD 67, so that would be the latest date that could be assigned. The letter was written between AD 64 and 67, with some preference being given to the earlier date.

The Historical Background. Since the time of the writing of 1 Timothy, Paul made further travels and then came to Rome and his second imprisonment. See this section under *1 Timothy.*

Theology. The letter is primarily pastoral rather than theological in emphasis. Yet Paul knows of the presence of heresy and wants to help Timothy avoid it and hold fast to the truths of orthodox Christianity. He attacks the errors of the heretics, but his primary emphasis is a positive presentation of the truth. This is found in the other Pauline letters and in the rest of the NT as well. The belief in a sovereign God is plain throughout the letter. Jesus is always the divine-human Savior, dying, rising, and coming again. There is a good balance between present duties and sufferings and the assured hope of a blessed eternity. Some have believed that Paul's statement "I have kept the faith" makes faith exclusively a body of orthodox creed, a concept too late for the time of Paul himself. But that is by no means a necessary interpretation. The word faith is a very broad one, going all the way from the dead faith which even the devils have (see Job) to the rich, full commitment to Christ that produces a transformed life and leads to the fullness of eternal life in heaven. Surely Paul was thinking about such a full view of faith—including and going beyond an orthodox creed. Paul had such an experience

of faith himself, and he wanted Timothy to have it too, and to share it with all the members of his church.

Content. *Salutation (1:1,2).* As was customary in ancient letters, the writer puts his name first. Then he gives a fuller identification of himself as apostle, one belonging to Jesus Christ, and one commissioned to tell the whole world about the eternal life which God has made available through faith in Jesus Christ. Thus Paul indicates his authority in writing and also gives a brief summary of the essence of the true Christian faith. All of this serves as an excellent preparation for the content of the letter.

The person to whom the letter is written is "Timothy, my beloved child."

Then follows a triple blessing, "Grace, mercy, and peace" from God the Father and his Son, Jesus Christ. As in all his letters Paul changes the rather colorless Greek salutation, "greetings," to one of the greatest theological concepts, "grace," and adds the Greek translation of the regular Hebrew salutation, "peace." Then he adds here the great word, "mercy," as he did in 1 Timothy.

Exhortations to Timothy to Be a Good Minister (1:3–2:13). Paul begins this section by telling Timothy how often he offered prayers of thanksgiving to God on his behalf, to the God of his fathers, to the one whom it was his chief purpose in life to please. Paul greatly desired to see Timothy, especially as he remembered their tearful parting.

Paul reminds Timothy of his great trust in the Lord, a trust which was passed on to him by two godly women, his mother Eunice and his grandmother Lois. Acts 16:1–3 states that Timothy's mother was a believing Jewess, and his father was a Greek, or Gentile. He had not allowed his son to be circumcised in infancy. But the believing mother had passed on her faith to her son. When Paul decided to take him along as an assistant on his second missionary journey, he had him circumcised so that he could work more effectively with the Jews. Thus Timothy had a great heritage from Lois, Eunice, and Paul himself.

"Hence I remind you to rekindle the gift of God that is within you through the laying on of my hands" (1:6). First Timothy 4:14 has, "when the council of elders laid their hands upon you." This looks very much like a formal service of ordination, when Timothy was set apart as a minister of the gospel by the laying on of hands with prayer. Timothy should never forget that solemn moment, and the memory should keep his life filled with strength and boldness. He was not just a man but truly a man of God, a man filled with the Spirit of God, and a man who is not afraid to do his Christian work. Timothy may suffer for his faith, but he can be encouraged as he remembers the sufferings and imprisonment of his spiritual father Paul. God will give Timothy strength to suffer as he had given to Paul.

Then Paul reminds Timothy of how God had saved him and Paul, how he had chosen them from all eternity to tell others of God's saving love through Jesus Christ, who came in time to work out that salvation, by breaking the power of death and showing the way to eternal life. God gave Paul a special charge to preach the gospel to the Gentiles.

Although Paul is in a Roman jail, he is not in the least ashamed: "For I know whom I have believed" (1:12). Paul knew, of course, what he believed, but more importantly he knew whom he believed, or trusted—Jesus Christ. And in spite of the many uncertainties that must have been in Paul's mind, he could be absolutely sure of Christ, and specifically that Christ would be "able to guard until that Day what has been entrusted to me." Paul was confident of that, and he wanted Timothy to have a similar assurance.

Paul urges Timothy to hold fast to the pattern of truth which Paul had taught him, that body of Christian doctrine, especially as it pertained to Jesus Christ and the faith and love in him. He should guard carefully the gift which the Holy Spirit had given him.

Paul shares with Timothy a great sorrow that had come to him. All the Christians of the Roman province of Asia, of which Ephesus was the chief city, had deserted Paul. Evidently the persecution was growing more intense, and they were not courageous enough to stay and endure it. Paul mentions two of the deserters by name, Phygellus and Hermogenes. Evidently Timothy knew who they were. In striking contrast, Paul mentions the good man Onesiphorus (also at 4:19), who had been such a wonderful and faithful helper of Paul, both in Ephesus and in Rome.

Paul again urges Timothy to be strong in the strength which Christ has given him (2:1). As Paul urges him to be strong so often, Timothy may have been somewhat timid.

Timothy should pass on the Christian truths to others and train them to pass them on to still others. Paul was probably thinking especially of the elders, or bishops, and deacons (cf. 1 Tm).

Paul used three effective illustrations to encourage Timothy to give his best in his Christian service. He was to fight and suffer as a good soldier, play the game well as a good athlete, and work hard as a good farmer. The rewards will come to all three if they perform their tasks well. All three illustrations were used by Jesus, Paul, and other NT writers.

There is a fine summary of true Christology (2:8–10). Jesus was truly man and truly God. It is heretical to deny either the full humanity or the full deity of Christ, even though no human mind can fully understand the mystery of the incarnation. And this divine-human being died and then rose again from the dead. Here is a wonderful summary of the essence of the true Christian faith.

Because Paul diligently preached this Christian faith, he was imprisoned in Rome. Paul is writing in hopes of inspiring Timothy to follow in his steps.

The Christian life may well be hard in this age, but all the sufferings will be more than worthwhile in the light of what God has in store in his heavenly home. If believers are faithful to Christ, they can be certain that he will always be faithful to them in this age and throughout all eternity.

Warnings Against Heresy (2:14–4:5). "Remind them of this, and charge them before the Lord to avoid disputing about words, which does no good but only ruins the hearers." There are heretical beliefs that should be definitely condemned, but Christians are warned against arguing among themselves about insignificant matters even in the Christian faith and losing sight of the important truths and duties. Christians can become angry with other Christians and spend time fighting one another rather than Satan himself.

Timothy was to strive to make himself a good servant, meriting the approval of his Master, knowing well the truths of his word. In that way he could combat the false teachings of the heretics.

Two of the heretics are mentioned by name, Hymenaeus and Philetus. Philetus is not mentioned again. Hymenaeus, though, was mentioned also in 1 Timothy 1:20 along with another heretic, Alexander; these two had been given over to Satan, or excommunicated, by Paul at that time. Their heresy was: "holding that the resurrection is past already" (2:18). This heresy was striking at the Christian hope of the final resurrection which would introduce all believers into God's eternal heaven. The heretics were denying the reality of that and redefining it as something which had already happened, possibly the experience that came to the Christian after accepting Christ. This taking away of the blessed hope was weakening the faith of those who followed the teaching of these heretics.

In various ways Paul urges Timothy to prove himself a true servant of God, one who is known by God and one who lives by the truths of God's word. He should avoid the evil thoughts that so often come to young men, and also the temptation to quarrel. Rather he should be gentle, patient, and humble as he seeks to help his people avoid the traps of Satan.

Second Timothy 3:1–9 gives Paul's strongest condemnation of the heretics in the church. They attend church, but they do not believe the Christian truths. They do not live Christian lives themselves, and strive to get others to follow their evil beliefs and practices; Paul likened the heretics of his day to the Egyptian magicians in Exodus 7, who were given the names by Jewish tradition, Jannes and Jambres. The modern heretics will fail in their attacks against the truth just as Jannes and Jambres failed in their attacks against God and his spokesman, Moses.

Paul contrasts his own life and beliefs with those of the heretics. He had been persecuted by heretics himself even on his first missionary journey, but he had continued to preach the truth and had brought many to accept Christ. Timothy should follow Paul's example.

The supreme way to overcome heresy is the diligent study of the Word of God. "All scripture is inspired by God and profitable for teaching, for reproof, for correction, and for training in righteousness, that the man of God may be complete, equipped for every good work" (3:16–17).

Paul gives Timothy a solemn charge to preach that word faithfully and diligently. Many will not be willing to listen to the truths of the Bible, but Timothy should try to correct and rebuke them, even though it may bring persecution upon himself.

Paul's Faith and Hope (4:6–18). Paul has been writing these very important injunctions to Timothy because he knows that he has very little time left here on earth: "For I am already on the point of being sacrificed; the time of my departure has come" (4:6). He can look back with satisfaction upon his past life, a life of true faith and service. So he can look forward in all confidence to his crown of victory in heaven. This kind of faith enabled Paul to face his death bravely, and it will do the same for all believing Christians for whom the second coming is a blessed hope.

Paul urges Timothy to come and be with him in Rome. Luke was the only one of his friends still with him. Paul tells Timothy about other friends who had been with him but who had left. One, Demas, had proved to be a failure. Crescens, Titus, and Tychicus had gone to other places. When Timothy comes to Rome, Paul asks him to bring his coat which he had left at Troas with Carpus, and also his books, especially those written on parchment, probably some rolls of Scripture. Paul warns Timothy against the evil man, Alexander the coppersmith (see 1 Tm 1:20).

At Paul's first trial, all of his friends had left him. But God has been with him and saved him. He had even had an opportunity of proclaiming the gospel for all the world to hear.

Concluding Greetings (4:19–22). Paul sends his greetings to a number of his friends in Ephesus. And he sends greetings to Timothy from some of the Roman Christians whom he evidently knew. He urges Timothy to try to come to him before winter, when traveling would be difficult or impossible. He concludes with a short benediction, "The Lord be with your spirit." SAMUEL CARTLEDGE

See TIMOTHY, FIRST LETTER TO; TITUS, LETTER TO; PAUL, THE APOSTLE.

Bibliography. J.H. Bernard, *The Pastoral Epistles;* P. Fairbairn, *Commentary on the Pastoral Epistles;* W. Henriksen, *Exposition of the Pastoral Epistles;* J.N.D. Kelly, *The Pastoral Epistles;* G.W. Knight, *The Faithful Sayings in the Pastoral Letters;* A. Plummer, *The Pastoral Epistles.*

Timothy, Timotheus (Person).

Paul's convert and companion, whose name means "one who honors God." His name is often spelled Timotheus in the KJV.

Timothy first appears in Acts 16:1–3 as Paul's disciple whose mother "was a believer; but his father was a Greek" (v 1). He was a third-generation Christian after his mother Eunice and grandmother Lois (2 Tm 1:5). The apostle Paul, undoubtedly Timothy's spiritual father, refers to him as "my true child in the faith" (1 Tm 1:2); he perhaps converted Timothy on his first or second missionary journey. The son of a Greek (or gentile) father, Timothy was yet uncircumcised; however, when Paul decided to take Timothy with him on the second journey, he had him circumcised, so as not to hinder their missionary endeavors among the Jews.

Timothy, who was "well spoken of by the brethren at Lystra and Iconium" (Acts 16:2), became Paul's companion and assistant on his second missionary journey at Lystra.

He traveled with Paul into Europe following the Macedonian vision. When Paul decided to go to Athens, he left Silas and Timothy at Beroea to better establish the church there (Acts 17:14). Timothy and Silas eventually joined Paul in Corinth (18:5). He next appears with Paul in Ephesus on his third journey (19:22), from where Paul sends Erastus and him into Macedonia ahead of himself. In the last mention of Timothy in Acts 20:4, he was included in the list of goodwill ambassadors who were to accompany Paul to Jerusalem with the offering for the Christian Jews.

Timothy is often mentioned in the Pauline letters. His name is included in the introductory salutations of 2 Corinthians, Philippians,

Colossians, 1 and 2 Thessalonians, and Philemon. Timothy's presence with Paul when he wrote these letters confirms the accuracy of the references to him in Acts. He was in Corinth on the second journey when Paul wrote 1 and 2 Thessalonians, at Ephesus on the third journey when Paul wrote 2 Corinthians, and in Rome during Paul's first Roman imprisonment, when he wrote Philippians, Colossians, and Philemon. He is mentioned in the introductions of 1 and 2 Timothy as the recipient of those two pastoral letters.

In the closing salutations of Romans 16:21, Timothy is listed along with others who send their good wishes to the believers in Rome. In 1 Corinthians 4:17 and 16:10, Paul speaks words of praise for Timothy as he sends him with a message to Corinth (see also Phil 2:19–23; 1 Thes 3:2–6). In 2 Corinthians 1:19 Timothy is named along with Paul and Silas as men who were telling about Jesus Christ.

In Hebrews 13:23 the author (Pauline authorship uncertain) tells his readers that Timothy has been released from prison, and hopes to come with Timothy to visit the readers of that letter.

Paul put Timothy in charge of the church at Ephesus and wrote him two pastoral letters addressed with his name to help him perform that responsible task.   SAMUEL CARTLEDGE

See TIMOTHY, FIRST LETTER TO; TIMOTHY, SECOND LETTER TO.

Tin. *See* MINERALS, METALS, AND PRECIOUS STONES.

Tiphsah. 1. City on the northeastern boundary of Solomon's empire (1 Kgs 4:24). It is most likely identified with Thapsacus, a town mentioned frequently in Greek and Roman texts. Though its precise location is unknown, it was an important trading center on the Euphrates River that dominated an east-west caravan route and also served as a northern terminal for river traffic.

2. KJV rendering of Tappuah, one of the towns conquered by Menahem after he deposed Shallum in Samaria (2 Kgs 15:16). Though many have argued that this is the same as #1 above, it is likely a separate location. Depending on the route selected, Tiphsah on the Euphrates would be 300 to 400 miles northeast of Tirzah where Menahem started his expedition. It appears that this Tiphsah (Tappuah) is located in Samaria proper, particularly since Menahem is condemned for the atrocities he committed there. Some have identified it with Khirbet Tafsah, six miles east of Shechem.

See TAPPUAH (PLACE) #2.

Tiras. Japheth's seventh son listed in the table of nations (Gn 10:2; 1 Chr 1:5). His descendants have been alternately linked to the Thracians, the Agathyrsi, the tribes of the Taurus mountain region, and the maritime Tyrrheni, but all of these identifications are purely speculative.

Tirathite. First of three families listed as scribes living at Jabez; perhaps belonging to the Kenite family (1 Chr 2:55).

Tirhakah. Ethiopian king who marched north to fight against the Assyrian army, thus diverting Sennacherib's siege of Jerusalem (2 Kgs 19:9; Is 37:9). The report of Tirhakah's intended invasion prompted the Rabshakeh's second threat against Jerusalem, Hezekiah's prayer for deliverance, and the subsequent divine destruction of the Assyrian army (2 Kgs 19:8–37). Tirhakah is almost certainly the Egyptian king Taharqa, who ruled from 689–664 BC during the 25th (Ethiopian) Dynasty. The reference to Tirhakah as "king" during this campaign (703–702 BC) creates potential chronological difficulties. Several suggestions have been made to solve the difficulty. It is possible that Tirhakah was king (regent) of Ethiopia prior to his accession as king of Egypt, though no record of this regency remains. Others have suggested that the biblical and Assyrian accounts of Sennacherib's Palestinian campaign actually combine two campaigns, the first in 702 BC and the second either by Sennacherib in 689 BC or by Esarhaddon in 675 BC (attested to in Egyptian records). While such a collation is not unprecedented, it does violate the apparent witness of the biblical text (cf. 2 Kgs 18:13; 19:36). A simpler and more likely solution is that Tirhakah served as commander of the army while he was crown prince so that the reference to him as "king" refers to his then future position.

Tirhanah. Hezronite and the second of Caleb's four sons by Maachah, his concubine (1 Chr 2:48).

Tiria. Jahallelel's son and a descendant of Judah through Caleb (1 Chr 4:16).

Tirshatha. KJV translation of a Hebrew word designating a title of authority with the connotation of "governor" (RSV). It is given after Zerubbabel's (Ezr 2:63) and Nehemiah's names (Neh 8:9; 10:1), who both held the office in Jerusalem during the postexilic period.

Tirzah (Person). One of the daughters of Zelophehad of Manasseh's tribe (Nm 26:33). Since her father had no sons, she and her sisters asked for and received their father's inheritance (Nm 27:1; Jos 17:3). This occasioned a law concerning inheritance rights with the stipulation that daughters who obtained their families' inheritance must marry within the tribe (Nm 36:11).

Tirzah (Place). Early capital city of the divided kingdom of Israel (1 Kgs 14:17; 15:21,33; 16:6–23). It was one of the cities captured by Joshua (Jos 12:24), but did not gain prominence until Jeroboam established it as his royal residence (1 Kgs 14:17). Although Baasha intended to move his capital to Ramah, he returned to Tirzah as a result of his war against Asa (1 Kgs 15:21). Tirzah also served as the capital for Elah, Zimri, and the first six years of Omri's reign. Omri built and established Samaria as his capital midway during his reign, resulting in the decline of Tirzah's significance. Perhaps as a result of the rivalry between Tirzah and Samaria, Menahem used Tirzah as his base to mount his revolt against Shallum in 753 BC (2 Kgs 15:14). Although it was known as a beautiful city located on a high hill (Sg 6:4), Tirzah's location has not been identified with precision. Several sites have been suggested but no conclusive evidence has been found.

Tishbe, Tishbite. Native city of Elijah the prophet and its inhabitants (1 Kgs 17:1; 21:17,28; 2 Kgs 1:3,8; 9:36). The Hebrew form of Tishbe in 1 Kings 17:1 prompted the KJV to translate the word as "of the inhabitants [of Gilead]." Most translations follow the Septuagint, however, in considering Tishbe a proper noun. This reading is also supported by the fact that Elijah is elsewhere called a Tishbite. If Tishbe is considered a proper name, it is likely identified with Thisbe, a town in Naphtali that is mentioned in Tobit 1:2.

Tishri. Hebrew month corresponding to about mid-September to mid-October.

See CALENDARS, ANCIENT AND MODERN.

Tithe, Tithing. Words deriving from Old English for "tenth," and representing a charge upon produce or labor levied for the maintenance mainly of religious activities. The custom is very ancient (Abraham paid tithe of spoil to Melchizedek, Gn 14:20; cf. 28:22), and widely practiced, being known in Athens, Arabia, Rome, Carthage, Egypt, Syria, Babylon, and China.

According to Deuteronomy (12:2–7,17–19; 14:22–29) the centralization of worship meant that the tithe was consumed annually at the sanctuary as a religious feast shared by priests and Levites. Corn, wine, oil, and flocks were tithed. If distance required, the value of the tithe could be carried and expended on arrival. Every third year, the Levites, aliens, fatherless, and widows were given the whole tithe in charity (cf. Dt 26:12).

According to Numbers 18:21–32 all tithe in Israel is given to the Levites forever in return for sanctuary service and in place of other inheritance in the land. A tithe of this tithe became a "heave offering" (offered toward, but not consumed upon, the altar) for the priests. In Leviticus 27:30–32 the holiness of the tithe is stressed, and herd and flock especially included.

The different regulations probably refer to different periods. The Numbers system is reflected in Nehemiah 10:37–39; 12:44; 13:5,12, and asserted for Hezekiah's time in 2 Chronicles 31:4–12. Amos includes "tithes every three days" in his ironic description of false religion (4:4).

Probably some motive of propitiation (Dt 14:23), even of payment, underlay the original custom. Proverbs 3:9 suggests that such gifts honor God (cf. Hebrews 7:4,7). Both the sage and the prophet Malachi (Prv 3:10; Mal 3:8–10), who scathingly declare the withholding of tithes to be "robbing God," promised full barns and vats, opened windows of heaven, outpoured blessing and deliverance from locusts, in return for faithful tithing. In the early tithe-feasts, thanksgiving for God's gifts would seem appropriate (cf. Gn 28:22), though not emphasized. Maintenance of the service of God remained the chief purpose of tithing, along with a wide charity. (For the secular tithe to maintain the king, see 1 Sm 8:15–17; perhaps Am 7:1).

Apart from recalling Melchizedek's tithe (Heb 7), tithing is mentioned in the NT only critically. In Matthew 23:23 and Luke 11:42 Jesus instances the meticulous payment of tithes of three small garden herbs, while neglecting three "weightier matters of the Law," namely, justice, mercy, and faith, as an example of the want of moral proportion, the lack of a right sense of priorities, which marked Pharisaism. The explicit rule, precisely observed, is so much easier and self-satisfying than the moral sensitivity which should govern all relations with others and with God. In Luke 18:12 the Pharisee, congratulating himself in prayer upon his superior virtues, mentions his tithing of all income among his claims to divine favor—the external, measurable, and well-remembered obedience to the rule again breeding religious self-esteem that is quite unaware of sinful self-righteousness. Christ sternly devalued the pride-filled performance, compared with that of the humble penitent, as availing nothing with God.

Jesus recommended payment of the temple tax without coercion (Mt 17:24–27), and especially praised the widow who gave not a tenth but her whole livelihood, though it made no appreciable difference to the temple's income (Lk 21:1–4). He also commanded that "those who proclaim the gospel should get their living by the gospel" (1 Cor 9:14, note 8–13), for the gospel's "laborer deserves his food" (Mt 10:10; cf. Gal 6:6). Yet nowhere in the NT is the tithing rule urged for this purpose or for charity. Instead, giving must be spontaneous, the amount governed by what a man has (2 Cor 8:1–15). As late as AD 180 Irenaeus still contrasts the tithing of the Jews with the greater generosity and joy of those who give all because of their greater hope (*Against Heresies*, 4.34).

R.E.O. WHITE

See SACRIFICES AND OFFERINGS.

Bibliography. R. de Vaux, *Ancient Israel*, pp 140–41, 379–82; 403–5; Y. Kaufman, *The Religion of Israel*, pp 189–93; L. Vischer, *Tithing in the Early Church*.

Titius Justus. Believer in Corinth with whom Paul stayed (Acts 18:7).

See JUSTUS #2.

Tittle. Tiny ornamental "horn" on certain Hebrew letters.

See JOT OR TITTLE.

Titus (Person). 1. One of Paul's converts— "my true child in a common faith" (Ti 1:4)— who became an intimate and trusted associate of the apostle in his mission of planting Christianity throughout the Mediterranean world (2 Cor 8:23; 2 Tm 4:10; Ti 1:5). Mentioned frequently in Paul's letters (eight times in 2 Cor, twice in Gal, once each in Ti and 2 Tm), his name occurs nowhere in Acts, a puzzling silence some have sought to explain with the fascinating, but uncertain, suggestion that he was a brother of Luke, the author of Acts.

Unlike Timothy, who was half Jewish, Titus was born of gentile parents. Nothing is recorded of the circumstances surrounding his conversion and initial encounter with Paul. He is first introduced as a companion of Paul and Barnabas on a visit to Jerusalem (Gal 2:3). The occasion appears to have been the Jerusalem Council, about AD 50, which Paul and Barnabas attended as official delegates from the church at Antioch not long after the apostle's first missionary journey (Acts 15).

With the hotly contested issue of compulsory circumcision of gentile converts to Christianity before the Council, Paul decided to make a test case of Titus. The Council decided in Paul's favor against the Judaizing party, and Titus was accepted by the other apostles and leaders of the Jerusalem church without submitting to the rite of circumcision. Thus Titus became a key figure in the liberation of the infant church from the Judaizing party.

Very likely Titus accompanied Paul from that time on, but he does not appear again until Paul's crisis with the church at Corinth during his third missionary journey. According to 2 Corinthians, while Paul was conducting an extended ministry in Ephesus, he received word that the Corinthian church had turned hostile toward him and renounced his apostolic authority. Other attempts at reconciliation, including a personal visit, having failed, he sent Titus to Corinth to try to repair the breach. When Titus rejoined Paul somewhere in Macedonia, where the apostle had traveled from Ephesus to meet him, he bore the good news that the attitude of the Corinthians had changed and their former love and friendship were now restored (2 Cor 7:6,7). In view of this development Paul sent Titus back to Corinth bearing 2 Corinthians and with instructions to complete the collection of the relief offering for the Jewish Christians of Judea which he had previously begun, but not finished (8:6,16). In this venture also Titus was apparently successful (Rom 15:26).

On the assumption that Paul was released after his first Roman imprisonment, recorded in the final chapters of Acts, it appears that Titus accompanied him on a mission to the island of Crete. On departing from Crete, Paul left Titus behind as his apostolic deputy to consolidate the new Christian movement there (Ti 1:5). The assignment was difficult, for the Cretans were unruly and the struggling church was already invaded by false teachers (vv 10–16). His handling of the Corinthian problem some years before, however, demonstrated that Titus possessed the spiritual earnestness, skillful diplomacy, and loving concern required to meet the present challenge, and Paul was confident that this new commission was therefore safe in his hands.

Paul's letter to Titus, one of his three pastoral letters, was written somewhat later to encourage Titus in his Cretan ministry. The letter closes with the apostle's request that Titus join him at Nicopolis, a town on the west coast of Greece, where he planned to spend the winter (Ti 3:12). Most likely it was from Nicopolis, or else later from Rome where the apostle was imprisoned again and eventually martyred, that Paul sent Titus on the mission to Dalmatia, a Roman province in what is now Yugoslavia, on which he had embarked when Paul wrote 2 Timothy, the last of his letters (2 Tm 4:10). If later tradition is correct,

The western interior view of the arch of Titus in Rome; it depicts the temple furnishings being carried away from Jerusalem.

Titus returned to Crete, where he served as bishop until advanced age.

See TITUS, LETTER TO.

2. Gentile proselyte in Corinth, to whose house Paul went after the Jewish community in general rejected his message. Some early NT texts read Titus (instead of Titius) Justus in Acts 18:7 (see ASV). Attempts to identify this man with Titus, the co-worker of Paul, are wholly unsatisfactory.

See JUSTUS #2.

3. Vespasian's son, and the emperor of Rome from 81 to 79 AD. RICHARD ALLEN BODEY

See CAESARS, THE.

Bibliography. J.H. Bernard, *The Pastoral Epistles*; P. Fairbairn, *Commentary on the Pastoral Epistles*; W. Hendriksen, *Exposition of the Pastoral Epistles*; J.N.D. Kelly, *The Pastoral Epistles*; G.W. Knight, *The Faithful Sayings in the Pastoral Letters*; A. Plummer, *The Pastoral Epistles*; V. Taylor, *Exposition of Titus*.

Titus, Letter to.

Authorship. This letter begins with the name and greeting of Paul (1:1–3), speaks of Titus' relationship to him (1:4), and the work the apostle gave him to do (v 5); in the end (3:12,13) there are further personal details and instructions. Its authorship has been questioned by modern scholars—on the grounds of its language and style, the church situation it presents, and the way that it sets forth Christian teaching. On the other hand, the fact that the Pauline authorship has been stoutly defended by eminent scholars and careful students of the letter shows that there is no overwhelming reason for thinking that, with some special purpose, this epistle was written in Paul's name, after the apostle himself had died, perhaps using fragments of letters that he had actually written. That the apostle may have used a secretary to convey in his own words his message to Titus is a possibility that has found some advocates.

Recipient. Titus appears to have been "one of the most trusted and valuable helpers of Paul" (Barclay). He speaks of him (2 Cor 8:23) as "my partner and fellow-worker." Strangely he is not mentioned in the Acts of the Apostles. According to 1:4 he owed his conversion to Paul. It is clear from Galatians 2:1–4 that he was a Gentile, as his was a test case whether gentile Christians should be compelled to be circumcised. At that time Titus was with Paul and Barnabas in Jerusalem. Much later, at the time of Paul's third missionary journey, he had two delicate missions to carry out for Paul in Corinth, the first concerned with the strained relationship of Paul with the Corinthian Christians, the second related to the gentile collection for the Jerusalem church (2 Cor 2:12,13; 7:5–16; 8:1–24). If 2 Timothy 4:9–18 deals with the end of Paul's life then Titus went to Dalmatia after the time of this letter.

Date. To date this letter with precision is difficult. Titus is left by the apostle in Crete to continue his work (1:5). Paul was there briefly in his voyage to Rome (Acts 27:7–13), but that could not have been the occasion referred to. In 3:12 Titus is called to come to Nicopolis (probably the Nicopolis in Epirus in Greece) as Paul had decided to winter there. Many have favored the view that after Paul's first imprisonment in Rome (Acts 28:16–31), he was released, carried out further ministry in various places (including Spain, Crete, and Greece), and then was arrested, imprisoned, and finally put to death. Those who do not accept Pauline authorship date this letter, like 1 and 2 Timothy, in the generation that followed Paul's death on the basis that the situation of the churches and their organization demand it.

Purpose and Teaching. Although this letter is addressed to an individual colleague of the apostle, it has a minimum of personal references and exhortations. The growing and developing churches are in view. There were the pressures of false teaching that appear to have had Jewish elements, possibly ascetic emphases and a great deal of speculative discussion (1:10,14,15; 3:9)—perhaps an early Jewish form of Gnosticism. Its advocates promoted this teaching "for base gain" (1:11). Titus and those whom he appoints as elders are to refute the wrong teaching and "give instruction in sound doctrine" (1:9). There is no detailed exposition of what Christians believe, but there are certainly clear statements of the saving grace of God in Christ, the renewing work of the Holy Spirit, and the future coming of the Lord Jesus (2:11,13; 3:4–7). There is constant emphasis on the life-style that bears out the truth of the gospel, and there is application to different groups in the Christian community, older men and women, young women, young men, slaves (2:2–10), to the way that Christians should relate to the state, and to qualities of their lives in society (3:1,2).

Content. *1:1–4.* Greetings from Paul whose apostleship is described as a stewardship of the gospel that promotes faith and strengthens the knowledge of the truth, hope of eternal life, and godliness of living—to Titus, spoken of as "my true son in our common faith."

1:5–9. Titus was left behind in Crete to continue Paul's work and to appoint elders in every church (cf. Acts 14:23). These elders are also called bishops (cf. Acts 20:17,28), that is, those with oversight. The necessary qualities of life for these are described (cf 1 Tm 3:2–7).

1:10–16. The closing words of the previous section speak about the responsibility of elders "to give instruction in sound doctrine and also to confute those who contradict it." Now this is spoken of as particularly necessary because of those who are upsetting people, indeed "whole families," by teaching what is neither true nor profitable. These false teachers are described in terms disparaging of Cretans, and as people who misrepresent Jewish tradition and the significance of circumcision, and whose lives do not demonstrate the knowledge of God that they profess to hold.

2:1–10. Titus has a particular responsibility to "teach what is in accord with sound doctrine." He should have relevant exhortation for older men (v 2), and for older women (v 3) who in turn will train younger women to live pure and loving lives in their homes "so that no one will malign the word of God" (vv 4,5). Younger men are to show self-control (v 6), and Titus himself is to be an example in word and life so that opponents may "have nothing bad to say about us" (vv 7,8). Finally, in this section slaves are taught to submit to their masters, to give good and honest service with the motivation "that in every way they will make the teaching about God our Savior attractive" (vv 9,10; cf. Eph 6:5–8; Col 3:22–25; 1 Pt 2:18–25).

2:11–15. What has been said leads now to a great statement of the purpose of the revelation of the grace of God in Jesus Christ: to bring salvation and to lead people to make a complete break with godless and sensual living so that they may live upright lives with the constant expectancy of the coming again of "our great God and Savior Jesus Christ," lives that show them to be "a people that are his very own, eager to do what is good." Titus' ministry is related to this great purpose of God in the gospel.

3:1,2. Christians also have a duty to submit to rulers (cf. Rom 13:1–7; 1 Pt 2:13–17) and to be available in the community "for any honest work." Again the quality of life-style is emphasized, in particular courtesy and the desire for peace in relationships with others.

3:3–8. The contrast with the past is again expressed, the transformation from lives that were pleasure-seeking and lacking in love, purity, and integrity—"being hated and hating one another." The means of that transformation is the saving work of God in Christ—not merited, but entirely of his mercy. He has brought cleansing from sin, "rebirth and renewal by the Holy Spirit." What is spoken of as a "trustworthy saying"(v 8) may come from an early baptismal hymn or a Christian liturgy. This may be so; at least it is a brief summing up of things that are at the heart of the gospel. Such things Titus is constantly to teach, and this teaching will lead to a life of good deeds.

3:9–11. On the other hand, unprofitable religious debate is to be shunned and the persistently divisive person is to be avoided.

3:12,13. Messages are given relating to Artemas and Zenas (not mentioned otherwise in the NT), Tychicus and Apollos (both known from other letters and the Acts of the Apostles). Titus himself is urged to come to Paul in Nicopolis.

3:14,15. Thus with a final exhortation to "good deeds" and to a spiritually fruitful life, and with greetings and prayer the epistle closes.   FRANCIS FOULKES

See PAUL, THE APOSTLE; TIMOTHY, FIRST LETTER TO; TIMOTHY, SECOND LETTER TO.

Tizite. Descriptive term of uncertain meaning applied to Joha, one of the outstanding warriors chosen by David for his personal bodyguard. It may designate his family background or the name of his village (1 Chr 11:45).

Toah. Kohathite Levite and Samuel's ancestor (1 Chr 6:34).

Tob. Place where Jephthah fled after his half-brothers threw him out for being illegitimate (Jgs 11:3,5). During the reign of David, the Ammonites hired 12,000 men from Tob as mercenaries to fight against David (2 Sm 10:6,8, KJV Ish-tob). It is probably the same as the Aramite kingdom named Tob which was located in the desert east or northeast of Gilead. During the Maccabean period, a Jewish colony was located in Tob but thus far no remains have been discovered.

Tobadonijah. One of the Levites under Jehoshaphat who went out into the cities of Judah to teach the Law (2 Chr 17:8).

Tobiah. 1. Forefather of a family of people that returned with Zerubbabel to Jerusalem following the exile, where they were unable to prove their Jewish descent (Ezr 2:60; Neh 7:62).
2. Member of a leading aristocratic family whose origin may be traced to an aristocratic family in Jerusalem which owned large estates in Gilead and played important roles in the political life of both Jerusalem and Gilead. "The son of Tabeel" (Is 7:6) may well have been a member of the Tobiah family.

Tobiah was a leading member of the family when Nehemiah arrived in Jerusalem about 445 BC. He was known as "the Ammonite servant" (Neh 2:10,19), a designation associated with a person of high office, such as a governor. He, together with Sanballat and Geshem, the other leading opponents of the reconstruction of the walls, were high-ranking officers in the Persian Empire. He married the daughter of Shecaniah the son of Arah, and his son Jehohanan married the daughter of Meshullam son of Berechiah (6:18). His marriage relations to an aristocratic Jerusalem family gave him strong ties with the Jerusalem aristocracy, which were strengthened by maintaining a regular correspondence with the nobles of Judah, who were "bound by oath to him" (6:17).

Nehemiah had to face the threat posed by Tobiah and his influential allies. He was charged with the intent of leading the Jerusalem population in a revolt against King Artaxerxes (2:19). As the work of rebuilding the wall progressed, Tobiah joined in the conspiracy of besieging Jerusalem (4:8). Nehemiah ordered the only defense of the Jews. They continued their labors of repairing the wall with the protection of armed guards, and when the enemy forces came closer, every worker held a weapon in addition to his trowel (4:7–19). They were encouraged by the belief that "our God will fight for us" (4:20). Tobiah also joined in the plot to assassinate Nehemiah after the walls were rebuilt (6:2–4). Nehemiah was further tested by libelous reports of insurrection (6:5–9) and by a Jerusalemite hired by the allies to seduce Nehemiah into entering the temple proper and thereby to discredit his standing among the faithful (6:10–13). Having been spared from many troubles, Nehemiah left Jerusalem in order to report to Artaxerxes. In his absence, Tobiah succeeded in reestablishing himself with those who had remained faithful to him. The priest Eliashib was also related to Tobiah and gave in to Tobiah by preparing a large room previously used for offerings in the temple (13:4,5). Tobiah used these quarters when visiting Jerusalem. One of Nehemiah's first acts upon his return was the expulsion of Tobiah from the temple (13:8,9) and the restoration of the room for its proper temple purposes.

Tobijah. 1. Levite sent by King Jehoshaphat to teach the Law in the cities of Judah (2 Chr 17:8).
2. One of four men who returned from Babylon to Jerusalem with gold and silver used to make a crown for the high priest Joshua (Zec 6:10,14).

Tochen. One of the villages settled by Simeon's tribe (1 Chr 4:32). The name does not appear in the parallel passage in Joshua, but does appear as Thokka in the Septuagint. Its location is unknown.

Togarmah. Third son of Gomer, a descendant of Japheth (Gn 10:3; 1 Chr 1:6). Beth-togarmah ("house of Togarmah") appears in Ezekiel's prophecy against the nations that opposed Israel (Ez 27:14; 38:6). Beth-togarmah was one of the principal trading partners of Tyre, providing war horses and mules. Since Togarmah is consistently linked with Javan, Tubal, Meshech, Dedan, and Tarshish, Ezekiel probably had the ethnographic lists of Genesis 10 in mind. As an ethnographic term, most have identified Togarmah with Armenia. The Armenians identify Togarmah (Thorgon) as the founder of their race.

Tohu. Kohathite Levite and Samuel's ancestor (1 Sm 1:1).

Toi. King of Hamath at the time David defeated the armies of Hadadezer (2 Sm 8:9,10; alternately called Tou in 1 Chr 18:9,10). He sent his son Joram to congratulate and give gifts to David. Many have suggested that Toi may have been a vassal of Hadadezer, so he would have been placating David.

Tokhath. Alternate form of Tikvah, the father-in-law of Huldah the prophetess, in 2 Chronicles 34:22.

See TIKVAH #1.

Tola. 1. One of the two sons of Issachar named among the 66 descendants of Jacob who accompanied him in the migration to Egypt to join Joseph (Gn 46:13); and the ancestor of the first of four families of the tribe of Issachar, as identified in the census of Israel undertaken by Moses and Eleazar (Nm 26:23). Tola's sons were Uzzi, Rephaiah, Jeriel, Jahmai, Ibsam, and Shemuel (1 Chr 7:2). The Israelite clan of the Tolaites took its name from him (Nm 26:23), and during the time of David the warriors of his family numbered 22,600 men (1 Chr 7:1,2).

2. One of the judges of Israel, the son of Puah and the grandson of Dodo (Jgs 10:1), of Issachar's tribe. Shamir, his home and burial place, was in the hill country of Ephraim; its precise site has not been identified. There he judged Israel for 23 years. Although he "delivered" Israel after the debacle of Abimelech's abortive attempt to establish a monarchy at Shechem, he receives notice in just two verses (Jgs 10:1,2). Like other "minor judges" mentioned only briefly (e.g., Jgs 12:8–15), he actually functioned in the judicial role—unlike some more prominent "judges" (e.g., Gideon and Jephthah) who were first, and perhaps solely, military heroes. It is not clear whether Tola's deliverance of Israel was military, political, or judicial.

There is a notable coincidence of names associated with the two Tolas. The son of Issachar had three brothers: Puvah, Jashub, and Shimron (Gn 46:13). The judge was the son of Puah (whose name is an alternate spelling of Puvah—1 Chr 7:1), and lived at Shamir. Since both men were descendants of Issachar, these names may have recurred commonly in the tribe. As the name of Issachar's eldest son has an animal association with the color red, so Puvah, the name of his second son, is Hebrew for "madder," a plant from which red dye is extracted. This correspondence is hardly an accident, but its intent is obscure.

See JUDGES, BOOK OF.

Tolad. Alternate form of Eltolad, a city in Simeon's territory, in 1 Chronicles 4:29.

See ELTOLAD.

Tolaite. Descendant of Tola from Issachar's tribe (Nm 26:23).

See TOLA #1.

Tomb. See BURIAL, BURIAL CUSTOMS.

Tongues, Speaking in. Ecstatic phenomenon traditionally associated with religious experiences. It has been practiced through the ages in various religious settings, both Christian and non-Christian, by individuals in private as well as by whole communities. When the apostle Paul mentions the use of tongues being a "sign not for believers but for unbelievers" (1 Cor 14:22), he refers to a view that was commonly held among the practitioners of ancient pagan religions, according to which glossolalia was a sign of the active presence of the gods. Thus, whenever the Oracle of Delphi became inspired, she would speak in tongues as an evidence of supernatural illumination. This interpretation of glossolalia as divine activity has been accepted by practitioners as diverse as medieval mystics, Huguenot sectarians, and oriental religionists, such as the Moslem Dervishes.

Glossolalia consists of a flow of unintelligible sounds that transcend the usual processes of verbal communication. As such, tongues are not languages. Referring to the Christian practice of glossolalia, Paul states "anyone who speaks in a tongue does not speak to men but to God. Indeed, no one understands him; he utters mysteries with his spirit" (1 Cor 14:2). Because the sounds uttered in glossolalia do not constitute intelligible language, they need interpretation (not translation) in order to be of use to the hearers (v 28). Apparently, this was not the case with the outburst of witness in foreign languages that immediately followed the event of Pentecost. According to Acts 2:8,11, the audience of the apostles in Jerusalem could understand them as they were communicating the gospel in the hearers' own languages. There was no need for interpretation.

According to Paul, glossolalia is to be used primarily as a private devotional exercise, for one's own edification. Since "anyone who speaks in a tongue does not speak to men but to God" (1 Cor 14:2), the benefits that may accrue from it are personal. Indeed, "he who speaks in a tongue edifies himself" (v 4). As a means of private worship, the practice of glossolalia is tantamount to speaking to oneself and to God (v 28). The apostle Paul referred to his own "closet" use of glossolalia only once in all his writings, and this under the pressure of his exhortation to the Corinthians (v 18). Obviously, he considered the private exercise of glossolalia a matter to be surrounded with discretion rather than to be boastfully paraded as a badge of spirituality.

However, under certain conditions formulated by Paul, glossolalia may become one of the spiritual gifts to be used in ministry to the church for the common good. In this case, the main concern is that the public use of glossolalia not be reduced to praying in tongues (vv 16,17) or speaking in tongues without interpretation (v 28). Glossolalia acquires validity in a congregational setting only if it is followed by interpretation so that it can contribute to the edification of the body. In this case, when it is duly interpreted, glossolalia becomes a prophetic ministry, that is, a communication in intelligible speech equivalent to teaching and preaching (vv 3,5). Paul's main requirement for the public exercise of glossolalia is that it be used for the common good and for the edification of the body (vv 4,5,6,9,12, 17,18,26,31). He strictly forbids individual praying and speaking in tongues within group situations as subjective experiences of individual piety (vv 17,28). Such practices belong in one's own private prayer closet, not in church.

In order to establish firmly the public practice of glossolalia as a ministry to the church and to prevent its abuse as a quest for personal fulfillment, Paul lays down a set of rules designed to control its corporate exercise (vv 27–33).

The word "if" at the beginning of verse 27 indicates that glossolalia is not an indispensable element of Christian worship. Paul placed glossolalia at the bottom of a hierarchical list of the gifts arranged by decreasing order of importance (1 Cor 12:28). The gifts he numbered first, second, and third are those requiring intelligible speech. They are designated as the "greater" or "higher gifts" and are the ministries to be especially desired (v 31).

A limit of one, two, or three persons is set for participation in tongues per worship session (1 Cor 14:27).

The one, two, or three tongues speakers are to make their contribution in sequence, "one at a time" or "in turn," never simultaneously (vv 27,30).

Before a worshiper decides to speak in tongues, he or she is to secure an interpreter. Should no such person be available, he or she is to refrain from speaking in tongues (vv 27,28). The person speaking in tongues should not be the one to provide the interpretation (1 Cor 12:10). If there are too many believers speaking in tongues and not enough interpreters, the former should pray instead for the power to interpret (1 Cor 14:13).

When the contribution in tongues has been interpreted in intelligible language, it becomes a prophecy that needs to be evaluated by the recipients (v 29). The genuineness of the experience is to be tested by those who have the "ability to distinguish between spirits" (1 Cor 12:10) so that they can test everything, hold fast what is good, and abstain from every form of evil.

Persons participating in worship should be in control of their conduct at all times. They may not appeal to ecstatic states to excuse disorderly conduct or infractions to the rules of worship (vv 32,40). Disorder and confusion are not inspired by God since he is a God of peace (v 33).

The gift of tongues is not to be desired or sought after. Only the "higher gifts" involving communication through directly intelligible speech are to be earnestly desired (v 39; cf 1 Cor 12:31; 14:1,5). However, should the gift of tongues be present, it should not be stifled (v 39), provided it can be used according to the rules and for the common good.

The dictum "do not seek; do not forbid" seems to summarize adequately the scriptural teaching on glossolalia. In the light of such teaching, two common errors should be avoided.

First, the biblical teaching on glossolalia does not support the view that speaking in tongues is an evidence of spirituality brought about by the baptism of the Holy Spirit. The Scripture teaches that all believers are baptized by the Spirit as they become integrated into the body of Christ, the church (1 Cor 12:13). It also teaches that not all believers speak in tongues (v 30). The genuine evidence of the work of the Holy Spirit is the "fruit of the Spirit" as defined in Galatians 5:22,23. According to this text, the sign of the impact of the indwelling Spirit upon human life is character and behavioral change. The quest for a liturgical substitute such as glossolalia to the process of sanctification cannot foster authentic spirituality.

The second error is to deny the current validity of glossolalia by relegating its relevance to the apostolic age. Paul's statements that "tongues will cease" (1 Cor 13:8) and that "when perfection comes, the imperfect disappears" (v 10) are sometimes adduced as evidence of the alleged obsolescence of glossolalia. However, Paul also writes that "knowledge will pass away" (v 8). Yet, no one insists that knowledge was valid only for the apostles' time. As a matter of fact, Paul states that knowledge and prophecy are imperfect, not tongues (v 9). They will all become obsolete at the end of the age, when perfection comes and believers understand fully (v 12). In the meantime, the Scriptures describe glossolalia as a means of private devotional practice, allowing its use for ministry in congregational settings provided it is practiced in accordance with carefully delineated regulations and contributes to the common good.   GILBERT BILEZIKIAN

See SPIRITUAL GIFTS; BAPTISM OF THE SPIRIT.

Bibliography. F.D. Bruner, *A Theology of the Holy Spirit;* L. Christensen, *Speaking in Tongues;* J.D.G. Dunn, *Baptism*

in the Holy Spirit; A.A. Hoekema, Tongues and Spirit-Baptism and What About Tongue-Speaking? W.H. Horton (ed.), The Glossolalia Phenomenon; M.T. Kelsey, Tongue Speaking; J.L. Sherrill, They Speak with Other Tongues; C.R. Smith, Tongues in Biblical Perspective; H.J. Stolee, Speaking in Tongues; M.F. Unger, NT Teaching on Tongues; B.B. Warfield, Miracles: Yesterday and Today; J.R. Williams, The Gift of the Holy Spirit Today.

Tongues of Fire. Phrase occurring only in Acts 2:3 describing the supernatural happenings on the Day of Pentecost. It describes the visible manifestation of the Spirit. The tongues of fire seem to be the fulfillment of John the Baptist's proclamation that the Coming One would baptize with the Holy Spirit and fire (Mt 3:11; Lk 3:16). Fire is often associated with the manifestation of God's presence in the OT, such as at the burning bush (Ex 2). This combines with the audible manifestation of a strong wind to speak of the Spirit's powerful presence on this historic day when the exalted Jesus poured out the Spirit on his disciples and other believers. The disciples are described as filled with the Holy Spirit—thus fulfilling the OT promise reiterated by John the Baptist and Jesus of the baptism of the Spirit.

Acts 2 describes the results of the Spirit's presence as a supernatural speaking in numerous languages. Verses 9–11 list about 16 nations whose representatives in Jerusalem hear the disciples speaking in their own language. The disciples are enabled by the Spirit to speak in these languages to symbolize a reversal of Babel (Gn 11) in which communication among men is restored, replacing the former confusion. There is probably an intended proclamation of the good news of God's salvation to the nations through their representatives assembled in Jerusalem.

This manifestation and miraculous speaking in various languages constitutes the fulfillment of God's promise to pour out his Spirit, as Peter affirms by his quotation of Joel's prophecy (Jl 2:28–32). This event, therefore, indicates the presence of the "last days" with all that this fulfillment means.

See PENTECOST.

Tools. Implement used for virtually any purpose. The earliest tools were not fashioned by man but were sharp pieces of flint, antler, or bone used as they were found. Because of the relative ease with which round flakes could be broken off a flint by striking one piece sharply against another, man discovered that flints could be made into more desirable shapes, and the first flint hand tools came into use. A sharp, well-designed hand ax designed to fit comfortably into the palm of the hand was discovered at Holon near Tel Aviv and has

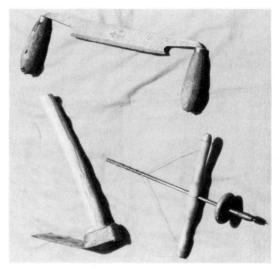

Ancient tools, now in the Tel Aviv Museum.

been dated to prehistoric times. Although in the period of prehistory flint was used predominantly for tools, wood, shell, horn, bone, and stone were also fashioned, particularly where a pointed or rounded tool was required. During the biblical period the manufacture of copper, bronze, and iron was responsible for the level of development of the nations, not only in the general standard of living, but particularly as regards their superiority in battle.

Flint. By striking off the small rounded fragments of the flint, which was a rock plentiful in chalk areas, a remarkably sharp-edged tool could eventually be made, as well as flint handaxes, scrapers, and sickle-shaped implements, which became the general-purpose tools for many millennia. Sharp instruments of this kind were essential in manufacturing processes, such as the cutting of cloth and the dressing of leather. The next development was a tool with a chopper action.

From Mesolithic (c. 8000 BC) sites in the Mt Carmel area have come flint tools used in hunting. The Natufians who lived in this region were skilled hunters. Sickles made of antler and bone with teeth of flint used for cutting grasses have also been recovered from the same sites. Agricultural implements from Tell es-Sultan (OT Jericho) have hafts decorated with carvings. Chisel-shaped flints from around 8000 BC have also been excavated. Irrigation farming was practiced in the Jordan Valley, and sites in the surrounding hills have yielded flint sickle blades and hoes. A relief from the 10th century BC discovered at Tell Halaf shows a leather sling in the form of a bag with a double thong threaded through it.

Earlier simple slings were made from stags' antlers.

Sites of Neolithic settlement, particularly in the Egyptian Fayyum, show patterns of established agriculture. The soil was prepared with stone hoes, and crops of wheat and barley were reaped with flint sickles. The cereal grains were ground into flour with a hand mill. There was primitive fishing using a bone hook and a line, as well as hunting with bows and finely fashioned flint-headed arrows. The setting of the tool into a bone or wooden handle ushered in the development of an increasing variety of implements, including stone hammers, sickles, hoes, polished stone axheads, and the shorter handled adzes, chisels, scrapers, arrowheads, and flint knives. The remains of hafted hammers have been found in flint, copper, and salt mines. The wooden handles, most of which have not survived, would have been held in place with fiber or sinew. Flint tools continued long after the introduction of copper and bronze. Flint knives were preferred for shaving because they retained their sharp edges, and they also remained in use for ceremonial and religious purposes. Zipporah, the wife of Moses, circumcised her son with a flint knife (Ex 4:25) in the traditional manner (cf. Jos 5:2,3).

As tools and skills for hunting and agriculture developed, time became available for more than sheer survival, and from around 5000 BC sherds of pottery were used as tools to make incised designs, sometimes resembling basketweave on pieces of pottery. Painted designs on pottery also occurred from the same period. Sharp splinters of antler or bone would have made perforations in leather and wood, but artifacts of shell, ivory, antler, bone, and tooth with holes bored in them have also been recovered. The holes were probably made by a stick twisted rapidly between the palms of the hands, the stick possibly having some abrasive such as sand placed beneath it. Some form of table bench made of a piece of board supported on four legs was in use from this time.

Metal. The next discovery came in the Middle East about 4000 BC when it was realized that certain pieces of what appeared to be rock did not respond by flaking when struck, but instead changed shape. Native gold and silver could be fashioned by hammering, but these metals were too soft to retain their shape if used as tools. They soon became popular for jewelry and all types of ornamental work. Natural copper, discovered at a similar time, was of much more practical use. It could be hammered into shape when cold, and would hold a sharp edge. Repeated beating, plunging into cold water, and hammering

could eliminate the brittleness of the copper, which was then hammered into arrowheads, knives, and other tools.

Meteoric iron, although not widespread, was recognized by the Sumerians and the Egyptians as "coming from heaven." Like copper, it was beaten into shapes for use as tools, although because of its rarity it was also used for jewelry. It was subsequently discovered that the heating, melting, and casting of gold, silver, and copper in a mold of pottery resulted not only in a more exactly reproducible shape, but also in the reuse of metal, particularly copper. It also meant that the size of any individual tool was no longer dependent upon the size of one piece of copper, but could be made of several molten chunks. It was approximately 1000 years later that man discovered the effects of high heat, charcoal, and wind on copper, and from this smelting came what was possibly the first accidental mixing of copper and tin, giving the first alloy, bronze. Early copper chisels were similar in design to the older flint ones, being quite long. The edges were sharpened and hardened by extensive hammering, and the tools were used for chiselling wood or the softer rocks. Marks indicating their use can be seen frequently on Egyptian sandstone and limestone.

As soon as the development of metal objects required high temperatures, tongs of some kind would have been required to lift the container holding the molten metal. At first bound branches or saplings would have been used, but these were doubtless replaced about 3000 BC by metal tongs, which would also have been necessary for handling hot coals.

Teleilat Ghassul, a village site in Jordan, yielded primitive copper axheads together with vast quantities of flint tools. Through the Bronze Age, copper continued to be the popular choice among metals for carpenters' saws and chisels, while the drills used were more complex implements made from a copper bit fixed to a wooden handle. Drills were operated by the use of a box and a leather thong, the latter giving the drill velocity. Metals did not completely supersede flint, particularly in the rural areas, for the next thousand years, although in prosperous trading and cultural centers it was accepted into everyday use much more quickly. At many sites copper dating to a period prior to 3500 BC has been excavated, showing that by then its use was increasing. Artifacts discovered at Ur near 2500 BC show that the development of skill in the use of bronze had already reached a very advanced level.

An Egyptian relief of around 2500 BC shows an ax of either copper or bronze with an unusual curved blade attached to a wooden handle. The shorter handled adze is shown frequently in the relief. Excavations also indicate that adzes and axes recovered from Mesopotamia dating from 2700 BC had a perforation in the head for the insertion of the handle. The hole was part of the design of the mold in which the head was formed. The double headed ax with a hole for the handle was cast in bronze from 2000 BC and continued in use through the later period.

A simple Egyptian bow drill dates also from an early period. The design was refined during the Bronze Age until the drill points with sharp edges took on the shape of an arrow with two fine cutting edges. The invention of the saw was a significant improvement over the previously used copper implements. Saws were used in Egypt during the building of the pyramids, and were employed extensively in all forms of woodworking during the Bronze Age. Bronze files were in use in Egypt in 1500 BC, while bronze chisels appeared in a shorter and handier form than their copper counterparts. In carpentry, the Egyptians acquired a high level of skill in the making of joints for any type of boxlike construction. The earliest form of plane was probably a smooth stone on some abrasive material such as sand which was rubbed along a piece of wood. Egyptian frescoes showed a length of wood lashed to an upright post, possibly a primitive vise.

The extensive hammering of metal required an anvil which would have been used from the Bronze Age. The level and the square were also employed as construction aids by the Egyptians. The earliest form of plow was a piece of wood with a metal edge of copper or bronze at the base (1 Kgs 19:19). Grains continued to be threshed with wooden sticks (Ru 2:17), while Deuteronomy 25:4 indicates that the hoofs of cattle were also used for that purpose. A type of shovel for turning the grain, and a fan for blowing away the hunks, were also part of threshing equipment (Is 30:24; Jer 15:7).

During the Bronze Age chariot wheels and potters' wheels also came into common use, the latter commonly being of stone. In the early 1970s Russian archaeologists made extensive discoveries in the area of Mt Ararat. They excavated numerous furnaces from near 2500 BC which had been used for smelting iron and zinc as well as copper and other metals. This may have been the center where Tubal-Cain (Gn 4:22) worked in metals. If iron, not meteoric iron, was in fact being smelted in this area, it was probably the earliest known example of iron smelting. This procedure required that a high temperature be maintained simultaneously with a strong draft of air. The actual method of smelting iron was similar to that used for copper and bronze. Both the abundance of iron and the strength of the metal made it popular for weapons and tools. The discovery in question dates from about 2500 BC and subsequently iron came into general use through the Hittites, about 1600 BC. By about 1200 BC the smelting of iron was further refined, and a steel casing could be made over the wrought iron.

The Israelites, not being in the forefront of the discovery of metals, found themselves at a distinct disadvantage in weaponry as their enemies' inventions became increasingly sophisticated. When the Philistines attacked Saul's army, they not only had heavy coats of mail, helmets, and shields, but also metal leg protectors. The weapons that gave them superiority in battle, however, were the iron-headed spear such as the one carried by Goliath (1 Sm 17:7), the lance, and the iron chariot (Jgs 1:19; 4:3). A dagger and a knife made of iron were found at Tell el-Far'a. In Gibeah, some iron weapons have been excavated, but the most important discovery was an iron plowpoint dated to the time of King Saul (c. 1000 BC), which has proved to be the earliest of its kind in Palestine.

By the beginning of the Israelite monarchy, tools which were not made of iron became increasingly obsolete. The Hebrews experienced some difficulty in obtaining them initially, because the Philistines controlled the manufacture and supply of iron weapons and tools (1 Sm 13:19–22). But Philistine power declined under David, and by the time of Solomon iron tools and weapons of war were plentiful (cf. 1 Chr 29:7).

With the dawn of the Iron Age, about 1300 BC, the tools familiar to artisans today were coming into increasing use. Iron saws (1 Kgs 7:9) were known from the 7th century BC. The iron anvil was essential for the large forge hammer (Is 41:7) used by the stonemason (for figurative use see Jer 23:29). Early ironsmiths had spring-back tongs similar to tweezers, and a hinged variety came into common use by about 500 BC.

The rule, the level, and the square were all construction tools used by builders and carpenters. They had marking tools, pairs of compasses, plumb lines (Am 7:7,8), a scraping implement similar to an early type of plane (Is 44:13), a variety of file, and wooden mallets (Jgs 5:26). Iron axheads (2 Kgs 6:5), tongs, and hammers (Is 44:12), together with more advanced chisels, awls (Ex 21:6; Dt 15:17, KJV aul), nails (Jer 10:4), and bow-drills were in common usage in Israel. In agriculture more elaborate plowshares (Jl 3:10) than the kind recovered from Gibeah, Saul's capital city, were used in tilling the land, and iron sickles

Model of a plowman with a two-animal plow.

had long replaced the earlier flint ones. Some iron sickles still retained a link with the past, however, in that the blade had an inset flint edge, which made for easy sharpening and enabled grain to be cut closer to the ground. Early varieties of ox-goads were developed in the Hebrew monarchy, and became tipped with iron.   HAZEL W. PERKIN

See AGRICULTURE; MINERALS, METALS, AND PRECIOUS STONES; TRADES AND OCCUPATIONS; WHEEL; INDUSTRY AND COMMERCE; ARMS AND WARFARE; ARCHITECTURE; HUNTING; HOMES AND DWELLINGS.

Bibliography. L. Aitchison, *A History of Metals,* 2 vols; D. Bayly, *The Geography of the Bible;* J. Bordaz, *Tools of the Old and New Stone Age;* R.J. Braidwood, *Prehistoric Man;* C.S. Chard, *Man in Prehistory;* R.J. Forbes, *Metallurgy in Antiquity;* and *Studies in Ancient Technology,* 1–4; F.C. Howell, *Early Man;* K.P. Oatley, *Man the Tool-Maker;* T.A. Rickard, *Man and Metals,* 2 vols; C. Singer, et al., (eds.), *A History of Technology,* vol 1.

Topaz. See MINERALS, METALS, AND PRECIOUS STONES.

Tophel. Place where Israel camped opposite the Jordan, "in the Arabah over against Suph between Paran and Tophel" (Dt 1:1). Tophel has been identified with et-Tafileh, east of the Dead Sea.

See WILDERNESS WANDERINGS.

Topheth, Tophet. Location within the Valley of Hinnom outside Jerusalem where Israel profaned the Lord by offering human sacrifices to Molech. As part of his religious reform, Josiah defiled Topheth and tore down its altars (2 Kgs 23:10). Josiah's reforms appear to have had only temporary impact, for the practice recurred under Manasseh (2 Chr 33:6), and was later condemned by Jeremiah (Jer 7:31,32; KJV Tophet). Jeremiah prophesied that the valley would be renamed the "Valley of Slaughter" because it would be the site where the Babylonians would rout Judah during their siege of Jerusalem (7:32). Jeremiah repeated

the prophecy during his parable of the potter's flask, emphasizing the fact that Jerusalem would be destroyed so thoroughly that it would resemble Topheth (19:12). By this time Topheth had evidently become a sort of city dump where broken pottery was thrown away and where burials that could not be accommodated in any of the city cemeteries would take place (19:11).

While Topheth is not mentioned in the NT, it is quite possibly referred to indirectly in references to Gehenna (Aramaic form of "Valley of Hinnom"). Gehenna refers to the place of destruction and is typically translated "hell" in the NT (Mt 5:22,29,30; 10:28; 18:9; Mk 9:43–47; Lk 12:5). It may also be obliquely referred to in the account of Judas Iscariot's betrayal of Jesus. The priests used Judas' betrayal money to purchase a potter's field where they could bury strangers (Mt 27:9,10; cf. Jer 19:1–13; 32:6–9; Zec 11:12,13). A notable similarity is the fact that Topheth is referred to as the "Valley of Slaughter" in Jeremiah, while the potter's field was called the "Field of Blood" (Mt 27:10; Acts 1:19); however, the latter's exact identification is uncertain.

Torah. Word translated "law" in the OT, derived from the Hebrew verbal root, *yarah,* which means "to throw" or "to shoot." The idea behind the word is to inform, instruct, direct, or guide. In Jewish tradition it is most frequently used to designate the text of the first five books of the Bible, also called the Pentateuch. Quite properly, however, the word has a wider meaning, acknowledged by OT usage, which embraces all directive from God. This is true in the NT as well where *Torah*—represented by the Greek, *nomos*—may refer to either the Mosaic legislation (Rom 7:14) or a broad behavioral principle (9:31).

For the Jew the Law includes what has been called the "Oral Torah," that is, the sayings of the rabbis and venerated fathers of Judaism throughout the centuries. Such verbal tradition, while not part of the canonical books of the OT, seeks to interpret the texts of the Law to enable men to comply with the will of God. Unfortunately, this method has often resulted in the accommodation of sinful man by lessening the demands of the Law through reinterpreting them. Without temple worship, priesthood, or sacrifice—all prescribed by the *Torah*—such compromise with the Torah's demands became inevitable. These oral traditions were firmly entrenched at the time of Christ's advent and were held by many Jews to have been implicit in the *Torah* given to Moses (cf. Mk 7:3).

The Pharisees believed that the failure of

the Jews to obey the *Torah* resulted in the great Babylonian captivity in the 7th century BC. Furthermore, it is commonly taught that until the *Torah* is rigorously subscribed to by all Jews the Messiah will not appear upon the earth.

For the Sadducees, the *Torah* represented the only part of the OT which they accepted as authoritative. Their tendency, however, was to de-emphasize the supernatural elements in the Pentateuch. Contrary to their viewpoint on resurrection, Jesus Christ quoted from the *Torah* to affirm eternal life (cf. Mt 22:31,32).

From the most ancient days the reading of the *Torah* in the synagogue has been accompanied by great ceremony. To be called upon to read from these sacred scrolls is a high honor. It is of course written in Hebrew by a highly skilled craftsman known as a *sofer*, or scribe. The *Torah* is found in the form of a roll, the scroll for which is of parchment taken from the skin of ceremonially clean animals. Rods around which the *Torah* is rolled are usually of wood, silver, or ivory. Ornately designed ends of the rods are magnificent aesthetic creations frequently wrought in precious metals and stones. A person reading from the scroll uses a delicate pointer, called a *yad*, to follow the words. Use of the pointer safeguards the scroll, which would soon be damaged by the constant running of fingers over the fine manuscript. Moreover, the *yad* minimizes the possibility for error in oral recitation by preventing the reader from losing his place and possibly skipping some words of God's sacred revelation.

Among the annual festivals of Judaism, *Simchath Torah*, rejoicing over the Law, is designed to demonstrate the Jewish people's joy over their possession of the *Torah* and the privilege of studying its contents. Jewish thinking claims the *Torah* and Israel to be the lamp of God upon the earth; a Jew with the knowledge of the *Torah* is a house full of light.

Among Jewish orthodoxy it is maintained that inasmuch as the *Torah* was the gift of God to Israel, the gentile nations are not required to submit to its regulations. Maimonedes, the medieval Jewish scholar, taught that Gentiles would have a share in the world to come by obeying the covenant God made with Noah. Seven commands are commonly linked to that agreement, namely, the abstaining from idolatry, incest, shedding of blood, profaning the name of God, injustice, robbery, and eating the flesh of live animals.

The new covenant maintains that the *Torah*, while a necessary stage in the outworking of redemption, was never given to enable individuals to receive salvation on the basis of obeying the Law. Although Leviticus 18:5 ap-

pears to hold out the possibility of working for righteousness, flawless obedience to God's will is beyond the reach of fallen humanity. The OT clearly bore witness to the role of grace in redemption by revealing the great patriarch Abraham to be justified by faith (Gn 15). Since that covenant preceded the *Torah* by four centuries, it presents an unalterable witness to the way in which God receives sinful people. A primary function of the Law is to reveal people's fallen spiritual condition and thereby serve as a tutor leading them to Christ (Gal 3:24). As a sinner is exposed to the demands of the Law he or she is convicted of great sinfulness (Rom 7:7) and consequently seeks the grace of God in Christ. It is clear that Jesus Christ held the *Torah* in high regard, the purpose of his ministry being the fulfillment of its contents. That great work of satisfying the demands of the Law is reckoned in the lives of all who entrust themselves to Christ; he is the end of the Law that everyone who has faith in him may be justified (Rom 10:4).

While it is true that every person must be saved by faith apart from the works of the Law, Jeremiah asserted that the salvation of the Messiah would be accompanied by the writing of the *Torah* upon the hearts of the people of God (Jer 31:31–34). Thus, it must be maintained that a forgiven Christian is not a lawless person. Although Christians are not bound to the minute details of the ceremonial law, they have been radically transformed by the regenerative work of Christ through the Holy Spirit which gives them an affinity for the will of God. What the letter of the Law could not accomplish for their hearts (2 Cor 3:6), the fruit of the Spirit achieves (Gal 5:22,23). All Christians should recognize and live in harmony with the truth that the ultimate intention of the Law is the motive to love (Gal 5:14).

See LAW, BIBLICAL CONCEPT OF; JUDAISM; TALMUD.

Bibliography. J. Neusner, *Judaism*, pp 167–229; and *The Way of Torah*.

Tortoise. *See* ANIMALS (LIZARD).

Tou. Alternate form of Toi, the king of Hamath, in 1 Chronicles 18:9,10.

See TOI.

Tower. *See* FORT, FORTIFICATION; WATCHTOWER.

Tower of Babel. *See* BABEL.

Tower of Shechem. *See* SHECHEM, TOWER OF.

Tower of Siloam. *See* SILOAM, TOWER OF.

Tower of the Furnaces. KJV translation for "Tower of the Ovens," a tower in Jerusalem, in Nehemiah 3:11.

See OVENS, TOWER OF THE.

Tower of the Hundred. *See* HUNDRED, TOWER OF THE.

Town Clerk. *See* TRADES AND OCCUPATIONS.

Trachonitis. One of the five Roman provinces east of the Jordan River along with Batanea, Gaulanitis, Auranitis, and Decapolis. The region of Trachonitis (apparently including Gaulanitis, Batanea, and Auranitis) was part of the tetrarchy of Philip, the brother of Herod (Lk 3:1). Trachonitis was an extremely desolate region northeast of the Sea of Galilee. Its name in Aramaic was Argob, which signified that the region was a "heap of stones." Other than the reference in Luke, Trachonitis is seldom mentioned in historical references. Josephus suggests that it was colonized by Uz, the son of Aram (cf. Gn 10:23). The Romans gained control of the region when Augustus deposed Zenodorus, a local robber-chieftain. Herod the Great was deeded the land on the condition that he control the local bandits. Philip received the land at the death of his father but apparently retained only nominal control over the region. The region is currently named el-Lejah and is located in southern Syria and northern Jordan.

Trader. *See* TRADES AND OCCUPATIONS (MERCHANT).

Trade Routes. *See* INDUSTRY AND COMMERCE; TRAVEL AND TRANSPORTATION.

Trades and Occupations. Numerous professions are represented in the Bible, many of which are still practiced in Near Eastern communities—some in a fashion similar to that of their ancestors.

Ambassador. In the OT, an ambassador was a messenger, envoy, or negotiator sent on a special, temporary mission as an official representative of the king, government, or authority who sent him. Examples include the ambassador of Pharaoh (Is 30:4), of the princes of Babylon (2 Chr 32:31), and of Neco, king of Egypt (2 Chr 35:21).

In the letters of Paul, the apostle included himself in a group of ambassadors for Christ, "God making his appeal through us" (2 Cor 5:20). As an apostle he represented the King of heaven in bringing the message of reconciliation to a world at enmity with God. From prison Paul asked for prayer that his witness would be bold as he communicated the gospel as an "ambassador in chains" (Eph 6:20).

See CHRISTIANS, NAMES FOR.

Archer. The archer used bow and arrows in peace and war. Nomads (Gn 21:20), hunters (Gn 27:3; Is 7:24), raiders (Gn 48:22; Jos 24:12), and warriors (Ez 39:9; Hos 1:7) used this weapon throughout the biblical period. The efficiency of the bow and the making of arrows improved tremendously over the centuries. The finest bow was the "composite bow" made from strips and bands of sinew glued to the parts furthermost from the core with animal horn glued to the inner surface. The best of these bows could fire arrows from 300 to 400 yards. The archer needed to be a strong person to string and operate it.

While the archer used the bow for hunting, it was particularly useful in war. Saul and Jonathan fought with sword and bow (1 Sm 18:4) and David's army contained skilled bowmen (1 Chr 12:2). The kings of Israel equipped their troops with bows (2 Chr 17:17). Israel's enemies, the Egyptians, Syrians, Assyrians, Babylonians, Persians, Greeks, and Romans, all had strong contingents of archers, with excellent pictures still available on some of their bas-reliefs. Often the archers worked in pairs, one to hold a shield and one to shoot the arrows. Sometimes archers operated from horseback or from chariots.

Job used the metaphor of God's archers round about him when describing his many bodily ailments (16:13). At times the archer's bow represents violence (Pss 11:2; 57:4) or divine judgment (Pss 7:13; 38:2; 64:7).

Archers, as such, are not referred to in the NT, although Roman archers were well known to the early Christians. They are not mentioned in Paul's picture of Christians who wear the armor of God (Eph 6:10–17).

See ARMS AND WARFARE.

Baker. The baker operated in the home (Gn 19:3), in the public bakery (Jer 37:21), and in the palaces of kings and nobles (Gn 40:1–22; 41:10,13; 1 Sm 8:13) preparing bread and cakes from the basic staples of oil and flour. The fleeing Israelites baked unleavened bread for their journey (Ex 12:39). The bread and cakes were baked in some kind of pan or oven (Lv 2:4; 26:26). As Israelite society developed, specialized bakers operated and formed guilds. Jeremiah was given his daily ration when in prison (Jer 37:21). Some have argued that Hosea was a baker because of his knowledge of baking techniques (Hos 7:4,6–8). In postexilic Jerusalem there was a fortress called the Tower of the Ovens (Neh 3:11; 12:38). Bakers

Roman flour mills in a bakery
at Pompeii.

are not referred to in the NT but ovens are mentioned (Mt 6:30; Lk 12:28).

See FOOD AND FOOD PREPARATION.

Banker. The professional banker was involved in the safekeeping of money and treasures, the exchange of money from one currency to another, and the provision of funds for large and small undertakings. His services were naturally available for a fee. In antiquity a barter system prevailed. For safekeeping people would bury their valuables (Jos 7:21) or deposit them with a neighbor (Ex 22:7). The

Code of Hammurabi (*c.* 1700 BC) had several laws concerning the safekeeping of deposits. With the increasing sophistication of societies, however, the professional banker appeared.

The development of interstate and international trade made it imperative to devise a method for facilitating the transfer of funds. The appearance of coinage in the 7th century BC brought the money changer into being. The royal monopoly in commerce (2 Sm 5:11; 1 Kgs 10:14–29) gave place to a system which resembled modern banking. Jews abroad became noted for their banking activities; a collection of financial documents from the house of the Jewish Murashu Brothers reveals the extent of Jewish involvement in banking in Babylonia during the postexilic era.

In NT times money changers represented one aspect of the banking system. They spent their time converting Roman money into orthodox coinage for the temple half-shekel (Mt 17:24; 21:12; 25:27; Mk 11:15; Lk 19:23; Jn 2:14,15).

Those who lent money (lenders) and those who gave credit in financial transactions (creditors) were protected by a system of guarantees such as pieces of movable property or a pledge of some kind. Interest was theoretically forbidden by Israelite law (Ex 22:25; Dt 15:1-21), although the Law was not always observed and exorbitant rates of interest were sometimes charged. Prophets and some national leaders deplored the practice (Ez 18:8, 13,17; 22:12; Neh 5:6-13). Often the people of Israel were afraid of their creditors (2 Kgs 4:1; Ps 109:11; Is 24:2; 50:1), who might invade their homes to recover a debt, even carrying off children as slaves (2 Kgs 4:1; Is 50:1). The parable of the creditor and the two debtors in Luke 7:41,42 represents a kindly creditor (cf. Mt 25:14-30; Lk 19:11-27).

See MONEY AND BANKING; MONEY CHANGER.

Barber. The barber cut hair and trimmed beards (Gn 41:14; 2 Sm 19:24). The barber's main tool was the razor (Ez 5:1). Levites and priests were forbidden to shave their heads or the edges of their beards (Lv 21:5; Ez 44:20); Nazirites were forbidden to remove their hair (Nm 6:3,18,19; Jgs 13:5; 16:17).

Carpenter. The carpenter worked in timber, setting up the framework of houses, the roofing, windows, and doors. Often small structures were erected by the householder, but temples and palaces required specialized artisans where carpenters worked alongside stonemasons (2 Kgs 12:11; 22:6; 1 Chr 14:1; 22:15; 2 Chr 24:12; 34:11; Ezr 3:7). Some of the delicate work for cedar linings, roofing, flooring, and the internal woodwork was undertaken by specialist carpenters (or joiners). Carpenters' tools of ancient times have been discovered in excavations. Some are referred to in the Bible (Is 44:13). They included compass, pencil, plane, saw, hammer, ax, adze, chisel, plumb line (Am 7:7,8), drill, file, and square. Carpentry is seldom referred to in the NT though it was the profession of Jesus and his father (Mt 13:55; Mk 6:3).

See INDUSTRY AND COMMERCE.

Caulker. The caulker repaired the seams of ships. The term occurs only once in the OT (Ez 27:9,27) in reference to Phoenician shipbuilders at Gebal (Byblos), but no details are given about their work. They probably used fibers and bitumen like modern caulkers. The people of Israel did not build large ships, yet caulkers would have been needed even for the small boats in use on the Sea of Galilee and on the Jordan River.

Chamberlain. Originally a chamberlain was a royal official in charge of the private quarters of the king. They sometimes had other significant tasks and had great influence with those in authority (Acts 12:20). The chamberlain Erastus (Rom 16:23 KJV) was actually the city treasurer. Nathan-melek the chamberlain (2 Kgs 23:11) was a court official at the time of Josiah. The Persian kings used eunuchs as chamberlains (Est 1:10,12,15; 2:3,14, 15; 4:4,5; 6:2,14; 7:9).

Cook. In addition to the cooking done by women in the home (Gn 18:6; 27:9; 2 Sm 13:8; cf. Jgs 19) people were employed as cooks in kings' palaces (1 Sm 8:13; 9:22–24). Cooks are not mentioned in the NT.

See FOOD AND FOOD PREPARATION.

Coppersmith. The coppersmith worked in copper and fashioned bronze and copper tools, implements, and ornaments (Ex 26:11,37; 27:2, 4,6,10; Jos 6:19,24; 1 Sm 17:5,6; 2 Sm 8:8, etc.). Only in the NT (2 Tm 4:14) is the term coppersmith used; however, the occupation was important throughout Bible history.

See MINERALS, METALS, AND PRECIOUS STONES.

Counselor. *See* COUNSEL, COUNSELOR.

Craftsman. The biblical craftsmen, sometimes called "artisans" (2 Kgs 24:14,16) and "artificers" (KJV in Gn 4:22; 1 Chr 29:5; 2 Chr 34:11; Is 3:3) were engaged in a wide range of activities including weaving and spinning (Ex 35:25), building (1 Kgs 5:18; 2 Kgs 12:11), stoneworking (1 Chr 14:1), and metalworking (Ex 35:31–33; 2 Tm 4:14). David and Solomon called in a wide range of craftsmen to the palaces and the temple. At times invaders even carried them off for work in their own lands (2 Kgs 24:16).

See INDUSTRY AND COMMERCE.

Cupbearer. Cupbearers frequented the courts of kings and high officials in antiquity (1 Kgs 10:5). Their primary duty was serving wine to the king to avoid the danger of assassination by poisoning. These men were close to those in authority and sometimes exercised considerable influence. Generally several of them served the king with the "chief cupbearer" (butler) at their head (Gn 40:1–23). Solomon's court included cupbearers (2 Chr 9:4), and Nehemiah was called "cupbearer to the king" (Neh 1:11–2:1); Rabshakeh may have been a cupbearer (2 Kgs 18:12–19; Is 36:2).

Custodian. The sons of noble families in Greece and Rome were placed in the charge of a slave until they reached maturity. These custodians supervised their moral conduct and general behavior. Their methods of persuasion varied from physical punishment to shaming. Paul regarded the Mosaic Law as a "school master" (KJV) or "tutor" (NASB) to lead us to Christ (Gal 3:24,25). To return to the Law represented a reversion to childhood.

Dyer. See DYE, DYER, DYEING.

Embroiderer. The embroidering of cloths and garments was an art practiced both in the home and as a profession; it was done on a loom or with needle. Delicate fabrics in the tabernacle and temple (Ex 26:1,31) and the garments of priests (Ex 28:6,8; 39:1) were beautifully embroidered. The art was practiced in Canaan (Jgs 5:30), Egypt (Ez 27:7), Syria (Ez 27:16), Babylonia (Jos 7:21), Assyria, and Persia (Est 1:6).

See CLOTH, CLOTH MANUFACTURING; FASHION AND DRESS.

Exorcist. The ability to expel or control demons was claimed by many in the ancient Near East. Only in Acts 19:13 is there a biblical reference to exorcism among the Jews, though in 1 Samuel 16:14–23 David functioned as an exorcist by playing a lyre to cast out an evil spirit from Saul.

Jesus often cast out demons (Mt 9:32–34; 12:22,23; cf. Lk 11:14); (Mk 1:21–28; cf. Lk 4:31–37); (Mk 5:1–20; cf. Mt 8:28–34; Lk 8:26–39); (Mk 7:24–30; cf. Mt 15:21–28); (Mk 9:14–29; cf. Mt 17:14–21; Lk 9:37–43). The power to exorcise in Jesus' name was in turn delegated to his disciples (Mk 3:14,15; 6:7; cf. Lk 9:1; 10:17–20; Mk 9:14–29; cf. Mt 17:14–21; Mk 16:17,18; Lk 9:37–43), and unsuccessfully attempted by nonChristians (Acts 19:13–17).

See DEMONS, DEMON POSSESSION.

Farmer. Israel was basically a farming and pastoral community. Israel's earliest memories were of farmers like Cain (Gn 4:2–8, a tiller of the ground) and Noah (Gn 9:20, a husbandman). Farmers are sometimes grouped with vinedressers and shepherds (2 Chr 26:10; Jer 31:24; 51:23; Jl 1:11–20; Am 5:16,17; Zec 13:5). The KJV substitutes "husbandman" for farmer in several places (2 Chr 26:10; Jer 31:24; 51:23; Am 5:16; 2 Tm 2:6; Jas 5:7).

Agricultural procedures are mentioned often in the OT. The plowman is sometimes called the husbandman in the KJV (2 Kgs 25:12; Jer 52:16; but plowman in Is 61:5; Am 9:13; 1 Cor 9:10). Jeremiah spoke of the difficulties of the plowman in a time of drought (Jer 14:4). Isaiah gives details of the farmer's task (Is 28:24–27). Amos gives a glowing picture of agriculture in the new age (Am 9:13). References also appear to reapers and reaping (Ru 2:3–7,14; 1 Sm 6:13; 2 Kgs 4:18; Am 9:13); threshing (Is 28:27; 41:15; Am 1:3; 1 Cor 9:10); threshing floors (Gn 50:10; Nm 15:20; 18:27,30; Ru 3:2;

A watchtower at Samaria.

1 Sm 23:1; 2 Sm 6:6; 24:16,18,21; 1 Chr 13:9; 21:15,18; 2 Chr 3:1; Jer 51:33), and winnowing (Jer 51:2). Grape culture and the vinedresser were important aspects of farming (2 Kgs 25:12; Is 61:5; Jer 52:16; Jl 1:11; Lk 13:7; Jn 15:1). When Jerusalem fell in 586 BC, Nebuchadnezzar left the farmers on the land (2 Kgs 24:14; Jer 41:4–8).

In the NT there are several references to farmers, vineyards, and flocks. The parable of Matthew 21:33–41 refers to the tenants of a vineyard whose owner was abroad (cf. Mk 12:1–9; Lk 20:9–16). Jesus in his discourse on the vine gave details of procedures in vine cultivation (Jn 15:1–6). An apt illustration of the rights of the farmer to have the first share of the crops occurs in 2 Timothy 2:6, and James urges Christians to await patiently the coming of the Lord like the farmer who waits for the precious fruit of the earth (Jas 5:7).

See AGRICULTURE.

Fisherman. Fishing was carried on by fishermen in the Holy Land from early times and is referred to in both the OT (Is 19:8; Jer 16:16; Ez 47:10) and the NT (Mt 4:18,19; Mk 1:16,17; Lk 5:2; Jn 21:7). Fishermen formed a distinct class in society. Jesus included several fishermen among his disciples (Mt 4:18–22; Mk 1:16–20; cf. Lk 5:2–11). Their work was strenuous (Lk 5:2–5) and not always rewarding (Lk 5:5; Jn 21:3). Jesus used the metaphor "fishers of men" of his disciples (Mt 4:19; Mk 1:17; Lk 5:10).

See INDUSTRY AND COMMERCE.

Fowler. The catching of birds for pets, food, and sacrifices was the business of the fowler. This was done by the use of a bow and arrow, a sling, or a net (Prv 1:17; Ez 12:13; 17:20; Hos 7:12). Other methods included the use of bird lime, a sticky substance to which birds adhere, and a throw stick which broke the birds' legs. Fowlers lay in wait near their trap, placing the captured birds in a basket (Jer 5:26,27). The term fowler appears also as a metaphor for wicked men who trap their fellows (Pss 91:3; 124:7; Jer 5:26; Hos 9:8).

See HUNTING.

Fuller. Fibers used for weaving were cleansed from oil and other impurities by a fuller. The cleansing materials were white clay, urine, and ashes of special plants. The fuller's plant lay outside the town because of offensive odors and because space was needed for spreading the fibers to dry, as was the case of the Fuller's Field outside Jerusalem in Isaiah's day (2 Kgs 18:17; Is 7:3; 36:2).

See FULLER'S FIELD; CLOTH, CLOTH MANUFACTURING.

Gatekeeper. Gates of the cities and doors of palaces, temples, and other large buildings were guarded by gatekeepers or doorkeepers who admitted or rejected visitors (2 Kgs 7:10,11; 11:4–9). In the Bible these men are variously named as gatekeeper, porter, doorkeeper, and guard. The temple gatekeepers, "priests who guarded the threshold" (2 Kgs 12:9) or "keepers of the threshold" (2 Kgs 22:4; Jer 35:4), formed a significant group. Postexilic writers saw these men as a special class (1 Chr 9:17–27; 23:5; Ezr 2:42; 7:24; Neh 7:45) who guarded the temple entrance (1 Chr 9:23–27; 2 Chr 23:19), cared for the ark (1 Chr 15:23), supervised the offerings (2 Chr 31:14), helped with purification services (Neh 12:45), and guarded the storehouses (Neh 12:25). In David's time there were 4000 of them (1 Chr 23:5), but only 172 in Nehemiah's day (Neh 11:19). In NT times the only references are to gatekeepers of private houses (Mt 13:34) or of a sheepfold (Jn 10:3). The girl who recognized Peter at the time of Jesus' trial was the "maid who kept the door" of the high priest's house (Jn 18:16,17).

Goldsmith. These were men who specialized in fine gold work. They fashioned costly and elegant idols for pagan worship (Is 40:19; 41:7; 46:6; Jer 10:9,14; 51:17), and prepared items and gold plating for the tabernacle (Ex 31:4; 35:32) and Solomon's temple (1 Kgs 6:20–35). They formed a guild in postexilic times and assisted in the restoration and repair of the temple (Neh 3:8,31,32).

See MINERALS, METALS, AND PRECIOUS STONES.

Handmaid, Handmaiden. Female servants were familiar members among many households in biblical days. The handmaid cared for the women and children of a family and served as the woman's personal attendant. She enjoyed the protection of the Law (Lv 25:6; Dt 5:14; 15:12–15), and as a free wife's maid, sometimes became a concubine in a childless marriage (Gn 30:3).

The term is also used to denote humility toward a man (Ru 3:9; 1 Sm 28:21) or toward God (1 Sm 1:11; Pss 86:16; 116:16; Acts 2:18).

Mary presents herself to the Lord as a handmaiden (Lk 1:38,48).

See MAID, MAIDEN.

Harlot. *See* HARLOT.

Herdsman. These men, variously known as herdsmen and shepherds, were keepers of small domestic animals such as sheep and goats (Gn 13:7,8; 26:20; 1 Sm 21:7). A special term occurring in Amos 7:14 suggests that the care of cattle represented another kind of herdsman. In the NT shepherds were well known. The metaphor of the shepherd and his sheep was used by Jesus (Jn 10:1–16). Some herdsmen kept swine (Mt 8:33; Mk 5:14; Lk 8:34). The owners of large flocks hired shepherds who led the flock from the front rather than driving them from behind (Jn 10:3–5,12–14). The shepherds knew their flock individually and counted them as they entered the sheepfold (Lv 27:32).

Interpreter. The interpreter facilitated communication between people who spoke different languages. Joseph pretended to need an interpreter to speak to his brothers (Gn 42:23). Also, dreams needed to be interpreted (Gn 40:22; 41:13; Dn 2; 4:6–9,18–24; 5:7,8,12–17; 7:16). The interpreter was sometimes one who acted as an intermediary (Jb 33:23). In NT times the interpreter explained the utterances of those who spoke in tongues (1 Cor 14:28), translated foreign languages (Acts 2:6), or expounded the Scriptures (Lk 24:27).

Ironsmith. The ironsmith was an artisan who normally worked in iron (Is 44:12). The first worker in iron recorded in the Bible is Tubal-cain (Gn 4:22). In Israel iron became widely known and used about the 11th century BC (Dt 3:11; Jos 6:19,24; 17:16; Jgs 1:19; 4:3,13). The craft developed in the days of the kings as the ironsmiths manufactured nails, tools, bars, chains, collars, and fetters (1 Kgs 6:7; 1 Chr 22:3; Pss 105:18; 107:10,16; 149:8); pagan ironworkers made idols (Is 44:12; Dn 5:4).

See MINERALS, METALS, AND PRECIOUS STONES.

Judge. The judge undertook a variety of tasks, mostly in legal and judicial areas but at times in political areas as well. In the patriarchal period the elders of the tribes decided disputes. Moses appointed other judges to assist him, taking only the difficult cases himself (Ex 18:13–26; Dt 1:9–17). Samuel went on circuit judging cases (1 Sm 7:16,17); his sons became judges, too (1 Sm 8:1). During the monarchy period the office of judge was well established. The king himself heard hard cases (1 Kgs 3:16–28; 7:7; 1 Chr 18:14; Prv 20:8). Some cases were heard at the city gate (Ex 18:13; Ru 4:11). Each party presented his plea to the judge (Dt 1:16; 25:1) and witnesses were called (Nm 35:30; Dt 17:6; 19:15). In difficult cases the judge sought for a word from God

(Lv 24:12; Nm 15:34). Absalom sought to usurp this right from David (2 Sm 15:2–6). Local courts developed in time (1 Chr 23:4; 26:29). Israel's problem was ensuring strict justice; the prophets often complained of bribery and corruption in this office (Is 1:23; 5:23; 10:1; Am 5:12; 6:12; Mi 3:11; 7:3).

In the NT era two kinds of courts operated in Palestine, the Jewish and the Roman. Capital cases were tried before a Roman judge. Witnesses were produced at trials (Mt 18:16; 2 Cor 13:1; 1 Tm 5:19). Jesus himself was tried before Pontius Pilate, the Roman procurator (Mt 27:11–25; Mk 15:2–5; Lk 23:2,3; Jn 18:29–40), and Paul before Felix (Acts 24:1–26) and Festus (Acts 25:1–26:32).

See CIVIL LAW AND JUSTICE; CRIMINAL LAW AND PUNISHMENT.

Magician. *See* MAGIC.

Maid. *See* MAID, MAIDEN.

Mason. The mason prepared stone from the quarry for use in building. In Israel's early days masons were brought from Phoenicia (2 Sm 5:11; 1 Kgs 5:17,18; 1 Chr 14:1), but later Israelite masons did their own work (2 Kgs 12:12; 22:6; 2 Chr 24:12; Ezr 3:7). The workmanship of ancient masons has been revealed by modern archaeology. Notable examples are the palace of Omri and Ahab in Samaria. Some of the finest masonry in Israel was that of Herod in Jerusalem, Hebron, Samaria, and elsewhere, some of which is still standing.

See ARCHITECTURE; INDUSTRY AND COMMERCE.

Merchant. The barter system of trade gave way in time to a system where professional merchants facilitated the exchange of goods. At first it was for payment in silver pieces (Gn 23:16) and then in coinage or some other medium of exchange. Merchants operated locally and internationally with Aramaeans (1 Kgs 20:34; Ez 27:16,18), Canaanites and Phoenicians (Is 23:2,8), Assyrians (Na 3:16), Babylonians, Persians, Greeks, and Romans. Some merchants traveled afar (Neh 13:16,20). Desert peoples with caravans traded their wares in many lands (Ez 27:15,20,23; 38:13). They operated in bazaars and set up shops for trade (1 Kgs 20:34; Neh 3:31; 13:19,20). Commodities were held in storehouses (Gn 41:49; 1 Kgs 9:19). The sons of Jacob traded in Egypt (Gn 43:11). In Solomon's day trade greatly expanded (1 Kgs 9:26,27; 10:28). During the exile, Jews became involved in merchant activity in Babylonia and many never returned to Palestine. In Jerusalem the merchants helped Nehemiah to rebuild the wall (Neh 3:31,32).

In the Roman world merchants were quite active (Mt 11:16; Rv 18:3,11,15,23). Some sought costly goods like pearls from afar (Mt 13:45). The activities of Jewish merchants were gov-

erned by Roman law, the Mosaic law, and the rabbinic law.

Money Changer. *See* MONEY CHANGER.

Musician. Musicians, both nonprofessional and professional, are as old as humanity. The earliest biblical reference is to Tubal, "the father of all who play the lyre and harp" (Gn 4:21). Instruments for home and village entertainment ranged from stringed to wind. Shepherds like David played the pipe or flute (Jgs 5:11). Musical instruments were important in war and peace. The trumpet blast was used to assemble citizens or to announce a march (Nm 10:2–10). David's playing on the harp calmed the troubled Saul (1 Sm 16:23). Musicians played an important part in temple worship. David organized the sons of Asaph, Heman and Jeduthun, to play harps, lyres, and cymbals (1 Chr 25:1–7). In the temple rituals music was in the care of the chief musicians to whom instructions appear at the head of over 50 psalms, the first of these being Psalm 4. There are biblical references to specific musicians such as trumpeters (2 Kgs 11:14; 2 Chr 5:12,13; 23:13; 29:28; Rv 18:22), harpists (Rv 14:2; 18:22), and pipers (1 Kgs 1:40; Mt 11:17; Lk 7:32; 1 Cor 14:7; Rv 18:22).

See MUSIC AND MUSICAL INSTRUMENTS.

Nurse. Nursing in ancient Israel was an honorable profession, and usually limited to the nursing and caring of infants. Women usually took care of their own children, such as Sarah (Gn 21:7) and Hannah (1 Sm 1:23). A wet nurse often held a significant place in the family circle. Rebekah had a nurse, whose death receives special mention in the biblical text (Gn 35:8). Moses' mother became his nurse, as arranged with Pharaoh's daughter (Ex 2:7).

Royal sons received special care and were under the supervision of a nurse after they had been suckled. Children were nursed up to the age of three (Gn 21:8; 1 Sm 1:23,24); and thereafter, a nurse-teacher took charge of the youngster. Mephibosheth was five years old when his nurse fell with him, causing his lameness (2 Sm 4:4). Joash was hidden with his nurse by Jehosheba his aunt (2 Kgs 11:2). In all probability male nurses were used as teachers for the young aristocrats (cf. 2 Kgs 10:1,5 where Ahab's children had "tutors"). In this sense Moses refers to himself as a "nurse": "Did I conceive all this people? Did I bring them forth, that thou shouldst say to me, 'Carry them in your bosom, as a nurse carries the sucking child, to the land which thou didst swear to give their fathers?' " (Nm 11:12). Paul saw himself, too, as a "nurse" to the church (1 Thes 2:7).

See MEDICINE AND MEDICAL PRACTICE.

Perfumer. The perfumer or apothecary (KJV) prepared oils, powders, and mixtures for medicinal use, for perfumes and cosmetics, and for religious use in incense. A wide variety of plants when crushed provided oils or powders giving off distinctive odors. Sometimes these were imported from foreign lands: caravans brought spices to Tyre (Ez 27:22); Ishmaelite spice merchants brought Joseph to Egypt (Gn 37:25); the Queen of Sheba and her retinue brought spices to Solomon (1 Kgs 10:10). Such trade was extensive in both the OT and NT periods when spices and aromatic materials were taken to Rome (Rv 18:13). The perfumer's products were used as cosmetics and for soothing the head (Mt 26:7), the feet (Lk 7:38), the hands (Sg 5:5), the body (Ru 3:3; Est 2:12). They were sprinkled on clothes or furniture (Ps 45:8; Sg 3:6; 4:11). The harlot sprinkled her bed with perfume (Prv 7:17).

Spices were used in wine (Sg 8:2). Myrrh was used as an anaesthetic in wine (Mk 15:23). Spices and oils were used in funeral ceremonies (Gn 50:2,3,26; 2 Chr 16:14; Jn 19:39,40). Not only in Israel but also in neighboring lands perfumes were featured in religious ceremonies. The sacred anointing oil in Israel consisted of myrrh, cinnamon, aromatic cane, and cassia (Ex 30:22–25,35; 37:29).

In postexilic times there were guilds of perfumers and apothecaries (Neh 3:8); yet even earlier there were professional perfumers who were employed by kings and nobles (1 Sm 8:13 KJV confectioners).

In Jesus' day spices were used to embalm bodies (Mk 14:8; 16:1; Lk 23:56; Jn 19:40). The ointments, balms, and oils of the apothecaries were applied to the body (Mk 6:13; Jas 5:14).

Physician. The physician tended to and repaired wounds and administered medicines to the sick. In early Israel the diagnosis and treatment of sick people was officially the concern of the priests although many nonprofessional people practiced the healing art in the small towns and villages. Jacob's body was embalmed by physicians for his burial (Gn 50:2). King Asa sought their help for his feet (2 Chr 16:12). Jeremiah inquired about physicians in Gilead (Jer 8:22). Job complained that his friends were useless physicians (Jb 13:4). Scientific medicine and the careful training of physicians awaited the rise of Greek medicine, which by NT times saw medical schools established in various countries in the Greco-Roman world. Remarkable collections of surgical instruments have come from places like Pompeii. The NT refers to a number of sicknesses and mentions Luke, the beloved physician (Col 4:14); the word physician occurs several times (Mt 9:12; Mk 2:17; 5:26; Lk 4:23;

5:31; 8:43). Physicians were not always able to effect a cure (Mk 5:26; Lk 8:43), but Jesus the healer succeeded where others failed.

See MEDICINE AND MEDICAL PRACTICE.

Potter. The potter made a wide variety of vessels out of clay which were then baked. Early potters worked by hand until the idea of rotating the vessel on a table was discovered. The early wheel was a simple round platform turned by hand (*tournette*). About 2000 BC two wheels were used; the bottom one was rotated by the potter's feet beneath the table and was connected by a spindle to the upper wheel where the clay was placed and manipulated by the potter. The considerable speed at which the wheels were rotated enabled the potter to produce symmetrical vessels quickly. This fast wheel came into use in Palestine in the Middle Bronze Age (*c.* 2000–1500 BC). Evidence of potters' factories has been found in excavations. While the art is ancient, the earliest biblical reference is to King David's potters (1 Chr 4:23). The Book of Isaiah mentions the potter and his clay (29:16; 30:14; 41:25; 64:8). Jeremiah used the potter's art to illustrate his preaching (18:2–6; 19:1,11). Lamentations compared the sons of Zion to the fine work of the potter (4:2). Zechariah referred to the man who threw down 30 pieces of silver in the potter's house (11:13), and Daniel referred to the toes of Nebuchadnezzar's image made partly of iron and partly of clay (2:41).

The NT has four references to the potter: two to the purchase of a potter's field by Judas (Mt 27:7,10), one to the power the potter has over his clay (Rom 9:21), and one as a metaphor for the breaking of the nations (Rv 2:27).

See POTTERY.

Priest. *See* PRIESTS AND LEVITES.

Prophet, Prophetess. *See* PROPHET, PROPHETESS.

Recorder. The title of a high public official from David's reign until the end of the Israelite monarchy. Though precise duties are never specified in the OT, the recorder probably kept the official log or ledger and advised the king from the information available to him. A recorder is mentioned with other leading officers in 2 Samuel 8:16; 20:24; and 1 Kings 4:3. The recorder spoke for Hezekiah in his dealings with Rabshekah (2 Kgs 18:18), and during Josiah's reign, supervised temple repairs (2 Chr 34:8).

Ruler. The term represents a number of different functions and translates 13 Hebrew and three Greek words. In a political sense a ruler was one who exercised political control over a state (2 Chr 7:18; Ps 105:20; Prv 23:1; 28:15; Eccl 10:4; Is 14:5; 16:1; 49:7; Jer 33:26; 51:46; Mi 5:2), or a state that exercised control over a subject people (Jgs 15:11). The usual term for ruler was "king," but because of its unsavory associations many in Israel preferred the Hebrew term translated "leader," meaning "one placed in front" (RSV prince). Samuel rejected the former term but used the latter (1 Sm 9:16; 10:1; 13:14; 25:30; 2 Sm 5:2; 6:21; 7:8). The word remained in use in some circles in Israel (1 Kgs 1:35; 1 Chr 5:2; 11:2; 17:7; 28:4; 2 Chr 6:5; 11:22). The same word was used of a person in charge of a specific religious or administrative area (1 Chr 9:11,20; 26:24; 27:4,16; 2 Chr 19:11; 31:12,13; 35:8; Neh 11:11).

In some passages the ruler represents someone who is raised up or lifted up over a group. Tribal leaders are sometimes called rulers (Ex 16:22; 22:28; 34:31; 35:27; Lv 4:22; Nm 13:2). The Hebrew term for "prefect" (KJV ruler) occurs frequently (Neh 2:16; 4:14,19; 5:7,17; 7:5; 12:40; 13:11; Jer 51:23,28,57; Ez 23:6,12,23). Other Hebrew words are translated ruler in the KJV. However, most modern translations prefer alternatives to this more generic term.

In the NT the Greek word regularly translated ruler refers to administrative or religious leaders (Mt 9:18,23; Lk 8:41; 18:18; 23:35; 24:20; Jn 3:1; 7:26,48; 12:31; Acts 3:17; 4:5,26; 7:27,35; 13:27; 14:5; 16:19; 23:5; Rom 13:3). Ephesians 6:12 mentions the rulers of the darkness of this world.

See KING, KINGSHIP.

Sailor. The people of Israel were not generally sea-faring and confined their activities on the water to the Sea of Galilee and the Jordan River. Occasionally they may have had contact with large ships (Gn 49:13; Jgs 5:17). Solomon had a fleet of ships at Ezion-geber on the Gulf of Aqaba (1 Kgs 9:26,28; 2 Chr 8:17,18; 9:21). Jehoshaphat, too, had a fleet at Ezion-geber which was wrecked (1 Kgs 22:48; 2 Chr 20:35–37). Ezekiel referred to Phoenician ships in some detail (27:5–9,25,26).

The NT frequently mentions ships and sailors—the numerous fishing boats on Galilee (Mt 14:22; Mk 1:19; 3:9; Lk 5:2; Jn 6:19,22–24; 21:8), and the large ships such as the one on which Paul traveled to Rome (Acts 27:6–44). Shipmen (KJV) or sailors are mentioned in Acts 27:27,30. The term "mariner" (KJV) refers to sailor (Ez 27:9,27,29; Jon 1:5). The officer in charge of the ship and its sailors in Revelation 18:17 is called the shipmaster (KJV).

See TRAVEL AND TRANSPORTATION.

Senator. Member of the council of Jewish leaders gathered together in Jerusalem to determine what action to bring against the apostles (Acts 5:21). In all probability this Jewish senate was equivalent to the Sanhedrin, the Jewish governing body in Palestine consisting of priests, elders, and scribes (cf. Acts 4:5). The

senates of Greece and Rome undoubtedly influenced the development of this Jewish assembly. During the first century, the Roman senate largely served as an advisory body to the Roman emperor.

Servant. The term is used in several different senses in the Bible. It represents a person of either sex who was under obligation to serve a master who would, in turn, provide a measure of protection. Some servants were slaves under legal bondage, others were voluntary. It is not always possible to distinguish "servant," "slave," "bondman," and "bondwoman." Several words in both Hebrew and Greek have been translated "servant," although newer translations sometimes prefer other words.

The Hebrew word for "lad," "youth," "boy" often means servant (Ex 33:11; Nm 22:22; 2 Kgs 4:12). Plural (KJV young man, Gn 14:24; 1 Sm 25:5; 2 Kgs 19:6) and feminine forms (KJV maid, damsel, Gn 24:16; Ru 2:5; Est 2:9) also occur. A free-born servant referred to the servants of the Lord, like the Levites (Ezr 8:17; Is 61:6; Ez 44:11) or priests (Ex 28:35; Jl 1:9; 2:17). Sometimes ministers of the king are called servants (1 Chr 27:1; Prv 29:12) as are angels who minister before the Lord (Pss 103:21; 104:4). The hired servant or hireling was also considered a free person (Ex 12:45; Jb 7:1; Mal 3:5).

The most common Hebrew term occurring nearly 800 times in the OT denotes a slave held in bondage (Gn 9:25; 12:16; Ex 20:17; Dt 5:15; 15:17, etc.). Yet the same word is used for people of noble rank, such as ministers and advisers to the king (2 Kgs 22:12; 2 Chr 34:20; Neh 2:10) or a servant of God (Gn 24:14; Nm 12:7; Jos 1:7; 2 Kgs 21:8), in such expressions as "Moses [or also David, Isaiah, Israel, Job, etc.] my servant." One of the noblest expressions is "The Servant of Yahweh [the Lord]" (Dt 34:5; Jos 1:13; 8:31–33; Is 49:1–6; 50:4–9; 52:13–53:12). The proper name Obadiah means "servant of Yahweh."

The NT variously defines servant as a hired servant or hireling (Mk 1:20; Lk 15:17,19; Jn 10:12–14), more widely as slave (Mt 8:9; 10:24,25; 13:27,28; Mk 10:44; 12:2,4; Lk 7:2,3,8,10; Jn 4:51; 8:34; 13:16; Eph 6:5; Col 1:7), and also as a domestic servant (Lk 16:13)—such a person could not serve two masters (Rom 14:4; 1 Pt 2:18).

See SLAVE, SLAVERY.

Shepherd. The task of the shepherd was to care for the flock, to find grass and water, to protect it from wild animals (Am 3:12), to look for and restore those that strayed (Ez 34:8; Mt 18:12), to lead the flock out each day going before it and to return the flock at the close of the day to the fold (Jn 10:2–4). At times the shepherd led the flock far from home and shel-

A sheepfold near Herodium, south of Bethlehem.

tered the animals by night in a cave or sheep-fold built of fieldstones; he would lie across the entrance. The shepherd was responsible to the owner for every sheep and was required to make restitution for losses (Gn 31:39; Ex 22:10–13). Shepherds and their flocks enjoyed a close relationship (2 Sm 12:3; Jn 10:3,4) giving them constant care (Ez 34:4,5; Mt 9:36; 26:31).

The figure of the shepherd and his sheep is important in the NT. Jesus is the Good Shepherd who gives his life for the sheep (Mt 18:10–14; Mk 6:34; Jn 10; Heb 13:20). The analogy of the shepherd and the flock finds rich expression in Psalm 23, Ezekiel 34, and John 10. God was the Shepherd of Israel (Gn 49:24; Pss 23:1; 80:1; Is 40:11). When unfaithful shepherds failed Israel, God intervened and appointed his servant David as a faithful shepherd over them (Ez 34:11–16,23,24).

Silversmith. The task of the silversmith was to refine silver-bearing ore, then cast it or beat it into the desired shape. Silversmiths produced musical instruments like trumpets (Nm 10:2), bases on which the frame of the tabernacle rested (Ex 26:19–25), and objects for use in the tabernacle and temple (Nm 7:13,19,25,31, etc.) as well as ornaments for private use. Silversmiths also made religious statues for false worship (Ex 20:23; Jgs 17:4). The silversmith Demetrius (Acts 19:24) made silver shrines for Artemis at Ephesus. The profession was well known in NT times (2 Tm 2:20; Rv 9:20).

See MINERALS, METALS, AND PRECIOUS STONES.

Singer. The professional singer was important in temple worship. David first organized singers for worship in the tabernacle (1 Chr 9:33; 15:16,19,27). Later, they ministered in Solomon's temple (2 Chr 5:12,13) and for other kings (2 Chr 20:21; 23:13; 35:15). After the exile the order of singers was again active (Ezr 2:41,70; Neh 7:1,44,73; 10:28,39). They sang psalms for temple worship (Pss 68:25; 87:7). Some were appointed "chief singers" (Hb 3:19). The sons of Asaph were prominent

among them. Some singers, male and female, were involved in secular entertainment. (Eccl 2:8).

See MUSIC AND MUSICAL INSTRUMENTS; SINGERS IN THE TEMPLE.

Slave. *See* SLAVE, SLAVERY.

Smith. An artisan who worked in metals. The earliest metal worker mentioned in the Bible is Tubal-cain (Gn 4:22). The term covers metal workers of all kinds: copper, bronze, iron, silver, and gold. Silversmiths are mentioned in Judges 17:4 and Acts 19:24. Iron-smiths were rare or even nonexistent in Israel up to the time of Samuel, and the Israelites had to go to the Philistine smiths to have their iron tools sharpened (1 Sm 13:19). In the days of the kings, Israelite smiths were active and were subsequently taken into captivity by Nebuchadnezzar (2 Kgs 24:14,16; Jer 24:1; 29:2). Details of the work of the smith are given in several accounts (Prv 25:4; Is 44:12; 54:16). The smiths in Zechariah 1:20 are probably ironsmiths (KJV carpenters).

See INDUSTRY AND COMMERCE; MINERALS, METALS, AND PRECIOUS STONES.

Soldier. The soldier was the individual unit in every army, whether a member of the infantry, cavalry, or part of the group engaged in siege warfare. There are only a few references to soldier as such in the OT but many references to army, whether of Israel or its enemies (Ex 14:9; Dt 11:4; 1 Sm 17:1; 28:1; 29:1; 1 Kgs 20:19,25; 2 Kgs 25:5,10,23–26; 1 Chr 11:26; 2 Chr 13:3; Neh 2:9; Is 36:2; 43:17; Jer 32:2; 34:1,7,21; Ez 17:17; 27:10,11; 38:4,15, etc.). Individual military units are also mentioned—the armor bearer (Jgs 9:54; 1 Sm 14:7,14,17; 16:21), the shield carrier (1 Sm 17:7,41), slingers (2 Kgs 3:25; Zec 9:15), spearmen (Acts 23:23), and swordsmen (2 Kgs 3:26). Sometimes soldiers are called "warriors" (1 Kgs 12:21; 2 Chr 11:1; Is 9:5). The soldiers of the Egyptians, Canaanites, Syrians, Assyrians, Babylonians, Persians, Greeks, and Romans all operated in Israelite territory at various times. The Roman army was well-known in Jesus' day. Roman soldiers crucified Jesus (Mt 27:27–37; Mk 15:16–25; Lk 23:33; Jn 19:16–18,23,24,32,34). Officers of the army, like centurions, encountered Jesus and the early Christians (Mt 8:5–13; Lk 7:1–10). Paul had extended contact with Roman soldiers (Acts 10:7; 12:4,6,18; 21:32,35; 23:23,31; 27:31,32,42; 28:16). For Paul, the equipment of a Roman soldier provided a picture of the Christian's armor (Eph 6:10–17). He referred to his friends Epaphroditus and Archippus as "fellow soldiers."

See ARMS AND WARFARE.

Spinner. Fibers were spun into yarn by women in all periods of Israel's history, but a class of professional spinners arose alongside them. Women spinners are mentioned in Exodus 35:25,26. Jesus spoke of the lilies of the field that did not need to spin (Mt 6:28; Lk 12:27). Among her other qualities the good wife of Proverbs 31 engaged in spinning (v 19).

See CLOTH, CLOTH MANUFACTURING.

Stonecutter. The stonecutter or stonemason removed stone from the quarry and squared it up for use in large buildings like palaces, the temple, administrative buildings, and large houses (1 Kgs 5:18; 2 Kgs 12:12; 1 Chr 22:2,15). At first the Israelites used Phoenician artisans, but soon learned the art and produced many fine buildings such as those in Samaria. Herod's masons left behind beautiful masonry in Jerusalem, Hebron, Samaria, and elsewhere. Some of these artisans produced fine work for the interior of buildings to be used in windows, doors, lintels, and capitals for pillars. One special class of stone cutters, the engravers (Ex 28:11), worked in precious stones to produce seals, ornamental pieces, and jewelry.

See ARCHITECTURE.

Tanner. The tanner converted hides and skins into leather by soaking them in lime and the leaves and juices of certain plants. Tanners lived outside the towns because of the foul smells produced from their vats. The tabernacle coverings were made from the skins of rams and goats (or perhaps sea cows). The leather was red in color either because of dye or as a result of the tanning process (Ex 25:5; 26:14; 35:7,23; 36:19; 39:34). The only biblical reference to a tanner is to Simon in Acts (9:43; 10:6,32). It was in his house that Peter had his vision of the great sheet filled with all manner of beasts and birds with the invitation to rise and eat (Acts 10:9–16).

See LEATHER.

Taskmaster. The taskmaster was an overseer of public works who enforced their performance. They are depicted on Egyptian bas-reliefs with whips in their hands to enforce discipline (Ex 1:11; 3:7; 5:6–14; Jb 3:18). The Hebrew verb means "to oppress." David and Solomon had such officers. Adoram was in charge of forced labor (2 Sm 20:24; 1 Kgs 4:6; 12:18; 2 Chr 10:18, KJV "tribute" means "forced labor"). The excesses of these men were a factor in the revolt of the northern tribes after the death of Solomon (1 Kgs 12:3–14). In the days of restoration Israel's taskmaster would be righteousness (Is 60:17).

Tax Collector. In NT times the Romans collected a variety of taxes. Their own officers undertook some of this work, but also delegated it to private individuals, Jews and others, who were required to return to the authorities an agreed sum. Dishonest individuals collected far more than they were required to

pay and became a hated group, especially the Jews among them. The Latin name *publicanus* gave rise to the name "publican." Zacchaeus, a Jew, was a "chief tax collector" who amassed considerable wealth in the Jericho area (Lk 19:2–10). Such men were regarded as sinners and were often linked in the phrase "tax collectors and sinners" (Mt 9:10,11; 11:19; Mk 2:15,16; Lk 5:30; 19:2–10).

See TAX, TAXATION.

Teacher. A teacher conserved the values and academia of a nation and passed them on to each new generation. In OT times the first teachers were often parents (Dt 6:7,20–25; 11:19–21). Leaders like Moses and Aaron were charged with teaching the people (Lv 10:11), and later, the priests and Levites had a teaching function (Dt 24:8; 33:8–10; 2 Chr 17:7–9; Ez 44:23; Mi 3:11). God himself was thought of as a teacher (Pss 25:8,12; 27:11; 32:8; 86:11; Is 2:3).

In the NT the Greek noun for "teacher" and verb "to teach" are widely used. John the Baptist was called a teacher (Lk 3:12). The term is used more than 30 times of Jesus (Mt 4:23; 5:2; 7:29; 9:35; 11:1; Mk 1:21; 2:13; 4:1,2; 6:2,6,34; Lk 4:15,31; 5:3; 6:6; Jn 6:59; 7:14,28, etc.). People recognized his teaching as authoritative (Mt 7:29; Mk 1:22; Lk 4:32). Even as a boy of 12 he met the teachers (KJV doctors) of the Law in the temple (Lk 2:46). These men were often associated with the Pharisees (Lk 5:17). Gamaliel was a Pharisee and a teacher of the Law (Acts 5:34). The term *rabbi* was often used to denote teacher. The rabbi was held in great honor. In the early church the teacher was widely recognized (Acts 13:1; 1 Cor 12:28,29; Eph 4:11; 2 Tm 1:11; Jas 3:1).

See GAMALIEL #2; PHARISEES; RABBI.

Tentmaker. These artisans made tents from a felted cloth of woven goats' hair. The Greek term for tentmaker may have served to denote a range of activities in cloth and leather. The single biblical reference (Acts 18:3) is to Claudius and Priscilla of Corinth who worked this trade. Paul joined them because he was trained in the same craft. He regularly earned his living at this trade during his missionary journeys (2 Cor 11:7–10; 1 Thes 2:9; 2 Thes 3:8).

See HOMES AND DWELLINGS.

Town Clerk. An official in the municipal administration, probably a secretary of the city. He published the decrees of the civic authority and acted as a liaison officer between the administration and the Roman provincial government. In Ephesus he was held responsible for the riotous assembly in Paul's day (Acts 19:35). He had the power to impose a severe penalty. Fortunately he was able to calm the assembly.

Treasurer. An officer in charge of financial matters. In OT times he had charge of the royal or sacred treasures which consisted of goods, documents, money, and jewels. He was steward of the king's possessions and overseer of the treasury. David appointed Azamaveth over the king's treasuries, Jonathan over the treasuries in cities and villages (1 Chr 27:25), and Ahijah over the temple treasuries (1 Chr 26:20). Solomon appointed Jehiel over the temple treasury (1 Chr 29:7,8). In Isaiah's day there was a steward over the household named Shebna (Is 22:15, KJV treasurer). An inscription found near Jerusalem may record his name.

Treasurers held positions in other lands too. Cyrus the Persian ruler entrusted the temple treasures to Mithredath (Ezr 1:8). Artaxerxes ordered the treasures of the province "Beyond the river" to supply funds to Ezra the priest (Ezr 7:21,22). Nehemiah appointed treasurers over the storehouses to distribute goods (Neh 12:44; 13:13).

In the NT, two treasurers are known. The Ethiopian eunuch was in charge of the treasury of Candace queen of Ethiopia (Acts 8:27), and Erastus was the city treasurer of Corinth (Rom 16:23; KJV chamberlain). An inscription left at Corinth by Erastus, a Roman treasurer, may be his.

See MONEY AND BANKING.

Watchman. Military or civil security person who had the responsibility to protect ancient towns or military installations from surprise attack or civil disasters (1 Sm 14:16; 2 Sm 18:24–27; 2 Kgs 9:17–20; Is 21:6–9). Watchmen also had the responsibility of announcing the dawning of a new day (Ps 130:6; Is 21:11,12). In a significant passage describing the function and responsibilities of the prophets, Ezekiel reports the watchman's parallel responsibility to warn of impending danger. If the watchman (or prophet) failed in his task the blood of the people would be on his head (Ez 33:2–9; cf. Ez 3:17; Jer 6:17; Hos 9:8). In contrast to the faithful prophets, Isaiah compares the leaders of Israel to blind watchmen who lacked the ability to even see Israel's danger, much less lead the people to repentance (Is 56:10; Mi 7:4). The prophets who served as Israel's watchmen were the ones who first saw the coming destruction of Israel and also the ones who first announced their return to the land (Is 21:11,12; 52:8).

Writer. The writer or professional scribe undertook a wide range of writing tasks in Israel and elsewhere. Often the scribe sat at the gate of the city or in an open area undertaking numerous kinds of writing tasks for illiterate citizens, correspondence, writing of receipts and contracts. More officially, he kept records and wrote annals. Religious scribes copied the Scriptures. Several of these men are mentioned in the OT, Shebna (2 Kgs 18:18,37), Shaphan (2 Kgs 22:8,10,12), Ezra (Ezr 7:6,11; Neh 8:1,9,13; 12:26,36), Baruch (Jer 36:26,32), and Jonathan (Jer 37:15,20). Many of the scribes exercised considerable influence.

In Jesus' day the scribes were highly trained in the art of writing and also in the Law. Jesus and the disciples had many contacts with them and their associates, the priests and Pharisees (Mt 2:4; 5:20; 7:29; 8:19; 9:3; 12:38; Mk 1:22; 2:6,16; 3:22; 7:1,5; 11:18; Lk 5:21,30; 6:7; 9:22; 11:53; Jn 8:3; Acts 4:5; 6:12; 23:9).

Paul made use of a scribe or amanuensis, but added his own name and final comments (Rom 15:15; 16:22; Gal 6:11; Phlm 19). John wrote to Christians (1 Jn 1:4; 2:1,7,8,12–14; 2 Jn 12; 3 Jn 9,13). The superscription over Jesus on the cross would have been written by a scribe (Jn 19:19). Scribes wrote on leather, papyrus, or on a writing table made of wax set in a wooden frame (Lk 1:63). JOHN A. THOMPSON

See SCRIBE; WRITING AND BOOKS.

Bibliography. A.C. Bouquet, *Everyday Life in NT Times* and *Everyday Life in OT Times;* M.P. Charlsworth, *Trade Routes and Commerce of the Roman Empire;* A. Edersheim, *Sketches of Jewish Social Life,* pp 182–212; M. Rostovtzeff, *The Social and Economic History of the Roman Empire;* A. van Deursen, *Illustrated Dictionary of Bible Manners and Customs.*

Tradition.

Respect for oral tradition was particularly strong among Jews during the period at the beginning of the Christian era. Among these traditions the most important collection was *Pirke Aboth* (traditions of the fathers). This consisted of comments by famous rabbis in explanation of the written law. This and a growing collection of other rabbinic traditions interpreting the Law became an authoritative commentary on the written code. This movement rapidly led to a position in which the oral law and the written code were virtually of equal standing. The Pharisees used the expression "tradition of the elders" (Mt 15:2; Mk 7:5), but Jesus in his response referred to the "traditions of men," thus drawing attention to their human origin. In fact, in Mark 7:8, he definitely set the commandment of God over these traditions.

The oral traditions developed in an attempt to prevent unwitting infringements of the Law of Moses but they had become a burden and tended to obscure rather than illuminate the written code. Jesus strongly criticized the scribes and Pharisees for the way these traditions were enforced (Mt 23). He noted that adherence to the tradition had become more important than the moral and personal effect of the teaching. The tradition of the elders had become merely an external set of rules, whereas Jesus was concerned about the motives which prompted men to observe the Law.

When Paul mentions his own zeal for "the traditions of my fathers" (Gal 1:14) before he became a Christian, he was no doubt thinking of his devotion to the oral tradition. Part of the wrong teaching he had to deal with at Colossae seems to have been connected with these same Jewish traditions (Col 2:8).

See PHARISEES; JUDAISM; LAW, BIBLICAL CONCEPT OF; TALMUD; TRADITION, ORAL; TRADITION CRITICISM.

Tradition, Oral. Oral tradition is both sharply distinguished from written tradition and yet closely connected with it. Many literary traditions are based on oral traditions, making it necessary to investigate how transitions were made from one to the other.

In the ancient Near East, all significant events were committed to writing by the scribes. At the same time, an oral version of the occurrences would enable the information to be disseminated in contemporary society, and perhaps also to subsequent generations. It is important to realize the coexistence of written and oral forms of the same material, so that the way in which material was transmitted will be understood properly.

Oral transmission was very important in Judaism, and one of the strongest characteristics of rabbinic theology is the importance attached to the oral law in addition to the written law. This oral law consisted of traditional interpretations which had been handed down from teacher to pupil. In the course of the passing on of the tradition, further explanations of basic principles were added. Rabbinic literature supplies many indications of the careful methods which were used in the schools for the study of the Law. The teacher's main aim was to ensure that the disciples accurately memorized the content of the teaching. There is no doubt that in rabbinic Judaism the passing on of the oral tradition had developed into a highly organized technique.

Such care is not surprising in view of the fact that the oral law carried equal weight with the written law. It was essential that the transmission of this tradition should not be left to chance. Authorized oral tradition was an essential feature of Jewish life. Yet in spite of its aim to explain the Law and preserve its true meaning, the oral law had frequently become a burden and as such was condemned by Jesus (Mt 15:3,6; Mk 7:8,9). He criticized those who attached more importance to the tradition of the elders than to the Law of God.

There are no parallels to the strong Jewish emphasis on oral tradition in the Hellenistic world, which had a more extensive literary tradition. Nevertheless, there were secret traditions which were at first orally transmitted, as for instance in the mystery religions. A similar appeal to secret oral traditions also occurs in Gnosticism, but much of this teaching soon found its way into documents attributed to apostles from whom the teaching was supposed to have been derived.

In the attempt to explain how the traditions about Jesus were preserved, there have been two major appeals to oral tradition. During the 19th century one of the earliest suggestions was the view that each of the Gospel writers drew his material from what was called the "oral gospel." There were several variations of this theory, but as the view that Matthew and Luke both used Mark and another source is preferred.

More recent studies have seen a revival of interest in the oral tradition. Form criticism has attempted to find out the forms in which the oral tradition was transmitted. The passing on of the material was possibly governed by laws of tradition. The most important of these may be the law of dissimilarity, in which only traditions which cannot be paralleled in Jewish literature or in early Christian teaching are considered genuine. The result has been a skeptical attitude toward the historical accuracy of the Gospels. But oral tradition cannot be readily reduced to laws, especially when the subject matter is the teaching of one who is unique. Yet in spite of the unsatisfactory nature of much form criticism, it has once again drawn attention to the importance of oral tradition and lessened reliance on source criticism.

There is little doubt that in the earliest period the words and works of Jesus were passed on by word of mouth. Whether Jesus himself followed the rabbinic teaching method is doubtful, but as much care went into preserving his teaching as the rabbis used in preserving their oral law.

See BIBLICAL CRITICISM, OLD TESTAMENT; BIBLICAL CRITICISM, NEW TESTAMENT; TRADITION; JUDAISM; PHARISEES; TALMUD; TRADITION CRITICISM; FORM CRITICISM.

Tradition Criticism. Biblical discipline also called "History of Tradition." This is a system for analyzing and distinguishing the traditions behind the biblical accounts and for determining the stages by which they developed to their final recorded form. The method evolved from the study of ancient folk literature and assumed that the biblical accounts also passed through similar periods of oral tradition to written form. Redaction criticism and tradition criticism complement each other in delineating the two foci of form criticism, the latter dealing with the development of the individual traditions and the former with the use of the traditions within the whole work.

General Presuppositions. The basic tenet of this school is that the historical narratives of the Bible took the form of "folk" stories and that the earliest stage of a folk story was distinguished by simplicity, that is, it tended to "float" in a basic form characterized by a simple plot and a minimum of characters. As the story was retold, details were then added to fit the needs of the audience. When it was recorded in the biblical account, it had passed through many stages. These can be determined by studying and classifying the literary forms themselves.

A second presupposition is that the complexity of the stories provides a key for denoting the stages through which it had passed. The stories are classified and their structures analyzed in order to discover recurring themes and to determine the original settings within which these themes were added to the stories.

Third, the various biblical stories may have followed the same process of development. Therefore, parallel themes point to the same original situation in the life of Israel or the early church.

Finally, dogmatic considerations are possibly the key to the original development of a tradition. Many assert that the deuteronomic corpus (Deuteronomy, Joshua–Judges, Samuel–Kings) originated in the 7th century, when the reform of Judah's King Josiah led to the centralization of worship, a new adherence to the covenant, and a resurgent nationalism. Also, stories like the miraculous catch of fish in Luke 5:1–11 are placed in a post-resurrection setting (note the parallel with Jn 21:1–8) and are seen to originate in the later church desire to see Jesus as a wonder-worker and divine man.

These presuppositions must be challenged. Tradition study has been unable to account for the presence of both simple and complex stories in the Gospels and OT historical books. Some seemingly went through a long process of adaptation (e.g., the temptation narratives) while others appear virtually untouched (e.g., the scene with Jesus' mother and brothers, Mk 3:31–35). The usual answer is that the simple story appeared late and did not have time to develop, but this is often circular reasoning. Also, dogmatic grounds are not a key to chronology. Many scholars have noted that the theology of Deuteronomy does not really show development from the Mosaic order seen in the

rest of the Pentateuch. Moreover, the high christology of a hymn like Philippians 2:6–11 is couched in such strong Semitic language that many believe it stems from the earliest Palestinian period. Tradition studies have tended to illustrate the preconceptions of the scholars rather than the original traditions themselves. Finally, the limitations of tradition criticism are most obvious in a tightly structured narrative like the Joseph chronicles or the passion narrative in which it is almost impossible to observe "stages" of development. The story itself seems a unified whole "composed" on a single occasion.

Methodology. A positive use of critical criteria to establish rather than deny authenticity and to illuminate the forms rather than strip them of traditional elements can sometimes be very helpful. With this in mind there are several positive criteria which enable the historian not only to evaluate but also to trace the development of traditions in the Bible. The following discussion covers these criteria in descending order, from the criterion which shows the greatest probability to the one which demonstrates tradition but cannot trace it back to its origin.

Statements or passages which are not characteristic of either Judaism or the later church may be regarded as authentic. Noting the limitations of this criterion, it still yields the most certain results with regard to critical questions. For example the "Amen" formula in Jesus' sayings and his "kingdom" teaching in the Synoptics cannot truly be paralleled in either branch. In OT tradition study, this criterion is more complex due to the multiplicity of periods involved. In fact, most today would point to a chain of traditions in the deuteronomic writings. The boundary descriptions in Joshua 13–19 are recognized as going back at least in part to Joshua's time.

Features which could not survive in the early church or OT setting unless they were genuine are also authentic. Sayings foreign to the intentions of the evangelists or early church fit into this category. Mark's emphasis on the obtuseness of the disciples and the fact that Jesus' relatives thought him insane (3:21) are examples, as well as Jesus' ignorance of the time of the eschaton (Mk 13:32). These seemingly cast Jesus and the disciples in an unfavorable light and, in fact, were excised by the other evangelists.

"Unintentional" signs of history, that is, those which would not appear as such to the author but clearly belong to the original setting, point to a high probability of authenticity. The difficulty comes in distinguishing "intentional" from "unintentional." Mark's details are a case in point. To some they point to an eyewitness account but to others are due to a master storyteller who adds details to strengthen the realism.

If there is no satisfactory setting for an episode in the life of the church or Israel, it may go back to the earliest period. For instance, the covenant structure of Deuteronomy fits the suzerainty treaty form from the Hittites of the 2nd millennium BC rather than the treaty formulae of the 7th century BC. Moreover, the absence of any reference to a king and the presence of the central shrine at Shechem rather than Jerusalem do not fit the situation of Josiah's day and point to the earlier period. One difficulty here is that periods tend to overlap, and it becomes difficult to isolate one particular setting. For instance, nonevangelicals have commonly attributed the Great Commission of Matthew 28:16–20 to the later gentile period, but there is no reason to deny that it would fit the proselyte theology within Judaism and probably stemmed from Jesus himself.

If the language and emphases are not characteristic of the author, it is a traditional passage. For example the so-called "hymns" of the NT (e.g., Phil 2:6–11; Col 1:15–20; 1 Tm 3:16) go far beyond their respective contexts both in language and theological themes and therefore stem from an earlier time. This criterion also helps to answer theories regarding a three-stage development of the Book of Jeremiah, from Jeremiah's original prophecies to additions by Baruch and finally by a deuteronomic editor.

Aramaic or Palestinian features may indicate an early origin. The problem is that the writer may well be following the language of the Septuagint rather than using tradition. Nevertheless, Semitic idiom, like Hebraic poetry, parallelism, and phrases, points to an early origin. For example, the "Maranatha" statement of 1 Corinthians 16:22 is Aramaic and may well be one of the earliest prayers in the NT.

Features which occur in more than one independent tradition (e.g., Mark and John) may be trustworthy. Of course, the difficulty is knowing which passages show dependence. For instance, the mission statements of Luke 24:44–49 and John 20:19–23 may be independent, but many believe that John knew Luke, especially in the passion narratives.

If an episode or saying is coherent with other authentic traditions on the basis of different criteria, it is probably also trustworthy. This cannot be a major test, since it depends on the accuracy of the other criteria. However, it can be useful, as in probing the synoptic "Son of man" sayings, which contain elements shown authentic in other passages and therefore are probably themselves authentic.

Conclusion. The judicious use of these criteria should aid the scholar in making historical decisions. Nevertheless, caution should be exerted when making value judgments. The criteria can do no more than show probability, but there is a strong basis for optimism in appraising the biblical documents. Two biblical controls are necessary for the use of the criteria.

First, the interpretation of the biblical authors must be based on the original words of the historical figure. For instance, the sayings of Jesus in John must be understood in light of 14:26, "The Holy Spirit . . . will bring to your remembrance of all that I have said to you." This was an internal control which John placed on himself. Second, there was no wholesale creation of stories in the early church. Luke's prologue (1:1–4) stresses the accuracy of his historical presentation and shows that he followed closely "the eyewitnesses and ministers of the word." GRANT R. OSBORNE

See BIBLICAL CRITICISM, NEW TESTAMENT; BIBLICAL CRITICISM, OLD TESTAMENT; DEMYTHOLOGIZATION; DOCUMENTARY HYPOTHESIS; FORM CRITICISM; MARKAN HYPOTHESIS; REDACTION CRITICISM; SOURCE CRITICISM; SYNOPTIC GOSPELS; TRADITION; TRADITION, ORAL.

Transfiguration. Event in Jesus' earthly ministry described in four passages in the NT (Mt 17:1–8; Mk 9:2–8; Lk 9:28–36; 2 Pt 1:16–18). According to Mark 9:2 and Matthew 17:1 the transfiguration took place "six days" after the confession of Peter at Caesarea Philippi, whereas in Luke 9:28 the temporal designation is "about eight days after." Quite possibly this difference is due to Matthew and Mark figuring the time exclusively and Luke having figured the time inclusively. The close temporal designation between these two events indicates not merely that the transfiguration and Peter's confession at Caesarea Philippi are associated together in time but also in meaning, for the transfiguration must be understood in the light of the events of Caesarea Philippi.

The Location of the Event. The exact site where the transfiguration took place is not given in the NT. Matthew 17:1 and Mark 9:2 simply state that it took place on a "high mountain." Various suggestions have been made as to which mountain, with the traditional site being Mt Tabor, a round hill located in the Plain of Esdraelon approximately 10 miles southwest of the Sea of Galilee. There are, however, two major problems with this suggested location. For one it is difficult to see how Mt Tabor can justifiably be called a "high mountain," for it is less than 2000 feet above sea level. Secondly, in the time of Jesus a Roman garrison was stationed on Mt Tabor, and thus it would be unlikely that Jesus would

Mt Tabor, the traditional site of the transfiguration.

and visionary but objective and historical. Furthermore, the temporal designation and especially Peter's words in the account clearly indicate that the event was historical.

According to the Gospel accounts, three things took place at the transfiguration.

"He was transfigured." The various accounts all witness to an unusual transformation of Jesus which took place. Jesus is transfigured; "his face shone like the sun, and his garments became white as light" (Mt 17:2); This transformation is described in Matthew and Mark by the verb *metamorpheō*, the root for the word "metamorphosis." This transformation furthermore involved not only the garments of Jesus but his very person.

Moses and Elijah appear and speak to Jesus. These men, who undoubtedly represent the Law and the Prophets, are said in Luke 9:31 to have spoken to Jesus of his "exodus" or departure. The term used in Luke 9:31 to describe Jesus' "exodus" or death is rather unusual and clearly sees the death of Jesus not as a tragedy or defeat but as a victorious event.

After Peter's remark that it was good for the three disciples to be present and witness this and his suggestion that they build three booths—one for Moses, one for Elijah, and one for Jesus—a voice comes from heaven which says, "This is my beloved Son; listen to him" (Mk 9:7). These words are clearly a rebuke. The first part is a rebuke not so much of an attempt by Peter to prolong this experience by making booths but rather of his placing Jesus on the same level as Moses and Elijah. To make three booths (one for Moses, one for Elijah, and one for Jesus) loses sight of who Jesus is, and the voice from heaven points out Peter's error. "This is my beloved Son!" As the writer of Hebrews 3:5,6 points out, "Now Moses was faithful in all God's house as a servant ... but Christ was faithful over God's house as a son." The voice from heaven points out this difference. The second part of this rebuke must be understood in the light of what Peter had said at Caesarea Philippi.

The Meaning of the Event. In order to understand the significance of the transfiguration it is important to contrast the voice which appears at the transfiguration with the voice which appears at the baptism. At the baptism both Mark 1:11 and Luke 3:22 indicate that the voice was addressed to Jesus: "Thou art my beloved Son." At the transfiguration, however, the voice is not addressed to Jesus but to Peter, James, and John: "This is my beloved Son" (Mk 9:7). Clearly the events of the transfiguration account are primarily directed toward the disciples rather than Jesus. "He was transfigured before them" (Mk 9:2); "And there appeared to them Elijah with

have walked with his disciples up this mountain. A second suggestion for the site is Mt Carmel, which is located on the coast, but this seems off the main route of Jesus' travel after the events of Caesarea Philippi. A third suggestion is Mt Hermon, which is over 9000 feet high and lies about 12 miles to the northeast of Caesarea Philippi. Mt Hermon is indeed a "high mountain" and has the additional advantage of being located near Caesarea Philippi. However, the early church and the writers of the Gospels were not oriented toward matters of precise historical detail. For them it was not important to know exactly where this event took place. What was important was the fact that a significant event took place.

The Event. Six days after the events of Caesarea Philippi, Jesus took Peter, James, and John to be alone with him on a high mountain. As in several other instances, these three disciples alone accompanied Jesus (cf. also Mk 5:35–43; 14:32–42). It has been suggested that what took place on the mountain was not so much an actual transformation of Jesus as a subjective vision on the part of the three disciples. In fact in Matthew 17:9 the incident is referred to as a "vision." Yet, a vision can refer to what is actually seen. In Deuteronomy 28:34,67, the Septuagint uses this very term to refer to "the sight which your eyes shall see," and the events referred to are not subjective

Moses" (Mk 9:4); "And a cloud overshadowed them . . . 'listen [you] to him'" (Mk 9:7); "And . . . they no longer saw any one with them but Jesus only" (Mk 9:8). Evidently from these references, the incident is not meant so much for Jesus' sake as for the disciples'. Coming so close after the events of Caesarea Philippi, God appears to affirm at the transfiguration what Peter has confessed at Caesarea Philippi. Jesus is indeed the Christ, the Son of God. This is revealed to the disciples by the transfiguration itself as well as the voice from heaven.

In 2 Peter 1:16–18 the writer associates the glory of Jesus at the transfiguration with the future glory of Christ at his second coming, (see esp. v 16). The transfiguration, at least according to 2 Peter 1:16–18, was an anticipatory glimpse of the future glory that Jesus would possess when he came as the Son of man "on the clouds of heaven with power and great glory" (Mt 24:30). On the other hand, some scholars have interpreted the transfiguration in the light of John 1:14 ("we have beheld his glory") and believe that this passage is an actual reference to the transfiguration. The transfiguration is interpreted according to this view as an instance in which the true form (*morphe*) of the Son of God temporally broke through the veil of his humanity and the disciples saw his preexistent glory. It may be wisest, however, to interpret the transfiguration from both of these perspectives. In this transformation of Jesus the three disciples witnessed something of both the preincarnate glory which the Son of God left behind at his incarnation as well as his future glory which he received at his resurrection and which all will see when he returns to judge the world. In this respect Philippians 2:6–11 may be a helpful commentary. In the transfiguration the disciples then saw for a moment the glory of him "who, though he was in the form of God . . . emptied himself" (Phil 2:6,7) as well as the glory of him whom "God has highly exalted . . . and bestowed . . . the name . . . above every name" (Phil 2:9).

The voice from heaven, "This is my beloved Son," rebuked Peter's words on the mountain. The second statement of the voice from heaven is also a rebuke. At Caesarea Philippi Peter received a rebuke for rejecting Jesus' words about his future death. It was inconceivable for him that the Messiah should die. As a result, Jesus rebuked Peter with the words "Get behind me, Satan!" (Mk 8:33). The voice from heaven at the transfiguration also rebukes Peter over this matter when he says, "listen to him." Since Jesus had not spoken on the mount of transfiguration, what the disciples are to listen to and heed must have previously

happened. This event, according to the chronological designation with which each of the synoptic accounts begins, is the confession of Peter at Caesarea Philippi and Jesus' subsequent rebuke. What the voice is saying to the disciples is that they are to listen to what the Son had said six days previous at Caesarea Philippi when he "began to teach them that the Son of man . . . must be killed, and after three days rise again" (Mk 8:31). At the transfiguration the voice affirms to Peter, James, and John, but especially to Peter, that Jesus' teaching concerning the necessity of his dying was indeed correct.

The Transfiguration as a Resurrection Account. There have been a number of scholars during the last century who have argued that the transfiguration was originally a resurrection account that was accidentally or intentionally read back into the ministry of Jesus. Usually Mark is the one suggested as having done this. Generally the arguments raised in support of this theory involve such issues as the vocabulary and the form of the account. Words such as "appeared," Mark 9:4, are frequently, but not always, associated with the resurrection. Other words such as "cloud," Mark 9:7, "high mountain," Mark 9:2, and "glory," Luke 9:32, are often associated with the risen Christ (cf. Acts 1:9; Mk 9:2; Mt 28:16, respectively). The transfiguration is supposedly more like a resurrection account than a story about the life of Jesus, the presence of Elijah and Moses is reminiscent of the angelic presence at the resurrection. Upon closer examination, however, it becomes quite clear that for several reasons the transfiguration could never have been a resurrection account. If this were a resurrection account Jesus would be referred to as "Lord" instead of "rabbi" (Mk 9:5), Jesus' appropriate address during his ministry. Second, a transformation such as the transfiguration might fit well in a resurrection context, but the loss of this "glory" is unexplainable in the case of the risen Lord. Such a temporary transformation fits into the ministry of Jesus. Another argument against this view is the reference to Peter, James, and John. On several occasions they were together with Jesus during his ministry (Mk 5:35–43; 14:32–42; cf. 1:16–20,29; 13:3), but never are the three involved in a resurrection appearance by themselves (cf. 1 Cor 15:3–8). Some scholars have therefore rewritten the transfiguration to omit James and John. Two final arguments against the view that the transfiguration was originally a resurrection account can be mentioned. One is that Matthew, Luke, and 2 Peter all agree that the transfiguration took place during the ministry of Jesus, which corroborates the Mark account. Finally, it is difficult to assume that Peter's error in equating Jesus with Moses and Elijah by suggesting the building of three booths could have taken place in a resurrection context, for he could not have mistaken the risen Lord as an equal of Moses and Elijah (Mk 9:5). In the ministry of Jesus this would be possible but not after the resurrection. All the evidence therefore clearly indicates that the transfiguration account was always understood as an event which took place in the life of Jesus and which furthermore was intimately connected to the events of Caesarea Philippi. ROBERT H. STEIN

See JESUS CHRIST, LIFE AND TEACHING OF.

Transgression. See SIN.

Transjordan. Territory on the east side of the Jordan River. Although this name does not appear in the Bible, numerous events took place there in biblical history. Today the area is roughly equivalent to the kingdom of Jordan. In biblical times the area would have comprised Bashan, Gilead, Ammon, Moab, Edom, and the desert regions further east. The expression "beyond the Jordan" is often used for the area (Gn 50:10,11; Dt 3:20; 4:47; Jos 9:10; 13:8; 18:7; Jgs 5:17), although the same expression is used occasionally for the area west of Jordan (Dt 3:25).

Geography. Transjordan is a relatively high plateau cut across by numerous wadis. Four major wadis divide the region: the Wadi Yarmuk which enters the Jordan just south of

A series of waterfalls near the Yarmuk River in Transjordan.

Galilee, the River Jabbok just over halfway between Galilee and the Dead Sea, the River Arnon which enters the Dead Sea about halfway down the east side, and the Brook Zered which enters the Dead Sea at its southern end. In antiquity these four territories comprised four small kingdoms. The region of Bashan lay north of the Wadi Yarmuk. Gilead occupied the central area between Galilee and the Dead Sea and was once the home of the Amorite kings Sihon and Og (Nm 21:21–26,33–35). The River Jabbok probably divided these two kingdoms. The kingdom of Ammon lay to the east of the southern arm of the Jabbok. Further south lay Moab as far south as the Brook Zered. It was divided by the River Arnon. South of the Brook Zered lay Edom. Gilead, Ammon, and Moab contain mountainous areas rising from 3000 to 4000 feet. Edom is situated on a high tableland reaching 5000 feet or more above sea level. A significant trade route ran throughout the area from the Red Sea to Damascus, known as the King's Highway (Nm 21:22; cf. Nm 20:19; Dt 2:27); the same highway seems to be implied in Genesis 14:5–12.

History. Human occupation in Transjordan began in the Paleolithic Age before 8000 BC and flourished until the Early Bronze Age (3000–2100 BC) when it came to an abrupt end. With the coming of the Late Bronze Age (1500–1200 BC) settlement began to increase, and by the Iron I Age (1200–1000 BC) small kingdoms emerged (Ammon, Moab, and Edom). The Israelites migrating from Egypt bypassed Edom and Moab but dispossessed the Amorite kings Sihon and Og (Nm 21) about 1250 BC. During the next four centuries Transjordan was subject to many invasions. Under David and Solomon, Israel ruled the whole area. After Solomon's death in about 930 BC the Syrians (Aramaeans) from Damascus encroached on the area, especially in the north, and many conflicts ensued. With the rise of Assyria, the whole region was either annexed or made tributary to Assyria. When Assyria fell Babylonians (604–539 BC) and Persians (539–332 BC) took control. Later, the Greeks settled colonists in the area of the Decapolis. Under the Maccabeans (164–37 BC) the northern areas came under Jewish rule. In NT times, these areas, known as Perea, were ruled by Herod Antipas and later by Agrippa I and Agrippa II until the end of the Jewish state in AD 73. Rome and Byzantium held sway from 63 BC until AD 636 when Moslems settled the area.

See PALESTINE.

Travel and Transportation.

Travel. In biblical times travelers found roads bad and often impassable. Sea voyages were made in comparatively small ships, usually by military and commercial personnel, and hardly ever for simple tourist traffic. With little reason to travel, ordinary citizens tended to remain in fairly limited areas. From time to time, there were group migrations, and sometimes people traveled for religious festivals or fled from war or famine.

Travel in OT Times. Several accounts depict the people of Israel moving over restricted areas to graze their flocks. Joseph's brothers took their flocks from the south of the land up to Shechem and then to Dothan (Gn 37:12–17)—but this was a mere 60 miles. David traveled around Palestine and even went to Moab (1 Sm 22:3). The Danites moved from their home southwest of Jerusalem to the north, just south of Mt Lebanon (Jgs 18). Examples of travel for pasturage, migration, and protection (but not normally for pleasure) could be multiplied. Such travelers would normally walk, though the ass was used both for riding and as a pack animal. The ox was employed for transporting heavy loads, but sometimes for people (Gn 46:5). Later the camel came into general use (1 Kgs 10:2; 2 Kgs 8:9).

In modern times travelers find rest and sustenance on their journey at hotels or motels, but little is known of resting places for travelers in OT times. The men of Gibeon who came to Joshua "from a very far country" brought their own provisions (Jos 9:9–13). There are references to an "inn" in the NT (Lk 2:7; 10:34); however, there are a few references to a "lodging place" (*malon*) in OT narratives (Gn 42:27; 43:21; Ex 4:24). But the roads were always indifferent in quality, and lodging places probably inadequate.

Ordinary people journeyed primarily on foot, even over long distances. There are, however, numerous references in the OT, to asses used to transport people. Balaam, the prophet from the Euphrates region, rode on an ass (Nm 22:21–33). Deborah addressed those who rode on asses (Jgs 5:10). The Shunammite woman rode on an ass to Elisha (2 Kgs 4:22–25). Abigail, wife of Nabal, rode on an ass to David (1 Sm 25:20,23,42). Shimei rode on an ass to recover his slaves (1 Kgs 2:40), and the old prophet of Bethel traveled by ass to call the man of God to his home (1 Kgs 13:13–32). These journeys and many others were very short.

Travel in NT Times. The advent of Roman peace and authority and the construction of well-made stone roads made travel relatively safe and quick. The modes of travel improved over that known in OT times. Long distances were traveled within the Roman Empire over good roads and in comparative safety. There were some hazards, notably in sea travel, from wind, storms, and pirates (Acts 15:39; 18:18–22; Rom 15:24,25; 2 Cor 11:25,26). Paul's journey to Rome was perilous indeed (Acts 27:1–28:14). But the NT mentions also a considerable number of journeys on foot. Mary journeyed from Galilee to Judea to visit Elizabeth (Lk 1:39,40,56). The baby Jesus was born in Bethlehem during the census (2:1–7). Jesus was brought to Jerusalem to comply with the Jewish purification law (v 22). Thus three trips were made from Nazareth to Jerusalem, a distance of about 70 miles, from the time of Jesus' conception to Mary's purification. The annual Passover visit was made by Joseph and Mary (vv 41–51). Other journeys are mentioned (Jn 2:13; 5:1; 7:1–14; 12:1). Jesus himself walked to Jericho from Galilee (Mk 1:1–11) and also to the region of Tyre and Sidon (7:24). He was in Samaria more than once (Lk 17:11; Jn 4:4). His last journey to Jerusalem was via Jericho and up through the hills to Jerusalem (Mk 10:1,46; 11:1). His last journey after the resurrection was to Emmaus (Lk 24:13–35).

Paul made many journeys on foot in Palestine, Asia Minor, and the Greek peninsula. He also went by sea on each of his missionary journeys (Acts 13:1–14:28; 15:41–18:22; 18:23–21:17), generally accompanied by friends. But not all travel was on foot in NT times. The ass, used for carrying loads, often carried people. Jesus once rode from Bethphage to Jerusalem, a short but highly symbolic journey (Mt 21:2,5,7; Mk 11:1–11; Jn 12:12–15). When Joseph traveled with his pregnant wife Mary to Bethlehem for the census at the time of Jesus' birth, Mary probably rode on an ass.

The Ethiopian eunuch was riding in a chariot after worshiping at Jerusalem and was joined by Philip traveling on foot (Acts 8:26–38).

Roman soldiers both marched and made wide use of horses. When Paul was brought to Caesarea from Jerusalem, mounts were prepared for him (Acts 23:23,24).

The Roman world knew a great deal of travel: to fulfill religious obligations at festival time, for trade, for government administration, for military purposes. Not the least among 1st-century wayfarers were the Christian evangelists.

Roads and Sea Lanes. The roads of biblical times figured prominently in the geography, topography, and history of Palestine—a land which served as a bridge between Egypt and centers of civilization and trade in the Middle East. Many of the roads were strategically important commercially and militarily. Some roads gained significance as pilgrim routes to facilitate travel to religious centers like Jerusalem. Roads in biblical times were of

three main types: long-distance international roads, medium distance intraregional roads, and a variety of roads inside each region or state.

Great International Roads. These linked the Mediterranean coast to the northern Tigris Valley and southern Mesopotamia. Some linked Mesopotamia to Asia Minor while others led south to Egypt, either along the coast, or east of the Jordan River and the Dead Sea and across the Sinai Peninsula. There were trade routes between Anatolia and Assyria early in the 2nd millennium BC. Apparently the military campaign referred to in Genesis 14 aimed to secure the great trade route, the King's Highway, from northern Mesopotamia to Egypt. Military invaders and travelers from Babylonia, Assyria, and Persia would head across the hinterlands of Syria toward the coast before turning south into Palestine and Egypt. The advent of European powers, Greece and Rome, into the Middle East opened up another vast network of international roads for the peoples of the East. Until Roman times these roads were not surfaced with stone but were cleared pathways. They were very rough, ungraded, and, in wet weather, impassable in many places. But they were evidently well defined by "waymarks" and "guideposts" (Jer 31:21). With the coming of the Romans, important roads were built with deep foundations and with large blocks of flat stone at the surface. The remains of these roads are still seen in many places in the Middle East and in Europe. Distance markers or milestones were regularly placed along the roads.

International North-South Roads in Palestine. The roads which linked countries to the north with Egypt passed through Palestine, a natural land-bridge. There were three major roads. The coastal road began in Damascus and passed via Hazor across the plain of Esdraelon, through the Megiddo pass, down the coast past Gaza and into Egypt. This was probably "the way of the sea" (Is 9:1). The Sinai road led from Egypt into the southern Negeb and then to Kadesh-barnea, Beersheba, Hebron, Jerusalem, Shechem to Acco, Tyre, and Sidon. The Red Sea road entered the Palestine area from the Gulf of Aqaba where the ancient port of Eloth and Solomon's port of Ezion-geber stood (Nm 33:35; 2 Chr 8:17). From there it led through the mountainous areas of Transjordan, crossing the deep wadis and then north through the Hauran region to Damascus. This was the road taken by caravans from southern Arabia to Damascus, the ancient King's Highway (Nm 20:17; 21:22).

There were other north-south roads of lesser importance. One coastal road led from

A Roman milestone.

pa to Shechem, across the Jordan at Adam (Jos 3:16) and into Gilead in Transjordan. Other roads led from Acco eastward to Galilee and also up the coast to Tyre and Sidon. There were, indeed, numerous east-west roads which provided contact between various parts of Palestine. In Roman times, when the speedy movement of armies was essential, some of the old roads were greatly improved and new ones built.

Sea Lanes. The people of Israel, unlike the Phoenicians, seldom used the sea lanes. When Solomon planned to send ships down the Red Sea to Ophir (1 Kgs 9:26–28), he used Phoenician seamen. Jehoshaphat planned a similar expedition but his ships were wrecked (1 Kgs 22:48,49). Coastal traffic in OT times was in the hands of Philistines and Phoenicians. There were several ports along the Mediterranean Sea coast such as Gaza, Joppa, Dor, and Acco, but none was very good. The story of Jonah tells of the departure of a ship from Joppa (Jon 1:3). But there were evidently well-known sea lanes linking the Mediterranean coast with Egypt and distant Tarshish, probably Spain.

The other coastal water was the Gulf of Aqaba with its two ports—Ezion-geber for Transjordan and Elath far west of the Jordan. Solomon's fleet used Ezion-geber as its home port.

In NT times things changed considerably. The Middle East produced commodities used by peoples further west, especially the Romans. Alexandria in Egypt and Antioch in Syria handled both cargo and travelers. Smaller ports like those in Palestine and many others round the coast of Asia Minor provided a haven for ships. One ingenious scheme to avoid a 200-mile journey round the Greek peninsula was to drag small boats across the five-mile wide isthmus at Corinth. Even the largest ship in NT times was in danger from wind and storm at sea (Acts 27), so that sea travel was undertaken preferably when the risk of storms was minimal, roughly from November to March. There was a lot of sea traffic in the

Joppa via Caesarea and Dor to Acco where it linked with the Sinai road. Evidently it was not very significant until Roman times, when the port of Caesarea was built. The marshes in the plain of Sharon posed many problems. The plain of Esdraelon was also marshy and interrupted the roads north in bad seasons. A raised road across the swampy sections was eventually constructed. Another road led north from Hazor, branching off the main trunk road to Damascus. The Jordan Valley road skirted the southwestern part of Galilee and led down the Jordan Valley to Jericho.

East-West Roads. Several important roads ran east-west, intersecting the bigger roads leading north. One such road led from Gaza to Beersheba and thence down the Arabah with an off-shoot to Petra. Another led from Ashkelon, via Gath to Hebron and on to En Gedi on the Dead Sea. Another road led from Joppa east up the Valley of Aijalon ("the way of the ascent to Beth-Horon," Jos 10:6–14) to Bethel and on to Jericho. A useful road led from Jop-

The docking area at Caesarea.

Mediterranean Sea at appropriate seasons, largely for trade. Grain ships crossed regularly from Rome to Egypt and to the east.

Ships were driven by sail power supplemented as necessary by oars operated by slaves. Some indication of the size of ships comes from the discovery of ancient wrecks and from Latin and Greek literature. An old dry dock 130 feet long found near Athens was once used for Greek war vessels which were smaller than the cargo vessels. The Roman writer Lucian refers to an Alexandrian grain ship 180 feet long, suggesting a capacity of about 1200 tons. Paul's ship carried 276 persons (Acts 27:37). Modern underwater archaeology is providing valuable information about these ancient ships.

Reasons for Travel. The most important reason for travel in NT times was for trade and commerce, which involved far more than merely transporting goods. There were agents, supervisors, insurers of cargoes, bankers, and a whole range of people involved in the acquisition and safe delivery of the cargo.

Military travel was considerable. A wide variety of tasks had to be undertaken in the way of reconnaissance, procuring of supplies, forward arrangements for the bivouacking of troops, and the transport of both troops and equipment.

Some travelers were tradesmen changing their place of employment, like Aquila and Priscilla (Acts 18:2). Aquila had traveled from Pontus on the Black Sea to Rome and then, in a time of persecution, he had fled to Corinth with his wife. He was a tentmaker and Paul, a fellow tentmaker, stayed with the couple (Acts 18:2). Many others traveled for similar reasons.

People on religious pilgrimage traveled by land or sea. Jews from many lands journeyed to Jerusalem for the annual Passover festival (Acts 2:5–11). Non-Jews went to religious centers at Ephesus, Athens, and Eleusis, where there were important temples. Many minor temples also attracted their quota of pilgrims. The construction of new temples and a variety of government administration buildings brought craftsmen from afar. Often the materials used in construction had to be transported to the site. Some people made trips for health reasons to temples famed for healing miracles or to enjoy the benefits of hot springs like Capernaum or Tiberias. Athletes traveled to centers for important contests like the Olympic games, and crowds of people flocked to witness the spectacle. Some travelers were students or teachers going to great centers of learning, the universities of those times. Yet others traveled as official emissaries bearing important government and commercial documents. Despite all this activity, vast numbers of ordinary citizens hardly ever moved more than a few miles from their homes.

Transportation. In the ancient Middle East both pack animals and vehicles carried loads. The ass or donkey caravan appeared very early in the history of the region. From 2000 to 1750 BC there was a considerable trade in western Asia between Anatolia and Assyria, between Mari on the Euphrates and states to the east and west of the Euphrates, and between western Asia and Egypt. Some of the donkey caravans were quite large, up to 500 animals, divided into smaller groups under the charge of individual attendants. After the 19th century BC the much stronger mules replaced donkeys, and by the 11th century BC camels replaced the mules. Documentary evidence verifies these caravans from Egypt and Assyria. One famous group of 37 Asiatics who visited Egypt about 1900 BC is portrayed on the tomb of Khnum-hotep at Beni-hasan. Genesis 37 mentions Ishmaelite caravan traders bearing gums, balm, and myrrh on their way to Egypt. They took Joseph as a slave and sold him in Egypt (Gn 37:25–28). Ass caravans are mentioned in Judges 5:6,10. The queen of Sheba visited Solomon with a great retinue and with camels bearing spices, gold, and precious stones. Such caravans carried the commodities of the Middle East throughout the biblical world.

Carts and wagons of various kinds were used for transport. Jacob and the family of Joseph came to Egypt in wagons sent by Joseph (Gn 45:19–27). The heavy items used in the tabernacle were carried by wagons (Nm 7:3–8). When the Philistines returned the ark to Israel, it was carried on a cart drawn by milk cows (1 Sm 6:7–18). David later carried the ark to Jerusalem on an ox cart (1 Chr 13:5–7). In the 8th century BC the ox cart carried loads of sheaves (Am 2:13). Egyptian paintings and Assyrian bas reliefs depict a variety of carts and wagons. One famous relief shows women and children in a cart being carried off by the Assyrians after the siege and capture of Lachish.

In NT times Greeks and Romans were using barges and wagons as well as asses, horses, and camels in the transport of heavy goods. Water transport remained significant outside Israel. In Assyria and Egypt, the great rivers were used to carry goods over considerable distances. Barges and boats tied up at quays after ferrying blocks of stone, timber, and other commodities. Boats also acted as a link in overland communications to ferry materials across rivers. At sea Greeks, Romans, Phoenicians, Egyptians, and others used their ships to transport grain, timber, and a host of other items. Ezekiel 27 gives some idea of the things the Phoenicians transported by sea and land. Other accounts of goods transported from one land to another are in 1 Kings 5:10,11 and 10:2,10–12,14,15. The list of ports of call for Phoenician mariners can be drawn from the Bible and from ancient writers.

The NT gives a few glimpses of the international traffic. Merchants prospered through cargoes drawn from many lands (Rv 18:11–13) and traveled the world in search of fine pearls (Mt 13:45). A few areas produced desirable items, like Thyatira, a center for "purple goods" (Acts 16:14). Classical writings relate that many items of interest to wealthy Romans were brought from distant lands like India, Arabia, and even China, by caravan. Among the items transported between countries were human beings, male and female slaves, who were marketed in the great cities of Greece and Rome.   JOHN A. THOMPSON

See TRADES AND OCCUPATIONS; INDUSTRY AND COMMERCE.

Bibliography. L. Casson, *Ships and Seamanship in the Ancient World* and *Travel in the Ancient World*; M.P. Charlsworth, *Trade Routes and Commerce of the Roman Empire*; A. Edersheim, *Sketches of Jewish Social Life*, pp 42–58; O.T. Mason, *Primitive Travel and Transportation*; J. Rougé, *Ships and Fleets of the Ancient Mediterranean*; C. Torr, *Ancient Ships*.

Treasurer. *See* TRADES AND OCCUPATIONS.

Tree. *See* PLANTS.

Tree of Knowledge of Good and Evil. Forbidden tree in Eden, whose fruit conferred knowledge but would entail death (Gn 2:9,15–17; 3:1–24). The tempting serpent promised equality with God if the fruit were eaten, insinuating that only divine jealousy prompted the prohibition. In the event, eating conferred sexual knowledge and shame, but not death. Banishment from Eden followed to prevent the eating of a second tree, "of life," which conferred immortality upon the disobedient.

The idea of attaining "knowledge of good and evil" recurs in Deuteronomy 1:39; Isaiah 7:15,16; and Hebrews 5:14, describing a stage in a child's passing from innocence to moral experience, which is also associated with sexual self-awareness. This suggests that the story came to symbolize the loss of innocence and divine companionship through deliberate disobedience in an attempt to attain godhood.

See TREE OF LIFE; ADAM (PERSON); EVE; GARDEN OF EDEN; FALL OF MAN.

Tree of Life. Tree placed by God in the midst of the garden of Eden (Gn 2:8,9). God told Adam that he could eat from every tree of the garden except the tree of the knowledge of

Apotheosis of Rameses II. He is seated on his throne while three gods (Amen-Ra-Tum, Safekh, and Tahut) inscribe his name on the fruits of the Tree of Life.

good and evil (vv 16,17). When Adam and Eve disobeyed God by eating from the tree of the knowledge of good and evil, they were expelled from the garden lest they "take also of the tree of life, and eat, and live for ever" (3:22).

The Genesis narrative suggests that God intended the tree of life to provide Adam and Eve with a sacramental symbol of life in fellowship with and dependence on him. Man's life, as distinguished from that of the animals, was much more than merely biological; it was also spiritual and found its deepest significance in fellowship with God. Life in the fullness of its physical and spiritual dimensions, however, could remain man's possession only so long as he remained obedient to God's command (Gn 2:17). It would seem unlikely that there was ever any intrinsic life-giving efficacy in the chemical properties of the fruit of the tree of life, but God made the fruit life-giving so far as he had sealed his grace to man in the use of it. When by disobedience man lost that which the tree of life signified, he also lost access to the symbol itself.

Apart from Genesis the only other OT occurrences of the phrase the "tree of life" are found in Proverbs where it symbolizes the enrichment of life in various ways. In Proverbs 3:18 wisdom is referred to as "a tree of life to those who lay hold of her"; in 11:30 "the fruit of the righteous is a tree of life"; in 13:12 a fulfilled desire is as "a tree of life"; and in 15:4 "a gentle tongue is a tree of life."

The Book of Revelation contains the only references to the tree of life in the NT (2:7; 22:2,14,19). The Bible begins and ends with a Paradise in the midst of which is a tree of life. The way to the tree of life which was closed in Genesis 3 is open again for God's believing people in Revelation. This has been made possible by the second Adam, Jesus Christ. Those who have washed their robes in the blood of Christ (cf. Rv 7:14), and have sought forgiveness of their sin through the redemptive work of Christ receive the right to the tree of life (22:14), but the disobedient will have no access to it.

See TREE OF KNOWLEDGE OF GOOD AND EVIL; ADAM (PERSON); EVE; GARDEN OF EDEN; FALL OF MAN.

Trespass. See SIN.

Trespass Offering. See OFFERINGS AND SACRIFICES.

Tribes, Territories of the. See CONQUEST AND ALLOTMENT OF THE LAND.

Tribulation. Word appearing some 45 times in the NT. It is variously translated in different versions of the Bible as tribulation, suffering, distress, affliction, trouble, or persecution. There exists a Hebrew equivalent that appears in four or five OT passages, never in the prophetic books. Therefore, it is appropriate to focus mainly on the NT for a definition of tribulation.

The NT contains a few references where the word "tribulation" is used to denote the hardships that occur in the lives of common mortals. The labor pains of a woman in childbirth (Jn 16:21), the worldly concerns that arise out of marriage in a world in crisis (1 Cor 7:28), and the affliction of widows (Jas 1:27) are all called "tribulation." In a more general way, a scourge like the famine that afflicted Egypt and Canaan during the patriarchal age is characterized as "great tribulation" (Acts 7:11).

In a more narrow sense, the word "tribulation" refers also to a specifically Christian experience. The teaching of Christ provides basic definitions for this meaning of "tribulation." Jesus established a strong association between the presence of the gospel in the world and the world's hostile response to it in the form of tribulation. Whenever the gospel is present in the world, tribulation becomes its unavoidable corollary. As the word of the gospel is sown, tribulation and persecution appear spontaneously (Mt 13:21).

This concept of the ineluctable presence of tribulation during the church age is carefully developed in Jesus' teaching on future events in the Olivet discourse (Mt 24,25; Mk 13; Lk 21). The teaching of Jesus provides the only explicit description of and clear chronological reference available in the Bible to the tribulation of his followers. In it, Jesus predicted the time of the beginning, the extent, and the end of tribulation. This teaching on the tribulation was handed down to the 12 disciples privately, as a matter directly relevant to their lives (Mt 24:3). Jesus told the 12 disciples that *they* would be delivered up to tribulation and that this tribulation would take the form of persecution to the death for his name's sake (v 9). The context of this teaching indicates that the tribulation taught by Jesus would affect Christians in many places throughout history. But the fact that Jesus predicted to the twelve that they would fall victim to the tribulation, at the very beginning of the sufferings (v 8), provides a clear reference to the starting point of the tribulation during the disciples lifetime.

Likewise, the same group of disciples were to be witnesses of the "great tribulation" that would befall Jerusalem as predicted by the prophet Daniel (vv 15–21). It is clear that, in the Olivet Discourse, Jesus was referring to the destruction of Jerusalem in AD 70. The fall of Jerusalem at the hands of the Roman legions was to be viewed as an archetypal representation of the perennial tribulation. This is attested by Matthew's parenthetical editorial comment in 24:15 ("let the reader understand"), intended to alert his original readers to the fulfillment of Jesus' prediction within their lifetime. Moreover, the parallel section in Luke 21:20–24 makes it clear that the desolation of Jewish Jerusalem would be followed by a long period of gentile domination, which is precisely what happened after AD 70.

The NT describes tribulation as the inevitable response of a sinful world dominated by Satan's power to the challenge of the gospel. Jesus had promised his disciples that, in this world, they would have tribulation (Jn 16:33). Not long after Jesus had uttered those words, the members of the early church community in Jerusalem were scattered because of the same tribulation that had claimed the life of Stephen (Acts 11:19). The apostle Paul experienced such tribulation in Asia that he became unbearably crushed, to the point of despairing of life as if he had received the sentence of death (2 Cor 1:8). Likewise, the churches established by him in Macedonia found themselves in the throes of a severe tribulation (2 Cor 8:2), similar to that of the Thessalonians who received the gospel in the midst of tribulation (1 Thes 1:6). The readers of the letter to the Hebrews had also been exposed to tribulation (Heb 10:33), and the apostle John writing to the seven churches reminded them that he was sharing with them both the tribulation and the kingdom (Rv 1:9). The fact that this tribulation was a contemporary reality for the churches is attested by Jesus' commendation of the church in Smyrna. Not only was this church suffering in tribulation (Rv 2:9), but the devil would intensify that tribulation for 10 days (v 10).

However, the victorious Christ is able to reverse affliction on the oppressors of believers (2 Thes 1:6). The false prophetess of Thyatira and her followers would, in turn, experience "great tribulation" (Rv 2:22). And, at the end, the innumerable multitude of the redeemed from every nation, tribe, people, and language that ever existed in the course of history will be gathered in heaven (7:9). They have come out of the "great tribulation," all those who, throughout history, have been adorned with the garments of redemption obtained by the blood of the Lamb (7:14). They will have been delivered from the tribulation that began with the death of Jesus' first disciples (Mt 24:9), the tribulation that will end when all the redeemed are gathered into eternal life at the second coming of Christ (vv 29–31). The great tribulation that occurred with the downfall of ancient Jerusalem in AD 70 was only a micro-cosmic example of the great tribulation that would be the lot of believers throughout the history of the church (v 21).

If the NT forewarns believers of the inevitability of tribulation, it also prescribes the appropriate response of Christians. They should rejoice because tribulation produces perseverance and strength of character (Rom 5:3). They should bear it patiently (12:12), knowing that God comforts the faithful in all tribulations (2 Cor 1:4) and that the present tribulation prepares incomparable glory in eternity (2 Cor 4:17).

Except for rare and exceptional circumstances that enable Christians to enjoy affluence and freedom, most believers throughout history have suffered tribulation. The normal vocation of the church has been to endure as a beleaguered and persecuted minority in a hostile world. For Christians providentially protected from tribulation, it is easy to relegate tribulation to a future period in history. For Christians suffering in the throes of opposition, however, the tribulation is an ever-present reality. The virulence and the severity of the tribulation may vary from time to time and from place to place, yet Christ's promise remains true, "In this world you will have tribulation. But be confident! I have overcome the world" (Jn 16:33).   GILBERT BILEZIKIAN

See AFFLICTION; ESCHATOLOGY; PERSECUTION.

Tribune.   Roman military official who served as the commander of a cohort (1000 men). In NT usage it designated the commander of the Roman garrison in Jerusalem (e.g., Acts 21:31; 22:24; 23:10; 24:22). Paul was placed under the tribune's protection after his arrest in Jerusalem (21:33).

Tributary, Tribute.   *See* TAX, TAXATION.

Trichotomy.   *See* MAN, DOCTRINE OF.

Trigon.   Triangular-shaped harp in Daniel 3:5,7,10,15.

See MUSIC AND MUSICAL INSTRUMENTS (SABCHA).

Trinity.   *See* GOD, BEING AND ATTRIBUTES OF.

Troas.   City in Turkey on the Aegean shore, 10 miles south of the ancient site of Troy, scene of the Trojan war immortalized by the poet Homer. Both the ancient city of Troy and the Roman city of Troas are on the Troad plain, an area about 10 miles in length bordering the sea. Paul sailed from Troas into Macedonia in response to the call, "come over to Macedonia and help us" (Acts 16:9).

The Seleucid king Antigonus founded the

Remains of the baths of Hadrian at Troas.

city about 300 BC and named it after himself. Later the name was changed to Alexandria Troas in honor of Alexander the Great who had passed through it in pursuit of the Persians. The city became a Roman colony when Roman influence replaced that of the Greeks. According to some scholars, Julius Caesar envisioned Troas as his eastern capital and Constantine considered making it his capital before deciding on Byzantium instead. It was an important seaport during the time of Paul because it was the easiest and shortest route from Asia to Europe. After Paul's visit, a great aqueduct, built by Herodes Atticus, brought water from Mt Ida, the sacred mountain a few miles to the east.

On the second missionary journey, Paul and Silas came to Troas after being forbidden to preach the Word of God in Asia (Acts 16:6). Although this trip to Europe is not stressed in Acts, many scholars believe this short voyage was as important historically as Caesar's invasion of Britain or even Columbus' discovery of the New World. After this vision Paul and Silas embarked, passed the island of Samothrace, and landed at Neapolis (modern Kavalla), their first stop in Europe (v 11).

Later, after his mission in Ephesus was finished, Paul stayed and preached the gospel here (2 Cor 2:12). On his way to Jerusalem for the last time, Paul preached until after midnight causing one of the young men to fall asleep and fall from a window to his death. But Paul called him back to life and continued the meeting until morning (Acts 20:6–12). There was an important church here from the earliest days.

Paul visited Troas again and left a cloak and parchments. These he wanted Timothy to bring to him at his prison in Rome (2 Tm 4:13).

Trogyllium. Rocky straits between Samos and Miletus through which Paul sailed on his trip to Jerusalem at the end of his third missionary journey (Acts 20:15 KJV; marginal reading in RSV; omitted in NIV). Most textual critics consider the phrase "after remaining at Trogyllium" to be a later insertion into the text. Whether or not it is original, Paul did actually sail past the rocky promontory at Trogyllium. The straits are quite narrow at this point, being only one mile in width, and therefore require precise navigation. Paul's ship probably anchored at a point just east of the ridge of Trogyllium at a harbor which bears the name St. Paul's Port.

Trophimus. One of the Asians who accompanied Paul on his final trip to Jerusalem (Acts 20:4). Because the Jews had seen Trophimus the Ephesian with Paul in Jerusalem, they incorrectly assumed that he had accompanied Paul into the temple (21:29). Since Trophimus was not a Jew, his alleged act of profaning the temple served as the pretense for Paul's arrest and subsequent imprisonment. Trophimus was traveling with Paul as one of the representatives of the Asian church who had been selected to superintend the collection for the Jerusalem church. Trophimus was probably one of the two brethren who accompanied Titus in the delivery of 2 Corinthians to Corinth (2 Cor 8:16–24).

One final mention of Trophimus in 2 Timothy potentially sheds light on the question of whether Paul had one or two imprisonments. Paul tells Timothy that he had left Trophimus ill at Miletus (2 Tm 4:20). If 2 Timothy was written shortly before Paul's death, then Paul likely was released from his first imprisonment since the passage fails to correlate with the events of Paul's first trip to Rome (Acts 27:1–12). Legend suggests that Trophimus was ultimately beheaded by the order of Nero.

Trumpet. See MUSIC AND MUSICAL INSTRUMENTS (HATZOTZROT).

Trumpets, Feast of. Day of solemn rest and remembrance of God's provision for his people through the Sinai covenant (Lv 23:23–25).

See FEASTS AND FESTIVALS OF ISRAEL.

Truth. The Bible does not provide a systematic account of the nature of truth in either its theological or philosophical dimensions. Nevertheless great prominence is given to the idea of truth in Scripture because God is the God of truth (Pss 31:5; 108:4; 146:6) who speaks and judges truly (Pss 57:3; 96:13). God is the God of all truth because he is the Creator, and it is impossible for him to lie (Heb 6:18).

All things exist because of his will (Eph 1:11). His will is the ultimate truth of every proposition or fact. Because of God's will the stars continue in their orbits (Ps 147:4) and Paul and his fellow voyagers arrive safely (Acts 27:24), even though God could have willed otherwise.

Whether God's creative power also extends to the truths of logic and mathematics has been the subject of controversy in Christian theology, some (e.g., Descartes and possibly Luther) claiming that two and two equals four only because God wills it, while the mainstream of Christian theology maintains that such a view is either speculative or incoherent.

While a general account of truth may be inferred from biblical data, the focus of Scripture is upon soteriology, the revealed truth in the gospel of God's redeeming grace through Christ. This is the truth which Christ and the apostles proclaimed (Jn 8:44–46; 18:37; Rom 9:1; 2 Cor 4:2), which was foreshadowed in the OT (1 Pt 1:10–12), and witnessed to by the Holy Spirit (Jn 16:13). God's revelation in Christ may be true in contrast to the OT teaching, not because the OT teaching is false, but because it is shadowy and incomplete in comparison with the NT. So Christ brings the truth (Jn 1:17) and the Holy Spirit leads into all truth (Jn 16:13).

The Christian gospel does not have a spiritual truth of its own, but contains truth-conditions familiar from other areas of human interest and inquiry, and embraces not only historical matters of fact, but metaphysical (Jn 1:14) and moral (Mk 1:15; Lk 13:3) truths. To restrict the scope of biblical truth or to contrast moral or spiritual truth with scientific or historical truth is a mistake. All truth is God's truth, and a moral truth (e.g., adultery is wrong) stands in the same objective sense as the historical fact that Jesus was crucified under Pontius Pilate. The popular idea that there is a characteristically Hebraic mode of truth, expressed particularly in the OT, which is contrasted with Greek ideas in Christian theology, should also be resisted. The difference between Hebrew and Greek thought forms lies not in the idea of truth but in the conflicting ideas of God, of human need, and of the way of salvation found in the two cultures. When Paul's hearers at Athens heard him say that what one of their poets had said was true (Acts 17:28), they were using the same idea of truth, even though they may not have fully understood the implications.

If there is a contrast at all between Hebrew and Greek thought, it is one of emphasis. Hebrew and biblical thought emphasize the personal source of truth (God and faithful men), while Greek thought emphasizes the truth of what is assented to or uttered. But even this difference must not be pressed too far, since the NT frequently employs Greek words for truth without any modification.

While the truth of God, backed by his authority, calls for a response (Rom 9:1) and is utterly trustworthy, defining truth in terms of reliability is a mistake. God's Word is true, therefore it is trustworthy.

By extension from these basic ideas about scriptural truth, Christ spoke of himself as the truth. Scripture elsewhere calls upon people to "do the truth" (Jn 14:6; Gal 3:1). Christ is the truth because, being God, his words carry divine authority. They are truth and life (Jn 6:63). In addition the life of Christ epitomized truthfulness and utter reliability. When people live in obedience to the truth, they are true and reliable.

Tryphaena, Tryphena. Christian woman of Rome who is referred with Tryphosa as "workers in the Lord" (Rom 16:12, KJV Tryphena). They may have been sisters, but were likely fellow deaconesses.

Tryphosa. Christian woman to whom Paul sent greetings in his letter to Rome (16:12).

Tsemed. Area measurement equivalent to about one-half acre.

See WEIGHTS AND MEASURES.

Tubal. Fifth of the listed sons of Japheth in the table of nations (Gn 10:2; 1 Chr 1:5). Tubal later gains significance in the prophetic writings of Isaiah and Ezekiel as one of the nations which would be judged for threatening God's people (Is 66:19; Ez 27:13; 32:26; 38:2,3; 39:1). Tubal is typically mentioned with Javan and Meshech as either nations of the north or nations of the coastlands (Is 66:19; Ez 38:2). The fact that Tubal traded with Tyre (Ez 27:13) supports the premise that Tubal was located in a coastland region. Beyond this sketchy evidence, it is difficult to determine Tubal's precise ethnic identification or location. It has been identified with the Scythians, the Iberians, the region between the Black and the Caspian Seas, Thessaly, and various Hittite tribes.

Tubal-cain. Son of Lamech by his wife Zillah (Gn 4:22). He was "a forger of all instruments of bronze and iron." Though the text does not claim that he was the first or the "father" of all ironworkers, many theorize that the text originally paralleled verses 20 and 21 to imply that he was the first. Some have suggested that Tubal-cain's invention of superior weapons motivated Lamech's concern for avenging blood. The derivation of the name is unknown.

Tulip. See PLANTS.

Tumbleweed. KJV rendering of "whirling dust" in Psalm 83:13 and Isaiah 17:13.

See PLANTS.

Tumor. Abnormal swelling or growth in any part of the body (KJV emerod). The only significant occurrence of these terms is in 1 Samuel 5 and 6. After the Philistines captured the ark of God from Israel, a painful lethal disease afflicted the population of the Philistine city that kept the ark. The swellings occurred "in their secret parts" (1 Sm 5:9 KJV), a reference to the groin, and was contagious, killing many (1 Sm 5:11,12). The disease was associated with the presence of "mice" (1 Sm 6:4,5). If these rodents that "mar the land" were not mice but rats, then the entire episode is consistent with the disease known as bubonic plague. In bubonic plague, the fleas of the rat are able to transmit to humans the pathologic bacteria, *Yersinia pestis*. The bacteria invade the human body, causing fever and buboes, which are large soft swellings in the armpit and groin. Without treatment, the mortality rate is 60 to 90 percent. The Philistines sent the ark of God back to Israel with handcrafted golden images of rodents and tumors (1 Sm 6:11,17,18). It was not until the 14th century that rats were associated with plague, and the exact role of the rat flea was not known until 1914.

See MEDICINE AND MEDICAL PRACTICE.

Turpentine Tree. Large tree that was prized for its longevity and resinous sap; also known as the terebinth tree (Is 6:13; Hos 4:13).

See PLANTS (TEREBINTH).

Turtle Dove. See BIRDS (PIGEON).

Tutor. NASB rendering of custodian in Galatians 3:24,25.

See TRADES AND OCCUPATIONS (CUSTODIAN).

Twelve, The. Designation for the 12 disciples/apostles in 1 Corinthians 15:5.

See APOSTLE, APOSTLESHIP.

Twin Brothers. Twin sons of Zeus whose images were the ship's figurehead on which Paul sailed to Rome (Acts 28:11).

See DIOSCURI.

Tychicus. One of the brethren who accompanied Paul in his deputation for the offering for the Jerusalem church (Acts 20:4). Determining whether Tychicus accompanied Paul all the way to Jerusalem or whether he stayed in Miletus when Paul stopped there to greet the Ephesian elders is difficult. Though Acts 21:8 speaks of "Paul's company" (KJV) as if all of the delegation remained with him, the fact that Tychicus is not mentioned with Trophimus in the Jews' charge against Paul would seem to indicate that Tychicus was not in Jerusalem (v 29). Since he is often mentioned with Trophimus, Tychicus was likely also a native of Ephesus. He served as the courier for Paul's letter to Ephesus (Eph 6:21), as well as Paul's letters to Philemon and the Colossians (Col 4:7). Most believe that he was also one of the two brethren (with Trophimus) who accompanied Titus in the delivery of 2 Corinthians (2 Cor 8:16–24). Paul mentions Tychicus twice in his later letters, first sending him to Crete to be with Titus (Ti 3:12), and later mentioning to Timothy that he had sent Tychicus to Ephesus so that he was no longer with him (2 Tm 4:12). Evidently Tychicus and Paul were close friends as well as fellow workers since Paul frequently refers to Tychicus as a "beloved brother."

Type, Typology. Branch of biblical interpretation in which an element found in the OT prefigures one found in the NT. The initial one is called the "type" and the fulfillment is designated the "antitype." Either type or antitype may be a person, thing, or event, but often the type is messianic and frequently refers to salvation. In working with types, the safest procedure is to limit them to those expressly mentioned in the Bible (cf. 1 Cor 4:6 NIV). On the other hand, it is argued that such an approach limits the legitimate use of types, for some obvious types are not mentioned in the NT. Further, the types given in the NT are examples which demonstrate how to find others in the OT.

Some examples may serve to identify some biblical types and antitypes: Jesus said to Nicodemus, "As Moses lifted up the serpent in the wilderness, so must the Son of Man be lifted up" (Jn 3:14; cf. Nm 21:9). The Passover lamb (Ex 12:1–13,49) is a type of Christ (1 Cor 5:7) The rock from which Israel drank in the wilderness (Ex 17:6) prefigures Christ (1 Cor 10:3,4).

The Book of Hebrews is replete with examples of types which represent the Messiah. All of the sacrifices ordained by the ritual law which God gave at Sinai typified some aspect of the person and work of Jesus. The blood that was sprinkled on the altar spoke of the blood of the one who was slain once for all (Heb 9:12–22).

In biblical study a type differs from allegory, which generally spiritualizes Bible history. In the early church this technique was carried to exaggerated lengths by Origen and followed by others. Galatians 4:22–31 states that Hagar and Sarah were a form of allegory in Paul's description of Law and grace.

A type also differs from a figure or a figure of speech. The Book of Hebrews declares that by faith Abraham offered up Isaac in expectation that God would immediately raise him from the dead. Abraham "figuratively" received Isaac as back from the dead when the Lord forestalled the sacrifice and provided a substitute (Heb 11:17–19). Baptism appears as a figure of salvation, not as physical cleansing but as the testimony of a forgiven conscience (1 Pt 3:21,22).

A parable is another rhetorical device for communicating spiritual truth. It is a kind of illustration, a brief story, told usually to illustrate a single point, although in some instances Jesus indicated specific meanings for various elements in the story. It is evident that a certain amount of contextual material must be inserted in a parable in order to make the story hold together; consequently, not every item in a parable is subject to interpretation.

A type can be distinguished from a symbol in that a symbol is a timeless sign. It can refer to past, present, or future, while a type always foreshadows that which is to come.

The English word type is derived from the Greek *tupos*, which has the basic meaning of "a visible impression or mark made by a blow or by pressure." In the Greek NT the word occurs 16 times, with various meanings. A type is formed as a copy, print, or a form cast in a mold. In Acts 7:43 it is applied to "figures" of idols or false gods. A type can be a pattern according to which something is made (e.g., the tabernacle, Acts 7:44; Heb 8:5). It is an example or model, whether of evil to be avoided (1 Cor 10:6,11) or of good to be emulated (Phil 3:17; 2 Thes 3:9; 1 Tm 4:12; Ti 2:7; 1 Pt 5:3). It is like a form for pouring concrete, which determines both shape and content of what is made. In this sense it is used of a letter written "to this effect" (RSV; "having this form" NASB Acts 23:25) and of a "standard" of teaching (RSV; "form" NIV Rom 6:17). A type is an OT element which prefigures one in the NT. The only time the translation "type" appears in the NT is in Romans 5:14, where Adam is called "a type of the one who was to come," that is, of Christ. This is taken up again in 1 Corinthians 15, where Adam is not named as a type, but both the resemblances and the dissimilarities between Adam and Christ are evident (1 Cor 15:22,45–49). This demonstrates that the type, like the illustration and the parable, cannot be pressed in all of its details.

On the other hand, there are details which are singled out as types. For example, in the directions for the celebration of the Passover, it is said of the roasted lamb, "you shall not break a bone of it" (Ex 12:46). This is repeated by the psalmist in Psalm 34:20 as a predictive prophecy. In the account of the crucifixion of Jesus (Jn 19:31–36), the Jews requested that the legs of the victims be broken to hasten their death so the bodies could be removed from the crosses before the sabbath. When the soldiers came to Jesus, they found that he was already dead and did not break his legs.

CARL E. DEVRIES

See BIBLE, INTERPRETATION OF THE; SIGN.

Bibliography. F.F. Bruce, *This Is That* and *The Time Is Fulfilled;* P. Fairbairn, *The Typology of Scripture;* F. Foulkes, *The Acts of God: A Study of the Basis of Typology in the OT;* L. Goppelt, *Typos: The Typological Interpretation of the NT;* A.T. Hanson, *Jesus Christ in the OT;* G.W.H. Lampe and K.J. Woolcombe, *Essays on Typology.*

Tyrannus, Hall of. Place in Ephesus where Paul taught daily for two years (Acts 19:9). Paul's ministry in Ephesus began at the synagogue, where he preached for three months. Finding increasing opposition there, Paul withdrew with his converts to the Hall of Tyrannus, where he began a ministry to both Jews and Greeks (Acts 19:10).

In Greek, the term "hall" literally means

"leisure" or "rest." It eventually became associated with the kind of activity carried on during times of leisure, that is, lectures, debates, and discussion. Finally, the term came to mean the place where these leisure activities occurred.

Virtually nothing is known about Tyrannus himself. Some scholars have suggested that he was a Greek rhetorician, possibly a sophist, sympathetic to Paul's preaching. This suggestion is made plausible by the addition of the Western text that states that Paul taught in the hall "from the fifth hour until the tenth," that is, from 11 AM until 4 PM. This would mean that Paul used the hall only during afternoon rest periods; for in all Ionian cities, work ceased at 11 AM and did not resume until late afternoon because of the intense heat. Possibly these rest periods made the hall available for Paul's use, and Tyrannus himself lectured there before and after these hours. There is no way to determine whether Paul was required to rent the hall or whether Tyrannus, in sympathy to Paul's work, simply made it available without cost.

If the western text is correct, it points to both the zeal of Paul for his ministry and the desire of his followers to learn. Undoubtedly, Paul and the Ephesian Christians rose early in the morning to engage in manual labor (Acts 20:34; 1 Cor 4:12). To follow this with five additional hours of teaching and dialogue (especially during a time when most of the city slept) is a testimony to the enthusiasm of this early Christian community and the priority they gave to the proclamation of the gospel.

Tyre. Ancient Phoenician city-state located on the Mediterranean coast 20 miles south of Sidon and 23 miles north of Acre. Tyre consisted of two major parts, an older port city on the mainland and an island city a half-mile from the coast where the majority of the population lived. According to Herodotus, Tyre was founded around 2700 BC. Its earliest historical attestations, however, are references in a 15th-century Ugaritic document and an Egyptian citation from the same period. Tyre first appears in the Bible in the list of cities that comprised Asher's inheritance (Jos 19:29). At that time it was already listed as a "strong city" and was evidently never conquered by the Israelites (2 Sm 24:7). Tyre was most significant as a mercantile center, with maritime contacts throughout the Mediterranean region and overland traffic with Mesopotamia and Arabia.

During the Davidic and Solomonic monarchies, Tyre (KJV Tyrus) was a strong commercial ally of Israel. Both David and Solomon contracted with Hiram of Tyre for timber, building materials, and skilled laborers, for

A Roman street and arch at Tyre.

which they provided Tyre with agricultural produce (2 Sm 5:11; 1 Kgs 5:1–11; 1 Chr 14:1; 2 Chr 2:3–16). After the division of the kingdom, Tyre evidently maintained friendly relations with Israel for some time. Ahab's wife Jezebel was the daughter of "Ethbaal king of the Sidonians," a king who is known elsewhere as Ithobal of Tyre (1 Kgs 16:31; cf. Menander). At some point, however, the pressure of Assyrian and Babylonian aggression dissolved the alliance, so that by the time of Samaria's fall, Tyre and Israel were no longer aligned and shortly thereafter became enemies.

During the later kingdom period, Tyre was the focus for some of the strongest prophetic denunciations recorded in Scripture (Is 23:1–18; Jer 25:22; 27:1–11; Ez 26:1–28:19; Jl 3:4–8; Am 1:9,10). Tyre's condemnation was justified for several reasons. Because of its commercial significance, Tyre was the focal point of Assyrian and Egyptian rivalries. Tyre managed, however, to play these rivals off against each other while building its wealth and exploiting its neighbors. Additionally, the city of Tyre was not only a city of unscrupulous merchants but also a center of religious idolatry and sexual immorality. Foremost among Tyre's sins was pride induced by its great wealth and strategic location.

Ezekiel's prophecy against Tyre offers a detailed picture of the city, its commercial empire, its sin, and its eventual demise (Ez 26:1–28:19; 29:18–20). Ezekiel's prophecy is significant for several reasons. First, Ezekiel prophesied that Tyre would be destroyed so thoroughly that it would be like "the top of a rock" and a place for the "spreading of nets" (26:4,5). While this prophecy was ultimately fulfilled, the final destruction of Tyre did not come for almost 1900 years (AD 1291), though it was besieged by Nebuchadnezzar for 13 years (587–574 BC), and conquered by Alexander the Great in 332 BC after a 7-month siege during which he built a causeway out to the island. Second, Ezekiel suggests that Nebuchadnezzar's failure to accomplish his objectives in Tyre was one of the reasons God permitted him to successfully attack Egypt (29:18–20). Third, the description of Tyre's arrogance has been compared to that of Satan, with Tyre's words "I am a god, I sit in the seat of God" (KJV) being the prototypical expression of the fall (28:2).

Despite Alexander's destruction of the city, Tyre had regained prominence by the NT period, being equal to or greater than Jerusalem in terms of population and commercial power. Jesus visited the region surrounding Tyre during his early ministry, healing the Syrophoenician woman's daughter (Mt 15:21–28; Mk 7:24–31). Jesus also compared the Galilean towns that had rejected him to Tyre and Sidon, suggesting that the Galileans would bear greater responsibility for their rejection because of the number of miracles that he had performed among them (Lk 10:13,14).

Tyropean Valley. Name given by Josephus to the central valley in Jerusalem that in ancient times divided Mt Moriah (the temple mount) and Mt Zion from the western ridge. The original Jebusite city as well as David's

The upper part of the Tyropean Valley.

Zion were located entirely on the eastern side of the central valley (the southeast hill), which either remained nameless or was biblical Hinnom. Jerusalem initially expanded to the north toward the current temple mount. It did not expand significantly west of the valley until the Late Kingdom period, an area which was not included within the city walls until the Hasmonean period (c. 150–100 BC). Once Jerusalem included the hills both east and west of the Tyropean Valley, the valley became significant to the topography of Jerusalem. At least two bridges ("Robinson's Arch" and "Wilson's Arch") spanned the valley, leading from the Hasmonean palace to the temple mount. Though the wall on the eastern side of the valley originally reached a height of 84 feet in places, the valley is presently filled in with a great amount of fill and debris so that much of the valley is presently level. The southern end of the temple wall, the Western or Wailing Wall, still remains and is one of the holiest shrines of Judaism.

See JERUSALEM.

Uu

Ucal. Disciple of Agur, the wise man whose sayings are recorded in the Book of Proverbs (Prv 30:1). The meaning of the passage is obscure. Many have suggested that the names Ithiel and Ucal are not proper nouns but should be translated, "I have wearied myself for God and fainted."

Uel. Bani's descendant and a priest who was encouraged by Ezra to divorce his foreign wife during the postexilic era (Ezr 10:34).

Ugarit. Capital city of a powerful city-state in northwest Syria during the 2nd millennium BC. Though the city is not mentioned in the Bible, it is a significant archaeological site that illuminates OT language and history. Ugarit, also known as Ras Shamra (Fennel Hill), was located just east of the Mediterranean coast approximately 175 miles north of Tyre, 60 miles northwest of Hamath, and 80 miles southwest of Aleppo.

Being known previously only from the Amarna letters, the ruins of Ugarit were discovered inadvertently by a peasant farmer in 1928. The resulting discoveries have been among the most important in the 20th century. Fifteen levels of occupation have been uncovered, dating from prepottery Neolithic (c. 6000 BC) to the early Roman period. Most significantly, Ugarit appeared to have reached its zenith politically and commercially during the Late Bronze Age (c. 1550–1180 BC), a period roughly contemporaneous with Israel's early settlement of Canaan. Excavations from this period have revealed a large palace (c. 950,000 square ft), several houses, a wealth of physical artifacts, and hundreds of cuneiform tablets. Among the tablets are commercial and diplomatic correspondence, including treaties whose form potentially parallels biblical treaty texts.

While the physical remains of Ugarit are archaeologically significant, its cultural and linguistic legacy have proven to be most valuable for biblical scholars. Since Ugarit was a political and cultural center, its scribes created and transcribed documents in a wide variety of Near Eastern languages, including a

Cretan vessels discovered at Ugarit.

language closely related to Hebrew that was written in an alphabetic cuneiform script. The discovery and subsequent deciphering of "Ugaritic" has influenced biblical studies both linguistically and culturally. Despite the fact that some have overemphasized the search for Ugaritic parallels, the study of Ugaritic has certainly illuminated some otherwise obscure Hebrew passages and given greater attestation to others. For instance, the terms used to describe each of the various sacrificial offerings are very similar in Hebrew and Ugaritic, though the sacrificial systems themselves vary quite dramatically. Hebrew and Ugaritic poetry are quite similar stylistically, thus assisting in the understanding of Hebrew verse and also increasing the appreciation of its ancient heritage. Books like Job that often have been dated late by biblical critics exhibit significant Ugaritic parallels in style, vocabulary, and occasionally in literary allusion as well (e.g., "flashing his lightning" Jb 37:2; "Leviathan" Jb 26:13). Similarities are most striking in the psalms and in the Wisdom literature (cf. Pss 29; 68; Prv 26:23). God's power over nature is described using motifs similar to those that appear in Ugaritic descriptions of Baal. Despite the similarity in metaphor, however, the differences in character between Baal and God are striking and are emphasized throughout the OT.

Perhaps the most significant contribution derived from the study of Ugaritic texts and cultural artifacts is the improved understanding of Canaanite culture and religion. The Ugaritic texts provide justification for the strongly negative assessment of Canaanite culture given in the Bible. Three principal religious epics have been discovered in the Ugaritic corpus, written in honor of Keret, Aqhat, and Baal, respectively. The Baal epic is most instructive. It describes the way in which Baal becomes lord of the earth after battling Yam, the god of the sea. The epics further reveal a great deal about Canaanite religious ritual, reinforcing biblical contentions concerning the sexual permissiveness and degradation of the society. The strong biblical injunctions against the worship of Baal and the Asherahs and the command to utterly destroy the Canaanites are more easily understood in the context of the Ugaritic religious epics.

Finally, the Ugaritic texts potentially illuminate some historical questions relating to the OT. For instance, when Hezekiah was sick with a boil, he was instructed by Isaiah to treat it with a poultice of figs (2 Kgs 20:7; Is 38:21). This procedure is attested to in a Ugaritic text that prescribes it as a treatment for boils that infected horses. The connection of Daniel with Job and Noah in Ezekiel 14:20

has troubled many. Possibly the Daniel referred to by Ezekiel was the Daniel mentioned in the Aqhat epic (Aqhat 1.i.23–25), since he would be a much closer contemporary of Noah and Job than would Ezekiel's younger contemporary, Daniel.   GARY N. LARSON

See INSCRIPTIONS.

Ulai.   River near the Persian capital city of Susa where Daniel had his vision concerning a ram, a goat, and the "abomination of desolation" (Dn 8:2,16). It is likely the same as the Eulaeus, which is described by both Greek and Roman geographers as a stream that flowed to the west of the citadel of Susa. Because of the frequent changes in the river channels of the seasonal streams in the region, identifying Ulai (Eulaeus) with any existing river or stream is difficult. Despite this difficulty, the Ulai was quite possibly a branch of the Kerkhah River which in ancient times flowed in a channel $1\frac{1}{4}$ miles east of its present course. In its ancient channel it would have flowed very near to the citadel of the city, thus fitting Daniel's description quite accurately. Gabriel is reported to have spoken from "between the banks of the Ulai" (v 16). While this may indicate that Gabriel was in the middle of the river, it is also possible that he was standing on the west bank between two branches of the river.

Ulam.   1. Clan in Manasseh's tribe (1 Chr 7:16,17).

2. Eshek's firstborn son and a mighty warrior in Benjamin's tribe (1 Chr 8:39,40).

Ulcer.   *See* SORE.

Ulla.   Family in Asher's tribe (1 Chr 7:39).

Ummah.   One of the villages inherited by Asher's tribe after the conquest of Canaan (Jos 19:30). Neither the location of Ummah nor the accompanying villages (Aphek and Rehob) are known.

Uncircumcision.   Natural state of the male, that is, with the prepuce covering his glans penis. Since the Jews, among many other peoples, surgically removed this as a sign of their covenant with God (Gn 17:9–14; Ex 12:48; Lv 12:3), the term came to designate "Gentile" or "non-Jew" (Philistines, Greeks, and Romans did not circumcise, but Egyptians and many Semitic peoples did). By extension it meant metaphorically "those outside the covenant," whether because they were Gentiles or because they were Jews living in disobedience to God.

The term "uncircumcision" occurs 20 times in the NT, most of the time meaning simply "Gentile" as opposed to Jew. In Act 11:3 the Jews are shocked that Peter entered the house of a (by definition ritually impure) Gentile. Paul, however, argued strongly against making such distinctions. For Paul, the attitude of the heart, obedience to God, was important and not ritual law, which had nothing to do with salvation. An obedient Gentile was as good as a circumcised Jew (Rom 2:25–27). Commitment to God, or faith, operates in the uncircumcised state as well as in the circumcised, as for example in the case of Abraham (Rom 3:30; 4:9–12). Formerly Gentiles were outside the people of God (Eph 2:11–12), but now Jew and Gentile believers have become one in Christ (Gal 2:7; 5:6; 6:15; Col 3:11). Paul refused to give way to those demanding circumcision for full church membership.

Yet Paul did not ignore the realities of culture. On the one hand, he advised uncircumcised Gentiles not to be circumcised upon conversion, for the operation was unnecessary; but on the other hand, Jewish believers could use their state in a mission to fellow Jews. A reversal operation was neither necessary nor useful (1 Cor 7:17–19).

In one passage (Col 2:8–15), Paul speaks of uncircumcision metaphorically, meaning a person's unregenerate state. Here uncircumcision is equivalent to "the flesh" (meaning one's evil impulse or natural state). As literal flesh is cut away in the rite of circumcision, so this "flesh" is cut away by Christ in conversion, as symbolized in baptism. The baptized person is one purified from "uncleanness" as a circumcised Gentile is purified from previous uncircumcised uncleanness.

See Baptism; Circumcision; Cleanness and Uncleanness, Regulations Concerning; Flesh.

Unclean, Uncleanness. *See* Cleanness and Uncleanness, Regulations Concerning.

Unforgivable Sin. *See* Unpardonable Sin, The.

Unicorn. KJV rendering for an animal called a "wild ox" in the RSV and most modern translations (Nm 23:22; 24:8; Dt 33:17; etc.). Unicorn is an unfortunate translation (following the Septuagint) considering that the animal possessed horns (plural), great strength, and ferocity.

See Animals (Wild Ox).

Unleavened Bread. Bread made without yeast (leaven). In ancient bread making, leaven was simply a piece of dough remaining from a former baking process which had fermented and developed a certain acid content—the yeast that caused bread to rise.

Bread used at the Jewish Passover and most other religious observances was, by the command of God, unleavened (Ex 12:15–20; 23:15). Only under certain conditions were the people permitted to use leavened bread for spiritual purposes (Lv 7:13; 23:17). This was largely owing to the fact that leaven generally symbolized evil: fermentation implied decay and corruption. Such feasts as the Passover and Unleavened Bread bore witness to the necessity of self-consecration to God and the putting away of the "leaven" of ungodliness.

With the exception of Jesus' teaching on the kingdom of God (Mt 13:33) the NT also speaks of leaven with a negative connotation. Jesus warns of the leaven of the Pharisees and Sadducees (Mt 16:6); Paul exhorts believers to guard against that tiny bit of yeast—unhealthy values—which can work through a whole batch of dough (1 Cor 5:6–8).

The most significant NT application of unleavened bread is found in the context of the Passover which Jesus celebrated with his disciples on the evening of his betrayal (Mt 26:17–29; Mk 14:12–25; Lk 22:7–23). There Jesus likened his body to the unleavened bread he broke in the presence of the 12. In view of the sinlessness of Christ this action was rich with meaning: he who was without "leaven" could alone offer himself up for the sins of his people. Christians feast upon the Christ who fulfills the hope of redemption linked to the unleavened bread of the Passover.

See Feasts and Festivals of Israel; Food and Food Preparation; Bread; Leaven.

Unleavened Bread, Feast of. *See* Feasts and Festivals of Israel.

Unni. 1. One of the musicians appointed by the chief of the Levites to sing and play the harp as part of the temple service during David's reign (1 Chr 15:18,20).

2. KJV spelling of Unno in Nehemiah 12:9. *See* Unno.

Unno. One of the Levites who participated in the temple service during the postexilic era (Neh 12:9, KJV Unni).

Unpardonable Sin, The. Attributing the righteous work of the Holy Spirit demonstrated through Jesus Christ to Satan. The unpardonable sin is not Israel's rebellion against God, even though this rebellion resulted in the eternal judgment of thousands and a temporary elimination of God's blessing.

The "sin unto death" (1 Jn 5:16,17) is not the unpardonable sin. It would be impossible for a person who has redemption and the forgiveness of sin (Eph 1:7), cleansing for present and future sin (1 Jn 1:7), and eternal life (Jn 3:16) to commit an unpardonable sin. But those who commit the "sin unto death" are all Christians. First John 5:16 says the person who commits the "sin unto death" is a "brother" in Christ.

The unpardonable sin is not rejection of the Lord Jesus, until the rejector dies in his unbelief. Such a sin will not be forgiven throughout eternity, but is not the same sin as that which Jesus condemned with the words: "It shall not be forgiven him either in this age, or in the age to come" (Mt 12:32). Numerous passages repeat the warning that unbelief in the Savior results in an eternal second death (Jn 3:18,36; 1 Jn 5:12; Rv 20:15; 21:8), but do not include the definition of the unpardonable sin. Jesus asserted that a person could be an unbeliever in him even to the degree of speaking against him, yet not be guilty of the unpardonable sin.

The unpardonable sin must be defined by its context (Mt 12:31,32; Mk 3:28–30). Jesus cast a demon from a blind-dumb man. Incontrovertible evidence of the power of God had occurred. The Pharisees with stubborn unbelief credited this display of God's power to Beelzebul, the devil (Mt 12:24). Several Scriptures reveal that many Jews practiced this sin (Mt 9:34; 11:18; Lk 7:33; 11:14–20; Jn 7:20; 8:48,52; 10:20). A group of Jews, mostly Pharisees, were guilty of attributing the righteous works of the Spirit demonstrated through the Lord Jesus, to the devil. They committed *the* unpardonable sin when they called the highest manifestation of holy labor by the most offensive opprobrium—the work of Beelzebul.

See Sin; Sin Unto Death; Justification.

Upharsin. Aramaic word interpreted as "divided" in Daniel 5:25 (KJV).

See Mene, Mene, Tekel, Parsin.

Uphaz. Region well known for its gold (Jer 10:9; Dn 10:5). Some contend that Uphaz is a scribal error for Ophir (only one consonant is different), another region famous for its fine gold.

See Ophir (Place).

Upper Gate. One of the gates leading to the temple mount in Jerusalem. It was built by Jotham (2 Kgs 15:35; 2 Chr 27:3), and served as the principal access between the royal palace and the temple area (2 Chr 23:30; Ez 9:2). It is possibly the same as the upper Benjamin Gate, where Jeremiah was beaten and placed in stocks because of his unfavorable prophecies against Jerusalem (Jer 20:2).

See Jerusalem.

Upper Room. Second-story room of a Hebrew or a Greek house; often like a tower, built on the flat roof of a Hebrew home for privacy, for comfort during the hot season, or for the entertainment of guests. In some instances it could accommodate large gatherings of people. In at least one instance, the room was on the third story (Acts 20:8). Eutychus, sitting in the window, went to sleep and fell three stories to the street below (v 10). It may have been a similar type of accident that caused Ahaziah's fatal injury when he fell through the latticework of his upper room (2 Kgs 1:2).

Elijah took the dead son of the widow of Zarephath to an upper room where he had been staying and raised him from the dead (1 Kgs 17:19,23). David went to an upper room for privacy to mourn the death of Absalom (2 Sm 18:33). The kings of Judah built strange altars near the upper room of Ahaz, which Josiah pulled down as part of his reform program (2 Kgs 23:12).

Jesus ate the Passover supper in an upper room with his disciples (Mk 14:15; Lk 22:12). The size of some of these rooms is evident from the fact that, after Jesus had left and ascended to heaven, the disciples went to the upper room where they all had been staying before. The congregation attending the meeting in Troas was not a small one either (Acts 20:8). It may have been to a room like this that Peter went to pray on the day when he had his vision of the sheet and the animals, teaching him that he should not call anything common or unclean, although the Scriptures only say that he went to the roof (Acts 10:9–16).

Dorcas was laid in an upper room after she had died; and later, Peter was taken up to the same room to pray for her restoration to life (Acts 9:36–41).

See Architecture; Homes and Dwellings.

Ur. Father of Eliphal, one of David's mighty men (1 Chr 11:35); probably the same as Ahasbai in the parallel passage (2 Sm 23:34).

Urbanus, Urbane. Believer greeted as one of Paul's fellow workers in Christ (Rom 16:9, KJV Urbane).

Uri. 1. Father of Bezalel from Judah's tribe, and a builder of the tabernacle (Ex 31:2; 35:30; 38:22; 1 Chr 2:20; 2 Chr 1:5).

2. Father of Geber, one of Solomon's officers in Gilead (1 Kgs 4:19).

3. One of the temple gatekeepers who put away his foreign wife at Ezra's request (Ezr 10:24).

Uriah. 1. Hittite who joined the people of Israel, became a leader in David's army, and was listed among the king's mighty men (2 Sm 23:39; 1 Chr 11:41). Uriah's wife was Bathsheba, whom David coveted and with whom he committed adultery while Uriah was fighting the Ammonites. Upon learning that she was pregnant, David summoned Uriah to Jerusalem, hoping that Uriah would sleep with his wife and consider himself the child's father. However, Uriah slept in the servants' quarters because he was unwilling to enjoy the comforts of home while his companions were at war. The second night David again tried to entice him to sleep with his wife. Even after falling into a drunken stupor, Uriah still could not be persuaded to go home; instead, he spent the night at the palace. To deepen the intrigue, David sent Uriah back to the battle, ordering him positioned at a vulnerable place where he was killed (2 Sm 11; Mt 1:6, KJV Urias).

See DAVID; GENEALOGY OF JESUS CHRIST.

2. Priest who built an altar at Jerusalem in imitation of an Assyrian model at King Ahaz of Judah's request (2 Kgs 16:10–16, KJV Urijah).

3. Meremoth's father. Meremoth weighed the silver, gold, and vessels for the temple (Ezr 8:33) and rebuilt portions of the Jerusalem wall during the days of Nehemiah (Neh 3:4,21, KJV Urijah).

4. One of the men who stood to Ezra's right when Ezra read the Law to the people (Neh 8:4, KJV Urijah). He is perhaps the same man as #3 above.

5. Priest whom Isaiah took as a witness (Is 8:2).

6. Prophet and Shemaiah's son from Kiriath-jearim. Uriah enraged King Jehoiakim by prophesying against Judah and Jerusalem. Fearing for his life, Uriah fled to Egypt, but was eventually abducted and brought back to King Jehoiakim, who subsequently put him to death (Jer 26:20–23, KJV Urijah).

Urias. KJV spelling (in Matthew 1:6) of Uriah, Bathsheba's husband, whom David had killed.

See URIAH #1.

Uriel. 1. Levite of the Kohathite branch who is listed as the son of Tahath and the father of Uzziah (1 Chr 6:24).

2. Levite who officiated over the moving of the ark from the house of Obed-edom to Jerusalem (1 Chr 15:5). He was a Kohathite clan chief in charge of 120 men who participated in the ceremony, and he was personally sanctified for the purpose of carrying the ark (v 11).

3. Grandfather of King Abijah of Judah, and the father of the queen mother, Micaiah, the favored wife of Rehoboam (2 Chr 13:2). There is potential difficulty in that Absalom is also called the father of Micaiah (Maacah) in 2 Chronicles 11:20. Josephus explained this discrepancy by suggesting that Micaiah's mother may have been Absalom's daughter Tamar, so that Uriel would be the father of Micaiah and Absalom the maternal grandfather. While many adopt this suggestion, others have posited that Absalom was known by two different names, particularly after he had been disgraced.

Urijah. KJV spelling of Uriah.

See URIAH #'s 2–4,6.

Urim and Thummim. Two untranslated Hebrew words which might mean "lights and perfections." They refer to some kind of stones or tokens which the ancient high priests of Israel used for discovering the will of God (Nm 27:21). Theories abound, but most guess they were something like dice or coins which had to land upright or upside down. According to Exodus 28:30, they were kept on or in the breastpiece of the high priest. They are not mentioned from the time of Saul (1 Sm 28:6) until the time of Ezra and Nehemiah (Ezr 2:63; Neh 7:65), when they were used for reaccrediting returned priests. In 1 Samuel 14:41 (RSV, NIV mg), the Greek translation preserves what may have been lost from the Hebrew original, a mention of them in connection with Saul's effort to determine guilt in his army. That they could give answers to true-false or yes-no questions is evident from this verse. Hence, the system was akin to casting lots.

Interestingly none of the major spiritual leaders (e.g., Abraham, Moses, David, or the prophets) ever used them for determining the will of God. So in the NT there is no mention of them. Such a means belonged to the nation Israel in its developing years, not when there were prophets and surely not once the Holy Spirit was available to believers.

See LOTS, CASTING OF.

Ur of the Chaldees. Hometown of Terah, the father of Abraham, and the birthplace of Abraham and Sarah. It is mentioned by name only four times in the Bible (Gn 11:28,31; 15:7; Neh 9:7), always with the full name, "Ur of the Chaldees." Although Stephen in his defense before the council does not refer to Ur by name, he makes it clear that God called Abraham before he lived in Haran and that Abraham "departed from the land of the Chaldeans, and lived in Haran," as an act of faith and obedience (Acts 7:2–4; cf. Heb 11:8).

The modern site is known as Tell el Muqayyar, "The Mound of Bitumen." The results of archaeological investigations demonstrate that Abraham came from a great city, cultured, sophisticated, and powerful.

The landscape was dominated by the ziggurat, or temple tower, and the life of the city was controlled by a religion with a multiplicity of gods. The chief deity was Nanna(r), or Sin, the moon god, who was also worshiped at Haran. Near his ziggurat was a temple dedicated to his consort, the moon goddess, Ningal.

Many clay tablets found at Ur tell of the business life of the city, which focused on the temples and their income. There were factories here, such as the weaving establishment for the manufacture of woolen cloth. Some tablets dealt with religion, history, law, and education. Students were instructed in reading and writing in cuneiform script. They were taught multiplication and division, and some were even able to extract square and cube roots.

Domestic architecture was highly developed. Houses had two stories and many rooms (10–20), sometimes with a private chapel. Small clay religious figures (teraphim or household idols) were discovered.

Many art objects made of precious metals and other costly materials were excavated especially in the royal tombs. These tombs also contained the remains of a number of retainers who were put to death at the time of the royal burials. Among the many finds of cultural and historical importance are the Stela of Ur-Nammu, the law code of Ur-Nammu, the "Standard" of Ur, exquisitely made harps and lyres, a gold dagger and sheath, fine gold vessels, various feminine headdresses (in particular that of Queen Shubad), and the famous statue of "a ram caught in a thicket."

Ur was not only a center of religion, culture, and economics; it was also a political power whose influence at times extended to northern Mesopotamia and even to Syria.

At Ur is a stratum of 8 to 11 feet of waterlaid clay which represented a flood of considerable magnitude. Some have associated this stratum with the flood of the Bible, but this is impossible, for most of the city escaped the devastation.

Uthai. 1. One who returned to Israel following the exile. He is listed as the son of Amnihud from the Perez branch of Judah's tribe (1 Chr 9:4).

Gold dagger and sheath from Ur.

2. One of Bigvai's sons who returned to Jerusalem with Ezra (Ezr 8:14).

Uz (Person). 1. Aram's firstborn son and a descendant of Shem (Gn 10:23). In the parallel passage in 1 Chronicles 1:17, Uz is linked directly to Shem without mention of Aram. He is perhaps the forefather of the Aramaean nation situated in the Damascene and Syrian desert regions.

2. Firstborn son of Abraham's brother Nahor by his concubine Milcah (Gn 22:21, KJV Huz).

3. Son of Dishan and the grandson of Seir the Horite (Gn 36:28; 1 Chr 1:42).

Uz (Place). Homeland of Job (Jb 1:1). It appears in parallels with Edom and is associated with the Uz in the family tree of the original Horites in Seir (Lam 4:21). Uz is referred to among the kings of the world (Jer 25:20) in an obscure geographical context. Uz is followed by Philistia and then by the Transjordanian nations of Edom, Moab, and Ammon.

The Book of Job does not locate the land of Uz but does ascribe it to the "sons of the East (Kedem)" (Jb 1:3). Uz is also close to the desert (v 15) and to the Chasdim (v 17).

The associations with Edom strongly suggest that the land of Uz was populated by descendants of the Horites of Seir. Further support for this view is a verse in the Greek version at the end of the Book of Job: "since he had lived in the land of Uz on the borders of Edom and Arabia."

Certain ancient traditions place the home of Job in Bashan. Josephus also says that Job lived in Trachonitis and Damascus (*Antiq.* 1.6.4) with reference to the Uz of the Aramaean genealogy (Gn 10:23). A ruler named Ayyabu is known from the Bashan area according to the el-Amarna letters dating to the 14th century BC. That city-state prince has the equivalent of the Hebrew name that comes into English as Job. There was also a place in Bashan called Udumu, which would be the equivalent of Hebrew Edom; it appears in the Amarna correspondence and in Egyptian texts. All this would dovetail with the allusion to the sons of the East (Kedem) in Job 1:3.

Uz was thus considered a source of wise men like Job. It was located to the east of the land of Israel, near the desert. One possibility is that there was more than one place by this name, perhaps a northern and a southern one. In any case, the land of Uz is not in any immediate contact with Israel or Judah. As the homeland of the ancient sage, Job, Uz would appear to belong to the earlier ethnographic sphere of places and peoples.

Uzai. Father of Palal, a repairer of the Jerusalem wall during Nehemiah's day (Neh 3:25).

Uzal (Person). Son of Joktan, a descendant of Eber through Shem's line (Gn 10:27; 1 Chr 1:21).

Uzal (Place). Place mentioned with Dan and Javan in an obscure passage (Ez 27:19). Both ancient and modern versions vary considerably in their rendering of the passage. Whereas the RSV translates Dan (wine) and Javan (exchanged) and considers Uzal to be a proper name, the KJV does exactly the opposite, translating Uzal ("going to and fro"), while considering Dan and Javan to be proper nouns. The ASV considers Uzal to be a common noun meaning "yarn."

Considering the wealth of allusions to the ethnological lists of Genesis 10 that are found in the passage, it is likely that Uzal is a proper name stemming from Uzal, Joktan's son (cf. Gn 10:27; 1 Chr 1:21). Assuming that Uzal is a place name, it is clearly identifiable with modern Sana (ancient Awzal), the capital of Yemen.

Uzza. 1. Owner or the initial planter of a garden that served as the burial place for kings Manasseh and Amon of Judah (2 Kgs 21:18,26). The "garden of Uzza" was apparently adjacent to Manasseh's royal residence. Some suggest that Uzza is the same person as King Uzziah (Azariah; 2 Kgs 15:1–6), but this is unlikely.

2. KJV spelling for Uzzah, Shimei's son, in 1 Chronicles 6:29.

See UZZAH #2.

3. Son of Heglam from Benjamin's tribe (1 Chr 8:7), listed as an ancestor of Mordecai in extrabiblical texts.

4. KJV spelling for Uzzah, Abinadab's son, in 1 Chronicles 13:7–11.

See UZZAH # 1.

5. Forefather of a family of temple servants that returned to Jerusalem with Zerubbabel following the exile (Ezr 2:49; Neh 7:51).

Uzzah. 1. Son of Abinadab who was killed while driving the cart that carried the ark of the covenant when it was returned from the Philistines (2 Sm 6:1–8; 1 Chr 13:7–11, KJV Uzza). He was struck dead by the Lord because he "took hold" of the ark while trying to steady it, thereby violating the proscriptions of Numbers 4:15. Uzzah's brother, Ahio, was apparently leading the oxen while Uzzah walked alongside. As a result of the incident, David renamed the site Perez-uzzah ("the breaking forth against Uzzah") and left the ark at the home of Obed-edom.

2. Levite from the clan of Merari who is listed as the son of Shimei and the father of Shimea (1 Chr 6:29, KJV Uzza).

Uzzen-sheerah, Uzzen-sherah. Town built by Sheerah, who was either the daughter or granddaughter of Ephraim (1 Chr 7:24, KJV Uzzen-sherah). Its site is unknown.

Uzzi. 1. Descendant of Eliezer who was in the direct ancestral line of high priests, though he apparently never served in that capacity (1 Chr 6:5,6,51). He is listed as the son of Bukki and the father of Zerahiah and a lineal ancestor of Zadok and later Ezra (Ezr 7:4).

2. Clan chief and mighty warrior of the tribe of Issachar. He was one of the six sons of Tola and the father of Izrahiah, his successor as clan chief (1 Chr 7:2,3).

3. Clan chief and mighty warrior of Benjamin's tribe, listed as one of the sons of Bela (1 Chr 7:7).

4. Head of one of the Benjamite clans that returned from Babylon, listed as the son of Michri and the father of Elah (1 Chr 9:8).

5. One of the overseers of the Levites in Jerusalem, listed as the son of Bani from the clan of Asaph (Neh 11:22).

6. Head of the priestly house of Jedaiah during the days of Joiakim the high priest (Neh 12:19).

7. One of the priests (or Levites) who participated in the dedication of the rebuilt temple (Neh 12:42). He may be the same as #6 above (or #5 above if 12:42a is connected with 12:42b rather than 12:41).

Uzzia. One of David's mighty men (1 Chr 11:44). He is described as an Asterathite, which probably means that he was from Ashtaroth, a town on the east side of the Jordan.

Uzziah. 1. Judah's king from around 792 to 740 BC (cf. 2 Kgs 14:21,22; 15:1–7; 2 Chr 26:1–23), the son of King Amaziah and Jecoliah of Jerusalem. Uzziah is the name he is called in Chronicles, but in Kings he is known as Azariah. Azariah means "the Lord has helped"; the meaning of Uzziah is "my strength is the Lord." Azariah may have been his given name and Uzziah was a throne name taken upon his accession. He came to the throne at the age of 16, upon the death of his father, who was assassinated in Lachish as a result of a conspiracy arising from his apostasy.

Uzziah was a capable, energetic, and well-organized person, with many diverse interests, all of which he handled admirably. The Lord blessed him in all of his undertakings, so that he prospered. He is characterized as one who "did what was right in the eyes of the Lord" (2 Kgs 15:3; 2 Chr 26:4). He determined to seek God and went to Zechariah for instruction in the fear of the Lord. Consequently, "as long as he sought the Lord, God made him prosper" (2 Chr 26:5). Nevertheless, the high places of false worship were not removed from the land (2 Kgs 15:4).

The prophets of the Lord were active during his reign. Isaiah, Hosea, and Amos began their prophetic work in the time of Uzziah (Is 1:1; Hos 1:1; Am 1:1).

The Bible reports the military victories of Uzziah before it tells of his military strength. His primary success was against Israel's strong historical enemy, the Philistines. He broke down the walls of Gath, Jabneh, and Ashdod, and built his own cities in Philistia. He also built many fortifications, such as fortified towers in Jerusalem and in the wilderness. He defeated some Arabs and also the Meunites, and brought the Ammonites under tribute (2 Chr 26:7,8).

Uzziah had an army "fit for war," which was drafted according to census and organized into divisions. There were 2600 officers, "men of valor," and 307,500 fighting men, "who could make war with mighty power." The army was well outfitted, with weapons, such as spears, bows, and slingstones, and with defensive equipment, including shields, helmets, and coats of armor (2 Chr 26:14). Second Chronicles 26:15 describes a kind of catapult, which was to be stationed on the towers and at the corners of walls for defensive purposes. This type of weapon could hurl arrows or large stones. Through his achievements and especially his military power, he became famous, "for he was marvelously helped."

In the Book of Kings the only achievement attributed to the reign of Uzziah is his building of Elath and restoring it to Judah. This port (modern Eilat) on the Gulf of Aqaba was near Ezion-geber, which Solomon used for trading expeditions by sea. No mention is made of similar commercial ventures by Uzziah, but evidently the possession of this city was advantageous for foreign trade.

As the downfall of his grandfather Joash came about by bloodguilt and that of his father resulted from apostasy, so the failure of Uzziah came because of pride, and serves as a good illustration of Proverbs 16:18. His pride became clearly evident when he usurped the function of a priest. Upon entering the temple to offer incense upon the altar of incense he was confronted by Azariah the priest and 80 other priests, "men of valor," who took him to task for his presumptuous behavior. When Uzziah became angry the Lord struck him with leprosy, so that he was forced to live in isolation and could not enter the temple. His son, Jotham, became acting head of state and then succeeded to the kingship at the time of Uzziah's death; he "did what was right in eyes of the Lord" (2 Chr 26:23; Mt 1:8,9; KJV Ozias)

The acts of the reign of Uzziah were recorded by the prophet Isaiah, the son of Amoz. When Uzziah died he was buried in Jerusalem with the earlier kings of Judah.

Perhaps the best-known verse associated with this king is Isaiah 6:1: "In the year that King Uzziah died I saw the Lord sitting upon a throne, high and lifted up."

See CHRONOLOGY, OLD TESTAMENT; ISRAEL, HISTORY OF.

2. Kohathite Levite and forefather of Samuel (1 Chr 6:24).

3. Father of Jonathan, overseer of David's treasuries throughout Judah (1 Chr 27:25).

4. One of Harim's five sons who was encouraged by Ezra to divorce his foreign wife during the postexilic period (Ezr 10:21; 1 Esd 9:21, Azariah).

5. Descendant of Perez from Judah's tribe (Neh 11:4).   CARL E. DeVRIES

Uzziel.   1. Youngest of the sons of Kohath of Levi's tribe who became the head of the Uzzielite division of the Kohathites (Ex 6:18; Nm 3:19,27,30; 1 Chr 26:23). He was Aaron's uncle, and his sons, Mishael and Elzaphan, carried Nadab and Abihu out of the camp when they rebelled against Aaron's authority (Ex 6:22; Lv 10:4). Several of his descendants were significant during Israel's history, including Amminadab, who officiated over David's transfer of the ark to Jerusalem, and Micah and Isshaiah, who were chiefs among the Levites during the reign of Solomon (1 Chr 15:10; 23:20).

2. Son of Ishi who was one of the leaders of the Simeonite warriors who defeated the Ammonites at Seir during the reign of Hezekiah (1 Chr 4:42). As a result of defeating the Amalekites, who had not been defeated earlier by Saul or David, the Simeonites inherited and dwelt in the land.

3. Benjamite clan chief who is listed as the son of Bela, the son of Benjamin (1 Chr 7:7).

4. Son of Heman of the Levite clan of Asaph (1 Chr 25:4). He may be the same as Azarel who was in charge of the 11th course (1 Chr 25:18). The spelling difference may be the same as the Azariah/Uzziah alternation.

5. Levite who participated in the reconsecration of the temple under Hezekiah (2 Chr 29:14), listed as the son of Jeduthun.

6. Goldsmith who worked on rebuilding the gates of Jerusalem (Neh 3:8). His name indicates that he was likely a priest who had the responsibility of making and repairing the temple instruments and vessels (cf. 1 Chr 9:29).

Uzzielite.   Descendant of Uzziel, Kohath's youngest son from Levi's tribe (Nm 3:27; 1 Chr 26:23).

See UZZIEL #1.

Vv

Vaizatha, Vajezatha. One of Haman's 10 sons, who was killed during the Jews' retaliation for Haman's plot to kill them (Est 9:9, KJV Vajezatha).

Vale of Siddim. KJV rendering of the Valley of Siddim in Genesis 14:3–10.

See SIDDIM, VALLEY OF.

Valley Gate. Gate from which Nehemiah went out to inspect the walls of Jerusalem and by which he reentered (Neh 2:13,14). It was on the west side of the city facing the Tyropean Valley. King Uzziah is said to have built and fortified a tower at this gate (2 Chr 26:9).

See JERUSALEM.

Valley of Craftsmen. Translation and alternate name for Ge-harashim in Nehemiah 11:35.

See GE-HARASHIM.

Valley of Decision. Valley near Jerusalem alternately called the Valley of Jehoshaphat in Joel 3:2,12.

See JEHOSHAPHAT, VALLEY OF.

Valley of Hinnom. Valley on the south side of Jerusalem, called Gehenna in the Greek NT.

See GEHENNA.

Valley of Jehoshaphat. See JEHOSHAPHAT, VALLEY OF.

Valley of Jezreel. See JEZREEL, VALLEY OF.

Valley of Rephaim. See REPHAIM, VALLEY OF.

Valley of Shaveh. Valley near Salem, also called the King's Valley in Genesis 14:17.

See KING'S VALLEY.

Valley of Siddim. See SIDDIM, VALLEY OF.

Vaniah. Bani's son and one of the priests who put away his foreign wife at Ezra's command (Ezr 10:36).

Vashni. KJV alternate name for Joel, Samuel's son, in 1 Chronicles 6:28.

See JOEL (PERSON) #2.

Vashti. Queen during the reign of Ahasuerus (Xerxes I) who was deposed for refusing to show herself to the guests at a royal banquet (Est 1:9–19; 2:1,4,17). Since neither she nor Esther is otherwise known in secular history, many have suggested that they were inferior wives or concubines who were simply dignified with the title "queen." According to Plutarch, Persian custom dictated that the kings would ordinarily eat with their legitimate wives, but when they wanted to "riot and drink" they would send their wives away and call in their concubines. While this citation is often used to support the judgment that Vashti was called because she was only a concubine, the opposite conclusion better explains Vashti's refusal to come. Vashti's importance is also indicated by the fact that she sponsored a banquet for the women, that seven chamberlains were sent to summon her, that she was supposed to appear with her "royal crown," that she was always called "queen" until the time of her dismissal, and the fact that her behavior could serve as an example for all the women in the kingdom.

Vegetable. See FOOD AND FOOD PREPARATION; PLANTS.

Veil. *See* FASHION AND DRESS.

Veil of the Temple. Curtain in the sanctuary separating the holy place from the most holy place (Ex 26:31–33).

See TABERNACLE, TEMPLE.

Vermilion. Red pigment used for painting.

See COLOR.

Vespasian. Roman general who entered Palestine in AD 66 to quell the rebellious Jews, and later became emperor of Rome (AD 69–79).

See CAESARS, THE.

Vestments, Biblical. *See* PRIESTS AND LEVITES.

Vine, Vineyard. Plant or place primarily referring to grape cultivation for the production of grapes, raisins, and wine. The grapevine is mentioned frequently in Scripture in a literal and a figurative sense. Probably originating in the Ararat region (Gn 9:20), the vine was also cultivated in ancient Egypt, where tomb murals depict the wine-making process. The Canaanites provided wine for Abraham (Gn 14:18), and Moses described the vineyards in the Promised Land (Dt 6:11). Excellent grapes from the valleys and plains (Nm 13:20,24; Jgs 14:5; 15:5; 16:4) provided fruit and wine to enhance the somewhat monotonous diet of the Hebrews. Wine was an extensive item of trade in the late monarchy (cf. Ez 27:18), and later in the Greek and Roman periods. For the Hebrews, an ideal picture of life was a sedentary one in which a man could remain peacefully in one place, cultivating his plot of land, and sitting under his vine (1 Kgs 4:25).

Christ frequently used the vineyard as a background for his parables (Mt 20:1–6; 21:28–43; Mk 12:1–11; Lk 13:6–9; 20:9–18). Wine-making methods were commonly known and understood, so that an allegory of placing new wine in old wineskins (Mt 9:17) was immediately familiar and significant. In a symbolic sense, Christ described himself as the true vine (Jn 15:1–11), and his blood became the sacramental wine of communion.

The typical vineyard was surrounded by a protective hedge or fence, and at harvest time the watchtower was manned to guard the crop from thieves (Jb 24:18; Is 1:8; Mk 12:1). The vines were planted in rows within the enclosed area, and as the plants grew the tendrils were trained along supports to raise the fruit-bearing branches off the ground (Ez 17:6). The vines were pruned and tended by vinedressers (Lv 25:3; Is 61:5; Jl 3:10; Jn 15:2), and at harvest time the mature fruit was picked and taken to the winepresses (Hos 9:2). A festive atmosphere accompanied the treading of the grapes (Is 16:10; Jer 25:30), and the fermenting juice was collected in new goatskin bags (Mt 9:17) or large pottery jars.

People working in the grape harvest were exempted from military service, which attests to its importance. Taxes and debts were often discharged by payments of wine, and the law provided for the poor to glean in the vineyards as in the wheat fields (Lv 19:9–10). Nonproductive vines were used for producing charcoal (Ez 15:4; Jn 15:6).

See AGRICULTURE; PLANTS (VINE).

Vinedresser. *See* AGRICULTURE; PLANTS (VINE); TRADES AND OCCUPATIONS (FARMER); VINE, VINEYARD.

Vinegar. *See* FOOD AND FOOD PREPARATION.

Vine of Sodom. Designation for a plant which produces an appetizing but inedible fruit in Deuteronomy 32:32.

See PLANTS (GOURD, WILD).

Vineyards, Plain of the. English translation of Abel-keramim, the name of a place of victory for the judge Jephthah in Judges 11:33.

See ABEL-KERAMIM.

Viol. KJV rendering of harp in Isaiah 5:12; 14:11; Amos 5:23; and 6:5.

See MUSIC AND MUSICAL INSTRUMENTS (NEBEL).

A grape vine near Hebron.

Violet. Color used in Jeremiah's denunciation of idols—they are described as wearing garments of violet and purple, colors indicative of wealth and royalty (Jer 10:9; KJV, NIV blue). The color, elsewhere rendered as "blue," was derived from a blue dye obtained from the cerulean mussel.

See COLOR.

Viper. *See* ANIMALS (ADDER).

Virgin. Word used only of women and (metaphorically) of places, nations, and the church. Literally, it describes a woman who has reached physical maturity but has not experienced sexual intercourse. Mary, mother of Jesus, is an obvious example (Mt 1:18–25).

The OT puts a very high value on premarital virginity. One of Rebekah's qualities which made her a suitable bride for Isaac was her virginity (Gn 24:16). The Law prescribed that priests, as men whose lives should conform most closely to God's standards, must marry only virgins (Lv 21:7,13,14).

Undoubtedly this reflects the whole Bible's teaching on marriage, with its ideal of exclusive faithfulness. The NT expresses that ideal by its ban on premarital intercourse (1 Cor 6:13,18), and by its use of "virgin" language to describe Christians who remain faithful to their Lord (Rv 14:4; cf. 2 Cor 11:2).

Negatively, the OT highlights the same principle in the penalties it lays down for the loss of a woman's virginity. If the man is morally responsible, he must either marry her or compensate her father (Ex 22:16,17). If the woman herself is to blame, the punishment is death (Dt 22:20,21).

The OT says little, however, to commend life-long virginity. Jeremiah was told not to marry, only to reinforce God's warning of coming judgment (Jer 16:2). From the woman's point of view, it was a tragedy to remain an unmarried virgin and therefore childless for life (cf. Jgs 11:37).

The NT echoes the value of marriage but brings out more clearly the advantages of a commitment to virginity for Christian men as well as women. Celibacy for some is God's gift, declares Paul, with positive gains for Christian service (1 Cor 7:7,25–38). And Jesus commends those who "make themselves eunuchs" for the kingdom of heaven's sake (Mt 19:12).

In praising the single life Jesus was, of course, drawing attention to his own example—denying the current misunderstanding that virgins can never experience human love and fulfillment.

See FAMILY LIFE AND RELATIONS; MARRIAGE, MARRIAGE CUSTOMS; SEX, SEXUALITY; VIRGIN BIRTH OF JESUS; WOMAN, DOCTRINE OF.

Virgin Birth of Jesus. Doctrine, from the birth narratives of Matthew 1 and Luke 1–2, which states that Jesus the Christ was conceived of the Holy Spirit and born of the virgin Mary. This doctrine has been at the heart of discussions involving the person and nature of Christ; the whole concept of the incarnation as well as of the divine and human natures focuses upon this historical event as its foundation. At the same time, rationalists and literary critics make this one of the first biblical events to be denied on the grounds of its obvious supernatural basis and so-called "mythical" form.

Pagan Parallels. The major pagan source is Greek mythology. Those who follow this theory argue that the early church first propounded the belief that Jesus was the Son of God and then proved it by using Hellenistic parallels. In Greek mythology Zeus as well as the other gods bore many children by human mothers, including Perseus and Hercules. These offspring were also men of heroic proportion. In addition, there were tales of the miraculous births of great historical figures, such as Plato (whose father was Apollo) or Alexander the Great (whose father, Philip of Macedon, was kept from consummating his marriage until the child, conceived of Zeus, was born). Interestingly, the church fathers often used these stories in their polemic against their Greek opponents to show that the idea of the virgin birth was not really so incredible to the Greek mind. However, the differences between the pagan and Christian forms are too great. For one thing, the lustful promiscuity of the gods starkly contrasts with the spiritual simplicity of the NT. Also, the concept of "virgin" hardly has any stress. In all cases, it is a physical union between god and human versus the spiritual conception of Jesus.

The same is true of the birth of Buddha, for the oldest records state that the entrance of the "white elephant" (representing the spirit of childbirth) into Gautama's mother took place in a dream, and the story of an actual virgin birth is post-Christian. As for the Persian myths of the birth of Zoroaster or the birth of Mithras from a rock, there is no concept of a virgin birth. Babylonian tales do involve the goddess-mother Ishtar, but again virginity has no emphasis and is actually doubtful. In conclusion, while there are slight analogical similarities between the virgin birth of Jesus and pagan parallels, one cannot establish any genealogical connection. The source of the doctrine is found in historical event, not literary parallels.

The Old Testament Prophecy. Isaiah 7:14 says that a "virgin" (or "young woman") shall "conceive and bear a son . . . Immanuel," and

Matthew 1:22,23 expressly states that this was fulfilled in Jesus' birth. This passage has been greatly debated, especially since the RSV changed the KJV "virgin" to "young woman." The term in the Hebrew original and the Septuagint is ambiguous. The Hebraic 'almah refers generally to a young girl who has passed puberty and thus is of marriageable age. Virginity was not stressed (Hebrew bethulah), but certainly was true in that culture. The Septuagint parthenos does denote a virgin, but there is no proof that the translator definitely understood this as a virgin birth.

From these linguistic considerations come the following theories. (1) The "virgin" (Is 7:14) was Ahaz's new wife and the son was Hezekiah; but the latter was nine years old when Ahaz began to reign, and this prophecy looks to the future. (2) She was Isaiah's wife and the son was Maher-shalal-hashbaz, which many deem probable since the definite article with 'almah seems to indicate that the woman was known to Isaiah and Ahaz and since verses 15,16 seem to state that the prophecy was to be fulfilled in Isaiah's time. The difficulty here is that Isaiah's wife already had a son and so could not be called 'almah.

(3) The prophecy is purely messianic. This is the traditional evangelical position, based on the naming of the child Immanuel, "God with us," and the reference (Is 9:6,7; 11:1–5) which points to a divine person. However, many evangelicals recently have opted for a fourth position, which fits the arguments for the historical and the futuristic positions, that is, multiple fulfillment. This view notes the historical fulfillment intended in verses 15,16 and yet realizes the future reference noted in Matthew 1:22,23.

The Gospel Records. Neither Mark nor John provides an account of the birth of Christ; the actual event is chronicled only in Matthew and Luke. Both agree that a "virgin," Mary, conceived of the Holy Spirit and bore a son, Jesus. Matthew's account is simpler and more direct, attributing the birth of the Messiah to divine origins and highlighting the christological significance. In the genealogy (1:1–17), Matthew uses a threefold pattern of 14 figures to stress the Davidic overtones of Jesus' messiahship (14 is the numerical sum of the Hebrew letters for "David"). In the birth scene (vv 18–25) Jesus is further connected to the exodus account and both the meaning ("savior," v 21) and significance stressing the divinity ("God with us") of the Christ is brought out. The scene where Joseph decides to privately divorce Mary is added to give even greater stress to the miraculous conception. The magi story (2:1–12) emphasizes the divine revelation behind the birth of the royal Messiah, and the malevolent plot of Herod (vv 13–23) brings out the divine protection and victorious power of God behind the birth. In short, Jesus is seen as Son of David and Son of God, revealed by the Father to Jew and Gentile (the magi) alike, and divinely protected in the midst of suffering. The unifying thread binding these themes is the fulfillment of Scripture, which again points especially to the divine ordination of the event.

Luke's chronicle is more complex, developing in several directions at the same time. Here the unifying theme is the witness of the Holy Spirit, used to show the true significance of the infant Messiah. A secondary motif is worship; the geographical core of the narratives is the temple, and Christ is pictured (throughout Luke–Acts) as fulfilling the temple worship system. Finally, Luke's account shows parallels between Jesus and John the Baptist. The first two scenes relate the annunciations of the Baptist (1:8–25) and of Jesus (vv 26–38), and the fourth and fifth scenes concern the birth, circumcision, and naming of the two (vv 57–66; 2:1–21). The middle episode, comprising the Magnificat (1:39–56), concerns the encounter of the two mothers. In so doing, the future ministry of the Messiah is set in bold relief by comparison with the one who would prepare the way. In every case Jesus is exalted to the higher place; John was born naturally to human parents, while in 1:27 Luke twice repeats the designation of Mary as a "virgin." The angelic messenger calls John "filled with the Holy Spirit" and "in the spirit and power of Elijah," while Jesus is "Son of the Most High," inhabiting "the throne of his father David . . . forever" (vv 15–17; cf. vv 32–33). At John's birth Zechariah praises God (vv 68–79, the Benedictus) but at Jesus' birth the "heavenly host" sings glory to God (2:13,14). The final act, the presentation in the temple (vv 22–40), sums up the theology contrasted in the preceding scenes. Both Simeon and Anna parallel Zechariah's previous prophecy of the Baptist's future ministry, but in so doing they are building on the angels' previous annunciation and so summarize the worship and exaltation aspects of the incarnation. Finally, Luke demonstrates that truly pious Israel worshiped at the feet of Jesus, seen in the shepherds as well as Simeon and Anna.

Modern Objections. Some scholars argue on literary grounds that the virgin birth represents a theological portrait of Jesus' significance rather than a historical event. There are two arguments: there are no corroborating witnesses, that is, no references in the epistles or eyewitnesses who saw the event; and there are conflicting details, such as the different episodes in the accounts (Matthew's magi and

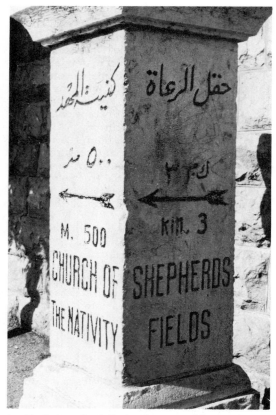

An old milestone directs the traveler to two of the most important Christian sites in the Holy Land.

flight into Egypt, Luke's annunciation scenes and presentation in the temple), as well as contrasts (the two genealogies, Luke's omission of their original home in Bethlehem) and historical errors (the massacre of the children, not mentioned in secular history; and the census, which Luke dates 10 years earlier than secular records). According to this approach, the infancy narratives do not attempt to provide factual history but are creative midrash stories which rewrite OT episodes (e.g., the magi story parallels the Balaam account; Herod's slaughter parallels Pharaoh; etc.).

Many evangelical works have been written to answer these objections. First, the so-called "silence" of the other NT works is not a final argument. While explicit allusions are missing, there are some implicit statements, such as Mark's "the carpenter" (6:3) and Matthew's "the carpenter's son" (13:55), or Paul's "born of a woman" (Gal 4:4). Many believe that strong incarnational hymns such as Philippians 2:6–8 assume the virgin birth. It is extremely doubtful that the other NT writers knew nothing of the doctrine; even liberal scholars admit that the doctrine was known

during Paul's ministry (and especially John's) and that the event was not discussed for other reasons, mainly because they were proclaiming theological meaning, the gospel, more than historical data. Second, the historical inconsistencies are a misreading of the evidence. It will suffice here to state that such pessimistic conclusions are not warranted. The historicity of the virgin birth can be reasonably affirmed.

Theological Implications. From the very beginning the doctrine of the virgin birth became the foundation of a high Christology. Many have pointed out that the earliest church fathers stressed this more perhaps than any other event as proof of the incarnation and deity of Christ. Justin Martyr and Ignatius defended the virgin birth against opponents at the beginning of the 2nd century, and even at that early date it appeared to be a fixed doctrine. In the acrimonious debates of the next three centuries, the virgin birth became a prominent issue. Gnostics (e.g., Marcion) contended that Christ descended directly from heaven and so was never truly human. On the other hand those groups which denied his deity, such as the Arians, concommitantly denied the virgin birth, stating that at his baptism Jesus was "adopted" as Son of God. The Council of Nicaea in AD 325 affirmed that Jesus was truly God, and then the Council of Chalcedon in AD 451 stated that Jesus was at the same time human and divine, a "hypostatic union" of the true natures. These were summarized in the Apostles' Creed of the 5th century, which declares "I believe in . . . Jesus Christ, his only Son, our Lord, conceived of the Holy Ghost, born of the Virgin Mary." In most of the creeds the virgin birth is also connected to Jesus' sinlessness, inasmuch as his incarnate, divine nature is the source of his sinlessness.

From the beginning, as attested in Matthew and Luke as well as the early patristic writers, the virgin birth has been a cardinal doctrine of the church. As such it is a living symbol of the twofold nature of our Lord, born of the Holy Spirit and of woman, and uniting the human and divine into the incarnate God-man, Jesus Christ. The teaching of the NT is clear on these aspects.   GRANT R. OSBORNE

See CHRISTOLOGY; JESUS CHRIST, LIFE AND TEACHING OF; INCARNATION; GENEALOGY OF JESUS CHRIST; VIRGIN.

Bibliography. T. Boslooper, *The Virgin Birth;* R.E. Brown, *The Virginal Conception and Bodily Resurrection of Jesus;* D. Edwards, *The Virgin Birth in History and Faith;* R.G. Gromacki, *The Virgin Birth: Doctrine of Deity;* J.G. Machen, *The Virgin Birth of Christ;* J. Orr, *The Virgin Birth of Christ;* H. von Campenhausen, *The Virgin Birth in the Theology of the Ancient Church.*

Vision. Visual experience of any kind. The term is sometimes used of dreams with no thought of supernatural revelation (see literal renderings of Jb 20:8; cf. 7:14; Is 29:7), but usually refers to the extraordinary religious experience of a prophet. In early OT prophecy there are cases of second sight, which was regarded as evidence of the visionary endowment of a prophet. Samuel was a "seer" or visionary, able to "see" the lost asses of Saul and to tell him their whereabouts (1 Sm 9:19,20). Elisha was able to follow Gehazi's wrongful actions "in spirit" and confront him on his return (2 Kgs 5:26). This psychic gift was evidently part of the divinely bestowed equipment of a "man of God" or prophet.

Apart from these visions of present happenings occurring elsewhere on earth, there are more complex series of visionary experience which give insight either into the future or into God's will for the person receiving the vision or for others under his responsibility. Visions are often closely coupled with dreams. Both experiences are regarded as legitimate channels of divine revelation, although the OT attests that counterfeit claims concerning both could be made. In Genesis 46:2 God speaks to Jacob "in a vision" (cf. Jb 33:15). In Numbers 12:6 normal prophetic revelation through the media of visions or dreams is contrasted with the yet higher form of communication enjoyed by Moses. Nor were God's servants the only recipients of this type of revelation: Nebuchadnezzar's "dream" or "night vision" of the tree in Daniel 4 is recognized as a medium of divine communication.

Presumably visions are distinguished from dreams as being daytime experiences. There are different types of revelatory vision. At one extreme is the ecstatic experience of Ezekiel, a psychic trance which could involve translation to other places (Ez 8:3; 40:2). Daniel's vision (Dn 8) was probably of the same type, and so perhaps was Jeremiah's experience (Jer 13:4–7). At the other extreme is what has been called symbolical perception. In this case a prophet sees an ordinary object which is part of the natural world, but sees it with a heightened significance beyond the normal. The basket of summer fruit which God "caused" Amos "to see" (Am 8:1,2) seems to fall into this category, and so probably do Jeremiah's visions of the almond branch and the tilting pot (Jer 1:11,13). An intermediate type includes the pictorial heavenly visions of 1 Kings 22:19–22 and Isaiah 6.

Prophecy could come via either an auditory or a visual experience. Typically in the course of a vision a verbal message was communicated, so that the seeing and hearing took place within the same supernatural experience. This is clearly so in the case of Isaiah's inaugural vision: the prophet both "saw the Lord" and heard his voice. Seeing a vision of God is paralleled with hearing his words in the case of Balaam in Numbers 24:4,16. In any vision the elements of seeing or hearing might come to the fore (cf. Gn 15:1). In fact an auditory experience could itself be called a vision, for the divine word is a revelation from God. It is often difficult to know whether the term "vision" includes a predominant element of hearing or is used in the wider sense of revelation (e.g., Ez 12:21–28).

Often "vision" is apparently used simply as a technical term for a verbal communication from God. Thus Samuel's call is literally called a vision (1 Sm 3:15), and the same term seems to have this auditory meaning (v 1). Some prophetic books are called "visions" in their headings (Is 1:1; Ob 1; Na 1:1). Nathan's prophecy of God's covenant with David is literally described as a vision (2 Sm 7:17; 1 Chr 17:15; Ps 89:19). In Daniel 9:24 "to seal both vision and prophet" means to authenticate the prophecy of Jeremiah referred to in verse 2. In the famous proverb traditionally rendered "Where there is no vision, the people perish," (Prv 29:18) the term "vision" refers to prophetic revelation, the divine gift of prophecy which was intended as a guiding influence upon Israelite society.

The OT recognizes that prophetic visions were not necessarily authentic. Although the recipient might sincerely understand them as divine revelations, their contents might brand them as false, or else time might reveal them to be purely subjective and arising solely from the subconscious human mind (Jer 14:14, 23:16; Lam 2:14; cf. Dt 18:20–22). This phenomenon was part of the larger issue of the necessity of discerning true and false prophecy, a concern of the NT (1 Jn 4:1; cf. 1 Cor 12:3).

See PROPHECY; DREAMS.

Vole. Small mouselike, burrowing animal (1 Sm 6:4,5).

See ANIMALS.

Vophsi. Man appointed by Moses from Naphtali's tribe to spy out the land of Canaan (Nm 13:14).

Vow. Serious promise or pledge. The making of vows to God is a religious practice which is frequently mentioned in Scripture. Most references to vows are found in the OT, especially in the psalms, but there are a few in the NT as well.

Unlike tithing, sacrifices and offerings, Sabbath-keeping, and circumcision, vow making was not something commanded by the Mosaic law. There are rules regulating the carrying out of vows which have been taken (even to the possible cancellation of a woman's careless vow by a discerning father or husband—Nm 30:5,8), but the making of them seems to be more a traditional and personal matter.

For example, Psalm 50:14 says, "Offer to God a sacrifice of thanksgiving; and pay your vows to the Most High." The command is to "pay," that is, to keep or fulfill a pledge that has already been made. No order is given to make such promises in the first place. The practice is accepted and regulated, but not demanded.

The purpose of a vow is either to win a desired favor from the Lord, to express gratitude to him for some deliverance or benefit, or else simply to prove absolute devotion to him by way of certain abstinences and nonconformities.

The NT information about vows sets the stage for reviewing the background information concerning what was by then a long-established custom. The term "vow" occurs just twice in the NT, both times in association with the apostle Paul (Acts 18:18; 21:23,24). But the same principle is involved in the case of the word "Corban" (Mk 7:11–13; cf. Mt 15:5,6). The Lord in these two passages severely rebukes those who have made a vow that served as a clever escape from meeting obligations to care for aged parents. A monetary figure was involved in such a "gift" or "offering." But Jesus declares that God does not want a gift which is designed to deprive someone.

In the case of Paul, he may have entered into his vows for the very purpose of forestalling objections which either antagonistic Jews or Jewish Christian believers had to his removing the yoke of Mosaic regulations from the shoulders of Gentile believers. At least he did not despise this practice of OT piety. This is especially true of the second of the two passages cited above. Paul was in Jerusalem under the keen surveillance of Jewish authorities. He made it a point to join with four other Jewish believers in the payment of vows in the temple. This action, however, was misconstrued by his enemies, who charged that he was bringing Gentiles into the holy temple.

Although vows seemed to be an important expression of spiritual commitment in OT times, there is little information and no real stress on vows in the NT. Spirituality is elevated to a higher plane for the Spirit-filled NT believer. Demonstration of devotion to the Lord is not an occasional thing. The all-pervasive reason for and measure of dedication to God in Christ is well summed up in 1 Corinthians 6:20: "You were bought with a price. So glorify God in your body."

The opening verses of Psalm 132 afford an excellent example of the expression of unselfish devotion on the part of David. He calls upon God to remember his strong determination to build a permanent home for the ark of the covenant, his determination to do something that expresses love for his great Redeemer. David exclaims, "I will not enter my house or get into my bed; I will not give sleep to my eyes or slumber to my eyelids, until I find a place for the Lord, a dwelling place for the Mighty One of Jacob" (Ps 132:3–5).

Dedication of self and separation to the Lord is the primary feature of the Nazirite vow. Samson, Samuel, and John the Baptist are the most familiar examples of this type of vow. Numbers 6:1–8 prescribes the conditions of this commitment, and verses 13–21 tell how release may be obtained by fulfillment and certain sacrifices. Women as well as men might take this vow of separation which could be of limited duration. The Rechabite clan pledged themselves to an ascetic and nomadic life. They constitute a compelling illustration of loyalty to the God of Israel (Jer 35).

Frequently, however, vows were taken as a type of bargain with God. At Bethel Jacob promised God worship and the tithe if he would protect him and supply his needs. Jephthah vowed to sacrifice whatever first met him on his return home victorious over the Ammonites (Jgs 11:30,31). Hannah offered to return her son to God (1 Sm 1:11,27,28). In the psalms, payment of vows is often associated with thanksgiving for deliverance from danger or affliction (e.g., 22:24,25; 56:12,13).

Most important is that once a vow is made, the obligation is serious. To refrain from making any vow is no sin (Dt 23:22), but once declared, the vow must be kept (Dt 23:21–23; see also Nm 30:2; Eccl 5:4–6).   MILTON C. FISHER

See COVENANT; OATH.

Vulture.   *See* BIRDS.

Ww

Wadi. Intermittent stream or torrent in the arid and semiarid regions of the Middle East. Although the stream beds were usually dry, they could attain flood proportions during spring runoff or after heavy rainfalls. The most significant wadi in the Bible was the Wadi of Egypt (NIV, RSV Brook of Egypt), which served as the southwestern border of Canaan according to God's instructions to Moses (Nm 34:5; Jos 15:4,47; 1 Kgs 8:65; Is 27:12). During the dry periods, wadis were important as roadways (e.g., Wadi Zin served as the route through the wilderness of Zin, Nm 27:14).

Wages. Payment received by a laborer in return for his work. Usually wages are calculated in terms of a medium of exchange, such as money, but they can be paid in any kind of goods or services. Jacob worked seven years in return for Laban's younger daughter, Rachel (Gn 29:18–20), and then had to work another seven years when Laban did not honor his agreement. Later, Jacob's wages were selected

A wadi in the Arabian Desert.

sheep and goats (30:31,32; 31:8). Nebuchadnezzar was given the country of Egypt as wages for his work in capturing the city of Tyre (Ez 29:18–20).

Usually wages were agreed upon by employer and employee (Gn 29:15–19; Mt 20:2), but sometimes the pay was at the discretion of the employer (Mt 20:4).

A fair wage for honest work is a biblical principle (Lk 10:7; 1 Tm 5:18). The Lord established laws to cover this principle and judged those who violated it. Wages were to be paid promptly (Lv 19:13); holding back of wages is condemned in the Scripture (Jas 5:1–6, esp v 4). The Lord declares that he will draw near for judgment and be a swift witness against various categories of evildoers, among whom he lists "those who oppress the hireling in his wages" (Mal 3:5).

Wages were often a source of discontent and dispute between employer and employee. When soldiers came to John the Baptist to be baptized and asked about their future conduct, he urged them to be "content with their wages" (Lk 3:14; cf. Heb 13:5). Jacob and Laban had disagreements about wages and twice Jacob complained, "You have changed my wages ten times" (Gn 31:7,41).

The earning of wages carries with it certain responsibilities before God. The prophet Haggai declared that "he who earns wages earns wages to put them into a bag with holes" (Hg 1:6). The Lord said: "You have looked for much, and, lo, it came to little; and when you brought it home, I blew it away" (v 9). The reason for this was their self-indulgence and neglect of the house and work of the Lord.

The Bible also speaks of ill-gotten wages. The wages of a prostitute could not be brought into the house of the Lord (Dt 23:18), and people are warned against the error of Balaam, who corrupted Israel because he "loved the wages of unrighteousness" (2 Pt 2:15 KJV).

There are wages which men do not wish to receive but payment is unavoidable; "the wages of sin is death, but the free gift of God is eternal life in Christ Jesus our Lord" (Rom 6:23).

See POOR, THE; RICHES; MONEY AND BANKING; WORK, BIBLICAL VIEW OF.

Waheb. Description of the borders of Moab in Numbers 21:14. The meaning of the expression is obscure. The KJV translates Waheb as a verb, "what he did in the Red Sea." The NIV also translates it as a verb with the more plausible, "I have been given from Suphah." Whether or not it is a proper noun, the location of either Waheb or Suphah is unknown.

See SUPHAH.

Wall. *See* ARCHITECTURE; ARMS AND WARFARE.

Walnut. *See* PLANTS.

Wanderings in the Wilderness. *See* WILDERNESS WANDERINGS.

War, Holy. Warfare as described in the Book of Deuteronomy, especially in chapter 20. Not merely a human enterprise fought by kings with trained soldiers and military equipment, it is God's war in which he himself is involved together with his covenant people who are selected to fight in his name. The size of the army is not important; indeed, often the numbers were pared down to dramatize the fact that the victory was gained, not by military superiority, but by the action of God against his enemies. When Israel lived in obedience to God as his covenant people and went into battle under his direction, war was within the will of God, commanded by him, and accomplished through trust in him. As already observed, God was known as "a man of war," and it is declared that "the battle is the Lord's" (1 Sm 17:47; cf. 18:17; 25:28). With this faith on the part of the Jews, it is easy to see how a concept of holy war developed, especially when they had the conviction that their enemies were God's enemies and that they were the people through whom God would effect his saving purposes for the world.

Moses believed that God declares war and sends his people into battle (Ex 17:16; Nm 31:3). On several occasions, at crucial points in warfare, the "terror of the Lord" fell upon the enemy, enabling the numerically inferior army of Israel to gain an easy victory over vastly superior forces (Jos 10:10–14; Jgs 4:12–

16; 2 Sm 5:24,25). In a time of acute military crisis Elisha is enabled to see the heavenly army of Jehovah drawn up on the hills around Samaria ready to defeat the fierce invading armies of Syria. In response to Elisha's prayer, the Syrian soldiers are struck with blindness and rendered helpless against the Israelites (2 Kgs 6:15–23). Various means were used to determine the will of God and to assure his active participation in war. In addition to the word of the prophet (1 Kgs 22:5–23), dreams, (Jgs 7:9–14), Urim and Thummim (Ex 28:30; Lv 8:8), the ephod (1 Sm 30:7), and the ark of the covenant were employed for this purpose. The leaders of God's troops were constantly to seek his direction for military strategy during the progress of battle, for no step was to be taken without divine approval and guidance (2 Sm 5:19–23).

Since God gave Palestine to the Jews as his own people, the land was indeed the Promised Land; it belonged by divine covenant to Israel and was in that sense "the Holy Land." Any defense of that land against foreign invasion was a holy war. The invading enemy was trespassing upon sacred territory that belonged to God's people by immutable decree and thus incurred the divine wrath. From this perspective the complete destruction of Israel's enemies is necessary, particularly when the enemy was pagan and morally corrupt. A characteristic Hebrew word used for this concept, *ḥērem*, originally meant "devoted" and came to mean "devoted to destruction" as something hostile to the rule of God (Jos 6:17,18). Means which may seem drastic and extreme were demanded in order to assure the success of God's holy, saving purposes for his chosen people and ultimately for the whole world. The divine plan must not be thwarted, obstructed, or aborted by any debasing idolatry or corrupting immorality (Dt 7:1–26). Enemy cities within the boundaries of the land promised to the Jews were to be utterly destroyed, a practice known as "the ban." Only silver, gold, and vessels of bronze and iron were to be spared. They were to be placed in the treasury of the Lord as sacred to him (Jos 6:17–21; 1 Sm 15:3). The whole city, including all life, was regarded as a sacrifice to Jehovah, emphasizing the sacrificial character of holy war. Fruit-bearing trees, however, were to be spared (Dt 20:19,20) as an example of the limitations placed upon wanton destruction of natural resources, which are God's gifts.

When Israel departed from God and forsook his holy ways, the Lord used its enemies to chastise and discipline, to bring it back to himself, and to bring to pass his sovereign purposes. Thus God used war as a punishment against his sinning people (Is 10; Jer 25; Ez 21;

Hb 1). At such a time the false prophet prophesies peace and security (Jer 28).

The fact that holy war was never engaged by means of military power and genius alone is characteristic of God's ways with his people. The commander and often his subordinates were viewed as elected by God and endowed by the Spirit of God with a special gift for their military roles (Jgs 6:34,35; 11:29–33). If this divine gift were lost or forfeited for any reason, the authority to lead or to command was also lost (Jgs 16:20,21; 1 Sm 16:14). Participation in holy war required complete surrender and dedication to the service of Jehovah. There was no place for the half-hearted, the fearful, or those distracted by other involvements or obligations (Dt 20:5–9). The presence of such persons in the army would affect the unity and singlemindedness of those who were wholly committed to the cause of the Lord.

The faithful soldier who offered himself willingly in response to the divine call was considered consecrated to God's service and was in a sense a holy servant of the Lord (Is 13:3). God is said to "walk in the midst of the camp," and therefore the camp should be holy "that he may not see anything indecent among you, and turn away from you" (Dt 23:14). Careful regulations were observed to guarantee the ritual cleanliness of the camp: any bodily contamination required a rite of purification and excrement was buried outside the camp (vv 9–13).

Victory in holy war was completely unrelated to military superiority, either with respect to armaments or numbers of soldiers (Jgs 7; 1 Sm 14:6–23), because "he who goes over before you as a devouring fire is the Lord your God; he will destroy them and subdue them before you; so you shall drive them out, and make them perish quickly, as the Lord has promised you" (Dt 9:3; cf. 20:4). God delivers the enemy into Israel's hand (Jgs 3:28; 7:15). He also cautions the Israelites not to think that their righteousness brought down their enemies in defeat and won the land, but that by God's own righteousness and judgment against the wickedness of the idolatrous nations he drove them out before the army of Israel. It was because of his faithfulness to the covenant which he swore to their fathers, to Abraham, Isaac, and Jacob (Dt 9:4,5). God reminds Israel of their unfaithfulness, stubbornness, and unrighteousness (vv 6–29), and exhorts them to fear the Lord their God and to walk in all his ways, to love him, to serve him with all their heart, and to keep all his commandments in order that he may bless them and give them peace in the land which he promised to their fathers (10:1–22). The Jews had to be reminded that it was for their disobedience and lack of faith in not going directly into the Promised Land at Kadesh-barnea that they were punished with 40 years of wandering in the Sinai wilderness (Nm 14:1–12).

In sharp contrast to such unbelief and failure to obey the will of God is the heroic example of Jonathan in his singlehanded attack against the Philistine garrison in the pass between Michmash and Geba (1 Sm 14). Convinced that the Lord would give the Philistines into his hand, Jonathan said to the young man who bore his armor, "Come, let us go over to the garrison of these uncircumcised; it may be that the Lord will work for us; for nothing can hinder the Lord from saving by many or by few" (v 6). Similarly, David's willingness to fight unassisted against the giant Goliath shows his firm trust in God— "Who is this uncircumcised Philistine, that he should defy the armies of the living God?" (17:26).

The idea of holy war was not exclusive to Israel. Other nations also believed that their gods fought for them in military conflicts, and usually the nation with the most powerful god won the battle. When the Philistines defeated the Israelites and captured the ark, they believed that they had won the conflict because their god Dagon was stronger than Israel's Jehovah. The biblical writer carefully makes clear that this is not the case. He explicitly points out the dramatic incident of Dagon falling on his face and being broken into pieces before the captured ark of God. In addition to this, the people of Ashdod were so terrified and afflicted with tumors that they cried, "The ark of the God of Israel must not remain with us; for his hand is heavy upon us and upon Dagon our god." Their panic and affliction continued until arrangements were made to return the ark with a guilt offering to the Israelites at Beth-shemesh (1 Sm 4–6). In the days of Mesha, king of Moab, the defeat of his army at one time was attributed to the weakness of his god Chemosh (2 Kgs 3:21–26), but his victory over the Israelites at a later time was attributed by him to the power of Chemosh. Sometimes the victory was determined by the particular place of battle, because the god of that locality was a god either of the hills, the valleys, or the plain (1 Kgs 20:28; 2 Kgs 18:33–35).

The idea of holy war was probably most intense during the time of the judges. Its centrality in the thinking of the nation of Israel diminished during the time of the monarchy. The progression of spiritual decline and apostasy brought a corresponding loss of trust in and expectancy of divine initiative and involvement in warfare. Considerations of political expediency overshadowed the holy war ideology.

In protesting this apostasy, the prophets viewed war as a divine judgment against the rebellious nation and also against the proud, defiant gentile powers. The tradition of holy war was preserved mostly among the ordinary, devout people rather than among the political and military leaders, and thus it survived throughout the time of the monarchy. For example, Uriah the Hittite seemed to be more faithful to the principles of holy war than King David, whose evil desires toward Bathsheba blinded him to divine regulations governing the affairs of war and even to the basic morality of the Decalogue (2 Sm 11).

There was a distinctly teleological aspect to the concept of holy war. It looked beyond the triumphs of God in specific battles to the conclusion of all hostilities and to a final time of peace which will vindicate the righteousness and sovereignty of God's saving purposes and display his concern and goal for his own people. Holy war is the instrument of the God of the covenant who has promised deliverance and eschatological victory. The final consummation will be preceded by a massive holy war, after which the weapons of warfare will be transformed into implements of peace (Is 2:4; Mi 4:3) under the reign of the Messiah, the Prince of Peace (Is 9:6), who will subdue all the enemies of Jehovah in a triumphant Day of the Lord (Ps 110; Dn 7; Zec 14).

RALPH E. POWELL

See ARMS AND WARFARE.

War, Warrior, Warfare. *See* ARMS AND WARFARE; TRADES AND OCCUPATIONS (SOLDIER).

Wars of the Lord, Book of. Literary work mentioned once in the OT (Nm 21:14); it is found in a description of Moab's border at the Arnon. The book was used as a source, but is no longer extant. It probably contained a record of Israel's conquest in Transjordan and may be identical to the "Book at the Upright [Jashar]" (Jos 10:13; 2 Sm 1:18). The passage in Numbers has a poetic style and pertains to Israel's conquest and warfare. However, the extent of the quotation is debatable. Some limit it to verse 14, others include verse 15, and others include verses 27–30. The finalized form of the work may be dated to the period of the wilderness wanderings.

The Septuagint and the Targums see in the word "book" a reference to the Law. This explains the Septuagint translation: "Therefore it is said in the Book: the wars of the Lord. . . ." However, most commentators look at the reference to the book as a separate composition from which the author of Numbers 21 quoted.

Watch. Principal unit for the division of the night in both the OT and NT. During the OT period, the night was divided into three military watches. The beginning or evening watch ran from sunset to roughly 10:00 PM (Lm 2:19); the middle or night watch was from 10:00 PM to 2:00 AM (Jgs 7:19); and the morning watch was from approximately 2:00 AM until sunrise (Ex 14:24; 1 Sm 11:11). During the Roman period, the number of watches was increased from three to four. These were either described by number (first, second, etc.) or as evening, midnight, cock-crowing, and morning (Mt 14:25; Mk 6:48). The respective watches ended at roughly 9:00 PM, midnight, 3:00 AM, and 6:00 AM. Since the watches were divided primarily for security and military purposes, the term "watch" was occasionally used to refer to the watchmen as well as the time during which they were watching (Jer 51:12).

Watchman. *See* TRADES AND OCCUPATIONS.

Watchtower. Platform from which farmers protected their land and livestock and soldiers guarded their cities. Watchtowers were built in the vineyards of Palestine. From the tower the watchman was assigned to oversee the vineyard, protecting it from wild animals and thieves (Is 5:2; Mt 21:33; Mk 12:1). Such structures are still used for similar purposes in Palestine and serve as the living quarters for the vineyard workers. Some watchtowers, like the tower of Eder (Gn 35:21), were constructed in wilderness areas. They provided a protected shelter for shepherds to watch their flocks and a fortified outpost for sentinels to guard a city and to safeguard its commerce from marauding bandits (2 Kgs 18:8; 2 Chr 20:24; Is 32:14).

See FORT, FORTIFICATIONS.

Water. One of the essentials of life which covers much of the earth's surface and is the primary component of the human body. Life cannot be sustained more than a few days without it.

In the beginning, when God first created the heavens and the earth, water was created before light, dry land, or vegetable, animal, and human life. The Lord declares that scoffers "deliberately ignore this fact, that by the word of God heavens existed long ago, and an earth formed out of water and by means of water" (2 Pt 3:5).

The amount of water and the relationship between water and land are important. The Lord used an overwhelming mass and movement of water to destroy "the world that then existed" (2 Pt 3:6), as punishment for its wick-

A watchtower on the south side of the Levonah Valley, in the mountains on the border between Samaria and Judea.

edness. On the other hand, extended drought also causes death.

When the Lord created the garden of Eden, he made a river to water it. This river divided into four rivers, of which two are identified with certainty, the Euphrates and the Tigris, which have sustained agricultural life in the Mesopotamian area both in antiquity and today (cf. Gn 2:10–14). The Bible also relates that early in the history of the earth there was no rain, but a mist that watered the earth (vv 5,6).

In the Near East, water is of special importance, for much of the area receives only moderate amounts of rainfall. In Egypt, for example, only two to four inches of rain falls in the area of Cairo, and at Aswan the average annual rainfall is zero. Egypt was dependent upon the Nile, which was sustained by equatorial rains. On the other hand, Palestine "drinks water by the rain from heaven" (Dt 11:10,11).

Water has many symbolic usages in Scrip-

A water fountain.

ture. It is used in ceremonies of purification and cleansing. The consecretion of the priests involved washing with water (Lv 8:6); parts of the animal sacrifices were washed (1:9,13).

The righteous man is like a tree planted by streams of water (Ps 1:3; Jer 17:8). The longing of the soul after God is likened to thirst for water: "My soul thirsts for thee; . . . as in a dry and weary land where no water is" (Ps 63:1). "My soul thirsts for thee like a parched land" (Ps 143:6). Jesus fulfills this need and declares, "If any one thirst, let him come to me and drink" (Jn 7:37). "Whoever drinks of the water that I shall give him will never thirst; the water that I shall give him will become in him a spring of water welling up to eternal life" (Jn 4:14).

The Word of God is presented as water by which spiritual cleansing is effected. The Lord speaks of the cleansing of the church by "the washing of water with the word" (Eph 5:26) and in Titus people are saved "by the washing of regeneration and renewal in the Holy Spirit" (3:5).

This renewing was symbolized by baptism, which was performed where "there was much water" (Jn 3:23). This figure is also used by Paul in Romans 6:3–4. Peter uses the escape of eight persons from the flood as a parallel to baptism, but "not as a removal of dirt from the body but as an appeal to God for a clear conscience, through the resurrection of Jesus Christ" (1 Pt 3:21).

The Holy Spirit himself is spoken of in terms of water. Jesus proclaimed, "He who believes in me, . . . 'Out of his heart shall flow rivers of living water' " (Jn 7:38) and the Gospel indicates that "this he said about the Spirit" (v 39).

In the closing chapters of the Bible the Lord declares: "To the thirsty I will give from the fountain of the water of life without payment" (Rv 21:6). Even in the description of the heavenly Jerusalem there is mention of water—the river of the water of life, "bright as crystal, flowing from the throne of God and of the Lamb through the middle of the street of the city" (22:1,2). The final invitation of Scripture is couched in similar terms: "And let him who is thirsty come, let him who desires take the water of life without price" (v 17).

CARL E. DEVRIES

Water Gate. One of the principal gates on the east side of Jerusalem. It was rebuilt during Nehemiah's day and served as the location for Ezra's reading of the Law (Neh 3:26; 8:3,16; 12:37).

See JERUSALEM.

Water Hen. Designation for several birds living near water such as the marsh hen, swan, or even the horned owl.

See ANIMALS; BIRDS.

Water Lily. See PLANTS.

Water of Separation. KJV translation of "the water for impurity," a water denoting cleansing from sin or impurity, in Numbers 19:9,13,20,21; 31:23.

See CLEANNESS AND UNCLEANNESS, REGULATIONS CONCERNING.

Waterpot. See POTTERY.

Waters of Chaos. See CHAOS, WATERS OF.

Waters of Merom. See MEROM, WATERS OF.

Wave Offering. See OFFERINGS AND SACRIFICES.

Way, The. One of the earliest names applied to the Christian community (Acts 9:2). It was apparently used by both the Jewish and the secular community and appeared in both positive and negative assessments of the church (19:9,23; 22:4; 24:14,22). Paul's use of the term in his defense before Felix suggests that the name had at least quasi-official acceptance (24:14,22).

In the OT, "way" was frequently used metaphorically to refer to modes of human behavior. While some references simply refer to behaviors without indicating whether they are good or bad, most references contain an ethical evaluation, contrasting the "good way" and the "evil way" (good—Ps 1:6; Prv 8:20; 12:15,28; evil—Pss 1:6; 119:101,104,128). "Way" is also frequently used to designate the ethical guidelines which God set forth for his people

(Gn 18:19; Ex 18:20; 32:8; Dt 8:6; 26:17). This "way" is distinguished from man's way, which inevitably leads him to sin (Jgs 2:19; Jb 22:15; Prv 12:15; 16:2).

Though the OT develops a rich repertoire for the term, its application to the NT derives primarily from Jesus' statement in John 14:6 that he was the "way." Though it was regularly used during the 1st century, it seems to have dropped out of general use shortly thereafter. Mohammed later appropriated the term in the Koran as a title for Islam.

See CHRISTIANS, NAMES FOR.

Wealth. Abundance, usually of money or material goods, whose value is ordinarily expressed in terms of some understood unit, such as a national currency. It is virtually synonymous with riches, and both may refer to family, friends, or even moral qualities, in addition to material possessions.

The Bible has much to say about material wealth and makes it clear that "a man's life does not consist in the abundance of his possessions" (Lk 12:15). Obviously God owns all wealth, for he is the creator and possessor of all that exists (Ps 50:10–12).

In the OT riches are a mark of favor with God (Ps 112:3) and he gives power to acquire wealth (Dt 8:18). Both the piety and the wealth of Job are well known (Jb 1:1–3). Solomon was perhaps the richest man who ever lived; God granted him "riches, possessions, and honor" because Solomon had asked for wisdom and discernment rather than material things (1 Kgs 3:10–13; 2 Chr 1:11,12).

Not all rich men were good. Nabal was "very rich," but he was "churlish and ill-behaved," stingy, and wicked (1 Sm 25:1–38). The affluent king of Tyre was the object of God's judgment (Ez 28), and many other rulers of the world fell under the same condemnation. In Isaiah 53:9 the prophecy concerning the Messiah links the wealthy with the wicked: "they made his grave with the wicked and with a rich man in his death."

In the NT wealthy men are often seen as godless, for example, the rich farmer (Lk 12:16–21) and the rich man with Lazarus (16:19–31). The wealthy are condemned for oppression and greed (Jas 5:1–6). Luke 6:24 pronounces woe against the rich, and all three synoptic Gospels speak of the dangers of riches (Mt 13:22; Mk 4:19; Lk 8:14).

Not all rich men were bad. Jesus was buried in the tomb of "a rich man from Arimathea, named Joseph" (Mt 27:57). Nicodemus, who provided lavishly for the burial of Jesus (Jn 19:39), was "a ruler of the Jews" (3:1) and probably a man of means.

See POOR, THE; RICHES; WAGES.

Weapons. *See* ARMS AND WARFARE.

Weasel. *See* ANIMALS.

Weaving. *See* CLOTH, CLOTH MANUFACTURING.

Wedding. See MARRIAGE, MARRIAGE CUSTOMS.

Weeds. *See* PLANTS (DARNEL GRASS).

Week. *See* CALENDARS, ANCIENT AND MODERN.

Weeks, Feast of. Celebration of the wheat harvest (Ex 23:14–17; Dt 16:16), occurring seven weeks after Passover on the sixth day of Sivan (June); also known as the Feast of Pentecost.

See FEASTS AND FESTIVALS OF ISRAEL.

Weights and Measures. Units of measure in the ancient world were largely based on practical standards: the length of an arm, a day's journey, how much a donkey could carry, and so forth. While this was a convenient system, it also suffered from a lack of standardization. Some arms were longer than others, and some donkeys could carry more than others. The history of weights and measures, therefore, becomes the story of seeking standards and precision. This was not achieved in the OT, but began to take place under Greek and Roman influences in NT times.

It must be understood, then, from the beginning, that any attempt to translate ancient measures into modern units can result only in approximations. In Egypt responsibility for weights and measures was the jurisdiction of a high administration official. In 1 Chronicles 23:29 the Levites are given this responsibility. Consistency, integrity, and general precision would be their concern. Even if standardization had been desired, the equipment did not exist to achieve or maintain precision. Any given locality in any given time period might use the same terms, but with slightly different values than other localities and other time periods. The attempt to identify which values any given biblical text had in mind becomes haphazard in that the text rarely offers any identification of measurement terms. The terms were known to the Israelite audience, so no explanation was considered necessary by the author.

As a result, it is difficult to be dogmatic about the exact nature of any given measurement in any specific passage. Usually, however, the approximations that can be made are sufficient to give an understanding of what is being communicated in the passage.

In the OT the measures that were used are

OT Measures

Linear Measures

Cubit	44.5 cm	17.5 in
Long cubit	52 cm	20.5 in
Finger/digit	1.85 cm	0.73 in
Handbreadth	7.4 cm	2.92 in
Reed	2.7 cm	104 in
Span	22.2 cm	8.75 in

Weight Measures

Shekel	12 gm	0.4 oz
Gera (1/20 shekel)	0.6 gm	.022 oz
Beka (1/2 shekel)	5.7 gm	0.2 oz
Pim (2/3 shekel)	7.6 gm	0.3 oz
Mina (50 shekels)	571 gm	1.26 lb
Talent (3000 shekels)	34.3 kg	75.6 lb

Dry Capacity Measures

Cor/homer	220 l	50 gal
Lethech (1/2 cor)	110 l	25 gal
Ephah (1/10 cor)	22 l	5 gal
Seah (1/3 ephah)	7.3 l	6.6 qt
Omer/issaron (1/10 ephah)	2.2 l	2.0 qt
Kab (1/18 ephah)	1.2 l	1.1 qt

Liquid Capacity Measures

Bath (1/10 cor)	22 l	5.8 gal
Hin (1/6 bath)	3.7 l	3.9 qt
Log (1/12 hin)	.31 l	.32 qt

NT Measures

Linear Measures

Cubit	44.5 cm	17.5 in
Fathom	1.8 m	6 ft
Stadium/furlong	170–90 m	189–215 yd
Mile	1480 m	1618 yd

Weight Measures

Same as OT		
Litra	327.5 gm	12 oz

Dry Capacity Measures

Choinix	1.1 l	1.2 qt
Saton	7.3 l	6.6 qt
Modius	7.4 l	7.7 qt

Liquid Capacity Measures

Bath	22 l	5.8 gal
Metretes	39 l	10 gal

frequently attested in Mesopotamian, Egyptian, and Canaanite literature as well. The Israelites did not have their own unique set of measurements. On the other hand, while the terms are shared, it is not unusual to find a particular term having one value in Israel and a noticeably different value in one of the other cultures.

By the time of the NT other variables were added. The Israelites of this period were still using many of the measures that had been used and developed throughout the OT period, but added to that were the Greek and Roman systems of measurement. Sometimes these terms are adopted wholesale, while at other times, Hebrew terms are adapted to Greco-Roman standards. On still other occasions, the Roman terms are apparently used when dealing with the government, whereas Hebrew terms are still used in everyday practice.

In most of the kinds of measurement, the base unit (i.e., the one that all of the others are fractions or multiples of) is the one about which there is the most uncertainty. So the cubit (length), the shekel (weight), the homer (dry volume), and the bath (liquid volume) are all to some degree controversial and uncertain. This makes all of the other measures which are based on them equally uncertain. In the following treatment every attempt is made to give ranges where possible and to try to represent a consensus of scholarship.

Linear Measures—Old Testament. Measurements of length and depth generally were derived from a part of the body used to make the measurement. The basic unit was the cubit and most others were related to it. Precise measurements of distance are lacking in the OT. Distance was most frequently stated in terms of the number of days it would take to arrive at a destination. A one day's journey was most likely 20 to 25 miles.

Cubit. The length from the tip of the forefinger to the elbow. There are both long and short cubits, which are used not only in Israel but in Mesopotamia and Egypt as well. Ezekiel 40:5 identifies the long cubit as being the equivalent of a cubit plus a handbreadth. The Egyptian cubit has been determined to be 17.7 inches with the long cubit being 20.65 inches. The Assyrian royal cubit (*khorsabad*) was 19.8 inches. Israel's standard cubit is similar to the Egyptian. The inscription found inside the Siloam tunnel built by Hezekiah (715–686 BC) indicates that the tunnel is 1200 cubits long. The actual length of the tunnel was determined to be 1749 feet. This would yield a cubit of 17.49 inches. All things considered, 17.5 inches is a good estimation of the length of the cubit in Israel. This would set the long cubit at approximately 20.5 inches.

The cubit is most frequently used to give the dimensions of buildings or objects (e.g., curtains, pillars, pieces of furniture, etc.). It is also the measure used to report the height of Goliath (1 Sm 17:4). The largest structure measured in cubits was the ark that Noah built, which was 300 cubits long (Gn 6:15). The largest number of cubits used in Scripture is 2000

cubits, which is the distance that was supposed to separate the Israelites from the ark of the covenant at the crossing of the Jordan (Jos 3:14). The eminent domain of the levitical cities is also 2000 cubits in each direction. This would equal approximately ⅔ mile.

Finger/digit. The width of a finger, equal to ¼ of a handbreadth, or ¾ inch. It is used only in Jeremiah 52:21 in the Bible (the thickness of a pillar), but is frequent in the Talmud.

Gomed. Measure occurring only in Judges 3:16, where it is the length of Ehud's dagger. By context it is generally considered to have been ⅔ of a cubit, or about a foot.

Handbreadth. The width of the hand at the base, equal to ⅙ a cubit, ⅓ a span, or just under 3 inches. The term is used only 5 times, and gives the width of the rim around the table of showbread (Ex 25:25) and Solomon's molten sea (1 Kgs 7:26).

Pace. The average distance of one man's stride or about one yard. It is used only once in the OT, when the ark was carried six paces from Obed-edom's house when David offered sacrifices to God (2 Sm 6:13).

Reed. One of the long, sturdy grasses growing by the river; it was considered the equivalent of 6 cubits, about 9 feet. In the OT it is used only in Ezekiel 40:3–5, where it is identified as a six-cubit measure, and in 42:16–19, where the measurements for the court of Ezekiel's temple are as 500 reeds on each side.

Span. The distance measured by the stretch of the hand from fingertip to fingertip, equal to ½ a cubit, or 8¾ inches. It is used only 7 times in the OT, and 4 of those are to describe the dimensions of the high priest's breastplate (Ex 28:16; 39:9). It is never used in the plural.

Linear Measurements—New Testament. In the NT some of the units of length and depth represent Greco-Roman standards, while others are those used in the OT.

Cubit. For the Romans, the cubit was set at 1.5 times their standard foot of 11.66 inches, equaling 17.5 inches, just as the OT cubit.

Fathom. The distance between the fingertips of the left and right hand when the arms were outstretched. It is used only in Acts 27:28, and is considered to be about 6 feet.

Measuring Rod. Equal to the reed in the OT, 6 cubits, 105 inches. It is used in Revelation 11:1 and 21:15 to measure the temple.

Like the OT, the NT frequently uses imprecise designations for distance, such as a stone's throw or a day's journey. There are, however, a few occurrences of precise terms borrowed from Roman culture.

Furlong/Stadium. The length of the ancient Greek race course, equal to ⅛ Roman mile, or a little over 200 yards. In half a dozen occurrences it is usually used to give approximate

Ancient scale for weighing gold.

silver or gold or any other trading commodity had to be weighed out so that bartering or purchasing could take place. This made the weights system the central core of the ancient economy. It also explains why the Scriptures inveigh so heavily against the use of false weights (Lv 19:36; Dt 25:13; Prv 16:11; 20:10,23; Mi 6:11; Hos 12:7; Am 8:5). This concern was not unique to the Israelites. As early as the 21st century BC Ur-Nammu, the founder of the Ur III dynasty in southern Mesopotamia, is said to have "standardized the mina-weight, and standardized the silver and stone shekel in relation to the mina" (Prologue to the *Law of Ur-Nammu*, ll 144–49).

Stone weights were used on a set of balances for conducting business in the ancient marketplace. In more sophisticated settings, the weights were crafted. But it would not be unusual to use unworked stones of approximately the agreed-upon weight.

Scales or balances are mentioned half a dozen times in the OT, but none of those are in actual economic contexts (Jb 6:2; 31:6; Ps 62:9; Is 40:12; Ez 5:1; Dn 5:27). The scales used were generally of the beam-balance type with dishes on each end.

Shekel. The basic unit of weight. Besides the regular shekel, there was a "heavy" or "royal" shekel (2 Sm 14:26). Calculating by weights which have been excavated and found labeled as "beka" (½ shekel), the shekel has been estimated to be about .4 ounce. However, other weights believed to be shekel weights range from .39 ounce all the way to .46 ounce. For example, the marked weights found at Tell Beit Mirsim average .4 ounce; while those found at El-jib, Megiddo, and Tell en-Nasbeh average .45 ounce.

The shekel is used in Scripture almost exclusively in contexts dealing with monetary value. Whether silver, gold, barley, or flour, the shekel valuation assigns the commodity a relative value in the economy. Exceptions to this are Goliath's armor and spear (1 Sm 17:5,7), which are described in terms of their shekel weight.

Beka. Seven stones inscribed with this label range in weight from .2 to .23 ounce. In Exodus 38:26 it is the amount levied on each individual for the census tax. There it is the equivalent of ½ shekel. The only other occurrence is in Genesis 24:22, where it is the weight of the gold nose ring given to Rebekah by Abraham's servant.

Gera. Equal to 1/20 of a shekel, or .022 oz. The term is used 5 times (Ex 30:13; Lv 27:25; Nm 3:47; 18:16; Ez 45:12), and on each occasion is used to give a valuation to the shekel. Its use is strictly monetary in these contexts.

Pim. The only reference to this unit is in

distances, but in Revelation 21:16 it is used to give the dimensions of the New Jerusalem and is measured with a measuring rod.

Mile. The only occurrence of this term, Matthew, 5:41, has reference to the Roman mile of 1620 yards, about 9/10 of a mile.

Weight Measurement. The terms used for weights have benefited most from archaeological attestation. Excavations provide stone weights which are occasionally inscribed with the unit which they represent. When the stones are weighed, they frequently give a range of weights which only have a general consistency. However, comparing this data with that provided by the text has given the basis for fairly accurate determinations. The relative scale in any given location is more important than absolute values.

There was standardization of weight measures, but precision was difficult to attain. The Israelite system is similar to that used by the Mesopotamians and the Canaanites. For most of the OT period, the weights system provided the monetary system. Minted coinage was the invention of the Persians. Up until that time,

A one-mina weight that dates back to the time of Nebuchadnezzar (605–562 BC).

1 Samuel 13:21, where it is the price charged to the Israelites by the Philistines for sharpening a plowshare. Excavated weights range from .25 to .3 ounce, suggesting that the pim was ⅔ of a shekel.

Mina. In the Canaanite material from Ugarit the mina equals 50 shekels, while in Babylon the mina equals 60 shekels. In Ezekiel 45:12 (KJV Maneh) the mina is set at 60 shekels, but it is unclear whether or not this represents a change from previous standards. In 1 Kings 10:17 3 minas of gold are used on each of 300 shields that Solomon made. In Ezra 2:69 and Nehemiah 7:71,72, contributions are given of 5000, 2200 and 2000 silver minas for the temple treasury.

Talent. Exodus 38:25,26 makes it clear that the talent was equal to 3000 shekels, but it is unclear how many minas were in a talent. As a result, it is unknown whether 3000 represents 60 minas of 50 shekels each, or 50 minas of 60 shekels each. Whichever the case may be, excavated talents weigh from about 65 to 80 pounds. In the OT the talent is only used for precious metals, usually silver or gold (but cf. Ex 38:29, bronze). In 1 Kings 10:14 the annual tribute income of Solomon's kingdom was 666 talents, which apparently was considered quite extravagant. David bequeathed 100,000 talents of gold and 1,000,000 talents of silver to Solomon for the building of the temple (1 Chr 22:14).

Qesitah. Weight occurring only 3 times (Gn 33:19; Jos 24:32; Jb 42:11). How much weight it represents is unknown. From the contexts its weight would be something between ½ and 1 shekel.

The NT uses the same weights that have already been identified in the OT usage, particularly shekel, mina, and talent. There is one additional unit used. The litra is used in John 12:3 and 19:39 with regard to spices. From Greek literature (including Josephus) it is approximately 12 ounces.

Capacity Measurement—Old Testament. Amounts of dry goods were oriented toward practical matters such as typical donkey loads, how much seed could be sown in a day, or how much seed would be needed to sow a certain size plot. As with the other types of measures these then became standardized along with their fractions and multiples.

Homer/Cor. The most common dry commodity measure and the equivalent of one donkey load. Estimates of its standard size vary greatly, ranging from 3.8 bushels to 7.5 bushels. Other than the 7 occurrences in Ezekiel 45:11–14, the term occurs only 4 times in the OT. Three of these contexts feature seed or barley (Lv 27:16; Is 5:10; Hos 3:2), while the fourth is in the context of Israelites gathering quail in the wilderness. A cor is used 9 times and occurs with a variety of commodities, including oil, flour, wheat, and barley, in multiples all the way up to 20,000 (1 Kgs 5:11).

Ephah. This is equal to ¹⁄₁₀ homer (Ez 45:11), or ⅜–⅔ bushel. The term occurs dozens of times with all sorts of agricultural products. It seems to have been the unit most used in trading and selling. In Zechariah 5:6–10 the ephah refers to a container which would hold an ephah of produce, much like the modern-day bushel basket.

Seah. If Isaiah 40:12 uses a variant name for the seah, as many would suggest, then the seah equals ⅓ of an ephah. Again this would be a fraction of the homer, which has a very wide range. Estimates of the seah usually identify it as something between ⅔ and 1 peck. The term occurs 9 times and is used with numbers from 1 to 5. It measures flour, seed, barley, and grain. It only occurs once outside of the books of Samuel and Kings, in Genesis 18:6, where Abraham uses 3 seahs of flour to prepare cakes for his 3 visitors.

Omer/Issaron. The omer occurs only in the account of the collecting of manna by the Israelites (Ex 16:22). It represents a day's ration of manna, and is identified as ¹⁄₁₀ of an ephah (Ex 16:36). The issaron is a term which means a tenth. Its 25 occurrences are all in Exodus, Leviticus, and Numbers (mostly in Nm 28, 29) and refer only to measures of fine flour.

Kab. This unit occurs in 2 Kings 6:25 (KJV cab). The estimate given by Josephus, ¹⁄₁₈ of an ephah, is usually accepted.

Lethech. Unit occurring only in Hosea 3:2. The early versions of the Bible identified it as ½ a cor, or homer.

Two basic measures were used for liquids in the OT.

Bath. The base unit for the measurement of liquids. The biblical data (Ez 45:11,14) sets it as the liquid equivalent to the dry measure, ephah. It is ¹⁄₁₀ of a homer. Archaeology has also been able to provide some data for this determination. Jars inscribed as "bath of the king" were found at Lachish and Tell en-Nasbeh, and jars marked "bath" were found at Tell Beit Mirsim. The jars are not complete, so their capacity must be calculated based on a reconstruction. Using this data, the bath was approximately 5.8 gallon. This estimate would provide acceptable results when factored into the information given in 1 Kings 7:23–26, where the "molten sea" of Solomon's temple is described as being 30 cubits in circumference, 10 cubits in diameter, 5 cubits deep, and capable of holding 2000 baths of water.

Hin. One-sixth of a hin of water was considered the minimum daily necessity for survival (Ez 4:11). A hin is equal to ⅙ of a bath, approximately 1 gallon. It is used for a measure of oil, wine, and water, but no context ever mentions more than one hin. Rather, fractions of a hin are used. Occurrences are limited to Exodus, Leviticus, Numbers, and Ezekiel, and are therefore most commonly attested in the context of sacrificial libations.

Log. This unit occurs only in Leviticus 14:10–24, and equals ¹⁄₁₂ of a hin, so about ⅔ pint or ⅓ liter.

Capacity Measurement—New Testament. The following dry measures are used in the NT.

Choinix. Occurring only in Revelation 6:6, the choinix is a little more than a quart. In Greek literature it was considered the amount of one man's daily allowance of corn.

Modius. This is the "bushel" under which one's lamp should not be hid (Mt 5:15; Mk 4:21; Lk 11:33). It is actually equal to about a peck, 7.68 dry quarts.

Saton. This is the equivalent of the OT seah, and can therefore also be approximated at about a peck. It is used only twice in the NT in parallel passages of the parable of the leaven which is like the kingdom of God (Mt 13:33; Lk 13:21).

The following liquid measures occur in the NT.

Bath. This is used only once (Lk 16:6), and is the same as the OT bath.

Xestes. Measurement used only in Mark 7:4 and thought to be about 1⅙ pints. It is a known Roman measure and occurs not only in Latin literature, but in Josephus as well. In Mark it may describe a cup (as it does outside of Scripture) rather than a specific measure.

Metretes. This is used only in John 2:6, where it describes the containers in which water was turned to wine. Josephus identifies it as equivalent to a Hebrew bath, but in Greek usage it was the equivalent of about 10 gallons. The KJV translates it as "firkin."

Area Measurement. *Tsemed.* The amount of land that a team of oxen could plow in a day (1 Sm 14:14; Is 5:10). It is usually translated "acre," though in Mesopotamia it was less than half an acre.

Ma'aneh. Measurement occurring in 1 Samuel 14:14 and Psalm 129:3 only. It may be the length of a furrow, perhaps 20 to 30 yards.

Well. Man-made reservoir fed either by subterranean springs or by rainwater. Because the majority of the biblical world ranges from arid to semiarid, wells were a critical source of water for humans, livestock, and the irrigation of crops. Unfortunately, most wells did not offer a reliable source of water, being dependent on the scarce rainfall or intermittent springs (Prv 25:26 NIV). The discovery of a reliable source of water was therefore the cause of much rejoicing (Nm 21:17,18) and frequent conflict as well (Gn 21:25–30; 26:19–22; 2 Kgs 3:19). Successfully digging a well and defending one's water rights often served as an important determinant of property rights (Gn 21:25–30; 29:2,3).

Good wells were generally considered signs of God's providence (Gn 16:14; 21:19; Nm 21:16–18). Biblical writers therefore often compared the water of spring-fed wells to God's provision of salvation for his people (Is 12:3; Jn 4:14). The distinction between the relatively poor quality of water in cisterns that captured rainwater and the high quality of those wells that tapped springs of "living" (i.e., flowing) water helps clarify the dialogue between Jesus and the Samaritan woman when Jesus offered her "living water" (Jn 4:10–15).

See CISTERN; JACOB'S WELL.

Western Sea. *See* MEDITERRANEAN SEA.

Whale. *See* ANIMALS.

Wheat. *See* AGRICULTURE; FOOD AND FOOD PREPARATION; PLANTS.

Wheel. Device originating in the region of Mesopotamia, probably dating from about 3500 BC. The earliest known form is the two-wheeled cart of Sumer. The first wheels were probably just discs cut from trees, but later

A well in the forum at Rome.

wheels were made by clamping three shaped planks together by copper clamps extending the length of the wheel. After 2000 BC wheels with spokes appeared in northern Mesopotamia.

In the Bible, four Hebrew words are used to identify a number of types and usages of the wheel. These include the potter's wheel (Jer 18:3), chariot wheels (Ex 14:25), and wheels for grinding grain (Is 28:28). The most frequent and most important usage of the word "wheel" in the Bible, however, is in connection with Ezekiel's vision of the chariot of God (chs 1,10; cf. Dn 7:9). Associated with the cloud appearing in a stormy wind (Ez 1:4) are fire, creatures, and wheels. Ezekiel draws the reader's attention to each of these phenomena. The wheels move in the direction the creatures take them. The significance of the wheel in Ezekiel is the shape. The wheel is compound, a wheel within a wheel. This is not to say that two wheels are on the same axis. It rather signifies a wheel set in a wheel in such a way that its rim makes a 90° angle with the rim of the wheel in which it is set. The wheel has mobility, as it can roll from east to west and from north to south. Wherever the creatures go it will follow. This speaks of God's universal judgment which no one can escape. Judah could not avoid the oncoming disaster, as God's judgment was pointed in its direction.

See Tools; Ezekiel, Book of.

Whirlwind. Term descriptive of any strong, potentially destructive wind (Jb 27:20; Ps 77:18; Dn 11:40). While whirlwinds are relatively common in the arid regions of the Mid- dle East (e.g., dust devils, sand columns), the apparent fury and destructiveness of the biblical "whirlwinds" makes it unlikely that the relatively harmless dust devils are intended (cf. Am 1:14; Hb 3:14). Sirocco winds from the eastern deserts are occasionally cyclonic in form, but the winds in Scripture may not be whirlwinds in the technical sense.

Biblical whirlwinds were often associated with divine activity. Elijah was taken into heaven by a whirlwind (one case where "whirlwind" may properly be translated as such; 2 Kgs 2:1,11). God frequently spoke out of the whirlwind (Jb 38:1; 40:6; Ps 77:18). The description of the sudden destruction of divine judgment was frequently associated with storms, tempests and whirlwinds (Hos 8:7; Am 1:14; Na 1:3; Hb 3:14). The movement of the invading armies that conquered Israel and Judah was compared to the relentless onslaught of the whirlwind (Is 5:28; 21:1; Jer 4:13).

White. *See* Color.

Whore. *See* Harlot.

Widow. A woman whose husband has died, and frequently classed with the fatherless and orphans (Dt 14:29; 16:11; 24:20; 26:12; Ps 94:6). Laws were passed to make special provision for this group and to protect them against the unscrupulous.

As the main purpose of the wife was to bear children, the childless widow, or the widow who had no son, was a person who had disgraced her family by not providing the male heir essential to the continuity of the family line. Probably for this reason the deceased man's brother was expected to marry the widow, whose firstborn son was then treated in all respects as the son of the deceased. This levirate marriage (cf. Dt 25:5–10), seen best in the Book of Ruth, may have originated as a form of inheritance, the brother-in-law taking by right the property of the deceased, including his widow. The idea of levirate marriage may have been altered by the Israelites so that the primary purpose was changed to that of the continuation of the family name, thereby perpetuating the memory of the ancestors.

Legally the widow was ignored for purposes of inheritance, and if her husband died prematurely, this was considered a judgment for the life he had led, and she became an object of reproach, partly for her inability to prevent his untimely death (Ru 1:20,21; Is 54:4). A childless widow who was the daughter of a priest could return home, where she again became subject to her father (Lv 22:13; cf. Ru 1:8). The only improvement in her legal status was that her oath was accepted, there being no husband to revoke it (Nm 30:9).

Remarriage was the ideal solution to the problem of widowhood, although priests were forbidden to marry widows (Lv 21:14; Ru 1:9, 13; 1 Sm 25:39; Ez 44:22; 1 Tm 5:14). It is possible that the widow may have worn special clothing forcing her to acknowledge her status (Gn 38:14).

The plight of the widow was recognized in the number of laws designed for her protection and even survival. God was her legal protector (Ps 68:5), and saw that she was provided with the essentials of food and clothing (Dt 10:18). Those who denied her justice were cursed by God (Dt 27:19). At harvest time the widow might glean the grain in the fields as well as some grapes and olives (Dt 24:19; Ru 2:2,7,15–19), and she was also eligible for some assistance from the third-year tithe. Nevertheless, the poverty of widows and the cruel treatment extended to them was so widespread that frequent reference is made to it (Jb 24:21; Ps 94:6; Is 1:23; Mal 3:5). A special law provided that the widow's garment could not be used as security for a loan (Dt 24:17).

In the early Christian church there was a recognized group of widows eligible to receive charity. They were generally those over 60 years of age who had only been married once, were in poverty, had no relatives to support them, and had lived blameless lives filled with Christian good works (1 Tm 5:9–16).

The figurative use of the term "widow" seems to indicate that it was the absolute depth to which one might fall. Isaiah 47:8,9 and Revelation 18:7 use the term with regard to the fate of Babylon, and the devastation of the once mighty and beautiful city of Jerusalem is likened to a wife who has become a widow (Lm 1:1).

HAZEL W. PERKIN

See FAMILY LIFE AND RELATIONS; MARRIAGE, MARRIAGE CUSTOMS.

Wife. See FAMILY LIFE AND RELATIONS.

Wilderness. Land that is basically wild, nonarable, and sparsely inhabited or unfit for permanent settlement. It may be desert, mountains, forest, or marsh.

In the Near East the wilderness is characteristically dry, desolate, and mostly rock and sand. It is rough, uneven, and interlaced with dry watercourses. The wilderness is not completely barren but provides seasonal pasture for flocks, depending on the former and latter rains.

Joel 2:22 declares that "the pastures of the wilderness are green"; and Psalm 65:12 states that the pastures of the wilderness drip (with richness). On the other hand, Jeremiah says that "the pastures of the wilderness are dried up" (23:10; cf. Jl 1:20).

Job refers to the wilderness as "a land where no man is" (38:26), it is a place for various animals and birds, such as wild asses, jackals, vultures, and owls (Ps 102:6; Jer 2:24; Is 13:22; 34:13–15).

Certain wilderness tracts are identified by name and are related to definite cities, persons, or events. Hagar wandered in the wilderness of Beersheba (Gn 21:14). In the exodus from Egypt, the Israelites traversed the following wildernesses: Shur (Ex 15:22), Etham (Nm 33:8), Sin (Ex 16:1), Sinai (Ex 19:1,2), Zin (Nm 13:21; 20:1), Paran (Nm 13:26), Kadesh (Ps 29:8), Moab (Dt 2:8), and Kedemoth (Dt 2:26).

When David was fleeing from Saul, David hid in the hill country of the wilderness of Ziph (1 Sm 23:14,15), in the wilderness of Maon (vv 24,25), and in the wilderness of En-gedi (24:1).

The descendants of Moses' Kenite father-in-law settled in the wilderness of Judah, "which lies in the Negeb near Arad" (Jgs 1:16).

The conflict between the men of Abner and those of Joab involved the wilderness of Gibeon (2 Sm 2:24). When the Lord delivered Judah from Moab and Ammon (2 Chr 20), the action occurred in the wilderness of Jeruel (v 16) and that of Tekoa (v 20).

In spite of the comparative desolation of the wilderness, villages or towns are sometimes associated with a wilderness setting. Joshua 15:61,62 lists the names of six cities and their villages "in the wilderness." The future joy of the towns of the desert is proclaimed by Isaiah (42:11).

The wilderness of Judea.

The wilderness is associated with both austerity and temptation. Elijah, by his way of life and his dress, is often thought of in connection with the wilderness. His successor, Elisha, had occasion to minister in the wilderness of Edom (2 Kgs 3:4–27; esp v 8).

Isaiah prophesied of the message of John the Baptist who preached in the wilderness of Judea (Is 40:3; Mt 3:1,3; Mk 1:2–4; Lk 3:1–6; Jn 1:23).

Jesus, full of the Holy Spirit, who led by the Spirit into the wilderness for 40 days. There he was tempted by the devil (cf. Lk 4:1,2) but there also angels ministered to him (Mk 1:13). The anchorites (hermits) of Egypt and the Qumran community near the Dead Sea used the wilderness as an escape from the evils of urban life. Jesus, however, used the wilderness as a place of prayer and communion with the Father (Lk 5:16).

The wilderness figures in both the warnings and promises of Scripture. The city or nation that refuses the message of salvation will be reduced to wilderness (cf. Ps 107:33,34), but for the faithful there will be restoration: "The wilderness and the dry land shall be glad, the desert shall rejoice and blossom" (Is 35:1).

See DESERT; WILDERNESS WANDERINGS.

Wilderness Wanderings.
When the Israelites came out of Egypt, they spent some 40 years wandering in the wildernesses of the Sinai peninsula and the Negeb. Then they moved on to conquer the Promised Land. The most significant events in this period are described in the books of Exodus, Leviticus, and Numbers.

According to the Bible, their experiences during these hard years in the desert molded the various tribes of former Egyptian slaves into a nation. In Sinai they became one people with one God and one national goal, the conquest of Canaan.

Chronology of the Wanderings. Numbers 14:34; 33:38 and Deuteronomy 1:3, describe the wilderness wanderings as lasting 40 years. Though 40 is sometimes used in the Bible as a large round number, the exactness of many of the dates in these narratives implies it should be taken literally. However, it is hard to know when this period began and ended.

According to 1 Kings 6:1 Solomon started to build the temple 480 years after the Israelites left Egypt. The building of the temple began about 950 BC, which would mean the exodus must have taken place about 1430 BC and the conquest about 1390 BC. However contemporary scholars generally date the exodus and conquest more than a century later (1290–1250 BC) on the grounds that this agrees with archaeological discoveries. But as yet, convincing proof for either position is lacking. Within the 40-year period of wanderings, there are full details of the first year and a half spent in the desert, from the exodus to the return of the spies (Ex 12:2–Nm 14), and of the final year or so that involved the conquest of Transjordan (Nm 20–Dt 34). Very little is known of the intervening years when the tribes camped in the desert near such oases as Kadesh-barnea. The episodes described in Numbers 15–17 presumably date from this little-known period.

The Route of the Wanderings. If it is difficult to locate the wanderings chronologically, it is even harder to be sure exactly what route the Israelites took through the Sinai peninsula. Though the Bible names many places in the wilderness where the tribes camped, few of them can be located with certainty today. This is because place names only survive if there is a continuity of settlement at the places concerned. But desert tribes come and go, and the names of different places are forgotten and change quite easily. Thus although Numbers 33 gives a detailed list of the places at which the Israelites stopped, scholars are uncertain where most are. However, Kadesh (vv 36,37) is most probably Ain el-Kudeirat, the largest spring in northern Sinai, and several of the places in Moab (vv 44–49) can be roughly located. The lack of agreement about the location of the Red Sea and Mt Sinai, where the most important events of all occurred, is striking.

According to the Bible the Israelites escaped from Egypt by crossing the Red Sea. Their Egyptian pursuers were drowned when the wind turned and the waters came back over them. The Israelites then made for Mt Sinai, where they spent nearly a year (Ex 19:1–Nm 10:11). From there they moved on to Kadesh, which served as their base till they set out on their campaign of conquest nearly 40 years later.

Traditionally the biblical Red Sea has been identified with the western branch of the Red

Sea, the Gulf of Suez. And Mt Sinai is supposed to be one of the high mountains in the south of the Sinai peninsula, perhaps Jebel Mousa (Arabic for Mountain of Moses). Because other evidence is lacking, such traditional identifications must be respected, but they do not amount to proof.

It is now generally agreed that in biblical times the Gulf of Suez extended as far north as the Bitter Lakes, and that is where the Red Sea was crossed. Here, before the Suez Canal was built, there was a shallow section some two miles wide which bedouin used to ford under favorable weather conditions. This fits Exodus 14:21, which states that "the Lord opened up a path through the sea, . . . a strong east wind blew all that night, drying the sea bottom."

Because of the distances involved and the scarcity of water, especially in the desert of Tih, which lies between Jebel Mousa and the Gulf of Suez, the location of Mt Sinai may have been further north. One alternative for Mt Sinai is Jebel Halal, quite near Kadesh. However, its nearness to Kadesh and distance from Egypt makes this unlikely, for Sinai is said to be three days' journey from Egypt and

11 days from Kadesh (Ex 5:3; Dt 1:2). The best recent suggestion is that Mt Sinai is Jebel Sin Bishar, a striking isolated peak in the Suder plain. Its Arabic name may mean "heralding of the law" or "the laws of man." It lies at the right relative distances from both the Egyptian border and Kadesh-barnea. There is sufficient water in the vicinity to sustain a large group of people such as the Israelite tribes.

Assuming that the Red Sea is identified with the Bitter Lakes, and Sinai with Jebel Sin Bishar, the other places mentioned in Exodus can also be located. Marah (Ex 15:23), reached three days after crossing the Red Sea, must be the place 25 miles south of the Bitter Lakes, which still has a salty well. (Marah means bitter in Hebrew). From there the Israelites came to Elim, which had springs and 70 palm trees (v 27) and which must be Ayoun Mousa (Wells of Moses). This still has 12 wells and a palm grove. Elim is 8 miles south of Marah.

From Elim the Israelites came to Rephidim, where water was scarce and they encountered the Amalekites (Ex 17). The shortage of water implies they had left the coast and moved toward the desert of Tih. Immediately

Arrangement of the Tribal Camps

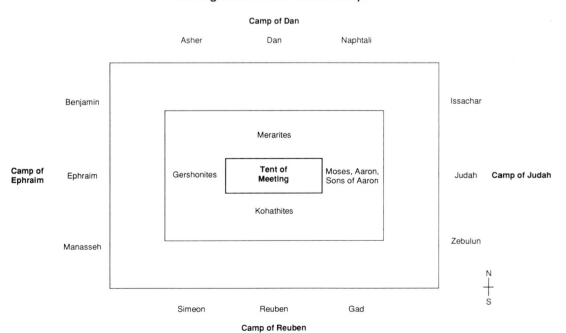

Camp of Dan

Asher   Dan   Naphtali

Benjamin   Issachar

Merarites

Camp of Ephraim   Ephraim   Gershonites   **Tent of Meeting**   Moses, Aaron, Sons of Aaron   Judah   **Camp of Judah**

Kohathites

Manasseh   Zebulun

N
S

Simeon   Reuben   Gad

Camp of Reuben

after Rephidim they came to Sinai (19:2). The valley in which Mt Sinai is located has some good pastureland, which had already attracted the Amalekites. They therefore came out to do battle with Israel to prevent their taking over the land. Israel's defeat of Amalek enabled them to camp at Sinai (17:8–13).

After a year at Sinai they moved on to Kadesh. During this period of about a month, there were bitter complaints about the food and Moses' leadership (Nm 11,12). This route took them them through the wilderness of Paran (10:12), the largest in the Sinai peninsula. It is covered with gravel; there is little vegetation and water. Deuteronomy 1:19 calls it "the great and terrible desert."

From Kadesh the spies set out to inspect the Promised Land. The gloomy report they brought back dismayed the people further, and they refused to believe that with God's help they could conquer the land. In punishment God condemned them to wander 40 years in the wilderness until the unbelieving adult generation had died (Nm 13,14). Unwilling to accept God's verdict, they tried to attack the Amalekites and Canaanites, but this time they were defeated and forced to wander between Kadesh and the Gulf of Aqaba, "the way to the Red Sea" (14:25).

At the end of their period of wanderings the Israelites made a second attempt to enter Canaan from the south. This time they clashed with the king of Arad (Nm 21:1–3). Another defeat prompted a change of strategy. The land was to be entered from the east across the Jordan River. They skirted the territory of the Edomites. But the kingdoms further north in Transjordan opposed them and were defeated. The tribes of Reuben, Gad, and half of Manasseh took over and settled this territory. These victories in Transjordan mark the end of the wanderings and the beginning of the conquest (21:10–36:13; Dt 1–3).

Major Events and Their Significance.
Whereas modern readers are interested in the when and where of past events, the Bible is much more concerned with the what and why. Four types of events from this period are specially stressed in the Bible, (a) the lawgiving at Sinai; (b) the establishment of worship; (c) miracles; (d) national rebellions.

Miracles. The period of wilderness wanderings was a time when God often spoke to his people. As elsewhere in the Bible, these revelations were frequently accompanied by miracles. These were of two sorts: miracles of provision and miracles of judgment. Food and water were often in short supply in the wilderness, and Exodus 16:2–17:7 and Numbers 11, 20 tell how God supplied the people's needs on a number of occasions. Quails are

still caught in northern Sinai at certain times of year, and what is often supposed to be manna, a sweet-tasting lichen, has been found there. What is striking about these miracles in the Bible is that these supplies were provided in answer to Moses' prayers and in great abundance.

In terrible contrast to these miracles, there were the numerous acts of judgment. The wanderings were made possible by a series of plagues against Egypt, climaxing in the drowning of the Egyptian army in the Red Sea (Ex 7–15). From then on the rebellious Israelites suffered sudden death for wickedness. Two of Aaron's sons were burned with fire for offering incense that the Lord had not commanded (Lv 10:1,2). Miriam, Moses' sister, was punished with a leprous-like skin disease for her grumblings (Nm 12:9–16). The rebels Korah, Dathan, and Abiram and their families were swallowed up by the ground caving in under their tents and 250 supporters were destroyed by divine fire (16:1–35). Twenty-four thousand died in a plague that struck the nation after their unfaithfulness at Baal-peor (25:1–9).

National Rebelliousness. The divine judgments just mentioned were provoked by the disobedience of Israel. But they are part of a much broader theme that runs through all the stories of the wanderings. Every step of the way the people were discontent or disobedient. From a human standpoint their complaints about lack of food and water and their questioning of Moses' judgment is understandable: the wilderness is a most inhospitable place and frightening to those unaccustomed to it. Yet these grumblings are seen as sinful, precisely because Israel had the visible sign of God's presence with them, the pillar of cloud and fire, and had no reason to fear.

Yet while Moses was on Sinai receiving the Law, the people down below were making a golden calf to worship (Ex 32). Though they knew God's promise that they would conquer the land, the report of the spies about the difficulties undermined their faith (Nm 14). Even the highest and holiest men in the nation, Aaron, the high priest, and Moses, the national leader, sinned and died before they enter the Promised Land (Nm 20:12,23–29; Dt 34). Of the spies who visited the land only Joshua and Caleb lived to settle there.

The wilderness wanderings are more than an interesting phase in the birth of Israel's national consciousness. It is a period when God fulfilled his promises despite human weakness and sin. These stories illustrate that man does not "live by bread alone, but by every word that proceeds from the mouth of God" (Dt 8:3; Mt 4:4). In quoting this text Jesus identified himself with ancient Israel. Like them he went

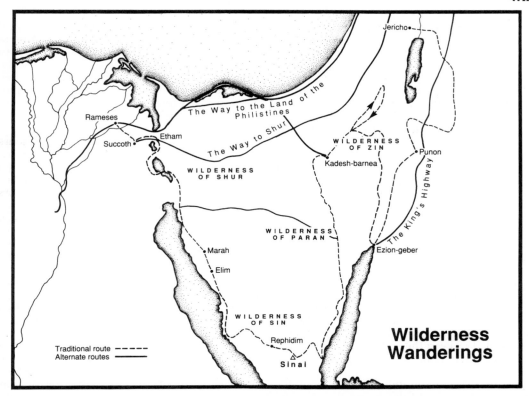

Jericho•

The Way to the Land of the Philistines

Rameses

The Way to Shur

Etham
Succoth•

WILDERNESS OF ZIN

Punon

Kadesh-barnea

The King's Highway

WILDERNESS OF SHUR

WILDERNESS OF PARAN

• Marah

Ezion-geber

• Elim

WILDERNESS OF SIN

Wilderness Wanderings

Rephidim

Traditional route —————
Alternate routes ——————

Sinai

into the wilderness to prepare for his life's work. So too Christians have recognized that they are called to follow in their Master's steps and live by faith in God's promises and obedience to his word, especially in times of difficulty and temptation. According to Paul the wilderness wanderings typify the life of the Christian believer and demonstrate the dangers of disobedience (1 Cor 10:1–11).

G.J. WENHAM

See CONQUEST AND ALLOTMENT OF THE LAND; COVENANT; EXODUS, THE; LAW, BIBLICAL CONCEPT OF; TABERNACLE, TEMPLE; TEN COMMANDMENTS, THE; ISRAEL, HISTORY OF; SINAI, SINA; ZIN, WILDERNESS OF; SIN, WILDERNESS OF; PARAN; CHRONOLOGY, OLD TESTAMENT; OFFERINGS AND SACRIFICES.

Wild Goat. *See* ANIMALS.

Wild Gourd. See PLANTS (GOURD, WILD).

Wild Grape. *See* PLANTS (VINE); VINE, VINEYARD; WINE.

Wild Ox. *See* ANIMALS.

Wild Vine. *See* PLANTS (VINE); VINE, VINEYARD; WINE.

Willow. *See* PLANTS (ASPEN).

Willows, Brook of the. Brook over which Moab's abundance would be carried off (Is 15:7). Isaiah's language suggests that it marked the southern border of Moab. It is possibly the Brook of the Arabah in Amos 6:14 (differing very slightly in the Hebrew). Several different identifications have been offered for the brook but none has gained general acceptance.

Wine. Beverage made from fermented grape juice.

Origin. Viticulture was known and wine was drunk in the prehistoric period of Mesopotamia and brought to Egypt before 3000 BC. Greek tradition speaks of the god Dionysus, who fled Mesopotamia in disgust because its inhabitants drank mostly beer, though wine was still a popular drink. Wine may have been produced first by Noah (Gn 9:21) on the slopes of Mt Ararat, but it did not stay confined to that region since Egypt, and later Greece, had a fondness for the juice.

The word "wine" may be identified with words for vine, vineyard, black grapes, and so forth. The vine, which brings forth the wine, was often identified in the Near Eastern world with the "tree of life." In both Egypt and Mesopotamia a goddess was thought to protect the vine. The "mistress of the heavenly tree of life," the goddess Siris, lived in the mountains of northwestern Assyria. Enoch 32:4 calls the vine the tree of knowledge. According to Jewish tradition the vine was saved from the flood by Noah.

Production of Wine. Few ancient documents are extant on the art of viticulture. Experience and the interests of a few early botanists appear to be the only source of knowledge available about the early winegrowers. Aristotle's most famous student, Theophrastus of Eresos, wrote a book entitled *Enquiry into Plants* showing a blend of practical experience and theory. Later he followed with *On the Life of Plants,* a work giving detailed observation of viticulture. His ideas on when to plant, how to prune, statements against grafting, and how to care for the vine in general demonstrate the Greek genius. They raised viticulture to a science that has changed little in the last 2200 years.

Great care was taken by Greek winegrowers to ensure the success of their crops. The vines were close to the ground instead of being propped. In view of this, mice and foxes were especially undesirable, and much hoeing was needed to keep the soil free of weeds. But their method, overall, was very effective.

In early September the grapes were collected in the plains, and at the end of the month in the hills. With an initial festival of song and dance the workers brought the bunches of grapes to the winepress, low cement vats inclined toward one corner. After this, workers trod the grapes. The first *must* (juice from the crushing) was especially valued since it provided the choicest wines. The remaining juice was extracted by wringing the trodden grapes in a bag-press usually made of cloth. A third class of wine was produced by mixing or even cooking the remaining grapes with some water and expressing the mixture. This type of wine was drunk only by the poor.

At a later time the Greeks invented a beam-press, in which a long beam having a turning portion at one end and heavy stones on the other compressed layers of grapes. The ancient Near East had these different methods of extracting wine, but the treading of grapes, even in Greece, was always the favorite method.

In Greece the fermentation period was usually six months, during which the liquid was constantly skimmed. However, in the ancient Near East the fermentation process was usually over in three or four days, the optimum growth temperature being 77°. The ancients knew that any further fermentation would produce acid.

After desired fermentation the wine was transferred to skins or pottery jars for transport or sale. The handles and stoppers were stamped to indicate the brand, the origin, and the vintage. At this time the wine was strained through perforated metal sieves or cloth to eliminate contaminates such as grit or insects.

At first, parts of Greece enjoyed a monopoly on wine and exported great quantities. Egypt was especially fond of Greek wine, the ancient Near East being famous for "froth-blowers" or beer.

Kinds of Wine. Ancient poets discuss many different brands of wine, with Athenaeus mentioning 85 different varieties. Galen cites 60, Pliny mentions 150, and Strabo 30. They are distinguished by different colors (black, red, white, or yellow), and by their taste (dry, harsh, light, or sweet). The biblical account enumerates various kinds of wine, such as the wines of Lebanon and Helbon. Hebron and Samaria were famous for viticulture. The Hebrew language has at least nine different words for wine, and the Greek has four that are mentioned in the NT.

Nature of Wine. Few would question that at least some wine of the OT was fermented. Some scholars argue, however, that certain forms of wine in the ancient world were unfermented. They contrast two Hebrew words for wine, concluding that one particular Hebrew word which refers to fresh wine meant only grape juice (Prv 3:10; Hos 9:2; Jl 2:24; Mi 6:15). The inconclusiveness of these arguments may be seen from the following points: (1) The Hebrew word is found in primarily neutral contexts; (2) often that particular word is found in contexts definitely including a fermented beverage (e.g., Gn 27:28; Hos 4:11; Mi 6:15); (3) the Ugaritic parallel to the term in question refers with certainty to a fermented wine (4) the Septuagint equivalents refer to fermented wine; (5) fermentation in the ancient Near East, unlike Greece, took only about three days, and (6) the Mishna provides no such evidence of the practice of having unfermented wine. There seems to have been no attempts to preserve wine in an unfermented state; it may have been a near impossible task. A careful examination of all the Hebrew words (as well as their Semitic cognates) and the Greek words for wine demonstrates that the ancients knew little, if anything, about unfermented wine.

Ample evidence is available to demonstrate that wine, though always fermented, was usually mixed with water in the classical and Hellenistic world. The wine was stored in large jugs called *amphorae,* from which the wine was poured through a strainer into a large mixing bowl call a *krater.* In the krater the wine was mixed with water. Then the drinking bowls or cups were filled.

The amount of wine per volume varied. The

A thermopolium (a bar that sells warm wine) in Herculaneum.

mixture that represented the greatest amount of water to wine was 20 to 1, apparently because the wine was so strong (Homer, *Odyssey* 10. 208f).

In the western Mediterranean world the term "wine" referred to the mixture of wine and water. If one desired to mention wine without water, it was necessary to add the word "unmixed." For the Greeks, to drink wine unmixed was regarded as barbaric. The evidence, however, seems to indicate that in the OT, wine was used without being mixed with water. The terminology of mixing water and wine is strikingly unattested. Wine diluted with water was symbolic of spiritual adulteration (Is 1:22). By Roman times this attitude changed. The Mishna assumes a ratio of two parts of water to one part wine; however, later Talmudic sources speak of three to one.

The strength of ancient wine is somewhat of a puzzle. A natural, nondistilled wine could reach as high as 15 percent alcohol content. If watered down 3 parts water to 1 part wine, the alcohol content would be 5 percent and still fairly potent. The difficulty arises in trying to understand how any naturally fermented wine could be so strong that as much as 20 parts of water were added to 1 part of wine. In addition Pliny speaks of fermenting wine having such a high alcohol content that it could burn. Laboratory experiments demonstrates that mixtures containing less than 30 percent alcohol will not burn instantly but will burn if a flame is applied persistently at room temperature, though a mixture at 20 percent alcohol is not flammable at room temperature. Thus the statement by Pliny suggests a very high alcohol content to some ancient wines. There is no proof of distillation in ancient records, though the evaporation of alcohol was understood.

Wine was mixed not only with water but also with other ingredients, similar to mixed drinks today. An example of this is seen in the Homeric "Hymn to Demeter," where the goddess rejects straight wine and desires the drink mixed with meal, water, and a soft mint. Often strong wine was mixed into weak wine, resulting in a stronger drink. This is what is meant by "mixture" in the Bible (Ps 75:8; Is 5:22; Rv 18:6; 19:13–15). At times the fresh wine, high in sugar content, was evaporated, and this concentrated must was mixed with wine to obtain a higher alcohol content.

The strong drink of the OT seems to be closely related to Mesopotamian date wine. This same date wine, high in sugar content, must have also been high in alcohol content. One Hebrew word is consistently used as strong drink (Lv 10:9; Dt 29:6; 1 Sm 1:15; Prv 20:1; 31:6; Is 5:22; 29:9). There is an equivalent word to this in Ugaritic, translated "drunk," which parallels the normal word for wine. Strong drink is usually condemned (Is 5:11,22; 28:7; 56:12) and is especially forbidden to priests on duty (Lv 10:9). It is commended for the weak and weary (Prv 31:6; Nm 28:7).

Old Testament and Wine. The evidence, as seen above, suggests that wine in the OT was not mixed with water and was looked on with favor when taken in moderation. Judges 9:13 presents wine as that "which cheers God and men." Psalm 104:15 portrays wine similarly, "And wine which makes man's heart glad" (cf. also Est 1:10; Eccl 10:19; Is 55:1,2; Zec 10:7). The temperate use of wine was a normal and accepted part of life (Gn 14:18; Jgs 19:19; 1 Sm 16:20). Levitical priests in service at the temple (Lv 10:8,9), Nazirites (Nm 6:3), and the Rechabites (Jer 35:1–3) were forbidden to drink wine.

Wine had many uses in the OT world. The "drink offering" was wine (Ex 29:40; Lv 23:13) and the worshiper regularly brought wine when offering sacrifice (1 Sm 1:24). In addition, a supply of wine was kept in the temple for sacrificial purposes (1 Chr 9:29). At times wine was used in helping the weak and sick (2 Sm 16:2; Prv 31:6). There is no mention of wine being administered to water to make it safe for drinking, as is commonly accepted. Modern examples of pollution were not common in the ancient world, although this problem appeared occasionally. Examples are myriad concerning the fresh wells, springs, and moving bodies of water in biblical times, and methods were available to purify any impure water.

Negative reactions to intemperate wine drinking abound in the OT. Isaiah condemned those who drank wine to excess (Is 28:1–8). Many admonitions of drinking wine in excess are given in the Scriptures (Prv 20:1; 21:17; 23:20,21; 23:32–34).

The New Testament and Wine. The intertestamental period serves as a backdrop for the NT period. Rabbinic sources reveal that wine was mixed with water (usually two parts of water to one of wine) in the Mishna, but later Talmudic material gives a three to one mixture. Prior to the NT era, wine was a normal part of the Passover ritual. The Mishna mentions drinking four cups of wine during the Passover meal, of which three were mixed with water.

Wine in the NT was a fermented beverage that was mixed with various amounts of water. It was also mixed with gall (Mt 27:34) and myrrh (Mk 15:23), and unmixed referred to God's wrath (Rv 14:10). Evidence strongly suggests that the wine used at the Lord's Supper was a mixture of water and wine, probably three to one in agreement with the dictates of the Mishna. The phrase "fruit of the vine" (Mt 26:27–29) is often interpreted to mean fresh grape juice. However, fresh grape juice would be all but impossible to find.

The NT, as the OT, argues forcefully against the unrestrained use of wine. The biblical admonition is not to be drunk with wine (Eph 5:18; 1 Pt 4:3). Leaders in the church were to practice moderation in the use of wine (1 Tm 3:3,8; Ti 1:7). In 1 Timothy 3:3 and Titus 1:7, the KJV implies that no wine is to be taken, whereas in 1 Timothy 3:8 not much is to be taken. In reality all these verses should be translated in the sense "not to be addicted to wine." Paul does urge believers to forego some things out of regard for an immature Christian's conscience, which may be offended by a mature Christian eating meat and drinking wine that was once offered to idols (Rom 14:21).

See FOOD AND FOOD PREPARATION.

Bibliography. H. Daniel-Rops, *Daily Life in Palestine in the Time of Christ*, pp 204–6; C. Seltman, *Wine in the Ancient World.*

Winepress. A sunken area (Jgs 6:11) into which the grape harvest was thrown, to be trodden with bare feet amid shouts of joy and traditional vintage worksongs (Jer 48:33; cf. Is 65:8). The red juice flowed through spouts into jars. Full winepresses meant prosperity; deserted ones underlined disaster. To tread grapes and remain thirsty showed extreme humiliation (Nm 18:27; Jb 24:11; Hos 9:2 NEB). The common winepress was a natural landmark (Jgs 7:25; Zec 14:10); a privately owned one indicated the special care and efficiency of the vineyard's owner (Is 5:2; Mt 21:33).

Grape treading provided a dramatic metaphor for ruthless trampling by invading armies (Lam 1:15). This vivid metaphor of battle is mingled with divine judgment (Is 63:1–6), and anticipates the final trampling of "the vintage of the earth" gathered by angels into "the winepress of the wrath of God."

See WINE; VINE, VINEYARD.

A winepress in Jerusalem.

Winnower. One who removes chaff from grain.

See AGRICULTURE; TRADES AND OCCUPATIONS (FARMER).

Wisdom, Wisdom Literature. Wisdom is a capacity of the mind; in the OT it involves both knowledge and the ability to direct the mind toward a full understanding of human life and toward its moral fulfillment. Wisdom is thus a special capacity, necessary for full human living, but one which can be acquired through education and the application of the mind.

The wisdom literature in the OT is that literature which has this special concept of wisdom as its central theme. It comprises principally the books of Job, Proverbs, and Ecclesiastes, and may also be found in portions of the psalms and prophets. The wisdom literature contains both the moral substance of true wisdom (Prv) and also the intellectual explorations of wise men seeking to understand the fundamental problems of human existence (Jb, Eccl).

The Wisdom of God. Although the term "wisdom" is used primarily in the OT with reference to human beings, all wisdom is ultimately rooted and grounded in God. Wisdom forms a central part of the nature of God. In wisdom God created the universe (Prv 3:19) and mankind (Ps 104:24). Those matters which are not understood by human beings or any other living creature are fully comprehended within the wisdom of God (Jb 28:12–23).

Thus wisdom, in its positive connotations, is something inherent in God, reflected in creation, and a part of the reason for human existence. Wisdom in creation is reflected in the form and order which emerged out of primeval chaos; the world may hold meaning for mankind only because it reflects in its structure the wisdom of God. The wisdom of God in the creation of mankind means that human life may also be marked by form and order, and that meaning in life may be found in the created world which contains the marks of wisdom. The wisdom of God is thus creative, purposeful, and good; it is not merely the intellectual activity of God. The potential for human wisdom is rooted in the creation of mankind. Created by divine wisdom, human beings have within them the God-given capacity for wisdom. Thus it is impossible to understand human wisdom without first grasping its necessary antecedent, divine wisdom.

The Wisdom of Man. The word wisdom, with reference to human beings, is used in a variety of different ways in the OT. The word is often used as virtually synonymous with the term "knowledge," but in its general and secular uses it commonly indicates applied knowledge, skill, or even cunning. Wisdom could be defined as either "superior mental capacity" or "superior skill." Thus wisdom is used to describe both the cunning of King Solomon (1 Kgs 2:1–6) and the craftsmanship or skill of the workman Bezalel (Ex 35:33). But it was also used to describe mental capacities and skills which had a moral component, the capacity to understand and to do the good. Thus, when Moses delegated some of his authority to newly appointed judges, he chose "wise, understanding, and experienced men" (Dt 1:13). It is from this latter sense that there emerged the central concept of wisdom and the wise man in ancient Israel. Human wisdom, in this special sense, was akin to the wisdom of God; it was not merely a gift from God, inherent at birth, but had to be developed consciously during life lived in relationship with God.

Thus this positive and special kind of wisdom in human beings cannot be understood apart from God. A frequent theme of the Wisdom Literature in the OT is that the "fear of the Lord is the beginning of wisdom" (Prv 9:10; see also Prv 1:7; 15:33; Jb 28:28; Ps 111:10). In several ways, this theme sets a perspective for understanding true human wisdom.

First, human wisdom is only possible because of the divine wisdom present in creation; the potential for wisdom exists only because God created it. Second, if wisdom is to be developed in a human being, the starting point must be God, specifically the reverence or fear of God. This Hebraic concept of wisdom is strikingly different from the Greek concept. The Ionian philosophers, with remarkable power, developed a system of thought which began without the assumption of the existence of god(s). They attempted to develop wisdom through human reason alone. But Hebrew wisdom, though it sought to develop both the reason and the intellect as did the Greeks, could start only with God. The mind and its capacities were God-given; thus, however secular in appearance the wisdom of the Hebrews might seem, it had God as its starting point. The reverence of God, namely the acknowledgment that God existed, created, and was important in human life, lay behind all the developments of Hebrew wisdom.

Human wisdom, in the Hebrew conception, is thus a development of the mind, an expansion of knowledge, and an understanding of both the meaning of life and how that life must be lived. It is thoroughly intellectual, but has a powerful moral content. Wisdom was not sought for its own sake, but always for its application to the meaning of life, for life—like wisdom—was God's gift. This thrust in Hebrew wisdom meant that the virtues of the wise man or woman were never described in intellectual terms alone. The wise are not the intelligentsia of Israelite society, but, as the Book of Proverbs makes clear, they were those whose lives were characterized by understanding, patience, diligence, trustworthiness, self-control, modesty, and similar virtues. In a word, the wise man was the God-fearing man; his wisdom lay not just in a static attitude of reverence, but rather in the conscious development of the mind toward wisdom in the context of reverence.

From this general conception of wisdom there emerged in ancient Israel a special category of men, the wise men. Wisdom was not limited to them, though in a special sense they were responsible for the growth and communication of wisdom in Israel. The wise men formed one of three classes of religious personnel. First, there were priests and Levites, whose responsibilities lay primarily within the context of established religion. They were the servants of the temple, the leaders of worship, and also had certain responsibilities in the area of religious education. Second, there were the prophets, the spokesmen of God to the people of God. Third, there were the wise men. From a certain perspective, they possessed the most secular task among the three groups. They were involved in a variety of tasks, from governmental administration to moral and secular education, yet in all their tasks wisdom was a necessary qualification. But it was from their role as moral educators that their wisdom has survived down into the modern world. They educated the young people of their day, not in how to make a living but in how to live, and something of their curriculum has survived in the Book of Proverbs. The books of Job and Ecclesiastes also reflect the thought of the wise men.

The Wisdom Literature. Wisdom literature forms an important part of the OT. It falls within the third division of the Hebrew canon, the Writings, and comprises basically three books: Proverbs, Ecclesiastes (or Qoheleth), and Job. There are also wisdom psalms (e.g., Pss 1,32,34,37) and wisdom-type passages in the prophets (such as the parables of Is: e.g., Is 5:1–7). In the Greek OT (and the English Apocrypha), two additional books of wisdom are found. There is Ecclesiasticus, a 2nd-century BC work of Joshua ben Sira, which has certain similarities to the Book of Proverbs, and the Wisdom of Solomon, an anonymous work more philosophical (or Greek) in style, representing the flowering of Jewish wisdom in the Hellenistic period.

The starting point for an understanding of OT wisdom literature is Proverbs. Its wisdom concerns morality, the knowledge of how to live properly. It has a theological foundation, though much of its wisdom is secular in form. The starting point, as for all wisdom, is the reverence of God. But for the most part, the concern of the book is to convey the fundamentals of morality, the virtues of integrity, discipline, justice, common sense, and the like, and to show by way of contrast the failure in life that awaits the fool. The book has a strongly didactic nature. Nowadays it can be read as a piece of literature, though its wisdom was designed to be learned, memorized even, by the young persons who received their education at the feet of the wise men. For those who learned its truth, for whom the short poetic sayings became a part of the subconscious mind, the wisdom of the proverbs served as a moral and spiritual guide throughout life. There was a way to live successfully, a way governed by morality, and success lay in the fact that the morally good life was the life lived according to the wisdom of the Creator of all life. Thus the wise men of the proverbs functioned as guides, in both their teaching and their writing; they provided no new philosophical theories, no advanced intellectual speculation, but communicated that most valuable of all human kinds of knowledge—how to live. Wisdom is "more precious than jewels, and nothing you desire can compare with her. Long life is in her right hand; in her left hand are riches and honor. Her ways are ways of pleasantness, and all her paths are peace" (Prv 3:15–17).

Yet there were two directions from which the relatively straightforward wisdom of proverbs was vulnerable. One was the attack of thoroughgoing skepticism; the other was the attack of such an awful experience of human life that the wisdom of proverbs seemed undermined to its very core. The attack from the perspective of skepticism is dealt with in Ecclesiastes; that from the direction of experience is examined in Job. Both these books have a more theoretical perspective than that of Proverbs; they teach, but in a simple didactic fashion and are both invaluable companions to the Book of Proverbs.

Ecclesiastes reflects the wisdom of a man who has lived long and seen the world from all perspectives. His faith, such as it is, is not the superficial faith of a man who lives easily and believes lightly. The man has seen through the façade of too simple a morality. It simply is not true that the righteous always prosper and the wicked suffer. Too often the righteous suffer, with no relief from their suffering, and the wicked enjoy their lives in carefree abandon. The writer of Ecclesiastes sought justice, but as he observed the world through honest and objective eyes, he could not see that justice was always done. More than justice, he sought truth, sought it with his rational mind, but even truth in its ultimate perspectives eluded him. All was vanity, a grasping after wind! Yet for all the skeptical and apparently negative tenor of Ecclesiastes, it is a magnificent monument of faith, a faith which held on to God despite the agony and pointlessness of a world filled with evil and vanity. This wise man could not soar with hope like that of the prophets, but he could hold on to the fundamental truth of God when all else, including understanding, failed. So the Book of Ecclesiastes may become an intimate companion to those who see the world as it really is, in all its agony and apparent vanity.

But whereas the writer of Ecclesiastes described the grief and sadness of the world from the perspective of an observer, Job grasps the problems from within, from the perspective of the sufferer. Job knows the wisdom of Proverbs and has lived his life by that wisdom, but he encounters an experience which calls into question the validity of the entire structure of conventional morality and wisdom. He was a pious man, an upright man, whose life embodied the precepts of Proverbs. Prior to his experience, he had no cause to doubt a simple interpretation of proverbial wisdom, namely that righteousness led to prosperity and happiness. But then Job's world collapsed, and with it the wisdom by which he had lived. The loss of possessions, property, and prestige; the death of his children; the pain and suffering of terrible illness—all these things conspired to raise an enormous question as to the validity of traditional morality. But the wisdom of the Book of Job raises an even more fundamental question than the validity of morality; Job questions the premise of all wisdom, God himself. In what sense can God be just in the face of such apparent injustice? In what sense can God be just, when unjust men flourish and prosper into the years of old age (Jb 21:7–15)? Does God's creation really reflect structure, order, and goodness, if the experience of Job is the measure of human life? Such are the radical questions evoked by Job and they receive no simple solution. Yet in the great climax of the Book of Job, namely the encounter between God and his servant (Jb 38–42), wisdom is set in its proper perspective. There remains always a mystery in God and in God's ways that lies beyond the grasp of the human mind. Wisdom is pursuit of the knowledge of God, but wisdom as intellectual knowledge can never grasp ultimate truth in all its depth, for God is always greater than the human mind and human wisdom. Yet Job

adds a further truth to the knowledge of conventional wisdom. While Job's questions were not explicitly answered, they were effectively removed; it was the encounter of God with Job which transformed the man. Thus, the ultimate wisdom lies not in finding an answer to the ultimate questions, but rather in the encounter with the living God.

The teaching of the wisdom literature has manifold dimensions and in its totality is a compound of the various perspectives on the truth contained in Proverbs, Ecclesiastes, and Job. There is a fundamental knowledge and morality which is vital to proper and successful living and which must be communicated to the young as their basic rule of life. It will lead not always to material prosperity, but to that more profound prosperity which transcends adversity; the prosperity of the person whose life is lived in reverence of God. With the passage of time and advancement of years, there comes to those educated in conventional wisdom the understanding that life and the world are not so simple. Faced with the temptation to jettison conventional morality and wisdom, a person may find that the more worldly wisdom of Ecclesiastes provides an anchor. Life may seem pointless, the world may seem to be essentially a place of vanity, but the truth of God and reverence for God must be maintained in the face of radical doubt (Eccl 12:13,14). To those who experience in some fashion the plight of Job, wisdom reaches its limits and points beyond itself; man cannot always find an answer to the questions, and the last resort is simply the experience of the living God.

Wisdom Literature in the Ancient Near East. Neither the concept of wisdom nor the literature of wisdom were unique to Israel in its ancient Near Eastern setting. Indeed, of all the types of literature found in the OT, wisdom literature is the most international and cosmopolitan in both form and content. There was a tradition of wisdom in most ancient civilizations, and the international character of wisdom is recognized within the OT itself. The proverbial wisdom of Solomon is said to have "surpassed the wisdom of all the people of the east, and all the wisdom of Egypt" (1 Kgs 4:30), and the same passage lists some of those wise men by name. And it was not just that wisdom existed in various places, but there was also conventionally an interchange of wisdom between the wise men of various countries: "men came from all peoples to hear the wisdom of Solomon, and from all the kings of the earth, who had heard of his wisdom" (1 Kgs 4:34). During the reign of Solomon and afterward, Jerusalem may have been a center in which the wise men of many lands gathered and exchanged insights on matters pertaining to wisdom. Thus, it should not come as any surprise that there are a number of close parallels between the OT wisdom literature and that of other Near Eastern countries.

The principal evidence of wisdom literature outside Israel comes from the literary sources of Egypt and Mesopotamia (Sumerian, Babylonian, and Assyrian civilizations). There are also a few wisdom texts from other places, including the ancient kingdom of Ugarit to the north of the Promised Land. This Near Eastern literature falls into the same two categories as does the biblical wisdom literature; some examples are of the proverbial or instructional type (parallel to Prv), while others are more theoretical in substance, directed toward specific problems (parallel to Eccl and Jb). As in Israel, this wisdom literature appears to have been the product of wise men who were engaged in some form of educational activity.

The proverbial and instructional type of wisdom literature was known in Egypt since the 3rd millennium BC, and continued to appear down to the latter half of the 1st millennium BC. The best-known text is the *Instruction of Amenemope*, dated early in the 1st millennium BC. This wisdom, expressed in the form of advice from a royal official to his son, makes extensive use of proverbial sayings and admonitions concerning how to live the good life. This text has some remarkably close parallels to the Book of Proverbs. Similar instructional material existed in the Babylonian wisdom literature; in a text entitled the *Counsels of Wisdom*, from the mid–2nd millennium BC, a man's son is warned against such potential dangers as dishonesty and unsuitable companions and wives.

The more theoretical type of wisdom literature was also known in Egypt. The *Song of the Harper* raises issues similar to those of Ecclesiastes, and the *Protests of the Eloquent Peasant* raises the questions of justice and injustice, though in a more superficial way than in Job. But it was Babylonia which produced the more significant theoretical wisdom literature. A text entitled *I Will Praise the Lord of Wisdom*, from the 2nd millennium BC, recounts in monologue form the plight of a man suffering from terrible illness and convinced that he was deserted by his gods. He felt that there was no justice and that traditional values had been turned upside down. Eventually the man is relieved of his suffering and restored to his former happy estate. Another work, commonly entitled the *Babylonian Theodicy*, records a debate between a sufferer and a wise man, in which the issues are the pain and apparent injustice which are present in the world. Both these writings have striking similarities to the Book of Job, though neither of them plumb the depths so profoundly and neither has quite the literary genius and power of the biblical book.

Many parallels exist between biblical and Near Eastern wisdom literature—some of a general kind and others so precise as to suggest some kind of interrelationship. But for all the parallels between parts of the wisdom literature (e.g., the precise parallels between Proverbs and Amenemope), there is a fundamental theological difference. The principle underlying the biblical wisdom, as noted above, is that the reverence or fear of God is the beginning of wisdom. Babylonian and Egyptian wisdom also has a theological foundation, but it is rooted in a different faith. In other words, the distinctive feature of Hebrew wisdom is not that it was rooted in God. The nature and identity of the God of Israel transformed Hebrew wisdom and imparted to it a timeless quality which is still evident in the modern world.

Wisdom in the New Testament. The word "wisdom" is used in the NT with a similar variety of nuances. The term is used both of the wisdom of God and the wisdom of man. With respect to human wisdom, the term may carry either positive or negative connotations. The continuation of the OT wisdom tradition is found in the NT uses of the word in conjunction with God and in the positive connotations of the word in relation to human beings. But the word may sometimes carry the negative overtones which depreciate human wisdom. Thus Paul describes his message as being "not in the plausible words of wisdom, but in demonstration of the Spirit and of power" (1 Cor 2:4); purely human wisdom has no ultimate merit of its own, and Paul quotes the OT to demonstrate that God would destroy human wisdom (1 Cor 1:19; cf. Is 29:14). A clear distinction between good and evil wisdom is provided in the Letter of James (3:13–18). A person whose life reflects jealousy and selfish ambition has not the true wisdom of God, but is earthly minded and unspiritual. But true, God-given wisdom is "first pure, then peaceable, gentle, open to reason, full of mercy and good fruits, without uncertainty or insincerity" (Jas 3:17). The fundamental wisdom is again that of God, which is rich and profound in all its fullness (Rom 11:33). The wisdom of God—which is relevant to all mankind, for God's wisdom concerns human beings—was to be revealed to the world as a whole through the life and ministry of the church (Eph 3:10). As wisdom was the primary possession of God, so too it was reflected in the life and ministry of Jesus. Jesus, during the years of his growth, reflected in his life the increase of wisdom (Lk 2:40,52), and his opponents, as well as his friends, recognized the wisdom in his teaching (Mt 13:54).

Since wisdom is rooted and grounded in God, true and spiritual wisdom was God's gift. It could be seen in the lives and words of the servants of God such as Stephen (Acts 6:10) and Paul (2 Pt 3:15). And just as wisdom had been required of men who were to assist Moses in his task in OT times, so wisdom was required of persons serving the early Christian church (Acts 6:3). Spiritual wisdom, which provided the knowledge enabling a person to live fully the life given by God, was to be desired for oneself and prayed for in others (Col 1:9).

But the most central aspect of wisdom in the NT is in the gospel of the crucified Christ. In his first letter to the Corinthian church, Paul contrasts vividly the positive and negative senses of wisdom in proclaiming the death of Jesus Christ. The world did not know God by their own wisdom (1 Cor 1:21); that is, the true revelation of God and his redemption of mankind were not revealed to those who sought such truth through wisdom alone, namely through the Greek approach to wisdom and philosophy. The gospel was declared in preaching, which was, from a strictly philosophical or wisdom perspective, a kind of foolishness. And yet the gospel of Jesus Christ was both the power of God and the wisdom of God (1 Cor 1:24). Jesus, for those who believed, became the ultimate source of that wisdom which could come from God alone (1 Cor 1:30).

Paul indicates that the wisdom of God is somehow intimately related to the death and resurrection of Jesus, which ties wisdom in the NT to one of the central passages concerning wisdom in the OT. The Book of Job ends, from a certain perspective, on an unsatisfactory note. The fundamental questions of wisdom concerning suffering, evil, and God, received no unambiguous and satisfying answer. All that is clear is that Job, in his encounter with the living God, somehow lost interest in the questions of wisdom. The encounter with God was in itself so overwhelming an experience that the questions of wisdom were no longer central. But for the person who does not encounter God in the whirlwind, as did Job, the persistent questions of OT wisdom remain. To this dilemma, the gospel offers a new wisdom and a new understanding. From a Christian perspective, the wisdom of Job functions as a signpost to a greater wisdom—the wisdom of God in the death and resurrection of Jesus Christ.

The way in which the wisdom of Job is superseded by that of the gospel may be seen partially in terms of the remarkable parallel between the experiences of Job and Jesus. Jesus, a good man, suffered, as did the righteous man Job. Jesus and Job suffered for no evil they had done, while evil men flourished and grew old in prosperity. Job felt deserted by the God whom he had known and served, as did Jesus on the cross: "My God, My God, why have you forsaken me?" But beyond the parallels, there lies a remarkable difference. In Job, we perceive the agonized face of humanity turned toward God and asking: "Why?" But on the cross, it is the agonized face of God himself which is revealed to mankind in the person of Jesus. The crucifixion no more provides a simple solution to the problems of wisdom than does the Book of Job, but it does provide the place where a solution may be found. For all those things which conspire against wisdom, the problems of pain and evil, even of God himself, are present in the crucifixion of Jesus. And while the answer to the question "Why?" remains partially a mystery, the resurrection of Jesus sets the questions in a different perspective. The Book of Job suggested that the resolution to the problems of wisdom was to be found in an encounter with the living God; the death of Jesus marks the place where that encounter may be made.

PETER C. CRAIGIE

See POETRY, BIBLICAL; PROVERBS, BOOK OF; JOB, BOOK OF; ECCLESIASTES, BOOK OF; GOD, BEING AND ATTRIBUTES OF; WISE MEN; APOCRYPHA, OLD AND NEW TESTAMENT; PSALMS, BOOK OF.

Bibliography. J.L. Crenshaw, ed., *Studies in Ancient Israelite Wisdom*; D.F. Morgan, *Wisdom in the OT Tradition*; M. Noth and D.W. Thomas, eds., *Wisdom in Israel and in the Ancient Near East*; W.O.E. Oesterley, *The Wisdom of Egypt and the OT.*; O.S. Rankin, *Israel's Wisdom Literature*; H. Ranston, *The OT Wisdom Books and Their Teaching*; J.M. Thompson, *The Form and Function of Proverbs in Ancient Israel*; R.L. Wilken, ed., *Aspects of Wisdom in Judaism and Early Christianity*.

Wise Men. Men appearing in Matthew 2:1–12 who, following a star, come to Jerusalem and then Bethlehem to pay homage to the newborn "king of the Jews." While Matthew tells nothing of their personal identity or positions and little of their nationalities, the account forms an appropriate introduction to his Gospel by drawing attention to the true identity of Jesus and by foreshadowing the homage paid by the Gentiles to Jesus throughout that Gospel.

The Role and Position in the Ancient World. Extrabiblical evidence offers various clues that shed light on the place of origin and positions held by the "wise men" of Matthew 2. The historian Herodotus mentions "magi" as a priestly caste of Media, or Persia, and, as the religion in Persia at the time was Zoroastrinism, Herodotus' magi were probably Zoroastrian priests. Herodotus, together with Plutarch and Strabo, suggests that magi were partly responsible for ritual and cultic life (supervising sacrifices and prayers) and partly responsible as royal advisers to the courts of the East. Believing the affairs of history were reflected in the movements of the stars and other phenomena, Herodotus suggests the rulers of the East commonly utilized the magi's knowledge of astrology and dream interpretation to determine affairs of state. The magi were therefore concerned with what the movement of the stars (as sign and portents) might signify for the future affairs of history. Such an interest could account not only for the wise men's association with the star in Matthew 2, but also their conclusion, shared with Herod, that the nova's appearance signified the birth of a new ruler of great importance (2:2). Several centuries before Christ a similar correlation was noted between a stellar phenomenon and the birth of Alexander the Great.

Identity in Matthew's Gospel. Matthew's infancy narrative contains little information concerning the identity of the magi. Matthew states only that the wise men were "from the East" (2:1,2), an ambiguous point of origin that left room for many subsequent hypotheses. Some church fathers proposed Arabia on the basis of where the gifts (gold, frankincense, and myrrh, 2:11) were likely to have originated. Other suggested Chaldea or Media/Persia, and, although certainty is impossible, Persia did certainly have a caste of priests (magi) which would fit the description in Matthew.

Interestingly, Matthew does not tell how many magi came to honor the infant Jesus. The Eastern church held that there were 12 travelers, although this may simply derive from the biblical penchant for that number (12 tribes of Israel, 12 disciples). The Western church settled on 3 wise men, based presumably on the 3 gifts brought in homage. The exact number is not known.

A similar silence exists in Matthew regarding the names of the wise men. The names Gaspar, Melchior (Melkon), and Balthasar are legendary and do not derive from Matthew. Similarly, the later tradition that Gaspar was a king of India, Melchoir a king of Persia, and Balthasar a king of Arabia has no basis in fact.

Importance for Matthew's Gospel. The visit of the wise men plays a significant role in introducing Matthew's Gospel. From the beginning it reveals the true identity of the infant as the long-expected and prophesied royal Messiah of Israel. This is brought out first in the appearance of the "star," which, as can be noted from Numbers 24:17 ("a star shall come forth out of Jacob, a scepter shall arise out of

Large pool in Herod the Great's palace at Herodium. At his own request, Herod was buried at Herodium, only 4 miles southeast of Bethlehem, the site of Jesus' birth and the slaughter of the infants (Mt 2).

Israel"), carried clear messianic connotations (see also Is 60:3). Second, the interchange between the magi, Herod, and the chief priests and scribes (2:2–6) reveals that Jesus is the fulfillment of the messianic prophecy of Micah 5:2, the ruler of Israel coming from the small village of Bethlehem. Third, the offering of the gifts (2:11) may also echo the possible messianic promises of Psalms 68:29 and 72:10.

In addition to confirming that Jesus is the long-awaited Messiah, the account of the magis' visit, as part of the introduction to Matthew's Gospel, introduces several prominent themes which reappear in subsequent chapters. First, the account establishes that Jesus' messiahship has bearing not only on the Jews, but on the gentile world (symbolized in the "wise men from the East"). The bowing homage of these gentile astrologers foreshadows the Great Commission directed to bring salvation to "all nations" (28:19; see also 8:11,12; 12:21). A second theme established in the account which surfaces later is the surprising gentile faith which is lacking among Jesus' own people. Even as the foreign magi honor the infant Messiah, Herod and possibly the chief priests and scribes of the people plot the baby's death (2:3–6,16). So also elsewhere in the gospel, Gentiles offer faith in Jesus which often contrasts markedly with the faith withheld by their Jewish counterparts (see 8:5–13; 15:21–28; 27:19,54). DAVID C. CARLSON

See WISDOM, WISDOM LITERATURE.

Withered Hand. *See* DEFORMITY.

Witness.
One who tells what he has seen or personally experienced in a court of law (cf. Jn 3:11). The term may also refer to the testimony which he has given. In the Bible a witness may also be a monument or memorial which signifies that a certain action has been taken or agreement made.

In the judicial procedure outlined in the OT one witness was not adequate for personal testimony against anyone, but two or three witnesses were required (Dt 17:6; 19:15). This principle was ingrained in Jewish law and is reiterated in the NT (cf. Mt 18:16; 2 Cor 13:1).

The truth of testimony is so important that the Bible expressly forbids false witness in the ninth commandment (Ex 20:16; Dt 5:20; cf. Mk 10:19; Lk 18:20). The practical wisdom of Proverbs speaks out frequently against the false witness (e.g., Prv 6:19; 14:5; 25:18). Nevertheless, false witnesses did arise (Pss 27:12; 35:11), and there are notable examples of the bribing of more than one witness in order to bring about the death of an innocent person. The case of Naboth and his vineyard is notorious; here Jezebel, wife of King Ahab, bribed two men to bear false witness against Naboth so that he would be stoned to death and her wicked husband could take the vineyard which he coveted so intensely (1 Kgs 21). In the illegal trial of Jesus, the chief priests sought testimony against him; there were false witnesses whose testimonies did not agree and were invalid (Mk 14:55–99).

Witnesses could be tested by the judges. If the testimony of an accuser was found to be false, that person was subjected to the punishment he had sought to have executed on the defendant (Dt 19:16–21). Proverbs also speaks of the punishment of the false witness (19:5,9; 21:28).

The OT records several accounts of legal proceedings in which witnesses are mentioned. Most of these involve the purchase or transfer of property. Ruth 4:7–12 relates the redemption of a field from Naomi by Boaz. Isaiah found "reliable witnesses" concerning a property title written on a large tablet (Is 8:1,2). To confirm the prophecy of the return of the exiles from Babylon, Jeremiah bought and paid for a field in the presence of witnesses, who also signed the deed for the property (Jer 32:6–15).

In the OT a monument often served as a witness to an event or an agreement. A heap of stones was piled up as a witness to a covenant between Jacob and Laban, and it was named "the heap of witness" in Aramaic and in Hebrew (Gn 31:44–50). When the Transjordanian tribes returned to their inheritance after helping their brethren subdue the land of Canaan, they built an altar of witness, which they named "Witness," to testify that they were a part of Israel (Jos 22:21–34; esp v 34).

At the conclusion of his farewell message at Shechem, Joshua declared that the Israelites themselves were witnesses that they had chosen to serve the Lord; then he set up a large stone and declared that it also was a witness (Jos 24:22–27).

The people of Israel themselves were declared God's witnesses (Is 43:10; 44:8,9). They were witnesses to the existence of God, to his uniqueness, holiness, power, and love. When they failed to acknowledge his uniqueness and holiness and turned to polytheism, he sent them into captivity, as he had warned, for they had failed in their witness and had given opportunity for the enemies of God to blaspheme.

In the NT the various words for witness are mainly related to the root *martureō*, "to bear witness, be a witness." The word "martyr" shows the ultimate form of witness in that one may be called upon to lay down his life as a witness to the truth or because of his witness for Jesus Christ.

John the Baptist was both a witness and a martyr. As the forerunner of the Messiah, his mission was to bear witness to the light and to identify the Lamb of God (Jn 1:7,8,19–36).

The followers of Jesus, and particularly the 12, were witnesses to the person and character of Jesus. They knew him intimately, heard his teachings, and observed his miracles; three were witnesses of his transfiguration (Mt 17:1, 2; 2 Pt 1:17,18) and many were witnesses to his resurrection (Lk 24:48; 1 Cor 15:4–8). They were specifically commissioned to be his witnesses at the time of his ascension (Acts 1:8), with the promise of the enabling of the Holy Spirit for this work (vv 4,8). The Book of Acts is replete with the accounts of that witness of the Holy Spirit through obedient believers.

God himself is the greatest of all witnesses. He describes himself as a "swift witness" against the workers of iniquity (Mal 3:5) and expressly mentions those who "swear falsely." The Father bears witness to the Son (Jn 5:37; 8:18). Jesus Christ is called the faithful witness (Rv 1:5) and his works are a witness to who he is (Jn 5:36). All of the prophets give witness to the salvation which is in Jesus (Acts 10:43). God bears witness to those who believe, by giving them the Holy Spirit (Acts 15:8), who bears witness with the spirits of believers that they are children of God (Rom 8:15–17; cf. 1 Jn 5:9–12).

CARL E. DeVRIES

Witness, Altar of. Altar built by the Reubenites, the Gadites, and the half tribe of Manasseh in the frontier of Israel near the Jordan (Jos 22:10–34). The building of the altar incited the remainder of Israel to threaten war for the presumed treachery. After the Transjordanian tribes explained their motives and Phinehas mediated the conflict, the altar was called "Witness" as a memorial of the resulting treaty.

Wizard. *See* MAGIC.

Wolf. *See* ANIMALS.

Woman, Doctrine of. The biblical teaching on women is a much debated issue in current biblical scholarship. Traditional values (or what people perceive to be "traditional") are pitted against the current radical ideas. Attitudes of male dominance are being challenged by those who argue for slight changes, as well as by those who make more radical demands for a rejection of scriptural portraits of God and a return to the mother-goddess cult. Meanwhile, women and men are more confused than ever about their relationship to one another, their roles in church and society, and even their interaction with God.

The biblical teaching on women is not the source of the problems in this area so much as the interpretation of the teaching. Traditionalists who wish to assert male-dominance models appear to have many passages to support their point of view. Those who argue for broader roles for women than are traditionally recognized believe that not all the biblical evidence has been adequately examined.

The place to begin the study of women is not in the letters of Paul, which treat the issue of women in church and family, but in the Torah, in which the foundational teachings are given on the nature of woman as God's creation.

Foundation Texts. Genesis 1:26–28 is the opening portrayal of the creation of the first man and woman. Here God created man in his image, as male and female. Hence, the female shares with the male the image of God, reflects his power and majesty on earth, and is commanded to multiply and bring dominion to the earth. From Genesis 1:26–28 there is no suggestion of inferiority of the female to the male, nor is there any suggestion of her submission to his dominance. Rather, they are pictured together, the male and the female, as the representation of their Maker.

Genesis 2:20–25 is the second portrayal of the creation of the first woman. In Genesis 2 the male was made before the female, a point that seems to give him some precedence. This may not be pressed too far, however, as the pattern in the creation texts is to move progressively from the lesser to the finer work! Yet it is because of his prior creation that the male is given the prerogative to name the female (Gn 2:23). In Semitic thought, the giving of names signifies dominion or ownership. This means that Adam's naming of his wife was an act of lordship. However, the name that he gives her is the equivalent to his own, meaning the male asserted her equality with him. Therefore this hierarchical relationship is a relationship of equals.

The situation in Genesis 1 and 2 reveals a balanced relationship between the man and the woman who are the parents of all mankind: two persons who are altogether equal in status as co-heirs of the mystery of the image of God, and yet who dwell in a delicate one-to-one relationship in which one is the leader of the other. In Eden before the fall this delicate balance was possible.

Trouble in Paradise. Genesis 3, the story of the fall of mankind, speaks of the breaking of the delicate balance between the man and the woman and the ensuing struggles that have been passed down to the present generation. In God's words to the woman, he announces the pain that will now attend her childbearing (Gn 3:16a) and the conflict of interests that will affect her relationship with her husband: "Your desire will be for your husband, and he will rule over you." The Hebrew term "desire" (*teshuqa*) is similarly used in Genesis 4:7b, where sin is pictured as crouching at Cain's door. He is told, "It desires to have you, but you must master it." The term "desire" in the Genesis 3 and 4 passages is not a sexual longing, but a desire to control, to master, to be in charge (the use of *teshuqa* meaning sexual desire is seen in Sg 7:10). Consequently, after the fall the desire of woman is to dominate her husband; her determination to reject his leadership in their relationship of equals is a breaking of the balance in their relationship. For his part, the man tends to tyrannize the woman.

Paul teaches about the tumbling of the male-female relationship of equals in Ephesians 5:22–33. To the woman who may attempt to dominate her husband the apostle says, "Wives, submit to your husbands as to the Lord" (v 22). Her natural inclination is to be transformed by her new relationship with the Savior. She is to see in her husband one who represents the Lord to her; as she submits to him she submits to the Lord. For, Paul argues, the husband is to the wife as Christ is to the church (v 23). Further, the man who may tend to tyrannize his wife has this inclination redirected because of his new relationship with the Savior. Husbands are exhorted to love their wives, "just as Christ loved the church and gave himself up for her" (v 25), and to love their wives "as their own bodies" (v 28). Even a casual observer may see that the greater command is upon the husband: to love as Christ loves.

By these words the apostle is presenting a means whereby couples may regain the bliss in their relationship that was the mark of Eden before the fall. Paul's citation of Genesis 2:24 in verse 31 is a case in point: here a couple may regain the original oneness that God intended for them. The relationship of equal persons in a hierarchy of responsiveness is stated in the context of mutual submission (v 21), which is a mark of their greatest submission to the Lord Jesus, who is the pattern for becoming truly human.

It appears, then, from both OT and NT that there is a gentle hierarchical relationship between the man and the woman, yet it is a relationship of equals. This is not far removed from the analogy of the holy Trinity, where three equal persons interrelate with one another in a determined hierarchical scheme (see 1 Cor 11:3). As Christ responds to the Father, so the wife responds to her husband; as the Father loves the Son, so the husband loves his wife. The hierarchy is not tyranny in either case; it is a mutual leadership of love and a mutual submission of one to the other.

Women in Biblical Culture. It is a minimizing of woman to think of her only in terms of home, babies, and the raising of children. The woman is a person in every respect as the man; she shares in the image of God and has the potential of varied ranges of response to culture, community, and life about her. Yet it

is a modern error of revisionists to attempt to think of woman altogether apart from tradiional familial ministries. It is a fact of Scripture that women are regularly associated with, and find their sense of worth in, childbearing. Yet the same Scriptures show that the nature of woman is not exhausted by associations with childbearing: she has her own identity in the community, in the cult, and before Yahweh in the whole of her life, not just when (or if) she bears and nourishes a child. Further, the biblical concept of childbearing always involves the husband, who is her partner at conception, at her side during delivery, and partner with her in the ongoing task of nourishing the child.

The image of the woman as the childbearer begins with the promise of God in Genesis 3:15, where he announces the ultimate victory over the evil one, Satan, by the offspring of the woman. This promise respecting the offspring of the woman became the universal blessing of God upon the woman as the childbearer. For ultimately, through one born of a woman, there would come the final deliverance. There is a sense in which each birth experience is a participation in the continuity of this blessing/ promise (see 1 Tm 2:15, and its possible relationship to this continuity of women, salvation, and childbearing).

Further, in the culture of the OT world, a woman's genuine worth was solely, or largely, perceived in terms of childbearing. Yet it is not in childbearing alone that she finds worth and dignity before God. For the woman, as for the man, the issue of faith in Yahweh is central. A woman who has a household of children, but no faith in God, might regard herself as a fulfilled person. Yet her care of her children is no substitute for piety to God. A woman who has no children, and perhaps no husband, may have her full identity and worth in her relationship with the God in whose image she is made and whose tasks she is commissioned by him to do. The harlot Rahab was justified before Yahweh because of her actions in protecting the Hebrew spies, not because of home and family (Heb 11:31). Moreover, the gifts of God in a woman's life may lead her to find opportunities in the community to express herself in praise to God. Women apparently had the same opportunities as men to take a Nazirite vow (Nm 6:2; see also ch 30).

Notable women whose public lives punctuate the male-dominated culture of ancient Israel include Miriam, the sister of Moses and Aaron (Ex 15:20,21), whose role as prophetess, worship musician, and national leader is tarnished by her jealousy over the more prominent role held by her younger brother, Moses (Nm 12). God judged her (Dt 24:9), but Israel

Egyptian bronze hand mirror with a handle in the form of a woman.

did not forget her superb gifts of leadership at the beginning of Israel's national experience. Long after her time, God spoke through his prophets of the gift he had given to Israel in the person of the national leader Miriam (Mi 6:4).

Other magnificent women whose lives were countercultural in this regard include Deborah, the prophetess of God and the only named woman judge of Israel (Jgs 4,5); Esther, the Hebrew queen of Xerxes who saved her people from the rash acts of the Persian king, a result of a frightful conspiracy; and Huldah, the prophetess who was the agent of Yahweh's word to Josiah at the inception of his revival (2 Chr 34:22–28). Huldah's reception and transmission of the word of Yahweh is the more remarkable because she was contemporary with Jeremiah and Zephaniah. In this case God chose to speak through a woman.

NT women who were released from cultural limitations on their public ministries include the daughters of Philip, Phoebe, Priscilla, Junias, Tryphena, Tryphosa, Persis, Euodia, and Syntyche. These women mark the beginning of the fulfillment of Joel's prophecy of a day in which women as well as men would be the instruments of the outpouring of the Holy Spirit (Jl 2:28,29).

Women such as Sarah, Ruth, and Hannah have exercised their faith to God in the context of the home and family as well. And pre-eminently there is Mary, mother of Jesus, in whom the ideal of womanhood is conjoined to the fulfillment of the ancient promise to Eve of a child who would one day be the great victor over the enemy of mankind.

Women Teachers. The Bible makes a number of implicit statements about women teachers. Miriam's sin was not being a leader of Israel, but jealousy against the special relationship her brother had with Yahweh. Priscilla was the teacher of a man; Philip's daughters hardly spoke to women's groups only, any more than did Huldah the prophetess.

Wisdom is personified as a woman in Proverbs 1–9. In fact, the culmination of the Book of Proverbs, the celebrated acrostic to the noble woman (31:10–31), shows the outworkings of biblical wisdom in the life of a person. Since wisdom is a woman in the first part of the book, how remarkably fitting that wisdom is found in a woman's personal, familial, and public life at the conclusion of the book.

The teaching and example of Jesus with respect to women is most countercultural. He reached out to them with the things of God in the most unlikely places (the well at Sychar, Jn 4), and he taught them in the crowds and in private places. The position of Mary at his feet in her home in Bethany is descriptive of a disciple; Martha was so busily occupied with the dishes she missed the greater reality (Lk 10:38–41).

The position of women in biblical history is subject to change. This appears to be the case in the story of the daughters of Zelophehad (Nm 27:1–11). These sisters had no brother, and their father's inheritance in the land was in jeopardy. They addressed Moses, he petitioned Yahweh, and they were given permission to inherit their father's land (with the later proviso that the land not pass from their tribal family, Nm 36:1–12). This passage indicates the beginning of a gradual movement for liberalizing laws and customs respecting women in ancient Israel. Growing slowly in Israel against significant resistance, the movement does proceed with the blessing of Yahweh (and the obedience of the women to his word, Nm 36:10).

Women and Church Leadership. The most difficult aspect of the biblical doctrine of women concerns their role and participation in the worship and leadership of the church. Certainly a casual reader of the pertinent NT texts might soon conclude that a woman is to be silent and submissive in the worship of the church of God, and that if she does speak at all, it has to be in very circumscribed circumstances. Many have concluded on the basis of close examination of these texts that this first impression of silence is the correct one. Arguments are made on the basis of God's order in creation (1 Tm 2:13), Eve's prior sin (v 14), and the subordination of the woman to the man (1 Cor 14:34). Since these are universal principles rather than cultural norms, it seems that this position is not open to varying interpretations.

Yet others look at these same verses and draw quite different conclusions. These texts may well have been designed to foster order and decorum in public worship at a time when women generally were not educated or prepared for public leadership roles in ministry. Women had been very active in the orgiastic cults of the cities in which the churches were being founded (e.g., Ephesus and Corinth). The tendency for newly converted but untaught women to lapse into error must have been enormous. Also, by their manner of immodest dress (1 Tm 2:9), they might attract men to their false views.

It may be suggested that the reason Eve first sinned was that she was the weaker of the two; since Adam had been created before Eve, he had had a longer association with God and a deeper understanding of the meaning of the things of God. Adam was not deceived; he sinned consciously. Eve, on the other hand, was deceived; she fell to the tempter's tricks.

So women in the early church needed time to learn; for the present they were to remain silent. The main verbal imperative of 1 Timothy 2:11–15 is not "be silent" (v 12) but "a woman should learn" (v 11).

The prophecy of Joel 2, the actions and teachings of Jesus, and the examples of Huldah and Priscilla suggest the coming fruition of the movement toward equality of personhood. Certainly the gifts of the Spirit are not gender related. If the Spirit gives gifts to women, and if women who are gifted receive the training necessary for ministries today, perhaps more doors will open for them in positions of shared leadership. The hierarchy aspect should not be stressed at the expense of the equality of mutual relationship.

The position of a woman of faith before God is assured on the same equal footing as any man of faith. In the Lord Jesus Christ there are no stratifications of sex, race, or social station, "for you are all one in Christ Jesus" (Gal 3:28). This verse speaks of justification, not socialization. In Paul's day there were still great differences based on sex, race, and social station. Within the assertion of justification in this verse are the seeds of change in socialization. Lines of race, of social station (slave and free) blur between those who know God. Debilitating lines of gender are beginning to blur as well. RONALD B. ALLEN

See EVE.

Bibliography. D.G. Bloesch, *Is the Bible Sexist?* S.B. Clark, *Man and Woman in Christ;* S. Foh, *Women and the Word of God;* E.M. Howe, *Women and Church Leadership;* J.B. Hurley, *Man and Woman in Biblical Perspective;* P.K. Jewett, *Man as Male and Female;* G.W. Knight, *The NT Teaching on the Role Relationship of Men and Women;* A. Mickelsen, *Women, Authority, and the Bible;* C.C. Ryrie, *The Place of Women in the Church;* A.B. Spencer, *Beyond the Curse: Women Called to Ministry;* L. Swidler, *Biblical Affirmations of Women;* P. Trible, *God and the Rhetoric of Sexuality.*

Wonders. *See* MIRACLE; SIGN.

Wood of Ephraim. KJV translation for "forest of Ephraim" in 2 Samuel 18:6.

See EPHRAIM, FOREST OF.

Woman drawing water from Jacob's well near Sychar.

Wool. Important commodity of the ancient Middle East. Woolen garments were commonly worn by the Israelites (Lv 13:47–59; Is 51:8; Hos 2:5,9). However, they were prohibited dress for Israelite priests serving in the sanctuary's inner court (Ez 44:17); woolen garments mingled with linen fabric were forbidden attire in Israel (Dt 22:11). Moses used wool in his levitical practice (Heb 9:19), and Gideon to test God's promise (Jgs 6:37). King Mesha of Moab, a sheep breeder, annually sent the wool of 100,000 rams as tribute to King Ahab of Israel (2 Kgs 3:4), and the people of Damascus traded wool with Tyre's merchants (Ez 27:18). Metaphorically wool symbolized whiteness and purity, as seen in Israel's redemption (Is 1:18), the hair of the Ancient of Days (Dn 7:9), and the hair and head of the Son of Man (Rv 1:14).

See CLOTH, CLOTH MANUFACTURING.

Word. In a mainly nonliterary society the dependability of the spoken word was all-important in law, trade, religion, marriage, and reputation. Receipts, agreements, and records had little general usefulness. Personal integrity and sincere speech were essential to communication, and for most people to self-expression and stable relationships. The words of poets, prophets, storytellers, and instructors were carefully preserved.

Words of Men. Words were therefore diligently tested. Foolish words, flattery, deceit, words spoken "while the heart was not with you," words of enticement, counsel given for the counselor's advantage, words of wisdom, lies, rumor, scandal, pious and blasphemous speech were all recognized. The oath had to be inviolable in commercial, judicial and civic affairs. The spoken blessing had power within itself and could not be withdrawn (Gn 27:30–38; Mt 10:12,13); so with the vow (Jgs 11:34,35) and the curse (Gn 27:12,13). Equally powerful was the word of command, of priestly, judicial, or royal authority (Eccl 8:4).

This estimate of human words lingers in the NT. The word reveals the inner self, and so every careless, hurtful, deceitful word will be judged (Mt 12:34–37; 5:22), as will blasphemy (Lk 12:10) and the misuse of the oath (Mt 5:34–37). Paul (Eph 4:29; 5:4) and James (3:1–12) preserve this Hebrew reverence for the spoken word.

Words of God. Against this background the utterance of God commanded extreme veneration. That God had spoken to the fathers and that his word was preserved in Scripture was a unique conviction of Israel, determining its character and history. God's word was discernible in nature (Pss 19:1–4; 29; cf. Acts 14:17; Rom 1:19,20) and in visions (dreams, Gn 15:1; 31:11; cf. Mt 1:20; Acts 9:10). His word "came" to and through prophets (1 Kgs 12:22; 1 Chr 17:3; cf. Lk 3:2), who spoke and acted "by the word of the Lord," and in the Law, which God "spoke" on Sinai (Ex 20:1)—hence statutes, commandments, precepts, and similar synonyms for God's "word" (e.g., Ps 119).

Periods when no such divine communication came constituted "famine" (1 Sm 3:1; Am 8:11). Mingled with warnings and injunctions were divine promises. All God's words were dependable, never "taken back" (Is 31:2) but firmly fixed in heaven (Ps 119:89; Is 40:8), being performed upon divine oath (Jer 1:12; Ps 110:4; Ez 12:25, 28). Many psalmists plead for the fulfillment of such promises "according to thy word." The integrity of God's spoken word is unquestioned; though certain military invasions and the Babylonian exile tested faith, the prophets could always assure Israel of the ultimate fulfillment of God's Law and promises.

This word expressing the divine mind was no mere threat or burden, but a delight, hope, joy, and protection against sin (Pss 1; 119: 11,49; Jer 15:16). Men live by it (Dt 8:3; Mt 4:4).

As with man in authority, so with God: his word has power to achieve, to execute his will. It will not return to him "empty" but accomplish that which he purposes (Is 45:23; 55:11). By speech alone God created the world, and his word upholds it (Gn 1; Ps 33:6; cf. Heb 1:3; 11:3; 2 Pt 3:5). He "sends his word," heals the sick, and melts the snow (Pss 107:20; 147:18).

Eventually, this continuing divine revelation is recorded in writings which also are "the word of God" (Mk 7:13; cf. Lk 16:29–31; Jn 5:39).

The same truth, authority, and power mark the divine word that came through Jesus. The church perpetuates this word in the gospel, the word God sent to Israel announcing peace through Christ (Acts 10:36). He was "mighty in word" (Lk 24:19); he taught with authority (Mk 1:22,27), exercising power over the sea, disease, demons, and death, even at a distance (Mt 8:8,13). His "word of the kingdom" is the living seed which in the good soil of receptive hearts bears fruit for God (Mt 13:19; Mk 4:14).

That word Christ "gives" to his disciples; it cleanses and frees them if they continue in it (Jn 8:31; 12:48; 15:3; 17:14), though they may be persecuted for their loyalty (Mt 13:21). For only those who are of God hear the words of God; but that same word will judge the world (Jn 12:48). To those who hear, Christ's words are spirit and life (Jn 5:24; 6:63).

The words of Christ, combined with the word about Christ, constitute "the word of Christ." The word of faith which the church preaches (Rom 10:8,9,17) is variously described as the word of this salvation, of grace, of reconciliation, of the truth of the gospel, of righteousness, and of life.

This "word of the gospel" (Acts 15:7) is not the word of men but of God; the "word that works" (1 Thes 2:13) is not fettered (2 Tm 2:9; cf. Acts 6:7; 12:24; 19:20). It is living and active, sharper than any double-edged sword to pierce the secrets of men (Heb 4:12). It is the only offensive weapon in the Christian's armor, "the sword of the Spirit" (Eph 6:17). Backed by prayer, it may "speed on and triumph" (2 Thes 3:1), and endures for ever (1 Pt 1:25).

The Word of God. First in the cluster of testimonies to Jesus in John 1 is that of the evangelist himself, who, deliberately recalling Genesis 1, designates Christ "the Logos" or "Word," who existed from the beginning, was divine, distinct from but in close relationship with God. Jesus is the source of all life and light, including the light inherent in every human soul. Long unknown within the world, the Word was made flesh, filled with grace and truth. Thus he perfectly revealed the invisible God, uttered God's mind, declared his purpose, and mediated his power—the functions of every "word" (Jn 1:18; cf. 3:34).

For this tremendous concept, John uses the term *logos*, familiar in Greek philosophy for the abstract principle of reason exhibited by an orderly universe, itself the source of the reason innate in man. By using this term, John relates Jesus to the culture prevailing beyond Jewry, to the popular cosmology current at the end of the 1st century.

But within Judaism it was becoming clear that the revelation of God's mind and will could not be complete through things (nature) or through sounds made by others (words). God is personal, and only through some quasi-personal intermediary could personality be fully known. So later Judaism had been working slowly toward the idea of a personal mediator (other than fallible human priests) between the transcendent God and the created world. Creative wisdom was spoken of in personal terms (Prv 8:12–31) that seem to go beyond poetry. And in the Targums as in rabbinic writings, a new term emerged, *Memra* (Aramaic for "Word") to indicate an intermediate agent between God and man. Thus the divine Memra created the world, appeared to Adam, Abraham, Moses, wrestled with Jacob, brought Israel from Egypt, and worked miracles.

Meanwhile, in Alexandria a Jewish apologist anxious to build bridges between Judaism and Greek culture, Philo, a contemporary of Jesus, had already identified the Wisdom discussed in Jewish theology with the Logos of Greek thought. Philo spoke of the Logos as divine mediator in creation, in revelation, and in all God's dealings with men, as the active agent of God's outgoing power. Even so, a convinced monotheist, Philo shrank from thinking of the Logos as fully personal.

Within this context John's declaration had relevance and persuasiveness for Jews and Greeks. The Logos, originally with God and divine, had become incarnate, full of divine grace and truth—the perfect personal expression of God's mind, agent of his will, and vehicle of his redeeming power. Behind this claim lay, of course, the lofty view of Jesus already reached in the apostolic church.

John's view of Jesus undoubtedly colors his whole Gospel, although the little "Logos" does not occur after 1:14. An attempt to recall John's claim for Jesus, while emphasizing that the foundation of Christian faith is neither philosophy nor theology but concrete history and personal experience, produces a broken and almost untranslatable sentence at 1 John 1:1–3. In Revelation 19:11–16 the Word once made flesh appears as the King of kings and Lord of lords, final Judge of all the earth.

R.E.O. WHITE

See LOGOS; BIBLE; REVELATION; JOHN, GOSPEL OF.

Bibliography. G. Bornkamm, *Early Christian Experience*, pp 1–13; R.E. Brown, *The Gospel According to John*, vol I, pp 519–24; R.G. Bury, *The Logos Doctrine and the Fourth Gospel*; W.F. Howard, *Christianity According to St John*.

Word of God, Word of the Lord. *See* BIBLE; BIBLE, CANON OF THE; BIBLE, INSPIRATION OF THE; REVELATION; WORD.

Work, Biblical View of.
The Bible views work in several different ways. Often the word has a very general meaning, referring either to God's activity in creating the world and redeeming his people, or to man's rebellious or obedient behavior. In the narrower sense of "regular occupation or employment" (the main theme of this article), work is highly regarded in Scripture.

The Value of Work. The Bible's positive outlook on work is rooted in its teaching about God. Unlike other ancient religious writings which regarded creation as something beneath the dignity of the Supreme Being, Scripture unashamedly describes God as a worker. Like a manual laborer, he made the universe as "the work of his fingers" (Ps 8:3). He worked with his raw material just as a potter works with the clay (Is 45:9). The intricate development of the unborn child in the womb and the vast, magnificent spread of the sky both display his supreme craftsmanship (Pss 139:13–16; 19:1). In fact, all creation bears witness to his wisdom and skill (Ps 104:24). The almighty Creator even had his rest day (Gn 2:2,3) and enjoyed job satisfaction when surveying his achievements at the end of the week (Gn 1:31).

This vivid biblical description of a working God reaches its climax with the incarnation of Jesus. The "work" which Jesus was given to do (Jn 4:34) was, of course, the unique task of redemption. But he was also a worker in the ordinary sense. His contemporaries knew him as "a carpenter" (Mk 6:3). In NT times carpentry and joinery were muscle-building trades. So the Jesus who stormed through the temple, overturning tables and driving out the men and animals, (Jn 2:14–16), was no pale weakling, but a working man whose hands had been hardened by years of toil with the ax, saw, and hammer. Hard, physical labor was not beneath the dignity of the Son of God.

If the Bible's teaching about God enhances work's dignity, its account of mankind's creation gives all human labor the mark of normality. God "took the man and put him in the garden of Eden to till it and keep it" (Gn 2:15). And God's first command, to "fill the earth and subdue it" (1:28), implied a great deal of work for both man and woman. In an important sense people today are obeying that command of their Creator when they do their daily work, whether they acknowledge him or not. Work did not, therefore, arrive in the world as a direct result of the fall into sin (though sin did spoil working conditions, Gn 3:17–19). Work was planned by God from the dawn of history for mankind's good—as natural to men and women as sunset is to day (Ps 104:19–23).

With this firm emphasis on the dignity and normality of labor, it is no surprise to find that Scripture strongly condemns idleness. "Go to the ant, O sluggard; consider her ways, and be wise" (Prv 6:6–11). Paul is equally blunt: "If any one will not work, let him not eat" (2 Thes 3:10–12). He set a good example (Acts 20:33–35; 1 Thes 2:9). Those who refuse to work, he insists, even for spiritual reasons, earn no respect from non-Christian onlookers by depending on others to pay their bills (1 Thes 4:11,12). Wage-earners, on the other hand, have the material resources of Christian service (Eph 4:28).

Vocation and Motivation. In biblical times the Greeks and Romans catalogued jobs according to importance or desirability. Routine manual labor, for example, was considered inferior to work involving mental activity.

Jewish teaching contrasts strongly with this attitude. "Hate not laborious work," taught the rabbis (Ecclus 7:15). Even the scholar had to spend some time in manual work. A few trades, like that of the tanner, were regarded as undesirable (a taboo broken very quickly by the early church—see Acts 9:43), but there is no indication in the Bible that some jobs are more worthwhile than others in God's sight. The Lord calls craftsmen (Ex 31:1–11) just as much as prophets (Is 6:8,9). So Amos was summoned from his fruit-picking to prophesy (Am 7:14,15), but with no suggestion that he was being promoted to a superior role. In much the same way Jesus called one tax collector to change his job (Mk 2:14) and allowed another to stay (Lk 19:1–10). The important thing was not the nature of the occupation but the readiness to obey God's call and to witness faithfully to him, whatever the job.

Some people, of course, could not choose their jobs. Among them were hired servants (Ex 12:45; Mk 1:20) and slaves (1 Sm 8:10–13; Eph 6:5). The latter, especially, had to obey orders or suffer the consequences. Some might find it impossible to view their work as a vocation at all. But Paul is absolutely sure that even forced labor is part of God's calling and should be accepted as such without any restless attempts at change (1 Cor 7:20–24).

Paul's advice to slaves and their masters pinpoints the incentive that should motivate all Christians to do their work well, according to the NT. Everything must be done for God. Those whose role it is to command and supervise should realize that they too have a Master (Eph 6:9). And those who have to carry out the orders must remember that they are really working for the Lord, whatever their specific tasks (Col 3:23–25). They should work conscientiously at all times (Eph 6:5–8). If they are

faithful in practical ways (by refusing to pilfer and by showing themselves trustworthy), others will be won over to the faith (Ti 2:9,10).

A slave's working environment was often far from congenial. He had no security against instant redundancy (or worse) and no redress against unscrupulous employers (1 Pt 2:18). The whole thrust of the Bible's teaching is that the Christian worker should be more highly motivated, not less.

Significantly, the Bible views so-called "creative" work with a degree of suspicion. Fine craftsmen may prostitute their talents by producing beautiful idols (Is 40:18,19). Farmers can become idolaters if they make work and its fruits the centerpiece of life (Lk 12:16–21). The fault does not lie in the craft, trade, or profession, but in the spirit that motivates the worker. In the Bible's view, *any* work gains value when done in a spirit of stewardship (cf. Mt 25:14–30); that is, when it is done for God and not for self or for a God-substitute. Inevitably, Paul made some of his worst enemies among businessmen whose motives and vested interests were challenged by the gospel he preached (Acts 16:16–21; 19:23–29; cf. Mk 11:15–17).

Working Relationships. Disruption in relationships at work is not just a modern problem. According to the Bible its roots go back to the beginning of human history. The dispute between Abel the herdsman and Cain the farmer illustrates sin's damaging influence in any situation where working people meet (Gn 4:2–8). And in particular, Scripture clarifies two key areas where the inroads of sin must be recognized and resisted.

First, there is the relationship between buyer and seller. The OT especially, has some harsh words for tradesmen who set out to cheat their customers. "All who cheat with unjust weights and measurements are detestable to the Lord your God" (Dt 25:16 LB). "Shall I acquit the man with wicked scales and with a bag of deceitful weights?" (Mi 6:11).

Second, the Bible has some pointed things to say about the relationship between employer and employee. Again, the OT prophets voice the strongest criticism. God is especially concerned to see that the weak get justice (Is 1:17; Mi 6:8). So naturally his spokesmen declare his anger when employers exploit their labor force and cheat them of their wages (Jer 22:13; Mal 3:5; cf. Jas 5:4). A man who wants to please God must "stop oppressing those who work for him and treat them fairly and give them what they earn" (Is 58:6 LB).

In Bible times the scales were weighted heavily in favor of the employer. But Scripture is not blind to the existence of selfish, greedy employees. Every worker deserves a just wage (Lk 10:7), but those with special power must not try to increase their pay by threats and violence (Lk 3:14). In this respect Christians who work for people who share their faith must be particularly careful not to exploit that special relationship (1 Tm 6:1,2).

Working for Christ. God is a working God who is pleased when his people work hard and conscientiously. That conviction lies at the heart of the Bible's teaching about Christian attitudes to secular employment. And quite naturally the NT extends the language of work, with the same positive emphasis, to cover all Christian service, paid or unpaid. The world is God's harvest field, said Jesus, waiting for Christian reapers to move in and evangelize (Mt 9:37,38). Paul takes up the same agricultural illustration and adds another from the building trade to describe the Lord's work of evangelism and teaching (1 Cor 3:6–15). Church leaders must work especially hard, he says (1 Thes 5:12), to stimulate *all* God's people to "abound in the Lord's work" (1 Cor 15:58).

No Christian, however, is self-employed in God's service. At best Christians are simply "God's co-workers" (1 Cor 3:9). Paul himself never forgot that however hard he toiled, he could achieve nothing unless God was working in and through him (1 Cor 15:10). "For this I toil, striving with all the energy which he mightily inspires within me" (Col 1:29).

DAVID H. FIELD

See TRADES AND OCCUPATIONS.

Bibliography. G. Baum, *The Priority of Labor;* A. Richardson, *The Biblical Doctrine of Work;* G. Rupp, *The Righteousness of God;* G. Wingren, *Luther on Vocation.*

World.

"World" in the NT is usually the Greek word *kosmos.* It is related to a verb which means "to set in order," or "to adorn, decorate." Greek lexicographers give five meanings for "world" (*kosmos*) in NT usage:

1. The universe created by God with design and order (e.g., Mt 13:35; Jn 17:24; Acts 17:24).

2. The planet earth (e.g., Jn 11:9). This includes the idea of earth as the dwelling place of human beings (16:21) and of earth as contrasted with heaven (6:14; 12:46).

3. The total of mankind (Mt 5:14; Jn 3:16; 1 Cor 4:13).

4. The total of human existence in this present life, with all of its experience, possessions, and emotions (Mt 16:26; 1 Cor 7:33).

5. The world order which is alienated from God, in rebellion against him, and condemned by nature and by godless deeds. It is "this world" (Jn 8:23; 12:25; 1 Cor 3:19) as opposed to "that which is to come"; "this world" in contrast with "the other, or heavenly world." The ruler of this world is the devil (Jn 12:31;

Clay tablet with an outline map of the regions of the world (the text below it relates to the conquests of Sargon of Agade).

14:30; 16:11; 1 Cor 5:10). "The whole world is under the control of the evil one" (1 Jn 5:19). On the other hand, the Christian is not of this world (Jn 15:19; 17:16), even though he is in the world and a participant in its activities (Jn 17:11). The believer is regarded as dead to the world (Gal 6:14; cf. Col 3:2,3). The Christian is to be separated from the world (Jas 1:27). Friendship with the world is enmity toward God (Jas 4:4). Relationship with the world is an indicator of relationship with God: "If anyone loves the world, love for the Father is not in him" (1 Jn 2:15). The Scripture points out that "all that is in the world, the lust of the flesh and the lust of the eyes and the pride of life, is not of the Father but is of the world" (1 Jn 2:16). The world and its desires or lusts are transient, passing away, but the doer of God's word abides forever (1 Jn 2:17; cf. 2 Cor 4:18).

The discourse of Jesus on the night before the crucifixion contains much teaching about the world. The world cannot receive the Spirit of truth (Jn 14:17). Christ gives a peace which the world cannot give (14:27). Jesus offers love, but the world gives hatred and persecution (15:19,20). The world's hatred of God is also directed against the followers of Christ (15:18–

21). Although the disciples of Jesus have tribulation "in this world," they are to be of good cheer, for Jesus has overcome the world (16:33).

Another Greek word sometimes translated "world" is *aiōn*, which emphasizes the temporal aspect of the world. It is used of time without end, eternity (e.g., Rom 1:25; 2 Cor 11:31; Phil 4:20). It is, however, also used of shorter time periods, such as the "age" and especially of "the present age." The god of this age is the devil (2 Cor 4:4). The cares of this age choke the word of the gospel as it grows (Mt 13:22; Mk 4:19).

The expression "this age" occurs frequently in contrast with that which is to come (cf. Mt 12:32; Eph 1:21; Heb 6:5). Christians are not to be conformed to this age (Rom 12:2), but they are to live "self-controlled, upright and godly lives" (Ti 2:12 NIV). Demetrius deserted Paul because he was in love with this present world (age) (2 Tm 4:10), but Jesus promised "I will never leave you nor forsake you" (Heb 13:5) and to be with his followers "always, to the very end of the age" (Mt 28:20 NIV).

The signification of the term "world" in the Bible is clear. The world of mankind is estranged from God, but can be reconciled to him (2 Cor 5:17–21). The world at enmity with God is condemned (Jn 3:18–21), without God and without hope (Eph 2:12). But Jesus came to redeem mankind from "the present evil age" (Gal 1:4) and to free them from "slavery under the basic principles of the world" (Gal 4:3 NIV).   CARL E. DEVRIES

Bibliography. G. Bornkamm, *Early Christian Experience*, pp 14–18; W.F. Howard, *Christianity According to St John*, pp 83–85; E.K. Lee, *The Religious Thought of St John*, pp 109–127; J.M. Robinson, "World in Modern Theology and in NT Theology" in *Soli Deo Gratia*.

Worm. *See* ANIMALS.

Wormwood.   Strong, bitter-tasting plant that symbolized bitterness and sorrow (Prv 5:4; Jer 9:15).

See PLANTS.

Worship.   Expression of reverence and adoration of God. The 1500 years from the days of Abraham to the time of Ezra (*c.* 1900–450 BC) saw many great changes in the form of worship in ancient Israel. Abraham, the wandering nomad, built altars and offered sacrifice wherever God appeared to him. In Moses' time the tabernacle served as a portable sanctuary for the Israelite tribes journeying through the wilderness. Solomon founded a lavish temple in Jerusalem which lasted more than three centuries until its destruction by the Babylonians in 586 BC. When the Jews returned from exile they built a new temple which, though less splendid than its predecessor, at least until Herod the Great renovated it, has served as the center of Jewish worship to this day. Though all the temple buildings were destroyed by the Romans in AD 70, the foundations remained, and by the western (wailing) wall the Jews still pray.

If the form of worship changed with times and situations, its heart and center did not. God revealed himself to Abraham, promising that his children would inherit the land of Canaan. Abraham demonstrated his faith through prayers and sacrifice. Throughout the biblical period listening to God's Word, prayer, and sacrifice constituted the essence of worship. The promises to Abraham were constantly recalled as the basis of Israel's existence as a nation and its right to the land of Canaan.

Modern people tend to restrict worship to what happens in church on Sunday. Ancient Israel had a much broader concept of worship, offering worship in the home as well as in the temple several times a day, not merely on the sabbath and at great festivals. Worship involved both the individual family and the whole nation.

In the Home.   The importance of constant meditation on the Laws of God is emphasized: "You shall talk of them when you sit in your house, and when you walk by the way, and when you lie down, and when you rise" (Dt 6:7). Children must be taught the Law and its significance must be explained to them (vv 7,20–25). But verbal reminders of the Law were only a beginning. The Israelites wrote verses from the Law on the doorposts of their houses. The Jewish custom of putting mezuzot (little boxes containing verses of the Law) on the door of the house is a survival of this OT law (v 9). Every garment had tassels at its corners to remind its weaver to obey the Law (Nm 15:38–40).

Many social customs had a religious significance in OT days. For example, the prohibition of mixtures (Dt 22:9–11), the food laws (Lv 11), and the insistence on ritual washing (Lv 15) symbolized Israel's calling to be a pure and holy people. Eating meat was only permitted if all the blood was drained out of the animal first (Lv 17:10–16; Dt 12:15,16). Keeping up these customs provided the faithful Israelite with occasions for worship each day and was a reminder of God's grace and demands.

The practice of saying grace before and after meals, which Jesus and later Jews followed (Lk 9:16; Jn 6:11), must go back to OT times, but it is not explicitly mentioned. However, the practice of personal prayer is. The great saints of the OT were people of prayer who interceded for the needs of others (Gn 18:23–32; Ex 32:11–13; 1 Sm 12:23; Ez 9:6–15). Daniel prayed three times a day (Dn 6:13), while the psalmist rose at midnight to praise God (119:62).

Family Worship in the Temple. From time to time every family visited the temple in Jerusalem. Eight days after a baby boy was born he was circumcised to mark his membership in Israel. Then a month or two later the baby's mother went to the temple to offer sacrifice (Lv 12; cf. Lk 2:22–24).

Animals were sacrificed in the lambing and calving season. The first lamb or calf born to every ewe or cow was presented in sacrifice (Ex 22:30). Similarly at the beginning of the harvest season a basket of the first fruits was offered, and at the end a tenth of all the harvest, the tithe, was given to the priests as God's representatives (Nm 18:21–32). Deuteronomy 26:5–15 gives a typical prayer for use on such occasions.

Sometimes a person would decide to offer a sacrifice for more personal reasons. In a crisis vows could be made and sealed with a sacrifice (Gn 28:18–22; 1 Sm 1:10,11). Then when the prayer was answered, a second sacrifice was customarily offered (Gn 35:3,14; 1 Sm 1:24,25). Serious sin or serious sickness also were occasions for sacrifice (Lv 4,5,13–15).

All the animals offered in sacrifice had to be unblemished. Only the best was good enough for God, and wild animals which cost the worshiper nothing were unacceptable. With the obligation to bring tithes and firstlings, worship in OT times could be extremely expensive.

It was also dramatic. The worshiper brought the animal into the temple court. Standing there before the priest he placed one hand on its head, thereby identifying himself with the animal, and confessed his sin or explained the reason for offering the sacrifice. Then the worshiper killed the animal and cut it up for the priest to burn on the great bronze altar. Some sacrifices (burnt offerings) involved the whole animal being burnt on the altar. In others some of the meat was set aside for the priests, and others the worshiper and his family shared. But in every case the worshiper killed the animal from his own flock with his own hands. These sacrifices expressed in a vivid and tangible way the cost of sin and the worshiper's responsibility. The animal represented the worshiper, dying that he might live. As the worshiper killed the animal, he recalled that sin would have caused his own death, had God not provided an escape through animal sacrifice.

National Worship in the Temple. Three times a year all adult men went to the temple to celebrate the national festivals (Ex 23:17; Dt 16:16): Passover (held in April), the Feast of Weeks (held in May), and the Feast of Booths (in October). When possible the whole family accompanied the men. But if they lived a long way from Jerusalem, they would only go up for one of the festivals (1 Sm 1:3; Lk 2:41).

These festivals were tremendous occasions. Hundreds of thousands of people converged on Jerusalem. They would stay with relatives or camp in tents outside the city. The temple courts would be thronged with worshipers. The temple choirs sang psalms appropriate for the festival, while the priests and Levites offered hundreds, and at Passover thousands, of animals in sacrifice. Groups of worshipers carried away with emotion would break forth into dancing. Those of more sober temperament were content to join in the singing, or simply pray quietly.

Joy was the keynote of the major festivals, for they celebrated the deliverance of Israel from Egypt. At Passover each family ate roasted lamb and bitter herbs to reenact the last meal their forefathers ate before leaving Egypt (Ex 12). At the Feast of Booths they built shelters of tree branches and lived in them for a week, as a reminder that the Israelites camped in tents during the 40 years of wandering in the wilderness (Lv 23:39–43). These great festivals served as reminders of how God had delivered them from slavery in Egypt and had given them the land of Canaan as he had promised to Abraham.

Each of these three festivals lasted a week, but there was one day in the year which was totally different, the Day of Atonement, when everyone fasted and mourned for their sins. On this day the high priest confessed the nation's sins as he pressed his hand on the head of a goat. Then the goat was led away into the wilderness, symbolizing the removal of sin from the people (Lv 16).

Priestly Worship in the Temple. At the festivals the temple services reached a great climax as the whole nation participated in worship. But every day in the temple priests offered sacrifices morning and evening, sacrificing extra animals on the sabbath and at the beginning of each month. Numbers 28,29 gives a full list of the sacrifices that had to be offered throughout the year. The priests also kept the lights on the golden candlestick burning and provided the loaves that sat on the golden table in the Holy Place (Lv 24). There was also a temple choir which sang as the sacrifices were offered (1 Chr 23:30,31).

The End of Temple Worship. Some time after the destruction of the first temple, synagogues developed for public worship. The services were more like modern church worship,

Monolith from the temple of Philoe, with two border designs from the same Egyptian temple.

consisting exclusively of prayer, Bible reading, and preaching without sacrifices. When the second temple was destroyed in AD 70, synagogues became the only places where Jews could worship in public. There were no more sacrifices. The NT sees this as fitting, for Jesus was the true Lamb of God (Jn 1:29). Thanks to his death there is no need for further animal sacrifice (Heb 10:11,12). The OT sacrifices illustrate Jesus' achievements in bringing peace between man and God (Heb 8:5). Yet Christians are still to meet together for public worship (Acts 2:46,47; Heb 10:25). The OT provides a model of true worship. Every home should be a church and every meal an act of worship. Each human family is a part of the greater family of God, who should meet together to celebrate their redemption from sin and the new life Christ has brought through his death and resurrection.　　　GORDON J. WENHAM

See PRAISE; PRAYER.

Bibliography. O. Cullmann, *Early Christian Worship;* D.G. Delling, *Worship in the NT;* A.S. Herbert, *Worship in Ancient Israel;* R.P. Martin, *Worship in the Early Church;* C.F.D. Moule, *Worship in the NT.*

Wrath of God.　Metaphor for God's displeasure with human beings and actions.

At a glance, the biblical teaching on the wrath of God seems inconsistent with the doctrine of God's love. Unfortunately, ignorance of the OT and a misunderstanding of the NT have resulted in a heretical view of the biblical canon (Marcionism), in which the OT reveals the God of wrath and the NT reveals the God of love. Contrary to popular misconception the NT, like the OT, also teaches the wrath of God in connection with his love. The biblical teaching on God's love cannot be appreciated unless it is seen in contrast with the biblical teaching on his wrath. The word "wrath" is a concept represented by many different words and idioms in the original languages of the Bible. The references to God's wrath are the most frequent—nearly three times as many as any other subject.

In the Old Testament. God in the OT may be angry with nations, sinners, and even with his covenant people and children. God's anger comes first to expression within the covenant community of Israel. The story of Israel's wilderness wanderings illustates how the Lord showed his wrath to Israel after they had been redeemed from Egypt, had received the Decalogue and the covenant, and had seen his glory (Nm 11:10; 12:9; 22:22; 32:10,13,14). The major reason for the Lord's anger in the OT was that his own people broke the covenant. They provoked him by their idolatry (Dt 2:15; 4:25; 9:7,8,19; Jgs 2:14; 1 Kgs 11:9; 14:9,15; 2 Kgs 17:18), by their mixing paganism with the worship of the Lord (Is 1:10–17; Jer 6:20; Hos 6:6; Am 5:21–27); by their wanton rebellion (1 Kgs 8:46), their unbelief (Nm 11:33; 14:11,33; Ps 95:10,11), and their disregard for his concern for love, justice, righteousness, and holiness (Ex 22:23; Is 1:15–17; Am 5:7,10–12; Mi 3:1).

The wrath of God also extends to all mankind (Na 1:2). The concept of the Day of the Lord was developed by the prophets to warn Israel and the nations that no one can escape the righteous expression of God's wrath (Am 5:18,20). The Day of the Lord is the day of his wrath (Zep 1:15).

The effects of his wrath are set forth in metaphorical language, associated with the semantic fields of *water and drink:* flood or river, Is 8:7,8; Na 1:8), a cup filled with wine (Is 51:17,22); of fire (Is 66:15,16; Jer 4:4; 21:12,14; Na 1:6), a fiery furnace (Ps 21:9); of *warfare* (Is 42:25; 63:3–6): rod (Is 10:5), physical hardship (Lam 3:5); and of *natural phenomena:* earthquake (Mi 1:3,4; Na 1:5,6), storm (Is 30:30; 66:15,16; Jer 30:23).

The OT holds the doctrine of the wrath of God in balance with three other doctrines: his forbearance, his love, and his readiness to forgive. First, God is patient. The Hebrew word for patient is related to the word for wrath, and means "length of wrath," that is, God does not quickly become angry. He is longsuffering (Ex 34:6). Second, God is full of compassion and fidelity (Ex 34:6). Even when his children sin against him, he is like a father who is full of compassion and love. He is always faithful to his children. Third, he is ready to forgive those who sin against him when they atone for and are cleansed from their sins (Ex 34:6). The pleasure of his love is so much greater than his wrath (Ps 30:5). Micah prayed that the Lord may soon forgive and restore his people on the ground that he cannot be angry forever (7:18; cf. Ps 89:46; Jer 3:5). In Psalm 103:8–13 the psalmist likens God's love and forgiveness

to that of a father who does not harbor his anger continually, nor does he vex his children with discipline, so great is his love for those who fear him.

The purpose of God's wrath is not to destroy mankind (Hos 11:9). His wrath is neither a vindictive, emotional overreaction, nor is it unpredictable. In his wrath he sovereignly imposes limits on nations (Babylon, Assyria), and disciplines his own people with the desired end that they return to him (Jl 2:13,14). The eschatological expectation of the OT concept of the Day of the Lord includes the restoration of the earth, when the whole earth will be filled with the knowledge (Is 11:9; Hb 2:14) and glory (Nm 14:21; Ps 72:19) of the Lord and wickedness will be no more (Is 65:25).

In the New Testament. The NT also teaches the wrath of God side by side with the doctrine of his grace, love, and forbearance (Mt 3:7; Lk 21:23; Jn 3:36; Rom 1:18; Eph 5:6; Rv 14:10). Faith in Jesus as the Messiah marks the difference in mankind, whether Jew or Greek. Those who do not profess faith in the risen Christ remain in their sins and fall under the wrath of God, whereas those who believe in him are delivered from God's wrath (Eph 2:3; 1 Thes 1:10). However, the faithful are reminded by the example of Israel that it is a terrible thing to fall into the hands of an angry God (Heb 10:31), because the God and Father of our Lord Jesus Christ is "a consuming fire" (12:29). The good news of the NT is that Jesus has come to deliver us from the wrath of God (Rom 5:9). Those who have been delivered are reconciled with God (Rom 5:10) because they no longer are under condemnation (Rom 8:1). The challenge of faith is to persevere in the Christian life so as not to give cause for God's wrath (Mt 18:34,35; 22:13,14).

WILLEM A. VAN GEMEREN

See DEATH; JUDGMENT; LAST JUDGMENT; ESCHATOLOGY; SECOND COMING OF CHRIST; HELL; LOVE; PROPITIATION.

Bibliography. G. Bornkamm, *Early Christian Experience,* pp 47–70; A.T. Hanson, *The Wrath of the Lamb;* L. Morris, *The Apostolic Preaching of the Cross;* R.V.G. Tasker, *The Biblical Doctrine of the Wrath of God.*

Writer. *See* LETTER WRITING, ANCIENT; TRADES AND OCCUPATIONS; WRITING AND BOOKS; "AUTHOR" SECTION FOR EACH BOOK OF THE BIBLE.

Writing and Books. Books have been written for many centuries, but have not always been produced in the familiar form in which they are known today. If a book is defined as any written record of thoughts or acts, the production of books then goes back to a very early period in the history of civilization. The Sumerians produced written documents and primers on clay tablets as early as 2500 BC.

Statue of Horemhab (then King Tutankhamen's commander-in-chief) with a scroll on his lap, reading a psalm to Thoth. On the base are prayers to Thoth and to other gods.

The Sumerian civilization went into decline after its conquest by the Akkadians (2300 BC). In the 21st century BC, however, there occurred a revival of Sumerian culture that produced a number of important literary works, including the first known written codified system of law.

Today a rich body of Sumerian material exists. It includes legal, mythological, and commercial documents, as well as written material produced in the process of training scribes.

A large collection of cuneiform tablets was found in the library of the Assyrian king Ashurbanipal which was established in the 7th century BC. The library contained many records of religious and scientific knowledge.

The scroll is also precursor of the modern book. The papyrus scroll of Egypt can be traced as far back as 2500 BC. One of the most famous literary productions of ancient Egypt is the Book of the Dead. Because of the damp climate of Palestine, comparatively little extra-biblical written material exists.

An important development in the evolution of book production occured with the advent of the codex. The codex is the modern form of the book, that is, a collection of leaves bound on one side. This was a revolutionary development, not only because it eliminated the use of cumbersome scrolls, but it enabled the writer to use both sides of a page.

Some Biblical Allusions to Books. The most important book to the ancient Hebrews was the Book of the Law (2 Kgs 22:8) because it came from God to Moses (Jos 23:6; Mk 12:26) and contained the record of the Mosaic covenant (e.g., Ex 20). God instructed Joshua to meditate on it day and night (Jos 1:8). The prophets appealed to it constantly, particularly to Deuteronomy. The discovery of the Book of the Law during the renovation of the temple in Josiah's reign led to important religious reforms (2 Kgs 22:8–13).

Some books specifically labeled as biblical source materials are the Book of the Wars of the Lord (Nm 21:14), the Book of Jashar (Jos 10:13; 2 Sm 1:18), the Book of the Acts of Solomon (1 Kgs 11:41), and the Book of the Chronicles of the Kings of Judah (1 Kgs 14:29). A number of prophetic works are cited in the books of Chronicles as sources for the material recorded in those books. Some of these are the Chronicles of Samuel the Seer, the Chronicles of Nathan the Prophet, the Chronicles of Gad the Seer (1 Chr 29:29), and the Prophecy of Ahijah the Shilonite (2 Chr 9:29). The fact that prophetic sources were used for Chronicles demonstrates that the Hebrew people regarded their history as the record of God's activity.

Writing Materials and Types of Books.
Stone and Metal. The metals used were gold, silver, copper, and bronze. The Ten Commandments were inscribed on two stone tablets (Ex 34:1). Job wished that his words protesting his innocence could be engraved in rock forever (Jb 19:24).

Clay. The Sumerian, Babylonian, and Assyrian clay tablets are well known. Baked clay tablets were preserved easily in almost any climate. They were suitable, however, only for a straight-line form of writing such as cuneiform, and were therefore not appropriate for the rounded Aramaic form of Hebrew script.

Papyrus. The papyrus rolls of Egypt have been used as a writing surface since the early 3rd millennium BC. The Greeks adopted papyrus around 900 BC and later the Romans adopted its use. However, the oldest extant Greek rolls of papyrus date from the 4th century BC. The inner pith of the papyrus plant was called *byblos*. From this comes the Greek word *biblion* ("book") and the English word "bible." The word "paper" is derived from "papyrus."

Unfortunately, papyrus is perishable, requiring a dry climate for its preservation. That is why so many papyri have been discovered in the desert sands of Egypt. Some papyrus fragments have also been found in the caves near the Dead Sea, where the climate is likewise sufficiently dry.

Potsherds. Broken pieces of pottery furnished an inexpensive writing material because the supply was so abundant. The Samaria and Lachish ostraca are examples.

Papyrus.

Wood. Wooden tablets covered with stucco or wax were sometimes used as a writing surface. A NT example is Luke 1:63.

Leather, Parchment, and Vellum. These are all made from animal skins. Leather (tanned skins), the forerunner of parchment, has been in use about as long as papyrus, but it was rarely used because papyrus was so abundant. The ancient Hebrews probably used leather and papyrus for writing materials. The Dead Sea Scrolls were sheets of leather sewed together with linen thread. Metal scrolls also existed (e.g., copper).

Parchment, made in the beginning from sheep and goat skins began to replace leather as early as the 3rd century BC, though actual parchment codices date from the 2nd century AD. To prepare parchment or refined leather, the hair was removed from the skins and the latter rubbed smooth. The most common form of book for OT and NT documents was evidently a roll or scroll of papyrus (2 Jn 12), leather, or parchment. The average length of a scroll was about 30 feet, though the famous Harris Papyrus was 133 feet long. Scrolls were often stored in pottery jars (Jer 32:14) and were frequently sealed (Rv 5:1).

Vellum had a finer quality than parchment and was prepared from the skins of calves, lambs, or kids. In the 4th century AD vellum or parchment as a material and the codex as a form became the norm.

Writing and Books

Paper. Paper, made from wood, rags, and certain grasses, began to replace vellum and parchment as early as the 10th century AD in the Western world, though it was used considerably earlier in China and Japan. By the 15th century paper manuscripts were common.

Scribes, Writing Implements, and Ink. Scribes were employed as secretaries in Palestine, Egypt, Mesopotamia, and the Greco-Roman Empire. Biblical examples are Baruch in the OT (Jer 36:4) and Tertius in the NT (Rom 16:22). Court scribes would sometimes rise to positions of social prestige and considerable political influence, much as a secretary of state today.

There were schools for the training of such scribes. To master the difficult art of writing on clay probably required as much time then as it takes students now to develop the ability to read and write. Would-be scribes could either enter a regular school or work as an apprentice under a private teacher, though most of them apparently followed the latter procedure. The schools were attached to the temples and were widely separated. Scribes who were willing to teach could be found everywhere—even in the smaller towns. In fact, most of the scribes had at least one apprentice, who was treated like a son while learning the profession. Such students learned not only from private tutoring but also from the example of their teacher. This kind of education was sufficient to equip young scribes for the normal commercial branches of the craft. They were fully prepared to handle the necessary formulas for the various kinds of legal and business documents, and they could easily take dictation for private correspondence. There are Assyrian reliefs picturing scribes taking dictation from an Assyrian monarch.

For additional study and training, however, it was necessary to attend the regular schools. For example, only the schools adjacent to the temples had the proper facilities to teach the sciences (including mathematics) and literature, which the more advanced scribes had to master. There a budding scribe could study to become even a priest or a "scientist." In the ruins of ancient cities archaeologists have discovered "textbooks" used by the pupils. Excavators have also uncovered schoolrooms with benches on which the students sat. Some of the ancient Near Eastern texts that have been unearthed are nothing but schoolboy exercises or student copies of originals. Naturally such copies are usually not as beautiful or as legible as the originals, which were written by master scribes.

When the teacher wanted to give the students an assignment, he had available in the temple school virtually every type of text imaginable. For elementary work he could have the students practice writing a list of cuneiform signs, much like our learning the letters of the alphabet—except that there were some 600 signs! Another simple assignment would have been to copy dictionaries containing lists of stones, cities, animals, and gods. After such preparatory work the students could then move to literary texts and, for example, accurately reproduce a portion of one of the great epics, a hymn, or a prayer.

Material recovered by archaeologists from the temple schools is very important because it almost always came from the classics and the manuals kept in the largest and best libraries. But such material often presents a special difficulty for the literary analyst or critic in

The writing equipment of an Egyptian scribe. An original palette (with two circular sections hollowed out) is attached to a writing reed and a water jar; the latter two objects are reconstructed.

that it is frequently found in piecemeal form. The specialist then faces the problem of attempting to reconstruct a given work into its unified, original shape. These fragments of stories have sometimes been misinterpreted by scholars who did not realize that they were only parts of a "book" and not stories complete in themselves. Most of the time other copies clarify the situation.

Thus, through arduous study and a lengthy program of instruction and practice, a gifted student could become qualified for scribal service in almost any field. Unfortunately, the masses did not have access to developing reading, writing, and professional ability.

Different kinds of writing implements were used, depending on the writing surfaces in use at various periods of history. Metal chisels and gravers were used for inscribing stone and metal. A stylus was used for writing cuneiform ("wedge-shaped" characters) on clay tablets. For writing on ostraca (potsherds), papyrus, and parchment, a reed was split or cut to act as a brush. In Egypt rushes were used to form a brush. Later, reeds were cut to a point and split like a quill pen. Apparently this was the type of pen or "calamus" used in NT times (3 Jn 13).

Ink (cf. 2 Jn 12) was usually a black carbon (charcoal) mixed with gum or oil for use on parchment or mixed with a metallic substance for papyrus. It was kept in an inkhorn as a dried substance, on which the scribe would dip or rub his moistened pen. It could be erased by washing (Nm 5:23) or with a penknife, which was also used for sharpening pens and trimming or cutting scrolls (Jer 36:23).

KENNETH L. BARKER & THOMAS E. MCCOMISKEY

See LIBRARIES, ANCIENT; LACHISH LETTERS; SCRIBE; LETTER WRITING, ANCIENT; ALPHABET.

Bibliography. D. Diringer, *Writing;* I.J. Gelb, *A Study of Writing;* W.J. Hoffman, *The Beginnings of Writing;* C.H. Roberts, "Books in the Graeco-Roman World and in the NT," pp 48–66 in *The Cambridge History of the Bible*, vol I, (eds. P.R. Ackroyd and C.F. Evans; B.L. Ullman, *Ancient Writing and Its Influence;* D.J. Wiseman, "Books in the Ancient Near East and in the OT," pp 30–48 in *The Cambridge History of the Bible*, vol I, eds. P.R. Ackroyd and C.F. Evans.

Xx

Xerxes. NIV rendering of Ahasuerus in Ezra 4:6 and Esther 1:1.

See AHASUERUS #1.

Xestes. Liquid measure equivalent to about 1 1/6 pints.

See WEIGHTS AND MEASURES.

Relief from a stairway of the Persian palace in Persepolis that shows Babylonians and Syrians bringing tribute.

Yy

Yahweh (YHWH). Most holy name for God in the OT, usually translated Lord or Jehovah. The name is also applied to Christ.

See GOD, NAMES OF.

Yard. Linear measure (Jn 21:8).

See WEIGHTS AND MEASURES.

Year. *See* CALENDARS, ANCIENT AND MODERN.

Yellow. *See* COLOR.

Yiron. One of the fortified cities of Naphtali's tribe (Jos 19:38, KJV Iron). Some have identified Yiron with the present village of Jarun, southeast of Bint Jebeil, but its precise location is unknown.

Yoke. Literally, the wooden bar that allowed two (or more) draft animals to be coupled so that they might effectively work together (Nm 19:2; 1 Kgs 19:19; Jb 1:3). In addition to this literal usage, the Bible frequently uses the term metaphorically to refer to work or bondage (Gn 27:40). The yoke of bondage was applied not only by foreign oppressors, but often by Israel's own kings as well (2 Kgs 12:4–14; 2 Chr 10:4–14). In prophetic writings, the yoke of bondage was generally associated with divine judgment (Lam 1:14), so that deliverance was represented as God breaking the yoke that had enslaved Israel (Is 9:4; 10:27; 14:25; 58:6; Jer 2:20; 5:5). The yoke of bondage figured prominently in Jeremiah's contest with Hananiah concerning Judah's imminent release from Babylonian captivity (Jer 27:8–11; 28:1–17). In the NT, Jesus transforms "yoke" into a positive term by calling on individuals to take up his yoke which was not burdensome (Mt 11:29,30).

Yom Kippur. One of the feast days of Israel involving atonement for the sins of the nation (Lv 23:26–32).

See FEASTS AND FESTIVALS OF ISRAEL.

Zz

Zaanaim. KJV spelling of Za-anannim in Judges 4:11.

See ZA-ANANNIM.

Zaanan. Village listed with Gath, Beth-le-aphrah, Shaphir, Beth-ezel, and Maroth in Micah's lament over Jerusalem ("the inhabitants of Zaanan do not come forth," Mi 1:11). Zaanan is probably a play on the Hebrew word *yatsah,* "to come forth." The village was in the Shephelah, but its precise location has not been identified. It is probably the same place as Zenan.

See ZENAN.

Za-anannim. One of the markers of the eastern border of Naphtali listed between Heleph and Adaminekeb (Jos 19:33). Za-anannim was near Kedesh. There Sisera visited the tent of Heber the Kenite and was killed by Jael (Jgs 4:11, KJV Zaanaim). While the precise location is not known, it was west of Lake el-Huleh (modern Merom) in a region that was probably marshy in ancient times. Though the KJV translates the text as "plain of Zaannannim" it is likely "oak of Za-anannim" (RSV, NIV). Since many terebinth trees are located in the region, the text is probably referring to a terebinth set aside as a sacred tree. Some have suggested that the text should read Bezaannannim, in which case it might be identified with Bessum, located halfway between Tiberias and Mt Tabor.

Zaavan. Second son of Ezer, a Horite clan chief (Gn 36:27; 1 Chr 1:42, KJV Zavan).

Zabad. 1. Son of Nathan and a descendant of Athlai the daughter of Sheshan (1 Chr 2:36,37).

2. Tahath's son and the father of Shuthelah from Ephraim's tribe (1 Chr 7:21).

3. One of David's mighty men, listed as a son of Athlai (1 Chr 11:41); he is perhaps the same as #1 above.

4. One of the conspirators against King Joash, listed as the son of Shimeath the Ammonitess (1 Chr 24:26). He is identical to Jozacar in 2 Kings 12:21. Zabad was a palace servant who was likely the agent of a powerful conspiracy against Joash.

See JOZACAR, JOZACHAR.

5,6,7. Three priests variously descended from Zattu, Hashum, and Nebo who renounced their foreign wives at Ezra's request during the postexilic period (Ezr 10:27,33,43).

Zabbai. 1. Bebai's son and one of the priests who divorced his foreign wife at Ezra's command (Ezr 10:28).

2. Father of Baruch. Baruch repaired a section of the Jerusalem wall during Nehemiah's day (Neh 3:20).

Zabbud. KJV form of Zaccur, Bigvai's descendant, in Ezra 8:14.

See ZACCUR #5.

Zabdi. 1. Zerah's son from Judah's tribe (Jos 7:1). Achan was a Zerahite of the Zabdi clan (Jos 7:17,18). He is alternately called Zimri (1 Chr 2:6).

2. Shimei's son and a descendant of Ehud from Benjamin's tribe (1 Chr 8:19).

3. David's officer over the produce of the vineyards for the wine cellars (1 Chr 27:27). He is called a Shiphmite, which likely means that he was a native of Shepham.

4. One of the temple musicians of the order of Asaph (Neh 11:17); alternately called Zichri (1 Chr 9:15).

Zabdiel. 1. Father of Jashobeam, the commander of the first division of David's army (1 Chr 27:2).

2. Priest and overseer of the mighty men of valor (Neh 11:14). The notation that he was a "son of Haggedolim" might indicate that he was a "son of the mighty men."

Zabud. Priest in Solomon's court and the "king's friend" (1 Kgs 4:5). The phrase "king's friend" may be an official title given to one of the king's advisers. Hushai the Archite had a similar title in David's court (2 Sm 15:37; 16:16).

Zabulon. KJV spelling of Zebulun in Matthew 4:13,15 and Revelation 7:8.

See ZEBULUN, TRIBE OF.

Zaccai. Forefather of a family that returned with Zerubbabel to Judah following the exile (Ezr 2:9; Neh 7:14).

Zacchaeus, Zaccheus. Jewish chief publican who hired assistants to collect taxes at Jericho. He perhaps secured this position by purchasing the exclusive right to collect revenue in that region or by working as a subcontractor for another affluent official. In either case Zacchaeus himself accrued great wealth (largely by illegitimate means) from his customs enterprise at Jericho, a significant center of commerce, stationed along a major trade route connecting Jerusalem and its environs with the lands east of the Jordan.

Luke in his Gospel records Zacchaeus' encounter with Jesus (Lk 19:2–8, NASB Zaccheus). Seeking Jesus but unable to see him over the crowd because of his small stature, Zacchaeus climbed a sycamore tree, near which Jesus would pass, to get a better view. To his astonishment, Jesus stopped under the tree and after ordering him down, invited himself to the publican's house for the night. Subsequently, Zacchaeus repented and followed Jesus, promising to restore fourfold to those whom he wrongfully exploited and give to the poor. According to Clement of Alexandria, Zacchaeus later became the bishop of Caesarea (*Hom.* 3. 63).

Zacchur. KJV spelling of Zaccur, Hammuel's son, in 1 Chronicles 4:26.

See ZACCUR #2.

Zaccur. 1. Father of Shammua, one of the 12 spies who represented Reuben's tribe in the reconnaissance of Canaan (Nm 13:4).

2. Simeonite who was the son of Hammuel and the father of Shimei (1 Chr 4:26, KJV Zacchur).

3. One of the sons of Merari in the record of the divisions of the priests (1 Chr 24:27). Apparently, Zaccur and his clan had only a minor priestly function (cf. 1 Chr 24:5,7,20).

4. One of the sons of Asaph who was assigned responsibility for the temple service (1 Chr 25:2). Zaccur and his sons and brethren were assigned the third lot among the various duties for the temple musicians (1 Chr 25:10). Descendants of Zaccur were present at the dedication of the city wall following the exile (Neh 12:35).

5. One of the descendants of Bigvai who returned to Jerusalem with Ezra (Ezr 8:14, KJV Zabbud).

6. Son of Imri who worked on repairing Jerusalem's wall in the vicinity of the Sheep Gate (Neh 3:2).

7. One of the Levites who signed Nehemiah's covenant to obey the law of God (Neh 10:12).

8. Son of Mattaniah and father of Hanan, the assistant to the storehouse treasurers during Nehemiah's time (Neh 13:13). Some have suggested that he is the same as #7 above.

Zachariah. 1. KJV spelling of Zechariah, king of Israel, in 2 Kings 14:29 and 15:8,11.

See ZECHARIAH (PERSON) #1.

2. KJV spelling of Zechariah, King Hezekiah's maternal grandfather, in 2 Kings 18:2.

See ZECHARIAH (PERSON) #2.

Zacharias. 1. KJV spelling of Zechariah, Jehoiada's son, in Matthew 23:35 and Luke 11:51.

See ZECHARIAH (PERSON) #14.

2. KJV spelling of Zechariah, John the Baptist's father, in Luke 1:5–67.

See ZECHARIAH (PERSON) #32.

3. KJV spelling of Zechariah, a proposed name for John the Baptist, in Luke 1:59.

See JOHN THE BAPTIST; ZECHARIAH (PERSON) #33.

Zacher. KJV form of Zechariah, Gibeon's son, in 1 Chronicles 8:31.

See ZECHARIAH (PERSON) #5.

NT Jericho, the home of Zacchaeus.

Zadok. Common OT name meaning "righteous."

1. David's priest, probably the most famous and influential of Israel's high priests apart from Aaron. He first appears at the time of Absalom's revolt, when he and his fellow priest, Abiathar, show their loyalty to David by coming to him with the ark, fully prepared to share his exile (2 Sm 15:24–29). David refused their offer and sent them back to Jerusalem to act in his interests.

In 2 Samuel 8:17, Zadok is listed as the son of Ahitub, who is elsewhere noted as the grandson of Eli (1 Sm 14:3). In the genealogies of Chronicles, Zadok's descent through Ahitub is traced back to Eleazar, the eldest son of Aaron (1 Chr 6:1–8,50–53; Ezr 7:2–5; 1 Esd 8:2), but with no reference to Eli. A slight problem emerges in that Zadok replaces the banished Abiathar, a descendant of Eli. This is regarded as the fulfillment of an earlier prophecy that the tenure of the high priestly office by Eli's family would be broken in favor of a different branch of Aaron's family (1 Sm 2:30–36; 1 Kgs 2:26,27). The crux of the problem is Eli's ancestry, which is not given in the OT. In the Apocrypha he is linked with Eleazar's line (2 Esd 1:1,2), but Josephus connects him with the line of another son of Aaron, Ithamar (*Antiq.* 5.11.5).

Largely on the basis of this uncertainty, some scholars have suggested that Zadok's origins were completely outside the family of Aaron, and that the genealogy was a fabrication designed to support his eventual position as high priest. Zadok also has been viewed as a young military hero (1 Chr 12:28), whose elevation to the priesthood was a reward for his outstanding services in David's cause. An obvious objection to this, and to the following views, is that David throughout appears concerned not to alienate the religious traditions of the tribal confederation. Such an appointment would surely have offended his own established priesthood. Another suggestion is that David appointed Zadok as priest in charge of a second major sanctuary at Gibeon (16:39–42), which is later called "the most famous of the hilltop altars" during Solomon's reign (1 Kgs 3:4). Zadok is thought to have been a Gibeonite priest whom David elevated to the high priesthood at Jerusalem in the furtherance of his centralization policy, the prominence given to the sanctuary at Gibeon being in the interests of national unity.

Equally conjectural is the view that Zadok was the leading priest of the Jebusite Jerusalem captured by David. Indeed, it has even been suggested that Zadok revealed to David the city's vulnerability if attacked via its water tunnel (2 Sm 5:8). The connection of the name Zadok with Melchizedek and Adonizedek, another king of Jerusalem (Jos 10:1), has led to the view that this was the traditional name of the chief priest or priest-king of the Jebusite city. David may have allowed Zadok to continue in office to facilitate Jerusalem's integration into his kingdom. There are many grave objections to this view. David's animosity to the Jebusites following their taunts is apparent (2 Sm 5:6–8). The adoption of the Jebusite cult and the elevation of its priest above the native Israelite priesthood would be a tactless action in a period when David displayed remarkable diplomacy in uniting the two sections of his kingdom. In fact when the ark was brought to Jerusalem, it was not placed in the Jebusite temple but in a tent shrine (6:17). Similarly, in David's elaborate plans for the building of the temple, there is no hint that the existing Jebusite temple cult had any part. When the temple was built, it was completely outside the walls of ancient Jerusalem, but within Solomon's extension of the city.

There is no valid reason why Zadok's Aaronic descent should be questioned. He is first introduced as senior partner to Abiathar, and David speaks principally to him. This implies that he was already well known. He was possibly the young hero of 1 Chronicles 12:28; the preceding verse may be taken as evidence that he was a descendant of Aaron. The considerable period of time until Absalom's rebellion allowed for the change from warlike to religious functions. By this time Zadok had a son, Ahimaaz, who together with Abiathar's son, Jonathan, acted as couriers between Hushai, their fathers, and David, warning the latter to cross the Jordan (2 Sm 15:36; 17:15–22). After the death of Absalom and the collapse of the rebellion, David complained to Zadok and Abiathar about the tardiness of the men of Judah in arranging for his victorious return as king (19:11–15).

In both summaries of David's court officials (8:17; 20:25), Zadok is listed as one of David's two principal priests, an office which was held throughout the latter part of David's reign. When David was near death, a power struggle over the throne was precipitated by Adonijah, David's oldest surviving son. With the support of Joab, the captain of the host, and the priest Abiathar, David's long-standing friend, Adonijah declared himself king (1 Kgs 1:5–10). Nathan the prophet promptly intervened with Bathsheba as Solomon's advocate. Zadok and Benaiah, the captain of the mercenary troops, supported Solomon (vv 11–27). Adonijah's cause was hopeless once David had indicated his approval of Nathan's plans (vv 28–53). Consequently, the discredited Abiathar was banished (2:26,27), leaving the loyal Zadok as Solomon's chief priest (2:35; 4:4). In the centuries that followed, the descendants of Zadok preserved this dominance, and as Jerusalem's prestige increased, so did their status. Azariah, the chief priest in Hezekiah's reign, was a Zadokite (2 Chr 31:10). Ezekiel restricted the main priestly functions to the "sons of Zadok," demoting the Levites generally to the rank of "temple caretakers" because of their apostasy during the monarchy (Ez 44:10–16). When the Jews came under Seleucid domination in the early 2nd century BC, the high priesthood, regarded as a political appointment, was taken away from the Zadokites. Conservative elements, however, like the Qumran covenanters, continued to look for its restoration.

See DAVID; ISRAEL, HISTORY OF.

2. Father-in-law of Uzziah and grandfather of Jotham, kings of Judah (2 Kgs 15:32,33; 2 Chr 27:1).

3. Descendant of Zadok, David's priest (1 Chr 6:12; 9:11; Neh 11:11). Note the similarity in names with the earlier generation (1 Chr 6:8).

4. Young man of exceptional courage, the leader of a substantial contingent which joined David at Hebron against Saul (1 Chr 12:28).

5. Son of Baana, who helped to repair the wall of Jerusalem in Nehemiah's time (Neh 3:4)

6. Son of Immer, who also shared in Nehemiah's rebuilding operations (Neh 3:29).

7. Signatory to Nehemiah's covenant (Neh 10:21) and perhaps identifiable with #5 or #6 above.

8. One of three treasurers appointed by Nehemiah during his second term of office, called the scribe (Neh 13:13).

9. Ancestor of Christ (Mt 1:14, KJV Sadoc).
ARTHUR E. CUNDALL

See GENEALOGY OF JESUS CHRIST.

Zaham. One of Rehoboam's sons by his wife Mahalath (2 Chr 11:19).

Zair. Place where Joram attacked and defeated the Edomites (2 Kgs 8:21). In the parallel passage of 2 Chronicles 21:9, the phrase "to Zair" is replaced by the phrase "with his commanders" (the Hebrew words are similar). Many have therefore suggested that a copyist revision appeared in 2 Chronicles because the location of Zair was unknown. Others have suggested that Zair should be identified with Zoar on the southeast end of the Dead Sea. In any case, it was located in Transjordan on a principal road to Edom.

Zalaph. Hanun's father. Hanun repaired a section of the Jerusalem wall during Nehemiah's day (Neh 3:30).

Zalmon (Person). Ahohite and one of David's mighty men (2 Sm 23:28); alternately called Ilai, the Ahohite, in 1 Chronicles 11:29.

Zalmon (Place). Mountain from which Abimelech took brush to burn down the Tower of Shechem (Jgs 9:48). Since the mountain obviously was close to Shechem, it tentatively has been identified with es-Sulemiyeh (the modern name for the southeastern portion of Mt Ebal) or one of its surrounding hills. Zalmon is also mentioned in connection with the defeat of Israel's enemies in Psalm 68:14 (KJV Salmon). Because of the mention of snowfall and the "mighty mountain of Bashan" in the following verse, the Septuagint and some commentators consider this Zalmon to be Mt Hermon in Lebanon. However, seasonal snowfalls also occur in the region of Mt Ebal.

Zalmonah. Place where the Israelites camped after they set out from Mt Hor (Nm 33:41,42). The precise location is unknown but may be the Wadi Ithm. The name suggests that it was a gloomy valley leading up to the Edomite plateau.

See WILDERNESS WANDERINGS.

Zalmunna. *See* ZEBAH AND ZALMUNNA.

Zamzummim. Ammonite name for the Rephaim, who are described as a "people great and many, and tall as the Anakim" (Dt 2:20). The Zamzummim were displaced by the Ammonites, just as the Horites were displaced by the Edomites and the Avvim by the Caphtorim (vv 12,23). The comparison with the Anakim, the Rephaim, and the Emim makes it evident that the Zamzummim were a race of giants who lived in Transjordan. While their precise origin is unknown, they probably resided in the vicinity of Rabbath-ammon. The similarity between the tribal lists of Genesis 14:5,6 and Deuteronomy 2:9–22 (e.g., Emim, Rephaim, Horites) suggests the possibility that the Zamzummim may be the same as the Zuzim of Ham (Ham-zuzim) who were defeated by Chedorlaomer (Gn 14:5).

See GIANTS; REPHAIM.

Zanoah (Person). Descendant of Caleb from Judah's tribe (1 Chr 4:18). Zanoah was the son of Jekuthiel and, depending on the translation of the Hebrew text, may have been related to

Bithiah, the daughter of Pharaoh (v 17). Some have interpreted the text as indicating that Jekuthiel was the founder or principal settler of the city named Zanoah. In any case, Zanoah's descendants may well have been connected with the city of that name.

Zanoah (Place). 1. One of the cities "in the lowland" that was part of Judah's inheritance (Jos 15:34). The inhabitants of Zanoah worked with Hanun to rebuild the Valley Gate as well as about 1500 feet of the city wall during the restoration of Jerusalem (Neh 3:13; 11:30). The city is probably identifiable with Zanu'a, which is located approximately 10 miles west of Jerusalem.

2. One of the cities in the Judean highlands south of Hebron that was part of Judah's inheritance (Jos 15:56). It is quite likely connected with the descendants of Zanoah, Jekuthiel's son.

Zaphenath-paneah, Zaphnath-paaneah. Name given to Joseph by Pharaoh when Joseph assumed his governmental responsibilities in Egypt (Gn 41:45, KJV Zaphnath-paaneah). While many suggestions have been made concerning the meaning of the name, it is most likely a Semiticized form of an original Egyptian name meaning, "says the god, he will live."

See JOSEPH #1.

Zaphon. Town located east of the Jordan River (Jos 13:27) and included as part of the inheritance of Gad's tribe (Jos 13:24). Egyptian records (13th century BC) refer to a town known as *dapuna*, while an Amarna text spells the name *sapuna*.

Modern sites proposed for the location of ancient Zaphon include Tel el-Qos and Tel es-Saidiyeh. Positive identification cannot be made for either site.

According to Judges 12:1, a group of Ephraimites camped near Zaphon and chastised Jephthah for not inviting them to participate in his fight against the Ammonites (see Jgs 11). Jephthah replied that he had asked for Ephraimite cooperation but had been refused. A fight ensued and the Ephraimites lost 42,000 soldiers in a crushing defeat.

Genesis 46:16 lists Ziphion as a "son" of Gad. Numbers 26:15 mentions Zephon as the head of a "family" known as the Zephonites. Connection between Zaphon and the Canaanite deity Baal-zephon has often been conjectured, but is not based upon any solid evidence.

Zara, Zarah. KJV alternate forms of Zerah, Judah's son, in Genesis 38:20; 46:12; and Matthew 1:3.

See ZERAH #2.

Zareah, Zareathite. KJV spelling of Zorah and Zorathite in Nehemiah 11:29 and 1 Chronicles 2:53, respectively.

See ZORAH, ZORATHITE.

Zared. KJV spelling of the Brook Zered in Numbers 21:12.

See ZERED.

Zarephath. Village where the woman who provided food and lodging for Elijah lived (1 Kgs 17:9,10; Lk 4:26, KJV Sarepta). Obadiah later prophesied that the Israelite exiles of Halah would "possess Phoenicia as far as Zarephath" (Ob 20). Zarephath was under the control of Sidon at the time Elijah visited, thus serving as a safe haven from King Ahab of Israel. Zarephath is likely identifiable with modern Surafend where a chapel marks the traditional site for the widow's house.

Zarethan, Zaretan. City or region near the Jordan River north of Jericho. It is first mentioned in connection with the "cutting off" of the waters of the Jordan which occurred at Adam, "the city that is beside Zarethan" (Jos 3:16, KJV Zaretan). Its location is more precisely defined in the list of Solomon's administrative districts as being in the vicinity of Beth-shean below Jezreel (1 Kgs 4:12, KJV Zartanah). Hiram cast the bronze vessels for the temple in the "clay ground" of the valley between Succoth and Zarethan (1 Kgs 7:46, KJV Zarthan). It is also likely that the Zeredah (NIV Zarethan; KJV Zeredathah) mentioned in the parallel passage in 2 Chronicles 4:17 is the same place as Zarethan. The precise identification of Zarethan is complicated by the large number of spelling variants. In addition to the references noted above, many have identified Zarethan as the same place as Zeredah, the birthplace of Jeroboam, mentioned in 1 Kings 11:26 (KJV Zereda) and Zererah, mentioned in connection with Gideon's defeat of the Midianites in Judges 7:22 (KJV Zererath). However, geographical details make it likely that only Zererah should be identified with Zarethan.

Zareth-shahar. KJV spelling of Zereth-shahar, a Reubenite city, in Joshua 13:19.

See ZERETH-SHAHAR.

Zarhite. 1. KJV rendering of Zerahite, a descendant of Zerah's family in Simeon's tribe, in Numbers 26:13.

See ZERAH #3.

2. KJV rendering of Zerahite, a descendant of Zerah's family in Judah's tribe, in Numbers 26:20.

See ZERAH #2.

Zartanah, Zarthan. KJV alternate forms of Zarethan in 1 Kings 4:12 and 7:46, respectively.

See ZARETHAN, ZARETAN.

Zatthu. KJV rendering of Zattu in Nehemiah 10:14.

See ZATTU #2.

Zattu. 1. Clan chief with whom 945 people returned with Zerubbabel (Ezr 2:8; Neh 7:13 cites 845 returnees). Of the priests who renounced their foreign wives, six are listed as "sons" of Zattu (Ezr 10:27).

2. One of the chiefs of the people who signed Nehemiah's covenant (Neh 10:14, KJV Zatthu); perhaps the same person as #1 above.

Zavan. KJV spelling of Zaavan, Ezer's son, in 1 Chronicles 1:42.

See ZAAVAN.

Zaza. Jonathan's son, in the family of Jerahmeel, a member of Judah's tribe (1 Chr 2:33).

Zealot. Term used for the second Simon among the twelve to distinguish him from Simon Peter (Lk 6:15; Acts 1:13; KJV Zelotes). Matthew (10:4) and Mark (3:18) use "Cananaean"—Greek and Aramaic equivalents for "zealous defender, enthusiast, one eager to acquire, fanatic" (from root words meaning "burn with zeal, or jealousy; desire eagerly"; Ex 34:14; 2 Mc 4:2). In this general sense, Christ showed zeal for God's house. Some were "zealots" for spiritual gifts, good works, goodness, and the Law, as Paul was for the tradition of the fathers and for God (Jn 2:17; Acts 21:20; 22:3; 1 Cor 14:12; Gal 1:14; Ti 2:14; 1 Pt 3:13). So, Simon was distinguished from Peter and the others by his religious zeal.

By the time Luke wrote, however, the title "Zealot" had become attached especially to a militant, anti-Roman, revolutionary faction, equally religious and political in motivation. This party may have been founded in AD 6 following the death of Herod the Great, by Judas the Galilean and Zadduk the Pharisee, but the movement was rooted in Maccabean resistance to foreign rule and infiltration (1 Mc 2:15–28 "zealous for the law"). Phinehas, renowned as "jealous with [God's] jealousy," "jealous for his God" in Moses' day (Nm 25:10–13; Ps 106:30,31), became with Elijah (1 Kgs 19:10,14) heroes of the movement (cf. 4 Mc 18:12 "Phinehas the Zealot," early 1st century AD).

Zealot opposition to Roman rule was rooted in zeal for the Torah, and for God the only King. The Zealot regarded himself as an agent of divine judgment and redemption, resolutely and fearlessly contending against idolatry, apostasy, and collaboration. Messiah would become their leader. Any closer link with the Qumran covenanters than shared zeal for the Torah is debatable.

As hostility between Rome and Judea sharpened, the religious motivation was channeled by nationalist feeling into a "holy war." Whereas the Maccabees had been forced to take arms in self-defense, the Zealots became increasingly militaristic. Josephus (*Antiq.* 18.1.1–6; *Wars* 4.3.9) with some prejudice calls them brigands and robbers. Their Latin name was *sicarii*, assassins, but supporters would call them patriotic guerrillas. They reached preeminence in the war with Rome (AD 66–70). Their last refuge and stronghold, at Masada, was overcome in AD 73, when the surviving 960 committed suicide.

Since by the time Luke wrote the meaning of the title was established, Simon probably was, or had been, a member of this movement's earlier phase, around AD 30. It is less probable that Judas Iscariot (possibly Sicarius) and the "sons of thunder" (Mk 3:17) were. Judas the Galilean (Acts 5:37,38), and even Paul (Acts 21:38), were considered Zealots.

See FIRST JEWISH REVOLT; JUDAISM.

Zealot, Simon the. *See* SIMON #5.

Zebadiah. 1. One of the sons of Beriah from Benjamin's tribe (1 Chr 8:15).

2. One of the sons of Elpaal from Benjamin's tribe (1 Chr 8:17).

3. One of the sons of Jeroham of Gedor, who came to David's support at Ziklag (1 Chr 12:7).

4. Korahite Levite descended from Asaph, third of Meshelemiah's seven sons and a temple gatekeeper (1 Chr 26:2).

5. Son of Asahel, Joab's brother, who was the commander of the fourth division of David's army (1 Chr 27:7).

6. One of the Levites sent by Jehoshaphat into the cities of Judah to teach the Law (2 Chr 17:8).

7. Ishmael's son and one of the rulers of the Levites whom Jehoshaphat appointed as governor of the house of Judah (2 Chr 19:11).

Masada, the last stronghold of the Zealots in AD 73.

8. Michael's son from Shephatiah's house who returned with Ezra to Jerusalem following the exile (Ezr 8:8).

9. One of the sons of Immer who renounced his foreign wife at Ezra's command (Ezr 10:20).

Zebah and Zalmunna. Two Midianite kings who slaughtered Gideon's brothers at Tabor (Jgs 8:18,19) and whom Gideon subsequently killed in order to avenge his brothers' deaths (v 21).

During Gideon's day, Midianite camel raiders annually made forays into Israelite territory at harvest time, stealing crops and livestock (6:3). So complete were their raids that nothing was left in Israel, including crops, sheep, oxen, or donkeys (v 4).

In this state of affairs God called Gideon to deliver Israel (6:16). His well-known victory over Midian near Mt Moreh was an important step toward realization of this divine commission (7:1–23). In the operations following the battle, Ephraimite warriors captured and assassinated two Midianite leaders named Zeeb and Oreb (7:24–8:3).

Gideon, however, determined to capture Zebah and Zalmunna, the kings of the Midianite forces. In tracking them down, he crossed the Jordan River and traveled more than 100 miles from the site of the original battle. Along the way two successive towns, Succoth and Penuel, refused to help Gideon and his men, doubtless fearing reprisal from the Midianite raiders should Gideon fail to defeat them (see 8:6,8).

Gideon routed the remaining Midianite warriors and captured Zebah and Zalmunna (8:12). Gideon later punished the uncooperative cities of Succoth and Penuel (vv 13,17). Because Zebah and Zalmunna had killed his brothers, Gideon slew the two Midianite kings (vv 19,21).

Psalm 83:11 indicates that Zebah, Zalmunna, and the Midianites were not merely the enemies of Israel but also of God.

Zebaim. KJV rendering of a place mentioned in Ezra 2:57 and Nehemiah 7:59.

See POCHERETH-HAZZEBAIM, POCHERETH OF ZEBAIM.

Zebedee. Father of the disciples James and John (Mt 26:37; Mk 3:17; 10:35). Zebedee was in the fishing business and may have been wealthy, considering that he had servants and apparent connections with the high priest (Jn 18:15). Although he personally appears only once in the narrative (Mt 4:21; Mk 1:19,20), his wife Salome appears frequently as one of the pious women who followed Christ.

Zebidah. Mother of Jehoiakim, king of Judah, Josiah's wife and the daughter of Pedaiah (2 Kgs 23:36, KJV Zebudah).

Zebina. Nebo's son, who obeyed Ezra's exhortation to divorce his foreign wife after the exile (Ezr 10:43).

Zeboiim. One of the "cities of the plain" that was destroyed with Sodom and Gomorrah (Dt 29:23; Hos 11:8; KJV Zeboim). Zeboiim is first mentioned, with Sodom, Gomorrah, and Admah, as one of the Canaanite cities in the table of nations in Genesis 10:19 (KJV Zeboim). It later appears confederated with the same states (including Zoar) in the battle against Amraphel king of Shinar, Arioch king of Ellasar, Chedorlaomer king of Elam, and Tidal king of Goiim (Gn 14:2,8).

As with the other "cities of the plain," identifying Zeboiim's location is the biggest difficulty. No ruins have been positively identified for Zeboiim, or for any of the other four cities in the confederation. Most scholars currently believe that the cities were located in the southeastern corner of the Dead Sea region and that their ruins may well be under the lake. Others have objected to this placement because of Zeboiim's apparent proximity to Zoar (Gn 13:10; Dt 34:3), which some have placed northeast of the Dead Sea.

See CITIES OF THE VALLEY, CITIES OF THE PLAIN.

Zeboim. 1. KJV spelling of Zeboiim in Genesis 10:19, Deuteronomy 29:23, and Hosea 11:8.

See ZEBOIIM.

2. Valley where one of the raiding parties of the Philistines turned toward the border of the wilderness (1 Sm 13:18). It may be identified with Shuk ed-Dubba.

3. One of the villages outside of Jerusalem where the Benjamites settled after the exile (Neh 11:34).

Zebudah. KJV spelling of Zebidah, King Josiah's wife, in 2 Kings 23:36.

See ZEBIDAH.

Zebul. Ruler of Shechem who served as an officer of Abimelech (Jgs 9:28,30). Zebul apparently obtained his position when Abimelech was crowned king at Shechem. When Gaal the son of Ebed incited the Shechemites to rebel against Abimelech, Zebul played an instrumental role in Abimelech's victory. After he goaded Gaal into attacking Abimelech outside of the city (vv 38,39), Zebul shut Gaal out of the city, preventing retreat into its confines (v 41). It is difficult to determine Zebul's fate when Abimelech later attacked and destroyed the city, but it is possible that he too met a treacherous fate.

Zebulun (Person). One of Jacob's 12 sons (Gn 35:23; 1 Chr 2:1). He was the sixth and last son borne to Jacob by Leah, who named the boy Zebulun, meaning "abode, dwelling," for she said, "Now my husband will *honor* [or *dwell with*, NASB] me, because I have borne him six sons" (Gn 30:19,20). Later, he settled his family in Egypt with Jacob and his brothers (Ex 1:3). Jacob foretold that Zebulun's descendants would become a maritime people with their border touching Sidon (Gn 49:13). Though Zebulun's tribe, after the conquest and allotment of land under Joshua (Jos 19:10–16), was separated from the Mediterranean by Asher's tribe and from the Sea of Galilee by Issachar, it prospered greatly in trade with the Canaanite cities of the coastal plains. Zebulun fathered three sons (Gn 46:14) and founded one of Israel's 12 tribes (Nm 1:30,31).

See ZEBULUN, TRIBE OF.

Zebulun, Tribe of. Tribe descended from Zebulun, the 10th son of Jacob and the 6th borne to him by Leah (Gn 30:19,20). His tribe was divided into 3 clans named after his 3 sons: the Sederites, the Elonites, and the Jaheelites (Gn 46:14; Nm 26:27). At the census taken on the Plains of Moab, the number of men in the tribe over 20 years of age and fit for military service was 60,500 (Nm 26:26,27).

The territory allotted to Zebulun's tribe was in central Canaan and included the Valley of Jezreel, but the boundary lines given in Joshua 19:10–24 are difficult to trace because only the tribe's southeastern and eastern borders are indicated. The western border on the Mediterranean side is not clearly defined. In the blessing of Moses (Dt 33:18,19) Zebulun, along with Issachar, "shall draw out [lit. suck] the abundance of the sea," which would seem to indicate that Zebulun would have access to the sea (Mediterranean) and, therefore, to the mercantile and maritime trade.

The boundary details, however, do not bring Zebulun in touch geographically with the sea, in apparent contradiction to Genesis 49:13. But this reference may not imply actual contact with the Mediterranean. Zebulun's position did enable it to profit by maritime trade because the great caravan route to the sea passed through Zebulunite territory. In addition, Zebulun's "lot," with its fruitful fields and valleys, ensured olive groves, vineyards, and splendid harvests. In 1 Chronicles 12:40 the tribe was able to provide rich provisions for David from its fertile lands. Throughout the centuries the tribe maintained its identity; its territorial borders are referred to by Isaiah (9:1) and Ezekiel (48:26,27).

Clearly, then, the tribe of Zebulun held a strong position among its tribal neighbors around Galilee and was settled more securely. In contrast to the tribes of Asher and Naphtali, who continued to "dwell among the Canaanites" (Jgs 1:32,33), the Canaanites constituted a minority in Zebulun. Throughout the period of the judges the tribe was very active. For example, the victorious army in the battle of Kishon was composed of men of Zebulun and Naphtali (Jgs 4:6,10); in the Song of Deborah, Zebulun is praised as "a people that puts its life in jeopardy to the point of death" (Jgs 5:18). In Judges 6:35 the men of Zebulun take part in Gideon's struggle with the Midianites on the Plain of Jezreel and fight with outstanding valor. The judge Elon belonged to the tribe of Zebulun (Jgs 12:11,12); and since Galilee was in the territory of Zebulun (Jos 19:15), Ibzan of Bethlehem was probably also a Zebulunite. Another indication of the strength and importance of Zebulun's tribe within the united kingdom period is found in the mention of Zebulun's fighting force as the largest of the western tribal armies that fought under King David (1 Chr 12:33). Isaiah refers to the land of Zebulun after the collapse of the northern kingdom of Israel when Assyria made Galilee a province in the empire (9:1). This may mean that the land of Zebulun suffered less than other regions after the fall of Samaria (2 Chr 30:6), and that the people of Zebulun were not uprooted to the same extent.

If this is a reasonable interpretation, then the people of Zebulun probably formed the core of the remnant that survived the Assyrian campaign against Samaria. This probably explains why the royal house of David, which ruled over the southern kingdom of Judah without interruption until the fall of Jerusalem, maintained close ties with the people of Zebulun. Also this may explain the pilgrimage from Samaria in the north to celebrate Hezekiah's Passover in Jerusalem (2 Chr 30:10,11).

Further evidence to strengthen this interpretation may be found in Manasseh's marriage with Meshullemeth of Jotbah (2 Kgs 21:19), a township which lay within the land of Zebulun). Meshullemeth's son, Amon, succeeded Manasseh as king in Jerusalem. In addition, King Josiah, son of Amon, married into the tribe of Zebulun. His wife was Zebidah, a native of Rumah and the mother of King Jehoiakim (2 Kgs 23:36).

In the lists of Jacob's sons Zebulun is always the last of Leah's group of six, after Issachar (Gn 35:23; 46:14; Ex 1:3; 1 Chr 2:1). Zebulun's tribe is closely connected with the tribe of Issachar: they were neighbors in southern Galilee (Jos 19:10–16,17–23) and the blessing of Moses refers to them together (Dt 33:18,19).

In the NT (KJV Zabulon), with the exception of the two references to Zebulun in Matthew 4:13,15, the name of the tribe appears only in the list of the 12 tribes in Revelation 7:8 after Issachar.   J. G. S. S. THOMSON

See ZEBULUN (PERSON).

Zebulunite.   Descendant of Zebulun, Jacob's son (Nm 26:27; Jgs 12:11,12).

See ZEBULUN, TRIBE OF.

Zechariah (Person).   Name frequently used in the Bible meaning "the Lord remembers."

1. Son of King Jeroboam II; the 15th king of Israel and the last of Jehu's dynasty. Beginning his rule in 753 BC, the 38th year of Azari-ah's reign in Judah (792–740 BC), Zechariah ruled in Samaria for only 6 months before he was murdered at Ibleam in a conspiracy masterminded by Shallum, his successor (2 Kgs 14:29; 15:8,11; KJV Zachariah). The Lord's promise to Jehu, that his descendants would rule to the 4th generation, was fulfilled with Zechariah's reign (2 Kgs 10:30).

2. Father of Abi (or Abijah, 2 Chr 29:1). Abi was the mother of Hezekiah, who later ruled Judah for 29 years (2 Kgs 18:2, KJV Zachariah).

3. Reubenite and leader of his tribe (1 Chr 5:7).

4. Korahite Levite, firstborn of Meshelemiah's seven sons and a wise counselor, selected by lot to oversee the gatekeepers of the sanctuary's northern entrance during David's reign (1 Chr 9:21; 26:2,14).

5. Benjamite and descendant of Jeiel (1 Chr 9:37). He is alternately called Zecher (KJV Zacher), perhaps an abbreviation of Zechariah, in 1 Chronicles 8:31.

6. One of the eight Levites assigned to play a harp before the ark of God in the procession led by David when the ark was brought from Obed-edom's house to Jerusalem (1 Chr 15:18, 20; 16:5).

7. One of the priests assigned to blow a trumpet before the ark in the procession led by David when the ark was brought to Jerusalem (1 Chr 15:24).

8. Levite and a descendant of Isshiah, who served in the sanctuary during David's reign (1 Chr 24:25).

9. Merarite Levite and Hosah's son, who served as one of the gatekeepers of the sanctuary's western entrance, at the gate of Hallecheth, during David's reign (1 Chr 26:11).

10. Father of Iddo. Iddo was the chief officer of the half-tribe of Manasseh in Gilead during David's reign (1 Chr 27:21).

11. One of the princes sent by King Jehoshaphat (872–848 BC) to teach the Law in the cities of Judah (2 Chr 17:7).

12. Gershonite Levite and Jahaziel's father. Jahaziel promised divine deliverance from Moab and Ammon to King Jehoshaphat and the people of Judah (2 Chr 20:14).

13. One of King Jehoshaphat's seven sons and the brother of Jehoram. Jehoram became sole regent of Judah (848–841 BC) at his father's death (2 Chr 21:2).

14. Son of Jehoiada the priest, who rebuked the princes of Judah for turning against the Lord and worshiping false gods. Enraged by Zechariah's rebuff, they conspired against him, and at King Joash's command, stoned him to death in the court of the sanctuary (2 Chr 24:20). The Lord, however, avenged Zechariah's death by allowing the Syrians to defeat Judah, kill the princes, and severely

wound Joash, who was subsequently killed by two of his own servants (vv 23–26).

Jesus in his diatribe against his generation of Jewish leaders, alluded to Zechariah's shameful murder in the temple's sacred precincts. He warned that retribution "from the blood of Abel to the blood of Zechariah, who perished between the altar and the sanctuary . . . shall be required of this generation" (Lk 11:51; Mt 23:35; KJV Zacharias). Abel was the first and Zechariah the last of the recorded prophets of God who were unjustly slain, according to the OT.

In the Matthew passage, Barachiah (KJV Barachias) is listed as Zechariah's father instead of Jehoiada. This perhaps reflects a later scribal error, where the copyist mistook him for the well-known postexilic prophet (cf. Berechiah's son, Zec 1:1).

15. Man who counseled King Uzziah of Judah to walk in the fear of God (2 Chr 26:5).

16. Abijah's father. Abijah was the mother of King Hezekiah of Judah (2 Chr 29:1).

17. Gershonite Levite descended from Asaph, who along with Mattaniah his kinsman was chosen by King Hezekiah to help cleanse the house of the Lord (2 Chr 29:13).

18. Kohathite Levite who was appointed to oversee the repair of the temple during King Josiah's reign (2 Chr 34:12).

19. One of the chief officers of the house of God who generously gave animals to the priests for the celebration of the Passover feast during King Josiah's reign (2 Chr 35:8).

20. Prophet, Berechiah's son and the grandson of Iddo, who began prophesying as a young man in 520 BC during the reign of King Darius I of Persia (Zec 1:1; cf. 2:4). Little is known about the prophet. He ministered with Haggai his contemporary in postexilic Jerusalem during the days of Zerubbabel, the governor, and Jeshua, the high priest (Ezr 5:1). He exhorted the Jews to finish building the second temple (Ezr 6:14), and headed Iddo's priestly family during Joiakim's term as high priest (Neh 12:16). Like Jeremiah and Ezekiel, Zechariah served as both priest and prophet (Zec 1:1,7; 7:1,8).

Numerous suggestions have been offered to resolve the discrepancy of Zechariah's pedigree; in the Ezra and Nehemiah passages, Iddo is listed as his father, whereas in Zechariah, Berechiah bears the name. Some conclude that Berechiah and Iddo were different names for the same person, or that Berechiah's name (Zec 1:1,7) was a later scribal emendation which confused Jeberechiah's son with Iddo's son (cf. Is 8:2). A more plausible theory identifies Iddo as Zechariah's grandfather, the renowned head of his family, who returned to Jerusalem from exile in 538 BC. Either by Bere-

chiah's early death or by the precedence of his grandfather's name, Zechariah was considered Iddo's successor.

See ZECHARIAH, BOOK OF; PROPHET, PROPHETESS.

21. Parosh's son and the head of his father's household. He returned with Ezra to Judah following the exile during the reign of King Artaxerxes I of Persia (Ezr 8:3).

22. Bebai's son and the head of a household. He returned with Ezra to Judah following the exile during the reign of King Artaxerxes I of Persia (Ezr 8:11).

23. One of the Jewish leaders whom Ezra sent to Iddo, the man in charge at Casiphia, to gather Levites and temple servants for the caravan of Jews returning to Palestine from Babylon (Ezr 8:16).

24. One of the six descendants of Elam who was encouraged by Ezra to divorce his foreign wife during the postexilic period (Ezr 10:26).

25. One of the men who stood to Ezra's left when Ezra read the Law to the people (Neh 8:4).

26. Descendant of Perez and an ancestor of a Judahite family headed by Athaiah living in Jerusalem during the postexilic period (Neh 11:4).

27. Descendant of Shelah and an ancestor of a Judahite family headed by Maaseiah living in Jerusalem during the postexilic era (Neh 11:5).

28. Priest, descendant of Malchijah and an ancestor of a family of Levites headed by Adaiah living in Jerusalem during the postexilic period (Neh 11:12).

29. Jonathan's son, a descendant of Asaph and one of the priestly musicians who played a trumpet at the dedication of the Jerusalem wall in Nehemiah's day (Neh 12:35).

30. Another priest who played a trumpet at the Jerusalem wall's dedication (Neh 12:41); perhaps the same person as #28 above.

31. Jeberechiah's son and undoubtedly a man of distinction who, along with Uriah the priest, publicly witnessed Isaiah's writing of the puzzling expression, "Maher-shalal-hashbaz," which later prophetically revealed God's intended judgment on Damascus and Samaria (Is 8:2).

32. John the Baptist's father, priest of Abijah's division, and the husband of Elizabeth, a woman of priestly descent. They lived in the Judean hill country during King Herod the Great's reign (37–4 BC; Lk 1:5). Zechariah (KJV Zacharias) and Elizabeth both lived righteous and pious lives; however, they were advanced in years and still had no children (vv 6,7).

As priest, Zechariah was one of the men chosen to represent his division in its yearly appointed session of service in the Jerusalem temple (the priests of Israel were divided into

24 orders, each being assigned an annual 2-week period of service in the temple). One day while serving in Jerusalem, Zechariah was selected by lot to burn incense in the temple's holy place, a privilege granted a priest only once in his lifetime. While performing this temple duty, the angel Gabriel appeared to him, telling him that Elizabeth his wife, though barren, would bear him a son, whose name would be called John (vv 12,13), and who would prepare the way for the Messiah. As a sign confirming the angel's report, Zechariah was struck dumb for his disbelief that, in their old age, he and Elizabeth would produce a child (v 18). When Zechariah returned to the temple court, the gathered multitude perceived that the gesturing priest had seen a vision (v 22).

Elizabeth became pregnant as promised, and in her sixth month was visited by her relative Mary, who was also with child (v 40). Later, shortly after the baby's birth, Zechariah affirmed that his son's name would be John, at which time his speech was restored and he was filled with the Holy Spirit, prophesying and praising God for the work that he was about to do in Israel (vv 62–64,67–79).

33. Original name proposed for John the Baptist after his father's name (Lk 1:59; KJV Zacharias). H. DOUGLAS BUCKWALTER

See JOHN THE BAPTIST.

Zechariah, Book of.

Longest book of the Minor Prophets and the most difficult to understand. One reason for this difficulty is the numerous visions which call for an interpreter. At times an interpreting angel is present to tell what the vision means (1:9,10,19,20; 4:1–4; 5:5,6), but at other times, when an interpretation is sorely needed, there is no angel to help. The obscure meaning of many passages has spawned numerous theories concerning the date, authorship, unity, and interpretation of this book. One thing that makes the Book of Zechariah significant for the Christian is its use in the NT. The last part of Zechariah (chs 9–11) is the most quoted section of the prophets in the Gospel passion narratives, and, other than Ezekiel, Zechariah has influenced the Book of Revelation more than any other OT book.

Author. The name Zechariah probably means, "the Lord remembers," or "the Lord is renowned." Zechariah is a common name in the OT and NT. At least 30 different people in the OT are named Zechariah. There is a problem in identifying the prophet's father. In Zechariah 1:1,7 the prophet is called "the son of Berechiah, the son of Iddo," but in Ezra 5:1 and 6:14 he is called simply "the son of Iddo." There was another Zechariah in Isaiah's time whose father was named Jeberechiah (Is 8:2). Another prophet by the name of Zechariah, the son of Jehoiada the priest, lived much earlier during the reign of Joash, king of Judah (835–796 BC). This prophet was stoned to death because he proclaimed that the Lord had forsaken his people because of their sins (2 Chr 24:20–22). Jesus seems to refer to this or a similar unrecorded incident, but he calls the prophet the son of Berechiah, the last of the martyrs among the prophets (Mt 23:35). However, Luke's account of what Jesus said about Zechariah (11:51) does not include the words, "the son of Berechiah." Since Jesus is quoting 2 Chronicles, which was the last book in the Hebrew Bible, he was simply indicating the sweep of time from the first murder (Abel) to the last (Zechariah, the son of Jehoiada). There is no evidence that the prophet of the Book of Zechariah was martyred; therefore, the best solution to the problem is to consider Berechiah the father, and Iddo the grandfather, of this prophet.

Date. The first part of the Book of Zechariah (chs 1–8) is well dated. The first date is in the first verse, "the eighth month of the second year of Darius." This was Darius, king of Persia (521–486 BC). The eighth month of Darius' second year would be October 520 BC. This date seems to be the first time the "word of the Lord" came to Zechariah. The second date in Zechariah is in 1:7: "On the twenty-fourth day of the eleventh month which is the month of Shebat, in the second year of Darius." This date would be February 15, 519 BC. The word of the Lord which came to Zechariah on this date seems to include the account of eight night visions along with some oracles from an angel who talked with him. The third date in Zechariah is in 7:1: "In the fourth year of King Darius . . . in the fourth day of the ninth month which is Chislev." This date would be the equivalent of December 7, 518 BC. This verse introduces a group of ethical and eschatological oracles (chs 7, 8) concerning the true meaning of fasting.

There are no dates in Zechariah 9–14. Zechariah's name is never mentioned, and neither is Darius or any king. A period of relative peace and stability gives place to war. The temple is standing (11:13; 14:20), and evidently Greek soldiers are present (9:13). Any attempt to assign specific dates to Zechariah 9–14 would be speculation.

Historical Background. The temple in Jerusalem was destroyed by Nebuchadnezzar, king of Babylon, in 586 BC. Nebuchadnezzar made several raids against Jerusalem before and after it fell, taking many captives to Babylon (cf. Dn 1:1; 2 Kgs 24:1–26). On two occasions Jeremiah had predicted that captivity

A Persian relief of Darius from Persepolis (c. 6th cent. BC).

would last 70 years (Jer 25:11; 29:10; cf. Dn 9:2). In the time of Zechariah, the period of 70 years since the fall of Jerusalem was coming to an end (1:12; 7:5). It had been 66 years since Jerusalem fell when the first "word of the Lord" came to Zechariah in the second year of Darius (520 BC). The Babylonian Empire had fallen to the Persians in 538 BC, and Cyrus the first king of Persia signed a decree permitting all captives to return to their homes (2 Chr 36:23; Ezr 1:1–4). Evidently the first contingent of Jewish captives returned to Jerusalem with Zerubbabel and Joshua the priest about 536 BC. One of the first objectives of the returnees was to rebuild the temple (Ezr 1:3). But internal strife and external opposition from the Samaritans prohibited the immediate rebuilding of the temple. After Darius I became king of Persia in 521 BC, a wave of expectation and enthusiasm swept over the Jewish communities in Jerusalem and Babylon. Two prophets possibly from the Babylonian exiles, Haggai and Zechariah, began preaching so powerfully that work on the second temple began in 520 BC and was finished in 516 BC (Ezr 5:1,14,15; Hg 1,2; Zec 1–8).

The Book of Zechariah opens in the second year of Darius (520 BC). Some of the captives had been back in Jerusalem for 16 years, but nothing was being done about rebuilding the temple. Zechariah's first message called for the people to repent and not repeat the mistake of their fathers whose sins and refusal to repent led to the exile and destruction of the temple (Zec 1:1–6). Then a series of eight night visions follows (1:7–6:8), assuring the people that the temple would be rebuilt by Zerubbabel (1:16; 4:9; 6:15). Two verses in Zechariah speak volumes concerning the hardships and difficulties in Jerusalem before the temple was rebuilt. "Thus says the Lord of hosts: 'Let your hands be strong, you who in these days have been hearing these words from the mouth of the prophets, since the day that the foundation of the Lord of hosts was laid, that the temple might be built. For before those days

there was no wage for man or any wage for beasts [widespread unemployment], neither was there any safety from the foe for him who went out or came in; for I set every man against his fellow [anarchy]" (8:9,10).

The first eight chapters of Zechariah are set against the social, political, and religious situations in Jerusalem from 520 to 518 BC. But beginning with chapter 9 historical moorings are lost. Chapter 9 opens with an oracle against Syria, including Damascus, Tyre, and Sidon, and against Philistia. Each of these places will be conquered, cleansed, and become like a clan in Judah (vv 1–8). There is the promise of a new king coming triumphantly to Jerusalem, yet humbly riding on an ass. His reign will be peaceful and universal (vv 9,10). The next oracle speaks of setting the captives free (v 11), but this may not refer to the Babylonian captives because of a reference to the Greeks (v 13). Zechariah 9–12 is primarily poetry rather than prose and is eschatological, almost wholly concerned with the future. Some scholars call this part apocalyptic literature. The nations attack Jerusalem and are defeated (chs 12,14). The temple is standing (11:13), but it does not seem to have a place of great prominence in the new Jerusalem and in the kingdom of God (14:6–9).

Purpose and Message. The purpose of the book is to reassure and encourage. The restored Jewish community of 520 BC needed the assurance that the temple would be rebuilt and later groups of God's people needed to know that ultimately the kingdom of God would come in its fullness. There are three messages in the Book of Zechariah: the need for repentance (1:1–6); the eight night visions (1:7–6:8) signifying that the temple would be rebuilt and God's glory would return to Jerusalem; and the coming kingdom of God (chs 9–14).

Content. The Book of Zechariah may be divided into two main parts: chapters 1–8 and 9–14. The first part is dated between 520 BC and 518 BC. It consists of oracles and visions of

Zechariah, the son of Berechiah. Mainly prose, its primary concern is to assure the restored Jewish community that the temple will be rebuilt. The second part (chs 9–14) is undated. There are no references to Zechariah. The temple is standing, and much of the language is eschatological and apocalyptic. The second part itself has two parts: chapters 9–11 and 12–14. Chapters 9 and 12 begin essentially the same way, "The burden [oracle] of the word of the Lord."

The first part of Zechariah (chs 1–8) has four main sections: superscription and first oracle (1:1–6); eight night visions and related oracles (1:7–6:8); the symbolic crowning of Joshua (6:9–15); and the question about fasting and morality (7:1–8:23).

The Superscription (1:1). This section is dated specifically "in the eighth month" of the Babylonian calendar, which was from mid-October to mid-November. The second year of Darius, king of Persia, was 520 BC. The date is important in relating the work of Zechariah to that of Haggai (cf. Hg 1:1,15; 2:1,10,18,20) and to the reconstruction of the temple under Zerubbabel. The first oracle concerns the need for repentance. The first message of Zechariah came between Haggai's second and third message. He, like Haggai, probably attributed the failure of the crops and other hardships to a failure to rebuild the temple (cf. Hg 1:6–11). Zechariah calls for the people to repent so that they can persevere with work on the temple.

The Eight Night Visions and Related Oracles (1:7–6:8). These visions that Zechariah saw in Jerusalem all seem to have been given on the night of the 24th day of the 11th month (Shebat) in the second year of Darius (mid-January to mid-February 519 BC). Seven of the eight visions have essentially the same form. Four of the visions begin with the words, "And I lifted up my eyes and saw and behold" (1:18; 2:1; 5:1; 6:1). One begins, "I saw in the night, and behold" (1:8). Another begins, "And the angel who talked with me came again and waked me . . . and said to me, What do you see? I said, I see and behold" (4:1,2). Still another (the seventh) vision begins, "Then the angel who talked with me came forward and said to me" (5:5). However, the fourth vision is different from the other seven. It begins, "Then he showed me" (3:1; cf. Am 7:1,4,7). This message in the third person contains no interpreting angel nor any direct message to Zechariah, as if he were merely an observer. This fourth vision is so different from the other seven that it was not a part of the original series of eight.

An overall pattern to the eight visions is not evident. Some scholars have seen some significance in the fact that the visions move from the evening or night in the first vision to the sunrise in the last vision. Others have detected some relationships in pairs of visions. The first and last visions speak about horses and riders or chariots. The second and third visions talk about restoring Judah and Jerusalem (1:18–21; 2:1–5). The fourth and fifth deal with the place of the two leaders in the restored community. Joshua will be cleansed and restored as the high priest (3:1–5) and Zerubbabel the governor will complete the temple (4:1–14). The sixth and seventh visions deal with the cleansing of the land. A flying scroll enters the house of every thief and false witness and consumes it (5:1–4). Wickedness personified as a woman will be carried in an ephah (basket) to the land of Shinar (5:5–11). Interspersed in the vision accounts are four oracles (1:14–17; 2:6–12; 3:6–10; 4:8–14). Each of these passages begins with the messenger formula "Thus says the Lord" or the expression "Cry out" (1:14,17). The first oracle assures the people that the temple, the cities, and the choice of Jerusalem will be renewed. The second oracle exhorts any exiles remaining in Babylon to return to Judah and Jerusalem (2:6–12). Zechariah 2:12, 13 are interesting. Verse 12 is the only OT reference to Palestine as "the Holy Land," and verse 13 is similar to the call to worship in Habakkuk 2:20: "The Lord is in his holy temple; let all the earth keep silence before him." The third oracle in the vision accounts concerns Joshua the high priest as a sign of the coming of God's servant, the Branch who removes the guilt of the land in a single day (3:6–10).

The Symbolic Crowning of Joshua (6:9–15). Zechariah is told to go into the house of Josiah son of Zephaniah, take silver and gold from some returnees from Babylon, make a crown, and put it on the head of Joshua the priest, as a symbol of the royal and priestly king, the Branch, the builder of the temple. After the ceremony the crown is to be hung in the temple as a memorial of those who gave the silver and the gold. The last verse (6:15) seems to say that just as gold and silver from exiles was used to symbolize the crowning of the coming king of the kingdom, exiles, "those who are far off," will also participate in the completion of the temple. Then Zechariah's hearers will know God sent him to prophesy. This will all take place when and if they will diligently obey the voice of the Lord.

The Question About Fasting and Morality (7:1–8:23). A delegation from Bethel (10 miles north of Jerusalem) came to Jerusalem in the 4th year of Darius (518 BC). Work on the temple had been going on for 2 years. The purpose of this visit was to entreat the favor of the Lord (7:2) and to ask the priests and the prophets if they should continue to fast as they have done since the temple was destroyed 70 years ago (v 3). The Lord told Zechariah to ask why they were fasting—for the Lord or for selfish motives. The answer to the question of fasting seems to be that God desires truth, justice, and covenant-love more than fasting. Zechariah reiterates the message the Lord had already given his people by the former prophets (vv 7–14). The last section in the first part of Zechariah is a decalogue of promises (8:1–23). The 10 promises begin with the words, "Thus says the Lord," or "The word of the Lord came to me" (vv 2–4,7,9,14,18,20,23). The last word of God is not judgment but promise, hope, forgiveness, and restoration.

The Oracles of the Lord (chs 9–12). The last half of the Book of Zechariah (chs 9–14) falls into two nearly equal parts: chapters 9–11 (46 verses) and chapters 12–14 (44 verses). Each part begins with the word "burden" (9:1; 12:1). Both "burdens" are primarily eschatological. The first part (chs 9–11) is concerned with the restoration of the tribes to Palestine (9:11–17; 10:6–12). In order to accomplish this, the Lord will rid Palestine and Syria of opponents to his rule (9:1–8; 11:1–3), remove the evil (rulers) shepherds (10:2b–5; 11:4–17), and the Prince of Peace will come (9:9,10). The last "burden" of Zechariah (12:1–14:21) is also eschatological. This time the concern is primarily that of Jerusalem and Judah. Twice Jerusalem is attacked by the nations (12:1–8; 14:1–5). Each time the Lord fights for Jerusalem, Judah, and the house of David. Jerusalem weeps and mourns for an unidentified martyr (12:10–14). The martyr could be called the "good" shepherd who is killed and his sheep scattered (13:7–9). Jesus referred to this passage in connection with his arrest (Mt 26:31; Mk 14:27). A fountain will be opened for the house of David, and the inhabitants of Jerusalem will be cleansed from sin, idolatry, and false prophets (13:1–6). The New Jerusalem will remain aloft on its site and the land around it will be turned into a plain (14:10,11). There will be no night nor extreme temperatures in the New Jerusalem. Living waters will flow from Jerusalem, and the Lord will become King of all the earth (vv 6–9). Those who fight against Jerusalem will be destroyed (vv 12–15), but those who survive will worship the Lord year by year by keeping the feast of booths (vv 16–19). The last scene in the Book of Zechariah is a picture of the world after Armageddon, a new world cleansed of sin. It will be a time of peace and security. When God comes to reign, everything will become holy. The war horses will become as holy as the priest's turban, and the ordinary cooking vessel will be as temple vessels. The Canaanite or trader will be elimi-

nated. There will be no difference between Jew and Gentile, or between the clean and the unclean. What matters will be whether or not one worships the Lord of Hosts as King.

RALPH L. SMITH

See POSTEXILIC PERIOD, THE; ISRAEL, HISTORY OF; PROPHECY; ZECHARIAH (PERSON) #20; PROPHET, PROPHETESS.

Bibliography. J.G. Baldwin, *Haggai, Zechariah, Malachi*; D. Baron, *Visions and Prophecies of Zechariah*; R.A. Mason, *The Books of Haggai, Zechariah, and Malachi*; G.A. Smith, *The Book of the Twelve Prophets*; M.F. Unger, *Zechariah*; C. von Orelli, *The Twelve Minor Prophets*; C.H.H. Wright, *Zechariah and His Prophecies*.

Zecher. Alternate form of Zechariah, Gibeon's son, in 1 Chronicles 8:31.

See ZECHARIAH (PERSON) #5.

Zedad. One of the geographical landmarks of Israel's northern boundary, mentioned between Hamath and Ziphron (Nm 34:8; Ez 47:15). Its precise location is unknown.

Zedekiah. 1. Judah's last king and a key political figure in the fateful final decade of the southern kingdom. His reign (597–586 BC) spanned Nebuchadnezzar's two attacks on Jerusalem, in 597 and 586. The first attack was in reprisal for the rebellion of Josiah's son Jehoiakim (609–598 BC) against Nebuchadnezzar; however, by the time his forces captured Jerusalem, Jehoiakim was dead and had been succeeded by his 18-year-old son Jehoiachin. Nebuchadnezzar deposed the young king and deported him to Babylon, along with the elite of the nation: government officials, army officers, and craftsmen. As Jehoiachin's replacement Nebuchadnezzar appointed his uncle Mattaniah, a younger brother of Jehoiakim and of the earlier, short-lived King Jehoahaz (609 BC). Mattaniah was thus the third son of Josiah to occupy the throne of Judah. The Babylonian king named Mattaniah, Zedekiah, which means, "the Lord is my righteousness," paralleling the way in which the Egyptian pharaoh nominated Eliakim ("God raises") as king of Judah and changed his name to Jehoiakim ("The Lord raises") 12 years earlier (2 Kgs 23:34). In each case a nationalistic-sounding name was bestowed upon the nominee by a foreign overlord. The magnificent trappings of kingship were thus granted, but in actuality the kings had little independent authority; their status was reduced to that of vassal king.

Zedekiah found himself in a difficult position as Judah's king. Many evidently still regarded Jehoiachin as the real king (cf. Jer 28:1–4). Certainly the Judeans deported to Babylonia dated events by reference to Jehoiachin (2 Kgs 25:27; Ez 1:2). Though the Babylonians exacted from Zedekiah an oath of loyalty (2 Chr 36:13; Ez 17:13–18), evidence suggests that they too viewed Zedekiah's predecessor as the legitimate king and Zedekiah as regent. They may have been holding him in reserve for possible restoration to power, should events require it.

Judah was filled with a false optimism which could hardly have helped the new king. It was confidently expected that the deportation of the leading citizens would be only temporary; prophets were guaranteeing that Babylon's power would be broken within two years (Jer 28:2–4). They were opposed by a few prophets led by Jeremiah, whose message found little support.

Pressure both from within the nation and from without was put on Zedekiah to change his political allegiance. In the fourth year of his reign (593 BC), the neighboring states of Ammon, Moab, Tyre, and Sidon formed a coalition to counter Babylonian hegemony and fight for independence. Envoys were sent to Zedekiah (Jer 27:1–4). However, Jeremiah advised the king not to get involved. In the same year according to Jeremiah 51:59, Zedekiah visited Babylon. He may have been summoned to affirm his loyalty and to explain his role in the political situation. The planned rebellion did not in fact occur, perhaps because aid from Egypt failed to materialize while Neco—earlier defeated by Nebuchadnezzar—was alive. However, his successor, Psammetichus II (594–589 BC), was more ambitious and hoped to gain a footing in Palestine.

Within the Judean court a strong pro-Egyptian party existed. This party saw Egypt as an ally for breaking away from their eastern master, just like the advisers of King Hezekiah a century before (cf. Is 31:1–3; 36:6). Zede-

kiah, finding it difficult to resist this political pressure, eventually transferred his allegiance to Egypt.

Hophra (589–570 BC), Psammetichus' heir to the Egyptian throne, organized a joint rebellion in the west against Babylon. According to Ezekiel 21:18–32 and 25:12–17, Judah and Ammon supported him, while Edom and Philistia shrewdly abstained. Zedekiah, prevailed upon to break with Babylon, was rebuked by the prophet Ezekiel (17:13–18) for breaking his oath to Nebuchadnezzar (cf. 2 Chr 36:13) and rebelling against him by sending envoys to Egypt to negotiate for military support.

In the face of this western uprising engineered by his Egyptian rival, Nebuchadnezzar was forced to march westward. Setting up headquarters at Riblah in northern Syria, he decided to make Jerusalem his prime target (Ez 21:18–23). The ensuing siege of Jerusalem was temporarily lifted due to an Egyptian attack, but afterward was resumed inexorably until the city fell. Zedekiah, fleeing eastward with his troops, was caught near Jericho and taken north to Nebuchadnezzar at Riblah. There he was put on trial for breaking his promises of vassalage. By way of punishment his sons were killed before his eyes. This tragic sight was the last he ever saw, since his eyes were then put out. He was taken in chains to Babylon, where he eventually died in prison (2 Kgs 25:5–7; Jer 39:7; 52:8–11; cf. Ez 12:13).

Zedekiah and Jeremiah were natural allies in their common political support of Babylon. However, with the Babylonians' laying siege to Jerusalem, King Zedekiah sent a two-man delegation to the prophet, asking for a divine message and hoping that God would intervene in a decisive way, as he had done in the past with his people (Jer 21:1–7; cf. Is 36,37). Unfortunately Jeremiah had to disappoint the

The Old City of Jerusalem, besieged and captured by Nebuchadnezzar during the reign of Zedekiah.

king. In God's name he proclaimed the coming total victory of Nebuchadnezzar as the manifestation of God's wrath against his sinful people.

In Jeremiah 34:1–7, Jeremiah offers Zedekiah seemingly cold comfort: his life would be spared, and he would enjoy an eventual peaceful death and an honorable royal burial. Woven into this assurance was the warning that his deportation to Babylon was inevitable. Because of the mixed nature of the message and the more natural conclusion that the royal funeral would take place in Jerusalem rather than in Babylon, a number of scholars have formed different interpretations. They conclude that verses 4,5 offer a happy alternative to the grim pronouncement of verses 2,3, on the condition that Zedekiah is obedient to God's word (see v 4), that is, by surrendering instead of continuing the struggle (cf. 38:17,18).

Later, the king sent another delegation to the prophet, this time asking him to intercede with God on the nation's behalf (Jer 37:3). At this time the military situation had improved temporarily as the Babylonian forces had withdrawn from the walls (v 5). The king's request was an indirect way of securing a favorable outcome with God's help, but unfortunately Jeremiah could lend no support to the optimism of the moment. He could only repeat the worst, that eventually the enemy would capture the city, after defeating the Egyptian expeditionary force.

Shortly afterward Jeremiah was arrested and beaten for supposedly deserting to the Babylonians. Zedekiah, sending for him in secret, again asked for a message from God (Jer 37:17). Jeremiah had to repeat his message of doom, but he took the opportunity to appeal his imprisonment to the king, requesting a transfer to royal custody to escape harsh and potentially fatal treatment at the hands of his political opponents. Zedekiah evidently felt himself powerless to order his release, but he did have him moved within royal jurisdiction. He also ensured for him a minimum daily bread allowance as long as the bread supply lasted in the beleaguered city (v 21).

Jeremiah 32:3–5 discloses that the underlying reason for Zedekiah's imprisonment of Jeremiah was the prophet's politically defeatist stand. The passage also summarizes the tenor of Jeremiah's prophetic messages at this time, including the divine forecast that Zedekiah would fall into Nebuchadnezzar's hands and be taken to Babylon "until I visit him," says the Lord" (v 5). The verse could be interpreted in a favorable sense in terms of God's intervention on Zedekiah's behalf (cf. the comments on 34:1–7 above). On the other hand it

was likely intended to have an ominous ring—visiting him with the ultimate punishment, death (cf. Nm 16:29).

Further information is given in Jeremiah 38 about Jeremiah's imprisonment and Zedekiah's secret interviews with the prophet. Scholars are uncertain whether the chapter is intended to follow the previous one in time or whether it is meant to supplement the same events. Jeremiah 38:5,24–26 reveals the king's weakness and nervous timidity before the officers of his administration. At the same time it is evident that Zedekiah held Jeremiah in deep respect and perhaps would have adopted the course to which the prophet directed him in God's name—had not political pressure barred the way. It was against his better judgment that the king regretfully refused to comply with Jeremiah's advice. From within the confines of a weak, indecisive personality and overbearing circumstances Zedekiah at least did his best to save God's servant from persecution and ill treatment. It is perhaps inevitable that posterity condemns him generally as a religious renegade and a coward. At least according to the standard of Matthew 25:35–40, he deserves a more sympathetic assessment.

Jeremiah 23:5,6 (cf. 33:15,16) contains a prophecy concerning the ideal king or Messiah of the Davidic line in whose reign all the old royal promises would come true. The kingly title "The Lord Our Righteousness" appears to be linked with the name "Zedekiah" ("The Lord is my righteousness/vindication"). Perhaps some invested Zedekiah with messianic expectations and the prophet was concerned to deny them. Certainly a contrast seems to be intended between Zedekiah's disastrous reign and that of the promised king who would truly live up to Zedekiah's own name.

See ISRAEL, HISTORY OF; CHRONOLOGY, OLD TESTAMENT.

2. Chenaanah's son and one of the prophets who spoke falsely to kings Ahab of Israel and Jehoshaphat of Judah, telling them that the Lord would give Ahab victory over the Syrians at Ramoth-gilead (1 Kgs 22:11). After hearing Micaiah's contrary prediction that Ahab would in fact be killed in the battle, Zedekiah, in anger, struck Micaiah (22:24).

3. Jeconiah's son and a descendant of David through Solomon's line (1 Chr 3:16).

4. Leading official who set his seal on Ezra's covenant during the postexilic era (Neh 10:1, KJV Zidkijah).

5. Maaseiah's son, who, according to Jeremiah, King Nebuchadnezzar of Babylon would kill by roasting in fire for his adultery and lying words (Jer 29:21–23).

6. Hananiah's son and a prince in Judah during King Jehoiakim's reign (Jer 36:12).

LESLIE C. ALLEN

Zeeb. One of two Midianite princes executed by Gideon's army (Jgs 7:25).

See OREB.

Zela, Zelah. City of Benjamin's tribe where the bones of Saul and Jonathan were buried (Jos 18:28; 2 Sm 21:14; KJV Zelah). Zela was probably the native town of Saul's father, Kish, and may well have been Saul's home before he was anointed king. Its site is unknown.

Zelek. Ammonite warrior among David's mighty men (2 Sm 23:37; 1 Chr 11:39).

Zelophehad. Hepher's son from Manasseh's tribe. He fathered five daughters but no sons (Nm 26:33). Because Zelophehad had no sons, his daughters petitioned Moses to give them their father's inheritance (27:1). Moses' subsequent ruling provided that daughters should receive the inheritance in such cases, providing that they marry within their tribe so that the tribal allotments would remain stable (27:7; 36:2; Jos 17:3).

Zelotes. KJV spelling of "Zealot," the surname of Simon, one of the twelve, in Luke 6:15 and Acts 1:13.

See SIMON #5.

Zelzah. Place near Rachel's tomb where Saul met the two men in fulfillment of Samuel's prophecy concerning the events which would confirm Saul's anointing (1 Sm 10:2). Rachel's tomb is traditionally located at the northern border of Benjamin, but no precise identification of Zelzah has been made. Some have argued that Zelzah and Zela are the same place, but this is unlikely.

Zemaraim. 1. Town near the northern border of the territory of Benjamin (Jos 18:22). The most likely location is Ras ez-Zeimara, about five miles northeast of Bethel in the hill country between et-Taiyibeh and Rammun.

2. Mountain in the hill country of Ephraim (2 Chr 13:4) and the scene of Abijah's speech of rebuke against Jeroboam and the Israelites.

Zemarite. One of the families of the Canaanites in the ethnological lists of Genesis 10 (v 18) and 1 Chronicles 1 (v 16). The Zemarites were a Hamitic tribe mentioned in connection with the Arvadites and the Hamathites. While their location has not been identified with certainty, their proximity to Ruad and Hamath suggests that they were located near the Mediterranean in the vicinity of Tripoli.

Zemer. Town from which skilled men emigrated to Tyre to serve as the pilots of the Tyrian ships (Ez 27:8). The Hebrew text and the KJV read "your wise men O Tyre" instead of "skilled men of Zemer." The RSV is perhaps influenced by the mention of "Zemer" with the Arvadites as in Genesis 10:18. The original reading is uncertain.

Zemirah, Zemira. Becher's firstborn son, from Benjamin's tribe (1 Chr 7:8, KJV Zemira).

Zenan. One of the cities of the Shephelah inherited by Judah (Jos 15:37); perhaps the same place as Zaanan, which is mentioned in the same connection by Micah (Mi 1:11). Its precise location is unknown.

See ZAANAN.

Zenas. Lawyer whom Paul requested Titus to send to him at Nicopolis (Ti 3:13). Zenas was probably a Jewish lawyer schooled in the Mosaic law prior to his conversion.

Zephaniah (Person). 1. Priest during the reign of Zedekiah who was executed at Riblah by the king of Babylon (2 Kgs 25:18; Jer 52:24). He was the second priest under Seraiah the chief priest and served as Zedekiah's envoy to Jeremiah during the period prior to the fall of Jerusalem (Jer 21:1; 29:25,29; 37:3).

2. Ancestor of Heman who was among the Kohathite Levites whom David placed in charge of the service of song in the house of the Lord (1 Chr 6:36). Zephaniah is listed as the father of Azariah and the son of Tahath.

3. Author of the Book of Zephaniah (Zep 1:1). Though little is known about Zephaniah, it is likely that his ancestor Hezekiah is the same as the king by that name.

See ZEPHANIAH, BOOK OF.

4. Father of Josiah in whose house Joshua was crowned as high priest (Zec 6:10,14).

Zephaniah, Book of. One of the books of the minor prophets in the OT.

Author. According to the editorial heading (1:1), Zephaniah prophesied during the reign of Josiah (640–609 BC). His family tree is given in an unusually full form. Some exegetes have suggested that his great-great-grandfather was King Hezekiah (715–686 BC). But remarkably there is no Jewish or Christian tradition to support the suggestion, which there probably would have been if it had been true. The last three names are probably supplied to make it clear that his father's name does not mean "Ethiopian," and so to establish that Zephaniah was a native Judean. His own name, meaning "he whom the Lord protects or hides," was not uncommon and was a testimony to the keeping power of God.

Date, Origin, and Destination. Zephaniah probably prophesied around 630 BC. The fall of Nineveh (612 BC) had not yet occurred (2:13–15). Josiah's reign falls into two periods, dividing at 622 BC. In that year, while the temple was being cleared of pagan articles, a scroll of the Law was found, which gave momentum to Josiah's religious reforms (2 Kgs 22). The obviously unreformed state of affairs described by Zephaniah (1:4–6,8–12; 3:1–4) points to a date before 622, at least for his denunciations. The prophet addresses Judah, the southern kingdom, and in particular the civil and religious authorities in Jerusalem. He most probably prophesied during the minority of Josiah, who came to the throne at the age of eight.

Scholars have been concerned to investigate the authenticity of the prophetic material throughout the book. Hesitation has been expressed mainly over the oracles against foreign nations in chapter 2 (apart from 2:13,14) and over the promises of 3:9–20. There is nothing in the foreign material that is inappropriate for the historical period of Zephaniah, nor can overwhelming objections be leveled against 3:9–20. But it is possible that 3:14–20 was a prophetic supplement added to round off the final literary edition of the book in exilic or postexilic times. The negative parts of the book concerning the sin and punishment of Judah—now fulfilled—would serve as a serious warning against disobedience to God. Moreover the fulfillment of Zephaniah's prophetic threats would serve to enhance the positive side of the book, confirming the hope of completion in the experience of a fresh generation of God's people.

Background. Politically, the Assyrian Empire had spread westward and held Palestine in its grip. The long reign of Manasseh (696–642 BC) had been a period of total subservience to Assyria. Political subservience as an Assyrian vassal meant religious subservience to the gods of Assyria, especially worship of the heavenly bodies (2 Kgs 21:5). Zephaniah complained of this sin (1:5). When the door opened to one foreign religion, others naturally came in. Once the exclusiveness of the worship of the God of Israel was abandoned, Palestinian cults were openly accepted. Thus the Canaanite Baal was blatantly worshiped (2 Kgs 21:3), as Zephaniah attested (1:4). Zephaniah condemned the worshipers of Molech (1:5), who sacrificed children to the Ammonite god (1 Kgs 11:7; 2 Kgs 23:10). International imperialism meant a weakening of national culture, so that foreign customs were practiced, probably with religious overtones (1:8,9).

The reign of Josiah brought changes, marking a political and religious turning point. Assyria, preoccupied with troubles on the eastern and northern frontiers and unable to consolidate its acquisitions, became unable to reinforce its authority in the west. This weakness induced Josiah to launch a national liberation movement. He threw off the yoke of Assyria and expanded his sphere of influence northward into the territory of the old northern kingdom. From a religious standpoint he completely dissociated himself and his country from the religions that prevailed in Judah and recalled the nation to a pure and exclusive faith in the God of Israel. The Book of Zephaniah shows that there was at least one person who shared his ideals. His prophetic ministry undoubtedly paved the way for Josiah's subsequent reformation. He was a contemporary of Jeremiah, at least for the early part of that prophet's career (Jeremiah began prophesying in 627 BC).

Scholars have suggested that Zephaniah's prophesying was prompted in part by attacks of the Scythians. The Greek historian Herodotus tells how the barbaric Scythians overran western Asia and reached as far south as the Egyptian frontier at about the time that Zephaniah prophesied. There is now much less inclination to believe Herodotus' tale and relate Zephaniah's prophetic ministry to it. There is no objective evidence for Scythian attacks on so large a scale as Herodotus claimed. Probably Zephaniah spoke simply out of a theological necessity, as he himself claimed (e.g., 1:17). From his inspired standpoint, he foresaw that a clash involving divine intervention and human downfall was unavoidable.

Purpose and Teaching. As Zephaniah prophesied in God's name, he denounced the religious sins of Judah and the corruption rampant among both civil and religious authorities. He foretold the downfall of the nation which actually occurred in 586 BC. The moral and religious landslide could only culminate in a political avalanche of destruction that would engulf the nation. This avalanche is called by Zephaniah "the Day of the Lord." It was not a new term, and the prophet knew that it would arouse terror in the hearts of his hearers. Amos used it, and even in his time it was well established (Am 5:18–20). Isaiah was the first to use the expression in the southern kingdom (Is 2:6–22, esp v 12). In this, as in a number of respects, Zephaniah was a latter-day Isaiah called by God to reapply truths earlier prophesied by Isaiah to a later generation.

The theme of the Day of the Lord refers to a time when the Lord would decisively intervene in the world to establish his sovereignty. Hostile elements would be swept aside. The enemies of God, sinners against his moral will, would be exposed and punished. It was associated with judgment upon those who did not acknowledge God's sovereignty—especially Gentiles, but also sinful Israel. The emphasis on the suffering of God's people was intended to correct the popular assumption that other nations would be the sole target of divine judgment.

The "day" also would vindicate those who were loyal to God. It guaranteed the rehabilitation of his oppressed supporters. Zephaniah develops this two-sided phenomenon in order to communicate the truth of God to his own generation. It is "a day of the wrath of God" (1:15,18; 2:2), when his reaction to human sin would be demonstrated. Its target was not only other nations, but Judah as well, both Jerusalem the capital (1:10–13) and the other cities of Judah (v 16).

The particular sins against which Zephaniah inveighed were first of all religious. Behind the prophet's attacks on the infiltration of foreign religions into Judah lies the first commandment, "You shall have no other gods before me" (Ex 20:3). The worship of Israel's God was exclusive. Zephaniah called Israel back to "the godly paths" they "used to walk in" (Jer 6:16). The prophet also attacked the authorities of Jerusalem for their abuse of positions of responsibility (1:8,9). Even religious leaders gave no moral leadership (3:3,4).

A fundamental sin which Zephaniah exposed was pride (3:11), a spirit of self-centeredness and self-sufficiency. Judah had know peace and calm—at a price—for 70 years. Other states around Judah had experienced military attack and destruction (v 6), but not Judah. The people of Judah had no sense of God's providential involvement in their lives (1:12). Other religions seemed to have better things to offer, and the worship of Israel's God appeared to have little contemporary relevance (1:6; 3:2). God would be forced to reestablish his authority and his position of sovereignty.

Zephaniah's God was essentially sovereign. The whole world lay in the power of the God of Israel. Past military defeat was attributed to his destroying agency (3:6). He would soon use military forces against Judah (1:13). The overall future of the nations lay in his hands; proud Assyria would be destroyed (2:13–15) along with the Philistines, Ammonites, and Moabites (2:4–10). In this respect Zephaniah had much to say that would delight a nationalistic Judean audience. But he preserved a theological balance: the time had come for judgment, and it must begin among God's own people (1 Pt 4:17). Another evidence of balance was the positive role assigned to nations other than Judah. Here he echoed the tradition preserved in Isaiah 2:2–4 of a world devoted to the worship of the God of Israel.

Zephaniah also had a positive message for the people of Judah. For the prophets, the message of salvation did not cancel the message of doom. Judgment would come first, then salvation would follow. But the period of tribulation could not be avoided. The prophet's grim descriptions of "the day of wrath" are interpreted as dire warnings and implicit pleas to the people of Judah to abandon their complacent, sinful ways. Zephaniah did not contemplate complete destruction, as 2:3 and 3:11–13 make abundantly clear. The bridge that Zephaniah erected between judgment and salvation was the idea of a remnant, another concept from Isaiah (3:12,13; cf. 2:3). As might be expected from Zephaniah's denunciation of pride and self-sufficiency, he valued humility before a sovereign God (2:3; 3:12). Humility in Zephaniah corresponds to faith in Isaiah. Another necessary qualification for inclusion in the remnant was practical righteousness, obedience to God who had revealed his moral will in his covenant with Israel (2:3).

Clearly Zephaniah's role under God was to reapply earlier truths sadly forgotten by his own generation. Zephaniah was able to foresee God's judgment of Judah and the world. But he also proclaimed permanent truths concerning the nature of God and his providential relationship to the world and concerning the responsibilities of the people of God.

The importance of the Book of Zephaniah for the NT lies in the phraseology about the Day of the Lord. There are a number of allusions to this aspect of his message (Mt 13:41 [Zep 1:3]; Rv 6:17 [1:14]; 14:5 [3:13]; 16:1 [3:8]). These echoes stress Zephaniah's importance beyond his own time. He contributed to the total biblical picture of a God who intervenes in human history and will establish his kingdom. Zephaniah's descriptions are a pattern for events that will mark the end of history.

Content. The heading (1:1) introduces Zephaniah, gives the historical setting, and above all stresses his meditation on the divine word.

The first major part of the book is 1:2–2:3. It subdivides into four units, verses 2–7, 8–13, 14–18; 2:1–3. Verses 2–7 include Judah in a forecast of universal destruction (see RSV for vv 2,3 and cf. 3:8). Zephaniah used traditional material to stress that God's people were by no means exempt, as they often chose to believe (cf. Am 5:18–20). The prophet undergirds his startling revelation with reasoned statements regarding the religious deviations practiced in Jerusalem. The image of sacrifice is used ironically, portraying Judah as the victim (v 7).

The national administration and members

of the royal family were guilty (1:8–13). Superstitions were punctiliously observed (v 9), yet basic divine commands against stealing and fraudulent gain went unheeded. Zephaniah responds in faith to the enemy attack on the north side of Jerusalem, using it as an illustration of God's punishment of dishonest traders (cf. Am 8:5,6; Mi 6:10,11). God would be behind the search parties sent through Jerusalem to root out people from their hiding places. Those hitherto indifferent to divine providence (cf. Jer 10:5) would find God intervening in their lives and would suffer "futility" curses (cf. Am 5:11).

There follows a shocking and terrifying description of the grimness of the coming "Day" (1:14–18). The prophet stirs up a complacent people who do not want to hear God's message. He frightens them into reality with a monotonous drumbeat of doom and destruction. Judah would be the demoralized target of God's wrath. Their wealth had secured luxurious imports (v 8), but could not prevent divine judgment (cf. Lk 12:15–21).

The prophet appropriately completes his sermon with an appeal for repentance (2:1–3). Having emotionally stirred his audience from their apathy, he is able to bring the good news that all was not yet lost. A penitential assembly at the temple (cf. Jl 1:14; 2:12–17) and the intercession of the spiritually minded and obedient among God's people might stem the tide of destruction (cf. Gn 18:23–26). Zephaniah cautiously used the prophetic "perhaps" (Jl 2:14; Am 5:15; Jon 3:9; cf. Acts 8:22; 2 Tm 2:25) that highlights the sovereignty of God and discourages human presumption.

God's punishment of foreign nations is described in the second main part of the book (2:4–15). Representative states are named to the west, east, south, and north of Judah. In the context of the previous material, it amplifies the universal nature of the Day of the Lord. Like the first part, it subdivides into four passages, 2:4–7, 8–11, 12, and 13–15.

The subject of the first passage is the Philistines. In the case of the cities of Gaza and Ekron, there is a play on words typical of Hebrew prophecy. Both names contain doom within their very sound. The Philistines are attacked as trespassers, illegal immigrants from Crete into the Promised Land intended for God's own people.

Moab and Ammon come under attack for their overbearing attitude and their annexation of Judean territory (2:8–11). God would come to the aid of his covenant people as their champion. He acts, not only because he is Israel's God, but also because he is God of all nations and by this means expresses his lordship (cf. Is 45:23).

Zephaniah prophesied the destruction of Assyria. This relief shows an Assyrian priest with an eagle's wings.

Zephaniah 2:12 ostensibly concerns the Ethiopians. Actually Egypt is in view. For a long period (about 716–663 BC) Egypt had been ruled by an Ethiopian dynasty of pharaohs (cf. 2 Kgs 18:21 with 19:9). Egypt entered into an alliance with failing Assyria to lend support against the growing power of the Medes and Babylonians. Therefore verse 12 is closely related to the next ones about Assyria.

More space is devoted to Assyria as Judah's enemy (12:13–15). Judah had suffered long at the hands of Assyria. As in Isaiah 10:13,14, Assyria is portrayed as a model of self-achievement and deification of human pride (cf. Is 45:9,22).

The first two main sections have spelled

out at length a message of judgment for both Judah and the surrounding nations. This two-fold message is now echoed in a much shorter form in the third main section (3:1–8). Zephaniah criticizes Jerusalem in its combined role of political capital and religious center. The responsibility of being God's representatives rested too lightly on the shoulders of government and temple officials. Civil leaders abused their powers by demanding bribes and even killing their political opponents (cf. 1 Kgs 21). Instead of being the shepherds of the people (cf. Ez 34), they were beasts of prey (cf. Ez 22:25,27). The prophets misused their gifts in their own selfish interests (cf. Mi 3:5; Jer 23:4; Ez 22:28), while the priests broke the strict regulations of the temple (cf. Ez 22:26). What made it more shocking was that they had before them the permanent model of the Lord's own high standards, set forth in the daily temple services that revealed and glorified him. Moreover the lessons of history went unheeded; they had not learned caution and reverence. The conclusion is clear: Judah could not escape punishment in the coming Day of the Lord, but would suffer with other nations.

The outworking of God's will for both Judah and the nations is in view in the final main section (3:9–20), but this time from a quite different aspect. Punishment was not God's last word for his own people or even for the nations at large. Ultimately God's will is not destruction but salvation (2 Pt 3:9). The tentative "perhaps" of 2:3 is now replaced by a positive affirmation concerning the period after the judgment. The section falls into three parts, 3:9–10, 11–13, and 14–20. Verses 9–10 deal with the conversion of the nations. This remarkable passage looks forward with divinely guaranteed certainty to the willing submission of Gentiles to the God of Israel. Their turning to God would not be based on human initiative, but would originate in the providential activity of God. Lips defiled by worship of pagan gods would be purified and devoted solely to the adoration of the God of Israel ("speech" in v 9 is lit "lip"; cf. Is 6:5–7). People from remote parts of the earth, here illustrated as the remote south beyond the Ethiopian Nile, would come as suppliants, as if they were scattered Jews returning home.

God's own people would be marked by a change of heart (3:11–13). By now they would have been purged of the proud who put themselves before God in the sphere of politics and religion. They would be a purified remnant characterized by humble trust in God (cf. Is 2:11,19). Theirs would be the blessings of Paradise (cf. Mi 4:4). The result would be a high level of community living based on mutual trust.

The last passage speaks of coming joys (3:14–20). The prophet projects himself into the future (cf. v 16), to the time when God's judgment was over and the ensuing time of salvation had dawned (cf. Is 40:2). God's people would rejoice in the presence of their Lord working out his sovereign will (cf. Ez 48:35). Fear and demoralization (cf. 1:17) would be cancelled by God's powerful presence and radiant joy. His joy would infectiously communicate itself to them so that they too will rejoice (vv 14,17). Moreover his joy would be a reaction to the transformation which he was lovingly working in the lives of his people (v 17; cf. RSV "he will renew you in his love"). A necessary part of this transformation would feature the vindication of God's suffering people. They would be brought to a position of honor, as the visible representatives of the God of glory. Ultimately God's power would be revealed through a people of power.

LESLIE C. ALLEN

See ISRAEL, HISTORY OF; JEREMIAH, BOOK OF; JEREMIAH (PERSON) #1; JOSIAH #1.

Bibliography. J.H. Eaton, *Obadiah, Nahum, Habakkuk, Zephaniah;* G.A. Smith, *The Book of the Twelve Prophets;* C. von Orelli, *The Twelve Minor Prophets;* J.D.W. Watts, *The Books of Joel, Obadiah, Jonah, Nahum, Habakkuk, and Zephaniah.*

Zephath. Canaanite city conquered by Judah and Simeon and subsequently renamed Hormah (Jgs 1:17). Zephath (Hormah) was the site of Israel's first abortive attempt to enter Canaan when they violated Moses' command and were, as a result, defeated by the Amalekites and the Canaanites (Nm 14:45).

See HORMAH.

Zephathah. Valley where Asa fought against and defeated Zerah the Ethiopian (2 Chr 14:10). The Valley of Zephathah is located in the vicinity of Mareshah and thus in southwestern Judah.

Zephi, Zepho. Eliphaz's son and a descendant of Esau (1 Chr 1:36); alternately spelled Zepho in Genesis 36:11,15.

Zephon (Zephonite). Firstborn son of Gad and the father of the Zephonite family (Nm 26:15); alternately called Ziphion in Genesis 46:16.

Zer. One of the fortified cities of Naphtali's tribe (Jos 19:35). From the surrounding names in the list it may be inferred that it was located on the southwest side of the Sea of Galilee.

Zerah. 1. One of the chiefs of the Edomites (Gn 36:17; 1 Chr 1:37), listed as the son of Reuel, Esau's son by his wife Basemath, and likely the ancestor of Jobab, who later assumed the position of king of the Edomites (Gn 36:13,33).

2. One of the twin sons of Judah by his daughter-in-law Tamar (Gn 38:30; 46:12, KJV Zarah; Mt 1:3, KJV Zara). Although Zerah thrust out his hand first, he retracted it, thus allowing his brother Perez to be born first. The descendants of Zerah (Zerahites) became one of the most influential clans of Judah (Nm 26:20, KJV Zarhites; Jos 7:1,18; 22:20; 1 Chr 2:4,6; 9:6). Because Ethan and Heman are listed as sons of Zerah in 1 Chronicles 2:6, the Ezrahites mentioned in 1 Kings 4:31 and the titles to Psalms 88 and 89 are also considered to be Zerahites. However, Ethan and Heman are listed as Levites in 1 Chronicles 15:17, thus making it more likely that the Ezrahites were a Levite clan.

3. One of the sons of Simeon from whom the Zerahite clan descended (Nm 26:13, KJV Zarhites; 1 Chr 4:24); alternately called Zohar in Genesis 46:10 and Exodus 6:15. Because Zerahite clans descended from both the tribes of Judah and Simeon, it is sometimes difficult to identify Zerahites with one tribe or the other (1 Chr 27:11,13).

4. One of the sons of Iddo, from the Gershonite branch of Levi's tribe (1 Chr 6:21).

5. One of the ancestors of Asaph from Levi's tribe, listed as the son of Adaiah and the father of Ethni (1 Chr 6:41). Several believe him to be the same individual as #4 above.

6. Commander of the Ethiopians (Cushites) who fought against Asa, king of Judah (2 Chr 14:9). It is difficult to identify this individual or the historical event with any certainty. The most common identification has been with Usarkon II of Egypt. The account of the battle agrees with the chronology of Usarkon's reign in Egypt, as do the number and nationalities of the troops involved in the conflict. Others have objected to the identification on etymological grounds, however, preferring to identify Zerah with some previously unknown military commander, either from Egypt or north Arabia.

Zerahiah. 1. Uzzi's son and ancestor of Ezra from the priestly line of Eleazar (1 Chr 6:6,51; Ezr 7:4).

2. Head of a family that returned to Jerusalem with Zerubbabel after the Babylonian exile (Ezr 8:4).

Zerahite. 1. Descendant of Zerah, Simeon's son (Nm 26:13).
See ZERAH #3.

2. Descendant of Zerah, Judah's son by Tamar (v 20).
See ZERAH #2.

Zered. Valley and brook by which the Israelites encamped, listed between Iye-abarim and a stopping place near the Arnon River to the north (Nm 21:12, KJV Zared). Though its exact location remains in question, Zered is probably identifiable with the modern Wadi el-Hesa, a stream bed that formed a natural border between the ancient countries of Moab and Edom, and, following a northwestward course, emptied into the southern end of the Dead Sea. The crossing of the Brook Zered by the Israelites marked 38 years since Israel rebelled against God at Kadesh-barnea (Dt 2:13,14).

Zereda. KJV spelling of Zeredah in 1 Kings 11:26.
See ZEREDAH #1.

Zeredah. 1. Birthplace (or hometown) of Jeroboam, Israel's first king during the period of the divided kingdom (1 Kgs 11:26, KJV Zereda).

2. Town near the site where Huram-abi (Hiram) cast the bronze vessels for the temple (2 Chr 4:17, KJV Zeredathah; NIV Zarethan); alternately called Zarethan in the parallel passage in 1 Kings 7:46.
See ZARETHAN, ZARETAN.

Zeredathah. KJV rendering of Zeredah in 2 Chronicles 4:17.
See ZEREDAH #2.

Zererah, Zererath. City in northern Ephraim mentioned in connection with Gideon's defeat of the Midianites (Jgs 7:22, KJV Zererath; RSV mg Zeredah); perhaps also identifiable with Zarethan.
See ZARETHAN, ZARETAN; ZEREDAH #2.

Zeresh. Wife of Haman the Agagite who advised him to build the gallows on which Mordecai was to be hung (Est 5:10,14). Upon learning that Mordecai was Jewish, she later warned that Haman would certainly fall before him (6:13).

Zereth. Asshur's son by his wife Helah from Judah's tribe (1 Chr 4:7).

Zereth-shahar. One of the cities inherited by Reuben's tribe (Jos 13:19, KJV Zareth-shahar), described as being on "the hill of the valley." Its precise location is unknown.

Zeri. One of the sons of Jeduthun who prophesied with the lyre in thanksgiving to the Lord (1 Chr 25:3). He is probably the same person as Izri (v 11).

Zeror. Benjamite, Becorath's son, the father of Abiel, and an ancestor of King Saul (1 Sm 9:1).

Zeruah. Mother of Israel's king Jeroboam I (1 Kgs 11:26).

Zerubbabel. Babylonian-born Jew who returned to Palestine in 538 BC to serve as governor of Jerusalem under Persian suzerainty. The name presumably means "seed [offspring] of Babylon," referring to someone born in Babylon.

The exact identity of Zerubbabel's biological father is uncertain. All biblical references except one mention Shealtiel as his father (Ezr 3:2,8; 5:2; Neh 12:1; Hg 1:1,12,14; 2:2,23; KJV Zorobabel in Mt 1:12,13; Lk 3:27). This would make Zerubbabel the grandson of the Davidic king Jehoiachin. However, 1 Chronicles 3:19 identifies Pedaiah, the brother of Shealtiel, as Zerubbabel's father.

Two solutions have been proposed. Many scholars have assumed that Shealtiel died before fathering an heir. His brother, Pedaiah, would then have fathered Zerubbabel by Shealtiel's widow. Hence, Zerubbabel would have retained the name of Shealtiel rather than Pedaiah in accordance with the law of levirate marriage (Dt 25:5–10). This solution is weakened by its lack of textual support; similarly, the Chronicler would hardly have failed to state such an important piece of information if he had been desirous of "correcting" an error pertaining to Zerubbabel's parentage.

A simpler solution is obtained by reading the Septuagint text of 1 Chronicles 3:19, which lists Salathiel (Shealtiel) as the father of Zerubbabel. In this way, the single reference to 1 Chronicles may be harmonized with the other verses cited above.

In either case, whether Shealtiel or Pedaiah was Zerubbabel's biological father, it is clear that Zerubbabel was of Davidic lineage and was viewed by members of the Isrealite community as a viable candidate for leading them back to a position of power.

Following the edict of Cyrus in 538 BC, Jews were permitted to return to Palestine and reclaim their former homeland. Zerubbabel was appointed governor, and probably by the decade of 529–520 had started work on the reconstruction of the Jerusalem temple. However, because of several discouraging events, little was accomplished until the year 520 BC.

The writings of Haggai and Zechariah reveal much information about Zerubbabel's standing in the community. These two prophets evidently viewed Jeshua and Zerubbabel as the two men chosen by God for the task. Accordingly, in many of their oracles, support for one or both men is openly stated (e.g., Hg 2:21–23; Zec 3:8; 4:6,7; 6:12). Though many scholars have overstated the conjecture that Haggai and Zechariah urged Zerubbabel to dream of a new era of Judean independence with himself, a descendant of David, on the throne, still a strong messianic element is undeniably present in the prophetic view of Jeshua and Zerubbabel's work.

This is most clearly seen in the vision of Zechariah (4:11–14). In the vision, two olive branches, one on either side of the lampstand, are identified as "the two anointed who stand by the Lord of the whole earth" (v 14). As the context clearly shows, none other than Joshua (Jeshua; named in 3:1–9) and Zerubbabel (named in 4:6–10) are meant.

Because of his association with the rebuilding of the temple in Jerusalem, Zerubbabel has been accorded a place of great honor in Jewish tradition. In Ecclesiasticus 49:11 he is listed among the most renowned of Jewish heroes. In 1 Esdras 3:1–5:6 Zerubbabel participates in a public contest to determine the wisest young man in the empire; he of course emerges victorious, in much the same way as Daniel (Dn 1:1–21). According to the legend, it was the display of wisdom given by Zerubbabel that influenced Darius to furnish financial support for the rebuilding of the temple. Despite the fact that this apocryphal account is in conflict with the biblical record offered in Ezra 6, the story in 1 Esdras illustrates the esteem in which Zerubbabel was held by later Judaism.

Zeruiah. Nahash's daughter and the sister of Abigail (2 Sm 17:25). In 1 Chronicles 2:16, David, Jesse's son, is listed as her brother. In reconciling this difference of paternity, some suggest that after the death of Zeruiah's father, her mother married Jesse and subsequently bore David, her brother; or that with her mother's marriage to Jesse, Zeruiah became David's step-sister; others less feasibly maintain that the listing of Nahash in 2 Samuel 17:25 was the result of a copying error that later crept into the text from verse 27.

Zeruiah eventually bore three sons: Joab, Abishai, and Ashahel, all of whom were David's intimates during his reign (2 Sm 2:18; 3:39; 8:16; 18:2).

Zetham. One of Ladan's sons of the Gershonite branch of Levites (1 Chr 23:8; 26:22). In the latter reference he is listed as Jehieli's son, but the text is difficult to reconstruct at that point.

Zethan. Bilhan's son from Benjamin's tribe (1 Chr 7:10).

Zethar. One of King Ahasuerus' seven chamberlains, who was commanded to bring Queen Vashti before the king for public display of her beauty (Est 1:10).

Zeus. Chief god of the Greek pantheon (Roman Jupiter). Zeus was initially worshiped as part of an animistic cult, as the sky god with thunder as his principal manifestation. Well before the time of Homer, however, Zeus had become the preeminent personal god of the Greek residents of Thessaly, with Mt Olympus serving as the focal point of the cult. By NT times, Zeus was considered the Greek father god who possessed supreme powers. The quotation Paul used in Acts 17:28 from Cleanthes (and/or Aratus) was originally ascribed to Zeus ("in him we live and move and have our being").

Zeus is most significant in biblical writings as a result of Paul and Barnabas' encounter with the priest of Zeus at Lystra (Acts 14:8–18). Because Paul and Barnabas had healed a lame man, the residents of Lystra attempted to worship them, identifying Barnabas with Zeus and Paul with Hermes, the messenger of the gods (v 12). It was not unusual that this misidentification should take place, since the Greek gods were frequently represented as taking on human appearances and intervening directly in human affairs. Unlike the true God, Zeus and his consorts were often viewed as capriciously bestowing favor or disfavor. The attribution of "divinity" to Paul and Barnabas allowed them to identify the key differences between Greek and Christian theology (vv 15–18).

See GREECE, GREEKS.

Zia. One of the clan leaders of Dan's tribe dwelling in Bashan (1 Chr 5:13).

Ziba. Former servant of Saul whom David commissioned to find survivors of the house of Saul so that he might "show them kindness" (2 Sm 9:2–12). In the period following Saul's death, Ziba apparently had not only gained his freedom but had also become a successful landowner (v 10). This status was lost as a result of the discovery of Mephibosheth, Jonathan's crippled son. Ziba later became involved in a controversy with Mephibosheth concerning Mephibosheth's failure to accompany David when he fled during Absalom's rebellion (16:1–4; 19:17,24–29). Most commentators have blamed Ziba with duplicity and slander in the affair, but the text allows no certain conclusion as to who was guilty. On Mephibosheth's behalf, it is unlikely that he would have believed that he could inherit the throne as Ziba had claimed (16:3). Mephibosheth also seems to have been loyal to David (though it is possible that David brought him to Jerusalem to ensure that he would be under protective surveillance). In Ziba's defense, it is notable that David did believe without question that Mephibosheth might have had aspirations for the throne (v 4). Ziba also appears consistently as a loyal supporter of David in spite of the fact that David's decision had cost him his independent status (16:1; 19:17). Of course, Ziba's displeasure at his loss of independence might have motivated him to defame Mephibosheth. In any case, David appears to have had reason to doubt both versions of the truth. Rather than supporting either claim, he chose to divide the land between them (19:29).

Zibeon. Ancestor of Oholibamah, the Canaanite wife of Esau (Gn 36:2,14). He is listed

Remains of a Corinthian column and capital of the temple of Zeus (Jupiter) in Athens.

as a Hivite in Genesis 36:2, but is probably the same as Zibeon the son of Seir the Horite (vv 20,29; 1 Chr 1:38). Possibly "Hivite" designated his tribal affiliation, while "Horite" indicated the fact that he dwelt in caves. It is also possible that "Hivite" is a transmission error in Genesis 36:2. Zibeon is also mentioned as the father of Anah, who discovered important hot springs in the wilderness (Gn 36:24; 1 Chr 1:40).

Zibia. One of the seven sons borne to Shaharaim by his wife Hodesh (1 Chr 8:9).

Zibiah. Mother of King Jehoash of Judah, from the town of Beersheba (2 Kgs 12:1; 2 Chr 24:1).

Zichri. 1. Kohathite Levite, Izhar's son, and the brother of Korah (Ex 6:21).

2. One of Shimei's sons from Benjamin's tribe (1 Chr 8:19).

3. One of Shashak's sons from Benjamin's tribe (1 Chr 8:23).

4. One of Jehoram's sons from Benjamin's tribe (1 Chr 8:27).

5. Ancestor of Mattaniah. Mattaniah returned with Zerubbabel to Israel following the exile (1 Chr 9:15); Zichri is probably identifiable with Zabdi in Nehemiah 11:17.

6. Descendant of Eliezer, the son of Moses. His son, Shelomoth, was in charge of the treasuries of the dedicated gifts (1 Chr 26:25).

7. Father of Eliezer, the chief officer of the Reubenites during David's reign (1 Chr 27:16).

8. Father of Amasiah, a volunteer in charge of 200,000 men during Jehoshaphat's reign (2 Chr 17:16).

9. Father of Elishaphat, a participant in the conspiracy against Athaliah led by Jehoiada (2 Chr 23:1).

10. Mighty man of Ephraim who participated in Pekah's subjugation of Judah. Zichri killed Ahaz' son Ma-aseiah, Azrikam the commander of the palace, and Elkanah the king's deputy (2 Chr 28:7).

11. Father of Joel, overseer of the Benjamites who returned to Jerusalem following the exile (Neh 11:9).

12. Levite who served as a priest and the head of the clan of Abijah during the days of Joiakim the high priest (Neh 12:17).

Ziddim. Fortified city in the land assigned to Naphtali's tribe (Jos 19:35). The Talmud suggests that the site be equated with Caphar Hittaia (modern Hattim el-Qadim) about eight miles northwest of Tiberias, but this remains unconfirmed.

Zidkijah. KJV form of Zedekiah, a prince of the Jews, in Nehemiah 10:1.

See ZEDEKIAH #4.

Zidon, Zidonian. KJV forms of Sidon and Sidonian, a city and its inhabitants in Asher's territory.

See SIDON, SIDONIAN (PLACE).

Zif. KJV form of Ziv, the name of the Hebrew month corresponding to about mid-May to mid-June (1 Kgs 6:1,37).

See CALENDARS, ANCIENT AND MODERN.

Ziggurat. Term meaning "temple tower"; a ziggurat was similar in profile to the step pyramid of Egypt and was used for worship. They were frequent in the major cities of Mesopotamia. The Tower of Babel (Gn 11:1–9) is believed to be of this construction. It was widely believed that deities dwelt above, in high places. Therefore worship was more appropriate on hills or mountains. There are no hills in Mesopotamia, nor is there building stone. Consequently the inhabitants built with mud brick. The ziggurats of mud brick were constructed as substitutes for hills, where the worshiper or priest could get closer to the gods. Like the pyramids of Egypt, these temple towers were four square. Instead of having sloping sides, there was a succession of terraces, each smaller than the one below. Access to each level was by stairways or ramps. The shrine or altar was on top, where the priests would officiate at sacrifices, incantations, and prayers. The great seven-story ziggurat at Babylon measured nearly 300 square feet at the base and rose to about the same height. Visitors to Babylon today find no tower there, but there is an impressive ziggurat at nearby Kish.

Ziha. 1. Ancestor of a family of temple servants that returned to Jerusalem with Zerubbabel after the exile (Ezr 2:43; Neh 7:46).

2. Overseer of the temple servants living at Ophel during the postexilic era (Neh 11:21). If Ziha is simply a family name, then this person is likely the same as #1 above.

Ziklag. Philistine city ruled by David for 16 months before he moved to Hebron to become the king of Judah. Ziklag was deeded to David by Achish of Gath, presumably to ensure David's continued neutrality (1 Sm 27:6; 1 Chr 12:1). The location of Ziklag is difficult to determine despite its prominence in the early history of Israel. In the record of the land allotments following the conquest, Ziklag appears to be located in the extreme south of Judah (Jos 15:31). It is later described as part of the

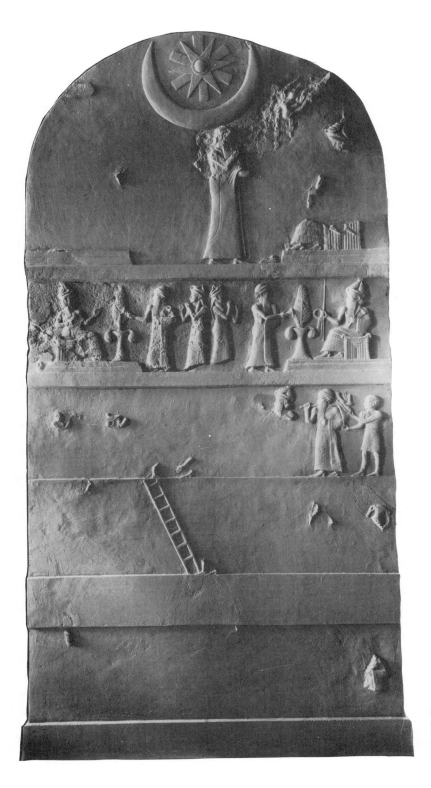

Stele that shows Ur-Nammu receiving directions for building a ziggurat; successive registers contain stages in the building process.

allotment within western Judah that was granted to Simeon (Jos 19:5; 1 Chr 4:30). Neither identification conclusively places Ziklag, however. It was most likely located somewhere on the frontier between Philistia and Judah, southeast of Gaza (possibly Tell el-Khuweilfeh). Ziklag is last mentioned as one of the cities that was inhabited by the settlers after the exile (Neh 11:28).

Zillah. Second wife of Lamech and mother of Tubal-cain and Naamah (Gn 4:19–23).

Zillethai. 1. One of Shimei's sons from Benjamin's tribe (1 Chr 8:20, KJV Zilthai).

2. One of the "chiefs of thousands" who deserted Saul and came to David at Ziklag (1 Chr 12:20, KJV Zilthai).

Zilpah. Mother of Jacob's sons Gad and Asher. Laban had given her to his daughter Leah as a handmaid (Gn 29:24; 46:18). Later, at Leah's insistence, she became Jacob's concubine for the purpose of bearing sons (30:9; 37:2).

Zilthai. KJV spelling of Zillethai in 1 Chronicles 8:20 and 12:20.

See ZILLETHAI #S 1 AND 2.

Zimmah. Gershonite Levite and ancestor of Joah (2 Chr 29:12).

Zimran. One of the sons of Abraham by Keturah (Gn 25:2; 1 Chr 1:32). Unlike the other sons of Abraham by Keturah, there is little evidence that Zimran is associated with a later tribal group. While efforts have been made to link Zimran with the Zimri of Jeremiah 25:25 or with the Zamereni, little consensus has been reached on these speculations.

Zimri (Person). 1. Clan chief of Simeon's tribe who was killed by Phinehas for consorting with a Midianite woman at Peor (Nm 25:14). Zimri's sin was magnified by the fact that he did it openly (v 6), that he was a leader within his tribe, and that the woman was the daughter of an important Midianite prince (v 18).

2. King of Israel for seven days (885 BC) following his assassination of Elah and the rest of the family of Baasha (1 Kgs 16:9–12). Zimri, commander of half of the chariot forces, failed to gain the support of the people, who supported Omri, the commander of the army. When Omri marched against Zimri at Tirzah, Zimri committed suicide by burning his palace down (1 Kgs 9:15–18). The cruelty of Zimri's coup is reflected in Jezebel's later taunt against Jehu, when she compared his duplicity to that of Zimri (2 Kgs 9:31).

3. One of the sons of Zerah, the son of Judah by Tamar (1 Chr 2:6); alternately called Zabdi in the parallel passage in Joshua 7:1,17.

See ZABDI #1.

4. Descendant of Saul from Benjamin's tribe, listed as the son of Jehoadda and the father of Moza (1 Chr 8:36). He is likely the same as Zimri the son of Jarah (9:42).

Zimri (Place). Place and peoples of the East, listed along with Elam and Media, against whom God's wrath would fall (Jer 25:25). Zimri's location and history are unknown; some identify its progenitor with Zimran, Abraham and Keturah's son (Gn 25:2).

Zin, Wilderness of. Area lying in the northern portion of the Sinai peninsula, while the wilderness of Sin lies in the southern portion. It is one of the four or five "wildernesses" of the Sinai peninsula, the others being the wilderness of Paran (Gn 21:21), the wilderness of Shur (Ex 15:22), the wilderness of Sin (Ex 16:1), and the wilderness of Sinai (Nm 9:1). These areas are not clearly defined, and there is probably some overlap.

The area identified as the wilderness of Zin is associated with the village of Zin (Nm 34:4). The wilderness was west of Edom, southwest of the Dead Sea, and south of Judah. Within this arid area were 4 copious springs or oases, including Kadesh-barnea. Most of the 38 years the Israelites spent in the Sinai desert were spent in this area. From the wilderness of Zin the spies were dispatched to spy out the land of Canaan (13:1–26; 32:8). Here also the rebels were sentenced to die because of their unbelief (14:22). Moses sinned by failing to give God the credit for bringing water out of the rock (20:1–13; 27:14) and Miriam, his sister, died and was buried here (20:1). This area was remembered as the "great and terrible wilderness" (Dt 1:19; 8:15).

See WILDERNESS WANDERINGS; SINAI, SINA.

Zina. Alternate form of Zizah, Shimei's son, in 1 Chronicles 23:10.

See ZIZAH.

Zinc. *See* MINERALS, METALS, AND PRECIOUS STONES.

Zion. Term also spelled Sion in KJV occuring over 150 times in the OT. It appears first as one of the names of the Jebusite fortress conquered by David. During subsequent biblical and postbiblical history, Zion was applied to other areas of Jerusalem and could be used as a designation of the entire city. Many theological motifs emphasize the city as the dwelling place of God.

Geographical Applications. *To the Jebusite Fortress.* The first occurrence of the word "Zion" is in the narrative of David's conquest of Jerusalem (2 Sm 5:6–10; 1 Chr 11:4–9). David captures the "fortress of Zion," which is thereafter known as the "city of David." The "fortress of Zion" may refer to the entire walled perimeter of the approximately 11-acre site on the southeastern ridge (the Ophel Ridge), or to a smaller fortified area within that site.

To the Temple Mount. Changes in the perimeter of the city by incorporating more territory within the walls extend the term Zion. When Solomon is building the temple and his palace and extends the walls north of the Ophel Ridge to encompass the threshing floor of Ornan the Jebusite (2 Sm 24:16,18; 1 Chr 21:15,18,28), the name Zion would be applied to these areas as well. The transfer of the ark "from the city of David which is Zion" (1 Kgs 8:1; 2 Chr 5:2) to the temple hill brought both an extension and a reduction of the territory embraced by the term "Zion"; the whole city could still be called Zion, but from this point on there would be a close identification between Zion and the temple hill. The temple precincts became the primary Zion; references to Zion in the poetic books and the preaching of the prophets are primarily to the temple area as the dwelling place of God.

To the Entire City. The word "Zion" can be used as a designation of the entire city or its population without any particular reference to the temple area. This use is clearest in poetic passages where Zion is the parallel term to Jerusalem (Pss 51:18; 76:2; 102:21; 135:21; 147:12; Is 2:3; 30:19; 33:20; 37:32; 40:9; 41:27; 62:1; Jer 26:18; 51:35; Am 1:2; Zep 3:14) or to the villages of Judah (Pss 69:35; 97:8; Is 40:9). The phrase "daughter of Zion" (2 Kgs 19:21; Ps 9:14; Is 1:8; Jer 4:31; Lam 1:6; Mi 1:13) is a common mistranslation of the Hebrew phrase which is better represented in English by the translation "Daughter Zion." The Hebrew use is a personification of Zion/Jerusalem as a young woman. The same poetic personification is also found in reference to Tarshish and Sidon (Is 23:10,12), Tyre (Ps 45:12), Babylon (Jer 50:42; 51:33), and other cities (Is 10:30; Jer 48:18). The plural "daughters of Zion" may be used as a reference to the inhabitants of the city (Sg 3:11; Is 3:16). When followed by a geographical name, "daughters" may also refer to the towns and villages near a major city (Nm 21:29; Jer 49:3; Ezk 16:27; Ps 97:8; Jos 17:11).

To the Southwestern Hill. The last use of the term "Zion" occurred early in the Christian era. From its application to the Ophel Ridge and the temple mount, the term came to be used of the southwestern hill of Jerusalem. The reason for this shift in the use of the term is not certain. Some authorities associate it with Herod's building projects that made that area of the city the most important part of Jerusalem; it was the residence of the aristocracy and the high priest. Others find the reason in the Christian shrines which were believed to be there, particularly the upper room of the last supper (Mk 14:15; Lk 22:12) and room where the disciples gathered after the Lord's ascension (Acts 1:13). After the destruction of the temple in AD 70, the prominence of the Christian shrines may have attracted the term "Zion" to this area of the city. By the 4th century a large basilica, "Holy Zion, Mother of All Churches," was built on the site of an earlier church. Tradition also attached the death of Mary to a site nearby. Despite the testimony of history, the name Zion to this day clings to the southwest hill.

View of Mt Zion from the Hill of Offense.

Theological Motifs. *In the OT.* Many theological motifs attach to the Zion theme as it develops in redemptive history. The dominant motif of Zion as the dwelling place of God, the place where God is in the midst of his people, is conjoined to the larger theme of Immanuel, "God in our midst." Just as the pillar of fire and cloud stood above the tabernacle during the wilderness wandering, so once Israel had attained the place of God's choosing (Dt 12:5–14), he would dwell there, "God with us." When Jerusalem became David's capital and Solomon had completed the temple, the glory cloud filled the temple (1 Kgs 8:10; 2 Chr 5:13,14) and Jerusalem became the dwelling place of God (Pss 74:2; 76:2; 135:21; Is 8:18; Jl 3:17,21). The Lord loved and chose Zion (Pss 78:68; 132:13). His glorious presence was there, and from there he would speak (Ps 50:1,2). His fire was in Zion, his furnace in Jerusalem (Is 31:8,9). There he was enthroned above the cherubim (Pss 9:11; 99:1,2) and ruled over his people and the nations (Is 24:23). His chosen king ruled from that holy hill (Pss 2:6; 48:1).

Though the size of the site of ancient Jerusalem is not particularly impressive and ordinarily would not be considered a large hill, for the psalmist Zion is God's holy hill (Ps 99:9). The prophets describe it as "chief among the mountains, raised above the hills" (Is 2:2; Mi 4:1). The Canaanite god Baal was thought to dwell on a great mountain to the north, Mt Zaphon; so the psalmist describes Zion as "beautiful in its loftiness, like the utmost heights of Mt Zaphon" (Ps 48:1,2). God's sanctuary is "like the high mountains" (Ps 78:68; Ez 40:2).

An adequate water supply has been a problem for Jerusalem throughout its history. During the OT period the city's water came from one small spring. But in the eyes of the poets and prophets, Zion is gladdened by a great river which brings life wherever it flows (Ps 46:4; Ez 47:1–12; Jl 3:18; Zec 13:1; 14:8; see Rv 22:1,2). The threatening waters of chaos cannot shake the city of God (Ps 46:1–3).

Because Zion is the city of God, it is the object of pilgrims, Jew and Gentile alike, who thirst to be in the presence of God in Zion's temple (Pss 42:1,2; 63:1,2). The pilgrim psalms give vivid expression to their longing (Pss 84; 122; 125–128). All mankind comes to God in Zion (Ps 65:1–4). The Gentiles will make annual pilgrimages bringing gifts (Ps 76: Is 18:7; Zep 3:9,10); even former enemies will be regarded as native-born citizens of Zion (Ps 87; Is 60:14; Zec 14:21). The nations will stream into Jerusalem to inaugurate an era of peace (Is 2:1–5; Mi 4:1–8). Year after year the feasts of Israel will be celebrated in Zion by Gentiles (Zec 14:16–19).

The doctrine of the "inviolability of Zion" is the natural consequence of its being the dwelling of God. The Lord is in the citadels of Zion and has shown himself to be its fortress; it is made secure forever (Ps 48:3,8) By God's help, it will not fall (Ps 46:5). The nations that plot against it do so in vain (Ps 2:1); all who hate Zion will be turned back in shame (Ps 129:5); foreign invaders will be repulsed (Jl 3:17).

Apart from the psalms, the clearest expression of the doctrine of Zion's inviolability is in the preaching of Isaiah set against the background of the Assyrian threat which had already carried away the northern kingdom. Though the armies of Assyria threaten, the Lord will fight for Zion (Is 31:4,5) and uphold its cause (34:8; see 46:13; 51:3,16). Zion is a tent that cannot be shaken; its stakes will never be pulled up nor its ropes broken (33:20). At the very time that enemy armies are encamped around the city, the Lord says of Sennacherib, king of Assyria, "he will not enter this city or shoot an arrow here. He will not come before it with shield or build a siege ramp against it. . . . I will defend this city and save it, for my sake and for the sake of David my servant" (Is 34:33–35).

It is easy to see how the doctrine of Zion's inviolability was perverted into a false sense of security and immunity from punishment. The popular theology of the Lord's eternal choice of Zion became for Israel a cause of presumptuous sin. On the eve of Nebuchadnezzar's invasion of Judah, the memories of how God had repulsed Sennacherib and the Assyrians because of his love for Zion led the populace of Jerusalem to think they could not be touched in spite of their transgressions. But God's choice of Zion would not be at the expense of his holiness and justice. The prophets who had preached the sanctity of Zion now inveighed against this misplaced confidence. Jeremiah's famous "temple sermon" (Jer 7:1–8:3) was intended to rid the people of their false expectations, for the Lord would abandon the city just as he had abandoned Shiloh and the ark (7:1–15; 26:1–6). Disaster is coming from the north, and Daughter Zion, once so beautiful and delicate, would be destroyed (Jer 6:1,2); a city so full of sin must be punished (6:6–8). Captivity is Jerusalem's fate (13:15–14:22); not even the intercession of Moses and Samuel could avert it (15:1–17:18). "Zion will be plowed like a field; Jerusalem will become a heap of rubble, and the temple hill a mound overgrown with thickets" (Jer 26:18; Mi 3:10–12).

Jeremiah's message should not have come as a surprise. Isaiah, who had so extolled the sanctity of Zion, could also foresee its destruction because of sin (64:8–12; see 2:6–3:26;

49:14). Joel had warned that the Day of the Lord would bring judgment to that holy hill (1:2–2:17). Amos too had warned those who were complacent in Zion (6:1). Micah viewed the sins of Jerusalem as requiring its overthrow (v 3). These warnings went unheeded; Israel persisted in sin, clinging to the lie that the mere presence of the temple on Zion would assure its safety (Jer 7:4). The Book of Lamentations gives the end result.

But the Lord had not cast off his people forever and forgotten Zion where he dwelt (Ps 74:1,2). Prophets before and during the exile looked to the restoration, the return to Zion, and the rebuilding of the temple. There was still hope for the future (Jer 30:17). The day would come when people would no longer have a vain trust in the ark, for it would not exist any longer, and no one would miss it. Jerusalem will again be the "throne of the Lord" (3:14–18). Babylon would be repaid for the harm done to God's people, who will return to Zion (50:5,28; 51:24,34,35). God will again rule from Zion over the nations (Mi 4). Jerusalem had thought it bereft of children, but it will have many descendants, Jew and Gentile alike (Is 49:19–23). In that day the Lord will lay a precious cornerstone in Zion (Is 28:16). During the exile Ezekiel, too, foresaw a glorious restoration of the city of God (Ez 42–48).

During the early years of the restoration God reaffirmed his love for Zion through the prophet Zechariah. The day of judgment would yet come against the nations (1:15,20,21; 2:7–9; 6:1–8; 12:1–9), for the Lord is still jealous for Jerusalem (1:14,16,17; 8:2). The Gentiles will make their pilgrimage to worship the Lord in Zion (2:10–13; 8:20–23; 14:16–21). The Lord says, "I will return to Zion and dwell in Jerusalem. Then Jerusalem will be called the City of Truth, and the mountain of the Lord Almighty will be called the Holy Mountain" (8:3).

In Extrabiblical Literature. The apocryphal and pseudepigraphal literature of the intertestamental period and the first Christian centuries exhibits the same uses of the term Zion as observed in the OT. The word can be used as a geographical name, again frequently in parallelism with Jerusalem (1 Mc 4:37; 5:54; 10:11; 2 Bar 7:1; 10:7–12; 13:1). Zion is mentioned in prophecies and in prayers for the well-being of the city (Jth 9:1–14; Ecclus 24:10,11; 48:17–25; 2 Bar 5:1–4).

But alongside this continuity with the OT there is a growing emphasis on an apocalyptic and eschatological understanding of the Zion theme, especially in the literature which followed the destruction of Jerusalem. The events of AD 70 brought a retheologizing of the Zion ideals. Expectations of historical realization of the promises to the prophets gave way to future projections of the city of God established unshakeable at the Day of Judgment. Moses himself understood that God had spoken of the eternal Zion which would come into existence with the renewal of heaven and earth (Jubilees 1:28,29; 4:26). Only after the coming judgment and the transformation of creation would Zion be built (2 Bar 22–32). The present city recently destroyed was not the city God had spoken of—earthly Jerusalem is destroyed to prepare for heavenly Jerusalem (2 Bar 4; 68;69). The glorification of the city will come in the messianic age (Pss Sol 11); "the future age is prepared . . . the city built" (4 Ezr 8:52).

In the New Testament. The NT further develops the emphasis on both the heavenly and the eschatological Zion.

In surveying the saints of the OT, the author of Hebrews speaks of their "looking forward to that city with foundations, whose architect and builder is God . . . longing for a better country, a heavenly one" (Heb 11:10,16), but none of them received the promises because God had planned something even better (11:39,40). The church now enjoys what believers of the old covenant could never know: unlimited access to the presence of God in that holy city, "Mt Zion, the heavenly Jerusalem, the city of the living God" (12:22; see 12:18–24). Earthly Zion was but a shadow of the heavenly reality. The present city of Jerusalem is likened to a slave woman, but the heavenly Jerusalem is free and the mother of both Jew and Gentile (Gal 4:21–27; see Is 49:14–23; 54:1). That river of life which the prophets of the OT envisioned flowing from the temple (Ps 46:4; Ez 47:1–12; Jl 3:18; Zec 13:1; 14:8) is seen in the NT as flowing from a man who was the temple incarnate (Jn 2:19–22; 4:11–14; 7:37–39; 19:34).

While the NT does emphasize the present reality of the heavenly Jerusalem, there is still the eschatological expectation of the re-creation of heaven and earth and the revelation of the new Jerusalem "coming down out of heaven from God as a bride beautifully dressed for her husband" (Rv 21:2). It is a city on a great high mountain (Rv 21:10; see Pss 48:1,2; 78:68; Is 2:2; Ez 40:2; Mi 4:1), and a river of life flows within (Rv 22:1,2). One conspicuous feature of the city is its lack of a temple (Rv 21:22); no longer is there any need for the expiation of sin. The city is in the shape of a perfect cube (Rv 21:15,16), the same shape as the Holy of Holies in the Mosaic tabernacle and the temple of Solomon, for the whole city has become the dwelling of God (Rv 21:3,22–27).

RAYMOND B. DILLARD

See JERUSALEM; JERUSALEM, NEW.

Zion, Daughter of. Term used primarily in prophetic literature to designate the inhabitants of Jerusalem (Zion) and its surrounding regions. The term was further applied to those in Babylon who had been exiled from Jerusalem and the Judean countryside (Is 1:8; Jer 4:31; 6:2,23). Since ancient cities were considered metaphorically to be the mother of their inhabitants, referring to the people of Jerusalem as "daughters of Zion" was entirely appropriate, particularly in poetic literature. While Israel was to be the "virgin daughter" of spiritual Zion (2 Kgs 19:21; Is 37:22; Lam 2:13), many of the prophetic contexts proclaim judgment on the unfaithful "daughters" (Is 3:16,17; 4:4; Mi 1:13). Although the "daughters of Zion" were judged for their unfaithfulness, the ultimate promise was that God would deliver them (Is 52:2; 62:11; Zec 9:9; Mt 21:5; Jn 12:15).

See ZION.

Zior. One of the cities of the hill country allotted to Judah's tribe for an inheritance (Jos 15:54). Since it is associated with Hebron in the text, Zior is likely identified with modern Sa'ir, the traditional location for Esau's tomb.

Ziph (Person). 1. Descendant of Caleb from Judah's tribe (1 Chr 2:42).

2. One of the sons of Jehallelel from Judah's tribe (1 Chr 4:16).

Ziph (Place). 1. One of the cities in the extreme south assigned to Judah's tribe for an inheritance (Jos 15:24).

2. One of the cities in the hill country belonging to Judah's tribe (Jos 15:55), mentioned with Maon, Carmel, Jezreel, and most prominently with Hebron (cf. 1 Chr 2:42). Ziph tentatively has been identified with a site three miles south of Hebron. The surrounding wilderness region is probably the "wilderness of Ziph" where David hid from Saul (1 Sm 23:14,15; 26:2). The Ziphites who betrayed David to Saul were residents of this city and surrounding region (1 Sm 23:19; 26:1; Ps 54 title, KJV Ziphims). Ziph is later mentioned as one of the cities fortified by Rehoboam (2 Chr 11:8).

Ziphah. Jehallelel's second son (or possibly daughter since the form is feminine), listed in 1 Chronicles 4:16. The genealogy is obscure.

Ziphims. KJV rendering of Ziphites, the inhabitants of Ziph, in the title of Psalm 54.

See ZIPH (PLACE) #2.

Ziphion. Alternate spelling of Zephon, Gad's firstborn son, in Genesis 46:16.

See ZEPHON.

Ziphite. Inhabitant of Ziph (1 Sm 23:19; 26:1; Ps 54 title).

See ZIPH (PLACE) #2.

Ziphron. Geographical landmark defining the northern boundary of the Canaanite land to be possessed by Israel (Nm 34:9). Its location is unknown.

Zippor. Father of the Moabite king Balak. Balak called on Balaam to curse Israel (Nm 22:2,4,10,16; 23:18; Jos 24:9; Jgs 11:25).

Zipporah. Wife of Moses and mother of his sons Gershom and Eliezer (Ex 2:21). Though she is listed as the daughter of Reuel (Ex 2:18), Reuel was probably the father of Hobab (Nm 10:29; also called Jethro, Ex 3:1; 4:18; etc.), who in turn was the father of Zipporah. Zipporah circumcised Gershom to prevent Moses' death prior to his return to Egypt (Ex 4:25). Apparently at that point Zipporah and the children left Moses and went back to live with her father, returning later during the wilderness wanderings (18:2).

Many have suggested that Zipporah was the Cushite (KJV Ethiopian) woman who furnished the pretext for Miriam and Aaron's criticism of Moses (Nm 12:1). While Cush and Midian are mentioned together in Habakkuk (700 years later), the identification does not fit the context of the passage, particularly since a long period would have elapsed between the marriage and the complaint.

Zithri. KJV spelling of Sithri, Uzziel's son, in Exodus 6:22.

See SITHRI.

The United Arab Republic, the Red Sea, and the Nile Valley (looking southeast)—the homeland of Zipporah.

Ziv. Name of the Hebrew month corresponding to about mid-May to mid-June (1 Kgs 6:1,37).

See CALENDARS, ANCIENT AND MODERN.

Ziz, Ascent of. Mountain pass going up from the Dead Sea to the Judean highlands. This ascent was the route used by the Ammonites and the Moabites prior to their defeat by Jehoshaphat as prophesied by Jehaziel (2 Chr 20:16). It is likely that Ziz should be identified with Ain Jidy, a pass which still provides an important route from the Dead Sea into the Judean interior.

Ziza. 1. Chief of Simeon's tribe descending from Shemaiah (1 Chr 4:37).

2. Son of Rehoboam and Maacah (2 Chr 11:20).

Zizah. Second of Shimei's sons and a clan chief within the Gershonite branch of Levi's tribe (1 Chr 23:11); perhaps the same as Zina in 1 Chronicles 23:10.

Zoan. One of the principal cities in the Delta region of ancient Egypt. Zoan, which was variously known as Zoan, Tanis, Avaris, and possibly Rameses (the towns were either the same or contiguous), was located on the south shore of Lake Menzaleh at the northeastern edge of the Egyptian Delta. Zoan was evidently an ancient city that was rebuilt during or shortly before the Hyksos period (c. 1730 BC; Nm 13:22). Because of its strategic location on the Tanitic branch of the Nile and near Egypt's northeastern frontier, Zoan was an important military and political base during the entire period of Egyptian native rule. It served as the capital city during the Hyksos period as well as serving as the effective capital during the 21st through the 23rd dynasties (c. 1090–718 BC) and as the northern capital during the 25th dynasty (c. 712–663 BC).

Zoan was significant to the Israelites during each of its periods of ascendancy. Whether the exodus occurred early (c. 1441 BC) or late (1290 BC), the Israelite settlement in Egypt would have been in the general vicinity of Zoan. The Israelites built the store cities of Pithom and Rameses, and possibly the latter should be identified with Zoan. In the account of the exodus in Psalm 78:12,43; the city of Zoan is poetically parallel to Egypt, indicating that it was either the capital or at least a significant city. During the period of Isaiah, Zoan was again significant, being designated as the home of the "princes" and "officials" of Egypt (Is 19:11,13; Ez 30:14).

See RAMESES (PLACE).

Zoar. One of the "cities of the plain" confederated with Sodom, Gomorrah, Admah, and Zeboiim (Gn 14:2,8). Zoar, also known by its earlier name Bela (v 2), is best known as the town which served as a temporary refuge for Lot and his daughters during the destruction of Sodom and the other cities of the plain (19:22,23,30). Despite the fact that Zoar was evidently a small town (19:22; Zoar means "little"), this place was evidently considered a significant geographical landmark in ancient times. When Abraham and Lot divided the land, Lot selected the land "in the direction of Zoar" (13:10). When Moses surveyed the Promised Land from Mt Pisgah, Zoar was reckoned as the southern terminus of the plain of the valley of Jericho (Dt 34:3). During the prophetic period Zoar was evidently considered to be on or just south of the southern boundary of Moab (Is 15:5; Jer 48:4,34).

As with the other "cities of the plain," the biggest difficulty comes in the identification of Zoar's location. Most scholars currently believe that the cities were located in the southeastern corner of the Dead Sea region and that their ruins may be located under the lake's surface. Some of the biblical references to Zoar potentially create problems for this view, however. Genesis 13 seems to identify Zoar (as well as Sodom and Gomorrah) with the Jordan River valley, which drains into the *northern* end of the Dead Sea (Gn 13:10,11). Deuteronomy 34 similarly places Zoar in "the valley of Jericho" (v 3). Scholars have further objected that Moses could not possibly have seen Zoar from Mt Pisgah, since the distance is too great and mountains intervene. If Zoar is located at the north end of the Dead Sea, Sodom and Gomorrah must also be located there, since Lot traversed the distance between Sodom and Zoar during the period between the first light of morning and sunrise (Gn 19:15,23). Both objections can be answered, however. In neither the case of Lot nor Moses does the text claim that they actually saw Zoar from their vantage points. Rather the text indicates that Zoar was the southernmost point of the region that they did see. The "plain" or "valley" of the Jordan evidently comprised the entire Jordan Rift, a geological feature that extends to the southern end of the Dead Sea. Furthermore, the prophetic references place Zoar on the southern frontier of Moab, which is accurately placed at the southern end of the Dead Sea. As a result, there is little cause to reject the consensus that the cities of the plain were at the southeast end of the Dead Sea.

See CITIES OF THE VALLEY, CITIES OF THE PLAIN.

Zobah, Zoba. Nation coming into contact with Israel during the early kingdom period.

King Saul defeated "all his enemies on every side" including "the kings of Zobah" (1 Sm 14:47). Soon after David became king of Israel he "defeated Hadadezer the son of Rehob, king of Zobah" and "took from him a thousand and seven hundred horsemen, and twenty thousand foot soldiers. . . . And when the Syrians of Damascus came to help Hadadezer king of Zobah, David slew twenty-two thousand men of the Syrians" (2 Sm 8:3–5,12; 1 Chr 18:3–10; Ps 60 title, Aram-Zobah). Later the Ammonites hired 20,000 "Syrians of Zobah" for an anticipated attack by David's forces. The coalition of Ammonites and hired mercenaries were defeated by soldiers led by Joab (2 Sm 10:6–14, KJV Zoba; cf. 1 Chr 19:6). When Hadadezer's army counterattacked, they were again defeated decisively by David (2 Sm 10:15–19; 1 Chr 19:16–19).

After Solomon had "turned away his heart from the Lord" (1 Kgs 11:9), another adversary appeared, a former vassal of Hadadezer, king of Zobah (vv 23–25). After Solomon's reign, Zobah passes from biblical history.

This small monarchy lay somewhere between Damascus and Hamath (Homs) in northern Syria. Zobah, along with its neighbors, same under the jurisdiction of Israel as David extended his conquests to the Euphrates River (2 Sm 8:3). But this jurisdiction was short-lived; after Solomon Zobah and other political entities in Syria rebelled.

Zobebah. One of the sons of Koz (or possibly a daughter since the noun is feminine) from Judah's tribe (1 Chr 4:8). The genealogy is obscure.

Zodiac. *See* Astrology.

Zohar. 1. Father of Ephron the Hittite. Abraham bought the cave of Machpelah from Ephron (Gn 23:8; 25:9).
2. Alternate spelling of Zerah, Simeon's son, in Genesis 46:10 and Exodus 6:15.
See Zerah #3.

Zoheleth, Stone of. KJV for "Serpent's Stone" in 1 Kings 1:9.
See Serpent's Stone.

Zoheth. Ishi's son from Judah's tribe (1 Chr 4:20).

Zophah. Helam's son from Asher's tribe (1 Chr 7:35,36).

Zophai. Alternate form of Zuph, one of 'amuel's ancestors, in 1 Chronicles 6:26.
See Zuph (Person).

Zophar. One of the "counselors" of Job who is listed as a Naamathite (Jb 2:11; 11:1; 20:1). He offers the most direct accusations against Job but later offers sacrifice for Job as commanded by the Lord (42:9). The location of his home country (Naamah) is unknown.

Zophim. Field from which Balaam pronounced his second blessing upon Israel (Nm 23:14). Zophim is associated with Mt Pisgah, but the precise location is unknown. Many have associated it with Tal'at es-Sufa on the northern ascent of Mt Nebo.

Zorah, Zorathite. One of the cities of the Shephelah attributed to both the tribe of Dan and of Judah (Jos 15:33; 19:41), because it was part of Judah's original allocation but was settled by Danites until they established their own territory near Laish (Jgs 18:11). Originally Zorah and nearby Eshtaol seem to have been settled by residents of Kiriath-jearim (1 Chr 2:53, Zorathites, KJV Zareathites; 4:2). The city was the home of Manoah, the father of Samson (Jgs 13:2). Samson's ministry was focused in the region surrounding Zorah and Eshtaol, and he was ultimately buried there (v 25; 16:31). Zorah is also mentioned as the home of the five spies whom the Danites sent out to search for a suitable inheritance (18:2,8). It is later listed among the towns that were fortified by Rehoboam and the villages outside of Jerusalem that were settled after the exile (2 Chr 11:10; Neh 11:29, KJV Zareah). Zorah is traditionally identified with Tell Sur'ah, which is strategically located at the entrance to a large valley leading toward the Mediterranean plain.

Zorites. Descendants of Salma from Judah's tribe (1 Chr 2:54). They possibly represent half of the Manahathite clan. Some have equated them with the Zorathites, but since the latter are mentioned in a different connection in the same genealogy (cf. v 53) this is unlikely.

Zorobabel. KJV form of Zerubbabel, Jerusalem's governor after the exile, in Matthew 1:12,13 and Luke 3:27.
See Zerubbabel.

Zuar. Father of Nethanel, the leader of Issachar's tribe at the start of Israel's wilderness wanderings (Nm 1:8; 2:5; 7:18,23; 10:15).

Zuph (Person). Ancestor of Elkanah, the father of the prophet Samuel (1 Sm 1:1). Zuph was a member of the Kohathite branch of Levites and is listed as the son of Elkanah (different than above) and the father of Toah (1 Chr 6:35). He is the same as Zophai listed in

Building over the traditional site of Rachel's tomb in Bethlehem, which was near the town of Zuph.

1 Chronicles 6:26. It is evident that Zuph was a Levite even though he is listed as an Ephraimite in the 1 Samuel passage. The seeming discrepancy results from Zuph's residence and his civil status. The Levites had no inheritance and civil status of their own but were reckoned with the tribe in whose territory they dwelt (Dt 18:1–8).

Zuph (Place). Place where Saul looked for his father's asses prior to his meeting with Samuel (1 Sm 9:5). It was near the tomb of Rachel, which is traditionally placed near the northern border of Benjamin. Zuph is apparently linked with Samuel, as one of his ancestors bore the name (see 1 Sm 1:1; Chr 6:35) and his native town was called Ramathaim-zophim. Its precise location remains unknown.

Zur. 1. Midianite prince who was the father of Cozbi, the Midianite woman who was killed by Phinehas for consorting with Zimri after the incident at Baal-peor (Nm 25:15). He was one of the five "kings" of Midian who with Balaam were later killed by the Israelites (31:8). Apparently he was a vassal of the Amorite king Sihon, since he is listed as one of his "princes" (Jos 13:21).

2. Son of Je-iel, the founder of Gibeon (1 Chr 8:30; 9:36). He was a Benjamite and a distant relative of Saul.

Zuriel. Son of Abihail and the head of the Merari family of Levites during the wilderness wanderings (Nm 3:35).

Zurishaddai. Father of Shelumiel, the leader of Simeon's tribe at the start of Israel's wilderness wanderings (Nm 1:6; 2:12; 7:36,41; 10:19).

Zuzim. One of the kingdoms attacked and defeated by Chedorlaomer's confederation (Gn 14:5), mentioned as residents of Ham, though the identification is obscure. They were likely located somewhere north of the Arnon River, since the general path of Chedorlaomer was from north to south along the Way of the Kings. Possibly these Ham-Zuzim are associated with the Zamzummim of Deuteronomy 2:20, since both are linked to the same geographical proximity. Furthermore, both passages speak of them in connection with races of giants, including the Horites, the Emim, and the Rephaim.

Illustration Credits

Illustrations in these volumes appear by permission of or courtesy of:

Alva Studios, 860 (right)

American Journal of Archaeology, 1631

Anrich, Erich, 738

Aramco World Magazine/Tor Eigeland, 650

Ashmolean Museum, 845

Athanassopoulou, Elly, 21

The Badè Institute of Biblical Archaeology, Pacific School of Religion, 1476

Louise M. Bauer, 1, 45, 52–53, 221, 240, 248, 393, 467, 509, 622, 673, 732, 777, 936, 1328, 1499, 1528–29, 1580, 1626–27, 1648–49, 1741, 1757, 1850–51, 2104, 2143, 2166, endsheets

V. Gilbert Beers, 138, 488–90, 927, 1126 (bottom right), 1256, 1643, 1673, 1677, 1905, 2037, 2107

British School of Archaeology in Jerusalem, 508

Brooklyn Museum, 66 (Charles Edwin Wilbour Collection), 1557 (gift of Hagob Kevorkian), 1917, 2193 (gift of Hagob Kevorkian)

Chase Manhattan Bank Money Museum, 1475, 1482

Consulate General of Israel, 151 (bottom), 678

John J. Davis, 1700 (left)

Drew-McCormick Archaeological Expedition/Lee C. Ellenberger, 628, 1011, 1942

Guy P. Duffield, 20, 164 (bottom), 727, 999, 1167 (bottom), 1192, 1645, 1795, 1966, 1995, 2009, 2067

Egyptian Museum, Cairo, 778, 1039, 2058

Endowment for Biblical Research, Boston, 161 (A. Marguerite Smith Collection), 1960

Jack Finegan, 1217

A. Gaddis, 408

George Weidenfeld and Nicolson Ltd., 1742

H. Gökberg, 706

Griffith Institute, Ashmolean Museum, 58

Clarence H. Hall, 154

Hart Picture Archives, *Designs of the Ancient World*, 200, 547, 674, 1689

Heirs of Charles F. Pfeiffer, 10, 871, 1040, 1215

Israel Department of Antiquities and Museums, 410, 595, 599, 600, 719, 721, 780, 1569, 1808, 1811

Israel Government Tourist Office, 405, 416 (bottom), 556, 618, 640, 813, 834, 983, 1056, 1130, 1260, 1313, 1353, 1411, 1532, 1535, 1817, 1897, 1976, 2029, 2059, 2126

Israel Information Services, 1338, 1599, 1779

Israel Office of Information, 596, 1412, 1836, 1982, 2097

Italian State Tourist Office, 1542, 1864

Jordan Tourist Department, 1668 (left)

Kelsey Museum of Archaeology, University of Michigan, 120 (top), 264, 1622, 1652

Homer A. Kent, Jr., 398, 569 (bottom), 1106, 1190, 1194, 1367

J. Carl Laney, 96, 249, 274, 435, 461, 525, 1436

Gerald A. Larue, 292 (bottom), 694, 839

Levant Photo Service, 2, 16, 29, 33, 35, 74, 112, 136, 146, 203, 284, 292 (top), 496, 530, 569 (top), 583, 604, 655, 657, 699, 703, 710, 762, 803 (bottom), 820, 828, 858, 977, 978, 992, 1063, 1122, 1140, 1149, 1184, 1238, 1304, 1309, 1460, 1473, 1543, 1603, 1623, 1668 (right), 1692, 1787, 1854, 1878, 1882, 1908, 2002, 2084, 2129, 2188, 2201

Los Angeles County Museum of Art, 1021 (detail; 66.4.5, county funds donated by Anna Bing Arnold)

John McGovern, 1783

John R. McRay, 37, 39, 63, 103, 143, 148, 151 (top), 164 (top), 166, 167, 169, 174, 182, 195, 204 (top), 230, 267, 268, 275, 277 (bottom), 286, 332, 348, 369, 371, 378, 390, 394, 395, 415, 420, 472, 479, 498, 513, 518, 555, 571, 584, 590, 597, 607, 625, 641, 714, 724, 767, 770, 774, 775, 786, 792, 803 (top), 805, 824, 835, 837, 844, 857, 860 (left), 898, 914, 930, 934, 943, 949, 954, 960, 963, 966, 968, 971, 975, 980, 995, 1015, 1026, 1031, 1045, 1066, 1119, 1126 (top; bottom left), 1127, 1136, 1146, 1148, 1150, 1151, 1163, 1174, 1180, 1199, 1203, 1208, 1224, 1228, 1251, 1252, 1280, 1305, 1331, 1364, 1374,

Illustration Credits

1398, 1403, 1404, 1414, 1420, 1423, 1431, 1446, 1488, 1500, 1536, 1578, 1585, 1587, 1634, 1660, 1684, 1695, 1705, 1710, 1718, 1719, 1720, 1721, 1725, 1727, 1729, 1746, 1765, 1803, 1827, 1842, 1849, 1866, 1870, 1885, 1886, 1888, 1893, 1911, 1920, 1952, 1954, 1964, 1977 (right), 2007, 2021, 2024, 2047, 2073, 2078, 2091, 2102, 2123, 2133, 2137, 2140, 2142, 2147, 2154, 2169, 2175, 2180, 2197, 2207

W. Harold Mare, 192, 194, 294, 360, 586, 891, 1034, 1089, 1098, 1134, 1153 (bottom), 1390, 1591, 2027

Matson Photo Service, 46, 85, 120 (bottom), 206, 271, 277 (top), 288, 325, 365, 387, 391, 427, 430, 748, 862, 867, 1082, 1103, 1124, 1210, 1211, 1218, 1220, 1289, 1356 (left), 1375, 1477, 1491, 1533, 1604, 1697, 1772, 1816, 1832, 2006, 2099, 2159

Metropolitan Museum of Art, 380, 389 (the Theodore M. Davis Collection, bequest of Theodore M. Davis, 1915), 559 (Rogers Fund, 1907), 669 (left), 889 (bottom; Fletcher Fund, 1924), 1510 (lyre, museum excavations, 1915–16; Rogers Fund, 1916), 2049, 2157 (gift of Miss Helen Miller Gould, 1910), 2168 (gift of Mr. and Mrs. V. Everit Macy, 1923), 2185 (Rogers Fund, 1945)

Michigan-Princeton-Alexandria Expedition to Mt Sinai, 316 (detail)

Musée du Louvre, 159, 881, 921

Museum of Fine Arts, Boston, 668 (gift of Miss Anna D. Slocum), 754, 1552 (gift of Edward W. Forbes)

National Aeronautics and Space Administration, 745, 756, 1356 (right), 1564, 2204

Nelson-Atkins Museum of Fine Arts, 152

North Wind Picture Archives, jackets, title pages (coin)

Oriental Institute, University of Chicago, 40, 47, 62, 157, 159, 177, 204 (bottom), 242, 244, 250, 578, 602, 669 (right), 735, 744, 752, 779, 889 (top), 921, 1004, 1345, 1427, 1479, 1681, 1762, 1906, 1977 (left), 2005, 2170, 2172

Pontifical Biblical Institute, 1395, 1636

Lisa Ramsey-Hershberger, 936, 1601, 1757, 1859

Religious News Service, 432, 842, 1094, 1321, 1384, 1620

Royal Ontario Museum, Toronto, 1700 (right)

Keith N. Schoville, 25, 1059, 1947

Lorraine O. Schultz, 1287

Staatliche Museen zu Berlin, 1115

Carl A. Stapel, 1064

N. Stoupnapas, 521, 633

Trans World Airlines Getaway Vacations, 142, 289, 503, 665, 1525, 1662

Trustees of the British Museum, 12, 67, 78, 107, 153, 188, 201, 215, 216, 245, 254, 256, 563, 564, 672, 715, 800, 923, 1004, 1048, 1051, 1108, 1308, 1377, 1503, 1739, 1925, 1935, 1956, 2062, 2081, 2138, 2163

Turkish Office of the Cultural and Information Attaché, 86, 129, 610, 615, 902

George A. Turner, 213, 418, 441, 701, 816, 917, 1041, 1087, 1157, 1161, 1209, 1221, 1242, 1272, 1385, 1413, 1455, 1495, 1777, 1792, 1986, 2013, 2024, 2111, 2112

UNESCO/Laurenza, 162

University Museum, University of Pennsylvania, 544, 864, 937, 2199

University of Chicago Press, 661

University of Cincinnati, 337

University of Wisconsin-Extension, Madison, 416 (top), 648, 851, 1038, 1665

Bastiaan Van Elderen, 1439, 1970

Howard F. Vos, 664, 743, 2148

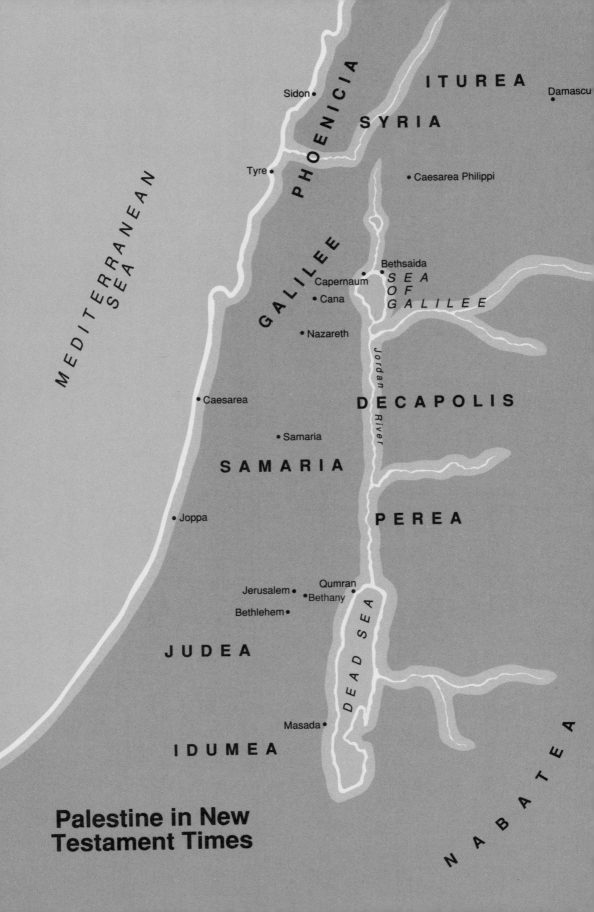

Palestine in New Testament Times

ATLANTIC
OCEAN

BELGICA

GAUL

SPAIN

ITALY

ADRIATIC SEA

ILLYR

CORSICA

Rome •

SARDINIA

Caesarea •

SICILY

MAURETANIA

MEDITER

AFRICA

The New Testament
World